The Breweries

Indexes & Further Information

Special thanks to 165,000 CAMRA members who carried out research for the pub entries; the Campaign's Regional Directors and Area Organisers, who co-ordinated the pub entries; the Campaign's Brewery Liaison Officers and Brewery Liaison Coordinators, who carried out research for the brewery entries; Paul Moorhouse for assembling the beer tasting notes; Rick Pickup for advising on new breweries; Michael Slaughter for advising on heritage pubs; Alex Presland for technical support; Nik Antona and Abi Newton for assistance co-ordinating the brewery entries; the publicans, breweries and others who kindly contributed their photographs; and CAMRA's National Executive for their support.

Thanks also to the following at CAMRA head office: Lauren Anderson, Steven Brooks, Matt Brown, Jill Burder, Claire Cain, Martin Clemmey, Caroline Clerembaux, Judy Collins, John Cottrell, Neil Cox, Helen Curnow, Gillian Dale, Catrin Davies, Aaron Dobbing, Rob Ferguson, Nick Forshaw, Gary Fowler, Anita Gibson, Faye Grima, Sarah Hall, Tony Jerome, Paul Kelly, Chris Lewis, Jonathan Mail, Tim Miller, Jay Norton, Marilyn O'Donoghue, Gary Ranson, Emily Ryans, Greg Rycroft, Nicky Shipp, Barnaby Smith, Tom Stainer, Ron Stocks, Claire-Michelle Taverner-Pearson, Neil Walker, Liz Wickham.

Photo credits: [Key: t = top; b = bottom; c=centre; l = left; r = right] p6: Shepherd Neame; p11: (tc) Bob Steel; p18: (l) Roger Protz, (t,b) Richard Brooks; p22: Cath Harries; p23: Thornbridge; p25: (tl) Tom Stainer, (tr) Valentyn Volkov/shutterstock, (bl) photowind/shutterstock, (br) Tom Stainer; p969: (main) Roger Protz.

Maps & illustrations: Cover illustration: © Claire Rollet; illustration p25: Mark Walker, MW Digital Graphics; Pubs section maps: David and Morag Perrot, PerroCarto.

Production: Cover design: Hannah Moore; colour pages design: Keith Holmes, Thames Street Studio; database, typesetting and indexes: AMA Dataset.

Printed and bound in the UK by William Clowes, Beccles, Suffolk.

Type set in Stag and Dax.

Published by the Campaign for Real Ale Ltd, 230 Hatfield Road, St Albans, Herts, AL1 4LW.
www.camra.org.uk

 ISBN 978-1-85249-320-2

All of the papers used in this book are recyclable and made from wood grown in managed, sustainable forests. They are manufactured at mills certified to ISO 14001 and/or EMAS.

About the Good Beer Guide

It's far more than just a pub guide

The *Good Beer Guide* is the essential compendium pointing to breweries, their ales and the essential outlets in towns and rural areas where you can enjoy them. For 42 years, the *Good Beer Guide* has celebrated two great British institutions: the pub and cask-conditioned real ale – cornerstones of our communities and our way of life.

More than just a pub guide

The *Good Beer Guide* is far more than a pub guide. Pubs are the central core – the essential outlets for real ale – but the *Good Beer Guide* has always walked tall on two feet, with its Breweries section complementing the pub listings by detailing all the producers of cask beer and their regular ales. As well as listing some 4,500 of the finest outlets for real ale and the ever-growing number of breweries, we also look at the modern threats to the pub and good beer and the exhilarating fight-back by consumers and publicans: see the Introduction on pages 6 to 9.

Comprehensive breweries section

The *Good Beer Guide* includes a comprehensive listing of all UK breweries and their core beers. Breweries are monitored on a regular basis, and each brewery is visited by CAMRA members, who speak to the brewer and check on the beers being produced before reporting to the Guide. As soon as a new brewery comes on stream, a liaison officer will be appointed to make sure the Breweries section of the Guide is updated every year and readers are aware of the increased choice available.

Democratically selected entries

The way in which pubs are chosen is equally meticulous and unique. Much of CAMRA's 165,000-plus membership is involved and those members who cannot be active or attend regular meetings are invited to recommend pubs via email or branch websites. Branch areas are broken down into smaller local areas so pubs can be more easily monitored. The quality of beer in each pub is checked using a meticulous 'beer scoring' system. Special branch meetings are convened once a year where members vote on the final selection for the Guide.

Regular inspections

The entries in most pub guides are chosen either by small editorial teams or by members of the public, whose recommendations are not necessarily checked. On the other hand, every pub that appears in this Guide has been visited frequently, often weekly, by CAMRA members. We offer full entries, with no unchecked 'lucky dip' sections of pubs sent in at random. Readers' recommendations for the Guide are passed to the local branch, who take this feedback on board during their surveying.

It's not only about quality beer

The key driving force of the *Good Beer Guide* – beer quality – has not changed over 42 years. However, the Guide also takes account of the history and architecture of pubs and such important aspects as food, family and disabled facilities, gardens, special events such as mini-beer festivals, and even the standard of the toilets. CAMRA's volunteer pub surveyors are called on to be minor essayists, describing in detail all aspects of the pubs they choose. We know, from the feedback we receive, that users of the Guide want as much information about pubs as possible before embarking on journeys to visit them.

Town & country pubs

In addition to full descriptions, users want a good spread of pubs. Unlike some guides that concentrate on rural pubs, we recognise that most people live in towns and cities and expect a good selection of pubs in those areas. But we don't neglect suburban and country pubs: on the contrary, CAMRA campaigns for the survival of rural pubs that are often vital hubs of their isolated communities.

We are at pains to ensure that all areas of the country are covered. Each county or region has an allocation of pubs based on a scientific calculation of population, number of licensed premises and the level of 'tourist penetration'. As a result, the Guide's reach is unparalleled.

Proudly independent

Unlike many of our competitors, **all of our entries are free**. CAMRA is a proudly independent organisation and there are no hidden costs of appearing in the *Good Beer Guide*. CAMRA is a broad church and the Guide reflects that by choosing pubs across a wide spectrum that will appeal to people from all walks of life, regardless of income and background.

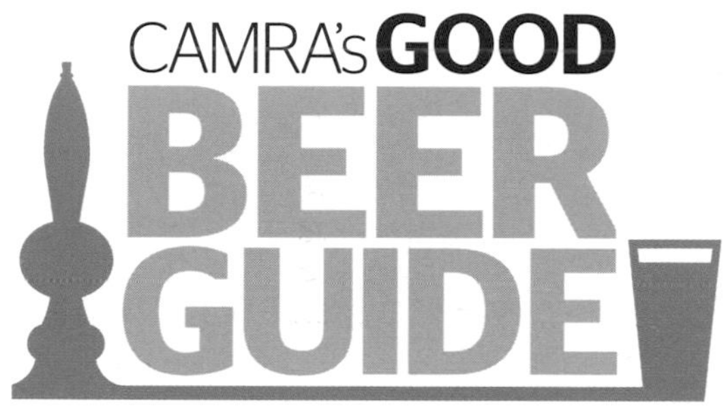

2015

Edited by Roger Protz

Project Manager Emma Haines

Assistant Editors Ione Brown, Katie Button, Simon Tuite

Head of Publishing Simon Hall

www.camra.org.uk

Contents

The *Good Beer Guide* celebrates Britain's pubs and cask-conditioned real ale

Keeping up to date

The Campaign has more than 200 branches. Each branch surveys the pubs in its area and regularly monitors not only the quality of the cask beer in each one but also watches for change of ownership or management that could affect the range of ale on offer, its quality and the overall standard of the pub. In addition, branch officers frequently liaise with local breweries and keep a close eye on the local brewing scene.

There is a cynical saying that 'all guide books are out of date as soon as they appear'. That's not the case with the *Good Beer Guide*. Thanks to modern technology, the Guide is checked and re-checked many times before publication and both pubs and breweries can be amended or even deleted at a late date. Checking doesn't stop there: both CAMRA's national website and its monthly newspaper *What's Brewing* publish regular information and updates about the Guide, including pubs that have closed or where beer quality has declined. These changes are also reflected in the Good Beer Guide Mobile app which, along with an e-book and sat-nav POI file, give readers access to the Guide in many different formats (see p973). This regular checking, along with the pubs and breweries databases underpinning the Guide, mean that CAMRA and the *Good Beer Guide* share an unrivalled electronic storehouse of information about pubs and breweries.

Additional resources

There are limits to the size of the *Good Beer Guide*. We believe – thanks to our members' efforts and the recommendations sent in by readers – that we offer a choice of the very best pubs throughout the country. But the Guide is complemented by other resources, including local pub guides produced by CAMRA branches and available at beer festivals, local outlets and **www.camra.org.uk/books**, and the online **www.whatpub.com** – CAMRA's official guide to all known real ale outlets in the UK.

National Beer Scoring Scheme

- Pubs are selected for the Guide by CAMRA branches who use the scores submitted by members to help them identify places that serve consistently good beer. The scheme uses a 0–5 scale that can be submitted online. Any CAMRA member can submit a beer score by going to CAMRA's online pub guide **www.whatpub.com**, logging in as a member and selecting 'Submit Beer Scores'.

Reader updates & feedback

- You can keep your copy of the Guide up to date by visiting the *Good Beer Guide* area of the CAMRA website: **www.camra.org.uk/gbg**. Click on 'Updates to GBG 2015' where you will find information about changes to pubs and breweries.
- The Guide is keen to hear from readers. If you wish to recommend a pub or feel that one you have visited fell below your expectations, then we would like to know. Please use the Readers' Recommendations and Have Your Say forms at the back of the book or contact the editor at **gbgeditor@camra.org.uk**.

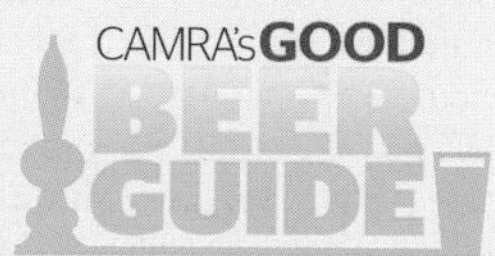

Introduction

The consumer is king

The 2015 *Good Beer Guide* – the 42nd edition – can proudly report positive gains for beer and pubs over the past 12 months, gains that could not have been achieved without the passion and commitment of the countless thousands who love real ale and good pubs.

In a beer world dominated by giant global players with deep pockets and vast advertising budgets, cask beer is almost an underground drink. With the exception of a few bigger British brewers, most producers cannot afford to advertise their beers. And yet real ale is the only success story in a declining beer market. As the Breweries section in this edition shows, new breweries, making handcrafted beers, continue to come on stream while many longer-running breweries are expanding with new equipment and even new premises. Cask beer has almost doubled its market share over the past decade as drinkers forsake both global lager brands and old-fashioned 'cream-flow' keg ales. Cask beer now enjoys a 55 per cent share of the total ale market.

Beer drinkers want products made from the finest grains and hops – and real ale fits the bill. It's not shipped thousands of miles round the world – clocking up enormous carbon footprints – nor given artificial 'shelf life' with the aid of foam enhancers, adjuncts, stabilisers and applied carbon dioxide. Cask beer has a short shelf life because it's a natural drink, rooted in the good husbandry of local brewers, barley growers and hop farmers.

The most invigorating aspect of real ale's success is its popularity among young people. The annual Cask Beer Report along with publicans' views and an analysis of those attending beer festivals show that more and more young people of both sexes are enjoying the multitude of choice and flavours delivered by the cask beer sector. That risible image of the 'typical' real ale drinker being an old man with a cloth cap and a whippet is as dead as the proverbial dodo.

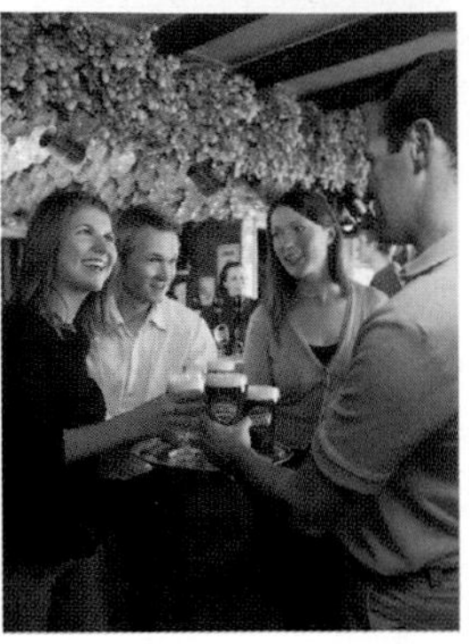

Real ale is reaching out to a younger, appreciative audience, proving it's not a type of beer drunk only by older people

Valiant Trooper

The astonishing success of one beer is proof of real ale's rip-roaring success with drinkers of all ages and backgrounds. Trooper is brewed by Robinsons of Stockport, a family-owned brewery founded in 1838 and an unlikely source for a beer that's proved a worldwide hit with lovers of heavy metal. The brewery, with 370 pubs in the North-west of England, is now in the hands of the sixth generation of the family and Oliver and William Robinson are determined to reach out to younger drinkers to invigorate sales.

They responded to a request from Bruce Dickinson, lead singer of Iron Maiden, who is a passionate real ale drinker, to devise a beer for the group and their worldwide legion of fans. The result was Trooper, a 4.7 per cent golden ale with an uncompromising hoppy aroma and palate from the use of Bobec, Cascade and Goldings hops. It's a long way removed from Eurofizz.

The success of the beer stunned Robinsons. In 2012 the company invested £6 million in a new, ultra-modern brewhouse that will enable it to brew between 85 and 90,000 barrels a year. Oliver Robinson says he expected to reach full capacity by around 2020 but in 2013 the new plant was already full – thanks to Trooper.

Singing the booze... Trooper, brewed as a collaboration between rock group Iron Maiden and Robinson's of Stockport, has been a world-wide success

The cask version of the beer has proved popular in Robinsons pubs while sales of the bottled version have reached the stratosphere. It follows Iron Maiden on tour and is drunk in large volumes in Australia, Brazil, Russia, Sweden and the United States. A bemused but delighted Oliver Robinson says: 'I can't believe it – we're selling ale in Brazil!'

Taxing the Government

As further proof of consumer power, beer drinkers have used their collective muscle to force the Government to reduce duty and lower prices – and now new legislation should ensure a better deal for landlords who work for giant pub companies.

In 2013 the Chancellor of the Exchequer George Osborne scrapped the Beer Duty Escalator, introduced by the previous government, which had almost doubled the price of a pint over a five-year period. As well as axing the escalator, the Chancellor also cut duty on beer by a penny. The two actions combined to bring much-needed relief to a pub trade reeling with 28 closures a week.

In 2014 the Chancellor acted again. It was predicted he would freeze beer duty in his Budget but once again he took the opportunity to cut it by a penny. It may sound like small beer but it stopped the tide of ever-rising beer prices that has closed pubs and sent drinkers into the arms of the supermarkets and their cut-price booze.

Most importantly, two years of positive action by the Government in support of beer has sent a signal that consumers have the power to change public policy. The present Government had been in office for four years and had done little to support beer and pubs until CAMRA supported an e-petition calling for the duty escalator to be axed. The Campaign won the necessary 100,000 signatures to the petition, which prompted a major debate in parliament and then the announcement by the Chancellor in 2013, followed by a further cut in duty in 2014.

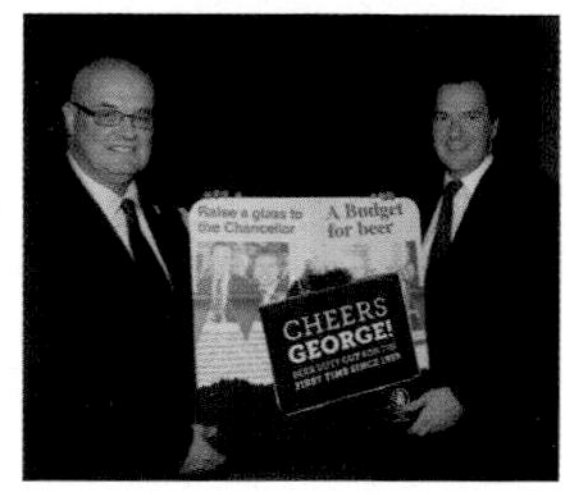

CAMRA's Julian Hough celebrating the cut in beer duty with Chancellor George Osborne. As a result of two successive cuts in duty and the axing of the Beer Duty Escalator in 2013, beer sales in pubs in 2014 increased by the highest rate this century

Tackling the pubcos

The most welcome news in 2014 came from Business Secretary Vince Cable, who announced sweeping measures to tackle the unbridled power of giant pubcos such as Enterprise Inns and Punch Taverns who burden their tenants with punitive rents and exorbitant beer prices. Dr Cable and his Government department had dragged their feet for months. Their proposals were delayed and were in danger of being stalled until both CAMRA and pub tenants' organisations pressured the government to act. The Campaign distributed beer mats and posters, sent 8,000 letters to MPs and promoted a petition signed by more than 40,000 pub users.

The terms of Dr Cable's proposals mean there will be a Statutory Code covering pubcos and their tenants while a Pubs Adjudicator – in effect, an Ombudsman – will be appointed to resolve disputes. Companies owning more than 500 pubs will have to offer rent assessments that will compare tied and free-of-tie costs to current and prospective tenants if negotiations break down.

But as CAMRA has stressed, there is still urgent work to be done to ensure a better deal for both publicans and beer drinkers. Missing from Dr Cable's proposals was the call to relax the beer tie, which would give tenants the right to buy beer from sources other than their pubco landlord, and a Market Rent Option. The option – supported by CAMRA, tenants and the Parliamentary Save the Pub Group chaired by Greg Mulholland MP – would allow publicans greater freedom to buy beers of their choice in return for a negotiated market rent.

Business Secretary Vince Cable (pictured with parliamentary secretary Tessa Munt MP) brought in a Bill with proposals to tackle the power of the giant pub companies in 2014

A petition with more than 44,000 signatures calling on the government to act on pub reforms was presented to parliament by pub tenants, MPs and CAMRA members

Greg Mulholland hailed the Government proposals as a huge win for campaigners and tied tenants but he added: 'It's vital the government goes further and makes the free-of-tie option mandatory.' He was echoed by CAMRA's Head of Public Affairs Jonathan Mail, who urged the Government to introduce a guest beer and market rent option.

The grip of companies such as Enterprise and Punch must be eased if pubs are to survive. The reason why so many pubs close is not because communities don't want them but because the pubcos sell them to ease their financial problems. Both Enterprise and Punch went on a wild buying spree in the early part of this century and then caught a heavy cold when the recession hit. As a result, they are saddled with debt, to such an extent that Punch Taverns spent many months in 2014 avoiding administration. It has debts of £600 million. As Carol Ross, tenant of the Roscoe Head in Liverpool, which has been in every edition of this Guide, says: 'It beggars belief how they have survived when they owe so much money. They'll only go on squeezing tenants to survive.'

Saving pubs

A simple equation: no pub = no real ale. Cask beer is a draught-only product, which is why the *Good Beer Guide* is committed to the pub's survival.

Pubs are vital community assets. People don't gather in supermarkets or betting shops for a chat, a drink or a meal. Too many pubs are being turned into retail stores and betting shops but strenuous efforts are being made to save pubs for local people. As the Guide shows on page 10 with the example of the Fox & Goose in Hebden Bridge, Yorkshire, pubgoers can pool their resources to stop their local from closing.

There are now several resources that can be used to save pubs. The Localism Act of 2011 has a provision known as the Community Right to Bid that enables a group to have a building listed by the local authority as an Asset of Community Value (ACV). This includes a six-month stay of execution: if a pubco wants to close and sell a pub to a speculative builder, for example, it can't do so while an ACV is in operation. This gives local people time to raise funds to buy the pub or look for an alternative buyer. To date, more than 430 pubs have been listed as ACVs: CAMRA has a target of 500 and is well on its way to achieving this figure.

For details of how to use the Localism Act, go to **www.gov.uk** and follow the link to 'A Plain English Guide to the Localism Act'.

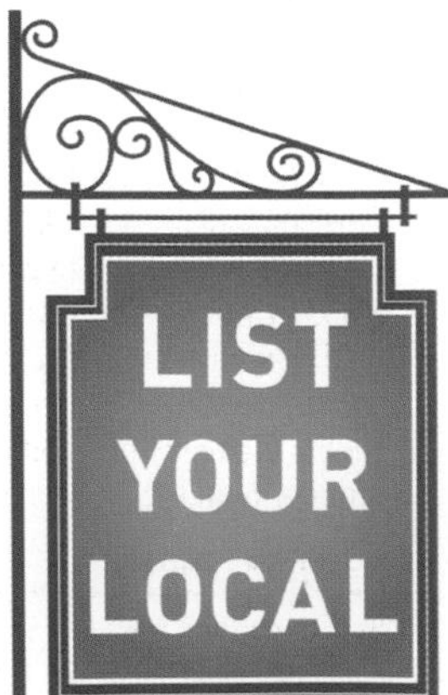

CAMRA's List Your Local campaign urges pub-goers to list pubs with local authorities to prevent pubcos from closing them

The *Good Beer Guide* salutes the work of Everards in Leicester (see page 10). This large family brewery has saved 30 pubs from closure or failure and leased them to smaller brewers, ensuring the pubs' survival and improved choice for locals. We encourage other brewers to follow Everards' public-spirited example.

Pub lovers in Maidenhead, Berkshire, were unable to save their local, the Golden Harp, which was turned into a Tesco Express

Explosion of choice

There are no boundaries in the world of real ale brewing. Brewers are endlessly seeking new aromas and flavours to entrance drinkers. Bitter remains overwhelmingly the most popular style of beer, but there's now a profusion of choice, with brewers daring to do the unexpected. No longer is brewing beer a simple matter of blending malt and hops: all manner of fruits, herbs and spices are also brought in to play.

Windsor & Eton's Kohinoor, an IPA brewed with the addition of jasmine petals, coriander and cardamom, may not be strictly true to the Victorian original but it gives fascinating new depths of flavour to the beer. The Berkshire brewery is not alone, with others using – to name but a few – chocolate, coffee beans, cherries, raspberries, ground ivy and yarrow.

Beers aged in whisky barrels have been popular for several years now, with the fumes of the distillate locked in the wood adding a warming and honey-sweet note to the beers. Now brewers have moved on to add the character of Bourbon, Cognac and rum to their brews with the use of oak casks brought from those industries.

The famous Belgian lambic and gueuze beers, brewed by 'spontaneous fermentation' with wild yeasts in the atmosphere, have inspired a number of brewers to make sour beer, inoculating their brews with a special Belgian 'wild' yeast culture. Elgoods in Cambridgeshire has gone the extra mile, brewing in true lambic style. A mash of malt and wheat is boiled with aged hops and then run in to open copper vessels known as coolships. Windows in the brewhouse are opened to encourage passing yeasts to enter and start fermentation. Finally, the beer is aged in wooden casks for several months and emerges with a complex aroma and taste of acidic fruit, oak, smoke, vanilla and rich grain.

Wood is back in fashion. One *Good Beer Guide*-listed pub, the Junction in Castleford, West Yorkshire (see page 551), buys oak casks from a specialist cooper and then gets local brewers to fill them with beer. Landlord Neil Midgley has a cellar packed with oak casks and hosts regular beer events where customers can taste the same beer from metal and oak containers.

He's not alone. Sam Smith's, Theakston's and Wadworth continue to supply beer in oak to outlets where publicans are convinced the wood gives an extra dimension to the beer. Theakston's, famous for its Old Peculier strong ale, took on an apprentice last year to learn the skills of cask building from the brewery's cooper, Jonathan Fenby. The brewery reports an increasing demand from publicans for beer from the wood. It's back to the future with a vengeance.

Wood you believe it... oak-aged beer is back in fashion. Theakston's cooper Jonathan Fenby is kept busy building casks for such popular beers as Old Peculier

On your guard

In the world of beer and pubs, nothing should be taken for granted. The history of CAMRA and this Guide is one of constant battles to save both breweries and pubs from takeover and closure. There are big players in the global world of brewing and pub retailing, and their interest lies in maximising profit, not in delivering choice for drinkers.

Support and defend your local brewery and local pub. Vigilance is the key to their success and survival.

Saving Pubs

Brewers and drinkers work to save at-risk pubs

A project between a regional brewer and smaller artisan breweries has helped save a number of closed and neglected pubs. And in West Yorkshire drinkers have come together to save a cherished local.

Project William

Collaboration between a major regional brewer and smaller artisan breweries has helped breathe life back into 30 failed pubs. The scheme is called Project William and is run by the family-owned Everards Brewery in Leicester.

The aim of Project William, according to Everards' managing director Stephen Gould, is to 'drive people back into pubs'. The project was the result of a meeting in 2006 between Gould and Keith Bott, founder of Titanic Brewery in Stoke-on-Trent. The result was the Greyhound in Newcastle-under-Lyne, which re-opened in 2007 with Titanic as tenant, after a major refurbishment following years of neglect under previous owners.

Everards now works with a total of 10 smaller breweries. The Leicester brewery buys and improves each pub and then leases it to one of its partners. Everards is paid rent for each pub and the agreement stipulates that while the partners can sell the full range of their beer they must also take at least one Everards' cask beer, usually its flagship Tiger Best Bitter.

Stephen Gould says 14 of the pubs that are part of Project William had closed when Everards bought them, while 13 others were trading so poorly they were unsustainable. To date, Everards has invested £11.5 million on the scheme – 'the biggest investment by any brewery in the country in pubs,' according to Gould.

The Old Fighting Cocks before and after...

In its early days, Project William was centred on pubs within Everards' immediate trading area. But it has spread it wings and now embraces breweries in Buckinghamshire, Derbyshire and Oxfordshire. It reaches as far as Shropshire, with two pubs in Telford. One, the Old Fighting Cocks in Oakengates, was brought out of administration at a cost of £95,000. The second, the Pheasant in Wellington, had been closed for three years and re-opened in spring 2014 with 10 handpumps on the bar and the relocated Ironbridge Brewery – renamed Wrekin Brewing Co – at the back.

The success of Project William can be measured by the fact that real ale represents 65 per cent of beer sales in the pubs: an astonishing proportion.

Friends of the Fox

A further heart-warming story of a pub being saved for its community comes from Hebden Bridge in West Yorkshire. The Fox & Goose, which dates from 1702, looked set to close in 2012 when landlady Julia Warren was forced to retire as a result of ill health. She was determined the pub wouldn't end up in the hands of a pubco and asked her customers to help.

They formed a steering group, Friends of the Fox, chaired by a local councillor, Dave Young, and sought advice from such experts in saving community assets as the Plunkett Foundation and Co-ops UK. Hebden Bridge is a former mill town but is now an alternative, vibrant community with local artists, writers, poets and media people involved in the campaign to save the pub and gain media support.

Members of the group visited Britain's first co-operatively-owned pub, the Old Crown in Hesket Newmarket, Cumbria, to learn from that experience. As a result, Friends of the Fox became a co-operative and eventually the shareholders raised £130,000, sufficient to buy the pub and pay for its refurbishment.

It re-opened in March 2014 and is trading briskly. Customers paraded through the streets and were 'danced in' by an all-woman Morris group. The Fox sells cask beers from breweries on both sides of the Pennines and even though it has neither draught lager nor keg beer it's attracting an enthusiastic young crowd.

Pub of the Year

Lancashire pub the best in Britain

A pub where the landlord speaks to his casks shows such commitment to good beer that it was named CAMRA's National Pub of the Year for 2014.

Steve Dilworth of the Swan with Two Necks in Pendleton says 'real ale is a living thing – like a butterfly, it enjoys only a short life span and needs careful care and attention'.

Steve and his wife Christine have run the pub for 27 years. It's called a 'hidden gem', in a delightful village with a stream running through it and surrounded by green fields. It stands at the heart of a rural community and, as well as offering a splendid range of beers from local breweries, serves generous portions of home-made food for locals and walkers.

Steve has been in the pub trade for 42 years. He learned bar and cellar skills in a Wadworth pub in Oxfordshire where the ale was stored in wooden casks. When the Dilworths took over the Swan it was a Whitbread pub and has changed hands several times since. But it's now a free house and Steve and Christine can support breweries of their choice. The regular beer on the bar is Golden Pippin from Copper Dragon and other breweries often found in the pub include Dark Star, Phoenix and Salamander.

In order to win the competition, the Swan with Two Necks had to win its local competition and battle through regional heats in order to go forward as one of four finalists. The entire process takes a full 12 months and hundreds of CAMRA volunteers act as judges.

Steve Dilworth said: 'Talking to the beer barrels has finally paid off! We're delighted to have been judged CAMRA's National Pub of the year. The Swan is a hidden gem and the award is a fantastic achievement not only for us but also for our dedicated staff – and it's a great boost for our community.'

CAMRA's National Pub of the Year competition analyses all the criteria that make up a good pub. The competition is judged by the Campaign's 165,000-plus members. Each branch selects its top pub. The branch winners are entered into 16 regional competitions, with the regional winners battling it out to reach the final stages of the competition. Look out for the 🏆 symbol against pub entries in the Guide and see 'Award winning pubs' on pages 965-966 for the winning branch pubs.

The three other finalists in the 2014 competition were:

Hope, Carshalton, Greater London (see p307)
The pub is owned by members of the local community and was CAMRA Greater London Pub of the Year in 2012 and local Pub of the Year in 2013. The pub holds regular community events and themed festivals and seven handpumps serve beers from smaller breweries.

Horse & Jockey, Stapleford, Nottinghamshire (see p382)
A carefully refurbished traditional ale house in the centre of town, known to locals simply as 'the Jockey', it serves 10 ever-changing cask beers along with traditional cider. Conversation flows, as the pub has no TVs, pool tables or fruit machines. It has its own house beer, brewed by nearby Full Mash brewery.

Old Spot, Dursley, Gloucestershire (see p174)
An award-winning free house dating from 1776. It's named after the local Old Spot pig and there's a porcine theme running through the pub. It's on the Cotswold Way and offers good home-cooked meals as well as a wide range of local ales, including Uley Brewery's Old Ric, which pays homage to a former landlord.

Beer Destinations

North, south, east and west... beer is best. In the early years of the *Good Beer Guide*, many parts of Britain were dubbed 'beer deserts' by CAMRA as real ale was in such short supply. But a thousand and more breweries have sprung up to water the deserts and choice is ensured wherever you travel. The Guide has chosen four cities where the grip of big brewers has been replaced by flourishing independent producers who offer choice in abundance.

ABERDEEN
LINCOLN
CARDIFF
BRISTOL

Aberdeen

The nickname 'Granite City' suggests a hard and forbidding place but Aberdeen's grey buildings, so different to those in most other Scottish towns and cities, have a certain elegance. Union Street, the main thoroughfare, is an architectural masterpiece, raised up and carried on a series of arches above the street below. The city's main industry today is oil but it's a place of culture, too, with two universities and annual literary and arts festivals. On the sporting front, Aberdeen Football Club is a major team in the Scottish Premiership while visitors from south of the border may be surprised and pleased to learn that the area has 25 cricket clubs that play in two leagues.

'The growth of new breweries in the surrounding area has enhanced its rich and varied pub scene'

Terry Lock, former chairman of the European Beer Consumers' Union

Aberdeen, like the rest of Scotland, was once in the sway of two brewing giants, Scottish & Newcastle and Tennent Caledonian. S&N is now a subsidiary of Heineken, which owns Caledonian brewery and the flagship Deuchars IPA, while Tennents, formerly Bass-owned, is part of the Irish Magners cider group and concentrates on lager production. Nowadays Aberdeen offers a good choice of beer from Scottish artisan breweries from as far south as Edinburgh, with new arrivals closer to home in the shape of Six° North in Stonehaven, Speyside Craft in Forres and the appropriately named Windswept in Lossiemouth. Among pubs to seek out, the **Brentwood Hotel's** basement bar, at 101 Crown Street, was a lone outpost for cask beer in the dog days of Scottish brewing. Not surprisingly, it has won many CAMRA awards for flying the real ale flag and today offers, alongside the ubiquitous Deuchars IPA, eight beers from a good number of smaller Scottish independents, including Houston, Highland and Kelburn. It's an elegant bar with comfortable couches and good food is available both in the bar and the main restaurant.

In sharp contrast to the mirrored elegance of the Brentwood, **Six Degrees North** in Littlejohn Street is a stripped-down, modern bar with granite walls, bare-boarded floor and wooden benches. It serves beers from the Stonehaven brewery that runs the pub, with a range of their craft cask ales and a large selection of both draught and bottled Belgian beers. Six Degrees North is a welcome newcomer to the Aberdeen drinking scene.

Two Wetherspoon's outlets offer contrasting styles if not beers. **Justice Mill** on Union Street is a Lloyd's No 1 with some quieter seating areas, including family facilities, away from the main bar and a range of guest beers to supplement the usual fare of Deuchars IPA and Greene King Abbot. Watch out for two unusual artefacts: the statue of an upside-down man and a fire behind glass.

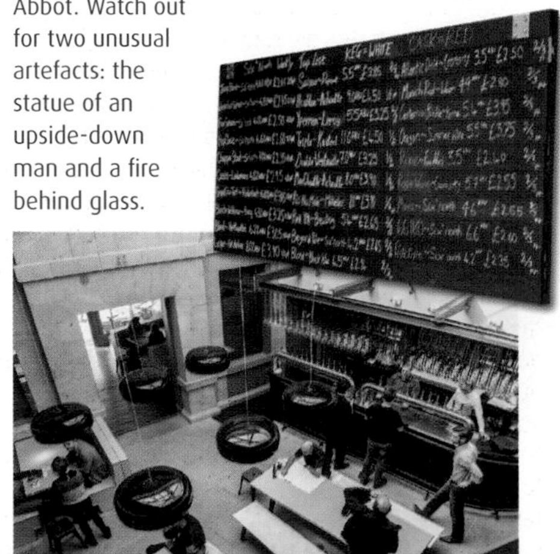

Six Degrees North has a modern feel

Archibald Simpson is a former bank

Archibald Simpson on Castle Street is named after the celebrated local architect and is based in the granite, high-ceilinged splendour of a former Clydesdale Bank. Twelve handpumps serve the stock Wetherspoon's ales along with a good range of beers from Scottish micros, including two specially brewed for the pub.

For a taste of old Aberdeen, visit the **Prince of Wales** in St Nicholas Lane, one of Scotland's True Heritage Pubs, with an impressive long bar counter dispensing a wide range of beers from both Scottish and English independent breweries and a house beer from Inveralmond. There are regular live folk nights and good-value food is served until 9pm.

Under the Hammer is the tongue-in-cheek name for a basement bar next to the city's auction rooms on North Silver Street, close to Union Street. It's a handy place for a beer before or after visiting the local Music Hall and His Majesty's Theatre and work by local artists is on display in the pub. Inveralmond Ossian accompanies Deuchars on the bar with a rolling list of guest beers from Scottish micros.

For more Aberdeen pubs see pages 612-613.

Bristol

Bristol is a major city, the sixth biggest in England, with a long history as a commercial centre based on its port and access to overseas markets. It also has a long association with brewing, with beer made both for the local population and for export. In the 18th century, Bristol became second only to London as a producer of porter, the dark beer style, the production of which created a commercial industry in order to keep pace with the insatiable demand for it from both industrial and agricultural workers. A Bristol porter brewery opened in the 1730s and was bought in 1788 by Philip George. Based on a three-acre site in the harbour area, George's was in a strong position to export its beers. It was always busy in the takeover market, acquiring a number of other breweries in the area until by the 20th century it owned 900 pubs. It became tempting bait for bigger brewers and in 1961 it was bought by the London-based Courage group. When Courage closed its London brewery, Bristol produced the legendary Courage Best and early editions of the *Good Beer Guide* listed pubs that predominantly sold Courage beers. But in 1991 Courage itself was taken over by Scottish & Newcastle, which closed the Bristol brewery four years later.

Tragic though the loss of such a historic brewery was, it did break the log-jam. New breweries started to emerge and today Bristol's pubs are well served by half-a-dozen local breweries, including the expanding Bath Ales and the award-winning Bristol Beer Factory.

Bristol's main business activities today are media and aerospace. It has a number of theatres, including the Old Vic and Theatre Royal and is famous for its associations with the indefatigable 19th century engineer Isambard Kingdom Brunel. He built the world-famous Clifton Suspension Bridge over the Avon Gorge, the Great Western railway line from London, and the *SS Great Britain*, a sailing ship with an iron hull that was for a time the longest ship in the world. It has been restored and is now a museum open to the public.

On the sporting front, Bristol has two football clubs, City and Rovers, a top Rugby Union team and is the headquarters of Gloucestershire County Cricket.

In a city bursting with pubs, a new entrant takes centre stage. The **Tobacco Factory Cafe Bar** in Raleigh Road, Bedminster, recalls one of Bristol's major but now lost industries and is also the home of the Bristol Beer Factory brewery. Its beers grace the bar in a modern building of bare-brick walls and metal pillars. Guest beers are also available, the food, including meze and tapas, is excellent and there is regular live music.

Close to Temple Meads, the **Cornubia** in Temple Street has long been a real ale institution. It's a small, narrow pub decorated with memorabilia, heated by open fires, with 10 handpumps serving an ever-changing range of beers from far and wide, ranging from gold to dark. Real cider is also served and live blues often features. The **Colston Yard** in Colston Street marks Butcombe brewery's entry into Bristol. It's based in the former Smiles brewery and it serves a good range of guest beers alongside the Butcombe range, as well as a wide selection of imported beers. Restaurant-standard meals are served.

Young's Highbury Vaults

The **Highbury Vaults**, St Michael's Hill, Kingsdown, is a rare West Country outlet for the London pub company Young's. As well as Young's, there are beers from the likes of Bath Ales and St Austell. With dark wood walls and dim lighting, it's an intimate pub popular with students and doctors from the nearby university and hospital. The pub achieved notoriety in 2008 when a mural appeared overnight on the outside wall, showing a graffiti artist climbing up Rapunzel's hair. It was thought at first to be an original Banksy but turned out to be the work of local artist Nick Walker.

The **Three Tuns** in St George's Road, Hotwells, is run by local Arbor Ales and as well as the brewery's own beers offers ales from many other small producers. The L-shaped pub has scrubbed tables, an outside patio and simple pub grub. Beer festivals are held twice a year and the Three Tuns' popularity is measured by the fact it was named local CAMRA Pub of the Year in 2012.

For more Bristol pubs see pages 168-172.

Cardiff

The Welsh capital was for many years dominated by just two breweries: the massive Hancock's plant near the railway station and the family-owned Brains. In the 1990 *Good Beer Guide* only three pubs out of a dozen entries for the city offered beers from other breweries, and one of those was Courage. Choice was severely limited. Hancock's was part of the Bass group and was renamed Welsh Brewers. When Bass left brewing in 2000 a game of brewery musical chairs followed, with Brains closing its own site and moving in to the Bass plant alongside the station. It remains in family hands and has added to its core range with a number of seasonal beers and one-off specials. It's one of the few large brewers in Britain to stay true to Dark Mild, a beery icon in the valleys. It owns 270 pubs in Wales and beyond and is a vigorous supporter of the local community, sponsoring rugby, football and cricket. Brains has been joined by new arrivals in the city and the country, giving drinkers the choice they were denied for decades.

Cardiff is the Welsh capital and seat of the National Assembly. Its vast wealth for centuries was built on coal, iron, steel and docks: Tiger Bay was once the biggest port in the world. With the decline of heavy industry, financial services and public administration are the major employers in the city. Tourism is a vital part of the economy: Cardiff is one of the most-visited cities in the UK and offers a cathedral and castle and the new Millennium Centre with a stadium that hosts both international rugby and football matches. Both sports are also played at Cardiff Arms Park while Glamorgan County Cricket Club's modern SWALEC Stadium in Sophia Gardens is host to Test and international matches.

Goat Major, handy for Cardiff Castle

At a cultural level, the Welsh National Opera is based in the capital, there are a number of theatres, including the New Theatre, and Cardiff is frequently host to the National Eisteddfod.

As Cardiff is a bilingual city, a review of some of the best pubs starts at **Mochyn Du** or the Black Pig. Based in Sophia Close, it's just a six hit from the cricket ground and is popular with sports fans and people enjoying the extensive gardens. There are many Welsh-themed events in the large, airy pub, which has spacious outside areas for good weather. The four house beers are brewed by Vale of Glamorgan, all with 'cwrw' in the name – the Welsh for ale. Other brewers often on tap include Bullmastiff, Tomos Watkin and Rhymney. Food – bar snacks and full meals – is of exceptional quality.

The **Andrew Buchan** in Albany Road, Roath, pays homage to the benefactor and manager of the Rhymney brewery in the 19th century, once the biggest brewery in South Wales. It had the misfortune to be taken over and closed by Whitbread in the 20th century. The current Rhymney brewery hangs a moosehead – the company logo – above the open fireplace. The full range of the brewery's beers, including Hobby Horse and Bevan's Bitter – is on tap.

The **City Arms** in Quay Street is a Brains house but with a vigorous guest beer policy that means drinkers can enjoy a wide range of ales. There's cider and

The City Arms serves a range of Brains beers

perry, too, and there are regular beer festivals and live music events. The **Goat Major** in the High Street is another Brains outlet handily placed opposite the entrance to the castle. It takes its names from the Keeper of the Goat, the mascot of the Royal Regiment of Wales. It's famous for its hearty, well-filled pies.

No visit to Cardiff pubs is complete without dropping in to the **Rummer Tavern** on Duke Street, also close to the castle. It's the oldest pub in the city and has wood-panelled walls and many snug areas. The beers include Wye Valley HPA and Hancock's HB: in the weird ways of big brewers, the Hancock's brands, formerly Bass, are now owned by Molson Coors in Burton upon Trent and brewed for the group by... Brains.

'Cardiff is up there with the best beer cities in the UK. Brains still runs many of the pubs but the selection of beers the brewery presents is so much greater today'
Jeff Evans, author of the Good Bottled Beer Guide

For more Cardiff pubs see pages 568-570.

Lincoln

A visit Lincoln in 2015 is timely as it's the 800th anniversary of the signing of Magna Carta in 1215, and one of the four original copies of the 'Great Charter' is held in Lincoln Castle and is on view to visitors. They can toast this historic occasion with a wide choice of beers in the city's pubs, many of them ancient and of historic interest.

Unlike the cities above, Lincoln never suffered from major brewery takeovers and closures but its pub trade for decades was based on beers produced by large outside breweries in Newark – where John Smith's of Tadcaster had a second plant – Nottingham and Sheffield. Batemans of Wainfleet has always had a presence in the county capital and it's been joined by many new arrivals in the region.

'One of the most picturesque yet vibrant cities in England, with pubs full of history and exciting beers'
Stuart Bateman, Batemans brewery

The city was a major Roman town that saw rapid growth during the Viking period when it became an important trading centre. The Norman castle was built in the 11th century and is close to the cathedral, which also dates from the same period. The majestic cathedral is famous for its towering twin spires while the great bulk of the castle is unusual in having two mottes or raised foundations. Lincoln's fortunes blossomed during the Industrial Revolution, with factories building ships, locomotives and later turbines. The first-ever tanks were built in the city during World War One. Today's economy is based on farming, public administration, information technology and tourism. On the sporting front, Lincoln City football club went into administration and was rescued by its fans: the club is now controlled by the supporters.

Visitors to Lincoln's pubs should be warned in advance of the city's steep hills. The **Adam & Eve Tavern** on Lindum Road, for example, requires a major clamber, but it's worth the effort to find this early 18th century alehouse with a plethora of seating areas and room for darts, meetings and musical events. The old tradition of beer coming from Nottingham survives here, but now it's the leading Castle Rock brewery. There are several guest beers on offer, too. Nearby, the **Jolly Brewer** on Broadgate has, for Lincoln, a surprising Art Deco design, with local artists' work displayed for sale. There are regular live music events while beer comes from a number of artisan brewers, including Tom Wood, and Welbeck Abbey.

The **Dog & Bone** on John Street and the **Golden Eagle** on High Street are both outlets for Batemans 'Good Honest Ales'. The Dog & Bone has an unusual design, with a central counter serving a large bar area and smaller lounge. There are regular live music events and quiz nights while customers can enjoy the full range of Wainfleet beers. The Golden Eagle is an old coaching inn with close connections to the football club, with old programmes and photos decorating the walls. There are occasional beer festivals and regular quiz nights. Batemans XB is joined by Castle Rock Harvest Pale and changing guest beers.

Be warned: the **Wig & Mitre** is on Steep Hill – and the street means what it says. It's close to the cathedral and castle and is in a building that dates from the 14th century. It has two floors, each with their own bars, and many head-cracking beams. It offers some of the best food in the city. Beers include Black Sheep, Everards and Oakham.

For more Lincoln pubs see pages 267-268.

Jolly Brewer: Art Deco design

CAMRA Beer Festivals

The Campaign For Real Ale's Beer Festivals are fizz-free and fun. They show cask beer in all its glory and underscore the brilliant choice now available to beer lovers. They are vital shop windows for independent breweries and turn the spotlight on great beers from different parts of the country that may be hard-to-find in the areas where festivals are based. Some festivals specialise in particular styles, such as winter beers or golden ales for summer. And most of them also offer cider and perry, along with food, live music and family entertainment.

Festivals range from such national events as the Great British Beer Festival (GBBF) in London Olympia in August and the National Winter Ales Festival in February, through large festivals in Bristol, Cambridge, Cardiff, Derby, Edinburgh, Leeds, Norwich and Peterborough to smaller ones in cities, towns and even villages. There are more than 200 festivals held every year and they stress that Britain today is awash with good ales, ranging from pale and gold to ruby and black in colour.

Festivals are run entirely by volunteers and an enormous commitment is needed. It's not a question of just putting up the beer casks and opening the doors to the public. Real ale is a living, breathing product and it needs careful handling and time to 'drop bright' before it's ready to serve.

Gantries and stillages have to be built to hold the beer casks. Food has to be booked from local suppliers, bands and other entertainers signed up. Security has to be planned. And once the event is over, the whole operation has to be taken down, with casks returned to breweries and metal structures taken back to suppliers.

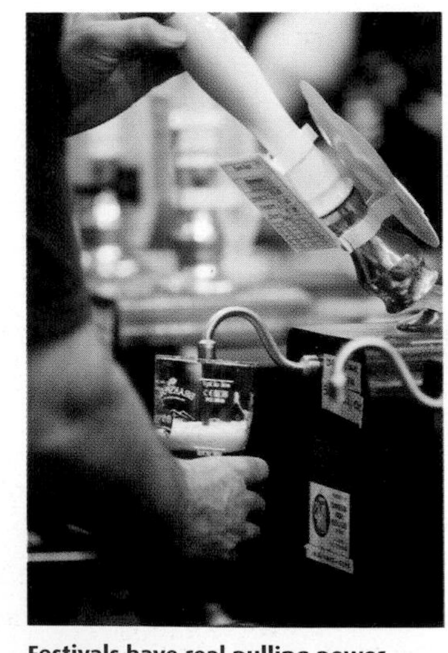
Festivals have real pulling power

Before the Great British Beer Festival, CAMRA's biggest event, volunteers are on site for the best part of a week, building the gantries, planning the stands and bringing in cooling equipment so beer is sold in the best possible condition. And when the week-long celebration is over, the volunteers' work isn't finished: they have to work flat out to clear Olympia so the next event can move in. Many of the volunteers donate their annual holidays to working at the festival.

FEST FACTS

One thousand CAMRA volunteers work at the Great British Beer Festival. In 2012, only one event had more volunteers than GBBF – the London Olympics.

Around 600,000 people attend CAMRA beer festivals every year. Approximately a quarter of those are members of the Campaign.

Bitter and best bitter remain the most popular beer styles, accounting for between 50 to 60% of sales.

Festivals are planned months in advance. Most are run by committees, made up of volunteers with expertise in such matters as ordering beer, food and entertainment, and arranging security. CAMRA members who work in the media or public relations have an important role to play, contacting the local media and writing and producing press releases and festival programmes. Trained professionals are needed to build the gantries that hold the heavy metal beer casks: the gantries have to be approved by Health & Safety officers: a collapsed gantry would be a disaster for both the beer and those working behind the bars.

Beer supplies are, of course, vital. Festival organisers will draw up a list of local and national breweries they want to invite to supply beer and will work out which can be picked up or booked through wholesalers. CAMRA

Broad appeal... festivals reach out to a wide spectrum of drinkers

members' cars and vans are called into play to help with deliveries. Once the beer has arrived on site, casks have to be hoisted into position and then 'tapped and spiled' to allow the beer to breathe and become clear as yeast and sediment settle. Most beer at festivals is drawn straight from casks, but if beer is served by handpumps, lines will have to be attached to the casks and the beer engines connected to the pumps. Beer has to be served cool – warm beer is strictly off-limits – and great attention is given to temperatures in the halls where festivals are staged. If air conditioning is not available, chiller units will have to be hired. Special 'in-cask' cooling devices can be inserted in to casks: they circulate cold water through tubes.

FEST FACTS

More than 320,000 glasses are bought at festivals every year and 50% of visitors take their glasses home with them.

Beer festivals are a major contributor to the economy with £3.5 million spent buying beer and cider from producers.

A showcase for beer and the Campaign

The way in which beer festivals can dramatically increase choice for drinkers is shown by the St Albans festival in Hertfordshire. When the local CAMRA branch suggested running a festival in the mid-1990s, critics said it wouldn't attract support as St Albans has the greatest number of pubs per square mile of any town or city in the country. But choice was restricted, with many of the 50-plus pubs owned by either Allied Breweries or Whitbread, with a handful run by local family brewer McMullen and few free houses.

CAMRA ignored the doomsayers and went ahead with its first modest festival in 1996. Today, while St Albans is a small market town, the annual festival is a major one on the festival circuit. In 2013, more than 10,000 people attended and drank 432 firkins (nine-gallon casks) of beer from 350 different breweries. There were also 50 ciders, 70 foreign beers and 30 bottle-conditioned ales.

Organiser John Bishop says that as well as offering a fine choice to drinkers, the festival acts as an important recruiter for the Campaign. It also gains a lot of media attention, not just through local radio, TV and newspapers but from national broadcasters. TV chef and food writer Sophie Grigson has filmed at the festival, as well as contestants from BBC's *The Apprentice*.

St Albans still has 50 pubs but real ale choice has blossomed. The big brewers have disappeared, McMullen is still prominent, and many pubs are now free houses or run by smaller pub companies offering a wide range of beers from smaller breweries.

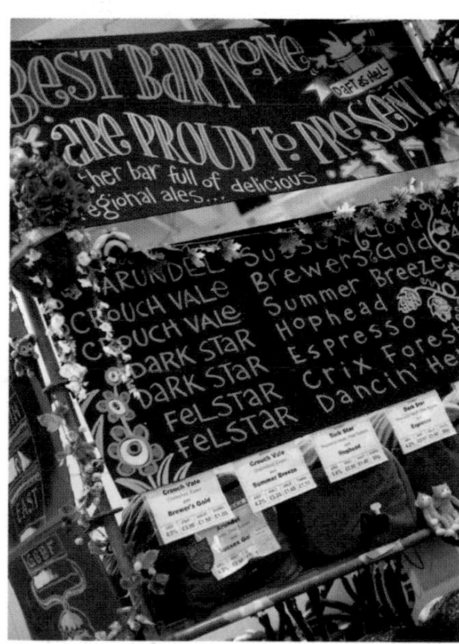

Festivals showcase a huge range of beers from around the country

CAMRA's beer festivals through the year

JANUARY
Atherton – Bent & Bongs Beer Bash
Cambridge – Winter
Colchester – Winter
Exeter – Winter
Manchester
Salisbury – Winter

FEBRUARY
Derby – National Winter Ales
Chappel – Winter
Chelmsford – Winter
Chesterfield
Darlington – Spring
Dorchester
Dover – White Cliffs Winter
Ely – Winter
Fleetwood
Gosport – Winter
Hucknall
Jersey – Winter
Liverpool
Luton
Pendle
Redditch
Stockton – Ale & Arty
Tewkesbury – Winter

MARCH
Bradford
Bristol
Bromley
Burton
Hove – Sussex
Leeds
Leicester
London Drinker
Loughborough
St Neots – Booze on the Ouse
Thanet
Walsall
Wigan
Winchester

APRIL
Barnsley
Bath
Bolton
Bury St Edmunds – East Anglian
Chippenham
Coventry
Doncaster
Farnham
Glenrothes – Kingdom of Fife
Gloucester
Hull
Isle of Man
Larbert – Falkirk
Maldon
Mansfield
New Mills
Newcastle upon Tyne
Oldham
Paisley
Stourbridge

MAY
Aberdeen
Banbury
Bexley
Cambridge
Clitheroe
Colchester
Dewsbury
Halifax
Kidderminster
Kingston
Lincoln
Macclesfield
Newark
Newport (Gwent)
Reading
Skipton
Stockport
Yapton
Yaxley – Mid Anglia

JUNE
Braintree
Bromsgrove
Cardiff – Great Welsh
Greater Manchester Cider & Perry Festival
Harlow – Gibberd Garden
Hitchin
Lewes – South Downs
Rugby
Salisbury
St Ives (Cornwall)
Southampton
Stratford-upon-Avon
Stowmarket
Tenterden – Kent & East Sussex Railway
Thurrock
Wolverhampton

JULY
Ardingly
Bishops Stortford
Canterbury – Kent
Chelmsford
Chorlton
Derby
Devizes
Ealing
Edinburgh – Scottish
Hereford – Beer on the Wye
Maidenhead
Plymouth
Winchcombe – Cotswold
Woodcote – Steam Fair
Wyke Regis –Wykefest

AUGUST
London – Great British
Clacton-on-Sea
Crewe – Rail Ale
Darlington
Grantham
Harbury
Manchester Velodrome
Morecambe
Peterborough
Stafford
Swansea
Worcester

SEPTEMBER
Belper – Amber Valley
Bridgnorth – Severn Valley
Bromley
Burnley
Cannock
Carmarthen
Chappel
Cockermouth – Taste Cumbria (Jennings)
Durham
East Malling (Kent)
Faversham – Hop
Hinckley
Jersey
Keighley
Lytham
Melton Mowbray
Minehead (West Somerset Railway)

Moreton-in Marsh – North Cotswolds
Portsmouth
St Albans
St Helens
Scunthorpe
Tamworth
Ulverston
Witham
York

OCTOBER
Alloa
Ascot
Barnsley
Basingstoke – Hampshire Octoberfest
Bedford
Birkenhead
Birmingham
Cambridge – Octoberfest
Carlisle
Chester
Chesterfield – Market
Croydon & Sutton – Wallington
Eastbourne
Egremont (Cumbria)
Falmouth
Gainsborough
Huddersfield – Oktoberfest
Kendal – Westmorland
Louth
Milton Keynes
Norwich
Nottingham
Oxford
Redhill
Richmond (North Yorkshire)
Sheffield
Solihull
South Woodham Ferrers
Southport
Spa Valley Railway (West Kent)
St Ives (Cambs) – Booze on the Ouse
Stoke-on-Trent – Potteries
Sunderland
Swindon
Troon – Ayrshire
Twickenham
Weymouth
Woolston – Southampton
Worthing

NOVEMBER
Belfast
Dudley
Heathrow
Poole
Rochford
Saltburn
Shrewsbury
Wakefield
Wantage
Watford
Woking

DECEMBER
Harwich & Dovercourt Bay
London – Pig's Ear

Let There Be Beer

Brewers have come together to celebrate the diversity of beer

We hardly need to tell you that beer is having a moment. By virtue of picking up this Guide you know that beer is currently being propelled from the ground up by the craft beer revival, both here and in the US. Beers of all styles are on the tip of our tongues literally and figuratively, as a growing numbers of breweries and beers spring up around us.

Innovation is in the air, and it seems that everyone is finally catching on to what we've always known – beer is great. Put simply, there's never been a more exciting time to be a British beer lover.

However, in some parts of the UK beer isn't seen to be the diverse and versatile drink we know it to be, or the first choice for discerning drinker of either gender. Old stereotypes hold us back, but we feel it's time for the world to understand that beer is just as interesting, varied and nuanced as wine.

Spreading the message

It's for this reason that last June the UK's largest brewers came together for the first time for the good of beer lovers everywhere. **Let There Be Beer** was born, and since then we've run glossy TV adverts, sponsored cooking programmes, got local landlords to interview celebrities like footballer Ian Wright and DJ Jo Whiley, had Channel 4's Tim Lovejoy create tantalising beer and food pairings, and amassed over 130,000 Facebook fans along the way.

In doing these things we've heard from beer aficionados up and down the country. We love nothing more than hearing that one of our recommendations has hit the spot, or that someone has discovered their new favourite brew because of us.

We've also listened to our community and the industry, and we've used this feedback as the foundation of a new campaign we've been working on over the summer. By the time you read this we will be putting the finishing touches to the campaign and preparing to launch. At the time of writing this, we've got a lot of Big Plans!

So, what *can* we tell you?

We can tell you that at the heart of our plans is the idea that there's more to beer – more to its flavour and taste, more to the styles, more to how it's made and more to the occasions that beer works so well with. Beer has got depth, character and a rich story behind it that deserves to be understood and enjoyed by more people.

It's also about variety and discovery. We want the UK to appreciate the full spectrum of beers, from Pilsners and pale ales to stouts and lambics.

But in celebrating the diversity of beer we don't want to overwhelm, which is why a key part of our plan is to educate and empower. We want to give everyone the tools to go on their own journey through the wonderful world of beer.

We also want to give those who are currently occasional beer drinkers the knowledge and confidence to ask questions. What's in my beer? Who made it, and where? What will it taste like? What would you recommend? What food will it go well with?

Ultimately, we want to get more people talking about and appreciating beer in all its forms. We want to re-ignite Britain's love of beer. It's because we're the first cross-industry group that **Let There Be Beer** really can be the champion of all beer, helping new and existing beer-lovers alike discover just how much more there is to beer. We couldn't do this without the support of many of the groups you already know and love – CAMRA, SIBA, Cask Marque and the British Beer and Pub Association, to name a few.

If you like the sound of what we're up to, then come and join us on Facebook or Twitter, and visit our website **lettherebebeer.com**. We'll be running regular competitions, including Hops and Dreams... a chance to win funding for your very own innovative beery project. Be it reviving a recipe from days gone by, setting up a new event for the beer lover's calendar or creating a beer gadget you're convinced the world needs, if you've been sitting on an idea the beer community would benefit from, now's your chance! Join us on Facebook to be the first to know when we launch this.

So, here's to beer! Here's to reaffirming an age-old British tradition at the heart of modern life. In some ways it feels like nothing's changed – but in others, the future looks incredibly new and exciting.

What's your favourite beer...?

...Dark and smoky or golden and grapefruity? Treacle, coffee, zesty grapefruit, biscuit, liquorice and marmalade are just some of the terms used by **Cyclops Beer** tasting notes to describe British beer.

Currently, there are over 1,800 beers that have been accredited by Cyclops Beer, including many of the beers in the *Good Beer Guide*, and the number is growing all the time. Cyclops provides beer tasting notes which are easy to understand, using symbols and simple descriptions so that you can see how a beer will look, smell and taste, and how bitter or sweet it is.

We also categorise beer by style, colour and ABV and include, where possible, details of the primary hops and malts used in each beer. This means that for many of the beers that you enjoy you will be able to see at a glance which hops and malted barley are used as part of the unique recipe for each one. You can also find out how a beer is dispensed, for example whether it is available in cask or is bottle conditioned.

The brewers send us samples of their beer to analyse and, working in our laboratory, our technicians run tests on each beer measuring its sweetness and bitterness, and taste each beer before putting together the descriptions for **www.cyclopsbeer.co.uk** and for the brewers to use on pump clips, on bottles and online. Each beer, therefore, has been independently tested and tasted by a third party so that you can rely on the notes that you see.

Cyclops® Beer
Discover your beer sense

Find out more by visiting **www.cyclopsbeer.co.uk** and search for the beers that you enjoy and find others which have a similar taste profile. Why not register and then rate your favourite beers? You can build up a list of beers that you have rated and discover more about your favourite tastes and flavours. Our Genius function will then recommend others that you may enjoy based on chosen beers. Once registered you can also gain badges based on your taste preferences or location such as the Happy Hopper or the Londoner.

The CaskFinder App is a free beer app for iPhone and Android that contains Cyclops Beer tasting notes. You can search for a beer, read the description and then find where to drink it. Armed with your *Good Beer Guide* and with access to **Cyclops Beer**, it's never been easier to enjoy real ales around the British Isles.

With so much choice for beer drinkers – especially with real ale – Cyclops Beer descriptions help consumers identify flavours they like and decide what to try next from the bar...

All About Beer

Real ale is the beer of the moment

The buzzword in the world of beer at the moment is craft. It's not a term that troubles the *Good Beer Guide* as it's committed – and has been for more than 40 years – to the finest-quality beer made from the best natural ingredients. Craft beer is a style of beer made by brewers who are by definition craftsmen and women.

But the word has become a catch-all. Large and even global brewers claim today to make craft beer. And a for a small number of brewers, the term means 'anything but real ale' in the mistaken belief that younger drinkers don't want to touch anything that comes out of a handpump and a cask.

The problem with 'craft beer' is that it has no industry definition. CAMRA's annual conference has agreed that 'while real ale is craft beer, not all craft beer is real ale' – an attitude that reaches out to all artisan brewers. The Campaign appreciates that not all outlets for beer are suitable for storing and serving cask-conditioned beer – though the problems can be exaggerated – and there is room in the market for new types of beer called 'craft keg'.

Modern keg beers have little in common with the risible beers of the 1960s and 70s, such as Red Barrel and Double Diamond, which gave rise to CAMRA's consumer backlash. Modern keg beers are filtered but not always pasteurised and, while served colder than real ale, are not heavily carbonated. In effect, they are identical to the draught beers produced by thousands of independent breweries in the United States. Several new beer festivals in Britain offer a range of craft keg beers but not exclusively so: some offer cask ale as well. Any events that bring people – especially those who have only recently reached legal drinking age – into the beer category are to be welcomed.

But in spite of the sound and fury generated by one or two craft keg brewers, it's important to keep its support in proportion. It's a small niche and the big success story of recent years is cask-conditioned real ale.

The *Good Beer Guide* remains committed to real ale not because we're hidebound but because we believe it's a beer style that's not only rooted in Britain's heritage and traditions but one that also offers the finest drinking experience for pubgoers. It's not a beer of the past but the beer of the moment.

Real ale reaches out to drinkers who seek beers made naturally from the finest ingredients. It's possible to make something called 'beer' with rice, maize and corn syrup, and flavoured with green juice squeezed from pulverised hops. But cask beer brewers prefer to use the finest malting barley along with hops left in their natural state. Real ale brewers may blend in darker malts and other grains, such as wheat or oats.

Consumers are increasingly concerned by the way food and drink are made. They don't want products that are shipped half-way round the world and are stuffed with preservatives to keep them in edible or drinkable condition. Neither are they impressed by dubious advertising that masks the fact that a 'Belgian' lager is brewed in Wales and 'Australian' and 'French' ones are manufactured in Manchester. The wine term 'terroir' has entered the beer world as drinkers seek confirmation that their beers are made locally from ingredients grown by farmers who use the finest forms of husbandry.

Thanks to the work of such companies as Warminster Maltings in Wiltshire and Branthill Farm in Norfolk, it's now possible to trace where barley is grown, down to the precise fields where it's harvested. Hop growers are developing new varieties that require fewer agri-chemicals.

As pub entry after pub entry in this Guide proves, publicans are opting for a good range of local cask beers. Their efforts are underscored by CAMRA's LocAle scheme that encourages publicans to source some of their beers from breweries within a 30-mile radius and reduce carbon footprints as a result. For more information on the scheme see **www.camra.org.uk/locale**.

The finished product is a beer that's neither filtered nor pasteurised and is pulled to the pub bar without the use of applied gas pressure. In all its forms – from the palest pale ale to the blackest stout – it's the perfection of beer.

How beer is brewed

Beer is the world's most complex alcoholic drink. Wine and cider are made from fruit juice. Flavourings are added late in the process to gin and some forms of vodka. Only beer has two contrasting raw materials that form its backbone: malted grain and hops. Add into the mix the purest water and carefully selected yeast strains and you have a drink of enormous depth and character.

Whether it's a summer refresher or a vintage ale designed for sipping, it deserves both respect and an understanding of the skill of the master brewers who make it. And those master brewers are restless people, constantly seeking out new recipes and new ingredients as well as digging deep into ancient logbooks to recreate great styles from the past. Today you will find beers made with the addition of fruits, herbs, chocolate, coffee, ginger, lemon grass, pumpkin, coriander and – tread carefully – chilli peppers.

Barley is beer's building block. Other grain can be used and many brewers blend in small amounts of wheat or oats and even rye, but barley is the preferred grain because it works in perfect harmony with hops and yeast.

But beer can't be made from barley. It has first to be turned into malt before the journey that creates beer can begin. Once it's harvested, barley is taken to specialist maltsters who thoroughly clean the grain, steeps it in water to absorb moisture, then spread it on heated floors or inside rotating drums where it starts to germinate.

Once germination is under way, with rootlets breaking through the husk, the grain is transferred to an oven known as a kiln. Heat dries the grain and, depending on the temperature, produces pale or darker malts.

All beer, regardless of colour, is made mainly from pale malt as it has the highest level of enzymes – natural chemical catalysts – that are crucial to the brewing process. Higher temperatures produce brown, black and chocolate malts used for colour and flavour in darker beers. Roasted barley, which is not malted, is often featured in stouts while a method similar to toffee making produces specialist crystal and caramalts for colour and flavour. Depending on the mix of malts, the grain will give aromas and flavours similar to Horlicks, Ovaltine, oatmeal biscuits, Ryvita, almonds and other nuts, honey, butterscotch, caramel, tobacco and vanilla.

MALT FLAVOURS

almonds, butterscotch, caramel, honey, Horlicks, nuts, Ovaltine, oatmeal biscuits, Ryvita, tobacco, vanilla

Pale malt that emerges from the kiln looks almost identical to barley but it has undergone an amazing transformation, with starch starting to turn into the sugar that is essential for fermentation.

The annual harvest has also produced beer's other key ingredient: hops. In common with grain, hops need good soil, in this case loamy or sandy soils that retain a good supply of water. Kent, Herefordshire and Worcestershire are the main hop-growing counties of England. Hops grow at great speed in the spring and summer and once harvested they are dried by warm air in special sheds or oast houses.

The brewing process

When malt reaches the brewery it's screened to clean it then ground in a mill into a powder called grist. Grist and pure hot water flow into the mash tun, where the porridge-like mixture of grain and water starts the process of being turned into beer. Pure water, called 'liquor' by brewers, can come from springs, bore holes or from the public supply. It will be thoroughly filtered, and brewers often add such sulphates as gypsum and magnesium to enhance the flavours of malt and hops. The mixture is left to stand in the mash tun for some two hours and during that time enzymes in the malt convert the remaining starch into fermentable sugar.

When starch conversion is complete, the brewer and his team will run the sweet extract, called wort, from the slotted base of the tun. The wort is pumped to a second vessel, the copper, where it's vigorously boiled with hops. The hops are usually added in stages: at the start of the boil, half way through and just before the end in order to extract the maximum combination of aroma and bitterness from the plants.

Adding hops for aroma and bitterness

The copper boil lasts between 1½ and two

hours. The hopped wort is passed through a cooler to lower the temperature and is then pumped to fermenting vessels. These can be open or closed, upright or horizontal, but it's here that the liquid starts the conversion to alcohol with the aid of yeast. Yeast is a type of fungus that feeds on sugary liquids. Every brewery will have its own yeast culture that's carefully guarded and stored, as it gives its own important 'house character' to the beer.

YEAST FLAVOURS
apples, banana, fresh leather, liquorice, molasses, oranges, pear drops

Ale fermentation is rapid and lasts for a week – it's a method known as 'warm fermentation' to distinguish it from the cold fermentation method used to make genuine lager. Yeast converts malt sugar into alcohol and carbon dioxide and creates a dense, rocky blanket on top of the liquid. It also produces natural chemical compounds called esters that give off aromas reminiscent of apples, oranges, pear drops, banana, liquorice, molasses and, in especially strong beers, fresh leather. These add to the complexity of the finished beer.

Eventually the yeast will be overcome by the alcohol it has created and the yeast blanket is skimmed from the vessel. The brewer measures the density of the 'green' or unfinished beer with a hydrometer to ensure the transformation of sugar to alcohol is complete: depending on the style of beer being produced, fermentation may be stopped earlier to leave some sugar in the beer to avoid it tasting too dry or astringent. The beer will rest for several days in conditioning tanks to mature and to purge unwanted rough alcohols and esters.

Then comes the major divide in the world of brewing. One route leads to filtered, pasteurised and carbonated beer. The other creates Britain's great contribution to the world of beer: cask-conditioned ale. Cask ale is unique as it's not finished in the brewery but in the pub cellar. From conditioning tanks, it's racked into casks. Finings, a natural clarifying agent, is added to encourage the beer to settle. Additional hops may also be placed in the casks for extra aroma and flavour and brewing sugar may also be added to encourage a strong secondary fermentation.

The beer that reaches the pub cellar is said to be 'still working' as remaining yeast turns the final sugars into alcohol and CO_2. Casks, set up on a cradle known as the stillage, have to be vented to allow the natural gas to escape. A cask has two openings: a bung at the flat end where a tap is inserted to serve the beer; and a shive hole on top. A soft porous peg of wood, a spile, is knocked into the shive, enabling some of the CO_2 to escape. As fermentation dies down, the soft spile is replaced after 24 hours by a hard one that leaves some gas in the cask: this gives the beer its natural sparkle, known as 'condition'.

Inside the cask the isinglass sinks to the floor, attracting yeast in solution. The publican will draw off small samples of the beer and when he or she is satisfied it has 'dropped bright', plastic tubes or 'lines' are attached to the tap and the beer is drawn by a suction pump activated by a handpump on the bar. The recommended serving temperature for real ale is 11 or 12 degrees C. Some golden summer beers are served between 8 and 10 degrees and they may go through a special cooler below the bar.

Hops & bitterness

Hops contain acids, oils and resins that deliver bitterness to beer along with fragrant aromas of spice, pepper, grass, cedar wood and citrus fruit. The oils and tannins in the plant help stabilise beer and prevent infection. Brewers often declare the 'units of bitterness' – measured as IBUs or EBUs (International or European Bitterness Units) – as a useful guide to their drinks. A mild ale will have IBUs in the low 20s, Bitter between 30 and 40 and a genuine IPA as much as 80 units.

HOP FLAVOURS
citrus, grapefruit, mango, pepper, spice, tropical fruits

English hops are prized for their spice and pepper notes. Fuggles and Goldings are the best known traditional varieties but new hops have been introduced in recent years, including First Gold, Boadicea and Endeavour: the last named is a cross between an English variety and the American Cascade and has a fine citrus character. American and New Zealand varieties, widely used by artisan brewers in Britain, give profound aromas and flavours of grapefruit, mango and tropical fruits.

Types of malt

All beer, regardless of colour, is made predominantly from pale malt. Other types of malt include crystal, which adds a nutty or toffee note, and such dark malts as black and chocolate that give notes of coffee, chocolate, burnt fruit and tobacco. Roasted barley is often used in porters and stouts. The finest malting barley is widely considered to be Maris Otter: though it's a 'low yielding' variety compared to more modern varieties, it's famous for the delicate biscuit note it gives to beer. But new varieties are now in great demand and include the appropriately named Tipple while Concerto allows brewers to play harmonious tunes in their mash tuns.

THE BREWING PROCESS

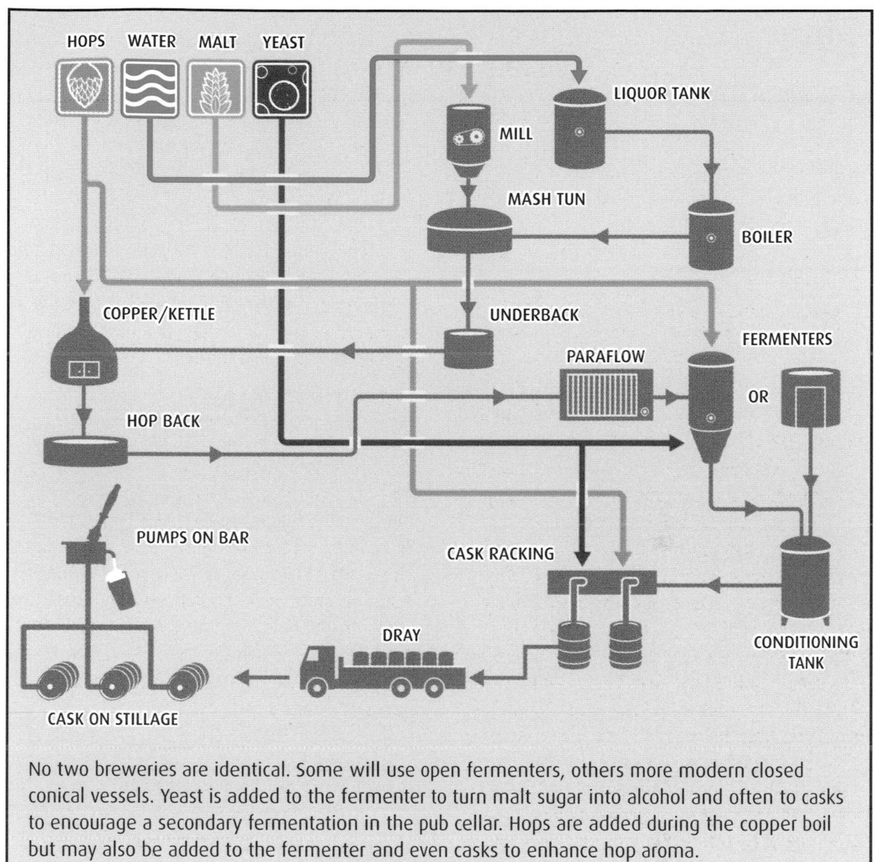

No two breweries are identical. Some will use open fermenters, others more modern closed conical vessels. Yeast is added to the fermenter to turn malt sugar into alcohol and often to casks to encourage a secondary fermentation in the pub cellar. Hops are added during the copper boil but may also be added to the fermenter and even casks to enhance hop aroma.

Beer is made from just four key ingredients:

1 HOPS: There are around two dozen hop varieties in England, ranging from the Golding and the Fuggle, first grown in the 18th and 19th centuries, to more modern ones, such as Boadicea and Endeavour. Hops can be used in the brewery either as whole flowers or ground and compressed into pellets.

2 WATER: Pure water, called 'liquor' by brewers, can come from springs, bore holes or from the public supply. It will be thoroughly filtered and brewers often add such sulphates as gypsum and magnesium to enhance the flavours of malt and hops.

3 MALT: Maltsters steep barley in water to absorb moisture, then spread it on heated floors or inside rotating drums where it starts to germinate. Once germination is under way, the grain is transferred to an oven known as a kiln. Heat dries the grain and, depending on the temperature, produces pale or darker malts.

4 YEAST: Yeast is a type of fungus that feeds on sugary liquids. Every brewery will have its own yeast culture that's carefully guarded and stored, as it gives its own important 'house character' to the beer. Brewers keep samples of their yeast cultures in a special bank in Norwich in case they need a fresh supply.

Beer Appreciation

Hops: the grapes of brewing

Sean Franklin, who played a pivotal role in the 'micro-brewing revolution' with Rooster's Brewery in Yorkshire in the 1980s, famously described hops as 'the grapes of brewing'. It was an expression that helped turn the spotlight on a plant that, until then, was thought to give just bitterness to beer. Thanks to Franklin and the legion of artisan brewers who followed him, beer drinkers now appreciate that hops also give a multitude of aromas and flavours to the finished product.

Hops are grown widely in both northern and southern hemispheres. The German Hallertau region in Bavaria is the world's biggest hop-growing region but is likely to be overtaken by both the United States and China. The Czech Republic is famous for its Zatec hops, better known by the German name of Saaz, while Slovenia, while a small country, is a major producer of Styrian Goldings, widely used in Britain. Poland has emerged as an important producer of fragrant hops and Ukraine also has a major hop industry.

Down Under, the challenging climate in Australia confines hop-growing to the south, Tasmania in particular. New Zealand has burst on to the world scene with a growing range of fruity hops. Many of its varieties originated in the northern hemisphere but have taken on their own distinctive character, many of them growing alongside the country's grapes.

English hops are famous for their robust, no-nonsense aromas and flavours. Bitter beer needs bitter hops and the varieties grown here rise to the challenge. Hops come in male and female form and much of the character of English hops is the result of the female hop being fertilised by the male. Only female hops are used in brewing and in most countries, lager brewers – who want delicate hop aroma in their beer – use only unfertilised plants. But in the English hop fields, the male plant is encouraged to have its wicked way with the ladies and the result is hops with pungent woody, peppery and spicy notes.

The English hop industry has been in steep decline for decades as a result of global brewers using imported 'high alpha hops', with bitterness but little aroma, and smaller artisan brewers switching to American and New Zealand varieties as a result of the profound fruity character they deliver.

But thanks to a vigorous campaign led by the British Hop Association, the industry is now showing signs of recovery. There are two dozen hop varieties grown here and the industry has led the way in developing hedgerow varieties, such as First Gold, that grow to only half the height of conventional hops, are easier to pick and are less prone to disease and pest attack.

Boadicea is a recent arrival and is the closest yet to an organic hop, requiring far fewer agricultural chemicals and fertilisers. Endeavour, introduced in 2013, is a cross between an American Cascade and an English variety and offers more of the citrus notes that many brewers look for.

In spring 2014, Hogs Back in Surrey planted 2½ acres opposite the brewery with Farnham White Bine. Chairman Rupert Thompson is a champion of locally-grown ingredients and he discovered that White Bine had been a leading variety in the 18th and 19th centuries and became known as the Golding when it was transported to Kent. The White Bine was wiped out by pests and disease 85 years ago but cuttings had been kept and they will produce a crop in 2015.

Know Your Hops

American hops, such as Amarillo, Cascade, Chinook, Citra and Simcoe are renowned for their 'catty' and citrus notes, with grapefruit to the fore. Citra in particular does what it says on the tin. The widely-used Willamette is more restrained, with a spicy profile: it's a descendant of the English Fuggle.

German hops are called 'noble' varieties and offer, in sharp contrast to American varieties, cedar wood, mint, pine kernels and lemon zest. Main varieties include Hallertau Mittelfrüh, Hersbrucker, Perle, Spalt and Tettnanger.

The leading English hops are Fuggles and Goldings – spicy and peppery – with Challenger, Target, Northdown offering woody, resinous notes with orange and lemon fruit. Bramling Cross has a pronounced blackcurrant character.

New Zealand hops have a vinous fruit character: one leading variety, Nelson Sauvin, is so-called as a result of flavours similar to Sauvignon wine. Motueka, an offshoot of Saaz, has lemon, lime and tropical fruit while Rakau has citrus and pine notes.

Tasting beer

We can increase the level of our appreciation of beer by sampling and tasting to pick out the different elements created by the brewing process. Gently swirl the liquid in the glass to release the aroma or the 'nose' and discover the malt, hop and fruit notes that emerge. Allow the beer to trickle over the tongue, which picks up bitterness, sweetness and salt, and enjoy the palate or 'mouthfeel' as the beer coats the cheeks. Finally, the beer passes down the back of the throat in what is known as the 'finish'.

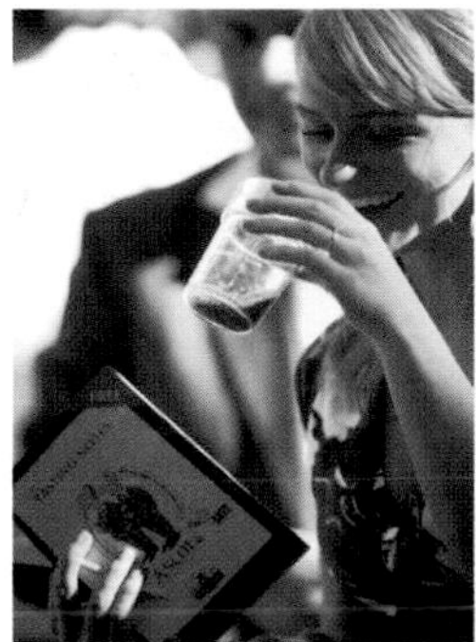

Many CAMRA festivals stage beer tastings

On the nose you may find a rich biscuit or Ovaltine-like malt character. Hops will add their own distinctive note (see box). Fruit may be detected and this comes from both hops and yeast. A sulphur or salty note may be detected: this is derived from the water, which will have had sulphates added to replicate the famous salty waters of Burton-on-Trent, home of classic pale ale brewing.

In the mouth, the malt may have a delicious juicy note while hop bitterness will build, balancing any fruitiness. Finally the finish, if the beer is well-balanced, will combine all the elements of malt, hops and fruit into a satisfying, dry finish. The flavour characteristics of a particular beer will depend on its style: see the Classic Beer Styles section that follows. Suffice it to say that a mild ale will offer a pronounced malt and caramel note, with restrained bitterness, while bitters and IPAs will have a robust hop character, porters and stouts a roasted and toasted grain note, while barley wines are fruity and vinous, and old ales will often have a slight hint of sourness allied to ripe malt, gentle hops and notes of leather and tobacco.

A tasting selection of different beers

Tasting beer can be carried out in the home but greater appreciation will emerge if a group of people take part.

Many pubs now stage regular beer festivals, with a wide choice of beers available. If festivals are not held in your local but it has a good range on the bar, ask whether a room or part of the bar could be set aside for a tasting event.

Glasses should be either half-pint beer glasses or the large ones used for red wine. You will need fresh water and a supply of crackers to allow tasters to clean their palates between beers. Scoring sheets add to the enjoyment of the event, especially if you want to name a 'best beer'. The sheets should be divided into marks out of 10 for appearance, aroma, palate and finish.

Depending on the availability of beer, you could base a tasting round just one style, such as mild, bitter or porter & stout. However, it's unlikely that many pubs would have six versions of a single style, so it's best to have a mixed event.

Marks for appearance will be based on the clarity of the beer when the glass is held up to the light. Does it have a good head of foam, which indicates the beer has what brewers call 'condition'. The absence of foam means the beer is flat. Some beers, such as wheat beers, are designed to have a cloudy appearance, and this should be born in mind when marking.

Marks for aroma will be based on the appeal of the beer as it's sniffed. Is there a good balance of malt, hops and fruit or is the beer overly malty or, conversely, too bitter? If you are judging bitter beers, including IPA, then expect to find the balance tilted toward hops and bitterness. Palate is based on the appeal of the beer in the mouth: you would mark down for cloying sweetness or harsh bitterness, and give higher marks when both characteristics are in balance. Finally, the finish: is the beer harmonious as it passes over the back of the tongue and down the throat, well-balanced between malt, hops and fruit, ending neither too malty nor too bitter. Again, marks in this section will be guided by the style of beer: you would expect a roasted grain character from a stout or porter.

If it's not possible to organise a tasting event of your own, bear in mind that many CAMRA festivals stage beer tastings, often hosted by experts in the field. Monitor the festivals listed in this Guide. The Great British Beer Festival, held in London every August, usually has beer tastings every day of the week: **www.gbbf.org.uk**.

Britain's Classic Beer Styles

FOR MANY PEOPLE, Britain's most famous beer style is bitter, a 20th century development of the pale ales brewed in Victorian times. Until the 1950s, mild ale matched bitter in popularity but then went into steep decline. Today there's far more to British beer than mild and bitter. Older styles, such as genuine IPAs, have reappeared while golden ale, fruit beer and wheat beer provide further choice for drinkers. In this briefing, **Roger Protz** gives an indication of some of the great beers available in British pubs and recommends some of his favourite versions of each style.

Porter & stout

Porter was a London beer that created the first commercial brewing industry in the world in the early 18th century. Its name came from its popularity with London porters who needed calories to help sustain them in their hard manual labour. The origins of the beer are disputed but the most recent research suggests porter, first called 'Entire', was blended in the brewery from pale, mild, and aged or 'stale' beer. The strongest version of porter was called stout porter, later shortened to just stout.

Porter and stout were exported from London to the rest of the British Isles and, as a result, Arthur Guinness built his own porter brewery in Dublin. During World War One, when the British government stopped brewers from using heavily-roasted malts in order to divert energy to the arms industry, Guinness and other Irish brewers came to dominate the market. In recent years, porter and stout have made a spirited comeback in Britain, the United States and Australasia, with brewers digging into old recipes books to create genuine versions of the style.

Look for a jet-black colour and expect a dark and roasted grain character with burnt fruit, espresso or cappuccino coffee, liquorice and molasses. The beer should have a deep bitterness to balance the richness of malt and fruit.

ROGER'S ROUND

AYR RABBIE'S PORTER
DUNHAM MASSEY DUNHAM PORTER
HEART OF WALES WELSH BLACK

Mild

Mild was once the most popular style of beer in Britain. It was developed in the 18th and 19th centuries as drinkers started to demand a slightly sweeter and less aggressively hopped beer than porter.
Mild ale was drunk primarily by industrial and agricultural workers who needed to refresh themselves after long hours of arduous labour. Early milds were much stronger than modern versions, which tend to fall into the 3% to 3.5% category though the likes of Bank Top and Cotswold Spring are among brewers bringing strength back to the style. Mild is usually dark brown in colour, due to the use of well-roasted malts or roasted barley, though there are paler versions such as Banks's Mild and Timothy Taylor's Golden Best. Look for a rich malty aroma and flavour, with hints of dark fruit, chocolate, coffee and caramel, with a gentle underpinning of hop bitterness.

ROGER'S ROUND

BANK TOP DARK MILD
COTSWOLD SPRING OLD SODBURY MILD
GREAT ORME WELSH BLACK

Old Ale

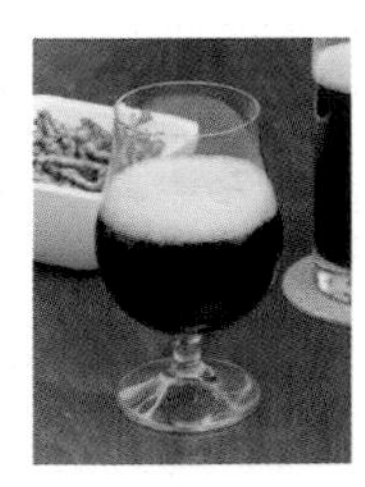

Old Ale is another style from the 18th century, stored for many months or even years in wooden vessels where the beer picked up some lactic sourness from wild yeasts and tannins in the wood. As a result of the sour taste, it was dubbed 'stale' by drinkers and the beer was one of the components of the early porters. In recent years, old ale has made a return to popularity, due primarily to the success of such beers as Theakton's Old Peculier and Gales' Prize Old Ale. Contrary to expectations, old ales do not have to be especially strong and can be no more than 4% alcohol. Neither do they have to be dark: old ale can be pale and bursting with lush malt, tart fruit and spicy hops. Darker versions will have a more profound malt character, with powerful hints of roasted grain, dark fruit, polished leather and fresh tobacco. The hallmark of the style is a lengthy period of maturation, often in bottle rather than cask.

ROGER'S ROUND

ADNAMS OLD ALE
BURTON BRIDGE TICKLE BRAIN
KINVER OVER THE EDGE

Barley Wine

Barley Wine dates from the 18th and 19th centuries when England was often at war with France and it was the duty of patriots, usually from the upper classes, to drink ale rather than French claret. Barley wine had to be strong – often between 10% and 12% – and was stored for as long as 18 months or two years. Fuller's Vintage Ale (8.5%) is a bottle-conditioned version of its Golden Pride and is brewed with four different varieties of malts and hops every year. Expect massive sweet malt and ripe fruit of the pear drop, mandarin orange and lemon type, with chocolate and coffee if darker malts are used. Hop rates are generous and produce bitterness and peppery, grassy and floral notes.

ROGER'S ROUND

DURHAM BENEDICTUS
BAREARTS BARLEY WINE
CHILTERN BODGER'S BARLEY WINE
CONISTON NO. 9

IPA

India Pale Ale changed the face of brewing in the 19th century. The new technologies of the Industrial Revolution enabled brewers to use pale malts to design beers that were pale bronze in colour. The first 'India ales' were brewed in London and were probably based on October beers that were matured for many months and were ideally suited to a long sea journey to India. But London was soon eclipsed by Burton upon Trent with its spring waters rich in minerals that brought out the fullest flavours of malt and hops. 19th century IPAs were high in both alcohol and hops to keep them in good condition during the journey to the colonies. Its life span was brief, driven out of Africa and India by German lager beer. But the style has made a spirited comeback in recent years and is now made in abundance in Britain, Australasia and the United States. Look for a big peppery hop aroma and palate balanced by juicy malt and tart citrus fruit.

ROGER'S ROUND

ACORN IPA
FULLER'S BENGAL LANCER
ST AUSTELL PROPER JOB

Burton Ale

As the name suggests, the origins of Burton Ale lie in Burton upon Trent, but the style became so popular in the 18th and 19th centuries that most brewers had 'a Burton' in their portfolio and the expression 'gone for a Burton' entered the English language. Bass in Burton at one time had six different versions of the beer, ranging from 6% to 11.5%: the strongest versions were exported to Russia and the Baltic States.

In the 20th century, Burton was overtaken in popularity by pale ale and bitter but it was revived with great success in the late 1970s with the launch of Ind Coope Draught Burton Ale. When Allied Breweries broke up, the beer moved first to Tetley's in Leeds and then to J W Lees in Manchester, where it's brewed in small batches but is worth seeking out: it's based on the recipe for a once famous beer, Double Diamond Export. Other versions of the style exist under different names: Young's Winter Warmer was originally called Burton. Bass No 1, brewed occasionally, is called a barley wine but is in fact the last remaining version of a Bass from Burton. Look for a bright amber colour, a rich malt and fruit character underscored by a solid resinous and cedar wood hop note.

ROGER'S ROUND

BURTON BRIDGE BRIDGE BITTER
DRAUGHT BURTON ALE
YOUNG'S WINTER WARMER

Pale Ale

According to a legend in the 19th century, when a sailing ship bound for India with a cargo of IPA foundered off the coast at Liverpool, the casks were brought ashore and news of both the colour and taste of pale ale spread throughout the country. IPAs were brewed for the domestic market as a result but the Burton brewers were keen to produce versions with lower alcohol and hop rates and which didn't need months to mature. The spread of the railway system allowed brewers in Burton to move beer around the country at speed and pale ale was dubbed 'the beer of the railway age' as a result. The clamour for pale ale was so great that brewers from London, Liverpool and Manchester opened second breweries in Burton to make use of the mineral-rich water to make their own versions of the style. From the early 20th century, bitter began to overtake pale ale in popularity and a result pale ale became mainly a bottled product. A true pale ale should be different to bitter, similar in colour and style to IPA and brewed without the addition of coloured malts. It should have a spicy/resinous aroma and palate with biscuit malt and tart fruit from the hops. Many beers called bitter today should properly be labelled pale ale.

ROGER'S ROUND

HAND DRAWN MONKEY PALE ALE
JOULE'S PALE ALE
MARSTON'S PEDIGREE

Bitter

At the turn of the 19th and 20th centuries, brewers built large estate of 'tied' pubs and they moved away from beers stored for months or years and developed 'running beers' that could be served after a few days of conditioning in pub cellars. Bitter was a new type of running beer: it developed from pale ale but was usually copper coloured or deep bronze due to the use of slightly darker malts, such as crystal, that gave the beer fullness of palate as thought it had enjoyed a longer period of conditioning. Best is a stronger version of bitter but there is considerable crossover. Bitter falls into the 3.4% to 3.95 band while best bitter is 4% upwards, though a number of brewers call their ordinary bitter 'best'. A further development of the style comes in the shape of strong bitter of 5% or more: Fuller's ESB and Greene King Abbot are well-known examples. With ordinary bitter, look for spicy, peppery and grassy hop character, a powerful bitterness, tangy fruit and juicy/nutty malt. With best and strong bitters, malt and fruit character will tend to dominate but hop aroma and bitterness are still crucial to the style, often achieved by 'late hopping' during the copper boil or by adding additional hops to casks as they leave the brewery.

ROGER'S ROUND

BUNTINGFORD TWITCHELL
HOBSONS BEST BITTER
SKINNER'S BETTY STOGS

Golden ale

Golden ales have become so popular with both drinkers and brewers of all sizes that the style now has its own category in the annual Champion Beer of Britain competition. Exmoor Gold, Hop Back Summer Lightning and Rooster's Yankee started the trend in the early 1980s and other brewers quickly followed in a rush to wean younger drinkers from mass-produced lager to the pleasures of cask ale. The style is different to pale ale in two critical ways: golden ale is paler, often brewed with lager malt or specially produced low colour ale malt and, as a result, hops are allowed to give full expression, balancing sappy malt with luscious fruit, floral, herbal, spicy and resinous notes.

While brewers of pale ale tend to use such traditional English hop varieties as Fuggles and Goldings, imported hops from North America, the Czech Republic, Germany, Slovenia and New Zealand give radically different notes to golden ale. As a result these beers offer a new and exciting drinking experience. They are often served colder than draught bitter and some brewers, such as Fuller's, have installed special cooling devices to ensure the beer reaches the glass at an acceptably refreshing temperature.

ROGER'S ROUND

BLUE MONKEY BG SIPS
FYNE JARL
OTLEY O2 CROESO

Wheat beer

Wheat beer is a style closely associated with Bavaria and Belgium and its popularity in Britain has encouraged many brewers to add wheat beers to their portfolios. The title is something of a misnomer as all 'wheat beers' are a blend of malted barley as well as wheat, as the latter grain is difficult to brew with and needs the addition of barley, which acts as a natural filter during the mashing stage. But wheat, if used with special yeast cultures developed for brewing the style, gives distinctive aromas and flavours, such as clove, banana and bubblegum that make it a complex and refreshing beer. The Belgian version of wheat beer often has the addition of herbs and spices, such as milled coriander seeds and orange peel – a habit that dates back to the time when Dutch traders brought exotic fruit and spices from the Far East.

ROGER'S ROUND

BRISTOL BEER FACTORY HEFE
LITTLE VALLEY HEBDEN'S WHEAT
ST AUSTELL CLOUDED YELLOW

Fruit/speciality beers

Brewers endlessly search for new flavours to reach out to a wider and more appreciative audience for their beers. The popularity in Britain of Belgian fruit beers has not gone unnoticed and now many domestic brewers are using fruit in their beer. Others have gone the extra mile and add honey, herbs, heather, spice and even spirits – brandy and rum feature in a number of speciality beers, while beers matured in Bourbon, whisky and Cognac casks has become a major development in both this country and the U.S. It's important to dispel the belief that fruit and honey beers are sweet: the ingredients add new dimensions to the brewing process and are highly fermentable, with the result that beers that use the likes of cherries or raspberries are dry and quenching rather than cloying.

ROGER'S ROUND

CONWY HONEY FAYRE/CWRW MEL
MARBLE GINGER
TITANIC CHOCOLATE + VANILLA STOUT

Scottish beers

Historically, Scottish beers tend to be darker and maltier than beers south of the border, the reflection of a colder climate where beer needs to be nourishing. It's an urban myth, though, that Scottish beers are less heavily hopped than English ones. The classic traditional styles are light, heavy and export, which are not dissimilar to mild, bitter and IPA. They are also known as 60, 70 and 80 shilling ales from a 19th century system of invoicing beers according to strength. A 'wee heavy' or 90 shilling ale, now rare, is the Scottish equivalent of barley wine: Traquair House Ale is a rare example of a Wee Heavy. Many of the newer brewers in Scotland are producing beers lighter in colour and with pronounced hop character.

ROGER'S ROUND

CAIRNGORM TRADE WINDS
FAN TEALLACH BEINN DEARG ALE
HIGHLAND DARK MUNRO
STEWART 80/-

Only accept perfect pints

Remember, you're the consumer, forking out a high price for beer, so don't be afraid to take your pint back to the bar if:

It's either too cold or too warm. Cask beer should be cool, not cold – but bear in mind that some golden ales are meant to be served at a lower temperature than milds and bitters. At the other end of the spectrum, it's a myth that real ale should be served at room temperature. Warm beer tastes bad, as the temperature creates unpleasant off flavours. If your beer smells of acetone, vinegar or stale bread, take it back.

The pint has no head, is totally flat and out of condition.

It's not only flat but hazy and has yeast particles or protein floating in the liquid.

If you get the response 'Real ale is meant to be warm and cloudy', invite the publican to join the 21st century. If the offending pub has a Cask Marque plaque, get in touch with Cask Marque. Otherwise, let us know at the Good Beer Guide – **camragbgeditor@camra.org.uk**.

And please go back to the bar if you are served a short measure – less than a pint (or half-pint) of liquid in the glass. Drinkers lose millions of pounds a year as a result of short measures. It's an outrageous rip-off. CAMRA beer festivals serve beer in oversize glasses that ensure drinkers always get the amount of beer they have paid for. Most pub owners refuse to use oversize glasses, preferring brim-measure glasses that allow them consistently to serve short measures. It's a scandal. Don't put up with it.

CAMRA's Beers of the Year

THE BEERS LISTED BELOW are CAMRA'S Beers of the Year. They were short-listed for the 2014 Champion Beer of Britain competition, held at the Great British Beer Festival in August, or the Champion Winter Beer of Britain Competition, held in February that year. Each beer was found by a panel of trained CAMRA judges to be consistently outstanding in its category and they all receive a 🍺 against their entry in the Breweries section. In the Champion Beer of Britain finals, the best beers from each category in both competitions are judged together to decide the overall national winner. For the full results, visit **www.camra.org.uk/cbob**.

BEST BITTERS

Ashover, Hydro
Bank Top, Flat Cap
Brains, Rev James
Butcombe, Gold
Elland, Beyond the Pale
Green Jack, Trawlerboys Best Bitter
Harveys, Sussex Best Bitter
Highland, Scapa Special
Isle of Skye, Red Cuillin
Langton, Inclined Plane Bitter
Leeds, Best
McMulllen, Country Bitter
Purity, Mad Goose
Purple Moose, Cwrw Glaslyn/ Glaslyn Ale
RedWillow, Directionless
Salopian, Darwin's Origin
St Austell, Tribute
Surrey Hills, Shere Drop

BITTERS

Acorn, Barnsley Bitter
Brewster's, Marquis
Flowerpots, Bitter
Hawkshea, Bitter
Mighty Oak, Captain Bob
Isle of Skye, Young Pretender
Otley, 01
Otter, Bitter
Otter, Amber
Purity, Pure Gold
Purple Moose, Cwrw Madog/ Madog's Ale
RedWillow, Headless
Salopian, Shropshire Gold
Scottish Borders, Game Bird
Sambrook's, Wandle Ale
Timothy Taylor, Boltmaker
Tydd Steam, Barn Ale
Whim, Hartington Bitter

BARLEY WINES & STRONG ALES

Darwin, Extinction Ale
Grainstore, Nip
Green Jack, Ripper
Heart of Wales, High as a Kite
Highland, Orkney Porter
Kinver, Over the Edge
Kissingate, 6 Crows
Lees, Moonraker
Moor, Old Freddie Walker

GOLDEN ALES

Brewster's, Hophead
Exmoor, Gold
Fyne, Jarl
Hawkshead, Cumbrian Five Hop
Leeds, Yorkshire Gold
Oakham, Citra
Salopian, Hop Twister
Tillingbourne, Falls Gold
Tiny Rebel, Fubar

MILDS

Bank Top, Dark Mild
Branscombe Vale, Mild
Byatt's, XK Dark
Castle Rock, Black Gold
Elgood's, Black Dog
Harveys, Sussex XX Mild Ale
Rhymney, Dark
Rudgate, Ruby Mild
Strathave, Craigmill Mild

OLD ALES & STRONG MILDS

Beowulf, Dark Raven
Bollington, Winter Reserve
Bragdy'r Nant, Mwnci Nel
Exe Valley, Winter Glow
Grainstore, Rutland Beast
Isle of Skye, Black Cuillin
Leeds, Midnight Bell
Palmers, Tally Ho!
Wolf, Woild Moild

PORTERS

Acorn, Old Moor Porter
Ayr, Rabbie's Porter
Batemans, Salem Porter
Dunham Massey, Dunham Porter
Enville, Old Porter
Fuller's, London Porter
Moonshine, Nightwatch Porter
RCH, Old Slug Porter

SPECIALITY BEERS

Bingham's, Vanilla Stout
Bullmastiff, Welsh Black
Cairngorm, Trade Winds
Moonshine, Chocolate Orange Stout
Offbeat, Way Out Wheat
Peak Ales, Chatsworth Gold
Salopian, Lemon Dream
Saltaire, Triple Chocoholic
Skinner's, Ginger Tosser

STOUTS

Ascot, Anastasia's Exile Stout
Cairngorm, Black Gold
Church End, Stout Coffin
Exeter, Darkness
Grainstore, Ratliffe's Stout
Hambleton, Nightmare
Heart of Wales, Welsh Black
Marble, Stouter Stout
Milton, Nero

STRONG BITTERS

Blue Monkey, Ape Ale
Church End, Fallen Angel
Greene King, Abbot
Kelham Island, Pale Rider
Loch Ness, HoppyNESS
Marble, Dobber
RCH, East Street Cream
Tiny Rebel, Urban IPA
Windsor & Eton, Conqueror

REAL ALE IN A BOTTLE

8 Sail, Victorian Porter
Burton Bridge, Bramble Stout
Burton Bridge, Empire Pale
Charles Wells, Young's Special London Ale
Dunham Massey, Chocolate Cherry Mild
Fuller's, 1845
Fuller's, Bengal Lancer
Fulstow, Sledgehammer Stout
Fyne, Sublime Stout
Grain, India Pale Ale
Kernel, Export Stout
Marble, Chocolate Marble
Marble, Lagonda IPA
Moor, Revival
Neath, Black
Neath, Firebrick
Neath, Gold
Old Bear, Black Mari'a
Old Bear, Goldilocks
Old Bear, Hibernator
Spire, Prince Igor
St Andrews, India Pale Ale
St Austell, Admiral's Ale
St Austell, Proper Job
Stewart, Embra
Woodforde's, Nelson's Revenge
Wye Valley, Butty Bach

CHAMPION WINTER BEER OF BRITAIN
Dunham Massey, Dunham Porter

CHAMPION BEER OF BRITAIN 2014
Timothy Taylor, Boltmaker

The Pubs

City Arms, Cardiff (p569)

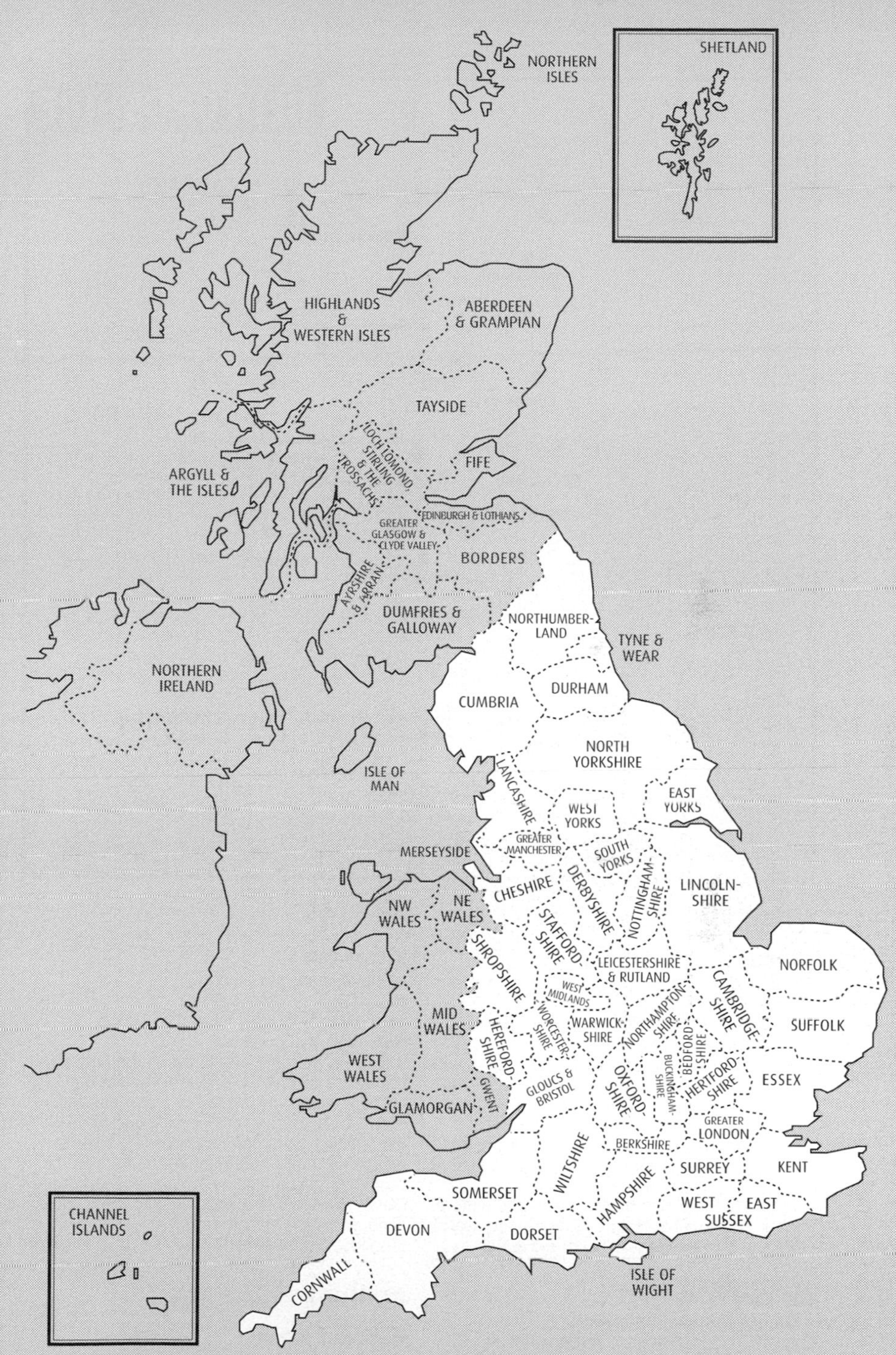
NORTHERN ISLES
SHETLAND
HIGHLANDS & WESTERN ISLES
ABERDEEN & GRAMPIAN
TAYSIDE
LOCH LOMOND, STIRLING & THE TROSSACHS
FIFE
ARGYLL & THE ISLES
EDINBURGH & LOTHIANS
GREATER GLASGOW & CLYDE VALLEY
BORDERS
AYRSHIRE & ARRAN
DUMFRIES & GALLOWAY
NORTHERN IRELAND
NORTHUMBER-LAND
TYNE & WEAR
DURHAM
CUMBRIA
NORTH YORKSHIRE
ISLE OF MAN
LANCASHIRE
WEST YORKS
EAST YORKS
GREATER MANCHESTER
SOUTH YORKS
MERSEYSIDE
CHESHIRE
DERBYSHIRE
NOTTINGHAM-SHIRE
LINCOLN-SHIRE
NW WALES
NE WALES
STAFFORD-SHIRE
SHROPSHIRE
LEICESTERSHIRE & RUTLAND
NORFOLK
WEST MIDLANDS
CAMBRIDGE-SHIRE
MID WALES
HEREFORD-SHIRE
WORCESTER-SHIRE
WARWICK-SHIRE
NORTHAMPTON-SHIRE
BEDFORD-SHIRE
SUFFOLK
WEST WALES
BUCKINGHAM-SHIRE
HERTFORD-SHIRE
ESSEX
GLOUCS & BRISTOL
OXFORD-SHIRE
GWENT
GLAMORGAN
GREATER LONDON
BERKSHIRE
WILTSHIRE
SURREY
KENT
SOMERSET
HAMPSHIRE
WEST SUSSEX
EAST SUSSEX
CHANNEL ISLANDS
DEVON
DORSET
CORNWALL
ISLE OF WIGHT

England

BEDFORDSHIRE

Ampthill

Albion 🏆 L

36 Dunstable Street, MK45 2JT

11.30-11 ☎ (01525) 634857

B&T Shefford Bitter, Golden Fox, Dragon Slayer; Everards Tiger; guest beers H

Narrow-fronted, traditional Victorian alehouse with one large bar and 12 handpumps serving a range of the local B&T beers as well as Everards Tiger and eight constantly changing ales, mainly from microbreweries. Two real ciders and a perry are also available. Beer and cider festivals are held at least once a year. Filled rolls are served at lunchtimes. There is a meeting room and patio garden. Music nights feature once a month. Local CAMRA Pub of the Year 2014.

Old Sun L

87 Dunstable Street, MK45 2NQ

12-11.30 (12.30am Fri & Sat) ☎ (01525) 405466

Adnams Southwold Bitter; St Austell Tribute; Sharp's Doom Bar; Wells Bombardier; guest beer H

Busy community pub on the town's main street, popular with a good mix of people. A selection of regular ales is available. There are two bars plus a games room, with a real fire adding a cosy feel in winter. Outside there are tables to the front, ample decked and grassed areas to the rear, and a function room in an outbuilding in the garden. Lots of events are arranged every year to raise money for charity.

Arlesey

Vicars Inn L

68 Church Lane, SG15 6UX

5-midnight; 12-4, 7-midnight Sat & Sun

☎ (01462) 731215

Wells Eagle IPA; guest beer H

A friendly welcome awaits you in the cosy front bar, which plays host to local dominoes and cribbage teams. At the rear is a spacious and comfortable lounge bar. Special events are held in the function room and an enclosed garden is popular in the summer months. At the bar, the Eagle IPA is accompanied by an ever-changing low gravity guest ale. The pub is opposite the church and just a short walk from the railway station and bus stop. **Q P** (72,97)

Bedford

Bedford Arms

2 Bromham Road, MK40 2QA (opp HM Prison)

12-midnight ☎ (01234) 214656

thebedfordarmsbedford.co.uk

Courage Directors; Wells Bombardier; Young's Bitter, Special; guest beers H

A Charles Wells Speciality Beer House offering three regularly changing guest beers and a changing guest cider as well as four regular Wells & Young's beers. Burgers, home-made chilli and Pieminister pies are available on Thursday and Friday evenings and noon to 10pm at weekends.

There is live jazz on Monday evening and Sunday afternoon, local bands on Sunday evening, traditional music on the first Thursday of the month and a book club on the second Thursday.

Burnaby Arms

66 Stanley Street, MK41 7RU (Prime Ministers area N of town centre)
5-11 (midnight Fri); 2-midnight Sat; 2-10.30 Sun
(01234) 330056 burnabyarmsbedford.co.uk
Courage Directors; Wells Eagle IPA; Young's London Gold; guest beer H
This two-room street-corner pub has rapidly become a hub of the local community. It hosts a well-attended fortnightly quiz while the darts team plays weekly. Hot pies and toasted sandwiches are available daily, and the monthly Pie Night is always popular. Sunday afternoon jazz and live music evenings feature monthly, and there are special events throughout the year. Local CAMRA Town Pub of the Year 2014. Q (10)

Cricketers Arms

35 Goldington Road, MK40 3LH (on A4280 near rugby ground)
5-11; 7-10.30 Sun (01234) 303958
cricketersarms.co.uk
Adnams Southwold Bitter; guest beers H
Also known as the Welsh Embassy, this welcoming one-bar pub near Bedford Blues rugby ground is popular with fans of the game and busy on match days. It opens at noon on Saturdays for Blues home games. Live rugby is shown (terrestrial TV only) and the pub opens early for live Six Nations games. Guest beers include brews from Brains and local breweries. There is a covered courtyard for smokers and drinkers. (5)

Devonshire Arms

32 Dudley Street, MK40 3TB (1 mile E of town centre S of A4280)
5 (4 Fri)-11; 12-11 Sat; 12-10.30 Sun (01234) 359329
devonshirearmsbedford.co.uk
Courage Directors; Wells Eagle IPA; Young's London Gold, Special; guest beers H
Pleasant Victorian LocAle pub in a residential area. Guest and seasonal ales are mainly from Wells & Young's, the two ciders and perry are from Westons. Pub festivals are held each year. The front bar has bare floorboards and an open fire, and there is a separate rear bar. The garden has a gazebo for smokers and a no-smoking paved area. A good range of wines is sold by the glass or bottle. Local CAMRA Pub of the Year 2013.
Q (4)

Three Cups

45 Newnham Street, MK40 3JR (200yds S of A4280 near rugby ground)
11-11; 12-10.30 Sun (01234) 352153
Greene King IPA, Abbot; Morland Old Speckled Hen; guest beers H
Comfortable inn dating from the 1770s, rebadged as a Greene King Local Hero pub, offering five guest ales, mostly from local microbreweries. Tasting thirds are available for all beers. Locally-sourced home-cooked food is served at lunchtimes. The old wood panelling has survived refurbishment, helping to retain some of the pub's original character. Situated five minutes from the town centre and close to the Peacock Auction Rooms and Bedford Blues rugby ground. P

Wellington Arms

40-42 Wellington Street, MK40 2JX (off A6 N of town centre)
12-11 (10.30 Sun) (01234) 308033
thewelly.wix.com/bedford
Adnams Southwold Bitter; B&T Shefford Bitter; Draught Bass; guest beers H
Winner of many awards, this street-corner local operated by B&T Brewery offers a wide selection of ever-changing regional and microbrewery beers from 12 handpumps. Westons and Thatchers ciders are served from two handpumps. A selection of draught Belgian and Dutch beers plus a wide range of bottled Belgian beers is also available. There is a courtyard for drinkers and smokers. A friendly pub with a mixed clientele, it can get very busy on Friday and Saturday evenings.

White Horse

84 Newnham Avenue, MK41 9PX
11 (12 Sun)-11 (01234) 409306
whitehorsebedford.co.uk
Wells Eagle IPA, Bombardier; guest beers H
Large, one-bar suburban pub a mile east of the town centre. Good value food is available, with a Sunday roast and regular themed and charity evenings. Monday is open mic night, Sunday and Tuesday are quiz nights, with an additional fundraising quiz on most Wednesdays. The pub has won several brewery and local business awards. A May Day weekend local beer, food and talent festival, and a November beer and banger festival, are held each year. P (4)

Biggleswade

Golden Pheasant

71 High Street, SG18 0JH
12-11.30 (midnight Fri); 11-midnight Sat; 1-11.30 Sun
(01767) 313653 goldenpheasantpub.co.uk
Courage Directors; Wells Eagle IPA; guest beers H
The licensee of this cosy one-bar pub was a founder member of the local CAMRA branch and the quality and variety of beers served reflect his enthusiasm for all styles of ale, with current beers and prices marked on blackboards. Two real ciders are also usually available, one from local Dunton Cider. Friendly conversation has priority over electronic diversions. Quiz night is the last Wednesday of the month. Outside is a large rear patio, popular for summer drinking.
Q

Pembroke Arms

29 Hitchin Street, SG18 8BE
12-11 (01767) 312490
Marston's EPA; guest beers H
Formerly called the Brown Bear, the Pembroke Arms has been refurbished with a bright and airy interior warmed by two open fires. The large L-shaped bar has up to six handpumps offering constantly changing ales. Guest beers are usually from the Marston's group including Banks's, Jennings, Ringwood and Wychwood. Meals are served every day, with the home-cooked Sunday

INDEPENDENT BREWERIES

B&T Shefford
Charles Wells Bedford
Potton Potton
White Park Cranfield

roast proving ever-popular. Occasional live music, quizzes and themed party events are hosted. There is a patio garden at the rear. Q

Wheatsheaf

5 Lawrence Road, SG18 0LS

11-4, 7-11.30; 11-midnight Fri & Sat; 12-11 Sun

(01767) 222220

Greene King IPA; guest beers H

A good example of the type of community local that is becoming more and more rare, with the emphasis on conversation, pub games and sport. The superbly kept beers, although limited to one or two guests from the Greene King approved list, are a reflection of the dedication and enthusiasm of the licensee to ensure top quality ales. The well-maintained rear garden is a pleasant place to relax in when the weather permits.

Bolnhurst

Plough

Kimbolton Road, MK44 2EX (on B660 S of village) TL088587

closed Mon; 12-3, 6.30-11; 12-3 Sun (01234) 376274

bolnhurst.com

Beer range varies H

Award-winning pub restaurant dating back to Tudor times, offering excellent food and beer. The main bar features a wood-burning stove, and a second room is set aside for dining and functions. Up to three real ales are offered, usually one from Adnams, one from Hopping Mad and a third from a local microbrewery. Outside is a large garden with decking beside a small pond. The pub is closed from Christmas until the second week of January each year. Q P

Broom

Cock ★

23 High Street, SG18 9NA

12-11 (11.30 Fri & Sat); 12-10 Sun (01767) 314411

thecockatbroom.co.uk

Greene King IPA; guest beers G

This Grade II-listed building, with its nationally important historic pub interior, is now a free house and features many charming rooms with flagstone floors and numerous fireplaces. There is no bar – the four ales are served directly from the cellar. At least two ciders are available, often from the local Potton Press. Pub games such as Northamptonshire skittles are played and occasional live music, quizzes, barbecues and mini beer festivals are hosted. Locally sourced pub food is served daily. Q P

Clophill

Stone Jug

10 Back Street, MK45 4BY (500yds off A6 at N end of village) TL083381

12-3.30, 6-11; 12-11 Fri & Sat; 12-10.30 Sun

(01525) 860526

B&T Shefford Bitter; Hopping Mad Brainstorm; Otter Amber; guest beers H

Originally three 16th-century cottages, this popular village local has an L-shaped bar that serves two drinking areas and a family/function room. Excellent home-made lunches are available Tuesday to Saturday. The two guest beers are often from local breweries, the cider is Westons. Picnic benches at the front and a rear patio garden offer space for outdoor drinking in fine weather. Parking can be difficult at busy times. Local CAMRA Pub of the Year 2014. Q P (44,81)

Dunstable

Gary Cooper

Grove Park, Court Drive, LU5 4GP

9am-midnight (2am Fri); 8am-2am Sat; 8am-midnight Sun

(01582) 471452

Greene King Abbot; Ruddles Best Bitter; guest beers H

This Wetherspoon bar, named after the Hollywood film star who attended a local grammar school, is situated in the Grove Park leisure area. A varying selection of ales, often from local breweries, and real cider are served along with all-day food. The pub tends to get very busy on Friday and Saturday evenings. The building is modern and spacious with toilets upstairs. Outside seating and a smoking area with parasols overlook a local park.

Globe

43 Winfield Street, LU6 1LS

12-11 (midnight Fri & Sat); 12-10.30 Sun

(01582) 512300

B&T Shefford Bitter, Golden Fox, Edwin Taylor's Extra Stout; Everards Tiger; guest beers H

A popular beer destination and community local where 13 handpumps dispense a good range of regular B&T beers and Everards Tiger plus five ever-changing microbrewery ales. There is also real cider and perry from Westons and Belgian bottled beers. Bare boards, bar stools and breweriana create a traditional town pub atmosphere that buzzes with conversation. Q

Pheasant

208 West Street, LU6 1NX

11-11 (11.30 Fri & Sat); 12-10.30 Sun (01582) 662706

the-pheasant-inn-dunstable.co.uk

Courage Directors; Sharp's Doom Bar; guest beers H

Free house situated a short walk west of the busier part of town. Six handpumps dispense the regulars and rotating guests often from micros. Flights of three thirds are available to enable wider tasting. The front bar is traditional while the large rear bar has pool and darts and doubles as a popular function room. Live sporting events are screened in both bars. There is free curry on Friday and free pizza on Saturday for drinkers. Outside are large covered and heated seating areas. P

Victoria

69 West Street, LU6 1ST

11-12.30am (1am Fri & Sat); 12-midnight Sun

(01582) 662682

Tring Victoria Bitter; guest beers H

Popular town-centre pub that usually offers four ales including a house beer, Victoria Bitter, from Tring Brewery. The varying guest ales are from micro and regional breweries, with one sold at a reduced price Monday to Friday. Good-value food is available until early evening Monday to Saturday and weekend lunchtimes. Darts, dominoes and crib are popular and televised sport feature in the bar. (34,61)

Dunton

March Hare

34 High Street, SG18 8RN

6-11 (midnight Fri); 12-midnight Sat; 12-10.30 Sun

(01767) 448093 duntonvillage.org.uk/pub/home.htm

Beer range varies

Village pub with a relaxed and welcoming atmosphere complemented by a beautifully kept range of four or five ales, always including one from Buntingford, and local Dunton Cider. Mini beer festivals are held irregularly and there are themed food nights as well as live music events. The pub is home to various clubs including the Hare Beer Bunch – a group of beer enthusiasts who meet monthly – and now houses the community shop. Q (188)

Eversholt

Green Man

Church End, MK17 9DU

12-2.30, 6 (5 Fri)-11; 12-midnight Sat & Sun

(01525) 288111 greenmaneversholt.com

Fuller's London Pride; Sharp's Doom Bar; guest beer

A genuine free house in Church End, one of the many 'Ends' that make up the village of Eversholt. The Victorian building features flagstone floors and exposed brick fireplaces, and has a large patio/garden. Freshly prepared, good-quality food, including an award-winning Sunday lunch, is served in the bar and restaurant. Ales vary and may include a beer from a local brewery. Conveniently placed for the popular tourist attractions of Woburn. P

Felmersham

Sun

Grange Road, MK43 7EU

4 (12 Sat)-11; 12-10 Sun (01234) 781355

thesuninn-felmersham.com

Wells Eagle IPA; guest beers

Pretty thatched community local reopened as a family-owned freehouse in 2013. Guest beers change weekly and normally include at least one from a local microbrewery. Traditional pub lunches and evening meals are served in both bars. The pub has a family-friendly rear garden and is convenient for visits to the historic parish church and a waterfowl nature reserve just across the river. Local CAMRA Most Improved Pub 2014. P (50)

Flitton

Jolly Coopers

Wardhedges, MK45 5ED

12-3 (not Mon), 5.30-11.30; 12-midnight Sat; 12-10.30 Sun

(01525) 303648 jollycoopersflitton.co.uk

Wells Eagle IPA; guest beers

Set in the hamlet of Wardhedges at the east end of Flitton, the landlord and lady take obvious pride in this wonderful country community pub. Two ever-changing and varied guest ales are available alongside the regular Eagle. Traditional British food is served in the bar and separate restaurant, with a choice of menus. There is a large garden to the rear and a patio with spectacular floral displays in the summer months. Dogs are welcome in the impressively flagstoned bar. P

Great Barford

Anchor Inn

High Street, MK44 3LF (by river bridge 1 mile S of village centre) TL134517

12-3, 6.30 (6 Fri)-11; 12-11 Sat; 12-10.30 Sun

(01234) 870364 anchorinngreatbarford.co.uk

Wells Eagle IPA; Young's Bitter; guest beers

Busy local inn next to the church, overlooking the River Great Ouse. At least two guest beers are usually available from an extensive range offered by the pub company. Good home-cooked food is served in the bar and restaurant, as well as a fine selection of wines. The pub is popular with river users in the summer. Occasional themed nights are hosted, mainly during the winter months. Q P (27)

Harlington

Carpenters Arms

Sundon Road, LU5 6LS

12-3.30, 6-midnight; 12-midnight Fri-Sun

(01525) 872384 thecarpentersarmsharlington.com

Greene King IPA; Woodforde's Wherry; guest beers

Situated in the heart of Harlington, this low-beamed, watch-your-head village inn was first licensed in 1790 and has listings of landlords from then until the present. The current landlord is a local who has always lived in the village. Two regular beers and two changing guests are available. Food is reasonably priced with good helpings. The railway station and occasional bus service along with a range of country walks make this a popular stop-off. Q P (42)

Old Sun

34 Sundon Road, LU5 6LS

12 (2 winter)-midnight; 12-1am Fri & Sat

(01525) 877330 theoldsunharlington.co.uk

Harveys Sussex Best Bitter; St Austell Trelawny, Tribute; guest beers

This traditional half-timbered building dates back to the 1740s and has been a pub since 1785. It has two separate bars and a side room. Three regular ales and one or two guest beers are on offer. Tuesday is steak night and Friday fish and chips night. Outside there is seating plus a children's play area. Situated just a short walk from the main-line rail station. Q P (42)

Heath & Reach

Axe & Compass

Leighton Road, LU7 0AA

11-midnight (01525) 237394

theaxeandcompass.co.uk

Beer range varies

Run by a resourceful new landlord, this village community pub is flourishing. The older front bar with its low wood beams serves as a lounge and dining area while the rear public bar has gaming machines, a pool table and TV screen. Local beers feature strongly from breweries such as Hopping Mad, Tring, White Park and Concrete Cow. The real ale loyalty card (buy six pints, get one free) is popular with regulars. Accommodation is available in a separate lodge. P (150)

Henlow

Engineers Arms

68 High Street, SG16 6AA
12-midnight (1am Fri & Sat) (01462) 812284
engineersarms.co.uk
Beer range varies
This multiple award-winning free house with 10 handpumps offers a wide range of beer styles, plus up to eight ciders and perries. The front bar has an open fireplace, brewery memorabilia and historical pictures. The lively back bar, popular with sports fans, has widescreen TVs, sporting pictures, occasional live music and disco evenings. The renowned October beer festival features over 100 real ales and there is a winter cider and country wine festival. Local CAMRA Pub of the Year 2014. (71,188)

Houghton Conquest

Knife & Cleaver

The Grove, MK45 3LA (opp parish church)
7am-midnight (7 Sun) (01234) 930789
theknifeandcleaver.com
Courage Directors; Wells Eagle IPA; guest beer
A smart pub/restaurant with accommodation, reopened by Charles Wells in January 2012 and run by licensees who previously operated a restaurant in France. Quality meals are made with fresh locally-sourced ingredients and the restaurant has an AA Gold Award for food in 2013 and 2014. Nine en-suite rooms are in a separate block behind the secluded rear garden. (42)

Kempston

Half Moon

108 High Street, MK42 7BN
12-3, 6 (5 Fri)-11.30; 12-11 Sat & Sun (01234) 852464
Wells Eagle IPA; guest beer
Popular community pub with a comfortable lounge and a public bar with games. The venue hosts a number of sports teams playing in local leagues. The large garden, which includes a children's play area, is busy in good weather. The River Great Ouse a short distance away offers a choice of attractive walks. No food is available on Sunday and evening meals must be booked in advance.

Leighton Buzzard

Golden Bell

4-6 Church Square, LU7 1AE
10-11.30 (midnight Fri & Sat); 11-11 Sun
(01525) 373330 thegoldenbell.co.uk
Tetley Golden Bell Bitter; Timothy Taylor Landlord; guest beers
With its front dating from the 18th century and Grade II-listing, this lively and welcoming community local has a single bar with low-beamed ceilings and sofas at one end. Food features fresh produce from local suppliers and is served throughout opening hours. Guest beers often include Adnams Broadside, Sharp's Doom Bar or St Austell Tribute, with one on gravity dispense. Sports are shown on four large screens and activities include a dominoes team and monthly themed quiz.

Red Lion

1 North Street, LU7 1EF
10-11 (midnight Fri & Sat); 11-11 Sun (01525) 374350
Banks's Bitter; Greene King Abbot; guest beer
This 17th-century building is a town-centre institution. An old-fashioned pub with old-fashioned values, the manager of 20 years offers a warm welcome. The public bar has all the traditional pub games; the main bar resembles a living room with comfy chairs, a large fish tank, TV and the pub's dogs wandering around. As well as the well-kept ales there is a selection of Irish and Scottish single malt whiskies.

Swan Hotel

High Street, LU7 1EA
7am-midnight (11.30 Sun) (01525) 380170
Greene King Abbot; Ruddles Best Bitter; guest beers
This former coaching inn, dating from the 17th century, was recently renovated by Wetherspoon. With good-value food and 39 guest rooms, the Swan is busy and bustling for much of the week. Friendly staff operate one long bar serving two rooms, a conservatory and a courtyard. Guest beers regularly come from local microbreweries such as Tring, Vale, Concrete Cow and Oxfordshire, and real cider is available. Events include beer festivals twice a year and occasional Meet the Brewer evenings.

Luton

Bricklayers Arms

High Town Road, LU2 0DD
12-11 Mon; 12-2.30, 5-11; 12-midnight Fri & Sat; 12-10.30 Sun (01582) 611017 bricklayersarmsluton.co.uk
Batemans XB; guest beers
The five busy handpumps serve a choice of light, amber or dark beer from an ever-changing range of guest ales from local and national breweries, often including a mild and an Oakham brew, with draught Belgian beers also available. This quirky town-centre pub has been run by the same landlady for 28 years. It is popular with Hatters fans on match days, with TVs in both bars. Quiz night is Monday. Lunchtime bar meals are served Monday to Friday.

English Rose

46 Old Bedford Road, LU2 7PA
12-11 (01582) 723889
Beer range varies
Traditional one-room, CAMRA-friendly street-corner pub which serves up to 600 different ales and ciders per year. A pub since 1845, it was originally called the Rabbit —this area was then called Coney Heath, coney being the old word for rabbit. In 1919 this was one of four pubs in which the dissidents met before marching into town and eventually ransacking and burning down the town hall. The pub is said to have been a haunt of celebrity actress Diana Dors who courted and then wed the landlord's son in the 1950s. (24,25)

London Hatter

46 Park Street, LU1 3ET
8am-midnight (1am Fri & Sat) (01582) 390920
Greene King Abbot; Ruddles Best Bitter; guest beers
Tasteful Wetherspoon conversion of a former nightclub at the university end of town, opened in

2011. Guest ales greet you on the first few pumps; the remaining pumps dispense the regular beers. One real cider is usually available on draught plus one or two ciders or perries from boxes in the fridge. The smart interior caters more for dining than partying, and local history, in pictures, adorns the walls. A supporter of the CLIC Sargent charity.
Q

Wigmore Arms

Wigmore Lane, LU2 9XG
11 (10 Sat & Sun)-11 ☎ (01582) 417343
Wells Bombardier; guest beers H
Lively and large two-bar modern pub in a residential area of Luton next to Asda supermarket. Beer festivals are held in April and October each year. The comfortable lounge includes a dining area where food is served all day every day. The sports bar has two large HD screens and 3D TV showing sports TV and the Luton Town channel. Live music features on the last Saturday of the month. A large function room is available.
P

Potton

Rising Sun

11 Everton Road, SG19 2PA
12-3, 5-11 (midnight Fri); 12-midnight Sat & Sun
☎ (01767) 260231 risingsunpotton.co.uk
Wells Bombardier, Eagle IPA; guest beers H
Large well-used community pub that offers an ever-changing range of four or five guest beers, always in good condition, alongside three from the Wells & Young's range. A blackboard indicates which beers are available with brief tasting notes. Beer festivals are held on the May and August bank holidays. The first floor terrace and patio tables outside are popular in the summer. Good home-cooked food is available until 9.30pm.
P (188,190)

Renhold

Polhill Arms

25 Wilden Road, MK41 0JP (at Salph End)
12-3, 5-11; 12-11 Fri & Sat; 12-10.30 Sun
☎ (01234) 771398 polhillarms.co.uk
Greene King IPA; H&H Bitter; guest beers H
One-bar family-friendly village local with a welcoming atmosphere and large garden, play area and restaurant. An interesting collection of pub and brewery artefacts is on view. Traditional pub food is served as well as fish and chips (not Sun and Mon eve). Live entertainment and quiz nights feature regularly, and darts and skittles are played. Three guest beers are usually available, with Olde Trip a popular choice. Four real ciders are now also on offer. P (27)

Salford

Red Lion Hotel

Wavendon Road, MK17 8AZ (2 miles N of M1 jct 13)
SP934389
11-2.30, 6.30-11; 12-2.30, 6-11 Sun ☎ (01908) 583117
redlionhotel.eu
Wells Eagle IPA, Bombardier H
Friendly, traditional country hotel serving a fine choice of home-cooked food in the bar and restaurant. The cosy bar is heated by an open fire in winter and offers a selection of interesting board games. The large garden includes a covered area and a secure children's playground. Six rooms are available for overnight accommodation.
Q P

> Give my people plenty of beer, good beer and cheap beer, and you will have no revolution among them. **Queen Victoria**

Sandy

Sir William Peel

39 High Street, SG19 1AG
12 (11 Sat)-midnight; 12-10.30 Sun ☎ (01767) 680607
sirwilliampeel.webs.com
Batemans XB; guest beers H
Set slightly back from the High Street, the tables and benches at the front of the pub are a popular suntrap in the summer, with more outdoor seating at the rear. Inside, the lighting is subdued and conversation lively around the U-shaped bar. An Oakademy of Excellence certificate is on display — an Oakham beer is always among the three guests. The pub hosts occasional live music and quizzes, and a beer and cider festival in spring. It supports the CLIC Sargent charity.
P (73,188)

Shefford

Brewery Tap

14 North Bridge Street, SG17 5DH
11.30-11; 12-10.30 Sun ☎ (01462) 628448
B&T Shefford Bitter, Dragon Slayer; Everards Tiger; guest beers H
Renamed by the nearby B&T Brewery in 1996, the Tap is primarily a drinkers' pub, offering three regulars plus two guests which tend to be stronger beers. Breweriana decorates the open-plan interior, which is divided into two distinct areas with a family room at the rear. Lunchtime pies and rolls are available. Darts, dominoes and cribbage teams are actively supported. The rear patio garden is heated on cool evenings. Car park access is through the archway next to the pub.
P (71,72)

Souldrop

Bedford Arms

High Street, MK44 1EY (½ mile W of A6)
closed Mon; 12-3, 6-11; 12-midnight Fri & Sat; 12-11 Sun
☎ (01234) 781384
Black Sheep Best Bitter; Greene King IPA; Phipps NBC Red Star; guest beers H
Large village pub created partly from a 17th-century hop and ale house. Guest beers are often from local microbreweries, cider is from local producer Eversheds. The restaurant has a central open fireplace and offers traditional pub favourites prepared to order, with daily specials and a roast on Sunday. A games room with skittles runs off the main bar. The spacious garden with pétanque is popular with families in summer. Local CAMRA Country Pub of the Year 2013.
P (26)

Toddington

Oddfellows Arms

2 Congar Lane, LU5 6BP

5 (1 Sat & Sun)-11 ☎ (01525) 872021

Adnams Broadside; Fuller's London Pride; guest beers

Attractive 700-year-old two-bar pub facing the village green with a heavily beamed and brassed bar featuring a vast collection of pumpclips, and a games room with a pool table. Two guest handpumps always provide a variety of ales. The regular real cider is Westons Old Rosie and various changing guests are also available. Outside, the patio garden is popular in summer and has shelter for smokers. (X31,42)

Totternhoe

Old Farm

16 Church Road, LU6 1RE

5-midnight Mon; 12-3; 12-10.30 Sun ☎ (01582) 674053

Fuller's London Pride, ESB; guest beers

Located in the conservation area of Church End, this charming village pub boasts two inglenooks. The public bar with its low-boarded ceiling is where you will find good conversation and traditional pub games. Dogs are welcome in the front bar and there is a child-friendly garden. Monday is folk music night. Tasty, home-cooked food is served including popular Sunday roasts (no food Mon or Sun eves). P

Whipsnade

Old Hunters Lodge

The Crossroads, LU6 2LN

11.30-2.30 (3 Fri & Sat), 6-11; 12-11 Sun

☎ (01582) 872228 old-hunters.com

Greene King Abbot; Tring Brock Bitter; guest beer

Beautiful 15th-century thatched inn set on the outskirts of Whipsnade village close to the world-renowned Whipsnade Zoo. A log fire warms the cosy main bar, where there is soft seating as well as traditional dining tables. The side bar retains many old features including the inglenook fireplace. Separate restaurant areas may be used as function rooms. The picturesque front garden is lovely for summer dining and drinking. Six guest rooms include a bridal suite.

QP(X31)

Wilstead

Woolpack

2 Bedford Road, MK45 3HW

12-3 (not Mon), 5-11; 12-11 Fri & Sat; 12-10.30 Sun

☎ (01234) 742318 woolpack-wilstead.co.uk

Greene King IPA, Abbot; H&H Olde Trip; guest beers

A friendly village local with a warm welcome to visitors. The open fire helps to create a cosy atmosphere and an old well in the corner adds further interest. The car park leads to a pretty patio garden. Good, home-cooked food with a gastro twist is served at lunchtime (no food Mon) and evening. From May to September the pub opens all day on Tuesday to Thursday.

P(44,81)

Wingfield

Plough

Tebworth Road, LU7 9QH

12-3, 5.30-midnight; 12-10.30 Sun ☎ (01525) 873077

theploughinn.com

Fuller's London Pride, ESB; Gales HSB; guest beer

Charming thatched village inn dating from the 17th century, decorated with paintings of rural scenes and ploughs. Beware the low beams! Good home-cooked food is served daily except on Sunday evening when a fortnightly quiz is held. There are tables outside at the front and to the rear is a conservatory and prize-winning garden, illuminated at night in the summer. Heated umbrellas are provided for smokers.

P(X31)

Wootton

Chequers

Hall End, MK43 9HP (NW edge of village) SP001457

12-11 ☎ (01234) 930464 chequerswootton.co.uk

Wells Eagle IPA; guest beers

Originally a farmhouse, this handsome old free house retains a wealth of heavy wooden beams and period features. A wide range of guest beers is offered, often from local microbreweries. An interesting, quality menu is served in the restaurant and good-value bar food is available throughout the pub (no food Sun eve). The large, pleasant garden is popular in fine weather.

QP(68)

Kitchen of an inn

In the evening we reached a village where I had determined to pass the night. As we drove into the great gateway of the inn, I saw on one side the light of a rousing kitchen fire beaming through a window. I entered, and admired for the hundredth time that picture of convenience, neatness, and broad honest enjoyment, the kitchen of an English inn. It was of spacious dimension, hung around by copper and tin vessels, highly polished, and decorated here and there with a Christmas green. Hams, tongues, and flitches of bacon were suspended from the ceiling; a smoke-jack made its ceaseless clanking behind the fireplace, and a clock ticked in one corner. A well-scoured deal table extended along one side of the kitchen, with a cold round of beef, and other hearty viands upon it, over which two foaming tankards of ale seemed mounting guard. Travellers of inferior order were preparing to attack this stout repast, while others sat smoking or gossiping over their ale, on two high-backed oaken settles beside the fire.

Washington Irving, Travelling at Christmas, 1884

Public transport information

Leave the car behind and travel to the pub by bus, train or tram

Using public transport is an excellent way to get to the pub, but many people use it irregularly, and systems can be slightly different from place to place. So, below are some useful websites and phone numbers where you can find all the information you might need.

Combined information

The national **Traveline** system gives information on all rail and local bus services throughout England, Scotland and Wales. Calls are put through to a local call centre and if necessary your call will be switched through to a more relevant one. There are also services for mobiles, including a next-bus text service and smart-phone app. The website offers other services including timetables and a journey planner with mapping:

- 0871 200 22 33
  www.traveline.org.uk

The **Transport Direct** website uniquely offers information for door-to-door travel by public transport, bicycle and car around England, Scotland and Wales. The site provides street-level mapping of transport stops and stations, places and addresses and can generate route maps for various types of journeys:

- **www.transportdirect.info**

LONDON

In London use Traveline or **Transport for London (TfL)** travel services. TfL provides information and route planning for all of London's transport networks, including London Underground and Overground, Docklands Light Railway, National Rail, buses, River Buses, Tramlink, Barclays Cycles and cycle routes. Detailed ticketing information helps you find the most cost effective ways to travel in London. There are also live departure boards, service and traffic updates; mobile services and more:

- 020 7222 1234
  www.tfl.gov.uk

Trains

National Rail Enquiries covers the whole of Great Britain's rail network and provides service information, ticketing, online journey planning and other information.

- 08457 48 49 50
  www.nationalrail.co.uk

Coaches

The two main UK coach companies are **National Express** and **Scottish Citylink**. Between them, they serve everywhere from Cornwall to the Highlands. Their websites offer timetables, journey planning, ticketing and route mapping, along with other useful information.

- National Express: 08717 81 81 81
  www.nationalexpress.com
- Scottish Citylink: 08705 50 50 50
  www.citylink.co.uk

Northern Ireland & islands

For travel outside mainland Britain but within the area of this Guide, information is available from the following companies:

NORTHERN IRELAND

- Translink: 028 9066 6630
  www.translink.co.uk

ISLE OF MAN

- Isle of Man Transport: 01624 662 525
  www.iombusandrail.info

JERSEY

- Liberty Bus: 01534 828 555
  www.libertybus.je

GUERNSEY

- Island Coachways: 01481 720 210
  www.buses.gg

Public transport symbols in the Guide

Pub entries in the Guide include helpful symbols to show if there are stations and/or bus routes close to a pub. There are symbols for railway stations (⇌); tram or light rail stations (🚊); London Underground, Overground or DLR stations (⊖); and bus routes (🚌). See the 'Key to symbols' on the inside front cover for more details.

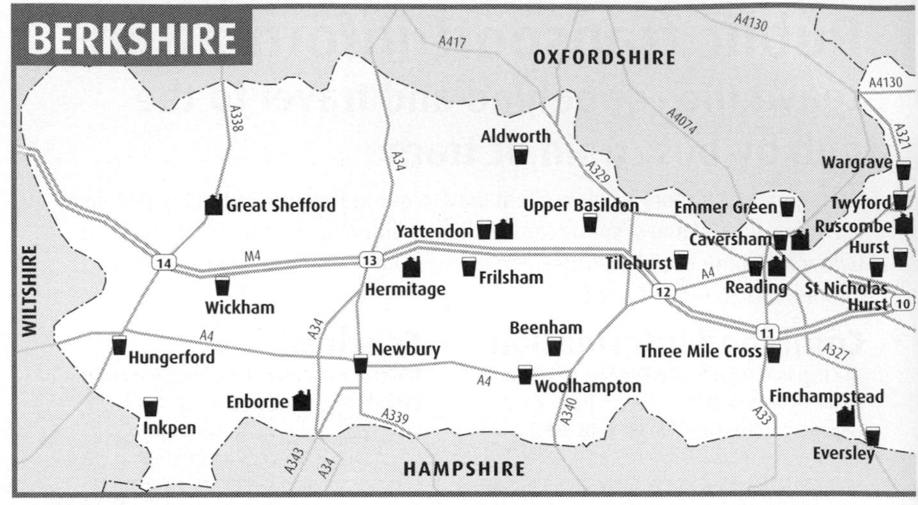

Aldworth

Bell Inn ★

Bell Lane, RG8 9SE (off B4009)

closed Mon; 11-3, 6-11; 12-3, 7-10.30 Sun

(01635) 578272

Arkell's 3B, Kingsdown Ale; West Berkshire Maggs' Magnificent Mild, Good Old Boy; guest beer H

Adjoining a cricket ground and an excellent stop-off for walkers on the nearby Berkshire Downs, this is an unspoilt gem of a pub with a sunny garden and a historic interior. Gentlemen will enjoy their own facilities known affectionately as the planetarium. The pub is famed for its hot filled rolls and its unique ale, Old Tyler. Formerly national, regional and branch CAMRA Pub of the Year, it sells Tutts Clump and Upton ciders. **QP**

Beenham

Six Bells

The Green, RG7 5NX (at Bucklebury end of main road through village)

12-2.30 (not Mon), 6-11; 12-2.30, 6.30-11 Sat; 12-3, 6.30-10.30 Sun (0118) 971 3368 thesixbells.co.uk

West Berkshire Good Old Boy; guest beers H

Welcoming local village pub with open fires in the winter and excellent walking year round. Four-bedroomed accommodation, good food and three ales from smaller breweries in Berks, Bucks and Hants make this a lovely out-of-town stopover. The two bars offer comfy seating and have a range of board games. The Wednesday pie and pudding club has been running for many years and is deservedly popular. **QP**(104)

Binfield

Jack o' Newbury

Terrace Road North, RG42 5PH

11-3, 5.30-11; 12-3, 7-10.30 Sun (01344) 454881

jackofnewbury.co.uk

Loddon Hoppit; West Berkshire Good Old Boy; Young's Special; guest beer H

This traditional family-run Victorian pub to the north of the village is a free house and multiple CAMRA branch Pub of the Year award winner. Visitors receive a friendly welcome. Four real ales are served —the house beer, Binfield Best (3.9% ABV), is popular. Good home-cooked food is available (no food Sun and Mon eves). The real fire is a particular joy. The pub may not open on Sunday evenings in the depths of winter. The adjacent building with skittle alley may be booked for events. **QP**

Victoria Arms

Terrace Road North, RG42 5JA

11.30-11 (midnight Fri & Sat); 12-11 Sun

(01344) 483856 victoriaarmsbinfield.co.uk

Fuller's London Pride, ESB, seasonal beers; Gales HSB H

A vibrant, welcoming pub situated in Binfield village, hosting charity events, quiz nights and occasional live music. It has seven handpumps presently serving five Fuller's ales, including seasonal beers. Outside is a beer garden and a covered, heated terrace, available for private functions. Food includes a children's menu and regular specials, with hog roasts and barbecues in summer. Children are welcome until 7pm. **QP**(53,153)

Bracknell

Cannie Man

Hanover Gardens, Hanworth, RG12 7PD

12-11 (10.30 Sun) (01344) 307620

Fuller's London Pride; guest beers H

A modern estate pub where visitors receive a friendly welcome from management, staff and customers alike. The three well-kept guest real ales include popular best bitters and one LocAle. The pub is consistently among the top three in the CAMRA branch beer-score list and is currently branch Most Improved Pub of the Year. It is well supported by the local community, running pool, darts and football teams, and has two TVs. Children are welcome until the early evening. **P**(100)

Green Man

Crowthorne Road, Wildridings, RG12 7DL

11.30-11; 11-11 Fri & Sat; 12-10.30 Sun

(01344) 423667

Wells Bombardier; guest beers H

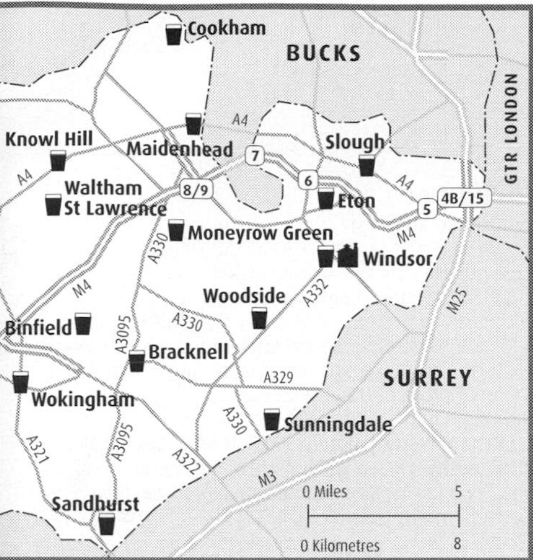

Reputedly a former 16th-century coaching inn, now surrounded by modern housing, the pub has a quiet lounge bar and a public bar with a pool table, dart board and sports TV. With little passing trade this pub depends on loyal locals who provide a good mix of clientele and a friendly atmosphere. The two or three guest beers are frequently from Wychwood and Triple fff breweries.
❀◑P🚌(108)📶

Old Manor 🄻

Grenville Place, RG12 1BP (at Met Office/College roundabout go on to Weather Way, then turn left, then sharp left into Grenville Place car park)
🕓 8am-midnight (1am Fri & Sat) ☎ (01344) 304490
Greene King Abbot; Ruddles Best Bitter; guest beers 🄷
Originally a Tudor manor house, this popular Wetherspoon pub has two bars linked by a half-timbered snug and the Monk's Room, which can be hired for parties and private functions. Eight different beers are served between the two bars, plus real cider. The six guests change constantly – a mix of national and LocAle. Steak, curry and chicken specials nights are held every week, plus roasts on Sunday. The pub has featured in the Guide every year since 2000. Q❀◑♿⇌🍎P🚌

Caversham

Baron Cadogan 🄻

22-24 Prospect Street, RG4 8JG
🕓 8am-11 (midnight Fri & Sat); 8am-10.30 Sun
☎ (0118) 948 1078
Loddon Ferryman's Gold; guest beers 🄷
A Wetherspoon venue on a more intimate scale than many, attracting a diverse crowd of customers since it first opened in 1997. (The Cadogan family seat was nearby.) Paintings by local artists adorn the walls, and TV screens on mute show news and occasional sporting events. The house beer is from the local Loddon Brewery and other microbreweries are also represented.
Q🛏◑♿🍎🚌📶

Fox & Hounds 🄻

51 Gosbrook Road, RG4 8BN
🕓 12-midnight (11 Sun) ☎ 07540 816293
Beer range varies 🄷
The pub offers a constantly changing range of real ales from local breweries and those from further afield. Real cider and perry are also available. 'Hound dogs' (hot dogs made with local sausages) are served at the weekend, plus traditional roast dinners on Sunday 1-5pm. A popular quiz night is hosted on Thursday. 🛏❀◐♣🍎P🚌🐾📶

Cookham

Bounty 🄻

Cock Marsh, SL8 5RG (over railway bridge from Bourne End or walk along Cookham towpath) SU 890872
🕓 12-11 ☎ (01628) 520056 🌐 thebountypub.com
Rebellion IPA, Mutiny; guest beer 🄷
Located on National Trust's Cockmarsh between Cookham village and Bourne End, this quirky, characterful pub is only accessible on foot or by boat. Dogs, walkers and children are made welcome. Bar billiards can be played while listening to '60s music. Live events feature throughout the summer, including the Mikron Theatre. Summer weekends can be busy. Food is served until 8pm. Note the reduced winter opening hours, noon-dusk weekends only.
🛏❀◑⇌(Bourne End)♣🚌🐾

Old Swan Uppers

The Pound, SL6 9QE
🕓 11.30-midnight (10.30 Mon; 11 Tue & Wed); 12-10.30 Sun
☎ (01628) 523573 🌐 theoldswanuppers.co.uk
Butcombe Bitter; Courage Best Bitter; Fuller's London Pride; guest beer 🄷
Friendly, cosy pub with low beamed ceilings, flagstone floors and a wood-burning stove, with a lovely homely feel throughout. Its name relates to the ancient activity of swan upping or marking of the swans on the River Thames. The front bar accommodates drinkers, with a separate restaurant and lounge to the rear. A tapas menu is available alongside traditional pub food.
❀◑⇌P🚌(37)🐾📶

Emmer Green

Black Horse

Kidmore End Road, RG4 8SE
🕓 11-11; 12-11 Sun ☎ (0118) 947 4111
Courage Best Bitter; Young's Bitter 🄷
The pub moved to its present site before 1870, allegedly to remove temptation from the adjacent chapelgoers at its original location in old Peppard Road. In Victorian times the pub yard doubled as the local fire station. Nowadays, this well-kept two-room local has pool and sports TV in its public bar, while the quieter lounge bar has a real fire. You can sit outside the front, or in the enclosed rear patio. Q❀🚌(2,24)

INDEPENDENT BREWERIES

Binghams Ruscombe
Butts Great Shefford
Hermitage Hermitage (NEW)
Siren Craft Finchampstead
Two Bridges Caversham (brewing suspended)
Two Cocks Enborne
West Berkshire Yattendon
Windsor & Eton Windsor
Zerodegrees Reading

Eton

Watermans Arms

Brocas Street, SL4 6BW
12-11.30 (midnight Sat); 12-11 Sun (01753) 861001
watermans-eton.com
Beer range varies
Welcoming, cosy pub located a few yards from Eton Bridge. The interior features rowing memorabilia and Olympic murals including a skiff from the now defunct Eton Boathouse. Secondhand books are on sale in aid of the local Swan Lifeline charity. A function room is available free of charge. Up to eight beers are on sale including at least one from Windsor & Eton and Binghams, local microbreweries and a house beer, Oar-Gasmic, brewed by Caledonian. The Sunday roasts are recommended. (Riverside) (60)

Eversley

Tally Ho

Fleet Hill, RG27 0RR (on A327 at jct of B3348 Fleet Hill just N of river)
11.30-11; 12-10.30 Sun (0118) 973 2134
tallyho.hcpr.co.uk
Phoenix Brunning & Price Original; guest beers
The Tally Ho has a large restaurant and smaller bar area. A large menu is available all day. Three of the five handpumps offer guest beers from many local brewers; the others are dedicated to beers from Phoenix brewery. The pub has a large car park, extensive gardens and a children's play area, all close to the river Blackwater. An ideal spot for outdoor dining in good weather.
Q P

Frilsham

Pot Kiln

RG18 0XX (on unnamed road between Yattendon and Bucklebury)
12-2.30, 6-10.30; closed Tue; 12-11 Sat; 12-9.30 Sun
(01635) 201366 potkiln.org
West Berkshire Mr Chubb's Lunchtime Bitter, Brick Kiln Bitter; guest beer
An 18th-century countryside pub with a cosy bar. The seasonal beer is the monthly speciality from West Berks, but may occasionally be drawn from its standard range to complement the guest selection from a regional brewery. Bar food is available, with venison Scotch egg a local favourite. On summer Sundays the outdoor pizza oven is put to work in the enclosed garden. A cribbage group meets on Friday. The adjoining restaurant is led by TV chef and owner Mike Robinson. Q

Hungerford

John o' Gaunt

Bridge Street, RG17 0EG
11-11 (midnight Fri & Sat); 12-10.30 Sun
(01488) 683535 john-o-gaunt-hungerford.co.uk
Milk Street Funky Monkey; Two Cocks 1643 Cavalier; guest beers
Reopened in 2013 as a free house and brewpub after an extensive refurbishment, this 16th-century listed building retains many original features. A changing selection of at least six real ales is regularly available, supplemented by four real ciders. One of the ales is brewed on the premises in Old Johnnies Brewery. Additionally, some 30 Belgian bottled beers are offered. Quality food, served lunchtimes, evenings and all day Sunday, is seasonal and locally sourced.
Q P

Hurst

Castle Inn

Church Hill, RG10 0SJ
5-11 Mon; 12-2.30, 5.30-11; 12-11 Sat; 12-10.30 Sun
(0118) 934 0034 castlehurst.co.uk
Binghams Twyford Tipple; guest beers
A classic country pub, owned by the church opposite, with parts dating back to the 10th century. First known as the Church House, it was the only place in Hurst where bread was baked — the original oven can still be seen in the snug. Unencumbered by brewery tie, at least one local brew is always available. A changing menu offers good pub food made with seasonal produce, locally sourced where possible. Q P (129)

Inkpen

Swan Inn

Craven Road, Lower Green, RG17 9DX
12-2.30, 7-11; 12-11 Sat; 12-4 Sun (01488) 668326
theswaninn-organics.co.uk
Butts Jester, Traditional; guest beers
A splendid traditional rural inn deep in the countryside run by the same proprietor for 18 years. The pub acts as the brewery tap for the local Butts organic brewery and serves excellent home-made organic food. Cosy tables are arranged on different levels, and there is a separate restaurant. Quiz nights and darts alternate every Thursday. An extensive terraced patio in front is popular with walkers, cyclists and others interested in rural pursuits and history, especially in summer. Ten quality bedrooms are all en suite.
Q P (3)

Knowl Hill

Bird in Hand

Bath Road, RG10 9UP (on A4 between Reading and Maidenhead)
11-11; 12-10.30 Sun (01628) 826622
birdinhand.co.uk
Beer range varies
This historic pub, with parts dating from the 14th century, has been owned by the same family for over 50 years. Hotel, restaurant and conference facilities are provided, along with up to five ever-changing real ales and real cider in summer. The bar fronts the comfortable, oak-panelled lounge area where meals can be enjoyed by the log fire in winter. Outside, there is a lovely beer garden for the warmer weather.
Q P (127,239)

Maidenhead

Bear

8-10 High Street, SL6 1QJ
8am-midnight (11 Sun) (01628) 763030
Greene King IPA, Abbot; guest beers
A short walk from the town hall, this large Wetherspoon pub, formerly a coaching inn, was refurbished in 2009. It has an open plan bar with several seating areas. A spiral staircase leads to an upper floor with an additional bar and comfy sofas.

The 10 handpumps dispense up to five guest ales, many from local breweries. Two or three ciders are often available, including Mr Whiteheads.

Grenfell Arms

22 Oldfield Road, SL6 1TW

12-11 (10 Sun) (01628) 620705

grenfellarmsmaidenhead.co.uk

Greene King IPA, Abbot, IPA Reserve; guest beers H

A welcoming two-room pub situated a short walk from the town centre and the River Thames, known affectionately as the Rat's Hole after the watermen who used to frequent it. The interior has recently been refurbished. There are eight handpumps on the bar divided between regular beers from the Greene King stable and four rotating guests often from local micros. Traditional pub food is served daily, with regular steak and curry nights during the week. QP

Maidenhead Conservative Club

32 York Road, SL6 1SF

11-11 (11.45 Fri & Sat); 12-11 Sun (01628) 620579

maidenheadconclub.co.uk

Fuller's London Pride; Gales Seafarers Ale; guest beers H

Friendly real ale outlet close to the station. The steward is a CAMRA member and the club was winner of the CAMRA Regional Club of the Year in 2013. Two guests ales from independent breweries plus a Fuller's seasonal are available, along with a selection of bottle-conditioned beers. Hot meals are served weekday lunchtimes. Crib and darts nights are held during the week. A public car park is close by. Show a CAMRA membership card for entry for a minimal fee.

Moneyrow Green

White Hart

SL6 2ND

12-11 (10 Sun) (01628) 621460

thewhitehartholyport.co.uk

Greene King IPA; Morland Old Speckled Hen; guest beers H

Charming, traditional two-bar pub half a mile south of the village. Full of character, the public bar has TV and traditional pub games including bar billiards. The smaller wood-panelled lounge bar has sofas and a real fire in winter. Guest ales often come from local breweries. Food is available daily except Monday. Regular quiz and live music evenings are held, plus a summer beer festival. Outside is a large, fenced garden with a children's play area and pétanque square. P(6)

Newbury

Hatchet Inn

12 Market Place, RG14 5BD

7am-midnight (1am Fri & Sat) (01635) 277560

Fuller's London Pride; Greene King Abbot; Ruddles Best Bitter; guest beers H

This Grade II-listed building in Newbury's market place has been a Wetherspoon since 2011. The pub celebrates the contributions made by local people throughout Newbury's history including local authors Michael Bond and Richard Adams, and displays a wood carving of the hatchet man by chainsaw sculptor Nick Speakman. Two Cocks and Wild Weather are just two of the local microbreweries that feature here. The pub is well positioned for public transport links. P

King Charles Tavern

54 Cheap Street, RG14 5BX

11-11 (midnight Fri & Sat) (01635) 42849

Greene King IPA; guest beers H

Under new management since mid-2013, this welcoming town-centre pub is known by the locals as the KC or KCT, and attracts a mixed clientele. It has three separate seating areas surrounding the central bar, with a fireplace in the main bar. Up to three guest ales are available, from breweries linked to Greene King such as Belhaven, and from independent breweries including Dark Star and Lancaster Brewery. Conveniently located close to the rail and bus stations.

Lock Stock & Barrel

104 Northbrook Street, RG14 1AA

11-11 (midnight Fri & Sat); 12-10.30 Sun

(01635) 580550 lockstockandbarrelnewbury.co.uk

Fuller's London Pride, Bengal Lancer, ESB; guest beer H

Popular, traditional town pub overlooking the Kennet & Avon Canal. It has a comfortably furnished open-plan interior, plenty of outside seating and a roof terrace. The regular beers are supplemented by a seasonal beer from Fuller's and a guest from West Berkshire Brewery. Fresh, home-made food is available daily until 9pm. The pub hosts a quiz night on Sunday, poker night on Tuesday and regular live music on Sunday afternoon.

Reading

Alehouse

2 Broad Street, RG1 2BH

11-11; 12-10.30 Sun (0118) 950 8119

hobgoblinreading.co.uk

Beer range varies H

The Alehouse has a unique atmosphere – the perfect antidote to town-centre bars. The pub champions many microbreweries, and the walls and ceiling are festooned with pumpclips reflecting the various ales dispensed over the years. It is the only pub in Reading that serves mead, as well as an excellent range of ciders and perries. Local CAMRA Cider Pub of the Year 2014.

Back of Beyond

104-108 King's Road, RG1 3BY

8am-midnight (0118) 959 5906

Fuller's ESB; Loddon Ferryman's Gold; Ruddles Best Bitter; guest beers H

This Wetherspoon pub stands on the site of a ginger beer factory, later used as a Salvation Army barracks. It has the usual Spoons mixture of tables, chairs and booths, and its long, rectangular lounge has windows spanning the back wall with views of the Kennet & Avon Canal. Prints of old Reading adorn the walls. Outside, there is a good-sized seating area. Stillaging is used in place of handpumps during the JDW beer festival. Q

Hop Leaf

163-165 Southampton Street, RG1 2QZ

12-11.30 (12.30am Fri & Sat) (0118) 931 4700

hopback.co.uk/our-pubs/the-hopleaf.html

Hop Back Golden Best, Redsells EKG, Crop Circle, Summer Lightning; guest beers [H]
A recently refurbished traditional local with an impressive sporting pedigree. Why not try your hand at one of the few bar billiards tables in Reading, or a game of crib or backgammon? The pub stocks an impressive selection of ciders and perries and an interesting variety of bar snacks. Fans of classic rock will enjoy the landlord's choice of music. A good range of daily newspapers is provided. ♣🍎🚌🐾

Nag's Head 🏆 L
5 Russell Street, RG1 7XD
12-11 (midnight Fri); 11-midnight Sat ☎ (0118) 957 4649
nagsheadreading.com
Beer range varies [H]
In seven years the Nags has established itself as a premier ale and cider venue, winning local CAMRA Pub of the Year multiple times. Pies and baguettes are available during the week, with a roast on Sundays. An eclectic mix of bottled beers is stocked. Numerous board games are available above the (tuned and working) upright piano. The pub gets busy on Reading FC match days.
❀◑≠(West)♣🍎P🚌🐾

Zerodegrees L
9 Bridge Street, RG1 2LR
12-midnight (11 Sun) ☎ (0118) 959 7959
zerodegrees.co.uk/reading
Zerodegrees Mango Wheat Ale, Wheat Ale, Black Lager, Pale Ale, Pilsner; guest beer [H]
Real ale continental style, brewed on-site by Angela, a German brewster; the stainless steel brewing plant, visible from the bar, is very much a feature of the establishment. Beer is served chilled, unfiltered and unpasteurised, direct from conditioning tanks. The large wood-fired oven bakes 24 types of pizza. ◑♿≠🚌

St Nicholas Hurst

Wheelwrights Arms
Davis Way, RG10 0TR (N from Winnersh, on B3030, turn right opp entrance to Dinton Pastures)
11.30-3, 5.30 (5 Fri)-11; 11.30-11 Sat; 12-10.30 Sun
☎ (0118) 934 4100 thewheelwrightsarms.co.uk
Wadworth Henry's IPA, Horizon, 6X, Bishops Tipple, Swordfish [A]**; guest beers** [H]
This former wheelwright's workshop is now a classic country pub, popular with locals, walkers and cyclists. It has two bars with low beams plus a dining area extension that can be booked for functions. Six or seven Wadworth beers, one or two guest ales and one real cider are provided. Good pub food is served lunchtimes and evenings (no food Sun eve). Families are welcome with children until 8.30pm, dogs too, and newspapers are provided. The garden has a heated, covered area with benches. Q❀◑♿🍎P🚌(128)

Sandhurst

Rose & Crown 🏆 L
108 High Street, GU47 8HA (on A321 less than 1 mile W of Sandhurst railway station)
12-11 (midnight Fri & Sat); 12-10.30 Sun
☎ (01252) 878938 roseandcrownsandhurst.info
Otter Bitter; guest beers [H]
This family-friendly pub has been an ale house since 1742. It takes pride in the regularly changing range of ales on offer, served via seven handpumps. Outside, there are front and rear decking areas with smoking spaces and a large garden with a children's play area. Beer festivals are held in March, June and October. Traditional pub food is served (no food Mon). Local CAMRA branch Pub of the Year 2014.
❀◑≠♣P🚌(194)🐾

Slough

Moon & Spoon L
86 High Street, SL1 1EL
8am-midnight (11 Sun) ☎ (01753) 531650
Greene King Abbot; Ruddles Best Bitter; guest beers [H]
This Wetherspoon establishment has 12 handpumps dispensing the two regular beers plus up to four constantly changing guest ales, always including one from a local brewery. A couple of ciders are also usually on offer, often Old Rosie and Black Dragon. The usual extensive all-day food menu is available. Soft lighting helps to give the pub a cosy ambience, especially at quieter times.
◑♿≠🍎🚌

Red Cow L
140 Albert Street, SL1 2AU
12-11 (midnight Fri & Sat) ☎ (01753) 522614
redcowpub.co.uk
Beer range varies [H]
A 17th-century listed building with two rooms separated by a large fireplace. The left room has a cosy feel with low beams, while the larger room on the right has a pool table and dartboard. The three real ales are generally sourced from local breweries. Food is served until 7pm, and on Sunday a roast lunch is available 1-4pm. The garden includes a children's play area. Live music features regularly. ❀◑♿♣P🚌(78,81)🐾

Rose & Crown L
312 High Street, SL1 1NB
11-midnight ☎ (01753) 521114
Beer range varies [H]
This small pub, tucked away at the quiet end of the High Street, has a pleasant local feel to it. The front bar and smaller rear bar both have plenty of TVs to allow for uninterrupted sports viewing. Three handpumps offer a constantly changing selection of well-kept ales, including the pub's house beer brewed by Vale. A covered area outside at the back offers comfy sofas, wood-burning stoves and another TV. ❀♣🚌

Sunningdale

Royal Oak L
19 Station Road, SL5 0QL
12-11 (1am Fri & Sat); 12-10.30 Sun ☎ (01344) 623625
oaksunningdale.co.uk
Greene King IPA, Abbot; guest beers [H]
A friendly pub in a village setting making its debut in this year's Guide. Six handpumps serve two regular and one guest beer from the Greene King range and three guest ales mostly from local breweries. Food is home cooked and locally sourced. The main bar has an open fire and a cosy feel, and the garden is great for children. Dogs are welcome too. Board games are available in the bar. Live music events are held on Saturday nights.
Q❀◑♿♣P🚌(1)🐾

Three Mile Cross

Swan L
Basingstoke Road, RG7 1AT
11-1, 2-11; 11-3, 7-11 Sat; 11-4 Sun ☎ (0118) 988 3674
Fuller's London Pride; Loddon Hoppit; Timothy Taylor Boltmaker, Landlord; Wadworth 6X H
Grade II-listed 17th-century inn, originally three timber-framed cottages, occupied by the current licensees for over 30 years. The nearest pub to the Madejski Stadium, the Swan attracts a large rugby/football crowd on match days. Locally produced hearty home-cooked food is served. Look out for the inglenook fireplace and the brass plaques in the loos, where famous visitors are recorded for posterity. ♨❀◑♿P🚌📶

Tilehurst

Fox & Hounds
116 City Road, RG31 5SB
11.30-11; 12-10.30 Sun ☎ (0118) 942 2982
foxandhounds-tilehurst.co.uk
Fuller's London Pride; Sharp's Doom Bar H**; guest beer** H/G
Situated near the western edge of Tilehurst, the Fox & Hounds has a country-pub feel. Licensees Garry and Julie have created a friendly community hostelry with a fishing club, weekly quiz, barbecues, beer festivals and other events throughout the year. Originally cottage-sized, a large conservatory has been added at the rear offering a light, airy space for dining and drinking. Guest beers are often served from gravity casks kept in the kitchen area. ♨❀◑♿♣P🚌(33)📶

Royal Oak
69 Westwood Glen, RG31 5NW
2-11; 12-midnight Fri & Sat; 12-11 Sun ☎ (0118) 941 6056
theroyaloak-tilehurst.co.uk
Beer range varies H
This charmingly quirky building has been frequently extended, and greatly improved by the present landlord and family. The building is a traditional 'bitsa' with all sorts of phases of construction, so one bar has you towering above the bar staff while the other bar is ground level. Show your CAMRA membership card for a discount on real ales. ❀◑♣P🚌(33)🐾

Twyford

Waggon & Horses
61 High Street, RG10 9AJ
5.30-11 Mon; 12-midnight; 12-11 Sun ☎ (0118) 934 0376
Fuller's London Pride; Sharp's Doom Bar; guest beers H
Located to the west of the village, the Waggon offers a good mix of country pub ambience – flagstone floor, low wood-beamed ceiling, big garden with an aviary and Wendy house and a modern outlook. Darts and crib are available to play. Hearty cooked food is served lunchtimes and evenings. A big screen is installed for sports events and there is ample parking.
❀◑⇌♣P🚌(127)🐾📶

> What care I how time advances: I am drinking ale today. **Edgar Allan Poe**

Upper Basildon

Red Lion L
Aldworth Road, RG8 8NG
11-3, 5-11; 12-10.30 Sun ☎ (01491) 671234
theredlionupperbasildon.co.uk
Courage Directors; Sharp's Doom Bar; West Berkshire Good Old Boy; guest beer H
This 17th-century pub welcomes locals and visiting real ale drinkers with an ever-changing selection of up to four ales, including at least two LocAles. The historic core has been extended to provide a restaurant area that doubles as a function room. Good-quality food is mainly traditional English, the ingredients largely sourced from local producers. In winter there is a welcoming open fire, in summer the large garden surrounded by village countryside is popular. ♨❀◑♣P🚌(132,133)🐾📶

Waltham St Lawrence

Bell L
The Street, RG10 0JJ
12-3, 5-11; 12-11 Sat; 12-10.30 Sun ☎ (0118) 934 1788
thebellwalthamstlawrence.co.uk
Beer range varies H
Dating back to the 14th century, this free house was originally a private dwelling, bequeathed to the village in 1608. It offers a changing range of mostly local ales and up to eight cask ciders and perries, served directly from the cellar. Food is taken very seriously – from the ketchup to freshly baked beer bread, hams and stocks, everything is made on site. Q♨❀◑🍎🚌(4)🐾

Wargrave

Wargrave & District Snooker Club
Woodclyffe Hostel, Church Street, RG10 8EP
7-11; closed Sat & Sun ☎ (0118) 940 1548
Beer range varies H
The Grade II-listed Woodclyffe Hostel, bequeathed to the village by a benefactor, houses the club and public library. At least one regularly changing ale from around the UK is always on handpump. Bar billiards, darts, chess, cards, books and TV are available in the bar area. Show this Guide or your CAMRA membership card to gain entry (£3 guest fee to use the snooker tables). Winner of local CAMRA branch Club of the Year for several years. ⇌♣🚌(850)

Wickham

Five Bells 🏆 L
Baydon Road, RG20 8HH
12-3, 5-11; 12-11 Sat; 12-10.30 Sun ☎ (01488) 657300
fivebellswickham.co.uk
Beer range varies H
Thatched village pub, now established as a real ale haven, with nine regularly changing real ales including at least one LocAle. Mark Genders, who has owned this free house since 2012, also keeps four ciders on draught, including some from local producers, and an extensive range of Belgian beers. Fortnightly brewing at weekends is planned for the new microbrewery, housed in a garden building, using the original Two Cocks Brewery brew-plant. Local CAMRA branch Pub of the Year 2014. Q♨❀🛏◑🍎P📶

Windsor

Acre 🄻

Donnelly House, Victoria Street, SL4 1EN
11-11 (midnight Fri & Sat); 12-10.30 Sun
(01753) 841083 theacrewindsor.com
Beer range varies 🄷
Formerly the Liberal Club but now a free house open to all. Three ales are on offer, one from the local Windsor & Eton brewery and two regularly changing guests. Live music is hosted every Saturday night plus an open mic night on Mondays. Two screens show live sporting events. Home-made Sunday roasts are served 1-4pm. Two function rooms are available for hire.
(Central) (77)

Carpenter's Arms

4 Market Street, SL4 1PB
11-11 (midnight Fri & Sat) (01753) 863739
Fuller's London Pride; Sharp's Doom Bar; guest beers 🄷
Nicholson's pub located in a narrow cobbled street near the castle. The tastefully decorated interior is split into three levels, the lowest reputedly containing an old passageway leading to the castle. Tiles on the entrance floor show that the pub was once an Ashby's house. Three regular beers including Nicholson's Pale Ale are supplemented by six guests – a large blackboard displays forthcoming ales. Local CAMRA Pub of the Year 2013. (Central) (71,702)

Two Brewers

34 Park Street, SL4 1LB
11.30-11 (11.30 Fri & Sat); 12-10.30 Sun
(01753) 855426 twobrewerswindsor.co.uk
Fuller's London Pride; St Austell Tribute; Sharp's Doom Bar 🄷
Small, cosy, wood-panelled 17th-century inn, close to the Cambridge Gate entrance to Windsor Great Park and an ideal place to stop after viewing the castle from Long Walk. Popular with locals and tourists alike, it is advisable to book a table if dining (note there is no food on Fri and Sat eves). Dogs are welcome but, due to its size, children are not allowed inside the pub. However, there are seats at the front if the weather permits.
Q (Central) (71,702)

Vansittart Arms 🄻

105 Vansittart Road, SL4 5DD
12-11 (midnight Fri); 10.30-midnight Sat; 10.30-11 Sun
(01753) 865988 fullers.co.uk
Fuller's London Pride, ESB; Gales Seafarers Ale; guest beer 🄷
Located a few minutes' walk west of the town centre, this popular and well-run Fuller's pub is a Guide regular. The ale range includes the current seasonal beer and often a guest from outside Fuller's. In addition to the main bar area there is a pool room to the rear with a small book swap library. Sport is keenly followed, with rugby taking priority. The large garden is ideal for summer barbecues and there is occasional live music.
(71,702)

Wokingham

Queen's Head 🄻

23 The Terrace, RG40 1BP
12-11 (12.30am Fri & Sat); 12-10.30 Sun
(0118) 978 1221
Greene King Abbot; Morland Old Golden Hen; Queen's Head Bitter; guest beers 🄷
A new manageress has transformed this Greene King Local Heroes pub, which now serves three GK ales and three beers from other breweries, mostly LocAle. It has a large, well-designed rear garden with a covered area and additional seating on the south-facing front terrace. There is a drop-down screen for sporting events, otherwise the pub is quiet. Children are welcome until 8pm. Food is served only on specials nights. CAMRA branch Pub of the Year runner-up 2014.
(144,190)

Woodside

Duke of Edinburgh

Woodside Road, SL4 2DP (near Ascot end of Woodside Road running through hamlet of Woodside) SU928709
11-11; 12-6.30 Sun (01344) 882736
thedukeofedinburgh.com
Arkell's 3B, Wiltshire Gold, Moonlight Ale, seasonal beer 🄷
Nick and Annie have managed this Arkell's tied house for over 15 years. Refurbished in 2013, it is very well run, with a friendly atmosphere, strong local support and a reputation for good food and great ales. Arkell's seasonal James' Real Ale has been well received. The bar has sports TVs and Chelsea memorabilia. Occasional football nights feature well-known Chelsea players from times gone by. P

Woolhampton

Rowbarge

Station Road, RG7 5SH
11.30-11 (11.30 Fri & Sat); 11.30-10.30 Sun
(0118) 971 2213 brunningandprice.co.uk/rowbarge
Beer range varies 🄷
The pub is situated alongside the towpath of the Kennet & Avon Canal. The large garden affords space for those arriving by bicycle, with tables on hard standing as well as grass. The building dates back to the 1850s; the interior offers a variety of nooks for intimate drinking, served by a single bar leading to a larger restaurant area. Six handpumps dispense a changing selection of ales from breweries within 60 miles.
(Midgham)P (A4)

Yattendon

Royal Oak 🄻

The Square, RG18 0UF
10-11; 12-10.30 Sun (01635) 201325
royaloakyattendon.co.uk
West Berkshire Mr Chubb's Lunchtime Bitter, Good Old Boy; guest beer 🄷
Effectively the brewery tap for the West Berkshire Brewery, the pub offers three ales as well as Isis Pilsner, all having travelled a matter of yards. There is a focus on dining, with good food made with local ingredients served in pleasant surroundings warmed by open fires. In summer months visitors can make use of seating outside at the front and the splendid garden to the rear. Private rooms can be hired for events and accommodation is available in several well-appointed rooms.
Q

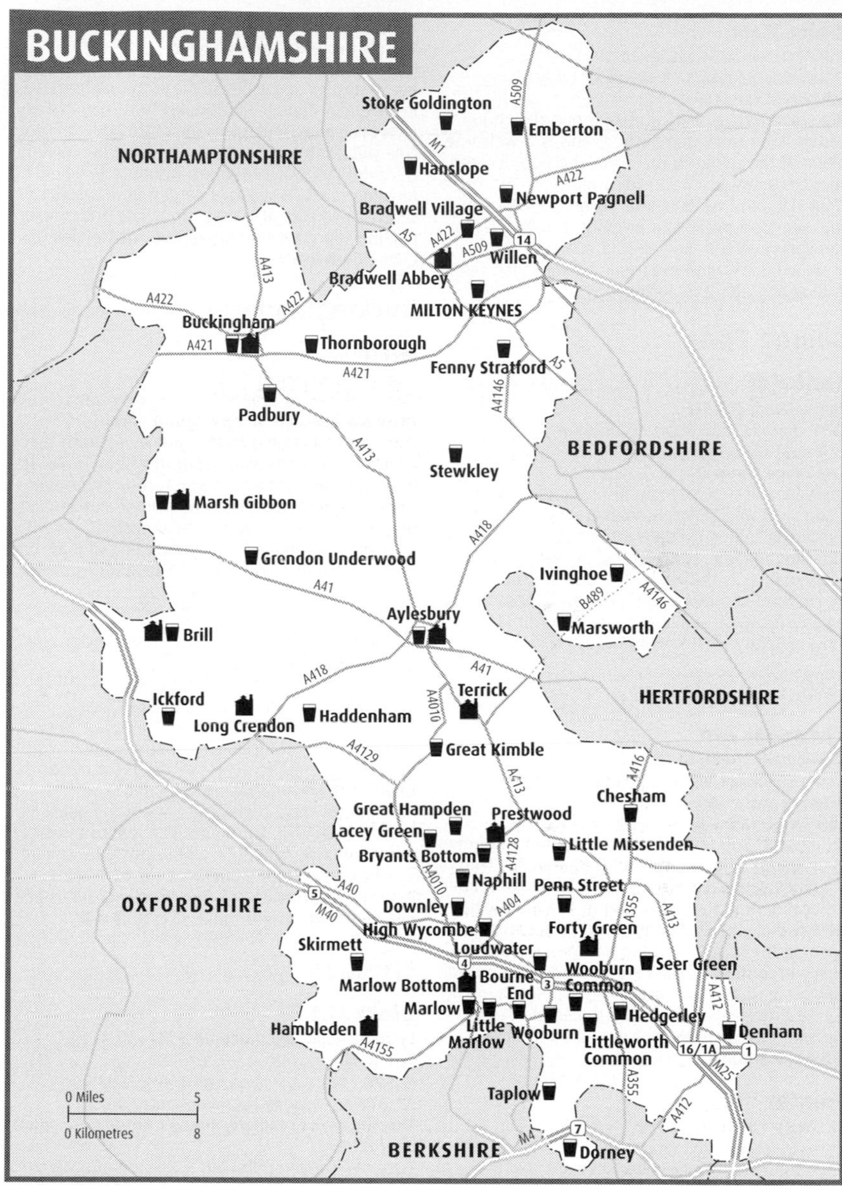

Aylesbury

Farmers' Bar at King's Head 𝕃

King's Head Passage, Market Square, HP20 2RW
11-11; 12-10.30 Sun ☎ (01296) 718812
farmersbar.co.uk
Chiltern Beechwood Bitter, Ale; guest beer Ⓗ
When Chiltern Brewery took over the running of the Farmer's Bar for the National Trust it became the first bar in the country to be no-smoking and free of piped music. Dating from circa 1455, this is the oldest courtyard inn in England and was donated by the Rothschild family in 1924. Ales are often used in cooking and lunches are made from ingredients freshly sourced from local suppliers. A former local CAMRA branch Pub of the Year.
Q

Hop Pole Inn 𝕃

83 Bicester Road, HP19 9AZ (near Gatehouse Industrial Area)
11-11 (midnight Fri & Sat); 11-10.30 Sun
☎ (01296) 482129
Aylesbury Pure Gold; Vale Best Bitter, Gravitas; guest beers Ⓗ
'Aylesbury's Permanent Beer Festival' is home to the Aylesbury Brewhouse and shop which opened in 2011. Their unique brews feature regularly in the pub, but may not last very long! This is Vale's sister brewery and the Hop Pole is the brewery's main outlet, featuring Vale beers plus a selection of guest ales. A friendly welcome as well as good food (no food Mon) add to the attraction.

White Hart
Unit 4, Exchange Street, HP20 1UR
8am-midnight (2am Fri & Sat) ☎ (01296) 468440
Beer range varies H
The White Hart is named after a pub that stood nearby, long since demolished, and is a welcome return of the name to the area. The pub, located opposite Aylesbury Waterside Theatre, used to be a night club, and continues to attract young people who like loud music late at night. During the day and early evening, however, it is a pleasant place to sit and relax, with the usual Wetherspoon range of food and ale.

Bourne End

Garibaldi
Hedsor Road, SL8 5EE
12-11 (midnight Fri & Sat); 12-10.30 Sun
☎ (01628) 522092 garibaldipub.co.uk
Beer range varies H
The Garibaldi is a cosy country pub, offering a warm welcome to locals, walkers, cyclists and families including children and dogs. The selection of quality real ale, typically five at any one time, is very good, as is the value. The pub was purchased by the local community in 2013 and needs all the support it can get while it finds its feet, which it most certainly will. P (37)

Brill

Pheasant Inn
39 Windmill Street, HP18 9TG
12-11 (midnight Fri & Sat) ☎ (01844) 239370
thepheasant.co.uk
Beer range varies H
Picturesque pub in Brill, a village famous for being the inspiration for the village of Bree in The Lord of the Rings and for its nickname Little London due to its location on the former end of the Metropolitan railway line. The Pheasant has been refurbished to open up the inside, creating a large, airy bar, with plenty of seating. Popular with walkers, the outside dining area has an attractive view past the windmill towards Oxford. The house ale, A Very Pleasant Pheasant Ale, is brewed by Skinner's.
Q

Pointer L
27 Church Street, HP18 9RT
12-11 (midnight Fri & Sat); 12-10.30 Sun
☎ (01844) 238339 thepointerbrill.co.uk
Beer range varies H
Extensive refurbishment has transformed the character of this pub. It is now decorated in a modern style that complements the original structure of the building. An open kitchen prepares wonderful food, served in a separate vaulted dining room. The main bar has both tables and couches, with plenty of room for drinkers and diners alike. An outbuilding has been converted into a butcher's (limited opening times). The pub supports the Brill beer festival in August.
Q

Bryants Bottom

Gate Inn
Bryants Bottom Road, HP16 0JS
11-11.30 (midnight Fri & Sat); 12-11 Sun
☎ (01494) 488632 thegateinnpub.co.uk
Fuller's London Pride; Greene King IPA Reserve; Sharp's Doom Bar; guest beer H
Dating from 1864, this traditional village free house nestles in a valley in the scenic Chiltern Hills. It currently offers four cask ales from national and local breweries, with plans for a fifth addition soon. Fine pub food is served lunchtimes and evenings (no food Sun eve). Facilities include a large function room, a spacious garden with a separate, secure children's play area, an aviary and ample parking space on site and on the road opposite.
Q P

Buckingham

Mitre L
2 Mitre Street, MK18 1DW
6 (12 Fri-Sun)-11 ☎ (01280) 813080 themitre.org.uk
Cotswold Lion Best in Show; guest beers H
This small, charming local is just away from the centre of town but well worth the short walk. The beer-only pub has a wonderful, cosy atmosphere with an open fire in the winter. Pool and darts are played in the bar, as well as board games. A variety of beers is available, usually including at least one Oakham ale. The house beer, The Mitre, is brewed by Silverstone. Q P

Woolpack
57 Well Street, MK18 1EP
11-11 (midnight Fri & Sat); 12-10.30 Sun
☎ (01280) 817972 buckinghamwoolpack.co.uk
Brains Rev James; Sharp's Doom Bar; guest beers H
This is a busy, attractively modernised pub which retains many old features, situated just out of the town centre with a riverside garden. Four handpumps serve two regular beers and guest ales from the SIBA list. Freshly cooked food is available, made with local produce where possible. Children are welcome in the large back room. Parking nearby can be awkward. The Woolpack holds beer festivals from time to time. Q

Chesham

Black Cat
Lycrome Road, Lye Green, HP5 3LF (off A416)
SP977034
9am-2.30, 5-11 (7 Mon); 9am-11 Sat; 12-11 Sun
☎ (01494) 773966 blackcatchesham.co.uk
Timothy Taylor Landlord; Young's Bitter H/G**; guest beer** H
Cosy, welcoming pub with a relaxed atmosphere. The single-bar interior has much black cat memorabilia and includes a collection of pumpclips. Generous portions of good food are served, both in the bar and the back room which doubles as a dining area, including excellent

INDEPENDENT BREWERIES
Aylesbury Aylesbury
Britannia Forty Green (brewing suspended)
Buckingham Buckingham
Chiltern Terrick
Concrete Cow Bradwell Abbey
Malt Prestwood
Old Luxters Hambleden
Oxfordshire Ales Marsh Gibbon
Rebellion Marlow Bottom
Vale Brill
XT Long Crendon

Sunday roasts. Families with well-behaved children are welcome and the spacious garden at the rear has a play area. Games are popular here, with darts, crib, dominoes and quiz nights. Breakfast is available from 9am-noon.
P (730)

Black Horse

Vale Road, HP5 3NS (at bottom of Nashleigh Hill turn right into Vale Rd and follow it for 1 mile) SP964046
12-3, 6-11; 12-6 Sun (01494) 784656
black-horse-inn.co.uk
Fuller's London Pride; Tring Side Pocket for a Toad; guest beers H
Situated in a beautiful valley, this traditional pub has something to offer all year round, with log fires to banish winter chills and a large garden pleasant for summer days. But the main draw is the beer – there are always four on offer, including two constantly changing guests. The pub holds a popular quiz on Monday and occasional beer festivals – bonfire night is a particular highlight. Children and dogs are welcome. Runner up local CAMRA branch Pub of the Year 2012.
Q P

Queen's Head

120 Church Street, HP5 1JD (in old town) SP956013
12-11 (10.30 Sun) (01494) 778690
queensheadchesham.co.uk
Brakspear Bitter; Fuller's London Pride, ESB; guest beer H
A traditional ale house and restaurant situated in the old part of town. This is a lovely old pub with the River Chess flowing past the entrance to its yard and under the corner of the public bar. First licensed in 1759, many of the building's original features have remained intact. There are two real fires. The Tour de Pednor charity cycle ride starts here and is usually linked with one of the pub's beer and cider festivals. Q P

Denham

Green Man

Village Road, UB9 5BH
11-11 (01895) 832760 greenmandenham.com
Fuller's London Pride; Greene King IPA; Rebellion Smuggler; guest beer H
With four real ales, tempting food menus and a Monday pie night, this friendly pub is popular with diners, families and drinkers alike. Free of tie, locals vote for the next guest ale. A coaching inn since 1780, the pub's front bar has beams, a real fire and flagged floors, opening out into a large conservatory and well-tended beer garden. Historic Denham is a rural village within the M25 boundary, a pleasant stroll from the Colne Valley Park Visitor Centre. (581)

Dorney

Palmer Arms

Village Road, SL4 6QW
11-11; 12-10.30 Sun (01628) 666612
thepalmerarms.com
Greene King IPA, Abbot; guest beer H
Large pub in a conservation village close to Eton Rowing Lake and the Jubilee River. The emphasis is on food but there is a dedicated area for drinkers with comfy chairs and sofas. Families are welcome and there is an enclosed children's play area in the large garden. The publicans are keen on promoting real ales and hold occasional beer festivals with live music. The guest ale comes from the Greene King list. P

Downley

De Spencers Arms

The Common, Wycombe, HP13 5YQ (across common from village on a flint track beyond the end of Plomer Green Lane)
12-11 (midnight Fri & Sat); 12-10.30 Sun
(01494) 535317 ledespencersarms.co.uk
Fuller's Chiswick Bitter, London Pride; guest beers H
A flint pub on Downley Common, accessible by car and just a mile by road or across the common from the village hall bus stop, with a welcoming atmosphere, open fire, rustic beams and stone-flagged floor. Serving home-cooked food, excellent real ales and wines, it is popular with locals, visitors, walkers and cyclists. Wednesday quiz night, music nights and beer and food events add to the attraction. This Fuller's Master Cellarmanship pub offers four ales including one regularly changing guest. P (31)

Emberton

Bell & Bear

12 High Street, MK46 5DH
12-3 (not Mon), 5-11; 11-3, 5-11 Fri & Sat; 12-10 Sun
(01234) 711565 bellandbear.net
Beer range varies H
A real village pub serving a variety of interesting beers and wonderful food. The landlord is a self-confessed foodie and real ale fan. There are usually three to four real ales, constantly rotating, with an emphasis on local breweries. Local ciders are also often available. The interesting old Grade II-listed building has a long bar and a separate restaurant. Parking is outside on the street. The pub gets busy in summer and at weekends – if you want to dine it is wise to book in advance. Q P

Great Hampden

Hampden Arms

HP16 9RQ
12-3.30, 6.30-midnight (11.30 Sun) (01494) 488255
thehampdenarms.co.uk
Fuller's London Pride; Rebellion IPA; guest beer H
Picturesque pub in the heart of the Chilterns offering excellent real ales and high quality food. Three ales are on handpump, with an emphasis on local breweries – Rebellion, Chiltern, Malt, Vale and Tring have all featured. The à la carte menu is complemented by specials and lunch snacks menus. The pub's large garden is a pleasant place to enjoy a beer in fine weather and is available for parties and events of all kinds. Q P

Great Kimble

Swan

Grove Lane, Smokey Row, HP17 9TR
12-3.30, 5-11 (7-10.30 Sun) (01844) 275288
Beer range varies H
A welcoming, family-run free house dating back to the 1840s, the Swan nestles on the village green in fine walking country at the foot of the Chiltern Hills. There are two separate drinking areas. The taproom features a roaring fire in colder months

while the lounge bar's rear doors open directly onto the enclosed beer garden, popular in summer. The pub is an enthusiastic supporter of LocAle with at least two well-kept ales usually on handpump from nearby breweries.
Q❀⇌◐◑≹(Little Kimble)♣P🚌(300)🐾📶

Grendon Underwood

Swan

Main Street, HP18 0SW
12-2.30 (not Mon & Tue), 5-11; 12-midnight Sat; 12-10 Sun
☎ (01296) 770242 🌐 theswanpub.org.uk
Vale Pale Ale Ⓗ
A traditional thatched village pub in the historic village of Grendon Underwood. The village, listed in the Domesday Book, once bordered the ancient forest of Bernwood, and was a travel stop on the Roman road, Akeman Street. The pub offers a warm welcome to drinkers and diners alike. The restaurant area is for diners only, specialising in tapas and Thai food. ❀◐◑P🚌(16,18)

Haddenham

Rising Sun L

9 Thame Road, HP17 8EN
12-2.30, 5-11; 12-1am Fri & Sat; 12-10.30 Sun
☎ (01844) 291744
Beer range varies Ⓗ
The Riser is a hive of activity throughout the year, with visiting pool and darts teams as well as Aunt Sally in the secluded garden for the summer months. Regular live music and poker on Tuesday evenings add to the pub's ever-expanding repertoire. Boasting Vale and XT ales straight from the cask and a regularly changing selection of guest ales, this little local is a jewel in Haddenham's crown and a friendly haven for regulars and visitors alike.
❀≹(Haddenham & Thame Parkway)♣●🚌(280)🐾📶

Hanslope

Watts Arms L

Castlethorpe Road, MK19 7LG
12-3, 5-11; 12-11 Sat & Sun ☎ (01908) 510246
🌐 thewattsarms.co.uk
Beer range varies Ⓗ
The landlord is a real ale enthusiast and this shows in the consistently excellent quality of his beers. The choice of guest ales is diverse and interesting. Home-cooked dishes freshly prepared using local produce are popular and it is wise to book in advance for Sunday lunch. Local CAMRA Pub of the Year in 2012, this is a traditional hostelry with a friendly welcome. 🐎❀◐◑🚌

Hedgerley

White Horse L

Village Lane, SL2 3UY (in old village, near church)
11-2.30, 5-11; 11-11 Sat; 12-10.30 Sun ☎ (01753) 643225
Rebellion IPA; guest beers Ⓖ
CAMRA branch Pub of the Year on numerous occasions, this village local offers an impressive range of real ales. Rebellion IPA is complemented by an Oakham or Mallinson's beer plus a further six from microbreweries. A draft Belgian beer and three real ciders are also available. This classic pub has a well-tended garden and a heated, covered patio area. Regular beer festivals are hosted, the largest is over the Whitsun weekend and is a must for real ale enthusiasts. Q🐎❀◐♣●P🐾

High Wycombe

Belle Vue

45 Gordon Road, HP13 6EQ
12-2, 4.30-11; 12-1am Fri & Sat; 12-10.30 Sun
☎ (01494) 524728 🌐 thebv.co.uk
Adnams Broadside; Sharp's Doom Bar; guest beers Ⓗ
Situated near the railway station, this friendly, traditional community pub has featured in the Guide for more than 10 years. It offers six ales and four ciders, and holds occasional beer festivals. There is a real fire, live music, regular quiz nights, literary society, knitting circle, ukulele club, vinyl night, folk sessions, charity events, film nights and even Christmas carol 'shouting'. There is also a permanent art exhibition. The ciders are from Westons. ❀⇌≹♣●🚌🐾📶

Falcon L

9 Cornmarket, HP11 2AX
8am-midnight (1am Fri; 2am Sat) ☎ (01494) 538610
Greene King Abbot; Ruddles County; guest beers Ⓗ
Historic ex-coaching inn in the centre of Wycombe. This is now a Wetherspoon pub with a great range of real ales – a welcome commitment to local beers ensures that there is always at least one ale from the area. The open-plan interior has an area reserved for diners and one for drinkers to enjoy the excellent ales. It can get crowded and noisy in the evenings. The cider is from Westons.
Q❀◐◑♿≹●🚌📶

Ickford

Rising Sun

36 Worminghall Road, HP18 9JD (close to M40 jct 8A)
12-2.30, 4-11; 12-11 Sat & Sun ☎ (01844) 339238
🌐 risingsunickford.com
Adnams Southwold Bitter, Broadside; Black Sheep Best Bitter; Hook Norton Hooky; guest beer Ⓗ
The Rising Sun is a traditional thatched pub dating back to the 15th century with exposed oak beams and a blazing real fire when it is cold outside. The pub serves good home-made food, sourcing ingredients locally, and offers four regular ales and a rotating guest. Dog-friendly and popular with ramblers, it hosts live music, quizzes, crib and Aunt Sally. The large beer garden features a children's play area and has a smokers' shelter.
Q❀◐◑♣P🚌🐾📶

Ivinghoe

Rose & Crown L

Vicarage Lane, LU7 9EQ
12 (5 Mon & Tue)-11 ☎ (01296) 668472
🌐 roseandcrownivinghoe.com
Butcombe Gold; Shepherd Neame Spitfire; Tring Side Pocket for a Toad; guest beer Ⓗ
Hidden away but clearly signposted, this is a traditional country pub with a surprisingly large and modern interior featuring an open fire and slate floors. A free house, it offers a good choice of regular beers and guests including those from local microbreweries. A quiet restaurant area to the rear leads to a courtyard patio with a covered area for smokers. Reasonably priced traditional British food is served Wednesday to Sunday. Live acoustic

music sessions feature on Sundays and a quiz night is held on the last Tuesday of the month. (61)

Lacey Green

Pink & Lily

Pink Road, Parsons Hillock, HP27 0RJ
12-midnight (10 Sun) (01494) 489857 pink-lily.com
Sharp's Doom Bar; guest beers
This 300-year-old historic pub, where WWI poet Rupert Brooke was a regular, reopened in 2013. It is now a locally-owned free house offering four real ales and fine food. The three guest ales are from local breweries, with XT Brewing Company a favourite. The garden includes a heated dining space, barbecue and children's play area. A games room is available for adults and children. Muddy boots and dogs are welcome. QP

Whip Inn

Pink Road, Loosely Row, HP27 0PG
11-11 (midnight Fri & Sat); 12-10.30 Sun
(01844) 344060 thewhipinn.co.uk
Beer range varies
High in the Chilterns and popular with ale aficionados, ramblers and cyclists, this pub is renowned for its variety of ales. More than 900 are served every year from the six handpumps, sourced from the many local breweries as well as other micros and nationals. Two real ciders are also kept, and the pub holds annual beer festivals in May and September. An attractive enclosed garden overlooks the Lacey Green Windmill and an excellent range of reasonably priced food is on offer. QP(300)

Little Marlow

King's Head

Church Road, SL7 3RZ
11-11; 12-10.30 Sun (01628) 484407
kingsheadlittlemarlow.co.uk
Adnams Broadside; Fuller's London Pride; Rebellion IPA; Timothy Taylor Landlord; guest beer
Wood-beamed 16th-century inn with three rooms spread over two buildings. With at least one fire in each room, this attractive pub offers a very warm welcome, while the large garden is an attractive option on a summer's evening. One room is dedicated to food, with a wide menu of traditional pub meals and light snacks, one is a function room and the other offers mixed drinking and dining. Ample parking is available. P

Little Missenden

Crown Inn

HP7 0RD (off A413, between Amersham and Gt Missenden) SU924989
11-2.30, 6-11; 12-3, 7-11 Sun (01494) 862571
the-crown-little-missenden.co.uk
Adnams Southwold Bitter; Rebellion IPA; St Austell Tribute; guest beers
This stalwart of the Guide never ceases to offer a good pint and a warm welcome. The clientele includes a good mix of regulars and those passing through, perhaps enjoying some of the local walks. The landlord is a real ale enthusiast and often rotates his beers, so it is a good idea to check if you are after a particular pint. The pub has three en-suite rooms available. QP(177)

Littleworth Common

Blackwood Arms

Common Lane, SL1 8PP SU 937863
closed Mon; 12-11; 12-9.30 (7 winter) Sun
(01753) 645672 theblackwoodarms.net
Brakspear Bitter, Oxford Gold; Wychwood Hobgoblin; guest beers
A delightful Victorian country pub brought back to life by an enthusiastic couple after a long period of closure. Close to Burnham Beeches and popular with walkers and diners, it has a roaring fire in winter and an attractive garden with plenty of seating for the summer. Three guest ales include one from the Marston's group and two free of tie. Traditional English pub food features on seasonal menus. Dog- and horse-friendly, hay is provided. QP

Loudwater

General Havelock

114 Kingsmead Road, HP11 1HZ
12-2.30, 5.30-11; 12-11 Fri & Sat; 12-10.30 Sun
(01494) 520391 generalhavelock.co.uk
Fuller's ESB, London Pride; Gales Seafarers Ale; guest beers
In its 26th consecutive year in the Guide, the General Havelock remains popular with all ages. Formerly three farmyard cottages supplying ale to farm workers, the interior features an eclectic selection of bric-a-brac and antiques. Run by the same family since Fuller's acquired it in 1986, it offers six ales including a range of seasonals and guests. Meals are served lunchtimes (not Sat) and Friday evenings. The pub has a cosy feel in winter while the garden is a peaceful haven in summer. P(35)

Marlow

Britannia

Little Marlow Road, SL7 1HL
11-11 (midnight Fri & Sat) (01628) 483852
mcmullens.co.uk/thebritannia
McMullen AK, Country Bitter
Following a transfer of ownership to McMullen, the Britannia has had a revamp. Its decor has been transformed to give a bright, modern feel, with comfortable furnishings. There is a strong emphasis on food, with meals served throughout the day. Beers are from McMullen, often including its seasonal offerings. Outside is a large decking and seating area for the warmer weather. Though a long way from the town centre, the pub is well connected by buses from Wycombe or Marlow town centre. P(800,850)

Royal British Legion

Station Approach, SL7 1NT (by train station)
7-11; 11-3, 7-midnight Fri & Sat; 11-4 Sun
(01628) 486659 rblmarlow.co.uk/index.html
Jennings Bitter; guest beers
Effectively a free house, this friendly club offers four ales from four independent breweries, with a Derbyshire beer usually available. Porter and stout are represented throughout the year for the discerning drinker. Home of the Marlow jazz club, music features regularly on a Saturday night. You will be welcomed to join in a game of pool, darts or crib. The recently refurbished hall is available for hire. Show a CAMRA membership card or a copy of this Guide for entry. P

Three Horseshoes 𝕃

Burroughs Grove Hill, SL7 3RA (on High Wycombe-Marlow Bottom road)
11.30-3, 5-11; 11.30-11 Fri & Sat; 12-5.30 Sun
☎ (01628) 483109
Rebellion IPA, Mutiny, Smuggler; guest beers Ⓗ
A large open-plan pub a short bus ride from both High Wycombe and Marlow. The extensive specials board, open fires and pleasant garden make this a popular destination for diners, drinkers and families. Close proximity to the Rebellion Beer Company means the six Rebellion ales on offer are always in great condition. Q❀◑◗P🚌(800,850)🐾

Marsh Gibbon

Plough Inn

Church Street, OX27 0HQ
4-midnight; 12-11 Sun ☎ (01869) 278759
theplough-marshgibbon.co.uk
Sharp's Doom Bar; guest beers Ⓗ
A quiet two-bar local in an attractive village on the Buckinghamshire/Oxfordshire border. The long-standing licensees will offer you a warm welcome and excellent ale. The public bar has a warming open fire, while the smaller, quieter room is for diners. Occasional live music and a pool table in an adjoining room provide additional entertainment. ❀◑◗♿♣P🚌(16)

Marsworth

Red Lion 𝕃

90 Vicarage Road, HP23 4LU (opp church)
11-3, 5-11; 11-11 Sat; 12-10.30 Sun ☎ (01296) 668366
redlionmarsworth.co.uk
Fuller's London Pride; guest beers Ⓗ
Traditional country pub in a rural village-green setting. The large public bar with an open fire is bustling and welcoming; the cosy snug leads to a quiet top bar with a wood-burning stove. Benches on the green and in the garden provide plenty of outdoor drinking space. Five guest beers are available and good-quality, value-for-money pub food is served lunchtimes and Tuesday to Saturday evenings. Bar billiards, shove-ha'penny, darts and dominoes are played. Local CAMRA and Buckinghamshire Pub of the Year 2013. Q❀◑◗♣🍎P🚌(61)🐾📶

Milton Keynes: Bradwell Village

Prince Albert

17 Vicarage Road, MK13 9AG
12-11 ☎ (01908) 226524 princealbertbradwell.co.uk
Wells Bombardier; Young's Bitter; guest beers Ⓗ
This friendly, Charles Wells tenancy pub, run by an experienced landlord, offers a selection of well-kept Wells and guest ales, and exceptionally good-value food. There is a pleasant, quiet garden at the back and, set in a peaceful location in the heart of the old village, it still feels like the traditional village inn it once was. ❀◑◗🍎P🚌

Milton Keynes: Central

Barn

800 Secklow Gate West, MK9 3BZ
12-11 (10.30 Sun) ☎ (01908) 663388
Beer range varies Ⓗ
Part of a Premier Inn, this pub, formerly called The Old Barn, is ideally placed for Milton Keynes city centre. It offers a changing selection of ales, often from the Marston's stable, and the usual Beefeater menu of reasonably priced food. Families are welcome. Be aware that daytime parking is on a meter. 🛏◑◗♿⇌P🚌

Wetherspoon's

201 Midsummer Boulevard, MK9 1EA
7am-11 ☎ (01908) 606074
Concrete Cow Bit o' Bully; Cotswold Cask; guest beers Ⓗ
Unbeatable for price and range of beers, this cavernous Spoons has been a local CAMRA Pub of the Year on two occasions. The usual Wetherspoon food menu is served until late. The pub can get extremely busy and service can be a bit tardy at times, but with 12 handpumps it offers the biggest variety of ales in Milton Keynes. ◑◗♿📶

Milton Keynes: Fenny Stratford

Red Lion

11 Lock View Lane, Simpson Road, MK1 1BY
12-11 (midnight Fri & Sat); 12-10.30 Sun
☎ (01908) 372317
Beer range varies Ⓗ
Tucked alongside a lock on the Grand Union Canal, this Grade II-listed gem promises friendly conversation with a real ale enthusiast landlord and a rolling choice of up to three ales, selected to contrast in style and strength. There is a main bar with TV and pool, a quieter lounge and a lock-side garden. ❀⇌♣P🚌🐾

Milton Keynes: Willen

Ship Ashore 🏆

Granville Square, MK15 9JL
11.30-11 (midnight Sat & Sun) ☎ (01908) 694360
Purity UBU; Woodforde's Wherry; guest beers Ⓗ
A smart, modern estate pub, part of the Ember Inns group, offering a constantly changing range of ales. The pub is food oriented but drinkers are always made welcome. It is located within a local centre not far from Willen and Tongwell Lakes and their recreational facilities. Ample free parking is available. Local CAMRA branch Pub of the Year 2014. ❀◑◗

Naphill

Wheel

100 Main Road, HP14 4QA
12 (4.30 Mon)-11; 12-10.30 Sun ☎ (01494) 562210
thewheelnaphill.com
Greene King IPA, IPA Reserve; guest beers Ⓗ
Traditional 18th-century village pub in the heart of the Chilterns with two bars and a recently added large dining area. It offers four excellent cask ales including two regularly changing guests, and good-quality home-cooked pub meals. Walkers, cyclists, families and dogs are all welcome, muddy boots too. There is a large garden at the front and a secluded, smoker-friendly courtyard at the rear. Two large beer festivals are held each year. ❀🛏◑◗♣P🚌(300)🐾📶

Newport Pagnell

Cannon

50 High Street, MK16 8AQ

11-11 (midnight Fri & Sat); 12-11 Sun ☎ (01908) 211495

Beer range varies

This family-run town-centre free house, a long-standing entry in the Guide, offers a good variety of keenly priced beers, often including LocAles. It has a heated area outside for smokers. The large car park is accessed from Union Street which runs behind the pub and the main street. P

Padbury

New Inn

London Road, MK18 2AW (on A413 Buckingham-Aylesbury road)

closed Wed; 5-11 (midnight Fri); 11-midnight Sat; 11-10 Sun ☎ (01280) 813173

Beer range varies

This free house is run by the third generation of the same family. It has three linked bars which are a blend of the old and the new, a smart dining room and a pleasant garden. The pub has retained its original genuine character but provides very modern facilities. The ales and food are always of excellent quality, with LocAles and local produce where possible. Q

Penn Street

Squirrel

HP7 0PX

12 (6 Mon)-11; 12-1am Fri; 12-10.30 Sun

☎ (01494) 711291 thesquirrelpub.co.uk

Rebellion IPA; Tring Side Pocket for a Toad; guest beers

The change in this village local over the last two years has been outstanding. The hard-working licensees have created a wonderful haven of good beer and great food. The main improvement is the beer range – the row of handpumps will bring joy to any ale lover, with four or five mostly LocAles alongside guests from further afield and real cider. The large award-winning garden area is great for families. The Squirrel hosts a beer festival in July in conjunction with another village pub offering more than 100 different beers. P

Seer Green

Jolly Cricketers

24 Chalfont Road, HP9 2YG

12-11.30 (midnight Fri & Sat); 12-10.30 Sun

☎ (01494) 676308 thejollycricketers.co.uk

Fuller's London Pride; Rebellion IPA; Vale Pale Ale; guest beers

A fine locals' village pub, usually busy, with a friendly clientele. Cricket memorabilia adorn the walls and ceiling. A free house, five ales are available, often local, and the house beer, Taverners, is brewed by Rebellion. Excellent food and snacks are made with fresh local and seasonal ingredients. Surrounded by wonderful walking countryside, dogs and muddy boots are welcome.

Q P (305)

Skirmett

Frog at Skirmett

RG9 6TG

11.30-3, 6-11; 12-10.30 (6 winter) Sun ☎ (01491) 638996

thefrogatskirmett.co.uk

Rebellion IPA; guest beers

Welcoming country pub nestled in the heart of the Hambleton Valley with an excellent reputation for fine food. Three handpumps serve two guest beers as well as the regular Rebellion IPA. A typical 18th-century coaching inn, where oak beams, bar and floorboards combine with comfortable furnishings to give a very homely feel. Off the beaten track but well worth making the effort to seek out.

Q P

Stewkley

Swan

1 Chapel Square, High Street North, LU7 0HA

5 (12 Sat)-midnight; 12-11 Sun ☎ (01525) 240285

Sharp's Doom Bar; Wells Bombardier; guest beers

This village local was originally three 16th-century cottages, later disguised by an 18th-century extension with a Georgian façade. Though much altered over the years, there is much of interest inside, and low beams and log fires add to the character. Three or four cask ales are usually available on handpump including guests from micros. Excellent Sunday roasts can be enjoyed in the separate restaurant area. The massive garden is a great attraction in summer with a play area, barbecues and other events.

P (152)

Stoke Goldington

Lamb

High Street, MK16 8NR

12-3 (not Mon), 5-11; 12-11 Sat; 12-7 Sun

☎ (01908) 551233 thelambatstokegoldington.co.uk

Beer range varies

The village is picture postcard-perfect and the Lamb is at its heart – a welcoming, friendly free house with a fine choice of unfailingly excellent ale, often including a LocAle, real cider and superb, generously portioned food. The pub has a cosy bar with a traditional Northampton skittle table and dartboard, restaurant and less formal dining room. Outside, the large garden has a stage area for live music events. Q

Taplow

Oak & Saw

Rectory Road, SL6 0ET

4-9.30 Mon; 12-11 (midnight Fri); 12-10.30 Sun

☎ (01628) 604074 oakandsaw.co.uk

Brakspear Bitter; Fuller's London Pride; guest beer

Situated opposite the village green and church in an idyllic setting, this pub offers three real ales including the monthly Rebellion. A selection of award-winning meat, fresh fish or vegetarian dishes is always on the menu plus chef's specials chosen to reflect seasonal local produce. The popular steak nights include a free bottle of wine. There are quizzes on the second and fourth Sunday of the month. A small garden at the rear has a covered smoking area. P

Thornborough

Two Brewers

Bridge Street, MK18 2DN

12-2 (Wed & Sat only), 6 (5 Sat)-11; 11.15-3, 7-10 Sun
(01280) 812020
Beer range varies H
Everyone's idea of an old country pub, run by the same friendly landlord for almost 30 years. Set in a tranquil village, it has a cosy snug with an inglenook fireplace and a larger main bar with a wood-burning stove, pool tables and darts. Closed weekday lunchtimes except Wednesdays when pensioners get half-price drinks. **QP**

Wooburn

Old Bell

Town Lane, HP10 0PL
12-11 (1am Fri & Sat); 12-6 Sun (01628) 523117
oldbellwooburn.co.uk
Rebellion IPA; Young's London Gold; guest beer H
Traditional 16th-century pub situated next to the church in the attractive conservation area of Wooburn Town. The wood-beamed interior is split between an area mainly for drinking and a dining area serving home-cooked favourites. A suntrap beer garden is popular in the summer for alfresco drinking. The two regular beers are complemented by a guest, usually a Rebellion Brewery seasonal. **QP** (36,37)

Wooburn Common

Royal Standard

Wooburn Common Road, HP10 0JS (follow signs to Odds Farm)
12-11 (10.30 Sun) (01628) 521121
theroyalstandard.biz
Caledonian Deuchars IPA H**; Hop Back Summer Lightning** G**; St Austell Tribute; guest beers** H
Ever-popular semi-rural pub with a congenial ambience in the bar, catering for diners and discerning drinkers alike. Ten real ales, five direct from the cask, alongside many real ciders, make this venue an important flagship pub in the area. There is always at least one dark beer on offer, either a stout, porter or dark mild. Two beer festivals are held, one over the May Day weekend, the other on the last weekend in October. Quiz night is the second Monday of the month.
QP

Squirrel, Penn Street (Photo: Katie Button)

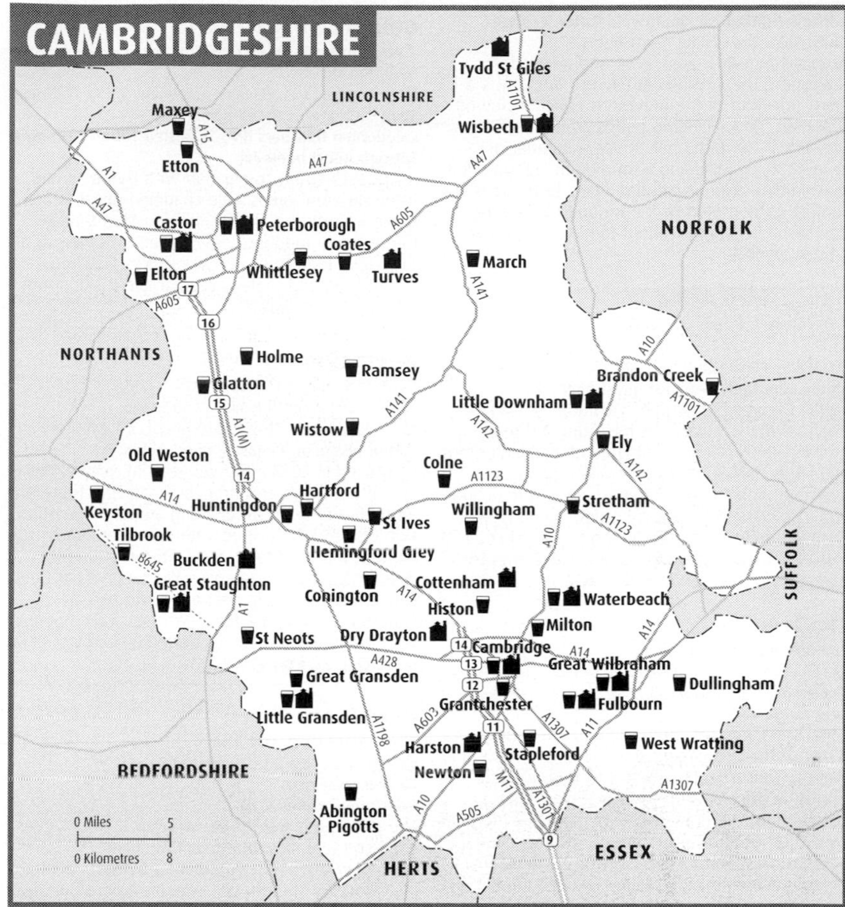

Abington Pigotts

Pig & Abbot

High Street, SG8 0SD (off A505 through Litlington)
✪ 12-3, 6-11; 12-11 Sat; 12-10.30 Sun ☎ (01763) 853515
🌐 pigandabbot.co.uk
Adnams Southwold Bitter; Fuller's London Pride; guest beers Ⓗ
A Queen Anne-period pub in a surprisingly remote part of the south Cambridgeshire countryside. The interior has exposed oak beams and two real fires, including a wood-burning stove in a large inglenook. A comfortable restaurant offers traditional home-made pub food, specialising in fresh fish and chips, steak and kidney puddings and pies. Two guest beers are stocked, often including a brew from Burton Bridge, Humpty Dumpty, Mighty Oak, Timothy Taylor or Woodforde's.
Q🛋✿◑♣P🐾

Brandon Creek

Ship

Brandon Creek Bridge, PE38 0PP
✪ 12-11 ☎ (01353) 676228 🌐 theshipbrandoncreek.co.uk
Beer range varies Ⓗ
A country pub with a comfortable bar, snug and restaurant plus a riverside seating area situated in a striking fork where the Great Ouse meets the Little Ouse on the Cambridgeshire/Norfolk border. At least three cask beers are available including a good selection of East Anglian ales, cider and even unusual local spirits. Locally-sourced food is served lunchtimes and evenings including a variety of gluten-free dishes. Regular Friday night live folk sessions and beer festivals add rustic charm.
✿◑🍎P🐾📶

Cambridge

Cambridge Blue 🄻

85 Gwydir Street, CB1 2LG
✪ 12-11 (10.30 Sun) ☎ (01223) 471680
🌐 the-cambridgeblue.co.uk
Beer range varies Ⓗ
Busy pub with a surprisingly large garden. Beers are from handpumps or the taproom. A huge selection of bottled beers, several German and Belgian beers on draught, a number of ciders and perries, plus mead are also on offer. Beer festivals are held in February, June and October. Wholesome home-cooked food is available all day.
Q🛋✿◑♣🍎🚌(Citi2)🐾📶

Castle Inn

38 Castle Street, CB3 0AJ
✪ 11.30-3, 5-11; 11.30-11.30 Fri & Sat; 12-11 Sun
☎ (01223) 353194 🌐 thecastleinncambridge.com

Adnams Lighthouse, Southwold Bitter, Explorer, Ghost Ship, Broadside; guest beers Ⓗ
Acquired by Adnams in 1994 and respectfully renovated, the Castle is family run and offers a great selection of the brewery's beers, including seasonals, and changing guests from other breweries. The large bar serves a number of drinking areas including a snug on the ground floor and another area on the first floor. To the rear is a suntrap garden next to the mound of the long-demolished castle. Excellent food is served every session.

Devonshire Arms

1 Devonshire Road, CB1 2BH
12-11 (midnight Fri & Sat); 12-10.30 Sun
(01223) 316610 individualpubs.co.uk/devonshire
Milton Minotaur, Pegasus; guest beers Ⓗ
Milton Brewery's first pub in Cambridge and impressively renovated, it has front and rear drinking areas offering a mixture of wooden booths and larger tables. Up to five Milton beers are available with three changing guests, a real cider and a selection of Belgian bottled beers. Good-quality food is on offer including pizzas cooked in a stone bake oven. A wood-burning stove warms the back room in winter. Q (Citi2)

Elm Tree

16a Orchard Street, CB1 1JT
11-11; 12-10.30 Sun (01223) 502632
theelmtreecambridge.co.uk
Beer range varies Ⓗ
At this relaxed back-street pub 10 handpumps dispense three changing ales from B&T, three from Wells & Young's, plus guest ales from myriad micros. A cider or perry is also served. To complement the draught brews there is a menu of over 100 bottled Belgian beers, with occasional beer tastings. Snacks are available at lunchtimes. Occasional live music – mainly folk and blues – and story-telling evenings are hosted.

Flying Pig

106 Hills Road, CB2 1LQ
12-11 (midnight Fri); 7-11 Sat & Sun (01223) 354623
Crouch Vale Brewers Gold; guest beers Ⓗ
Cosy, friendly, L-shaped pub, with a local feel despite being on a main road. The walls and ceiling are decorated with an eclectic collection of old posters and pig paraphernalia. Basic pub grub is served weekday lunchtimes only. In the evenings the intimate lighting is enhanced by candles. Local beers are regularly available, as well as two draught beers from Freedom Brewery. Live acoustic music features most Tuesday/Wednesday evenings and some Saturdays. CAMRA branch Pub of the Year 2013.

Free Press

7 Prospect Row, CB1 1DU
12-2, 6-11; 12-11 Fri & Sat; 12-2.30, 7-10.30 Sun
(01223) 368337 freepresspub.com
Greene King XX Mild, IPA, Abbot; guest beers Ⓗ
Intimate, friendly pub named after a temperance movement newspaper which lasted for just one edition. It serves high-quality food and great beer, including the rare XX Mild. Guests are from Greene King's seasonal and guest lists. A pub for over 120 years, only the tiny snug remains from the original building – the rest is a loving reconstruction. An intimate walled garden is at the rear.
Q

Geldart

1 Ainsworth Street, CB1 2PF (off Mill Road via Kingston & Sturton streets)
closed Mon; 5-11.30 (1am Fri); 12-1am Sat; 12-11.30 Sun
(01223) 314264 the-geldart.co.uk
Caledonian Deuchars IPA; St Austell Tribute; Young's Special; guest beers Ⓗ
Large back-street corner pub with two bars and three different areas. Five changing guest beers come from Punch Finest Cask and SIBA Direct. Home-made food includes hot rocks – diners cook their own meat on a volcanic stone. Functions are catered for, and there is regular live music, from folk to jazz.

Haymakers

54 High Street, CB4 1NG
12-11 (midnight Fri & Sat); 12-10.30 Sun
(01223) 311077 individualpubs.co.uk/haymakers
Milton Justinian, Pegasus; guest beers Ⓗ
Reopened in 2013 after two years of closure, this is Milton Brewery's second pub in the city. There are a number of separate drinking areas —one either side of the door, a snug with bar access and another room off to one side. The food menu includes pizzas to take away. The car park has been converted into the largest pub cycle park in Cambridge, leaving a few spaces for cars. Popular with locals and employees from the nearby science park. Q P (Citi2)

Hopbine

11-12 Fair Street, CB1 1HA
11-11 (12.30am Thu-Sat) (01223) 367204
thehopbine.co.uk
Beer range varies Ⓗ/Ⓖ
The Hopbine is free of tie, with up to seven ever-changing real ales, often East Anglian microbrewery beers. Continental bottled beers are also stocked. The interior includes a bare-boarded area with a pool table, but the rest of the pub is more comfortably furnished. The food ranges from pub classics and burgers to snacks and hot rock menus. Quiz night is Sunday.

Kingston Arms

33 Kingston Street, CB1 2NU
12-3, 5-11; 12-midnight Fri; 11-midnight Sat; 11-11 Sun
(01223) 319414 kingston-arms.co.uk

INDEPENDENT BREWERIES

Bexar County Peterborough
BlackBar Harston
Calverley's Cambridge (NEW)
Cambridge Cambridge (NEW)
Castor Castor
Crafty Beers Great Wilbraham
Draycott Buckden
Elgood's Wisbech
Fellows Cottenham
Lord Conrad's Dry Drayton
Mile Tree Wisbech
Milton Waterbeach
Moonshine Fulbourn
Oakham Peterborough
Red Great Staughton
Son of Sid Little Gransden
Three Blind Mice Little Downham (NEW)
Tydd Steam Tydd Saint Giles
Xtreme Turves (NEW)

Crouch Vale Brewers Gold; Oakham Bishops Farewell; Thornbridge Jaipur IPA; Timothy Taylor Landlord; Woodforde's Wherry; guest beers Ⓗ
Classic side-street pub just off Mill Road. Eleven handpumps serve regular and changing guest beers plus a changing cider and Broadoak Perry. A large selection of Belgian and other bottled beers is stocked and monthly beer festivals are held in the warmer months. Good food is available at all sessions including a recession menu of cheap eats. The walled garden has canopies and heaters and is popular all year round. Free newspapers are available. Q❀◐⇌♣●🚌(Citi2)🐾📶

Live & Let Live 𝕃

40 Mawson Road, CB1 2EA
⏲ 11.30-2.30, 5.30 (6 Sat)-11; 12-3, 7-11 Sun
☎ (01223) 460261
Nethergate Umbel Ale; Oakham Citra; guest beers Ⓗ
Wood panelling and railway and beer memorabilia add to the atmosphere at this discreet corner local just off Mill Road. Up to seven handpumps present an array of ever-changing guest ales ranging from session bitters to strong ales and generally including a dark beer. The eighth handpump dispenses local Cassells cider. There is an outstanding collection of rums from around the world, and occasional rum festivals take place. Snacks are available – the pork pies and Scotch eggs are excellent. Q⇌♣●🍷🚌(Citi2)🐾

Maypole 𝕃

20a Portugal Place, CB5 8AF
⏲ 11.30-midnight (2am Fri & Sat); 12-11.30 Sun
☎ (01223) 352999 🌐 maypolefreehouse.co.uk
Beer range varies Ⓗ
The Castiglione family, who have run this city-centre pub for over 30 years, bought the freehold from Punch Taverns in 2009. It has since become a showcase for quality beers and won the first CAMRA branch Real Ale Champion award in 2010. Up to 16 beers are on offer including local ales. The interior comprises two rooms either side of the bar plus a large upstairs function room. A pleasant suntrap patio has covered space for smokers. The food menu focuses on home-cooked Italian dishes. ❀◐●🚌(Citi I,Citi2)📶

Mill 𝕃

14 Mill Lane, CB2 1RX
⏲ 11-11 (midnight Thu-Sat) ☎ (01223) 311829
🌐 themillpubcambridge.co.uk
Beer range varies Ⓗ
Set in a honeypot location next to the Mill Pond, the pub has been recently refurbished – improvements include an attractive wood-panelled side room. The bar has eight handpumps, including one for cider. There is a strong commitment to locally brewed beers from Milton, Fellows, BlackBar, Moonshine and Lord Conrad's, plus beers brewed at sister pub the Cambridge Brew House. An Adnams' beer is generally available, and a polypin of local cider often sits behind the bar. Q🐴◐●🐾

St Radegund 𝕃

127 King Street, CB1 1LD
⏲ 5 (12 Sat)-11; 12-10.30 Sun ☎ (01223) 311794
Beer range varies Ⓗ
The smallest pub in Cambridge, near the Four Lamps roundabout. A unique free house, it offers up to seven real ales including LocAles. The interior is packed with local sporting memorabilia and has a rain check tree, enabling you to pay for a pint for someone to drink later. In tribute to the Eagle pub, the ceiling is covered in inscriptions. The pub has its own rowing and cricket teams and is the home of the infamous Hash House Harriers. Q🚌

Castor

Prince of Wales Feathers 𝕃

38 Peterborough Road, PE5 7AL
⏲ 12-11.30 (1am Fri & Sat); 12-midnight Sun
☎ (01733) 380222 🌐 princeofwalesfeathers.co.uk
Adnams Broadside; Woodforde's Wherry Ⓗ**; guest beers** Ⓗ/Ⓖ
This 17th-century stone-built inn has an open-plan layout with different areas including the bar and a TV area with leather sofas. Six real ales – one served from the cellar – a real cider and a perry are available at all times. Lunches are available daily, evening meals on weekdays only. Live music is hosted every Saturday and a quiz night on Sunday. There is an annual beer festival in May.
❀◐♣●🍷🚌(4P,9)🐾

Coates

Vine 𝕃

4 South Green, PE7 2BJ
⏲ 3-11; 12-midnight Fri & Sat; 12-10.30 Sun
☎ (01733) 840343 🌐 vinefreehouse.wordpress.com
Beer range varies Ⓗ
Traditional English country free house overlooking the green. It has a lively bar/lounge and a separate restaurant with its own bar. Good pub food is served lunchtimes and evenings. The varying beer list includes a LocAle. The large outdoor area includes a pétanque court. Local buses pass in front of the pub. Q❀◐P🚌(33,701)🐾📶

Colne

Green Man 𝕃

East Street, PE28 3LZ
⏲ 12-2.30 (not Mon), 5-11; 12-11 Fri-Sun ☎ (01487) 840368
🌐 greenmancolne.co.uk
Elgood's Cambridge Bitter; Oakham Inferno; Sharp's Doom Bar; guest beers Ⓗ
Picturesque 17th-century village local in an old Fenland fruit-growing area. This busy, friendly pub provides a public bar with pool, darts and TV, and a warm, sociable lounge with a modern dining area extension serving good food. Quiz nights are held fortnightly. Outside, the garden has a children's play area and hosts barbecues in summer. There is camping nearby at Earith Lakes.
🐴❀◐♿⛺♣P🐾📶

Conington

White Swan

Elsworth Road, CB23 4LN
⏲ closed Mon; 12-3, 6-11 (10.30 Sun) ☎ (01954) 267251
🌐 whiteswanconington.com
Adnams Southwold Bitter, Ghost Ship; guest beers Ⓖ
Sturdy 18th-century brick building fronted by an impressive sward for alfresco drinking and children's amusement. The main bar has a tiled floor and a brick fireplace occupied by a fine cast-iron stove. It has been extended into the old cellar, the real ales being served by gravity from behind the new bar. The food menu offers quality and value (no meals Sun eve). Q🐴❀◐♣●P🐾

Dullingham

Boot

18 Brinkley Road, CB8 9UW

❂ 11.30-2.30, 5-11; 11.30-11.30 Sat; 11.30-10.30 Sun
☎ (01638) 507327

Adnams Southwold Bitter; Greene King IPA; guest beers [H]

Traditional village inn rescued by a villager, it is now a vibrant and welcoming community local where something is always going on. The pub is home to darts, crib and pétanque teams, and hosts regular live music and beer festivals twice a year. Simple, good-value pub food is served lunchtimes (no food Sun), and fish and chips on Wednesday evenings. Children are welcome until 8pm. Around a mile from Dullingham railway station. ❀◑♣P🐾

Elton

Crown Inn L

8 Duck Street, PE8 6RQ

❂ 12 (5 Mon)-11 ☎ (01832) 280232 🌐 thecrowninn.org

Greene King IPA; Phipps NBC IPA; guest beers [H]

Sixteenth-century stone pub with a thatched roof. It has one main bar, a small dining area to the front and a restaurant to the rear. Six real ales are usually on offer via handpump including the house beer, Golden Crown Ale, brewed by Tydd Steam. There is a dedicated handpump for real cider. No bar food is served Saturday evening or Sunday. Five-star B&B accommodation is available.
❀🛏◑●P🚌 (X4,24)🐾📶

Ely

Liberty Belle

29a Forehill, CB7 4AA

❂ 5.30-10 Mon; 5 (4 Thu)-10.30 (10 Tue); 12.30-10.30 Sat; 12.30-10 Sun 🌐 libertybelleely.co.uk/liberty-belle-the-real-ale-bar

Beer range varies [G]

Small, welcoming micropub, opened in 2013. Six real ales are usually available, mostly sourced from local microbrewers. The cellar is in a back room and beer is usually delivered to your table. Two local ciders are also available. The pub hosts Super 8 Cine nights and some small live music events. Limited food is available. Open weekday lunchtimes during the summer. ⇌●

Prince Albert L

62 Silver Street, CB7 4JF (opp cathedral car park)

❂ 12-3, 5-11.30; 12-11.30 Sat; 12-10.30 Sun
☎ (01353) 663494

Greene King XX Mild, IPA, Abbot; guest beers [H]

Classic small back-street local with friendly staff and locals situated a short walk from Ely Cathedral. It has 10 handpumps and is a rare outlet for XX Mild. Usually up to five guest beers are available and a guest cider. No music, TV or fruit machine distract from the pleasant bar room banter. A beautiful walled garden is ideal for relaxing in the summer. Q❀◑⇌●🚌🐾📶

Etton

Golden Pheasant L

1 Main Road, PE6 7DA

❂ 12-2.30 (not Mon), 5-11; 12-11 Fri-Sun ☎ (01733) 252387
🌐 thegoldenpheasant.net

Beer range varies [H]

An impressive stone-built Grade II-listed former manor house, with five handpumps dispensing changing and mostly local beers in the recently enlarged bar. There is ample parking, a large garden, a children's play area, and a permanent marquee with bar for functions. A separate restaurant seats up to 30. It is on the Green Wheel route from Peterborough. Live music features most Saturday nights, and it is a meeting place for several local groups. Q❀◑♣●P🚌 (22)

Fulbourn

Six Bells

9 High Street, CB21 5DH

❂ 11.30-3, 5-11; 11.30-11 Fri-Sun ☎ (01223) 880244
🌐 thesixbellsfulbourn.co.uk

Adnams Southwold Bitter, Broadside; Greene King IPA; Woodforde's Wherry; guest beers [H]

Traditional thatched village pub, previously a coaching inn. The main bar has low ceilings, a real fire and many cosy corners. The food is locally sourced and home-cooked and may be eaten in the bar or the separate dining room (no food Sun or Mon eve). The function room hosts a trad jazz club on the first and third Wednesdays of the month. A regular in the Guide.
🐴❀◑♿♣●P🚌 (Citi1,Citi3)🐾📶

Glatton

Addison Arms L

Sawtry Road, PE28 5RZ

❂ 11-3, 5-11; 11-11 Fri-Sun ☎ (01487) 830410
🌐 addisonarms.co.uk

Adnams Broadside; guest beers [H]

Built at the start of the 18th century, the pub is named after the playwright and politician Joseph Addison (co-founder of The Spectator), who was a relative of the first landlord. At least three real ales and a real cider are on offer, with a focus on local producers, alongside good food prepared from fresh locally-sourced supplies. The Sunday night quiz is popular. The house beer, Addison Ale, is Digfield Shacklebush. Q❀◑♣●P🐾

Grantchester

Blue Ball Inn

57 Broadway, CB3 9NQ

❂ 2-11; 12-midnight Sat; 12-10 Sun ☎ (01223) 840679

Adnams Southwold Bitter; guest beer [H]

Small, authentic local built in 1893 and retaining its original two-bar layout and many old fittings (including the landlord). No lager, no TV, no children – good beer, good conversation and old pub games are the order of the day. The piano is still played and there is live music every Thursday. At the back is a small walled garden with a heated 'smokeatorium'. Try your hand at ringing the bull.
Q❀♣🚌 (18)🐾

Great Gransden

Crown & Cushion L

2 West Street, SG19 3AT

❂ closed Mon; 3 (12 Sat)-11; 12-10 Sun ☎ (01767) 677214
🌐 crownandcushion.com

Beer range varies [H]

Picture-postcard village pub with a thatched roof and oak beams. The lounge and dining area feature a large fireplace with wood-burning stove. This

busy village pub has much to offer including live music on Wednesdays and Thursdays. An interesting menu focusing on Indonesian cuisine is available Friday to Sunday and at other times by prior arrangement. Three guest beers are mainly from Adnams and Oakham.
Q🐴❀◑▲♣P🚌(18)📶

Great Staughton

White Hart

56 The Highway, PE19 5DA (on B645)
⏲ 12-2.30, 4-11 (midnight Fri); 12-11 Sat & Sun
☎ (01480) 861131 🌐 whitehartgreatstaughton.co.uk
Batemans XB, XXXB; guest beer Ⓗ
A former coaching inn dating back to the 16th century; although extended and altered it still warrants a Grade II-listing. The interior comprises a main bar, a small room at the front and a restaurant to the rear. Traditional pub food is served lunchtimes and evenings Thursday to Saturday, lunchtime only on Sunday.
Q🐴❀◑P🚌(156)🐾📶

Great Wilbraham

Carpenters Arms Ⓛ

10 High Sreet, CB21 5JD
⏲ 11.30-3, 6.30-11; closed Tue; 11.30-3 Sun
☎ (01223) 882093 🌐 carpentersarmsgastropub.co.uk
Crafty Beers Carpenter's Cask; guest beers Ⓗ
The Carpenters has its own microbrewery in the old stables at the rear and offers one or two of its own beers plus occasional guest ales. The pub serves both traditional pub food and a menu reflecting the owners' previous experience running an award-winning restaurant in France. Parts of the building date back to the 17th century. The bar billiards table is in regular use. ❀◑♿♣P📶

Hartford

King of the Belgians 🏆 Ⓛ

27 Main Street, PE29 1XU
⏲ 11-11 (midnight Fri & Sat); 12-10.30 Sun
☎ (01480) 52030 🌐 kingofthebelgians.com
Beer range varies Ⓗ
Sixteenth-century pub in a picturesque village setting. A genuine community pub, it offers an ever-changing selection of four real ales and good-value food every day including a traditional Sunday roast. Oak beams and a copper-topped bar are features of the public bar and there is a separate dining area. It holds regular quizzes, games nights and an open mic night on the first Monday of the month. Do not miss the beer festival at the end of May. 🐴❀◑♣●P🚌(1a)🐾

Hemingford Grey

Cock Ⓛ

47 High Street, PE28 9BJ (off A14, SE of Huntingdon)
⏲ 11.30-3, 6-11; 11.30-11 Sat; 12-10.30 Sun
☎ (01480) 463609 🌐 cambscuisine.com
Brewsters Hophead; Nethergate IPA; guest beers Ⓗ
This village pub and restaurant has won local, regional and national awards. The cosy interior has been recently refurbished to provide more comfortable facilities and is popular with locals and diners who enjoy the well-kept locally-sourced beers, and real Cromwell cider produced in the village. For the separate restaurant booking is essential at all times. During the summer, occasional beer festivals are held in the garden.
Q❀◑▲●P🚌(5)🐾

Histon

Red Lion

27 High Street, CB24 9JD
⏲ 10.30-11 (midnight Fri); 12-11 Sun ☎ (01223) 564437
🌐 theredlionhiston.co.uk
Adnams Ghost Ship; Batemans XB; Oakham Bishops Farewell; Tring Blonde; guest beers Ⓗ
The two bars of this free house are adorned with a wonderful collection of breweriana and historic photos. The beer range includes five changing guests, Belgian and German beers on draught plus a range of continental bottles. A mild is usually available, plus up to three ciders and a perry. Breakfast is served from 10.30am on Saturday. Two beer festivals are held each year – an Easter aperitif, then the main event in September.
🐴❀◑♿♣●P🚌(Citi8)📶

Holme

Admiral Wells Ⓛ

41 Station Road, PE7 3PH (jct of B660 and Yaxley Rd)
⏲ 11-2.30, 5-11; 11-11 Sat; 11-10.30 Sun ☎ (01487) 831214
🌐 admiralwells.co.uk
Adnams Southwold Bitter, Broadside; Digfield Shacklebush; Oakham JHB; guest beers Ⓗ
Victorian inn named after one of Nelson's pall bearers and officially the lowest ground-level pub in the UK. It has two drinking areas in a modern contemporary style, and a function room at the rear. Next to the old Holme railway station and the East Coast mainline, the walls are adorned with photographs from the steam railway days. Up to seven real ales and a cider are usually available and the pub serves excellent food. Quiz night is Tuesday. Q🐴❀◑♿♣●P🐾

Huntingdon

Old Bridge Hotel

1 High Street, PE29 3TQ (at S end of High St on ring road, by river)
⏲ 11-11; 12-10.30 Sun ☎ (01480) 424300
🌐 huntsbridge.com
Adnams Southwold Bitter; guest beers Ⓗ
Handsome ivy-clad 18th-century building set in a prominent position on the banks of the River Ouse. Diners can enjoy imaginative, high-quality food on the patio, while drinkers can relax in the bar or lounge area. The hotel hosts occasional beer tastings presented by local and regional brewers, and the Old Bridge Wine Shop offers tutored wine tastings. The bus station is a short walk away.
Q🐴❀🛏◑P🚌🐾📶

Keyston

Pheasant Ⓛ

Loop Road, PE28 0RE (on B663, 1 mile S of A14, E of Thrapston)
⏲ closed Mon; 12-3, 6-11; 12-11 Fri & Sat; 12-5 Sun
☎ (01832) 710241 🌐 thepheasant-keyston.co.uk
Adnams Southwold Bitter; guest beers Ⓗ
The village is named after Ketil's Stone, probably an Anglo-Saxon boundary marker. Created from a row of thatched cottages in an idyllic setting, the pub offers high-quality food, fine wines and well-

kept cask ales. There is a splendid lounge bar and three dining areas. Regularly changing guest beers are offered, usually from Nene Valley or Digfield. One of the few pubs in this Guide that have featured regularly since the first edition in 1972.
Q P

Little Downham

Plough

106 Main Street, CB6 2SX (W end of village)
12-3 (not Mon), 6-11; 12-midnight Fri & Sat; 12-3, 6-10.30 Sun (01353) 698297
Beer range varies
An early Victorian Grade II-listed pub, well preserved in character and charm. Three cask-conditioned ales are usually on handpump, often from Cambridgeshire and East Anglian breweries. Thai cuisine is served, also available to take away. The annual Plough beer festival is held in early September. The pub stays open all day at weekends if busy and children are welcome until 9pm. P

Little Gransden

Chequers

71 Main Road, SG19 3DW
12-2, 7-11; 12-11 Fri & Sat; 12-6, 7-10.30 Sun
(01767) 677348 chequersgransden.co.uk
Beer range varies
This village pub has been owned and run by the same family for more than 60 years, and has featured in the Guide for 20 years. The unspoilt middle bar, with its wooden bench seating and roaring fire, is a favourite spot to catch up on local gossip. The pub's Son of Sid brewhouse supplies the pub and local beer festivals. Fish and chips are a highlight on Friday night (booking essential). Pickled Pig cider is nearly always available. The pub is the winner of numerous CAMRA awards.
Q P (18A)

March

Hippodrome

Dartford Road, PE15 8AQ
8am-midnight (1am Fri & Sat) (01354) 602980
Adnams Broadside; Greene King Abbot; Ruddles Best Bitter; guest beers
Originally a cinema that became a bingo hall, it closed in 2009 but reopened in 2011 as a Wetherspoon pub after a major refurbishment. Vintage cinema posters adorn the walls and a large, impressive work of art, The March Montage, is on the wall above the bar, and there are circle seats above the drinking area. Ten handpumps serve the two regular beers plus changing guests.
(33)

Rose & Crown

41 St Peters Road, PE15 9NA
12-11 (11.30 Thu; midnight Fri & Sat) (01354) 652077
the-rose-and-crown-march.co.uk
St Austell Trelawny; guest beers
Traditional family-run 150-year-old free house. This is a community pub with low-beamed ceilings in both rooms and a real fire. Up to six handpumped real ales, mainly from micros, often include an Oakham ale and a West Country beer, plus a real cider and/or perry. The pub also holds a regular Easter beer festival. Good-quality food is served lunchtimes and evenings. Quiz night is Thursday and occasional live music features on Saturday.
Q P (33,46)

Ship Inn

1 Nene Parade, PE15 8TD
11-11 (12.30am Fri & Sat); 11-10.30 Sun
(01354) 607878
Tydd Steam Barn Ale; Woodforde's Wherry; guest beers
Built in 1680, this Grade II-listed thatched riverside pub has extensive boat moorings. The unusual carved beams are said to have 'fallen off a barge' during the building of Ely Cathedral. Full of character, note the collection of pumpclips and the quaint wobbly floor and wall leading to the toilets, and to a small games room. Following a major refit the pub reopened in 2010 as a free house.
Q (33,46)

Maxey

Blue Bell

39 High Street, PE6 9EE
5.30 (1 Sat)-11.30; 12-11.30 (12-7, 8.30-11.30 winter) Sun
(01778) 348182
Abbeydale Absolution; Fuller's London Pride; Woodforde's Wherry; guest beers
This multi-award-winning stone-built free house has been run by the same landlord for over 12 years. Originally a barn, it was converted many years ago and reflects the rural setting in which it is found. Paraphernalia of countryside living adorn the walls and shelves of the two-roomed interior. Nine handpumps dispense a range of ales from large and small breweries from far and wide. A popular meeting place for groups including birdwatchers and golfers. Q P (413)

Milton

Jolly Brewers

5 Fen Road, CB24 6AD
12-midnight (1am Fri); 12-10.30 Sun (01223) 863895
jollybrewersmilton.co.uk
Elgood's Cambridge Bitter; Greene King IPA; guest beers
This refurbished pub and restaurant reopened in 2012. The timber-framed building dates back to 1700 and had its own brewery until 1925. There is a small bar to the left of the entrance, with the restaurant to the right. At the rear is a courtyard which includes an outside seating area, a children's playground and B&B accommodation (four en-suite rooms). Guest beers include ales from the local Milton Brewery. (9)

Newton

Queen's Head

CB22 7PG
11.30-2.30, 6-11; 12-2.30, 7-10.30 Sun (01223) 870436
Adnams Southwold Bitter, Broadside; guest beers
This village local is one of a handful to have appeared in every edition of this Guide. The list of landlords since 1729, displayed on the wall in the simply furnished public bar, has just 18 entries. The cosy lounge has a welcoming fire in the colder months. Simple but excellent food, served evenings, centres on soup and sandwiches. Guest beers are from the Adnams' seasonal range.
Q P (31)

Old Weston

Swan

Main Street, PE28 5LL (on B660, N of A14)
⏲ 6.30-11; 12-2.30, 7-11 Sat; 12-3.30, 7-10.30 Sun
☎ (01832) 293400
Greene King Abbot; Timothy Taylor Landlord; guest beer Ⓗ
Dating from the 16th century, this oak-beamed building started life as two private houses. At the end of the 19th century the pub had its own brewery. There is a central bar with a large inglenook, a dining area and a games section offering hood skittles and pool. At weekends a varied menu of traditional pub food is available, including home-made puddings. Q◑♣P🐾

Peterborough

Charters 🄻

Town Bridge, PE1 1FP (down steps at Town Bridge)
⏲ 12-11 (midnight Fri & Sat); 12-10.30 Sun
☎ (01733) 315700 🌐 charters-bar.com
Oakham JHB, Inferno, Citra, Bishops Farewell; guest beers Ⓗ/Ⓖ
The converted Dutch grain barge from circa 1907 sits on the River Nene near to the city centre. An oriental restaurant is on the upper deck and food is also served in the bar. A large garden with a marquee, bar and landing stage for boats is popular in summer. Up to 12 beers are on offer plus cider. Live music plays some weekends inside and outside the pub. Busy on football match days. Close to the Nene Valley Railway. ❀◑♣🍎P🚌🐾

Coalheavers Arms

5 Park Street, Woodston, PE2 9BH
⏲ 12-2 (not Mon-Wed), 5-11; 12-11 Fri & Sat; 12-10.30 Sun
☎ (01733) 565664 🌐 individualpubs.co.uk/coalheavers
Milton Justinian, Sparta; guest beers Ⓗ
This friendly one-room back-street community pub dates back to the 1850s. Up to four guest ales, cider, Belgian bottled beers and an English unpasteurised lager are stocked. The house beer is Bombers Drop, brewed by Milton. Home-made pies are available all week, with fresh rolls on Friday. Beer festivals are held in the spring and autumn and the large garden is popular in the summer with families. A free quiz is hosted on Sunday nights. Very busy on football match days.
Q❀♣🍎🚌🐾

Dragon 🄻

Hodgson Centre, Hodgson Avenue, Werrington, PE4 5EG
⏲ 4-11.30; 12-midnight Fri & Sat; 12-11 Sun
☎ (01733) 578088 🌐 thedragon-werrington.co.uk
Beer range varies Ⓗ
Opened in 1988, this community pub hosts four darts teams, three pool teams and a crib team. Traditional pub food is served Thursday to Saturday afternoons and Sunday lunchtime. A charity beer festival and fun day is held in April to raise money for the troops abroad. Live music or karaoke is hosted on Friday and Saturday nights. Six real ales include four changing guests. A quiz features on Sunday night and league poker on Mondays and Tuesdays. Children are welcome. Local CAMRA Gold Award winner in 2013. ❀◑♿♣P🚌(1)

Draper's Arms 🄻

29-31 Cowgate, PE1 1LZ
⏲ 8am-midnight (1am Fri & Sat) ☎ (01733) 847570
Courage Directors; Greene King Abbot; Ruddles Best Bitter; Theakston Old Peculier; Woodforde's Wherry; guest beers Ⓗ
A converted former draper's shop circa 1899, the pub is one of two Wetherspoon establishments in the city. The beer range, including many local microbrews, is dispensed through 10 handpumps. The spacious split room includes more intimate wood-panelled spaces. Food is served all day and regular beer and wine festivals are held throughout the year. Quiz night is Wednesday. A regular top-10 listed real ale pub within the Wetherspoon chain. Close to bus and rail stations. Q◑♿⇌🍎🚌

Hand & Heart ★ 🄻

12 Highbury Street, PE1 3BE
⏲ 3-11.30; 2-midnight Fri; 12-midnight Sat; 11.30-11.30 Sun
☎ (01733) 564653
Beer range varies Ⓗ
This 1930s back-street pub features in CAMRA's National Inventory of Historic Pub Interiors for its unspoilt interior. There is a main bar to the front and a quiet room to the rear connected by a drinking corridor. Five handpumps often feature some hard-to-find real ales. The large garden has an outside bar and stage used for beer festivals and music events. Live music plays on Thursday nights, with a Cheese Club on the last Thursday of the month. Saturday is quiz night. Q❀♣🚌(1)🐾

Ostrich 🄻

17 North Street, PE1 2RA
⏲ 11-11 (1am Fri & Sat); 12-11 Sun ☎ (01733) 746370
Oakham JHB; guest beers Ⓗ
A relaxing side-street pub off the main drag. The one-roomed interior has a U-shaped bar and is decorated with many pictures and posters of bygone breweries and famous acts who appeared in the city. Up to five regularly changing beers are on offer, many from local breweries. Live music plays most weekends. The small enclosed patio is a sun trap at the rear. ❀♿⇌♣🚌

Palmerston Arms 🄻

82 Oundle Road, PE2 9PA
⏲ 3-11, 12-midnight Fri & Sat; 12-10.30 Sun
☎ (01733) 565865 🌐 palmerston-arms.co.uk
Batemans XXXB, Salem Porter Ⓖ**; Castle Rock Harvest Pale; Oakham Citra** Ⓗ/Ⓖ**; guest beers** Ⓖ
Popular 400-year-old listed stone-built locals' pub. Owned by Batemans, three of its beers sit alongside nine or more real ales, which include some from Oakham Ales. Most beers are served straight from the cellar, which can be seen through a large glass viewing window at the back of the bar. Traditional ciders, perries and an extensive range of malt whiskies are also available. Rolls and a variety of snacks tempt customers. Live music and psycho nights are hosted some weeks.
❀♣🍎🚌(1,24)

Ploughman 🏆 🄻

1 Staniland Way, Werrington, PE4 6NA
⏲ 2-11; 12-midnight Fri & Sat; 12-11 Sun ☎ (01733) 327696
🌐 theploughman-werrington.co.uk
Beer range varies Ⓗ
This rejuvenated two-roomed community pub has been brought to the forefront of the city's real ale outlets by the enthusiastic licensee. Ten handpumps serve beers from both local breweries and from afar. An annual beer festival is held early in July. Many activities are hosted including charity events, and live music plays at weekends. Part of

the pub was converted into community tea rooms, which open at 10am on some days. Local CAMRA branch Pub of the Year in 2014. ❀♣P🚌(1,22)

Ramsey

Jolly Sailor 🄻

43 Great Whyte, PE26 1HH

⏲ 11 (12 Sun)-midnight ☎ (01487) 813388

Greene King Abbot; St Austell Tribute; Sharp's Doom Bar; guest beers 🄷

This Grade II-listed building has been a pub for 400 years. The three linked rooms feature wooden beams dating from various periods. Ramsey history is depicted in pictures and artefacts adorning the walls. A welcoming, friendly pub, it attracts a mixed clientele of all ages and hosts occasional charity nights and acoustic music sessions. Guest beers are available at the weekend. Good-value home-cooked food is served.
Q❀◖◗♿♣P🚌(31)📶

St Ives

Royal Oak 🄻

13 Crown Street, PE27 5EB

⏲ 10-11 (2am Fri & Sat); 12-midnight Sun ☎ (01480) 462586

Oakham Inferno; Sharp's Doom Bar; Wychwood Hobgoblin; guest beers 🄷

Busy town-centre pub, one of a number of historic listed inns in St Ives, whose most famous inhabitant was Oliver Cromwell. The room layout and character were happily preserved in a sensitive renovation in the 1990s. A changing range of guest beers keeps the customers happy; quizzes, card nights, karaoke and live music provide the entertainment. Traditional, freshly prepared food is served at lunchtime. 🐴◖♿🍎🚌🐾

St Neots

Hog & Partridge 🄻

25 Russell Street, PE19 1BA

⏲ closed Mon-Wed; 6 (4 Fri)-12.30am; 12-12.30am Sat; 1-7 Sun ☎ (01480) 406330

Beer range varies 🄷/🄶

A small, traditional back-street pub with the comfortable feel of a lounge bar. Up to five guest beers are offered, usually including two from Batemans, and others from local microbreweries. Also available are two real ciders, Trappist beers on tap and a good range of UK and foreign bottled beers and ciders. Tapas are served Thursday to Saturday evenings. Q🐴❀◗🍎P🍺🚌(X5)📶

Olde Sun 🄻

11 Huntingdon Street, PE19 1BL

⏲ 12-11 ☎ (01480) 216863 🌐 yeoldesun.moonfruit.com

Woodforde's Wherry; guest beers 🄷

Low-beamed, traditional town-centre pub with two large inglenook fireplaces, three bar areas, a dining area and a secluded patio. It has a lively atmosphere and a jukebox but there are also quiet areas for conversation. Shove-ha'penny and bar billiards are played. Five constantly changing guest beers come from various regional breweries including Adnams, Elgood's, Marston's, Thwaites and Woodforde. ❀◖◗♣🚌(X5)🐾

Pig 'n' Falcon 🄻

9 New Street, PE19 1AE (behind Barretts department store)

⏲ 11-midnight (2.30am Fri & Sat) ☎ 07951 785678

🌐 pignfalcon.co.uk

Greene King Abbot 🄶**; Oakham Inferno; Potbelly Best** 🄷**; guest beers** 🄶

This busy town-centre free house has up to eight real ales and four real ciders, focusing on microbreweries and unusual beers including milds, porters and stouts. A good range of bottled ciders and UK and foreign bottled beers including Trappist ales is also stocked. Four beer festivals are held each year. Live blues and rock nights are hosted on Wednesday, Friday, Saturday and Sunday. Outside is a large covered and heated beer garden.
🐴❀♿♣🍎🍺🚌(X5)🐾📶

Stapleford

Three Horseshoes

2 Church Street, CB22 5DS

⏲ 12-2.30, 5-11; 12-midnight Fri & Sat; 12-10.30 Sun ☎ (01223) 503402

Oakham Inferno; guest beers 🄷

The pub has three drinking areas, with the main bar facing the entrance, a small room to the left and a large room to the right with access to the garden. The new management also runs the Cambridge Blue in Cambridge, and follows a similar formula here. There are eight handpumps and a selection of bottled beers, with an emphasis on Belgian beers. A beer festival is held annually.
🐴❀◖◗♿⇌(Shelford)♣🍎P🚌(Citi7)🐾📶

Stretham

Lazy Otter

Cambridge Road, CB6 3RU

⏲ 10-11; 11-10 Sun ☎ (01353) 649780 🌐 lazy-otter.com

Beer range varies 🄷

Spacious free house on the banks of the River Great Ouse, conveniently close to the riverbank footpath for walkers and cyclists. It has a modern feel with a large bar area and an extensive restaurant serving locally-sourced food. Up to five real ales are available, constantly changing. Outside there is plenty of room to relax and a children's play area. Five moorings are available if visiting by boat.
🐴❀🛏◖◗🍎P🐾

Tilbrook

White Horse 🄻

High Street, PE28 0JP

⏲ 12 (5.30 Mon)-11 ☎ (01480) 860764

🌐 whitehorsetilbrook.com

Wells Eagle IPA, Bombardier; Young's Bitter; guest beer 🄷

Two-roomed village pub partly dating back to 1735 and surrounded by large gardens and open fields. The public bar is furnished with sofas and bar stools and provides darts and hood skittles. There is also a large lounge, dining area and bright conservatory with further seating. Traditional, locally-sourced food is served lunchtimes and evenings (no food Mon and eve Sun). The garden has swings and slides for children and a petting zoo featuring ducks, chickens, sheep, goats and a goose.
🐴❀◖◗♣P🚌(150)🐾📶

Waterbeach

Sun Inn

Chapel Street, CB25 9HR

⏲ 5-11; 12-midnight Fri-Sun ☎ (01223) 861254
Woodforde's Wherry; guest beers 🄷
The small, cosy lounge is dominated by a huge fireplace while the simply appointed public bar, with its wood-block floor, is always lively. There is also a small meeting room and a function room upstairs which hosts regular gigs. Beer and music festivals feature on the May and August bank holiday weekends. No food is available Monday or Sunday evenings. The pub is now home to the local CJs Café, which operates here from 9am Friday and Saturday (bar open from noon).
❀◑♿⇌♣●🚌(9)📶

West Wratting

Chestnut Tree 🏆
1 Mill Road, CB21 5LT
⏲ 12-3, 5.30-11.30; 12-midnight Fri & Sat; 12-10.30 Sun
☎ (01223) 290384 🌐 chestnuttreepub.co.uk
Greene King IPA; guest beers 🄷
Welcoming two-bar locals' pub with ample car parking and an attractive garden at the rear. The pub is now free of tie – the guest beers are mainly from micros, including local brewers. A changing real cider is also kept. The public bar is basically furnished, with an extension housing a pool table. The saloon bar is more comfortable. The pub hosts darts and pool teams and has a small lending library. Regional CAMRA Pub of the Year 2014.
Q❀◑♣●P🚌(19)🐾

Whittlesey

Boat Inn 🄻
2 Ramsey Road, PE7 1DR
⏲ 4 (11 Fri-Sun)-midnight ☎ (01733) 202488
🌐 quinnboatinn.wordpress.com
Elgood's Black Dog, Cambridge Bitter, Golden Newt; guest beers 🄶
This 11th-century inn is mentioned in the Domesday Book. It attracts locals, anglers and visitors, who all receive a warm welcome. The lounge has an unusual boat-shaped bar and hosts a whisky club that meets on the second Friday of every month. Up to five traditional ciders and perries supplement the real ales that are all served direct from the cask. Open mic music nights feature on some Tuesdays and Fridays. Outside is a pétanque terrain. Good value accommodation is offered. 🐴❀🛏♿♣●P🚌(31,33)🐾

George Hotel 🄻
10 Market Place, PE7 1AB
⏲ 8am-midnight (1am Fri & Sat) ☎ (01733) 359970
Courage Directors; Oakham Bishops Farewell; Ruddles Best Bitter; Woodforde's Wherry; guest beers 🄷
Built in the late 1700s, the building was significantly altered in the mid-19th century before receiving a Grade II-listing in 1974. Once a popular locals' haunt with a basic bar and comfortable lounge, it was closed and unloved until Wetherspoon refurbished and reopened it in 2010. Now once again a local favourite, it offers a large selection of real ales and Wetherspoon's good-value food menu. Q🐴❀◑♿●P🚌📶

Letter B 🄻
53-57 Church Street, PE7 1DE
⏲ 5-11; 3.30-midnight Fri; 12-midnight Sat; 12-11 Sun
☎ (01733) 206975 🌐 theletterbpublichouse.co.uk
Tydd Steam Barn Ale; guest beers 🄷
Reputed to have been named the Letter B because there were so many pubs in Whittlesey that they ran out of names, the name was then changed to the Bee for a while but is now back to the Letter B. This 200-year-old local community pub offers a warm welcome to all and hosts popular charity events and quiz nights. An annual beer festival is held in the spring. Q❀🛏♣●🚌🐾📶

Willingham

Bank Micropub
High Street, CB24 5ES
⏲ closed Mon; 6 (5 Wed & Thu)-11; 12-2, 5-11 Fri & Sat; closed Sun ☎ (01954) 260331 🌐 thebankmicropub.co.uk
Beer range varies 🄶
Part of the growing micropub movement, the Bank was converted from a former village bank branch. Although not a full-size pub, 'micro' is perhaps a misnomer here. The small space has been well used, with an L-shaped drinking area around a shortish bar which, along with some of the furniture, was rescued from a closed pub and renovated. The walls are decorated with photos of local interest. Between three and six real ales are usually on at once and local beers feature strongly.
Q●🚌(Citi5)

Wisbech

Red Lion 🄻
32 North Brink, PE13 1JR
⏲ 11.30-3, 6-11; 11.30-3, 7-midnight Sat; 12-11 Sun
☎ (01945) 582022
Elgood's Black Dog, Cambridge Bitter; guest beer 🄷
The nearest Elgood's pub to the brewery. The Red Lion is a friendly and comfortable inn which caters equally well for both drinkers and diners. The fine ales, including a seasonal beer from the Elgood's range or a guest, are complemented by excellent home-cooked food served seven days a week. Weekday lunch specials are good value. Children are welcome. Wheelchair access is from the rear, where there is an outdoor drinking area for warmer weather. Q❀◑♿P🚌(X1)📶

Wistow

Three Horseshoes
Mill Road, PE28 2QQ
⏲ 6-10 Mon; 12-3, 6-11; 12-10 Sat; 12-4 Sun
☎ (01487) 822270
Adnams Southwold Bitter, Ghost Ship 🄷
Multi-roomed brick-and-thatch 18th-century pub opposite the village church. It was once also a blacksmith's and in the 18th century provided accommodation for workers employed in major church rebuilding work. Traditional pub food is available daily. Quizzes are held once a month. Families are welcome to use both bars. There is a covered area outside for smokers.
🐴❀◑♿⛺♣P🚉🚌(30)📶

> Good ale is the true and proper drink of Englishmen. He is not deserving of the name of Englishman who speaketh against ale, that is good ale. **George Borrow, Lavengro**

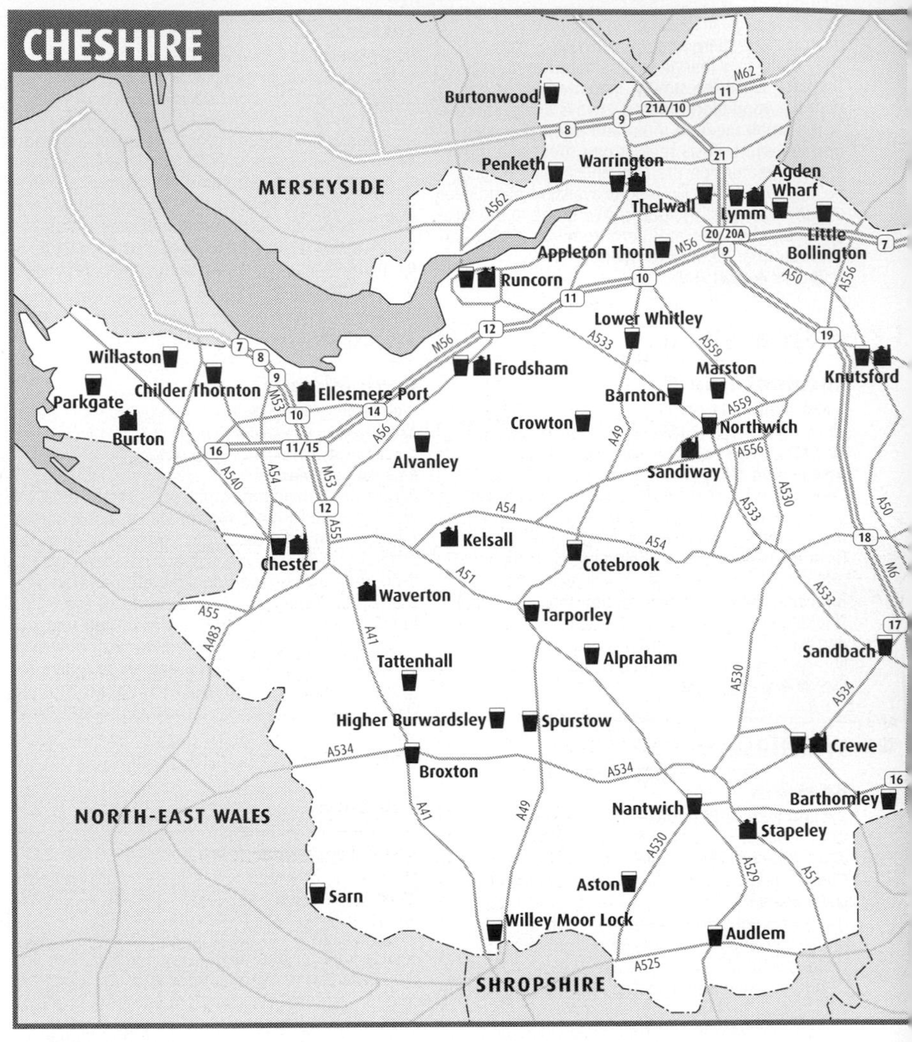

Agden Wharf

Barn Owl 🄻

Warrington Lane, WA13 0SW (on Bridgewater Canal)
⚙ 11-11 ☎ (01925) 752020 🌐 thebarnowlinn.co.uk
Thwaites Original, Wainwright, Lancaster Bomber; guest beers 🄷
Situated alongside the Bridgewater Canal, both the pub and canalside patio enjoy views across the Cheshire countryside. A favourite with locals as well as canal trippers, the Barn Owl is renowned for both its ale and food. The three regular beers are complemented by up to four guest ales, sourced mainly from independent breweries. Freshly cooked dishes made with mainly local produce are popular and the pub is especially busy at meal times. ⛴❀◑♿♣P

Alpraham

Travellers Rest ★ 🄻

Chester Road, CW6 9JA (A51, on N outskirts of village)
⚙ 6.30-11; 12-5, 6-11 Sat; 7-10.30 Sun ☎ (01829) 260523
Tetley Bitter; Weetwood Eastgate Ale 🄷
Featuring in CAMRA's National Inventory of Historic Pub Interiors, the Travellers Rest is a must for those who seek a traditional English pub, an increasing rarity today. A classic gem, it has been owned and run by the same family for over 110 years, and retains the ambience of a pub from early last century. Well kept by friendly, unpretentious staff, it has four rooms, although only two are usually used. Prices are keen for the regular beers and it is worth the effort to get here. Q❀♣P🚌(84)🐾

Alsager

Lodge 🄻

88 Crewe Road, ST7 2JA
⚙ 4-11 (midnight Fri); 2-midnight Sat; 2-11 Sun
☎ (01270) 873669
Beer range varies 🄷
Friendly family-run two-room pub with a genuine community feel. Although a popular locals' establishment, the casual visitor is warmly welcomed – this is a place for conversation. A choice of up to eight ever-changing real ales is always available including brews from Goodall's

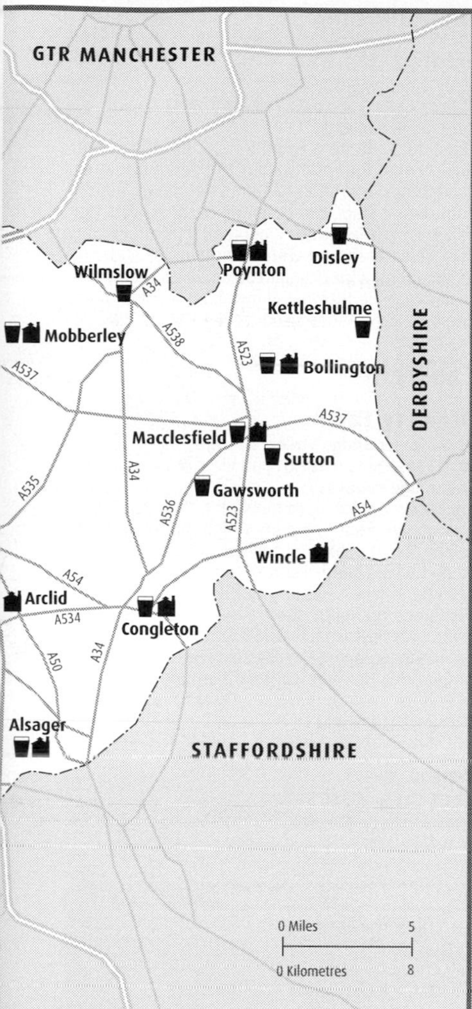

Brewery – a 2.5-barrel plant is located at the back of the pub. The quiet beer garden provides a pleasant seated area in summer. Q P (20)

Alvanley

White Lion

Manley Road, WA6 9DD (opp church)
12-11 (10.30 Sun) (01928) 722949
whitelionalvanley.co.uk
Hartleys Cumbria Way; Robinsons 1892 Dark; guest beer
Bustling and busy rural village inn, one of a group of Robinson's pubs run by an enterprising licensee. Once part of a farm, it continues its diverse activity today with the operation of an on-site coal supply business. The food is excellent, with extensive specials boards dotted around the room. The well-appointed and extensive gardens can be hired for marquee functions. Events are held throughout the year including a beer festival, and the pub raises funds for the local Alvanley Charity. Q P

Appleton Thorn

Appleton Thorn Village Hall

Stretton Road, WA4 4RT
closed Mon-Wed; 7.30-11.30; 1-4, 7.30-10.30 Sun
(01925) 261187 appletonthornvillagehall.co.uk
Beer range varies
Previous CAMRA National Club of the Year winner, the building used to be the village school and features a large function room and a smaller members' lounge. Up to seven ever-changing real ales are available, mostly from microbreweries, and up to 10 draught ciders. Light lunches are served on Sundays 1-3pm. Quizzes, live music and an annual beer festival are hosted in the function room. Q P (10,10X)

Aston

Bhurtpore

Wrenbury Road, CW5 8DQ (just off A530 jct)
12-2.30, 6.30-11.30; 12-midnight Fri & Sat; 12-11 Sun
(01270) 780917 bhurtpore.co.uk
Hobsons Mild; guest beers
Now featuring in the Guide for its 22nd consecutive year, the Bhurtpore has been owned and run very successfully by Simon and Nicky since 1992. A great range of ales is available, mainly from small and micro breweries, including mild, stout or dark, premium and session ales, from the 11 handpumps, plus an excellent range of malt whiskies. There are four distinct drinking areas and a separate restaurant. Locally sourced and home-prepared food – curries a speciality – are well worth sampling. Q P (72)

Audlem

Lord Combermere

The Square, CW3 0AQ
12-12.30am (01270) 812277
thelordcombermere.co.uk
Greene King IPA; Salopian Shropshire Gold; Timothy Taylor Boltmaker; guest beers
A friendly hub in the centre of the town, this modern, airy, open-plan pub is full of natural light, with an area for dining at one end, a TV area at the other and an attractive bar in between. The beer range, a mixture of national and local brews, is sourced from breweries including Salopian, Merlin and Wincle. The food menu includes a full gluten-free range. Quiz night is Tuesday, live music features on Thursday. P (73)

Barnton

Barnton Cricket Club

Broomsedge, Townfield Land, CW8 4QL (200yds from A533 via Stoneheyes Lane)
6.30-11.30 (11 Wed; 12.30am Thu; midnight Fri); 4-midnight Sat; 12-11 Sun (01606) 77702
barntoncc.co.uk
Theakston Best Bitter; Thwaites Nutty Black, Original; guest beers
CAMRA National Club of the Year for 2014, this popular and multi-award-winning club provides many real ales sourced from microbreweries from all over the country. A beer festival is held every November. Many sports are played here including cricket, squash, poker, darts and dominoes. Food is available Wednesday to Sunday evenings plus Sunday lunchtime. P (4)

Barthomley

White Lion Inn ★
Audley Road, CW2 5PG
☼ 11.30-11; 12-10.30 Sun ☎ (01270) 882242
🌐 whitelionbarthomley.com
Banks's Bitter, Sunbeam; Jennings Cocker Hoop, Sneck Lifter; Marston's EPA, Burton Bitter 🄷
Following a devastating fire in April 2013, this thatched inn reopened the following July and, like the phoenix rising from the ashes, it is back better than ever. The three-roomed building, full of rustic charm with beamed ceilings, is at the hub of this beautiful historic Cheshire village, and is extremely popular with locals and travellers. Friendly staff work hard to ensure the comfort and happiness of their customers. Q❀◐♣P🐾📶

Bollington

Poachers Inn 𝕃
95 Ingersley Road, SK10 5RE
☼ 12-2 (not Mon), 5.30-11; 12-11 Sun ☎ (01625) 572086
🌐 thepoachers.org
Storm Beauforts Ale; Weetwood Old Dog Bitter; guest beers 🄷
Friendly and welcoming family-run free house near the Gritstone Trail. The interior is divided into comfortable seating/dining areas; a real coal fire adds warmth in winter. Offering five real ales, the licensee enthusiastically supports local breweries, including nearby Happy Valley. Real cider is on handpump, world beers in bottles. Popular, good-value, home-prepared food is sourced locally. Events include a Wednesday pie night and a monthly quiz for local charities. The suntrap garden is busy in summer. ❀◐◑●P🚌(10,392)🐾📶

Vale Inn 𝕃
29-31 Adlington Road, SK10 5JT
☼ 12-2.30, 5-11; 12-11 Fri & Sat; 12-10.30 Sun
☎ (01625) 575147 🌐 valeinn.co.uk
Beer range varies 🄷
Dating from the 1890s, this single-room family-run free house is the tap for the Bollington Brewing Company. It features five of its beers plus a guest and at least two real ciders/perries. Seasonal mini beer festivals are hosted. The home-cooked food is excellent and the pub is popular with the local community as well as walkers and bikers using the nearby canal and Middlewood Way footpath. The beer garden overlooks the cricket ground and is the perfect place to enjoy the sound of leather on willow. ❀◐◑●P🚌(10,392)📶

Broxton

Sandstone 𝕃
Nantwich Road, CH3 9JH (A534, E of A41)
☼ 12-3, 6-11; 12-11 Sat; 12-10.30 Sun ☎ (01829) 782333
🌐 thesandstone.co.uk
Beer range varies 🄷
Popular 17th-century rural inn ideally situated for refreshment following a walk in the countryside around the Sandstone Trail. The landlord and friendly staff are keen to promote the pub's four real ales; the range includes a regular beer from Stonehouse Brewery and others from local microbrewers. Superb food is sourced from within the local community, served both in the main bar and the separate conservatory dining room. Well-behaved children and dogs are welcome.
Q❀◐◑♿P🐾📶

Burtonwood

Fiddle i' th' Bag
Alder Lane, WA5 4BJ
☼ 12-3, 4.45-11; 12-11 Sat & Sun ☎ (01925) 225442
Beer range varies 🄷
Standing alone on a country road, this long-term Guide entry dispenses changing beers from three handpumps as well as unfailing hospitality from its enthusiastic staff. The eccentric decor reflects the proximity of the former World War II US airbase, but this theme is shared with a chimpanzee and mannequins who change costumes to keep customers – be they passing walkers, cyclists, horse riders or locals – bemused. ❀◐◑♿P🚌(329)🐾

Chester

Brewery Tap 𝕃
52-54 Lower Bridge Street, CH1 1RU
☼ 12-11 (10.30 Sun) ☎ (01244) 340999 🌐 the-tap.co.uk
Beer range varies 🄷
Reached via steps from the street, the inn occupies a Jacobean great hall with a high, barrel-vaulted ceiling, ornate sandstone fireplace, tapestries and stone floors. Charles I stayed here before the battle of Rowton Moor. Spitting Feathers beers, plus numerous changing guest ales, including many from local micros, are available. The menu focuses on freshly prepared, locally-sourced food. A winner of CAMRA's Heritage Conservation and Conversion to Pub Use award, this is a must-visit for visitors to Chester. Q◐◑♣●🚌🐾📶

Cellar 🏆
19-21 City Road, CH1 3AE
☼ 4-midnight (2.30am Fri); 12-2.30am Sat; 12-midnight Sun
☎ (01244) 318950 🌐 thecellarchester.co.uk

INDEPENDENT BREWERIES

2 & Nine Warrington (NEW)
4Ts Runcorn
Beartown Congleton
Blakemere Sandiway
Blueball Frodsham
Bollington Bollington
Borough Arms Crewe
Britman Burton (NEW)
Cheshire Brew Brothers Ellesmere Port (NEW)
Cheshire Brewhouse Congleton
Coach House Warrington
Frodsham Frodsham
Front Row Congleton
Goodall's Alsager
Happy Valley Bollington
Lymm Lymm (NEW)
Merlin Arclid
Mobberley Mobberley
Norton Runcorn
Offbeat Crewe
Pied Bull Chester
Redball Chester (NEW)
RedWillow Macclesfield
Spitting Feathers Waverton
Storm Macclesfield
Tatton Knutsford
Tipsy Angel Warrington
Weetwood Kelsall
Wincle Wincle
Woodlands Stapeley
Worth Poynton

Beer range varies
Despite its name, this lively, open-plan bar is actually at street level. The enthusiastic staff ensure an interesting range of beer is always on offer. Events include Monday £1 off cask ales, Tuesday quiz night, Friday and Saturday music nights and monthly Beer Club meetings. CAMRA members receive a 10 per cent discount on cask beers Sunday to Thursday. TV screens show sport. Simple, home-made bar snacks are available, with free bacon sandwiches on Sundays. Weekday closing times are flexible.

Cross Keys

2 Duke Street, CH1 1RP
12 (5 Mon winter)-11 (11.30 Fri & Sat); 12-10.30 Sun
(01244) 344460 crosskeyschester.co.uk
Joule's Blonde, Pale Ale, Slumbering Monk; guest beer
Attractive, Victorian red-brick building, featuring a stylishly refurbished interior with etched mirrors, oak floors, wood panelling and a log fire. Specially commissioned stained glass windows depict other hostelries in the Joule's estate. A large upstairs room, named the Slaughtered Lamb, is available for functions. Joule's ales plus a guest are on offer, with food available Tuesday to Sunday. A small beer terrace in front of the building catches the afternoon sun.

Lodge Bar

8-10 Hoole Road, Hoole, CH2 3NH
11-11 (midnight Fri & Sat) (01244) 324971
lodgebar.co.uk
Beer range varies
Lounge-style bar, part of the Bawn Lodge Hotel, situated half a mile from Chester Railway Station in the suburb of Hoole. The bar at the entrance leads to intimate alcove seating and a large side lounge. Three handpumps serve a changing range of ales at competitive prices, and good-value food is available all day. The large beer garden is popular in summer. One of few pubs where traditional bagatelle is played.

Old Harkers Arms

1 Russell Street, CH3 5AL (down steps off City Road to canal towpath)
11.30-11; 12-10.30 Sun (01244) 344525
harkersarms-chester.co.uk
Phoenix Brunning & Price Original; Weetwood Cheshire Cat; guest beers
Upmarket pub converted from the ground floor of a former Victorian canalside warehouse. Timber flooring, traditional wooden furniture and cast iron pillars are a reminder of its former use. Blackboards list real ales with tasting notes – usually nine are available including a selection of bitters, stouts, milds and porters, many from local breweries. Ciders are listed separately and served from the cellar. Food is served all day (booking advised for busy weekend periods). There is outside seating alongside the canal. Q

Olde Cottage Inn

34-36 Brook Street, CH1 3DZ
4-11 (midnight Fri); 2-midnight Sat (01244) 324065
oldecottagechester.co.uk
Timothy Taylor Golden Best; guest beers
Popular with locals who help to generate a lively and welcoming atmosphere, this pub is a refreshing contrast to the mock drawing-room hostelries that can be found nearby. Two long open rooms, one with two dartboards, a pool table and a bagatelle table, are served by a central bar. Beers are always competitively priced, and there is a discount loyalty scheme.

Pied Bull

57 Northgate Street, CH1 2HQ
10-11 (midnight Fri & Sat) (01244) 325829
piedbull.co.uk
Adnams Broadside; guest beers
Home to the only microbrewery inside the city walls, the Pied Bull attracts a lively mix of locals and visitors. Up to three of the six cask ales on offer come from a range of eight regular house brews. The knowledgeable staff organise occasional beer festivals, often in association with other northern breweries. A competitive quiz is hosted on a Thursday. High-quality pub food made with locally sourced ingredients is available all day.

Telford's Warehouse

Canal Basin, Tower Wharf, CH1 4EZ
12-12.30am (11 Mon & Tue); 12-2am Fri & Sat; 12-1am Sun
(01244) 390090 telfordswarehousechester.com
Thwaites Original; Weetwood Cheshire Cat; guest beers
Converted Georgian warehouse boasting original features, industrial artefacts and a glass frontage overlooking the canal basin. Three regular ales are available plus a varying range of guests, usually seasonal and often local. A specialised live music venue; check the website for details as admission charges may apply. Regular salsa/Latin dance classes are hosted as well as open mic sessions and an annual beer festival. Quality food is served and there is an outside drinking area next to the canal. Families are welcome upstairs. P

Childer Thornton

White Lion

New Road, CH66 5PU (off A41 between Great Sutton and Hooton)
11.30-11.30 (11 Sun) (0151) 339 3402
Thwaites Original, Wainwright, Lancaster Bomber; guest beers
This friendly village local has been an inn since 1724. The bar area features an original fireplace, with a small snug and a separate cosy room adjoining it. Two regular guest beers often include a Thwaites' seasonal. Good-value home-cooked meals are available all day until 8pm (5pm Sun). There are two pleasant outdoor drinking areas at the front and rear of the pub, with a children's play area adjoining the rear one. Curry night is held on a Tuesday and quiz night is on a Thursday.
P

Congleton

Beartown Tap

18 Willow Street, CW12 1RL
4 (12 Fri & Sat)-11; 12-10.30 Sun (01260) 270775
Beartown Best Bitter, Bear Ass, Kodiak Gold, Bearskinful; guest beers
A leading real ale outlet in Congleton since 1999, this is, as the name suggests, the brewery tap for Beartown. Twice CAMRA Regional Pub of the Year, at least five real ales are always available. There are three rooms downstairs and a function room upstairs, and the outdoor patio area has benefited

from recent investment. A community pub for conversation, games and occasional music.
Q❀🍏🚌(39,99)🐾📶

Lord Mountbatten 𝕃

70 Mill Street, CW12 1AG (off Mountbatten Way)
⏲ 4 (12 Fri-Sun)-midnight ☎ 07811 199902
Beer range varies Ⓗ
This Congleton pub offers a wide range of changing beers from microbreweries, dispensed through five handpumps. New breweries always get a welcome here. The focus is clearly on the beer, with rugby and football TV viewing also popular. The owner manages and runs the pub and is always available to advise on beer choice, with detailed knowledge of existing and new local brewers. Pub games include pool, darts and backgammon.
❀♣P🚌(38,42)🐾

Queen's Head Hotel 𝕃

Park Lane, CW12 3DE
⏲ 12-midnight (1am Fri & Sat) ☎ (01260) 272546
🌐 queensheadhotel.org.uk
Black Sheep Best Bitter; Draught Bass; Greene King IPA, Abbot; Joule's Pale Ale; guest beers Ⓗ
Probably the most improved privately-owned pub in town, with eight handpumps offering a mix of mainstream and microbrewery ales, served by knowledgeable and friendly bar staff. The kitchen has been refurbished and meals are cooked to order. Darts and pool teams are flourishing. Outside, the gardens have been redesigned with the addition of a boules court – probably the only one in Cheshire. Your first stop before delving into Congleton's other hostelries.
🐴❀🛏◑🚆♣🍏P🚌(99,99A)🐾📶

Young Pretender 🏆 𝕃

30-34 Lawton Street, CW12 1RS
⏲ 12-midnight (1am Thu-Sat) ☎ (01260) 273277
🌐 youngpretenderbeerparlour.co.uk
Beer range varies Ⓗ
Branch Pub of the Year for 2014, this conversion of a former toy shop now brings the community together for films, quizzes, open mic and other music evenings, Meet the Brewer, foreign language conversation and much more. A chess evening is the latest innovation. An excellent selection of real ales, craft and foreign bottled beers is on offer and artisan pies are served throughout the day. 🐴◑♿P🚌🐾📶

Cotebrook

Fox & Barrel 𝕃

Foxbank, CW6 9DZ (On A49)
⏲ 12-11 (10.30 Sun) ☎ (01829) 760529
🌐 foxandbarrel.co.uk
Caledonian Deuchars IPA; Weetwood Eastgate Ale; guest beers Ⓗ
Friendly country pub with a welcoming, relaxed atmosphere and helpful staff. Dating from 1730, it was sensitively refurbished in a traditional style several years ago. A central bar serves a number of rooms and alcoves, with dining and drinking throughout. Guest beers come from local breweries and further afield. Good food is served all day until 9.30pm (9pm Sun). The bar area is warmed by an open fire and outside is a terraced area and beer garden; handy for Oulton Park race circuit.
Q🐴❀◑♣P🐾📶

Crewe

Borough Arms 𝕃

33 Earle Street, CW1 2BG (on Earle St railway bridge, entrance up steps in adjoining Thomas St)
⏲ 5 (12 Fri & Sat)-11; 12-10.30 Sun
🌐 borougharmscrewe.co.uk
Beer range varies Ⓗ
Popular ale-led pub a short walk from the town centre, also home to the Borough Arms Brewery. Nine handpumps on one bar serve a wide range of constantly changing real ales. A second bar on a lower level dispenses a good selection of Belgian beers. Due to the lack of electronic gizmos, this is a pub for genuine conversation. A large downstairs room leads out to the pleasant beer garden.
🐴❀♣🍏P

Gaffers Row 𝕃

48 Victoria Street, CW1 2JE (opp Les's Fish Bar)
⏲ 8am-11 (midnight Thu; 1am Fri & Sat) ☎ (01270) 503820
Greene King Abbot; Ruddles Best Bitter; guest beers Ⓗ
A busy town-centre pub, this Wetherspoon establishment opened in 2003 in a former furniture showroom. The interior is mainly open plan with a large bar and a family area. Two TV screens show news channels with subtitles throughout the day. There are 10 handpumps dispensing the regular beers and six rotating guests from local and national breweries. 🐴◑♿🍏🚌📶

Hops 🏆 𝕃

Prince Albert Street, CW1 2DF (opp Forge Street car park)
⏲ 11 (5 Mon)-11; 12-11 Sun ☎ (01270) 211100
Beer range varies Ⓗ
Friendly, family-run free house with a downstairs bar, more seating upstairs, and outside space with tables and chairs. There are five handpumps, one serving the house beer, Enigma, brewed locally by Townhouse. A comprehensive range of Belgian beers, bottled and draught, is always available. CAMRA members receive a discount on cask ale on Monday night. Current Local CAMRA Pub of the Year. Q🐴❀◐♿♣🍏P🚌🐾📶

Crowton

Hare & Hounds

Station Road, CW8 2RN (jct of B5153 and Bent Lane)
⏲ 12-3 (not Tue), 5-11; 12-11 Sat; 12-3, 7-10.30 Sun
☎ (01928) 788851 🌐 harenhounds.co.uk
Greene King IPA; guest beers Ⓗ
Quiet country pub and restaurant. In winter there are warm open fires with free toast and forks on Tuesday evenings. A variety of changing guest beers is offered from the Punch list. The annual Easter duck race on the garden stream raises thousands of pounds for local charities. Joe the landlord can usually be spotted as he will be wearing his chef's uniform. For the hardy smoker there is a covered table outside with space heating. No meals on Tuesday. Q❀◑♣P🚌(48)📶

Disley

White Lion 𝕃

135 Buxton Road, SK12 2HA
⏲ 12 (6.30 Mon)-11; 12-12.30am Sat & Sun
☎ (01663) 762800
Beer range varies Ⓗ

Situated on the A6 towards the easterly end of the village, although now painted white, the building was the 'red house' that gave its name to the adjacent side road. It offers eight real ales, many from micros, constantly changing and selected from SIBA member breweries. The contemporary interior includes a separate dog room – water bowls and canine dinners available. A comprehensive and varied food menu is served until 9pm (no food Mon). A short walk from the Peak Forest Canal (bridge 26). ❀◑P🚌(199)🐾

Frodsham

Helter Skelter 🏆 L

31 Church Street, WA6 6PN

⏲ 11-11 (11.30 Fri & Sat); 12-10.30 Sun ☎ (01928) 733361

🌐 helterskelter-frodsham.co.uk

Weetwood Best Bitter; guest beers Ⓗ

A haven for discerning real ale drinkers, this single-roomed bar has seven handpumps offering a budget-priced local house bitter alongside a varying beer range mainly from local and national micros. A guest cider and an array of imported bottled beers is also available. The relaxed atmosphere encourages conversation during the day but the pub gets lively on weekend evenings and even the central standing area can fill at busy times. Excellent home-cooked food is served in the bar and upstairs restaurant. Local CAMRA branch Pub of the Year 2013 and 2014.
◑⇌🍎▯🚌(48,X30)🐾📶

Gawsworth

Harrington Arms ★ L

Church Lane, SK11 9RR (off A536)

⏲ 12-3, 5-11.30 (midnight Fri); 12-11.30 Sat; 12-11 Sun

☎ (01260) 223325

🌐 harringtonarmsgawsworth.robinsonsbrewery.com

Robinsons 1892, Dizzy Blonde, Unicorn, seasonal beer Ⓗ

Former working farmhouse/pub dating from 1710, this Grade II-listed building is a superb example of a largely unspoilt country pub and features in CAMRA's National Inventory of Historic Pub Interiors. Full of traditional character, a number of small rooms are furnished with simple wooden tables and chairs, with original tiled floors and open fires. Home-cooked food is on offer lunchtimes and evenings, made with locally-sourced produce where possible. The bus stop is 100 yards from the pub. A former local CAMRA Pub of the Year. Q🐴❀◑♿♣🚌(38)🐾

Higher Burwardsley

Pheasant Inn L

CH3 9PF

⏲ 11-11; 12-10.30 Sun ☎ (01829) 770434

🌐 thepheasantinn.co.uk

Weetwood Eastgate Ale; guest beer Ⓗ

Tucked away in the Peckforton Hills, this charming 300-year-old inn has stunning views over the Cheshire plain to the Welsh hills. A popular stop-off for walkers on the Sandstone Trail and visitors to the nearby candle workshops, the inn usually has three Weetwood beers on offer plus one guest ale. Quality locally-sourced food is served in the main bar and separate dining room. Accommodation is in 12 en-suite rooms in either the main building or nearby converted stable block. Q❀🛏◑♿P🐾📶

Kettleshulme

Swan Inn

Macclesfield Road, SK23 7QU

⏲ 12 (5.30 Mon)-11; 11-11 Fri; 12-8.30 Sun

☎ (01663) 732943 🌐 verynicepubs.co.uk/swankettleshulme

Marston's Burton Bitter; guest beers Ⓗ

Small, idyllic 15th-century inn with timber beams, an open log fire in winter and two patios for warmer weather. Two ever-changing guest beers often come from local micros. A beer festival is held in September. A varied menu of high-quality food always includes a range of speciality fish dishes (booking advisable; no food Mon). Situated in the Peak District National Park and surrounded by good walking country, families and walkers are welcome. Worth a visit for the new toilets alone.
Q🐴❀🛏◑P🚌🐾📶

Knutsford

Lord Eldon L

27 Tatton Street, WA16 6AD

⏲ 11-11 (midnight Thu-Sat); 12-10.30 Sun

☎ (01565) 652261

Tetley Bitter; guest beers Ⓗ

This 300-year-old inn has an attractive exterior with a sundial and hanging baskets. Surprisingly spacious inside, it has a bar room with real fire and three further rooms. Low beams, brasses and pictures create a cosy feel. A popular locals' venue, there is plenty of support when darts or dominoes are in progress. Live music and a quiz feature regularly. One of the guest ales is usually a Cheshire LocAle and Tetley is reduced in price up to 7pm on weekdays. Q🐴❀⇌♣🚌🐾

Little Bollington

Swan with Two Nicks L

Park Lane, WA14 4TJ (signed off A56)

⏲ 12-11 (10.30 Sun) ☎ (0161) 928 2914

🌐 swanwithtwonicks.co.uk

Black Sheep Bitter; Coach House Swan with Two Nicks; Timothy Taylor Landlord; guest beers Ⓗ

Welcoming country pub on the fringes of the Dunham Massey National Trust property. The rustic interior comprises several rooms with a central bar. Local beers feature on the seven beer engines, two usually from Dunham Massey Brewery. A varied food offering, including gluten-free dishes, is available all day until 9pm (8pm Sun), served in both the pub and restaurant. Handy for boaters on the canal. 🐴❀◑P🚌🐾

Lower Whitley

Chetwode Arms

Street Lane, WA4 4EN (off A49)

⏲ 12.30 (5 winter)-11; 2.30-8 Sun ☎ (01925) 730203

🌐 chetwode-arms.co.uk

Adnams Broadside; Marston's Pedigree; guest beer Ⓗ

Picturesque 17th-century former coaching inn, Grade II-listed, retaining many original features. The menu includes exotic meats of South African origin plus traditional British cuisine, and specialises in hot rocks for cooking your own meat at your table. Seating outside overlooks the pub's own bowling green, built in 1928. Home to bowling, dominoes and darts teams.
Q🐴❀◑🍎P🐾📶

Lymm

Brewery Tap

18 Bridgewater Street, WA13 0AB

12-11 (midnight Fri & Sat); 12-10.30 Sun

(01925) 755451 lymmbrewing.co.uk

Lymm Bitter, Bridgewater Blond; guest beers H

Modern venue, opened in 2013, in the red brick former post office near the canal. The well-lit bar is complemented by a tastefully decorated front room with subdued lighting, comfy armchairs and a wood-fired stove. Five guest ales are often either from the microbrewery under the pub or nearby Dunham Massey, and two rotating real ciders are available. No food is served but you can bring your own pies and sandwiches from the deli next door. Free newspapers are on offer to while away the day. (5,37)

Macclesfield

Macc

Mill Green, SK11 7PE

4-11.30; 12-12.30am Fri & Sat; 12-11.30 Sun

(01625) 423704 maccbar.co.uk

Beer range varies H

Situated on the way from central Macclesfield to the football ground, this is a large two-room pub with the lounge bar divided into smaller areas. An excellent free house, staff here are passionate and knowledgeable about cask beer. The range includes a house beer, Macclesfield Bitter, from the local RedWillow Brewery, and five varying guests from the country's more innovative brewers. An extensive list of bottled world beers is also kept. Food is available Friday to Sunday noon-9pm, other days 4-9pm. (9,14)

Park Tavern

158 Park Lane, SK11 6UB

4 (12 Sat & Sun)-11; 12-11 Sun (01625) 667846

park-tavern.co.uk

Beer range varies H

Just five minutes' walk from the town centre, the Park Tavern is a must on any Macclesfield visit. One of three pubs owned by Bollington Brewing, it has a modern interior with separate rooms and drinking areas, and hosts numerous events including quizzes and a Sci Bar. Upstairs it has its own cinema. Roasts are served on Sundays.

RedWillow Bar

32A Park Green, SK11 7NA

closed Mon; 4-11 (midnight Thu); 12-midnight Fri & Sat; 12-10.30 Sun (01625) 503253 redwillowbar.com

RedWillow Headless; guest beers H

Opened in 2013, this is the first outlet owned by the local RedWillow brewery. Sensitively converted from former shop premises, original windows and parquet flooring contrast nicely with modern wood fittings and a copper bar servery. Copper also features throughout the bar area and in the toilets. Five handpumps dispense RedWillow beers and changing guests from other micros. Snacks such as cheese and charcuterie are available lunchtimes and evenings. (10,38)

Treacle Tap

43 Sunderland Street, SK11 6JL

12-11 (midnight Thu-Sat) (01625) 615938

thetreacletap.co.uk

Beer range varies H

All the values of a traditional pub packed into a small modern bar. The Treacle is home to language conversation groups, stitch and bitch, chess club and a weekly Sunday night quiz. An interesting, ever-changing range of three casks beers is on offer from some of the best micros, served by friendly, helpful staff. Bottled Belgian, American and world beers are also kept. A good selection of locally made pies, cold platters and snacks is available. Q

Waters Green Tavern

96 Waters Green, SK11 6LH

12-3, 5-11; 12-4, 7-11 Sat; 12-4, 7-10.30 Sun

(01625) 422653

Beer range varies H

Overseen by long-established landlord Brian, and assisted by his son Steve since 2013, this multi-award-winning free house serves a varying range of up to seven beers, usually from northern breweries, with pale beers predominating. Real cider and perry are also available and good-value home-cooked lunches are served (no food Sun). The pub is open plan with two distinct seating areas, one with a real fire, and a pool room. Close to rail and bus stations.

Wharf

107 Brook Street, SK11 7AW

12-midnight (01625) 261879 thewharfmacc.co.uk

St Austell Dartmoor Best Bitter; guest beers H

Cheshire CAMRA Pub of the Year 2013. This friendly community free house has a cosy, secluded fireside area offering newspapers, books and games, and a more open space for darts, skittles, pool, quizzes, widescreen TV and, mainly on Fridays, live music. A dark beer is always among the four rotating guests, and a draught cider and a good selection of bottled beers is also available. The landlord is a committed beer enthusiast and has recently opened an artisan bottled beer shop, Brewtique, in Macclesfield town centre. (1,58)

Marston

Salt Barge

Ollershaw Lane, CW9 6ES

12-3, 5-11 (11.30 Fri); 12-11.30 Sat; 12-10.30 Sun

(01606) 43064 thesaltbarge.co.uk

Merlin Merlin's Gold, Excalibur; Tatton Best H

Multi-roomed pub built in 1861 offering good food and a warm welcome to all; home to monthly quiz nights and music events every other Friday. Situated opposite the Lion Salt Works, which is due to reopen in 2015, the history of salt and salt mining is featured in the bar. Also close to Marbury Country Park, the Trent & Mersey Canal and not far from the Anderton Boat Lift, the location has plenty to offer all tastes. P

Mobberley

Bull's Head

Mill Lane, WA16 7HX

12-10.30 (11 Wed, Thu & summer); 12-midnight Fri & Sat; 12-10.30 Sun (01565) 873395 thebullsheadpub.co.uk

Weetwood Cheshire Cat; guest beers H

Excellent country inn that bills itself 'a real pub – local and proud'. The cobbled frontage is a promise of the delights within – three open fires, stone floor, candlelit tables, low beams, exposed Cheshire brick and an old back-to-back fireplace.

Seven Cheshire beers are part of the ethos of the pub. The house beers are brewed by Weetwood. Each handpump has tasting notes and tasters are provided to help you decide. Much of the good freshly-cooked food is locally sourced.
P (88)

Nantwich

Black Lion

29 Welsh Row, CW5 5ED (opp Cheshire Cat)
12-3 (not Mon), 5-11; 12-11 Sat; 12-10.30 Sun
(01270) 628711 blacklion-nantwich.co.uk
Weetwood Best Bitter, Cheshire Cat, Old Dog Bitter; guest beers H
A traditional inn dating back to the 17th century, this black-and-white-fronted pub stands among the historic buildings of Welsh Row. The beautiful plaster and wood-beamed interior features the requisite bowed walls and creaking floorboards. An open fire welcomes you into an open plan area which in the past would have been three separate rooms. There is a covered beer garden to the side and an additional small room warmed by a pot-bellied stove. Q

Crown L

High Street, CW5 5AS
10-11.15 (11 Tue) (01270) 625283
crownhotelnantwich.com
Salopian Shropshire Gold; guest beers H
This Grade II-listed building, burnt down in the Great Fire of Nantwich in 1583, was quickly rebuilt. The traditional bar offers a regularly changing range of guest beers, often LocAle, and a house ale brewed by Salopian. A classical and jazz pianist plays regularly during the week and occasional entertainment upstairs includes a monthly film night and live music. The pub hosts an annual Easter jazz and blues festival and in 2013 held its first beer festival. Sky Sports is available.
P (84)

Northwich

Penny Black L

110 Witton Street, CW9 5AB
8am-midnight (1am Fri & Sat) (01606) 42029
Greene King Abbot; Ruddles Best Bitter; guest beers H
Wetherspoon has done an excellent job bringing this Grade II-listed former post office, dating from 1914, back to life. Large and mainly open plan, TVs screen news channels with subtitles throughout the day. LocAle accredited, Cheshire-brewed beers are often to be found on the bar as well as at least one darker beer – a mild, stout or porter. The car park is behind the pub off Meadow Street immediately after the Royal Mail sorting office. Former local CAMRA Pub of the Year.
Q P (289)

Parkgate

Red Lion

The Parade, CH64 6SB
10.30-11 (midnight Fri & Sat); 12-11 Sun
(0151) 336 1548 theredlionparkgate.wix.com/theparade
Courage Best Bitter; Tetley Bitter; Wychwood Hobgoblin H
Excellent multi-roomed traditional inn on the edge of the River Dee Marshes. The oldest unchanged pub in Parkgate, dating from 1822, it is decorated throughout with beams and bric-a-brac. One central bar serves both the public bar and cosy lounge where panoramic views can be enjoyed towards Wales and the Dee Estuary. There is a large, attractive beer garden at the rear, with waiter service. Guest beers feature occasionally.
Q (22,487)

Penketh

Ferry Tavern

Station Road, WA5 2UJ (park in car park before railway crossing; pub is on opp side of railway and canal)
12-3, 5.30-11 (11.30 Fri); 12-11.30 Sat; 12-10.30 Sun
(01925) 791117 theferrytavern.com
Jennings Cumberland Ale; Ruddles County; Timothy Taylor Landlord; guest beers H
Lying between the River Mersey and the St Helens Canal, the Ferry was first licensed in 1762. A single bar serves up to three guest ales plus three regular beers and a large selection of whiskies. To the right of the bar, the quiet lounge features photographs and information about the pub's 250-year history, mostly compiled by present licensee Andy. With the Transpennine Trail nearby, it is a popular stop-off for walkers and cyclists. P (32)

Poynton

Poynton Royal British Legion

Georges Road West, SK12 1JY
11-11 (midnight Sat); 12-11 Sun (01625) 873120
poyntonlegionclub.co.uk
Worth Anson; guest beers H
Spacious private members' club offering a minimum of four beers, two from the on-site Worth Brewery and two from microbreweries. A quiet lounge drinking area is complemented by a public bar area with two snooker tables and a large-screen TV. A function room and bowling green are available for hire. Folk, quiz and jazz nights are hosted. For free entry show a CAMRA membership card or a copy of this Guide. The club is the winner of several awards. P

Runcorn

Lion Hotel

100 Greenway Road, WA7 5AG
5-11 (midnight Fri); 12-midnight Sat; 12-10.30 Sun
(01928) 574129
Beer range varies H
Situated 200 yards from Runcorn station, on the edge of the Old Town, this former Greenall's outlet is a fine example of what can be done to bring these old pubs up to modern day standards and give them a new lease of life. What was once a two-roomed keg pub is now a bright, airy, open room with a horseshoe bar and four handpumps featuring a regularly changing range of ales.
(10)

Norton Arms

125-127 Main Street, WA7 2AD
12-11 (01928) 567642 thenortonarms.co.uk
Beer range varies H
Two-roomed, ex-Greenalls, oak-beamed pub in the centre of Halton Village. The licensees have recently shown their dedication to cask ale by

increasing the number of handpumps from two to four, with third-of-a-pint taster glasses available. One of the few pubs in the area to have a bowling green, entertainment includes a quiz, live music and open mic nights. Food is sourced locally.

Prospect

70 Weston Road, WA7 4LD
12-11 (10.30 Sun) ☎ (01928) 561280
folkattheprospect.co.uk
Adnams Broadside; Timothy Taylor Landlord; guest beers H
On the outskirts of Weston village overlooking the Castner-Kellner chemical works, this traditional two-roomed pub has four handpumps including one for cider. The lounge features local memorabilia, while the bar is decorated with old vinyl 45s. A winner of numerous awards including local CAMRA Pub Of The Year 2012, the Prospect prides itself on sourcing local produce for meals and is committed to supporting local businesses whenever possible.

Sandbach

Old Hall

High Street, CW11 1AL
11.30-11; 12-10.30 Sun ☎ (01270) 758170
oldhall-sandbach.co.uk
Phoenix Brunning & Price Original; guest beers H
Grade I-listed building dating from 1656, once home to the lords of the manor of Sandbach. An extension was added in the 18th century when it was known as the Three Tuns, and it was further extended in the 19th century to accommodate coach travellers. Used as a billet for American officers during WWII, it was then allowed to decay by previous owners, but brought back to life when bought by Brunning & Price. Carefully restored and tastefully refurbished in 2010, it reopened in 2011. Well worth a visit. QP

Sarn

Queen's Head

SY14 7LN (off B5069 in Sarn)
closed Mon; 6 (5 Fri & Sat)-midnight; 12-11 Sun
☎ (01948) 770244 queensheadsarn.co.uk
Timothy Taylor Golden Best; guest beer H
A rural pub right on the Welsh border. The central lounge has a real fire, and quality home-cooked food is served in the adjacent dining area, with popular Sunday lunches from 12 noon to 6.30. The former taproom houses a pool table and dartboard. The partially covered patio garden overlooks Wych Brook and a disused corn mill, with a fish ladder currently being constructed. Timothy Taylor Golden Best is the regular beer, with varying guests. Open bank holiday Mondays. QP

Spurstow

Yew Tree

Long Lane, CW6 9RD
12-11; 11-10.30 Sun ☎ (01829) 260274
theyewtreebunbury.com
Stonehouse Station Bitter; guest beers H
A multi-award-winning pub/restaurant with a part black and white frontage, closed for a while then restored to its former glory by the current owners. The horseshoe-shaped bar has a central island displaying many spirits and cocktails. The real ale handpumps dominate the bar counters. Outside there are areas for alfresco dining and drinking, and plenty of parking. A bit off the main highways, this pub is a must visit. Regular beer festivals take place throughout the year. P

Sutton

Church House

Church Lane, SK11 0DS
12-midnight ☎ (01260) 252436
Banks's Bitter; Robinsons Unicorn; guest beers H
A friendly pub, popular with locals for good food and a selection of beers supplied by national and local breweries. A real fire provides warmth on winter days and is much appreciated after a walk or cycle ride in the surrounding Macclesfield Forest. A children's play area is at the rear of the building. There is a campsite for Camping and Caravan Club members only a short walk down the hill.
P(14)

Tarporley

Swan Hotel

50 High Street, CW6 0AG
8am-11 (10.30 Sun) ☎ (01829) 733838
theswantarporley.co.uk
Timothy Taylor Landlord; Weetwood Best Bitter, Cheshire Cat, Eastgate Ale; guest beer H
Historic coaching inn dating from 1565 and extensively rebuilt in Georgian times. The Swan has a stone-flagged tap room and numerous rooms and alcoves for dining and drinking. Friendly and efficient staff dispense five cask ales and good food throughout the day in a convivial atmosphere. Upstairs, the hunt room, dating from 1762, houses original works of art. Mini beer festivals are staged. Disabled access is through the car park at the rear. Use on-street parking when the car park is full.
QP(20)

Tattenhall

Sportsman's Arms

High Street, CH3 9QF
12-11 (10.30 Sun) ☎ (01829) 770233
sportsmanstattenhall.co.uk
Thwaites Original, Wainwright, Lancaster Bomber; guest beer H
Attractive white-painted traditional terrace pub in the centre of the village. The cobbled frontage leads to a welcoming and cosy interior featuring low beams and scrubbed pine tables. A central bar serves several distinct drinking areas, one of which was formerly the butcher's shop next door. Thwaites' regular beers are usually supplemented by its seasonal offerings and a guest beer. Reasonably priced, high-quality food is available and sports fans can enjoy BT and Sky.
P

Thelwall

Little Manor

Bell Lane, WA4 2SX
10.30-11; 10.30-10.30 Sun ☎ (01925) 212070
littlemanor-thelwall.co.uk
Coach House Cromwells Best Bitter; guest beers H
Recently refurbished by Brunning & Price, Little Manor is set in pleasant grounds, with a relaxed

ambience. Committed to locally brewed beers, it offers three guest ales alongside the house beer, brewed by Phoenix, and two regular beers, always including one from Wincle. Traditional pub fare is high quality and made with local, fresh ingredients. A community pub, it supports local parish activities and the village rose fête. Dogs are welcome in the main bar. Q≋❀◐◑♿P🚌🐾📶

Warrington

Bull's Head

33 Church Street, WA1 2SX
⏲ 12-11 ☎ (01925) 635680
Beer range varies Ⓗ
This is a very old building at the heart of old Warrington. The pub was renovated back in the 1990s, but retains a few discrete rooms and its essential character. There is usually a choice of three real ales – typically including Greene King IPA and Sharp's Doom Bar. A dartboard, pool table and two TVs are fairly unobtrusive. The local quiz league committee meets here. There is a separate function room and a bowling green outside. ≋❀⇌(Central)♣🚌

Friar Penketh Ⓛ

4 Barbauld Street, Friars Gate, WA1 1EX
⏲ 8am-midnight (1am Fri & Sat) ☎ (01925) 237320
Greene King Abbot; Ruddles Best Bitter; guest beers Ⓗ
Warrington's first Wetherspoon pub, built on the site of an old friary, with the remains visible through a section of glass floor. This is one of the better pubs in the chain, with a strong emphasis on well-kept ale. The downstairs bar usually has up to 10 real ales available including several from local breweries; the real cider is upstairs. Meet the Brewer events are hosted occasionally. Q≋❀◐◑♿⇌(Central)🍎🚌📶

Lower Angel Ⓛ

27 Buttermarket Street, WA1 2LY (in pedestrianised town centre)
⏲ 11-11 (midnight Fri; 12.30am Sat); 12-10 Sun
☎ (01925) 653326 🌐 lowerangel.co.uk
Tetley Bitter; Tipsy Angel Angelic Mild; guest beers Ⓗ
Town centre Victorian gem with two rooms – vault and lounge – and a rear beer garden. It is the tap for the Tipsy Angel Brewery behind the pub. Eight handpumps serve up to six guest beers alongside the two regulars. A vast selection of malt whiskies is available, some quite rare. Walkers Brewery memorabilia decorates the pub walls. ❀⇌(Central)🚌

Tavern Ⓛ

25 Church Street, WA1 2SS
⏲ 2-11; 12-midnight Fri & Sat; 12-11 Sun ☎ (01925) 747463
Beer range varies Ⓗ
The tap for 4T's Brewery, the Sports Bar features up to eight beers and two real ciders. Four more beers can usually be found in the Music Bar next door at weekends – a covered rear courtyard connects the two bars. Bottled ciders and Belgian beers are also available. Sport features on many screens, the bar getting busy when Warrington Wolves are at home. The 4T's mini brew kit was relocated to the Music Bar in 2014. ❀⇌(Central)♣🍎🚌📶

Willaston

Nag's Head

Hooton Road, CH64 1SJ
⏲ 11-11 (midnight Fri & Sat); 11-10.30 Sun
☎ (0151) 328 0808 🌐 thenagswillaston.co.uk
Otter Bitter; Wells Bombardier; York Guzzler; guest beer Ⓗ
Nestled in historic Willaston village, famous for its mill and the preserved station of Hadlow Road, the Nag's Head has risen from obscurity to a well-established local at the heart of the community. Refurbished extensively in 2011, the pub offers good food and great beer in warm, relaxing surroundings. Food is available all day, ranging from light bites to full meals. Popular with locals, tourists and walkers from the nearby Wirral Country Park footpath. Q≋❀◐◑♣P🚌🐾

Willey Moor Lock

Willey Moor Lock Tavern

Tarporley Road, SY13 4HF (400yds off A49)
⏲ 12-2.30, 6-11; 12-3, 7-10.30 Sun ☎ (01948) 663274
🌐 willeymoorlock.co.uk
Beer range varies Ⓗ
This family-run free house is reached from the car park by a footbridge over the Llangollen Canal. Situated by a lock and on the Sandstone Trail, it is popular with boaters and walkers. Outside seating is available by the canal and in the garden. Inside, the pub has a real fire and is decorated with local watercolours and a large collection of teapots. Three changing beers are available, increasing to six in summer, at least one from a local micro. Q≋❀◐◑P

Wilmslow

Bollin Fee Ⓛ

6-12 Swan Street, SK9 1HE
⏲ 8am-midnight (2am Sat) ☎ (01625) 441850
Greene King Abbot; Sharp's Doom Bar; Thornbridge Jaipur IPA; guest beers Ⓗ
Comfortable Wetherspoon's pub in the town centre just two minutes from the railway station. There is a central airy bar with raised tables and stools, plus other areas for family dining or relaxed fireside drinking. Local beers feature and there are regular Meet the Brewer events on Friday evenings. Saturday is DJ night, with the pub open till 2am. Look for the wall panel featuring the life of mathematician Alan Turing, who lived nearby. ≋❀◐◑♿⇌🍎🚌🐾📶

By George!

It was my Uncle George who discovered that alcohol was a food well in advance of modern medical thought.

P G Wodehouse, The Inimitable Jeeves

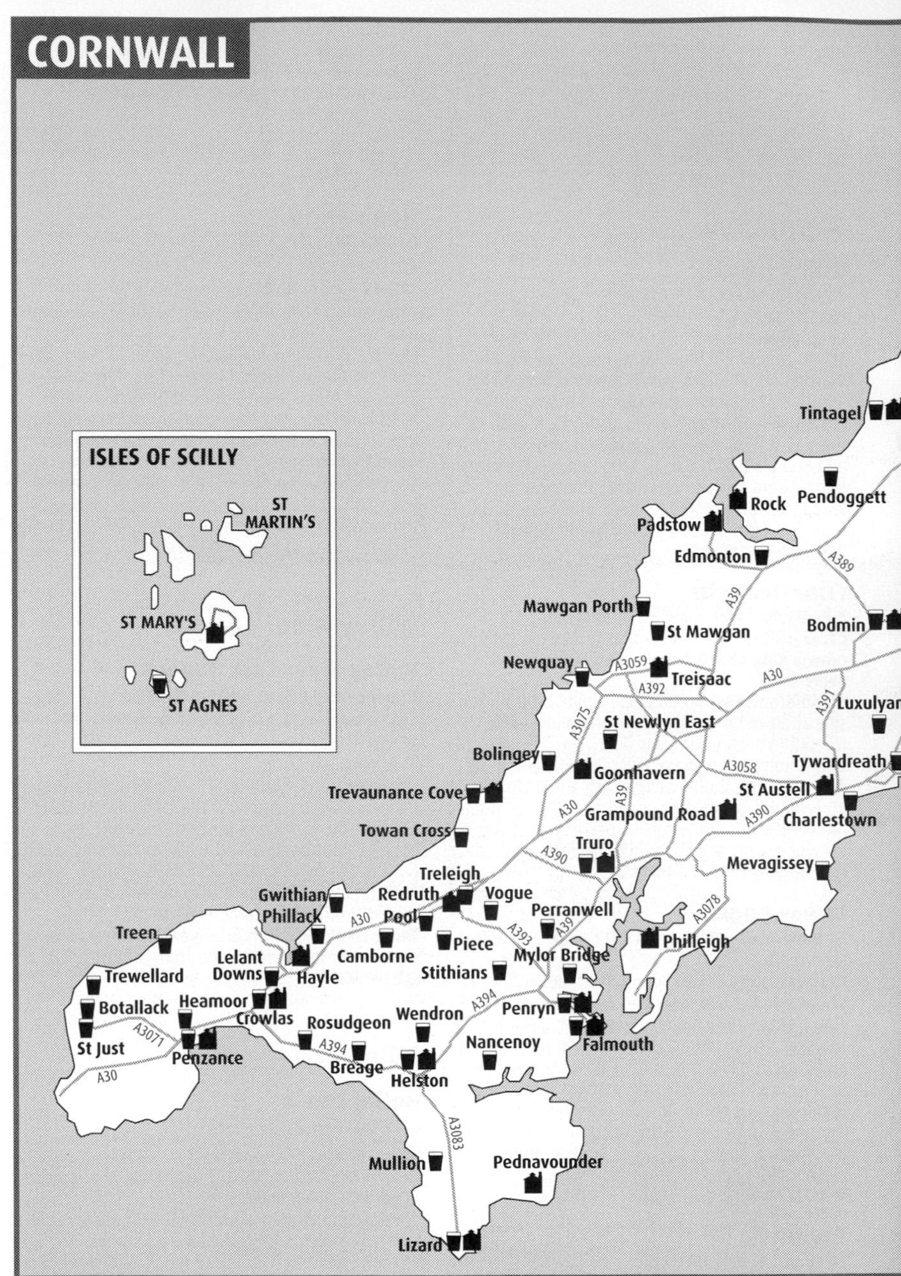

Altarnun

Rising Sun 🄻

PL15 7SN (1¼ miles NW of village) SX215825

🕒 12-2.30, 5.30-11; 12-11 Sat; 12-10.30 Sun

☎ (01566) 86636 🌐 therisingsuninn.co.uk

Penpont St Nonna's, Shipwreck Coast; Skinner's Betty Stogs; guest beers Ⓗ

A pub for 150 years, this characterful building on the outskirts of Altarnun enjoys good community support, and is the tap for the nearby Penpont Brewery. The interior is cosy, with beamed ceilings, an open fireplace, antique guns and various pictures on the walls. Deceptively spacious, there is ample seating in the bar, two small annexes for pool and drinkers, and a separate restaurant. Outside is a large patio and grassed area for games. Food is home cooked using locally-sourced ingredients. **Q**❀◐◑♿⅄♣●**P**⊡🚌(225)🐾

Blisland

Blisland Inn 🄻

The Green, PL30 4JF (off A30 NE of Bodmin) SX100732

🕒 11.30-11; 12-10.30 Sun ☎ (01208) 850739

Beer range varies Ⓗ/Ⓖ

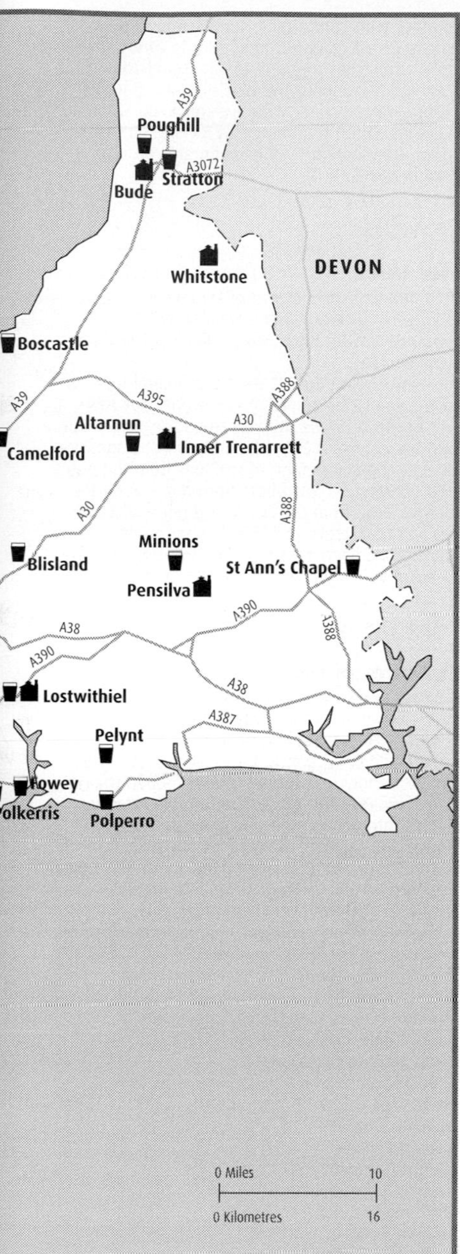

Friendly rural community pub by the village green, the Blisland retains its reputation as a real ale centre of excellence on the edge of Bodmin Moor. More than 3,000 different real ales have been served here; six or seven beers are usually available with at least two brewed locally, and frequently changing draught ciders include more unusual examples. Freshly prepared food features local produce. Popular with walkers and cyclists, well-behaved children and dogs are all welcome.
Q

Bodmin

Chapel an Gansblydhen

Fore Street, PL31 2HR
8am-midnight (11 Sun) ☎ (01208) 261730
Greene King Abbot; Ruddles Best Bitter; guest beers H
This busy town-centre pub has been beautifully converted from a former Methodist chapel, with many original features restored or retained. Four real ales are on offer, mostly from Cornish microbreweries, with two draught ciders also available. The pub pioneered the Wetherspoon Ale Club which meets every Wednesday and includes events such as Meet the Brewer evenings, tutored tastings and beer quizzes. Two beer festivals and a real cider festival are held annually, and a popular quiz night each Sunday. Q

Bolingey

Bolingey Inn

Penwartha Road, TR6 0DH (near B3284) SW763532
11-midnight (1am Fri & Sat); 12-11 Sun ☎ (01872) 571626
Sharp's Doom Bar; guest beers H
Quaint two-roomed village inn where a warm welcome awaits and conversation is the primary entertainment. Four beers are on offer throughout the year, boosted by beer festivals in April, August and October. Substantial home-cooked meals are served, made with local produce wherever possible. Well worth seeking out, the pub is not far from the brighter lights of Perranporth and its excellent golden sandy beach. An hourly bus service passes a short (but hilly) distance away.
Q ♣P (588)

Boscastle

Napoleon Inn

High Street, PL35 0BD (top of village) SX099907
11 (12 Nov-Mar)-11 ☎ (01840) 250204
napoleoninn.co.uk
St Austell Trelawny, Tribute, HSD G
Whitewashed stone inn dating from the 16th century in upper Boscastle, reputedly haunted and once a recruiting centre for press gangs. The St Austell Trelawny may alternate with Dartmoor Best Bitter. Several drinking areas on different levels cluster around the central bar. One room is simply furnished with settles, tables, chairs and a dartboard. The larger beamed lounge comprises four more areas including a separate restaurant. Screens are provided for sporting occasions. Local singers perform on Tuesdays, and there is live music on Friday evenings.
Q ♣P (595)

Botallack

Queen's Arms

St Just, TR19 7QG (just off Lands End-St Ives road)
12-11.30 (12.30am Fri & Sat) ☎ (01736) 788318
queensarms-botallack.co.uk
Sharp's Doom Bar; Skinner's Heligan Honey; guest beers H
Charming family-friendly granite free house in the heart of tin-mining country offering a warm welcome to all. Popular with coastal path walkers, its cosy single bar features an open fire and several distinct drinking and dining areas, with a family room at the rear. The homely decor depicts old

local mining scenes. Imaginative meals are served with up to four ales offered, usually from Cornish microbreweries. An annual August beer festival is held in the spacious rear beer garden.
Q🐴❀🛏◐◑⛺P🚌(10,300)🐾📶

Breage

Queen's Arms

TR13 9PD (off A394 Helston-Penzance road)
🕓 11-midnight; 12-11 Sun ☎ (01326) 573485
🌐 queensarmsbreage.co.uk
St Austell Tribute; Sharp's Doom Bar; guest beers Ⓗ
Comfortable and lively family-run village pub at the heart of the community, built originally to house artisans constructing the church across the road. The single long bar has an open fireplace at one end, a stove at the other, and a games room around the corner with a pool table and sports TV available; the dining room is at the rear. Outside seating includes some tables across the lane in an enclosed garden, with a safe play area for children.
🐴❀◐◑♿⛺♣P🚌(2,2A)🐾📶

Camborne

John Francis Bassett

21 Commercial Street, TR14 8JZ
🕓 8am-midnight (1am Fri & Sat) ☎ (01209) 721720
Greene King Abbot; Ruddles Best Bitter; guest beers Ⓗ
Wetherspoon pub in the centre of town, in the former market house built by architect William Bond in 1866. Previous uses of the building have included a cinema, night club and a pub called the Corn Exchange. Named after a prominent former local mine owner, it is a large, airy, open-plan venue with high ceilings, tall windows and a single long bar offering an impressive selection of guest beers. Q🐴❀◐◑♿⇌🚌📶

Camelford

Masons Arms

11 Market Place, PL32 9PB (on A39)
🕓 11-midnight ☎ (01840) 213309
St Austell Trelawny, Tribute, Proper Job Ⓗ
Community pub dating back 300 years with open stone walls and low-beamed ceilings, floored with a mix of wood, tiles and flagstones. Many interesting knick-knacks adorn the interior including long-vanished domestic products in display cases, toys and an eclectic collection of old glass bottles, banknotes and sheet music suspended from the beams. An ancient flowmeter presides over the passageway to the garden. Home-cooked meals include a selection of fresh fish. The beer choice is reduced during winter.
Q🐴❀◐◑⛺♣🚌🐾📶

Charlestown

Harbourside Inn

Charlestown Road, PL25 3NJ (on harbour front)
🕓 11-11 (midnight Fri & Sat); 12-11 Sun ☎ (01726) 68051
🌐 pierhousehotel.com
Draught Bass; St Austell Tribute; Sharp's Doom Bar; Skinner's Betty Stogs, Cornish Knocker; guest beer Ⓗ
Former harbourside warehouse, now a modern, lively sports-oriented free house attached to the Pier House hotel. Its charming single-bar interior features exposed stonework, slate and wooden flooring, with comfortable furnishings throughout. An expansive glass frontage affords views of the historic tall ships moored nearby. Good-value food is served throughout the day. Popular sporting events are screened, with live music on Saturday evenings. Often frequented by TV and film crews on location, drawn by the seven ales on offer.
❀🛏◐◑⛺🚌(524)📶

Crowlas

Star Inn

TR20 8DX (on A30, 3 miles E of Penzance)
🕓 11.30-11; 12-10.30 Sun ☎ (01736) 740375
Penzance Crowlas Bitter, Potion No 9, Brisons Bitter; guest beers Ⓗ
Cornwall CAMRA Pub of the Year several times in recent years, this impressive red-brick roadside free house is an ale drinkers' paradise. The single long bar is festooned with handpumps, dispensing an ever-changing range of real ales from the pub's own brewhouse plus beers from the around the country. Free from music, TV and noisy machines, this is a real locals' pub where beer quality reigns supreme and conversation abounds. Best to come by bus – you will stay a while. Q❀⛺♣🍎P🚌🐾

Edmonton

Quarryman Inn

PL27 7JA (just off A39 near Royal Cornwall showground)
🕓 12-11 ☎ (01208) 816444 🌐 thequarryman.co.uk
St Austell Proper Job; guest beers Ⓗ
Conversation and banter thrive at this convivial, family-friendly free house, where mobile phones are prohibited. The quiet, comfortable interior divides into a slate-floored public bar, carpeted lounge and separate dining area. The eclectic decor features local art. A varying beer menu offers four ales, served alongside good-quality meals

INDEPENDENT BREWERIES

Ales of Scilly St Mary's
Allsaints Redruth
Atlantic Treisaac
Black Flag Goonhavern (NEW)
Black Rock Falmouth (NEW)
Blue Anchor Helston
Bude Bude (NEW)
Castle Lostwithiel
Coastal Redruth
Cornish Chough Lizard
Cornish Crown Penzance
Driftwood Trevaunance Cove
Granite Rock Penryn (NEW)
Harbour Bodmin
Hardhead Pensilva (NEW)
Keltek Redruth
Lizard Pednavounder
Longhill Whitstone
Padstow Padstow
Paradise Hayle
Penpont Inner Trenarrett
Penzance Crowlas
Rebel Penryn
Roseland Philleigh
Sharp's (Molson Coors) Rock
Skinner's Truro
St Austell St Austell
Tintagel Tintagel
Wooden Hand Grampound Road

featuring locally-sourced produce. Near the county showground, it is well worth making a diversion to this ever-popular pub, frequented by locals and tourists alike. Dogs are allowed in the public bar only. Q

Falmouth

Beerwolf Books

3-4 Bells Court, TR11 3AZ
10-midnight; 11-11 Sun (01326) 618474
beerwolfbooks.com
Penzance Crowlas Bitter; guest beers H
According to taste, this is either a pub with books or a bookshop with beer. The spacious former maritime store loft, with wooden floor and open rafters, is divided into two distinct areas. The bar offers six changing real ales from microbreweries nationwide and a selection of four varying ciders and a perry from a bank of handpumps behind. The books area has shelves neatly stacked with many good-quality volumes to browse. No food is available but you may bring your own.
Q(Town)

Boathouse

Trevethan Hill, TR11 2AG (top of High Street)
12-11 (midnight Thu-Sat) (01326) 315425
Beer range varies H
Large family-oriented pub on two levels, up a short but steep hill on the edge of the town centre. The interior is decorated like a wooden boat and the decked balcony affords impressive river views. There is a small family room on the lower level but most of the action takes place upstairs where a single bar faces a long wood-floored room of unusual shape. The real ales vary but at least two are locally brewed. The real cider changes frequently. (Town)

Seven Stars Inn ★

The Moor, TR11 3QA
11-11; 12-10.30 Sun (01326) 312111
Draught Bass; St Austell Proper Job; Sharp's Special; Skinner's Porthleven; guest beer G
Grade II-listed, unspoilt town-centre drinkers' pub, run by the same family for several generations. Identified by CAMRA as having a nationally important historic pub interior, it has a narrow taproom at the front where you can watch your beer being drawn from the cask, or a quieter snug beyond a passageway with an original bottle and jug hatch. The bar top is a mixture of warped wood, marble and formica. No food, but you may bring your own to eat on benches outside.
Q(Town)

Fowey

Galleon Inn

12 Fore Street, PL23 1AQ
10 (12 Sun)-midnight (01726) 833014
galleon-inn.co.uk
Sharp's Cornish Coaster, Doom Bar; guest beers H
Riverside pub in the town centre dating back 400 years, now fully modernised, and reached off Fore Street through a glass-covered corridor with a colourful marine life mural. The only free house in Fowey, it features mainly Cornish ales and boasts delightful harbour views from the main bar and conservatory. Tables outside overlook the water and there is a heated, sheltered courtyard. A wide range of meals is available daily. Accommodation is en suite, some rooms affording river views.
(524,526)

Gwithian

Red River Inn

Prosper Hill, TR27 5BW
12-11 summer; closed Mon; 12-2, 5.30-11; 12-11 Sat & Sun winter (01736) 753223 red-river-inn.com
Sharp's Own; guest beers H
Named after the nearby river, this family-friendly and community-oriented free house is worth seeking out. Its pleasant single-bar interior features wood flooring and furnishings throughout, with wood-burning stoves adding winter warmth. The atmosphere is quiet and relaxing, and conversation thrives. Freshly cooked meals, using local produce, are served daily in separate dining areas. Up to four real ales are offered alongside the Sharp's Own, two generally from Cornish breweries. Live music plays every Saturday evening. An Easter beer festival is held annually.
P(515,547)

Heamoor

Sportsman's Arms

Carmen Square, TR18 3HH (on B3312)
12-midnight (01736) 364217
Beer range varies H
Comfortable, family-friendly village pub on the edge of Penzance. This is essentially a drinkers' pub, although food is available daily except Monday – Wednesday is curry night. The large L-shaped bar area is carpeted throughout and tastefully decorated with modern furniture. There are generally three real ales available, although there may be fewer at quiet times of year, always including one local Cornish brew and others sourced from various microbreweries. A small bar extension room hosts the pool table; quiz night is Friday. (10,10A)

Helston

Blue Anchor

50 Coinagehall Street, TR13 8EU
10-midnight (1am Fri & Sat) (01326) 562821
spingoales.com
Blue Anchor Flora Daze, Jubilee IPA H**, Ben's Stout** G**, Spingo Middle, Spingo Special** H
Rambling, unspoilt 15th-century thatched granite building with its own brewery at the rear, one of Britain's oldest brewpubs. Entry is through an arched passageway; there are two small bars to the right, a snug on the left, and an indoor skittle alley with bar at the back. Well-worn stone floors throughout and interesting bar room furniture are in keeping with the pub's antiquity; a mural in the front bar depicts former regulars and the licensees. The brewery is open to visitors. Q

Henlys

2 Church Street, TR13 8TG
11-midnight (1am Fri & Sat); closed Sun
(01326) 561141 henlysbarandrestaurant.co.uk
St Austell Tribute; Sharp's Doom Bar; guest beer H
Modern but tasteful pub in a converted former clothing shop in the centre of town. The single granite-topped bar is fronted with slate, the floor is wood parquet throughout, and seating includes

tables by the windows for people-watching. One area is furnished with sofas, and a comfy alcove is Moorish in style. Opposite the bar are a large mirror and drinking perches, and TVs hang in all areas. Home-cooked food is available in the restaurant upstairs or in the bar. ♘◐◑♿🚌🐾

Lelant Downs

Watermill Inn

TR27 6LQ (off A3074, on secondary St Ives road)
⏲ 12-11 ☎ (01736) 757912
Sharp's Doom Bar; Skinner's Betty Stogs; guest beer ⓗ
Standing in beautiful surroundings, this former 18th-century mill house is now a family-friendly, two-storey free house. Downstairs is a comfortable traditionally styled lounge bar, separated into drinking and dining areas, where a creative menu is served, and home to the original working watermill complete with millstones. Upstairs, the former mill loft functions as a stylish evening-only restaurant. Annual June and November beer festivals are held in the extensive beer garden straddling the mill stream. Live music features on Friday nights.
Q♘❀◐◑⛺≠(Lelant Saltings)P🚌🐾📶

Lizard

Witch Ball

Lighthouse Road, TR12 7NJ
⏲ 12-11 (midnight Fri & Sat) ☎ (01326) 290662
🌐 witchball.co.uk
Cornish Chough Kynance Blonde, Fire Raven; St Austell Tribute; Skinner's Betty Stogs ⓗ
Small, low-beamed single-bar pub offering cosy seating space to the right of the bar area and a larger dining annexe housing the witch ball, used to ward off evil spirits. A stove warms the bar area, and there are working wells behind and to the front of the pub, where there is also a large beer garden. The Cornish Chough beers are indicative of the range and may vary. A charity beer festival is held every August. It's the most southerly pub in Britain. ♘❀◐◑⛺🚌(37)🐾📶

Lostwithiel

Globe Inn 🄻

3 North Street, PL22 0EG
⏲ 12-2.30, 6-11 (midnight Fri & Sat) ☎ (01208) 872501
🌐 globeinn.com
Otter Ale; Sharp's Doom Bar; Skinner's Betty Stogs; guest beer ⓗ
Cosy 13th-century free house situated near the railway station in the narrow streets of this old stannary town. A charming, somewhat rambling pub, it has a single bar with several drinking and dining areas, and to the rear an intimate restaurant and sheltered suntrap patio. The varied food menu, prepared from local seasonal produce, features fish and game specials. A guest beer, generally from a microbrewery, is added in the summer. Accommodation is en-suite. Q❀🛏◐◑⛺≠♣🐾📶

Luxulyan

King's Arms

Bridges, PL30 5EF SW048580
⏲ 10.30-11 (midnight Sat); 11-11 Sun ☎ (01726) 850202
St Austell Trelawny, Tribute, HSD; guest beer ⓗ
Although the King's Arms is located on the outskirts of the village, it is very much a local community pub. Its large single bar is divided into drinking, dining and games areas. The pub is a short walk from the delightful Luxulyan Valley and is next to the railway station, featured on the local Atlantic Coast Rail Ale Trail. One of the few pubs in Cornwall that still has a skittle alley regularly used by locals in the summer. Q♘❀◐◑♿⛺≠♣P🚌(423)🐾📶

Mawgan Porth

Merrymoor

TR8 4BA (on B3276 coast road, opp beach)
⏲ 10-11.30 ☎ (01637) 860258 🌐 merrymoorinn.com
St Austell Tribute; Sharp's Doom Bar, Own; guest beer ⓗ
Atmospheric pub run by the same family since 1961. The spacious main bar with its picture windows overlooking the beach just 50 yards away is supplemented by a separate family room and a large beer garden. Locally-sourced food is cooked on the premises, with a carvery on Sundays. This pub is at the heart of the local community and raises large sums for charity every year. Accommodation is in seven en-suite rooms, and there is ample parking. Q♘❀🛏◐◑♿⛺P🚌(556)

Mevagissey

Fountain Inn

3 Cliff Street, PL26 6QH
⏲ 12-midnight ☎ (01726) 842320
St Austell Dartmoor Best Bitter, Tribute, HSD ⓗ
Friendly two-bar 15th-century inn near the harbour, with slate-flagged floors, exposed stone walls and low beamed ceilings. The decor includes historic photographs and paintings of old Mevagissey. The back Smugglers Bar once housed a pilchard press; a glass plate in the floor covers the former fish-oil sump, which also served as a store for contraband. The menu offers a range of home-cooked dishes. Nearby buses connect with St Austell and the Lost Gardens of Heligan.
Q♘🛏◐◑♿⛺♣🚌(524,525)📶

Minions

Cheesewring Hotel

PL14 5LE (off A38, N of Liskeard) SX261712
⏲ 12-midnight (10.30 Sun) ☎ (01579) 362321
🌐 cheesewringhotel.co.uk
Sharp's Doom Bar; guest beers ⓗ
Former paymaster-general's house for the nearby mines, this claims to be the highest pub in Cornwall at close to 985 feet above sea level. Named after a local rock formation, it is a homely family-owned hostelry at the centre of an area of Bodmin Moor of remarkable heritage interest. It has two bar rooms, one mainly for diners, and painted ceilings, wooden furniture and carpeted floors. A newly excavated cellar ensures the beer is kept in perfect condition. Traditional pub food is served.
Q♘❀🛏◐◑♿⛺♣P🍺🐾📶

Mullion

Mounts Bay Inn

Churchtown, TR12 7HN
⏲ 11-11 (midnight Fri & Sat); 12-10.30 Sun
☎ (01326) 240221 🌐 mountsbaymullion.co.uk
Sharp's Doom Bar; guest beers ⓗ

Light and airy traditional village pub with a modern bar leading through to a sun-trap garden and deck, offering views across Mounts Bay. Recently refurbished and opened up, the decor includes wooden floors, comfy leather sofas and plenty of seating at rustic tables. The two guest beers are mainly from Cornish microbreweries and dispensed through handpumps with polished steel handles. A separate restaurant is to the right; accommodation is next door. P (37)

Mylor Bridge

Lemon Arms

Lemon Hill, TR11 5NA (off A393 from Penryn)
11-3, 6.30-11; 12-3, 7-11 Sun ☎ (01326) 373666
St Austell Trelawny, Tribute, Proper Job

There has been a hostelry on this site since 1765. Once called the Griffin Inn, it became the Red Lion in 1829 and took its present name in 1837. A friendly one-bar pub in the centre of the village, it is home to local sports teams. Good home-cooked food is available – booking for the popular Sunday lunches is advisable. Families are made most welcome. Daytime buses run from Falmouth during the week. P (69)

Nancenoy

Trengilly Wartha Inn

TR11 5RP (off B3291 near Constantine) SW732283
11 (12 Sun)-3.15, 6-11 ☎ (01326) 340332
trengilly.co.uk
Penzance Potion No. 9; guest beers

Versatile inn in extensive grounds including a lake, in an isolated steeply wooded valley – the pub's name means 'settlement above the trees'. Originally a farmhouse, it has a variety of rooms, the wood-beamed bar displaying pictures by local artists. A conservatory extension serves as the family room. The real ales are mainly from local microbreweries, with real cider on offer in summer. A wide-ranging and imaginative food menu uses mostly fresh local produce.
Q P

Newquay

Towan Blystra

Cliff Road, TR7 1SG
8am-midnight (1am Fri & Sat) ☎ (01637) 852970
Greene King Abbot; Ruddles Best Bitter; guest beers

When three shops were converted into the town's first Wetherspoon outlet, it transformed the real ale scene in Newquay. In traditional Wetherspoon style, one long bar serves separate dining and drinking areas, offering an impressive range of beers mainly from Cornish microbreweries, generally including brews from Atlantic, Crown, Coastal or Tintagel. A drinking terrace overlooks the main street, while disabled access is via an alley off Springfield Road at the rear. Food is served until 11pm. Q

Pelynt

Jubilee Inn

Jubilee Hill, PL13 2JZ (on B3359)
12-11 ☎ (01503) 220312 jubilee-inn.co.uk
St Austell Black Prince, Tribute, Proper Job, HSD

Once called the Axe, this 17th-century village inn was renamed in 1887 to celebrate Queen Victoria's Golden Jubilee. Inside are oak-beamed ceilings, antique furniture, a Delabole slate floor and a wood-panelled bar with a huge burnished copper hood, plus a collection of Victorian jubilee and other royalty-related memorabilia. An extensive restaurant menu features freshly cooked locally-sourced produce. The beer range usually reduces to two in the winter, and one of the regular brews may be replaced by a St Austell seasonal beer.
Q P (573)

Pendoggett

Cornish Arms

St Kew, PL30 3HH (on B3314)
11-11 summer; 11-2.30, 5-midnight Mon & Fri; 11-midnight Sat winter ☎ (01208) 880263
cornisharms.com
Beer range varies

A former 16th-century coaching inn, this picturesque family-run free house is welcoming and family friendly. Full of charm and character, its atmospheric interior accommodates a bar, snug, two drinking/dining areas and a restaurant offering English and Thai cuisine. Flagstone floors, open beams, wood panels, partitions and furnishings reflect the pub's origins. Local caricatures adorn the walls, and handbells hang over the bar. An open fire adds warmth to the quiet, cosy atmosphere. The beer menu always includes one from Tintagel Brewery.
Q P

Penryn

Seven Stars

73 The Terrace, TR10 8EL
11 (12 Sun)-11 ☎ (01326) 373573
Blue Anchor Spingo Middle; guest beers

The nearest Penryn has to an ale house, this single-bar pub is run by a jovial Dutchman. Decorated with foreign cash, postcards and beer-related clippings, its spacious interior has a raised drinking annexe at the rear, dominated by a large ship's wheel. The pub is home to Penryn Community Theatre, who entertain with plays and pantos. A piano is available for competent pianists and live music features occasionally. Guest beers are usually from nearby brewery Rebel or other Cornish micros.

Penzance

Crown

Victoria Square, TR18 2EP SW474306
12-11.30 (10.30 Sun) ☎ (01736) 351070
thecrownpenzance.co.uk
Cornish Crown St Michael's, Causeway, SPA; guest beer

Locals' pub on a Victorian residential square off the town centre, and Cornish Crown Brewery tap – the beer selection may vary according to availability. Essentially a one-room pub, it is tidily furnished with upholstered window bench seats and a huge mirror covering one wall, though there is a cosy two-table snug at the back, available for an intimate meal or drink (booking for meals advised). There is a small patio outside for warmer weather. Live entertainment is on Monday, a quiz on Tuesday. Q

Perranwell

Royal Oak 𝕃

TR3 7PX

⏲ 11-3, 6-11 ☎ (01872) 863175

St Austell Tribute; Sharp's Doom Bar; Skinner's Betty Stogs; guest beer Ⓗ

At first sight this looks more a restaurant than a pub, but do not be put off. Although food is important here, this friendly 18th-century cottage-style inn is also a thriving village hub where drinkers are made welcome, the small bar area becoming quite crowded in the evenings. Quality food and wine are served alongside good beer – the guest ale varies and is usually from a microbrewery. On the Maritime Line Rail Ale Trail. Q❀◐◑⇌P🚌(46,82)🐾

Phillack

Bucket of Blood

14 Churchtown Road, TR27 5AE

⏲ 12-4, 6-11 (midnight Sat); 7-10.30 Sun ☎ (01736) 752378

🌐 bucketofblood.co.uk

St Austell Black Prince, Tribute, Proper Job, HSD Ⓗ

Named after a local gory legend, this historic, reputedly haunted pub is both family- and dog-friendly. Its comfortable single-bar interior separates into cosy drinking and dining areas. Low beamed ceilings, slate flooring and wooden furnishings, mainly settles, create character and an open fire adds warmth. The decor includes a St Ives Bay wall mural and pictures of local railway scenes. The HSD is always available but other St Austell beers may vary. Meals are available April to October only. Situated close to Hayle Towans. Q❀◐◑ÅP🐾

Piece

Countryman Inn

TR16 6SG (on Four Lanes-Pool road) SW679398

⏲ 11-11 (midnight Sat); 12-11 Sun ☎ (01209) 215960

Courage Directors; Sharp's Doom Bar, Own; Skinner's Betty Stogs, Heligan Honey; Theakston Old Peculier; guest beer Ⓗ

Residents of nearby towns are irresistibly drawn to this lively stone-built pub, a former miners' shop, set among the old copper mines near the distinctive landmark of Carn Brea. The larger bar is dominated by a granite fireplace and massive cast-iron cooking range, the smaller room has a public-bar feel and welcomes families. The pub hosts live entertainment most nights and Sunday lunchtimes, when there is also a raffle to support local charities. ❀◐◑Å♣P🚌(442)🐾

Polkerris

Rashleigh Inn 𝕃

PL24 2TL (off A3082 Par-Fowey road) SX093521

⏲ 11-11 ☎ (01726) 813991

🌐 therashleighinnpolkerris.co.uk

St Austell HSD; Timothy Taylor Landlord; guest beers Ⓗ

Former 18th-century pilchard boathouse, now an excellent family-run free house beside a secluded beach near the Saints Way footpath. Its atmospheric interior features exposed stonework, wooden flooring, beamed ceilings, open fires, comfortable furnishings and a splendid slate-topped bar. Up to six ales are available, and quality meals are served in the bar and split-level restaurant. The bar bay window and sheltered terrace offer panoramic views of St Austell Bay. Well-behaved dogs on leads are allowed in the bar only. Q❀◐Å♣P🐾📶

Polperro

Crumplehorn Inn 𝕃

The Old Mill, Crumplehorn, PL13 2RJ (on A387)

⏲ 11-11; 12-10.30 Sun ☎ (01503) 272348

🌐 crumplehorn-inn.co.uk

St Austell Tribute; Sharp's Doom Bar; Tintagel Castle Gold, Harbour Special Ⓗ

Once a mill and mentioned in the Domesday Book, this historic inn at the entrance to the village still has a working waterwheel outside. The split-level bar is divided into three comfortable areas with low ceilings and flagstone floors, and outside the spacious patio by the millstream has tables with large umbrellas providing shade. A varied menu includes locally caught fish. The buses turn round opposite the pub; in summer catch the milk float 'tram' down to the harbour. Accommodation is B&B or self-catering.

Q❀🛏◐◑ÅP🚌(572,573)🐾

Pool

Plume of Feathers

Fore Street, TR15 3PF (on A3047)

⏲ 11.30-11.30; 12-midnight Sat; 11.30-10.30 Sun

☎ (01209) 713513

Beer range varies Ⓗ

Cosy old granite inn on the main road, with low beams and several drinking areas around a central bar. The ever-changing beer range comes mainly from Cornish and south-west microbreweries, with three brews always available and occasional cider. A beer festival is held in summer. Family-friendly, with an outdoor play area, it is also a meeting place for clubs. Once used as a mortuary for a local mining disaster, the pub is home to two ghosts. No food Sunday evening. Q❀◐◑♣P🚌🐾📶

Poughill

Preston Gate Inn

Poughill Road, EX23 9ET (on Sandymouth Bay Road)

⏲ 11-11 ☎ (01288) 354017 🌐 prestongateinn.co.uk

Sharp's Doom Bar; guest beers Ⓗ

Originally two cottages, this 16th-century building became a single-room village pub in 1983. The spacious U-shaped room hosts the dartboard at one end of the bar, with more seating and a roaring log fire at the other end. Meals include popular Sunday roasts and monthly themed nights, and breakfast is available 10am-noon during the summer months. Conversation rules here, and the pub supports darts and quiz teams. The name Preston comes from the Cornish word for priest. Q◐◑Å♣P🚌(219)🐾

Rosudgeon

Falmouth Packet 𝕃

TR20 9QE (on A394 Penzance-Helston road)

⏲ 12-3, 5.30-11 (midnight Sat); 11-midnight Fri; 12-11 Sun

☎ (01736) 762240 🌐 falmouthpacketinn.co.uk

Penzance Crows-an-Wra; guest beers Ⓗ

Vibrant family-run free house enjoying a flourishing reputation for fine ales and cuisine. Its comfortable, quiet single-bar interior divides into

drinking and dining areas, with an open fire, exposed stonework, slate floors and wooden furnishings adding character. Additional drinking/dining space is provided by an adjoining conservatory. An imaginative food menu uses locally sourced seasonal produce. The pub is community-oriented and supports a local clubhouse. A Penzance ale, Tater Du, is brewed especially for the pub. A holiday let is available.
Q❀⊟◐♿⛺♣P🚌(2)🐾📶

St Agnes (Isles of Scilly)

Turk's Head

TR22 0PL (close to quay)

☉ 11 (12 Sun)-4.30, 7-11 (10.30 Sun); 11 (12 Sun)-11 Jul & Aug ☎ (01720) 422434

St Austell Tribute; guest beers Ⓗ

The island's only pub, near the jetty, with an outdoor drinking area unrivalled for its scenic views. Opening hours may vary slightly according to boat times – you can watch your boat approaching from the bar. Evening trips to sample the ale and food run from St Mary's in summer. The Tribute is badged as house beer Turk's Ale, while two guest ales are usually selected from the Ales of Scilly, Skinner's or Sharp's ranges. Order lunchtime pasties early. ❀◐⛺🐾

St Ann's Chapel

Rifle Volunteer Inn

PL18 9HL (on A390)

☉ 11.30-11; 11-11.30 Sat; 12-10.30 Sun ☎ (01822) 833038

🌐 theriflevolunteer.co.uk

Sharp's Doom Bar; Tintagel Cornwall's Pride; guest beer Ⓗ

Former mine captain's house built around 1800 and converted to a coaching inn during the mid 19th century. The larger open-plan bar accommodates a modern conservatory, popular with diners for its views over the garden. A small public bar caters for drinkers and hosts the pool table, dartboard and church settles. There is also a skittle alley. On the Tamar Valley Rail Ale Trail, the pub offers panoramic views across the Tamar Valley and is in good walking country.
Q❀◐♿≈(Gunnislake)♣P🚌(79)

St Just

Star Inn

1 Fore Street, TR19 7LL

☉ 11.30-midnight (11.30 Sun) ☎ (01736) 788767

🌐 thestarinn-stjust.co.uk

St Austell Dartmoor Best Bitter, Tribute, Proper Job Ⓗ

Ever-popular 18th-century granite inn, reputedly the oldest in town, its atmospheric single bar interior reflecting a long association with tin mining and the sea. Celtic flags adorn the beamed ceilings, with wooden furnishings and an open fire creating character and warmth. A separate snug functions as a meeting or family room. Up to five St Austell ales are served, but no food – this is a proper drinkers' pub, a timeless place where conversation and singing are the primary entertainment. Q❀♿⛺♣🚌(10,300)🐾

St Mawgan

Falcon Inn L

TR8 4EP (near Newquay airport)

☉ 11-11 summer; 11-3, 5.30-11 winter; 11-midnight Fri & Sat; 12-11 Sun ☎ (01637) 860225

🌐 thefalconinnstmawgan.co.uk

Beer range varies Ⓗ

This charming, family-friendly, 16th-century free house offers a quiet retreat, despite the proximity of Newquay airport. The relaxed interior features a cosy single bar with large open hearth and adjoining stylish restaurant. Four ales are on offer from a varying menu and excellent home-cooked food is served daily; the extensive well-kept gardens are perfect for alfresco dining and drinking. Nestling in the Lanherne Valley, this picturesque pub supports numerous local charity events. An annual beer festival is held in July.
Q❀⊟◐⛺♣P🚌(556)🐾📶

St Newlyn East

Pheasant Inn L

Churchtown, TR8 5LJ

☉ 12-3, 6-midnight; 12-midnight Fri, Sat & summer; 12-11 Sun ☎ (01872) 510237

St Austell Tribute; Sharp's Doom Bar; Skinner's Betty Stogs; guest beer Ⓗ

Easy to find opposite the church, this is a real community local at the centre of a thriving village, where darts, euchre and football teams are all supported. Two bar areas supply the Cornish beers, and an annual beer festival takes place in October. Good-value pub food uses local produce including meat raised and supplied by the village butcher, who is a regular. The car park to the rear is entered via a narrow lane. ❀◐♣P🚌(586)🐾📶

Stithians

Seven Stars Inn

Church Road, TR3 7DH

☉ 12-11 (midnight Fri & Sat) ☎ (01209) 860003

St Austell Trelawny, Tribute; guest beer Ⓗ

Lively and friendly cottage-style village local, popular with a broad cross-section of the community and supportive of local events and sports teams. The pub was originally purpose built as an extension to a farmhouse, to serve the drinking needs of local tin miners at the end of the 19th century. The original bar and lounge have been opened out to form one L-shaped drinking area. A more modern extension towards the rear houses the pool table. Q❀◐♣🚌(82,442)🐾📶

Stratton

King's Arms L

Howells Road, EX23 9BX (on A39)

☉ 12-11 ☎ (01288) 352396

Sharp's Doom Bar; Tintagel Cornwall's Pride; guest beers Ⓗ

Popular locals' local in the heart of this ancient market town, a 17th-century former coaching inn whose name reflects the town's loyalties after the Civil War. The pub has many original features including two simply furnished bars, and well-worn Delabole slate flagstone and wood floors. During renovation work, a small bread oven was exposed in the lounge. The two guest beers usually include one from a Cornish brewery and one from Devon. Four letting rooms are available, one en suite.
Q❀⊟◐♿♣🍎P🚌🐾

Tintagel

King Arthur's Arms

Fore Street, PL34 0DA
9am-midnight ☎ (01840) 770831
kingarthursarms.co.uk
St Austell Tribute; Sharp's Doom Bar; Tintagel Harbour Special; guest beers H
Modernised 14th-century granite inn with beamed ceilings, situated opposite the National Trust Old Post Office. The unusually shaped main bar area is large and open plan. A fourth Cornish beer appears in winter, usually from Tintagel Brewery, and six beers are available in summer. Food is served until 9pm, with breakfast from 9am. Good facilities are on offer for families of all ages, with an outside area and large interior for the summer trade offering various pub games. There are 13 B&B rooms. (595)

Towan Cross

Victory Inn

TR4 8BN
11-midnight ☎ (01209) 890359
thevictoryinncornwall.co.uk
St Austell Tribute; Skinner's Betty Stogs; guest beers H
Traditional family-friendly free house situated high on the cliff top above Porthtowan. With a restful atmosphere, the open-plan single-bar interior is comfortably furnished throughout, and accommodates separate dining and games areas. An adjoining conservatory doubles as a family or dining room. At the rear are a large beer garden, ample parking and camping facilities. The four ales on offer are mainly from the Skinner's range, while an interesting good-value menu features local produce. QP (304)

Treen (Zennor)

Gurnard's Head Hotel

TR26 3DE (on B3306, Lands End-St Ives coast road)
10-11.30 ☎ (01736) 796928 gurnardshead.co.uk
St Austell Tribute; Skinner's Betty Stogs; guest beers H
Enjoying a well-earned reputation for fine ales and excellent cuisine, this impressive free house draws custom from near and far. The characterful, expansive wood-floored interior accommodates a spacious single bar, cosy snug and stylish dining room. The attractive decor features local art, and comfy sofas and wooden furnishings help to create a relaxed ambience. The extensive locally sourced food menu changes daily. An Ale & Games Club evening is held on Thursday, when substantially discounted beers are on offer. A beer festival features in May. QP (300)

Treleigh

Treleigh Arms

Basset Road, TR16 4AY (beside old Redruth bypass A3047)
11-2.30, 5-11; 11-11 Fri & Sat; 11-10.30 Sun
☎ (01209) 315095 treleigharms.com
Draught Bass; Sharp's Doom Bar; Skinner's Betty Stogs; guest beer H
Expect warm, friendly service at this single-bar granite-built pub to the east of Redruth. The large, comfortable bar room features exposed stone walls and a woodburner. The emphasis is on Cornish ales, with real cider in summer. There is a separate dining room offering mainly locally-produced food including coeliac (gluten-free) and vegetarian menus, also speciality coffee and locally grown tea. Well-behaved dogs are welcome. No TV or games machines. Quiz night is Tuesday and pétanque is available. QP (14,18)

Keep your Good Beer Guide up to date by visiting the CAMRA website **camra.org.uk**, then Good Beer Guide, then Updates.

Trevaunance Cove

Driftwood Spars

Quay Road, TR5 0RT
11-11 (1am Fri & Sat) ☎ (01872) 552428
driftwoodspars.com
Driftwood Red Mission, Montol, Lou's Brew; guest beers H
Dedicated to promoting real ale, this outstanding coastal free house offers a range of eight ales plus real cider. The nautical-themed brewpub boasts three different bars, a sea view dining room and sun terrace, and two beer gardens. Local seasonal produce is emphasised in a creative food menu. Vibrant and family-friendly, it is a popular wedding venue, with entertainment including live music and occasional theatre. Annual March and May beer festivals are held, as well as tutored tastings. QP

Trewellard

Trewellard Arms

Trewellard Road, TR19 7TA (on B3318/B3306 jct)
12-11 (midnight Sat) ☎ (01736) 788634
goodpubfoodlandsend.co.uk
Beer range varies H
Near Geevor Mine, this was formerly the mine owner's home and is now a thriving, family-run free house. Its cosy interior accommodates a spacious open-beamed single bar, dining area and secluded cellar seating area. Welcoming and family-friendly, its comfortable furnishings and open fires enhance the homely atmosphere. Home-cooked meals are good value and the ever-changing beer menu offers up to six, generally local, ales. An annual beer festival is held each May. A drinking patio and ample parking are at the front of the pub. P (10,300)

Truro

City Inn

Pydar Street, TR1 3SP (N edge of city centre, through railway arch)
12-11.30 (12.30am Fri & Sat) ☎ (01872) 272623
Otter Bitter; Sharp's Doom Bar; Skinner's Betty Stogs; guest beer H
Situated near the city centre by the railway viaduct, this two-bar community-focused pub has the atmosphere of a village local. Its welcoming wood-beamed interior includes a front bar with several drinking and dining areas, and an impressive water jug collection. The sports-oriented back bar has a pool table and TV. Good-value home-cooked meals are served daily. Regular charity events include the

annual conker and hog's pudding championships. To the rear is a suntrap garden where occasional beer festivals are held. Q

Old Ale House

7 Quay Street, TR1 2HD

11-11 (1am Fri & Sat); 12-10.30 Sun ☎ (01872) 271122

Skinner's Betty Stogs, River Cottage EPA, Lushingtons, Cornish Knocker H; guest beers H/G

This two-storey pub's façade belies its short history. The atmospheric ground floor bar features wooden flooring, beams, uprights and furnishings; various old artefacts adding character. The stylish upper Hop Store Bar doubles as a function room. Leased by Skinner's Brewery, it is effectively the brewery tap but the eight ales include ever-changing guest brews and six ciders. Freshly cooked good-value food is served as well as free monkey nuts. Live music plays on Friday and Saturday evenings. The bus station is close by. Q

William IV

Kenwyn Street, TR1 3DJ

11-11 (midnight Fri & Sat); 12-10.30 Sun

☎ (01872) 273334 thewilliamivtruro.co.uk

St Austell Trelawny, Tribute, Proper Job, HSD H

Large city-centre pub just off Victoria Square, catering for business people and shoppers at lunchtime and a younger clientele in the evenings. The beers may vary, but there are usually four available from St Austell Brewery. The split-level, open-plan bar includes sofas beside a real fire, and there is an airy conservatory and a pleasant beer garden. Food is available all day, with a carvery on Sunday. Live bands or a disco entertain on Friday and Saturday evenings.

Tywardreath

New Inn

Fore Street, PL24 2QP

12-11 ☎ (01726) 813901

Draught Bass G; St Austell Trelawny, Tribute, Proper Job H; guest beer G

Classic village pub built in the mid-18th century by mine owners, a perfect example of a community local. Groups are supported and meet here, and fêtes are held in the extensive gardens. Although tied to the brewery, the landlord takes every opportunity to serve guest beers, as well as Draught Bass which the pub is covenanted to sell in perpetuity. Pub games and good conversation provide the entertainment, backed up by regular live music by talented local bands.

Q (Par) P (524,526)

Vogue

Star Inn

TR16 5NP (on St Day-Redruth road)

12-midnight (1am Fri & Sat); 11-11 Sun

☎ (01209) 820242 starinnvogue.biz

Beer range varies H

True village local, full of character and with a strong community focus – it hosts a council library, hairdressing salon and a vintage motor club in the large car park. The homely interior accommodates a spacious bar for drinking and dining, a quiet lounge and a separate restaurant. Home-cooked food is served daily – book for Sunday lunch. The ever-changing beer menu features local microbreweries and popular national brews. Entertainment includes live music weekends and an annual June beer festival.

P (47)

Wendron

New Inn

Redruth Road, TR13 0EA (on B3297)

Closed Mon winter; 12-3, 6-11; 12-3, 7-10.30 Sun

☎ (01326) 572683

St Austell Tribute; guest beers H

Sitting near the village church, this comfortable, welcoming country pub caters for locals and visitors alike. The cosy, homely bar is dominated by paintings of horses and hunting scenes, and an interesting woodcarving of the Four Horsemen of the Apocalypse. Food is prepared by the landlady and her daughter; the separate restaurant is accessed through the bar. The two guest beers usually include a Skinner's brew and one from another local microbrewery.

Q P (2A,34)

Of Ale

Ale is made of malte and water, and they the which do put any other thynge to ale than is rehersed, except yest, barme or godisgood (other forms of yeast) do sofysticat (adulterate) theyr ale. Ale for an englysshe man is a natural drynke. Ale must have these propertyes, it must be freshe and cleare, it must not be ropy (cloudy) or smoky, nor it must have no welt nor tayle (sediment or dregs). Ale should not be dronke under V days olde. Newe ale is unholsome for all men. And soure ale and deade ale the which doth stande a tylt is good for no man. Barley malte maketh better ale then oten malte or any other corne doth, it doth engender grosse humoures, but yette it maketh a man stronge.

Of Bere

Bere is made of malte, of hoppes, and water, it is a natural drinke for a dutche man. And nowe of late dayes it is moche used in Englande to the detryment of many englysshe men, specyally it kylleth them the which be troubled with the colycke and the stone & strangulion (quinsy), for the drynke is a colde drynke: yet it doth make a man fat and doth inflate the bely, as it doth appere by the dutche mens faces & belyes. If the beer be well served and be fyned & not newe, it doth qualify ye heat of the lyver.

Andrew Boorde (c.1490-1549), A 'Compendyous Regyment' or 'a Dyetary of Helth', 1542

CUMBRIA

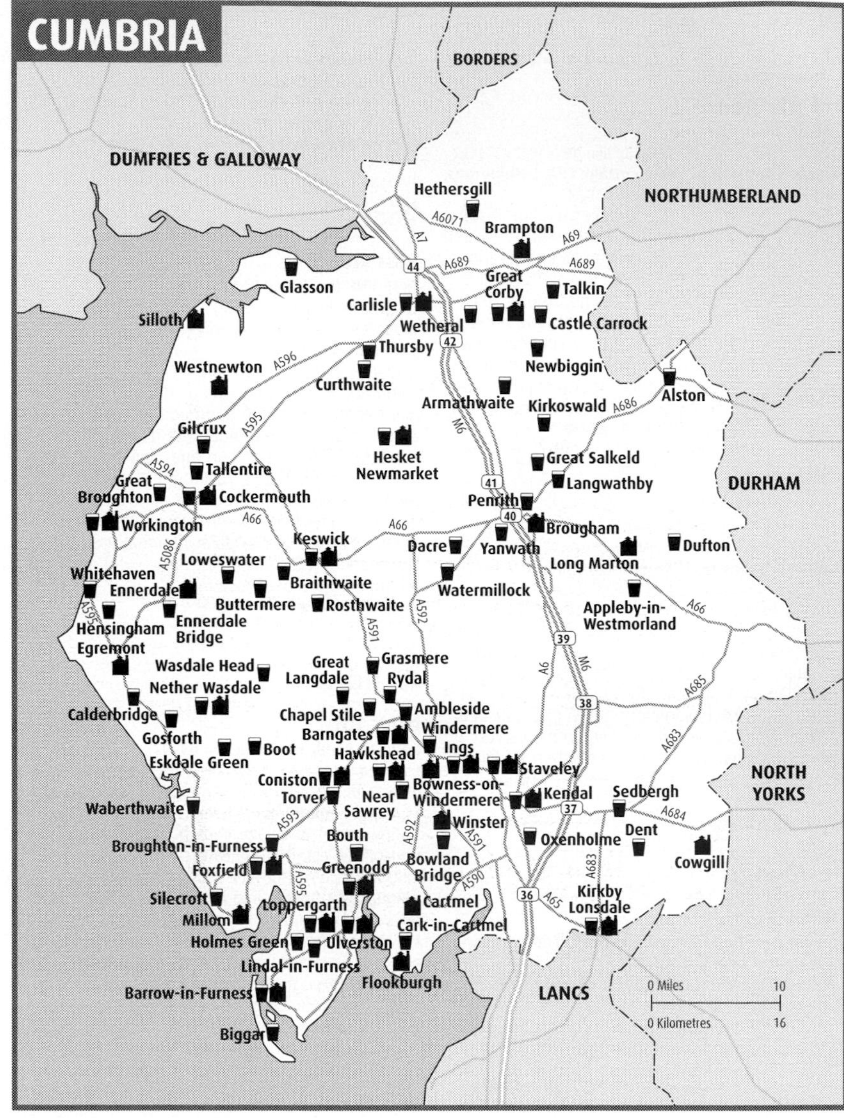

Alston

Cumberland Inn L

Townfoot, CA9 3HX

12-11 ☎ (01434) 381875 alstoncumberlandhotel.co.uk

Yates Bitter; guest beers H

A family-run 19th-century inn overlooking the South Tyne River. Close to the Coast-to-Coast cycle route and Pennine Way, it is an ideal base to explore the highest market town in England. Meals are available in the bar throughout the week, with roasts on Sundays. The house beer is Yates Bitter, with guests from Geltsdale, Hesket Newmarket, Allendale, High House Farm and Mordue, as well as further afield. Old Rosie and occasional Cumbrian ciders and perry are stocked. Local CAMRA Cider Pub of the Year 2013. Q P

Ambleside

Lily L

12-14 Lake Road, LA22 0AD

12-11 (midnight Fri & Sat) ☎ (01539) 433175
thelilybar.co.uk

Cumbrian Legendary Loweswater Gold; guest beers H

Popular town centre bar with three ever-changing guest beers from local Cumbrian breweries, often Barngates and Cumbrian Legendary Ales. Large, comfortable seating and solid wooden tables abound here, with a mixture of slate and wood floors. Live music is performed at weekends, with occasional open mic and comedy nights. Accommodation is available at the separate Ambleside Central situated above the bar and restaurant.

Appleby-in-Westmorland

Golden Ball

High Wiend, CA16 6RD

11 (12 Sun)-midnight ☎ (017683) 51493

Marston's Burton Bitter; guest beers

A traditional side-street pub which has changed little over the years. The lounge is on the left of the entrance and the bar is on the right, with TV and an excellent rock jukebox. Both bars are served from a central back-to-back counter with up to six real ales. As well as a strong local following, the pub also attracts visitors including railway enthusiasts using the Settle to Carlisle line. The patio has a large covered area. (563)

Midland Hotel

25 Clifford Street, CA16 6TS

closed Mon; 11-5 Tue & Wed; 11.30-11 ☎ (017683) 51524

themidlandhotelappleby.co.uk

Beer range varies

The Midland is set in the beautiful Eden Valley between the Lake District and the Yorkshire Dales National Parks, adjacent to the station on the Settle & Carlisle railway. The building has been extensively refurbished and much improved, now having a light modern feel. Three handpumps offer beers from both local and national microbreweries, and real cider and perry are often available. Excellent locally-sourced food is served in this local CAMRA Pub of the Year. P (563)

Armathwaite

Fox & Pheasant

CA4 9PY

11-11 ☎ (016974) 72400 foxandpheasantinn.co.uk

Robinsons Dizzy Blonde, Cumbria Way, Unicorn, seasonal beer

Atmospheric 17th-century coaching inn overlooking the River Eden. The main bar has a flagstone floor and inglenook fireplace. The former stables have been converted into a bar and dining area. Original wooden beams, exposed stonework and stable stalls all add to the ambience. Friendly, welcoming service is assured. The guest beer is the Robinsons seasonal ale. An ideal base for exploring the Eden Valley and popular with walkers and anglers. P

Barngates

Drunken Duck Inn

LA22 0NG (signed off the B5286 Hawkshead to Ambleside road) NY351013

11.30-11; 12-10.30 Sun ☎ (015394) 36347

drunkenduckinn.co.uk

Barngates Cat Nap, Cracker, Tag Lag; guest beer

Home of Barngates Brewery, the Duck always serves four of the 10 beers brewed here and brewery tours can be arranged. The bar has been extensively renovated to create a pleasing mix of local and modern styles. Lunchtime bar meals and the à la carte menu available in the dining room in the evening are of an exceptionally high standard. The outside seating area at the front offers magnificent views of the fells to the north-east.

Q P

Barrow-in-Furness

Furness Railway

76-80 Abbey Road, LA14 1PQ

8am-midnight (1am Fri & Sat) ☎ (01229) 820818

Courage Directors; Greene King Abbot; Ruddles Best Bitter; guest beers

On the ground floor of the old central Co-op department store, divided into four distinct drinking areas, the pub is a fine example of early 20th-century commercial architecture and a credit to Wetherspoon, who have given this building a new lease of life. It can be busy throughout the day but particularly at weekends, when it is a popular starting point for the town-centre circuit. Good-value food is served all day.

King's Arms

Quarry Brow, Hawcoat, LA14 4HY

5.30-11; 4-midnight Fri; 12.30-midnight Sat; 1-11 Sun

☎ (01229) 828137

Beer range varies

Popular local pub with friendly staff selling beer mainly from local micros, including Barngates, Bowness Bay, Copper Dragon, Cumberland, Cumbrian Legendary and Lancaster breweries. Seasonal ales also feature, with a beer menu on a chalkboard listing forthcoming attractions. The landlord and landlady are cask beer enthusiasts who have increased their real ale availability to six handpumps. There has been a pub on these premises since the 1860s. The interior comprises two rooms, one being dog friendly.

Q (1,6)

INDEPENDENT BREWERIES

Abraham Thompson Barrow-in-Furness
Barngates Barngates
Beckstones Millom
Blackbeck Egremont
Bowness Bay Winster
Brewshine Kendal (NEW)
Carlisle Carlisle (NEW)
Coniston Coniston
Cumberland Great Corby
Cumbrian Legendary Hawkshead
Dent Cowgill
Derwent Silloth
Eden Brougham
Ennerdale Ennerdale
Fell Flookburgh
Foxfield Foxfield
Geltsdale Brampton
Greenodd Greenodd
Hardknott Millom
Hawkshead Staveley
Healey's Loppergarth
Hesket Newmarket Hesket Newmarket
Jennings (Marston's) Cockermouth
Kendal Kendal
Keswick Keswick
Kirkby Lonsdale Kirkby Lonsdale
Mitchell Krause Workington
Strands Nether Wasdale
Stringers Ulverston
Tirril Long Marton
Ulverston Ulverston
Unsworth's Yard Cartmel
Watermill Ings
Wild Boar Bowness-on-Windermere (NEW)
Winster Valley Winster
Yates Westnewton

Biggar

Queen's Arms 𝕃

Biggar Village, Walney Island, LA14 3YG
⏲ closed Mon; 6-11.30 Tue; 12-10.30 Wed & Thu; 12-midnight Fri & Sat; 12-10.30 Sun ☎ (01229) 471880
🌐 thequeensarmsbiggar.co.uk
Beer range varies H
Situated in the ancient village of Biggar, the Queen's Arms retains its unique character and style, and now has a restaurant attached serving local produce. Several draught beers are available and there is always a warm welcome. The beer range varies from week to week and the menu changes seasonally. The pub hosts a variety of events including a book club, jam sessions, quizzes and occasional beer festivals in the large courtyard. Live music features every Saturday.
Q♨❀⇌◑◐P▯🐾📶

Boot

Brook House Inn 🏆 𝕃

CA19 1TG (200yds from Dalegarth Station – La'al Ratty)
⏲ 9am-11 ☎ (019467) 23288 🌐 brookhouseinn.co.uk
Cumbrian Legendary Ales Langdale; Hawkshead Bitter; guest beers H
In the heart of the western Lake District in beautiful Eskdale, close to the terminus of the Ravenglass & Eskdale miniature railway, this popular family-run tourist pub is renowned for good food and a wide range of well-kept cask ales. Together with other nearby pubs in the Eskdale valley, the Brook House Inn provides the focal point for an annual beer festival held in June.
Q♨❀⇌◑◐♿⛺⇌(Dalegarth)🍎P🐾📶

Woolpack Inn 𝕃

CA19 1TH (¾ mile E of Boot village on approach to Hardknott Pass) SD192011
⏲ 9am-11 ☎ (019467) 23230 🌐 woolpack.co.uk
Hardknott Continuum; Jennings Cumberland Ale; Theakston Best Bitter; guest beers H
An iconic Lakeland pub on the approach to Hardknott Pass, surrounded by stunning scenery, this popular, family-run, tourist local is renowned for good food and well-kept cask ales. The lounge/walkers' bars offer an attractive mix of traditional and modern styles with wood-burning stoves in both areas. Together with other nearby pubs in the Eskdale valley, the Woolpack participates in the annual Boot beer festival held in June. Families are welcome. **Q♨❀⇌◑◐⛺🍎P▯🚌🐾📶**

Bouth

White Hart Inn 𝕃

LA12 8JB (off A590, 6 miles NE of Ulverston)
⏲ 12-11 (10.30 Sun) ☎ (01229) 861229
🌐 whitehart-lakedistrict.co.uk
Black Sheep Best Bitter; Jennings Cumberland Ale; Tetley Bitter; guest beers H
A 17th-century inn with old farming and hunting implements adorning the walls, horse brasses and hops on beams, slate-flagged floors and a wood-burning stove adding to the atmosphere. A high standard of food is available, using locally-sourced ingredients, served in the bar, upstairs dining area or on the terrace. The guest ales are often from local breweries. A 20-minute walk is rewarded by magnificent views of the Rusland Valley and Coniston Old Man. **Q♨❀⇌◑◐P**

Bowland Bridge

Hare & Hounds Inn

LA11 6NN
⏲ 12-11; 12-10.30 Sun ☎ (015395) 68333
🌐 hareandhoundsbowlandbridge.co.uk
Thwaites Wainwright; guest beer H
A welcoming 17th-century coaching inn nestled within the tiny hamlet of Bowland Bridge in the beautiful Winster Valley. It lies between the shores of Windermere and Kendal. The bar is an eclectic mix of old and new, with log fires and black slate floors. Very much part of the local community, the pub is renowned for its consistently good beers and the quality of its bar meals. A summer beer festival is held in the grounds. **Q♨❀⇌◑◐P🐾📶**

Braithwaite

Middle Ruddings Country Inn 𝕃

CA12 5RY (W end of village, just off A66)
⏲ 10.30-11 ☎ (017687) 78436 🌐 middle-ruddings.co.uk
Beer range varies H
Country inn close to the A66 with great views of Skiddaw, family run and family friendly, with children and dogs welcome. It has three handpumps and only sells Cumbrian beers. The landlord visits the breweries before taking the beers, and hosts annual beer lovers' and cider lovers' dinners. The hostelry offers a range of real ciders and a selection of bottled world beers. There is a restaurant which also promotes local produce. CAMRA branch Pub of the Year in 2013.
Q♨❀⇌◑◐♿🍎P▯🚌(X5)🐾

Broughton-in-Furness

Manor Arms 𝕃

The Square, LA20 6HY
⏲ 12-11.30 (midnight Fri & Sat); 12-11 Sun
☎ (01229) 716286 🌐 manorarmsthesquare.co.uk
Cumberland Corby Blonde; Hawkshead Windermere Pale; Yates Bitter; guest beers H
An outstanding free house owned by the Varty family for more than 25 years; Scott has been in charge for over five years since David and Christine's retirement. It is the winner of numerous CAMRA awards, including Cumbria CAMRA Pub of the Year 2013. A comprehensive, frequently changing choice of up to eight real ales is served – with a range to suit all tastes. Up to six traditional ciders and perries are also available. Like a mini beer festival all year round. **Q♨⇌♣🍎▯🚌🐾📶**

Buttermere

Bridge Hotel

CA13 9UZ
⏲ 10.30-11 (10.30 Sun) ☎ (01768) 770252
🌐 bridge-hotel.com
Jennings Cumberland Ale H
The hotel sits at the head of Buttermere on the site of a former mill. It has a cosy bar area and a popular walkers' bar frequented by tourists (dogs are allowed in this bar only). A guest beer is sourced mainly from a Cumbrian brewery. There is no wheelchair access to the hotel. Set between Buttermere and Crummock Water in an Area of Outstanding Natural Beauty, the seating area outside enjoys stunning views of the Buttermere Fells. **♨❀⇌◑◐⛺P🚌🐾📶**

Calderbridge

Stanley Arms
CA20 1DN (on the A595)
12-11 ☎ (01946) 841235 stanleyarmshotel.com
Cumbrian Legendary Loweswater Gold; Thwaites Wainwright; guest beers Ⓗ
A small hotel, just inside the Lake District National Park, with probably the best beer garden in Cumbria, alongside the River Calder; the hotel has fishing rights. Four real ales, usually from Thwaites and Cumbrian breweries, are regularly on offer in the two-room bar. Booking is advised for meals in the separate dining room; food is locally sourced. Local attractions include the riverside walk to the ruins of 12th-century Calder Abbey.
Q ♣P (X6)

Cark-in-Cartmel

Engine Inn
LA11 7NZ
11.30-1am (midnight Sun) ☎ (015395) 58341
engineinn.co.uk
Unsworth's Yard Pride of Cartmel 1643; guest beers Ⓗ
Run by enthusiastic CAMRA members, this 17th-century inn, a short walk from the station, makes an excellent end to the walk from Grange described in CAMRA's Lake District Pub Walks book. Beers from the Punch range are supplemented by ales from local breweries. The pub features an open bar area with a cosy fire, separate rooms away from the bar, and a riverside beer garden. The building was extensively and tastefully refurbished in 2012, retaining the separate restaurant and games room.
♣P (532,530)

Carlisle

Crown & Thistle
53 Church Street, CA3 9DS
10-midnight ☎ (01228) 532965
Sharp's Doom Bar; guest beer Ⓗ
A real old-fashioned locals' pub, refurbished and with a separate bar and lounge. Outside is a smoking area with further seating which is well used on hot summer days. Strong support for the city football team ensures it gets busy after a home game. Darts, dominoes and whist and, on Thursday, a popular quiz night attract a varied mix of customers. Horse racing and other sports are shown on TVs, which are not left on longer than necessary. ♣P (76,62)

King's Head
Fisher Street, CA3 8RF
10 (12 Sun)-11 ☎ (01228) 533797
kingsheadcarlisle.co.uk
Yates Bitter; guest beers Ⓗ
An excellent city-centre pub, winner of many CAMRA awards. In addition to the Yates Bitter it offers a range of guest ales from four handpumps. Pictures of old Carlisle adorn the internal walls and outside is an explanation of why the city is not in the Domesday Book. Good-value meals are served at lunchtime. Children and dogs are not allowed. The spacious covered courtyard has a large-screen TV and regularly features live music. A frequent CAMRA City Pub of the Year, most recently in 2013.
♣

Spinners Arms
Cummersdale, CA2 6BD
6 (5 Fri; 12 Sat)-midnight; closed Sun ☎ (01228) 532928
thespinnersarms.org.uk
Carlisle Spun Gold, Magic Number, Flaxen Ⓗ
The pub is the home of the Carlisle Brewing Co, which started production in summer 2013. The cosy, family-friendly hostelry, an original Redfern pub with unique and classic features, is less than half a mile from Carlisle's south-western boundary, close to the Cumbrian Way and National Cycle Route 7, which run alongside the picturesque River Caldew. There is regular live music, with Irish music sessions every first and third Wednesday. Children are welcome until 9pm and well-behaved dogs are permitted. ♣P (75)

William Rufus
10-16 Botchergate, CA1 1QS
8am-1am (3am Fri & Sat); 8am-midnight Sun
☎ (01228) 613310
Cumberland Corby Ale, Corby Blonde; Ruddles Best Bitter; guest beers Ⓗ
Typical Wetherspoon Lloyds No.1 bar open from breakfast until late, named after the designer and builder of Carlisle Castle. It is popular with shoppers and families but can get noisy at nights and weekends, and is the venue for watching sporting events on its numerous TV screens. Food is served all day and there is a separate dining area. Children are welcome but with restrictions. It is two minutes from the railway station.

Woodrow Wilson
48 Botchergate, CA1 1QS
8am-midnight (12.30am Fri & Sat) ☎ (01228) 819942
Cumberland Corby Ale; Greene King Abbot; Jennings Sneck Lifter; Marston's Old Empire; Ruddles Best Bitter; Sharp's Doom Bar; guest beers Ⓗ
A Wetherspoon pub in a refurbished Co-op building named after the former US president, whose mother was born in Carlisle. Up to 12 handpumps offer the largest range of real ales to be found in Carlisle, usually including many LocAle beers. Food is available all day till 10pm. At the rear there is a spacious outdoor seating area, heated patio and smokers' area. Children are welcome in some areas until 8pm. Five minutes' walk from the railway station and city centre. P

Castle Carrock

Duke of Cumberland
CA8 9LU
12-11.30 (midnight Fri & Sat) ☎ (01228) 670341
thedukeofcumberlandinn.com
Geltsdale Cold Fell; guest beers Ⓗ
At the heart of this charming local village, the Duke reopened in 2009 and is now successfully re-established. A local following also sees it as the centre for the annual Marr Folk Festival in July. At the foot of the northern Pennines, it is ideally located for outdoor activity enthusiasts, who can enjoy real ale from the local Geltsdale Brewery and sample the home-made food which has a growing reputation. The layout separates the games/TV area from the dining area. Q P

Chapel Stile

Wainwrights' Inn
LA22 9JH

11.30-11; 12-11 Sun ☎ (015394) 38088
langdale.co.uk/dine/wainwrights
Jennings Cumberland Ale, Sneck Lifter; guest beers Ⓗ
Originally a farmhouse near the former gunpowder works, it then became a hotel. The building was converted in the late '80s to a pub which is now well known for its location in one of the most popular Lakeland valleys, as well as for its quality of service and variety of real ales. The stone-flagged bar area, where customers with dogs are welcome, has four guest beers which are usually from Cumbrian or small northern breweries.
P (516)

Cockermouth

Bush
Main Street, CA13 9JS
11-11 (midnight Fri & Sat) ☎ (01900) 822064
Jennings Bitter, Cocker Hoop, Sneck Lifter; guest beers Ⓗ
A popular pub with a friendly welcome on the main street in this historic gem of a town, serving a wide range from Cockermouth's Jennings Brewery. It has two bars with slate and wood floors and original features, warmed by a wood-burning stove. Wall plaques note the water levels reached inside the pub in the devastating floods of November 2009. Home-cooked meals are available at lunchtimes. The TVs in the back bar screen major sporting fixtures and local bands play every Thursday. The pub is child and dog friendly.
P

Castle Bar
14 Market Place, CA13 9NQ
11 (11.30 Sun)-11 ☎ (01900) 829904
Cumbrian Legendary Loweswater Gold; Jennings Bitter; guest beers Ⓗ
Busy pub in the town's market place. Refurbished and commended in CAMRA's Pub Design Awards 2009, the modern interior retains many historic features of this fine old building. Three floors house a bar, with five handpumps serving mainly Cumbrian ales, a restaurant on the first floor, and a relaxing second floor room with comfy leather sofas. The terraced courtyard beer garden is popular in summer. Large TV screens show sport. Private functions for family celebrations and events can be arranged.

Coniston

Black Bull Inn & Hotel
LA21 8DU
8.30am-11 ☎ (015394) 41335 blackbullconiston.co.uk
Coniston Oliver's Light Ale, Bluebird Bitter, Bluebird Premium XB, Special Oatmeal Stout, Old Man Ale, No.9 Barley Wine Ⓗ
A 16th-century coaching inn serving good food in traditional and comfortable surroundings and the tap house for the on-site Coniston Brewing Company. The six regular beers (available from 11am) are supplemented by other beers from the brewery on a rotation basis. The spacious bar and lounge are always well frequented by tourists in this hugely popular area. The outside seating area is perfect for the summer months, in a spectacular location near Coniston Old Man.
Q P (X12,505)

Sun
LA21 8HQ
11-11 (12-11 winter) ☎ (015394) 41248
thesunconiston.com
Barngates Tag Lag; Black Sheep Ale; Coniston Bluebird Premium XB; Copper Dragon Golden Pippin; Cumbrian Legendary Loweswater Gold; Hawkshead Bitter; guest beers Ⓗ
Take the Walna Scar road up from Coniston village, or down from Coniston Old Man, to visit this 16th-century pub and hotel. The recently refurbished dual-level bar area has atmosphere and character, with slate flooring and abundant exposed beams, all heated by a large open range. The slate-topped bar offers up to eight cask ales, mostly from local brewers. The conservatory and terrace complete the picture, with delightful views over the garden.
Q P

Curthwaite

Royal Oak
CA7 8BG
12-2, 5-11 (10.30 Sun) ☎ (01228) 710219
Beer range varies Ⓗ
The Royal Oak is a popular, welcoming traditional country inn less than a mile south of Thursby, fairly well catered for by public transport. The pub has a deserved reputation for excellent food with an emphasis on local produce. Three changing real ales are available and these are usually sourced from local breweries including Cumberland, Eden, Geltsdale, Hesket Newmarket and Jennings. Well-behaved dogs are welcome in the bar. A CAMRA award winner. P

Dacre

Horse & Farrier
CA11 0HL (1 mile S of the A66)
12-11 ☎ (017684) 86541
Jennings Cumberland Ale; guest beers Ⓗ
A lovely 300-year-old village pub just to the north of Ullswater. The cosy bar has an old black range, and there are separate dining and pool rooms. There is always a cheery welcome from the landlady, Susie, and her regulars. Good-value home-made food and proper puddings are served. One of the few remaining true locals pubs in the area, everyone is encouraged to come and join in the craic. Dogs and muddy boots are welcome.
Q

Dent

George & Dragon
Main Street, LA10 5QL
12-11 (midnight Fri & Sat); 12-10.30 Sun
☎ (015396) 25256 thegeorgeanddragondent.co.uk
Dent Golden Fleece, Aviator, Ramsbottom Strong Ale, Kamikaze, T'Owd Tup Ⓗ
The Dent Brewery tap showcases all its own beers plus real ciders, and was runner-up in the CAMRA National Cider and Perry Pub of the Year competition. The mahogany panelled walls are increasingly covered with awards for both the pub and brewery. Set on the cobbled main street in this attractive village, the pub has two bars that welcome all. It has a separate games room and downstairs dining room. There is a local bus on Wednesdays and Saturdays.
Q P (564a)

Dufton

Stag Inn
CA16 6DB
12-3, 5-11.30; 12-11.30 Sat; 12-11 Sun ☎ (017683) 51608
thestagdufton.co.uk
Beer range varies [H]
Fell-side pub in a picturesque village on the Pennine Way. It has two bar areas with open fires and four changing local ales, always including one from Eden Brewery. Good-value, imaginative food is served, and the separate dining room affords views to the Pike. There is a popular beer festival each August. Walkers and tourists join the locals to enjoy the lively atmosphere in this dog-friendly pub. Q⚘❀◐◑ÅP🐾

Ennerdale Bridge

Fox & Hounds Inn
CA23 3AR
11-11 (11.30 Sat, 9.30 Mon & Tue winter); 11-11.30 Sun ☎ (01946) 861373 foxandhoundsinn.org
Ennerdale Blonde, Darkest, Wild Ennerdale; Jennings Bitter; guest beer [H]
A first or last Coast-to-Coast walk destination makes this Lake District inn a perfect stopover, a historic community-run pub with good food and locally-sourced ingredients. In a picturesque setting with a large beer garden, there are exposed beams, an L-shaped bar, and a cosy inglenook fireplace at the entrance with a larger dining/drinking area to the rear. Weekly meetings of a craft group, book club and library are held in the pub. May close early Friday and Saturday in winter. Q⚘❀🛏◐◑♿Å●P🍺🐾📶

Eskdale Green

George IV Inn
CA19 1TS (400yds E of outward bound centre)
11-midnight (1am Fri & Sat) ☎ (019467) 23470
kinggeorge-eskdale.co.uk
Beer range varies [H]
In a prominent roadside position at the head of the main Eskdale valley amid beautiful scenery, this popular tourist pub with oak beams and flagged floors is renowned for its pub food and wide range of well-kept cask ales. The inn runs its own beer festival in the peak tourist period (date varies). Q⚘❀🛏◐◑♿Å⇌P🚌🐾📶

Foxfield

Prince of Wales 🏆
LA20 6BX
closed Mon & Tue; 2.45 (12 Fri & Sat)-11; 12-10.30 Sun ☎ (01229) 716238 princeofwalesfoxfield.co.uk
Foxfield Dark Mild; guest beers [H]
Honoured among CAMRA's Top 40 campaigners, Stuart and Lynda are testament to what is achievable through passion and hard work at this splendid pub. The guest ales come from the pub's two house breweries – Foxfield and Tigertops – plus others nationwide. The range will always include a mild. Beer and cider festivals throughout the year are an added bonus. A discount on B&B is offered to CAMRA members. Bus and rail stops are outside. Q⚘❀🛏♿⇌♣●P🍺🚌(7)🐾📶

Gilcrux

Barn Bistro
CA7 2QX (5 miles N of Cockermouth off A595)
closed Mon; 12-11 ☎ (016973) 23289 barnbistro.co.uk
Jennings Bitter; guest beer [H]
Four miles from Aspatria, the village of Gilcrux hosts a pub and this restaurant-bar, with a growing reputation for excellent ales and locally-sourced food. Renamed and reopened in 2010, it is still known to some as the Beeches (being next to the Beeches caravan park). The mainstay Jennings Bitter is the landlord's favourite and two other handpumps showcase Cumbria's many other breweries, with over 100 different brews having been served in the Barn's first three years.
Q⚘❀◐◑P🐾

Glasson

Highland Laddie
Water Street, CA7 5DT
12-midnight ☎ (016973) 25007
highlandladdieinnglasson.co.uk
Greene King IPA; Morland Old Speckled Hen; Timothy Taylor Landlord [H]
Popular village local close to the Solway Firth and a bird reserve, and the only pub in the area open all day for people walking the Hadrian's Wall route. Meetings are held in the pub for the fishermen who follow the ancient occupation of haaf net fishing, unique to the Solway. The licensee has gained a reputation for providing excellent food, locally sourced, including delicacies such as sea salmon, sea bass and sea trout. Usually, three ales are available. Q⚘❀🛏◐◑♣🐾

Gosforth

Gosforth Hall Inn
Wasdale Road, CA20 1AZ (from A595 follow road signed to Wasdale)
3 (12 Sat & Sun)-midnight ☎ (019467) 25322
gosforthhallhotel.co.uk
Yates Golden Ale; guest beers [H]
An inn with many attractions in addition to its four popular cask ales, usually Cumbrian, and its beer festival in May. This former 17th-century farmhouse is Grade II-listed, boasts a priest hole and the widest single sandstone hearth in England. There is a boules pitch in the large landscaped garden. Adjacent to St Mary's Church.
Q⚘❀🛏◐◑♿Å♣P🐾📶

Grasmere

Tweedies Bar (Dale Lodge Hotel)
Langdale Road, LA22 9SW
12-11 (midnight Thu-Sat) ☎ (015394) 35300
tweediesbargrasmere.co.uk
Beer range varies [H]
Popular with locals and tourists alike, this large bar is part of Dale Lodge Hotel, situated in the middle of Grasmere. Up to 10 changing beers are served, always including three or four ales from local breweries. The main bar with a stone-flagged floor and welcoming wood-burning stove has a side room leading off. A quiz night is held on Thursday and there is live music at weekends; an annual beer festival is hosted in September.
⚘❀🛏◐◑●P🚌(555,599)🐾📶

Great Broughton

Punch Bowl Inn

19 Main Street, CA13 0YJ

closed Mon-Wed; 8-11 Thu; 6-11 Fri & Sat; 1-3, 8-11 Sun

Beer range varies H

This small, welcoming, 18th-century inn is now a community venue. Very much a drinkers' pub, it is run by a committee that includes a number of CAMRA members. It has two handpumps serving beer from a choice of three Cumbrian breweries. The bar is adorned with sporting memorabilia and a selection of water jugs. You can play darts and dominoes here. **QP**(35,77)

Great Corby

Corby Bridge Inn

CA4 8LL

3-11 (01228) 560221 corbybridgeinn.org.uk

Thwaites Wainwright, Lancaster Bomber H

Sitting on the level crossing of the Tyne Valley Line, this open-plan village pub is just a short walk from Wetheral station, across the stunning rail and footpath viaduct that spans the River Eden. Good home-cooked food is served Thursday-Saturday evenings and on Sunday lunchtime, pool and darts are available and a large outdoor drinking area affords fine views of the beautiful surrounding countryside. (Wetheral)**P**

Great Langdale

Old Dungeon Ghyll Hotel

LA22 9JY

11-11; 11-10.30 Sun (015394) 37272 odg.co.uk

Black Sheep Ale; Cumbrian Legendary Esthwaite Bitter; Jennings Cumberland Ale; Theakston Old Peculier; Yates Bitter; guest beers H

A traditional walkers' and climbers' bar set in the magnificent Langdale valley, it is part of the hotel and there is a separate residents' bar. An old range in the main bar always has a welcoming real fire, much needed after a long day on the fells in winter. There is always a good selection of local ales, with several guest beers in the summer months. The two charity folk festivals are popular. **QP**(516)

Great Salkeld

Highland Drove L

CA11 9NA

12-2.30 (not Mon), 6-midnight; 12-midnight Sat (01768) 898349 highland-drove.co.uk

Eden Gold; Theakston Black Bull Bitter; guest beer H

Just off the main road through this attractive village, everything here is of a high standard. Entering into the exceptionally well-stocked bar you will find a lounge and a games room either side, with the award-winning Kyloes restaurant upstairs, all with well-chosen decor featuring exposed timber and brickwork, embellished with Highland-style soft furnishings, brass and copper ornaments. The excellent food is available daily and themed nights have recently been introduced. Watch out for the Highland cows.
QP

Greenodd

Ship L

Main Street, LA12 7QZ

closed Mon; 5-11; 12-midnight Sat; 12-10.30 Sun (07782) 655294

Greenodd Blonde, Citra, Best Bitter; guest beers H

A traditional locals' village inn and the tap house for Greenodd Brewery, where visitors are made most welcome. Beers are predominantly from the Greenodd range but guest ales are also served. The characterful open-plan interior includes slate floors, wooden beams, rustic stone walls and real fires. There is a separate quiet room through the back, and check out the quirky grotto, with seats and a table, in the car park area. An expanding menu includes an intriguing range of pizzas.
P(X12)

Hawkshead

King's Arms Hotel L

The Square, LA22 0NZ

11-midnight (015394) 36372 kingsarmshawkhead.co.uk

Cumbrian Legendary Loweswater Gold; Hawkshead Bitter; guest beers H

Popular 500-year-old inn with an open fire and traditional beamed ceilings, one of which is held up by a life-size monarch, hand carved by local artist Jimmy (The Whistle) Whitworth. There is a separate dining room and bar area, and the seating area outside fronts onto the village square. Occasional live music plays. Ales are predominantly sourced locally. (505)

Hensingham

Globe Inn L

95 Main Street, CA28 8QX

closed Mon; 5-11; 12-11 Sat & Sun (01946) 590772 theglobehensingham.co.uk

Beer range varies H

A cosy and welcoming, beautifully refurbished, community pub with a homely family atmosphere. The smallish bar constantly serves two changing ales, mostly Cumbrian, with an enticing list of 'what's-in-the-cellar'. Reasonably priced, home-cooked food with hand cut chips is tasty and hugely popular; gluten-free choices are available. Sunday lunches are best booked though. Eat in the bar or the upstairs dining room. Watch out for owls. The motto here is: strangers leave as friends.
(32,30)

Hesket Newmarket

Old Crown Inn L

CA7 8JG

5.30-11; 12-12.30am Fri; 12-midnight Sat; 12-2.30, 5.30-10.30 Sun (016974) 78288 theoldcrownpub.co.uk

Hesket Newmarket Helvellyn Gold, High Pike, Haystacks, Doris's 90th Birthday Ale, Blencathra Bitter, Black Sail H

Sitting in the heart of this lovely fell-side village, the Old Crown is a showcase for the Hesket Newmarket Brewery, which is immediately behind the pub. It is well known as the first co-operatively owned pub in the country and is popular with locals and visitors alike, with Prince Charles and Sir Chris Bonington among its supporters.
Q

Hethersgill

Black Lion Inn

CA6 6EH
3.30-11; 12.30-1am Fri & Sat; 12.30-11 Sun
(01228) 675318
Beer range varies
Warm and welcoming village inn at the centre of the community. Although the pub is open plan it has the feel of three separate rooms. This is a place with lots going on, including live music, bingo and quiz nights, a large assortment of pub games and an annual beer festival over the August bank holiday. Excellent bar meals are available during opening hours. The real ale range varies and includes local breweries such as Cumberland, Derwent and Geltsdale. ♣P

Holmes Green

Black Dog Inn

Broughton Road, LA15 8JP (from Dalton 1 mile past South Lakes Wildlife Park) SD233761
closed Mon; 5-midnight; 1-midnight Fri & Sat; 12-9 Sun
(01229) 227982
Beer range varies
With six real ales on offer, and hospitable new owners, the Black Dog makes a welcome return to the Guide. Local breweries are represented, including Abraham Thompson (can you spot him in the pub?). Regulars and visitors share good conversation in the quarry-tiled snug located in front of the bar. Good quality food is available Thursday, Saturday and Sunday. Two real fires, outdoor picnic benches and regular live music including open mic nights, add to the attraction.
Q♣P

Ings

Watermill Inn

LA8 9PY
11-11 (10.30 Sun) (01539) 821309
watermillinn.co.uk
Coniston Bluebird; Theakston Old Peculier; Watermill Collie Wobbles, A Bit'er Ruff, Isle of Dogs, Wruff Night; guest beers
An award-winning family-owned pub and brewery with a relaxed and friendly atmosphere, offering up to 16 real ales including those brewed on site. An extensive range of foreign bottled beers is also kept. The two separate bars are served from a central counter, and viewing windows look into both the cellar and brewery. A wide selection of meals is available daily until 9pm, while dogs are provided with biscuits and water.
Q♣P(555)

Kendal

Rifleman's Arms

4 Greenside, LA9 4LD
6.30 (4.30 Fri)-midnight; 12-midnight Sat & Sun
(01539) 723224
Greene King Abbot; guest beers
A true community pub on the edge of town, with the Vaux motif still etched on the windows. Numerous local groups meet here, with popular live folk music sessions on Thursdays. It is dog-friendly and has a quiet atmosphere, with a Sunday quiz and traditional pub games. There are always five real ales available including local beers. The pub looks out onto a pleasant green and is often involved with events taking place there.
Q♣(44,48)

Romney's

72 Milnthorpe Road, LA9 5HG
11-11; 12-10.30 Sun (01539) 720956
romneyskendal.co.uk
Bowness Bay Swan Blonde; guest beers
A welcome entry to the Kendal ale and pub scene, the pub is situated on the main road into Kendal from the south, a place with something for everyone. It has a relaxed and welcoming modern bar area, as well as a large restaurant with a comprehensive menu and a four-meat carvery. Events include regular steak and quiz nights, and there is an outdoor play area for children.
P

Keswick

Dog & Gun

2 Lake Road, CA12 5BT
12 11.30 (017687) 73463
Keswick Thirst Session, Thirst Run; Theakston Old Peculier; Yates Bitter; guest beers
You will get the best selection of real ale in Keswick here. Full of character, with flagged floors and low beamed ceilings, this venue is famed for its Hungarian goulash and Old Peculier stews. Dogs are welcome and there is a special menu and doggy bags for them. The beer badged as Landlord's Choice is Keswick Thirst Gold, 3.6% ABV.

Kirkby Lonsdale

Orange Tree

9 Fairbank, LA6 2BD
11-11 (midnight Fri & Sat) (015242) 71716
theorangetreehotel.co.uk
Kirkby Lonsdale Tiffin Gold, Ruskins Bitter, Monumental Blonde; guest beers
The Kirkby Lonsdale Brewery tap is just up the road from the church in this lovely market town. Friendly, enthusiastic staff ensure a warm welcome here. The front bar has old photographs and rugby prints, and there is a separate dining area to the rear, where good wholesome meals are served, with most ingredients from local suppliers. There are always three Kirkby Lonsdale beers on, and up to three guest ales. ♣(567)

Kirkoswald

Fetherston Arms

The Square, CA10 1DQ
4-midnight; 12-midnight Sat & Sun (01768) 898284
fetherston-arms.com
Beer range varies
The Fethers is situated in the centre of this historic village. Extensive alterations and the friendly enthusiasm of the family owners have helped convert it into a truly outstanding pub, with a deservedly excellent reputation for superb food. Its commitment to real ale is borne out by the annual beer festival (usually the first weekend in July). Four changing real ales are available from breweries such as Cross Bay and Hesket Newmarket. Check ahead for winter opening hours. Q

Langwathby

Shepherds Inn L

The Village Green, CA10 1LW
11.30-11 (1am Fri; midnight Sat) ☎ (01768) 881463
shepherds-inn.co.uk
Beer range varies H
A welcoming country pub at the heart of the community, this 18th-century inn was totally refurbished in 2012. The bar is made of local stone to resemble a sheep fold, the lounge is bright and comfortable and there is a games area in the snug. Real cider is available and the three real ales come from local microbreweries such as Eden and Tirril. The Shepherds has a well-deserved reputation for excellent food. Booking is advised, but not essential. ❀♿♣P (130-140,R12)

Lindal-in-Furness

Railway Inn L

6 London Road, LA12 0LL
closed Mon & Tue; 12-2, 5 (4 Fri & Sat)-11; 12-7.30 Sun
☎ (01229) 462889
Beer range varies H
A friendly open-plan, single-room pub with a beamed ceiling and slate floor. At one end is a comfortable lounge area with a woodburner. Adding to the character is a centrally positioned bar made from old church pews, with up to five handpumps active, and a local beer always available. Food is served including Sunday lunches (booking advisable). Visitors are also welcome at the quiz night on Thursday. ❀ (6,6A)

Loppergarth

Wellington Inn L

Main Street, LA12 0JL (1 mile from A590 between Lindal and Pennington)
6-11 (1am Fri & Sat); closed Sun ☎ (01229) 582388
Beer range varies H
Superb village local with its own working microbrewery – a custom-made stainless steel plant which is viewable from the games room. Four handpumps primarily dispense beers brewed on the premises. These include a blonde, a golden bitter and a traditional darker best bitter. Wood-burning stoves make this a cosy pub, with games, books and good conversation. There is a quiz on alternate Saturdays. Dogs on leads are welcome.
❀♣

Loweswater

Kirkstile Inn L

CA13 0RU (off B5289, S from Cockermouth, through Lorton) NY140210
11-11; 11-10.30 Sun ☎ (01900) 85219 kirkstile.com
Cumbrian Legendary Esthwaite Bitter, Langdale, Grasmoor Dark Ale, Loweswater Gold, American Invasion; guest beer H
Providing food and shelter since Tudor times, a short stroll from lakes Loweswater and Crummock, this pub has six handpumps, two seating areas and a reputation for good food (it can get busy at meal times). It is the brewery tap for Cumbrian Legendary Ales. Winner of local CAMRA branch Pub of the Year five times in recent years and runner-up in 2013. Q❀♿P

Near Sawrey

Tower Bank Arms L

LA22 0LF (on B5285 2 miles S of Hawkshead)
11-11; 12-10.30 Sun ☎ (015394) 36334
towerbankarms.co.uk
Barngates Cat Nap; Hawkshead Bitter, Brodie's Prime; guest beers H
All the features of a 17th-century Lakeland inn are found here: slate floor, oak beams and an open fire set in a range. It is next to Hill Top (Beatrix Potter's former home). Food of a high standard is served in the bar and the restaurant, and children and dogs are welcome. Beers are sourced (very) locally, and cider and perry are also served. There is a bus service in summer – the Cross Lakes Experience. Afternoon opening may be variable in winter, phone to check. Q❀♣P

Nether Wasdale

Strands Inn L

CA20 1ET
11 (12 Sat)-11; 12-10.30 Sun ☎ (019467) 26237
thestrandsinn.com
Strands Pied Piper, Brown Bitter, Errmmm..., T'errmmm-inator H
This inn, originally a 17th-century post house, sits at the entrance to Wasdale, famed for its view of England's deepest lake and highest mountains. Five beers are regularly offered, chosen from over 20 produced by the inn's microbrewery, which also brews its own cider. A range of these beers is available in bottle. The annual beer festival in May usually attracts a troupe of morris dancers. There is an open mic night on the first Wednesday of every month. Q❀♣P

Newbiggin

Blue Bell Inn L

Heads Nook, CA8 9DH (8 miles S of Brampton just off B6413)
6 (7 Mon)-midnight; 6-1am Fri; 12-3, 6-1am Sat; 12-3, 6-midnight Sun ☎ (01768) 896615
bluebellinnnewbiggin.co.uk
Geltsdale Cold Fell; guest beer H
Nestled in the North Pennines Area of Outstanding Natural Beauty, this small country pub is used mainly by locals. It is also popular with holidaymakers and walkers needing refreshment, with food served every evening and lunchtimes at weekends. Traditional pub games and pool can be enjoyed. Its regular ale, Cold Fell, is brewed locally in Brampton and named after a nearby hill. Look out for the naughty gnomes. ❀♣P

Oxenholme

Station Inn

LA9 7RF
12-midnight (11 Sun) ☎ (01539) 724094
stationinnoxenholme.co.uk
Hawkshead Bitter; Moorhouse's Pride of Pendle, Blond Witch; guest beer H
Originally a farmhouse on the edge of Kendal, in a beautiful rural setting, the pub is near the main line railway station. Outside there is a large garden complete with crazy golf and a large children's play area. The recently refurbished main bar serves an extensive menu along with daily specials which use many locally-sourced ingredients. The inn is

close to one of the Coast-to-Coast cycle routes. There is hard standing for caravans on site.
Q

Penrith

Agricultural Hotel

Castlegate, CA11 7JE
11-11 (midnight Fri & Sat); 12-10.30 Sun
(01768) 862622 the-agricultural-hotel.co.uk
Jennings Bitter, Sneck Lifter, Cumberland Ale; guest beers H
The hotel is built from local sandstone and the bar and dining room are open plan, with steps from one to the other. There is also a small reception area. It has a Victorian shuttered bar of sash screens, with six handpumps selling Jennings and guest beers. Food is served in the large dining area, as well as in the bar at quiet times. Convenient for the railway station and nearby bus stops. Local CAMRA Pub of the Year 2013. P

Moo Bar

52 King Street, CA11 7AY
12-12.30am (01768) 606637
Beer range varies H
A small and intimate venue in the centre of Penrith on three floors which was only converted into a pub two years ago. Since then it has rapidly built up a reputation for serving a changing range of guest beers. There is always a variety of local ales as well as brews from further afield. Real cider is often available as well as small brewery keg beers. There is also a large choice of bottled beers from around the world.

Rosthwaite

Scafell Hotel

Borrowdale, CA12 5XB (on B5289)
12-11.30 (10.30 Sun) (017687) 77208 scafell.co.uk
Copper Dragon Best Bitter; Jennings Bitter, Cumberland Ale, Sneck Lifter; guest beers H
Primarily a walkers' bar, with slate flags and a coal fire. Six handpumps offer a variety of well-kept ales which enhances an impressive selection of bar food. In good weather relax in the riverside garden and take in the superb mountain views. In bad weather enjoy the warmth of the bar and the river view. The pub sponsors a fell race on the first Saturday in August – see the race board for the times of the runners. P(78)

Rydal

Badger Bar (Glen Rothay Hotel)

LA22 9LR
10-11; 10.30-11 Sun (01539) 434500
theglenrothay.co.uk
Barngates Goodhew's Dry Stout; guest beers H
A popular bar, part of the Glen Rothay Hotel situated on the main road between Ambleside and Grasmere. Being almost directly opposite Rydal Water and Loughrigg Terrace means this pub is a haven for walkers and visitors alike. The four varying guest ales are mainly Cumbrian beers; the Goodhew's stout has become the only stout on the bar. The bar offers good-value meals, especially the lunches. Q P(555,599)

Sedbergh

Red Lion Inn

Finkle Street, LA10 5BZ
closed Mon; 11.30-3, 6-midnight; 11.30-12.30am Sat; 11.30-11.30 Sun (015396) 20433
theredlionsedbergh.co.uk
Jennings Cumberland Ale; guest beers H
Town-centre pub popular with the locals, opposite the parish church of St Andrew's, serving a wide range of beers from the Marston's group of breweries. The open-plan bar area has several quiet areas and a large open fire. Fresh local produce is used in many of the items on the good-value menu. (564)

Silecroft

Miners Arms

Main Street, LA18 5LR
6 (12 Sat & Sun)-midnight (01229) 772325
minersarmssilecroft.com
Beer range varies H
The Miners Arms is a traditional country pub situated 50 yards from Silecroft train station and less than a mile from one of west Cumbria's loveliest beaches. There are three handpumps on the bar offering locally-produced ales. The business underwent a complete refurbishment in 2013, which added four en-suite guest bedrooms to accompany the new surroundings. The owners have introduced a new menu which features many excellent examples of local Cumbrian produce.
P

Staveley

Beer Hall

Mill Yard, LA8 9LR
12-6 (5 Mon); 12-11 Fri & Sat; 12-8 Sun (01539) 822644
Hawkshead Windermere Pale, Bitter, Red, Lakeland Gold, Brodie's Prime, Cumbrian Five Hop H
The Hawkshead tap next door to the brewery, on two storeys; on both floors there is a mix of comfy sofas and solid wooden furniture. The food menu now includes a good selection of tapas to complement the brewery's beers. Spring and summer beer festivals are held, with up to 60 beers to sample. The beer shop has a range of bottled Hawkshead and foreign beers. CAMRA members and train users get a 10 per cent discount. Q P(555)

Eagle & Child Inn

Kendal Road, LA8 9LP
11-11; 12-10.30 Sun (01539) 821320
eaglechildinn.co.uk
Beer range varies H
In winter there are log fires to keep you warm and in summer riverside tables and a garden to enjoy. The five changing beers are mainly from Cumbria or north Lancashire, often including Yates. The pub has an interesting arrangement of artefacts around the walls. There are great meal deals including a two-course Sunday lunch. An entertaining Thursday night quiz is popular with locals and visitors alike.
Q P(555)

Talkin

Blacksmiths Arms

CA8 1LE

12-3, 6-11 ☎ (016977) 3452 blacksmithstalkin.co.uk
Geltsdale Tarn; Yates Bitter; guest beers Ⓗ
Since taking over in 1997, the present owners have made this probably the most popular pub in the vicinity. The winning formula includes four real ales, a superbly stocked bar, friendly efficient staff, no TV and meticulous attention to detail. With a golf course and country park within two miles and plenty of other outdoor activities available locally, and set on the edge of an Area of Outstanding Natural Beauty, it attracts visitors from far outside the north Cumbria area. **Q** **P**

Tallentire

Bush Inn
CA13 0PT
closed Mon; 6-midnight; 12-2, 7-11 Sun
☎ (01900) 823707
Beer range varies Ⓗ
A good old-fashioned pub that always serves at least one ale from a Cumbrian brewery. The hub of the community, it is home to the local cricket team and hosts a traditional music session on the last Wednesday of the month. With its exposed beams and stone floor, the pub also has a sensitive exterior in keeping with the character of the village. Dogs are welcome as long as they are well behaved. **P** (58)

Thursby

Ship Inn
Church Lane, CA5 6PE
12-2 (not Mon), 5.30-11; 12-2, 5.30-12.30am Fri; 12-12.30am Sat; 12-11 Sun ☎ (01228) 710600
shipinnthursby.co.uk
Beer range varies Ⓗ
The Ship Inn dates from the 18th century and is famously the birthplace of Sir Thomas Bouch, a great Victorian engineer. Situated on the edge of the green in a quiet village off the bypass, a warm welcome is assured by staff and locals, giving a friendly atmosphere to this pub. Food is served every day except Monday. Up to three different real ales are on sale. **P**

Torver

Wilson Arms Ⓛ
LA21 8BB
8.30am-11 ☎ (015394) 41237 thewilsonsarms.co.uk
Coniston Bluebird Premium XB; Cumbrian Legendary Loweswater Gold; guest beers Ⓗ
Extensively refurbished pub with large gardens and an emphasis on good-quality food (including breakfast from 8.30am). The pub incorporates the Wilson's Deli, a shop catering for villagers and tourists alike. It is easily reachable by walkers from Coniston following the shore of the lake. Beers are all sourced from local breweries. A quiz night is held every Sunday. The seven rooms at the hotel are supplemented by luxury holiday cottages. **P** (X12)

Ulverston

Devonshire Arms Ⓛ
Braddyll Terrace, Victoria Road, LA12 0DH (next to railway bridge in town centre)
4 (3 Fri)-11; 12-midnight Sat; 12-11 Sun
☎ (01229) 582537
Lancaster Amber; guest beers Ⓗ
Conveniently situated between the bus and train stations, the Dev is a large single-room pub which is divided into distinct areas with comfortable seating. Two TVs show major sporting events, and pool, darts and dominoes are played here. This is a real locals' pub, with a welcoming atmosphere. Six handpumps serve superb ales from near and far. The bar and the cellar are powered by solar panels. **P**

Mill Ⓛ
Mill Street, LA12 7EB
11-11 (1am Fri & Sat); 11-10.30 Sun ☎ (01229) 581384
mill-at-ulverston.co.uk
Lancaster Amber, Blonde, Black, Red; guest beers Ⓗ
A converted flour mill in a town-centre location with many interesting features including a restored waterwheel. The main bar has 10 handpulls dispensing six guest beers alongside the Lancaster Brewery range. There are two wood-burning stoves plus a first-floor outdoor patio area with seating, and picnic tables to the front. Quality food is popular, served in the bar and upstairs restaurant (booking recommended). Live music features every Wednesday and Friday. Occasional beer festivals are held.

Stan Laurel Inn Ⓛ
31 The Ellers, LA12 0AB
7-11 Mon; 12-2.30, 6-11 (midnight Fri & Sat); 12-11.30 Sun
☎ (01229) 582814 thestanlaurel.co.uk
Thwaites Original; Ulverston Flying Elephants; guest beers Ⓗ
Just off the centre of Stan Laurel's home town, the Stan offers a warm welcome to locals and visitors alike. Six handpulls serve a variety of beers, mainly locally brewed. Excellent-value quality food is available Tuesday to Sunday. Adjacent to the bar is a large room with pool and darts, and a smaller room primarily used by diners. In winter a log-burning stove adds to the pub's comfortable ambience. Well-behaved dogs are welcome. **P** (6,6A)

Swan Inn Ⓛ
Swan Street, LA12 7JX
3.30-11; 12-midnight Thu-Sat; 12-11 Sun
☎ (01229) 582519
Beer range varies Ⓗ
Located on the edge of the town centre overlooking the A590, the pub has a single bar serving three drinking areas, one with a real fire. Ten handpulls offer a wide range of beers sourced from near and far, representing a full range of styles and strengths. Live music is a regular weekend feature. Additional entertainment includes a jukebox, BT sport and a Thursday night quiz. The beer garden behind the pub is particularly popular in summer. Occasional beer festivals are planned. (6,X6)

Waberthwaite

Brown Cow Inn Ⓛ
LA19 5YJ (on A595)
11.30-1am; 12-midnight Sun ☎ (01229) 717243
thebrowncowinn.com
Ennerdale Blonde; Hawkshead Bitter; guest beers Ⓗ
This 100-year-old pub, a centre of activity in the village, regularly rings the changes on its seven real ales, to the delight of the local ale tasting society. Beers are usually from Cumbrian and north

Lancashire breweries, and two changing ciders are also on offer. Good food uses locally-sourced ingredients. Live music features once a month at weekends, regular quiz nights take place, and there are annual beer festivals in June and October. There is easy access from here to the western fells, coastline and Eskmeals nature reserve.
Q🛏❀⇌◑⅄♣●P🚌(X6)🐾📶

Wasdale Head

Wasdale Head Inn 𝕃

CA20 1EX (at head of Wasdale, 9 miles from A595)
⏲ 11 (12 Sun)-11 ☎ (019467) 26229 🌐 wasdale.com
Beer range varies Ⓗ
After a winter's day on the fells, tuck into a hearty bar meal in Ritson's Bar, with seven mostly Cumbrian real ales, a cosy log-burning stove, and Abraham Brothers photos commemorating this birthplace of British rock-climbing. In summer, enjoy attractive views of the fells from the garden tables alongside Mosedale Beck. In the nearby churchyard of England's smallest church, St Olaf's, are gravestones of early climbers; present day adventurers benefit from the hamlet's camping ground and well-stocked shop for walkers, climbers and campers. Q🛏❀⇌◑♿⅄♣●P🍺🐾📶

Watermillock

Brackenrigg Inn

CA11 0LP (on A592)
⏲ 12-11; 12-10.30 Sun ☎ (017684) 86206
🌐 brackenrigginn.co.uk
Black Sheep Best Bitter; guest beers Ⓗ
A large roadside inn with outstanding views of Ullswater and the north-eastern Lake District fells, attracting both locals and tourists with a friendly atmosphere and real fires; there are distinct areas for drinking and eating. The landlord keeps three guest ales in winter and up to seven in the summer, mainly from local breweries. There is a great range of locally-sourced food and cheeses.
Q🛏❀⇌◑♿⅄●P🚌(108)🐾

Wetheral

Wheatsheaf Inn 𝕃

CA4 8HD
⏲ 12-11 (midnight Fri & Sat) ☎ (01228) 560686
Beer range varies Ⓗ
Early 19th-century village inn, just a few minutes' walk from the village green and railway station. Deservedly popular with locals and visitors, three cask ales are usually available, with a house beer, Wheatsheaf Ale, brewed locally. Good-value bar meals are served Wednesday to Sunday. Regular Tuesday quiz nights are well supported. The pub is a former CAMRA award winner.
🛏❀◑⇌♣P🚌(75)🐾📶

Whitehaven

Bransty Arch 𝕃

9 Bransty Row, CA28 7XE
⏲ 8am-11 ☎ (01946) 517640
Greene King Abbot; Hawkshead Windermere Pale; Yates Golden Ale; guest beers Ⓗ
Wetherspoon pub in the historic port of Whitehaven convenient for the harbour, marina, shops, and bus and railway station. The modern sea-themed interior offers plenty of seating, and windows are open during summer to create an alfresco feeling. The pub often stocks real ales from local breweries, with regular rotating guest ales. Three annual festivals showcase beers from around the world. It is handy for a bite to eat, but can get busy at weekends. 🛏◑♿⇌●🍺🚌📶

Windermere

Elleray Hotel

Cross Street, LA23 1AE
⏲ 12-11 (midnight Fri & Sat) ☎ (015394) 43120
🌐 elleraywindermere.co.uk
Copper Dragon Golden Pippin; Cumbrian Legendary Loweswater Gold; Jennings Cumberland Ale, Sneck Lifter; Wychwood Hobgoblin Ⓗ
A friendly locals' pub with a good visitor following, consisting of a large bar and separate dining room. There is a wide choice of both local and national beers, the menu is varied, with good value-meals, especially at lunchtimes, and there is a carvery on Sundays. An annual beer festival is held each autumn. There is a welcoming log fire in winter and the rear patio is a suntrap in the better weather. 🛏❀⇌◑♿⇌🚌(555,599)🐾📶

Workington

Henry Bessemer 𝕃

New Oxford Street, CA14 2NA
⏲ 8am-11 (midnight Thu-Sat) ☎ (01900) 734650
Greene King Abbot; Ruddles Best Bitter; Yates Golden Ale; guest beers Ⓗ
A spacious, high-ceilinged pub with a few cosy corners, occupying an old cinema building and named after a steel-making pioneer whose Bessemer Converter functioned in the local steelworks until 1981. With dependable standards for ale and food, it offers a wide-ranging menu at competitive prices, and there are themed food nights for curry, steak and fish. Q🛏◑♿🚌📶

Yanwath

Gate Inn

CA10 2LF
⏲ 12-11 (10.30 Sun) ☎ (01768) 862386
🌐 yanwathgate.com
Beer range varies Ⓗ
Cosy inn in a village three miles south of Penrith with an intimate bar, open fire and candles on the tables. This Cumbrian dining pub affords a warm welcome to everyone and their dogs. Drinkers can sample three different local ales and some uncommon foreign beers on draught. The superb wine list includes 12 served by the glass. There is a lovely garden and a well-appointed self-catering cottage. Q🛏❀◑♣●P🚌(108)🐾

A glass of bitter beer or pale ale, taken with the principal meal of the day, does more good and less harm than any medicine the physician can prescribe. **Dr Carpenter, 1750**

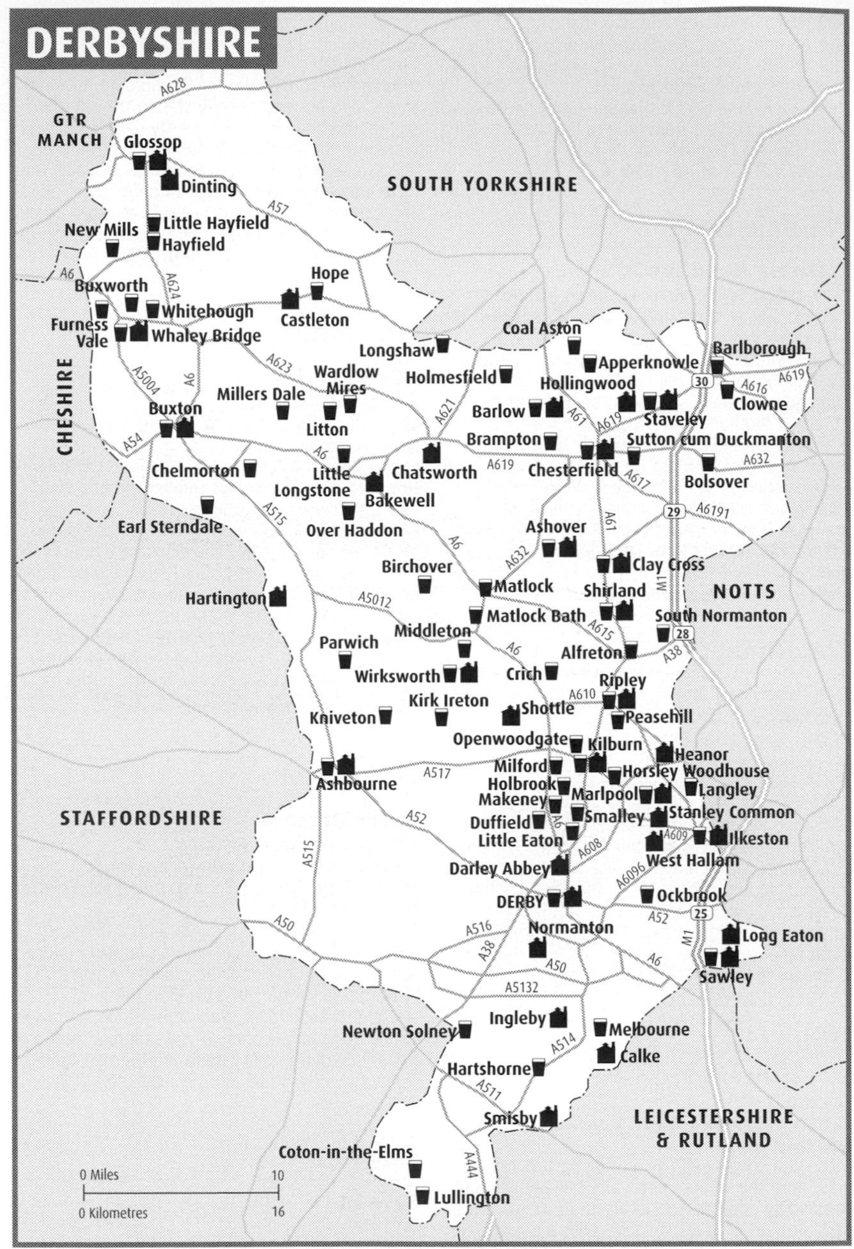

Alfreton

Waggon & Horses 𝕃

9 King Street, DE55 7AF

✪ 8am-midnight (1am Fri & Sat) ☎ (01773) 545890

Greene King Abbot; Ruddles Best Bitter; Wychwood Hobgoblin; guest beers Ⓗ

Centrally located, opposite the war memorial, this Wetherspoon house is deceptively large with an elongated bar and an open-plan layout with some cosy corners. The Waggon is LocAle accredited, often featuring beers from several Derbyshire breweries. Meet the brewer nights are also a feature here. Q

Apperknowle

Travellers Rest 🏆

High Street, S18 4BD SK384782

✪ 12-11 ☎ (01246) 460169

Abbeydale Moonshine; John Smith's Bitter; Timothy Taylor Landlord Ⓗ**; guest beers** Ⓗ/Ⓖ

This top-quality pub is the best place for music for miles around. The beer is always in A1 condition and CAMRA members get a 20p per pint discount on production of a current membership card. The Travellers is the current local Cider Pub of the Year, as well as the local 2014 Pub of the Year.
QP

Ashbourne

Smith's Tavern 🏆

36 St John Street, DE6 1GH
12-11 (midnight Fri & Sat) ☎ (01335) 300809
Banks's Sunbeam; Marston's EPA, Pedigree; Ringwood Fortyniner; guest beer 🄷
Small, highly traditional pub, possibly the oldest in town, with as many as seven real ales on. Marston's portfolio of beers features, from which the landlord selects as widely as possible. He is also allowed one free choice guest ale, served at weekends, always from a local brewery. This venue was selected as local CAMRA Pub of the Year for the second successive year in 2014. Q♣🚌🐾📶

Ashover

Old Poets' Corner 🄻

Butts Road, S45 0EW (downhill from church)
12-11 ☎ (01246) 590888 🌐 oldpoets.co.uk
Ashover Light Rail, Poets' Tipple; guest beers 🄷
Home of the award-winning Ashover Brewery, this large brewers' Tudor pub is a frequent local CAMRA Pub of the Year. The staff welcome walkers and dogs and provide excellent food and beer. Choose from up to 10 ales, including Ashover beers, along with a range of guest ales, traditional ciders, bottled Belgian beers and country wines. The pub hosts three beer festivals a year, weekly quizzes and live music. Q❀🛏◑◗♿♣●P🚌(63,64)🐾

Barlborough

Royal Oak 🄻

High Street, S43 4EU
12-3, 5-midnight; 12-midnight Fri & Sat; 12-8 Sun
☎ (01246) 570818 🌐 royaloakbarlborough.co.uk
Beer range varies 🄷
Within half a mile of M1 junction 30, this pub is ideal for passing motorists and locals alike. The building was completely refurbished in 2011 to create a traditional village hostelry with a contemporary twist. The three areas – restaurant, lounge and bar – provide a variety of options, from traditional British cuisine in the restaurant to bar snacks in the main bar or lounge.
Q🛋❀◑◗♣●P🚌🐾📶

Barlow

Hare & Hounds 🄻

32 Commonside Road, S18 7SJ (from B6051, turn up hill at Commonside Rd)
12-11 ☎ (0114) 289 0464
Barlow Dark Horse, Three Valleys IPA; guest beers 🄷
Friendly, traditional village pub with three rooms around a central bar, plus a separate games room. The tap for Barlow Brewery, this pub has a strong community feel, though all are made welcome. In summer, Barlow Brewery's Carnival Ale is very popular. Views over the countryside can be enjoyed from the back room. A tiny terrace area with colourful windowboxes and planters is to the front of the pub. The landlord has been here for over 30 years. Q🛋❀♣P🚌(16,16A)🐾

Birchover

Druid Inn 🄻

Main Street, DE4 2BL
12 (5 Mon & Tue Jan 12-10.30 Sun ☎ (01629) 653836
🌐 druidinnbirchover.co.uk
Beer range varies 🄷
Traditional country free house with the main room featuring open fires at both ends. Both landlord and landlady are passionate about beer, with the central bar offering four real ales, usually from breweries that include Abbeydale, Blue Monkey, Oakham and Sarah Hughes. The pub has a mixed clientele of locals plus tourists visiting the Peak District National Park. Excellent home-cooked food is served in both the bar and separate restaurant. Q🛋❀◑◗♿⛺P🚌(172)🐾📶

Bolsover

Fidlers Rest 🄻

Craggs Road, S44 6BQ (just off A632, Bolsover Hill)
5 (12 Sat & Sun)-11 ☎ (01246) 828300
Beer range varies 🄷
This place was built as a private residence in 1812 by Peter Fidler, the famous explorer who mapped

INDEPENDENT BREWERIES

Amber Ripley
Ashover Ashover
Barlow Barlow
Bottle Brook Kilburn
Brampton Chesterfield
Brown Clay Cross (NEW)
Brunswick Derby
Bumpmill Shirland
Buxton Buxton
Coppice Side Heanor
Dancing Duck Derby
Derby Derby
Derventio Darley Abbey
Falstaff Derby: Normanton
Globe Glossop
Hartshorns Derby
Haywood Bad Ram Ashbourne
Heath Village Heath (NEW)
Hope Valley Castleton
Howard Town Glossop
Instant Karma Clay Cross (NEW)
John Thompson Ingleby
Leadmill Heanor
Leatherbritches Smisby
Marlpool Marlpool
Middle Earth Derby
Mouselow Farm Dinting
Mr Grundy's Derby
Muirhouse Ilkeston
North Star Ilkeston
Nutbrook Stanley Common/West Hallam
Old Sawley Sawley
Peak Chatsworth
Pigeon Fishers Hollingwood (NEW)
Raw Staveley
Rowditch Derby
Shiny Derby
Shottle Farm Shottle
Songbird Long Eaton (NEW)
Spire Staveley
Tap House Smisby
Thornbridge Bakewell
Tollgate Calke
Townes Staveley
Wentwell Derby
Whaley Bridge Whaley Bridge (NEW)
Whim Hartington
Wirksworth Wirksworth

the Canadian wilderness for the Hudson Bay Company. Guest beers are sourced mainly from local micros and are served alongside regular ales from Northumbria and Yorkshire. The modern interior has fine views over Bolsover Castle and the Peak District. Q❀♣🚌🐾📶

Brampton

Peacock Inn

412 Chatsworth Road, S40 3BQ

12-11.30 (11 Sun) ☎ (01246) 275115

thepeacockinnbrampton.co.uk

Bradfield Farmers Blonde; Castle Rock Harvest Pale; guest beer H

This local is popular with CAMRA members in the area. It has open fires and a warm, friendly welcome, with a quiz night on Monday. There are two rooms – the tap room with leather seating and a dartboard, and the best room with comfortable seating. Outside, there is a new marquee and decking area to the rear, with a children's play area. Q❀♣P🚌🐾

Rose & Crown

104 Old Road, S40 2QT

12-11 (midnight Fri & Sat) ☎ (01246) 563750

roseandcrownbrampton.co.uk

Brampton Golden Bud, Best, Impy Dark, Tudor Rose; Everards Tiger; guest beers H

Everards' Project William renovation enabled the Brampton Brewery to open its first tied house. A compact snug provides room for groups, while the main room has plenty of quiet corners. Memorabilia from the original brewery festoon the walls. Good-value food is served. Quiz night is Tuesday, and jazz features on the first Sunday of the month, from 4pm. A music quiz takes place on the last Sunday of the month. A drinking area to the rear can be accessed through the pub.
❀◐♣P🚌(170)📶

Tramway Tavern

192 Chatsworth Road, S40 2AT

4-11; 12-midnight Fri & Sat; 12-11 Sun ☎ (01246) 200111

tramwaytavern.co.uk

Brampton Golden Bud, Griffin, Best, Impy Dark; Everards Tiger; guest beers H

Local CAMRA Pub of the Year 2014, this is the Brampton Brewery tap. There are eight beers on the bar: four from Brampton, one Everards and three guests. A selection of Belgian and world beers, along with traditional ciders and perries, is also available. A popular Bring Your Vinyl night is held every Wednesday evening. An area is dedicated to pictures and history of the old Chesterfield tram service that once passed by. There is a courtyard to the rear. ❀🚌📶

Buxton

Cheshire Cheese

37-39 High Street, SK17 6HA

12-11 (midnight Fri & Sat) ☎ (01298) 212453

Everards Tiger; Titanic Steerage, Iceberg, White Star, Plum Porter, Captain Smith's Strong Ale; guest beers H

A double-fronted building of considerable age that, after refurbishment, reopened under the management of Titanic in autumn 2013. The pub is essentially open plan but split into several distinct areas. Low ceilings with original beams add to the cosy atmosphere. There is a quiet area at one end which features an open fire. The bar boasts an impressive array of 10 handpulls – no keg fonts – serving a range of Titanic beers and guests.
Q❀◐♿▲P🚌(199)🐾📶

Buxworth

Navigation Inn

Brookside, SK23 7NE (off B6062)

12-11 ☎ (01663) 732072

Black Sheep Best Bitter; Timothy Taylor Landlord; guest beers H

Multi-roomed 18th-century pub in attractive countryside in Buxworth village. It caters for all tastes; families and walkers are welcome. There is a pleasant outdoor drinking area and a children's play area. Good-value food and real fires complement a warm and welcoming atmosphere. The guest beers tend to be sourced from micros. The pub stands alongside the renovated Peak Forest Canal Basin, once the terminus of the limestone-carrying Peak Forest Tramway from the quarries at Dove Holes. ❀◐♣P🐾

Chelmorton

Church Inn

Main Street, SK17 9SL

12-3, 6-11; 12-11 Fri-Sun ☎ (01298) 85319

thechurchinn.co.uk

Adnams Southwold Bitter; Marston's Burton Bitter, Pedigree; guest beers H

Set in beautiful surroundings opposite the local church, this traditional village pub caters both for locals and walkers. The main room is laid out for dining, and good home-cooked food is on offer; however, a cosy pub atmosphere is maintained, with a low ceiling and real fire. Guest beers are usually from local micros. There is an excellent patio area outside. Parking is available at the end of the road in front of the pub. Monday is quiz night. Q❀◐▲♣

Chesterfield

Derby Tup

387 Sheffield Road, Whittington Moor, S41 8LS

12-3 (not Wed), 5-11; 12-midnight Fri & Sat; 2-11 Sun ☎ (01246) 454316

Castle Rock Harvest Pale, Screech Owl; Timothy Taylor Landlord; guest beers H

Ten handpumps offer beers from near and far, with a stout or porter usually available, as well as Westons Old Rosie cider. The main bar has a real fire, a variety of wooden settles and etched glass windows dating from its original incarnation as the Brunswick Hotel. There is also a small snug. The pub is popular with followers of Chesterfield FC, whose stadium is close by. Dogs are welcome, and quiz night is on Thursday. ♣🚌(43,50)🐾📶

Market Pub

95 New Square, S40 1AH

11-11 (midnight Fri & Sat) ☎ (01246) 273641

themarketpub.co.uk

Kelham Island Easy Rider; Timothy Taylor Landlord; guest beers H

Popular, friendly town-centre pub, serving up to nine real ales. Beer festivals are held throughout the year, as are speciality food evenings and wine and whisky tastings. The Market is deservedly popular and well known for its food served lunchtimes and early evenings. Quiz night is on Thursday and live music features on Sunday evening. ❀◐◑⇌●▭ᯤ

Rutland Arms 𝕃

23 Stephenson Place, S40 1XL

11.30-11.30 (12.30am Thu-Sat); 12-11 Sun ☎ (01246) 205857

Greene King Abbot; Sharp's Doom Bar; Thornbridge Jaipur IPA; guest beers Ⓗ

Popular town-centre pub next to the famous Crooked Spire parish church. The hostelry is distinguishable by its castellated roof line and, inside, it has two areas divided by steps, with subdued lighting and wooden panelling. As well as the regular beers there are five guests; the landlord likes to choose unusual ales. Westons Old Rosie cider is available. The food is recommended and is good value. There are occasional beer festivals. ❀◐◑⇌●▭ᯤ

White Swan 𝕃

16 St Mary's Gate, S41 7TJ

12-midnight (1am Fri & Sat) ☎ (01246) 229570

rawbrew.com/whiteswan

Raw Blonde Pale; guest beers Ⓗ

Affectionately known as the Mucky Duck, this pub is going from strength to strength. With a spacious all-in-one room, it is the Raw Brewing Company tied house, offering 12 cask ales including house beer Mucky Duck and a wide range of local and national guest beers. There are also up to seven real ciders and an impressive selection of bottled beers. Home-made food is served all day Monday to Saturday and Sunday lunchtimes. An upstairs function room is available for hire. ❀◐◑♿⇌●▭ᯤ

Clay Cross

Rykneld Turnpyke 𝕃

4 John Street, S45 9NQ

12-midnight ☎ (01246) 250366

Instant Karma Test Brew Number One!, Bramling Porter; Thornbridge Jaipur IPA; guest beers Ⓗ

Formerly the Egstow Working Men's Club, the Rykneld Turnpyke (named after Rykneld Street, the old road between Chesterfield and Derby) has one large room divided into different areas, with comfortable seating. There is an excellent choice of up to 12 reasonably priced beers, mostly from local brewers. You will often see a game of cribbage or dominoes, and may hear a pianist in the evening. The on-site Instant Karma brewery can be seen through a viewing panel at the rear. ♣●▭❀

Clowne

Clowne Community Centre 𝕃

Recreation Close, Villa Park, S43 4PL

7-11 ☎ (01246) 819546

Beer range varies Ⓗ

A council-run community centre widely used by the locals for functions. The Rock & Blues Club has live bands every Sunday and there is a popular quiz night on Tuesday, with free food. The place is well cared for, with a relaxed and friendly atmosphere, and it has a beer festival in May. There is a Timothy Taylor changing house beer, plus guests. Ample car parking is available. Q❀♿P▯▭

Coal Aston

Cross Daggers 𝕃

Brown Lane, S18 3AJ

4 (5 Sat)-11.30; 12-3 Sun ☎ (01246) 412728

Abbeydale Moonshine; Bradfield Farmers Blonde; Tetley Bitter; guest beer Ⓗ

The Cross Daggers is a 19th-century pub which has been home to landlord Anthony Hutchinson since 2000. It proudly carries the Cask Marque accreditation for excellent beer management. Q❀♣P▭❀

Coton-in-the-Elms

Black Horse 🏆

17 Burton Road, DE12 8HJ (in centre of village)

4-11 (midnight Fri); 1-midnight Sat; 12-10.30 Sun ☎ (01283) 762947 theblackhorsederbyshire.co.uk

Draught Bass; Joule's Pale Ale; Marston's Pedigree; guest beer Ⓗ

This Guide regular of some 30 years ago was revived in 2009 as a lively and popular free house after more than a decade of neglect. Tastefully renovated with extensive use of wood, the bright and airy main room is divided into bar and lounge areas by glass-topped wood partitions. A small snug, served through a hatch, features a bar billiards table. The guest beer often comes from a local microbrewery. The real cider is Woody's. Quiz night is Tuesday, with occasional live music Sundays. ❀♣●P▭(22)❀

Crich

Cliff Inn 𝕃

Town End, DE4 5DP (150yds from Crich Tramway Village)

5 (7 Mon)-11; 12-11 Sat & Sun ☎ (01773) 852444

Blue Monkey Sanctuary; Buxton Moor Top; Dancing Duck Ay Up; Sharp's Doom Bar; guest beer Ⓗ

Traditional gritstone free house at the top of the village just below the National Tramway Museum. Built in about 1800, the two rooms are largely unchanged since the 1960s. There are logburners in both rooms. It has five handpumps, of which four normally dispense LocAles. Home-made food is served Tuesday-Friday evenings and weekend lunchtimes. Q❀◐◑▲♣P▯▭❀

Derby

Alexandra Hotel 𝕃

203 Siddals Road, DE1 2QE

12-11 (midnight Fri); 11-midnight Sat ☎ (01332) 293993

alexandrahotelderby.co.uk

Castle Rock Harvest Pale; guest beers Ⓗ

The Alex, once the Midland Coffee House, is a Castle Rock establishment serving Harvest Pale and the brewery's seasonal beers. It offers up to eight guest ales including a mild, a stout/porter, and LocAles. There are also more than 50 UK and continental bottled beers of varying styles. The bar is adorned with railway memorabilia, and the lounge with breweriana. A Class 37 locomotive cab resides in the car park. The pub was the birthplace of Derby CAMRA in 1974. Q❀🛏♿⇌♣●P▭❀ᯤ

Babington Arms 𝕃

11-13 Babington Lane, DE1 1TA

8am-midnight (1am Fri & Sat) ☎ (01332) 383647

Greene King Abbot; Kelham Island Pale Rider; Marston's Burton Bitter, Pedigree; Ruddles Best Bitter; Theakston Old Peculier; guest beers H

With possibly the best real ale range of any Wetherspoon pub, it has won the company's prestigious Cask Ale Pub of the Year and local CAMRA City Pub of the Year awards twice. It offers an amazing range of 16 beers on handpump as well as four or five traditional ciders. The drinks are listed on a TV screen. The pub participates in the bi-annual Wetherspoon beer festivals which showcase unusual beers, including some from overseas brewers. Q

Bell & Castle

92-96 Burton Road, DE1 1TG

12-midnight (1am Fri & Sat) (01332) 209808

Beer range varies H

New ownership and a complete redesign have restored this pub to real ale after many years of neglect. The interior layout is contemporary open plan, with offset spaces that partition the room. A large garden hidden away at the rear is a welcome extension of the drinking area in good weather. Food is a feature of the pub, from home-made, stone-baked pizzas to a full menu. Real cider is always available.

Coach & Horses

Mansfield Road, Little Chester, DE1 3RF

12-midnight (1am Sat) (01332) 258901

Draught Bass; Exmoor Gold; guest beers H

Welcoming pub in Little Chester, the oldest part of Derby and dating back to Roman times. Focused on the local community, there is a games room for pool and darts, events including popular Sunday night quizzes, support for local charities and a book exchange. The two guest beers are from the SIBA range. Live music features on bank holidays alongside a larger range of beers. A discount is available for card-carrying CAMRA members.
P (H1)

Exeter Arms L

13 Exeter Place, DE1 2EU

11-11 (11.30 Wed & Thu; midnight Fri & Sat); 12-10.30 Sun
(01332) 605323 exeterarms.co.uk

Dancing Duck Ay Up, Nice Weather, Dark Drake, Gold; Marston's Pedigree; guest beers H

A remarkable transformation in recent times by the licensees and Dancing Duck Brewery earned the venue local CAMRA Pub of the Year 2013. The Ex simply oozes old world charm and features a small bar with an open fire, partitioned lounges and a wooden settled snug with an old-fashioned range. The adjoining atmospheric cottage dating from about 1815 has been incorporated into the pub, and the rear garden houses a stable-type bar which opens for beer festivals.

Falstaff L

74 Silverhill Road, New Normanton, DE23 6UJ

12-11 (midnight Fri & Sat) (01332) 342902
falstaffbrewery.co.uk

Falstaff Fist Full of Hops, Phoenix, Smiling Assassin; guest beer H

A 20-minute walk from the city centre rewards you with this atmospheric and reputedly haunted free house. Originally a coaching inn before the neighbourhood was built up, it is now the Falstaff Brewery tap and has long been the best real ale house in the Normanton area of Derby. The curved bar has a small lounge on one side where Offiler's Brewery memorabilia is displayed. Other collectables can be viewed throughout the games room and second bar room. Q

Five Lamps L

25 Duffield Road, DE1 3BH

12-11 (midnight Fri & Sat) (01332) 348730
fivelampsderby.co.uk

Derby Five Lamps; Everards Tiger; Peak Ales Chatsworth Gold; Whim Hartington IPA; guest beers H

Since it reopened in 2010, the pub has gone from strength to strength thanks to the dedication of the licensees and staff, which culminated in local CAMRA Pub of the Year 2012. Fourteen handpumps showcase many local ales from breweries such as Derby, Buxton, Peak and Whim. The Lamps is essentially open plan, but has many little nooks and crannies to give it a homely feel. It has been tastefully refurbished with wood panelling and leather seating in a traditional style.
Q P

Flowerpot L

23-25 King Street, DE1 3DZ

12-11 (11.30 Wed & Thu; 12.30am Fri & Sat)
(01332) 204955 flowerpotderby.co.uk

Black Iris Sunflower; Blue Monkey BG Sips; Oakham Bishops Farewell; Whim Hartington IPA; guest beers H/G

Dating from around 1800 but much expanded from its original premises, this pub reaches back from the small roadside frontage and divides into several interlinking rooms. One room provides the stage for regular live bands, and another has a glass cellar wall revealing rows of stillaged firkins, which can be seen from the bar and from the road outside. Eight real ales are usually available and it is now the home of the Black Iris Brewery.
Q

Furnace Inn L

Duke Street, DE1 3BX

4 (12 Fri & Sat)-midnight; 12-11 Sun (01332) 385981

Beer range varies H

Since it reopened in 2012 the pub has been transformed into a real ale mecca, which has culminated in the local CAMRA Pub of the Year award for 2014. A former Hardys & Hansons pub and now the tap for the Shiny Brewing Company, it serves up to eight real ales and three ciders/perries, with guest beers from all over. It is open plan with two distinct sides off a central bar. Open mic, poker and cheese nights feature, with regular beer festivals held throughout the year.
Q

Greyhound L

76 Friar Gate, DE1 1FN

12-11 (midnight Thu; 1am Fri); 11-1am Sat; 11-11 Sun
(01332) 344155 greyhound-dbc.co.uk

Derby Business As Usual; guest beers H

An old coaching inn that has been restored to a high standard by Derby Brewing Company. It has a walled beer garden which is a boon in fine weather, as well as a roof terrace open in summer. Modern art adorns the walls in this vibrant establishment which caters for a mixed clientele. Up to seven beers from the Derby Brewing range and up to three guests are on offer as well as a draught cider.

Horse & Groom

48 Elms Street, West End, DE1 3HN

12-11 horseandgroomderby.co.uk

Draught Bass; guest beers H

Situated in the city's old West End, the pub dates from around 1850. A complete refurbishment has restored the building back to a thriving community local, with ladies' and gents' darts teams and two pool teams. The regular Bass is accompanied by three changing guests, often from Thornbridge, Ossett or Whim. There is regular live music at the weekend, jazz on the last Wednesday of the month, and a folk and blue-grass jamming session most Sunday evenings.

Little Chester Ale House L

4a Chester Green Road, Little Chester, DE1 3SF

3 (12 Fri-Sun)-10 07584 244726

Wentwell seasonal beer; guest beers H

Derby's first micropub was voted local CAMRA City Pub of the Year runner-up in 2014. On the edge of a tree-lined conservation area, the pub is in the historic Little Chester part of the city, site of Roman Derventio where two Roman wells can still be seen nearby. This former shop has one small main room and a passageway leading to a tiny rear room. It offers four changing beers, including at least one from local Wentwell Brewery, the pub's owner. Q

New Zealand Arms L

2 Langley Street, New Zealand, DE22 3GL

12-midnight (01332) 384945 newzealandarms.com

Beer range varies H

Popular local brewery Dancing Duck has taken on another pub near the city centre, and six of its ales plus guests and draught ciders are on offer here. Comfortable surroundings, pleasant staff and a good choice of home-cooked food have helped to re-establish it as a pub to visit in this part of the city after a period of closure. Quiz night is Wednesday, music nights are Monday, Thursday and Saturday. Food is served Wednesday to Friday evenings and Saturday and Sunday lunchtimes.
(28,29)

Peacock Inn L

87 Nottingham Road, DE1 3QS

11-11 (midnight Fri & Sat); 12-10.30 Sun
(01332) 583308

Draught Bass G**; Leatherbritches Peacock Pale Ale; Marston's Pedigree; Oakham Bishops Farewell; Whim Arbor Light; guest beers** H

Attractive 18th-century stone-built roadside pub that used to be a staging post on the main coach road out of Derby, which ran alongside the now filled-in old Derby Canal. Two rooms on different levels are divided by a central bar and feature wooden floors, stove burners, photos of old Derby and Derby County memorabilia. Up to nine real ales and two ciders and/or perries are on offer; beer festivals are held in the large, covered garden area to the rear. Q

Rowditch Inn

246 Uttoxeter New Road, DE22 3LL

12-2 (not Mon-Fri), 7-11 (01332) 343123

Marston's Pedigree; guest beers H

A plain-fronted but warmly welcoming roadside hostelry with an unexpectedly deep interior, which divides into two drinking areas and a small snug. The rear garden is a peaceful haven in warmer weather. Pumpclips adorning the walls of the bar are evidence of myriad guest ales. The output of the pub's brewery is almost exclusively consumed on the premises. Well worth the walk or the five-minute bus ride from the city centre.

Smithfield L

Meadow Road, DE1 2BH

12-midnight (01332) 370429

Derby Smithy Ale; Draught Bass; Whim Arbor Light; guest beer H

This local is a short walk down-river from the Tap or across Bass Rec from the Brunswick. Once a sister pub of the Flowerpot, the new owner has completely refurbished the pub, upgrading it and giving it a modern, contemporary interior. The main bar is complemented by a small, more intimate back lounge. The rear patio overlooks the river. Good-value home-cooked food is available every lunchtime. P

Duffield

Pattenmakers Arms

4 Crown Street, DE56 4EY

12-2, 5-midnight; 12-midnight Fri-Sun (01332) 842844
pattenmakersarms.co.uk

Draught Bass G**; Marston's Pedigree; guest beers** H

A pleasant Edwardian pub – its motto: Enter a stranger and leave as a friend – tucked away behind the main road. A traditional, welcoming and customer-focused local, it has retained much of its original character, with quarry-tiled and parquet floors and stained/etched glass windows. Skittles, darts, dominoes and quiz teams meet here, and there are Sunday quizzes and weekend meat raffles. Good-value wholesome food is served every lunchtime, and breakfast from 10am on Saturday. Ecclesbourne Valley Heritage Railway is close by. P

Earl Sterndale

Quiet Woman

SK17 0BU (off B5053)

7-11; 4-11 Sat; 5-11 Sun (01298) 83211

Jennings Dark Mild; Marston's Burton Bitter; guest beer H

Unspoilt basic local with an unusual name and sign set in the heart of the Peak District National Park, opposite the church and village green. A low-beamed room has a real fire on the left and a small bar to the right. There is a separate games room with a pool table. Local fresh eggs and traditional pork pies can be purchased at the bar. The pub offers its own selection of bottle-conditioned beers from Leek Brewery. Q P (442)

Furness Vale

Soldier Dick Inn

150 Buxton Road, SK23 7PH

12-11 (01663) 611010

Thwaites Wainwright; guest beers H

A busy and comfortable pub in the centre of Furness Vale, close to the railway station and Peak Forest Canal. It caters for all tastes, and walkers and families are welcome. A real fire and good-value dining add to the warm and friendly atmosphere. There is occasional live entertainment and accommodation is available.
P (61,199)

Glossop

Crown Inn ★

142 Victoria Street, SK13 8JF (on Hayfield road out of town centre)

⏲ 5 (12 Fri & Sat)-11; 12-10.30 Sun ☎ (01457) 862824

Samuel Smith Old Brewery Bitter [H]

End-of-terrace local, a few minutes from the town centre and railway station, built in 1846 and the only Smith's house in the High Peak area since being acquired by the brewery in 1977. An attractive curved bar serves two side snugs, each with real fires in winter, and a pool/games room. Pictures of bygone Glossop add to the traditional character. Prices are keen and the brewery's bottled beers are available. An enclosed outdoor drinking area is provided in the rear yard.
Q❀♿⇌♣🚌

Queen's Arms

1 Shepley Street, SK13 7RZ

⏲ 12-midnight ☎ (01457) 853005

🌐 queens-arms-hotel-old-glossop.co.uk

Holt Bitter; Morland Old Speckled Hen; Robinsons Unicorn; Thornbridge Jaipur IPA; Thwaites Wainwright [H]

A traditional, warm and welcoming pub in the original heart of Glossop – now Old Glossop – it is an ideal stopping off point for walkers from the popular hill-walking areas close by, and is well used by locals and visitors from far and wide. It carries a good range of real ales in excellent condition. Upstairs is the popular Coriander Indian restaurant and takeaway. Regular music events are held on Tuesday and Saturday evenings. Coach parties are welcome by arrangement.
❀◐♿🚌(390)🐾📶

Star Ale House

2 Howard Street, SK13 7DD (next to railway station)

⏲ 4 (2 Thu)-11; 2-midnight Fri; 12-midnight Sat; 12-10.30 Sun ☎ (01457) 853072

Timothy Taylor Landlord; guest beers [H]

Highly popular town-centre pub, run by a dedicated CAMRA member, adjacent to the railway station. A large comfortable main room where conversation predominates is complemented by a smaller room to the rear. Guest beers come mainly from local microbreweries, and real draught cider is regularly available – all dispensed by handpump. Regular beer and cider festivals are held throughout the year. The town is ideally situated for walking within the Dark Peak area. **Q⇌🍎🚌**

Hartshorne

Admiral Rodney Inn

65 Main Street, DE11 7ES (on A514)

⏲ 6-11; 5.30-11.30 Fri; 4-11 Sat; 12-midnight Sun ☎ (01283) 216482

Exmoor Gold; Marston's Pedigree; guest beers [H]

A traditional village pub dating back to the early 19th century, but rebuilt and extended in the late 20th century to provide an open-plan L-shaped drinking area while retaining the original oak beams in the former snug. Up to three guest beers are available, usually from SIBA members. A Cheese Society meets here monthly on a Monday evening. Quiz night is Friday, karaoke Sunday. The grounds include a cricket pitch, home of Hartshorne Cricket Club. Saturday opening hours are 12-midnight during the season. **❀♿♣P🚌(61)🐾📶**

Hayfield

Royal Hotel

Market Street, SK22 2EP

⏲ 11-11 ☎ (01663) 742721

Hydes Original Bitter; guest beers [H]

An imposing stone pub near the church, cricket ground and River Sett. The interior boasts oak panels and pews, creating a relaxing atmosphere; real fires burn in winter. Four guest beers from local micros are always available and an annual beer festival is hosted in October. A restaurant and function room complete the facilities (food is available all day in summer). The village is the base for many leisure activities in the Dark Peak and was the birthplace of actor Arthur Lowe.
Q❀🛏◐♿⛺P🚌(61,358)📶

Holbrook

Dead Poets Inn

38 Chapel Street, DE56 0TQ

⏲ 12-2.30, 5-11; 12-11 Fri & Sat; 12-10.30 Sun ☎ (01332) 780301

Draught Bass; Greene King Abbot; Marston's Pedigree [G]**; guest beers** [H]

Built in 1800 and formerly known as the Cross Keys, the pub has undergone a remarkable transformation to create an inn with a real medieval feel inside. There is a delightful snug, and the main bar has high-backed pews, stone-flagged floors, a real fire and an inglenook fireplace. Around 25 guest beers feature during the week (six at any one time), usually including at least one from Abbeydale and Whim breweries. It is a great destination in summer and winter.
Q❀◐♿🍎P🚌

Holmesfield

Rutland Arms 𝕃

96 Main Road, S18 7WT

⏲ 12-11.30 ☎ (0114) 289 0374

Black Sheep Best Bitter; Bradfield Farmers Blonde; Castle Rock Harvest Pale; Sharp's Doom Bar; Theakston Best Bitter; guest beer [H]

A traditional country pub with open fires and low beams, it has a relaxing, warm and cosy atmosphere. Up to six handpulled cask ales are served. The pub has numerous accreditations for cask ales, and was awarded local CAMRA Country Pub of the Year in 2012. **Q❀◐♣🍎🚌(15)🐾📶**

Hope

Cheshire Cheese

Edale Road, S33 6ZF

⏲ closed Mon; 12-3, 6-11; 12-11 Sat; 12-9 Sun ☎ (01433) 620381 🌐 thecheshirecheeseinn.co.uk

Bradfield Farmers Blonde; Peak Ales Swift Nick; guest beers [H]

A cosy country inn dating from 1578, with an open-plan bar area and a smaller room at a lower level that was probably originally designed to house animals, but is now mainly used as a dining area. It is situated in good walking country but parking is limited and the road outside is narrow. The pub can arrange outdoor activities for guests.
Q❀🛏◐⛺P🐾📶

Horsley Woodhouse

Old Oak Inn

176 Main Street, DE7 6AW (on A609)
⏲ 4 (3 Thu & Fri; 12 Sat)-11; 12-10.30 Sun ☎ (01332) 881299
Bottle Brook Charlatan ⊞; Draught Bass ⊞/Ⓖ; Leadmill Arc-Light; Marston's Pedigree; Timothy Taylor Boltmaker; guest beers ⊞
Flagship of the Leadmill Brewery, featuring a mouthwatering variety of its beers, plus a couple of guests. This traditional pub boasts four rooms of differing character, some with open fires. At weekends drinkers can enjoy the RuRAD bar – effectively a mini beer festival offering gravity-dispensed ales from craft brewers near and far, alongside the familiar Leadmill and Bottle Brook beers. Homely, welcoming and excellent value for money, this roadside tavern enjoys extensive views. ❀◐◑♿●P🚉🚌🐾

Ilkeston

Brewery Tap Ⓛ

24 South Street, DE7 5QE
⏲ 12-11 ☎ (0115) 837 6886 🌐 muirhousebrewery.co.uk
Beer range varies ⊞
A micropub belonging to the Muirhouse Brewery, it opened in 2013 and is a converted shop, with additional seating in a function room upstairs. The ground floor is double fronted and maintains its large glazed shop front. There is a step up to the raised bar area where six handpumps dispense two ales from the award-winning Muirhouse range, two guest ales from microbreweries, and two real ciders. This family run hostelry is a welcome addition to the expanding Ilkeston real ale scene. Q●🚌🐾📶

Dewdrop Ⓛ

24 Station Road, DE7 5TE
⏲ 4 (3 Fri; 12 Sat)-11; 12-10.30 Sun ☎ (0115) 932 9684
Bob's White Lion; Oakham Bishops Farewell; guest beers ⊞
This Victorian multi award-winning Guide regular is a haven for fine ale and conversation. There is a cosy lounge with a roaring fire, a family room, and a bar with a pool table and classic oldies jukebox. Hearty cobs are made fresh to order. Outdoors there is a heated, covered smoking area. The range of up to eight fine ales is sourced from near and far, often including beers from Blue Monkey and Acorn. Two ciders are also kept. A nearby station is due to open in December 2014. Q❀◐●🚌🐾

Spanish Bar Ⓛ

74-76 South Street, DE7 5QJ
⏲ 10-11 (midnight Fri & Sat); 10-10.30 Sun
☎ (0115) 930 8666
Whim Hartington IPA; guest beers ⊞
This bustling town-centre pub is popular with all ages. A long main bar with a log-burner extends into a second room at busy times. Up to six handpumps often feature beers from local micros, and several ciders are also kept. This true community gem supports darts and skittles teams and holds weekly quiz, cards and dominoes nights. Outside there is a popular award-winning garden with long alley skittles and a heated, covered smoking area. Q❀♿●🚌🐾

Kilburn

Hunters Arms

Church Street, DE56 0LU
⏲ 2-11; 12-11 Fri-Sun and summer ☎ (01332) 781518
Marston's Pedigree Ⓖ; Oakham Bishops Farewell; guest beers ⊞
Named after the owners of nearby Kilburn Hall when the pub was built in 1879, it was rescued from closure in 2009, and won the local CAMRA Pub of the Year award in 2012. There is a pleasant, opened-out interior with fire, TV and free Wi-Fi. Six guest beers are sourced from smaller breweries, often featuring Thornbridge, Blue Monkey and Dancing Duck. Food is served Tuesday to Saturday only. Q♿●P🚌📶

Kirk Ireton

Barley Mow Inn

Main Street, DE6 3JP (off B5023) SK266501
⏲ 12-2, 7-11; 12-2, 7-10.30 Sun ☎ (01335) 370306
Whim Hartington IPA; guest beers Ⓖ
Set in a charming village overlooking Ecclesbourne Valley, this gabled Jacobean building houses an old-fashioned down-to-earth pub, of the type that is increasingly hard to find. Several interconnecting rooms of different character have low beams, mullioned windows and well-worn woodwork, and there is a welcoming open fire in the main bar. A small serving hatch reveals a stillage with up to six gravity beers. Local breweries such as Blue Monkey, Dancing Duck, Burton Bridge, Thornbridge and Peak Ales often feature. Q❀⛺✚●🐾

Kniveton

Red Lion

Main Street, DE6 1JH
⏲ 12-11 (midnight Fri & Sat); 12-10.30 Sun
☎ (01335) 345554
Marston's Pedigree; Sharp's Doom Bar; guest beer ⊞
Attractive stone pub in the middle of this small village, it has a good, well-kept range of beers, mainly from established regionals, but occasionally featuring a local brewery. The staff are friendly and welcoming, and the venue does a good range of food, with several different speciality events such as pie nights and curry nights. Awarded Most Improved Pub in the local CAMRA awards for 2014. ◐◑P

Langley

Butchers Arms 🏆 Ⓛ

127 Hands Road, Heanor, DE75 7HB
⏲ 4 (3 Fri & Sat)-midnight; 12-midnight Sun
☎ (01773) 713316
Bottle Brook Rapture; Coppice Side Owd Miner, Ninkasi; guest beers ⊞
Friendly local pub with 11 handpumps specialising in beers from the local Leadmill and Bottle Brook breweries; it is also the brewery tap for the Coppice Side Brewery. The main bar is simply furnished and has a log-burning fire; there is no jukebox or gaming machine. The pub is a listed building dating from the early 1830s; it has a large car park to the rear, and beer gardens to the front and back. Families and dogs are welcome. Q❀♣●P🚌🐾

Little Eaton

Queen's Head

131 Alfreton Road, DE21 5DF
11-11 (midnight Fri & Sat) (01332) 986065
queenshead-dbc.co.uk
Derby Business As Usual, Dashingly Dark; Everards Tiger, Original; guest beer H
A historic Derbyshire stone inn boasting some original features including low-beamed ceilings. The main entrance has been renovated and the bar relocated to create a welcoming and stylish interior. There is an attractive patio garden to one side for warmer summer days. There are normally nine real ales, five of which are from Derby Brewing Company. The menu selection includes home-made, locally-sourced food, all prepared and cooked on site. P

Little Hayfield

Lantern Pike

45 Glossop Road, SK22 2NG (10 minutes' walk from Hayfield towards Glossop)
12-3 (not Mon), 5-11; 12-11 Sat & Sun (01663) 747590
lanternpikeinn.co.uk
Timothy Taylor Landlord; guest beer H
Picturesque ivy-clad pub nestling in a small hamlet within the Dark Peak area. The comfortable lounge bar, with a real fire in winter, connects to separate informal dining areas. There is a traditional pub menu featuring home-made dishes, with specialist lunches on Sundays. Coronation Street originator Tony Warren once lived nearby and wrote early episodes of the soap while in the pub. There are superb views from the rear patio area. Hikers welcome. P(61)

Little Longstone

Packhorse Inn

Main Street, DE45 1NN
12-3, 5-11; 12-11 Sat & Sun (01629) 640471
packhorselongstone.co.uk
Black Sheep Best Bitter; Thornbridge Wild Swan, Lord Marples, Jaipur IPA; guest beers H
A small pub that began life as two miners' cottages but which has been welcoming drinkers since 1787. Situated just a short walk from stunning views of Monsal Head, dogs and walkers are welcome. Fresh local produce is a passion, an ethos also extended to the beers, which always include a choice from the nearby Thornbridge Brewery. The beer garden features a barbecue in summer, and food is served all day at weekends.
(173)

Litton

Red Lion

Main Street, SK17 8QU
12-11 (midnight Fri & Sat); 12-10.30 Sun
(01298) 871458 theredlionlitton.co.uk
Abbeydale Absolution; Peak Ales Bakewell Best Bitter; guest beer H
Nestling on the green and the only pub in the village, the Red Lion is a welcome refuge for locals and visitors alike. There is a large fireplace serving several rooms off a central passageway. The house beer, Litton Pride, is from Wincle Beer Co, with guest ales mostly from local breweries. The annual Wakes Week at the end of June is not to be missed, with events including a well dressing on the village green. No food Mondays in January and February.
QP(65,66)

Longshaw

Grouse

S11 7TZ
12-3, 6-11; 12-11 Sat & Sun (01433) 630423
thegrouseinn-derbyshire.co.uk
Banks's Bitter; Marston's EPA, Pedigree; guest beer H
In the same family for 50 years, this free house stands in isolation on bleak moorland south-west of Sheffield, and is a welcome refuge for walkers as well as climbers from the nearby Fraggatt Edge. The walls are decorated with photos of local scenes and a large collection of international banknotes. The comfortable lounge and bar are at the front with a separate room at the rear reached through the conservatory. No food Monday evenings. A self-catering holiday flat is available.
QP

Lullington

Colvile Arms

Main Street, DE12 8EG (centre of village)
6-11; 12-3, 7-10.30 Sun (01827) 373212
Draught Bass; Marston's Pedigree; guest beer H
Leased from the Lullington Estate, the seat of the Colvile family until the early 1900s, this popular 18th-century free house is at the heart of an attractive hamlet at the southern tip of the county. The public bar comprises an adjoining hallway and snug, each featuring high-backed settles with wood panelling. The bar and a comfortable lounge are on opposite sides of a central serving area. A second lounge/function room overlooks the beer garden and lawn. P

Makeney

Holly Bush ★

Holly Bush Lane, DE56 0RX
12-11; 12-10.30 Sun (01332) 841729
Fuller's London Pride; Greene King Abbot; Marston's Pedigree H**; Ruddles County** G**; Timothy Taylor Landlord; guest beers** H
Late 17th-century Grade II-listed pub oozing character. It was once a farmhouse with a brewery on the Strutt Estate and stood on the Derby turnpike before the new road opened in 1818; Dick Turpin drank here. Identified by CAMRA as having a nationally important historic pub interior for its enclosed wooden snug sandwiched between two bars with real fires. Beer festivals are held in March and October. The Milford bus stop on the A6 is a 10-minute walk. QP

Marlpool

Marlpool Ale House

5 Breach Road, Heanor, DE75 7NJ
closed Mon-Thu; 2-10 Fri; 12-10 Sat & Sun
(01773) 711285 marlpoolbrewing.co.uk
Marlpool Blind Boris, Otters Pocket, Scratty Ratty; guest beers H/G
Micropub and brewery tap for the Marlpool Brewery. A former butcher's shop, it comprises a cosy bar area, a small room at the rear with open fire and an outside seating area. The bar is a pulpit reclaimed from a Methodist chapel, and is now

adorned with four handpumps. Further ale and ciders are brought up from the cellar. The small size encourages conversation. Opening hours are restricted but include all bank holidays. Q

Matlock

MoCa Bar

77 Dale Road, DE4 3LT

11-10.30; 11-11 Fri & Sat (01629) 258084

Beer range varies [H]

Winners of the CAMRA Matlock and Dales Pub of the Year in 2013 and 2014, this relatively new addition to the Matlock pub scene has a sophisticated big-city-cafe feel. Open plan and urbane, with music memorabilia adorning the walls, the MoCa Bar has seven handpulls featuring ales from six dedicated breweries (Abbeydale, Blue Monkey, Brampton, Dancing Duck, Kelham Island and Oakham) and one rotating guest. There is a reduction in the price of real ales Monday-Wednesday.

Thorn Tree Inn

48 Jackson Road, DE4 3JQ (up Bank Rd, left into Smedley St, 2nd right up Smith Rd, 1st left)

12-2 (not Mon), 6-11; 12-2, 5-midnight Fri; 12-midnight Sat; 12-11 Sun (01629) 580295

thorntreeatmatlock.co.uk

Draught Bass; Ruddles Best Bitter; Timothy Taylor Landlord; guest beers [H]

Perched high above Matlock town, this two-roomed traditional pub enjoys beautiful views from the heated patio area. Children and dogs are welcome although cat-swinging is not recommended due to the compact nature of the establishment. Reputedly, a haunted wall clock hangs in the lounge, where regulars, ramblers and real ale enthusiasts convene to enjoy the atmosphere. Three permanent real ales are complemented by four changing guests. Home-made food is served Tuesday-Friday lunchtimes, and pie night is on Wednesday 6-8pm.
Q

Matlock Bath

Fishpond

204 South Parade, DE4 3NR

11-midnight (11 Sun) (01629) 55006

thefishpondmatlockbath.co.uk

Beer range varies [H]

At the south end of this historic spa town and set into the limestone cliff face, this recently refurbished free house has not lost any of its traditional character. Woodburners bookend the cavernous interior, adding to the congenial atmosphere. The changing selection of ales and ciders has a strong focus on LocAle, and is complemented by an interesting menu featuring artisan bread from the pub's own bakery. It regularly hosts live music and comedy plus special events, including the local CAMRA beer festival.
P

Melbourne

Blue Bell Inn

53 Church Street, DE73 8EJ

11-11; 12-10.30 Sun (01332) 865764

thebluebellinnmelbourne.co.uk

Shardlow Golden Eye, Reverend Eaton; guest beers [H]

This is the brewery tap for Shardlow Brewery – a range of its beers is on offer, including Reverend Eaton, with guest beers mainly from local breweries. Real cider is sold and there are two beer festivals each year. Run on traditional lines, the bar has a sporting emphasis and the restaurant serves classic pub fare. The pub is popular with walkers and is well located for visitors to Melbourne Hall and the 12th-century Norman parish church.
(61)

Middleton

Nelson Arms

The Green, Main Street, DE4 4LU

5 (12 Sat)-midnight; 12-11 Sun (01629) 825154

nelsonarmsmiddleton.co.uk

Marston's Pedigree; guest beers [H]

A friendly family-owned free house at the top of the village. A small comfortable bar is located to the left as you enter; a large beamed room to the right has a welcoming fire and an interesting array of pictures, artefacts and curious ornaments that adorn the walls. A separate pool/function/family room is to the rear of the pub, along with an outdoor drinking area. Real cider complements the choice of two guest ales. P (6.1)

Milford

King William IV

The Bridge, DE56 0RR

5-11.30; 12-11.30 Sat; 12.30-11 Sun (01332) 840842

kingwilliam1v.co.uk

Greene King Abbot; Sharp's Doom Bar; Timothy Taylor Landlord; guest beers [H]

Heading north on the A6, this stone-built Georgian inn, dramatically situated at the foot of sandstone cliffs, hoves into view. Within, an open fire at one end of the elongated bar adds to the ambiance of the cosy interior in the winter. Period furniture and quarry tiled flooring are from the same period as the building. Regular beer festivals, featuring interesting beers from around the UK, are a feature of this pub.

Millers Dale

Angler's Rest

SK17 8SN

12-3, 6.30-11; 12-midnight Sat; 12-9 Sun

(01298) 871323 theanglersrest.co.uk

Adnams Southwold Bitter; Storm Silk of Amnesia; guest beers [H]

An ivy-clad inn dating from 1753 on the bank of the River Wye, handy for the spectacular walk along the Monsal trail. It is a multi-room pub including a cosy lounge with real fire and a comfortable dining area. Walking boots and dogs are welcome in the hikers' bar. Good, traditional pub food is served daily and the guest beers are mostly LocAle. A self-catering apartment is available. Q P (65)

New Mills

Pack Horse Inn

Mellor Road, SK22 4QQ

12-11; 12-10.30 Sun (01663) 742365

Phoenix Arizona; Tetley Bitter; guest beers [H]

Stone-built pub occupying an elevated position on the New Mills to Mellor road, with magnificent views across the Sett Valley to Kinder Scout and beyond. The main room is comfortable, with the buzz of conversation the predominant feature. Guest beers are listed on a blackboard. Food is a major attraction, with a separate restaurant to one side of the bar. Good-quality accommodation is provided. The stone-flagged rear courtyard has plenty of seating and is popular in the summer months. Q❀◐P

Newton Solney

Brickmakers Arms

9 Main Street, DE15 0SJ (on B5008, opp jct with Trent Lane)

5-11; 12-11 Sat & Sun ☎ (01283) 703170

Burton Bridge Golden Delicious, Bridge Bitter, Burton Porter, Stairway to Heaven; guest beer Ⓗ

Acquired by the Burton Bridge Brewery in 2011, this comfortable, cosy local is at the end of an 18th-century terrace of cottages, but was converted into a pub in the early 19th century for workers at a nearby brickworks. Internally, it features a narrow central bar leading at one end to a room served through a hatch, and at the opposite end to an impressive oak-panelled room. Quiz night is Monday, bingo Tuesday. An interesting range of books is available. Q❀♣P(V3)

Ockbrook

Royal Oak

55 Green Lane, DE72 3SE

11.30-2.30, 5-11 (11.30 Fri); 11.30-3, 5-11.30 Sat; 12-11 Sun ☎ (01332) 662378 royaloakockbrook.com

Draught Bass; guest beers Ⓗ

An attractive 18th-century pub with a number of small rooms. Run by the Wilson family since Coronation year, they have brought about many improvements while retaining the original character and features. Excellent home-cooked food is served every lunchtime and Monday to Friday evenings (no food Tue eve). A large function room allows the pub to host many community and public events including live music and open mic nights. Outside there are two pleasant gardens, one with a play area for children.

Q❀◐♿♣P(9,9A)

Openwoodgate

Black Bull's Head

2 Kilburn Lane, DE56 0SF

12-11 (10.30 Sun) ☎ 07860 757741

blackbullshead.com

Greene King Abbot; Oakham Bishops Farewell; guest beers Ⓗ

Two-roomed former Greene King pub, now a welcoming free house serving up to eight real ales plus ciders. Four additional real ales and four ciders are served in the Bedlam Bar, which is open Friday-Sunday. The Black Bull's Head was crowned local CAMRA Pub of the Year in both 2013 and 2014.

Q♿♣P

Over Haddon

Lathkil Hotel

School Lane, DE45 1JE

11-11; 12-10.30 Sun ☎ (01629) 812501 lathkil.co.uk

Everards Tiger; guest beers Ⓗ

This pub overlooks a masterpiece of Peak District scenery, marvellous in any weather. Walking in, one side is an old-fashioned bar room with a real fire and oak beams, while the larger room opposite, again with a log-burning fire, is where diners enjoy superb home-cooked meals. The covered beer garden is the perfect place to while away summer evenings with a pint. Dogs are welcome in the bar, but walkers should please remove their boots at the door.

Q❀◐P(178)

Parwich

Sycamore Inn

DE6 1QL (near church) SK187543

12-2, 7 (6 Thu & Fri)-11; 12-11 Sat & Sun

☎ (01335) 390212

Robinsons Double Hop, Old Tom Ⓗ

A true hub in the centre of a picturesque village that feels remote, though is only 15 minutes' drive from Ashbourne. The landlady took on the village store a few years back and runs it from a side room off the bar corridor, as well as serving well-kept beers from Robinsons, including Old Tom when in season. It has a small single-room bar, although side rooms are in use occasionally. It regularly features in the local CAMRA Pub of the Year awards. Q❀◐♣P

Ripley

Beehive Inn

151 Peasehill Road, Peasehill, DE5 3JN

5.30-11; 4.30-midnight Thu & Fri; 12-midnight Sat & Sun

☎ (01773) 749593

Beer range varies Ⓖ

On the edge of town, this three-roomed free house is a hub for local rugby and pub league teams. Since 2012, the opening of a bar in a building at the top end of the garden called the Honey Pot has proved popular, with up to four real ales and several ciders always on the go there. The Beehive is the winner of the first-ever local CAMRA Cider Pub of the Year competition. ❀♣P

Red Lion

Market Place, DE5 3BS

8am-midnight (1am Fri & Sat) ☎ (01773) 512875

Greene King Abbot; Marston's Pedigree; guest beers Ⓗ

Dating from the 1960s, this former home brewery house faces the fine Victorian town hall, and is at the heart of a vibrant, well-pubbed market town. Now a Wetherspoon outlet, its comprehensive selection of seven guest beers should satisfy the most ardent ale enthusiast. You have to pay to use the adjoining car park. Q◐♿P

Talbot Taphouse

1 Butterley Hill, DE5 3LT

5-11; 12-11.30 Fri & Sat; 12-11 Sun ☎ (01773) 742626

amberales.co.uk/brewerytap

Amber Derbyshire Gold, Original Black Stout, Barnes Wallis; guest beers Ⓗ

The eye-catching Amber Ales tap occupies a flat-iron site, and sits handily between the town centre and Midland Railway heritage centre. Renovated in 2009, the Victorian former Shipstone's house is blissfully free of electronic accoutrements, with the traditional games of bar billiards and table skittles holding sway. Innovation in brewing is the name of the game here, with experimental brews frequently featured, and beer safaris organised by the nearby brewery. Q♣●P🚌(91,92)🐾📶

Sawley

Nags Head Inn

Wilne Road, NG10 3AL

🕐 11-11.30 (midnight Fri & Sat); 12-11 Sun

☎ (0115) 973 2983

Marston's Burton Bitter, Pedigree; guest beer Ⓗ

Early 19th-century inn close to Sawley Marina in the historic area of Old Sawley, with friendly staff serving handpumped ales from the Marston's range. A flagstone floor and low ceilings help to create a lively atmosphere in the rustic bar, with a quieter ambience in the intimate lounge. Good-value home-cooked food with changing specials is served lunchtimes and early evenings Monday to Saturday. ❀◑◐♿♣P🚌🐾

White Lion Ⓛ

Tamworth Road, NG10 3AT

🕐 2-11.30; 12-midnight Fri-Sun ☎ (0115) 946 3061

Blue Monkey BG Sips; Draught Bass; guest beers Ⓗ

An 18th-century pub that reopened as a free house in 2011 after extensive refurbishment. It is a traditional two-room venue with a central bar, and serves up to six draught beers, including some from its own microbrewery. Up to four real ciders are also available. Close to the thriving Sawley marina and historic church, the pub boasts a large rear garden and boules pitch. Open fires add warmth during the winter months. There are no gaming machines or jukebox.

Q❀♣●P🚌(15)🐾📶

Shirland

Shoulder of Mutton Ⓛ

Hallfieldgate Lane, DE55 6AA (on B6013, Wessington-Shirland crossroads)

🕐 5-11; closed Tue; 11-11.30 Fri & Sat; 11-10.30 Sun

☎ (01773) 834992

Beer range varies Ⓗ

Eclectic, 16th-century traditional drinking den, nestling on the edge of Amber Valley. The beer garden offers spectacular views and sunsets. It is a true free house where real people enjoy real ale from small breweries; there is no beer list on the wall because the ales change daily. The regular customers are drawn from far and wide, fuelling the unique, easy atmosphere created by the irrepressible landlord and landlady. Dogs and hikers are welcome. Check out the teacups.

Q❀▲♣P🐾📶

Smalley

Bell

35 Main Road, DE7 6EF (on A608)

🕐 12-2.30, 5-11; 11.30-11 Fri-Sun ☎ (01332) 880635

🌐 thebellsmalley.co.uk

> Not all chemicals are bad. Without chemicals such as hydrogen and oxygen, for example, there would be no way to make water, a vital ingredient in beer.
> **Dave Barry**

Castle Rock Harvest Pale; Marston's Pedigree; Sharp's Doom Bar; guest beers Ⓗ

Near Shipley Country Park, this mid-19th century inn has three rooms in which brewing and other memorabilia adorn the walls. A drinkers' pub, it serves three regular beers plus guests, but is also renowned for food, with a good and varied menu including daily home-made specials (no food Sun eves). Accommodation is in three self-catering apartments in converted stables, and there is a large attractive garden. Weekday opening hours may be extended in the summer. Quiz night is Wednesday. Q❀🛏◑◐P🚌(H1,AMB)📶

South Normanton

Clock Inn

107 Market Street, DE55 2AA

🕐 4-11 (midnight Fri); 12-midnight Sat; 12-11 Sun

☎ (01773) 811396 🌐 theclockinn.co.uk

Jennings Cumberland Ale; Peak Ales Swift Nick; guest beer Ⓗ

A multiple-roomed pub, with lounge and public bar areas both served by a central bar. It has a pleasant garden to the rear with seating, and a covered smoking area. Sky Sports is available in both rooms on large projection screens. Look out for the Clocktober Fest. Dogs are welcome in one room.

❀♣P🚌(9.1,9.2)🐾📶

Devonshire Arms 🏆

137 Market Street, DE55 2AA

🕐 12-midnight ☎ (01773) 810748

Beer range varies Ⓗ

Genuine free house which offers up to five real ales and three real ciders/perries. A home-cooked food menu is available every day except Sunday, when a popular carvery is offered. Vegetarians, vegans and coeliacs are all catered for, and specials are available each day. Sky Sports and BT Sport are shown on up to four big screens. Local CAMRA Pub of the Year for the past few years.

◑◐♿♣●P🚌(9.1,9.2)🐾📶

Villager Ⓛ

Church Street, DE55 2DH

🕐 3-11; 12-1am Fri & Sat; 12-11 Sun ☎ (01773) 861798

Dancing Duck Abduction; Sharp's Doom Bar; Welbeck Abbey Henrietta; guest beers Ⓗ

Two-room hostelry with a central connecting bar. An additional pool room is to the rear with a free jukebox. Food is served every day. There is a quiz on Sunday night and live entertainment on Saturday night. Two LocAles are usually on handpump, with Dancing Duck, Welbeck Abbey, Lincoln Green and Spire Brewery all featuring recently alongside the house beer, Doom Bar. With the collectors' card you buy 10 pints and get one free. The pub is child-friendly week nights, and until 9pm at weekends. There is ample car parking.

Q❀◑♣P🚌(9.2,9.1)📶

Staveley

All Inn Ⓛ

Lowgates, S43 3TX (on A619)

🕐 5-11.30 (1am Fri); 1-1am Sat; 1-11.30 Sun

☎ (01246) 473303

Raw Blonde Pale; guest beers Ⓗ

Family-run, friendly pub which has deservedly become popular with the local community. It has a central bar flanked by a smart lounge area to the left and, to the right, a larger sports bar where pub games are played. These include dominoes, pool, darts and poker, while widescreen TVs feature sports events. Usually there are two beers from the nearby Raw Brewing Company on the bar, plus two guests from other micros, often unusual for the area. ❀♿♣P🚌📶

Sutton cum Duckmanton

Arkwright Arms 𝕃

Chesterfield Road, S44 5JG (A632 between Chesterfield and Bolsover)

🕐 11-11.30 (midnight Thu-Sat); 11-11 Sun

☎ (01246) 232053 🌐 arkwrightarms.co.uk

Beer range varies Ⓗ

A free house with a 'Brewers' Tudor' front. A changing range of 10 guest ales, many from local micros, is complemented by 12 ciders and four perries. Beer festivals are held at Easter and bank holidays, with mini events throughout the year. Quality food is served until 8pm Monday to Saturday, and until 3pm Sunday. The spacious beer garden has play equipment for children. A winner of numerous local CAMRA awards, including Cider Pub of the Year and Pub of the Year.
❀◑♣●P🚌🐾📶

Wardlow Mires

Three Stags' Heads ★

SK17 8RW (jct A623/B6465)

🕐 closed Mon-Thu; 7-11 Fri; 11-11 Sat; 12-10.30 Sun

☎ (01298) 872268

Abbeydale Brimstone, Absolution; guest beer Ⓗ

A quaint 300-year-old pub with two small rooms, stone-flagged floors and low ceilings. Unspoilt, it is one of the few pubs in the area identified as having a nationally important historic interior. An ancient range warms the bar and the house dogs – the house beer, Black Lurcher, is named after one of them. The food is locally sourced, with game a speciality in season. Q❀◑Ä●P🚌(173)🐾

Whaley Bridge

Shepherds Arms

7 Old Road, SK23 7HR

🕐 3 (12 Sat)-midnight; 2-midnight Sun ☎ (01663) 732840

Marston's Burton Bitter, Pedigree; guest beers Ⓗ

This little gem of a pub nestling close to the centre of the village is an attractive, whitewashed, stone building which has been preserved unspoilt, conveying the feel of the farmhouse it once was. The unchanged taproom is a delight, with an open fire, flagged floor and scrubbed tabletops. Additionally, there is a comfortable lounge also with an open fire in winter. The changing guest beers are selected from the Marston's range. In attractive walking country, hikers are welcome.
Q❀⇌♣P🚌(199,60)

Whitehough

Old Hall Inn 🏆 𝕃

Chinley, SK23 6EJ (750yds off B6062)

🕐 12-midnight ☎ (01663) 750529 🌐 old-hall-inn.co.uk

Marston's Burton Bitter; guest beers Ⓗ

The 14th-century Whitehough Hall forms part of this quintessential country inn which has won the Great British Pub award for best cask pub in the region for several years and is a regular entry in this Guide. Eight ales, including seven changing guests from quality local micros, complement those available at the adjacent Paper Mill Inn (under the same ownership). A popular menu features dishes using local produce. Well-attended beer festivals run in September and February.
🐎❀🛏◑Ä⇌(Chinley)●P🚌(189,190)🐾📶

Wirksworth

Royal Oak

North End, DE4 4FG

🕐 8-11.30 (midnight Fri & Sat); 12-3, 8-11 Sun

☎ (01629) 823000

Draught Bass; Timothy Taylor Landlord; Whim Hartington IPA; guest beers Ⓗ

Excellent, ultra-traditional local near the marketplace, highlighted at night by rows of fairy lights. The bar features old pictures of local interest and there is also a pool room and smoking grotto. The Oak enjoys a long-standing reputation for Draught Bass, and always has five ales from which to choose, including a LocAle. The Ecclesbourne Valley Railway visitor attraction is close by, and this former lead mining town is an architectural gem with much to interest the historian. Q❀🚌(6.1)🐾

Beers suitable for vegetarians and vegans

A number of cask and bottle-fermented beers in the Good Beer Guide are listed as suitable for vegetarians and vegans. The main ingredients used in cask beer production are malted grain, hops, yeast and water, and these present no problems for drinkers who wish to avoid animal products. But most brewers of cask beer use isinglass as a clearing agent: isinglass is derived from the bladders of certain fish, including the sturgeon. Isinglass is added to a cask when it leaves the brewery and attracts yeast cells and protein, which fall to the bottom of the container. Other clearing agents – notably Irish moss, derived from seaweed – can be used in place of isinglass and the Guide feels that brewers should take a serious look at replacing isinglass with plant-derived finings, especially as the sturgeon is an endangered species.

Vegans avoid dairy products: lactose, a by-product of cheese making, is used in milk stout, of which Mackeson is the best-known example. Some beers are brewed with honey, which is also unacceptable to vegans.

A number of entries in the Guide refer to the pubs' support for the LocAle scheme. The aim of the scheme is to get publicans to stock at least one cask beer that comes from a local brewery no further than 20 miles away. It also encourages publicans to use the Direct Delivery Scheme run by SIBA, the Society of Independent Brewers (see p662). SIBA members deliver direct to pubs in their localities instead of going through the central warehouses of pub-owning companies.

The aim is a simple one: to cut down on 'beer miles'. Research by CAMRA shows that food and drink transport accounts for 25 per cent of all HGV vehicle miles in Britain. Taking into account the miles that ingredients have travelled on top of distribution journeys, an imported lager produced by a multi-national brewery could have notched up more than 24,000 'beer miles' by the time it reaches a pub.

Supporters of LocAle point out that £10 spent on locally-supplied goods generates £25 for the local economy. Keeping trade local helps enterprises, creates more economic activity and jobs, and makes other services more viable. The scheme also generates consumer support for local breweries.

Support for LocAle has grown at a rapid pace. It's been embraced by pubs and CAMRA branches throughout England and has now crossed the borders into Scotland and Wales.

For more information, see the CAMRA website www.camra.org.uk and type 'locale' into the search window.

What is CAMRA LocAle?

- An initiative that promotes pubs which sell locally-brewed real ale.
- The scheme builds on a growing consumer demand for quality local produce and an increased awareness of 'green' issues.
- The LocAle scheme was created in 2007 by CAMRA's Nottingham branch which wanted to help support the tradition of brewing within Nottinghamshire, following the demise of local brewer Hardys & Hansons.

Everyone benefits from local pubs stocking locally brewed real ale...

- Public houses, as stocking local real ales can increase pub visits
- Consumers, who enjoy greater beer choice and locally brewed beer
- Local brewers, who gain from increased sales and get better feedback from consumers
- The local economy, because more money is spent and retained in the local economy
- The environment, due to fewer 'beer miles' resulting in less road congestion and pollution
- Tourism, due to an increased sense of local identity and pride – let's celebrate what makes our locality different.

DEVON

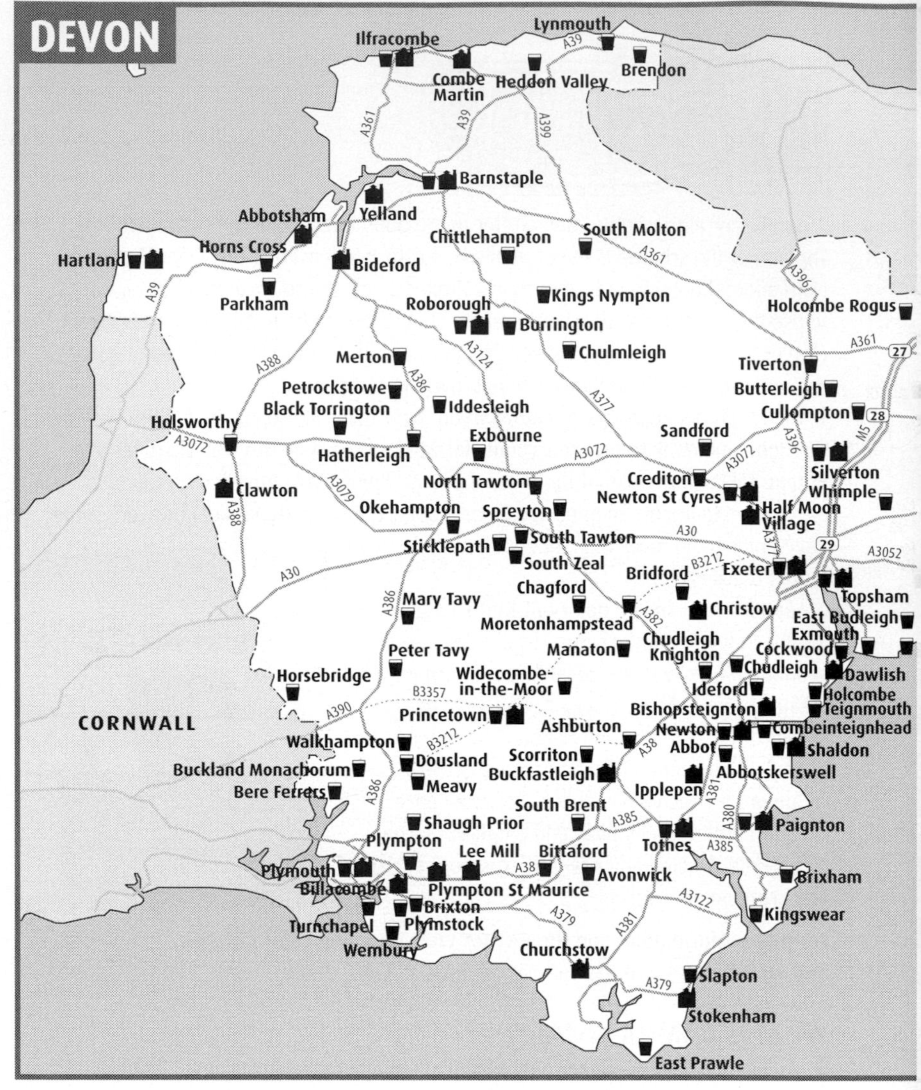

Abbotskerswell

Court Farm Inn

Wilton Way, TQ12 5NY

11-11 (01626) 361866 courtfarminn.com

Draught Bass; Otter Bitter; St Austell Tribute; guest beer H

Nestling in the centre of the village, this listed 17th-century Devon longhouse was converted from a farm around 50 years ago. The lounge bar has flagged floors, beamed ceilings and stone walls. The long bar has four handpumps. Pool and darts are played in the public bar and an upper room is used as an additional dining area and function room. Food is served lunchtimes and evenings Monday-Wednesday, all day Thursday-Sunday. The garden is popular in summer and has a heated smoking area. Dogs are welcome in the public bar. P (177)

Ashburton

Dartmoor Lodge Hotel

Peartree Cross, TQ13 7JW

11-11; 12-10.30 Sun (01364) 652232 dartmoorlodge.co.uk

Beer range varies H

A good selection of local real ales, including some from Butcombe and Dartmoor breweries, is served at this 24-bedroom roadside hotel on the edge of the Dartmoor National Park and the town of Ashburton. There is a friendly, comfortable atmosphere in the oak-beamed bar and restaurant area which, in winter, has a welcoming log fire. Good-quality local food is served all day every day. The location makes it an ideal base for walkers, cyclists and canoeists, and rooms are available for meetings. Ashton Still cider is sold. Q P (88,X38)

Exeter Inn 🄻

26 West Street, TQ13 7DU (on main road through centre of Ashburton opp church)

11-2.30, 5-11 (midnight Fri & Sat); 12-3, 7-10.30 Sun

☎ (01364) 652013

Dartmoor IPA, Legend 🄷

The oldest pub in Ashburton, built in 1131, with additions in the 17th century. A friendly local that originally housed the workers constructing the nearby church, it was used by Sir Francis Drake on his journeys to London. There are seated drinking areas either side of the entrance hall in the main bar, which is L-shaped, rustic and wood panelled, with a canopy. There is another bar at the rear served via a small hatch and counter. Local Thompstone's cider is on sale.

Q ♣ (88,X38)

Ashill

Ashill Inn

EX15 3NL

12-2.30 (not Mon), 5.30-11.30; 12-4, 6.30-10.30 Sun

☎ (01884) 840506 ashillinndevon.co.uk

Otter Bitter; guest beers 🄷

A Grade II-listed inn, built in 1835, and located down narrow lanes in the Culm Valley. It is a charming small pub. The comfortable bar serves local South-west brewery ales. There is a large stone alcove fireplace at one end of the main room, with a separate restaurant area to one side. Good-value food is available, with produce mainly sourced from local farms. Live music and special events are often featured. Q♣P

Avonwick

Avon Inn 🄻

TQ10 9NB

11-10.30 ☎ (01364) 73475 avon-inn.co.uk

Dartmoor Legend, Jail Ale; Hunter's Half Bore; Otter Bitter 🄷

The Avon is at the crossroads in the centre of the village, and is open until at least 10.30pm daily, but may close later. The lounge is now the restaurant. The pub is the centre of the community, hosting various events including quizzes and live music. Up to eight ciders are on offer from Ashridge, Countryman, Sandford Orchards and Westons. No food Sunday evenings.

♿♣P(91)

INDEPENDENT BREWERIES

Barum Barnstaple
Bays Paignton
Beer Engine Newton St Cyres
Black Tor Christow (NEW)
Branscombe Vale Branscombe
Bridgetown Totnes
Clearwater Bideford
Combe Martin Combe Martin
Country Life Abbotsham
Dartmoor Princetown
Devon Earth Buckfastleigh
Exe Valley Silverton
Exeter Exeter
Fat Pig Exeter (NEW)
Forge Hartland
Garage Plympton St Maurice (brewing suspended)
Hanlons Half Moon Village
Holsworthy Clawton
Hunter's Ipplepen
Isca Dawlish
Jollyboat Bideford
New Lion Totnes (NEW)
Noss Beer Works Lee Mill
Otter Luppitt
Platform 5 Newton Abbot
Plymouth Plymouth
Quercus Churchstow
Red Rock Bishopsteignton
South Hams Stokenham
Summerskills Billacombe
Tavy Roborough
Teignworthy Newton Abbot
Topsham Topsham
Two Beach Shaldon (NEW)
Wizard Ilfracombe
Yelland Manor Yelland (NEW)

Axminster

Axminster Inn

Silver Street, EX13 5AH

10.30-1am (midnight Sun & Mon) (01297) 34947
axinn.co.uk

Palmers Copper Ale, Best Bitter, 200, Tally Ho! H

A friendly traditional pub, lying just off the town centre, with a real log fire and lovely enclosed beer garden. It offers a good range of Palmer's ales. Good-value home-cooked food, often locally sourced, is served lunchtimes and evenings, including a roast on Sundays. Live music is featured at least four times a week. Free Wi-Fi is available, and there is a skittle alley and dartboard. Children are welcome, and the pub is dog-friendly. Sheppy's real cider is served.

Barnstaple

Reform Inn

Reform Street, Pilton, EX31 1PD

11.30-11 (midnight Fri & Sat); 12-11 Sun
(01271) 323164

Barum Original, EPA; guest beer H

Well-established popular community local and the brewery tap for Barum Brewery. From the main road, look above roof level to locate the pub sign. The skittle alley is home to the annual Green Man beer festival in July, and other regular beer festivals are held during the year. In the public bar, where there is a pool table, open mic evenings are held on Mondays, with bands playing on alternate Fridays. The lounge bar is quieter.

Bere Ferrers

Olde Plough Inn

Fore Street, PL20 7JG (close to church and river)

11-3, 6-11; 11-11 Sat; 12-11 Sun (01822) 840358

Penpont An Howl; Sharp's Doom Bar, Own; guest beer H

A 16th-century village inn with outstanding views over the River Tavy from the beer garden, and only a 15-minute walk from the station on the picturesque Tamar Valley line. Inside, there are flagstones, exposed stonework, beams, real fires and a welcoming atmosphere popular with both locals and visitors. Live music, acoustic and jam sessions feature, along with fish and chip suppers and curry nights. Up to four ales are sourced from local and popular national brewers. Real cider is available in summer. Q (87)

Bittaford

Horse & Groom

Exeter Road, PL21 0EL

12-11 (midnight Fri & Sat) (01752) 892358

Dartmoor Jail Ale; Hunter's Half Bore; guest beers H

A family-owned pub that does good home-cooked food and boasts six pumps, with Jail Ale and Horse & Groom Ale as the regulars. The other pumps predominantly serve ales from local breweries in south Devon and Cornwall. Real ciders are also available. The venue has a long bar and a separate dining area. Quiz night is Friday, and a summer beer festival is held on the first weekend of July, supporting local charities. Third-pint tapas are available. Q P

Black Torrington

Torridge Inn

Broad Street, EX21 5PT SS465056

12-3 (not Tue), 6.30-11; 12-11 Sat; 12-10.30 Sun
(01409) 231243 thetorridgeinn.co.uk

St Austell Tribute; guest beer H

Friendly village local dating from the 18th century and close to both the Tarka Trail and the Ruby Trail walks. A large log fire welcomes in winter, while in summer the pleasant beer garden affords attractive views of the Torridge Valley. At least two real ales are always available (with a discount scheme for CAMRA members), together with Sam's cider from Winkleigh. A good selection of home-cooked locally-sourced food is served, with Sunday lunches particularly popular.
Q P (639,642)

Brendon

Staghunters Inn

EX35 6PS SS767481

12-11 (01598) 741222 staghunters.com

St Austell Trelawny, Proper Job; guest beers G

The Staghunters is a historic building on the site of an old abbey within the Exmoor National Park, and is an ideal base for exploring the local area. Up to five regularly changing real ales are served on gravity, with the emphasis on West Country brewers. A wide range of locally-sourced food is available, and the venue also has 14 well-appointed rooms. Dogs are welcome in the bar and allowed to stay overnight for a nominal charge.
Q P

Bridford

Bridford Inn

EX6 7HT

12-11 (midnight Sat & Sun) (01647) 252250
bridfordinn.co.uk

Dartmoor Jail Ale; guest beers H

A 17th-century Devon longhouse within the Dartmoor National Park which was converted to a pub in 1968 and now also houses a village shop. It has a spacious open-plan interior for both drinkers and diners, with old oak beams and an inglenook fireplace complete with old bread oven and a woodburner. Fresh home-cooked quality food is served to order. Outside there is a beer garden with picnic tables and stunning views. Traditional ciders from Sandford Orchards are always available.
Q P (360,361)

Brixham

Queen's Arms

31 Station Hill, TQ5 8BN

4-11; 2-midnight Fri; 12-midnight Sat; 12-11 Sun
(01803) 852074 thequeensarmsbrixham.co.uk

Beer range varies H

Away from the town centre up a short hill, this end-of-terrace pub is well worth seeking out. A friendly one-roomed bar with stone walls and discounted ale (£2.50 a pint), it supports many community activities including live music at weekends, ale events and pub sports teams. One beer each from Hunter's and Oakham take up two of the six handpumps, with the others sourced countrywide, but mainly from Devon. South Devon CAMRA Pub of the Year 2014.

Brixton

Foxhound Inn 🏆 L
PL8 2AH
⏲ 11-11 (midnight Fri & Sat); 12-11 Sun ☎ (01752) 880271
🌐 foxhoundinn.co.uk
Courage Best Bitter; guest beers Ⓗ
An 18th-century former coaching house in a rural village just east of Plymouth, well served by a frequent daytime bus service. The pub has two separate bars and a small restaurant. Traditional English meals are home cooked using locally sourced ingredients from a nearby National Trust farm. Look out for Red Coat, an ale crafted by the landlord, among four guest ales. A monthly charity quiz night is held. Local CAMRA Country Pub of the Year 2014. **Q🍼❀◑▲♣●P🚌**(93,94)🐾

Broadhembury

Drewe Arms
EX14 3NF
⏲ 12-11 (10.30 Sun) ☎ (01404) 841267
🌐 drewearmsinn.co.uk
Bays Gold; Exeter County Best; Otter Amber; guest beers Ⓗ
A Grade II-listed 15th-century thatched pub, with a secluded garden, set in a picturesque estate village within the Blackdown Hills. This is a friendly and welcoming family-run venue, with the emphasis on local real ales and produce. Good-value food is served lunchtimes and evenings every day, and a takeaway menu is always available. The pub holds an annual beer festival over the Easter weekend.
Q🍼❀◑▲♣●P🐾

Buckland Monachorum

Drake Manor Inn L
PL20 7NA
⏲ 11.30-2.30, 6.30-11; 11.30-11.30 Fri & Sat; 12-11 Sun
☎ (01822) 853892 🌐 drakemanorinn.co.uk
Dartmoor Jail Ale; Sharp's Doom Bar; guest beer Ⓗ
A cosy and friendly pub, dating from the 16th century, in a pleasant village on the edge of Dartmoor. It attracts a regular clientele who are happy to be assisted with the daily crossword. The inviting traditional interior features an intimate meeting area, a public bar, and a restaurant area in which to sample the good food. The garden, with a stream, is an enjoyable suntrap. Good-value food is served both lunchtimes and evenings.
Q🍼❀🛏◑♣●🚌🐾📶

Budleigh Salterton

Salterton Arms L
22 Chapel Street, EX9 6LX
⏲ 11-11.30; 12-11 Sun ☎ (01395) 445048
Otter Ale; St Austell Dartmoor Best Bitter; guest beer Ⓗ
A local pub with a decor of Cotswold stone floors and bare wood. A large variety of meals is available, served in both the main bar and the upstairs mezzanine area. The three TVs in the bar are well spaced apart as occasionally they show different sporting events. In addition to the regular beers there is a continually changing guest ale, and real cider from Green Valley. Euchre is played and the local ukulele group meets Monday evenings.
◑♿♣●🚌(157,357)🐾📶

Burrington

Portsmouth Arms
EX37 9ND (on A377 approx 4 miles S of Umberleigh)
⏲ 4-11; 12-11 Fri-Sun ☎ (01769) 561117
Otter Bitter; Skinner's Betty Stogs Ⓗ**; guest beer** Ⓖ
A former coaching inn in the heart of the Taw Valley, making it an ideal base for walking and fishing. The front bar area, with original oak beams and a woodburner, provides a warm and welcoming atmosphere in winter, while in summer stunning views are afforded from the decked rear veranda. There is good accommodation and ample parking. The pub serves well-sourced local food every day until 9pm. Well-behaved children and dogs welcome. **Q🍼❀🛏◑⇌♣P🐾📶**

Butterleigh

Butterleigh Inn L
The Green, EX15 1PN (opp church)
⏲ 12-2.30 (not Mon), 6-11; 12-2.30, 6-midnight Fri & Sat; 12-3 Sun ☎ (01884) 855433 🌐 butterleighinn.co.uk
Cotleigh Tawny Owl; Dartmoor IPA; Otter Ale; guest beer Ⓗ
Situated in this small, quaint village, the Butterleigh is an excellent country pub, with a mixed clientele creating a great atmosphere with diverse conversation. Good-value home-cooked food is served lunchtimes and evenings, Tuesday to Saturday, with a carvery Sunday lunchtime. There is always a choice of four real ales, one being a LocAle, plus three real ciders: Sandford Orchards' Devon Scrumpy, Winkleigh Sam's Medium plus a rotating guest. There is a main bar, lounge and a modern dining room. **Q🍼❀🛏◑♿♣●P🐾📶**

Chagford

Globe Inn L
9 High Street, TQ13 8AJ
⏲ 11-11.30 (midnight Fri & Sat); 12-10.30 Sun
☎ (01647) 433485 🌐 theglobeinnchagford.co.uk
Dartmoor IPA; Otter Bitter Ⓗ**, Ale; guest beer** Ⓖ
Overlooking the parish church in this historic stannary town, the Globe was once a coaching inn and coopery. It has evolved into a focal point for the town, providing good food, music evenings, a cinema club and numerous other events and functions – winning the South West Community Hero Award in 2012. It has a splendid traditional public bar and another separate bar, both with big open fires. A small courtyard garden is at the rear and a car park is nearby. The cider is Westons Old Rosie. **Q🍼❀🛏◑♣●P🚌🐾📶**

Sandy Park Inn L
Sandy Park, TQ13 8JW (on A382 Moretonhampstead-Whiddon Down road)
⏲ 11-11 (4-11 Mon & Tue winter); 12-10.30 Sun
☎ (01647) 433267 🌐 sandyparkinn.co.uk
Dartmoor IPA, Jail Ale; Otter Bitter Ⓗ
A thatched free house thought to be 17th century, the bar has a large open fireplace, ancient beams, stone floor and high-backed wooden bench seating. Beyond is a small snug set around a large table. There is a separate room beyond the front door and a small car park at the front with the garden reached by steps at the side of the building. Castle Drogo (NT), Fingle Bridge and the moorland town of Chagford are nearby. Good home-cooked food is served (not Sun eve or Mon). The cider range varies. **Q🍼❀🛏◑●P🚌🐾📶**

Chardstock

George Inn 𝕃
EX13 7BX
⏲ 12-3, 6-10; 12-4 Sun ☎ (01460) 220241
🌐 georgeinnchardstock.co.uk
Otter Ale; guest beers 🄷
An attractive 15th-century thatched church house in the heart of a rural village near the Devon, Somerset and Dorset borders. It is Grade II-listed. The layout provides two bar areas, a dining room and a pool table, with a dartboard up some stairs. A varied menu caters for all tastes and is sourced locally, with Sunday lunch offering traditional roasts. There are four en-suite rooms. Look out for the superb linenfold panelled screen and centuries-old graffiti. Q🛋❀🛏◑◗♣P🐾📶

Chittlehampton

Bell Inn 𝕃
The Square, EX37 9QL (opp St Hieritha's parish church) SS636254
⏲ 11-3, 6-midnight; 11-midnight Fri & Sat; 12-11 Sun
☎ (01769) 540368 🌐 thebellatchittlehampton.co.uk
Exmoor Ale; Otter Bitter; guest beers 🄷
This popular village local has been in the same family for more than 30 years. Before entering, note the etched window commemorating its local CAMRA Pub of the Year win in 2007. As well as the regularly changing selection of ales on handpump, more may be available on gravity – check the blackboard on the right-hand side of the bar. There are two patios, a conservatory, and an orchard which is home to alpacas. Well-behaved children and dogs welcome. 🛋❀◑◗♿♣🚌(658,859)🐾📶

Chudleigh

Bishop Lacy Inn 𝕃
Fore Street, TQ13 0HY
⏲ 12-midnight (1am Fri & Sat) ☎ (01626) 854585
Beer range varies 🄷
A warm welcome is assured from the ebullient landlady at this Grade II-listed building opposite the church, named after the Bishop of Exeter 1420-1455. The active public bar is dominated by an enormous fireplace, with hooks for hanging hams, and doll witches suspended from the bar. Beers are always West Country and sometimes very local, from Hunter's or Exeter. The other bar is more food/family oriented, serving excellent home-cooked fare. Sambuca, the pub dog, welcomes other sensible canines. 🛋◑◗⛺♣🚌(39,182)🐾📶

Chudleigh Knighton

Anchor Inn
Plymouth Road, TQ13 0EN (on old A38)
⏲ 12 (11 Fri & Sat)-11; 12-10.30 Sun ☎ (01626) 852366
Beer range varies 🄷
On the old A38 and opposite the village hall, this was once a coaching inn on the Exeter to Plymouth turnpike. The beers are mainly West Country and dispensed from three handpumps in a delightful, and largely unspoilt, small public bar. The larger saloon has a big open fireplace and was once a vet's surgery, but now offers coffee and meals including an all-day breakfast and Sunday carvery (12-2pm). To the rear is a smoking area, leading to a pleasant garden. Q🛋❀◑◗♿♣🚌(39,182)🐾📶

Chulmleigh

Old Court House
South Molton Street, EX18 7BW
⏲ 11-11 ☎ (01769) 580045 🌐 oldcourthouseinn.co.uk
Dartmoor IPA; Exmoor Ale; guest beer 🄷
Grade II-listed historic local with three handpumps and Thatchers Traditional Dry cider. A wall in one of the bedrooms still bears the coat of arms that marks the time when Charles I stayed here in 1634. The real fire adds to the warm welcome in the bar and there is a separate restaurant to the rear. A CAMRA discount of 10p per pint is available to members. The Thursday evening quiz supports local charities. 🛋❀🛏◑◗♿♣🚌(377)🐾📶

Cockwood

Anchor Inn 𝕃
EX6 8RA (just off A379, outside Starcross, next to Cockwood harbour) SX976807
⏲ 11-11; 11.30-10.30 Sun ☎ (01626) 890203
🌐 anchorinncockwood.com
Otter Ale; St Austell Tribute; guest beers 🄷
On picturesque Cockwood harbour, this 450-year-old inn and former seaman's mission has many old settles, timber panelling, low beams and snugs, with an impressive display of old nautical memorabilia all around. It has an extensive award-winning seafood menu, with mussels the speciality. Haunted by a friendly ghost and his dog, this is a really atmospheric Devon gem. Being close to the main GWR line, it is a steam train spotters' paradise. Guest ales are all LocAle. Limited parking, with a bus stop over the bridge.
Q❀◑◗♿⛺♣P🚌(2)🐾

Ship Inn
Church Road, EX6 8NU (just off A379, outside Starcross, close to Cockwood harbour)
⏲ 11-11; 12-10.30 Sun ☎ (01626) 890373
🌐 shipinncockwood.co.uk
Dartmoor Jail Ale; Exmoor Ale; St Austell Tribute; Sharp's Doom Bar; guest beers 🄷
A busy family-run pub, close to the pretty harbour at Cockwood, with a large beer garden with views of the estuary, and a roaring log fire for the winter. The Ship is popular with drinkers and diners alike, offering a choice of four regular ales, and an excellent food menu. Meals are made with local produce where possible, including a varied choice of locally caught fish. Q🛋❀◑◗⛺♣P🚌(2)🐾📶

Colyton

Gerrard Arms 𝕃
St Andrew's Square, EX24 6JN
⏲ 12-3, 5.30-11 (1am Fri); 12-3, 6-midnight Sat; 12-3, 7-10.30 Sun ☎ (01297) 552588 🌐 thegerrardarms.co.uk
Branscombe Vale Branoc; Draught Bass; Otter Ale; guest beer 🄷
Busy one-bar pub dating back to 1506 and next to the church in this delightful little town with lots of lovely old cottages and tangled narrow streets and alleyways. There is a safe courtyard at the back. The home-made food is good value but only served on Friday and Saturday, with a traditional roast lunch available on Sundays. In summer, the lunchtime session may run on. Colyton station on the Seaton Tramway is a level walk.
Q🛋❀◑◗⛺♣🚌(885,20)🐾

Combeinteignhead

Wild Goose

TQ12 4RA (between Newton Abbot and Shaldon on S side of river)
11-3, 5.30-11; 12-3, 7-11 Sun ☎ (01626) 872241
thewildgooseinn.co.uk
Beer range varies H
Charming 17th-century pub and restaurant with a cosy and welcoming atmosphere. A changing range of ales is offered, plus a selection of continental beers, with traditional cider coming from various producers, mainly in the South-west. Food is sourced locally. Friday night music is eclectic but good, while the Saturday night quiz is popular. An attractive garden at the rear abuts a 14th-century red sandstone church. Two holiday cottages are available to rent.
P

Crediton

Crediton Inn

28a Mill Street, EX17 1EZ (near A377 and station)
10-11; 12-3, 7-10.30 Sun ☎ (01363) 772882
crediton-inn.co.uk
Hanlon's Yellow Hammer; guest beers H
The framed deeds date this inn to 1878, with windows etched with the ancient town seal. It is a genuine free house, well supported by the locals. The handpumps have increased to 10, served by local breweries, with an ale festival in November. The skittle alley doubles as a function room. Good home-cooked food is available at weekends, with snacks and renowned Scotch eggs at other times. The bubbly owner is the longest-serving landlady in Crediton. P

Cullompton

Pony & Trap

10 Exeter Hill, EX15 1DJ (on B3181 S of town)
12-2, 5-11.30; 12-5, 8-11 Sun ☎ (01884) 34182
ponyandtrapcullompton.co.uk
Butcombe Bitter; Dartmoor IPA, Jail Ale; Otter Bitter; guest beers H
A traditional local with a good atmosphere and mixed clientele. It has a smart interior featuring a logburner, making it cosy in winter; flowers and ornaments add a homely feel. Six real ales are always on during the week, seven at weekends. Food is available Tuesday to Sunday lunchtimes, and in the evenings on request in advance. Outside is a seating area and garden. Live music features once a month, and pub games are played. Local CAMRA branch Pub of the Year 2014.
Q (1)

Dousland

Burrator Inn

PL20 6NP
11-11 (12.30am Sat); 12-11 Sun ☎ (01822) 853121
theburratorinn.com
Dartmoor IPA, Jail Ale; St Austell Tribute; Sharp's Doom Bar H
Substantial pub on the road between Yelverton and Princetown, close to the picturesque Burrator Reservoir. It has a pool table, two dartboards and a separate dining room. Home-made food and pies are produced from local suppliers and are served throughout the day. There is ample parking and a large enclosed beer garden incorporating a children's play area. A beer festival is held annually in September; a Sunday quiz night, live music and other entertainment feature regularly.
Q P

East Budleigh

Sir Walter Raleigh Inn

22 High Street, EX9 7ED (off B3178 opp Hayes Lane)
12-2.30, 6-11; 12-2.30, 7-10.30 Sun ☎ (01395) 442510
sirwalterraleighinn.co.uk
Beer range varies H
Set in the middle of the delightful village of East Budleigh, the birthplace of Sir Walter Raleigh, this free house is a truly welcoming 16th-century country inn. Good-quality pub food is served lunchtimes and evenings, and normally there are four real ales to choose from. Originally two cottages, it was then converted into a Jacobean-style hostelry. There are original wood beams throughout the two different areas. This gem is well worth a visit for good quality real ale.
Q (157)

East Prawle

Pig's Nose Inn

TQ7 2BY
12-2.30, 6-11 (closed Sun eve winter) ☎ (01548) 511209
pigsnoseinn.co.uk
Otter Ale; South Hams Devon Pride, Eddystone G
An old three-bedroomed smugglers' inn on the village green, popular with bird-watchers and coastal walkers. Gravity beers are stored on a specially made rack behind the bar. Home-cooked locally-sourced food is served. Children and dogs are welcome and have their own menus. The maritime-themed interior is cluttered with objects, children's games and knitting for adults. Local CAMRA Pub of the Year 2013. There are occasional live music events in a hall adjoining the pub.
Q

Exbourne

Red Lion

High Street, EX20 3RY (200yds N of jct with A3072) SS602018
12-11 ☎ (01837) 851551 theredlionexbourne.co.uk
Dartmoor IPA, Legend; guest beer G
Village local with an L-shaped single bar that refuses to serve any draught lagers. Casks are set at the end of the bar on stillage, along with Sam's cider from nearby Winkleigh. There is a small drinking area in front of the bar with high tables and chairs, and excellent locally-sourced food is served all day in the adjacent cosy dining area. Three charity beer festivals are held during the year. North Devon CAMRA Pub of the Year 2014.
Q P

Exeter

Fat Pig

2 John Street, EX1 1BL (behind Fore St)
5 (12 Sat)-11; 12-5 Sun ☎ (01392) 437217
fatpig-exeter.co.uk
Beer range varies H
Formerly the Coachmakers Arms, this Victorian corner local has been brought back to life as a traditional inn, featuring a range of locally-sourced

food, including the pub's own sausages, cured hams and belly pork from its herd of rare breed pigs. In addition to producing its own cider since 2013, it has become the only brewpub in the city, with a large range of styles. There are weekly quiz nights, malt whisky evenings and a home-brew competition. (Central)

Great Western Hotel

St David's Station, EX4 4NU

10-midnight (1am Fri & Sat) (01392) 274039
greatwesternhotel.co.uk

Branscombe Vale Branoc; Dartmoor Jail Ale; RCH PG Steam, Pitchfork; guest beers H

Adjacent to Exeter mainline station, this hotel is ideal for stopovers, offering a variety of 35 en-suite rooms. The Loco Bar has a good community spirit, with the enthusiastic manager's large range of ales. It has won the CAMRA branch Pub of the Year accolade twice. The Brunel restaurant has an extensive à la carte menu, while the bar serves good-value meals. The hotel also hosts conferences, meetings, parties and weddings. Q(St David's)(H)

Hour Glass Inn

21 Melbourne Street, St Leonards, EX2 4AU (approx 300yds from Exeter quayside)

12-3, 5-11 (midnight Sat); 12-10.30 Sun
(01392) 258722

Beer range varies H

A traditional pub in the back streets of Exeter, in the hub of the local area close to the quay and about five minutes' walk from the main city centre. The pub has two restaurants and a bar, serving contemporary and continental food. It is very traditional in its features, with a mixture of live entertainment including light theatre and music, which has proved popular with its eclectic group of customers. Q(S,T)

Imperial

New North Road, St David's, EX4 4AH

8am-midnight (1am Fri & Sat) (01392) 434050

Greene King Abbot H**; Ruddles Best Bitter** H/G**; guest beers** H

Large Wetherspoon pub near the university. Its spacious sunny garden offers plenty of tables and seating. Ten beers are usually available, plus guest ales, often from local breweries. Good-value food is served all day. Built in 1810 as Elmfield House, then changed to the Imperial Hotel in 1923, its attractive architecture and orangery are still there to be enjoyed. Beer festivals are regularly held throughout the year, with some showcasing local breweries. Q(St David's)P(D,50)

Mill on the Exe

Bonhay Road, St David's, EX4 3AB

10.30-11 (01392) 214464 millontheexe.co.uk

St Austell Dartmoor Best Bitter, Tribute, Proper Job; guest beer H

Beautiful riverside pub, formerly a paper mill, with a welcoming and vibrant atmosphere. It has two bars over two floors, each boasting four handpumps, with St Austell brews, seasonal and guest ales. It also stocks a selection of bottled ales, including Clouded Yellow, with more guest brewery ales to come in the future. Quality home-cooked food is served noon-9pm daily. The large garden has stunning views of Blackaller Weir. Children and dogs are welcome.
(St Thomas)P

Oddfellows

60 New North Road, EX4 4EP

12-3 (not Mon-Wed), 5-11; 12-1am Fri & Sat; 12-8 Sun
(01392) 209050 theoddfellowsbar.co.uk

St Austell Tribute, Proper Job H**; guest beers** H/G

The narrow frontage at the end of a Victorian terrace belies a deep interior and features the original 19th-century conservatory. Its cellar benefits from backing onto the old city wall. It is divided into small areas and alcoves, with sofas and rustic furniture. A friendly gastro-style pub with a varied clientele, it has weekly open mic and acoustic music nights. CAMRA members receive a 50p discount on a pint. The open kitchen enables you to watch your food being cooked.
Q(Central)

Royal Oak

79-81 Fore Street, Heavitree, EX1 2RN

11.30-11 (midnight Fri & Sat); 12-4, 7-11 Sun
(01392) 254121 heavitreeroyaloak.co.uk

Otter Amber, Ale; Young's Bitter; guest beers H

Traditional family-run pub on several bus routes, with ample parking nearby. Three regular ales, plus three guests, are usually on offer. Good-value pub food is served lunchtimes, with a traditional roast on Sundays; no food is served evenings, except for a steak/fish night on Thursdays. With a large comfortable main bar and smaller side room, the pub has a real community feel, while remaining welcoming to visitors. It has front and rear beer gardens with a covered smoking area.

Exmouth

First & Last Inn

10 Church Street, EX8 1PE (off B3178 Rolle St)

11-11 (11.30 Sat); 12-10.30 Sun (01395) 263275

Courage Best Bitter; Otter Ale H**; guest beers** H/G

Victorian hostelry near the town centre, with a public car park opposite. It is a genuine free house, with three distinct drinking areas and a patio with heated awnings. Games include pool and darts, and there is a skittle alley. Televised sport is prominent in the pub. Well-behaved dogs are welcome. Two or three guest beers are sold, usually from the West Country, and three real ciders: Green Valley, Old Rosie and Thatchers Dry. The pub has air conditioning.
(57,157)

Grapevine

2 Victoria Road, EX8 1DL

12-11 (midnight Fri & Sat); 12-4 Sun (01395) 222208

Beer range varies H

A stylish free house with a continental café ambience, which stocks a changing range of real British ales (over 100 last year) along with continental lagers and bottled beers. Green Valley Cyder is also sold. The excellent food with a regularly changing dish of the day makes the pub the ideal place for people looking for something special. Monday is quiz night, Friday sees live music, and an informal chess club has started on Tuesdays. (57,97)

Holly Tree

161 Withycombe Village Road, Withycombe Raleigh, EX8 3AN (leave A376 at Gipsy Lane lights, then turn left)

11 (12 Sun)-midnight (01395) 273440

Draught Bass; Greene King Abbot; St Austell Dartmoor Best Bitter, Proper Job; Wells Bombardier; guest beer H

A popular inn that does not sell food but concentrates on serving good beer. Although owned by St Austell, the other regular ales are sourced from a variety of breweries. The pub is well supported by the local community, with two ladies' and two gents' darts teams, six pool teams, two euchre teams and a Sunday night quiz. Dogs are welcome at all times, and families until 7pm. P (97)

Powder Monkey

2-2a The Parade, EX8 1RJ

8am-midnight (1am Fri & Sat) ☎ (01395) 280090

Greene King Abbot; Ruddles Best Bitter; guest beers H

A Wetherspoon pub named after Nancy Perriam, whose sewing skills earned her a berth in the navy where she also acted as a powder monkey. Nancy lived in nearby Tower Street. 'Powder monkey' was naval slang for boys and girls who filled shells and cartridges with gunpowder on board ships of war. The building was converted from local newspaper offices. The bar is adjacent to the central seating areas, with a number of rooms off it. Q (57)

Hartland

Hartland Quay Hotel

Hartland, EX39 6DU (head W from Hartland, through Stoke, for about 2 miles to Hartland Quay)

11-11 ☎ (01237) 441218 hartlandquayhotel.com

Dartmoor Legend; St Austell Tribute; guest beer H

Run by the same family for more than 50 years, the hotel boasts fabulous coastal views. In what was the old stables, the Wreckers' Retreat bar contains relics and pictures of wrecks, together with lifelike models of the local sea fish. Accommodation extends to 13 rooms and a cottage, with free parking for residents. Three real ales are available and good-value food is served both lunchtimes and evenings. The adjacent Hartland Quay Museum is well worth a visit. Q P

Hatherleigh

Tally Ho!

14 Market Street, EX20 3JN (opp church)

12 (11 Tue)-11 ☎ (01837) 810306

tallyhohatherleigh.co.uk

Clearwater Devon Dympsy; St Austell Tribute; guest beer H

Oak-beamed 15th-century inn with a single bar which has two wood-burning fires. There are three real ales on tap that are significantly reduced on Tuesday market day from 11am to 3pm. Special prices also apply from 3pm to 6pm on weekdays. Good-quality food made with local produce is served in the bar or separate dining room. Outside there is a pleasant garden, with a covered smoking area. A disused railway line is available nearby for walkers. P (118,51)

Heddon Valley

Hunters Inn

EX31 4PY (signposted from A399) SS655481

10-11 ☎ (01598) 763230 thehuntersinn.net

Exmoor Ale, Stag, Gold; guest beers H

Popular inn set in the beautiful Heddon Valley, with a large front beer garden and more gardens to the rear, where peacocks wander freely. Several real ales are on offer, including up to three brewed for the pub by Country Life Brewery. The cider is Sam's Medium from Winkleigh. Walkers, cyclists, families and dog owners are all attracted here and there are 10 rooms for accommodation. A three-day beer and music festival takes place in September. Q P

Holcombe

Smugglers Inn

27 Teignmouth Road, EX7 0LA (on A379 between Dawlish and Teignmouth)

11-11 ☎ (01626) 862301 thesmugglersinn.net

Dartmoor Legend; Teignworthy Reel Ale; guest beer H

With splendid coastal views, this roadside free house has an excellent reputation. Good food is served lunchtimes and evenings, including a popular carvery. There are two regular ales and one varying guest. The bar area has a wood-burning stove. The outside area, with separate smokers' canopy, is popular throughout the seasons. A mini beer festival is held towards the end of January, usually featuring around 14 ales, and regular entertainment is hosted. There is a car park, and buses pass the door. P (2)

Holcombe Rogus

Prince of Wales Inn

TA21 0PN

5.30-10 Mon; 12-3, 5.30-11 (midnight Fri); 12-midnight Sat; 12-10 Sun ☎ (01823) 672070

theprinceofwales-uk.com

Otter Bitter; Sharp's Doom Bar; guest beers H

A 19th-century country pub, lying close to the Grand Western Canal and Somerset border. The area is popular with walkers and cyclists. Inside, the bar features unusual cash register handpumps. Home-cooked food, including vegetarian options and a carvery on Sundays, is served, and regular food-themed nights are held. A large log-burning stove warms the pub in winter. There is a darts and games area, live music features, and a beer festival is hosted in September. The attractive walled garden is popular in summer. Q P

Holsworthy

Golden Fleece

EX22 6BB

11-11; 12-10.30 Sun ☎ (01409) 253263

Dartmoor IPA; guest beer H

This is a busy free house, just off the centre of a historic market town mentioned in the Domesday Book. The pub itself dates back to Tudor times and is oak panelled throughout. There are two connected bar areas, featuring old beams and an open fire. The regular Dartmoor IPA is joined by a regularly changing guest ale, which is often sourced locally. Q

Old Market Inn

Chapel Street, EX22 6AY (on A388 S of town square)

11-midnight (1am Fri & Sat); 12-11 Sun

☎ (01409) 253941 oldmarketinn.co.uk

Holsworthy Ales Old Market Monk; Otter Bitter H**; guest beers** G

Local CAMRA Pub of the Year in 2012. This family-run free house has stillage for six casks at the end of the single bar, plus four handpumps and Autumn Scrumpy cider from Winkleigh. Locally-sourced food is served in the spacious rear restaurant. Local comedy club acts appear regularly, and during St Peter's Fair week in July a mini beer festival is held. Wednesdays are busy thanks to a thriving local livestock and food market.
P (X9,X90)

Honiton

Holt

178 High Street, EX14 1LA
closed Sun & Mon; 11-3, 5.30-11 (01404) 47707
theholt-honiton.com
Otter Bitter, Amber, Bright, Ale, Head [H]
The Holt has a slate floor and ochre walls, which makes for a smart decor, with lots of exposed wood. The kitchen is fully open, allowing you to watch the chefs preparing their delicious award-winning main meals and tapas. The pub is the first to be opened by Otter Brewery and is also the brewery tap; this is reflected by the five handpumps and the innovative taster racks – third-of-a-pint measures are also available.

Horns Cross

Coach & Horses

EX39 5DH (on A39 between Bideford and Clovelly)
11-2.30 (not Mon), 5-11; 12-11 Sat & Sun
(01237) 451214 thebestpubindevon.co.uk
Sharp's Doom Bar; guest beers [H]
Friendly 17th-century roadside inn with a single bar, a separate children's room with pool table, and three en-suite B&B rooms. It is ideally situated for exploring the local north Devon coast and is close to Peppercombe beach. Up to five real ales are served, together with Sam's Medium cider from Winkleigh. Good-quality food is sourced from local suppliers. Q P (319)

Horsebridge

Royal Inn

PL19 8PJ (off A384 Tavistock-Launceston road)
12-3, 7-11 (10.30 Sun) (01822) 870214
royalinn.co.uk
Dartmoor Legend; St Austell Proper Job [G]**; Skinner's Betty Stogs** [H]**; guest beers** [G]
Originally built as a nunnery in 1437 by French Benedictine monks and reported to have been visited by Charles I, the pub overlooks an old bridge on the River Tamar, connecting Devon and Cornwall. It features half-panelling, stone floors and traditional styling in the bar and lounge, with a further larger room off the lounge. It has a terraced garden with sheltered seating and free Wi-Fi. Most beers are served on gravity. The locally-sourced food is recommended. Q P

Iddesleigh

Duke of York

EX19 8BG (off B3217 next to church) SS570083
11-11; 12-10.30 Sun (01837) 810253
dukeofyorkdevon.co.uk
Adnams Broadside; Cotleigh Tawny Owl; guest beer [G]
A 15th-century inn, close to the Tarka Trail, where village resident Michael Morpurgo was inspired to write his famous book, War Horse. In the atmospheric bar, with its inglenook fire and old beams, at least three real ales are served straight from the cask. Food is available from noon until 9.30pm (9pm Sun). There are seven en-suite rooms, while the pub also runs a courtesy bus service from local camp sites, B&Bs and neighbouring villages. (The 648 bus only runs Thursdays.) Well-behaved dogs welcome.
Q (648)

Ideford

Royal Oak Inn

TQ13 0AY
12-2.30 (not Mon), 6-11; 12-3, 7-11 Sun
(01626) 852274
Courage Directors; guest beers [H]
A traditional thatched 17th-century inn, set in an ancient Saxon village nestling under Haldon Moor. The small cosy bar, with its flagstone floor and beamed ceilings, is festooned with historic memorabilia of Nelson and Trafalgar. At the rear is a small sheltered patio area, with more tables across the road by the pub car park. Children and dogs are welcome. The venue is not only popular with locals but also with hashers, cyclists and walkers. P

Ilfracombe

Ship & Pilot

10 Broad Street, EX34 9EE
11-midnight; 11.30-11 Sun (01271) 863562
Draught Bass [G]**; St Austell Trelawny; guest beers** [H]
Close to the harbour and pier, with a distinctive bright yellow painted front, this thriving and friendly local offers a choice of six real ales, including Draught Bass on gravity. At least three real ciders and a perry are also available. Although only bar snacks are served, food may be brought in and consumed on the premises if a drink is purchased to accompany it. Local CAMRA Pub of the Year 2013 and Cider Pub of the Year 2014.
(21,300)

Kilmington

Old Inn

EX13 7RB
11-3, 6-11; 12-3, 7-10.30 Sun (01297) 32096
oldinnkilmington.co.uk
Branscombe Vale Branoc; Otter Bitter; guest beers [H]
Thatched 16th-century inn on the A35. The Cricketers' bar, a lounge with a log fire, and a restaurant area are complemented by a suntrap patio and raised lawn. Food, served lunchtimes and evenings (not Sun eve), is sourced locally, including good mussels, and many specials are changed daily. See the website for more about beer festivals held at the end of May and August, bonfire night in November, and regular themed nights. A loyalty card system operates, earning points towards meal vouchers. Q P (380)

Kings Nympton

Grove Inn

EX37 9ST SS683194
12-3 (not Mon), 6-11; 12-4, 7-10 Sun (01769) 580406
thegroveinn.co.uk
Exmoor Ale; guest beers [H]

A 17th-century, Grade II-listed thatched pub that keeps four real ales, a local cider and over 65 single malt whiskies from around the world. The single bar has low beams from which bookmarks hang, while the adjacent dining area, in which award-winning food is served, has an open fire in winter. Children and dogs are welcome in the pub and the self-catering cottage nearby. Q

Kingswear

Ship Inn

Higher Street, TQ6 0AG
12-3, 6-midnight; 12-midnight Sat, Sun & summer
(01803) 752348
Adnams Southwold Bitter; Otter Bitter, Ale, seasonal beer; St Austell Trelawny; Skinner's Betty Stogs; guest beers H
Popular village inn with a well-deserved reputation for food, particularly fish dishes, offering up to six ales in summer. The building is 15th century with thick stone walls, warmed by two big fires in winter and decorated in a nautical theme. There are lovely river views from the restaurant and patio. Beer festivals take place in conjunction with Dartmouth food and sailing festivals. A previous South Devon CAMRA Pub of the Year and runner-up in 2014. Q

Lynmouth

Blue Ball Inn

Countisbury Hill, Countisbury, EX35 6NE (on A39, 1 mile E of Lynmouth) SS747496
11-11 (01598) 741263 blueballinn.com
Clearwater Proper Ansome; St Austell Tribute; guest beer H
Privately owned and run old coaching inn, which is open every day of the year. It has low ceilings, blackened beams and a large 13th-century inglenook fire near the bar. Four real ales are usually available, including one guest. Food is served all day from an extensive menu, both in the bar and the large dining area. It is ideal for walking and other outdoor pursuits and dog friendly. A beer festival is held in late November.
Q P (300)

Manaton

Kestor Inn

TQ13 9UF (on main road through village)
11-11 (01647) 221626 thebullersarms.co.uk
Dartmoor Legend; Otter Bitter; guest beer H
Spacious local village inn on Dartmoor with a large open-plan L-shaped bar with plenty of seating, including alcoves. There is also a separate pool room and a long dining room, which can be used for functions. It has a friendly atmosphere, and a good selection of local real ales is on offer. The lobby area of the pub has been turned into a small shop selling basic items, and a book exchange scheme is in operation. Sam's Medium Cider is sold. Q P (271,671)

Mary Tavy

Mary Tavy Inn

Lane Head, PL19 9PN
12-3, 6-11 summer; closed Mon; 12-2.30, 6-11; 12-2.30, 5-midnight Fri; 12-11 Sat & Sun winter (01822) 810326
themarytavyinn.co.uk
Dartmoor Jail Ale; St Austell Proper Job; guest beers H
A traditional roadside inn where families, visitors and locals are welcome. The popular bar area accommodates pool, darts, TV and a large fire, and up to four real ales. This is complemented by a spacious restaurant and garden with open views to Dartmoor. Music nights, charity events, quizzes, a Sunday carvery and a Whitsun bank holiday beer festival feature in the pub's calendar. Modern B&B accommodation is available in the adjacent building. The pub closes on Mondays in winter.
Q P (118)

Meavy

Royal Oak

PL20 6PJ (on village green)
11-11; 11-10.30 Sun (01822) 852944
royaloakinn.org.uk
Dartmoor IPA, Jail Ale; guest beer H
An iconic English village inn, dating from the 16th century, next to the church and overlooking the green, where the eponymous tree stands. The lounge has a restaurant serving home-cooked food, complemented by an eclectic wine list. Up to four local ales figure prominently, and there is a good range of ciders. The public bar provides a return to its history and agricultural roots: flagstone floor, large open fire, and photos of times past. Local CAMRA branch Country Pub of the Year runner-up 2014. Q

Merton

Malt Scoop Inn

EX20 3EA (on A386, 7miles S of Great Torrington) SS527121
12-3, 6-midnight (1am Fri); 12-1am Sat; 12-10.30 Sun
(01805) 603924 themaltscoop.co.uk
St Austell Dartmoor Best Bitter, Tribute, HSD H
Originally part of a farm and built in the 1700s, the Malt Scoop became a coaching inn during the 19th century and has been in the same family for more than 100 years. The horseshoe-shaped bar, with inglenook fire, has adjacent seating areas and leads through to the restaurant. This friendly local tends to concentrate on beers from St Austell, together with ciders from Devon and Cornwall. Good-quality modern British food is sourced locally.
Q P (118)

Moretonhampstead

Union Inn

10 Ford Street, TQ13 8LN (on A382 heading out of town toward Chagford)
11-11; 12-10.30 Sun (01647) 440199
theunioninn.co.uk
Fuller's London Pride; Red Rock Lighthouse IPA, Red Rock, Break Water H
Traditional 16th-century village-centre free house with a beamed and panelled bar with adjoining pool room displaying old photographs of the village. The function room has its own bar and skittle alley and is reached via a corridor with artefacts relating to the inn's history. The Red Rock beers are given house names and good-value home-cooked pub food is served, with a carvery on Sunday lunchtime. There is outside seating on the decking next to the small car park.
Q

Newton Abbot

Richard Hopkins

34-42 Queen Street, TQ12 2EW

8am-midnight (01626) 323930

Greene King Ruddles Best Bitter, Abbot; guest beers H

A large, welcoming town-centre Wetherspoon venue which was converted from a drapery store in 2003 and named after a local baker and landowner. The spacious wood-panelled interior is divided into several seating areas and has displays depicting local history and people. Guest ales come from local breweries. There is outdoor covered seating at the front of the premises, and disabled access is good.

Teign Cellars

67 East Street, TQ12 2JR

10.30 (11.30 Sun)-11 (01626) 337653

teigncellars.co.uk

Beer range varies H/G

A wonderful reincarnation of the previous Green Man, used by paupers in the 19th century from the workhouse opposite. It has one bar, wooden flooring and walls adorned with beer mats, posters and mirrors. Four draught beers, often of the unusual kind, including hoppy and unfined ones, are served, plus one good-value beer from either Bays or Teignworthy. You can also find eight real ciders, including some from local producers Hunt's and Reddaway's, and a further 170 bottled beers at the bar or from the shop behind. Superb food.

Q

Newton Poppleford

Cannon Inn

High Street, EX10 0DW

11-2.30, 6-11 (5.30-midnight Thu-Sat); 12-2.30, 6-10.30 Sun (01395) 568266 pubindevon.com

Otter Amber; guest beer G

A cheery welcome greets you as you enter this two-bar pub, with dining tables in the lounge bar and restaurant, or bar stools for those who wish to sit and watch the action. Real ales are served by gravity from stillage behind the bar. This is a friendly locals' pub, but with a busy passing trade. Good-value home-cooked food is served lunchtimes and evenings. Well-behaved dogs are allowed in the lounge bar.

P (52,157)

Newton St Cyres

Beer Engine

EX5 5AX (beside railway station N of A377)

11-11; 12-10.30 Sun (01392) 851282

thebeerengine.co.uk

Beer Engine Rail Ale, Silver Bullet, Piston Bitter, Sleeper Heavy H

A Georgian pub, built in 1850, on the Exeter to Barnstaple Tarka Line. Popular with drinkers and diners alike, it is well frequented by locals, visitors and the cricket team. The dining area adjoining the bar serves its own bread made with beer yeast, along with locally-sourced food, available lunchtimes and evenings. The pub brews its own ales whose names, like the pictures and old pub signs, have a railway theme. QP

North Tawton

Railway Inn

Whiddon Down Road, EX20 2BE (1 mile S of town, just off A3124) SS666000

12-3 (not Mon & Thu), 6-11; 12-3, 7-11 Sun

(01837) 82789 therailwaynorthtawton.co.uk

Teignworthy Reel Ale; guest beers H

Next to the former North Tawton station (closed in 1971), the Railway has numerous old station photos and memorabilia in evidence. This traditional single-bar local is well worth seeking out, with a warm welcome always assured. The regular beer is usually joined by guest ales from other West Country breweries, together with a real cider in summer. The dining room is popular in the evening (no food Thu), with light meals served at lunchtime. No dogs allowed except guide dogs.

QP

Okehampton

Plymouth Inn

26 West Street, EX20 1HH (W end of town near West Okement bridge)

11-midnight (01837) 53633

Beer range varies H

Old coaching inn and friendly village-style local dating from the 17th century. The constantly changing ales are mainly from West Country brewers, with different local ciders kept during the summer months. Two popular beer festivals take place in the function room: one coinciding with the Ten Tors Challenge in May, and the other with the Baring Gould Folk Festival in October. Reasonably priced, locally-sourced food and snacks are served. Children and dogs welcome.

(X9,510)

Ottery St Mary

Volunteer Inn

Broad Street, EX11 1BZ

12-11; 12-10.30 Sun (01404) 814060

thevolunteerinn-ottery.co.uk

Otter Bitter, Ale G**; guest beers** H

Located in the centre of the town, this lively venue is popular with the younger folk. All real ales are served by gravity, and good pub food is available seven days a week, with a traditional roast on Sunday. The Volunteer is family friendly, and has a beer garden towards the rear of the building.

Paignton

Henry's Bar

53 Torbay Road, TQ4 6AJ

11-11 (midnight Fri & Sat) (01803) 551190

Dartmoor IPA; Sharp's Doom Bar; Skinner's Betty Stogs; guest beer H

A traditional-style pub situated among arcades and gift shops, deceptive from the exterior but welcoming and friendly inside. It has a long bar with ample seating. The decor has a nautical feel, with branded mirrors and old beer adverts. Outside is a pleasant covered pavement seating area. Food is available all day and is reasonably priced. Children are welcome until 9pm. Sam's Dry cider is available on handpump, together with several other West Country ciders served from polyboxes.

Q

Isaac Merritt

54-58 Torquay Road, TQ3 3AA
8am-midnight ☎ (01803) 556066
Dartmoor Jail Ale; Greene King Abbot; Ruddles Best Bitter; guest beers H
Community-oriented Wetherspoon just five minutes' walk from both the bus and railway stations. Popular with locals and visitors alike, it has a well-deserved reputation for the quality and choice of both real ales and traditional ciders. The interior is themed around Isaac Merritt Singer, the inventor of the Singer sewing machine. It has seated alcoves, a separate family dining area, an external smokers' area, and has access and toilet facilities for the disabled. Q

Parkham

Bell Inn

Rectory Lane, EX39 5PL (½ mile S of the A39 at Horns Cross) SS387212
12-2 (not Fri), 5-11; 5.30-midnight Sat; 12-3, 6-midnight Sun ☎ (01237) 451201 thebellinnparkham.co.uk
Sharp's Doom Bar; guest beers H
Historic 13th-century thatched inn with traditional oak beams, cob walls and open fires, which was originally a forge and two farmers' cottages. The single bar has up to four real ales available, one a local guest. A beer festival takes place in early June, and summer spit roasts have become a popular feature. Locally-produced food is served lunchtimes and evenings daily, in both the bar area and the raised dining room. P (372)

Peter Tavy

Peter Tavy Inn

Lane Head, PL19 9NN
12-3, 6-11; 12-3, 6.30-10.30 Sun winter; 12-11 (10.30 Sun) summer ☎ (01822) 810348 petertavyinn.com
Dartmoor Jail Ale; Tavy Ales Ideal Pale Ale; guest beers H
In a quiet village on the edge of Dartmoor, a varying range of up to five local beers can be found in the pub's small central bar. Traditionally attired throughout, there are also two larger rooms, one for families. A patio and hidden garden are added attractions. The pub is renowned for its food, but drinkers are made welcome. Summer hours are extended. The inn is on the No. 27 cycle route, near a caravan and camping site.
Q P (118)

Petrockstowe

Laurels Inn

EX20 3HJ (S of church on main road through village) SS513091
12-3 (not Mon), 6-midnight; 12-1am Fri & Sat; 12-midnight Sun ☎ (01837) 810578
Otter Bitter; Sharp's Doom Bar; guest beer H
In a picturesque village with several chocolate box cottages, this 17th-century coaching house has historic links to the Civil War. The single bar has three handpumps, with the guest ale often tending towards the stronger side. There is a cosy restaurant offset near the entrance and a pool table in the bar area. Outside there are wooden benches and tables for eating and drinking alfresco. The Tarka Trail, convenient for walkers and cyclists, is a mile away. The bus runs Thursday and Friday only. P (386)

Plymouth

Brass Monkey

12-14 Royal Parade, PL1 1DS
9am-11 (midnight Wed-Sat; 7 Sun) ☎ (01752) 260442
thebrassmonkeyplymouth.co.uk
Hunter's Half Bore, Black Jack; guest beers H
Typical, modern, bustling city-centre pub with a wide clientele. It offers up to eight real ales, including two house beers brewed by Hunter's, and two real ciders. Conveniently situated, there is easy access to shopping, buses, the Hoe and the Barbican. Several TVs are balanced by photographs of pre-war Plymouth. Good-value family meals are served by friendly and efficient staff. Several ale festivals are held each year. On a number of bus routes.

Britannia Inn

2 Wolseley Road, Milehouse, PL2 3BH
8am-midnight (1am Fri & Sat) ☎ (01752) 607596
Dartmoor Jail Ale; Greene King Abbot; Ruddles Best Bitter; guest beers H
A large pub built in the 1830s which retained its name when it became a Wetherspoon in 1999, close to the football ground. (It can get busy on match days.) There are 10 pumps, one of which always dispenses a real cider. Being on the main road, it is on numerous bus routes from the train and bus stations, and city centre. There is free Wi-Fi, a display of Good Beer Guides and a map of Devon breweries. Q

Dolphin Hotel

14 The Barbican, PL1 2LS
10-11 (midnight Thu-Sat); 11-11 Sun ☎ (01752) 660876
Draught Bass; St Austell Tribute; guest beers G
An unpretentious hostelry steeped in history, the Dolphin is a Plymouth institution. A makeunder has left the character thankfully untouched, with tiled floors, well-used wooden benches, together with a real open fire, all adding to the ambience. The walls are adorned with paintings by local artist, the late Beryl Cook, who painted many of the characters she encountered in the Dolphin. The best Bass in the West Country is served straight from the cask here, with up to seven guest beers as well. Q (25)

Fawn Private Members Club

39 Prospect Street, Greenbank, PL4 8NY
3 (2 Fri)-11; 12-11 Sat & Sun ☎ (01752) 226385
Bays Topsail; guest beers H
The club is named after the now scrapped HMS Fawn. CAMRA members are welcome with a current membership card; regular visitors will be required to join. The club is popular for rugby and other televised sports, and supports multiple dart and euchre teams. Four guest ales from the local area are generally available, as well as a rotating range of local cider. The smoking area is on the patio and is covered. Local CAMRA Club of the Year 2014.

Ferry House Inn

888 Wolseley Road, Saltash Passage, PL5 1LA
12-midnight ☎ (01752) 361063
Dartmoor Jail Ale; St Austell Tribute; Sharp's Doom Bar; guest beer H
This picturesque riverside pub is on the River Tamar, which separates Devon from Cornwall. There is a decking area outside, giving spectacular views of Brunel's iconic railway bridge, which

dates from 1859. Good home-cooked food is served, and uses locally-sourced ingredients, with a daily specials board also featuring. The bars display photos of Brunel's bridge dating back to the turn of the 20th century, and photos of the pub, and the Saltash foot ferry, after which it was named. ≈(St Budeaux)(13)

Fortescue Hotel

37 Mutley Plain, PL4 6JQ

11-midnight; 12-11 Sun (01752) 660673

Bays Devon Dumpling; St Austell Proper Job; Skinner's Betty Stogs; guest beers H

The landlord is a real ale enthusiast and the bar has nine handpumps, with one dedicated to a real cider; the rest serve a changing range of ales. There are several local ales always available, and up to seven real ciders/perries. There is a long main bar, a cellar bar and a covered beer garden. Traditional roasts are served on Sundays only, washed down with Spingo beer. Local CAMRA Pub of the Year 2013 and 2014.

Lord High Admiral

33 Stonehouse Street, PL1 3PE

8am-11; 9am-10.30 Sun (01752) 256881

St Austell Tribute, HSD; guest beer H

A back-street pub set close to Millbay Docks ferry port. It is a friendly community local which has been revitalised over the past couple of years. Good-value food is served from breakfast time until 2pm and again in the early evening. Free tapas are served with the well-kept St Austell ales. It has a large-screen TV for sporting enthusiasts. The real fire adds to the ambience in winter.

Lounge

7 Stopford Place, Devonport, PL1 4QT

11.30-3 (not Mon), 6-11; 11.30-3, 6-midnight Fri; 11.30-11 Sat; 12-11 Sun (01752) 561330

Draught Bass; guest beers H

In a quiet residential area, this street-corner local is near to Devonport Park, and offers a warm welcome. The wood-panelled bar is comfortable and relaxing, although it may be busy at times with Plymouth Albion RFC's ground nearby. One weaker, one stronger than the regular Bass is the rule for guest beers, with lighter and darker brews also alternating. A secluded garden at the front offers a retreat for smokers. Food is only available at lunchtimes. Q≈P(32,34)

Minerva Inn

31 Looe Street, Barbican, PL4 0EA

11.30-11.30 (midnight Wed; 12.30am Thu & Fri); 12-12.30am Sat; 1-10.30 Sun (01752) 223047

minervainn.co.uk

St Austell Tribute, HSD; guest beers H

Plymouth's oldest pub, dating from about 1540, and within easy walking distance of the city centre and the historic Barbican. The pub has a long and narrow bar, leading through to a cosy seating area at the rear. Two guest beers are supplemented by spring and autumn beer festivals, where beer could, and does, come from all over the country. Live music takes place Thursday-Sunday evenings, and Sunday lunchtime. The pub benefits from a varied clientele. Q

Stoke Inn

43 Devonport Road, Stoke, PL3 4DL

12-midnight (1am Fri & Sat) (01752) 515749

stokeinnplymouth.co.uk

Dartmoor Jail Ale; guest beer H

Traditional family-friendly pub in the village suburb of Stoke. It is close to the city centre and has a large garden. Four beers are available, with an emphasis on local ales. Pub food is served during the week, with traditional roasts on Sundays. Sport is shown on TV, with occasional live music events held in the garden. Traditional pub games are played, including Scrabble. Two function rooms are available for hire, with parking for motorhomes by prior arrangement.
≈(Devonport)P(32,34)

Plympton

George Inn

191 Ridgeway, PL7 2HJ

11.30-11 (midnight Fri & Sat); 12-11 Sun

(01752) 342674 thegeorgeplympton.co.uk

St Austell Dartmoor Best Bitter, Tribute, HSD; guest beer H

A warm welcome awaits you in this 17th-century former coaching house, which is situated on the old Plymouth-Exeter road. Roaring fires warm the flagstone-floored bar in winter, and there is a spacious dining room area as well. The floral-bedecked patio is popular during fine weather. The St Austell ales are complemented by an extensive food menu – booking at weekends is advisable. A popular quiz is held on the second Sunday of the month. Dogs on leads are welcome.
QP

London Inn

8 Church Road, Plympton St Maurice, PL7 1NH

12-11 (midnight Fri & Sat) (01752) 657045

Beer range varies H

A friendly 16th-century pub next to the church, the epitome of a typical village inn. The cosy lounge bar is adorned with a large collection of Royal Naval memorabilia, while the public bar boasts a pool table, dartboard and TVs for sports enthusiasts. It is the brewery tap for the Garage Brewery, whose ale is supplemented by up to three other beers and several ciders. The pub is allegedly haunted by Captain Hinds. QP

Union Inn

17 Underwood Road, PL7 1SY

4-11 (11.30 Fri); 12-midnight Sat; 12-11 Sun

(01752) 336756 unioninnplympton.com

Beer range varies H

This traditional, cosy, 19th-century pub is a family-run community hostelry that offers a warm welcome to all who enter. The landlord's passion for ale is evident, as up to four beers vary to provide a year-round beer festival. There are also four real ciders served on gravity. All meals are freshly prepared using local produce, and booking is advisable. Lunchtime meals are only available at weekends. Dogs on leads are welcome. CAMRA branch Cider Pub of the Year 2013 runner-up.
QP

Plymstock

Morley Arms

4 Billacombe Road, PL9 7HP (E end of Laira Bridge)

11.30-2.30, 5-11; 12-9 Sun (01752) 401191

morleyarms.co.uk

Morland Old Speckled Hen; Sharp's Doom Bar; guest beers H

The building was constructed in 1824 to house the workers who built the original Laira Bridge, which nearly bankrupted the Morley family, and was then converted into a pub. Most of the rooms have been opened out, but retain the wall beams, giving a cosy feel to a visually open area. Home-cooked food is served which has an excellent local reputation, and up to five ales are served. There are open fires in winter. Live music features weekly and morris men visit on occasion.
P

Princetown

Plume of Feathers Inn

Plymouth Hill, PL20 6QQ
10.30 (midnight Fri & Sat) (01822) 890240
theplumeoffeathersdartmoor.co.uk
Dartmoor IPA, Jail Ale; St Austell Tribute; guest beers
Princetown's oldest building (1785) features granite walls, slate floors and slate-topped tables. A later addition is the large family/function room with its own bar. Food is served all day, with a carvery in the family room on weekend lunchtimes. There is ample outdoor seating on the spacious patio, and a children's play area. There is also a large car park, campsite and camping barn on site. Three local ales complement the three regulars. There is an infrequent bus service from Tavistock. Q P (98)

Roborough

New Inn

West Road, EX19 8SY (100yds W of the parish church)
SS575170
12-3 (not Mon & Tue), 5-11 (01805) 603247
thenewinnroborough.co.uk
Bays Gold; guest beers
A 16th-century thatched village pub that locals have been heard to describe as like walking into your own living room. The single bar serves up to three real ales, two of which come from local breweries, plus Winkleigh's Autumn Scrumpy cider. Good-quality pub food is served from a regularly changing menu offering traditional and seasonal dishes using local produce. Fresh bread is baked daily. Live music events are held regularly along with impromptu jam sessions. Well-behaved children are welcome. Q P

Sandford

Lamb Inn

The Square, EX17 4LW
10.30-11 (01363) 773676 lambinnsandford.co.uk
Otter Bitter; guest beers
A traditional 16th-century free house in the village centre, with a warm, welcoming atmosphere. It is well-supported by locals and visitors alike, enjoying award-winning food, West Country ales, and Sandford Orchards cider. Skittles is played four nights a week in the alley-cum-cinema-cum-conference venue. There are open mic music and comedy evenings. Six B&B rooms are available and children and dogs are welcome. It is frequented by the village football, squash and cricket teams.
Q (369)

Scorriton

Tradesman's Arms

TQ11 0JB
12-3, 6-11; 12-midnight Sun (01364) 631206
thetradesmansarms.co.uk
Dartmoor IPA; guest beers
On the edge of Dartmoor, the Tradesman's reopened after it was bought by four locals who drank here prior to its demise. It was renovated and updated, and has an L-shaped main bar with plenty of seating in a long alcove to one side, with a conservatory open to the pub at the other. There is a friendly atmosphere, and good local food is served together with local Thompstone's cider. One of the guest beers is from Hunter's. Accommodation is available.
Q P

Seaton

King's Arms

55 Fore Street, EX12 2AN
11-2.30, 6-11; 11-11 Sat; 12-11 Sun (01297) 23431
Branscombe Vale Branoc
A traditional locals' pub just out of town, near the cricket ground and popular with visitors staying at the nearby caravan park. Real ales come mainly from Branscombe Vale Brewery. It has a reputation for good-quality home-cooked food, served lunchtimes and evenings. It can get very busy, especially on Sundays (pre-booking advisable). A large beer garden at the rear, with tables, play equipment and two boules pitches, overlooks the estuary to Axmouth.

Shaldon

Clifford Arms

34 Fore Street, TQ14 0DE
11-2.30, 5-11 (11.30 Fri & Sat); 11.30-3, 5.30-10.30 Sun
(01626) 872311
Dartmoor IPA, Jail Ale; guest beers
In the centre of a pretty coastal village, this pub has an attractive modern interior, and a warming log fire in winter. The guest and seasonal beers are sourced mainly from West Country breweries. The low-level restaurant at the rear serves good-quality food every day, and leads out onto a sunny decked patio. Special menus are available for modern jazz evenings on Mondays, monthly Sunday lunchtime jazz sessions, and numerous charity events.
Q (11)

Shaldon Conservative Club

Dagmar Street, TQ14 0DU
12-3, 5-11; 12-11 Sat & Sun (01626) 873667
Teignworthy Reel Ale; guest beers
Situated in the centre of the village, the club offers two real ales and a real cider at reasonable prices. The single bar has comfortable seating and is home to snooker, darts and euchre teams. At the the hub of the community, this venue hosts charity fundraising events, wakes and private parties. Live music features regularly and includes open mic nights. Televised rugby is also popular. CAMRA members with a current membership card are welcome. (11)

Shipwrights Arms

Ringmore Road, TQ14 0AG
5-11; closed Tue; 12-11 Sat; 12-10.30 Sun
(01626) 873232

Hunter's Half Bore; Otter Ale; Teignworthy Reel Ale [H]
A locals' pub on the banks of the River Teign which dates back to the time when Shaldon had shipyards. Two cosy bars, both with open fires, serve three real ales from local breweries. An attractive walled garden at the rear has river views. Good pub food is on offer, as is a takeaway service for real ale and still cider. There is live music on Saturdays and open mic on alternate Thursdays. P (11)

Shaugh Prior

White Thorn Inn

PL7 5HA (on Cornwood to Bickleigh road, S of Yelverton)
12-3, 6-11; 12-10.30 Sun (01752) 839245
white-thorn-inn.co.uk
Beer range varies [H]
Very much a community village pub, situated a mile from the Plym Valley Foot and Cycle Path. It serves three varying beers from Devon and Cornwall in a large open-plan bar with a central fireplace. Regular entertainment is on offer, including quizzes, local events and a spring beer festival. There is a large car park and children's play area at the rear, overlooking Bickleigh Vale. The food menu is excellent, with deals for the over-60s. The local bus does not operate evenings and Sundays. P (59)

Sidmouth

Swan Inn

37 York Street, EX10 8BY
11-11; 12-11 Sun (01395) 512849
Young's Bitter, Special; guest beer [H]
Traditional and quiet back-street inn, established around 1770, which lies just off the centre of this quaint town, a short walk from the sea front and bus terminus. An old-style wood-panelled bar with an open fire leads to a dedicated dining area serving good food, attracting a strong local trade. Three beers, all from the Wells' range, are normally available. Dogs, but not children, are welcome indoors. Find out about the King of Chit – a traditional competition. Q (52,157)

Silverton

Lamb Inn

Fore Street, EX5 4HZ
11.30-2.30, 6-midnight; 11.30-midnight Sat; 12-11 Sun
(01392) 860272 thelambinnsilverton.co.uk
Exe Valley Dob's Best Bitter; guest beers [G]
Popular family-run village-centre pub with stone floors, stripped timber and old pine furniture, as well as a real fire. A fine display of old pumpclips jogs your memory of ales long gone. At least three beers are served by gravity from a temperature-controlled stillage behind the bar, at very competitive prices. There is a well-used function room and skittle alley. Good-value home-cooked food is available lunchtimes and evenings, plus a popular Sunday roast. Q (55B)

Slapton

Queen's Arms

TQ7 2PN
12-3, 5.30-11; 12-3, 6-10.30 Sun (01548) 580800
queensarmsslapton.co.uk
Dartmoor Jail Ale; Otter Bitter, Bright; guest beer [H]
A 14th-century village-centre pub. Its large open fire welcomes you in the bar, which has numerous photographs depicting the WWII evacuation. The large gardens and patio at the rear are filled with flowers, and children and dogs are made welcome both inside and out. An extensive menu is available with daily specials; the chef is particularly known for his home-made pies. During the winter months Sunday roasts are served (booking recommended). A food takeaway service is also provided. Q P (93)

South Brent

Oak

Station Road, TQ10 9BE
12-2, 4-midnight; 12-midnight Sat; 11.30-11 Sun
(01364) 72133 oakonline.net
Dartmoor IPA; Teignworthy Gun Dog; guest beers [H]
Village-centre pub on the edge of Dartmoor. The wood-panelled, L-shaped bar is surrounded by a large open-plan area with plenty of seating. An excellent range of real ales is available. At the rear a restaurant serves good-quality food, and a new function room can be found upstairs, which is available for meetings. There is a no-smoking courtyard outside and accommodation is offered. Occasional beer festivals are held, with a discount on real ales for CAMRA members.
Q P (X38,X80)

South Molton

Town Arms Hotel

124 East Street, EX36 3BU (100yds E of town square)
11-midnight; 12-midnight Sun (01769) 572531
Exmoor Ale; Sharp's Doom Bar; guest beer [H]
Main-street local with interesting old photographs on the walls. This small historic market town is ideally situated for exploring Exmoor and north Devon. There is one main bar, containing a pool table and an open fire, plus a quieter back room. The pub can get quite lively on occasions, particularly on market day (Thursday). There is a strong commitment to real ale, with a CAMRA discount scheme in operation. Well-behaved dogs are welcome. P (X7,155)

South Tawton

Seven Stars

EX20 2LW
12-3 (not Mon), 6-11; 12-11 Fri & Sat; 12-10.30 Sun
(01837) 840292 thesevenstarssouthtawton.co.uk
Dartmoor IPA; Otter Bitter [G]**; guest beer** [H]
In the centre of a pretty and unspoilt village on the edge of Dartmoor, this creeper-clad Victorian pub is a delight to visit, with a wonderful Art Deco theme. Antiques sales are held every two months, but if you like something, make an offer. Three real ales are served, while the food menu changes weekly and is based on locally-sourced seasonal ingredients. There is a two-hourly bus service between South Tawton and Okehampton.
Q

South Zeal

Oxenham Arms

EX20 2JT (on main road through village at lower end)
12-3, 6-11 (10.30 Sun) (01837) 840244
theoxenhamarms.co.uk

Beer range varies Ⓗ

The pub was once described as the stateliest and most ancient abode in the hamlet. The original hamlet has since grown into a village but the Oxenham retains its grandeur. It has the unspoilt atmosphere of an old country inn, with low beams, flagged floors, open fires and mullion windows. In the small lounge behind the bar monastic builders incorporated a prehistoric standing stone into the wall. Two guest beers, frequently from local breweries, join the regular Oxy Ale house beer. Q🐴❀🛏◐◑♿♣🍎P🚌(178)🐾📶

Spreyton

Tom Cobley Tavern Ⓛ

EX17 5AL (off A3124 in village)

⏲ 6.30-11 Mon; 12-3, 6-11 (1am Fri & Sat); 12-4, 7-11 Sun

☎ (01647) 231314 🌐 tomcobleytavern.co.uk

Beer range varies Ⓗ/Ⓖ

A choice of 14 real ales, all from West Country brewers, together with real ciders and delicious home-cooked food, make this a gem of a pub. It was a finalist for CAMRA National Pub of the Year in 2012, testifying that this is a true community local. Children and dogs are welcome in the bar, and the garden is a delight on warm sunny days. Six comfortable guest rooms are available for night stops. A warm and friendly pub. Q❀🛏◐◑♣🍎P🐾

Sticklepath

Taw River Inn Ⓛ

EX20 2NW (on old A30 road through village) SX642941

⏲ 12-midnight (11 Sun) ☎ (01837) 840377

🌐 tawriver.co.uk

Dartmoor Jail Ale; St Austell Tribute; Sharp's Doom Bar; guest beers Ⓗ

A former 17th-century manor house, this oak-beamed pub is popular with locals and visitors alike. Set in an attractive village on the edge of Dartmoor, it is ideally situated for exploring the area or visiting the Finch Foundry Museum (National Trust) opposite. Holiday cottage accommodation is available. The varied real ales are competitively priced, and good-value pub food is served in both the bar area and adjacent dining room. Well-behaved children and dogs are welcome. 🐴❀◐◑♿♣P🚌(X9)🐾📶

Teignmouth

Blue Anchor Inn Ⓛ

Teign Street, TQ14 8EG

⏲ 12-midnight (11 Mon-Wed) ☎ (01626) 772741

Beer range varies Ⓗ

Grade II-listed former City Ales and Devenish outlet on the edge of a conservation area and close to the docks, with a VR letterbox in the wall outside. One bar is quiet during the day but is likely to be more lively during the evenings and at weekends, given the jukebox. Seven handpumps serve mainly West Country beers, with an eighth for real cider (from Westons or more local producers). Beer festivals are held outside during bank holidays and in September. Q❀♿⥂♣🍎🚌(2,11)🐾

Brass Monkey Ⓛ

Hollands Road, TQ14 8SR

⏲ 11-midnight; 12-11 Sun ☎ (01626) 773961

St Austell Tribute, HSD Ⓗ

Formerly known as the Half Moon and situated halfway between the railway station and the towns bus stops, this pub is an ideal waiting room. The long-standing and award-winning licensees offer a warm welcome to a community-oriented pub. Sporting events are shown on the TV screens and the pub has a Tuesday quiz, Friday night karaoke, Sunday meat draw and early evening happy hours. No food other than a Sunday roast. Q♿⥂♣🚌(2,11)🐾

Tiverton

Goldy's Ale & Cider Bar

10 Newport Street, EX16 6NH

⏲ closed Mon; 12-11 (midnight Fri & Sat); 12-7 Sun

Otter Amber; guest beers Ⓖ

A micropub, opened in 2012 in a former pet shop, and named after a relative of one of the joint owners. The original large glass windows have been etched with local brewery motifs. There are four casks of real ale on racks behind the compact wooden bar area, plus four real ciders, all from the South-west. Two ales are from Otter and Hunter's breweries. Another small carpeted area is off to one side of the bar. Toilet facilities are limited. Q🍎🐾

Topsham

Bridge Inn ★ Ⓛ

Bridge Hill, EX3 0QQ

⏲ 12-2, 6-10.30 (11 Fri & Sat); 12-2, 7-10.30 Sun

☎ (01392) 873862 🌐 cheffers.co.uk/bridge

Branscombe Vale Branoc; guest beers Ⓖ

Historic, cosy, 16th-century inn run by six generations of the same family since 1897, with a varying range of ales from local breweries and further afield. This hostelry is a delight for fans of real ale, in a traditional setting overlooking the banks of the River Clyst. The inn was visited by the Queen in 1998. Nine beers are usually available, all dispensed by gravity straight from the cellar. Snacks are available lunchtimes and until 8.30pm in the evening. Q❀◐◑⥂P🚌(57,T)🐾

Exeter Inn Ⓛ

68 High Street, EX3 0DY

⏲ 11-11 (midnight Fri & Sat); 12-10.30 Sun

☎ (01392) 873131

Sharp's Special; Teignworthy Beachcomber; guest beers Ⓗ

Originally a 17th-century coaching house, the partially thatched building is now a welcoming community pub. There are two regular ales plus two more handpumps dedicated to rotating guest beers. Real cider from Green Valley is also available. Three TVs show sporting events, and pool, darts and euchre are played. Live music and a quiz evening are hosted once a month. Well-behaved dogs are welcome. ❀⥂♣🍎🚌(57,T)🐾📶

Totnes

Bay Horse Inn Ⓛ

8 Cistern Street, TQ9 5SP

⏲ 12-11.45 ☎ (01803) 862088 🌐 bayhorsetotnes.com

Dartmoor Jail Ale; Otter Bitter; Teignworthy Reel Ale; guest beers Ⓗ

A 15th-century coaching inn, this quaint pub at the top of the picturesque town serves a minimum of three ales throughout the year. The pub is the tap for the New Lion Brewery and guests are mainly from South-west breweries. Live music features two or three times a week, including jazz, folk and acoustic sessions. A beer festival in the first week of September coincides with the Totnes festival. The large, attractive rear garden has disabled access. Q

Turnchapel

Clovelly Bay Inn

1 Boringdon Road, PL9 9TB

12-3 (not Mon-Thu), 6-11; 12-4, 7-10.30 Sun winter; 11-3, 6-11; 12-11 Sat; 12-4, 7-10.30 Sun summer
(01752) 402765 clovellybayinn.co.uk

Beer range varies

Family-run free house nestled in a picturesque village on the South-West Coast Path. It has an enthusiastic landlord with a passion for real ales and ciders, with up to 10 on tap. It holds a variety of festivals throughout the year, with an emphasis on local produce and a willingness to source beers and ciders from further afield. The pub is also renowned for its wonderful food. Local CAMRA branch Pub of the Year runner-up 2012 and 2013. Q (2)

Uplyme

Talbot Arms

Lyme Road, DT7 3TF

11-11 (01297) 443136 talbotarms.com

Otter Bitter; guest beers

Friendly brick-built pub near the Dorset border. There is a cosy lounge and a separate dining area. Toilets, games/family room and access to a large patio are all down steepish stairs (difficult for the disabled). TVs show all the major sporting fixtures. Good locally-sourced food is served, with a Sunday lunchtime carvery. A summer beer festival is held in a marquee towards the end of July/early August. Mighty Hop Talbot Tap is another regular beer. Opening hours vary during the winter.
Q P (31)

Walkhampton

Walkhampton Inn

PL20 6JY

12-3 (not Mon winter), 5-11 (8 Mon; 10 Tue); 12-11 Fri & Sat; 12-10 Sun (01822) 855345
thewalkhamptoninn.co.uk

Dartmoor Jail Ale; St Austell Proper Job; guest beers

Set in the centre of the village, this welcoming local displays traditional features throughout the bar, dining areas and snug. Up to five real ales are on offer. A courtyard beer garden hosts summer events. There are quiz, live music and open mic nights throughout the year, with an annual cider festival. Dogs are welcome but not in the dining areas while serving. If the pub appears to be closed during opening hours, then a notice will invite you to ring the bell. Q P (55)

Wembury

Odd Wheel

Knighton Road, PL9 0JD

12-3, 5-midnight; 12-midnight Fri-Sun (01752) 863052
theoddwheel.co.uk

Dartmoor Jail Ale; St Austell Tribute; Sharp's Doom Bar; guest beers

Friendly country pub which was tastefully refurbished several years ago, and is at the northern end of this picturesque village. It is only a short distance from many walking routes, including the South-West Coast Path. The three regular beers are supplemented by up to three guests, mainly from Devon and Cornwall. Regular beer festivals are held. Food is served daily, with ingredients from locally-sourced suppliers. Outside, there is a terraced garden and play area for children.
P (48)

Whimple

New Fountain Inn

Church Road, EX5 2TA

12-2 (not Mon), 6.30-11; 12-3, 6.30-11 Sat; 12-3, 7-10.30 Sun (01404) 822350

Teignworthy Reel Ale; guest beers

Converted from cottages in about 1890, this pub has changed little over the years, although modern toilets were added in an extension to one of the bars in 2009, and it has featured in every edition of the Guide since 1993. The other bar retains many original features including a real fire in winter. In this genuine free house the handpumps are decorative – ale is fetched from the cellar. Good-value home-cooked food is served. The village heritage centre in the car park is worth visiting.
Q P

Widecombe-in-the-Moor

Rugglestone Inn

TQ13 7TF (¼ mile from village centre)

11.30-3, 6-11.30 (5-midnight Fri); 11.30-midnight Sat; 12-11 Sun (01364) 621327 rugglestoneinn.co.uk

Dartmoor Legend; guest beers

Unspoilt pub in a splendid Dartmoor setting. This Grade II-listed building was converted to an inn back in 1832. The stone-flagged bar area has seating, with beer also served through a hatch in the passageway. An open fire warms the lounge. A wide selection of home-cooked food is available. Across the stream is a large grassed seating area. Local farm cider is sold, and the house beer is from Teignworthy. The pub's car park is just down the road. Q P

Drunken primates

Brehm asserts that the natives of north-eastern Africa catch the wild baboons by exposing vessels with strong beer, by which they are made drunk. On the following morning they (the baboons) were very cross and dismal; they held their aching heads with both hands, and wore a most pitiable expression: when beer was offered them, they turned away in disgust.

Charles Darwin, The Origin of Species, 1859

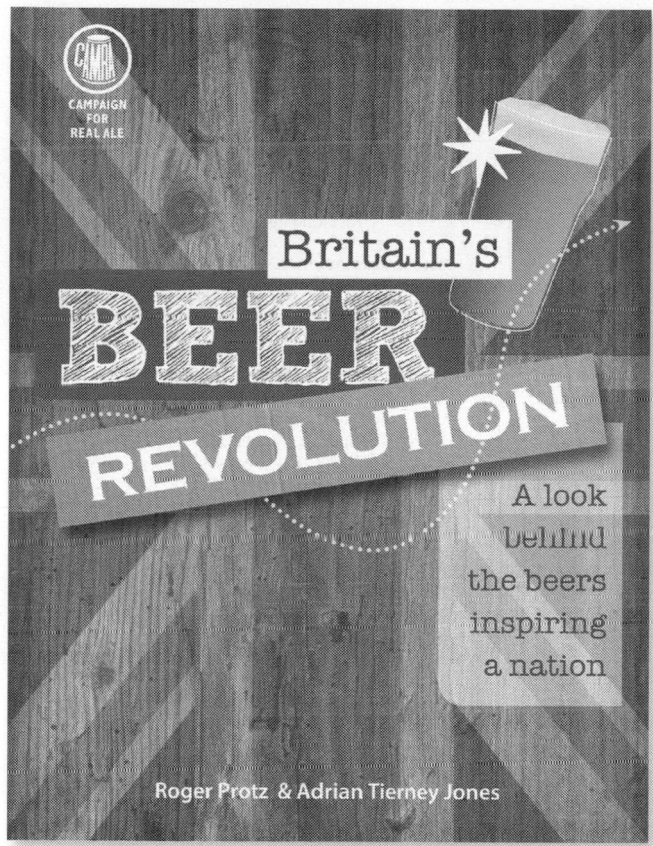

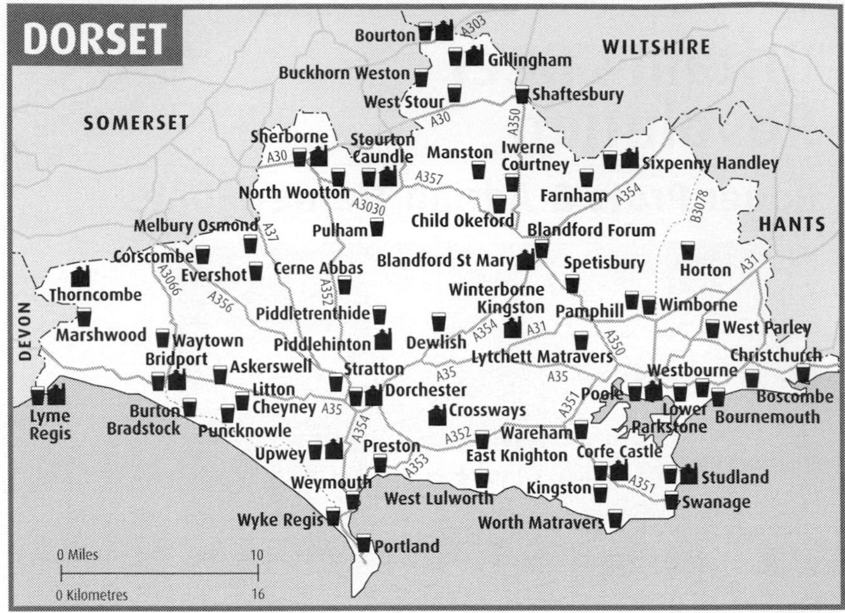

Askerswell

Spyway Inn 𝕃

DT2 9EP

⏲ 12-3, 6-11 ☎ (01308) 485250 🌐 spyway-inn.co.uk

Otter Bitter, Ale 🄷

Family-friendly 16th-century smugglers' inn perched on a hill outside Askerswell on the road to Eggardon Hill fort. From March to October there is usually a local cider on draught as well as the Otter beers on gravity. The lounge bar has beams and a woodburner; a further bar has tables for dining. The menu features dishes made with locally-produced ingredients. The garden is popular with locals, walkers and dog owners, and has a play area for families. Q❀⛺●P

Blandford Forum

Dolphin 𝕃

42 East Street, DT11 7DR

⏲ 11-11 (midnight Fri & Sat) ☎ (01258) 456813
🌐 thedolphinblandford.co.uk

Dorset Piddle Piddle, Slasher; Timothy Taylor Landlord; guest beers 🄷

Originally the White Hart, the pub was rebuilt as the Dolphin after the great Blandford fires of 1731. Now owned by the Dorset Piddle Brewery, it retains much of its historical feel and cosy atmosphere. The bar features a prominent selection of Piddle beers, with plenty of room for regular and seasonal guests and a real cider. Popular for lunches and evening meals, reservations are recommended for Sunday lunch. Dogs are welcome and even have their own meal on the menu. ◑●🚌🐾ᯤ

Boscombe

Chaplin's & The Cellar Bar 🏆

529 Christchurch Road, BH1 4AG

⏲ 9am-midnight (2am Thu-Sat) ☎ (01202) 251953
🌐 chaplins-bar.co.uk

Beer range varies 🄷/🄶

This bar, restaurant and live music venue was local CAMRA Pub of the Year in 2013. Upstairs, the Chaplin-themed bar is decorated with memorabilia and screens silent films. It serves one beer and excellent food all day, locally sourced and organic where possible. Downstairs, the Cellar Bar, artfully decorated with suitably moody lighting, opens from 4pm (noon Sat and Sun). It hosts live music every night on a small stage. Up to six beers from local breweries are available here. The unexpected garden helps make this a venue not to be missed. ❀◑♣●🚌ᯤ

Bournemouth

Cricketers Arms

41 Windham Road, BH1 4RN

⏲ 11-11 (10.30 Sun) ☎ (01202) 551589

Fuller's London Pride; guest beers 🄷

This unspoilt Victorian gem dating back to 1847 is one of the oldest pubs in Bournemouth and retains many original features including internal stained glass windows and superb gents' urinals. The vaulted upper section of the lounge was converted from a gym where the legendary world champion boxer Freddie Mills once trained. Entertainment includes occasional live music, card bingo on Friday and a popular annual beer festival. Sunday lunch is available, served in generous portions at a reasonable price. ❀♣●P🚌🐾ᯤ

Bourton

White Lion

High Street, SP8 5AT

⏲ 12-2.30, 5-11; 12-11 Fri & Sat; 12-10.30 Sun
☎ (01747) 840866 🌐 whitelionbourton.co.uk

Otter Amber; guest beer 🄷

The White Lion is a traditional inn dating from 1763. Originally separate rooms, the cosy flagstoned bar has been opened out but there is always a quiet corner to be found. It has a comfortable, intimate restaurant and, to the rear, a large beer garden. The pub is set back from the B3081 with parking opposite as well as in the car park. ❀🛏◑🍎P🚌(158)📶

Bridport

Crown Inn 🄻

56 West Bay Road, DT6 4AX

⏲ 11.30-11 (1am Fri & Sat); 11.30-10.30 Sun ☎ (01308) 422037

Palmers Copper Ale, Best Bitter, 200, Tally Ho! 🄷

Welcoming single-bar establishment on the A35 roundabout between Bridport and West Bay. The Crown is a popular locals' pub, but families, parties and travellers are all made to feel at home. The full range of Palmer's beers is available and good food is served noon-9pm. Large TV screens show sport, and there is a thriving live music scene here at weekends. Outside is a beer garden and large car park. ♉❀◑♣P🚌🐾📶

Ropemakers Arms 🄻

36 West Street, DT6 3QP

⏲ 11-11 (12.30am Fri); 10-12.30am Sat; 12-3 Sun ☎ (01308) 421255 🌐 theropemakers.com

Palmers Copper Ale, Best Bitter, seasonal beer 🄷

Deceptively large pub situated in the centre of town serving the full range of Palmer's ales, with Dorset Gold in the summer and Tally Ho! in the winter. The interior has lots of separate themed areas decorated with memorabilia and local history. Outside is a large partially covered courtyard; disabled access is via the back door. Quality home-cooked food features ingredients sourced from local suppliers, with breakfast served 10-11.30am on Saturday mornings. Live music is hosted on Friday and Saturday evenings. Q❀◑♣🍎🚌

Tiger Inn

16 Barrack Street, DT6 3LY

⏲ 12-11 (midnight Fri & Sat) ☎ (01308) 427543

Butcombe Adam Henson's Rare Breed; Grays Best Bitter; Sharp's Doom Bar; guest beers 🄷

Bright, cheerful Victorian ale house offering six real ales including three guests mainly from West Country breweries. The single split-level bar has TV for major sports events, plus pub games and a skittle alley. Children are allowed in the top bar. There is a pretty garden and a heated courtyard. B&B is offered in five en-suite rooms. Close to the town centre shops, the Tiger is a well-hidden secret worth seeking out. ❀🛏♣🚌🐾📶

Buckhorn Weston

Stapleton Arms

Church Hill, SP8 5HS (between A303 and A30) ST75652462

⏲ 11-3, 6-11; 11-11 Sat & Sun ☎ (01963) 370396 🌐 thestapletonarms.com

Butcombe Bitter; Moor Beer Revival; guest beers 🄷

Imposing village pub with a large car park and secluded garden. The two guest beers often reflect the seasons and are frequently from local breweries. Excellent food is served as well as classic bar snacks such as hand-made pork pies, Scotch eggs and chutney. Children, dogs and muddy boots are welcome. Modern en-suite accommodation completes the 'Drink, Eat, Sleep' motto. Q♉❀🛏◑🍎P🐾📶

Burton Bradstock

Three Horseshoes 🄻

Mill Street, DT6 4QZ

⏲ 12-3, 5-11; 12-11 Sat; 12-10.30 Sun ☎ (01308) 897259 🌐 3hsbb.co.uk

Palmers Copper Ale, Best Bitter, Dorset Gold, 200, Tally Ho! 🄷

Thatched 300-year-old pub and restaurant with suntrap seating at the front and in the beer garden. A popular refreshment stop for families using the beach, it serves good food featuring local produce. The full Palmer's beer range is kept and this is one of the few Palmer's pubs that regularly stocks Tally Ho! Q♉❀◑♿♣P🚌(X53)🐾

Cerne Abbas

Royal Oak Inn 🄻

23 Long Street, DT2 7JG

⏲ 11-3, 6-11 ☎ (01300) 341797 🌐 royaloakcerneabbas.co.uk

Hall & Woodhouse Badger First Gold, seasonal beers 🄷

Delightful thatched pub in the heart of the village, built in 1540 using stone and other building materials from the abbey, which was largely destroyed following the Dissolution of the Monasteries. The interior, made up of three interconnecting rooms, has a cosy feel. Good wholesome food is served lunchtimes and evenings with daily specials. The pub may open all day during the summer. Q♉❀◑♿♣🐾📶

Child Okeford

Saxon Inn

Gold Hill, DT11 8HD

⏲ 12-3, 6-11 ☎ (01258) 860310 🌐 saxoninn.co.uk

Butcombe Bitter; Otter Ale; guest beer 🄷

This traditional village pub is situated at the north end of the village, close to the iron age hill forts of Hambledon and Hod Hill near the Stour Valley Way. Converted from three farm cottages in the 1950s, a corner bar serves the comfortable main room with an open fire and low beams, and an adjoining panelled lounge with a wood-burning stove. A delicious food menu is offered including daily specials. The large, quiet garden with a covered patio is at the rear. Q♉❀🛏◑♣P🐾📶

INDEPENDENT BREWERIES

Blackmore Stourton Caundle
Bournemouth Poole (NEW)
Brewhouse & Kitchen Dorchester (NEW)
Corfe Castle Corfe Castle
Dorset (DBC) Crossways
DT Upwey
Gyle 59 Thorncombe (NEW)
Hall & Woodhouse (Badger) Blandford St Mary
Isle of Purbeck Studland
King Alfred Bourton (NEW)
Palmers Bridport
Piddle Piddlehinton
Sherborne Sherborne (brewing suspended)
Sixpenny Sixpenny Handley
Small Paul's Gillingham
Southbourne Lyme Regis (NEW)
Sunny Republic Winterborne Kingston
Town Mill Lyme Regis

Christchurch

Thomas Tripp

10 Wick Lane, BH23 1HX

⌚ 11-11; 12-11.30 Sun ☎ (01202) 490498

🌐 thomastripp.co.uk

Ringwood Best Bitter, Fortyniner; guest beer Ⓗ

Making a welcome return to the Guide, this historic inn, named after a local smuggler, has been refurbished by the enthusiastic landlord. Situated just off the High Street, near the historic priory, quay and preserved trolley bus turntable, it is popular with young and old. Live music features on several nights a week, bar food is served lunchtimes, and there is a barbecue on the patio in summer. A covered area for smokers is available. ❀◐♿🚌📶

Corfe Castle

Royal British Legion Club

70 East Street, BH20 5EQ (off A351)

⌚ 12-2.30, 6-11; 12-11 Sat & Sun ☎ (01929) 480591

Ringwood Best Bitter; Timothy Taylor Landlord; guest beer Ⓗ

Built in Purbeck stone, this friendly club has a bar area with upholstered bench seating, wooden tables and chairs. An upstairs meeting room can be hired. Major sporting events are shown on TV, and darts, shove-ha'penny and occasional live music are played. Filled rolls are available at lunchtime. The lovely garden has a boules court and views over the Purbecks. Show a CAMRA membership card or a copy of this Guide for entry. ❀♣P🚌(40)

Corscombe

Fox Inn Ⓛ

DT2 0NS

⌚ closed Mon & Tue; 12-2, 7-11 (10.30 Sun)

☎ (01935) 892381 🌐 foxinncorscombe.com

Dartmoor Legend; Sharp's Doom Bar; guest beers Ⓗ

Traditional family-run village pub in ramblers' countryside with a thatched roof and unspoilt interior boasting a slate bar, flagstone floors and a lovely old inglenook fireplace. The food appeals to all tastes, with pub classics and a main menu featuring local seasonal produce, served in the conservatory. There are two changing guest beers from breweries such as Yeovil and Exmoor, and two ciders. The pub hosts many events including regular live music. Q♨❀◐◑♣🍎P🐾📶

Dewlish

Oak at Dewlish

DT2 7ND

⌚ 12 (11 Fri)-2.30, 6-11; 12-2.30, 7-11 Sun

☎ (01258) 837352 🌐 oakpub.co.uk

Beer range varies Ⓗ

Unpretentious village inn with two or three ever-changing ales, mainly from West Country breweries such as Cotleigh, Isle of Purbeck and Dartmoor. The horseshoe-shaped bar has a dining area and opens onto a patio and large garden. To the rear is a separate room with a pool table. A varied food menu offers good home-cooked dishes made with local produce. Two B&B rooms and self-catering accommodation are available in an adjacent converted coach house. Dogs and children welcome. Q♨❀🛏◐◑♣🚌(311)🐾

Dorchester

Blue Raddle Ⓛ

8 Church Street, DT1 1JN

⌚ 11.30-3 (not Mon), 6.30-11; 12-3, 7-10.30 Sun

☎ (01305) 267762 🌐 blueraddle.co.uk

Branscombe Vale Branoc; Dartmoor IPA; St Austell Trelawny; guest beers Ⓗ

Popular, genuine, town-centre free house with friendly staff and an enthusiastic landlord. In addition to the regular beers, guest ales and local ciders are also on offer. Good locally-sourced food is served lunchtimes (no food Sun) and Thursday, Friday and Saturday evenings. The pub takes part in local events and hosts regular folk music sessions. Piped comedy shows and Private Eye are available in the conveniences. No children, but dogs are welcome. Q◐◑⇌(West)♣🍎🚌🐾📶

Tom Browns Ⓛ

47 High East Street, DT1 1HU

⌚ 11-11 (2am Fri & Sat); 12-11 Sun ☎ (01305) 264020

Dorset Goldfinch Tom Brown's, Jurassic; guest beers Ⓗ

Previously home to the Goldfinch Brewery, this is now the Dorset Brewing Company tap. The full range of Goldfinch, DBC and interesting guests rotate round the eight handpumps, and a local cider is also available. Refurbished but retaining the feel of a town-centre ale house, the pub hosts mini beer festivals, live music and other events. It has a fully functional skittle alley and large riverside garden. Food includes award-winning pies. ♨❀◐⇌(West)♣🍎🚌🐾📶

East Knighton

Countryman Inn Ⓛ

Blacknoll Lane, DT2 8LL

⌚ 7.30-11 ☎ (01305) 852666

🌐 thecountrymaninndorset.com

Fuller's London Pride; Ringwood Best Bitter, Fortyniner; St Austell Tribute, Proper Job; Sharp's Doom Bar; guest beer Ⓗ

Large village pub situated just off the A352 between Dorchester and Wool. It has an open plan layout with a restaurant area which serves a carvery six days a week as well as an extensive menu and daily specials. The Ringwood Fortyniner is rebadged as Countryman's Ale. The garden has a play area and there is a nine-hole crazy golf course between the car park and the pub. Dog-friendly – dogs are allowed in the accommodation. ♨❀🛏◐◑♿♣P🚌(X53)🐾📶

Evershot

Acorn Inn Hotel Ⓛ

28 Fore Street, DT2 0JW

⌚ 11 (12 Sun)-11 ☎ (01305) 262360 🌐 acorn-inn.co.uk

Beer range varies Ⓗ

Small, attractive, 16th-century hotel mentioned in Thomas Hardy's Tess of the d'Urbervilles as the Sow & Acorn. The large flagstoned village bar at the back has a wood-burning stove. A smaller bar and restaurant are at the front. Two ales are always available, usually from Dartmoor, Dorset Brewing Company, Otter Brewery or Yeovil Ales. A third ale and local cider are added in the summer. The skittle alley can be hired for functions. Winner of a Taste of the West Gold Award in 2014. ♨❀🛏◐◑♣🍎P🐾📶

Farnham

Museum 𝕃

DT11 8DE (off A354)

⏲ 12-11 ☎ (01725) 516261 🌐 museuminn.co.uk

Fuller's London Pride; Sixpenny 6D Best Bitter; guest beer Ⓗ

Set in tranquil Dorset countryside, this 17th-century, part-thatched country inn has a cosy, intimate feel. Refurbished in 2012, the interior is open plan but divided into four distinct areas. Some original features have been retained including the flagstone floor in the bar area, large inglenook and window seat. The pub is predominately food oriented but welcoming to those who just want a drink. Excellent locally-sourced food is served all day from a good varied menu. Q⛭❀🛏◑◗♿P🐾

Gillingham

Phoenix

High Street, SP8 4AW

⏲ 10-3, 6-11 (not Mon eve); 10-11 Fri; 11-midnight Sat; 11-3, 6-11 Sun ☎ (01747) 823277

St Austell Tribute; Sharp's Doom Bar Ⓗ

Originally built in the 15th century as a coaching inn, with its own brewery and stables, the pub was rebuilt in the 17th century following a fire, hence the Phoenix. It has an open-plan layout with a dining area to one side serving good-value pub grub. There are two public car parks within walking distance. ◑◗⇌🚌(158)

Horton

Drusilla's Inn

Wigbeth, BH21 7JH

⏲ 10-11 ☎ (01258) 840297 🌐 drusillasinn.co.uk

Flack Manor Flack's Double Drop; Ringwood Best Bitter; guest beer Ⓗ

Attractive thatched pub with leaded windows and olde worlde charm, offering views over the rolling Dorset countryside and Horton Folly. Decorated with brasses, rural prints and an inglenook fireplace with logburner, it has a traditional atmosphere. Well-kept ales, delicious meals and friendly, welcoming staff make this a pub to return to. The secure garden has a play area for children. Accommodation is offered in stylish traditional Dorset shepherds' huts. Q⛭❀🛏◑◗P🐾

Iwerne Courtney (Shroton)

Cricketers

Main Street, DT11 8QD (off A350 N of Stourpaine)

⏲ 12-3, 6-11; 12-10.30 Sun ☎ (01258) 860421

🌐 thecricketersshroton.co.uk

Butcombe Bitter; guest beers Ⓗ

Situated in the picturesque north-east Dorset village of Shroton, and convenient for walks around Hambledon Hill, the Cricketers is a community pub popular with locals and tourists alike. The open-plan centre bar serves a bustling drinking area and a dining area at the rear. An extensive menu offers local specialities and traditional pub food. In the summer the tranquil garden is popular, while the woodburner adds warmth in winter. Q⛭❀◑◗P📶

Kingston

Scott Arms

West Street, BH20 5LH

⏲ 11-11 ☎ (01929) 480270 🌐 thescottarms.com

Dorset Jurassic; Ringwood Best Bitter; guest beers Ⓗ

This imposing Virginia Creeper-covered corner pub has an upper and lower bar, the upper part being a series of cosy interconnected rooms, and a garden with unrivalled views across Corfe Castle to Poole Harbour. Two guest beers are kept, often from Butcombe or Otter, and the pub serves local cider produced just down the hill. Excellent home-cooked food with some exotic dishes is served lunchtimes and evenings.
⛭❀◑◗Λ♣🍎P🚌(40,44)

Litton Cheney

White Horse Inn 𝕃

DT2 9AT

⏲ 12-3, 6-11; 12-11 Sat & Sun ☎ (01308) 482539

🌐 thewhitehorseinndorset.co.uk

Palmers Copper Ale, Best Bitter, 200 Ⓗ

A traditional British pub with a restaurant serving home-cooked food. The single-room inn is on the southern edge of the village, not far from the spectacular coastline and Chesil Beach. Popular with walkers, it is dog-friendly. There is a stream-side garden for those summer days and a welcoming fire in winter. Live music nights are a regular feature. Closed Mondays in autumn and winter. Q⛭❀◑◗♣🍎P🐾

Lower Parkstone

Bermuda Triangle

10 Parr Street, BH14 0JY

⏲ 12-3, 5-11; 12-midnight Fri & Sat; 12-11 Sun

☎ (01202) 748047

Beer range varies Ⓗ

This busy pub is decorated to reflect the Bermuda Triangle story. The single-room bar is on three levels, with the walls and ceiling displaying a range of artefacts relating to ships and planes including maps, newspaper cuttings and ship and aircraft fittings. Run by the same owner for 24 years, the bar has four handpumps offering an ever-changing range of ales sourced locally and throughout the UK as well as speciality lagers and foreign beers.
❀⇌(Parkstone)P🚌(M1,1B)

Poole Ex-Servicemen's Club (RBL)

66 North Road, BH14 0LY

⏲ 6-11 Mon & Tue; 12-3, 6-midnight; 12-midnight Fri-Sun

☎ (01202) 744515

Beer range varies Ⓗ

Winner of Wessex CAMRA Club of the Year 2013, this social club is affiliated to the Royal British Legion. Visitors are welcome with a CAMRA membership card or a copy of this Guide. Three ever-changing ales from breweries across the country as well as a real cider are on offer. Beer festivals are held in summer and winter. The club has a large main room, meeting rooms, pool tables, eight dartboards and a beer garden. A snooker room is upstairs.
⛭❀◑♿⇌(Parkstone)♣🍎P🚌(M2)📶

Lyme Regis

Volunteer 𝕃

31 Broad Street, DT7 3QE

⏲ 11-11 (10.30 Sun) ☎ (01297) 442214 🌐 thevoli.co.uk

Branscombe Vale Best Bitter Ⓖ**; St Austell Tribute; guest beers** Ⓗ

Old two-room pub in the heart of this historic town, close to the seafront, and popular with locals. The house beer, Donegal, is Branscombe Vale Best and is stillaged behind the bar. A rotating choice of two West Country guest ales is on offer, alongside local ciders. Food is served at weekends only in winter. Dogs are allowed in the main bar and families in the refurbished left-hand room.
Q (31,X53)

Lytchett Matravers

Rose & Crown

178 Wareham Road, BH16 6DT
12-11 (2am Fri & Sat); 12-10.30 Sun ☎ (01202) 625325
roseandcrownlytchett.co.uk
Sharp's Doom Bar; guest beers H
The Rose & Crown is a welcoming, friendly, two-bar free house. Doom Bar is the regular beer on handpump, along with up to three guests, often from local breweries. Real cider is kept in the public bar, where there is a dartboard and an open fire. Excellent home-cooked food is available. The lawned garden has a covered arch for smokers. The pub hosts regular comedy and live music events on site and at the village hall, plus a village beer festival. P (X8,387)

Manston

Plough Inn

Shaftesbury Road, DT10 1HB (on B3091 2 miles NE of Sturminster Newton) ST81351611
11.30-2.30, 6-11; 12-3 Sun ☎ (01258) 472484
theploughinn.co.uk
Fuller's London Pride; Palmers Copper Ale; Sharp's Doom Bar; Timothy Taylor Landlord; guest beer H
This 450-year-old stone-built country inn has a single large bar with oak beams and unique plaster decorations on the ceiling and bar front, thought to be harvest fertility symbols. There is a large conservatory dining area, covered patio, garden complete with pétanque court and campsite. Live music features every Saturday night.
P

Marshwood

Bottle Inn

DT6 5QJ (on B3165 nr Devon border)
12-10.30 ☎ (01297) 678484 bottle-inn.net
Beer range varies H
The pub has two rooms served by a single bar, with a family room and skittle alley at the rear. A large garden overlooks Marshwood Vale. Six ales are served, usually including two from local micros such as Mighty Hop, together with interesting guests from afar. Around 20 ciders and perries, plus foreign beers, are available. The pub holds a nettle eating competition in June incorporating a beer festival. Local CAMRA branch Pub of the Year 2014.
Q P

Melbury Osmond

Rest & Welcome

Yeovil Road, DT2 0NF (on A37 Yeovil-Dorchester road)
11.30-11; 12-10 Sun ☎ (01935) 83248
the-rest-and-welcome-inn.co.uk
Beer range varies G
Split-level two-roomed roadside pub on the main Dorset artery offering a welcome break to seaside-bound travellers. On the Thomas Hardy trail, the inn featured as the Sheaf of Arrows in the author's Interlopers at the Knap short story of 1884. The home-cooked food is locally sourced. Three varying guest beers are served direct from the cask. A skittle alley doubles as a function room.
Q P (212)

North Wootton

Three Elms Inn

DT9 5JW
11-11; 12-10.30 Sun ☎ (01935) 812881
thethreeelmsinn.co.uk
Beer range varies H
This enterprising rural free house is not only a thriving pub but also the village shop and post office. The comfortable L-shaped bar offering two real ales and traditional pub food is popular with drinkers and diners alike (no food Mon). The ales change every week and are rarely repeated, although they are not over 5% ABV. West Dorset CAMRA Rural Pub of the Year 2013.
Q P

Pamphill

Vine Inn ★

Vine Hill, BH21 4EE (off B3082)
11-3, 7-10.30 (11 Thu-Sat); 12-3, 7-10.30 Sun
☎ (01202) 882259
Beer range varies H/G
With a nationally important historic pub interior and winner of many local CAMRA awards, this pub has been run by the same family since 1900. Bought by the National Trust in 1989 and built into Vine Hill, access is via stone steps from the road. It has a small public bar, upstairs taproom and cosy lounge. The simple bar counter serves two beers. The suntrap garden features a veranda that supports an impressive vine. Ploughman's lunches and sandwiches are served lunchtimes only.
Q P

Piddletrenthide

Poachers Inn

DT2 7QX
12-11.30 ☎ (01300) 348358 thepoachersinn.co.uk
Butcombe Bitter; St Austell Tribute; Sharp's Doom Bar H
A quiet family pub with a friendly welcome and three permanent real ales, renowned for its good food sourced from local suppliers. It has a traditional yet modern bar on split levels, a 17th-century restaurant, riverside garden and 21-room accommodation arranged around a central courtyard. A swimming pool is available during the summer months. There is disabled access and plenty of parking. P (307)

Poole

Blue Boar

29 Market Close, BH15 1NE
12-11 (midnight Fri & Sat) ☎ (01202) 682247
blueboarpoole.co.uk
Fuller's London Pride, ESB; Gales Seafarers Ale; guest beer H
Popular Fuller's pub, located near the town centre, with four handpumps, the guest beer often not from the Fuller's range. The L-shaped bar is

adorned with pictures and artefacts with either a military or local theme, while the cellar bar, a converted air raid shelter, offers an interesting alternative and hosts occasional live music at weekends. An excellent first-floor function room is available for hire. The home-cooked food is worth investigating, lunchtimes only on Sunday because of the evening quiz. ⛺❀◐⇌🚌(9,52)🐾

Bournemouth Brewing Company Ⓛ

Unit 12, 4-6 Abingdon Road, Nuffield Industrial Estate, BH17 0UG

⏲ closed Mon-Wed; 12-7 Thu & Fri; 10-5 Sat; closed Sun
☎ (01202) 280405 ⊕ bournemouthbrewery.co.uk

Beer range varies Ⓗ/Ⓖ

A bar/brewery shop set in this microbrewery which opened mid-2013. The small bar has limited facilities but it has become popular with locals working on the industrial estate and and now attracts custom from further afield. Enjoy a pint served directly from the cask while admiring the brewery behind the bar. An old family recipe is displayed that dates back to 1928 – the brewer used this as the base for Wessex Wobble beer. P

Brewhouse

68 High Street, BH15 1DA

⏲ 11-11; 12-10.30 Sun ☎ (01202) 685288

Milk Street Beer; guest beers Ⓗ

Popular, bustling town-centre local owned by the Milk Street Brewery of Frome, Somerset. The split-level interior has a bar at street level with two pool tables at the rear. Beers include Mermaid, which is almost exclusively brewed for the people of Poole, along with two other Milk Street beers and one well-chosen guest and real cider. Sit out front and watch the world go by, or enjoy the patio at the back. ❀⇌♣🍎🚌🐾

Portland

George Inn

133 Reforne, Easton, DT5 2AP

⏲ 12-11 ☎ (01305) 820011 ⊕ thegeorgeinn.org

Ringwood Best Bitter Ⓗ**; guest beers** Ⓗ/Ⓖ

A friendly, family-oriented local dating from the mid-18th century. It has four separate bar and dining areas, and a large enclosed beer garden. Food is available every day and the substantial Sunday roasts are popular. There are usually three ales on offer on both handpump and gravity, typically Black Sheep Best Bitter and St Austell Tribute. A popular beer festival is held annually around St George's Day. Q❀◐♣🚌(1)🐾

Royal British Legion

3 High Street, Fortuneswell, DT5 1JQ

⏲ 11.45-3, 7.30 (7 Thu)-11; 11.45-3, 6.30-11.15 Fri; 11.30-11.30 Sat; 11-11 Sun ☎ (01305) 821207

Exmoor Ale; guest beers Ⓗ

Popular members' club with a large downstairs bar serving three ales on handpump, including two guests usually selected from St Austell, Dartmoor, Skinner's, Sharp's, Exmoor, Yeovil and Piddle breweries. The upstairs function room is available for hire and there is a skittle alley, pool table, Sky Sports showing all major events and free WiFi. Live music features every Saturday evening and some bank holiday Sundays. Meat and alcohol raffles are held every Sunday lunchtime. Show your CAMRA membership card to be signed in as a guest. ⛶♣P🚌(1)📶

Preston

Spice Ship

240 Preston Road, DT3 6BH

⏲ 11.30-midnight summer; 12-11 Sun & winter
☎ (01305) 834651 ⊕ spiceship.co.uk

Ringwood Best Bitter; Sharp's Doom Bar; Timothy Taylor Landlord; guest beer Ⓗ

Grade II-listed coaching house with a lively public bar and a separate dining area serving excellent food. The guest beer rotates between Butcombe Bitter, Dartmoor Jail Ale and Otter Bitter, plus DBC Jurassic in the summer. Screens show televised sports events and live music draws a crowd. Outside is a large grassed area with tables and a safe children's play area. Car parking and overnight accommodation are available.
Q⛺❀🛏◐⛶♣P🚌(4A,X53)🐾📶

Pulham

Halsey Arms

DT2 7DZ

⏲ 11-2.30, 6-midnight; 11-midnight Fri-Sun
☎ (01258) 817344

Ringwood Best Bitter; guest beers Ⓗ

Family-friendly pub with a snug and main bar. Home-cooked and locally-sourced food is served in the restaurant, and bar snacks are also available. It gets popular with diners on a Sunday lunchtime. Live music and quizzes take place throughout the month, and there is a beer garden and children's play area. Weddings and conferences are catered for in the function room.
Q⛺❀🛏◐♿⛶♣🍎P🚌(307)🐾📶

Puncknowle

Crown Inn Ⓛ

Church Street, DT2 9BN

⏲ 11-3, 5.30-10.30; 11-11 Sat; 10-6 Sun ☎ (01308) 897711
⊕ thecrowninndorset.co.uk

Palmers Copper Ale, Best Bitter, Dorset Gold, 200, Tally Ho! Ⓗ

Attractive thatched inn with an extensive menu including vegetarian dishes, plus pizzas to eat in or take away. The two bars are comfortably furnished and heated by three log fires; there is also a comfortable family room. An acoustic music session is held on the first Monday of every month. A small village shop in an old store room at the rear of the building stocks a wide range of basic provisions. The village name is pronounced 'Punnel'. Q⛺❀🛏◐⛶♣P🐾

Shaftesbury

Ship Inn

24 Bleke Street, SP7 8JZ

⏲ 12-midnight (1am Fri & Sat) ☎ (01747) 853219
⊕ shipinnfreehouse.co.uk

Beer range varies Ⓗ

The 17th-century Ship has four bars – the main bar, a games room with pool, darts, fruit machine and jukebox, a snug with an open fire and a newly refurbished lounge bar. Outside, there is space to sit in the sun or shelter in the covered smoking area. No food is served but staff will order food for you from local takeaways or you can bring in your own. Rumoured to be home to a ghost. ❀🍎🚌🐾📶

Sherborne

Digby Tap

Cooks Lane, DT9 3NS

11 (12 Sun)-11 ☎ (01935) 813148 digbytap.co.uk

Beer range varies H

The Digby Tap is an institution in west Dorset. Hidden away between the railway station and the abbey, it is worth seeking out for the building alone. The interior feels like stepping back in time, yet the pub remains popular with all ages. Four or five ales from across the West Country are always available. Bought by the pint or jug, they offer superb value. Reasonably priced pub food is served at lunchtime. Q

Sixpenny Handley

Sixpenny Tap

The Dairy Building, Manor Farm, SP5 5NU (turn off B3018 onto unclassified road ¼ mile S of village, signed behind farm buildings) ST99811663

closed Mon & Tue; 4.30-6 Wed & Thu; 4-6.30 Fri; 11.30-1 Sat; closed Sun ☎ (01725) 726006 sixpennybrewery.co.uk

Sixpenny 6D Best Bitter, Gold, IPA, 106 Jack FM Ale, seasonal beer H/G

This bar attached to the brewhouse is also the brewery shop. Seasonal and occasional ales are often available. Opening hours are restricted due to the terms of the lease but the bar is busy and popular. Beers are available direct from the cask or by handpump, by the glass or in take-home disposable containers. P(184)

Spetisbury

Woodpecker

High Street, DT11 9DJ (A350)

12-3, 6-11; 12-3, 7-10.30 Sun ☎ (01258) 452658

Beer range varies H

An imposing free house situated in the heart of the picturesque village of Spetisbury. This comfortable open-plan pub offers four ever-changing ales from the surrounding area, three real ciders and three perries. Good-quality food is available (no food Sun and Mon eve). Bar billiards and shove-ha'penny can be played. The spacious garden is home to an annual cider festival and is the perfect place for whiling away an afternoon. Winner of local CAMRA Rural Pub of the Year 2012. P(X8)

Stourton Caundle

Trooper

Golden Hill, DT10 2JW (1½ miles E of A357) ST71491495

closed Mon; 12-2.30 (3.30 Sun), 7-11 ☎ (01963) 362405 thetrooperinn.co.uk

Blackmore Ale; guest beers H

Stone-built single-room community pub with a separate function room/skittle alley. There is an attached camping and caravan site and children's play area next to the beer garden. Good food is available lunchtimes and early evenings including popular Friday fish and chips. Two guest ales are offered and a farmhouse cider, with beers from the pub's own brewery when available. An annual beer festival is held in the spring. Dogs and walkers are welcome. CAMRA Regional Pub of the Year 2013. QP

Stratton

Saxon Arms

Dorchester Road, DT2 9WG

11-2.30, 5.30-11; 11-midnight Fri & Sat; 12-midnight Sun ☎ (01305) 260020 thesaxon-stratton.co.uk

Ringwood Best Bitter; Timothy Taylor Landlord; guest beers H

Newly built in 2001, this flint and thatch pub has the feel of a country inn. Outside, a patio area overlooks the green and village hall. The bar is divided into three areas including a dining space serving quality food from locally-sourced producers. In addition to the two regular beers, two guest beers from breweries such as Otter, Town Mill and Wychwood are available. This busy pub with helpful staff is an integral part of the local community. QP

Studland

Bankes Arms L

Watery Lane, BH19 3AU

11-11 ☎ (01929) 450225 bankesarms.com

Isle of Purbeck Best Bitter, Fossil Fuel, Solar Power, Studland Bay Wrecked, Purbeck IPA; guest beers H

This National Trust-owned country inn is over 200 years old and has been in the same family for 27 years. Situated in a picturesque village in the heart of the Purbecks, it is also home to Isle of Purbeck Brewery whose beers are dispensed through nine handpumps alongside guest ales and real cider. An annual beer festival is held in August. Delicious home-cooked food features on an ever-changing blackboard menu. The huge cliff-top garden offers attractive views over Poole Bay.
Q(50)

Swanage

Ship Inn L

23a High Street, BH19 2LR

12-11 ☎ (01929) 423855 theship-swanage.co.uk

Palmers Dorset Gold; Ringwood Best Bitter, Fortyniner H

Substantial bustling Victorian pub standing proudly in the heart of the High Street. Convenient for the beach, pier, Swanage Steam Railway and the South West Coast Path, this pub caters for all. The interior is open plan with a contemporary feel, featuring Purbeck stone walls and comfortable sofas. It is served by one large bar divided into three areas. Sporting events are shown on two TV screens and there is occasional live music. In summer enjoy the suntrap tiered seating area at the rear.
(Swanage Steam Railway)(40,50)

Upwey

Royal Standard L

700 Dorchester Road, DT3 5LA

11.30-3, 5.30-11; 11-midnight Fri & Sat; 12-11 Sun ☎ (01305) 812558 theroyalstandardupwey.co.uk

Yeovil Star Gazer; guest beers H

Situated on the outskirts of Weymouth and popular with locals and visitors alike, the pub has a U-shaped wood-panelled bar with a cosy lounge on one side and a seating area on the other. Two regular and two ever-changing locally-sourced guest beers are offered from breweries such as Piddle, Sixpenny and Sunny Republic. The on-site microbrewery supplies DT3 and DT4 ales, and the pub hosts an annual beer festival and sausage and cider festival. No food served on Monday. Q❀◑♣●P🚌(31)🐾

Wareham

King's Arms

41 North Street, BH20 4AD

⏲ 11-11; 12-10.30 Sun ☎ (01929) 552503

Ringwood Best Bitter; guest beers Ⓗ

A traditional thatched inn that has its roots in the 1500s and survived the great fire of 1762. This multi-roomed establishment has a flagstone-floored public bar, real fire, a drinking corridor and one room exclusively for dining. To the rear is a large garden with a covered area for smokers. A good range of reasonably priced home-cooked food is served. Three guest beers from the southern counties are on offer alongside the Ringwood Best Bitter. Q❀◑⇌●P🚌(40,X53)🐾

Quay Inn

The Quay, BH20 4LP

⏲ 8am-midnight (1am Fri & Sat) ☎ (01929) 552735

🌐 thequayinn.com

Ringwood Best Bitter; Timothy Taylor Landlord; guest beer Ⓗ

Much-acclaimed, award-winning, 18th-century pub, it offers a sumptuous freshly cooked steak and seafood menu alongside a fine selection of real ales, including a local Purbeck brew, and a good range of ciders, all served in front of a cosy open fire. Live music features at weekends, and there are also regular events on the quay and a Saturday market to enjoy. En-suite B&B rooms overlook the River Frome. ❀🛏◑▲P🚌(40,X53)🐾

Waytown

Hare & Hounds 𝕃

DT6 5LQ

⏲ 11.30 (12 Sun)-3, 6-11 ☎ (01308) 488203

Palmers Copper Ale, Best Bitter, 200, seasonal beer Ⓗ

Hidden down winding lanes, this unspoilt gem is well worth seeking out. The garden, with stunning views, has a play area and space for children to let off steam. Bridge Farm cider is a regular and the food menu features home-cooked meals. A quiz replaces food on Sunday evenings in winter. Palmers Dorset Gold is available in the summer and Tally Ho! in the winter. The pub may close earlier on quiet nights or stay open later if busy. Q❀◑♣●P🐾

West Lulworth

Castle Inn 𝕃

Main Road, BH20 5RN

⏲ 11-11 ☎ (01929) 400311

🌐 thecastleinn-lulworthcove.co.uk

Palmers Best Bitter Ⓗ**; guest beers** Ⓗ/Ⓖ

Winner of local CAMRA Rural Pub of the Year 2013, this enchanting 16th-century thatched inn close to Lulworth Cove has two comfortable bars, one with a low ceiling, both beamed. Six mostly local ales and 13 or more traditional ciders are served alongside an extensive food menu offering good-value home-made dishes in generous portions. Board games are available inside and at the rear is a tiered garden with a giant chess set. The inn has 15 bedrooms, 14 en-suite, and is dog-friendly. Q❀🛏◑♣●P🚌(103)🐾

West Parley

Owl's Nest

196 Christchuch Road, BH22 8SS

⏲ 11.30-3, 5 (6 Sat)-11.30; 12-3, 6-10 Sun

☎ (01202) 572793 🌐 theowlsnest-westparley.com

Otter Ale; guest beers Ⓗ

Tudor-style building with beamed ceilings and a woodburner, with a welcoming, comfortable ambience. The two-room interior is decorated with a number of collections, Toby jugs, military hats above the bar and many owls strategically positioned around the walls. Four handpumps serve a selection of locally-sourced beers. The pub offers a range of excellent home-cooked food, with pies a speciality. A monthly Irish music night and an annual beer festival are both popular. Q◑♿P🚌(13,57)

West Stour

Ship Inn

A30, SP8 5RP

⏲ 12-3, 6-11; 12-11 Sun ☎ (01747) 838640

🌐 shipinn-dorset.com

Beer range varies Ⓗ

Once a coaching inn, this popular roadside pub has views across the Blackmore Vale. The public bar features a flagstone floor, while the separate restaurant area is light and airy with stripped oak floorboards. There is a patio and large garden to the rear. A friendly, welcoming establishment, it is renowned for superb home-cooked food (no meals Sun eve) and comfortable accommodation. Three changing beers are always available and a beer festival is held in July. Dogs are welcome in the bar. Q❀🛏◑♣●P🐾

Westbourne

Porterhouse

113 Poole Road, BH4 9BG

⏲ 11-11 (midnight Fri & Sat); 12-11 Sun ☎ (01202) 768586

🌐 theporterhouse.com

Ringwood Best Bitter, Fortyniner, Old Thumper; guest beer Ⓗ

Previously known as the Old Thumper, this friendly wood-panelled one-bar local is popular with regulars, shoppers and office workers. Formerly a Ringwood pub and now owned by Marston's, the Porterhouse serves ales from Ringwood Brewery plus a guest from the Marston's family. A simple menu is available at lunchtimes, plus a roast on Sunday and an interesting range of bar snacks. With no music the conversation is lively, and board games and cards are available. Easy access by bus, train and taxi. Q◑⇌(Branksome)♣●🚌🐾

Weymouth

Boot Inn

High Street, DT4 8JH

⏲ 11-11 (midnight Fri & Sat); 12-11 Sun ☎ (01305) 770327

Ringwood Best Bitter, Fortyniner; guest beers Ⓗ

Weymouth's oldest pub has a single bar area leading to rooms at both ends, warmed by a roaring fire in winter. The Ringwood beers are complemented by guests from the Marston's group and Cheddar Valley cider. No meals are served except large pork pies but there is an impromptu banquet on Sundays when the fare is provided by both landlord and customers. It is a conversation-dominated venue, with customers spilling outside when the weather is clement. Live music Tuesdays, a quiz on Wednesdays. Q❀♿♣●🚌🐾

Globe Inn

24 East Street, DT4 8AS
⏲ 11-1am (midnight Sun) ☎ (01305) 786061
🌐 theglobeweymouth.co.uk
Dartmoor Jail Ale; Ringwood Old Thumper; St Austell Tribute; Sharp's Doom Bar; guest beers Ⓗ
Welcoming street-corner free house near Weymouth harbour and the town bridge, within walking distance of the town centre, main beach and esplanade. Four regular real ales are served plus two guests and a real cider. The separate games room has a pool table, darts and pub games. Reasonably priced accommodation is available in four letting rooms. A recent innovation is a fun quiz on Sunday afternoons for those days when the seaside sun does not shine. 🛏♣●🚌

Wimborne

Green Man

1 Victoria Road, BH21 1EN
⏲ 10-11.30 (1.30am Fri & Sat); 10-12.30am Sun
☎ (01202) 881021 🌐 greenmanwimborne.com
Wadworth Henry's IPA, 6X, seasonal beer Ⓗ
Note the green man in the floor when entering this traditional 18th-century one-bar pub, favoured by locals and providing a homely atmosphere. Famous for its summer floral displays, and woodburner to keep you snug and warm in the winter while enjoying the papers and books provided, this truly is a pub for all. Excellent food is served at lunchtimes. A quiet pub at times, but karaoke and live music feature at weekends. An ideal location for exploring the historic town and model village. ❀◐♣●P🚌🐾📶

Man in the Wall

10 West Borough, BH21 1NF
⏲ 8am-midnight (1am Fri & Sat) ☎ (01202) 639800
Courage Directors; Greene King Abbot; Ruddles Best Bitter; guest beers Ⓗ
Look for the man in the wall in this excellent refurbishment of a former Conservative Club. A listed building, it is near to the town centre and handy for the Tivoli Theatre. There are three separate rooms, decorated with antique books, pictures of Kingston Lacy, a map of the Wessex region and a Thomas Hardy quote. The usual Wetherspoon beers are available plus three guests and a house special brewed by Sixpenny.
Q❀◐◑♿🚌📶

Worth Matravers

Square & Compass ★

Weston Road, BH19 3LF (off B3069)
⏲ 12-3, 6-11; 12-11 summer & Fri-Sun ☎ (01929) 439229
🌐 squareandcompasspub.co.uk
Palmers Copper Ale; guest beers Ⓖ
This iconic multi-award-winning pub with a nationally important interior has appeared in every edition of the Guide. Two rooms either side of a serving hatch convey an impression that little has changed in many years. The sea-facing garden offers fantastic views across the Purbecks and fossils from the nearby coast are displayed in the small adjacent museum. Pasties are always available along with a choice of beers, and cider produced by the pub. Beer and cider festivals are held in October and November respectively.
Q❀⛺●P🚌(44)🐾

Wyke Regis

Wyke Smugglers

76 Portland Road, DT4 9AB
⏲ 12-midnight (1am Fri & Sat) ☎ (01305) 760010
Morland Old Speckled Hen; St Austell Proper Job; guest beer Ⓗ
A large and popular local, home to many teams including cricket, football, darts and skittles. A disco or live music feature on most Saturday nights, when the pub can get busy. The main dining area, warmed by a woodburner, offers a menu of good-quality locally-sourced food. Guest beers are from southern breweries and the Punch Finest Cask range. The large skittle alley doubles as a function room, and has a pool table. ❀◐◑♿♣P🚌(1)🐾

Life, liberty – and beer

Beer, happy produce of our Isle
Can sinewy Strength impart,
And wearied with Fatigue and Toil
Can cheer each manly Heart.

Labour and Art upheld by Thee
Successfully advance,
We quaff thy balmy juice with Glee
And Water leave to France.

Genius of Health, thy Grateful Taste
Rivals the Cup of Jove,
And warms each English generous Breast
With Liberty and Love.

Verses by James Townley to accompany William Hogarth's engraving, Beer Street, 1751

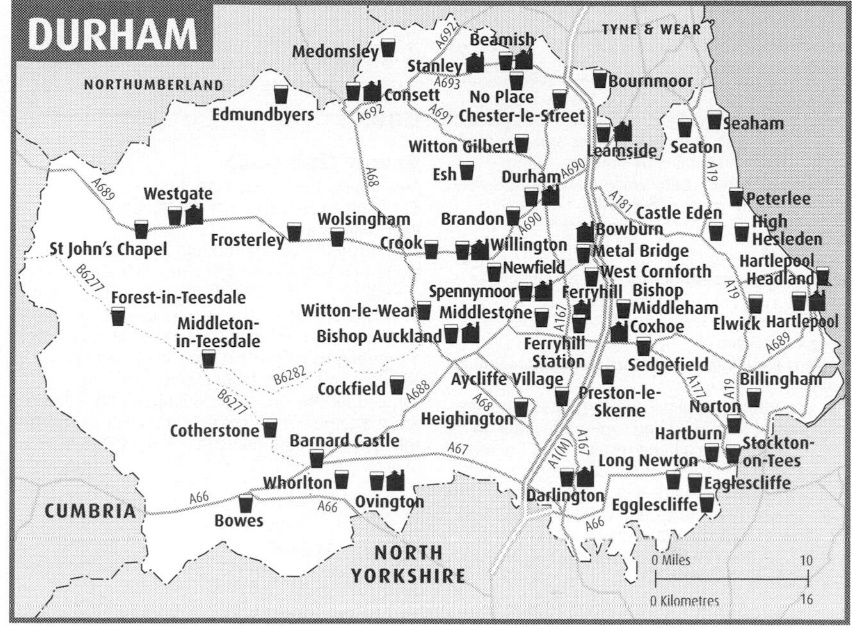

Co Durham incorporates part of the former county of Cleveland

Aycliffe Village

County

13 The Green, DL5 6LX
12-3, 6-11; 12-11 Sun ☎ (01325) 312273
thecountyaycliffevillage.com
Beer range varies Ⓗ
Overlooking the award-winning green in a picturesque village, this cream-coloured country free house was originally three 17th-century cottages. It is now open plan, with the bar and three dining areas unified by bright modern decor, complemented by older beams and log fireplaces. The current owners took over in 2008 and have a passion to marry good food with excellent beers. Up to four guests come from northern micros. Sunday is quiz night. There is accommodation in seven rooms. **Q** P (7)

Barnard Castle

Old Well Inn L

21 The Bank, DL12 8PH
12-11 ☎ (01833) 690130 theoldwellinn.co.uk
Courage Directors; Timothy Taylor Landlord; guest beers Ⓗ
The boundary of this 17th-century town-centre inn incorporates part of the medieval castle wall. The pub has a cosy front bar and a comfortable lounge, a separate restaurant and a conservatory, plus an enclosed garden. At least five beers are available including three guests from local micros. Excellent food is served daily, and there is accommodation in 10 rooms. Two 10-day beer festivals are held at Easter and in October. The Castle Players meet here. **Q** (75,76)

Beamish

Stables Bar & Restaurant L

Beamish Hall Country House Hotel, DH9 0YB
11-11 (midnight Fri & Sat); 11-10.30 Sun
☎ (01207) 288750 beamish-hall.co.uk/stables
Stables Beamish Hall Best Bitter, Old Miner Tommy, Bobby Dazzler, Silver Buckles, Beamish Burn, Bell Tower Ⓗ
The Stables is attached to Beamish Hall Country House Hotel, and has its own microbrewery. Stone floors, old beams, solid furniture and crackling log fires in winter help to create a relaxing environment. Outside is a courtyard seating area and, behind the pub, an extended play area for children. Beer festivals are hosted in September and January. The pub is also a popular live music venue. An extensive menu of locally-produced food is served. **Q** **P**

Billingham

Greenholme Catholic Club

37 Wolviston Road, TS23 2RU (on E side of old A19, just S of Roseberry Road roundabout, next to bus stop)
7-midnight (2am Fri); 12.30-2am Sat; 12-midnight Sun
☎ (01642) 901143 thecatholicclub.co.uk
Beer range varies Ⓗ
A genuine welcome awaits at this friendly private members' club, renowned for its vibrant R&B/rock scene. Dedicated and enthusiastic volunteers ensure that the club's reputation for serving 150 different beers annually continues. Three beers, one usually from Maxim, three ciders and a perry are normally offered, with up to 10 beers available during regular beer/music festivals, held over bank holiday weekends. The Monday Club offers heavily discounted prices. CAMRA branch Club of the Year 2014. **P** (35,36)

Bishop Auckland

Bay Horse

38-40 Fore Bondgate, DL14 7PE (50yds N of bus station)

11-11 (1am Fri & Sat); 12-11 Sun ☎ (01388) 609765
bayhorse-pub.co.uk
Timothy Taylor Landlord; guest beer Ⓗ
At the heart of Bishop's pub scene since 1530, this welcoming hostelry is a haven from shopping during the week, and a joyfully boisterous place on a weekend, with Friday live bands and Saturday night karaoke. It retains its roots as a long-established, proper pub, while featuring televised sports and pub games.

Pollards

104 Etherley Lane, DL14 6TU (400yds W of railway station)
12-2, 5.30-11; 12-3, 6-11 Sun ☎ (01388) 603539
thepollardsinn.co.uk
Jennings Cumberland Ale; Marston's Pedigree; guest beers Ⓗ
Four separate but linked drinking areas form the main part of this bright and comfortable pub on the edge of town, with a large restaurant to the rear. A popular quiz is hosted on Sunday evening, with supper included. Pollards has a reputation for good food, served lunchtimes and evenings, including the renowned Sunday carvery. A genuine pub offering seven well-kept ales and good conversation. QP

Stanley Jefferson

5 Market Place, DL14 7NJ
8am-midnight (1am Fri & Sat) ☎ (01388) 452830
Greene King Abbot; Ruddles Best Bitter; guest beers Ⓗ
All the usual Wetherspoon facilities are on offer at this interesting conversion of former solicitors' offices. Several separate but linked drinking areas and a glass-roofed bar area provide the opportunity for privacy or company. Close to the Bishop of Durham's palace and park, the pub takes its name from locally schooled Mr Jefferson – better known as Stan Laurel. There is a large walled garden to the rear and a small pavement patio to the front. Quiz night is Wednesday.

Bishop Middleham

Cross Keys

9 High Street, DL17 9AR (1 mile from A177)
12 (5 Mon)-11 ☎ (01740) 651231 crosskeyspub.net
Beer range varies Ⓗ
A busy family-run village pub with a good reputation for food. It has a bar with a real fire, a lounge and a large restaurant at the back. The pub is opposite the remains of Fosters Brewery, which closed in 1913, and may well have been its tap house. The village has a series of walks through beautiful countryside and to the ruins of Bishop Middleham Castle. Q

Bournmoor

Dun Cow

Primrose Hill, DH4 6DY
12-11 ☎ (0191) 385 2631 theduncowbournmoor.co.uk
Beer range varies Ⓗ
Welcoming 18th-century pub, reputedly haunted by an oft-seen Grey Lady ghost. It offers a varying beer range, good-value pub food served in the lounge and bar, and an à la carte menu in the Lambton restaurant. There is also a large function room. The pub is family-friendly, with extensive gardens. Beer festivals showcasing local ales are held in March and October. Music festivals on the first Saturday in June and last in September feature local folk and rock bands. P

Bowes

Bowes Club (CIU)

Arch House, The Street, DL12 9HR
7 (3 Sat & Sun)-midnight ☎ (01833) 628431
Beer range varies Ⓗ
Previously the village lock-up, this 18th-century stone building is now a thriving club which hosts community events including quoits. There are two downstairs rooms – one with pool and darts, the other with a cosy fire in the fine old fireplace – and a meeting room upstairs. The single handpump features an ever-changing guest beer, often sourced locally. Guests including CAMRA members are welcome – if in the area you must experience this gem. Opening hours may vary. Q

Brandon

Morley Wood

Winchester Drive, DH7 8UG
12-11 ☎ (0191) 447 5995 themorleywood.co.uk
Black Sheep Best Bitter; Timothy Taylor Landlord; guest beers Ⓗ
Large, modern, family-focused pub serving a range of ales and a selection of reasonably priced food. It has a lively atmosphere and ample comfortable seating. Activities include pool, darts and dominoes. Live music plays occasionally on Friday or Saturday nights and there is a pub quiz on Thursday. Outside, there is a good-sized enclosed beer garden and ample parking.
P(46)

Castle Eden

Castle Eden Inn

Stockton Road, TS27 4SD
12-11 ☎ (01429) 835137 castleedeninn.com
Timothy Taylor Landlord; guest beers Ⓗ
Castle Eden village is famous for the former Castle Eden Brewery. This recently refurbished old coaching inn has a large bar offering a good selection of ales. The lounge has a spacious and comfortable seating area. Quality food featuring local produce is served in the bar, lounge or the more formal restaurant. There is also a private function room. P

INDEPENDENT BREWERIES

Black Paw Bishop Auckland
Blackhill Stanley
Camerons Hartlepool
Consett Ale Works Consett
Crafty Pint Darlington (NEW)
Durham Bowburn
Four Alls Ovington
Gambling Man Willington
Hill Island Durham
Just A Minute Spennymoor
Leamside Leamside
Sonnet 43 Coxhoe
Stables Beamish
Weard'ALE Westgate
Yard of Ale Ferryhill

Chester-le-Street

Butchers Arms

Middle Chare, DH3 3QD (off Front St)
🕘 11-11 (midnight Fri & Sat) ☎ (0191) 388 3605
🌐 butchersarms.org.uk
Jennings Cumberland Ale; Marston's Pedigree; guest beers Ⓗ
A cosy pub in the centre of town acknowledged for the quality and quantity of its beers – the landlady has now increased the number of cask ales to seven. The pub is also noted for its food, with home cooking a speciality – Sunday lunches are popular and good value. Teas and coffees are also served. Convenient for the railway station and all buses through the town.
Q (21)

Chester-le-Street Cricket Club

Ropery Lane, DH3 3PF
🕘 11-11 (midnight Fri-Sun) ☎ (0191) 388 3684
🌐 chesterlestreet-cc.com
Cumberland Corby Ale; guest beer Ⓗ
A splendid club house with two main rooms downstairs and an area outside for warm-weather drinking – all with fine views over the cricket ground. Sandwiches and pies are available from the bar on most days. Functions for up to 100 people (including wheelchair users) can be accommodated in the well-appointed function room on the first floor. Local CAMRA Club of the Year a number of times – runner up in 2013.
P (21)

Lambton Worm

North Road, DH3 1AJ
🕘 11.30-11 (midnight Fri & Sat); 12-10.30 Sun
☎ (0191) 387 1162 🌐 thelambton.com
Sonnet 43 Steam Beer, Blonde Beer, Bourbon Milk Stout, India Pale Ale, Brown Ale, American Pale Ale; guest beers Ⓗ
Sonnet 43 Brew House tap with a bar at the front and gastro restaurant at the back matching traditional English food with Sonnet 43 beers. Experimental and limited edition beers are offered here alongside the core range, complemented by ever-changing guest ales from regional microbreweries. A relaxed ambience, friendly staff, spacious bar area and plenty of tucked-away areas for seating add to the enjoyment. P (21)

Cockfield

Queen's Head

106 Front Street, DL13 5AA
🕘 5 (11 Sat)-11; 12-11 Sun ☎ (01388) 710981
Beer range varies Ⓗ
Towards the north end of the village, this cosy, welcoming and popular pub serves two constantly changing beers from the Marston's range. It has an open-plan interior with various seating areas and tables outside at the front of the building. A proper community local, it is very handy for the historic Cockfield Fell and associated industrial archaeology. Well worth a visit. Q P (6,8)

Consett

Company Row

Victoria Road, DH8 5BQ
🕘 8am-11 ☎ (01207) 585600
Courage Directors; Greene King Abbot; Ruddles County; guest beers Ⓗ
Modern pub named after the row of houses built by the Derwent Iron Company for its workers. This spacious and well-decorated Wetherspoon establishment is a real asset to Consett town centre. A varied beer selection and good food make this social pub popular with a wide clientele of all ages. P

Grey Horse

115 Sherburn Terrace, DH8 6NE
🕘 12-12.30am (midnight Sun) ☎ (01207) 502585
🌐 thegreyhorse.co.uk
Consett Steel Town Bitter, White Hot; guest beers Ⓗ
Traditional pub dating back to 1848. The interior comprises a lounge and L-shaped bar with a wood-beamed ceiling. Consett Ale Works Brewery is located at the rear. Beer festivals are held twice a year, live entertainment is hosted on Thursday and a quiz on Wednesday. The coast-to-coast cycle route is close by. P

Cotherstone

Red Lion

Main Street, DL12 9QE
🕘 12-3 (not Mon-Fri), 7-11; 12-4, 7-10.30 Sun
☎ (01833) 650236 🌐 theredlionhotel.blogspot.com
Yorkshire Dales Best Bitter; guest beers Ⓗ
An 18th-century Grade II-listed coaching inn, built in stone and set in an idyllic village. Simply furnished, this homely local with two open fires has changed little since the '60s. There is no TV, jukebox or one-armed bandit, just good beer and conversation. Children, dogs and clean boots are welcome. Local CAMRA Community Pub of the Year, the venue is used by various local clubs, and the small garden is a suntrap. Guest beers regularly come from local Mithril Ales. Q P

Crook

Horse Shoe

4 Church Street, DL15 9BG
🕘 8am-midnight ☎ (01388) 744980
Greene King Abbot; Ruddles Best Bitter; guest beers Ⓗ
Wetherspoon refurbishment of a pub and butcher's shop, with a nod to its previous use in the metal bar top. Four interlinked drinking areas make up the main part of the pub, with a pleasant patio to the side. Local history is reflected in the decor, with a surprise at the top of the stairs in the shape of old mining equipment. (1)

Darlington

Darlington Snooker Club

1 Corporation Road, DL3 6AE (corner of Northgate)
🕘 12-11 (1am Sat) ☎ (01325) 241388
Beer range varies Ⓗ
First-floor, family-run and family-oriented private snooker club offering a warm welcome. Four guest beers from micros countrywide are stocked. A cosy, comfortable TV lounge is available for those not playing on one of the 10 top-quality snooker tables. Twice-yearly, the club plays host to a professional celebrity, and two beer festivals are held annually. Frequently voted CAMRA Regional Club of the Year, and a finalist for National Club in 2014, it welcomes CAMRA members on production of a membership card.

Half Moon

130 Northgate, DL1 1QS

12 (5 Wed)-11 (01325) 469965 thecraftypint.co.uk

Beer range varies

Across the ring road from the town centre, this local reopened in 2013 as a real ale pub following a long period of closure. There is a relaxed and welcoming atmosphere, where the seven guest beers include ones from micros unusual for the area as well as from the on-site Crafty Pinto nano brewery. You have a choice of two ciders. The Crafty Pint bottled beer shop is also incorporated here, offering a large selection of bottled beers from regional micros.

Number Twenty 2

22 Coniscliffe Road, DL3 7RG

12-11 (9 Mon); closed Sun (01325) 354590

villagebrewer.co.uk/our-pubs/number-twenty-2

Village White Boar, Bull, Old Raby; guest beers

Town-centre ale house with a passion for cask beer and winner of many CAMRA awards. Ales are dispensed from up to 16 handpumps, including a stout or porter, plus two real ciders and 10 draught European beers. Huge curved windows, stained glass panels and a high ceiling give the interior an airy, spacious feel. Sandwiches and light bites are served 12-7. This is the home of Village Brewer beers, commissioned from Hambleton by the licensee. Q

Old Vic

95a Victoria Road, DL1 5JQ

11 (1 Sun)-11 (01325) 251199

Beer range varies

This upstairs pub was formerly the Victoria Social Club, situated on the corner of Victoria Road and Backhouse Street. Perfect for a pint on your way to or from the train station, once you have negotiated the stairs you will be welcomed by an enthusiastic landlady. A range of up to four real ales is sourced from local breweries including Mithril and Truefitt. A real cider is also kept. Every Friday the pub hosts open mic sessions for local performers.

Old Yard Tapas Bar

98 Bondgate, DL3 7JY

11-11; 12-10.30 Sun (01325) 467385 tapasbar.co.uk

John Smith's Bitter; Theakston Old Peculier; guest beers

Interesting mixture of a bar and Mediterranean taverna offering real ales alongside a fascinating blend of international wines and spirits in a friendly setting. Four guest beers from local micros and countrywide are stocked, with two more added on Thursday for the weekend. Although this is a thriving restaurant you are more than welcome to pop in for a pint and tapa. The pavement café is popular in good weather. The TV is for sport only. Q

Quakerhouse

2 Mechanics Yard, DL3 7QF (off High Row)

11 (12 Sun)-midnight (01325) 245052

Beer range varies

Eleven times local CAMRA Town Pub of the Year and North-East Pub of the Year 2013, this gem of a pub is located in one of the town's historic yards. The lively bar offers 10 handpulled guest beers from local and regional breweries and Westons Old Rosie cider. A popular music venue, it caters for all tastes from acoustic to rock – on Wednesday there is a door charge after 8pm. P

Tanners Hall

63-64 Skinnergate, DL3 7LL

8am-midnight (1am Sat) (01325) 369939

Greene King Abbot; Ruddles Best Bitter; guest beers

A popular Wetherspoon pub named after the local 18th-century leather trade that dominated the town. Its 12 handpumps provide a good selection of real ales including up to seven guests, often from local micros. The spacious interior makes it an ideal venue for beer festivals and Meet The Brewer nights as well as the chain's national events. Reasonably priced food is served until 10pm with a 20 per cent discount for CAMRA members. Q

Voodoo Café

Skinnergate, DL3 7LX

10-5 Mon; 10 (9am Wed)-11.45; 12-5 Sun

(01325) 467555 voodoocafe.co.uk

Beer range varies

Mexican/South American-themed café which stocks a large range of bottled beers from around the world. Downstairs is a simply furnished, colourful bar area, serving handpulled beers from microbreweries. Upstairs is a vibrant restaurant. During warmer weather there is seating out on the street. It is a popular Latin dance venue offering salsa lessons. There is a 50p/pint discount for card-carrying CAMRA members.

Durham

Bishop Langley

Framwellgate Bridge, North Road, DH1 4PW

10-11 April-September; 12-11 October-March

(0191) 386 4779 bishoplangleydurham.co.uk

Sharp's Doom Bar; guest beers

A city-centre gastropub with a large, heated roof terrace overlooking the River Wear with views of Durham Castle. A selection of changing cask ales is available alongside Doom Bar. The pub serves food all day and is open until late each evening, offering a 50p discount on a pint and 10 per cent off food to CAMRA members. Quiz night is Monday.

(20,64)

Court Inn

Court Lane, DH1 3AW

11-11.30 (11 Sun-Tue) (0191) 384 7350

courtinn.co.uk

Beer range varies

Up to six real ales are on offer here as well as a real cider. An extensive selection of bottled beers from local micros is also available. There is a heavy emphasis on good food using locally-sourced produce (served 11am-10.20pm daily with a 20 per cent discount Sun-Tue eves). The decor reflects the location of the pub near to the Crown Courts, with exposed brickwork and original artwork. Given its location it is popular with students and prison staff.

(6)

Dun Cow

37 Old Elvet, DH1 3HN

11-11.30; 12-10.30 Sun (0191) 386 9219

Black Sheep Best Bitter; Camerons Castle Eden Ale

In 995AD Lindisfarne monks were searching for a resting place for the body of St Cuthbert when they came across a milkmaid looking for her lost cow. She directed them to Dun Holm (Durham). This Grade II-listed pub, dating back to the 16th century in parts, is named after the historic animal. There is a friendly front snug and a larger lounge to the rear. The story of the monks' legendary journey is told on the corridor wall. Q🐎◑♿⛺🍺📶

Durham City Rugby Football Club

Hollow Drift, Green Lane, DH1 3JU

🕒 12-2, 7-11 (not Wed eve); 12-11 Sat; 12-10 Sun

☎ (0191) 386 1172

Black Sheep Best Bitter; Timothy Taylor Landlord 🄷

Set in a great position near the banks of the River Wear just outside the city centre, this rugby club provides a quality pint and a friendly atmosphere. It can get busy depending on games and other activities. Lunch is always available, as are the Landlord and Black Sheep. Local CAMRA branch Club of the Year in 2013. 🐎◐♿P🐾

Half Moon Inn 🄻

86 New Elvet, DH1 3AQ

🕒 11-11 (midnight Fri & Sat); 12-11 Sun ☎ (0191) 374 1918

🌐 thehalfmooninndurham.co.uk

Draught Bass; guest beer 🄷

This city-centre pub is a regular in the Guide, named after the crescent-shaped bar that runs from the front room through to the lounge area. Run by the son of the landlord who managed the pub for 30 years, the interior is largely unchanged, with traditional decor throughout and interesting photos of the building at the beginning of the 20th century. It has a large garden next to the river. The guest beer is from Durham Brewery. ❀◐🍺🚌(6,21)📶

John Duck 🄻

91a Claypath, DH1 1RG

🕒 11-12.30am (11 Sun)

Beer range varies 🄷

A good city ale house with a wide selection of real ales and cider. There are multiple screens for sporting events and a popular pub quiz takes place on Thursdays at 8pm. Live music plays on Friday nights. This pub is in the same Durham City pub group as Ye Old Elm Tree. 🐎♿≹

Market Tavern 🄻

27 Market Place, DH1 3NJ

🕒 11-1am (midnight Tue & Thu); 12-11 Sun

☎ (0191) 386 2069

Beer range varies 🄷

Situated in Durham's historic marketplace, this single-roomed, L-shaped bar offers an array of six ales from all over Britain. The management makes full use of its guest list and has featured Mordue, Hydes, Beartown and Oakleaf breweries, to name a few. One of the most-improved venues in town, it serves good food until 9pm. The interior is of basic wooden alehouse appearance, with friendly staff providing a warm welcome to both the regular and casual visitor. Q🐎◑⛺≹📶

Olde Elm Tree 🄻

12 Crossgate, DH1 4PS

🕒 12-11; 11-midnight Fri & Sat; 12-10.30 Sun

☎ (0191) 386 4621

Caledonian Deuchars IPA; Wychwood Hobgoblin; guest beers 🄷

One of Durham's oldest pubs, dating back to at least 1600. As befits its age, it is reputed to have two ghosts. The interior comprises an L-shaped bar room and a top room linked by a set of stairs. A popular pub, it attracts a good mix including students, locals and bikers. Enjoy excellent home-cooked food, the Wednesday quiz (arrive early) and a folk group on Monday and Tuesday. Ask the landlord for details of the next Elm beer festival. Q❀◑⛺≹P🍺

Tap & Spile 🄻

Front Street, Framwellgate Moor, DH1 5EE

🕒 6-11; 12-3, 5-11 Fri; 12-3, 6-11 Sat; 12-3, 7-10.30 Sun

☎ (0191) 386 5451

Beer range varies 🄷

One of the last survivors of the old Cameron's chain, the inn has two bars at one side, while the other side can be partitioned into two. Families are welcome in the back room until 9pm. A local CAMRA award winner, it has a varied selection of ales from near and far, with eight constantly changing handpumps. The pub has a welcoming atmosphere, with friendly bar staff. Folk music nights are a weekly event. 🐎♿🍎P🚌(21)🐾

Victoria Inn 🏆 ★ 🄻

86 Hallgarth Street, DH1 3AS

🕒 11.45-3, 7-10.30 ☎ (0191) 386 5269

🌐 victoriainn-durhamcity.co.uk

Big Lamp Bitter; guest beers 🄷

This welcoming Grade II-listed, three-room Victorian pub has remained almost unaltered since it was built in 1899. The quaint decor, coal fires, tiny snug and a genuine Victorian cash drawer help create an olde-worlde feel. Ales are mainly from local breweries and a wide selection of single malt whiskies is on offer. No meals are served but toasties are available. Voted local CAMRA Pub of the Year for the seventh time in 2012. 🐎🛏◐♿🍎P🚌(21)🐾

Water House 🄻

65 North Road, DH1 4SQ

🕒 8am-11.30 ☎ (0191) 370 6540

Greene King Abbot; Ruddles Best Bitter; guest beers 🄷

Situated in former water board offices and a short distance from the bus station, this pub is popular with young and old alike and extremely busy at weekends. The modern decor is complemented by coal-effect open fires. Good-value food is served. An excellent Wetherspoon pub. Q🐎◑≹🍎🚌📶

Eaglescliffe

Cleveland Bay

718 Yarm Road, TS16 0JE (jct of A67 and A135)

🕒 11-1am ☎ (01642) 780275 🌐 clevelandbay.co.uk

Timothy Taylor Landlord; guest beers 🄷

This popular locals' pub and previous CAMRA branch Community Pub of the Year is under the stewardship of an enthusiastic licensee who has established an enviable reputation for serving a fine range of premium bitters, in oversized glasses, as well as a free Sunday lunch buffet. The main bar, with four handpumps, has two sports TVs, and there is also a quieter lounge and a function room where live bands play on Friday evenings. Third-of-a-pint glasses and tasting notes are available. Q❀♿≹♣P🍺🚌(7,17)🐾📶

Edmundbyers

Punch Bowl 🄻

DH8 9NL (2½ miles W of A68)

🕒 11-11; 12-10.30 Sun ☎ (01207) 255545

🌐 thepunchbowlinn.info

Beer range varies Ⓗ
Set in a lovely rural location close to Derwent Reservoir, fishing permits can be arranged. Three handpumps dispense an ever-changing range of local ales, and quality home-made food includes puddings and ice creams. The pub has three smartly furnished, comfortable rooms, with roaring log fires in the winter months. There is also an attractive tea room and a local shop. Q❀⇔◐▶P🐾

Egglescliffe

Pot & Glass

Church Road, TS16 9DQ (300yds E of A167, opp parish church)
⏲ 12-2 (not Mon & Tue), 6-11; 5.30-midnight Fri; 12-midnight Sat; 12-11 Sun ☎ (01642) 651009
Draught Bass; Caledonian Deuchars IPA; Black Sheep Best Bitter; guest beers Ⓗ
A previous local CAMRA award winner, this old-fashioned and ever-popular multi-roomed 17th-century village local is situated in a quiet cul-de-sac. Former licensee and cabinet maker Charlie Abbey, whose last resting place overlooks the pub, fashioned the ornate bar fronts from old country furniture. Tasting notes are available for the seven handpumps, which include four guests. Outside is a large south-facing garden. Themed food evenings complement the good-value home-cooked menu.
Q♉❀◐▶♿⇌♣P🚌(7,577)

Elwick

McOrville Inn

34 The Green, TS27 3EF (300yds E of A19)
⏲ 11-11; 12-10.30 Sun ☎ (01429) 273344 🌐 mcorville.co.uk
Tetley Bitter; guest beers Ⓗ
Sixteenth-century traditional inn, situated on the village green and named after a local horse that won the 1802 St Leger. Deep, cool cellars help to ensure the regular beers, together with two local guests, are always in fine form. A quality menu that supports local suppliers and farmers – including real home-made chips served in a pint pot – is available all day every day and offers good value. A secret secluded garden, and a more extensive beer garden, both face south. Q❀◐▶♿P

Esh

Cross Keys 𝕃

Front Street, DH7 9QR (3 miles W of A691 via Langley Park)
⏲ 12-2, 5.30 (6 Sat)-11; 12-2, 7-10.30 Sun
☎ (0191) 373 1279
Big Lamp Prince Bishop Ale; Black Sheep Best Bitter; guest beers Ⓗ
Pleasant 18th-century pub offering a varied food menu including vegetarian and children's choices. A comfortable locals' bar is complemented by a lounge/restaurant overlooking the Browney Valley. Delft racks display porcelain artefacts, some of which portray the old locality. The village is commonly known as Old Esh to distinguish it from nearby Esh Winning. Q❀◐▶♿♣P

Ferryhill Station

Surtees Arms 𝕃

Chilton Lane, DL17 0DH
⏲ 4-11; 12-midnight Sat; 12-11 Sun ☎ (01740) 655724
🌐 thesurteesarms.co.uk
Yard of Ale Black as Owt Stout, One Foot in the Yard, Surtees Gold; guest beers Ⓗ
Traditional multi-roomed pub serving locally and nationally sourced ales and ciders as well as beers from the on-site Yard of Ale Brewery (est 2008). Annual beer festivals are held in the summer and at Halloween. Live music and charity nights are regular events. A large function room is available for private gatherings. Lunches are served on Sunday only. ♉▶♿⛺●P🍺🐾📶

Forest-in-Teesdale

Langdon Beck Hotel

DL12 0XP (on B6277, 8 miles NW of Middleton-in-Teesdale)
⏲ 11-10.30 (closed Mon Nov-Easter); 12-10.30 Sun
☎ (01833) 622267 🌐 langdonbeckhotel.com
Jarrow Rivet Catcher; Ringwood Best bitter; guest beer Ⓗ
Known as the Sportsman's Rest in the early 1800s, this pub is situated in the North Pennines, three miles from the spectacular High Force and Cauldron Snout waterfalls and close to the Pennine Way. The welcoming inn has long been a destination for walkers, fishermen and those seeking hospitality in scenic and peaceful surroundings, whether staying overnight or just long enough to enjoy the excellent food and drink. A beer festival is held over the late May bank holiday weekend.
Q♉⇔◐▶♿⛺♣🐾

Frosterley

Black Bull 𝕃

Bridge End, DL13 2SL
⏲ closed Mon-Wed; 11-11 (5 Sun) ☎ (01388) 527784
🌐 blackbullfrosterley.com
Beer range varies Ⓗ
A truly unique, family-run pub next to the Weardale Railway and river, with four guest ales usually from local brewers, and up to four ciders and perries. High-quality, locally-sourced produce features in the popular food menu. Bare boards, stone flags, all manner of artefacts and antique furniture create a wonderful ambience, with music, plays and storytelling the regular entertainment. The outbuilding houses a peal of bells, visited by enthusiasts from far and wide.
Q❀◐▶♿♣●P🚌(101)

Hartburn

Parkwood Hotel

64-66 Darlington Road, TS18 5ER (on A67, 1 mile W of Stockton town centre)
⏲ 12-11 (midnight Fri & Sat) ☎ (01642) 587933
🌐 theparkwoodhotel.com
Greene King Abbot; Camerons Strongarm; guest beers Ⓗ
This magnificent red-brick Victorian building, built in 1865, is the former home of the Ropner family – shipbuilders, shipowners and civic benefactors. Set in its own grounds, it features an imposing porch, tiled hallway, staircase and public rooms. The licensee is a real ale enthusiast. A local CAMRA branch award winner, it offers two regular beers supplemented by three guests, one sourced under the SIBA scheme. The ciders are Westons Old Rosie/Thatchers Traditional Scrumpy. There are six high quality en-suite bedrooms.
Q♉❀⇔◐▶●P🍺🚌(588,589)🐾📶

Hartlepool

Brewery Tap
Stockton Street, TS24 7NU (on A689)
11-4; closed Sun ☎ (01429) 868686
cameronsbrewery.com
Camerons IPA, Gold Bullion, Strongarm; guest beer H
When Camerons Brewery discovered that it owned a somewhat derelict pub, the former Stranton's future was secured – it was converted into the brewery tap, museum and visitors' centre. Strongarm, Camerons' flagship brand, and two new beers, Gold Bullion and IPA, are always available, together with the monthly special. The bar also acts as the starting point for brewery tours. Meetings and conferences, evening opening and other social events can be arranged.
P (1,36)

Causeway
Vicarage Gardens, Stranton, TS24 7QT (beside Camerons Brewery)
11.30-11 (11.30 Thu; midnight Fri & Sat); 11-11 Sun
☎ (01429) 273954
Banks's Bitter; Camerons Strongarm; guest beers H
Marvellous multi-roomed, red-brick Victorian building, dating from 1862 and Cameron's unofficial brewery tap for more than a century. The Causeway is now owned by Marston's, though the sales of banked Strongarm remain huge. A CAMRA multi-award-winning pub, it gets a mention in Hansard for the quality of its Strongarm. The licensee hosts an eclectic mix of live music most evenings, and a quiz night on Tuesdays. Three guest beers are sourced from the Marston's range. Good-value bar snacks are available.
(1,36)

Rat Race Ale House
Hartlepool Rail Station, Station Approach, TS24 7ED (on Platform 1 of railway station)
closed Mon; 12-2.15, 4-8.15; 12-9 Sat; closed Sun ☎ 07903 479378 ratracealehouse.co.uk
Beer range varies H
A recent CAMRA Regional Cider Pub of the Year and Branch Pub of the Year, the station's former newsagent's is now an ale lovers' paradise, with 200 different ales featuring annually. Its opening/closing times coincide with the arrival/departure of the coast trains. No fizzy lager, beer nor cider, no spirits nor alcopops, no food, no TV/jukebox, no one-arm bandit nor quiz machine, no bar! Just four ever-changing real ales, cider and perry, served in oversized glasses to your table. Perfect.
Q

Hartlepool Headland

Fisherman's Arms
Southgate, TS24 0JJ (on headland close to Fish Quay)
5-11.30; 4-midnight Sat; 3.30-11.30 Sun
☎ (01429) 266029 thefishermans.co.uk
Jennings Cumberland Ale; guest beers H
The Fish, local CAMRA Pub of the Year 2014, is a friendly, family-run, one-room locals' pub. Four handpumps offer Cumberland Ale and three guests from the Punch Taverns list. Three third-of-a-pint tasters are available to help you make up your mind. Westons Rosie's Pig and a guest cider are also served. Popular music sessions are well supported, with quizzes on Tuesday and Sunday. Two beer and two cider festivals are held annually.
Q (7)

Globe
Northgate, TS24 0LJ (on headland, towards Fish Quay)
11.30 (11 Sun)-11 ☎ (01429) 860097
Camerons Strongarm H
Opposite the port that was once bustling with fishing boats, coal staithes and pit props, this family-run, friendly community pub, comprising a main public bar and a smaller quieter lounge, is under the stewardship of licensees celebrating 29 years of service to the trade. The posh ladies' loo could win prizes apparently. The price of the Strongarm (ask for a Hartlepool Head) reflects the pub's freehold status – savings negotiated with Camerons have been passed on to the customer.
Q (7)

Heighington

George & Dragon
4 East Green, DL5 6PP
12-11 (midnight Fri & Sat); 12-10.30 Sun
☎ (01325) 313152
Black Sheep Best Bitter; John Smith's Bitter; Wells Bombardier; guest beers H
A warm and welcoming pub in a picturesque village, situated in a fine position on the smaller green. An old coaching inn, it has been refurbished in a modern style. The main bar, with real log fire, serves a regular real ale, up to four guests and a real cider, ensuring its popularity with lovers of good beer. A separate bar has a large-screen TV for sporting events. Excellent food is available daily in the lounge and conservatory-style restaurant area.
Q (1,16)

High Hesleden

Ship Inn
Mickle Hill Road, TS27 4QD (signed from B1281, between A19 and Blackhall)
closed Mon; 12-3 (not Tue-Fri), 6-11; 12-9 Sun
☎ (01429) 836453 theshipinn.net
Beer range varies H
Now in its 14th year of continual family ownership, complete satisfaction is guaranteed at this nautical-themed rural gem. The landlord serves seven ever-changing real beers, sourced mainly from local microbreweries, and real cider. His wife runs the superb restaurant offering top-quality food at reasonable prices, including mid-week early-doors two-course specials. Six motel-style chalets and the Crow's Nest flat provide highly recommended good-value accommodation. There are stupendous coastal views from the well-kept gardens. CAMRA Regional Pub of the Year 2012.
Q P (206)

Leamside

Three Horseshoes L
Pit House Lane, DH4 6QQ (½ mile N of A690, just outside West Rainton)
11 (12 Sun)-11 ☎ (0191) 584 2394
threehorseshoesleamside.co.uk
Leamside Adventure, Alexandrina; Timothy Taylor Landlord; guest beers H
A country pub with an excellent restaurant (the Back Room – booking advisable). The traditional bar has open fires in winter and a large TV for sport. The recently attached Leamside Brewery provides up to five real ales, with Timothy Taylor Landlord always available. The Leamside beers are named

after local geographical features, with a map in the corner of the room pointing out their location. The pub is home to local cycle and clay pigeon clubs.
Q◑♿P🚉📶

Long Newton

Vane Arms

Darlington Road, TS21 1DB (W end of village, close to A66 jct)
⏲ 12-2 (not Mon), 5-11; 12-2, 5-midnight Fri & Sat; 12-11 Sun
☎ (01642) 580401 🌐 vanearms.com
Beer range varies Ⓗ
This lovely village pub, comprising a public bar and restaurant, was left abandoned for 898 days before a local couple, new to the trade, bought the freehold. They quickly established an enviable reputation for serving four microbrewery sourced beers, together with freshly home-made and reasonably priced top-quality restaurant meals. The licensees celebrated their second 898-days period of tenure with the opening of four newly refurbished en-suite letting bedrooms. Various community events are hosted.
Q🐴❀🛏◑♿♣P🚉🚌(87A)📶

Medomsley

Royal Oak 🄻

7 Manor Road, DH8 6QN
⏲ 11.30-3, 5.30-11; 11-11 Sat; 12-11 Sun ☎ (01207) 560336
🌐 theroyaloakmedomsley.co.uk
Hadrian Border Tyneside Blonde; guest beers Ⓗ
The Royal Oak is a traditional country-style pub which has recently been refurbished to create a warm, welcoming country feel. It has a large bar with a selection of seating including soft sofas and leather chairs, and plenty of dining space. Outside, there is a large, attractive garden at the back and ample parking to the front. An excellent, friendly local, it offers a rotation of excellent beers as well as good food. Quiz night is Sunday. Q🐴❀◑P🐾

Metal Bridge

Old Mill Hotel

Thinford Road, DH6 5NX (off A1M jct 61, follow signs on A177)
⏲ 12-11 (10.30 Sun) ☎ (01740) 652928
🌐 oldmilldurham.co.uk
Beer range varies Ⓗ
Originally built as a paper mill in 1813, this spacious inn is now the venue of choice for discerning locals and visitors alike. It offers good-quality food and well-kept ales – three handpumps serve a changing range, with the nearby Durham Brewery often supplying one of the beers. The food menu is extensive, with daily specials written on a board above the bar. Larger groups are welcome in the conservatory. Accommodation is of a high standard, with all rooms en suite.
Q🐴🛏◑⛺P🚉🐾

Middlestone

Ship Inn 🏆 🄻

Low Road, DL14 8AB (between Coundon and Kirk Merrington)
⏲ 4 (12 Fri-Sun)-11 ☎ (01388) 810904
🌐 shipinnmiddlestone.co.uk
Beer range varies Ⓗ
At the heart of a small village, the Ship draws its regulars from far and wide. It has a three-part bar warmed by an open fire, and a large function room upstairs which is home to twice-yearly beer festivals. The rooftop patio has spectacular views, and there is always an event either in the offing or taking place. Various pieces of Vaux memorabilia are on display, and are one of the many subjects of conversation. Sunday lunches are popular.
Q🐴❀◑♿♣🍎🐾

Middleton-in-Teesdale

Teesdale Hotel

Market Place, DL12 0QG
⏲ 11 (12 Sun)-11 ☎ (01833) 640264 🌐 teesdalehotel.co.uk
Black Sheep Best Bitter; guest beers Ⓗ
A former coaching inn updated to provide excellent accommodation. This is a popular village local as well as a resting place for Pennine walkers. Middleton-in-Teesdale is often referred to as the capital of Upper Teesdale, with High Force and Cauldron Snout nearby. Up to two guest beers, often from local micros, are served. Meals can be enjoyed in the main bar or the comfortable restaurant. A farmers' market is held on the last Sunday of the month. Q🐴🛏◑P🚉🚌(95,96)🐾

Newfield

Newfield Inn

Front Street, DH2 2SP
⏲ 4 (12 Sat & Sun)-11.30 ☎ (0191) 370 0565
Maxim Ward's Best Bitter; guest beers Ⓗ
A friendly two-roomed pub in the centre of the village, now owned by Maxim brewery from nearby Houghton-le-Spring, with two of its beers and a guest available. The pub offers accommodation, fortnightly live music entertainment, quiz nights and TV football among other attractions. Families are welcome and there is a beer garden. 🐴🛏♿♣P

No Place

Beamish Mary Inn

DH9 0QH (follow signs to No Place off A693 from Chester-le-Street to Stanley)
⏲ 12-11 (10.30 Sun) ☎ (0191) 370 0237
🌐 beamishmaryinn.co.uk
Big Lamp Sunny Daze, Lamp Light; Consett White Hot, Red Dust; guest beers Ⓗ
A former local CAMRA Pub of the Year. This pub, full of character, is well respected for its warm welcome, generously portioned pub grub and ample choices of well-kept real ale. Accommodation is available including twin, double and family rooms. The location is handy for visitors to the nearby world-renowned Beamish Open Air Museum. Q🐴❀🛏◑♿P🚉🚌(8,78)🐾📶

Norton

George & Dragon 🏆

109 High Street, TS20 1AA (100yds S of duck pond)
⏲ 12-midnight (11 Mon & Tue) ☎ (01642) 554150
Greene King Abbot; guest beer Ⓗ
Traditional, ornate and unobtrusive, the George & Dragon has been described as 'how pubs used to be and how pubs ought to be'. It has a bar where drinkers sit on leather benches and muse over photographs of yesteryear, a lounge/restaurant

and a games room. The guest beer, always a stronger premium bitter, is chosen by customers. Excellent value home-made meals, including a whopping 10-item breakfast, are served. Going home thirsty or hungry is not an option. Local CAMRA Community Pub of the Year 2014.
Q (35,37)

Ovington

Four Alls

The Green, DL11 7BP (2 miles S of Winston and A67)
7 (6 Fri; 4 Sat)-11; 7-10.30 Sun (01833) 627302
thefouralls-teesdale.co.uk
Beer range varies
Friendly 18th-century inn opposite the village green in what is known as the maypole village. A Victorian sign denotes the four alls: 'I govern all (queen), I fight for all (soldier), I pray for all (parson), I pay for all (farmer).' The pub has a hop-adorned bar, games room and restaurant serving excellent value food. One guest beer is brewed in the pub and one comes from Mithril Ales. Accommodation is available in seven rooms in a lovely setting. Q P

Peterlee

Five Quarter

Units 3B-3C Hailsham Place, SR8 1AB
8am-11 (midnight Fri & Sat) (0191) 518 5880
Maxim Double Maxim; Morland Old Speckled Hen; guest beers
This well-presented Wetherspoon bar is an oasis of real ale in the area. Good food is available and a TV shows sport. Nearby is Horden Colliery, which at one time was the biggest pit in Britain, where miners worked the High Main, Five Quarter and Yard seams – from where the pub took its name.

Preston-le-Skerne

Blacksmiths Arms

Ricknall Lane, DL5 6JH (1 mile E of A167 at Gretna Green)
closed Mon; 11.30-2, 6-11 (6.30 winter); 12-11.30 Sun
(01325) 314873 blacksmithsarms-pls.co.uk
Beer range varies
Welcoming free house, known locally as the Hammers, situated in a rural location near Newton Aycliffe. A long corridor separates the bar, restaurant and a beamed lounge furnished in farmhouse style. The pub has an excellent reputation for home-cooked food, and up to three guest beers are available, mainly from local micros. A former local CAMRA Rural Pub of the Year, it even has a helicopter landing pad. Q

St John's Chapel

Blue Bell Inn

Hood Street, DL13 1QJ
5 (12 Sat & Sun)-1am (01388) 537256
Beer range varies
Originally a pair of cottages, the Blue Bell is a friendly, cosy pub with a bar across the front of the building leading to a small pool room, and garden to the rear. Right on the A689, it serves the local community and those who holiday in Upper Weardale. Pub games are popular and there are plenty of books to choose from. Q (101)

Seaham

Crow's Nest

Featherbed, East Shore Village, North Road, SR7 7XR
11-11 (11.30 Fri); 9am-11.30 Sat; 9am-11 Sun
(0191) 581 4927 crowsnestpub.co.uk
Banks's Bitter; Marston's Pedigree; Wychwood Hobgoblin; guest beers
A light and airy pub from the Marston's group with an excellent position on Seaham seafront at the head of East Shore Village. The site was originally part of Vane Tempest pit. It reopened in December 2013 after major refurbishment, with six handpumps. It offers a cask platter of three one-third pints. It opens at 9am at weekends for breakfasts (although no alcohol is sold until 11am) and has an extensive menu and weekend carvery.
P (202,238)

Hat & Feathers

57-59 Church Street, SR7 7HF
8am-11 (1am Fri & Sat) (0191) 513 3040
Greene King Abbot; Ruddles Best Bitter; guest beers
This Wetherspoon pub derives its name from the milliners shop that was next door and from the Doggarts store that occupied the site from the 1920s to the 1980s which had a department selling hats and feathers. Upstairs are old photographs depicting the headgear of the best-dressed ladies of the time. The furnishings are a mix of modern and traditional styles, with a selection of wooden chairs and deep comfortable settees. Outside is a plaque giving a history of the building.

Seaton

Dun Cow

The Village, SR7 0NA
4 (5 winter)-midnight; 12-midnight Fri-Sun
(0191) 513 1133
Beer range varies
Excellent, friendly, unspoilt inn on the village green with a public bar and lounge areas. A pub for good conversation or a game of darts, the TV is only turned on for special events. No meals are served but toasties are always available. The guest beer selection changes but usually includes two light and two dark beers to suit all tastes.
P (238)

Sedgefield

Dun Cow

43 Front Street, TS21 3AT
11-3, 6-11; 12-11 Sat & Sun (01740) 620894
duncowinn.co.uk
Black Sheep Best Bitter; Theakston Best Bitter; guest beers
Run by the same landlord for nearly 40 years, this large and comfortable 18th-century inn has an excellent county-wide reputation for good food. It was the scene of a historic George Bush and Tony Blair lunch in 2003. There are three bars including a farmers bar-cum-snug and restaurant. Four real ales are always on including at least one local beer.
Q P (X1)

Spennymoor

Frog & Ferret

Coulson Street, DL16 7RS

⏲ 3 (12 Fri & Sat)-11; 12-10.30 Sun ☎ (01388) 818312
Beer range varies Ⓗ
Friendly, family-run free house offering four constantly changing real ales, sourced from far and wide, with local and northern microbreweries well represented. A welcoming atmosphere greets you on arrival at the three-sided bar in the comfortably furnished lounge, with brick, stone and wood cladding. Darts and dominoes are played and bar snacks are available. Well-behaved children are permitted until 4pm. The pub hosts a quiz on Sunday evening, and a music quiz on the first Wednesday evening of the month. ◗⛺●▯🐾

Stockton-on-Tees

Sun Inn
2 Knowles Street, TS18 1SU
⏲ 11-11; 12-10.30 Sun ☎ (01642) 611461
Draught Bass Ⓗ
This popular traditional town-centre drinkers' pub is reputed to sell more Draught Bass than any other pub in the country. It was rescued from an uncertain future 11 years ago by a regular who became the licensee and who quickly established record sales of banked Bass. The pub supports darts, football teams and various charitable causes. It has been home to the famous Monday evening Stockton Folk Club for the last 44 years. ⇌🚌🐾

Thomas Sheraton
4 Bridge Road, TS18 3BW (at S end of High St)
⏲ 8am-midnight (11 Sun) ☎ (01642) 606134
Greene King Abbot; Ruddles Best Bitter; guest beers Ⓗ
This previous local CAMRA Pub of the Year is a fine Wetherspoon conversion of the Victorian law courts and named after one of the country's great Georgian cabinet makers, born in the town in 1751. The interior comprises several dining/drinking areas, with a balcony and patio upstairs. Six guest beers are mainly sourced locally, and real cider is kept. Meet the Brewer, beer festivals and a January sale are all supported. Q🐴❀◐◗♿⇌●🚌📶

West Cornforth

Square & Compass Ⓛ
7 The Green, DL17 9JQ (off Coxhoe-W Cornforth road)
⏲ 7 (12 Sat & Sun)-11 ☎ (01740) 653050
Beer range varies Ⓗ
A proper drinking pub and friendly local on the village green in the old part of Doggy (the village's local nickname). It has sold real ale for over 30 years and hosts darts, dominoes and chess clubs. The pub has good views over to Wear Valley and Durham City. 🐴❀♣P🐾

Westgate

Hare & Hounds Ⓛ
24 Front Street, DL13 1RX
⏲ closed Mon; 12-3.30 (not Tue-Fri), 6.30-11; 12-3.30, 6.30-9 Sun ☎ (01388) 517212
🌐 hareandhoundswestgate.blogspot.co.uk
WeardAle Fell Over, Challenger, Gold, Dark Nights; guest beers Ⓗ
On the main road up Weardale, with the river at the bottom of the garden, the spacious stone-flagged bar is partially fitted out with furniture and other items salvaged from the former village chapel, and the restaurant has a patio overlooking the Wear. Catch up on the local news over a pint brewed only a few feet below you, while watching the pub's poultry in the rear garden. Food is locally sourced, including the famous Sunday carvery. Q🐴❀◗♿⛺♣P🚌(101)

Whorlton

Bridge Inn
The Green, DL12 8XD (1 mile S of A67)
⏲ 12-11 (11.45 Sat) ☎ (01833) 627341
🌐 thebridgeinn-whorlton.co.uk
Theakston Best Bitter; guest beers Ⓗ
Named after the Whorlton Suspension Bridge, the pub is set in a quintessential English village surrounded by riverside walks, and is a welcoming stop-off for ramblers. The Bridge is a traditional country pub and tearoom with a light, modern feel. The food menu is classic British, all made with the best ingredients. Beer is a passion, with one from local Mithril Ales always on, and regular special food nights and drink events are hosted. Monday is quiz night. 🐴❀◐◗♣P🐾📶

Willington

Black Horse
42 Low Willington, DL15 0BD
⏲ 6 (12 Sat & Sun)-11 ☎ 07727 280196
Beer range varies Ⓗ
A tasteful refurbishment a couple of years ago created a spacious, open-plan pub while maintaining separate drinking areas. Beers are mostly from local brewers, pub games are regularly played, and sport is popular on the large screens. Local car clubs use the Black Horse as a base, and the pub enthusiastically supports the local ladies' football team. Handily placed between Durham and Weardale. ♣P🚌(46,50)

Witton Gilbert

Glendenning Arms
Front Street, DH7 6SY (off A691 bypass)
⏲ 4 (12 Sat & Sun)-11 ☎ (0191) 371 0316
Black Sheep Best Bitter; guest beer Ⓗ
A typical village community local and Guide regular with a small, comfortable lounge and lively, welcoming bar with a real open fire. The bar is attractively decorated in a contemporary style and still sports the original Vaux 1970s red and white handpulls. The lounge remains more traditional. The pub runs darts, dominoes and football teams. A classic car club meets monthly, as does a classic motorcycle club. Situated on the village main road, with ample parking. Q🐴❀♿♣P🚌(14,X25)🐾

Witton-le-Wear

Dun Cow
19 High Street, DL14 0AY
⏲ 6 (1 Sat)-11; 12-11 Sun ☎ (01388) 881711
Beer range varies Ⓗ
Dating from 1799, this comfortable and welcoming pub is set back from the road through the village. The single room has an open fire at both ends, one guarded by a sleeping fox who always seems to have just closed his eyes, and the other by an impressive set of horns. A seating area to the front offers pleasant views, with bench seats to the left of the bar. The decor includes some interesting football memorabilia. Q❀♣P

Victoria

School Street, DL14 0AS

6-11 Mon, Wed & Thu; closed Tue; 12-midnight Fri & Sat; 12-10.30 Sun ☎ 07779 128024

Beer range varies H

Pleasant village pub with a central bar serving a small pool room and a split-level bar that includes a raised dining area. The bar has great views over Wear Valley from the rear and the church from the front. Real ale is enthusiastically promoted, with beers coming from the Marston's range and local independents. Thursday is beer discussion night. Food is served Friday to Sunday. The patio to the rear overlooks the car park. ❀◗♣P

Wolsingham

Black Bull

27 Market Place, DL13 3AB

12-11 (11.30 Sun) ☎ (01388) 527332

Caledonian Deuchars IPA; guest beer H

Refurbishment has not diminished the attractions of this welcoming Weardale institution. Situated opposite the town hall, it has a snug bar, lounge, and formal dining room offering good food. To the rear is a south-facing garden, and there are tables to the front. Close to the Weardale Way, the pub is the base for the local cricket team, and hosts social events. Q❀⇌(◗♣(101)

Black Lion L

21 Meadhope Street, DL13 3EN (50yds N of Market Place)

6.30 (6 Fri)-11; 12-11 Sat; 12-10.30 Sun
☎ (01388) 527772

Beer range varies H

Hidden away a minute from the Market Place, this friendly and comfortable gem is a great place to relax. The open fire is a focus in the single, open-plan room, with a pool table to the rear and bar with TV sport to the front. Regular beer festivals are often held in the suntrap rear garden, and local charities benefit from the fundraising efforts of the pub. Ask for the cider menu, as more than six can be on offer. North-East Cider Pub of the Year 2013. Q❀♿♣●(101)

Rat Race Ale House, Hartlepool (Photo: Tom Stainer)

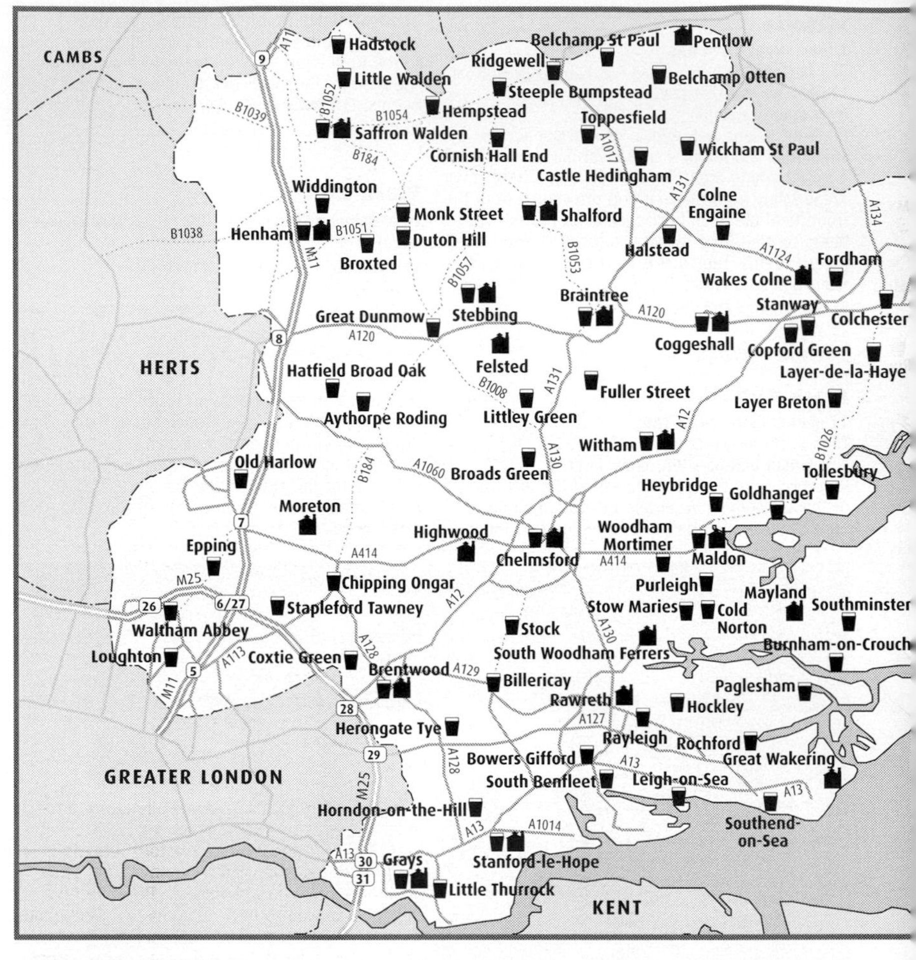

Aythorpe Roding

Axe & Compasses 🄻

Dunmow Road, CM6 1PP (on B1845 5 miles SW of Dunmow) TL594154

☼ 11-11 (midnight Fri & Sat); 12-10.30 Sun

☎ (01279) 876648 ⊕ theaxeandcompasses.co.uk

Adnams Lighthouse, Broadside; Sharp's Doom Bar 🄷**; guest beer** 🄶

An 18th-century thatched pub set in open countryside, frequented by a mixed clientele of drinkers, diners and local farming folk. Quality ales and good locally-sourced food are always available, with friendly and efficient service. Guest beers are often from regional brewers. In winter there is a log fire and on fine days the garden offers views across the fields to the windmill. Quizzes and themed nights are popular, as are the seasonal food offers. Q❀◑●P🚌(17,18)📶

Belchamp Otten

Red Lion

Fowes Lane, CO10 7BQ (on a very small single track lane, signed by the duck pond) TL799415

☼ closed Tue; 12-2.30, 5.30-11; 12-11 Fri & Sat; 12-7 Sun

☎ (01787) 278301 ⊕ ottenredlion.co.uk

Adnams Southwold Bitter; guest beers 🄷

Lovely local pub hidden away in the smallest of the Belchamps. The owners provide a warm welcome, with an open fire in winter. Local artwork on display is for sale. Pub games include bar billiards and darts. Live music is scheduled on the last Saturday of the month in summertime. Reasonably priced, wholesome, home-cooked food is available at lunchtimes, evenings, and to take away too (no food Mon and Tue). There are excellent views, good walks and cycle rides from here. Q❀◑♣●P🐾

Belchamp St Paul

Half Moon

Cole Green, CO10 7DP TL792423

☼ 12-3, 6-midnight (11 Mon & Tue); 12-midnight Sat & Sun

☎ (01787) 277402 ⊕ halfmoonbelchamp.co.uk

Greene King IPA; guest beers 🄷

Friendly thatched rural pub dating from about 1685, opposite the village green. Three beers are available and guest beers change regularly. The pub is popular with locals and has an excellent choice of bar and restaurant meals (no food Sun eve). There are chickens in the back garden. In the past the pub provided one of the locations for the first Lovejoy TV series. Outside there is a separate smoking area. Q🐴❀◑♣P📶

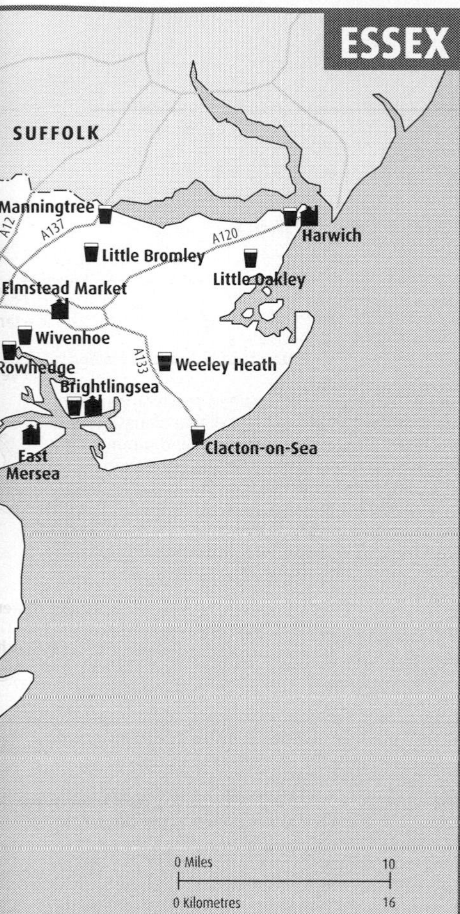

Billericay

Blue Boar 🄻

39 High Street, CM12 9BA
8am-11 ☎ (01277) 655552
Greene King Abbot; Ruddles Best Bitter; guest beers Ⓗ
A popular Wetherspoon pub, especially at weekends, with the usual suspects on handpump, plus guests from microbrewers, often sourced locally. Breakfast is available until midday, plus main meals and snacks until 10pm. There is no music but there are fruit machines and muted TVs. An outside area at the rear is designated for drinking and smoking. The pub has a Pay & Display car park at the rear, and the train station and bus stops are nearby. Q❀◐♿≋●P🚌(100)

Coach & Horses

36 Chapel Street, CM12 9LU
11-11; 12-10 Sun ☎ (01277) 622873
thecoachandhorses.org
Black Sheep Best Bitter; Greene King IPA; Sharp's Doom Bar; guest beers Ⓗ
Close to the High Street, this welcoming one-bar pub with an inviting atmosphere is a regular in the Guide. Guest beers, from the Gray's portfolio, change weekly. Good-quality food is available lunchtimes and evenings, with curry night (including Thai and Goan) on Wednesday and fish night on Friday. The bar and food service is efficient and friendly. The walls are adorned with prints and decorative plates, and a fine collection of jugs hangs from the ceiling. Q❀◐≋P🚌(100)

Bowers Gifford

Gun

London Road, SS13 2DU (on old A13)
11-10 (11 Wed & Thu; 11.30 Fri & Sat); 12-10 Sun
☎ (01268) 551506 thegunpub.co.uk
Fuller's London Pride; Sharp's Doom Bar; guest beers Ⓗ
Community pub with a friendly and inviting atmosphere for all age groups. Two beer festivals are held each year, in May and August. Many events are organised including pub outings and rock & roll bingo for charity. It has a separate Persian restaurant (the menu can be served in the pub), as well as good-value pub classics and Sunday roasts in the pub. Several awards have been won for customer service. Well-behaved children are welcome until 9pm. Dogs are allowed on leads in the garden; water is provided.
❀◐♿♣●P

Braintree

King William IV 🄻

114 London Road, CM77 7PU
3-midnight; 12-midnight Fri-Sun ☎ (01376) 567755
kingwilliamiv.co.uk
Beer range varies Ⓖ
Warm and friendly traditional free house serving a changing range of real ales, usually featuring a Sharp's beer and some from Essex microbreweries. Three or four ciders include Westons and other interesting selections. There is a main bar and a small back bar with a dartboard. The extensive gardens are used to host many events throughout the year including beer festivals and musical events. This is a traditional drinking pub that does not offer cooked meals. ❀♣●P🚌(70,352)🐾

Brentwood

Rising Sun 🄻

144 Ongar Road, CM15 9DJ (on A128, at Western Rd jct)
3-11.30 (midnight Fri); 12-midnight Sat; 12-10.30 Sun
☎ (01277) 213749
Fuller's London Pride; Sharp's Cornish Coaster; Timothy Taylor Landlord; guest beers Ⓗ
Splendid community local with five real ales. There are charity quizzes on Monday evenings and frequent darts matches in the public bar, as well as occasional chess evenings. Five handpumps in the saloon bar dispense three regular ales plus a beer from Brentwood Brewery and a guest from anywhere. Framed prints of the local area decorate the walls. Outside is a covered heated smokers' area and patio. Q❀♿♣P🚌

Brightlingsea

Railway Tavern 🄻

58 Station Road, CO7 0DT
5 (4 summer)-10; 3-11 Fri; 12-11 Sat; 12-3, 7-10.30 Sun
Crouch Vale Essex Boys Best Bitter; guest beers Ⓗ
A brewpub that has been a CAMRA favourite for several years. It has a basic interior; drinkers mainly

sit on pews donated several years ago by a priest from St James Church. Beers come from the pub's own brewery or local brewers, usually including a dark beer. A cider festival takes place the first May weekend, with music including the pub band, The Railwailers, who practise from January. The pub raises money for the local museum and football team. Q (78)

Broads Green

Walnut Tree

CM3 1DT (turn off B1008 at Ash Tree corner, signposted Great Waltham; after ¼ mile turn left into Larks Lane and continue for ¾ mile) TL694125

12-11 ☎ (01245) 360222

Morland Original Bitter; Ruddles Best Bitter; guest beer G

Handsome Victorian pub overlooking the green. The front door opens into what was the bottle and jug but is now a small snug. To the left is the wood-panelled public bar, little changed since 1888. To the right is the slightly more modern saloon bar. Outside there is seating in front of the pub, a children's play area and a large garden. There is no food, the landlord preferring to concentrate on his beers and to maintain a traditional atmosphere. Q P

Broxted

Prince of Wales

Brick End, CM6 2BJ

closed Mon; 11.30 (12 Sun)-11 ☎ (01279) 850256

Greene King IPA; guest beers H

In the southern part of Broxted, this former Charrington's inn, for many years in the doldrums, has been transformed into a welcoming community pub after the current landlords took over in late 2011. It has a comfortable split-level bar, an adjoining room with two woodburners and a large conservatory. Generously portioned pub grub, mostly locally sourced, will satisfy the most demanding appetite. There is a small garden to the rear. Four beers are always available, with LocAle from Bishop Nick. Local CAMRA Pub of the Year 2014. Q P (5)

Burnham-on-Crouch

New Welcome Sailor

Station Road, CM0 8HF

12-11 ☎ (01621) 784778

Dark Star Hophead; Sharp's Doom Bar; Wibblers Dengie IPA; guest beer H

This is a spick and span community local which is very comfortable and friendly, only 400 yards from the railway station. Within the large, single-room, L-shaped interior there are traditional pub games and Sky TV. Two darts teams play in the local league. A spacious function room is available for special events. No food is served. The guest ales (summer only) may well come from any of the four local breweries. Q P

Queen's Head

26 Providence, CM0 8JU

2 (5 Mon)-11; 12-11 Fri-Sun ☎ (01621) 784825

Dark Star Hophead; Wibblers Dengie IPA; guest beers H

A Gray's house tucked away in a side street opposite the town's clock tower. Four cask beers are always available, often including a stout or porter, one of which could well be from Red Fox brewery. Two ciders and a perry complement the beer range. The huffer bread rolls are made in the pub's kitchen or you could try the home-made curried goat for a taste of the Caribbean. An annual beer festival takes place over the August bank holiday. (31X)

Castle Hedingham

Bell

10 St James Street, CO9 3EJ

11.45-3, 6-11; 12-midnight Fri & Sat; 12-11 Sun
☎ (01787) 460350 hedinghambell.co.uk

Adnams Southwold Bitter; Mighty Oak IPA, Maldon Gold; guest beer G

Fifteenth-century Gray's-owned coaching inn with small rooms for drinking and dining alongside two main bars. Beer is cask-dispensed and summer and winter beer festivals are held. Jazz is played lunchtimes on the last Sunday of the month, while local musicians perform on Friday evenings and Sunday is quiz night. Locally-sourced food includes Turkish specials prepared in a wood-fired stone oven, and a barbecue fish menu on Monday evening. Q P (89)

Chelmsford

Ale House

24-26 Viaduct Road, CM1 1TS

11-11 (midnight Fri & Sat); 12-10 Sun ☎ (01245) 260535
the-ale-house-chelmsford.co.uk

Beer range varies H

Real ale pub situated in three railway arches beneath Chelmsford station. Each week there is a selection of 12 real ales, always including dark beers and stronger brews, and up to 12 real ciders. Although the range is continuously changing, it usually includes beers from Adnams, Black Sheep, Hepworths and Oakham. There are also imported

INDEPENDENT BREWERIES

Bishop Nick Braintree
Brentwood Brentwood
Brightlingsea Brightlingsea
Colchester Wakes Colne
Crouch Vale South Woodham Ferrers
Deverell's Grays
Dominion/Pitfield Moreton
Felstar Felsted
George's/Hop Monster Great Wakering
Hart of Stebbing Stebbing
Harwich Town Harwich
Highwood (Cann Do Beers) Highwood
Hope Stanford-le-Hope (NEW)
Indian Summer Saffron Walden
Maldon Maldon
Mersea Island East Mersea
Mighty Oak Maldon
Nethergate Pentlow
Railway Tavern Brightlingsea
Red Fox Coggeshall
Round Tower Chelmsford
Saffron Henham
Shalford Shalford
Sticklegs Elmstead Market
Vens Rawreth (brewing suspended)
Wibblers Mayland
Witham Witham (NEW)

German lagers on tap and a wide choice of bottled beers from around the world. Pizzas are available all day, other food just lunchtimes.

Barista

44-45 Duke Street, CM1 1JA

11.30-11; 11-midnight Wed & Thu; 11-2am Fri & Sat; closed Sun (01245) 493333 baristachelmsford.com

Beer range varies

Small contemporary bar with comfortable leather furniture and subdued lighting close to the railway and bus stations. It is slightly surprising to find three well-kept real ales which are served by gravity from the first floor cellar. Outside, there is a small cordoned-off area with tables and chairs allowing customers to drink alfresco. Popular beer festivals are held at least twice a year. Food is served weekday lunchtimes. All ages from 21 upwards are welcome.

Endeavour

351 Springfield Road, CM2 6AW

11-11; 11-10.30 Sun (01245) 257717

Greene King IPA; McMullen AK; Mighty Oak IPA; Sharp's Doom Bar; guest beer

Fifteen minutes' walk from the city centre, this busy and friendly pub has three rooms, one used for early evening dining on Friday (fish night) and Saturday (steak night); bookings are required for these and Sunday lunch. There are no evening meals on other days. All food is locally sourced and home cooked. Bar snacks are also available. It is a true community pub with a darts team, weekly poker nights and charity events. The pub also shows BT Sport. (54,71c)

Ivory Peg

7 New London Road, CM2 0NA

8am-midnight (1am Fri & Sat) (01245) 253130

Greene King Abbot; Ruddles Best Bitter; guest beers

Town-centre pub with a single open-plan area at ground level featuring large windows onto the street, and toilets upstairs with a good collection of old photographs on the walls. Excavations prior to its building produced an ivory tuning peg from a medieval musical instrument (now in Chelmsford Museum). Food is served all day, with alcohol available from 9am. As with other Wetherspoon pubs, beer festivals are held twice a year, with a cider festival in the summer.

Oddfellows Arms

195 Springfield Road, CM2 6JP

12-11 (midnight Fri & Sat) (01245) 490514

theoddfellowsarms.com

Mighty Oak Maldon Gold; Sharp's Doom Bar; Wibblers Dengie IPA; guest beers

Refurbished in 2012, this is a pub with a modern wood interior but maintaining the feel of a local. There is a large U-shaped bar area with a back room containing a pool table leading out to the garden/smoking area. Beer festivals are held annually. There is monthly live music, and poker nights are held Tuesday and Wednesday. Extensive home-made food is served lunchtimes and evenings weekdays, and all day at weekends up to 9pm. Sport is screened on TV.

Orange Tree

Lower Anchor Street, CM2 0AS

12-11; 12-11.30 Fri & Sat (01245) 262664

the-ot.com

Dark Star Hophead; Mighty Oak Oscar Wilde; Shalford Barnfield Pale Ale; guest beers

The Orange Tree is one of the best real ale pubs in Chelmsford and was voted local CAMRA Pub of the Year 2014. It is a place for conversation and meeting friends. There is a public bar plus a large saloon. The guest beers, served from handpump or on gravity, normally include a stout or porter. Ciders are Westons Old Rosie and from the Gwynt y Ddraig range. Lunchtime food is served, including Sunday roasts, with a curry night Thursday evenings.

Plough

28 Duke Street, CM1 1HY

11-11 (01245) 250145

theoriginalploughchelmsford.co.uk

Adnams Southwold Bitter; Fuller's London Pride; Greene King IPA; Sharp's Doom Bar; guest beers

Conveniently located close to both railway and bus stations, this pub is now one of M&B's Oak Tree brand. Eight handpulls are available to serve beers, with eight more repeating the same range further along the bar. This is an open-plan pub with several distinct areas. Toilets are upstairs. Good-value pub food is served all day, starting with breakfast. Large screens show news and sporting events.

Queen's Head

30 Lower Anchor Street, CM2 0AS

12-11 (11.30 Fri & Sat) (01245) 265181

queensheadchelmsford.co.uk

Crouch Vale Essex Boys Best Bitter, Brewers Gold, Yakima Gold; guest beers

Crouch Vale Brewery's only pub, the Queen's Head sells three of its beers permanently, with four guests which may include a Crouch Vale seasonal and always a dark beer. The Victorian L-shaped pub has bare board flooring and comfortable bench seating. Two fires make it cosy in winter. This popular local can be busy when there is a match at the nearby county cricket ground. The Essex Beard Club meets here once a year in February.

Railway Tavern

63 Duke Street, CM1 1LW

12-11 (11.30 Fri & Sat); 11-4 Sun (01245) 280679

Greene King Abbot; McMullen AK; Mighty Oak IPA; Sharp's Special; guest beers

A Tardis-like corner pub outside Chelmsford station – a little oasis in a concrete jungle. There is even a small garden where you can listen to the station announcements. Not surprisingly, a railway theme dominates. This is a long, narrow pub with banks of handpumps at opposite ends of the central bar counter, a TV at one end for sporting events, and seating towards the rear laid out like a railway carriage. It does a good range of quality lunchtime meals (no food Sun).

Royal Steamer

1 Townfield Street, CM1 1QJ

11 (12 Sun)-11 (01245) 258800

Fuller's London Pride; Greene King IPA; Timothy Taylor Landlord; Wibblers Dengie Gold; guest beer

A small wedge-shaped traditional pub in a residential area behind the railway station. Its name is believed to be unique in the UK. Two street doors lead to an opened-up pub (ostensibly public and saloon bars) with two bar counters, each with three handpumps. It does a lunchtime menu.

A separate function room is available for hire, and there is a small secluded courtyard garden at the rear. It is a games-oriented pub with pool table, darts, a golf society, large-screen TV and regular quiz nights. ❀◖≋♣🚌📶

White Horse 🅛

25 Townfield Street, CM1 1QJ

✪ 11.30-11 (12.30am Fri & Sat); 12-10.30 Sun
☎ (01245) 269556 🌐 whbl.co.uk

Mighty Oak Oscar Wilde, Captain Bob; guest beers Ⓗ

The pub is situated behind the railway station at the end of a delightful road of two-storey terraced cottages. It has been a long-time CAMRA favourite but the present owners have given it a new lease of life – traditional with a contemporary twist. One of the longest bars in Chelmsford leads to a lounge area with comfy armchairs and sofas. Mighty Oak beers feature regularly among a changing selection. Large screens show news and sport. Occasional live music, discos and beer festivals take place. ◖≋🍎🚌

Chipping Ongar

Cock Tavern 🅛

218 High Street, CM5 9AE

✪ 11-midnight (3am Fri & Sat); 12-midnight Sun
☎ (01277) 362615 🌐 cocktavernongar.co.uk

Adnams Southwold Bitter; guest beers Ⓗ

Located at the north end of the High Street near the preserved railway station, next to the library and close to public car parks, the Grade II-listed building is constructed with timber frames, part plasterboard and part weatherboard. Three rotating guest ales are on handpump, normally from local breweries. Live music plays every Saturday night. A spacious function room is available.
Q◖◗≋P🚌🐾📶

Clacton-on-Sea

Moon & Starfish

1 Marine Parade East, CO15 1PT

✪ 8am-11 (12.30am Fri & Sat) ☎ (01255) 222998

Greene King Abbot; Ruddles Best Bitter; guest beers Ⓗ

A Wetherspoon pub on Clacton seafront, frequented by both locals and holidaymakers. It is handy for the traditional seaside amusements, the pier rides, and close to the town centre shops. It is also well served by public transport, being on or near many bus routes, and only a short walk from Clacton railway station. There is an area set aside for dining and an outside space with seating that overlooks the sea, perfect for fine weather.
Q🚼❀◖◗♿≋🍎🚌(74,76)📶

Old Lifeboat House 🏆

39 Marine Parade East, CO15 6AD

✪ 11-10.30; 12-10.30 Sun ☎ (01255) 476799

Beer range varies Ⓗ

A family-run pub that continues to grow in popularity, with plans to extend the premises. It was voted local CAMRA Pub of the Year 2012, 2013 and 2014. Food is served Wednesdays only, lunchtime and evening. Up to six ciders and perries are usually available. Beer festivals are held during the last weekends of April and October. A St Austell beer is normally served, with up to four other guest beers, all on handpump. ◖◗≋🍎P🚭🚌(74,76)🐾📶

Coggeshall

Chapel Inn 🅛

4 Market Hill, CO6 1TS

✪ 12-11 ☎ (01376) 561655 🌐 thechapelinn.com

Adnams Ghost Ship; Red Fox Coggeshall Gold; Sharp's Doom Bar; guest beer Ⓗ

Built on the site of an early chapel and licensed in 1554, the pub overlooks the Market Square, selling up to five consistently well-kept ales, with beers from the local Red Fox Brewery always available. Despite having a fairly large seating area it retains a cosy and welcoming feel, with beams separating the various drinking and dining areas. The pub hosts a popular weekly quiz every Sunday night. Exact closing times may vary day to day.
❀◖◗P🚌(70)

Colchester

Ale House 🅛

82 Butt Road, CO3 3DA

✪ 3-11 (midnight Fri); 12-11 Sat; 12-10 Sun
☎ (01206) 573464

Ale House Bitter; guest beers Ⓗ

A free house with one bar at the end of the long pub. Beers are mostly from local breweries and always include a dark ale. Real cider is also on handpump. Comfortable seating is available inside and there is a lovely relaxing garden to the rear. Darts is popular in the pub and there is also a crib board, plus a rare bar billiards table. Quiz night is the third Wednesday of the month.
🚼❀≋(Town)♣🍎🐾📶

Bricklayers Arms

27 Bergholt Road, CO4 5AA

✪ 11-3, 5.30-11; 11-midnight Fri; 11-11 Sat; 12-7 Sun
☎ (01206) 852008

Adnams Southwold Bitter, Broadside; guest beers Ⓗ

Flagship Adnams' pub close to the main railway station, attracting commuters and locals alike. A range of up to nine ales is available, with a wide variety of guests plus the regular Adnams' range. Up to four real ciders are also kept, with Crones always on. A large lounge bar is complemented by a traditional public bar, pool table and dartboard, plus a large beer garden with cycle racks. Excellent food is served at lunchtime (no food Sat), with great-value roasts on Sunday. A popular monthly quiz is held. Q◖◗≋(North)🍎P🚭🚌(66)

Britannia Gurkha Restaurant & Bar

42 Meyrick Crescent, CO2 7QY

✪ 3.30-11; 2-11 Fri (midnight Sat); 12-11 Sun
☎ (01206) 76100 🌐 britanniagurkharestaurant.co.uk

Colchester Metropolis, Colchester No. 1; guest beer Ⓗ

Family-run pub and restaurant not far from Colchester town centre. The traditional bar features both a pool table and dartboards, with a large-screen TV catering for sports fans. Do take time to look at the Ghurkha memorabilia and read about the incredible bravery of those awarded the Victoria Cross. By contrast, the restaurant is pleasantly relaxed and a great place to enjoy the highly-rated Nepalese cuisine. Booking is recommended to avoid disappointment.
◗≋(Town)♣P🚌

British Grenadier 🅛

67 Military Road, CO1 2AP

✪ 12-3 (not Mon-Wed), 5-11.30; 12-3, 5-midnight Fri & Sat; 12-3, 7-11.30 Sun ☎ 07832 215118

Beer range varies Ⓗ
Traditional two-bar corner pub with a large front bar warmed on cold winter nights by an open fire, plus a small back bar containing a pool table; there is also an outside seating area. Formerly Adnams tied, the handpumps now offer a changing selection of up to four local and national beers plus at least two real ciders and perries. Darts and pool are regularly played, with a quiz night every Sunday. The pub hosts two beer festivals annually. ❀≈(Town)♣●▯🚌

Hospital Arms

123-125 Crouch Street, CO3 3HA
12-11 (midnight Fri & Sat); 12-10.30 Sun
☎ (01206) 542398 🌐 colchester-hospitalarms.co.uk
Adnams Southwold Bitter, Broadside; guest beers Ⓗ
Located opposite the Essex County Hospital and known locally as Ward, the Hospital Arms makes a welcome return to the Guide. The pub comprises three separate bar areas and a beer garden to the rear. Good-quality lunchtime food is a big feature. It is a friendly and busy venue with a good mix of customers. A regularly changing selection of guest ales is offered to complement the permanent Adnams' house beers. Q❀◐

Odd One Out 🄻

28 Mersea Road, CO2 7ET
4.30-11; 12-11 Fri & Sat; 12-10.30 Sun ☎ (01206) 513958
Mauldons Silver Adder; guest beers Ⓗ
Colchester's original multi-award-winning free house, it celebrates 30 years in 2015 and is the current local CAMRA Cider Pub of the Year. Up to seven ales are on offer, primarily from micros, and at least one is usually a dark beer. Four real ciders along with over 50 scotch malt whiskies can be enjoyed. Without a TV, jukebox or fruit machines, it has just two lovely open fires to complement the atmosphere. The garden is situated to the rear, plus there is a separate back bar which hosts meetings for many local groups.
Q❀≈(Town)●🚌(8,67)🐾📶

Purple Dog 🄻

42 Eld Lane, CO1 1LS
11-11 (1am Thu); 10-1am Fri; 10-2am Sat; 11.30-10.30 Sun
☎ (01206) 564995
Crouch Vale Brewers Gold; Sharp's Doom Bar; Woodforde's Wherry; guest beers Ⓗ
Vibrant town-centre pub, popular with younger folks and seasoned drinkers alike. A single large bar serves various drinking areas, including a pleasant courtyard. Up to six ales are available on handpull and two from the cask, usually from local breweries. Regular beer festivals are also held along with a monthly quiz. A menu of excellent-value home-cooked food is served to supplement the fine ales on offer. ❀◐◑≈(Town)📶

Victoria Inn 🏆 🄻

10 North Station Road, CO1 1RB
12-11 (midnight Fri & Sat); 2-11 Sun ☎ (01206) 514510
🌐 victoriainncolchester.co.uk
Maldon Pucks Folly; guest beers Ⓗ
A warm welcome awaits at the local CAMRA and Essex County Pub of the Year for 2014. Five real ales are on handpump, from both local and smaller brewers around the country, one usually being a dark ale. Craft keg beer is also available, plus up to nine real ciders. A large courtyard caters for alfresco drinking and also hosts the annual beer festival. Live music is played on Sundays, and vintage Space Invaders plus an excellent jukebox complement the entertainment. The pub has a function room. ❀≈(North)●🚌🐾

Cold Norton

Norton 🄻

Latchingdon Road, CM3 6JB
4.30 (12 Thu)-11; 12-midnight Fri & Sat; 12-11 Sun
☎ (01621) 826948 🌐 savethenorton.org
Mighty Oak Captain Bob; guest beers Ⓗ
A friendly village pub, rescued from closure and run by a committee of local people. Guest beers are sourced from all over the UK. Live music can be experienced twice-monthly and an open mic night, bingo or a quiz take place most Thursdays. Local walks, finishing at the pub, are organised on the second Saturday of each month. The pub's annual beer festival is over the May Day weekend. Good home-cooked food is served in the attractive new restaurant. ❀◐◑♿♣●P▯🚌🐾📶

Colne Engaine

Five Bells

Mill Lane, CO6 2HY
12-3, 6-11; 12-11 Thu; 12-1.30am Fri; 12-12.30am Sat; 12-10 Sun ☎ (01787) 224166 🌐 fivebells.net
Adnams Southwold Bitter; guest beers Ⓗ
A 16th-century free house on the Essex-Suffolk border in the heart of the village, with fine views over the Colne Valley, offering a range of ales, mostly from East Anglia, with local breweries regularly featuring. There are both dining and drinking areas and a separate restaurant. Outside is a terrace with a covered and heated area for smokers. There is an annual beer festival and live music features regularly. A large TV in one bar shows sport or music. The bus stop is about a mile away. ◐◑♿P🚌(88)🐾📶

Copford Green

Alma 🄻

School Road, CO6 1BX
12-3, 5-10.30 (11 Thu & Fri); 12-11.30 Sat; 12-10.30 Sun
☎ (01206) 210607 🌐 thealma.org.uk
Greene King IPA, Abbot; Red Fox Hunter's Gold; guest beer Ⓗ
Pleasant country pub with one bar serving various drinking and dining areas, with real fires in winter. Four ales are regularly available from Greene King and Red Fox breweries, and there is an annual spring bank holiday beer festival. The pub is a meeting place for classic car and motorcycle enthusiasts. A large garden at the rear has ample seating and garden games. Quiz night is the first Thursday of each month, and a good-value menu of home-cooked food is available.
Q❀◐◑♿♣P🐾📶

Cornish Hall End

Horse & Groom

CM7 4HF (on the B1057) TL683366
closed Mon; 12-midnight ☎ (01799) 586306
🌐 thehorseandgroom.org
Greene King IPA; guest beers Ⓗ
A pleasant village pub, opposite the parish church, with a restaurant and garden. It runs beer festivals and events and is a warm and friendly place, with beers that change frequently. It is the social centre

of this village, supporting many charities too. It offers good food, and special lunches, carveries and fish and chips nights are regularly held. These can be so popular they need booking. Poker is played every Friday evening.

Coxtie Green

White Horse

173 Coxtie Green Road, CM14 5PX (1 mile W of A128, at jct with Mores Lane) TQ564959

11.30-11 (midnight Fri & Sat); 12-11 Sun

(01277) 372410 whitehorsebrentwood.co.uk

Beer range varies H

Excellent country free house with a relaxed, friendly atmosphere. There is a large comfortable saloon bar with an extension leading through to the public bar, with Sky TV and a dartboard. The 10 handpumps offer three or four beers from Brentwood Brewery and six or seven guests. The pub is now badged as the Brentwood Brewery tap. It has a large garden with a children's play area. There is a beer festival in July each year and occasional smaller events. Bus service is limited, but reliable. P (72)

Duton Hill

Three Horseshoes

CM6 2DX (1 mile W of B184) TL606268

12-2.30 (not Mon-Thu), 6-11; 12-3, 6-11 Sat; 12-3, 7-10.30 Sun (01371) 870681

Mighty Oak Captain Bob; guest beers H

Cosy village local with a garden, wildlife pond and terrace overlooking the Chelmer Valley and farmland. The landlord hosts a weekend of open-air theatre in July. A millennium beacon in the garden, breweriana and a remarkable collection of Butlins memorabilia are features. A beer festival is held on the late spring bank holiday in the Duton Hill Den. Look for the pub sign depicting a famous painting, Our Blacksmith, by former local resident Sir George Clausen. P (313)

Epping

Forest Gate Inn

111 Bell Common, CM16 4DZ (turn off main road opposite Bell Motel S of town; pub is 500yds away on bend)

10-2.30, 5-11; 12-3.30, 6.30-10.30 Sun (01992) 572312

haywardsrestaurant.co.uk

Adnams Southwold Bitter, Broadside; Nethergate IPA H**; guest beers** H/G

On the edge of Epping Forest, a mile from Epping Underground station, this is an old-fashioned pub in a 17th-century building with low ceilings and flag floors. It is frequented by locals, walkers and their dogs. Bar snacks are available in the pub as well as full meals in the adjacent new Haywards restaurant. Another new addition is B&B with four rooms. The pub concentrates on real ale in a traditional setting, with a large outside seating area at the front. Q P (213,541)

Fordham

Three Horseshoes

Church Road, Colchester, CO6 3NJ

closed Mon; 12-3, 5-11; 12-midnight Sat; 12-8 Sun

(01206) 240195 threehorseshoes-fordham.co.uk

Red Fox Bitter, Three Horseshoes Bitter, Coggeshall Gold; guest beer H

Vibrant 16th-century village pub with two bars, plus a separate dining room. The interior is heavily timbered, with a large brick fireplace, woodburner and comfortable sofas. Several Red Fox beers are served, plus one guest ale. Tuesdays are steak nights and Thursdays are curry nights. Occasional live music is hosted, along with an annual beer festival. The pub's latest acquisition is a bright pink pool table. P

Fuller Street

Square & Compasses

CM3 2BB TL748161

11.30-3, 5.30-11; 12-midnight Sat; 12-11 Sun

(01245) 361477 thesquareandcompasses.co.uk

Beer range varies G

A 17th-century free house known locally as the Stokehole. Set in attractive countryside and handy for the Essex Way long distance footpath, this is a small, well-looked-after country pub. It has exposed beams throughout, with two wood-burning stoves in inglenook fireplaces. Old local woodworking tools adorn the Taproom Bar. Up to four real ales and Westons cider and perry are served. Fresh locally-sourced home-cooked food is available daily, including game from the surrounding estates (no food Sun eves). P

Goldhanger

Chequers

The Square, CM9 8AS

11-11; 12-10.30 Sun (01621) 788203

thechequersgoldhanger.co.uk

Adnams Ghost Ship; Crouch Vale Brewers Gold; Sharp's Doom Bar; Young's Bitter; guest beers H

Charming 15th-century inn in an attractive village, with timbered rooms including a snug and games room with bar billiards. The guest beer list is varied, often featuring local ales. Beer festivals are held in March and September. An extensive food menu offers superb quality meals made with local produce. The courtyard is a real suntrap in the summer, while real fires in two of the bars provide warmth in winter. The pub is a short walk from the River Blackwater. Q P (95)

Grays

Theobald Arms

141 Argent Street, RM17 6HR (about 7 minutes' walk from Grays rail and bus station, down Kings Walk)

11-11; 11-midnight Fri & Sat; 12-11 Sun

(01375) 372253 theobaldarms.com

Beer range varies H

Genuine, traditional pub with a public bar that has an unusual hexagonal pool table. The changing selection of four guest beers showcases local independent breweries, and a range of British bottled beers is also stocked. Regular St George's weekend and summer beer festivals are held in the old stables and on the rear enclosed patio. Lunchtime meals are served Monday to Friday. Darts and cards are played. A former local CAMRA Pub of the Year. P

White Hart

Kings Walk, Argent Street, RM17 6HR (about 7 minutes' walk from Grays rail and bus stations, down Kings Walk)
12-midnight (12.30am Fri & Sat); 12-11.30 Sun
☎ (01375) 373319 whitehartgrays.co.uk
Crouch Vale Brewers Gold; Sharp's White Hart Ale; guest beers
Traditional local just outside the town centre, rejuvenated since it was taken over in 2006. Two regular ales, including the house beer, are supplemented by three guests (one usually dark) and a selection of bottled Belgian beers. There is a meeting/function room and a large, secluded beer garden. Live music plays fortnightly, the pub supports pool and darts teams, and sport is screened on TVs. A beer festival is held in February/March. ❀⇌♣P

Great Dunmow

Angel & Harp

Church End, CM6 2AD
9am-11 (11.30 Fri & Sat); 9am-10.30 Sun
☎ (01371) 859259 angelandharp.co.uk
Nethergate IPA; guest beers
The pub has refurbished its building and restaurant to increase its business. There is a substantial garden area, a patio and a large car park. It has a function room and runs occasional beer festivals. Local ales regularly feature as guest beers, alongside the Nethergate IPA which is always available. This pub is on the north-east side of Great Dunmow and accommodates families and large parties, although the drinking area is small. Q❀P

Hadstock

King's Head

Linton Road, CB21 4NU TL559449
12-2 (not Mon), 5-11; 12-2, 5-midnight Fri; 12-midnight Sat; 12-8 Sun ☎ (01223) 893473 kingsheadhadstock.co.uk
Mighty Oak IPA; guest beers
The most northern pub in north-west Essex, this is an old village local with a darts teams, good cheap food and excellent local beers. Set in the centre of the village, it has a garden at the rear. Popular with walkers, support for the pub is growing as many football teams also use it as a social base. Pensioners' meals are reduced in price here on some weekdays. Q❀♣P

Halstead

Three Pigeons

6 Mount Hill, CO9 1AA
4.30-11.30; 12-midnight Fri-Sun ☎ (01787) 274392
Beer range varies
Friendly pub with wooden floors, beams and a real fire. It comprises two separate drinking areas, plus a well-maintained garden which is also home to the pub's beer festivals. There is a large-screen TV for watching football. This is the pub's first appearance in the Guide, and it usually has three different guest ales, with an emphasis on local brewers. A traditional meat raffle is held every Sunday. ❀♣P(88)

Harwich

Alma Inn

25 Kings Head Street, CO12 3EE
12-11 (midnight Fri & Sat) ☎ (01255) 318681
almaharwich.co.uk
Adnams Southwold Bitter, Broadside; guest beers
Now in its fifth year under freehold ownership, this increasingly vibrant pub bucks the trend by increasing its footfall, catering for traditional beer drinkers and family diners, and offering Adnams' beers and changing guests. Real cider is also available. Freshly-cooked meals are served at all times in the bar and in the separate dining areas. Music, quizzes and gourmet evenings are among the in-house attractions and the Alma is always involved in community events.
❀⇌(Town)(102,103)

New Bell Inn

Outpart Eastward, CO12 3EN (off King's Quay St)
11-3, 7-11 (midnight Fri & Sat); 12-4, 7-11 (12-11 summer) Sun ☎ (01255) 503545
Greene King IPA; Mighty Oak Oscar Wilde; guest beers
Traditional pub that is very community focused, with many local events being conceived and organised under its roof. The front bar is a great place to practise the art of conversation and enjoy the selection of real ales, while the rear bar and seating area offer a place to relax with friends or enjoy the hearty lunchtime food. There is a small walled garden at the rear and the pub manages to be both cosy in winter and airy in summer.
Q❀⇌(Town)P

Hatfield Broad Oak

Cock Inn

High Street, CM22 7HF
12-11 (midnight Fri & Sat); 12-10.30 Sun
☎ (01279) 718306 thecockinn-hatfieldbroadoak.co.uk
Adnams Southwold Bitter; Wells Eagle IPA; Woodforde's Wherry; guest beer
A real village local in a picturesque central location. It is close to Hatfield Forest and popular with walkers. The building is 16th century and Grade II-listed, a former coaching inn, now decorated in a sympathetic yet elegant style. Sensibly priced but generous meals are cooked to order using local produce; unusual desserts are a feature. A second bar has a dartboard and TV, while a third room is a quiet area or is used for larger groups. QP

Hempstead

Bluebell Inn

High Street, CB10 2PD (on B1054)
closed Mon; 11-3, 6-11; 11.30-11 Sat; 12-7 Sun
☎ (01799) 599199 thebluebellinn.co.uk
Adnams Lighthouse, Southwold Bitter, Broadside; Woodforde's Wherry; guest beers
Late 16th-century village pub with 18th-century additions, reputed to be the birthplace of Dick Turpin; the bar displays posters about his life. Six beers are usually available. The restaurant serves excellent meals from an extensive menu and the large bar has a log fire. Ample seating is provided outside, plus a children's play area. Folk nights are hosted on Tuesdays and some other evenings.
Q❀♣P(18)

Henham

Cock Inn 𝕃

Church Street, CM22 6AL (1 mile off B1051) TL545286
🕔 12-3, 5-11; 12-midnight Thu-Sat; 12-11 Sun
☎ (01279) 850347 🌐 thecockinnhenham.co.uk
Greene King IPA; Sharp's Doom Bar; guest beers [H]
Traditional village pub in residential surroundings with outdoor seating at the front and a garden at the rear. The main and snug bars both have open fires. The snug has a large TV which screens major sporting events, and there is a large separate dining room next to the bar. The Saffron Brewery is 100 yards away and one of its beers is normally available here. There are regular quiz nights. No food Sunday evenings. **Q**⛯❀◐◑**P**🚌(7,7a)🐾

Herongate Tye

Olde Dog Inn 𝕃

129 Billericay Road, CM13 3SD (E of A128) TQ641909
🕔 11.30-11; 12-11 Sat; 12-10.30 Sun ☎ (01277) 810337
🌐 theoldedoginn.co.uk
Crouch Vale Brewers Gold [G]; **Greene King Abbot** [H]; **guest beers** [G]
Family-owned and family-run free house with a beer garden that dates from the 17th century. Six real ales are always available including three regularly changing guest beers of varying styles from countrywide microbreweries and national brands; the Olde Dog IPA house beer is from local brewery Crouch Vale. As well as the period decor, a variety of beer mats and oddities adorns the walls and ceilings. Food is available at the bar and in the separate restaurant area lunchtimes and evenings.
❀◐◑♿**P**

Heybridge

Maltsters' Arms

Hall Road, CM9 4NJ
🕔 12-midnight; 12-1am Fri & Sat ☎ (01621) 853880
Greene King IPA, Abbot [H]; **guest beers** [H]/[G]
This friendly Gray's local is a little like somebody's comfortable front room converted into a bar. The pleasant atmosphere is enhanced by a collection of mirrors and some breweriana. Three guest beers are usually available, one from a local brewery. Filled rolls are served lunchtimes. The rear patio, with plenty of tables and chairs, can be a real suntrap in summer. The pub is popular with ramblers walking the nearby Chelmer and Blackwater Navigation towpath. **Q**⛯❀◐♣🚌🐾📶

Hockley

White Hart

274 Main Road, SS5 4NS
🕔 11-11; 12-10.30 Sun ☎ (01702) 203438
🌐 whiteharthockley.co.uk
Beer range varies [H]
A well established, friendly local dating from the 18th century, facing the village green. The pub is community oriented and supportive of local charities through its quiz nights and music events. Up to three changing guest ales are served. Lunchtime food is available all week, including roasts on Sunday, with evening meals served Tuesday to Saturday. There is a large rear garden with seating and a patio area, plus picnic tables at the front. A beer festival is held every spring.
⛯❀◐◑⇌**P**🚌(7,8)📶

Horndon-on-the-Hill

Bell Inn

High Road, SS17 8LD (near centre of village, almost opp Woolmarket and Orsett Road)
🕔 11-11; 12-10.30 Sun ☎ (01375) 642463 🌐 bell-inn.co.uk
Crouch Vale Brewers Gold; Greene King IPA; Sharp's Doom Bar; guest beers [H]
Popular 15th-century coaching inn, where beamed bars feature wood panelling and carvings, run by the same family since 1938. Note the hot cross bun collection; a bun has been added every Good Friday for more than 100 years. Three regular beers are on handpump, plus two guests, including ales from Essex breweries. The award-winning restaurant is open daily, lunchtimes and evenings, offering a daily changing menu, using seasonal and local produce (booking is advisable). Accommodation is available in individually styled bedrooms.
Q❀🛏◐◑♿🍎**P**🚌(374)

Layer Breton

Hare & Hounds

Crayes Green, CO2 0PN
🕔 9am (10am Sun)-midnight ☎ (01206) 330459
🌐 thehareandhound.co.uk
Adnams Southwold Bitter; Greene King IPA, Abbot; guest beer [H]
A community pub with separate areas for drinking and dining. A large real fire warms the bar area, which also sells newspapers and an assortment of grocery items. Three beer festivals a year are held, including one for St George's Day. Quiz night is the first Wednesday and live music the last Friday of each month. A menu of good-quality home-cooked food is served. The large garden hosts a bouncy castle and an annual Easter egg hunt.
⛯❀🛏◐◑▲**P**🚌(75)🐾📶

Layer-de-la-Haye

Layer Fox 𝕃

2 Malting Green Road, CO2 0JH
🕔 8.30am-11 (midnight Fri & Sat); 8.30am-10 Sun
☎ (01206) 738723 🌐 thelayerfox.co.uk
Red Fox Bitter; guest beers [H]
Friendly country pub with a single bar serving various seating areas on different levels. Four ales are usually on tap, primarily from local breweries. A good-value menu of home-cooked food is served and the Sunday roasts are famous for their Yorkshire puddings. The pub is open from 8.30am as a delicatessen and village shop, with a paypoint and cash machine. Accommodation is available in the Sleepy Fox B&B chalets.
Q⛯❀🛏◐◑♿♣**P**🚌(50)🐾📶

Leigh-on-Sea

Crooked Billet

51 High Street, SS9 2EP
🕔 12-11 (10.30 Sun) ☎ (01702) 480289
Adnams Southwold Bitter, Broadside; Fuller's London Pride; St Austell Nicholson's Pale Ale; Sharp's Doom Bar; guest beers [H]
Situated in Old Leigh fishing village overlooking the Thames Estuary, this 16th-century pub has two small bars, with bare floorboards and beamed ceilings. The walls are decorated with local village and fishing pictures. Beer sampling evenings take place once a month. It has a small garden to one

side and a larger seating area to the front which is shared with a seafood merchant. It is 10 minutes' walk from Leigh station. Popular in the summer. Q

Elms

1060 London Road, SS9 3ND (on A13)
8am-11 (1am Fri & Sat) ☎ (01702) 474687
Greene King Abbot; Ruddles Best Bitter; guest beers H
An old coaching inn converted by Wetherspoon into a large, open pub decorated with photos of the local area. Breakfast is available until noon, with main meals and snacks until 10pm. Children are admitted until 9pm. Six changing guest ales and up to three real ciders are served. There is no music but there are fruit machines and muted TVs. Outside is a paved, heated and covered area for smokers, and the pub also has a hedged front garden. P

Mayflower

5-6 High Street, Old Leigh, SS9 2EN (far end of Old Leigh from station behind chip shop)
11 (12 Sun)-11 summer; 11-9; 12-11 Thu-Sun winter
☎ (01702) 478535 mayfloweroldleigh.com
Crouch Vale Brewers Gold; George's Cockleboats; guest beers H
Single-bar hostelry that adjoins a fish and chip restaurant. The popular food menu, unsurprisingly, consists mainly of fish dishes. Two permanent Essex ales are served: George's Cockleboats and Crouch Vale Brewers Gold, with up to four guest ales usually from East Anglia. One wall depicts the passenger manifest of the Pilgrim Fathers who sailed on the Mayflower. The pub has a drinking/smoking terrace with views across the estuary. Local CAMRA Pub of the Year 2014.

Little Bromley

Haywain

Bentley Road, CO11 2PL
closed Mon; 12-2.30 (not Tue), 6-10.30; 12-2.30, 6-11 Fri & Sat; 12-5 Sun ☎ (01206) 390004 thehaywain.co.uk
Adnams Southwold Bitter; guest beers H
A traditional 18th-century roadside inn with exposed interior beams and two real fires. As a true community pub, it is a regular venue for the village amenities committee. There is an additional function room with a self-contained bar. A good menu of home-made locally-sourced food, including a number of vegetarian dishes, is provided by landlady Dawn, and three to four real ales are always available, sourced from local breweries, their good condition ensured by landlord Andy. No buses on Sunday.
Q P (2)

Little Oakley

Olde Cherry Tree

Clacton Road, CO12 5JH
12-3, 5-11; 12-midnight Fri-Sun ☎ (01255) 886290
yeoldecherrytree.com
Adnams Southwold Bitter; guest beers H
A recently refurbished family-run pub with four real ales on handpump on most occasions and one real cider. It has a cosy and welcoming main bar with a large brick fireplace, a snug with sofas and chairs, a restaurant and a games area for darts and cribbage. It serves up good home-cooked food, including the popular traditional Sunday lunch, prepared by the resident chef. The pub runs its own summer beer festival held in the garden, with food and live music on some evenings during the festival.
P (3,4)

Little Thurrock (Grays)

Ship

16 Dock Road, RM17 6ES (on A126)
12-11.30; 12-10.30 Sun ☎ (01375) 371121
Wadworth 6X; guest beers H
Since it was taken over in 2011, this pub has been rejuvenated and it now offers one regular beer and three guest ales. A separate restaurant serves good-value food, with a popular carvery on Thursdays and Sundays – booking is recommended for Sunday lunch. A large, secluded, south-facing garden is at the rear of the building. Live bands perform twice a month at weekends – check out the information board at the front of the pub.
P (22A,66)

Traitor's Gate

40-42 Broadway, RM17 6EW (on A126)
12-11; 12-10.30 Sun ☎ (01375) 372628
Beer range varies H
This is the brewery tap for Deverell's Brewing, since being taken over in autumn 2013. Five handpumps offer a rotating selection of Deverell's and Mighty Oak beers, plus other guest ales, with an emphasis on Essex breweries. For details of forthcoming beers, look at the chalkboards above the bar. Draught cider from New Forest Cider is also available. A 10 per cent discount on real ales is offered to card-carrying CAMRA members. Live music features on Thursdays with an open mic night, plus fortnightly bands. Local CAMRA Pub of the Year 2014. (22A,66)

Little Walden

Crown

High Street, CB10 1XA (on B1052)
11.30 (11 Sat)-2.30, 6-11; 12-10.30 Sun
☎ (01799) 522475 thecrownlittlewalden.co.uk
Adnams Broadside; Greene King Abbot; Woodforde's Wherry; guest beer G
Charming 18th-century beamed country pub in a quiet hamlet, featuring a large walk-through fireplace. The pub is popular with diners, especially at weekends, when booking is advisable. Evening meals are served Tuesday to Saturday. An excellent range of beers is dispensed direct from the cask, which can be enjoyed on the covered patio area in warmer weather. The pub hosts traditional jazz on Wednesday evenings and has a function room for club meetings and private parties.
Q P

Littley Green

Compasses

CM3 1BU
12-3, 5.30-11.30; 12-11.30 Thu-Sun ☎ (01245) 362308
compasseslittleygreen.co.uk
Bishop Nick Ridley's Rite; guest beers G
Formerly Ridley's brewery tap, this is a picturesque Victorian country pub in a quiet hamlet. A wood-panelled bar has benches around the walls and a tiled floor. Beers are drawn direct from casks in the half-cellar. Renowned filled huffers (giant baps)

are available lunchtimes and evenings, plus other traditional dishes. There are seats and tables outside and in the large gardens. Five high-quality rooms are available. CAMRA Essex Pub of the Year 2012 and 2013 and East Anglian Pub of the Year 2012. Q❀◑♣P

Loughton

Victoria Tavern

165 Smarts Lane, IG10 4BP

11-3, 5-11; 11-11 Sat; 12-10.30 Sun ☎ (020) 8508 1779
victoriatavern.co.uk

Adnams Southwold Bitter; Greene King IPA; Sharp's Doom Bar; Timothy Taylor Landlord; guest beer [H]

This is an old-fashioned, traditional pub that prides itself on real ale and conversation. It is on the edge of Loughton and Epping Forest, a 10-minute walk from the Underground station. It has a small, well-kept garden and is popular with locals and walkers; well-behaved dogs are welcome. The pub is family friendly and serves generous portions of traditional home-cooked food in the raised restaurant area. There is a lively atmosphere and quizzes and charity fundraisers are hosted. Q❀◑♿⊖P

Maldon

Carpenters' Arms

33 Gate Street, CM9 5QF

11-11; 11-midnight Fri & Sat ☎ (01621) 859896
thecarpentersarmsmaldon.co.uk

Adnams Southwold Bitter; Mighty Oak Kings; Red Fox IPA; Theakston Old Peculier [H]**; guest beers** [H]/[G]

A back-street gem at the top end of historic Maldon, and a pub since 1847. Its dimly lit interior, low wood beams and warm, welcoming atmosphere make this Gray's community pub more country than town, with a wide range of well-kept real ales and ciders from around the UK and the four local microbreweries. It has two comfortable bars, an attractive side garden, thriving darts and dominoes teams, regular beer festivals and quizzes. The Maldon Brewing Company's brewery and shop are a stone's throw away.
Q❀♿♣

Manningtree

Red Lion

42 South Street, CO11 1BG

12-3, 5-11 (midnight Fri); 12-midnight Sat; 12-11 Sun
☎ (01206) 391880 redlionmanningtree.co.uk

Adnams Southwold Bitter; guest beers [H]

Manningtree's oldest pub has been recently refurbished without losing its character. Three or four real ales – Southwold Bitter and guests – generally with an East Anglian connection, are all on handpump. Landlord Tom intends to have all the beers on gravity shortly. The venue does not do food, but is takeaway-friendly – menus, cutlery and crockery are provided for those who like a good pint with their takeaway. The courtyard garden is a suntrap in summer. A runner-up in the Observer Food Monthly Awards Best Place to Drink (East) in 2013. ❀♣(102,103)

Monk Street

Farmhouse Inn [L]

CM6 2NR (off B184, 2 miles S of Thaxted) TL614288

11-midnight; 11-11 Sun ☎ (01371) 830864
farmhouseinn.org

Greene King IPA; Mighty Oak Maldon Gold; guest beer [H]

Built in the 16th century, this former Dunmow Brewery pub has been enlarged to incorporate a restaurant and accommodation; the bar is in the original part of the building. The quiet hamlet of Monk Street overlooks the Chelmer Valley, two miles from historic Thaxted. A disused well in the garden supplied the hamlet with water during World War II. The pub has a rear patio, front garden and a top field. Draught cider from Westons is usually sold in summer.
Q❀◑♿P(313)

Old Harlow

Crown [L]

40 Market Street, CM17 0AQ

12-11 (2.30am Fri & Sat); 12-10.30 Sun ☎ (01279) 868969

Greene King IPA, Abbot; guest beers [H]

A 16th-century building houses this former coaching inn, with many original beams. The smaller part of the pub was a grocer's shop until about 20 years ago. When removing the connecting wall, a 17th-century floral wall painting was discovered, now preserved in the side room. The large garden is popular in summer. The pub is a favourite meeting place for a varied clientele. The tenants pride themselves on having no TV but just occasional acoustic afternoons.
◑♿⇌(Harlow Mill)

Paglesham

Punch Bowl

Church End, SS4 2DP (Paglesham is signed from Rochford)

11.30-11 (10 Mon); 12-10 Sun ☎ (01702) 258376

Adnams Southwold Bitter; Sharp's Doom Bar; guest beers [H]

Facing south in a quiet one-street village, this 16th-century building (formerly a baker's and a sailmaker's), clad in white Essex board, is reputed to have once been used by smugglers. A pub since the 1800s, it has a single low-beamed bar adorned with a large display of mugs, brassware and old local pictures. A small, cosy restaurant next to the bar serves excellent, reasonably-priced food. Picnic tables are to the front of the pub. Q❀◑P

Purleigh

Bell

The Street, CM3 6QJ

closed Mon; 11.30-3, 6-11; 12-4, 6-11 Sat; 12-6 Sun
☎ (01621) 828348 purleighbell.co.uk

Adnams Southwold Bitter; Mighty Oak Captain Bob; guest beers [H]

With commanding views of the Blackwater Estuary from its hilltop location, this 14th-century village pub provides a warm welcome. The interior includes an open fire in a large inglenook, three heavily beamed seating areas and a hop-decorated bar. Up to four ales are usually on offer, with guests often from local microbreweries. It has a good reputation locally for its excellent food. The Prince of Wales and Duchess of Cornwall paid a visit to the Bell in 2014. Q❀◑♣P

Rayleigh

Roebuck

138 High Street, SS6 7BU
8am-midnight (1am Fri & Sat) (01268) 748430
Courage Directors; Greene King Abbot; Ruddles Best Bitter; guest beers [H]
Friendly Wetherspoon pub in Rayleigh High Street with a varied selection of guest beers from around the UK and sometimes the U.S. – as well as Westons Old Rosie and Wyld Wood cider on draught. Families are welcome in a sectioned-off area. Breakfast is served 8am-midday, with the main menu available 9am-11pm. There are patio areas to the front and side for smoking and drinking, with heaters when it gets cold.

Ridgewell

White Horse Inn L

Mill Road, CO9 4SG (on A1017) TL735408
12 (5 Mon & Tue)-11 (01440) 785532
ridgewellwhitehorse.com
Mighty Oak Oscar Wilde; guest beers [G]
CAMRA award-winning real ale pub set in a pretty village which was home to the American 381st Heavy Bomb Group during WWII. At least one dark beer is always available here. Annual beer festivals are held in early March and early August on the patio behind the pub. As well as a choice of excellent real ale, this pub offers 4-star accommodation and an interesting selection of good quality wines to suit a variety of tastes.
Q P

Rochford

Golden Lion L

35 North Street, SS4 1AB
11-midnight; 11-1am Fri & Sat (01702) 545487
goldenlionrochford.co.uk
Adnams Southwold Bitter; Greene King Abbot; Mighty Oak Maldon Gold; guest beers [H]
Multi award-winning pub within the town centre conservation area. This is a small 16th-century, traditional Essex weatherboarded free house with stained glass windows. The decor includes hops above the bar and a fireplace with a traditional logburner. It has a pretty patio garden to the rear – look for the vintage petrol pump water feature. Seven ales are always on offer, including three changing guests (one usually a dark beer) from local micros. Sandwiches and rolls are usually available. A true community local.

Horse & Groom L

1 Southend Road, SS4 1HA
12-11 (01702) 544015
horseandgroomrochford.co.uk
Mighty Oak Maldon Gold; guest beers [H]
A Guide regular and frequent winner of local CAMRA awards. This welcoming and friendly pub is a few minutes' walk from Rochford town centre or the railway station. Six handpumps are in use and the range of quality real ales changes on a regular basis. The restaurant is managed by Harrisons of Hockley and food is served lunchtimes and evenings. A function room is available for hire.
P

Rowhedge

Olde Albion

High Street, CO5 7ES
12-3, 5-11 Tue & Wed; 12 (5 Mon)-11; 12-10.30 Sun
(01206) 728972
Beer range varies [H]
Friendly one-bar pub located on the waterfront at Rowhedge. It has a split-level interior with a wooden floor. The bench seating is arranged to create a cosy, intimate atmosphere, enhanced by a logburner during the winter months. There is a changing range of up to four quality real ales. The pub hosts annual St George's, Halloween and Rowhedge Regatta beer festivals. The external seating offers picturesque views across the River Colne towards Wivenhoe. Q (66)

Saffron Walden

King's Arms

10 Market Hill, CB10 1HQ
12-midnight (11 Mon); 12-12.30am Fri & Sat; 12-11 Sun
(01799) 522768 thekingsarmssaffronwalden.co.uk
Adnams Southwold Bitter; Sharp's Doom Bar; Woodforde's Wherry; guest beers [H]
Venerable, multi-roomed pub, just off the market square (market days are Tuesday and Saturday). Five handpumps feature the regular beers augmented by two guest beers, often including a mild in winter. There is live music at weekends, acoustic music on Thursdays and a monthly quiz. Welcoming log fires in the winter and a pleasant patio for alfresco dining and drinking are particular features. Home-cooked food is served at lunchtimes and some evenings. Q P

Old English Gentleman

11 Gold Street, CB10 1EJ (E of B184/B1052 jct)
11-midnight (11 Mon; 1am Fri & Sat); 11-11 Sun
(01799) 523595 oldenglishgentleman.com
Adnams Southwold Bitter; Woodforde's Wherry; guest beers [H]
An 18th-century town-centre pub with log fires and a welcoming atmosphere. It has a traditional main bar, opening out to a spacious area with tables and plenty of seating. A selection of guest ales is on offer alongside an extensive menu of bar food and sandwiches. Traditional roasts and chef's specials are available on Sunday, served in the bar and dining area, where a variety of works of art is displayed. There is a pretty patio garden with heating at the rear. Saffron Walden is busy on Tuesday and Saturday market days. Local CAMRA Pub of the Year 2012.

Temeraire

55 High Street, CB10 1AA
8am-midnight (1am Fri); 9am-1am Sat; 9am-midnight Sun
(01799) 516975
Greene King Abbot; Ruddles Best Bitter; guest beers [H]
Fine Georgian building that was once a working men's club, featuring photographs of the old club and historic Saffron Walden. Local management have either a Nethergate or Shalford beer available most of the time. Regular Wetherspoon beer and cider festivals take place. A former regional Wetherspoon food award winner, it hosts a Monday quiz night and always stocks draught ciders. Families are welcome and there is a large garden and a covered smoking area.
Q P

Shalford

George Inn 🄻

The Street, CM7 5HH

✪ 12-3 (not Mon), 6-11; 12-4, 6-11 Sat; 12-6 Sun
☎ (01371) 850207 🌐 thegeorgeinnshalford.co.uk

Fuller's London Pride; Shalford 1319 Mild, Stoneley Bitter; Young's Bitter; guest beers 🄷

Traditional, attractively beamed 15th-century inn, at the centre of village life. In summer it is pleasant to sit outside on the patio, while in winter the roaring log fire draws you inside. A true local, it attracts both drinkers and diners, and has a separate à la carte restaurant area. Various clubs and social events feature throughout the year, including a summer beer festival. Shalford Brewery beers are always available.
Q🐴❀◐◑♿♣P🀫🚌(9,10)🐾

South Benfleet

Hoy & Helmet

24-32 High Street, SS7 1NA

✪ 11.30 (12 Sun)-11 ☎ (01268) 792307

Adnams Broadside; Courage Directors; Greene King IPA; guest beer 🄷

This 500-year-old pub is a Grade II-listed building, warmed by a large open fire, with many small rooms with low-beamed ceilings, plus a separate pool room. Guest beers are from the Brewmasters Choice list. Food is served all day from a wide-ranging menu. Dogs are only allowed in the large rear garden. Payment for parking at the rear is refundable against your first order at the bar. A separate room is available for private functions.
🐴❀◐◑P📶

South Benfleet Social Club 🄻

8 Vicarage Hill, SS7 1PB

✪ 11 (7 Mon)-11 ☎ (01268) 206159

Beer range varies 🄷

A new entry to the Guide, this friendly and spacious club welcomes all members of the family. Two beer festivals are held each year. CAMRA members are welcome; just show your membership card or a copy of the Guide. It has a separate function room and hosts many events including a family day and barbecues in summer. Quiz night is on Thursday and pool on Tuesday, with live music most Saturday evenings. Screens show football and other sports. Bar snacks are available all day.
🐴❀◐♿⇌P🚌📶

Southend-on-Sea

Last Post 🄻

Weston Road, SS1 1AS

✪ 8am-midnight (1am Fri & Sat) ☎ (01702) 431682

Courage Directors; Greene King Abbot; Ruddles Best Bitter; Sharp's Doom Bar; guest beers 🄷

Large Wetherspoon pub in an old post office, with knowledgeable and friendly staff, close to two railway stations and the bus station. There are two bars – and when the beer festival is on, a third is set up to serve ales direct from the cask. There are usually nine or ten real ales, with at least three from national breweries and the rest from regionals. Wibblers, Brentwood, Nethergate and Adnams' beers are often featured. Up to six real ciders are also available.
Q🐴◐◑♿⇌(Central/Victoria)🍎🚌📶

Olde Trout Tavern 🄻

56 London Road, SS1 1NX

✪ 11-11 (midnight Fri & Sat); 12-11 Sun ☎ (01702) 337000
🌐 theoldtrout.webs.com

George's Trout Ale; guest beers 🄷

A modern town hostelry within walking distance of Southend High Street and both mainline railway stations. The house beer, George's Trout Ale, is from the local brewery – and two other guests are complemented by Westons Rosie's Pig on draught. Strong bottled beer is also available. Hot meals and snacks are served lunchtimes. A quiz night is held fortnightly on Sundays. An interesting selection of clocks adorns the walls. Local CAMRA Pub of the Year 2013. Q◐⇌(Victoria/Central)🍎🚌

Southminster

Station Arms

39 Station Road, CM0 7EW

✪ 12-2.30, 6 (5.30 Fri)-11; 2-11 Sat; 12-4, 7-10.30 Sun
☎ (01621) 772225 🌐 thestationarms.co.uk

Adnams Southwold Bitter; guest beers 🄷

An attractive weatherboarded pub which has featured in the Guide for the past 24 years. The guest beers always include one from George's Brewery (Hop Monster). Beer festivals are held in January and May. The extremely pleasant courtyard is a great place to sit and sample the good range of beers – weather permitting. Live music takes the form of blues nights on the third Saturday and a monthly folk club. A real gem, which is well worth the journey. Q❀⇌♣🍎🚌

Stanford-Le-Hope

Rising Sun 🄻

Church Hill, SS17 0EU (opp church and near A1014)

✪ 3-10.30 (11 Wed); 12-midnight Thu-Sat; 12-10.30 Sun
☎ (01375) 671097

Beer range varies 🄷

Much-improved two-bar traditional town pub in the shadow of the church. The five guest beers are mainly from independent breweries and include LocAles, and up to three ciders or perries are stocked. Freshly prepared, locally-sourced food is served at Sunday lunchtime in the back bar (booking advisable). Regular monthly live music is hosted. Beer festivals are held three times a year in spring, summer and winter. A back bar is available for private functions. Local CAMRA Pub of the Year 2012 and 2013. 🐴❀◐⇌🍎P🚌📶

Stanway

Live & Let Live 🄻

12 Millers Lane, CO3 0PS

✪ 12-11 (midnight Fri & Sat) ☎ (01206) 574071

Wibblers Isla Rose; guest beers 🄷

Traditional welcoming local with a quiet homely saloon bar and separate public bar that offers a pool table, dartboard and large-screen TV for sport. Beers from local breweries such as Mersea, Bishop Nick, Mauldons, Red Fox and Colchester are often available, plus a selection of bottled ales and take-out containers for off-sales. A menu of good-value home-cooked food is available and, twice a year, in summer and winter, a popular Sausage & Beer Festival is held. ❀◐◑♣P🚌🐾

Stapleford Tawney

Moletrap

Tawney Common, CM16 7PU (3 miles E of Epping, in the middle of nowhere!) TL500013

11.30-2.30, 6-11; 12-3, 7-10.30 Sun ☎ (01992) 522394

themoletrap.co.uk

Fuller's London Pride; guest beers Ⓗ

A 200-year-old pub, set in beautiful countryside, difficult to locate but well worth the effort. It offers a good selection of varying guest ales, which normally includes one dark ale, and serves good-value home-cooked food (no food Sun or Mon eves). There is a cosy bar with a real fire. Well-behaved children are allowed, and dogs at the landlord's discretion. It has plenty of outside seating and an extensive beer garden with amazing views of the countryside. Q❀◑P🐾

Stebbing

White Hart 𝕃

High Street, CM6 3SQ

11-3, 5-11; 11-11 Sat; 12-10.30 Sun ☎ (01371) 856383

hartofstebbingbrewery.co.uk

Hart of Stebbing Hart IPA; Wells Eagle IPA; guest beer Ⓗ

Friendly 15th-century timbered inn in a picturesque village, featuring exposed beams, an open fire, eclectic collections from chamber pots to cigarette cards, an old red post box on an interior wall, and a selection of exposed lath and plaster wall behind a glass screen. The Hart of Stebbing microbrewery is in the garage, producing beers currently only available here and at beer festivals. Good value food is served daily. There is a patio and a covered heated gazebo. Q❀◑♣P (16)

Steeple Bumpstead

Fox & Hounds

3 Chapel Street, CB9 7DQ

12-3, 5-11; 12-midnight Fri & Sat; 12-11 Sun

☎ (01440) 731810 foxinsteeple.co.uk/contact.html

Greene King IPA; guest beers Ⓗ

A 500-year-old pub featuring a main bar with an open fire, two other rooms used mainly for dining, and a rear courtyard garden. Four beers are on offer from local and national breweries. The locally-sourced food ranges from bar snacks to a full à la carte menu. Live music plays on occasional Friday evenings and quizzes are hosted on some Sunday nights. Reduced price beer and wine plus free cheese are on offer on Wednesday evenings, and Thursdays are steak nights.

Q❀◑♣P (18)🐾

Stock

Hoop

High Street, CM4 9BD

11-11 (midnight Fri & Sat); 12-10.30 Sun

☎ (01277) 841137

Adnams Southwold Bitter; guest beers Ⓗ

> When you have lost your inns, drown your empty selves, for you will have lost the last of England. **Hilaire Belloc, The Four Men, 1912**

This traditional weatherboarded pub has been an ale house for about 450 years. The heavily beamed interior has lots of character and the pub welcomes drinkers and diners alike. It is a long-standing Guide entry, with a number of CAMRA awards. Three guest beers are available and a cider or perry is usually also on offer. Home-made food is served in the bar, or upstairs in the Oak Room, at lunchtimes, evenings and all day Saturday. A beer festival is held over the May bank holiday.

Q❀◑♿ (100)🐾

Stow Maries

Prince of Wales 𝕃

Woodham Road, CM3 6SA

11-11 (midnight Fri & Sat); 12-10.30 Sun

☎ (01621) 828971 prince-stowmaries.net

Dark Star Hophead; guest beers Ⓗ

This classic weatherboarded pub boasts several characteristic drinking areas with open fires, and an old bread oven which is used for baking pizzas in the winter months. The extensive garden, courtyards and terraces provide plenty of options for outside drinking. Good food is available made with local produce. The excellent guest ale selection is supplemented with a range of Belgian and German bottled beers. RHS Hyde Hall and Stow Maries WWI airfield are nearby. Local CAMRA Pub of the Year for 2012 and 2013.

Q❀◑♿P (99,593)

Tollesbury

King's Head

1 High Street, CM9 8RG

12-11 (midnight Fri & Sat); 12-10.30 Sun

☎ (01621) 869203

Adnams Southwold Bitter; Bishop Nick Ridley's Rite; guest beers Ⓗ

In the heart of a village with a long yachting heritage, this welcoming pub offers excellent value. The public bar has pool and darts and the lounge bar boasts many historic yachting photographs and paintings. Popular with the boating fraternity, it also caters for birdwatchers, walkers, their dogs and casual drinkers. The pub retains some original etched windows from the days of Russell's Gravesend Brewery. No food is served except at Friday lunchtimes. A selection of bottled beers is available. Q❀◐♣P🐾

Toppesfield

Green Man 𝕃

Church Lane, CO9 4DR

4-midnight; 12-1am Fri & Sat; 12-midnight Sun

☎ (01787) 237418 thegreenmantoppesfield.co.uk

Greene King IPA; guest beers Ⓗ

A village community-owned pub purchased by 150 investors and run by locals. It was bought from Admiral Taverns and is now free of tie and has the same landlord as before. The variety of guest beers is expected to increase and the pub will be running beer festivals and events throughout the year. Darts and pool are played in the public bar. Special meals are served on Thursday evenings and Sunday lunches need to be pre-booked as they are popular. Q❀◑♣P🐾

Waltham Abbey

Woodbine Inn 𝕃

Honey Lane, EN9 3QT

11.30-11 (2am Fri & Sat); 11-9.30 Sun ☎ (01992) 713050

thewoodbine.co.uk

Dominion Woodbine Racer; Greene King Abbot; Sharp's Doom Bar; guest beers H

Situated in Epping Forest and close to junction 26 of the M25, the pub is ideally located. The new restaurant is a great addition, though the pub concentrates on real ale. It caters for walkers, is dog-friendly, and is patronised by many locals. The guest beers are from local breweries, including the house beer. The food is prepared on the premises using local suppliers, with home-cooked ham and sausages as specialities. The Ale Sampling Society meets monthly here. ♣P (255)

Weeley Heath

White Hart

Clacton Road, CO16 9ED (on B1441, 1 mile from Weeley station)

12-2.30, 4-11 (10 Mon); 12-11 Fri & Sat; 12-10.30 Sun

☎ (01255) 830384

Beer range varies H

Run by a friendly couple, it does good-quality beer, hence it is a regular Guide entry, and is a hit with the local community, with its own pool and darts team. Sporting events shown on TV make for a busy pub. Real ciders are available, and it has its own beer club. Greene King XX Mild is often available. Weeley train station is about a mile away, and there is a bus stop nearby (although the No. 2 does not run Sundays). ♣P (2,76)

Wickham St Paul

Victory Inn

The Green, CO9 2PT

12-11 (midnight Fri & Sat) ☎ (01787) 269364

thevictoryinn.com

Beer range varies H

This attractive traditional pub in an idyllic village green location is the focus for many sporting activities including darts and pool. A Gray's pub, it has a public bar area with games and a projection TV for sport. Food is available both at lunchtimes and evenings (not Sun eve), with a fish and chips takeaway on Fridays 5-7pm. The pub also offers pensioner lunches on weekdays. Occasional beer festivals are held here. ♣P

Widdington

Fleur de Lys

High Street, CB11 3SG TL538316

12-3 (not Mon), 6-11; 12-11.30 Fri & Sat; 12-10.30 Sun

☎ (01799) 543280 thefleurdelys.co.uk

Adnams Southwold Bitter; Sharp's Doom Bar; guest beers H

Rumours of a ghost abound at this welcoming 400-year-old village local, which boasts a large open fireplace and beams. The games room has a full-sized pool table, football table and dartboard. This was the first pub to be saved from closure by the local branch of CAMRA after its formation. Quality meals are offered made with local ingredients. The source of the River Cam and Prior's Hall Barn, an English heritage site, are both nearby.

Q ♣P (301)

Witham

Battesford Court

100-102 Newland Street, CM8 1AH

8am-midnight (1am Fri & Sat); 8am-11 Sun

☎ (01376) 504080

Greene King Abbot; Ruddles Best Bitter; guest beers H

Large Wetherspoon conversion of a former hotel of the same name. The 16th-century building was previously the courthouse of the manor of Battesford. It has distinct areas, with wood panelling and oak beams, and there is a family area. Four to six guest beers are served including something local, usually from Nethergate or Shalford, plus up to four ciders and perries from the Westons, Sandford Orchard and Gwynt Y Ddraig ranges. The usual Wetherspoon's food offering is available. Q

Woolpack

7 Church Street, CM8 2JP

11.30-11 (midnight Fri & Sat); 12-11 Sun

☎ (01376) 511195

Greene King IPA H**; Witham No Name** G**; guest beers** H

Home to the Witham Brewery, the Woolpack is a traditional local pub. Set in a conservation area, the building probably dates from the 15th century. It has two rooms with low wooden beams, and a real log fire during the winter. Two to four guest beers are served, always from the local area. There is a quiz night every second Sunday. Note the extensive collection of glass soda siphon bottles displayed in one of the windows.

Wivenhoe

Horse & Groom

55 The Cross, CO7 9QL

10.30-3, 5.30 (6 Sat)-11; 12-4, 7-10.30 Sun

☎ (01206) 824928

Adnams Southwold Bitter, Broadside; guest beer H

This friendly Adnams' local is divided into two bars, both offering ample seating in traditional public/lounge style. The public bar features a well-used dartboard. Two Adnams' guest or seasonal ales complement the regular Bitter and Broadside. Good-value lunches are a popular feature too (no food Sun). There is a large garden to the rear of the building. Excellent bus links from Colchester pass the pub on a frequent basis. ♣P

Woodham Mortimer

Hurdlemakers Arms 𝕃

Post Office Road, CM9 6ST

12-11; 12-9 Sun ☎ (01245) 225169

hurdlemakersarms.co.uk

Beer range varies H

A 400-year-old traditional country Gray's pub with a good range of beers, including specials from local breweries. Excellent home-cooked food is served daily. There are various monthly events including quiz nights. The pub boasts a spacious beer garden with a barbecue and children's play area along with a small barn and marquee for hire. It is popular with walkers, cyclists, locals and families. An annual beer festival is held in June. Local CAMRA Pub of the Year 2014.

♣P

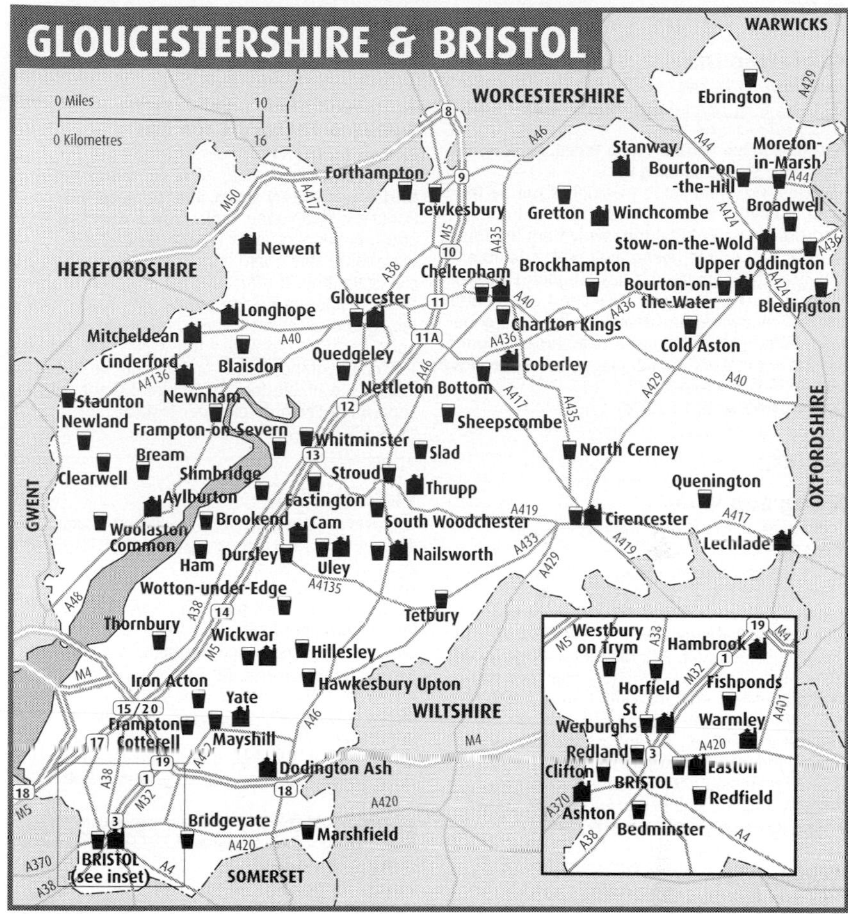

Blaisdon

Red Hart 🄻

GL17 0AH (centre of village, signed from A4136 E of Longhope or N of A48)

⏲ 12-3, 6 (7 Sun)-11 ☎ (01452) 830477 🌐 redhartinn.co.uk

Young's Bitter; guest beers 🄷

Local CAMRA Pub of the Year, this attractive old inn with flagstone floors, low oak beams and an open fire has a welcoming atmosphere, aided by chatty staff and regulars. Most guest beers are LocAle, particularly Bespoke, with either a perry or cider also available. The selection of good-quality food is popular, with dining often spreading into the bar area, so be prepared to mix it with a rack of lamb. There is a large, family-friendly garden, and barbecues are hosted on the patio throughout the summer. ♉❀◑♿⛺♣🍎P

Bledington

King's Head 🄻

The Green, OX7 6XQ (4 miles from Stow-on-the-Wold, off B4450)

⏲ 12-3, 6-11 ☎ (01608) 658365 🌐 kingsheadinn.net

Brakspear Oxford Gold; Butcombe Adam Henson's Rare Breed; Hook Norton Hooky Lion 🄷

Delightful 16th-century stone inn overlooking the village green. Originally built as a cider house, the pub retains the old beams, low ceilings, nooks and crannies and inglenook log fire, and is furnished with high-back settles. This free house, with 12 comfortable letting rooms, is famous for its wide range of ale and food. There are good local walks to nearby villages, with Kingham station close by. The guest beers are selected from local brewers in Gloucestershire and Oxfordshire. A former CAMRA award winner. Q♉❀🛏◑≢(Kingham)♣P

Bourton-on-the-Hill

Horse & Groom 🄻

GL56 9AQ (on A44 at top of hill)

⏲ 11-2.30, 6.30-11 ☎ (01386) 700413

🌐 horseandgroom.info

Goff's Jouster; Prescott Hill Climb; guest beer 🄷

Grade II-listed Georgian stone inn that has been family-run since 2005. It serves three local real ales - Goff's and two local guests – with award-winning contemporary food in an attractive dining area. The light and airy bar has been tastefully modernised with bar stools and an open fire. Ideal for visits to nearby Moreton-in-Marsh and the Batsford Arboretum, the pub has five en-suite rooms. The delightful sheltered garden has plenty of seating, with stunning views over the Cotswold countryside. ♉❀🛏◑♣P🚌

Bourton-on-the-Water

Mousetrap Inn

Lansdowne, GL54 2AR
11.30-3, 6-11; 12-3, 6-11 Sun (01451) 820579
mousetrap-inn.co.uk
Butcombe Adam Henson's Rare Breed; Hook Norton Old Hooky; Stroud Budding
Attractive Cotswold stone free house run by the same family for several years and in the quieter Landsdowne part of Bourton, away from the tourist areas. It has a large dining area with a feature fireplace. This popular pub has 10 good-value en-suite rooms. Three regular local beers are on offer, and it is renowned for friendly service and good-value home-cooked meals. A patio area in front of the pub with tables and hanging baskets provides a suntrap in the summer.
Q P (801,855)

Bream

Rising Sun

High Street, GL15 6JF (opp war memorial)
SO6032305812
4.30 (6 Mon)-midnight; 12-midnight Sat; 12-3, 6.30-midnight Sun (01594) 564555
Butcombe Bitter; St Austell Tribute; guest beer
With spectacular views of the forest and opposite the village cenotaph, this rambling 300-year-old stone building houses a friendly main bar with overspill into several adjoining rooms, complete with two restaurants and a large function room that has its own bar. An enclosed garden with seating provides a pleasant venue in the summer. Several years ago a 100ft tunnel was found connected to the pub cellar. Food is by arrangement only. P (23)

Bridgeyate

White Harte

111 London Road, BS30 5NA (on A420 jct wth A4175 E of Bristol)
11-11; 12-10.30 Sun (0117) 967 3830
Butcombe Bitter; Courage Best Bitter; Marston's Pedigree; guest beers
A traditional pub dating from 1860, extended in 1987. It is often called the Inn on the Green because of the large village green at the front. An unusual bar counter incorporates old wooden spice drawers. Reasonably priced food attracts lunchtime diners, and the pub also gets busy in the evening. Two guest beers generally come from well-known brands, and Black Rat cider is served. A quiz features on Monday evening. There is extra parking to the rear. Q P (634,635)

Bristol: Bedminster

Hare

51 North Street, BS3 1EN
5-11; 4-midnight Fri; 3-midnight Sat; 3-11 Sun
(0117) 966 5740 theharepub.co.uk
Beer range varies
Formerly the Full Moon, and a pub since at least 1822. Three changing guest beers are sold which are often unusual in this area, with regular brews from New Bristol and Box Steam breweries. The compact bar attracts a mixed clientele, many of them relatively young. A steep flight of stairs leads to a rear garden/patio area above the pub which is used for barbecues in the summer. Bar snacks are available. There is no connection with Bath Ales, despite the name. (24,25)

Tobacco Factory Café Bar

Raleigh Rd, BS3 1TF
12-11 (midnight Fri & Sat); 10-11 Sun (0117) 902 0060
Bristol Beer Factory Seven, Sunrise; guest beer
Popular with a young, funky crowd as well as locals and theatregoers, with an interior that is warehouse chic – bare brick walls, metal pillars and clever lighting. It offers a great selection of drinks and a restaurant-quality menu, with mezze and tapas both excellent value. The outside yard is open from mid-April. Live music plays on Sundays, Tuesday evenings are DJ nights, and the Green Room is available for private hire. Do not miss the September Factoberfest beer festival.
(24,25)

Victoria Park

66 Raymend Road, BS3 4QW (250yds off St Johns Lane)
11-11 (11.30 Fri & Sat); 11-10.30 Sun (0117) 330 6043
thevictoriapark.co.uk
Wye Valley Butty Bach; guest beers
A thriving, red-brick pub in a residential area. The interior has something of a gastro-pub feel but drinkers are most welcome. There is a large garden/patio area to the rear which features a wood-fired pizza oven. Three pumps serve quality beers, usually including a dark offering. The interesting all-day menu is displayed on a chalkboard and a large drop-down screen shows some major sports events.

INDEPENDENT BREWERIES

Arbor Bristol
Ashley Down Bristol: St Werburghs
Bath Ales Bristol: Warmley
Battledown Cheltenham
Bespoke Mitcheldean
Bristol Beer Factory Bristol: Ashton
Ciren Cirencester
Corinium Cirencester
Cotswold Bourton-on-the-Water
Cotswold Lion Coberley
Cotswold Spring Dodington Ash
Donnington Stow-on-the-Wold
Force Cirencester (NEW)
Freeminer Cinderford
Gloucester Gloucester
Goff's Winchcombe
Great Western Bristol: Hambrook
Halfpenny Lechlade
Hillside Longhope
Moor Bristol
Nailsworth Nailsworth
New Bristol Bristol (NEW)
Prescott Cheltenham
Rocket Science Yate
Severn Vale Cam
Stanway Stanway
Stroud Thrupp
Terrace Aylburton
Towles' Bristol: Easton
Uley Uley
Whittingtons Newent
Wickwar Wickwar
Wiper and True Bristol: St Werburghs (NEW)
Zerodegrees Bristol

Windmill

14 Windmill Hill, BS3 4LU (100yds uphill from Bedminster station)
12-11 (midnight Fri & Sat); 12-10.30 Sun
(0117) 963 5440
Bath Ales Gem; Bristol Beer Factory Sunrise; guest beers
With pastel colours and wooden flooring throughout, the pub is on two levels, with a family room on the lower area where children are welcome until 8pm. There are two changing guest ales, as well as real cider and foreign bottled beers. One beer from the nearby Bristol Beer Factory is always on offer. Good food is served all day until 10pm and Sunday roasts too. An old 1970s jukebox features. Outside is a small patio area to the front.

Bristol: City Centre

Bank Tavern

8 John Street, BS1 2HR (take lane by arcade in All Saints Lane)
12-midnight (1am Thu-Sat) (0117) 930 4691
banktavern.com
Beer range varies
Popular, compact one-bar pub, in the city centre yet well hidden away. The four beers are often from South-west microbrewers and can be of any style. Two real ciders change constantly. Very quirky humour and many varied events define the pub. Live music plays Wednesdays and Thursdays. Look out for the summer fête and Christmas party. The place is a great alternative to the more predictable establishments all around. Quality food is served 12-4pm (booking advisable Sun).

Barley Mow

39 Barton Road, BS2 0LF (400yds from rear exit of Temple Meads station over footbridge)
12-11 (11.30 Fri & Sat); 12-10 Sun (0117) 930 4709
barleymowbristol.com
Beer range varies
Completely refurbished in early 2013 and now relaunched as Bristol Beer Factory's flagship pub. Eight handpulls offer two from the brewery plus six different guests from only the highest-quality UK breweries. There are also 10 changing specialist beer fonts and an extensive bottled beer list. Beer-related events are regularly hosted. A small range of frequently changing quality food dishes is offered lunchtimes and evenings. Sundays roasts are served 12-5pm.
(Temple Meads) (506)

Beer Emporium

13-15 Kings Street, BS1 4EF
12 (11 Sat)-2am; 12-midnight Sun (0117) 379 0333
thebeeremporium.net
Beer range varies
The Beer Cellar Bar opened in 2013 and is set in three tunnels: one containing the bar and seating, one with seating only, and the third housing the kitchens. A lift makes it all accessible. Up to 12 changing real ales are served plus keg beers and a wide range of world bottled beers. Indeed, a new bottle shop has opened just inside the entrance. Regular beer-related events feature. Quality food is offered lunchtimes and evenings, all day at weekends.

Bell

16-18 Hillgrove Street, BS2 8JT (just off Jamaica Street)
12-midnight (1am Fri); 4-1am Sat; 1-midnight Sun
(0117) 909 6612 bell.butcombe.com
Bristol Beer Factory Sunrise; Butcombe Bitter, Blond; guest beer
Pleasant, eclectic, two-roomed pub where DJs often spin their discs from 10pm in the back room. Friday evenings attract drinkers on their way to nearby clubs, while local workers are regular customers for the lunchtime and early evening food. Sunday lunches are popular. A surprising feature is the pleasant rear garden with a patio, which is heated in cold weather. Local art on the wood-panelled walls adds a bohemian feel.
(Montpelier)

Bridge Inn

16 Passage Street, BS2 0JF
12-11.30 (midnight Fri & Sat); 6-11 Sun
(0117) 929 0942 bridgeinnbristol.co.uk
Bath Ales Gem; Dark Star Hophead; guest beers
Tiny pub close to the station, yet only a short walk from the city centre. Music industry memorabilia features, along with a selection of board games. Occasional live music takes place and there is free Wi-Fi. Guest beers are adventurous, with two from high-quality microbreweries. Lunch is served 12-3pm weekdays only. Outside tables increase capacity in good weather. It now stocks a range of UK and US bottled beers, plus over a dozen Scottish single malt whiskies.
(Temple Meads) (8,9)

Canteen

80 Stokes Croft, BS1 3QY
10-midnight (1am Fri & Sat); 10-11 Sun
(0117) 923 2017 canteenbristol.co.uk
Beer range varies
On the ground floor of a '70s office block, now a cultural/community centre. The name is fitting as the place is open plan, with plywood tables and steel tube chairs. The long bar offers up to five real ales, many sourced locally, of all strengths and styles. An open kitchen serves a range of locally-sourced food. At the other end of the room is a stage, with nightly music. There is a large covered patio and a good deal of cycle parking.
(Montpelier)

Cornubia

142 Temple Street, BS1 6EN (opp fire station by former Courage Brewery)
12-11 (11.30 Thu-Sat); closed Sun (0117) 925 4415
thecornubia.co.uk
Beer range varies
A cosy small pub with two linked rooms adorned with much patriotic memorabilia as well as countless pumpclips. Eight real ales plus several ciders are always on, and a small but interesting range of bottled and speciality beers is also stocked. A wide range of board games and books is available. Live blues features on Thursday evenings when anyone can come along and jam, and live bands some Saturdays. A CAMRA discount is offered. The outside area has been enclosed, developed and expanded in recent years.
(Temple Meads)

Gryphon

41 Colston Street, BS1 5AP
1-11 (1am Fri & Sat); 6-11 Sun 07894 239567
gryphonbristol.co.uk

Beer range varies Ⓗ
A shrine to dark beer and great rock/heavy metal music. Posters, guitars and many pumpclips adorn the walls. Triangular in shape due to its corner plot and just a few yards uphill from the Colston Hall, up to six handpumps dispense rapidly changing brews, many dark and often strong. Live bands sometimes play upstairs and there are beer festivals in March and September. Good food is served. May open earlier than shown.

Highbury Vaults

164 St Michael's Hill, BS2 8DE
12-midnight (11 Sun) ☎ (0117) 973 3203
highburyvaults.com
Bath Ales Gem; St Austell Tribute; Young's Bitter, London Gold; guest beers Ⓗ
In the same hands, and this Guide, for many years, this pub is popular with university and hospital staff. Dating from the mid-19th century, its interior is dark and dimly lit, with a small front snug bar, main drinking area and a bar billiards table. Outside, there is a large heated patio and garden. Good-quality food is served every lunchtime and weekday evenings. The pub is owned by Young's but is allowed some freedom with guest beers. Toilets are down steep stairs.
Q ≹(Clifton Down) (8,9)

Hillgrove Porter Stores

53 Hillgrove Street North, BS2 8LT
4-midnight (1am Fri); 2-1am Sat; 2-midnight Sun
☎ (0117) 924 9818
Dawkins Bristol Blonde; guest beers Ⓗ
The first of the Dawkins Taverns, the brainchild of a local entrepreneur who also bought Matthews Brewery in 2009. An excellent community pub, it usually dispenses up to seven guest ales, including dark beers and rare styles, plus Ashridge cider. The interior is horseshoe-shaped, with a wonderfully comfortable lounge area hidden behind the bar, and a pleasant patio. Mini beer festivals are held in conjunction with the other Dawkins pubs.
≹(Montpelier)

Kings Head ★

60 Victoria Street, BS1 6DE
11 (12 Sat)-11.30; 12-2.30, 6.30-11.30 Sun
☎ (0117) 929 2338
Butcombe Gold; Fuller's London Pride; Sharp's Doom Bar; Skinner's Betty Stogs Ⓗ
Classic small pub, dating from around 1660 and identified by CAMRA as having a nationally important historic interior. A narrow area around the bar leads to the tramcar snug at the rear. Pictures of old Bristol make fascinating viewing. An earlier landlady is reputed to haunt the pub. Popular food is served weekday lunchtimes only. Quiz night is the third Thursday of the month. The beer range changes occasionally. There are tables outside in summer. Handy for Temple Meads station and buses. Q ≹(Temple Meads)

No 1. Harbourside

1 Canons Road, BS1 5UH
10-midnight (11 Sun & Mon; 1am Fri & Sat)
☎ (0117) 929 1100 no1harbourside.co.uk
Beer range varies Ⓗ
Refurbished pub/diner located on the covered walkway on the quayside of the floating harbour. With early opening it is ideal for morning coffee, snacking or a naughty early beer. Five handpumps usually feature two Bristol Beer Factory beers and three guests, many from Arbor, and are supplemented by a good selection of bottled beers and changing ciders. Food is served all day and there are some tables outside. Free live music features (Wed-Sat eves).

Seven Stars

1 Thomas Lane, BS1 6JG (just off Victoria St)
12-11 (10.30 Sun) ☎ (0117) 927 2845 7stars.co.uk
Beer range varies Ⓗ
Many who live miles away call this their local. This small free house offers generous discounts for CAMRA members at all times and for others in happy hour. Features are a pool table, a rock-oriented jukebox and outdoor seating. Eight pumps dispense a full range of styles and strengths, plus ciders and perries. Quality acoustic acts play on weekend afternoons. Beeriodicals are held on the first Monday to Thursday of every month, with 20 beers from a different county each time.
≹(Temple Meads)

Three Tuns

78 St George's Road, BS1 5UR (300yds from Bristol Cathedral towards Hotwells)
12-2.30, 4-11; 12-midnight Fri & Sat; 4-10.30 Sun
☎ (0117) 907 0689 threetunsbristol.co.uk
Arbor Brigstow Bitter; guest beers Ⓗ
Run by Arbor Ales, this is independent beer nirvana. Seven pumps dispense the full range of beer styles, with two or three from Arbor and the rest from top-rated British brewers, plus many unusual bottled beers and several ciders. The L-shaped interior has scrubbed wooden tables and mixed seating, plus a covered heated rear patio. Food is limited to rolls and bar snacks. It hosts occasional beer festivals.

Volunteer Tavern

9 New Street, BS2 9DX (very close to main Cabot Circus car park across carriageway from shops)
12-11 (midnight Fri & Sat) ☎ (0117) 955 8498
volunteertavern.co.uk
Beer range varies Ⓗ
Tucked away in a side street, it is convenient for Old Market and its bus interchange. Dating from 1670 and listed, this venue reopened in 2011 and has quickly become popular on the local scene. It always serves six changing beers including dark options, plus two changing ciders. It stages regular beer festivals with 25 plus ales, and live music events. There is a large, fully enclosed paved garden. Food is served every day and is hugely popular on Sundays – book ahead.

Bristol: Clifton

Eldon House

6 Lower Clifton Hill, BS8 1BT (off top of Jacobs Wells Road)
12-3, 5-midnight; 12-1am Fri & Sat; 12-midnight Sun
☎ (0117) 922 1271 theeldonhouse.com
Bath Ales Special Pale Ale, Gem; guest beers Ⓗ
A tasteful extension in 2009 has not detracted from the traditional look and feel of this cosy end-of-terrace pub, which lies close to the busy Clifton Triangle area. Get off a bus near the top of Park Street and head a short way down Jacobs Wells Road. The four or five beers include guests from well-chosen independent brewers, often local, and occasionally from further afield. Good-quality food is served daily and Sunday roasts are popular. Many events are hosted.

Hope & Anchor

38 Jacobs Wells Road, BS8 1DR (between Anchor Rd and top of Park St)
12-11; 12-10.30 Sun ☎ (0117) 929 2987
hopeandanchor.net
Beer range varies Ⓗ
Popular and friendly city local offering up to six changing real ales, mostly from West Country microbreweries. The pub has achieved a happy balance between those who come to eat the high-quality food, served all day, and those who just want a pint. Subdued lighting, candles on the tables and hanging hop bines over the bar create atmosphere. On summer days the terraced garden at the rear is very pleasant. Street parking is limited.

Lansdown

8 Clifton Road, BS8 1AF
4-11; 12-midnight Fri & Sat; 12-10.30 Sun
☎ (0117) 973 4949 thelansdown.com
St Austell Tribute; guest beers Ⓗ
Traditional pub with a strong real ale offering, mainly from South-west breweries. Beers from GWB and Cheddar Ales are normally among the five or six on offer, which change every few months, and there is usually an excellent mix of styles. All beers are sold at similar upper-end prices irrespective of strength. An upstairs lounge/dining room is available for functions. Good food is available weekend lunchtimes and Monday-Saturday evenings. The courtyard garden is heated and covered in winter. (8,9)

Portcullis

3 Wellington Terrace, BS8 4LE (close to Clifton side of Suspension Bridge)
4.30 (12 Sat)-11; 12-10.30 Sun ☎ (0117) 908 5536
Dawkins Bristol Blonde, Bristol Best; guest beers Ⓗ
A pub since 1821, rescued by Dawkins in 2008, with a downstairs bar and a quieter upstairs lounge (also used for functions) with a supply of board games. Seven handpumps usually dispense three or four Dawkins beers and a range of interesting guests from other micros. All styles and strengths are showcased. Real ciders and good-value tapas-style nibbles are usually on offer. Several mini beer and cider festivals per year take place. The rear garden is accessed from upstairs. Q

Quinton House

2 Park Place, BS8 1JW (just off top of Park St)
4 (12 Fri & Sat)-midnight; 12-11 Sun ☎ (0117) 909 3857
quintonhousebristol.co.uk
St Austell Tribute; Sharp's Doom Bar; guest beers Ⓗ
Reopened in 2009 as a genuine free house, this small pub lies hidden in a residential area just a few yards from the top of Park Street, with its many shops and bus routes. It overlooks a grassy area and an ancient yew tree. The cosy interior has a coal-effect gas fire and a selection of pictures and old brewery signs. The range of four cask ales changes occasionally, and Thatchers Heritage cider is sold. Traditional board games are available.

Victoria

2 Southleigh Road, BS8 2BH (off St Pauls Rd)
4 (12 Sat)-11; 12-10.30 Sun ☎ (0117) 974 5675
Dawkins Bristol Blonde, Bristol Best; guest beers Ⓗ
Small 19th-century, Grade II-listed Dawkins' tavern, tucked away just off the bottom of Whiteladies Road next to the Clifton Lido. Six pumps offer changing independent beers and ciders, always including two or more from Dawkins Brewery. The walls are adorned with pumpclips and brewery mirrors, plus an amusing collection of obsolete keg fonts on a mantelpiece. Regular events, including beer festivals and quizzes, are held. An ever-increasing stock of bottled Belgian beers is available. Parking close by is difficult.
Q ≹ (Clifton Down)

Bristol: Easton

Chelsea Inn

60-62 Chelsea Road, BS5 6AU
1-midnight ☎ (0117) 329 1316 thechelseabs5.co.uk
Beer range varies Ⓗ
Street-corner community local with one large room and a collection of vintage sofas, armchairs and other furniture. Pictures from local artists are for sale or commission. In a cosmopolitan area, the pub attracts a varied crowd, many relatively young. A small book exchange library is available. Up to four changing beers are served and two ciders. Live music plays on Tuesday (jazz), Wednesday and Saturday. Look for the interesting graffiti in the garden. ≹ (Stapleton Rd) (6,7)

Bristol: Fishponds

Van Dyck Forum

748-756 Fishponds Road, BS16 3UA
8am-midnight (1am Fri & Sat) ☎ (0117) 965 1337
Greene King Abbot; Ruddles Best Bitter; guest beers Ⓗ
Originally a 1926 movie theatre, the Van Dyck Picture House, it became a bingo hall in 1973 before being converted by Wetherspoon. A large, high-ceilinged, single-bar pub, it has a mixture of wooden seating, carpeting, and a slightly more formal dining area to the rear, and is popular with local residents and shoppers. There is a large screen at the back of the pub for showing sport. A good selection of guest beers is always on offer.

Bristol: Horfield

Annexe

Seymour Road, BS7 9EQ (directly behind Sportsman pub near county cricket ground)
11.30-3, 5-11.30; 11.30-11.30 Sat; 12-11 Sun
☎ (0117) 949 3931 the-annexe.co.uk
Butcombe Gold; Dartmoor Legend; St Austell Tribute; Sharp's Doom Bar; Wye Valley HPA; guest beers Ⓗ
Community pub not far from the Memorial Stadium. Inside is a converted skittle alley and a large conservatory/family room to one side. Several TVs show live sport, including one on the partially covered patio outside. Good wholesome food is served, plus quality pizzas, which are available until 10pm. No dogs are allowed, even on the patio. It serves one or two guest beers which can be fairly adventurous.

Bristol: Redfield

Old Stillage L

145-147 Church Road, BS5 9LA (on A420)
3 (12 Mon)-11; 3-midnight Thu; 12-midnight Fri & Sat; 12-10.30 Sun ☎ (0117) 939 4079
Beer range varies Ⓗ

Arbor's first tied pub is just a few hundred yards from the brewery and is the testing ground for its many one-off and trial brews. It now offers four changing Arbor beers and two guest brews. A new café bar has been added recently to the side of the main pub and food is an increasing feature. There is a pool table, dartboard and large rear patio. Many events, including live music, are held. ❀◑⇌(Lawrence Hill)♣🚌

St George's Hall

203 Church Road, BS5 9HL (on A420)
⏲ 9am-midnight ☎ (0117) 955 1488
Greene King Abbot; Ruddles Best Bitter; Sharp's Doom Bar; guest beers Ⓗ
Bustling suburban Wetherspoon pub popular with the locals, on the main A420 towards the east of the city. Up to seven guest ales are on tap, with a leaning towards stronger ones – Thornbridge Jaipur is a frequent visitor. A suggested guest beer list is on the bar and drinkers are encouraged to participate. Several ciders, including Westons, add to the appeal. Every Wednesday all real ale is currently discounted. There is a small patio area outside to the right as you enter.
Q⛄❀◑♿⇌(Lawrence Hill)●🚌📶

Bristol: Redland

Cambridge Arms

Coldharbour Road, BS6 7JS
⏲ 12-11 (11.30 Fri & Sat) ☎ (0117) 973 9786
🌐 cambridgearms.co.uk
Butcombe Bitter; Fuller's London Pride; Gales Seafarers Ale; guest beer Ⓗ
Large, red-brick Edwardian Fuller's house, not far from the Downs, with an L-shaped bar, wooden floors and pastel walls. The pub can get busy with diners and those seeking refreshment after sporting exertions. There is a large south-facing garden at low level behind the pub. Fuller's seasonal beers and those from the former Gales brewery are often available. Sunday roast is popular but you cannot book ahead. There is a quiz on Sundays at 8.30pm. ❀◑P🚌(505)🐾📶

Bristol: St Werburghs

Miners Arms

136 Mina Road, BS2 9YQ (400yds from M32 jct 3)
⏲ 4-11 (midnight Fri); 2-midnight Sat; 2-11 Sun
☎ (0117) 907 9874
Dawkins Bristol Best, Miners Gold; guest beers Ⓗ
Close to St Werburghs City Farm and Bristol Climbing Centre, this is an excellent three-roomed street-corner local, part of the local Dawkins chain and free of previous beer ties. There are usually four guest beers and two from Dawkins, along with Westons cider. Another small, quiet bar lies to the side, and a larger pool room to the rear. Children and dogs are welcome. The function room can be booked. Thursday is quiz night. Note the antique cigarette machine. ❀♣●🚌(5,25)🐾

Bristol: Westbury on Trym

Victoria

20 Chock Lane, BS9 3EX (in small lane behind churchyard)
⏲ 12-2.30, 6-11; 12-3, 7-10.30 Sun ☎ (0117) 950 0441
🌐 thevictoriapub.co.uk
Butcombe Bitter; Wadworth Henry's IPA, 6X; guest beer Ⓗ
Once a courthouse, this traditional, relaxed and welcoming Wadworth-owned pub has been in the Guide for many years. A raised garden to the rear is a suntrap in summer. Pictures of Westbury as a village adorn the walls. Popular home-cooked food is available lunchtimes and evenings (no food Sun eve). Entertainment includes quizzes, themed meals and regular pub outings. Various societies meet here. Bonus card offers are now available if you provide your email address.
Q⛄❀◑🚌(1,20)🐾

Broadwell

Fox Inn Ⓛ

The Green, GL56 0UF (off A429 Fosse Way)
⏲ 11-2.30, 6-11; 12-3, 7-10.30 Sun ☎ (01451) 870909
Donnington BB, SBA Ⓗ
Attractive stone-built hostelry overlooking the village green. The Donnington beers are good value, brewed only a few miles away, and popular with visitors. A family-run local, it offers good company and quality home-cooked food. There are flagstoned floors in the bar area, jugs hanging from the beams and Aunt Sally is played in the garden. At the back is a camping and caravan site. Ideally placed for visiting the nearby Chastleton House.
Q⛄❀🛏◑▲♣●P🚉🚌🐾

Brockhampton

Craven Arms Ⓛ

Kingsbury Street, GL54 5XQ (off A436 in centre of village in cul-de-sac)
⏲ 12-3, 6-11 ☎ (01242) 820410 🌐 thecravenarms.co.uk
Butcombe Bitter; Otter Bitter; guest beer Ⓗ
Spacious 17th-century free house set in an attractive hillside village with truly outstanding views and walks. It has a bar area with an open fire and an excellent dining room separated by church-style stone windows. Three or four carefully selected beers are kept by the fastidious owner-chef. A beer festival is held in July in the garden. It is a regular local CAMRA award winner and a well-managed gem, with a really friendly family who organise functions for locals each month.
Q⛄❀🛏◑▲♣P🐾📶

Brookend

Lammastide Inn Ⓛ

GL13 9SF (off B4066) SO6842202062
⏲ 12-3, 7 (6 Fri)-midnight; 12-midnight Sat; 12-11 Sun
☎ (01453) 811337 🌐 lammastideinn.co.uk
Draught Bass; Wye Valley Bitter; guest beers Ⓗ
Built in 1932, this imposing, single-bar pub has six beer engines, and a raised seating area in the bay window (the only part not wheelchair-friendly). The large dining area overlooks the raised decking in the garden that has children's play equipment, plus fine views towards the River Severn and Forest of Dean. Wye Valley beers plus occasional guests from Gloucestershire brewers feature at present. The pub opens at 6.30pm on Monday and Tuesday to serve take-away fish and chips.
Q⛄❀◑♿♣P🚌🐾📶

Charlton Kings

Royal

54 Horsefair Street, GL53 8JH (in centre of village opp church)
11-11 (midnight Fri); 10-midnight Sat; 12-10.30 Sun
(01242) 228937 royalpub.co.uk
Beer range varies H
Popular village pub, on the eastern fringe of Cheltenham, which underwent a major refurbishment a few years ago in a contemporary style. The central bar has a lounge to the left and a restaurant area to the right, with comfy sofas in cosy corners. Live music, quizzes and Meet the Brewer evenings feature regularly. Four ales are usually available, typically from Hogs Back, Dartmoor, Severn Vale, Bespoke, Wye Valley, Bath and Butcombe breweries. Outside is a large garden with patio areas. No food Sunday evening.
QP

Cheltenham

Cheltenham Motor Club

Upper Park Street, GL52 6SA (off Hales Road – access from A40 via Crown Passage)
6 (12 Sat)-midnight; 7-midnight Sun (01242) 522590
cheltmc.com
Salopian Oracle; Stroud Tom Long; guest beers H
CAMRA members are welcome at this friendly club just east of the town centre in the former Crown pub. It was National Club of the Year winner 2013 and has multiple county and regional awards. Three changing ales from microbreweries across the country complement the regulars plus Thatchers Heritage cider. At least two beer festivals are held annually, and regular Meet the Brewer evenings are hosted. The club is home to local league quiz, darts and pool teams.
Q(B)

Greatfield

Caernarvon Road, Up Hatherley, GL51 3BW (by Morrisons supermarket)
11.30-11 (11.30 Tue; midnight Wed-Sat)
(01242) 863149
Butcombe Bitter; guest beers H
A modern Ember Inn next to Morrisons in the south-western suburbs, with a meandering open-plan layout and many cosy corners. It is popular both locally and from a wider area for its good-value quality food and beer. Five ales are generally available, with the guest options changing almost daily. You can choose your next guest ale from its seasonal list. Regular quiz nights feature, as well as live music. Q(D)

Jolly Brewmaster

39 Painswick Road, GL50 2EZ (off A40 Suffolk Rd)
2.30 (12 Sat)-11; 12-10.30 Sun (01242) 772261
Beer range varies H
Frequent local CAMRA Pub of the Year and runner-up 2012 South-West Regional Cider Pub of the Year. Thirteen handpumps feature a changing range of seven ales and six ciders, sourced locally and across the country. Relaxed and friendly, this busy community hub features original etched windows, a horseshoe bar and open fire. The attractive courtyard garden serves as an extra room in the summer, with regular barbecues. Quiz and music nights are hosted weekly.
Q(10,94)

Moon Under Water

16-28 Bath Road, GL53 7HA
8am-midnight (1am Fri & Sat) (01242) 583945
Greene King Abbot; Ruddles Best Bitter; guest beers H
Open-plan Lloyds No.1 just off the east end of the pedestrianised high street (Strand). A decked area at the back overlooks the River Chelt and Sandford Park. Some five changing guest ales from local to countrywide breweries supplement the standard beers, plus Westons Marcle Hill and Old Rosie ciders. The dance floor is only used Friday and Saturday from 8pm, with a generally quiet atmosphere at other times. Food is served all day.

Morans Eating House

123-129 Bath Road, GL53 7LS (½ mile from centre at town end of Bath Road shopping area)
10-11; closed Sun (01242) 581481
moranseatinghouse.co.uk
Beer range varies H
Highly regarded for its restaurant, the separate attractive bar has become a popular ale and wine bar for socialising and currently serves two ales. Timothy Taylor Landlord is usually available plus a beer from Wye Valley, Purity, Box Steam or Bespoke breweries. The interesting bar menu includes tapas, platters, speciality sandwiches and home-made cakes. There is a pleasant conservatory to the rear and covered outdoor seating to the front. Closed on bank holidays.
Q(F,46)

Royal Union Inn

37 Hatherley Street, GL50 2TT (just off A40, S, near Westal Green roundabout)
12 (4 summer)-11 (midnight Fri & Sat); 11-11 Sun
(01242) 519098 theroyalunion.com
Beer range varies H/P
At least eight guest ales from near and far are on offer at this friendly corner local. More than 20 malts and wines are also available. The former skittle alley is now a contemporary dining and drinking area. Home-made food, ranging from lunchtime snacks to evening sharing dishes, is available all day (not Mon and Tue eve), with brunch on Sunday. Live acoustic music features two or three times a week. Q(94,94U)

Sandford Park Alehouse

20 High Street, GL50 1DZ (E end of High St, past Strand on right, no hanging pub sign)
12-11 (midnight Wed-Sat) (01242) 574517
spalehouse.co.uk
Oakham Inferno, Citra; guest beers H
Current CAMRA Cheltenham sub-branch Pub of the Year, this smart new alehouse has a U-shaped main bar area with bar billiards, a cosy front snug room with fire, an upstairs lounge with sport TV (also used for occasional meetings and functions), and a large south-facing patio/garden area which hosts regular barbecues in summer. Sixteen speciality lagers and craft beers are on offer in addition to the ales on 10 handpumps (the website keeps you informed), plus many bottle-conditioned Belgian ales. Q

Cirencester

Corinium Hotel

12 Gloucester Street, GL7 2DG (off A435 to N of town centre)

11-11; 11-10.30 Sun ☎ (01285) 659711

coriniumhotel.co.uk

Wickwar Cotswold Way; guest beers H

Entered via an attractive, narrow courtyard, this agreeable 2-star hotel has a slightly idiosyncratic interior, with a comfortable lounge area complete with comforting woodburner. The varying thickness and layout of the walls hint at its heritage as an Elizabethan wool merchant's house. The guest ales usually include at least one from a microbrewery, often LocAle. A modern vestibule leads into a smart dining room and the pleasant suntrap of a garden at the rear of the premises. P

Drillman's Arms

34 Gloucester Road, GL7 2JY (on old A417, 200yds from A435 jct)

11-2.30, 5.30-midnight; 11-midnight Sat; 12-4.30, 7-11 Sun ☎ (01285) 653892

Sharp's Doom Bar; guest beers H

A great community hub, this busy roadside hostelry features low-beamed ceilings and a wood-burning stove which, allied to great staff, creates a warm and welcoming atmosphere. Popular with darts, pool and skittles teams, its three guest beers change regularly for those who welcome something different to sample. The lunchtime menu is well priced and there is a smaller rear bar adjacent to the combined skittle alley/function room. A popular beer festival is hosted over the August bank holiday weekend. P

Marlborough Arms

Sheep Street, GL7 1QW

12-midnight ☎ (01285) 713540

Box Steam Piston Broke; North Cotswold Windrush Ale; guest beers H

Opposite the old GWR Station, and local CAMRA Pub of the Year, this wooden-floored venue has been transformed into a real ale haven. Offering eight beers, plus ciders, from both regionals and microbreweries, for the discerning drinker it is a rare outlet for Corinium Ales. Brewery memorabilia adorn the walls, with pews and a deep-set fireplace adding character. The ceiling is disappearing behind the encroaching pumpclip collection. The patio at the back is used for barbecues during beer festivals.

Clearwell

Lamb Inn

The Cross (Newland Road), GL16 8JU (signed from North Nibley – OS map recommended) SO5704508170

closed Mon & Tue; 12-3 (not Wed & Thu), 6-11; 12-4, 7-10.30 Sun ☎ (01594) 835441

Wye Valley Bitter; guest beers G

Former iron miners' pub and over 200 years old, this welcoming village local has two bars – a tidy snug with a woodburner and a main bar with an open fire. The main room has large, attractive settles alongside tables flanking the open fireplace, making an ideal setting for family or group occasions. The beer selection is indicated on defunct handpumps as all ales are poured straight from the casks in the cellar behind the bar. Beers are mostly sourced from local and regional brewers. Q P

Cold Aston

Plough Inn

GL54 3BN

12-3 (not Mon), 6-11; 12-11 Fri-Sun ☎ (01451) 822602

coldastonplough.com

Cotswold Spring Stunner H**; Prescott Hill Climb; Stroud Budding** G**; guest beer** H

A transformed stone-flagged country pub high in the Cotswolds. The attractive village went by the name of Aston Blank as far back as the Domesday Book. Reopened in 2013 by new enthusiastic owners, it has three letting luxury bedrooms in an innovative internal extension of the original 17th-century cottage. The emphasis is on real ale and good, interesting food. Look out for three local beers from award-winning Gloucestershire brewers, two served directly from the cask. Local CAMRA Pub of the Year 2014.
Q P

Dursley

Old Spot Inn

2 Hill Road, GL11 4JQ (by bus station and free car park)

11-11; 12-11 Sun ☎ (01453) 542870 oldspotinn.co.uk

Uley Old Ric; guest beers H

Dating from 1776, this free house serves up to eight independent ales. Named after the Gloucestershire Old Spot pig, a porcine theme blends with the extensive brewery memorabilia; low ceilings, log fires and welcoming staff create a convivial atmosphere. The attractive garden has a heated, covered area. Wholesome, freshly prepared dishes complement the pub's enthusiasm for real ale. On the Cotswold Way, it hosts regular beer festivals. CAMRA National Pub of the Year runner-up 2014. Q P

Eastington

Old Badger Inn

Alkerton Road, GL10 3AT

12-11 (10.30 Sun) ☎ (01453) 822892

oldbadgerinn.co.uk

Moles Tap Bitter; Wye Valley HPA; guest beers H

Formerly the Victoria, the pub was rescued, renovated, renamed and reopened as a free house after being closed by Punch Taverns in 2010. The large single bar features a wood-burning stove, with smaller rooms on either side plus a restaurant area. The walls are covered with brewery and other memorabilia. Outside there is a covered and heated patio and a large garden with a children's play area. Very dog-friendly: quarry-tiled floors, water bowls and a biscuit await every four-legged visitor. Q P (21)

Ebrington

Ebrington Arms

GL55 6NH (off B4035 by village green)

12-11 ☎ (01386) 593223 theebringtonarms.co.uk

Prescott Hill Climb; Stroud Organic Ale; guest beers H

A regular winner of CAMRA awards, this 17th-century Cotswold-stone-built pub is set in a beautiful village with excellent walks. The cosy bar has a lovely open fireplace and six handpumps, with three dispensing the pub's own Yubby beers and three others, usually from Gloucestershire. An excellent range of food from local suppliers is on offer. There are five en-suite rooms, one with a

four-poster bed. The pub is usually closed Mondays except on folk nights and bank holidays.
Q P

Forthampton

Lower Lode Inn

GL19 4RE (follow sign to Forthampton from A438 Tewkesbury to Ledbury) SO8788231809
12-midnight (2am Fri & Sat); 12-11 Sun
(01684) 293224 lowerlodeinn.co.uk
Donnington BB; Malvern Hills Black Pear; Sharp's Doom Bar; guest beers H
An attractive brick-built 15th-century coaching inn; note the stained glass before admiring the three acres of lawned frontage looking across the River Severn to Tewkesbury Abbey, complete with moorings and a private slipway. This is a licensed touring park site, with en-suite accommodation, day-fishing licences and a separate function room. Regional ales are complemented by changing guests (two in winter, three in summer). The annual beer festival takes place in September. A small ferry operates Easter to October.
Q P

Frampton Cotterell

Globe Inn

366 Church Road, BS36 2AB
12-11 (10.30 Sun) (01454) 778286
theglobeframptoncotterell.co.uk
Butcombe Bitter; Fuller's London Pride; guest beers H
Independent free house on the Frome Valley Walkway, which links the Cotswolds with the Avon Valley Walkway. An open-plan venue with a separate pavilion which can be hired for functions, it specialises in home-made food using local produce. The pub has an active golf society, a Tuesday quiz and caters for children with an excellent play area. Three guest beers are normally on handpump, including many local brews. Moles Black Rat cider is served. P

Rising Sun

43 Ryecroft Road, BS36 2HN
11.30-11.30 (midnight Fri & Sat); 12-11 Sun
(01454) 772330 risingsunframpton.co.uk
Draught Bass; Great Western Maiden Voyage, Classic Gold; guest beer H
Brewery tap for Great Western Brewing and an excellent free house owned by the same family for many years. Two or more Great Western beers and at least one guest are available. The three-roomed interior comprises the main bar, a small snug and a conservatory/restaurant. Food is served all day (until 8pm Sun). There is also a skittle alley and function room, and an enclosed child-safe beer garden. The pub has featured in almost every edition of this Guide. Q P (482,581)

Frampton-on-Severn

Three Horseshoes

The Green, GL2 7DY (off B4071)
11.30-2, 5.30-11 (1am Fri); 11.30-1am Sat; 11.30-11 Sun
(01452) 742100 threehorseshoespub.co.uk
Sharp's Doom Bar; Timothy Taylor Landlord; Uley Bitter H
A 19th-century two-bar rural community pub built by a farrier at the south end of England's longest village green. Locally-sourced food is home-made, especially the unique 3-Shu pie, which is freshly baked to order. Both bars have coal fires; dogs are welcome in the public bar, and children are permitted until 8.30pm. Evening jamming sessions are popular, as are pasty baking competitions, conker contests and veggie olympics. A double boules court hosts annual championships.
Q

Gloucester

Fountain Inn

53 Westgate Street, GL1 2NW
11-11 (midnight Fri & Sat); 12-11 Sun (01452) 522562
Butcombe Bitter; Dartmoor Jail Ale; Otter Ale; guest beers H
A 17th-century inn on a site where ale was almost certainly being served in 1216. The Cathedral Bar has a panelled ceiling, carved stone fireplace and log fire while the Orange Room acts as a function room or bar overflow. Another function room is available upstairs. Home-cooked food is served lunchtimes and evenings (all day Sat, until 4pm Sun). Local morris men meet here regularly, with folk music featured most Tuesdays. The young landlord looks for quality in his four guest beers.
Q

King Edward VII

47 Old Cheltenham Road, Longlevens, GL2 0AN
11.30-11 (midnight Thu-Sat) (01452) 381273
Bath Ales Gem; Wadworth 6X; guest beers H
This Edwardian red-brick pub was built by Mitchells & Butlers in 1907 and renamed for the king's visit to Gloucester in 1909. Given a total refit in 2001, the interior features modern styling with a central bar and a real fire. It is a popular pub, with excellent offerings of food and ale. Quiz nights are held Wednesday and Sunday. The three guest beers are from the Ember Inns cask list. In summer a real cider displaces one of the beers on handpump. P (94)

Linden Tree

73-75 Bristol Road, GL1 5SN (on A430, S of docks)
11.30-2.30 (not Mon), 6-11; 11.30-11.30 Fri & Sat; 12-11 Sun (01452) 527869 lindentreegloucester.co.uk
Wadworth Henry's IPA, Horizon, 6X, Swordfish, seasonal beers; guest beer H
Set back from a busy thoroughfare, this end property of a Grade II-listed terrace has a country feel inside. Its entrance is modest, but the open log fire, warm colour scheme and eccentric decorative features contribute to a homely atmosphere. The skittle alley opens up to provide extra space when required. Up to three guest beers are from family brewers. Substantial home-cooked meals are offered (no food Sat and Sun eves), and accommodation is reasonably priced.
Q (12)

Pelican Inn

4 St Mary's Street, GL1 2QR (WNW of cathedral)
11-11.30 (01452) 387877
Wye Valley Bitter, Butty Bach, Dorothy Goodbody's Wholesome Stout, seasonal beers; guest beer H
Licensed as an alehouse in the 17th century, some of its beams may have come from Drake's Golden Hind, which began life as the Pelican. The single bar is dominated by conversation; there is a smaller room to the side and an attractive garden area. Ciders and perry come from Olivers and Westons. Always popular, especially on match

days, it is the current local CAMRA Pub of the Year. Annual beer festivals take place in June and winter. Q❀⇌♣●🐾

Gretton

Royal Oak L

Gretton Road, GL54 5EP (E end of village, 1½ miles from Winchcombe)
11-11; 12-10.30 Sun ☎ (01242) 604999
royaloakgretton.co.uk
Marston's EPA; Ramsbury Gold; Wye Valley HPA; guest beers H
A warm welcome is assured from the local owners of this popular Cotswold pub set in two acres. All the regular beers are from local breweries or Marston's. The home-cooked food can be eaten in the L-shaped bar or in the conservatory with its outstanding views across the Vale of Evesham. The Royal Oak dates from about 1830, and the large garden includes a children's play area and a tennis court. The Gloucestershire-Warwickshire railway runs past the garden. ❀◐♿♣P🐾

Ham

Salutation Inn 🏆 L

Ham Green, GL13 9QH (from Berkeley take the road signposted to Jenner Museum)
12-2.30 (not Mon), 5-11; 12-11 Sat; 12-10.30 Sun
☎ (01453) 810284 the-sally-at-ham.com
Butcombe Bitter; guest beers H
Local CAMRA Pub of the Year, this rural gem is in the Severn Valley, within walking distance of the Jenner Museum, Berkeley Castle and Deer Park. The enthusiastic landlord keeps an inspired selection of ales and eight real ciders and perries. The pub has two cosy bars with a log fire and a skittles alley. Food is available lunchtimes and Monday evening only. Live folk music and piano singalongs regularly occur. Shove-ha'penny and table skittles are played. Q❀◐♿♣●P🐾

Hawkesbury Upton

Beaufort Arms L

High Street, GL9 1AU (off A46, 6 miles N of M4 jct 18)
12-11; 12-10.30 Sun ☎ (01454) 238217
beaufortarms.com
Bath Ales SPA; Bristol Beer Factory No. 7; guest beers H
Attractive Grade II-listed Cotswold-stone free house built in 1602 and close to the historic Somerset Monument. Complete with separate public and lounge bars, dining room and skittle alley/function room, this warm, welcoming pub contains an ever-increasing plethora of ancient brewery and local memorabilia. It serves up to five ales and traditional cider on handpump. There is an attractive garden with a barbecue, which is used for local community activities.
Q❀◐♿Ă♣●P🐾

Hillesley

Fleece Inn L

Chapel Lane, GL12 7RD (between Wotton-under-Edge and Hawkesbury Upton)
11-11 (midnight Fri & Sat) ☎ (01453) 520003
thefleeceinnhillesley.com
Butcombe Bitter; guest beers H
An attractive 17th-century whitewashed pub, owned by the community. It has a single bar with a separate lounge/dining room and a snug area. An extensive food menu is largely sourced from local produce. The pub offers a 10 per cent discount for CAMRA members on real ales, which are mainly sourced from local micros. Thatchers Heritage cider is on handpump. Children are welcome and the garden has a safe play area with limited access to the large car park. Q❀◐♣●P🐾

Iron Acton

Lamb Inn

Wotton Road, BS37 9UZ (opp school at one end of village)
11-midnight (1.30am Fri & Sat); 12-11 Sun
☎ (01454) 228265 ironacton.net
Butcombe Bitter; Courage Best Bitter; guest beers H
A coaching house since 1690 and a listed building; it is claimed William of Orange stayed here. The central bar is the hub; children's swings, a stream and a covered veranda feature in the garden to the rear. Another area upstairs has pool, darts and TV. A skittle alley and function room are available. Food is served lunchtimes and evenings and all day at weekends – look out for great-value offers. The two guest beers are mainly local. B&B is available.
❀◐♣●P🐾

Marshfield

Catherine Wheel

39 High Street, SN14 8LR (if using postcode in sat nav check it is not showing Colerne)
12-11 ☎ (01225) 892220 thecatherinewheel.co.uk
Butcombe Bitter; Cotswold Spring Stunner; Sharp's Doom Bar; guest beer H
An impressive stone building with a charming Georgian dining room, beamed bars, wood fires, friendly staff and chatty locals. This owner-operated free house provides real ales, home-cooked food, and accommodation in three comfortable en-suite guest rooms. Its location, close to Bath and on the edge of the Cotswolds, is ideal for sightseeing in Somerset, Wiltshire and Gloucestershire, and for visits to races and horse trials. Well-behaved dogs are welcome in the bar, back room and the well-tended garden.
Q❀◐♿♣●P🐾

Mayshill

New Inn

Badminton Road, BS36 2NT (on A432 between Coalpit Heath and Nibley)
11.45-3, 5.30-10.30 (11 Wed & Thu); 11.45-11 Fri & Sat; 12-10 Sun ☎ (01454) 773161 newinn-mayshill.co.uk
Beer range varies H
A 17th-century inn hugely popular for its food (including gluten-free options), so book ahead. Three guest beers come from far and wide – one of them usually dark – plus a changing cider. The main bar is warmed by a real fire in winter, and the rear area is more of a restaurant. Children are welcome until 8.45pm. The garden, with play area, is pleasant in summer. Generous beer discounts are given to CAMRA members Sunday and Monday evenings. Q❀◐●P🐾

Moreton-in-Marsh

Inn on the Marsh

Stow Road, GL56 0DW (on A429, at S end of town)
⏲ 12-2.30, 7-11 ☎ (01608) 650709
Marston's Burton Bitter, Pedigree; guest beers H
This charming pub is a rare outlet in the area for Marston's beers and guest ales such as Ringwood. A former bakery, it features woven hanging baskets. There is a comfortable locals' bar and a large, attractive conservatory and dining area suitable for parties. Within the garden area competition for nesting sites is at a premium between the resident ducks who live on the pond next door. It is one of the best pubs in Moreton and holds an annual beer festival.
Q❀◑◗♿⚠≠♣●P🚌🐾

Nailsworth

George Inn L

GL6 0RF (15 mins' walk uphill from town centre)
⏲ 11-3, 6.30-11 ☎ (01453) 833228
Stroud Tom Long; Timothy Taylor Landlord; Uley Pig's Ear H
Traditional Cotswold-stone local overlooking the Newmarket valley. Originally three cottages, the interior still has a cosy, homely feel. It became a pub in 1820 and was renamed in 1910 to honour the incoming King George V. The pub is south facing so the popular outdoor seating areas to the front and side are both suntraps. Footpaths radiate in all directions, including one up the hill behind the pub to the Forest Green Rovers' ground (a 15-minute walk). Q❀◗P

Nettleton Bottom

Golden Heart L

Birdlip, GL4 8LA (on A417)
⏲ 10.30-3, 5-11; 10.30-11 Fri-Sun ☎ (01242) 870261
🌐 thegoldenheart.co.uk
Brakspear Bitter; Cotswold Lion Best in Show; Otter Bitter; guest beer H
A 400-year-old haven of peace beside the single carriageway section of the Swindon to Gloucester road. Its large log fire, bare stone walls, mixed furniture and assorted mementos ooze rustic charm. The finest locally-sourced produce contributes to the national award-winning food (served all day Sat and Sun), and children are fully catered for. To the rear, a large stone-paved patio and lawn abut a cow pasture. Two en-suite bedrooms are available, and caravan parking is permitted. Q❀🛏◑◗♣P🐾📶

Newland

Ostrich

GL16 8NP (on B4231 opp church)
⏲ 12-2.30, 6.30-11 ☎ (01594) 833260 🌐 theostrichinn.com
Wye Valley Butty Bach; guest beers H
Set in a beautiful village, this largely unspoilt traditional English hostelry sits at the western edge of the Forest of Dean, opposite the church known as the Cathedral of the Forest. Inside there is a wealth of flagstones, beams and period features to admire. The large fireplace dominates the bar, where up to eight ales can feature at busy times, most of them regional offerings (Exmoor and Uley are popular). A wide-ranging menu normally features some more unusual items. Q❀◑◗⚠●

Newnham

Railway Inn L

Station Road, GL14 1DA (turn off A48 at clock tower)
⏲ 12-11.45 ☎ (01594) 516317
Butcombe Bitter; Greene King Abbot; guest beer H
Regional CAMRA Cider Pub of the Year 2013, this friendly community hub offers over 60 ciders and perries (14+ straight from the box) from different areas, but focuses on the six local producers who frequent the pub themselves. Real ales also feature, as does the Indian restaurant upstairs. Hidden at the back is a continental-style decked garden. Railway memorabilia predominate inside, and you can roast your chestnuts in the log fire. Live music and quiz nights are hosted regularly.
❀◗⚠♣●

North Cerney

Bathurst Arms L

GL7 7BZ (on A435)
⏲ 12-11 ☎ (01285) 831281 🌐 bathurstarms.com
Hook Norton Hooky; guest beers H
Built in 1699, this old wheelwright's house (an original template still adorns the garden) has been selling ale since the Beer Act 1830. Bordering the River Churn, this spacious hostelry has two main areas: the left side of the building for LocAle-seeking drinkers, featuring flagstone floors and an inglenook fireplace, the other half given over to the restaurant and dining areas. Four beer festivals are hosted each year, and offerings from Cotswold Spring and Ramsbury often appear on the bar.
Q❀🛏◑◗⚠P🚌(52)🐾📶

Quedgeley

Haywain

Bristol Road, GL2 4PE (on B4008)
⏲ 11.30-11; 12-10.30 Sun ☎ (01452) 720124
🌐 haywainpubquedgeley.co.uk
Banks's Bitter; Marston's Pedigree; Ringwood Fortyniner; guest beer H
Spacious, modern pub in the middle of Quedgeley that was built in 1985. A reproduction of the Constable masterpiece greets customers upon entry, and a portrait of the artist complements framed pictures throughout. A horseshoe bar takes centre stage, and prominent pillars help to create some discrete seating areas with table service for food. A quality two-for-one menu is available. It is ideal for families, with its internal and external children's play areas and large outdoor seating area. Q❀◑◗♿♣P📶

Quenington

Keepers Arms

Church Road, GL7 5BL (from Fairford turn right at village green)
⏲ 12-3 (not Mon & Tue), 7-11; 12-3, 7-10.30 Sun
☎ (01285) 750349 🌐 thekeepersarms.co.uk
Beer range varies H
Wonderful community local, whose owners have upgraded even more of this lovely free house. Dogs, children and cricketers are still welcome in the lovingly refurbished oak bar, which has a varying selection of ales from regional brewers. Its unpretentious menus are popular (no food Mon and Tue), with regular food theme nights, quizzes and occasional live music. The petite front garden

of this picturesque hostelry is popular with cyclists and ramblers in summer. Three swish en-suite rooms are available. P

Sheepscombe

Butchers Arms

GL6 7RH (signed off A46 N of Painswick, or off B4070 N of Slad) SO8911610434

11.30-3, 6.30 (6 Fri)-11; 11.30-11 Sat; 12-10.30 Sun

(01452) 812113 butchers-arms.co.uk

Butcombe Adam Henson's Rare Breed; Moles Bitter; guest beer

Popular 17th-century Cotswold-stone pub basking in a picturesque village in one of the combes north of Stroud. Its inn sign, a painted three-dimensional carving of a butcher quaffing ale while tethered to a pig, is world famous. Inside, the pub benefits from a high-quality inter-war refurbishment, including generous bay windows, leaded panes and parquet flooring. A wood-burning stove provides warmth in winter and the pub's orientation means the forecourt tables and steeply sloping side garden are suntraps in summer. Q P

Slad

Woolpack

GL6 7QA (on B4070)

12-midnight (01452) 813429

Stroud Budding; Uley Bitter, Old Spot, Pig's Ear; guest beer

Popular 17th-century inn made famous by the book Cider With Rosie (author Laurie Lee was a regular all his life). Only one room deep, the pub offers superb views over the Slad Valley, and has been thoughtfully restored – the built-in dark wooden settles in the end rooms are recent. The bar runs the length of the building, extending into all four rooms. Westons Old Rosie cider and Country Perry are sold, and Wilce's cider. Dogs and walkers welcome. Q

Slimbridge

Tudor Arms

Shepherd's Patch, GL2 7BP (from A38 1 mile beyond Slimbridge village)

11-11; 12-10.30 Sun (01453) 890306

thetudorarms.co.uk

Palmers Dorset Gold; Uley Bitter, Pig's Ear; Wadworth 6X; Wye Valley HPA; guest beer

Winner of local CAMRA awards for seven consecutive years, this large family-owned and operated free house is near the Wildfowl and Wetlands Trust site. Two bars and five dining areas are constantly being improved, and excellent home-cooked food is available all day. A modern lodge alongside offers high-class accommodation, and a separately owned caravan and camping park is immediately behind. A LocAle guest ale complements up to nine ciders and perries. Children and dogs are welcome. Q P

South Woodchester

Ram Inn

Station Road, GL5 5EQ (signed off A46) SO8395202189

11 (12 Sun)-11 (01453) 873329

Butcombe Gold; Gloucester Gold; Otter Amber; Wickwar Cotswold Way; guest beers

Much altered and extended 400-year-old Cotswold stone inn tucked into the hillside, commanding fine views over the Nailsworth Valley towards Amberley and Minchinhampton Common from a suntrap front terrace. Inside, three interconnecting rooms (one with a log fire) are grouped around a long stone-built bar. Popular with locals and visitors alike, it is situated in superb walking country near Woodchester Mansion. Beers are competitively priced. The car park at the front is on two levels. Q P (46,93)

Staunton

White Horse Inn

Staunton Road, GL16 8PA (on A4136)

closed Mon; 6.30-11 Tue; 12-3, 6-11; 12-10.30 Sun

(01594) 834001 whitehorseinnstaunton.co.uk

Beer range varies

Billed as the last pub in England, this cracking village inn has taken on many aspects of a village shop as well. The real ales here all come from local breweries, with none of them a permanent fixture on the bar. There is a welcoming wood-burning stove in the bar, with the back of the room dedicated to groceries and other basic shopping requirements. The menu options are home cooked from fresh, locally-sourced ingredients wherever possible. Q P

Stroud

Ale House

9 John Street, GL5 2HA (opp Cornhill farmers' market)

12-3, 5-11; 12-midnight Fri; 10.30-midnight Sat; 12-11 Sun

(01453) 755447

Cotswold Lion Golden Fleece; Dark Star Hophead; Stroud Budding; guest beers

Built in 1837 for the Poor Law Guardians, this Grade II-listed building hosts an all-year-round beer festival, and is local CAMRA Pub of the Year. The bar occupies the double-height top-lit former boardroom, where a varied range of beers, ciders and perries is dispensed from a bank of 12 handpumps. Opposite is a blazing log fire flanked by a leather sofa (frequently occupied by Finbar, the landlord's Irish wolfhound). Two smaller rooms adjoin this principal space. Home-made curries are a speciality. Q

Crown & Sceptre

98 Horns Road, GL5 1EG

3 (12 Fri-Sun)-11 (01453) 762588

crownandsceptrestroud.com

Stroud Budding; Uley Bitter, Pig's Ear; guest beer

Lively back-street pub that is the beating heart of the local community, a genuine free house where Blue Anchor beers are regular guests. An eclectic selection of framed prints and posters graces the walls. A large oak table in a side room is popular with local groups, including a knitting circle, and the pub also has its own motorcycle society. Sky Sports is screened in the back bar. A terrace at the rear offers panoramic views over Stroud. P (8,227)

Prince Albert

Rodborough Hill, GL5 3SS (corner of Walkley Hill)

4-11.30 (12.30am Thu & Fri); 12-12.30am Sat; 12-11 Sun

(01453) 755600 theprincealbertstroud.co.uk

Otter Bitter; Stroud Budding; Timothy Taylor Landlord; guest beers
This lively, cosmopolitan, stone-built pub near Rodborough Common is simultaneously bohemian, homely and welcoming, with an eclectic mix of furniture, fittings and memorabilia, an open log fire, and walls covered with film and music photos, posters and handbills. The pub hosts a May beer festival, art exhibitions, live music and stand-up comedy. Some events are ticketed (phone or check website). Friday is pizza night, every other night bring your own food or phone for a takeaway. Children, dogs and walkers are welcome.
(36)

Tetbury

Royal Oak

1 Cirencester Road, GL8 8EY (on B4067)
11-11 (11.30 Fri & Sat); 12-11 Sun ☎ (01666) 500021
theroyaloaktetbury.co.uk
Bath Ales Gem; Stroud Tom Long; guest beers
Clever design options make this totally renovated pub (it is not often that both buildings get re-roofed) feel welcoming and modern. The expanse of wooden surfaces and a small fireplace give the place a warm feeling. Six handpumps greet the eye; offerings include Severn cider and an ale from Moor – chosen to match the vegan option on the ever-varying menu. The hearty one pot stew is always popular. Upstairs dining facilities and six letting rooms are available, with acoustic music on Sunday evenings. P

Tewkesbury

Nottingham Arms

129 High Street, GL20 5JU (on A38 in town centre)
11-11 (midnight Thu-Sat); 12-midnight Sun
☎ (01684) 276346
St Austell Tribute; Sharp's Doom Bar; Wye Valley HPA, Butty Bach; guest beers
A 14th-century town-centre pub with two welcoming rooms, both with timber predominating: a bar at the front and a restaurant behind. Framed photographs of old Tewkesbury adorn the walls. Four real ales are usually offered, one LocAle, plus Westons Old Rosie cider. The pub is noted for its excellent, well-priced contemporary cuisine, served lunchtimes and evenings. Knowledgeable staff will happily tell you about the resident ghosts. Live music is hosted most Sunday evenings and Thursday is quiz night.

Olde Black Bear

68 High Street, GL20 5BJ (on A38, top of High St near river bridge)
11-11 ☎ (01684) 292202
Adnams Broadside; Greene King IPA; guest beers
Built in 1308, this ex-coaching house is the oldest inn in Gloucestershire. As might be expected in such an historic building, the interior is rich in timber, both frames and beams. Allegedly haunted by three ghosts, including a cavalier and an old lady, it was used as a hospital during the Wars of the Roses. Quiz nights are Sunday and Wednesday, with Sky TV screened inside and outside in the riverside beer garden. Private moorings and fishing are available.

Royal Hop Pole

94 Church Street, GL20 5RS (centre of town between Abbey and Cross)
7am (8am Sun)-11 ☎ (01684) 274039
Greene King IPA; Ruddles County; guest beers
Town-centre landmark that is an amalgamation of historic buildings dating from the 15th and 18th centuries, gaining its name after a visit from Princess Mary of Teck (Queen Mary, Royal Consort of George V) in 1891. Mentioned in The Pickwick Papers, this current local CAMRA Pub of the Year is not short of interior space, and features generous swathes of wood panelling. The popular multi-roomed drinking establishment has an attractive garden and patio at the rear. Local beers are often among the guests. Q P

Theoc House

85 Barton Street, GL20 5PY (on A438, 50yds from the Cross)
8.30am-11 ☎ (01684) 296562 theochouse.co.uk
Beer range varies
This fully refurbished town-centre hostelry is a wonderful blend of pub, café and coffee lounge with a truly relaxed atmosphere created by the owners. As the venue competes with a certain national pub chain, it is open all day to serve good-value breakfast, brunch and evening meals. Only two real ales are regularly available, one often a stout, but there are plans to offer more. Sunday is quiz night, with jazz evenings on the second and fourth Wednesdays of the month.
Q P (42)

White Bear

Bredon Road, GL20 5BU (off N end of High Street)
10-midnight ☎ (01684) 296614
Draught Bass; guest beers
On the north-western edge of the town centre, this good-value, family-run pub attracts a varied clientele. Being located close to Tewkesbury Marina, it is popular with river users. The open-plan L-shaped bar offers room to play pool, cribbage and darts; there is also a skittle alley. Live music is hosted every Sunday evening. All three guest beers change frequently and are often sourced from smaller microbreweries, while a range of three traditional Thatchers ciders is also offered.
P

Thornbury

Anchor Inn

Gloucester Road, Lower Morton, BS35 1JY
11-11 ☎ (01454) 281375 theanchorthornbury.co.uk
Draught Bass; guest beers
Licensed since 1695 and the second oldest pub in Thornbury, this friendly, traditional inn has one regular beer and five changing guests, mostly of low to medium strength, with occasional milds – plus a real cider. Good home-cooked food is served daily. There are two large rooms, one with a central fireplace. The pub has its own darts, crib, dominoes and cricket teams and angling syndicate. The garden includes a boules piste and children's play area. P

Uley

Old Crown

17 The Green, GL11 5SN (on B4066 at top end of village)

12-11 ☎ (01453) 860502 theoldcrownuley.co.uk
Uley Bitter, Pig's Ear; guest beers H
A 17th-century whitewashed coaching inn situated in this pretty village on the steep Cotswold scarp. It has an attractive walled garden and, as well as being the village local, it is popular with passing walkers traversing the Cotswold Way footpath. The low-beamed single bar has a welcoming fire. The guest ales are usually from microbreweries. The establishment offers four en-suite double bedrooms and food is served 12-2pm and 7-9pm. There is a covered smoking area.
Q

Upper Oddington

Horse & Groom

GL56 0XH (top of village signed off A436 E of Stow)
12-3, 5.30-11 ☎ (01451) 830584
horseandgroom.uk.com
Prescott Hill Climb; Wye Valley Bitter, HPA; guest beer H
Attractive, privately owned 16th-century inn run by friendly licensees who have won many CAMRA awards. It has an extended bar area for locals with its own sitting room linked by a real open log fire in an inglenook setting. Wye Valley beers are served, plus a weekly changing guest from a Gloucestershire brewery. There is a large car park, garden and patio area. The pub is in good walking country and is close to Stow. Eight letting bedrooms are available. Q P

Whitminster

Old Forge Inn

Bristol Road, GL2 7NY (On A38 at south end of village – near M5 jct 13)
12-11 ☎ (01452) 741306
Greene King IPA; St Austell Tribute; guest beers H
Records for this largely timber framed building go back to 1535, but some roof trusses are thought to be Saxon. It's thought to have been a Drovers' resting place en-route from Wales to Lechlade. The small bar serves two carpeted areas, one with comfortable armchairs and a TV for sport. Home-cooked food is available lunchtimes and evenings. Dart teams have been reinstated and the weekly pub lotteries are proving popular. Guest ales are from the Punch list. Q P (12,91)

Wickwar

Buthay

15 High Street, GL12 8NE (close to traffic lights)
closed Mon; 12-11 (midnight Fri & Sat) ☎ (01454) 299083
thebuthay.com
Beer range varies H
Enjoying a new lease of life, this friendly family-run 16th-century coaching inn attracts a varied clientele. It has a welcoming single bar main drinking area with a log fire. The large dining room specialises in authentic Italian food cooked fresh to order by Peppe. There is a skittles alley/function room, and to the rear is a large enclosed garden with a well-equipped children's play area. Well-behaved dogs are welcome in the bar area.
P

Woolaston Common

Rising Sun

The Common, GL15 6NU (1 mile off A48 at Woolaston)
SO5901500924
12-2.30 (3 Sun), 6.30-11; 12-3, 6.30-midnight Sat
☎ (01594) 529282
Butcombe Bitter; Wye Valley Bitter; guest beer H
Blessed with spectacular views over the Forest of Dean, this 350-year-old stone-built hostelry is well worth seeking out, and is a popular stopping point with walkers travelling through this lovely area. The real fire is a draw in the large main bar and the cosy snug is rarely empty. The walls are adorned with various artefacts, including banknotes. The food is home cooked, using local produce where possible (no food lunchtimes Mon and Tue). The cribbage league meet here on Tuesdays.
Q P

Wotton-under-Edge

Falcon Inn

20, Church Street, GL12 7HB (Bottom of Long St shopping area)
12-11.30; 12-11 Sun ☎ (01453) 521005
Great Western Maiden Voyage G**; Stroud Tom Long; guest beers** H
A free house built in 1659, the interior has rooms on several levels. The cosy single bar has an open fire. Off this is a snug with a flagstone floor and there is a dining area, which specialises in locally-sourced food; the steaks come from the family farm situated a mile away. The beers are selected by customer vote from breweries within a 25-mile radius. A popular pub with both locals and Cotswold Way walkers.

Royal Oak Inn

3-5 Haw Street, GL12 7AG (on B4060)
12-midnight ☎ (01453) 844366 royaloakwotton.com
Cotswold Spring Codger; Fuller's London Pride; Wye Valley HPA; guest beer H
A large coaching inn with a friendly atmosphere. It has two comfortable bars, both featuring real open fires, plus a spacious dining room. There is a full-size snooker table upstairs which is very popular. This pub supports the local community and offers a warm welcome to walkers using the Cotswold Way. At the rear is a car park and enclosed garden containing a well-equipped children's play area, originally occupied by stables, pigsty and a poultry house. Q P

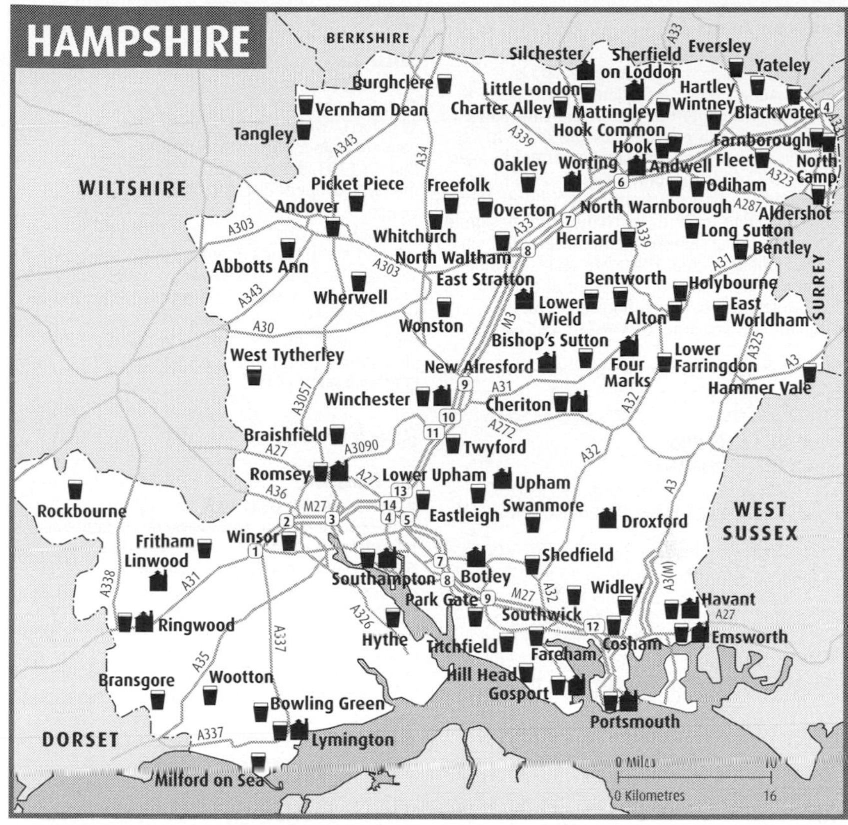

Abbotts Ann

Eagle Inn L

High Street, SP11 7BG

11.30-11; 12-10.30 Sun ☎ (01264) 710339

eagleabbottsann.co.uk

Skinner's Betty Stogs; guest beers H

Located in a picturesque village just two miles south west of Andover, this pub is at the heart of the community. Friendly conversation rules the house. The regular Betty Stogs is supplemented by three changing beers, often from local breweries, plus up to four real ciders. A beer festival with live music is held in summer. The public bar has a pool table and there is a skittle alley at the rear. Food is served lunchtimes and evenings (no food Tue and Sun eves). Q❀◑♣●P🚌(77,87)🐾

Aldershot

White Lion L

20 Lower Farnham Road, GU12 4EA

1-11 (10.30 Mon; midnight Fri); 12-midnight Sat; 12-10.30 Sun ☎ (01252) 323832

Triple fff Alton's Pride, Moondance; guest beers H

Traditional two-bar pub built shortly after the army arrived in 1854. Cut-down church pews, a real fire and dartboard are in the main bar. The back bar is generally quieter. One of only two Triple fff pubs, pub dog Millie welcomes away fans when Aldershot Town are at home. The A5 Scooter Club meets here on a Sunday. There is a pub quiz and rock & roll bingo on alternate Thursdays, and occasional live music. ❀♣🚌(3,20)🐾

Alton

Eight Bells

Church Street, GU34 2DA (opp St Lawrence Church)

11-11; 12-10.30 Sun ☎ (01420) 82417

Bowman Swift One; Sharp's Doom Bar; guest beers H

Popular free house, dating from circa 1640, just outside the town centre. Opposite lies the Church of St Lawrence, site of the Civil War Battle of Alton. The pub has an original oak-beamed interior with a main bar and smaller drinking area, plus a restored listed smoking shelter incorporating a 17th-century well in a secluded paved garden. Sandwiches and soup and a roll are available Monday to Friday from 12.30pm. Look out for Nigel's not-so-secret beer festival following the late summer holiday. Q❀⇌🚌(13,64)🐾

George 🏆

Butts Road, GU34 1LH

11-11 (10.30 Sun) ☎ (01420) 82331

thegeorgealton.co.uk

St Austell Tribute; Sharp's Doom Bar; guest beers H

Grade II-listed pub dating from 1745, also the courthouse famed for the trial of the murderer of Sweet Fanny Adams. Previously the Duke's Head, it is back under Jason and Suzie's stewardship; they run a friendly local with two regular beers and two guest ales from the SIBA list. Excellent snacks and main meals are served to suit all tastes. Music features on the first Sunday of each month – check the website for visiting bands. ❀◑P🚌(64)🐾

Railway Arms 🄻

26 Anstey Road, GU34 2RB (opp Station Approach)
12-11; 11-midnight Fri & Sat ☎ (01420) 82218
Triple fff Alton's Pride, Moondance; guest beers Ⓗ
Friendly pub close to the Watercress Line and mainline station. It is owned by the Triple fff Brewery, whose beers are supplemented by ales from a host of micros. Bottled cider is from Mr Whitehead's. A rear function room, with its own bar, is available for hire. The patio area, designed with a traditional railway theme, incorporates a covered smoking area. There are tables outside at the front under a striking sculpture of a steam locomotive. Well-behaved dogs and CAMRA members are welcome. ❀≥♣⊟(64,65)🐾

Andover

John Russell Fox

10 High Street, SP10 1NY
7am-midnight (1am Fri & Sat) ☎ (01264) 320920
Greene King Abbot; Ruddles Best Bitter; guest beers Ⓗ
A High Street Wetherspoon pub in former offices of the Andover Advertiser, founded by John Russell Fox. A large entrance area leads to the bar with 10 handpumps. Several references to print and newspapers adorn the pub. A separate raised seating and eating area is to the rear where families are welcome. Note the Time Ring in the pavement outside. ◐♿●P⊟

Bentley

Star 🄻

Main Road, GU10 5LW
9am (11 Sat)-midnight; 11-11 Sun ☎ (01420) 23184
thestarinnbentley.co.uk
Sharp's Doom Bar; Triple fff Moondance; guest beer Ⓗ
Recently extensively refurbished, creating a pleasant imbibers' environment. From the station follow signs to Bentley Village or local footpaths. The 65 bus stops nearby (outside from the Alton direction). This hostelry opens at 9.30am for breakfast and is licensed from 11.30am. There is a price premium for half pints – check the price board above the bar. It does excellent food, much of which is locally sourced – the licensee is also a local farmer. He has an interesting beer range, often from Tillingbourne, which is well worth tasting.
Q❀◐P⊟(65)🐾

Bentworth

Star Inn 🄻

Village Street, GU34 5RB (opp village crossroads)
12-11.30 ☎ (01420) 561224 star-inn.com
Fuller's London Pride; Palmers Copper Ale; Triple fff Alton's Pride, Moondance Ⓗ
At the crossroads in the centre of Bentworth, this pub is a real hub for the local community but equally welcoming to visitors. As well as offering well-kept real ale and excellent food, the pub puts on quiz nights, regular live music with a blues theme on Friday nights, and a jam session on Sundays. At other times there is unobtrusive music in the bar and a separate quiet dining area. It also holds regular cinema events and a popular annual blues festival. Q❀◐♿▲♣P⊟🐾

Bishop's Sutton

Ship Inn

SO24 0AQ (on B3047)
12-2.30 (not Mon), 6-11; 12-3, 7-10.30 Sun
☎ (01962) 732863
Palmers Copper Ale; guest beer Ⓗ
Built in 1753, this pub was on the main road before the bypass opened; today, it is the hub of the village. A split-level bar with a log fire provides a cosy, relaxing atmosphere, with pictures of notable sail and steam ships adorning the walls. There are separate areas for pub games, families and dining; food is home-cooked, with daily specials (no food Mon lunchtime). The regular Winchester/Alton bus service stops outside and the Watercress Line preserved steam railway is nearby.
Q❀◐♣P⊟(64)

Blackwater

Mr Bumble

19 London Road, GU17 9AP
12-11 (midnight Fri); 11-midnight Sat; 12-10.30 Sun
☎ (01276) 32691
Fuller's London Pride; guest beers Ⓗ
Formerly the Red Lion, this free-of-tie pub has been run by landlady Philippa for 20 years, with the lease recently renewed, and her efforts were rewarded by entry in the 2014 Guide. This is very much a community pub, with three pool tables, darts, and live bands on Saturdays. Of the three guest ales, at least one is normally a local beer, and the pub featured in the CAMRA branch's Locale Trail in 2013. ❀≥♣P⊟(3)

Bowling Green

Wheel Inn 🄻

Sway Road, SO41 8LJ
12-midnight (11 Tue); 12-1am Fri & Sat
☎ (01590) 676122 thewheelinnpub.co.uk
Ringwood Best Bitter; guest beers Ⓗ

INDEPENDENT BREWERIES

Alfred's Winchester
Andwell Andwell
Botley Botley
Bowman Droxford
Brewhouse & Kitchen Portsmouth (NEW)
CrackleRock Botley (NEW)
Dancing Man Southampton
Emsworth Emsworth
Flack Manor Romsey
Flowerpots Cheriton
Fulflood Arms Winchester (brewing suspended)
Havant Havant
Irving Portsmouth
Itchen Valley New Alresford
Longdog Worting
MASH East Stratton (NEW)
Oakleaf Gosport
Queen Inn Winchester (NEW)
Red Cat Winchester (NEW)
Red Shoot Linwood
Ringwood (Marston's) Ringwood
Sherfield Village Sherfield on Loddon
Triple fff Four Marks
Upham Upham
Vibrant Forest Lymington
Wild Weather Silchester

Victorian-built family pub set in a former pottery and blacksmith's, which sources unusual, mainly local, beers. It serves award-winning Thai food in the lounge/restaurant, Tuesday to Sunday, with takeaways available. Although it has a pool table and background music plus an acoustic singaround on Mondays, this is mainly a pub for conversation. It has camping facilities (caravans only). Q❀◑♿▲♣P🚌(X2)🐾ᯤ

Braishfield

Dog & Crook

Crook Hill, SO51 0QB

11.30-3, 5.30-11; 11.30-11 Fri & Sat; 11.30-11 Sun winter; 11.30-11 summer ☎ (01794) 368530 🌐 dogandcrook.co.uk

Bowman Wallops Wood; Ringwood Best Bitter; guest beer H

Friendly village pub on the southern edge of the village, convenient for visitors to the nearby Hillier's arboretum and gardens. This free house has two regular beers and one guest beer (usually a local ale) on handpump. An excellent and varied menu is served in the restaurant, bar or large garden, lunchtimes and evenings (no food Sun eve). There has been a pub here since at least 1871, when it appeared on a map of the village. Quiz night is Tuesday. Q❀◑♿♣P🐾ᯤ

Bransgore

Three Tuns

Ringwood Road, BH23 8JH (between Burley Road and Harrow Road)

11.30-11; 12-10.30 Sun ☎ (01425) 672232

🌐 threetunsinn.com

Otter Bitter; Ringwood Best Bitter, Fortyniner; guest beers H

Charming 17th-century thatched former coaching inn serving three regular and two local guest ales. Inside you will find a well-kept bar area with exposed beams, open fires and chatty locals, run by a hardworking friendly team. Food is important here, locally sourced with a strong focus on fish, as the pub nestles between the coast and the New Forest. Outside are extensive gardens with stunning views over open fields, and a large patio; pétanque is popular. Q❀◑♿▲♣●P🐾ᯤ

Burghclere

Carpenters Arms

Harts Lane, RG20 9JY (off A34 at Tothill Services, follow signs to Sandham Memorial Chapel)

11 (12 Sun)-11 ☎ (01635) 278251

🌐 carpentersarms-burghclere.co.uk

Arkell's 3B, Kingsdown Special Ale, seasonal beer H

Warm and welcoming local village pub with views over Watership Down from the patio and garden. Arkell's beers are served from three handpumps. Popular with both walkers and cyclists, children and dogs are welcome. There is a wide selection of good honest pub food on offer, including traditional roast meals on Sundays (no food Sun eve). Accommodation consists of six comfortable rooms in a separate cottage adjacent to the pub. Q❀🛏◑P🚌(21,22)🐾

Charter Alley

White Hart

White Hart Lane, RG26 5QA (1 mile W of A340, opp turning for Little London)

7-11 Mon; 12-2.30, 7 (5.30 Thu & Fri)-11; 12-3, 6.30-11 Sat; 12-4, 7-10.30 Sun ☎ (01256) 850048

🌐 whitehartcharteralley.com

Triple fff Moondance; guest beers H

Cosy inn, built in 1819, the epicentre of this rural village, where all comers are assured of a friendly greeting. Welcoming features include log fires, oak beams and a capacious restaurant, serving a variety of quality food and home-made pies. The breweriana-decorated main bar has six pumps dispensing an array of ales that changes so frequently that an email notification service is available by subscription. It has been a stalwart Guide entry for over 20 years. No food Sunday and Monday evenings. Q❀🛏◑P🐾ᯤ

Cheriton

Flowerpots Inn

Brandy Mount, SO24 0QQ (½ mile N of A272 between Winchester and Petersfield) SU581283

12-2.30 (3 Sat), 6-11; 12-3, 7-10.30 Sun

☎ (01962) 771318 🌐 flowerpots-inn.co.uk

Flowerpots Perridge Pale, Bitter, Goodens Gold, seasonal beer G

Excellent two-bar pub in an attractive village. The public bar has a 19th-century well and log fire. The lounge is small and cosy. In summer there is plenty of seating in the well-kept garden. It is the home of Flowerpots Brewery, located across the car park. Good home-cooked food is served daily (no food Sun eve), while Wednesday is curry night. There are many good walks nearby and the Watercress steam railway is situated three miles away. Three B&B double rooms are available.

Q❀🛏◑●P🚌(67)🐾

Cosham

First Post

High Street, PO6 3AG

8-11 ☎ (023) 9221 0331

Courage Directors; Greene King Abbot; Ruddles Best Bitter; guest beers H

As much a community venue as a Wetherspoon pub, it offers several traditional pub games and shows Racing UK daily. It also screens Sky and BT sport. This establishment is a committed supporter of local beers, with at least two always available. Fundraising events are frequently held here for local schools and charities. ❀◑⇌♣●🚌ᯤ

East Worldham

Three Horseshoes

Cakers Lane, GU34 3AE

11.30-3, 5.30-10.30; 11.30-11 Sat; 11.30-5 Sun

☎ (01420) 83211 🌐 threehorseshoesalton.co.uk

Fuller's London Pride, seasonal beer; Gales Seafarers Ale, HSB H

Once a Gales house, part of the building dates back over 300 years and is allegedly haunted. Mine hosts John and Gill are rapidly gaining an excellent reputation for their food as well as their ales. Very much a community pub, it is the place to go to for details of local events, while their website lists pub events. Quiz night is the last Thursday of the month; special events take place on the last Saturday of the month – murder mystery, and so on. Q❀◑▲P🚌(13)📶

Eastleigh

Wagon Works

28 Southampton Road, SO50 9FJ

⌚ 7am-midnight (1am Fri & Sat) ☎ (023) 8062 2670

Greene King Abbot; Itchen Valley Pure Gold; Ruddles County; Sharp's Doom Bar; Shepherd Neame Spitfire; Wychwood Hobgoblin; guest beers H

Smaller than most Wetherspoon houses, this cosy corner pub is an ideal place to wait for a train as it is directly opposite the railway station. It serves food all day from 7am, alcohol is licensed from 9am. There is a good-sized paved area at the rear of the pub which is a suntrap in the summer months, and it has a heated, covered seating area. Four guest beers are usually from local breweries. Black Dragon cider is on gravity.
Q❀◑♿≠🍎🚌📶

Emsworth

Coal Exchange L

21 South Street, PO10 7EG

⌚ 10.30-3, 5-11; 10.30-midnight Fri & Sat; 12-11 Sun
☎ (01243) 375866 🌐 thecoalexchange.co.uk

Fuller's London Pride; Gales Seafarers Ale, HSB; guest beers H

A comfortable single-bar pub close to the harbour. Its name is derived from the custom of local farmers trading produce for coal delivered by sea – which is now commemorated on the pub sign. Although no longer commercial, the harbour is a popular venue for sailing and coastal walks. Award-winning food is served at lunchtimes, with themed evening meals including Monday burger night, Tuesday curries and an international menu on Thursday. Live music features on Wednesday and Saturday. ❀◐≠♣🚌(700)🐾

Eversley

Golden Pot L

Reading Road, RG27 0NB

⌚ 11.30-3, 5.30-11; 12-3.30 Sun ☎ (0118) 973 2104
🌐 golden-pot.co.uk

Beer range varies H

Picture-postcard village pub that was formerly two red-brick cottages dating back to the 18th century. The pub is supplied by 14 different microbreweries on rotation, eight of which are local, including Andwell, Siren and Longdog. High-quality wholesome food is served, which is also available in small plate options, and there is a rosti menu on Mondays. Another delightful feature is the Snug and Vineyard garden at the rear of the pub. Opening hours may vary on midweek evenings.
Q❀◑P🐾📶

Fareham

Crown

40 West Street, PO16 0JW

⌚ 7am-midnight (1am Fri & Sat) ☎ (01329) 241750

Greene King Abbot; Ruddles Best Bitter; guest beers H

This town-centre Wetherspoon outlet is in a pedestrianised street convenient for the bus station and shopping centre. Wall-mounted portraits with brief histories of famous local figures add to the character of the premises. The three guest beers normally include one from a local brewery, and the occasional specialist beer from an American brewer visiting this country. Near each handpump is an indicator giving the colour of the beer. Real cider is available occasionally and may become a regular feature. Q❀◑🚌📶

Golden Lion

28 High Street, PO16 7AE

⌚ 11.30-11 (9 Mon); 12-3.30 Sun ☎ (01329) 234061
🌐 thegoldenlionfareham.info

Fuller's London Pride; Gales Seafarers Ale, HSB; guest beer H

A well-presented Grade II-listed pub at the northern end of the High Street conservation area where the licensees are Cask Marque and Fuller's Master Cellarman-accredited. Every Thursday an additional guest ale is on offer to coincide with the charity quiz night. Home-cooked, locally-sourced food is available and pre-booking is recommended for the popular steak nights on Fridays and Saturdays as well as the roasts on Sunday lunchtimes. Folk musicians entertain on the last Tuesday of every month. Q❀◑P🚌📶

Farnborough

Prince of Wales 🏆 L

184 Rectory Road, GU14 8AL

⌚ 11.30-2.30, 5.30-11; 11.30-11 Fri & Sat; 12-10.30 Sun
☎ (01252) 545578 🌐 theprinceinfarnborough.co.uk

Dark Star Hophead; Fuller's London Pride; Hop Back Summer Lightning; Ringwood Fortyniner; Young's Bitter; guest beers H

Featuring in the Guide for more than 30 years, this cosy freehold pub is well known to beer lovers throughout the area, and was the local CAMRA branch Pub of the Year in 2014. Of the 10 cask ales, five are guests, including a monthly special at a reduced price and, generally, at least one qualifying as LocAle. It is popular for its lunches (plus Monday pie night), and also for the annual beer festival in October. The pub is around the corner from Farnborough North station.
❀◐≠(North)P🚌(31)🐾📶

Tilly Shilling

Unit 2-5, Victoria Road, GU14 7PG

⌚ 7am-midnight (1am Fri & Sat) ☎ (01252) 893560

Greene King Abbot; Ruddles Best Bitter; guest beers H

Town-centre aero-themed pub opened in 2011 and named after an engineer at the nearby RAE factory which designed a major improvement to Rolls-Royce Merlin engines that powered many RAF fighter planes during WWII. The large rectangular open-plan lounge features a glass frontage that opens in good weather, extending the pub onto the pavement. Ten handpumps leave plenty of space for regular and guest beers. Real cider is available from polypins at the end of the bar. Alcohol is on sale from 9am.
◑♿≠(Main)🍎🚌📶

Fleet

Prince Arthur L

238 Fleet Road, GU51 4BX

⌚ 8am-midnight (1am Fri & Sat) ☎ (01252) 622660

Greene King Abbot; Longdog Brindle Bitter; Ruddles Best Bitter; guest beers [H]
Wetherspoon pub named after Queen Victoria's third son, Prince Arthur, Duke of Connaught, who lived in Fleet while he was commander of the Aldershot garrison. Two LocAle beer festivals take place every year. Real cider is Gwynt y Ddraig Black Dragon or Westons Old Rosie, available from refrigerated polypins kept behind the bar. The house beer, Winning Co-ALE-ition, is Longdog Brindle Bitter, renamed in association with the Official Monster Raving Loony Party whose leader lives locally and is a regular. Q❀◐♿●🚌📶

Freefolk

Watership Down Inn L

Freefolk Priors, RG28 7NJ (just off B3400)
12-3, 6-11 (10 Mon; midnight Fri); 12-midnight Sat; 12-10 Sun ☎ (01256) 892254 🌐 watershipdowninn.com
Itchen Valley Godfathers, Pure Gold; guest beers [H]
Built in 1840, in the Upper Test Valley, and still affectionately known locally as the Jerry, the pub has been named in honour of local author Richard Adams' book Watership Down, set in the downland to the north of the pub. Outside there is an extensive garden, patio and family area. Each May a beer festival is held and occasional live music evenings are arranged.
Q❀◐●P🚌(76,86)🐾📶

Fritham

Royal Oak L

SO43 7HJ (W end of village) SU232141
11-3, 6-11; 11-11 Sat; 12-10.30 Sun ☎ (023) 8081 2606
Bowman Wallops Wood; Flack Manor Double Drop; Ringwood Best Bitter; guest beers [G]
Thatched gem at the end of a New Forest track. A main bar leads to two connected areas featuring low beams and doors, colourwashed walls, log fires and wooden floors, both served via a hatchway. Guest ales are from small local brewers – the house beer, Royal Oak, is Wallops Wood. Simple but excellent lunches include local cheeses. The vast garden has many tables and hosts barbecues and hog roasts. It warmly welcomes walkers, cyclists and equestrians (facilities provided); dogs abound. Q❀◐🐾

Gosport

Junction Tavern

1 Leesland Road, Camden Town, PO12 3ND
11-11.30 (midnight Fri & Sat); 12-10.30 Sun ☎ (023) 9258 5140 🌐 junctiontavern.com
Beer range varies [H]
A relatively small pub on the site of Brockhurst Junction, on the Fareham to Gosport railway line, now a cycle track and footpath. The seating once consisted of old railway carriage seats. Deana, the licensee, introduced real ale when she took over a few years ago. The three real ales are from independent breweries and two real ciders and a real perry are also available. Beer festivals take place over the Easter and August bank holiday weekends. ❀♣●🚌(E1)

Queen's Hotel L

143 Queens Road, Forton, PO12 1LG
11.30-2.30 (not Mon-Thu), 5-11; 11.30-11 Sat; 12-3, 7-10.30 Sun ☎ 07974 031671
Oakleaf India Pale Ale; Ringwood Fortyniner; Young's Bitter; guest beers [H]
Under the same management for over 30 years, this award-winning free house is sought after by locals and visitors from all over the country. The focal point is a real fire with a carved wood surround. Three guest beers are available, from independent breweries and micros. A regular beer festival takes place in October. Snacks are served Friday lunchtimes, and weekend opening times are often extended by up to half an hour. ❀♣●🚌

Hammer Vale

Prince of Wales

Hammer Lane, GU27 1QH (Enter Hammer Ln from Haslemere end due to width restriction at Liphook end)
11 (12 Sun)-11 ☎ (01428) 652600
Fuller's London Pride, seasonal beers; Gale's HSB [H]
Although tucked away it's well worth a visit in order to sample the beers. It boasts a huge outside seating area and is well-sited for walkers and campers. Nick and Heidi provide excellent meals and the lunchtime baguettes will hit the spot. There are many stories (mostly apocryphal) as to how such a large 1927-built roadhouse was sited away from the main road. Check the stained glass windows, one for Amey's of Petersfield.
Q❀◐♿Ʌ♣P🐾📶

Hartley Wintney

Cricketers

The Cricket Green, RG27 8QB (next to cricket pitch behind High Street)
12-11 ☎ (01252) 842166
🌐 thecricketers-hartleywintney.co.uk
Thwaites Wainwright; guest beers [H]
A lovely traditional English pub in a fantastic cricketing location, this hostelry is in the heart of the community. It offers great locally-sourced food, brilliant ales and a fabulous wine list. With open fires in the winter and a village-green life in the summer, you are always wrapped up in a friendly, welcoming atmosphere. Monthly wine dinners take place. Q❀◐♿P🚌(100,72)📶

Waggon & Horses

High Street, RG27 8NY
11-11 (midnight Fri & Sat); 12-11 Sun ☎ (01252) 842119
Courage Best Bitter; Gales HSB [H]**; guest beers** [G]
A village pub whose landlord of 30 years has won several local CAMRA awards. HSB and Courage Best are regularly served alongside changing guest beers. The pub's lively public bar contrasts with a quieter lounge. Tables outside on the pavement enable guests to enjoy the atmosphere of the village, renowned for its antique shops. At the rear is a pleasant courtyard garden and a heated, covered smokers' area. Food is served lunchtimes only, not Sundays. Q❀◐♿●🚌(100,72)🐾

Havant

Old House at Home

2 South Street, PO9 1DA
11-11; 12-10.30 Sun ☎ (023) 9248 3464
🌐 old-house-at-home-havant.co.uk
Fuller's London Pride; Gales Seafarers Ale, HSB; guest beers [H]
Formerly five cottages, this is one of only two buildings to survive the great fire of Havant. Beams

recovered from the Spanish Armada were used in the construction, although the date inscribed in the front is about 200 years too early. The pub is reputed to have exhibited the last dancing bear in England. Behind the building is a large hidden garden and the lounge has the remains of an old bakery oven, indicating another of its former uses.

Robin Hood

6 Homewell, PO9 1EE

11-11; 12-10.30 Sun (023) 9248 2779

Fuller's London Pride, seasonal beer; Gales Seafarers Ale, HSB

Originally this pub was more like someone's front room and had no keg beer; it has since expanded considerably. The bar is divided into two areas: the front has bare flagstones and the rear is carpeted, with comfortable seating. At the back is a small garden and smoking area. The low beams, open fireplaces and cosy interior add to the appeal of this hidden gem in the centre of town.

Herriard

Fur & Feathers

Back Lane, RG25 2PN (on old Basingstoke-Alton road, parallel to A339)

closed Mon; 12-3, 5-11; 12-11 Fri & Sat; 12-6 Sun

(01256) 384170 franskitchen.co.uk

Sharp's Doom Bar; guest beers

Victorian ale house built for local farmworkers in 1880, now open plan with a central bar area. The two guest beers are often from local breweries including Hogs Back, Flack Manor and Andwell. The two dining areas either side of the bar area provide a pleasant atmosphere in which to enjoy the mouthwatering menu. Q P (13)

Hill Head

Crofton

48 Crofton Lane, PO14 3QF

11-11; 12-10.30 Sun (01329) 314222

thecrofton.co.uk

Oakleaf Hole Hearted; Sharp's Doom Bar; guest beers

This 1960s estate pub is one of the more successful Punch Taverns outlets, and the premises were extended in 2012. Six real ales are normally on handpump, including beers from SIBA breweries and interesting brews from the Punch portfolio. The function room with skittle alley is popular and gets booked up well in advance. A beer festival takes place in November. The home-cooked food is served all day Friday to Sunday.

Q P (21)

Holybourne

Queen's Head

London Road, GU34 4EG

12-11 (12.30am Fri & Sat); 12-10.30 Sun (01420) 86331

queensheadalton.co.uk

Greene King IPA; Hardys & Hansons Bitter; guest beers

Traditional, friendly pub offering an interesting selection of local and guest ales. The Queen's comprises three refurbished rooms plus a covered and heated smoking area. Home-made hearty food is served daily featuring the pub's famous pies. There is regular live music throughout the year, with the charity music and beer event, Altonbury, on the first Saturday in July. An extensive beer garden features a children's play area and dogs are permitted on a short lead. Happy hour is Monday-Friday 4.30-6.30pm. Q P (65)

Hook

Hogget

London Road, RG27 9JJ (M3 jct 5, A30 just S of Hook)

12-3, 5.30-11; 12-11 Fri & Sat; 12-10.30 Sun

(01256) 763009 hogget.co.uk

Ringwood Best Bitter; guest beers

Situated on the junction of the A30 and A287 just to the south west of Hook, this recently refurbished pub offers a good choice of home-cooked dining options. There is a small bar area usually offering a range of three real ales, one of which will be a guest ale. Ample car parking is at the rear and there is a covered patio at the front. P (30)

White Hart Hotel

London Road, RG27 9DZ (5 mins from M3 jct 5, next to Hook Texaco garage)

11-11; 12-10.30 Sun (01256) 762462

Sharp's Doom Bar; guest beers

You will always get a warm welcome at the White Hart, a 16th-century coaching inn. Recently refurbished, it has a spacious bar area, oak beams and some nooks where you can sit. The bar area is busy and has softly piped music and TVs showing sport; the opposite end is much quieter and ideal for enjoying a meal. There is an extensive beer garden to the side and a large car park behind.

P (30)

Hook Common

Crooked Billet

RG27 9EH

11.30-3, 6-midnight; 11.30-midnight Sat; 12-11 Sun

(01256) 762118 thecrookedbilletpub.co.uk

Courage Best Bitter; guest beers

The Crooked Billet is on the London Road just outside Hook and has been a free house under the same ownership for 28 years. In the summer you can enjoy the pleasant riverside garden or the air-conditioned bars, restaurant or snug. In winter, warm up around one of the traditional log fires. Good food and ales are always available here. An annual beer and rock music festival is held over the August bank holiday weekend. Q P

Hythe

Ebenezers

18A Pylewell Road, SO45 6AR (a few yards SW of the pier)

11-2.30, 5.30-11; 11-11.30 Fri & Sat; 12-11 Sun

(023) 8020 7799

Flack Manor Double Drop; Greene King Abbot; guest beer

This delightful little pub, built in 1845 as a Baptist chapel, has also been a school, a store for flour and furniture, and now serves some of the best local ales in the area. The open-plan bar is modern, but with a traditional feel that attracts seekers of conversation. Home-made pub food is available lunchtimes and evenings. Outside is a large covered smoking area. Nearby is the world's oldest pier railway, connecting with the Southampton ferry. Q

Little London

Plough Inn

Silchester Road, RG26 5EP
12-3, 5.30 (6 Sat)-11; 12-3, 7-10.30 Sun
☎ (01256) 850628
Palmers Dorset Gold; Ringwood Best Bitter; guest beers G
Wonderful village pub and recent CAMRA Regional Pub of the Year, where in winter you can enjoy a glass of beer in front of one of the log fires or play a game of bar billiards. A good range of baguettes is available (no food Sun eve). There is a secluded garden at the side of the pub. It is ideal for ramblers and cyclists visiting Pamber Wood or the extensive Roman ruins at nearby Silchester.
Q❀♣P(14)

Long Sutton

Four Horseshoes

The Street, RG29 1TA (follow brown signs from B3349 Odiham to Alton Rd) SU748470
12-3 (not Mon & Tue), 6.30-11; 12-5 Sun
☎ (01256) 862488 fourhorseshoes.com
Beer range varies H
Set in the rolling open countryside of the Hampshire Downs between Long Sutton village and the hamlet of Well. The single bar is spacious yet cosy, with two real fires. Horse brasses, a few old farm implements and pictures of old Odiham decorate the walls. Two low-strength beers tend to come from small breweries across southern England and the Midlands. Food is home-cooked English fare, with a popular roast on Sundays.
Q❀ÅP

Lower Farringdon

Golden Pheasant L

Fareham Road, GU34 3DJ (at Farringdon crossroads on A32)
12-11 (10.30 Sun) ☎ (01420) 588255
Courage Best Bitter; Hancock's HB; Hogs Back TEA; guest beers H
A free house serving up to five cask ales, often including one from the Flowerpots brewery. The Hancock's HB is badged as Pheasant Ale. Mine host is renowned in the local area for his excellent food, locally sourced, which includes diabetic ice cream. Candlelit dining to piano accompaniment is available every third Friday (booking required). Fresh fish is on offer daily. The first Sunday in the month is curry club (from Odiham Spice) after 6.30pm. It has a large bar area, a separate dining room, and ample parking. Q❀♣P

Lower Upham

Woodman Inn

Winchester Road, SO32 1HA (on B2177, 200yds E of B3037)
12-3, 7.15-11; 12-3, 5.15-midnight Fri; 12-6.45, 7.45-11.30 Sat; 12-6.45, 7.45-10.30 Sun ☎ (01489) 860270
Beer range varies H
Run by members of the same family for five decades, the Woodman offers a changing selection of two real ales (three at weekends), with the emphasis on local independent breweries. The otherwise contrasting bars share a liking for beams, Toby (and other) jugs and hunting scenes; the public has a woodburner, the lounge an open fireplace. Fans of the Water of Life may choose from over 180 whiskies. Live music (blues) is hosted on the first Wednesday of the month.
Q❀♣P(69)

Lower Wield

Yew Tree L

SO24 9RX SU636398
closed Mon; 12-3, 6-11; 12-10.30 Sun ☎ (01256) 389224
the-yewtree.org.uk
Triple fff Alton's Pride; guest beer H
Out-of-the-way rural local set in picturesque rolling Hampshire countryside, with an old yew tree growing outside (hence the name), situated on a quiet lane opposite the local cricket pitch. The house beer is Triple fff Alton's Pride and the guest usually comes from a local brewery. All real ales are sold at reasonable prices. The pub has a separate dining area where locally renowned, good-value food is served. The nearest bus stop is Medstead 1½ miles away. Q❀P

Lymington

Borough Arms

39 Avenue Road, SO41 9GP (on B3054, N edge of town centre)
4-11 Mon; 5-10.30; 12-2, 4-11 Thu; 12-midnight Fri & Sat; 12-10.30 Sun ☎ (01590) 672814
Ringwood Best Bitter, Fortyniner; guest beers H
Friendly local with a loyal clientele of all ages, close to the town centre, St Barbe Museum, the town hall and the community centre, with ample parking. It has a carpeted and separate seating area away from the bar, a jukebox, a pool table and occasional TV. Attractive features include stained glass windows, a large mirror and fireplace. Forthcoming guest ales, ciders and brewers are shown on a blackboard above the bar. Check opening hours before travelling as it closes lunchtimes early in the week.
Q❀(Town)♣P

Mattingley

Leather Bottle L

Reading Road, RG27 8JU
11.30-11 (10.30 Sun) ☎ (0118) 932 6371
leatherbottle.hcpr.co.uk
Beer range varies H
The Leather Bottle is a classic village inn dating back to the 18th century, with a beautiful old tiled roof sheltering mellow Hampshire brick. Queen Anne had just died when the pub opened to serve local people and travellers on the road from Reading to Southampton. Inside you will find comfortable, relaxed surroundings and a warm, friendly atmosphere – a great place to meet for a chat over a pint or two, a quick lunchtime bite to eat, or a good dinner with friends and family.
Q❀♿P

Milford on Sea

Red Lion

32 High Street, SO41 0QD
11.30-2.30, 5.30-11; 11-11 Fri & Sat; 12-10.30 (6 winter) Sun ☎ (01590) 642236 theredlionmilford.co.uk
Ringwood Best Bitter; guest beer H
Spacious extended former coaching inn on split levels with much natural light, catering for local

and visiting trade. Open plan, it has a large central fireplace for winter warmth, a separate area for pool and darts, and a large garden for families. Close to the Danestream riverside path, it is 700 yards from the beach and bracing cliff-top walks. Guest ales, independently sourced, increase to two in summer and busy periods, and real cider is always available.
Q⛵❀⛟◑♿⛺♣●P🚌(X1)🐾📶

North Camp

Squirrel 𝕃

125 Park Road, GU14 6LR (½ mile N off A3011 jct with A331)
⏲ 11.30-11.30 (12.30am Thu-Sat) ☎ (01252) 523980
🌐 thesquirrelfarnborough.co.uk
Fuller's London Pride; Greene King IPA; Sharp's Doom Bar; guest beers Ⓗ
Recently refurbished pub in a quiet residential area offering spacious and comfortable areas for drinkers and diners alike. A welcoming community local, there is something here for everyone, with good-value food, a popular weekly quiz and a changing ale selection. Competition for the five handpumps is keen and the regular beers are often outnumbered by guests from the likes of Hogs Back, Hammerpot and Dorset Brewing, to name a few. There is a large patio and beer garden.
❀◑♿P🚌(41)📶

North Waltham

Fox 𝕃

Popham Lane, RG25 2BE (off Frog Lane, between village and A30, M3 jct 7)
⏲ 11-11 (midnight Fri & Sat); 12-10.30 Sun
☎ (01256) 397288 🌐 thefox.org
Brakspear Bitter; Sharp's Doom Bar; West Berkshire Good Old Boy; guest beer Ⓗ
A lovely country pub, overlooking farmland. The place is divided into two – a popular restaurant, and a public bar where food is also served (booking advisable). Outside there is an extensive beer garden and a children's adventure play area. Once a year the pub holds a charity oyster festival, with a beer tent and many other stalls and attractions. The original Ushers signage remains on the rear of the pub. Q⛵❀◑♿P🐾

North Warnborough

Anchor Inn

The Street, RG29 1BE
⏲ 5 (5.30 Mon)-11; 12-4, 7-10.30 Sun ☎ (01256) 702740
Courage Best Bitter; guest beer Ⓗ
Traditional local family pub owned by Enterprise Inns. There are two separate bars, saloon and public. There is a large beer garden with plenty of parking to the rear. It is worth checking opening times as the pub is usually closed on weekday lunchtimes. The food is reasonably priced and there is a real fire during the winter months.
Q⛵❀◑⛺♣P🚌(30)🐾📶

Oakley

Barley Mow 𝕃

19 Oakley Lane, RG23 7JZ
⏲ 12-11 ☎ (01256) 782591
Sharp's Doom Bar; guest beers Ⓗ
The Barley Mow, a traditional English pub, is situated in the pleasant village of Oakley. There is a quiz each Tuesday night and a music quiz on the first Saturday of each month. Beers from SIBA and Punch Finest Cask are available as guests.
Q⛵❀P🚌(8)🐾📶

Odiham

Odiham & Greywell Cricket Club 𝕃

King Street, RG29 1NF (approx ¾ miles along King Street from village centre) SU751462
⏲ 5-9 (10 Fri); 2-9 Sat; 1-8 Sun ☎ (01256) 703749
Andwell Gold Muddler, King John; guest beer Ⓗ
The first recorded match at this club was in 1764, making it one of the oldest cricket clubs in the country. Set in countryside just south of the village, the timber building closed in 2011 following a fire, and the new well-appointed replacement opened in 2013 with a single modern lounge bar. It has three handpumps, normally serving two Andwell beers and a guest. Although a private members' club, CAMRA members and visitors are welcome. Check for seasonal opening times. ⛵❀♿P🐾📶

Overton

Red Lion 𝕃

37 High Street, RG25 3HQ
⏲ 11.30-3, 6-11 (midnight Fri & Sat); 12-10.30 Sun
☎ (01256) 773363 🌐 redlion-overton.co.uk
Flowerpots Bitter; Sharp's Doom Bar; guest beer Ⓗ
Close to the village centre, the Red Lion styles itself as a gastro-pub, with a good reputation for high-quality, freshly cooked food and well-kept local ales at reasonable prices. Three smartly decorated areas include a restaurant, main bar and snug with upholstered bench settees. There is a car park at the rear and a partially covered patio area. A function room/skittle alley is available for private parties. Q❀◑P🚌(76,86)📶

Park Gate

Village Inn

67 Botley Road, SO31 1AZ
⏲ 11.30-11 (midnight Fri & Sat) ☎ (01489) 573223
Ringwood Best Bitter; Sharp's Doom Bar; Wadworth 6X; guest beers Ⓗ
The Village Inn was for many years keg only, but then reopened as a gastro-pub with a good selection of real ales. Although the beer range is limited to the Ember Inns portfolio, the three guest beers are normally of varying styles from interesting breweries, and tasting notes are available. Food is served all day until 10pm. Occasional live music takes place on Saturday evenings. Q❀◑⇌(Swanwick)●P🚌

Picket Piece

Wyke Down

SP11 6LX
⏲ 11-2.30, 6 (5 Fri)-11; 12-2.30, 5-11 Sat; 12-3.30, 6-10.30 Sun ☎ (01264) 352048 🌐 wykedown.co.uk
Fuller's London Pride; guest beers Ⓗ
A family-run pub and restaurant in a 19th-century barn overlooking its own spacious campsite and the scenic north Hampshire countryside. The main bar is adorned with farming implements and signs from its early era, while there is an ample conservatory. Outside is a small swimming pool

and the pub runs a 300-yard golf driving range and a small farm. Special events are often arranged including a Vehicle Meet. ♘❀◐▲♣P

Portsmouth

Apsley House

Auckland Road West, Southsea, PO5 3NY

🕐 3-11.30 (12.30am Fri & Sat); 12-11.30 Sun

☎ (023) 9282 1294

Hop Back Summer Lightning; guest beers 🄷

Back-street pub just off Southsea sea front with one big bar catering for a varying clientele and which can be busy at weekends. A patio drinking area outside the front of the pub is popular in the summer months. The pub has darts and pool and three real ales. ♣🚌🐾📶

Artillery Arms 🄻

Hester Road, Milton, PO4 8HB

🕐 12-11.30 (midnight Fri & Sat); 12-11 Sun

☎ (023) 9273 3610

Bowman Swift One; Ringwood Fortyniner; guest beers 🄷

Traditional split-level locals' pub serving both local ales and several from further afield. It has a large garden with lots of play equipment for children. Supporting both darts and pool teams, several other traditional pub games are played. Only five minutes' walk from Fratton Park, it can get busy on match days, but is welcoming to away supporters. ❀◐♣P🚌🐾

Barley Mow

39 Castle Road, Southsea, PO5 3DE

🕐 12 (11 Sat)-midnight; 12-11 Sun ☎ (023) 9282 3492

🌐 barleymowsouthsea.co.uk

Fuller's London Pride; Gales HSB; guest beers 🄷

Friendly two bar community pub that offers a selection of seven ales including a mild, stout or porter. There is an impressive array of events including live music, meat raffles, quizzes, pool, darts, and golf teams, bar billiards, chess league, and monthly druid moots, all listed on the pub's website. The garden is a real gem, with some hidden treasures, and has won awards in its own right. Children are welcome until 8pm. ❀♣🍎🚌🐾📶

Bridge Tavern

54 East Street, Old Portsmouth, PO1 2JJ

🕐 11-11; 12-10.30 Sun ☎ (023) 9275 2992

🌐 bridge-tavern-portsmouth.co.uk

Fuller's London Pride; Gales Seafarers Ale, HSB; guest beers 🄷

Situated in the heart of the Camber Docks, this is the only surviving pub in East Street. Surrounded by fishing boats, it is not surprising that fish features heavily on the menu. The single downstairs bar is welcoming and divided into several areas. Outside seating provides a pleasant spot to enjoy the sea air and the bustle of a small fishing port. ♘❀◐P🚌(16,19)📶

Golden Eagle

1 Delamere Road, Southsea, PO4 0JA

🕐 3-midnight (1am Fri); 12-1am Sat; 12-11 Sun

☎ (023) 9282 1658 🌐 goldeneaglesouthsea.co.uk

Fuller's London Pride; Gales Seafarers Ale, HSB; guest beers 🄷

A surprisingly large two-bar street-corner local, this pub is a popular music venue with live entertainment at weekends. The small garden has its own TV for watching sporting events on warm summer days. The bars are somewhat unusual in that the public bar is carpeted and the lounge has bare boards and a pool table. ❀⇌(Fratton)♣🚌📶

Hole in the Wall 🏆

Great Southsea Street, Southsea, PO5 3BY

🕐 4-11; 12-midnight Fri; 4-midnight Sat; 2-11 Sun

☎ (023) 9229 8085 🌐 theholeinthewallpub.co.uk

Oakleaf Hole Hearted 🄶**; guest beers** 🄷

The Hole is one of the smallest pubs in Portsmouth but, a genuine free house, it offers a wide range of beers from a changing selection of microbreweries (check website for current beer range). Oakleaf Hole Hearted, originally brewed for this pub, is on gravity. Real ciders are always available. Food, in the form of quality sausages and suet puddings, is available 5-8pm Tuesdays-Saturdays, also 12-2pm Fridays. It opens Saturdays 12-2pm for Pompey home games. No admittance after 11pm. Local CAMRA branch Pub of the Year 2014. Q◗🍎🚇🚌(7,15)📶

Lawrence Arms

63 Lawrence Road, Southsea, PO5 1NU

🕐 2-11.30 (12.30am Fri); 11-12.30am Sat; 11-11 Sun

☎ (023) 9282 1280 🌐 lawrence-arms-portsmouth.co.uk

Sharp's Doom Bar; guest beers 🄷

Dating back to 1887, this street-corner pub's exterior retains some traditional tiles and lanterns. Inside, the L-shaped bar faces a large lounge area. Very much a friendly community pub, there are darts, pool and football teams, weekly meat raffles, quizzes and themed days. Guest ales are Irving seasonals, another local beer plus one other. It has a good cider selection too, with Westons plus boxed and bottled ciders, with as many as 20 in the summer. Food includes tasty gourmet toasties. ♘❀⇌(Fratton)♣🍎🚌

Leopold Tavern 🄻

154 Albert Road, Southsea, PO4 0JT

🕐 10-11 (midnight Fri & Sat); 12-11 Sun ☎ (023) 9282 9748

Beer range varies 🄷

A former Portsmouth & Brighton United Breweries pub with a green tiled exterior, it now has a single bar and a light, airy interior. With 10 handpumps, over 100 bottled beers from around the world, and several ciders and perries on offer, this pub is well worth a visit no matter what your drinking taste. A popular quiz is held on Monday evenings and the small patio garden is overlooked by the pub's own Tardis. ❀🍎🚌📶

Nell Gwynne 🄻

70 Jessie Road, Southsea, PO4 0EN

🕐 2 (12 Mon)-11; 12-midnight Fri & Sat; 12-11 Sun

☎ (023) 9283 2751

Beer range varies 🄷

Saved from years of being a keg pub, it now sells a range of four to six ales from near and far but always has at least one LocAle beer on handpump. A former local CAMRA Cider Pub of the Year, up to 25 ciders are also available. It can get quite noisy on music nights but has a friendly atmosphere. ⇌(Fratton)🍎🚌(15,18)🐾

Northcote Hotel 🄻

35 Francis Avenue, Southsea, PO4 0HL

🕐 11-midnight (1am Fri & Sat); 12-midnight Sun

☎ (023) 9282 8852 🌐 northcotehotel.co.uk

Hop Back Summer Lightning; Irving Invincible; Timothy Taylor Landlord; Wadworth 6X 🄷

A large back-street local with two bars and a sizeable heated patio garden. The lounge bar is decorated with film memorabilia going back to the comedians of the silent era and the most famous of all fictional detectives, Sherlock Holmes. The bar back is somewhat unusual, having glass instead of mirrors, allowing you to watch a game of darts in the public bar from the comfort of the lounge.

Old Customs House

Gunwharf Quays, PO1 3TY

9am-midnight (10.30 winter; 2am Fri & Sat); 12-midnight Sun (023) 9283 2333 theoldcustomshouse.com

Fuller's London Pride, ESB, seasonal beer; Gales Seafarers Ale, HSB H

Proclaiming itself the only traditional pub in the Gunwharf Quays retail complex, this Grade II-listed building retains the layout of the former naval offices of HMS Vernon. There is a heated rear patio area, and seating at the front which is ideal for people-watching during the summer. As well as offering seasonal ales, the pub hosts a couple of beer festivals, including a regular Easter event, and a number of the food dishes include local ales in their recipes. (Harbour)

Old House at Home

104 Locksway Road, Milton, PO4 8JR

12-11.30 (1am Fri & Sat) (023) 9273 2606

Beer range varies H

Large two-bar community pub with a varied range of three beers during the week and up to six at weekends. It is active in the community, with pool and darts teams and an annual Easter beer and music festival (and planning a winter one), plus family events in its large enclosed garden. Cider is an important aspect, with 40 available year round, including perries – this is recognised by being a previous local CAMRA Cider Pub of the Year.
P

Pembroke

20 Pembroke Road, Old Portsmouth, PO1 2NR

10-midnight (1am Fri & Sat); 12-4, 7-11 Sun
(023) 9282 3961

Draught Bass; Fuller's London Pride; Greene King Abbot H

Dating back to 1711, and under this name since 1900, this single-room venue reflects the street-corner aspect with an L-shaped bar decorated with naval memorabilia. A rare place to find a good pint of Bass makes it worth seeking out, just a short distance from the cathedral. It is home to a darts team and hosts live music at weekends and occasionally during the week.

Phoenix L

13 Duncan Road, Southsea, PO5 2QU

10-midnight (1am Fri & Sat); 12-midnight Sun
(023) 9282 1189

Beer range varies H

This hidden gem is a popular two-bar community local just off Albert Road. The public bar has memorabilia relating to Portsmouth FC and often hosts live music. The lounge is adorned with photos of many of the celebrities who have appeared at the nearby Kings Theatre (including three Goons). There is also a quirky patio garden which separates the bars from the games room, which is itself part of the former Dock End brewery. The house beer is by Tetley.

Rose in June L

102 Milton Road, Milton, PO3 6AR

12-midnight (1am Fri & Sat) (023) 9282 4191
theroseinjune.co.uk

Gales HSB; Irving Frigate; Ringwood Best Bitter; Thwaites Lancaster Bomber; guest beer H

About 10 minutes' walk from Fratton Park, this two-bar pub is popular with football fans. It hosts plenty of events such as a quiz on Thursday, occasional comedy nights and a curry night on the first Wednesday of the month. It is home to pool and darts teams. The extensive garden has a play area and is made use of for barbecues and a popular summer beer festival. Ciders include Cheddar Valley, Old Rosie and Black Rat, plus a perry and a regular mild.

Sir John Baker L

80 London Road, North End, PO2 0LN

7am-11 (11.30 Thu; 12.30am Fri & Sat)
(023) 9262 7960

Courage Directors; Greene King Abbot; Ruddles Best Bitter H

In a busy high street and named after a local dignitary, this Wetherspoon pub has a large single bar with a family area at the rear (children welcome until 9.30pm). There are five guest handpumps, usually offering beer from microbreweries in Hampshire, West Sussex and the Isle of Wight, plus an occasional American craft beer. Local breweries are showcased monthly. Meals are served until 11pm. At least three real ciders are available from Gwynt Y Ddraig and Westons. Well served by buses. Q

Sir Loin of Beef

152 Highland Road, Eastney, PO4 9NH

11-11.30 (midnight Fri & Sat); 12-11.30 Sun
(023) 9282 0115

Beer range varies H

Large single-bar pub with an almost Mediterranean café feel. The walls are decorated with submarine paraphernalia and a klaxon is used to call time. A good selection of bottle-conditioned ales is stocked to supplement the eight fine ales on draught. The pub hosts live entertainment on Sunday lunchtimes and the ever-popular meat raffle.

White Swan L

26 Guildhall Walk, Landport, PO1 2DD

10-11 (023) 9289 1340

Beer range varies H

Distinctive from the outside with its Tudor timber-framed Grade II-listed façade and hanging baskets, you enter to the sight of gleaming copper and, possibly, brewing aromas; this pub brews its own beer in a 2.5 barrel plant. The regular beer, Mucky Duck, harks back to previous incarnations of the pub. There are usually six of its own beers plus guests and many bottles. You can meet the brewer every Wednesday (there are other monthly brewing events). Food is locally sourced and tasty. (Southsea)

Winchester Arms L

99 Winchester Road, Buckland, PO2 7PS

3 (4 Mon)-11; 12-11 Sat & Sun (023) 9266 2443

Oakleaf Hole Hearted; Robinsons Trooper; guest beer H

The Winch is a proper back-street local, offering two regular beers and a varying guest. Every third Sunday evening of the month is open mic night with music and comedy, and there is live music on the other Sundays. A beer festival is held over the spring bank holiday weekend. The garden has a covered smoking shelter. It may stay open until midnight Friday/Saturday if busy. Dogs are welcome, but beware the cat. Ciders are available during the summer.

Ringwood

Inn on the Furlong

12 Meeting House Lane, BH24 1EY

9.30am-11 (midnight Fri & Sat); 10-11 Sun

(01425) 475139

Marston's Old Empire; Ringwood Best Bitter, Boondoggle, Fortyniner; guest beer [H]

An efficiently run pub, enviably located between the bus station and town centre. Good breakfasts feature, lunch is available until 3pm or later, and Wednesday to Friday evenings have themed food (curries, fine dining and tapas respectively) in addition to a standard menu. The raised bar serves several cosy interlinked rooms, including a family area and conservatory. There are several patios, including one with weatherproofed TV. There is also a games room reserved for members of the pub's games club.

Railway Hotel

35 Hightown Road, BH24 1NQ SU152048

11.30-11; 12-10 Sun (01425) 473701

ringwoodrailway.com

Beer range varies [H]

Traditional two-bar pub with a small rear snug, leading to an enclosed beer garden. Its name recalls the now demolished railway station, which succumbed to Beeching in 1964. The décor features photographs, maps and posters of the railway plus a tribute to Peter Austin, microbrewing pioneer and founder of close-by Ringwood Brewery. Reasonably priced home-cooked food is available all day. The three beers, from the Admiral list, usually include one LocAle. Castleman's Corkscrew Trailway, nearby, follows the disused railway line. Q P (175,B)

Rockbourne

Rose & Thistle

SP6 3NL

11-3, 6-10.30; 11-11 Sat; 12-8 Sun (01725) 518236

roseandthistle.co.uk

Butcombe Gold; Ringwood Best Bitter; Sharp's Doom Bar; guest beer [H]

Delightful 16th-century thatched building in a pretty village with a Roman villa and a part-Norman church. Originally three cottages, it became a pub in the 1890s after serving as a bakery which branched out into liquor retailing. It was saved from closure in the 1990s by a local consortium which later sold it to a private owner. It has fully functioning fireplaces in both the rustic bar and cosy restaurant. Food includes local game and fish, and home-made desserts (no food Sun eve). P

Romsey

Bishops Blaize

4 Winchester Road, SO51 8AA

12-11 (midnight Fri & Sat); 12-10.30 Sun

(01794) 511777

Beer range varies [G]

This modest, welcoming, family-run local is on the main bus route east of Romsey centre. A long single bar has a woodburner at one end and a large TV at the other; this plus another TV in the smart patio garden show a lot of sport. There are crib and darts teams, and live music every Saturday and summer Sundays. The constantly varying beers are always a good reason to visit, with all beers and ciders served by gravity. P

Old House at Home

62 Love Lane, SO51 8DE (NE of town centre, adjoining Waitrose car park)

11-11 (11.30 Fri & Sat); 12-10.30 Sun (01794) 513175

theoldhouseathomeromsey.co.uk

Fuller's London Pride; Gales Seafarers Ale, HSB; guest beer [H]

The welcoming and efficient OHAH, a former Fuller's Pub of the Year and three times Best Town Local, is timber framed and part thatched. Its beamed interior comprises three discrete areas: a comfortable bar with booths, a cosy restaurant, separated from the bar by a brick and wood-beamed fireplace, and a bar-cum-dining-area with banquettes. The heated patio leads to a gravelled and planted garden. Food is excellent, and snacks are available noon-6pm. Live folk/acoustic music plays on Mondays. No under-18s after 9pm. P

Romsey Beer Emporium

15 Bell Street, SO51 8GY

closed Mon; 10-6; 11-3 Sun (01794) 517764

romseybeeremporium.co.uk

Beer range varies [G]

This off-licence opened in 2011 and is going from strength to strength. Real ale is dispensed from casks to take away, with local beers featuring frequently, alongside a fine range of bottle-conditioned ales from across the UK. Continental and North American beers, plus ciders and perries, can also be found here. A selection of home-brew supplies, glasses, books and T-shirts is available.

Shedfield

Wheatsheaf Inn

Botley Road, SO32 2JG (on A334)

12-11 (10.30 Sun) (01329) 833024

Flowerpots Perridge Pale, Bitter, Goodens Gold; guest beers [G]

Popular, award-winning pub with a lively public bar, warmed by a wood-burning stove in winter. The home-cooked food is excellent (available every lunchtime, but only Tue and Wed eves). Beers are served on gravity and come mainly from the Flowerpots brewery; there is also at least one real cider from Thatchers. Blues, jazz or folk music is played live most Saturday evenings, and a beer festival is held over the late spring bank holiday weekend. The garden's flowers are delightful in summer. Q P (69)

Southampton

Bitter Virtue

70 Cambridge Road, SO14 6US (jct with Alma Road)

closed Mon; 10.30-8.30 (2 Sun) (023) 8055 4881

bittervirtue.co.uk

Beer range varies [G]

A corner shop-style off-licence run by a pair of long-standing ale enthusiasts. The shop is stocked with a constantly updated range of more than 500 bottled beers from around the globe, breweries from the UK, Belgium and the US being particularly well represented. A four-cask stillage usually has at least two ales available for take-out. Some real ciders are stocked in bottle and cask. A varied selection of breweriana is also sold.

Giddy Bridge

10-16A London Road, SO15 2AE

8am-11.30 ☎ (023) 8033 6346

Greene King Abbot; Ruddles County; guest beers H

Wetherspoon pub on the edge of the city centre, previously a furniture shop. It has a large single bar on the ground floor with additional seating upstairs and an unusual secluded roof terrace for when it is sunny. Covered tables and chairs are outside on the pavement. Food is served all day, alcohol from 9am. The large range of guest beers often includes those from local breweries, and there are usually two draught ciders. Close to Southampton Solent University. Q

Guide Dog

38 Earl's Road, SO14 6SF

12-11 (10.30 Sun) ☎ (023) 8022 5642

theguidedogsouthampton.co.uk

Flowerpots Goodens Gold; Fuller's ESB; guest beers H

This single-room back-street pub is regularly voted local CAMRA Pub of the Year and is a mecca for real ale fans. Up to seven guest beers, often local, are available in thirds, halves, two-thirds, pints and half-gallons, all clearly listed on an enormous price list. Good-value rolls are sold for lunch (no food Sun). Close enough to St Mary's Stadium, it welcomes visiting fans, if you can squeeze in. Other attractions include the Friday meat draw and dog-related charity events.

Hop Inn

Woodmill Lane, SO18 2PH

12 (11 Sat)-11; 12-10.30 Sun ☎ (023) 8055 7723

Bowman Swift One; Gales HSB; Sharp's Doom Bar H

The unassuming Hop Inn could be easily overlooked, but step inside the lounge bar and it instantly feels like home. A long L-shaped bar sits one side with seating on the other. The public bar is reached through a separate entrance and houses bar games and a jukebox. A quiz is held on the first Sunday of the month; competitors receive complimentary cheese and biscuits. Although food is not regularly served, Wednesday night is supper night. P

Junction Inn

21 Priory Road, SO17 2JZ

12-11 (midnight Fri & Sat) ☎ (023) 8058 4486

thejunction-inn.co.uk

Greene King XX Mild, IPA, Abbot; guest beers H

One of only a handful of Greene King Local Hero pubs in this area, this popular community local offers a good range of beers including the rarely seen XX Mild. It serves freshly cooked traditional meals including Sunday roast lunches and dishes from a specials board. Live music takes place once a month, a quiz every Friday, and ukulele jam sessions on Wednesday evenings. It has three darts and two crib teams, and a bar billiards table. Saints' St Mary's Stadium is a 15-minute walk along the Itchen Boardwalk.

≹(St Denys) (16,7)

Obelisk Hotel

108 Obelisk Road, SO19 9DP (jct with Bedford Avenue)

12-11 (midnight Fri & Sat) ☎ (023) 8044 4271

obeliskhotel.co.uk

Draught Bass; Ringwood Best Bitter; Sharp's Doom Bar; guest beers H

Large two-bar street-corner pub that has seen impressive changes to the beer quality and choice. Regular entertainment is hosted, from quizzes on Tuesday nights to karaoke on Sunday nights. All Premier League Saints home and away games are shown live on big screens, and live music is usually a feature on Friday nights. A large function room is available for events and meetings.

≹(Woolston)P

Park Inn

37 Carlisle Road, SO16 4FN (frontage in Shirley Park Road)

12-11.30 (midnight Fri & Sat) ☎ (023) 8078 7835

theparkinnshirley.co.uk

Wadworth Henry's IPA, 6X, Old Timer, seasonal beer H

Classic Victorian street-corner local. Parking is very difficult, especially during the working day. A single-bar pub, it retains two entrances and its two-bar feeling; many brewery themed mirrors adorn the walls. Six handpumps serve the Wadworth range, including seasonal and guest beers. A paved area with seating caters for outside drinkers/smokers. Sundays are busy, with a lunchtime meat draw and a popular evening quiz. There are two annual beer festivals.

Q

Platform Tavern

Town Quay, SO14 2NY

12-11 (midnight Thu-Sat) ☎ (023) 8033 7232

platformtavern.com

Fuller's London Pride; Gales Seafarers Ale; guest beers H

This is the home of the Dancing Man microbrewery, which provides up to three of the five beers on handpump. Interior decoration is an eclectic mix of African and cosy pub, with masks and relics alongside fireside leather sofas. Part of the old town wall is exposed in the bar. Food is of high quality and good value. Live music features on Thursday and Friday evenings and Sunday lunchtimes. Pavement tables allow outside drinking given the right weather. Beer festivals are frequently arranged.

Rockstone

63 Onslow Road, SO14 0JL

11-midnight (1am Fri & Sat) ☎ (023) 8063 7256

therockstone.co.uk

Beer range varies H

A busy, lively free house run by Max and his team. Up to eight guest beers, mainly from the region, are served alongside real ciders and a vast selection of rums, whiskies, gins and bourbons. Beer and cider festivals in March and October are complemented by themed nights throughout the week. Open mic night is Monday. Voted one of the Top 21 Burger Venues of the UK, the extensive menu features a film theme throughout and offers huge portions.

South Western Arms

38-40 Adelaide Road, SO17 2HW

12-11 (midnight Fri & Sat) ☎ (023) 8032 4542

southwesternarms.com

Beer range varies Ⓗ
Corner pub with a single bar and a raised seating area on the ground floor; more seating, pool and football tables are in the gallery upstairs. At the rear is a walled garden with covered smoking area which is an oasis in the summer. It is so close to St Denys station that the garden is almost on the platform. Mini beer festivals are held each year. There are normally nine real ales and up to 20 foreign bottled beers available.
Q🐴❀⇌(St Denys)**♣●P🚌**(16,7)**🐾📶**

Talking Heads

320 Portswood Road, SO17 2TD
⏲ 6-2am; 5-3am Fri; 2-3am Sat; 2-2am Sun
☎ (023) 8067 8446 🌐 thetalkingheads.co.uk
Longdog Lamplight Porter; Triple fff Alton's Pride; Upham Punter; guest beers Ⓗ
A highly successful pub and music/comedy establishment near Southampton University. The front bar has interesting antique armchairs and original windows. It is a popular meeting place for university clubs, and bikers meet on Monday nights. It doesn't do food but the Frying Druid food van can be found in the back car park most nights to cater for empty stomachs. Womble, the van's owner, is himself a qualified preaching druid. A full monthly list of gigs is a testament to the Talking Heads' popularity. **🐴❀♣P🚌🐾📶**

Waterloo Arms

101 Waterloo Road, SO15 3BS
⏲ 12-11 (midnight Fri & Sat) ☎ (023) 8022 0022
Downton IPA; Hop Back Golden Best, Crop Circle, Entire Stout, Summer Lightning; guest beer Ⓗ
Erected in the 1930s, this pub became Hop Back's second house in 1991. It has a single L-shaped bar with a rear conservatory and paved garden with seating. Eight handpumps serve the Hop Back range, plus seasonal and guest beers. Families are welcome up to 8pm in the conservatory. Lunchtime and evening meals are served daily (no food Wed) and Sunday roasts are popular. Tuesday is quiz night and Friday evening has a meat draw. Old Rosie cider is served. Regular beer festivals take place. **❀◐◑⇌**(Millbrook)**♣●🚌🐾📶**

Wellington Arms Ⓛ

56 Park Road, SO15 3DE (on corner of Park Road and Mansion Road)
⏲ 12-11.30 (12.30am Fri & Sat) ☎ (023) 8022 0356
🌐 wellingtonarmssouthampton.co.uk
Fuller's London Pride, ESB; guest beers Ⓗ
Truly a unique pub, it is Redonda's only consulate. Situated in a residential area, the dimly lit, two-bar pub contains plenty of Iron Duke memorabilia. Eleven handpumps dispense many local brews as well as those from further afield. The public bar has a bartop embedded with old coins, polished smooth after years of service. A popular quiz takes place every Thursday evening and live music is on Tuesday evenings. The garden is reached via a third, quiet, room. **Q❀🚌🐾📶**

Southwick

Golden Lion Ⓛ

High Street, PO17 6EB
⏲ 12-3, 5.30-11; 12-midnight Sat; 12-7 Sun
☎ (023) 9237 9134
Suthwyk Old Dick, Skew Sunshine Ale; guest beers Ⓗ
Free house with historic connections in a village still privately owned. The D-Day landings were partially planned by Montgomery and Eisenhower in the back bar. In the car park is the brewhouse museum, and the house beer, Old Dick, is named after the last brewer. The award-winning food can be enjoyed in the bar or separate dining room. Tuesday is jazz night. Guest beers usually come from within 30 miles. **Q🐴❀◐◑♣●P🐾**

Swanmore

Rising Sun

Hill Pound, SO32 2PS (on Droxford Rd)
⏲ 11.30-3, 6-11; 12-3.30, 6-10.30 Sun ☎ (01489) 896663
🌐 risingsunswanmore.co.uk
Irving Type 42; Sharp's Doom Bar; guest beers Ⓗ
This family-run free house features beers from Irving, Oakleaf, Suthwyk, Andwell, Itchen Valley and Palmers breweries. Built in 1672, the former coaching inn has exposed beams from 16th-century ships, with an open log fire and arched dining section. If you smell snuff, Harold the resident ghost is present. A good range of pub food is served daily featuring local produce. There is a beer festival in August and the pub has plans to brew its own beer. **Q🐴❀◐◑P⊟🚌**(17)**🐾**

Tangley

Cricketers Arms

SP11 0SH (towards Lower Chute)
⏲ 11-3 (Fri & Sat), 6-11; 12-3, 7-10.30 Sun
☎ (01264) 730283 🌐 thecricketers.eu
Bowman Swift One, Wallops Wood Ⓖ
Set in attractive countryside, this 16th-century drovers' inn sits below the Berkshire Downs. The two Bowman ales, served from stillage behind the bar, may be supplemented by a local guest in summer months. The front bar, with its huge inglenook fireplace, is used mainly for drinking, while traditional home-cooked food is available in the flagstoned dining area at the rear. Accommodation is provided in 10 en-suite rooms in the separate building at the rear of the pub.
Q🐴❀🛏◐◑♿♣P🚌(C6)**🐾**

Titchfield

Wheatsheaf Inn Ⓛ

1 East Street, PO14 4AD
⏲ 12-11 (midnight Fri & Sat) ☎ (01329) 842965
🌐 wheatsheaftitchfield.co.uk
Flowerpots Bitter; Palmers Best Bitter; guest beers Ⓗ
This welcoming 17th-century free house continues to grow in popularity for its excellent ales and high-quality food. A real fire and cosy snug add to the friendly atmosphere. Food is available every day in the bar and separate restaurant. Curries feature on Monday evenings, steaks on Tuesday evenings and roasts are served every Sunday. Folk musicians entertain on the second Monday evening of each month and beer festivals are held in summer and winter. **Q🐴❀◐◑♿●P🚌🐾**

Twyford

Phoenix Inn Ⓛ

High Street, SO21 1RF
⏲ 11.30-2.30, 6-11; 11.30-11 Fri & Sat; 12-10.30 Sun
☎ (01962) 713322 🌐 thephoenixinn.co.uk
Flowerpots Bitter; Hardys & Hansons Bitter; Morland Old Speckled Hen; guest beers Ⓗ

Originally a 17th-century inn on the old Winchester/Portsmouth turnpike. The large, long bar is multi-level, and a popular skittle alley/function room is to the rear. An impressive bank of eight handpumps delivers four Greene King beers and four LocAle guests. Traditional pub food is served, with additional themed nights: burgers Wednesdays and fish and chips Thursdays. A projection TV shows major sporting events. Occasional live music and quiz nights take place. The house beer is Hardys & Hansons Bitter.
Q❀◑♣P🚌(69,E1)

Vernham Dean

George Inn
SP11 0JY
12-11 (5 Sun) ☎ (01264) 737279
thegeorgeatvernhamdean.co.uk
Flack Manor Double Drop; Greene King Abbot; Hop Back Crop Circle; guest beer 🄷
Beautiful old-fashioned village pub dating back to the 17th century, with eyebrow windows, in the upper reaches of the Bourne Valley. Numerous footpaths and cycling routes lie nearby, including to Fosbury Camp hillfort. Outside there is an enclosed beer garden and seating to the front. Inside are oak beams and fireplaces. Freshly cooked food is served throughout the day and themed nights feature regularly. A beer festival takes place in August, with camping available.
Q❀◑P🐾

West Tytherley

Black Horse 🄻
North Lane, SP5 1NF
12-3 (not Mon-Wed), 6-11; 12-8 (4.30 winter) Sun
☎ (01794) 340308 theblackhorsepublichouse.co.uk
Hop Back Golden Best; guest beers 🄷
Dating from the 17th century, the Black Horse is all a village inn should be. The main bar with old farming paraphernalia is complemented by a second, predominantly tabled, dining room plus a hireable function room/skittle alley. The pub sports its own football team and its own skittle league. Locally-sourced produce, including game and even buffalo, feature on the menu. Guest beers often come from Palmers, Bowman and Flowerpots plus another local brewery. Opening hours may increase in summer – check ahead.
Q❀◑♣🍎P🚌(37)🐾

Wherwell

White Lion
Winchester Road, SP11 7JF
7.30am (8am Sat & Sun)-11 ☎ (01264) 860317
thewhitelionwherwell.co.uk
Flowerpots Bitter; Sharp's Doom Bar; Timothy Taylor Landlord; guest beers 🄷
Pleasant former coaching inn at the centre of a historic and idyllic thatched village alongside the River Test, world famous for its trout fishing. The venue was built in 1611 and hit by a cannon ball in the Civil War, which still hangs on the bar today. Now the pub is used by the village community and walkers on the Test Way. It opens for breakfasts to non-residents and lunch hampers can be provided. No food Sunday. Q❀🛏◑🍎P

Whitchurch

Bell Inn
Bell Street, RG28 7DD
10-11; 12-10.30 Sun ☎ (01256) 893120
thebellwhitchurch.co.uk
Fuller's London Pride; Gales Seafarers Ale; Sharp's Doom Bar 🄷
The 15th-century, half-timbered Bell oozes the character of a traditional pub. Look carefully for the wooden nail in the timber work. Conversation rules in both bars, while an area off the lounge with exposed beams provides space for a quiet pint or a meeting. Local musicians feature regularly on Sunday afternoons. There is a pool table, and a book library raises funds for charity. A small patio is accessible through the pub, which has an electric car charging point. Q❀🛏◐≉♣P🚌(76,86)🐾

Widley

George Inn
Portsdown Hill Road, PO6 1BE
11 (12 Sun)-11 ☎ (023) 9237 6756
Adnams Broadside; Fuller's London Pride; Greene King Abbot; Morland Old Speckled Hen; Ringwood Best Bitter; guest beer 🄷
Situated on top of Portsdown Hill alongside the old London to Portsmouth road, this pub also used to be a stop on the Portsdown & Horndean Light Railway. The guest beer is often from a local micro. The patio garden in front of the pub offers excellent views of Portsmouth and the Isle of Wight.
❀◐♣P🚌

Winchester

Albion
2 Stockbridge Road, SO23 7BZ
12-11 (midnight Fri & Sat); 12-10 Sun ☎ (01962) 864259
Beer range varies 🄷
Small cosy hostelry, at the bottom of Station Hill, the closest pub to Winchester rail station. The acute street-corner location at a busy intersection gives it an unusual shape, and makes it an ideal place from which to watch the world go by. It has a pleasant plain interior with a wood-burning stove. Antipasti snacks are served. The range of ales varies but there is often one from Dark Star, plus an interesting foreign bottled beer selection.
Q≉🚌🐾

Black Boy 🄻
1 Wharf Hill, SO23 9NQ (just off Chesil Street, B3404)
12-11 (midnight Fri & Sat); 12-10.30 Sun
☎ (01962) 861754 theblackboypub.com
Alfred's Saxon Bronze; Bowman Swift One; Flowerpots Bitter; Itchen Valley Pure Gold; guest beer 🄷
Centuries-old rambling building, its many interconnected rooms resembling an over-stocked folk museum. Serviced from a central bar, one room simulates a country kitchen complete with Aga, another a butcher's with papier mâché joints, while other areas are tradesmen's workshops. Taxidermy surprises are everywhere. Pub food is served Tuesday evening to Sunday lunchtime. (The Black Rat restaurant, opposite, has the same ownership.) The beer range emphasises local breweries. Ten B&B rooms have recently been created. Note the splendid medieval-style smoking shelter. Q❀🛏◑🍎🚌(4)🐾

Fulflood Arms

28 Cheriton Road, SO22 5EF

4-11; 11-midnight Fri & Sat; 12-10.30 Sun

(01962) 842996

Triple fff Moondance; guest beers H

The original dark-green tiled façade and etched windows are evidence of this 19th-century inn's former Winchester Brewery ownership. In a quiet residential conservation area, this is a comfortable pub with a single bar, sofas and newspapers. It has a good atmosphere, with friendly staff and locals, and serves a superb selection of real ales from mainly local breweries. Outside, drinkers and smokers have small patios front and rear. Available before 4pm for private functions.

Q (4)

Hyde Tavern

57 Hyde Street, SO23 7DY

5-11; 12.30-2, 5-11 Thu; 12-midnight Sat; 12-11 Sun

(01962) 862592 hydetavern.co.uk

Flowerpots Bitter; Harveys Sussex Best Bitter H**; guest beers** G

A fine double gable dominates the exterior of this small, medieval, timber-framed building. The two-roomed interior is below street level – beware of low doors and ceilings, and undulating floors. A cellar is used for many regular events, from storytelling to ukulele classes. Up to seven beers from small local breweries feature, usually including a mild or stout; real cider is also available. There is no regular food, but customers may order takeaways and a barbecue is available for hire. Outside is a delightful secluded garden.

Q (67)

Old Gaolhouse

11A Jewry Street, SO23 8RZ

8am-midnight (1am Fri & Sat) (01962) 850095

Fuller's ESB; Greene King Abbot; Marston's Burton Bitter; Ringwood Fortyniner; guest beers H

A popular split-level Wetherspoon in the city centre, convenient for most Winchester buses. The narrow seating area outside the attractive blue frontage is ideal for people-watching, but unfortunately drinking is not allowed there. The core beers are supplemented by guest ales chosen by the manager after consultation with regular drinkers. The pub was originally a Governor's House, which was the central building in the old debtor's prison. It later became one of the UK's earliest libraries, then an ironmonger's, and finally a high-class furniture store. Q (1,69)

Old Vine

8 Great Minster Street, SO23 9HA

11-11 (10.30 Sun) (01962) 854616

oldvinewinchester.com

Ringwood Best Bitter; guest beers H

Attractive, vine-clad 18th-century inn, with stunning views across to the cathedral. Its medieval cellars are said to have two ghosts who haunt the premises. The single, cosy, oak-beamed bar has an adjoining restaurant serving home-cooked food made using much local produce. There are three guest beers, with a strong LocAle emphasis. The rear courtyard has a terrace, which is smoke-free, and an inviting courtyard garden room. Superior accommodation is available in six stylish en-suite guest rooms.

(1,69)

Keep your Good Beer Guide up to date by visiting the CAMRA website **camra.org.uk**, then Good Beer Guide, then Updates.

St James Tavern

3 Romsey Road, SO22 5BE

12-11 (midnight Fri & Sat); 12-10.30 Sun

(01962) 861288 saintjamestavernwinchester.co.uk

Wadworth Henry's IPA, Horizon, 6X, Bishops Tipple, seasonal beer H

An acutely angled end-of-terrace pub on the steep Romsey Road hill. Inside is a single split-level L-shaped bar, with lots of wood and dark walls, giving a restful feel. Outside at the rear is a smart patio and garden. A good food menu, friendly staff and free newspapers make this an ideal lunch spot, with special events adding to a lively evening and weekend ambience. Live music features on the first and last Sundays in the month. The cider is Westons Old Rosie.

Wykeham Arms

75 Kingsgate Street, SO23 9PE (immediately outside the city's ancient Kingsgate)

11-11 (01962) 853834

wykehamarmswinchester.co.uk

Flowerpots Goodens Gold; Fuller's London Pride; Gales Seafarers Ale, HSB; guest beer H

Dating from 1755, this is a Georgian inn in a historic street between the Cathedral Close and the college. Many interlinked rooms are crammed with memorabilia, much of it Nelsonian, and old school desks masquerade as bar tables. It can become crowded but never loses its civilised, conversational atmosphere; booking for meals is advisable at busy times. Although a Fuller's house, one Flowerpots beer is always offered, often alongside a second local ale. A winner of many awards, the pub offers highly rated accommodation in 14 rooms. Q (1,69)

Winsor

Compass Inn

Winsor Road, SO40 2HE

12-11 (023) 8081 2237 compassinn.co.uk

Flack Manor Double Drop; Gales HSB; Sharp's Doom Bar; Young's Bitter H

Easily found at the east end of Winsor village, the Compass is a cosy, wood-floored, three-roomed pub, comprising a bar, a lounge with bare brick walls, lots of polished brass and a woodburner, and an adjoining dining room; to the left of the bar is a third dining area. Outside is a colourful garden with lots of shelter. Group dog walks are organised twice a month, with a snack beforehand and Sunday lunch afterwards. Q P (T3,T4)

Wonston

Wonston Arms

Stoke Charity Road, SO21 3LS

4 (12 Fri & Sat)-11; 12-10.30 Sun (01962) 760288

Beer range varies H

This no-frills village pub serves well-kept ales, mainly from local breweries. The regular community activity nights include a cheese and port club. The interior decor resembles a cosy front room including sofas, but with the benefit of a well-stocked bar and a pool table. It is

approximately a 15-minute walk from Sutton Scotney and the nearest bus stop.
Q❀♣P🚌(800)🐾📶

Wootton

Rising Sun

Bashley Common Road, BH25 5SF (on B3058, 1½ miles SE of A35)
⏲ 10-11 (10.30 Sun) ☎ (01425) 610360
Flack Manor Double Drop; Sharp's Doom Bar; guest beer Ⓗ
Prominent, spacious roadside pub adjacent to open forest, with an abundance of attractive stained glass, old prints, photographs and artefacts. Its large family room and adventure playground are separate from the main dining and drinking area. Food for all tastes is available all day from an extensive menu, with daily specials including many smaller appetite options. A discount food scheme operates for regular customers. Ample parking includes electric car charging points and equine tethering posts. The guest ale, usually from an independent brewery, changes regularly.
Q🐎❀◐◑♿P🚌(C32,C33)🐾📶

Yateley

White Lion

104-108 Reading Road, GU46 7RX
⏲ 11.30-11.30 (10.30 Sun) ☎ (01252) 890840
Fuller's London Pride; Wadworth 6X; guest beer Ⓗ
Originally an old coaching inn, this pub has been extensively refurbished over the years, and is now a Vintage Inn within the Mitchells & Butlers portfolio. The sizeable floor space is split into several smaller areas, and two log fires give a distinctly cosy atmosphere in wintry weather. The guest ale can be from anywhere in the country. A popular pub, with good meals available throughout the day. Q❀◐◑♿P🚌(3)🐾📶

Carpenters Arms, Burghclere

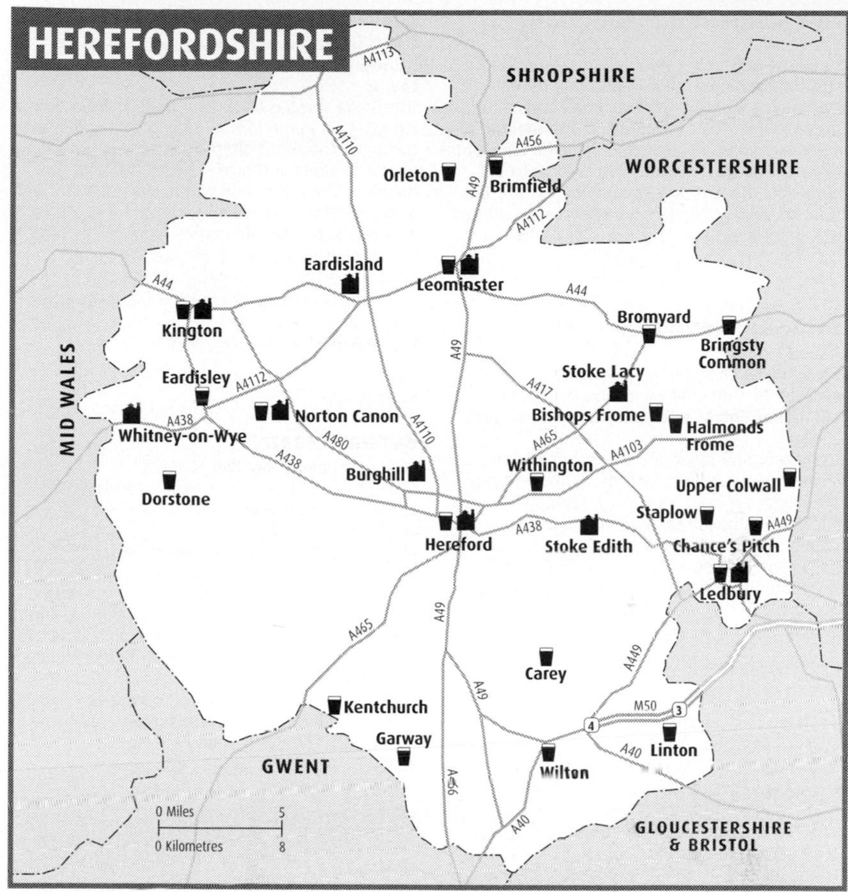

Bishops Frome

Green Dragon 𝕃

WR6 5BP (just off B4214)
⌚ 5 (4 Fri)-11.30; 12-11.30 Sat; 12-4, 7-11 Sun
☎ (01885) 490607
Otter Ale; Purple Moose Cwrw Eryri (Snowdonia Ale); Theakston Best Bitter; Timothy Taylor Golden Best; Wye Valley Butty Bach; guest beers Ⓗ
A welcome return to the Guide for the Green Dragon, now under new management. With a warren of flagstone-floored rooms and low beams in abundance, this 17th-century award winner boasts a real fire in every bar, plus a patio area to the rear. Six handpumps dispense a range of local and regional beers, supplemented by real cider and perry. Bar meals are served in the evenings Tuesday to Saturday, plus lunchtimes Saturday and Sunday. Q P (469,672)

Brimfield

Roebuck 𝕃

SY8 4NE (just E of A49 and S of A456)
⌚ 12-3, 7-11 summer; 12-2.30 (not Mon), 6-11; 12-3 Sun winter ☎ (01584) 711827
Hobsons Best Bitter; guest beers Ⓗ
The Roebuck has a community-oriented emphasis, albeit with good food always on offer. Pleasantly reappointed, the large front room features interesting old maps, while the more traditional oak-panelled back room is now the restaurant. Meals range from bar snacks to full à la carte, all locally sourced. Guest beers are from local breweries. The village store is attached to the pub. Q P

Bringsty Common

Live & Let Live 𝕃

WR6 5UW (off A44, at cat & mouse sign follow right-hand track down onto common) SO699547
⌚ closed Mon; 12-11 (10.30 Sun); 12-2.30, 6-11 Tue-Thu winter ☎ (01886) 821462 🌐 liveandletlive-bringsty.co.uk
Wye Valley Butty Bach; guest beers Ⓗ
Threatened with conversion into a dwelling, the present owners rescued the pub and are to be commended for transforming this isolated Grade II-listed building into the delightful venue it is today. The only thatched inn in Herefordshire, its renovation is to a high standard, featuring exposed timbers, flagstone floors, a fine fireplace and oak-back settles. Quality locally-sourced food is available in the bar and upstairs restaurant. Q P (420)

Bromyard

Rose & Lion 𝕃

5 New Road, HR7 4AJ

🕐 11-11 (midnight Fri & Sat) ☎ (01885) 482381
Wye Valley Bitter, HPA, Butty Bach Ⓗ
One of the expanding Wye Valley estate, the Rosie enjoys a loyal local following, and is never anything but friendly. The two small original rooms are complemented by a further bar to the rear plus an annexe with fully equipped disabled toilets and a pleasant garden. Furnished in a modern but appropriate style, it acts as a venue for live folk music on Sunday nights – there is always a real buzz about the place. **Q❀♿♣P🚌**(420)🐾

Carey

Cottage of Content

HR2 6NG
🕐 closed Mon & winter Tue; 12-2, 6-10.30 (11 Fri & Sat); 12-3 Sun ☎ (01432) 840242 🌐 cottageofcontent.co.uk
Hobsons Best Bitter; Wye Valley Butty Bach; guest beer Ⓗ
A truly beautiful black and white building in delightful surroundings, with parts dating from 1485. There are two bars and a separate restaurant. Although food of high quality predominates (booking is advised at most times), drinkers are welcome. There is a large garden on the hillside to the rear. Dogs are allowed in the bar only. The pub may close for short holidays in winter. **Q❀🛏◐●P🐾**

Chance's Pitch

Wellington Inn

WR13 6HW (on A449, near B4218 jct)
🕐 closed Mon; 12-3, 6.30-11; 12-4 Sun ☎ (01684) 540269
🌐 thewellingtoninnmalvern.co.uk
Goff's Tournament; guest beers Ⓗ
A landmark venue standing alone on the main Ledbury-Malvern road, this is a much-extended multi-level pub. While majoring on food, the drinking trade is well catered for. A comfortable and plainly decorated drinkers-only bar area has a traditional feel, and the lounge on the lower level offers views across open country. Two restaurant areas to the rear serve a wide range of often locally-sourced meals, from sandwiches to full à la carte. The guest beer is normally from a Gloucestershire micro. **Q🐴❀◐P🐾**

Dorstone

Pandy Inn

HR3 6AN (signed off B4348)
🕐 closed Mon; 12-3, 6-11; 12-11 Sat; 12-3, 6.30-10.30 Sun
☎ (01981) 550273 🌐 pandyinn.co.uk
Three Tuns XXX; Wye Valley Butty Bach Ⓗ
Set opposite the village green, the Pandy has a history dating back to the 12th century. Although opened out, the interior has a welcoming feel with exposed stone walls, timber framing and a huge fireplace. The garden includes a children's play area. The pub caters equally for drinkers and diners, with an interesting range of dishes including vegetarian meals. Bottled local cider is available. Live music is hosted monthly on Fridays. Accommodation is in an exciting new timber eco-house at the rear. **Q🐴❀🛏◐●P🚌**(39,39A)🐾

Eardisley

Tram Inn

HR3 6PG (on A4111)
🕐 closed Mon; 12-3, 6-midnight (12.30am Fri & Sat); 12-3, 7-10.30 Sun ☎ (01544) 327251 🌐 thetraminn.co.uk
Hobsons Best Bitter; Wye Valley Butty Bach; guest beer Ⓗ
This Grade II-listed black and white half-timbered inn takes its name from a long-gone horse-drawn tramway. The much-altered 16th-century building retains its original charm – a cosy bar with traditional floor tiles and woodwork contrasts with a larger bar with panelled walls and a grand bay window, plus a simple games room to the rear. Locally-sourced freshly made pub meals including Sunday roasts are available (no food Sun eve). Draught Dunkertons and bottled Orgasmic and Gwatkins ciders are stocked.
Q❀◐⛺♣●P🚌(446,462)🐾📶

Garway

Garway Moon

Garway Common, HR2 8RQ SO465227
🕐 closed Tue; 12-3 (not Mon & Wed), 6-midnight; 12-midnight Sat & Sun ☎ (01600) 750270
🌐 garwaymooninn.co.uk
Wye Valley HPA, Butty Bach; guest beers Ⓗ
A remote but popular pub overlooking the delightful village green and cricket pitch, with a lounge and public bar plus a separate snug/family room and garden. Beers are from regional and local breweries. Traditional, good-value, home-prepared bar and restaurant meals are served including vegetarian options. Pizza night is Wednesday; curry night Thursday and roasts on Sunday. Beers are mainly from Wye Valley and Butcombe.
🐴❀🛏◐♿⛺♣●P🚌(412)🐾

Halmonds Frome

Major's Arms

WR6 5AX (¾ mile N of A4103 at Bishops Frome) SO675481
🕐 5 (4 Fri; 3 Sat; 12 Sun)-11 ☎ (01531) 640261
Purity Pure Gold; Wye Valley Bitter; guest beer Ⓗ
Housed in what was once an old cider mill, this small, isolated pub has a simple, high-ceilinged bar with bare stone walls and a large woodburner. From the patio there are superb views over west Herefordshire and into Wales – the sunsets are stunning. Occasional live music is hosted. Although food is not normally served, events can be catered for. Local Henney's Cider is available.
🐴❀⛺♣●P🐾

Hereford

Barrels

69 St Owen Street, HR1 2JQ

INDEPENDENT BREWERIES

Arrow Kington
Hereford Hereford
Jones the Brewer Whitney-on-Wye (NEW)
Ledbury Ledbury
Mayfields Leominster
Mulberry Duck Burghill
Saxon City Stoke Edith (brewing suspended)
Shoes Norton Canon
Simpsons Eardisland
Wobbly Hereford
Wye Valley Stoke Lacy

11-11.30 (midnight Fri & Sat); 12-11.30 Sun
(01432) 274968
Wye Valley Bitter, HPA, Butty Bach; guest beers H
Winner of Herefordshire CAMRA Pub of the Year six times, it keeps true to its soul as a community pub. There are no meals or gimmicks here, but tons of character across five different bars. With the TV only turned on for major sports events, conversation and good times still hold sway. A charity beer and music festival is hosted in the cobbled courtyard each August bank holiday weekend.

Beer in Hand

136 Eign Street, HR4 0AP
closed Mon; 12 (4 Tue & Wed)-11; 11-10.30 Sun
(07443) 487124 beerinhand.co.uk
Beer range varies G
Herefordshire's first foray into the genre of the micropub is not actually that small. Converted from a launderette, this edge-of-city-centre venue is decorated in contemporary but unpretentious style. It typically offers six interesting beers, rising to 12 at weekends, all served from an impressive purpose-built chilled racking system behind the bar. It also offers five ciders, wine and a limited range of hot and cold snacks. Herefordshire CAMRA Cider Pub of the Year 2013. Q

King's Fee

49-53 Commercial Road, HR1 2BJ
8am-midnight (1am Sat) (01432) 373240
Greene King Abbot; Ruddles Best Bitter; guest beers H
An award-winning Wetherspoon conversion of an old supermarket. The large open-plan main bar, with numerous alcoves, leads to an elevated family seating area (children welcome until 8pm) and courtyard. The decor is contemporary in style, featuring local history panels and woodcut prints by a local artist. Good-value food is served all day, and alcohol from 9am. Voted Herefordshire CAMRA Cider Pub of the Year 2012, it serves five mainly local ciders on handpump. Q

Volunteer Inn

21 Harold Street, HR1 2QU
11-11 (midnight Fri & Sat); 12-11 Sun (01432) 276189
Greene King Abbot; Otter Ale; Wye Valley HPA; guest beer H
There is always a friendly atmosphere at this keenly run, community focused, back-street pub, which boasts two main bars and a fabulous little snug off the main corridor. Unusually, a skittle alley to the rear has survived. Regular events include a quiz on Monday, curry and a pint on Wednesday, a local farmers' vegetable sale on Thursday, and an acoustic music night on the second Tuesday of the month. Food is traditional with plenty of vegetarian options, along with popular Sunday lunches.
Q (76)

Kentchurch

Bridge Inn

HR2 0BY (on B4347)
closed Tue; 12-2.30 (not Mon), 6-11; 12-11 Sat summer; 12-5 Sun (01981) 240408 bridgeinnkentchurch.co.uk
Otter Bitter; guest beers H
Beautifully situated close to the Welsh border on the banks of the River Monnow, the building probably dates from the 14th century. It has a welcoming single front bar and a restaurant with excellent views, and boasts riverside gardens and a pétanque piste for summer days. The freshly prepared food ranges from bar snacks to full à la carte. Guest beers are from regional and local breweries, usually including one from Wye Valley. A beer festival is held in May. Q P

> For we could not now take time for further search (to land our ship) our victuals being much spent especially our beer. **Log of the Mayflower**

Kington

Olde Tavern ★

22 Victoria Road, HR5 3BX
6.30-10.30 (midnight Wed & Thu); 3.30-midnight Fri; 12-midnight Sat & Sun (01544) 239033
Hobsons Mild; Ludlow Best; Wye Valley Butty Bach; guest beer H
Diminutive Grade II-listed two-room time warp with an entrance lobby, still with its off-sales hatch, leading to a main bar with many original features, alcove seating and fascinating curios. The old smoke room to the right has a flagstone floor and bench seating, plus a serving hatch to the bar. Regulars take pride in the pub's activities, including the annual beer festival on the spring bank holiday.
Q

Ledbury

Prince of Wales

Church Lane, HR8 1DL
11-11 (10.30 Sun) (01531) 632250 powledbury.com
Butcombe Bitter; Hobsons Best Bitter; Ledbury Dark; Otter Bitter; Wye Valley HPA, Butty Bach; guest beer H
Set in a delightful cobbled alley leading up to the imposing church, this 16th-century timber-framed pub boasts two bars and a discrete alcove where a folk jam session is held every Wednesday evening. Herefordshire CAMRA Pub of the Year 2013, it is a true community pub, bustling with locals and visitors. Westons draught cider is stocked, together with an extensive range of draught and bottled foreign beers. The bar meals are excellent value, with roasts on Sunday.

Talbot Hotel

14 New Street, HR8 2DX
11-11 (midnight Fri & Sat) (01531) 632963
visitledbury.co.uk/talbot
Wadworth Henry's IPA, 6X; Wye Valley Butty Bach; guest beer H
An outstanding black and white half-timbered hotel and bar dating back to the 1590s with direct links to the Civil War. Various comfortably-furnished seating areas, with discreet nooks and corners, surround an island servery facing a splendid fireplace. The restaurant, with its superb wood-panelling, offers affordable fine cuisine using locally-sourced ingredients, while conventional bar snacks are also available in the bar. The guest beer is from Wadworth's seasonal range or Red Shoot subsidiary.

Leominster

Grape Vaults

2-4 Broad Street, HR6 8BS
11-11 ☎ (01568) 611404 thegrapevaults.co.uk
Ludlow Best, Gold; guest beers H
Do not be put off by the rather ordinary façade. In the distant past this was a hardcore cider house, but today is a real gem of a pub, with a welcoming fireplace, bench seating and much original woodwork. Typical pub food is served at reasonable prices (no food Sun eve). The guest beers are usually local. Live music features on Sunday afternoons. Q

Linton

Alma Inn

HR9 7RY (off B4221) SO659255
12-3 (not Mon-Fri), 6-11; 12-3, 7-10.30 Sun
☎ (01989) 720355 lintonfestival.org/about/the-alma-inn
Butcombe Bitter; Ludlow Gold; Malvern Hills Black Pear; Oakham Bishops Farewell H
This outstanding, multi-award-winning free house is currently Herefordshire CAMRA Country Pub of the Year. Run with real passion, the Alma is living testament to the fact that village pubs do not have to sell food to thrive. It has a conventional front bar, complete with a real fire, and a pool room at the back. Events include a major music festival in June and summer sessions in August, both held in the extensive grounds, with accompanying beer festivals. Q ♣P

Norton Canon

Three Horseshoes

HR4 7BH (on A480)
12-3 (Wed only), 6-11; 12-3, 7-10.30 Sun
☎ (01544) 318375
Shoes Norton Ale, Canon Bitter, Peploe's Tipple, Farrier's Ale H
Traditional early Victorian red-brick roadside pub of timeless rural character, home to the Shoes Brewery located at the rear of the premises. It is one of only a handful of pubs to still have a shooting gallery. With a small but loyal following, the atmosphere is friendly and welcoming. A cosy and comfortable lounge, furnished with an eclectic collection of old chairs and sofas, contrasts with a more traditional public bar, both inviting gentle conversation. Q ♣P (461,462)

Orleton

Boot Inn

SY8 4HN (off B4361)
12-3, 5.30-11; 12-11.30 Sat; 12-11 Sun ☎ (01568) 780228
thebootinnorleton.co.uk
Hobsons Best Bitter; Wye Valley HPA; guest beer H
Comfortable and welcoming 16th-century black and white village pub with a large inglenook fireplace and original oak beams. A charity quiz is held on the second Tuesday of the month in winter and a beer and cider festival in July in the large beer garden. Home-prepared food ranges from bar snacks to interesting gourmet meals. The Mortimer Trail passes about a mile away and walkers are welcome. Bus service 492 stops outside.
Q P (492)

Staplow

Oak Inn

HR8 1NP (on B4214)
12-11 (10.30 Sun) ☎ (01531) 640954
oakinnstaplow.co.uk
Bathams Best Bitter; Ledbury Gold; Wye Valley Bitter; guest beer H
A stylishly renovated and well-run roadside country inn that offers exceptional food, good beer and quality accommodation overlooking nearby hop yards. The contemporary public area neatly divides into three – a reception bar area with modern sofas and low tables, a snug and a main dining area featuring an open kitchen. At the rear is another room with scrubbed tables. Booking ahead is essential for both food and accommodation.
Q P (417)

Upper Colwall

Chase Inn

Chase Road, WR13 6DJ (off B4218, turn at upper hairpin bend signed British Camp) SO766431
12-3, 5-11; 12-11 Sat; 12-10.30 Sun ☎ (01684) 540276
thechaseinnuppercolwall.co.uk
Bathams Best Bitter; Sharp's Doom Bar; guest beers H
Conversation rules at this two-bar free house tucked away in a quiet wooded backwater on the western slopes of the Malvern Hills. It comprises a small lounge for informal dining, where good, hearty food is served, and a narrow bar very much for drinkers. The walls are adorned with interesting paraphernalia. The suntrap rear garden commands views across Herefordshire to the Welsh Hills. A beer festival is held each June and a cider festival in October. Q ♣P (675)

Wilton

White Lion

Wilton Lane, HR9 6AQ (just off B4260)
12-11 (10.30 Sun) ☎ (01989) 562785
whitelionross.co.uk
Wye Valley Bitter; guest beer H
This pleasant riverside inn commands fine views from its patio and garden across the River Wye to Ross and the surrounding countryside. The 16th-century building has a single opened-out main bar area, complete with original beams, stonework and fireplace. Upstairs is the bistro-style Gaol Restaurant, originally part of a neighbouring prison house, but now for enjoying traditional English meals made with locally-sourced produce.
♣P (32)

Withington

Cross Keys

HR1 3NN (on A465 in Withington Marsh)
5 (12 Sat)-11; 12-10.30 Sun ☎ (01432) 820616
Otter Ale; Wye Valley Butty Bach; guest beer H
Run by the same landlord for over 40 years, this cracking old inn is a favourite for its atmosphere. A long, narrow single bar divides into two drinking areas, each with original beams, exposed stonework, a woodburner and basic bench seating. A folk jam session is held on the last Thursday of the month. Filled rolls are available on Saturdays.
Q ♣P (420)

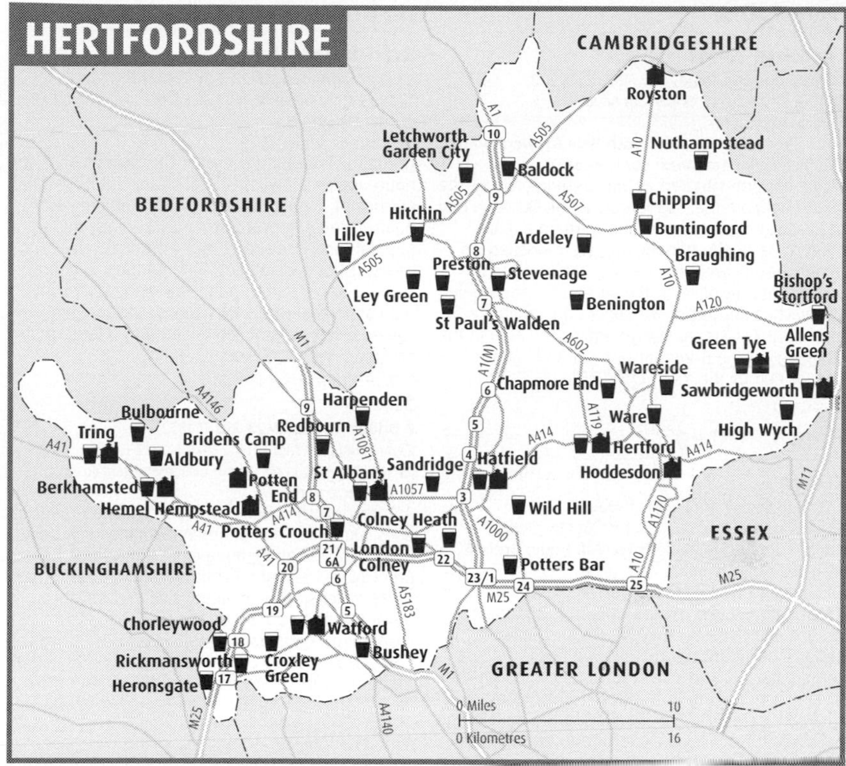

Aldbury

Valiant Trooper L

Trooper Road, HP23 5RW SP964123

11 (12 Sun)-11 ☎ (01442) 851203 valianttrooper.co.uk

Chiltern Beechwood Bitter H; Dark Star Original G; Fuller's London Pride; Tring Side Pocket for a Toad H/G; XT Six G; guest beers H

Edge-of-village local dating from the 17th century in a popular walking area. The beamed bar gives way to a spacious food area, but beer is the focus here, with larger micros and LocAle breweries supported. Good British pub food made with locally-sourced ingredients is served in the bar and garden. With an enthusiastic landlord and friendly staff, the Trooper has featured in the Guide for many years and is a must-visit for serious pubgoers. Q P (30,31)

Allens Green

Queen's Head L

CM21 0LS TL455170

12-2.30 (not Mon & Tue), 5-11; 12-10.30 Sun

☎ (01279) 723393 shirevillageinns.co.uk

Fuller's London Pride G; Mighty Oak Maldon Gold; guest beers H

Popular village inn, well-worth seeking out for its constantly changing range of four beers. Mighty Oak and other East Anglian brewers often feature. Mini beer festivals are held on the third weekend of the month and over bank holiday weekends, utilising gravity stillage to bring the number of beers up to 10 or more. Hot snacks are available unless the pub is exceptionally busy. Local CAMRA Pub of the Year six times. Q P

Ardeley

Jolly Waggoner

SG2 7AH (off B1037 between Walkern and Cottered) TL311271

12-11.30 (12.30am Fri & Sat); 12-11 Sun

☎ (01438) 861350 thejollywaggoner.co.uk

Buntingford Highwayman; guest beers H

This 16th-century pub was once farmworkers' cottages. Now managed by the nearby Church Farm, the Jolly Waggoner has a reputation for fine food, most of it sourced from the farm itself or local suppliers. Real ale is sourced locally, too, from Buntingford, Red Squirrel and Nethergate. Regular events include speciality food evenings, guest landlords and a beer festival in August. P

Baldock

Orange Tree L

Norton Road, SG7 5AW TL242339

12-2.30, 4.30-11; 12-midnight Thu-Sat; 12-10.30 Sun

☎ (01462) 892341 theorangetreebaldock.com

Greene King XX Mild, IPA, Abbot; guest beers H

This is not a typical Greene King pub, with 10 guest beers all from small brewers, including two from the award-winning Buntingford Brewery, as well as four real ciders, two from local producer Apple Cottage. Quiz night is Tuesday, folk music features on a Wednesday and a popular beer festival is hosted annually. Good home-made food is served. Local CAMRA Pub of the Year 2013. P (94)

Benington

Lordship Arms

42 Whempstead Road, SG2 7BX TL307228
12-3, 6 (7 Sun)-11 ☎ (01438) 869665
lordshiparms.com
Black Sheep Best Bitter; Crouch Vale Brewers Gold; Timothy Taylor Landlord; guest beers H
Single-bar pub situated at the southern end of the village with a fantastic 21 years in the Guide. A tidy bar is decorated with telephone memorabilia – even some of the handpumps are modelled on telephones. A well-maintained garden sports superb floral displays in the summer. Good-quality sandwiches and other bar snacks are available at lunchtime. Classic car club meetings are held in the summer. A repeat winner of local and county CAMRA Pub of the Year. Q❀◐P🚌(384)

Berkhamsted

Crown

145 High Street, HP4 3HH SP992077
8am-midnight (1am Fri & Sat) ☎ (01442) 863993
Adnams Broadside; Fuller's London Pride; Greene King IPA; Sharp's Doom Bar; guest beers H
The building was first recorded as the Crown in the 18th century. Now owned by Wetherspoon, it divides into several different sections including an atmospheric front room and snug to the right, a conservatory to the side, and a more modern area at the back leading to a terraced patio garden. Disabled access is down an alley to the right of the pub. Two guest ales include one from a local brewery, and the cider is Westons Old Rosie. ❀◐◑♿≠🚌(500)

Lamb

277 High Street, HP4 1AJ SP987080
11-11 (midnight Fri & Sat) ☎ (01442) 862615
Adnams Ghost Ship; Fuller's London Pride; Tring Side Pocket for a Toad, Ridgeway H
Traditional roadside pub that is over 300 years old. The two entrances lead into separate sides connected by a narrow section in front of the bar. The walls are adorned with old photographs of the town, many of which feature pubs. A door with stained glass panels leads to the small patio at the rear. A variety of seats and tables is scattered throughout including tall tables and chairs, and bench seating. Food is only served weekday lunchtimes. ❀◐≠♣🚌(500,501)

Rising Sun

1 Canal Side, George Street, HP4 2EG (at lock 55 on Grand Union Canal) SP997077
3-11; 12-midnight Fri & Sat; 12-10.30 Sun
☎ (01442) 864913 theriserberko.net
Tring Ridgeway; guest beers H
Traditional pub which adopted the environs of lock 55 in 2013. The four changing guest beers and 15 real ciders/perries are accompanied by bottled French ciders, snuff, cigars, unusual spirits and liqueurs. Three inside areas, canalside seating and a sunken patio make this a pub for any time of the year. Many events feature throughout the year including beer festivals, quizzes and a cheese club. Food is restricted to the renowned ploughman's. CAMRA members receive a discount. Local CAMRA Pub of the Year/Cider Pub of the Year 2014. Q❀◐≠♣🚌(500,501)

Bishop's Stortford

Bricklayers Arms

61 Hadham Road, CM23 2QY TL482214
12 (5 Mon)-midnight; 12-1.30am Fri & Sat; 12-11.30 Sun
☎ (01279) 657803
Beer range varies H
Landlords Ivor and Rose own this former Benskins house which showcases local beers, often featuring Colchester, Nethergate or Mighty Oak breweries. Built on the site of a former brickworks, this popular local has served the community for 150 years. It has a quiet, comfortable lounge and a lively sports-oriented public bar and pool room with several satellite TV screens. Outside is a covered, heated smokers' patio and a large but secluded deck. Q❀P

Star

7 Bridge Street, CM23 2JU TL487214
11-midnight (2am Fri); 12-2am Sat; 12-6 Sun
☎ (01279) 654211 thestar-bishopsstortford.co.uk
Beer range varies H
A 17th-century town-centre pub that caters for all ages. On Friday and Saturday evenings it is busy with a young crowd, but a quiet pint can be had on other nights and at lunchtimes. The range of three beers is constantly changing and well balanced, often including a mild or porter. The food is a big draw here – good-value traditional fare such as fish and chips is served at lunchtime, and pizzas can be made to order at any time. ❀◐≠🚌

Braughing

Golden Fleece

20 Green End, SG11 2PG
11.30-3, 5.30-11; 11.30-11 Sat; 12-10.30 Sun
☎ (01920) 823555 goldenfleecebraughing.co.uk
Adnams Southwold Bitter; guest beers H
A large rural pub built in the early 1700s, with wooden floors, beams and a large fireplace. It closed as a pub in 2003 but reopened in 2010 after extensive remodelling of the interior layout. Guest ales come from local breweries such as Buntingford, Nethergate and Saffron. The food available is all gluten-free, and includes a changing range of daily specials, plus monthly tapas nights and themed food evenings.
Q❀◐◑P🚌(331,386)

Bridens Camp

Crown & Sceptre

Red Lion Lane, HP2 6EY (from A4146 at Water End take Red Lion Lane up hill for ½ mile) TL044111

INDEPENDENT BREWERIES

3 Brewers Hatfield
Big Ears Green Tye (NEW)
Broxbourne Hoddesdon
Buntingford Royston
Haresfoot Berkhamstead (NEW)
McMullen Hertford
Mix Hemel Hempstead (NEW)
Old Cross Hertford
Pope's Yard Watford
Red Squirrel Potten End
Sawbridgeworth Sawbridgeworth
Tring Tring
Verulam St Albans

☉ 12-3, 5.30-11; 12-11 Sat & Sun ☎ (01442) 234660
🌐 crownandsceptrepub.co.uk
Greene King IPA, Abbot; guest beers Ⓗ
This popular country pub dates from 1839 – mind the beams if you are tall. Seven handpumps are on two sides of the U-shaped bar, so there are more ales to choose from than first meets the eye. The pub has a patio and beer garden, with an outside bar available for beer festivals and functions. Quiz nights are hosted on Sundays in winter. Situated on the Chiltern Way, it is popular with walkers and cyclists. Great Gaddesden Cricket Club is opposite.
Q❀◑♣●P🚌(X31)

Bulbourne

Grand Junction Arms

Bulbourne Road, HP23 5QE (next to Grand Union Canal bridge 138) SP932135
☉ 12-11 (10.30 Sun) ☎ (01442) 891400
🌐 grandjunctionarms.co.uk
Sharp's Doom Bar; Tring Side Pocket for a Toad; guest beers Ⓗ
This canalside pub boasts a clean, spacious and modern interior with local artwork displayed for sale. Extensive home-made menus serve all tastes, with daily specials and Monday steak night. Music sessions are hosted on the first Tuesday of the month and Sunday is curry and quiz night. The large family-friendly garden is next to the canal and features a wild flower orchard. During busy periods a downstairs bar serves the garden, notably during bank holiday music festivals.
Q🐴❀◑♿P🚌(61)🐾📶

Buntingford

Brambles 𝕃

117 High Street, SG9 9AF TL360298
☉ 12-11 (10.30 Sun) ☎ (01763) 273158
Buntingford Twitchell; Fuller's London Pride; guest beers Ⓗ
Brambles has two bars, both warmed by real fires, and up to eight handpumps dispensing the ales. Fuller's London Pride is always available, alongside other regular ales from Buntingford Brewery or Church End. Pool and darts are played, and there is occasional live music. The clientele is varied and can get exuberant at weekends.
🐴❀♣🚌(331,700)🐾📶

Bushey

Swan

25 Park Road, WD23 3EE TQ132954
☉ 11-11; 12-10.30 Sun ☎ (020) 8950 2256
🌐 swanpubbushey.co.uk
Greene King Abbot; Sharp's Doom Bar; Timothy Taylor Landlord; Young's Bitter Ⓗ
A small and friendly single bar in a residential street off the High Street. Photos of life in the village and sporting achievements adorn the walls and there is a plaque celebrating the pub's entry in the first 10 editions of the Guide. Four regular ales are offered and toasties and rolls are available all day. Three TV screens show selected sports events and two real fires add to the warm welcome. The Ladies is in the back garden. ❀♣🚌📶

Chapmore End

Woodman

30 Chapmore End, SG12 0HF (off B158 between Bengeo and A602 roundabout) TL328164
☉ 12 (5 Mon)-11; 12-10.30 Sun ☎ (01920) 463339
Greene King IPA, Abbot; guest beers Ⓖ
Classic two-bar country pub in a quiet hamlet off the B158, popular with walkers and the local shoot. At this totally unspoilt gem the beer is served straight from cooled casks in the cellar behind the bar. Recent improvements have been made to the gardens and a new conservatory has been added at the rear. A pétanque pitch is available to book. A beer and music festival is held once a year.
Q🐴❀P🐾📶

Chipping

Countryman

Ermine Street, SG9 0PG TL356319
☉ closed Mon-Thu; 12-11 (10.30 Sun) ☎ (01763) 272721
Beer range varies Ⓗ
Built in 1663, and a pub since 1760, the Countryman has a one bar, split-level interior. The room boasts some well executed carvings on the bar front, an impressive fireplace and some obscure agricultural implements. Three varying real ales and a cider are usually available. A pub for conversation. Note the restricted opening hours.
Q🐴❀●P🚌(331)🐾

Chorleywood

Rose & Crown 𝕃

Common Road, WD3 5LW TQ027963
☉ 11.30-3, 5.30-11; 11.30-11.30 Sat; 12-10 Sun
☎ (01923) 283841 🌐 roseandcrownchorleywood.co.uk
Fuller's London Pride; Young's Bitter; guest beers Ⓗ
A friendly one-bar pub opposite the common with a popular restaurant. Guest beers usually come from local breweries such as Vale, XT and Tring, but beers from breweries further afield, such as Loose Cannon, do appear. The homely drinking area can get crowded, and can operate as a restaurant overspill in the evenings. Children are not allowed in the bar. ❀◑⇌⊖♣P🚌(336)🐾📶

Colney Heath

Crooked Billet 𝕃

88 High Street, AL4 0NP TL202060
☉ 11-2.30, 4.30-11; 11-11 Fri & Sat; 12-10.30 Sun
☎ (01727) 822128
Tring Side Pocket for a Toad; guest beers Ⓗ
Popular and friendly cottage-style village pub dating back over 200 years. A genuine free house, it stocks three to five guest beers from national, regional and microbreweries. A wide selection of good-value home-made food is served lunchtimes and Friday and Saturday evenings. Summer barbecues and Saturday events are held occasionally. This is a favourite stop-off for walkers on the many local footpaths. Families are welcome in the bar until 9pm and in the large garden where there is play equipment. 🐴❀◑♣P🚌(304)🐾

Croxley Green

Sportsman 𝕃

2 Scots Hill, WD3 3AD (at A412 jct with the green) TQ069953

⌚ 12-11 (10.30 Sun) ☎ (01923) 443360
Beer range varies H
A pub with a real ale focus, it offers an ever-changing selection of up to eight ales in a range of styles to suit all tastes, alongside a real cider. If you cannot make up your mind, try the tasting rack of six beers first. The pub has a community feel, with regular quizzes and beer festivals, live music on Saturday, social activities including a book club and jazz group, and games including darts and pool. ❀♣P▯🚌(320,324)

Green Tye

Prince of Wales L

SG10 6JP TL444184
⌚ 12-3, 5.30-11; 12-11 Sat; 12-10.30 Sun ☎ (01279) 842139
🌐 thepow.co.uk
Abbeydale Moonshine; Wadworth Henry's IPA; guest beers H
A traditional and friendly 19th-century village local, well worth a visit whether you are a walker, cyclist, dog owner or just plain thirsty. The Green Tye Brewery at the back of the pub is undergoing some updating – owners Rob and Jane are planning to reopen the brewery shortly, making the Prince of Wales the brewery tap. Great-value traditional pub grub is available. There is a small garden for fine weather. Q❀♿P🐾

Harpenden

Cross Keys L

39 High Street, AL5 2SD (opp war memorial) TL133144
⌚ 11.30-11; 12-10.30 Sun ☎ (01582) 763989
🌐 cross-keys-harpenden.co.uk
Rebellion IPA; Timothy Taylor Landlord; Tring Side Pocket for a Toad H
Tucked in among the shops in the town centre, this two-bar pub has retained its traditional charm with a rare fine pewter bar top and flagstone floors. The original oak-beamed ceiling has tankards from past and present customers hanging from it. In spring and summer, enjoy your pint in the secluded, attractive rear garden, and in autumn or winter relax in front of the saloon bar's fire. Traditional home-cooked lunches are served Monday to Saturday. Q❀♿≠♣🚌🐾

Hatfield

Horse & Groom

21 Park Street, AL9 5AT TL233086
⌚ 11.30-11 (midnight Fri & Sat); 12-10.30 Sun
☎ (01707) 264765
Black Sheep Best Bitter; Greene King Abbot; guest beers H
This supposedly haunted, 16th-century, Grade II-listed building, formerly timber-framed and later brick-clad, is thought to house a priest hole. The pub serves up to five real ales and hosts three beer festivals a year. Tuesday is bangers and mash night, Saturday is chilli and rice night – purchase an ale for a free portion. In the heart of Old Hatfield, railway and bus stations are just a few minutes' walk away. Q❀≠♣🚌🐾

Heronsgate

Land of Liberty, Peace & Plenty 🏆 L

Long Lane, WD3 5BS (off M25 jct 17) TQ023949
⌚ 12-11 (midnight Fri & Sat); 12-10.30 Sun
☎ (01923) 282226 🌐 landoflibertypub.com
Beer range varies H
Welcoming pub with historic connections to the Chartists who had a short-lived rural community nearby. Popular with walkers, cyclists, locals and real ale enthusiasts, six to eight beers are usually offered, all from microbreweries, in a range of styles and strengths. Ciders, perries and malt whiskies are always stocked. Beer festivals, tastings and other regular events are held throughout the year. Bar snacks are available all day. Outside is a large pavilion for families. Current local CAMRA Pub of the Year. ❀♣P▯🚌(R4)🐾

Hertford

Black Horse L

29-31 West Street, SG13 8EZ TL324123
⌚ 12-midnight (11 Mon; 11.30 Tue); 12-1am Fri & Sat; 12-10.30 Sun ☎ (01992) 583630 🌐 theblackhorse.biz
Beer range varies H
Community-focused timbered free house, dating from 1642 and situated in one of Hertford's most attractive streets, near the start of the Cole Green Way. The well-kept garden has a separate safe children's area. The interesting food menu features game, and the pub now has its own bakery. Handy for Hertford Town FC supporters and now the only pub in Britain with a rugby team affiliated to the RFU. ❀♣🚌🐾

Hertford Club

Lombard House, Bull Plain, SG14 1DT
⌚ 12-3 (not Mon & Tue), 5-11; 12-11 Fri & Sun; 11-11 Sat
☎ (01992) 421422 🌐 hertfordclub.co.uk
Beer range varies H
Dating from the 15th century with later additions, Lombard House, on the River Lea, was built as an English Hall House and is one of the oldest buildings in Hertford. It has been the home of this private members' club since 1897. CAMRA members are welcome and can be signed in on production of a membership card. You will find three ever-changing beers and real cider, which in summer can be enjoyed in the delightful walled garden. An open acoustic club on Sunday evenings is well supported. ❀≠(East)♣🚌

Old Barge

2 The Folly, SG14 1QD (ask for Folly Island) TL326128
⌚ 11-11 (midnight Fri & Sat); 12-11 Sun ☎ (01992) 581871
🌐 theoldbarge.co.uk
Dark Star Hophead; St Austell Tribute; Sharp's Doom Bar; guest beers H
A free house on Folly Island pleasantly situated canalside on the River Lee, offering not only a good selection of beers – usually including a dark mild, stout or porter – but also four real ciders/perries, together with locally-sourced home-cooked food. The pub hosts regular beer festivals and a popular Sunday night quiz. Live jazz features every second Thursday of the month. Look out for August's crayfish festival for children under 12. Watch the narrowboats as you enjoy your pint.
❀≠(East)♣🚌

Old Cross Tavern L

8 St Andrew Street, SG14 1JA TL323126
⌚ 4.30 (12 Fri & Sat)-11; 12-10.30 Sun ☎ (01992) 583133
Old Cross Gertcha!; Timothy Taylor Landlord; guest beers H

Superb town free house offering a friendly welcome. Up to eight real ales, usually including a dark beer of some distinction, come from brewers large and small, including the pub's own microbrewery, and there is a fine choice of Belgian bottle-conditioned beers. Two beer festivals are held each year – one over the spring bank holiday, the other in October. No TV or music here, just good old-fashioned conversation. Home-made pork pies are available. Q≷(North)♣🚌(395)🐾

White Horse

33 Castle Street, SG14 1HH TL326124

⏲ 12-midnight ☎ 07454 781261

Adnams Southwold Bitter; Butcombe Bitter; Fuller's London Pride, ESB; Gales Seafarers Ale, HSB; guest beers Ⓗ

Charming old timber-framed building with two bars and extra rooms upstairs, popular with community groups. One room features bar billiards and others are family rooms where children are welcome. The Horse is a pub for conversation and a must-see for visitors to Hertford, with up to 10 beers available including a wide Fuller's range and additional guests. Two beer festivals are held each year. Thursday is tapas night. Dogs are welcome, even the resident canine pub ghost.
Q♘☋❀◐≷(East)♣●🚌🐾ᯤ

High Wych

Rising Sun 🏆

High Wych Road, CM21 0HZ TL463141

⏲ 12-2.30 (not Tue), 5.30-11; 12-3, 7-10.30 Sun

☎ (01279) 724099

Courage Best Bitter; Mighty Oak Maldon Gold; Oakham Jeffrey Hudson Bitter; guest beers Ⓖ

This friendly village local has never used handpumps – a range of four or five beers is served on gravity, often from East Anglian breweries such as Mighty Oak and Oakham. Although recently refurbished, the original character of the building has been preserved, with a stone floor, attractive fireplace and wood panelling. Popular with locals and walkers, it holds a monthly quiz and an annual vegetable competition. Parking is in the village hall car park opposite. Q❀♣P🚌(347)🐾

Hitchin

Half Moon 🏆 Ⓛ

57 Queen Street, SG4 9TZ TL186288

⏲ 12-midnight (1am Fri & Sat); 12-11 Sun

☎ (01462) 452448 🌐 thehalfmoonhitchin.co.uk

Adnams Southwold Bitter; Young's Bitter; guest beers Ⓗ

Split-level single-bar pub dating from 1748, once owned by Hitchin brewer W&S Lucas. It sells two regular and six guest beers, often from local breweries, plus two regular ciders, a perry and four guest ciders. Home-prepared food including tapas is served daily. Monthly quiz nights and speciality food events are popular in this friendly community pub. Cribbage is played during the summer. Former Hertfordshire CAMRA Pub of the Year and local Pub of the Year 2014. ☋❀◐◑♣●P🐾ᯤ

Nightingale Ⓛ

Nightingale Road, SG5 1RL TL192293

⏲ 3 (2.30 Tue & Wed)-11; 12-midnight Thu-Sat; 12-10.30 Sun

☎ (01462) 457448 🌐 nightingalehitchin.co.uk

Tring Colley's Dog; guest beers Ⓗ

Community pub hosting darts, pool, dominoes and cricket teams. Tring Colley's Dog is a permanent fixture, alongside four SIBA guest ales and a real cider. Thursday is open mic night and live music also features on some Saturdays. Behind the pub is a large patio area complete with pond and goldfish. Those interested in local brewing history should note the Fordham's Ales & Stout sign in the brickwork on the front of the pub. ☋❀≷♣●P🐾

Radcliffe Arms Ⓛ

31 Walsworth Road, SG4 9ST TL190295

⏲ 8am-11; 9am-midnight Sat; 9am-11 (4 winter) Sun

☎ (01462) 456111 🌐 radcliffearms.com

Buntingford Twitchell; guest beer Ⓗ

This independent gastro-pub continues to go from strength to strength. While much of the pub is given over to dining, there is a bar area open to drinkers which sports two handpumps, usually supplying LocAle beers from Buntingford or guest beers sourced via Buntingford. The Radcliffe also offers an eclectic range of lagers and fruit beers, and an extensive wine list. Excellent food is served in the restaurant. ☋❀◐◑♿≷P▯🐾ᯤ

Victoria

1 Ickleford Road, SG5 1TJ (off A505) TL186298

⏲ 12-11 (midnight Fri); 11-midnight Sat ☎ (01462) 432682

🌐 thevictoriahitchin.com

Greene King IPA, Abbot; guest beers Ⓗ

Popular and busy community pub dating from 1865, offering two regular Greene King beers and two interesting guests. It hosts a wide range of events from quiz nights and live music to comedy and cabaret, as well as an annual beer and cider festival and the Vic Fest music festival. Good-value home-made modern British food is served every day, plus Sunday roasts and regular pie nights. The historic barn is available for community use and live events. ☋❀◐◑♿≷♣🚌ᯤ

Letchworth Garden City

Three Magnets Ⓛ

18-20 Leys Avenue, SG6 3EW TL219326

⏲ 9am-midnight (1am Fri & Sat) ☎ (01462) 681093

Greene King Abbot; Ruddles Best Bitter; guest beers Ⓗ

Built in 1924 as a furniture shop, the building was converted by Wetherspoon in 1996. The chain aims to be all things to all people and this pub focuses on food and ales. It is a family pub during the day and early evening, a social club later, a quiet pub except during major national and international sports events (the TVs are silenced at other times), and a restaurant serving competitively priced food all day. Many old photographs of early Letchworth generate much interest among visitors.
Q☋❀◐◑♿≷🚌ᯤ

Ley Green

Plough

Plough Lane, SG4 8LA (look for brown pub signs at end of Plough Lane) TL162243

⏲ 4-11 Mon & Tue; 12-midnight (11 Wed); 12-10.30 Sun

☎ (01438) 871394

Greene King IPA, Abbot; guest beer Ⓗ

An ale house as far back as 1846, this warm and friendly traditional pub is set in rolling farming country. The large patio has idyllic views across the Beds/Herts countryside – look out for red kites. Hot

and cold snacks are available throughout the week. Visitors are welcome to join in acoustic music sessions on Tuesday evenings. The snug bar can be booked for small functions. The Plough is a popular stop-off for walkers and cyclists.
(88)

Lilley

Lilley Arms

41 West Street, LU2 8LN (just off village green) TL117264
12-11 (10.30 Sun) (01462) 768371 lilley-arms.co.uk
Greene King IPA, Abbot; guest beer H
Former coaching inn dating back 300 years, set in the beautiful surroundings of the Hertfordshire countryside in an ideal location for horse riding, cycling and walking. This traditional country pub is included in one of the Chiltern pub walks. The restaurant is popular so booking is advised. There is additional seating in the attractive garden for warmer days, home to chickens, ducks and goats.
P (101,102)

London Colney

Bull

Barnet Road, AL2 1QU TL182037
12-11 (midnight Thu-Sat) (01727) 823160
thebullatlondoncolney.co.uk
Black Sheep Best Bitter; St Austell Trelawny H**; guest beers** G
Lovely old 17th-century timbered building near the River Colne with a cosy lounge and original fireplace, offering a range of real ales. The large public bar features darts, pool and TV. Evening events include a quiz on Sunday and live music on Saturday. Good-value home-made meals are served Monday to Saturday lunchtimes. Wednesday is food night and curry evenings are held monthly. There is a children's play area outside. P

Nuthampstead

Woodman

Stocking Lane, SG8 8NB TL412344
4-8 Mon; 11.30-11; 12-7 Sun (01763) 848328
thewoodman-inn.co.uk
Adnams Southwold Bitter; Buntingford Twitchell; Greene King IPA; guest beer G
Seventeenth-century free house with an L-shaped bar and a wonderful open fire. The restaurant offers à la carte meals as well as house specials and snacks. Beer is dispensed under gravity from casks behind the bar. The TV is restricted to major sports events. During WWII the USAF 398th Bomber Group was based nearby and much memorabilia is displayed here. Ideally located for visiting local attractions such as Duxford Imperial War Museum.
Q P

Potters Bar

Admiral Byng

186-192 Darkes Lane, EN6 1AF (corner of Byng Drive) TL251015
10-midnight (12.30am Thu-Sat) (01707) 645484
Courage Directors; Greene King Abbot; Ruddles Best Bitter; guest beers H
A friendly community Wetherspoon pub with a display of two model sailing ships and other memorabilia celebrating the exploits and downfall of the unfortunate Admiral Byng, who was executed for 'failing to do his utmost' to save Minorca from falling to the French in 1756 (the family estate is located nearby between Potters Bar and Barnet). In summer the frontage of the pub is opened onto the street, with additional seating provided. (84,610)

Old Manor

Wyllyotts Place, Darkes Lane, EN6 2JD (opp Wyllyotts Centre round corner from railway station) TL249012
11-11 (midnight Fri & Sat); 12-10.30 Sun
(01707) 650674 the-old-manor.co.uk
Caledonian Deuchars IPA; Courage Directors; Fuller's London Pride; guest beers H
Extremely popular dining and drinking venue close to the railway station, frequented by all age groups. Dating back to the 13th century, the building is the surviving part of an old manor house and opened as a pub in its present form in 2000. The large adjoining galleried restaurant offers a wide menu. It gets busy before and after events at the theatre/leisure centre opposite. Tastefully refurbished in 2008, the pub now displays an interesting collection of photos of bygone Potters Bar. P

Potters Crouch

Holly Bush

Bedmond Lane, AL2 3NN (at jct of Potters Crouch Lane and Ragged Hall Lane) TL116052
12-2.30, 6-11; 12-3, 7-10.30 Sun (01727) 851792
thehollybushpub.co.uk
Fuller's London Pride, ESB; Gales Seafarers Ale H
An attractive early 17th-century family-run pub in rural surroundings, beautifully and tastefully furnished to a high standard and boasting large oak tables, antique dressers and period chairs. Spotless throughout, there are no jukeboxes, slot machines or TVs to disturb the drinker in any of the three separate areas. The food menu is not extensive but is of high quality. The garden is ideal in summer – children are not permitted inside.
Q P (300,301)

Preston

Red Lion L

The Green, SG4 7UD (on green at crossroads) TL180247
12-2.30 (3.30 Sat), 5.30-11; 12-3.30, 7-10.30 Sun
(01462) 459585 theredlionpreston.co.uk
Fuller's London Pride; Young's Bitter; guest beers H
This attractive free house standing on the village green was the first community-owned pub in Great Britain. An ever-changing list of beers includes many from small breweries. Ray and Jo prepare fresh home-made food using locally-sourced ingredients where possible. The pub hosts the village cricket teams and fundraises for charity. Local CAMRA Pub of the Year 2012.
Q P

Redbourn

Cricketers L

East Common, AL3 7ND TL104119
12-11 (midnight Fri & Sat); 12-10.30 Sun
(01582) 620612 thecricketersofredbourn.co.uk
Greene King IPA; guest beers H

Redbourn's only free house dates back to 1725. Five real ales and a cider are always available and the food is excellent. The pub is opposite Redbourn's common and historic cricket pitch, making it a perfect setting for a drink on a sunny day. In winter a wood-burning stove creates a cosy atmosphere. Beer festivals showcasing local beers are held in marquees in the car park in the summer. Quiz nights feature on a regular basis, raising funds for local organisations.
Q✿⇔◑♿●P🚌🐾ᯤ

Rickmansworth

Feathers

Church Street, WD3 1DJ TQ060942
⏲ 12-11 (midnight Fri & Sat); 12-10.30 Sun
☎ (01923) 770081 🌐 thefeathers.co.uk
Castle Rock Harvest Pale; Fuller's London Pride; guest beers Ⓗ
This comfortable, rambling building has been a pub for over 200 years. An upmarket and food-oriented venue, a full menu is available daily until 10pm. Beer pricing reflects the consistent high quality of the ales, table service for drinkers and the candlelit atmosphere. The pub is the only one in the area with Harvest Pale permanently on handpump alongside two carefully chosen guest beers. There are weekly quiz evenings and occasional beer festivals. A separate room is available for hire.
✿◑♿⇌⊖♣P🚌ᯤ

St Albans

Blacksmiths Arms

56 St Peters Street, AL1 3HG TL150075
⏲ 11-11 (12.30am Fri & Sat); 12-10.30 Sun
☎ (01727) 868845
Sharp's Doom Bar; guest beers Ⓗ
A large, welcoming high-street pub with an open-plan bar and an extensive beer garden to the rear. One regular ale, along with up to seven guest beers from around Britain, are offered, and one handpump specialises in cider. Regular real ale festivals are held during the year in the main and garden bars. Good-quality reasonably priced pub grub is served. Sport is screened on TV.
✿◑♿♣●🚌🐾ᯤ

Boot Inn

4 Market Place, AL3 5DG TL147072
⏲ 12-midnight (12.45am Fri & Sat); 12-11.30 Sun
☎ (01727) 857533 🌐 thebootstalbans.com
Beer range varies Ⓗ
Situated in the centre of the city, this one-bar pub has a welcoming atmosphere. It can be busy on weekend evenings and Wednesday and Saturday market days. The Clock Tower and Abbey are nearby and it is a short walk to Verulamium Park. The bar features a real fire, exposed beams, low ceiling and wood flooring. Families are welcome until 6pm. Three real ciders are available alongside a changing range of ales. Live music features on Wednesday and Sunday evenings. Curry night is the first Tuesday of the month.
◑⇌(Abbey)●🚌🐾ᯤ

Farriers Arms

32-34 Lower Dagnall Street, AL3 4PT (off A5183 Verulam Rd) TL145073
⏲ 12-2.30 (not Mon), 5.30-11; 12-11 Sat; 12-10.30 Sun
☎ (01727) 851025
McMullen AK, Country Bitter; guest beers Ⓗ
Originally a grocer's and butcher's shop, the building was converted to a pub in the 1920s. The Farriers is a classic back-street local, becoming a free house in 2013 – it is the only pub in the city never to have forsaken real ale. A plaque outside commemorates the first meeting of the Hertfordshire branch of CAMRA. The split-level interior has an area fronting the bar for stand-up drinking, darts and cards, and a back room with comfortable seating. Sport is shown on TV. Parking can be difficult. ◑♣🚌🐾ᯤ

Garibaldi

61 Albert Street, AL1 1RT TL149068
⏲ 12 (2.30 Mon)-11; 12-11.30 Thu; 12-midnight Fri & Sat; 12-10 Sun ☎ (01727) 894745 🌐 garibaldistalbans.co.uk
Fuller's Chiswick Bitter, London Pride, ESB; Gales Seafarers Ale, HSB; guest beer Ⓗ
Larger inside than its frontage suggests, this is a classic example of a quality back-street local, in the heart of Sopwell. Named after the 19th-century Italian patriot, the Garibaldi offers an extensive range of Fuller's ales and excellent home-cooked food, with a fine Sunday roast particularly recommended. Regular live music, poker nights, quizzes, darts, twice-monthly karaoke, food nights and charity events, combined with hospitable staff, give the place a homely, community feel.
✿⇔◑♿⇌(Abbey)♣🚌🐾ᯤ

Lower Red Lion

34-36 Fishpool Street, AL3 4RX TL143072
⏲ 12-11 (10.30 Sun) ☎ (01727) 855669
🌐 thelowerredlion.co.uk
Oakham JHB; St Austell Tribute; guest beers Ⓗ
Both bars of this classic pub have plenty of character and history. Located in a conservation area and between the city centre and the site of Roman Verulamium, the pub stands in one of the city's most picturesque streets. The Lower Red was an early champion in the real ale revival movement and has featured a good range of beers ever since. One handpump dispenses real cider.
Q✿⇔◑♣●P🐾ᯤ

Mermaid

98 Hatfield Road, AL1 3RL (between City station and town centre) TL152074
⏲ 12-11 (midnight Wed, Fri & Sat); 12-10.30 Sun
☎ (01727) 568912
Oakham Citra; guest beers Ⓗ
Located between the main railway station and the city centre, this friendly free house features seven real ales, usually from microbreweries, plus a range of 12 ciders and perries, as well as foreign bottled beers. Try the six mixed thirds of cider or ale. Live music features on Wednesday nights. Wetherspoon CAMRA vouchers are accepted. Hertfordshire CAMRA Cider and Perry Pub of the Year 2013. ◑♿⇌(City)♣●P🚌🐾ᯤ

Six Bells

16-18 St Michael's Street, AL3 4SH TL137074
⏲ 12-11 (midnight Fri & Sat); 12-10.30 Sun
☎ (01727) 856945 🌐 the-six-bells.com
Oakham JHB; Timothy Taylor Landlord; Tring Ridgeway; guest beers Ⓗ
This 16th-century free house is a traditional ale drinker's haven with three regular beers and two changing guests – at least one from a Hertfordshire brewer. it is the only licensed premises within the walls of Roman Verulamium and within walking

distance of the city centre, cathedral, park and museum. Occasional quiz nights and live music are hosted. Good home-cooked food is served lunchtimes and evenings (no food Sun eve). The pleasant patio area is popular in summer. (300,301)

White Hart Tap

4 Keyfield Terrace, AL1 1QJ TL150069
12-11 (01727) 860974 whitehart tap.co.uk
Castle Rock Harvest Pale; Fuller's London Pride; Sharp's Doom Bar; Timothy Taylor Landlord; guest beers H
Welcoming, one-bar, back-street local with four regular beers and three guests from the Punch Taverns range. Good-value home-prepared food, featuring fresh vegetables from the pub's own allotment, are served every lunchtime and Monday-Saturday evenings, with curries on Monday, fish and chips on Friday and roasts on Sunday. Quiz night is Wednesday. Live music plays occasionally on Saturday. Outside is a large garden and separate heated, covered smoking area. Barbecues are held in summer and beer festivals hosted throughout the year. A public car park is opposite the pub. (Abbey/City)

St Paul's Walden

Strathmore Arms

London Road, SG4 8BT TL193222
6-11 Mon; 12-2.30, 5-11; 12-11 Fri & Sat; 12-10.30 Sun (01438) 871654 thestrathmorearms.co.uk
Buntingford Strathmore Bitter; guest beers H
This pub on the Bowes-Lyon estate caters for drinkers and lunchtime diners. Obscure breweries are a speciality on the ever-changing rota of guest beers, and regular beer festivals are hosted. Unusual bottled beers are stocked along with a real cider and perry. The pub keeps a full collection of Good Beer Guides dating from 1976 and is renowned locally for raising funds for charities. A former local CAMRA Pub of the Year and Community Pub of the Year.
QP(304)

Sandridge

Green Man

31 High Street, AL4 9DD TL169104
11-11 (midnight Fri & Sat); 12-11 Sun (01727) 854845
Black Sheep Best Bitter; Greene King IPA, Abbot G
In the centre of Sandridge, this family-run pub extends a warm welcome to all ale and cider drinkers alike. The landlord has been in residence for over 25 years. All ales are available straight from the cask, and up to six real ciders from Westons and Millwhites are also served. On the doorstep of the newly established 850-acre Heartwood Forest, the pub is an ideal place for refreshment after a stroll in the woods. Dogs are welcome in the conservatory and garden.
QP

Rose & Crown

24 High Street, AL4 9DA TL170104
11-11; 12-10.30 Sun (01727) 859739
roseandcrownpubsandridge.co.uk
Sharp's Doom Bar; Tring Ridgeway; Young's Special; guest beers H
Seventeenth-century inn with oak beams, an inglenook fireplace and several areas for drinking and dining. There is a large car park to the rear and a garden where barbecues are held. The pub was reopened in 2010 following redecoration, and has been tastefully modernised, enhancing the traditional interior with additional seating and new dining areas. QP

Sawbridgeworth

Gate

81 London Road, CM21 9JJ TL481150
11.30-2.30, 5.30-11 Mon; 11.30-11 (2 Wed; 2.30 Tue & Thu); 12-11 Sun (01279) 722313 thegatepub.com
Rebellion IPA; guest beers H
A lively hostelry with a huge collection of pumpclips adorning the beams. A pub for sports fans, several satellite TVs screen games and the bar is home to darts, football and cricket teams. A range of up to six beers is offered, typically three from the small Sawbridgeworth Brewery at the back of the pub together with three guests from near or far. A beer festival is held on the Easter and August bank holidays. No dogs are allowed in the pub. P

Old Bell

38 Bell Street, CM21 9AN TL484148
11-11 (1am Fri & Sat); 12-11 Sun (01279) 721050
theoldbellpublichouse.co.uk
Adnams Southwold Bitter; Woodforde's Wherry; guest beers H
An attractive 16th-century timber-framed former coaching house, this comfortable town-centre pub with friendly staff is popular with the locals. The cosy main bar benefits from exposed beams and a fine open fireplace. An additional bar doubles as a dining area. At the back, the courtyard and garden accommodate both smokers and summer sun-seekers. Quiz night is Sunday and a jam session is hosted every other Monday.
QP(333,510)

Stevenage

Our Mutual Friend

Broadwater Crescent, SG2 8EH TL249226
12-11 (11.30 Fri & Sat) (01438) 312282
omfpub.co.uk
Beer range varies H
Thriving community pub on the southern side of Stevenage serving an ever-changing selection of cask beer. Since being rescued from the cask ale graveyard back in 2002, it has featured in the last 12 editions of the Guide. Ten or more real ciders and perries are offered alongside the ales, and regular beer festivals are held throughout the year. The pub can be busy on Stevenage FC match days. Winner of many local CAMRA awards including Pub of the Year. QP(4,5)

Tring

Anchor

73 Western Road, HP23 4BH SP919111
12-11 (11.30 Fri & Sat) (01442) 823280
Greene King IPA; Tring Side Pocket for a Toad, Deacon Dog, Ridgeway; guest beers H
Situated 10 minutes' walk west of the town centre, this welcoming pub, refurbished in 2012, has a spacious bar with tall tables in the two front bay windows and more conventional seating at the rear. There are pictures of local scenes and,

unusually, wine crates on one wall, TVs for sports viewing, and the bar sides are faced with reclaimed door and floor timbers. Fresh filled rolls made with local bread from the bakery opposite are available on the bar. (61,500)

Castle

Park Road, HP23 6BN SP923110
3-11; 12-11.30 Fri & Sat; 12-11 Sun ☎ (01442) 823552
Vale Wychert Ale, Special; guest beer H
Situated on the southern fringe of Tring, close to the Rothschild Zoological Museum, this friendly Victorian corner pub is owned by Vale Brewery. A genuine single-room drinkers' pub, it has comfortable, upholstered bench seating and TVs for sports viewing. Three handpumps dispense well-kept local ales – the guest is invariably a Tring beer. No food is served. The attractive rear open courtyard has some covered seating. A thriving local, it is home to two darts teams.

Robin Hood

1 Brook Street, HP23 5ED (B4635/B486 jct) SP925116
11.30-3, 5.30-11; 11.30-11.30 Fri; 12-11.30 Sat; 12-11 Sun
☎ (01442) 824912 therobinhoodtring.co.uk
Fuller's Chiswick Bitter, London Pride, Bengal Lancer, ESB; Gales Seafarers Ale; guest beer H
This fine 17th-century Fuller's pub situated on the edge of the town has the atmosphere of a country pub, with low-beamed ceilings and two wood-burning stoves adding to the warm, friendly feel. The bar area opens up into a light and airy conservatory which leads out to an open patio and heated, covered area. Six well-kept ales are on handpump, freshly prepared food is available all week and a Thai menu is offered on Sunday evening. Q P (61,500)

Ware

Crooked Billet

140 Musley Hill, SG12 7NL (via New Rd from High St) TL362150
5.30-11 (midnight Fri); 12-midnight Sat; 12-11.30 Sun
☎ (01920) 462516
Hook Norton Hooky; guest beers H
Stuart and Sue have presided over the Billet for more than 20 years. The pub has stocked over 400 different ales since it was acquired by Admiral, fully utilising the local SIBA Direct Delivery Scheme to provide an ever-changing range of four or five ales, always including a mild, porter or stout. An annual spring beer and cider festival is held. This gem of a community pub has two small bars featuring TV sport, pool and darts. Carlisle United and Ware FC fans are assured of a warm welcome. (395)

Wareside

Chequers

Ware Road, SG12 7QY (B1004) TL395156
12-3 (3.15 Wed), 6-11; 12-4, 6.30-10.30 Sun
☎ (01920) 467010
Adnams Southwold Bitter; Buntingford Highwayman; guest beer H
A rural free house dating from the 15th century, the Chequers was originally a coaching inn and has three distinct bars plus a restaurant. The rotating range of three beers features both local brewers such as Buntingford and breweries from outside the area. All food is home made and there are many vegetarian options. Walkers and cyclists are welcome, making this a good base for a ramble. No machines, no music, and there is a ban on swearing. Q P (M3,M4)

Watford

West Herts Sports Club

8 Park Avenue, WD18 7HP TQ103964
4-11; 12-11.30 Fri; 12-11 Sat; 12-10.30 Sun
☎ (01923) 229239 westhertssports.co.uk
Young's Bitter; guest beers H
This comfortable members' bar is a multiple winner of CAMRA East Anglian Club of the Year. Up to three regularly changing guest beers are on offer alongside a house beer from Wells. The bar is tastefully decorated with sporting memorabilia and major sporting events are screened. A separate function room, home of the Watford Beer Festival, is available to hire. Show a CAMRA membership card or copy of this Guide for entry up to four times a year. P

Wild Hill

Woodman

45 Wildhill Road, AL9 6EA (between A1000 and B158) TL264068
11.30-2.30, 5.30-11; 12-2.30, 7-10.30 Sun
☎ (01707) 642618
Greene King IPA, Abbot; guest beers H
Winner of local CAMRA Pub of the Year 10 times and Hertfordshire Pub of the Year four times, this excellent village hostelry extends a warm welcome to a varied clientele of all ages. Six beers are available, with four guests from regional and micro breweries, usually including one from Hertfordshire. Good pub grub is served at lunchtime (no food Sun). The large garden is ideal in summer. An all-round superb boozer – but look out for God's Waiting Room. P

Cask breather

Where an entry states that some beers in a pub are served with the aid of cask breathers, this means that demand valves are connected to both casks and cylinders of gas; as beer is drawn off, it is replaced by applied gas (either carbon dioxide, nitrogen or both) to prevent oxidation. The method is not acceptable to CAMRA as it does not allow beer to condition and mature naturally. The Campaign believes brewers and publicans should use the size of casks best suited to the turnover of beer in order to avoid oxidation. If a pub in the Good Beer Guide uses cask breathers, we list only those beers that are free of the device.

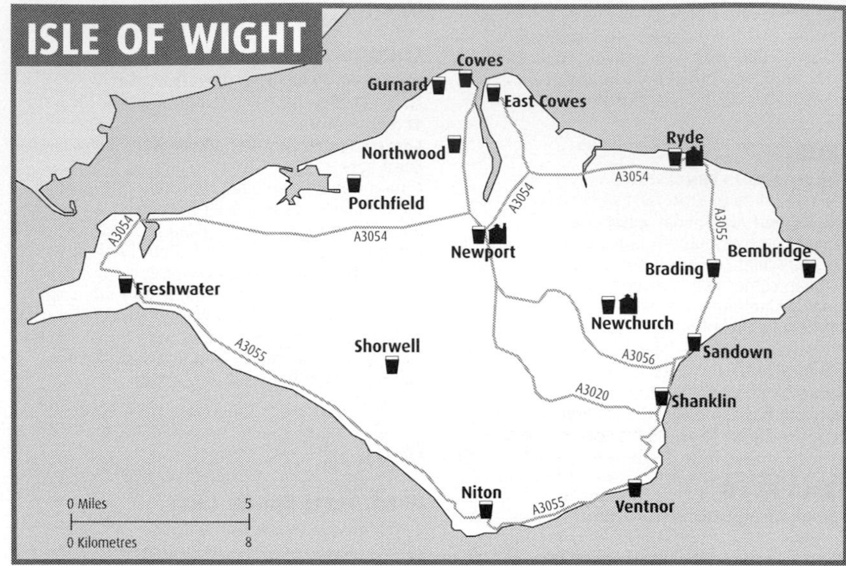

Bembridge

Old Village Inn

61 High Street, PO35 5SF
12-11 ☎ (01983) 872616 yeoldevillageinn.co.uk
Beer range varies H
The Old Village Inn Steak & Ale House is the latest addition to the Bembridge scene, specialising in local meat and fish dishes. A fine choice of real ales and selected wines is served in a refined and relaxed atmosphere. Food is available 12-3pm and 5-9pm. Live music plays on occasional Fridays and a popular quiz is held on the first Monday of the month. There is a patio area to the rear and a pétanque terrain. Q ♣P (8)

Brading

Yarbridge Inn

Yarbridge, PO36 0AA (on main Brading to Sandown road) SZ60448642
11-11 ☎ (01983) 406212
St Austell Tribute; Sharp's Doom Bar; guest beers H
Previously known as the Anglers, this is a pleasant single-bar pub with a changing range of four beers. The dining area offers a fixed menu plus a specials board, and a choice of roasts on Sunday. Outside is a safe area for children and a paved area with parasols. Live music is hosted occasionally.
Q P (2,3)

Cowes

Anchor Inn

1 High Street, PO31 7SA (opp Sainsbury's)
11-11 (midnight Fri & Sat); 12-10.30 Sun
☎ (01983) 292823 theanchorcowes.co.uk
Adnams Southwold Bitter; Fuller's London Pride; Goddards Fuggle-Dee-Dum; guest beers H
This high-street pub, originally the Trumpeters back in 1704, is close to the marina, tempting visiting yachtsman for their first pint ashore. The recent conversion has integrated the stables and created a pleasant beer garden. A good selection of beer is on offer, including one Island ale and two guests. A varied food menu is available, served in prodigious quantities. Frequent live entertainment is provided. Accommodation is in seven comfortable rooms.
(1)

Bertie's

High Street, PO31 7RR
11-midnight (1am Fri & Sat) ☎ (01983) 200666
Beer range varies H
Part wine bar, part café, part traditional pub and part jazz club. There are three handpumps, each with a beer from one of the three Island breweries. Live entertainment includes a jazz jam session on Thursdays, and more music on Fridays and Saturdays. Children are welcome during the day. Furnishings are comfortable, newspapers are provided and tasty nibbles are served. ♣ (1)

Union Inn

Watch House Lane, PO31 7QH (just off Parade)
11-midnight; 12-10.30 Sun ☎ (01983) 293163
unioninncowes.co.uk
Fuller's London Pride; Gales Seafarers Ale, HSB; guest beer H
A haven for yachting enthusiasts, locals and holidaymakers, one three-sided bar serves the lounge, snug, dining area and airy conservatory. A roaring fire in winter adds to the cosy atmosphere. Delicious family meals are served, with portions for children and ingredients sourced from local suppliers. The pub may close at 11pm but frequently stays open later. There is pay parking on the Parade 25 yards away, free later in the day. A popular quiz evening is hosted on the first three Wednesdays of the month. Q ♣ (1)

INDEPENDENT BREWERIES

Goddards Ryde
Island Newport
Yates' Newchurch

East Cowes

White Hart Inn

Dover Road, PO32 6RG (opp ferry terminal building)
12 (11 Sat)-11 ☎ (01983) 280230
Beer range varies H
Originally built in 1748, and rebuilt in 1890, this is an imposing, street-corner local with a friendly atmosphere and well-chosen and kept beers. It is conveniently placed for the first or last drink on the Island (the ferry is only 30 yards away). Keep an eye open for the alleged ghost in the lounge bar. Q (4,5)

Freshwater

Prince of Wales

Princes Road, PO40 9ED
3-11; 12-11.30 Fri & Sat; 12-11 Sun ☎ (01983) 753535
Ballard's Midhurst Mild; guest beers H
Fine, unspoilt gem of a town pub run by possibly the longest-serving landlord on the Isle of Wight. Just off the main Freshwater shopping centre, it has a large garden and pleasant public and lounge bars. Along with the two regular beers there are four frequently changing guests including one from a local brewery, so there is always something new to try. Q P (7,12)

Gurnard

Portland Inn

2 Worsley Road, PO31 8JN (opp church) SZ47909530
12-11 (10.30 Sun) ☎ (01983) 292948
Beer range varies H
Pleasant and friendly village local, previously the baker's, grocer's and hardware store. It has a comfortable, upmarket single bar and a secluded garden. Three ales are available from the well-run cellar. Sadly, the old Gurnard Hotel opposite, a hugely popular pub in its day, was demolished many years ago, but now the Portland provides a focal point for the community. Q (1)

Newchurch

Pointer Inn

High Street, PO36 0NN (next to church)
11-11; 12-10.30 Sun ☎ (01983) 865202
pointerinn.com
Fuller's London Pride; Gales HSB; guest beer H
Ancient village local where families are welcome. The home-cooked food is prepared by a chef with a vast experience of Island trade (booking is essential). Food is served until 9.30pm (9pm Sun). A highchair and toys are always available for children. The large garden has a pétanque terrain and a covered area for smokers. Awards include Fuller's Best Country/Village Pub and a Certificate of Excellence by Trip Advisor.
Q P (23)

Newport

Prince of Wales

36 South Street, PO30 1JE (opp bus station)
10.30-11; 12-10.30 Sun ☎ (01983) 525026
Beer range varies H
This mock-Tudor single-bar street-corner local has a fine reputation for well-kept ale, with up to three available from the Punch list. Located opposite the bus station and Morrisons, this is very much a locals' venue and retains the feel of a public bar. The pub stages an annual beer festival, and has a good games following. Food is restricted to tasty, wholesome sandwiches, pies and mother's home-baked specials. A real gem. Q P

William Coppin

Furlongs, PO30 2TA (at bottom of town, part of multiplex cinema complex)
8am-midnight (2am Fri; 3am Sat) ☎ (01983) 556030
Greene King Abbot; Ruddles Best Bitter; guest beers H
A former nightclub, and still acting as one at weekend evenings, this Wetherspoon pub has a large, modern interior with panelling, big mirrors and subdued colours. The beer range is not as extensive as at other pubs in the chain, but includes an interesting selection of guests, all in excellent condition. The origin of the pub's name and lots of local history feature on the walls. Close to the bus station. P

Niton

Buddle

St Catherine's Road, Niton Undercliff, PO38 2NE (follow signs to St Catherine's Lighthouse) SZ50207580
11-10.30 (11.30 Fri & Sat); 12-10.30 Sun
☎ (01983) 730243 buddleinn.co.uk
Beer range varies H
This 16th-century pub was built as a farmhouse but reputedly became a smugglers' inn during the 18th century. Extensively refurbished, it retains its ancient flagstones and beams, inglenook fireplace and many interesting photographs. A popular destination dining pub, serving good locally-sourced food, it also has a strong real ale following, with six ales on handpump. Close to the lighthouse, the pub has many links to Trinity House. Q P (6)

Northwood

Travellers Joy

85 Pallance Road, PO31 8LS (on Northwood-Porchfield road) SZ48009360
11-11 summer; 12-2.30, 5-11; 12-11 Thu-Sat; 11-11 Sun winter ☎ (01983) 298024 thetravellersjoy.co.uk
Island Wight Gold; guest beers H
Offering one of the best choices of cask ale on the island, this long-standing old country inn was the Island's first beer exhibition house. Up to seven varied and interesting ales rotate to supplement the Island's Wight Gold. A real cider is also available. A good range of home-cooked food is served lunchtimes and evenings. The pub is a thriving venue for real ale followers, the local community and visitors seeking a friendly and amenable base. Q P (1)

Porchfield

Sportsman's Rest

Main Road, PO30 4LP (on main Cowes-Yarmouth road)
12-3, 6-11; 12-6 Sun ☎ (01983) 522044
sportsmansrest.co.uk
Beer range varies H
Popular village inn of some character, with a splendid family garden. Recently purchased by a local couple, it is fast gaining a reputation for good food and ale. The St Lawrence steak & ale pie is a house speciality. Three real ales are available

including one from an Island brewery. A rural pub with fine walks nearby, including the coastal path.
Q❀◑♿⛺♣P🐾📶

Ryde

Railway

68 St John's Road, PO33 2RT (by St John's station)
12-midnight summer; 3-11 winter ☎ (01983) 566651
Goddards Ale of Wight; guest beers
This pleasant town local has seen several changes of ownership in the past few years before becoming a free house. The new owner has refurbished it to a high standard, while retaining flagstone floors, beams and plenty of wood. Horticulturalists will be interested in the Ginkgo biloba tree in the garden, a species whose ancestry can be traced back over 200 million years. Close to the station, it is handy for visitors from Portsmouth in search of quality real ale.
❀♿⇌(St John's Road)♣🚌(2,3)🐾📶

S Fowler & Co

41-43 Union Street, PO33 2LF (top of Union St)
7am-midnight (1am Fri & Sat) ☎ (01983) 812112
Courage Directors; Greene King Abbot; Ruddles Best Bitter; guest beers
A Wetherspoon conversion of a drapery store offering a varied range of well-kept beers. The pub is in the centre of town, with a bus stop conveniently outside. The pub's name came at the suggestion of the local CAMRA branch; not only is it the name of the former store, but also that of the first local CAMRA chairman and revered early campaigner. The upstairs restaurant is family-friendly. Q◑♿⇌(Esplanade)🍎🚌📶

Simeon Arms

21 Simeon Street, PO33 1JG (short walk from Canoe Lake)
11-11.45 (11.30 Mon; 11 Tue & Wed); 12-11.30 Sun
☎ (01983) 614954
Courage Best Bitter; Goddards Ale of Wight; guest beer
Thriving yet unlikely gem tucked away in a Ryde back street with a Tardis-like interior and annexed function hall. The pub is immensely popular with the local community who come to participate in various leagues including shove-ha'penny, darts, crib and pool, and pétanque on the enormous floodlit terrain in summer. You can always expect to find a local ale. Live music plays on Saturday and Sunday nights. The smoking area outside is heated and covered. ❀◑⇌(St John's Road)♣🚌📶

Sandown

Castle Inn

12-14 Fitzroy Street, PO36 8HY (off High St)
11-11 (midnight Fri); 10.30-1am Sat; 10.30-midnight Sun
☎ (01983) 403169 sandowncastle.co.uk
Young's Special; guest beers
The Castle is an excellent town free house and locals' pub with crib and two darts teams. Six real ales are on offer including the best from local breweries. There is a children's room at the back and a patio for warm weather. The TV is not allowed to intrude, but is turned on for special occasions. Happy hour is popular, as is the Sunday quiz. Beer festivals are held several times a year, usually featuring local ales and cider.
Q❀♿⇌♣🚌(3,8)🐾📶

Shanklin

Chine Inn

1 Chine Hill, PO37 6BW (up hill at end of Esplanade)
closed Mon; 11.30-11; 12-10.30 Sun ☎ (01983) 865880
chineinn.co.uk
Sharp's Doom Bar; Timothy Taylor Boltmaker; guest beer
This inn with magnificent views of the bay is a classic. The building, which has been standing since 1621, must be one of the oldest pubs with a licence on the Island. Completely refurbished, it has retained plenty of its original charm. Live music features on Saturday night and Sunday afternoon. The Chine Inn ghosts – a girl in blue and an old man in the corner – have been seen by small children. Ask to see the opening hours notice.
Q❀◑🍎🚌(2,3)🐾

King Harry's Bar

6 Church Road, PO37 6NU (on edge of Old Village towards Ventnor)
11 (12 winter)-11; 12-10.30 Sun ☎ (01983) 863119
kingharrysbar.co.uk
Fuller's ESB; guest beers
Charming 19th-century thatched property with two established Tudor bars, restaurants, decked gardens and the Chine walk, plus car parking front and rear. Up to three guest beers are offered, chosen for their originality. Food is only served in the summer months commencing Easter – the long-established Henry VIII kitchen specialises in steaks to die for. Function facilities and entertainment are provided and accommodation is available. Q❀◑⛺♣🍎P🚌(2,3)🐾

Shorwell

Crown Inn

Walkers Lane, PO30 3JZ
10.30 (11.30 Sun)-11 ☎ (01983) 740293
crowninnshorwell.co.uk
Adnams Broadside; Goddards Fuggle-Dee-Dum; St Austell Tribute; Sharp's Doom Bar; guest beers
Expansive 300-year-old hostelry in the picturesque village of Shorwell, with a central multi-sided bar and traditional bar areas. It offers a range of four to six beers and a good home-cooked pub menu, available all day. The pub has a trout stream running through the garden, ducks in abundance to keep the children amused, and plenty of car parking. Q❀◑♿♣P🚌(12)🐾📶

Ventnor

Volunteer

30 Victoria Street, PO38 1ES (50yds from bus terminal)
11 (12 Fri-Sun)-midnight ☎ (01983) 852537
Courage Best Bitter; guest beers
Built in 1866, the Volunteer is one of the smallest pubs on the Island. A past winner of local CAMRA Pub of the Year, up to six beers are available including an occasional local brew. No chips, no children, no fruit machines, no video games – just a pure adult drinking house and one of the few places where you can still play rings and enjoy a traditional games night. Live music features on Sunday afternoon. Westons Old Rosie cider is available. Q♿♣🍎🚌(3,6)🐾

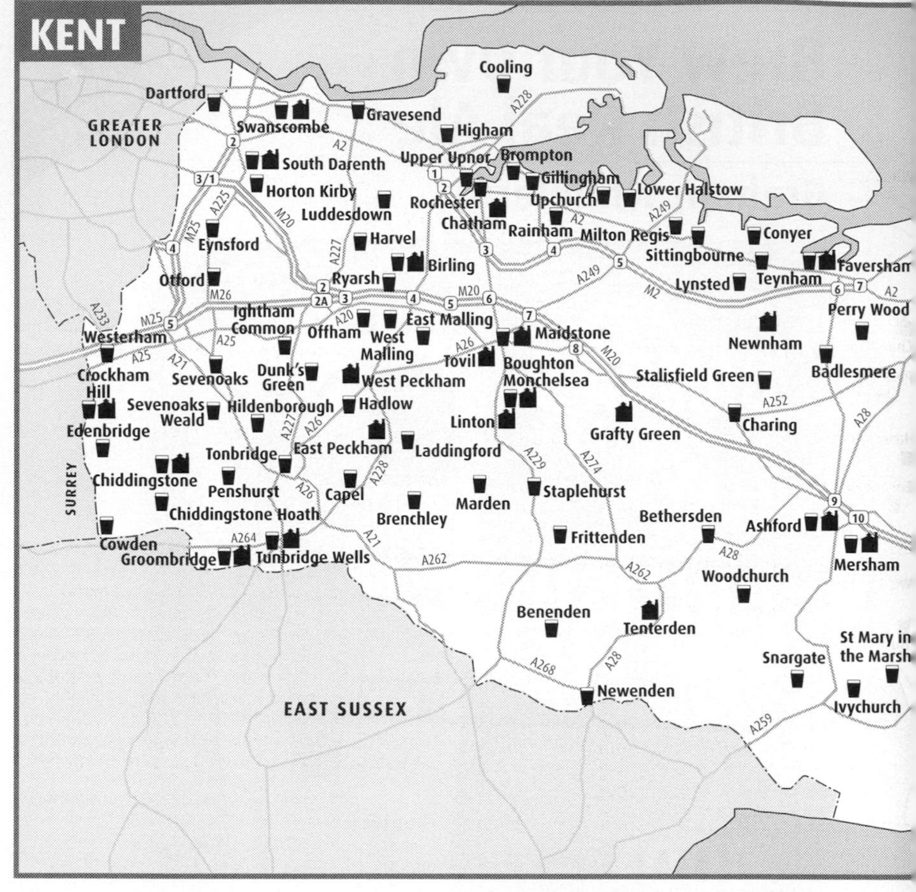

Ashford

County Hotel

10 High Street, TN24 8TD

8-11 (midnight Thu; 1am Fri & Sat) ☎ (01233) 646891

Greene King Abbot; Ruddles Best Bitter; guest beers Ⓗ

A spacious Wetherspoon pub in the centre of Ashford. The 18th-century red-brick building has seven bays and a tile-hung top storey. There are two bars with three separate seating areas; note the distinctive metal statue. Two real ciders are available, dispensed from polypins in the fridge. Food is available every day from 8am to 10pm. Children are welcome until 9pm.

(International) P

Badlesmere

Red Lion

Ashford Road, ME13 0NX (on A251)

12-11 (9 Mon; midnight Fri & Sat); 12-7 Sun

☎ (01233) 740320 redlionbadlesmere.co.uk

Shepherd Neame Spitfire; guest beers Ⓗ

Traditional country pub with many public bridleways and footpaths in its vicinity. The selection of ales usually includes several local beers, often from Ramsgate (Gadds) and Millis. The pub offers a range of home-cooked food and can cater for functions and parties. Regular live music from local bands can be enjoyed here. Camping facilities are available in the pub's own paddock.

P (666)

Benenden

Bull

The Street, TN17 4DE

12-midnight ☎ (01580) 240054

thebullatbenenden.co.uk

Dark Star Hophead; Harveys Sussex Best Bitter; Larkins Traditional Ale; guest beer Ⓗ

Free house overlooking the village green where you can watch the local cricket team. The building dates from the 17th century and features wooden floors, oak beams and an inglenook fireplace. Meals may be enjoyed in the separate restaurant or the public bar (no food Sun eve). Booking is advisable for the Friday fish and chips evening and Sunday lunchtime carvery. An acoustic music club is held monthly on a Thursday and there is live music most Sunday afternoons. Q P (297)

Bethersden

George Inn

The Street, TN26 3AG (off A28 between Ashford and Tenterden in centre of village)

⏲ 12-11.30 (5 Sun) ☎ (01233) 820235
Brakspear Bitter; Harveys Old Ale; Morland Old Speckled Hen; guest beer Ⓗ
Two-bar free house in a pretty Kentish village decorated with pictures of local life. The public bar is a reminder of what village inns used to be like, with pub games, jukebox and good conversation. The former saloon now doubles as a restaurant. Food is served every day (not Mon lunch and Sun eve), with carveries on Wednesday evening and Sunday lunchtime. Beer festivals are held around St George's Day and in July. Buses from Ashford and Tenterden stop outside. ❀◗●P⊟(2)🐾

Birchington-on-Sea

Wheel Alehouse

60 Station Road, CT7 9RA
⏲ 12-2, 5-9; closed Sun eve & Mon ☎ (07826) 130927
🌐 thewheelalehouse.co.uk
Beer range varies Ⓖ
This pub, converted from a shop, has been a welcome addition to the village's beer scene. A nautical theme runs throughout. The beers are served direct from the cask from a temperature-controlled stillage room behind a small bar counter. At the rear is a steep flight of stairs leading to the Upper Deck, where toilets and further seating can be found. Q⇌●⊟(33,34)

Birling

Nevill Bull 𝕃

1 Ryarsh Road, ME19 5JW
⏲ 11-3, 6-11; 12-11 Sat; 12-6 Sun ☎ (01732) 843193
🌐 nevillbull.co.uk
Kent Pale; guest beers Ⓗ
A village-centre pub with a quirky interior, displaying an ever-changing eclectic collection of china, glass and other items. The name was changed in 1953 and honours a local landowner's son, Lt Michael Nevill, killed in WWII. A beer from the close-by Kent Brewery is normally available. Hearty food, sourced from local producers, may be found every day, with a pig roast on Sunday. The restaurant can be used for meetings and is fitted with audio-visual equipment. ❀◗P⊟(58)🐾

Boughton Monchelsea

Cock Inn 𝕃

Heath Road, ME17 4JD TQ776512
⏲ 11-11; 12-10.30 Sun ☎ (01622) 743166
Shepherd Neame Master Brew, Spitfire, seasonal beers; guest beers Ⓗ
A 16th-century coaching inn built to provide lodgings for Canterbury pilgrims, full of character, with oak beams and an inglenook fireplace. An excellent menu specialising in seafood is served in both bar and restaurant (no food Sun eves). Darts and board games are available, and quiz nights are held monthly. There is a large patio area. This dog-friendly pub is situated near to the Greensand Way and walkers are welcome. Q❀◗♣P⊟(59)🐾

Bramling

Haywain 𝕃

Canterbury Road, CT3 1NB
⏲ 7-11 Mon; 12-3, 6-11; 12-4 Sun ☎ (01227) 720676
Fuller's London Pride; Wells Bombardier; guest beers Ⓗ
Classic and friendly country pub which features hanging hop bines and assorted curios. The cosy snug is used mainly for dinners and meetings. Traditional games include darts and bat and trap. Mondays feature a quiz night, Wednesday evenings crib. One of the two guest beers is usually from a Kent brewery. An annual beer festival is hosted over the spring bank holiday weekend in a marquee in the attractive garden. Excellent home-cooked food, using local produce, is served (no food Mon). Q❀◗♣P⊟(13,14)🐾

Brenchley

Halfway House 𝕃

Horsmonden Road, TN12 7AX (½ mile SE of village)
⏲ 12-11 (10.30 Sun) ☎ (01892) 722526
🌐 halfwayhousebrenchley.co.uk
Goacher's Fine Light Ale; Rother Valley Smild; guest beers Ⓖ
This award-winning rural free house is full of character and serves eight to ten competitively priced beers direct from the cask together with Kentish Chiddingstone Cider. The expansive gardens, including one dedicated to families and children, come into their own on Whitsun and August bank holidays when festivals are held

featuring up to 75 ales. Meal choices are chalked up in the bar (no food Sun eve). A half-hour bus ride from Tunbridge Wells will drop you outside the the front door. Q❀◐P (297)

Bridge

White Horse Inn L

53 High Street, CT4 5LA

11.30-11 ☎ (01227) 830845 whitehorsebridge.co.uk

Ringwood Best Bitter; Timothy Taylor Landlord H; **guest beers** H/G

A 16th-century half-timbered coaching inn with superb beamed ceilings and two wide fireplaces in which wood fires burn in winter. The two guest beers usually include one from Ramsgate (Gadds) Brewery. The restaurant is well known for its freshly-prepared food, mostly from local sources. The specials menu lists imaginative combinations of seasonal foods. There is a classy gin and vodka menu on a chalkboard in the bar.
❀◐P (17,18)

Broadstairs

Four Candles Alehouse

1 Sowell Street, St Peter's, CT10 2AT

5-10.30 (11.30 Fri); 12-3.30, 5-11.30 Sat; 12-3.30, 5-10.30 Sun ☎ 07947 062063 thefourcandles.co.uk

Beer range varies G

This converted shop has been a welcome addition to the local micropub scene. Maintaining its basic shop-like interior, it is furnished with high tables and bar stools and decorated with pumpclips of various beers that have been served. Beer comes from a temperature-controlled stillage in an adjoining room. Named after the famous Two Ronnies sketch which was reportedly modelled on a local shop, there is a distinctive pair of fork handles above the door. Q (56)

Thirty-Nine Steps Alehouse

5 Charlotte Street, CT10 1LR

12-11 thethirty-ninesteps.co.uk

Beer range varies G

One of Thanet's many micropubs, this former shop has been tastefully converted and furnished with heavy wooden high tables and bench seating. The three changing beers are dispensed from a glass-fronted cooled stillage cabinet behind the bar. The enthusiastic and knowledgeable landlord is keen to source interesting and unusual brews from around the country and the place has become a popular destination for discerning local ale drinkers, as well as offering a pleasant alternative to the town's tourists. Q (56)

Brompton

King George V L

1 Prospect Row, ME7 5AL

11.45-11; 12-10.30 Sun ☎ (01634) 842418 kgvpub.com

Adnams Southwold Bitter; guest beers H

A 17th-century free house decorated with military memorabilia, it has three connected areas and a covered and heated space outside for smokers. Four guest ales from local microbreweries feature as well as from further afield, always including a mild, plus a wide variety of Belgian beers, malt whiskies, rums and ciders. Food is served every lunchtime and evening, Tuesday to Saturday, with themed pizza, curry, tapas and steak nights. Sunday roasts are recommended. Four guest rooms are available. ❀◐ (101,182)

Burmarsh

Shepherd & Crook L

Shear Way, TN29 0JJ (follow signposted road from A259 to E of Dymchurch) TR101320

11.30-11 (10 Mon & Wed); closed Tue; 11.30-6 Sun ☎ (01303) 872336 shepherdandcrook.co.uk

Old Dairy Red Top; guest beers H

A friendly family-run free house on the Romney Marsh Cycle Route. The pub has a separate dining room and single bar where ring the bull can be played. Frequently changing guest ales are always available. Traditional home-cooked English meals utilising local ingredients, where possible, are available lunchtimes and evenings (no food Sun). The interesting adjacent medieval church has a Norman doorway within a 16th-century porch and is well worth a visit. Q❀◐ (111)

Canterbury

Bottle Shop

The Goods Shed, Station Road West, CT2 8AN

closed Mon; 12-10.30 (11 Sat); 12-4 Sun ☎ (01227) 656280 bottle-shop.co.uk

Beer range varies H

Located in the Goods Shed, an acclaimed permanent farmers' market and food hall, the shop specialises in bottled beers from the UK and all over the world. Choose from over 400 beers, many rarely found in the UK, to take home or enjoy on the premises. A selection of ales is also served from mini-casks, and bottled ciders, home-brew

INDEPENDENT BREWERIES

Black Cat Groombridge
Canterbury Ales Chartham
Canterbury Brewers Canterbury
Caveman Swanscombe
Farriers Arms Mersham
Goacher's Tovil
Goody Herne
Hop Fuzz West Hythe
Hopdaemon Newnham
Kent Birling
Larkins Chiddingstone
Mad Cat Faversham
Maidstone Maidstone (NEW)
Millis South Darenth
Musket Linton (NEW)
Nelson Chatham
Old Dairy Tenterden
Pig & Porter Tunbridge Wells (NEW)
Ramsgate (Gadds) Broadstairs
Ripple Steam Sutton
Rockin' Robin Boughton Monchelsea
Shepherd Neame Faversham
Spencer's Ashford
Swan West Peckham
Tír Dhá Ghlas Dover
Tonbridge East Peckham
Wantsum Hersden
Westerham Crockham Hill
Whitstable Grafty Green

kits and gift vouchers are available. The website has details of regular tasting events, the board game club and discounts for students and CAMRA members. Q⚘♿⇌(West)P🚌(4,6)

Dolphin 🄻

17 St Radigund's Street, CT1 2AA

12-12.30am ☎ (01227) 455963

thedolphincanterbury.co.uk

Sharp's Doom Bar; Timothy Taylor Landlord; guest beers 🄷

Friendly local decorated with 1950-1970 memorabilia and free of TV screens. Good pub food in generous portions is served daily, with roasts on Sundays. There is a comprehensive collection of board games and free internet access. The attractive verandah is popular with diners, and there is a large suntrap garden.

⚘⇌(West)🐾

Eight Bells

34 London Road, CT2 8LN

3-11; 12-midnight Fri & Sat; 12-10.30 Sun

☎ (01227) 454794

Wells Bombardier; Young's Bitter 🄷

Small, traditional local dating from 1708 and rebuilt in 1902, retaining original embossed windows and decorated with memorabilia. There is live music fortnightly on Fridays, and a quiz, usually on the last Wednesday of the month. Five darts teams play every week and their trophies are on display. Roast lunches are served on Sundays and simple meals at other times. There is an attractive small walled garden and a comfortable heated smoking area. ⚘⇌(West)♣🚌(3,6)🐾

Foundry Brew Pub 🄻

White Horse Lane, CT1 2RU (just off High Street)

12-midnight (3am Fri & Sat); 12-11 Sun

☎ (01227) 455899 thefoundrycanterbury.co.uk

Canterbury Foundryman's Gold, Foundry Torpedo, Streetlight Porter; guest beers 🄷

The home of Canterbury Brewers, this former 19th-century foundry is on two floors. Seven ales are usually offered, including one Kent guest beer, plus local ciders. The brewery's own bottled ale can be bought to take away. Good-value pub food is available until 6pm (8pm Thu-Sat). A DJ plays upstairs on Friday and Saturday nights. There is a pleasant patio. ⚘♿⇌(East/West)🚌

King's Head 🄻

204 Wincheap, CT1 3RY (on A28 S of city centre)

12-2.30, 4.45-midnight; 12-midnight Fri & Sat; 12-11.30 Sun ☎ (01227) 462885

Greene King IPA; Harveys Sussex Best Bitter; guest beers 🄷

Friendly 15th-century traditional local, worth the short walk from the city centre. Two guest beers are sold, one usually from a local microbrewery, plus Kentish Pip cider and Westons perry. Bar billiards and darts are played, and bat and trap in the garden in the summer. There is a quiz night on the first Sunday in each month, and a curry night every Thursday. Good-value pub food is available every evening, plus Saturday and Sunday lunchtimes. ⚘⇌(East)♣P🚌(1,28)🐾

New Inn

19 Havelock Street, CT1 1NP (off ring road near St Augustine's Abbey)

12-2, 6-11; 12-midnight Fri & Sat ☎ (01227) 464584

newinncanterbury.co.uk

Greene King IPA; guest beers 🄷

Victorian back-street terraced house close to the cathedral, St Augustine's Abbey and the bus station. The main bar has red walls, a wooden floor and a jukebox. At the back is a long conservatory with two cosy alcoves, one known as the Library. Usually four guest beers, mostly from microbreweries, plus Biddenden cider are on sale. Beer festivals are held on Whitsun and August bank holiday weekends. Disabled access is through the attractive garden via Old Ruttington Lane. No food Mondays. ⚘♿♣🚌🐾

Unicorn Inn 🏆 🄻

61 St Dunstan's Street, CT2 8BS

11.30-11 (midnight Fri & Sat) ☎ (01227) 463187

unicorninn.com

Sharp's Doom Bar; Shepherd Neame Master Brew; guest beers 🄷

Comfortable 1604 pub near the historic Westgate, with an attractive suntrap garden. Bar billiards is played and a quiz, set by regular customers, is held weekly on Sunday evening. One of the guest beers is often from a Kent microbrewery, and beer updates are posted on Twitter. Food is good value, with a Two Meals for £10 special offer on selected meals (no food Sun eve). Sporting events (not Sky) are televised unobtrusively. Local CAMRA branch Pub of the Year 2014.

Q⚘⇌(West)♣🚌🐾

Capel

Dovecote Inn

Alders Road, TN12 6SU (½ mile W of A228 towards Tudeley)

5.30-9.30 Mon; 12-3, 5.30-11; 12-10.30 Sun

☎ (01892) 835966

Gales HSB; Harveys Sussex Best Bitter; guest beers 🄶

Excellent country inn with a homely interior, hung with hops and beautifully decorated with flowers and bunting. Old shotguns add an antique feel. Westons Old Rosie cider and a varied range of four to five ales are served straight from the cask. Good pub food is available (not Sun and Mon eves). Live music features monthly on a Sunday. Outside are a shaded patio with plenty of seating, a children's play area, and the garden where you can try your hand at a game of bat and trap.

Q⚘♿♣P🚌(6A)

Charing

Bowl Inn

Egg Hill Road, TN27 0HG (signposted from A20 and A251)

4-11; 12-midnight Fri & Sat; 12-10.30 Sun

☎ (01233) 712256 bowlinn.co.uk

Fuller's London Pride; guest beers 🄷

A 16th-century free house located on the top of the North Downs in an Area of Outstanding Natural Beauty, and signposted from the A20 and A251. A large inglenook fire warms the bar. The pub is a popular stop-off point for walkers and cyclists and offers five rooms; camping is also available. In summer it opens from noon Monday to Saturday. An annual beer festival is held.

⚘♿ΔP🐾

Chiddingstone

Castle Inn 🄻

TN8 7AH (turn of B2027 approx 1 mile W of Penshurst station)

☼ 10-11; 12-10.30 Sun ☎ (01892) 870247

🌐 castleinn-kent.co.uk

Harveys Sussex Best Bitter; Larkins Traditional Ale; guest beer 🄷

Rambling, impressive stone inn in the centre of a picture-postcard village. Different areas of the pub have distinct characters. The black and red tiled floor of the public bar, complete with wood-burning stove, is home to locals and possibly the Larkins brewer sampling his wares. Other areas are popular with the many visitors drawn by the village, nearby Hever and Chiddingstone castles, and Penshurst Place. Relax awhile in the secluded courtyard garden or dine in the restaurant. **Q🐴❀◑♣🐾ᯤ**

Chiddingstone Hoath

Rock 🄻

TN8 7BS (1½ miles S of Chiddingstone)

☼ 12-11 (10.30 Sun) ☎ (01892) 870296

Larkins Traditional Ale; guest beer 🄷

A characterful old drovers' inn frequented by characters itself, popular with locals and visitors despite its remote nature. Extensively beamed, the main focuses of this brick-floored gem are the wood-burning stove and the game of ring the bull. Beers come from Larkins Brewery up the road, with guests from the landlord's old stamping ground of the West Country, such as Cotleigh. Good food is served but do book. The garden tucked around the corner is a secluded suntrap. **Q🐴❀◑♣P🐾ᯤ**

Coldred

Carpenters Arms 🄻

The Green, CT15 5AJ

☼ 6 (7 Sun)-11 ☎ (01304) 830190

Beer range varies 🄷/🄶

Overlooking the village green and duck pond, this is a superb no-frills community pub dating from the 18th century. In 2013 it celebrated 100 years in the Fagg family. Inside, many of the traditional features of this village pub have remained unchanged for 50 years, including the handpumps and till. There is usually one real ale from a Kent microbrewery alongside Westons cider. One local quoted: 'Do not go putting the Carpenters in the Guide; it is our best-kept secret!' **Q🐴❀♣●P🚌**(88A,89A)**🐾**

Conyer

Ship

Conyer Quay, ME9 9HR TQ962648

☼ 12-3, 6-11 (midnight Fri); 11-11.30 Sat; 10-9.30 Sun ☎ (01795) 520778 🌐 shipinnconyer.co.uk

Adnams Southwold Bitter; Shepherd Neame Master Brew; guest beers 🄷

Well-renovated 18th-century free house in this isolated hamlet. The pub is owned by Swale Marina and is known for good-quality food. Primarily a gastro-pub, the Ship serves up to four beers, often sourced from Old Dairy or Whitstable breweries. This venue has a real fire and a garden overlooking the creek. Its location next to the Saxon Shore Way makes it popular with walkers and cyclists. **Q🐴❀◑P🚌**(344)**ᯤ**

Cooling

Horseshoe & Castle 🄻

Main Road, ME3 8DJ

☼ 11.30-3, 5.45-11 Tue; 11.30 (5.45 Mon)-11; 12-10.30 Sun ☎ (01634) 221691 🌐 horseshoeandcastle.com

Shepherd Neame Master Brew; guest beer 🄷

Welcoming free house nestling in a quiet village on the Hoo peninsula. The restaurant specialises in seafood (closed Mon). Accommodation of a high standard is available for those who wish to explore the area. The village has two main points of interest: the local church and graveyard, which was used in a film version of Great Expectations, where Pip met Magwitch, and the nearby ruined castle. The guest beer is normally from a Kent microbrewery. Good-value Sunday lunches are served. **Q❀◑♿P🐾**

Cowden

Fountain

30 High Street, TN8 7JG (1 mile W of B2026)

☼ 12-3, 6-midnight; 12-11 Sun ☎ (01342) 850528

🌐 fountain-cowden.com

Harveys Hadlow Bitter, Sussex Best Bitter; guest beer 🄷

This excellent village community pub dates in parts from the 18th century, possibly earlier. Owned by Harveys of Lewes, it is one of just a handful of its pubs in west Kent. Home to a golfing society and the Muckspreaders Society (ask!), it is popular for its fine food served in generous portions. A large conservatory has recently been added, leading to a suntrap garden. The railway station is a mile away. This pub is a gem worth seeking out. **🐴❀◑♣P🚌**(234)**🐾ᯤ**

Crockham Hill

Royal Oak 🄻

Main Road, TN8 6RD (on B2026 jct with B269)

☼ 11-3, 5-11; 11-11 Sat; 12-10.30 Sun ☎ (01732) 866335

🌐 royaloakcrockhamhill.co.uk

Westerham Finchcocks Original, British Bulldog; guest beer 🄷

Village pub belonging to Westerham Brewery, close to Chartwell, former home of Winston Churchill, and well supported by villagers, walkers and cyclists. The smart modern interior with subdued lighting and open fires comprises one room, although one side, where dogs are allowed, retains the feel of a traditional bar. An excellent menu, including light bites, is served by friendly management and staff (no food Sun eve). A secluded wooded garden to the rear is perfect for relaxing after a good walk. **Q❀◑♣●P🚆🚌**(236)**🐾ᯤ**

Dartford

Foresters

15 Great Queen Street, DA1 1TJ

☼ 12-11.30 (11 Sun) ☎ (01322) 223087

Adnams Ghost Ship; Harveys Sussex Best Bitter; guest beer Ⓗ
Typical side-street local dating from 1869 and a five-minute walk to the town centre. Opposite is St Edmunds Pleasance burial ground, which contains the unmarked pauper's grave of famed steam pioneer Richard Trevithick. The pub has a U-shaped bar with an open wood/coal fire. The guest beer is a regularly changing seasonal brew. A large paved beer garden and covered smoking area lies to the rear, while adjacent is the car park. ❀⇌♣P🚌📶

Ivy Leaf Ⓛ

72 Darenth Road, DA1 1LS
⏲ 12-11; 12-10.30 Sun ☎ (01322) 220993
Sharp's Doom Bar; Wells Bombardier; guest beers Ⓗ
Medium-sized pub with a single U-shaped bar with wood/coal fires at each end. Situated halfway between East Hill and Princes Road, there is a Fastrack B bus stop by the pub, and it is a five-minute walk from Dartford football ground. Four guest ales are on offer, with at least one brewed locally. Home-made food and sandwiches are served lunchtimes. There is a covered smoking area and a grassed beer garden. Music plays on Thursday and Saturday evenings. ❀◐⇌P🚌(B)

Malt Shovel

3 Darenth Road, DA1 1LP
⏲ 12 (3 Mon)-11; 12 midnight Sat ☎ (01322) 224381
St Austell Tribute; Young's Bitter; guest beer Ⓗ
Country pub in central Dartford dating from 1673. It has two bars, with the low-ceilinged taproom featuring an 1880s Dartford Brewery mirror. A large conservatory attached to the bar leads to a beer garden with views across Dartford. Opposite the beer garden is a Fastrack bus stop, with other stops close by. Food is served every day except Monday, and barbecues are hosted in the summer. Live entertainment features on a regular basis with an open quiz on Monday evening. ❀◐◑⇌♣P🚌

Deal

Alma

126 West Street, CT14 6EB
⏲ 11-11 (11.30 Sat); 12-11 Sun ☎ (01304) 369349
Harveys Sussex Best Bitter; Thwaites Wainwright; Timothy Taylor Landlord; guest beer Ⓗ
Large, friendly, unassuming hostelry a stone's throw from Deal town centre and railway station. Entering the pub you come upon the imposing central bar, featuring four real ales, usually including one from Ripple Steam. During the month this community venue hosts many events ranging from live music, quiz nights and sports TV to a Sunday carvery, and is home to darts and pool teams. The rear courtyard has a smoking area. A large function room is available, which is used for charity events. ⛵❀◐⇌♣🚌🐾📶

Just Reproach Ⓛ

14 King Street, CT14 6HX
⏲ closed Mon; 12-2, 5-9 (11 Fri); 12-3.30, 5-11 Sat; 12-4 Sun
🌐 thejustreproach.co.uk
Beer range varies Ⓖ
Micropub just off the High Street that takes everything back to the absolute fundamentals: no keg, no spirits, no fruit machines, no music and fines levied for using a mobile phone. Its friendly welcome, high benches and table service make for a convivial atmosphere, whether you are there for a sociable chat or just to read the paper. Kent breweries and cidermakers feature strongly in the pub's offerings and snacks include Kentish Ashmore cheese. Q⇌♣🍏🚌🐾

Mill Inn

78-80 Mill Hill, CT14 9ER
⏲ 12-midnight (10 Sun) ☎ (01304) 449643
Sharp's Doom Bar; guest beers Ⓗ
Large housing estate pub with a friendly community spirit which has just celebrated its 80th anniversary. It has a substantial main bar and a smaller side bar. It hosts pool and darts teams, has sports TV and holds regular fundraisers supporting local charities. Home-made pies are cooked to order. Live music events feature every Saturday with a weekly meat raffle. It has a good-sized garden with a bouncy castle in the summer. ⛵❀◐◑♣🍏🚌(14,15)🐾📶

Prince Albert

187-189 Middle Street, CT14 6LW
⏲ 6 (12 Sun)-11 ☎ (01304) 375425
Beer range varies Ⓗ
A Victorian pub just off the seafront. Walk through the unique curved doors into a cheerful, welcoming and well-kept local. The cosy bar offers a varied range of three real ales from smaller, often local, breweries. Evening meals are served Wednesday to Saturday and roast lunches on Sunday. The small, sheltered courtyard garden is ideal in summer. This pub is a 10-minute walk north of the town centre and railway station. ⛵❀◐◑🐾

Ship Inn Ⓛ

141 Middle Street, CT14 6JZ
⏲ 11 (12 Sun)-11 ☎ (01304) 372222
Caledonian Deuchars IPA; Dark Star Hophead, American Pale Ale; Ramsgate Gadds' No. 7 Bitter Ale, Gadds' Seasider; guest beer Ⓗ
In Deal's historic conservation area, this unspoilt traditional pub with its dark wooden floor and subdued lighting is well worth a visit. The pub's nautical theme further complements the warm, comfortable atmosphere and the fire is welcome in winter. Beers from Ramsgate and Dark Star feature on the bar. The small snug at the back overlooks the patio garden, which is accessed by a staircase. Occasional live music is hosted. It is a 10-minute walk from the town centre. ❀⇌🚌🐾

Dover

Eight Bells Ⓛ

19 Cannon Street, CT16 1BZ
⏲ 8am-midnight ☎ (01304) 205030
Adnams Broadside; Fuller's London Pride; Sharp's Doom Bar; guest beers Ⓗ
Probably selling more real ale than any other Wetherspoon in South-east Kent, this bustling pub is celebrating its sixth year in the Guide. Located on Dover's main shopping street, it was once a cinema and the name is linked to the Dover parish church opposite. The large open-plan single-room interior includes a raised restaurant area. Twelve handpumps adorn the long bar, with 10 normally in use, featuring at least one Kent microbrewery. Outdoor seating overlooks the pedestrian precinct. ⛵❀◐♿⇌(Priory)🍏🚌📶

Louis Armstrong

58 Maison Dieu Road, CT16 1RA

2-11; 7-11 Sun ☎ (01304) 204759

Hopdaemon Skrimshander IPA; guest beers H

A renowned music venue and down-to-earth pub located on Dover's ring road. The main bar has up to four real ales, mostly from Kent microbreweries. Through the arch to the right is a second room and stage, set with old music posters, bench seating and a mirrored wall. There is a fine garden at the back. Good-value food is served Wednesday evenings. There is a large car park opposite.

Rack of Ale

7 Park Place, CT16 1DF

12 (1 Sun)-10.30 ☎ 07703 059201 rackofale.co.uk

Beer range varies G

Opened in October 2013, this new pub brings the micropub concept to Dover. A modern one-roomed venue, with simple but quirky decor, it encourages conversation, reading a paper or book, or playing pub games while enjoying a pint or two of real ale. The selection includes beers from Kent microbreweries and cider from Kentish Pip. A tasting tray is available. Opening hours can be flexible, depending on how busy it is.

Q (Priory)

Dunk's Green

Kentish Rifleman

Roughway Lane, TN11 9RU (jct with Dunk's Green Rd, 4 miles N of Tonbridge off A227)

11.30-3, 6-11; 11.30-11 Sat; 12-11 Sun ☎ (01732) 810727

thekentishrifleman.co.uk

Harveys Sussex Best Bitter; Whitstable Native Bitter; guest beers H

Situated directly on the Greensand Way long-distance footpath, in excellent walking and cycling country, this delightful 16th-century inn provides an ideal refreshment stop. The cosy oak-beamed Rifle bar leads through comfortable dining areas to a tranquil cottage garden at the rear. Kentish beers are well represented, with guests often sourced from the Tonbridge and Westerham breweries. Good home-made dishes are served (no food Sun and Mon eves) and Sunday lunch booking is essential. A twin-room B&B is available.

Q P (222)

East Brabourne

Five Bells Inn

The Street, TN25 5LP (sat nav recommended; in lanes from A20 via Smeeth and Brabourne Lees, or via Stowting from the B2068)

11.30-11.30 ☎ (01303) 813334

fivebellsinnbrabourne.com

Beer range varies H

A 16th-century rural inn modernised without losing any of the architectural features. Locally grown, farmed and prepared food is served lunchtimes and evenings, along with Kentish ales and ciders. The inn is popular with walkers, motorists and locals. It incorporates a shop selling local produce, and a large garden is suitable for alfresco dining. The pub hosts acoustic evenings on Tuesdays and the Vintage and Racing Club meets on the fourth Sunday of the month. Q P

East Malling

King & Queen

1 New Road, ME19 6DD

11 (12 Sat)-11; 12-6 Sun ☎ (01732) 842752

kingandqueeneastmalling.co.uk

Harveys Sussex Best Bitter; Kent Pale; Sharp's Doom Bar; guest beer H

A 16th-century beamed inn noted for the quality of its meals and snacks, which are served all day. At either end of the main bar there are quieter rooms. The garden is pleasant for summer days and dogs are welcome. The guest beer changes monthly, supplementing the three regular ales. A popular quiz is held monthly and there are occasional music or comedy nights on Sunday evenings. Accommodation is available at the rear, with three well-appointed rooms.

Q P (58)

Rising Sun

125 Mill Street, ME19 6BX

12-11 (10.30 Sun) ☎ (01732) 843284

Fuller's London Pride; Goacher's Fine Light Ale; guest beer H

Community free house run by the same family for over 24 years. Its low prices and quality ales are greatly appreciated. Guest beers may be local or national. Food is served weekday lunchtimes. It has a large patio garden to the rear for summer drinking. Sport is popular here and all major football matches and other sports events are shown on large TVs. The pub is home to several teams including darts, football and cricket. A lunchtime meat raffle is held on Sundays.

(58)

Eastry

Five Bells

The Cross, CT13 0HX

11-11.30 (1am Fri & Sat) ☎ (01304) 611188

thefivebellseastry.com

Greene King IPA; guest beer H

Community pub sitting at the heart of the village, well served by local buses. There is a comfortable lounge bar and a public bar with pool, darts and sports TV. The old fire station, with historic memorabilia, is used as a function room/restaurant. Food is served all day. Events include quiz nights, live music and an Easter beer festival. You can sit on the rear patio or at the front just watching village life.

P (14,87)

Edenbridge

Old Eden Inn

121 High Street, TN8 5AX (by roundabout just S of river)

12-11 (midnight Fri & Sat); 11-11 Sun ☎ (01732) 862398

theoldeden.com

Timothy Taylor Landlord; Westerham 1965; Young's Bitter; guest beers H

A 15th-century building on the edge of town close to the River Eden. The rear garden with a partially covered terrace is a pleasant refuge in which to enjoy alfresco drinks or the popular meals. Inside, exposed beams, brickwork and real fires, and a more private restaurant upstairs, provide for atmospheric dining (no food Sun eve). Sunday

lunch booking is advisable. The pub is a strong supporter of local Westerham beers including its specially brewed house beer, Old Eden.
❀◑◗ ⇌(Town)♣●P🚌(231,233)

Elham

King's Arms 🄻

The Square, CT4 6TJ (in village square near church, just off main road)
🕐 11-11.30; 12-10.30 Sun ☎ (01303) 840242
🌐 kingsarmselham.com
Harveys Sussex Best Bitter; Hopdaemon Golden Braid, Skrimshander IPA 🄷
Overlooking the village square and the fine medieval church, this pub is the focal point for social activities across the area and provides a friendly atmosphere for regulars, visitors and walkers from the Elham Valley alike. Customers are always guaranteed a good pint of Kentish ale and a hearty meal, with discounted food available to senior citizens Monday to Friday lunchtimes. Parking is in the square. ❀◑◗♿♣🚌(17)🐾

Eynsford

Five Bells

High Street, DA4 0AB
🕐 4 (12 Sat)-11; 12-10.30 Sun ☎ (01322) 863135
Dark Star Hophead; Harveys Sussex Best Bitter; Sharp's Doom Bar; guest beer 🄷
Popular traditional pub in an attractive village. The public bar has been retained, with wooden tables and a wood-burning fire. A separate saloon bar has a dartboard. There is a large lawned back garden. A quiz is held on the third Thursday of each month. Regular ales are supplemented by a guest from one of various small breweries. Dogs are welcome in the public bar. Q❀♣P🚌(421,478)🐾📶

Faversham

Bear Inn

3 Market Place, ME13 7AG
🕐 10.30-11; 12-10.30 Sun ☎ (01795) 532668
Shepherd Neame Master Brew; guest beer 🄷
A 16th-century pub located in Faversham's historic Market Square, boasting a traditional interior with three separate bar areas running the length of the building. The lunchtime menu is popular, and a general knowledge quiz is held on the last Monday of the month. The pub often features the seasonal Shepherd Neame beer and is popular with visitors to Faversham and locals alike. Q◑⇌♣🚌🐾📶

Elephant 🄻

31 The Mall, ME13 8JN
🕐 closed Mon; 3 (12 Sat)-11; 12-7 Sun ☎ (01795) 590157
Beer range varies 🄷
Voted local CAMRA Pub of the Year on seven occasions, this traditional beer house features a range of five real ales, usually including a mild. Local real cider is normally available on handpump. Beers are mainly sourced from microbreweries and two beer festivals are held during the year. The pub features a log fire and an enclosed rear garden. Regular music nights take place and dogs and children are welcome. ❀⇌♣●🚌🐾📶

Phoenix Tavern

98/99 Abbey Street, ME13 7BH
🕐 12-11 (midnight Fri & Sat) ☎ (01795) 591462
🌐 thephoenixtavernfaversham.co.uk
Harveys Sussex Best Bitter; Timothy Taylor Landlord; guest beers 🄷
A 14th-century traditional English pub set in the heart of Faversham and close to Faversham Creek. The range of ales usually includes well-known national brands such as Timothy Taylor, Harveys and Otter. A separate restaurant serves a varied menu and a bar menu of West Country pies is available. The pub boasts two open fires and hosts regular meetings of the Timothy Taylor Appreciation Society. Q❀◑◗⇌●P🚌🐾📶

Shipwright's Arms 🄻

Hollowshore, ME13 7TU (over 1 mile N of Faversham at the confluence of Faversham and Oare creeks) TR017636
🕐 6-11 summer; 11-3, 6-10 (closed Mon eve); 12-4, 6-11 Sat; 12-4, 6-10.30 winter Sun ☎ (01795) 590088
🌐 theshipwrightsathollowshore.co.uk
Goacher's Real Mild Ale, Special/House Ale; guest beers 🄶
Remote 300-year-old family-run free house with a jolly, welcoming, old-style landlord – a good pub to relax in after a 45-minute walk across the marshes from Faversham. The wooden-clad building's interior reflects its nautical heritage, with many ornaments and pictures on display or tucked into nooks and crannies. The large garden at the rear is open spring to autumn, with outside seating at the front in all seasons. In severe winter weather telephone to check opening times. Q❀◑◗P🐾

Vaults Cask & Kitchen 🄻

75 Preston Street, ME13 8PA
🕐 11-11 (10.30 Sun) ☎ (01795) 591817
🌐 theoldwinevaults.com
Beer range varies 🄷
Recently renamed, this large inn is on the main route from the railway station to the market square. The pub has a house beer from the local Mad Cat Brewery and often serves another of its beers. Further ales are from a mixture of national and regional breweries. The Vaults has an extensive menu, regular live music and a large beer garden. It hosts occasional beer festivals.
❀◑◗⇌●🚌🐾

Finglesham

Crown Inn 🄻

The Street, CT14 0NA
🕐 12-11 (10 Sun) ☎ (01304) 612555
🌐 thecrownatfinglesham.co.uk
Dark Star Hophead; guest beers 🄷
Traditional rural pub offering a warm and friendly welcome. Three to four real ales are on offer, often from Kent microbreweries. Freshly cooked home-made food is served lunchtimes and evenings, all day on Friday and Saturday, and there is a traditional roast on Sunday; it has barbecues in the summer. Eat in the bar or the pleasant restaurant which opens out onto the large garden, with a children's play area. Community and charity events, live music and bat and trap keep the pub busy. ❀◑◗⛺♣P🚌🐾📶

Folkestone

East Cliff Tavern

13-15 East Cliff, CT19 6BU (from harbour, up hill past lifeboat and second right; from Dover Road looking S, turn left at Raglan, first left, down hill, footpath across railway – no trains – and it is in front of you)
5-11; 12-11 Sat & Sun ☎ (01303) 251132
Beer range varies H
Friendly terraced back-street pub, near a footpath across the railway line, a short walk from the harbour. The main bar is to the right and there are usually two beers, often from local breweries, with Biddenden cider on gravity behind the bar. Old photographs of Folkestone decorate the walls, and community events include weekly raffles. The television is in the saloon bar. Opening hours may vary; check if making a special visit. Q

Firkin Ale House

18 Cheriton Place, CT20 2AZ
closed Mon; 12-9 (10 Fri & Sat); 12-3 Sun
☎ (07894) 068432
Beer range varies G
Folkestone's first micropub, selling up to four cask beers with at least one from a Kent microbrewery. No lager, keg beers, alcopops or spirits here, but it has a limited wine selection, Kentish cheeses and basic bar snacks. You will not find music or pub games, only good company and conversation, making the Firkin a place to relax in and enjoy a quality ale. Mobile phones are prohibited and their use incurs a minimum donation of £1 to charity. Local CAMRA branch Pub of the Year for 2014.
Q(Central)

Fordwich

Fordwich Arms

King Street, CT2 0DB
11-midnight (1am Fri & Sat); 12-11 Sun
☎ (01227) 710444 fordwicharms.co.uk
Adnams Southwold Bitter; Sharp's Doom Bar; Shepherd Neame Master Brew H
Classic 1930s building opposite the tiny town hall in England's smallest town, overlooking the River Stour. The large bar has a lovely open fireplace and there is a separate oak-panelled dining room (no food Sun eves). The pub hosts regular themed food evenings including the popular pudding club, usually on the second Wednesday of the month (booking essential). A folk club meets every second and fourth Sunday night. Live jazz is played in the garden once a month on summer Sunday afternoons. Q(Sturry)P

Frittenden

Bell & Jorrocks

Biddenden Road, TN17 2EJ TQ815412
12 (11 Sat)-11; 12-10.30 Sun ☎ (01580) 852415
thebellandjorrocks.co.uk
Adnams Southwold Bitter; Woodforde's Wherry; guest beers H
The only pub in the village and very much the centre of the local community. It provides good pub grub including menus for children, as well as a more gourmet specials board. A bar billiards table is kept in the small side room which is dominated by a Heinkel 111 propeller from a German WWII bomber shot down locally. An annual beer festival is held in the old stables at the rear of the pub.

Gillingham

Frog & Toad

38 Burnt Oak Terrace, ME7 1DR
1 (2 Mon)-11; 12-11 Fri-Sun ☎ (01634) 852231
Fuller's London Pride; guest beer H
A typical back-street corner one-bar pub and former winner of the local CAMRA Pub of the Year. To the rear is a large patio area and garden with covered tables and bench seating, plus an outside bar for beer festivals held during bank holidays. Two beers are regularly on offer, with the guest ale coming from the Cottage Brewery. The pub hosts occasional entertainment at weekends and provides Sunday lunches for which a booking is required. Q

Marquis of Lorne

9 Mill Road, ME7 1HL
11-11; 12-10.30 Sun ☎ 07825 599566
Beer range varies H
Located at the far end of the High Street, opposite Medway Park sports centre, this small one-bar local with four handpumps is dedicated to serving a variety of guest beers, both from Kentish and nationwide breweries, at competitive prices. It also stocks imported German and Belgian beers. The landlord provides free savouries and snacks on the bar at most times.

Will Adams

73 Saxton Street, ME7 5EG
12.30-4 (not Mon-Fri), 7-11; 12.30-3, 8-11 Sun
☎ (01634) 575902 thewilladams.co.uk
Beer range varies H
A real oasis for 20 years, the Will Adams serves two to three guest ales along with cider and perry, including Old Rosie. Pete welcomes both home and away fans on Gillingham FC home games, typically opening early and getting busy. Will Adams was a mariner born in Gillingham who opened up Japan to the West and became a Samurai, this being the theme of the mural on the pub's walls. It is open weekday evenings and weekends.

Gravesend

Crown & Thistle

44 The Terrace, DA12 2BJ
12-11; 12-10.30 Sun ☎ (01474) 332387
Young's Bitter; guest beers H
Small Georgian terraced pub, originally two fishermen's cottages. The name symbolises the union of England and Scotland, ratified on 1 May 1707, and the pub is believed to have opened in 1847. The convivial atmosphere is free from amplified music and gaming machines. Four guest beers are on handpump. Double Vision and Westons cider are also available. Indian and Chinese takeaways can be ordered and eaten in the pub. Former CAMRA National Pub of the Year.
Q

Jolly Drayman

1 Love Lane, Wellington Street, DA12 1JA
12-11.30; 12-11 Sun ☎ (01474) 352355
Dark Star Hophead; St Austell Tribute; guest beers H

Comfortable and cosy character pub with consistently good ale, to the east end of the town on the site of the former Wellington Brewery. Four beers are available. It has a quirky low ceiling and a relaxed atmosphere with no gaming machines and a TV that is muted. Daddlums (Kentish skittles) is played on alternate Sundays. There is a large, tidy outdoor area. Beer festivals take place twice-yearly in May and November. Dogs are allowed in the garden only. Q❀🛏♿⇌♣P🚌🐾📶

Robert Pocock

181-183 Windmill Street, DA12 1AH
8am-midnight (1am Fri & Sat) ☎ (01474) 352765
Greene King Abbot; Ruddles Best Bitter; guest beers Ⓗ
A large and busy Wetherspoon venue on two levels in the town centre, now open for 15 years, in a building that was previously a retail bed centre. There is no music and the gaming machines and TV are muted. Families are encouraged. Food is served from 8am until 10pm Monday-Saturday and until 9pm Sunday. A changing range of well-kept guest beers, including one local ale plus two ciders, is always available. Guide dogs only.
🐴◑♿⇌🍎🚌📶

Rum Puncheon Ⓛ

87 West Street, DA11 0BL (on one-way system, next to Tilbury Ferry)
11 (12 Sat)-11; 12-10.30 Sun ☎ (01474) 353434
rumpuncheon.co.uk
Beer range varies Ⓗ
A large riverside building near the town pier with good views from its rear terrace. It has two function rooms upstairs with a bar. The L-shaped main bar with chandeliers and log fire has no TV or gaming machines. Live music plays Friday or Saturday evenings and jazz occasionally on Sunday lunchtimes. Eight real ales rotate frequently, often including Betty Stogs and at least one from Kent. A quiz is hosted on the last Wednesday of the month. Lunchtime meals and tapas are served Friday and Saturday evenings. Q❀◑♿⇌♣🚌🐾

Ship & Lobster Ⓛ

Mark Lane, Denton, DA12 2QB (E of town; follow Ordnance Rd and Norfolk Rd into Mark Lane)
11-11 ☎ (01474) 324571 shipandlobster.co.uk
Beer range varies Ⓗ
The pub is in an industrial area and is reputed to be the Ship in Dickens' Great Expectations. It is also on the Saxon Shore Way and is popular with walkers and anglers. Internally it has a nautical theme, with pictures of shipping. The pub can be busy when there are angling competitions. There is an outside drinking area on the sea wall with views of the Thames. Three ales are available, usually including one from a Kent brewery. ❀◐🍎P🐾

Groombridge

Crown Inn

Groombridge Hill, TN3 9QH (on village green)
11-11; 12-10.30 Sun ☎ (01892) 864742
thecrowngroombridge.com
Black Cat Original; Harveys Sussex Best Bitter; Larkins Traditional Ale; guest beer Ⓗ
Family-run 16th-century free house, oozing charm and enjoying a sunny outlook over the village green and church. In fine walking country and a short stroll from Groombridge Place, the pub is a regular outlet for Black Cat beers, brewed in the village. Quality food is available for patrons, and biscuits for their dogs. It gets cosy in winter with beams, a snug and inglenook fireplace. The Tunbridge Wells bus drops you outside the door, or you could arrive via the Spa Valley Railway.
Q🐴❀🛏◑⛺♣P🚌(291)🐾

Hadlow

Two Brewers

Maidstone Road, TN11 0DN (on A26)
12-3, 5-midnight Mon & Tue; 12-midnight (1am Fri & Sat); 12-11.30 Sun ☎ (01732) 850267
thetwobrewershadlow.co.uk
Harveys Sussex XX Mild Ale, Hadlow Bitter, Sussex Best Bitter; guest beer Ⓗ
Under Harvey's brewery ownership for a decade, this pub is popular with locals and visitors passing through this bustling town. Wood abounds – flooring, tables and bar – and attractive etched glass partitions are decorated with the brewery logo. Hadlow was a brewing and malting centre and brewery memorabilia such as photos and bottles are on display throughout. A range of up to six ales, including the Hadlow Bitter (Sussex Pale) using locally grown hops, is complemented by occasional festivals held in the garden.
❀◑♿♣P🚌(7,77)🐾📶

Harvel

Amazon & Tiger Ⓛ

Harvel Street, DA13 0DE
4 (6 Mon)-11; 12-11 Fri & Sat; 12-10.30 Sun
☎ (01474) 814705
amazonandtiger-harvel.webeden.co.uk
Beer range varies Ⓗ
Situated in a remote village close to the North Downs/Pilgrims Way and popular with walkers, the pub was built in 1914 on the opposite side of the road to the original inn and designed to blend in with the village houses. In two distinct bar areas modern furnishings combine with flagstones and wood floors. The village cricket team can be watched from the garden. It has a bar billiards table and a separate TV area, and a good range of beers, usually including an ale from Kent Brewery.
🐴❀🛏◑♿⛺♣P🐾📶

Hastingleigh

Bowl Inn Ⓛ

The Street, TN25 5HU TR095449
closed Mon; 5 (12 Sat)-11.30; 12-10.30 Sun
☎ (01233) 750354 thebowlonline.co.uk
Beer range varies Ⓗ
This lovingly restored listed village pub retains many period features, including a taproom used for playing pool, and is free from jukebox and games machines. It was local CAMRA Pub of the Year in 2012. Quiz night is Tuesday and the lovely garden is home to a tame European eagle owl. A beer festival is held on August bank holiday Monday. Excellent sandwiches and baguettes are available at the weekend. Q🐴❀◐♣🍎P

Herne

Butcher's Arms

29A Herne Street, CT6 7HL (opp church)
closed Mon; 12-1.30, 6-9; 12-2 Sun (01227) 371000
micropub.co.uk
Adnams Broadside; Fuller's ESB; Kent Session Pale; Old Dairy Copper Top; guest beers G
Britain's first micropub, opened in 2005, is a real ale gem and the inspiration for other micropubs. Once a butcher's shop, it still has the original chopping tables. There is seating for 10 customers and standing room for 20 – the compact drinking area ensuring lively banter. Customers can also buy beer to drink at home. Snack food includes local Ashmore cheeses. The pub has won many CAMRA awards and the landlord was voted one of CAMRA's top 40 campaigners. Q(4,6)

Herne Bay

Bouncing Barrel

20 Bank Street, CT6 5EA
6-9 Mon; 12-2, 5-9; 12-11 Sat; 12-2 Sun 07777 630685
bouncingbarrel.com
Beer range varies G
Friendly welcoming micropub with bench seating for 20 customers around old workshop tables. The beer range changes regularly and usually includes four ales, mainly from microbreweries, with at least one from a Kent brewery. Local cheeses and other snacks are available. The pub is named after the bombs used in the Dambuster raids, which were tested off the coast nearby, and features a mural of a bomber flying past the Reculver Towers. Q

Firkin Frog

157 Station Road, CT6 5QA
12-3, 5-9; closed Sun eve & Mon 07460 895527
Beer range varies G
The front bar of this micropub has comfortable seating, and the ceiling is decorated with English county flags. There is a small snug where a wide range of board games can be played. Between three and five beers are served, mostly from Kent and Sussex microbreweries. Bar snacks include a fine cheeseboard, pork pies and Scotch eggs. There is a monthly quiz, usually on the last Wednesday in the month, and a pie-making competition. Charity fundraising includes fining mobile phone users. Q(4,6)

Higham

Gardeners Arms

2 Forge lane, ME3 7AS
11-11; 12-11 Sun (01474) 823901
gardenersarmshigham.com
Shepherd Neame Master Brew, Kent's Best, Spitfire, Bishops Finger; guest beer H
Quiet pub situated in Upper Higham with a clock that goes backwards. Other than the four beers listed, a fifth handpump is reserved for a guest ale, not always from Shepherd Neame. The food in the restaurant is sourced locally and represents good value. The garden is secluded, with a raised patio which backs onto a small car park. Q

Hildenborough

Plough

Leigh Road, TN11 9AJ (½ mile S of Hildenborough at Powdermills)
closed Mon; 12-3, 6-11; 12-5 Sun (01732) 832149
theploughatleigh.com
Harveys Sussex Best Bitter; guest beers H
Low-ceilinged 16th-century inn, attractive inside and out. The open-plan, heavy-beamed interior is scattered with wooden tables on a flagged floor. Particularly notable is a large open-sided fireplace for warming weary walkers. The extensive garden by a stream accommodates a children's play area and garden furniture. The pub keenly supports local breweries so both Tonbridge and Westerham beers are served, sometimes including a cask on the bar. The Great Barn can be hired for functions. Opening times may extend in summer.
P(210)

Horton Kirby

Bull

Lombard Street, DA4 9DF
12-11 (10.30 Sun) (01322) 867662
Dark Star Hophead; Oakham Citra; Rudgate Ruby Mild; guest beers H
Friendly one-bar village pub with a large garden affording views across the Darent Valley. The bar supports six handpumps, with three rotating guest ales. The landlord is a member of the Oakham Oakademy cellarmanship award scheme. Food is served Tuesday-Sunday lunchtimes. Cribbage is played on Tuesday evenings, darts on Wednesdays and poker on Thursdays. (414)

Hythe

Three Mariners

37 Windmill Street, CT21 6BH
4-10 Mon; 12-11; 12-midnight Fri & Sat (01303) 260406
Young's Bitter; guest beers H
Hidden away in a side street not far from the Royal Military Canal, this refurbished traditional pub is well worth visiting. Friendly staff and local customers are always happy to have a chat with you. With no food available, it attracts its clientele due to the quality and selection of real ales on offer; these can be enjoyed in one of the two bars or the outside area that is partly heated and popular with smokers.

Ightham Common

Old House ★

Redwell Lane, Redwell, TN15 9EE (½ mile SW of Ightham village, between A25 and A227) TQ590558
7-11 (9 Mon & Tue); 12-3, 7-11 Sat & Sun
(01732) 886077
Beer range varies G
Located down a narrow, secluded country lane, this is a Grade II-listed Kentish cottage. Red-brick built and tile-hung, it comprises an entrance lobby and two separate bars. The public bar features a Victorian wood-panelled counter, parquet flooring and an imposing inglenook fireplace. The parlour bar houses a chaise longue. Up to six beers are dispensed by gravity from the taproom, always

including at least one bitter, a golden ale and a dark beer, all from an impressive range of breweries. Parking is available on a small forecourt. Q❀⛺♣P🐕📶

Ivychurch

Bell Inn

Ashford Road, TN29 0AL (signposted from A2070 between Brenzett and Hamstreet, 1 mile from A259/ A2070 roundabout at Brenzett) TR028275
🕐 12-11; 12-10.30 Sun ☎ (01797) 344355
🌐 thebellinnromneymarsh.co.uk
Sharp's Doom Bar; St Austell Trelawny; Wadworth Henry's IPA; guest beers Ⓗ
Like many Romney Marsh pubs, a warm welcome awaits, at this inn adjacent to the church. It is popular for its excellent ales and ciders as well as the selection of food. The current licensees have gained an enviable reputation for the establishment, achieving the honour of CAMRA branch Pub of the Year in 2013 and runner-up in 2012. Well worth finding, it was once a centre for the Romney Marsh Owlers (smugglers).
❀◑♿♣🍎P🐕📶

Kingsdown

Zetland Arms 𝕃

Wellington Parade, CT14 8AF
🕐 10-11.30 (10.30 Sun) ☎ (01304) 370114
Shepherd Neame Master Brew, Whitstable Bay Pale Ale, Spitfire; guest beer Ⓗ
The pub, on the beach front, was sympathetically refurbished in 2013. It is now a relaxing place to eat and drink, with lots of wood and pastel colours. The varied menu is available seven days a week, from sandwiches through to seafood. A good range of Shep's ales is available, including the occasional seasonal, and guests from other breweries. There is plenty of seating on the front and a suntrap walled garden to the rear. Do not forget the pub dog.
❀◑⛺P🚌(82)🐕📶

Laddingford

Chequers

The Street, ME18 6BP TQ689481
🕐 12-3, 5-11; 12-11 Sat & Sun ☎ (01622) 871266
🌐 chequersladdingford.co.uk
Adnams Southwold Bitter; guest beers Ⓗ
An attractive, community-spirited, oak-beamed pub, dating from the 15th century. A warm welcome is assured in the simply furnished bar and split-level dining area. A beer festival is held in late April. Food theme nights include Sausage Thursdays and Pie Days on the first Tuesdays and Wednesdays of the month. There is a large rear garden with children's play equipment. One double letting room is available. Buses stop outside and Beltring Halt is a 20-minute walk away.
Q❀🛏◑♣P🚌(23,26)🐕📶

Lower Halstow

Three Tuns 𝕃

The Street, ME9 7DY
🕐 12-11 (midnight Fri & Sat); 12-10.30 Sun
☎ (01795) 842840 🌐 thethreetunsrestaurant.co.uk
Goacher's Real Mild Ale; Millis Kentish Best; guest beers Ⓗ
True family village pub with a friendly, cheerful atmosphere and lively conversation. The owners actively support real ale, offering mainly local Kentish ales and a local cider. It does a quirky range of bar snacks, has an award for best pub chips and a local reputation for good food. Events including quizzes are held throughout the year. A function room, games room, log fires, sofa seating, brick walls and beams add character. It has a large garden with stream-side decking.
❀◑♿♣🍎P🚌

Luddesdown

Cock Inn 𝕃

Henley Street, DA13 0XB TQ664672
🕐 12-11 (10.30 Sun) ☎ (01474) 814208
🌐 cockluddesdowne.com
Adnams Lighthouse, Southwold Bitter, Broadside; Goacher's Real Mild Ale; St Austell Trelawny; Truman's Swift; guest beers Ⓗ
Rural free house dating from 1713, under the same ownership since 1984, offering a large range of real ales and quality German beers. It harbours an enchanting warren of cosy rooms with log fires, and has a peaceful atmosphere dedicated to conversation, traditional pub games and relaxation. All around are fascinating curios, memorabilia, photographs and lots more on walls and in cabinets. A function room hosts many clubs and societies. There is a heated smoking area. Beware the quiz on Tuesdays. Q❀◑♿♣P🍺🐕

Lynsted

Black Lion 𝕃

The Street, ME9 0RJ
🕐 11-3, 6-11; 12-3, 7-10.30 Sun ☎ (01795) 521229
Goacher's Real Mild Ale, Fine Light Ale, Best Dark Ale; guest beer Ⓗ
Welcoming village local frequented by the discerning drinker. Although the pub is a free house it offers four Goacher's beers including rarely seen occasionals such as Old Ale and Imperial Stout. The characterful and jovial landlord holds court with a cluster of regulars and always has a story to tell. The pub, with a large garden, has bar billiards and serves regular home-cooked food.
Q❀🛏◑♣P🚌(345)🐕

Maidstone

Flower Pot 𝕃

96 Sandling Road, ME14 2RJ
🕐 12 (11 Sat)-11; 12-10.30 Sun ☎ (01622) 757705
🌐 flowerpotpub.com
Goacher's Gold Star Strong Ale; guest beers Ⓗ
A real ale lover's paradise, this street-corner pub has nine handpumps. TV screens display the current beers along with their strength and price, plus forthcoming events such as music every other Saturday and jam nights every Tuesday. Four ciders are regularly on offer and beer festivals are held in May and August. The pub is five minutes' walk from the local football ground. The landlord is a partner in the Maidstone Brewing Company. This place is a must-visit when in the county town.
❀◑⇌(East)♣🍎🍺🚌(101,155)🐕

Olde Thirsty Pig

4a Knightrider Street, ME15 6LP
4-1am; 12-2am Fri; 12-3am Sat; 12-1am Sun
(01622) 299283 yeoldethirstypig.com
Beer range varies H
This 15th-century street-corner local is Grade II-listed, with the original beams throughout. Beware of low ceilings and doorways, especially upstairs where the floor slopes. Four handpumps dispense ales, mainly from Kent microbreweries. There is also an array of bottled beers to choose from including several foreign ones. Another room has more comfortable chairs, and directly above that is a meeting room. Outside is a heated and covered courtyard area. A free jukebox is provided. Q

Rifle Volunteers L

28 Wyatt Street, ME14 1EU
11-3, 6 (7 Sat)-11; 12-3, 7-10.30 Sun (01622) 758891
Goacher's Real Mild Ale, Fine Light Ale, Crown Imperial Stout H
A stone-built, single-bar, street-corner pub located a short walk away from Maidstone's main shopping area. It is one of only two Goacher's tied houses and has had the same landlord since 1978. The interior, which retains many of its original features, is somewhat spartan in appearance but is comfortable enough. A place for a quiet drink or conversation, the pub has no fruit machines, jukebox or piped music. Q(East)

Society Rooms

Brenchley House, Week Street, ME14 1RF
7am-midnight (1am Fri & Sat) (01622) 350910
Courage Directors; Greene King Abbot; Ruddles Best Bitter; guest beers H
A light and airy Wetherspoon outlet opposite Maidstone East station, occupying the site of a former newspaper printing works. The pub is named after the efforts of William Shipley, who founded the Royal Society of Arts and the Maidstone Society for Promoting Useful Knowledge. There is a large, covered outside drinking/smoking area. Food is available all day. (East)(101,155)

Swan L

2 County Road, ME14 1UY
12-11 (midnight Fri & Sat) (01622) 751264
theswaninnmaidstone.co.uk
Shepherd Neame Master Brew, Kent's Best, Spitfire, seasonal beers; guest beer H
Welcoming traditional locals' pub, just a two-minute walk from Maidstone East station and opposite Maidstone Prison. Three regular well-kept Shepherd Neame beers plus seasonal ales and quarterly mini beer festivals can be enjoyed here. The pub, with a swan-adorned interior, dates back to 1840 and was extended in the 1960s by incorporating the adjoining property. It hosts monthly folk nights, fortnightly Wednesday fun quiz nights and occasional live music at weekends. Bar meals are served 12-2pm daily and 5-7pm week nights. (East)

Marden

Stile Bridge L

Staplehurst Road, TN12 9BH (on A229 just before jct with B2079)
11-11 (10 Sun) (01622) 831236 thestilebridge.co.uk
Shepherd Neame Master Brew; guest beers H
Five real ales and three ciders await visitors to this large roadside pub. It has a welcoming atmosphere with a good mixture of drinking and dining areas, all with pub and drinking memorabilia on the walls. Local microbreweries are supported as well as a good selection of genuine continental and US beers and lagers. Spring and summer bank holidays see beer and music festivals; live music and comedy feature at other times. Maidstone CAMRA branch Pub of the Year 2014. P(5)

Margate

Northern Belle

Mansion Street, CT9 1HE
12-11; 11-11 Sat; 12-10.30 Sun 07810 088347
Shepherd Neame Master Brew H
This iconic regular Guide local dates from 1680, when it was built from two cottages; its present name derives from the wreck of an American cargo ship in 1857. It has a cosy maritime theme and is close to the Stone Pier, Turner Contemporary Art Centre and the old town area. Live music takes place on Sunday afternoons. A second Shepherd Neame beer rotates with the Master Brew and the pub participates in Shepherd Neame's regular beer festivals. Q

Mersham

Farriers Arms L

The Forstal, TN25 6NU (through village turn right into Church Rd, pub is on left after approx ½ mile)
12-midnight; 11-1am Fri & Sat; 11-11.30 Sun
(01233) 720444 thefarriersarms.com
Farriers Arms Farriers 1606; guest beers H
Community-owned Grade II-listed pub dating back to 1606. Its own five-barrel microbrewery produces Farriers 1606 and seasonal ales. An annual beer festival takes place in late July and there are many other events throughout the year. Food is available at the Barn in Anvil restaurant lunchtimes and evenings Monday to Thursday, and all day Friday to Sunday. The local bus does not run at weekends. QP(125)

Milton Regis

Three Hats

93 High Street, ME10 2AR
11-11 (10 Sun) (01795) 427645
Beer range varies H
Popular and friendly local in historic Milton Regis. The open-plan interior has low beams and a large rear lounge bar area. The landlord serves a selection of national beers from the Enterprise range including ales rarely available in this part of Kent, from breweries such as Dartmoor and Windsor & Eton. Two beer festivals are held each year and occasional quizzes and live music events take place. CAMRA local Pub of the Year 2013. A CAMRA discount is offered. (347)

Minster-in-Thanet

Minster & Monkton Royal British Legion Club

Clements House, 61 Augustine Road, CT12 4DH

11-11 (midnight Fri & Sat); 12-11 Sun ☎ (01843) 821471
rblminster.org/index
Courage Best Bitter; guest beers H
Friendly British Legion club that has plenty of room, with a main bar, side room and a separate bar full of naval memorabilia for all to enjoy. Darts and pool can be played, with bingo, quizzes and other social events regularly planned. Guest beers are often from the local Ramsgate (Gadds) brewery. The beer is well kept and sells quickly. Entry is permitted on production of a CAMRA membership card, the current Guide or the phone app.
(11,42)

Newenden

White Hart

Rye Road, TN18 5PN (on A268 in centre of village)
TQ834273
11-11; 12-11 Sun ☎ (01797) 252166
thewhitehartnewenden.co.uk
Harveys Sussex Best Bitter; Rother Valley Level Best; guest beers H
This historic 16th-century weatherboarded building includes old oak-beamed bars and an inglenook fireplace. The pub provides good-quality home cooked food and has six en suite rooms. Conveniently situated for the Kent & East Sussex Railway and several National Trust properties, it is an ideal location for exploring the Rother Valley.
P (340,341)

Offham

King's Arms

Teston Road, ME19 5NR
12-midnight ☎ (01732) 845208
kingsarmsoffham.co.uk
Beer range varies H
Originally two 16th-century farm cottages, it has two drinking areas plus a restaurant. The former sports bar has been newly refurbished, making a comfortable drinking area with a variety of games. A warm atmosphere prevails, with six well-kept ales from Kent, Tonbridge, Adnams and Ramsgate (Gadds) breweries, to name a few. The pub has quarterly beer festivals, and live music features monthly. Home-made pies are a speciality. Thai food is served on Friday evenings and roasts on Sunday. QP (70)

Otford

Crown

10 High Street, TN14 5PQ (adjacent to village duck pond)
12-11 (11.30 Fri & Sat) ☎ (01959) 522847
crownpubotford.co.uk
Beer range varies H
A cottage-style pub close to the only Grade II-listed duck pond in England. Very much at the heart of village life, activities include darts, live music, open mic nights, quiz nights and comedy evenings. Supernatural nights have also been held, with some interesting revelations from the pub ghosts. Home-cooked food is served lunchtimes, as well as Wednesday to Saturday evenings. Crown Ale is a blend of Westerham's Finchcocks and Freedom beers. Beer festivals are held in April and October.
(431,432)

Penshurst

Spotted Dog

Smarts Hill, TN11 8EP (turn off B2188 S of Penshurst)
11.30-11 (3 Mon); 12-9 Sun ☎ (01892) 870253
spotteddogpub.co.uk
Harveys Sussex Best Bitter; Larkins Traditional Ale; guest beers H
A 15th-century weatherboarded country inn where families, walkers and dogs are all welcome. In winter log fires add to the cosy feel, and in summer terracing affords elevated views over some fine countryside. Larkins Brewery, only three miles down the road, often supplies a seasonal ale as well as the regular Trad, while a beer from another local brewer, Black Cat, may also be found alongside a guest from further afield. Try the three third-of-a-pint tasting glasses for variety.
P (231)

Perry Wood

Rose & Crown

Crown Hill, ME13 9RY TR042552
closed Mon; 11.30-3, 6.30-11; 11.30-11 Sat; 12-10 Sun
☎ (01227) 752214 roseandcrownperrywood.co.uk
Adnams Southwold Bitter; Harveys Sussex Best Bitter H
A 16th-century free house, reputedly haunted and formerly a woodcutter's cottage. The pub is popular with walkers and prides itself on its green reputation. The bar is adorned with old woodcutting tools and there is a large inglenook fireplace. It has an extensive garden with a children's play area. Food is produced using locally-sourced ingredients, served in the bar or the separate restaurant area. The pub hosts regular beer festivals, quizzes and live music.
P

Petham

Chequers

Stone Street, CT4 5PW
12-3 (not Mon), 6-11; 12-4, 7-10.30 Sun
☎ (01227) 700734
Dark Star Hophead, Partridge Best Bitter; Oakham Citra; Sharp's Doom Bar; guest beers H
On the Roman road from Canterbury to Hythe, the Chequers was built around 1830. The bar area has comfortable leather sofas. A spacious dining area and restaurant is at the back, with a tempting menu including a popular carvery on Sunday lunchtime and Wednesday evening. Darts and pool are played in a small side bar. Up to six beers are served at busy times. A green hop festival is planned for October. P (620,18)

Rainham

Three Sisters

Otterham Quay Lane, ME8 8QR (jct B2009, Lower Rainham Road, and Otterham Quay Lane)
12-midnight (2am Fri & Sat) ☎ (01634) 231991
threesistersrainham.com
Beer range varies H
Vibrant country pub on the edge of Rainham serving four beers and a cider. The pub has a full-length bar with an open fire and a pool table to the

rear. There is entertainment on some Fridays and Saturdays. It also has a separate function room where beer festivals are held during the year, and an outside drinking area. ❀♣🍎P🚌(327)🐾📶

Ramsgate

Artillery Arms

36 Westcliff Road, CT11 9JS

🕐 12-11 (midnight Fri-Sun) ☎ (01843) 853202

Beer range varies Ⓗ

Celebrated ale house a short walk from the town; it is popular and attracts a diverse clientele. The lower bar area with stairs leads to an upper area with more seating. The landlord maintains a long tradition of stocking a carefully considered range of real ales. Doom Bar is the house bitter but other handpumps serve a selection of beers from Kent and beyond. Interesting old painted windows depict battle scenes and the theme is continued with displays of other militaria. ♣🚌

Churchill Tavern

18-20 Paragon, CT11 9JX

🕐 12-11 (1am Fri & Sat) ☎ (01843) 587862

Greene King IPA; guest beers Ⓗ

Spacious pub overlooking the Royal Marina, with superb views across the English Channel. Built in 1816 as the Paragon Hotel, it has seen a number of changes through the centuries. It offers a variety of ales in a warm, welcoming atmosphere. A good selection of meals is available in the pub or separate dining area. It has a small outdoor roof terrace. Live bands play most Saturday evenings and Sunday afternoons, and a popular quiz night is held on Monday evenings. ◐♣🚌(34,88)

Conqueror Alehouse

4c Grange Road, CT11 9LR

🕐 closed Mon; 11.30-2.30, 5.30-9.30; 12-3 Sun ☎ 07890 203282 🌐 conqueror-alehouse.co.uk

Beer range varies Ⓖ

Welcoming micropub with room for about 20 customers, offering a cosy and pleasant music- and TV-free environment. Opened in a former retail outlet, it offers three changing real ales, served straight from the cask, as well as a local cider and a perry. It is named after a two-funnelled paddle steamer that operated excursions from the town in the early 1900s, pictures of which adorn the walls. A finalist in CAMRA's National Pub of the Year 2013. Q⛺♣🍎🚌

Hovelling Boat

12 York Street, CT11 9DS

🕐 11.30-9.30 (11 Fri & Sat); 12-4 Sun ☎ 07974 613030 🌐 hovellingboatinn.co.uk

Beer range varies Ⓖ

Sympathetic shop conversion micropub opened Easter 2013 in a handy town-centre location that is proving to be a welcome addition to the burgeoning real ale scene in Ramsgate. It was to have had another name until the landlord discovered it had originally been the Hovelling Boat pub, which ceased trading in 1909. Features are exposed brickwork and a display of breweriana. Four different beers from Kent and beyond are served at your table by friendly staff. Cold snacks, tea and coffee are also available. Q☕❀🍎🚌🐾

Montefiore Arms

Trinity Place, CT11 7HJ

🕐 12-2.30 (not Wed), 7-11; 12-4.30, 7-11 Sat; 12-3, 7-10.30 Sun ☎ (01843) 593265 🌐 montefiorearms.co.uk

Ramsgate Gadds' No. 7 Bitter Ale; guest beers Ⓗ

A long-established regular in this Guide, the Monte enjoys a good reputation with real ale drinkers in the Thanet area. Most shifts at this friendly back-street local just off Hereson Road are presided over by the consummately professional landlord, serving an excellent and competitively priced Gadds' bitter, two changing guest ales and Biddenden cider. Sunday lunchtimes are particularly well patronised, with a popular high-rolling meat raffle as the climax. During the week quiz and darts teams play league matches. ♣🍎🚌

Rochester

Britannia Bar Café Ⓛ

376 High Street, ME1 1DJ (½ mile E of railway station)

🕐 10-11 (9 Mon); 12-9 Sun ☎ (01634) 815204

Goacher's Fine Light Ale; guest beers Ⓗ

Situated between Rochester and Chatham railway stations, customers will find this bar a combination of a traditional English public house and a continental café bar. Breakfast and an extensive lunchtime menu are available, with a traditional roast offered on Sundays. Fish and chips are served on Thursday evenings. The stylish bar leads to a small walled garden at the back. No jukeboxes or fruit machines. Q❀◐➡(Chatham)🚌

Coopers Arms

10 St Margaret Street, ME1 1TL

🕐 11-11 (midnight Fri & Sat) ☎ (01634) 404298

Courage Best Bitter; Young's Special; guest beers Ⓗ

A one-minute stroll past Rochester cathedral and castle, this charming inn, originally dating from 1199, is one of the oldest in Kent. The front bar has beamed ceilings, and a couple of impressive fireplaces. A passageway leads to a more modern rear bar and out into a well-kept garden area, popular on sunny days. This venue features up to seven real ales, Sunday roasts and lunchtime specials. ❀◑➡

Eagle Tavern

124 High Street, ME1 1JT

🕐 12-midnight (9 Mon; 11 Tue & Wed); 12-8 Sun ☎ (01634) 409040 🌐 theeagletavern.org.uk

Harveys Sussex Best Bitter; St Austell Tribute; Sharp's Doom Bar; Wychwood Hobgoblin; guest beer Ⓗ

A pub that describes itself as Rochester's premier music venue, with jam nights on Wednesdays, a band on Thursday evenings and jazz on Sunday lunchtimes. Situated in the middle of historic Rochester High Street, things are usually a lot quieter during the day. This single-room hostelry can be found opposite a large car park and has a big garden at the back that gives a view of the old city wall. A varied menu is offered lunchtimes (no food Sun). ❀◐♿➡🚌

Good Intent

3 John Street, ME1 1YL

🕐 12-midnight ☎ (01634) 843118

Beer range varies Ⓖ

A back-street pub for real ale enthusiasts, with a gravity-fed system for dispensing up to three beers. The casks can be seen clearly in the public bar, which has a pool table and a large-screen TV for major sports fixtures. The back bar is accessed via a garden gate and has a much quieter atmosphere. A monthly quiz is held in this local, as well as live music events. There are regular beer festivals. Q❀≋♣●P🚌

Man of Kent 𝕃

6-8 John Street, ME1 1YN (200yds left off A2 from bottom of Star Hill)

⏲ 2 (3 Mon)-11; 2-midnight Fri; 12-1, 2-midnight Sat; 12-1, 2-11 Sun ☎ 07772 214315

Goacher's Fine Light Ale, Gold Star Strong Ale; guest beers Ⓗ

All the draught ales from the 11 handpumps on the bar come from Kent breweries only. An extensive range of Kent wines and cider is also stocked, while a number of German and Belgian beers are offered on draught and in bottles. Live music features on Wednesday and Thursday, a jam night on Sunday, a ukulele jam night on the first Tuesday, and a quiz night on the third Tuesday. An enclosed garden allows for pleasant drinking in summer. ❀≋▯🚌

Two Brewers

113 High Street, ME1 1JS

⏲ 11-11 (midnight Fri & Sat); 12-7.30 Sun ☎ (01634) 812448 🌐 twobrewersrochester.com

Shepherd Neame Master Brew, Spitfire, Bishops Finger; guest beer Ⓗ

Rochester castle and cathedral are both within walking distance of this cosy and friendly pub situated in the High Street. The Two Brewers dates back to 1683 but has had extensive alterations. Despite its small size it hosts live music every Sunday afternoon and a blues nights on the first Thursday of each month. Large-screen TVs show all the major sporting fixtures. The full range of Shepherd Neame products is available. ≋🚌

Who'd Ha' Thought It

9 Baker Street, ME1 3DN

⏲ 12-11.30 (midnight Fri & Sat) ☎ (01634) 830144 🌐 whodha.co.uk

Beer range varies Ⓗ

A charming back-street local off Rochester's Maidstone Road, offering three rotating ales. This is a friendly free house with a wood-panelled bar, log fire, large TV with satellite sport and a snug bar to the rear. A range of events is held, including live music and a monthly charity quiz evening. There is a well-maintained family and dog-friendly garden where barbecues and beer festivals are held. Bar snacks include rolls and pizzas. ♉❀♣🚌(134,155)

Ryarsh

Duke of Wellington 𝕃

The Street, ME19 5LS

⏲ 11-11; 12-10.30 Sun ☎ (01732) 842318 🌐 dukeofwellingtonryarsh.com

Harveys Sussex Best Bitter; Sharp's Cornish Coaster; Westerham Grasshopper Kentish Bitter; guest beer Ⓗ

A 16th-century building occupying a prominent position in this small village at the foot of the North Downs. There are two distinct bars, one mainly for dining, divided by a magnificent fireplace. Food, including a tapas menu, is available all day Friday-Sunday, and at lunchtimes and evenings on all other days. One or two of the beers may change from time to time. Live music features on the first Thursday of the month. ♉❀◐◑♣P🚌(58)🐾📶

St Mary in the Marsh

Star Inn

TN29 0BX (From New Romney turn by the Plough into St Mary's Road; after 1¼ miles bear left at signpost for ½ mile, then turn right at end of road; the Star is on right opp church) TR065279

⏲ 12-11 (11.30 Fri-Sun) ☎ (01797) 362139 🌐 thestarinn-themarsh.co.uk

Young's Bitter, Special; guest beers Ⓗ

Warm, traditional pub with an open fire. It still has a bar billiards table to accompany the excellent beer and good food. It was built in the reign of Edward IV, and Noel Coward used to live in an adjacent cottage, where he wrote his first play. Edith Nesbit, author of The Railway Children, is buried in the graveyard at St Mary the Virgin church opposite. ♉❀🛏◐♿♣●P🚌(11A)🐾📶

Sandgate

Ship Inn 𝕃

65 Sandgate High Street, CT20 3AH (on A259)

⏲ 11-11.30 (12.30am Fri & Sat) ☎ (01303) 248525

Dark Star Hophead; Greene King IPA, Abbot; Hop Back Summer Lightning; Hopdaemon Incubus Ⓗ**; guest beers** Ⓖ

Narrow pub on a corner fronting onto the High Street, part of it dating from 1798, with a front bar and a back room, plus a restaurant with sea views and an upstairs top deck for drinkers, both added in 2010. Nautical maps and pictures featured on the walls reflect the landlord's naval interests. Biddenden ciders are always available and an August bank holiday beer festival is held. No food is served Sunday evenings. ❀🛏◐◑♣●🚌🐾

Sandwich

Crispin Inn 𝕃

4 High Street, CT13 9EA

⏲ 11-11; 12-10.30 Sun ☎ (01304) 621967 🌐 sandwichpubs.co.uk

Adnams Broadside; Sharp's Doom Bar; guest beers Ⓗ

A 15th-century public house by the Barbican and old toll bridge. Its low ceilings and wooden beams create a cosy atmosphere for locals and visitors alike. Sit in the lounge, with its comfortable sofas, or the rear courtyard overlooking the river, an added attraction in summer. Occasional live music is hosted. The house beer is from the Mad Cat Brewery and real cider is from Westons or Thatchers. A good range of home-cooked food and bar snacks is available. ♉❀◐◑⛺≋♣●🚌🐾📶

George & Dragon 𝕃

24 Fisher Street, CT13 9EJ

⏲ 11-11; 11-4.30 Sun ☎ (01304) 613106 🌐 georgeanddragon-sandwich.co.uk

Shepherd Neame Master Brew; guest beers Ⓗ

A wood-floored bar area, beamed ceilings and exposed brickwork welcome you as you walk into this 15th-century pub and restaurant. The restaurant's varied menu is complemented by superb home-made bar snacks. Wantsum and Hopdaemon are some of the Kentish ales you will find on the bar. A small rear courtyard offers a pleasant place to sit in summer. The pub is located in the back streets of Sandwich, a short walk from bus and railway services. ♉❀◐◑⛺≋🚌🐾📶

Red Cow

12 Moat Sole, CT13 9AU
11-11 (midnight Fri & Sat) ☎ (01304) 613399
Sharp's Doom Bar; guest beers H
The large red cow on the front of this timber-framed building is testament to its past; it served traders from the local cattle market into the 1980s. Inside, this family-run pub is divided into three distinct areas accommodating drinkers, diners and bar billiards players alike. The real ale line-up always includes one from the Ramsgate (Gadds) Brewery. The cider is from Broomfield. There is a popular quiz on Sunday evenings. At the back is a pleasant suntrap garden.

Sevenoaks

Anchor

32 London Road, TN13 1AS
11-3, 6-11; 10.30-11 Fri; 10.30-4.30, 7-11 Sat; 12-11 Sun
☎ (01732) 454898 anchorsevenoaks.co.uk
Harveys Sussex Best Bitter; Sharp's Doom Bar; guest beer H
One of the last real traditional pubs in the area and Barry, the inimitable landlord, is the longest serving. A pub full of friendly banter and mickey-taking makes for a unique experience, while enjoying one of three exceptionally well-kept real ales. The changing guest ale usually comes from a local microbrewery. An established venue for live music, twice-monthly blues and open mic nights are held. Darts, poker and pool are played and there is a weekly meat raffle.

Chequers

73 High Street, TN13 1LD
11-11; 12-10.30 Sun ☎ (01732) 450144
chequerssevenoaks.co.uk
Harveys Sussex Best Bitter; St Austell Tribute; Tonbridge Copper Nob, Rustic; guest beers H
A 16th-century traditional pub with some grim history – records of hangings and even a drowned landlord. Thankfully these days it is a social hub and the visitor will be greeted by hop-strewn oak beams, an open fire and comfortable seating. A U-shaped bar, sporting handpumps, delivers top-quality guest beers, including three local brews and Westons Old Rosie cider. There is a discount promotion on ales, and pie and mash on Monday evenings, live music is performed fortnightly and weekly quiz nights are held.

White Hart

Tonbridge Road, TN13 1SG
11-11; 12-10.30 Sun ☎ (01732) 452022
whitehart-sevenoaks.co.uk
Harveys Sussex Best Bitter; Old Dairy Blue Top; guest beers H
Acquired by a small north-west pub company a few years ago, this attractive 17th-century coaching inn has seen a new lease of life. Appropriately, the house beer comes from Manchester's Phoenix Brewery, accompanying many local guest ales and good-quality food. Real Kent cider is served at the end of the front bar. The whitewashed exterior leads to an open-plan wood-floored interior containing many cosy corners. A lovely sunny patio and garden is tucked away at the back.
QP(401,402)

Sevenoaks Weald

Windmill

1 Windmill Road, TN14 6PN
12 (5 Mon)-11; 10-11 Sat ☎ (01732) 463330
wealdwindmill.co.uk
Larkins Traditional Ale; guest beers H
Following a recent chequered history, the Windmill, now under welcome new ownership, offers an excellent selection of five to six top-notch ales, three Kentish ciders, and continental draught lagers, together with a comprehensive menu and basket meals (no food Sun eve). The homely interior features wooden settles, a log-burning stove, etched windows, porcelain and pub memorabilia, while a quiet, colourful garden is available for warmer times. Live acoustic music is performed every Sunday evening and a quiz night is held monthly. (401,402)

Sittingbourne

Paper Mill

2 Charlotte Street, ME10 2JN (N of Sittingbourne station, almost in Milton Regis, at the corner of Church St and Charlotte St)
12-2 (not Mon), 5-9; 12-9 Sat; 12-6 Sun ☎ 07927 073584
Goacher's Real Mild Ale; guest beers G
The first micropub to open in Swale is located close to Sittingbourne town centre and railway station. This one-room venue has bench seating around four large wooden tables. Three to four beers are available, with Goacher's supplying the regular beer, mild, and an occasional house beer – Gremlins. Other regular breweries include Hopfuzz, Hopdaemon, Wantsum and Kent. The pub also serves several real ciders.
Q(334,347)

Summoner

Units 1-3 Bell Shopping Centre, High Street, ME10 4AY
8am-midnight (1am Fri) ☎ (01795) 410158
Greene King IPA, Abbot; guest beers H
As with many in the JD Wetherspoon chain, this is a conversion into a pub; it has a large open area, while more private booths are on a raised platform. The Summoner is a character from Chaucer's Canterbury Tales, who promises to 'telle tales of friars, ere I come to Sittingbourne'. (In medieval times the town was on the pilgrims' route to Canterbury.) The pub serves a range of guest beers which will often include local ales. Q

Snargate

Red Lion ★

TN29 9UQ (on B2080, 1 mile NW of Brenzett) TQ990285
12-3, 7-11 (not Mon eve); 12-3, 7-10.30 Sun
☎ (01797) 344648
Goacher's Best Dark Ale; guest beers G
Superb multi-roomed 16th-century pub which has been in the same family for over 100 years and is universally known as Doris's. It is decorated inside with posters from the 1940s and the Women's Land Army, it has a nationally important historic pub interior. It is on the road that separates Walland Marsh from Romney Marsh. Beers from small breweries including Goacher's are served. A beer festival is held in June, with a mini festival in October. QP(11B)

South Darenth

Queen 𝕃

58-62 New Road, DA4 9AR

✪ 2-11; 12-11.30 Sat; 12-10.30 Sun ☎ (01322) 862430

Kent Session Pale; guest beers Ⓗ

Friendly back-street local once serving the nearby, recently closed, paper mill. It was extended in 1988 to incorporate a former shop and given a contemporary interior. It has two separate bars, one adorned with photographs of 1960s/70s London football teams. This genuine free house promotes beers from Kent Brewery and various guests, including Dark Star. Substantial free bar food is available Sunday lunchtimes. Children are welcome until 8.30pm, and there is a garden with a covered area. ♨❀🛏♣🚌(414)🐾📶

Stalisfield Green

Plough Inn 𝕃

ME13 0HY

✪ 12-3, 6-11; 12-11 Sat; 12-6 Sun ☎ (01795) 890256

Beer range varies Ⓗ

A large country pub, situated high on the North Downs, serving three real ales, mostly from Kent breweries. Meals are available lunchtimes and evenings; families are welcome in the front bar and dogs in the main bar. The pub has a large car park and garden. The 660 bus runs infrequently from Faversham. The pub is popular with walkers and cyclists. ♨❀◐◑♿⛺●P🚌(660)🐾

Staplehurst

Lord Raglan 𝕃

Chart Hill Road, TN12 0DE (½ mile N of A229 at Cross at Hand) TQ786472

✪ 12-3, 6.30-11; closed Sun ☎ (01622) 843747

Goacher's Fine Light Ale; Harveys Sussex Best Bitter; guest beer Ⓗ

Twenty consecutive years in the Guide is the proud achievement for this popular and unspoilt free house. It retains the atmosphere of a country pub from bygone days. The bar is hung with hops and warmed by two log fires and a stove. The large orchard garden catches the evening sun. Excellent snacks and full meals are always available. The guest beer changes regularly and local Double Vision cider is sold. Well-behaved children and dogs are welcome. The nearest bus stop is on the A229. Q❀◐◑●P🐾

Swanscombe

George & Dragon 🏆 𝕃

1 London Road, DA10 0LQ

✪ 12 (4 Mon & Tue)-11; 12-10.30 Sun ☎ (01322) 386440

🌐 georgedragonswanscombe.co.uk

Beer range varies Ⓗ

Local CAMRA Pub of the Year 2013 and 2014, this enterprising former Victorian coaching inn has been quickly established as a must-visit for quality real ales and food. A horseshoe-shaped bar supports nine handpumps; chilled local ciders are also available. It is home to the Caveman Brewery, now established in the pub cellar, and offers an interesting whisky cabinet and chilled bottles from UK and international specialist brewers. The restaurant is open Wednesday to Saturday lunchtimes and evenings, plus Sunday lunchtime for traditional roasts – recommended. ❀🛏◐◑⇌♣●P🚌🐾📶

Tankerton

Tankerton Arms 𝕃

139B Tankerton Road, CT5 2AW

✪ closed Mon; 12-2, 5-9 (11 Fri & Sat); 12-2 Sun ☎ 07532 025626 🌐 thetankertonarms.co.uk

Beer range varies Ⓖ

Micropub with a firm policy of supporting microbreweries, mainly from Kent. The pleasant, airy room is lined with high wooden tables and benches, which encourage the art of conversation. Mobile phones are banned. The walls are decorated with pictures of Thames sailing barges. Snacks include local cheeses and Scotch eggs from the butcher's shop opposite. There is some seating outdoors on the tree-shaded pavement. Q❀●🚌(4,6)🐾

Teynham

Swan 𝕃

78 London Road, ME9 9QH

✪ 4-midnight (2am Fri); 12-2am Sat; 12-midnight Sun ☎ (01795) 521218 🌐 swanteynham.co.uk

Beer range varies Ⓗ

Large roadside pub on the A2, situated 950 yards from Teynham railway station. Two real ales are served, often from Kent breweries, as well as real cider, usually from Dudda's Tun. The pub hosts darts teams and shows sporting events on TV. Live music features on most weekends. A large function room is available for hire and hosts the pub's annual beer festival. Good hearty Sunday lunches are served 12-3pm. ♨❀◐●P🚌(333,344)

Tonbridge

Humphrey Bean

94 High Street, TN9 1AP

✪ 7am-midnight (1am Fri & Sat) ☎ (01732) 773850

Adnams Broadside; Greene King Abbot; Ruddles Best Bitter; guest beers Ⓗ

Ever-popular Wetherspoon house close to Tonbridge Castle and the River Medway, with ample space and an extensive flower-adorned garden. An interesting range of six guest beers from breweries such as Long Man, Adnams, Hogs Back and Dark Star illustrates the commitment to real ale, enhanced by occasional events showcasing a brewery's beers. Ask for the current choice of ciders supplementing Westons Old Rosie, kept behind the bar. Food is served from 7am for breakfast until 11pm for late meals. Q♨❀◐◑♿⇌●P🚌📶

Tunbridge Wells

Bedford 𝕃

2 High Street, TN1 1UX

✪ 12-11 (midnight Fri & Sat); 12-6 Sun ☎ (01892) 510133

🌐 thebedfordtw.co.uk

Greene King IPA, Abbot; Morland Old Golden Hen, Old Speckled Hen; guest beers Ⓗ

Bustling pub acting as a surrogate waiting room, with the railway station opposite, for thirsty travellers. Its choice of 10 handpumps and several real ciders makes the Bedford a magnet for drinkers near and far. Specialising in Kent and Sussex brews, the house beer is from Turners of Ringmer. Sandwiches and English tapas are served every lunchtime. Three third-of-a-pint glasses on a beer bat can complement a three-tapas dish deal. A discount Cask Ale Club operates Wednesdays 5-8pm. ◐⥲♣●🚌🐾📶

Grove Tavern 🄻

19 Berkeley Road, TN1 1YR

☺ 12-11 ☎ (01892) 526549

Harveys Sussex Best Bitter; Timothy Taylor Landlord; guest beers 🄷

Only five minutes' walk from the railway station, this small pub, probably the oldest in town, is popular with locals and beyond. It does not serve food but your dog will be happy as dog biscuits and a water bowl are provided. You may also see regulars bringing their own snacks in to share. It is a pub where customers' conversation happily coexists with darts and pool players and those enjoying their beer while watching sport shown on terrestrial TV. ⛾⥲♣🚌🐾📶

Ragged Trousers

44 The Pantiles, TN2 5TN

☺ 12-11 ☎ (01892) 542715

Larkins Traditional Ale; Long Man Brewery Long Blonde; guest beer 🄷

Long, narrow café-style pub on the famous Georgian Pantiles area of the town. In clement weather the front seating provides an enviable position to observe passers-by and activity around the local traders' market. Inside, scrubbed wooden tables, candles and low lighting create a cosy feel, contrasting with the vibrant atmosphere. Three handpumps dispense the local Larkins and Long Man ales and a guest, frequently from Dark Star brewery. The daily lunchtime menu runs from sandwiches to international cuisine. ❀◐⥲♣🚌🐾📶

Royal Oak 🄻

92 Prospect Road, TN2 4SY

☺ 12-11 (10.30 Sun) ☎ (01892) 542546

Harveys Sussex Best Bitter; guest beers 🄷

Large but homely pub a short walk from the town centre. Six handpumps mainly dispense beers from Kent and Sussex breweries, such as Larkins and Dark Star, on a rolling basis. Ciders are from Biddenden or Dudda's Tun. Occasional beer/cider festivals are held. The Oak is used by clubs and societies and in 2013 was awarded Asset of Community Value status. Ample space is available in which to enjoy live music, regular quizzes or a game of bar billiards. ⛾❀◐◑⥲♣●P🚌(6,285)🐾

> Charles Collins liveth here;
> Sells rum, brandy, gin and beer;
> I make this board a little wider
> To let you know I sell good cyder.
> **17th-century notice at the Arrow, Knockholt, Kent**

Upchurch

Brown Jug

76 Horsham Lane, ME9 7AP

☺ 12-10 ☎ (01634) 366543

Greene King IPA; Harveys Sussex Best Bitter; guest beers 🄷

Welcoming little pub on the outskirts of the village, unpretentious with good service and a friendly atmosphere. Sold off by Shepherd Neame, this is now a true free house with a strong liking for Harveys of Lewes. A bar menu is available during the week until 9pm – meat or fish pie, toasties and ploughmans, all nice and fresh. Weekends after 7pm a comprehensive menu is offered, and on Sunday lunchtimes there is a choice of four roasts. When busy the pub may close later, especially at weekends. ⛾❀◐◑♿♣P🚌(327)🐾📶

Upper Upnor

King's Arms 🏆

2 High Street, ME2 4XG

☺ 11.30-11; 12-11 Sun ☎ (01634) 717490

🌐 kingsarmsupnor.co.uk

Beer range varies 🄷

The pub is set at one end of the scenic cobbled High Street, which leads to the River Medway and a historic castle. This village local is the current CAMRA branch Pub of the Year, the third time that it has won. There are usually four guest beers on offer, plus cider and perry, and a good range of European bottled beers. The pub is well known for its food, which ranges from home-cooked traditional fare to an à la carte menu. Q⛾❀◐◑●🚌(197)

Walmer

Berry 🏆 🄻

23 Canada Road, CT14 7EQ

☺ 11 (2 Tue; 12 Thu)-11.30; 11.30-11 Sun

☎ (01304) 362411 🌐 theberrywalmer.co.uk

Dark Star American Pale Ale; Harveys Sussex Best Bitter; Time & Tide Spratwaffler Pale Ale; guest beers 🄷

If you like real ale this is a must-visit. A traditional back-street ale house with friendly and knowledgeable staff, it has 11 handpumps, two ciders and perries, and KeyKeg from Time & Tide. The family-run pub has won multiple CAMRA awards including Kent CAMRA Pub of the Year 2013. Real ale festivals are held in February and July, a cider festival in May, and an Oktoberfest. Entertainment includes darts, pool, a monthly charity quiz and occasional live music. ❀♣●🚌🐾

West Malling

Bull 🄻

1 High Street, ME19 6QH

☺ 12-2.30, 4-11; 12-11 Fri & Sat; 12-10.30 Sun

☎ (01732) 842753 🌐 thebullinnwestmalling.com

Timothy Taylor Landlord; Young's Bitter; guest beers 🄷

A two-room free house at the north end of the village by the railway line. Considerable renovation and decoration have been undertaken by the owner, although care has been taken to preserve the character of the main bar with its wood panels, hops on the beams and log fire. There are now eight handpumps, with two regular and six changing guest ales, plus a local cider, on handpump. Good pub meals are served in both bars but the left side is mainly for dining. Q❀◑♣🍎🚌(72,151)🐾📶

Westerham

General Wolfe

High Street, TN16 1RQ (W end of town on A25)
🕐 12-11 (midnight Fri & Sat); 12-10.30 Sun
☎ (01959) 562104 🌐 generalwolfepubwesterham.co.uk
Greene King IPA, Abbot; guest beers Ⓗ
Picturesque weatherboarded pub named after a famous town resident, General Wolfe of Quebec, and formerly serving as the old Black Eagle Brewery tap. Participating in the Local Hero scheme, the two guest beers come from the likes of Tonbridge, Westerham or Cronx breweries. Good-value locally-sourced food is available, including Sunday roasts and Friday night curries. Live entertainment takes place most Saturday nights, with open mic on Sunday nights – outside on the decking in summer. A log fire creates a cosy atmosphere in winter. Q❀◑♣P🚌(401,246)🐾📶

Westgate-on-Sea

Bake & Alehouse 🏆

21 St Mildred's Road, CT8 8RE (down alleyway between bookmakers and Carlton cinema on left opp United Services club)
🕐 closed Mon; 12-2, 5.30-9; 12-2 Sun ☎ 07581 468797
🌐 bakeandalehouse.co.uk
Beer range varies Ⓖ
One of the earliest of a burgeoning number of micropubs in this part of east Kent. This former baker's shop has been sensitively managed to create an intimate and friendly community atmosphere, and has room for around 20 people. Four predominantly Kentish ales and real cider are usually available. Food comprises local pork pies and cheese, which seems to keep regulars and visitors alike satisfied. CAMRA branch Pub of the Year 2014. Q⇌♣🍎🚌🐾

Whitstable

Ship Centurion Ⓛ

111 High Street, CT5 1AY
🕐 11-11; 12-7 Sun ☎ (01227) 264740
Adnams Southwold Bitter; Elgood Black Dog; Young's Special; guest beer Ⓗ
A friendly and traditional town-centre pub, which gets busy at weekends. Colourful hanging baskets add to its charm in summer. Pictures of Whitstable hang in the bar. A mild is always served; the home-cooked bar food often includes authentic German dishes, and there is schnitzel on Saturdays (no food Sun). Live music plays on Thursday evenings (except in January) and Friday lunchtimes. There is a summer cider festival and an October beer festival. ◑⇌🚌🐾📶

Woodchurch

Six Bells Ⓛ

Bethersden Road, TN26 3QQ (close to village green opp church)
🕐 12-midnight ☎ (01233) 860246 🌐 6-bells.co.uk
Fuller's London Pride; Harveys Sussex Best Bitter; Hopdaemon Golden Braid; Timothy Taylor Landlord; guest beers Ⓗ
Unspoilt and friendly village local which has a separate public bar and a saloon bar with a dining area, but with plenty of bar space for drinkers. Beer festivals are held several times through the year. A good range of freshly prepared meals is available seven days a week, including all day Sunday. There are gardens to the front and rear of the pub, with the large enclosed garden at the rear being ideal for families. Q🐴❀◑♿♣🍎P🚌(2A)🐾📶

Worth

Blue Pigeons Ⓛ

The Street, CT14 0DE
🕐 12-11 (10 Sun) ☎ (01304) 613233
🌐 thebluepigeons.co.uk
Beer range varies Ⓗ
The pub is an imposing Georgian building opposite St Nicholas Church. The front door leads you into the main bar area, wood-floored and decorated in neutral colours. The small snug has a discreet sports TV. There are normally three real ales, with one from a Kent brewery, typically Wantsum or Canterbury Ales. A varied menu of home-made food is available in the vaulted restaurant. The rear patio looks out onto a large garden with a gazebo and climbing frame. 🐴❀🛏◑P🚌(13,14)🐾📶

The village inn

The village inn, the dear old inn,
So ancient, clean and free from sin,
True centre of our rural life.
Where Hodge sits down beside his wife
And talks of Marx and nuclear fission
With all a rustic's intuition.

Ah, more than church or school or hall,
The village inn's the heart of all.

Sir John Betjeman, 1906-1984, former Poet Laureate

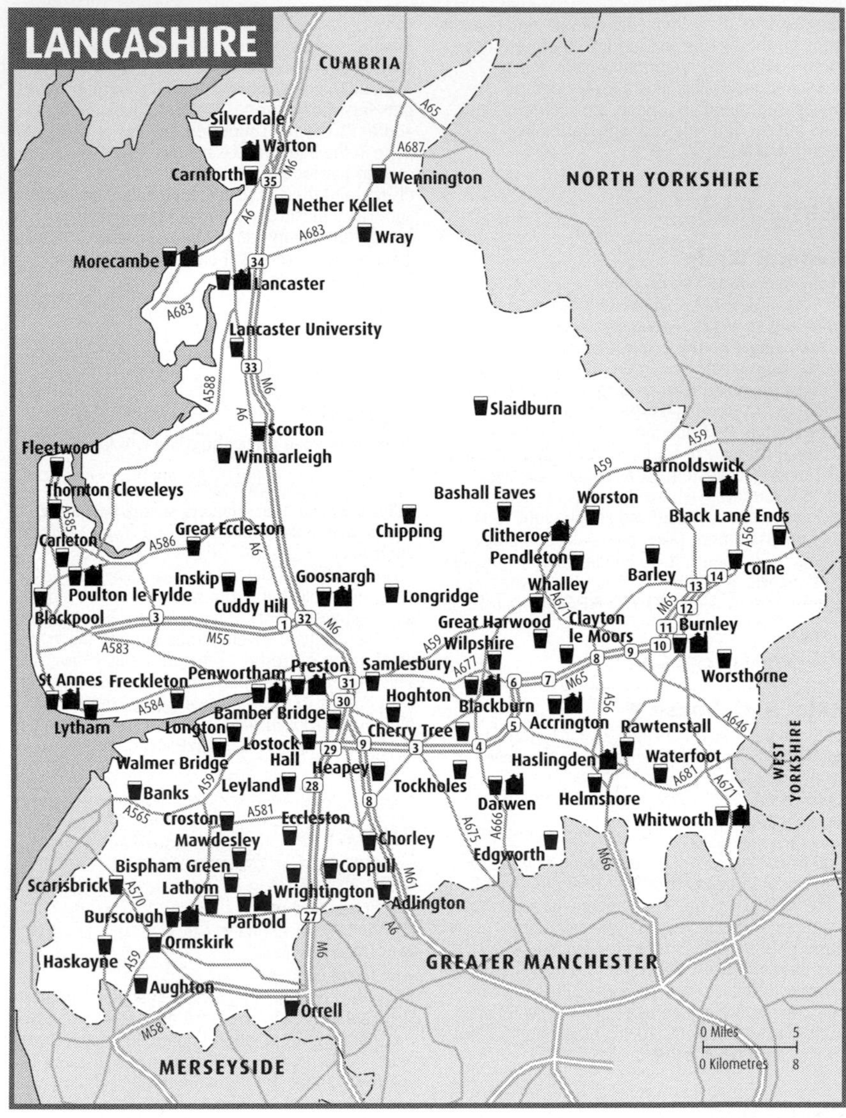

Accrington

Commercial Hotel

1 Church Street, BB5 2EN

✪ 8am-11 ☎ (01254) 300140

Greene King Abbot; Ruddles Best Bitter; guest beers Ⓗ

An open-plan pub in the typical Wetherspoon tradition, the Commercial contains many local features with more than a nod to the local Tiffany glass collection. It is adjacent to the bus station and markets and only a short walk to the railway station. The pub supports LocAle, with six of the 10 handpumps given over to guest beers, alongside two ciders. Q◑♿⇌●🚌📶

Grants

1 Manchester Road, BB5 2BQ

✪ 12-11 ☎ (01254) 393938 🌐 grantsbar.co.uk

Beer range varies Ⓗ

A large, imposing building on the edge of the town centre. Thoroughly modern on the inside, it is something of a place to be seen at weekends. The pub is home to the Big Clock Brewery, which can be viewed from the main drinking area. Up to seven real ales are sold from breweries such as Pennine, Oakham, Bank Top and Reedley Hallows, as well as real cider. There is a separate function room upstairs for hire (no disabled access). ⇌P🚌

Peel Park Hotel

Turkey Street, BB5 6EW

✪ 12-11.30; 12-10.30 Sat & Sun ☎ (01254) 235830

Tetley Bitter; guest beers Ⓗ

A true free house opposite the site of the old Stanley football ground. Six beers are sold, mainly from micros such as Three B's and Slaters, and regional brewers like Robinsons. The main bar is a large, open front room which is split into two sections. There is a separate small pool room and a room used for functions and meetings. An annual beer festival is held over the spring bank holiday. ≑P

Adlington

Spinners Arms

23 Church Street, PR7 4EX
12-11 (midnight Fri & Sat); 12-10.30 Sun
☎ (01257) 483331
Thwaites Wainwright; Timothy Taylor Dark Mild; guest beers Ⓗ
The pub is known as the Bottom Spinners to differentiate it from the other Spinners Arms in the village. Welcoming and friendly, a single bar serves three seating areas and there is a pleasant outdoor drinking area to the front. It has no pool table or gaming machine, just an open log fire. The bar menu offers home-cooked food with weekend specials. Five alternating guest beers are served, often sourced from local breweries. Small functions are catered for. ≑P (3)

Aughton

Derby Arms

Prescot Road, L39 6TA (at Bowker's Green on B5197)
11.30-midnight (1am Fri & Sat); 12-midnight Sun
☎ (01695) 422237
Tetley Mild, Bitter; guest beers Ⓗ
Friendly country pub with a long award-winning heritage; one wall proudly displays around 20 CAMRA awards. The interior is both atmospheric and intimate, with locals and staff offering a warm welcome to all. Five handpumps dispense two Tetley beers and an interesting range of guest ales. Quiz nights are held Tuesdays and Thursdays and there are regular charity events. Excellent-value food is available throughout the day; the popular pub breakfast is served from 9am till late on Saturdays. ♣P

Stanley Arms

24 St Michael Road, L39 6SA (off A59 at Aughton Springs) SD391055
12-11 (midnight Fri & Sat) ☎ (01695) 473241
thestanleyarmsaughton.com
Marston's Pedigree; Tetley Mild, Bitter; Timothy Taylor Landlord; guest beers Ⓗ
Situated beside a historic Norman church, the Stanley has distinctive 18th-century architecture. Decorated throughout with Tudor-style woodwork, there are several side rooms containing brewing memorabilia placed around the central bar, which dispenses from five handpumps. Immaculately kept both inside and out, the pub is exceptionally popular for its excellent home-cooked and locally-sourced food. Beer and jazz festivals are held twice-yearly, with proceeds going to kidney research. ♿P

Bamber Bridge

Withy Arms

Station Road, PR5 6QP
11-midnight (1am Fri); 10.30-1am Sat; 10.30-midnight Sun
☎ (01772) 697706 withyarms.com
Beer range varies Ⓗ
On the main crossroads and 15 minutes' walk from the railway station, this pub was reopened in 2011 after previously being bought by a local business for the office space. The open-plan bar has a slightly continental feel and there is an impressive counter featuring six handpumps. Guest beers are usually from local breweries, with Prospect or Moorhouse's often featuring. The house beer, WA Cask Bitter, is brewed by Thwaites. Quiz night is Tuesday. ≑P

Banks

New Fleetwood

1 Hoole Lane, PR9 8BD (corner of Hoole Lane and Ralph's Wife's Lane)
12-11 (1am Fri & Sat) ☎ (01704) 620127
Southport Golden Sands; guest beer Ⓗ
A former Tetley Walker establishment dating from the 1960s, this friendly community pub retains many original features in both the comfortable lounge and tiled public bars. The excellent home-cooked food and weekly theme nights (live music, quiz, karaoke) attract a wide clientele. The pub has Sky TV and a pool table, and supports darts and dominoes teams. It has struggled over recent years but was reopened in 2012 on a free house lease and is now a focal point for the community.
P (2,47)

Barley

Pendle Inn

Barley Lane, BB12 9JX
12-3, 5-10; 12-midnight Fri & Sat; 12-10 Sun
☎ (01282) 614808 pendle-inn.co.uk
Corby Blonde; Moorhouse's Pride of Pendle; guest beers Ⓗ
An impressive stone-built pub nestling resplendently in the lap of Pendle Hill in historic Pendle Witch country. The central bar provides a setting in which locals can tell improbable tales. There is a pool room, quiet room and a large dining room. Guest beers might be from Moorhouse's, Bowland, Bank Top and Three B's.
QP

INDEPENDENT BREWERIES

Arkwright's Preston
Barlick Barnoldswick
Big Clock Accrington (NEW)
Bishop's Crook Penwortham (NEW)
Bluestone Whitworth
Borough Lancaster (NEW)
Bowland Clitheroe
Burscough Burscough
Chapel Street Poulton-le-Fylde (NEW)
Cross Bay Morecambe
Fuzzy Duck Poulton-le-Fylde
Goosnargh Goosnargh
Hart of Preston Preston
Hopstar Darwen
Lancaster Lancaster
Lytham St Annes
Moonstone Burnley
Moorhouse's Burnley
Old School Warton
Problem Child Parbold (NEW)
Reedley Hallows Burnley
Rossendale Haslingden
Snaggletooth Darwen (NEW)
Three B's Blackburn
Thwaites Blackburn
Worsthorne Burnley

Barnoldswick

Fountain Inn

14 Church Street, BB18 5UT
12-11 (midnight Thu-Sat) (01282) 813412
fountaininnbarnoldswick.com
Dark Horse Hetton Pale; Tetley Bitter; Thwaites Wainwright; guest beers
This free house has become very popular since it was bought from a pubco chain. The landlady has transformed the pub into a real ale haven in the centre of town, and has kept to a policy of offering rotating guest beers from breweries like Prospect and Three Peaks. There is often also a real cider (usually Thatchers). It has a relaxing bar/lounge area with logburner, and a separate dining area. (29,215)

Greyhound

61 Manchester Road, BB18 5PW
5-11; 2-11 Sat & Sun (01282) 850670
thegreyhoundbarnoldswick.co.uk
Moorhouse's Blond Witch, Pride of Pendle; Thwaites Wainwright; guest beer
Traditional community local run by a syndicate and now the home of Barlick microbrewery, the first brewery in Pendle for many years. The three-storey stone building is in the old part of town close to Bancroft Steam Mill. It has a separate games room for pool, darts and dominoes, with a real fire in the main room. Guest beers might come from breweries such as Saltaire, Worsthorne and Reedley Hallows. Live music takes place at weekends and a quiz on Wednesday. P

Bashall Eaves

Red Pump Inn

Bashall Eaves, BB7 3DA
closed Mon & Tue; 12-2.30, 6-9; 12-6 Sun
(01254) 826227 theredpumpinn.co.uk
Hawkshead Windermere Pale; Moorhouse's Broomstick Bitter; guest beer
Within the Forest of Bowland Area of Natural Beauty, with great views of Pendle Hill, this country pub has a flagged bar area, where dogs are welcome. There is a separate dining room and function room, ideal for private parties. Home-made food is locally sourced wherever possible, and includes robust fare such as rabbit and venison. Guest ales may come from Ilkley, Black Sheep, Corby and Deeply Vale. There are also three comfortable guest rooms. Please ring beforehand to confirm opening times. Q P

Bispham Green

Eagle & Child

Malt Kiln Lane, L40 3SG
12-11; 12-10.30 Sun (01257) 462297
Southport Carousel; guest beers
An 18th-century pub with cheerful staff. Eight handpumps showcase local ales; Southport Carousel is always available and a variety of guest ales includes Allgates, Prospect and Moorhouse's. This busy classic country pub is the Lancashire Dining Pub of the Year for the fifth time, so book early for a table. The beer garden, with its wildlife area and great views, hosts a beer festival on the May bank holiday. Quiz night is every Monday. P

Black Lane Ends

Black Lane Ends

Skipton Old Road, BB8 7EP (off A56 2 miles E of Colne golf club)
12-11; 2-10.30 Sun (01282) 863070
Black Sheep Best Bitter; Lancaster Blonde; Taylor Golden Best
Previously named the Hare & Hounds, this isolated pub is situated on the old road between Colne and Skipton overlooking Pennine moorland. High-quality food is served all day every day in the two rooms either side of the central bar. Specials boards supplement the printed menu. Guest beers are often from Marston's. There is no nearby public transport. Q P

Blackburn

Black Bull

Brokenstone Road, BB3 0LL
closed Mon & Tue; 4-11 (midnight Fri); 12-midnight Sat; 12-10.30 Sun (01254) 581381 threebsbrewery.co.uk
Beer range varies
Originally a Thwaites' outlet, the pub was purchased by Three B's brewery as its first tied house. It serves the complete range of the brewery's beers plus its seasonal beers, and is the only place you can try Black Bull Bitter. Those wishing to sample several beers can try the three thirds-of-a-pint offer. An occasional guest or cider is on one of the handpumps. The pub enjoys great views looking west and south, but is only a few miles from Blackburn town centre. Q P

Blackpool

Bispham Hotel

68 Red Bank Road, FY2 9HY
12 (11 Sat)-11; 12-10.30 Sun (01253) 351752
Samuel Smith Old Brewery Bitter
Despite being only 100 yards from the promenade and a 10-minute tram ride from the Tower, this 1930s Art Deco pub is quite different to the stag and hen party image of Blackpool. It is a pub for a pint and chat. It is child, music, TV and food free. Behind the main room with its U-shaped bar is a smaller vault. Quizzes are held twice weekly. An upstairs meeting room is available. Q (3,4)

Blackpool Cricket Club

Barlow Crescent, West Park Drive, FY3 9EQ (follow signs to Stanley Park)
4.30-11; 12-midnight Sat; 12-11 Sun (01253) 393347
blackpoolcricket.co.uk
Thwaites Wainwright; guest beers
Part of Stanley Park, the club hosts numerous local sports teams that play on the nearby pitches. Large-screen TVs show all sports events and an upstairs room is available for social events. The club has its own squash courts and holds quiz and entertainment nights. It is the West Pennines CAMRA Club of the Year, and the home of the Bass Appreciation Society for the area. Dogs are permitted outside food service hours.
P (4,16)

Layton Rakes

17-25 Market Street, FY1 1ET
8am-midnight (1am Fri & Sat) (01253) 743710
Greene King Abbot; Ruddles Best Bitter; guest beers

Opened in 2011, this three-storey pub includes a roof terrace and two bars. Tastefully decorated, it features snippets of the resort's heritage including a carousel horse sculpture, a waltzer car, and a wall artwork immortalising one of Blackpool's adopted sons, Charlie Cairoli, the famous Blackpool Tower Circus clown. A total of 11 handpumps offer eight beers on the ground floor bar and three on the first floor. A good selection of guest beers is always available. ≋(North)

Shovels

260 Common Edge Road, FY4 5DH (on B526, ½ mile from A5230 jct)

12-11 (midnight Fri & Sat) ☎ (01253) 762702

Wells Bombardier; guest beers Ⓗ

A spacious open-plan roadside venue which has won local CAMRA Pub of the Year more than once. The pub is home to many sports clubs and has a large plasma screen for sporting events. Good food is served all day. With six handpumps, the beer range varies and comes mainly from microbreweries. The manager offers a warm and friendly welcome to all customers. Buses are daytime only. ♣P (10,17)

Burnley

Bootleggers Music Bar

Boot Way, BB11 2EE

11-11 ☎ (01282) 830111

Copper Dragon Golden Pippin; Courage Directors; guest beer Ⓗ

An interesting change of use from a Pentecostal chapel to a sports and music bar. TVs dominate this small, narrow bar, with a massive example above the entrance door which can be viewed from an upper level. This is definitely not a family pub but is purely for drinkers who enjoy TV sport and loud music. One unusual item of furniture is the (unused) pole dancing pole. The guest beers tend to be from local microbrewers. ≋(Central)

Bridge Bier Huis

2 Bank Parade, BB11 1UH

closed Mon & Tue; 12-midnight (1am Fri & Sat); 12-11 Sun ☎ (01282) 411304 thebridgebierhuis.co.uk

Moorhouse's Premier Bitter; guest beers Ⓗ

Free house with a large open-plan bar area and a small snug to one side. Alongside the Moorhouse's, three guest beers are offered, usually from microbreweries, plus a real cider or perry. More than 60 foreign bottled beers are available as well as seven draught foreign beers, usually including two rare German ones. Wednesday is quiz night and live music is hosted on occasional weekends. It opens at 5pm on Tuesdays if Burnley FC are playing at home. ≋(Central)

Brun Lea

31-39 Manchester Road, BB11 1HG

8am-midnight (1am Fri-Sun) ☎ (01282) 463700

Greene King Ruddles Best; Moorhouse's Pendle Witches Brew; guest beers Ⓗ

This large Wetherspoon venue in the town centre was formerly an office block and now bears a striking resemblance to an airport lounge. As with any Wetherspoon, good beer and food are on offer all day every day, and excellent local breweries vie with great beers from further afield. This pub does have loud music on weekend evenings, when it can be busy with the young at heart enjoying themselves. ≋(Central)

Rifle Volunteer

1 Smalley Street, BB11 3HH

2 (12 Sat)-11; 12-10.30 Sun ☎ (01282) 453839

Draught Bass; guest beers Ⓗ

A rare outlet in this area for Draught Bass, this free house is a supreme example of the street-corner local. No jukebox disturbs the quiet ambience of this friendly pub where the emphasis is on good beer and conversation. The Vols is an award-winning pub and currently local CAMRA Pub of the Year. The guest beer generally comes from the Burnley-based Reedley Hallows brewery. Check out the very rare Ducketts urinals. Q

Talbot

65 Church Street, BB11 2RU

5-midnight; 4-1am Fri; 12-1am Sat; 12-midnight Sun ☎ (01282) 412074

Copper Dragon Golden Pippin; guest beers Ⓗ

A free house that dates back to the 1800s, with a landlord who is a real ale enthusiast and offers four guest beers alongside the regular brews listed above. Guest beers are often local to east Lancashire but can come from much further afield. The central bar area has several separate seating areas. Live bands play every weekend and also one Wednesday each month. The pub has pool tables and a widescreen TV. Four guest bedrooms are available. ≋(Central)♣P

Burscough

Hop Vine

Liverpool Road North, L40 4BY (on A59 near bridge)

10.30-midnight (12.30am Fri & Sat) ☎ (01704) 893799

thehopvine.co.uk

Burscough Priory Gold, Mere Blonde, Ringtail; guest beers Ⓗ

This spacious former coaching house is now a thriving community brewpub renowned for its friendly atmosphere and popular for its exceptional ale and food. The classic country pub interior has wood panelling and wood/tile flooring throughout, and is decorated with historic local maps, photographs and vintage bottled ales. The award-winning Burscough Brewery operates from the attractive floral courtyard at the rear. Catering for all age groups, it offers great-value meals, live music, twice-yearly beer festivals and other seasonal events. ≋(Bridge)P (2A)

Carleton

Castle Gardens

10 Poulton Road, FY6 7NH

11.30-11 (midnight Fri & Sat); 12-11 Sun ☎ (01253) 890015

Moorhouse's Pendle Witches Brew; Thwaites Original, Wainwright; guest beers Ⓗ

Once the centre of a Victorian pleasure garden, this historic pub is now owned by Ember Inns and is Casque Mark accredited. Dining is popular because of the quality food served, and the choice and standard of its six real ales are good. CAMRA members receive a discount. The Cask Club offers cut prices on Mondays, along with a popular quiz. Add the friendly and knowledgeable staff and this community pub becomes a popular family venue. P

Carnforth

Snug

Unit 6, Carnforth Gateway Building, LA5 9TR (at N end of former mainline up platform)
closed Mon; 12-2, 5-9; 12-3 Sun ☎ (01524) 735677
Beer range varies H
Described as a micropub, both in the sense of being very small (which it is) and also of being a minimalist concept. The only beverages are ale, cider, wine and a few soft drinks, the only food is a few light snacks, while the only sounds are conversation and the roar of passing trains. The decor is similarly stripped back in the modern style – just painted walls, bare floorboards and chunky tall tables. Parking is on the station car park, for which there is a charge. Q

Cherry Tree

Station Hotel

391 Preston Old Road, BB2 5LW
3-12.30am; 11-1.30am Fri & Sat; 11-12.30am Sun
☎ (01254) 201643
Thwaites Nutty Black, Original, Wainwright, Lancaster Bomber; guest beer H
A noisy pub on the main road to Blackburn, with the full range of Thwaites' beers on the bar. A good mixture of young and old enjoys this pub. Darts, pool and dominoes are played. A large projection screen is the main feature, along with satellite for a variety of sporting events. Close to Cherry Tree station. P (124,152)

Chipping

Tillotsons Arms

18 Talbot Street, PR3 2QE
closed Mon; 12-3, 5-midnight; 12-midnight Sat; 12-11 Sun
☎ (01995) 61568 thetillotsonsarms.co.uk
Beer range varies H
In a picturesque village in the Forest of Bowland, this two-roomed, beamed pub built in 1836 has between two and four real ales – often from local micros, with Bowland, Copper Dragon and Hawkshead featuring regularly. Child and dog friendly, it has two real fires and a garden at the rear. Locally sourced home-cooked food is served lunchtimes and evenings, and all day at weekends. The pub is on the SIBA direct delivery scheme.
Q P (4)

Chorley

Malt 'n' Hops

50-52 Friday Street, PR6 0AH
4.30 (2 Fri)-11; 12.30-11 Sat; 1-10.30 Sun
☎ (01257) 260967
Beer range varies H
Converted to its current use from an old shop in 1989, the pub is handily situated for both the railway and bus stations. With a single L-shaped bar on two levels, the decor is very much of the Edwardian period. The friendly chat of the locals is complemented by the noise of the vocal parrot. Now a genuine free house, there are up to seven guest ales, usually sourced from local micros, and a cider. Home-made hot pot is provided on Wednesday quiz nights. May close early midweek if quiet.

Potters Arms

42 Brooke Street, PR7 3BY (next to Morrisons)
3-11.30 (midnight Fri); 12-4, 7-midnight Sat; 12-5, 7-11 Sun ☎ (01257) 267954
Black Sheep Best Bitter; Three B's Doff Cocker; guest beer H
A small free house named after the owners, at the bottom of Brooke Street alongside the railway bridge. The central bar serves two games areas, while two comfortable lounges are popular with locals and visitors alike. The pub displays a fine selection of photographs from the world of music, as well as vintage local scenes. Regular darts and dominoes nights are well attended and the chip butties go down a treat. The smoking area is covered. P

Prince of Wales

9-11 Cowling Brow, PR6 0QE
12-11 ☎ (01257) 260815
Banks's Sunbeam; Jennings Dark Mild, Cumberland Ale; guest beers H
A friendly multi-roomed local. The central bar serves a taproom, large lounge and pool room, with a further room off the entrance hall. There are real fires in both lounges and a beer garden to the rear. Sandwiches and pies are available lunchtimes. It is close to the Leeds and Liverpool Canal, with access nearby. Dogs are welcome and treats provided. Live music plays on Sundays, otherwise the pub is quiet. A range of eight beers from the Marston's stable is usually on offer plus varying guests. Q

Railway

20 Steeley Lane, PR6 0RD (under subway from train station)
12-midnight (1am Fri & Sat) ☎ (01257) 411449
therailwayhotelchorley.com
Banks's Sunbeam; Jennings Cumberland Ale; Wychwood Hobgoblin; guest beers H
Adjacent to the railway station and 100 yards from the bus station, this is a community local that offers a changing range of up to five real ales from the Marston's portfolio. Darts, dominoes and pool are popular with the locals, along with seasonal music festivals and Saturday night concerts. Open mic sessions on the first Sunday of the month are well attended, with the pub providing its own instruments and PA system to make participation easier.

Rose & Crown

15 St Thomas's Road, PR7 1HP (on A581 just outside pedestrian area)
12-11 (midnight Fri & Sat); 12-10.30 Sun
☎ (01257) 368022
Jennings Cumberland Ale; Thwaites Wainwright; guest beers H
Stone-built pub with a central bar covering two drinking areas, along with the former stables to the rear of the pub courtyard. There is a mixed age range, with youth in the majority at weekends when it is busy and lively, but there are plenty of bar staff. All major sporting events are shown on wall-mounted TV screens and there are occasional live music nights. Good-value food is served lunchtimes Monday to Friday.

White Bull

135 Market Street, PR7 2SG
12-11 (midnight Fri); 11-midnight Sat ☎ (01257) 232745

Courage Directors; Thwaites Wainwright; Wells Bombardier; guest beer H
This single-bar pub is a beacon for real ale in an area where so many pubs around it are closing. The games room is partitioned to the right of the comfortable L-shaped lounge. The walls are adorned with memorabilia from the landlord's favourite football team – Preston North End. Pies are served all day. Children are permitted in the beer garden if supervised. The guest beer is often from Bank Top Brewery.

Clayton le Moors

Forts Arms

1 Lower Barnes Street, BB5 5TA
4-midnight (1am Thu); 2-2am Fri & Sat; 2-midnight Sun
(01254) 433713
Beer range varies H
Partially opened out in a modern style, the pub boasts a function suite. A regular bus service stops at the end of Sparth Road 300 yards from the building. There are up to six real ales available, with at least two normally from local breweries; the beers on offer are usually new to the pub. Examples of breweries that you might find include Newby Wyke, Naylors and Bowness Bay. Four beer festivals are hosted each year. P (6,7)

Colne

Admiral Lord Rodney L

Mill Green, BB8 0TA
4-midnight (2am Fri); 1-2am Sat; 1-midnight Sun
(01282) 866206
Osset Silver King; guest beers H
Traditional local drinkers' hostelry in South Valley, perhaps all that remains of the old industrial heart of Colne. The stone floor includes mosaics in parts, and there are beautiful tiles up the inner staircase. The pub has become the meeting place for a number of clubs, impeccably serving many of the local beers, plus ales from the likes of Ilkley, Reedley Hallows, Bowland or Worsthorne. The music is lively, relatively traditional, but not always. There is a pool table. Excellent simple pub food is now available. Q

Wallace Hartley L

35-37 Church Street, BB8 0EB
8am-11 (midnight Thu; 1am Fri & Sat); 8am-11.30 Sun
(01282) 857990
Greene King Abbot; Ruddles Best Bitter; Wychwood Hobgoblin; guest beers H
Named after a local hero, the band leader on the ill-fated Titanic, this medium-sized Wetherspoon offers a relaxed, welcoming drinking place for all ages. The oak-panelled interiors are often favoured by mature drinkers. Friendly bar staff serve up to 10 real ales. The venue has several distinct seating areas. In addition to the exhibits associated with Wallace Hartley and the Titanic, photographs of old Colne can be found.

Coppull

Red Herring

Mill Lane, PR7 5AN
3-11; 12-11.30 Fri-Sun (01257) 470130
Beer range varies H
Real ale hostelry in the former offices of the next-door mill. It was converted to a pub some years ago; the bar area comprises a large single room plus an extension. Up to four beers, often from micros, are usually served, with ales from Moorhouse's and Three B's often available. TV sports fans are catered for, as are anglers who use the pond opposite. The pub hosts regular music nights and barbecues, and has a large first-floor function room. P (362)

Croston

Crown L

80 Station Road, PR26 9RN
12 (10 Sat & Sun)-11 (01772) 972785
crowncroston.co.uk
Thwaites Original; guest beers H
A comfortable traditional open-plan village pub with a large garden to the rear where boules can be played. The front door into the bar has glass engraved with the logo of Massey's Burnley Brewery. The guest ales are from the Thwaites Cask Club range, with an emphasis on the beers from its microbrewery. A 20p-a-pint discount is available to CAMRA members on production of a membership card, and third-of-a-pint taster trays are available.
Q P

Wheatsheaf

Town Road, PR26 9RA
12-11 (midnight Fri); 10-midnight Sat; 10-11 Sun
(01772) 600370 wheatsheaf-croston.com
Beer range varies H
On the main road and overlooking the village green, this recently refurbished pub has a contemporary feel. There is a distinct area for dining as well as a comfortable drinking area with sofas and chairs. The large outdoor space at the front is used to hold an annual beer festival during October. Up to five varying ales are served, sourced from the SIBA list, with Hawkshead Windermere Pale regularly available. P (7,112)

Cuddy Hill

Plough at Eaves Inn

Eaves Lane, PR4 0BJ (1 mile off B5269)
12-3, 5.30-11; 12-midnight Sat; 12-11 Sun
(01772) 690233
Thwaites Original, Wainwright, Lancaster Bomber; guest beer H
Located on an old drovers' road near the site of a Civil War battle where Scottish forces were defeated by Cromwell in 1648, the Plough is both one of the Fylde's oldest and hardest-to-find pubs. The long whitewashed building contains an old bar with low beams, flagstone floor and a blazing fire in winter, a restaurant, piano room and conservatory. Outside there is a pleasant beer garden and a children's play area. Food is served daily. Q P

Darwen

Number 39 L

39-41 Bridge Street, BB3 2AA
12-11 (01254) 704305
Hopstar Dizzy Danny Ale, Lancashire Gold, Smokey Joe's Black Beer; guest beers H
A good LocAle bar in the centre of town, formerly a Thai restaurant and now the brewery tap for Hopstar – its new brews are tried here first. Three beers from Hopstar and a guest are always on, as

well as real cider, a large variety of continental and world bottled beers, and draught Timmermans from Belgium. Live music night is every Thursday, featuring jazz and live bands, with tapas on Friday. (1,22)

Eccleston

Original Farmers Arms

Towngate, PR7 5QS
12-midnight (11.30 Sun) (01257) 451594
originalfarmersarms.co.uk
Black Sheep Best Bitter; Greene King IPA; Robinsons Dizzy Blonde; Thwaites Wainwright; guest beers
A white-painted village inn that has expanded over the years into the cottage next door, adding a substantial dining area. However, the original part of the pub is still used mainly for drinking. The three rotating guest beers are predominantly sourced from local breweries large and small. Meals are available all day every day, and there is accommodation in four good-value guest rooms. P(113,347)

Edgworth

White Horse

2-4 Bury Road, BL7 0AY
12-3 (not Mon & Tue), 5-11; 12-midnight Sat; 12-11 Sun
(01204) 852929
Bank Top Flat Cap; Moorhouse's Pendle Witches Brew; Thwaites Wainwright; guest beers
This particular White Horse has heraldic origins dating back to the 18th century – white being the colour of peace, and a horse representing stead, readiness-for-all-events-in-the-name-of-the-king (a wall plaque outside explains more). The range of real ales on six handpumps includes some from LocAle breweries. Situated prominently at the Bolton-Bury crossroads, this local is a large corner building. The impressively decorated interior has dining for locals and tourists, who come to enjoy excellent cuisine. QP

Fleetwood

Strawberry Gardens

Poulton Road, FY7 6TF (on A587 and near to Fisherman's Walk tram stop)
12-11 (1am Fri & Sat) (01253) 771991
strawberrygardensfleetwood.co.uk
Banks's Sunbeam; Cross Bay Halo; guest beers
Free house with up to 18 beers, and Old Rosie and three other ciders. Quiz night is held on Wednesday and live music on Friday and Saturday nights. A beer festival is hosted at the end of May. A past winner of local CAMRA Pub and Cider Pub of the Year, card-carrying members receive a discount. Food is served daily from noon. Away fans are welcome when playing Fleetwood Town. Dogs on leads are allowed in the vaults bar. P(14,82)

Thomas Drummond

London Street, FY7 6JE
8am-11 (midnight Thu-Sat) (01253) 775020
Greene King Abbot; Ruddles Best Bitter; guest beers
A Wetherspoon pub named after the builder who helped construct the town; it also displays details of the town's founder, Sir Peter Hesketh Fleetwood, and architect Decimus Burton. Food is served daily all day, and children are welcome until 9pm. Eight guest beers, which are sourced from an extensive catchment area and constantly rotated, are available. Two draught ciders are also rotated. Three beer festivals and two cider festivals are run each year. Q(1,14)

Freckleton

Ship Inn

Bunker Street, PR4 1HA (off Preston Old Road)
12-11 (midnight Fri & Sat); 12-10.30 Sun
(01772) 632393 theshipinnfreckleton.co.uk
Moorhouse's Pride of Pendle; guest beers
Known to have been licensed since 1677, but probably dating from the 14th century, the Ship may be the oldest pub on the Fylde. It formerly served local maritime trade and was reported to be involved in smuggling. The beer garden at the rear has wildlife identification guides and enjoys extensive views over Freckleton Marsh and the Ribble Estuary. Food is served lunchtimes and evenings daily, all day at weekends. This local is Cask Marque accredited, and families are welcome here. QP(68,78)

Goosnargh

Horn's Inn ★

Horns Lane, PR3 2FJ (corner of Inglewhite Rd, 2 miles NE of village)
11.30-3 (not Mon), 6-11; 12-9 Sun (01772) 865230
hornsinn.co.uk
Goosnargh Truckle, Gold; guest beer
Country pub close to the Forest of Bowland dating from 1782. There are five rooms, including a rare snug, one of only three in the country, where customers sit behind a bar counter while staff serve from the same area. Although marked private, it is open to all. Goosnargh Brewery operates on site. There is a 50p CAMRA members' discount on pints of Goosnargh beers. This local does good food using locally-sourced ingredients. Accommodation is in a converted barn at the rear. QP

Great Eccleston

White Bull Hotel

The Square, PR3 0ZB (in village square)
11-midnight; 12-11.30 Sun (01995) 670203
Black Sheep Best Bitter; Copper Dragon Golden Pippin; Everards Tiger; St Austell Tribute; Thwaites Wainwright; guest beers
A genuine local, this historic coaching inn is set in the heart of the village. A family-friendly, welcoming pub, it has flagged floors, an unspoilt atmosphere, and a room with pool, darts and the usual pub games. Three quieter rooms are for talking, drinking and dining. Locally-sourced home-cooked meals are good quality and excellent value (no food Mon and Tue lunchtimes). Interesting guest ales come from breweries on the SIBA list. There is free public parking in front of the pub. QP

Great Harwood

Victoria ★

St Johns Street, BB6 7EP
3-11 (midnight Fri & Sat); 12-10.30 Sun (01254) 885210

Black Sheep Bitter; Bowland Gold; Timothy Taylor Landlord; guest beers 🄷
Welcoming pub built in 1905 by Alfred Nuttall, with cream and green Art Nouveau tiling and etched windows. The central horseshoe-shaped bar serves a main bar area and five further rooms including a small snug, a darts room with original wooden lathe bench seating and a comfortable lounge. In addition to the three regulars, you might find beer from breweries such as Goose Eye, Saltaire and Irwell Valley. There is a popular weekly quiz night and an annual beer festival in the autumn.
Q⛾❀⛺🍎

Haskayne

Ship Inn

6 Rosemary Lane, L39 7JP
⌚ 12-midnight ☎ (01704) 840077
Lees Bitter; guest beers 🄷
The Ship was constructed in 1787 and claims to be the first hostelry to be built beside a canal. Nowadays, passing trade is more likely to come from the nearby M57/M58 interchange, the building being just off the A5147. Guest beers tend to come from breweries such as Burscough, Saltaire and Phoenix, with more available in summer. A previous winner of local CAMRA Pub of the Year, this pub has an attractive beer garden with play area. **Q⛾❀◐◑♿♣P🚌**(300)🐾

Heapey

Top Lock

Copthurst Lane, PR6 8LT (next to Leeds-Liverpool canal at Johnson's Hillock)
⌚ 11-11 (10.30 Sun) ☎ (01257) 263376
Beer range varies 🄷
A popular canalside pub with a large single room at the top of the Johnson's Hillock locks. Nine real ales are served, mainly from micros. Always available are beers from Coniston and Timothy Taylor, a mild and a stout or porter, plus up to three ciders on gravity. Curry night is on Tuesday and fish and chips on Wednesday. Monday is quiz night, with live music most Thursdays. An annual beer festival is held in October with up to 100 real ales.
Q⛾❀◐◑🍎P🚉🚌(124)

Helmshore

Robin Hood Inn 🄻

280 Holcombe Road, BB4 4NP
⌚ 4 (12 Fri-Sun)-11 ☎ (01706) 213180
Beer Studio Crystal Chestnut, Burnt Vienna; Hydes Original; guest beers 🄷
Traditional stone-built village pub that retains the original Glentop Brewery windows. Although the pub has been partly opened up, it still has three small rooms, two of which have open fires. Hydes Original is the main beer, but brews from Hydes' separate micro, the Beer Studio, can often be found here. Quiz night is Thursday. The small, hidden beer garden can be found via steps at the side of the pub, overlooking the textile museum. **Q❀♣🚌🐾**

Hoghton

Royal Oak 🄻

Blackburn Old Road, Riley Green, PR5 0SL
⌚ 11.30-11 ☎ (01254) 201445 🌐 dininginns.co.uk/royaloak/index.htm
Thwaites Nutty Black, Original, Wainwright, Lancaster Bomber; guest beers 🄷
Stone-built pub on the old road between Preston and Blackburn, near the Riley Green basin on the Leeds and Liverpool Canal. Popular with diners and drinkers alike, a dining room and alcoves radiate from the central bar while low beamed ceilings and horse brasses give the pub a rustic feel. This Thwaites' tied house is a regular award winner and acts as an outlet for its seasonal beers and guest range from the Thwaites Cask Club.
Q⛾❀◐◑P🚌(152)🐾📶

Inskip

Derby Arms

Carrs Green, PR4 0TJ
⌚ 5.30 (5 Thu)-midnight; 5-1am Fri; 12-midnight Sat & Sun
☎ (01772) 690168
Beer range varies 🄷
Once a well-known motoring inn on the edge of the village, this is now a free house close to the prominent radio masts of HMS Inskip. There is a small bar at the front of the pub, a games room behind where pool and darts teams play two or three times a week, and a separate restaurant serving food in the evenings and weekend lunchtimes. Two marquees in the garden to the rear may be hired for events.
⛾❀◐◑♿♣P🚌(80,82)

Lancaster

Borough 🄻

3 Dalton Square, LA1 1PP (near town hall)
⌚ 12-11.30 (12.30am Fri); 11-12.30am Sat; 11-11.30 Sun
☎ (01524) 64170 🌐 theboroughlancaster.co.uk
Borough Bitter, Pale, Wintertime Dark; guest beers 🄷
An upmarket town house built in 1824 but with a Victorian frontage. Now a pub, it succeeds in appealing both to food lovers and ale aficionados. The front area resembles a gentlemen's club, with deep-buttoned chairs and chandeliers; the large back room is a restaurant and the bar is in a passage between them. Outside is a sheltered patio with a covered smoking area. A comedy club takes place on Sunday evening.
❀🛏◐◑♿⇄🚌🐾📶

Merchant's

27 Castle Hill, LA1 1YN
⌚ 11.30-11 (midnight Fri & Sat); 12-11 Sun
☎ (01524) 66466 🌐 merchants1688.co.uk
Beer range varies 🄷
Converted wine merchants' cellars built in 1688, with an extensive outdoor drinking area, creating a peaceful haven away from the hubbub of the city centre. The main drinking areas are in three separate tunnels, with a fourth forming the entrance and bar area. Quiz night is Sunday. Look out for the stoneware bottles used in the construction of the cellar walls. **❀◐◑⇄🚌📶**

Tap House 🄻

2 Gage Street, LA1 1UH
⌚ 4-midnight; 2-1am Fri; 12-1am Sat; 12-11 Sun
☎ (01524) 842232 🌐 taphouselancaster.co.uk
Beer range varies 🄷
A place that describes itself as a world beer shrine, selling as it does a number of international ales, unusual bottles and keg beers. This small pub was completely refurbished in 2012 and features some

bare brickwork, a lot of visible wood (including old beer casks incorporated into the furnishings) and otherwise a white and grey colour scheme. A range of paninis, sandwiches and snacks is available.

Three Mariners

Bridge Lane, LA1 1EE (near Parksafe car park entrance)
11-midnight (1am Fri & Sat) (01524) 388957
thethreemarinerslancaster.co.uk
Everards Beacon; Hawkshead Windermere Pale; York Guzzler; guest beers
Commonly claimed to be the oldest pub in Lancaster, it certainly looks aged, inside as well as out, and many of the beams and stones are quite ancient. However, it has suffered some rebuilding, and had a comprehensive revamp in 2004. Built into the side of Castle Hill, the cellar is excavated at first-floor level. Bluegrass is played on Wednesdays, and folk on the first Friday of the month. Beacon is badged as Mariner's Gold. There is limited parking. Q

Water Witch

Tow Path, Aldcliffe Road, LA1 1SU (on canal towpath near Penny Street bridge)
11-midnight (11 Sun) (01524) 63828
thewaterwitch.co.uk
Beer range varies
The Water Witch was a passenger packet boat that once plied the Lancaster Canal. The building, originally a stable block, assumed its present name and use in 1978 – the first true canalside pub on this stretch of water. Wedged between the towpath and a retaining wall, it is long and narrow, with bare stone walls and floors. A mezzanine floor and the space underneath it are used mainly for dining. There are seats on the towpath. Quiz night is Thursday.

White Cross

Quarry Road, LA1 4XT (behind town hall, on canal towpath)
11.30-11 (12.30am Fri & Sat); 12-11 Sun (01524) 33999
thewhitecross.co.uk
Sharp's Doom Bar; Theakston Old Peculier; Timothy Taylor Landlord; Tirril Old Faithful; guest beers
A recent renovation of an old canalside warehouse converted to a pub in 1988, with an open-plan interior and a light, airy feel. French windows open onto extensive canalside seating, making this a popular location for summer afternoons and evenings. There is a well-attended Tuesday night quiz, and a beer and pie festival each April. Much of the custom comes either from the residential areas up the hill or from the nearby workplaces (including the Adult College). P

Lancaster University

Graduate College Bar

Bailrigg, LA1 4ZA (on pedestrian square in Alexandra Park; Graduate College is signposted)
7 (5 Fri & Sat term time)-11.30 (midnight Thu-Sat); 8-11 Sun (01524) 592824
Beer range varies
The Graduate College bar is much pubbier and attracts a higher age range than the usual student watering hole. The choice of beer is good, with eight handpumps. There is a beer fest in June and a cider fest in October. Curry night is Friday, and an open mic night alternates with live bands on Thursdays. (3,4)

Lathom

Ring o' Bells

Ring o' Bells Lane, L40 5TF (take A5209 from Burscough, turn left at Ring o' Bells crossroads)
11-11; 11-10 Sun (01704) 893157
Thwaites Nutty Black, Wainwright; guest beers
Impressive country pub in large rural grounds only 20 minutes' walk along the Leeds and Liverpool Canal from Burscough village. Reopened in 2011 by a local pubco, the huge split-level interior boasts stone and wood floors and offers a separate locals' area and family area with playpen. Six handpumps serve Thwaites' and local microbrewery beers. The outstanding food is well priced and locally sourced (beef is company farmed and slaughtered). An upstairs private function room and 24-hour canal moorings are also available.
Q P (3A,337)

Leyland

Leyland Lion

60 Hough Lane, PR25 2SA
8am-11.30 (12.30am Fri & Sat); 9am-11.30 Sun
(01772) 643990
Greene King Abbot; Ruddles Best Bitter; guest beers
Opened in 2011, this conversion of a town-centre post office is smaller than most Wetherspoon pubs. A central log fire is also unusual for this operator. The pub's name commemorates one of the types of bus that made this town famous, which were built a few yards up the road. Six guest beers are usually available, often coming from local breweries, plus a real cider. It is handy for the Commercial Vehicle Museum. The house beer, Leyland Lion, is brewed by Moorhouse's.

Railway at Leyland

1 Preston Road, PR25 4NT
4-11.30 (midnight Wed-Thu); 12-2am Fri (1.30am Sat); 12-midnight Sun (01772) 458427
therailwayatleyland.co.uk
Beer range varies
Since its refurbishment in 2007, this pub has led the way as Leyland has been transformed into a town much more attractive to the real ale drinker. The bright and airy interior makes it a welcoming hostelry, with four changing cask ales always available from breweries all over the country. Although a large pub, it can get extremely busy on weekend evenings when there is live entertainment. A first-floor function room can accommodate up to 100 people.
P (109,111)

Longridge

Corporation Arms

Lower Road, PR3 2YJ (near B5243/B6245 jct)
11-midnight (1am Fri & Sat); 12-10.30 Sun
(01772) 782644 corporationarms.com
Beer range varies
A substantial 18th-century stone-built inn close to the Longridge reservoirs on the road to Ribchester and handy for local walks. This free house has a reputation for excellent ale, food, service and accommodation. Four handpumps serve beers sourced from local breweries, with Bowland, Copper Dragon and Moorhouse's among the favourites. Real cider is normally only available

during summer months. There is an annual beer festival on the spring bank holiday weekend. Q❀⇌◐◑♿⛺●P🚌(3,3A)ᯤ

Longton

Dolphin 🄻

Marsh Lane, PR4 5JY

⌚12-11 ☎(01772) 612032

Beer range varies 🄷

Isolated country pub at end of a lane on Longton Marsh. The handpumps are in the wood-floored public bar, and there is a comfortable lounge and a restaurant in the rear conservatory. A large and varied menu covers everything from sandwiches to 'man versus food' challenges, all imaginatively presented. Up to five real ales and one cider are available. The selection changes, with an emphasis on local micros, and often includes a mild or dark beer. ⚇❀◐◑♿●P🐾

Lostock Hall

Anchor

Croston Road, PR5 5LA (300yds from B5254 alongside Preston-Blackburn railway line)

⌚4.30-11.30; 12-midnight Fri & Sat; 1-11.30 Sun

☎(01772) 335637 🌐 theanchorinnlostockhall.co.uk

Beer range varies 🄷

Just a short distance from the Tardy Gate shopping area and alongside the Preston to Blackburn railway line, this friendly community pub offers five changing cask ales from the Heineken Cellarman's Reserve list, with LocAle beers often available. In May and September a beer festival is held in marquees on a large grassy area adjacent to the pub. To the rear is a boules pitch used in summer. A traditional roast is available on Sundays only, 3-5pm. Q⚇❀♿⇌♣P🚌(111,113)🐾

Lytham

Railway Hotel 🄻

Station Road, FY8 5DH (next to fire station on B5259)

⌚8am-midnight ☎(01253) 797250

Fuller's London Pride; Ruddles Best Bitter; Moorhouse's C & S Ale; guest beers 🄷

A recent acquisition by Wetherspoon on the Fylde coast. A former pub, it has a new-look interior, a large beer garden at the front and a novel no-smoking beer garden at the side. Three distinct themed drinking areas feature golfing memorabilia, railway signage and old photographs from the '50s depicting Lytham's halcyon days. Five varying guest beers are available, plus the permanent Moorhouse's C & S Ale, brewed from a local defunct brewery recipe. The venue is Cask Marque accredited. Parking is limited. Q⚇❀◐◑♿⛺⇌●P🚌ᯤ

Taps 🏆 🄻

Henry Street, FY8 5LE

⌚11-11 (midnight Fri & Sat) ☎(01253) 736226

🌐 thetaps.net

Greene King IPA; guest beers 🄷

A former branch CAMRA Pub of the Year and once again winner in 2014, this small and cosy pub has also twice been a national finalist. Red-bricked and wood-floored, with a real fire in winter, it offers a good selection of beers from microbreweries, as well as a mild and two changing ciders, with warm and friendly service by a knowledgeable staff. Locally-sourced home-made dishes are served 12-3pm Monday-Saturday, with locally made pies always available. Monday is quiz night, and dominoes and darts can be played. Q❀◐♿⇌♣●🚌

Mawdesley

Red Lion

68 New Street, L40 2QP (on main road in centre of village)

⌚12 (3 Mon)-11; 12-midnight Fri & Sat ☎(01704) 822208

🌐 redlionmawdesley.com

Beer range varies 🄷

Small white-painted pub at the centre of the village and gaining a growing reputation for food, which is served in the attractive conservatory at the rear of the pub as well as in the lounge bar. There is a small public bar where sport can be watched on TV. Guest beers are from the Enterprise list and include ales from local breweries. Copper Dragon Golden Pippin alternates with Wye Valley HPA. ⚇❀◐◑♿♣P🚌(337,347)🐾ᯤ

Morecambe

Eric Bartholomew

10 Euston Road, LA4 5DD

⌚9-11 (midnight Fri & Sat) ☎(01524) 405860

Greene King Abbot; Ruddles Bitter; guest beers 🄷

Opened in 2004, this Wetherspoon pub is dedicated to Eric Morecambe (born Eric Bartholomew). The building, situated near the seafront, functions on two levels, with an upstairs lounge and dinner area. The long bar services an open-plan room decorated with pictures of 19th-century Morecambe and some artwork with a Morecambe and Wise theme. There is outside seating at the front for smokers but no drinking is allowed. Close to shops and a public car park. Q◐◑♿⇌●🚌ᯤ

Palatine

The Crescent, LA4 5BZ (overlooking prom opp clock tower)

⌚11.30-midnight (1am Fri & Sat); 11.30-11 Sun

☎(01524) 410503 🌐 thepalatine.co.uk

Lancaster Red, Blonde, Black, Amber; Thwaites Wainwright; guest beers 🄷

An Edwardian seafront mid-terrace pub. The ground floor was completely transformed in late 2008 with much bare stone and woodwork now on show. The bar room is quite small, with some intimate corners. An upstairs room is rather different. Cosy and carpeted, many of the fittings – leaded lights, shelving and fireplace – appear to be original. Enjoy the spectacular views across the bay, especially at sunset. There are seats on the pavement in front. ❀◐◑♿⇌🚌ᯤ

York

87 Lancaster Road, LA4 5QH (where B5321 crosses railway)

⌚11-midnight ☎(01524) 425353

🌐 yorkhotelmorecambe.co.uk

Everards Beacon; guest beers 🄷

Large Victorian community pub on the edge of the town centre, with several rooms and some original plasterwork ceilings. It is the headquarters of Morecambe Royal British Legion, and St George's Day and Remembrance Day are celebrated. On Morecambe FC match days away fans can relax with the locals in this football-friendly pub. A large function room (with catering if required) and a patio complete the picture. Quizzes take place on Thursdays, and all ales are £2 a pint on Tuesdays.

Nether Kellet

Limeburners Arms

32 Main Road, LA6 1EP

7.30 (2 Sun)-midnight (01524) 732916

Beer range varies H

The building here is early 19th century. Once – within living memory – most country pubs were like this: no food, no jukebox, plain and simply furnished. Minor improvements have not changed the character of the place. Unsurprisingly, most of the customers are locals; the landlord himself is a local farmer and his family have run the place for 80 years. The old photos in the bar make a rewarding study. **QP** (51)

Ormskirk

Farmers Club

65 Burscough Street, L39 2EL

12-11 (midnight Fri & Sat) (01695) 572172

Tetley Bitter; guest beer H

Housed in an impressive Georgian building, the grand portico entrance leads into an equally splendid interior. The club has active snooker and darts teams, and screens live football matches, often laying on free refreshments. The two Cask Marque-accredited ales have resulted in the club being voted local CAMRA Club of the Year for the past few years. Visitors are asked to show a current copy of the Guide or CAMRA membership card for entry. **Q**

Hop Inn Bier Shop

Burscough Street, L39 2EG

11-11 (01695) 575907

Burscough Priory Gold; guest beer H

A former shop recently converted into a plush Belgian-style single-room bar. It features an extensive range of foreign bottled beers (Lambic, Trappist, fruit beers) which can be perused in the beautiful menus or the tasteful wall-mounted cabinets. The bar serves authentic foreign lagers, a real cider, and at least three real ales including beers from nearby Burscough Brewery. A Bavarian night and quiz during the week and live music at weekends make this a popular venue. **Q**

Orrell

Delph Tavern

Tontine Road, WN5 8UJ

11.30-midnight; 12-12.30am Fri & Sat; 12-11.30 Sun
(01695) 622239

Thwaites Wainwright; guest beers H

A real community pub with a wide range of regular customers. Its evening activities cover a broad choice – pool, darts, TV sport on several large screens, quizzes and live music. It has a varied menu of traditional tasty pub grub and a nice refurbished dining area. A good selection of local ales is served – if you can elbow your way past the keen real ale drinkers to the pumps. Used by many Orrell families for special occasions. **P**

Parbold

Stocks Tavern

16 Alder Lane, WN8 7NN

12-11.30 (midnight Fri & Sat); 12-11 Sun
(01257) 462874 thestockstavern.co.uk

Beer range varies H

Refurbished in 2009 but retaining its original charm, with low-beamed ceilings, a wooden floor and wood panelling, this inn offers two real fires and a quirky public bar, with a small annexe containing leather sofas. The pub attracts canal enthusiasts, walkers and cyclists as well as locals. Good-value food is served lunchtimes Monday to Friday, all day Saturday and Sunday. Five handpumps dispense mainly local beers. There is a small car park and a disabled WC with baby-changing facilities. **QP**

Wayfarer Inn

1-3 Alder Lane, WN8 7NL

12-3, 5-11 (midnight Fri & Sat); 12-11 Sun
(01257) 464600 wayfarerparbold.co.uk

Beer range varies H

You will find at least one Problem Child beer on the six handpulls here, plus a range of locally brewed ales and a real cider. The Il Viandante Italian bistro was built onto the Wayfarer. There are now three menus to choose from: bar food, restaurant and Italian. It has low beamed ceilings with cosy little nooks and crannies, and is a popular stop in the summer being close to the Leeds-Liverpool Canal and Parbold Hill with its panoramic views. **QP**

Pendleton

Swan With Two Necks

Main Street, BB7 1PT

closed Mon; 12-2.30, 6-11; 12-11 Sun (01200) 423112
swanwithtwonecks.co.uk

Copper Dragon Golden Pippin; guest beers H

CAMRA National Pub of the Year in 2014, this amazing establishment is run by two CAMRA members who thoroughly deserve all the awards they have received. Four handpulls serve a varying selection of guest beers from breweries such as Phoenix, Old School, Hopback, Caledonian and Fyne. Mild and stronger beers can often be available, and a real cider is also on handpull. Food is good value and of excellent quality. Note the huge collection of teapots. **QP**

Penwortham

Black Bull Inn

83 Pope Lane, PR1 9BA

11-11 (midnight Fri & Sat); 12-11 Sun (01772) 752953
blackbull-penwortham.co.uk

Greene King IPA; Theakston Lightfoot; guest beers H

Attractive cottage-style inn dating back to the 1800s, which retains a village pub atmosphere. On entering, a narrow passageway leads through to a central bar serving a number of drinking areas including a separate public bar. A friendly community venue, the many social events include a popular Thursday quiz, while local charities are actively supported. Two guest beers are always available. A 20p discount is offered on production of a CAMRA membership card. TV sport is Sky and BT. **QP** (3,3A)

Poulton le Fylde

Grapevine

19-21 Market Place, FY6 7AS
closed Mon & Tue; 6-1am (2am Fri & Sat); 3-midnight Sun
☎ (01253) 896700
Thwaites Original, Wainwright; guest beers Ⓗ
Spread over three floors of a former ironmongers' shop, the Grapevine has something for everyone. Steep narrow stairs lead to the first floor, which has the main bar and seating area. The second floor has a small gallery area with ancient exposed roof beams and comfortable settees, plus a cocktail bar with more seating. With a late licence, live music features on Thursdays and a DJ on Fridays and Saturdays. ⇌🚌(2,42)

Old Town Hall Tavern

5 Church Street, FY6 7AP
11-11 (11.30 Thu; midnight Fri & Sat); 12-11 Sun
☎ (01253) 892257
Beer range varies Ⓗ
A range of five beers, mainly from brewers within a 50-mile radius, are served in this hostelry which, as the name suggests, served for many years as the town hall, although it was an inn before that. Many TVs show live sport, and the rear of the pub is decorated with football memorabilia. Live bands play most Saturdays. An upstairs function room/bar is available. ◐◑♿⇌🚌

Thatched House Ⓛ

30 Ball Street, FY6 7BG
11.30-11 (11.30 Thu; midnight Fri & Sat); 12-11 Sun
☎ (01253) 891063 🌐 thatchedhousepoulton.co.uk
Tetley Bitter; guest beers Ⓗ
Mock-Tudor style pub built in 1910 on the site of a predecessor pub, possibly medieval, in the corner of a Norman churchyard right in the centre of Poulton. Many pictures of sporting heroes decorate the wood-panelled walls, and there are three wood-burning fires. Regular beer festivals are held in every season, and a microbrewery is due to open in 2014 in the coach house. Regular guest beers include two from Saltaire, Rooster's, Belhaven and Lytham Stout.
Q♿⇌♣●🚌(2,2A)🐾📶

Preston

Anderton Arms

Longsands Lane, Fulwood, PR2 9PS
11.30-11 (11.30 Wed & Thu; midnight Fri & Sat); 12-11 Sun
☎ (01772) 700104
Moorhouse's Pendle Witches Brew; Thwaites Original, Wainwright; guest beers Ⓗ
Up to five real ales at this friendly local are sourced from over 90 breweries from a seasonal cask menu that changes every quarter. Meals are served all day, with children welcome with parents if dining up to 8pm. Discounts on drinks include Sunday evening wines, and cask ales on Monday. Quiz night is Wednesday. The pub is home of the local Sunday Bake Off competition. ❀◐◑♿P🚌📶

Black Horse ★

166 Friargate, PR1 2EJ
10.30-11 (midnight Fri & Sat); 12-10.30 Sun
☎ (01772) 204855 🌐 blackhorse-preston.co.uk
Robinsons Dizzy Blonde, Hartleys XB, Cumbria Way, Unicorn, Double Hop; guest beers Ⓗ
Classic Grade II-listed pub in the main shopping area close to the historic open market. With its tiled bar and walls and mosaic floor, it has a nationally important historic pub interior. The two front rooms, with real log fires, bear historic photos of old Preston; the famous hall of mirrors seating area is to the rear, and memorabilia of a previous landlord is displayed. Up to eight Robinson's beers are regularly on offer. The covered smoking area is upstairs. ❀◐⇌●🐾

Continental

South Meadow Lane, PR1 8JP
12-11.15 (12.30 am Fri & Sat) ☎ (01772) 499425
🌐 newcontinental.net
Beer range varies Ⓗ
Beside the River Ribble, the main railway line and Miller Park, the pub has a main bar area plus a lounge with a real fire in winter and a conservatory overlooking the garden. Live music and theatre regularly feature in a separate arts/events space that is also used for beer festivals. Seven microbrewery beers are on offer, including the house ale from Marble and a dark beer. Freshly cooked meals are served daily (no food Mon). A two-times winner of local CAMRA Pub of the Year.
Q❀◐◑♿●P🚌(3A)🐾

Grey Friar

144 Friargate, PR1 2EJ
8am-midnight (1am Fri & Sat) ☎ (01772) 558542
Beer range varies Ⓗ
Modern open-plan Wetherspoon with raised areas to the side and rear. Preston's students and citizens, both young and old, appreciate the range of ales and food at good prices, with up to eight guests beers on sale. The social mix creates a bustling atmosphere and the bar can get extremely busy at weekends. The pub plays an active role in local CAMRA recruiting. There are two beer festivals a year, when casks are set up on extra stillages alongside the bar. ❀◐◑♿⇌🚌📶

Market Tavern

33-35 Market Street, PR1 2ES
10.30-9 (midnight Fri & Sat); 12-10.30 Sun
☎ (01772) 822455 🌐 themarkettavernpreston.co.uk
Beer range varies Ⓗ
Three handpumps serve guest beers from all over the country, usually from micros but with no particular emphasis. A small, popular, city-centre local with two intimate seating booths, it is in a pedestrianised area overlooking the historic Victorian outdoor market and is a former local CAMRA Pub of the Year. A selection of imported bottled beers is also on offer, plus German Weisse [wheat] beers on draught. Outside seating is available in summer. No food is served but you are welcome to bring your own. ❀⇌🚌

Old Black Bull

35 Friargate, PR1 2AT
10.30-11 (midnight Fri & Sat); 12-10.30 Sun
☎ (01772) 823397
Beer range varies Ⓗ
Mock-Tudor city-centre pub with a tiled exterior. A small front vault, main bar with distinctive black and white floor tiles, and two comfortable lounge areas combine to make this a popular venue. There is also a patio to the rear. Live music plays on Saturday evenings and all televised sport is shown. It is now completely free of tie for cask beers. Nine guests ales from micros or small independents are sourced from all over Britain. ❀♿⇌♣🚌

Old Vic 🄻

78 Fishergate, PR1 2NJ
✪ 11.30-11 (midnight Fri; 1am Sat); 12-midnight Sun
☎ (01772) 254690
Courage Directors; guest beers 🄷
Opposite the railway station and on bus routes into the city, this is a popular pub that can get busy at weekends. Seven handpumps offer the widest range of LocAle beers in the area, with several microbreweries usually represented. A number of TVs show sporting events while the pub hosts thriving pool and darts teams. To the rear is an outdoor decked smoking area and a car park that is only available on Sunday and in the evenings. ❀◐⇌♣P🚌📶

Olde Dog & Partridge

44 Friargate, PR1 2AT
✪ 11-11.30; 11-2, 4-11.30 Tue; 11-1am Sat; 12-midnight Sun
☎ (01772) 252217
Holt Bitter; Tetley Mild; Timothy Taylor Landlord; guest beers 🄷
Down-to-earth city-centre pub that specialises in rock music. Five real ales include two guest beers from the SIBA direct delivery scheme. There is also a real cider. The landlord has been at the pub for more than 30 years. There is a monthly live music night, a weekly quiz on Thursday and a rock DJ on Sunday evening. Excellent-value pub lunches are served (no food Sun) and a covered smoking area is provided at the rear. ❀◐⇌♣🍎🚌

Wheatsheaf 🄻

50 Water Lane, Ashton-on-Ribble, PR2 2NL (on way to Preston marina, 1 mile from city centre)
✪ 11-11 (11.30 Fri & Sat); 12-10.30 Sun ☎ (01772) 725917
Beer range varies 🄷
Guest beers include at least one from Moorhouse's and often Courage Directors, otherwise they come from anywhere in the country. Third-of-a-pint tasting racks are available. At least two beer festivals are held a year in a marquee at the rear. This Victorian local's beer prices are among the lowest in the area. It is big on TV sport, and live music plays Friday and Saturday nights. There is disabled access through the courtyard.
❀♿♣🍎🚌(68,35)

Rawtenstall

Buffer Stops 🄻

Bury Road, BB4 6DD
✪ closed Mon & Tue; 12-8 (10 Fri); 10-10 Sat; 12-8 Sun
☎ (0161) 764 7790 🌐 eastlancsrailway.org.uk/food-drink/buffer-stops
Outstanding Piston Broke; guest beers 🄷
As its name suggests, the Buffer Stops is on the platform at Rawtenstall station, part of the East Lancs steam railway. This unique one-roomed bar has five handpulls, with a variety of guest beers, usually including a stout or a porter. It also sells a real draught cider and continental bottled beers. It is handy for Rossendale ski slope, the Weavers Cottage and the museum, which are all a short distance away. Q🝊♿⇌🍎P🚌🐾

Craven Heifer

264 Burnley Road, BB4 8LA
✪ 4-midnight; 1-11 Sat & Sun ☎ (01706) 214757
Moorhouse's Premier, Pride of Pendle, Blond Witch 🄷
Originally two cottages, this is a stone-built two-roomed pub, part of which is over the Limy Water. There are six handpulls in this Moorhouse's tied house, with the full range of its beers and an occasional guest ale. In winter a log-burning fire greets you in the main bar. The Pendle Witches vintage velo cycle race is hosted every Easter. There is live entertainment on Friday nights. Rossendale ski slope and the East Lancs steam railway are not far away. 🝊❀🚌(X43)

White Lion 🄻

72 Burnley Road, BB4 8EW
✪ 4.30 (2 Fri; 12 Sat)-11; 1-11 Sun ☎ (01706) 213117
Copper Dragon Golden Pippin; Moorhouse's Pride of Pendle; guest beers 🄷
There has been a public house on this site since 1816, when it was formed from a row of four cottages, and it has been substantially enlarged since then. There is a fourth handpull that regularly has beers from micros such as Prospect, Hopstar, Reedley Hallows, Salamander and Acorn. There is a quiz night weekly on Tuesday, and live entertainment on Friday and Saturday. Handy for the ski slope and preservation railway.
❀♣P🚌(X43)

St Annes

15s of St Annes 🄻

42 St Annes Road West, FY8 1RF
✪ 11-11 (11.30 Fri; midnight Sat); 12-11 Sun
☎ (01253) 725852 🌐 fifteensstannes.com
Beer range varies 🄷
Situated in the heart of St Annes Square, this gem of a pub has lit up and added to the real ale scene. A former Lloyds Bank, it is a watering hole that has its own style; its vault is a must-see. Recently CAMRA branch Pub of the Year, it continues to provide a delightful selection of wonderfully kept beers, including two house ales. Live sport and occasional live music/DJs enhance this pub's appeal. Two real ciders are available and a CAMRA discount applies. ♿⇌🍎🚌🐾📶

Trawl Boat 🄻

36-38 Wood Street, FY8 1QR (in side street off St Annes Square)
✪ 8am-midnight (1am Fri & Sat) ☎ (01253) 783080
Greene King Abbot; Ruddles Best Bitter; guest beers 🄷
A Wetherspoon pub that was originally a solicitors' office, situated 400 yards from the seafront. Its tasteful decor with a natural fire creates a good, warm atmosphere. It has eight guest beers on at any one time, and supports local breweries. Just off St Annes Square, the name comes from an old pub closed many years ago. It is handy for the shops and railway station and caters for young and old alike, with a designated area for families.
Q🝊❀◐◑♿⇌🚌📶

Samlesbury

Nabs Head 🄻

Nabs Head Lane, PR5 0UQ
✪ 12-3 (not Mon), 5-11; 12-3, 4.30-midnight Fri; 12-12.30am Sat; 12-11 Sun ☎ (01254) 851416 🌐 thenewnabshead.co.uk
Thwaites Original, Wainwright; guest beers 🄷
Isolated two-roomed country pub in a picturesque setting. A central bar serves two distinct drinking areas. There is an extensive food menu including lunchtime senior citizens' deals, with food from local suppliers wherever possible. Quiz night is on

Tuesday. Guest beers come from the Thwaites Cask Club selection. A 20p a pint discount for CAMRA members operates on production of a membership card. Open mic sessions take place once a month in winter, and there is TV sport from BT and ESPN. Q

New Hall Tavern

Cuerdale Lane, PR5 0XA (on B6230)
12-11 (midnight Thu-Sat) (01772) 877942
Copper Dragon Best Bitter; guest beers H
On a crossroads just off junction 31 of the M6, this pub has a large car park and a heated outdoor smoking area. Indoors it is divided up by wood and glass panels, providing separate areas for dining. Up to six real ales are served, often from local micros. Home-cooked food is sourced from local suppliers where possible. Old photos and prints give an insight into the history of the area, which includes nearby Samlesbury Hall.

Scarisbrick

Heatons Bridge Inn

2 Heatons Bridge Road, L40 8JG
12-midnight (01704) 840549
Black Cat Black Cat; guest beers H
A traditional country inn on the Leeds and Liverpool Canal, it was built in 1837 as offices for the canal freight business and retains many original features. Three handpulls dispensing a mixture of local and national beers, and traditional home-cooked food, make this an ideal place to stop after a canalside stroll. Military displays are held twice-yearly and the pub often serves a Pillbox Ale to commemorate the World War II lookout post in the grounds.
(375)

Scorton

Priory

The Square, PR3 1AU
12-9 (11 Thu-Sat); 9am-11.30 Sun (01524) 791255
theprioryscorton.co.uk
Bowland Nicky Nook; Thwaites Lancaster Bomber; guest beer H
Scorton has no recognised tourist attractions, yet trippers regularly converge on the place, many ending up in the Priory. This is first and foremost a restaurant, but the former blacksmith's shop at one end of the rambling range of buildings houses a fully licensed bar (signed Stout's Bar), where the furniture is mostly dining room-style. In the evenings a fair number of locals gather. There is generally no music or amusements, so nothing interrupts the flow of conversation.
Q

Silverdale

Woodlands

Woodlands Drive, LA5 0RU
5-11; 12-midnight Sat; 12-11.30 Sun (01524) 701655
Beer range varies H
Large country house from about 1878, converted to a pub with only minimal alterations. Most of the trade is provided by locals. The bar has a large fireplace as big as the counter, and great views across Morecambe Bay. Beer pumps are in another room with a list of the four available ales in the bar. Home-made sandwiches are served at weekends. There is a beer festival of 30 ales in October, and a quiz on the last Sunday of the month. Q (33,51)

Slaidburn

Hark To Bounty

Townend, BB7 3EP
12-11 (10.30 Sun) (01200) 446246
harktobounty.co.uk
Moorhouse's Pride of Pendle; Theakston Best Bitter; guest beers H
Dating in parts from the 13th century, this former coaching inn has four large adjoining rooms, real fires and four handpumps. Dark wood beams, polished copper kettles and taxidermied critters lend a convivial ambience. Guest beers might be from Moorhouse's, Tirril or Brains, and delicious local food is served. At the rear is a pleasant beer garden with picnic benches and views. The pub makes an ideal base for exploring the Forest of Bowland, fishing, walking and cycling. Eight guest rooms are available, with dogs permitted.
P

Thornton Cleveleys

Victoria Hotel

183 Victoria Road West, FY5 3PZ (approx ¼ mile from town centre on B5412)
11-11; 12-10.30 Sun (01253) 853306
Samuel Smith Old Brewery Bitter H
Large main road pub on a corner in a residential area, a short walk from shops, food and the Blackpool-Fleetwood tramway. Wood beams, leaded windows and open fires feature in the comfortable, spacious lounge. The popular, well-appointed vaults have their own entrance. This local is known for low-priced ale drawn from oak casks. There is no music, food or TV to distract from quiet conversation or reading. A separate meeting room is available. Q

Tockholes

Royal Arms

Tockholes Road, Rydal Fold, BB3 0PA
closed Mon; 12-11; 12-10.30 Sun (01254) 705373
Beer range varies H
An old, traditional free house formed from two cottages knocked together. It is small but has a great atmosphere within its four back-to-back rooms, where the original stone walls have been retained, with flagged and wooden floors and three real fires. Beers are usually from local microbreweries Three B's or Rossendale. On the edge of the West Pennine Moors, it is close to Darwen Tower and overlooks Roddlesworth Woods. The pub welcomes walkers with dogs and offers good meals Wednesday and Sunday.
P

Walmer Bridge

Walmer Bridge

Liverpool Old Road, PR4 5QE
4 (1 Sat & Sun)-midnight (01772) 612296
Beer range varies H
Village local comprising two rooms, from either of which you have to go through four doors to reach the bar. The comfortable lounge contains photographs of bygone Walmer Bridge and

Longton. The vault is popular with the sporting fraternity, while outside there is a large garden with a children's play area. Bingo takes place on Monday and quiz night on Thursday. Up to three changing beers are available from the Punch portfolio, with an emphasis on pale and golden beer. ♣P (2,2A)

Waterfoot

Jolly Sailor

Booth Place, BB4 9BD

12-midnight (11 Sun) (01706) 226340

jolly-sailor.co.uk

Copper Dragon Golden Pippin; Moorhouse's Pride of Pendle; guest beers

With five handpulls on the bar and a friendly atmosphere, this stone-built village local is deservedly popular both with locals and visitors. Guest beers can come from breweries such as St Austell or Scottish Borders, to name just a couple. Food is served 12-8pm weekdays, 12-6pm at weekends, and comes from an extensive menu. Live entertainment takes place every Friday night. The pub is Cask Marque accredited.

Q (464,483)

Roebuck

482 Burnley Road East, BB4 9JR

4.30 (2.30 Fri; 12 Sat)-midnight; 12-10.30 Sun

(01706) 223550

Bowland Gold; Thwaites Original; guest beer

Still retaining some of the original stone-flagged floor, this large stone-built pub is on the main road through Waterfoot to Burnley. It has been opened out inside over the years and a central bar serves three distinct areas. The Roebuck is a free house, and although beers from Bowland and Thwaites dominate, there are occasional guest beers on. It is a welcoming, friendly pub with a large beer garden at the rear. P (483)

Wennington

Bridge

Tatham, LA2 8NL (on B6480 S of Wennington)

12-11; 12-2.30, 5-11 Wed & Thu; 12-10.30 Sun

(015242) 21326

Black Sheep Best Bitter; Tetley Bitter; York Guzzler; guest beer

Two linked buildings, one dating from 1642, the other from 1744, make up a small bar, cosy and low beamed, and two dining rooms. Set in an isolated spot south of Wennington, it attracts a surprisingly large number of local customers, as well as walkers in the summer months. Quiz night is Friday. The pub features in a Turner painting. There is an associated caravan park and helipad. Note that the pub closes in the afternoon on Wednesday and Thursday.

Q ♣P (80,81b)

Whalley

De Lacy Arms

61 King Street, BB7 9SP

2-midnight; 1-1am Fri; 12-1am Sat & Sun

(01254) 823197

Theakston Best Bitter; guest beers

Named after a 13th-century nobleman, this comfortable locals' pub is in the centre of the village. It has a large-screen TV for football and rugby, and it can get busy on a local match day. A yard at the rear caters for smokers and summertime drinkers. Up to three ales are served, usually including a LocAle from brewers such as Bowland, Thwaites or Bank Top. Excellent locally made hot pies are often available.

Dog Inn

55 King Street, BB7 9SB

11-11 (midnight Fri & Sat); 12-11 Sun (01254) 823009

Beer range varies

One of four pubs serving real ale in the centre of the village. The curved central bar provides a convivial drinking area, while cosy seating spaces are partly screened off and give the pub a homely feel. The back yard has been converted for outdoor drinking. Bar meals are served at lunchtime. The varied range of up to six real ales often includes a beer from Moorhouse's, but you could find brews from Mordue, Cottage, Dunscar Bridge or Prospect.

Whitworth

Sportsman

464 Market Street, OL12 8QN

12-midnight (01706) 854402

Tetley Bitter; guest beers

A friendly, family-run pub with a good selection of real ales, which reopened after refurbishment by the current landlord in 2010. A welcoming open fire greets you in winter. It has ties with Whitworth Spartans Rugby League team, and has pool and boules teams. An AA 3-star award was given in 2012 for the quality of its accommodation. The location is very handy for Healey Dell nature reserve. ♣ (464)

Wilpshire

Rising Sun

797 Whalley New Road, BB1 9BE

2.30-11.30 (midnight Fri); 12-11.30 Sat & Sun

(01254) 247379

Theakston Best Bitter; guest beer

Two miles from Blackburn town centre, this pub is a former Matthew Brown house, with memorabilia and photos of old Blackburn and its pubs from the early 1900s. The guest beers are often from local breweries such as Thwaites, Moorhouse's and Three B's. In the lounge a real fire is great on cold winter nights. Cards and dominoes are played in the public bar; there is a piano in one room which is used for the Saturday night singalong session.

Q (25)

Winmarleigh

Patten Arms

Park Lane, PR3 0JU (on B5272 3 miles N of Garstang)

4-11; 12-midnight Sat; 12-10 Sun (01524) 791484

Jennings Cumberland Ale; Thwaites Wainwright; guest beers

Genuine, isolated free house situated away from villages on a B road, yet enjoying regular local custom. Dating from the 19th century, this Grade II-listed building has a single bar with a country-pub feel, high-backed bench seats, cream-painted walls and open fires. There is a separate restaurant, and terraced seating overlooking a bowling green.

♣P

Worsthorne

Crooked Billet

1-3 Smith Street, BB10 3NQ

⏲ 7 (6 Thu)-midnight; 4.30-1am Fri; 12-1am Sat; 12-12.30 Sun ☎ (07766) 230175 🌐 crookedbilletworsthorne.co.uk

Tetley Bitter; Timothy Taylor Boltmaker, Landlord; guest beers Ⓗ

Rescued from the clutches of the pubcos, this superb free house is situated just off the village square and is handy for walking the nearby moors. The interior retains its wood panelling and has a fine bar with a snug to one side. This pub is the real hub of the community and holds various themed events such as acoustic or Thai nights plus a quiz night every Wednesday. Local CAMRA Pub of the Year 2013. **Q🐴❀◖♿♣P🐾📶**

Worston

Calf's Head 𝕃

West Lane, BB7 1QA

⏲ 10-11 ☎ (01200) 441218 🌐 calfshead.co.uk

Black Sheep Best Bitter; Moorhouse's Blond Witch; Thwaites Wainwright; guest beers Ⓗ

A country house hotel in a tranquil setting on the side of Pendle Hill. It boasts a scenic conservatory overlooking the brook at the bottom of the extensive garden, and 11 en-suite bedrooms. Good-value meals are available all day and there is a large dining room suitable for functions. The popular Sunday carvery is served 12-3pm. It is child friendly, and cosy open fires in the bar provide a warm welcome. There is a regular quiz night on alternate Tuesdays. **Q🐴❀🛏◖◗P📶**

Wray

George & Dragon

Main Street, LA2 8QG (off B6480)

⏲ 6-11 Mon; 12-2.30, 5-midnight; 12-midnight Sat; 12-11 Sun ☎ (015242) 21403

Everards Beacon; guest beers Ⓗ

A genuine village local with an excellent reputation for its food. Inside, there are two bar rooms of quite different sizes and a restaurant. Unusual pub games are available and there is a Wednesday night quiz. The extensive beer garden has an aviary, as well as a covered but unheated smoking area. Wray hosts a popular scarecrow festival in May. **Q❀◖◗♣🚌**(80,81B)📶

Wrightington

White Lion

117 Mossy Lea Road, WN6 9RE

⏲ 11.30-11 (midnight Fri); 10-midnight Sat; 10-10.30 Sun ☎ (01257) 425977 🌐 thewhitelionlancs.co.uk

Banks's Bitter; Jennings Cumberland Ale; guest beers Ⓗ

This extremely popular country pub attracts many locals, with a good range of food and beers for diners and drinkers. Eight handpumps are in constant use, serving six guest ales and two from Marston's. There is a weekly quiz on Tuesday, a poker league on Thursday, and themed evenings in the restaurant. The pub is family friendly, with a large garden area, and community oriented, running the village scarecrow festival, snail racing and more on St Patrick's Day, plus brewery trips. ❀◖◗♿P🚌(113)

Swan With Two Necks, Pendleton

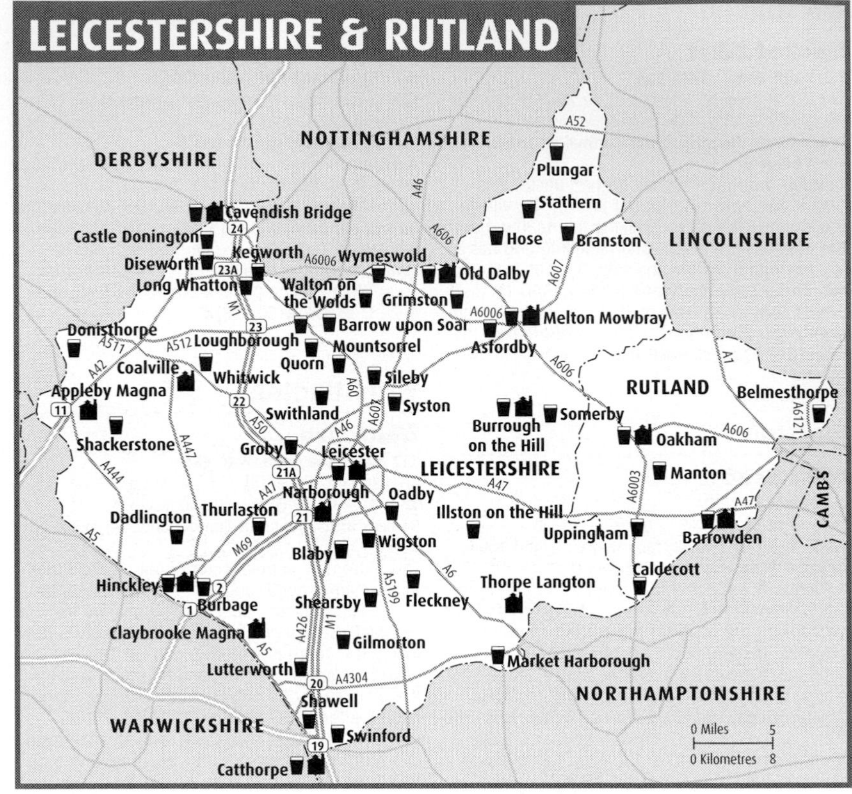

Asfordby

Horse Shoes

128 Main Street, LE14 3SA

12-11 (midnight Fri & Sat) ☎ (01664) 813392

Batemans Black & White, XB; guest beer H

A single-roomed pub at the heart of the village, the Horse Shoes compensates for its plain and simple decor with a warm welcome for all. This community inn is home to darts teams and has a skittle alley. This is the only local Bateman's house with at least two of the brewery's real ales available, as well as a seasonal beer. ♣🚌(5)

Barrow upon Soar

Soar Bridge

29 Bridge Street, LE12 8PN

12 (4 Mon)-11; 12-10.30 Sun ☎ (01509) 412686

Castle Rock Elsie Mo; Everards Beacon Bitter, Tiger, Original; guest beers H

Situated next to the bridge that gave it its name, this pub is popular with walkers, boaters and drinkers. The large single-room interior divides into distinct areas, with a separate restaurant, function room and skittle alley. Outside there is a floodlit pétanque court, beer terrace and garden. Well-behaved dogs and children are welcome. Home-made food is served Tuesday to Sunday, with a different theme each evening.

Q❀◑♿⛺≠♣●P🚌(2,27)🐾

Barrowden

Exeter Arms L

28 Main Street, LE15 8EQ

12-2.30 (not Mon), 6-11; 12-3.30, 6-11 Sat; 12-5 Sun ☎ (01572) 747247 🌐 exeterarmsrutland.co.uk

Barrowden Pilot, Beech, Own Gear, Hop Gear H

Collyweston slate-roofed pub with a fine view over the valley and village duck pond. It offers a warm welcome and serves highly regarded food. Pétanque is played here in the summer and dominoes in the winter. Barrowden Brewery is situated in a barn to the rear.

Q❀🛏◑♿⛺♣●P🚌🐾

Belmesthorpe

Blue Bell L

Shepherds Walk, PE9 4LG

12-2.30 (not Mon), 6-11; 12-2, 5-11 Fri; 12-11.30 Sat; 12-11 Sun ☎ (01780) 753081

Abbeydale Absolution; Hop Back Summer Lightning; Oakham Bishops Farewell; guest beers H

The Blue Bell is a historic village pub. Low ceilings, a roaring fire and stone walls are part of its charm. Six handpulls offer a wide range of guest beers, including at least one LocAle and real cider. Dogs on leads are welcome in the bar area. Good honest home-made pub food is available Tuesday to Sunday lunchtimes (booking advisable). Local CAMRA Pub of the Year 2013.

Q❀◑♿⛺♣●P🐾

Blaby

Bull's Head

22 Lutterworth Road, LE8 4DN
⏲ 12-11 (10 Mon); 12-midnight Fri & Sat; 12-10 Sun
☎ (0116) 278 9799
Adnams Southwold Bitter; Grainstore Rutland Panther; guest beers Ⓗ
As well as the traditional Bull's Head pub sign, an impressive bull's head adorns the pub's frontage, situated immediately above the front door. Two or three guest beers are always available, sourced through the Punch list and SIBA Direct. A former long alley room is now a function room which is also used for table skittles and darts matches. This is mainly a drinkers' pub, although reasonably priced cobs are always available. ❀♣●P🚌📶

Branston

Wheel 𝕃

Main Street, NG32 1RU
⏲ closed Mon; 11-11; 12-10.30 Sun ☎ (01476) 870376
🌐 thewheelinnbranston.co.uk
Batemans XB; guest beers Ⓗ
This attractive stone-built 18th-century pub houses a small bar with some seating and a larger restaurant area, sympathetically renovated. The deceptively large outdoor area is quiet and relaxing in the summer months, with traditional outbuildings used to host festivals and regular live music. The Wheel boasts an extensive lunch and evening food menu using locally-sourced ingredients where possible, including produce from the nearby Belvoir Estate. Cask cider is usually available on the bar. Q❀◐◑♿♣●P🐾📶

Burbage

Lime Kilns

Watling Street, LE10 3ED
⏲ 12-3, 5.30-11; 12-11 Sat; 12-10.30 Sun ☎ (01455) 631158
Jennings Cocker Hoop; Marston's Burton Bitter, Pedigree; guest beer Ⓗ
Situated alongside the Ashby Canal and the A5, the pub was originally an 18th-century coaching inn. It offers free moorings, a large canalside beer garden and a children's play area. The first floor lounge has canal views and an open fire in winter. Guest beers change regularly and real ciders include Thatchers Traditional, Cheddar Valley and Heritage. Traditional food is served, with special deals including Monday curry night and pie and a pint on Wednesday. Q🛏❀◐◑♿♣●P📶

Burrough on the Hill

Grant's Free House 𝕃

4 Main Street, LE14 2JQ
⏲ 12-2.30 (not Mon), 5-11; 12-midnight Sat; 12-11 Sun
☎ (01664) 452141
Oakham Citra; Parish PSB, Burrough Bitter Ⓗ
Formerly an inn known as the Stag & Hounds, dating from the 16th-century, Grant's Free House is now firmly established as the home of the Parish Brewery which is located in an adjacent out-building. New licensees redecorated and refurbished the pub in 2013 and reopened the restaurant to the rear of the building. The bar is on two levels surrounding a central servery on three sides and a games room on the fourth.
Q🛏❀◐◑♿♣P🚌(113)🐾📶

Caldecott

Plough Inn

16 Main Street, LE16 8RS
⏲ 11-3.30 (Sat & Sun only), 6-11 ☎ (01536) 770284
Grainstore Rutland Bitter; Langton Angler; guest beers Ⓗ
Attractive sandstone inn on the village green. A welcoming, traditional, open-plan pub, it has a bar area, restaurant and a relaxing snug area. To the rear is a large garden and there is a terrace to the front. Beers are often sourced from local breweries Grainstore and Langton. Q🛏❀◐◑♿⛺P🚌🐾

Castle Donington

Jolly Potters

36 Hillside, DE74 2NH
⏲ 12-11 (midnight Fri); 11-midnight Sat; 12-10.30 Sun
☎ (01332) 811912
Draught Bass; Fuller's London Pride; Marston's Pedigree; Sharp's Doom Bar Ⓗ
Traditional, friendly pub, built at the turn of the 20th century. The open-plan front room divides into bar and lounge areas – the basic stone-floored bar has traditional wooden pews and there is a back room with jukebox, TV and dartboard. A collection of framed beer mats and cards decorates the walls, and cups, jugs and tankards hang from the ceiling. ❀♿♣

Catthorpe

Cherry Tree 🏆

Main Street, LE17 6DD
⏲ 12-2.30 (not Tue-Thu), 5-11; 12-2.30, 5-12.30am Fri; 12-12.30am Sat; 12-11 Sun ☎ (01788) 860430
🌐 cherrytree-pub.co.uk
Jennings Bitter; guest beers Ⓗ
Welcoming two-roomed free house and hub of the community. Four beers are usually on offer including a mild and changing guests, often from Dow Bridge Brewery based in the village. The excellent bar menu features local produce, with Sunday roasts a highlight. Aviation and railway memorabilia cover the walls. Outside, the south-facing patio and garden are busy in summer and during the twice-yearly beer and music festivals. Camping is available with the landlord's permission. Q❀◐◑⛺♣●P🐾

Cavendish Bridge

Old Crown

DE72 2HL (off A6)

INDEPENDENT BREWERIES

Barrowden Barrowden
Belvoir Old Dalby
Dem Bones Leicester (NEW)
Dow Bridge Catthorpe
Elliswood Hinckley
Everards Narborough
Gas Dog Melton Mowbray
Golden Duck Appleby Magna
Grainstore Oakham
Langton Thorpe Langton
Long Lane Coalville
Parish Burrough on the Hill
Pig Pub Claybrooke Magna
Shardlow Cavendish Bridge

⏲ 11 (3 Mon)-11; 11-midnight Fri & Sat; 11-10.30 Sun
☎ (01332) 792392 🌐 oldcrownshardlow.co.uk
Banks's Sunbeam; Marston's EPA, Pedigree, Old Empire; guest beers Ⓗ
Coaching inn dating from the 17th century with the original oak-beamed ceiling displaying an extensive collection of old jugs. The cosy open-plan interior is divided into two areas, with a large inglenook on the right. The walls are covered with pub mirrors, brewery signs and railway memorabilia. Good-value food includes fish and chips on Friday evening. Quiz night is Monday and live music features on Tuesday. A former local CAMRA Pub of the Year. ❀◑♣●P🚌🐾ᯤ

Dadlington

Dog & Hedgehog 𝕃
2 The Green, CV13 6JB
⏲ 12-11 (5 Sun) ☎ (01455) 213151
Elliswood Just One More; Quartz Extra Blonde; Tunnel Nelson's Column Ⓗ
This friendly free house continues to build on its reputation for good ales, as well as serving the best in locally-produced food in its fine restaurant. In a picturesque location, the terrace and beer garden overlook the Ashby Canal and site of the famous Battle of Bosworth (1485). The bar boasts three LocAles, all rebadged for the pub – Henry Tudor is Tunnel Nelson's Column, Dadlington Hamlet is Quartz Crystal and Bridge 30 is Elliswood Just One More. Q🐎❀◑♿P🚌(86)🐾

Diseworth

Plough
33 Hall Gate, DE74 2QJ
⏲ 11.30-11 (midnight Fri & Sat); 12-10.30 Sun
☎ (01332) 810333 🌐 theploughdiseworth.com
Draught Bass; Greene King Abbot; Marston's Pedigree; Sharp's Doom Bar; guest beer Ⓗ
Situated in a village with many half-timbered buildings, this is a cosy, multi-roomed pub with parts dating back to the 13th century. Low-beamed ceilings and exposed brickwork are just some of the original features discovered during renovation work in the 1990s. There is an interesting display of old photographs of the area. Tasty home-made food is served. The spacious, well-presented beer garden is popular in summer. Joint local CAMRA Village Pub of the Year 2011. Q❀◑♿▲●P🚌ᯤ

Donisthorpe

Halfway House
65 Church Street, DE12 7PX
⏲ 12-11 (midnight Fri & Sat) ☎ (01530) 588783
🌐 halfwayhousedonisthorpe.com
Draught Bass; Marston's Pedigree; guest beers Ⓗ
Traditional village inn set in the heart of Donisthorpe. One of the three oldest buildings in the village, the pub dates back hundreds of years. Recently refurbished to a high standard, it now comprises a public bar, lounge bar and a separate dining room, with beamed ceilings and a wood-burning fire. Home-made food is served Tuesday to Saturday. Three guest beers are on offer, usually including one from Burton Bridge, and can be served in a taster selection of three third-of-a-pint measures. Q❀◑●P🚌🐾ᯤ

Fleckney

Golden Shield 𝕃
46 Main Street, LE8 8AN
⏲ 4 (12 Wed & Thu)-11; 12-midnight Fri & Sat; 11.30-11 Sun
☎ (0116) 240 2366
Banks's Bitter; Greene King IPA, Abbot; Timothy Taylor Landlord; guest beers Ⓗ
Village pub in the heart of Leicestershire serving six real ales, including ever-changing LocAles and microbrewery beers. Home-cooked and à la carte meals are available lunchtimes Wednesday to Sunday and evenings Tuesday to Saturday – Sunday lunches are always popular. A pétanque court is available. ❀◑♣P🚌(44,49B)

Gilmorton

Red Lion
Main Street, LE17 5LT
⏲ 12-2 (not Mon), 5-11; 12-9 Sun ☎ (01455) 203564
🌐 theredliongilmorton.co.uk
Banks's Mild; Marston's Pedigree; guest beers Ⓗ
Marston's National Cask Ale Pub of the Year 2012, this village bistro pub is popular with both locals and visiting diners. Open plan, bright and spacious, the interior has a welcoming and modern feel. The two regular beers are usually complemented by three guest ales from the Marston's list. Food is prepared and cooked on the premises and made from local produce where possible, including herbs from the garden, home-made bread and ice creams. ❀◑♿Pᯤ

Grimston

Black Horse
3 Main Street, LE14 3BZ
⏲ 12-3, 6-11; 12-6 Sun ☎ (01664) 812358
🌐 theblackhorsegrimston.com
Adnams Southwold Bitter; Marston's Pedigree; guest beers Ⓗ
The pub overlooks the village green and is busy both lunchtimes and evenings, with a reputation for good food and ale. The single-roomed interior is divided into three sections on two separate levels, warmed by a real fire. Outside, the garden has patio heaters and a pétanque court where local teams compete. Two regular and two guest real ales are usually available. ❀◑♣🚌(23)

Groby

Stamford Arms
2 Leicester Road, LE6 0DJ
⏲ 10-11 ☎ (0116) 287 5616 🌐 stamfordarms.co.uk
Everards Beacon Bitter, Tiger, Original; guest beers Ⓗ
At the heart of Groby and the home of the Everard family until 1921, the pub was extensively refurbished in 2013, enhancing all aspects of the main house while developing the annexe into a large restaurant. Freshly made local food is available all day. The house ale, Lady Jane, is a zesty pale ale with floral character, brewed by Everards, which complements the cask ales. 🐎❀◑♿♣●P🚌🐾ᯤ

Hinckley

Ashby Road Sports Club 𝕃
Hangmans Lane, LE10 3DA

5-11 (11.30 Fri); closed Tue; 12-11.30 Sat; 12-11 Sun
(01455) 615159
Sharp's Doom Bar; guest beers H
A regular in the Guide since 2008 and frequently CAMRA branch Club of the Year, this private members' club welcomes CAMRA members. Sharp's Doom Bar is always available plus two changing guest ales, local and national, from Wednesday to Sunday. Facilities include free Wi-Fi, satellite TV for sporting fixtures, traditional games, camping, caravanning and large function rooms for hire. Easily accessible, the club has a large car park and is on three bus routes.

New Plough Inn
Leicester Road, LE10 1LS
4.45-11; 12-midnight Fri-Sun (01455) 615037
thenewploughinn.co.uk
Marston's Burton Bitter, Pedigree; guest beers H
Victorian building boasting original wood settles, comfortable lounge areas and a traditional and cosy ambience with rugby-themed memorabilia. Darts, dominoes and skittles are played in the games room. Outside is a sheltered beer garden and heated, covered smokers' area. The landlady, a CAMRA member, runs a charity pub quiz on the last Thursday of the month, chairs the annual town carnival and sponsors the local rugby club. Local CAMRA Pub of the Year 2012. P (159)

Queens Head
Upper Bond Street, LE10 1RJ
5 (3 Fri)-11; 12-11 Sat; 12-7 Sun 07887 770038
thequeensheadinn.co.uk
Beer range varies H
A comfortable, family-run free house near the town centre, on bus routes and 15 minutes from the railway station. This modernised pub retains many Victorian features in its four rooms and bar, with open fires and a working Victorian range in the newly restored snug. Four ever-changing real ales are available from national award-winning brewers. Local CAMRA Pub of the Year 2013, it always offers a warm welcome. (48,158)

Hose

Rose & Crown
Bolton Lane, LE14 4JE
6-10 Mon & Tue; 12-3, 6-11 (midnight Fri); 12-midnight Sat; 12-10 Sun (01949) 869458
theroseandcrownhose.co.uk
Tetley Bitter; guest beers H
Set in the heart of the Vale of Belvoir, this renowned 200-year-old country pub has undergone a new lease of life over the past few years. Six cask ales are offered, with no smooth beer, and a wide-ranging food menu featuring local produce. The pub has a large, comfortable bar and seating area, and a separate restaurant. Outside is an attractive and spacious deck plus a paddock. Regular live music events are held throughout the year. Local CAMRA Pub of the Year 2013 and 2014. QP

Illston on the Hill

Fox & Goose
Main Street, LE7 9EG
6 (11 Sat & Sun)-midnight (9 Sun winter)
(0116) 259 6340
Everards Beacon Bitter, Tiger; guest beers H
Unique gem of a pub unscathed by the passing of time, with many artefacts including hunting scenes, McLachlan cartoons, farming implements and taxidermy exhibits. In 1997, when major structural work was undertaken, photographs were taken so that each item could be put back in its original place. A conkers contest and an onion competition are held annually to raise funds for charities. Evening meals are served Thursday to Saturday. Cider is available in summer.
Q

Kegworth

Red Lion
24 High Street, DE74 2DA
11.30-11; 12-10.30 Sun (01509) 672466
redlionkegworth.com
Adnams Southwold Bitter; Castle Rock Harvest Pale; Draught Bass; Gales HSB; guest beers H
Georgian building standing on the 19th-century route of the A6, with four rooms served from one bar. There are bench seats and original features including coal fires. Eight cask ales and real cider are available plus a good selection of malt whiskies. Food is served every lunchtime and weekday evenings. Outside is a large car park and garden plus a pétanque court and children's play area. En-suite accommodation is available. A former local CAMRA Pub of the Year.
QP

Leicester

Ale Wagon
27 Rutland Street, LE1 1RE
11-11; 7-10.30 Sun (0116) 262 3330 alewagon.co.uk
Hoskins HOB Bitter, IPA; guest beers H
Run by the Hoskins family, this city-centre pub with a 1930s interior, including an original oak staircase, has two rooms with tiled and parquet floors and a central bar. There is always a selection of Hoskins Brothers ales and guests available. The pub is popular with visiting rugby fans and real ale drinkers. A function room is available to hire. Handy for the nearby Curve Theatre.

Black Horse
65 Narrow Lane, Aylestone, LE2 8NA
12-11 (midnight Fri & Sat) (0116) 283 7225
blackhorse-aylestone.co.uk
Everards Beacon Bitter, Tiger, Original; guest beers H
Welcoming, traditional, three-roomed Victorian pub in a village conservation area with a distinctive bar servery. Eight real ales are always available and home-cooked food is served lunchtimes and evenings Monday to Friday, all day at weekends. Coaches are welcome by prior arrangement. The skittle alley and function room can be hired and live music and comedy feature regularly. Beer festivals and community events are hosted. Quiz night is Sunday. There is a large beer garden and children's play area. Q

Black Horse
1 Foxon Street, Braunstone Gate, LE3 5LT
12-midnight (11 Sun) (0116) 254 0446
Everards Beacon Bitter, Sunchaser Blonde, Tiger, Original; guest beers H
The only remaining traditional pub in a street of youth-oriented bars, with two rooms separated by a central bar, wood-panelled walls and practical

furniture. A genuine community pub with a comfortable ambience, it hosts live music four nights a week and a quiz night on Wednesday. The guest beers are sourced through Everards and the cider is Westons Old Rosie. A large selection of whiskies and rare spirits is also available.

Criterion

44 Millstone Lane, LE1 5JN

12-11 (10.30 Sun) (0116) 262 5418

Beer range varies H

Two-roomed 1960s city-centre pub offering up to 12 guest ales from micros and regionals. Beer festivals are held regularly, with many beers on gravity from the cellar. More than 100 international bottled beers are stocked. Darts and dominoes are played in the bar. A general knowledge quiz is hosted on Wednesdays, live music on some Fridays, and it is a venue for Leicester Comedy Festival. Pub food is available on Sunday, with Italian-style pizzas Monday to Saturday. It closes on some Sundays in summer.

High Cross

103-105 High Street, LE1 4JB (400yds from Clock Tower on corner of High Street)

8am-midnight; 9am-11 Sun (0116) 251 9218

Grainstore Ten Fifty; Greene King Abbot; Marston's Pedigree; Purity Pure Ubu; Ruddles Best Bitter; guest beers H

Named after the nearby cross marking the centre of medieval Leicester, this is a Wetherspoon conversion of a former shop. The large L-shaped open-plan room divides into different areas on several levels. Guest ales include a mild and beers from local breweries.

King's Head

King Street, LE1 6RL

12-midnight (0116) 254 8240

thekingsleicester.co.uk

Black Country Bradley's Finest Golden, Pig on the Wall, Fireside; guest beers H

A traditional one-room city centre local owned by Black Country Ales. Ten handpulls serve five regularly changing guest ales and at least two varying ciders. With an open fire and roof terrace it is popular throughout the year, attracting real ale enthusiasts and visitors to the local football and rugby grounds. Two changing craft beers are complemented by a range of bottled beers, and seasonal beer festivals are held. Screens show Sky and BT sport. Access can also be gained from New Walk.

Marquis Wellington

139 London Road, LE2 1EF

12-midnight (1am Fri & Sat); 12-11 Sun

(0116) 254 0542 themarquiswellington.com

Everards Beacon Bitter, Tiger, Original; guest beers H

The historic pub with a richly decorated façade stands out on the London Road thoroughfare. The pub is popular with local workers, shoppers and students. Monday is quiz night in term time and acoustic music is played on Tuesday. A good range of real ales and hearty food is available. The large attractive garden features beach huts, heated on cooler nights.

Old Horse

198 London Road, LE2 1NE

11-11.30 (midnight Fri & Sat); 11-11 Sun

(0116) 254 8384 oldhorseleicester.co.uk

Everards Beacon Bitter, Sunchaser Blonde, Tiger, Original; guest beers H

Nineteenth-century coaching inn, handy for dog walkers, students and sports supporters. There are four monthly changing guest beers. Tasty and good-value food is served. Behind the pub is the largest pub garden in Leicester, complete with children's play equipment and pétanque court. Regular quiz nights, karaoke and other special events take place. Note the unique coffee table and butler.

Pub L

12 New Walk, LE1 6TF

12-11 (midnight Fri & Sat); 11-8 Sun

Blue Bee Nectar Pale; guest beers H

Showcasing the widest range of real ales in Leicester, 14 ever-changing microbrewery guest beers are on handpump. A wide range of continental draught and bottled beers is also kept. The home-cooked food menu is available every day, ever-popular with local diners. Regular beer festivals are hosted and a pub quiz is held every Wednesday. Live sport is shown on multiple TV screens. The pub is home to rugby and football fans and also the Leicester Morris Men.

Salmon

19 Butt Close Lane, LE1 4QA

12-11 (10.30 Mon); 12-11.30 Fri & Sat; 12-6 Sun

(0116) 253 2301 thesalmon.org.uk

Beer range varies H

Victorian back-street free house with a friendly welcome. It has a strong sports following, especially for rugby. The large, open, U-shaped bar offers a selection of beers from six handpumps, mainly from microbreweries. It is the brewery tap for the new Dem Bones Brewery and regularly sells Raw Brewery beers. Cellar runs are offered. Two real ciders are always available. The Salmon has been a regular local CAMRA Pub of the Year winner in recent years. Close to St Margaret's bus station.

Sir Robert Peel

50 Jarrom Street, LE2 7DD

12-11 (midnight Fri & Sat); 12-7 Sun (0116) 254 0715

sirrobertpeelleicester.co.uk

Everards Tiger; guest beers H

Named after the 19th-century prime minister, this has been an Everard's house since 1901 and was refurbished by the brewery in traditional style in 2013. Up to five guest ales are on sale, frequently including a dark beer. Good lunchtime food includes tasty pub favourites such as pork pies, sausage rolls and freshly filled cobs. A short walk from Leicester's rugby and football stadiums.

Slug & Lettuce L

27 Market Street, LE1 6DP

10-11 (1am Fri & Sat) (0116) 255 5370

slugandlettuce.co.uk/leicester

Wells Bombardier; guest beers H

A welcoming family-friendly city centre establishment, the Slug appeals to a mixed clientele of all ages. It is a passionate supporter of LocAle, with four guest ales usually available, often from microbreweries. Regular beer festivals have established it as a firm favourite for real ale drinkers in Leicester and beyond. An extensive food menu is available all day and includes many special offers. Within easy walking distance of the city's sporting venues, sporting fixtures are shown on TV screens.

Swan & Rushes

19 Infirmary Square, LE1 5WR
12-11 (midnight Thu-Sat); 12-11.30 Sun
(0116) 233 9167 swanandrushes.co.uk
Batemans XB; Oakham JHB, Bishops Farewell; guest beers H
Comfortable, triangular, two-roomed pub in the city centre with a relaxed atmosphere, with some breweriana and framed photographs on the walls. Up to nine real ales are available plus a changing real cider and a range of bottled beers including international classics. Several food-linked beer festivals are held each year plus cider and cheese events. Thursday is quiz night, open mic is the second Wednesday of the month, and live gigs feature on some Saturdays. Home-made pizzas are served.

Tom Hoskins

131 Beaumanor Road, LE4 5QE
12-11.30 (midnight Fri); 10.30-midnight Sat; 10.30-11.30 Sun (0116) 266 9659
Greene King IPA; John Smith's Bitter; M&B Brew XI; Tetley Mild; guest beers H
Hospitable two-room city-suburbs pub catering for the mature drinker. Between four and six ales are always available including a mild and changing guest beers. If you are hungry there are freshly made cobs. Darts is played in the bar and the pub is popular with local football and rugby teams. Regular Sunday evening quiz nights are held. A barber is available Thursday and Friday afternoons and Saturday and Sunday mornings. P

Western

70 Western Road, LE3 0GA
12-midnight (1am Fri & Sat) (0116) 254 5287
steamin-billy.co.uk/western
Steamin' Billy Tipsy Fisherman, Bitter, Skydiver; guest beers H
Traditional local in a residential location close to football and rugby grounds on the edge of the city centre. The bar and lounge are popular with a mixed clientele of all ages. Up to four guest beers are available, mainly from microbreweries. Old pub signs decorate the pub and beer garden. There are regular music and beer festivals and the pub is home to a theatre and theatre groups.

Long Whatton

Royal Oak

26 The Green, LE12 5DB
12-11 (midnight Fri & Sat) (01509) 843694
theroyaloaklongwhatton.co.uk
Draught Bass; St Austell Tribute; Sharp's Doom Bar; guest beer H
Tastefully modernised, award-winning gastro-pub welcoming real ale drinkers and diners alike. Regularly changing guest beers usually include one from Blue Monkey. The owners are passionate about their ale and hold two beer festivals a year. Local produce features in an interesting food menu including 'nip & tuck' – four nips of beer and locally-produced nibbles on a platter. Convenient for East Midlands airport and Donington race circuit, accommodation is available in a separate building. Local CAMRA Village Pub 2011. Q P

Loughborough

Generous Briton

85 Ashby Road, LE11 3AB
12-11 (midnight Fri & Sat) (01509) 263565
thegbpub.com
Draught Bass; Nottingham Legend; Oakham JHB; guest beers H
Reopened in 2011 as a genuine free house, the GB is ideally situated between the town centre and university. The traditional bar has a dartboard and features old local photographs; the lounge has a pool table and jukebox. Satellite sport is shown throughout. A limited food menu is available but customers are welcome to bring their own. Families are welcome until 7.45pm and there is an enclosed beer garden to the rear. Local CAMRA Town Pub 2013 and Pub of the Year 2012. (126)

Organ Grinder

4 Woodgate, LE11 2TY
12-11 (midnight Fri & Sat); 12-10.30 Sun
(01509) 264008
Blue Monkey 99 Red Baboons, Infinity; guest beers H
Previously known as the Pack Horse, bought by Blue Monkey in 2012, the building has received a top-to-bottom renovation, uncovering lots of interesting original features. The new stable bar at the back reflects the pub's past life as a coaching inn. Eight cask ales are always available alongside a choice of two real ciders and a perry, and a range of Belgian bottled beers. Bar snacks include interesting pork pies. CAMRA branch Most Improved Pub 2012 and Pub of the Year 2013.

Tap & Mallet

36 Nottingham Road, LE11 1EU
7 (5 Tue & Thu; 12 Sat; 3.30 Sun)-2am
Batemans XB; guest beers H
Genuine free house specialising in beers from microbreweries not commonly found in the Loughborough area, plus seasonal brews from Abbeydale and Salopian. The large single-room interior is divided into two distinct drinking areas – a public bar with pool table, darts and boxed games, and a quieter lounge area which can be partitioned off for functions. Outside there is a large, secluded, lawned garden, patio area and pets' corner.

White Hart

27 Churchgate, LE11 1UD
11-midnight; 12-11 Sun (01509) 236976
Draught Bass; Shipstones Bitter; Timothy Taylor Landlord; guest beers H
Reopened in 2013 as a free house after extensive refurbishment, the pub has a secluded patio and beer garden to the rear. Regularly changing guest beers often come from local breweries such as Alchemist and Belvoir, with one dark and one light beer always available. Bar snacks and cobs are available, and there are plans for a more substantial food menu. Live music plays on Friday evenings and Sunday afternoons. Local CAMRA branch Most Improved Pub in 2013.

Lutterworth

Fox

34 Rugby Road, LE17 4BN
12 (5 Mon)-midnight; 12-1am Fri & Sat (01455) 550935

Draught Bass; Salopian Shropshire Gold; Sharp's Doom Bar; guest beer H
Situated half a mile from junction 20 of the M1 and close to the Sir Frank Whittle jet monument, the Fox has an L-shaped open-plan interior warmed by a real fire. Four real ales are available including one regularly changing guest. Food is served lunchtimes, with Thai meals in the evening in a separate function room. Outside is an attractive drinking area and landscaped garden.
P

Unicorn
29 Church Street, LE17 4AE
10.30-11 (midnight Thu-Sat); 12-11 Sun
(01455) 552486
Adnams Broadside; Draught Bass; Greene King IPA; guest beer H
Town-centre street-corner local built in 1919 on the site of an 18th-century coach house. A busy and friendly two-room community pub, it has an open fire in the public bar area and traditional games are played. The comfortable lounge features many photographs of old Lutterworth and doubles as a family-friendly dining area for lunchtime meals. The menu includes vegetarian options. P

Manton

Horse & Jockey L
2 St Marys Road, LE15 8SU
11 (10 Sat)-11; 10-10 Sun (01572) 737335
horseandjockeyrutland.co.uk
Grainstore Cooking; Morland Old Golden Hen; guest beer H
Situated in a wonderful location near Rutland Water, the pub gets busy in the summer. Good-quality home-cooked food is available every day. Ales include Fall at the First, brewed for the pub by Grainstore. Dominoes and quiz nights feature regularly. The pub is home to Rutland Morris and Jason, the landlord, is a tourism representative for the county. A popular stop-off for cyclists, it is on the Rutland Water Cycle Route. Q P

Market Harborough

Admiral Nelson
49 Nelson Street, LE16 9AX
12-2, 5-midnight; 12-midnight Fri & Sat; 12-11 Sun
Wells Eagle IPA, Bombardier; guest beer H
Friendly locals' pub, built in 1900, a short stroll from the centre of the historic market town. Just off the beaten track, this pub is the town's best-kept secret, offering a lounge with TV (where they like their rugby) and a bar with darts, pool, jukebox and another TV. A function room is available. Outside is a heated and covered smoking area with seating.
P

Melton Mowbray

Boat
57 Burton Street, LE13 1AF
11-3 (not Mon), 5-midnight; 11-midnight Thu-Sat; 12-midnight Sun (01664) 500969
Draught Bass; Theakston Best Bitter; Wells Bombardier; guest beer H
A traditional single-room pub that takes its name from a canal basin that was once adjacent. The walls are decorated with old pictures of the town and a map of the old Melton-Oakham canal whose workers this establishment once served. The pub is always busy with mature drinkers and the local darts teams who enjoy good conversation with their pint. A range gives plenty of warmth and adds to the atmosphere in winter. CAMRA branch Pub of the Year 2012 and 2013. Q (5,5A)

Kettleby Cross L
Wilton Road, LE13 0UJ
7am-midnight (01664) 485310
Greene King Abbot; Ruddles Best Bitter; guest beers H
The Kettleby Cross is a Wetherspoon new-build, opened in 2007 as a flagship eco pub complete with a prominent wind turbine on the roof. The pub stands close to the bridge over the nearby River Eye and is named after the cross that once directed travellers in the direction of Ab Kettleby. The large single-room interior is on two levels. Dan the manager supports local breweries and hosts an occasional local beer festival.
Q P (5,5A)

Noel's Arms L
31 Burton Street, LE13 1AE
12 (4 Mon)-11; 12-midnight Fri & Sat; 12-7 Sun
(01664) 562363
Beer range varies H
A welcome return to the Guide after a long absence for this popular single-roomed town pub. The Noel's became a free house in 2013 and shows a commendable commitment to real ale, with microbreweries featuring prominently. The pub is the tap for the Gas Dog Brewery and offers a discount to CAMRA members. A live music venue, there is always something going on at the Noel's, with darts, pool and cribbage all popular. CAMRA branch Pub of the Year 2014. (5)

Mountsorrel

Swan
10 Loughborough Road, LE12 7AT
12-2.30, 5.30-11; 12-11 Sat; 12-10.30 Sun
(0116) 230 2340 the-swan-inn.eu
Black Sheep Best Bitter; Morland Old Speckled Hen; Theakston XB; guest beers H
Grade II-listed, 17th-century coaching inn. The traditional split-level interior has open fires, stone floors and low ceilings, and includes a small dining area with a polished wood floor. Good-quality, interesting food is cooked to order, the menu changing weekly, and there are regular themed menus. Outside is a secluded riverside garden with moorings. Q P

Oadby

Cow & Plough
Gartree Road, LE2 2FB
11-11 (0116) 272 0852 steamin-billy.co.uk/cowplough
Fuller's London Pride; Steamin' Billy Bitter, Skydiver; guest beers H
Situated in a former farm building with a conservatory, the pub is decked out with breweriana. It is home to Steamin' Billy beers, named after the owner's now departed Jack Russell who features on the logo and pumpclips. A mild and cider are always available. A restaurant has been added in the former dairy buildings.
P

Lord Keeper of the Great Seal

96-100 The Parade, LE2 5BF

7am-midnight (0116) 272 0957

Greene King Abbot; Ruddles Best Bitter; guest beers

Named after Sir Nathan Wright, a local landowner who held this position in the 17th century, this typical Wetherspoon conversion of a row of shops stands on the site of Sandhurst Infants School. It features pictures of old buildings and industries of Oadby and a varied library of books. Regular beer festivals and charity events are held. Families are welcome until 9pm.

Oakham

Grainstore Brewery Tap

Station Approach, LE15 6EA

11-11 (midnight Fri); 9am-midnight Sat; 9am-11 Sun
(01572) 770065 grainstorebrewery.com

Grainstore Rutland Panther, Cooking, Triple B, Ten Fifty

A pub and brewery in a cleverly converted small warehouse over four floors, retaining some original features. Brewery tours are available but must be booked in advance. The beer range always includes a mild, and a range of bottle-conditioned Belgian beers is also stocked. Home-made food is served at lunchtime. Live bands feature regularly during the month. An annual beer festival is held over the August bank holiday. Walkers and their dogs are welcome. Q P

Lord Nelson

Market Square, LE15 6SJ

11-11 (midnight Fri & Sat); 11-10.30 Sun
(01572) 868340 thelordnelsonoakham.com

Castle Rock Harvest Pale; Fuller's London Pride; guest beers

A sympathetic refurbishment of Nick's Restaurant in the corner of the marketplace. Part of the Thurlby Group of pubs, the Lord Nelson is a traditional-looking example of a pub in a historic town. It serves good quality beer and has become a new addition to the county's real ale circuit. Good-quality home-cooked food is available daily. A regular quiz night is hosted. Q

Old Dalby

Sample Cellar

Station Road, LE14 3NQ

12-10 (8 Sun) (01664) 823455 belvoirbrewery.co.uk

Belvoir Dark Horse, Whippling, Star Bitter, Beaver Bitter, Oatmeal Stout, Old Dalby

The brick-fronted Sample Cellar on the outskirts of the village incorporates a bar, function room and visitors' centre, with brewery tours available by arrangement. The comfortable, spacious interior, filled with brewing artefacts, has a traditional bar area, with room for long alley skittles and a bar billiards table. Two large internal windows provide views into the brewery. A full menu is served daily, with the focus on good wholesome food made with local produce. P

Plungar

Anchor

Granby Lane, NG13 0JJ

12-3 (not Mon-Fri), 6-11; 12-10.30 Sun (01949) 860589

Beer range varies

This brick building in the middle of a small Leicestershire village dates from 1774 and at one time was the local courtroom. The pub now houses a large bar and lounge area, a separate restaurant and a pool room. Outside is an attractive beer garden and seating area. The Anchor has developed a reputation for fine food using locally-sourced ingredients and a good range of quality cask ales. At least one but sometimes all the beers come from local breweries. Q P

Quorn

Royal Oak

2 High Street, LE12 8DT

5.30-11 (01509) 413506

Timothy Taylor Landlord; guest beers

Traditional village inn in the centre of the village. The building has been an inn for around 160 years and was originally three terraced cottages. The internal walls were removed long ago to open up the interior but it retains many original features, including beamed ceilings and an open log fire. There is a sheltered, covered courtyard to the side. Q

Shackerstone

Rising Sun

Church Road, CV13 6NN

12-3, 6.30-midnight; 11.30-midnight Sat & Sun
(01827) 880215 risingsunpub.com

Marston's Pedigree; Timothy Taylor Landlord; Wychwood Hobgoblin; guest beer

Traditional family-owned free house located in the heart of Shackerstone village near the Ashby Canal and the preserved Battlefield Railway. It has a wood-panelled bar serving traditional ales, a restaurant, pool room with Sky Sports, family-friendly conservatory and an attractive garden. The pub, popular with locals and visitors alike, is renowned for the quality and variety of its ales and serves good pub food – the ideal hub for visiting this rural part of Leicestershire. P

Shawell

White Swan

Main Street, LE17 6AG (off roundabout on A5/A42)

11-11 (10.30 Sun & Mon) (01788) 860357
whiteswanshawell.co.uk

Dow Bridge Acris, Gladiator, Fosse Ale; guest beer

Centrally located in a rural village just off the Watling Street Roman road, the main building dates from the 17th century. The pub has been extensively refurbished and was the winner of a CAMRA pub design award in 2013. The spacious bar retains character with a stone floor, exposed beams and a woodburner. There is a separate lounge and an excellent restaurant serving an à la carte menu featuring local produce. A bar menu is also available. Local beers are from nearby Dow Bridge Brewery and guests from Churchend and Adnams. Q P

Shearsby

Chandlers Arms

Fenny Lane, LE17 6PL

7-11 Mon; 12-3 (4 Sat), 6-11; 12-10.30 Sun
(0116) 247 8384 chandlersatshearsby.co.uk

Dow Bridge Acris; guest beers

Classic, quaint old country pub overlooking the village green. Popular with walkers, cyclists, diners and visitors from the city, it also has strong local support. It was the first pub in CAMRA's Leicester branch to be accredited to the LocAle scheme. Microbrewery beers are always on the bar, often locally sourced. Draught cider is available in summer. No food is served Sunday evening or Monday. Local CAMRA Country Pub of the Year 2014 – for the sixth year in succession.

Sileby

Free Trade

27 Cossington Road, LE12 7RW
11.30-2.30 (not Mon), 5-11; 11.30-midnight Fri & Sat; 12-11 Sun ☎ (01509) 814494 thefreetradeinn.co.uk
Everards Beacon Bitter, Tiger, Original; guest beers H
Sixteenth-century thatched pub with a resident ghost. The comfortable front lounge with low beams and lots of nooks and crannies leads to a more open area at the back, with plenty of room to get together after a rugby match. Two guest beers are always available as well as real cider and perry. Regular beer festivals and charity events are hosted throughout the year. Local CAMRA branch Village Pub 2013 and branch Pub of the Year 2014.
P

Horse & Trumpet

4 Barrow Road, LE12 7LP
1-11 (midnight Fri & Sat); 12-11 Sun ☎ (01509) 812549
steamin-billy.co.uk/horse-trumpet
Steamin' Billy Tipsy Fisherman, Bitter, Skydiver; guest beers H
This multi-room pub with open fires has undergone a huge transformation since becoming part of the Steamin' Billy chain. Two guest beers are on offer plus a real cider and perry. No hot food is served but cobs are available, and there is a monthly curry club. Open mic nights feature weekly and jazz nights monthly. A function room is available. Dogs are welcome in the bar and seating area outside.
QP (2)

Somerby

Stilton Cheese L

High Street, LE14 2QB
12-3, 6-11; 7-11 Sun ☎ (01664) 454394
stiltoncheeseinn.co.uk
Grainstore Ten Fifty; Marston's Burton Bitter; guest beers H
Late 16th-century pub built in local ironstone, like most of the buildings in the village. The interior comprises two bars and a function room/restaurant upstairs. On purchasing their drinks, tall customers should take care not to bump their heads on the low beam adorned with a wide range of pumpclips. Look for the large stuffed pike mounted on the wall. Four ales are usually available; local breweries are well represented. An ideal place to stop for lunch while walking the Leicestershire Round. QP (113)

Stathern

Plough L

Main Street, LE14 4HW
12-11 (10.30 Sun) ☎ (01949) 860411
theploughstathern.com
Belvoir Star Bitter; Greene King Abbot; guest beer H
A large free house situated centrally in Stathern, in the heart of the Vale of Belvoir, well-located for the castle. This is a popular stop-off both for visitors to the Vale and for locals. The large bar is home to the pool table and other pub games, plus a large collection of football scarves. There is a more traditional lounge and dining area where home-cooked food is served every day. CAMRA members receive a generous discount on real ale.
P

Swinford

Chequers

High Street, LE17 6BL (near church)
12-2.30 (not Mon), 6-11; 12-3, 6-11 Sat; 12-3, 7-11 Sun
☎ (01788) 860318 chequersswinford.co.uk
Adnams Southwold Bitter; guest beers H
Smart wood-floored family-run village inn conveniently placed for the A14 M6/M1, popular with locals and visitors alike. Bar meals are served in a separate dining area, with vegetarian and children's menus available. The guest beer range regularly includes a mild. Skittles and darts are played. Outside is a children's play area and a marquee where a summer beer festival is held. The 16th-century Stanford Hall is nearby and there is a caravan park a mile away which hosts regular rallies. P

Swithland

Griffin Inn

174 Main Street, LE12 8TJ
9am-11 ☎ (01509) 890535 griffininnswithland.co.uk
Adnams Southwold Bitter; Everards Tiger, Original; guest beers H
Friendly and welcoming local with three comfortable rooms. Three guest ales are usually on offer, chosen from the Everard's list —one may be replaced by a traditional cider. Alongside the regular food menu, light snacks are available every afternoon including Melton Mowbray pork pies. Set in the heart of Charnwood Forest, there are many walking and cycling routes nearby. Swithland Reservoir, Bradgate Park and the preserved Great Central Railway are all close.
P (123,154)

Syston

Syston & District Social Club L

36 High Street, LE7 1GP
7.30-11; 12-2.30, 5.30-midnight Fri; 12-midnight Sat; 12-4, 7-11 Sun ☎ (0116) 260 9086 systonsocial.co.uk
Banks's Mild, Bitter; Marston's Pedigree; guest beers H
This former pub is home to many local societies and sports clubs including darts, skittles, chess and crib, and has a large function room available for hire. The range of six beers includes three regularly rotating guests. An annual beer festival is held in June. Show a CAMRA membership card or a copy of this Guide for entry. CAMRA East Midlands Club of the Year 2013.

Thurlaston

Elephant & Castle L

26 Main Street, LE9 7TP

🕓 6.30-11 Mon & Tue; 12-2.30, 6-11 Wed-Fri; 12-3, 6-11.30 Sat; 12-3, 7-10.30 Sun ☎ (01455) 888213

Everards Beacon Bitter, Tiger, Original; guest beers Ⓗ

A regular in the Guide, this friendly inn is set in the heart of the village. The pub's ales benefit from the landlord's national awards in cellarmanship. Three Everard's beers and two guests are on offer plus two real ciders. The refurbished front lounge has a logburner and to the rear is a restaurant/lounge. The landlady's home-made pies and good-value Sunday lunches are a treat. Outside is a children's play area and patio. Walking and cycling routes pass the pub. Q✿◐♿♣🍎P🚌(X55)🐾📶

Uppingham

Crown Inn 🏆

19 High Street East, LE15 9PY

🕓 11-11; 11.30-10.30 Sun ☎ (01572) 822302

🌐 thecrownrutland.co.uk

Everards Tiger, Original; guest beer Ⓗ

A warm welcome is assured at this traditional market town pub dating from 1739. It offers up to seven ales, many from Everards, and good-quality home-cooked food in the bar and restaurant. Live music plays regularly and a beer festival is held every April on St George's Day. The pub is home to a local dominoes team. En-suite accommodation is available. Winner of many CAMRA awards including local CAMRA Pub of the Year 2014.
✿🛏◐♿♣🍎P🚌🐾📶

Walton on the Wolds

Anchor

2 Loughborough Road, LE12 8HT

🕓 12-3, 6-11; 12-10.30 Sun ☎ (01509) 880018

Adnams Southwold Bitter; Fuller's London Pride; Timothy Taylor Landlord Ⓗ

The Anchor is situated in the centre of a small village within easy reach of Leicester and Nottingham. It is a popular venue for walkers who stop for a well-earned home-cooked lunch in front of the log fire. There is a menu to suit all tastes plus an extensive specials board. Outside is an elevated seating area to the front and a garden and large car park to the rear. En-suite B&B accommodation is available. Q✿🛏◐P🚌

Whitwick

Three Horseshoes ★

11 Leicester Road, LE67 5GN

🕓 11-3, 6.30-11; 12-2, 7-10.30 Sun ☎ (01530) 837311

Draught Bass; Marston's Pedigree Ⓗ

Identified by CAMRA as having a nationally important historic pub interior, the Three Horseshoes is nicknamed Polly's after a former landlady, Polly Burton. The pub was originally two separate buildings but now has two rooms. To the left is a long bar with a quarry-tiled floor and open fires, wooden bench seating and pre-war fittings; to the right is a similarly furnished small snug. 🚌

Wigston

William Wygston

84 Leicester Road, LE18 1DR

🕓 9am-midnight ☎ (0116) 288 8397

Greene King Abbot; Ruddles Best Bitter; guest beers Ⓗ

A classic Wetherspoon establishment named after William Wygston (1456-1536), an extremely wealthy wool merchant, philanthropist, MP, and twice mayor of Leicester. Staffed by an efficient, friendly and helpful team of employees, it offers an ever-changing array of guest beers, often from local breweries Grainstore, Langton and Shardlow. Interesting pictures depicting bygone Wigston and Leicester adorn the walls. ◐♿🍎🚌📶

Wymeswold

Three Crowns

45 Far Street, LE12 6TZ

🕓 12-midnight ☎ (01509) 880153

Adnams Southwold Bitter; Draught Bass; Sharp's Doom Bar; guest beer Ⓗ

Late 18th-century pub standing opposite the church. This friendly village local features a beamed ceiling in the bar and a split-level snug/lounge. Guest beers are usually from local breweries including Castle Rock, Belvoir or Nottingham. Evening meals are available Thursday to Saturday. There is a regular daytime bus service.
Q✿◐♿⛺♣🍎P🚌🐾📶

What is real ale?

Real ale is also known as cask-conditioned beer or simply cask beer. In the brewery, the beer is neither filtered nor pasteurised. It still contains sufficient yeast and sugar for it to continue to ferment and mature in the cask. Once it has reached the pub cellar, it has to be laid down for maturation to continue, and for yeast and protein to settle at the bottom of the cask. Some real ale also has extra hops added as the cask is filled, a process known as 'dry hopping' for increased flavour and aroma. Cask beer is best served at a cellar temperature of 11-12 degrees C, although some stronger ales can benefit from being served a little warmer. Each cask has two holes, in one of which a tap is inserted and is connected to tubes or 'lines' that enable the beer to be drawn to the bar. The other hole, on top of the cask, enables some carbon dioxide produced during secondary fermentation to escape. It is vital that some gas, which gives the beer its natural sparkle or condition, is kept within the cask: the escape of gas is controlled by inserting porous wooden pegs called spiles into the spile hole. Real ale is a living product and must be consumed within three or four days of a cask being tapped as oxidation develops.

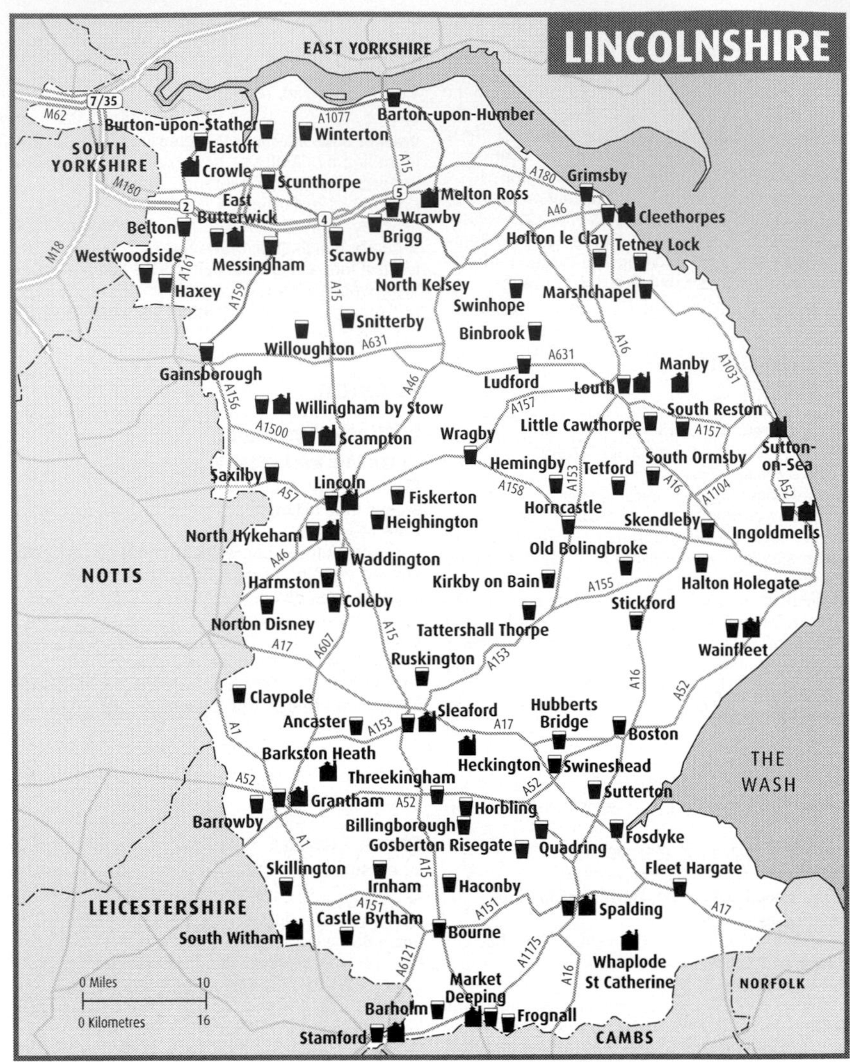

Ancaster

Ancaster Social Club

Ermine Street, NG32 3PW

7 (12 Sat)-11; 12-10.30 Sun ☎ (01400) 230896

John Smith's Bitter; guest beer [H]

This village club is home to numerous sporting teams and hosts local cup finals. The excellent John Smith's is supplemented by different guest ales. There is an airy conservatory and an outside seating area overlooking the sports fields. Voted local CAMRA Club of the Year 2012, 2013 and 2014, and Lincolnshire Club of the Year 2013. ❀♣P

Barholm

Five Horseshoes [L]

PE9 4RA

4 (1 Sat)-11; 12-10.30 Sun ☎ (01778) 560238

Adnams Southwold Bitter; Oakham JHB; guest beers [H]

An 18th-century stone-built traditional pub, comprising two bars, two side rooms and a TV/pool room. A welcoming wood fire burns throughout the winter. Stuffed birds and enamelled adverts adorn the walls. Outside there is a garden, kids' play area and car park. Barbecues and music events are held in the summer. A regularly changing range of beers from local and regional microbreweries is available from six handpumps. Pizzas are served on Fridays. The pub supports the Macmillan Nurses charity.

Q❀P

Barrowby

White Swan

Main Street, NG32 1BH

12-midnight (1am Fri & Sat) ☎ (01476) 562375

Adnams Southwold Bitter; Sharp's Doom Bar; guest beers [H]

The landlord is a long-standing member and active supporter of CAMRA, and runs a traditional old-style village pub with separate bar and lounge areas, which is well frequented by the locals. It is also an ideal spot to break a journey, being next to

the A1 and A52. As well as the regular beers on offer there is always at least one guest ale chosen from a varied countrywide selection.
Q❀◐♣P🚌🐾📶

Barton-upon-Humber

Sloop Inn 🄻

81 Waterside Road, DN18 5BA (follow Humber Bridge viewing signs)
⏲ 11.30 (3.30 Mon)-11; 12-10.30 Sun ☎ (01652) 637287
Tom Wood's Lincoln Gold, Bomber County; guest beer 🄷
A welcoming pub with nautical-themed decoration and areas named after parts of a ship. The central bar serves a games area, a drinking/dining area and two further rooms, one with an original Delft tiled fireplace. Real ales are from the local Tom Wood's Brewery, plus guest beers often from Cottage Brewery. A wide range of home-cooked food is on offer, with many specials. Far Ings nature reserve, Waters Edge visitor centre, Ropewalk and the Humber Bridge are nearby.
❀◐◑♿⛺≈♣●P🚌(250,350)🐾

Stables 🄻

6A Holydyke, DN18 5PS
⏲ 12-2, 5-11; 12-11 Sat & Sun ☎ (01652) 660789
🌐 stablesinbarton.co.uk
Beer range varies 🄷
Although predominantly a dining establishment, this bistro is definitely worth a visit to sample the well-kept and interesting ales. The enthusiastic manager sources the varied and changing guest beers locally, and also offers a range of bottled Belgian beers. The upper level is dedicated to relaxed dining while the lower level offers some seating for drinking, particularly around the bar area. Be warned: weekend evenings are busy and standing may be the only option. ◐◑⛺≈🚌

Belton

Crown Inn

Church Lane, Churchtown, DN9 1PA
⏲ 1 midnight; 12-1.30am Fri & Sat; 12-midnight Sun
☎ (01427) 872834
Batemans XB; Bradfield Farmers Blonde; Brakspear Bitter; Jennings Cocker Hoop; guest beers 🄷
Difficult to find, but well worth the effort. This pub is a haven for the discerning drinker, with a long history of offering quality cask ales. Six are available, always including a rotating guest beer from the nearby Glentworth Brewery. Quizzes, pub games and live music are a feature of this friendly local, which also holds occasional beer festivals. Winner of a number of awards, including local CAMRA Pub of the Year in 2013. ❀●P🍺🐾📶

Billingborough

Fortescue Arms

27 High Street, NG34 0QB
⏲ 12-3, 5.30-11; 12-11 Sat & Sun ☎ (01529) 240228
🌐 fortescuearms.co.uk
Greene King Abbot; Oldershaw Heavenly Blonde; guest beers 🄷
Fine, Grade-II listed inn with an interesting multi-roomed interior and a rustic feel. It is popular with diners and has a large patio to the rear. Nearby is the site of Sempringham Priory and its monument to Gwenllian, daughter of the Prince of Wales, who was confined to the priory in the 12th century. Stone from the priory was used to build part of the inn. Guest beers are usually from micros.
Q❀◐◑♿P

Binbrook

Plough

Market Place, LN8 6DE
⏲ 12-11 (12.30am Fri & Sat) ☎ (01472) 398808
Wells Bombardier; guest beers 🄷
Three-roomed pub situated in a Lincolnshire Wolds village close to the former RAF Binbrook station (featured in the movie Memphis Belle). Numerous Lightning jet and other aircraft memorabilia are on display. The chef relies upon fresh, local produce for steak pie or fish and home-cooked chips. Guest beers from independent breweries feature regularly. A pool league is hosted and a darts team.
Q❀◐◑♣P🐾📶

Boston

Eagle

144 West Street, PE21 8RE
⏲ 11-11 (11.30 Thu; midnight Fri & Sat) ☎ (01205) 361116
Castle Rock Black Gold, Harvest Pale, Preservation Fine Ale, Elsie Mo; guest beers 🄷
Part of the Castle Rock chain, the Eagle is known as the real ale pub of Boston. This friendly two-roomed hostelry has an L-shaped bar with a large TV screen for big sports events. The small cosy lounge has an open fire. The pub stocks a wide range of guest ales, and at least one cider. A function room upstairs is home to Boston Folk Club. Thursday is quiz night – allegedly the hardest in town. Q❀♿≈♣●🚌🐾

Golden Lion

46 High Street, PE21 8SP
⏲ 6 (12 Sat & Sun)-midnight ☎ (01205) 352745
Brains The Rev James; Theakston Best Bitter; Thwaites Lancaster Bomber 🄷

INDEPENDENT BREWERIES

8 Sail Heckington
Austendyke Spalding
Axholme Crowle
Bacchus Sutton-on-Sea
Batemans Wainfleet
Black Horse Louth
Blue Bell Whaplode St Catherine
Blue Cow South Witham
Brewster's Grantham
Cathedral Heights Lincoln
DarkTribe East Butterwick
Firehouse Manby (NEW)
Fulstow Louth
Grafters Willingham by Stow
Greg's Scampton (NEW)
Hopshackle Market Deeping
Leila Cottage Ingoldmells
Melbourn Stamford
Newby Wyke Grantham
Oldershaw Barkston Heath
Poachers North Hykeham
Riverside Wainfleet
Sleaford Sleaford
Star Market Deeping (NEW)
Tom Wood's Melton Ross
Willy's Cleethorpes

Low-beamed ceilings and wood panelling mark out this pub on the old High Street away from the main shopping thoroughfares. It has recently reopened, serving a good range of beers, and has active teams who play traditional games. Old fishing boat nameplates hang above the bar as a reminder of the history of Boston as a fishing port.

Indian Queen & Three Kings

4 Dolphin Lane, PE21 6EU

11-11 ☎ (01205) 354221

Batemans Black & White, XB, XXXB; guest beers H

Recently restored to a Victorian theme, this is now an attractive hostelry with wood panelling, mirrors, retro-style electric lighting and even a pub piano. There are no keg dispensers on the bar, only handpulls, but keg beer is discreetly served from small taps at the back of the bar. Originally known as the Three Kings of Cologne, the pub has been rebuilt and renamed at least three times and is thought to be the oldest in Boston. Q

Moon Under Water

6 High Street, PE21 8SH

9am-midnight (1am Fri & Sat) ☎ (01205) 311911

Greene King Abbot; Ruddles Best Bitter; guest beers H

A large, lively, town-centre Wetherspoon pub near the tidal section of the River Witham. Formerly a government building, an imposing staircase leads from the lounge up to the toilets. A spacious conservatory-style dining area is supplemented by a second child-friendly dining room adjacent to the lounge. The pub offers a good number of guest ales and a large range of continental bottled beers. Local history photographs and information boards highlight important people associated with Boston.

Bourne

Smith's

25 North Street, PE10 9AE

10-11 (midnight Fri & Sat); 11.45-11 Sun

☎ (01778) 426819 smithsofbourne.co.uk

Castle Rock Harvest Pale; Fuller's London Pride; guest beers H

A successful conversion from an old grocery store to a highly atmospheric public house. The main bar at the front serves six beers, mostly from independent brewers, via handpump, as well as a maze of interconnecting rooms over a further two floors. Outside to the side there is a well-equipped patio leading to a large beer garden at the rear. The pub hosts an annual beer festival in July and cider and sausage festival in August.

Q

Brigg

Black Bull

3 Wrawby Street, DN20 8JH

11-3, 7-11 Mon & Tue; 11-11; 12-11 Sun

☎ (01652) 652153

Everards Tiger; John Smith's Bitter; guest beer H

Comfortable town-centre pub, open plan in design. It has two dining/drinking areas decorated in traditional village-inn style with old pictures and brass wall plates. There is also a separate raised dining area, with good home-cooked meals served throughout, including steak nights Tuesday-Saturday. Quiz night is Wednesday. Two regular real ales are supplemented by a rotating guest beer. A smoking area is provided at the rear of the building. Q P (4)

Yarborough Hunt

49 Bridge Street, DN20 8NS (across bridge from market place)

11-11; 10-midnight Thu; 11-midnight Fri; 10-midnight Sat

☎ (01652) 658333

Tom Wood's Best Bitter, Lincoln Gold, Bomber County; guest beers H

This former Sergeants Brewery tap was built in the 1700s and retains original rustic features. It was recently extended to form an extra room. Simply furnished with warming open fires in three of its four rooms, four Tom Wood's beers are generally on, supplemented by three guest beers and draught Westons Old Rosie cider. A good selection of bottled beers and ciders is stocked, plus a wide selection of malt whiskies and wines. The smoking area is covered and heated. Q (4)

Burton-upon-Stather

Ferry House Inn

Stather Road, DN15 9DT (follow campsite signs through village; down hill at church)

6-11; 12-11 Sat & Sun ☎ (01724) 721783

ferryhousepub.co.uk

Beer range varies H

Friendly village local by the River Trent which has been in the same family for 54 years. The pub brews its own beer (check for availability) as well as offering rotating guest ales. Real cider is also sold. Food is served Thursday-Sunday. Features include a large outdoor children's play area and occasional live music, while a beer festival is generally held over the August bank holiday weekend. The pub is a meeting place for local heritage groups. P

Castle Bytham

Castle Inn L

High Street, NG33 4RZ

6-11; 10-3 Sun ☎ (01780) 410504

castleinnbytham.co.uk

Star Astral; Woodforde's Wherry; guest beers H

One of the original public houses in a historic village, this 17th-century gem has Star Brewery beers permanently on the bar, along with regularly changing guest ales sourced both locally and nationally. A traditional cider is also on offer. An excellent menu offering home-made food is available every evening and Sunday lunchtime.

Q P

Fox & Hounds

6 High Street, NG33 4RZ

12.30-2.30 (not Mon-Wed), 6-11.30; 12-2.30, 5-11.30 Sun

☎ (01780) 410336

Marston's Pedigree; Oakham Bishops Farewell; guest beers H

A welcoming and friendly village local which has been in the same family for 16 years. Marston's Pedigree and Oakham Ales are always available, plus two changing guest ales. A regular quiz night is held on the first Sunday of the month. There is excellent home-cooked food to be enjoyed, including a curry night on the first Thursday of the month, bought in from the award-winning Bengal Clipper in Stamford. P

Claypole

Five Bells 𝕃
95 Main Street, NG23 5BJ
⏲ 11 (4 Mon)-11; 10-10.30 Sun ☎ (01636) 626261
🌐 thefivebellsclaypole.co.uk
Greene King IPA; guest beers Ⓗ
Traditional village pub with four beers and two ciders always available at the bar. The guest ales come predominantly from local microbreweries, with small jars displaying the colour of the beers. There is a large public bar, a small lounge, and a restaurant serving home-cooked food. Outside there is a spacious beer garden and children's play area. The pub has four en-suite rooms. Local CAMRA Pub of the Year 2012 and 2013, and county CAMRA Pub of the Year 2013.
Q≋❀⛟◐◑♿♣●P🚌🐾📶

Cleethorpes

No. 2 Refreshment Room
Railway Station, DN35 8AX
⏲ 6-1am ☎ 07905 375587
Hancock's HB; Rudgate Ruby Mild; guest beers Ⓗ
A small, single-roomed pub on the station concourse underneath the last remaining wooden railway clock tower. With a mix of young and not-so-young regulars, it is always welcoming. It now serves two regular beers (one is a mild) and four changing guests. Thursday is quiz night and a free buffet is provided on Sunday evenings. ❀⇌🚌🐾📶

Nottingham House 🏆
7 Seaview Street, DN35 8EU
⏲ 12-11 (midnight Thu; 1am Fri & Sat) ☎ (01472) 505150
Tetley Mild, Bitter; Timothy Taylor Landlord; Wychwood Hobgoblin; guest beers Ⓗ
Traditional local with three rooms, situated at the highest point in town. Some alterations took place pre-war and the pub has been extended, but it keeps a standard public bar to the left and a splendid lounge to the right, both with open fireplaces. At the rear is a snug with unusual all-round banquette seating, while upstairs there is a restaurant serving lunches Wednesday-Sunday and evening meals Wednesday-Saturday. Food can be served in any of the bars. Q⛟◐◑⇌♣●🚌🐾📶

Willy's
17 High Cliff, DN35 8RQ
⏲ 11-11 (2am Fri & Sat); 11-midnight Sun ☎ (01472) 602145
Draught Bass; Willy's Original; guest beers Ⓗ
With views overlooking the River Humber and beach through a glass frontage, drinkers can take in the sights while enjoying their beers. Willy's Original is brewed on the premises and the brewery can be seen from the bar. Food is served lunchtimes and there are Tuesday and Thursday evening supper clubs. Extensive camping facilities are available at nearby Meridian Park. The two real ciders can include Moles Black Rat and Gwynt y Ddraig Black Dragon. There is a covered smoking area at the rear. ≋❀◐◑⇌●🚌🐾📶

Coleby

Tempest Arms
Hill Rise, LN5 0AG
⏲ 12 (4 Mon)-11; 12-midnight Fri & Sat; 12-10.30 Sun
☎ (01522) 810258 🌐 the-tempest.co.uk
Castle Rock Harvest Pale; Fuller's ESB; Greene King Abbot; Thwaites Original, Lancaster Bomber Ⓗ
A friendly village pub, with its Victorian faux-Tudor decor that oozes ale-thusiasm. The separate dining area affords views over the terraced beer garden to the farmlands of the Witham Valley below. Meals and snacks are served lunchtimes and evenings Wednesday to Saturday until 9pm, with a carvery on Sunday lunchtimes. The comfortable lounge, with its stone fireplace, wraps around the well-stacked bar. It is a useful respite from the Viking Way outside. Q≋❀◐◑Å●P🚌(1)🐾📶

East Butterwick

Dog & Gun 𝕃
High Street, DN17 3AJ (off A18 at Keadby Bridge, E bank)
⏲ 5 (12 Sat & Sun)-11 ☎ (01724) 782324
DarkTribe Sternwheeler, Old Gaffer Ⓗ
Village community pub alongside the River Trent. It has three rooms, with a drinking area and picnic-style bench seating on the river bank outside. Three beers from the house DarkTribe microbrewery are always on sale, and occasional seasonal ales are also produced. Quiz night is Tuesday, and during the warmer months motorsport meetings are held for motorcycles and vintage cars. A nearby cycle club holds time trials in the summer, starting outside the pub, which is on a national cycle route. ≋❀♿♣P🚌🐾

Eastoft

River Don Tavern
Sampson Street, DN17 4PQ (on A161 Goole-Gainsborough road)
⏲ 3.30 (12 Sun)-11 ☎ (01724) 798040
🌐 riverdontavernandlodge.co.uk
Batemans Yella Belly Gold; guest beers Ⓗ
Refurbished traditional village local on the main road. The bar serves a single spacious room, with two distinct drinking areas, the larger one also used for dining. Meals are available every evening, plus a superb carvery from noon on Sunday. One or two rotating guest ales are sold, generally from Yorkshire and Lincolnshire breweries, including local micro Axholme. A large orchard is set out with tables for alfresco drinking in summer. Accommodation is available in four lodges at the rear. ❀◑♿♣●P🚌(356)

Fiskerton

Carpenters Arms
High Street, LN3 4HF
⏲ 6-10.30 Mon; 12-2, 6-11; 12-10.30 Sun ☎ (01522) 305509
Batemans XB; guest beers Ⓗ
A free house with a spacious public bar which hosts pool, darts and crib teams. The smaller lounge has information on RAF Fiskerton – the pub was popular with personnel from the wartime airfield. Award-winning food is served in the large dining area. To the rear is a patio and grassed beer garden. Guest beers are generally light or amber coloured. The pub is favoured by walkers and cyclists using the nearby riverside trail. ❀◐◑♿♣P🚌(15,15A)📶

Fleet Hargate

Rose & Crown
Old Main Road, PE12 8LH
⏲ 12-3, 6-11; 12-midnight Fri & Sat; 12-4, 7-11 Sun
☎ (01406) 422165

Elgood's Cambridge Bitter; Tetley Bitter; guest beer
A friendly welcome awaits in this village local as you step down into its U-shaped bar/lounge. The beamed ceiling and bay windows suit the building, and the neat rear garden has an attractive summer house. The pub engages in various activities supporting the local community. The landlord favours Elgood's beers and often has one of its seasonal or special ales available as a guest.
Q P (505)

Fosdyke

Ship Inn

Moulton Washway, PE12 6LH
11.30-10 (11 Fri & Sat) (01205) 260764
shipinnfosdyke.co.uk
Adnams Southwold Bitter, Broadside; Batemans XB
This venue is just outside Fosdyke when travelling from Boston on the main A17, next to the bridge. As its name suggests, this former Bateman's hostelry is dedicated to all things maritime – maps, photographs, charts and model ships of every description are in plentiful supply. The week's tide table is also detailed on a blackboard. The inn is near to the busy Fosdyke Marina and boaters and landlubbers are well catered for with excellent home-cooked food and a welcome cheer.
Q P

Frognall

Goat

155 Spalding Road, PE6 8SA
12-3, 6-11.30; 12-11.30 Sat; 12-10.30 Sun
(01778) 347629 thegoatfrognall.com
Beer range varies
Large single-bar pub with a number of dining areas. There are six handpumps serving a range of regional and micro beers, usually incorporating local beers from Hopshackle and a strong ale. In addition to the handpumps there are two real ciders on gravity. A large selection of malt whiskies is available. A popular beer festival is held in summer, and the good-quality food is all home cooked. The large garden has a play area for children and one for toddlers.
Q P (100)

Gainsborough

Blues Club

Northolme, North Street, DN21 2QW
7-midnight; 5-1am Fri; 12-1am Sat; 12-midnight Sun
(01427) 613688
Beer range varies
The club has a bar area with several TVs showing sport, a quieter lounge and a large function room which hosts regular live entertainment (admission charges may apply). Two changing real ales are usually available and details of forthcoming beers can be emailed to customers on request. CAMRA guests are always welcome on production of a membership card or a copy of the Guide.
(Central)

Canute

12-14 Silver Street, DN21 2DP
9am-11 (midnight Thu; 1am Fri & Sat); 11-11 Sun
(01427) 678715 canutegainsborough.co.uk
Courage Best Bitter; guest beers
A typical town-centre pub where Courage Best Bitter is a permanent feature. Landlord Neil is keen to provide a varying range of other beers; there are usually five real ales on handpump. Good-quality food is served and live sport is shown. The pub can be busy on Friday and Saturday nights.
(Central)

Eight Jolly Brewers

Ship Court, DN21 2DW
11 (12 Sun)-midnight 07926 797767
Glentworth Lightyear; guest beers
The branch's flagship real ale haven and in the Guide since 1995, the pub is based in a 300-year-old Grade II-listed building. Eight varying beers, at least one at a discounted price, are always on sale, many from northern micros, but new breweries from all areas feature. Real cider and continental bottled beers are also on sale. There are fortnightly Wednesday evening quizzes and quality live music plays every Thursday. Customers bring in food to share on Sunday lunchtimes.
Q (Central) P (200)

Elm Cottage

138 Church Street, DN21 2JU
11.30-midnight; 12-11.30 Sun 07590 806584
Beer range varies
This pub, close to Gainsborough Trinity's football ground and the Blues Club, is making a welcome return to the Guide. There are six changing beers, some from the Marston's portfolio, but often from microbreweries. Good-value food is available Tuesday to Saturday. The pub is popular with local amateur sports teams. Weekly live music is featured. Q (Central) P

Sweyn Forkbeard

22-24 Silver Street, DN21 2DP
8am-midnight (01427) 675000
Ruddles Best Bitter; Wychwood Hobgoblin; guest beers
It is good to see this town-centre Wetherspoon establishment in the Guide again. Three rotating guest beers often feature some oddities for this part of the country. Customers can ask for their favourite beer and it often appears. The pub is named after the Danish King of England from 1013, whose son Canute is rumoured to have stopped Aegir, Norse god of the sea. Good, well-priced food is available until 11pm. (Central)

Gosberton Risegate

Duke of York

106 Risegate Road, PE11 4EY
12 (6.30 Mon)-11; 11-3, 7-10.30 Sun (01775) 840193
Batemans XB; St Austell Tribute; guest beers
A friendly pub and a long-standing entry in the Guide, with a deserved reputation for value-for-money ale and food. As well as the regular beers there are guests from a range of independent brewers. A wide choice of cooked food is available with portions to suit the largest appetite. Local community life is supported through charities, sports teams and other social events. Visitors can expect an enthusiastic welcome from the two pub dogs. P

Grantham

Lord Harrowby

65 Dudley Road, NG31 9AB

3 (12 Sat & Sun)-11 (01476) 563515

Oldershaw Heavenly Blonde; guest beers

This back-street hostelry, surrounded by chimney pots, is a friendly locals' pub, and a real gem in today's world. It has two rooms – a modern lounge and a traditional bar of Victorian style where darts and cribbage are played. A great choice of real ales for tickers is available as well as two ciders. Two real ale and cider festivals are held each year, and a real log fire in the winter creates a cosy and warm ambience. Q

Nobody Inn

9 North Street, NG31 6NU (opp Asda car park)

12-11 (10.30 Sun) (01476) 565288 nobodyinn.com

Wells Bombardier; guest beers

A superbly run independent town pub and local CAMRA Pub of the Year 2014, selling a range of six beers, also featuring LocAles from Newby Wyke, with Grantham Gold brewed exclusively for the pub. A seventh handpump dispenses Old Rosie cider. Popular with drinkers and sports fans, it has five screens around the bar showing different sporting events. Allow time to find the hidden entrance to the toilets and look out for the spider.

Tollemache Inn

17 St Peter's Hill, NG31 6PY

8am-midnight (1am Fri & Sat) (01476) 594696

Adnams Broadside; Fuller's London Pride; Greene King Abbot; Ruddles Best Bitter; Sharp's Doom Bar; guest beers

A Wetherspoon venue, one of the first to be opened outside London, occupying the old Co-op building and a former local CAMRA Pub of the Year. Ideally situated in the town centre and next to the museum and arts centre, it always has a large selection of national and guest ales on handpump; especially noteworthy is that there is always one beer on from each of Grantham's award-winning and renowned microbreweries – Brewster's, Newby Wyke and Oldershaw.

Grimsby

Barge

Riverhead, DN31 1NH

10-midnight (2am Tue, Fri & Sat); 12-11 Sun (01472) 340911 thebargegrimsby.co.uk

Wells Bombardier; Wychwood Hobgoblin

This venue is an old converted grain barge and has had a slight tilt for over 25 years. In the afternoons custom is quieter and tends toward those seeking food, popular with a mixed age range. In the evening the jukebox is turned up and the bar takes on a rock/student feel. Monday is quiz night. The cider is from Skidbrooke.

Rose & Crown

Louth Road, DN33 2HR

11-11 (midnight Fri & Sat); 11.30-11 Sun (01472) 278517

Abbeydale Moonshine; Tetley Bitter; guest beers

An Ember Inn, well appointed and friendly, with an emphasis on good, reasonably priced food but rightly proud of its real ales. One large bar serves several seating areas. Monday is pie night, Tuesday is burger night, Wednesday is sausage night and Thursday char grill night. There is a seated and heated area at the front and a grassed seating area to the side which will serve to accommodate the smoker. P (8,51)

Spiders Web

180 Carr Lane, DN32 8LN

12-midnight (11 Mon-Wed) (01472) 692065 thespiderswebgy.co.uk

Black Sheep Best Bitter; John Smith's Bitter; Timothy Taylor Landlord; guest beer

Friendly family-run pub with a bar, quiet lounge and a function room which holds frequent folk, blues and local band nights. The rotating guest beer is chosen by the regular customers. A large, grassed area is a suntrap, with a separate smoking area. Traditional pub games can be played in the bar and poker (league and non-league) in the lounge. P (14)

Wheatsheaf

Bargate, DN34 5AD

11-11 (midnight Thu-Sat); 12-11 Sun (01472) 246821

Abbeydale Moonshine; Adnams Broadside; Everards Tiger; guest beers

A popular Ember Inn with five real ales in addition to good, affordable food. The split-level layout has various seating areas and a function room is available. Monday is pie night, Tuesday is burger night, Wednesday is sausage night and Thursday chargrill night. Quizzes are held on Sunday and Thursday nights. There is a heated patio at the rear and another with a grassed area at the front which can accommodate smokers. P

Haconby

Hare & Hounds

2 West Street, PE10 0UZ

12-2, 6-11 (10.30 Mon); 12-11 Sat; 12-10.30 Sun (01778) 570521

Marston's EPA; guest beer

This low-beamed pub built around 1600 has comfortable settees in the back room and is a popular dining hostelry. Walking groups frequent the place and there is live music on the first and second Sundays and third Mondays in the month. Guest ales are from the Marston's stable, usually two and changing regularly. Q P

Halton Holegate

Bell Inn

Spilsby Road, PE23 5PA

12-3 (not Mon & Tue), 6-11; 12-3, 5-11 Thu & Fri; 12-11 Sat & Sun (01790) 753242 thebell.me.uk

Beer range varies

A 16th-century country inn with low beamed ceilings in a quiet village. Pictures of the Dambusters adorn the small cosy lounge. The friendly, welcoming landlord has a keen interest in beers and the three guests are often from small breweries within the county. No food is served Mondays or Tuesdays. A recently formed computer club meets Sunday evenings. Q P

Harmston

Thorold Arms

High Street, LN5 9SN

closed Mon & Tue; 12-3 (not Wed-Fri), 6-11; 12-3, 7-11 Sun (01522) 720358 thoroldarms.co.uk

Beer range varies Ⓗ
A stone building with a modern bar, open fire, sofas and traditional tables and chairs. Oldershaw beers are the regular choice, with at least three other guest ales, often originating from Lincolnshire breweries. A real cider is on offer, changing on a regular basis. A separate dining room serves evening meals from Wednesday to Saturday and the pub is renowned for its fine Sunday lunches. Q❀◐♿♣●P🚌(1)📶

Haxey

Loco

31-33 Church Street, DN9 2HY (on B1396)
⏲ 4-11 (midnight Fri); 12-11 Sat; 1.30-11 Sun
☎ (01427) 752879 🌐 thelocohaxey.co.uk
Beer range varies Ⓗ
Former village chippie converted into a railway-themed pub during the 1980s. Refurbished since then, only a locomotive smokebox remains of the railway memorabilia. The pub has gained a reputation for quality English and Asian food and also offers 4-star en-suite accommodation. Up to three cask ales from micros are served, with Poachers and Milestone breweries often featured. This hostelry participates in the local Haxey Hood game each January. Q♨🛏◑♿🚌(399)🐾

Heighington

Butcher & Beast

High Street, LN4 1JS
⏲ 12-11; 12-10.30 Sun ☎ (01522) 790386
🌐 butcherandbeast.co.uk
Batemans Black & White, XB, XXXB; guest beers Ⓗ
A welcoming Bateman's village pub. Outside, this old stone building has beautiful hanging baskets in summer and a large garden with pétanque. Inside are distinct drinking areas, a real fire and delightful historic local photographs on the walls. The six handpumps also offer changing guest beers. Ciders are available, plus a splendid range of rare malt whiskies. A good food menu includes themed nights (Monday steak, Tuesday fish, Thursday curry), with roast lunch on Sundays (no food Sun eve). Q♨❀◐♣●P🚌(2)🐾📶

Hemingby

Coach & Horses 🄻

Church Lane, LN9 5QF (1 mile from A158 at Baumber)
⏲ 12-2 (not Mon & Tue), 6-11; 12-2, 7-11 Sat; 12-3, 7-10.30 Sun ☎ (01507) 578280
Beer range varies Ⓗ
Set against a backdrop of the Lincolnshire Wolds, this pub has been owned by the same couple for over 20 years. Low wooden beams run throughout the building and an impressive fireplace separates the main bar from the darts/pool area. Three beers are available with a dedicated pump for a mild. Excellent home-cooked food is served at reasonable prices. Q♨❀◐⛺♣P🐾

Holton le Clay

Royal Oak

Louth Road, DN36 5AB
⏲ 12-11 (11.30 Fri & Sat) ☎ (01472) 828583
Black Sheep Best Bitter; St Austell Tribute; Sharp's Doom Bar Ⓗ
A friendly village local. There is a standard public bar with TV, pool, darts and dominoes. The lounge is a lovely haven of peace; a glass-roofed extension has been seamlessly added and has the feel of a living room. The pub serves a good selection of food lunchtimes daily and evenings Monday-Saturday. A quiz is hosted during the week and live entertainment once a month on a Saturday. ♨❀◐♣P🚌(51)🐾📶

Horbling

Plough Inn

4 Spring Lane, NG34 0PF
⏲ 11.30-2.30, 6.30-11.30; 11.30-midnight Fri & Sat; 12-10.30 Sun ☎ (01529) 240263 🌐 theploughinnhorblingltd.co.uk
Adnams Ghost Ship; guest beers Ⓗ
A low-beamed true community pub, built in 1832 and owned by the parish council, in a quiet village. In addition to the lounge and bar, its snug is surely one of the smallest and most intimate of its kind. Beers are often from microbreweries, and change regularly. Home-cooked meals are available in the bar and restaurant. Spring wells are a feature just a few yards down the lane. ♨❀◐♿♣●P🐾

Horncastle

King's Head

16 Bull Ring, LN9 5HU
⏲ 12-midnight (11 Mon; 2am Fri & Sat); 12-1am Sun
☎ (01507) 523360
Batemans XB; guest beers Ⓗ
A comfortable and friendly pub with a single bar/lounge that nevertheless accommodates two separate drinking areas. Three beers from Batemans are mostly on handpump. Unusually for this locality, the building has a thatched roof, hence its local name, the Thatch. Reputedly the pub inspired an 00 gauge Hornby model, an example of which is displayed behind the bar. In summer the exterior is bedecked with hanging baskets and it has won Bateman's Floral Display competition. ♨❀🚌🐾📶

Hubberts Bridge

Wheatsheaf Inn

Station Road, PE20 3QR
⏲ 12-2 (not Mon-Wed), 5-10.30; 12-2 Sun
☎ (01205) 290347 🌐 thewheatsheafinn.org
Batemans XB; Sharp's Doom Bar; guest beer Ⓗ
Standing on the banks of the South Forty Foot Navigation, with moorings nearby, this free house has been a pub for over 100 years and is run by a family partnership. It is planned that the waterway will eventually link with the entire Midland canal system; currently access is via the River Witham at Boston. Occasional beer festivals are held and there is regular live music throughout the year. Food is sourced locally. Opening hours are extended during the summer. Q❀◐⛺≹♣P

Ingoldmells

Countryman 🄻

Chapel Road, PE25 1ND
⏲ 12-midnight (winter hours vary) ☎ (01754) 872268
🌐 countryman-ingoldmells.co.uk
Leila Cottage Leila's Lazy Days, Ace Ale, Lincolnshire Life; guest beer Ⓗ

The privately owned Countryman appears to be a modern building but it incorporates the early 19th-century Leila Cottage, which gives its name to the brewery behind the pub. A notorious smuggler, James Waite, used to reside here when Ingoldmells was a wild and lonely place, but he certainly wouldn't recognise the current holiday coast, with Skegness, Butlin's and Fantasy Island nearby. Noticeboards give brewery, pub and beer information for visitors. The pub is on northern bus routes from Skegness.

Irnham

Griffin Inn

15 Bulby Road, NG33 4JG
closed Mon & Tue; 11-3, 6-11; 12-3, 6-10.30 Sun
(01476) 550201 thegriffinirnham.co.uk
Oakham JHB; guest beers H
A recently refurbished 200-year-old stone-built property with a bar area serving Oakham JHB and two changing personally sourced microbrewery beers. It has two separate dining rooms offering a wide selection of food, from the traditional to the innovative. Vintage and classic car evenings take place on the first Wednesday of the month from April to September. Awarded Best UK B&B by Les Routiers in 2012. QP

Kirkby on Bain

Ebrington Arms

Main Street, LN10 6YT
12-2 (not Mon), 6-11 (01526) 354560
ebringtonarms.com
Adnams Broadside; Batemans XB; Black Sheep Golden Sheep; Sharp's Doom Bar; guest beers H
Attractive country pub close to the River Bain and dating from 1610. World War II airmen used to slot coins into the ceiling beams to pay for beer when they returned from missions over Germany. Sadly, many of these coins are still in situ and make a unique memorial to the dead. The restaurant offers good food made with local produce (booking advised). There is a handy caravan site within a mile of the pub. QP(65)

Lincoln

Adam & Eve Tavern

25 Lindum Road, LN2 1NT
12-11 (midnight Fri & Sat) (01522) 537108
adamandevelincoln.co.uk
Castle Rock Harvest Pale; Greene King Abbot; guest beers H
Situated in between the city's cathedral and cultural quarters, the Adam & Eve dates back as far as the 1700s, reputedly making it one of Lincoln's oldest taverns. The pub has various seating areas: one for meetings or gatherings, one for darts, one for pool and, in the main bar, a large TV for sporting events. Live music features on a Saturday. If you are heading to the pub from town, prepare yourself for the hill. P

Dog & Bone

10 John Street, LN2 5BH
4.30-11; 12-11 Fri-Sun (01522) 522403
dogandbonelincoln.co.uk
Batemans Black & White, XB, Yella Belly Gold; guest beers H
A warm and welcoming community pub with a traditional character. The bar counter is in the centre of the pub, with the main bar area to one side and a slightly smaller lounge opposite. Books and art grace the walls and add to the surroundings. Outside to the rear is a charming garden which is a delightful place to drink in the warmer months. Regular events, including live music and pub quizzes, take place throughout the year. Q(4)

Golden Eagle

21 High Street, LN5 8BD
11-11 (11.30 Fri & Sat); 12-11 Sun (01522) 521058
Batemans XB; Castle Rock Harvest Pale; Fuller's London Pride; guest beers H
Formerly an old coaching inn, this two-roomed establishment sometimes has as many as nine changing guest beers and Castle Rock ales on offer, plus up to three ciders. The bar can get busy, especially on match days. The lounge is quiet and cosy, with photos and football programmes on the walls. A first-class beer garden awaits outside, with covered seating, lighting and heating. Occasional beer festivals feature, live music most weekends, and a Friday night quiz. Food is served throughout the day (lunchtime only Sun). P

Jolly Brewer

27 Broadgate, LN2 5AQ
12-11 (midnight Fri & Sat); 12-8 Sun (01522) 528583
jollybrewer.org
Tom Wood's Lincoln Gold; Welbeck Abbey Henrietta, Portland Black; guest beers H
Situated near the foot of Lindum Hill, this free house has a warm welcome for all drinkers. Quirky Art Deco is used throughout the building. The walls usually display artworks, often available for purchase. Live music and music-themed events are hosted inside at weekends, or outside in the beer garden during the summer months. Real perry and ciders are always available, as is a small range of home-made food. P

Morning Star

11 Greetwell Gate, LN2 4AW
11-midnight; 12-11 Sun (01522) 527079
Draught Bass; Ruddles Best Bitter; Timothy Taylor Golden Best; Wells Bombardier; guest beers H
A long-established real ale pub dating back to the 1700s and located just a few minutes' walk from Lincoln Cathedral. A lengthy bar greets you on entry, with a cosy fire to the right. Pictures of historic Lincoln adorn the walls. The pubs hosts occasional live music while a quiz is held every Tuesday evening. Two changing guest beers are available. QP

Strugglers Inn

83 Westgate, LN1 3BG
12-1am (11 Mon & Tue; midnight Wed); 12-11 Sun
(01522) 535023
Timothy Taylor Landlord; guest beers H
Located in Lincoln's cathedral quarter at the base of the castle walls is this small and popular pub, a winner of many awards and recently registered as a community asset. Eight handpumps serve a changing and interesting selection usually featuring local brewery and rare beers. Upcoming ales are listed on a chalkboard above one of the two fireplaces and pumpclips of previous ales cover the walls. The beer garden in the rear is a summer suntrap. Q(7,8)

Victoria
6 Union Road, LN1 3BJ
11-midnight (1am Fri & Sat); 12-midnight Sun
(01522) 541000
Batemans XB, Yella Belly Gold; Castle Rock Harvest Pale; Timothy Taylor Landlord; guest beers H
Below the castle walls, this hostelry was built in the 1800s during the Industrial Revolution. Now in its 31st consecutive year in this Guide, this small and friendly pub with a long narrow bar and cosy lounge offers four regular and three guest ales, plus ciders and perry. Live music plays on most Saturday evenings in the bar, or occasionally outdoors in the pleasant seating area during the summer months. Q

Wig & Mitre
30 Steep Hill, LN2 1LU
8.30am-11 (9.30 Sun) (01522) 535190
wigandmitre.com
Black Sheep Best Bitter; Everards Tiger; Oakham JHB; guest beer H
Located towards the top of the historic and aptly named Steep Hill, the Wig is close to the cathedral, castle and Bailgate shopping area. It occupies buildings dating from the 14th century. The spacious, beamed interior comprises characterful rooms, with a bar on each of the two floors. A free house, it is renowned for the quality of its food but happily welcomes drinkers. The pub is family-friendly throughout and dogs are welcome downstairs. Q

Little Cawthorpe

Royal Oak Inn (Splash)
Watery lane, LN11 8LZ (right off main road to Legbourne then left onto Buston Lane, through ford and turn left)
11-midnight (01507) 600750 royaloaksplash.co.uk
Black Sheep Best Bitter; Greene King IPA; guest beers H
Known locally as the Splash because of the picturesque ford nearby, this 400-year-old inn is situated in its own large lawned gardens on the edge of the Lincolnshire Wolds near Louth. Four beers are regularly available, and often a guest ale from a local brewery. Three restaurants cover most culinary requirements and themed evenings are popular. The en-suite rooms are often used by visitors to Cadwell Park or explorers of the Wolds.
P

Louth

Boar's Head
12 Newmarket, LN11 9HH
closed Mon; 11-11 (01507) 603561
Batemans XB, XXXB; guest beer H
The Boar's Head is a traditional three-room inn just outside the centre of the market town of Louth. It is well known locally for its real ales. Pub games include darts, dominoes and pool. Thursday is Cattle Market day, when the pub opens early. Lunches are served daily (bookings are sometimes required for Sunday lunchtime).

Brown Cow
133 Newmarket, LN11 9EG (top of Newmarket on jct of Church St)
5-11; 12-3 Fri; 12-11 Sat & Sun (01507) 605146
Adnams Broadside; Black Sheep Best Bitter; Castle Rock Harvest Pale; Fuller's London Pride; guest beer H
Friendly town pub with a lively atmosphere and, most importantly, great beer. A free quiz is held every Sunday night and the local folk club meets here on a Tuesday evening. The popular bistro serves traditional home-cooked meals, made with locally-sourced products (food is available Thu-Sun). The pub is a great community meeting place.
QP(51)

Cobbles Bar
New Street, LN11 9PU (off Cornmarket)
10-midnight 07736 275262
Black Sheep Ale; Marston's Pedigree; guest beer H
Traditional pub-style bar based in the centre of town, with friendly staff at all times. This small but accommodating venue has multiple personalities, from a bustling coffee shop serving light lunches to a busy pre-club local with a DJ and live music at weekends. It has a good beer trade, with two contrasting cask ales, as well as a huge selection of exotic spirits. Disabled access is right through the front doors.

Gas Lamp Lounge
13 Thames Street, LN11 7AD (bottom of Thames St by factories)
5 (12 Sat & Sun)-11 (01507) 607661
fulstowbrewery.com/News.html
Fulstow Common, Marsh Mild, Northway IPA; guest beer H
A unique bar – one of only 22 in the UK lit by gas lamps. It has no music or bandits, just good pub traditions, serving four regular beers from the upstairs brewery, plus a guest ale. There are outdoor canalside benches for enjoying a drink during the summer, and inside is a roaring logburner to sit beside in the winter months.
QP

Joseph Morton
Pawnshop Passage, LN11 9EZ (small alley off Mercer Row)
8am-midnight (1am Fri & Sat) (01507) 353700
Batemans XB; Greene King Abbot; Ruddles County; guest beers H
A Wetherspoon pub, opened in 2011, just off the town centre, offering good-value food and drink every day. The former warehouse was built between 1808 and 1834, with cast-iron wall plates bearing the name of the local ironmonger, Joseph Morton.

Ludford

White Hart
Magna Mile, LN8 6AD
closed Mon; 12-2 (not Tue-Thu), 6-11; 11-2, 6-11 Sat; 12-3.30, 7-11 Sun (01507) 313489
Beer range varies H
A flagship ale pub where Mick and Jenny do their best to get as many beers behind the bar as possible. Formerly a coaching house, dating from the 18th century, this two-roomed, rural village inn is close to the Viking Way and popular with hikers and ramblers. Four different guest beers are offered. The licensees pride themselves on serving real ale from microbreweries. All food is home made using ingredients from local suppliers, and meals are available lunchtimes and evenings.
QP

Market Deeping

Vine Inn 𝕃

19 Church Street, PE6 8AN

4-11; 12-11.30 Fri; 12-11 Sat & Sun ☎ (01778) 218622

Sharp's Doom Bar; Wells Eagle IPA; guest beers Ⓗ

A free house since 2011, this small and friendly two-bar pub was once a Victorian school. The bar features oak beams and stone floors. There is a large patio at the rear. Five handpumps dispense two regular beers and a constantly changing range of guests, usually including a strong ale and local Hopshackle beers. No food is served but free nibbles are provided Sunday lunchtime and early during the week. The TV is only used for major sporting events. ❀P🚌(101)🐾📶

Marshchapel

White Horse

Seadyke Way, DN36 5SX

4-11; 12-midnight Fri-Sun ☎ (01472) 388280

Beer range varies Ⓗ

A traditional pub just outside Grimsby. It is a jewel in the countryside, and people travel from afar for the well-kept beers and home-cooked food. It has large gardens, a children's play area and there is a large car park at the front. Two varying guest beers include the likes of Ruddles County and Moorhouse's Black Cat. Bingo is held on the last Saturday of the month, while there is a Friday free quiz and a regular musicians' open night.
❀◑◐♣P🚌(50)📶

Messingham

Pooleys

46 High Street, DN17 3NT

closed Mon; 6-11; 7-11 Sun ☎ (01724) 762220

Batemans XB; guest beers Ⓗ

Pooleys is an attractive, well-appointed village tea room by day and a busy licensed bar in the evenings, popular with local drinkers and visitors alike. It has four rooms, heated by log-burning stoves in the colder months. The bar area serves Batemans XB as a stock beer plus three rotating guests, always including one golden beer. Fifty-two malt whiskies are also stocked to add to the choice available. The Stagecoach Scunthorpe to Lincoln bus route passes through the village.
Q♿🚌(100,103)📶

North Hykeham

Centurion

Newark Road, LN6 8LB

11-11 (midnight Thu-Sat) ☎ (01522) 509814

Abbeydale Moonshine; Tetley Bitter; Wells Bombardier; guest beers Ⓗ

Ales feature strongly in this community local, with regularly changing guests; you can even try before you buy, within reason. Comfortable seating and modern decor give a cosy home-away-from-home feel. This is a pub for all seasons, with its spacious garden patio and roaring fires. Food is a staple, but you are more than welcome to pop in for a pint or two. Children are permitted in the family dining area for well-priced bar meals.
❀◑◐♿⇌(Hykeham)♣P🚌(27,46)📶

North Kelsey

Butchers Arms

Middle Street, LN7 6EH (off main road through village)

4-midnight (1.30am Fri); 12-1.30am Sat; 12-midnight Sun ☎ (01652) 678002

Ruddles County; Tom Wood's Best Bitter; guest beer Ⓗ

This is the epitome of a traditional village pub, open plan in design, with a polished wood bar and overhanging hop bine. Simply but comfortably furnished in rustic style, it has a welcoming real fire. Beers from the Tom Wood's and Greene King ranges are usually available, supplemented by an occasional guest beer. Weekly quiz nights are held, and a games area is used for darts. The pub has an attractive beer garden framed by mature trees. A hidden gem worth finding. ❀♿♣P

Norton Disney

Green Man 𝕃

Main Street, LN6 9JU

12-3, 5.30-11; 12-11 Sat; 12-10 Sun ☎ (01522) 789804

Black Sheep Ale; guest beers Ⓗ

At the heart of the village, the interior is modern and cosy with a real fire and TV in the bar area. Black Sheep is the regular beer, alongside three guest ales, sometimes sourced from Lincolnshire breweries. At least 12 real ciders are also served and these too change on a regular basis. There is a separate room for diners; bar snacks are also available. Outside is a large car park and garden.
Q❀◑◐♿♣🍎P🐾📶

Old Bolingbroke

Black Horse Inn

Moat Lane, PE23 4HH

closed Mon; 8.30am-11 Tue; 12-3, 7-11 ☎ (01790) 763388

Milestone Black Pearl; Young's Bitter; guest beers Ⓗ

In a splendid walking area, this fine old country inn has 14th-century origins but was largely rebuilt in 1930. Henry IV was born at nearby Bolingbroke Castle, which was besieged during the Civil War. Still part of the Duchy of Lancaster, the Black Horse is a great place to visit when exploring the Lincolnshire Wolds. Friday fish night is a speciality, and there are also themed food nights. Lunchtime meals are served at the weekend only.
Q❀◑◐♿⛺♣🍎P🐾📶

Quadring

White Hart

7 Town Drove, PE11 4PU

12-3 (not Tue-Thu), 6.30-11; 5-11 Fri ☎ (01775) 822178

Greene King IPA Ⓗ

Friendly low-beamed village inn, popular with locals. One end of the pub was previously a small shop and at the rear the large attractive garden once housed a bakery. It serves just one, occasionally changing, real ale at a time, always in excellent condition. Buses from Boston and Spalding stop at the nearby crossroads (not evenings or Sundays). Pool and darts are played in the bar – the landlord often joins in the pool.
Q❀♿♣P🚌(59)🐾

Ruskington

Shoulder of Mutton

11 Church Street, NG34 9DU

⏲ 12-11 ☎ (01526) 832220

John Smith's Bitter; Sharp's Doom Bar; Wells Bombardier; guest beer 🄷

A popular and thriving pub in the heart of the village that attracts customers of all ages. It has low wooden ceilings in its two main rooms and is probably one of the oldest buildings in the village; reputedly it once housed a butcher's shop, hence the name. Although additions have been made in recent years they have not spoilt the essential character. There is a separate pool room. ❀♿⇌♣P🚌(31)🐾📶

Saxilby

Anglers

65 High Street, LN1 2HA

⏲ 11.30-12.30am; 12-midnight Sun ☎ (01522) 702200

Greene King IPA; Theakston Best Bitter; guest beers 🄷

In the same hands for over 20 years, this village hostelry is home to various pub sports teams, giving it a lively atmosphere at times. The lounge bar is quieter and has many old photographs of the village. The two guest beers are from the pubco list. No food is served, but there is a chip shop across the road. The station and bus stops are close by, as are visitor moorings on the Fossdyke, the country's oldest canal. ❀⇌♣P🚌(100,105)

Scampton

Dambusters Inn 🄻

23 High Street, LN1 2SD

⏲ 5-9.30 Mon; 12-3, 5-10 Tue (11 Wed & Thu; 12.30am Fri); 12-12.30am Sat; 12-6 Sun ☎ (01522) 731333

🌐 dambustersinn.co.uk

Poachers Shy Talk Bitter; Thwaites Lancaster Bomber; guest beers 🄷

Is this a pub or a museum? Both! Dambusters memorabilia and ephemera cover the walls, while the bar boasts at least five beers and two ciders and perries; two ales are from Greg's Brewery behind the pub. Add in good food and you see why the place is popular. Beer festivals are in May (around the anniversary of the Dambusters raid) and autumn. The pub is at the end of RAF Scampton's runway – look out for the Red Arrows. Q🐴❀◑♣P🚌(103)

Scawby

Sutton Arms

10 West Street, DN20 9AN (on main road through village)

⏲ 11.30-midnight ☎ (01652) 652430

Theakston Best Bitter; guest beers 🄷

Well-appointed village local with a strong emphasis on food. A central bar serves an open-plan dining area with a small snug on one side, the latter used mostly for drinking. There is an extensive menu plus daily specials available lunchtimes and evenings. Steak night is Wednesday. The Theakston beer is supplemented by three rotating guest ales, often from Axholme, Batemans, Grafters, Milestone and Tom Wood's. There is a quiz on Sunday evening and live music once a month. ❀◑P

Scunthorpe

Berkeley Hotel ★

Doncaster Road, DN15 7DS (½ mile from end of M181)

⏲ 11.30-2.30, 5-11; 12-11 Fri & Sat; 12-10.30 Sun ☎ (01724) 842333

Samuel Smith Old Brewery Bitter 🄷

A roomy Samuel Smith's pub, identified by CAMRA as having a nationally important historic interior for its 1930s Art Deco interiors. The landscaped front entrance opens into a large lobby area, leading to two bars. The main lounge bar has a real fire, the second is a spacious room with a ballroom leading off. A side entrance provides access to the public bar and rear beer garden. The pub is five minutes' walk from Glanford Park football ground. Q🐴❀🛏◑♿♣🍎P🚌

Blue Bell

1-7 Oswald Road, DN15 7PU (at town centre crossroads)

⏲ 8am-midnight (1am Sat) ☎ (01724) 863921

Greene King Abbot; Ruddles Best Bitter; guest beers 🄷

Popular Wetherspoon pub with an open-plan layout on two levels. The upper level is a family and dining area with a guarded fire; the lower level, also used for dining, has wooden and carpeted floors with a mix of high and low seating. There is a small heated patio area at the rear for smokers. Beer festivals are held regularly and events such as Burns Night and Valentine's Day are celebrated. A muted TV screens sport/news. 🐴◑♿🚌📶

Malt Shovel 🍷 🄻

219 Ashby High Street, Ashby, DN16 2JP (in Ashby Broadway shopping area)

⏲ 10-11 (midnight Fri & Sat); 12-11 Sun ☎ (01724) 843318

Exmoor Gold; Tom Wood's Best Bitter; guest beers 🄷

Comfortably furnished single-room pub with a conservatory dining/drinking area and the widest choice of beer and cider in the town. It is one of only a handful of pubs elevated to the prestigious Oakademy of Excellence, awarded for perfectly served permanent Oakham ales. It gets busy at lunch and teatimes thanks to its good-value home-cooked food. Magazines, newspapers, a book swap and members-only snooker facilities are available. Quizzes are on Tuesdays and Thursdays, with live music on alternate Saturdays and a monthly folk night on Sundays. ❀◑🍎🚌

Skendleby

Blacksmiths Arms

Main Road, PE23 4QE

⏲ 12-3 (not Mon), 5.30-11; 12-4 Sun ☎ (01754) 890662

Batemans XB; guest beers 🄷

A traditional country pub, dating back to the 18th century, nestling on the south-east edge of the Lincolnshire Wolds. Ducking beneath the low door lintel, you discover the gem of a small quarry-tiled snug, complete with range and settles, with the cellar visible through a glass panel behind the bar. The dining room at the rear incorporates the building's former well. There is a newly refurbished restaurant and a conservatory. On the last Sunday in the month it is open 7am until late with live music. Q🐴❀◑♣P🚌(96)🐾📶

Skillington

Cross Swords 🏆

The Square, NG33 5HB
⏲ 12-2 (not Mon), 7-11; 12-2, 6-11 Fri & Sat; 12-2 Sun
☎ (01476) 861132 🌐 thecross-swordsinn.co.uk
Phipps NBC IPA; guest beer [H]
Impressive stone-built pub dating from the early to mid-1800s and voted local CAMRA Country Pub of the Year 2014. The current hosts, Harold and Linda, have owned the inn since 1991, with the ales on the bar supplied by Grainstore Brewery and other local brewers. Quality pub food is always available and the pub boasts three letting cottages.
❀🛏◑◐P

Sleaford

Carre Arms Hotel

Mareham Lane, NG34 7JP
⏲ 10-11 ☎ (01529) 303156 🌐 carrearmshotel.co.uk
Beer range varies [H]
A privately run hotel previously owned by Bass, adjacent to the Bass Sleaford maltings complex which is now awaiting a regeneration scheme. It has a comfortable bar area with two rooms, offering two or three real ales which change regularly. Draught cider is often available on handpump. An extensive food menu is served in the bar area or restaurant. 🐴❀🛏◑◐♿⇌🍎P🚌

Packhorse Inn

7 Northgate, NG34 7BH
⏲ 8am-midnight ☎ (01529) 308730
Courage Directors; Greene King Abbot; Ruddles Best Bitter; guest beers [H]
An 18th-century coaching inn on the London to Lincoln road that has had several names during its lifetime, reverting to the original name when taken over by Wetherspoon a few years ago. Despite being remodelled as partly open plan, it retains an intimate atmosphere. As the Lion Hotel it hosted the opening dinner for the Sleaford Railway, an event that marked the start of the decline in the coaching trade. Q🐴❀◑◐♿⇌🍎🚌📶

Snitterby

Royal Oak

High Street, DN21 4TP (1½ miles from A15)
⏲ 5 (12 Sat)-midnight; 12-9 Sun ☎ (01673) 818273
Rooster's Buckeye; Thwaites Original [H]**; guest beers** [H]/[G]
Traditional family-run community pub in a village setting. It was selected for the UK Top 150 Local Real Ale Pubs in 2014, and was local CAMRA branch Pub of the Year in 2013. Up to eight real ales are on tap, more on bank holidays. In 2013 alone 138 guest ales from 63 breweries were served. The interior is light and airy with wooden floors and real fires, and has recently been sympathetically extended. Outside, a seating area overlooks a stream. Q🐴❀🍎P📺🐾

South Ormsby

Massingberd Arms

Brinkhill Road, LN11 8QS (1 mile off A16)
⏲ closed Mon; 12-2.30, 6-11; 12-11 Sun ☎ (01507) 480492
Thwaites Original; guest beer [H]
An old, traditional country pub situated in the heart of the Lincolnshire Wolds, a designated Area of Outstanding Natural Beauty. It does home-cooked food and holds a quiz for charity every Wednesday night. The recently upgraded dining room now has a wood-burning fire. The pub closes on a Monday. Set in a beautiful location, walkers are welcome.
Q🐴❀◑◐♿P

South Reston

Waggon & Horses

Main Road, LN11 8JQ
⏲ 11-11 ☎ (01507) 450364
🌐 waggonandhorsesreston.co.uk
Batemans XB; Marston's Burton Bitter; guest beer [H]
A great country pub that is warm and inviting, standing in the small village of South Reston not far from one of the rare hedgehog sanctuaries. Open fires greet you in a setting that is a mixture of modern and new. The Waggon & Horses serves excellent ales, including many from local micros. High quality food is available every day. A large dining room is located to the rear (booking for meals is advisable). Q◑◐♿♣🚌(9)

Spalding

Priors Oven

1 Sheep Market, PE11 1BH
⏲ 12-midnight; 12-11 Sun
Beer range varies [G]
The first micropub to be opened in Lincolnshire. The building has quite a history and is believed to be 800 years old; it was originally the prison of the local priory. Its more recent use was as a bakery and it then became a pub in mid-December 2013. The ground floor bar has a domed ceiling, and a stone spiral staircase leads up to a comfortable lounge room. Q⇌🍎🚌

Red Lion Hotel

Market Place, PE11 1SU
⏲ 10-midnight ☎ (01775) 722869
🌐 redlionhotel-spalding.co.uk
Draught Bass; Fuller's Bengal Lancer; Greene King Abbot; Wells Bombardier [H]
A cosy and welcoming one-room traditional hotel bar popular with locals and visitors, overlooking the marketplace, with tables and chairs outside in the fine weather. It is a regular entry in the Guide due to its consistently well-kept range of cask ales, which the bar staff take great pride in serving in top condition. It is a rare outlet for Bass in the locality. 🐴🛏♿⇌P🚌🐾📶

Stamford

Green Man [L]

29 Scotgate, PE9 2YQ
⏲ 11 (12 Sun)-midnight ☎ (01780) 753598
Castle Rock Harvest Pale; Fuller's London Pride; guest beers [H]
Dating from 1796, this stone-built former coaching inn comprises an L-shaped split-level bar, with a real fire. Up to eight ales and seven ciders, complemented by a good range of European bottled beers, are on offer. Two beer festivals are held, at Easter and September, on the secluded patio, which has one of only five stepping stones from the inn's coaching days. A regular entry in the Guide, the pub has much beer memorabilia adorning the walls. ❀🛏◑♣🍎📺🚌(201)🐾📶

Jolly Brewer 𝕃

1 Foundry Road, PE9 2PP

11-midnight; 12-11.30 Sun ☎ (01780) 755141

jollybrewer.com

Oakham JHB; Sharp's Doom Bar; guest beers 🄷

This pub, with a stone-built exterior and an L-shaped room around the bar, dates from 1830. An adjoining small room serves as a dining area. The home-cooked food is locally sourced. It is home to pool, darts, crib and domino teams from the local community, and offers beers from six handpumps from local and countrywide brewers. One handpump serves traditional cider, and a good range of malt whiskies is available. There are plans for a small brewery on site.
Q❀◐♣●P🚌(9,202)🐾📶

Tobie Norris

12 Saint Paul's Street, PE9 2BE

11.30-11; 12-10.30 Sun ☎ (01780) 753800

tobienorris.com

Adnams Southwold Bitter; Castle Rock Harvest Pale; guest beers 🄷

The building, parts of which date back to 1280, was bought by Tobie Norris in 1617 and used as a bell foundry. Immediately before its award-winning conversion into a pub it was the RAFA Club, and it was then split into many small rooms with real fires, stone floors and low beams. Five handpumps serve beers from local and countrywide brewers. Specialities of the house include pizzas with unusual toppings. Two beer festivals are held each year. Q❀◐♣●🚌(202,203)🐾

Stickford

Red Lion Inn 𝕃

Church Road, PE22 8EP

closed Mon & Tue; 7-11; 4-11.30 Fri & Sat; 12-10.30 Sun ☎ (01205) 480395 redlionstickford.co.uk

Batemans XB; guest beer 🄷

This pub name is the most common in England, and is frequently found hereabouts because the red lion was a heraldic emblem of the 14th-century John of Gaunt, Earl of Lancaster and Lord of the Manor at nearby Bolingbroke Castle. This two-bar cosy, friendly pub has a small room used as a restaurant and for private functions. Food is served evenings and Sunday lunchtimes using local produce, such as rabbit pie. Beer festivals are held. There are two en-suite letting bedrooms.
Q❀🛏◐⛺♣●P🚌(113)🐾📶

Sutterton

Thatched Cottage

Pools Lane, PE20 2EZ

11.30-11.30 ☎ (01205) 460870

thatchedcottagerestaurant.co.uk

Batemans XB; Greene King IPA; Morland Old Speckled Hen; guest beer 🄷

Picturesque thatched 17th-century listed building, a rarity in fen country, which was a private house until 1985. Although extended and modernised to the rear, the bar and separate dining room exhibit a wealth of ancient timbers and inglenook fireplaces. Tall people beware! Behind the pub is a country farm store, and meat is butchered and cured on the premises. Outside is an area for giant chess, pétanque and quoits, together with a country park containing a natural burial ground and arboretum. Q🔥❀◐♿♣P🚌(113)📶

Swineshead

Pig & Whistle

Market Place, PE20 3LJ

5.30-11; 12-11 Sat; 12-4, 7.30-11 Sun ☎ (01205) 821381

Banks's Mild; Fuller's London Pride; guest beers 🄷

Years ago the pub was called the Green Dragon; its fortunes gradually declined, it became run down and, despite a change of name, eventually closed. Now the current owners have brought it back to life as a vibrant and thriving village local, successfully blending old and new to recreate a genuine community pub with an emphasis on beer and traditional pub games. Guest beers come from a wide range of breweries and the food comprises home-made pizzas and bar snacks. ❀♣●P🚌(K59)

Wheatsheaf

Market Place, PE20 3LJ

12-3 (not Mon), 6-11; 12-11 Fri-Sun ☎ (01205) 820349

wheatsheafhotel.co.uk

Batemans XB; guest beers 🄷

The Wheatsheaf is a friendly local which can trace its origins back 300 years to Georgian times. The comfortable bar has an oak-beamed ceiling and a real fire in winter. The Sports Bar is a lively location for traditional games and sports fixtures on TV. The restaurant offers a varied menu for lunch and evening meals (closed Mon). There are tables in the garden to enjoy the sun.
🔥❀🛏◐♿♣P🚌(K59)🐾📶

Swinhope

Click 'em Inn

Binbrook Road, LN8 6BS (2 miles N of Binbrook on B1203)

12-3 (not Mon-Wed), 5-11; 12-11.30 Fri & Sat; 12-10.30 Sun ☎ (01472) 398253 clickem-inn.co.uk

Timothy Taylor Landlord; guest beers 🄷

Formerly the Talbot, this Lincolnshire Wolds pub derives its name from a clicking gate for sheep. It is renowned for its traditional pub food and is popular with walkers and cyclists. Continuous Guide entries and CAMRA Country Pub of the Year awards stand as testament to the landlord's commitment to real ale. Five handpulls feature beers from independent and small regional brewers (updates are available on the pub website). The house beer, Terry's Tipple, is from Batemans. ❀◐♣P🐾📶

Tattershall Thorpe

Blue Bell Inn

Thorpe Road, LN4 4PE

closed Mon; 12-3, 6-11; 12-4 Sun ☎ (01526) 342206

bluebell-inn.com

Batemans XB; Tom Wood's Bomber County; guest beers 🄷

This ancient building, in a delightful location, has 13th-century origins and is one of Lincolnshire's oldest inns. It has a large open fire and beamed ceilings that are covered in signatures and photographs of airmen from World War II RAF squadrons who used the pub, including the 617 Dambusters and 627 Pathfinders. King Henry VIII reputedly visited the Blue Bell and there is a ghost in residence. Q🔥❀◐♿⛺♣P📶

Tetford

White Hart

East Street, LN9 6QQ

12-3 (not Mon), 5-11 ☎ (01507) 533255

Brains The Rev James H; guest beers H/G

A historic village hostelry where Tennyson and Johnson have both stayed, offering real ale, good food and a friendly and relaxed atmosphere. A traditional country pub and restaurant, it is nestled in the heart of the Lincolnshire Wolds between Horncastle and Louth, and ideally positioned for Cadwell Park race track.

Tetney Lock

Crown & Anchor

Lock Road, DN36 5UW

12-11 ☎ (01472) 388291

Sharp's Doom Bar; guest beers H

Overlooking the historic but now defunct Louth Navigation Canal, this is a convenient watering hole for lovers of outdoor pursuits. Dogs are welcome in the public bar, which has a cosy open fire. Outside, there is a pleasant garden and children's play area at the rear, while at the front there is a patio overlooking the canal and an awning suitable for smokers. Please note that on Sundays only the traditional roast lunch is served. Q P

Threekingham

Three Kings Inn

Saltersway, NG34 0AU

closed Mon; 12-3, 6-11 (10.30 Sun) ☎ (01529) 240249
thethreekingsinn.com

Draught Bass; Timothy Taylor Landlord; guest beer H

A classic country inn with charm and character. Its bright and comfortable lounge bar with attractive rural prints, and panelled dining room serving locally-sourced food, are deservedly popular with locals and visitors. Guest beers are usually from independent brewers. There is a pleasant beer terrace and garden for the summer months and a large function room. The pub's name refers to the slaying, by the Saxons, of three Danish chieftains in battle in 870 at nearby Stow; look for the effigies above the entrance. P

Waddington

Three Horseshoes

High Street, LN5 9RF

12 (3 Mon)-midnight; 11-midnight Sat; 12-11 Sun
☎ (01522) 720448

John Smith's Bitter; guest beers H

A small community pub in the middle of the village just a short bus journey from Lincoln. The four frequently changing guest beers are mainly sourced from microbreweries. The main bar area is the heart of the pub and is complemented by a smaller lounge, with a real fire in winter. Various sports teams have made the pub their own and have been joined by poker players on Thursday evening and televised sport, giving the bar a lively ambience. (1,13)

Wainfleet

Batemans Brewery Visitors Centre

Salem Bridge Brewery, Mill Lane, PE24 4JE

11.30-4 (closed Mon & Tue Oct-Apr); closed Jan
☎ (01754) 882009 bateman.co.uk

Batemans Black & White, XB, Yella Belly Gold, XXXB; guest beer H

Visiting the brewery's visitors centre provides the chance to experience the blend of Bateman's proud 140-plus years of craft brewing tradition with its forward-looking outlook. Mr George's Bar, within the iconic windmill, is the ideal venue to sample a range of the beers. Further entertainment is to be found with brewery tours, featuring the Theatre of Beers, and in the pleasant beer garden with its games. A good range of Lincolnshire food is served 12-2pm. Tours are at 12.30pm and 2.30pm in summer, 2.30pm in winter.
Q P (7)

Westwoodside

Carpenter's Arms

Newbigg, DN9 2AT

4 (2 Sat)-11.30; 12-10.30 Sun ☎ (01427) 752416

Black Sheep Best Bitter; Brains The Rev James; Caledonian Deuchars IPA; guest beers H

This popular village local takes an active part in local community life and has raised significant sums of money for charity. Under the present licensees the pub has become a regular in this Guide. Five ales are usually on offer, including two from micros. The Carpenter's hosts a variety of community events and also participates in the local Haxey Hood game each January. Q P

Willingham by Stow

Half Moon

23 High Street, DN21 5JZ

12-2 (not Mon & Tue), 6-11; 12-11 Sat; 12-10.30 Sun
☎ (01427) 788340 graftersbrewery.com

Beer range varies H

Home to Grafters Brewery, this popular village pub goes from strength to strength. It offers four varied Grafters' beers, and four additional pumps serve rotating guests, mainly from micros. Seasonal Grafters' beers are also sold when brewed. The renowned home-cooked fish and chips are a must, available lunchtimes and evenings, Tuesday to Friday, all day Saturday, and Sunday lunchtimes (booking recommended). Brewery tours, including food and a tasting session, can be arranged by appointment. Q

Willoughton

Stirrup Inn

1 Templefield Road, DN21 5RZ

5 (3 Sat)-midnight; 12-11.30 Sun ☎ (01427) 668270

Black Sheep Best Bitter; guest beer H

Built from local Lincolnshire limestone, this hidden gem in an out-of-the-way location is well worth seeking out, and you can be sure of a warm welcome. The pub oozes character, with a roaring log fire in winter, and is popular with locals and folk from further afield. A choice of ales is always available, with Black Sheep Best Bitter a permanent fixture, plus two changing guests. Quizzes are well supported and traditional pub games are played. Q P

Winterton

George Hogg

25 Market Street, DN15 9PT

2-11 (midnight Fri); 9.30am-midnight Sat; 9.30am-11 Sun

(01724) 732270 thegeorgehogg.co.uk

Batemans XB; Tom Wood's Best Bitter; York Guzzler; guest beer H

Popular Grade II-listed marketplace pub and local CAMRA award winner. It has a large lounge/dining area and a separate public bar, both with real fires. Good-value locally-sourced food is served, plus home-made snacks. The pub is open for Sunday breakfast from 9.30am. Guest beers come from a local brewery. There is an annual beer festival, and football teams and the local supporters' club meet here. An upstairs restaurant plus tea and coffee are also available. Q♣(350)

Wragby

Ivy

Market Place, LN8 5QU

12-12.30am (1am Sat) (01673) 858768

theivy.vpweb.co.uk

Black Sheep Best Bitter; guest beers H

This free house is situated by the town's market place. The building dates from the 17th century and the large bar area retains original beams and a fireplace with log-burner. A smaller side room accommodates diners, offering a menu featuring local produce. Upstairs are six B&B rooms. The beer garden has a large decked area and outside bar. The pub's crib team plays in the local league, and weekly quiz nights are held. Q❀♿(6,10)

Wrawby

Jolly Miller

Brigg Road, DN20 8RH

12-11; 11.30-midnight Fri; 11.30-1am Sat; 11.30-11 Sun

(01652) 655658

Greene King IPA; guest beers H

Refurbished village local open again after a period of closure, with a large lounge set out for dining at one end, plus a games room with pool table and TV sport. Outside is a spacious covered and heated dining area known as Millers Store. Extensive lunchtime and evening menus are available Monday-Saturday, plus Sunday lunches. Three real ales are served, two of which are rotating guest beers, often from Batemans and Tom Wood's. Meet the Brewer nights and beer festivals are hosted from time to time. ❀♣P

Wig & Mitre, Lincoln

London index

*** Shown on Inner London map**

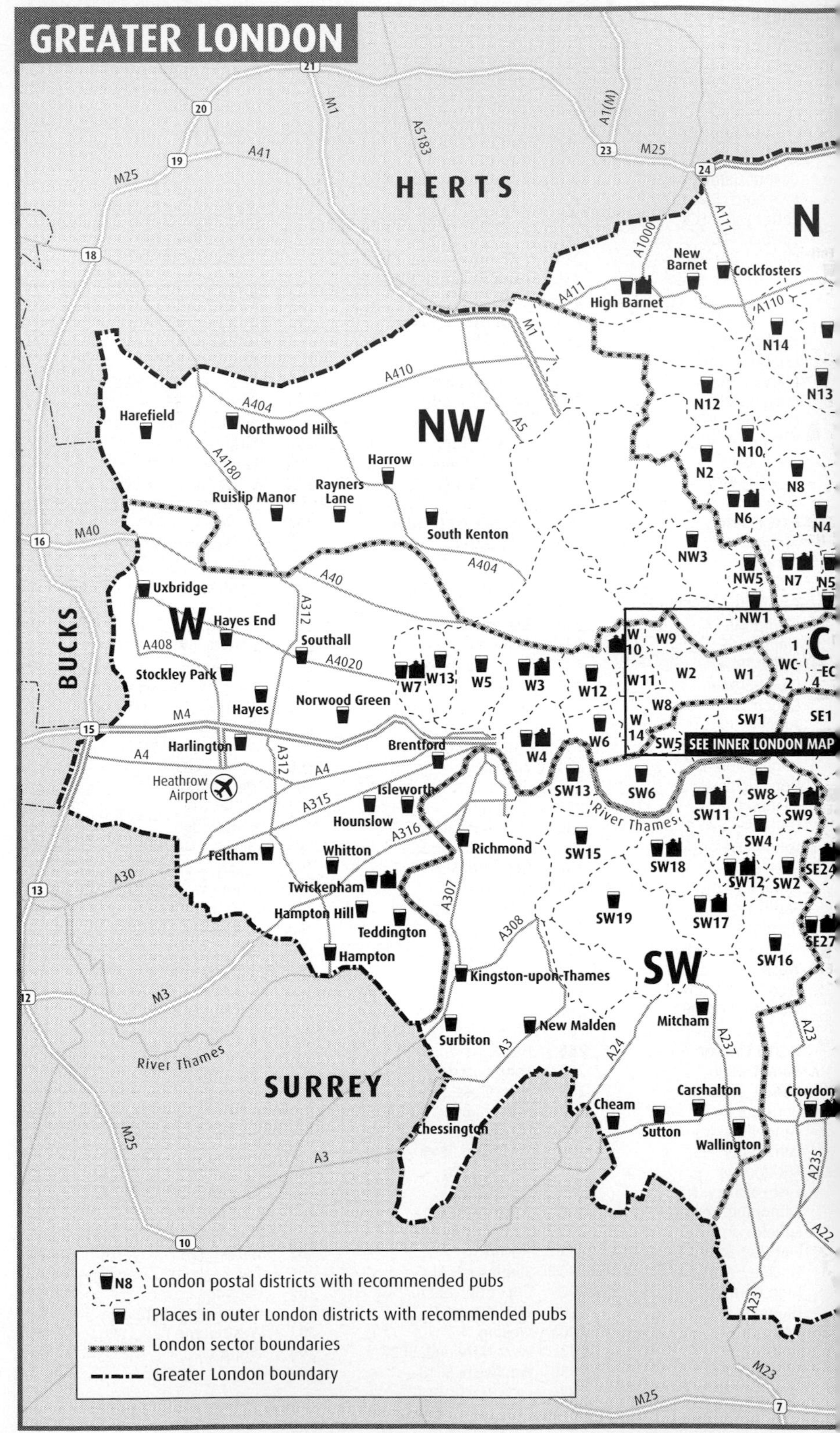
GREATER LONDON
HERTS
BUCKS
SURREY
NW
W
SW
N
C
Harefield
Northwood Hills
Harrow
Ruislip Manor
Rayners Lane
South Kenton
Uxbridge
Hayes End
Southall
Stockley Park
Hayes
Norwood Green
Harlington
Brentford
Heathrow Airport
Isleworth
Hounslow
Feltham
Whitton
Twickenham
Hampton Hill
Teddington
Hampton
Richmond
Kingston-upon-Thames
Surbiton
New Malden
Chessington
Cheam
Sutton
Carshalton
Wallington
Mitcham
Croydon
High Barnet
New Barnet
Cockfosters
N14
N13
N12
N10
N2
N8
N6
N4
NW3
NW5
N7
N5
NW1
W10
W9
W2
W1
W11
W8
W14
SW5
SW1
SE1
WC1
WC2
EC4
W7
W13
W5
W3
W12
W6
W4
SW13
SW6
SW8
SW11
SW9
SW4
SW15
SW18
SW12
SW2
SE24
SW19
SW17
SE27
SW16
SEE INNER LONDON MAP
River Thames
A41
M25
M1
A5183
A1(M)
A1000
A111
A411
A110
A410
A404
A4180
A5
A40
A312
A408
A4020
M40
M4
A4
A315
A316
A30
A307
A308
A3
A24
A237
A23
A235
A22
M3
M23
21
20
19
23
24
18
16
15
13
12
10
7
N8 London postal districts with recommended pubs
Places in outer London districts with recommended pubs
London sector boundaries
Greater London boundary

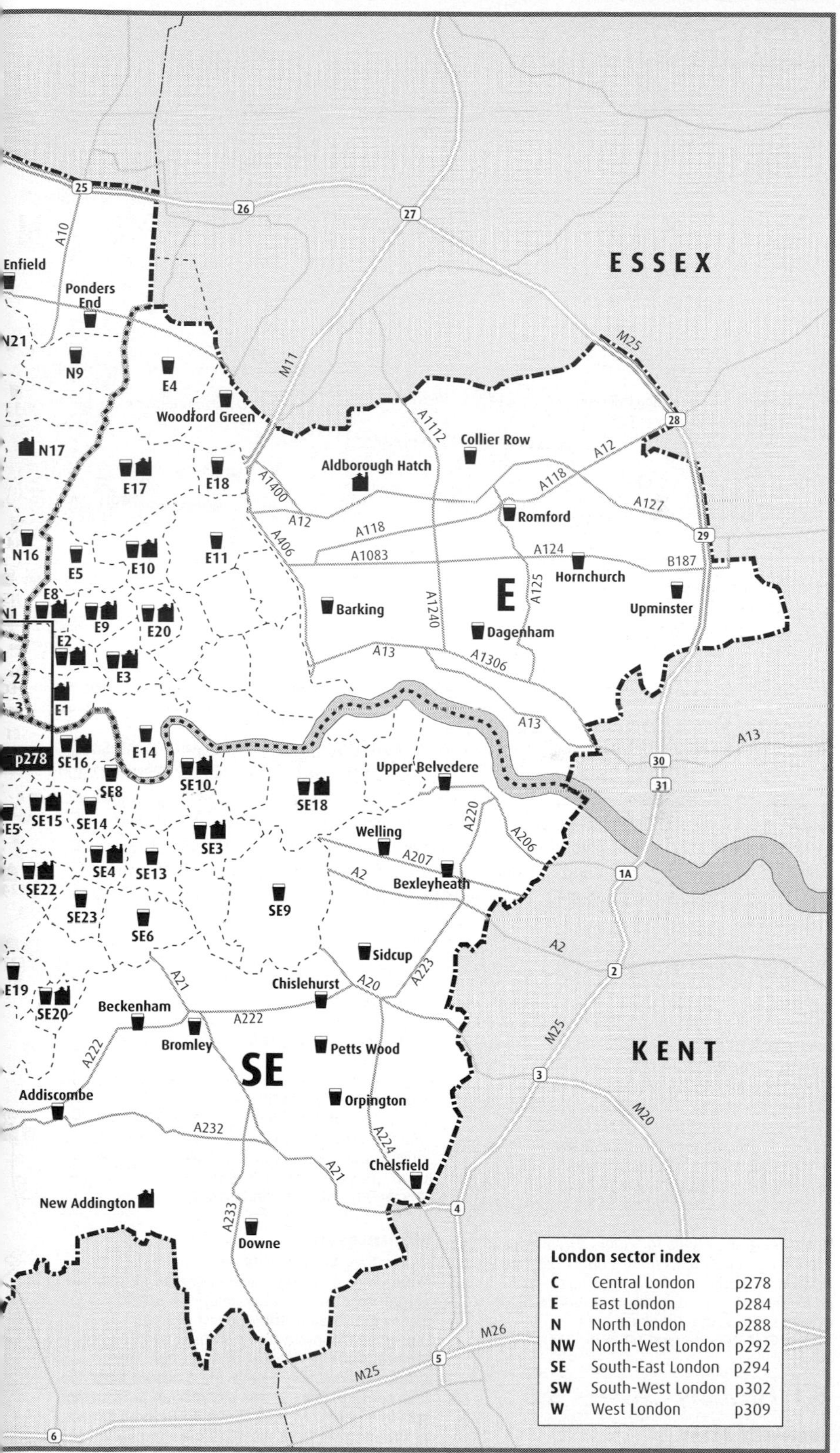

London sector index

C	Central London	p278
E	East London	p284
N	North London	p288
NW	North-West London	p292
SE	South-East London	p294
SW	South-West London	p302
W	West London	p309

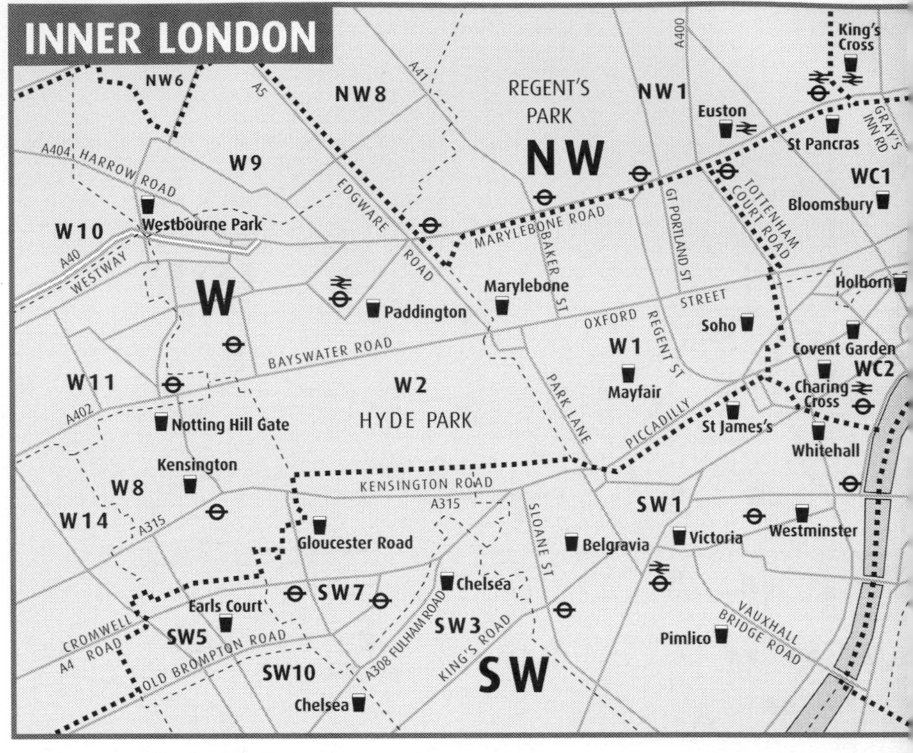

How to find London pubs

Greater London is divided into seven sectors: Central, East, North, North-West, South-East, South-West and West, reflecting postal boundaries. The Central sector includes the City (EC1 to EC4) and Holborn, Covent Garden and the Strand (WC1/2) plus W1, where pubs are listed in postal district order. In each of the other six sectors the pubs with London postcodes are listed first in postal district order (E1, E2 etc), followed by those in outer London districts, which are listed in alphabetical order (Barking, Chadwell Heath etc) – see Greater London map. Postal district numbers can be found on every street name plate in the London postcode area.

CENTRAL LONDON

EC1: Clerkenwell

Gunmakers L

13 Eyre Street Hill, EC1R 5ET

12-11; closed Sat & Sun ☎ (020) 7278 1022

thegunmakers.co.uk

Harveys Sussex Best Bitter; guest beers H

Busy pub just off the Clerkenwell Road. Five handpumps offer a variety of beers, frequently from Ascot, Purity or Windsor & Eton, alongside the Harveys, generally including at least one LocAle, often from Portobello or Redemption. There are two more handpumps for ciders, usually from the Westons' range. The kitchen is open 12-3pm and 6-9.30pm. In addition, wood-fired pizzas are available in the yard at the rear, which also provides a smoking/drinking area.

Q◑⊖(Farringdon)

EC1: Finsbury

Exmouth Arms L

23 Exmouth Market, EC1R 4QL

11-midnight (1.30am Fri & Sat); 11-10.30 Sun

☎ (020) 3551 4772 exmoutharms.com

Beer range varies H

This free house, formerly a Courage pub dating from 1915, has been completely refurbished under new ownership since 2012. Probably three rooms originally, it now has one bar with wooden flooring and fittings, and exterior green tiling. Four beers are served including local London brews. A large range of bottled beers is also on sale. Food is served until 10pm, with roast dinners on Sundays. It can get very busy at weekends.

◑♿⊖(Angel/Farringdon)

Wilmington

69 Rosebery Avenue, EC1R 4RL

8am-11 (midnight Fri); 9am-midnight Sat; 10-10.30 Sun

☎ (020) 7837 1384 wilmingtonclerkenwell.com

Greene King Stay & Griffin; guest beers H

Closed for complete refurbishment in 2013, this pub reopened in October of that year. Work included reinstating a large glass atrium from the 19th century. Prior to this it had been a music pub with live bands. As well as the house beer brewed by Greene King, four guest ales are available, usually including local brews. There is a large

ENGLAND

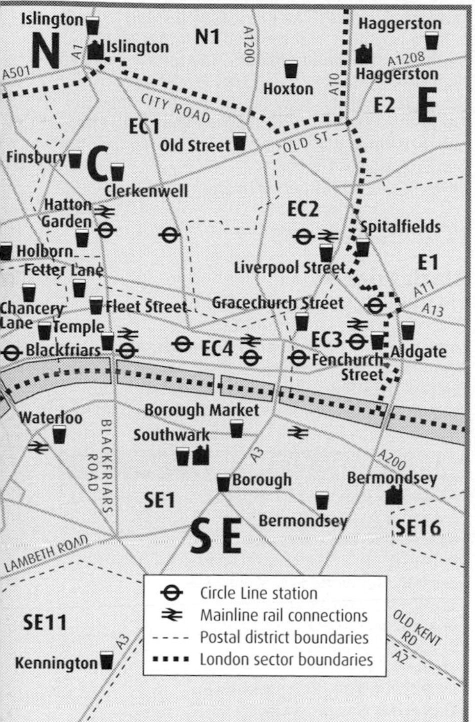

dining area with an open-plan kitchen. It gets busy at lunchtimes and early evenings.
◑♿⇌⊖(Angel/Farringdon)🚌🐾📶

EC1: Hatton Garden

Argyle

1 Greville Street, EC1N 8PQ

11 (12 Sat)-11; closed Sun ☎ (020) 7405 0999

theargylelondon.co.uk

Sharp's Doom Bar; guest beers H

In a modern building just off Leather Lane, this Stonegate establishment is popular with a City clientele on weekdays. Of the three guest beers, one normally comes from a London brewery. Traditional pub food is served until 9pm. The main bar is on the ground floor; there is also an intimate cellar bar and an upstairs bar that includes a terrace, with rugs available in winter.
❀◑⇌(Farringdon)⊖(Chancery Lane)♣🚌📶

Craft Beer Co L

82 Leather Lane, EC1N 7TR

12-11 (10.30 Sun)

Kent Craft Pale; guest beers H

One of five Craft Beer Co houses, this mecca for aficionados in Leather Lane is always busy and attracts a mix of local workers and beer buffs from wider afield. It has 16 handpumps and also 21 keg fonts for unusual British and imported beers. Snacks such as pork pies and Scotch eggs are served and recommended. As well as the traditional bar downstairs, there is more seating upstairs. Unlike many pubs in the City, it is open seven days a week. **Q**⇌⊖(Farringdon)🍎🍺🚌

Olde Mitre 🏆 ★ L

1 Ely Court, Ely Place, EC1N 6SJ

11-11; closed Sat & Sun ☎ (020) 7405 4751

Adnams Broadside; Caledonian Deuchars IPA; Fuller's Discovery; Gales Seafarers Ale; guest beers H

Multi award-winning pub with a history going back nearly 500 years and a nationally important historic pub interior. It is renowned for its wide selection of quality real ales and ciders, along with its bar snacks – no chips are sold here. There is extensive wood panelling in the main bar, the seating area and the snug. A function room upstairs is available for overspill or hire. Closed on bank holidays.
Q❀⇌(City Thameslink)⊖(Chancery Lane/Farringdon)🍎🚌🐾

EC1: Old Street

Old Fountain L

3 Baldwin Street, EC1V 9NU

11-11; 12-11 Sat & Sun ☎ (020) 7253 2970

oldfountain.co.uk

Fuller's London Pride; guest beers H

A traditional pub with entrances from two streets, owned and run by the same family for 50 years. With a dartboard in one bar and an attractive roof terrace, it is popular with office workers and locals of all ages. Seven guest beers often hail from up-and-coming breweries and there is a large range of bottles from London, Denmark and the US. Open now at weekends, it has live music on Saturday evenings and serves Sunday roasts.
❀◑⇌⊖♣🍎🚌📶

EC2: Liverpool Street

Hamilton Hall

Unit 32, The Concourse, Liverpool Street Station, EC2M 7PY

7am (9am Sun)-11.30 ☎ (020) 7247 3579

Greene King IPA, Abbot; guest beers H

This Wetherspoon pub, by the entrance to Liverpool Street Station, was once a ballroom. Renovation restored the fantastic gilded ceiling and moved the downstairs Gents nearer the bar, releasing more seating. With 10 handpumps downstairs and five more repeated upstairs, you usually find at least one local ale on the guest list. Enjoy service with a smile as this station pub can get busy. TV screens show train departures and arrivals. **Q**◑♿⇌⊖🍎🚌

Lord Aberconway

73 Old Broad Street, EC2M 1QS

11-11; 12-9.30 Sat; closed Sun ☎ (020) 7929 1743

Fuller's London Pride; St Austell Nicholson's Pale Ale; Sharp's Doom Bar; guest beers H

Named after a chairman of the old Metropolitan Railway, this Victorian pub has fine traditional fittings including some cosy booths. An M&B Nicholson's establishment, it is popular both with City workers and tourists. Three changing guest beers complement the three regulars. A traditional pub menu is served until 10pm and, in addition to the ground floor, a gallery area is also used for dining. ◑⇌⊖🚌

Woodins Shades

212 Bishopsgate, EC2M 4PT

11-1am ☎ (020) 7247 4324

Fuller's London Pride; St Austell Nicholson's Pale Ale; guest beers H

One of the M&B owned Nicholson's chain, the pub is named after a certain William Woodin who bought it in the mid-19th century. Seven handpumps dispense the two regulars and five changing guest beers. It can get extremely busy, especially early evenings when drinkers spill out onto the pavement, although seating can be found upstairs. Food is served until 10pm daily. Music is kept at background level and there is TV for major sporting events. ◑♿⇌⊖🚌

EC3: Fenchurch Street

East India Arms

67 Fenchurch Street, EC3M 4BR

11.30-11; closed Sat & Sun ☎ (020) 7480 6562

Shepherd Neame Kent's Best, Whitstable Bay, Spitfire 🄷

One of only two pubs recalling the East India Company, this small Shepherd Neame house close to Fenchurch Street station is a Grade II-listed red-brick building dating from the 1820s. Originally with two bars, it now has just one, with bare wooden floors and half-walled wooden panelling along with framed old photographs. It can get busy with office workers and tourists spilling out onto the pavement. An award-winning pub for the quality of its beers. ⇌⊖(Aldgate/Tower Hill)🚌

Peacock 𝕃

41 Minories, EC3N 1DY

12-1am; closed Sat & Sun ☎ (020) 7488 3630

Ringwood Fortyniner; Timothy Taylor Golden Best; guest beers 🄷

In the corner of the Grade II-listed Ibex House, possibly the largest survivor of Streamline Moderne (a short-lived form of Art Deco) and reputed to have been earmarked for Gestapo HQ had we lost World War II. Now a darts players' haven with seven dartboards and over 20 teams playing, it can get busy during darts night. The landlord is passionate about real ale, so check the guest beers, and especially for local brews.
⇌⊖(Aldgate/Tower Gateway)♣🚌

EC3: Gracechurch Street

Crosse Keys

7-12 Gracechurch Street, EC3V 0DR

8am-11 (midnight Fri); 9am-10 Sat; 9am-8 Sun
☎ (020) 7623 4824

Fuller's London Pride; Greene King IPA; Sharp's Doom Bar; guest beers 🄷

A grand Wetherspoon free house that opened in 1999 in the former Hong Kong and Shanghai Bank, complete with marble pillars and cupolas. A larger than normal range of beers is served from 24 handpumps on the central bar; check the plasma screens for the list of current beers. Look out for special themed festivals as well as the regular Wetherspoon beer festivals. Large TVs show muted news except for major sporting events.
Q◑♿⇌(Cannon Street)⊖(Bank/Monument)
🍎🚌📶

Old Tom's Bar

10-12 Leadenhall Market, EC3V 1LR

11-11; closed Sat & Sun ☎ (020) 7626 2454
oldtomsbar.co.uk

Wells Bombardier; Young's Bitter; guest beer 🄷

A tiny bar under the same management as the Lamb Tavern above it, in florid late-Victorian Leadenhall Market. The name (see painted legend) is from a gander that escaped slaughter and became a familiar local figure. The brick vaults and utilitarian clean and green tiles lend credence to the belief that this may be the place of slaughter before the poultry was displayed in butchers' shops above. Painted glass shows the former bar use. The pub is available for hire.
◑⇌(Fenchurch Street)⊖(Monument)🚌

EC4: Blackfriars

Black Friar ★

174 Queen Victoria Street, EC4V 4EG

10-11; 12-10.30 Sun ☎ (020) 7236 5474

Fuller's London Pride; Sharp's Doom Bar; guest beers 🄷

Built in 1875 but substantially altered in 1905, creating a nationally important historic pub interior

INDEPENDENT BREWERIES

Anspach & Hobday/Bullfinch SE1: Southwark (NEW)
Barnet High Barnet
Beavertown N17: Tottenham Hale
Belleville SW12: Wandsworth Common
Brew By Numbers SE16: Southwark
Brick SE15: Peckham (NEW)
Brixton SW9: Brixton (NEW)
Brockley SE4: Brockley
Brodie's E10: Leyton
By the Horns SW17: Summerstown
Clarence & Fredericks Croydon
Clarkshaws SE22: East Dulwich (NEW)
Crate E9: Hackney Wick
Cronx New Addington
Dragonfly W3: Acton (NEW)
Earls N1: Islington
East London E10: Leyton
Five Points E8: Hackney Downs
Florence (A Head in a Hat) SE24: Herne Hill
Fourpure SE16: Bermondsey (NEW)
Fuller's W4: Chiswick
Gipsy Hill SE27: West Norwood (NEW)
Ha'penny Aldborough Hatch
Hackney E2: Haggerston
Hammerton N7: Barnsbury (NEW)
Hop Stuff SE18: Woolwich (NEW)
Howling Hops E8: Hackney
Kernel SE16: Bermondsey
Laine E9: Hackney (NEW)
Laine W3: Acton (NEW)
Late Knights SE20: Penge
London Beer Factory SE27: West Norwood (NEW)
London Brewing N6: Highgate
London Fields E8: Hackney
Meantime SE10: Greenwich
Moncada W10: Kensal Town
One Mile End E1: Whitechapel (NEW)
Partizan SE16: South Bermondsey
Portobello W10: Kensington
Pressure Drop E8: Hackney
Redchurch E2: Bethnal Green
Redemption N17: Tottenham
Rocky Head SW18: Southfields
Sambrook's SW11: Battersea
Strawman SE15: Peckham (NEW)
Tap East E20: Stratford
Truman's E3: Hackney Wick
Twickenham Twickenham
Weird Beard W7: Hanwell
Wild Card E17: Walthamstow
Zerodegrees SE3: Blackheath

in now a rare Art Nouveau style. Friars in marble and brass carouse their way around the pub, and the grotto (dining area) is clad in Italian marble topped with Romanesque ceiling gold leaf. A sight to behold! A lively city pub welcoming office workers and tourists. Breakfasts are served 10am-noon and a variety of meals noon-10pm.

EC4: Fetter Lane

Castle

26 Furnival Street, EC4A 1JS
11-11; closed Sat & Sun (020) 7405 5470
Fuller's London Pride; Nethergate Red Car Best Bitter; guest beers H
Part of the small Red Car pub chain, this Victorian pub is popular with a City clientele. Eight handpumps offer six rotating guests alongside the two regular beers. The lunchtime menu comprises pub favourites; snacks are served in the evening. Seating in the downstairs bar is mainly stools, but there is also an upstairs bar/dining room with tables and chairs. The downstairs bar has a real fire.
(City Thameslink) (Chancery Lane)

EC4: Fleet Street

Old Bell

95 Fleet Street, EC4Y 1DH
11-11; 12-8 Sat; 12-5 Sun (020) 7583 0070
Fuller's London Pride; St Austell Nicholson's Pale Ale; Sharp's Doom Bar; guest beers H
An M&B Nicholson's pub with a central bar with bare wooden floors and half-wall panelling, giving it a warm and cosy feel. The walls are adorned with pictures, old press cuttings and announcements. Eight handpumps serve up to five guest beers alongside the three regulars. The pub has two entrances: one from Fleet Street and the rear entrance from an alley off Bride Lane.
(City Thameslink) (Blackfriars)

WC1: Bloomsbury

Calthorpe Arms

252 Grays Inn Road, WC1X 8JR
11-11.30; 12-10.30 Sun (020) 7278 4732
Young's Bitter, Special, seasonal beer; guest beer H
Unusual double doors lead into this single-bar corner local. With no music and an unobtrusive corner TV, it is easy either to strike up a conversation sitting at the bar or take one of the tables along the sides for more privacy. The upstairs dining room opens for lunch (12-2.30pm) but can be booked at other times. Evening meals are served 6-9.30pm. Young's bottle-conditioned beers are stocked, and guest beers come from Young's list. There is pavement seating outside.
(Russell Sq)

Lamb

94 Lambs Conduit Street, WC1N 3LZ
12-11 (midnight Thu-Sat); 12-10.30 Sun
(020) 7405 0713
Redemption Trinity; Young's Bitter, Special, seasonal beers; guest beers H
Beautifully preserved, Grade II-listed and with a regionally important historic pub interior, including a small snug and etched glass snob screens in place above the bar. The Empire Bar and restaurant are upstairs. The glorious Victorian history of the pub and area is commemorated by a working polyphon (predecessor to the gramophone). Among nine handpumps, three or four guest beers usually include one brewed for the pub by Redemption. At the back is a small walled garden.
Q (Russell Sq)

Swan

7 Cosmo Place, WC1N 3AP
12-11 (midnight Fri & Sat); 12-10.30 Sun
(020) 7837 6223
Fuller's London Pride; St Austell Tribute; guest beers H
Real ale and family-oriented pub among the tourist hotels on Southampton Row. There is a single long room, and tables in front on a pedestrian passage. The pub is popular with visitors to Great Ormond Street Children's Hospital. There are eight handpumps, two serving real cider in summer. Guest ales are mainly from London breweries. Pub grub and snacks are served until 10pm every day. A large-screen TV shows live sporting events.
(Russell Sq)

WC1: Holborn

Penderel's Oak

286-288 High Holborn, WC1V 7HJ
8am-11 (midnight Thu; 1am Fri & Sat); 10-11 Sun
(020) 7242 5669
Fuller's London Pride; Greene King IPA, Abbot; Sharp's Doom Bar; guest beers H
Large, busy Wetherspoon pub offering up to six guest beers. Tables at the front lead to the bar and a raised seating area. There is also a back room, and various settees and high stools; low-key lighting adds to the atmosphere. A cellar bar (with music on screens), available for hire, is popular with younger visitors; it opens later than the main bar. Food is served until 10pm. Children are welcome during the day. There is a small walled garden at the rear.
Q (Chancery Lane/Holborn)

WC1: St Pancras

Mabel's Tavern

9 Mabledon Place, WC1H 9AZ
11-11 (midnight Thu-Sat) (020) 7387 7739
Shepherd Neame Master Brew, Kent's Best, Whitstable Bay, Spitfire, Bishops Finger H
Originally owned by Whitbread and called the Kentish Arms (note the plaque on the outside wall), the pub was renamed for landlady Mabel Macinelly, who is said to haunt these cosy premises. Up to the left of the bar is a snug, and a raised area at the back has a traditional fireplace with a large TV screen above it. Various prints and old photos adorn the walls. Food is served until 10pm (9pm Fri-Sun). Handy for the British Library.
(King's Cross/St Pancras)

Queen's Head

66 Acton Street, WC1X 9NB
12-midnight (11 Mon); 12-11 Sun (020) 7713 5772
queensheadlondon.com
Redemption Trinity; guest beers H
Narrow, late-Georgian premises with a single bar, smoking patio at the rear and benches in front. The piano is used for jazz and blues on Thursdays. Guest beers are from microbreweries and include one dark beer. One handpump serves cider, with three

more real ciders and a range of keg and bottled beers on offer. Sharing platters of snacks are served at this comfortable pub, popular with locals and occasional tourists off the Gray's Inn Road. Closing time can be flexible.
(King's Cross/St Pancras)

WC2: Chancery Lane

Seven Stars

53-54 Carey Street, WC2A 2JB
11-11; 12-11 Sat & Sun (020) 7242 8521
Adnams Southwold Bitter; guest beers H
Dating from 1602 and formerly known as the League of Seven Stars, this pub has a historic interior of regional importance. The bar, with its decorative Victorian bar-back, sits in the narrow space between two distinctive drinking areas. Located near the Royal Courts of Justice, the pub sports a legal theme, with one of the drinking areas named the Wig Box. The landlady favours Adnams' beers. The pub is also home to Ray Brown, the resident cat. Q

WC2: Charing Cross

Harp

47 Chandos Place, WC2N 4HS
10-11; 12-10.30 Sun (020) 7836 0291
harpcoventgarden.com
Dark Star Hophead, American Pale Ale; Harveys Sussex Best Bitter; Sambrook's Wandle Ale; guest beers H
Small, friendly, independent free house which has become a haven for beer choice, generally offering a mild or porter and London microbrewery seasonals. A fine range of real ciders is also available. The narrow bar is adorned with mirrors and portraits. There is no intrusive music or TV, and a cosy upstairs room provides a refuge from the busy throng. Its numerous awards included, in 2010, the ultimate accolade: CAMRA National Pub of the Year. Q

WC2: Covent Garden

Coach & Horses

42 Wellington Street, WC2E 7BD
11-11; 12-10.30 Sun (020) 7240 0553
Courage Best Bitter; Shepherd Neame Spitfire H
A small and traditional independent pub with a lot of Irish influence, very much used by locals but also some tourists; this house has a fantastic collection of around 70 Irish whiskeys and Scotch whiskies. Food is served 11-3.30pm Monday to Saturday and sometimes also Sunday lunchtime. There are photos of Gaelic football teams, and the sport of hurling also features, plus theatre posters. Note the beautiful front windows. Q

Cross Keys

31 Endell Street, WC2H 9BA
11-11; 12-10.30 Sun (020) 7836 5185
crosskeyscoventgarden.com
Brodie's Bethnal Green Bitter, seasonal beers; guest beer H
Built in the mid-1840s when Endell (formerly Belton) Street was widened as part of clearing the St Giles Rookery (slum). An ornate façade reveals a long, welcoming bar, subdued lighting, comfortable banquette seating and tables and chairs. Copper kettles, pans, street signs, stuffed fish, framed pictures, photographs and Beatles memorabilia adorn the place, plus a fine Truman, Hanbury, Buxton & Co mirror. Families are welcome (over 12s only) until 7pm unless it is busy, but no dogs. ()

Nell of Old Drury

29 Catherine Street, WC2B 5JS
12-3, 5-11.30; 12-midnight Sat; closed Sun
(020) 7836 5328 nellofolddrury.com
Adnams Broadside; Sambrook's Wandle Ale H
Originally licensed as the Lamb, and renamed by 1965 after the orange seller and mistress of King Charles II, this pub was a location in Hitchcock's film Frenzy. The cosy small bar, decked with theatre bills and photographs, is a popular haunt for theatregoers who pre-order interval drinks. The large bay window with cushion-strewn ledge gives a good view of the Drury Lane Theatre. Upstairs is additional seating. Dogs are allowed, but no children, and no food is served.

Salisbury ★

90 St Martin's Lane, WC2N 4AP
11-11 (11.30 Thu; midnight Fri & Sat); 12-10.30 Sun
(020) 7836 5863
Fuller's London Pride; St Austell Tribute; Timothy Taylor Landlord; Wells Bombardier; guest beer H
Grade II-listed and with a nationally important historic pub interior, this is a Victorian gem. Its predecessor, licensed in 1694, was the Coach & Horses until 1866. The sign shows the Marquess of Salisbury, Prime Minister three times in the 19th century, whose family once owned the freehold. The interior is spectacular, with an island bar, cut and etched glass, large mirrors and Art Nouveau light fittings. It featured in the 1961 film Victim.
(Charing Cross) (Leicester Sq)

White Swan

14 New Row, WC2N 4LF
10-11 (11.30 Fri & Sat); 12-10.30 Sun (020) 3077 1129
Adnams Explorer; Fuller's London Pride; Sharp's Doom Bar; guest beers H
Once owned by the famous London banking firm Hoare & Co and formerly an O'Neills outlet, this Grade II-listed building is now an M&B Nicholson's pub with eight handpumps. Just a stone's throw from Covent Garden, it is popular with tourists. It has been tastefully refurbished with a small bar, limited seating in the bar area but with more room past a partition. The first-floor dining room can be booked for functions.
(Charing Cross) (Leicester Sq)

WC2: Holborn

Shakespeare's Head

Africa House, 64-68 Kingsway, WC2B 6BG
7am-midnight (1am Fri); 8am-midnight Sat; 8am-1am Sun
(020) 7404 8846
Fuller's London Pride; Greene King IPA, Abbot; guest beers H
A 1998 Wetherspoon conversion from a bank, taking its name from a famous pub located nearby until that entire street (Wych Street) was demolished over 100 years ago. This large pub is nearly always busy with shoppers, tourists, local office workers and students from the nearby London School of Economics during term time. A convenient place for a couple of pints after your cultural sojourn at the British Museum. Alcohol is served after 9am. (91)

Ship Tavern

12 Gate Street, WC2A 3HP
11-11 (midnight Thu-Sat); 12-10.30 Sun
(020) 7405 1992 theshiptavern.co.uk
Butcombe Bitter; Caledonian Deuchars IPA; St Austell Tribute; guest beers H
In a passage behind Holborn Station, a pub has been on this site since 1549. It used to be one of the few Younger's pubs in London. Decor is a mix of alcoves and stools, with mahogany-coloured walls and prints of early 20th-century ships. Six handpumps serve regional beers including two changing guest ales. Food is available all day, with a traditional roast on Sunday as well as live jazz. The Oak Room restaurant upstairs is available for booking.

WC2: Temple

Devereux

20 Devereux Court, WC2R 3JJ
12-11; closed Sat & Sun (020) 7583 4562
St Austell Tribute; Sharp's Doom Bar; guest beers H
Attractive Grade II-listed pub built in 1844; part of the site was once the Grecian Coffee House. The comfortable lounge with wood panelling has a bar with five handpumps. Prints on the walls show local places of interest and historic figures, the judges and wigs reflecting proximity to the law courts. Upstairs is a restaurant available for hire. Ale drinkers enjoy up to five changing guest beers.
Q

Edgar Wallace

40 Essex Street, WC2R 3JF
11-11; closed Sat & Sun (020) 7353 3120
Beer range varies H
There has been a pub here since 1777. Now leased from Enterprise, this one has so far collected about 140 of the 170-odd books written by Edgar Wallace. The comfortable downstairs room has a fine wooden bar with eight handpumps and there is also seating upstairs. The pub operates a try-before-you-buy policy but, to compensate for this, half pints may be charged at a premium rate. Look out for beer festivals. Q

W1: Marylebone

Carpenters Arms

12 Seymour Place, W1H 7NE
11-11; 12-10.30 Sun (020) 7723 1050
Harveys Sussex Best Bitter; guest beers H
A sister pub to the Market Porter in SE1 but with a smaller range of guest beers, this establishment is a haven from the bustle of Edgware Road. Many local people enjoy watching TV sport and playing darts in the rear alcove. A sensitive refurbishment has preserved the mosaics. On the side wall is a display of facsimiles of woodworking tools. The food menu consists entirely of pork pies, and the upstairs function room is available for hire.
(Marble Arch)

W1: Mayfair

Clarence

4 Dover Street, W1S 4LB
10-11.30 (midnight Thu-Sat); 10-11 Sun
(020) 7491 3607
Fuller's London Pride; St Austell Nicholson's Pale Ale; Sharp's Doom Bar; Windsor & Eton Knight of the Garter; guest beers H
Licensed in 1724 as the Coach & Horses and rebuilt in 1892 and 1953, The Duke of Clarence became King William IV in 1830. Its smallish frontage belies a much larger area extending back. It has a convivial atmosphere after its refurbishment in 2012, with a pleasant, quieter upstairs bar. The pub is close to the Ritz hotel in Piccadilly.
(Green Park)

Coach & Horses

5 Bruton Street, W1J 6PT
11.30-11; 12-8 Sat; 12-midnight Sun (020) 7629 4123
Brains SA Gold; Fuller's London Pride; guest beer H
An excellent refuge from the nearby Bond Street shopping area. First licensed in 1738, it was rebuilt in 1933 and has an imposing mock-Tudor exterior. Inside, the atmosphere is traditional, with wooden beams and panelling. Pictures on the walls feature caricatures of 19th-century politicians and clerics. Four handpumps dispense a changing series of guest ales. The small dining room with bar upstairs is available for private functions.
Q (Green Park)

Windmill

6-8 Mill Street, W1S 2AZ
11-11; 12-4.30 Sat; closed Sun (020) 7491 8050
windmillmayfair.co.uk
Wells Bombardier; Young's Bitter, London Gold, Special; guest beers H
In adjoining buildings previously housing a nightclub and an escort agency, this pub has a well-furnished lounge bar with wood panelling, decorative ceilings and frieze. There is a restaurant on the first floor. Pies are a speciality; the Pie Club claims 6,000 members, who enjoy changing monthly specials such as beef & stilton. A roof garden bar and restaurant are recent additions.
Q (Oxford Circus)

W1: Soho

Argyll Arms ★

18 Argyll Street, W1F 7TP
10-11.30 (midnight Fri & Sat); 10-11 Sun
(020) 7734 6117
Brains SA Gold; Fuller's London Pride; St Austell Nicholson's Pale Ale; Windsor & Eton Knight of the Garter; guest beers H
Victorian M&B Nicholson's house with a nationally important historic pub interior and Grade II*-listed. Three snugs are separated by etched-glass partitions; note the remarkable Bass mirror. The bar-back is impressive, and next to that is a rare survivor, a manager's office with etched glazing. The magnificent saloon is decorated with ornate mirrors. With eight of the 16 handpumps in regular use, enjoy guest ales from brewers including Adnams, Harviestoun and Thwaites.
(Oxford Circus)

Dog & Duck ★

18 Bateman Street, W1D 3AJ
10-11 (020) 7494 0697
Fuller's London Pride; St Austell Nicholson's Pale Ale; guest beers H
In the heart of Soho, this Grade II-listed Nicholson's outlet, built in 1897, has a nationally important historic pub interior. An elaborate mosaic depicts dogs and ducks, and wonderful advertising mirrors

adorn the walls. Changing guest beers may include, for example, Sambrook's Wandle and Orkney Dark Island. The upstairs Orwell Bar can be hired for functions. The pub is small and so popular, especially with media people, that it is not just smokers who have to drink outside.
(Tottenham Court Rd)

Queen's Head

15 Denman Street, W1D 7HN
11-11.30 (midnight Fri & Sat); 12-10.30 Sun
(020) 7437 1540 queensheadpiccadilly.com
Fuller's London Pride; Sambrook's Wandle Ale; guest beers H
Dating from 1738, the pub takes its name from Queen's Street, renamed Denman Street in 1862 in honour of a Lord Chief Justice born there. In the 1840s it was known as the Couriers Club, trading in wine, brandy and coal. Later, reduced in size, it became part of the Piccadilly Theatre site. With the main bar on the ground floor and more accommodation upstairs, it is a rare free house in central London for pre-theatre dining and drinks.
(Piccadilly Circus)

EAST LONDON

E1: Aldgate

Dispensary

19A Leman Street, E1 8EN
11.30-11; closed Sat & Sun (020) 7977 0486
thedispensarylondon.co.uk
Dark Star Hophead; Harveys Armada Ale; Vale Pale Ale; guest beers H
This former local CAMRA Pub of the Year was originally constructed in 1858 to house the Eastern Dispensary, which provided medical treatment to the poor of the area. When converted to a pub in 1998, original features were sympathetically repaired, including the Victorian tiled floor in the entrance, renovated to its former glory. As well as the great beers there is modern British cuisine prepared by an award-winning chef. The Wellington room on the first floor offers private dining facilities.
Q(Fenchurch St)(Aldgate East/Tower Gateway)

E1: Spitalfields

Williams Ale & Cider House

22-24 Artillery Lane, E1 7LS
11-11 (midnight Thu-Sat); closed Sun (020) 7247 5163
williamsspitalfields.com
Greene King IPA; Truman's Swift; guest beers H
Fourteen handpumps grace the bar of this pub in a lane off Bishopsgate – one for Greene King IPA (badged as Spitalfields Brew), three for ciders and the rest for guest beers, many from London breweries such as Hackney, London Fields and Truman's. It is comfortably furnished and has photographs of old Truman's pubs and brewery posters on the walls. There are live jazz and blues performances on Friday and Saturday nights. Food is served noon-9pm. (Liverpool St)

E2: Cambridge Heath

Sebright Arms

31-35 Coate Street, E2 9AG
5-11 (midnight Thu-Sat); 12-10.30 Sun
(020) 7729 0937 sebrightarms.co.uk
Beer range varies H
A two-roomed pub with wood panelling, reopened in 2011 after being closed for three years. The building was saved after planning permission for flats was refused. Once attached to a Victorian music hall, it has been a heavy metal, disco and cabaret venue. Live music continues most nights in the downstairs room. Four handpumps mainly serve local beers such as Five Points and Hackney, and a range of over 40 bottled beers includes British bottle-conditioned brews. It can get very busy at weekends.

E2: Haggerston

Albion in Goldsmith's Row

94 Goldsmith's Row, E2 8QY
12-11 (1am Fri & Sat); 12-10.30 Sun (020) 7739 0185
thealbioningoldsmithsrow.co.uk
Caledonian Deuchars IPA; Timothy Taylor Landlord; guest beers H
Previously the Duke of Sussex, this friendly locals' pub changed its name when the current owner, a West Bromwich Albion supporter, bought it in 1985. Built in 1926, it was owned by West's Brewery which was on the site of nearby Hackney City Farm. It now has one room, full of football memorabilia, and there is even a TV in the window so you can sit outside and watch the footie. The pub hosts a Thursday quiz and live music outside in summer. (Cambridge Heath)

E3: Bow

Eleanor Arms

460 Old Ford Road, E3 5JP
4 (12 Fri-Sun)-11 (020) 8980 6992
eleanorarms.co.uk
Shepherd Neame Kent's Best, Whitstable Bay; guest beers H
Built in 1879 and close to Victoria Park, this single-room bar has two distinct areas, the rear one offering a pool table and a large-screen TV for major sporting events. Two real fires have been reinstated. On the first Thursday of each month is a quiz, with jazz every Sunday and music from the landlord's vast, eclectic record collection on Fridays and Saturdays.
(Bow Church/Bow Rd)(8)

Palm Tree

127 Grove Road, E3 5RP (in Mile End Park; road access via Haverfield Rd)
12.30-midnight (2am Sat); 12-midnight Sun
(020) 8980 2918
Beer range varies H
Standing isolated in Mile End Park, this pub has been run by the same family for nearly 40 years and retains a regionally important historic pub interior with two separate bars. It gets busy on Friday-Sunday nights, with live jazz and floor singers; at other times music is kept at background level. Two changing real ales are served. Outside drinking is in the park. Sandwiches are usually on offer weekday lunchtimes. Knock if it is not open on time. (Mile End)P

E4: Chingford

King's Ford

250-252 Chingford Mount Road, E4 8JL
8am-midnight (1am Fri & Sat) (020) 8523 9365

Adnams Broadside; Greene King Abbot; Ruddles Best Bitter; guest beers H

A spacious Wetherspoon conversion, the long single room has the bar halfway down on the right-hand side. There are 10 handpumps, four on the front serving regular ales and six serving the cider and guest beers, including at least one from a local brewery. As well as the two main Wetherspoon beer festivals, it also holds local beer festivals and Meet the Brewer nights. Two large screens are mute except for major sporting events.

King's Head

2B Kings Head Hill, E4 7EA

12-11 (midnight Fri & Sat) ☎ (020) 8529 6283

thekingsheadchingford.co.uk

Fuller's London Pride; Morland Old Speckled Hen; St Austell Tribute; Sharp's Doom Bar; guest beers H

A popular and welcoming Stonegate pub in leafy north Chingford. It is roomy, with various seating areas, a small garden and a car park. The number of handpumps has recently increased to 10, to include one real cider, four regular beers (selected by customer vote) and five guest ales, often one from a local brewery. Food is served all day from a wide-ranging menu. Quiz nights are Sunday and Wednesday. Q P

E5: Clapton

Clapton Hart

231 Lower Clapton Road, E5 8EG

4-11; 12-midnight Thu-Sat; 12-11 Sun ☎ (020) 8985 8124

claptonhart.com

Beer range varies H

After being closed for too many years, this pub has taken on a new lease of life. On the eight handpumps there is a range of ales from microbreweries such as Magic Rock, Moor and Siren, and LocAles from brewers including London Fields. The decor in this multi-roomed pub is the usual distressed style that is the Antic way, with grass covering the floor and tables for an annual cider festival. The changing food menu often has real ale in the recipes.

Crooked Billet

84 Upper Clapton Road, E5 9JP

4-11; 12-midnight Fri & Sat; 12-11 Sun ☎ (020) 8291 8649

e5crookedbillet.co.uk

Beer range varies H

An absolute gem of a pub since reopening in 2013; friendly locals and chatty, helpful bar staff always ensure a warm welcome. The five handpumps offer a range of local ales and sometimes a Dark Star beer appears. The large car park has turned into a lawned area with deckchairs. The remaining outdoor area has booths and an outside bar. Inside are open fires. Traditional English food is served, including popular Sunday roasts.

E8: Hackney

Cock Tavern

315 Mare Street, E8 1EJ

12-11 (1am Fri & Sat); 12-10.30 Sun ☎ (020) 8533 6369

thecocktavern.co.uk

Beer range varies H

Single-room bar in the middle of Hackney with one of the smallest gardens in the area, which accommodates in its cellar the excellent Howling Hops brewery. The 16 handpumps divide into eight for Howling Hops and guest beers – mostly brewed within a few miles – and eight for real cider. The bar has a rustic feel, with bare wooden floors and wood panelling. Take a look at the welcome board depicting when the brews are available.

(Hackney Downs) (Hackney Central)

Pembury Tavern

90 Amhurst Road, E8 1JH

12-11 (midnight Fri & Sat) ☎ (020) 8986 8597

Milton Minotaur, Pegasus, Nero, Cyclops; guest beers H

Large one-room bar with 16 handpumps offering the Milton range of beers, changing guest ales and two ciders. Bar billiards, pool and board games are available. Freshly made pizzas are served all day alongside a full Italian menu (12-3pm, 6-9pm); on Sundays there are traditional roasts instead until 4pm. Monday is quiz night. Beer festivals are held at the start and end of the summer.

Q (Hackney Downs) (Hackney Central)

E8: London Fields

Dove Free House & Kitchen

24-28 Broadway Market, E8 4QJ

12-11 (midnight Fri & Sat) ☎ (020) 7275 7617

dovepubs.com/contact

Crouch Vale Brewers Gold; East London Brewing Company Pale Ale; Timothy Taylor Landlord; guest beers H

The Goring Arms until 1990 when acquired by Elizabeth Grogan, this pub comprises a front bar and four other rooms (two for dining) and feels in parts like a Belgian brown bar. Three changing guest beers usually come from the same brewery. The many bottled beers are mostly Belgian and Belgium's national day is celebrated with Belgian brewers. Home-made food, Thai and Sunday roasts are served. It has an annual cider festival, a quiz on Wednesday and jazz on Sunday evenings.

(236,394)

London Fields Brewery Tap Room

365-366 Warburton Street, E8 3RR

11-midnight ☎ (020) 7241 5983

londonfieldsbrewery.co.uk/tap-room

Beer range varies H

Just off Mare Street is the Tap Room of London Fields Brewery, serving its beers on six handpumps and 12 keg taps. The evolving new bar has bare wooden floors, plenty of plain wooden panels (to be decorated) and hanging hops, and you can see through glass into the brewery. Check for the quiz night once a month and the menu for food cooked with London Fields beers. Book a brewery tour Saturday to Wednesday.

E9: Hackney Wick

Crate Brewery & Pizzeria

Unit 7, White Building, Queen's Yard, White Post Lane, E9 5EN (down steps by canal bridge)

12-11 (midnight Fri & Sat) ☎ 07834 275687

cratebrewery.com

Crate Best Bitter, Stout; guest beers H

Opened in 2012 in an old warehouse, as part of the Olympic legacy. The furniture is hand-made from recycled items; some of the lampshades are made from springs. A larger brewery is now at the back, but the original brewery is still in use. Bottled foreign beers and wine are available but no spirits. You can also sit in moored boats to drink your beer. Food is served until 10pm (11pm Fri & Sat). (276,488)

E10: Leyton

Drum

557-559 Lea Bridge Road, E10 7EQ

8am-midnight (1am Fri & Sat) (020) 8539 9845

Greene King Abbot; Ruddles Best Bitter; guest beers H

An early Wetherspoon pub and one of the smaller outlets. The 10 handpumps (split into two banks of five) usually offer at least one local ale and one cider. The single TV, showing 24 hour news, faces the bar and is normally muted, although the sound comes on for major sporting events, and there is ample seating to the rear away from it. There is an enclosed garden at the back. Regular Wetherspoon beer festivals and special mini festivals are held during the year. (Midland Rd)

Leyton Orient Supporters Club

Matchroom Stadium, Oliver Road, E10 5NF

12.30-8 Sat match days; from 5.30 weekdays (not during game) (020) 8988 8288 orientsupporters.org

Mighty Oak Oscar Wilde; guest beers H

This may be the best clubhouse in the football league. Serving real ale since 1995, it now usually offers a range of seven, and one or two ciders or perries, with bar snacks and rolls available. Closed during matches, it reopens afterwards. Two beer festivals are held each season, plus special brewery-themed nights. Free entry is permitted with a CAMRA membership card or a copy of this Guide.

Leyton Technical

265B High Road, E10 5QN

4-11 (11.30 Fri); 12-11.30 Sat; 12-11 Sun (020) 8558 4759 leytontechnical.com

Beer range varies H

Originally operated as a pop-up pub during the 2012 Olympics, it now has a permanent licence. It is in what was previously Leyton Town Hall, an 1896 building that became a technical college. Eight beers are usually served, including local brews. There are two spacious rooms, filled with Antic's typically eclectic furniture and fittings. Quiz night is every Wednesday and comedy every second Thursday of the month.

E11: Leytonstone

Red Lion

640 High Road Leytonstone, E11 3AA

12-11 (midnight Thu; 2am Fri & Sat) (020) 8988 2929 theredlionleytonstone.com

Beer range varies H

One of the jewels in Antic's crown. Handpumps dispense up to 10 changing guest ales from breweries such as London Fields, Otley, Summer Wine and Thornbridge. In addition there is a wide range of bottled beers including offerings from London, the rest of the UK and America. Scotch eggs and sausage rolls are available as well as main meals and Sunday roasts (no food Sun eves). Quiz night is Monday. (257,W14)

E14: Crossharbour

George

114 Glengall Grove, E14 3ND

11-midnight (020) 7987 4433

Fuller's London Pride; Sharp's Doom Bar; Timothy Taylor Landlord; Young's Bitter H

Dating from 1864, this welcoming Enterprise pub has a rich history linked to the docks and the local community, as well as a regionally important historic pub interior. The present early-1930s building has three distinct bars, each with its own special character, a large conservatory, and an award-winning patio garden. The walls are adorned with pictures of local dock scenes and characters. An excellent choice of food (served weekdays until 8pm; lunchtimes at weekends) includes vegetarian choices.

E17: Walthamstow

Bell

617 Forest Road, E17 4NE

11-midnight (11 Mon; 1am Fri & Sat); 12-11 Sun (020) 8523 2277 belle17.com

Hogs Back TEA; Timothy Taylor Landlord; guest beers H

Large Victorian pub refurbished and reopened in 2012. The interior is open plan but has two distinct areas. It is comfortably furnished and often very busy. Eight handpumps serve a range of ales from regional and local breweries. Tuesday is quiz night, DJs provide entertainment Friday and Saturday evening, and live jazz is performed on Sunday evening. Children are allowed until 8pm. The smoking area is spacious, with extra seating during summer. There are no TV screens. (Central)

Nag's Head

9 Orford Road, E17 9LP

12-11 (10.30 Sun); 12-10.30 Sun (020) 8520 9709 thenagsheade17.com

Mighty Oak Oscar Wilde, Maldon Gold; guest beers H

A cat-friendly pub in the heart of Walthamstow Village conservation area. Seven handpumps serve a varied range of ales. This community pub has many events including wine tastings and Pilates upstairs, and on Fridays and Saturdays an extra quiet bar serves spirits and bottled beers. Outside seating is at the front and a covered patio at the rear. Food is now Italian and available all day. Themed beer festivals are held through the year. (Central) (W12)

Olde Rose & Crown

53-55 Hoe Street, E17 4SA

10-11 (midnight Fri & Sat); 12-11 Sun (020) 8509 3880 yeolderoseandcrowntheatrepub.co.uk

Beer range varies H

This large friendly community venue starts serving beer from noon. Six handpumps deliver changing beers from SIBA and local brewers, and there are usually two ciders in addition. Food is available alternate Mondays and Tuesday-Saturday, with various pop-up restaurants plus Sunday roasts. The theatre upstairs has regular productions and the bar has live music events, plus a 78s night on the second Wednesday of the month. Look out for special beer festivals. (Central)

ENGLAND

E18: South Woodford

George

70-74 High Road, E18 2QL
11-11.30 (midnight Fri & Sat); 12-11 Sun
(020) 8532 2441 georgesouthwoodford.co.uk
Fuller's London Pride; Greene King IPA; Sharp's Doom Bar; guest beers H
A real ale haven in South Woodford, this old coaching house is a listed building – a pub has been here since 1657. Full of friendly locals, it has one welcoming bar with wood-panelling, divided into three distinct areas. The regular ales rotate and local beers from East London breweries are always among the guest beer range. The usually silent TVs show sport and news. St George's Day is celebrated with morris dancers and the like.

E20: Westfield Stratford City

Tap East L

Montfichet Road, 7 International Square, E20 1EE
11-11; 12-10 Sun (020) 8555 4467 tapeast.co.uk
Tap East Tonic Ale, JWB; guest beers H
In Westfield shopping centre, Tap East is the only cask ale brewpub in a shopping mall in the UK. Six handpumps dispense three house beers and three guests. Occasional beer festivals are held, and sometimes other breweries collaborate to produce special one-off brews. Pizzas, burgers and the like are served and there are numerous dining places nearby. Music is played and occasionally sport is shown.
(Stratford/Stratford International)

Barking

Barking Dog

61 Station Parade, IG11 8TU
8am-11 (10.30 Sun) (020) 8507 9109
Greene King Abbot; Ruddles Best Bitter; Wychwood Hobgoblin; guest beers H
A Wetherspoon pub, close to Barking station and numerous bus routes. Popular with locals and passing commuters alike, it can be boisterous at times. A range of handpumps serves up to six continually changing guest beers of varying types and strengths, plus three regular beers and two Westons ciders. Food is available all day (breakfasts from 8am) and alcohol from 9am. Muted TV screens show rolling news. Framed prints feature local scenes and historic figures such as Captain Cook and Vera Lynn.

Collier Row

Colley Rowe Inn

54-56 Collier Row Road, RM5 3PA (on B174)
9am-midnight (1.30am Fri & Sat) (01708) 760633
Fuller's London Pride; Greene King Abbot; Ruddles Best Bitter; guest beers H
Pleasant Wetherspoon shop conversion with some cosy alcoves. It is often lively around the bar, but quieter at the rear. Up to four well-chosen guest beers are normally on tap, often including Wibblers from Essex, plus two real ciders from Westons and a perry. Food is served all day, every day. The Colley is a 10-minute bus ride from Romford railway station (on three bus routes and near three others). There is a segregated smoking area on the pavement. Q

Dagenham

Eastbrook ★

Dagenham Road, RM10 7UP (nr jct with Rainham Rd South)
11-11 (midnight Fri & Sat) (020) 8592 1873
Beer range varies H
This Grade II-listed 1930s hostelry is a welcoming community local with a large function room/restaurant and two bars. The main bar is the Walnut Room, with extensive panelling; the second, the Oak Room, used for functions, can be visited on request. Beers are from the Brakspear range and change monthly. The pub is the local for Dagenham & Redbridge FC supporters, particularly when their team is at home. Football memorabilia adorn the pub. P

Hornchurch

JJ Moons

48-52 High Street, RM12 4UN (on A124)
8am-11.30 (12.30am Fri & Sat) (01708) 478410
Adnams Ghost Ship; Greene King Abbot; Ruddles Best Bitter; guest beers H
Busy Wetherspoon high-street pub, popular with all age groups, featuring a changing selection of ales with an emphasis on breweries from London and the south-east. Watercolour paintings of local scenes provide the main decoration, with the usual local interest panels to the rear of the pub. Families are welcome until 6pm. Alcohol is sold from 9am. Local CAMRA Pub of the Year 2014.
Q(Emerson Park)

Romford

Moon & Stars

99-103 South Street, RM1 1NX
8am-midnight (1am Thu-Sat) (01708) 730117
Courage Directors; Greene King Abbot; Ruddles Best Bitter; guest beers H
Enjoy guest ales from the current Wetherspoon list, while real cider, usually Old Rosie and Black Dragon, is served from containers in coolers behind the bar. There are local history display panels and shelves of assorted books. Children are allowed in the raised area at the rear until 6pm. On Thursday and Friday evenings it can get quite busy. Photo ID is required for all customers on Thursday, Friday and Saturday evenings. Close to Romford railway station and buses. Q

Upminster

Huntsman & Hounds

2 Ockendon Road, Corbets Tey, RM14 2DN (on B1421)
11-11 (midnight Fri & Sat) (01708) 221672
Beer range varies H
Much extended local with a good real ale choice, including seasonal guest beer selections from numerous microbreweries. A range of meat, seafood and vegetarian food offerings is available through the day until 10pm, including a set-price buffet and daily specials. Weekly quiz nights take place. The pub has a south-facing beer garden and a large car park. P(370)

Woodford Green

Cricketers L

299-301 High Road, IG8 9HQ (on A1099)

11.30-11 (midnight Fri & Sat); 12-11 Sun
(020) 8504 2734
McMullen AK, Cask Ale, Country Bitter
Warm, comfortable two-bar local with a dartboard in the public bar and plaques in the saloon for all 18 first class cricket counties, together with photographs of former MP Sir Winston Churchill, whose statue stands almost opposite. Good-value food is served Monday to Friday lunchtimes (special offers for pensioners Mon-Thu). There are picnic tables on the front patio and a covered smoking area with seats at the rear. Boules is played on a pitch at the back.
QP(179,W13)

Travellers Friend
496-498 High Road, Woodford Wells, IG8 0PN (on slip road off A104)
12-midnight (020) 8504 2435
Adnams Broadside; Courage Best Bitter; Fuller's London Pride; Sharp's Doom Bar; Wells Bombardier; guest beers
Now owned and run by two local families, this friendly, comfortable pub has a regionally important historic pub interior with oak-panelled walls and rare original snob screens. East London Brewery supplies one of the two guest beers. As far as is known, the pub has never sold keg bitter. At the rear is a large heated patio and smoking area, plus a small car park. In front are picnic tables; a new side garden is planned. QP

NORTH LONDON
N1: Barnsbury

Barnsbury
209-211 Liverpool Road, N1 1LX
4.30 (12 Fri & Sat)-11.30; 12-11.30 Sun
(020) 7607 5519 thebarnsbury.co.uk
Dark Star Hophead; Skinner's Betty Stogs; guest beers
Traditional, friendly local with a separate dining area and rear garden terrace. A large free house, it offers up to four changing real ales ranging from light to dark. There are regular pub favourites on the menu as well as more modern food; the various Sunday roasts are popular with locals. Recent refurbishment has subtly lifted the interior, which is comfortable and bright, with an interesting take on chandeliers. A relaxing refuge away from the busy drag of Upper Street.
(Angel)

N1: Canonbury

Hops & Glory
382 Essex Road, N1 3PF
4.30-11 (midnight Thu); 12-2am Fri & Sat; 12-10.30 Sun
(020) 7226 2277 hopsandglory.co.uk
Redemption Big Chief; Weird Beard Mariana Trench; guest beers
Popular, privately owned free house offering a fine selection of cask ales, other beers and ciders. It has an open-plan public area with a high ceiling and the usual Islington mix of mismatched tables, chairs and sofas. With a heated patio garden, it is family-friendly, and dogs and cyclists are welcome. Live piano music features on Thursdays. The beers available are likely to change regularly; there are plans to launch its own microbrewery.
(Essex Rd)P

N1: Hoxton

Baring
55 Baring Street, N1 3DS
12-11 (10.30 Sun) (020) 7359 5785
thebaringpub.co.uk
Shepherd Neame Spitfire; guest beers
A corner pub just off New North Road, offering welcome seating with settees in the corner. An interesting selection of books is available, along with board games and a big-screen TV for sport. There is a garden to the rear. Thatchers cider is served and lunchtime and evening meals are provided. The pub has its own football and cricket teams. Two guest beers are on handpump, with at least one LocAle. (Essex Rd)

Howl at the Moon
178 Hoxton Street, N1 5LH
4-11 (1am Fri); 12-1am Sat; 12-11 Sun (020) 7339 9221
Hackney Best Bitter; guest beers
Attractive conversion of a disused pub in a once run-down but now revived area. Five real ales are served from smaller breweries across the UK with one real cider on tap, plus two cider boxes behind the bar. The pleasant staff offer tastings. A superb selection of music is played. Mixed seating consists of sofas and chairs around the bar and numerous interesting items adorn the walls. Real English food is served at reasonable prices, and live blues features on Friday.

Wenlock Arms
26 Wenlock Road, N1 7TA
4-11 (midnight Thu); 12-1am Fri & Sat; 12-11 Sun
(020) 7608 3406 wenlockarms.com
Beer range varies
Saved from closure by a vigorous local campaign, this free house has 10 handpumps featuring beers from all across the UK, concentrating on small and medium-sized breweries, usually including a mild ale. With up to six ciders and perries and a small snacks menu headlined by salt beef sandwiches, this is a truly welcoming street-corner local with an international reputation. Jazz is played in the bar on Thursday nights. (Old St)

N1: Islington

Charles Lamb
16 Elia Street, N1 8DE
12 (4 Mon & Tue)-11; 12-10.30 Sun (020) 7837 5040
thecharleslambpub.com
Dark Star Hophead; Windsor & Eton Windsor Knot; guest beers
Charming, deservedly busy little pub serving four real ales, all from independent brewers and always in perfect condition, and occasionally cask cider. Service is fast, friendly and efficient. There is also a worthwhile range of bottle-conditioned ales. Food is a point of pride, but all seating is available to non-diners. The decor is traditional, with bare floorboards. There is some outside seating in a quiet street. Close to Regent's Canal.
(Angel)

Craft Beer Co
55 White Lion Street, N1 9PP
4-11 (midnight Thu); 12-1am Fri & Sat; 12-10.30 Sun
(020) 7278 4560
Beer range varies
Multi-room pub with a wooden bar displaying 10 handpumps, all dispensing ales from independent

brewers, and multiple keg fonts. Green curtains and red carpet give some warmth to the main bar, which has two Victorian pillars, a wooden floor, raised tables and stools, all overseen by Winston Churchill. A cosy room, with subtle lighting and settees, is to the left, and there is a smaller room to the back. To the side of the pub is a small garden. ❀◐◑⊖(Angel)🚌

Earl of Essex

25 Danbury Street, N1 8LE

2-11.30 Mon; 12-11.30 (12.30am Fri & Sat); 12-11 Sun
☎ (020) 7424 5828 🌐 earlofessex.net

Earls Earl, Pale Ale; guest beers H

Brewpub in Islington whose brewery currently produces two beers. Rather than using pumpclips, it has a large beer board showing the day's beers. Oddly, it does not list the one traditional cider served (from Gwatkin) but ask and you will get. There is a beer garden at the back. The six handpumps serve a rotating range of beers, usually from modern micros. Food is served until 9pm but the kitchen is closed 3pm-5pm Tuesday-Friday. ❀◐◑⊖(Angel)🍎🚌📶

New Rose

84-86 Essex Road, N1 8LU

12-11 (midnight Thu; 2am Fri & Sat); 12-10.30 Sun
☎ (020) 7226 1082 🌐 thenewrose.co.uk

Portobello VPA; guest beers H

Spacious and friendly pub, traditional but quirky, in the heart of Islington. As well as a changing range of four quality real ales (light through dark) from London breweries and further afield such as Hogs Back and Hanlons, there are American bottled beers. It does a tempting menu of pub favourites from locally-sourced ingredients; home-cooked pizzas are a speciality. Enjoy a pint in the small rear garden or on a bench at the front, or catch the big game on TV. ❀◐◑⇌(Essex Rd)🍎🚌📶

North Pole

188-190 New North Road, N1 7BJ

11-11 (midnight Fri & Sat); 11-10.30 Sun
☎ (020) 7354 5400 🌐 thenorthpolepub.co.uk

Hackney American Pale Ale; Redemption Pale Ale; guest beers H

A modern, spacious free house with a homely feel. Your first impression is of the dazzling array of 10 handpumps offering a wide selection of eight real ales (from Arbor to Wild Beer) and two ciders. Added to this are another 12 keg beers to complement the freshly prepared home-cooked food ranging from burgers, ribs and pizzas to pub classics and Sunday roasts, served all day. Seating is in abundance, indoors or out to suit. ❀◐◑⇌(Essex Rd)♣🍎🚌🐾📶

N1: King's Cross

Parcel Yard

Unit 8, Shared Service Yard, Goods Way, King's Cross Railway Station, N1C 4AH

8am-11; 9am-10.30 Sun ☎ (020) 7713 7258
🌐 parcelyard.co.uk

Fuller's Chiswick Bitter, Discovery, London Pride, ESB; Gales HSB; guest beers H

Large pub approached by stairs at the end of the new concourse, converted from a station parcel office. Used by local workers, commuters and for meetings, as well as bars on two levels there are semi-private rooms converted from offices (which can be booked) and an indoor balcony. The lower bar has 12 handpumps, the upstairs bar fewer. Minimal decor and rescued furniture feature, and there is no music. Breakfast is served until 11.45am, main meals 12-10pm. Disabled access is by lift. There are no smoking facilities. ❀◐◑♿⇌⊖(King's Cross/St Pancras)🚌📶

N2: East Finchley

Bald Faced Stag

69 High Road, N2 8AB

12-11 (midnight Fri & Sat) ☎ (020) 8442 1201
🌐 thebaldfacedstagn2.co.uk

Beer range varies H

A short walk from East Finchley underground station, this large and busy open-plan pub has a three-sided bar affording a friendly welcome. A separate area can be hired for functions or meetings. The house beer is from Greene King but beers from small independents are often featured, and beer festivals held twice a year. Bar meals are served, with a large, busy restaurant area at the rear. It is popular with patrons from the nearby Phoenix cinema. Over-21s only. ❀◐◑⊖P🚌

N4: Stroud Green

Old Dairy

1-3 Crouch Hill, N4 4AP

12-11 (midnight Thu; 1am Fri & Sat); 12-10.30 Sun
☎ (020) 7263 3337 🌐 theolddairyn4.co.uk

Portobello APA; Sambrook's Battersea Rye; guest beers H

Popular in the evenings, this Greene King Metropolitan outlet was built as a dairy, and outer wall decorations on Crouch Hill feature all of its previous dairy activities. The cavernous space is divided between a sit-down restaurant and two large rooms served by the bar, with a menu of British standards common to both (no food Mon lunchtimes). Four or five ales are served, including a house beer from Greene King, and a real cider in summer. ◐◑♿⊖(Crouch Hill)🚌

N5: Canonbury

Snooty Fox 🏆

75 Grosvenor Avenue, N5 2NN

4-11 (1am Fri); 12-1am Sat; 12-10.30 Sun
☎ (020) 7354 9532 🌐 snootyfoxlondon.co.uk

Otter Ale; guest beers H

Vibrant, spacious pub with 1960s icons depicted throughout and a 45rpm jukebox giving a retro feel. The light, airy lounge leads to a small patio, a pleasant spot to enjoy one of up to four real ales and watch the world go by. There is an occasional DJ for music, and several seasonal beer festivals feature up to 30 beers. Good modern British food is cooked to order, including Sunday roasts; table bookings are welcome. Local CAMRA Pub of the Year 2014. ❀◐◑⊖🚌

N6: Highgate

Bull

13 North Hill, N6 4AB

12-11.30 (midnight Fri & Sat); 12-11 Sun
☎ (020) 8341 0510 🌐 thebullhighgate.co.uk

London Brewing Company High Rise, Beer Street, Waterlow Gold, Vista, Ginger, Skyline H

Home to the London Brewing Company, this brewpub has five of its regular beers available plus a seasonal offering and a rotating cider on handpump. Now resurrected, it was formerly a restaurant for 15 years, and offers a fine menu, served in the dining area to the left, but is determined to attract beer drinkers from near and far into its remodelled bar area – as you enter and to the right. There is seating outside on the front terrace. (143,603)

Prince of Wales

53 Highgate High Street, N6 5JX

12-11 (midnight Fri & Sat) (020) 8340 0445

Butcombe Bitter; guest beers

Situated in the centre of the village at the top of the High Street, this traditional pub serves three guest ales, often from West Country brewers. A Thai menu is available lunchtimes, evenings and all day at weekends, along with Sunday roasts. The pub holds a challenging quiz on Tuesdays and also sponsors a cricket team, whose highest scores are celebrated on bats displayed in the bar. A rear outdoor area offers smoking and drinking overlooking Pond Square.

Wrestlers

98 North Road, N6 4AA

4.30-midnight (1am Fri); 12-1am Sat; 12-11 Sun

(020) 8340 4297 thewrestlershighgate.com

Fuller's London Pride; St Austell Tribute; guest beers

Near the top of North Hill, noted for the ancient ceremony of Swearing on the Horns dating from 1623. A large wood-burning fireplace dominates the front end of the bar, above which sit the said horns. Dark wood panelling sets a traditional tone. Early evening drinkers give way to diners later. The menu offers suggestions for drinks with each dish. Busy at weekends, it has a large TV screen for major sport and a heated outdoor yard at the rear. (143,603)

N7: Holloway

Coronet

338-346 Holloway Road, N7 6PA

8am-midnight (020) 7609 5014

Greene King IPA, Abbot; guest beers

Impressive Wetherspoon conversion of an old cinema, the Savoy, designed by William Glen, which showed its last film in 1983 and is now adorned with large prints of movie stars and former local entertainers. An old projector is the centrepiece of a raised dais towards the rear. Up to six guest ales are frequently served, with single brewery festivals at times. Expect plastic glasses and higher prices when Arsenal are playing at home. There are tables outside on the pavement and at the rear. Q (Holloway Rd)

N8: Hornsey

Three Compasses

62 High Street, N8 7NX

11-11 (midnight Fri & Sat); 12-11 Sun (020) 8340 2729

threecompasses.com

Fuller's London Pride; Redemption Pale Ale; Timothy Taylor Landlord; guest beers

Large front windows contribute to an airy, bright feel in the front bar of this award-winning community pub, a popular after-work venue for local young professionals and those heading for events at nearby Alexandra Palace. The rear bar is much larger, with daylight from a skylight roof, a pool table, two dartboards, a large-screen TV at the end and occasional live music. Three changing guest ales are served on the front bar. (141,144)

N9: Lower Edmonton

Beehive

24 Little Bury Street, N9 9JZ

12-midnight (1am Fri & Sat); 12-11 Sun

(020) 8360 4358 thebeehiveedmonton.co.uk

Adnams Southwold Bitter, Ghost Ship; Sharp's Doom Bar; guest beer

Tucked away in semi-detached suburbia, this imposing pub, rebuilt in 1929, usually has four real ales, kept in tip-top condition by the keen landlord. The all-through bar has a games area at one end and a dining area at the other, popular with a good mix of local customers. Quiz night is Tuesday. Fresh daily specials as well as traditional pub grub are available lunchtime and evening.

P

Stag & Hounds

371 Bury Street West, N9 9JW

12-midnight (11 Mon); 12-10.30 Sun (020) 8360 7412

Adnams Broadside; guest beers

A spacious M&B Ember Inns pub/restaurant towards the edge of Enfield with many distinct seating areas and a large garden. Popular with all age groups and families, it is mainly food oriented. Three quickly rotating seasonal guest beers are available at reasonable prices, with try-before-you-buy offers on all ales. The TV is always mute, showing news with subtitles. Tuesday is quiz night. The garden is gated and therefore child-friendly.

P

N10: Muswell Hill

John Baird

122 Fortis Green Road, N10 3HN

11-11 (midnight Fri & Sat); 12-10.30 Sun

(020) 8444 8830 thejohnbaird.co.uk

Purity Mad Goose; Redemption Trinity; Sharp's Doom Bar; guest beers

A mecca for real ale and cider fans in this part of north London, sporting up to six ales and a couple of ciders. One wing of this large pub is home to an excellent Thai restaurant, and the other provides ample space for drinkers and those wanting to watch major sporting events in comfort. A sizeable outside smoking and drinking area is provided at the rear. Quiz night is Tuesday. Children are allowed in the bar until 7pm, restaurant until 9pm. (102,234)

N12: North Finchley

Elephant Inn

283 Ballards Lane, N12 8NR

11-11 (midnight Fri & Sat); 12-10.30 Sun

(020) 8343 6110 elephantinnfinchley.co.uk

Fuller's London Pride, ESB; guest beers

Large wood-panelled pub with a U-shaped bar split into three distinct drinking areas, one a quiet zone free of TV screens. Bar meals focus on Thai food; the upstairs restaurant is open 6-10.30pm. The two guest beers are from the Fuller's portfolio, likewise the wide range of bottled beers. Numerous pub games are available, including darts and dominoes.

There is a patio with umbrellas at the front where you can watch traffic go by.
✿◑⊖(West Finchley)♣🚌🐾

N13: Palmers Green

Alfred Herring

316-322 Green Lanes, N13 5TT
🕐 8am-11 (midnight Thu-Sat) ☎ (020) 3232 1083
Courage Directors; Greene King Abbot; Ruddles Best Bitter; guest beers Ⓗ
A busy Wetherspoon shop conversion in the heart of Green Lanes shopping area, opened in 2006, comprising a large open area with booths to the side. Six of the 10 handpumps offer a varied range, with the manager regularly obtaining beers from the expanding list of London breweries. There is a resident darts team. The pub is named after a local First World War soldier, awarded the Victoria Cross for his heroic action in France in 1918. Q◑⇌🚌📶

N14: Southgate

New Crown

80-84 Chase Side, N14 5PH
🕐 8am-11.30 (12.30am Fri & Sat) ☎ (020) 8882 8758
Greene King Abbot; Ruddles Best Bitter; guest beers Ⓗ
A well-run Wetherspoon pub with polite, helpful and knowledgeable staff, minutes away from the tube. Formerly a Sainsbury's store, it has a large open-plan interior with spacious toilets. A range of 10 cask ales including eight changing guests is offered, all kept in good condition by keen staff. The manager aims to have two ales from small local breweries. Sparklers may be used; if concerned, please ask for them to be removed. Alcohol is served from 9am. ☕◑♿⊖🍎🚌🐾📶

N16: Stoke Newington

Jolly Butchers 🄻

204 Stoke Newington High Street, N16 7HU
🕐 4-midnight (1am Fri); 12-1am Sat; 12-11 Sun
☎ (020) 7241 2185 🌐 jollybutchers.co.uk
Redemption Trinity; Windsor & Eton Knight of the Garter; guest beers Ⓗ
A classic Art Deco-style bar boasting elaborate ironwork and glass, with a lively modern feel and the enviable status of being a true free house. Nine handpumps offer six different real ales, usually from microbreweries (the beers listed are just examples of what might be found), and three ciders or perries. The ale is complemented by great food, served Saturday and Sunday lunchtimes and every evening. ✿◑⇌🍎🚌🐾📶

Railway Tavern Ale House 🄻

2 St Jude Street, N16 8JT
🕐 4-11 (midnight Fri); 12-midnight Sat; 4-10.30 Sun
☎ (020) 0011 1195
Adnams Broadside; Redemption Trinity; guest beers Ⓗ
A gem of a pub well worth visiting, a stone's throw from busy Dalston. It has six varied and interesting cask ales to suit all tastes, including one from Adnams and a LocAle, plus exceptional bottled beers, such as Kernel. A Thai menu and Sunday roasts complete the offering. It is full of character, and a perfect venue to relax away from the sports crowd, with good beer and good company.
◑♿⊖(Dalston Jct/Dalston Kingsland)🚌🐾📶

N21: Winchmore Hill

Dog & Duck

74 Hoppers Road, N21 3LH
🕐 12-11.30 (12.30am Fri & Sat) ☎ (020) 8886 1987
🌐 dogandduckwinchmorehill.co.uk
Fuller's London Pride; Greene King IPA; Timothy Taylor Landlord; Young's Bitter Ⓗ
Traditional small one-bar pub, popular with football fans and the golfing fraternity. A corner is devoted to golf trophies and memorabilia, while other walls are adorned with local history pictures. Fortnightly quiz nights are held and sport is shown on TV. The patio-style walled garden courtyard at the rear welcomes dogs at quiet times; there is also a covered area. The pub has now been in this Guide for 11 years. ✿🚌(W9)

Orange Tree

18 Highfield Road, N21 3HA
🕐 12-midnight (12.30am Fri & Sat) ☎ (020) 8360 4853
🌐 the-orange-tree-pub.co.uk
Greene King IPA; Morland Old Speckled Hen; guest beers Ⓗ
This old-fashioned, original back-street local just a few yards from the New River Walk has been in the Guide for 21 consecutive years. Originally a Taylor Walker house with the sign still outside, it is now a well-established free house. Live sport is shown and the two guest beers are often sport related. A Redemption beer is frequently available. Always welcoming, with friendly staff, it has two darts teams, a fortnightly quiz, and holds barbecues in summer in the award-winning garden.
☕✿◑⇌♣P🚌(329)🍷

Cockfosters

Cock & Dragon

Chalk Lane, EN4 9HU
🕐 11-11 (11.30 Fri & Sat); 11-10.30 Sun ☎ (020) 8449 7160
🌐 cockanddragon-cockfosters.co.uk
Greene King IPA; guest beers Ⓗ
Set back from the main road and a short stroll from Cockfosters station, the London Loop passes close by, with Trent Park a few minutes' walk away. Guest beers are from the Punch Finest Cask list. The main bar has several alcoves with comfortable seating, and an area to the right of the bar for TV sport. Thai food is served, with an English menu option at lunchtime. The pleasant rear garden has a large decked area. ☕✿◑⊖♣P🚌(298)

Enfield

Moon Under Water 🄻

115-117 Chase Side, EN2 6NN
🕐 9am-11 (10.30 Sun) ☎ (020) 8366 9855
Greene King Abbot; Ruddles Best Bitter; Shepherd Neame Spitfire; guest beers Ⓗ
Long-established Wetherspoon pub converted from a dairy, within easy reach of both Enfield Chase and Gordon Hill stations. The building has a church-like appearance: light floods in on three sides and note the large stained-glass window. Popular with all age groups, it has a dedicated area for families until 8.30pm. Westons Old Rosie is invariably available. Breakfast is served until noon and meals until 10pm. Sparklers may be used; if concerned, ask for them to be removed.
☕✿◑♿⇌(Chase)🍎P🚌(191,W9)📶

Wonder 𝕃

1 Batley Road, EN2 0JG

⊛ 11-11 (12.30am Fri & Sat); 12-11 Sun ☎ (020) 8363 0202

McMullen AK, Cask Ale, Country Bitter; guest beer Ⓗ

A great, old-fashioned back-street local. The separate public bar has a real fire, dartboard, fruit machine and piano. There is honky tonk music Saturday evenings and Sunday afternoons, jamming sessions the last Wednesday of the month and a quiz night the first Wednesday. A meat raffle is held weekly. The landlord prints a monthly What's On newsletter, also available on Facebook. The paved seating space outside includes a heated area for smokers. Pies are served all day – mushy peas optional.
Q❀◐♿⇌(Gordon Hill)♣P🚌(191,W8)📶

High Barnet

Black Horse

Wood Street, EN5 4HY

⊛ 12-midnight (1am Fri & Sat); 12-11 Sun
☎ (020) 8449 2230 🌐 blackhorsebarnet.co.uk

Beer range varies Ⓗ

Drinkers are always made most welcome in this pub, reopened in 2012, tastefully extended into an open-plan area and now food-oriented. The Barnet Brewery, located at the rear of the pub, can be viewed through glass doors. Eight handpumps normally offer up to three of the brewery's beers, plus one from Purity and regional and local ales from around the country. There is an extensive side garden and a paved area at the back, in front of the microbrewery. ♘❀◐◑♿⊖●🚌📶

Misty Moon

148 High Street, EN5 5XP

⊛ 11-11 (midnight Fri & Sat); 12-midnight Sun
☎ (020) 8441 9476

St Austell Tribute; guest beers Ⓗ

Long, narrow, former 1987 Wetherspoon conversion, but now a free house, offering a changing range of four ales, some of them sourced from SIBA. The landlord is passionate about serving a great pint, and has been awarded a Certificate of Recognition from St Austell Brewery. The pub is popular with sport fans as all live football games are now shown. Open mic night features on Sunday and occasional live music on Saturday.
❀◐⊖♣🚌

Olde Mitre Inne 🏆

58 High Street, EN5 5SJ

⊛ 12-11 (1am Fri & Sat) ☎ (020) 8449 5701

Adnams Southwold Bitter; guest beers Ⓗ

The oldest coaching inn in Barnet; there has been a pub here since 1553. Beams, exposed brickwork, wood panelling and an open fire give an authentic feel. The enthusiastic landlord offers three or four house regulars, one or two national brands, one or two SIBA ales and one or two special seasonal beers from a list that changes every eight weeks. A new corridor allows easy access to further rooms and outside is a well-maintained courtyard drinking area. ♘❀◐◑⊖♣●🚌🐾📶

New Barnet

Railway Bell

13 East Barnet Road, EN4 8RR

⊛ 8am-11 (midnight Thu-Sat) ☎ (020) 8449 1369

Greene King Abbot; Ruddles Best Bitter; Shepherd Neame Spitfire; guest beers Ⓗ

A Wetherspoon pub that unusually was previously neither a shop nor a showroom. Extensively refurbished in 2013, it is a bright place where families are well catered for. However, the manager is keen on showcasing her beer and 10 well-kept ales are always available, often including local London brews. The car park has gone, replaced by a larger garden now divided into smoking and no smoking areas, the latter having pretend grass. ♘❀◐◑♿⇌🚌📶

Ponders End

Picture Palace 𝕃

Howard Hall, Lincoln Road, EN3 4AQ

⊛ 9am-11 (midnight Fri & Sat) ☎ (020) 8344 9690

Greene King Abbot; Ruddles Best Bitter; guest beers Ⓗ

A sympathetic Wetherspoon conversion of a 1920s cinema with some architectural features preserved; the spacious main hall has film murals above the bar and there are two smaller areas to the front and side. There is also an outdoor patio area. A huge screen is available for showing sport or films in silent mode. LocAle is provided by London microbreweries. Sparklers may be used; if concerned, please ask for them to be removed.
❀◐◑♿⇌(Ponders End/Southbury)●P🚌📶

NORTH-WEST LONDON

NW1: Camden Town

Tapping the Admiral 𝕃

77 Castle Road, NW1 8SU

⊛ 12-midnight (11 Mon & Tue); 12-10.30 Sun
☎ (020) 7267 6118 🌐 tappingtheadmiral.co.uk

London Fields Love not War; Redemption Big Chief; Twickenham Naked Ladies; Windsor & Eton Canberra; guest beers Ⓗ

A community pub to enjoy, where friendly and knowledgeable staff offer a warm welcome. Eight handpumps dispense a variety of high-quality guest ales, mainly from local breweries, and two serve real cider or perry. The food offering is from a Thai menu, with great-value lunches. The beer garden is well designed. There is a Wednesday quiz and live music weekends including traditional Irish music on Sunday nights. Local CAMRA Pub of the Year 2013. ❀◐◑⊖(Kentish Town West)●🚌

NW1: Euston

Bree Louise 𝕃

69 Cobourg Street, NW1 2HH

⊛ 11.30-11.30; 12-10.30 Sun ☎ (020) 7681 4930
🌐 thebreelouise.com

Redemption Trinity; Sambrook's Junction Ale; Windsor & Eton Knight of the Garter, Guardsman; guest beers Ⓗ

One-bar corner pub, busy with locals and Euston commuters. A cooled gravity stillage, complemented by handpumps, provides a large and changing range (beers listed are to give an indication of what you may find), alongside up to 11 ciders and perries. Regular beer festivals are held. Pumpclips festoon the walls, there is no music, just conversation, but occasional sport on TV (usually at the weekend). Outdoor seating is on the pavement. Closing time may be later on weekdays.
❀◐◑⇌⊖(Euston/Euston Sq)●🚌🐾📶

Doric Arch 🄻

Euston Station Colonnade, 1 Eversholt Street, NW1 2DN
10-11 (10.30 Sun) ☎ (020) 7383 3359 doric-arch.co.uk
Fuller's Discovery, London Pride, ESB; guest beers 🄷
Formerly the Head of Steam, this pub has been in the Guide for many years. Up a flight of stairs, the window allows for a view of the busy urban world below. The pub is right next to Euston Station and is used extensively by commuters. The excellent staff are helpful and informative about ale. Toilets are at entrance level. Brewery and railway memorabilia adorn the walls. LocAles will come from London breweries, guests from around the country.

Euston Tap

West Lodge, 190 Euston Road, NW1 2EF
12-11.30 (10 Sun) ☎ (020) 3137 8837 eustontap.com
Beer range varies 🄷
Fronting the main station building, an impressive Grade II-listed Portland stone lodge, this is one of the few relics from the original 1830s station. Up to eight changing beers are pumped up to taps behind the bar. Space is rather limited although there is a large outside drinking area as well as seating up a wrought-iron spiral staircase. The lodge opposite, the Cider Tap, opening at 3.30pm (not Sun), features six real ciders. Food can be ordered from various takeaway menus.
Q(Euston/Euston Sq)

Royal George 🄻

8-14 Eversholt Street, NW1 1DG
11-11 (2am Fri & Sat); 12-10.30 Sun ☎ (020) 7387 2431
Fuller's London Pride; London Fields Love Not War; guest beers 🄷
Large late-Victorian pub, arranged as interconnecting rooms facing the three street frontages, with a modern central bar. An unusual fireplace with marquetry work on its surrounds is on one side of the pub. Opposite Euston Station, it is named after HMS Royal George, a flagship vessel for the Royal Navy in the 1800s, and the front of the pub looks like the rear of the ship. Local breweries can be London Fields, Hackney, By the Horns and Portobello.

NW3: Hampstead

Duke of Hamilton 🄻

23 New End, NW3 1JD
12-11 (10.30 Sun) ☎ (020) 7794 0258
thedukeofhamilton.com
Dark Star Hophead; Fuller's London Pride, ESB; guest beers 🄷
An old favourite, saved from conversion into flats in 2010, this historic back-street pub still serves a range of ales, but has lost its kitchen. Named after a Civil War royalist, it has been in the Guide for two decades. Its origins date back over 250 years. The main bar has a TV screen and quieter areas. The cellar is now a theatre, where music and plays are performed occasionally. There are outside areas front and rear. (268,603)

NW5: Kentish Town

Pineapple 🄻

51 Leverton Street, NW5 2NX
12-11 (10.30 Sun) ☎ (020) 7284 4631
Adnams Broadside; Redemption Trinity; guest beers 🄷
A real community pub, saved from closure by the locals, Grade II-listed and with a regionally important historic pub interior notable for its mirrors and splendid bar-back. There is comfortable seating around tables in the front bar and to the rear an informal conservatory overlooking the patio garden. A Thai kitchen and traditional Sunday roasts feature. LocAles can come from across London and, the pub being free of tie, the beer range changes regularly. Local CAMRA Pub of the Year 2012.

Southampton Arms

139 Highgate Road, NW5 1LE
12-midnight thesouthamptonarms.co.uk
Beer range varies 🄷
A past winner of CAMRA awards, this pub does what it says on the sign outside: Ale, Cider, Meat. On and behind the bar, 18 handpumps serve almost equal amounts of cider and a whole range of beers from microbreweries across the UK. Snacks include pork pies, cheese and meat baps. Music on vinyl is played and the piano is in regular use. At the rear is a secluded patio.
(Gospel Oak/Kentish Town)

Harefield

Harefield

41 High Street, UB9 6BY
12-11 (10.30 Sun) ☎ (01895) 820003
Sharp's Doom Bar; Timothy Taylor Landlord; guest beers 🄷
Built in 1801, this pub spent many years as a beer house and butcher's. Originally the King's Head, it has had several name changes before settling on the current one in 2007 after a complete refurbishment and the introduction of an over-21s policy. It is well known for its friendly welcome and good food made with fresh local produce. There is discounted beer every Wednesday. It has an outside patio, but parking is limited. Quiz nights are the first and third Thursdays of the month.
P(331,U9)

King's Arms

6 Park Lane, UB9 6BJ
11-11 (midnight Fri & Sat) ☎ (01895) 822131
Adnams Broadside; Fuller's London Pride; Young's Bitter; guest beer 🄷
Parts of this heavily beamed hostelry are said to be 15th century, forming one of the wings when it was rebuilt in the 17th century. Although there is only one bar, there are many discrete areas in which to lose yourself and possibly enjoy Thai food in the evenings. Quiz nights are Wednesday and Sunday. The guest beer is often from Vale.
P(331,U9)

Old Orchard 🄻

Jacks Lane, UB9 6HJ (off Park Lane)
11.30-11 (10.30 Sun) ☎ (01895) 822631
oldorchard-harefield.co.uk
Mighty Oak Oscar Wilde; Phoenix Brunning & Price Original; Tring Side Pocket for a Toad; guest beers 🄷
Formerly a country house before becoming a restaurant, this is now a Brunning & Price establishment. Refurbished in 2010, the pub is lined with bookcases and pictures, and has an unfussy array of mismatched tables and chairs; there are three welcoming real fires in the colder

months. Three guest beers are usually available, mostly from local breweries. There are great views of the Colne Valley from the terrace and beer garden. Q (U9)

Harrow

Castle ★
30 West Street, HA1 3EF
12-11 (midnight Fri & Sat) (020) 8422 3155
castle-harrow.co.uk
Fuller's London Pride, ESB, seasonal beer; Gales Seafarers Ale; guest beer H
In the heart of historic Harrow-on-the-Hill, this is a popular and friendly Fuller's house. Built in 1901 and Grade II-listed, it has a nationally important historic pub interior. Food is served until 9pm every day; reservations are recommended for Sunday lunchtime. Three real coal fires help to keep the pub warm and cosy in the colder months and a secluded beer garden is popular during the summer. Q (258,H17)

Moon on the Hill
373-375 Station Road, HA1 2AW
8am-midnight (12.30am Fri & Sat) (020) 8863 3670
Greene King Abbot; Ruddles Best Bitter; guest beers H
Small, busy Wetherspoon pub close to Harrow-on-the-Hill station and served by numerous bus routes. Offering food all day, it is popular with price-conscious regulars, office workers and students from the nearby University of Westminster. The pub gets extremely busy when there are sporting events on at nearby Wembley Stadium and plastic glasses may be used on these occasions. Alcohol is served from 9am.
(Harrow-on-the-Hill)

Northwood Hills

William Jolle L
The Broadway, 53 Joel Street, HA6 1LL
8am-midnight (1am Fri & Sat) (01923) 842240
Greene King Abbot; Ruddles Best Bitter; Sharp's Doom Bar; guest beers H
Once a car showroom and before that a furniture showroom, this venue was converted to a Wetherspoon pub in 1998. It provides a large open interior, with some booths on the left and towards the right of the bar. The patio is heated. Local beers are usually from Rebellion or Tring. Alcohol is served from 9am. Q

Rayners Lane

Village Inn
402-408 Rayners Lane, HA5 5DY
8am-11 (midnight Thu; 12.30am Fri & Sat)
(020) 8868 8551
Sharp's Doom Bar; Greene King Abbot; Ruddles Best Bitter; guest beers H
Another split-level, double-fronted shop conversion. The rear of the pub, accessed down a few steps, sports the traditional Wetherspoon booths with a row of tables down the centre. A terraced area behind has a variety of large potted plants among the picnic tables. The front pavement has a few tables and chairs for that alfresco moment. The pub has a good cross-section of clientele who mingle quite happily. Alcohol is served from 9am. Q

Ruislip Manor

JJ Moons L
12 Victoria Road, HA4 0AA
8am-midnight; 9am-1am Fri & Sat; 8am-11 Sun
(01895) 622373
Courage Best Bitter; Fuller's London Pride; Greene King Abbot; Ruddles Best Bitter; guest beers H
Opened in 1990 in a former Woolworths and still with the same licensee, this busy Wetherspoon pub has a range of ales plus two ciders on draught. A real ale club meets on a Wednesday evening, advising the manager which guest beers to stock, and participating in a cellar dash when up to 16 ales can be tried. Additional beer festivals are held throughout the year as well as the chain's regular bi-annual events. Alcohol is served from 9am.
Q

South Kenton

Windermere ★
Windermere Avenue, HA9 8QT
12-11.30 (12.30am Fri); 11-12.30am Sat; 11-11.30 Sun
(020) 8904 7484 windermerepub.com
Courage Best Bitter; Young's Special H
A genuine community pub with a nationally important historic pub interior, next to South Kenton station. Built in 1939, it has three bars, the public bar now only used for functions. The saloon and lounge retain many original features including the large inner porches, bar counters, back-fittings, wall panelling and fireplaces. A quiz night is held on alternate Thursdays and live entertainment takes place on a regular basis. A guest ale is usually on the bar on special occasions.
P (223)

SOUTH-EAST LONDON
SE1: Bermondsey

Simon the Tanner
231 Long Lane, SE1 4PR
12 (5 Mon)-11; 12-10.30 Sun (020) 7357 8740
simonthetanner.co.uk
Beer range varies H
Offering a peaceful oasis away from the Bermondsey crowds, the Simon is a modestly sized mid-terrace pub which is Grade II-listed, mainly for its exterior. Inside are bare floorboards and a nice mix of traditional and contemporary decor. Three changing real ales are available, often from London breweries. Food is a quality take on standard dishes like pies, burgers and soups. A quiz is held on Tuesday evenings and the upright piano is put through its paces every Wednesday.
(London Bridge)

SE1: Borough

Royal Oak
44 Tabard Street, SE1 4JU
11 (12 Sat)-11.30; 12-9 Sun (020) 7357 7173
Harveys Sussex XX Mild Ale, Sussex Best Bitter, Armada Ale, seasonal beers; guest beer H
A back-to-basics drinkers' pub with charm and history, separated into two sections by the bar. You cannot help but fall in love with the quaintness of the book and games library, or the friendliness of the staff. Once inside, you could be forgiven for thinking you are in an old country pub, and the high ceilings and quirky decorations add to the

atmosphere. Many regulars come from miles away to spend time here, as should you.
Q◑≋(London Bridge)⊖♣●▭

Ship

68 Borough Road, SE1 1DX
✪ 12-11 (midnight Fri & Sat); 12-10.30 Sun
☎ (020) 7403 7059 🌐 shipborough.co.uk
Fuller's London Pride, Bengal Lancer, seasonal beers; Gales Seafarers Ale; guest beer Ⓗ
Halfway between Borough and Elephant & Castle, this is a great example of a pub that brilliantly combines good beer, good food, sport and music. As part of the local Victorian landscape, the building is long and thin, and the bar runs most of its length along one side, with larger spaces at the front and rear. As with all Fuller's pubs, the menu is hearty and a pie is always the perfect accompaniment to a pint.
❀◑≋(London Bridge)⊖♣▭ᯤ

SE1: Borough Market

Market Porter

9 Stoney Street, SE1 9AA
✪ 6am-9am, 11-11; 12-11 Sat; 12-10.30 Sun
☎ (020) 7407 2495
Harveys Sussex Best Bitter; guest beers Ⓗ
A classic market pub serving up to 12 changing ales and ciders. Attached to the walls and ceiling is a vast range of pumpclips showing those ales that have previously been on sale. It can get busy, with drinkers spilling out on to the street, especially on market days. A small air-conditioned seating area is at the rear. An upstairs restaurant serves lunches and is available for private hire in the evenings.
◐≋⊖(London Bridge)●▭

Old King's Head

45 Borough High Street, SE1 1NA
✪ 11-midnight (1am Fri & Sat); 12-midnight Sun
☎ (020) 7407 1550 🌐 theoldkingshead.uk.com
Harveys Sussex Best Bitter; St Austell Tribute, Proper Job; Sharp's Doom Bar; Wells Bombardier Ⓗ
Down a narrow, cobbled road off Borough High Street lies this traditional pub. The stained glass windows hint at a bygone era and the pictures adorning the walls tell the story of a pub, and an area, that has a rich history. The layout inside is simple, with an L-shaped bar in one corner usually offering five or six real ales on handpump. The clientele is a mix of tourists, office workers and market-goers. ◑♿≋⊖(London Bridge)▭

Rake

14 Winchester Walk, SE1 9AG
✪ 12 (11 Fri; 10 Sat)-11; 12-8 Sun ☎ (020) 7407 0557
Beer range varies Ⓗ
If you were to start a library of bottled beers, this pub, operated by Utobeer of Borough Market, would be about the best reference point. Alongside its vast range of bottles, it packs three handpumps and five taps into just 4ft of bar. For unusual guest ales, a world tour of beer and knowledgeable staff, this is an ideal place to visit. A heated patio doubles the area available, with overspill into the market when busy.
Q❀♿≋⊖(London Bridge)▭ᯤ

Sheaf

24 Southwark Street, SE1 1TY
✪ 11-11 (midnight Fri); 12-11 Sat; 12-10.30 Sun
☎ (020) 7407 9934
Fuller's London Pride; Young's Bitter; guest beers Ⓗ
Situated beneath the old Hop Exchange, this pub is remarkably bright and airy for a basement bar, and offers an oasis from the bustle of the nearby market. The recent contemporary refurbishment contrasts with the more traditional surroundings of nearby establishments. The retro benches, stools and tables are complemented by modern partitioning and flat-screen TVs showing popular sporting events. With 10 handpumps, up to seven guest ales are available in addition to the regulars, including the house Red Car Bitter.
◑≋⊖(London Bridge)♣▭🐾ᯤ

SE1: Southwark

Charles Dickens

160 Union Street, SE1 0LH
✪ 12-11 (7 Sun) ☎ (020) 7401 3744
🌐 thecharlesdickens.co.uk
Beer range varies Ⓗ
A classic 19th-century back-street pub, tucked away from the hustle and bustle of the surrounding area. It boasts a lively atmosphere in the evenings, two screens for sport, a partially covered beer garden and an unpretentious local quality. Sunday afternoons are a more chilled affair, with a roast available. Up to six constantly changing real ales, often from Adnams plus interesting microbreweries, are advertised on a blackboard. There is a pub quiz on Wednesday evenings.
Q♨❀◑≋(Waterloo East)⊖▭🐾ᯤ

SE1: Waterloo

King's Arms

25 Roupell Street, SE1 8TB
✪ 11 (12 Sat)-11; 12-10.30 Sun ☎ (020) 7207 0784
Adnams Southwold Bitter; guest beers Ⓗ
Here is a back-street corner treasure worth seeking out. Seating is at a premium, however, and it is not unusual to find as many people drinking and chatting in the street as inside. Up to nine varied real ales are available, including house beer Ale of Kings, brewed by Sharp's. The two separate sides of the central bar allow for a change of scene without leaving the pub. To the rear is a Thai food restaurant. ◑≋(Waterloo/Waterloo East)⊖●▯▭

SE3: Blackheath

Hare & Billet

1a Eliot Cottages, Hare & Billet Road, SE3 0QJ
✪ 11-11 (midnight Thu-Sat); 12-10.30 Sun
☎ (020) 8852 2352 🌐 hareandbillet.com
Beer range varies Ⓗ
Popular pub on the edge of Blackheath village overlooking the open expanse of the heath itself; it was tastefully refurbished in 2013 with a rustic feel. There are now 10 handpumps, with an emphasis on London microbreweries, and several ciders. A selection of US and Belgian bottled beers is also available. After tasting sessions, a self-styled Blackheath Beer Council can choose some of the future beers to be stocked. It is more expensive than other local pubs. ♨◑♿≋●▭🐾ᯤ

Royal Standard

44 Vanbrugh Park, SE3 7JQ
✪ 11 (12 Sun)-11 ☎ (020) 8858 1533
Fuller's London Pride; guest beers Ⓗ

Giving its name to the local vicinity, this pub attracts a mixed crowd in a good-natured atmosphere. Up to three guest beers change weekly; pumpclips displayed around the bar illustrate the wide range sold since 2008. London microbreweries regularly supply guest ales, as does Cottage. Boxed real cider is also served. The pub hosts monthly Meet the Brewer events, occasional live music, a poker evening on Monday and a Thursday night pub quiz.
(Westcombe Park) P

SE4: Brockley

Talbot

2-4 Tyrwhitt Road, SE4 1QG
12-11 (midnight Fri & Sat); 11-10.30 Sun
(020) 8692 2665
Harveys Sussex Best Bitter; guest beers
A fine Victorian suburban pub on two floors which has built up a good reputation since reopening a few years ago and is popular with all ages. The decor sets a nice balance between old and new, and there is a large outdoor seating area. As well as the regular beer, up to three guest ales are usually on offer, plus a tasty food menu. Regular events include a quiz night on Tuesday and live music. **Q** (St Johns) (Elverson Rd)

SE5: Camberwell

Stormbird

25 Camberwell Church Street, SE5 8TR
4-midnight (1am Fri & Sat) (020) 7708 4460
thestormbirdpub.co.uk
Beer range varies
This is the sister pub of the Hermit's Cave across the road and offers a slightly more contemporary feel, attracting a mixed but generally younger crowd. There is a huge range of beers of all types available, including three regularly changing real ales on handpump and an extensive keg and bottled beer selection, with brews from the UK, continental Europe and the US. Draught beers can be enjoyed in third-of-a-pint measures.
(Denmark Hill)

SE5: Denmark Hill

Fox on the Hill

149 Denmark Hill, SE5 8EH
8am-midnight (12.30am Fri & Sat) (020) 7738 4756
Greene King Abbot; Morland Old Speckled Hen; Ruddles Best Bitter; guest beers
Spacious and welcoming Wetherspoon pub at the top of a steep hill. Inside are a number of cosy, low-screened booths, while outside is a large garden, smokers' terrace and front lawn with picnic tables. Wall displays depict the history of the local area, including well-known Victorian former resident John Ruskin, after whom the nearby park is named. Up to seven guest beers are usually available and the pub hosts regular Meet the Brewer events. Alcohol is served from 9am.
P

SE6: Catford

London & Rye

109 Rushey Green, SE6 4AF
8am-11 (020) 8697 5028
Greene King Abbot; Ruddles Best Bitter; guest beers
Converted by Wetherspoon from a former DIY shop in 2000, this pub takes its name from its location on the old coaching route between London and Rye in Kent. Displays feature historic figures with local connections, ranging from singer Tommy Steele to nursery education pioneers Rachel and Margaret McMillan, the statesman Herbert Morrison and the tragic love poet Ernest Dowson. Guest beers often come from microbreweries. Alcoholic drinks are served from 9am, with food through until 11pm.
Q (Catford/Catford Bridge)

SE8: Deptford

Dog & Bell

116 Prince Street, SE8 3JD
12-11.30 (midnight Fri & Sat) (020) 8692 5664
Fuller's London Pride, Bengal Lancer; guest beers
A traditional and welcoming pub tucked away down a side street near the centre of Deptford, offering four or five excellent beers and simple, tasty meals. It has a lively bar, a real fire in winter, and a good mix of clientele including locals, cyclists and those taking a stroll along the nearby Thames Path. Charlie and Eileen have run the pub since 1988 and proudly display the many awards and citations they have won over the years.
Q

SE9: Eltham

Howerd Club

447 Rochester Way, SE9 6PH
12-4 (not Mon-Fri), 7.30-11; 12-4, 7.30-10.30 Sun
(020) 8856 7212
Fuller's London Pride; guest beers
A warm welcome awaits at this tiny social club tucked away at the back of a community hall. A former CAMRA National Club of the Year, it serves London Pride and two other changing ales, one Fuller's and one usually from Shepherd Neame. Children are welcome until 8.30pm. The decor includes memorabilia linked to former local celebrity Frankie Howerd, and a copy of every Guide since 1996 is also to hand. CAMRA members are admitted on showing their membership card.
(132,286)

Park Tavern

45 Passey Place, SE9 5DA
12-11 (020) 8850 3216 parktaverneltham.co.uk
Beer range varies
Attractive traditional Victorian pub with a tiled frontage and historic Truman's signage. The stylish interior has elegant drapes, bar lamps and chandeliers, an impressive wooden bar and a real log fire. Decorative plates and pictures line the walls. Jazz and light classical background music complements the atmosphere. An impressive selection of up to eight real ales is on sale, alongside whiskies and wine. Outside is a well-kept heated rear garden, and additional seating at the front and side. **Q**

SE10: East Greenwich

Pelton Arms

23-25 Pelton Road, SE10 9PQ

12-midnight (1am Fri); 11-midnight Sat; 12-11 Sun
(020) 8858 0572 peltonarms.com
Adnams Broadside; Greene King IPA; Wells Bombardier; guest beers
Popular and spacious back-street pub a short stroll from Greenwich town centre. It has an L-shaped bar, eclectic furnishings and soft lighting, giving the place a welcoming feel. Very much at the heart of the local community, it hosts varied live music four nights a week, plus a quiz on Tuesdays; the Pelton knitters get together on Wednesdays. Up to seven changing guest ales are offered. There are also five B&B rooms available.
(Maze Hill) (177,188)

SE10: Greenwich

Old Loyal Britons

62 Thames Street, SE10 9BX
12-11 (10.30 Sun) (020) 3601 8941 ewbrewery.com
Beer range varies
Friendly independent bar and restaurant renovated and reopened in what is believed to have originally been a fire station. Local artists' work is displayed throughout. Comfortable armchairs and traditional bar furniture lead to the dining area with old pews. The food speciality is raclette – a table-top grill for locally-sourced smoked and cured meats, cheese and potatoes. Up to four real ales are served, with an on-site brewery planned.
Q (Cutty Sark)

SE11: Kennington

Oaka at the Mansion House

46 Kennington Park Road, SE11 4RS
12-midnight (1.30am Fri & Sat) (020) 7582 5599
oakalondon.com
Oakham JHB, Inferno, Citra, Scarlet Macaw, seasonal beers
Opened in 2013, this is Oakham Ales' flagship pub in London, offering an impressive range of its beers on handpump. The decor is contemporary, with subdued lighting, a water feature and background music. The bar area on the right has a mix of sofas and table seating. To the left is the restaurant which serves a varied menu of pan-Asian cuisine.
(Elephant & Castle)

SE13: Hither Green

Station

14 Staplehurst Road, SE13 5NB
12-11 (10.30 Sun) (020) 8463 0367
stationhotelhithergreen.co.uk
Castle Rock Harvest Pale; Harveys Sussex Best Bitter; Purity Mad Goose; Sambrook's Wandle Ale; Timothy Taylor Landlord; guest beers
A stone's throw from the railway station and hence attracting a varied clientele, this pub is housed in a beautiful and imposing Victorian-style building dating from 1906. The interior is now open plan with tasteful contemporary decor, following a comprehensive refurbishment in 2012. Inside is a spacious L-shaped bar at the front and a restaurant area to the rear. An impressive 11 handpumps offer up to 10 real ales plus real cider. There is a regular quiz night. (273)

SE14: New Cross

Royal Albert

460 New Cross Road, SE14 6TJ
4-midnight (1am Fri); 12-1am Sat; 12-midnight Sun
(020) 8692 3737 royalalbertpub.com
Beer range varies
An Antic pub with a moustache logo and a relaxed, homely ambience – almost romantic come evenings. An L-shaped bar leads to a conservatory and an open-to-view kitchen. The decor includes two impressive stuffed birds. Up to four guest beers come from microbreweries such as By the Horns, Kent, Purity and Thornbridge. The menu includes steaks, chops, pies and game. The clientele is a mixture of academia, musicians and people out for an enjoyable time. A front patio offers outside drinking.
(Deptford Bridge)

SE15: Nunhead

Ivy House

40 Stuart Road, SE15 3BE
12-11 (midnight Fri & Sat); 12-10.30 Sun
(020) 7277 8233 ivyhousenunhead.com
Brockley Pale Ale; Truman's Runner; guest beers
London's first co-operatively run pub, rescued from closure in 2012 by local community action. Built by Truman's Brewery, it is now Grade II-listed and winner of the English Heritage Angel Award, a wonderful example of the 1930s 'improved public house' initiative and with a regionally important historic pub interior. Visit the pub's website for information about its 1970s pub rock history, community events and live music gigs. Five guest beers are generally sourced from small London breweries. (343,484)

SE15: Peckham

Gowlett Arms

62 Gowlett Road, SE15 4HY
12-midnight (1am Fri & Sat); 12-11.30 Sun
(020) 7635 7048 thegowlett.com
Beer range varies
Situated in a back street on the Peckham and Dulwich border, this pub is popular with people of all ages, and their dogs. It has a C-shaped bar with attractive wood-panelled walls at one end, a mix of table seating and sofas, and a real fire in winter months. Usually four changing real ales are available, along with great pizzas. On Thursday nights you can play your own 7in records, and a DJ spins the discs on Sunday evenings.
(E Dulwich) (Peckham Rye) (37,484)

Kentish Drovers

71-79 Peckham High Street, SE15 5RS
8am-midnight (020) 7277 4283
Beer range varies
A former bank in the heart of Peckham, now a popular Wetherspoon pub with a clientele that reflects the multicultural locality. Its name harks back to when livestock were driven to London from Kent. There is a lovely mosaic floor as you enter, and two drinking areas, one opposite the bar and another to the rear leading to a small courtyard. Five changing real ales are usually sold, plus a range of ciders, and occasionally a Jamaican stout. Alcohol is served from 9am.
(Peckham Rye)

SE16: Rotherhithe

Surrey Docks

185 Lower Road, SE16 2LW

✪ 8am-midnight (1am Fri & Sat) ☎ (020) 7394 2832

Fuller's London Pride; Greene King Abbot; Ruddles Best Bitter; guest beers Ⓗ

Modern Wetherspoon pub which commemorates the Surrey Commercial Docks that operated here from 1807 to 1970. Information panels on the walls chart the history of the area and some of its more famous residents. Up to six real ales and at least one real cider make this pub a must, as do the friendly and helpful staff and characterful local clientele. The pub is well served by public transport, including the London Overground station opposite. No alcohol before 9am. ❀◐◑♿⊖(Surrey Quays)🍎🚌📶

SE18: Plumstead

Star Inn

158 Plumstead Common Road, SE18 2UL

✪ 11-11 (midnight Fri & Sat); 12-11 Sun ☎ (020) 8854 1524

Courage Best Bitter; Sharp's Doom Bar; guest beer Ⓗ

Close to Plumstead Common, this pub has a regionally important historic interior. Retaining Victorian features from its predecessor, it has three separate bars, a rare surviving example of such a pub in this part of London. The saloon bar on the left is more contemporary, following its inter-war rebuilding. In bygone days, when the forerunner to Woolwich Arsenal played their football matches on the common, the Star was used as a changing room. Good honest-value lunches are available Monday to Saturday. ◐♣🚌

SE18: Woolwich

Prince Albert (Rose's)

47-49 Hare Street, SE18 6NE

✪ 11-11; 12-6 Sun ☎ (020) 8854 1538

Beer range varies Ⓗ

The nearest real ale house to the Woolwich Ferry, this friendly single-bar pub was rebuilt in 1928 with 12ft-high ceilings, giving a spacious feel. The interior is traditional and uncluttered, with wood panelling, banquette seating and matching furniture. Up to three varying real ales are available from the likes of Hogs Back and Westerham, and occasional beer festivals are held. Often called Rose's, echoing a predecessor establishment. Two lizards in a vivarium keep their beady eyes on proceedings. ⇌⊖(Woolwich Arsenal)♣🚌🐾📶

SE19: Crystal Palace

Postal Order

33 Westow Street, SE19 3RW

✪ 8am-midnight ☎ (020) 8771 3003

Greene King Abbot; Ruddles Best Bitter; guest beers Ⓗ

Occupying the site of the former Royal Mail sorting office, this popular Wetherspoon one-bar pub is at the heart of the thriving Crystal Palace triangle area. The decor includes local pictures. Frequented by a loyal local customer base, it provides a contrast to some of the area's pricier establishments for both ale lovers and cider fans. Up to seven beers are on sale at any time, including a changing selection of guests from local and national brewers. Q◐◑♿⇌(Gipsy Hill)🍎🚌📶

Westow House

79 Westow Hill, SE19 1TX

✪ 5.30-midnight Mon; 12-midnight (2am Fri & Sat); 12-11 Sun ☎ (020) 8670 0654 🌐 westowhouse.com

Beer range varies Ⓗ

A popular Antic pub with vintage retro furniture and artwork. The changing selection of seven real ales is drawn mostly from microbreweries, often including those from within the Greater London area. Occasional Meet the Brewer events are held. Lunchtime and evening meals are served daily. There is regular live music, often on a Thursday, and a quiz night on Tuesday. At the front is a large outside drinking area. ❀◐◑⇌⊖🍎🚌🐾📶

SE20: Penge

Moon & Stars

164-166 High Street, SE20 7QS

✪ 9am-11 (10.30 Sun) ☎ (020) 8776 5680

Dark Star Hophead; Greene King Abbot; Ruddles Best Bitter; Thornbridge Jaipur IPA; guest beers Ⓗ

A popular high street Wetherspoon pub, with a large L-shaped interior with a raised seating area at the rear and many alcoves suitable for small groups. The bar has 17 handpumps, often showcasing beers from local microbreweries including the nearby Late Knights. The pub hosts regular mini festivals and other beer-related events.
🐴❀◐◑♿⇌(Kent House)🚋(Beckenham Rd)
🍎🚌(227,358)📶

SE22: East Dulwich

East Dulwich Tavern

1 Lordship Lane, SE22 8HJ

✪ 12-midnight (1am Fri & Sat) ☎ (020) 8693 1316

🌐 eastdulwichtavern.com

Adnams Lighthouse; guest beers Ⓗ

Spacious and popular Victorian corner pub sitting proudly at the head of Lordship Lane. It is operated by Antic and furnished in its typical eclectic style, with an amazing tiled floor in the main bar area. There is a large first-floor function room and pavement seating outside at the front. Up to five real ales are on offer, with four changing regularly, along with a good-quality food menu. The pub hosts monthly film club and jazz nights.
🐴◐◑⇌♣🚌🐾📶

Flying Pig

58-60 East Dulwich Road, SE22 9AX

✪ 12-11 (midnight Fri & Sat); 12-10.30 Sun

☎ (020) 7732 7575 🌐 theflyingpiglondon.com

Beer range varies Ⓗ

Craft beer and barbecue bar, opened in the summer of 2013 in former restaurant premises. It has a small bar at the front with a large seating area and an open-to-view kitchen to the rear, plus outdoor seating on the front terrace. There are six varying real ales from around the country on handpump plus two real ciders in polypins and up to 12 more beers on tap. The range includes ales from various small breweries plus American and European brews. 🐴◐◑⇌🍎🚌

SE23: Forest Hill

All Inn One

53 Perry Vale, SE23 2NE

3-11 Mon; 12-11 (midnight Fri & Sat) (020) 8699 3311
allinnone.org.uk
Brains SA; Caledonian Deuchars IPA; guest beers
Formerly the Foresters Arms, this large red-brick pub is located behind Forest Hill station and can be reached via a subway under the railway line. It is roomy, comfortable and open plan, with a C-shaped bar that extends through into the rear wood-panelled function room. A spacious garden with children's play equipment and smoking area is a haven in the summer. Live music features twice monthly, plus a weekly quiz night on Wednesdays. Two changing guest beers are usually on the bar.

Blythe Hill Tavern

319 Stanstead Road, SE23 1JB
11-11.30 (midnight Thu-Sat); 12-11 Sun
(020) 8690 5176
Courage Best Bitter; Dark Star Hophead; Fuller's London Pride; Harveys Sussex Best Bitter; guest beers
A friendly local, rooted in the community, this Victorian corner pub has a regionally important historic interior for its interesting three-room layout and 1920s panelling. The barmen wear traditional collar and tie. There are TV screens often showing sport in two bars. Quiz nights are Mondays from September to April, traditional Irish music plays on Thursdays. The garden includes a children's play area and is abloom with flowers in summer. Local CAMRA Pub of the Year 2012.
Q (Catford/Catford Bridge) (171,185)

Capitol

11-21 London Road, SE23 3TW
8am-midnight (1am Fri & Sat) (020) 8291 8920
Greene King Abbot; Ruddles Best Bitter; guest beers
This J Stanley Beard-designed Art Deco building dates from 1929 and was originally a cinema, then later a bingo hall, and is now a popular Wetherspoon pub. Tours of the upper circle and other parts of the reputedly haunted building can be arranged for groups. Four or five changing guest beers are usually on offer in addition to the two regulars. Drinkers can vote for their favourite beer to appear the following week. Alcohol is served from 9am.

Sylvan Post

24-28 Dartmouth Road, SE23 3XU
4-11 (midnight Fri); 12-midnight; 12-11 Sun
(020) 8291 5712 sylvanpost.com
Beer range varies
An Antic pub that was a 1960s post office, it retains many original features including the strong room, now transformed into a snug, and the original exterior. Two more quiet snug rooms contain old post office equipment and the walls are hung with postal memorabilia. Up to three changing real ales are sold. Music in the main room can be loud. It is family-friendly, with board games suitable for children. Food is good quality, with Sunday lunch a speciality. Quiz night is Tuesday.
Q

SE27: West Norwood

Hope

49 Norwood High Street, SE27 9JS
11-11.30 (midnight Fri & Sat); 12-11 Sun
(020) 8670 2035
Young's Bitter, Special, seasonal beer; guest beer
A comfortable, traditional Young's pub, dating from 1840, serving a diverse local and wider community around a central bar. Pleasant, relaxed and welcoming, it has a lovely walled, terraced beer garden with a fish pond and covered, heated bench seating around tables. It hosts a quiz night and monthly live music, and boasts 3D sports TV, with screens in the garden during the summer also used for film nights. Children and dogs are welcome. An autumn beer festival is held.

Addiscombe

Claret Free House

5 Bingham Corner, Lower Addiscombe Road, CR0 7AA
11.30-11 (11.30 Thu; midnight Fri & Sat); 12-11 Sun
(020) 8656 7452
Palmers Best Bitter; guest beers
Small, family-owned free house in a row of shops, convenient for the tram stop. The rather dimly lit interior is decorated in mock-Tudor style. The house beer, Palmers Best Bitter, has sold over one million pints. Five varying guest ales, mainly from microbreweries, come from all over the UK. Beers on and coming next are shown on a board facing the bar. Cider is fetched from the cellar. The Claret has featured in the Guide continuously for 27 years.
(289,367)

Cricketers

47 Shirley Road, CR0 7ER
12-midnight; 12-11 Sun (020) 8655 3507
Harveys Sussex Best Bitter; guest beers
This popular Brewers' Tudor community pub has recently received an external spruce-up. The single-room interior has a comfortable, lived-in atmosphere, with three real fires. Up to four guest beers come from microbreweries and the Enterprise list. Food is available all day and regular curry nights and quiz nights are held along with occasional beer festivals. Televised sport is popular, especially when Crystal Palace are playing.
P (130,367)

Beckenham

Bricklayers Arms

237 High Street, BR3 1BN
11-11; 12-10.30 Sun (020) 8402 0007
bricklayersarms.co
Harveys Sussex Best Bitter; St Austell Tribute; Young's Special; guest beer
A traditional, family-friendly, high-street pub attracting a clientele of all ages. Three regular ales plus a rotating guest are always on. Home-cooked food is provided, with Thai specialities. There is an open log fire in winter and covered outdoor seating. Customers are welcome to bring their dogs. (Jct)

Jolly Woodman

9 Chancery Lane, BR3 6NR
12 (4 Mon)-11 (020) 8663 1031
Harveys Sussex Best Bitter; Timothy Taylor Landlord; guest beers
Family-run traditional local in a narrow back street. With a cosy, cheerful atmosphere and welcoming staff, it is popular with a mixed clientele of all ages. The pub comprises a single L-shaped room with a small front-of-bar area, more seating towards the rear, and outdoor benches at the front and in the

rear courtyard. Up to four guest beers are on tap. Home-made hot food and sandwiches are available at lunchtimes. Q❀◐⇌⊟(Jct)♣●⊟🐾ᯤ

Bexleyheath

Earl Haig

The Pantiles, Little Heath Road, DA7 5HH
11.30-midnight ☎ (01322) 449463
Fuller's London Pride; Harveys Sussex Best Bitter; Young's Bitter; guest beers Ⓗ
A 1930s Charrington pub, currently with 11 handpumps covering major and smaller producers. The clientele already know it as a dining venue. Ember Inns foresee deeper involvement in real ale, with enthusiastic management leading staff ale champions to take up Marston's cellarmanship training. Cheaper real ale is available on Monday evenings. The pub offers periodic cabaret and twice-weekly quizzes. Q❀◐◑♿P⊟

Robin Hood & Little John 𝕃

78 Lion Road, DA6 8PF
11-3, 5.30 (7 Sat)-11; 12-4, 7-10.30 Sun
☎ (020) 8303 1128 🌐 robinhoodbexleyheath.co.uk
Adnams Southwold Bitter, Broadside; Brains Rev James; Fuller's London Pride; Harveys Sussex Best Bitter; Sharp's Doom Bar; guest beer Ⓗ
This back-street local pub dates from the 1830s when it was surrounded by fields. Eight real ales are on offer, mostly from independent breweries. It has a reputation for its home-cooked food at lunchtimes and evenings (until 8.30pm Mon-Thu), with Italian specials, which can be eaten at tables made from old Singer sewing machines. A regular CAMRA branch Pub of the Year and regional winner three times. Over-21s only. Q❀◐◑⊟(313)🐾

Wrong 'Un 𝕃

234-236 Broadway, DA6 8AS
8am-midnight ☎ (020) 8298 0439
Fuller's London Pride; Greene King Abbot; Ruddles Best Bitter; guest beers Ⓗ
Bexleyheath's first Wetherspoon pub, opened in 1994 in a single-storey former furniture store. There are records of cricket being played locally since 1746 and the unusual pub name is an alternative expression for a googly. Westons Old Rosie cider is served on handpump. Alcohol is available from 9am and food is served until 11pm daily. There are comfortable booths to sit in as well as an open-plan area. Q◐◑♿⇌●⊟ᯤ

Bromley

Partridge

194 High Street, BR1 1HE
12-11.30 (12.30am Fri & Sat); 12-11 Sun
☎ (020) 8464 7656 🌐 partridgebromley.co.uk
Fuller's Discovery, London Pride, ESB, seasonal beer; Gales Seafarers Ale; guest beer Ⓗ
Former NatWest bank, now a Fuller's ale and pie house, which has retained many original features including high ceilings and chandeliers. There are two smaller snug rooms at either end of the main bar. As well as Fuller's regular range, seasonal guest beers are available. It has an extensive food menu. The pub is popular with shoppers and can also get crowded when football is shown.
❀◐◑♿⇌(North/South)⊟

Red Lion

10 North Road, BR1 3LG
11 (12 Sun)-11 ☎ (020) 8460 2691
Greene King IPA, Abbot; Harveys Sussex Best Bitter; guest beers Ⓗ
The Red Lion has been a regular Guide entrant for more than 20 years and is well worth seeking out in the quiet back streets north of Bromley town centre. Five handpumps include two for changing guest beers. The pub hosts three darts teams and boasts an extensive library of donated books. Original tiling is a feature. Staff are knowledgeable and carry-out containers are available. Local CAMRA Pub of the Year in 2012.
Q❀◐◑⇌(North)♣⊟

Shortlands Tavern

5 Station Road, BR2 0EY
12-11.30 (midnight Fri & Sat); 12-11 Sun
☎ (020) 8466 0202
Beer range varies Ⓗ
A comfortable pub in the heart of the local community and convenient for trains and buses. It has recently been refurbished and now sells an excellent choice of real ales and food. Local beers and microbreweries are normally well represented on the four handpumps. Quiz nights and live band performances take place regularly. Upstairs is a smart function room and there are several different cosy areas in the main bar.
Q❀◐◑⇌(Shortlands)♣⊟

Chelsfield

Five Bells

Church Road, BR6 7RE
11.30-11; 12-10.30 Sun ☎ (01689) 821044
🌐 thefivebells-chelsfieldvillage.co.uk
Courage Best Bitter; Sharp's Doom Bar; guest beers Ⓗ
A regular Guide entry for many years, this popular village pub still has a public bar. Around the corner, a separate entrance gives access to the saloon and dining area where dogs are also welcome outside mealtimes. A quarterly guide gives details of events including a weekly quiz night and live music evenings. The guest beers are predominantly from the West Country. The R3 bus service from Orpington stops outside the door.
❀◐◑♣P⊟(R3)🐾ᯤ

Chislehurst

Imperial Arms

1 Old Hill, BR7 5LZ
12-11 (11.30 Thu; midnight Fri & Sat); 12-10.30 Sun
☎ (020) 3605 7899 🌐 imperialarms.co.uk
Harveys Sussex Best Bitter; Sharp's Doom Bar; guest beer Ⓗ
A stylish and comfortable pub which was expensively refurbished in 2012. Now the two bars combine space for social drinkers with tables for diners. The publican is enthusiastic about his beers, and fresh home-made food is prepared daily, with roasts on Sunday. Live music is hosted on Saturday and Sunday evenings. The final stage of the pub's rejuvenation – the reopening of the Coach House function room – was completed in 2014.
Q❀◐◑⇌⊟(162,269)🐾ᯤ

Croydon

Builders Arms

65 Leslie Park Road, CR0 6TP

12-11 (midnight Fri & Sat) ☎ (020) 8654 1803

buildersarmscroydon.co.uk

Fuller's Chiswick Bitter, London Pride; Gales HSB; guest beer Ⓗ

A traditional back-street local opened in the 19th century to serve builders working on nearby railways. The two bars each have their own character. At the back of the larger saloon bar is a pleasant garden with games available during the warmer months, and at the front a TV for sport. In the public bar there is a larger screen and dartboard. Tuesday night is quiz night. This pub holds Fuller's Master Cellarman accreditation.

♿≉(East)(Lebanon Rd)♣

Dog & Bull

24 Surrey Street, CR0 1RG

11-11 (11.30 Fri & Sat); 12-10.30 Sun ☎ (020) 8667 9718

Young's Bitter, Special; guest beers Ⓗ

A historic Grade II-listed pub in the middle of the daily street market. You will feel at home as soon as you enter. It has a classic layout – an island bar with rooms and seating around the sides. There is an attractive courtyard garden with bedding plants and seasonal baskets, and a function room upstairs. This is the pub that Young's used for their publicity shot of Prince Charles pulling a pint.

Q≉(East/West)(George St/Reeves Corner)

George

17-21 George Street, CR0 1LA

10am-midnight (1am Fri & Sat); 8am-midnight Sun

☎ (020) 8649 9077

Greene King IPA, Abbot; Thornbridge Jaipur IPA; guest beers Ⓗ

Large town-centre pub, open plan, with two bars serving a wide range of real ales. The usual Wetherspoon decor encompassing local historical information teaches us that this pub and street are named after an ancient 15th-century inn. A large central screen shows sport, and smaller ones show a subtitled news channel with the sound turned off. On weekend evenings it can get noisier, with a younger crowd in attendance.

♿≉(East/West)(George St)

Green Dragon

58 High Street, CR0 1NA

10-midnight (1am Fri & Sat); 12-10.30 Sun

☎ (020) 8667 0684

Beer range varies Ⓗ

A lively street-corner pub near the market, popular with all ages. Six handpumps and two gravity casks dispense a changing range of beers including those from local breweries. Through the day the atmosphere is quiet and friendly; in the evenings and at weekends the place is livelier, with a wide variety of music and other events taking place. Traditional, good-quality pub food is served at reasonable prices. Voted local CAMRA's Pub of the Year 2013.

♿≉(East/West)(George St)♣

Oval Tavern

131 Oval Road, CR0 6BR

12-11 (midnight Fri & Sat); 12-10.30 Sun

☎ (020) 8686 6023 theovalcroydon.co.uk

Thwaites Wainwright; Timothy Taylor Landlord; guest beers Ⓗ

Popular back-street family pub with a growing reputation for live music. Good home-made food is always available – the huge Scotch eggs and sausage rolls are especially recommended. Children and dogs are welcome and there is a large garden and barbecue area to the rear. The decor is unusual; the half-timbering creates an interesting interior with a rural atmosphere. The pub has been under new management since 2013, with a greater emphasis on cask ale.

♿≉(East)♣

Skylark

34-36 South End, CR0 1DP

8am-midnight (1am Fri & Sat) ☎ (020) 8649 9909

Fuller's London Pride; Greene King Abbot; Dark Star Hophead; guest beers Ⓗ

Enthusiastic two-storey Wetherspoon pub in the south-end restaurant quarter, a short walk from the town centre. Interesting local and microbrewery guest beers feature regularly, and festivals and Meet the Brewer events are held. The pub's name is inspired by a work of the Victorian poet Gerard Manley Hopkins, who was a regular visitor to Croydon. Internal decoration includes a focus on the history of London's first airport, located in Croydon on what is now the A23 Purley Way.

♿≉(South)

Spreadeagle

39-41 Katharine Street, CR0 1NX

11-11 (midnight Fri & Sat); 12-10.30 Sun

☎ (020) 8781 1134

Fuller's London Pride, ESB; Gales Seafarers Ale, HSB; guest beer Ⓗ

Occupying former bank premises next to the town hall, the Spreadeagle combines good food and ales with film and theatrical performances, filling a gap created by the closure of other venues locally. Guest ales are often from local breweries, and an extensive range of Fuller's bottled beers is available. The pub is proud of its Fuller's Master Cellarman accreditation. TV screens show sporting events and quiz night is Sunday. Two function rooms upstairs can be used for meetings.

♿≉(East/West)(George St)

Downe

Queen's Head

25 High Street, BR6 7US

12-11 (11.30 Fri & Sat); 12-10.30 Sun ☎ (01689) 852145

queensheaddowne.com

Harveys Sussex Best Bitter; Sharp's Doom Bar; guest beers Ⓗ

A classic family-run village pub and former coaching stop dating back to 1565, convenient for country walks and visiting Charles Darwin's Down House. The bar and dining rooms are full of old-world charm, with open fires and cosy sofas. Guest beers are mostly from local microbreweries and the menu uses many locally-sourced ingredients. Local CAMRA branch Pub of the Year 2014, the pub is home to the local cricket club and golf society.

(146,R8)

Orpington

Orpington Liberal Club

7 Station Road, BR6 0RZ

1-3 (not Mon-Thu), 8-11; 12-3, 7-11 Sat; 8-10.30 Sun
(01689) 820882 orpingtonliberalclub.co.uk
Beer range varies H
Free-of-tie club concentrating on LocAle, as well as regional and national microbreweries. Real cider and perry are always stocked. The Bromley and Greater London CAMRA Club of the Year 2013 and a National Club of the Year 2014 finalist, it has regular live music, runs beer festivals twice a year, holds Meet the Brewer and beer launch events and has started collaboration brewing with microbreweries. A CAMRA or National Union of Liberal Clubs membership card is required for entry. Q P

Petts Wood

Sovereign of the Seas L
109-111 Queensway, BR5 1DG
9am-11 (midnight Thu & Fri) (01689) 891606
Greene King Abbot; Ruddles Best Bitter; Sharp's Doom Bar; guest beers H
A large and popular Wetherspoon pub centrally located in a shopping area. It boasts 12 handpumps, with six or more offering a changing range of guest beers. The pub has an intimate atmosphere with different styles of seating including snug alcoves. A community noticeboard is prominently placed, and local historic photos line the walls, including those of William Willett, the daylight-saving campaigner, and the ship after which the pub is named.

Sidcup

Tailor's Chalk
47-49 High Street, DA14 6ED
8am-11 (020) 8308 6880
Courage Best Bitter; Greene King IPA, Abbot; guest beers H
Situated in the middle of Sidcup's shopping parade, this unusually compact Wetherspoon has lots of nooks and crannies. The large internal support pillars can make it seem fuller than it really is. There are the usual changing guest ales, often from local breweries. News is always on the TV screen by the main door.

Upper Belvedere

Prince of Wales L
13a Woolwich Road, DA17 5EE
2-10.30 Mon & Tue; 12-11 Wed & Thu; 12-midnight Fri & Sat; 12-11 Sun (01322) 433737
Sharp's Doom Bar; Young's Bitter; guest beers H
Built around 1863, this small pub with a horseshoe-shaped bar stands on what was once Lessness Heath. All beers are generally below 4.5% ABV and are £2.50 a pint between 1-5pm. Sports fans can watch the action on large-screen TVs. Made-to-order snacks and meals are available, with Sunday roasts (served 1-6pm) and a well-priced Thursday meal deal. There is entertainment on Saturday nights and a quiz on Sunday evenings.
(99,401)

Welling

Door Hinge
11 Welling High Street, DA16 1TR
closed Mon; 3-9; 12-10 Fri & Sat; 12-3 Sun 07956 845509 thedoorhinge.co.uk
Beer range varies G
Opened in 2013 in part of a former electrical wholesalers, London's first permanent micropub is a welcome breath of fresh air on the local pub scene, stocking over 300 real ales in its first year. Normally at least three beers are on, dispensed from within a glass-fronted cold room. The cosy bar seats 22 patrons, encouraging conversation among strangers. Welling United and Erith & Belvedere football grounds are just a couple of minutes away.
Q

New Cross Turnpike L
55 Bellegrove Road, DA16 3PB
8am-midnight (020) 8304 1600
Greene King Abbot; Ruddles Best Bitter; Shepherd Neame Spitfire; guest beers H
The pub takes its name from its location on what was once one of many private toll roads. It is an attractive Wetherspoon establishment on four levels including a gallery and two patios. Opened in 1998, it was previously a NatWest bank. Disabled access includes two wheelchair lifts and a ground floor toilet. Up to eight guest ales are served by the helpful staff from 9am onwards. The management aim to ensure that local beers are always on offer. Q

SOUTH-WEST LONDON

SW1: Belgravia

Antelope
22-24 Eaton Terrace, SW1W 8EZ
12-11 (11.30 Fri); 12-10 Sun (020) 7824 8512
antelope-eaton-terrace.co.uk
Fuller's London Pride, Bengal Lancer, ESB; Gales Seafarers Ale H
Dating back to 1827, this pub is now operated by Fuller's after many years as a Nicholson's pub. Preserved original features include etched glass windows, the central bar and a side room used as a snug. This is very much an upmarket house and the clientele consists mainly of local professionals. The upstairs bar and side room can be hired for functions. The pub plays cricket matches against the Churchill Arms (Notting Hill).
Q (Sloane Square)

Star Tavern L
6 Belgrave Mews West, SW1X 8HT
11 (12 Sat & Sun)-11; 11-10.30 Sun (020) 7235 3019
star-tavern-belgravia.co.uk
Fuller's London Pride, ESB, seasonal beer; Gales Seafarers Ale H
A charming mews pub rich in the history of the powerful, famous and infamous; it is rumoured that the Great Train Robbery was planned here. Now it is a popular Fuller's pub where local residents, business people and embassy staff rub shoulders with casual visitors. Sometimes a special Fuller's beer can be found. Upstairs is a dining room, also bookable for functions. This pub is one of the select few that has featured in every edition of this Guide.
Q (Hyde Park Corner/Knightsbridge)

SW1: Pimlico

Cask Pub & Kitchen L
6 Charlwood Street, SW1V 2EE

12-11 (10.30 Sun) ☎ (020) 7630 7225
caskpubandkitchen.com
Dark Star Hophead; guest beers H
Formerly the Pimlico Tram and converted to a beer destination pub by owners who have since acquired and converted several more premises in the south-east. Ten handpumps serve real ales from many microbreweries such as Arbor Ales and Dark Star, and a vast range of bottled beers from the UK and around the world complements some unusual keg choices. Burgers feature on the weekday menu, with Sunday roasts until late afternoon. A regular local CAMRA Pub of the Year contender. Q(Victoria)

Constitution

42 Churton Street, SW1V 2LP
11-11; 12-10.30 Sat & Sun ☎ (020) 7834 3651
theconstitution.co.uk
Greene King IPA; guest beers H
Unspoilt and comfortable wood-panelled venue, the first Italianate, ornate tavern in Pimlico, built by Richard Lacy in 1842 and named after a sailing ship. Many nautical pictures and photographs adorn the walls of this single-bar pub, with models on shelves. A fine mirror hangs above the fireplace. Upstairs, the restored Churton Room is available for hire. Traditional British food includes Cumberland sausages, fish and chips and a popular Sunday roast. No food on Saturdays. (Victoria)

SW1: St James's

Red Lion ★

2 Duke of York Street, SW1Y 6JP
11.30-11; closed Sun ☎ (020) 7321 0782
redlionmayfair.co.uk
Fuller's Chiswick Bitter, Discovery, London Pride, ESB, seasonal beer; Gales Seafarers Ale H
Close to the upmarket shops in Jermyn Street, this is a deservedly celebrated little gem, worth visiting just for its spectacular Victorian interior of etched mirrors and glass. The Grade II-listed building dates from 1821 and was given a new frontage in 1871; it has a tiny, nationally important historic pub interior and visitors often spill onto the pavement outside. Mind the precipitous steps down to the toilets. (Green Park/Piccadilly Circus)

SW1: Victoria

Cask & Glass

39 Palace Street, SW1E 5HN
11-11; 12-8 Sat; closed Sun ☎ (020) 7834 7630
Shepherd Neame Master Brew, Kent's Best, Spitfire, seasonal beer H
First licensed in 1862 as the Duke of Cambridge, this attractive small one-room pub on the route between Buckingham Palace and Westminster Cathedral, adorned with flowers in summer, is a haven for tourists, office workers and local residents. The wood-panelled bar has pictures of local scenes and politicians. Look out for the bull's eye windows and the paintings of the pub on the way to the toilets. A cosy place for a pint after (or instead of) visiting the sights.
Q(St James's Park)

Wetherspoon's

Unit 5, Upper Concourse, Victoria Station, Terminus Place, SW1V 1JT
7am-11 (midnight Fri & Sat) ☎ (020) 7931 0445
Fuller's London Pride, ESB; Greene King IPA, Abbot; guest beers H
Overlooking the station concourse and accessed mainly by escalators, this pub has recently been refurbished in a bright café-bar design. The interior features blue and cream tiling, two curved bars with marble-style tops and the welcome addition of banquettes along the opposite side. Twelve handpumps dispense regular beers and changing guest ales, which often come from local brewers like Portobello. TV screens show times of train departures. Note that British Transport police sometimes close the bar when football fans are due. Q

SW1: Westminster

Buckingham Arms

62 Petty France, SW1H 9EU
11-11 (6 Sat); closed Sun ☎ (020) 7222 3386
buckinghamarms.com
Wells Bombardier; Young's Bitter, Special, seasonal beer H
Said to have once been a hat shop, this pub was opened in the 1720s as the Bell and renamed the Black Horse in the 1740s, rebuilt in 1898 and renamed the Buckingham Arms in 1901. Substantially renovated in recent years, it has appeared in every edition of this Guide. A mix of modern and traditional seats and tables, high and low, draws civil servants and visitors alike, plus the occasional Member of Parliament.
(St James's Park)

Sanctuary House Hotel

33 Tothill Street, SW1H 9LA
8am-11 (10.30 Sun) ☎ (020) 7799 4044
sanctuaryhousehotel.co.uk
Fuller's Chiswick Bitter, Discovery, London Pride, ESB; guest beer H
A Fuller's Ale & Pie House and hotel, mainly drawing office workers and visitors to Westminster Abbey and other nearby attractions. On ancient marshland and Tothill Fields, scene of trials by combat and 18th-century duels, this converted early 20th-century office building has housed publishers and politicians. Now in quieter times it offers warmth and hospitality. The fields were within the limits of Sanctuary at the Abbey, hence the medieval-style mural on the back wall.
Q(St James's Park)

Speaker L

46 Great Peter Street, SW1P 2HA
12-11; closed Sat & Sun ☎ (020) 7222 1749
Timothy Taylor Landlord; Young's Bitter; guest beers H
This comfortable wood-panelled one-bar local dates from at least 1729 when it was the Castle, renamed Elephant & Castle around 1800, and then the Speaker in 1999. The area was the Devil's Acre, a notorious slum and next to the world's first public gas works. The pub, decorated with parliamentary caricatures, now welcomes residents from local estates and workers from government offices and Channel 4, who enjoy the range of five beers and home-made food; no music, TV or children.
Q(St James's Park)

SW1: Whitehall

Lord Moon of the Mall

16-18 Whitehall, SW1A 2DY

8am-11.30 (midnight Fri & Sat); 8am-11 Sun
(020) 7839 7701

Fuller's London Pride; Greene King IPA, Abbot; guest beers

A 1995 Wetherspoon conversion, the building was designed by Richard Coad and built in 1870. Formerly a bank, the pale pink sandstone, dark-wood panelling, high ceilings and arched windows would still be recognisable to the Victorian clerks. It is entirely open plan, with a family dining area to the rear where children are welcome until 9.30pm. Alcoholic drinks are served from 9am and meals all day. There are up to seven rotating guest beers. Note Wetherspoon founder Tim Martin's portrait on the pub sign. Q (Charing Cross)

SW2: Streatham Hill

Crown & Sceptre

2A Streatham Hill, SW2 4AH

9am-midnight (1am Fri & Sat) (020) 8671 0843

Greene King Abbot; Ruddles Best Bitter; Sambrook's Wandle Ale; guest beers

A landmark building situated where the South Circular crosses the A23, this ex-Truman's pub was the earliest Wetherspoon conversion in south-west London. With an energetic young manager of many years' standing, it sells more cask beer than lager – four or five changing guests generally encompassing a wide range of strengths and styles. As well as the original Truman's façade and tiling outside, it has kept a pub atmosphere and is decorated with unusual framed floral artwork on the walls. Q P

SW3: Chelsea

Hour Glass

279-283 Brompton Road, SW3 2DY

12-11 (11.30 Fri & Sat); 12-10.30 Sun (020) 7589 2840

Fuller's London Pride; guest beers

Narrow single bar rebuilt in 1936 with a tiled exterior. First licensed in 1852 as a beer house, it later became part of the Goring & Jenkins Lion Brewery Estate. Alongside the London Pride, the pub offers a semi-resident ale which rotates every three months, and a weekly guest, fresh every Wednesday night, showcasing regional brewers and little-known microbreweries.
(South Kensington)

SW4: Clapham

Prince of Wales

38 Old Town, SW4 0LB

5-11 (midnight Thu; 1am Fri); 1-1am Sat; 1-11 Sun
(020) 7622 3530

Harveys Sussex Best Bitter; guest beers

Narrow corner pub picked out at night by the neon letters POW and decorated inside with an extraordinary collection of bric-a-brac, such as traffic lights, stuffed animals and model aircraft – an experience not to be missed. Alongside the Harveys, a local Sambrook's beer, sometimes Taylor Landlord, and Millwhites Rum Cask cider are all served on handpump, with other real ciders from boxes behind the bar. Pizzas are available in the evenings. (Clapham Common)

Windmill on the Common

Clapham Common South Side, SW4 9DE

11-midnight; 12-11 Sun (020) 8673 4579
windmillclapham.co.uk

Wells Bombardier; Young's Bitter, Special, seasonal beer

A sprawling, landmark public house dating from 1665 with mainly 18th and 19th century extensions. Among several distinct drinking areas, the domed room has a whispering gallery effect to rival that of St Paul's Cathedral. Quiz night is Sunday. The quality of the Young's beers here is consistently impressive. Entrance to the 29-bedroom hotel is around the corner in Holly Lodge. (Clapham Common/Clapham South) P

SW5: Earls Court

King's Head

17 Hogarth Place, SW5 0QT

11-11 (10.30 Sun) (020) 7373 5239

Beer range varies

Dating from the 17th century, this inn is the oldest surviving licensed premises in the area. Rebuilt in 1937, it is now a friendly corner pub off the busy Earl's Court Road, recently refurbished in a modern style with a wooden floor and coloured tiling around the bar. Expect to find Portobello and Westerham beers among the four on handpump. Quiz night is Monday, and there is occasional live music on special days.
(West Brompton)

SW6: Parsons Green

White Horse

1-3 Parsons Green, SW6 4UL

9.30am-11.30 (midnight Thu-Sat) (020) 7736 2115
whitehorsesw6.com

Adnams Broadside; Oakham JHB; guest beers

Destination M&B pub which normally boasts five guest beers and an attractive selection of international bottled beers. Regular beer and food matching events take place as well as four annual beer festivals, including the not-to-be-missed Old Ale Festival in late November when the Coach House, normally reserved for dining, has a stillage. The pub can get busy when Chelsea FC are playing at home, but the upstairs area is a good place to escape the crowds. Q (22)

SW7: Gloucester Road

Queen's Arms

30 Queens Gate Mews, SW7 5QL

12-11 (10.30 Sun) (020) 7823 9293
thequeensarmskensington.co.uk

Fuller's London Pride; Sharp's Doom Bar; guest beers

Lovely corner mews pub well worth seeking out for its real ales and further wide range of interesting beers, malt whiskies and other spirits. Note the unusual curved doors. The L-shaped room has wood floors and panelling. The clientele reflects the location: well-heeled locals, students from Imperial College and musicians from, and visitors to, the nearby Albert Hall. The food menu and specials are of superior quality. Q

SW8: South Lambeth

Priory Arms 🄻

83 Lansdowne Way, SW8 2PB

5 (12 Sat)-11.30; 12-10.30 Sun ☎ (020) 7622 1884

theprioryarms.com

Beer range varies 🄷

Award-winning free house with an attractive frontage and an extensively modernised interior, serving a wide choice of beers and home-cooked food. Guest ales, from breweries such as Dark Star, Downton and Northumberland, change almost daily. Around 40 German and Belgian bottled beers are usually on offer. The pub has a community feel with events including a Sunday evening quiz, and is home to a cricket team. Upstairs is a function room used for occasions such as live comedy nights. ⊖(Stockwell)

SW9: Brixton

Craft Beer Co

11-13 Brixton Station Road, SW9 8PA

4.30-11 (midnight Thu; 1am Fri); 11.30-1am Sat; 11.30-10.30 Sun ☎ (020) 7095 9129

Kent Craft Pale; guest beers 🄷

Opened in 2012, this café-style pub has 10 handpumps. Alongside the house beer, and often a brew from the nearby Brixton Brewery, there are eight varying guest ales from the likes of Dark Star, Magic Rock, Otley and Thornbridge, plus an array of 18 other British, continental and American beers on draught. There is more room upstairs, and some seating under umbrellas outside, but it can be crowded before gigs at the nearby O2 Academy.

Trinity Arms

45 Trinity Gardens, SW9 8DR

11-11 (midnight Fri); 12-midnight Sat; 12-11 Sun

☎ (020) 7274 4544 trinityarms.co.uk

Young's Bitter, London Gold, Special, Winter Warmer 🄷

A friendly traditional inn tucked away in a quiet square off the busy Acre Lane and Brixton High Road. Drinking areas comprise three sides of a horseshoe-shaped bar, and outside are a front patio and a back garden that features a wishing well and covered smoking area. The pub is popular in the evening and busy on Brixton Academy nights. Well-kept real ale is a big attraction. Families are welcome until 7.30pm, with food served until 10pm. Q

SW9: Stockwell

Crown & Anchor

246 Brixton Road, SW9 6AQ

4.30-midnight (1am Fri); 12-1am Sat; 12-11 Sun

☎ (020) 7737 0060 crownandanchorbrixton.co.uk

Beer range varies 🄷

A modernised gastro-pub, in something of a pub desert, that offers seven changing real ales, sometimes from London micros, as well as four ciders from Sandford. A wide range of keg and bottled beers, the latter including many from the US and Belgium, amplify the drinker's choice. Meals are available every evening and also at lunchtime at the weekend. There are tables outside but no heating or cover for smokers.

SW10: Chelsea

Sporting Page

6 Camera Place, SW10 0BH

11-11 (10.30 Sun) ☎ (020) 7349 0455

Beer range varies 🄷

Rebuilt in 1974 as the Red Anchor on the site of the Odell Arms (1856-1971) and renamed in 1989, this pub is now part of the Food & Fuel chain. A comfortable one-bar gastro-pub with a friendly feel, it offers real ales on six handpumps, often including local brews from Moncada and Truman's. An interesting wine selection complements the food offering. Sporting themed prints and memorabilia adorn the walls. Quiz night is Sunday. Q

SW11: Battersea

Eagle Ale House 🄻

104 Chatham Road, SW11 6HG

3 (12 Sat)-11; 12-10.30 Sun ☎ (020) 7228 2328

eaglealehouse.co.uk

Surrey Hills Shere Drop; guest beers 🄷

A resolutely traditional pub just up the hill from fashionable Northcote Road, the Eagle has a slightly ramshackle interior decorated with old bottles and books plus film and sporting pictures. Around seven real ales are usually available, many from London microbreweries and often one from Downton. Real cider appears occasionally. Weekend beer festivals are held on the spring and August bank holidays. In the garden is a heated marquee. Local CAMRA Pub of the Year 2012. (319,G1)

Falcon ★ 🄻

2 St John's Hill, SW11 1RU

10-11.30 (midnight Thu-Sat); 10-11 Sun

☎ (020) 7228 2076

Beer range varies 🄷

Landmark building sitting prominently on the street corner and dating from 1887, with a nationally important historic pub interior noteworthy for its extensive Victorian island servery, screens and glasswork. Twenty two handpumps usually dispense a wide range of ales from the M&B Nicholson's list, often from London microbreweries and sometimes including dark beers. The pub's location at the Clapham Junction crossroads means that it is usually busy. The rear seating area is mostly reserved for dining. ⊖(Clapham Jct)

Fox & Hounds

66-68 Latchmere Road, SW11 2JU

12-3 (not Mon), 5-11; 12-11 Fri & Sat; 12-10.30 Sun

☎ (020) 7924 5483 thefoxandhoundspub.co.uk

St Austell Tribute; Sambrook's Wandle Ale; guest beers 🄷

Prominent street-corner pub that sits well among the Victorian streets down from Lavender Hill, and reflects their gentrification. It is deservedly popular for its food, especially with families. The decor features brewery mirrors, art prints and Orlando the Marmalade Cat. You may also catch sight of Charlie and Melton, the resident pub cats. Guest beers usually include a Dark Star brew. The yard at the rear has a heated and covered area. No food weekday lunchtimes. ⊖(Clapham Jct)

Lighthouse 🄻

441 Battersea Park Road, SW11 4LR

12-11 (midnight Fri & Sat); 12-10.30 Sun

(020) 7223 7721 thelighthousebattersea.com

Beer range varies 🄷

Styled as a pub and kitchen, this is an open and airy family-friendly single bar with bare boards, cream and green decor and an attractive split-level patio. Three guest beers are offered, from Adnams and local breweries such as Belleville, By the Horns and Sambrook's. Movie nights alternate with eclectic live music on Sundays, and music also features one Friday a month. Board games are available. The menu includes octopus, fowl terrine, red mullet and chocolate truffles.

Powder Keg Diplomacy

147 St John's Hill, SW11 1TQ

4-11 Mon-Wed; 12-midnight Thu & Fri; 10-midnight Sat; 10-10.30 Sun (020) 7450 6457

powderkegdiplomacy.co.uk

Beer range varies 🄷

An immensely popular gastro-pub kitted out in colonial style. Three handpumps dispense real ale from innovative brewers such as Head in a Hat, Oakham and Windsor & Eton, and Meet the Brewer events are held from time to time. Keg beers come from the likes of Kernel, and around 50 bottled beers are expertly chosen from around the world. To the rear, a high-class yet reasonably priced restaurant offers immaculate service. Could this be the future of the British pub?

(Clapham Jct)

SW12: Balham

Nightingale 🄻

97 Nightingale Lane, SW12 8NX

12-midnight; 11-11 Sun (020) 8673 1637

Young's Bitter, Special; guest beers 🄷

Tucked away among the grand houses of Nightingale Lane, this popular community local almost has the feel of a country pub. It is famous for its charity walk in aid of Guide Dogs for the Visually Impaired. Other events include a spring arts and crafts fair and a Scotch egg and sausage roll baking challenge. Outside seating is on the rear patio and out on the pavement. A frequent local CAMRA Pub of the Year finalist.

Q (Wandsworth Common) (Clapham South) (G1)

SW13: Barnes

Red Lion

2 Castelnau, SW13 9RU

11-11; 12-10.30 Sun (020) 8748 2984

red-lion-barnes.co.uk

Fuller's Chiswick Bitter, London Pride, ESB, seasonal beer; guest beer 🄷

Large Victorian landmark pub at the entrance to the Wetland Centre. It has been opened out in recent years although the rear room, with its ornate fireplace, chandelier, dark-wood panelling and pillars, still has a more exclusive feel. Beyond is a decked patio and a spacious no-smoking garden. The landlords are three-times winners of the Fuller's Cellarman of the Year award. Excellent food is available from a varied, modern menu, and children are welcome during the day.

P

SW15: Putney

Bricklayer's Arms

32 Waterman Street, SW15 1DD

12-11 (10.30 Sun) (020) 8789 0222

bricklayers-arms.co.uk

Beer range varies 🄷

The oldest pub in Putney (1826), this welcoming family-owned free house usually features a rotating range of microbrewery beers, often several from just one brewer. Shove-ha'penny and bar skittles are played and the pub runs a cricket team. Regular beer festivals bring a stillage to the patio. Its popularity with Fulham FC supporters tends to reduce the beer range after home matches. Twice CAMRA's Greater London Pub of the Year. (Putney Bridge)

SW16: Streatham

Railway 🄻

2 Greyhound Lane, SW16 5SD

12-11 (midnight Thu; 1am Fri & Sat) (020) 8769 9448

therailwaysw16.co.uk

Beer range varies 🄷

A restored community pub with four handpumps showcasing London breweries including By the Horns, Redemption, Sambrook's and Twickenham. The front bar has a high ceiling, large windows, low-level lighting and a wine bar atmosphere. The rear bar hosts comedy shows on the last Sunday of the month and can be hired. Behind is a concreted area used for dining in warm weather and a twice-monthly farmers' market. There are quiz nights, food nights, regular craft workshops and no TV.

(Streatham Common) (60,118)

SW17: Tooting

King's Head ★

84 Upper Tooting Road, SW17 7PB

12-midnight (11 Sun) (020) 8767 6708

Fuller's London Pride; guest beers 🄷

This local landmark has a nationally important historic pub interior dating from 1896, featuring wonderful cut and etched glass screens as well as tiling in the side passages. Real ale has made something of a comeback here, with three changing guest beers from the Taylor Walker list, often including a local one. In warmer months patrons may enjoy sitting on the front or rear patio.

(Tooting Bec/Tooting Broadway) P

SW18: Southfields

Pig & Whistle 🄻

479-481 Merton Road, SW18 5LD

12-midnight (10.30 Sun) (020) 8874 1061

Young's Bitter, Special; guest beers 🄷

Converted from retail premises in 1974, this corner local has a split-level interior decorated in contemporary style with old photos and posters. It won the Kennel Club's 2013 Open for Dogs award and offers a doggie menu, including pig's ears, while humans can enjoy home-made pork scratchings. Four guest beers include one each from Sambrook's and Twickenham. There is seating outside at the front and in the yard at the rear.

(Earlsfield) (Wimbledon Park) (156)

SW18: Wandsworth

Grapes

39 Fairfield Street, SW18 1DX
12-11 (midnight Fri & Sat); 12-10.30 Sun
(020) 8874 3414
Young's Bitter, Special H
A gem of a street-corner local providing an oasis of calm from the traffic on the manic Wandsworth one-way system. Always friendly and welcoming, the well-decorated bar offers unobtrusive TV sport, and outside there is both a heated patio for smokers and a suntrap secret garden for everyone. A former local CAMRA Pub of the Year, this pub serves excellent beer as well as good-value lunches during the week. A seasonal ale is occasionally on offer.
(Wandsworth Town)

Old Sergeant

104 Garratt Lane, SW18 4DJ
12-11 (midnight Fri & Sat) (020) 8874 4099
Sambrook's Wandle Ale; Young's Bitter, Special; guest beers H
Given the Best Community Pub award for 2012, this friendly and impressively refurbished local has also been voted the best place to bring your dog for a drink. Table menus for the excellent food include an informative beer list. The John Young Room upstairs displays treasured memorabilia of the late chairman and the Wandsworth brewery. Quiz night is Monday. Local CAMRA Pub of the Year runner-up for 2013. (44,270)

Royal Standard

1 Ballantine Street, SW18 1AL
3 (1 Fri; 12 Sat)-11; 1-10.30 Sun (020) 8877 3766
Sambrook's Junction Ale; Sharp's Doom Bar H
A small and welcoming back-street corner pub, redecorated in recent years to give a light and airy feel. The attractive exterior features pretty stained glass top lights. Quiz night is every other Thursday and board games and glossy magazines are available. No food is served but menus, plates and cutlery are provided so customers can order takeaways to eat at this delightful pub.
(Wandsworth Town)

SW19: Wimbledon

Hand in Hand

7 Crooked Billet, SW19 4RQ
11-11 (midnight Fri & Sat); 12-11 Sun (020) 8946 5720
thehandinhandwimbledon.co.uk
Young's Bitter, Special, seasonal beers; guest beers H
Celebrated single-bar ale house on the edge of Wimbledon Common with separate drinking areas and a variety of seating. Three or more guest beers usually include at least one each from Sambrook's and Twickenham. Paddles of three thirds-of-a-pint are available. This is a great place to eat, with beer included in several recipes. There is poker on Mondays and a quiz on Tuesdays. Local CAMRA Pub of the Year 2013. Q (200)

Carshalton

Hope

48 West Street, SM5 2PR
12-11 (10.30 Sun) (020) 8240 1255
hopecarshalton.co.uk
Downton New Forest Ale; Windsor & Eton Knight of the Garter; guest beers H
Ground-breaking pub that celebrates the current revolution in cask beer. Two regular beers are complemented by a constantly changing selection on five further handpumps, including a dark, hoppy and strong beer, served in lined third, half, two-thirds and pint glasses. Innovative festivals showcase specific beer styles or breweries, and foreign and key-keg beers are stocked. A food menu is available at lunchtime, with pot meals served until 10pm (9.30pm Sun). CAMRA Greater London Pub of the Year for 2012 and 2013.
Q P

Sun

4 North Street, SM5 2HU
5-11 Mon; 12-11 (midnight Fri & Sat); 12-10.30 Sun
(020) 8773 4549 thesuncarshalton.com
Sharp's Doom Bar; guest beers H
Imposing street-corner building dating from 1870 with a contrasting contemporary one-bar interior. Five handpumps are in use and the guest beers will probably include one from Brighton Bier. Good pub food is served lunchtimes and evenings, and throughout the day at weekends. Accompanied children are catered for, and welcome until 7pm. There is an attractive garden, and also an upstairs dining area and a function room, available for hire. Quiz night is Tuesday.

Windsor Castle

378 Carshalton Road, SM5 3PT
11-11 (11.30 Fri & Sat); 12-10.30 Sun (020) 8669 1191
windsorcastlepub.com
Long Man Best Bitter; Shepherd Neame Master Brew, Kent's Best, Spitfire, Bishops Finger; guest beers H
A roomy and popular landmark pub to the west of the town centre, on the main road to Sutton. It serves a range of guest beers and holds an annual beer festival in May. An outside courtyard leads to a well-hidden but spacious garden. Regular events include live music on Saturdays, which can fill the pub to capacity. There are restaurant and bar food menus, and a carvery on Sundays.
(Carshalton Beeches) P

Cheam

Railway

32 Station Way, SM3 8SQ
12-11 (midnight Thu-Sat) (020) 8395 5393
Courage Best Bitter, Directors; guest beers H
A local landmark for over 150 years, in 2012 this cosy drinkers' pub close to Cheam station saw in new management. Since then it has enjoyed a steady programme of tasteful redecoration and refurbishment while retaining its warmth and charm. The ever-friendly staff are happy to pour tasters, and well-behaved dogs are welcome. Up to three guest ales are usually available. There are regular quiz and poker nights and occasional evenings of live music.

Chessington

North Star

271 Hook Road, Hook, KT9 1EQ (on A243)
12-midnight (11 Mon) (020) 8391 9811
Fuller's London Pride; Greene King IPA; Sambrook's Junction Ale; guest beers H
Dating back over 150 years, this large locals' pub is popular with all ages. There are several distinct drinking areas and a garden to the rear. Guest

beers are from the Ember Inns list, which changes monthly, and can be from regionals or the larger micros. Food is served every day until 10pm, with Wednesday Sausage Night and Thursday Grill Night.

Kingston-upon-Thames

King's Tun

153-157 Clarence Street, KT1 1QT
8am-midnight (1am Fri & Sat) (020) 8547 3827
Fuller's London Pride; Greene King IPA, Abbot; Sharp's Doom Bar; guest beers H
Large Wetherspoon pub on the one-way system near railway and bus stations. A long bar runs along the rear with two separate seating areas leading to the front. The smaller side with raised seating is usually quieter. The larger side, giving panoramic views of the traffic racing by, was originally the Empire Theatre, whose name is still high on the side of this rather grand-looking building. There is also a good-sized bar upstairs. Alcohol is served from 9am.

Willoughby Arms

47 Willoughby Road, KT2 6LN
10.30 (12 Sun)-midnight (020) 8546 4236
thewilloughbyarms.com
Fuller's London Pride; Robinsons Trooper; Sharp's Doom Bar; guest beers H
Friendly Victorian back-street local, divided into a sports bar with games and large-screen TV, and a quieter lounge area. At least one of the guest beers is locally brewed. An upstairs function room, where the Yardbirds rehearsed in the '60s, can be hired. Pizzas and pies are cooked to order. Beer festivals are held around Valentine's Day, St George's Day and Halloween. The spacious garden includes a smoking area with a large TV screen. Quiz night is Sunday. Q (371,K5)

Mitcham

Windmill

40 Commonside West, CR4 4HA
12-11.30 (midnight Thu); 11.30-1.30am Fri & Sat; 11.30-midnight Sun (020) 8685 0333
Young's Bitter; guest beers H
A warm, friendly, independent free house facing the common, with stained glass windmills in attractive bow windows. This is very much a community pub, with terrestrial TV for sports highlights, popular live music on Fridays and a monthly acoustic session. There is sometimes a second guest beer. Bar snacks include roast potatoes and cocktail sausages on Sundays. At the side are covered patio tables for smokers.

New Malden

Woodies

Thetford Road, KT3 5DX
11-11; 12-10.30 Sun (020) 8949 5824
woodiesfreehouse.co.uk
Adnams Broadside; Fuller's London Pride, ESB; Young's Bitter; guest beers H
This free house is a former sports pavilion adorned with theatrical and sporting memorabilia. The three guest ales usually come from small breweries and are always changing; check the website for what is in the cellar. Home-cooked lunches are served daily, with a carvery on Sundays and weekend barbecues during the summer. A beer festival is held in August. P (265)

Richmond

Red Cow

59 Sheen Road, TW9 1YJ
11-11 Sun & Mon; 11-11.30 (midnight Fri & Sat)
(020) 8940 2511 redcowpub.com
St Austell Tribute; Young's Bitter, Special; guest beers H
Dating back at least 200 years, this popular community local maintains a traditional atmosphere despite extensive changes over the years. The Victorian painted glass panels can still be seen behind the bar. A changing menu of home-cooked food is served until 10pm (no food Sun eve). Tuesday is quiz night and live music is performed regularly. The pub, with front patio area, is prominently situated between converging roads. B&B accommodation is available.

Roebuck

130 Richmond Hill, TW10 6RN
12-11 (midnight Fri & Sat); 12-10.30 Sun
(020) 3582 3827
Fuller's London Pride; guest beers H
Close to Richmond Park Gate, this 200-year-old pub overlooks the World Heritage view of Petersham Meadows and the River Thames. Air conditioned and now Taylor Walker-branded, it has eight regularly rotating guest beers and one real cider on tap. There is an upstairs bar (weekends only) and a large function room. The terrace across the road can also be used by patrons. Food is available until 10pm. A former CAMRA Greater London Pub of the Year. Q (65,371)

Surbiton

Cap in Hand

174 Hook Rise North, KT6 5DE (jct A3/A243)
9am-midnight (020) 8397 3790
Fuller's London Pride; Greene King Abbot; Ruddles Best Bitter; Sharp's Doom Bar; guest beers H
An enthusiastic manager and friendly staff make for a pleasant visit to this large Wetherspoon pub. Open plan, it has many different areas, including an airy conservatory at the front, all served by one long bar. The decor features wood panelling, with photos and text of local interest. Guest beers are sourced from local micros and further afield. The pub holds mini festivals in addition to the national ones, and organises Meet the Brewer nights and brewery trips. Q P

Lamb

73 Brighton Road, KT6 5NF
12-11 (midnight Thu-Sat) (020) 8390 9229
lambsurbiton.co.uk
Surrey Hills Ranmore Ale; guest beers H
A small family-run free house at the heart of the local community. The pub was built in 1850 and formerly divided into four separate rooms. It still retains the original horseshoe-shaped bar. Guest beers are from micros, sometimes local, and family brewers. Specialist cheeses are always available. Music and other events are regularly held throughout the year. Local CAMRA Pub of the Year 2012 and 2014.

Sutton

Grapes

198 High Street, SM1 1NR
8am-11 (020) 8722 0170
Greene King Abbot; Ruddles Best Bitter; guest beers
The smaller of the two Wetherspoon pubs in the town, the Grapes is at the northern end of the shopping area, close to the market and well served by bus routes. The pub is popular with shoppers and locals. The single long room has windows along its length, giving an airy appearance, with comfortable seating and attractive light fittings. There is a large patio area. Three beer festivals are held each year. Q

Little Windsor

13 Greyhound Road, SM1 4BY
12-11.30 (midnight Fri & Sat); 12-11 Sun
(020) 8643 2574
Fuller's London Pride, ESB; guest beers
A small back-street corner local in the New Town area, east of Sutton town centre. The pub is popular with locals, especially in the evenings and at weekends. Sport is shown on TV and quizzes are held on Sundays. The L-shaped bar leads to a heated, covered terrace and garden. A discount is available on four-pint jugs of beer. Children are welcome until 9pm.

Robin Hood

52 West Street, SM1 1SH
11-11 (midnight Fri & Sat); 12-11 Sun (020) 8643 7584
robinhoodsutton.com
Young's Bitter, Special; guest beers
Traditional English local, with home-cooked food including curries, vegetarian lasagne and burgers. As well as a children's play area (with high chairs and baby-changing facilities available), it offers a large function room, a piano, books, and a good variety of local historic photographs. Quiz night is every Monday, and cribbage every Tuesday. Other events, including some for charity, are hosted throughout the year. The pub is home to football and darts teams. (West)

Wallington

Whispering Moon

25 Ross Parade, SM6 8QF
8am-11 (midnight Fri & Sat) (020) 8647 7020
Greene King Abbot; Ruddles Best Bitter; guest beers
A smallish Wetherspoon pub located on the high street near the station, handy for Wallington Hall, home of the local CAMRA October beer festival. The drinking area is L-shaped and, apart from a small raised dining area, all facilities are on the same level. The walls are hung with historic pictures of the local area including one of the building in its Odeon cinema days. Guest beers include one from the brewer of the month.

WEST LONDON

W2: Paddington

Mad Bishop & Bear

Upper Level, Paddington Station, W2 1HB
8am-11; 10am-10.30 Sun (020) 7402 2441
madbishopandbear.co.uk
Fuller's Chiswick Bitter, Discovery, London Pride, ESB, seasonal beer; guest beer
Above the shopping complex just behind the station concourse, the traditional pub interior features a long bar, mirrors, good prints and a rather grand chandelier, with train information screens and two TVs for sport. The raised area can be hired for events and there are café-style seats outside. It does not get too crowded, even in the rush hour. Note that the bar may close early if there are football crowds passing through.

Victoria ★

10A Strathearn Place, W2 2NH
11-11; 12-10.30 Sun (020) 7724 1191
victoriapaddington.co.uk
Fuller's Chiswick Bitter, Discovery, London Pride, ESB, seasonal beer
There is plenty to admire in the nationally important historic pub interior of this Grade II-listed mid-Victorian inn, including ornately gilded mirrors above a crescent-shaped bar, painted tiles in wall niches and numerous portraits of Queen Victoria. The walls display cartoons, paperweights and a Silver Jubilee plate. A recessed area at the back is furnished with a leather bench seat. Upstairs, via a spiral staircase, there is a library and Theatre Bar available for public use. Tuesday is quiz night.
Q (Lancaster Gate/Paddington)

W3: Acton

Aeronaut

264 High Street, W3 9BH
12-midnight (1am Thu; 2am Fri & Sat) (020) 8993 4242
Laine Acton Ale, Random Pale Ale, Porter, IPA, seasonal beers
Commemorating locally born pioneer aviator George Lee Temple, this recently refurbished establishment is part pub, part brewery and part circus. Traditional English meals are served daily. The function area is designed like a circus with a variety of acts performing on Friday and Saturday nights. The garden contains carnival booths. Six beers brewed on site or at other Laine breweries are regularly available. (Town)

West London Trade Union Club

33-35 High Street, W3 6ND
7-midnight (020) 8992 4557 wltuc.com
Beer range varies
Small and friendly club, run as a co-operative, which combines excellent real ale with a busy cultural and social life. One or two beers are normally served, either from the Nelson Brewery range or from another small independent brewery. The Acton Community Theatre is upstairs, and the club hosts regular special events including summer barbecues in the courtyard. The local CAMRA branch is an associate member; show a CAMRA membership card or this Guide for entry.
Q (Central)

W4: Chiswick

Fox & Hounds/Mawson Arms

110 Chiswick Lane South, W4 2QA
10.30-8; closed Sat & Sun (020) 8994 2936
mawsonarmschiswick.co.uk
Fuller's Chiswick Bitter, London Pride, Bengal Lancer, ESB, seasonal beer; Gales Seafarers Ale

On the corner of the Griffin Brewery, and its de facto brewery tap, this listed pub is the start for the Fuller's brewery tour. The unusual double naming is a historic relic of separate licences needed for beer and spirits. The pub is well known for its quality food, and hot meals can be ordered until 7pm. Brewery memorabilia on the walls include ancestral portraits of the Fuller, Smith and Turner families. It opens at weekends for functions only. Q (190)

George IV

185 Chiswick High Road, W4 2DR
11.30-11 (1am Fri & Sat); 12-11 Sun (020) 8994 4624
georgeiv.co.uk
Fuller's Chiswick Bitter, London Pride, ESB, seasonal beer H
In the heart of Chiswick, this is one of Fuller's Ale & Pie pubs and proud of its fresh-food policy. There has been a pub here since 1777 and the present one is reputed to have its own ghost, George. The purpose-built Headliners Comedy Club within the pub plays host to a variety of events including top-class comedians, salsa dancing, jazz nights and silent movies. It is also available for private hire for parties and conferences.
(Turnham Green)

Old Pack Horse

434 Chiswick High Road, W4 5TF
11-midnight (1am Thu; 2am Fri & Sat); 12-midnight Sun
(020) 8994 2872 oldpackhorsechiswick.co.uk
Fuller's Chiswick Bitter, London Pride, Bengal Lancer, ESB; Gales Seafarers Ale; guest beer H
A Grade II-listed corner pub last rebuilt in 1910 but claiming to date back to 1747. Refurbished recently, it has a beautiful frontage often featured in local photographs, and a view across Turnham Green. With ornate woodwork and glasswork including some stained glass panels, it has a regionally important historic pub interior. Five drinking areas include a snug and a Thai restaurant towards the back. A bar sign refers to the long-gone Chiswick Empire, and walls display theatre memorabilia.
(Chiswick Park/Gunnersbury)

Tabard L

2 Bath Road, W4 1LW
12-11 (midnight Thu-Sat) (020) 8994 3492
Beer range varies H
The pub dates back to 1880 and was built as part of the Bedford Park estate, the first London garden suburb. Notable features include the swing sign painted by TM Rooke, tiling by William de Morgan and Walter Crane, and Arts & Crafts mirrors and pictures. Ten handpumps serve cider and eight or nine changing guest ales – a permanent beer festival that always includes local beers. The intimate first-floor fringe theatre has hosted the likes of Al Murray and Russell Brand.
(Turnham Green)

W5: Ealing

Grove

1 Ealing Green, W5 5QX
10-11; 11-10.30 Sun (020) 8567 2439
thegrovew5.co.uk
Beer range varies H
Large one-bar pub owned by Greene King's Metropolitan PubCo division, with many semi-private areas. Since its rebranding, the range of beers has improved dramatically and focuses on local microbreweries such as Truman's, Sambrook's, Vale and Windsor & Eton. The food offer has also moved up a notch. Large heated front and side gardens are popular. Regular beer festivals and Meet the Brewer events are held.
(Broadway)

Questors Grapevine Bar L

12 Mattock Lane, W5 5BQ
7-11; 12-2.30, 7-10.30 Sun (020) 8567 0011
questors.org.uk
Fuller's London Pride; guest beers H
Friendly theatre bar set opposite Walpole Park just south of the centre of Ealing. It regularly serves guest beers, usually including one from a local brewery, and also runs CAMRA-themed festivals twice a year. Books are available, as are Belgian beers and obscure whiskies. The club is run by enthusiastic volunteers and was the 2012 national CAMRA Club of the Year.
Q (Broadway) P

Red Lion

13 St Marys Road, W5 5RA
12-11 (midnight Thu & Fri); 11-midnight Sat
(020) 8567 2541 redlionealing.co.uk
Fuller's Chiswick Bitter, London Pride, ESB, seasonal beer; guest beer H
A great local, affectionately known as Stage 6, opposite Ealing Studios. Black and white photographs of TV and film stars associated with the studios are on display along with memorabilia of their films. It was taken over and refurbished by the Lee family in 2001, maintaining the original character of the pub. There is a heated, covered patio at the back. Good real food is cooked to order and the friendly bar staff espouse the spirit of the Lee family.
Q (Broadway) (Broadway/South Ealing) (65)

Sir Michael Balcon

46-47 The Mall, W5 3TJ
8am-11.30 (020) 8799 2850
Greene King IPA, Abbot; Sharp's Doom Bar; guest beers H
Located on the Uxbridge Road east of Ealing town centre, this became a Wetherspoon pub in 2008, named after the legendary Ealing Studios producer whose life and films form the basis of many of the wall displays. It is split level, with a raised area at the rear and a glass-covered area at the front for smokers. Guest ales are often from Adnams or Hogs Back. Alcohol is sold from 9am.
Q (Broadway)

Wheatsheaf

41 Haven Lane, W5 2HZ
11-11; 12-10.30 Sun (020) 8997 5240
wheatsheaf-ealing.co.uk
Fuller's Chiswick Bitter, London Pride, ESB, seasonal beer H
Tucked away up a side street just north of Ealing town centre, the pub has a deceptively large interior which appears to have been constructed almost entirely of wood. The main saloon connects to an open-plan room at the rear. There is also a small area at the front, Rugby Corner, frequented by devotees of the oval ball. Several screens show televised sport, and quiz nights are held on Mondays. (Broadway)

W6: Hammersmith

Andover Arms

57 Aldensley Road, W6 0DL

12-midnight ☎ (020) 8748 2155

andover-arms-hammersmith.co.uk

Fuller's Chiswick Bitter, London Pride, seasonal beer; guest beer H

A frequent entry in this Guide, tucked away in the side streets of Hammersmith, this popular local is an enduring real ale champion. The kitchen offers a wide range of lunchtime and evening meals. Major sporting events are shown on terrestrial TV and traditional pub games such as dominoes are available. The pub holds regular quiz and live music nights. Guest ales are a recent innovation and drinkers can sup beers from brewers such as Brains or Long Man.

Q (Ravenscourt Park)

Dove

19 Upper Mall, W6 9TA

11-11; 12-10.30 Sun ☎ (020) 8748 9474

dovehammersmith.co.uk

Fuller's London Pride, ESB, seasonal beer; Gales Seafarers Ale H

Traditional Fuller's pub, a Grade II-listed building overlooking the Thames and hence often crowded in summer. With a regionally important historic pub interior, it also holds the Guinness world record for the smallest bar area. Classic food with a twist is served every day; meals can take a little time to arrive at busy times but are worth the wait. Dylan Thomas, Ernest Hemingway and Alec Guinness have reputedly enjoyed a pint or two here.

(Ravenscourt Park)

Swan

46 Hammersmith Broadway, W6 0DZ

10-11 (11.30 Thu; midnight Fri & Sat); 10-10.30 Sun

☎ (020) 8748 1043

Fuller's London Pride; Windsor & Eton Knight of the Garter; guest beers H

Wood predominates in this bustling M&B Nicholson's pub, handily placed opposite Hammersmith Broadway and claimed to be on the site of the first coaching stop after leaving the City. Ornate stairs lead to a first-floor restaurant and bar (and the toilets). It is well worth breaking your journey here to or from Heathrow Airport. Guest beers are often from regional brewers such as Adnams, Elgood's and Thornbridge. Note the fine tessellated gables.

W7: Hanwell

Fox L

Green Lane, W7 2PJ

11-11; 12-10.30 Sun ☎ (020) 8567 4021

thefoxpub.co.uk

Fuller's London Pride; Sharp's Cornish Coaster; Timothy Taylor Landlord; guest beers H

Wonderful back-street free house in the welcoming town of Hanwell, as popular with walkers, cyclists and other nearby canal users as with locals. A good range of beers, with changing guest ales from independent breweries, is complemented by excellent, inexpensive food, including a popular Sunday lunch (booking recommended). Add in beer festivals and occasional jazz, and it is no surprise that the Fox has often been local CAMRA Pub of the Year, most recently in 2013.

P (195,E8)

W8: Kensington

Elephant & Castle

40 Holland Street, W8 4LT

10-11 ☎ (020) 7937 6382

Fuller's London Pride; St Austell Nicholson's Pale Ale; Sharp's Doom Bar; guest beers H

Licensed in 1865 as a beer house in what were two adjacent properties and tucked away north east of the town hall, this cosy, wood-panelled pub is a welcome refuge from the hurly-burly of Kensington High Street. There are strong journalistic connections: witness the notable framed newspapers in the back bar. Guest beers are from the wide-ranging M&B Nicholson's portfolio. Food is served all day.

(High Street Kensington)

W8: Notting Hill Gate

Churchill Arms

119 Kensington Church Street, W8 7LN

11-11 (midnight Thu-Sat); 12-10.30 Sun

☎ (020) 7727 4242 churchillarmskensington.co.uk

Fuller's Chiswick Bitter, Discovery, London Pride, ESB, seasonal beer H

Long-serving landlord Gerry keeps standards high at this multi-award-winning pub with its regionally important historic pub interior. Churchillian and Irish memorabilia hang from the panelled ceiling, and plaques at the bar commemorate former drinkers. There is a Thai restaurant in the rear conservatory. It is often very busy, both inside and on the pavement, with drinkers standing below the hanging flower baskets that create a striking visual landmark. Local CAMRA 2013 Pub of the Year.

Q

Uxbridge Arms

13 Uxbridge Street, W8 7TQ

12-11 (10.30 Sun) ☎ (020) 7727 7326

Fuller's London Pride; Harveys Sussex Best Bitter; St Austell Tribute H

A world away from nearby Portobello Road, manager Linda and her team run a great pub here. Now part of the Enterprise estate, it dates from 1836, starting as a beer house. Carpeted throughout, the bar has a welcoming appeal. Together with the plates, the Lt Colonel's tunic has been part of the fabric for a number of years now.

Q

W9: Westbourne Park

Union Tavern L

45 Woodfield Road, W9 2BA

12-11 (midnight Fri & Sat); 12-10.30 Sun

☎ (020) 7286 1886 union-tavern.co.uk

Fuller's London Pride, seasonal beer; guest beers H

A radical departure by Fuller's, this is an unbranded beer house offering international keg beers alongside cask ales produced only within 30 miles and, with one brewery exception, from London. The mainly young crowd enjoys reduced beer prices on Monday, a weekly quiz, and Meet the Brewer events on the last Tuesday of the month. Good-value food is another plus, with traditional Sunday lunch a feature. The canalside terrace comes into its own on a warm, sunny day.

W12: Shepherds Bush

Defector's Weld

170 Uxbridge Road, W12 8AA
12-midnight (2am Fri & Sat); 12-11 Sun
(020) 8749 0008 defectors-weld.com
Adnams Southwold Bitter; guest beers H
Downstairs, the large horseshoe-shaped main bar has five handpumps and a mix of sofas, tables and chairs. Frequently rotating guest beers include at least one from Moncada, Redemption, Sambrook's or Twickenham. An upstairs bar is available for hire. DJs play music Thursday to Sunday evenings (no admission after midnight Fri and Sat). On QPR match days the pub is for home fans only, but card-carrying CAMRA members not wearing team colours are welcome.
Q(Shepherd's Bush Market)

W13: West Ealing

Forester ★

2 Leighton Road, W13 9EP
11-11.30 (midnight Wed & Thu; 1am Fri & Sat); 11-11 Sun
(020) 8567 1654 theforesterealing.com
Fuller's London Pride, ESB, seasonal beers; guest beers H
Built in 1909 from designs by Nowell Parr for the Royal Brewery of Brentford and bought by Fuller's in 2012, this pub has a nationally important historic interior. Thai and English food are available daily except Sundays, when the traditional carvery is served until 6pm. Wednesdays are quiz nights and on Thursdays there are poker tournaments. Two guests beers are supplemented by two additional beers from Fuller's (often Gales HSB). Several beer festivals a year are held.
(Northfields)(E2,E3)

Brentford

Magpie & Crown

128 High Street, TW8 8EW
12-midnight (1am Thu-Sat) (020) 8560 4570
Beer range varies H
This mock-Tudor free house is a popular haunt for beer lovers, with six eclectic guest ales, a cider and a perry, three strong keg beers and a range of continental and American bottled beers, all served by enthusiastic and knowledgeable staff. There are tables and a cycle rack at the front, and a rear patio with covered smokers' tables. Food is available lunchtimes and evenings daily, with roasts on Sunday.

Feltham

Moon on the Square

Unit 30 The Centre, High Street, TW13 4AU
8am-midnight (10.30 Sun) (020) 8893 1293
Courage Best Bitter; Greene King Abbot; Ruddles Best Bitter; guest beers H
A real ale oasis that continues to flourish in Feltham. The interior is early Wetherspoon – wood panelling and glass-partitioned booths, with pictures and local history displays. A range of eight real ales features continually varying guests including local brews, with a bar-top gravity cask on tap during beer festivals (April and October). Westons cider is available. Food is served all day, alcoholic drinks from 9am. Families with children are welcome until 6pm.

Hampton

Jolly Coopers

16 High Street, TW12 2SJ
11-11 (midnight Fri & Sat); 12-10.30 Sun
(020) 8979 3384 squiffysrestaurant.co.uk
Caledonian Deuchars IPA; Courage Best Bitter; Hop Back Summer Lightning; guest beers H
A popular traditional community pub proud of its heritage; a wooden wall panel lists landlords from 1727 to the present owners who took over in 1986. The small horseshoe bar features five handpumps. The walls display water jugs, old pub photographs and local memorabilia as well as the tools coopers use to make casks. An extensive menu of tapas and traditional food, including Sunday lunches, is served in the bar, Squiffy's restaurant beyond and, weather permitting, on the sun patio outside.

Hampton Hill

Roebuck

72 Hampton Road, TW12 1JN
11-11 (11.30 Fri & Sat); 12-4, 7-10.30 Sun
(020) 8255 8133
St Austell Tribute; Sambrook's Junction Ale; Young's Bitter; guest beers H
It is impossible to do justice in a few words to the extensive and eclectic collection that fills this comfortable Victorian local. The wickerwork Harley-Davidson hanging from the ceiling is most notable but do not miss the real miniature steam locomotive or the cigar store Indian. Traffic lights in the bar and award-winning garden (with gazebo for smokers) mark closing time. There is a summer house for cooler evenings, available for hire. The two guest beers change regularly.
(Fulwell)

Harlington

White Hart

158 High Street, UB3 5DP
11-11 (11.30 Thu; midnight Fri & Sat); 12-11 Sun
(020) 8759 9608 whitehartharlington.co.uk
Fuller's London Pride, ESB, seasonal beer; guest beer H
Large Grade II-listed Fuller's pub standing proud at the north end of the village. A single bar provides access to an open-plan area for sport on large TV screens, through to seating favoured by diners. The interior was refurbished in 2009 to improve facilities and create the open feel it now has. Local history is the theme of the wall displays enjoyed by locals and visitors from nearby Heathrow Airport. Quiz night is Thursday. P

Hayes

Botwell Inn

25-29 Coldharbour Lane, UB3 3EB
8am-midnight (020) 8848 3112
Greene King Abbot; Ruddles Best Bitter; guest beers H
A large Wetherspoon pub opened in 2000 following a shop conversion from furnishers S Moore & Son, with several areas for dining and drinking. There is a fenced paved area to the front and a patio at the rear with large market-style parasols with heaters. Guest beers are usually from Adnams, Nelsons and Windsor & Eton, and at least

ENGLAND

one Westons cider is served. Several beer festivals are held annually. Alcohol is available from 9am. Q🝡❀◑♿⇌(Hayes & Harlington)●🚌📶

Hayes End

Angel ★

697 Uxbridge Road, UB4 8HX
11-midnight (1am Fri & Sat) ☎ (020) 8848 8020
angelpub.net
Fuller's Chiswick Bitter, London Pride; Gales HSB; guest beer Ⓗ
A real community local containing three bars, with the large rear bar mostly used for functions. The small saloon bar is quiet and the traditional atmosphere is maintained in the larger public bar, which has a pool table annexe. The pub takes part in darts and pool leagues and sponsors Hayes Angels football team. Regular events include jazz, film, jam and comedy nights and Sunday bingo. The historic pub interior is now recognised as of national importance. Q🝡❀◑♿♣P🚌🐾📶

Hounslow

Moon Under Water

84-88 Staines Road, TW3 3LF (W end of High St)
9am-12.30am ☎ (020) 8572 7506
Greene King Abbot; Ruddles Best Bitter; guest beers Ⓗ
Early Wetherspoon shop conversion in original style, still displaying many local history panels and photos. Very popular, it is a regular venue for the town's beer lovers, also attracting others from surrounding areas. Up to five guest ales are often locally sourced, with many more at festival times when all 12 handpumps are put to work. The cider is usually Westons Old Rosie, again with others during festivals. Children are welcome until 8.30pm. Q🝡❀◑♿⇌⊖(Central)●🚌📶

Isleworth

London Apprentice

62 Church Street, TW7 6BG
11-11 (midnight Fri & Sat) ☎ (020) 8560 1915
thelondonapprentice.co.uk
Adnams Ghost Ship; Fuller's London Pride; guest beers Ⓗ
Famous Grade II*-listed former Isleworth Brewery riverside pub in old Isleworth, with a unique name and interesting history. The interior is classic traditional, although opened out, with an upstairs Riverview Room. The large patio has many tables with more on the riverbank. Four guest ales are regularly on offer, plus a cider, as well as excellent food. With music most Monday evenings, Thursday poker and a Sunday quiz, it is well worth the short walk here from the nearest bus stop.
🝡❀◑♿●P🚌(H37)

Red Lion

92-94 Linkfield Road, TW7 6QJ
12-11.30 (11 Tue; midnight Fri & Sat); 12-11 Sun
☎ (020) 8560 1457 red-lion.info
Morland Original Bitter; guest beers Ⓗ
Spacious and traditional two-bar free house with a strong community focus. There is often an event taking place: a performance by its own theatre group, the Thursday quiz, live music throughout the week. Up to eight beers complement the regular bitter, and up to four ciders or perries. Twice-yearly beer festivals feature champion beers; weekend festivals have regional themes. Bar snacks are available. Dogs are welcome if on a lead.
🝡❀⇌●🚌🐾

Norwood Green

Plough

Tentelow Lane, UB2 4LG
11 (12 Sun)-midnight ☎ (020) 8574 7473
ploughinnnorwoodgreen.co.uk
Fuller's London Pride; Gales Seafarers Ale; guest beers Ⓗ
A 17th-century Grade II-listed building, with exposed wooden beams and low ceilings, and Fuller's oldest pub. The company acquired it in 1816 and it is now run by a splendid landlord who takes pride in the friendly service all customers receive. A traditional menu is available in the bar lunchtimes and evenings, all day on Saturday, until 5pm Sunday, and Italian food in the Positano Restaurant (open 6-10pm Tue-Sat). Music on Tuesdays is folk and country, on Fridays other styles. 🝡❀◑♿♣🚌(120)🐾📶

Southall

Southall Conservative & Unionist Club 𝕃

Fairlawn, High Street, UB1 3HB
11.30-2.30, 7-11; 11.30-3, 6-11 Fri & Sat; 12-3, 7-10.30 Sun
☎ (020) 8574 0261
Rebellion IPA, seasonal beers Ⓗ
Virtually the last real ale outlet in this historic market town, situated behind the former town hall. Access can be gained with this Guide or a CAMRA membership card. A selection of beers from the Rebellion range is to be found inside. Meals are served some lunchtimes and various events are held most evenings. It is an ideal meeting place before enjoying a curry in one of the many local restaurants. 🝡❀◐⇌♣P🚌📶

Stockley Park

White House

The Arena, Bennetsfield Road, UB11 1AA
7am-10 (11 Thu-Sat) ☎ (020) 8589 7870
Fuller's London Pride; Sharp's Doom Bar; guest beers Ⓗ
A fairly modern Lloyds No.1 bar set in a small commercial complex servicing the Stockley Park business community and golf course. At the end of a long bar/restaurant, a charming conservatory leads out onto a decked area overlooking a small lake with several species of waterfowl – lovely on a summer's day. There is a patio with heaters and a large grassed area. A Westons cider is also on handpump. 🝡❀◑♿●P🚌📶

Teddington

Masons Arms

41 Walpole Road, TW11 8PJ
12-11 (11.30 Fri & Sat); 12-10.30 Sun ☎ (020) 8977 6521
the-masons-arms.co.uk
Sambrook's Junction Ale; Tillingbourne AONB; guest beers Ⓗ
Back-street community free house built in 1860. The pictures and paraphernalia adorning the walls leave you in no doubt that the publican is a beer enthusiast. Worth noticing are the four bespoke

turned wooden handles on the handpumps and the unusual painted pub sign. There is a log-burning stove, a dartboard and a small, secluded rear patio. Occasional quiz and music nights take place. Guest beers change frequently, coming from a wide range of independent brewers across the UK.

Twickenham

Crown

174 Richmond Road, St Margarets, TW1 2NH
11-11 (11.30 Fri & Sat); 11-10.30 Sun (020) 8892 5896
crowntwickenham.co.uk
Harveys Sussex Best Bitter; Sharp's Cornish Coaster; Surrey Hills Shere Drop; guest beer H
Spacious pub built around 1730 and Grade II-listed, now extensively but tastefully refurbished. The Victorian hall at the rear has been opened up for dining and a courtyard garden has been attractively remodelled. Inside are various seating areas and three fireplaces, one with a real fire. Several windows and doors and the bar floor are original. Food is served 12-9.30pm every day (to 10pm Fri & Sat). Acoustic music plays on Thursday evenings. Q (St Margarets)P

Fox

39 Church Street, TW1 3NR
11-11.30 (12.30am Fri & Sat) (020) 8892 1535
thefoxpubtwickenham.co.uk
Fuller's London Pride; Sharp's Doom Bar; Twickenham Naked Ladies; guest beers H
The Fox has been at the heart of Twickenham for over 300 years. The street is now higher than when the pub was first built, so customers step down into the bar. A major restoration has retained its character and original features, including two open fires. The restaurant area offers British-based food, and a private oak-panelled dining room is available. Live local bands are popular at weekends. Quiz night is Sunday. There is an attractive beer garden.

Prince of Wales

136 Hampton Road, TW2 5QR
11-11 (midnight Thu-Sat); 11-10.30 Sun
(020) 8894 5054 princeofwalestwickenham.co.uk
St Austell Proper Job; guest beers H
The final staging post on the Windsor to London stagecoach route; original stables survive and are listed. Once an Isleworth Brewery pub, this unspoilt, two-room community inn now always serves a Twickenham beer. It offers French-style cuisine, with Friday steak night and an excellent, popular Sunday roast (12-6pm). Acoustic music plays on Tuesday and quiz night is Thursday. Outside is an attractive garden.
(Strawberry Hill)

Rifleman

7 Fourth Cross Road, TW2 5EL
12-11 (10.30 Sun) (020) 8893 3836
theriflemantwickenham.co.uk
Butcombe Bitter; Ringwood Best Bitter; Timothy Taylor Landlord; Young's Bitter; guest beer H
A late-Victorian traditional pub, originally a beer house, commemorating riflemen billeted nearby in Napoleonic times. It benefits from a small beer garden, a front patio and close proximity to seven bus routes. No main meals are served, but toasties are available up to 7pm. Very much a community hub, it has board games, darts and TV sports. On Thursday it hosts a lively open mic night. Twickenham Stadium and Harlequins rugby club are a 15-minute walk.
(Strawberry Hill)P

Sussex Arms

15 Staines Road, TW2 5BG
12-11 (10.30 Sun) (020) 8894 7468
thesussexarmstwickenham.co.uk
Beer range varies H
Sensitively restored in 2011, this traditional pub with two real fires is now a beer-lovers' favourite. Eighteen handpumps showcase independent UK breweries, including Twickenham, and six ciders and perries. Acoustic blues and Irish music feature regularly, and music is played from vinyl LPs. Food includes Anthea's famous pies. Every tenth pint of ale is free with the pub's loyalty card. CAMRA Greater London Cider Pub of the Year 2012 and local Pub of the Year 2012 and 2013.
(Strawberry Hill)

William Webb Ellis

24 London Road, TW1 3RR
9am-11 (020) 8744 4300
Adnams Broadside; Greene King IPA, Abbot; Sharp's Doom Bar; guest beers H
Twelve handpumps are in constant use in this imaginative Wetherspoon conversion of a historic town-centre building that was for 100 years Twickenham's post office. In the home town of English rugby, this pub is large and spacious, with live news and sport on silent screens. The rear patio is open until 9pm, food is served all day and children are welcome until 8pm. A Monday ale club offers reduced prices and third-of-a-pint glasses.

Uxbridge

Queen's Head

54 Windsor Street, UB8 1AB
11-11 (midnight Fri & Sat); 12-10.30 Sun
(01895) 258750
Beer range varies H
In the old part of town, opposite the church, visitors have to step down from the street into this attractive, Grade II-listed, mid 19th-century pub, tastefully decorated and furnished. There is just one, irregularly shaped bar, with bay windows, wooden floorboards, walls mainly of exposed brick, and low ceilings. On the walls are old photographs and prints of hop-picking and beer-making. Guest beers rotate.

Whitton

Admiral Nelson

123 Nelson Road, TW2 7BB
11-11 (midnight Fri & Sat); 12-10.30 Sun
(020) 8894 9998 admiral-nelson-whitton.co.uk
Fuller's Chiswick Bitter, London Pride, ESB, seasonal beer; guest beer H
A former beer house, fully licensed in 1861 and rebuilt in the 1930s, this large landmark pub has a small patio area on the side and stands in a prominent position on the crossroads at the end of the high street. It has both a Nelsonian and a rugby theme; near to Twickenham Stadium and Twickenham Stoop, it is a haven for fans on match days. Large TVs provide sports coverage. Sunday is quiz night.

London Pub Walks – 2nd Edition

Bob Steel

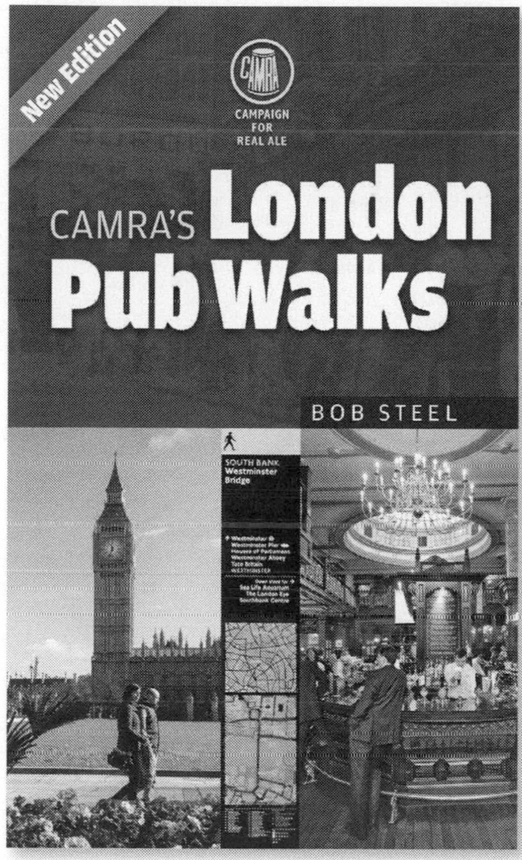

CAMRA's pocket-size walking guide to London is back. This fantastic second edition is packed with interesting new routes, fully updated classic routes from the first edition, new pubs and a special selection of routes that take full advantage of London's public transport network. With 30 walks around more than 190 pubs, **CAMRA's London Pub Walks** enables you to explore the entire city while never being far from a decent pint.

£9.99 ISBN 978-1-85249-310-3 CAMRA members' price £7.99 192 pages

For this and other books on beer and pubs visit CAMRA's online bookshop at www.camra.org.uk/books or call 01727 867201

GREATER MANCHESTER

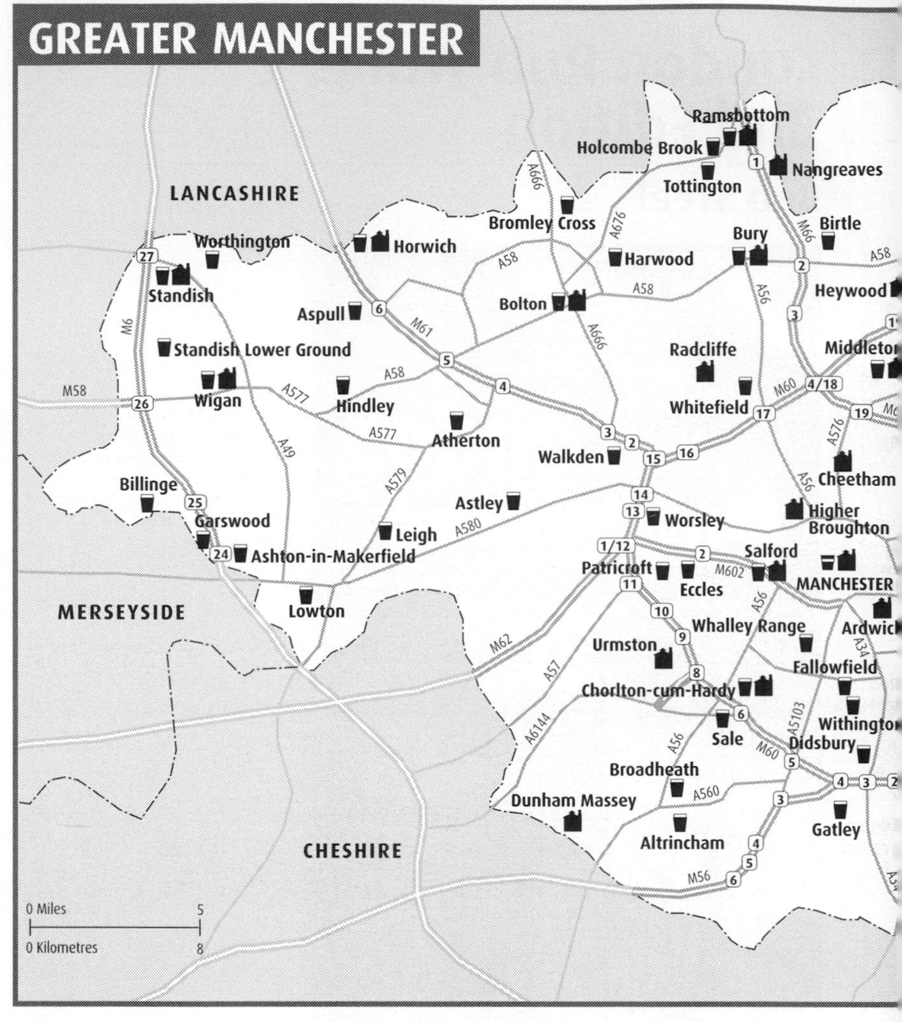

Altrincham

Costello's Bar

18 Goose Green, WA14 1DW (down pedestrian road oppjct of Stamford New Rd & Regent Rd)
12-11 (midnight Fri & Sat); 12-10.30 Sun
(0161) 929 0903 costellosbar.co.uk
Dunham Massey Big Tree Bitter, seasonal beers H

This is Dunham Massey Brewing Company's brewery tap, situated in Altrincham's attractive Goose Green behind the new hospital. The small bar has a modern feel and is popular with locals and visitors alike. The brewery has over 25 different recipes and showcases them all in the bar over time on seven handpumps. A perry and three real ciders are also available. Local CAMRA Pub Of The Year 2012 and 2013.

Old Market Tavern

Old Market Place, WA14 4DN (on A56)
12-midnight (11 Mon & Tue); 12-11 Sun
(0161) 927 7062 omt123.co.uk
Caledonian Deuchars IPA; George Wright Northern Lights; Phoenix Arizona; Timothy Taylor Landlord; guest beers H

Large black and white former coaching inn, the OMT is renowned for both its excellent range of real ales and live music. Eleven handpumps dispense up to six regular beers plus five guests from mostly local breweries. A large whiteboard lists the available beers. Real cider is also served and a range of bottled beers. Rock bands feature on Friday and Saturday evenings. Wednesday is quiz night. Q

Pi (Altrincham)

18 Shaws Road, WA14 1QU
11-11 (11.30 Wed & Thu; midnight Fri & Sat); 12-11 Sun
(0161) 929 9098 abarcalledpi.com
Tatton Blonde; guest beers H

An intimate bar over two floors with four handpumps serving three real ales and a guest cider or perry alongside world beers on draught and an extensive foreign bottle collection. Guest beers are sourced from micros as well as more established breweries including RedWillow, Saltaire and First Chop. Pieminister pies and mash are served until 11pm daily. Service is always friendly, with little touches like blankets for those outside.

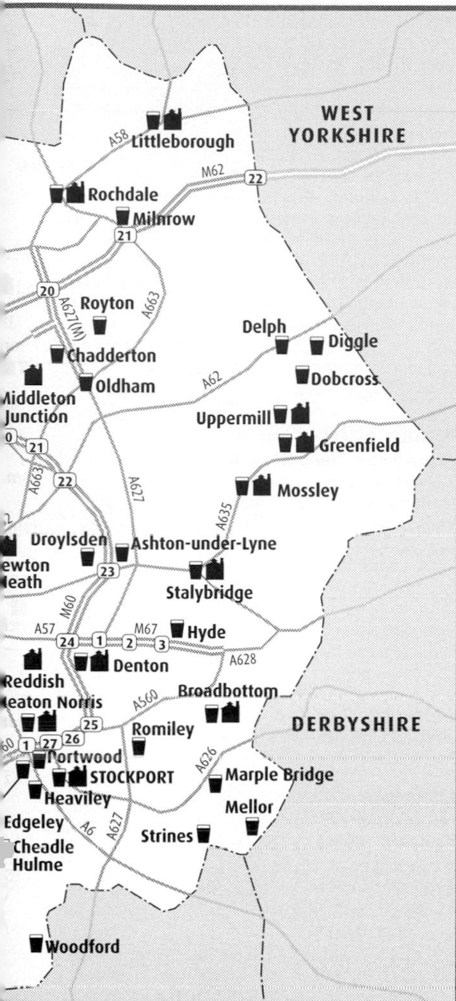

Ashton-in-Makerfield

Sir Thomas Gerard 𝕃

2 Gerard Street, WN4 9AA

⏲ 8am-midnight (1am Wed & Thu; 2am Fri & Sat)
☎ (01942) 713519

Marston's Pedigree; guest beers Ⓗ

CAMRA award-winning Wetherspoon pub close to Haydock Park Racecourse. There are 12 handpumps with local ales from Coach House, George Wright and Phoenix among others. As well as the national beer festivals, other themed festivals are held during the year. There is a beer garden for the hot summer months and during the winter the pub has a cosy atmosphere. The usual good-value Wetherspoon food menu is served all day.
❀◑♿P🚌 (320,600) 📶

Ashton-under-Lyne

Ash Tree

9-11 Wellington Road, OL6 6DA

⏲ 8am-midnight ☎ (0161) 339 9670

Greene King Abbot; Ruddles Best Bitter; guest beers Ⓗ

Directly facing the Victorian Market Hall and square, this pub has become one of the premier real ale destinations in the town centre and is easily accessible by bus and train. Families are welcome in the lower level; above are the bar and lounge/dining area which leads to the rear entrance and outdoor smoking area. Wetherspoon's usual good value applies to the beers and food. Two real ale festivals are run each year. TV screens have the sound turned off.
Q🐴❀◑♿⇌🚏🚌📶

Dog & Pheasant

528 Oldham Road, OL7 9PQ

⏲ 12-11 (11.30 Fri & Sat); 12-10.30 Sun ☎ (0161) 330 4894

Banks's Mild, Sunbeam; Marston's Burton Bitter, Pedigree; guest beers Ⓗ

Known as the Top Dog, this popular, friendly local near the Medlock Valley Country Park has been a regular Guide entry since 1992. It has a large bar serving three distinct areas, plus another room at the front. The beer range is supplemented by two guests from the Marston's portfolio. A menu of good-value food includes vegetarian options. Quiz night is Thursday. The pub is home to a local hiking group known as the Bog Trotters.
❀◑P🚌 (409,419)

INDEPENDENT BREWERIES

AllGates Wigan
Bank Top Bolton
Blackedge Horwich
Blackjack Manchester
Boggart Hole Clough Manchester: Newton Heath
Bootleg Chorlton-cum-Hardy
Brightside Radcliffe
Craftsman Manchester (NEW)
Deeply Vale Bury
Dunham Massey Dunham Massey
Dunscar Bridge Bolton
First Chop Salford
Fool Hardy Heaton Norris
Green Mill Broadbottom
Greenfield Greenfield
Hay Rake Littleborough
Holt Cheetham
Hornbeam Denton
Hydes Salford
Irwell Works Ramsbottom
Lees Middleton Junction
Leyden Nangreaves
Marble Manchester
Millstone Mossley
Outstanding Bury
Phoenix Heywood
Pictish Rochdale
Privateer Manchester: Ardwick
Prospect Standish
Quantum Stockport
Ramsbottom Ramsbottom
Ringway Reddish
Robinsons Stockport
Rtwo Dtoo Urmston (NEW)
Runaway Manchester (NEW)
Saddleworth Uppermill
ShinDigger Bury (NEW)
Silver Street Bury (NEW)
Six O'Clock Manchester (NEW)
Star Inn Higher Broughton
Ticketybrew Stalybridge (NEW)
Wilson Potter Middleton

Aspull

Gerrard Arms

615 Bolton Road, WN2 1PZ

12 (4 Mon & Tue)-11; 12-midnight Fri & Sat

(01942) 832346 thegerrard.com

Prospect Silver Tally; guest beers

One-room, open-plan, cosy pub with a light and airy interior, comfortable seating and retaining the original Boddington and Smoke Room windows. It has six handpumps, with Tetley and Prospect beers the regulars plus varying guests. Two TV screens show sport. Located on the edge of Borsdane Wood, a local nature reserve, it makes an ideal refreshment stop. Food is served lunchtimes and evenings, and all day at weekends.

Victoria

50 Haigh Road, Haigh, WN2 1YA

4 (2 Sat & Sun)-midnight (01942) 830869

AllGates Ostara; guest beers

Traditional two-room local and AllGates Brewery's first pub. The smart yet intimate lounge displays photographs depicting the history of Aspull and Haigh. Large screens cater for sports fans, although the TV in the lounge is rarely switched on. The pub is not far from Haigh Hall Country Park and halfway between Bolton Wanderers and Wigan Athletic football grounds. Guest beers come from AllGates and other microbreweries. There is a covered smoking area. LocAle beers are among the guests.

Astley

Miners' Welfare Institute

Meanley Road, Gin Pit Village, M29 7DW

12-midnight (01942) 883067 ginpitclub.com

Beer range varies

Social and sports club with a cricket pitch in Gin Pit Village. This is the hub of the community and home to many clubs including karate and amateur radio. An annual beer festival is held in February and various events are hosted throughout the year.

P

Old Boat House

Higher Green Lane, M29 7JB

12-midnight (01942) 883300

Ruddles County; guest beers

Situated on the towpath of the Bridgewater Canal, the pub is located off Higher Green Lane. It was originally built with stabling for horses that pulled the barges. There is an old fashioned taproom with pictures of the area past and present, and a spacious lounge with wood decor, with big tables where you can spread out the newspapers. Good ales are served alongside excellent food. Live music features most weekends. P

Atherton

Atherton Arms

6 Tyldesley Road, M46 9DD

12-midnight (01942) 882885

Holts Mild, Bitter; guest beers

Traditional public house with a great atmosphere and facilities, including a full-sized snooker table and function room. The pub is known for its superb beer garden, which has TV screens and heaters. The beer is competitively priced and promotions change on a monthly basis, with happy days Monday to Friday. Mid-week, the pub offers a wide range of entertainment. Friday and Saturday is Steve's Karaoke and there is live entertainment every Sunday. P

Jolly Nailor

20 Market Street, M46 0DN

12-midnight (01942) 792640

AllGates California, Pretoria; guest beers

The Jolly Nailor is a revitalised local situated on the main Market Street in Atherton. The pub was purchased by AllGates in early 2010 and refurbished with the addition of six handpumps selling a range of cask beers plus draught cider. The interior is divided into three areas for live music, TV sport and the weekly quiz. There is still space for the ladies' and men's darts teams.

Pendle Witch

2-4 Warburton Place, M46 0EQ

12-midnight (01942) 884537

Moorhouse's Black Cat, Premier Bitter, Pride of Pendle, Blond Witch, Pendle Witches Brew; guest beers

A real gem hidden down a narrow alley. The entrance, part of a conservatory, leads to an open-plan bar that serves the full range of Moorhouse's beers plus up to two guests. The games area has a pool table and large-screen TV. Regular rock nights are hosted and occasional beer festivals are held. Food is served during the day, with a cheese night on Thursday. There is a well-kept garden for summer. Close to town-centre parking.

Billinge

Masons Arms

99 Carr Mill Road, WN5 7TY

2-11.30; 12-midnight Sat & Sun (01744) 603572

masonsarmsbillinge.co.uk

Beer range varies

Built in 1779 and run by the same family for over 200 years, the pub is well placed for walking or cycling in the local area. Five handpumps offer regularly changing guest beers. Folk and quiz nights are hosted mid-week. The luxurious smoking shelter boasts a bison's head and logburner, and the beer garden overlooks fields to the rear. Just the place for a quiet chat – Sky Sports is screened but usually without the volume.

P

Birtle

Church Inn

Castle Hill Road, BL9 6UH

closed Mon; 12-2.30, 5-midnight Tue & Wed; 12-midnight Thu-Sat; 12-2am Sun (0161) 764 2857

thechurchinnbirtle.co.uk

Timothy Taylor Landlord; guest beers

Spacious 17th-century inn commanding terrific views due to its elevation. The interior is divided in two by the bar, with two rooms to the left for dining or drinking, and another room to the right leading to the restaurant. There is more than adequate seating outside. The building was formerly used as a law court – the condemned were led away for prompt punishment at the gallows in the barn still atop Gallows Hill, opposite.

P

Bolton

Alma Inn

152-154 Bradshawgate, BL2 1BA
12 (4 Mon)-11; 12-2am Fri & Sat; 4-11 Sun
☎ (01204) 364113
Beer range varies H
Originally in the right-hand building, the pub was extended into next door, creating a split-level interior. Three changing beers from the Marston's range and one real cider are dispensed from the handpumps. There are some interesting decorative features – the old cast-iron range and even a tricycle hanging from one of the walls. The Alma is both a welcoming local pub and a venue for regular weekend gigs and music festivals, popular with rock and metal fans. ❀≋♣●⊟

Bank Top Brewery Tap 🏆 L

68-70 Belmont Road, Astley Bridge, BL1 7AN
12-11 (11.30 Fri & Sat) ☎ (01204) 302837
banktopbrewery.com
Bank Top Dark Mild, Flat Cap, Gold Digger, Old Slapper, Pavilion Pale Ale, Port o' Call; guest beer H
Although a basic two-room street-corner local, this is an extremely popular venue and a deserved winner of various local CAMRA awards including Pub of the Year 2014. It is immaculately kept with superb service, and the eight rotating Bank Top beers are fairly priced. A guest beer, real cider and a wide selection of bottled Belgian beers are available. The brewery owner and staff are regulars and, with a good mixed clientele, everyone feels at home. ❀♿♣●⊟🐾

Barristers Bar

2-4 Churchgate, BL1 1HJ (entrance on Deansgate in passageway at rear of Swan Hotel)
12-1am (2am Fri-Sun) ☎ (01204) 365174
Black Sheep Best Bitter; Moorhouse's Blond Witch; Tetley Bitter; guest beers H
Barristers Bar is part of the Swan Hotel, a listed building dating from 1845. The wood-panelled interior has been tastefully decorated to recreate a traditional pub atmosphere. The regular range of cask beers is supplemented by five or six guests, usually including some from local small breweries. A heated courtyard with tables is used as a smoking area. Disabled toilet facilities are available. ❀◐≋●⊟

Bob's Smithy L

1448 Chorley Old Road, Heaton, BL1 7PX
4.30 (12 Wed & Thu)-11; 12-11.30 Fri & Sat; 12-10.30 Sun
☎ (01204) 842622 bobs-smithy.com
Bank Top Flat Cap; Thwaites Original, Wainwright; Timothy Taylor Boltmaker; guest beers H
This comfortable 200-year-old hostelry on the edge of the moors has panoramic views over the south Lancashire plain. It is handy for walkers as well as visitors to the Macron Stadium two miles away. The inn is named after the blacksmith who allegedly spent more time in the pub than in his smithy across the road. Guest beers are from small breweries far and wide. There is a new Old Forge restaurant and extra seating on the patio area. ❀◐◑P⊟(125,126)🐾

Bolton Ukrainian Social Club L

99, Castle Street, BL2 1JP
3.30 (12 Fri-Sun)-11 ☎ (01204) 526038
Beer range varies H
Large, imposing building to the east of town with a comfortable and well-laid-out two-room bar. Two of the three handpumps dispense beers from Bank Top or Blackedge, and a guest from further afield features on the third one. The Bolton CAMRA beer festival is held here in April. The club is home to several societies including brass band and bagpipes. Greater Manchester CAMRA Club of the Year in 2013. Q♣●P⊟

Dog & Partridge L

22-26 Manor Street, BL1 1TU
5-3am; 4-4am Sat ☎ (07708) 377229
Bank Top Flat Cap; Thwaites Wainwright; guest beers H
Traditional multi-roomed free house just off Bolton town centre, popular with both young and old. The guest ale selection champions local breweries such as Blackedge, and usually includes a dark ale. Look for the Cornbrook Ales etched glass window and large stencils in each room of famous musicians and DJs. Bands play most weekends and there is an excellent outdoor staged area that hosts popular summer gigs. ❀≋♣●P

Spinning Mule

Unit 2 Nelson Square, BL1 1JT
8am-11 (midnight Thu, Fri & Sun; 1am Sat)
☎ (01204) 533339
Greene King Abbot; Ruddles Best Bitter; guest beers H
Opened in 1998, this large town-centre pub has an open-plan split-level interior with a separate comfortable dining area. It is named after Samuel Crompton's Mule, a revolutionary invention in cotton spinning that made Bolton famous worldwide. In 1862 a statue of Samuel Crompton was erected in the square in front of the pub. Moorhouse's beers are usually available plus others from local breweries on the nine guest beer handpumps. Two or three ciders are usually served. Q◐◑♿≋●⊟

Broadbottom

Harewood Arms 🏆 L

2 Market Street, SK14 6AX
3-11 (midnight Fri); 2-midnight Sat; 2-11 Sun
☎ (01457) 762500 greenmillbrewery.co.uk
Green Mill Gold, Talisman, Big Chief; guest beers H
Taken over in 2013, the Green Mill brewery has moved from Rochdale to the cellar of the Harewood Arms and the pub is now essentially the brewery tap. A range of continental bottled beers and a guest handpull cider complement the Green Mill beers. This large open-plan community pub is warmed by open fires, helping to create a friendly atmosphere. There is a pool table and elevated darts area to the rear. Convienently located for the railway station. ❀◑♿Å≋♣●⊟🐾

Broadheath

Old Packet House

1 Navigation Road, WA14 1LW
12-11 (midnight Fri); 11-midnight Sat; 12-10.30 Sun
☎ (0161) 929 1331
Dunham Massey Little Bollington; Timothy Taylor Golden Best H
Dating back to the 18th century, this pub was once the second inn on the journey from Manchester along the Great Bridgewater Canal which runs just

behind the building. The main bar area is divided by an impressive central chimney with a real fire in winter, and leaded and stained glass feature on the back bar and partitions around the interior. Home-cooked food is popular with local office workers at lunchtimes. Quiz night is Monday and karaoke is hosted every Friday. P

Railway ★

153 Manchester Road, WA14 5NT (adj to retail park)
12-11 (midnight Fri & Sat) (0161) 941 3383
Holt Mild, Bitter H
This Grade II-listed Victorian pub features on CAMRA's National Inventory of Historic Pub Interiors. Once a row of terraced cottages running alongside the local railway, it has multiple rooms, with a hallway leading to the bar and a taproom and bar parlour either side. There are two further rooms to the rear. The outside drinking area has a gas lampost and an original red telephone box.
Q

Bromley Cross

Dunscar Arms L

547 Darwen Road, BL7 9ED
3-11; 12-midnight Sat & Sun (01204) 778782
Beer range varies H
A traditional stone-built end-of-terrace local. The small interior has a single drinking area around a prominent central bar. The motto on the pub sign outside invites passers-by to come in for a drink. Two guest beers frequently come from Copper Dragon, Hopstar or Moorhouse's. The pub's house beer, Pride of Dunscar, is brewed by Moorhouse's.

Flag Inn

Arnold Road, Egerton, BL7 9HL (off B6472)
11-11 (midnight Fri & Sat) (01204) 598267
Greene King IPA; guest beers H
This popular local is well over 200 years old, with timber decor, low ceilings and stone-flagged floors helping to give a traditional feel. Ales are dispensed from the viewing cellar – the seven guest beers are often from Phoenix, Hopstar or Moorhouse's breweries. With great service and good food, it is an ideal stop-off after a walk over the local moors or a visit to the nearby Last Drop Village. The licensee is restoring the pub to its former glory as a cask beer drinkers' mecca.
(533,537)

Bury

Automatic Café & Malt Real Ale Bar L

Derby Hall, 36 Market Street, BL9 0BW (250yds N from Bury Interchange)
10-11 (midnight Fri & Sat); 12-10.30 Sun
(0161) 763 9399 automaticcafe.com
Outstanding Silver Fox; guest beers H
This welcoming independent bar and restaurant shares the Derby Hall with two theatres. The Malt Bar gives a complete view of the beer cellar and its small electric hoist and pulley system, and also provides an overspill at busy times for the dining area. In the evening it becomes a lovely, quiet, cosy space to enjoy a pint. Relaxed, safe and comfortable, this a popular choice for all. Silver Fox is also served upstairs in the theatre bar.
(Bolton St)

Black Bull

8-10 Lowercroft Road, Starling, BL8 2EY
12-midnight (1am Fri & Sat) (0161) 761 5961
theblackbullbury.co.uk
Thwaites Nutty Black, Original, Wainwright, Lancaster Bomber; guest beer H
This family-run local offers a warm and friendly welcome to drinkers and diners alike. Winner of Thwaites Pub of the Year 2012 and Thwaites Best Pint Award 2013, it is also Cask Marque accredited and takes great pride in serving the perfect pint. Guest beers are from the Thwaites 1807 Cask Club range. Excellent meals are served daily, prepared using locally-sourced top-quality produce (booking is recommended). P (486,510)

Lamb Inn L

533 Tottington Road, Woolfold, BL8 1UB
4.30-11 (midnight Fri); 1-midnight Sat & Sun
(0161) 764 2714
Beer range varies H
Originally a coaching inn built in 1831, this is a popular family-run local with a warm welcome for young and old alike. The landlord, Roger Elliot, is passionate about his real ales and a keen supporter of local microbreweries. Excellent food made with local produce is served at weekends. There is a good-sized beer garden where dogs are allowed. Sky Sports is screened on four TVs.
P (468,469)

Robert Peel L

10 Market Place, BL9 0LD
8am-midnight (1am Fri & Sat) (0161) 764 7287
Greene King Abbot; Ruddles Best Bitter; guest beers H
Situated in Bury's cultural quarter, the Robert Peel is well established, popular and has the largest open public drinking area in Bury, with a mixture of tables and booths. This Wetherspoon pub bears the name of the man who was twice UK prime minister and founder of the modern police force; he was born in Bury. The decor also celebrates other local worthies including Richmal Crompton, the author of the Just William books. Ciders are from Gwynt y Ddraig, Westons and Thatchers.
(Bolton St)

Trackside Bar L

Bolton Street Station, BL9 0EY (Platform 2 East Lancs Railway)
12-midnight Mon & Tue; 9am-12.30am (midnight Wed & Thu) (0161) 764 6461 eastlancsrailway.org.uk
Outstanding Piston Broke; guest beers H
A small buffet bar renowned for its range of nine ever-changing real ales and a house beer, Piston Broke, from Bury's Outstanding Brewery. The bar also stocks a selection of continental beers and some fine malt whiskies together with up to four real ciders/perries. Winner of CAMRA branch and regional Cider Pub of the Year 2013. A great venue for a drink while reliving the days of steam.
(Bolton St) P

Chadderton

Rose of Lancaster

7 Haigh Lane, OL1 2TQ
11.30-11 (11.30 Fri & Sat); 12-11 Sun (0161) 624 3031
roseoflancaster.co.uk
Lees Brewer's Dark, Manchester Pale Ale, Bitter, seasonal beer H

Situated by the Rochdale Canal and overlooking open countryside to the rear, the Rose is a popular pub with a separate vault and a conservatory restaurant. It attracts a good mix of people and is one of Lees' busiest pubs, with a high ale turnover. The covered patio is popular during the summer months, and an open fire adds warmth in winter. Friendly management and a buzzy atmosphere always ensure a convivial visit. Buses and trains are nearby. ❀◐◑♿⇌(Mills Hill)♣P🚌(59,64)📶

Cheadle Hulme

John Millington

67 Station Road, SK8 7AA (on A5149)
⏲ 12-11 (midnight Fri & Sat); 12-10.30 Sun
☎ (0161) 486 9226
Hydes Manchester's Finest, Original Bitter, seasonal beer; guest beers Ⓗ
The interior of the Grade II-listed former Millington Hall is pleasantly rambling with a variety of rooms and areas around a central L-shaped bar. The pub is something of a flagship for Hydes and features its seasonal and one-off beers alongside guests from other breweries, usually micros. Periodic beer festivals are also hosted. The well-regarded food ranges from snacks to full meals, served every day until 9pm. The cider is usually from Gwynt-y-Ddraig. ❀◐◑♿⇌🍎P🚌(X57,313)📶

Chorlton-cum-Hardy

Bar Ⓛ

533 Wilbraham Road, M21 0UE (opp Morrisons)
⏲ 12-11.30 (midnight Thu; 12.30am Fri); 11.30-12.30am Sat; 11.30-11.30 Sun ☎ (0161) 861 7576 🌐 barchorlton.co.uk
Castle Rock Harvest Pale; Marble Ginger; guest beers Ⓗ
The Bar has eight handpumps dispensing seven real ales (beware, one handpump is for non-real cider), with beer blackboards listing the current selection. Regular beers are from a number of local breweries as well from further afield. At least one beer of every style – golden, porter, mild – should be available at any one time. Foreign and craft beers are also well represented. New to Chorlton are Epicurean Nights, popular at sibling The Knott. 🐎❀◐◑⚐♣🚌🐾📶

Beech Inn

72 Beech Road, M21 9EG
⏲ 4-11; 12-midnight Fri & Sat; 12-11 Sun ☎ (0161) 312 0309
Black Sheep Best Bitter; Copper Dragon Golden Pippin; Timothy Taylor Golden Best, Landlord; guest beers Ⓗ
The Beech is one of Chorlton's few remaining traditional pubs. Recent changes have smartened up the pub and garden, which now houses the Hungry Gecko caravan from which MasterChef finalist Jackie Kearney serves excellent Asian street food (largely Thai). Alternatively there are some bar snacks or the staff are happy for you to bring in your own food from one of the local takeaways. Live music features on Mondays and Wednesdays and traditional games such as bridge are played. Q🐎❀◑⚐♣🚌(276)🐾📶

Electrik

559 Wilbraham Road, M21 0AE
⏲ 12-12.30am (1.30am Fri); 10-1.30am Sat; 11-12.30am Sun
☎ (0161) 881 3315 🌐 electrikbar.co.uk
Thwaites Wainwright; guest beers Ⓗ
Central Chorlton café bar with excellent food including locally renowned breakfasts and good coffee. In addition it offers a rotation of guest ales in a range of styles from dark to IPA, and has an enviable bottle selection. Fairly regular music nights are hosted. During the week this is a delightful place for lunch or to read a book with a decent pint; at weekends the bar gets more lively. There is a secret garden to the rear and terrace at the front. 🐎❀◐◑♿⚐♣🐾📶

Font

115-117 Manchester Road, M21 9PG
⏲ 11-12.30am (1am Fri & Sat) ☎ (0161) 871 2022
🌐 thefontbar.wordpress.com
Beer range varies Ⓗ
Opened in early 2013, this new addition to the Font group hit the ground running with eight cask ales and up to eight ciders. Featuring breweries such as Dark Star, RedWillow, Magic Rock, Tickety Brew and others, plus a wide range of bottles and craft keg, there is plenty of choice. A small open kitchen showcases the chefs' skills, with excellent food served daily until 10pm. DJs provide the musical background on Friday and Saturday. CAMRA members receive a 25 per cent discount on ales and ciders. 🐎❀◐◑⚐🍎🚌(84,86)🐾📶

Marble Beer House Ⓛ

57 Manchester Road, M21 9PW
⏲ 12-midnight (11 Mon-Wed) ☎ (0161) 881 9206
🌐 marblebeers.com/beerhouse
Marble Pint, Manchester Bitter, Ginger; guest beers Ⓗ
The Beer House is a stalwart of the Chorlton bar scene and a mecca for cask ale lovers since it opened over 15 years ago. The knowledgeable team offers a warm welcome and serves a rotating and varied range of beers from Marble and guest breweries. A good choice of bottled beers (Marble and a host of others) is also available. There are occasional music and quiz nights. Though dogs are still welcome, look out for the new addition, Igloo the cat! Q🐎❀⚐♣🍎🚌🐾

Parlour Ⓛ

60 Beech Road, M21 9EG
⏲ 12-11.30 (12.30am Fri & Sat) ☎ (0161) 881 3871
🌐 theparlour.info
Beer range varies Ⓗ
Winner of awards for both food and excellent ale, the Parlour has become a favourite. A café-style bar with a warm welcome for all, it has comfy sofas inside and a quaint set of pavement tables for when the sun shines. The good British food menu features ingredients from local independent suppliers. RedWillow provides the regular beers and there is usually a dark beer among the range. 🐎❀◐◑⚐🍎🚌🐾📶

Pi (Chorlton) Ⓛ

99 Manchester Road, M21 9GA (500yds from B5217/A6010 jct)
⏲ 11-11 (11.30 Wed & Thu; midnight Fri); 12-midnight Sat; 12-11 Sun ☎ (0161) 882 0000 🌐 abarcalledpi.com
Tatton Blonde; guest beers Ⓗ
Popular café bar with friendly service to the north of Chorlton's main drag. Five handpumps serve four real ales and a guest cider or perry alongside a selection of 10 world beers on draught – no mainstream brands here. An impressive menu of 80 bottled beers from around the world is also offered. Gourmet Pieminister pies with trimmings are served until 11pm daily. 🐎❀◐◑⚐🍎🚌🐾📶

Sedge Lynn 🄻

21a Manchester Road, M21 9PN (next to library)
9am-11 (midnight Fri & Sat) ☎ (0161) 860 0141
Brightside Medlock Madness; Greene King Abbot; Ruddles Best Bitter; Moorhouse's Blond Witch; Phoenix Wobbly Bob; guest beers 🄷
Built by Norman Evans as a billiard hall for the temperance movement, this Grade II-listed building, with a barrelled roof and Art Deco styling, is well worth a look. This Wetherspoon establishment provides a typical selection of ales — the manager's aim is to ensure there is a range of light to darker beers available on the 10 handpumps, with five changing guests.
Q

Delph

Royal Oak (Th' Heights)

Broad Lane, OL3 5TX (Via Thame Lane, off main Delph-Denshaw road)
closed Mon; 7 (5 Thu & Fri; 12 Sat)-11; 12-7.30 Sun
☎ (01457) 874460
Beer range varies 🄷
Isolated 250-year-old stone-built pub on a packhorse route overlooking the Tame Valley. In a popular walking area, it benefits from outstanding views. The pub comprises a cosy bar and three rooms, each with an open fire. The refurbished side room boasts a hand-carved stone fireplace, while the comfortable snug has exposed beams and old photos of the inn. A Millstone beer is always available and the house beer is from Moorhouse's. A regular in the Guide for 23 consecutive years.
QP

Denton

Lowes Arms

301 Hyde Road, M34 3FF
12-11 ☎ (0161) 336 3064
Beer range varies 🄷
Built in 1824 to serve the new Manchester Road, this thriving local has a reputation for quality beers and good-value food. Beers from Hornbeam and Conwy breweries feature regularly among the range of frequently changing guest ales. The comfortable lounge to the left is the main food area. To the right is the vault, with a wooden floor and a pool table. The pub is home to local darts, dominoes and pool teams. P(201)

Didsbury

Fletcher Moss

1 William Street, M20 6RQ (off Wilmslow Rd, A5145 via Albert Hill St)
12-11 (midnight Fri & Sat) ☎ (0161) 438 0073
Beer Studio seasonal beer; Hydes Manchester's Finest, Original Bitter, seasonal beers; guest beers 🄷
Named after the alderman who donated the nearby botanical gardens to the city, this thriving community local attracts people of all ages and drinking tastes, engaged in lively conversation without having to compete with piped music. The front encompasses two traditional snugs, full of Hydes memorabilia, while the rear opens up into a large conservatory. Beyond that is a neat garden. A quiz features every Tuesday and acoustic music on alternate Mondays. Board games are available. The cider is Gwynt-y-Ddraig. Q(42,142)

Gateway

882 Wilmslow Road, M20 5PG (jct Kingsway)
8am-11 ☎ (0161) 438 1700
Greene King Abbot; Ruddles Best Bitter; guest beers 🄷
This large late-1930s roadhouse built near the site of an old toll bar was acquired by Wetherspoon in 2011. The company has done an excellent job in improving the comfortable interior, with various lounges surrounding an island bar. Although often busy, there are sufficient separate areas to enable you to have a quiet drink and a chat. Handily located for the popular Parrs Wood leisure complex opposite and its public transport terminus, which features in the pub's decor.
(East Didsbury)P(42,50)

Milson Rhodes

School Lane, M20 6RD (off Wilmslow Rd, A5145)
8am-11.30 (12.30am Fri & Sat) ☎ (0161) 446 4100
Greene King Abbot; Ruddles Best Bitter; guest beers 🄷
Smart Wetherspoon pub near Didsbury metro station, named after Dr Milson Rhodes who treated local people suffering from learning difficulties and epilepsy. The pub has a main bar downstairs and a slightly smaller upstairs room. There is more space outside in a drinking area at the front and on the balconies. Two regular beers plus seven guests and a different locally brewed house beer every six months are offered. Look out for the regular beer and cider festivals. The pub can be busy with all age groups. QP(42,142)

Diggle

Diggle Hotel 🄻

Station Houses, OL3 5JZ (½ mile off A670)
12-midnight (11.30 Sun) ☎ (01457) 872741
digglehotel.com
Black Sheep Best Bitter, Golden Sheep; Millstone Tiger Rut; Timothy Taylor Landlord; guest beer 🄷
Stone pub in a pleasant hamlet near the Standedge Canal Tunnel under the Pennines. Built as a merchant's house in 1789, it became an alehouse and general store in 1834. Affording fine views of the Saddleworth countryside, this makes a convenient base in a popular walking area. The pub was totally revamped in 2013, and has a bar area and two rooms with open fires and a Yorkshire range. The accent is on home-cooked food served all day. QP(184)

Dobcross

Navigation Inn 🄻

21-23 Wool Road, OL3 5NS
12-2.30, 5-11 (midnight Fri); 12-11 Sat; 12-10.30 Sun
☎ (01457) 872418
Millstone Tiger Rut; guest beers 🄷
A popular family-run watering hole for Huddersfield canal boaters and walkers, this stone-built pub of 1806 slaked the thirst of navvies cutting the Standedge Tunnel. It comprises an open-plan bar and L-shaped interior, with four handpumps offering a variety of guest beers. People come for the freshly prepared food, with special offers Monday-Saturday and occasional themed evenings. Food events raise funds for local charities. It is a venue for the popular Saddleworth Rushcart Festival in August. Dog-friendly, and families welcome at all times. Q(184,350)

Swan Inn (Top House)

The Square, OL3 5AA
12-3 (not Mon), 5-11; 12-3, 5-midnight Fri; 12-midnight Sat; 12-11 Sun ☎ (01457) 873451 theswandobcross.com
Banks's Sunbeam; Jennings Cumberland Ale; Marston's Pedigree; guest beer H
A focal point for the local community, this rejuvenated stone pub overlooks the attractive village square. Built in 1765, the building has been tastefully renovated with three separate rooms, each with an open fire. The function room hosts entertainment including theatre, poetry readings and music. A home-cooked menu features dishes from around the world. Annual events such as the Whit Friday Brass Band Contest, Rushcart Festival and Yanks Weekend are popular. Voted Marston's Pub of the Year in 2013. Q (184,354)

Droylsden

Beehive

145 Market Street, M43 7AR
12-11 (midnight Fri & Sat) ☎ (0161) 292 2302
Beer range varies H
This lively two-room suburban community pub close to the town centre and Droylsden FC was built in 1870. It has a small public bar and a larger lounge on two levels. One handpull dispenses alternating beers from local micros including Hornbeam and Boggart Hole Clough. The lounge has brass ornaments, a quiz machine and free jukebox. There is a Monday Club 3-7pm every week with a singer and bingo.

Eccles

Lamb Hotel ★

33 Regent Street, M30 0BP (opp Metrolink station)
11.30-11 (11.30 Sat); 12-11 Sun ☎ (07877) 850252
Holt Mild, Bitter; guest beer H
One of the best of Holt's Edwardian monumental houses, the building was painstakingly restored a few years ago, retaining most of its original features including a billiards room. There are four separate rooms and an ornate central bar, with much polished mahogany, etched glass and original tiling in evidence. The pub is popular with a wide cross-section of customers of all ages. The landlady hosts a quiz on Wednesdays and a lively karaoke on alternate Friday evenings.
P

Fallowfield

Friendship

353 Wilmslow Road, M14 6XS (B5093, jct Egerton Rd)
12-11 (12.30am Fri & Sat) ☎ (0161) 224 5758
Hydes 1863, Original Bitter, Manchester's Finest, seasonal beers; guest beers H
Impressive Victorian mansion in a busy student area. This is not purely the domain of the young, however, as it attracts a good mix of folk. A large horseshoe bar serves a variety of areas on different levels – some quiet. The rear extension has created the space for food service including interesting and popular oriental food (takeaways available). Many TVs show sport. Nine handpumps offer the Hydes' range, as well as varying guest ales. The cider is Gwynt-y-Ddraig. P (42,43)

Garswood

Railway Hotel

4 Station Road, WN4 0SA
2-11 (11.30 Thu); 12-midnight Fri & Sat; 12-11 Sun
☎ (01942) 745187
Beer range varies H
Family-friendly pub with a large beer garden and children's area. The central bar has three handpumps serving varying guest ales from the Punch Taverns range. Outside, there is a large heated smoking area and car park to the rear. Access to the beer garden is via a gate at the front of the pub. A community establishment, it regularly holds charity events, and was a previous winner of local CAMRA Community Pub of the Year.
P

Gatley

Horse & Farrier

144 Gatley Road, SK8 4AB (jct Church Rd)
11-11 (midnight Fri & Sat); 12-10.30 Sun
☎ (0161) 428 2080
Beer Studio seasonal beers; Hydes 1863, Original Bitter, seasonal beers; guest beers H
Formed from three cottages which were later rendered to look like stone, and with a mock-Tudor upper floor, this Hydes Heritage house has a central bar and a food bar at the rear. Meals are served 12-3pm (5pm Sat & Sun). A couple of seats are set cosily under the stairs that lead to the Martingale function room. There is an outside smoking area past rooms on the left. Quarterly beer festivals are held each year. Real cider is available during festivals. Q P (11A,44)

Greenfield

Railway Inn L

11 Shawhall Bank Road, OL3 7JZ (opp station)
12-midnight (1am Thu & Fri); 11.30-1am Sat
☎ (01457) 872307
Copper Dragon Golden Pippin; Millstone Tiger Rut; Theakston Old Peculier; Wells Bombardier; guest beers H
Unspoilt pub comprising a central bar, lounge, games area and tap room with a log fire and old photos of Saddleworth. The Railway is a popular venue for all styles of live music on Thursday, Friday (unplugged night) and Sunday. It is also a stop-off on the Transpennine Real Ale Trail. In a picturesque area, the pub affords beautiful views across Chew Valley and is a great base for outdoor pursuits. Various ciders are served on gravity.
P (180,184)

Wellington Inn L

29 Chew Valley Road, OL3 7AF (near Tesco)
3-10 Mon; 12 (3 Tue)-11; 12-10.30 Sun
Thwaites Nutty Black, Original, Wainwright; guest beers H
Friendly village local on the end of a terrace, now a free house. It has a small bar area, an open-plan room catering for diners and a separate sports room with Sky TV, cribbage and a dartboard. Good home-made food features pies, puddings and real chips, served on Tuesday and Wednesday evenings and all day Thursday to Sunday, with fish specials on Friday. Up to three guest beers are available and real cider in summer.

Harwood

House Without a Name

75 Lea Gate, BL2 3ET

12-midnight (1am Fri & Sat) ☎ (01204) 433568
housewithoutaname.co.uk

Courage Best Bitter; Lancaster Straw; Robinsons Unicorn; guest beers H

This terraced pub, originally licensed in 1832, has been recently refurbished. It has a lounge area with a real fire and a smaller snug with a dartboard, both with TV screens showing BT Sport and Sky. There are six handpumps with guests from local breweries including Bank Top, Blackedge and Phoenix. A full food menu is available daily until 7pm, later a more limited selection. Live music features on Sunday. The outside area catches the late evening sun. (507)

Hindley

Hare & Hounds

31 Ladies Lane, WN2 2QA

4 (2 Fri; 12 Sat & Sun)-midnight ☎ (01942) 702227

AllGates Napoleon's Retreat, Pretoria; guest beers H

This small but traditional pub located between the railway station and town centre has a large cosy lounge and a distinct bar/vault area. The lounge displays pictures from bygone Hindley and has a large-screen TV for sport. This is an AllGates pub serving its own beers and a range of guests including LocAles. The pub is popular for darts and both men's and women's teams play in the local league. Quiz night is Thursday.
Q (559)

Holcombe Brook

Hare & Hounds

400 Bolton Road West, BL0 9RY (on A676 at jct with Longsight Rd)

12-11 (midnight Thu-Sat) ☎ (01706) 822107
aleatthedogs.co.uk

Beer range varies H

There has been an inn on this site for over 100 years. Ten ever-changing beers are available, sourced from all around the country, especially from new breweries. Beer festivals are held throughout the year, and the landlord sources ales from around the country. The pub has its own pool and quiz teams. Excellent food is served until 9pm. This multi-award-winning pub is currently local CAMRA Pub of the Year 2014.
P (472,474)

Horwich

Bowling Green

175 Lee Lane, BL6 7JD

4 (12 Sat & Sun)-midnight ☎ (01204) 413449
bowlinggreenhorwich.co.uk

Beer range varies H

This former Tetley Walker street-corner pub is now free from tie and offers four ever-changing beers, often including some from AllGates and Cross Bay breweries. The original green tiles feature in the long, narrow vault. Rock bands play once a week, usually on Friday evening. On the edge of the West Pennine Moors, families, hikers and dog walkers are all welcome. (125)

Crown

1 Chorley New Road, BL6 7QJ (on B6226, 200yds from A673)

11-11 (midnight Fri & Sat); 12-11.30 Sun
☎ (01204) 693109

Holt Mild, IPA, Bitter; guest beers H

A grand local landmark near the Macron Stadium, Rivington Park and the West Pennine Moors. Lever Park across the road was a gift from Lord Leverhulme, the soap magnate and great benefactor to his home town. Darts and dominoes teams play on Tuesday and Thursday evenings in the vault and games areas. Various artists provide entertainment on Sunday evenings. Children are welcome at lunchtimes when dining. A Holt seasonal beer is usually among the guest ales.
Q P (125,575)

Victoria & Albert

114 Lee Lane, BL6 7AF

4-11 (midnight Fri); 12-midnight Sat; 12-11 Sun
☎ (01204) 770837 vicandalbert.co.uk

Holt Bitter; guest beers H

Formerly the Albert Arms, the pub is situated across the road from Horwich Public Hall. Recently refurbished, it is now a modern and comfortable lounge-style venue with three separate seating areas. Now officially the Blackedge Brewery tap, beers from the Blackedge range will be among the six guests. The pub is handy for the West Pennine Moors and walkers are always welcome. Over 21s only. Local CAMRA Pub of the Year 2012 and 2013.
Q (125)

Hyde

Cheshire Cheese

407 Stockport Road, Gee Cross, SK14 5RY

4-midnight (1am Fri); 12-1am Sat; 12-11.30 Sun
☎ (0161) 368 6406

John Smith's Bitter; guest beers H

Comfortable and welcoming pub with a loyal group of regulars. Beer is the thing here – there is no food. Four constantly changing guests (all over 4% ABV) are sourced from all over the country to complement the regular John Smith's Bitter. The pub is a member of the Ossett Beer Excellence Club so there is every chance of finding an unusual Ossett beer here. An outside seating area to the front features a retractable canopy to protect customers in wet weather.

Cheshire Ring Hotel

72-74 Manchester Road, SK14 2BJ

4 (12 Sat)-11; 12-10.30 Sun ☎ 07917 055629

Beartown Ambeardextrous, Kodiak Gold, Bearskinful; guest beers H

One of the oldest pubs in Hyde, the building was comprehensively overhauled several years ago by Beartown. Seven handpumps offer a range of Beartown ales and guests from micros, in addition to ciders, perries and continental beers. A selection of bottled beers is also stocked and occasional beer festivals boost drinking choice. Gentle background music plays. Home-made curries are available on Thursday evenings. The opening hours vary with the season. (Central) P (201)

Godley Hall

Godley Hill, SK14 3BL

4 (12 Fri-Sun)-midnight ☎ (0161) 368 4415

Sharp's Doom Bar; Theakston Best Bitter; guest beer Ⓗ
Not easy to find but this comfortable pub is well worth the effort to seek out. From Godley station go up Kerry Way into the works. Turn left in front of the main building and continue up the hill. Turn left at the top to find a converted farmhouse built in 1718 and used as a pub since 1830, retaining many original features. A warm and friendly welcome is assured. The guest beer changes weekly, but is often from Hornbeam. Outside seating is available.
Q⚘◑⇌(Godley)P🚌(201,202)

Sportsman Inn 🄻

57 Mottram Road, SK14 2NN (by Morrisons car park)
☼ 12-midnight ☎ (0161) 368 5000
Rossendale Floral Dance, Glen Top, Halo Pail, Pitch Porter, Sunshine; Thwaites Wainwright; guest beer Ⓗ
Rossendale Brewery tied house, close to Hyde town centre, offering the full range of its Pennine Ales plus up to three guests from micros. Real cider is also kept. Bar snacks are served and there is a restaurant upstairs specialising in genuine home-cooked Cuban food and tapas. This former CAMRA Pub of the Region is popular with locals and retains its character. The rear patio includes a covered and heated smoking area.
⚘◑⇌(Newton for Hyde)♣●P🚌(201,202)
🐾📶

Leigh

Thomas Burke 🄻

Leigh Road, WN7 1QR
☼ 12-midnight ☎ (01942) 609144
Greene King Abbot; Ruddles County; guest beers Ⓗ
Popular with all ages, this Wetherspoon pub is named after a renowned Leigh tenor, known as the Lancashire Caruso. The pub divides into three areas: the main long bar, a raised dining area and, in what was once a cinema foyer, lounge-style seating. Ten handpumps offer a changing range of beers from local and distant breweries.
Q⚘◑♿🚌📶

White Lion 🏆 🄻

6a Leigh Road, WN7 1QL
☼ 12-midnight ☎ 07814 575883
AllGates California, Pretoria; guest beers Ⓗ
Fully refurbished and reopened in 2011, the White Lion is situated opposite the historic parish church just a few minutes' walk from Leigh's centre. A friendly town-centre pub, you can choose whether to enjoy the comfort of the main bar, bar games in the vault, or the quiet of the snug. Six handpumps dispense a selection of AllGates real ales plus guests, and draught Gwynt y Ddraig cider. Local CAMRA Pub of the Year 2012.
Q⚘♿♣●🚌(12,582)🐾📶

Littleborough

Red Lion 🄻

6 Halifax Road, OL15 0HB
☼ 2-midnight; 12.30-1am Fri & Sat; 1-midnight Sun
☎ (01706) 378195
Lees Bitter; Timothy Taylor Landlord; guest beers Ⓗ
Detached stone-built pub, nestling between the railway and canal (yet older than both). Four distinct rooms, each different in character, offer beer and conversation throughout. The main room is large and homely, while the adjacent snug has comfortable high-backed chairs. Two rooms are for games and TV sport. Up to six guest beers supplement the two regulars; the house beer is from Phoenix. German and Belgian beers are also available on draught, with traditional ciders from Thatchers and Westons. Q⇌♣●P🚌(528,590)

White House 🄻

Blackstone Edge, Halifax Road, OL15 0LG
☼ 12-3, 6.30-midnight; 12.30-10.30 Sun ☎ (01706) 378456
🌐 thewhitehousepub.co.uk
Black Sheep Best Bitter; Theakston Best Bitter; guest beers Ⓗ
Originally built in 1691 and named the Coach & Horses, the White House stands on the Pennine Way. At over 1300ft it commands outstanding views over the local countryside. A family-run inn for 30 years, it offers a warm and friendly welcome to all, with two bars, both warmed by log fires. Four handpumps serve two regular and two guest beers, and a wide range of bottled beers, cider and wine is also stocked. An excellent food menu is available, served all day on Sunday.
Q⚘◑⛺P🚌(528)🐾

Lowton

Travellers Rest

443 Newton Road, WA3 1NZ
☼ 12-11 (midnight Fri & Sat); 12-10.30 Sun
☎ (01925) 293222 🌐 travellersrestlowton.com
Theakstons Best Bitter; Thwaites Wainwright; guest beers Ⓗ
Comfortable, friendly roadside local. The low ceiling lounge contains various discrete seating areas with the bar as the social focal point. Families are welcome with well-behaved children up until 8.30pm. There is a separate restaurant with an emphasis on local produce. At the rear of the pub is the large beer garden with plenty of seating.
Q⚘◑♿P🚌📶

Manchester: City Centre

Angel

6 Angel Street, M4 4BQ (corner Rochdale Rd)
☼ 11.30-12.30am (2am Fri & Sat); 12-11 Sun
☎ (0161) 833 4786 🌐 theangelmanchester.com
Bob's White Lion; guest beers Ⓗ
A free house five minutes' walk from the city centre's Northern Quarter. A wide range of ever-changing real ales and ciders from far and wide is served via 12 handpumps. The bar is on the left as you enter, serving the main downstairs drinking area, with patio doors leading to a small garden. Upstairs is the restaurant. ⚘◑⇌(Victoria)🚊●🚌📶

Bar Fringe

8 Swan Street, M4 5JN
☼ 12-midnight (12.30am Fri & Sat) ☎ (0161) 835 3815
Beer range varies Ⓗ
This is a popular and well-established Belgian-style bar on the edge of the city's Northern Quarter. The long narrow room is served by the bar on the left, where you will find five real ales from near and far as well as a range of draught and bottled continental beers. There is a beer garden at the rear with some covered seating. The décor is quite eclectic ranging from cartoons to rats and even a motorbike. ⚘◑⇌(Victoria)🚊●🚌

Bull's Head

84 London Road, M1 2PN (jct of Fairfield St)

11.30-11; 12.30-10 Sun ☎ (0161) 236 1724

Banks's Mild, Sunbeam; Jennings Cumberland Ale; Ringwood Boondoggle; guest beers H

Situated across the road from Piccadilly Station's taxi rank, the pub attracts both travellers and locals. While the interior is basically open plan it nevertheless manages to generate the atmosphere of cosy intimacy that you might expect to find in a more suburban location. Run with superb professionalism across the board, the Bull's Head never disappoints and is a beacon for quality. The guest beers are from the Marston's list but the licensee has a free hand in choosing the real cider. Q(Piccadilly)(1,3)

Cask Bar

29 Liverpool Road, M3 4NQ

12-11 (10.30 Sun) ☎ (0161) 819 2527 caskmanc.co.uk

Beer range varies H

Despite the name, Cask specialises in imported beers, with a number available on tap and a wider selection in bottles. The four real ale pumps tend to have at least one Pictish beer, often joined by a Hornbeam or a Phoenix. Sited just off the main Deansgate route, Cask has been in business for 12 years, with a friendly attitude, and is a relaxed sanctuary away from the centre of Manchester. Patrons may bring in their own food.
(Deansgate)

Castle Hotel

66 Oldham Street, M4 1LE

12-1am (2am Fri & Sat) ☎ (0161) 237 9485

thecastlehotel.info

Robinsons Dizzy Blonde, Unicorn; guest beers H

Robinsons' only pub in the city centre serves four of its beers and four guests, plus real cider. This fine Grade II-listed building underwent a major but sympathetic refurbishment in 2010. The bar serves the small front room and there is a more intimate middle room and a larger back room where regular live music is performed. The back room has a splendid skylight which was restored to its former glory during the refurbishment.
(Victoria)

City Arms

46-48 Kennedy Street, M2 4BQ

12-11 (midnight Fri & Sat); 12-8 Sun ☎ (0161) 236 4610

Moorhouse's Pride of Pendle; guest beers H

Multi-award-winning pub tucked away on a back street close to Albert Square, with two traditional rooms and many original features. The City Arms has featured in the Guide for many years, with six handpumps always serving a full range of beer styles in excellent condition. Saturday evenings are Northern Soul nights, but mostly the pub is noisy with the sound of convivial conversation.
Q(Oxford Rd)(M3)

Crown & Kettle

2 Oldham Road, M4 5FE

12-midnight ☎ (0161) 236 2923

Ossett Silver King; guest beers H

This fascinating Grade II-listed building on the edge of the city centre has three contrasting rooms served from a central bar – a small snug, comfortable lounge and a larger vault with an ornate ceiling. There are currently six handpumps, with two usually selling milds, porters or stouts. More handpumps are planned and up to five ciders are available. Beer festivals are held periodically, a quiz on Wednesday and open mic night on Thursday. (Victoria)

Knott Bar

374 Deansgate, M3 4LY

12-11.30 (midnight Thu; 12.30am Fri & Sat)

☎ (0161) 839 9229 knottbar.co.uk

Castle Rock Harvest Pale; Marble Ginger; guest beers H

Award-winning pub famous for its real ales and an extensive range of foreign beers alongside British keg. Two regular ales and four guests come from breweries including RedWillow, Magic Rock and Pictish. Real cider is also available from a box on the back bar (ignore the handpump serving non-real cider). Excellent transport links make this an ideal start/end point for a crawl. Meals are served until 8pm daily, with all food cooked fresh and interesting vegetarian and vegan options available.
(Deansgate)

Marble Arch ★

73 Rochdale Road, M4 4HY

12-11.30 (12.30am Sat); 12-midnight Sun

☎ (0161) 832 5914 marblebeers.com/marble-arch

Marble Best, Ginger; guest beers H

This pub with a nationally important historic interior held its 125th birthday celebrations in 2013. Situated a 10-minute walk from the city centre, close to the Marble Brewery, it offers the Marble house ales alongside many guest beers. Good food is served in a separate restaurant area, and there is a pleasant beer garden. Admire the floor and ceiling mosaics uncovered in the early 1980s. This north Manchester favourite was awarded the local CAMRA branch's Neil Richardson Traditional Pub Award in 2014.
Q(Victoria)

Micro Bar

Unit FC16, Arndale Market, M4 3AH (in Arndale food market)

11-6; 12-5 Sun ☎ (0161) 277 9666

boggart-brewery.co.uk

Beer range varies H

This unusual market stall bar is owned by Boggart Hole Clough Brewery and sells two of its beers plus two guests. There is also an extensive range of bottled beers, British and foreign, for drinking in or taking away. Despite its location, the bar exudes the friendly atmosphere of a local. There is a choice of food from many nations at nearby market stalls.
(Victoria)

Molly House

26 Richmond Street, M1 3NB (jct Sackville St)

12-1am (midnight Mon & Tue; 2am Fri & Sat)

☎ (0161) 237 9329 themollyhouse.com

Beartown Ginger Bear; guest beers H

A comfortable yet modern pub set in the heart of Manchester's gay village. This has fast become a destination for the more discerning/older village devotees. The welcoming ground floor has a bar and a small restaurant (tapas a speciality) as well as papers and a small library. The larger upper floor holds another bar, comfy sofas and a terraced smoking area where drinkers congregate in fine weather. The house beer range is from Beartown plus Hornbeam, Dunham Massey, RedWillow and other local brewers. (Oxford Rd)(1,3)

Paramount

33-35 Oxford Street, M1 4BH (jct Portland St)
7am-midnight (1am Fri & Sat); 7am-midnight Sun
☎ (0161) 233 1820
Adnams Broadside; Elland Paramount Porter; Moorhouse's Pendle Witches Brew; Robinsons Trooper; Sharp's Doom Bar; Thwaites Wainwright; guest beers H
This large and extremely popular Wetherspoon house has a pleasant, lively atmosphere. What really sets it apart, however, is the enthusiasm of the management team for its wide and interesting range of cask beer. Located in Manchester's old theatreland – hence the name – photos of closed theatres and cinemas adorn the walls. Nowadays it is handy for a pint when visiting one of the many modern-day venues nearby, including the Bridgewater Hall, Palace Theatre and Manchester Central. (Oxford Rd) (1,3)

Piccadilly Tavern

71-75 Piccadilly, M1 2BS (opp Hope St)
8am-11 (midnight Thu; 1am Fri & Sat); 9am-11 Sun
☎ (0161) 236 9622 thepiccadillytavernmanchester.co.uk
Greene King IPA; Moorhouse's Pendle Witches Brew; Wells Bombardier; guest beers H
Large split-level pub with a keen manager committed to real ale who ensures the beers are served in excellent condition. The bar is at the front of the pub on the lower level, with a large raised area to the rear. Good-value food is served and the pub can get busy on football match days, due to its proximity to transport termini. Guest beers come from various micro and regional breweries.
(Piccadilly)

Port Street Beer House

39-41 Port Street, M1 2EQ
closed Mon; 4 (2 Fri)-midnight; 12-1am Sat; 12-midnight Sun ☎ (0161) 237 9949 portstreetbeerhouse.co.uk
Beer range varies H
This back-street Northern Quarter bar opened in early 2011 in former shop premises. There are seven handpumps providing an always interesting range of beers. A wide selection of other draught beers and bottled beers is also available, often from the US. The bar is on the ground floor with a beer garden at the rear. There is also an upstairs room displaying changing pictures from different artists. Regular Meet the Brewer events are popular. (Piccadilly)

Sandbar

120-122 Grosvenor Street, M1 7HL (off Oxford Rd A34)
12-midnight (1am Thu; 2am Fri & Sat) ☎ (0161) 273 1552
Facers Clwyd Gold; Phoenix Arizona; Privateer Tarantula; guest beers H
Excellent conversion of 18th-century town houses into a quirky and bohemian bar. In the heart of Manchester's student land, the bar is popular with both student and university staff alike. Exhibitions of photographs and paintings adorn the walls and DJs do their thing at weekends. A good range of foreign beers complements the seven handpulled cask ales; the changing guest cider often comes from a smaller producer. Beers from First Chop and Privateer are usually available.
(Oxford Rd) (42,43)

Soup Kitchen

31-33 Spear Street, M1 1DF
12-11 (1am Thu; 4am Fri & Sat) ☎ (0161) 236 5100
soup-kitchen.co.uk
Beer range varies H
Soup Kitchen is a communal canteen-style bar with bench seating and menus mainly focusing on a wide variety of soups. Up to five real ales and one cider are available, ever changing and from far and wide, served by friendly, knowledgeable staff with a genuine appreciation of real ales. The basement is a popular live music venue, so at night it can get busy. Close to Stevenson Square bus terminus.
(Piccadilly) (X35,131)

Waterhouse L

67-71 Princess Street, M2 4EG (opp town hall)
9am-midnight ☎ (0161) 200 5380
Greene King Abbot; Phoenix Wobbly Bob; Roosters Buckeye; Thwaites Wainwright; guest beers H
Standing adjacent to the town hall designed by Albert Waterhouse, this Wetherspoon outlet has a split interior with several areas for drinking and dining. The four regular beers are complemented by an ever-changing choice of six guest ales, often from local micros. Meet the Brewer nights feature regularly and such is the relationship between the cellar team and local breweries that the pub often stocks beers that have been produced in collaboration between the two.
Q (Oxford Rd)

Wharf L

6 Slate Wharf, Castlefield, M15 4ST
11-11 (midnight Fri & Sat); 11-10.30 Sun
☎ (0161) 220 2960 brunningandprice.co.uk/thewharf
Phoenix Brunning & Price Original; Weetwood Cheshire Cat; guest beers H
Impressive pub with a large outdoor terrace overlooking the Castlefield Basin where the Bridgewater and Rochdale canals meet. The bar boasts 12 handpumps, nine serving guest beers including a stout/porter and one serving a real cider. The knowledgeable staff can advise on a wide range of wines and whiskies. A popular mooring point for leisure boaters.
Q (Deansgate) P

Marple Bridge

Hare & Hounds

19 Mill Brow, SK6 5LW (from A626 Lane Ends along Ley Lane for ¾ mile)
5-10 (midnight Wed & Thu); 12-3, 5-midnight Fri; 12-midnight Sat & Sun ☎ (0161) 427 4042
hareandhoundsmillbrow.co.uk
Robinsons 1892, Dizzy Blonde, Unicorn; guest beer H
This pub is a hidden gem in the beautiful hamlet of Mill Brow. Extensively refurbished to a high standard, this excellent country pub, with a great atmosphere and a roaring fire in winter, is the perfect place for both discerning drinkers and diners. The menu is inventive and food is locally sourced and freshly prepared. A genuine local that caters for everyone, including walkers, with some of the best views in the area.
Q P (394)

Norfolk Arms

2 Town Street, SK6 5DS
12-11 (10.30 Sun) ☎ (0161) 427 8090
Beer range varies H
A recently refurbished stone-built pub that sits in an attractive urban setting. The atmosphere is warm and friendly with good-value food available and four real ales, often from microbreweries. Comfortably furnished with a real fire, it attracts a

wide clientele by catering for all tastes. The beer range is a good addition to the choice in the area. Live music plays on Thursdays. Well served by public transport. ❀◑♿⇌(Marple)🚌🐾

Mellor

Oddfellows Arms

73 Moor End Road, SK6 5PT

closed Mon; 4 (12 Fri-Sun)-11 ☎ (0161) 449 7826

oddfellowsmellor.com

Marston's Pedigree; guest beers H

This elegant stone-built pub is tucked away in a dip in the road in the old part of the village. The smart but traditional interior is enhanced by beams and flagged floors, with blazing real fires in winter. Guest beers are often sourced from micros such as Marble and Bollington. Sought-after food comes from a realistic menu with a gourmet twist. The 375 bus service passes the door but runs only infrequently. ❀◑♿ÅP🚌(375)

Middleton

Ring o' Bells L

St Leonards Square, M24 6DJ

5-midnight; 12-1am Fri & Sat; 12-midnight Sun

☎ (0161) 654 9245 ringobellsmiddleton.co.uk

Lees Bitter, seasonal beer H

Situated to the rear of Jubilee Park and opposite the historic parish church, this old pub has a strong place in the community. It hosts an annual Maypole event on May bank holiday Monday and a unique Pace Egg play on Easter Monday. Live music also features as do popular quizzes. One main room is divided by stairs leading to an upstairs function room decorated with old collages made from butterflies. At the rear is a covered smoking area. ❀♣P🚌

Tandle Hill Tavern

14 Thornham Lane, M24 2SD (1 mile on unmetalled road from either A664 or A627)

closed Mon; 5 (12 Sat & Sun)-midnight ☎ (0161) 376 4492

Lees Bitter, seasonal beers H

Set on the top of a hill in the Tandle Country Park, this neat little pub nestles among a number of farms. It comprises a main bar and lounge area with a quieter side room. In summer the walled rear beer garden is a suntrap, with benches to the front and side providing more outdoor seating. The pub is popular with walkers, farmers and locals, and dogs are welcome (biscuits and water provided). Food is limited to toasties. Q❀🐾

Milnrow

Waggon Inn

31 Butterworth Hall, OL16 3PE

12 (4 Mon & Tue)-midnight; 12-11 Sun ☎ (01706) 648313

Banks's Bitter; guest beers H

A true family hostelry welcoming young and old, the Waggon dates back to 1782 and with its mullioned windows has the appearance of a real village pub. The beer range, supplied by Marston's, changes monthly. A broad variety of live musical acts features at weekends, which draws a crowd. A quiz is hosted on Thursday evenings. The pub is now within walking distance of the new Manchester Metro tramline. ◑♣P🚌(181,182)

Mossley

Britannia Inn

217 Manchester Road, OL5 9AJ

2-midnight; 12-1am Fri & Sat; 12-midnight Sun

☎ (01457) 832799

Marston's Burton Bitter; guest beers H

The Britannia is an imposing gritstone building, acquired by Marston's in 1961 when it bought it from Rothwell's (who had in turn obtained it from Shaw & Bentley in 1902). The Brit is now in the hands of a pubco and offers a range of beers that rivals many free houses. There is a secluded dining area, with meals served from opening time until 7.30pm (5pm Sun). Smokers may use the covered seating area at the front of the pub. ❀◑⇌♣🚌(343,350)🐾

Church Inn

82 Stockport Road, OL5 0RF

4-midnight; 1-1am Fri & Sat; 2-midnight Sun

☎ (01457) 831513

Thwaites Original, Wainwright; guest beer H

Once the Hardman's Arms, the pub now takes its name from the nearby St John's Church. This traditional local has a separate games room – effectively a public bar – and its own pool team. There is some splendid tile work just inside the front door, a veranda to the rear for smokers and a pavement patio at the front, used in warmer weather. Food is served 4-7pm (not Tue, Fri & Sat). Dogs are welcome, but they will be directed to the games room. ❀◗♣P🚌(353)🐾

Commercial Hotel

58 Manchester Road, OL5 0AA

12-11 (midnight Fri & Sat) ☎ 07849 186285

Millstone Tiger Rut; guest beers H

The Commercial was the first pub in Bottom Mossley. For a time it was a stopping place on the coach route between Lancashire and Yorkshire (until the railways came). It was bought by Gartsides in 1895, and the company was taken over by Bents of Liverpool in 1939. Today, this is a lively, semi open-plan pub with a pool room and a stage. A disco and/or a live act is hosted on Saturday. The darts team plays on Tuesday and there is poker on Thursday. ❀⇌♣🚌(343,350)🐾

Rising Sun

235 Stockport Road, OL5 0RQ

12-midnight ☎ (01457) 238236 risingsunmossley.co.uk

Millstone Tiger Rut, Stout, Rising Sunsation; guest beers H

This true free house is nearly a mile from the station, but a good deal higher up (by the 1904 tram terminus). The pub has views over the Tame Valley. The regular beers are augmented by an ever-changing selection of six guests. The pub is semi open-plan, but has a games room (used by the local Blue Grass Boys on Tuesdays and a folk club on alternate Wednesdays). Home-made pizzas are served Wednesday to Sunday, 6-9pm. ❀◗♣●P🚌(353)🐾

Oldham

Ashton Arms L

28-30 Clegg Street, OL1 1PL

11.30-11 (11.30 Fri & Sat); 11.30-8.30 Sun

☎ (0161) 630 9709

Beer range varies H

Extremely popular town-centre free house overlooking the old town hall, serving an excellent range of four to seven rotating beers from both new and long-established breweries. It specialises in local micros and LocAles, with themed beer festivals throughout the year. Traditional cider and perry are sold all year round as well as a good selection of Belgian and German bottled beers. Good-value food is available weekdays until 6pm (3pm Fri). The pub is 100 yards from Oldham Central tram stop.

Carrion Crow

271 Huddersfield Road, OL4 2RJ

12-midnight ☎ (0161) 633 4490

Beer range varies

Dating from 1796, the Crow is a vibrant community pub selling a range of ever-changing beers from Marston's breweries through six handpulls. CAMRA Oldham Pub of the Year 2014, the licensee is a real ale aficionado and the pub is Cask Marque accredited. Pub food featuring local ingredients is served daily, with popular home-cooked roasts on Sunday (book ahead). Football and quiz teams use the pub as a base. Quiz night is Thursday. An annual Christmas fair and St George's Day walk are held. P (81A,82)

Royal Oak Hotel ★

178 Union Street, OL1 1EN

11 (12 Sun)-midnight ☎ (0161) 633 2642

Robinsons Cumbria Way, Unicorn, Trooper, Old Tom, seasonal beers

An early 20th-century brick building with a quality refit in 1928, including the addition of a splendid glazed servery and lots of wall tiling which remain to this day. The pub has kept a traditional multi-roomed layout with a pool room. The landlord is an avid real ale fan and offers four handpumps dispensing the Robinson's range, including Old Tom in winter. Tea, coffee and bar snacks are available most of the day. Handy for the Mumps tram stop. Q

Up Steps Inn

17-23 High Street, OL1 3AJ (between town square and Tommyfield market)

8am-midnight ☎ (0161) 627 5001

Greene King Abbot; Ruddles Best Bitter; guest beers

Traditional town-centre Wetherspoon pub on the main shopping street near the bus station and market. There are usually two regular beers and six to eight rotating guests on offer, including several from nearby breweries under the LocAle scheme. The pub also hosts beer festivals featuring specially brewed beers and ciders. Food is available all day from 8am, beer from 9am. The cider is often from Westons, with more choice available at festival times.

Patricroft

Bird in Hand

304 Liverpool Road, M30 0RY (adjacent to Eccles Fire Station)

11-midnight (1am Fri); 11-12.30am Sat; 11-11.30 Sun ☎ (0161) 211 6478

Holt Mild, Bitter; guest beer

Purchased by Holt in 1885, the original building first became a pub in 1839. Previously it was part of a farm and served as a coaching house to accommodate the gentry. The coachmen and servants would stay at the nearby Golden Cross (now demolished). The interior comprises two separate rooms at the front and a lounge and pool room at the rear. Reputedly there are tunnels leading to the old police station but there is little evidence. A friendly pub with a lively atmosphere. P

Queen's Arms

Green Lane, M30 0SH

7 (5 Fri)-11; 12-11 Sat & Sun ☎ (0161) 789 2019

Thwaites Original; guest beer

Built in 1828 for the arrival of the Liverpool and Manchester railway, the Queen's Arms is one of the world's earliest railway pubs. Three unspoilt rooms are served from a central bar, well cared for by proud licensees (a guest beer is only on at weekends). Known locally as the Top House, the pub was Grade II-listed at the instigation of the local CAMRA branch. Travel back in time here. Q P (67,100)

Wangies

303 Liverpool Road, M30 0QN

2 (12 Sat)-midnight; 12-11 Sun ☎ (0161) 787 8995

Beer range varies

Originally The Oddfellows but known locally as Wangies, hence the name change. Real ale was reintroduced a couple of years ago and there are now up to three beers available. Live alternative music is supported with regular weekend gigs, and a DJ on a Friday. The pub is separated into four areas, with two lounges at the front, a pool table in one back room and a dartboard in the other. It can be noisy but is always friendly, with a mixed clientele.

Ramsbottom

First Chop

43 Bolton Street, BL0 9HU

4-midnight; 12-1am Fri & Sat; 12-midnight Sun ☎ (01706) 827722 thefirstchop.co.uk

Beer range varies

This friendly bar is set over two floors and has a passion for beer, food and music. It specialises in real ale, with four handpumps usually supplying two of its own First Chop beers plus other ales from the north of England. Up to six real ciders are also available. Food is locally sourced and home prepared. Live music also features. The bar offers a buy-five-get-one-free deal and CAMRA members receive a 20 per cent discount on food and beer. (East Lancs) (472,474)

Irwell Works Brewery Tap

Irwell Street, BL0 9YQ

closed Mon & Tue; 12-11 ☎ (01706) 825091 irwellworksbrewery.co.uk

Irwell Works Tin Plate, Copper Plate, Richard Mason 1888, Steam Plate, Iron Plate; guest beers

The Irwell Works Brewery is situated in the former Irwell Steam, Tin, Copper and Iron Works foundry. The building was used as an engineering works until a few years ago and now houses a six-barrel brewery. The bar sells its own range, guest beers and locally produced Ribble Valley Gold cider on draught. A minimum of 10 beers is always on. Small plates of food are served at lunchtimes. Brewery tours are available by request. (East Lancs) (472,474)

Major Hotel L
158 Bolton Street, BL0 9JA
⏲ 3-11 Mon & Tue; 12-midnight ☎ (01706) 826777
Bank Top Flat Cap; St Austell Tribute; guest beers Ⓗ
Now in its eighth year under the current owners, the stone-buillt Major prides itself on being a traditional local. There is a large logburner in the main lounge and the central bar features Sky TV, pool, darts and dominoes. Four real ales are sold, from local breweries and further afield. Unpretentious and reasonably priced food is served, ranging from snacks to full meals. The pub has a large car park next door and is a short walk from the local steam railway.
❀◐≹(East Lancs)♣P🚌(472,474)🐾📶

Rochdale

Baum L
35 Toad Lane, OL12 0NU
⏲ 11.30-11 (midnight Fri & Sat); 11.30-10.30 Sun
☎ (01706) 352186 🌐 thebaum.co.uk
Beer range varies Ⓗ
A hidden gem within a conservation area, the Baum occupies part of the Rochdale Pioneer Museum building on an isolated part of Toad Lane, just south of the bypass. A split-level inn with old world charm, the conservatory at the rear overlooks a large beer garden and smoking area. Friendly staff serve seven real ales, a cider, a large selection of worldwide bottled beers and continental lagers on draught. Good, reasonably priced fresh food is available daily until 9pm (6pm Sun). ❀◐🍎🚌🐾📶

Cemetery Hotel ★
470 Bury Road, OL11 5EU (on B6222 Bury Rd)
⏲ 12-11 (1am Thu-Sat) ☎ (01706) 645635
Beer range varies Ⓗ
This pub next to Rochdale Cemetery has a nationally important historic interior for its excellent Edwardian décor. It has three separate rooms off the main bar area, with impressive tiles, woodwork and a fire in the front room helping to create a cosy ambience. Rochdale AFC is close by and the pub is popular on match days, with one room displaying club memorabilia. Four real ales are always available, often six or seven later in the week. ❀◐♣🍎P🚌(468,469)🐾📶

Flying Horse Hotel L
37 Packer Street, OL16 1NJ
⏲ 11-midnight (1am Fri & Sat); 12-midnight Sun
☎ (01706) 646412 🌐 theflyinghorsehotel.co.uk
Timothy Taylor Landlord; guest beers Ⓗ
Situated in the Town Hall Square, this impressive Edwardian stone-built free house and B&B has many original architectural features including log fires. Live sports events are shown on TV. Live music plays most Thursdays, Fridays and Saturdays. The food menu features meat from a local butcher and pies made on the premises. A function room is available for hire and there is a heated smoking area outside. Parking is Pay & Display, free after 3pm weekdays and at weekends.
🛏◐≹🍎P🚌🐾📶

Healey Hotel
172 Shawclough Road, OL12 6LW
⏲ 11.30-11.30 (midnight Fri & Sat); 12-11.30 Sun
☎ (01706) 645453
Robinsons Unicorn; guest beers Ⓗ
The pub is situated close to Healey Dell Nature Reserve. A major enlargement and refit in 2013 have taken this always excellent pub to a new level. The original tiling and bar were retained. It now sells four Robinson's beers, two ever-changing guests and a cider. The beer garden has a decked and covered area with a pétanque piste and there is a separate covered smoking area. Excellent food is served lunchtimes and evenings (until 6pm Sun). Q❀◐♣🍎🚌(446,466)🐾📶

Regal Moon L
The Butts, OL16 1HB
⏲ 9am-midnight (1am Fri & Sat) ☎ (01706) 657434
Ruddles Best Bitter; Thwaites Wainwright; guest beers Ⓗ
Large and imposing former cinema in the town centre, handy for the tram and bus interchange. The pub has an open-plan interior divided into discrete drinking areas. Eighteen handpumps dispense a wide variety of ales and ciders, with local and West Yorkshire microbreweries featured. The cider is usually from Westons, with occasional guests. The pub has recently been refurbished, but the mannequin organist remains on his perch above the bar. There is a patio to the rear for smokers. Q◐♿🍎🚌📶

Romiley

Duke of York
Stockport Road, SK6 3AN (on B6104, 100yds from bridge 14 on Peak Forest canal)
⏲ 12-midnight (11.30 Mon & Tue); 12-11.30 Sun
☎ (0161) 406 9988
Black Sheep Best Bitter; John Smith's Bitter; Thwaites Wainwright; Wells Bombardier; guest beer Ⓗ
Built in 1786 and extensively refurbished, this traditional village pub retains its character and historic feel. Good-quality food is served both in the main bar and the separate upstairs restaurant. A free-to-enter quiz is held every Wednesday evening, with all teams winning a prize. Beer festivals feature throughout the year, the bigger ones in summer and autumn. Q❀◐≹P🚌📶

Platform 1
6 Stockport Road, SK6 4BN
⏲ 12-11 (10.30 Mon; midnight Fri & Sat); 12-10.30 Sun
☎ (0161) 406 8686
Beer range varies Ⓗ
The pub is next to Romiley railway station and within a conservation area close to the village centre. It opened in 2012 as a free house and wine bar following major refurbishment. Six real ales are on offer, usually including beers from local micros such as Hornbeam and RedWillow, served in the large bar situated down the side of the mainly open-plan lower floor. A separate restaurant area on the first floor (named Platform 2) serves food 12-8pm. ❀◐≹🚌📶

Royton

Puckersley Inn
22 Narrowgate Brow, OL2 6YD (off A671 via Dogford Rd & Fir Lane)
⏲ 12-midnight ☎ (0161) 652 2834
Lees Brewer's Dark, Bitter, seasonal beers Ⓗ
Popular, detached, stone-fronted pub situated on the edge of the green belt, with panoramic views over Royton, Shaw and Oldham. This welcoming

local has a traditional vault and a comfortable lounge. The dining extension serves an excellent range of well-prepared meals, lunchtimes and evenings until 9pm. Cosy corners provide plenty of space to chat and chill out over a pint or two. A garden area is available for warmer weather. ❀◖◗♣P🚌(408)

Sale

J P Joule 𝕃

2A Northenden Road, M33 3BR
⏲ 8am-midnight (1am Fri & Sat) ☎ (0161) 928 9889
Greene King Old Speckled Hen, Abbot; Ruddles Best Bitter; guest beers Ⓗ
Situated yards from Sale Metrolink station, this is an extremely popular Wetherspoon pub named after the famous physicist, frequented by people of all ages from both near and far. The pub is spread over two floors connected by a stunning staircase, each floor having its own extensive bar hosting a total of 14 handpumps. Look for the CAMRA noticeboard at the far end of the bar where drinkers are invited to post nominations for guest ales. Q❀◖◗♿🚊●🚌📶

Volunteer Hotel 𝕃

81 Cross Street, M33 7HJ
⏲ 12-11.30 (midnight Fri-Sun) ☎ (0161) 973 5503
Holt Mild, Bitter Ⓗ
Large late-Victorian establishment on the main A56 road with friendly and welcoming staff. The ground floor has been opened out to create one large room, with a pool table and darts on one side and seating on two levels on the other. Upstairs is a wood-panelled room used for functions and meetings. A quiz is held every Thursday in the main lounge. For the exterior and upstairs panelled room the pub was recently Grade II-listed. ❀♿🚊♣P🚌📶

Salford

New Oxford

11 Bexley Square, M3 6DB
⏲ 12-midnight ☎ (0161) 832 7082 🌐 thenewoxford.com
Beer range varies Ⓗ
Popular Salford free house situated on a corner of the historic Bexley Square. This is a smart two-room pub dedicated to the worship of beer. It serves up to 16 real ales and two or more real ciders from far and wide. Twelve draught foreign beers and a selection of over 100 bottled beers from around the globe are also stocked. Food is available in the afternoons. Outside is a small area of tables and chairs overlooking Bexley Square. ❀◖⇌(Central)●🚌

Salford Arms

146 Chapel Street, M3 6AF
⏲ 12-midnight (11 Sun) ☎ (0161) 288 8883
🌐 salfordarmshotel.co.uk
Beer range varies Ⓗ
Street-corner hotel reopened under new ownership in 2012. Now its five handpumps dispense an array of real ales from near and far, including a house beer from Blackjack Brewery. A side room to the right provides additional space when the main bar is busy. Various events are held including a popular quiz night, and good food is served lunchtimes and evenings (until 9pm). Just across the road from Salford Central station. ❀🛏◖◗⇌(Central)♣●🚌🐾📶

Stalybridge

Old Hunters Tavern

51 Acres Lane, SK15 2JR
⏲ 12-midnight ☎ (0161) 303 9477
Robinsons 1892, Unicorn; guest beer Ⓗ
Traditional characterful two-roomed pub, just outside the town centre, which appeals to all. The main room features unusual brass poles with circular shelves for holding pints, and there is a smaller room off to the side. Football matches are shown in both main rooms. The Manchester log end ladies' darts team meets every Tuesday and a golf society meets monthly. Quiz night is Thursday. There is a covered, heated area outside for smokers. No food is served at weekends. ❀◖P🚌

Society Rooms

49 Grosvenor Street, SK15 2JN
⏲ 8am-midnight ☎ (0161) 338 9740
Greene King Abbot; Ruddles Best Bitter; guest beers Ⓗ
This Wetherspoon pub is named after the former Co-op store premises it now occupies in the town centre. It has two elevated sections either side of the entrance and a typically large main area. Enthusiastic management and a strong focus on real ales dispensed from 10 handpumps have made this a favourite destination for local drinkers. Beer-oriented events such as Meet the Brewer nights, and ale requests by customers, have helped to boost the pub's reputation. Real ciders are always available. ❀◖◗♿⇌●🚌

Stalybridge Buffet Bar ★

Platform 1, Stalybridge Railway Station, Rassbottom Street, SK15 1RF (access from station platform)
⏲ 11-midnight; 12-10.30 Sun ☎ (0161) 303 0007
🌐 stalybridgebuffetbar.co.uk
Timothy Taylor Landlord; guest beers Ⓗ
Featured in many beer publications and on TV, this enduring Victorian gem is worth missing a train for. Sympathetic refurbishment has allowed expansion of the food menu, which includes home-cooked meals. Nine handpumps dispense a variety of beers, many locally sourced, plus at least one real cider or perry. A good range of bottled beers is also available. Events including live music and Meet the Brewer nights are held in the function room. Monday is quiz night. Q◖◗♿⇌♣●P🚌

Stalybridge Labour Club

Acres Lane, SK15 2JR
⏲ 7.30-11.30; 12-midnight Fri-Sun ☎ (0161) 338 4796
Thwaites Wainwright; guest beers Ⓗ
Recently reopened following refurbishment, this large club, close to the town centre, boasts a welcoming lounge, a separate large function room (available for hire), and a games room with a full-sized billiard table. At least two rotating guest beers are offered, sourced from the Thwaites' list. Catering is available on request. For entry to the club show a copy of this Guide or a CAMRA membership card. ♿P🚌

Standish

Silver Tally

41 Shevington Moor, WN6 0SQ
⏲ 12-11 ☎ (01257) 472733 🌐 silvertally.co.uk
Prospect Silver Tally; Thwaites Wainwright Ⓗ
Reopened in 2012 as the Silver Tally, Prospect brewery's first pub is both the brewery bar and

beer tap. It has been totally refurbished, with a modern but traditional feel, and has three main areas for games, drinking and dining. High-quality home-cooked pub favourites are served from a simple food menu. Q (113)

Standish Unity Club

Cross Street, WN6 0HQ
7.30-11 (midnight Fri & Sat) (01257) 424007
standishunityclub.com
Prospect Silver Tally; guest beers H
Established for 11 years, this is an independent, non profit-making club open to all. A welcoming and thriving venue, it has a comfortably furnished bar and function room (available for hire) with a separate pool/snooker room. Live music and quizzes feature regularly. Prospect Unity Gold is usually available along with other beers from local breweries. The club hosts an annual beer festival and CAMRA members are welcome at all times. Local CAMRA Club of the Year 2013. Q P

Standish Lower Ground

Crooke Hall Inn

Crooke Road, WN6 8LR
12-midnight (01942) 204451
AllGates Napoleon's Retreat; guest beers H
Multi-roomed pub with a refurbished cellar bar owned by AllGates Brewery, featuring ales from the brewery and guests. An excellent food menu including good vegetarian options is available lunchtimes and evenings, seven days a week. The pub is home to men's and ladies' darts teams, a ukulele club on Wednesday and a folk night on Thursday. There is a beer garden and children's play area overlooking the Leeds-Liverpool Canal at the rear. P

Stockport: Centre

Arden Arms ★

23 Millgate, SK1 2LX (jct Corporation St)
12-11 (0161) 480 2185 ardenarms.com
Robinsons 1892, Dizzy Blonde, Double Hop, Unicorn H**, Old Tom** G**, seasonal beer** H
This Grade II-listed building close to Stockport market has a nationally important historic pub interior. The multi-roomed interior centres around one main serving area; to reach the tiny rear snug you must walk through the bar. Many Victorian features remain, making this an unmissable gem. It is said that the cellar once served as a mortuary and still retains body niches in its walls. Lunches are available daily, evening meals Wednesday to Sunday 5.30-8pm. A former CAMRA branch Pub of the Year. (300,384)

Boar's Head

2 Vernon Street, Market Place, SK1 1TY
11-11; 12-6.30 Sun (0161) 480 3978
Samuel Smith Old Brewery Bitter H
A town-centre multi-roomed pub with a genuine, cosy feel. Owners Samuel Smith spent a fair sum restoring this pub to how it may have once looked like. The front room on the right is a sparsely furnished public lounge; on the left is a more substantial, comfortably furnished room with cushioned pews, high-back chairs and stools. To the rear is a second lounge (formerly the music room) leading to a decked area outside. Q

Crown Inn

154 Heaton Lane, SK4 1AR (under viaduct)
12-11 (10.30 Sun) (0161) 480 5850
Beer range varies H
A former CAMRA National Pub of the Year runner-up, the Crown offers around 16 ever-changing beers – with helpful and knowledgeable staff to advise those confused by the choice. Pictish and Bollington beers are regulars, and there is always a mild, stout/porter and four ciders. Four rooms radiate from the busy bar – two compact snugs, a large lounge and a stand-up bar. Food is served until 3pm weekdays. Live music features, with the rear yard showcasing local bands at weekends. Q P (192)

Red Bull

14 Middle Hillgate, SK1 3AY
12-11 (10.30 Sun) (0161) 480 1286
redbullstockport.robinsonsbrewery.com
Robinsons 1892, Dizzy Blonde, Unicorn, seasonal beers H
Situated 400 yards uphill from Robinsons brewery, the Red Bull aims to maintain its flagship operation within the Robinson's estate and usually showcases the seasonal beers. Refurbished and enlarged in 2008, the pub retains a homely, rustic atmosphere. Numerous dining and drinking areas radiate from a large central bar area, with a wooden and tiled floor. Full lunchtime and evening menus are provided plus daily specials at competitive prices. Outside are a cobbled courtyard and small car park. Q P (310,314)

Robinsons Brewery Visitors Centre

Apsley Street, SK1 1YE
closed Mon; 10.30-6; 10.30-5 Sun (0161) 612 4100
robinsonsvisitorscentre.co.uk
Robinsons 1892, Dizzy Blonde, Trooper, Unicorn, seasonal ale H
The former Robinsons brewery Unicorn Room reopened in 2013 as a fully-fledged visitors' centre with a bar open to the public. The reception area features a huge display of brewery memorabilia tracing Robinson's history from 1838 to the present day. Steps lead you down to a bar to the right and a café to the left. A great place to visit, and a good place to sample the seasonal beers while enjoying a light lunch. Book ahead for a brewery tour. Q P (314,300)

Swan with Two Necks ★

36 Princes Street, SK1 1RY (jct Hatton St)
10.30-7 (11 Fri & Sat); 10.30-6 Sun (0161) 480 2341
swanwithtwonecksstockport.robinsonsbrewery.com
Robinsons 1892 Dark, Old Tom, Unicorn, seasonal beers H
Narrow-fronted with a mock-Tudor façade, the building was bought by Robinsons in 1924. Rejuvenated by a young couple, it is impressively panelled in light oak throughout in familiar Robinson's style, with labelled doors to match. The front door leads to a vault, then the bustling bar corridor, beyond that a cosy snug with an attractive skylight, and at the rear a small lounge and diner. Outside is a compact, walled drinking area. Quality lunchtime meals are served Monday-Friday. Cider is Westons Scrumpy. (300,330)

Stockport: Edgeley

Armoury

31 Shaw Heath, SK3 8BD (on B5465)
11.30-midnight (1am Fri & Sat) ☎ (0161) 477 3711
Robinsons 1892, Dizzy Blonde, Trooper, Unicorn, seasonal beer Ⓗ
Comfortable, recently refurbished, multi-roomed local with a strong community involvement and friendly service. The pub caters for a varied clientele from sports watchers to darts teams (with two leagues often playing on the same night) to quiet bookworms alike. The lounge walls feature memorabilia of the Cheshire Regiment. There is a pleasant beer garden, quite a suntrap in summer months. Handy for the train station and football ground, the pub opens at 11am if Stockport County are at home. Q❀♿⇌♣🚌(310,369)

Olde Vic

1 Chatham Street, SK3 9ED
closed Mon; 5 (7 Sat & Sun)-midnight ☎ (0161) 480 2410
yeoldevic.com
Beer range varies Ⓗ
Once visited, never forgotten. This gem of a local, containing a fascinating array of bric-a-brac, games and reading matter, hides behind an unkempt exterior. However, a friendly and sometimes surprising welcome awaits. Landlord Steve will tease you given the chance, while you can be sure of a warm and cheery welcome from Jo. Six handpumps dispense a changing variety of beers from micros far and near, building on the Olde Vic's reputation as Stockport's first pub to offer a continuous rotation. Last entry is 10.30pm. Q❀⇌♣🍎🚌(310,369)

Stockport: Heaton Norris

Hope Inn 🏆

118 Wellington Road North, SK4 2LL (N of Belmont Way)
12-11 (midnight Fri & Sat) ☎ (0161) 637 6191
thehopestockport.co.uk
Fool Hardy Rash Dash, Reckless Danger, Risky Blonde, seasonal beer; Outstanding 3.9, IPA; guest beers Ⓗ
A full refurbishment and installation of the new Fool Hardy Ales brewery has turned a dead duck into a real gem – winning CAMRA branch Pub of the Year just 12 months after reopening. This speciality free house comprises two large rooms: to the right is the cask ale side with 11 handpumps serving at least four of the brewery's own beers, two regulars from Outstanding, plus changing guests; the left side is dedicated to foreign beers and real ciders. An extensive bottled beer range and beer festivals also feature. Q❀☽♣🍎P🚌(22,192)

Magnet

51 Wellington Road North, SK4 1HJ
4 (12 Fri-Sun)-11 ☎ (0161) 429 6287
themagnetfreehouse.co.uk
Beer range varies Ⓗ
A focus on quality and choice quickly gained the Magnet full acclaim. It boasts 14 handpumps for beer and a draught cider, complemented by a large foreign bottled range. There is a bustling vault to the left, leading to a lower pool room, and a series of rooms separated by arched magnet doorways on the right. A beer terrace and function room upstairs are also busy. Monday cheese night is popular. An in-house brewery is in development. Q❀♣🍎P🚌(22,192)

Stockport: Heaviley

Blossoms

2 Buxton Road, SK2 6NU (at A6/A5102 jct)
12-11 (10.30 Sun) ☎ (0161) 429 8128
Robinsons 1892, Dizzy Blonde, Trooper, Unicorn, seasonal beer Ⓗ
An excellent, welcoming local with the vault, front lounge and cosy snug set around the central curved bar. The Grade II-listed former coaching house was given a makeover by Robinsons in 2012, turning it into one of its Ale Shrine pubs, retaining the original small, intimate rooms, striking decor and air of elegance. At the rear, the now disused cobbled street has benches for outside drinking, while the former outside toilet is now the smoking area. Food is served lunchtimes Monday to Friday. Well worth a visit.
Q❀☽⇌(Davenport)♣🍎P🚌(192,199)

Fairway

137 Higher Hillgate, SK1 3HR
closed Mon; 12-11 (midnight Fri); 3-midnight Sat; 12-10.30 Sun ☎ (0161) 474 1082
Beer range varies Ⓗ
Formerly a Robinson's house (the Flying Dutchman), it was purchased and reopened in autumn 2012 by Stuart and Emma, who have run pubs in the north-west for many years. The building now boasts a newly refurbished interior, smart smoking and drinking area outside and upgraded cellar facilities. Six constantly rotating handpulled beers, many from local microbreweries, are offered alongside quality meals available lunchtimes and evenings (no food Mon). Local CAMRA 2014 Pub of the Year runner-up. Q❀☽⇌♣🍎🚌(192,199)

Stockport: Portwood

Railway

1 Avenue Street, SK1 2BZ
12-11 (10.30 Sun) ☎ (0161) 429 6062
Moorhouse's Pride of Pendle, Railway Witch; Outstanding Blonde, Red; Pictish Brewers Gold; Rossendale Floral Dance; guest beers Ⓗ
Bustling, street-corner house with 15 handpumps showcasing the ranges of Rossendale, Outstanding and Pictish breweries, plus guests. A changing mild and a real cider are always stocked, plus a wide selection of Belgian, German and other bottled beers. Occasional beer and cider festivals are also hosted. Note the model railway atop the bar canopy, alongside much railway-related memorabilia. A bar billiards table is well used, while the outside yard is a suntrap in summer. A former local CAMRA Pub of the Year.
Q❀♣🍎🚌(325,330)

Strines

Sportsman 🄻

105 Strines Road, SK6 7GE (on B6101)
12-3, 5-11; 12-11 Sat & Sun ☎ (0161) 427 2888
the-sportsman-pub.co.uk
Beer range varies Ⓗ
Splendid white pub standing alone on the edge of the Goyt Valley, popular with local drinkers and diners. The comfortable lounge has large picture windows giving superb views over the wooded valley to the hills beyond. A monumental fireplace accommodates log fires in winter and there is a separate taproom. Five guest beers, mainly from

micros, are available. Outside, a terrace and balcony are popular in summer, and the pub is close to the Peak Forest Canal.
❀◐◑♿▲♣P🚌(62,358)🐾

Tottington

Dungeon Inn

9 Turton Road, BL8 4AW
⌚ 5-11 (12.30am Fri); 2-1am Sat; 2-10.30 Sun
☎ (01204) 887068 🌐 thedungeontottington.co.uk
Thwaites Original, Wainwright, Lancaster Bomber; guest beer 🄷
A well-maintained example of an Edwardian Bury Brewery pub offering comfortable surroundings and a great ambience. Five handpumps feature Thwaites' ales plus guests, and an extensive range of wines is available by the glass. The open fireplace is a real attraction in winter while the south-facing beer garden woos locals and walkers alike in summer. All cask ales are discounted on Mondays and Dungeon Platters – a selection of cheeses, meats, quiches, olives and chutneys – are served every day. Live entertainment and a quiz feature weekly. Q♨❀♣P🚌🐾📶

Uppermill

Cross Keys Inn

Running Hill Gate, OL3 6LW (off A670 up Church Rd)
⌚ 12-midnight ☎ (01457) 874626 🌐 crosskeysinn.co.uk
Lees Brewer's Dark, Manchester Pale Ale, Bitter, seasonal beer 🄷
Overlooking Saddleworth Church, this attractive 18th-century stone building has exposed beams throughout. The public bar features a stone-flagged floor and Yorkshire range. Home-cooked food includes puddings, pies and real chips. Outside is a children's play area and a covered, heated smoking area. Live folk music plays on Wednesday and Sunday nights. Annual events including the Rushcart Festival and Wartime Weekend are popular. The pub is the centre for Mountain Rescue and Saddleworth Runners. A regular in the Guide for 40 years. Q♨❀◐◑P🐾📶

Walkden

Bull's Head

12 High Street, M28 3NJ
⌚ 8am-midnight ☎ (0161) 702 5350
Greene King Abbot; Ruddles Best Bitter; guest beers 🄷
Large pub on the main road through Walkden, now in its third year as a Wetherspoon venue. The spacious ground floor is loosely divided into smaller seating and dining areas, with a long bar featuring 10 handpumps running the length of one wall. Up to six guest beers and two ciders complement the two regular ales. Food is served all day and the pub is family-friendly. There is a beer garden to the rear, but no parking facilities.
Q♨❀◐◑♿⇌🍎🚌🐾📶

Whalley Range

Hillary Step 𝕃

199 Upper Chorlton Road, M16 0BH
⌚ 4-11.30; 3-12.30am Fri; 12-12.30am Sat; 12-11.30 Sun
☎ (0161) 881 1978 🌐 thehillarystep.co.uk
Beer range varies 🄷
A modern bar in a small strip of shops and bars just north of Chorlton centre. Three handpumps are dedicated to Thwaites, Phoenix and Thornbridge breweries, with two more serving guest ales, alongside a good range of draught and bottled continental beers plus around 20 malt whiskies. Cheese boards and charcuterie snacks are popular, with a choice of other nibbles (olives, salami, nuts) also on offer. Live jazz features on Sunday evening and a quiz the first Tuesday of the month. Children are not permitted. ❀◐◑🚊♣🚌🐾

Whitefield

Eagle & Child

Higher Lane, M45 7EY
⌚ 12-11 (midnight Fri & Sat) ☎ (07827) 85022
Holt Mild, IPA, Bitter, seasonal beer 🄷
Traditional black-and-white-timbered double-fronted inn built in 1936 on the site of the original pub dating from the 1800s. It has a spacious lounge and a vault served by a central bar, plus a separate front room, ideal for meetings and private parties. Home to darts, dominoes and cribbage teams, it hosts live acts every Friday and a quiz-and-curry night fortnightly on a Tuesday. The pub is family-friendly and dogs are allowed on a lead in outside areas. A large floodlit bowling green is open April to September and is available for hire.
Q♨❀♿🚊♣P🚌(98,135)📶

Wigan

Anvil 𝕃

Dorning Street, WN1 1ND
⌚ 11-11; 12-10.30 Sun ☎ (01942) 239444
AllGates California; guest beers 🄷
Popular town-centre pub close to the bus station, a frequent winner of local CAMRA seasonal and Pub of the Year awards – note the array of certificates adorning the wall of fame. Seven handpumps offer ales from the nearby AllGates brewery plus guests. Six draught continental ales and a range of bottled beers are also on offer. Close to the DW Stadium, the pub can be busy on match days. It has a heated smoking terrace. ❀⇌(Wallgate/N-Western)🚌

Berkeley 𝕃

27-29 Wallgate, WN1 1LD
⌚ 11.30-11.30 (midnight Fri & Sat); 12.30-10.30 Sun
☎ (01942) 242041
Prospect Silver Tally; guest beers 🄷
The Berkeley is a former coaching house opposite Wallgate rail station and three minutes from Wigan North-Western. The large bar hosts a range of rotating guests, including LocAle beers. Food is served daily 12-7pm. Watch your favourite sporting event on the massive projector screen or one of the eight large flatscreen TVs. A first-floor function room is available for hire. ◐◑⇌(Wallgate/N-Western)🍎🚌

Boulevard 𝕃

17a Wallgate, WN1 1LD
⌚ 4-3am; 2-5am Fri & Sat; 2-4am Sun ☎ (01942) 497165
🌐 boulevard-wigan.co.uk
Beer range varies 🄷
This is a surprisingly large basement pub with a large back room that is home to regular live entertainment. Live music features on Fridays and Saturdays. Two ciders, one permanent Moorhouse's beer and three guest beers are

available. Open until late, the bar is close to Wigan Wallgate and North-Western train stations. A former winner of Local CAMRA New Cask Outlet. ≠(Wallgate/N-Western)♣●🚌📶

Brocket Arms 𝕃

58 Mesnes Road, WN1 2DD

7am-midnight (1am Fri & Sat) ☎ (01942) 403500

Thwaites Wainwright; guest beers Ⓗ

In a residential area just 15 minutes' walk from the town centre, the Brocket is also a Wetherlodge. The interior is large and open plan with two bars and intimate booths. Two conference rooms are available for private hire. Guest beers are always on offer. In addition to the usual Wetherspoon menu there is a popular Sunday carvery. A patio area to the front has benches and cover for smokers. Fundraising events are often held to support various charities. ♿P🚌📶

Raven Hotel

5 Wallgate, WN1 1LD

11-11 ☎ (01942) 239764 🌐 theravenwigan.com

Beer range varies Ⓗ

The Raven reopened in all its glory after a full refurbishment in 2012. A superb example of an early 1900s commercial hotel, many original features have been retained including the windows, wood panelling and proper coal fires. It is well worth a visit for the building alone. A good range of quality real ales is available on five handpumps, mainly from local breweries, alongside tasty home-made pub grub including the renowned Raven Pies. ≠●🚌📶

Withington

Victoria

438 Wilmslow Road, M20 3BW (on B5093)

11.30-11 (midnight Thu-Sat); 12-11 Sun

☎ (0161) 434 2600

Hydes Original Bitter, Owd Oak, seasonal beers; guest beers Ⓗ

A recent refurbishment has turned this once ordinary pub into a thriving real ale venue, selling the full range of Hydes ales' alongside its own pilot-plant Beer Studio beers, plus four guests and two rotating ciders (usually from Westons). The large single-roomed interior is partitioned into separate spaces, belying the building's true size. Very much a community pub, the Victoria is popular with all ages. Look out for occasional beer festivals, live bands, quizzes and regular karaoke. ♿♣●🚌(42,43)🐾📶

Woodford

Davenport Arms (Thief's Neck)

550 Chester Road, SK7 1PS (on A5102)

11-11; 12-10.30 Sun ☎ (0161) 439 2435

Robinsons 1892, Dizzy Blonde, Unicorn, seasonal beer Ⓗ

The Thief's Neck has long had a reputation for serving Robinson's ales in peak condition. It has been run by the same family for more than 80 years and this is its 28th consecutive Guide listing. In 2014 it underwent a major refurbishment, but retains the original cosy feel with a variety of areas all warmed by real fires in winter. Excellent home-made lunches are served daily, plus evening bar tapas. There are extensive drinking areas outside at the front and rear. Q♿♣P🚌(X57,157)🐾📶

Worsley

Barton Arms

2 Stablefold, M28 2ED (off Barton Rd)

11.30 (12 Sun)-11 ☎ (0161) 728 6157

Black Sheep Best Bitter; Thwaites Original, Wainwright; guest beers Ⓗ

This modern and comfortable pub close to the centre of the village and next to the Bridgewater Canal serves three guest ales from the interesting and varied Ember Inns cask ale list, usually including a dark ale. The enthusiastic management has built up cask ale sales and offers a discount on beers on a Monday. Classic pub food is served until 10pm throughout the pub. ♿P🚌(33,68)🐾📶

Bridgewater Hotel

23 Barton Road, M28 2PD

11-11 ☎ (0161) 794 6206

Greene King IPA; guest beers Ⓗ

Large, imposing building, built in 1903, with a black and white timber front, situated across from the Bridgewater Canal, considered the first true canal in England. It has a large bar area with many smart rooms and alcoves radiating from it. Food is prominent, served until 9pm. Six handpumps often feature beers from Robinsons and Moorhouse's. Note there is a charge for daytime weekday parking, refundable for customers at the bar. ♿P🚌(33,68)📶

Worthington

Crown Hotel 𝕃

Platt Lane, WN1 2XF

12-11 (11.30 Fri & Sat); 12-10.30 Sun ☎ (01257) 421354

🌐 thecrownatworthington.co.uk

Beer range varies Ⓗ

Privately owned free house in a country location with en-suite bedrooms and function rooms. High-quality, home-cooked food is served in the bar and conservatory restaurant, and outside on the decked sun terrace at the rear. Up to 10 ales are offered and up to three ciders and perries, with as many as 16 different beers on offer weekly. An extensive selection of bottled beers is also stocked and beer festivals are hosted throughout the year. Winner of multiple CAMRA awards. Q●P🚌📶

Good old ale

When schoolboy friends meet once again, who have not met for years,
Say, over what will they sit down, and talk of their careers.
Your 'wishy washy' wines won't do, and fiery spirits fail,
For nothing blends the heart of friends like good old English ale.

J Caxton, circa 1880

MERSEYSIDE

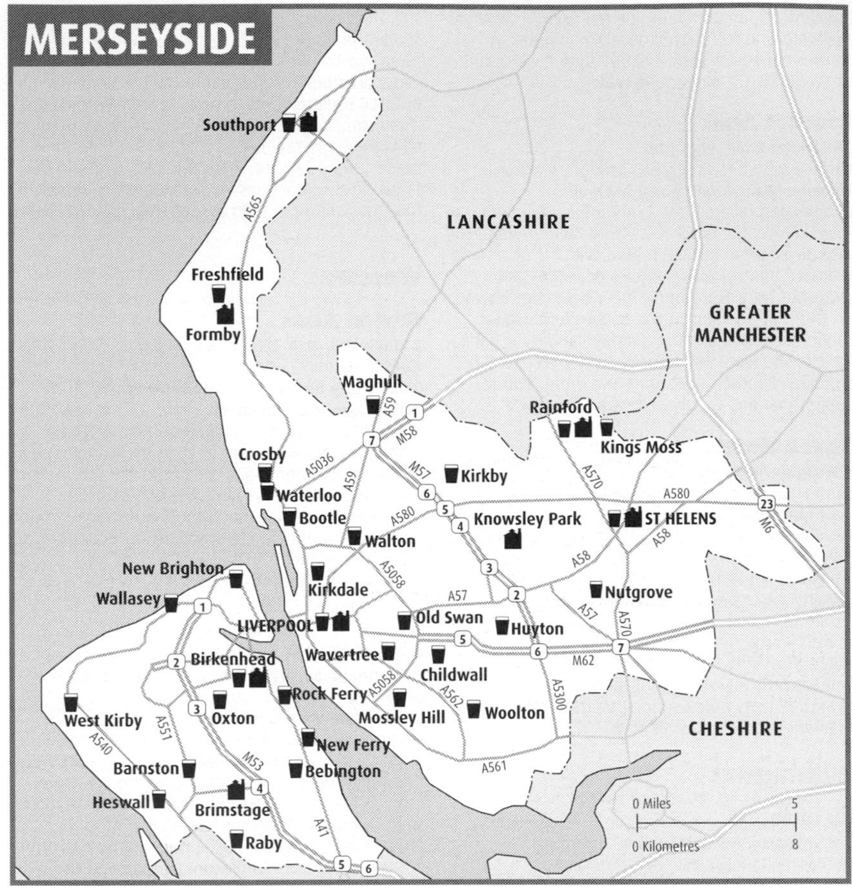

Barnston

Fox & Hounds

107 Barnston Road, CH61 1BW (on A551)
11-11; 12-10.30 Sun ☎ (0151) 648 7685
the-fox-hounds.co.uk
Brimstage Trappers Hat Bitter; Theakston Best Bitter, Old Peculier; guest beers H
Village pub with a bar, lounge and snug full of bric-a-brac, local photos and other memorabilia. The lounge, converted from tea rooms, is quiet with no music or games machines. The pub retains its original character including real fires in the bar and snug. The stone courtyard is a profusion of colour in the summer. Popular for its cask ales and good food, it offers a fish dish of the day, daily specials and traditional Sunday roasts (no eve meals Sat, Sun or Mon). Q P

Bebington

Rose & Crown

57 The Village, CH63 7PL
12-midnight (1am Fri & Sat) ☎ (0151) 643 1312
Thwaites Nutty Black, Original, Wainwright, Lancaster Bomber H
Former coaching inn built in 1732, adjacent to Mayer Park and now a thriving suburban pub with a bar and games room. Satellite TV sport is prominent. Nearby is Port Sunlight Village, founded by William Hesketh Lever in 1888 to house his soap factory workers. In the village is the Lady Lever Art Gallery, home to one of the most beautiful collections of art in the country.
(Port Sunlight) P (410,487)

Birkenhead

Gallaghers Pub & Barbers

20 Chester Street, CH41 5DQ
12 (4 Mon)-11; 12-midnight Fri-Sun ☎ (0151) 649 9095
gallagherspubandbarbers.com
Brimstage Trappers Hat Bitter; guest beers H

INDEPENDENT BREWERIES

Brimstage Brimstage
Evening Star St Helens
George Wright Rainford
Liverpool Craft Liverpool
Liverpool One Liverpool
Liverpool Organic Liverpool
Mad Hatter Liverpool
Melwood Knowsley Park
Parker Formby (NEW)
Peerless Birkenhead
Southport Southport
Stamps Liverpool
Wapping Liverpool

Multi-award-winning genuine free house close to the famous Mersey ferries, resurrected after closure and refurbished in 2010 by a former Irish Guardsman as a unique pub with barber's shop. Decorations include a fascinating range of military memorabilia and a collection of shipping images. Six handpumps feature guest beers often from Rat, Salopian and Hawkshead, plus a real cider and perry in summer. The pub runs a green hop beer festival in autumn. ❀⇌(Hamilton Sq)●🚌🐾📶

Crosby

Liverpool Pigeon 🏆 L

14 Endbutt Lane, L23 0TR

closed Mon; 4 (12 Sat)-9; 12-5 Sun

liverpoolpigeon.co.uk

Beer range varies H

Merseyside's first micropub and, true to the formula, it serves no spirits, alcopops or keg beers. Belgian bottled beers are available, and usually two boxed ciders. There is no music, just good conversation, as well as board games and a library of beer books and guides. The pub is named after an extinct pigeon called the Liverpool or Spotted Green Pigeon, of which the only known specimen is in the World Museum, Liverpool. Local CAMRA Pub of the Year 2014. Q♿●🚌(47,54)

Stamps Bar L

5 Crown Buildings, L23 5SR

12-11 (midnight Fri & Sat) ☎ (0151) 286 2662

stampsbar.co.uk

Beer range varies H

Real ale, real food, real music is the Stamps motto. At least one beer from the local Stamps microbrewery is always available, plus five changing guests, often from other local brewers. Home-produced food is served 12-7pm Tuesday to Sunday. Local musicians play live Friday to Sunday, with music ranging from jazz and blues to rock. There is an upstairs lounge away from the bustle of the main bar. A popular loyalty card scheme is offered. 🚌(47,54)📶

Freshfield

Freshfield 🏆 L

1 Massams Lane, L37 7BD

11-11 (midnight Fri & Sat) ☎ (01704) 874871

Greene King IPA, Abbot; guest beers H

A great example of a community local where the emphasis is on beer quality. A Greene King pub, it offers up to 14 ales including 10 guests. The pub also has a growing reputation for good food served in the restaurant. Following a successful CAMRA-led campaign, the stone floored bar area has been retained. Families are welcome. An enlightened management with engaging staff help to ensure a welcoming pub experience. CAMRA Regional Pub of the Year 2013. ❀♿⇌♣●P🚌🐾

Heswall

Dee View Inn L

Dee View Road, CH60 0DH

12-midnight (11 Sun) ☎ (0151) 342 2320

Brimstage Trappers Hat Bitter; Fuller's London Pride; Timothy Taylor Landlord; Wells Bombardier; guest beers H

Homely, traditional local built in the late 1800s, offering a warm welcome. Redecorated in 2008, it has retained its character and friendly atmosphere. It sits on a hairpin bend by the war memorial and famous mirror, with views over the Dee Estuary and close to the Wirral Way path. A popular and entertaining quiz night is held on Tuesday and live music is a frequent attraction. Traditional home-cooked food is served and children are welcome if dining. ♣P🚌

Johnny Pye

Pye Road, CH60 0DB (next to bus station)

11-11 (11.30 Thu; midnight Fri & Sat); 12-11 Sun

☎ (0151) 342 8215

Banks's Bitter; Marston's Pedigree; Wychwood Hobgoblin; guest beers H

Situated on the site of an old bus depot, this lively, modern open-plan pub is named after a local entrepreneur, Johnny Pye, who was responsible for starting the local bus service. There is a strong community focus here, with real ale and music events raising money for local charities. Following the success of Thursday open mic nights, live music is now a regular feature. ❀♿♣P🚌📶

Huyton

Barkers Brewery L

Archway Road, L36 9UJ

8am-11 (midnight Fri & Sat) ☎ (0151) 482 4500

Adnams Broadside; Fuller's London Pride; Greene King Abbot; Ruddles Best Bitter; Sharp's Doom Bar; guest beers H

A large, airy Wetherspoon pub with a traditional feel. A good selection of beer is available including at least one local and one dark beer. The pub is on the site of the old Huyton Brewery, founded in 1825, and managed by the Barker family over four generations until 1925. A sculpture of Richard Barker can be found near the bar. The main dining area leads to the beer garden at the rear. Q❀♿⇌●P🚌📶

Kings Moss

Colliers Arms

Pimbo Road, WA11 8RD

11-11 (10.30 Sun) ☎ (01744) 892894

Black Sheep Best Bitter; guest beers H

Situated in the rural hamlet of Kings Moss at the foot of Billinge Hill, the pub is part of a row of former miners' cottages near the site of the former Hillside Colliery. The interior comprises four distinct areas served from a central bar. Books, mining memorabilia and photographs decorate the walls. Outside, there is a pleasant children's play area and beer garden. Good quality home-cooked food is served. ❀🚌

Kirkby

Gold Balance L

6-10 Newton Gardens, L32 8RR

8am-midnight ☎ (0151) 548 7939

Adnams Broadside; Fuller's London Pride; Sharp's Doom Bar; guest beers H

The name of this open-plan Wetherspoon establishment recalls Reverend Thomas Wilkinson, who was vicar at St Chad's, Kirkby, in the 1760s. Buried in Kirkby, he invented the gold balance and the pocket balance for weighing sovereigns. The pub is busy during the daytime. ❀♿🚌(14,19)📶

Liverpool: Bootle

Merton Inn L
42 Merton Road, L20 3BW
🕘 8am-midnight (1am Fri & Sat) ☎ (0151) 934 7790
Adnams Broadside; Fuller's London Pride; Greene King Abbot; Kelham Island Pale Rider; Sharp's Doom Bar; guest beers [H]
The Merton Inn was formerly two villas, combined to become a hotel in the 1930s. Used as a hospital during World War II, it was converted into a pub in the 1970s. This spacious multi-level venue, with wood panelling and subdued lighting, retains some of the character of its villa origins. The pub also boasts some specially commissioned abstract paintings depicting the local landscape.
♨◐♿≈(Oriel Rd)P🚌(53,55)📶

Wild Rose L
2a & 1b Triad Centre, L20 3ET
🕘 7.30am (8am Sat & Sun)-midnight (1am Fri & Sat)
☎ (0151) 922 0828
Adnams Broadside; Fuller's London Pride; Greene King Abbot; Ruddles Best Bitter; Sharp's Doom Bar; guest beers [H]
The name of this large, open-plan Wetherspoon pub relates to a reference made by William Gladstone, the 19th-century prime minister and MP for Liverpool, who spent part of his childhood on Merseyside. He recollected: 'I have seen wild roses growing on the very ground which is now the centre of Bootle.' The pub is popular with locals, shoppers and workers alike.
♨◐♿≈(New Strand)🚌(53,55)📶

Liverpool: Childwall

Childwall Fiveways L
179 Queens Drive, L15 6XS
🕘 8am-11.30 ☎ (0151) 738 2100
Adnams Broadside; Fuller's London Pride; Greene King Abbot; Sharp's Doom Bar; guest beers [H]
A former Higsons tied house, this large single-roomed pub opened as a Wetherspoon in 2010. Located in a leafy suburb, it has good motorway and public transport links. The refurbished interior is decorated with wood panelling, and outside there is a beer garden. A popular establishment, it can get busy, especially at weekends.
♨✿◐♿🍎P🚌(79,81)📶

Liverpool: City Centre

Augustus John L
Peach Street, L3 5TX (off Brownlow Hill)
🕘 11.30 (12 Sat)-11; closed Sun ☎ (0151) 794 5507
Tetley Bitter; guest beers [H]
Opened in 1901 and run by the University of Liverpool, the Augustus John is an open-plan pub popular with students, lecturers and locals. Up to four guest beers are available and a number of ciders – the pub is a recent winner of local and regional CAMRA Cider Pub of the Year awards. Pizza is served at all times, sport is screened and there is a jukebox. Closed over Christmas and the New Year. ◐🍎🚌

Baltic Fleet L
33 Wapping, L1 8DQ
🕘 12 (11 Sat & Sun)-11 ☎ (0151) 709 3116
Beer range varies [H]
Located near the Albert Dock, Liverpool's only brewpub is in a Grade II-listed building based on the flat-iron principle, with interior decoration on a nautical theme. Six handpumps serve beer from the Wapping Brewery in the cellar, plus occasional guests. Pies and home-cooked scouse are regularly available. Tunnels in the cellar have led to some speculation of a dark period in the pub's history involving smuggling and press gangs.
◐≈(James St)🍎🚌

Belvedere L
8 Sugnall Street, L7 7EB
🕘 12-11 ☎ (0151) 709 0303
Beer range varies [H]
Hidden in the Georgian area of the inner city, this small two-roomed community pub is a free house serving four rotating beers usually from local microbreweries. Rescued in 2006 from closure for housing development, this Grade II-listed building retains many original fixtures and interesting etched glass features. Attracting a mixed local clientele, including thirsty members of the Royal Liverpool Philharmonic Orchestra, this is a pub that offers a warm welcome and good conversation.
Q🍎🍺🚌🐾

Blackburne Pub & Eatery L
24 Catherine Street, L8 7NL
🕘 12 (9am Fri & Sat)-midnight; 12-11 Sun
☎ (0151) 709 9159 🌐 the blackburne.co.uk
Beer range varies [H]
A popular, open-plan, village-style pub in the heart of the Georgian Quarter – a short bus ride or a walk of 15 or 20 minutes from Lime Street station. Attractive decor helps to create a relaxed, welcoming and homely atmosphere. The lounge area is the perfect place to enjoy a beer or real cider from one of the four handpumps, with a LocAle always among the range. Food offers are available every day except Saturday. The sign outside is a reminder of the pub's connection to Higsons Brewery. Q♨🛏◐🍎🚌📶

Bridewell
1 Campbell Square, L1 5FB
🕘 12-11 (midnight Fri & Sat) ☎ (0151) 709 7000
Beer range varies [H]
Grade II-listed building dating from the mid-19th century when it was a police bridewell. The original cells provide unusual seating areas. Changing beers from Liverpool One and Lancaster breweries are served, together with Lees Governor. Three handpumps are in regular use, with two more in busy periods, and a selection of continental bottled beers is kept. An upstairs function room (available to hire) hosts music and cultural events. Food is served Tuesday to Sunday. There is small patio area at the front. Q◐≈(Central)🚌

Clove Hitch L
23 Hope Street, L1 9BQ
🕘 11-11 (4.30 Mon; midnight Fri & Sat); 11-10 Sun
☎ (0151) 709 6574 🌐 theclovehitch.com
Beer range varies [H]
The Bistro is a ground-floor restaurant serving meals all day, with a small bar area and garden. Downstairs is the 23 Club, a basement bar open from 4.30pm (1pm Sat) providing more drinking space. Beers are provided by the Liverpool Craft Brewery, a mixture of its own beers and swaps from other smaller breweries. A good selection of bottled ales and ciders is also kept. Popular with theatre and concert goers. ✿◐≈(Central)🍎🚌

Cracke 🄻
13 Rice Street, L1 9BB
12-11.30 (midnight Fri & Sat) ☎ (0151) 709 4171
Thwaites Original; guest beers Ⓗ
Characterful multi-roomed back-street pub with two bars. In the 1900s War Office – a tiny snug – a plaque states that this is where drinkers discussed Britain's overseas military operations. There are pictures of John Lennon in the public bar showing him outside the pub, from the time he attended the nearby art college. One room is used as a gallery by local artists. The beer range may include LocAles and beers from microbreweries, and farmhouse ciders are available.
Q❀⇌(Central)●🚌(86)

Crown Hotel ★
43 Lime Street, L1 1JQ
11-11 ☎ (0151) 707 6027 🌐 thecrownliverpool.co.uk
Greene King IPA; guest beers Ⓗ
Just a few seconds' walk from Lime Street station, this Grade II-listed building boasts an Art Nouveau-style interior with ornate plasterwork ceilings and has been identified by CAMRA as having a nationally important pub interior. Many original features are retained in the two downstairs rooms, including some impressive wood panelling and original push bells. There is also an ornate glass dome above the staircase. Food is served all day until 10pm. The outside of the pub is adorned with a stucco Walkers Ales, Warrington frieze.
◐⇌(Lime St)●🚌

Dispensary 🄻
87 Renshaw Street, L1 2SP
12-11 (midnight Fri & Sat) ☎ (0151) 709 2160
George Wright Mild; guest beers Ⓗ
This lively local in the city is a haven for real ale drinkers of all ages. The licensee's impeccable attention to beer quality shines through, and there is an ever-changing and imaginative choice of local and other interesting microbrewery beers, offering a good range in terms of both style and strength. Mark's Mild is dedicated to the much-loved barman who passed away in 2012. The attractive bar area has Victorian features, with a raised wood-panelled area to the rear. ⇌(Central)🚌

Flute 🄻
35 Hardman Street, L1 9AS
11-midnight (2am Fri & Sat); 11-11 Sun
☎ (0151) 707 6485 🌐 fluteliverpool.co.uk
Greene King IPA; Wells Bombardier; guest beers Ⓗ
Large, busy pub, 10 minutes' walk from Lime Street station. A combination of good-value food, drink offers, multiple large screens and pool tables makes this venue popular with students. The pub can get particularly busy when live football is shown. National beers are available alongside at least one local ale. There is a Cask Card deal and CAMRA members receive a 10 per cent discount on ale. Various themed nights are held throughout the week. ◐⇌(Central)🚌(86,86A)

Fly in the Loaf
Hardman Street, L1 9AS
12-11 (midnight Fri & Sat) ☎ (0151) 708 0817
Okells Bitter; guest beers Ⓗ
A former bakery, the name comes from the slogan 'no flies in the loaf'. Owned by Isle of Man brewer Okells, it serves up to four of its beers alongside a changing range of guests from around the country, many from microbreweries, and a good selection of foreign beers. Recently refurbished, it has a light and airy frontage with attractive wood-panelled areas towards the rear. There is a function room upstairs. Food from the popular Baltic Bakehouse is served, in line with its Beer and Bread theme.
❀◐♿⇌(Central)🚌(86,86A)

Grapes 🄻
60 Roscoe Street, L1 9DW
1-1am (2am Thu-Sat) ☎ (0151) 709 3977
🌐 thegrapesliverpool.co.uk
Beer range varies Ⓗ
This corner local dates back to 1804 and retains its original Mellors signage outside. There is a total of nine handpumps, with a large number of beers coming from local microbreweries such as Liverpool Organic and Liverpool Craft. The cosy beer garden at the rear is popular with smokers. Live jazz is hosted every Sunday night from 9pm.
❀⇌(Central)●🚌(82,84)

Hub 🄻
12 Hanover Street, L1 4AA
10-11 (midnight Thu & Fri); 9am-midnight Sat; 9am-11 Sun
☎ (0151) 709 2401 🌐 thehub-liverpool.com
Lancaster Amber; Liverpool Organic 24 Carat Gold; guest beer Ⓗ
Serving interesting European-style food and good real ales, this Grade II-listed ale house and kitchen occupies the Casartelli Building, built in 1760. Initially an Italian family-run scientific manufacturing business, it was latterly a wine warehouse. A period of decay led to dismantling in 2001. A campaign to Stop the Rot led to reconstruction using as many original materials as possible. The house beer is Liverpool Organic 24 Carat and a rotating Lancaster Brewery beer is also offered. ◐⇌(Lime Street)🚌(1)

Lion Tavern ★ 🄻
67 Moorfields, L2 2BP
11 (12 Sun)-midnight ☎ (0151) 236 1734
🌐 liontavern.com
Young's Bitter; guest beers Ⓗ
The Lion was named after the locomotive that worked the Liverpool to Manchester railway. Grade II-listed and featuring in CAMRA's National Inventory of Historic Pub Interiors, it has exquisite artwork and intricately etched and stained glass. Regular society meetings and occasional Meet the Brewer events take place. Meals are served at lunchtimes with speciality pork pies available at all times. The house beer, brewed by George Wright, is called the Lion Returns, and the cider is from Westons. ⇌(Moorfields)●🚌

Peter Kavanagh's ★ 🄻
2-6 Egerton Street, L8 7LY
12-midnight (1am Fri & Sat) ☎ (0151) 709 3443
Greene King Abbot; guest beers Ⓗ
A splendid back-street local, this gem is situated in the Georgian area of Liverpool and has been identified by CAMRA as having a nationally important historic pub interior. Murals by Eric Robinson adorn the walls, thought to have been commissioned to cover a debt. There are fine stained-glass windows with wooden shutters and two snugs with wooden benches – note the carved armrests, allegedly caricatures of the politically incorrect Peter Kavanagh. Up to four rotating guest beers are available. Q◐🚌(75,86)

Richard John Blackler

Units 1 & 2 Charlotte Row, L1 1HU
8am-midnight (11 Mon & Tue); 10-1am Sun
(0151) 709 4802
Adnams Broadside; Fuller's London Pride; Greene King Abbot; Sharp's Doom Bar; guest beers
This Wetherspoon pub is the ground floor of the former Blacklers department store which opened in 1908 and finally shut in April 1988. The Beatles' George Harrison served his electrician's apprenticeship here. The rocking horse is a replica of one ridden by children who visited the store – the original is at Alder Hey Children's Hospital. Close to the bus station, St John's shopping centre and Liverpool One, the pub is busy, but it is a good place to take a break. (Central)

Richmond Pub & Hotel

32 Williamson Street, L1 1EB
10-11; 11-midnight Fri-Sun (0151) 709 2614
Draught Bass; guest beers
Lively family-run pub in a pedestrianised shopping area, offering up to three guest ales from local and regional breweries. Formerly a Bass house, the original Bass mirror remains. More than 50 malt whiskies are usually available, sports fixtures are shown and there are occasional beer festivals and Meet the Brewer events. The pub sign, simply saying Richmond Pub, depicts World War II veteran Paddy Golden, a much missed regular and one of the first to land on the Normandy beaches.
(Central)

Roscoe Head

24 Roscoe Street, L1 2SX
11.30 (12 Sun)-midnight (0151) 709 4365
Jennings Bitter; Tetley Bitter; guest beers
One of the Magnificent Six pubs that have been in every edition of the Guide. This is a cosy four-roomed pub where conversation and the appreciation of real ale rule. Run by members of the same family for over 30 years, the name commemorates William Roscoe, a leading campaigner against the slave trade. Six handpumps feature two regular beers plus four changing guests, mostly from small breweries from the Finest Cask list. Food is served Monday to Friday lunchtimes. **Q**(Central)(80,86)

Vernon Arms

69 Dale Street, L2 2HJ
11.45-11.30 (12.30am Fri & Sat) (0151) 236 6132
Boggart Hole Clough Rum Porter; Brains Rev James; guest beers
Situated close to the business district, the Vernon retains the feel of a street-corner local. The single long-roomed bar serves three drinking areas including a back room with frosted glass windows advertising the Liverpool Brewing Company which used to serve the pub. The main bar has wood panelling, several large columns and a small snug area. The regular Boggart Rum Porter is popular with many, and real cider on handpull is unusual for the city centre. **Q**(Moorfields)

Liverpool: Kirkdale

Thomas Frost

177-187 Walton Road, L4 4AJ
8am-11.30 (0151) 207 8210
Adnams Broadside; Fuller's London Pride; Greene King Abbot; Sharp's Doom Bar; guest beers
This Wetherspoon pub occupies the ground floor of a Grade II-listed building, the former Thomas Frost Drapery Store dating from 1885. The pub is near both the Everton and Liverpool football grounds and gets very busy on match days. It has a spacious open-plan layout with a large family area.
(20,21)

Liverpool: Mossley Hill

Pi (Rose Lane)

106 Rose Lane, L18 8AG
11-11 (11.30 Fri & Sat) (0151) 222 0443
pi-roselane.co.uk
Tatton Blonde; guest beers
A café-style bar in premises that was previously a shop, near to Mossley Hill railway station. The beer range always includes a LocAle. The bar also has a number of foreign beers on tap and stocks dozens of bottled beers. A simple hot food menu – real pies with sides – is available all day. The extension into next door has now been completed and provides more space. (61,80)

Liverpool: Old Swan

Navigator

694 Queens Drive, L13 5UH
8am-11.30 (0151) 220 2713
Adnams Broadside; Fuller's London Pride; Greene King Abbot; Ruddles Best Bitter; Sharp's Doom Bar; guest beers
This branch of Wetherspoon, named after St Brendan the Navigator, patron saint of sailors and travellers, occupies a former showroom. The open-plan layout is punctuated with alcoves along one side. The pub is a welcome oasis on the edge of a busy shopping area, with a raised area set aside for families. (8,9)

Liverpool: Walton

Raven

72-74 Walton Vale, L9 2BU
8am-midnight (1am Fri & Sat) (0151) 524 1255
Adnams Broadside; Fuller's London Pride; Greene King Abbot; Ruddles Best Bitter; Sharp's Doom Bar; guest beers
An open-plan Wetherspoon pub, popular with locals, particularly at weekends. It is themed on Edgar Allan Poe's The Raven, after a local, James William Carling, produced illustrations for the famous poem in the late 19th century. Born in 1857, Carling became a pavement artist at the age of five, later went to America, and is buried in Walton Cemetery. Aintree, the home of the world-famous Grand National, is less than a mile away.
(Orrell Park)

Liverpool: Wavertree

Edinburgh

4 Sandown Lane, L15 8HY
2 (12 Fri-Sun)-midnight (0151) 733 3533
Liverpool Organic Cascade, Liverpool Pale Ale; St Austell Proper Job; guest beer
A cosy pub at the end of a Victorian terrace with a small bar area, a separate 'front room' and a space for drinking outside. One of the regular beers may be replaced by a guest. Irish music night on Monday is popular and there is a Tuesday quiz.
Q(Technology Park)(78,79)

Liverpool: Woolton

Gardeners Arms

101 Vale Road, L25 7RW

4 (2 Fri)-11.30; 12-11.30 Sat; 12-11 Sun

(0151) 428 1443

Greene King IPA; Timothy Taylor Landlord; guest beers H

Friendly, one-room, community village pub situated over the hill from Woolton village and separated from Menlove Avenue by blocks of flats. It now serves evening food in the form of a curry club. A popular quiz is held on Tuesday evening, and live music hosted monthly. Sky Sports is shown. There are numerous sports teams based at the pub. Recently awarded Cask Marque accreditation. Q(76,77)

Maghull

Frank Hornby L

38 Eastway, L31 6BR

8am-11.30 (midnight Fri & Sat) (0151) 520 4010

Adnams Broadside; Fuller's London Pride; Sharp's Doom Bar; guest beers H

Wetherspoon pub named after local businessman and politician Frank Hornby, the inventor of the famous Hornby train set. Unsurprisingly, samples of his work including Meccano and Dinky Toys are on display inside the pub. Situated in a surburban street, the pub has a light and spacious interior, and there is a decked area at the front for outside drinking. The ever-changing selection of guest ales includes some from local breweries.

QP

New Brighton

Perch Rock Hotel

7 Grosvenor Road, CH45 2LW

11-12.30am (midnight Sun) (0151) 639 5236

Otter Bitter; Wells Bombardier H

Welcoming, unspoilt street-corner pub with a strong local following. It has a long front bar with a TV often showing horse racing, and two side rooms which appear to have remained unchanged since the 1960s. Situated 200 yards from the Marine Promenade and the mouth of the River Mersey, it is also convenient for the Floral Pavilion Theatre.

Queen's Royal L

Marine Promenade, CH45 2JT

10.30-11 (10.30 Sun) (0151) 691 0101

thequeensroyal.com

Hawkshead Windermere Pale, Bitter; guest beers H

An airy, modern bar in an imposing Victorian building, close to the Floral Hall Theatre and overlooking Marine Promenade, Marine Lake and Fort Perch Rock. The drinking area outside affords superb views over Liverpool Bay. Snacks are available in the bar Monday and Tuesday until 9pm and good-value hot meals including breakfast from 8am Wednesday to Sunday.

Stanley's Cask

212 Rake Lane, CH45 1JP

11-midnight (11 Mon & Wed) (0151) 691 1093

Beer range varies H

This ever-popular local continues to thrive, due in no small part to the landlady who has a track record for serving good beer. Up to four guest ales are offered, mainly from national and regional breweries. A traditional, single-roomed community local, it hosts various sports teams, quiz nights and regular live music. (410)

New Ferry

Freddies Club L

36 Stanley Road, CH62 5AS

7 (5 Fri & Sat)-11; 12-11 Sun

Brimstage Trappers Hat Bitter; guest beer H

A popular social club, formerly a Conservative Club, now converted into a comfortable lounge bar with adjoining snooker room with two full-size tables. It is situated in a residential street just a short walk from New Ferry shopping centre. Two handpumps serve mainly local beers and there is regular live entertainment. A former local CAMRA Club of the Year, show a CAMRA membership card or a current copy of the Guide for entry.

Q(Bebington)P(401)

John Masefield

70-72 New Chester Road, CH62 5AD

8am-11 (11.30 Fri & Sat) (0151) 644 4250

Greene King Abbot; Ruddles Best Bitter; guest beers H

Open-plan Wetherspoon pub in a former bicycle shop. Named after a former poet laureate with local links, controversy surrounded the opening when locals suggested that the portrait on the pub's sign looked more like Adolf Hitler – judge for yourself. Two banks of handpumps often include beers from local microbreweries and further afield. The pub features Wetherspoon's meal deals, a Wednesday night quiz and regular vintage bus pub trips. (Bebington)

Oxton

Oxton Bar & Kitchen

2 Claughton Firs, CH43 5TQ

12-midnight (11 Mon; 1am Fri & Sat); 1-11 Sun

(0151) 651 2535 oxtonbar.co.uk

Beer range varies H

Situated in the centre of attractive Oxton village among shops, bars and restaurants, this former John Smith's pub has been tastefully converted into a smart, comfortable, single-room lounge bar. There is a strong emphasis on quality food, ranging from sandwiches and snacks to full meals. Guest beers are usually from local microbreweries.

P

Raby

Wheatsheaf Inn L

Raby Mere Road, CH63 4JH

11.30-11 (midnight Fri & Sat); 12-10.30 Sun

(0151) 336 3416 wheatsheaf-cowshed.co.uk

Brimstage Trappers Hat Bitter; Tetley Bitter; Thwaites Original, Wainwright; Timothy Taylor Landlord; guest beers H

An inn for 350 years, this is Wirral's oldest pub. The thatched building was rebuilt following a fire in 1611 and is reputed to be haunted by Charlotte, who died here. The walls are decorated with old photographs of Raby. The bar has nine handpumps serving two rooms and a restaurant in a converted cowshed. Four guest beers are often from local breweries. Food is served in the bar until 5pm and in the restaurant Tuesday to Saturday evenings.

QP(85)

Rainford

Star Inn 🄻

Church Road, WA11 8PX

11-11; 12-10 Sun ☎ (01744) 882639

starinnrainford.co.uk

Coach House Postlethwaite; guest beers Ⓗ

Situated towards the edge of the village of Rainford, the pub has a cosy lounge and a restaurant to the rear. Beers are sourced from local microbreweries, always including a dark brew. The comfortable bar is at the front of the building. Meals are served Wednesday to Sunday in the restaurant to the rear. P

Rock Ferry

Refreshment Rooms

Bedford Road East, CH42 1LS (off B5136, take Rock Lane East, then 4th right and over bridge)

12-11 (1am Fri & Sat) ☎ (0151) 644 5893

refreshmentrooms.info

Beer range varies Ⓗ

Refurbished and reopened in 2012 under its original name, the pub was built in the 1880s for ferry passengers to Liverpool. Although the ferry terminal is long gone, this off-the-beaten-track establishment is well worth seeking out, with excellent views over the Mersey. One central bar services two rooms, with local beers often from Liverpool Organic and Peerless breweries. The house beer, HMS Conway, is from Lees. Excellent-quality reasonably priced food is served daily until 9pm. Live music features every Friday evening.

St Helens: Central

Cricketers Arms 🏆 🄻

Peter Street, WA10 2EB

2-11; 12-1am Fri & Sat; 12-11 Sun ☎ (01744) 361846

George Wright Drunken Duck, Blonde Moment; guest beers Ⓗ

Now in the hands of new owners, the Cricketers has introduced cask ale for the first time in many years. There are seven handpumps on the bar dispensing beers from local microbreweries. Situated on the edge of the town centre, this is a local community pub and home to darts and pool teams. Entertainment features at the weekend. P

Duke of Cambridge

Duke Street, WA10 2JE

2.30-11 (2am Fri); 12-2am Sat; 12-11 Sun ☎ (01744) 602663

Beer range varies Ⓗ

A small local pub on the edge of the town centre, providing a welcome real ale outlet among the many keg-only bars of Duke Street. Two handpulls feature Moorhouse's beers and guest ales often from local micros. Entertainment features highly on the pub's list of attractions, with live bands at weekends and a jam night on Wednesday. (Central)

Phoenix 🄻

Canal Street, WA10 3LL

2-11; 12-1 Fri & Sat; 12-11 Sun ☎ (01744) 751890

Beer range varies Ⓗ

Built in 1903, the pub has its name in mosaic tiles on an outer wall, and a mosaic tile floor. A community local, the small bar is home to pool, darts and dominoes, and the spacious lounge is more comfortable. Up to six beers are available, mostly from local microbreweries. Sky Sports is shown on numerous TVs. Music dominates, with karaoke on Friday night and live Irish bands on Saturday. A yard at the back has been converted into a heated smoking area. (Central)

Sportsman's Inn 🄻

Duke Street, WA10 2JG

4-11 (1am Fri); 12-1am Sat; 12-11 Sun ☎ (01744) 738848

George Wright Drunken Duck, Cheeky Pheasant; guest beers Ⓗ

Friendly town-centre venue with pictures of St Helens RFC on the wall reflecting the town's sporting heritage. The pub is divided into two areas – a public bar and a comfortable lounge. It has recently become free of tie and now offers a growing range of cask beers. At the weekends the focus is on entertainment, in line with many of the other pubs on Duke Street. P

Turk's Head 🄻

Morley Street, WA10 2DQ

2 (12 Sat & Sun)-11 ☎ (01744) 751289

Beer range varies Ⓗ

A short distance from town, this popular pub was a previous CAMRA National Pub of the Year runner-up. Half-timbered, with etched glass windows, it was built in the 1870s by Ellis Warde Brewery. It offers a constantly changing beer range, with 12 handpulls in use over the weekend, six at other times. Draught and bottled continental beers are also stocked. Thursday is curry and jazz night, and on Tuesday night there is a free quiz. Darts and dominoes are played.

St Helens: Nutgrove

Brown Edge

229 Nutgrove Road, WA9 5JR

11-11 ☎ (01744) 607113 brownedgepub.co.uk

Banks's Sunbeam; Marston's Pedigree; guest beers Ⓗ

Situated on the main road between St Helens and Rainhill, this is a comfortable suburban pub. It has two main areas – a public bar at the front of the building with pub sports such as darts and live sport on TV, and a comfortable lounge at the rear leading to a bowling green. Live bands and beer festivals are hosted at various times of the year. (Thatto Heath)P

Southport

Baron's Bar

239 Lord Street, PR8 1NZ

11-11 (11.30 Fri & Sat); 12-11 Sun ☎ (01704) 543000

Moorhouse's Black Cat; Tetley Bitter; guest beer Ⓗ

Set within the Scarisbrick Hotel on Lord Street, the Baron's Bar is an atmospheric single-roomed bar with a long tradition of showcasing real ale. In 2012 Britannia Hotels acquired the venue and has strongly supported the bar. The range, quality and value of the selection of local and national beers across 10 handpumps is excellent, and there is one real cider. QP

Bold Arms

59-61 Botanic Road, Churchtown, PR9 7NE (adjacent to botanic gardens)

11-11 (midnight Fri & Sat); 12-11 Sun ☎ (01704) 228192

Tetley Bitter; Thwaites Wainwright; guest beers Ⓗ

The Bold Arms is situated in the the tranquil village of Churchtown on the northern fringes of Southport, which is mentioned in the Domesday book. The pub dates back to at least the 1600s – a former landlord, William Sutton, was the founder of the present-day town of Southport. It has retained many rooms for drinking and dining, and plenty of nooks and crannies. Freshly prepared pub food is available daily.

Fishermen's Rest

3 Weld Road, Birkdale, PR8 2BX
11-11 (midnight Fri & Sat) ☎ (01704) 569986
Caledonian Deuchars IPA; Theakston Best Bitter; Thwaites Wainwright; guest beer H
The Fishermen's Rest gets its name from the infamous Mexico disaster of 1886. The event is still commemorated every December by crews from the local Southport Lifeboat station. The pub was originally part of the Palace Hotel and was renamed after the bodies of the brave sailors and lifeboat crews were laid out in the building. Home to two teams in the Southport & Formby quiz league, the pub is also close to the Sefton coastal footpath. P

Guest House

16 Union Street, PR9 0QE
11.30-11 (11.30 Fri & Sat); 12-10.30 Sun
☎ (01704) 537660
Adnams Southwold Bitter; Caledonian Deuchars IPA; Jennings Cumberland Ale; Ruddles Best Bitter; Theakston Traditional Mild, Best Bitter; guest beer H
Close to fashionable Lord Street, the pub sports an impressive half-timbered Edwardian frontage and an unspoilt wood-panelled interior with three separate drinking areas. The bar boasts 11 handpumps, at least one serving a local microbeer, and stocks a good range of malt whiskies. A Thursday quiz and acoustic folk club on the first and third Monday of the month attract a mixed clientele. There is outside seating to the front and a pleasant courtyard at the rear. Q

Inn Beer Shop

172 Lord Street, PR9 0AW
11-10 (10.30 Fri & Sat); 12-10 Sun ☎ (01704) 533054
Southport Golden Sands H**; guest beers** G
Friendly café bar offering a huge selection of local, national and foreign bottled beers for takeaway or consumption on the premises. The bar now sports a second handpump and also serves real ciders and draught foreign lagers. Snacks and a tea/coffee service with cakes are available throughout the day. The long interior is lined with bottles and continental-style seating, leading to a comfy area with games. Outside seating is on Lord Street. The bar can get busy at weekends.

Sandgrounder L

137-141 Lord Street, PR8 1PU
9am-midnight (1am Fri & Sat) ☎ (01704) 549271
Beer range varies H
A relatively new free house, this large, split-level pub offers a range of seating areas from restaurant tables to comfy couches, as well as outside seating on Lord Street. Four handpulls provide exclusively local micro beers at exceptional prices. A range of themed nights includes live and open mic music events. Very popular when sporting events are held, the pub features several large TV screens and supports darts and pool teams. Regular food deals are available.

Sir Henry Segrave L

93-97 Lord Street, PR8 1RH (S end of Lord Street)
8am-midnight (1am Fri & Sat) ☎ (01704) 530217
Moorhouse's Pendle Witches Brew; Phoenix Wobbly Bob; Ruddles Best Bitter; Thwaites Wainwright; guest beers H
Named after the former land speed world record holder who used to race on Southport flats, this is a spacious Wetherspoon pub with an attractive 19th-century exterior. The manager is a strong supporter of real ale and runs regular beer festival trips and occasional Meet the Brewer evenings. The 12 handpumps offer the best all-round choice of microbrewery beers in Southport – regular orders are placed with Phoenix, Saltaire, Titanic and Hawkshead. There is outside seating on Lord Street.

Willow Grove L

387-389 Lord Street, PR9 0AG (on A565)
8am-midnight (1am Fri; 2am Sat) ☎ (01704) 517830
Greene King Abbot; Ruddles Best Bitter; Thwaites Wainwright; guest beers H
A Lloyds No.1 bar situated on the town's famous Victorian Lord Street opposite the impressive 1920s war memorial. The large L-shaped interior leads to a brightly lit bar and contains a mixture of tall buffet chairs, restaurant tables and comfy sofas. The manager is a keen supporter of real ale and the nine handpumps serve a good selection of microbrewery beers, both local and from further afield. The pub can get busy on Friday and Saturday nights.

Zetland

53 Zetland Street, PR9 0RH
12-midnight (11.30 Sun) ☎ (01704) 808404
Jennings Cumberland Ale; guest beers H
Situated in a residential area just 10 minutes from Lord Street, the Zetland is a local community hostelry offering amazingly low-priced home-cooked food in a friendly atmosphere. The pub shows live sport and hosts bowling competitions, with one of the finest crown green facilities in the north-west. A large pub with several side rooms, it offers excellent buffets and can cater for parties of up to 100. P

Wallasey

Cheshire Cheese L

2 Wallasey Village, CH44 2DH
12-11 (midnight Fri & Sat) ☎ (0151) 638 3641
Wells Bombardier; guest beers H
This friendly local is Wallasey's oldest licensed premises, with a separate bar, snug and lounge. Outside is a walled garden where regular beer festivals are held. The handpumps are located in the lounge, with guest beers usually including a local ale, often from Liverpool Organic Brewery. Excellent home-cooked meals are served until early evening (no food Thu). Quiz nights are Monday and Wednesday, and the pub hosts a golf society and football, darts and bowls teams.
Q (Village) (124,423)

Farmers Arms

225 Wallasey Village, CH45 3LG
11.30-11 (11.30 Fri & Sat); 12-11 Sun ☎ (0151) 638 9345
Adnams Southwold Bitter; Greene King IPA; Jennings Cumberland Ale; Sharp's Doom Bar; Tetley Mild; guest beer H

Excellent, friendly local near the centre of Wallasey Village, convenient for local rail stations. Popular with all sections of the community, the pub has a multi-room layout with a traditional small public bar, cosy snug and large lounge, all served from a central bar. Sunday lunches are available 12-4pm. The guest beer is often from a local microbrewery. Q❀◐⇌(Village)🚌

Waterloo

Old Bank

34 South Road, L22 5PE

11-midnight (11 Mon); 12-midnight Sun

☎ (0151) 928 7020

Beer range varies H

Four handpumps dispense a range of beers, both local and from across the North West. A quiet oasis on weekday afternoons, the pub is a hive of activity most evenings and weekends, with a strong commitment to live music and football. Music memorabilia adorn the walls, and a book swap library and games are available. A courtyard at the back of the pub provides an outdoor drinking area for warmer days, and the marina and beach are nearby. ❀⇌🚌(53)🐾📶

Queen's Picture House

47-49 South Road, L22 5PE

9am-11 (11.30 Fri & Sat) ☎ (0151) 949 2070

Adnams Broadside; Fuller's London Pride; Greene King Abbot; Ruddles Best Bitter; Sharp's Doom Bar; guest beers H

The pub takes its name from a cinema that once stood on the site, although the current building is a converted furniture store. The bright and functional main room and bar area are furnished with high tables and chairs, with some lower seating close to the fireplace. To the right is a long room ideal for dining. The decor reflects the site's former use as a cinema, and also pays homage to local shipping and aviation links. ❀◐◑♿⇌🍎🚌(53)📶

Stamps Too

99 South Road, L22 0RL (opp Waterloo station)

12-11 (11.45 Fri & Sat) ☎ (0151) 280 0035

Beer range varies H

Local CAMRA branch Pub of the Year in 2013, and its first accredited LocAle pub in 2009. This friendly café-style pub, where lively banter often prevails at the bar, continues to serve mainly local beers, in particular from Liverpool Organic, Brimstage, Southport and AllGates breweries, with occasional beers from further afield. A sixth handpump dispenses real cider. The pub is a popular live music venue, with local musicians and bands Thursday through to Sunday evenings. ♿⇌🚌(53,53A)

Volunteer Canteen ★

45 East Street, L22 8QR

2-11; 12-midnight Fri & Sat; 12-10.30 Sun

☎ (0151) 928 4676

Sharp's Doom Bar; guest beers H

A Grade II-listed terraced building nestling in the back streets of Waterloo, this cosy, traditional pub still provides table service. The Volly, as it is known locally, dates back to 1871 and until the 1980s was owned by Higsons – evidence of which can be seen etched into its windows. Small breweries around Merseyside and North Wales often supply guest ales. Pies, pate, olives and a variety of nuts are available at all times. Q❀⇌♣🚌(53,53A)🐾📶

West Kirby

White Lion

51 Grange Road, CH48 4EE

12-11 (10.30 Sun) ☎ (0151) 625 9037

Black Sheep Best Bitter; Courage Best Bitter; guest beers H

Traditional local free house in a 200-year-old sandstone building close to West Kirby centre. The pub is a five-minute walk from fine views of the Welsh hills, and Marine Lake, the promenade and beach are also within easy walking distance. The White Lion is a warm, welcoming retreat, especially in the colder months with a real fire by the bar – perfect after that Wirral Way ramble. An ever-changing range of guest beers is on offer. Quiz night is Monday. No food on Sunday. Q❀◐⇌🚌(22,437)

The beauty of hops

When Sean Franklin, who runs Roosters Brewery in Yorkshire, described hops as the 'grapes of brewing' he opened a debate that has led to a much greater appreciation of the role of the small green plant in brewing.

There are many varieties of hops: global brewers use 'high alpha' varieties (high in alpha acids) purely for bitterness. Craft brewers prefer to use varieties that deliver aroma and flavour as well as bitterness. The two most widely used English hops are Fuggles and Goldings, often blended together in the same beer, the Fuggle primarily for bitterness but with earthy and smoky notes, the Golding for its superb resiny, spicy and peppery character. Bramling Cross delivers rich fruity (blackcurrant) notes, Challenger has a citrus/lime edge while the workhorse of the hop fraternity, Target, offers citrus and pepper. First Gold is the most successful of the new 'hedgerow' varieties that grow to only half the height of conventional hops and are therefore easier to pick. It offers piny and apricot notes. American varieties used in Britain include Willamette (an offshoot of the Fuggle) and Cascade, both of which give rich citrus/grapefruit aromas and flavours. The Styrian Golding, renamed Bobek, (actually a type of Fuggle) from Slovenia is widely used as an aroma hop in Britain for its luscious floral and citrus character.

The Beer Select-O-Pedia

NEW TITLE

Michael Larson

Michael Larson
THE BEER
SELECT-O-PEDIA
CAMRA
CAMPAIGN FOR REAL ALE
THE AUTHORITY ON BEERS
WHAT TO DRINK NEXT

The Beer Select-O-Pedia is a an enthusiast's guide through the delicious world of beer, demystifying scores of traditional and innovative new styles from Britain & Ireland, Continental Europe and America. Organised into families of beer styles according to their origins, it is easy to look up the style of beer you are drinking and discover more. Much more than a list of recommended brews and breweries, this book gives beer lovers all the information they need to navigate the ever-expanding world of beer and find new brews to excite their tastebuds.

£12.99 ISBN 978-1-85249-310-3 CAMRA members' price £10.99 224 pages

For this and other books on beer and pubs visit CAMRA's online bookshop at www.camra.org.uk/books or call 01727 867201

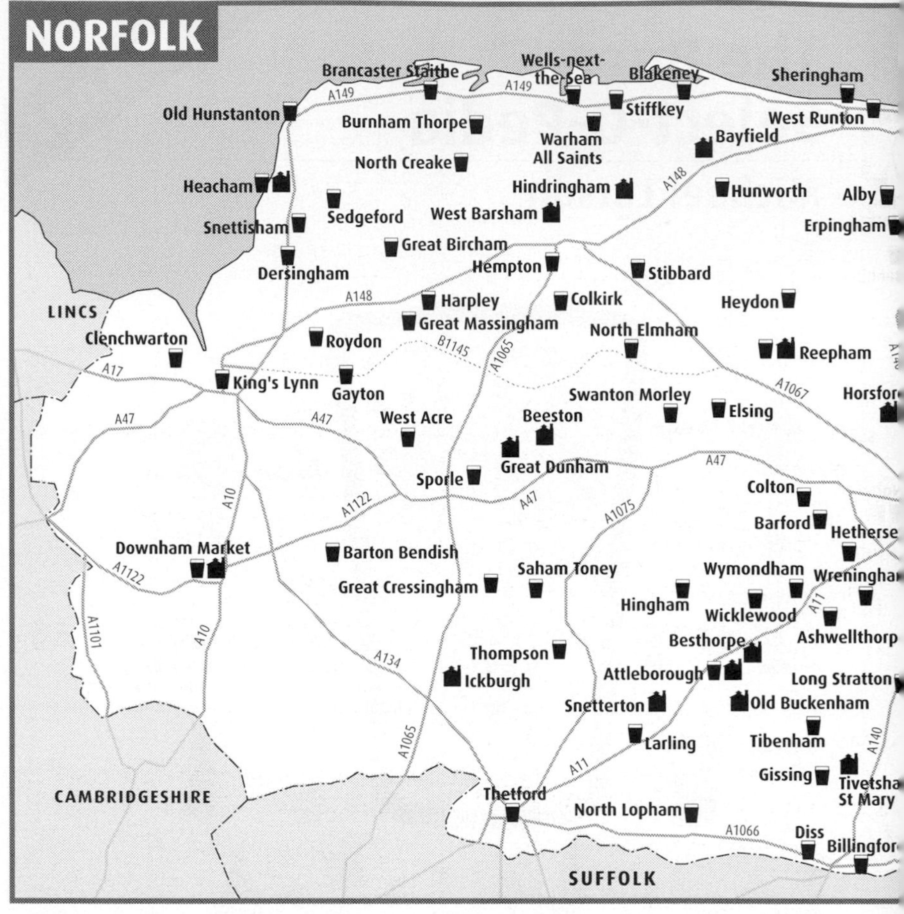

Alby

Horseshoes 𝕃

Cromer Road, NR11 7QE

✪ closed Mon; 12-2.30, 6.30-11; 12-4.30 Sun

☎ (01263) 761378 🌐 albyhorseshoes.co.uk

Adnams Southwold Bitter; Woodforde's Wherry; guest beers Ⓗ

A 19th-century inn that offers four real ales, always from local breweries. There are two bars, a wood-burning stove, and a dining room. Traditional games of ring the bull and twister are located in the ceiling. Pictures of old cars adorn the walls; the landlord is a classic car enthusiast. Live music is '50s, '60s and traditional country, with a touch of local folk. Locally-sourced home-cooked food is served. Outside is a patio area and garden with tables and umbrellas. ❀🛏◑♿♣P🚌(44,50)

Ashwellthorpe

King's Head

The Turnpike, Norwich Road, NR16 1EL (on B1113)

✪ 12-11 (10.30 Mon & Tue); 12-3, 7-10.30 Sun

☎ (01508) 489419

Woodforde's Wherry; guest beers Ⓗ

Family-run pub with a spacious open-plan interior and a dining area to one side. Round to one side of the main bar, overlooking the large back garden, is a games area with a pool table and dartboard which is guarded by a parrot. There is always one interesting rotating guest beer available in addition to the Woodforde's Wherry. Good-quality home-cooked food is offered at reasonable prices. 🛏◑♣P

Attleborough

London Tavern 𝕃

Church Street, NR17 2AH

✪ 11-11 (1.30 Fri & Sat) ☎ (01953) 457415

Beer range varies Ⓗ

Family and dog friendly pub in the town centre, close to public transport. The house beer is from Wolf, and the range of five guest beers, normally from microbreweries, comes from all over the UK. The pub has a dining room and serves breakfast and lunch every day. A beer festival takes place over the August bank holiday weekend. The microbrewery at the rear of the pub started brewing in 2014. CAMRA members receive a discount. ♞❀◐♿⇌P🐾ᯤ

Banningham

Crown Inn 𝕃

Colby Road, NR11 7DY (about 2 miles E of A140, opp church)

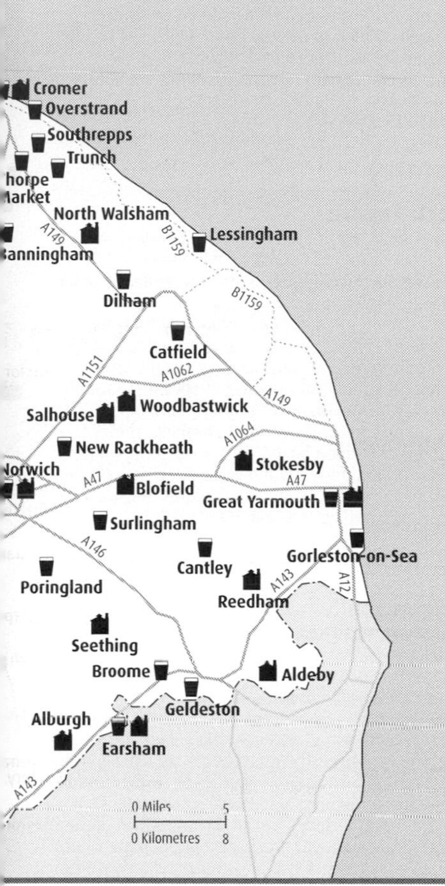

⏲ 12-2.30, 6-11 (12.30am Fri); 12-11 Sat; 12-10.30 Sun
☎ (01263) 733534 🌐 banninghamcrown.co.uk

Adnams Broadside; Greene King IPA, Abbot; guest beers Ⓗ

Traditional, friendly free house in the heart of the village, opposite the parish church and village green, which has been run by the same family since 1991. Interior features include beams and a large working fireplace, in a building that has housed an inn since the 17th century. There is a patio with a covered smoking shelter, garden and barbecue area. Quality food, often made with locally-sourced produce, is available. Monthly quiz nights and other regular special events are held.
Q❀◑⛺♣P🚌(18)📶

Barford

Cock Inn 🄻

Watton Road, NR9 4AS (on B1108)
⏲ closed Mon-Wed; 5.30 (12 Sat)-8.30; 12-4 Sun
☎ (01603) 757747

Beer range varies Ⓗ

Situated on the main road through the village, the pub has two rooms. The entrance door leads into the larger room which has settles, pub games and a real fire in winter. The other is a long, thin room with the bar at one end and the entrance to the restaurant at the other. ❀◑♣P🐾

Barton Bendish

Berney Arms

Church Road, PE33 9GF
⏲ 12-11 (10 Sun) ☎ (01366) 347995
🌐 theberneyarms.co.uk

Adnams Southwold Bitter, Broadside; guest beers Ⓗ

A smart village local which serves excellent food in the dining room and the bar. The midweek specials are good value and a step up on average pub food. The beers are from Adnams, with a couple of its seasonal beers normally found alongside the regular offerings. An interesting selection of pictures decorates the walls of the bar.
Q❀🛏◑♿⛺♣P🐾📶

Billingford

Horseshoes

Lower Street, IP21 4HL (on A143 between Scole and Harleston)
⏲ 11-11; 12-10 Sun ☎ (01379) 740414
🌐 thehorseshoes-billingford.co.uk

Adnams Southwold Bitter; guest beer Ⓖ

On the A143 Diss to Lowestoft road, this is an old hostelry that relies on passing trade but attracts locals for its beers. Handpumps advertise the ales on offer but all are dispensed straight from the cask in the taproom. Adnams Southwold Bitter is ever-present, with one or two guest beers, depending on the season. It stays open long hours, with breakfast served 7-11am and meals from lunchtimes through to the evening.
Q❀🛏◑♿♣P🚌(580)

INDEPENDENT BREWERIES

Beeston Beeston
Buffy's Tivetshall St Mary
Chalk Hill Norwich
Elmtree Snetterton
Fat Cat Norwich
Fox Heacham
Golden Triangle Norwich
Grain Alburgh
Humpty Dumpty Reedham
Iceni Ickburgh
Jo C's West Barsham
Lacons Great Yarmouth
Norfolk Hindringham
Norfolk Square Stokesby
Norwich Bear Norwich
Ole Slewfoot North Walsham
Opa Hay's Aldeby
Panther Reepham
Poppyland Cromer
Redwell Norwich (NEW)
S&P Horsford (NEW)
Stumptail Great Dunham
Taylors Attleborough (NEW)
Tindall Seething
Tipples Salhouse
Tombstone Great Yarmouth (NEW)
Two Rivers Downham Market
Uncle Stuarts Blofield
Wagtail Old Buckenham
Waveney Earsham
Why Not Norwich
Winter's Norwich
Wissey Valley Downham Market
Wolf Besthorpe
Woodforde's Woodbastwick
Yetman's Bayfield

Blakeney

King's Arms

Westgate Street, NR25 7NQ

9.30am-11; 12-10.30 Sun ☎ (01263) 740341

blakeneykingsarms.co.uk

Adnams Explorer; Marston's Pedigree [H]; Woodforde's Wherry, Sundew, Nelson's Revenge [G]; Wychwood Hobgoblin; guest beers [H]

Close to the harbour in one of Norfolk's most picturesque coastal villages, this old building was originally three fishermen's cottages. The interior comprises a series of interconnecting rooms, and there is a large garden to one side. Around five to six real ales are available, dispensed either by handpump or gravity, including at least one from Woodforde's. Cooked breakfasts are now served 9.30-11.30am, which is handy for campers and walkers. Children and dogs are welcome and en-suite accommodation is offered.
Q❀🛏◐◑♿P🚌(3)🐾

Brancaster Staithe

Jolly Sailors

Main Road, PE31 8BJ

11-11; 12-10.30 Sun ☎ (01485) 210314

jollysailorsbrancaster.co.uk

Adnams Broadside; Brancaster Best; Woodforde's Wherry; guest beer [H]

A cosy inn with several small drinking areas and two dining rooms, convenient for the Norfolk coast path and Brancaster Staithe harbour. It has a garden and play area, is family and dog friendly, and has an ice cream hut. Brancaster beers are produced by a local brewery to the pub's recipes and at least one is always available. Food offerings include local seafood and stone-baked pizza, with the oven visible from the bar. Coasthopper buses stop outside. Q🐎❀◐◑♿▲♣P🚌(2)🐾📶

Broome

Artichoke

162 Yarmouth Road, NR35 2NZ (just off A143, on road through village)

closed Mon; 12-3, 5-11 (12-11 Tue-Fri Apr-Sep); 12-midnight Sat; 12-11 Sun ☎ (01986) 893325

theartichokeatbroome.co.uk

Adnams Southwold Bitter [H], Broadside [G]; Woodforde's Mardler's [H]; guest beers [G]

A community-oriented village local made special by the people who run it. Delicious home-cooked food is served lunchtimes and evenings, which can be eaten in the separate dining area, the main bar near a roaring log fire, or in the garden in summer. A range of up to 10 beers is offered, with emphasis on local ales dispensed either by handpump in the bar or by gravity from the taproom. The pub has around 100 malt whiskies.
Q🐎❀◐◑♿P🚌(580,588)🐾

Burnham Thorpe

Lord Nelson

Walsingham Road, PE31 8HN (off B1355)

11.45-3, 6-10.30; 11.45-4 Sun ☎ (01328) 738241

nelsonslocal.co.uk

Greene King Abbot; Woodforde's Wherry; guest beer [G]

A 17th-century pub in the village where Nelson was born and the first pub to be named in his honour after Trafalgar; it is full of Nelson memorabilia. The beer is all served by gravity through a hatch to the taproom, which still has the original settles. This local participates in the Britstop campervan scheme. Opening hours are extended in summer – check with the pub.
Q🐎❀◐♿▲♣P🐾📶

Cantley

Cock Tavern

Manor Road, NR13 3JQ (1½ miles N of village centre)

11-3, 6-11.30; 11-11 Sun ☎ (01493) 700895

Adnams Southwold Bitter, Broadside; Fuller's London Pride; guest beers [H]

Old roadside inn situated a little way from the village of Cantley. It has a rambling interior with several rooms and some original beams visible. Although fairly food-oriented, it sells a range of five cask ales, with prices displayed prominently on the pumpclips, and over 100 whiskies. The restaurant is open seven days a week serving home-cooked food, with bargain specials including fish and chips on Fridays. Quiz nights are on selected Mondays. 🐎◐◑♣P🚌(730)🐾

Catfield

Crown Inn

The Street, NR29 5AA (in centre of village, S of A149, E of Stalham)

12-2.30, 7 (5 Fri)-11; 12-3, 7-midnight Sat; 12-3, 7-10.30 Sun ☎ (01692) 580128 catfieldcrown.co.uk

Belhaven Black; guest beers [H]

Tastefully furnished 300-year-old village inn with a real fire in winter. The guest beers are usually from local micros such as Green Jack, Wolf, Grain, Norfolk Brewhouse, Lacons, Woodforde's and Buffy's. A varied menu includes Italian dishes, which are a speciality, made with fresh local ingredients where possible. Takeaway fish and chips are served from 5pm on Fridays. There is a separate function/dining room and a secluded garden for summer. Accommodation is in a detached building that was once the doctor's surgery. Q❀🛏◐◑P🚌(12/12A)

Clenchwarton

Victory Inn

243 Main Road, PE34 4AQ

12-11 (midnight Fri & Sat) ☎ (01553) 775668

Elgood's Cambridge Bitter; guest beers [H]

An Elgood's house which usually offers a couple of guest beers alongside the regulars, some of which come from the Elgood's seasonal range. There are interesting pub games on the tables in the bar, or you can try the hearty, good-value food served in the separate dining room. Outside, there is a garden and a smoking area. Look out for the beer festivals and events such as the regular quiz nights.
🐎❀🛏◐◑♿♣🍎P🚌(505)🐾📶

Colkirk

Crown

Crown Road, NR21 7AA

closed Mon Oct-Mar; 11-3, 5-11; 11-11 Sat & Sun ☎ (01328) 862172 colkirk-norfolk.co.uk/crown.htm

Greene King IPA; guest beer [H]

Welcoming, popular, two-bar pub with an attractive dining room and an open fire in a brick inglenook. A range of pub games is provided, along with occasional live music, and good food. Dogs are allowed but only in the bar area. The guest beer is from Greene King, either Abbot or Old Speckled Hen. The pub was owned by the parish from 1767 until 1952, when it was sold to Greene King for £1,500. Q❀◐♣P🐾

Colton

Ugly Bug Inn

High House Farm Lane, NR9 5DG (2 miles from S of A47 Norwich southern bypass)
12-2.30 (not Tue), 5-10.30; 12-2.30, 5-11 Fri & Sat; 12-3, 7-10 Sun ☎ (01603) 880794 uglybuginn.co.uk
Beeston Worth the Wait, The Dry Road, Village Life; guest beers H
A pub that is well worth finding, a short drive off the A47 in Colton. It is large and has a beer garden, with a friendly and relaxing atmosphere. Good-quality food is served in the dining room, and there are monthly jazz evenings. The landlord cellars his beers well, and always has at least two beers on handpump, from local Beeston and Humpty Dumpty breweries. The pub is closed on a Tuesday lunchtime. Eight en-suite bedrooms are available. Q❀◐♿♣P

Cromer

Red Lion Hotel

Brook Street, NR27 9HD (behind church on clifftop)
11-11 ☎ (01263) 514964 redlion-cromer.co.uk
Adnams Southwold Bitter; Woodforde's Wherry; guest beers H
Splendidly situated with views of Cromer pier and the sea, the 19th-century Red Lion has retained many of its original features, including panelling, a Victorian tiled floor and open wood fires. The work of local artists decorates the walls of the two bar areas. Up to four guest ales are usually available, often from local breweries such as Humpty Dumpty and Wolf. Beer festivals are held in the summer. The award-winning restaurant offers an extensive menu. Q◐♿P(3)🐾

Dersingham

Coach & Horses

77 Manor Road, PE31 6LN
12-11.30 ☎ (01485) 540391 thecoachpub.com
Woodforde's Wherry; guest beers H
Busy 19th-century carrstone pub close to Sandringham offering three changing guest ales plus one constant, all at reasonable prices. It is popular for home-made traditional meals (check for winter availability). Entertainment includes quiz nights, a piano and a pool table, plus live music on Friday nights and some Sundays. The large garden includes a children's play area. There are three en-suite B&B rooms. An October beer festival offers around 20 real ales plus cider. Dogs on leads are welcome. CAMRA branch Pub of the Year 2014. Q❀◐P(11,10)🐾

Dilham

Cross Keys

The Street, NR28 9PS (E of A149 Stalham-North Walsham road – look for Amenities sign)
12-11 (10.30 Sun) ☎ (01692) 536398
crosskeysdilham.co.uk
Greene King IPA; guest beers H
Traditional local in an attractive setting with an excellent reputation for top-quality home-made meals using local ingredients where available, and a good choice of ales. In summer food and drinks may be enjoyed on the south-facing terrace; in winter there are log fires in both restaurant and bar. There are games in a separate room. It is the most northerly pub on the Broads and just a short walk from quiet moorings on the River Ant. A beer festival is hosted in summer. ❀◐♿♣P🐾

Diss

Waterfront Inn

43 Mere Street, IP22 4AG (lower end of main street, backing onto mere)
11-11 (midnight Fri & Sat) ☎ (01379) 652695
Greene King IPA, Abbot; guest beers H
Listed town-centre pub in a great position at the lower end of the main street and backing onto Diss Mere. The main bar is cosy and atmospheric, with oak beams and fireplaces. The rear has been extended to create a comfortable dining area, but the outside space is the main feature. In better weather enjoy the large decking area next to and overlooking the lovely mere, while trying some of the brews from the new Greene King microbrewery, and take in the views. ❀◐♿P

Downham Market

Crown Hotel

12 Bridge Street, PE38 9DH
9.30am-11 ☎ (01366) 382322
Adnams Southwold Bitter; Greene King IPA, Abbot H
An unspoilt 17th-century coaching inn at the heart of the town. Enter through a room with a lovely staircase to the bar with a beamed ceiling and large fireplace, where a good selection of ales is served. There is a restaurant and separate function room that caters for parties and weddings, and plenty of outside seating. Q❀◐≋P

Railway Arms

Platform 1, Railway Station, Railway Road, PE38 9EN (entrance on platform remains open when station office is closed)
10-12, 3.30-5.30 (9.30 Thu); 10-10.30 Fri; 10-1, 6-10.30 Sat; 12-2.30 Sun ☎ (01366) 386636 railway-arms.co.uk
Beer range varies G
A micropub selling two real ales on the platform at Downham Market railway station. A varying range of beers is sourced from around the country, including some local ales. Five ciders/perries are also available – the pub was voted CAMRA National Cider Pub of the Year in 2013. Ciders are similarly from both national and local producers, often including nearby Pickled Pig. It is advisable to call and check opening hours if you are travelling a long way. Q≋♣P🐾

Earsham

Queen's Head

Station Road, NR35 2TS (just W of Bungay)
12-11; 12-10.30 Sun ☎ (01986) 892623
Waveney East Coast Mild, Lightweight; guest beers H
On the Norfolk-Suffolk border, near the Suffolk town of Bungay, this busy 17th-century locals' pub has a large front garden overlooking the village green. The main bar has a flagstone floor, wooden

beams and a large fireplace with a fire in winter. It is home to the Waveney Brewing Co selling a range of – usually – four beers, with at least one guest beer from another brewer. There is a separate dining area serving food at lunchtimes (no food Mon and Tue). ❀◖♿♣P🚌(580)📶

Elsing

Mermaid Inn

Church Street, NR20 3EA

⏲ 12-3 (not Mon), 7-11; 5-midnight Fri; 6-midnight Sat; 12-3, 6-midnight Sun ☎ (01362) 637640

🌐 elsingmermaidinn.co.uk

Adnams Broadside; Woodforde's Wherry Ⓖ**; guest beers** Ⓗ

A 17th-century pub opposite the village church. The large single room has a log-burning fire at one end and a pool table at the other. Cask ales sold here are mainly, though not exclusively, from local brewers, typically Humpty Dumpty and Batemans, and are dispensed by gravity. The menu features curries, steaks and pie specials. Books and pub games are available for patrons' use, and the 12-mile Wensum Way walk passes the door. Lined glass are available on request.
🐴❀◖◗♿⛺♣P🍺🐾📶

Erpingham

Erpingham Arms Ⓛ

The Street, NR11 7QA

⏲ 12-3 (11.30 Fri & Sat); 12-10.30 Sun ☎ (01263) 761591

Woodforde's Wherry, Nelson's Revenge; guest beers Ⓗ

Newly refurbished pub tracing its history back to the 1720s, it features a cosy main bar with wood-burning stoves, a small restaurant and a function room. The food is locally sourced where possible and includes recipes that historically have a strong Norfolk connection. Guest ales are usually from Norfolk brewers, while beer festivals are held annually and also feature beers from Norfolk. There are quiz nights monthly and other themed events throughout the year. 🐴❀◖◗⛺♣P🚌(18)🐾

Gayton

Crown Inn

Lynn Road, PE32 1PA (on B1145)

⏲ 12-11 ☎ (01553) 636252

Greene King XX Mild, IPA, Abbot; Morland Old Speckled Hen; guest beer Ⓗ

Originating from the 13th century, the Crown Inn combines a charming historic feel with a friendly atmosphere. It is a rare outlet for the dark XX Mild as well as an occasional interesting guest beer. There are several drinking areas and an outside patio for the summer with attractive flowerbeds. The restaurant serves locally-sourced food including game dishes and does a popular Sunday carvery. Q❀🛏◖◗♿⛺♣P🚌(48)🐾

Geldeston

Locks Inn Ⓛ

Locks Lane, NR34 0HW (around 800yds along track from Station Road)

⏲ 12 (9 Sat)-11 (closed Mon-Wed in winter); 9-11 (7 winter) Sun ☎ (01508) 518414 🌐 geldestonlocks.co.uk

Green Jack Orange Wheat Beer, Trawlerboys Best Bitter; guest beers Ⓗ

On the north bank of the River Waveney, the pub is accessed by a long meandering track between dykes and marshes. The small main bar, with low ceiling beams and clay floor, retains an authentic feel, with candlelight adding atmosphere. The pub is owned by Green Jack Brewery, whose beers are supplemented by guest ales, real ciders and perries. Live music features in summer. The building may flood in winter. Note: use postcode NR34 0HS for your sat nav. Q❀◖◗♣🍎P🐾

Gissing

Crown Inn

Lower Street, IP22 5UJ (approx 5 miles N of Diss, 3 miles from A140)

⏲ 11.30-2.30, 6.30-midnight; 11.30-2.30, 6-1am Fri; 11.30-1am Sat; 12-midnight Sun ☎ (01379) 677718

🌐 gissingcrown.co.uk

Adnams Southwold Bitter; Woodforde's Kett's Rebellion; Young's Special; guest beers Ⓖ

There is a friendly, welcoming atmosphere in this tucked-away, oak-beamed, 16th-century pub near the ancient round-towered church. It offers good food, with fish and chips every Friday and curry night on the first Wednesday of the month. Differing guest ales are always on, with four at weekends and all served straight from the cask.
Q🐴❀◖◗♿♣P🚌🐾📶

Gorleston-on-Sea

Oddfellows Arms

43 Cliff Hill, NR31 6DG

⏲ 4-11 (midnight Fri); 3-11 Sat; 12-10 Sun ☎ 07584 355161

🌐 oddiesgy.co.uk

Beer range varies Ⓗ

A well-refurbished two-bar town pub tucked away a short distance from the harbour mouth. Jazz nights are a speciality, and there are always four beers on tap, mostly bitters or golden ales at 3.5-4% ABV. Free peanuts are often provided on the bar in glass carafes. It has a pleasant outdoor seating area for fine summer evenings, but limited parking at the rear. P🐾📶

Great Bircham

King's Head Hotel

Lynn Road, PE31 6RJ (on B1153)

⏲ 11-11; 12-10.30 Sun ☎ (01485) 578265

🌐 the-kings-head-bircham.co.uk

Morland Old Speckled Hen; Woodforde's Wherry; guest beers Ⓗ

Enter this Grade II-listed building in rural Norfolk to find a comfortable contemporary bar and lounge area. Four ales on handpump are on offer plus a quality restaurant serving seasonal local dishes such as hare or mussels, along with fish and chips and speciality sandwiches. Themed evenings and quiz nights are popular with the local community. For visitors, the boutique hotel provides a base close to the Sandringham Estate, walking trails, the Norfolk coast and other memorable west Norfolk attractions. Q🐴❀🛏◖◗♿P🐾📶

Great Cressingham

Windmill Inn

Water End, IP25 6NN (off A1065 S of Swaffham)

⏲ 11-11 ☎ (01760) 756232 🌐 oldewindmillinn.co.uk

Adnams Southwold Bitter, Broadside; Greene King IPA; guest beers H
Run by a local family for three generations, the Windmill is a maze of rooms of differing sizes and a conservatory. A rolling list of guest beers sometimes surprises. Real cider has been a popular feature for several years. A range of games is available and popular music nights are held. The food ranges from real sophistication to great-value lunches, all supervised by the daughter of the family. Modern accommodation is on offer, with a caravan site opposite. Q☋❀🛏◑♿▲♣●P🐾

Great Massingham

Dabbling Duck L

11 Abbey Road, PE32 2HN
⚙ 12-11; 12-10.30 Sun ☎ (01485) 520827
🌐 thedabblingduck.co.uk
Adnams Broadside; Beeston Worth the Wait; Woodforde's Wherry; guest beer H
Situated in an attractive village, the pub features bar areas with a roaring fire in the winter and an extensive garden. There is a separate restaurant for the many customers attracted by the excellent food, but also ample room for those who just wish to try one of the five or six beers on offer. There is accommodation, and guides are available from the bar featuring details of local walks.
☋❀🛏◑♣P🐾📶

Great Yarmouth

Mariners L

69 Howard Street South, NR30 1LN (behind both Palmers and Star Hotel)
⚙ 11-11; 12-11 Sun ☎ (01493) 332299
Beer range varies H
Traditional two-bar pub in the town centre, this local stocks up to 10 ales and eight real ciders/perries – visitors could be excused for thinking that a beer festival is always in progress, given the range and choice from all over the country. However, regular beer festivals are hosted throughout the year, including one at Easter, and when the town's maritime festival is held in early September. Most local buses stop nearby.
Q☋◐▲♣●P📶

Red Herring L

24-25 Havelock Road, NR30 3HQ (at back of Time & Tide Museum)
⚙ 12-3, 6-midnight; 12-midnight Sat & Sun
☎ (01493) 853384
Beer range varies H
Formerly the Derby Wine Vaults, this back-street corner local is close to the award-winning Time & Tide Museum and spectacular sections of the medieval town wall. It has a relaxed, comfortable atmosphere and the pool table and TV are tucked away in a room separated from the bar by folding doors. There are many photos of old Yarmouth during its fishing days when the town was invaded by many Scottish herring boats. The cider is Westons Old Rosie. ♣●

Harpley

Rose & Crown

Nethergate Street, PE31 6TW
⚙ closed Mon; 12-3.30 (not Tue), 6.30-10.30; 12-5 Sun
☎ (01485) 521807
Woodforde's Wherry; guest beers H
An attractive 17th-century pub in the centre of an unspoilt village close to Houghton Hall. It features open bar areas with a stylish and comfortable feel, and has log fires in winter. Outside is a beer garden for summer drinking. It is welcoming to families and dogs, and there is an extensive menu serving good food. Q☋❀◑P🚌(X8)🐾📶

Heacham

Fox & Hounds L

22 Station Road, PE31 7EX
⚙ 12-11; 12-10.30 Sun ☎ (01485) 570345
Adnams Broadside; guest beers H
Popular with locals and visitors, this is the home of the Fox Brewery. There are eight beers to choose from including a selection from Fox, whose bottled beers are also sold, plus a range of imported beers. The restaurant offers beer recommendations to match the food. There is live music on Tuesday evenings (mainly blues) and a quiz on Thursdays. Beer festivals are hosted throughout the year. It is on the King's Lynn-Hunstanton bus route.
☋❀◑♿♣P🚌🐾📶

Hempton

Bell

27 The Green, NR21 7LG
⚙ 11-2.30 (not Tue), 5-midnight; 11-midnight Sat; 12-midnight Sun ☎ (01328) 864579 🌐 hemptonbell.co.uk
Sharp's Doom Bar; Woodforde's Wherry; guest beer H
A family-run village pub with a relaxed, friendly atmosphere. It retains a traditional two-bar layout little altered since the early 1970s. Pub games include dominoes, cribbage and poker dice – you will be welcome to get involved. Changing guest beers are from micros or independent breweries and are typically over 4% ABV. Open mic folk sessions take place on the second Tuesday of the month and regular quizzes are held. ◐P🐾

Hethersett

King's Head L

36 Old Norwich Road, NR9 3DD
⚙ 11-11 (midnight Fri & Sat); 12-11 Sun ☎ (01603) 810206
Adnams Southwold Bitter; Shepherd Neame Spitfire; Timothy Taylor Golden Best; guest beer H
The pub is one of the oldest in Norfolk, with some parts of the building dating back to the 1600s, and has a regionally important historic interior for its gem of a snug bar. The saloon bar is beamed, comfortable, and has a real fire in winter in the inglenook fireplace. It also boasts a suit of armour. There is a separate dining room and an outside smoking shelter. Q❀◑P

Heydon

Earle Arms

The Street, NR11 6AD
⚙ closed Mon; 12-3, 6-11; 12-11 Sun ☎ (01263) 587376
🌐 theearlearms.com
Adnams Southwold Bitter; guest beers H
Lovely 16th-century former coaching inn opposite the green, in the centre of a privately owned picture-postcard village that is often used as a film location. The bar is mainly candlelit, with a welcoming atmosphere and a log fire in winter; it also has an interesting collection of horse racing

memorabilia. The food is seasonal and locally sourced, cooked to order and of the highest quality – booking is advisable. Real cider is available in the summer. The guest beer is from Woodforde's.
Q⇄◑♣P ᯤ

Hingham

White Hart Hotel

3 Market Place, NR9 4AF
⏲ 11-11 (midnight Fri & Sat); 12-10 Sun ☎ (01953) 850214
🌐 whitehartnorfolk.co.uk
Jo C's Bitter Old Bustard, Knot Just Another IPA, Norfolk Kiwi; guest beer Ⓗ
Friendly hostelry with an imposing façade and a statue of a white hart as the pub sign. The pub describes itself as a restaurant, and has a front and rear area laid for dining either side of the central bar, with a raised dining floor at the far end of the rear area. A further dining room is to the left of the entrance hall, with yet another two dining rooms on the upper floor. It is smart and comfortable throughout. **Q◑P**

Hunworth

Hunny Bell

The Green, NR24 2AA
⏲ 11-3, 5.30-11; 11-11 Sat & Sun ☎ (01263) 712300
🌐 thehunnybell.co.uk
Adnams Southwold Bitter; guest beers Ⓗ
A 300-year-old pub overlooking the village green with a warm, friendly atmosphere, enhanced by a log fire in winter. The interior, and the large barn conversion to the rear, feature exposed brickwork and oak beams, with quality finishes evident throughout. Outside there is a dining terrace and garden for the summer. Excellent locally-sourced food is served, including game from the nearby Stody Estate, and there are always three or four well-kept ales on the bar, from breweries such as Wychwood and Marston's. **Q❀◑♿P🚌(X6)🐾**

King's Lynn

Crown & Mitre

Ferry Street, PE30 1LJ (just off Tuesday Market Place)
⏲ 12-2.30, 6-11 ☎ (01553) 774669
Beer range varies Ⓗ
A treasure trove of interesting objects, many with a maritime or railway connection, can be found here. It has a gallery and a garden overlooking the river. Good-value food is served alongside a selection of five or six guest beers. There is no pub car park, but plenty of public ones close by. Note that the pub closes during the annual Mart, for two weeks from around February 14th. **Q❀◑≢🐾**

Lattice House

Chapel Street, PE30 1EG
⏲ 9am-11 (1am Fri & Sat) ☎ (01553) 769585
Beer range varies Ⓗ
Some of the regular Wetherspoon features will be familiar here, such as the menu and the frequent beer and cider festivals. However, this pub is elevated by its architecture – the 15th-century building retains many original features. There are three bars and lots of small rooms. It is worth visiting to experience the cosy atmosphere which is enhanced by the absence of TV screens.
Q◑≢● ᯤ

Stuart House Hotel

35 Goodwins Road, PE30 5QX (up gravel drive off Goodwins Road)
⏲ 6-11; 7-10.30 Sun ☎ (01553) 772169
🌐 stuart-house-hotel.co.uk
Beer range varies Ⓗ
Tucked away down a gravel drive not far from the Walks park and football ground, this former private residence, dating back to Victorian times with many additions, is now a hotel. The bar features two or three guest beers. There is an annual beer festival, usually in the last week in July, and regular events such as live music and murder mystery evenings. Note that the bar opens evenings only, except by arrangement. **❀⇄◑≢♣P🐾ᯤ**

Larling

Angel

NR16 2QU (1 mile SW of Snetterton racetrack, just off A11)
⏲ 10-midnight; 11-11 Sun ☎ (01953) 717963
🌐 angel-larling.co.uk
Adnams Southwold Bitter Ⓗ
Norfolk CAMRA Pub of the Year 2013, five real ales are on handpump here, always including a mild. Over 100 whiskies are also stocked, with one featured each week. The lounge and bar have open fires. There is a dining room which boasts excellent home-made fare. The friendly atmosphere is enjoyed by locals, passers-by, campers and rallyists, who use the Angel's campsite. A long-running summer beer festival showcases more than 70 ales. The local rail service is infrequent.
Q❀⇄◑♿⛺P▯

Lessingham

Star Inn 𝕃

Star Hill, NR12 0DN (just off main B1159, corner of High Rd and Star Hill)
⏲ closed Mon; 12-3, 4-11 ☎ (01692) 580510
🌐 thestarlessingham.co.uk
Adnams Southwold Bitter; Buffy's Bitter; Woodforde's Once Bittern; guest beer Ⓖ
Excellent village local that serves well-kept beers to regulars from near and far, and has a relaxed, welcoming atmosphere. Situated near the north-east Norfolk coast, it is convenient for those visiting nearby East Ruston Old Vicarage garden. The large beer garden is perfect for summer drinking. The cider is Westons Old Rosie. Dogs are welcome in the bar. Bar snacks and freshly prepared high-quality lunches and dinners are available daily (but no food Sun eve and Mon).
Q❀⇄◑●P🚌(34,36)🐾

Long Stratton

Swan Hotel

The Street, NR15 2XG (in centre of village on A140)
⏲ 11-2.30 (3 Fri), 6-11; 12-10.30 Sun ☎ (01508) 530200
Adnams Southwold Bitter; Fuller's London Pride; guest beers Ⓗ
Large 500-year-old roadside pub with a ghost. It was once a coaching inn on the busy A140, and now has two bars serving two regular ales plus two changing guests, including at least one from a local brewery. The pub has a wheelchair ramp and a separate disabled WC. Crib and whist are played.
⇄◑♿♣P🚌(3)

New Rackheath

Sole & Heel

2 Salhouse Road, NR13 6QH

⏲ 12 (5 Mon)-11; 12-10 Sun ☎ (01603) 720146
🌐 soleandheel.co.uk

Greene King IPA [G]; guest beers [H]

A warm and welcoming single-bar pub with two restaurant areas for about 25 diners in each. Beers often include interesting non-local micros, and are served on gravity from the cellar, alongside one or more real ciders. The restaurant has a large choice of fresh home-cooked and locally-sourced food, including seasonal evening specials. There is a pleasant garden with decking, a children's play area and regular live music and events.
🐴❀◑♿♣🍎P🚌(123,14)📶

North Creake

Jolly Farmers

1 Burnham Road, NR21 9JW

⏲ closed Mon & Tue; 11-2.30, 7-11; 12.30-2.30, 7-10.30 Sat; 12-7 Sun ☎ (01328) 738185 🌐 jollyfarmersnorfolk.co.uk

Woodforde's Wherry, Nelson's Revenge; guest beer [G]

Comfortable chairs, open fires and excellent food from the finest ingredients combine to create a great atmosphere in this unchanging local pub. You are as likely to meet locals as tourists straying from the nearby north Norfolk coast. Dogs and walkers are welcome. The friendly landlords make this a lovely pub – but note that it is closed on Mondays, Tuesdays and late Sunday evenings. **Q🐴◑♣P🐾**

North Elmham

Railway Hotel [L]

40 Station Road, NR20 5HH

⏲ 11.30-midnight; 11-10.30 Sun ☎ (01362) 668300

Beer range varies [H]/[G]

A fine example of a rural community pub, set in central Norfolk. A rotating choice of ales is available, dispensed by handpump or gravity. The range favours local brewers such as Wolf, Panther and Beeston, but beers from Somerset brewer Cottage also feature regularly. There is an adjacent function room that hosts many music events. Home-cooked meals using mainly locally sourced ingredients are available. The pub now offers B&B and has a campsite at the rear.
Q🐴❀🛏◑♣P🐾📶

North Lopham

King's Head

16 The Street, IP22 2NE (2 miles N of A1066)

⏲ 5-11 Mon; 11.30-3, 5-11 (midnight Thu & Fri); 11.30-midnight Sat; 12-10.30 Sun ☎ (01379) 688007
🌐 lophamkingshead.co.uk

Adnams Southwold Bitter; Woodforde's Wherry; guest beer [H]

Two-bar timber-framed pub dating from the 16th century, set back from the main road through the village. The public bar has an inglenook fireplace and a pool table, while the comfortable saloon and dining area have a woodburner. The guest beer varies but is normally over 4% ABV. Food is served lunchtimes and evenings Wednesday to Saturday, and Sunday lunchtime. The pub has its own crazy golf course – clubs can be borrowed free of charge.
Q🐴❀◑♿♣P🚌🐾📶

Norwich

Alexandra Tavern

16 Stafford Street, NR2 3BB (on corner of Stafford St and Gladstone St, off Dereham Rd)

⏲ 12-11 (midnight Thu); 10.30-midnight Fri & Sat
☎ (01603) 627772 🌐 alexandratavern.co.uk

Chalk Hill Tap Bitter, CHB, Gold; guest beers [H]

Popular, bustling and friendly, this pub is a little gem found just outside the city centre. The interior is brightly decorated, with the walls featuring pictures and articles about the landlord's charity achievements. The bar regularly serves three Chalk Hill Brewery beers as well as guest ales, along with a good variety of food including a soup menu. There is a pool table, dartboard and lots of board games to choose from. ◑♣▯🚌

Beehive [L]

30 Leopold Road, NR4 7PJ

⏲ 5-11; 11-midnight Fri; 12-midnight Sat; 12-3, 7-11.30 Sun
☎ (01603) 451628 🌐 beehivepubnorwich.co.uk

Fuller's London Pride; Green Jack Golden Best; guest beers [H]

The Beehive is home to three darts, football and korfball teams and serves up to five guest ales, mainly from East Anglia. The two-bar pub is popular with the local community and has a weekly quiz on Wednesday and a monthly folk night. Free Wi-Fi and pub games are available. The beer festival, held in the first week of July, is popular, as are regular charity barbecues, also hosted during the summer months. Food is served lunchtimes only. **Q❀◐♿♣P**

Duke of Wellington [L]

91/93 Waterloo Road, NR3 1EG

⏲ 12-11.30 (midnight Fri & Sat); 12-10.30 Sun
☎ (01603) 441182 🌐 dukeofwellingtonnorwich.co.uk

Fuller's London Pride [H]; Oakham JHB, Bishops Farewell [G]; Wolf Brewery Golden Jackal, Wolf in Sheep's Clothing, Silver Fox [H]; guest beers [G]

One of the city's premier real ale establishments, offering a wide selection of beers from around the country, with many served from the small taproom, which can be seen from the bar area. The revamped patio garden area holds the pub's annual beer festival during the late summer bank holiday and is picturesque in the sunshine. There is no food available but customers may bring their own – plates, cutlery and condiments will be supplied by the friendly staff. ❀♿♣P🚌(9A,16)📶

Earlham Arms [L]

41 Earlham Road, NR2 3AD

⏲ 10-11 (midnight Fri & Sat); 9.30am-10.30 Sun
☎ (01603) 622993 🌐 earlhamarmsnorfolk.co.uk

Jo C's Norfolk Kiwi, Bitter Old Bustard, Knot Just Another IPA; guest beers [H]

Large pub and restaurant which reopened after a refurbishment; the focus is on quality food but beer drinkers are welcome. Beer from Jo C's Norfolk Ale is always available, alongside up to 12 guest beers from Norfolk and Suffolk, both on handpump and on gravity from the cellar – CCTV means you can watch your pint being poured on a big screen behind the bar. Excellent and good-value food and bar snacks/tapas are served. ❀◑♿P🚌📶

Eaton Cottage

75 Mount Pleasant, NR2 2DQ

⏲ 12-11 (midnight Fri & Sat) ☎ (01603) 453048

Fuller's London Pride; Tipples Moonrocket; Wolf Brewery Golden Jackal; guest beers H
A large and friendly local pub close to the shops in the Golden Triangle, with a number of seating areas inside and out, serving an interesting variety of ales from local breweries such as Tipples and Wolf, plus beers from other UK breweries large and small. Sport is are shown on TV but the screens do not dominate (except in one small area).
(25)

Fat Cat L

49 West End Street, NR2 4NA
12-11 (midnight Thu & Fri); 11-midnight Sat
(01603) 624364 fatcatpub.co.uk
Adnams Southwold Bitter; Crouch Vale Yakima Gold; Fat Cat Bitter; Fuller's ESB; Oakham Bishops Farewell; Timothy Taylor Landlord H**; guest beers** G
An outstanding example of what a real ale pub should be, with excellent service, ales from the Fat Cat range, plus about 10 regular and 20 guest beers from all over the UK, including many dark and stronger ales, real ciders, and foreign beers on draught and in bottle. These complement the brewery memorabilia around the pub. Food is limited to excellent-value rolls and pies. A beer lover's paradise that no visitor to Norwich should miss, and CAMRA national Pub of the Year twice.
Q

Fat Cat & Canary L

101 Thorpe Road, NR1 1TR
12-11 (midnight Fri); 11-midnight Sat (01603) 432393
fatcatcanary.co.uk
Fat Cat Bitter; guest beers H
A new, third member of the Norwich-based Fat Cat mini-chain, about one and a half miles from the centre of the city. The pub serves most of the Fat Cat brewery's ales, and up to 10 guests from around the UK, together with continental beers and real ciders. There is a small TV to the rear of the main bar, a large car park and terraces to the front and rear, the latter being heated. Home-made rolls are available. P

Fat Cat Tap L

98/100 Lawson Road, NR3 4LF
12-11 (midnight Fri); 11-midnight Sat; 12-10.30 Sun
(01603) 413153 fatcattap.co.uk
Adnams Southwold Bitter; Fat Cat Bitter, Honey Cat H**, Marmalade Cat** G**; Harviestoun Bitter & Twisted** H**; guest beers** G
A 1970s estate pub dropped unsympathetically into Victorian suburbs, the Tap has blossomed since becoming the northernmost of the three Cats and home of the Fat Cat Brewery. The single drinking area showcases extensive breweriana; the impressive bar hosts a selection of beers and ciders on gravity and handpump, complemented by a worldwide selection of bottled beers. Closing time is indicated by a set of traffic lights suspended from the ceiling. There is live music twice a week and a challenging quiz fortnightly. P(11,11A)

Jubilee L

26 St Leonards Road, NR1 4BL
12-11 (midnight Fri & Sat); 12-10.30 Sun
(01603) 618734
Hop Back Summer Lightning; Sharp's Doom Bar; Woodforde's Wherry, Sundew, Nelson's Revenge; guest beer H
An attractive Victorian corner pub with a warm welcome. There is a choice of two bars and a comfortable conservatory and enclosed patio garden. Many of the well-kept ales are local and this is also reflected in the range of lagers available. This popular pub at the heart of the community caters for all tastes, from sports fans to those who enjoy local history talks, and has a village feel though within easy reach of the city centre.

King's Arms

22 Hall Road, NR1 3HQ (city end of Hall Rd)
11 (11.30 Fri & Sat); 12-10.30 Sun (01603) 766361
kingsarmsnorwich.co.uk
Batemans XB, XXXB; Beeston Worth the Wait; Hop Back Summer Lightning; guest beers H
A friendly Bateman's house serving an extensive range of guest ales to complement the Bateman's beers, usually including a stout or porter. It is to the south of the city centre. The only food served is Sunday roast, but the pub allows customers to bring their own food from various nearby takeaways (plates and condiments provided). The pub hosts monthly quiz nights, poker evenings and live music, and Westons Old Rosie cider is often available. Busy on match days. Q

King's Head L

42 Magdalen Street, NR3 1JE
12 (midnight Fri & Sat); 12-10.30 Sun (01603) 620468
kingsheadnorwich.co.uk
Beer range varies H
This award-winning pub offers a dozen quality real ales, but no keg beers at all. The beers are mainly from Norfolk microbreweries, plus a rotating range from East Anglia. The house beer, KHB, is brewed by Winter's. A range of continental bottled beers is also available, plus draught Kingfisher cider. The pub plays host to the Norwich bar billiard league, with the table situated in the rear drinking area.
Q

Murderer's L

2-8 Timber Hill, NR1 3LB
12-11; 12-10.30 Sun (01603) 621447
themurderers.co.uk
Beer range varies H
Deceptively large multi-level pub with an attached café-bar (open lunchtimes only). Up to a dozen ales from micros around the country are stocked, including the house beer brewed by Coors. It is popular with shoppers and office workers during the day and the younger set in the evening. The real name of the pub is the Gardeners Arms, but it is far better known as the Murderer's after a 19th-century landlord who was convicted of murdering his wife.

Plasterers Arms L

43 Cowgate, NR3 1SZ
12-midnight (1am Fri & Sat) (01603) 387525
Oakham JHB; guest beers H
This is a traditional corner local with an excellent range of both local and national microbrewery beers. It stages occasional beer tasting evenings, and stocks specialist keg beers from real ale breweries. A 10 per cent discount is offered to CAMRA members, available to all on Mondays. Local bands play live music on most Sunday afternoons. The pub was refurbished in 2011, giving it a brighter feel but still retaining its idiosyncratic layout from yesteryear. Q

Plough

58 St Benedict Street, NR2 4AR
12-11 (midnight Fri & Sat); 12-10.30 Sun
(01603) 626333 theploughnorwich.co.uk
Beer range varies H

Popular pub in one of the city's oldest areas near the Arts Centre. As the Grain Brewery tap, it offers the full range of ales and the occasional guest. The two-bar interior is fairly small, with wooden chairs and tables, and a roaring log fire in winter. The large Mediterranean-style courtyard garden is a fine place to while away a summer's evening. Excellent cocktails and spirits are also available, along with Vicky's special sausage pie, and barbecues in summer.

Reindeer L

10 Dereham Road, NR2 4AY
closed Mon; 12-11 (midnight Fri & Sat); 12-8 Sun
(01603) 762223 thereindeerpub.co.uk
Crouch Vale Brewers Gold; Elgood's Black Dog, Cambridge Bitter; Humpty Dumpty Little Sharpie; Thornbridge Jaipur IPA; guest beers H

Spacious single roomed public house serving a variety of guest ales as well as Elgood's own range including its monthly specials and one-off brews. The food is excellent and varied, ranging from gourmet bar snacks to roasts on Sundays. The former brewing room is now a separate dining area. Patio decking has been constructed at the rear, and there are benches at the front of the building. Q (21,22)

Ribs of Beef L

24 Wensum Street, NR3 1HY
12-11; 12-10.30 Sun (01603) 619517
ribsofbeef.co.uk
Adnams Southwold Bitter; Wolf Brewery Golden Jackal; Woodforde's Wherry; guest beers H

Traditional and well-decorated pub overlooking the River Wensum. A welcoming row of nine handpumps dispenses a large selection of local ales, with foreign beers and real cider also available. The pub is popular with visitors and the kitchen offers a great selection of meals made with locally-sourced ingredients. The atmosphere is relaxed and friendly, with a room downstairs as well as a big screen that regularly shows major sporting events. Just the place to watch the boats go by.

Sir Garnet L

36 Market Place, NR2 1RD
11-midnight (2am Fri & Sat); 12-10.30 Sun
(01603) 615892 sirgarnet.wordpress.com
Beer range varies H

Interesting old pub overlooking the city-centre market place. Tastefully refurbished in 2012 by the owners of the nearby Birdcage, it has rooms on four or five different levels. The pub was originally named after Field Marshall Garnet Wolseley, a celebrated army officer who served in Burma and the Crimean War. Gourmet burgers and other excellent food is served, alongside ales on handpump and gravity from local brewers such as Lacons and Adnams, and quality spirits.

Take 5 L

17 Tombland, NR3 1HF
11-11 (midnight Fri); closed Sun (01603) 763099
Beer range varies H

A range of around five real ales is available from Norfolk and Suffolk breweries in this Grade II-listed building, which dates in parts from the 15th century. Quality home-cooked food is sold all day, all sourced locally. A function room with a small terrace is upstairs, plus a cellar downstairs. Real cider and a selection of bottled beers and organic wines are also available. Prior to 2004 it was named the Louis Marchesi, after the founder of the Round Table.

Trafford Arms L

61 Grove Road, NR1 3RL
11-11; 12-10.30 Sun (01603) 628466
traffordarms.co.uk
Adnams Southwold Bitter; Tetley Bitter; Woodforde's Wherry; guest beers H

Close to the city centre, a warm welcome is assured at this public house run by the same licensees for over 20 years. A wide range of beers is available, usually including a mild, and Kingfisher Farm cider. Excellent home-cooked food includes pie, curry and fish evenings each week. Monthly quiz nights are popular. A former CAMRA Pub of the Year, the annual Valentine's beer festival is one of the biggest in the country, with 70-plus ales.
Q (9,17)

Vine L

7 Dove Street, NR2 1DE
11-11; closed Sun (01603) 627362 vinethai.co.uk
Oakham JHB; guest beers H

Located just off the marketplace, Norwich's smallest pub is a gem in the heart of the city, serving up to four quality ales plus traditional Thai cuisine in a winning combination. The restaurant is upstairs, although customers often eat downstairs in the bar area. The pub also boasts a range of bottled ciders and world beers. Extra tables and chairs are set outside in the pedestrianised street. Beer festivals held in January and late June are highlights. Q

Whalebone

144 Magdalen Road, NR3 4BA
11-11 (midnight Fri & Sat); 12-11 Sun (01603) 425482
whalebonefreehouse.co.uk
Adnams Southwold Bitter; Fuller's London Pride; Oakham JHB; Woodforde's Bure Gold, Wherry; guest beers H

A community local with eight beers, conveniently situated just to the south of Sewell Park. The pub has three separate areas: the original front and rear bars plus a newly refurbished area leading to a covered and heated terraced patio, which is very popular and used for summer barbecues. The pub holds an annual beer festival in July and supports three cricket teams as well as a golf society. Wine and beer tasting evenings are hosted occasionally.
P (10,18)

White Lion

73 Oak Street, NR3 3AQ
12-11; 12-10.30 Sun (01603) 632333
Milton Dionysus, Justinian, Pegasus, Sparta, Nero; guest beers H

A friendly three-roomed local pub serving an extensive range of over 20 ciders and perries, plus beers from the Milton Brewery, and two or three guests from good non-local microbreweries. Since reopening in 2008, the pub, under its current stewardship, won CAMRA Cider Pub of the Year for East Anglia four years later. The food served is varied and of excellent value. An annual beer festival is held in the autumn, and bar billiards and darts are played. Q◑♣●🐾📶

Wig & Pen 🄻

6 St Martin-at-Palace Plain, NR3 1RN

⏲ 11.30 (midnight Fri & Sat); 11.30-6 Sun ☎ (01603) 625891

🌐 thewigandpen.com

Adnams Southwold Bitter; Fuller's London Pride; Oakham JHB; Woodforde's Wherry; guest beers 🄷

Friendly 17th-century free house with a spacious patio immediately opposite the Bishop's Palace and with an impressive view of Norwich Cathedral spire. Three permanent ales and three guests are always available, usually including two local beers. The small back room can be used for meetings. Major sporting events are shown on two TVs. Good-quality food is available lunchtimes and evenings. The pub is a short walk from Tombland, where there are bus stands for several bus routes. ◑♿⇌♣

Old Hunstanton

Ancient Mariner

6 Golf Course Road, PE36 6JJ (within Le Strange Arms hotel complex)

⏲ 11-11 ☎ (01485) 534411

Adnams Southwold Bitter, Broadside; guest beers 🄷

A popular pub adjoining the Le Strange Arms Hotel, with a large beer garden leading down to the beach. The inn was originally the old barns and stables, and has a family room and restaurants. At least four ales are available and live music nights are held every month. Old Hunstanton is on the east coast facing west and the pub offers superb views of spectacular sunsets over the sea from the decking at the rear. Q👶❀🛏◑♿P🚉🚌(2)🐾📶

Overstrand

White Horse

34 High Street, NR27 0AB

⏲ 11-11 ☎ (01263) 579237 🌐 whitehorseoverstrand.co.uk

Woodforde's Wherry; guest beers 🄷

The White Horse is situated in the centre of the coastal village of Overstrand, yards from a sandy beach. Behind its Edwardian exterior lies a recently refurbished pub offering excellent beer as well as outstanding food and accommodation. A spacious modern bar serves up to four guest ales, usually from local Norfolk breweries such as Humpty Dumpty, Grain, Buffy's and Wolf. Outside is a large beer garden with play equipment, where occasional beer festivals are hosted in the summer. Q👶❀🛏◑♿P🚌(5,36)🐾📶

Poringland

Royal Oak 🄻

44 The Street, NR14 7JT

⏲ 11-11 (midnight Fri & Sat); 12-11 Sun ☎ (01508) 493734

🌐 poringlandroyaloak.com

Woodforde's Wherry; guest beers 🄷

A comfortable country pub with welcoming bar staff. The interior is divided into several small seating areas, one of which features memorabilia of the former RAF radar station that was situated nearby. A good selection of local real ales is stocked, supplemented by others from around the country, plus real ciders from Westons. No food is served but customers are welcome to bring in fish and chips from the shop next door. No dogs allowed, even in the garden.
Q❀♣●P🚉🚌(87,88)📶

Reepham

King's Arms 🄻

Market Place, NR10 4JJ

⏲ 11.30-3, 5.30-11; 11.30-11 Sat; 12-10.30 Sun

☎ (01603) 870345

Adnams Southwold Bitter; Greene King Abbot; Panther Golden Panther; Woodforde's Wherry, Once Bittern; guest beer 🄷

A former coaching inn, dating back to 1667, in the picturesque square of this small market town. Extended sympathetically in the 1990s, original beams, Norfolk brickwork and open fires have been retained, providing several drinking and dining areas. At least one ale from the local Panther Brewery is always on handpump. The ingredients for the comprehensive menu are from nearby butchers and bakers. Jazz bands play in the rear courtyard on summer Sundays, and a bar billiards table is available. Q👶◑♣🐾

Roydon

Union Jack

30 Station Road, PE32 1AW (off A148)

⏲ 12 (4 Tue-Thu)-midnight ☎ 07716 60439

Beer range varies 🄷

A popular village drinking pub, voted local CAMRA Pub of the Year in 2012. Four handpumps dispense a variety of ales, and beer festivals are held over the Easter and August bank holidays, with local breweries often featuring. There is live music each month, regular bingo and quizzes, and weekly support for darts, crib and dominoes.
❀♣P🚌(48)🐾

Saham Toney

Old Bell

1 Bell Lane, IP25 7HD

⏲ 11-11 (10.30 Sun) ☎ (01953) 884934

Adnams Southwold Bitter; Greene King IPA; guest beers 🄷

In a lane off the main street in Saham, the Bell boasts four guest beers of good quality. The lovely old building comprising a long bar room and restaurant is situated right next to Saham Mere. Small beer festivals are staged occasionally and the pub is engaged in a lot of local fundraising. Food is available daily from midday. ◑♿⛺♣P

Sedgeford

King William IV

Heacham Road, PE36 5LU (off B1454)

⏲ 11 (4 Mon)-11; 12-10.30 Sun ☎ (01485) 571765

🌐 thekingwilliamsedgeford.co.uk

Adnams Southwold Bitter; Greene King Abbot; Woodforde's Wherry; guest beers 🄷

A large well-appointed village pub, popular for its locally-produced food. Known by the locals as the King Willie, it has an excellent reputation for quality food but still retains a pub atmosphere that attracts local drinkers. There are two bars and a restaurant divided into four areas. A large garden at the rear has a superb outdoor covered drinking/dining area. Nine luxury rooms are available. Both bars are dog-friendly. Q👶❀🛏◑♿P🐾

ENGLAND

Sheringham

Windham Arms

15-17 Wyndham Street, NR26 8BA (on Lifeboat Plain, less than 100yds from seafront)
12-11 (12.30am Sat); 12-9 Sun ☎ (01263) 822609
thewindhamarms.co.uk
Beer range varies H
This cosy and welcoming local is close to the beach and promenade. It has a public bar and a lounge with a restaurant offering high-quality, good-value food including authentic Greek specials. Meals are served evenings plus summer lunchtimes. Outside is a partly covered drinking area with sea views. At least four Norfolk real ales are regularly on offer (six in summer) from Elmtree, Beeston and Humpty Dumpty among others. Beer festivals are held on local festival days and bank holidays. Q P

Snettisham

Rose & Crown

Old Church Road, PE31 7LX (off B1440)
11-11 (10.30 Sun) ☎ (01485) 541382
roseandcrownsnettisham.co.uk
Adnams Southwold Bitter, Broadside; Sharp's Doom Bar; Woodforde's Wherry; guest beer H
A popular traditional village inn with cosy bars, exposed beams, a real fire and a dining room. Head through the narrow passage to find a larger bar and dining areas with a contemporary feel. The pub is well known for traditional and exciting local seasonal fare; the bars also remain popular with local drinkers. The garden and play area make it appealing to families. Accommodation is available in 16 stylish bedrooms for those who wish to remain longer in this beautiful area. Q P (10,11)

Southrepps

Vernon Arms

2 Church Street, NR11 8NP (on A149 from North Walsham to Cromer; after Thorpe Market turn right at crossroads; continue into Southrepps and pub is on left past post office) TG2563636583
11-11.30; 12-10.30 Sun ☎ (01263) 833355
vernonarms.com
Adnams Southwold Bitter; Woodforde's Wherry; guest beers H
Traditional Norfolk brick and flint free house set in the heart of a vibrant village community. Regular ales are augmented by a variety of guest beers. It is popular with diners who appreciate fine food, locally-sourced ingredients (where possible), the variety of dining areas, candlelit tables and excellent service. Takeaway fish and chips are served 6-8pm Tuesday-Saturday. There is a log fire in winter and a heated smoking area outside. A beer festival with music is staged in July (request your favourite beer in June). P

Sporle

Peddars Inn

70 The Street, PE32 2DR
closed Mon; 11-3 (not Tue), 6-10.30; 11-3, 6-11 Fri; 12-11 Sat; 12-6 Sun ☎ (01760) 788101 thepeddarsinn.com
Adnams Southwold Bitter; guest beers H
A traditional village local with a comfortable bar warmed by a log fire in winter. It has a conservatory where freshly cooked food is served, and a private dining room for group bookings. There is plenty of entertainment here, with events such as music, discos and quizzes. The pub is handy for the Peddars Way long distance footpath, from where it gets its name. No food is available on Tuesday. P

Stibbard

Ordnance Arms

Guist Bottom, NR20 5PF (on A1067)
5.30-midnight; 11.30-2.30, 5-11 Sat; 12-11 Sun
☎ (01328) 829471
Adnams Southwold Bitter; guest beers H
A roadside pub with a small but comfortable front bar, a larger back bar with hatch service, stone flooring and simple wooden furnishing, and a pool room between the two. Both bars have real fires. The pub is named after its use as a base for the first ordnance survey of Norfolk, and a number of maps adorn the walls. Adjacent to the pub is a popular Thai restaurant (open Tue-Sat eves), food from which may be eaten in the bar. Q P (X29)

Stiffkey

Red Lion

44 Wells Road, NR23 1AJ (on A149)
11-11 ☎ (01328) 830552 stiffkey.com
Woodforde's Wherry G**, Nelson's Revenge** H
Beamed building from circa 1670 in the beautiful coastal village of Stiffkey, with several drinking areas of character, four log fires, an original stone floor and a covered patio at the rear. Today's pub is a food-oriented establishment serving an extensive menu. The pub also offers 10 en-suite rooms with eco-friendly roofs in a block behind the pub. Close to both Blakeney and Holkham nature reserves. Q P (3)

Surlingham

Ferry House

Ferry Road, NR14 7AR (follow signs to Surlingham Ferry; from Bramerton Rd continue to Pratts Hill, keep left at fork; Pratts Hill turns slightly left and becomes Ferry Rd)
11-11; 12-11 Sun ☎ (01508) 538659
Adnams Broadside; Humpty Dumpty Little Sharpie; Woodforde's Wherry; guest beer H
A rambling old characterful riverside country inn which is popular with boaters during the summer months. The spacious interior has a large brick fireplace in the centre of the room. Three cask ales are always on plus an occasional guest in high summer. High-quality home-cooked food is served all day. Occasional live music and quiz nights take place. P

Swanton Morley

Angel Inn

66 Greengate, NR20 4LX
12-11; 12-10 (6 winter) Sun ☎ (01362) 637407
theangelpub.co.uk
Hop Back Summer Lightning; Woodforde's Wherry; guest beer H
Dating back to 1610, this inn boasts a connection with Abraham Lincoln's family. The owners are keen CAMRA members and three beers are usually available. It has a spacious main bar with a real fire, hop-draped ceilings, and a dining room. There

are themed food nights and a live folk group plays on the first Wednesday of each month. The garden includes a bowling green. An annual beer festival is held, usually at Easter. Q🐎❀◐◑♣P🚌(4)🐾📶

Darbys

1 Elsing Road, NR20 4NY
⏲ 11.30-3, 6-11; 11.30-11 Fri & Sat; 12-10.30 Sun
☎ (01362) 637647 🌐 darbysfreehouse.com
Adnams Southwold Bitter, Broadside; Woodforde's Wherry; guest beers [G]
Originally a row of cottages which, around 20 years ago, was converted into a public house. There is one large long bar plus a split-level dining area, and a function room upstairs. An extensive food menu is available both lunchtimes and evenings, and customers may now order their meals via email before visiting. There is a large garden and car park, and the 12-mile Wensum Way passes the door. Q🐎❀◐◑♿P🚌(4)🐾📶

Thetford

Albion

93-95 Castle Street, IP24 2DN (opp Castle Park and Hill)
⏲ 11-11 Mon & Sat (11.30 Thu; midnight Fri); 11-3, 6-11 Tue & Wed; 12-3, 7-11 Sun ☎ (01842) 752796
Greene King IPA, Abbot [H]
Refurbished by Greene King a few years ago, the Albion now features a much longer bar. It offers the brewery's beers at very good prices. Run by the same family for several generations, the Albion is a classic town pub. There is seating outside and you can see the 1,000-year-old castle mound and its surrounding Iceni hill fort from here. Although food is not available you are welcome to order in from one of the food outlets in the town. Q❀◐◑♿♣P

Red Lion Ⓛ

Market Place, IP24 2AL
⏲ 8am-11 (1am Fri & Sat) ☎ (01842) 757210
Adnams Broadside; Greene King IPA, Abbot; guest beers [H]
Reopened in 2012 as a Wetherspoon pub, the Red Lion is a large town-centre venue with a range of drinking and dining areas decorated in a traditional style with plenty of information on local history and attractions. It was once a Lacons house and the plaque can still be found on the wall outside. Three guest beers feature plus the usual Wetherspoon regulars. It sits on the market square made famous as a location for Dad's Army. 🐎❀◐◑⇌📶

Thompson

Chequers Inn

Griston Road, IP24 1PX
⏲ 12-3, 6.30-11; 11.30-11 Sun ☎ (01953) 483360
🌐 thompsonchequers.co.uk
Greene King IPA, IPA Gold; Woodforde's Wherry [H]
A 16th-century gem in this pretty village, near Watton, featuring a steep thatched roof and timber-framed interior. Stooping to a 16th-century height will keep your head from the beams. With an excellent reputation for food, there are two rooms for dining, and a small area and another small room for drinking. It is much better to drink outside on sunny days. Guest beers are often from Wolf. Separate accommodation is available.
🐎❀🛏◐◑♿P

Thorpe Market

Gunton Arms Ⓛ

Cromer Road, NR11 8TZ (on W of A149 Cromer-North Walsham road SE of Thorpe Market, look for hanging sign, lit at night)
⏲ 12-11 (10.30 Sun) ☎ (01263) 832010
🌐 theguntonarms.co.uk
Adnams Southwold Bitter, Broadside; Woodforde's Wherry; guest beer [H]
Award-winning inn situated in the beautiful grounds of Gunton Park with its deer herd, featuring tasteful decor, comfortable furnishings and log fires in winter. East Anglian ales predominate, with regular guests. The first-class restaurant features some dishes cooked in the vaulted main dining room. Accommodation is sumptuous and cosy; most rooms overlook the restored parklands and the deer. Interesting art and artefacts abound for the connoisseur. A high-quality pub worthy of an early visit.
Q🐎❀🛏◐◑♿♣P🐾📶

Tibenham

Greyhound

The Street, NR16 1PZ (300yds from church)
⏲ 12-3 (not Tue), 6.30 (6 Fri)-midnight; 12-midnight Sat & Sun ☎ (01379) 677676 🌐 the-greyhound-tibenham.co.uk
Adnams Southwold Bitter, Broadside; Fuller's London Pride; guest beer [H]
Friendly local community pub in the heart of the south Norfolk countryside offering beers from Adnams and Fuller's plus rotating guests. The interior has many old beams and comprises a lounge, bar area and a small games room with pool table. There is a large car park, and a four-acre field at the rear which hosts many transport-themed events throughout the summer season. The field also provides an ideal base for campers and caravanners, complete with electric hook-ups.
Q◑⛺♣P

Trunch

Crown

Front Street, NR28 0AH (opp parish church)
⏲ 11.45-3 (not Mon), 5.30-11; 12-11 Sat; 12-10.30 Sun
☎ (01263) 722341
Batemans XB, XXXB; Greene King IPA; guest beers [H]
Set in the middle of a charming north Norfolk village with fine old flint cottages, close to the coast, this is Bateman's only pub in the area, offering an excellent choice of beers and a friendly atmosphere. XXXB is often replaced by a Bateman's seasonal beer; the cider is from Westons. A quiz night is held on the second Tuesday of every month. Dogs are welcome in the bar. The pub may close early on weekday evenings – ring ahead to check. Q❀◐◑♿⛺🍎P🚌(5,34)🐾

Warham All Saints

Three Horseshoes

69 The Street, NR23 1NL (2 miles SE of Wells)
⏲ 12-2.30 (3 Sat), 6-11 ☎ (01328) 710547
🌐 warhamhorseshoes.co.uk
Woodforde's Wherry [G]**; guest beers** [H]
A real pub in every sense of the word, with the perfect atmosphere for a quiet drink and conversation. The interior comprises three connected rooms that are filled with a fascinating

collection of antiques and pictures, including the traditional game of Norfolk twister. In winter months customers can warm themselves by a log fire in the main bar. The beer garden provides a quiet haven in the summer. The pub is renowned for good traditional cooking, featuring soups, pies and puddings. Q

Wells-next-the-Sea

Albatros

The Quay, NR23 1AT

12-11 (10.30 Sun) ☎ 07979 087228 albatros.eu.com

Woodforde's Wherry, Sundew G**, Nelson's Revenge** H**; guest beers** G

Possibly one of the Guide's most unusual entries, the Albatros is a Dutch North Sea clipper that is moored on the quayside of Wells harbour. The bar is in the hold of the 19th-century vessel and is adorned with nautical memorabilia, including many shipping maps. It sells up to four Woodforde's beers on gravity. Dutch pancakes are a speciality, and live bands perform each Friday and Saturday night, as well as Sunday afternoons in high season. Q (2,3)

Crown Hotel

The Buttlands, NR23 1EX

12-11 (10.30 Sun) ☎ (01328) 710209

thecrownhotelwells.co.uk

Jo C's Norfolk Kiwi, Bitter Old Bustard; Woodforde's Wherry H

A former coaching inn whose interior has been much modernised, overlooking the picturesque Buttlands Green. Inside are a bar and two restaurants, one of which looks out onto the rear garden. Despite the light, airy, modern feel, a sense of history remains about the place, and old photographs of the hotel are all around the bar. There are usually up to two beers from local East Barsham-based Jo C's brewery, plus up to two rotating guest ales. (2,3)

West Acre

Stag

Low Road, PE32 1TR

closed Mon; 12-3, 6.30 (5 Fri)-11 ☎ (01760) 755395

westacrestag.co.uk

Beer range varies H

The pub is a strong supporter of local ales and maintains a high standard; it serves three varying beers and also hosts excellent beer festivals. The Stag is at the east end of picturesque West Acre, popular with walkers, cyclists and riders. The restaurant offers a wide choice of freshly prepared food. There is a monthly quiz on Sunday nights. Q P

West Runton

Village Inn

Water Lane, NR27 9QP

12-11 ☎ (01263) 838000 villageinnwestrunton.co.uk

Adnams Southwold Bitter, Ghost Ship; Grain Oak; Lacons Affinity; Wolf Golden Jackal H

A large pub a short distance from the station and beach, set in pleasant gardens in the centre of this quiet coastal village. Up to six well-kept and mostly local ales are stocked. Excellent home-cooked meals can be enjoyed in the dining areas or outside in the spacious gardens. In the 1970s rock bands such as Deep Purple played secret gigs at the Pavilion which was at the rear of the pub (sadly now demolished). (3)

Wicklewood

Cherry Tree

116 High Street, NR18 9QA

5 (3 Fri)-11; 12-11 Sat & Sun ☎ (01953) 606962

wicklewoodcherrytree.co.uk

Buffy's Norwegian Blue, Bitter, Polly's Folly, Ale H

Buffy's tied house, with all the beers originating from the brewery. The pub is divided into three: the bar, a lounge separated from the bar by a fireplace, and a dining room. The bar counter is formed from naturally curved planks of solid oak, so take care when putting down your glass. Home-cooked food is served at all sessions, and features a range of pies with imaginative fillings. A quiz night is held on the first Wednesday of the month. P

Wreningham

Bird In Hand

Church Road, NR16 1BJ (on B1113)

11.45-11; 12-11 Sun ☎ (01508) 489438

birdinhandwreningham.com

Woodforde's Wherry; guest beers H

The original bar of this roadside pub has been converted into the Victorian Dining Room, and large extensions have been made to the side and rear of the building to make this a spacious, if somewhat food-oriented, pub. There is a drinking area adorned with interesting old photos depicting scenes of local village life. Occasional quiz nights are held. Access to the pub is via the car park to the rear of the building. P

Wymondham

Feathers Inn

13 Town Green, NR18 0PN

11-2.30, 7-11; 11-2.30, 6-midnight Fri & Sat; 12-2.30, 9-11 Sun ☎ (01953) 605675

Adnams Southwold Bitter; Fuller's London Pride; Greene King Abbot; guest beers H

The 18th-century Feathers is an excellent example of a community town local. It has a cosy bar with many separate drinking areas. Alcoves and walls are adorned with posters, pictures and memorabilia, including an old bike. There is a large patio garden at the rear with a smoking shelter. Reasonably priced food is available lunchtimes and evenings. Folk evenings are hosted on the last Sunday of the month. The house beer is by Nethergate. (14,15)

Green Dragon

6 Church Street, NR18 0PH

12-11 (midnight Fri & Sat); 12-10.30 Sun

☎ (01953) 607907 greendragonnorfolk.co.uk

Beer range varies H

A remarkable box construction, half-timbered inn, formerly a medieval merchant's shop and converted in the 16th century. The interior has two bars and a snug that retain many of their original beamed timbers. The medieval carved figures in the mantelpiece serve to emphasise its history. A rotating range of four ales includes brews from Green Jack, Nethergate, Wolf and Humpty Dumpty, and quality food is on offer. A mix of locals and tourists creates a vibrant feel. Q (14,15)

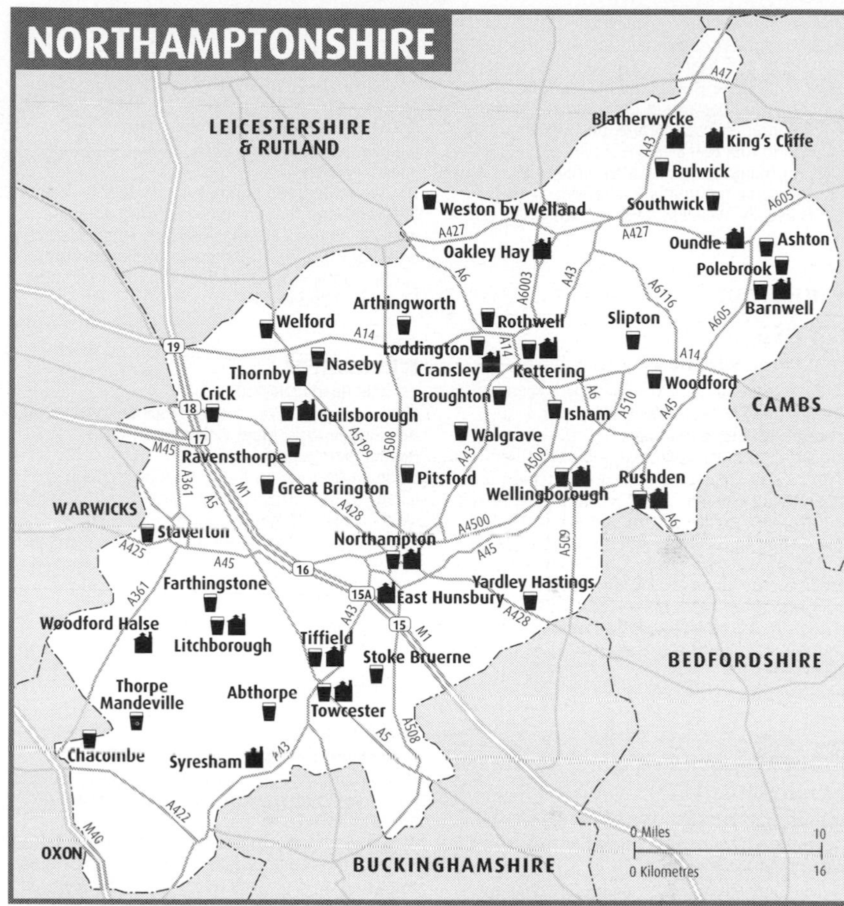

Abthorpe

New Inn

Silver Street, NN12 8QR

12-2.30 (not Mon & Tue), 6-11; 12-11.30 Fri & Sat; 12-10.30 Sun (01327) 857306 newinnabthorpe.co.uk

Hook Norton Hooky; guest beers

A tranquil country hostelry, hidden up a cul-de-sac off the corner of the village green. This mellow sandstone local with its inglenook fireplace and low-beamed ceilings is welcoming to all, offering high-quality meals cooked to order and served from the open kitchen, with much of the food locally sourced, including meat from the owner's farm. Hook Norton seasonal beers feature as guests. Q

Arthingworth

Bull's Head

Kelmarsh Road, LE16 8JZ (off A508)

12-3, 6-11; 12-11 Sat & Sun (01858) 525637 thebullsheadonline.co.uk

Thwaites Original; guest beers

This 19th-century former farmhouse is situated in rolling countryside. The pub has an opened-up bar with several cosy drinking areas and a restaurant to the front serving home-cooked fresh food from local producers. Ideal for ramblers and cyclists, this is a good place to finish a walk in the local area, or stay over in one of the annexe rooms. A beer festival is held over the August bank holiday on the suntrap patio. Three regular guest ales are kept, sparklers removed on request.

Q

Ashton

Chequered Skipper

The Green, PE8 5LD

11.30-3, 6-11.30; 11.30-11 Sat & Sun (01832) 273494 chequeredskipper.co.uk

Brewster's Hophead; guest beers

The centrepiece of the Rothschild's model village of Ashton, this thatched stone-built pub was rearranged internally in 1997 following a fire. There have been recent extensions to the side adding a coffee bar and a large function room. Regular events include at least two beer festivals each year. Up to four real ales are on offer including regularly changing guest beers from local microbrewers. Q (C24)

Barnwell

Montagu Arms

PE8 5PH

12-3 (not Mon), 6-11; 12-11 Sat; 12-10.30 Sun (01832) 273726

Adnams Southwold Bitter; guest beers Ⓗ
Sixteenth-century stone-built inn with a public bar at the front and a large restaurant and car parking to the rear. There is disabled access to the dining room only. The bar area is busy and attractive with large original exposed beams on the ceiling and walls. Up to four real ales are served via handpump including many from local microbreweries. A large play and camping area is to the rear. A Digfield beer is usually available. Q❀◑♿▲♣●P🚌(24)🐾

Broughton

Red Lion Ⓛ

7 High Street, NN14 1NF (off A43)
12-2.30 (not Mon), 5-11; 12-midnight Fri & Sat; 12-11 Sun ☎ (01536) 790239 🌐 redlionbroughton.co.uk
St Austell Tribute; guest beers Ⓗ
Large 18th-century ironstone pub with three main rooms: a bar, lounge and open-plan dining area. Six changing ales are on offer and there are two beer festivals a year. On the bar are two totem poles listing forthcoming beers. The landlady is a fan of dark ales and ensures that a mild, porter or stout is on the bar to accompany the home-cooked, locally-produced food. Many social events are hosted. The community-focused pub was local CAMRA Rural Pub of the Year 2013.
Q❀◑♿♣●P🚌(39)🐾

Bulwick

Queen's Head Ⓛ

Main Street, NN17 3DY
closed Mon; 12-3, 6-11; 12-7 Sun ☎ (01780) 450272
🌐 thequeensheadbulwick.co.uk
Digfield Barnwell Bitter; Oakham JHB; Shepherd Neame Spitfire; guest beers Ⓗ
Seventeenth-century stone pub with a Collyweston slate roof on the main street opposite the church. Inside, it has low ceilings, exposed beams and a single bar with five handpumps serving a range of ever-changing beers, often from local micros. There are three separate rooms for diners and a patio with a leafy pagoda outside. The high-quality locally-sourced food is thoroughly recommended (booking advisable). Winner of CAMRA local branch Pub of the Year 2013. Q❀◑♣●P🐾📶

Chacombe

George & Dragon

1 Silver Street, OX17 2JR (1 mile from M40 jct 11)
12-11 (10 Sun) ☎ (01295) 711500
🌐 georgeanddragon.org
Everards Tiger, Original; guest beer Ⓗ
This 17th-century stone-built pub is situated in front of the village green. Full of character, there are oak beams aplenty and a brass bar with one end dominated by a glass-topped 26ft well. The interior comprises one small area for drinkers and three for diners. Outside, there is a pleasant patio where Aunt Sally is played in summer. Folk music features on the last Friday of the month. Winner of Northamptonshire Food & Drink Award Rural Community Pub of the Year 2013/14.
Q🐴❀◑♿●P🚌(500)🐾📶

Crick

Royal Oak

22 Church Street, NN6 7TP (200yds from A428 past church)
4-11 (10 Sun & Mon) ☎ (01788) 822340
Oakham Jeffrey Hudson Bitter, Bishops Farewell; guest beers Ⓗ
The wood-beamed pub has a cosy feel with open fires warming the two main drinking areas. An ever-changing beer range features 10 guests every week. Skittles, darts and pool are played in the games room. A separate function room can be booked. Q🐴❀♣P🚌

Wheatsheaf Ⓛ

15 Main Road, NN6 7TU
12-midnight (1am Fri & Sat); 12-11 Sun ☎ (01788) 823824
Dow Bridge Acris; Nene Valley Bitter; Wells Bombardier; guest beer Ⓗ
Large corner pub on the main road through the village. It has a main lounge bar at the front with a smaller bar with games at the rear. A large restaurant is available for functions. The landlord organises regular themed nights with menus to match. Four beers are always available at this community local. The owners have recently opened up rooms for B&B. 🐴❀🛏◑♣P🚌

Farthingstone

King's Arms

Main Street, NN12 8EZ (opp church)
closed Mon; 7-11; 6.30-midnight Fri; 12-4, 7-11 Sat; 12-4, 8.45-11 Sun ☎ (01327) 361604 🌐 farthingstone.org.uk
Beer range varies Ⓗ
A quintessentially English 18th-century free house in delightful countryside in the heart of the county. The listed building with its inglenook fireplace and warming log fires has a unique and fascinating secret garden. A separate games room has Northants skittles. The pub is a retail outlet for fine cheeses and Cornish fish. Lunchtime food is served only at weekends, although speciality food evenings with entertainment are held monthly. The garden is beautiful in summer.
Q🐴❀◑♿♣P🚌🐾📶

INDEPENDENT BREWERIES

Brigstock Kettering
Copper Kettle Rushden
Digfield Barnwell
Frog Island Northampton
Great Oakley Tiffield
Gun Dog Woodford Halse
Hart Family Wellingborough
Hunsbury Craft East Hunsbury
Julian Church Cransley
King's Cliffe King's Cliffe (NEW)
Latimer Oakley Hay
Merrimen Litchborough (NEW)
Nene Valley Oundle
Nobby's Guilsborough
Phipps Northampton
Potbelly Kettering
Rockingham Blatherwycke
Silverstone Syresham
Tom Smith Oakley Hay
Towcester Mill Towcester (NEW)
Whistling Kite Kettering

Great Brington

Althorp Coaching Inn (Fox & Hounds) 𝕃

Main Street, NN7 4JA
☼ 11-11.45; 12-10.30 Sun ☎ (01604) 770651
🌐 althorp-coaching-inn.co.uk
Fuller's London Pride; Greene King IPA; Hook Norton Old Hooky; St Austell Tribute; guest beers Ⓗ
Lovely thatched country pub dating back to 1765 close to Althorp House, home of the Spencer family. The interior features flagstone floors and a lounge with a large inglenook fireplace and oak beams, while outside there is a courtyard, barn and enclosed garden. Excellent food is served in the bar and separate restaurant. A beer festival is held in August. Up to four guest ales are available. Q❀🛏◐◑♣●P🚌(G1)🐾📶

Guilsborough

Ward Arms 𝕃

High Street, NN6 8PY
☼ 12-2 (not Mon & Tue), 5-11; 12-midnight Fri & Sat; 12-10 Sun ☎ (01604) 740265
Nobby's Best, Guilsborough Gold; guest beers Ⓗ
This 17th-century whitewashed pub, built from local ironstone with a thatched roof, is situated at the heart of a historic rural village. Downstairs is the lounge and restaurant, while the upper reaches contain the main bar. The stable has incorporated Nobby's Brewery and visitor centre, and Nobby's beers including seasonals feature heavily on the bar. Traditional home-cooked food is locally sourced. Live music is hosted on the last Saturday of the month. Northants skittles and pool are played. Q🐴❀◐◑♣P🚌(60)🐾📶

Isham

Lilacs

39 Church Street, NN14 1HD (off A509 at church)
☼ 12-midnight ☎ (01536) 723948
Greene King 1799; H&H Olde Trip; guest beers Ⓗ
Named after a breed of rabbit - despite the new pub sign depicting flowers - this hard-to-find village pub is at the heart of the community, popular with locals, diners and drinkers alike. it has a lounge and a cosy snug to the front, complemented by a large games room towards the rear with two pool tables, darts and Northants skittles. Quiz and live music nights are held regularly. The guest beers are from the Greene King guest list. Q🐴❀◐◑♣P🚌(X4)🐾📶

Kettering

Alexandra Arms 𝕃

39 Victoria Street, NN16 0BU
☼ 12-11.30 (midnight Fri & Sat); 12-11 Sun
☎ (01536) 522730
Beer range varies Ⓗ
Traditional town-centre street-corner local where you will always find a beer from an unknown brewery. The landlord takes great pride in searching out new beers and breweries, with over 8,000 different beers from over 800 breweries served over an 11-year period on the 14 handpumps. Two opened-out rooms contain a piano and settee, while the rear bar has a TV and Northants skittles. The outdoor patio area to the rear features an aviary. Q❀♣●🚌🐾

Cherry Tree 𝕃

Sheep Street, NN16 0AN (opp church)
☼ 12-midnight (1am Fri & Sat) ☎ (01536) 514706
Hop Back Summer Lightning; Potbelly Best, Bellowhead Hedonism; Wells Bombardier; guest beers Ⓗ
The oldest pub in town, this low-ceilinged building has the feel of a traditional village local. The interior was opened out a few years ago and is served by a central L-shaped bar. The focus is now on live music, with rock bands on Friday and Saturday and jam sessions on other nights. The music starts from 9.30pm and the volume is loud. Guest ales always include an Oakham beer. Happy hour is 4-6pm, with 30p off a pint. ♿⇌●🚌🐾

Three Cocks 𝕃

48 Lower Street, NN16 8DJ
☼ 12-11.30 (11 Sun) ☎ 07909 698798
Mighty Oak Maldon Gold, Kings; guest beers Ⓗ
A pleasant edge-of-town pub with an L-shaped servery at the centre serving two main bar areas, furnished with comfortable armchairs and high-backed stools. On an upper level is a games area featuring Northants skittles and darts, and a shove-ha'penny board is available. Well-filled cobs are on offer for the peckish. Four beer festivals are held in the rear function room over the solstice and equinox weekends. Q◐◑♿♣●🚌🐾

Litchborough

Old Red Lion 𝕃

4 Banbury Road, NN12 8JF (opp church)
☼ 12-11 (10.30 Sun) ☎ (01327) 830064
🌐 oldredlionlitchborough.co.uk
Great Oakley Wagtail; Hopping Mad Brainstorm; Phipps Red Star; guest beers Ⓗ
A traditional stone-built village pub worth seeking out. The bar area has flagstone flooring and a large inglenook with seating inside. A small passage leads to two further cosy rooms. Recently extended, a barn has been converted into a restaurant and it has a shop selling local farm produce. A wide range of locally brewed bottled beers is stocked, with Merrimen Brewery a short distance away. Near to the Knightly Way footpath, the pub is popular with walkers and cyclists. Q🐴❀◐◑♿P🚌🐾📶

Loddington

Hare at Loddington 𝕃

5 Main Street, NN14 1LA
☼ 12-3, 5.30-11; 12-midnight Sat & Sun ☎ (01536) 710337
🌐 thehareatloddington.com
Greene King Abbot; Sharp's Doom Bar; Wells Bombardier; guest beer Ⓗ
Set in a conservation area, the Hare is a listed building in this picturesque village built from local ironstone. It stands in the middle of Main Street surrounded by listed houses. Formerly the Chequered Flag, the pub has been refurbished by the new owner. Now more open plan, it still comprises four areas – one is a dining space where good home-cooked food made with local produce is served. The guest beer is often from Julian Church or Langton. Q🐴❀◐◑♿●P🐾📶

Naseby

Royal Oak

Church Street, NN6 6DA (on B4036)
⌚ 4 (12 Sat)-11; 12-7 Sun ☎ (01604) 743310
Oakham Bishops Farewell; Sharp's Doom Bar; guest beers [H]
A rural village pub close to the Naseby battlefield, scene of the first English Civil War in 1645. The L-shaped single room is divided into three areas, with a real fire in the wall between the main bar and games room. Northants skittles and darts are played. Two guest ales are served, often including one from Oakham Ales. Q♘❀▲♣P🚌🐾📶

Northampton

Cordwainer

The Ridings, NN1 2AQ
⌚ 8am-midnight (1am Thu; 3am Fri & Sat)
☎ (01604) 609000
Greene King Abbot; Ruddles Best Bitter; guest beers [H]
Large, popular Wetherspoon Lloyds No.1 town-centre pub on two levels. A choice of five different real ales is always available, along with three real ciders. The upper floor can be hired for private functions. There is a large, paved outdoor drinking area to the rear. DJs play Thursday, Friday and Saturday evenings. Two annual beer festivals are held. ♘❀◐♿●🚌🐾📶

Lamplighter 🏆 [L]

66 Overstone Road, The Mounts, NN1 3JS
⌚ 12-midnight (1am Fri & Sat); 12-11 Sun
☎ (01604) 631125 🌐 thelamplighter.co.uk
Phipps IPA; Vale Pale Ale; guest beers [H]
A delightful, traditional, street-corner pub just off the town centre. Five changing guest beers are from established micros, along with a selection of bottled beers. Home-cooked food is served until 9pm (7pm weekends) and children are welcome during meal times. There is a roaring fire in the bar and a courtyard outside, heated in colder weather. The pub hosts open mic and quiz nights, a disco on Friday and live music on Saturday. Local CAMRA Pub of the Year 2013. ♘❀◐♿♣🚌

Malt Shovel Tavern [L]

121 Bridge Street, NN1 1QF
⌚ 11.30-3, 5-11; 11.30-11 Fri & Sat; 12-10.30 Sun
☎ (01604) 234212 🌐 maltshoveltavern.com
Elgood's Black Dog; Hook Norton Lion; Nobby's Best, T'owd Navigation; Oakham Bishops Farewell; Phipps IPA; guest beers [H]
This popular pub has won many awards over the years including local CAMRA Pub of the Year on numerous occasions. Thirteen beers including five guests are available alongside real cider, LocAle, Belgian draught and bottled beers. Two beer festivals are held each year on bank holidays, with live bands. Blues bands play on Wednesday nights. The pub has a strong rugby following. Home-made lunches are served Monday to Saturday.
❀◖♿⇌♣●🚌

Moon on the Square

6 The Parade, NN1 2EA (on Market Square)
⌚ 8am-11 (midnight Thu; 1am Fri & Sat) ☎ (01604) 634062
Adnams Broadside; Batemans XXXB; Greene King Abbot; guest beers [H]
Opposite the largest historic marketplace in the country, this pub conversion from 1996 is two-tiered, with a quiet conservatory area to the rear. It offers a good selection of ales and ciders, and holds two beer festivals a year. Food is served all day, every day. There are TV screens with the volume turned down. Busy at weekends. ♘◐♿●🚌

Olde England [L]

199 Kettering Road, The Mounts, NN1 4BP
⌚ 12-midnight (11 Mon); 12-11 Sun ☎ 07742 069768
🌐 theoldeengland.com
Great Oakley Wagtail [G]**, Wot's Occurring; Potbelly Bellowhead Hedonism; St Austell Trelawny; Vale Gravitas; guest beers** [H]
An end-of-terrace Victorian building converted into a welcoming pub on three floors. The ground and first floors have a medieval theme and solid fuel burners. The cellar bar is contemporary in style and more intimate. Over 20 beers from local micros and regional breweries are served by gravity and handpump as well as 20 ciders. Various board games, cards and dominoes are provided. Quiz night is Wednesday, live folk music is Thursday. No food Sunday. The racecourse car park is nearby.
Q♘◐♣●🚌🐾📶

Queen Adelaide [L]

50 Manor Road, Kingsthorpe, NN2 6QJ (off A5199)
⌚ 11-11.30; 12-10.30 Sun ☎ (01604) 714524
🌐 queenadelaide.com
Adnams Southwold Bitter, Broadside; Elgood's Black Dog; Moorhouse's Pride of Pendle; Nobby's Guilsborough Guzzler; St Austell Tribute; guest beers [H]
This well-established pub in Kingsthorpe village was voted local CAMRA Pub of the Year in 2012. An 18th-century stone-built listed local, it has low beams and an uneven floor in the main bar, a small snug furnished with leather sofas, and a further lounge bar to the rear. A friendly pub, it is popular with rugby followers. The Sunday roasts are exceptional (booking advised). Up to four guest beers are often from local microbreweries. A beer festival is held in early September.
♘❀◐♿♣●P🚌📶

Road to Morocco [L]

Bridgwater Drive, Abington Vale, NN3 3AG
⌚ 12-11 (midnight Fri & Sat); 12-10.30 Sun
☎ (01604) 632899
Greene King IPA, Abbot; Theakston Old Peculier; guest beers [H]
A 1960s brick-built estate pub, it has two connected but distinctly different rooms. The bar area is quite lively, particularly if there is a sporting event on TV, and is home to darts and pool. The homely lounge is the quieter area of the pub. Quiz night is Tuesday. ♘❀♿♣●P🚌(5)🐾📶

Wheatsheaf [L]

126 Dallington Road, Dallington, NN5 7HN
⌚ 11.30-11 (11.30 Fri & Sat); 12-10.30 Sun
☎ (01604) 758871
Everards Sunchaser Blonde, Tiger; guest beers [H]
An attractive stone and thatched two-roomed pub with an unspoilt frontage tucked away in the conservation area of Dallington opposite the 13th-century village church. The bar room has a partly flagstoned floor and hosts live music on Saturday nights, open mic on alternate Sundays. The lounge/dining room is a large, quiet area. A veterans' lunch is served on Tuesdays. Up to four guest ales and two real cider are available.
♘❀◐♿♣●P🚌(7)🐾

Wig & Pen

19 St Giles Street, NN1 1JA
10 (11 Sat)-11; 12-10.30 Sun ☎ (01604) 622178
thewigandpennorthampton.com
Adnams Ghost Ship; Elgood's Black Dog; Fuller's London Pride; Greene King IPA; guest beers H
A 300-year-old town-centre pub near the town hall. A long L-shaped bar counter serves up to nine guest ales, cider and a wide range of bottled beers. There is a new retractable cover providing shelter in the garden, where jazz bands play on Tuesday nights and live bands on Sunday afternoons. Good home-cooked food features locally-sourced ingredients. Local CAMRA Pub of the Year 2012, it offers 10 per cent discount on ales to CAMRA members.

Pitsford

Griffin

25 High Street, NN6 9AD (off A508)
6-11; 5-midnight Fri; 6-midnight Sat; 12-2.30, 7-11 Sun
☎ (01604) 880346 griffinpitsford.co.uk
Greene King Abbot; Morland Old Speckled Hen; Potbelly Best; guest beer H
Formerly cottages, this Grade II-listed 17th-century ironstone pub is family run and owned. The charming pub has retained most of its original character and is festooned with fascinating artefacts in both the cosy bar room and larger comfortable lounges to the rear. The guest beer is often from Potbelly. Sunday is quiz night. Ideally situated for Pitsford Reservoir and Brixworth Country Park. QP

Polebrook

King's Arms

Kings Arms Lane, PE8 5LW
12-3, 6-11; 12-11 Sat & Sun ☎ (01832) 272363
thekingsarms-polebrook.co.uk
Digfield Barnwell Bitter; guest beers H
Situated in the centre of the village, this traditional stone-built thatched inn has a main bar, three areas for diners and a small garden. Five real ales are on offer at weekends including two from the nearby Digfield Brewery. Third-of-a-pint glasses are available to allow customers to try a wider variety of beer. There is an annual themed beer festival in mid-September and regular food and beer pairing evenings. Beers from Adnams are usually available. QP(25)

Ravensthorpe

Chequers

Church Lane, NN6 8ER (off A428, opp church)
12-3, 6-midnight; 12-midnight Sat & Sun
☎ (01604) 770379 chequersravensthorpe.co.uk
Oakham Bishops Farewell; Sharp's Doom Bar; Thwaites Original; guest beer H
The hosts have enjoyed more than 23 years at this friendly pub, popular with locals, walkers and fishermen alike. The brick-built Grade II-listed free house has an L-shaped bar and a restaurant serving excellent home-cooked food. Outside is a children's adventure play area and a separate building for Northants skittles. P

Rothwell

Rowell Charter Inn

Sun Hill, NN14 6AB
12-11 (10.30 Sun) ☎ (01536) 710453
Fuller's London Pride; Sharp's Doom Bar; guest beers H
Dating from 1642 and built from Northants ironstone, rooms have been added to the building in a piecemeal fashion, resulting in different levels with low door lintels and ceilings. The name commemorates the granting of the Charter by King John in 1204 to hold a market and fair in the town each year. Before the annual beer festival the Bailiff of Rothwell rides out and reads a proclamation. Seven beers and two ciders prove popular. QP(18,19)

Woolpack

Market Hill, NN14 6BW
2-10 (1am Fri & Sat) ☎ (01536) 710284
Phipps IPA; Potbelly Beijing Black; guest beers H
Seventeenth-century ironstone pub with three low beamed open-plan rooms – a games room with a pool table, an L-shaped bar and a lounge to the rear. This inn was believed to have been the place where wool was sold on the medieval market since the granting of the 1204 Charter. One of the guest beers is from Potbelly – either Hedonism or Pigs Do Fly. QP(18,19)

Rushden

Rushden Historical Transport Society

Station Approach, NN10 0AW (on ring road)
6 (7.30 Mon & Tue)-11; 4.30-11 Fri; 12-11 Sat & Sun
☎ (01933) 318988 rhts.co.uk
Phipps IPA; Oakham Bishops Farewell; guest beers H
Former Midland Railway station serving seven real ales including a dark beer. Not to be missed, the bar occupies the gas-lit former ladies' waiting room, with walls adorned with enamel advertising panels and railway photos plus many CAMRA awards. On the platform, carriages provide a meeting room, Northants skittles and a buffet. Numerous open days are held in the summer, with steam and diesel train trips. A beer festival is hosted in September. Day membership is £1 except on open days. Q(X46,M50)

Slipton

Samuel Pepys

Slipton Lane, NN14 3AR
12-3, 5-11; 12-11 Sat; 12-7 (10 summer) Sun
☎ (01832) 731739 samuel-pepys.com
Digfield Fools Nook; Greene King IPA H**; guest beers** H/G
Set in a picturesque thatched village, this lovely 16th-century ironstone pub has a low-beamed and brick-floored traditional bar to the front where locals and visitors can chat or relax in cosy armchairs in front of a real fire. The stone-built dining/lounge bar and conservatory restaurant are decorated and furnished in a smart modern style. Three guest beers often come from local micros, with Nene Valley always featured, and in summer a real cider is also available. No food Sunday evening. QP

Southwick

Shuckburgh Arms L

Main Street, PE8 5BL
4 (12 Fri & Sat)-11; 10-11 Sun ☎ (01832) 272044
shuckburghpub.co.uk
Brewster's Hophead; Nene Valley Bitter H/G; guest beers H
Adjacent to the village hall and cricket pitch, this stone-built thatched pub has a front bar and side room. Outside there is a covered patio area with a bar. The large enclosed garden at the rear is the venue for the World Conker Championships in October. A three-day music festival is held in July and the pub cricket team plays throughout the summer. The main bar has five handpumps selling regular brews from Elgood's and Oakham plus local microbrewery guests. Q P (C24)

Staverton

Countryman L

Daventry Road, NN11 6JH (on A425 just outside village)
12-3, 6-11; 12-10 Sun ☎ (01327) 311815
thecountrymanstaverton.co.uk
Beer range varies H
The last remaining of three pubs in this lovely village. The L-shaped bar, with wood beams throughout, serves four areas, some set aside for diners, and an open hearth fire between the spaces provides some seclusion. The enthusiastic landlord offers a wide choice of reasonably priced food, sourced locally whenever possible. The three changing guest beers are listed on the website and include a locally brewed beer. Q P (66)

Stoke Bruerne

Boat Inn

Shutlanger Road, NN12 7SB
9.30am-11 (10.30 Sun) ☎ (01604) 862428
boatinn.co.uk
Jennings Cumberland Ale; Marston's EPA, Old Empire; Ringwood Best Bitter; Wychwood Hobgoblin H
Family-owned since 1877, this long narrow pub is situated on the banks of the Grand Union Canal opposite the National Canal Museum and next to the locks. The delightful tap bar's interconnecting rooms have canal views, open fires, original stone floors and window seats, while an adjoining room has Northants skittles. Popular with diners, the lounge, restaurant and bistro are in a large extension. A canal boat is available for parties to hire. The cider is Thatchers Heritage.
Q P (86)

Thornby

Red Lion L

Welford Road, NN6 8SJ (on A5199)
5-9 Mon; 12-2, 5-11; 12-10.30 Sun ☎ (01604) 740238
redlionthornby.co.uk
Beer range varies H
An impressive whitewashed village pub situated on the old A50 dating back more than 400 years. The compact bar has two drinking areas with a wood-burning open fire in the lounge. To the rear is the restaurant, which occupies two linked rooms, one heavily beamed. Four guest beers are usually from local breweries including Oakham and Dowbridge. A beer festival is held in late July/ August. Q P

Thorpe Mandeville

Three Conies L

Banbury Lane, OX17 2EX
10-11; 11-10 Sun ☎ (01295) 711025
threeconiesinn.co.uk
Hook Norton Hooky Mild, Hooky, Old Hooky H
Located on the edge of the village, the building dates back to the 18th century when it was a drovers' inn. Today this ironstone pub is noted for its meals, available throughout the day, with breakfast from 10am. The beamed interior has open fires at both ends of the bar. The pub hosts an annual beer festival and a cider festival, and is home to a Northants Skittles team. The large garden is ideal for families. Q P

Tiffield

George L

21 High Street North, NN12 8AD
12-3 Mon; 7-11 Tue; 12-3, 6-11; 12-11 Sat; 12-7 Sun
☎ (01327) 350527 thegeorgeattiffield.co.uk
Great Oakley Wot's Occurring; Vale Pale Ale; guest beers H
A true community pub involved in many village activities, dating from the 16th century with Victorian and more modern additions. It has a cosy bar, games room with Northants skittles and back room restaurant which can also be booked for small functions. Three changing guest beers include one from Great Oakley, who brew close to the village. Live music features on Wednesday night. Two annual beer festivals are hosted. Northamptonshire Food & Drink Awards 2012/13 Rural Community Pub of the Year.
Q P

Towcester

Plough L

96 Watling Street, NN12 6BT
11-midnight (10.30 Sun) ☎ (01327) 350738
theploughinn.biz
Wells Bombardier; Young's Bitter; guest beers H
Situated in the centre of this racecourse town, the Plough features a cosy front bar with stone floors and a large bay window overlooking the main street, and a larger lounge bar/restaurant to the rear. A wide corridor runs from the front to the back of the pub, and outside is a small drinking area. Two constantly changing guest beers are available. No food on Monday. Q

Walgrave

Royal Oak

Zion Hill, NN6 9PN (off A43)
11.30-2.30, 5.30-11; 12-10.30 Sun ☎ (01604) 781248
royaloakatwalgrave.co.uk
Adnams Southwold Bitter; Greene King Abbot; guest beers H
A mid-19th-century ironstone pub set back from the main road. The low-beamed front bar is semi-open plan with a drinking area to the left of the bar, dining spaces either side and a stone inglenook fireplace. To the rear is a small bar, cosy lounge and a function area. Outside there is a room for Northants skittles and children's play equipment in the garden. Three changing guest beers are available. Q P

Welford

Wharf Inn 𝕃

NN6 6JQ (on A5199 by canal basin)
12-11 ☎ (01858) 575075 wharfinn.co.uk
Marston's Pedigree; guest beers Ⓗ
Located on the Leicestershire border, this red-brick inn is at the start of several walks – ask the landlord for a leaflet. The pub is popular with narrowboaters, walkers and locals alike. Inside is a small bottom bar, while up a couple of steps is the main bar, with an inglenook separating the drinking area from the restaurant. Six handpulls offer an Oakham beer and others from established micros. Food is served all day at the weekend. **QP**

Wellingborough

Coach & Horses 𝕃

17 Oxford Street, NN8 4HY (800 yards from Market Square)
12-11 (11.30 Fri & Sat); 12-6 Sun ☎ (01933) 441848
coachandhorseswellingborough.co.uk
Beer range varies Ⓗ
Town-centre local with an enthusiastic landlord fully committed to offering a constantly changing choice of 12 beers and 12 ciders, including two or more local ales. The single L-shaped room has cosy corners. Traditional home-cooked food is served (no food Sun eve, Mon or Tue), with pies the speciality. The pub quiz is every other Wednesday. A former CAMRA East Midlands Regional Pub of the Year runner-up. (X4,X46)

Golden Lion 𝕃

19 Sheep Street, NN8 1BN
11-11 (midnight Fri & Sat); 12-7 Sun ☎ (01933) 223206
thegoldenlionwellingborough.co.uk
Adnams Ghost Ship; guest beers Ⓗ
This magnificent Grade II-listed Tudor inn dates from 1540 and is one of the oldest buildings in the area. Many original features remain including The Hall —a restaurant/dining room with a vaulted ceiling, exposed beams and minstrels' gallery. There is also a comfortable lounge area warmed by open fires in winter, and outdoor seating for clement days. Service is always friendly, with up to seven guest beers available alongside a good seasonal menu lunchtimes and evenings.
Q

Locomotive 𝕃

Finedon Road, NN8 4AL
11-11; 12-10 Sun ☎ (01933) 276600
Sharp's Doom Bar; guest beers Ⓗ
A popular locals' pub on the outskirts of the town featuring an extensive collection of railway memorabilia including a display of classic 00-gauge locomotives behind the bar and a model railway running above the servery. There are three rooms – the front bar has armchairs, sofas and a piano, while the games area features bar billiards, darts and Northants skittles. A large selection of beers is served including three from Julian Church and others from micros. **QP** (45)

Old Grammarians 𝕃

46 Oxford Street, NN8 4JH (opp Morrisons car park)
12-11 (11.30 Fri); 11.30-11 Sat; 12-10.30 Sun
☎ (01933) 226188 wellingborough-ogs.org
Courage Directors; Oakham JHB; Young's Bitter; guest beers Ⓗ
Established in 1934 as a rugby club, this is now a flourishing sports and social club with over 2,000 members. The headquarters is located close to Wellingborough town centre, with a large main bar, spacious function room and sports bar featuring Sky Sports on a large plasma screen. The club hosts several events each month, including fun quiz nights, bingo and live artists. Happy hour is 6.30-7.30pm. Non-members must be signed in.
P (X4,X46)

Weston by Welland

Wheel & Compass

Valley Road, LE16 8HZ
12-11 ☎ (01858) 565864 thewheelandcompass.co.uk
Greene King Abbot; Marston's Burton Bitter, Pedigree; St Austell Tribute; Sharp's Doom Bar; guest beer Ⓗ
A rural pub in the picturesque Welland Valley with a cosy bar/lounge and a large extended dining room. An outside drinking area offers good views and is an ideal play space for children. The pub is a good stop-off for walkers on the Jurassic Way which runs close by. The Wheel & Compass is one of the five founding pubs hosting the Welland Valley Beerfest – now supported by 12 pubs – held annually in June. **QP** (67)

Woodford

Duke's Arms 𝕃

83 High Street, NN14 4HE (off A510)
12-11 ☎ (01832) 732224
Digfield Fools Nook; Greene King Abbot; Oakham JHB; guest beers Ⓗ
Originally a 17th-century manor, the pub was renamed in honour of the Duke of Wellington, who was a frequent visitor to the village. Overlooking the green, it has two main bars, plus a rear games room with 3D TV and an upstairs restaurant. Very much a community focused pub, it holds a Whitsun bank holiday beer festival and August bank holiday music festival, plus an open mic night on Thursday, disco and karaoke on Friday and acoustic session on Sunday night. Traditional pub food is available alongside pizza and chilli.
P (16)

Yardley Hastings

Rose & Crown 𝕃

4 Northampton Road, NN7 1EX
12 (5 Mon)-11; 12-10 Sun ☎ (01604) 696276
roseandcrownbistro.co.uk
Greene King IPA, Abbot; Phipps Diamond Ale; guest beers Ⓗ
A lovely ironstone pub extensively refurbished in the 1980s and now a single large room in olde-worlde style. It retains stone-flagged floors and beamed ceilings throughout, and has a small drinking area in the bay window. The emphasis is on traditional home cooking with a menu that changes daily. Regular live music events range from jazz to rock to blues. The house beer is from Hart Family. The landscaped gardens are wonderful in summer. Northamptonshire Food & Drink Award Food Pub of the Year 2013/14. **P** (41)

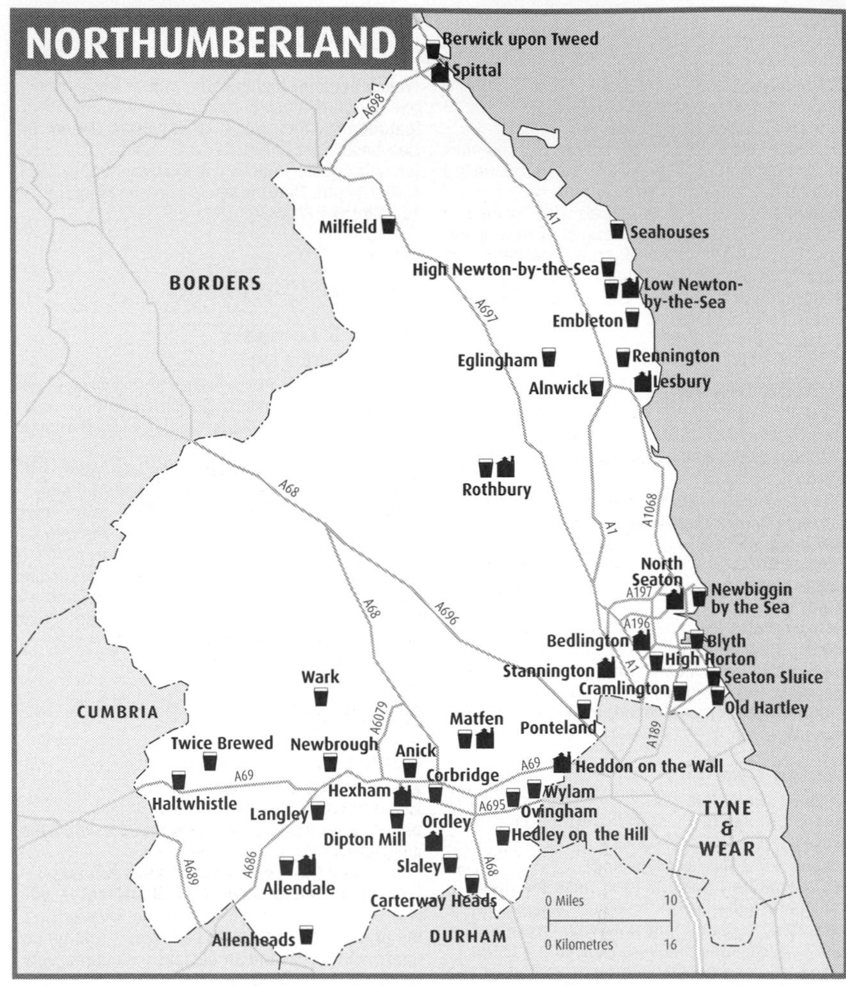

Allendale

Golden Lion Hotel L

Market Place, NE47 9BD

12-1.30am (1am Wed); 12-2.30am Fri-Sun

(01434) 683225 goldenlionhotel.net

Timothy Taylor Landlord; Wylam Gold Tankard; guest beers H

Friendly and hospitable pub in the centre of town, patronised by locals and tourists. The walls are adorned with photographs of the annual tar barrel procession, an experience in itself, and local landscapes. Allendale's local choir practises here on Tuesday evening, and live Irish music features on the last Wednesday of the month. Two regular beers and three guests are on handpump, including a choice of local ales. Good home-cooked food is served. (688)

King's Head

Market Place, NE47 9BD (opp Co-op)

12-11 (01434) 683681 thekingshead-allendale.co.uk

Jennings Cumberland Ale; guest beers H

A welcoming, upmarket inn situated in the main square of this small market town, next door to the Golden Lion. The area is renowned for countryside walks, and the pub is popular with locals, tourists, ramblers and day trippers. The refurbished bar retains original features including an open log fire. Traditional pub food is served all day. Bingo is hosted on Sunday evening. Allendale is easily accessible by rail and bus, and the town is well worth a visit. Q (688)

Allenheads

Allenheads Inn L

NE47 9HJ

INDEPENDENT BREWERIES

Acton North Seaton
Allendale Allendale
Anarchy Stannington
Bear Claw Spittal
Bondgate Hexham (NEW)
Coquetdale Rothbury
Hexhamshire Ordley
High House Farm Matfen
Northumberland Bedlington
Ship Inn Low Newton-by-the-Sea
VIP Lesbury
Wylam Heddon on the Wall

4 (12 Sat)-11; 12-10.30 Sun (01434) 685200
allenheadsinn.co.uk
Black Sheep Best Bitter; Mordue Northumbrian Blonde; guest beers H
Superb 18th-century rural inn with a public bar with log fire, games room and dining room. It is on the Coast-to-Coast cycle route and popular with cyclists, ramblers and tourists. Good bar meals are available at a decent price. Originally the home of Sir Thomas Wentworth, the premises are bedecked with memorabilia and knick-knacks from a bygone age. The pub will open early on request for coach parties and rambling groups.
P (688)

Alnwick

John Bull Inn

12 Howick Street, NE66 1UY
12-3 (not Mon-Fri), 7-11; 12-3, 7-10.30 Sun
(01665) 602055 john-bull-inn.co.uk
Beer range varies H
Many time local CAMRA Pub of the Year winner, this 180-year-old inn thrives on its reputation as a back-street ale house. The landlord offers a wide range of cask-conditioned ales at varying ABVs, real cider, the widest range of bottled Belgian beers in the county and over 120 single malt whiskies. Darts teams compete in the local league and the pub upholds the North East tradition of an annual leek show. There is a cheese competition on Saturday night. Q (505)

Tanners Arms

2-4 Hotspur Place, NE66 1QF
5-11 (midnight Fri & Sat); 5-10.30 Sun (01665) 602553
tannersarms.com
Beer range varies H
Ivy-covered stone-built inn just off Bondgate Without and a short distance from Alnwick Garden. The rustic-style single room has a tree beer shelf in the middle and a flagstone floor. Acoustic music nights are hosted regularly and open mic on the last Friday of the month. The ever-changing real ales frequently come from North Eastern and Scottish Borders microbreweries. (505)

Anick

Rat Inn

NE46 4LN (signed at Hexham A69 roundabout)
12-3, 6-11; 12-11 Sat; 12-10.30 Sun (01434) 602814
theratinn.com
Timothy Taylor Landlord; guest beers H
Superb 1750 country inn with spectacular views across Tyne Valley. The pub has a welcoming and friendly feel to it, with an open log fire and several chamber pots hanging from the ceiling. It has an excellent local reputation for good food prepared with locally-sourced ingredients and appears in several food guides. The first Thursday of the month is singers/poetry night. Bottled beers are stocked to complement the handpumped ales. Well worth the short taxi ride from Hexham rail station. Q P

Berwick upon Tweed

Barrels Ale House

59-61 Bridge Street, TD15 1ES (in old Berwick, at town end of original bridge)
12 (3 winter)-midnight (01289) 308013
Jarrow Rivet Catcher; guest beers H
There is an Old Curiosity Shop-ambience to this pub, located in the old part of Berwick next to the original road bridge over the Tweed. The excellent real ale no doubt helps customers brave the 'dentist's chair' at the side of the bar. A downstairs bar is used by DJs and bands at weekends. Outside is a unique open drinking area surrounded by high walls. A former winner of CAMRA Pub of the Year awards.

Pilot

31 Low Greens, TD15 1LZ
12 (11 Sat)-midnight; 12-11 Sun (01289) 304214
Caledonian Deuchars IPA; guest beers H
Well patronised by locals and sought out by train trippers who have heard about this gem. This stone-built end of terrace pub dates from the 19th century and has a regionally important historic interior. It retains the original small room layout and boasts several nautical artefacts over 100 years old. The pub runs a darts team and hosts music nights. The bar staff are welcoming and friendly.

Blyth

Olivers

60 Bridge Street, NE24 2AP
4 (12 Sun)-11 (01670) 368346
Anarchy Blonde Star; Caledonian Deuchars IPA; Morland Old Speckled Hen; Ruddles County H
This warm and friendly one-roomed hostelry was converted from a former newsagent's and is a welcome real ale outlet within a beer desert. Well supported by locals, it is close to the regenerated quayside. Complementary food is served on Saturday afternoons. Three real ales are available, one usually locally sourced. Bus 308 passes outside but the bus station for other services to Blyth is only a five-minute walk. (308)

Carterway Heads

Manor House Inn

DH8 9LX (on A68 S of Corbridge)
11 (12 Mon)-11; 11-11.30 Thu; 12-10.30 Sun
(01207) 255268 themanorhouseinn.com
Morland Old Speckled Hen; guest beers H
Warm and hospitable country inn with three open fires, situated just off the A68, 10 miles south of Corbridge. A glazed window in the bar wall allows customers to view the well-maintained cellar. Proper home-cooked food is on offer and is popular with both tourists and locals. Excellent accommodation is available. Derwent Reservoir is nearby. P

Corbridge

Angel Inn

Main Street, NE45 5LA
11 (12 Sun)-11 (01434) 632119
theangelofcorbridge.com
Cumberland Corby Ale; Hadrian Border Tyneside Blonde; guest beers H
Superb former 1726 coaching inn located on the main road with good transport links. Seven handpulls offer a range of ales and a wonderful selection of malt whiskies is also kept. Family-friendly with a reputation for good food, the pub is popular with tourists, ramblers and locals. A

separate lounge area has comfy leather seating and outside is a relaxed seating area. The town has strong links with the Romans and Hadrian's Wall is nearby. QP(10,685)

Dyvels Inn

Station Road, NE45 5AY (adjacent to Tynedale Rugby Club)

12-11 ☎ (01434) 633633

Beer range varies

Situated next to Corbridge station, this country pub is cosy in winter yet light and airy in summer. It has a public bar, a pool room to the rear leading to a secluded area outside, and a popular meeting room. Food is served throughout, but check availability first on Mondays January to March. Three letting rooms are an ideal base for exploring this lovely town and the many country walks on the doorstep. P(10,685)

Cramlington

Plough

Middle Farm Buildings, NE23 1DN

11-11 (midnight Fri & Sat); 12-11 Sun ☎ (01670) 737633

theploughcramlington.co.uk

Cullercoats Jack the Devil; Harviestoun Bitter & Twisted; guest beers

Converted farm buildings in the old village make up this Sir John Fitzgerald outlet, which is arranged in the style of a traditional pub with separate bar and lounge areas. Alongside the core range of local beers, an excellent range of ales from local microbreweries is on continual rotation, backed by a commitment to sourcing the best ales from across the UK. Under-18s are permitted in bar areas daytime only, and families are always welcome in the function room upstairs.

Q♣P

Dipton Mill

Dipton Mill Inn

Dipton Mill Road, NE46 1YA

12-2.30, 6-11; 12-3 Sun ☎ (01434) 606577

diptonmill.co.uk

Hexhamshire Devil's Elbow, Shire Bitter, Blackhall English Stout, Devil's Water, Whapweasel, Old Humbug

The tap for Hexhamshire Brewery, this small inn is run by a keen landlord who brews his own excellent beers – Blackhall English Stout has proved so popular it has ousted the Guinness. To complement the ales there is fine home-cooked food – Saturday is curry night. A cosy atmosphere and a warm welcome make this pub well worth seeking out. The large garden has a stream running through it and there is plenty of countryside to explore. QP

Eglingham

Tankerville Arms

15 The Village, NE66 2TX

6-11 Mon & Tue; 12-2, 6-midnight; 12-3, 6-11 Sun

☎ (01665) 578444 tankervillearms.com

Hadrian Border Tyneside Blonde, Farne Island Pale Ale; guest beer

Well-appointed, traditional country pub dating from 1851. The bar serves three locally sourced beers and has several framed pictures that enhance the surroundings. There is an excellent open-beam restaurant and a tranquil beer garden at the rear with superb rural views. The pub hosts meetings for the local golf and cricket clubs and is popular with tourists and ramblers – families are welcome. En-suite accommodation is available and River Breamish Caravan Club is nearby.

QP

Embleton

Greys Inn

Stanley Terrace, NE66 3UZ

12-11 (10.30 Sun) ☎ (01665) 576983

Beer range varies

Pleasant, traditional pub in a lovely seaside hamlet, just a short walk from a wonderful beach. It has three open fires and a framed 1904 grocery list hangs on the wall. The pub is an excellent venue to enjoy a bite to eat washed down with a locally sourced real ale, sitting outside on the superb patio in good weather. It is home to a ladies' darts team, clay pigeon club and golf club.

♣(501)

Haltwhistle

Black Bull

Black Bull Lane, Market Square, NE49 0BL (down a cobbled lane)

12-11 (midnight Fri & Sat); 12-10.30 Sun

☎ (01434) 320463

Caledonian Deuchars IPA; guest beers

Warm, welcoming, two-room pub close to Hadrian's Wall, located just off the marketplace down a cobbled lane. A low-beamed timber ceiling, open fire and horse brasses contribute to the traditional ambience. With six handpulls, the pub is popular with locals as well as ramblers. The friendly licensee treats customers as people not as a source of income. Regular themed nights are held. Ring to check winter hours – meal times can vary. Q(685)

Milecastle Inn

Military Road, NE49 9NN (on B6318 Military Road)

12-11 ☎ (01434) 321372 milecastle-inn.co.uk

Big Lamp Sunny Daze, Bitter, Prince Bishop Ale

This 1600s pub adjacent to Hadrian's Wall only sells ale from Newburn-based Big Lamp Brewery. Located a mile and a half north of Haltwhistle, the rural pub has a homely feel, attracting ramblers and tourists. Food is locally sourced and customers travel from as far as Newcastle and Carlisle. Two comfy holiday cottages are available. Check opening times from November to Easter. The Hadrian's Wall bus stops outside April-October.

QP(AD122)

Hedley on the Hill

Feathers

NE43 7SW

12 (6 Mon)-11; 12-10.30 Sun ☎ (01661) 843607

thefeathers.net

Beer range varies

Much-acclaimed country pub in a pleasant hamlet with superb views. It has a comfy feel with exposed stone walls and beams. Welcoming staff serve high-quality home-cooked food that complements the real ales (booking advised for Sunday lunch). The pub has won awards for food quality. Locally-sourced real ales are always

available. Folk night is the first Sunday of the month. A beer festival is held at Easter with an uphill barrel race on Easter Monday.
Q P

High Horton

Three Horse Shoes L

Hathery Lane, NE24 4HF (off A189 N of Cramlington, follow A192) NZ277793
11-11 (midnight Fri & Sat); 12-11 Sun (01670) 822410
threehorseshoes-horton.co.uk
Greene King Abbot; Tetley Bitter; guest beers H
Extended former coaching inn at the highest point in the Blyth Valley, with views of the Northumberland coast. The pub is open plan with distinct bar and dining areas plus a conservatory. Dedicated to real ale, there are regular beer festivals. Ten guest ales are sourced from local microbreweries and from further afield. An extensive range of meals and snacks is available lunchtimes and evenings, all day Friday-Sunday. Licensed for weddings and civil ceremonies.
P (X5)

High Newton-by-the-Sea

Joiners Arms

Town Square, NE66 3EA (on B1340)
12-11 (10.30 Sun) (01665) 576112 Joiners-arms.com
Hadrian Border Tyneside Blonde; guest beer H
Eighteenth-century former manor house tastefully restored and refurbished following closure for two years. The house ale, Anarchy St Marys, is named after the local church – for every pint sold a donation is made towards the church's upkeep. Set in a typical Northumbrian hamlet, the pub's seating area at the front overlooks a small picturesque green. Five en-suite bedrooms are fitted out to a high standard. P (X18)

Langley

Carts Bog Inn L

NE47 5NW (3 miles off A69 on A686 to Alston)
closed Mon; 12-2.30 (2 Wed), 5-11; 12-11 Sat; 12-10.30 Sun (01434) 684338 cartsbog.co.uk
Beer range varies H
Excellent rural pub serving the Langley community and tourists. The building dates from 1730 and was built on the site of an ancient brewery (circa 1521). Carts really did get bogged down here. A large open fire divides the two-room interior and the walls proudly display pictures of bygone days. Good locally-sourced food including meat from a nearby farm is served (booking essential for Sunday lunch). Three real ales from local breweries are usually available, and a beer festival is held in August. Home to three quoits teams.
Q P (688)

Low Newton-by-the-Sea

Ship Inn L

Newton Square, NE66 3EL (off B1340 between Seahouses and Craster)
11-11; 12-10.30 Sun (01665) 576262
shipinnnewton.co.uk
Ship Inn Sandcastles at Dawn, Sea Coal, Sea Dog, Sea Wheat, Ship Hop Ale H
Small pub nestling in the corner of a three-sided square of former fishermen's cottages only a few yards from the beach. It is often busy with beer drinkers seeking ales from the in-house microbrewery, walkers and diners – the excellent menu uses fresh local ingredients. The pub is a short walk from the public car park at the top of the hill (there is no customer parking). Note that opening times may vary in winter so phone ahead if travelling any distance. Q

Matfen

High House Farm Visitor Centre L

NE20 0RG
closed Wed; 10.30-9 (5 Sun-Tue) (01661) 886192
highhousefarmbrewery.co.uk
High House Farm Auld Hemp, Nel's Best, Matfen Magic; guest beer H
All real ales are sourced from the brewery, with tours available (book ahead). The visitor centre includes an award-winning restaurant offering a daytime menu, evening meals and Sunday lunches. A tearoom in a converted barn complements the traditional ambience. There is a children's play area outside. Situated one and a half miles from the Military Road and not far from the Roman wall, it has a caravan and camping field. Licensed for weddings and popular for wedding receptions. Q P

Milfield

Red Lion Inn

Main Road, NE71 6JD
11-2, 5-11, 11-11 Sat & Sun (01668) 216224
redlionmilfield.co.uk
Black Sheep Best Bitter; guest beers H
A true local pub at the heart of the village, just eight miles inside the border, dating back to the mid-1700s. Rescued by the current licensee from the tight grip of S&N, the Red Lion is a proper free house, with many varied guest beers served through the third handpump. Freshly prepared food is available, with blackboards proudly displaying where the local produce is sourced. Home to the local leek growing club.
Q P (267)

Newbiggin by the Sea

Queen's Head

7 High Street, NE64 6AT
10-midnight (01670) 817293
Beer range varies H
Single-room building with the bar, lounge and snug all together. Rebuilt in 1909, some Edwardian features have been retained, including the curved bar counter. The owner sells competitively priced real ales at advantageous opening times and displays an ever-growing, impressive collection of guest beer pumpclips on the walls. Just one beer is usually available, varying weekly and often sourced locally. This no-nonsense pub is popular with locals and visitors alike.

Newbrough

Red Lion

Stanegate Road, Hexham, NE47 5AR
12-11 (10.30 Sun) (01434) 674226
redlionnewbrough.co.uk
Beer range varies H

The road outside was first laid down by the Romans back in 71AD, long before Hadrian's Wall was built. The building reputedly dates back to the 13th century, featuring many flagstones and beams plus much old stonework. Popular with cyclists, Route 72 of the National Cycle Network runs alongside and the pub operates a pick-up, drop-off luggage service. Opening hours and food service are liable to change in winter. An ale from a local brewery is always available.
❀⛟◑ ♣P🚌(683)📶

Old Hartley

Delaval Arms

NE26 4RL (jct of A193/B1325 S of Seaton Sluice)
12-2.30, 6-11; 12-11 Fri-Sun winter; 12-11 summer
☎ (0191) 237 0489 thedelavalarms.wordpress.com
Beer range varies H
Multi-roomed Grade II-listed building dating from 1748, with a listed WWI water storage tower behind the beer garden. It is the first pub in Northumberland for those following the coastal route. Good quality, affordable meals complement the beer, with guest ales coming from local micros. To the left as you enter is a room served through a hatch from the bar and to the right is a music room where children are welcome.
Q❀◑P🚌(308,309)🐾

Ovingham

Bridge End Inn

West Road, NE42 6BN
4 (12 Sat)-11.30; 12-3.30, 7-11 Sun ☎ (01661) 832219
thebridgeendinn.co.uk
Tetley Bitter; Timothy Taylor Landlord; Wylam Gold Tankard, Collingwood; guest beer H
Superb traditional family-run hostelry with the same licensee for 38 years. The back door opens onto the village green. A popular stop-off for day trippers including Whistle Stops visitors, children are welcome until 9pm. Access to the pub from Prudhoe is over a bridge via a pedestrian walkway. Folk night is the third Wednesday of the month. An allotment club meets monthly. Visitors are made welcome by the friendly pub regulars.
Q♿⇌(Prudhoe)♣P🚌(X84,686)

Ponteland

Blackbird

North Road, NE20 9UH
12-11 (midnight Fri & Sat) ☎ (01661) 822684
theblackbirdponteland.com
Beer range varies H
This pub goes back over 500 years – part of the building is the remains of Ponteland Castle. A blend of old and new, the Blackbird is central to village life, with a good mixed clientele. The popular Big Bird Quiz features every second Sunday of the month. An annual New Year's Day wheelbarrow race starts and finishes at the pub. Two local beers are always available as well as two nationally sourced guest ales. ❀◑♿P🚌(X77,X78)📶

Rennington

Horseshoes Inn

6 Rennington Village, NE66 3RS
closed Mon; 12-3; 6.45-11; summer hours vary
☎ (01665) 577665 thehorseshoesrennington.co.uk
Hadrian Border Farne Island Pale Ale; guest beer H
Superb traditional family-run village pub dating from 1841, with its history detailed on the chimney breast. The bar is warm and friendly, free from TV and jukebox, with a log fire; dry hops hang over the serving area. The large restaurant has an excellent reputation. The pub hosts a scarecrow competition every August bank holiday Saturday and is home to two darts teams. There is a pleasant beer garden at the front. Q❀◑♣P

Rothbury

Queen's Head

Townfoot, NE65 7SR
11-1am (midnight Sun) ☎ (01669) 620470
queensheadrothbury.com
Beer range varies H
Friendly hotel dating from 1756 on the main street, popular with locals, tourists and ramblers. Live folk music features on the first Tuesday and last Thursday of the month (there is a charge and it often sells out). The hotel has pool and darts teams competing in local leagues. Four guest beers come from the SIBA Direct Delivery Scheme and Punch Finest Cask. All bedrooms are en suite. There is an hourly bus service. ⛟◑♣P🚌(14,X14)📶

Seahouses

Olde Ship Hotel

7-9 Main Street, NE68 7RD
11 (12 Sun)-11 ☎ (01665) 720200 seahouses.co.uk
Black Sheep Best Bitter; Courage Directors; Hadrian Border Farne Island Pale Ale; Morland Old Speckled Hen; Ruddles County; Theakston Best Bitter; guest beers H
This 1745 farmhouse was converted to the licensed trade in 1812 and has a regionally important historic pub interior. It has been family-owned since 1910. Three fascinating bars are adorned with a veritable treasure trove of 19th- and 20th-century maritime memorabilia. Fully residential, the pub offers a unique menu of fresh fish, crab meals and snacks (no chips served).
Q❀⛟◑♿♣P🚌(501)

Seaton Sluice

King's Arms

The Harbour, NE26 4RD (on cliff top to E of main road)
12-11 (11.30 Fri & Sat); 12-10.30 Sun ☎ (0191) 237 0275
thekingsarms-ne.co.uk
Caledonian Deuchars IPA; Greene King Abbot; guest beers H
Traditional pub dating from the 1700s, sitting majestically next to the man-made harbour constructed by the famous Delaval family. The pub is set back from the road, with extensive views of Seaton Sluice beach. It has an excellent reputation for good food made using local ingredients (booking is advised). There are five handpulls dispensing a range of ales sourced nationally. Live bands play on Sunday evening.
Q❀◑♿P🚌(308,309)🐾

Melton Constable

Beresford Road, NE26 4QL
12-11 (10.30 Sun) ☎ (0191) 237 7741
Black Sheep Best Bitter; Morland Old Speckled Hen; Thwaites Wainwright; Wychwood Hobgoblin; guest beers H

Large roadside pub a few minutes' walk from the beach and local history sights. It is named after the southern seat of Lord Hastings, a member of the Delaval family – Delaval Hall is close by. The pub hosts a nighttime fishing club and the BSA owners' club on the first and third Thursdays of the month. Tuesday is steak night, Wednesday is quiz night, Sunday evening features live music.
P (308,309)

Slaley

Travellers Rest

NE46 1TT (on B6306 1 mile N of village)
12-11 (10.30 Sun) ☎ (01434) 673231
travellersrestslaley.com
Black Sheep Best Bitter; Caledonian Deuchars IPA; guest beer H
Former farmhouse dating from the 16th century, licensed for over 150 years. The pub has an excellent reputation for good food and accommodation. The bar has a large open fire, stone flag floor and comfortable furniture. Children are welcome and there is a safe play area alongside. Note the beautiful wine rack skilfully carved from a large piece of wood. The pub is typically quiet. P

Twice Brewed

Twice Brewed Inn

Miltary Road, Bardon Mill, NE47 7AN (on B6318)
11-11 (10.30 Sun) ☎ (01434) 344534
twicebrewedinn.co.uk
Beer range varies H
Superb remote inn close to Hadrian's Wall, patronised by tourists and ramblers. It has its own well supplying water. Yates Twice Brewed Bitter is the house beer and a range of bottled beers named Beers of the World is kept. The pub is home to two quoits teams. The inn acts as a rural transport interchange and has full disabled access and 16 bedrooms, seven en suite.
Q P

Wark

Battlesteads Hotel L

NE48 3LS
11-11; 12-10.30 Sun ☎ (01434) 230209
battlesteads.com
Beer range varies H
Welcoming, well-appointed, former farmhouse dating from 1747 with a superb rear walled garden, restaurant, large conservatory and accommodation. The five handpulls provide an excellent choice of beer, all in tip-top condition. Ingredients for the excellent food menu, including home-grown fruit and vegetables, are sourced from a 25-mile radius. Accommodation includes ground floor rooms with disabled access. Handy for the PlusBus via Hexham Rail Station.
P (880)

Wylam

Black Bull L

Main Street, NE41 8AB
4 (12 Fri & Sat)-11 ☎ (01661) 853112
blackbull-wylam.co.uk
Wylam Gold Tankard; guest beers H
Cheerful pub with a friendly landlord and staff located on the main street in Wylam, popular with the locals. Real ale is now available on six handpulls, the beers mainly from the nearby Wylam brewery. Food includes local home-cooked specialities, steak night on Wednesday, fish night on Friday and curry night on the last Thursday of the month. Regular themed nights are hosted, many raising funds for charities. Nearby is Wylam Waggonway, a popular walk that passes George Stephenson's cottage.

Boathouse Inn L

Station Road, NE41 8HR
11-11 (midnight Sat); 12-10.30 Sun ☎ (01661) 853431
boathousewylam.info
Beer range varies H
Superb two-roomed pub with 15 handpulls, three dedicated to cider, with more ciders served from the cellar. Beers are sourced locally and nationwide, and on bank holidays themed beer festivals are held. Sunday roasts are popular, with lunchtime and early evening meals available throughout the week. The pub is a popular stopping-off point for Whistle Stops II travellers. Fifteen CAMRA awards cover one wall. Saturday afternoons and the first Wednesday evening of the month are for buskers. Q P

The sign of the Bell

Mr Jones and Partridge travelled on to Gloucester. Being arrived here, they chose for their house of entertainment the sign of the Bell; an excellent house, and which I do most seriously recommend to every reader who shall visit this ancient city. The master of it is brother to the great preacher, Whitfield, but is absolutely untainted with the pernicious principles of Methodism, or of any other heretical sect. He is indeed a very honest, plain man, and in my opinion not likely to create any disturbance either in Church or State. His wife hath, I believe, had much pretension to beauty, and is still a very fine woman. Her person and deportment might have made a shining figure in the politest assemblies; but though she must be conscious of this and many other perfections, she seems perfectly contented with, and resigned to the state of life to which she is called – To be concise, she is a very friendly, good-natured woman; and so industrious to oblige that the guests must be of a very morose disposition who are not extremely well satisfied in her house.
Henry Fielding (1707-54), The History of Tom Jones, 1749

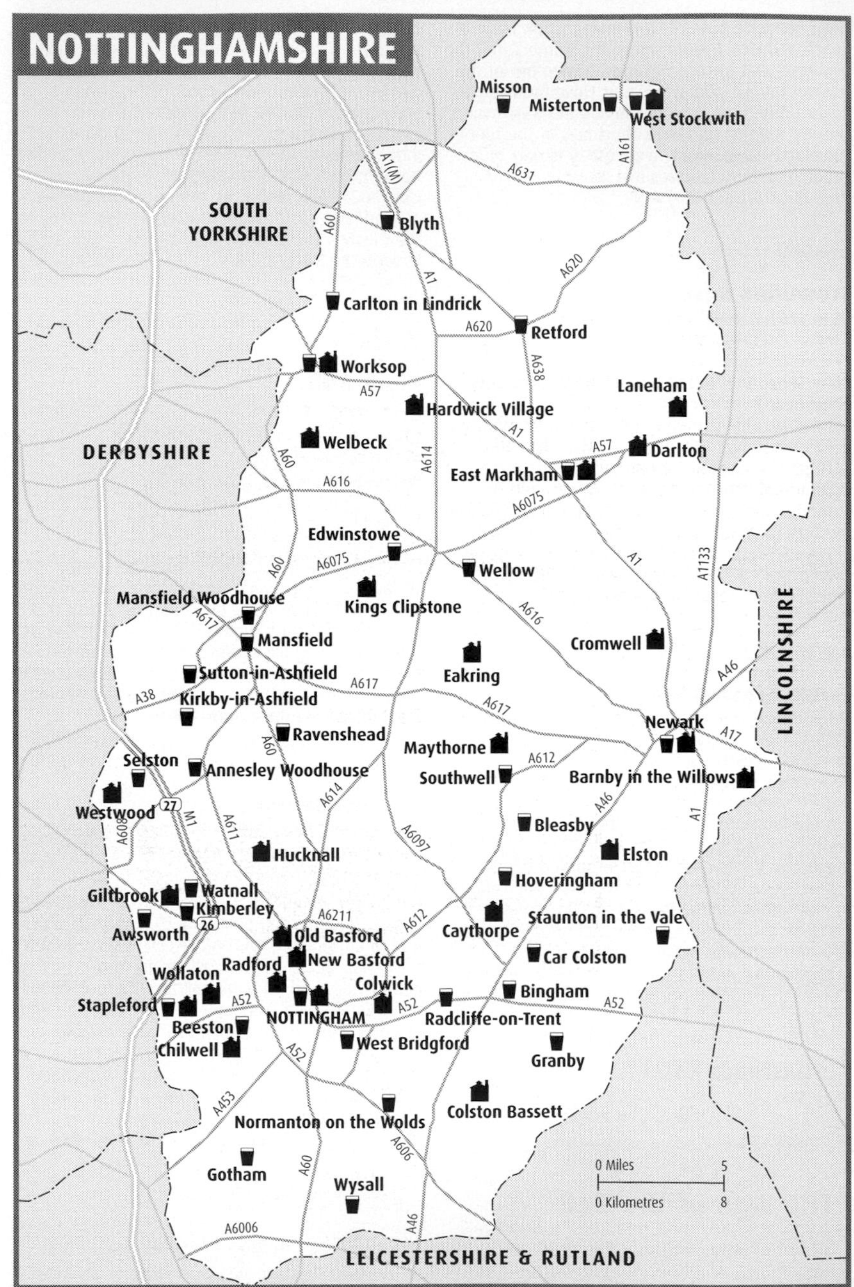

Annesley Woodhouse

Badger Box

Derby Road, NG17 9BX

11-11.30 (11 Mon); 11.30-11.30 Sun ☎ (01623) 752243

Greene King XX Mild, IPA, Abbot; H&H Bitter; Morland Old Speckled Hen; guest beers Ⓗ

Hungry Horse-branded pub restaurant with the same landlord for the past 34 years. Six handpumps dispense the usual Greene King range plus two guests. Food is served all day – look for the daily menu offers. Large-screen TVs show sport and outside is a spacious fenced beer garden with a children's play area. The large car park is on two sides of the pub. Greene King Hungry Horse Pub of the Year in 2013. P

Awsworth

Gate Inn

Main Street, NG16 2RN

12-midnight ☎ (0115) 932 9821

Burton Bridge XL Bitter; guest beers Ⓗ

Deemed to be unviable and sold by the pub's former owners, the Gate reopened in 2010 as a free house and has quickly established itself as a quality real ale outlet, winning LocAle Pub of the Year in 2013. A truly welcoming and friendly local, this late-19th-century inn has a bar and a lounge. The current owners are gradually renovating the building and have added a skittle alley and a courtyard. ♿♣🍎P🚌(TBR1,27)🐾

Beeston

Crown Inn 🄻

Church Street, NG9 1FY

⏲ 12-11.30 (11 Sun) ☎ (0115) 925 4738

🌐 crowninnbeeston.co.uk

Brown Inception, The Shining; Everards Sunchaser Blonde, Tiger; Leatherbritches Scoundrel; guest beers 🄷

Grade II-listed pub dating to 1830 as an ale house. Restored by Everards, it now offers 14 ales and several real ciders and perries. A cosy atmosphere is created by five distinct drinking areas including a snug and a three-seat 'confessional', once used as a hideaway by the local vicar. Breweriana from days past decorate throughout. The beer garden regularly hosts events. Snacks are available daily. Q✿♿⇌♣🍎P🚌🐾

Victoria Hotel 🄻

85 Dovecote Lane, NG9 1JG

⏲ 10.30-11 (midnight Fri & Sat); 12-11 Sun

☎ (0115) 925 4049 🌐 victoriabeeston.co.uk

Castle Rock Harvest Pale; Everards Tiger; Kelham Island Best Bitter; guest beers 🄷

A Victorian masterpiece with something for everyone. A genuine free house, up to 16 ales – a taster tray of three third-of-a-pints is offered to help you decide – and two ciders are kept alongside 110 whiskies. The VicFest in July and beer festivals throughout the year are held in the impressive beer garden, which has a heated, covered area and ample seating. CAMRA and NUS discounts are available Sunday to Thursday. High-quality food includes vegan and vegetarian options. Q✿◐◑♿⇌🍎P🚌🐾

Bingham

Horse & Plough

Long Acre, NG13 8AF

⏲ 11-11 (11.30 Fri & Sat); 12-11 Sun ☎ (01949) 839313

🌐 horseandploughbingham.com

Caledonian Deuchars IPA; Thwaites Lancaster Bomber; guest beers 🄷

Situated in the heart of a busy market town, this warm, friendly, one-room free house is a former Methodist chapel and has a cottage-style interior and flagstone floor. Six cask ales are served including four guests, with a Try Before You Buy policy, and a cider from Westons. Freshly prepared food is served weekday lunchtimes and evenings in the bar, and the first floor à la carte restaurant offers a varied seasonal menu. A regular local CAMRA Pub of the Year winner. ◐◑♿⇌🚌🐾📶

White Lion 🏆

Nottingham Road, NG13 8AT

⏲ 11 (11.30 Sun)-11 ☎ (01949) 875541

Theakston Best Bitter; guest beers 🄷

The White Lion is a typical local with a loyal following of regulars. Recently refurbished, it now serves up to four cask ales. Basic good-value meals are available lunchtimes and evenings. Home to pool and darts teams, it hosts a popular quiz night every Sunday. The bar has a big screen showing all major games on Sky Sports. There is a large car park plus a good-sized decked area for outdoor drinking. Local branch CAMRA Pub of the Year 2014. ✿◐◑♿⇌♣P🚌

Bleasby

Waggon & Horses 🄻

Gipsy Lane, NG14 7GG

⏲ 12-2 (not Mon-Wed), 5-11; 12-midnight Sat; 12-11 Sun

☎ (01636) 830283

Blue Monkey BG Sips; Mallard Specduckular; Sharp's Doom Bar; guest beers 🄷

Thriving village free house offering six real ales, featuring award-winning Blue Monkey beers alongside others from micros. Real cider is also kept. This is a true village pub overlooking the church and green with no gimmicks or electronic games, just good conversation and banter. To the rear is a conservatory and a small restaurant. Well worth finding in a lovely Trent Valley village close to Southwell Minster and races. Walkers with muddy boots and dogs with muddy paws all welcome. Q✿◐◑⛺⇌♣🍎P🚌🐾📶

Blyth

Red Hart 🄻

Bawtry Road, S81 8HG

⏲ 2.30-11.30 Mon; 11.30-midnight ☎ (01909) 591221

🌐 redhart.co.uk

INDEPENDENT BREWERIES

Alcazar Nottingham: Old Basford
Black Iris Nottingham: New Basford
Blue Monkey Giltbrook
Castle Rock Nottingham
Caythorpe Caythorpe
Copthorne Darlton
Double Top Worksop
Dukeries Worksop
Flipside Colwick
Full Mash Stapleford
Funfair Elston
Grafton Worksop
Handley's Barnby in the Willows
Idle West Stockwith
Kings Clipstone Kings Clipstone
Lincoln Green Hucknall
Magpie Nottingham
Mallard Maythorne
Maypole Eakring
Medieval Colston Bassett
Milestone Cromwell
Naked Brewer Westwood
Navigation Nottingham
Newark Newark
Nottingham Nottingham: Radford
Pheasantry East Markham
Prior's Well Hardwick Village (brewing suspended)
Reality Nottingham: Chilwell
Robin Hood Nottingham: New Basford
Scribbler's Stapleford (NEW)
Springhead Laneham
Totally Brewed Nottingham (NEW)
Welbeck Abbey Welbeck
Wollaton Wollaton

Sharp's Doom Bar; guest beers Ⓗ
An attractive former 17th-century coaching inn in the centre of the village with a reasonably large lounge, traditional taproom and an attractive dining room. The walls in the lounge are decorated with photographs and paintings from nearby locations. Restaurant-quality food is served daily at pub prices. This CAMRA award-winning pub has been in the Guide for the past eight years and runs an annual beer festival.
Q♨❀🛏◐◑♿♣P🚌(25,29)🐾📶

Car Colston

Royal Oak

The Green, NG13 8JE
⏲ 11.30-3, 5.30-11; 11.30-11 Fri & Sat; 12-10.30 Sun
☎ (01949) 20247 🌐 brilliantpubs.co.uk/royaloaknotts
Marston's Burton Bitter; Ringwood Best Bitter; Wychwood Hobgoblin; guest beer Ⓗ
Impressive country inn situated on one of England's largest village greens. The two-room interior includes a lounge and restaurant on one side and bar with comfortable seating on the other. Note the bar's vaulted brickwork ceiling – a legacy from the building's previous life as a hosiery factory. Good-quality, traditional food is served lunchtimes and evenings. There is a skittle alley to the rear. The landlord maintains his 100 per cent record for entries in the Guide. ❀◐◑♿⛺♣P

Carlton in Lindrick

Grey Horses Ⓛ

The Cross, S81 9EW (in centre of old village)
⏲ 12 (11 Sun)-11 ☎ (01909) 730252 🌐 greyhorsesinn.com
Welbeck Abbey Henrietta, Red Feather, Cavendish; guest beers Ⓗ
The Grey Horses is the brewery tap for Welbeck Brewery and is situated in the heart of the village within the conservation area. It has a front bar accessible from the street where locals gather to play cards and dominoes, and a large lounge bar area. A former CAMRA award winner, it holds beer festivals in conjunction with the Welbeck Abbey Brewery featuring ales on up to 12 handpulls as well as cider and perry.
Q♨❀◐◑♿♣🍎P🚌(21,22)🐾📶

East Markham

Queen's Hotel 🏆

High Street, NG22 0RE
⏲ 12 (2 Mon)-11 ☎ (01777) 870288
🌐 queenshoteleastmarkham.co.uk
Adnams Southwold Bitter; Everards Beacon Bitter, Sunchaser Blonde, Tiger; guest beers Ⓗ
Situated on the village main street, this cosy public house has a friendly atmosphere enhanced by an open fire in winter. A single bar serves the lounge, pool room and dining area. Food ranges from hot and cold snacks to full home-cooked meals. There is a large garden area at the rear where you can enjoy a drink on a warm summer's day. Local CAMRA Pub of the Year for 2013.
Q♨❀◐◑♿🍎P🚌(36,37)🐾

Edwinstowe

Forest Lodge

2-4 Church Street, NG21 9QA
⏲ 11.30-3, 5.30 (5 Fri)-11; 12-3, 6-10.30 Sun
☎ (01623) 824443 🌐 forestlodgehotel.co.uk
Welbeck Abbey Forest Lodge English Pale Ale; Wells Bombardier; guest beers Ⓗ
Family owned and run for the past 10 years, this 18th-century coaching inn in the heart of Sherwood Forest offers a range of ever-changing guest beers, sourced from breweries near and far. The house beer is supplied by local Welbeck Abbey Brewery. The high-class restaurant offers a large choice of daily specials, featuring local produce wherever possible. Private functions can be catered for. Accommodation is four-star AA rated.
♨❀🛏◐◑P🚌📶

Gotham

Sun Inn

1 The Square, NG11 0HX
⏲ 12-11 ☎ (0115) 878 9047 🌐 suninngotham.co.uk
Everards Beacon Bitter, Sunchaser Blonde, Tiger, Original; guest beers Ⓗ
Traditional village two-roomed pub opposite St Lawrence's Church. Pub games such as darts and dominoes are played in the public bar, while the lounge is also used for dining. Food is served lunchtimes Wednesday to Sunday and Friday evening. A regional winner of a best-kept cellar award in 2013, nine handpumps serve at least five real ales plus three ciders from Westons. There is a bright and colourful garden area to while away the hours in summer. Q❀◐♿♣🍎P🚌(NCT1)🐾📶

Granby

Marquis of Granby

Dragon Street, NG13 9PN
⏲ 4-11 (midnight Fri); 12-midnight Sat; 12-11 Sun
☎ (01949) 859517
Brewster's Hophead, Marquis; guest beers Ⓗ
Believed to be the original Marquis of Granby, dating back to 1760 or earlier, this small two-roomed pub is now the brewery tap for Brewster's. York stone floors complement the yew bar tops and wood-beamed rooms, period wallpaper features throughout and the lounge has a welcoming open fire in winter months. Guest beers served alongside the Brewster's range usually come from micros, and include a mild, stout or porter. Fish and chips night is Friday. ❀♿♣P🚌🐾

Hoveringham

Reindeer Ⓛ

Main Street, NG14 7JR
⏲ 12 (5 Mon & Tue)-11.30; 12-2, 5-11.30 Wed
☎ (0115) 966 3629 🌐 thereindeerinn.com
Black Sheep Best Bitter; Castle Rock Harvest Pale; Woodforde's Wherry; guest beers Ⓗ
Genuine free house in a pleasant country village with traditional beams and a log fire for cold winter nights. A central servery divides the bar and restaurant areas of the pub. Well-kept ales are offered alongside a good range of home-cooked food including vegetarian and vegan choices. The outside drinking area is served through the pub window and overlooks the village cricket pitch for those who like the sound of leather on willow as they drink. Q❀◐◑♣P🚌(103)🐾

Kimberley

Stag Inn

67 Nottingham Road, NG16 2NE

5 (1.30 Sat)-11; 12-10.30 Sun ☎ (0115) 938 3151

Adnams Southwold Bitter; Timothy Taylor Landlord; guest beers H

This wattle and daub Tudor-style house dates from 1737 and is near the town centre. It has two rooms linked by a central bar, furnished with an eclectic mix of seating, including wooden settles. Table skittles and dominoes are played, but at most times conversation reigns. The spacious rear garden includes a children's play area and ample seating. The annual charity beer festival is held in late May. Guest beers always include a brew from a lesser-known local brewery.
Q P (TBR1)

White Lion

74 Swingate, NG16 2PQ

4 (12 Sat & Sun)-11.30 ☎ (0115) 938 3193

whitelionswingate.co.uk

Castle Rock Black Gold, Harvest Pale; Sharp's Doom Bar; guest beers H

The owners of the White Lion have turned what was once a failing pub into a venue that is fast becoming the place to visit. Set in a residential area, the two-roomed pub has been newly refurbished with a modern décor. It now offers up to six cask beers, mainly from local microbreweries. No cooked food is served but sandwiches are available on request. There is a large garden to the rear and walkers and their dogs are welcome. Q P (TB27)

Kirkby-in-Ashfield

Regent

Kingsway, NG17 7BQ

8am-midnight (1am Fri & Sat) ☎ (01623) 687630

Courage Directors; Greene King Abbot; Ruddles Best Bitter; Shepherd Neame Spitfire; Wychwood Hobgoblin; guest beers H

A former cinema on the corner of Kingsway converted by Wetherspoon. There is a big emphasis on cask ales here, with up to 10 available at any one time, including a house beer brewed exclusively for the pub by Funfair. The usual excellent-value range of Wetherspoon meals is served every day until 11pm. Families are welcome.

Mansfield

Bold Forester

Botany Avenue, NG18 5NF

11-11.30 (12.30am Fri & Sat); 12-11.30 Sun
☎ (01623) 623970

Greene King IPA, Abbot; H&H Bitter, Olde Trip; Morland Old Speckled Hen; guest beers H

Hungry Horse split-level pub and restaurant, run by the same landlord for the past 15 years. A wide choice of real ales is offered, usually six from Greene King and up to six guests. Food is served all day until 9pm. The spacious open-plan interior has large-screen TVs showing all major live sport. Outside, there is a beer garden with a covered smoking area and TV. P

Court House

Market Place, NG18 1HX (next to town hall)

9am-11 (midnight Fri & Sat) ☎ (01623) 412720

Greene King Abbot; Ruddles Best Bitter; guest beers H

Friendly community pub in the town centre overlooking the market place. A range of at least five cask ales is available, often from local microbreweries including Lincoln Green and Milestone, plus two real ciders. The usual good-value Wetherspoon meals are served every day until 11pm. The pub is a winner of numerous local branch CAMRA awards and families are welcome.
Q

Railway Inn

9 Station Street, NG18 1EF

11-11 ☎ (01623) 623086

Beer range varies H

A true community pub situated near the railway and bus stations. Three constantly changing real ales, including at least one LocAle, are available in the main bar, and two additional quiet rooms are popular with diners. Real cider and bottled beer are also on offer. Home-cooked food is served all day at reasonable prices. A popular music night is held on the third Thursday of every month. Outside is a small walled garden and smoking area.
Q

Redgate

189 Westfield Lane, NG19 6EH

12-11 ☎ (01623) 624406 redgateinn.co.uk

Beer range varies H

Thriving community-focused pub with a spacious lounge/public bar and a separate restaurant, the Best Side, serving quality home-cooked food lunchtimes and evenings. Darts and dominoes are played and the pub has a skittles alley. Local sports memorabilia is displayed in the public bar where a quiet TV shows news and sport. Up to five ever-changing beers are regularly available, usually including at least one from a local microbrewery.
Q P

Stag & Pheasant

4 Clumber Street, NG18 1NU

8am-midnight (1am Thu; 2am Fri; 3am Sat)
☎ (01623) 412890

Greene King Abbot; Ruddles Best Bitter; guest beers H

A spacious Lloyds No.1 bar not far from the town centre. It gets busy at weekends, with music after 6pm and a DJ after 9pm on Friday and Saturday (an entry charge applies). Two regular cask ales and three rotating guests are usually available, plus two real ciders. The usual range of excellent-value Wetherspoon meals is served until 11pm every day. There is a large covered smoking area to the front.

Widow Frost

41 Leeming Street, NG18 1NB

8am-midnight (1am Fri & Sat) ☎ (01623) 666790

Greene King Abbot; Ruddles Best Bitter; guest beers H

This spacious pub, situated not far from the town centre, gets busy, especially at weekends. The full range of Wetherspoon meals is served until 11pm every day, with a separate family dining area. Up to six real ales are available, plus two real ciders.
Q

Mansfield Woodhouse

Greyhound Inn

82 High Street, NG19 8BD
⏲ 12-11 (midnight Fri & Sat); 12-10.30 Sun
☎ (01623) 464403
Adnams Broadside; Caledonian Deuchars IPA; guest beers [H]
A regular in the Guide for the past 21 years, this two-room pub has been run by the same licensee for 31 years. Quiz nights are Monday and Wednesday. Pool, darts and dominoes are played in the public bar. No hot food is served but a range of bar snacks is available. Two mini beer festivals are held a year. Dogs are welcome in the taproom. ❀♣●P🚌(1)🐾

Misson

Angel Inn

Dame Lane, DN10 6EB
⏲ 4-11 (midnight Fri); 12-midnight Sat; 12-11 Sun
☎ (01302) 711761 🌐 angel-misson.co.uk
John Smith's Bitter; Theakston Lightfoot; York Guzzler; guest beers [H]
This village pub is well worth seeking out. You can be sure of a friendly greeting when you walk into the pleasant bar. The beers are well kept and there is an excellent menu of high-quality home-made food for diners. Accommodation is available and the pub is handy for Robin Hood Airport. A recent CAMRA award winner. Q❀🛏◐♿P🚌📶

Misterton

Haxey Gate Inn Ⓛ

Haxey Road, DN10 4BA (on road to Epworth)
⏲ 12-11 ☎ (01427) 890746 🌐 haxeygate.co.uk
Batemans XB; Welbeck Abbey Henrietta, Red Feather, Cavendish; guest beers [H]
Occupying an idyllic position beside an ancient bridge over the River Idle, the Haxey Gate is a friendly local specialising in good, wholesome, reasonably priced food and well-kept beer. Diners can enjoy their refreshments throughout the inn, but the front-facing conservatory is popular, with plenty of seating. A choice of four real ales is available. Golfers can enjoy a game on the adjacent course. ≋❀🛏◐♿ÅP🐾📶

Newark

Castle Ⓛ

5 Castle Gate, NG24 1AZ
⏲ 11-midnight (1am Thu-Sat); 12-midnight Sun
☎ (01636) 640733
Oldershaw Posh Blonde; Sharp's Doom Bar; guest beers [H]
A long one-roomed pub on different levels offering a good range of real ales, with guest beers often sourced from microbreweries. A live music venue, jazz, blues and acoustic music are hosted throughout the week in a friendly atmosphere. No food is available here but sister pub, the Mayze next door, serves a good range of meals. CAMRA members receive a discount on real ale.
⇌(Castle)🚌🐾📶

Castle Barge

Town Wharf, NG24 1EU
⏲ 11-11 (midnight Fri-Sun) ☎ (01636) 677320
🌐 castlebarge.co.uk
Beer range varies [H]
The Castle Barge was a Spillers grain barge plying its trade between Hull and Gainsborough. Situated on the River Trent at the Town Wharf in the centre of Newark, it was converted into a public house in 1980. Children are allowed on the top deck and there is an outdoor drinking area adjacent to the barge. Curry night is Tuesday and quiz night is Wednesday. Three handpulls generally serve LocAles including brews from Full Mash and Lincoln Green. ≋❀◐⇌(Castle)🚌(28,29)

Fox & Crown Ⓛ

4-6 Appleton Gate, NG24 1JY
⏲ 10.30-11 (midnight Fri & Sat); 10-11 Sun
☎ (01636) 605820
Castle Rock Sheriff's Tipple, Harvest Pale, Preservation Fine Ale, Elsie Mo; Everards Tiger; guest beers [H]
Popular, friendly, town-centre local opposite the parish church, offering a good range of real ales, imported beers and wines. The open-plan interior has a central bar and three side rooms, decorated with brewery pictures, posters, mirrors and old photos of Newark. Freshly cooked, locally-sourced food is served daily, with themed food nights weekly, and there are food promotions for seniors. Live music is hosted on Friday nights. A former local CAMRA award winner.
Q≋❀◐♿⇌(Castle)♣🚌(1,2)🐾📶

Just Beer Micropub 🏆 Ⓛ

32A Castlegate, NG24 1BG (in Swan & Salmon Yard, off Castlegate)
⏲ 1-11; 11-midnight Fri & Sat; 12-10 Sun ☎ (07983) 993747
🌐 justbeermicropub.biz
Beer range varies [H]
One-bar pub, opened in 2010 by four local beer enthusiasts. Four ever-changing ales are usually available, all from microbreweries, with an emphasis on one-offs and new breweries – over 2,300 beers have featured over the years. Two real ciders and a limited range of wines and soft drinks are offered but no keg, bottles or spirits. Food includes local pork pies, bar snacks and pickled eggs. Pub games such as darts and dominoes are played, plus a selection of board games. Local CAMRA Pub of the Year 2012, 2013 and 2014.
Q♿Å⇌(Castle)♣●▯🚌🐾

Prince Rupert Ⓛ

46 Stodman Street, NG24 1AW
⏲ 11-midnight (1am Fri & Sat); 12-midnight Sun
☎ (01636) 918121 🌐 theprincerupert.co.uk
Brains Rev James; Oakham JHB; guest beers [H]
This Grade II-listed building dates back to 1452 and has been lovingly restored. It has several rooms and snugs both downstairs and up – where the beamed, vaulted ceiling of the original Wealden House can be seen. Six handpumps dispense an ever-changing range of ales plus a real cider. An extensive food menu is available. Live music is a frequent attraction. Q❀◐⇌(Castle)●🚌🐾📶

Normanton on the Wolds

Plough Inn

Old Melton Road, NG12 5NN (off A606 Melton Road)
⏲ 11-11 (midnight Fri & Sat); 12-11 Sun ☎ (0115) 937 2401
🌐 theploughatnormanton.co.uk
Black Sheep Best Bitter; Castle Rock Harvest Pale; Fuller's London Pride; Wells Bombardier; guest beer [H]

Traditional dining pub in an ivy-clad brick building, situated on the main street of this well-heeled sleepy village. Inside, to the right is a comfortable lounge bar area with a real fire, while to the left is a smaller bar linked to the restaurant through an archway. In the summer, many events are hosted in the huge garden including a beer festival.
Q P (19)

Nottingham: Central

Canalhouse

48-52 Canal Street, NG1 7EH
11-11 (midnight Thu; 1am Fri & Sat); 11-10.30 Sun
(0115) 955 5060 thecanalhouse.co.uk
Castle Rock Harvest Pale, Preservation Fine Ale, Elsie Mo; guest beers H
Uniquely converted from an old Waterways Warehouse, with the adjacent canal running into the building and resident narrowboats moored inside. The pub is quiet and relaxed during the day, with home-made meals complementing the range of Castle Rock beers and guests. There is a good selection of ciders and perries, and 120 bottled world beers kept in large fridges. Outside is a generously sized patio overlooking the canal – popular on warm sunny days.
P

Falcon Inn

1 Alfreton Road, NG7 3JE
5-10 (11 Thu); 12-11 Fri & Sat; 12-10 Sun
(0115) 924 4635 thefalconinn.co.uk
Beer range varies H
Purchased by Lincoln Green Brewing Company in 2013, this prominently positioned pub was extensively refurbished after a long period of closure. The pub has two small rooms, with a function room/restaurant area upstairs. Eight handpumps serve a selection of mainly local ales, always including a dark beer, and one real cider. Meals are served on Sundays only, although large parties can be catered for at other times by prior arrangement, otherwise bar snacks are available.
Q

Fellows, Morton & Clayton

54 Canal Street, NG1 7EH
11-11 (midnight Fri); 10-midnight Sat; 11-10.30 Sun
(0115) 950 6795 fellowsmortonandclayton.co.uk
Black Sheep Best Bitter; Fuller's London Pride; Sharp's Doom Bar; Timothy Taylor Landlord; guest beers H
Red-brick pub opposite the Broadmarsh bus station with an attractive frontage featuring colourful floral displays in summer. There are several drinking areas on different levels, as well as a conservatory and small garden. A rear two-floored room with a spiral staircase is used as a restaurant and small function room. Beers are mainly well-kept national offerings, but there will always be a local ale, often from Lincoln Green. Sport is shown on a large screen and three TVs.

Hand & Heart

65 Derby Road, NG1 5BA
12-midnight (11 Mon); 12-1am Fri & Sat; 12-11 Sun
(0115) 958 2456 thehandandheart.co.uk
Maypole Little Weed; guest beers H
A traditional pub steeped in history, it has a sandstone cave at the back and a Victorian front, contrasting with a glass conservatory on top, built in the 1980s and converted to include an open balcony in 2012. This contrast of old and new offers a unique experience for both drinkers and diners. Eight beers are on handpump, more during beer festivals, and a range of real ciders and perries. The high-quality food menu features home-cooked English food. Music is hosted on Sundays and Thursdays.

Kean's Head

46 St Mary's Gate, Lace Market, NG1 1QA
11.30-11 (12.30am Fri & Sat); 12-10.30 Sun
(0115) 947 4052
Castle Rock Harvest Pale, Preservation Fine Ale, Screech Owl; guest beers H
Cosy one-room pub opposite the imposing St Mary's Church in the historic Lace Market district – the building was once a lace factory. Named in honour of the 19th-century actor Edmund Kean, it is busy at weekends and attracts a diverse and varied clientele. Owned by the Castle Rock group, it serves inventive, freshly-prepared traditional English and European food from an ever-changing menu. Three guest ales are usually available, often including a dark beer.

King William IV

6 Eyre Street, Sneinton, NG2 4PB
12 (2 Mon)-11; 11-11 Sat; 12-10.30 Sun
(0115) 958 9864
Oakham JHB, Bishops Farewell; guest beers H
Nicknamed the King Billy, this cosy Victorian gem nestling on the edge of town is just a stone's throw from the Capital FM Arena. A family-run free house that oozes charm and character, it is a haven for real ale drinkers, with a choice of seven microbrewery ales from near and far, as well as a cider. Occasional live music and televised sport feature. A fine selection of rolls is available. Not to be missed on a visit to Nottingham.
Q (43)

Lincolnshire Poacher

161-163 Mansfield Road, NG1 3FR
11-11 (midnight Thu & Fri); 10-midnight Sat; 12-11 Sun
(0115) 941 1584
Castle Rock Harvest Pale, Elsie Mo, Screech Owl; Everards Tiger; guest beers H
Thirteen handpumps offer a wide selection of ales, mainly from microbreweries. A mild, stout or porter is always available, as are real ciders/perries, continental bottled beers and a fine selection of whiskies. Meals are made with locally-sourced ingredients. The interior is split level with a snug, conservatory and enclosed courtyard. The decor includes artwork celebrating the pub's twinning with In de Wildeman bar in Amsterdam and various memorabilia of local and international interest. Live music is showcased on Sundays and Wednesdays. Q

Major Oak

24-26 Pelham Street, NG1 2EG
10-midnight (1am Thu-Sat) (0115) 958 4825
majoroak-nottingham.co.uk
Amber Barnes Wallis; guest beers H
This modern real ale pub, formerly a Hogshead, serves a variety of beers often unusual for Nottingham. Stretching between two roads either side of the Council House, the interior is split level with a long bar running down one side of the room. You cannot avoid the sport shown on several TV screens. There is a pool table in the middle of the pub. Food is served daily 10am-10pm.

Malt Cross

16 St James's Street, NG1 6FE

11-11 (1am Fri & Sat); 11-6 Sun ☎ (0115) 941 1048
maltcross.com

Beer range varies Ⓗ

This Grade II-listed former Victorian music hall, built by Edwin Hill in 1877, is owned by a charitable trust. An upstairs gallery overlooks the ground floor area from all sides. The guest beer range often includes a Glastonbury ale, alongside others from local microbreweries. Monday is quiz night and live music plays on Tuesday evening. Food is served until 8pm (5pm Sun).

Organ Grinder

21 Alfreton Road, Canning Circus, NG7 3JE

12-11 (11.30 Thu; midnight Fri & Sat) ☎ (0115) 970 0630

Batemans XB; Blue Monkey BG Sips, Guerrilla; guest beers Ⓗ

Previously the Red Lion, this pub was bought and refurbished by Blue Monkey Brewery to act as its brewery tap. The single-roomed, multi-level pub boasts a wood-burning fire. To the rear is a small courtyard, leading to a raised decked area and the first floor function room where there is a TV. The guest beers are sourced mainly from small breweries and up to three real ciders/perries are available. No meals, but bar snacks such as Scotch eggs and pork pies are on offer.

Vat & Fiddle

Queens Bridge Road, NG2 1NB

11-11 (midnight Thu-Sat) ☎ (0115) 985 0611

Castle Rock Sheriff's Tipple, Black Gold, Harvest Pale, Preservation Fine Ale, Elsie Mo, Screech Owl; guest beers Ⓗ

This is the brewery tap for the adjacent Castle Rock Brewery, a minute's walk from the station. Tours (Monday to Saturday, book in advance) end in Golding's Room, which opened in 2011. Twelve handpumps mostly serve the Castle Rock range, with guests from local and new breweries completing the selection. A seating area at the front allows patrons to admire the Art Deco frontage and floral displays in summer. Hot food is served all week, with roasts on Sundays.
Q

Nottingham: East

Bread & Bitter

153-155 Woodthorpe Drive, Mapperley, NG3 5JL

10-11 (midnight Thu-Sat); 11-11 Sun ☎ (0115) 960 7541

Castle Rock Black Gold, Harvest Pale, Preservation Fine Ale, Elsie Mo, Screech Owl; Fuller's London Pride; guest beers Ⓗ

Castle Rock pub built in 2007 on the premises of the old Judge's bakery on Mapperley Top. The original baker's oven fronts are still embedded in an inside wall, giving the place a warm and welcoming feel. The pub started a revival of real ale outlets in Mapperley. Twelve beers including a mild and rotating guests are available, along with an extensive foreign bottled beer list. Food is all home cooked and varies frequently – look for the specials board. Q (25,45)

Inn for a Penny

146 Burton Road, Carlton, NG4 3GP

10-11 (midnight Fri & Sat) ☎ (0115) 961 7233
innforapenny.co.uk

Castle Rock Harvest Pale; guest beers Ⓗ

Friendly traditional roadside pub on the outskirts of Nottingham, now totally refurbished with a fresh, airy feel. The L-shaped room has distinctive areas either side of the bar, which serves up to six beers, mainly from national brewers. A dartboard is tucked away on the left and TVs show sport. Children are welcome at mealtimes (until 8pm, 7pm weekends) and there is a play space beyond the large rear seating area outside.
(Carlton) P (100)

Nottingham: North

Gladstone Hotel

45 Loscoe Road, Carrington, NG5 2AW

5-11 (midnight Thu); 4-midnight Fri; 12-midnight Sat; 12-11 Sun ☎ (0115) 912 9994

Castle Rock Harvest Pale; Fuller's London Pride; Oakham Scarlet Macaw; Timothy Taylor Landlord; guest beers Ⓗ

This friendly back-street local sits in the middle of a Victorian terrace, just north of Nottingham, with memorabilia decorating the walls in the bar alongside traditional bar games. The lounge features old brasswork, ornaments, pictures and a large collection of books, with drinkers encouraged to browse. Outside, the secluded garden offers a haven in summer, winning many a Nottingham in Bloom award. The function room has hosted the Carrington Folk Club for 25 years, meeting each Wednesday.

Horse & Groom

462 Radford Road, New Basford, NG7 7EA

4 (12 Thu)-11; 12-11.30 Fri; 11-11.30 Sat; 12-11 Sun
☎ (0115) 970 3777 horseandgroombasford.com

Belvoir Shipstones Bitter; Castle Rock Harvest Pale; guest beers Ⓗ

This is a friendly and popular pub sitting in the shadow of the defunct Shipstones Brewery. There are steps up to the front door but wheelchair access to the function room is available via a ramp towards the rear on request. The pub has a cosy lounge with a real fire and a separate open taproom area where you will find nine handpumps. Beers mainly come from microbreweries, including a mild and at least one local guest, plus a real cider. Q

Hotel Deux

2 Pelham Road, Sherwood Rise, Carrington, NG5 1AP

5-11 (11.30 Thu & Fri); 6-11.30 Sat; 6-11 Sun
☎ (0115) 985 6724 theguitarbar.co.uk

Beer range varies Ⓗ

Formerly a hotel, now a pub with a friendly, comfortably furnished main bar overlooking the front garden. The range of four ales varies, but usually includes a beer each from Whim and Blue Monkey. Off the main bar is the Guitar Bar, featuring live entertainment at weekends from local, national and sometimes international artists (see the website for details). A separate function room is much used by the local community. Board games are available. P

Nottingham: West

Johnson Arms

59 Abbey Street, Lenton, NG7 2NZ

12-midnight (11 Fri); 4-11 Sat ☎ (0115) 978 6355
johnsonarms.co.uk

Adnams Southwold Bitter; Sharp's Doom Bar; guest beers Ⓗ
Popular two-room pub close to the University of Nottingham and QMC hospital. This former Shipstone's house retains the original etched windows, complemented by a green-tiled frontage. Annual highlights include beer festivals, Johnsonbury and Eurovision night. The Johnnos is a regular supporter of both the Nottingham CAMRA Stout & Porter Stroll and Mild Trail. Traditional home-cooked food includes JA burgers. The magnificent beer garden, with a pétanque court, is not to be missed. Q❀◑♣●🚌(13)🐾📶

Plough Inn 🄻
17 St Peter's Street, Radford, NG7 3EN
🕐 12-11 (midnight Thu-Sat) ☎ (0115) 970 2615
Nottingham Rock Ale Bitter Beer, Rock Ale Mild Beer, Legend, Extra Pale Ale; guest beer Ⓗ
Linked with the old Nottingham Brewery since 1887, the Plough is now the brewery tap for the revived company. A full range of Nottingham beers is served, four regular and four rotating. The present building, a 1932 two-room house with a central servery, is largely unchanged. Attracting regulars from a wide area, this 'village pub in the city' has retained its local feel in a period of rapid change, offering real fires, an outside skittle alley and a popular quiz night. Q❀♿♣●P🚌🐾📶

Radcliffe-on-Trent

Horse Chestnut 🄻
49 Main Road, NG12 2BE
🕐 12 (5 Mon & Tue)-11; 12-11.30 Fri & Sat
☎ (0115) 933 1994 🌐 horsechestnutradcliffe.com
Castle Rock Harvest Pale; Everards Tiger; St Austell Tribute; guest beers Ⓗ
Previously known as the Cliffe Inn, this LocAle-accredited pub was totally refurbished in 2006 with a smart 1920s-style décor. Six real ales are served including three ever-changing guests. Casual dining is offered, with fresh local food plus stone-baked pizzas from the pizza oven. Very much a smart local pub that serves food, rather than a restaurant that serves beer. ❀◑♿≠●P🚌🐾📶

Ravenshead

Larch Farm
2 Mansfield Road, NG15 9HA
🕐 12-11 (10.30 Mon); 11.30-11 Sat ☎ (01623) 491987
Timothy Taylor Landlord; guest beers Ⓗ
Situated at a busy crossroads on the main road between Nottingham and Mansfield, Larch Farm, a converted farm building, is hard to miss. Three real ales are on offer at all times alongside home-cooked meals lunchtimes and evenings. A popular destination with a large garden in the area that used to be the farmyard, it gets especially busy at weekends. B&B accommodation is available.
Q🔥❀🛏◑♿P🚌

Retford

Brick & Tile Inn 🄻
81 Moorgate, DN22 6RR
🕐 1-3 (5 Sat; 4 Sun), 7-11 ☎ (01777) 703681
Dukeries Baronet; Idle Golden Crown; guest beers Ⓗ
A quiet pub situated on the main road between Retford and Gainsborough. A choice of two real ales is always available here – one light and the other dark – usually from local breweries Idle, Springhead and Milestone. Accommodation is available in two twin rooms and two single rooms. The pub is a recent local CAMRA branch award winner. Q🔥🛏♿♣P▯🚌🐾📶

Rum Runner 🄻
Wharf Road, DN22 6EN (by fire station)
🕐 12-midnight (1am Fri & Sat) ☎ (01777) 860788
Batemans XB; Castle Rock Harvest Pale; guest beers Ⓗ
Formerly home to the now-closed Broadstone Brewery, the interior comprises a long room warmed by a real fire and a second room with its own serving hatch through to the bar, which can be used for meetings. A quiz is held on Wednesday evening, frequent music nights are hosted and mini beer festivals are a regular feature. Outside is a large enclosed beer garden.
Q🔥❀◑♿≠♣●🚌🐾📶

Turk's Head 🄻
39 Grove Street, DN22 6LA
🕐 11-2.30, 5-11; 11-11 Sat; 12-11 Sun ☎ (01777) 702742
Black Sheep Best Bitter; John Smith's Bitter; Sharp's Doom Bar; Tetley Bitter; Young's Special; guest beer Ⓗ
Situated close to the main Market Square, entry to this pub is via two large oak doors, which both lead into an open-plan area served by an L-shaped bar. The room features plenty of oak panelling and has a large warming open fire. At the far end is a pool table. Four real ales are served. ♣P🚌

Selston

Horse & Jockey 🏆 🄻
Church Lane, NG16 6FB
🕐 12-3.30, 5-1am; 12-4, 7-1am Sun ☎ (01773) 781012
Greene King Abbot; Timothy Taylor Landlord; guest beers Ⓗ
A drinkers' gem dating from 1664 with wooden bench seating, large open fires and flagstone floors. Up to six real ales are available, two served from the jug including a LocAle. A real cider or perry is also always kept. Quiz night is Sunday and folk night every Wednesday. Look out for the Selstock Beer and Music Festival in July. No hot food is served. A winner of many CAMRA awards including Pub of the Year 2014.
Q🔥❀♿♣●P🚌(90,331)🐾

Southwell

Final Whistle
Station Road, NG25 0ET
🕐 12-11.30 (11 Sun) ☎ (01636) 813094
🌐 finalwhistlepub.co.uk
Everards Beacon Bitter; Fuller's London Pride; guest beers Ⓗ
Formerly known as the Newcastle Arms, which served the old station, this pub was extensively modified, and reopened in 2011. A superb reconstruction of a 1920s railway station, it has three main drinking areas full of railway memorabilia, wood panelling, settles and fireplaces. The beer garden is styled as a platform, with seating and the old railway track. Bar snacks are available and there are quizzes on Tuesday and Sunday. The house beers are from Brown Ales.
🔥❀♿♣P🚌🐾

Old Coach House

69 Easthorpe, NG25 0HY
5 (4 Fri)-midnight; 2-midnight Sat; 12-midnight Sun
(01636) 813289
Black Sheep Best Bitter; Oakham Citra; guest beers
Genuine old-fashioned public house on the edge of the village built in the 17th century. Recently refurbished, it has five open areas with oak beams and three real fires including a cast-iron range. There is live jazz one Sunday a month, and regular music festivals.

Stapleford

Horse & Jockey

20 Nottingham Road, NG9 8AA
12-11 (midnight Fri & Sat) (0115) 875 9655
horseandjockeystapleford.co.uk
Full Mash Horse & Jockey; guest beers
Known locally as the Jockey, the pub was refurbished and turned into a traditional ale house in 2012. It offers a choice of 10 ever-changing real ales, including five LocAles, plus local ciders. There are two rooms —a main bar and a function room — free of fruit machines, pool tables and TVs. Pictures of local landmarks decorate the pub alongside water jugs for whisky and welcomes in many different languages. CAMRA national Pub of the Year finalist 2014. **Q P**

Staunton in the Vale

Staunton Arms

NG13 9PE
12-11; 11-midnight Fri & Sat; 11-10 Sun
(01400) 281218 stauntonarms.co.uk
Castle Rock Harvest Pale; guest beers
Two hundred-year-old listed pub in the far north of the Vale of Belvoir, carefully restored to retain its original character. The large bar offers comfortable seating for drinkers and diners, with a further separate raised restaurant area. The pub serves freshly prepared meals lunchtimes and evenings and three cask beers, one always a LocAle. Mini festivals are held occasionally, with upcoming events publicised on the website. CAMRA branch Pub of the Year 2013. **Q P**

Sutton-in-Ashfield

Masons Arms

Unwin Road, NG17 4NB
12-11 (01623) 472704 themasonsarmspub.co.uk
Beer range varies
A thriving community pub with a lounge and public bar served from a central servery dispensing two ever-changing real ales, one a LocAle, and one cider. Darts and dominoes are popular. A conservatory has been added at the rear leading to a garden and smoking area. Mini beer festivals are held twice a year. **Q P**

Picture House

Forest Street, NG17 1DA
8am-midnight (01623) 554627
Greene King Abbot; Ruddles Best Bitter; guest beers
A popular Wetherspoon pub near the bus station. Open plan and Art Deco in style with a high ceiling, the building was originally the King's Cinema in 1932, then it closed and reopened in 1967 as the Star Bingo and Social Club. The bingo hall survived until the 1990s and, more recently, it became the Picture House Night Club. Meals are available until 11pm every day. Sky Sports and ESPN are shown on a huge screen above the front door.

Watnall

Queen's Head

40 Main Road, NG16 1HT
12-11; 11.30-midnight Thu-Sat; 12-midnight Sun
(0115) 938 6774 thequeensheadwatnall.co.uk
Adnams Broadside; Everards Tiger, Original; Morland Old Speckled Hen; Wells Bombardier; guest beer
A 17th-century rural gem with a lounge/dining space, a small snug hidden behind the bar and an unusual locals' area with a grandfather clock. The extensive garden has children's play equipment and a marquee, making the pub popular all year round. The internal fittings around the bar are original, and photos of locals adorn the walls. Home-cooked English food is served all day. The pub is reputedly haunted. Occasional beer festivals and live music feature. **Q P**

Wellow

Olde Red Lion

Eakring Road, NG22 0EG
12-11 (01623) 861000
Maypole Wellow Gold; Welbeck Abbey Red Feather; Wells Bombardier; guest beers
This 400-year-old village pub is opposite the village green with its maypole and participates in a large event on May Day. The traditional wood-beamed interior includes a restaurant, lounge and bar areas, with photographs and maps depicting the history of the village. Situated close to both Sherwood Forest and Clumber Park. **Q P**

West Bridgford

Poppy & Pint

Pierrepont Road, NG2 5DX
9.30am (10 Sun)-11 (0115) 981 9995
Castle Rock Sheriff's Tipple, Black Gold, Harvest Pale, Preservation Fine Ale, Screech Owl; guest beers
This former British Legion Club, converted in 2011 to become Castle Rock's largest pub, has three areas, one raised, and a family room (until 9pm) with a café bar. Look for the old snooker table ends on one wall. A large function room is upstairs and the beer garden overlooks a bowling green. Twelve handpumps on the large bar dispense Castle Rock beers plus guests. There are usually two real ciders, and excellent food is served. The pub is motorhome friendly. **P**

Stratford Haven

2 Stratford Road, NG2 6BA
11-11 (midnight Fri & Sat); 12-11 Sun (0115) 982 5981
Adnams Broadside; Batemans XB; Castle Rock Harvest Pale, Elsie Mo, Screech Owl; guest beers
A former pet shop, the pub has a single narrow bar with a larger seating area at the back and a secluded snug to one side. Up to 12 cask ales plus a cider are available at any one time, including LocAles from owner Castle Rock's portfolio. A wide range of food includes curry night on Monday and pie night on Tuesday. Sunday is silent quiz night and new-brew day is the first Thursday of the month. **Q**

Trent Bridge Inn

2 Radcliffe Road, NG2 6AA

8am-midnight ☎ (0115) 977 8940

Adnams Broadside; Greene King Abbot; Marston's Pedigree; Nottingham Rock Ale Mild Beer, Trent Bridge Inn Ale; Ruddles Best Bitter; guest beers H

This large, prominent, Victorian corner pub reopened in 2011 under the Wetherspoon banner to much acclaim, including a CAMRA branch award in 2012. A number of inter-connected, wood-panelled rooms include cosy booths, comfy sofas, an open fireplace and an array of mainly cricket-themed sporting memorabilia. Pleasant staff will be happy to pull a sample of one of the 12 real ales and two real ciders usually available, from several bars, including those in the function rooms.

West Stockwith

White Hart

Main Street, DN10 4EY

11-11 ☎ (01427) 890176

whitehartinnweststockwith.co.uk

Idle Golden Crown, Black & Tan, Black Abbot; guest beer H

Small country pub with a little garden overlooking the River Trent, Chesterfield Canal and West Stockwith Marina. One bar serves the through bar, lounge and dining area. A range of five real ales is usually on tap including three from The Idle Brewery, situated in outbuildings at the side of the pub. The area is especially busy during the summer, due to the canal and river traffic.

(97)

Worksop

Grafton Hotel

157-161 Gateford Road, S80 1UQ

3 (12 Fri-Sun)-midnight ☎ (01909) 530470

Beer range varies H

The brewery tap for the Grafton Brewing Company, at least three of its beers are always available at reasonable prices as well as guests from other local breweries. A lively community pub, it has a spacious bar area and a restaurant serving good-value food. It is situated close to the railway station and Worksop Town Football Club and offers good accommodation. CAMRA branch Pub of the Year 2013.

Mallard

Station Approach, S81 7AG (on railway platform)

12 (5 Mon)-11; 11-11 Fri & Sat; 12-10.30 Sun ☎ 0797 352 1824

Double Top Bad Boy; guest beers H

Formerly the Worksop station buffet, the Mallard is situated within the railway station buildings, with access from the car park. The pub offers a warm welcome as well as four real ales, usually including one from the Double Top Brewery, a selection of foreign bottled beers and country fruit wines. A further room is available downstairs for special occasions – such as the three beer festivals the pub holds each year.

Shireoaks Inn

Westgate, S80 1LT

11.30-4, 6-11; 11.30-11 Sat; 12-10.30 Sun

☎ (01909) 472118 shireoaksinn.co.uk

Beer range varies H

Warm, friendly pub converted from cottages. The public bar houses a pool table and large-screen TV, and the comfortable lounge bar has a separate dining area. Tasty home-cooked food is good value for money. The two handpulls dispense regularly changing guest ales. A small outside area with tables is available in the summer. It is the sister pub to the Station Hotel.

Station Hotel

Carlton Road, S80 1PS

11 (12 Sun)-11 ☎ (01909) 474108

thestationhotelworksop.co.uk

Acorn Barnsley Bitter; guest beers H

The pub is situated opposite Worksop railway station on the edge of the town centre. Four regularly changing real ales are available alongside the Barnsley Bitter. One long bar serves a large bar area with a separate dining room, and there is a further small room suitable for functions and meetings. Food is served lunchtimes and evenings and accommodation is offered.

Q (5)

Wysall

Plough

Main Street, Keyworth Road, NG12 5QQ

12-midnight ☎ (01509) 880339

Draught Bass; Greene King Abbot; Timothy Taylor Landlord; guest beers H

A busy country pub dating back more than 150 years, and for the past 14 years owned by the same family. This pleasantly updated village free house retains many period features and much original character, with an attractive beer garden at the front. A sensibly priced menu of traditional home-cooked pub favourites is available at lunchtime. Dogs are welcome after 2.30pm when food service is finished. There is a separate area for pool, and a quiz is hosted on Tuesday.

Q (63)

Noted ales

At one time or another nearly every county town in England of any size has been noted for its beers or ales. Yorkshire claims not only stingo but also Hull and North Allerton ales whilst Nottingham, Lichfield, Derby, Oxford and Burton have almost branded their ales. During the eighteenth century the fame of Dorchester beer almost equalled the popularity of London porter.

Frank A. King, Beer has a History, 1947

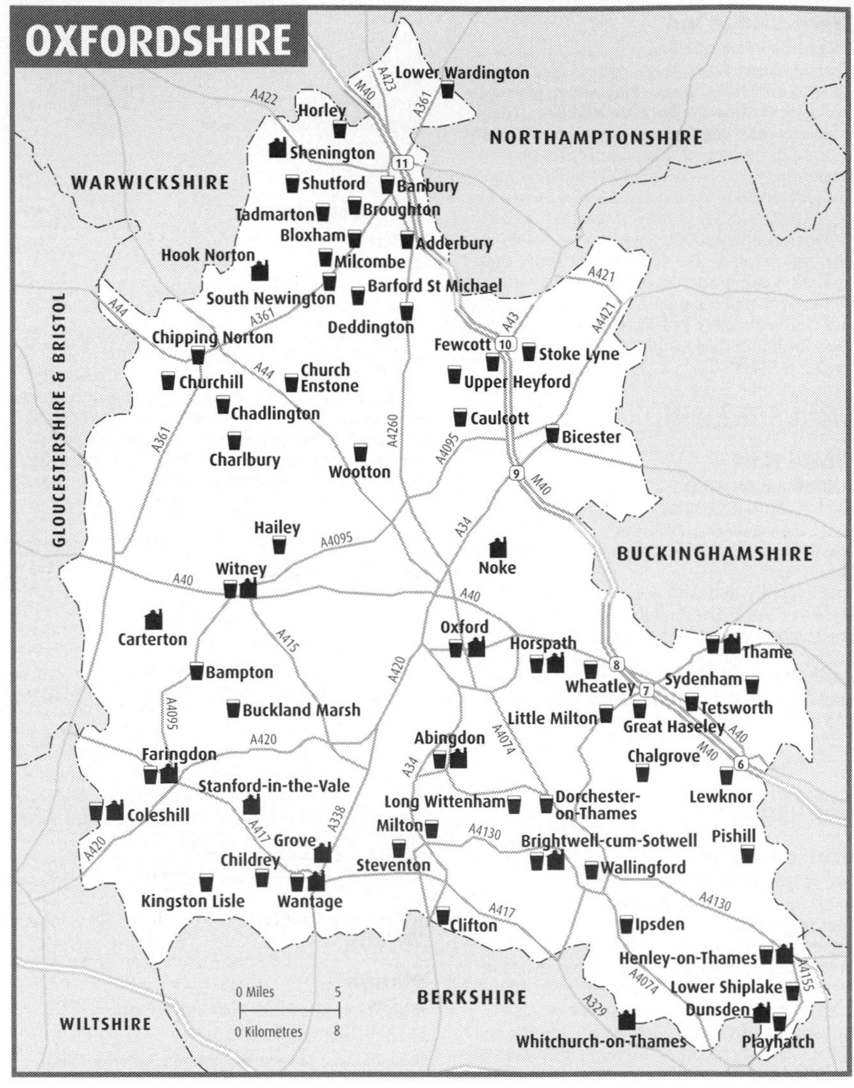

Abingdon

Brewery Tap

40-42 Ock Street, OX14 5BZ

11-11.30 (1am Fri & Sat); 12-11 Sun ☎ (01235) 521655
thebrewerytap.net

Morland Original Bitter; guest beers H

Morland created a tap for its brewery in 1993 by converting three Grade II-listed town houses. The brewery closed in 2000, following a takeover by Greene King, but the pub, run by the same family since it opened, has thrived. There are usually four regularly changing guest beers, including local ales not from the Greene King list. The pub holds three beer festivals a year. Local CAMRA Town & Village Pub of the Year 2012. Q P

King's Head & Bell

10 East St Helen Street, OX14 5EA

12-11 Mon-Wed; 11-midnight Thu (1am Fri & Sat); 12-10.30 Sun ☎ (01235) 525362
kingsheadandbell-abingdon.com

Beer range varies H

First recorded in 1554 and at one time a coaching inn, there are still traces of the building's historic origins in this much renovated and restored pub. It has a number of rooms including two meeting rooms upstairs available for hire, one with a bar. Outside is a pleasant garden in the old courtyard. Guest beers often come from local breweries. The food is home cooked using ingredients sourced from local farms and shops. CAMRA members get a discount on ale. Q

Nag's Head on the Thames

The Bridge, OX14 3HX

11-11.30 (12.30am Fri & Sat); 12-10 Sun
☎ (01235) 524516 thenagsheadonthethames.co.uk

Beer range varies H

Set on an island right on Abingdon Bridge, the pub is split over two levels with a large garden area next to the river and lovely views of the countryside and the town's historic buildings. A free house, it offers eight regularly changing beers,

mostly local. Good food is available all day. Live music plays at weekends and some weekdays. Salter's Steamer cruises from Oxford pass by twice a day in summer. CAMRA members get a discount. Local CAMRA Town & Village Pub of the Year 2013 and Pub of the Year 2014.
(X3,X13)

Adderbury

Pickled Ploughman

Aynho Road, OX17 3NL
10.30-11 (10.30 Sun) (01295) 810327
thepickledploughman.co.uk
Hook Norton Hooky; Ringwood Best Bitter; guest beers H
Following a tasteful and extensive refurbishment in 2012, this free house has built and maintained a reputation not only for an extensive menu of locally-sourced dishes but also for its four well-kept ales on handpump. A decked patio area to the rear is attractive in the summer. The nearby camping and caravan site provides a pleasant base for exploring this picturesque ironstone village with its morris dancing heritage.
QP(S4,81)

Bampton

Morris Clown

High Street, OX18 2JW
5 (1 Sat)-11; 12-10.30 Sun (01993) 850217
Beer range varies H
This single-bar, simply furnished free house, run by the same family for two generations, is heated in the winter by a huge log fire. Bar billiards is played, while Aunt Sally features in the sprawling rear garden. Three guest ales are on handpump, often local, and real cider is available in the summer months. The pub's name change from New Inn by former owners Courage in 1975 proved controversial as morris dancing teams feature a fool, not a clown – this led to a boycott for 25 years.
QP(RH18)

Banbury

Olde Reindeer Inn

47 Parsons Street, OX16 5NA
11 (12 Sun)-11 (01295) 270972
yeoldereindeer.co.uk
Hook Norton Hooky Mild, Hooky, Lion, Old Hooky; guest beer H
This traditional old English pub first became an inn in 1570, and features original wood panelling dating from the English Civil War. It is reported to be the location where Cromwell's men met to plan the Battle of Edge Hill and the siege of Banbury Castle. The pub is adorned with many items of interest including a large selection of pub jugs and other brewery artefacts. Food is served lunchtimes and evenings —see the blackboard for good-value meals. QP

Barford St Michael

George Inn

Lower Street, OX15 0RH (off B4031)
7-11; 12-4 Sun (01869) 338226
Beer range varies H
This quirky thatched free house dates from 1672. Landlord Martin, ably assisted by Dillon the labrador, provides a friendly welcome and a changing range of ales plus cider and perry from Westons and others. No food is served, but patrons may bring their own or takeaways can be ordered in. A beer festival is usually held in summer. Weddings and functions are catered for in a marquee in the garden. Opening hours can vary to suit visitors on request. QP(90)

Bicester

Bure Farm

Barberry Place, OX26 3HA
11.30-11 (01869) 327578 burefarmpub.co.uk
Marston's Pedigree; Ringwood Old Thumper; guest beers H
Family-oriented Marston's inn, well situated on the outskirts of Bicester between two housing estates. Tables are set for diners, but drinkers are made welcome by the friendly staff. There are four handpumps, two reserved for guest ales supplied by Marston's. Seasonal beers, especially those with a sports theme, are always in demand. A wide range of food is available throughout the day including rotisserie meals. There are children's play areas and an attractive beer garden.
Q(North)P

Plough Inn

63 North Street, OX26 6NB
12 (4 Tue)-11; 12-11.30 Fri & Sat; 12-8 Sun
(01869) 388101 theploughbicester.co.uk
Greene King IPA; guest beers H
Traditional Greene King pub situated near the town centre. Angie and Shaun (also the chef) have been at the helm for three years and have built up a regular clientele. In addition to the permanently discounted IPA, up to three other guest ales are offered, with golden ales featuring regularly. Excellent food is served throughout the day (booking recommended for the Sunday carvery). A real log fire is a welcome sight on a cold winter's evening. (North)P

White Hart

4 Sheep Street, OX26 6TB
12-12.30am (1.30am Thu); 10-3am Fri & Sat; 12-1am Sun
(01869) 242734

INDEPENDENT BREWERIES

Adkin Wantage
Appleford Brightwell-cum-Sotwell
Bell Street Henley-on-Thames
Bellinger's Grove
Brakspear (Marston's) Witney
Cats Shenington (NEW)
Compass Carterton
Faringdon Faringdon
Fisher Noke
Hen House Whitchurch-on-Thames
Henley Henley-on-Thames
Hook Norton Hook Norton
Loddon Dunsden
Loose Cannon Abingdon
Old Bog Oxford
Old Forge Coleshill
Shotover Horspath
Thame Thame
Turpin Hook Norton (NEW)
White Horse Stanford-in-the-Vale
Wychwood (Marston's) Witney

Black Sheep Best Bitter; Sharp's Doom Bar [H]
A vibrant town-centre pub which underwent extensive renovation in 2013. During the refurbishment a well was discovered and this has been developed into an attractive feature. Superb outdoor facilities include a bar for summer use and a covered pool table, pinball and gaming machines. Three real ales are permanently on handpump, one the house beer. No meals are available but during the day the front bar serves as a coffee house with sandwiches for sale.
❀♿⇌(Town)♣P🚌🐾📶

Bloxham

Elephant & Castle
Humber Street, OX15 4LZ (off A361)
⏲ 10-3, 6 (5 Fri)-11; 10-11 Sat; 12-10.30 Sun
☎ (01295) 720383 🌐 bloxhampub.co.uk
Hook Norton Hooky; guest beer [H]
This 17th-century coaching inn seems to face the wrong way as the turnpike once ran through the car park and its carriage entrance. More historic features, including a bread oven and photographs of old Bloxham, lie within. In the hands of the same family for 40 years, a warm welcome awaits. Two Hooky beers and one guest are served, plus up to eight ciders and perries. Home-made food is served at lunchtimes (not Sun).
❀🛏◐♣🍎P🚌(488,489)🐾📶

Brightwell-cum-Sotwell

Red Lion L
Brightwell Street, OX10 0RT (off A4130)
⏲ 12-3, 6-11.30; 12-9 Sun ☎ (01491) 837373 🌐 redlion.biz
Loddon Hoppit; West Berkshire Good Old Boy; guest beers [H]
A welcome return to the Guide for this popular pub in a quiet village, now under new management. The traditional half-timbered thatched inn dates from the 16th century, with a comfortable bar featuring wood beams and exposed brick leading to a restaurant area off to one side. Beers are usually from local breweries, and good-quality reasonably priced pub food is served.
Q❀◐◑🍎P🚌(X2,131)🐾📶

Broughton

Saye & Sele Arms
Main Road, OX15 5ED
⏲ 11.30-2.30 (3 Sat), 7-11; 12-5 Sun ☎ (01295) 263348
🌐 sayeandselearms.co.uk
Adnams Southwold Bitter; Sharp's Doom Bar; guest beers [H]
Imposing village pub built of Hornton stone at the edge of Broughton Castle grounds. This friendly and welcoming hostelry is popular for its beer, food and friendly welcome. The beamed and flagstoned bar is ideal for sampling the four ales. Food is locally sourced, and Danny's pie of the day should not be missed. There is an attractive beer garden for summer drinking and dining, and the pub holds regular events including a monthly quiz. Well worth a visit. Q❀◐◑♿♣P🚌(50A)

Buckland Marsh

Trout Inn at Tadpole Bridge L
SN7 8RF
⏲ 11.30-3, 6-11; 11-11 Fri & Sat; 12-10.30 Sun
☎ (01367) 870382 🌐 trout-inn.co.uk
Ramsbury Bitter; Young's Bitter; guest beers [H]
Located in an idyllic setting by the upper reaches of the Thame, this former toll house for the adjacent ancient humpback bridge has a light interior and features much woodwork. The decor includes stuffed fishes in glass cases, reflecting the popularity of this stretch of the river with anglers. Although there is an emphasis on food, for which the pub is acclaimed, drinkers popping in for a pint are welcomed, with two regular ales supplemented by two changing guests.
Q🔥❀🛏◐◑♿P🐾📶

Caulcott

Horse & Groom
Lower Heyford Road, OX25 4ND
⏲ 12-3, 6-11 (not Mon eve); 12-3, 7-10.30 Sun
☎ (01869) 343257 🌐 horseandgroomcaulcott.co.uk
White Horse Bitter; guest beers [H]
A small pub with a big welcome, this genuine free house offers three guest ales, often from local micros and Cornish brewers. The French landlord/chef serves excellent food (booking recommended, especially for Thursday steak night and Sunday lunch). The Bastille Day beer festival is not to be missed. No dogs or under-sevens permitted inside. The good-sized garden is popular in summer. Car parking is available nearby. Q❀◐◑P📶

Chadlington

Tite Inn
Mill End, OX7 3NY
⏲ 11.30-11 (10.30 Sun) ☎ (01608) 676910
🌐 thetiteinn.co.uk
Sharp's Doom Bar; guest beers [H]
Welcoming community pub serving one regular and two ever-changing guest ales alongside Westons Old Rosie cider on handpump. The pub name is taken from the old Oxfordshire dialect for 'spring' – water runs under the pub and through the beautiful hillside garden, which is an idyllic setting for a summer evening pint. Inside you can relax in comfortable surroundings and there is a logburner for colder nights. Excellent, affordable food is served in the bar and restaurant.
Q🔥❀◐◑⛺🍎P🚌(S3,X9)🐾📶

Chalgrove

Red Lion L
115 High Street, OX44 7SS
⏲ 11.30-3, 6-11; 12-11.30 Sun ☎ (01865) 890625
🌐 redlionchalgrove.co.uk
Butcombe Bitter; Fuller's London Pride; Rebellion Mild; guest beers [H]
Church-owned village local run by a friendly husband and wife team, both trained chefs. Good food is a speciality at this picturesque 16th-century inn. The two guest beers are usually from small breweries such as Rebellion and West Berks. The interior is divided into several distinct areas and the pub is used by a wide cross-section of the community. You can drink outside in both front and rear gardens, while a real fire awaits inside in the winter months. Q🔥❀◐◑♿♣🚌🐾📶

Charlbury

Rose & Crown

Market Street, OX7 3PL
12-11 (1am Fri); 11-1am Sat (01608) 810103
roseandcrown.charlbury.com
Beer range varies [H]
Well-respected, traditional ale house boasting eight draught beers plus real cider, perry and a Belgian beer selection. On average, 15 beers a week are on offer here, sourced from all corners of the UK, with at least one handpump dedicated to beer from Wye Valley. There is an established winter beer festival on the last weekend of January, and fortnightly Saturday night live blues featuring international artists.

Childrey

Hatchet Inn

Main Street, OX12 9UF (on B4001)
12-2.30 (not Mon & Tue; 3 Sat), 7-11; 12-3.30, 7-10.30 Sun
(01235) 751213
Morland Original; guest beers [H]
A split-level, single-bar, family-run local, host to a variety of village sports teams. The landlord is well known for his commitment to cask ale, and the pub is famed among cognoscenti for its large assortment of crisps and other packeted delights. The large garden has children's climbing frames. A previous winner of local CAMRA branch Pub of the Year. P (38,67)

Chipping Norton

Chequers

Goddards Lane, OX7 5NP (next to theatre, on corner of Spring St)
11-11 (midnight Fri & Sat) (01608) 644717
chequers-pub.com
Fuller's Chiswick Bitter, Discovery, London Pride, London Porter, ESB; Gales HSB; guest beers [H]
The Chequers is renowned for its choice and quality of beer. Eight handpumps serve the whole Fuller's range and changing guests. The bar area is free of machines and TV. There is a spacious and airy restaurant to the rear where top-quality food is served. The function room hosts eclectic community and interest groups. The pub is popular with theatregoers next door. Watch out for the badgers and the legendary home-made Scotch eggs. CAMRA branch Pub of the Year 2013.
Q

Red Lion

Albion Street, OX7 5BJ
9.30 (10 Mon)-11; 11-11 Sun (01608) 644641
Hook Norton Hooky, Lion, Old Hooky; guest beer [H]
The smallest pub in Chipping Norton, dating back to 1684, although in its present location since 1898. Hooky is always available plus a seasonal ale from Hook Norton or an occasional guest. There is a roaring fire in winter and a suntrap garden for summer. The pub's annual charity three-legged race is well supported along with the beer festival. Traditional pub games include Aunt Sally and cribbage. Sky Sports is screened.
Q P

Church Enstone

Crown Inn

Mill Lane, OX7 4NN (off A44, on B4030)
12-3, 6-11; 12-4 Sun (01608) 677262
crowninnenstone.co.uk
Hook Norton Hooky; guest beers [H]
This enchanting 17th-century Cotswold stone village inn features an inglenook fireplace and wooden beams, and old local photos on the stone walls. It is popular with both locals and visitors, an ideal destination following a walk in the countryside. The award-winning menu offers food made with locally-sourced ingredients, and two varying guest ales are available. A pub for conversation, there is no jukebox or games machine. Families welcome. Q P (S3)

Churchill

Chequers

Church Road, OX7 6NJ
11-midnight (01242) 822937
thechequerschurchill.co.uk
Bath Barnsey; Hook Norton Hooky; guest beers [H]
Attractive 18th-century stone-built pub with later additions and extensions, situated opposite the village church. The traditional interior is divided into different areas with stone-flagged and bare-wood floors and exposed beams aplenty, together with interesting and quirky decorations. The emphasis is on good food, but the drinker is far from forgotten, with the bar supporting six handpumps and an impressive brushed metal tube with an array of taps for ciders and other beers. Families are welcome. P

Clifton

Duke of Cumberland's Head

Main Street, OX15 0PE
12-11 (01869) 338534 cliftonduke.com
Hook Norton Lion; Sharp's Doom Bar; guest beers [H]
This thatched Elizabethan coaching inn in a quiet village beside the River Cherwell has been in the same family for 19 years. It offers four ales on handpump and a monthly changing menu which attracts diners from far and wide. The tranquil ambience can be enjoyed beside the log fire in winter or outside in the large garden in summer, where the local game Aunt Sally is played. Dogs are welcome in the bar area and the accommodation. Q P (81)

Coleshill

Radnor Arms [L]

32 Coleshill, SN6 7PR
12-11 (10.30 Sun) (01793) 861575
radnorarmscoleshill.co.uk
Old Forge Anvil Ale, Blacksmiths Gold, Hammer and Tongs, Sledgehammer [H]/[G]**; guest beer** [G]
Set in a beautiful National Trust village, the 18th-century building was the former smithy to the Coleshill estate. Old blacksmith's tools are displayed in the split-level two-room interior; one room has its own snug. This is the brewery tap for the on-site Old Forge Brewery. Beers are dispensed by gravity and handpump, to be enjoyed with traditional home-cooked pub fare. Walkers, children and well-behaved dogs are welcome.
Q P

Deddington

Crown & Tuns

New Street, OX15 0SP (beside A4260)
12-3 (not Mon), 5.30-11; 12-10.30 Sun ☎ (01869) 337371
puddingface.com
Hook Norton Hooky, Old Hooky; guest beer Ⓗ
You will be warmly welcomed at this 16th-century coaching inn beside the main Oxford to Banbury road. The building has been magnificently adapted into a bistro-style award-winning Hook Norton outlet. Affectionately known locally as 'the pie place', the menu consists mainly, but not exclusively, of delicious pies with puff/short pastry alternatives. A good range of Hook Norton beers is available. The peaceful rear terraced patio is attractively decked, and Aunt Sally is played. Q (S4)

Dorchester-on-Thames

George Hotel

High Street, OX10 7HH (opp church lychgate)
11-midnight ☎ (01865) 340404
thegeorgedorchester.co.uk
Brakspear Bitter; Butcombe Bitter; Wadworth 6X; guest beer Ⓗ
One of the oldest in the country, this coaching inn was built in 1495, situated in a historic village opposite Dorchester Abbey and museum. Inside, there is a friendly front bar, lounge and restaurant, complete with oak beams and inglenook fireplaces. Liaan, the landlord, is passionate about serving real ale in perfect condition. Three regular ales and one guest are on offer at £2.35 between 5 and 7pm, but CAMRA members receive a 50p per pint discount at other times. QP

Faringdon

Swan

1 Park Road, SN7 7BP
4.30-midnight; 3.30-2am Fri, 12-2am Sat; 12-midnight Sun
☎ (01367) 241480
Faringdon Folly Ale; guest beers Ⓗ
The Swan was completely renovated in 2010. Up to six real ales are available including a range from the on-site Faringdon Brewery plus a wide choice of guests sourced locally and from further afield. Live music and folk jamming sessions keep the ever-increasing regular clientele entertained. Pub games include bar billiards, table skittles, bagatelle and others. Q (66)

Fewcott

White Lion

Fritwell Road, OX27 7NZ (1 mile from M40 jct 10)
7 (5.30 Fri)-11; 12-11 Sat; 12-6.30 Sun ☎ (01869) 346639
Beer range varies Ⓗ
A true free house, offering a constantly changing selection of three ales, mainly from micros, with a stout, porter or mild often available. This popular village pub is the hub of the community, ideal for enjoying conversation and watching sport on TV, though it can get busy on darts and quiz nights. The large garden is popular in summer.
Accommodation is a single en-suite room (early booking recommended).
P (81,81A)

Great Haseley

Plough

Rectory Road, OX44 7JQ (off B480)
12-3, 5-11; 12-midnight Sat; 12-11 Sun
☎ (01844) 279283 ploughpub.com
Sharp's Doom Bar; guest beers Ⓗ
Thriving community-owned pub, close to the M40, sympathetically extended and refurbished in 2013. It retains a traditional, cosy and friendly atmosphere, with a thatched roof and exposed original stonework and beams. The main bar at the front offers at least two beers from local microbreweries, with XT and Vale often featured. The separate dining room, in the new extension to the rear, has an interesting and well-priced menu featuring locally-sourced produce.
QP (103,124)

Hailey

Bird in Hand

White Oak Green, OX29 9XP (near Witney)
8am-11 ☎ (01993) 868321 birdinhandinn.co.uk
Brains SA; Hook Norton Hooky; guest beer Ⓗ
This Cotswold country inn near Hailey has a comfortable bar area with many period features including wooden beams and an inglenook fireplace. Three handpumps offer beers from the local area plus Brains SA. The owner's enthusiasm for Welsh rugby is clear – a wealth of memorabilia festoons every corner. A popular destination for diners, all food is freshly cooked and locally sourced, from as nearby as the pub's vegetable garden. Accommodation is available, and function rooms can be booked. QP (X9)

Henley-on-Thames

Bird in Hand

61 Greys Road, RG9 1SB
12-2, 5-11; 12-11 Sat; 12-10.30 Sun ☎ (01491) 575775
Brakspear Bitter; Fuller's London Pride; Hook Norton Hooky Mild; guest beers Ⓗ
The Bird is a genuine community local, run by the same couple for over 20 years. It is a frequent winner of local CAMRA Pub of the Year, including in 2014, and a regular in the Guide. Two ever-changing guest beers, often from local micros, complement the three regulars. The pub hosts darts and cribbage teams, and regular quiz nights. The family room leads onto a delightful rear garden with a pond and aviary, very popular in summer. TVs show sporting events. Q

Henley Brew House

38 Market Place, RG9 2AH
12-11 (midnight Fri & Sat) ☎ (01491) 576561
henleybrewhouse.com
Henley Jail House, Temple Island; guest beers Ⓗ
Housed in what was formerly a Victorian police station, this lively free house in the centre of the market town is home to the Henley Brewing Company microbrewery. The brewery is visible through glass in the centre of the pub and at least two of its beers are always available. Other local guest beers are usually among the range on the six handpumps. The restaurant to the rear has dining alcoves in the former prison cells.

Horley

Red Lion

Hornton Lane, OX15 6BQ

closed Mon; 6-11; 12-6 Sun (01295) 730427

horleyvillage.co.uk

Hook Norton Hooky; Purity Mad Goose; Sharp's Doom Bar [H]

A traditional pub at the heart of the community, this village local offers a friendly welcome to visitors, dogs and walkers. The garden is a tranquil area for a summer's evening tipple. Three handpumped ales are available. The annual beer festival around St George's Day has become a must with locals and visitors alike. Darts and dominoes are played, and a TV shows live sporting events. A wet sales-only hostelry. (504)

Horspath

Queen's Head [L]

26 Church Road, OX33 1RU

12-3 (not Mon), 5-11; 12-11 Fri-Sun (01865) 875567

thequeensheadhorspath.co.uk

Fuller's London Pride; Shotover Prospect, Scholar; guest beer [H]

A traditional, friendly, family-run pub, and a local outlet for Shotover beers, brewed just down the road. There are steps up from the street – to the right is a lively bar with a lower pool room area, to the left is a comfortable lounge. There is also a restaurant and a large rear courtyard garden. Live music is hosted on most Saturdays. The pub has five letting rooms, including one with full disabled access. P (103,104)

Ipsden

King William IV

Hailey, OX10 6AD (follow brown signs off A4074) SU641859

11.30-3, 5.30-11; 11.30-11 Fri & Sat; 11.30-10.30 Sun

(01491) 681845 kingwilliamipsden.co.uk

Brakspear Bitter; guest beer [G]

Breathtaking views over the Oxfordshire countryside and the lambs in springtime can be enjoyed from the large garden area of this idyllic country pub. The beers are dispensed by gravity from the single bar, with a guest from the Brakspear pubco approved list, and there is an extensive food menu with daily specials. In addition to the area by the bar, warmed by an open fire, there are two other contiguous areas for drinkers and diners. A popular destination for cyclists and walkers, also for those who choose to drive. Q P

Kingston Lisle

Blowing Stone Inn [L]

OX12 9QL

12-midnight (2am Fri & Sat) (01367) 820288

theblowingstone.co.uk

Morland Original Bitter; Sharp's Doom Bar; guest beers [H]

Large, friendly, relaxed free house in the shadow of Uffington White Horse. The building was totally refurbished in 2009 and the bars now feature contemporary decor and modern, comfortable furnishings. There is a separate conservatory, a large beer garden and an award-winning restaurant. A good mixture of locals and diners frequent the pub. Two regular ales are supplemented by two changing guest beers, locally sourced. P

Lewknor

Leathern Bottle

1 High Street, OX49 5TW (off B4009 near M40 jct 6)

11-2.30 (3 Sat), 5.30-11; 12-3, 7-10.30 Sun

(01844) 351482 theleathernbottle.co.uk

Brakspear Bitter; Marston's Pedigree; guest beer [H]

This classic 17th-century inn has featured in all but one edition of the Guide. The pub has a reputation for great ale, good home-cooked food featuring locally-sourced meats, log fires, a warm welcome and a family-friendly garden. Popular with walkers from the nearby Ridgeway, it is easily reached by car, or a short walk from the Oxford Tube and the airline coach stop at junction 6. The guest beer comes from the Brakspear pubco approved list. Q P

Little Milton

Lamb

High Street, OX44 7PU (on A329)

12-3, 6.30-midnight; 12-10.30 Sun (01844) 279527

lambinnlittlemilton.co.uk

Brakspear Bitter; guest beers [H]

Thatched 16th-century stone pub situated on the main road through the village. The attractive, welcoming split-level bar features plenty of original beams, with seating areas for those who just want a drink, as well as for diners enjoying the high-quality pub food. To the rear there is a patio and a quiet garden where a beer festival is held in July. Brakspear Bitter is the regular ale, plus two changing guests. P

Long Wittenham

Plough

24 High Street, OX14 4QH

11-11 (01865) 407738 theploughinnlw.co.uk

Butcombe Bitter; guest beers [H]

The Plough is Grade II-listed and dates back to the 17th century – you may need to duck when you enter the bar to avoid the wooden beams. There are two cosy bars and a restaurant. The long garden is a great place to visit in summer – go past the children's play area and you will find it stretches right down to the River Thames. Ever-changing guest ales are sourced from breweries and microbreweries in the South East. P (97)

Lower Shiplake

Baskerville [L]

7 Station Road, RG9 3NY

11-11; 12-10.30 Sun (0118) 940 3332

thebaskerville.com

Loddon Hoppit; Sharp's Doom Bar; Timothy Taylor Landlord; guest beer [H]

Popular food-oriented pub located at the heart of this riverside village. The wood-panelled bar features many rowing artefacts and rugby memorabilia from national and local teams, in particular the pub's own team – the Hounds. The enclosed garden has a children's play area and hosts regular summer barbecues. Convenient for the Henley Regatta Railway Line and an ideal stop-off for walkers on the Thames Path, it offers accommodation in four en-suite rooms. Q(Shiplake)P(800)

Lower Wardington

Hare & Hounds

Edgecote Lane, OX17 1SH
12-3, 5-11; 12-midnight Fri & Sat; 12-8 Sun
(01295) 750645
Hook Norton Hooky; guest beer H
With over 20 years' experience in the trade, Carol and Jamie have established this Hook Norton tied house, 50 yards off the A361, at the heart of the local community. It raises around £10,000 annually for a different charity each year, selected by customers, and is a former Hook Norton Community Pub of the Year. Annual fundraising events include a sponsored cycle ride over the spring bank holiday and a beer and music festival in July. QP(200)

Milcombe

Horse & Groom

Main Road, OX15 4RS
12-3, 6-11; 12-5 Sun (01295) 722142
thehorseandgroominn.co.uk
Beer range varies H
Convivial 17th-century coaching inn made from local stone, warmed by a log fire in the inglenook fireplace. The interior comprises a bar with a flagstone floor and traditional furnishings, a snug and a more contemporary dining room. Three handpumps dispense a range of ales, and a regularly changing food menu features locally-sourced ingredients. Set on the edge of the Cotswolds, it is an ideal place to end a walk, and has an attractive enclosed patio area – families are welcome. QP(488)

Milton

Plum Pudding

44 High Street, OX14 4EJ
11.30-2.30, 5-11; 11.30-11.30 Fri & Sat; 12-11 Sun
(01235) 834443 theplumpuddingmilton.co.uk
Brakspear Oxford Gold; Ringwood Plum Pudding Best Bitter; guest beers H
Plum Pudding actually refers to the Oxford Sandy and Black pig, one of the older and rarer British breeds, so it is no surprise to see pork featuring on the food menu here. Until autumn 2013 this was a Greene King pub, but it is now owned by Mandy and Jez, who have an excellent record of running Guide pubs. A great village local, it is close to the thriving Milton Business Park. Plum Pudding Best Bitter is the pub's house beer, brewed by Ringwood. P

Oxford

Chequers

130a High Street, OX1 4DH
11-11.30 (12.30am Fri & Sat); 11-11 Sun
(01865) 727463
Brakspear Bitter, Oxford Gold; St Austell Nicholson's Pale Ale; guest beers H
Down a narrow medieval passageway off the High Street, the Chequers is a fine old inn, much of it dating back to the 16th century when it was converted from a money lender's tenement to a tavern. Note the fine carvings and the ceiling in the lower bar. Up to five frequently changing guest beers are available, with tasting notes provided, and interesting food is served. A cobbled courtyard provides alfresco drinking, dining and smoking facilities. Q

Far from the Madding Crowd

10-12 Friars Entry, OX1 2BY (alley between Magdalen St and Gloucester Green)
11.30-11 (midnight Thu-Sat); 12-10.30 Sun
(01865) 240900 maddingcrowd.co.uk
Brakspear Bitter; guest beers H
An award-winning free house, with six handpumps and a beer choice that changes daily, one always offered at a discount. Four beer and two cider festivals are held annually, and real cider is always available. A quiz and curry night is hosted on Sunday, Monday is open mic (no food), and pizza night on Thursday is popular. The pub is handy for the city's theatres and cinemas. Local CAMRA City Pub of the Year 2012.

Grapes

7 George Street, OX1 2AT
11-11 (midnight Fri & Sat); 12-11 Sun (01865) 793380
Bath Gem, Golden Hare, Barnsey; guest beers H
First built in 1820 and rebuilt in 1879, this is a rare Victorian pub situated opposite the New Theatre in the city centre – the traditional exterior stands out from the surrounding chain bars and restaurants. The single narrow, panelled room has the bar on one side and seating on the other, with glazed timber screens. There is some original tiling in the entrance. This is the only outlet for Bath Ales in Oxfordshire. Q

Lamb & Flag

12 St Giles, OX1 3JS
12-11 (10.30 Sun) (01865) 515787
Palmers Best Bitter; Skinner's Betty Stogs; Theakston Old Peculier; guest beers H
Grade II-listed building run by St John's College as a free house. Some of the profits from the pub support student scholarships. Beers from the south-west feature – the house beer Lamb & Flag Gold is brewed by Palmers of Bridport. Two real ciders or perries are always available and beer festivals are held three or four times a year. Believed to be the setting for the inn in Thomas Hardy's novel Jude the Obscure, it has other literary links. Q

Masons Arms L

2 Quarry School Place, Headington Quarry, OX3 8LH
5 (7 Mon)-11; 12-11 Sat; 12-4, 7-10.30 Sun
(01865) 764579 themasonsarmshq.co.uk
Dark Star Hophead; Rebellion Mutiny; West Berkshire Good Old Boy; guest beers H
Family-run community pub full of character, hosting many pub games leagues, including bar billiards and Aunt Sally. The guest ales are varied and regularly come from the Old Bog Brewery (named after the original purpose of the building behind the pub where it is located). A range of local and foreign bottled beers is stocked. The pub is home to the Headington beer festival in September. A heated decking area and garden lead to the function room. Events include twice-monthly music nights. P(H2)

Rose & Crown L

14 North Parade Avenue, OX2 6LX (½ mile N of city centre, off Banbury Road)

⏲ 11-midnight (1am Fri & Sat); 12-midnight Sun
☎ (01865) 510551 🌐 roseandcrownoxford.com
Adnams Southwold Bitter; Hook Norton Hooky; guest beer Ⓗ
Now a free house, this popular Victorian local on a vibrant north Oxford street is a time capsule with two small rooms and many original features. No intrusive music or mobile phones are permitted. A friendly community pub, there are books and local business cards to peruse. Landlords Andrew and Debbie celebrated 30 years here in 2013 and the pub's fame has even spread to Everest – see the photo on wall. To the rear is a heated, covered patio. Children are welcome until 5pm.
Q❀◑♣🚌

Royal Blenheim Ⓛ
13 St Ebbes Street, OX1 1PT
⏲ 11-11 (11.30 Wed & Thu; midnight Fri & Sat); 10-11 Sun
☎ (01865) 242355 🌐 royalblenheim.co.uk
White Horse Bitter, Village Idiot, Wayland Smithy; guest beers Ⓗ
Street-corner, single-room, Victorian pub with a bright, airy interior, next to the Museum of Modern Art. The pub is owned by Everards but leased to the White Horse Brewery. Ten handpumps dispense a full range of White Horse beers plus guests (including one from Everards) and a real cider. Good food includes vegetarian and gluten-free options on the menu. Opens for breakfast at 10am on Sunday. ◑♿⇌♣🍎🚌

St Aldates Tavern Ⓛ
108 St Aldate's, OX1 1BU
⏲ 11.30-11 (midnight Thu-Sat) ☎ (01865) 241185
🌐 staldatestavernoxford.co.uk
Beer range varies Ⓗ
Refurbished for its reopening in 2012, this friendly pub in the centre of Oxford features a range of six real ales including at least three from local breweries such as XT and Rebellion. Good-quality, freshly cooked food is served lunchtimes and evenings (all day at weekends), made with locally-sourced ingredients where possible. There is an attractive function room upstairs, available to hire, with its own bar and toilets. ◑🚌🐾

White Hart
12 St Andrew's Road, Headington, OX3 9DL
⏲ 12-11 (midnight Fri & Sat) ☎ (01865) 761737
Everards Sunchaser Blonde, Tiger; guest beer Ⓗ
This friendly 17th-century establishment is located in the picturesque, Cotswold-stone area of Old Headington opposite the 12th-century church of St Andrew. In the 16th century it was an ale house/brothel run by the notorious Joan of Headington (see the framed poem on the wall). To the rear is a large and attractive walled garden, home to the spring beer festival. The food is traditional and home-made, with pies a speciality. Local CAMRA City Pub of the Year 2013. ❀◑🍎🚌🐾

Pishill

Crown Inn
RG9 6HH (on B480) SU724900
⏲ 12-3, 6-11; 12-3, 7-10 summer Sun ☎ (01491) 638364
🌐 thecrowninnpishill.co.uk
Brakspear Bitter; guest beer Ⓗ
An ale house has stood on this site since the 11th century, originally serving a monastic community with links to the nearby Stonor manor house. The current building dates from the 15th century, boasting a wealth of exposed brickwork, beams and log fires. The emphasis is on well-kept beer and quality food. A beautifully renovated 400-year-old thatched barn is available for functions, including a beer festival each September. Accommodation is in a one-bedroom self-catering cottage, with views over Stonor Valley.
Q❀🛏◑P🐾

Playhatch

Flowing Spring
Henley Road, RG4 9RB (on A4155)
⏲ closed Mon; 12-3, 5-midnight; 12-midnight Fri-Sun
☎ (0118) 969 9878 🌐 theflowingspringpub.co.uk
Fuller's London Pride, ESB; Gales Seafarers Ale; guest beer Ⓗ
Popular 18th-century country pub featuring Fuller's ales plus occasional guests. The large stream-side garden has two slides and is overlooked by a heated covered balcony. The pub serves home-made food and specialises in gluten-free, dairy-free, vegetarian and vegan options. Events are held all year round including astronomy nights, comedy nights, murder mysteries, an annual ferret show, and a beer festival with live music in summer. Look out for Quirky Corner and its collection of weird and wonderful artefacts. ❀◑♣P🚌(800)🐾

Shutford

George & Dragon
Church Lane, OX15 6PG
⏲ 12-2.30 (not Mon-Thu), 6-11; 12-11 Sat; 12-10.30 Sun
☎ (01295) 780320 🌐 thegeorgeanddragon.com
Beer range varies Ⓗ
This popular and welcoming 13th-century village pub nestles into the hillside beside the church. The free house has a lively bar with an inglenook fireplace, tiled floor and a well-stocked bar with a Hook Norton ale and four guest beers. The restaurant serves British food that is home-cooked from scratch and uses local ingredients. The pub hosts traditional games including darts and Aunt Sally. There is a separate TV room with Sky and BT Sports. Q❀◑♣🍎📺🚌(269)

South Newington

Duck on the Pond
Main Street, OX15 4JE
⏲ 11-3, 5-11; 11-11 Sat & Sun ☎ (01295) 721166
🌐 duckonthepond.com
Hook Norton Hooky; guest beers Ⓗ
Parts of this attractive village pub, on the main road from Banbury to Chipping Norton, date from the 16th century. Originally built from local stone, it has been lovingly renovated, retaining many original features including oak beams and a bread oven behind the large open fire. A spacious patio area overlooks the pond, where ducks and fish coexist, with picturesque views beyond. There are regularly changing guest ales and a varied menu featuring locally-sourced produce. ❀◑♣P🚌

Steventon

North Star ★ Ⓛ
2 Stocks Lane, OX13 6SG (end of the Causeway off B4017)
⏲ 5 (3 Fri)-11; 12-11.30 Sat; 12-11 Sun
Morland Original; guest beers Ⓖ

Identified by CAMRA as having a nationally important historic pub interior and next to the Causeway, a listed ancient monument, this wonderful, unspoilt village inn has been run by the same family for 160 years. Popular with locals and visitors, it hosts many village clubs and social events. Inside it has a function/games room and two additional rooms, one with a snug space with three settles around an open fireplace. Beers are served through a stable door or hatch. An ideal stop-off for walkers and their dogs. **Q❀▲♣P🚌🐾**

Stoke Lyne

Peyton Arms

OX27 8SD

⏲ closed Mon; 12-2, 5-9 Tue & Fri; 5-11 Wed & Thu; 12-7 Sat & Sun ☎ (01869) 345285

Hook Norton Hooky, Old Hooky [G]

Prepare to step back in time when you enter this good old-fashioned hostelry. Set in a farming community, the bar has no handpumps – two local Hook Norton ales are served direct from the cask. The hosts are local legends, very much a part of the character of the pub. The bar, a great place for conversation, is for adults only. Simple rolls are available. Close to junction 10 of the M40, phone ahead for weekday opening hours. **Q❀P🚌**(37,81)

Sydenham

Inn at Emmington 🄻

Sydenham Road, OX39 4LD

⏲ 12-2 (not Mon & Tue), 4-11; 12-11 Fri & Sat; 12-9 Sun ☎ (01844) 351367 🌐 theinnatemmington.co.uk

Fuller's London Pride; Rebellion IPA; guest beer [H]

The Inn, renowned for its cask ales, convivial atmosphere and excellent food, is just off junction 6 of the M40, with the proximity to the Chiltern Hills also a big draw. Those looking to explore the local ales should book a stay in one of the seven guest rooms, some with views over the Oxfordshire countryside. Lunch and evening menus change frequently depending on the fresh local produce available. A 150-year-old English walnut tree presides over the large well-kept garden. **❀🛏◑♣🍎P🚌**(40)🐾📶

Tadmarton

Lampet Arms

Main Street, OX15 5TB

⏲ 12-2, 4.30-11; 11-11 Sat; 12-5 Sun ☎ (01295) 780070

Hook Norton Hooky; guest beers [H]

The Lampet Arms was built in the Victorian era as a railway tavern in a village where the railway was expected but never actually arrived. Walkers, hikers and their dogs are greeted with a warm welcome, and a choice of four handpumped beers and one cider. With home-cooked food, a function room, TV for major sporting events, coffee mornings and accommodation, this pub has become a focal point for the village. **🐴🛏◑♣🍎P🚌**(50A)🐾📶

Tetsworth

Old Red Lion

40 High Street, OX9 7AS

⏲ 11-10 (midnight Fri); 12-4 Sun ☎ (01844) 281274 🌐 theoldredliontetsworth.co.uk

Beer range varies [H]

The Old Red Lion is situated on the Oxford side of the quiet village of Tetsworth, opposite the village green. It has a warm and friendly atmosphere, with a cosy log fire in the winter time. Two well-kept real ales are served, one from a local brewery. Traditional pub food is available all day in the bar, and in the more formal restaurant. Home to the village shop. **Q❀◑♿🍎P🚌**(124,275)🐾

Thame

Cross Keys 🏆 🄻

1 Park Street, OX9 3JS

⏲ 12-2, 5-11; 12-11 Sat; 12-10.30 Sun ☎ (01844) 218202

XT Four; guest beers [H]

Transformed from a failing keg-only dive, this fantastic pub serves plentiful ales to a discerning drinker. Usually busy, the bar will see at least two beers change every day over the weekend, and more during the week. Keep a close eye on Twitter for unusual beers, especially those from the Thame brewery at the back of the pub – but be warned, they will go quickly. With cribbage and other bar games available, you can easily while an afternoon and evening away. **Q❀♣🍎🚌**(280)🐾📶

Upper Heyford

Barley Mow

Somerton Road, OX25 5LB

⏲ 12-2.30, 5-11; 12-11 Sat; 12-3.30, 7-10.30 Sun ☎ (01869) 232300 🌐 barley-mow-upper-heyford.co.uk

Fuller's Chiswick Bitter, London Pride; guest beer [H]

A warm welcome is assured at this family-run, community-focused local situated near to the end of the runway at the now-closed RAF base. The landlord is a Fuller's Master Cellarman, and his guest beer is either a Fuller's seasonal or from a local brewer. There is a large open bar and a separate dining area where home-made food is cooked to order. Aunt Sally can be played in the garden. Close to the canal, moorings are available. **🐴❀◑♿♣P🚌**(25A)🐾

Wallingford

Town Arms 🄻

102 High Street, OX10 0BL

⏲ 12-midnight (1am Thu-Sat); 12-11 Sun ☎ (01491) 837773 🌐 thetownarms.com

Loose Cannon Abingdon Bridge; West Berkshire Good Old Boy; guest beers [H]

A remarkable turnaround for this two-room pub, which has quickly established a reputation for good-value local real ale and pub food. Three local ales are usually served, although six handpumps are available for busier periods. The bars have been refurbished to make more space for drinkers, with an open fire in winter. There is a pool table and a dartboard. Located close to the River Thames, the pub is ideally situated for walkers and boaters. **❀◑♣P🚌**

Wantage

Royal Oak 🄻

Newbury Street, OX12 8DF (S of Market Sq)

⏲ 5.30-11; 12-2.30, 7-11 Sat; 12-2, 7-10.30 Sun ☎ (01235) 763129 🌐 royaloakwantage.co.uk

Wadworth 6X [H]/[G]**; West Berkshire Maggs' Magnificent Mild, Dr Hexter's Wedding Ale, Dr Hexter's Healer; guest beers** [G]

This multi-award-winning street-corner pub is a mecca for the discerning drinker and a meeting place for many local clubs. Photographs of ships bearing the pub's name adorn the walls. The lounge bar features wrought-iron trelliswork covered in pumpclips. The pub is the primary outlet for West Berkshire ales in the area – two beers carry the landlord's name – together with more than 30 ciders and perries. National Cider and Perry Pub of the Year in 2012.

Shoulder of Mutton

38 Wallingford Street, OX12 8AX (E of Market Sq)
11-11 (10.30 Sun) ☎ 07870 577742 themutton.co.uk
Betjeman Wantage Bells; guest beers
Corner pub renovated by the enthusiastic landlord. The constantly changing range of 10 beers has a strong emphasis on LocAle and the pub is the main outlet for Betjeman beers brewed by the landlord. The interior comprises public and lounge bars, a small cosy snug and a 'lay-by' leading to an outdoor patio and function room. The pub specialises in vegetarian food. Regular folk music evenings and a weekly raffle are hosted. Regional Pub of the Year 2012, county Pub of the Year 2013 and local CAMRA Pub of the Year 2014.
Q

Wheatley

Cricketer's Arms

38 Littleworth, OX33 1TR
12-3 (not Wed & Thu), 6-11; 12-11 Fri; 7-10.30 Sun
☎ (01865) 872738 cricketers-arms.co.uk
Hook Norton Hooky; Shotover Scholar; guest beer
A friendly, family-run free house offering three cask ales from local breweries, frequently dark ales. A huge range of local bottled beers is also available and real cider. Great-value home-cooked food is served, locally sourced wherever possible, and themed nights are hosted. Walkers, dogs and children are welcome. Beer and sausage festivals are held in February and September.
Q P (103,104)

Witney

Eagle Tavern

22 Corn Street, OX28 6BL
11-3, 5-midnight (2am Fri); 11-2am Sat; 12-midnight Sun
☎ (01993) 700121
Hook Norton Hooky, Lion, Old Hooky; Wychwood Hobgoblin; guest beer
Following acquisition and an excellent refurbishment by Hook Norton Brewery, this wood-panelled and stone-floored building has won a number of awards including Hook Norton Best Kept Cellar 2011 and local CAMRA Town & Country Pub of the Year twice. The landlord has been running pubs in Corn Street for 20-odd years. An unobtrusive jukebox, friendly locals, welcoming staff and quality beer all add up to a must-visit pub. Wychwood Brewery is just around the corner.
(S1,S2)

New Inn

111 Corn Street, OX28 6AU
5-midnight; 12-1am Sat; 12-midnight Sun
☎ (01993) 703807
Sharp's Doom Bar; Tring Side Pocket for a Toad; guest beers
Traditional old pub with an excellent choice of six real ales, including two guests from microbreweries. Just out of the town centre, it can be quiet mid-week but is always busy when major rugby tournaments are televised. Take a seat at the bar, where you will be welcome to engage in a full and frank exchange of views with the friendly locals. There is live music every Saturday night and the jukebox has an eclectic mix of music.
P (S1,S2)

Wootton

Killingworth Castle

Glympton Road, OX20 1EJ
9am 11 ☎ (01993) 811401 thekillingworthcastle.com
Beer range varies
This three-storey stone coaching inn on the ancient Worcester to London road was discovered to date back to 1637 during sensitive renovation under new owners. The frontage features a fine Morland brewery plaque. At the front is a small dining area and the bar, warmed by a wood-burning stove. Four handpumps usually serve three house ales from sister company Yubberton Brewing and one guest from a local micro. To the rear in a later extension is the larger restaurant area serving award-winning food. Q P (220,224A)

Spores for thought

Yeast is a fungus, a single cell plant that can convert a sugary liquid into equal proportions of alcohol and carbon dioxide. There are two basic types of yeast used in brewing, one for ale and one for lager. (The yeasts used to make the Belgian beers known as gueuze and lambic are wild spores in the atmosphere). It is often said that ale is produced by 'top fermentation' and lager by 'bottom fermentation'. While it is true that during ale fermentation a thick blanket of yeast head and protein is created on top of the liquid while only a thin slick appears on top of fermenting lager, the descriptions are seriously misleading. Yeast works at all levels of the sugar-rich liquid in order to turn malt sugars into alcohol. If yeast worked only at the top or bottom of the liquid, a substantial proportion of sugar would not be fermented. Ale is fermented at a high temperature, lager at a much lower one. The furious speed of ale fermentation creates the yeast head and with it the rich, fruity aromas and flavours that are typical of the style. It is more accurate to describe the ale method as 'warm fermentation' and the lager one as 'cold fermentation'.

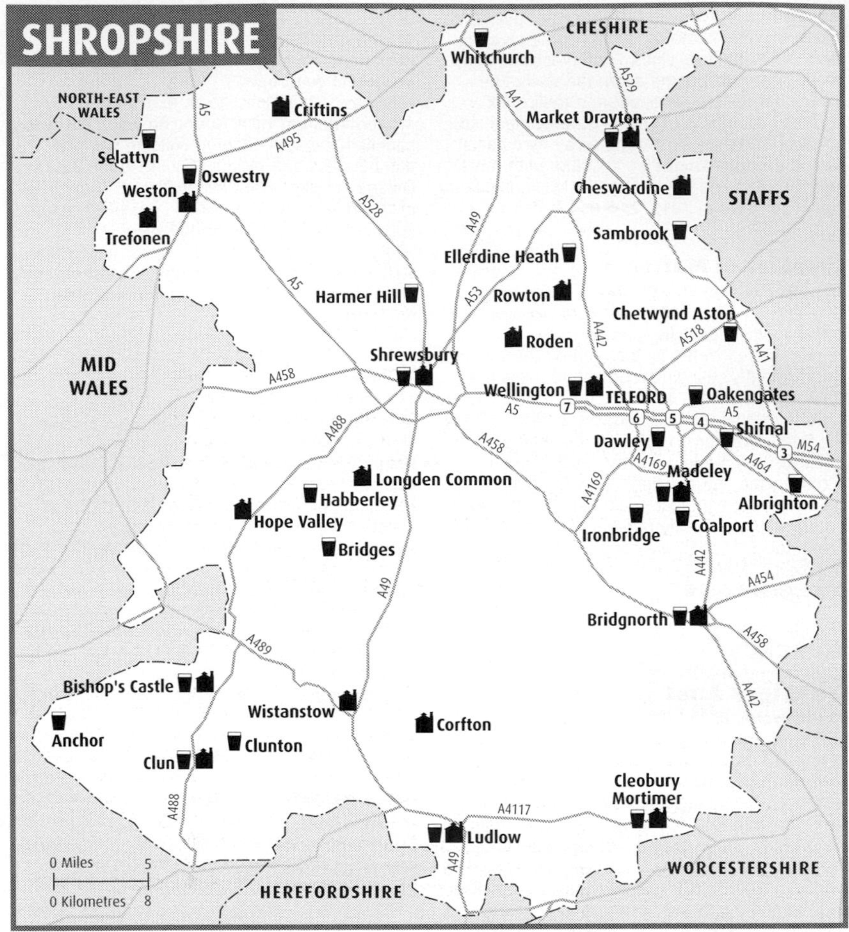

Albrighton

Harp Hotel

40 High Street, WV7 3JF
12-11 (1am Fri & Sat) (01902) 374381
jazzclub90.co.uk
Beer range varies H
A family-owned free house with a superb range of constantly changing beers, and at least one real cider. Jazz sessions feature on Sunday lunchtimes and Tuesday evenings at this internationally known live music venue, plus open mic on Monday, easy listening on Wednesday, and rock on the last Friday or Saturday of the month. A lively pub, it has a lounge and separate bar with pool table, dartboard and jukebox, and a covered smoking area in the yard at the rear.

Anchor

Anchor

SY7 8PR (on B4368 Clun-Abermule road)
7-11 (01686) 670900
Hobsons Best Bitter; Six Bells Big Nev's H
The pub is situated at just under 1,300 feet above sea level at the head of the Clun Valley in the most remote part of Shropshire and close to the Welsh border. The bar room has a wood-burning stove and a pool table, with another cosy room on the other side of the bar. Opening hours can vary by arrangement. **QP**

Bishop's Castle

Six Bells L

Church Street, SY9 5AA
12-2.30 (not Mon), 5-11; 12-11 Sat & Sun
(01588) 638930 sixbellsbrewery.co.uk
Beer range varies H
The tap for the Six Bells Brewery, re-established on the site of the original brewery which closed in the early 1900s. A friendly place and full of character, it has a wood-beamed and stone-walled bar. Three regular and one seasonal Six Bells beer are on handpump, plus cider in summer. The lounge doubles as a dining room (no food Mon all day, Sun and Tue eves). The pub participates in the town's beer festival in July, with around 20 ales available. Sunday hours may vary. **Q** (553)

Three Tuns L

Salop Street, SY9 5BW
12-11 (10.30 Sun) (01588) 638797
thethreetunsinn.co.uk
Theakston Best Bitter; Three Tuns 1642 Bitter, XXX, Stout, Cleric's Cure H

A truly historic pub, this is one of the Famous Four brewpubs that were still brewing in the early 1970s. The brewery is now separately owned. Refurbished and enlarged, the pub has been extended into four rooms – on one side is the lounge, on the other, the ever-popular front bar leading to the central snug and the extended timber-framed glass-sided dining room. A function room is available for hire. Q❀◐◑⛺♣🚌(553)🐾

Bridges

Bridges 🄻

SY5 0ST (on back road from Shrewsbury to Bishop's Castle via Longden)
⏲ 11-11 ☎ (01588) 650260 🌐 thebridgespub.co.uk
Three Tuns XXX, Stout, Cleric's Cure 🄷
Formerly the Horseshoe, the pub is one of two tied houses belonging to the Three Tuns Brewery. A long, low building of some age, it nestles on the western edge of the Long Mynd on the banks of the River East Onny. Inside, there is a large dining area to the left, a bar area to the right, and beyond that a newly constructed room with a woodburner, used primarily for drinking. Six Three Tuns beers are regularly on offer. Walkers are welcome.
Q🐎❀🛏◐◑♣P🚌🐾

Bridgnorth

Golden Lion 🄻

83 High Street, High Town, WV16 4DS
⏲ 11.30-2.30, 5-11; 11-11 Fri & Sat; 12-10.30 Sun
☎ (01746) 762016 🌐 goldenlionbridgnorth.co.uk
Greene King IPA; Hobsons Town Crier; Wye Valley HPA; guest beers 🄷
Traditional 17th-century coaching inn in Bridgnorth's High Town. There are two cosy lounge areas where old photographs of the local area and a vast array of pumpclips are displayed. The public bar has a sports TV. Home-cooked meals are served at lunchtime. Five cask ales, including two guest ales, are on offer. An outdoor smoking area and car park are at the rear. B&B is available in en-suite rooms. Q🛏◐♿⇌♣P🚌🐾

King's Head 🄻

3 Whitburn Street, High Town, WV16 4QN
⏲ 11-11 (midnight Fri & Sat); 12-10.30 Sun
☎ (01746) 762141 🌐 kingsheadbridgnorth.co.uk
Hobsons Twisted Spire, Town Crier; guest beers 🄷
A Grade II-listed 16th-century coaching inn complete with timber beams, flagstone floor, leaded windows and roaring log fires in winter. Two regular and two guest beers are offered. The menu includes a pub grub section and daily specials featuring locally-sourced produce. To the rear the Stable Bar, open in the evenings and when the pub is busy, has four handpulls and hosts live music on Fridays. The courtyard has a pleasant seated area. Q❀◐◑♿⇌🚌🐾📶

Old Castle 🄻

10/11 West Castle Street, WV16 4AB (between Severn Valley Railway and town centre)
⏲ 11.30-11 ☎ (01746) 711420 🌐 oldcastlebridgnorth.co.uk
Hobsons Town Crier; Sharp's Doom Bar; Timothy Taylor Landlord; Wye Valley HPA; guest beer 🄷
This popular pub dates from the 1600s. A dining area to the front serves good tasty meals lunchtimes and evenings, and to the rear is a conservatory/games room, with pool table and dartboard, and a small function room. The bar area has four handpumps offering a range of local and regional real ales. The garden has fine views over Bridgnorth, an ideal spot for dining on a summer's day. 🐎❀◐◑♿⇌♣🚌(436,890)🐾📶

Railwayman's Arms 🄻

Severn Valley Railway Station, Hollybush Road, WV16 5DT (follow signs for SVR, pub is on Platform 1)
⏲ 11.30 (11 Sat)-11; 11.30-10.30 Sun ☎ (01746) 764361
🌐 svr.co.uk
Bathams Best Bitter; Hobsons Mild, Best Bitter, Town Crier; guest beers 🄷
A licensed refreshment room since 1861, this popular pub attracts locals and visitors. The eight handpumps offer a selection of local and national real ales, two dispensing cider but one perry in summer. The landlord is proud of his cellarmanship and keeps a good pint of real ale. A CAMRA beer festival is held here every September. The bars are full of railway memorabilia, and the platform is the perfect place to soak up the atmosphere of a steam railway. Q🐎❀⇌🍎P🚌🐾📶

White Lion 🄻

3 West Castle Street, WV16 4AB
⏲ 11 (12 Sun)-11 ☎ (01746) 763962
🌐 whitelionbridgnorth.co.uk
Hop & Stagger Golden Wander, Pure Amber; Ludlow Gold; guest beers 🄷
A warm welcome awaits locals and visitors to this 18th-century inn, with six handpumps offering Hop & Stagger brews alongside local and national beers. Sam and Bob have converted a room in the grounds into their own brewery, producing a good selection of beers. A wide range of snacks includes popular home-made Scotch eggs. A folk club, quizzes and music all feature here. Bridgnorth scenes are depicted in murals on the bar and garden walls. 🐎❀🛏◐◑⇌♣🍎🚌(436,890)🐾📶

Chetwynd Aston

Fox

Pave Lane, TF10 9LQ (½ mile W of A41)
⏲ 11-11.30 (10.30 Sun) ☎ (01952) 815940
🌐 fox-newport.co.uk

INDEPENDENT BREWERIES

Chapel Criftins (NEW)
Clipper Bridgnorth (NEW)
Clun Clun
Corvedale Corfton
Dickensian Roden
Hobsons Cleobury Mortimer
Hop & Stagger Bridgnorth
Joule's Market Drayton
Lion's Tale Cheswardine
Longden Longden Common (NEW)
Ludlow Ludlow
Offa's Dyke Trefonen
Rowton Rowton
Salopian Shrewsbury
Shires Madeley
Six Bells Bishop's Castle
Stonehouse Weston
Three Tuns Bishop's Castle
Tunnfield Hope Valley (brewing suspended)
Wood Wistanstow
Wrekin Telford: Wellington

Phoenix Brunning & Price Original; Three Tuns XXX; Wood Shropshire Lad; guest beers Ⓗ
This large and imposing roadside house belongs to the Brunning & Price chain of hostelries and is a popular venue. Although predominantly a food outlet, it has much on offer for the cask ale drinker too. Up to six beers are available, with Shropshire breweries always represented. The car park is large and there is an extensive garden area with good views over the surrounding countryside. The national sports centre at Lilleshall is close by.
Q❀◐♿♣P

Cleobury Mortimer

King's Arms Ⓛ
6 Church Street, DY14 8BS
10-11 (midnight Thu-Sat); 10-10.30 Sun
☎ (01299) 271954 🌐 kingsarms-cleobury.co.uk
Hobsons Mild, Twisted Spire, Best Bitter, Old Prickly, Town Crier Ⓗ
Set in a market town known as 'the gateway to the Shropshire Hills', this welcoming 15th-century pub is the brewery tap for Hobsons' award-winning ales. Comfy sofas and a central log-burning fire provide the perfect setting to enjoy the beers on five handpumps. An excellent menu of locally-sourced food always has traditional home-made pies available. Breakfasts are served from 10am. There is a heated, covered terrace for smokers. A mini beer festival is held in September.
❀◐♿♣🚌(292)🐾

Clun

White Horse Ⓛ
The Square, SY7 8JA
12-midnight ☎ (01588) 640305 🌐 whi-clun.co.uk
Clun Loophole, Pale Ale, Citadel; Hobsons Best Bitter; Wye Valley Butty Bach; guest beers Ⓗ
Sixteenth-century inn and post house standing in the old market square at the centre of a timeless town, described by AE Housman as 'one of the quietest places under the sun'. Inside is an L-shaped bar with low beams, and adjoining dining room serving excellent, reasonably priced food. The pub has its own nano brewery which has now grown up. Rotating real ciders are stocked. Outside is a secluded garden. Jam nights are held once a month. **❀◐♣🍎🐾**

Clunton

Crown Ⓛ
SY7 0HU
4 (5 Tue; 12 Fri & Sat)-midnight; 12-11 Sun
☎ (01588) 660265 🌐 crowninnclunton.co.uk
Hobsons Best Bitter; Stonehouse Station Bitter; guest beer Ⓗ
Set in the Clun Valley, a designated area of outstanding natural beauty, this community-owned inn, now run by a local family, has three rooms including a smart restaurant. It hosts a popular fish and chips night every Wednesday (including takeaways), an acoustic folk night on the third Wednesday of the month, and takes part in the annual Clun Valley Beer Festival. **Q❀◐♣🍎P**

Ellerdine Heath

Royal Oak Ⓛ
Hazles Road, TF6 6RL (2 miles off A442 towards A53)
SJ603226
12-11 ☎ (01939) 250300
Hobsons Best Bitter; Purity Pure Gold; Wye Valley HPA; guest beers Ⓗ
Also known as 'The Tiddly', this friendly rural pub welcomes locals, visitors, families and dogs. Six handpulls dispense three regular beers and up to three guests, and real cider is usually available. A cosy separate dining room with an open fire offers generous portions of locally-sourced food, and parties can be catered for. The pub hosts a folk night every third Tuesday, French conversation group Tuesday lunchtime, seasonal music nights, a biennial charity dog-walk and a cider festival on the last Saturday in July. **Q❀◐♿♣🍎P🐾**

Habberley

Mytton Arms 🏆 Ⓛ
SY5 0TP
4 (12 Fri-Sun)-11 ☎ (01743) 792490
Hobsons Best Bitter; Three Tuns XXX; guest beers Ⓗ
Situated in a small village on the edge of the south Shropshire hills and somewhat off the beaten track, this popular pub is worth seeking out. There are three low-beamed rooms and a friendly rustic atmosphere – beer and conversation predominate. Outside are seats to the front and a paved area with a vine-covered pagoda to the side. A well-known local character and pub regular features on the inn sign. The South Shropshire Hills shuttle bus provides transport in summer. **Q❀♣P🚌🐾**

Harmer Hill

Red Castle
SY4 3EB
12-4, 6-midnight; 12-midnight Fri-Sun ☎ (01939) 291071
Hobsons Mild, Best Bitter; Sharp's Doom Bar; guest beer Ⓗ
A successful village local, under the same ownership for some 20 years. There are two public rooms, the larger one mainly used for dining. The community aspect is reflected in the stock of books (including some for children) and videos, participation in the local darts league, and a substantial amount of money raised for charity. Smokers will need to be persistent in finding the smoking area, the route being rather obscure.
❀◐♿♣P🚌(501)🐾

Ludlow

Church Inn
Buttercross, SY8 1AW
10-11.30 (midnight Fri & Sat); 11-11.30 Sun
☎ (01584) 872174 🌐 thechurchinn.com
Hobsons Town Crier; Ludlow Gold, Black Knight, Boiling Well; Wye Valley Bitter; guest beers Ⓗ
Situated in the centre of Ludlow, close to the castle and market square, the church is the only free house within the town walls and now has a residential ale conner to ensure the quality of the beer. The landlord, a former mayor of Ludlow, is a great advocate of real ale. Guest ales are usually from national microbreweries. Nine guest rooms are available, some with views over the town.
❀◐⇌🚌🐾

Queens

113 Lower Galdeford, SY8 1RU (Just off town centre,Just off town centre,Just off town centre, opposite Co-op)
12-11; 12-midnight Fri & Sat; 12-10.30 Sun
(01584) 879177 thequeensludlow.com/
Hobsons Best Bitter; Ludlow Ludlow Best, Gold; Wye Valley Butty Bach
Popular pub/cafe bar with a decent range of local ales. The light and airy L-shaped bar has two distinct areas with dining down a short flight of steps. Good value quality meals are freshly cooked from locally-sourced food for which booking is advised at weekends. Live music features regularly. Large enclosed patio style garden with views over Ludford. Home of the Ludlow venison pie and regular award winner at Ludlow Festival. It is a family run, friendly local. Dogs are allowed.

Railway Shed

Station Drive, SY8 2PQ
10-5 (6 Fri; 4 Sat); closed Sun (01584) 873291
theludlowbrewingcompany.co.uk
Ludlow Ludlow Best, Gold, Black Knight, Boiling Well, Stairway
Brewery and bar/lounge located in a converted railway shed, handy for the railway station. Open during the day, it offers five house beers and extensive off-sales, and brewery visits are welcome. The spacious venue has ample, comfortable seating on two levels overlooking the modern brewing plant. State-of-the-art underfloor heating, recycling of rainwater, low energy lighting and solar panels make for super energy efficiency. It hosts beer festivals, live music and private functions. Q P

Market Drayton

Red Lion

Great Hales Street, TF9 1JP
11-11 (midnight Fri & Sat) (01630) 652602
joulesbrewery.co.uk
Joule's Blonde, Pale Ale, Slumbering Monk
This Joule's brewery tap was formerly a coaching inn, built in 1623. Unique features include an illuminated well in the main bar and the Mouse Room – a Robert Thompson-inspired function room with carved mice. Log fires and oak beams help to create a comfortable atmosphere. Locally-sourced food can be enjoyed from an extensive menu along with the Joule's range of beers produced in the adjacent brewery. Q P

Oswestry

Oak

Church Street, SY11 2SZ
12 (11.30 Sat & Sun)-midnight (01691) 659254
Draught Bass; Salopian Shropshire Gold; Stonehouse Station Bitter, Cambrian Gold; guest beer
An early 18th-century listed building opposite the parish church, formerly the coach house of the hotel next door. This unspoilt pub is close to the town centre and is one of Oswestry's many free houses. It has a public bar at the front and a larger, comfortable lounge to the back with TV screens for sports events. The lounge is accessed via a passage that runs down the side, which also leads to a covered area outside.

Sambrook

Three Horseshoes

TF10 8AP (½ mile E of A41)
12-2 (not Mon), 4.30-11; 11-11 Sat & Sun
(01952) 551133 theshoes-sambrook.co.uk
Hobsons Mild; St Austell Tribute; Salopian Shropshire Gold; guest beers
A friendly, welcoming rural pub in a small village on the eastern side of the county. The quarry-tiled bar area is heated by a wood-burning stove – good-value home-cooked food can be enjoyed here or in the lounge or dining room. The pub is home to dominoes and darts teams, and young farmers and music groups visit regularly. One of the guest beers is from Joule's brewery. Travel here by bus from Newport on weekdays. Q P (19)

Selattyn

Cross Keys ★

SY10 7DN
closed Mon & Tue; 7 (6 Fri)-11; 12-5, 7-10.30 Sun
(01691) 650247 thecrosskeys-selattyn.co.uk
Stonehouse Station Bitter; guest beers
This 17th-century building has been a pub since 1840 and has a nationally important historic interior. It is situated next to the church in a village close to the Welsh border and Offa's Dyke. The small bar has a quarry-tiled floor, real fire and a large topical cartoon; there are two further rooms and function room. Accommodation is in a self-catering cottage next to the pub. The pub opens lunchtimes Monday to Saturday by arrangement. The landlord is a keen campanologist. Q P

Shifnal

Anvil

22 Aston Road, TF11 8DU
5-11.30 (10 Tue & Wed; 11 Sat); 12-10 Sun
(07923) 250268
Everards Tiger; Exmoor Gold; guest beer
A warm welcome awaits you at this cosy old-fashioned family-run pub. Located off the high street, a five-minute walk from Shifnal railway station, this 17th-century former coaching house has tiled floors, timber beams and an open fire. It is proud to be TV-sport free. A small patio garden has abundant flowers, outside toilets (with a ghost) and a covered smoking area. A guest beer makes an occasional appearance. Q

Odfellows Wine Bar

Market Place, TF11 9AU
12-11 (01952) 461517 odleyinns.co.uk
Salopian Shropshire Gold, Oracle; guest beers
Set in a town whose buildings many believe were the basis for Dickens' Old Curiosity Shop, this popular gastro-pub overlooks Market Place, and is handy for the railway station. A range of mainly local beers is available including Best Odley Bitter, a house brew by Odley Ales served only in its own pubs. Beer festivals feature each year in May and September. Food is of good quality and made with locally-sourced ingredients whenever possible. P

Plough

26 Broadway, TF11 8AZ
12-11 (10.30 Sun) (01952) 463118 artybars.co.uk
Hobsons Best Bitter; Shires Best Bitter; Three Tuns 1642 Bitter; guest beers

Cosy 17th-century free house offering a wide selection of beers, focusing on ales from local breweries and some national favourites, as well as traditional pub meals (no food Mon). The Plough has an extensive beer garden at the rear which is popular in summer. A weekly quiz is held on Tuesday, live Irish folk music on the first Monday of the month. The walls are decorated with work by local artists, available for sale. The large function room can be hired. 🛏❀◐◑⇌●🚌(891,892)🐾

White Hart L

High Street, TF11 8BH

⌚ 12-11 ☎ (01952) 461161

Enville Ale; Greene King Abbot; Holden's Black Country Mild; Salopian Shropshire Gold; Wye Valley HPA, Butty Bach; guest beers Ⓗ

Timber-framed two-bar free house with something for everyone in a pleasant small market town. Many CAMRA awards are proudly on display. Eight handpulls dispense superbly kept beers at keen prices, earning top marks from Cask Marque, with guest brews often local or nationally renowned. Good home-made lunches are available Monday to Saturday. There is a sunny patio to the rear and a separate beer garden popular with families. The pub is a supporter of fundraising events. Q❀◐⇌♣P🚌

Shrewsbury

Admiral Benbow L

24 Swan Hill, SY1 1NF (off main square)

⌚ 5 (12 Sat)-11; 7-10.30 Sun ☎ (01743) 244423

Ironbridge Gold; Ludlow Gold; Six Bells Cloud Nine; Slater's Top Totty; Wye Valley HPA; guest beers Ⓗ

Spacious free house offering a range of Shropshire and Herefordshire beers – often including a brew from Titanic – ciders from Rosie's including Black Bart, Wicked Wasp and Triple, and a good choice of Belgian beers. A small room off the bar can be used for private functions, and there is a seating and smoking area outside at the rear. Children are not permitted. Q❀⇌♣●🚌🐾

Coach & Horses

Swan Hill, SY1 1NF

⌚ 11.30-midnight (12.30am Fri & Sat); 12-11.30 Sun

☎ (01743) 365661 🌐 odleyinns.co.uk

Salopian Shropshire Gold, Oracle; Stonehouse Station Bitter; guest beers Ⓗ

Set in a quiet street off the main shopping area, the Coach & Horses provides a peaceful haven, with magnificent floral displays in summer. Victorian in style, it has a wood-panelled bar, a small side snug area and a large lounge where meals are served lunchtimes and evenings. Bar snacks are available at lunchtimes. Cheddar Valley cider is sold on handpull. Q◐◑♿⇌●🚌🐾📶

Dolphin L

48 St Michaels Street, SY1 2EZ

⌚ 12-11 (10.30 Sun) ☎ (01743) 247005

🌐 thedolphinalehouse.com

Joule's Blonde, Pale Ale, Slumbering Monk; guest beers Ⓗ

Part of the Joule's sponsored estate, this end-of-terrace ale house is within easy walking distance of the railway station. A sympathetic refurbishment has retained a traditional atmosphere, with wooden floors, internal gas lighting and open fires. A pub for the community, folk music is hosted on the first and third Thursdays of the month, quiz and open mic sessions on the second and fourth Thursdays. A cider, often Westons, is served. Newspapers are usually available.

Q❀◐◑⇌♣●🚌🐾📶

Loggerheads ★ L

1 Church Street, SY1 1UG

⌚ 11-11.30 (1.30am Thu-Sat); 12-11.30 Sun

☎ (01743) 362398

Banks's Bitter; Jennings Dark Mild; Marston's Pedigree; guest beers Ⓗ

This 18th-century Grade II-listed town-centre pub has a nationally important historic interior. It has a small bar, servery and three further rooms. The bar to the left – gents only until 1975 – is furnished with scrubbed tables and has a shove-ha'penny board. Folk music plays on Sunday and Thursday evenings. Good food made with locally-sourced produce is available all week. Q◐◑⇌♣🚌🐾

Montgomery's Tower L

Lower Claremont Bank, SY1 1RT

⌚ 9am-midnight (1am Wed & Thu; 2am Fri & Sat)

☎ (01743) 239080

Salopian Shropshire Gold; Wood Shropshire Lad; guest beers Ⓗ

Close to the Quarry Park and handy for Theatre Severn, this Lloyds No.1 offers a choice of two bars. To the left is a large open area rich in natural light, with a smoking area to the rear. The bar to the right provides quieter surroundings and subdued lighting, except on Friday and Saturday when there is a DJ. Gwynt y Ddraig cider is usually available. The walls display prints illustrating local history and famous Salopians. Food is served 9am-11pm.

🛏❀◐◑♿⇌●🚌📶

Nag's Head

22 Wyle Cop, SY1 1XB

⌚ 11.30-midnight (1am Fri & Sat); 12-midnight Sun

☎ (01743) 362455

Caledonian Deuchars IPA; Hobsons Best Bitter; Sharp's Doom Bar; Timothy Taylor Landlord; Wychwood Hobgoblin; Wye Valley HPA; guest beer Ⓗ

Situated on the historic Wyle Cop, the main features of this timber-framed building are best appreciated externally – in particular the upper storey jettying and to the rear the timber remnants of a 14th-century hall house including a screened passage which provided protection from draughts (and now offers shelter for smokers). The old-style interior has remained unaltered for many years. The pub is said to be haunted and features on the Shrewsbury Ghost Trail. ❀⇌♣🚌

Prince of Wales L

30 Bynner Street, Belle Vue, SY3 7NZ

⌚ 5 (12 Fri-Sun)-midnight ☎ (01743) 343301

🌐 princeofwaleshotel.co.uk

Greene King IPA; St Austell Tribute; Salopian Golden Thread; Thwaites Wainwright; guest beer Ⓗ

Welcoming two-roomed community pub with a heated smoking shelter and a large suntrap deck adjoining a bowling green. The green is overlooked by a 19th-century maltings. Darts, dominoes and bowls teams abound. Beer festivals take place each year in February and May. Shrewsbury Town FC memorabilia adorn the building both inside and out, with some of the seating from the old Gay Meadow ground skirting the bowling green. Meals are served Friday to Sunday lunchtimes.

🛏❀◐♿♣●P📺🚌(27)🐾

Salopian Bar

Smithfield Road, SY1 1PW

11-11 (midnight Wed); 11-midnight Fri & Sat
(01743) 351505 thesalopianbar.co.uk

Salopian Oracle; Stonehouse Off the Rails; guest beers

The bar's dedicated management strives to increase the beer, cider and perry range to satisfy public demand. Regular cider and perry is provided by Westons and Thatchers, and an impressive range of Belgian and American bottled beer is also available. Coverage of major sports events is shown on large-screen TVs. Local artwork is on display and for sale. A regular winner of local CAMRA branch Pub of the Year awards.

Three Fishes

Fish Street, SY1 1UR

11.30-3, 5-11; 11.30-11.30 Fri & Sat; 12-10.30 Sun
(01743) 344793 realaleshrewsbury.co.uk

Sharp's Doom Bar; Stonehouse Station Bitter; Three Tuns Stout; Timothy Taylor Landlord; guest beers

Fifteenth-century building standing in the shadow of two churches, St Alkmund's and St Julian's, within the maze of streets and passageways in the town's medieval quarter. Freshly prepared food is available at lunchtimes and early evenings Monday to Saturday. The pub offers a range of up to six local and national ales, usually including some dark beers, and a choice of real ciders and perries. A former local CAMRA Pub of the Year.
Q

Vaults

16 Castle Gates, SY1 2AB

12-11 (2am Fri & Sat) (01743) 358807
the-vaults.co.uk

Hobsons Town Crier; Stonehouse Station Bitter; guest beer

Situated in a prominent position adjacent to the railway station and a few minutes' walk from the town centre, this free house is part of Shrewsbury's vibrant weekend entertainment scene. It has an open-plan layout with separate seating areas, and for the summer there is a courtyard and roof garden in the shadow of the castle. The guest beer is usually from a local brewery.

Woodman

32 Coton Hill, SY1 2DZ

4 (12 Sat & Sun)-midnight (01743) 351007

Salopian Shropshire Gold, Oracle; Wye Valley Butty Bach; guest beers

Half-brick and half-timbered black and white corner pub originally built in the 1800s, destroyed by fire in 1923 and rebuilt in 1925. The wonderful oak-panelled lounge has two real log fires and traditional settles, and the separate bar has the original stone-tiled flooring, wooden seating, log fire and listed leaded windows. The courtyard has a heated smoking area and seating.
Q (501)

Telford: Coalport

Shakespeare

High Street, TF8 7HT (near Tar Tunnel and China Museum)

5 (12 Sat & Sun)-11 (01952) 580675
shakespeare-inn.co.uk

Everards Tiger; Hobsons Twisted Spire; Ludlow Gold; guest beers

A warm, welcoming family-run pub with wonderful views of the Severn gorge and river. Ideally located for the Coalport China and Tar Tunnel museums, it is also close to the Silken Way leading to Blists Hill museum. A good selection of guest ales, often from local breweries, includes favourites Exmoor Gold and Three Tuns XXX. The tempting menu of excellent home-cooked dishes is always popular (advance booking advisable). The garden is tiered and has children's play equipment.
Q P

Woodbridge Inn

Coalport Road, TF8 7JF

11-11 (10.30 Sun) (01952) 882054
woodbridge-coalport.co.uk

Ironbridge Gold; Phoenix Brunning & Price Original; Three Tuns XXX; guest beers

The Woodbridge is on the banks of the River Severn, a mile downstream from Ironbridge. It was built around 1785 and named after the wooden bridge that connected the pub to Coalport, which was constructed at the same time. Inside, there are open areas as well as many interesting nooks and crannies. A substantial raised deck at first floor level provides an outside drinking and dining area, and there is a garden room overlooking the river. Six ales, including the pub's own brews, are on offer. Q P

Telford: Dawley

Elephant & Castle

1 High Street, TF4 2ET

5-10 (11 Thu); 4-11 Fri & Sat; 4-10 Sun (01952) 610888
elephantdawley.net

Hobsons Mild; Joule's Pale Ale; Purple Moose Cwrw Madog/Madog's Ale, Ochr Tywyll y Mws/Dark Side of the Moose; Wood Quaff; guest beers

Extensive Grade II-listed inn, recently restored to a high standard. Notable features include 16th-century beams, oak bars, real fires, a conservatory and a large sunny garden. Beers are dispensed from 12 handpulls, plus two more in one of several function rooms. A morris group meets on most Mondays and a comedy night is held on the last Friday of the month. The pub is half a mile from the Telford Steam Railway and two miles from Ironbridge Gorge. The sister pub to the Crown in Oakengates, joint beer festivals are held early in May and October. Q (11,22)

Telford: Ironbridge

Robin Hood Inn

33 Waterloo Street, TF8 7HQ

12-11; 11-midnight Fri & Sat; 11-11 Sun
(01952) 433071 yeolderobinhoodinn.co.uk

Holden's Black Country Mild, Black Country Bitter, Golden Glow, Special; guest beer

In a superb setting on the edge of Ironbridge with views over the River Severn, a recent refurbishment has maintained the charm and character of this traditional Holden's pub. Quality home-cooked food is available throughout the day, including a great range of vegetarian dishes. The pleasant outside seating area is popular in summer with both locals and tourists, and families are always made welcome. Comfortable en-suite accommodation is available.
P (88,89)

Telford: Madeley

All Nations

20 Coalport Road, TF7 5DP (signed off Legges Way, opp Blists Hill museum)
12-11 ☎ (01952) 585747 shiresbrewery.co.uk
Shires Best Bitter; guest beers H
A historic brewhouse, an icon of home-brewing history, is still working at the back of the building. Regulars and visitors love this pub for its cosy interior and ubiquitous friendliness. Four real ales including home-brew Dabley Ale and a cider or perry are available. Freshly prepared bar snacks are on offer – the black pudding and cheese toastie is a favourite with the locals. Visitors can browse books from the window ledges and newspapers from a rack. A TV appears only for international Rugby Union matches. QP

Telford: Oakengates

Crown Inn

Market Street, TF2 6EA
12-11 ☎ (01952) 610888 crown@oakengates.net
Hobsons Twisted Spire, Best Bitter; Joule's Pale Ale; guest beers H
The front bar of this traditional three-roomed inn has been refurbished with a new oak bar and floor, but nothing else has changed. Cask Marque-accredited, it has three regular beers, 10 ever-changing guests and a cider from the Ross-on-Wye range on handpull. Continental bottled beers and interesting whiskies are also kept. At the heart of the community and welcoming to strangers, there is always something happening here: live bands, acoustic and blues jam evenings, comedy and curry nights, regular quizzes and beer festivals.
P

Old Fighting Cocks

48 Market Street, TF2 6DU
12-11 ☎ (01952) 615607 oakengatespicturehouse.com
Everards Tiger; Ironbridge Pale Ale, Gold; guest beers H
Jointly owned by Ironbridge and Everards, the building was sympathetically restored and reopened in 2010. It swiftly became a local favourite, helped by occasional beer festivals, keen prices and good staff. The busy well-appointed multi-roomed pub offers a varied and ever-changing selection of beers from both breweries, plus plenty of guests, on its 10 pumps, alongside Scrambler from the Bottle Kicking Cider Co. Bring your own food – irons and plates provided. There is a 32-seat cinema above, for hire.
Q

Station Hotel

42 Market Street, TF2 6DU
10-11; 10.30-3.30, 7-11 Sun ☎ (01952) 612949
Beer range varies H
This no-nonsense three-roomed local majors on Yorkshire breweries along with an ever-present Salopian beer. With eight handpulls there is always something unusual for the area to discover, plus a changing cider. The tiled front room has a real fire, bench seating and blackboards listing current and forthcoming beers; two further rooms are more comfortable with easy chairs. The rolls and pies are legendary, and the Wednesday curry night has a big following. Q

Telford: Wellington

Cock Hotel

148 Holyhead Road, TF1 2GA
4 (12 Thu)-11.30; 12-midnight Fri & Sat; 12-4, 7-11 Sun
☎ (01952) 244954 cockhotel.co.uk
Hobsons Mild, Best Bitter; guest beers H
This much-loved multi-award-winning old coaching inn has four distinct drinking areas, plus a semi-covered courtyard used as a smoking area. All areas are served from the main bar, the hop-festooned Wrekin tap. Seven handpulls offer an ever-changing selection of beers, usually from local breweries, and one handpull is for cider. A comprehensive international bottle list is also available. No music, just the hum of good conversation and customers ordering another beer.
QP

Railway Inn

42-44 Mill Bank, TF1 1SD
4.30 (11 Fri-Sun)-11 ☎ (01952) 259212
Wye Valley HPA, Butty Bach; guest beers H
This new entry into the Guide was totally refurbished in 2012. A traditional locals' pub, it is only a few minutes from Wellington town centre, close to the Cock Hotel and AFC Telford. The interior is semi-open plan but retains a friendly intimacy. It is home to darts, dominoes and crib teams, and has TV screens for sport. Live music plays at Sunday teatime. The two guest beers are usually from local breweries such as Ironbridge, Joule's, Ludlow or Salopian. QP(44,55)

William Withering

43-45 New Street, TF1 1LU
8am-midnight (1am Fri & Sat) ☎ (01952) 642800
Greene King Abbot; Ruddles Best Bitter; Salopian Shropshire Gold; guest beers H
Named after a local physician and geologist, this large open-plan Wetherspoon pub mixes period 1700s features with a typical modern bar. The 10 handpulls provide three house beers and seven constantly changing ales from up and down the country, with the focus on ales from the local area. There are also four real ciders, mostly from Westons. Good-value food is available until 11pm in a relaxed atmosphere.

Whitchurch

Black Bear

High Street, SY13 1AZ
12-3, 6-11; 12-11 Sat & Sun ☎ (01948) 663800
blackbearpub.co.uk
Phoenix Monkeytown Mild; guest beers H
This tastefully renovated black and white corner pub lies opposite the historic St Alkmund's church. The ornate bar has six handpulls serving beers from both local and lesser-known national microbreweries, with pumpclips adorning the walls, ceiling and bar area. Cider is served on gravity. The pub has two separate dining areas offering locally-sourced home-cooked food from an ever-changing menu. QP

Good Bottled Beer Guide – 8th Edition

Jeff Evans

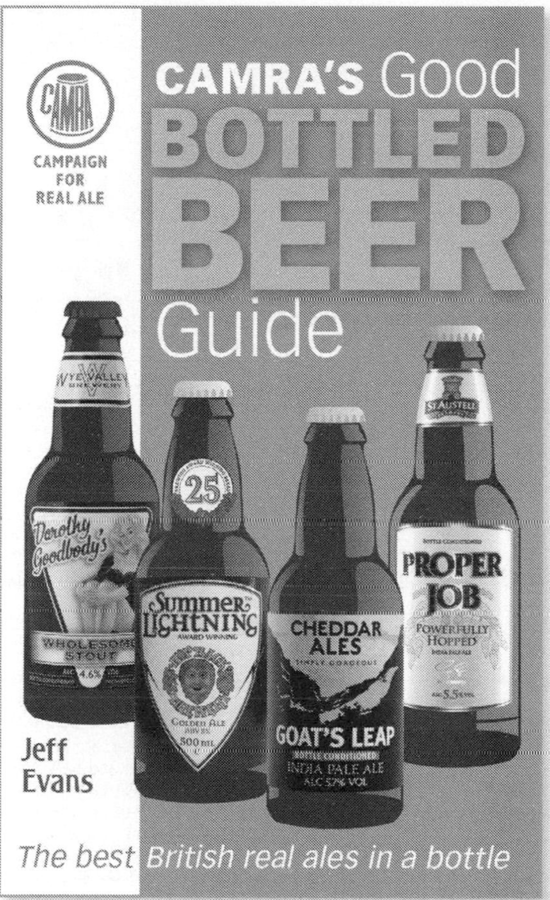

A pocket-sized guide for discerning drinkers looking to buy bottled real ales and enjoy a fresh glass of their favourite beers at home. The new 8th edition of the **Good Bottled Beer Guide** is completely revised, updated and redesigned to showcase the very best bottled British real ales now being produced, and detail where they can be bought. Everything you need to know about bottled beers; tasting notes, ingredients, brewery details, and a glossary to help the reader understand more about them.

£12.99 ISBN 978-1-85249-309-7 CAMRA members' price £10.99 440 pages

For this and other books on beer and pubs visit CAMRA's online bookshop at www.camra.org.uk/books or call 01727 867201

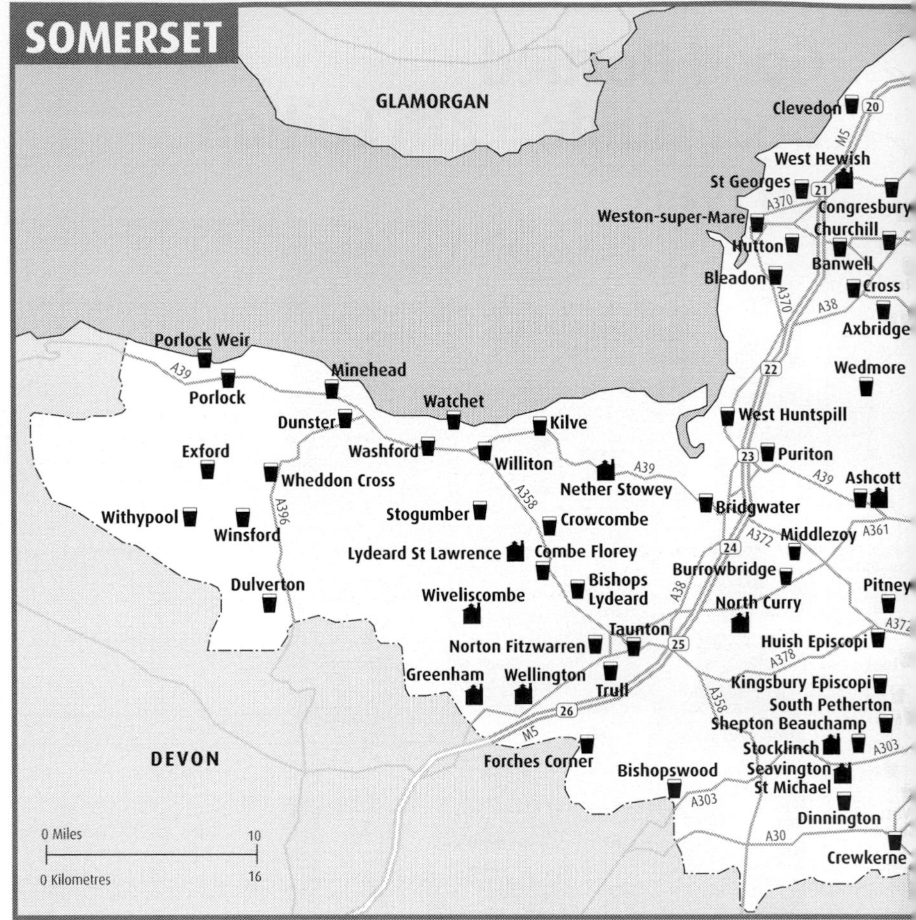

Ash

Bell Inn 𝕃

3 Main Street, TA12 6NS

⏲ 12-11 (midnight Sat); 12-10.30 Sun ☎ (01935) 822727
🌐 thebellinnash.co.uk

Beer range varies Ⓗ

The Bell is a well-run village pub with a changing choice of up to four, mainly Somerset, ales on handpump and Old Rosie cider. Good, reasonably priced, home-cooked food, made from locally-sourced ingredients, is available (no food Mon). Live music nights and a Sunday quiz are popular. Unusual belfry items adorn the walls. An open log fire makes it a cosy place for a quiet drink or a family occasion for locals or passing visitors.
Q🚸❀◑♿♣🍎P🚌(N9,N9A)🐾

Ashcott

Ring o' Bells

16 High Street, TA7 9PZ

⏲ 12-2.30, 7-11 (10.30 Sun) ☎ (01458) 210232
🌐 ringobells.com

Beer range varies Ⓗ

A former Somerset CAMRA award winner, this family-run free house has three bars on split levels. Old beams and fireplaces enhance the bar and dining area. Families are welcome and there is an enclosed garden. Two or three real ales from microbreweries, and Wilkins cider, are served. The food is excellent, and both food and beer are available to take away. Live music plays on the first Saturday and third Wednesday of the month. A large skittle alley/function room is available. The pub is situated central to many of Somerset's nature reserves. Q🚸❀◑♿⛺♣🍎P🚌

Axbridge

Lamb

The Square, BS26 2AP

⏲ 11.30-11 (midnight Fri & Sat); 12-11 Sun
☎ (01934) 732253 🌐 lamb.butcombe.com

Butcombe Bitter, Gold; Fuller's London Pride; guest beer Ⓗ

Butcombe-owned Grade II-listed coaching house in the village square. The National Trust's medieval King John's Hunting Lodge lies directly opposite. There is a large low-beamed bar area and several smaller, quieter areas leading off from it, and space to drink outside to the front and rear. Lunchtime and evening meals are served (not Sun eve). Butcombe seasonals are occasionally replaced by a guest beer and the cider is Thatchers. The Weston to Wells 126 bus stops nearby during the day.
Q❀◑♣🍎🚌(126)🐾📶

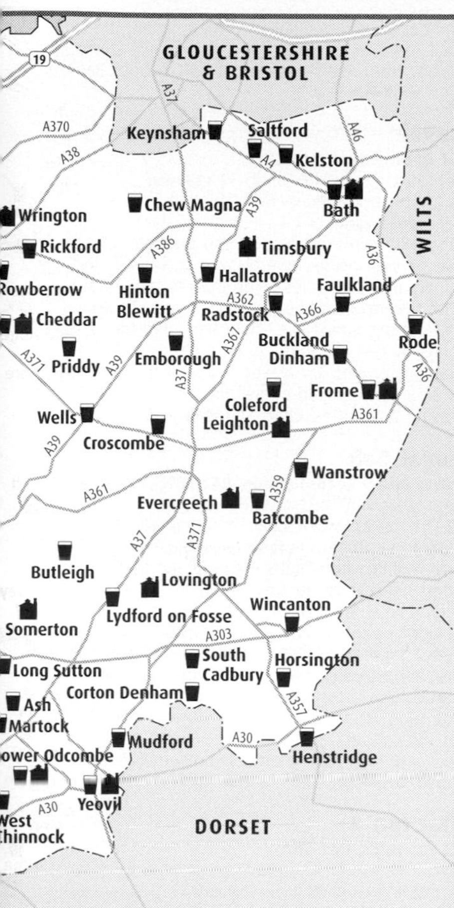

Banwell

Bell Inn

1 The Square, BS29 6BL

5-11 ☎ (01934) 822330

Butcombe Bitter; St Austell Proper Job; guest beer H

Village pub being slowly and lovingly restored after years of neglect. The guest beer is sometimes joined by a second one. A real fire warms the front bar and a small patio is used for outside drinking. There is a quiz on Thursdays, board games are available and occasional live music is hosted. Despite the address, the pub is on a blind right-angled bend on the busy main road, so extra care is needed outside. Banwell Castle is nearby.

Batcombe

Three Horseshoes Inn

BA4 6HE (off Back Lane) ST69023908

11-3, 6-11; 11-11 Sat; 12-10.30 Sun ☎ (01749) 850359

thethreehorseshoesinn.co.uk

Butcombe Bitter; guest beers H

The Three Horseshoes is a 400-year-old country pub which has a spacious bar with an inglenook fireplace and beamed ceiling, a stunning dining room with a vaulted ceiling, and a lawned garden overlooked by the church tower. Open to all, it welcomes drinkers, foodies, walkers, children (with colouring books and games provided to keep them entertained) and dogs. Q P

Bath

Bath Brew House

14 James Street West, BA1 2BX

10-11 (midnight Fri & Sat) ☎ (01225) 805609

thebathbrewhouse.com

James Street Gladiator, Emperor; guest beers H

A major refurbishment in 2013 saw the former Midland Hotel transformed into a City Pub Company brewpub. The on-site James Street Brewery produces two regular beers, the refreshing and malty Gladiator (3.9% ABV) and the hoppier, citrussy Emperor (4.4% ABV), and rotating seasonal beers. Four guests, usually from nearby micros, are complemented by four craft beers. An L-shaped bar leads to a dining area and beer garden. The upstairs room hosts TV sport, quizzes, comedy and more. (Spa)

Bell

103 Walcot Street, BA1 5BW

11.30-11; 12-10.30 Sun ☎ (01225) 460426

Abbey Bellringer; Bath Ales Gem; Butcombe Bitter; Hop Back Summer Lightning; RCH Pitchfork; Stonehenge Danish Dynamite; guest beers H

Owned by 536 of its regulars, fans and staff following a community buy-out in 2013, the Bell has seven real ales plus two varying guests from micros near and far. Live music is a mainstay, with bands playing Monday and Wednesday evenings and Sunday lunchtimes and, in the separate Love Lounge to the rear, open mic nights on Thursday evenings. Features include bar billiards, board games and even a tiny launderette. At the rear is a walled garden with covered seating.

Coeur de Lion

17 Northumberland Place, BA1 5AR

11-11.30 (12.30am Sat); 12-11 Sun ☎ (01225) 463568

coeur-de-lion.co.uk

Abbey Bellringer; guest beer H

In a passageway opposite the Guildhall in the centre of town, this pub claims to be the smallest in Bath – with just four tables in the small bar, this may well be true. Seating capacity is increased in summer by placing tables outside. There is also an upstairs room used mainly for dining – traditional pub food is served at lunchtimes. The pub's unique feature is the fine stained glass window that forms its frontage. Q (Spa)

Garrick's Head

8 St John's Place, Saw Close, BA1 1ET

12-11 (midnight Sat); 12-10.30 Sun ☎ (01225) 318368

garricksheadpub.com

Butcombe Bitter; guest beers H

A theatre pub for over 200 years but originally the town house of Beau Nash, Bath's 18th-century Master of Ceremonies, this local is reputedly the most haunted pub in the city. Three or four real ales, mostly from local microbreweries, include some rarities, while local ciders are often complemented by a perry. Traditional food made from local ingredients is served lunchtimes and evenings. Tables in the pedestrianised area outside are ideally placed for watching the world go by.

Griffin Inn

Monmouth Street, BA1 2AP

12-11; 12-10 Sun (01225) 420919

thegriffinbath.co.uk

Butcombe Bitter; guest beers H

Grade II-listed inn refurbished with a modern minimalist feel. The bar offers up to four real ales, many from regional microbreweries, and draught cider in summer. The two rooms provide ample space and reveal the internal fabric of this Georgian building. Popular with a varied clientele, it has an urban café bar feel mixed with that of a friendly local. Four-star accommodation includes seven, mostly en-suite, bedrooms.

Hop Pole

7 Albion Buildings, Upper Bristol Road, BA1 3AR

12-11 (midnight Fri & Sat) (01225) 446327

Bath Ales Special Pale Ale, Gem, Barnsey; guest beer H

A Bath Ales pub a half-mile west of the city centre, close to Royal Victoria Park and the River Avon. Five real ales are available including four from Bath Ales. The enclosed and spacious beer garden is popular with families. Food is served lunchtimes and evenings Monday to Friday, all day on Saturday and until 4pm on Sunday. Home-made bar snacks – nuts, pork scratchings and Scotch eggs – are also on offer. Q(Oldfield Park)

Old Green Tree ★

12 Green Street, BA1 2JZ

11-11; 12-3 Sun (01225) 448259

RCH Pitchfork; guest beers H

A classic, unspoilt pub in a 300-year-old building. The three oak-panelled rooms include a superb northern-style drinking lobby. Although it can get crowded, there is often space in the comfortable back bar. Guest beers generally come from local microbreweries, with a stout or porter usually on offer in the winter months. A local farmhouse cider is also served, along with a range of fine wines and malt whiskies. Winter Sunday hours may be longer. Q(Spa)

Pig & Fiddle

2 Saracen Street, BA1 5BR

11-11.30; 12-10.30 Sun (01225) 460868

Butcombe Bitter; Fuller's London Pride; guest beers H

This large and busy town-centre pub has a varied clientele and a friendly atmosphere. One end is an old shop front, the other a courtyard with drinking benches and covered heaters. The decor is an esoteric collection of art displays and sporting memorabilia. Up to three guest beers come from local breweries. Table football is played, and there are regular live music and open mic nights. The pub is popular with rugby fans and has several large TV screens. (Spa)

Pulteney Arms

37 Daniel Street, BA2 6ND (corner of Daniel St and Sutton St)

12-3, 5-11 (midnight Thu); 12-midnight Fri & Sat; 12-10.30 Sun (01225) 463923 thepulteneyarms.co.uk

Fuller's London Pride; Otter Bitter; Timothy Taylor Landlord; guest beers H

Tucked away near the end of Great Pulteney Street, this venue has been open since 1792. The cat symbol on the pub sign refers to the Pulteney coat of arms. There are five gas light fittings (now sadly condemned) above the bar. The decor has an emphasis on sport, particularly rugby. An extensive and deservedly popular food menu is on offer (no food Sun eves). Two or three guest beers are kept, usually from nearby micros and often from Bath Ales.

Raven

6-7 Queen Street, BA1 1HE

11.30-11 (midnight Fri & Sat); 12-10.30 Sun

(01225) 425045 theravenofbath.co.uk

Beer range varies H

Busy 18th-century free house in the heart of Bath. The six ales include two brewed exclusively by Blindmans. Guest ales come from far and wide, with several mini beer festivals a year. The main bar and the quieter first-floor bar serve the same range of ales. Famous for its sausages and Pieminister pies, the Raven is one of the few pubs in Bath serving food on Sunday evening. It's on several bus routes. (Spa)

Royal Oak

Lower Bristol Road, Twerton, BA2 3BW (on A36 at intersection with road to Windsor Bridge)

4-11; 12-midnight Fri-Sun (01225) 481409

Butts Jester, Barbus Barbus; guest beers H

Two regulars from Butts Brewery and up to five guest beers from microbreweries near and far are served here, alongside an equally interesting range of ciders, perries and bottled British and Belgian beers. There are folk music sessions (alternating Irish and English) on Wednesday evenings, and live music plays most weekends. Tuesday evening is quiz night. Outside is a secluded garden and small on-site car park. A discount of 50p per pint is available to CAMRA members on some of the range. (Oldfield Park)P

Star Inn ★

23 Vineyards, BA1 5NA

12-2.30, 5.30-11; 12-midnight Sat; 12-10.30 Sun

(01225) 425072 star-inn-bath.co.uk

Abbey Bellringer H**; Draught Bass** G**; guest beers** H

A main outlet for Abbey Ales, this classic town pub was fitted out by specialist beer equipment manufacturer Gaskell & Chambers in 1928. Its four small rooms have benches around the walls, wood

INDEPENDENT BREWERIES

Abbey Bath
Blindmans Leighton
Butcombe Wrington
Cheddar Cheddar
Cotleigh Wiveliscombe
Cottage Lovington
Dawkins Timsbury
Exmoor Wiveliscombe
Glastonbury Somerton
James Street Bath (NEW)
Kubla Lydeard St Lawrence
Masters Greenham
Milk Street Frome
North Curry North Curry
Odcombe Lower Odcombe
Ordnance City Ashcott
Quantock Wellington
RCH West Hewish
Stocklinch Stocklinch
Stowey Nether Stowey
Twisted Oak Wrington
Wild Beer Evercreech (NEW)
Windy Seavington St Michael
Yeovil Yeovil

panelling and roaring fires. The smallest room has a single bench, called Death Row, while the pub itself, which dates from around 1760, is coffin shaped. Bass is served from the cask and complementary snuff is available. There is a Friday night folk session and a monthly quiz.
Q♣●🚌🐾📶

Bishops Lydeard

Bird in Hand 🄻
34 Mount Street, TA4 3LH
⏲ 12-11 (10 Sun) ☎ (01823) 432090
🌐 thebirdinhand34.com
Cotleigh Tawny Owl; Exmoor Gold; guest beers 🄷
This free house is very much a community pub, set at the centre of the village and 10 minutes' walk from West Somerset Railway. Four ales are served, mainly from local and south-west breweries. The slate-floored bar is warmed by an open fire in winter. Good locally produced and home-cooked food is served in the refurbished dining room. The skittle alley accommodates functions. Families and dogs are welcome in the large garden. Weekly quiz nights and frequent mini beer festivals take place.
Q❀◑♣P🚌(18,28)🐾📶

Bishopswood

Candlelight Inn
TA20 3RS (off A303 between Newton and Marsh)
⏲ closed Mon; 12-2.30 (3 Sat & Sun), 6-11
☎ (01460) 234476 🌐 candlelight-inn.co.uk
Otter Bitter; guest beers 🄶
Popular and friendly country pub set in a pretty village in the Blackdown Hills. Features include flint walls, wooden floors and open fires, as well as a lovely garden for those warm summer days. Good food is served lunchtimes and evenings, made using local ingredients wherever possible. Beers come mainly from West Country breweries and there is usually a selection of real ciders on offer. The large dining room is available for private functions and large parties. Q❀◑●P

Bleadon

Queen's Arms
Celtic Way, BS24 0NF (off A370)
⏲ 11.30-11; 12-10.30 Sun ☎ (01934) 812080
🌐 queensarms.butcombe.com
Butcombe Bitter, Gold; guest beer 🄷
A 17th-century stone-built pub in the centre of the village. Three rooms converge on the bar, the largest is the main dining area. Food sales are strong, but not at the expense of ale drinkers – the pub is owned by the local Butcombe Brewery. Thatchers cider is also sold. Two real fires and exposed beams add to the cosy atmosphere. There is a garden/patio with a sales hatch. Families are welcome. Regular buses serve the village from Weston. Q❀◑●P🚌(83)🐾📶

Bridgwater

Carnival Inn 🄻
37-39 St Mary Street, TA6 3LX
⏲ 8am-midnight (1am Fri & Sat) ☎ (01278) 726180
Greene King Abbot; Ruddles Best Bitter; guest beers 🄷
This town-centre Wetherspoon takes its name from Bridgwater's famous carnival. Steak night is on Tuesday, chicken club on Wednesday, curry club on Thursday, and fish on Friday. A cider festival is held in September. The venue offers a good range of Somerset ales. There is a large bar area, with another room off to one side. At the back of the bar is a family area. The garden at the rear has space for smokers. Q🐎❀◑♿⇌●🚌

Fountain Inn 🄻
1 West Quay, TA6 3HL (corner of town bridge and Fore Street)
⏲ 11-11 ☎ (01278) 444951
Moles Best Bitter; St Austell Proper Job; Sharp's Doom Bar; guest beers 🄷
Traditional pub in a town-centre location, next to the River Parrett, with a wood-burning stove to give it a cosy feel. Its large, friendly open bar has a library with many books and a selection of newspapers on display, where you can relax and read in comfortable surroundings. You can expect a warm welcome from the landlord and landlady. This locally owned free house offers excellent-value real ales. Light snacks are available.
❀⇌♣●🚌

Buckland Dinham

Bell Inn
High Street, BA11 2QT
⏲ 12-3 (not Mon & Tue), 6-midnight ☎ (01373) 462956
🌐 bellatbuckland.com
Butcombe Bitter; guest beers 🄷
This warm and friendly pub is strongly community-focused – it has produced a village recipe book and holds film nights. It also offers a facility to order and pay for beer online. A good range of guest beers is kept. A three-day summer beer festival with live music is run in August and a cider festival in October. Local beers feature in home-prepared dishes. The pub has its own large campsite (featuring a collection of bikes), attracting CAMRA members from all over the UK.
🐎❀◑⛺●P🚌(414,424)📶

Burrowbridge

King Alfred Inn 🄻
TA7 0RB (on A361 9 miles from Taunton)
⏲ 5.30-8 Mon; 12-3, 5.30-11; 12-9 Sun ☎ (01823) 698379
🌐 kingalfredinn.com
Butcombe Bitter; Otter Amber; guest beers 🄷
A friendly free house by the River Parrett and believed to be close to where King Alfred burnt the cakes. This Grade II-listed hostelry has stone flag floors and offers two West Country beers as guests plus local real cider. Its good home-cooked food, locally sourced, has an excellent local reputation. A beer festival takes place in late August. An upstairs outside patio area provides peaceful views. The pub featured on TV news during the floods of early 2014. 🐎❀🛏◑⛺♣●P🚌(29)🐾📶

Butleigh

Rose & Portcullis
Sub Road, BA6 8TQ
⏲ 12-2.30, 5.30-11; 12-2.30, 7-10.30 Sun ☎ (01458) 850287
🌐 rose-and-portcullis.co.uk
Otter Bitter; guest beers 🄷
Butleigh nestles in the low hills, south of Glastonbury, and the pub's blue lias stonework is typical of the area. The interior was renovated in

2011, becoming open plan and adding a dining area. The feel of the old Rugby Bar has been retained, and an ancient Courage ales cockerel, sometimes adorning the exterior and now painted in local colours, is proudly displayed when Butleigh wins the local grudge match against the Tor. Since 2011, 300 different real ales have been served. Q❀◐◑♣●P🚌(667)🐾📶

Cheddar

Riverside Inn

Cliff Street, BS27 3PX (next to public car park)
⏲ 9am-11 (midnight Fri & Sat) ☎ (01934) 742452
🌐 riversidecheddar.co.uk
Cheddar Potholer; guest beers Ⓗ
Large and tastefully decorated pub at the bottom end of the gorge. The public bar has sofas and high stools, with TVs offering a choice of sporting events. The lounge leads to a 90-seat restaurant and a huge beer garden bordering the River Yeo, with sheltered areas and a heated space for smokers. There is a well-equipped play area for children. Two guest beers, usually of session strength, and Thatchers cider, are served, as is food, all day from 9am breakfast.
Q❀◐◑♿♣●P🚌(126)🐾📶

Chew Magna

Pelican

10 South Parade, BS40 8SL
⏲ 12-midnight (6 Sun) ☎ (01275) 331777
🌐 pelicanchewmagna.com
Butcombe Bitter; St Austell Tribute; guest beer Ⓗ
An imposing double-gabled, whitewashed pub in the centre of the village. It has an elaborate porch entrance marked by two fine but unobtrusive pieces of privet topiary. An upmarket food menu is served in comfortable surroundings and there is a suntrap courtyard and garden. The pub is now in the hands of the former owner of the nearby Bear & Swan before it was sold to Fuller's some years ago. The one guest beer can be interesting and unusual. No food Sunday evening.
❀◐◑♣●P🚌🐾📶

Churchill

Crown Inn

The Batch, Skinners Lane, BS25 5PP (off A38, 400yds S of A368 jct)
⏲ 11-11 (10.30 Sun) ☎ (01934) 852995
Draught Bass; RCH Hewish IPA, PG Steam; St Austell Tribute; guest beers Ⓖ
Long-time Guide regular and winner of many CAMRA awards, tucked away down a small lane yet close to the village centre. Several small rooms with stone-flagged floors are warmed by two log fires and offer an assortment of seating. Excellent lunchtime food is provided, featuring local ingredients. Up to eight beers, usually local, are served on gravity. There are outside drinking areas to the front and rear. A classic unchanged old pub.
Q❀◐⛺P🚌(121)🐾

Clevedon

Royal Oak

35 Copse Road, BS21 7QN (behind ice cream parlour near pier)
⏲ 12-11 (midnight Fri & Sat) ☎ (01275) 547420
Butcombe Bitter; Fuller's London Pride; Sharp's Doom Bar; guest beer Ⓗ
Lively, friendly, mid-terrace inn close to the seafront and connected via an alley. It has a large front window and a Tardis-like interior with many rooms. This community pub is home to cribbage and cricket teams. The winner of various awards, it hosts many events including cooking competitions and dancing, ranging from morris dancing through to belly dancing and Zulu. There is a quiz on Monday and folk music on Wednesday. Thatchers cider is sold. Q♣●🚌

Coleford

King's Head

BA3 5LU
⏲ 12-midnight ☎ (01373) 812346
Butcombe Bitter; guest beers Ⓗ
In the heart of the old part of the village, the King's Head was rebuilt after a fire in 1830. This rambling old inn offers a welcome for walkers and regulars. The flagstone-floored main bar has a roaring fire and there is a separate games room. The weekend after August bank holiday is the busiest of the year, when the pub hosts an Irish music festival, with up to eight different beers. The cider is Thatchers Cheddar Valley. Q❀◐♿♣●P🐾📶

Combe Florey

Farmers Arms Ⓛ

TA4 3HZ (on A358 between Bishops Lydeard and Williton)
⏲ 12-11.30 (10.30 Sun) ☎ (01823) 432267
🌐 farmersarmsatacombeflorey.co.uk
Cotleigh Tawny Owl; Exmoor Ale, Gold; St Austell HSD Ⓗ
An old thatched inn off the A358 next to the Quantock Hills, it has a small public bar, a large log fire and a restaurant area. Four regular ales are available, three of them local. The pub overlooks a scenic garden and stream. The West Somerset Railway passes on an embankment at the rear. While the inn is deservedly known for its excellent locally-produced food, it was the national Innserve Best Cellar UK 2013 winner. Q❀◐◑⛺P🚌🐾

Congresbury

Plough 🏆

High Street, BS49 5JA (off A370 at B3133 jct)
⏲ 11.30-2.30, 4.30-11; 11.30-midnight Fri; 11.30-3, 5-11 Sat; 12-3, 7-11 Sun ☎ (01934) 877402 🌐 the-plough-inn.net
Butcombe Bitter; St Austell Tribute; Twisted Oak Fallen Tree; guest beers Ⓗ
Characterful village pub with flagstone floors and many original features, decorated with interesting local artefacts. Three guest beers are served from a row of old cask heads behind the bar, mainly from local breweries. Thatchers cider is also stocked. Food is available lunchtimes and evenings, except Sunday night when the quiz is hosted. The pub has real fires and a large garden, and Mendip morris men meet here. Local CAMRA Pub of the Year 2013 and 2014. Q❀◐◑♣●P🚌(X1,353)🐾

Corton Denham

Queen's Arms Ⓛ

DT9 4LR (3 miles S of A303)

⏲ 10-11 (midnight Fri & Sat); 11-11 Sun ☎ (01963) 220317
🌐 thequeensarms.com
Beer range varies [H]
Cosy, friendly pub with two real fires in an idyllic setting. Beers from Moor and Exmoor breweries are always available – the house ale is Queen's Revival. Local ciders are also served – the Queen's Arms was Somerset CAMRA Cider Pub 2012. Food ranges from snacks to quality main meals, and many food awards have been won. The pub opens for breakfast at 8am. Special events including quizzes and food nights are held. The accommodation is highly rated, with the garden overlooking rolling countryside.
Q❀🛏◐◑♿🍎P🐾📶

Crewkerne

King William Inn

Barn Street, TA18 8BP (last turning on left off A30 towards Chard)
⏲ 5 (12 Sat)-midnight; 12-4 Sun ☎ (01460) 74492
Butcombe Bitter, Brunel IPA; guest beers [H]
Just off the main shopping area of Crewkerne, a short uphill walk takes you to a well-hidden proper pub. The King William specialises in real ales, plus local cider from Perry's. Popular with the locals, a TV shows horse racing unless a local team is playing football. The pub is always busy on Mondays, when there is a happy hour and the reasonably priced real ale is keenly discounted.
Q🐎❀♣🍎P🚌 (99,99A)

Croscombe

George

Long Street, BA5 3QH (on A371 between Wells and Shepton Mallet)
⏲ 12-3, 6-11 ☎ (01749) 342306 🌐 thegeorgeinn.co.uk
Beer range varies [H]/[G]
Attractive 17th-century inn refurbished by the owner, serving at least four guest ales from West Country independents and hosting two beer festivals a year. Blindmans King George is exclusively brewed for the pub. It has a large main bar, a snug with fireplace, a family room and a separate dining room. Food is home-cooked using locally-sourced ingredients. Regular steak, curry and pizza nights feature. A skittle alley is to the rear, and it has a large garden with a covered terrace. Q🐎❀🛏◐◑♿♣🍎P🚌🐾📶

Cross

New Inn

Old Coach Road, BS26 2EE (on A38/A361 jct)
⏲ 12-11 (midnight Fri & Sat) ☎ (01934) 732455
🌐 newinncross.co.uk
Otter Ale; Sharp's Cornish Coaster; guest beers [H]
This roadside inn on the A38 is close to the historic medieval town of Axbridge. Popular for its extensive food menu served all day until 9pm (8pm Sun) and beer festivals at Easter and the August bank holiday, it usually has three guest beers that can often be adventurous. There is a function room on the first floor. A large hillside garden with children's play facilities offers a fine view of the Mendip Hills and Somerset Levels. Ale is discounted on Thursdays. ❀◐◑♣P🚌 (126)🐾📶

Crowcombe

Carew Arms 𝕃

TA4 4AD (village is signed off A358)
⏲ 12-11 summer; 12-3, 5-11 winter ☎ (01984) 618631
🌐 thecarewarms.co.uk
Exmoor Ale; Otter Bright; Quantock Wills Neck; St Austell Proper Job; guest beers [H]
A classic rural pub in the village at the foot of the beautiful Quantock Hills. The flagstoned public bar has a historic inglenook, and the large garden looking towards the Brendon Hills makes this popular with locals, walkers and dogs. Four to five guest ales come from local microbreweries. The bar/restaurant serves locally-sourced food. The skittle alley doubles as function room. A local beer festival is held in August. Comfortable accommodation is available in six rooms, ideal for walkers and bikers.
Q🐎❀🛏◐◑♿⛺♣🍎P🚌 (18,28)🐾📶

Dinnington

Dinnington Docks

TA17 8SX (approx 3 miles E of Ilminster off Crewkerne Rd)
⏲ 11.30-3.30, 6-midnight; 11-midnight Sat; 12-10.30 Sun
☎ (01460) 52397
Butcombe Bitter; Teignworthy Gun Dog; guest beers [H]
One of those step-back-in-time establishments with a really warming atmosphere, ancient wood enhancing it, and well worth navigating the narrow lanes to visit it. Curiously, as it would appear the village only boasted a level crossing, various railway memorabilia is displayed. Meals are made with local produce wherever possible, with fresh fish from Dorset on the menu on Fridays. Please ask your children to be nice to the dogs who litter the floor. ❀◐◑♿♣🍎P🐾

Dulverton

Bridge Inn 𝕃

20 Bridge Street, TA22 9HJ
⏲ 12-11 summer; 12-3, 6-11 (not Mon); 12-11 Fri-Sun winter
☎ (01398) 324130 🌐 thebridgeinndulverton.com
Exmoor Ale; guest beers [H]
Close to the River Barle, this warm, welcoming pub dating from 1845 has a cosy single-room bar with a wood-burning stove and surrounding memorabilia. A wide range of excellent food is available lunchtimes and evenings. The Bridge holds a Green Tourism Award in recognition of the environmentally friendly way it is run. An annual beer festival coincides with the local folk festival over the Whitsun holiday.
Q🐎❀◐◑⛺♣P🚌 (25,398)🐾📶

Dunster

Luttrell Arms

36 High Street, TA24 6SG
⏲ 10-11.30 ☎ (01643) 821555
Exmoor Ale; Otter Amber; Sharp's Doom Bar; guest beers [H]
The Luttrell Arms occupies the site of three ancient houses dating back to 1443. The back bar with its open log fire is a gem. The garden offers great views of Dunster Castle. This 15th-century inn has 28 unique bedrooms, an à la carte restaurant and private function rooms, with many unusual

features in some of the suites. The inn features some of the oldest glass windows in Somerset and some fine plaster work on the lounge ceiling. Q

Emborough

Old Down Inn

BA3 4SA

12-2.30, 6.30-11.30; 12-11 Sun ☎ (01761) 232398

Butcombe Bitter; Draught Bass [G]**; guest beers** [H]/[G]

A free house first licensed in 1640, this establishment was once an important coaching inn. The spirit of the past lives on in the main bar, where beer is served straight from the cask. Two guests from local breweries are generally available. The bar snacks are excellent value, and likewise the main meals. This friendly and popular hostelry is a classic example of a traditional Somerset inn and is the centre of many local community activities. Q (173)

Exford

Exmoor White Horse Inn

TA24 7PY (on B3224)

11-11 ☎ (01643) 831246 exmoor-whitehorse.co.uk

Exmoor Ale, Gold; guest beers [H]

This pub hotel is a real gem. In its long bar furnished with large benches, alongside a choice of ales, 100 malt whiskies are available. There are also tables outside set on the bank of the River Exe. Set right in the heart of Exmoor, it offers 28 en-suite rooms, some with four-poster beds, and a honeymoon suite. An Exmoor safari in the inn's own eight-seater Land Rover can be arranged. The restaurant offers local trout, salmon and lobster, as well as game dishes. Q P

Faulkland

Tucker's Grave ★

BA3 5XF

12-3 (not Mon), 6-11; 12-3, 7-10.30 Sun

☎ (01373) 834230

Butcombe Bitter, seasonal beer [G]

A gem from a bygone age and with a nationally important historic pub interior, this inn was built in the mid-17th century and has changed little since. It was named after Tucker, who hanged himself and was buried at the crossroads outside, and featured in a song by 1970s punk band The Stranglers. There is no bar – beers and Thatchers cider are served from an alcove. Shove-ha'penny is played and there is a skittle alley. Camping is available in the grounds. Q P

Forches Corner

Merry Harriers

EX15 3TR (3 miles SE of Wellington)

12-3, 6.30-11 (closed Sun eve & Mon) ☎ (01823) 421270

merryharriers.co.uk

Otter Head; guest beers [H]

Friendly, family-owned, award-winning free house on the Blackdown Hills bordering Somerset and Devon. The bar separates the lounge from the dining area, where excellent meals featuring fresh fish, meat and game are served. Guest beers are usually from local breweries, and locally made Bollhayes cider is also served. Although in a somewhat remote location, the pub has a thriving trade. There is a large, pleasant garden in which to enjoy the warm summer sunshine.
Q P

Frome

Griffin

Milk Street, BA11 3DB

5-11; 4-1am Fri & Sat; 1-9 Sun ☎ (01373) 467766

Milk Street Funky Monkey, The Usual, Beer; guest beers [H]

In the part of Frome known as Trinity or Chinatown, the Griffin is the brewery tap for Milk Street Brewery at the back. A wide range of ales is produced along with seasonals and specials. The single bar retains original features such as etched windows, a wooden floor and a stained glass griffin behind the bar. Regular quiz nights and live music take place. The small garden is open all year but food is limited to summer barbecues and Sunday lunches. P

Old Bath Arms

1 Palmer Street, BA11 1DS

11-midnight ☎ (01373) 465045 theoldbatharms.co.uk

Draught Bass; Fuller's London Pride; guest beers [G]

The landlord here champions beer on gravity – up to six ales are served directly from the cask. This multi-faceted town-centre pub consists of a lively real ale bar, a lounge, cocktail bar, restaurant and beer garden. Food encompasses traditional pub fare, steaks, tapas, paella, Sunday roasts and pizzas cooked in a wood-fired oven. Guests are usually from local micros but sometimes further afield. The seven ciders come from Westons, Orchard Pig and Moles. Entertainment includes a pub pianist.
P

Hallatrow

Old Station

Wells Road, BS39 6EN

12-3, 5-11; 12-11 Fri & Sat; 12-10.30 Sun

☎ (01761) 452228 theoldstationandcarriage.co.uk

Brains Rev James; Butcombe Bitter; guest beers [H]

Unusual eclectic pub noted for its high-quality food at reasonable prices as well as its totally eccentric decor. A bewildering array of unexpected items appears throughout. An old GWR railway carriage serves as a dining room and the pub has its own crazy golf course. Owned by Brains brewery, it often serves the small batch one-off beers from its in-house microbrewery. Book ahead to dine at weekends. Children are welcome, and there are five ground floor en-suite rooms available.
P (376)

Henstridge

Bird in Hand

Ash Walk, BA8 0QD

11-2.30, 5.30-11; 11-11 Sat; 12-10.30 Sun

☎ (01963) 362255

Butcombe Bitter; guest beers [H]

Old stone village pub with low ceilings, beams, a fireplace at each end of an attractive long bar, and a games room housing a TV. There is an adjoining skittle alley. Excellent-quality ales and good-value snacks help make a visit to this friendly establishment worthwhile. At the heart of most village activities, this is a true community pub.
Q P (58)

Hinton Blewitt

Ring o' Bells

Upper Road, BS39 5AN (2 miles W of Temple Cloud from A37) ST594569
12-3, 5-11 (midnight Fri); 12-midnight Sat; 12-11 Sun
(01761) 452239 ringobellshinton.butcombe.com
Butcombe Bitter; Fuller's London Pride; guest beer H
Butcombe pub dating from the 19th century, a dining/function room with its own garden was recently added, and blends nicely with the cosy bar and snug. Quality food is served, using local produce when possible. Local sports clubs meet here and much memorabilia is on show, particularly cricket-related. Cyclists, walkers, children and dogs are all most welcome. Ashton Still cider is served. QP

Horsington

Half Moon Inn

Duck Lane, BA8 0EF
12-2.30, 6-11; 12-4 Sun (01963) 370140
Fuller's London Pride; Wadworth 6X; guest beers H
Owned and run by the same couple for over 20 years, this pub is the focal point of a lovely village. Up to three guest beers are available, and over 1,000 different ales have been served so far. There are gardens to the front and rear, a separate skittle alley, a large function room, an ample car park and 10 letting rooms. Reasonably priced food is available at all sessions. The annual beer festival is well worth a visit. Closed Monday and Tuesday in winter. QP(58)

Huish Episcopi

Rose & Crown ★ L

TA10 9QT (on A372)
11.30-2 (not Mon), 5.30-11.30; 11.30-midnight Fri & Sat; 12-10.30 Sun (01458) 250494
Teignworthy Reel Ale; guest beers H
Grade II-listed 17th-century thatched inn, known locally as Eli's. Having a nationally important historic pub interior, this quaint free house is unusual in having no bar counter in the flagstoned taproom – only 10 of these remain country-wide. Generations of the same family have served patrons with good food and ale here, to be enjoyed in the relaxed atmosphere of the various small rooms. Bus 54 stops a 20-minute walk away. No food Sunday evenings. P(54)

Hutton

Old Inn

Main Road, BS24 9QQ
11.30-11 (midnight Fri & Sat); 12-11 Sun
(01934) 812336
Butcombe Gold; Fuller's London Pride; St Austell Tribute; guest beers H
Genuine free house owned by a long-standing Guide landlord, and now a thriving local, set right at the heart of the local community. The pub is extremely popular for its excellent and great-value food, particularly the Sunday carvery. Dogs are welcome in the bar. The car park to the rear is accessed by narrow one-way lanes either side. Food is served lunchtimes and evenings except Sunday, which is quiz night. Up to two guest beers are available. P(5,5A)

Kelston

Old Crown

Bath Road, BA1 9AQ (3 miles from Bath on A431)
11.30-11; 12-10.30 Sun (01225) 423032
oldcrown.butcombe.com
Butcombe Bitter; Draught Bass; Fuller's London Pride; guest beer H
Attractive multi-roomed 18th-century coaching inn owned by Butcombe Brewery. The rare cash register handpumps, flagstone floors, open fires and settles all help create a convivial atmosphere. In summertime, barbecues and live musical events are occasionally held in the large, attractive garden. Sunday is quiz night and occasional themed food events are hosted. Butcombe's own Ashton Still cider is sold. Take care crossing the busy road to the car park. Buses 319 and 37 stop directly outside. QP(319,37)

Keynsham

Lock Keeper

Keynsham Road, BS31 2DD (on A4175)
11-midnight; 12-11 Sun (0117) 986 2383
lockkeeperbristol.com
Bath Ales Gem; Young's Bitter, Special; guest beer H
Multi-roomed Young's pub, noted for its food, by Keynsham lock on the River Avon. The original 17th-century cottage once brewed its own beer and was named the White Hart. It divides into two parts, with the older bar facing the canal, while the large conservatory and heated veranda overlook the river, pétanque pitches and the popular garden. Families are welcome. Occasional live music features in summer. The pub may stay open later when busy. QP

Kilve

Hood Arms L

TA5 1EA (on A39)
11-11 (01278) 741210 thehoodarms.com
Exmoor Gold; Otter Head; guest beers H
Former 17th-century coaching inn set beside the main road, near a beach frequented by fossil hunters. It has oak beams and an open fireplace, a comfortable bar and separate restaurant. Outside is a walled garden where boules is played in the summer. There are 12 en-suite rooms and a lodge available to rent. The pub is an ideal base for walkers, with easy access to the Quantock Hills and the Coleridge Way. It offers good food and wines and welcomes dogs. QP(14)

Kingsbury Episcopi

Wyndham Arms L

Folly Road, TA12 6AT
12-midnight (1am Sat & Sun) (01935) 823239
wyndhamarms.com
Butcombe Bitter; guest beers H
This pub is around 400 years old, with a log fire in the bar and a comfy dining room. Antique settles make for a relaxed drinking atmosphere, and the beers are well kept to Cask Marque standard. Outside is a skittle alley that doubles as a function room, and a heated smoking area with a full-size pool table. Another room upstairs is used for music nights and meetings. Good home-made meals are served. Once visited you will go back again.
QP

Long Sutton

Devonshire Arms Hotel

Cross Lane, TA10 9LP

12-3, 6-11 (10.30 Sun) ☎ (01458) 241271

thedevonshirearms.com

Beer range varies [H]

This fine old Grade II-listed building opposite the village green houses a well-appointed contemporary bar and restaurant, furnished with comfy chairs and glass-topped tables, and warmed by a real log fire. The bar mostly serves real ale from Somerset breweries, but always offers beers from Moor, which is only a couple of minutes from the pub. Drinkers can use the walled garden, the courtyard or the terrace overlooking the village green. En-suite accommodation is available. Q❀♿P

Lower Odcombe

Masons Arms

41 Lower Odcombe, BA22 8TX (off Yeovil to Montacute road)

12-2.30, 6-midnight ☎ (01935) 862591

masonsarmsodcombe.co.uk

Odcombe No.1, Spring [H]

A pretty thatched pub with its own microbrewery, well situated for campers and caravanners to explore the areas of natural beauty nearby. The brewery supplies some excellent beers, two regulars and often seasonal brews. Food is also high quality, made with local produce. Various local events are held on the pub field. B&B rooms are offered and the pub campsite at the rear has hook-ups, showers and laundry room. Children and dogs are welcome. Q❀P(81)

Lydford on Fosse

Cross Keys Inn [L]

TA11 7HA (next to A37 from Yeovil-Shepton Mallet crossroads)

11.30-3, 5-11; 11.30-midnight Fri; 11.30-3, 5-midnight Sat; 12-4, 7-11 Sun ☎ (01963) 240473 thecrosskeysinn.net

Dark Star Hophead; Exmoor Gold; Hogs Back TEA; Yeovil Star Gazer; guest beers [G]

First mentioned by name in 1759 when it was a tavern, the pub has expanded over the years, but was in need of the complete renovation it recently underwent. Following the official grand opening in September 2013, the Cross Keys has quickly established itself as a public house specialising in real ales, excellent food and accommodation in comfortable surroundings. Keep an eye on its website for beer festivals and music. Q❀♿♣P(667)

Martock

White Hart Hotel [L]

East Street, TA12 6JQ

12-3 (not Mon), 5.30-11; 12-3 Sun ☎ (01935) 822005

whitehartholelmartock.co.uk

Otter Bitter; Sharp's Doom Bar; guest beers [H]

Family-run hotel, built in 1735 and Grade II-listed, in an attractive hamstone-built village. It has a main bar for drinks and meals and a restaurant for table service, offering a comprehensive menu and bistro board. A function room/skittle alley can be rented when not in use for skittles. There are 10 guest rooms. Three real ales are available, rotating through 10 choices. Local clubs meet here including the monthly 41 club, and bi-monthly film and music clubs. Q❀♿♣P(N9,N10)

Middlezoy

George Inn [L]

42 Main Road, TA7 0NN (off A372, 1 mile NW of Othery, 5 miles E of Bridgwater)

closed Mon; 12-3, 7 (6.30 Fri & Sat)-midnight; 12-4, 7-10 Sun ☎ (01823) 698215 thegeorgeinnmiddlezoy.co.uk

Cheddar Gorge Best; guest beers [H]

Friendly 17th-century free house with stone-flagged floors and exposed beams. Beers are mainly from the south-west, and one local real cider is always on sale. Excellent locally-sourced food is served Wednesdays to Saturdays. The landlord keeps his beers in top condition and runs an annual beer festival at the Easter weekend. This village pub may be a little remote but it is well worth finding. Q❀♣P(16)

Minehead

Kildare Lodge

Townend Road, TA24 5RQ

11-3, 6.30-11; 12-5 Sun ☎ (01643) 702009

kildarelodge.co.uk

St Austell Dartmoor Best Bitter; guest beers [H]

Close to Minehead town centre, this Grade II-listed building in the Arts & Crafts style retains many interesting features. There is a small bar, two separate lounges and a dining room. It offers quality ales at low prices. The pub participates in the local boules and quiz leagues. It is an ideal base for exploring Exmoor and nearby Dunster, and close to the West Somerset Railway. Accommodation includes 12 en-suite rooms and a bridal suite with a four-poster bed. Q❀♿♣P

Old Ship Aground

Quay Street, TA24 5UL (beside harbour)

11-11 (midnight Fri & Sat) ☎ (01643) 703516

oldshipaground.com

Marston's Pedigree; Ringwood Best Bitter, Boondoggle; guest beers [H]

A 1906 pub with 12 en-suite rooms plus a function room, set in the picturesque part of Minehead between the harbour and the lifeboat station, with fantastic views over the Bristol Channel. This hostelry offers local and national beers and locally-sourced food, with a diverse carvery on Sundays, and curry on Tuesdays. It has open log fires. The West Somerset Railway and the town centre are a short walk away, with Exmoor a 20-minute drive. ❀♿♣P

Mudford

Half Moon Inn

Main Street, BA21 5TF (on A359 between Yeovil and Sparkford)

12-11 (10.30 Sun) ☎ (01935) 850289

thehalfmooninn.co.uk

Beer range varies [G]

Welcoming 17th-century village roadside inn, extensively restored in traditional style, always busy with diners and drinkers. It has a single bar divided into several cosy areas. The menu is written on blackboards, and snacks and daily specials are available. Real ales are from RCH

Brewery and are served from a stillage behind the bar; cider is also on offer. An outside courtyard is pleasant on warm days. The pub has 14 letting rooms. Guide dogs only. Q❀🛏◐◑♿🍎P🚌(1)📶

Norton Fitzwarren

Cross Keys 𝕃

TA2 6NR (at A358/B3227 jct, W of Taunton)
⏲ 11-11; 12-10.30 Sun ☎ (01823) 333062
Beer range varies Ⓗ
Busy 19th-century former coaching inn and stables converted into a pub and restaurant, comprising several separate seating areas with open fires and exposed beams. There is a large garden to the rear and a covered outside seating area, with a big car park to the side. Four changing real ales from local, regional and national breweries are usually sold, plus Westons Old Rosie cider. A large menu, offering traditional pub food, is served all day, and there is a skittle alley and regular live music. 🐴❀◐◑♿🍎P🚌📶

Pitney

Halfway House 𝕃

Pitney Hill, TA10 9AB (on B3153)
⏲ 11.30-3, 5.30-11 (midnight Fri & Sat); 12-11 Sun
☎ (01458) 252513 🌐 thehalfwayhouse.co.uk
Butcombe Bitter; Hop Back Summer Lightning; Otter Bright; Teignworthy Reel Ale; guest beers Ⓖ
This pub offers eight to 10 local ales on gravity, often including beers from the nearby Moor brewery, alongside many international bottled beers. It is a basic but buzzing pub deserving its many accolades – it was a former Somerset CAMRA Pub of the Year – and also the distinction of being in the Guide continuously for 23 years. Superb home-cooked food is based on local produce, including the roast lunch served on Sundays (no food Sun eve). Local ciders are from Wilkins and Gold Rush. Q❀◐◑♣🍎P🚌(54)🐾

Porlock

Ship Inn 𝕃

High Street, TA24 8QD
⏲ 11 (12 Sun)-midnight ☎ (01643) 862507
🌐 shipinnporlock.co.uk
Exmoor Beast; Otter Bitter; guest beers Ⓗ
At the bottom of the notorious Porlock Hill, this pub is known locally as the Top Ship. Dating from the 13th century, it featured in RD Blackmore's Lorna Doone. It still has flagstone floors and an inglenook fireplace. In the summer up to eight real ales are served, plus local cider. This CAMRA award-winning pub has a three-tiered patio garden, skittle alley and en-suite rooms. Beer festivals are staged. Well-behaved children and dogs are welcome. Q🐴❀🛏◐◑♿⛺♣🍎P🚌(10,39)🐾

Porlock Weir

Ship Inn 𝕃

TA24 8PB (take B3225 from Porlock)
⏲ 11-11; 12-10.30 Sun ☎ (01643) 863288
🌐 thebottomship.co.uk
Exmoor Ale, Stag; St Austell Tribute, Proper Job; guest beers Ⓗ
A 400-year-old pub in Exmoor National Park next to the old harbour, with possibly some of the best views of any Somerset pub, overlooking the Bristol Channel towards south Wales. It is well known for good food, served by friendly staff. The pub is ideal for walkers and close to Porlock village, and can be busy in the holiday periods. A joint beer festival with the Ship Inn at Porlock is held. The large car park is opposite. Q❀◐◑♿⛺♣🍎P🚌(10,39)🐾

Priddy

Hunters Lodge

Hillgrove Road, BA5 3AR (isolated crossroads 1 mile from A39 close to TV mast) ST549500
⏲ 11.30-2.30, 6.30-11; 12-2, 7-11 Sun ☎ (01749) 672275
Butcombe Bitter; Cheddar Potholer; guest beers Ⓖ
Timeless, classic roadside inn near Priddy, the highest village in Somerset, popular with cavers and walkers. The landlord has been in charge for well over 40 years. Three rooms include one with a flagged floor and all beer is served direct from casks behind the bar. Local cider is served. The simple home-cooked food is excellent and exceptional value. A folk musicians' drop-in session is held on Tuesday evening. The garden is pleasant and secluded. Mobile phones are not welcome. Q🐴❀◐◑🍎P🐾

Queen Victoria Inn

Pelting Drove, BA5 3BA
⏲ 12-11 ☎ (01749) 676385 🌐 queenvictoria.butcombe.com
Butcombe Bitter; Fuller's London Pride; guest beers Ⓗ
Creeper-clad inn, a pub since 1851, with four rooms that feature low ceilings, flagged floors and log fires. A wonderfully warm and relaxing haven on cold winter nights, it is popular during the Priddy Folk Festival in July and the annual fair in August. Reasonably priced, home-cooked food is a speciality. Children are welcome and there is a play area by the car park. Cheddar Valley and Ashton Still ciders are sold. It may close briefly on some afternoons. Q❀◐◑⛺♣🍎P🐾

Puriton

37 Club 𝕃

1 West Approach Road, Woolavington Road, TA7 8AD (between Puriton and Woolavington)
⏲ 6 (5 Fri)-11.30; 12-midnight Sat; 12-10.30 Sun
☎ (01278) 685190 🌐 37club.co.uk
Butcombe Gold; guest beers Ⓗ
Formerly the social club of the Royal Ordnance factory whose allocated number was 37, this large venue offers many facilities to members (with non-members welcome). Two skittle alleys, pool, snooker and football can be enjoyed, and a separate function room is available for up to 150 people. Food varies from steaks with a starter to just a bowl of chips. Thursday night is curry night, and there is free entertainment once a month. Members can use the fishing club lakes. RCH beers are sold. 🐴❀◐◑⛺♣🍎P🚌

Radstock

Fromeway

Frome Road, BA3 3LG
⏲ closed Mon; 12-3, 6-11; 12-11 Sun ☎ (01761) 432116
🌐 fromeway.co.uk
Butcombe Bitter; Wadworth 6X; guest beers Ⓗ
This friendly free house has been in the same family for five generations. The present landlord has been in charge for more than 36 years and produces his own sausages, faggots and home-

cured hams for the excellent bar and restaurant meals. Popular with locals, the Fromeway has a warm and relaxing atmosphere. A single bar serves three regular ales, and there are weekly guest beers. The pub organises many functions, quizzes and walks for charity. Three charming bedrooms are available. Q❀🛏◑◐●P🚌(768,178)🐾

Rickford

Plume of Feathers

Leg Lane, BS40 7AH (off A368, 2 miles from A38; approaching from Churchill, the left U-turn into Leg Lane is extremely tricky)

🕘 12-11 ☎ (01761) 462682 🌐 theplumeoffeathers.com

Butcombe Bitter; Cheddar Potholer; guest beers 🄷

A 17th-century building that has been a pub since the 1800s, the interior is divided into several areas including a restaurant with a real fire. A popular local, it also provides a pleasant and convenient base from which to walk, fish or explore the Mendips. It has a garden at the rear and a stream running along the front, leading to a ford. Parking is limited. Butcombe seasonal beers often feature among the two guests. A charity duck race is staged in July. Q❀🛏◑◐♣P🚌(791)🐾

Rode

Cross Keys

20 High Street, BA11 6NZ

🕘 11.30-3, 6-11.30; 11.30-11.30 Sat; 11.30-10.30 Sun

☎ (01373) 830900 🌐 crosskeys.butcombe.com

Butcombe Bitter; guest beers 🄷

Reopened in 2004 after 10 years of closure, this was originally the brewery tap for the long-closed Fussell's Brewery, and more latterly a Bass depot. Sympathetically restored, it has succeeded in bringing back a strong village trade. A passageway featuring a deep well links two bars. There is also a large restaurant. The two guest beers can come from almost anywhere and encompass major brands, like London Pride, but equally breweries otherwise unknown in the area (Red Squirrel for example). Q❀🛏◑◐♿♣●P🚌🐾

Rowberrow

Swan Inn

Rowberrow Lane, BS25 1QL

🕘 12-3, 6-11; 12-11 Sat; 12-10.30 Sun winter; 12-11 (10.30 Sun) summer ☎ (01934) 852371 🌐 swan.butcombe.com

Butcombe Bitter; guest beers 🄷

Believed to date from around the late 17th century, this Butcombe Brewery-owned country pub enjoys an attractive setting, nestling beneath the Dolebury Iron Age hill fort. A convenient stop for walkers on the Mendip Hills, the emphasis is on home-cooked food with unusual specials, but customers who just want a drink are welcome. There is a collection of artefacts around the walls and a grandfather clock. The large, attractive beer garden and car park are opposite. Q❀◑◐●P🐾

St Georges

Woolpack

Shepherds Way, BS22 7XE (very close to M5 jct 21 – take A371 towards Weston)

🕘 11-11; 12-10.30 Sun ☎ (01934) 521670

🌐 woolpack.butcombe.com

Butcombe Bitter, Gold; Fuller's London Pride; guest beer 🄷

A 17th-century coaching house which was once a packing station that baled wool for local farmers. Owned by Butcombe since 2006, it has two bar areas, a conservatory and a separate carvery. The pub is in the much-expanded St Georges area just off the M5 at junction 21, and within walking distance of Worle station. It has an extensive menu and daily specials. A discount on real ale is offered to CAMRA members. ❀◑◐♿⇌(Worle)P🚌

Saltford

Bird in Hand

58 High Street, BS31 3EJ

🕘 11-11 ☎ (01225) 873335 🌐 birdinhandsaltford.co.uk

Butcombe Bitter; Sharp's Doom Bar; guest beers 🄷

Characterful and smart traditional country inn dating from 1869, 400 yards from the A4, and close to the Bristol to Bath cycle path and the River Avon. There is a long, L-shaped bar and a pleasant conservatory with fine views across the garden to the hills beyond. Old photographs feature and there is a small family area. Food is served lunchtimes and evenings and all day at weekends. Two guest beers and Thatchers traditional cider are sold. It has a pétanque piste.
❀◑◐♿♣●P🚌🐾

Shepton Beauchamp

Duke of York 🄻

North Street, TA19 0LW

🕘 12 (5.30 Mon; 3.30 Tue & Wed)-midnight; 12-10.30 Sun

☎ (01460) 240314 🌐 thedukeshepton.co.uk

Otter Bright; Teignworthy Reel Ale; guest beers 🄷

A charming 17th-century free house in the centre of a pretty Somerset village, with excellent en-suite rooms. At the front there are tables on the raised pavement to allow patrons to observe the leisurely life of the locals. Good food is served in both the bar and restaurant, which helps attract visitors from the surrounding villages (no food is available Sun eves or Mon). Children and dogs are welcome. ❀🛏◑◐♣P🐾

South Cadbury

Camelot 🄻

Chapel Road, BA22 7EX (just off A303 between Sparkford and Wincanton)

🕘 11-midnight (closed 3-5 winter); 11.30-11 Sun

☎ (01963) 440448

Beer range varies 🄷

A large, attractive pub in the centre of this pleasant village, with flagstoned floors throughout and log fires at both ends. A display case contains information about the nearby Cadbury Castle (reputed to be King Arthur's Camelot) and artefacts found in the various excavations. Beers are mainly from local breweries such as Yeovil Ales, and cider is from the next village. Excellent home-cooked food is served at all sessions and friendly staff make for a pleasant visit. Q❀◑◐♿♣●P🐾

South Petherton

Brewers Arms 🄻

18-20 St James Street, TA13 5BW (½ mile off A303)

🕘 11.30-2.30, 6-11; 11.30-midnight Fri & Sat; 12-11 Sun

☎ (01460) 241887 🌐 the-brewersarms.com

Butcombe Bitter; Otter Bitter; guest beers 🄷
A regular finalist for the Somerset CAMRA local Pub of the Year, this pub has sold some 2,300 different ales during the landlord's 20-year tenure. Good food at reasonable prices and helpful, knowledgeable staff, also help ensure visitors make a return visit to this lively village inn. Should you happen to call in during one of the two annual beer festivals you might want to stay in one of the en-suite rooms. (81)

Stogumber

White Horse Inn

High Street, TA4 3TA (turn left off A358 at Crowcombe)
12-11 ☎ (01984) 656277 whitehorsestogumber.co.uk
Otter Bitter; St Austell Proper Job; guest beers 🄷
Traditional free house opposite the church in this picturesque village lying between the Quantock and Brendon Hills, near the West Somerset Railway. It is popular with railway buffs, ramblers and locals alike. The pub has a skittle alley, which doubles as a music venue, and a music festival is held in September. Locally-produced food is served in the lounge and restaurant, and most of the real ales come from West Country breweries. Pétanque is played in summer. P

Taunton

Coal Orchard

Bridge Street, TA1 1UD
8am-midnight (1am Fri & Sat) ☎ (01823) 447330
Greene King Abbot; Ruddles County; guest beers 🄷
An Art Deco style conversion of a former hardware store, set in the town centre. One level is open plan, with good disabled access. It is family-friendly and there is a small garden at the rear. Food is served until 11pm (with a discount for card-carrying CAMRA members). There are usually three guest beers from local breweries. Beer festivals are held in spring and autumn. Two large screens show major sporting events. Q

Ring of Bells

16-17 St James Street, TA1 1JS
11-11 (10 Mon); 9am-11 Sat; 12-6 Sun ☎ (01823) 259480
theringofbellstaunton.co.uk
Beer range varies 🄷
Under new ownership in 2013, this town-centre pub has gone from strength to strength. There are two bar areas with wooden floors, a downstairs dining area, an upstairs restaurant and a large outside courtyard. Four handpumps dispense local and south-west microbrewery beers alongside three keg craft beers, and there are regular beer festivals. Excellent locally-produced food is served, from light snacks to full meals. Somerset cricket ground is close by. Somerset CAMRA Pub of the Year 2014.

Trull

Winchester Arms

8 Church Road, TA3 7LG
12-3, 6.30-11 (10.30 Sun) ☎ (01823) 284723
winchesterarmstrull.co.uk
Beer range varies 🄷
Thriving family-run community pub on the outskirts of Taunton, near to the Blackdown Hills. The comfortable bar is separated from the long dining area by an impressive coal-effect fireplace. Three ales are mainly from south-west breweries. Real cider is served in summer only. The locally-sourced home-cooked food is excellent (booking is advised at popular times). The stream-side gardens, perfect for families and dogs, are the venue for entertainment and barbecues. Accommodation is available. Q P (97)

Wanstrow

Pub at Wanstrow

Station Road, BA4 4SZ (midway along main road running through village)
6 (6.30 Mon)-11; 12-2.30, 6-11 Sat & Sun
☎ (01749) 850455
Blindmans Golden Spring; Draught Bass; guest beers 🄷
An absolute gem, this friendly village local has a lounge bar with an open fire and flagstone floors, leading to a small restaurant. It serves two regular and up to three guest beers, from almost anywhere, along with ciders from Thatchers and Rich's. Games include skittles, bar billiards and ring the bull. A small but imaginative menu is offered and all food is home cooked. The pub opens evenings only during the week. Q P

Washford

White Horse Inn

Abbey Road, TA23 0JZ (off A39)
12-11 ☎ (01984) 640415 exmoorpubs.co.uk
Beer range varies 🄷
Only 500 yards from the ruins of Cleve Abbey and close to the Torre Cider Farm, this riverside free house is an ideal base for visits to the coast, Exmoor National Park, the Quantock Hills and the West Somerset Railway. You can relax on the riverside balcony in summer, or by the fire in winter. Food includes locally-sourced produce when possible. There is en-suite accommodation available. Voted Pub of the Year by the local press in 2012. Q P (18,28)

Watchet

Esplanade Club

5 The Esplanade, TA23 0AJ (opp marina)
12-3 (Sun only), 7-midnight ☎ (01984) 634518
Beer range varies 🄷
Three times Somerset CAMRA Club of the Year, this major music venue has great views over the marina and the Bristol Channel. It displays old photographs and memorabilia. Built in the 1860s as a sailmaking factory, it has been a club since the 1930s. There are folk nights in the week, and live music every weekend. It is home to the boat owners' club, and a short walk from the West Somerset Railway. CAMRA members are welcome.

Star Inn

Mill Lane, TA23 0BZ
12-3.30 (4 Sun), 6.30-midnight ☎ (01984) 634518
thestarinnwatchet.co.uk
Beer range varies 🄷
This friendly local offers four changing real ales, and was twice voted Somerset CAMRA Pub of the Year. It has darts, quiz and boules teams, and is home to the Sunday night Bad Boys Club. It also hosts port and cheese nights, and has run over 50 beer trips. Festivals and music nights are held in

the marquee in summer. Good local food is served, including seafood. Close to the marina and West Somerset Railway, it is handy for the Quantock Hills and Exmoor. ❀◑♿⛺♣●🚌🐾📶

Wedmore

New Inn

Combe Batch, BS28 4DU

12-2.30 (not Mon), 5-midnight; 12-2am Fri; 12-1am Sat; 12-10.30 Sun ☎ (01934) 712099

Butcombe Bitter; guest beers [H]

Traditional village inn famous for many local events, including the annual turnip prize, conkers, spoof, apple bobbin and penny chuffin. The public bar, lounge and dining areas are complemented by beer gardens to the front and back. Forthcoming ales are listed on a chalkboard, and are mainly from south-west micros, all on handpump. There is a skittle alley/function room. Food is home cooked and good value, with theme nights and a takeaway menu. Q❀◑⛺♣●P🚌(668,670)

Wells

City Arms

69 High Street, BA5 2AG

10-11; 9am-midnight Fri & Sat; 10-10.30 Sun ☎ (01749) 673916

Butcombe Bitter; Glastonbury Hedge Monkey, Golden Chalice; Goff's White Knight; Quantock Rorke's Drift [H]

In 1810 the City of Wells jail closed and later became the City Arms. The main bar retains the small barred windows and low-vaulted ceilings of its former existence. The building encloses a courtyard on three sides, with outdoor seating. There is an extensive food menu available in the bar, bistro and restaurant, with meals made to order using fresh local produce. Between five and seven beers are normally available, mainly from local brewers, with a Molson Coors rebadged beer, Cathedral City. Q🛏◑♿●🐾📶

West Chinnock

Muddled Man

Lower Street, TA18 7PT

11-2.30, 7-11; 11-midnight Fri & Sat; 12-11 Sun ☎ (01935) 881235

Beer range varies [H]

This is a popular, family-run, traditional free house in a picturesque village, offering a warm welcome to visitors and locals. The beer garden at the rear catches the sun throughout the day, while the hanging baskets and troughs are a sight to see. Regularly changing ales from local breweries are pulled from three handpumps. Good home-cooked food is served lunchtimes and evenings (Sunday lunch must be pre-booked). Q❀🛏◑♿♣●🐾

West Huntspill

Crossways Inn

Withy Road, TA9 3RA (on A38)

12-midnight (11.30 Sun) ☎ (01278) 783756 crosswaysinn.com

Cheddar Gorge Best; RCH Double Header; guest beers [H]

Somerset CAMRA Pub of the Year 2013, this 17th-century inn offers up to six real ales, including guest beers. It has several bar areas, two fireplaces with log fires during winter, an outside fireplace to keep smokers warm, a dining room and a skittle alley which can be used as a function room. A good food menu is available plus daily specials boards. Breakfast is served 7.30-11am (available to all) and there are seven en-suite rooms. ❀🛏◑♿⛺♣●P🚌(15,21)🐾📶

Weston-super-Mare

Cabot Court Hotel

Knightstone Road, BS23 2AH (300yds N of main pier)

7am-midnight (1am Fri; 2am Sat) ☎ (01934) 427930

Greene King Abbot; Ruddles Best Bitter; guest beers [H]

Large Wetherspoon conversion on the seafront between the Grand Pier and the Winter Gardens. On four levels, each has a distinctive style. There are bars on the ground and second floors with different guest ales in each. The first floor room is particularly comfortable, with sofas and a real fire in winter – a refuge from the TVs and speakers in the other rooms. Local breweries are supported, with Exmoor and GWB breweries often featured. It has 21 letting rooms. Q❀🛏◑♿●🚌📶

Criterion

45 Upper Church Road, BS23 2DY

12-midnight (1am Fri & Sat); 12-10.30 Sun ☎ 07527 425795 criterioninns.co.uk/the-criterion

St Austell Tribute [G]**; guest beers** [H]

Genuine free house and traditional community pub, just off the seafront in the Knightstone area. Believed to be one of the oldest pubs in town, it has interesting local photos on the walls. Pub games feature strongly, with darts, bar billiards and table skittles, plus a quiz on Tuesday. Bar snacks are available, including filled rolls at lunchtime. Guest ales come in various styles, with local breweries well supported. Thatchers cider is often served, but sometimes replaced by another. ♣●🚌(1,4)🐾

Regency

22-24 Lower Church Road, BS23 2AG

10-11.30 (midnight Fri & Sat); 10.45-11.30 Sun ☎ (01934) 633406 theregencyinn.co.uk

Butcombe Bitter; Draught Bass; Flowers IPA; Wells Bombardier; guest beer [H]

Comfortable and friendly town-centre local, attracting a mixed clientele and popular with students at lunchtime. The pub has pool, skittles and crib teams, but also offers a quiet refuge for conversation. The pool room with TV and jukebox is separate from the main bar area, and children are welcome here. Home-cooked food at keen prices is served lunchtimes plus Wednesday (curry) and Thursday (grill) evenings. There are patios to the front and rear. Monthly mini beer festivals feature, plus occasional live bands. ❀◑♣🚌

Waverley

69 Severn Road, BS23 1DR

12-11

Greene King Abbot; St Austell Tribute; guest beers [H]

Genuine old-fashioned community free house in an area with few pubs, to the south of the town centre but walkable from the station. Two guest beers are usually on, often unusual ales. Thatchers ciders are served. A weekly quiz features, as does live music some weekends in what is known as the Brig, a former air raid shelter to the rear. It also stages a regular farmers' market. Food is limited to basic snacks. ❀≠●🚌(7)🐾📶

ENGLAND

Wheddon Cross

Rest & Be Thankful Inn

TA24 7DR

11.30-2, 6-midnight ☎ (01643) 841222

restandbethankful.co.uk

Exmoor Ale; St Austell Tribute; guest beers

This 19th-century coaching inn, at the heart of Exmoor National Park, is at the crossroads of Exmoor's highest village. It is close to the highest point in Somerset, Dunkery Beacon, and near Snowdrop Valley. The interior includes a skittle alley, pool table, dartboard and private function room. A carvery is served on Sundays and Wednesdays. The pub is also a lively music venue. Eight comfortable en-suite rooms are available, all with TV, ideal for cyclists and ramblers. Q❀🛏◑♿♣●P🚌(398)🐾

Williton

Mason's Arms

2 North Road, TA4 4SN

11-2.30, 6-11; 12-3, 7-10.30 Sun ☎ (01984) 639200

themasonsarms.com

Sharp's Doom Bar; Skinner's Betty Stogs; guest beers

Beautiful thatched 16th-century inn with oak beams throughout, offering five en-suite rooms in the adjoining annexe. Outside is a pleasant beer garden where locals and visitors alike sit and relax. The pub hosts quiz teams and plays in the local boules league. It has a good reputation for its food and the quality of its ales – Rich's cider is always available. Close to the West Somerset Railway, Quantock Hills and the coast, and a short drive from Exmoor National Park. Q❀🛏◑♿♣●P🚌(18,28)

Wincanton

Nog Inn

South Street, BA9 9DL

10.30-11 (midnight Fri & Sat); 12-11 Sun

☎ (01963) 32998 thenoginn.com

Otter Bitter; Sharp's Own; guest beers

Attractive listed pub with a striking Georgian façade fronting a long, narrow building with parts dating back to the 16th century. A secluded sunny garden with covered seating can be found at the far end of the property. The guest ales are often seasonal and an extensive range of continental draught beers is always available, as are real ciders. CAMRA members receive a 10p discount on real ale. ❀◑♣●P🚌(58)🐾

Winsford

Royal Oak Inn

Halse Lane, TA24 7JE

11-3, 6-11; 11-midnight Sat; 11-11 Sun

☎ (01643) 851455 royaloakexmoor.co.uk

Exmoor Ale, Gold; guest beers

Originally a 12th-century farmhouse, this beautiful thatched pub claims to be England's most photographed inn. It has eight en-suite rooms and features in the Michelin Guide, Taste of the West and Best Loved Hotels of the World. Well-behaved dogs are made welcome in the bar. It is also proud of its Cask Marque accreditation for its real ales. The Win brook runs past the pub and over the ford that leads up to Exmoor and Tarr Steps.

Q❀🛏◑♿▲♣P🚌🐾

Withypool

Royal Oak Inn

TA24 7QP

12-11 ☎ (01643) 831506 royaloakwithypool.co.uk

Exmoor Ale, Gold; guest beers

For over 300 years the Royal Oak, set in a tiny village in the heart of Exmoor, has been providing great local ale and food. It has two bars, a dining room and en-suite rooms. It offers game shooting, riding and fishing, and Exmoor safaris can be arranged to see the ponies and deer. Two cottages near the pub are for hire. An open fire and logburners feature in winter, with a few tables outside for summer. Q❀🛏◑▲♣●P🐾

Yeovil

Quicksilver Mail

168 Hendford Hill, BA20 2RG (at jct of A30 and A37)

10.30-midnight (1am Sat); 12-11 Sun ☎ (01935) 424721

quicksilvermail.com

Butcombe Bitter; Dartmoor Jail Ale; Sharp's Doom Bar

Friendly and comfortable, this was once a stop for the horse-drawn mail service from Exeter to London. Historic photos and pictures of pop stars and sports personalities adorn the walls. Various local groups meet here regularly including retired teachers, railway enthusiasts, badminton players and motorcyclists. There is a TV in the bar and low ambient music. A function room offers live pop, rock, jazz and folk music. Good-value food is served including Sunday lunchtime roasts. Well-behaved children and dogs are welcomed.

❀🛏◑♣P🚌(47,99)🐾

Fishing for beer

Ah! My beloved brother of the rod, do you know the taste of beer – of bitter beer – cooled in the flowing river? Take your bottle of beer, sink it deep, deep in the shady water, where the cooling springs and fishes are. Then, the day being very hot and bright, and the sun blazing on your devoted head, consider it a matter of duty to have to fish that long, wide stream. An hour or so of good hammering will bring you to the end of it, and then – let me ask you avec impressement – how about that beer? Is it cool? Is it refreshing? Does it gurgle, gurgle and 'go down glug' as they say in Devonshire? Is it heavenly? Is it Paradise and all the Peris to boot? Ah! If you have never tasted beer under these or similar circumstance, you have, believe me, never tasted it at all.

Francis Francis, By Lake and River, 16th century

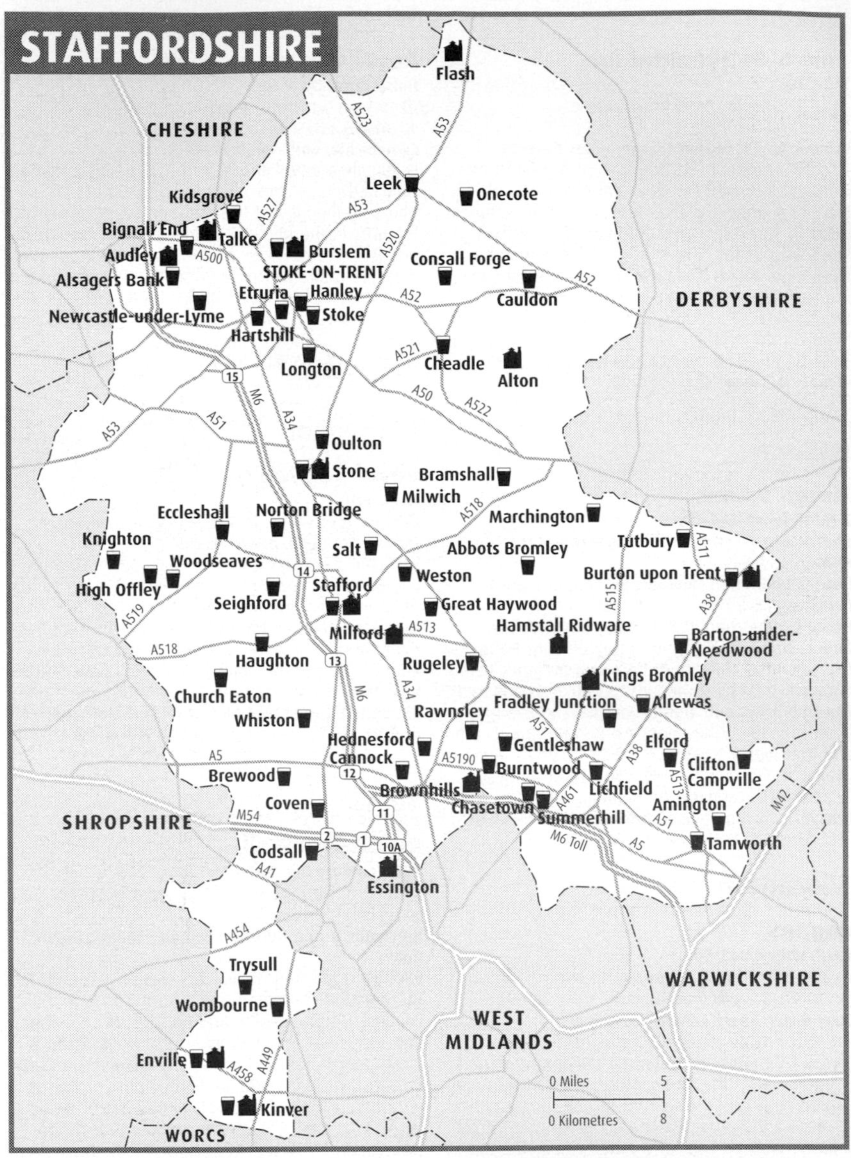

Abbots Bromley

Coach & Horses

High Street, WS15 3BN (on B5014, at E end of village)
12-2.30 (not Mon), 5.30-midnight; 12-midnight Sun
(01283) 840256 coachandhorsesabbotsbromley.co.uk
Marston's Pedigree; St Austell Tribute; guest beer
Grade II-listed coaching inn dating back to 1745, although the building is even older, with links to Burton Abbey. The interior has recently been substantially refurbished, the extended bar area retaining some old wooden beams and an assortment of memorabilia. Beyond the bar is a large lounge/dining room – the pub is gaining a reputation for fine food. Occasional live music features, and Abbots Bromley is world famous for its annual Horn Dance. P (428)

Goat's Head

Market Place, WS15 3BP (on B5014)
12-midnight (01283) 840254 thegoatshead.co.uk
Greene King Abbot; St Austell Tribute; Sharp's Doom Bar; Timothy Taylor Landlord; guest beers
Attractive timber-framed 16th-century building facing the Market Place and Butter Cross. Dick Turpin reputedly stayed here. Tudor-styled outside, it is a conventional two-roomed pub internally, featuring a wood-panelled public bar and a wood-panelled lounge with beamed ceiling, the latter used primarily for dining (no meals Sun eve). The large beer garden at the rear comprises a patio, decking and lawn. Public car parking is nearby. An annual beer festival takes place on the spring bank holiday weekend. (428)

Alrewas

George & Dragon

120 Main Street, DE13 7AE

11 (12 Sun)-11 ☎ (01283) 791476

georgeanddragonalrewas.co.uk

Jennings Cumberland Ale; Marston's Burton Bitter, Pedigree; guest beer H

Imposing, three-storey, welcoming village local, thought to be a former coaching inn and dating back to the early 1700s. The comfortable main bar area is split into three distinct sections, and there is a separate lounge/dining room to one side (no meals Sun eve). Monthly live musical entertainment takes place. The Trent & Mersey canal runs along the edge of the village, about 300 yards distant, and the National Memorial Arboretum is a mile to the east. P (7,7E)

Alsagers Bank

Gresley Arms

High Street, ST7 8BQ (on B5367 4 miles N of Newcastle-under-Lyme)

12 (3 Mon-Wed)-11 ☎ (01782) 722469

gresleyarms.co.uk

Draught Bass; guest beers H

Sitting at a height of 700 feet above sea level, the Gresley Arms commands views over Cheshire, Shropshire and the Wirral. The pub is also close to two country parks. Eight varied real ales are on offer, plus four real ciders and a huge range of imported bottled beers. Good-value meals are served four nights a week, plus Sunday lunch. A regular folk and blues festival, including a beer festival, takes place in May every year. A gem. P (94,94A)

Amington

Gate Inn

Tamworth Road, B77 3BY

11-11 (11.30 Fri & Sat) ☎ (01827) 63189

gatepubtamworth.co.uk

Marston's Pedigree; guest beers H

Busy and welcoming canalside pub, popular with boat users during the summer. The multi-level lounge is mostly used for dining, while the separate bar is accessible through the lounge. At least five guest ales from the Marston's portfolio are offered, and beer festivals are held twice a year. The garden features a raised beer terrace and separate children's play area. Karaoke takes place every second and fourth Sunday of the month, and open mic every first Sunday. Tuesday is quiz night. P (785,5)

Barton-under-Needwood

Royal Oak

74 The Green, DE13 8JD (½ mile from B5016 via Wales Lane)

12-midnight (1am Fri & Sat); 12-11 Sun ☎ (01283) 713852

Marston's Pedigree; guest beers H/G

Bustling, community local on the southern edge of the village, home to many traditional pub games teams and an over-40s football team. While parts of the building date back to the 16th century, the pub has only existed since the mid-1800s. Public bar and lounge customers are served from a central sunken bar, its floor being below the level of the rest of the ground floor. Beers are available on handpump or by gravity, direct from the cask, on request. Q P

Bignall End

Bignall End Cricket Club

Boon Hill, ST7 8LA (400yds from B5500)

7 (12 Fri-Sun)-midnight ☎ (01782) 720514

bignallend.play-cricket.com

Draught Bass; guest beers H

Popular club now run as a pub, with great views over the Cheshire Plain. Summer and winter beer festivals take place in the upstairs function room. There is also a snooker room while the busy bar with TV caters for sports fans. Three or four beers are on draught including Bass and different guests from smaller breweries. Covered outside seating is by the cricket pitch, where it is lovely to sit in good weather and watch the sun go down. P (34)

Bramshall

Old Bramshall Inn

Stone Road, ST14 5BG

12-midnight ☎ (01889) 563634 bramshallinn.co.uk

Marston's Pedigree; Sharp's Doom Bar; Timothy Taylor Landlord; guest beers H

Whether it be a drink with friends (and everyone at the pub is a friend), a light snack at lunchtime or a full evening à la carte meal, the Old Bramshall Inn provides it all with warmth and friendliness. There are five handpumps on the bar, with beers from local breweries such as Slater's and Titanic always available. Food is high quality and locally sourced wherever possible, served lunchtimes and evenings (12-6pm Sun). One of Titanic Brewery's Blue Riband Inns of Excellence. P

Brewood

Swan Hotel

15 Market Place, ST19 9BS

11.45-midnight ☎ (01902) 850330

Caledonian Deuchars IPA; Courage Directors; Theakston Black Bull Bitter; Wye Valley HPA; guest beers H

INDEPENDENT BREWERIES

Beowulf Brownhills
Black Hole Burton upon Trent
Blythe Hamstall Ridware
Burton Bridge Burton upon Trent
Burton Old Cottage Burton upon Trent
Enville Enville
Flash Flash
Gates Burton Burton upon Trent
Kinver Kinver
Lymestone Stone
Marston's Burton upon Trent
Morton Essington
Peakstones Rock Alton
Quartz Kings Bromley
Shugborough Milford
Slater's Stafford
Talke O' Th' Hill Talke
Titanic Burslem
Tower Burton upon Trent
Townhouse Audley
Worthington's (Molson Coors) Burton upon Trent

A regular CAMRA award winner, this comfortable old coaching inn, with low-beamed ceilings and seasonal log fires, is five minutes' walk from the Shropshire Union Canal and the Staffordshire Way. Cosy snugs displaying early prints of the area flank the central bar and there is a traditional skittle alley upstairs. Three of the six handpumps feature LocAle and there is a selection of over 70 malt whiskies. Cheese and ham baguettes are served weekday lunchtimes and afternoons.
Q❀♿♣P🚌🐾📶

Burntwood

Drill Inn

33 Springlestyche Lane, WS7 9HD (left off northbound Rugeley Road out of Burntwood) SK061101
⌚ 12-midnight; 12-10.30 Sun ☎ (01543) 675799
🌐 drillinnburntwood.co.uk
Beer range varies Ⓗ
Vibrant and friendly pub tucked away down a country lane. The homely, sprawling main room is partnered by a small, quiet snug. Three varying ales are offered, plus occasional beer festivals. There is a large elevated beer garden to the rear, plus a children's play area. Well-behaved children and dogs are welcome at all times. Good food is a draw here, supplemented by themed dining nights (no food served Mon). There is clay pigeon shooting on alternate Sunday mornings.
Q🛋❀◐◑♣P🐾📶

Burton upon Trent

Burton Bridge Inn

24 Bridge Street, DE14 1SY (on A511, at town end of Trent Bridge)
⌚ 12-2.30, 5-11; 11.30-11.30 Fri & Sat; 12-3, 7-11 Sun
☎ (01283) 536596 🌐 burtonbridgeinn.co.uk
Burton Bridge Golden Delicious, Sovereign Gold, Bridge Bitter, Burton Porter, Festival Ale; guest beer Ⓗ
This 17th-century pub is the flagship of the Burton Bridge Brewery estate and fronts the brewery itself. Two rooms are served from a central bar: a smaller front room, with wooden pews and a display of awards and brewery memorabilia, and a back room featuring oak beams and panels. The beer range is usually supplemented by a special Gold Medal Ale, plus a selection of malt whiskies and fruit wines. A dining/function room and a skittle alley are upstairs. No lunches Sunday-Tuesday. Q❀◐♣🚌🐾

Coopers Tavern ★

43 Cross Street, DE14 1EG (off Station St)
⌚ 5 (3 Tue & Wed; 12 Thu)-11; 12-11.30 Fri & Sat; 12-11 Sun
☎ (01283) 532551 🌐 cooperstavern.co.uk
Draught Bass Ⓖ**; Joule's Blonde, Pale Ale, Slumbering Monk** Ⓗ**; guest beers** Ⓗ/Ⓖ
Classic, unspoilt 19th-century ale house, once the Bass Brewery tap and now part of the Joule's estate. The intimate inner taproom has barrel tables and bench seating, with the beer served from a small counter by cask stillage. The more comfortable lounge leads to a third small room. Up to four varying ciders/perries plus fruit wines are also available. Local folk musicians meet here on Tuesday evenings, and there is live music on some weekends. Q❀≉🍎🚌🐾

Devonshire Arms

86 Station Street, DE14 1BT
⌚ 12-3 (not Mon), 5-11; 12-11 Fri & Sat; 6-11 Sun
☎ (01283) 562392 🌐 thedevonshire.co.uk
Burton Bridge Golden Delicious, Bridge Bitter, Damson Porter, Stairway to Heaven, Festival Ale; guest beer Ⓗ
Popular old pub, dating from the 19th century and Grade II-listed, and one of the five Burton Bridge Brewery hostelries in the area. It comprises a public bar at the front, and a larger, more comfortable, split-level lounge to the rear. Note the 1853 map of Burton, old photographs, and unusual arched wooden ceilings. An enclosed rear patio features flower borders and hanging baskets. Some continental bottled beers and English fruit wines are also stocked. Lunches Tuesday-Saturday only. ❀◐≉♣P🚌🐾

National Brewery Centre (Brewery Tap)

Horninglow Street, DE14 1NG (on A511, at Guild St jct)
⌚ 11-11 (6 Mon & Tue); 11-6 Sun ☎ (01283) 532880
🌐 nationalbrewerycentre.co.uk
Sharp's Doom Bar; Worthington's Red Shield, E, White Shield; guest beer Ⓗ
Formerly the Bass Museum/Coors Visitor Centre, the associated Brewery Tap showcases beers from the William Worthington's brewery, usually including a seasonal Shield beer. The comfortable single-room bar features an illuminated ice-block-look counter with chrome fonts and traditional handpumps. Food is served in the bar and the adjacent restaurant, while an L-shaped conservatory overlooks the garden and children's play area. The NBC organises numerous events throughout the year, including live music.
🛋❀◐◑♿P🚌(1)

Old Cottage Tavern

36 Byrkley Street, DE14 2EG (off Derby St, A5121, behind town hall)
⌚ 12 (11.30 Sun)-11 ☎ (01283) 511615
Burton Old Cottage Oak Ale, Stout, Halcyon Daze; guest beers Ⓗ
No longer owned by the brewery but leased from the Tadcaster Pub Company, this traditional local continues to operate as the Burton Old Cottage brewery tap. The public bar at the front, with a cosy snug to one side, and the wood-panelled lounge to the rear, are served from a central bar. There is also a games/function room (with demountable skittle alley) upstairs. Guest beers are usually from other SIBA members. It hosts the Brewtown Folk Club and Spoken Word events. Q🛋❀🛏≉♣🚌📶

Roebuck Inn 🏆

101 Station Street, DE14 1BT (on corner of jct with Mosley St)
⌚ 12-midnight (1am Fri & Sat) ☎ (01283) 511213
Draught Bass; Draught Burton Ale; Greene King Abbot; Marston's Pedigree; guest beer Ⓗ
A Victorian corner-terrace pub near the railway station, this friendly local was once the Ind Coope brewery tap and is sited opposite the former brewery. Draught Burton Ale was launched here in 1976. Inside, there is a long, narrow single room with dark wood panelling and the bar counter down one side. A small patio at the rear can be used for outdoor drinking, plus a few tables and chairs outside at the front in summer. Live music plays early on Sunday evenings. ❀🛏≉♣🚌📶

Cannock

Linford Arms

79 High Green, WS11 1BN

8am-12.30am (1am Fri & Sat) ☎ (01543) 469360

Greene King Abbot; Ruddles Best Bitter; guest beers H

Although close to Cannock Chase, this Wetherspoon pub on two levels is in an ideal town-centre location, and handy for the main bus station. Up to eight real ales are sold, including guests from local breweries. The pub name originates from the builders' merchants that formerly occupied the premises. Historic photographs and prints of local interest decorate the walls. It can get lively at weekends but there are quiet areas away from the main bar.

Cauldon

Yew Tree Inn

ST10 3EJ (1 mile S of A523 at Waterhouses)

6 (12 Sat)-midnight; 12-11 Sun ☎ (01538) 309876

yewtreeinncauldon.co.uk

Burton Bridge Bridge Bitter; Rudgate Ruby Mild; guest beers H

The pub, overlooked by the beautiful yew tree, has been standing for over 300 years and has been run by the same family since 1961. Entering here is like walking into an Aladdin's cave, with a unique collection of antiques and curios on display. You can enjoy one of four real ales, dispensed through brass Gaskell handpulls dating from 1926, while sitting on a church pew and listening to the pianola. The beer choice is based on customers' requests. Q P

Chasetown

Uxbridge Arms

2 Church Street, WS7 3QL SK045080

12-midnight (1am Fri & Sat) ☎ (01543) 677852

Beer range varies H

The five ales are forever changing in this deservedly long-standing Guide entry. A wide range of country wines and malt whiskies is available, plus a varying real cider. Sport is popular here, with bowls, darts and football teams. Chasewater Country Park and the associated heritage railway are close by. Good food is served in the lounge and upstairs restaurant (no food Sun eve). Children are allowed until 9pm, and dogs are welcome in the bar. P

Cheadle

Huntsman

The Green, ST10 1XS

12-midnight ☎ (01538) 750502

thehuntsmancheadle.com

Castle Rock Harvest Pale; Joule's Slumbering Monk; Marston's Pedigree; guest beers H

A family-oriented pub on the edge of Cheadle, close to attractions like Alton Towers and the Churnet Valley. It was local CAMRA Pub of the Year in 2013. A varied range of beers from independent breweries is offered, with an ale from the local Peakstones Rock usually on. Excellent locally-sourced food is served. A beer festival is held at the end of May and a cider festival is staged in the autumn. The pub cat is very happy.

P (X51)

Church Eaton

Royal Oak

High Street, ST20 0AJ (signed from A518 at Haughton) SJ932019

5 (12 Sat)-11; 12-9 Sun ☎ (01785) 823078

theroyaloakchurcheaton.co.uk

Banks's Bitter; guest beers H

Once threatened by closure but saved by a local consortium, the Royal Oak is now a thriving pub at the centre of the community. The interior is split into a lounge, a restaurant and an area with a dartboard and a pool table The pub is about a mile north-east of the Shropshire Union Canal at High Onn Bridge. Q P (482)

Clifton Campville

Green Man

Main Street, B79 0AX

12-2.30, 5.30-11; 12-11 Fri & Sat; 12-10.30 Sun

☎ (01827) 373262

Marston's Pedigree; guest beers H

Grade II-listed, this old village pub dates from the 18th century but has a 15th-century core. The right side of the pub offers a lounge-cum-restaurant, while the main entrance takes you into a low-beamed bar warmed by a coal fire. The three guest ales are always different. There is a pool table to the rear, plus a Devil Among the Tailors board in the bar. A terrace is to the front, a beer garden at the rear, and a large function room is available.

Codsall

Codsall Station

Chapel Lane, WV8 2EJ

11.30-2.30, 5-11; 11.30-11.30 Fri & Sat; 12-10.30 Sun

☎ (01902) 847061

Holden's Black Country Mild, Black Country Bitter, Golden Glow, Special; guest beers H

Sensitively converted from the waiting room, offices and stationmaster's house, the Grade II-listed building comprises a bar, lounge, snug and conservatory, and displays worldwide railway memorabilia. A raised terrace overlooks the working platforms. Bar meals are served all week except Sunday, when the Sunday Sandwich menu is available until 5pm. Two guest beers are kept and the mild is often replaced by Holden's Old Ale in winter. Beer festivals are held in May and the weekend after the August bank holiday.

Q P (5,10B)

Firs Club

Station Road, WV8 1BX (entrance along drive from shared Co-op car park)

7.30-11 (midnight Fri); 12-midnight Sat; 12-11 Sun

☎ (01902) 844674

Banks's Mild, Bitter P**; guest beers** H

Formerly the Conservative Club, this venue has a bar area, lounge and sports lounge with a pool table, dartboard and card table. Interesting photos of old Codsall and surrounding areas are displayed on the walls. Up to three guest ales are served, often from local breweries, and a beer festival is held in November. A large function room is available for hire. Show this Guide or a current CAMRA membership card to be signed in.

Q P (5,10B)

Consall Forge

Black Lion Ⓛ

Wetley Rocks, ST9 0AJ (off A522 follow signs to Consall Gardens, then Nature Reserve on hairpin bend; go straight on, ignore No Vehicular Access sign; at bottom of hill go left along track to car park)
🕘 12-11 ☎ (01782) 550294 🌐 blacklionpub.co.uk
Draught Burton Ale; Peakstones Rock Black Hole; Welbeck Abbey Henrietta; guest beers Ⓗ
A destination pub in the Churnet Valley, accessed by car, barge, steam train or on foot. Regular beer festivals are held in February, July and at Christmas, often in conjunction with the Churnet Valley Railway which runs past the front door. A free house, beers are sourced from breweries near and far, and a selection of ciders and perries is also available. Food portions are large, and there are regular hog roasts and barbecues.
🐴❀◐◑⛺♣🍎P🐾

Coven

Harrows Inn Ⓛ

School Lane, WV9 5AW
🕘 12-11 (midnight Fri & Sat) ☎ (01902) 790055
🌐 theharrowsinn.co.uk
Three Tuns XXX; guest beers Ⓗ
Privately owned, this pub has been a free house since 2012. Two refurbished rooms are served by a central counter; one room is used for dining and the other is a public bar with old beams, pool table, dartboard and piano. Both rooms have wood floors and log-burning stoves. Home-cooked meals are served all day (until 4pm Sun). Six real ales and up to 10 real ciders are usually stocked. The house bitter is brewed by Broughs.
🐴❀◐◑♿♣🍎P🚌(76)🐾📶

Eccleshall

Royal Oak Ⓛ

25 High Street, ST21 6BW
🕘 11-11 (midnight Fri & Sat); 12-11 Sun ☎ (01785) 859065
🌐 royaloakeccleshall.co.uk
Joule's Blonde, Pale Ale, Slumbering Monk Ⓗ
Fully refurbished by Joule's of Market Drayton, featuring light oak and specially commissioned stained glass windows and panels, this venue reopened in 2011. Portraits of past generations of the Joule family adorn the walls together with old brewery advertisements. Sir Geoff Hurst, of the 1966 World Cup winning team, ran the pub from 1974 to 1984, on retirement from football. The first floor has meeting and function rooms.
Q🐴❀◐◑♿P🚌(350,432)🐾

Star Inn Ⓛ

Copmere End, ST21 6EW (leave Eccleshall on B5026 and turn left at sign for Copmere End; follow road – pub is on crossroads)
🕘 closed Mon; 12-3, 6-11; 12-11 Sat & Sun
☎ (01785) 850279 🌐 thestarinn-eccleshall.co.uk
Draught Bass; Joule's Pale Ale; Titanic Anchor Bitter; Wells Bombardier; guest beer Ⓗ
A thriving 100-year-old pub in the heart of the beautiful Staffordshire countryside, adjacent to Copmere Lake. There are numerous walks around the area. The pub has become an integral part of this rural community, holding charity auctions and events. The extensive garden with play area is ideal for families. An excellent selection of bar meals and an à la carte menu are offered lunchtimes and evenings. The beer complements the award-winning locally-sourced food.
Q🐴❀◐◑♿⛺♣P🚌(436)🐾

Elford

Crown Inn Ⓛ

The Square, B79 9DB (600yds E of A513) SK189106
🕘 6-11; 12-midnight Fri & Sat; 12-11 Sun ☎ (01827) 383602
Burton Bridge Sovereign Gold; Draught Bass; guest beer Ⓗ
Welcoming and cosy village pub, with a bar, lounge, dining room and a separate pool room with its own serving hatch. In the 18th century the upstairs rooms were used as a courthouse, and today's dining room once served as the cells. Beamed ceilings feature throughout, with real fires in the bar and lounge. Food is served until 9pm Wednesday to Saturday, until 4pm on Sunday. Bar snacks are available at all times. No evening bus service. ◐◑♣P🚌🐾📶

Enville

Cat Inn 🏆 Ⓛ

Bridgnorth Road, DY7 5HA (on A458)
🕘 12-2.30 (not Mon), 5-11; 12-11 Fri & Sat; 12-6 Sun
☎ (01384) 872209 🌐 thecatinn.com
Enville Ale, Ginger Beer; guest beers Ⓗ
Parts of this traditional country pub date back to the 16th century. It has three oak-beamed rooms, all with real fires. The Garden Room has been refurbished and there is a function room upstairs. Hanging baskets adorn the beer garden and courtyard during the summer months. Regular Enville beers are on offer plus three guests, usually from local breweries. Home-made dishes and daily specials, using local produce whenever possible, are served. Joint winner of South Staffordshire CAMRA branch Pub of the Year in 2014, and winner in 2013. Q🐴❀◐◑🍎P🚌(585,588)🐾📶

Fradley Junction

Swan Inn

DE13 7DN (by Trent & Mersey canal, about 1 mile W of Fradley village) SK140140
🕘 11-11 (midnight Sat); 12-10.30 Sun ☎ (01283) 790330
Greene King Abbot; Marston's Pedigree; guest beers Ⓗ
Known locally as the Mucky Duck, this late 18th-century Grade II-listed mid-terrace pub overlooks the Trent & Mersey/Coventry canal junction. There is a basic but cosy public bar and a smaller lounge on opposite sides of a central serving area, plus a cellar room with a vaulted brick ceiling beyond the lounge. Guest beers come mainly from Midlands microbreweries. Real cider (Holden's Summat Else) is served in summer only. Folk night is Thursday, open mic night Sunday. Walkers and boaters are welcome. Q🐴❀◐◑♣🍎P🐾

Gentleshaw

Olde Windmill

Windmill Lane, WS15 4NF SK051118
🕘 12-midnight ☎ (01543) 682468 🌐 yeoldewindmill.co.uk
Draught Bass; guest beers Ⓗ
Welcoming 400-year-old country pub, with smartly attired staff and equally sharp food and drink offerings. Free of tie, the two guest ales are usually interesting microbrews. The cosy bar is dog-

friendly, while the wood-panelled lounge offers freshly cooked meals including interesting specials. Both rooms feature old beams (some cleverly fake) and open fires. A number of teams use the crown bowling green. The pub is 100 yards from the stump of an old disused windmill.

Great Haywood

Clifford Arms

Main Road, ST18 0SR (off A51, 4 miles NW of Rugeley)
12-11.30 (midnight Fri & Sat); 12-11 Sun
(01889) 881321 thecliffordarms.co.uk
Adnams Broadside; Draught Bass; Morland Old Speckled Hen; guest beers H
Village-centre inn with a large bar providing plenty of seating and a restaurant adorned with past photos of the pub. It is home to cribbage, dominoes and quiz teams, as well as a tug o' war team. It is also popular with walkers, cyclists, boaters and visitors to the nearby Shugborough Estate (National Trust). The Staffordshire Way and bridge 73 of the Trent & Mersey Canal are 200 yards along Trent Lane. The pub is dog-friendly.
QP(841)

Haughton

Bell Inn

Newport Road, ST18 9EX (on A518)
12-3, 5-midnight; 12-midnight Fri-Sun (01785) 780301
thebellhaughton.co.uk
Marston's EPA, Pedigree; Timothy Taylor Landlord; guest beers H
The L-shaped interior includes a restaurant at the rear that serves really good, locally-sourced food. At the front is a small, well-run, friendly bar with bar snacks on offer. As well as running charity events, the pub has six dominoes teams. The guest beer changes regularly and comes from the SIBA list, often from local brewers. Booking is recommended for dining.
P(481)

Hednesford

Cross Keys Hotel

42 Hill Street, WS12 2DN
12-midnight (01543) 879534
Brains The Rev James; Draught Bass; Holden's Golden Glow; Morland Old Speckled Hen; Salopian Oracle; guest beers H
Former coaching inn dating back to 1746 serving up to eight real ales, including several changing guests. Hednesford Town football club was originally based behind the pub, and strong connections remain as the licensee is an ex-player and now assistant manager. Sporting and historic photographs decorate the walls, and monthly quiz nights are held. It is rumoured that the highwayman Dick Turpin stopped here on his famous ride to York. Local CAMRA Pub of the Year 2013. P

High Offley

Anchor Inn ★

Peggs Lane, Old Lea, ST20 0NG (by bridge 42 of the Shropshire Union Canal) SJ775256
12-3, 7-11 (01785) 284569
Wadworth 6X H
On the Shropshire Union Canal, this Victorian two-bar inn is a rare example of an unspoilt country pub. It has been run by the same family since 1870, when it was called the Sebastopol. It has a lovely, award-winning garden. About two miles from the A519, the pub is not easily found, but is well worth the journey. Winter hours and Monday to Thursday lunchtime opening may vary, so check ahead. QP

Kidsgrove

Blue Bell

25 Hardingswood, ST7 1EG (off A50 near Tesco)
closed Mon; 1-4 (not Tue-Fri), 7.30-11; 12-10.30 Sun
(01782) 774052 bluebellkidsgrove.co.uk
Beer range varies H
Genuine free house with the same owners for 16 years and in every Guide since 2000. There are no TV or games machines, just lively conversation. Occasional impromptu folk music takes place on Sunday evenings. The pub attracts customers from a wide area. Six handpumps offer beers from microbreweries, plus Belgian and German ales, as well as real cider and perry. Easily reached by bus, train or boat on the Trent & Mersey and Macclesfield canals, which meet a few yards away.
QP(20,20A)

Kinver

Cross Inn

Church Hill, DY7 6HZ
12-11 (midnight Fri & Sat) (01384) 878481
Black Country Bradley's Finest Golden, Pig on the Wall, Fireside; guest beers H
This recently refurbished 19th-century pub is a few hundred yards from the Staffs & Worcester Canal. It brewed its own beers in the 19th century and still retains a strong community feel. It has a large L-shaped room with a log-burning fire at one end. The adjacent Tudor house is of particular architectural note as it has been faithfully restored and is an award winner. The 228 bus does not run on Sundays or evenings. P(228)

Kinver Constitutional Club

119 High Street, DY7 6HL
5 (12 Wed & Thu)-11; 12-midnight Fri; 11.30-midnight Sat; 12-10.30 Sun (01384) 872044
kinverconstitutionalclub.co.uk
Enville Ale; Hobsons Best Bitter, Town Crier; Olde Swan Bumble Hole Bitter; Wye Valley HPA; guest beers H
Built in 1902 on the site of an old pub, this converted hotel has three main areas and the bar dispenses up to 18 real ales. The club enjoys an enviable sporting reputation. Card-carrying CAMRA members are welcome but must be signed in; groups should book ahead. Buses to the village run from Stourbridge (except evenings or Sundays). A frequent local and regional CAMRA Club of the Year. P(228)

Knighton

Haberdasher's Arms

Knighton, ST20 0QH (between Adbaston and Knighton) SJ753275
12.30 (7 Wed & Thu)-midnight; 12.30-1am Fri & Sat
(01785) 280650 haberdashersarms.com
Banks's Mild; guest beers H

Traditional country pub, built about 1840, offering a warm and friendly welcome. It has four compact rooms, all served from a central bar. The extensive collection of oil lamps is not just for decoration; on monthly Lamp Nights the electric lights are switched off and the lamps are lit, creating a special relaxed atmosphere. The pub hosts a range of events in its large garden including the annual Potato Club Show and music festivals.
Q🐴❀⛺♣P🐾

Leek

Cock Inn

19 Derby Street, ST13 6HN (top of main street, near Market Square)
⏲ 10-11 (midnight Fri & Sat); 12-10.30 Sun
☎ (01538) 388013
Joule's Blonde, Pale Ale, Slumbering Monk; guest beers [H]
Traditional town-centre local owned by Joule's Brewery of Market Drayton, benefitting from a beautifully refurbished interior with ample seating including several intimate alcoves and a raised area reserved for diners. A smart beer garden to the rear is adorned with flowers; further seating opens out onto the main town-centre car park. At least three Joule's beers are served plus up to two guests, and a guest cider is always on offer. Food is served all day. There is entertainment on Saturday evenings. Q🐴❀◑◐P🚌📶

Roebuck [L]

18 Derby Street, ST13 5AB (on main shopping street)
⏲ 10-11 (midnight Fri & Sat); 12-11 Sun ☎ (01538) 385602
Everards Tiger; Titanic Steerage, Anchor Bitter, Iceberg, White Star, Captain Smith's Strong Ale; guest beers [H]
Half-timbered former 17th-century coaching inn, sympathetically refurbished by Titanic Brewery in 2011. A smart lounge, bar and two smaller snug areas are served from a central bar. Ten handpulls deliver six Titanic ales plus four changing guests. Two real ciders are always on offer as well as an adventurous range of foreign lagers from 10 taps protruding from a copper wall feature of the main bar. It has an attractive outdoor seating area, dogs are welcome, and a function room is available.
Q🐴❀◑◐🍎P🚌(16,18)🐾📶

Wilkes Head [L]

15 St Edward Street, ST13 5DS
⏲ 12 (3 Mon)-midnight; 12-11 Sun ☎ 07976 592787
Whim Arbor Light, Hartington Bitter, Hartington IPA, Flower Power; guest beers [H]
A regular entry in the Guide and one of the oldest hostelries in Leek; the site's documented origins date back to 1296. It is a true free house and the only outlet in town to offer ales from Whim Brewery of Derbyshire. Seven handpulls serve at least three Whim beers plus up to four guests. A range of real cider is always on sale. Live music, including folk nights, features regularly and summer events take place in the walled beer garden; the landlord is a professional musician.
Q❀♣🍎P🚌🐾

Lichfield

Bowling Green

Friary Road, WS13 6QJ
⏲ 11-midnight ☎ (01543) 257344
Marston's Pedigree; Sharp's Doom Bar; Timothy Taylor Landlord; guest beers [H]
Sprawling mock-Tudor pub sitting on a large roundabout 10 minutes' walk from the city centre. In typical Ember Inns style, the place is full of cosy dining spaces (food is served until 10pm), but it also has a plush area dedicated to drinkers. Quiz nights are held every Sunday and Wednesday. Discounts operate for CAMRA members, and on Monday evenings all cask ales are sold at a reduced price. At least three guest ales are usually available. Parking is Pay & Display.
🐴❀◑◐♿⇌(City)P🚌📶

Duke of Wellington [L]

Birmingham Road, WS14 9BJ
⏲ 4 (12 Sat)-11; 12-10.30 Sun ☎ (01543) 256584
Fuller's London Pride; Holden's Golden Glow; Marston's Pedigree; Wye Valley HPA; guest beer [H]
This former canalside pub, noted for good ale quality, is well worth the 15-minute trek from the city centre. The split-level, open-plan interior comprises three distinct drinking areas, one with a real fire. Live sport is shown on three separate screens. The pub is dog-friendly and during the summer months the large back garden is popular. A bar snack menu that includes locally-produced pork pies is on offer during all sessions.
❀♿♣P🚌(112)🐾📶

Duke of York

23-25 Greenhill, WS13 6DY
⏲ 12-11 (midnight Fri & Sat) ☎ (01543) 300386
Joule's Blonde, Pale Ale, Slumbering Monk; guest beer [H]
Tastefully restored Grade II listed pub with a split-level bar, separate lounge, and a multi-purpose room called the Courtyard. All three have real fires. Good-quality food is served lunchtimes 12-2.30pm Monday to Saturday, and pork pies are available during all sessions. A Joule's seasonal beer is served alongside the three regulars, and a dark ale often features as the guest. A comprehensive malt whisky and country wine selection can also be enjoyed. Dogs are welcome except in the lounge.
Q❀◑⇌(City)♣🍎P🚌🐾📶

George & Dragon

28 Beacon Street, WS13 7AJ
⏲ 11-midnight (1am Fri & Sat); 12-11.30 Sun
☎ (01543) 254854
Banks's Mild, Bitter; Brakspear Oxford Gold; Marston's Pedigree; Wychwood Hobgoblin; guest beers [H]
A friendly atmosphere greets all at this traditional local which is located a short distance from the historic Erasmus Darwin house. The interior comprises a public bar and cosy lounge where a small but tempting menu of bar snacks is served at all times. Outside is a large beer garden where a plaque marks the spot where an artillery battery was used to bombard the cathedral during the Civil War. Darts, dominoes and board games are available. ❀⛺♣P🚌🐾📶

Horse & Jockey [L]

8-10 Sandford Street, WS13 6QA
⏲ 12-11 (midnight Fri & Sat); 12-10.30 Sun
☎ (01543) 410033
Fuller's London Pride; Holden's Golden Glow; Marston's Pedigree; Timothy Taylor Landlord; Wye Valley HPA; guest beers [H]

This genuine free house is deservedly one of the most popular pubs on Lichfield's real ale circuit. Up to three guests, mainly from micros, complement the regular ales. There is a cosy snug and a separate games room at the back of the large open-plan bar. Home-cooked food is served Wednesday to Saturday lunchtimes and pork pies are always available. Dogs are welcome but note there is an over-21 entry policy for humans. Sport is shown on muted TV screens.
❀◐⇌(City)♣P🚌🐾📶

Marchington

Dog & Partridge

Church Lane, ST14 8LJ

12-3, 6-11.30; 12-11 Sun ☎ (01283) 830394

dogandpartridgemarchington.co.uk

Draught Bass; guest beers H

Formerly a restaurant, the premises were closed for some time and reopened as a pub in 2012. Landlord Paul restored a bar area for drinkers and now puts on his own beer festivals in the village hall. Beers are served by handpump without a sparkler – ask for a sparkler if you really want one. A loyalty card scheme is operated – buy eight pints and get one free. Q◐◑♿P🚌📶

Milwich

Green Man L

Sandon Lane, ST18 0EG (on B5027)

12-2 (not Mon-Wed), 5-11; 12-11 Fri & Sat; 12-10.30 Sun

☎ (01889) 505310 greenmanmilwich.com

Adnams Southwold Bitter; Draught Bass; Sharp's Doom Bar; guest beers H

An inn since 1775 and known as the Green Man since 1815, this free house offers guest beers from regional brewers. It is the licensee's 25th year at the pub and a record of previous landlords dating back to 1792 is displayed. A venue popular with walkers and cyclists, the bar has a real fire. Home-cooked food is served in the bar or in the separate small restaurant area (no food Mon-Wed). The cider is from Westons or Thatchers. Well-behaved dogs are welcome in bar. Q❀◐◑♿♣🍎P🐾📶

Newcastle-under-Lyme

Castle Mona

4 Victoria Street, ST5 1NT

4 (12 Sat)-midnight; 12-11.30 Sun ☎ 07895 555598

Castle Rock Harvest Pale; Sharp's Doom Bar; Skinner's Cornish Knocker; Wells Bombardier; guest beers H

Only five minutes' walk along the A34 from Newcastle town centre, this hostelry has a wooden-panelled lounge with a woodburner, and a traditional bar area where the regulars provide their own entertainment, with hours of chatter, banter and games of bar skittles and pool. Outside there is a lovely well-kept beer garden for the summer evenings. It is a real traditional English pub, which always offers a warm welcome and has a sense of community spirit. ❀♣🚌(101)

Freebird

96 Liverpool Road, ST5 2AX

5-11 (midnight Fri); 2-midnight Sat; 2-11 Sun ☎ 07714 782599

Beer range varies H

Named after the Lynyrd Skynyrd song, the Freebird is a real ale and music pub. The bar sports a friendly atmosphere, a pool table and plenty of lively conversation. A second room to the other side of the bar is used for live entertainment and other functions. Eight varying real ales are usually on tap, from breweries both near and far, with many unusual offerings to be discovered; a beer festival is held on the spring bank holiday. ♿♣🍎P🚌🐾

Lymestone Vaults L

Pepper Street, ST5 1PR

10-11 (midnight Fri & Sat); 11-10.30 Sun

☎ (01782) 615801

Lymestone Stone Cutter, Stone Faced, Foundation Stone, Ein Stein, Stone the Crows; guest beers H

This Staffordshire Environmental Quality Mark pub is a brewer-owned tap for the Lymestone Brewery in Stone. It offers eight real ales including two guests; additionally, seasonal beers are usually available. Two local lagers are also served on draught, and eight real ciders. The pub won the public-voted Staffordshire Tourism Pub of the Year Award in 2013, and is Taste of Staffordshire-registered for its quiet, bright, open bar and lounge with civilised leather sofas, newspapers and wooden benches. ◐♿♣🍎🚌🐾📶

Victoria

62 King Street, ST5 1HX

2-11 Mon & Wed; 2-midnight Tue & Thu; 12-midnight Fri & Sat; 12-11 Sun ☎ (01782) 631505

Draught Bass; Salopian Shropshire Gold; guest beers H

Reopened in 2012 following a five year period of closure, this pub has risen like a phoenix from the ashes. Hugely successful in its first year, it was awarded the local CAMRA branch Pub of the Year merit award due to the outstanding quality and selection of its beers and also its warm and friendly atmosphere. A traditional pub with Victorian-style decoration, it has an amazing wooden bar, a beautiful open fire and an outside drinking area. Q⚡♣🚌(34,34A)

Onecote

Jervis Arms

ST13 7RU (on B5053 N of A53 Leek-Ashbourne road)

12-3, 6-midnight; 12-midnight Sun ☎ (01538) 304206

Wadworth 6X; guest beers H

A genuine free house in the Peak District with a long-serving landlord. The ceiling is adorned with pumpclips from breweries far and wide, soon to be added to when the pub opens its own Nixon Grange brewery. The beer garden by the river can get busy on a hot summer's afternoon. Situated close to Alton Towers, it has a good-sized car park. A long-standing entry in the Guide, this rural gem is well worth a visit. Q❀◐◑♿⛺♣🍎P🐾📶

Oulton

Brushmakers Arms

8 Kibblestone Road, ST15 8UW (500yds W of A520, 1 mile NE of Stone)

12-midnight (1am Fri & Sat) ☎ (01785) 812062

Thwaites Original, Lancaster Bomber; guest beer H

Named after a local cottage industry, the Brush is a pub where time stands still. It has a traditional quarry-tiled floor to the bar and a small ornate lounge. Pictures and postcards adorn the walls, reflecting a bygone era. The small rear paved garden is a real suntrap and doubles as the

smoking area. With no games machines or jukebox, conversation rules in this excellent village local. Well-behaved dogs welcome.
Q🐴❀♿▲♣P🚌(250)🐾📶

Rawnsley

Rag
Ironstone Road, WS12 0QD
⌚ 11-11; 12-10.45 Sun ☎ (01543) 277491
🌐 theragatrawnsley.co.uk
Fuller's London Pride; Greene King IPA; guest beers Ⓗ
A free house set in three acres of grounds with an award-winning 100-seat restaurant and seven en-suite rooms. There is a bowling green at the rear of the building, along with six recently installed camping pods. Regular summer barbecues are held. An ideal base for visiting local attractions such as Lichfield Cathedral, Trentham Village and Monkey Forest, and Chasewater Light Railway.
❀🛏◐◑♿▲P🚌

Rugeley

Plaza 🄻
Horsefair, WS15 2EJ
⌚ 9am-11.30 (12.30am Fri & Sat) ☎ (01889) 586831
Greene King Abbot; Ruddles Best Bitter; guest beers Ⓗ
Previously a cinema dating from the 1930s, this spacious Wetherspoon pub retains much of the cinematic atmosphere and Art Deco flourishes of the period. The light and airy interior allows for three widely separated levels, and the outside drinking areas are multi-level too, with a balcony, terrace and lawned beer garden. Around five guest ales are offered, with micros such as Salopian or Slater's proving popular. The small car park is Pay & Display. Q🐴❀◐◑♿⇌(Town)●P🚌📶

Salt

Holly Bush Inn
ST18 0BX (turn W off A518 opp Weston Hall) SJ959277
⌚ 12-11 (10.30 Sun) ☎ (01889) 508234
🌐 hollybushinn.co.uk
Adnams Southwold Bitter; Marston's Pedigree; guest beers Ⓗ
The pub claims to have origins as far back as 1190 and is reputed to be the second oldest inn to be granted a licence. The original part of the building retains a thatched roof. Extensions and alterations over the centuries have created three distinct areas: a bar area, dining room and snug. Many awards have been won for the superb-quality meals. Guest beers come from the SIBA range.
Q🐴❀◐◑P🚌📶

Seighford

Hollybush Inn
Main Road, ST18 9PQ
⌚ 12-3, 5-11; 12-11.30 Fri-Sun ☎ (01785) 281644
🌐 hollybushseighford.co.uk
Everards Tiger; Titanic Steerage, Iceberg; guest beers Ⓗ
Formerly an inn and converted to an Indian restaurant in 2010, it was purchased by a village group in 2012 and restored to a drinking establishment. The premises are leased by the community pub company to Titanic Brewery, its first venue in a village. There are a number of spaces and rooms in the original half-timbered building, and large dining areas in the extensions. Note that not all 490 buses go to Seighford.
Q🐴❀◐◑♿P🚌(490)🐾

Stafford

Greyhound 🄻
12 County Road, ST16 2PU (off A34, opp jail)
⌚ 4-11.30 (midnight Fri); 12-midnight Sat; 12-11 Sun
☎ (01785) 222432 🌐 greyhoundfreehousestafford.co.uk
Wells Bombardier; guest beers Ⓗ
Less than a five-minute walk from the centre of Stafford, this two-room free house is well worth a visit. The pub dates from 1831 and a newspaper article from the day it opened can be seen above the bar. Today the pub offers a changing range of eight ales, often from breweries in Yorkshire. If you arrive during opening hours and the front door is locked walk around the back to Sash Street for entry. Q❀♿♣P🚌🐾

Olde Rose & Crown
10 Market Street, ST16 2JZ
⌚ 12-11 (midnight Fri & Sat); 12-10.30 Sun
☎ (01785) 251343
Joule's Blonde, Pale Ale, Slumbering Monk Ⓗ
Extensively refurbished at the end of 2011, this comfortable Joule's house is right in the heart of Stafford and is much larger than it looks from the outside. Three handpumps serve Joule's ales alongside a cider. Situated next to the Gatehouse Theatre, the pub is a favourite of theatregoers and is frequented by cast members enjoying an after-show pint. An acoustic night is held every Wednesday, and the fourth Tuesday of the month is storytelling night. ❀◐♿⇌●🚌🐾📶

Spittal Brook 🄻
106 Lichfield Road, ST17 4LP (1 mile SE of centre off A34 at Queensville Bridge)
⌚ 12-3, 5-11; 12-11 Fri; 9am-11 Sat & Sun
☎ (01785) 245268 🌐 thespittalbrook.com
Draught Bass; Sharp's Doom Bar; Wye Valley HPA; guest beers Ⓗ
A thriving and traditional two-roomed alehouse within walking distance of the town centre. Entertainment includes a folk night on Tuesday, a quiz on Wednesday and a cheese night on the last Sunday of the month (bring your own cheeses to share with others). The pub holds beer and cider festivals in July and October. A guest real cider is always on tap. Dogs can stay overnight with their owners. Breakfast is available 9am-noon Saturday and Sunday. Q🐴❀🛏◐◑♿▲♣●P🚌🐾📶

Sun 🄻
7 Lichfield Road, ST17 4JX
⌚ 11.30-11 (midnight Fri & Sat); 12-11 Sun
☎ (01785) 248361 🌐 thesunstafford.co.uk
Everards Tiger; Titanic Steerage, Anchor Bitter, Iceberg, White Star, Captain Smith's; guest beers Ⓗ
One of Titanic Brewery's fleet, it has been plain sailing for this popular pub following an extensive refurbishment in 2010; it was voted local CAMRA branch Pub of the Year in 2012. Twelve handpumps offer a constant choice of beers from Titanic, a changing range of guest ales, and cider. Food is served throughout the day, using ingredients sourced as locally to the pub as possible. Keep an eye out for the original pub sign now hanging inside. Q🐴❀◐◑⇌♣●P🚌🐾📶

Swan Hotel

46 Greengate Street, ST16 2JA

10-11 (midnight Fri & Sat); 11-10.30 Sun

(01785) 258142 theswanstafford.co.uk

Marston's EPA, Pedigree; guest beers H

This 18th-century coaching inn has been a part of Stafford's history for over 300 years. It has a coffee shop and a long bar extending through two rooms which allows one to be set aside for functions. Monthly themed food events include a food and matched beer night. It offers a 10 per cent discount to CAMRA members and also runs a beer club – buy nine pints and get a free 10th pint of beer or real cider. P

Stoke-on-Trent: Burslem

Bull's Head

14 St John's Square, ST6 3AJ

3-11 (11.30 Wed & Thu); 12-midnight Fri & Sat; 12-11 Sun

(01782) 834153

Titanic Steerage, Anchor Bitter, Iceberg, White Star, Plum Porter; guest beers H

Titanic's brewery tap in the centre of Burslem, only 10 minutes' walk from Port Vale's ground and welcoming to all supporters, home and away. It is a two-roomed pub with an island bar, up to 10 real ales on tap and seven or more real ciders and perries, all straight from the cellar, alongside draught and bottled Belgian beers. Bar billiards, table skittles and an old jukebox operate in the public bar. CAMRA Regional Cider Pub of the Year 2012 and Bronze award winner 2013.

Duke William

2 St Johns Square, ST6 3AJ

11.30-11 (midnight Fri & Sat); 12-10.30 Sun

(01782) 814809 dukewilliamburslem.com

Joule's Slumbering Monk; Morland Original Bitter; Oakham Citra; Springhead Roaring Meg; guest beers H

An imposing pub that has undergone a sympathetic restoration, with most of the original features intact, including the horseshoe-shaped bar and its heated foot rail, bell push-buttons in the lounge, serving hatch and leaded windows. Eight handpumps serve up to four house beers, three guest ales and a real cider. There is also a smoking area to the rear and a restaurant upstairs with an English menu and its own bar. A beer festival is held each year. (98)

Post Office Vaults

3 Market Place, ST6 3AA

11-11 (1am Fri & Sat); 12-10.30 Sun (01782) 811027

Greene King Abbot; Oakham Bishops Farewell; Wye Valley Dorothy Goodbody's Wholesome Stout; guest beers H

A small one-roomed pub in the centre of Burslem, popular with the local football club and community. The handpumps dispense three house beers and two guest ales from a variety of microbreweries. Real cider is also served. Sport and live music feature on the array of TV screens, and there is a heated and lit smoking area to the rear with its own TV. Post Office memorabilia adorn the walls, including a factory clocking-in machine.

Stoke-on-Trent: Etruria

Holy Inadequate

67 Etruria Old Road, ST1 5PE

4-11; 12-midnight Fri-Sun 07771 358238

Joule's Pale Ale; guest beers H

Current local CAMRA branch and Staffordshire Pub of the Year, the Holy continues on its journey of excellence. The pub's continuing support of quality ales and microbrewers is enhanced by the growing range of British and world bottled beers it now stocks. Six beers and four ciders are on the bar, with beer festivals held every bank holiday, when up to 26 ales are served from the stillage room. A friendly welcome is extended to all. Locally sourced bar snacks are available. Q (34,34A)

Stoke-on-Trent: Hanley

Coachmakers Arms ★

65 Lichfield Street, ST1 3EA (off A5008 Potteries Way ring road)

4 (12 Thu-Sat)-midnight; 12-11 Sun (01782) 860438

Draught Bass; guest beers H

The Coach, as it is affectionately known by locals, is a regular and well-deserved entry in this Guide. A Victorian multi-roomed pub serviced by a central bar with corridor hatch, this gem has been under threat of demolition for several years. It is rightly recognised by CAMRA as having a nationally important historic pub interior. The absence of TV or loud music gives this unique place a traditional drinking ambience that is fast disappearing elsewhere. Up to four guest beers including a mild or stout are served. Q P

Victoria Lounge Bar

5 Adventure Place, ST1 3AF

11-11 (01782) 273530 thereardon.com

Draught Bass; Timothy Taylor Landlord; guest beers H

The Victoria Lounge Bar, known locally as Reardons (it is connected to the Reardon snooker club) is a well-deserved new entry in this Guide, situated behind Hanley's bus station. A smart, modern and comfortable interior is deceptively spacious and can get busy at lunchtimes – a home-cooked carvery is served every day. Six handpulls dispense the regular beers, plus four changing guests from local and national brewers. A self-contained function room is available for hire. P

Stoke-on-Trent: Hartshill

Greyhound

67 George Street, ST5 1JT

12-11.30 (midnight Wed & Thu; 12.30am Fri & Sat)

(01782) 635814

Everards Tiger; Titanic Steerage, Iceberg, White Star, Plum Porter; guest beers H

Just 10 minutes' walk from Newcastle town centre, on the Newcastle/Stoke-on-Trent border area known locally as Top of Castle, the pub has handpulls dispensing at least four of the Titanic fleet, Everards Tiger and a range of guest ales from breweries across the country. Two pumps offer cider and perry, and bottled Belgian beers are also available. The Sunday quiz is always a winner. Irish folk music nights are staged. Q

Stoke-on-Trent: Longton

Congress Inn

14 Sutherland Road, ST3 1HJ (opp police station)
12-midnight ☎ (01782) 763667 thecongressinn.co.uk
Wadworth Henry's IPA, 6X; guest beers H
Spacious two-roomed pub likened to Dr Who's Tardis – with so much going on, it must be bigger on the inside. Drawing a loyal clientèle from a wide area, the pub has won many awards including CAMRA Potteries and Staffordshire Pub of the Year. Up to nine beers are on handpump plus four ciders, and a large selection of bottled Belgian beers is stocked. A beer festival is held every May, with 30 ales plus ciders on gravity. Traditional pub games include table skittles.

Stoke-on-Trent: Stoke

Glebe

35 Glebe Street, ST4 1HG
12-11 (11.30 Fri & Sat); 12-10.30 Sun ☎ (01782) 860670
Joule's Blonde, Slumbering Monk; guest beer H
A short walk from the rail station, this superb Joule's Brewery establishment has justifiably become one the must-visit pubs in the city – its impressive features, including the beautifully restored stained glass windows, plus candlelit tables, all add to the welcoming atmosphere. The two mainstay Joule's beers are supplemented by one handpulled cider. Home-made meals served lunchtimes and early evenings are of a high standard, with Staffordshire cheese platters and pork pies also on offer.

Wheatsheaf

84-92 Church Street, ST4 1BU
8-midnight (1am Fri & Sat) ☎ (01782) 747462
Greene King Abbot; Ruddles Best Bitter; guest beers H
Town-centre Wetherspoon pub, a regular Guide entry, and regarded as one of the best in the local chain. It is popular with its many regulars and visitors alike, proud of its strong community links, and often customer-led in its choice of beers. Apart from the usual house beers, five rotating guest ales are to be found on the bar, with Lymestone always a favourite. Food is now served from 8am to 11pm. Q

White Star

63 Kingsway, ST4 1JB (off Church St, close to King's Hall)
11-midnight; 12-11 Sun ☎ (01782) 848732
Everards Tiger; Titanic Steerage, Iceberg, White Star, Plum Porter, Captain Smith's; guest beers H
Situated conveniently in the town centre, this multi award-winning Titanic Brewery pub is a popular and busy establishment. A spacious and well-furnished split-level interior is enhanced with a bar that, apart from serving five of Titanic's excellent range of local beers, also stocks Everards Tiger, plus four rotating guest ales. An extensive menu of quality home-cooked food is served from opening till 9pm. A function room is available.
Q

Stone

Langtrys

1-3 Oulton Road, ST15 8EB
12-midnight ☎ (01785) 286609
Castle Rock Harvest Pale; Flowers Original; Purity Pure Ubu; Sharp's Doom Bar; guest beer H
A friendly corner local comprising a comfy bar with a coal fire and a double-room lounge area with wood and stained glass panelling. The landlady and staff are committed to real ale – the range and quality make this pub well worth the short walk out of Stone town centre. Langtrys hosts darts and cribbage teams and is committed to totally-locally dealings for its food. Good B&B accommodation is offered. Children are welcome during food-service hours. P (250)

Royal Exchange

Radford Street, ST15 8DA (on corner of Northesk St and Radford St)
12-11.30 (midnight Fri & Sat) ☎ (01785) 812685
Everards Tiger; Titanic Steerage, Iceberg, White Star, Captain Smith's; guest beers H
Although one room, there are four distinct drinking areas in this friendly pub, with real fires at either end. Three guest ales, mainly from micros, are always served, along with a real cider. There are no TVs or piped music, just good craic. Acoustic music nights feature, and many clubs, including backgammon, knitting, French, reading and Stone Jazz Club, meet here. The ingredients in the expanding food range are totally local. Well-behaved dogs are welcome, as are children until 9pm. Q

Swan Inn

18 Stafford Street, ST15 8QW (on A520 near Trent & Mersey Canal)
12-1am (11 Mon; midnight Tue & Wed); 12-11 Sun
☎ (01785) 815570 swaninnstone.co.uk
Beer range varies H
A thriving free house in a carefully renovated Grade II-listed building, with nine handpulls featuring Coach House Old Priory Ale and eight others – the beer range can change daily. You can even put in a request for your favourite beer to be put on. Four real ciders and bottled varieties are always available. An annual beer festival is held each July, with up to 80 beers on tap. Live music features twice a week. Strictly over-18s only.

Summerhill

Boat

Walsall Road, WS14 0BU
12-3, 6-11; 12-11 Sun ☎ (01543) 361692
oddfellowsintheboat.com
Beer range varies H
This is a free house for real ale and a haven for lovers of gourmet food. Relax in the reception area and peruse the extensive chalkboard menu while watching the cooking. There is no processed or pre-cooked food and all ingredients are delivered daily. A Cottage beer is generally featured, plus two changing ales which are usually interesting and frequently local. There is a large enclosed garden area next to the car park. Q P

Tamworth

Market Vaults

7 Market Street, B79 7LU
12 (1 Mon)-11.30; 12-12.30am Fri & Sat ☎ (01827) 66552
marketvaults-tamworth.co.uk
Joule's Pale Ale, Slumbering Monk; guest beers H
Featuring in several episodes of TV's Most Haunted, this traditional two-roomed town-centre hostelry

dates back to the 14th century. Near the Norman castle and town hall, this vibrant pub offers up to three guest ales plus a Joule's seasonal beer. Light snacks are available, with traditional lunches served on Sunday afternoons. The heated, covered beer garden becomes a suntrap in summer, while wood-burning stoves create a cosy atmosphere in winter.

Sir Robert Peel

13-15 Lower Gungate, B79 7BA
2-11 (midnight Fri); 12-midnight Sat; 12-11 Sun
(01827) 300910
Beer range varies H/G
This long-standing Guide entry is a popular free house in the centre of town. It serves up to seven ales, including two straight from the cask. The house beer, Apeeling, is provided by Church End Brewery. Oakham ales, including one-off specials, feature regularly. Bustling at the weekend in contrast to the relaxed midweek atmosphere, this pub is well known for its excellent ale quality and condition. Two real ciders are also available.

Trysull

Bell Inn

Bell Road, WV5 7JB SO852940
11.30-3, 5-11 (midnight Fri); 11.30-midnight Sat; 12-11 Sun (01902) 892871
Bathams Best Bitter; Holden's Black Country Mild, Black Country Bitter, Golden Glow; guest beers H
A fine 18th-century building next to the village church, comprising a small but cosy bar, pleasant lounge and a large restaurant/dining room (lunchtime and Early Bird deals are popular). As well as the Holden's range, Bathams Best Bitter is a regular, together with a varying guest, often from a microbrewery. A patio area is to the front of the building. The pub is popular with walkers – the Staffordshire & Worcestershire Canal is a 15-minute walk away. QP

Tutbury

Leopard Inn

Monk Street, DE13 9NA (near centre of village, on jct with Castle St)
12-10 (1am Fri & Sat); 12-11 Sun 07854 080852
Marston's Pedigree; guest beers H
End-of-terrace, friendly, community-focused pub, formerly four cottages, dating back to the late 1800s. The long single room is raised at one end and has a pool table at the other; it features photos of old Tutbury. Regular live music, karaoke and quiz nights are hosted. There is decking at the rear for warmer weather and a few benches are placed outside at the front in summer. The pub has no car park, but the main Tutbury public car park is just across the road.

Weston

Woolpack Inn

The Green, ST18 0JH (off A518)
11-11 (midnight Fri & Sat); 11.30-11 Sun
(01889) 270238 woolpackpubweston.co.uk
Banks's Bitter; Marston's Pedigree; Ringwood Old Thumper; guest beers H
Known locally as the Inn on the Green, this welcoming village pub has an extensive dining area and a space for dominoes and darts. Over the years the low-ceilinged interior has been thoughtfully extended while retaining the original bar area – four bays inside reflect the pub's origins as a row of cottages and blacksmith's shop. The property is recorded as being owned by the Bagot family in the 1730s. Guest beers are from the Marston's family. QP(X1)

Whiston

Swan Inn

ST19 5QH (in Penkridge turn W off A449 at roundabout near Texaco garage onto Bungham Lane, cross Cuttlestone Bridge and follow signs to Whiston) SJ895144
12-3 (not Mon), 5-11; 12-11 Sat; 12-10.30 Sun
(01785) 716200 swanwhiston.co.uk
Holden's Black Country Mild, Black Country Bitter; guest beers H
Although remotely situated, this pub continues to thrive thanks to its high-quality, well-kept ales and superb food. Built in 1593, burnt down and rebuilt in 1711, the oldest part today is the small bar housing an inglenook fireplace. The lounge features an intriguing central double-sided log fire. Six acres of grounds include a children's obstacle course, aviary and rabbits. A discount on ales is offered to CAMRA members.
QP(88,88A)

Wombourne

New Inn

1 Station Road, WV5 9EY (jct of Station Rd and Ounsdale Rd)
12-11 (11.30 Thu; midnight Fri & Sat) (01902) 892037
newinnpubwolverhampton.co.uk
Banks's Mild, Bitter H/P**, Sunbeam; Jennings Cocker Hoop; guest beer** H
Comfortable open-plan pub with a strong emphasis on good-quality food sold at reasonable prices. The lounge is mainly used for dining while drinkers use the bar area, but both areas are served from the central horseshoe-shaped bar. The landlord is a real ale enthusiast who sells guest beers from the Marston's stable. A spacious garden is at the rear and a patio, especially busy in summer, at the front. There is a large TV in the bar for occasional sport. A CAMRA discount is offered from 6pm on Mondays. QP(255,256)

Woodseaves

Cock Inn

Newport Road, ST20 0NP (just N of jct of A519 and B5405)
4 (12 Fri-Sun)-11 (01785) 284343
Banks's Mild, Bitter; Holden's Golden Glow; Marston's Pedigree; guest beer H
After a few uncertain years the Cock reopened in 2012 as a free house. It has one large, comfortable room with two open fires. The pub has darts and dominoes teams, no TV or gaming machines, and is dog-friendly. As well as a good selection of ales, a wide range of malt whiskies is stocked – 52 at the last count. There are plans to build a restaurant on the back of the building. The Shropshire Union Canal is within half a mile.
P(432)

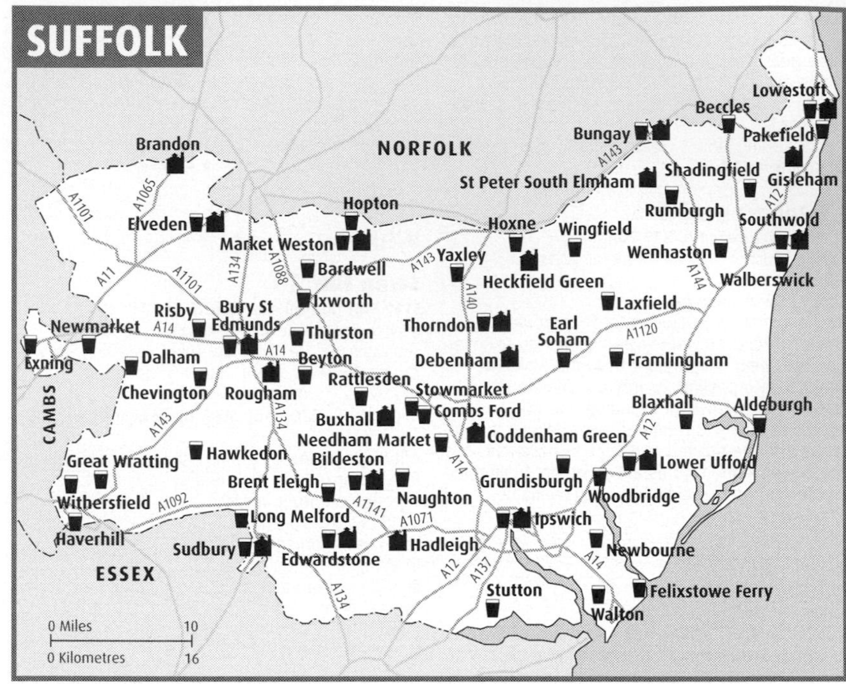

Aldeburgh

White Hart

222 High Street, IP15 5AJ

11.30-11; 12-10.30 Sun (01728) 453205

Adnams Southwold Bitter, Ghost Ship, Broadside; guest beers

Lively and friendly establishment close to the town's renowned fish and chip shop. The single-room bar was formerly a public reading room. Drinkers can buy fish and chips from next door and eat them in the garden in fine weather. Occasional live music is hosted. There is new covered seating outside, with pizzas cooked in the wood-fired oven available from Easter until mid-September. Families are welcome in the garden in summer.

Bardwell

Dun Cow

Up Street, IP31 1AA (1 mile off A143 at Stanton)

11.30-2.30, 5-midnight; 12-1am Sat; 12-10.30 Sun (01359) 250806

Greene King IPA; guest beers

A traditional pub in a pleasant village set in the Suffolk countryside. The pub has two bars and offers speciality food nights. Party bookings are taken and coaches are welcome if booked in advance. Outside is a covered smoking area and a large family area in the garden. The restored village windmill makes for attractive photos and has occasional open days. Q P

Beccles

Caxton Club

Gaol Lane, NR34 9SJ

12-1.30 (not Tue), 7-11; 12-2, 6.30-11 Fri; 12-11 Sat; 12-10.30 Sun (01502) 712829

Theakston Black Bull Bitter; guest beers

Spacious club conveniently situated a short walk from bus and train stations and the town centre. All members and guests are warmly welcomed (there is a small charge for CAMRA members to sign in). Four beers are available, some locally sourced, plus Westons ciders. To one side of the main bar is a lounge with a TV screen and dartboard and a separate snooker room. There is also a large function room with its own bar. CAMRA Regional Club of the Year 2013. P

Beyton

Bear

Tostock Road, IP30 9AG

12-2, 5-11; 12-4, 7-10.30 Sun (01359) 270249

thebearinnbeyton.co.uk

Adnams Broadside; Woodforde's Wherry; guest beer

Rebuilt in 1900 after the original thatched premises perished by fire during a July thunderstorm – a full account of this traumatic event can be found in the bar. The pub has been run by the same family since 1922. It has a traditional interior with a public bar with an open fire, and a separate bar with a restaurant serving excellent food (Fri-Sun lunchtimes, Thu-Sat eves). A separate function room is available. Children are welcome in the beer garden. Q P (384)

Bildeston

King's Head

132 High Street, IP7 7ED

closed Mon & Tue; 6 (4 Sat)-midnight; 12-10.30 Sun (01449) 741434 bildestonkingshead.co.uk

King's Head Bildeston Best; guest beers

Home of the King's Head Brewery since 1996, the building's large carved timbers indicate its history as part of a larger complex dating from around 1530. Now a single bar with a large inglenook fireplace, a friendly ale house atmosphere has evolved, with food available at the weekends only. There is a fully enclosed rear garden with a covered patio area, lawns and play equipment for children. The late May bank holiday beer festival is well established and popular.

Blaxhall

Ship

School Road, IP12 2DY

12-3, 6-11.30; 12-midnight Fri & Sat; 12-10.30 Sun

(01728) 688316 blaxhallshipinn.co.uk

Adnams Southwold Bitter; Woodforde's Wherry; guest beers

A cosy two-roomed 16th-century pub on the edge of Suffolk Sandlings, with a reputation for traditional singing in the bar. The menu now offers a wide choice of home-made dishes and daily specials using locally-sourced ingredients, with various German options (book for breakfast from 10.30am during the summer months). Live music is hosted at least once a week including regular folk sessions, often on bank holiday weekends. Letting chalets are available beside the pub and camping at the nearby village hall is by arrangement. P

Brent Eleigh

Cock ★

Lavenham Road, CO10 9PB

12-4, 6-11; 12-11 Fri & Sat; 12-10.30 Sun

(01787) 247371

Adnams Southwold Bitter; Greene King Abbot; guest beer

Unspoilt gem identified by CAMRA as having a nationally important historic pub interior. In winter both bars are snug and warm; in summer with the doors open the bar is at one with its surroundings. Hungry walkers and cyclists exploring the area will be pleased to know that landlady Deborah is a great cook and that food is available at all times. Separate B&B accommodation is available to the rear of the pub. The real cider is usually Castling's Heath Cottage. Q P (111)

Bungay

Green Dragon

29 Broad Street, NR35 1EE

11 (12 Sat)-midnight; 12-5 Sun (01986) 892681

Green Dragon Chaucer Ale, Gold, Bridge Street Bitter; guest beer

Bungay's only brewpub, located on the northern edge of town; the Green Dragon ales are brewed in outbuildings adjacent to the car park to the rear of the building. The pub is popular and a regular entry in the Guide. It has a public bar and a separate spacious lounge with a side room that welcomes families. Outside, the small garden is surrounded by a hop hedge. During the summer opening hours can be flexible. P (580,588)

Bury St Edmunds

Beerhouse

1 Tayfen Road, IP32 6BH

5 (12 Sat)-11; 12-10 Sun (01284) 766415

burybeerhouse.co.uk

Brewshed Pale Ale, Best Bitter, American Blonde; guest beers

Unusual semi-circular brick-built pub, formerly called the Ipswich Arms, close to the railway station. The building was refurbished in 2010 prior to reopening in 2011 as a traditional ale-focused pub. The single bar has eight handpumps providing an ever-changing selection of real ales from local and national brewers and four ciders. Tasty bar snacks are available. An outside yard has extensive seating alongside the Brewshed building. P

Dove

68 Hospital Road, IP33 3JU

5-11; 12-3, 6-11 Sat; 12-3, 6-10.30 Sun (01284) 702787

thedovepub.co.uk

Woodforde's Wherry; guest beers

East Anglian CAMRA Regional Pub of the Year in 2013, in a back street just five minutes from the town centre. This community pub has six handpumps and a good selection of real ciders, and staff are knowledgeable about the changing range of ales. The venue is traditionally basic, with no lager, TVs or gaming machines, with a main bar of scrubbed floorboards and a parlour – how pubs used to be. Q P

Oakes Barn

St Andrews Street South, IP33 3PH

11-11 (4 Sun) (01284) 761592 oakesbarn.co.uk

Adnams Southwold Bitter; Crouch Vale Brewers Gold; Woodforde's Wherry; guest beers

This real ale pub, which opened in 2013, is a new-build but it has retained some period features and historic links to the medieval town. A traditionally run one-bar establishment, it serves up to six beers by handpump plus three cask ciders. Light snacks and soups are available. There is a covered smoking area outside, and a beer garden is planned. Children are welcome daytime and early evening. A meeting room is available free of charge to local community groups and can be hired for private functions.

INDEPENDENT BREWERIES

Adnams Southwold
Bartrams Rougham
Brandon Brandon
Brewshed Bury St Edmunds
Briarbank Ipswich (NEW)
Calvors Coddenham Green
Cliff Quay Debenham
Cox & Holbrook Buxhall
Dove Street Ipswich
Earl Soham Debenham
Elveden Elveden
Green Dragon Bungay
Green Jack Lowestoft
Greene King Bury St Edmunds
Hektor's Southwold
Hellhound Hadleigh
Hoxne Heckfield Green (NEW)
Kings Head Bildeston
Mauldons Sudbury
Mill Green Edwardstone
Old Cannon Bury St Edmunds
Old Chimneys Market Weston
Shortts Farm Thorndon
St Peter's St Peter South Elmham
Trinity Gisleham
Uffa Lower Ufford

Rose & Crown

48 Whiting Street, IP33 1NP

11.30-11.30; 11.30-3, 7-11.30 Sat; 12-2.30, 8-11.30 Sun
(01284) 755934

Greene King XX Mild, IPA, Abbot; guest beers H

In sight of Greene King's Westgate Brewery, this is a traditional pub with two bars and a separate off-sales hatch. The present tenants have run this house for over 25 years, succeeding the landlady's father. Good-value wholesome food is served at lunchtimes (no food Sun). Children are not allowed in the bars but are welcome in the garden. The pub is a listed building located within the conservation area of Bury St Edmunds, and has a regionally important historic interior. Q

Chevington

Greyhound

2 Chedburgh Road, IP29 5QS

12-2.30, 7 (6 Fri & Sat)-11; 12-2.30, 7-10.30 Sun
(01284) 850765 chevingtongreyhound.co.uk

Adnams Southwold Bitter H**; guest beers** H/G

Run by the same family for over 25 years, this village pub has a nice sideline in authentic Indian cuisine, to eat in or take away, available alongside an extensive menu of traditional English food. Beers from the Mersea Island Brewery are often to be found, thanks to an Essex connection. The bar has an open fireplace, and there is a pool table in the adjacent lounge. The large garden is welcoming to children. Q P

Combs Ford

Magpie

Combs Road, IP14 2AP

closed Tue; 12-11 (midnight Fri & Sat); 12-10.30 Sun
(01449) 612727

Adnams Southwold Bitter; Greene King IPA; Sharp's Doom Bar; guest beers H

Large two-bar free house serving at least six real ales including changing guests. The previously run-down pub has now been fully refurbished by new owners and offers friendly service and a good food menu including a traditional roast carvery every Sunday. Live entertainment features regularly, ranging from jazz, soul, Motown, reggae and rock to karaoke on Thursdays, and occasional Sunday afternoon jazz. P

Dalham

Affleck Arms

1 Brookside, CB8 8TG

closed Mon & Tue; 5 (12 Sat & Sun)-11 (01638) 500306

Beer range varies H

Situated in the most thatched village in Britain, this beautiful 16th-century river-fronted free house, with a thatched roof, original wood beams and a roaring fire, is a real gem. Family run, it is a proper traditional community inn with a welcoming atmosphere and quality local ales. A large car park is at the rear. Q P (225,312)

Earl Soham

Victoria

The Street, IP13 7RL

11.30-3, 5.30-11 (11.30 Fri & Sat); 12-10.30 Sun
(01728) 685758

Earl Soham Sir Roger's Porter, Brandeston Gold; guest beer H

Popular, traditional Victorian pub with two small bars and an open fire in winter months, which has changed little over the years —it still has an outside toilet. An ever-changing food menu with daily specials is offered lunchtimes and evenings, all home cooked. The pub gets busy at weekends, especially on sunny days when even a seat in the garden can be hard to find. Dogs and children are welcome. The Earl Soham Brewery was originally located behind the pub. Q P

Edwardstone

White Horse Inn

Mill Green, CO10 5PX

12-3, 5-11; 12-midnight Fri & Sat; 12-11 Sun
(01787) 211211 edwardstonewhitehorse.co.uk

Mill Green Mawkin Mild, White Horse Bitter, Green Goose; guest beers H

Well off the beaten track in rural countryside, this is a traditional Suffolk free house with its own Mill Green microbrewery. Six or seven beers are usually available plus three or four ciders including Castling's Heath Organic. Two small holiday cottages and a campsite are within the grounds. The pub and brewery are eco-friendly, using solar and wind power, their own borehole for water, and burning local coppice wood for heating. Home-prepared food uses mainly locally-sourced and home-grown ingredients.
Q P

Elveden

Elveden Inn

Brandon Road, IP24 3TP (50yds from A11)

7.30am-midnight (11 Sun) (01842) 890376
elvedeninn.com

Adnams Southwold Bitter; guest beers H

Located on the historic country estate of the Earl of Iveagh (a direct descendant of the Guinness family), this traditional country inn is truly the home of Guinness in England. It offers a varying range of fine local ales including its own seasonal pump and bottle ales. The traditional food menu features home-grown produce, served all day every day. Family- and pet-friendly, the extensive garden is popular in warmer weather. AA England Pub of the Year 2013-14, accommodation is five-star. Q P

Exning

White Horse

23 Church Street, CB8 7EH

12-midnight (01638) 577323

Beer range varies H

Mentioned in the Domesday Book, this fine free house has been run by the same family since 1923. With a public bar, cosy lounge and separate restaurant, the pub has comfortable authenticity. An excellent menu of home-cooked food includes seafood, steaks and classic British dishes (booking advisable). Happy hour is 5.30-6.30pm, extended to 7pm on Friday. A private room can be hired.
Q P (10,10a)

Felixstowe Ferry

Ferry Boat Inn

Ferry Road, IP11 9RZ

11-3, 5.30-11; 11-11 Sat; 12-10 Sun (01394) 284203

ferryboatinn.org.uk

Adnams Southwold Bitter; Woodforde's Wherry; guest beer H

Popular coastal pub set in a small hamlet one mile north of the main town. The split-level bar has old stone-flagged flooring and traditional seating around a large fireplace with a woodburner. Food is mostly locally sourced and freshly prepared on the premises, including fish from nearby fishermen's huts. Daily specials, gluten-free dishes and vegetarian options are available lunchtimes and evenings. A room to the rear can cater for private functions, while the large garden to the front is busy in summer months.

Framlingham

Station Hotel

Station Road, IP13 9EE

12-3, 5-11; 10-3, 7-10.30 Sun (01728) 723455

thestationhotel.net

Earl Soham Gannet Mild, Victoria Bitter, Brandeston Gold; guest beer H

Cosy three-bar pub set in a former station buffet (the branch line closed in 1963). It enjoys a good reputation for food, made with locally-sourced ingredients and prepared on the premises. An ever-changing menu is displayed on chalkboards. On Sundays, brunch and beers are available from 10am. Beers and a guest cider are dispensed from a set of Edwardian German silver handpumps. A beer festival is held over the third weekend in July. The garden bar has a wood-fired pizza oven. Child and dog friendly. Q

Great Wratting

Red Lion

School Road, CB9 7HA

11-2.30, 5-11; 11-1.30am Sat; 12-3, 7-10 Sun (01440) 783237

Adnams Southwold Bitter, Broadside; guest beer H

A whale's jawbones frame the doorway to this village local dating from the 17th or 18th century, making an unusual and amusing entrance. An Adnams' tied house, it offers quality beer, good food and conversation as its mainstay. Locals love this pub and are passionate supporters of the activities overseen by an enthusiastic landlord of long experience. Quiz nights and a darts league thrive here. Q

Grundisburgh

Dog

The Green, IP13 6TA

closed Mon; 12-3, 5.30-11; 12-11 Fri-Sun (01473) 735267 grundisburghdog.co.uk

Adnams Southwold Bitter; Earl Soham Victoria Bitter; Woodforde's Wherry; guest beer H

Traditional two-room pub serving good beer and great food. The public bar has a fine beamed ceiling, flagstone flooring and comfortable seating, and offers a selection of pub games including darts and dominoes. The lounge bar is set for dining, with a varied menu of home-cooked meals and snacks made with locally-sourced ingredients, including gluten-free options. Monthly themed food evenings are a highlight. Outside, there are seating areas to the front and rear and a children's play area. (171)

Haverhill

Royal Exchange

69 High Street, CB9 8AH

11-11; 12-10.30 Sun (01440) 702155

Greene King IPA, Abbot; Morland Original Bitter, Old Speckled Hen; guest beer H

Town-centre local in a classic street-corner location. This Greene King-managed house has had the full refurbishment treatment with scrubbed floors and old-style furnishings. It can be boisterous when sports fans are watching on five TVs including 3D — free goggles supplied. A swift turnover on beer ensures the quality is always good.

Hawkedon

Queen's Head

Rede Road, IP29 4NN

5 (12 Sat)-11; 12-10.30 Sun (01284) 789218

Adnams Southwold Bitter; Woodforde's Wherry; guest beers H

Fifteenth-century free house off the beaten track with an unspoilt interior including a huge fireplace with a stove in the bar. Real cider, perry and Belgian beers are on tap alongside the ale. Locally sourced home-cooked food of high quality is available Friday-Sunday. The pub holds a beer festival in July and is a meeting place for classic car clubs. A butcher's shop on the premises is another string to its bow. A rural gem and local CAMRA Pub of the Year in 2014. Q

Hopton

Vine

High Street, IP22 2QX

3 (12 Fri-Sun)-11 (01953) 681908

Greene King IPA; Woodforde's Wherry; guest beers H

Located on the main road near the church, this village local has been revitalised by an enthusiastic landlord since it was taken over in 2013. Five ales including a selection of local and regional guests are currently offered at reasonable prices, with plans for more. The pub has a pool table in one of its three areas. Outside is a play area for children. A welcoming inn with friendly staff, popular with locals and visitors. (100)

Hoxne

Swan

Low Street, IP21 5AS

12-3, 6-11; 11-3, 5-11 Fri; 11-3, 6-11 Sat; 12-11 Sun (01379) 668275

Adnams Southwold Bitter; Woodforde's Wherry; guest beer G

Good food made with fresh, seasonal, locally-sourced ingredients is served alongside a selection of fine real ales. The timber-framed Grade II country pub was built in 1480 by the Bishop of Norwich and is full of history. It has three main rooms including a front bar with a large fireplace and high-beamed ceiling. The spacious garden backs onto the river and is close to where King Edmund, last Saxon king of East Anglia, was killed by the invading Danes.

Ipswich

Brewery Tap

Cliff Quay, IP3 0AT
11-3, 6-11; 11-11 Sat; 11-10.30 Sun ☎ (01473) 225501
thebrewerytap.org
Cliff Quay Classic Bitter, Tolly Roger; Earl Soham Victoria Bitter; guest beers H
Old brewer's house located close to the former historic Tolly brewery with a large central bar area and various drinking and dining spaces. Alongside mainly locally brewed beers is an extensive food menu with home-produced fare. Themed food nights, home-made pickled eggs and bar snacks are offered. There are fine views of the River Orwell through a bay window in the bar, despite new sea defences being recently added. Live music is a regular feature. Three private function rooms are available and a secluded garden.

Briarbank Tap

70 Fore Street, IP4 1LB
12-11 ☎ (01473) 284000
Briarbank Dark Knight, Cardinale Wolsey, Perpendicular, Old Spiteful; guest beer H
This smart, modern, first-floor drinking bar opened in 2013 above the new Briarbank Brewery. The building was derelict for many years but was originally used as a bank. Many beers from the brewery are also available as craft keg. The bar operates a card membership scheme but offers free entry to visiting CAMRA members and drinkers carrying a copy of this Guide – buzz at the door for attention. P

Cricketers

51 Crown Street, IP1 3JA
8am-midnight (12.30am Fri & Sat) ☎ (01473) 225910
Greene King IPA, Abbot; guest beers H
Situated opposite the Tower Ramparts bus station, this large 1930s town-centre pub was once one of the Tolly Follies. Now run by Wetherspoon, it has various seating areas set around a central bar and kitchen. Popular at most times of day, it offers a choice of 12 ever-changing beers on handpump. Regular beer festivals add to the range. The patio area to the side includes a heated smoking area. Q P

Dove Street Inn

76 St Helen's Street, IP4 2LA
12-midnight (10.30 Sun) ☎ (01473) 211270
dovestreetinn.co.uk
Adnams Broadside; Crouch Vale Brewers Gold; Fuller's London Pride H**; guest beers** H/G
Popular multi-roomed pub serving a large selection of real ales including milds, plus ciders and continental beers. Some ales are from the adjacent brewery, located behind the brew shop. Home-cooked food and bar snacks are served at all times. Well-behaved dogs and children are welcome during the day. The green room, a large covered and heated seating area outside, is available for events and private hire. Three beer festivals are held annually. Letting rooms are available above the brewery. Last admission is 10.45pm.

Fat Cat

288 Spring Road, IP4 5NL
12-11 (midnight Fri & Sat) ☎ (01473) 726524
fatcatipswich.co.uk
Adnams Southwold Bitter H**; Crouch Vale Brewers Gold; Fuller's London Pride; Woodforde's Wherry; guest beers** G
Cosy drinking pub with no background music or games machines. Enamel signs, posters and brewery artefacts adorn the walls. Up to 16 gravity beers are dispensed from the taproom behind the bar, and one or two ciders. Outside is a heated area for smokers and a secluded garden and patio, providing extra space on sunny afternoons. Snacks are available at lunchtimes, and in the evenings customers are welcome to order in takeaways (not Fri or Sat eve). No children or dogs. Local CAMRA Pub of the Year 2012 and 2013. Q

Mulberry Tree

5 Woodbridge Road, IP4 2EA
12-11 (1am Fri & Sat) ☎ (01473) 225776
Adnams Southwold Bitter H**; guest beers** H/G
This large, imposing pub was bought in 2012 by the current owner and refurbished as a free house after several years of neglect. It now has woodblock flooring throughout and a large open fire in the main bar. Beers are served in oversized glasses. Live music features on Friday and Saturday evenings. Dogs and children are welcome. There are plans for new outdoor seating to provide more alfresco drinking. Local CAMRA Cider Pub of the Year 2013 and 2014. P

St Jude's Brewery Tavern

69 St Matthew's Street, IP1 1EW
4-11; 12-midnight Thu-Sat ☎ (01473) 413334
stjudestavern.com
Beer range varies G
Small, friendly, Gothic-themed bar close to the town centre with sawdust on the floor and various quirky artefacts. Formerly a photographic studio, it opened in 2011 as a tribute to 19th-century back-street beer houses. It is the only pub owned by the former St Jude's Brewery (which may be resurrected). Up to 20 changing beers and four ciders are served from a gravity stillage alongside some imported lagers. Live acoustic music plays occasionally and sport is screened on TV. Themed nights include Gothic fancy dress, Halloween and pirate nights. Local Pub of the Year 2014.

Thomas Wolsey

9-13 St Peters Street, IP1 1XF (300yds from bus station)
4.30-midnight; closed Sun ☎ (01473) 210055
Adnams Ghost Ship; Crouch Vale Brewers Gold; Woodforde's Wherry; guest beer H
Large single-room lounge bar set in a historic Grade II-listed building. It has a patio area to the side and two nicely furnished function rooms upstairs, used for a wide variety of events including story-telling nights, charity quizzes and private meetings. Jazz and R&B feature twice a month on Thursday evenings. Over 40 quality wines are stocked (20 sold by the glass). Games are available including darts. Home supporters only on football match days.

Ixworth

Greyhound

49 High Street, IP31 2HJ
11.30-2.30, 6 (5 Fri & Sat)-11; 12-3, 7-11 Sun
☎ (01359) 230887
Greene King XX Mild, IPA, Abbot; Ruddles Best Bitter; guest beer H

Situated on the town's pretty high street, this traditional inn has three bars, one a lovely central snug. The heart of the building dates back to Tudor times. The pub is a rare outlet for XX Mild. Good-value lunches and early evening meals are served in the restaurant. Dominoes, crib, darts and pool are played in leagues and for charity fundraising. ❀◑▲♣P🚌🐾

Laxfield

King's Head ★ 🄻

Gorams Mill Lane, IP13 8DW

🕘 12-3, 6-11; 12-midnight Sat; 12-8 Sun ☎ (01986) 798395

🌐 laxfieldkingshead.co.uk

Adnams Southwold Bitter, Ghost Ship, Broadside; guest beer 🄶

This thatched inn is often called the Low House and has changed little over the years. A warren of small rooms, with high-back settles and beers served straight from casks in a taproom with no bar counter, make this a unique pub. Traditional home-cooked food features seasonal local ingredients, with special themed evenings. A large garden to the rear has croquet and pétanque, and hosts an annual beer festival. Self-catering accommodation and camping are available by arrangement. Q🛋❀🛏◑♣P🚌(182,183)🐾

Long Melford

Crown Inn

Hall Street, CO10 9JL

🕘 11.30-11; 12-10.30 Sun ☎ (01787) 377666

🌐 thecrownhotelmelford.co.uk

Adnams Southwold Bitter, Ghost Ship; Greene King IPA; Mauldons Silver Adder 🄷

This traditional 17th-century family run free house stands on the main street. It has a central bar with four real ales, leading to the lounge and restaurant. Pub favourites are served in the bar and an excellent seasonal menu offered in the restaurant. The large patio garden is popular for summer drinking and dining. Accommodation is available in 12 guest bedrooms. The village has many antique shops and close by are the 16th-century Kentwell and Melford halls. Q❀🛏◑♿P🚌🐾

Lower Ufford

White Lion

Lower Street, IP13 6DW (between church & river)

🕘 closed Mon; 11-3.30, 6-11; 11-4 Sun ☎ (01394) 460770

🌐 uffordwhitelion.co.uk

Adnams Southwold Bitter; guest beer 🄶

Cosy, small, single-bar pub in a meadowside setting with a quarry-tiled interior offering various home-brewed beers on gravity stillage. Food is all locally sourced and freshly prepared on the premises. The large garden leads to the River Deben and includes a substantial marquee used for many events on summer days including car rallies, an annual beer festival over the August bank holiday, themed balls, quiz nights, hog roasts and various private events. Camping is available by arrangement. Q🛋❀◑▲P🐾

Lowestoft

Mariners Rest

60-62 Rotterdam Road, NR32 2HA

🕘 11-midnight (2 Fri & Sat); 12-11.30 Sun ☎ (01502) 218077

Beer range varies 🄷/🄶

Welcoming community local on the west side of the town centre, a 15-minute walk from the railway station. It has an open-plan interior with TVs showing sports events. Part of the Mariners pub chain, the owners have plans for extensive refurbishment of the bar and taproom. A large selection of real ales and ciders is always available including mild, stout and porter, either handpulled or gravity fed. Local CAMRA Cider Pub of the Year 2014. ❀♣🍎🐾

Norman Warrior 🄻

Fir Lane, NR32 2RB

🕘 11-11.30 (12.30am Fri & Sat); 12-11.30 Sun

☎ (01502) 561982 🌐 thenormanwarrior.co.uk

Greene King IPA; guest beers 🄷

Large estate pub on the northern side of town with ample parking, 20 minutes' walk from Oulton Broad North train station. The public bar has a pool table and dartboard, leading to the terraced garden where an annual beer and cider festival with live music is held over the August bank holiday weekend. The comfortable lounge area leads to a spacious restaurant serving home-cooked meals daily. 🛋❀◑♿⇌♣🍎P🚌(101)🐾📶

Oak Tavern 🄻

71 & 73 Crown Street West, NR32 1SQ

🕘 10.30-11; 12-10.30 Sun ☎ (01502) 537246

Adnams Southwold Bitter; Greene King Abbot; guest beers 🄷

Popular with all ages, this well-run, lively community pub has an open-plan bar divided into two areas, one festooned with Belgian brewery memorabilia and the other for pool and darts. A TV screen shows sporting events and there is a patio and car park to the rear. Four real ales are always available, often including a beer brewed locally and a dark beer in winter months. A beer festival is held in July. ❀♣P🚌🐾

Stanford Arms 🏆 🄻

Stanford Street, NR32 2DD

🕘 4-midnight; 12-1am Fri & Sat; 12-midnight Sun

☎ (01502) 587444 🌐 stanfordarms.co.uk

Green Jack Golden Best, Orange Wheat Beer, Trawlerboys Best Bitter, Lurcher Stout, Rising Sun; guest beers 🄷

The Green Jack Brewery tap, situated a five-minute walk from the brewery and Lowestoft FC or 10 minutes from the train station. An array of handpumps dispenses ales from the Green Jack range plus one guest and a real cider. The spacious open-plan bar leads to a large courtyard with a wood-fired pizza oven. Friday is pizza night, spice night every other Friday and curry club on Saturday. A fine collection of beer trays adorns the walls. Live music is hosted on Saturday evening. Local CAMRA Pub of the Year in 2014. 🛋❀◗⇌🍎🐾📶

Triangle Tavern 🄻

29 St Peters Street, NR32 1QA

🕘 11-11 (midnight Thu; 1am Fri & Sat); 12-10.30 Sun

☎ (01502) 582711 🌐 thetriangletavern.co.uk

Green Jack Golden Best, Orange Wheat Beer, Trawlerboys Best Bitter, Gone Fishing ESB; guest beers 🄷/🄶

This lively town tavern is the flagship for the Green Jack Brewery. The characterful front bar is decorated with many brewery and pub awards and is home to live music every Friday evening. The back bar has a central pool table and is more popular with a younger clientele. Alongside the full Green Jack range are guest ales, real ciders and occasional continental craft beers, with quarterly beer festivals held. Customers are welcome to bring in their own food.

Market Weston

Mill

Bury Road, IP22 2PD

11-3 (not Mon), 5-11; 12-3, 7-11 Sun (01359) 221018

Adnams Southwold Bitter; Greene King IPA; Old Chimneys Military Mild, Golden Pheasant; guest beer H

Striking white brick and flint-faced inn standing at a crossroads. It is the closest outlet to the Old Chimneys Brewery, located on the other side of the village. Run by the same landlady for more than 18 years, it offers an excellent choice of beers complemented by a good menu of home-cooked meals. QP

Naughton

Wheelhouse

Whatfield Road, IP7 7BS (450yds off B1078 close to former airbase)

5-11 (9 Mon; 8 Tue); 6-11 Sat; 12-10.30 Sun

(01449) 740496 thewheelhouseatnaughton.co.uk

Beer range varies H

The main bar has a welcoming fire on cold nights, but please mind your head when entering this small rural thatched pub with low beams. The traditionally tiled floor is a foot lower than it once was and is now below ground level. A larger public bar is brighter and more modern, and leads to the games room with pool table and dartboard. Opening times vary to suit local demand. A delightful, friendly pub, well worth seeking out. QP(111)

Needham Market

Rampant Horse

Coddenham Road, IP6 8AU

12-3, 5-11; 12-11 Sat & Sun (01449) 722044

therampanthorse.co.uk

Woodforde's Wherry; guest beer H

Calvors Brewery purchased and reopened this pub at the end of 2012, selling a wide range of locally-sourced food and drink including its own high-quality lagers. Recently Calvors started brewing ale too, now also available on the bar. Beer festivals feature occasionally and live music is hosted. The pub is close to an area previously known as 'camping land', the local pitch for an ancient ball game called Campball – a precursor to football dating back to at least the 17th century. P(87,88)

Newbourne

Fox Inn

The Street, IP12 4NY

11-11; 12-10.30 Sun (01473) 736307

debeninns.co.uk/fox

Adnams Southwold Bitter; guest beers H

Picturesque timber-framed, two-bar village local with a large garden, popular with ramblers and cyclists. A wide range of local food is home cooked and served every day, with an à la carte menu, gluten-free options and daily specials. The garden has a large pond and a shed housing an old skittle alley – the only one currently active in Suffolk. QP(179)

Newmarket

Golden Lion

44 High Street, CB8 8LB

8am-11 (01638) 672040

Adnams Ghost Ship; Greene King Abbot; Nethergate Old Growler; Ruddles Best Bitter; guest beers H

This is one of Wetherspoon's finest —a large, bustling, 18th-century town pub, situated on the main street. Knowledgeable and efficient staff serve up to seven real ales at any one time including up to three guests. Real cider is also available. The pub's name is thought to have originated from King Henry I —it is also known as the Lion of Justice. Children are welcome until 9pm in the family area. The pub is particularly popular with the local horse racing community. P

Pakefield

Oddfellows

6 Nightingale Road, NR33 7AU

11-11; 12-10.30 Sun (01502) 538415

Adnams Southwold Bitter; guest beers H

Small, cosy pub close to the cliff top and popular with locals, holidaymakers and those walking the Coastal Heritage Path. The interior comprises three open-plan areas, one reserved for diners. A central fireplace separates the other two spaces, with TV screens showing sporting events. Up to four beers are available, usually including one or two from Green Jack Brewery. Two beer festivals are held each year. Local CAMRA Pub of the Year 2013.

Rattlesden

Five Bells

High Street, IP30 0RA

12-12.30am (11.30 Sun) (01449) 737373

Beer range varies H

Set on the high road through a picturesque village, here is a good old Suffolk drinking house – few of its kind still survive. Three well-chosen ales on the bar are usually sourced direct from local breweries. The cosy single-room interior has a games area on a lower level and there is occasional live music. Pub games include shut-the-box and shove-ha'penny plus pétanque in the garden in summer. A dog-friendly pub. Q

Risby

Crown & Castle

South Street, IP28 6QU

12-3, 5 (6.30 Sat; 7 Sun)-11 (01284) 810393

crownandcastle.com

Greene King IPA H**; guest beer** G

This attractive flint-faced building opened as a pub and shop in the late 19th century. A 120ft deep unrecorded well was discovered during alterations in recent times and is now a feature beneath a grille in the entrance lobby. The pub has classic bars to the back and front, with food served in both. The back bar is the public, with games and conversation dominating – dogs are also allowed in here outside food service times. QP

Rumburgh

Buck

Mill Road, IP19 0NT
11.45-3, 6.30-11; 12-3, 7-10.30 Sun (01986) 785257
rumburgh-buck.co.uk
Adnams Southwold Bitter; guest beers [H]
Popular local at the heart of village life, full of character and charm. Interlinked rooms have been added to the historic 17th-century core, which retains its timber frame and flagstone floor. There are two dining rooms serving good food, plus a bar and games room. Guest beers and ciders are often locally sourced. Home to the famous Old Glory Morris Dancers, folk music and craft events are regularly hosted. Local CAMRA Cider Pub of the Year 2013.

Shadingfield

Fox

London Road, NR34 8DD
closed Mon; 12-3, 6-11; 12-11 Sat & Sun
(01502) 575100 shadingfieldfox.co.uk
Fuller's London Pride; guest beers [H]
A charming and cosy rural inn just a short drive from busy Beccles. This refurbished 16th-century building has retained the original arched doors and carved fox heads on the beams. The interior comprises a bar with comfortable seating, a conservatory and restaurant. Outside is a small garden and a sun terrace with umbrellas and chimenea heaters. Two beer festivals are held, one over the Father's Day weekend and the other close to Guy Fawkes Night. (524)

Southwold

Lord Nelson

42 East Street, IP18 6EJ
10.30-11; 12-10.30 Sun (01502) 722079
thelordnelsonsouthwold.co.uk
Adnams Southwold Bitter, Gunhill, Explorer, Broadside; guest beer [H]
Always busy and lively, the pub is popular with locals and visitors enjoying coastal views from the nearby cliff top. With a flagstone floor and warmed by an open fire in winter months, the large central bar offers the full range of Adnams' beers. Children are welcome in the side room and the partly covered and heated patio area to the rear. Decorated throughout with naval and seafaring memorabilia, the pub is timeless in an ever-changing world.

Stowmarket

King's Arms

Station Road, IP14 1RQ
11 (10.30 Sun)-11 07852 497412
Woodforde's Wherry; guest beers [H]
Multi-roomed hostelry, just a short walk from the historic railway station and town centre. Pub games are popular, and occasional live music and barbecues are hosted. Food is available until 4pm including snacks, stews, hotpots, chilli and omelettes. The patio to the rear leads to a smoking room and various other spaces used for live music and private parties. There is a new children's play area and dogs are welcome when the pub is not busy. Two or three beer festivals are held each year. The cider is usually Old Rosie.

Royal William

53 Union Street East, IP14 1HP
11 (12 Sun)-11 (01449) 674553
Greene King IPA; Woodforde's Wherry; guest beers [G]
Tucked away down a side street, just a short walk from the town centre, this is a real gem of a pub. An end-of-terrace back-street bar, it is well supported by locals and visitors alike. All ales are served by gravity dispense from the cellar behind the bar, with up to eight guest beers. There is a games room, home to regular dominoes, darts and crib matches, and a smoking area in an enclosed garden to the rear. Traditional music features once a month. Various home-made bar snacks are offered.

Stutton

Gardeners Arms

Manningtree Road, IP9 2TG
12-3, 6-11; 12-11 Sat; 12-10.30 Sun (01473) 328868
thegardenersarms.net
Adnams Southwold Bitter; guest beers [H]
Cosy two-bar pub set on the edge of a small village, close to the River Stour and just four miles from the historic Flatford Mill. An interesting collection of bric-a-brac adorns the walls, including saddlery, musical instruments and various framed posters. An interesting and varied menu is available with most food prepared on the premises. A bridge club is hosted on Wednesday evening and crib and darts are played. Children are welcome in the pub and large patio garden to the rear of the building.

Sudbury

Brewery Tap

21-23 East Street, CO10 2TP (200yds from marketplace)
11-11 (midnight Fri & Sat); 12-10 Sun (01787) 370876
blackaddertap.co.uk
Mauldons Moletrap Bitter, Silver Adder, Suffolk Pride [H]**; guest beers** [H]/[G]
Sudbury-based Mauldons Brewery's first tied pub, this street-corner local is just outside the town centre one-way traffic system. The bars are clean and comfortable in traditional beer house style. Pies, filled rolls and soup are available, takeaways can be ordered in. Popular events include beer festivals in April and October, regular live music nights and a monthly breakfast club. West Suffolk CAMRA Pub of the Year 2012.

Thorndon

Black Horse

The Street, IP23 7JR
12-3, 5-11; 12-3, 6-midnight Sat; 12-10.30 Sun
(01379) 678523 theblackhorsethorndon.co.uk
Adnams Broadside; Shortts Farm Skiffle; guest beers [H]
Traditional country pub in the heart of a pretty village. Dating back to the 1600s and full of character, it has many historic photos of the village on display. The central bar has a log fire and two adjoining restaurant areas. Two guest ales are usually on offer, typically local and often from Brandon, Grain or Woodforde's breweries. At lunchtime there is a carvery and evening meals are served daily. Dogs on leads are welcome in the main bar area.

Thurston

Fox & Hounds

Barton Road, IP31 3QT
⏲ 12-2.30, 5-11; 12-midnight Fri & Sat; 12-10.30 Sun
☎ (01359) 232228 🌐 thurstonfoxandhounds.co.uk
Adnams Southwold Bitter; Greene King IPA; guest beers Ⓗ
A listed building, this busy local pub sits in the middle of the village and is the centre of local life. The restaurant, serving good home-cooked food, is within the public bar area but separated by uplights from an original wall. There is a separate bar for pool and darts. On bank holidays and special occasions live music is performed. A conker competition features in the autumn. B&B accommodation is available. ❀🛏◐▲⇌♣P🚌🐾

Walberswick

Anchor 🄻

The Street, IP18 6UA
⏲ 11-4, 6-11; 11-11 Sat; 12-11 Sun ☎ (01502) 722112
🌐 anchoratwalberswick.com
Adnams Southwold Bitter, Broadside; guest beer Ⓗ
Situated in an idyllic coastal village, this hotel caters for holidaymakers and locals alike. It has two cosy alcove areas, heated by a real fire on both sides, with a side room for families, plus a spacious restaurant serving local produce. The pub is accessible from Southwold via footbridge or ferry. As well as the Adnams' ales, it stocks an extensive range of global bottled beers and craft ales. Accommodation is available in the main building or garden chalets. Q🐴❀🛏◐♿▲P🐾

Walton

Half Moon

303 High Street, IP11 9QL
⏲ 12-2.30 (not Mon), 5-11; 12-11 Sat; 12-3, 7-10.30 Sun
☎ (01394) 285586
Adnams Southwold Bitter, Ghost Ship, Broadside; guest beer Ⓗ
A meeting place for local groups of all kinds, this excellent, traditional, two-bar community pub has quiz nights, darts and a selection of books for customers to read. There are no gaming machines or music. Recent improvements to the garden include demolishing the long-disused outside toilets and store to provide space for a new pagoda. Food is now available at lunchtimes. 🐴❀◖♿♣P🚌🐾

Wenhaston

Star Inn 🄻

Hall Road, IP19 9HF
⏲ 12-3, 6-11; 12-11 Sun ☎ (01502) 478240
🌐 wenhastonstar.co.uk
Adnams Southwold Bitter; guest beers Ⓗ
Located outside the village with fine views of the Blyth Valley, the pub is popular with walkers and cyclists, and dogs and muddy boots are welcome. It is now a free house since it was bought from Adnams by the current landlords. Three small public rooms overlook a large lawn. The front bar is a gem with old enamel advertising signs, and there are open fires on cold evenings and a working pianola in a back room. Good home-cooked food is made with local produce. Q🐴❀◐♣P🚌(520)🐾

Wingfield

De La Pole Arms

Church Road, IP21 5RA (follow brown tourist signs to Wingfield Barns)
⏲ 12-3, 5-11; 12-11 Sat; 12-10.30 Sun ☎ (01379) 384545
Adnams Southwold Bitter; guest beers Ⓗ
Traditional village pub in a lovely setting opposite the church where Elizabeth of York and a Duke of Suffolk are buried. Wingfield College stands next to the church with Wingfield Barns arts centre alongside. Extensively and lovingly restored in the mid-1990s, the pub is full of character, with oak beams and log fires in the bars. Dogs are welcome in the public bar and food is served in both the saloon bar and the restaurant area with its vaulted ceiling. Q🐴❀◐♿♣P🐾📶

Withersfield

White Horse

Hollow Hill, CB9 7SH
⏲ 11-11; 12-10.30 Sun ☎ (01440) 706081
🌐 whitehorsewithersfield.co.uk
Greene King IPA; guest beers Ⓗ
The village is on a Roman road heading south-eastwards from Cambridge. The pub originates from the 1600s and was probably once a coaching inn on this ancient route. There is a public bar with a huge fire in winter, a restaurant and a large garden for summer drinking, popular with families. Cricket buffs will be interested in the pub's connection with Sir Donald Bradman and should read the story displayed in the bars. Five B&B rooms are available for those wanting to stay and explore the area. Q🐴❀🛏◐♿P🚌(16)

Woodbridge

Angel

2 Theatre Street, IP12 4NE
⏲ 12-3, 5-11 (midnight Fri); 12-midnight Sat; 12-10.30 Sun
☎ (01394) 383808 🌐 theangelwoodbridge.co.uk
Adnams Southwold Bitter; guest beers Ⓗ
Five or six changing beers and over 200 different gins are on offer at this popular and lively 16th-century inn, just off the market square. One bar is used for dining and occasional private hire, with home-made food on offer and themed food evenings. The pub hosts monthly gin tasting evenings, live music every other Monday and monthly open mic nights. The bar areas are furnished in a homely style and there is additional seating outside under cover. 🐴❀◐⇌♣P🐾📶

Cherry Tree

73 Cumberland Street, IP12 4AG
⏲ 10.30-11 ☎ (01394) 384627 🌐 thecherrytreepub.co.uk
Adnams Southwold Bitter, Ghost Ship, Broadside; Elgood's Black Dog; guest beers Ⓗ
Spacious bar with a large central counter and several distinct seating areas. Eight beers are usually on offer and two annual beer festivals hosted. Food is served all day, all locally sourced and home cooked, including some gluten free options. Board games are available to play. The large garden has play equipment to the rear. Accommodation is offered in a converted barn beside the garden and car park. Wheelchair-, child- and dog-friendly. Breakfast is available from 7.30am (9am Sun). 🐴❀🛏◐⇌♣P🐾📶

Old Mariner

26 New Street, IP12 1DX

11-3, 5-11; 11-11 Fri & Sat; 12-9 Sun ☎ (01394) 382679
theoldmariner.co.uk

Adnams Ghost Ship; Black Sheep Best Bitter; Fuller's London Pride; Woodforde's Wherry; Young's Bitter; guest beer H

Traditional two-roomed pub close to the town centre, offering food including tapas, sandwiches and specials alongside a regular range of well-presented ales. The Sunday roast is popular. The front bar with scrubbed tables and a low ceiling is lively, while the rear bar is usually quieter. The back room has a TV turned on only for rugby and major events, and can be booked for private parties. The garden has a patio and smoking area, and leads to the car park (off Castle Street).
♣P

Olde Bell & Steelyard

103 New Street, IP12 1DZ

12-3, 6-11.30 (12.30am Fri & Sat); 12-3, 7-11 Sun
☎ (01394) 382933 yeoldebellandsteelyard.co.uk

Greene King IPA, Abbot; guest beers H

Large multi-roomed pub with oak beams in two bars and a separate function room. The steelyard – a former cart weighbridge that still works and dates from 1650 – was on show at the Great Exhibition in 1851. Traditional games include bar billiards, chess and bar skittles. Live rugby is shown on TVs in the bar area. The food menu offers home-made seasonal dishes using fresh locally-sourced ingredients wherever possible. To the rear of the building is a large heated and covered patio area.
♣

Yaxley

Cherry Tree L

Old Norwich Road, IP23 8BH

closed Mon; 12-3, 6-midnight; 12-7 Sun
☎ (01379) 788050

Woodforde's Wherry; guest beers H

Unusual community village local incorporating a post office and shop, with a large enclosed garden to the rear. Four handpumps feature three rotating ales from East Anglia and one foreign beer from outside the area. Beer festivals are held twice a year, and barbecues on bank holiday Mondays. Historic photos of the village are displayed in the front bar and a vast collection of pumpclips in the back bar. The games room has pool and darts. There is a covered and heated area outside for smokers. Q ♣P

Cricketers, Ipswich

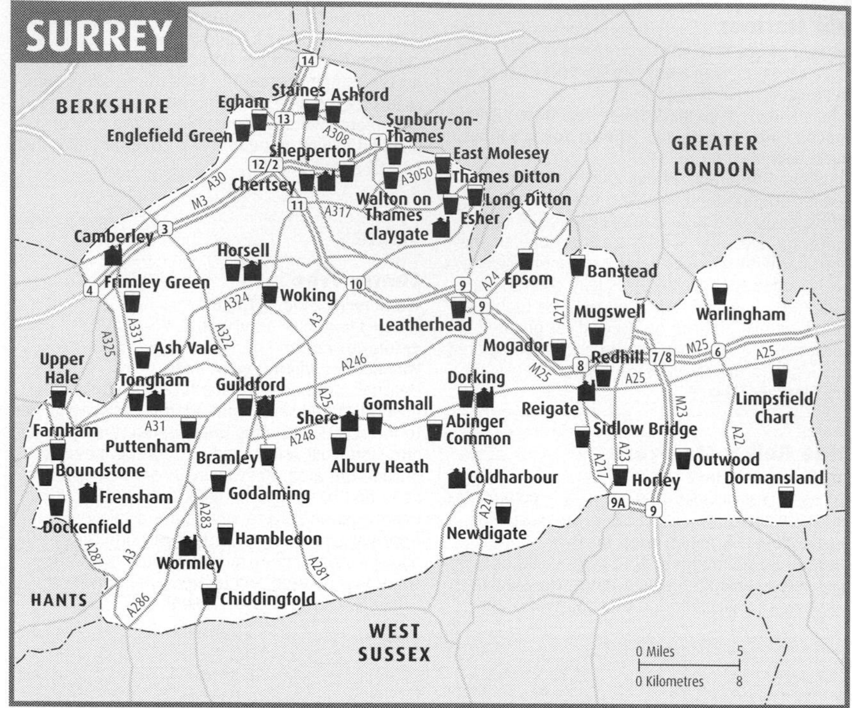

Abinger Common

Abinger Hatch

Abinger Lane, RH5 6HZ TQ11574596
☼ 11-11.30; 12-10.30 Sun ☎ (01306) 730737
🌐 theabingerhatch.com
Beer range varies Ⓗ

The interior of this attractive 17th-century inn, situated opposite a church in the lovely Surrey Hills, rambles over three levels. The lowest area has large flagstones on the floor, the others have bare boards. There are four or five beers served from the beautiful English oak bar, mainly from regional brewers, usually including Ringwood and often a local ale. Good food, served all day, is a feature, with a varied menu on offer. Outside are large gardens. **Q⛀✿◐◑P🚌**(22)🐾📶

Albury Heath

William IV 𝕃

Dark Lane, Little London, GU5 9DG TQ06554673
☼ 11-3, 5.30-11; 11-11 Sat; 12-11 Sun ☎ (01483) 202685
🌐 williamivalbury.com
Hogs Back TEA; Surrey Hills Ranmore, Shere Drop; Young's Bitter Ⓗ

Set on a quiet lane adjoining extensive woodland, the area is popular with walkers. This part 16th-century building features beams, flagstones and a large fireplace where a welcoming wood fire burns brightly in winter. There are two traditional bars with a dining room where excellent home-made meals are served (no food Sun eve). Dishes include Gloucester Old Spot pork from the pigs kept in the field behind the pub. Shove-ha'penny can be played. **Q✿◐◑♣P🐾**

Ash Vale

Swan 𝕃

Heathvale Bridge Road, GU12 5ET
☼ 9am-11.30; 10.30-10.30 Sun ☎ (01252) 325212
Courage Directors; Fuller's London Pride; Hogs Back TEA; guest beers Ⓗ

An old but modernised pub by the Basingstoke canal with an outside seating area leading to the canal and boat moorings. The large interior has four main seating areas and two fireplaces. Mock wood panelling and a beamed ceiling give it a country feel. A wide selection of food is available including brunch in the morning. Beer is served from 10am Monday to Saturday. There is a large car park with overflow capacity nearby. **Q⛀✿◐◑♿⇌P🚌**(3)

Ashford

King's Fairway 𝕃

91 Fordbridge Road, TW15 2SS (on B377)
☼ 11.30-midnight ☎ (01784) 423575
Fuller's London Pride; Sharp's Doom Bar; guest beers Ⓗ

Popular, rambling, modern pub in a cosy, traditional style. Six handpumps dispense two regular real ales and four frequently changing guests from the Ember Inns seasonal selection, all good value for money. Food is also reasonably priced (children are welcome in the dining area). Two gas fires provide winter comfort. Quiz nights are Wednesday and Sunday and curry night Thursday, with additional themed food evenings. There is a small TV area for sport and a heated and covered smokers' refuge alongside the patio. **Q✿◐◑♿P🚌**(290)

Banstead

Woolpack

186 High Street, SM7 2NZ
11-11; 12-10.30 Sun ☎ (01737) 354560
thewoolpackbanstead.co.uk
Shepherd Neame Master Brew, Spitfire, Bishops Finger; guest beers H
Brick and tile building with a front patio and lawned back garden. Although a Shepherd Neame pub, there are two true guest beers which almost always come from smaller breweries in the south-east and are often local. An annual beer festival is held over the August bank holiday. Food, using local ingredients whenever possible, is served all day except Sunday evening. Children are welcome when dining and there is a separate restaurant area. ❀ ♿P

Boundstone

Bat & Ball

15 Bat & Ball Lane, Upper Bourne Lane, GU10 4SA (off Sandrock Hill Rd via Upper Bourne Lane) SU833444
11-11; 12-10.30 Sun ☎ (01252) 792108
thebatandball.co.uk
Bowman Swift One; Hogs Back TEA; guest beers H
A popular family-owned free house offering six interesting beers mainly from adjoining counties, alongside excellent reasonably priced food. The beer range is clearly displayed with strengths and prices. A family-friendly front room complements the beamed, panelled and log-fired bar – a cosy inner sanctum for adults. The garden, with children's playground, hosts an annual beer festival. Open mic night is the last Thursday of the month and other live music features occasionally.
Q❀ ♿P(16,17)

Bramley

Jolly Farmer

High Street, GU5 0HB
11 (12 Sun)-11 ☎ (01483) 893355 jollyfarmer.co.uk
Young's Bitter; guest beers H
A privately owned free house, this traditional pub in the village centre is full of character with oak beams and heavy decoration creating a cosy, welcoming ambience. High-quality food is served and a children's menu is available. Booking is essential for the Sunday lunchtime carvery. Up to six guest beers are from small breweries, often including some from Sussex. A dark beer is usually available, and lagers are imports only. Dogs are welcome in the bar but not the restaurant.
❀ ♣P(53,63)

Chertsey

Coach & Horses

14 St Ann's Road, KT16 9DG (on B375)
12-11 (8 Sun) ☎ (01932) 563085
coachandhorseschertsey.co.uk
Fuller's London Pride, ESB; Gales Seafarers Ale H
Attractive, tile-hung, busy community local, close to the town's cricket and football grounds, dedicated to three Fuller's cask ales. This perennial Guide entry has London Pride people travel miles for. Good-value English food is available weekdays (no food Mon eve) but the landlady likes to keep a 'proper pub' for beer and conversation at weekends. League darts is played. There is an awning for smokers at the front. Frequent buses to Staines and Woking stop nearby.
❀ ♣P(451,446)

Golden Grove

Ruxbury Road, KT16 9EN (off Twynersh roundabout at foot of St Ann's Hill)
11-midnight (11 Sun-Tue) ☎ (01932) 562132
thegoldengrovepub.co.uk
Fuller's London Pride; Sharp's Doom Bar; guest beers H
This pleasant rambling old pub was once one of Chertsey's many coaching inns. It has seven handpumps with up to three constantly changing guest beers, a real cider and a house beer brewed by Cottage alongside the regular ales. The extensive garden has a children's play area. Wednesday night is quiz and ale club with 50p off cask beers from 5pm. Occasional live music events are hosted, usually tribute acts. The pub offers a loyalty card scheme (buy nine pints, get one free).
❀ ♿P

Thyme at the Tavern

20 London Street, KT16 8AA (jct of London St and Heriot Rd)
12 (5 Mon)-midnight; 12-1am Fri & Sat; 12-midnight Sun
☎ (01932) 429667 thymeatthetavern.co.uk
Courage Best Bitter; St Austell Tribute; guest beers H
This genuine free house was local CAMRA Pub of the Year in 2014. Alongside the two regular cask beers, two guests, usually from Surrey or neighbouring county microbreweries, are available. Occasional beer festivals – often LocAle themed – are held. The pub is heavily involved in local charity fundraising. Live music is hosted on Friday nights. Good food is served (no food Mon or Sat) but diners have to fit in with drinkers. The comfortable marquee provides a smokers' refuge.
❀ ♿♣

Chiddingfold

Swan Inn

Petworth Road, GU8 4TY
11-11 ☎ (01428) 684688 theswaninnchiddingfold.com
Adnams Southwold Bitter; Surrey Hills Shere Drop; guest beer H
Lively modern inn in the centre of the village. The focus is on dining but drinkers are welcome. The regularly changing guest beer is usually from a local brewery. A feature fireplace, logburner and wooden beams all add to the atmosphere, and various pictures adorn the walls. An annual beer festival is held in a marquee.
❀ ♿P(71)

INDEPENDENT BREWERIES

Abbey Ford Chertsey (NEW)
Ascot Camberley
Brightwater Claygate
Dorking Dorking
Frensham Frensham (NEW)
Hogs Back Tongham
Hoptimists Wormley (NEW)
Leith Hill Coldharbour
Little Beer Guildford
Pilgrim Reigate
Surrey Hills Dorking
Thurstons (Horsell) Horsell
Tillingbourne Shere

Dockenfield

Bluebell L

Batts Corner, GU10 4EX SU820410
12-3, 5.30-11 Mon-Wed; 12-11; 12-7 Sun
☎ (01252) 792801 bluebell-dockenfield.com
Hogs Back TEA; Triple fff Moondance; guest beers H
Set in a quiet rural area about three-quarters of a mile from Dockenfield village, the pub has a smart wooden and slate interior furnished with sofas and warmed by a real fire. There is an open-plan bar and dining area, and freshly-prepared food ranges from bar snacks to an à la carte menu. Outside there is plenty of parking and a garden with a children's play area for the warmer weather.
♿▲♣P

Dorking

Cobbett's Real Ales L

23 West Street, RH4 1BY (on A25 one-way system eastbound)
12 (10 Fri & Sat)-8; 12-6 Sun ☎ (01306) 879877
cobbettsrealales.com
Beer range varies G
A must-visit when in the area, this excellent off-licence, with a hidden-away micro bar, offers quality beers at fair prices. Two cask beers are usually on tap at the beginning of the week, four at weekends including a hop monster on Friday. Additionally, two beers are sold from KeyKegs. At least one draught cider is available plus perry in summer. A large number of interesting bottled beers and ciders are also stocked. CAMRA members receive a five per cent discount (10 per cent discount for all on Tuesday).
Q ≠(West)

Cricketers L

81 South Street, RH4 2JU (on A25 one-way system westbound)
12-11 (midnight Thu & Sat; 12.30am Fri)
☎ (01306) 889938 cricketersdorking.co.uk
Fuller's Chiswick Bitter, London Pride, ESB, seasonal beer; guest beer H
Small bare-brick pub with a good mixed clientele. A walled Georgian garden at the back is used for beer festivals on the first May bank holiday and in the autumn. The fourth pump either has a Fuller's seasonal beer or a guest from an independent brewery. Major sporting events are shown on terrestrial TV, especially rugby – it is standing room only when England are playing. Children are welcome until early evening and basic lunches are available weekdays. ♣

Red Bar & Lounge L

45 Dene Street, RH4 2DW
12-11 (midnight Fri & Sat); 12-10.30 Sun
☎ (01306) 882222
Surrey Hills Ranmore, Shere Drop; guest beer H
This smart and comfortable bar, just off the High Street, attracts a good variety of customers. The guest beer is often from a local microbrewery; the cider tends to be from one of the larger producers. Excellent food is available (no food Sun eve). A comedy night is hosted every two months (entry charge applies) and music nights feature two or three times a month, usually on a Saturday. The garden is closed in winter. P

Dormansland

Old House At Home

63 West Street, RH7 6QP
12-midnight (1am Fri & Sat) ☎ (01342) 836828
Shepherd Neame Master Brew G**, Kent's Best, Spitfire, seasonal beer** H
A friendly old local hidden away on the west side of the village, signposted from adjoining roads. The pub was originally a pair of Victorian cottages but now has a bar room, with darts played in a small room to the left, and a separate dining room serving home-cooked meals lunchtimes and evenings. Pizzas are available at all times. Some beers are sold direct from casks behind the bar. Quiz night is the first Monday of the month.
Q ♿♣P

East Molesey

Albion

34 Bridge Road, KT8 9HA (off B3379)
11.30-midnight (11.30 Sun) ☎ (020) 8783 9342
Fuller's London Pride; Sambrook's Junction Ale; Young's Bitter; guest beers H
Open-plan locals' pub, part of the Ember Inns estate. The central bar serves separate drinking and dining areas, with comfortable seating throughout. Reasonably priced food including vegetarian options is available from opening time until 10pm each day. The pub is a short walk from Hampton Court Palace and the River Thames. Four guest beers in a wide variety of styles and a cider are usually available, with occasional mini festivals adding to the range. Various deals are offered on food and drink.
♿≠(Hampton Court)

Europa

171 Walton Road, KT8 0DX (on B369)
11-11 (midnight Fri & Sat); 12-11 Sun ☎ (020) 8979 5396
Courage Best Bitter; Sharp's Doom Bar; guest beer H
Friendly local with several bars and a play area in the garden for children. The convivial public bar is traditional in style and has a dartboard surrounded by white-painted wood panelling. There is a quiet snug called the Cabin, decorated with photographic memories of Hurst Park racecourse which closed in 1962, and a comfortable lounge. The pub attracts all age groups. Guest beers are usually from larger breweries or more established micros. No food on Sundays. Q ♣P(411)

Egham

United Services Club L

111 Spring Rise, TW20 9PE (close to A30 Egham Hill)
12-11 (midnight Fri & Sat) ☎ (01784) 435120
eusc.co.uk
Rebellion IPA; Surrey Hills Ranmore; guest beers H
A mecca for the discerning real ale or cider drinker and a strong local brewery supporter. Ten handpumps offer an ever-changing range of five guest ales plus three ciders. Three beer festivals per year attract visitors from far and wide to enjoy the eclectic range of ales, mostly from some of the newest micros around. Satellite TV and free Wi-Fi are available and most Saturday evenings feature live music. A copy of this Guide or CAMRA membership card secures entry.
♿≠♣P(71,441)

Englefield Green

Beehive

34 Middle Hill, TW20 0JQ (200yds N of A30 Egham Hill)
12-11 (midnight Fri & Sat); 12-10.30 Sun
(01784) 431621 beehiveegham.co.uk
Fuller's London Pride; Gales Seafarers Ale, HSB; guest beer
This small pub dating from the 1870s is now open plan with a light and airy feel. It passed through the hands of a number of local breweries including Ashby's before becoming an outlier of the Gale's estate before the Fuller's takeover. It now hosts an interesting variety of Fuller's ales including those under the Gale's badge and a single guest from elsewhere. Freshly cooked food is available throughout the day. Events include regular quiz nights and occasional live music.
P(71,441)

Happy Man

12 Harvest Road, TW20 0QS (off A30)
12-11.30 (midnight Fri & Sat); 12-10.30 Sun
(01784) 433265
Hop Back Summer Lightning; guest beers
Originally two Victorian cottages, the building was converted to a pub to serve the workers building Royal Holloway College. Recently refurbished but virtually unchanged, it is now a popular haunt of students and locals. Four handpumps dispense a changing range of guest ales from microbreweries around the country and sometimes additional beers on gravity from the cellar. Darts and quiz nights are hosted, and food is available all day. The attractive rear garden has a heated smokers' refuge. (71,441)

Epsom

Barley Mow

12 Pikes Hill, KT17 4EA (off A2022)
12-11 (midnight Fri & Sat); 12-10.30 Sun
(01372) 721044 barley-mow-epsom.co.uk
Fuller's London Pride, ESB; guest beers
This good sized, popular pub, hidden off Upper High Street, was originally three cottages. One bar serves many alcoves and other seating areas, with traditional wooden furnishings and leaded windows. The garden room is available to hire. A secluded garden at the rear has access from the nearby public car park. Guest ales are usually from Fuller's or another family brewer. A beer festival is held every July. (166)

Jolly Coopers

84 Wheelers Lane, KT18 7SD (off B280 via Stamford Green Road)
12-11 (midnight Fri & Sat); 12-10.30 Sun
(01372) 723222 jollycoopers.co.uk
Beer range varies
More than 200 years old, this traditional independent three-bar pub lies half-a-mile west of Epsom town centre. It has a quiet lounge with a real fire, a sports bar with TVs and darts, and a small snug in between. Five ales come mainly from Surrey and Sussex, plus occasionally from the West Country. Meals are served all day with traditional roasts on Sunday and barbecues in summer. Music jam night is every Thursday. Children are allowed until 8pm. Local CAMRA Pub of the Year 2012.
QP(E9)

Esher

Albert Arms

82 High Street, KT10 9QS (on A307)
10-1am (01372) 465290 albertarms.com
Fuller's London Pride; Sharp's Doom Bar; guest beers
Handily situated just off the main crossroads at Esher, the pub has a wooden U-shaped bar at the front and a long narrow restaurant to the rear. The interior features bare wood floorboards and wood panelling, with framed rugby shirts on the walls. Children are welcome in the dining area until 10pm. Occasional music nights are held and big matches on Sky Sports are screened. The guest beers are normally from micros, often locally brewed. There is a roof garden. Over-21s only.

Wheatsheaf

40 Esher Green, KT10 8AG
11-11 (midnight Thu-Sat) (01372) 464014
wheatsheaf-esher.co.uk
Fuller's London Pride; Sharp's Doom Bar; Surrey Hills Shere Drop
Traditional community pub, about 400 years old, opposite Esher Green. Decorated in a rustic theme with heavy wood beams, it has the feel of a village local despite being just a short walk from Esher town centre. There is an L-shaped bar leading to a lower area at the front, decorated with various old framed pictures on the walls. Families are welcome until 8pm. Quiz night is every Tuesday and live music events feature occasionally. Accommodation is in two double rooms. P

Farnham

Farnham Conservative Club

Ivy Lane, GU9 7PQ (off Downing St)
11-3 (3.30 Fri), 5-11; 11-11 Sat; 12-4 Sun
(01252) 723712 farnhamconservativeclub.org.uk
Fuller's London Pride; Triple fff Alton's Pride; guest beers
This is a private members-only club, situated in a large Grade II-listed Queen Anne house hidden away down a narrow side street in the centre of Farnham. CAMRA members are welcome and can be signed in at the bar. The club is popular with diners and snooker players. A large function room with its own bar is available upon request. The patio area at the rear of the premises is a perfect suntrap in summer. CAMRA branch Club of the Year 2014. QP

Hop Blossom

50 Long Garden Walk, GU9 7HX (between Waitrose and Castle St)
12-11.30 (12.30am Fri & Sat); 12-11 Sun
(01252) 710770 hopblossom.co.uk
Fuller's Chiswick Bitter, London Pride, ESB; guest beers
A Victorian corner pub with traditional furniture and decor, bare wooden floorboards, an open log fire in winter and dried hops above the bar. The good-sized back room can be used for private functions, and there are benches outside where customers sit in summer. Lunchtime meals range from sandwiches to burgers and pasta. A popular pub with friendly and welcoming staff, it can be very busy on Friday nights. Q

Jolly Sailor 🄻
64 West Street, GU9 7EH
12-11 (1am Fri & Sat); 12-10.30 Sun ☎ (01252) 719139
jollysailorfarnham.com
Greene King IPA; guest beers Ⓗ
Welcoming community pub that has been recently refurbished with a subtle nautical theme. The single bar room, warmed by an open fire in cold weather, is divided into two, with a quieter area by the bay window. A map of Farnham from the 1890s is on the ceiling. The outside terrace is comfy and a perfect place to relax on a warm summer's evening. Good, freshly prepared pub food is served lunchtimes and Monday to Thursday evenings.
P (65)

Nelson Arms 🄻
50-52 Castle Street, GU9 7JQ
12-11 (midnight Fri & Sat); 12-10.30 Sun
☎ (01252) 712554 nelson-arms.co.uk
Andwells Gold Muddler; Hogs Back TEA; Timothy Taylor Landlord; guest beer Ⓗ
Originally three farm cottages belonging to the Bishop of Winchester's estate, this pub has plenty of history. It is named after Admiral Horatio Nelson, who is reputed to have stayed here while visiting Lady Hamilton, who lived nearby. Nowadays, a friendly welcome awaits in traditional surroundings, with an open fireplace and original wooden beams. Good food is served as well as good beer, and there are regular quiz nights, pudding nights and even a gin night.

Queen's Head
9 The Borough, GU9 7NA
10-11 (11.30 Thu; 12.30am Fri & Sat) ☎ (01252) 726524
queens-head-farnham.co.uk
Fuller's London Pride; Gales HSB; guest beers Ⓗ
Situated in the centre of Farnham, with a bus stop right outside, the Queen's Head is a friendly pub with tasteful decor. On entering the pub you are greeted by a row of four handpumps in their own serving area, offering a range of Fuller's beers including a seasonal and a guest ale. Food is available lunchtimes and on Tuesday burger night and Wednesday steak night. Thursday's entertainment alternates between open mic and quiz night. Live music is hosted every Sunday evening.

Frimley Green

Rose & Thistle
1 Sturt Road, GU16 6HT
12-11 (midnight Thu; 12.30am Fri & Sat); 12-10.30 Sun
☎ (01252) 834942 theroseandthistlefrimleygreen.co.uk
Fuller's London Pride; Sharp's Doom Bar; guest beers Ⓗ
A large open-plan pub divided into separate areas with a more secluded conservatory dining space. The regular beer alternates between London Pride and Doom Bar. Up to three guest ales are available at any one time, often from distant microbreweries. Food is served throughout the day until 9pm (10pm weekends), featuring both pub classics and more inventive dishes. The pub aims to be the hub of the local community with live music and an enthusiastic darts scene.
Q P (3,11)

Godalming

Jack Phillips 🄻
48-56 High Street, GU7 1DY
8am-midnight (1am Wed & Thu; 2am Fri & Sat)
☎ (01483) 521750
Greene King Abbot; Ruddles Best Bitter; guest beers Ⓗ
This Wetherspoon pub, converted from a shop in 2000, has a light airy interior, styled to look like an Art Deco passenger saloon on an ocean liner. It is named after local hero Jack Phillips who was the radio operator on the Titanic. Four or more guest beers supplement the regulars, usually including at least one from a local brewery, and two or more real ciders are often available. There is a small patio area at the front. Q

Star Inn
17 Church Street, GU7 1EL
12-11 Sun & Mon; 11-11 (11.30 Thu; midnight Fri & Sat)
☎ (01483) 417717 thestargodalming.co.uk
Greene King St Edmunds Ⓗ**; guest beers** Ⓗ/Ⓖ
Dating from the 1830s or earlier, the Star has a small public bar at the front, the main rooms to the side leading to a patio and smoking area, and a separate lounge. Up to eight real ales are stocked and beer festivals are held at Easter and Halloween. Renowned for cider and perry, with four to six available, it was CAMRA Surrey & Sussex Regional Cider Pub of the Year for 2013.

Gomshall

Compasses 🄻
50 Station Road, GU5 9LA
11-11; 12-10.30 Sun ☎ (01483) 202506
thecompasses-gomshall.co.uk
Surrey Hills Ranmore, Shere Drop, seasonal beer Ⓗ
This 19th-century roadside pub stands between the A25 and the River Tillingbourne. It has a traditional bar with three handpumps, decorated with old farming and other tools on its wooden pillars and beams. There is a garden and seating beside the stream. Home-made meals are served in the bar and separate dining room. Live music plays every Friday, with a music festival over the August bank holiday. B&B is in two en-suite rooms.
P (25,32)

Gomshall Mill 🄻
52 Station Road, GU5 9LB (on A25)
12-11 (10.30 Sun) ☎ (01483) 203060
gomshallmill.hcpr.co.uk
Beer range varies Ⓗ
Spanning the River Tillingbourne, the pub is within a 17th-century timber-framed and timber-clad watermill. While the emphasis is on excellent dining, with food available all day, the comfortable bar serves four constantly changing brews, usually including two LocAles, one from Tillingbourne. Dining areas are spread across several levels around two waterwheels, formerly used to produce flour, and these may be viewed as the stream races beneath your feet. There is a pleasant garden by the mill pond.
P (25,32)

Guildford

Keystone 🄻
3 Portsmouth Road, GU2 4BL

7am-11 (1am Fri & Sat) (01483) 575089
Otter Ale; St Austell Tribute; guest beers
Conveniently tucked away just out of sight of the madding crowds, this pub offers something for everyone, with monthly scientific discussions, live music, pub quizzes and sport, especially rugby, on TV. It has a modern, relaxed interior, with sofas, table seating and bar stools. Large blackboards advertise food, drink and events, and the walls display contemporary art. A raised rear patio features a wood-burning chiminea. Open for breakfast from 7am, with food served all day (until 4pm Sun). Licensed from 11am.

King's Head

27 King's Road, GU1 4JW (on A320 Stoke Road)
11-11 (1am Fri & Sat); 12-10.30 Sun (01483) 568957
kingsheadguildford.co.uk
Fuller's Chiswick Bitter, London Pride, ESB, seasonal beers; guest beer
A mid-Victorian street-corner pub, extended over time, with many different drinking and dining areas served from a centre bar. The subtle Alice in Wonderland theme celebrates Charles Dodgson's association with the town. Alongside a Fuller's seasonal beer, the guest ale is from a local brewery, usually Surrey Hills or Tillingbourne. A range of Belgian bottled beers is also available. Acoustic music features on Tuesday and open mic on Thursday. Food is served until 10pm (9pm Sun). (London Rd) P

Rodboro Buildings

1-10 Bridge Street, GU1 4SB (opp Friary Centre)
8am-midnight (1am Mon; 1.45am Fri & Sat); 9am-10.30 Sun (01483) 306366
Fuller's London Pride; Greene King IPA; Hogs Back TEA; Sharp's Doom Bar; guest beers
A Grade II-listed building constructed in 1900 for the Dennis Car Company and then used by the Rodboro Boot and Shoe Company for 11 years until 1928. It survived demolition to become a Wetherspoon pub in 1998 and is now a Lloyds No.1. The cavernous factory interior extends over two floors and is usually busy and noisy. A good selection of local beers is stocked.

Row Barge

7 Riverside, GU1 1LW
12-11 (midnight Fri & Sat) (01483) 570242
therowbargeguildford.com
Ascot On the Rails, Alligator Ale; Dartmoor Jail Ale; St Austell Tribute; Surrey Hills Shere Drop; guest beer
Built in 1856 and extended for the post-war Bellfields Estate, this two-bar pub with pool room is 1½ miles along the River Wey towpath from the town centre, close to the A320 Woking Road. Day and night moorings are available to customers and a cycle rack is provided. Poker night is Thursday and live music features on Friday and Saturday. Food is served until 7pm (5pm Sun).
P (3,34)

Royal Oak

Trinity Churchyard, GU1 3RR
12-11; 11-11 (11.30 Thu; 12.30am Fri & Sat); 12-10.30 Sun
(01483) 459023 royaloakguildford.co.uk
Fuller's London Pride, seasonal beers; Gales HSB; guest beers
Originally the rectory of Holy Trinity Church and the largest house in an early 17th-century terrace, it was converted to a pub in about 1870 with the two front sitting rooms becoming bars – now knocked into one. Comfortable seating helps to create a homely atmosphere and the beers benefit from a cellar that is larger than the pub. Current beers can be viewed in sample jars. Three beer festivals are held each year, one just before Christmas. Food is served lunchtimes and evenings (not Sun eve).

Stoke

103 Stoke Road, GU1 4JN
10-midnight (01483) 504296 thestoke.co.uk
Beer range varies
Large Victorian pub 10 minutes' walk from the town centre with a central bar divided into various areas for dining and for relaxing in comfy chairs. The four beers are from independent breweries near and far. Food, including breakfast, is served all day, with pizzas from a proper oven the speciality. There are toys and games for children. Other entertainment includes a piano, pinball machine, two pool tables and several TV screens. Regular live music events and quizzes are held.
(London Rd) P

Hambledon

Merry Harriers

Hambledon Road, GU8 4DR SU967391
11-2.30, 5.30-11; 11-11 Sat; 11-8 Sun (01428) 682883
merryharriers.com
Pilgrim Progress; Surrey Hills Shere Drop; Tillingbourne Falls Gold; guest beers
A stylish yet traditional 16th-century establishment with a warm welcome for all. The main bar has an inglenook fireplace and is flanked by a small quiet side room and a restaurant and function room. All food, except fish, and ales are sourced from within a 25-mile radius. Live music features on the last Saturday of the month. Accommodation is either in the converted barn or the camping field. Llamas can be admired from the garden or even taken for a walk. Q P

Horley

Jack Fairman

30 Victoria Road, RH6 7PZ
8am-midnight (1am Fri & Sat) (01293) 827910
Greene King Abbot; Ruddles Best Bitter; guest beers
Conveniently situated close to the station and the town centre, this Wetherspoon Lloyds No.1 pub occupies a former Kwik-Fit tyre centre, originally built in the 1930s as Fairman's Garage. Jack Fairman was an early racing driver and his history is displayed inside. The bar has an industrial look to it with large pipes coming from the ceiling. Three large screens show televised sport. Food is available all day.

Horsell

Crown

104 High Street, GU21 4ST
12-11 (midnight Fri); 11-midnight Sat (01483) 771719
thecrownhorsell.co.uk
Beer range varies
A rare find in this area, this is a traditional 'wet' pub – the only food on offer is pizza. A short walk from Woking, the Crown is popular with both locals and visitors from afar who come to sample the beers from Thurstons Brewery next door. Thurstons

beers alternate with other locally brewed ales so check the website to see what is currently on offer and what is coming up. An annual beer festival is held at Easter. The large garden has a pétanque piste. Live music plays occasionally. Q🍼❀♣P🚌(48)🐾📶

Leatherhead

Edmund Tylney

30-34 High Street, KT22 8AW

8am-11 (midnight Thu; 1am Fri & Sat) ☎ (01372) 362715

Greene King Abbot; Ruddles Best Bitter; Young's Special; guest beers Ⓗ

Formerly a Woolworths store, this typical Wetherspoon has multiple levels around a large staircase. The spacious interior has a bar area with high tables and chairs and a raised area with more comfortable seating. There are also separate, more private booths divided by glass partitions. Children are allowed until 8pm if dining. At least six guest beers, including locally brewed ones, are on offer, and two or three ciders and perries. Edmund Tylney, a Leatherhead man, was Master of the Revels to Queen Elizabeth I. 🍼❀◐♿⇌🍎🚌📶

Running Horse 🏆 L

38 Bridge Street, KT22 8BZ (Off B2122)

11.30-11; 12-10.30 Sun ☎ (01372) 372081

Shepherd Neame Master Brew, Kent's Best, Spitfire, Bishops Finger; guest beer Ⓗ

Grade II*-listed pub dating back to 1403, overlooking the River Mole. John Skelton (Poet Laureate to Henry VIII) wrote about Elinour Rumming brewing 'nappy ale' here. The lounge has low ceilings, exposed beams and a real fire, the public bar has TV, pool table and dartboard. Home-made meals use many local ingredients and the guest beer is usually Ranmore from Surrey Hills. A quiz night is held every alternate Tuesday, live bands play monthly, and a charity event is hosted on May Day. Children are allowed until 9pm. Call in advance for disabled access. Q🍼❀◐♿⇌♣P🚌

Limpsfield Chart

Carpenters Arms L

12 Tally Road, RH8 0TG

11-3, 5-11; 11-11 Sat; 12-10.30 Sun ☎ (01883) 722209

carpenterslimpsfield.co.uk

Westerham Finchcocks Original, British Bulldog, Spirit of Kent, 1965, seasonal beer Ⓗ

This Westerham Brewery tied house features the full range of its beers. The L-shaped bar has parquet flooring and a dartboard on one side, and provides ample room for drinkers and diners. Good home-made food is served daily (no food Sun eve). The monthly quiz is popular. The pub is located adjacent to National Trust land, attracting walkers and horse riders. The locals take great pride in this friendly pub. 🍼❀◐♣P🚌(594)🐾📶

Long Ditton

Ditton

64 Ditton Hill Road, KT6 5JD

12-11 (10 Sun) ☎ (020) 8339 0785 theditton.co.uk

Sharp's Doom Bar; guest beers Ⓗ

A former Hodgsons pub, previously known as the Plough & Harrow, this popular local has been consistently improving its beer range over the years. Guest beers are increasingly sourced from local microbreweries. A relaxed public bar at the front leads through to a more formal dining room at the rear, overlooking the huge south-facing garden. Families are welcome throughout, and traditional pub games are available including a skittle alley. 🍼❀◐♿♣P🚌(K3)🐾📶

Mogador

Sportsman

Mogador Road, KT20 7ES (off A217) TQ23985316

12-11 (10.30 Sun) ☎ (01737) 246655

timewellspent.info

Sharp's Doom Bar; Young's Bitter; guest beers Ⓗ

Food-oriented pub situated in a lovely position on the edge of Walton Heath. It can get busy, especially on warm weekends. Built as a lodge on royal hunting grounds, parts date from the 16th century, although most of the building is of later construction. There is a restaurant, a large garden to the side and another at the front. Guest beers come from both large and small brewers and may be local —anything from Greene King to Clarence & Fredericks. ❀◐P🐾📶

Mugswell

Well House Inn L

Chipstead Lane, CR5 3SQ (off A217) TQ25845526

12-11 (10.30 Sun) ☎ (01737) 830640

wellhouseinn.co.uk

Adnams Southwold Bitter; Fuller's London Pride; Surrey Hills Shere Drop; guest beers Ⓗ

Grade II-listed building dating from at least the 16th century. In the garden is St Margaret's Well or Mag's Well, mentioned in the Domesday Book, which gives the area its name. There are three bars, all with their own fires, and a conservatory. The two guest beers change frequently and are usually from local microbreweries. The cider may be from Westons or a smaller producer. Dogs are welcome in two of the bars. Good pub food is available (no food Sun and Mon eves). 🍼❀◐♣🍎P🐾📶

Newdigate

Surrey Oaks 🏆 L

Parkgate Road, Parkgate, RH5 5DZ TQ20524363

11-2.30, 5.30-11; 11-3, 6-11 Sat; 11-9 Sun

☎ (01306) 631200 surreyoaks.co.uk

Harveys Sussex Best Bitter; Surrey Hills Ranmore; guest beers Ⓗ

Attractive 16th-century inn renowned for its commitment to real ale, a frequent winner of local CAMRA Pub of the Year including 2014. Hoppy beers are particularly popular and third-of-a-pint glasses are available. The pub features low beams, flagstones and an inglenook fireplace. Outside there are two boules pistes in the large garden and a skittles alley in the barn. Good food is served in the bar and restaurant (no food Sun or Mon eves). Beer festivals are held on the late spring and August bank holidays. Q🍼❀◐♣🍎P🚌(22,29)🐾

Outwood

Castle L

Millers Lane, RH1 5QB TQ31764534

12-3, 5.30-11; 12-11 Sat; 12-8 Sun ☎ (01342) 842754

castleoutwood.co.uk

Harveys Sussex Best Bitter; Pilgrim Progress; guest beers Ⓗ
This pub has three distinct drinking areas and a small snug warmed by real fires. Good food is served in the restaurant (no food Sun eve) but this is also a drinkers' pub, welcoming locals and visitors. There are four pumps on the front bar and another couple round the side. One of the three guest beers is always from Pilgrim, the other two are from larger breweries. The garden has a children's play area and covered decking. A disabled toilet is available. ❀◑♣P🚌(315)📶

Puttenham

Good Intent

60-62 The Street, GU3 1AR
⌚ 12-3, 6-11.30 (11 Mon); 12-11.30 Sat; 12-10.30 Sun
☎ (01483) 810387 🌐 thegoodintentpub.co.uk
Otter Bitter; Sharp's Doom Bar; Timothy Taylor Landlord; guest beers Ⓗ
A 16th-century inn situated in an attractive village on the North Downs Way. The cosy bar with oak beams and an inglenook fireplace is decorated with hops and hop-growing equipment which serve as a reminder that the last hop field in Surrey is just 500 yards along The Street. Three guest beers are normally available. Food is served daily (but not Sun and Mon eves), with fish and chips night on Wednesday and curry night on the last Thursday of the month. Q❀◑⛺P🐾📶

Redhill

Garland

5 Brighton Road, RH1 6PP (on A23 south of town)
⌚ 11.30-11.30 (12.30am Fri; midnight Sat); 12-11.30 Sun
☎ (01737) 760377
Harveys IPA, Sussex Best Bitter, Armada Ale, seasonal beer Ⓗ
A classic Victorian street-corner local dating from 1865, the Garland is just south of the town centre. There are usually a couple of seasonal beers on offer as well as Imperial Extra Double Stout in bottles. Darts is popular here, with two boards, and there is also a bar billiards table – the pub fields teams in local leagues. Good-value food is sold lunchtimes (no food Sat lunch) plus Friday evening. ❀◑⇌♣P🚌🐾

Hatch

44 Hatchlands Road, RH1 6AT (on A25 W of town)
⌚ 11-midnight (12.30am Fri & Sat); 12-midnight Sun
☎ (020) 3588 4400 🌐 thehatchpub.co.uk
Shepherd Neame Master Brew, Kent's Best, Spitfire, Bishops Finger, seasonal beer; guest beer Ⓗ
This comfortable pub dates from the 17th century and is a former workhouse with a hayloft for horses. The landlord is extremely proud of his beer and tries to offer additional ales from the Shepherd Neame microbrewery whenever he can. Good home-cooked food is served each day (no food Sun or Mon eves). There is also a good selection of wines on offer, plus a choice of teas and coffees. ❀◑♿♣🍏🚌📶

Sun Ⓛ

17-21 London Road, RH1 1LY
⌚ 8am-midnight (1am Sat) ☎ (01737) 766886
Fuller's London Pride; Greene King Abbot; Ruddles Best Bitter; guest beers Ⓗ
When the Sun opened on 14 August 1996, it was Wetherspoon's 150th pub - named to commemorate local astronomer Richard Carrington who wrote Observations of the Spots on the Sun in 1861. It is a huge brick building with a long bar serving one vast open space. A raised dining area is to the left of the bar, with food served all day from 8am-11pm. Up to six guest beers are available. ❀◑♿⇌🍏🚌📶

Shepperton

Barley Mow Ⓛ

67 Watersplash Road, TW17 0EE (off B376 in Shepperton Green)
⌚ 12-11 (10.30 Sun) ☎ (01932) 225326 🌐 themow.co.uk
Hogs Back TEA; Hop Back Summer Lightning; guest beers Ⓗ
Friendly side-street local in Shepperton Green, west of the main village centre. Five handpumps adorn the horseshoe bar, serving beers from the likes of Hogs Back, Windsor & Eton, King Beer and other local or more distant microbreweries. Past CAMRA awards are displayed on one of the beams along with a mass of pumpclips. Live rock 'n' roll or R&B plays on Friday and Saturday, jazz on Wednesday, and quiz night is Thursday. Outside is a covered and heated patio area for smokers. ❀♣🍏P🚌(438,458)🐾📶

Sidlow Bridge

Three Horseshoes Ⓛ

Ironsbottom, RH2 8PT (off A217)
⌚ 12-11 (8 Sun) ☎ (01293) 862315
🌐 thethreehorseshoes-pub.co.uk
Dark Star Hophead; Fuller's London Pride, ESB; Pilgrim Surrey Bitter; guest beers Ⓗ
Just a short distance from the A217, the Shoes is a good stopping place when heading for Gatwick Airport. Formerly a coaching inn on the original London-Brighton road, parts of the building date back 300 years. A section of the single bar area was once a forge, hence the name. Good-quality meals are served daily except Sunday evening and a beer festival is held over the first May bank holiday. The pub has a large garden. ❀◑🍏P🚌(433)📶

Staines

Bells

124 Church Street, TW18 4ZB (off B376)
⌚ 12-3, 5-11 (midnight Fri); 12-midnight Sat; 12-10.30 Sun
☎ (01784) 454240 🌐 thebellspub.co.uk
Young's Bitter, Special; guest beer Ⓗ
Friendly, comfortable, 18th-century pub opposite St Mary's Church close to the Thames Path and within easy walking distance of the town centre. Regular beers and seasonals from Wells & Young's are available plus up to two guests from microbreweries around the country. Noted locally for the quality of its food, it is often busy in the evenings. The pleasant rear patio garden, with a large heated smokers' canopy, is especially popular in summer, attracting local workers and shoppers. Q❀◑♿🚌(305)

Wheatsheaf & Pigeon Ⓛ

Penton Road, TW18 2LL (off B376, corner of Wheatsheaf Lane and Penton Rd)
⌚ 12-11 (10.30 Sun) ☎ (01784) 452922
🌐 thewheatsheafandpigeon.co.uk

Fuller's London Pride; Otter Ale; Sharp's Doom Bar; guest beers Ⓗ
Welcoming and friendly community local between Staines and Laleham, a short walk signposted from the Thames Path and Staines Town FC. Ales often include local micro or West Country guests, and good-value food is served every day except Monday and Sunday evening. There is seating outside for the warmer months plus a covered smoking area, and families are welcome. Quiz night is Sunday and beer festivals are held. The pub is particularly busy on football match days. The bus stops in Laleham Road. P (458)

Sunbury-on-Thames

Magpie

64 Thames Street, TW16 6AF
12 (11 Fri & Sat)-11; 12-10.30 Sun ☎ (01932) 782024
magpiesunbury.com
Beer range varies Ⓗ
Recently refurbished rambling old pub on two levels with a Greene King seasonal ale and up to five regularly changing real ales, usually from London or other local microbreweries, available in the downstairs bar along with draught Budvar and other exotics. An extensive food menu offers traditional pub classics, seasonal dishes and daily specials. The outside drinking area overlooks the Thames. The pub was once the headquarters for the Grand Order of Water Rats showbusiness charity —the founders had a horse called the Magpie, described as 'looking like a water rat', after whom the pub was later renamed.
(216)

Thames Ditton

Olde Swan

Summer Road, KT7 0QQ
11-11 (10.30 Sun) ☎ (020) 8398 1814
Greene King IPA, Abbot; Morland Old Speckled Hen; guest beers Ⓗ
Although much altered, this large pub backing on to the Thames can trace its history back to the 13th century and was once used as a hunting lodge by Henry VIII. The multi-roomed interior has a stylish yet traditional feel with stone walls, black flagstones around the bar area and wooden floorboards in the seating area. Guest beers are supplied by Greene King but can be from other brewers. Access is from the riverside, not the street. (514,515)

Red Lion

85 High Street, KT7 0SF
11-11 (midnight Fri); 10-midnight Sat; 10-10.30 Sun
☎ (020) 8398 8662
Beer range varies Ⓗ
In new hands since autumn 2012, this quirkily decorated pub, divided into distinct areas, is situated close to the river and just away from the village centre. Old doors, some retaining their locks, make up the front of the bar. The two handpumps mainly dispense locally brewed beers. Food is served all day. P (514,515)

Tongham

White Hart

76 The Street, GU10 1DH
11-11.30 (midnight Fri & Sat); 12-10.30 Sun
☎ (01252) 782419 thewhiteharttongham.co.uk
Hogs Back TEA; guest beers Ⓗ
A friendly family-run pub with a central bar area serving three rooms: the lounge bar with a relaxed atmosphere and wood fire, the quiet saloon bar suitable for dining, and the sports bar, with the usual activities. Home-made food is served Tuesday to Sunday, plus bar snacks. The beer garden has decking and a covered smoking area. There is a monthly live band and Tuesday evening quiz. Four guest beers are offered and two beer festivals are held each year.
P (3,20)

Upper Hale

Alfred Free House

9 Bishops Road, GU9 0JA
5 (12 Sat)-11; 12-10.30 Sun ☎ (01252) 820385
thealfredfreehouse.co.uk
Beer range varies Ⓗ/Ⓖ
A friendly street-corner local tucked away in a residential area, popular with locals and visitors alike. An interesting choice of ales is available, with ever-changing guests on gravity dispense. For the hungry there is an excellent choice of snacks and main meals, all prepared on site using locally-sourced ingredients. The pub holds two beer festivals a year, often with a themed selection, and hosts occasional live music.
Q P (4,5)

Walton on Thames

Ashley Park

Ashley Park Road, KT12 1JP (Off B365)
11 (11.30 Sun)-midnight ☎ (01932) 220196
Fuller's London Pride; Sharp's Doom Bar; guest beers Ⓗ
Conveniently situated opposite the railway station, this popular Ember Inns pub is decorated in the usual cosy, comfortable style. The interior is quite rambling with various tucked-away areas between the pillars and walls, and a mixture of carpet and wood flooring. To the rear is a quieter dining area. Accommodation is in the adjoining Premier Inn.
P (458,555)

Regent

19 Church Street, KT12 2QP (On A3050)
8am-midnight (1am Fri & Sat) ☎ (01932) 243980
Adnams Broadside; Greene King Abbot; Ruddles Best Bitter; Sharp's Doom Bar; guest beers Ⓗ
An attractive Wetherspoon conversion of the former Regent cinema, the pub is tastefully decorated in Art Deco style with wood surround panelling under the curved ceiling and period lighting. The walls are decorated with lots of photos of old Walton plus relics of local connections with the film industry. At the far end, steps lead up to a small seating area for customers seeking a more secluded spot, albeit on the way to the toilets. Alcohol is served from 9am.
Q (461,564)

Warlingham

White Lion

3 Farleigh Road, CR6 9EG (on B269)
11.30-midnight ☎ (01883) 625085

Adnams Broadside; Fuller's London Pride; Harveys Sussex Best Bitter; Ringwood Best Bitter; guest beers Ⓗ

Parts of this historic Ember Inns pub date from 1467. The interior is a warren of rooms, both ancient and modern, and there are some low beams so beware. There is a modern dining area to the rear. An impressive display of pumpclips reflects the wide range of guest beers available from far and wide. CAMRA members receive a discount on cask ales. ❀◑♿♣P🚌(403,409)

Woking

Herbert Wells

51-57 Chertsey Road, GU21 5AJ

8am-midnight (1am Fri & Sat) ☎ (01483) 722818

Courage Best Bitter, Directors; Greene King Abbot; Hogs Back TEA; guest beers Ⓗ

Six guest beers are usually available in this popular town centre Wetherspoon pub. Eight real ciders are also on offer along with an interesting selection of bottled beers. Alcohol is served from 9am and children are welcome when dining until 6pm daily. Note the novel nod to the pub's namesake dotted around the walls and ceiling. Q◑♿🚌

Woking Railway Athletic Club

Goldsworth Road, GU21 6JT

10.30-11 (11.30 Fri & Sat); 12-10.30 Sun

☎ (01483) 598499

Beer range varies Ⓗ

Friendly and lively social club tucked away near Victoria Arch, serving two ever-changing ales, often from local breweries. One side of the bar is sports oriented, with darts, pool and Sky Sports, while the other side is quieter. Beyond the bar is a large function room. Children are welcome at all times. Filled rolls are available on Saturday afternoon. For entry show a CAMRA membership card or copy of this Guide. ♣🚌

Rose & Thistle, Frimley Green (Photo: Jack Dicken)

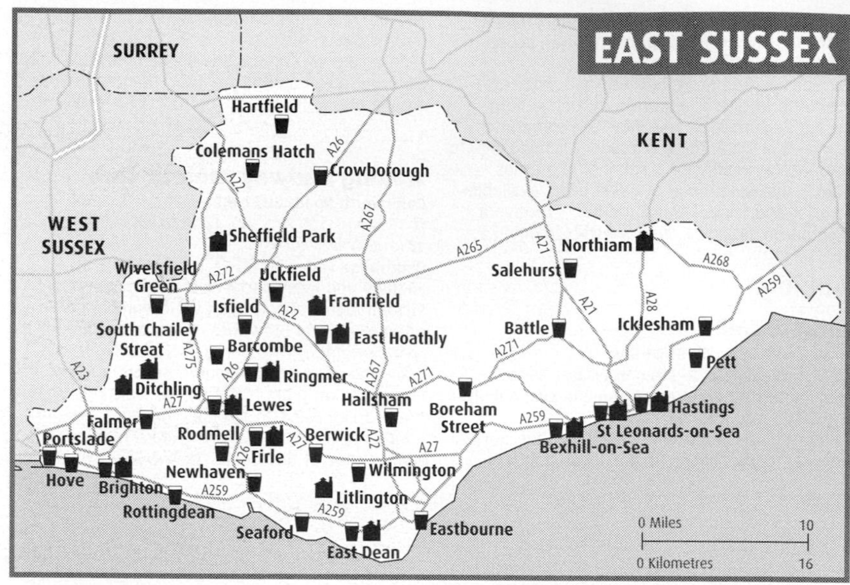

SUSSEX (EAST)

Barcombe

Royal Oak 𝕃

High Street, BN8 5BA

10 (12 Sun)-11 ☎ (01273) 400418

royaloakbarcombe.co.uk

Harveys Sussex XX Mild Ale, Sussex Best Bitter; guest beer Ⓗ

This hostelry lies in the centre of the small village of Barcombe, north of Lewes. Two regular ales are supplemented by other beers from Harveys, such as the relatively new Sussex Wild Hop. Old Ale is usually on in winter. There is a small car park in front and a garden at the rear. The pub has a skittle alley, and there is a real fire in the main bar. Good-value food is served lunchtimes and evenings. **Q**(125)

Battle

Bull Inn 𝕃

27 High Street, TN33 0EA

11-11.30 (12.30am Fri & Sat); 11-10.30 Sun

☎ (01424) 775171 thebullinn.co.uk

Harveys Sussex Best Bitter; guest beer Ⓗ

Fine old 17th-century coaching inn in the middle of Battle High Street with a large single bar with two inglenook fireplaces and a clientele of mixed ages. The house beer, Top Bull, is brewed by Old Dairy; guest ales are usually from local microbreweries, and a fourth handpump is due to be installed. Live music is played here on a regular basis. Five en-suite rooms are available. **Q**

Berwick

Cricketers' Arms 𝕃

BN26 6SP (S of A27)

11-3, 6-11 (11-11 summer); 11-11 Sat; 12-10.30 Sun

☎ (01323) 870469 cricketersberwick.co.uk

Harveys Sussex Best Bitter, Armada Ale Ⓖ**; guest beer** Ⓗ

Just off the South Downs Way, this Harveys tied house is a traditional country pub, converted from two flint-walled cottages. Two regular ales and at least one seasonal beer are served from a cellar room behind the bar. The well-kept gardens make this a great place to stop in the summer, with real fires inside in the winter. Good-quality, home-produced food is on sale all day. **Q P**

Bexhill-on-Sea

Albatross Club (RAFA) 𝕃

15 Marina Arcade, TN40 1JS (on seafront 200yds E of De La Warr Pavilion)

11.30-2.30, 7 (5 Thu)-11; 12-2.30 Sun ☎ (01424) 212916

bexhillrafa.co.uk

Beer range varies Ⓗ

Local CAMRA branch Club of the Year 2012-2014, and regional Club of the Year 2013. An extremely friendly place with a comprehensive collection of flying and RAF memorabilia. The changing ales are from local and national microbreweries. Beers in the cellar are listed on a board behind the bar. In a separate TV room major sporting events are shown. Twice-yearly beer festivals are held in April and September, and live jazz on the fourth Tuesday evening of the month. **Q**

Boreham Street

Bull's Head 𝕃

Boreham Hill, BN27 4SG

12-3, 6-11; 12-11 Fri & Sat ☎ (01323) 831981

bullsheadborehamstreet.co.uk

Harveys Sussex Best Bitter; guest beer Ⓗ

This village pub, the first ever Harveys tied house from the early 19th century, has a simple interior of wooden floors, tables and chairs, and an ambience that makes the visitor feel immediately at ease. The range of Harveys ales includes the house beer, Bull's Head Bitter. A variety of home-prepared food can be enjoyed at all sessions (no food Sun eves and Mon). The pub has its own campsite, a large car park and outside seating. **Q P**(98)

Brighton

Barley Mow

92 St George's Road, Kemp Town, BN2 1EE
11 (12 Sun)-midnight ☎ (01273) 682259
Beer range varies H
Small free house in the Kemptown area of Brighton with an eclectic mix of customers, serving five ales from Sussex and a real cider. There is a large courtyard to the rear of the pub with heaters for the chilly months. It holds popular quiz nights every Thursday, has books you can borrow, and there are a couple of games on every table. Home-made food is served all day. (37)

Basketmakers Arms

12 Gloucester Road, BN1 4AD
11-11 (midnight Fri & Sat); 12-11 Sun ☎ (01273) 689006
basket-makers-brighton.co.uk
Fuller's London Pride, Bengal Lancer; Gale's Seafarers Ale, HSB; guest beers H
Two-room street-corner pub on the edge of Brighton's famous North Laine district. Eight handpumps serve the Fuller's/Gale's range plus guests. Locally-sourced home-made food is on offer every day including at least one vegetarian option. The walls are adorned with old metal signs and tobacco tins containing messages, secrets and codes written by customers over the years. Around 100 whiskies are stocked and there is a Malt of the Month. Sister pub to the Lewes Arms.

Constant Service

96 Islingword Road, Hanover, BN2 9SJ
3-midnight; 4-1am Fri & Sat; 12-midnight Sun
☎ (01273) 607058
Harveys Sussex Best Bitter, Armada Ale; guest beer H
One-bar pub in residential Hanover offering a warm welcome to regulars and newcomers alike. A fantastic selection of vinyl, and friendly and enthusiastic staff, make for a great atmosphere. Bands play regularly, and two TV screens show sport. An award-winning beer garden at the rear catches the sun all day. A range of well-kept Harveys beers is offered. Good-quality hearty pub grub is on offer weekday evenings and all day Saturday – pies are a speciality, with roasts on a Sunday.

Craft Beer Co

22-23 Upper North Street, BN1 3FG (short walk from Churchill Square shopping centre)
3-11 (11.30 Thu); 12-midnight Fri; 12-1am Sat; 12-10.30 Sun ☎ (01273) 735799
Kent Pale; guest beers H
A lively corner pub with at least six real ales on handpump, including a few from local breweries, as well as bottled beers. Cask ales are priced according to strength and cost about average for Brighton. The popular pub has plenty of seating at tables, and a range of bar snacks is on offer including cheese, sausage rolls and pork pies. Lined glasses ensure there are no short measures.

Evening Star

55-56 Surrey Street, BN1 3PB (200yds S of station)
12-11 (midnight Fri); 11.30-midnight Sat
☎ (01273) 328931
Dark Star Hophead, American Pale Ale; guest beers H
As close to beery heaven as it is to Brighton station, the Evening Star is a local pub with a sense of community, and a hostelry for travellers, welcoming to all who appreciate excellent beer. Wooden and uncluttered inside, with seven handpumps, the Star shines because of its beers and ciders, and the conducive space it provides for drinkers to enjoy the experience without distractions. The staff are knowledgeable and helpful to both the knowing and the naive, and the regulars are friendly.

Hand in Hand

33 Upper St James's Street, Kemptown, BN2 1JN
12-midnight; 12-11.30 Sun ☎ (01273) 699595
Beer range varies H
A fairly small but perfectly formed pub, like entering someone's front room, with a bar, fairy lights, piano, lots of photographs and pictures. Up to six handpumps offer beers from Kemptown Brewery (situated at the back of the pub), Brighton Bier Company (same brewer but various locations), sometimes Dark Star, and interesting guests. This is the Kemptown Brewery tap and, after a few years in the wilderness, the beers are good enough for the pub to re-enter the Guide. Food, served 12-5pm, is from a nearby café. (37,47)

Mitre Tavern

13 Baker Street, BN1 4JN
10.30-11.30 (midnight Fri & Sat); 12-10.30 Sun
☎ (01273) 683173 mitretavern.co.uk
Harveys Sussex XX Mild Ale, Sussex Best Bitter, Armada Ale; guest beer H
Close to many London Road and Open Market bus routes, this back-street corner pub has a long, narrow bar with a real fire and a cosy snug. Old Ale is stocked in the winter months and Olympia in summer, as well as the monthly seasonal. Two ciders are usually available. The good-value lunchtime food comes from a nearby café.

North Laine

27 Gloucester Place, North Laine, BN1 4AA
11-12.30am (2.30am Thu-Sat); 11-11.30 Sun
☎ (01273) 683666
Beer range varies H
A large pub on the edge of Brighton's famous North Laines, with its own brewery behind the bar. On a weekday the brewer, Dallas, can be seen making one of the pub's own beers. It brews seven ales, six of which are made on the premises. Large tables add to the party atmosphere and there is a

INDEPENDENT BREWERIES

1648 East Hoathly
360° Sheffield Park (NEW)
Beachy Head East Dean
Brighton Bier Brighton
Burning Sky Firle (NEW)
FILO Hastings
Franklins Bexhill-on-Sea
Goldstone Ditchling (NEW)
Harveys Lewes
Hastings St Leonards-on-Sea
Isfield Framfield
Kemptown Brighton
Kitchen Garden Sheffield Park (brewing suspended)
Laine Brighton
Long Man Litlington
Rectory Streat
Rother Valley Northiam
Turners Ringmer

photo booth to record the fun. Food is served all day. Regular live bands and DJs feature.

Prestonville Arms

64 Hamilton Road, BN1 5DN (in back street E of Seven Dials)
5-11; 12-midnight Fri & Sat; 12-11 Sun (01273) 701007
theprestonvillearms.co.uk
Fuller's London Pride; guest beer
It can be a bit hard to find, but a sign at the road end points you up Hamilton Road to this excellent back-street pub. There is a horseshoe-shaped bar with a wooden floor. Work by local artists is displayed on the mezzanine level. Beers from the Fuller's range supplement the Pride, and a genuine guest beer, often from Butcombe, is usually on handpump. The nearest buses are at Seven Dials.

Prince Albert

48 Trafalgar Street, BN1 4ED
12-midnight (12.30am Fri & Sat) (01273) 730499
Harveys Sussex Best Bitter; guest beers
Close to Brighton station and several bus routes, this pub serves up to six real ales – the guest beers are from Sussex breweries. At least one of Burning Sky's beers is usually available, and a cider is sold. Food is served from noon-9pm (until 3pm Fri). Families are welcome until 6pm. There are a number of rooms off the main bar and outside seating is in front of the pub.

Southover

58 Southover Street, Hanover, BN2 9UF
3-midnight (1am Fri); 12-1am Sat; 12-midnight Sun
(01273) 601419 thesouthoverbrighton.co.uk
Beer range varies
The pub is at the top of the steep hill of the same name, and anyone less than fit is advised to use the bus. Survivors of the climb will find a friendly, roomy venue offering a range of bottled beers in addition to those on the five pumps. Mostly local ales are stocked, with a weekend guest from further afield. Prices are reasonable for the area but a premium is charged on halves. A range of food is served in the evenings, and roasts on Sunday. (20,23)

Victory Inn

6 Duke Street, BN1 1AH
12-midnight (2am Fri & Sat) (01273) 326555
Beer range varies
A small, cosy, traditional inn in the heart of Brighton's famous Laines. One of the city's oldest hostelries, it retains many original features. Further seating is upstairs and outside in the enclosed courtyard. It offers four real ales from Sussex breweries and a real cider. CAMRA members receive a discount on pints of ale on production of their membership card. Good pub grub is available all day. DJs feature at the weekend and open mic on Thursdays.

Colemans Hatch

Hatch Inn

Kidds Hill, TN7 4EJ
11.30-3, 5.30-11; 11-11 Sat; 12-11 Sun (01342) 822363
hatchinn.co.uk
Black Cat Original; Harveys Sussex Best Bitter; Larkins Traditional Ale; guest beer
A 15th-century pub that can be hard to find, but is well worth the effort. Popular with walkers and diners, the interior has low-beamed ceilings. There are two garden areas and picnic tables on the forecourt, ideal for summer drinking and dining. The daily food menu includes locally-sourced food. The pub has featured in TV dramas. The Ashdown Forest visitor centre is nearby and Poohsticks Bridge is five minutes away in Upper Hartfield.
Q P (291)

Crowborough

Coopers Arms

Coopers Lane, TN6 1SN
12-2.30 (not Mon), 5-11; 12-11 Sat & Sun
(01892) 654796
Dark Star Partridge Best Bitter; guest beers
A long bar forms the main drinking area, with a separate restaurant and a side bar for games. This friendly, traditional pub offers two changing guest beers from Sussex and beyond and real cider in the summer. Beer festivals are normally held at Easter and late winter, with all beers served from the 12 available handpumps. A selection of bottled beers is also kept. Home-prepared food is served.
Q P

Wheatsheaf

Mount Pleasant, Jarvis Brook, TN6 2NF
12-11 (10.30 Sun) (01892) 663756
wheatsheafcrowborough.co.uk
Harveys Sussex XX Mild Ale, Sussex Best Bitter, Armada Ale
Unspoilt early Victorian local with an unusual split-level three-sided bar. This tied house always has a good range of Harveys beers on hand, which can be enjoyed in any of the three distinct drinking areas or the garden. Real cider is served periodically. Two beer festivals are usually held each year, in May and October. The lower bar area has a rare copper fireplace originally designed for a yacht. Q P (228,229)

East Dean

Tiger Inn

The Green, BN20 0DA
11-11 (01323) 423209
Beachy Head Beachy Original, Legless Rambler; Harveys Sussex Best Bitter; Long Man Brewery Long Blonde; guest beer
Quaint 15th-century smugglers' inn sitting on a traffic-free village green near the South Downs Way. The cosy main bar has wooden beams and a wood-burning stove, and there is a smaller bar and an extended dining area; freshly cooked meals are popular. There is plenty of outdoor seating on the green and at tables. The pub offers luxury accommodation, making it popular with walkers and cyclists, and is the brewery tap for the nearby Beachy Head Brewery. Q P

East Hoathly

Foresters Arms

6 South Street, BN8 6DS
6-10 Mon; 11.30-3, 6-11; 11.30-11 Sat; 12-10 Sun
(01825) 840208 theforesterseasthoathly.co.uk
Harveys Sussex Best Bitter, Old Ale; guest beer
A Harveys tied house with a large L-shaped bar split by wooden and carpeted areas. The elevated

floor of the front bar helps to give a bright aspect, while wood panelling and bay windows lend a bygone Victorian charm to the dining area. A pleasant restaurant area accessed through an archway adds to the ambience. Outside is a beer garden with children's play area. Level access is available to the side. Toad in the Hole is played here. Q(54)

King's Head

1 High Street, BN8 6DR

12-11; 11-midnight Fri & Sat; 12-10.30 Sun

(01825) 840238

1648 Triple Champion, Signature; Harveys Sussex Best Bitter; guest beer H

Traditional 17th-century pub that was once the village school. The old stables and forge next door, which once served the London stagecoach, have become home to the local 1648 Brewing Company. The pub sells a range of 1648 beers as well as a guest. Fresh food is served lunchtimes and evenings, with locally-sourced products on offer. There is a walled garden to the rear and seating to the front, and two function rooms for all occasions. QP(54)

Eastbourne

Buccaneer

10 Compton Street, BN21 4BW

11-11; 12-10.30 Sun (01323) 732829

Arundel Buccaneer Ale; Harveys Sussex Best Bitter; guest beers H

Situated by the theatres and near the seafront, this pub has a large L-shaped bar with some partitioned seating. Old theatre posters decorate the walls and a raised rear area overlooks the Devonshire Park tennis courts. Good-value food is available each day, all day, and five ales are on offer, including three frequently changing guests. Arundel Brewery provides the house beer, with 10p per pint sold going to the pub's charity, Canine Partners. (3)

Crown

22 Crown Street, Old Town, BN21 1PB

11-11 (midnight Fri & Sat); 12-11 Sun (01323) 724654

Dark Star Hophead G**; Harveys Sussex Best Bitter; Shepherd Neame Spitfire; Wadworth 6X** H**; guest beer** G

Family-friendly community pub in the heart of Old Town, just 15 minutes' walk from Eastbourne station. There are two bars, one with a log fire, and a separate pool room at the back. The large enclosed rear garden has regular barbecues and children's play equipment during the summer months. A weekly guest beer is sold and there are regular beer festivals. Excellent traditional bar snacks are available, with complementary snacks and ale discounts on Sunday lunchtimes. Occasional live music features.

Dew Drop Inn

37-39 South Street, BN21 4UP

12-midnight (1 Fri & Sat) (01323) 723313

Beer range varies H

Friendly Greene King pub offering at least two guest beers, usually including one from Dark Star. The horseshoe-shaped bar area is divided in two, with ample comfortable seating, and there is a small rear garden. The place is popular with all ages, but evenings attract mainly a younger crowd – there are occasional special events, DJ nights and sometimes live bands. Beer and cider festivals are held. A range of pub food, including speciality burgers, is served until 9pm. (3,3A)

Dolphin

14 South Street, BN21 4XF

11-11 (midnight Fri & Sat); 12-10.30 Sun

(01323) 746622

Harveys Sussex Best Bitter; guest beers H

Popular Brakspear town-centre pub in the Little Chelsea area. Five ales are on offer, one from Brakspear, with guests usually coming from Sussex breweries. The front bar has a friendly atmosphere which attracts drinkers of all ages, and features an open fire. There is a small bar to the rear and a larger room mainly used by diners, with an outside patio area. Good-quality food cooked to order is available. Beer club meetings are held monthly. Convenient for Saffrons sports ground. Q

Eagle

57 South Street, BN21 4UT

11-11 (12.30am Fri & Sat) (01323) 417799

Harveys Sussex Best Bitter; guest beers H

Single-bar former Kemptown Brewery pub featuring some fine internal decoration and a small roof terrace. Sport is shown on several TVs, including a 100in HD projection screen, and there is a pool table and dartboard. Four beers from local breweries are regularly served, together with Westons Old Rosie cider. An excellent range of pub food is on offer all day until 9pm. Regular beer festivals are held. CAMRA members receive a discount of 10p per pint.

London & County

46 Terminus Road, BN21 3LX

8am-midnight (1am Fri & Sat) (01323) 746310

Greene King Abbot; Ruddles Best Bitter; guest beers H

Occupying the original 1880 London & County Bank building, this Wetherspoon Lloyds No.1 Bar is in the town centre, opposite the railway station and convenient for all local bus routes. Two regular ales, five different guest beers and a real cider are on handpump, and good-value food is served each day, all day and evenings. There is a small upper room for functions, muted TV screens provide daily news updates, and music is played in the evenings.

Victoria Hotel

27 Latimer Road, BN22 7BU (behind TAVR Centre from seaside)

11-11 (midnight Fri & Sat); 12-10.30 Sun

(01323) 722673 victoriaeastbourne.co.uk

Harveys Sussex Best Bitter, Armada Ale, seasonal beer H

Friendly family-run local, just 20 minutes' walk from Eastbourne station, serving all Harveys seasonal ales, including Old Ale or Olympia, and Westons Old Rosie cider. The large front bar, with ample comfortable seating, features Victorian portraits and brewery memorabilia, while the smaller back bar has darts, pool and Toad in the Hole. Excellent, good-value, home-made food is on offer lunchtimes (Thu-Sun) and evenings (Thu-Sat). The garden is furnished for alfresco dining. A popular beer festival is held over the Easter weekend.

Falmer

Swan Inn

Middle Street, BN1 9PD (just off A27 N of village)
12-11 (4 Mon); 12-10.30 Sun ☎ (01273) 681842
theswanfalmer.co.uk
Palmers Best Bitter, Tally Ho!; guest beers H
Cosy, traditional family-run free house in the village of Falmer near the universities. It has three bar areas and a German model railway runs above the bar in the narrow middle room. Good-value food is served at lunchtimes and Thursday and Friday evenings. Being close to the Amex Stadium, the pub gets busy on days when Brighton & Hove Albion play at home – only home fans tend to be allowed entry and there is no parking available. A small courtyard area sits to the rear of the building. **Q**P(28,29)

Firle

Ram Inn

The Street, BN8 6NS
11.30-11; 9am-11 Sat & Sun ☎ (01273) 858222
raminn.co.uk
Harveys Sussex Best Bitter; guest beers H
Village pub convenient for walkers on the South Downs Way. Up to two guest beers will often be from local breweries and a Westons cider and/or perry is usually available. There is a games room where various pub games can be played including crib, scrabble and Toad in the Hole. Families are welcome but children are not allowed in the bar area. A restaurant-style menu is offered. Outside seating is at the front and rear.
P(25,125)

Hailsham

George Hotel

1 George Street, BN27 1AD
8am-11 (midnight Fri & Sat) ☎ (01323) 445120
Greene King Abbot; Ruddles Best Bitter; guest beers H
Conveniently located in the town centre opposite the restored picture palace, the Hailsham Pavilion. Wetherspoon tastefully converted the George Hotel in 2010, opening up the interior to create a spacious area with an L-shaped bar. There is also a small raised alcove, plus a beer garden to the rear, and outside seating on the terrace by the side entrance. A selection of carefully chosen and reasonably priced guest beers is available, including at least one from a local Sussex microbrewery. The usual good-value Wetherspoon food menu is available all day.

Hartfield

Anchor Inn

Church Street, TN7 4AG
11-11; 12-10.30 Sun ☎ (01892) 770424
anchorhartfield.com
Harveys Armada Ale; Larkins Traditional Ale; guest beers H
The Anchor was built in 1465 as a manor house. By the 1800s it was a workhouse but started selling beer in the 1860s. It is in the centre of this Ashdown Forest village, close to the church. The interior includes two bars, the rear one with an inglenook, and a restaurant, used during busy periods. The wooden-beamed front bar is decorated with an interesting selection of old pictures. Food is served all day at weekends in summer. **Q**P(291)

Hastings

Dolphin

11-12 Rock-A-Nore Road, Old Town, TN34 3DW
11-11 (midnight Sat) ☎ (01424) 431197
Dark Star Hophead; Harveys Sussex Best Bitter; Young's Special; guest beers H
With six handpumps, this cosy Old Town pub is the current CAMRA South East Sussex Pub of the Year. Decorated with fishing memorabilia, it gets particularly busy at weekends and holidays. Good speciality seafood platters are served lunchtimes all week and also on Monday evenings. There is live music on Tuesdays, Fridays and Saturdays, and a quiz night on Thursday. An outside seating area overlooks the historic fishermen's huts on the Stade. **Q**(20,100)

First In Last Out

14-15 High Street, Old Town, TN34 3EY (near Stables Theatre)
12-11 (midnight Fri & Sat) ☎ (01424) 425079
thefilo.co.uk
FILO Mike's Mild, Crofters, Churches Pale Ale, Old Town Tom, Cardinal; guest beer H
Dating back to the 1500s, this building has been an inn since 1896. Formerly home to the FILO Brewery, which is now 300 yards away, the popular pub has a large bar warmed by a central open fire. Five beers are generally available. Beer festivals are held over most bank holiday weekends, with real cider also sold. Monday is tapas night. Although Ore station is closer than Hastings, it is a more difficult walk and has a less frequent service. **Q**(20,100)

General Havelock ★

27 Havelock Road, TN34 1BP
11-midnight (2am Thu-Sat); 12-midnight Sun
☎ (01424) 719048
Dark Star Hophead; Harveys Sussex Best Bitter; Timothy Taylor Landlord; guest beers H
Situated in the town centre, the pub is near local bus routes and a short walk from the railway station. The building has recently undergone a refurbishment, but it retains all the features that classify it as having a nationally important historic pub interior, in particular the exceptional large tiled paintings of scenes of local interest. The two guest beers change weekly and a good-value lunchtime menu is served. **Q**

Jenny Lind

69 High Street, Old Town, TN34 3EW
12-11 (midnight Fri & Sat) ☎ (01424) 421392
jennylindhastings.co.uk
Theakston Old Peculier; guest beers H
Next door to the Old Town Hall Museum of Local History, this popular pub serves a good range of beers from six handpumps, including two or three guest ales and two from Hastings Brewery. Live music is performed at weekends, while Sunday night is vinyl night, where customers can bring their own records and take turns to be DJ for a few minutes. The pub acts as the brewery tap for Hastings Brewery and a loyalty card scheme operates. **Q**(20,100)

White Rock Hotel

White Rock, TN34 1JU (opp pier)
10 (12 Sun)-11 (01424) 422240
thewhiterockhotel.com
Beer range varies H
A stylish, contemporary bar with ample seating, and a terrace overlooking the seafront and the pier, are the main features for non-residents in this large, friendly hotel adjacent to the theatre of the same name. Four beers on offer are always from independent Sussex breweries, and a good range of freshly prepared food is available until 10pm. Many of the en-suite guest rooms have sea views – the best are on the first floor with balconies.
Q

Hove

Neptune Inn

10 Victoria Terrace, BN3 2WB (on coast road E of King Alfred leisure complex)
12-1am (2am Fri & Sat); 12-midnight Sun
(01273) 736390 theneptunelivemusicbar.co.uk
Greene King Abbot; Harveys Sussex Best Bitter; guest beers H
Five handpumps serve regular favourites plus frequently changing guest ales, always in good condition. This traditional single-bar pub is frequented by a local clientele. Live music is strongly supported, with blues and rock every Friday and jazz on Sunday, together with open mic and vinyl nights on the second and fourth Mondays. This pub is on the Brighton to Shoreham coast road near central Hove. Interior features are music-related pictures, posters and other memorabilia. (700)

Sussex Cricketer

Eaton Road, BN3 3AF
11-midnight (01273) 771645
Arundel Sussex Gold; Harveys Sussex Best Bitter; guest beers H
A stylish single-bar Ember Inn sitting at the entrance to the Sussex cricket ground. There are normally at least five real ales on offer, including beers both from local breweries and from wider afield. It offers frequent food and drink promotions, including a discount for CAMRA members, and on Monday all ales are reduced. Quizzes are held on Tuesday and Sunday. Food is well presented and there is a large garden. P

Icklesham

Queen's Head

Parsonage Lane, TN36 4BL (opp village hall)
11-11; 12-10.30 Sun (01424) 814552
queenshead.com
Greene King IPA, Abbot; Harveys Sussex Best Bitter; guest beers H
Early 17th-century inn, beginning its fourth consecutive decade in this Guide, serving guest beers from local breweries and from further afield. It stocks five beers - often eight to 10 at weekends – and a real cider. In winter three log fires warm the five interior areas. A spacious garden with a children's play area gives fine views towards Winchelsea and Rye. Home-made affordable food is served and live music is performed 4-6pm on Sundays. The autumn beer festival offers Sussex and Kent beers. Q P (100)

Robin Hood

Main Road, TN36 4BD (on A259 at W end of village)
11-3, 6-11; 11-11 Fri & Sat; 12-4, 7-10.30 Sun
(01424) 814277
Beer range varies H
Local CAMRA branch Pub of the Year 2012, this 17th-century inn offers six or seven beers, always including a low ABV beer and some from local brewers. At least two ciders are on tap, often including the local Battle Pink cider. A separate dining area serves home-cooked food. Each July a successful village beer festival is held in an adjacent field. There is a pool table and the large rear garden has a pétanque piste.
Q P (100)

Isfield

Laughing Fish

Station Road, TN22 5XB (off A26 between Lewes and Uckfield)
11.30-11 (3 Mon) (01825) 750349
laughingfishonline.co.uk
Greene King IPA; Hardys & Hansons Olde Trip; guest beers H
The pub, next to the preserved Lavender Line, is now the unofficial Isfield Brewery tap. A good range of beers is on the pumps, always including at least one from Isfield. A warm welcome greets you from tenants Andy and Linda. Good-quality pub food is served. Bar billiards, Toad in the Hole and darts are all played. There is a pub quiz on the first Sunday of the month, an Easter beer race, and an outdoor play area for children.
P (29,29B)

Lewes

Brewers Arms

91 High Street, BN7 1XN (near Lewes Castle)
10-11; 12-10.30 Sun (01273) 475524
brewersarmslewes.co.uk
Beer range varies H
Genuine family-run free house catering for most tastes in its two bars, offering up to six real ales. At the front, the comfortable saloon has a range of seating with books and games. The rear bar has a pool table, and two TVs show sporting events. It is popular on match days with Lewes FC, Brighton & Hove Albion and away fans. Food, including traditional breakfasts, is served until 8pm. The exterior proclaims the former owners, Page & Overton's, Brewers of Croydon.
Q (28,29)

Elephant & Castle

White Hill, BN7 2DJ (off Fisher St, near old police station)
11.30-11 (midnight Fri & Sat); 12-11 Sun
(01273) 473797 elephantandcastlelewes.com
Harveys Sussex Best Bitter; Timothy Taylor Landlord; guest beers H
Built in 1838 to provide accommodation and stabling for a new road into the town, the Ellie is a spacious community-based pub, home to one of the famous Lewes bonfire societies and a Saturday folk club. Major sporting events including the Six Nations Rugby are shown on a large-screen TV. The pub has a good-sized function room available for hire. The changing guest beers are usually from Sussex brewers and the food is locally sourced.
(127)

Gardener's Arms 🏆 L

46 Cliffe High Street, BN7 2AN
11-11; 12-10.30 Sun ☎ (01273) 474808
Harveys Sussex Best Bitter; guest beers H
Small, genuine free house in the heart of Lewes, near Harveys brewery. Five changing guest ales are on offer, generally from small breweries countrywide, and bottled and draught cider. Harveys seasonal ales and one-off brews often feature. Locally made pies and pasties are available. A Guide and ale trail regular, the pub is popular with Brighton and Lewes FC fans on match days. Customers' canine friends are made welcome with water and dog treats. No children allowed. CAMRA branch Pub of the Year 2014.
(28,29)

Lewes Arms

1 Mount Place, BN7 1YH
11-11 (midnight Fri & Sat); 12-11 Sun ☎ (01273) 473152
Fuller's London Pride; Gale's HSB; Harveys Sussex Best Bitter; guest beer H
In the heart of the county town, this is a traditional alehouse with six handpumps, popular with visitors and locals alike. Fuller's beers are served plus Harveys Best and a guest. It is home to the world pea-throwing championship, dwyle flunking, spaniel racing and other unusual events. A three-day music festival is hosted in August and an annual pantomime in March in the upstairs function room, in aid of a local charity. Home-made food is served every day (times vary).
Q(28,29)

Snowdrop Inn L

119 South Street, BN7 2BU
12-midnight (11 Sun) ☎ (01273) 471018
thesnowdropinn.com
Harveys Sussex Best Bitter; guest beers H
A genuine free house and the unofficial brewery tap for the nearby Burning Sky brewers, this pub offers six real ales and a real cider. Popular with families, it also serves good-quality food made with local free-range ingredients. The two outside areas are suntraps in the summer, while a large upstairs space is cosy in the winter. It hosts regular live bands and a beer festival every October, and the Alternative Miss Snowdrop competition in August is always entertaining.
(28,29)

Newhaven

Hope Inn

West Pier, BN9 9DN (close to Newhaven Fort)
11-11 (10.30 Sun) ☎ (01273) 515389
Harveys Sussex Best Bitter; guest beers H
Spacious pub at the far end of Newhaven with a covered balcony overlooking the harbour entrance. The interior has a timber-panelled and beamed ceiling, a panelled bar, walls and polished wood floors. Look out for the stained glass panels, the multitude of nautical-themed pictures and the flag signals on the ceiling beams. Heed the sign warning you against feeding the pub dog. Quiz night is Wednesday. Home-cooked food is available every day. A raised patio smoking area is at the front. P

Pett

Royal Oak

Pett Road, TN35 4HG
11-11; 12-10.30 Sun ☎ (01424) 812515
royaloakpett.com
Beer range varies H
Village free house refurbished by the new owners in 2011, serving up to four real ales, often from local breweries. There are two fires, one set in a large open fireplace. The interesting and varied food menu, sourced locally, is served throughout the pub. The highlight of an excellent selection of traditional pub games is an antique bagatelle board, the forerunner of modern bar billiards. Events include a quiz and occasional live music. The pub has real character, with friendly staff, and is very welcoming. QP(347)

Two Sawyers

Pett Road, TN35 4HB
12-1am (midnight Sun) ☎ (01424) 812255
twosawyers.co.uk
Ringwood Fortyniner; guest beers H
A 17th-century village pub with friendly staff and two main bars, a separate restaurant and smaller dining areas, and open fires. Up to four beers are on offer, with guest ales often from local breweries. Good locally-sourced food is served from an extensive menu each session and all day Sundays. A collection of antique saws decorates the pub, reflecting the pub's name. Be aware that it may close early if there are no customers.
QP(347)

Portslade

Stanley Arms

47 Wolseley Road, BN41 1SS (on corner of Stanley Rd)
3 (4 Mon & Tue)-11; 12-11 Sat; 12-10.30 Sun
☎ (01273) 430234 thestanley.com
Beer range varies H
Genuine family-run free house. Beer festivals are held in spring, summer and autumn, with reduced price Cellar Nights with free nibbles every second Monday. A varying range of beers is served from seven handpumps. The pub has a football team and shows matches on HD TV. Quiz and crib evenings are organised, plus occasional live music and talks by sports personalities. It is named after Henry Morton Stanley, the man who found Doctor Livingstone. There is a stained glass tiled canopy over the bar. Q(Fishersgate)

Ringmer

Cock Inn L

Uckfield Road, BN8 5RX (1 mile from village on slip road off A26)
11-3, 6-11; 11-11 Sun ☎ (01273) 812040
cockpub.co.uk
Harveys Sussex Best Bitter; guest beers H
A traditional family-run pub offering an extensive menu of quality food with vegetarian, vegan and gluten-free options. Harveys Best Bitter is always served, plus two seasonal local ales (from Harveys, Hammerpot, WJ King, Isfield or Dark Star). There is also a comprehensive range of Harveys bottled beers. The bar has a large inglenook fireplace, exposed beams and a flagstone floor. There is a large dining area, a well-furnished beer garden and plenty of car parking space.
QP(29,29B)

Rodmell

Abergavenny Arms
Newhaven Road, BN7 3EZ
12-11.30 (01273) 472416 abergavennyarms.com
Harveys Sussex Best Bitter; guest beers
A large roadside pub in a small village near Lewes, with some original features including a spectacular fireplace. It is popular with walkers on the South Downs Way and visitors to the nearby Monks House, the former home of author Virginia Woolf. It has a lovely, sunny courtyard to the rear. Home-made food is served lunchtimes and evenings, with a popular steak and a drink deal on Thursdays. P (123,130)

Rottingdean

Queen Victoria
54 High Street, BN2 7HF
12-11 (midnight Fri & Sat); 12-10.30 Sun
(01273) 302121
Harveys Sussex Best Bitter; Long Man Brewery Long Blonde; guest beers
At the bottom of the High Street you will find this welcoming one-bar pub with a mock-Tudor frontage, real fire and a cast-iron stove. Decorated with William Morris wallpaper and elegantly lit with numerous chandeliers, gentle jazz music plays in the background. Built in the 1930s, it replaced the original pub situated opposite. On Saturday afternoons the jazz is live. Look out for the 19th-century harmonium and old photographs of Rottingdean. Excellent food is on the menu, locally sourced where possible. The staff are knowledgeable and passionate about the beer they serve.

St Leonards-on-Sea

North Star Inn
Clarence Road, TN37 6SD
11-midnight (1am Fri); 12-midnight Sun
(01424) 436576
Harveys Sussex Best Bitter; Timothy Taylor Landlord; guest beers
This friendly local is just off the main Bohemia Road. The large U-shaped bar has an open fire and is decorated with railway memorabilia. There is a meat raffle on Sundays, a cheese raffle on Saturdays, a monthly bingo night and quiz night, and occasional live music. Three changing guest beers are on offer, often from local microbreweries. Although food is not usually served, a popular curry evening is hosted on Wednesdays. Q (99,100)

St Leonard
16-18 London Road, TN37 6AN
closed Mon & Tue; 5-11; 3-9 Sun (01424) 272332
thestleonard.co.uk
Beer range varies
Tastefully refurbished, this pub attracts a mixed crowd of discerning drinkers. There are three varying beers, often from local breweries, an excellent wine list, and quality bar snacks using local ingredients where possible. There is a raised bar area and plenty of tables and chairs, and a warm welcome is offered to all, making this reopened pub well worth visiting. Do note the reduced opening times.
(Warrior Square)

Tower
251 London Road, TN37 6NB
11-11.30 (12.30am Fri & Sat); 11-11 Sun
(01424) 721773
Dark Star Hophead, American Pale Ale; guest beers
The Tower is a free house offering reasonably priced real ales, mostly pale in colour, with two changing guest beers. Entertainment includes live sporting events on HD TV, themed events, a well-stocked jukebox and monthly meat raffles. The decor is plain, but the wood-burning stove and friendly staff help to create a warm atmosphere. For those who knew the pub before its conversion to five real ales, a pleasant surprise awaits you.

Salehurst

Salehurst Halt
Church Lane, TN32 5PH (by church)
closed Mon; 12-11 (01580) 880620
salehursthalt.co.uk
Harveys Sussex Best Bitter; guest beers
A welcoming, traditional family-run pub which is popular with walking groups and locals. It is adjacent to a disused railway halt on a former hop-picking line. Guest beers are often from local microbreweries and up to three ciders are served in the summer. Good-quality, locally-sourced food features strongly. The large garden has views over the beautiful Rother Valley. Inside there is a selection of board games, and live music is performed every second Sunday of the month.
Q

Seaford

Wellington Hotel
33 Steyne Road, BN25 1HT
12-11 (midnight Fri & Sat) (01323) 899517
thewellington-hotel.com
Beer range varies
A Greene King house close to the seafront with three bars, one with sports TV and games, one comfortably furnished and featuring ornate ceiling mouldings, and the third which also acts as a restaurant. Ten real ales are served from Greene King and other local and national breweries, with a board in the main bar giving detailed descriptions of the beers that are on. Various food deals feature on weekday evenings as well as daily specials. Three-star B&B accommodation is available. Q

South Chailey

Horns Lodge
South Street, BN8 4BD (on A275)
11.30-2.30 (not Tue), 5.30-11; 11.30-11 Sat; 12-10.30 Sun
(01273) 400422 hornslodge.com
Harveys Sussex Best Bitter; guest beers
On the A275 north of Lewes, this pub is popular with locals and visitors alike. Guest beers come from breweries anywhere in the country and at least one cider is always available. The pub has been awarded Country Pub of the Year and Cider Pub of the Year by the local CAMRA branch. Various pub games are played including bar billiards and Toad in the Hole. Food is served daily except Tuesdays. Annual beer, cider and sausage festivals are held. P (121)

Uckfield

Alma 𝕃

65 Framfield Road, TN22 5AJ (on B2102)
11-11 (11.30 Fri & Sat); 12-10.30 Sun ☎ (01825) 762232
alma-arms.co.uk
Harveys Sussex XX Mild Ale, Sussex Best Bitter; guest beer Ⓗ
A Harveys pub about five minutes' walk from the town centre, station and buses. The large main bar has smaller seating areas and there are independent meeting/function rooms. A separate part houses a number of traditional games including Toad in the Hole. Thai food is served on Saturday evenings and on Sundays a selection of roasts is on offer 12-4pm (no food Mon or Tue). XX Mild is available all year round and the cider is Thatchers Heritage. Q❀◑♿⇌♣●P🚌(318)🐾

Wilmington

Giant's Rest 𝕃

The Street, BN26 5SQ (off A27)
12.30-3, 6-10; 11.30-11 Sat; 12-10 Sun ☎ (01323) 870207
giantsrest.co.uk
Long Man Brewery Best Bitter; guest beer Ⓗ
This Victorian hostelry is located within a short walk of the Long Man, a chalk figure now reinforced by concrete blocks, cut into the side of Windover Hill. The pub is a free house and currently serves three beers from its local brewery. It was originally a village cottage, converted in the 1920s and now a busy establishment noted for its food. A popular pub with locals, walkers and tourists alike. Q❀🛏◑●P🚌(126)🐾📶

Wivelsfield Green

Cock Inn 𝕃

North Common Road, RH17 7RH (900yds E of B2112)
12-11 (10.30 Sun) ☎ (01444) 471668
cockinn-wivelsfield.co.uk
Harveys Sussex Best Bitter; guest beers Ⓗ
A two-bar pub on the eastern edge of the village, popular with walkers, cyclists and locals alike. A more frequent bus service is available at the other end of the village on routes 40/40X. Two guest ales supplement the Harveys beer. In summer real cider is also available. There is a large garden/seating area to the front and a smaller outdoor area to the side. The recently refurbished lounge bar has a timber-panelled bar counter. Look out for the cow bell. Q🐴❀◑♣P🚌(166,824)

SUSSEX (WEST)

Alfold Bars

Sir Roger Tichborne 𝕃

Loxwood Road, RH14 0QS (2 miles S of A281)
11-midnight; 12-11 Sun ☎ (01403) 751873
thetichborne.co.uk
Young's Bitter; guest beers Ⓗ
This beautiful old country pub is stunning. It oozes charm, from the low ceilings, slate floors and inglenook fireplaces to its breathtaking views onto the South Downs. Helpful staff serve beers from local breweries on five handpumps, including the tasty 4.3% ABV Firebird Tich unique to the pub. Cider is on gravity. The atmosphere is friendly and the landlord is passionate about local ales and locally-sourced food. Q🐴❀◑♿●P🚌(63)🐾📶

Angmering

Spotted Cow

1 The High Street, BN16 4AW (E from village centre along B2225; where B2225 turns S, bear E along unclassified road for about 100yds)
11-3, 5.30-11; 11-11 Fri & Sat; 12-10.30 Sun
☎ (01903) 783919 spottedcowangmering.co.uk
Greene King Abbot; Timothy Taylor Landlord; guest beers Ⓗ
A delightful pub at the end of a lane away from the centre of Angmering and looking out over the South Downs. The large 18th-century building has a fascinating history, which includes serving for generations as a meeting place for smugglers, commemorated in the form of a Spinning Jenny hanging from the bar ceiling. The restaurant serves a wide variety of locally-sourced food. The pub is handily situated for visitors to Worthing Rugby Club. Q🐴❀◑⛺P🚌(9)🐾

Bognor Regis

Hatters

2-10 Queensway, PO21 1QT (at W end of High St opp Iceland)
8am-midnight (1am Fri & Sat) ☎ (01243) 840206
Courage Directors; Greene King Abbot; Ruddles Best Bitter; guest beers Ⓗ
This large town-centre Wetherspoon was formerly a Sainsbury's store, part of a concrete 1960s retail development at one end of the main shopping street. The usual Wetherspoon beer range of regulars and changing guests, mainly from local micros, can be found, plus good-value food all day. There is an outside drinking and smokers' area in a small patio garden at the rear. Public parking is available in Queensway car park or the adjacent multi-storey. 🐴❀◑♿⇌●🚌📶

Bolney

Bolney Stage 𝕃

London Road, RH17 5RL
11-11 (10.30 Sun) ☎ (01444) 881200
bolneystage.hcpr.co.uk
Beer range varies Ⓗ
The pub dates back to the 16th century, and is on the old A23 coaching route. It has a large bar area with three separate dining areas and a beer garden. The rooms feature huge inglenook fireplaces, ancient flagstones, open-timbered ceilings and crooked beams, together with comfy old furniture. The blackboard by the bar gives tasting notes on the four regularly changing beers, mainly from Sussex breweries.
🐴❀◑♿P🚌(89,273)🐾📶

Burgess Hill

Quench Bar & Kitchen 𝕃

2-4 Church Road, RH15 9AE
9am-11 (12.30am Thu & Fri; 1am Sat); 10-10.30 Sun
☎ (01444) 253332 quenchbar.co.uk
Harveys Sussex Best Bitter; guest beers Ⓗ
This conversion of a former corner shop, although a bar, has a definite pub-like atmosphere. In addition to the three guest beers – mostly, but not exclusively, from Sussex independent brewers and often featuring Dark Star seasonals or beers from Downlands – there is an eclectic selection of imported bottled beers. A limited number of tables

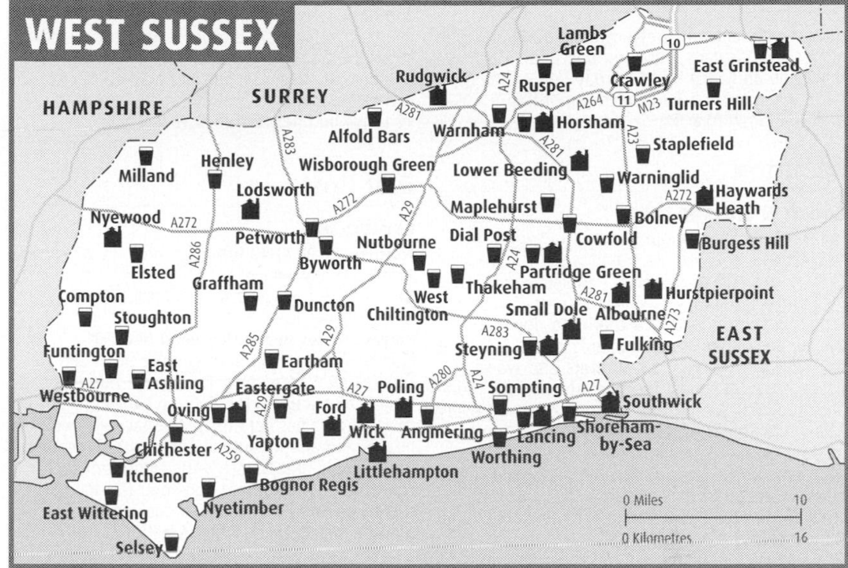

and chairs are provided outside. Sunday lunches are served from noon, breakfast from 9am. All buses that serve Burgess Hill pass the door.
◑≠🚌 ᯤ

Byworth

Black Horse Inn 🄻

GU28 0HL (leave Petworth eastwards on A283 for about 1 mile, then turn left into The Street)
⏲ 12-11 ☎ (01798) 342424 🌐 theblackhorseatbyworth.com
Flowerpots Bitter; Fuller's London Pride; guest beers 🄷
Friendly and welcoming old-style village pub, dating from the 16th century. The cosy bar area has a large open log fire, wood floors throughout, wattle and daub walls and large beams. It serves good real ales, and guest beers are LocAle. Excellent locally-sourced seasonal food is available, with secluded dining areas overlooking the large steeply terraced garden at the back, which has stunning views over a beautiful valley. An iron staircase leads to an upstairs function room. Regular darts and quiz nights take place.
Q❀◑♣P🚌(1)🐾

Chichester

Bell Inn

3 Broyle Road, PO19 6AT (on A286 just N of Northgate)
⏲ 11.30-2.30, 5-midnight; 12-3, 7-11 Sun
☎ (01243) 783388 🌐 thebellinnchichester.com
Beer range varies 🄷
Cosy and comfortable city local with a traditional ambience enhanced by exposed brickwork, wood panelling and beams. A rear suntrap garden has a covered smoking area heated by a coal stove in winter. The pub tends to become busiest after 10pm, when the nearby Festival Theatre empties out. The beer selection usually includes two from the Enterprise range and one from a local micro, complemented by an extensive food menu chalked up on the blackboard (no food Sun eve).
Q❀◑♣P🚌(60)🐾ᯤ

Bull 🄻

4 Market Road, PO19 1JW (at Eastgate opp market)
⏲ 11.30 (11 Wed)-11; 11.30-midnight Fri; 11-midnight Sat; 12-10.30 Sun ☎ (01243) 792432
Beer range varies 🄷
Situated opposite the market car park at Eastgate, this airy and friendly city local sells up to seven beers, mostly from local microbreweries. The famous O'Hagan's sausages are always available in bar meals or to take away. The landlord's sense of humour is evident in the forever growing display of potato mashers on one of the high beams. A meeting room is available and there is a covered garden and smoking area behind the pub.
Q❀◑≠🚌🐾ᯤ

Chichester Inn 🄻

38 West Street, PO19 1RP (at Westgate roundabout)
⏲ 12-11.30 (midnight Fri & Sat); closed 3-5.30 Mon-Thu Jan-Apr; 12-10.30 (7 Jan-Apr) Sun ☎ (01243) 783185
🌐 chichesterinn.co.uk
Dark Star Hophead; Harveys Sussex Best Bitter; guest beers 🄷
In this pleasant two-bar pub the front lounge has a log fire with comfy chairs around it plus a mixture of seating and tables. A larger public bar to the rear features live music on Friday, Saturday and Wednesday evenings. Outside, you can enjoy your beer in the attractive walled garden or in the heated and covered smoking area. Two guest beers from local micros are stocked. Food includes Sunday lunches. Two B&B rooms are available.
❀🛏◑≠♣P🚌🐾ᯤ

Eastgate

4 The Hornet, PO19 7JG (500yds E of Market Cross)
⏲ 12 (11 Wed)-11; 10-12.30am Sat; 12-11.30 Sun
☎ (01243) 774877 🌐 theeastgate.co.uk
Fuller's London Pride; Gale's Seafarers Ale, HSB; guest beers 🄷
Welcoming town establishment with an open-plan bar and an area for diners. Good-quality traditional pub meals are served daily. There is a heated patio garden to the rear, which is the venue for a beer festival in July. The pub attracts locals,

holidaymakers and shoppers from the nearby market with its warm welcome and traditional pub games such as darts, cribbage and pool. Music is turned up on Friday and Saturday late evenings, while live bands perform once a month.
❀◐◑♣🚌(51,700)🐾📶

Compton

Coach & Horses 🄻

The Square, PO18 9HA (on B2146)
closed Mon; 12-3, 6-11; 12-3, 7-10.30 Sun
☎ (023) 9263 1228 coachandhorsescompton.com
Beer range varies Ⓗ
Sixteenth-century pub in a charming downland village, popular with walkers and cyclists. The front bar, with internal window shutters and wooden floors, has a traditional feel. An adventurous menu of high-quality locally-sourced food is served every day, while at least three, and up to five, beers are on offer from independent breweries. The occasional house beer, Coach & Horses, is a dry-hopped version of Ballards Best Bitter. Outside seats and limited public parking are available in the square. Q❀◐◑⛺♣🍎🚆🚌(54)🐾

Cowfold

Hare & Hounds 🄻

Henfield Road, RH13 8DR
12-3, 5-11; 12-11 Sat & Sun ☎ (01403) 865354
hareandhoundscowfold.co.uk
Dark Star Hophead; Harveys Sussex Best Bitter; Sharp's Doom Bar Ⓗ
Convivial village local where you can be sure of a warm welcome. It has a large stone-flagged bar area, a separate carpeted dining space, and an adjacent area for families and bar games. The log fire is the main focal point in winter. This free house frequently offers Dark Star beers along with other local ales, milds and dark beers. There are regular jazz, comedy and quiz nights, and an annual beer festival is held in July. Food is served during all sessions. Q👶❀◐◑♿♣P🚌🐾📶

Crawley

Brewery Shades 🄻

85 High Street, RH10 1BA
10-11.30 (1am Fri & Sat); 10-10.30 Sun ☎ (01293) 514105
Greene King Abbot; Morland Old Speckled Hen; guest beers Ⓗ
Arguably the oldest building in Crawley High Street, dating back to the 1400s and complete with two active ghosts. The pub is wet-sales led. The licensee has a true passion for the trade, demonstrated by the inspired range of guest ales and ciders which are always in excellent condition. The haunted upstairs room is now available for meetings. Good food is served during the day and evening – check the specials board or try the mixed grill. ❀◐◑⇌🍎🚌📶

Swan 🄻

1 Horsham Road, West Green, RH11 7AY
12-11 (1am Fri & Sat) ☎ (01293) 527447
theswanpubcrawley.co.uk
Fuller's London Pride; Sharp's Doom Bar; guest beers Ⓗ
Superb example of a bustling street-corner local, situated conveniently close to the town centre and with good transport links. This is a drinkers' pub and no food is served, but you are free to bring in your own. The changing beers frequently include strong brews. Live music is hosted regularly and two or three beer festivals are held each year. The pub supports CAMRA's Mild Day in May, with up to 12 milds on offer. ❀🛏♿⇌♣🍎🚌(23)

Dial Post

Crown Inn 🄻

Worthing Road, RH13 8NH (signed off the A24 approx 10 miles N of Worthing)
12-3, 6-11; 12-3 Sun ☎ (01403) 710902
floatingcrown.co.uk
Harveys Sussex Best Bitter; guest beers Ⓗ
Charming family-run 16th-century pub keen to support local breweries. The superb home-cooked food is also sourced locally wherever possible. The cosy bar area has kept its traditional style, with oak beams and a woodburner. There is a choice of three dining areas, each with a different feel: conservatory, restaurant and snug (no food is served on Sun eve). This is a dog- and walker-friendly pub. Q👶❀🛏◐◑♿⛺🍎P🚌(23,108)🐾

Duncton

Cricketers 🄻

High Street, GU28 0LB (on A285 about 5 miles S of Petworth)
11-11 (10.30 Sun) ☎ (01798) 342473
thecricketersduncton.co.uk
Beer range varies Ⓗ
Friendly, family-run, 16th-century coaching inn, said to be haunted, in the heart of the West Sussex countryside and close to Goodwood racecourse. It has wooden beams throughout, with a solid oak wooden bar and a large inglenook fireplace. Good real ales and Thatchers draught cider are served. The excellent menu offers locally-sourced, seasonal, home-cooked food, including fish and game whenever possible. A separate function room can be hired and there is a large secluded garden to the rear. Families are welcome.
Q👶❀◐◑P🚌(99)🐾

INDEPENDENT BREWERIES

Adur Steyning
Anchor Springs Wick
Arundel Ford
Ballard's Nyewood
Baseline Small Dole
Bedlam Albourne
Dark Star Partridge Green
Downlands Small Dole
Firebird Rudgwick (NEW)
Goldmark Poling
Gribble Oving
Hammerpot Poling
Hepworth Horsham
High Weald East Grinstead
Hurst Hurstpierpoint
King Beer Horsham
Kissingate Lower Beeding
Langham Lodsworth
Lister's Littlehampton (NEW)
Naked Beer Lancing (NEW)
Pin-Up Southwick
Top-Notch Haywards Heath (NEW)
Weltons Horsham

Eartham

George 𝕃

PO18 0LT

⏲ closed Mon; 11.30-11; 12-7 Sun ☎ (01243) 814340

🌐 thegeorgeeartham.com

Beer range varies Ⓗ

A spacious old village pub whose landlord's passion for the best of English, and especially Sussex, extends to the whole of the drinks and food menu. Two house bitters, and typically both guest beers, are LocAles. Usually, one is a hoppy golden ale while the other is porter, old ale or mild. The food menu features locally-sourced ingredients. Popular with walkers and cyclists, the pub holds a garden beer festival each April featuring 21 West Sussex ales and live music. Q🐴❀◑◗♿P🚌(99)🐾📶

East Ashling

Horse & Groom 𝕃

PO18 9AX (on B2178 in village)

⏲ 12-11 (6 Sun) ☎ (01243) 575339

🌐 thehorseandgroomchichester.co.uk

Burning Sky Plateau; Dark Star Hophead; Hop Back Summer Lightning; Sharp's Doom Bar; Young's Bitter Ⓗ

An inn for over 200 years, set between the downs and the sea, this fine country free house has a compact bar featuring flagstones, settles, half-panelled walls and a fine old range. Sympathetically extended, it remains unspoilt. The beers are meticulously presented and sold at consistently good-value prices. A blackboard reveals the diverse, high-quality menu of home-made dishes, all sourced locally (no food Sun eve). En-suite accommodation is dog-friendly, some in a converted 17th-century oak beamed flint barn. Q❀🛏◑◗♿⛺♣P🗑🚌(54)🐾📶

East Grinstead

Ounce & Ivy Bush 𝕃

Little King Street, RH19 3DJ

⏲ 8am-11.30 (10 Sun) ☎ (01342) 335130

Adnams Broadside; Greene King Abbot; Ruddles Best Bitter; guest beers Ⓗ

This Wetherspoon conversion of a former bowling alley is conveniently situated in the town centre. Its name recalls one of the town's former inns of the same name, and the coat of arms (which featured an ounce – a wild cat) of the Sackville family, who were leading local landowners. This spacious and family-friendly pub serves food all day and is LocAle accredited, showcasing a local brewery each month. Q🐴◑◗♿⇌🚌📶

East Wittering

Shore 𝕃

Shore Road, PO20 8DZ (50yds from sea)

⏲ 11-11 (10.30 Sun) ☎ (01243) 674454

🌐 theshorepub.co.uk

Dark Star Hophead, American Pale Ale; Palmers Copper Ale, Dorset Gold; Sharp's Cornish Coaster, Doom Bar Ⓗ

Friendly beachside town pub popular with the locals (particularly dog owners) and the many summer visitors. There are two main bars, a children's room and a fair-sized decked area for outside drinking as well as smoking. The good-quality lunchtime menu can be enjoyed either in the bar or restaurant. Evening meals are only available on Thursday (locals' night) and Friday (fish night), when extremely inviting menus are on offer at fair prices. Live music features occasionally. Q🐴❀◑◗♿♣P🚌(52,53)🐾📶

Eastergate

Wilkes' Head 🏆 𝕃

Church Lane, PO20 3UT (off A29 in old village, 350yds S of B2233 roundabout, 1⅓ miles W of Barnham Station) SU943053

⏲ 12-11 ☎ (01243) 543380 🌐 wilkesheadeastergate.co.uk

Adnams Southwold Bitter; guest beers Ⓗ

Small Grade II-listed red-brick pub, built in 1803 and named after 18th-century radical John Wilkes. There is a cosy lounge left of the central bar, to the right a larger room with an inglenook fireplace, flagstones and low beams, and a separate restaurant. At the rear is a permanent marquee with seating, a heated smokers' shelter and a large garden. There are five well-chosen guest beers, and regular beer festivals are held. Local CAMRA Pub of the Year 2014. Q❀◑◗♣●P🚌🐾📶

Elsted

Three Horseshoes

Lower Elsted, GU29 0JY (E end of village)

⏲ 11-2.30, 6-11; 12-3, 7-10.30 Sun ☎ (01730) 825746

Bowman Wallops Wood; Flowerpots Bitter; Young's Bitter; guest beers Ⓖ

Old and cosy rural inn divided into small rooms, including one reserved for dining and one with a blazing log fire in winter. Outside, the large, pleasant garden enjoys superb views of the South Downs. In summer there are five beers, mainly from local micros, and three in winter, all served by gravity from a stillage alongside the bar. Meals are substantial and of high quality. This is a popular and homely pub that you will be reluctant to leave. Q❀◑◗♣P🐾

Fulking

Shepherd & Dog 𝕃

The Street, BN5 9LU

⏲ 11-10.30; 12-8 Sun ☎ (01273) 857382

🌐 shepherdanddogpub.co.uk

Downlands Truleigh Gold, Ruskin's Ram; guest beers Ⓗ

The pub, comprising a large traditionally styled room with low beams, plenty of tables and a patio area, is the brewery tap for the nearby Downlands Brewery and usually stocks three of its ales plus a guest beer. Nestling as it does at the foot of the South Downs, it is particularly popular with walkers, and dogs are made most welcome. It has a large garden, making it a favourite with families, and is known for its good-quality food. Q🐴❀◑◗♿⛺●P🐾📶

Funtington

Fox & Hounds

PO18 9LL (on B2146)

⏲ 10 (9am Sat)-11; 9am-10.30 Sun ☎ (01243) 575246

🌐 foxandhoundsfuntington.co.uk

Dark Star Hophead; Timothy Taylor Landlord; guest beers Ⓗ

This welcome new entrant to the Guide is now free of tie and has re-emerged in its old guise as a

country village pub serving good food and concentrating on local, regional and microbrewery beers. Customer recommendation is sought when choosing guest beers. There are two real fires providing warmth in winter and a warm welcome from the enthusiastic landlord all year round. Beer festivals are held twice a year.
Q P (54)

Graffham

Foresters Arms

The Street, GU28 0QA (3 miles W of A285) SU930177
closed Mon winter; 12-3, 6-11; 12-3, 6-10.30 (closed eve winter) Sun (01798) 867202 forestersgraffham.co.uk
Dark Star Hophead; Harveys Sussex Best Bitter; guest beers H
Fine Grade II-listed pub originally built in 1609. An attractive garden and an impressive log fire in winter help make this a popular venue, as does its proximity to fine walking country. Up to two guest beers are sourced from local independent breweries. There are three en-suite rooms in the adjoining converted stables. The 99 bus runs two and a half miles away but will divert if booked ahead. An extensive food menu is available in the restaurant (booking recommended).
Q P (99)

Henley

Duke of Cumberland

GU27 3HQ (off A286, 3 miles N of Midhurst) SU894258
11-11; 12-10.30 Sun (01428) 652280
dukeofcumberland.com
Harveys Sussex Best Bitter; Langham Hip Hop, Best; guest beer G
Stunning 15th-century inn nestling against the hillside in 3½ acres of terraced gardens with extensive views. The rustic front bar has scrubbed-top tables and benches, plus a log fire at both ends, while to the rear is a dining extension that blends in perfectly with the original pub and offers much-needed additional space. Outside is a smokers' shelter with its own woodburner. A former local CAMRA Pub of the Year, this is a rural gem. It may close on Sunday evenings in winter.
Q P (70)

Horsham

Beer Essentials

30a East Street, RH12 1HL
closed Sun & Mon; 10-6 (7 Fri & Sat) (01403) 218890
thebeeressentials.co.uk
Arundel Sussex Gold; guest beers G
A mecca for the connoisseur, this shop opened in Horsham following the demise of the King & Barnes Brewery in 2000. Up to seven cask ales are served on gravity to take away in two, four and eight pint containers, along with JB Medium cider and occasional perry. The shop also stocks over 150 bottled beers from near and far. A popular beer festival is organised each September in the nearby Drill Hall. Every town should have a shop like this!

Malt Shovel

15 Springfield Road, RH12 2PG
11-11 (1am Fri & Sat); 12-midnight Sun (01403) 252302
Robinsons Trooper; Timothy Taylor Landlord; guest beers H
Situated near to the town centre, the pub has a pleasant, warm and bright interior. It usually offers up to six real ales and one cider on draught. Ales come from the Enterprise list, but with one guest. The venue features live music on most Friday and Saturday nights and hosts regular open mic evenings. P

Itchenor

Ship

The Street, PO20 7AH (100yds from waterfront)
11-11 (10.30 Sun) (01243) 512284
theshipinnitchenor.co.uk
Arundel Castle; Ballard's Best Bitter; King Beer Horsham Best Bitter; Langham Hip Hop H**; guest beer** G
Popular pub in an attractive village on the shore of picturesque Chichester harbour. A cosy bar decorated with yachting memorabilia adds to the pub's character and is complemented by a pleasant patio, a suntrap in summer. The separate restaurant area offers a wide range of traditional meals, including locally landed fish. Accommodation includes a self-contained three-bed cottage and separate B&B rooms. Buses 52 and 53 stop on the B2179 1½ miles away, but the occasional 150 stops opposite the pub.
Q P

Lambs Green

Lamb

RH12 4RG (2 miles N of A264)
11.30-3, 5.30-11; 11.30-11 Fri; 9.30am-11 Sat; 9.30am-10.30 Sun (01293) 871336
Dark Star Hophead; guest beers H
Lovely old pub with a mixture of flagstones and wood floors interspersed with wrought-iron work, low-beamed ceilings and exposed brick walls. Furnishings include high-backed settles and soft sofas, and a real fire adds warmth in winter. This welcoming pub with a friendly landlord and staff is committed to LocAle – all beers come from within 25 miles, and customers elect the guest beer. Lunchtime and evening food is served daily using quality home-made and locally-sourced food, and breakfast is available at weekends.
Q P (52)

Lancing

Crabtree Inn

140 Crabtree Lane, BN15 9NQ (head N from Lancing station and turn left at Crabtree parade of shops; pub is about ½ mile further on)
11-11 (12.30am Fri & Sat) (01903) 755514
Fuller's London Pride; guest beers H
Traditional Kemptown Brewery house which offers a wide-ranging selection of real ales. The large public bar has darts, pool and table football; the recently refurbished lounge bar offers a quieter, more relaxed experience, and can be booked for functions. Live music is featured monthly. The garden is spacious, child and dog friendly, and includes a covered smoking area. The menu specialises in home-made pies and there is a Sunday carvery. Recent investment has modernised the pub without sacrificing its traditional ambience. P

Maplehurst

White Horse L
Park Lane, RH13 6LL
12-2.30 (not Mon), 6-11 (11.30 Fri & Sat); 12-3, 7.30-11 Sun ☎ (01403) 891208
Harveys Sussex Best Bitter; Weltons Pride 'n' Joy; guest beers H
Under the same ownership for 32 years, this splendid and welcoming country pub has featured in the Guide 29 times. Popular with locals, cyclists and walkers, the cosy interior, with its unusually large wooden bar, boasts real fires and many interesting artefacts and bric-a-brac. While good honest pub fare is provided, the emphasis is on beer and conversation. Many local beers feature, including a good selection of dark ales. Local JB cider is also stocked. Q P

Milland

Black Fox L
Portsmouth Road, GU30 7JJ (on B2070) SU829291
12-2 (not Mon), 6-11; 12-3 Sun ☎ (01428) 723218
theblackfoxinn.co.uk
Bowman Swift One; Young's Special; guest beers H
On the B2070 and the West Sussex Border Path, this comfortable free house has an air of spaciousness about its L-shaped bar, high ceilings and brick arches. Food from an extensive menu can be enjoyed in the restaurant overlooking the patio and the enclosed garden with children's playhouse. There is also a skittle alley for hire, four B&B rooms and a covered smoking area to the rear. Up to two guest beers usually come from Hants and Sussex micros. Q P

Nutbourne

Rising Sun
The Street, RH20 2HE (turn left off A283 just before bridge over River Chilt)
11-11 ☎ (01798) 812191 therisingsunnutbourne.co.uk
Beer range varies H
This attractive stone building is a true village pub which has been in the same family for many years and is the centre of village activity, also serving as the local polling station and used for WI meetings. The bare wooden boards of the bar contrast with the smart restaurant. It features a changing beer range with at least two local brews always on offer. The garden has a listed outdoor privy.
Q P (1)

Nyetimber

Inglenook
255 Pagham Road, PO21 3QB
11-11 (midnight Fri & Sat) ☎ (01243) 262495
the-inglenook.com
Fuller's London Pride; Young's Special; guest beers H
A 16th-century Grade II-listed hotel, restaurant and free house, which has been owned and run by the Honour family and their experienced staff for over 35 years. The hotel is open to non-residents, and has facilities for conferences, functions and wedding receptions. There is always a selection of excellent real ales available, which can be enjoyed in the bar areas, restaurant and front or back gardens. Guest beers, which change weekly, tend to be on the strong side. P (60)

Oving

Gribble Inn L
Gribble Lane, PO20 2BP (W end of village)
11 (12 Sun)-11 ☎ (01243) 786893 gribbleinn.co.uk
Gribble Ale, Fuzzy Duck, Reg's Tipple, Plucking Pheasant, Pig's Ear H
Once home to a Miss Gribble, this attractive thatched cottage has been a traditional village inn for over 30 years. The Gribble Brewery is on site and the pub also serves as the village shop. A wide range of regular Gribble beers, complemented by its seasonal brews, is always on offer. Ever cosy, with log fires in winter, the pub serves good home-made food in the bar/restaurant. In summer a large attractive garden offers occasional weekend barbecues, and the skittle alley is available for functions. Q P (85,85A)

Partridge Green

Partridge L
Church Road, RH13 8JS (jct of High St and Church Rd)
11-11; 12-10.30 Sun ☎ (01403) 710391
Dark Star Hophead, Partridge Best Bitter; guest beers H
The Dark Star brewery tap, this former railway hotel is next to the popular Downs Link Trail, which follows the old Guildford to Shoreham line. The spacious wood-panelled family lounge leads out to a pleasant patio and garden with playground, while the smaller front bar has a display of local photographs and offers darts and pool. The menu features locally-sourced produce (no food Sun, or Mon eves). Daily buses run from Brighton and Horsham. P (17,108)

Petworth

Angel Inn L
Angel Street, GU28 0BG (three mins' walk W from centre of town)
10.30-11; 11.30-10.30 Sun ☎ (01798) 344445
angelinnpetworth.co.uk
Langham Best; guest beers H
Steps lead from the main road to this handsome part timber-framed building in a small market town, possibly dating back to the 14th century, which has been lovingly restored to reveal its former glory. A large single bar with various nooks and crannies gives a welcoming, homely feel, and a large sunny courtyard is popular in the summer months. Six en-suite bedrooms make the pub an excellent base for exploring Petworth House, Cowdray Park and the surrounding countryside.
Q (1,99)

Stonemasons L
North Street, GU28 9NL (just N of village on A283)
12-midnight (10.30 winter); 12-10.30 Sun
☎ (01798) 342510 thestonemasonsinn.co.uk
Sharp's Doom Bar H**; guest beers** H/G
A 17th-century pub on the north side of Petworth, sympathetically extended, featuring original beams and an inglenook. It has a restaurant serving fine local produce, and five pumps showcasing largely local ales under the care of its new landlords. On the edge of the South Downs National Park and close to Goodwood, Arundel and Chichester, this family-friendly establishment makes a pleasant, homely diversion from the rush and bustle of modern life for the drinker or the tourist. Q P (1,99)

Rusper

Royal Oak

Friday Street, RH12 4QA (on Langhurstwood Rd off A264 N of Horsham)
12-2.30, 5-9; 12-9 Sat; 12-7 Sun ☎ (01293) 871393
theroyaloakrusper.webs.com
Surrey Hills Ranmore; guest beers H
This traditional country pub is an absolute gem, with seven handpumps always offering at least one dark beer. Cheddar Valley cider is usually available and others seasonally. Food is freshly cooked from locally-sourced ingredients and available every lunchtime – book ahead for evenings and weekends. The emphasis here is on good banter and conversation, enhanced by the lack of music and slot machines. The pub supports local community charities with regular fundraising activities. Q P

Selsey

Seal

6 Hillfield Road, PO20 0JX (on B2145, 600yds from sea)
10.30-midnight; 12-11 Sun ☎ (01243) 602461
the-seal.com
Dark Star Hophead; Greene King Abbot; Young's Bitter; guest beers H
A real community hub, family-run for 43 years, and recently refurbished throughout. It has a spacious public bar with a pool table at one end and a comfortable lounge with an extended restaurant featuring quality home-cooked food, including locally-caught fish (booking advised). The guest beers are mostly from local micros. Acoustic live music often features on Sunday. Umbrellas on the patio cater for smokers. Camping is available nearby at West Sands caravan park. The 13 en-suite B&B rooms are popular. Q P (51)

Shoreham-by-Sea

Duke of Wellington

368 Brighton Road, BN43 6RE (on A259)
12-11 (1am Fri & Sat) ☎ (01273) 441297
dukeofwellingtonbrewhouse.co.uk
Dark Star Hophead; guest beers H
Formerly a Dark Star pub, the Welly is now a free house serving six beers and one real cider on handpump, together with a selection of continental bottled beers. Of interest are the stained glass windows of the old Kemptown Brewery, which date from 1929 when the pub was extended. The pub hosts regular live music together with ukulele, sea shanty and quiz nights. There are plans for an on-site brewhouse operated by the new owner.

Piston Broke

88 High Street, BN43 5DB
11-11; 12-10.30 Sun ☎ (01273) 441622
Box Steam Golden Bolt; Harveys Sussex Best Bitter; Long Man American Pale Ale H**; guest beers** H/G
Facing the Ropetackle roundabout, this is a rare outlet for gravity dispensed beers in a town awash with good pubs. The brown and cream decor has a wine-bar feel, and if there is a theme it is motor racing, but not oppressively so. Indeed, there is a decent wine list, and simple bar food can come, like at Wetherspoon's, with a pint at a bargain price. Previously called the Lazy Toad, the new owners downsized from a larger pub across the river.

Sompting

Gardeners Arms

West Street, BN15 0AR (in village, on B2222, just S of A27 and 200yds from Marquis of Granby)
11-11 (midnight Fri & Sat); 12-11 Sun ☎ (01903) 233666
Harveys Sussex Best Bitter; Sharp's Doom Bar; guest beers H
Vibrant, friendly, 19th-century free house in the original village main street. A unique feature is the 1962 British Rail passenger carriage built onto the side of the pub. The name of the pub remains unchanged from 1858, when market gardens were the main local employer. Five handpumps feature the regulars, plus a mild and a guest ale. Tuesday is quiz night. Quality home-cooked food is served daily – the amazing Sunday roasts are renowned. Q P (7,16)

Staplefield

Jolly Tanners

Handcross Road, RH17 6EF
11-3, 5.30-11; 11-11 Fri-Sun ☎ (01444) 400335
jollytanners.com
Fuller's London Pride; Harveys Sussex Best Bitter; guest beers H
Independently run free house on the north corner of the cricket green, which takes great pride in providing a wide selection of real ale and cider, and tasty food made using local ingredients where possible. This is a friendly place and well worth a visit. A roaring fire welcomes you in winter and open mic evenings are hosted on Tuesdays. Beer festivals are held regularly during the year with an excellent range of ale to be enjoyed. CAMRA branch Pub of the Year 2013.
Q P (271)

Steyning

Norfolk Arms Hotel

13 Church Street, BN44 3YB (to E of village centre, two mins' walk N from White Horse roundabout)
12-2, 6-11 (midnight Fri & Sat); 12-2, 7-10.30 Sun
☎ (01903) 812215
Adnams Broadside; Harveys Sussex Best Bitter; guest beers H
A traditional beer drinkers' pub set back off the main street in Steyning, a pleasant market town north of Worthing. An alehouse since at least 1880, the building is over 350 years old and original beams are evident, as are real open fires. The pub is home to cricket and rugby teams, and offers a changing selection of (mostly local) ales and a friendly ambience. A welcome throwback to a style of English pub that has become a rare and precious commodity. Q

Stoughton

Hare & Hounds

PO18 9JQ (off B2146, through Walderton) SU803115
11-3, 6-11; 11-11 Fri & Sat; 12-10.30 Sun
☎ (02392) 631433 hareandhoundspub.co.uk
Dark Star Hophead; Flack Manor Flack's Double Drop; Harveys Sussex Best Bitter; Otter Amber; guest beer H
An ideal base for walking, this is a traditional country pub in a beautiful setting. A large dining room serves fresh local produce while the public bar, with racing car pictures and its own open fire,

is the locals' choice. Three open fires, stone-flagged floors and simple furniture create a wonderful atmosphere. Outside is a paved drinking area and a garden at the back. The 54 bus stops on the B2146, a mile away. The cider is Westons First Quality. Q❀◑♿⛺♣●P📶

Thakeham

White Lion Inn 𝕃

The Street, RH20 3EP (N of village)
11-11; 12-10.30 Sun ☎ (01798) 813141
whitelion-thakeham.co.uk
Beer range varies Ⓗ
An ivy-clad 15th-century pub with stone steps leading up from the street. Previously a coaching house, there are three separate bar areas, with a restaurant serving top-quality food. The open fire is used to smoke locally bought hams. Four real ales are served including a changing guest. Hosting monthly music and quiz nights, the White Lion is a perfect example of an English country pub with a lovely nostalgic ambience. Q❀◑P🚌🐾

Turners Hill

Crown

East Street, RH10 4PT
11-11; 11.30-10.30 Sun ☎ (01342) 715218
thecrownturnershill.co.uk
Harveys Sussex Best Bitter; St Austell Tribute; guest beers Ⓗ
A tastefully decorated 16th-century farmhouse, together with a 17th-century barn with Jacobean oak beams, make up this pub which converted to an inn during 1706. It holds a St George's Day celebration, a beer festival to coincide with the London to Brighton cycle ride, and a 30-ale festival in October. Leather settees surround a large open fire in the bar area, with another open fire in the restaurant, which serves traditional English dishes.
Q🐴❀◑♿●P🚌🐾📶

Red Lion 𝕃

Lion Lane, RH10 4NU
11-3, 5-11; 11-11 Sat & Sun ☎ (01342) 715416
redlionturnershill.com
Harveys Sussex XX Mild Ale, IPA, Sussex Best Bitter, Armada Ale; guest beer Ⓗ
Still very much a village local, offering a warm welcome to all who enter, it's a split-level pub with a large inglenook fireplace. It has recently had a tasteful extension to the dining area. Good-value, high-quality lunchtime food is served. Children and dogs are welcome and there is a fortnightly quiz. North Sussex CAMRA held its first meeting here in 1974 and a beer festival was staged to celebrate its 40th anniversary in March 2014.
Q🐴❀◖♿♣●P🚌(82,84)🐾📶

Warnham

Sussex Oak 𝕃

2 Church Street, RH12 3QW
11-11 (10.30 Sun) ☎ (01403) 265028
thesussexoak.co.uk
Fuller's London Pride; Harveys Sussex Best Bitter; Timothy Taylor Landlord; guest beers Ⓗ
Popular village pub with a separate dining area. Six handpumps dispense three regular beers and up to three guests. LocAle is actively supported. Two handpumps offer real cider and perry in the summer months. An extensive menu of high-quality, reasonably priced food is available. There is a large garden and dogs are welcome. Quiz nights are hosted fortnightly and jazz nights on the last Thursday of the month, while beer festivals are held on bank holidays. Q🐴❀◑♿♣●P🚌🐾📶

Warninglid

Half Moon 𝕃

The Street, RH17 5TR
11.30-3, 5.30-11; 11.30-11 Sat; 12-5 Sun
☎ (01444) 461227 thehalfmoonwarninglid.co.uk
Harveys Sussex Best Bitter; Morland Old Speckled Hen; guest beer Ⓗ
Large village pub dating back in parts to the 16th century. The entrance leads straight into the bar with oak beams, wooden floors and an open fire. To the right are two further rooms with fires and a large smartly furnished restaurant featuring a covered and illuminated well that's flush with the floor. The cellar was upgraded in 2014 with auto-tilt stillage. Regular events take place, including a cheesecake charity event each June.
Q🐴❀◑P🚌(89)🐾📶

West Chiltington

Five Bells 𝕃

Smock Alley, RH20 2QX (S of W Chiltington)
12-3, 6-11; 12-3, 7-10.30 Sun ☎ (01798) 812143
thefivebellsinn.com
Palmers Copper Ale; guest beers Ⓗ
Bill and Joan have been welcoming drinkers, diners, walkers and dog lovers to this charming family-run village free house since 1983. It has a cheery and friendly spacious bar with a big, open, copper-hooded fireplace, and large conservatory dining areas. Excellent beers, often LocAles and almost always including a mild, are on handpump, alongside a draught Kentish cider. Fantastic locally-sourced home-cooked food is available every day (no food Sun eve). The accommodation is dog-friendly. Q🐴❀🛏◑♣●P🚌(1,74)🐾

Westbourne

Stag's Head 𝕃

The Square, PO10 8UE (on B2147, in village centre)
12-11; 12-10.30 Sun ☎ (01243) 372393
stagsheadwestbourne.co.uk
Greene King IPA; Harveys Sussex Best Bitter; Irving Admiral Stout; Oakleaf Hole Hearted Ⓗ
An early 19th-century pub built on the site of the village market and subsequently extended into a neighbouring shop. The newer area is mainly used for dining (no food Sun eves and Mon Sept-April), leaving the remainder of the L-shaped bar with its real fire for drinkers. There is an outside bar in the yard which comes into its own during beer festivals, when the list can feature ales from far and wide. Occasional cider festivals are also held.
❀◑♣🚆🚌

Wisborough Green

Three Crowns

Billingshurst Road, RH14 0DX
11-11; 12-10.30 Sun ☎ (01403) 700239
thethreecrownsinn.com
Bedlam Hoppy Golden Ale; Hogs Back TEA; guest beer Ⓗ

A warm welcome awaits at this cosy village pub next to the cricket green. A fireplace with a woodburner creates an inviting atmosphere. The pub serves a selection of hand-picked local ales including Three Crowns Crowning Glory Ale by Downland, and home-cooked food made from local produce within a 20-mile radius. Regular music is hosted on a Tuesday night and a seven-course food and beer matching evening was introduced in 2013. Well worth a visit.
Q ♿ ♣ P

Worthing

Castle Tavern

1 Newlands Road, BN11 1JR (just E of roundabout on A24 at southern foot of railway bridge)
5-11 (midnight Fri); 6-midnight Sat; closed Sun
(01903) 601000
Dark Star Hophead; Harveys Sussex Best Bitter; guest beers H
A short walk from Worthing town centre or station, this imposing corner pub is now a free house. The L-shaped bar has games at one end, while at the other end is a comfortable candlelit area in which to relax. A changing range of six beers along with a menu of proper pub food are available. On Saturday evenings the bar offers a growing selection of chilli products for the unsuspecting to sample, watched over by the knowledgeable landlord and locals. Q

Parsonage Bar & Restaurant

10 High Street, Tarring, BN14 7NN
12-11 (7 Mon; midnight Fri & Sat); 12-7 Sun
(01903) 820140 theparsonage.co.uk
Dark Star Hophead; Harveys Sussex Best Bitter; guest beers H
A welcome addition to Worthing's real ale scene, this 15th-century establishment was originally three cottages, saved from demolition in 1927 when it was bought by a local resident for £900. Once the Museum of Sussex Folklore, this Grade II-listed building has been a restaurant for 26 years, serving up food of the highest quality and now offering beers of similar distinction. At least two guest LocAles are always available, served by gravity from an outside cold store.
Q (West) (7,16)

Selden Arms

41 Lyndhurst Road, BN11 2DB
11-11 (11.30 Fri); 12-11.30 Sat; 12-10.30 Sun
Kent Beyond the Pale; guest beers H
A regular in the Guide, this 19th-century free house has a small, single bar with six handpumps, at least one of which dispenses a dark ale. Belgian and German draught and bottled beers are also on sale. A beer festival is held at the end of January and there is occasional live music. The pub supports a darts team. Photographs of old Worthing hostelries adorn the walls, as well as a chalkboard displaying a list of forthcoming ales. No food is served on Sunday. Q ♿ (106)

Swan Inn

79 High Street, BN11 1DN
11-11 (midnight Fri & Sat); 12-11 Sun (01903) 232923
Harveys Sussex Best Bitter; guest beers H
A town-centre pub with a village feel to it. A long, attractive U-shaped bar dominates the single room, and various regimental badges adorn the frontage immediately above. A large collection of copper and brasses hangs from the beamed ceiling. Bar billiards, darts and cribbage are all played here. Music is a regular attraction, with blues every Wednesday, an open mic session on Sunday, and DJs at the weekend. The final Tuesday of each month features a folk music singaround.
Q

Wandering Goose

18A Marine Parade, BN11 3PT (150yds E of Worthing pier)
12-midnight (01903) 203851
thewanderinggoose.co.uk
Dark Star Hophead; guest beers H
Worthing's newest pub gives the impression of having been a fixture for years, with a clever mix of traditional ambience and modern management and cellaring. Nathan, ex-landlord of the Geese in Brighton, emphasises quality above all in his beer and food, and welcomes the discerning pubgoer. With a seafront location and tables outside, this is a pub for the local drinker, the tourist and those in search of interesting beers to enjoy in a calm and conversational atmosphere.

Yapton

Maypole

Maypole Lane, BN18 0DP (off B2132 1 mile N of village; pedestrian access across railway from Lake Lane, 1¼ miles E of Barnham station) SU978042
11.30-11 (midnight Fri & Sat); 12-11 Sun
(01243) 551417
Dark Star Hophead; guest beers H
Small flint-built free house hidden away from the village centre, down a narrow lane that ends in a pedestrian crossing over the railway. The cosy lounge boasts two open fires and a row of eight handpumps, dispensing up to four guest beers and real cider. It has a traditional public bar and a skittle alley/function room. Bar snacks are served lunchtimes. There is a new outside seating area.
Q ♿ ♣ P (66,700)

Choosing pubs

CAMRA members and branches choose the pubs listed in the Good Beer Guide. There is no payment for entry, and pubs are inspected on a regular basis by personal visits; publicans are not sent a questionnaire once a year, as is the case with some pub guides. CAMRA branches monitor all the pubs in their areas, and the choice of pubs for the guide is often the result of democratic vote at branch meetings. However, recommendations from readers are welcomed and will be passed on to the relevant branch: write to Good Beer Guide, CAMRA, 230 Hatfield Road, St Albans, Hertfordshire, AL1 4LW; or send an email to: **gbgeditor@camra.org.uk**

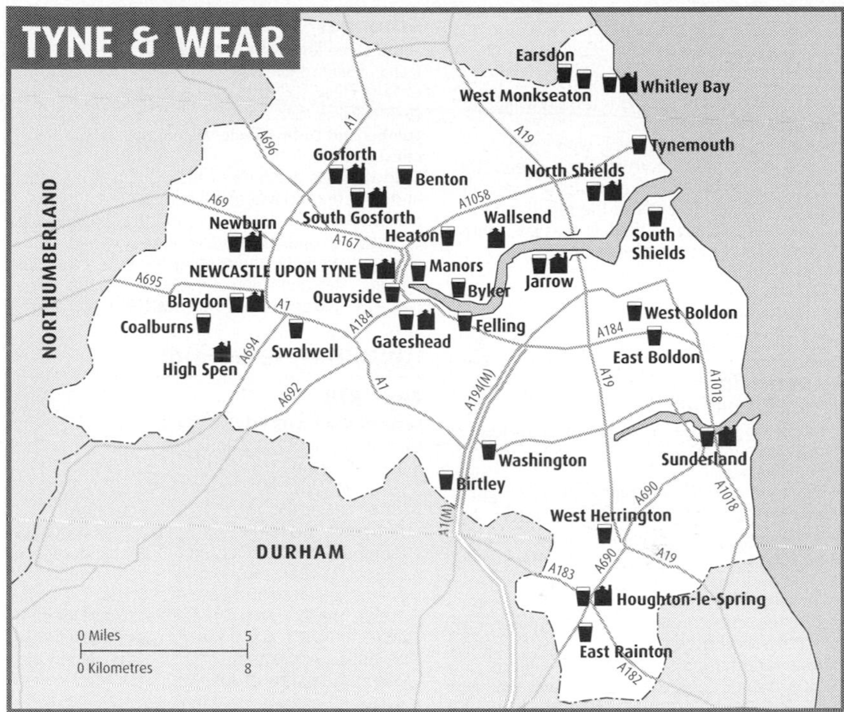

Birtley

Barley Mow Inn 🄻

Durham Road, DH3 2AG (jct of Durham Rd and Vigo Lane)

11-midnight; 10-11.30 Sun ☎ (0191) 410 4504

thebarleymowinn.co.uk

Harviestoun Bitter & Twisted; Rudgate Viking; guest beers Ⓗ

A 1930s roadhouse-style pub on the southern edge of the town, with up to seven guest beers, often from northern microbreweries, alongside two regulars. There is a public bar, split-level lounge and a separate dining area. The seasoned tenants run a weekly quiz and the pub is home to darts and dominoes teams. Regular and varied live music takes place plus two music and beer-themed festivals each year, in February and August.

Blaydon

Black Bull

Bridge Street, NE21 4JJ

2-11; 12-midnight Fri & Sat; 12-11 Sun ☎ (0191) 414 2846

blackbull-blaydon.co.uk

Black Sheep Best Bitter; Caledonian Deuchars IPA; guest beer Ⓗ

Two-roomed pub with traditional values —'no pool table, no jukebox, no bandit' boasts the proud landlord. Entertainment includes two folk nights weekly, buskers' night, quiz night and live bands once a month. Barbecues are held in the superb rear beer garden during the summer months. The pub enjoys excellent views of River Tyne and Tyne Valley. Blaydon has recently benefited from a much improved rail service and there are now 10 trains per day in each direction calling at Blaydon Station. Q

Coalburns

Fox & Hounds

NE40 4JN

4.30-9 Mon; 4-11; 11.30-10.30 Sun ☎ (0191) 413 2549

coalies.co.uk

Hadrian Border Tyneside Blonde; Harviestoun Bitter & Twisted; guest beers Ⓗ

Welcoming, traditional pub with friendly management and bar staff on the outskirts of Greenside. Dating from 1795, the walls and ceilings are decorated with memorabilia from the local industries of centuries ago, and there is a log-burning stove. The pub has been running an annual leek show since 1979 and also hosts a folk club on Sunday, quiz night on Wednesday and live music on Saturday. There is a superb beer garden at the rear. Q

Earsdon

Beehive 🄻

Hartley Lane, NE25 0SZ

12-11 (10.30 Sun) ☎ (0191) 252 9352

beehiveearsdon.co.uk

Hadrian Border Tyneside Blonde; Mordue Workie Ticket; guest beers Ⓗ

This 18th-century Grade II-listed building has been an inn since 1896. The superb three-room country pub is now back to its best and the new owners take great pride in the quality of the real ale. A range of blonde, pale and dark beers is usually available. Excellent food is served, made with ingredients sourced from local suppliers. The car park has now been extended and there is a mini goat area, children's secret garden, a picnic site and extra seating.

East Boldon

Grey Horse
Front Street, NE36 0SJ
12-11; 11-midnight Fri & Sat ☎ (0191) 519 1796
Beer range varies [H]
Distinctive mock-Tudor building with separate lounge and bar areas. There are large-screen TVs in the bar for football and other sports. A folk club meets on the first Tuesday of the month and the Boldon History Society on the last Tuesday. There is a separate first-floor function room.
Q❀◑P🚌(9,30)

East Rainton

Old Ships Inn
Durham Road, DH5 9QT
12-11 Fri-Sun & summer; 4-11 (closed Mon) winter
☎ (0191) 584 0944
Beer range varies [H]
Traditional, family-friendly pub with a welcoming atmosphere, popular with locals and visitors alike. The large open-plan L-shaped room has a nautical theme with walls covered in marine charts and many framed photographs of Sunderland shipbuilding. There are no gaming machines or jukebox, just unobtrusive background music. The pub hosts a local cricket team and book club and is a regular stop for local walkers. Quiz night is Tuesday. Freshly cooked, traditional pub food is served until 9pm (4pm Sun). ◑♣P🚌(20,20a)

Felling

Wheatsheaf [L]
26 Carlisle Street, NE10 0HQ
5 (3 Thu; 12 Fri & Sat)-11; 12-10.30 Sun
☎ (0191) 597 2981 🌐 wheatsheaf-felling.co.uk
Big Lamp Bitter, Prince Bishop Ale; guest beer [H]
Welcoming street-corner pub owned by Big Lamp Brewery, popular with a loyal band of regulars who often travel quite a distance to drink here. The pub features some original details, mismatched furniture and, when needed, real coal fires, and outdoor toilets have original Victorian urinals. There is a fortnightly Monday night quiz, traditional folk music featuring keen local musicians on Tuesday night and Wednesday is dominoes night. An original CAMRA clock keeps time behind the bar.
⇌(Heworth)♣🚌🐾

Gateshead

Central ★ [L]
Half Moon Lane, NE8 2AN
10-11 (10.30 Sun) ☎ (0191) 478 2543
🌐 theheadofsteam.co.uk/gateshead
Anarchy Blonde Star; guest beers [H]
Mid-19th-century Grade II-listed wedge-shaped building, identified by CAMRA as having a historic pub interior of national importance. It has a revamped public bar, two function rooms, and there is a terrace on the roof of this four-storey venue. However, the main attraction is the quite magnificently restored Buffet (closed when quiet; ask to view). It is fitted out circa 1900 with a carved U-shaped counter and bar back, plasterwork frieze and panelling. Live music is a regular feature.
◑♿♣🚌🐾

Schooner
South Shore Road, NE8 3AF (vehicular access only from E end of South Shore Rd)
12-11 (10.30 Sun) ☎ (0191) 447 7404
🌐 theschooner.co.uk
Cumberland Corby Blonde; Maxim Double Maxim; guest beers [H]
Following the purchase of the Schooner, husband and wife team David and Julie have breathed new life into the pub. There are currently six handpulls for cask ales and one for cask cider – the beer range changes regularly, showcasing the best local and national ales and ciders. Regular live music features at weekends. ◑♿P🚌(93,94)

Houghton-le-Spring

Copt Hill [L]
Seaham Road, DH5 8LU (on B1404)
11 (11.30 Sun)-11.30 ☎ (0191) 584 4485
🌐 thecopthill.co.uk
Beer range varies [H]
With a spectacular vista over the Houghton countryside, this former Vaux pub has six handpulls offering a changing selection of ales, half local and half from a wider area. Excellent food including breakfast is served all day from an extensive menu – booking for the recently refurbished restaurant is advisable, as it can get busy at evenings and weekends. A variety of party nights is held in the function room. Q❀◑ΔP🚌(20)

Jarrow

Robin Hood [L]
Primrose Hill, NE32 5UB (on old road parallel to A194)
12-11 (11.30 Fri & Sat) ☎ (0191) 428 5454
🌐 jarrowbrewery.co.uk
Jarrow Bitter, Rivet Catcher, McConnells Irish Stout, Westoe IPA; guest beer [H]
Originally a coaching inn dating back to 1824, the Robin Hood is tastefully decorated and retains its old charm. A previous CAMRA local Pub of the Year, and the original home of the Jarrow Brewery, it is adorned with awards for both the brewery and the pub. It has three function rooms, live entertainment every Friday and Sunday, and a good range of award-winning Jarrow ales constantly on offer plus one guest. QΔP🐾

INDEPENDENT BREWERIES
Big Lamp Newburn
Cullercoats Wallsend
Darwin Sunderland
Delavals Whitley Bay (suspended production)
Firebrick Blaydon
George N Porter Whitley Bay (brewing suspended)
Hadrian Border Newburn
Jarrow Jarrow
Leazes Lane Newcastle upon Tyne (NEW)
Maxim Houghton-le-Spring
Mordue North Shields
Northern FC Newcastle: Gosforth
Olde Potting Shed High Spen (NEW)
Ouseburn Valley Newcastle: South Gosforth
Out There Newcastle upon Tyne
Rail Ale Gateshead
Tavernale Newcastle upon Tyne (NEW)
Temptation Houghton-le-Spring
Three Kings North Shields
Tyne Bank Newcastle upon Tyne

Newburn

Keelman

Grange Road, NE15 8NL
11-11; 12-10.30 Sun ☎ (0191) 267 1689
keelmanslodge.co.uk
Big Lamp Sunny Daze, Bitter, Summerhill Stout, Prince Bishop Ale; guest beer H
This pub is the brewery tap for the Big Lamp Brewery, set in a tastefully converted Grade II-listed former pumping station. A conservatory restaurant serves excellent food and quality accommodation is provided in the adjacent Keelman's Lodge and Salmon Cottage. Attractively situated by Tyne Riverside Country Park, the Coast-to-Coast cycleway and Hadrian's Wall National Trail. P (22)

Newcastle: Benton

Benton Ale House

Front Street, NE7 7XE
11-11 (11.30 Wed); 11-midnight Fri & Sat; 12-11 Sun
☎ (0191) 266 1512
Banks's Bitter; Jennings Cumberland Ale; Ringwood Boondoggle, Fortyniner; guest beers H
Traditional, well-appointed pub with a horseshoe bar, run by a friendly manager and staff. Large bay windows give a light and airy feel to the lounge at the front, and the public bar is to the rear. Reasonably priced good-quality food is served – the food menu proudly announces 'fresh meat in home-made dishes and Sunday lunches supplied by Lemington butchers' (booking essential for Sunday lunches). Quiz night is Wednesday. Interesting abstract art is displayed in the back bar. Families welcome. P (1,353)

Newcastle: Byker

Cluny

36 Lime Street, NE1 2PQ
12-11 (10.30 Sun) ☎ (0191) 230 4474
theheadofsteam.co.uk/newcastle-outlets-the-cluny
Beer range varies H
Large, former industrial building converted into a pub, art gallery and live music venue. The pub runs frequent themed beer festivals and always has a good selection of British and foreign draught and bottled products available. The art gallery shows work of all kinds ranging from final degree shows to local independent established artists in all media, with the displays changing monthly. Live music sessions are held most evenings and include a wide range of British, European and American musicians. Q

Cumberland Arms

James Place Street, NE6 1LD (off Byker Bank)
3-11 (midnight Fri); 12-midnight Sat; 12-11 Sun
☎ (0191) 265 1725 thecumberlandarms.co.uk
Beer range varies H
Three-storey venue rebuilt over 100 years ago and relatively little changed since. It stands in a prominent position overlooking the lower Ouseburn Valley. The pub is home to dance and music groups and its house beer, Rapper from Wylam Brewery, is named after the traditional rapper sword dance. A multiple winner of CAMRA regional Cider Pub of the Year awards, it generally offers up to six ciders or perries. Winter and summer beer festivals are held each year. Closing time may vary. Q P

Free Trade Inn

St Lawrence Road, NE6 1AP
11-11 (midnight Fri & Sat); 12-10.30 Sun
☎ (0191) 265 5764
Mordue IPA; guest beers H
This unique former S&N pub was CAMRA Tyneside Pub of the Year in 2013. It has wonderful views of the bridges over the Tyne, and the Newcastle and Gateshead quaysides. A range of up to nine interesting beers from far and wide, as well as two ciders, is available on the bar, with cellar runs willingly offered. Service is with a smile, friendly and knowledgeable. Tasty sandwiches are supplied by a long-established local delicatessen. The jukebox is classic and free. There is an excellent beer garden across the road.
Q (Q2,106)

Newcastle: City Centre

Bacchus

42-48 High Bridge, NE1 6BX
11.30-midnight; 12-11 Sun ☎ (0191) 261 1008
thebacchusnewcastle.co.uk
Beer range varies H
Local CAMRA Pub of the Year four years running, this smart, comfortable city-centre pub boasts nine handpumps offering a wide range of rapidly changing guest beers, with one handpump dedicated to cider and another to beer from Orkney's Highland Brewing Company. A seasonal house beer is brewed by Yorkshire Dales brewery, and a large range of draught and bottled foreign beers is available. Photographs and posters on the walls show the industries in which this region used to lead the world. (Central)

Bodega

125 Westgate Road, NE1 4AG
11-11 (midnight Fri & Sat); 12-10.30 Sun
☎ (0191) 221 1552 thebodeganewcastle.co.uk
Big Lamp Prince Bishop Ale; Durham Magus; guest beers H
Two fine stained-glass domes are the architectural highlights of the pub, which stands next to the Tyne Theatre and is popular with football and music fans. TVs show sporting events and the pub can be busy on match days. The interior offers a number of standing and seating areas with separate booths for more intimate drinking. Several old brewery mirrors adorn the walls. A good selection of foreign bottled and draught beers is available.
(Central)

Bridge Hotel

Castle Square, NE1 1RQ
11.30-11 (midnight Fri & Sat); 12-10.30 Sun
☎ (0191) 232 6400 bridgehotelnewcastle.co.uk
Black Sheep Best Bitter; Caledonian Deuchars IPA; guest beers H
This large Fitzgerald pub is situated next to Stephenson's spectacular High Level Bridge; the rear windows and the patio have views of the city walls, River Tyne and Gateshead Quays. The main bar area, adorned with many stained-glass windows, is divided into a number of seating areas with a raised section at the rear. Guest beers come from far and wide. Among the live music events held in the upstairs function room is what is claimed to be the oldest folk club in the country.
(Central)

Duke of Wellington

High Bridge, NE1 1EN
11-11 (midnight Fri & Sat); 12-11 Sun (0191) 261 4050
thedukeofwelly.co.uk
Beer range varies H
An L-shaped ale house situated in Newcastle's premier real ale street with nine handpulls, two serving cider. Recent tasteful refurbishments have given the pub a modern look, and it can be busy on match days and during racing festivals. Rhythm 'n' Booze every Thursday is a jazz/soul vinyl record DJ night. Vintage classic movies are screened.
(Central)

Hotspur

103 Percy Street, NE1 7RY (opp Haymarket Metro)
11-11 (1am Tue; midnight Fri & Sat); 12-10.30 Sun
(0191) 232 4352
Beer range varies H
Traditional double-fronted city-centre pub opposite Haymarket bus station and Eldon Square, with the universities close by. The Hotspur is a popular pub and especially busy on match days. Quiz night is Monday and Newcastle University Folk Club plays on Tuesday nights. The interior has been refurbished and is much enhanced without losing character. Eight handpulls adorn the bar, six serving guest beers and two serving real cider.
(Central)

Lady Grey's

20 Shakespeare Street, NE1 6AQ (opp Theatre Royal)
12-11 (0191) 232 3606 ladygreys.co.uk
Mordue Northumbrian Blonde; guest beers H
Close to the historic Theatre Royal and busy shopping areas, this pub, formerly the Adelphi, is a welcome addition to the city centre real ale scene. Recent refurbishment has added two more handpumps for beer and two for real cider. Beers are mainly from local brewers Mordue, Hadrian & Border, Allendale and Wylam, with guests from all over the country. Food is served all day.
(Central)

Pleased To Meet You

High Bridge, NE1 1EW
11-1am (2am Fri & Sat) (0191) 241 4395
ptmy-newcastle.co.uk
Mordue Five Bridges; guest beers H
Totally refurbished to a high standard and serving a multitude of drinks, this gin and real ale eatery has a busy mixed clientele. Situated on Newcastle's premier real ale street, it offers six handpulls serving a variety of brews, both local and national, with a trend towards the out-of-the-ordinary. The outdoor smoking cabins, installed for Christmas, have been a success and will remain in place throughout the year. (Central)

Trent House

1-2 Leazes Lane, NE1 4QT
12-11 (0191) 261 2154
Beer range varies H
The world-famous Trent House is situated by Leazes Park, Newcastle University and the RVI. Friendly and laid-back, the pub is popular with students. The Trent is home to the best jukebox in town, featuring an eclectic mix of classic rock, jazz and electronica. Board games are available from the bar. The pub has a nightly happy hour 8pm-9pm, with cask ales priced at £2 per pint. Occasional beers are brewed on the premises.
(32,32A)

Newcastle: Gosforth

County

High Street, NE3 1HB
12-11 (10.30 Sun) (0191) 285 6919
Caledonian Deuchars IPA; Fuller's London Pride; Jarrow Rivet Catcher; Wells Bombardier; Wylam Bitter; guest beers H
The large L-shaped bar attracts a variety of visitors, from office workers to students, and can get very busy, especially at weekends. A separate quiet room at the back offers respite from the hustle and bustle of the main bar, and also doubles as a small meeting or function room. Several guest beers are available. P

Gosforth Hotel

High Street, NE3 1HQ
10-11 (midnight Fri); 11-midnight Sat; 11-11 Sun
(0191) 285 6617 gosforthhotelnewcastle.co.uk
Caledonian Deuchars IPA; Fuller's London Pride; Mordue Northumbrian Blonde, Workie Ticket; Timothy Taylor Landlord; guest beers H
On the corner of a busy junction at the top of the High Street, this is a stalwart of the Gosforth pub scene. Popular with a wide clientele, from nearby office workers to locals and students, the pub often gets busy. Three ales are regularly available along with the occasional guest beer. A quieter adjoining bar opens occasionally at busier times and also serves as a function room.

Job Bulman

St Nicholas Avenue, NE3 1AA
8am-11 (0191) 223 6230
Greene King Abbot; Mordue IPA; Ruddles Best Bitter; guest beers H
Popular Wetherspoon pub located just off the High Street, which strives to serve a wide range of real ales at all times. Aside from the two core beers, up to six guests may be available, often from local established breweries or micros. There is a raised area to the right set aside for families and diners.

Queen Victoria

206 High Street, NE3 1HD
12-11 (midnight Fri); 11-midnight Sat (0191) 285 8060
Copper Dragon Golden Pippin; Sharp's Doom Bar; guest beers H
Popular pub located on a busy corner of Gosforth High Street. Part of the Leopard Leisure group, the premises have benefited from major refurbishment. Meals and snacks are reasonably priced and the pub does a decent cheeseboard. Guest ales are sourced from the Punch list and local breweries. Sunday is buskers' night, Wednesday evening folk night and Thursday quiz night.

Newcastle: Heaton

Chillingham

Chillingham Road, NE6 5XN
11-11 (midnight Fri & Sat); 12-11 Sun (0191) 265 3992
thechillinghamnewcastle.co.uk
Black Sheep Best Bitter; Jarrow Rivet Catcher; Mordue Workie Ticket; guest beers H
A large two-roomed pub with contrasting styles – the public bar in traditional dark wood with panelling and a historic mirror recalling the past glories of nearby Wallsend, and the lounge with a contemporary feel, flatscreen sports TVs and

artwork depicting the sights of Newcastle. Appealing to the widest possible customer base, it offers an excellent choice of local microbrewery beers, as well as bottled beer, whisky and wine. ◑⚲♣P🚌(62,63)📶

Newcastle: Manors

New Bridge 🄻

2-4 Argyle Street, NE1 6PF

🕘 11-11 (11.30 Thu); 12-10.30 Sun ☎ (0191) 232 1020

🌐 thenewbridgenewcastle.co.uk

Tyne Bank Monument Bitter; guest beers 🄷

Just east of Newcastle city centre, well-served by buses and the metro, this pub has no regular beers but offers an ever-changing choice from independent brewers. It is very much a locals' venue, but all are made welcome. The building is next to a business park and facing a large new extension to Northumbria University, so attracts a mixed lunchtime and early evening crowd enjoying the beer and home-made food.

◑⇌(Manors)⚲🍎🚌📶

Newcastle: Quayside

Bridge Tavern 🄻

7 Akenside Hill, NE1 3UF

🕘 12-midnight (1am Fri & Sat); 12-11 Sun

☎ (0191) 261 9966 🌐 thebridgetavern.com

Beer range varies 🄷

A trendy Newcastle pub with its own microbrewery – the Bridge Tavern's plant brews a range of beers under the Tavernale name. Food ranging from bar snacks to evening meals to Sunday roasts is prepared on site using locally-sourced seasonal produce. There has been an ale house here for over 200 years – the original building was demolished in 1925 and a new premises built following the construction of the town's most famous landmark, the Tyne Bridge. Children are welcome until 7pm.

🐴❀◑◐♿⇌(Central)⚲🍎🚌(Q1,Q2)🐾📶

Broad Chare 🄻

25 Broad Chare, NE1 3DQ

🕘 11-11 (10 Mon) ☎ (0191) 211 2144

🌐 thebroadchare.co.uk

Beer range varies 🄷

A warm welcome awaits in this cosy bar just off Newcastle's historic, bustling Quayside. Stripped floors and exposed brickwork make this a comfortable, quiet bar to relax in and enjoy a pint. Bar food is served all day and there is a restaurant upstairs if you wish to dine in style. The house beer is The Writer's Block from Wylam.

◑◐⇌(Manors)⚲🍎🚌(Q2)📶

Crown Posada ★ 🄻

33 Side, NE1 3JE

🕘 12 (11 Thu)-11; 11-midnight Fri; 12-midnight Sat; 12-10.30 Sun ☎ (0191) 232 1269 🌐 crownposadanewcastle.co.uk

Beer range varies 🄷

An architecturally fine pub, listed in CAMRA's National Inventory of historic pub interiors. Behind the narrow street frontage with two impressive stained-glass windows lie a small snug, bar counter and a longer seating area. There is an interesting coffered ceiling, as well as local photographs and cartoons of long-gone customers and staff on the walls. Small brewers are enthusiastically supported, with three regular local ales.

Q⇌(Central)⚲🚌(Q1,Q2)📶

Newcastle: South Gosforth

Brandling Villa

Haddricks Mill Road, NE3 1QL

🕘 12-11 (midnight Fri & Sat) ☎ (0191) 284 0490

🌐 brandlingvilla.co.uk

Harviestoun Bitter & Twisted; Timothy Taylor Landlord; guest beers 🄷

Large double-fronted pub with keen, enthusiastic staff. The pub offers a constantly changing selection of 10 beers – available in third-of-a-pint tasting glasses if you cannot make up your mind – plus two ciders on handpump. The imaginative manager organises various well-attended, beer-related events, including brewery takeovers, local sausage and pie festivals, music, cinema and beer festivals. The house beer, Frank & Bird, is from Hadrian Border Brewery and is a special brew, not a rebadge. 🐴❀◑◐♿⚲♣P🐾📶

Millstone

Haddricks Mill Road, NE3 1QL

🕘 12-11 (midnight Fri & Sat) ☎ (0191) 285 3429

Draught Bass; Hadrian Border Tyneside Blonde; guest beers 🄷

Refurbished by a new entrepreneurial pub group, this is a modern, stylish, two-roomed pub with the lounge to the front and a small public bar to the rear. The enthusiastic CAMRA licensee sources beers from local microbreweries as well as offering national favourites. Bass has been the regulars' top choice for many years. The function room upstairs, also recently renovated, hosts CAMRA events.

🐴❀◑◐⚲P

North Shields

Low Lights Tavern 🄻

Brewhouse Bank, NE30 1LL

🕘 10-2.30am ☎ (0191) 257 6038 🌐 lowlightstavern.co.uk

Draught Bass; guest beers 🄷

Believed to have been an ale house for over 400 years, this is possibly the oldest pub in the area. The Grade II-listed tavern is now a free house offering a range of guest ales. Three rooms make up the public area, with the bar in the central room. Monday is buskers' night, Thursday acoustic music, and more live music is hosted over the weekend. A genuine community pub where the locals get involved in many events.

🐴◑◐♿♣🚌(333)🐾📶

South Shields

Alum Ale House

Ferry Street, NE33 1JR

🕘 11-11 (midnight Fri & Sat); 12-11.30 Sun

☎ (0191) 427 7245

Banks's Mild, Bitter; Jennings Cumberland Ale, Cocker Hoop; Marston's Pedigree; Wychwood Hobgoblin; guest beers 🄷

Small, traditional pub situated on the south bank of the River Tyne, next to the ferry landing and close to the marketplace. The open-plan bar, with its eight handpumps, is the venue for a fortnightly buskers' night on alternate Thursdays and a lively Irish music session on the first Sunday of the month. The pub offers traditional bar games such as dominoes, hosts a regular chess club and organises quiz nights. Beers are all from the Marston's stable. 🐴❀⚲♣🍎🥛

Maltings

9 Claypath Lane, NE33 4PG (off Westoe Rd)
12-11.30 (midnight Fri & Sat) (0191) 427 7147
Jarrow Rivet Catcher; guest beers
The Maltings is situated on the first floor of the former Co-op Dairy which became the second home of the Jarrow Brewery in 2008. The full range of Jarrow ales is available but only Rivet Catcher is always on. Thai food is served Tuesday to Saturday and there are quizzes on Wednesday and Sunday. Q P

Stag's Head ★

45 Fowler Street, NE33 1NS
12-11 (midnight Fri-Sun) (0191) 427 2911
Draught Bass; guest beers
Traditional single-room town-centre pub dominated by an attractive alcove back bar. Listed on CAMRA's National Inventory of Historic Pub Interiors, it has retained many original design features including colourful entrance tilework and a wide acid-etched bay window at the front. Three beers are usually available, always including Bass. This popular local can get busy at times. Upstairs is an extra room complete with its own small bar – available to hire for private functions. Karaoke features on Sunday.

Steamboat

Mill Dam, NE33 1EQ (follow signs for Customs House)
12-11 (midnight Thu-Sat); 12-11.30 Sun
(0191) 454 0134
Beer range varies
Under the same management for the past 25 years, the Steamboat has one of the largest selections of cask ales in South Shields. Eight handpumps dispense a range of beers from small and family brewers across the country, and Meet the Brewer events and beer festivals take place throughout the year. The split-level bar is decorated with a nautical theme. The pub is a short walk from the Shields Ferry and Customs House Theatre.

Wouldhave

16 Mile End Road, NE33 1TA
8am-midnight (0191) 427 6014
Greene King Abbot; Ruddles Best Bitter; guest beers
This Wetherspoon pub is in the town opposite the rear entrance to South Shields metro station and close to the main bus stand. The bar is on the ground floor with plenty of seats and tables; there is another area upstairs where children are welcome until 7pm. Six handpumps offer two regular beers and four guest beers or ciders. Wetherspoon's popular beer and cider festivals are held regularly. Reasonably priced food is available all day from breakfast until late. Q

Sunderland

Avenue

Zetland Street, Roker, SR6 0EQ (just off Roker Avenue)
12.30-11.30; 11-midnight Fri & Sat; 11-11 Sun
(0191) 567 7412 theavenuepub.net
Beer range varies
Close to the Stadium of Light and Roker seafront, this is a popular local and home to entertainment such as live music, quiz nights and bingo evenings. With a ground-floor lounge, bar, function room, and a games room with a full-size snooker table upstairs, there are plenty of options for relaxing with one or two of the handpulled real ales. (E1,E6)

Fitzgeralds

12-14 Green Terrace, SR1 3PZ
11-11 (1am Fri & Sat); 12-10.30 Sun (0191) 567 0852
Fyne Ales Jarl; Jarrow Rivet Catcher; Timothy Taylor Boltmaker; guest beers
One of Sunderland's largest ranges of cask beers can be found at this busy city-centre pub run by the real-ale-friendly Sir John Fitzgerald group. There are two separate rooms, with the smaller Chart Room quieter than the main bar. The pub is an enthusiastic supporter of North East microbreweries, with eight guest beers usually on offer. Quizzes are held on Tuesday and Thursday. CAMRA members receive a discount on ale. It was the local CAMRA Pub of the Year in 2013. Q P

Harbour View

Harbour View, Roker, SR6 0NU
10.30-11.30 (midnight Fri & Sat) (0191) 567 3878
Caledonian Deuchars IPA; Timothy Taylor Landlord; guest beers
A modern, open-plan bar with good views of the River Wear and the sea. It offers two regular ales alongside a choice of four guests. Quiet during the week, the pub is livelier at weekends – match days are best avoided if you like a peaceful pint as it can get hectic.

Isis

26 Silksworth Row, SR1 3QJ
12-11 (11.30 Fri & Sat) (0191) 514 7684
Jarrow Rivet Catcher, Red Ellen, Isis; guest beers
Originally dating back to 1885, the pub was tastefully and extensively renovated when reopened by Jarrow Brewery in 2011, after lying dormant for more than two years. A long and narrow wood, chrome and glass bar holds 12 handpulls serving three changing Jarrow beers and six guests, plus two ciders and a perry. There is a long, narrow lounge to the side of the main bar. Pub photographs abound throughout the building, upstairs and downstairs. Local CAMRA branch Pub of the Year for the past two years. P (10,11)

Ivy House

Ashbrooke, SR2 7AW
11-11; 12-10.30 Sun (0191) 567 3399
Beer range varies
Tucked away but close to the bus and metro interchange, the Ivy is well worth seeking out. The music is more 6 Music than Top 20. Five ever-changing guest ales usually include one from a local brewery. An extensive range of bottled Belgian beers is also kept. Home-made pizzas and burgers are prepared in an open kitchen. Quiz night is Wednesday. P

King's Arms

Beach Street, Deptford, SR4 6BU
4.30 (4 Wed & Thu)-11; 12-midnight Fri & Sat; 12-11 Sun
(0191) 567 9804
Timothy Taylor Landlord; guest beers
Established in the Deptford area of Sunderland in 1834, the King's Arms is a traditional pub with an L-shaped bar featuring eight handpulls, one regularly dispensing Timothy Taylor's Landlord and another a real cider. The guest beer range is sourced from

local breweries and beyond. There is a small snug and a marquee outside where live music is hosted. A quiz is held every Sunday and curry night is Thursday. Bar snacks are available.
P(10,11)

Museum Vaults

33 Silksworth Row, SR1 3QJ
12 (3 Tue & Thu; 12 Wed)-11; 12-midnight Fri & Sat; 12-10.30 Sun (0191) 565 9443
Beer range varies H
This former Vaux pub has been managed by the same family for over 40 years. It was the subject of a recent fly-on-the-wall documentary about 'a proper British pub and the people who drink there'. A welcoming community local, its walls and shelves are adorned with Sunderland memorabilia. Three handpulled beers are available, one usually from Maxim Brewery, the others alternating between local and national microbrews. Bottled beers and real ciders are also usually available.
P(10,11)

R Bar

Roker Terrace, Roker, SR6 9ND
11-11 (1am Fri & Sat) (0191) 577 6767
tavistockleisure.com/r-bar.htm
Sonnet 43 Steam Beer, Blonde Beer, Bourbon Milk Stout, India Pale Ale, Brown Ale, American Pale Ale H
The R Bar is part of the Roker Hotel, with fine views of the mouth of the River Wear and seashore. All six of the Sonnet 43 core beers are on offer, served in tall glasses. The decor is a blend of modern and traditional, and there are separate areas for dining with wood-panelled ceilings and comfortable seating. Meal deals are offered Monday to Friday. Disabled access is to the left of the hotel reception.
P

William Jameson

32 Fawcett Street, SR1 1RH
8am-midnight (0191) 514 5016
Greene King Abbot; Ruddles Best Bitter; guest beers H
Sunderland's first Wetherspoon pub is at the heart of the city centre in a former department store under the City Library and Arts Centre and opposite the Winter Gardens. All the usual features associated with the chain can be found is this busy venue. Twelve handpumps offer up to four guest beers to complement the regular range. The pub is a keen supporter of local brewers. Good-value food is served all day. Q

Swalwell

Sun Inn

Market Lane, NE16 3AL (just off roundabout at end of Front St)
11 (12 Sun)-11 (0191) 488 7783
Marston's Pedigree; guest beers H
Situated in the heart of the historic village that spawned many internationally renowned engineers and industrialists, and of course the famous Swalwell cabbage. This truly no-nonsense community pub provides good company for locals and strangers alike. Sword dancers, darts, domino handicaps, a monthly pie competition and Saturday buskers' nights all feature. Bar food and snacks are available and free on Sundays. There is a regular bus service here from Newcastle.

Bread is the staff of life, but beer is life itself. **Traditional**

Tynemouth

Hugo's at the Coast

29 Front Street, NE30 4DZ
11-11 (midnight Fri & Sat); 11-10.30 Sun
(0191) 257 8956 hugostynemouth.co.uk
Beer range varies H
A tasteful conversion of a former restaurant with pleasing décor – the walls are adorned with local photographs of yesteryear, Tynemouth beach and pony rides. Popular with locals and tourists, the weekends are extremely busy. The men's darts team plays on Tuesday night, quiz night is Wednesday and live music features on the last Thursday of the month. A constantly changing range of guest ales usually includes a Three Kings beer. (306)

Tynemouth Lodge Hotel

Tynemouth Road, NE30 4AA
11-11; 12-10.30 Sun (0191) 257 7565
tynemouthlodgehotel.co.uk
Caledonian Deuchars IPA; Draught Bass; Mordue Northumbrian Blonde; guest beer H
This attractive externally tiled 1799 free house, situated next to a former house of correction, has featured in every issue of the Guide since 1983. The comfortable pub has a U-shaped lounge with the bar on one side and a serving hatch on the other, and is noted in the area for the quality of its Draught Bass. A popular stopping-off point for those completing the Coast-to-Coast cycle route.
QP(1,306)

Washington

Courtyard

Biddick Lane, NE38 8AB
11-11 (midnight Fri & Sat); 12-11 Sun (0191) 417 0445
Timothy Taylor Landlord H
Located within the lively arts centre, this light and airy café/bar offers a warm welcome to drinkers and food lovers alike. Eight handpumped beers, one real cider, one perry and a range of bottled Belgian beers are available. An extensive range of food is served throughout the day, with early evening specials. The pub hosts a weekly quiz and buskers' nights. Outdoor seating is within the spacious courtyard. Two popular beer festivals are held annually, on the Easter and August bank holidays. QP

Sir William de Wessyngton

2-3 Victoria Road, Concord, NE37 2SY (opp bus station)
7am-11 (0191) 418 0100
Greene King Abbot; Ruddles Best Bitter; guest beers H
The only establishment in Concord selling cask ale, the pub was converted from a former billiard hall and offers everything you come to expect from a Wetherspoon hostelry including excellent value-for-money beer. Guest ales frequently come from North East microbreweries and the pub hosts regular Meet the Brewer events and brewery visits.
QP

West Boldon

Black Horse

Rectory Bank, NE36 0QQ (off A184)
✪ 11-11 (11.30 Sun) ☎ (0191) 536 1814
Jennings Cumberland Ale; guest beer Ⓗ
An old-fashioned pub with unusual bric-a-brac adorning the walls and candles on the tables. The photographs on display are by the talented chef, and prints are available for sale. The pub has one small L-shaped bar and, with a popular restaurant serving high-quality food, can get busy in the evenings and at weekends. Live music features on Sunday night. **Q◗🂠**

West Herrington

Stables

DH4 4ND (off B1286)
✪ 12-midnight ☎ (0191) 584 9226
Black Sheep Best Bitter; Timothy Taylor Landlord; guest beer Ⓗ
Located just off the main road, at first sight this pub looks like a private dwelling, as there is no pub sign. The small beer garden leads to a converted stable block, with low ceilings, a flagstone floor and welcoming peat fire in winter. The main area is open plan, with a cosy snug behind the bar. Three ales are offered including one changing guest. Quality food is served until 3pm. **♘◗▲🚌**(35)

West Monkseaton

Beacon Hotel

Earsdon Road, NE25 9PT
✪ 11-midnight ☎ (0191) 253 6911
Caledonian Deuchars IPA; guest beers Ⓗ
A superb modern pub set back from the main road, popular with locals. The manager likes to source a wide range of ales and there is a quick turnover. Customers can order a rack of ale with three third-of-a-pints for variety. The cellar has dedicated lines so the ale is served at the right temperature. There are themed food nights Monday to Thursday and chef's specials Friday and Saturday. Quiz nights are Sunday and Wednesday. **Q❀◖◗♿🚉P🚌**(51)

Whitley Bay

Briar Dene 𝕃

71 The Links, NE26 1UE
✪ 11-11; 12-10.30 Sun ☎ (0191) 252 0926
🌐 thebriardenewhitleybay.co.uk
Black Sheep Golden Sheep; Timothy Taylor Landlord; guest beers Ⓗ
This Fitzgerald's pub has a large, attractive lounge with sea views of the links and St Mary's lighthouse, and a more compact rear bar with widescreen TV, pool and darts. The pub is well known for its food, with local fish and chips a speciality. Guest beers change regularly and are well-advertised on chalkboards. Children are welcome in a family area in the lounge. There is seating outside at the front of the pub. Thursday is grill night. **Q♘❀◖◗♿♣●P🚌**(308,309)📶

Rockcliffe Arms

Algernon Place, NE26 2DT
✪ 11-11 (11.15 Fri & Sat) ☎ (0191) 253 1299
🌐 rockcliffearmswhitleybay.co.uk
Beer range varies Ⓗ
Outstanding back-street Fitzgerald pub, a few minutes' walk from the metro station. This one-room establishment has distinct bar and lounge areas with a snug in between. There are four constantly changing guest beers, with tasting notes on notices above the dividing arch. Regular darts and dominoes matches are held in the snug. Well-patronised by locals and real ale drinkers. **❀🚉♣**

Bridge Hotel, Newcastle (Photo: Cat Button)

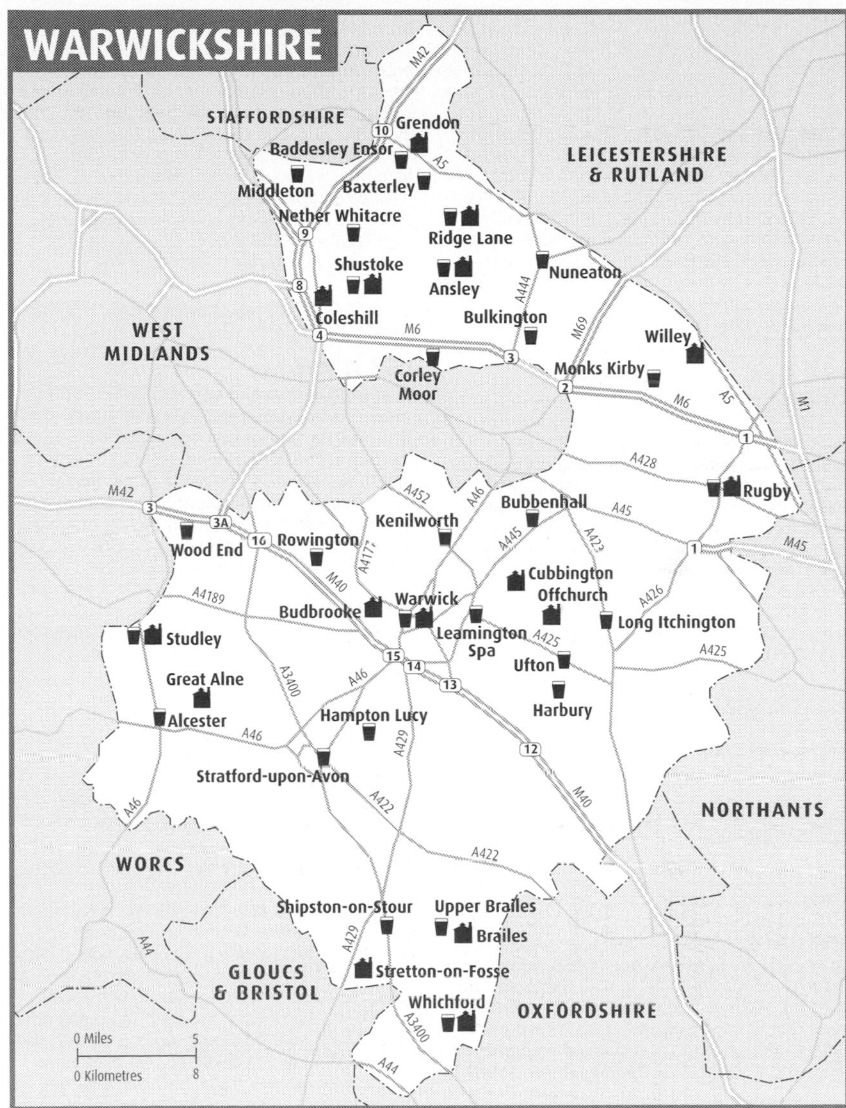

Alcester

Holly Bush 🏆

37 Henley Street, B49 5QX (behind church)
12-11 ☎ (01789) 762482 🌐 thehollybushalcester.co.uk
Black Sheep Best Bitter; guest beers Ⓗ
This traditional 17th-century local is a frequent CAMRA branch Pub of the Year. Restoration has preserved its five rooms and many original features, including a function room and pretty walled garden. Up to four guest ales are available and a beer festival is held in June. Both traditional English and à la carte menus are offered (no food Sun eve). Folk sessions are held monthly and music may strike up at any time. White Hart Morris Men practise here.

Turk's Head

4 High Street, B49 5AD (near church)
12-11 ☎ (01789) 765948 🌐 theturkshead.net
Wye Valley HPA; guest beers Ⓗ
A central location helps make this a popular place. The publican is a cask ale enthusiast, staging beer festivals during the summer months. Four handpumps offer beers sourced as locally as possible and a good range of changing bottled beers is also available, with the most popular making it to draught on occasion. The pub is divided into two rooms with real fires and serves traditional pub food – booking advisable. A quiz and open mic night are regular attractions. Well worth a visit.

Ansley

Lord Nelson Inn 🏆 L

Birmingham Road, CV10 9PQ
12-11 (10.30 Sun) ☎ (024) 7639 2305
🌐 thelordnelsoninnansley.co.uk

Marston's Pedigree; Victory Head Hunter, Band of Brothers, Third Party, Thick as Thieves; guest beers Ⓗ
This old historic building is thought to date back to the late 16th century. Run by the Sperrin family since 1974, it has featured in the Guide for 21 consecutive years. Nine handpulls dispense the family's own Sperrin brews under the name of Victory Brewery plus beers from other local breweries and some not so local. An extensive food menu is available. The pub is nautically themed throughout and has a courtyard garden where beer festivals and barbecues are hosted. ❀◐◑P🚌

Baddesley Ensor

Red Lion

The Common, CV9 2BT SP273983
⌚ 7 (4 Fri)-11; 12-3, 7-11 Sat; 12-3, 7-10.30 Sun
☎ (01827) 718186
Everards Tiger; Marston's Pedigree; guest beers Ⓗ
Busy community local, now the only pub in this former mining village, with comfortable seating and a log fire. Food and music do not feature, just ale and conversation. Four guest ales are served, often from major concerns such as Greene King and Everards, but sometimes from small local breweries. The sparkler is willingly removed on request. Off-road parking is available opposite the pub. Q♣●🚌(766)🐾

Baxterley

Rose Inn

Main Road, CV9 2LE (off B4116, W of Atherstone) SP278969
⌚ 12-3, 6-11; 12-11 Fri-Sun ☎ (01827) 713939
🌐 roseinnbaxterley.com
Draught Bass; St Austell Tribute; Wells Bombardier; guest beer Ⓗ
Classic country pub in a former pit village with a picturesque duck pond setting. The Rose is well known for its excellent food, but remains a community drinkers' pub where real ale outsells lager by a factor of three to one. Guest ales are from the Wells seasonal portfolio. The bar has an open coal fire and welcomes dogs. There are three further intimate areas, a restaurant with a scenic view, and a skittle alley. ❀◐◑♿♣P🚌(766)🐾📶

Bubbenhall

Malt Shovel 🄻

Lower End, CV8 3BW
⌚ 12-11 ☎ (024) 7630 1141
Greene King Abbot; Wells Bombardier; guest beers Ⓗ
Friendly village free house in a 17th-century Grade II-listed building comprising a large L-shaped lounge bar at the front and a small public bar to the rear. Outside is a small front patio and behind the spacious car park lies a large walled garden and adjacent bowling green, with access to the woods in summer. Home-cooked food is available. The two guest beers are usually LocAles, often from Church End or Purity. A LocAle beer festival is held in the autumn. Q❀◐◑♣P🚌(539,580)🐾

Bulkington

Weavers Arms

12 Long Street, CV12 9JZ
⌚ 1 (4 Mon & Tue)-11; 12-11 Sun ☎ (024) 7631 4415
Draught Bass; guest beers Ⓗ
This family-owned two-room traditional village pub was converted from weavers' cottages. It has a wood-panelled games room, log-burning fireplace and a slate floor. Up to two guest ales are available, with beers from Wood Farm regularly featured. An extensive well-kept beer garden hosts barbecues in the summer. Children are welcome, private functions are catered for and the pork pie club, weavers, walkers and hillbilly golf society hold regular meetings here. Often open after 11pm, but no later than 1am. ❀♣🚌

Corley Moor

Bull & Butcher

Common Lane, CV7 8AQ SP279850
⌚ 9am-midnight (1am Fri-Sun) ☎ (01676) 540241
Draught Bass; Greene King IPA, Abbot; guest beer Ⓗ
The Bull & Butcher has featured in the Guide for more than 10 years, run by the same family throughout. This multi-roomed traditional pub has a large conservatory for family dining, offering good-value food all day every day. Cask Marque-accredited regular beers are accompanied by one varying guest. The pub has a cosy feel with real fires in the bar and adjoining snug. The decking area and garden with imaginative play equipment are popular with families in the summer. Q❀◐◑♿P🐾📶

Hampton Lucy

Boar's Head 🄻

Church Street, CV35 8BE
⌚ 12-10 (midnight Fri & Sat) ☎ (01789) 840533
🌐 theboarsheadhamptonlucy.co.uk
Church End Gravediggers Ale; Ringwood Best Bitter; guest beers Ⓗ
A deservedly popular village pub dating back to the 17th century. Situated on a Sustrans route and close to the River Avon, it is popular with cyclists, walkers and visitors to nearby Charlecote Park. At least five ales are served including one LocAle, often from Church Farm Brewery. The menu offers fresh, locally-sourced, home-made food with daily specials. Outside is a sheltered rear garden. An annual themed beer festival is held. A former Warwickshire CAMRA County Champion Pub of the Year. Q❀◐◑♣P🚌📶

INDEPENDENT BREWERIES

Atomic Rugby
Church End Ridge Lane
Church Farm Budbrooke
Griffin Shustoke
Long Itch Offchurch
Merry Miner Grendon
North Cotswold Stretton-on-Fosse
Old Pie Factory Warwick
Patriot Whichford
Purity Great Alne
Red Even Coleshill (NEW)
Slaughterhouse Warwick
Sperrin (Victory Beers) Ansley
Tunnel Ansley
Warwickshire Cubbington
Weatheroak Studley
Whale Brailes
Wood Farm Willey

Harbury

Old New Inn

Farm Sreet, CV33 9LS
4.30 (12 Fri & Sat)-midnight; 12-11 Sun (01926) 614023
Church End Goats Milk; guest beers
This stone pub on the edge of the village was once a farmhouse and a bakery. It has a splendid family garden at the rear. Inside, the two rooms have low ceilings reflecting the age of the building. The beer range changes regularly but Purity and Wye Valley are often featured. Sport is popular here with major fixtures screened on TV. The pub's darts, dominoes and pool teams are well supported. There is plenty of space in the car park. P(65,66)

Kenilworth

Green Man

Warwick Road, CV8 1HS
11.30-midnight (01296) 863061
M&B Brew XI; Purity Pure Ubu; guest beers
Welcoming pub with a central bar and various seating options. Drinkers can sample the different beers by choosing three thirds for the price of a pint, and locals are encouraged to vote weekly for their favourite ales. An increase to the beer range is planned. The food menu changes twice yearly for light and dark nights and there are food-themed evenings. Quiz nights are Sunday and Thursday, and open mic is hosted monthly. CAMRA members receive a discount on beer.
P(11,X17)

Old Bakery

12 High Street, CV8 1LZ (near A429/A452 jct)
5.30 (5 Fri & Sat)-11; 12.30-10.30 Sun (01926) 864111
theoldbakery.eu
Wye Valley Bitter, HPA; guest beer
Located in the picturesque High Street, a short walk from Kenilworth Castle, this two-roomed hostelry offers ales in tip-top condition for the discerning drinker. Rustic décor and friendly service contribute to a convivial ambience. Monday is fish and chips night and a range of unusual nuts and snacks is offered. Accommodation is in 14 en-suite rooms.
QP(11)

Royal Oak

New Street, CV8 2EZ (250yds from A429/A452 jct)
4 (12 Sat)-11; 12-10.30 Sun (01926) 856906
Adnams Southwold Bitter; Sharp's Doom Bar; Timothy Taylor Landlord; guest beer
This traditional Grade II-listed pub is situated close to the crossroads at the heart of old Kenilworth and attracts a diverse clientele. Darts, pool, poker and chess are played, with occasional karaoke nights. A pleasant patio and garden are to the rear. The number 11 Coventry to Leamington bus stops outside the front door. (11)

Virgins & Castle

7 High Street, CV8 1LY (A429/A452 junction)
11-midnight (11 Sun) (01926) 853737
virginsandcastle.co.uk
Everards Beacon Bitter, Sunchaser Blonde, Tiger, Original; guest beer
Located in Kenilworth's picturesque High Street, this multi-roomed, split-level pub has a central L-shaped bar, three snugs and a function room. The pub is the oldest in town, dating from 1563. English and Filipino cuisine is served lunchtimes and evenings (no food Sun eve). A guest cider changes twice weekly. Beer festivals are held at the end of May and October. There is limited parking in front of the pub and a public car park is nearby.
Q(11)

Leamington Spa

Benjamin Satchwell

112/114 The Parade, CV32 4AQ (opp town hall)
7-midnight (1am Fri & Sat) (01926) 883733
Greene King Abbot; Ruddles Best Bitter; guest beers
Town centre Wetherspoon pub converted from two shops, stretching from The Parade right through to Bedford Street at the rear. The pub is named after a former Leamington benefactor who discovered the second of the springs that made the town a popular spa in Regency times. On the walls are panels depicting the history of Leamington and its benefactors. The impressively long bar has 12 handpumps, two for guest ciders.

Jug & Jester

11 Bath Street, CV31 3AF
8am-midnight (1am Fri & Sat) (01926) 331820
Fuller's London Pride; Greene King Abbot; Ruddles Best Bitter; guest beers
Formerly the Theatre Royal, this interesting Wetherspoon establishment has four distinct drinking areas on varying levels reflecting the layout of the original rooms. Pictures depicting the heritage of the town together with an eclectic mix of furniture help to create a comfortable ambience that attracts a mixed clientele of all ages. Look for the unusual collection of stoneware vats on the high shelf in the middle room. Convenient for a beer before a gig at the nearby Assembly.
Q

Talbot Inn

34 Rushmore Street, CV31 1JA
12-11 (midnight Fri & Sat) 07933 855377
Oakham JHB; Wye Valley Butty Bach; guest beers
This Victorian local is situated in a quiet backwater on the south-east side of town near the canal. The gable end of the building features a large, colourful mural. Inside is a spacious bar area and a smaller lounge. Sport is shown on TV at all times but without the volume. An eclectic collection of music plays in the background. A rare sight is the battered honky-tonk piano – it just needs a player. All real ales and ciders are served without sparklers.

Long Itchington

Green Man

Church Road, CV47 9PW
5-11.30 (midnight Fri); 12-midnight Sat; 12-10.30 Sun
(01926) 812208 greenmanlongitchington.co.uk
Black Sheep Best Bitter; Fuller's London Pride; Purity Mad Goose; St Austell Tribute; guest beer
Dating back to the 1700s in parts, this country inn is divided into linked drinking areas, some with open fires. The pub is home to dominoes and crib teams, plus a knitting group. There is a function room available to hire, a quiet garden at the rear, patio tables to the front plus a field at the back which can be used for camping. The Green Man takes part in the annual Long Itchington Beer Festival.
QP(64)

Harvester 🄻

6 Church Road, CV47 9PE (off A423 at village pond, then first left)

12-2.30, 6-11; 12-3, 7-10.30 Sun ☎ (01926) 812698

theharvesterinn.co.uk

Hook Norton Hooky; guest beers 🄷

Simon and the family have presided over this wholly unpretentious pub since 1984, set in a Warwickshire village boasting six hostelries. A regular Guide entry, the Harvester is central to the May bank holiday beer festival supported by the pubs in the village. Two guest ales are usually available and there is now an unfiltered continental beer to complement the dark version. In the separate restaurant, the locally supplied steaks are highly recommended.

(64)

Middleton

Green Man

Church Lane, B78 2AN

11-11 (10.30 Sun) ☎ (0121) 308 6580

thegreenmanmiddleton.co.uk

Purity Pure Ubu; Sharp's Doom Bar; guest beer 🄷

Spacious upmarket village pub with a number of intimate drinking and dining areas radiating from the central bar. Dating from 1866, it has been refurbished to a high standard in old-fashioned style. Soft lighting, open fires and leather chairs enhance the cosy atmosphere, but watch out for the low beams. The pleasant hedged beer terrace is ideal for alfresco dining. There is plenty of car parking.

Monks Kirby

Denbigh Arms

Main Street, CV23 0QX

5.30-11 (midnight Fri); 12-midnight Sat; 12-11 Sun

☎ (01788) 832303

Greene King Abbot; Sharp's Doom Bar; Timothy Taylor Landlord; guest beer 🄷

The landlord is a cask ale enthusiast and tries to include one local ale among the four beers on handpump. This welcoming multi-roomed village pub is renowned for its home-cooked locally-sourced food and monthly themed nights. Sunday lunch is a must. Traditional pub games include table skittles and darts. Outside drinking and a small garden for summer days make this a shining example of how a village pub should be.

Q

Nether Whitacre

Gate Inn

Gate Lane, B46 2DS SP231926

12-11 (10.30 Sun) ☎ (01675) 481292

Banks's Mild, Bitter, Sunbeam; Marston's Pedigree; Ringwood Boondoggle, Fortyniner; guest beer 🄷

Convivial rural ale house with a strong sense of community. Diners tend to favour the conservatory and large lounge while drinkers gravitate to the dog-friendly bar. Both main rooms feature solid fuel stoves. Try before you buy is offered on ales. The guest beer is from the interesting end of Marston's portfolio. To the rear is a large, child-friendly garden, plus a separate beer garden for adults. Local eggs are sold at the bar.

Nuneaton

Crown

10 Bond Street, CV11 4BX

12-11 (midnight Fri & Sat) ☎ (024) 7637 3343

Oakham JHB; guest beers 🄷

Close to the railway and bus stations, this Guide regular boasts ten handpulls dispensing seven real ales and three ciders, a large selection of malt whiskies and a choice of foreign bottled beers. Live music plays on Saturday nights. A function room is available for hire and there is a large garden to the rear. Beer festivals are held in June and December. Food is available Friday to Sunday, including popular Sunday lunches. A discount is offered to CAMRA members.

Felix Holt 🄻

3 Stratford Street, CV11 5BS

8am-midnight (1am Wed & Thu; 2am Fri & Sat)

☎ (024) 7634 7785

Greene King Abbot; Ruddles Best Bitter; Thornbridge Jaipur IPA; guest beers 🄷

Large Wetherspoon outlet situated in the town centre. The pub takes its name from the George Eliot novel and the literary theme is reflected in the decor, with books and pictures illustrating local history. The regular ales are complemented by a further six handpulls providing an interesting range of local and guest ales. The pub offers a discount to CAMRA members. Food is served from 8am to 10pm. Outside is a heated area for smokers.

Q

Rose Inn

Coton Road, CV11 5TW (opp Our Lady of the Angels church)

11.30-11.30 (11 Sun) ☎ 07957 376787

Banks's Mild; Marston's Burton Bitter, Pedigree 🄷

This is the pub where CAMRA held its first AGM in the 1970s. An account of the occasion hangs on the wall, as does a commemorative brass plaque. The L-shaped lounge features a large collection of clocks and the front bar has a pool table and dartboard. At the back is a covered and heated area for smokers. The pub is across the road from Riversley Park and Nuneaton's museum.

(41,48)

Ridge Lane

Church End Brewery Tap 🄻

CV10 0RD (2 miles SW of Atherstone)

closed Mon-Wed; 6 (12 Fri & Sat)-11; 12-10.30 Sun

☎ (01827) 713080 churchendbrewery.co.uk

Church End Poachers Pocket, Gravediggers Ale, What the Fox's Hat, Fallen Angel 🄷

The Brewery Tap is hidden from the road – access is signposted by a board positioned at the entrance. Once inside, the brewery can be seen from the bar area. Eight handpulls serve the bar and vestry – the mild is ever present but other beers change regularly. Various ciders are dispensed direct from the barrel. Children are not allowed inside but there is a large meadow with ample seating. A folk night is held on the third Monday of the month.

Q

Rowington

Rowington Club 🄻

Rowington Green, CV35 7DB (E of B4439, opp village hall) SP1988070150

2 (12 Sat & Sun)-midnight (01564) 782087
Sharp's Doom Bar; Wye Valley HPA; guest beers H
Busy and thriving community club, popular with locals, also open to non-member visitors (free entry for CAMRA members). Frequent entertainment is provided plus seasonal events such as Ladies' Day, August beer and music festival, Marrow Sunday and game fair. Four real ales are on offer at all times plus traditional ciders. Bar snacks are available but no meals. The large beer garden overlooks the village cricket ground and the club is handy for local walking and cycling. Always friendly – well worth seeking out.
P

Rugby

Alexandra Arms L
72 James Street, CV21 2SL (next to John Barford car park)
11.30-11.30 (midnight Fri & Sat); 12-11.30 Sun
(01788) 578660 alexandraarms.co.uk
Abbeydale Absolution; Atomic Strike, Half life; Fuller's London Pride; guest beers H
Bought in 2011 by Atomic Brewery, this town centre pub has a comfortable newly refurbished lounge bar where good-value pub food is served at lunchtime. A popular local, it offers a range of ales including a number from Atomic. The large back bar accommodates a pool table, skittles table and the best jukebox in the county. A summer beer festival is held in the garden and the brewery is at the back in the garden. Seven times CAMRA local Pub of the Year. Q

Merchants Inn L
5-6 Little Church Street, CV21 3AW (behind Marks & Spencer)
12-midnight (1am Fri & Sat) (01788) 571119
merchantsinn.co.uk
Batemans XB; Oakham Bishops Farewell; Purity Mad Goose; guest beers H
Nine real ales are always available in this gem of a pub. Flagstone floors, comfortable seating and an open fire make this a welcoming place to enjoy real ales or a selection of ciders, perries and foreign beers. Excellent home-cooked food is served at lunchtime. The walls are covered in an impressive range of pub and brewery memorabilia. Rugby and cricket feature on the big screen. There are regular beer festivals, theme nights and quizzes.

Raglan Arms
50 Dunchurch Road, CV22 6AD
4-midnight (1am Fri); 12-1am Sat; 12-midnight Sun
(01788) 544441
Greene King Abbot; guest beers H
Opposite Rugby School playing fields, the Raglan is a long time Guide regular and winner of numerous CAMRA awards. The interior comprises a bar, lounge and small snug, popular for meetings, and outside is a covered courtyard with tables. All main sporting fixtures are shown on TV – rugby is ever-popular. Up to 10 beers are on handpump, mostly from Greene King, Fuller's, Oakham and Abbeydale. Real cider and excellent snacks are always available. QP

Rugby Tap L
3 St Matthews Street, CV21 3BY
10-6 (7 Thu-Sat); 11-4 Sun (01788) 576767
rugbytap.co.uk
Beer range varies G
Opened in 2012, this off-licence offers real ale and more. A huge selection of bottled beers both foreign and British is stocked alongside cider, fine wines, spirits and malt whiskies. In addition there are up to six mostly local cask ales to take home. An even larger range is available on the website. Occasional tasting evenings and brewery visits are hosted.

Seven Stars
40 Albert Street, CV21 2SH
12-11 (midnight Fri & Sat); 12-10.30 Sun
(01788) 546611
B&T Shefford Bitter, Golden Fox, Dragon Slayer; Everards Tiger; guest beers H
Quintessential back street local benefiting from a recent substantial refurbishment, with a smart, traditional bar, comfortable lounge, snug and conservatory. The pub has plenty of charm and character, and offers a warm and friendly welcome. It is free from electronic games and music, making conversation a delight. The bar boasts 14 handpumps, with a mild and two ciders always on offer. Live music evenings feature occasionally. A former Rugby, Warwickshire and West Midlands CAMRA Pub of the Year.
Q

Squirrel Inn L
33 Church Street, CV21 3PU
12-11; 4-10.30 Sun (01788) 578527
Marston's Pedigree; guest beers H
A warm welcome awaits all at this fine real ale emporium where an eclectic mixed clientele makes lively bar banter unavoidable. The guest ales change regularly but always include a LocAle, usually from Dow Bridge. Two cask ciders from the Westons range are also available. Home-made jams and chutney are on sale along with bar snacks. Live acoustic music is a highlight on Wednesday and Saturday evenings. Darts is played along with a wide selection of table-top games.
Q

Victoria Inn L
1 Lower Hillmorton Road, CV21 3ST
12 (4 Mon-Wed)-midnight (01788) 544374
downthevic.com
Atomic Strike, Fission, Half life; Hook Norton Hooky; guest beers H
A traditional Victorian real ale pub with friendly, efficient staff owned by Atomic Brewery. Fourteen handpumps offer rapidly changing ales and real cider, and a selection of foreign beers is available. It has a lively, bustling period lounge and a traditional bar which doubles as a games room with darts and pool. The courtyard hosts themed beer festivals twice a year. Sports TV is screened at the weekend. Rugby CAMRA branch Pub of the Year 2013.

Shipston-on-Stour

Black Horse L
Station Road, CV36 4BT (120yds from A3400 via Watery Ln)
12-3, 6-11 Tue & Wed; 12 (6 Mon)-11; 12-10.30 Sun
(01608) 238489 blackhorseshipston.com
Purity Mad Goose; Wye Valley HPA; guest beer H
This ancient stone-built 16th-century hostlelry is the oldest pub and the only thatched building in Shipston. The licence dates back to 1540. With two

rooms, the main bar is cosy and welcoming, with a large inglenook log fireplace. The other bar has a log fire, wooden beams and a dartboard. CAMRA members receive a 10p discount. There is free Wi-Fi, and Thai food is available in any room.
Q

George Hotel
High Street, CV36 4AJ
11-11 (11.30 Fri & Sat) (01608) 661453
georgehotelshipston.com
St Austell Tribute; guest beers H
Centrally located Grade II-listed coaching inn built in 1820, featuring original oak beams, wood flooring and a marble bar. The airy, contemporary interior comprises several rooms including a snug warmed by a large open fire. A function room is available for hire and the hotel can arrange local brewery tours. Food is classic to contemporary. There is a happy hour on Friday evening, with a sporting theme during major events.
P

Shustoke

Griffin Inn
Church Road, B46 2LB (on B4116)
12-2.30, 7-11; 12-10.30 Sun (01675) 481205
griffininnshustoke.co.uk
Hook Norton Old Hooky; Jennings Dark Mild; Marston's Pedigree; RCH Pitchfork; Theakston Old Peculier; guest beers H
Ever-popular family-run Guide regular with its own brewery next door. Five guest ales are offered, usually including a Griffin Inn beer and an ever-changing ale from the Oakham specials range. A real cider is also available. The low-beamed interior is blessedly music and TV-free. Winter is superbly cosy with log-burning stoves roaring away. Children are permitted in the conservatory, beer terrace and meadow-style garden. No food is served Sunday. Dogs are welcomed with free biscuits. QP

Plough
The Green, B46 2AN
12-2.30, 5.30-11; 12-11 Sat; 12-10.30 Sun
(01675) 481557
Draught Bass; guest beers H
This classic country pub is the focal point of the village but also draws much passing trade. Popular for food, its many rooms are often busy with diners. The small bar area has a limited amount of seating. There is a separate room for pool and darts. Three guest ales are usually available, a mix of micro and mainstream. Children will like the feathered and furry pets area to the rear, while the front has a tidy beer terrace. P

Stratford-upon-Avon

Bear at the Swan's Nest Hotel
Swan's Nest Lane, CV37 7LT (S end of Clopton Bridge)
12-11 (midnight Fri & Sat) (01789) 265540
thebearfreehouse.co.uk
Castle Rock Harvest Pale; Hook Norton Old Hooky; North Cotswold Windrush Ale; Wye Valley Butty Bach; guest beers H
Historic pub in a waterside location, five minutes' walk from the town centre. It serves eight real ales with the focus on local and regional brewers such as Wye Valley, Hook Norton and Whale Ale, with seasonal beers available. The Bear has a warm, friendly, welcoming atmosphere, and features a pewter bar and much wood panelling; outside there are picnic tables for riverside drinking. Excellent, home-made bar meals are served and board games and newspapers are available. Local CAMRA branch Pub of the Year 2013.
P(23)

New Bulls Head
9 Bull Street, CV37 6DT
11.30-11; 12-10.30 Sun (01789) 268832
thenewbullshead.co.uk
Timothy Taylor Landlord; guest beers H
A family-run community pub located in the heart of Old Town, a short walk from Holy Trinity and the town centre. Between four and six beers are always on offer in a wide range of ABVs and a broad spectrum of styles. Food is served lunchtimes and evenings – Sunday lunch is a highlight, with vegetarian options. Daily newspapers are available. Outside is a large patio area.

Studley

Victoria Works
33 Redditch Road, B80 7AU
12 (4 Mon)-11 (0121) 445 4411
the-victoria-works.co.uk
Weatheroak St Udley Mild, Light Oak, Weatheroak Ale, Victoria Works, Redwood, Keystone Hops; guest beers H
Formerly the Nags Head, this pub has become Weatheroak brewery's tap house. The horseshoe-shaped interior has separate comfortable seating areas on different levels. The full range of the brewery's beers is always available, with a changing guest ale and a real cider. No food is available but you are welcome to bring your own. Live music evenings and open mic feature now and again and a quiz on the first Sunday of the month.
P

Ufton

White Hart
White Hart Lane, CV33 9PJ SP378622
11.30-3, 6-11; 11.30-5 Sun (01926) 612976
thewhitehartufton.com
Purity Pure Ubu; Slaughterhouse Saddleback Best Bitter; guest beer H
A 16th-century coaching inn featuring oak beams throughout. The free house offers a warm welcome, with historic photos of the pub and the village on display in the hallway. The garden has magnificent views over Warwickshire, and the Malvern Hills can be seen on a clear day. The pub is an ideal starting or finishing point for walkers. Ufton Fields Nature Reserve is nearby. Thatchers Heritage cider is available.
QP(63)

Upper Brailes

Gate at Brailes
OX15 5AX
12-2 (not Mon), 5-10.30; 12-3, 5-10.30 Sat; 12-4, 6-10.30 Sun (01608) 685212 thegateatbrailes.co.uk
Hook Norton Hooky Mild, Hooky, Old Hooky; guest beer H

Historic village pub set in a quiet Cotswolds location with a traditional unspoilt lounge. The publican is a keen CAMRA member and former local brewer, and has been awarded many accolades. Four real ales are kept including one on gravity. The spiritual home of the Brailes Cycling Club and close to many walking routes, it is a place to relax and enjoy old-fashioned banter. Music night is the first Sunday of the month and acoustic mic on the third Thursday. Aunt Sally is played here. The pub is a former CAMRA award winner. Q (50A)

Warwick

Cape of Good Hope

66 Lower Cape, CV34 5DP (off Cape Road)

12-11 (midnight Fri-Sun) (01926) 498138

thecapeofgoodhopepub.com

Church Farm Harry's Heifer; Hook Norton Hooky; Wye Valley Butty Bach; guest beers H

Friendly and characterful pub on the Grand Union Canal with plenty of moorings. It has two drinking areas – a front bar with sports TV and a comfortable quiet lounge – decorated throughout with canal memorabilia. Good food is available every day. Children are welcome and dogs are permitted in the front bar on a lead. Seating is available outside next to the towpath. Take care when entering the bar from the rear corridor when darts is being played. Q P (G1)

Punch Bowl

1 The Butts, CV34 4SS

closed Mon; 12-11 (midnight Fri & Sat); 12-10 Sun

(01926) 403846 punchbowlwarwick.co.uk

Beer range varies H

One of the oldest pubs in the town, this popular free house offers five constantly changing real ales. Good food, including Sunday roasts, is served lunchtimes and early evenings. The large bar area hosts live music on Thursdays and major sporting events are shown on a big screen. The pub is a 15-minute walk from Warwick bus and train stations. P (X17)

Wild Boar

27 Lakin Road, CV34 5BU

12-11.30 (12.30am Fri & Sat); 12-10.30 Sun

(01926) 499968 thewildboarwarwick.co.uk

Everards Tiger; Slaughterhouse Saddleback Best Bitter; guest beers H

A friendly, traditional pub with a separate cosy snug. It is the brewery tap for Slaughterhouse with a microbrewery on site. Hops grown in the patio garden are used in a green hopped brew. Ten handpumps on the bar offer four house beers, five varying guests and a cider. Home-made lunches are served daily, with beer bites and pie meals available all day. A large function room at the rear hosts regular skittles nights and international rugby match screenings. Q (X17)

Whichford

Norman Knight

CV36 5PE (opp village green)

11-11 summer; 7-11 Mon; 12-3, 6-11 winter; 12-midnight Sun (01608) 684621 thenormanknight.co.uk

Hook Norton Hooky, Lion; Patriot Morris, Bulldog; guest beers H

A traditional Cotswolds pub on the village green, serving a wide range of beers from nine handpumps including Patriot ales brewed next door and beers from several local breweries, plus three ciders and perries. Imported beers are also served on draught. The pub has a phenomenal local following and welcomes walkers and their dogs. It hosts regular classic car meets and music nights. Excellent food is cooked by an award-winning French chef. Warwickshire CAMRA County Champion Pub of the Year 2012.

Q P

Wood End

Warwickshire Lad

Broad Lane, B94 5DP

12 (11.30 Sat & Sun)-11 (01564) 742346

thewarwickshirelad.co.uk

St Austell Tribute; guest beers H

Country pub and restaurant offering excellent freshly prepared food featuring local produce. Beers are available from the local Whitworth Brewing Company including The Lad – a beer commissioned by the pub. Children and dogs on leads are welcome, and there is a garden and outside decking area. A log fire blazes in winter months. P

The praise of Yorkshire ale

It warms in winter, in summer opes the pores,
'Twill make a Sovereign Salve 'gainst cuts and sores:
It ripens wit, exhillerates the mind,
Makes friends of foes, and foes of friends full kind;
It's physical for old men, warms their blood,
Its spirits makes the Coward's courage good:
The tatter'd Beggar being warmed with Ale,
Nor rain, hail, frost, nor snow can him assail,
He's a good man with him can then compare,
It makes a Prentise great as the Lord Mayor;
The Labouring man, that toiles all day full sore,
A pot of ale at night, doth him restore,
And makes him all his toil and paines forget,
And for another day's work, he's then fit.

GM Gent, York, 1697

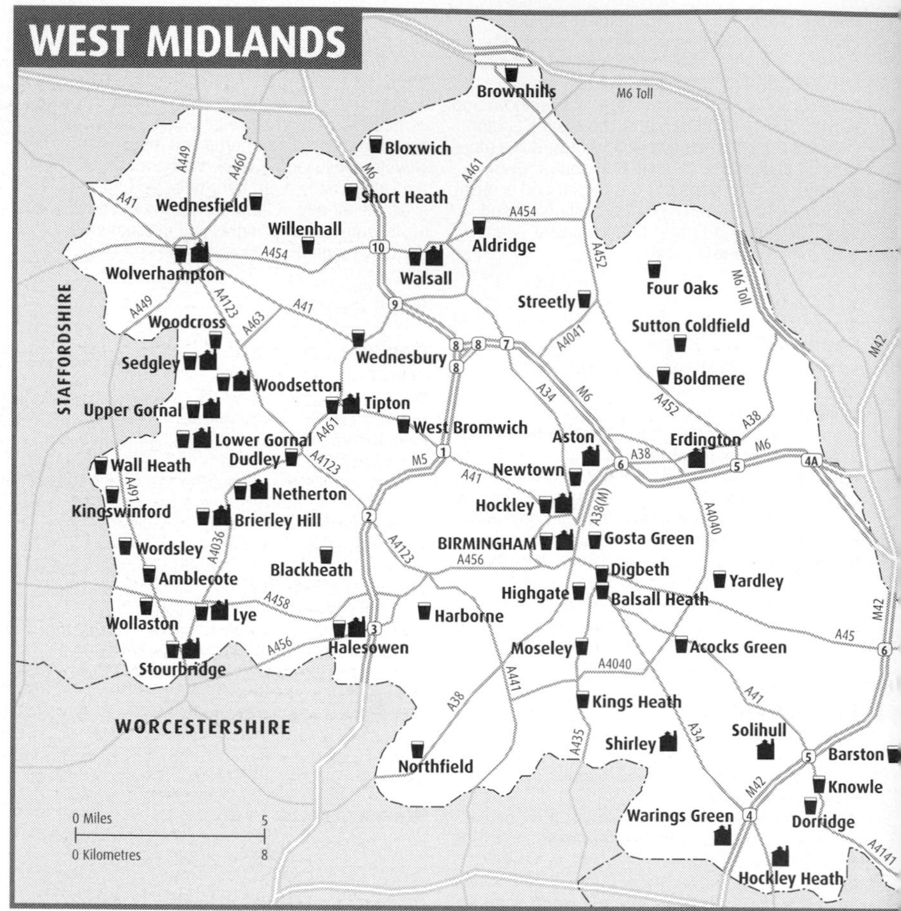

Aldridge

Avion

19 Anchor Road, WS9 8PP

8am-midnight (1am Fri & Sat) ☎ (01922) 749810

Adnams Broadside; Greene King Abbot; Ruddles Best Bitter; guest beers Ⓗ

A recent Wetherspoon conversion of the former Avion Cinema, with two outside drinking areas at the front and rear. The large single bar supplies the usual range of Wetherspoon ales along with many guests. Posters from its former incarnation adorn the walls, including many featuring George Formby, who opened the cinema in 1938. The cinema closed in 1967 and the building was then used as a bingo hall until 2009, after that it remained empty until the current conversion in 2013. Q

Lazy Hill Tavern

196 Walsall Wood Road, WS9 8HB

6-11; 12-2.30, 7-10.30 Sun ☎ (01922) 452040

Blythe Staffie; Greene King IPA, Abbot; Holden's Golden Glow; Wye Valley Butty Bach; guest beer Ⓗ

Large and welcoming family-run free house which has had the same licensee for over 30 years. Originally a farmhouse, it next became a country club, then finally a pub in 1986. Four separate rooms are all similarly and comfortably furnished, with logburners in two. The spacious 160-seater function room is used midweek by local sports and community organisations and can be booked for weddings and other events. QP

Amblecote

Maverick Drinking House

1 High Street, DY8 4BX (on jct of A491 and A461)

12-11.30 (midnight Wed; 12.30am Fri & Sat); 11.30-11 Sun ☎ (01384) 824099

Jennings Cumberland Ale; guest beers Ⓗ

Large corner establishment and former CAMRA branch Pub of the Year. It has a Wild West theme and is a live music venue for blues, folk, rock and more. Four beers are on handpump including three guests – two from local breweries. BT Sports, ESPN and Racing Channel are shown in a separate area when no music is on. There is a covered, heated smoking area and a small garden. Occasional beer festivals take place, locally advertised. Q

Robin Hood

196 Collis Street, DY8 4EQ (on A4102 one-way street off Brettell Lane A461)

12-3 (not Mon & Tue), 5-11; 12-midnight Fri & Sat; 12-11 Sun ☎ (01384) 821120

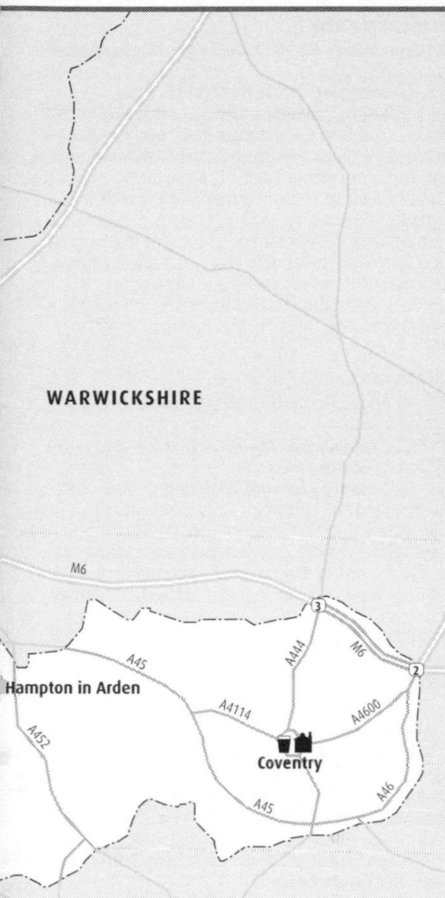

Bathams Best Bitter; Enville Ginger Beer; Holden's Golden Glow; Kinver Light Railway; Olde Swan Bumble Hole Bitter; guest beers Ⓗ
Fine ales, high quality food and a warm welcome – what more could you ask from a Black Country local? Recent enhancements to the pub along with its forward-looking approach have surely strengthened its grasp on traditional values. The front rooms house a wonderful beer bottle collection including international as well as historic brews. The pub hosts a popular beer and music festival in October and is now showcasing more beers from local breweries.

Starving Rascal

1 Brettell Lane, DY8 4BN
4 (12 Sat & Sun)-11 ☎ 07843 670163
starvingrascal.co.uk
Enville White, Ale; Salopian Oracle; guest beers Ⓗ
An external restoration has completed the transformation of this friendly local. With five ales on handpump, this is a pub for beer enthusiasts, with bottles and images creatively displayed among the oak features, hanging hops and memorabilia. TV sport is shown in the front bar, with a quiet rear lounge and separate pool room. Over 60 whiskies from around the world are stocked. A large cellar bar is available for hire. CAMRA branch Pub of the Year 2013. ♣P (246)

Barston

Bull's Head

Barston Lane, B92 0JU (in village opp church)
SP2073378090
11-2.30, 5-11; 11-11 Fri & Sat; 12-11 Sun
☎ (01675) 442830 thebullsheadbarston.co.uk
Adnams Southwold Bitter; Purity Mad Goose; guest beers Ⓗ
A true countryside local, formerly a coaching inn dating back to 1490, reflected in its three beamed rooms. It has two comfortable bars with real fires and racing memorabilia, plus a small, intimate restaurant. Seasonal home-cooked food is served alongside a standard menu (no food Sun eve). Cask Marque and LocAle accredited, it has two regular ales and two guests, and has frequently featured in this Guide. With a secluded beer garden and a warm welcome, it is definitely worth a visit.
QP

Birmingham: Acocks Green

Inn on the Green

2 Westley Road, B27 7UH
10-11 (midnight Fri-Sun) ☎ (0121) 708 0108
innonthegreenpub.co.uk
Beer range varies Ⓗ
Big former M&B roadhouse in the heart of Acocks Green, run by a keen landlord who is an active CAMRA member, with friendly and knowledgeable staff. The ales are always interesting and this local is well worth visiting. It holds regular karaoke evenings, shows live sport and hosts live music on weekends in the function room. Excellent beer festivals are staged four times a year. A CAMRA branch 2013 Pub of the Year finalist.
P

Birmingham: Balsall Heath

Old Moseley Arms

53 Tindal Street, B12 9QU (400yds off Moseley Rd)
12-11 (midnight Fri & Sat) ☎ (0121) 440 1954
Enville Ale; Wye Valley HPA, Butty Bach; guest beers Ⓗ
Current CAMRA branch Pub of the Year, this traditional 19th-century former Ansells local is a welcoming establishment. The main bar on the left shows sport while the bar on the right has a classic jukebox. There are comfy sofas in the covered garden/smoking area. A superb tandoori menu is served Monday-Friday 12-2.30pm, every evening from 6pm and all day Sunday. Regular beer festivals are held offering 10 ales, ciders and perries. Live music featuring local talent takes place upstairs every Sunday evening. ♣

Birmingham: City Centre

Craven Arms

47 Upper Gough Street, B1 1JG (in side street near the Mailbox)
12-11 (midnight Fri & Sat) ☎ (0121) 643 6756
Black Country Bradley's Finest Golden, Pig on the Wall, Fireside; guest beers Ⓗ
Early 19th-century former Holden's pub, recently restored by Black Country Ales, which sports an attractive blue tiled exterior and a cosy interior. In addition to three permanent Black Country beers, between six and eight changing guest casks are available from breweries often new to

Birmingham. An interesting range of bottled beers is offered plus real cider. Beer festivals are held regularly and customers are welcome to bring their own food. ≋(New St)🍎📶

Old Contemptibles 𝕃

176 Edmund Street, B3 2HB (100yds from Snow Hill station)

⏲ 11 (12 Sat)-11; 12-6 Sun ☎ (0121) 200 3310

St Austell Nicholson's Pale Ale; guest beers Ⓗ

Red-bricked corner establishment, part of the Nicholson's chain, named after the famous World War I soldiers. The place resembles a Victorian public house, with chandeliers, a wood-panelled bar and a comfortable snug at the rear. Good-quality food is served. The guest ales come from the Nicholson's range and there is an impressive wine list. Popular with local office workers, it has been known to close early if there is not much custom. ◑≋(Snow Hill/New St)🍎

Old Fox

54-56 Hurst Street, B5 4TD (opp Hippodrome Theatre)

⏲ 11.30-midnight (2am Fri & Sat); 12-midnight Sun ☎ (0121) 622 5080

Morland Old Golden Hen; St Austell Tribute; guest beers Ⓗ

The Old Fox dates from 1891 and stands on the edge of the Historic and Chinese Quarters. The pub has two rooms – a comfortable carpeted lounge where families are welcome and food is served until 7.30pm, and a more basic bar, which is awash with wood and stained glass. Up to four guest ales are served from a large range of breweries, along with a real cider. Opposite the Hippodrome, the place can be busy at interval time.
◑♿≋(New St/Moor St)🍎(45,47)📶

Post Office Vaults 𝕃

84 New Street, B2 4BA (entrances on both New St and Pinfold St)

⏲ 11-11 (midnight Fri & Sat); 12-11 Sun ☎ (0121) 643 7354

🌐 postofficevaults.co.uk

Hobsons Mild; Salopian Oracle; guest beers Ⓗ

Just a minute's walk from the Navigation Street entrance to New Street station, with an excellent range of eight real ales, this subterranean pub is a great place for lovers of traditional ale. At least 300 different bottled beers are always available from all over the world from staff who really know how to advise you, plus a rotating range of a dozen or more ciders and perries. This was CAMRA West Midlands Cider Pub of the Year 2013.
Q≋(Moor St/New St/Snow Hill)♣🍎📶

Queen's Arms

150 Newhall Street, B3 1RY

⏲ 12-11 (10.30 Sun) ☎ (0121) 236 3710

🌐 queensarmsbar.co.uk

Wye Valley HPA; guest beers Ⓗ

Classic Grade II-listed Victorian corner pub with tiled signage outside. Its interior is open plan, with a central bar, but retains its heritage. Comfortable seating is found at both ends and there is a sheltered smoking area at the rear. Quality pub food is served alongside a good selection of pizzas. A quiz is held every Thursday and sporting events are shown on screens. The pub is just outside the city centre, on the edge of the Jewellery Quarter.
◑

Shakespeare 𝕃

31 Summer Row, B3 1JJ (200yds from city end of Broad St)

⏲ 10-11 (midnight Fri & Sat) ☎ (0121) 236 8702

St Austell Nicholson's Pale Ale; guest beers Ⓗ

Glorious red-bricked Victorian local, part of the Nicholson's chain. It is near Broad Street and the new Library of Birmingham. The traditional bar has a small hatch to serve the rear snug, which is normally reserved for diners. There is a decorated patio garden to the rear and seating at the front. It is popular with office workers and students from the nearby University College Birmingham. Regularly changing guest ales feature, with a good selection of pub food. ❀◑♿≋(Snow Hill)📶

Victoria 𝕃

48 John Bright Street, B1 1BN (next to stage door of Alexandra Theatre)

⏲ 12-midnight (1am Thu; 2am Fri & Sat) ☎ (0121) 633 9439

🌐 thevictoriabirmingham.co.uk

Wye Valley Butty Bach; guest beers Ⓗ

The locally-based Bitters & Twisted chain has resurrected this 19th-century theatre bar. It gets busy before theatre performances and gigs at the nearby O2 Arena. One regular beer and three rotating guests are served, alongside food with an American Deep South flavour and a twist on the classic British roast. Quiz night is Tuesday and music features on Thursday, Friday and Saturday. The pub is reportedly haunted. ◑≋(New St/Moor St)📶

Wellington 𝕃

37 Bennetts Hill, B2 5SN (5 mins from New St and Snow Hill stations)

⏲ 10-midnight ☎ (0121) 200 3115

🌐 thewellingtonrealale.co.uk

Black Country Bradley's Finest Golden, Pig on the Wall, Fireside; Oakham Citra; Titanic Plum Porter; Wye Valley HPA; guest beers Ⓗ

Recently refurbished and extended, with an additional upstairs bar and roof-terrace beer garden, this multiple award-winner is a veritable beer festival every day. Sixteen ales and three traditional ciders are on handpump, and a wide

INDEPENDENT BREWERIES

Angel Halesowen
Backyard Walsall
Banks's (Marston's) Wolverhampton
Bathams Brierley Hill
Beer Geek Birmingham: Aston
Black Country Lower Gornal
Blue Bell Brewhouse Warings Green (NEW)
Broughs Wolverhampton
Byatt's Coventry
Craddock's Stourbridge
Fownes Upper Gornal
Frothblowers Erdington (NEW)
Green Duck Stourbridge
Hearsall Coventry
Holden's Woodsetton
Olde Swan Netherton
Rock & Roll Birmingham
Sadler's Lye
Sarah Hughes Sedgley
Shed Brewery Hockley Heath
Silhill Solihull
Toll End Tipton
Two Towers Birmingham: Hockley
Whitworth Shirley

selection of bottled beers and whiskies is served to a varied clientèle by knowledgeable staff. Regular quizzes, cheese nights and darts competitions are held. No food is served but you are welcome to bring your own – plates, cutlery and condiments are provided. Q❀≢(New St/Snow Hill)♣●

Birmingham: Digbeth

Anchor ★ 𝕃

308 Bradford Street, B5 6ET (next to Digbeth coach station)

11-midnight (2am Fri & Sat); 12-11.30 Sun

☎ (0121) 622 4516 anchorinndigbeth.co.uk

Hobsons Mild; guest beers H

A four-times winner of local CAMRA branch Pub of the Year and a current finalist, the Anchor is a must-visit for the ale enthusiast. Grade II-listed and with a nationally important historic pub interior, it has been run by the Keane family for over 40 years, bringing a local pub feel to a city-centre location. There is a changing beer range with new breweries often featuring, along with regular beer festivals. The pub is busy when Birmingham City play at home. Q❀♿≢(New St/Moor St)♣●

Spotted Dog

104 Warwick Street, B12 0NH

5-11; 3-1am Fri; 12-1am Sat; 12-midnight Sun

☎ (0121) 772 3822 spotteddog.co.uk

Holden's Black Country Mild; guest beers H

Traditional multi-roomed establishment with an Irish feel that is well worth a visit. There is a large covered garden/smoking area with heaters and a barbecue area. Traditional Irish music alternates with a film screening celebrating Irish cinema on Monday nights, and jazz is hosted on Tuesday nights. Sport is shown on a large screen, especially rugby. Lashford's pork pies with home-made pickles, and excellent Scotch eggs, including vegetarian versions, are on sale. The pub can be busy when Birmingham City are at home. ❀♿≢(Bordesley)

Woodman ★ 𝕃

New Canal Street, B5 5LG (opp old Curzon St by Millenium Point)

11-11 (midnight Fri & Sat) ☎ (0121) 643 4960

thewoodmanbirmingham.co.uk

Castle Rock Black Gold, Harvest Pale; guest beers H

Recently given an environmentally friendly refurbishment, the pub is Grade II-listed and has a nationally important historic pub interior. It has a red-bricked tile and terracotta exterior, with an L-shaped bar which is tiled above a wooden dado. A tiled lobby on Albert Street leads to an attractive small drinking area, with a hatch to the servery, warmed by a real fire. The third plain room on the left now makes for a pleasant dividing area. Good food is served daily, there is a quiz night every Wednesday, and an outside seating/dining area. Q❀◑♿≢(Moor St)♣●

Birmingham: Gosta Green

Sacks of Potatoes 𝕃

10 Gosta Green, B4 7ER

11 (12 Sun)-11 ☎ (0121) 503 5811

Beer range varies H

A lively pub on the Aston University campus, with leaded windows and wooden floors. The main bar has a variety of seating and outside tables that offer views overlooking the campus. The pub is popular with students and local office staff. Alongside guest ales there is always a rotating LocAle and real cider or perry. Good-value food is available at reasonable prices and silent TV screens show sports coverage. Beer festivals are held throughout the year.
❀◑♿≢(Snow Hill)●P(66)

Birmingham: Harborne

Harborne Club 𝕃

39 Albany Road, B17 9JX (200yds down road, last house on left)

12.30-3.30 (not Mon-Fri), 5.30-midnight; 12.30-3.30 Sun

☎ (0121) 427 1638 theharborneclub.co.uk

Beer range varies H

CAMRA members are always made to feel welcome at this private members' club – please sign the attendance book on entry. Its inconspicuous exterior belies a friendly interior, with a small bar and comfortable, homely décor. One LocAle is usually on plus another guest. A snooker room is upstairs for members, and TVs show major sporting events. Occasional quiz nights and guest speaker evenings are held. The club does not open until 5.30pm during the week. ♣

White Horse 𝕃

2 York Street, B17 0HG

11 (12 Mon)-11.30; 11-12.30am Fri & Sat; 12-11.30 Sun

☎ (0121) 427 8004 whitehorseharborne.com

Beer range varies H

A much-improved and extended free house with a great emphasis on real ale, just off the busy high street. There is an island bar with a front snug and a rear heated area. Regular live music nights are hosted on Fridays and Saturdays, with a monthly open mic night on the last Wednesday. Quiz nights are held every Tuesday and Thursday. A basic food menu is available. The artworks on the walls are by local artists, including the landlord. ❀◑●

Birmingham: Highgate

Lamp Tavern 𝕃

157 Barford Street, B5 6AH (500yds from A441 Pershore Rd near bottom of Hurst St)

12.30-11 ☎ (0121) 688 1220

Everards Tiger; Hobsons Mild; Stanway Stanney Bitter; guest beers H

A warm welcome awaits from Eddie, a landlord of more than 20 years standing, at this characterful, single-roomed, street-corner local. It is home to the rooftop Rock and Roll Brewery and its only regular outlet, with one beer from its range always available. This is also the only Birmingham pub to supply Stanway Stanney Bitter. A Guide regular, the pub won the Silver award in the local CAMRA branch Pub of the Year 2013 competition.

Birmingham: Hockley

Black Eagle 𝕃

16 Factory Road, B18 5JU (turn right out of Soho Benson Road metro station, cross road and walk 200yds)

11.30-3, 5.30-11; 11.30-11 Fri; 12-3, 7-11 Sat; 12-3 Sun

☎ (0121) 523 4008 theblackeaglepub.co.uk

Bathams Best Bitter; Marston's Pedigree; Timothy Taylor Landlord; guest beers H

Traditional award-winning multi-room pub with a restaurant to the rear. While slightly off the beaten track, this real ale oasis is well worth seeking out for its excellent range of beers and good-value food. Three guest beers are always on handpump and an annual beer festival is held in the summer. Barbecues feature occasionally. Real cider and perry usually come from Gwynt y Ddraig and Westons.

Lord Clifden

34 Great Hampton Street, B18 6AA

10-midnight (2am Fri & Sat) ☎ (0121) 523 7515

thelordclifden.com

Wye Valley HPA; guest beers Ⓗ

An unassuming exterior belies the depth of activities that take place here, with a public bar at the front, a rear lounge, and a permanent outside bar in the superb, spacious, heated beer garden. Its extensive award-winning food menu includes excellent Sunday roasts and daily specials, and barbecues in the garden. The pub is renowned for the collection of urban street art that adorns its walls. Live DJs feature at weekends, when food is served until 10pm, and a quiz night is held every Thursday. A good range of bottled beers is stocked. (Jewellery Quarter)

Red Lion

95 Warstone Lane, B18 6NG

10-midnight (2am Fri & Sat) ☎ (0121) 233 9144

theredlionbirmingham.com

Wye Valley Butty Bach; guest beers Ⓗ

Traditional two-roomed pub that is rich both in local heritage and modern art. There is a lively front bar and a cosy back lounge. A good-sized club room is upstairs and there is a sheltered patio and smoking area to the rear. An excellent extensive food menu is served all day, with a Cow Club for steak lovers on Mondays. There are three changing guest beers and two changing ciders. Regular quiz nights are held and large screens show sporting events. (Jewellery Quarter)

Birmingham: Kings Heath

Kings Heath Cricket & Sports Club

Charlton House, 247 Alcester Road South, B14 6DT

12-midnight ☎ (0121) 444 1913

kingsheathsportsclub.co.uk

Wye Valley HPA, Butty Bach; guest beers Ⓗ

CAMRA members are welcome at this friendly sports club – show your membership card for entry (maximum 10 visits per year). The club has two rooms: the comfortable lounge for relaxed drinking, and another for watching sporting events on large screens and also housing two full-size snooker tables. The beer range always includes two rotating guest ales, with a minimum of five real ales available. Varying social events are held throughout the year including live music.

P

Birmingham: Moseley

Prince of Wales

118 Alcester Road, B13 8EE

12-11.30 (1am Fri & Sat) ☎ (0121) 449 4198

theprincemoseley.co.uk

Castle Rock Harvest Pale; Oakham Bishops Farewell; Purity Mad Goose, Saddle Black; Sharp's Doom Bar; Timothy Taylor Landlord; guest beers Ⓗ

Serving cask ales since 1861, this three-bar pub is a real community local. The front bar boasts an authentic Victorian bar-back and there are two further bars at the rear, leading to a beer garden and cigar smoke room that boasts the largest collection of Cuban cigars in the country. Two ciders are on sale, alongside a good selection of whiskies and interesting cocktails. There is a TV for sport, a real fire and a quiz night every Tuesday.

Birmingham: Newtown

Bartons Arms ★

144 High Street, B6 4UP

12-11 (10.30 Sun) ☎ (0121) 333 5988

bartons-arms.co.uk

Oakham JHB, Inferno, Citra, Bishops Farewell; guest beer Ⓗ

A stunning red-bricked pub run by Oakham Brewery from Peterborough. The 1901 interior is Grade II-listed and has a nationally important historic pub interior. The Bartons has ornate Minton tiles throughout, including a central tiled staircase, original stained glass windows and snob screens on the bar. Superb Thai food is served in the lounge. A range of Oakham Ales is available, usually plus one guest and a cider. Quiz nights are on Mondays and regular music and beer festivals are held. P

Birmingham: Northfield

Black Horse ★

Bristol Road South, B31 2QT (opp Sainbury's)

8am-11 (1am Fri & Sat); 8am-midnight Sun

☎ (0121) 477 1800

Greene King Abbot; Purity Pure Ubu; Ruddles Best Bitter; Sharp's Doom Bar; guest beers Ⓗ

Large inter-war mock-Tudor roadhouse offering the only extensive real ale choice in this part of the city, transformed from being an undesirable local to a popular pub serving consistently good quality beer. Unusually for Wetherspoon, this venue has a multi-room layout and bars on two levels. It still retains the original baronial hall entrance but the bar has been tastefully refurbished with an etched glass entrance door. There is a bowling green with original outbuildings to the rear.

P

Birmingham: Yardley

William Tyler

140 Church Street, B25 8UT

8am-11 ☎ (0121) 789 5860

Greene King Abbot; Ruddles Best Bitter; guest beers Ⓗ

This Wetherspoon pub was formerly a Woolworths store and has been excellently converted. Historical murals adorn the walls and on the ceiling are paintings of Nigel Mansell, Murray Walker and Tony Hancock. There are books for customers to read while enjoying their beer, and the light arrangements are made of bottles and wine glasses – a must-see from an architectural point of view. It is a great example of a community local in an area that is sparsely populated with pubs.

Blackheath

Britannia

124 Halesowen Street, B65 0ES

8am-midnight (1am Fri & Sat) ☎ (0121) 559 0010
Greene King Abbot; Ruddles Best Bitter; guest beers Ⓗ
Briefly known as the Traveller's Rest, this friendly, popular, community pub is open-plan and comfortable. The walls are adorned with pictures of local historic figures detailing the area's industrial history. Up to seven guest beers are available at any given time. The pub gets busy at weekends and is readily accessible by buses from Birmingham, Dudley and West Bromwich, which stop nearby. A garden area at the back provides a pleasant drinking area. Cider festivals are run twice a year. (Rowley Regis)P

Waterfall

132 Waterfall Lane, B64 6RG
12-midnight (11 Sun) ☎ (0121) 559 9198
Bathams Best Bitter; Enville Ginger Beer; Holden's Golden Glow, Special; guest beers Ⓗ
Characterful, homely, community-centred pub owned by Holden's Brewery. It is close to Blackheath town centre or a steep 10-minute walk uphill from Old Hill station. Basic, good-value food is served from Anne's Kitchen and it has up to six guest beers, mostly on the strong side and usually from Burton Bridge and Olde Swan breweries. The outside drinking area affords wonderful views in summer due to its elevation. The pub can get crowded at weekends.
(Old Hill)P(4M)

Bloxwich

Wheatsheaf

35 Field Road, WS3 3JL
11-11 ☎ (01922) 279799
Banks's Mild, Bitter; guest beers Ⓗ
A welcoming family-run pub which has four handpulls with regularly changing guest ales from the Marston's family of breweries. A real log fire helps create a friendly atmosphere in the bar. There is a snug available for private functions. The Wheatsheaf plays host to traditional pub games, dominoes, crib, pool and darts teams. Inn Stitches 2, the knitting club, meets on Tuesdays. Live music takes place every Saturday and there are regular quizzes. The pub has a good-sized covered smoking area and garden. Q(301,302)

Boldmere

Bishop Vesey

63 Boldmere Road, B73 5UY
8am-11 (midnight Fri & Sat) ☎ (0121) 355 5077
Backyard Blonde; Greene King Abbot; Purity Mad Goose; Ruddles Best Bitter; guest beers Ⓗ
This sprawling Wetherspoon pub has an open-plan layout with upstairs seating and an outside patio/smokers area. Boasting 14 consecutive years in the Guide, it is a frequent Pub of the Year for the local CAMRA branch. The loyal local clientèle includes a thriving darts team. Children are welcome in the family area until 9pm. Up to seven guest beers, many from local micros, together with regular beer festivals, make this a venue not to miss.

Brierley Hill

Vine

10 Delph Road, Delph, DY5 2TN
12-11; 12-10.30 Sun ☎ (01384) 78293
Bathams Mild Ale, Best Bitter Ⓗ
Classic, unspoilt brewery tap with an ornately decorated façade proclaiming the Shakespearean quotation: 'Blessing of your heart, you brew good ale'. Step inside and enter an elongated pub with a labyrinthine feel. The rooms have contrasting characters. The front bar is staunchly traditional while the larger rear bar with its own servery and leather seating houses the dartboard at the far end. On the other side of the central passageway is a homely lounge partly converted from former brewery offices. QP(X96)

Brownhills

Swan

Pelsall Road, WS8 7DL
4 (2 Fri; 12 Sat & Sun)-midnight ☎ (01543) 820628
Holden's Golden Glow; guest beers Ⓗ
A traditional pub with two rooms served by a central bar. The main drinking area is to the right of the front entrance, with a lounge area to the left. Beyond the lounge, a separate area houses the pool table. There is an outside drinking area at the front of the pub. The Swan has been refurbished throughout and is a comfortable and welcoming venue for both locals and visitors. Up to two guest beers supplement the regular beer. P

Coventry

Boat

31 Shilton Lane, Walsgrave, CV2 2AB
11-11.30 (midnight Fri & Sat); 12-11.30 Sun
☎ (024) 7661 2191
Draught Bass; Thwaites Original; guest beers Ⓗ
Charming Victorian pub sympathetically refurbished nine years ago. Two regular and up to five guest ales are on in the public bar and lounge. There are two additional rooms: one was once used for smoking meat (the meat hooks are still visible), the other is a quiet snug. Pictures adorn the walls, which adds to the Victorian character. The venue hosts darts and dominoes teams in local leagues. Children are welcome when dining until 9.30pm; no food Sunday evenings.
P(30)

Broomfield Tavern

14-16 Broomfield Place, Spon End, CV5 6GY (next to rugby ground but hidden from main road)
12-midnight (2am Fri); 12-2am Sat; 12-midnight Sun
☎ (024) 7663 0969
Beer range varies Ⓗ
A Victorian pub with on-street parking next to the park. All keg fonts have been removed to accommodate more handpumps. The beer range usually includes one from Church End plus an interesting variety of different beers on draught, as well as a selection of bottled beers from around the world. Live music on Fridays often features well-known musicians. Otherwise, lively conversation dominates with no electronic sources of noise. The pub opens at 4pm weekdays in winter.

City Arms

1 Earlsdon Street, Earlsdon, CV5 6EP (on roundabout at centre of Earlsdon)
8am-midnight (1am Fri & Sat) ☎ (024) 7671 8170

Greene King Abbot; Ruddles Best Bitter; guest beers Ⓗ
Large mock-Tudor pub in the centre of Earlsdon, a Wetherspoon outlet with a high volume of real ale sales; it has been in the Guide for 10 years. Usually one LocAle from Purity or Byatts is on handpump, with up to seven other guest beers. The largely open-plan seating areas are served from a long central bar. Ciders usually come from Westons or Gwynt y Ddraig. The pub attracts a varied clientèle and can get busy at weekends. Food is available all day until 11pm.
P(5,12)

Establishment

The Old County Hall, 51 Bayley Lane, CV1 5RN (between the cathedral and Holy Trinity church)
11-11 (midnight Thu; 2am Fri & Sat); 10-11 Sun
(024) 7622 2727 establishmentbars.co.uk
Byatt's Coventry Bitter; Sharp's Doom Bar; guest beer Ⓗ
Interesting bar which has been fashioned from the old courthouse. Many features of its former life are much in evidence. Note the glass panel over the steps from the dock (which has been moved to create a DJ booth) to the cells. The rear part used to be the exercise yard. Daytime trade tends to be food-driven, with office staff and shoppers. Evenings are more raucous, especially at weekends. The guest beer is usually from a LocAle brewery, Byatts.

Gatehouse Tavern

46 Hill Street, CV1 4AN (close to Belgrade Theatre and Spon St, near jct 8 of ring road)
11-11 (midnight Thu-Sat); 12-10.30 Sun
(024) 7663 0140 gatehousetavern.com
Beer range varies Ⓗ
The building was converted in the 1990s from the former gatehouse of textile company Leigh Mills. It is now a thriving free house, serving a changing range of real ales, including LocAles. The garden is the largest within the city centre. The stained glass windows depict the Six Nations, indicating the sporting interests of the pub, with major events shown. The meals are served in ample portions and are good value.

Greyhound Inn

Sutton Stop, Hawkesbury Junction, CV6 6DF (off Grange Rd at jct of Coventry and Oxford canals)
11-11; 12-10.30 Sun (024) 7636 3046
greyhoundinn.org
Draught Bass; Marston's Pedigree; Theakston Traditional Mild; guest beers Ⓗ
Canalside pub, and winner of many local and CAMRA awards. Dating back to the 1830s, it sits at the junction of two canals. Inside are separate restaurant and bar areas serving an extensive range of freshly cooked food. To the front, an outside drinking area overlooks the canals. At the rear is a beer garden bar, also serving real ale, which is open most weekends in the summer and for some sporting events. Occasional beer festivals are held. Q P

Nursery Tavern

38-39 Lord Street, Chapelfields, CV5 8DA (1 mile W of city centre, off Allesley Old Rd)
12-11.30 (midnight Fri & Sat); 12-11 Sun
(024) 7667 4530
Courage Best Bitter; Fuller's London Pride; Hook Norton Hooky Mild; guest beers Ⓗ
Community pub comprising three rooms, the front two both served by a central bar. The rear room is used for a variety of events including monthly quizzes, society and club meetings, and music nights featuring local talent. It also serves as a restaurant on Sunday lunchtimes, providing excellent-value traditional roast meals. The pub displays a collection of Rugby Union and Formula 1 paraphernalia. Beer festivals are held in the garden every June and December.
Q (Canley)

Old Windmill

22-23 Spon Street, CV1 3BA (in a medieval street, behind IKEA)
12 (3 Mon)-midnight; 12-1am Fri & Sat
(024) 7625 1717
Morland Old Speckled Hen; Sharp's Doom Bar; Theakston Old Peculier; Timothy Taylor Landlord; Wychwood Hobgoblin; guest beers Ⓗ
The pub dates from 1472 and so has naturally undergone many alterations. The most recent changes, in the 1980s, increased the areas with public access while retaining a lot of the original room structure, and exposed an old fireplace with an adjoining entrance to a priest hole. One guest is usually a local ale; the other is frequently RCH Old Slug Porter. The garden is only open in the summer. Hand-made pork pies are usually sold.

Open Arms

Daventry Road, CV3 5DP
11.30-midnight (11 Mon & Tue; 11.30 Wed); 11.30-11 Sun
(024) 7650 5129
M&B Brew XI; Marston's Pedigree; Purity Pure Ubu; guest beers Ⓗ
A post-war family-friendly Ember Inn in an area of the city devoid of real ale pubs. It is only about a mile from the city centre, near the War Memorial Park. The LocAle is usually from Purity. Although a single bar, there are several separate areas. A number of events are hosted, including live music, especially at weekends. To the rear are a large garden and car park. P(9,9A)

Town Crier

Corporation Street, CV1 1PB
11-11 (1am Thu-Sat); 12-6 Sun (024) 7663 2317
thetowncriercoventry.com
Marston's Burton Bitter, Pedigree; guest beers Ⓗ
Modern pub located in the city centre, with a single bar serving a large open-plan room. The landlord promotes traditional ales and has increased the number of real ales available from two to four. Two regular beers are supplemented by changing guest beers from the Marston's stable. An open mic evening is held every Thursday and live bands feature on Saturday nights. Good-value home-made meals are served. Families are welcome until early evening. There is an outdoor patio with benches.

Town Wall Tavern

Bond Street, CV1 4AH (behind Belgrade Theatre)
12-11 (midnight Fri); 11.30-midnight Sat; 12-10 Sun
(024) 7622 0963 townwalltavern.co.uk
Adnams Southwold Bitter, Broadside; Caledonian Deuchars IPA; Draught Bass; guest beers Ⓗ
Traditional pub with three bars, up to three guest ales, and Westons Old Rosie cider. The public bar is decorated with sheet music and mirrors. The extended lounge has cosy bays and corners, and is

popular with theatregoers from the nearby Belgrade; the pictures on the walls have a theatrical theme. The donkey box is a snug for people and donkeys alike. Food is a delight (not available Sun eve or all day Mon). There is a small smoking patio. No under-18s.

Whitefriars Olde Ale House

114-115 Gosford Street, CV1 5DL

12-midnight (1am Fri & Sat); 12-11 Sun

☎ (024) 7625 1655

Beer range varies

A 14th-century building once part of the Whitefriars monastery, subsequently a butcher's shop, before being renovated and made into a pub. The small front room used to be the friars' kitchen, retaining the open fire. Beer is served from between five and nine handpumps, depending on season. Live music is played on some evenings. Beer festivals include cider and perry and also feature live music. No food served Sundays. (8,9)

Dorridge

Forest Hotel

25 Station Approach, B93 8JA (directly opp railway station)

11-11 (midnight Thu-Sat); 11-10 Sun ☎ (01564) 772120

forest-hotel.com

Hook Norton Hooky; Wye Valley HPA; guest beer

This Victorian hotel has a bar decorated in a contemporary, eclectic style with polished wooden tables, comfortable armchairs and sofas. The restaurant specialises in fine dining – meals are also available in the bar. There is a large, partly covered, outdoor seating area with several patio heaters. A cider and ale festival is held in July and a real ale festival in November. Voted Most Improved Pub 2012 by the local CAMRA branch.

P(S2,S3)

Dudley

Court House

30 New Street, DY1 1LP (a short walk from bus station towards police station)

12-11 (10.30 Sun) ☎ (01384) 240062

Black Country Bradley's Finest Golden, Pig on the Wall, Fireside; guest beers

Run by Black Country Traditional Inns as a specialist real ale pub, the regular beers come from the company's own brewery accompanied by a large selection of guest ales from across the country. The pub has developed a reputation for offering a dark beer. Cider drinkers are well catered for, with four to choose from. The small snug and the large upstairs function room complement the facilities. CAMRA Cider Pub of the Year 2012 and 2013.

Q(1,126)

Lamp Tavern

116 High Street, DY1 1QT

12-11 (10.30 Sun) ☎ (01384) 254129

Bathams Mild Ale, Best Bitter

A classic Bathams pub with a large front bar with traditional games and a cosy back room with a more relaxed feel. The old Queens Cross Brewery has been converted into a large function room, used for staging music nights and also available for hire. B&B accommodation is in the adjacent Lamp Cottage (a discount is available for CAMRA members – ring for details). An outside area for drinking overlooks the southern area of the Black Country to the Clent Hills beyond.

P

Four Oaks

Butlers Arms

444 Lichfield Road, B74 4BL (near corner with Butlers Lane)

12-11 (midnight Fri & Sat); 12-10.30 Sun

☎ (0121) 308 0765 butlersarms.co.uk

Beer range varies

This attractive suburban pub has a strong local following, but visitors also make use of the nearby bus stop and rail station. The interior is an eclectic mix of styles with lamps, mirrors and curiosities. The four guest ales vary but usually include a Caledonian beer plus Greene King Abbot. The chalkboard menu is full of fish specials, with meat and vegetarian alternatives. This is a family-run pub with great staff and a comfortable, friendly feel. Q(Butlers Lane)P

Mare Pool

297 Lichfield Road, B74 2UG (behind shops on E side of Lichfield Rd)

8am-midnight (1am Fri & Sat) ☎ (0121) 323 1070

Greene King Abbot; Ruddles Best Bitter; Sharp's Doom Bar; guest beers

The usual Wetherspoon food offerings and its family-friendly policy attract a younger daytime clientele. The name refers to one of the many pools that used to surround Sutton, and the watery theme includes hundreds of hanging glass droplets. The interior features an unusual canopied gas fire and outside there is a suntrap beer terrace. There are occasional showings of big-screen sport. The five guest ales often showcase Backyard and Purity beers. QP

Halesowen

Somers Sports & Social Club

2 Grange Hill, B62 0JH (at A456/B4551 jct)

12-2.30, 6-11; 12-11 Sat & Sun ☎ (0121) 550 1645

somersclub.co.uk

Bathams Best Bitter; Enville Ale; Holden's Black Country Bitter; Olde Swan Original; Wye Valley HPA; guest beers

Grade II*-listed building set in landscaped grounds. Its long bar features five regular beers and six guests, many local, usually including an Oakham ale. The lounge overlooks the large garden, which has a children's play area and a crown green bowling court. It is a three-times winner of CAMRA's National Club of the Year, and is current branch Club of the Year. CAMRA members are welcome; large groups should phone ahead. Lunchtime pub food is served (not Sun). Regular evening entertainment is hosted.

QP(9,241)

Waggon & Horses

21 Stourbridge Road, B63 3TU (on main A458, ½ mile from bus station)

12-11.30 (12.30am Fri & Sat) ☎ (0121) 550 4989

Bathams Best Bitter; Bob's White Lion; Holden's Golden Glow; Nottingham Extra Pale Ale; Oakham Inferno; guest beers

A thoroughly welcoming pub with an enviable reputation for its wide selection of expertly kept beers. Fourteen ales are always available, usually including stout or mild, plus real cider and draught Belgian beers. The traditional interior comprises a long bar flanked by quieter seating areas at both ends. Top-quality home-made hot and cold food is now served Monday to Saturday 12-6.30pm – later on Mondays and Wednesdays – with regular steak and curry nights held on Mondays. Q◐⬤🚌(9)🐾

Hampton in Arden

White Lion

10 High Street, B92 0AA (opp church) SP2025080820
12-midnight (10.30 Sun) ☎ (01675) 442833
thewhitelioninn.com
Banks's Sunbeam; Castle Rock Harvest Pale; Hobsons Best Bitter; M&B Brew XI; Purity Pure Ubu; Sharp's Doom Bar Ⓗ
A charming 17th-century timber-framed building with Grade II-listed status, the White Lion has been licensed since 1838. It has an L-shaped lounge and dining area with a separate public bar, with finereal fires. The dining area is light, airy and open plan. Quality British pub food is available lunchtimes and evenings. The landlord's wife is from Brittany and the pub often serves galettes and crepes on weekday lunchtimes. Six regular ales are on handpumps. Q🔥❀🛏◐♿⇌P🚌🐾

Kingswinford

Park Tavern

182 Cot Lane, DY6 9QG (on corner of Cot Lane and Broad St)
11-11 (midnight Fri & Sat) ☎ (01384) 287178
Bathams Best Bitter; Enville Ale, Ginger Beer; Timothy Taylor Landlord; guest beers Ⓗ
Popular lively old pub in the back streets of Kingswinford, currently serving six real ales. Opened as the Brickmakers Arms in 1855, it changed to the Park Tavern in 1859. The bar and lounge each have their own feel, but TV does dominate when there are sporting events on. For the peckish try the selection of cobs. There is a patio at the rear for smokers and sports enthusiasts alike. ❀♣⬤P🚌(226)🐾

Knowle

Red Lion

1672 High Street, B93 0LY (opp church)
12-11 (midnight Fri & Sat) ☎ (01564) 771522
Greene King IPA; Purity Pure Ubu; guest beers Ⓗ
This large, 17th-century Grade II-listed building has a single bar servicing a number of secluded areas within the pub. The interior has been extensively modernised while still retaining some of the original character, including exposed beams and a cast-iron fireplace dating from 1779. Three coal-effect gas fires add to the ambience. Up to five varying guest ales are on offer along with standard Ember Inns food, served until 10pm daily. Q❀◐♿P🚌

Vaults

St John's Close, B93 0JU (off High St A4141)
12-2.30, 5-11; 12-11.30 Thu-Sat; 12-11 Sun
☎ (01564) 773656
Adnams Lighthouse; St Austell Tribute; Sharp's Doom Bar; Tetley Bitter; guest beers Ⓗ
A traditional pub that can be relied on for a wide range of quality real ales, as well as Biddenden's real cider. A regular winner of the local CAMRA branch Pub of the Year, it has also achieved more than 20 Guide entries. It is a popular meeting place for those visiting the many local restaurants. Major sporting events are shown on BT Sport TV. Light meals are served 12-2pm Monday to Saturday. ◐⬤P🚌(S2,S3)

Lower Gornal

Black Bear

86 Deepdale Lane, DY3 2AE
5 (4 Fri)-11; 12-11 Sat; 12-10.30 Sun ☎ (01384) 253333
Beer range varies Ⓗ
Once a farmhouse and now a traditional Black Country pub, serving at least four guest beers. Subsidence has taken its toll and there is a distinct slope to the split-level interior; large buttresses support the downhill exterior walls. The views from the garden are stunning and dogs are welcome here. There are bus stops close by or you could choose to walk uphill from the Gornal Wood bus station. The bar has interesting local history prints around the walls. ❀♣🚌(27,257)🐾

Five Ways Inn

375 Himley Road, DY3 2PZ (jct of B4176/4175, 3 mins from Gornal Wood bus station)
12-midnight; 9am-1am Fri & Sat; 9am-midnight Sun
☎ (01384) 252968
Bathams Best Bitter; guest beer Ⓗ
Family-friendly Gornal Wood corner house. Its one J-shaped room divides the bar into two distinct areas. It has a cottage-like feeling, with a carpeted floor and mugs hanging from the ceiling. There is a raised concrete decking area overlooking the car park at the back. Buses 257 and 297 pass close by. 🔥♣P🚌(257,297)🐾

Fountain

8 Temple Street, DY3 2PE (on B4157 5 mins from Gornal Wood bus station)
12-11 (10.30 Sun) ☎ (01384) 242777
fountaininnrealale.co.uk
Greene King Abbot; Hobsons Town Crier; Morland Old Speckled Hen; RCH Pitchfork; guest beers Ⓗ
Serial Guide entry and twice winner of local CAMRA Pub of the Year. This excellent free house serves eight real ales accompanied by draught Belgian beers, a real cider and 12 fruit wines. The busy, vibrant bar is complemented by an elevated dining area serving excellent food lunchtimes and evenings Monday-Friday, all day Saturday, and Sunday lunches until 5pm. During the summer months the rear garden is a suntrap and a pleasant area to while away an hour or two. 🔥❀◐♣⬤P🚌(27,297)🐾

Red Cow

84 Grosvenor Road, DY3 2PR
4 (12 Sat & Sun)-midnight ☎ 07943 189351
Holden's Golden Glow; Wye Valley Butty Bach; guest beers Ⓗ
An early 19th-century hostelry in a cul-de-sac that is part of Grosvenor Road. This community pub supports numerous pub games teams. The narrow bar is to the left, while the cosy lounge to the right is divided in two by a large chimney breast, with openings either side to afford passage between them. There is a large garden at the rear. A real cider accompanies the six beers. The pub is five minutes' walk from the bus stop in Corncrake Road. CAMRA county and branch Pub of the Year 2013. 🔥❀♣⬤P🚌(257)🐾

Lye

Windsor Castle Inn L

7 Stourbridge Road, DY9 7DG (at Lye Cross)
12-11 ☎ (01384) 897809
Sadler's Red House Mild, Mellow Yellow, Worcester Sorcerer, Thin Ice, Hop Bomb, Mud City Stout; guest beers H
Tap house for the family-owned Sadler's Ales since 2004, showcasing its full range of regular beers along with monthly specials. The modern yet cosy interior creates an atmosphere that is relaxed and laid back during the week, livening up at weekends. Tasty home-made food is served daily from a varied award-winning menu or, alternatively, purchase a two-pint carry-out container if you are frequenting one of the many local curry houses for which Lye is famed. Q❀◑♿⇌●P🚌(9,276)

Netherton

Olde Swan ★ L

89 Halesowen Road, DY2 9PY (on Dudley-Old Hill road)
11-11; 12-4, 7-11 Sun ☎ (01384) 253075
Olde Swan Original, Dark Swan, Entire, Bumble Hole Bitter, seasonal beer H
One of the last four remaining English home-brew pubs from 1974, deservedly on CAMRA's National Inventory of Historic Pub Interiors and home to the Olde Swan Brewery. The bar is an unspoilt treasure and there is a cosy snug. A fifth beer is often available from the on-site brewery. Food is available in the lounge Monday-Saturday lunchtimes and Monday evening. The upstairs restaurant is highly regarded for its à la carte menu (open Tue-Sat). Sunday lunches are also served, with booking essential. Q❀◑♿♣P🚌🐾📶

Sedgley

Beacon Hotel 🏆 ★ L

129 Bilston Street, DY3 1JE (A463)
12-2.30 (3 Fri), 5.30-11; 12-3, 6-11 Sat; 12-3, 7-10.30 Sun
☎ (01902) 883380 🌐 sarahhughesbrewery.co.uk
Sarah Hughes Pale Amber, Sedgley Surprise, Dark Ruby Mild; guest beers H
In the shadow of Sedgley beacon, this hotel has sat virtually unchanged for decades. It is a Grade II-listed building with a nationally important historic pub interior, where time has stood still. At its heart is a central servery with snob screens. There are four rooms, including one for families. The Sarah Hughes brewery lives in a tower at the back and supplies the pub. The Beacon lives up to its name – it shines. Q🐴❀⇌(Coseley)P🚌(229,223)

Mount Pleasant

144 High Street, DY3 1RH (A459)
6.30 (7 Mon & Tue)-11; 12-3, 7-10.30 Sun ☎ 07950 195652
Beer range varies H
Known locally as the Stump by its many regulars, this friendly, popular, free house serves an interesting selection of eight beers. It possesses a Tardis-like interior and a mock-Tudor frontage. The front bar has a convivial and warm atmosphere while the lounge has a more intimate feel, with its two rooms on different levels housing various nooks and crannies to hide away in and two real coal stoves. Food is limited to ham or cheese cobs. The pub is five minutes' walk from Sedgley. Q❀♣P🚌(1)🐾

White Lion

104 Bilston Street, DY3 1JF
12-3, 6-11; 12-4, 7-11 Sun ☎ (01902) 685232
Dark Star American Pale Ale; Oakham Bishops Farewell; guest beers H
A warm welcome awaits in this old pub with a comfortable modern interior. The meals are excellent, in the traditional English style – you will not leave hungry, and an extension is planned to accommodate the increasing number of diners. The guest ales are pale and hoppy. Occasional live music is hosted. The south-facing beer garden makes a lovely suntrap in the right weather. Children under eight are welcome only when dining. 🐴❀◑P🚌📶

Short Heath

Duke of Cambridge L

82 Coltham Road, WV12 5QD
12-11 ☎ (01922) 712038
Black Country Bradley's Finest Golden, Pig on the Wall, Fireside; guest beers H
A traditional welcoming pub converted from 17th-century cottages about 200 years ago. There are three comfortable rooms including a tastefully refurbished lounge/family room with a pool table. The public bar has a solid fuel burner and one room features the original wood beams. A quiz is held every other Wednesday. Local CAMRA Pub of the Year in 2013. Q🐴❀♣●🚌(341,369)🐾

Stourbridge

Duke William L

25 Coventry Street, DY8 1EP (corner of Coventry St and Duke St)
12-11 (11.30 Fri & Sat) ☎ (01384) 440202
Craddock's Saxon Gold, Crazy Sheep, Lion's Pride, Capra, Troll; guest beers H
Locally listed Edwardian town-centre pub and home of the Craddock's Brewery. It has a main bar with a real fire and an adjacent snug; upstairs is a function room with a bar. Traditional pie and mash (with a choice of eight varieties) is served Monday-Thursday lunchtimes and evenings, and lunchtimes Friday-Sunday, alongside a range of cold snacks. Regular events and brewery tours can be arranged. There are summer festivals with a choice of over 50 ales and ciders. US and continental beers are also available. Q❀◑♿⇌(Town)●🍺🚌🐾📶

Edward Rutland L

77-78 High Street, DY8 1DX (next to bus/rail interchange)
8am-midnight (2am Thu & Fri; 2.30am Sat)
☎ (01384) 445670
Greene King Abbot; Ruddles Best Bitter; guest beers H
A Wetherspoon/Lloyds No.1 conversion from a catalogue bargain store – the dark decor and lack of natural light is made up for by the keen managers and their staff, who always welcome suggestions from customers on local and guest beers to be stocked. There is a passageway to another bar and additional seating at the rear. Background music plays after 5pm, with Lloyds-style music from 10pm onwards Thursday-Saturday. The standard Wetherspoon menu of pub food is served. 🐴◑♿⇌(Town)🚌📶

Royal Exchange 🄻

75 Enville Street, DY8 1XW (on A458 just off ring road)
⏲ 1 (12 Sat)-11; 12-10.30 Sun ☎ (01384) 396726
Bathams Mild Ale, Best Bitter 🄷
A pub with a busy traditional bar to the front and a small cosy lounge to the rear, accessed through a side passage. The bar is decorated with whisky bottles and boxes, pewter tankards and foreign banknotes. The ale is good value and served in handled beer glasses on request. A public car park is directly opposite. There is a covered and heated smoking area within the large beer garden to the rear. A function room is available upstairs and may be booked for free. Q❀♣P🚌

Streetly

Queslett

Queslett Road East, B74 2EY
⏲ 11.30-11 (midnight Thu-Sat) ☎ (0121) 580 8123
M&B Brew XI; Marston's Pedigree; Purity Pure Ubu; guest beers 🄷
This refurbished Ember Inn now boasts a large front patio. The open-plan interior is split into a variety of comfortably furnished areas, enhanced by flaming gas fires. Well-presented food is served daily until 10pm. Four guest beers from the Ember seasonal range are offered, usually providing interesting choices. Ales are reduced in price to all on Cask Ale Mondays. Quizzes are held on Tuesdays and Sundays. ❀◑◗♿♣P🚌

Sutton Coldfield

Horse & Jockey

90 Birmingham Road, B72 1LY
⏲ 11.30-11.30 (midnight Thu-Sat) ☎ (0121) 321 2412
Marston's Pedigree; Purity Pure Ubu; Sharp's Doom Bar; guest beers 🄷
This mock-Tudor multi-gabled street-corner pub is a typical Ember Inn. It features deep bay windows, elaborate hanging lamps and a trio of flaming gas fires. An ever-popular food-oriented establishment, it also has a good range of ales, with three regular beers complemented by two changing guests selected from the Ember Inns portfolio. Pictures of old Sutton adorn the walls. Children are welcome until 9pm in a designated dining area. The car park is Pay & Display. ❀◑◗♿⇌(Wylde Green)P🚌

Three Tuns

19 High Street, B72 1XS (up hill N from town centre)
⏲ 11.30-midnight (11 Mon; 11.30 Tue; 1am Fri & Sat); 11.30-11 Sun ☎ (0121) 355 2996 🌐 threetuns.net
Thwaites Original, Wainwright, Lancaster Bomber; guest beer 🄷
A 16th-century coaching inn, said to be haunted. The central coach track is still evident, now a courtyard sheltered by a glazed canopy. There are four rooms – one for quiet contemplation, a bar for chat, a lounge for food and regular live music, and a games room with Sky Sports. Sometimes the guest ale is a special from Thwaites. Food is served noon-9pm (to 8pm Sun and Mon) and children are welcome until 9pm. Q◑◗♿⇌♣P🚌🐾

Tipton

Fountain

51 Owen Street, DY4 8HE
⏲ 11-11 ☎ (0121) 522 3606
Banks's Mild; Wye Valley HPA; guest beers 🄷
Featuring in the Guide for the first time, this canalside pub has a central bar with a good range of ales. It is children-friendly and serves a range of good-value pub meals and curries lunchtimes and evenings, as well as roasts on Sunday lunchtimes. Guest beers are sourced through the Punch Taverns Finest Cask Ales scheme. ❀◑◗⇌♣P🚌🐾

Rising Sun 🄻

116 Horseley Road, DY4 7NH (off B4517)
⏲ 12-midnight ☎ (0121) 557 1940
Black Country Bradley's Finest Golden, Pig on the Wall, Fireside; guest beers 🄷
A former CAMRA National Pub of the Year, it reopened in 2013 following a superb refurbishment by Black Country Ales. This imposing Victorian hostelry has two distinct rooms warmed by open fires. For the summer there is a tidy yard at the back. Five changing guest beers are available and one real cider, usually Black Rat. Cobs and snacks are served. The pub is 10 minutes' walk from Great Bridge bus station, which has frequent services to Dudley, West Bromwich and Birmingham. ❀♣🚌(310)🐾

Tamebridge

45 Tame Road, Great Bridge, DY4 7JA (off A461)
⏲ 12-11 ☎ (0121) 557 2496
RCH Pitchfork; Wye Valley HPA; guest beers 🄷
Situated alongside the Oldbury arm of the River Tame, the Tamebridge stands out with its bright red painted brickwork. The bar, which has a large coal fire, leads onto a small, cosy snug area. There is also a family room, all rooms having a large-screen TV. Outside is a covered and heated smoking area and garden. The pub has a separate toilet for wheelchair users. It currently serves four real ales, including two varying guests. ❀⇌(Dudley Port)P🚌(74)🐾

Upper Gornal

Britannia ★ 🄻

109 Kent Street, DY3 1UX (on A459)
⏲ 12-11 (10.30 Sun) ☎ (01902) 883253
Bathams Mild Ale, Best Bitter 🄷
The Britannia has a nationally important historic pub interior for the taproom at the rear, with its wall-mounted handpumps, named after legendary former landlady Sally Perry. Service can be obtained from the front bar, itself a very comfortable place to be, with both areas warmed by a roaring open fire. There is also a family/games room with TV. Behind the pub is the former brewhouse and a delightful garden. A good selection of bar snacks is available. Bathams XXX is sold in winter. Q❀♣🚌(1)🐾

Jolly Crispin 🄻

25 Clarence Street, DY3 1UL (A459)
⏲ 4 (12 Fri & Sat)-11; 12-10.30 Sun ☎ (01902) 672220
🌐 thejollycrispin.co.uk
Fownes Crispin's Ommer; guest beers 🄷
This lively pub on the main route from Dudley to Sedgley was an 18th-century shoemaker's house. It hosts a festival of beer – every day. The pub features regular ales from the on-site Fownes Brewing – Crispin Ommer is the house beer, and up to eight guest pulls are complemented by a real cider. A twice-yearly cider festival is held in the garden. The No.1 bus from Dudley to Wolverhampton stops outside. CAMRA branch Cider Pub of the Year 2014. Q❀♣P🚌(1)🐾

Wall Heath

Wall Heath Tavern 🄻

14 High street, DY6 0HA (on A449)
⏲ 12-midnight (1am Thu-Sat) ☎ (01384) 287319
Enville Ale, Ginger Beer; Holden's Golden Glow; Sharp's Doom Bar; Timothy Taylor Landlord; guest beers 🄷
A bustling pub on the road approaching Wall Heath village centre. Serving up to 10 real ales, with a major emphasis on Enville Ales, it can get busy, particularly at weekends, with a sports TV in the bar. The lounge is predominantly used for the enjoyment of good-value food, especially in the evenings when tables can be reserved. There is a large patio area at the rear, which is busy in the summer months. A CAMRA discount is available on production of a membership card.
🐴❀◐◑♿●P🚌(256,257)🐾📶

Walsall

Black Country Arms 🏆 🄻

High Street, WS1 1QW (in market area, opp Asda)
⏲ 11-11 (midnight Fri); 12-midnight Sat; 12-11 Sun
☎ (01922) 640588 🌐 blackcountryarms.co.uk
Black Country Bradley's Finest Golden, Pig on the Wall, Fireside; guest beers 🄷
A large, imposing establishment on three levels – part of the building was originally the Green Dragon Inn, dating back to the 18th century. The pub lay empty for 70 years until extensive refurbishment saw it reopen in 1987. The impressive bar boasts 16 handpumps serving up to 11 guest ales, mainly from microbreweries, with two real ciders always on tap. Live music features frequently. Current local CAMRA Pub of the Year.
🐴❀◐⥈♣●P🚌📶

Fountain 🄻

49 Lower Forster Street, WS1 1XB (off A4148 ring road)
⏲ 12-2.30, 4.30-11; 12-midnight Fri & Sat; 12-11 Sun
☎ (01922) 633307
Backyard The Hoard, Blonde, Gold; guest beers 🄷
The brewery tap for Backyard Brewhouse, with up to eight real ales available. This recently refurbished pub has a friendly atmosphere and welcoming staff. Bar snacks include cobs and pork pies. A vinyl night takes place once a month, craft night on a Wednesday, jam night every other Sunday, and film night every Monday. The pub supports local artists but keeps a traditional feel.
Q🐴◐◑⥈♣●🚌(394,977)

Longhorn

255 Sutton Road, WS5 3AR
⏲ 11-midnight (11 Sun & Mon) ☎ (01922) 625065
Greene King IPA; Purity Pure Ubu; guest beers 🄷
Large 1930s roadside inn with a real community feel. The rear of the pub is given over to diners while drinkers tend to occupy the front section. The Longhorn hosts many charity events throughout the year, with quiz nights on Sundays and Wednesdays. Regular food and drinks deals are on offer. There is a function area available to hire free of charge. Up to six guest ales can be enjoyed.
🐴❀◐◑♿P📶

Lyndon House Hotel 🄻

9-10 Upper Rushall Street, WS1 2HA (between market and St Matthew's church)
⏲ 11-11 (1am Fri & Sat); 12-11 Sun ☎ (01922) 612511
🌐 lyndonhousehotel.co.uk
Bathams Best Bitter; Burton Bridge Golden Delicious; Caledonian Deuchars IPA; Greene King Abbot; Holden's Golden Glow; guest beers 🄷
A pub that is part of a hotel complex. The bar was converted in the 1980s, incorporating old brick and many old timbers to warm and cosy effect. The luxurious hotel was formerly a Salvation Army hostel and leather factory. Popular with business people, its clientèle are drawn from all over the town to give a slice of Walsall life. Occasional live entertainment takes place. Lunchtime meals are available all week, with a carvery on Sunday, evening meals Monday-Thursday only.
Q❀🛏◐◑♿P🚌(51,377)

Pretty Bricks 🄻

5 John Street, WS2 8AF (near magistrates court, off B4210)
⏲ 12-11 ☎ (01922) 612553
Black Country Bradley's Finest Golden, Pig on the Wall, Fireside; guest beers 🄷
Small and friendly hostelry dating from 1845. Cosy and comfortable, the bar has a wood fire, lounge, an upstairs function room and a small blue-brick yard. Officially called the New Inn, its name derives from a part-glazed frontage. This is where one of the first branches of CAMRA was formed in 1972, driven by an early campaigner, the late Peter Linley. It was given an initial brief to cover the country from here north to John o'Groats.
Q❀◐◑⥈♣●🚌(301)

St Matthew's Hall

Lichfield Street, WS1 1SX
⏲ 8am-midnight (2am Fri & Sat) ☎ (01922) 700020
Adnams Broadside; Greene King Abbot; Ruddles Best Bitter; Sharp's Doom Bar; guest beers 🄷
A stunning Grade II-listed Wetherspoon outlet with two log fires and music playing daily from noon onwards. There are large beer gardens to the front and rear, including a sheltered area. A selection of local and national guest ales supplements the two regular offerings. The licensee is always interested in hearing customers' views on the ales available, or ones they would like to see served. There is a DJ every Friday and Saturday till 2am.
🐴❀◐◑♿⥈●🚌

Walsall Cricket Club

Gorway Road, WS1 3BE (off A34, by university campus)
⏲ 8-10.30; 12-11 (4-10.30 winter) Sat; 12-11 (8 winter) Sun
☎ (01922) 622094 🌐 walsallcricketclub.com
Wye Valley HPA; guest beers 🄷
The club has been on its Gorway site since 1909 and has a comfortable single-roomed lounge displaying cricket memorabilia and two large screens for sporting events. The bar is manned by members. On match days the cricket can be viewed through panoramic windows, while in good weather the lounge is opened onto the patio area. On a summer's evening this feels like a rural retreat in the heart of town. Rooms here are available for functions. CAMRA members are welcome – show your membership card.
🐴❀♿♣P🚌(51)📶

Wheatsheaf 🄻

4 Birmingham Road, WS1 2NA
⏲ 3-11 Mon-Wed; 1-midnight Thu; 12-1am Fri & Sat; 12-11 Sun ☎ (01922) 636687 🌐 wheatsheafwalsall.com
Brains SA Gold; Holden's Golden Glow; Salopian Oracle; Wye Valley Butty Bach; guest beers 🄷

Friendly open-plan community local with live music most weekends. Tuesday is jam night and monthly quiz nights are held. Steak night is on a Thursday and traditional lunches on Sunday. Up to eight ales are served, with a real cider. The building has been a pub since at least 1801, formerly in the hands of historic brewers Allsopp and then Ansells. It became the Flock & Firkin in the 1980s before restoration in 2007. The current licensees have been in place since late 2012.
(51)

Wednesbury

Bellwether

3-4 Walsall Street, WS10 9BZ

7am-midnight (1am Fri & Sat) ☎ (0121) 502 6404

Greene King Abbot; Morland Old Speckled Hen; Oakham Jeffrey Hudson Bitter; guest beers H

Just off the marketplace and main shopping area, this pub attracts a varied patronage. It has one large L-shaped room, on a split level, with open-plan tables and chairs in front of the bar and more intimate bench seating at the rear. It is decorated throughout with historic events and characters associated with the town. There is a split-level garden area at the rear offering a tranquil oasis in the town. Ten handpumps serve a large selection of guest ales. **Q**

Cottage Spring

106 Franchise Street, WS10 9RG

2-11.30; 12-12.30am Fri & Sat; 12-11.30 Sun

☎ (0121) 526 6354

Holden's Black Country Bitter; guest beers H

An 18th-century two-roomed inn with a public bar that features one of the early editions of a red telephone box, and photographs from the 1950s and '60s. The family lounge, where Sunday lunches are served, has old advertisements on the walls. On Friday night and Saturday there is karaoke. Up to three real ales are sold, all from the Holden's range. **Q P**

Old Blue Ball

19 Hall End, WS10 9ED (just off B4200 Whitley St)

12-3, 5-11; 12-11 Fri-Sun ☎ (0121) 556 0197

Brains The Rev James; Everards Original; Olde Swan Original; Wye Valley Butty Bach; guest beers H

The small bar is adorned with chamber pots, jugs and advertising mirrors. Darts is played in the lounge. Old canal maps and a history of cock fights are on display, while the cosy snug is decorated with a sketch of the pub plus paintings on the walls, and the popular stand-up passage has artists' impressions of old Wednesbury. The large split-level garden includes a TV and children's play area. **Q** (311A,313)

Olde Leathern Bottel

40 Vicarage Road, WS10 9DW (just off A461)

12-2.30 (not Mon), 6-11; 12-3, 6-11.30 Fri; 11-11.30 Sat; 12-4, 7-11 Sun ☎ (0121) 505 0230

Beer range varies H

The bar and snug of the Bottel are set in cottages dating from 1510, with a later extension housing the lounge. It has four rooms adorned with old photos, including a snug which is also used as a function room. The small bar features a photo of the pub from about 1887 and a map of Wednesbury from 1845. At the rear is a pleasant benched area with plant pots. There is a quiz on Sunday evenings. **Q P** (311)

Wednesfield

Vine ★

35 Lichfield Road, WV11 1TN

12-11 (midnight Fri & Sat) ☎ (01902) 733529

Black Country Bradley's Finest Golden, Pig on the Wall, Fireside; guest beers H

Built in 1938, this Grade II-listed community local is a rare intact example of a simple inter-war working-class pub. It has been identified by CAMRA as having a nationally important historic pub interior for retaining its original bar, lounge and snug. Guest beers from all over the country are available alongside the regular beers and other LocAles. A covered smokers' shelter and a beer garden provide outdoor drinking areas. Excellent home-cooked food is served (no food Mon or Sun eve). **Q P** (59,89)

West Bromwich

Old Hop Pole

474 High Street, B70 9LD

12-3, 5-11; 12-1am Fri & Sat; 12-11 Sun ☎ 07946 579957

Wye Valley HPA; guest beers H

A friendly and popular local just outside the town centre. The central serving area supplies a busy front bar and a quieter rear room. There are up to three changing guest ales together with the regular beer, Wye Valley HPA. Cards, darts and dominoes are frequently played at a competitive level. Live music or a disco is staged most Saturday nights. It gets extremely busy when West Bromwich Albion are at home. (74,79)

Vine

152 Roebuck Street, B70 6RD

11.30-2, 5-11; 11.30-11 Fri & Sat; 12-10.30 Sun

☎ (0121) 553 2866 thevine.co.uk

Beer range varies H

From the street this appears to be a traditional corner pub, but be prepared for a surprise. The standard interior comprises three small rooms off a corridor. But continue further and the building opens up into a large dining area where an extensive range of Indian meals is available, together with more usual British fare and vegetarian options – all excellent value. Two guest ales are regularly on tap. It can get busy, especially when West Bromwich Albion are at home.
(Smethwick Galton Bridge) (74)

Willenhall

County

7 Walsall Street, WV13 2ES

12-11 (midnight Fri & Sat); 11-11 Sun ☎ (01902) 608283

Wye Valley HPA; guest beers H

Situated on the main Walsall road out of town, the County is a large street-corner pub dating from 1834. The venue includes a comfortable wooden-beamed lounge and a more basic public bar with a pool table and darts. The three handpumps are found in the lounge. Home-cooked food is served in the lounge daily and the Sunday lunches are popular. There is a beer garden at the rear.
(529)

Falcon

77 Gomer Street West, WV13 2NR (off B4464, behind flats)

12-11; 12-10.30 Sun ☎ (01902) 633378

Exmoor Gold; Hop Back Summer Lightning; Olde Swan Dark Swan, Bumble Hole Bitter; Salopian Oracle; guest beers Ⓗ
The Falcon, built in 1936, is situated just off the town centre and has been run by the same family for over 30 years, with a strong local following. A true Black Country local, it has two rooms, a lively front bar and a quieter lounge at the rear. Seven keenly priced beers are served. Old pub memorabilia adorn both rooms.
Q (525,529)

Malthouse

The Dale, New Road, WV13 2BG
8am-midnight (1am Fri & Sat) ☎ (01902) 635273
Greene King Abbot; Ruddles Best Bitter; Sadler's Hop Bomb Ⓗ**; guest beers** Ⓗ/Ⓖ
Formerly a cinema and bingo hall, the Malthouse stands on the site of an old maltings associated with the nearby Dale House. It consists of a single L-shaped room, with a rear patio area accessible via stairs from within the pub or via an external gate at ground level. Wheelchair access is by means of a lift at the front entrance. At least two traditional ciders are served.

Wollaston

Graham's Place

73 Bridgnorth Road, DY8 3PZ (on A458 towards Bridgnorth, just before Wollaston)
11-11 ☎ (01384) 440315 grahams-place.co.uk
Salopian Shropshire Gold, Oracle, Hop Twister; guest beers Ⓗ
A single-room pub with a modern, clean style of decor and a variety of different feels within the bar area. Freshly prepared meals from locally-sourced ingredients are served in the conservatory to the rear, with a more intimate, cosy drinking area to the front and a long bar between the two. Up to seven real ales are on handpull. There is also a covered smoking area and patio. Tuesday is quiz night. CAMRA branch Pub of the Year 2014.
P

Unicorn

145 Bridgnorth Road, DY8 3NX (on A458 towards Bridgnorth)
12-11; 12-4, 7-10.30 Sun ☎ (01384) 394823
Bathams Mild Ale, Best Bitter Ⓗ
A former brewhouse purchased by Bathams, it has barely altered in appearance since the Billingham family sold up in the early 1990s. The brewhouse is still there but is not used any more. The pub is renowned for serving one of the best pints in the area. A traditional two-bar local, it has a small back room where children are welcome. The pub is popular with all age groups and conversation is the order of the day. Fresh cobs are available on request. QP

Wolverhampton

Chindit

113 Merridale Road, WV3 9SE
4 (12 Sat & Sun)-11 ☎ 07986 773487 thechindit.co.uk
Castle Rock Harvest Pale; Hop Back Summer Lightning; Wye Valley HPA; guest beers Ⓗ
Street-corner local, built in the 1950s originally as an off-licence. It is thought to be the only pub in the country named after the Chindits, a special force who fought in Burma in World War II – their history is displayed on the wall in the lounge. The bar is extensively decorated with music memorabilia and hosts live music every Friday evening. The beers are almost exclusively light in colour and often come from local brewer Broughs.
P (3,4)

Combermere Arms

90 Chapel Ash, WV3 0TY (on A41 Tettenhall Rd)
12-3, 5-11; 12-midnight Fri & Sat; 12-10.30 Sun
☎ (01902) 421880
Banks's Mild; guest beers Ⓗ
Lovely old-fashioned pub with heaps of character, including the tree in the Gents. It has three rooms with cosy fires, a wealth of humorous pictures, and pub and football memorabilia. Live entertainment features on Saturday evenings throughout the summer and occasionally in winter. The pub is clean and friendly, with good wholesome food served weekdays 12-2pm. Local ales and changing guest beers are displayed on the bar chalkboard. A short walk from the city centre and served by four buses. QP

Dog & Gun

1 Wrottesley Road, Tettenhall, WV6 8SB (off A41 Wergs Rd)
11.30-11 (midnight Fri & Sat) ☎ (01902) 747943
Banks's Bitter; Purity Pure Ubu; guest beers Ⓗ
Recently refurbished, this comfortable, welcoming Ember Inns pub has individual seating areas around a large U-shaped bar. It attracts a wide age range, including a local writers' group and a rambling club who meet here regularly. Food quality, a varied range of LocAle beers and an imaginative choice of guest beers, often dark, ensure a busy and friendly atmosphere, particularly on weekend evenings. There is a patio for outside drinking and a covered, heated area for smokers. P (1,891)

Great Western

Sun Street, WV10 0DJ (via subway from high level rail station and city centre)
11-11 (10.30 Sun) ☎ (01902) 351090
Bathams Best Bitter; Holden's Black Country Mild, Black Country Bitter, Golden Glow, Special; guest beers Ⓗ
A previous CAMRA National Pub of the Year, this historic and listed pub gets its name from the adjacent former low-level railway station. Plenty of railway memorabilia is on display and cosy real fires blaze in the winter. Good-value meals are served at lunchtime and snacks are available until 10pm. Free nibbles are offered on Sunday evenings. It is popular with Wolverhampton Wanderers fans, and gets busy on match days.
P

Hail to the Ale

2 Pendeford Avenue, Tettenhall, WV6 9EF (on Claregate island)
closed Mon-Wed; 5-10 Thu & Fri; 12-10 Sat; 12-5 Sun ☎ 07846 562910 hailtothealemicropub.co.uk
Beer range varies Ⓗ
Converted from a vacant shop, the West Midlands' first micropub was opened by Morton Brewery. Two Morton beers are normally on offer along with two different guest beers, usually LocAle, and a real cider. Bar snacks such as pork pies and cheese cobs are served. The pub is available for private functions on Wednesday evenings. The Wolverhampton to Codsall bus stops nearby and there is a car park at the front. QP (5,5A)

Hog's Head 𝕃

186 Stafford Street, WV1 1NA

10-midnight (1am Fri & Sat) ☎ (01902) 717955

hogsheadwolverhampton.co.uk

Beer range varies Ⓗ

Large city-centre pub built in the 19th century, locally listed for its terracotta exterior. A stained-glass window above the front door reveals its original name, the Vine. The single room interior divides into many areas featuring large-screen TVs, including one in the smokers' courtyard, showing sport and music videos. It was a deserved winner of local CAMRA Pub of the Year in 2013 for its wide range of real ales, including local beers from microbreweries, making it popular with all ages.

Lych Gate Tavern 🏆 𝕃

44 Queen Square, WV1 1TX

11-11 (midnight Fri & Sat) ☎ (01902) 399516

lychgatetavern.co.uk

Black Country Bradley's Finest Golden, Pig on the Wall, Fireside; guest beers Ⓗ

A real ale pub converted from offices by Black Country Traditional Inns in 2012. One of the oldest buildings in the city centre, the Georgian frontage dates from 1726, while the timber-framed rear dates back to around 1500. The bar area is reached by a short flight of stairs down from street level, and there is a function room with a bar upstairs. A changing range of six guest beers and a real cider is served. Q

Moon Under Water 𝕃

53-55 Lichfield Street, WV1 1EQ (opp Grand Theatre)

7am-midnight (1am Fri & Sat) ☎ (01902) 422447

Banks's Mild; Greene King Abbot; Ruddles Best Bitter; guest beers Ⓗ

Since opening in the former Co-op building in 1995 this Wetherspoon pub has thrived, attracting a varied clientele from around the area. Old pictures of Wolverhampton decorate the walls and there is a stained-glass pattern in the ceiling around one of the pillars. It is handy for the Grand Theatre and is also near the bus and railway stations. You are welcome to try before you buy if you can't decide which beer to order.

Newhampton 𝕃

19 Riches Street, Whitmore Reans, WV6 0DW

11-11 (midnight Fri & Sat); 12-11 Sun ☎ (01902) 680766

Caledonian Deuchars IPA; Courage Best Bitter; Enville Ale; Fuller's London Pride; Timothy Taylor Landlord; Wye Valley HPA Ⓗ

A street-corner local with a bar, smoke room (quiet room) and a pool room with a jukebox. It has eight handpumps, seven for beer and one for real cider. The upstairs room hosts the local folk club on Saturdays. The large garden includes a children's adventure playground, a crown green for bowls and a covered smoking area. The bowls pavilion has one wall devoted to small cupboards for keeping the bowls in.

Posada 𝕃

48 Lichfield Street, WV1 1DG (opp art gallery)

12-11 (1am Fri & Sat)

Castle Rock Harvest Pale; Sharp's Doom Bar; guest beers Ⓗ

A splendid Victorian Grade II-listed city-centre pub. It is much altered but retains some of its original features, notably the tiling. It attracts a varied customer base, quiet during the day and busier in the evening and weekends, especially when Wolverhampton Wanderers are at home. There is a courtyard to the rear and a smoking area. Two real ciders are served.

Royal Oak 𝕃

70 Compton Road, WV3 9PH (on A454 300yds from Chapel Ash jct)

11.30-11 (midnight Fri & Sat) ☎ (01902) 422845

Banks's Mild, Bitter; guest beers Ⓗ

Historic local pub, a short walk from the city centre, with a lively and friendly atmosphere in its single-bar room. Winning an industry award for the quality of its ales, the three changing guest beers are from a Marston's-owned brewery. There is an open mic night every Wednesday, and local music acts regularly feature on Saturday evenings. A large patio, covered at one end, provides ample shelter for smokers, and stages live music in the summer. P (10,890)

Stile Inn 𝕃

3 Harrow Street, Whitmore Reans, WV1 4PB (off Newhampton Rd East/Fawdry St)

11.30-11 (midnight Fri; 1am Sat) ☎ (01902) 425336

thestileinn.co.uk

Banks's Mild, Bitter, Sunbeam; guest beers Ⓗ

This late-Victorian multi-room pub is probably best known for its unusual L-shaped bowling green. It has a good reputation for its food, and in particular Polish dishes. The club room caters for darts and dominoes. There are comedy nights on Fridays and karaoke on Saturdays. Sky Sports is shown in all rooms. It is close to the Wolverhampton Wanderers ground and gets busy on match days. (5,6)

Swan (at Compton) 𝕃

Bridgnorth Road, Compton, WV6 8AE (at Compton Island A454)

12-11 (11.30 Thu; midnight Fri & Sat) ☎ (01902) 754736

swanpubwolverhampton.co.uk

Banks's Mild, Bitter; guest beers Ⓗ

A Grade II-listed inn on the main road and close to the Staffordshire & Worcestershire Canal. The Swan has a basic charm with a warm, friendly atmosphere and an interior that has not been tampered with. Guest ales come from the Marston's range. The separate public bar has exposed beams, wooden settles and a humorous collection of placards around the serving area. A function room is used by local groups for meetings. The heated patio is partially covered for smokers. Q P (10,890)

Woodcross

Horse & Jockey 𝕃

64 Robert Wynd, WV14 9SB

12-11 (11.30 Fri & Sat) ☎ (01902) 662268

horseandjockeywoodcross.co.uk

Greene King Abbot; Hobsons Twisted Spire, Town Crier; St Austell Tribute; Tetley Bitter; guest beers Ⓗ

Friendly, family-owned community local run by real ale enthusiasts. Good-value, home-cooked food is served daily, with vegetarian options, until 8.30pm (4pm Sun). A regular quiz night is on Tuesday and spice night on Wednesday. The bar has a dartboard and TV. Under-18s are allowed in the lounge area and garden until 8pm. A smoking area is provided at the front and a pleasant enclosed garden at the rear. Cask Marque and LocAle accredited. Q P (81)

Woodsetton

Park Inn 𝕃

George Street, DY1 4LW (on A457, 200yds from A4123)

12-11 (10.30 Sun) ☎ (01902) 661279

Holden's Black Country Mild, Black Country Bitter, Golden Glow, Special; guest beer Ⓗ

Vibrant suburban brewery tap, held by the Holden family since 1915. Radiating out from the spacious main bar are a small games room, raised dining area and separate conservatory. Functions are catered for and reasonably priced food is served 12-8pm (till 4.30pm Sun). There is a 10p discount on a pint for card-carrying CAMRA members. The new brewery centre is on the right of the car park.

♣P (81,126)

Wordsley

New Inn 𝕃

117 High Street, DY8 5QR (A491)

12-11 (10.30 Sun) ☎ (01384) 295614

Bathams Mild Ale, Best Bitter Ⓗ

The building has an imposing three-storey Victorian façade. One of the Bathams 11, it has become extremely popular and can be busy. An L-shaped bar serves a single room that has a small annexe at one end, with a patio area and newly refurbished garden outside. A variety of cobs is served. The pub has the feel of a proper local. Bathams XXX is on in winter. Children are not permitted inside but there is a play area outside available in summer.

♣P (256,257)

Black Horse, Birmingham: Northfield

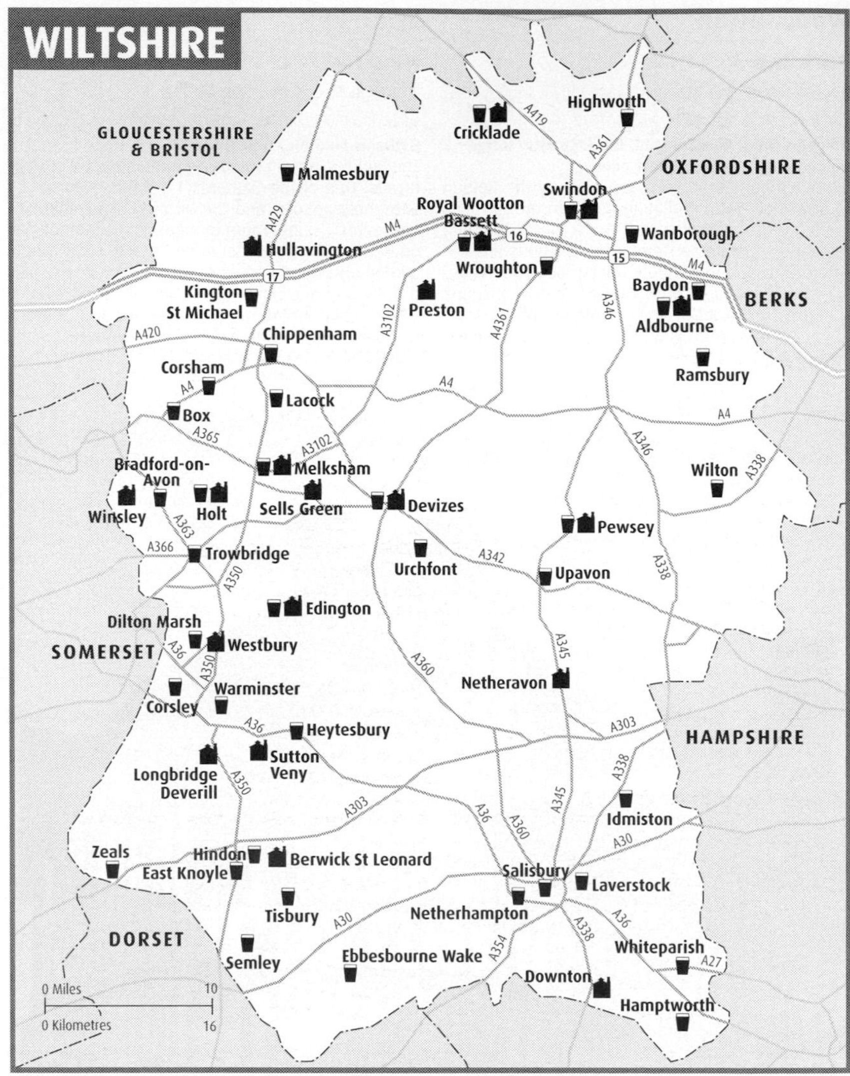

Aldbourne

Crown Hotel

The Square, SN8 2DU

☉ 12-midnight (10.30 Sun) ☎ (01672) 540214

🌐 thecrownaldbourne.co.uk

Sharp's Doom Bar; Shepherd Neame Spitfire; guest beers Ⓗ

The Crown – probably a former coaching inn – is set in the middle of the village opposite the duck pond. Much improved in recent years, it has a relaxed and pleasant atmosphere. The main bar is stylishly refurbished with a welcoming fire during the colder seasons. The smaller bar shows films on Monday night. The restaurant serves freshly prepared food with daily specials until 10pm. There are four en-suite bedrooms. Entertainment includes quiz nights and live music.
❀🛏☽▲🚌(46,48)📶

Baydon

Red Lion 𝕃

Ermin Street, SN8 2JP

☉ 12-11 (midnight Fri & Sat); 12-10 Sun ☎ (01672) 541224

🌐 redlionbaydon.co.uk

Box Steam Tunnel Vision; Ramsbury Bitter, Gold; guest beers Ⓗ

Mark and Julie celebrated the reopening of the Red Lion as a free house with a beer festival, and now hold two festivals every year. Most of the beers are local, from microbreweries such as Box Steam, Ramsbury and Malmesbury. Three ciders are also available. The Red Lion has established itself as a popular local with quality ales and good home cooking. Quiz night is Wednesday and live music features once a month. Cyclists, walkers and dogs are welcome. ❀☽🍎P🚌(46,48)

ENGLAND

Box

Quarryman's Arms 𝕃

Box Hill, SN13 8HN
⏲ 10 (11 Mon)-11; 10-midnight Fri; 11-midnight Sat; 11-11 Sun ☎ (01225) 743569 🌐 quarrymans-arms.co.uk
Butcombe Bitter; Moles Best Bitter; Wadworth 6X; guest beers Ⓗ
Tucked away off the main routes, the Quarryman's is a steep uphill walk from the nearest bus stop, but this 300-year-old miners' inn is well worth the effort. A friendly welcome is assured and the pub is renowned for high-quality food and ales, served in the bar, restaurant or garden. Quiz night is every second Wednesday, and county-themed beer festivals are held regularly.
Q🛋❀🛏◐◑♿⛺♣🍎P📶

Bradford-on-Avon

Castle Inn

Mount Pleasant, BA15 1SJ
⏲ 9am-11; 10-10.30 Sun ☎ (01225) 867280
🌐 flatcappers.co.uk/the-castle-inn
Three Castles Barbury Castle, Vale Ale; guest beers Ⓗ
A popular, comfortable pub commanding splendid views across the town towards Salisbury Plain. The recent refurbishment by Flatcappers earned a national CAMRA award. A wide range of handpulled real ales is complemented by excellent food, served all day until 9pm. The three guest beers are usually sourced from micros in Wiltshire and east Somerset. B&B is available, with four luxury double bedrooms. 🛋❀🛏◐◑♿⇌P🚌📶

Rising Sun

231 Winsley Road, BA15 1QS
⏲ 12 (4 Tue)-11; 12-10.30 Sun ☎ (01225) 862354
Courage Best Bitter; guest beers Ⓗ
Popular local with two bars: a small, quiet lounge and a more spacious, livelier saloon with TV screens. Behind is a walled beer garden with patio. The pub is home to darts, quiz, crib, pool and football teams, and hosts regular live music including a Rhythm & Booze beer festival over the August bank holiday. The two guests change week by week and the cider is Thatchers Cheddar Valley. The pub's ancient spaniel is still there, ready to welcome you. 🛋❀⇌♣🍎🚌📶

Chippenham

Gladstone Arms

34 Gladstone Road, SN15 3BW (by bus station)
⏲ 5.30-10.30 Mon; 11.30-3, 5.30-11 Tue-Thu; 11-midnight Fri & Sat; 12-11 Sun ☎ (01249) 660535
🌐 thegladstonearms.co.uk
Bath Ales Gem; St Austell Tribute; Sharp's Doom Bar Ⓗ
This popular pub is conveniently situated just out of the town centre, close to the bus station. Three real ales are available in the bistro-style bar. The walls are decorated with a variety of music-themed photographs – and look for the unique stools at the bar. High-quality food is served in the bar and restaurant, and in the largest pub garden in town during the summer. Sunday is quiz night.
🛋❀◐◑⇌P🚌🐾📶

Old Road Tavern

Old Road, SN15 1JA (over bridge from railway station)
⏲ 11-11.30 (12.30am Fri & Sat); 12-11 Sun
☎ (01249) 652094
Bath Ales Gem; Hop Back Summer Lightning; Otter Bitter; Wye Valley HPA; guest beer Ⓗ
This Grade II listed community local is over 140 years old. Frequently changing guest beers are sourced from breweries both nearby and further afield. The barn regularly hosts local bands and comedy nights, and is a popular venue during the Chippenham Folk Festival held over the spring bank holiday weekend. Bar food is served Thursday to Saturday lunchtimes. The large garden is popular in summer. Lively and friendly, this is an all-round top pub. ❀◐♿⇌♣🍎🚌🐾📶

Three Crowns 🏆 𝕃

18 The Causeway, SN15 3DB (E of town centre)
⏲ 5 (12 Thu)-11; 12-midnight Fri & Sat; 12-11 Sun
☎ (01249) 449029 🌐 threecrownschippenham.co.uk
Beer range varies Ⓗ
Originally an 18th-century wagon inn on the London to Bath road, with a large extension added in the 19th century. A free house, it offers seven cask beers sourced from local microbreweries as well as from further afield. The range always includes two dark beers and one strong brew. Three ciders are also on offer, mainly from Wiltshire producers, and a perry. CAMRA members receive a discount. Four beer festivals are held each year. Branch CAMRA Cider Pub of the Year.
Q🛋♣🍎P🥛🚌🐾

Corsham

Hare & Hounds

Pickwick, SN13 0HY
⏲ 11-11 ☎ (01249) 701106
🌐 hareandhoundscorsham.co.uk
Bath Ales Gem; Sharp's Cornish Coaster; guest beers Ⓗ
Originally a coaching inn on the London to Bath road, this large two-bar hostelry is proud to serve locally-produced food to accompany its fine ales. A popular pub with locals, it hosts a quiz night every Tuesday. It is situated close to the bus stop and has a large car park. It is said that Charles Dickens developed his ideas for Pickwick Papers during a stay here. Q🛋❀◐◑P🚌 (X31)

INDEPENDENT BREWERIES

Arkell's Swindon
Box Steam Holt
Braydon Preston
Downton Downton
Flying Monk Hullavington (NEW)
Hop Back Downton
Hop Kettle Cricklade
Kennet & Avon Sells Green (NEW)
Keystone Berwick St Leonard
Malmesbury Royal Wootton Bassett (NEW)
Moles Melksham
Plain Sutton Veny
Ramsbury Aldbourne
Shed Ales Pewsey
Stonehenge Netheravon
Three Castles Pewsey
Three Daggers Edington
Twisted Westbury (NEW)
Wadworth Devizes
Weighbridge Swindon
Wessex Longbridge Deverill
Willy Good Ale Winsley
World's End Pewsey

Two Pigs L

Pickwick, SN13 0HY
7-11; 12-2.30, 7-10.30 Sun ☎ (01249) 712515
thetwopigs.co.uk
Stonehenge Pigswill, Danish Dynamite; guest beers H
A long-standing entry in the Guide, this is a drinkers' pub with no food. It has a large single bar with a flagstone floor and ample wooden seating. Pigswill was originally brewed for the pub before becoming part of the Stonehenge range. Background music is usually blues, and live music on Monday is predominantly blues, or blues-influenced rock or jazz. If you're looking for the landlord, he's wearing a loud shirt. Q (231)

Corsley

Cross Keys Inn

Lye's Green, BA12 7PB
12-3, 6-11; 12-11 Sun ☎ (01373) 832406
Wadworth Henry's IPA, 6X; guest beers H
Always worth a visit, this rural gem has a large open fire and a warm, welcoming ambience. It offers a good portfolio of guest beers along with excellent bar food and restaurant meals. There is a function room and an attractive, award-winning garden for outside drinking. The pub actively supports the local cricket team and is situated in good walking country close to Cley Hill and Longleat House and Safari Park. P

Cricklade

Red Lion L

74 High Street, SN6 6DD
12-11 (10.30 Sun) ☎ (01793) 750776
theredlioncricklade.co.uk
Butcombe Bitter; Wadworth 6X; guest beers H
Friendly, popular and comfortable inn, parts of which are quite ancient – the old Saxon town wall passes through the building. The pub is home to the Hop Kettle Brewing Co which started brewing in 2012. Ten real ales – two regular, four from Hop Kettle and four guests – are on handpump, plus real cider. Food is served lunchtimes and evenings Monday-Saturday, lunchtime only on Sunday. There is a large garden at the back. Five rooms are available for B&B. A beer festival takes place in June. Q (51,53)

Devizes

British Lion

9 Estcourt Street, SN10 1LQ (on A361)
11-11 (midnight Fri & Sat); 12-11 Sun ☎ (01380) 720665
britishliondevizes.co.uk
Beer range varies H
The Lion has been the essential port of call in town for 20 years. What you see is what you get – a wooden floor, comfy benches and settles, a three-sided bar and an eclectic and friendly bunch of locals. There are four handpumps with an ever-changing range of ales, usually from West Country breweries, plus a good selection of seasonals. A superb pub, not to be missed. P (49)

Southgate Inn

Potterne Road, SN10 5BY
4-11; 12-midnight Fri & Sat; 12-11 Sun ☎ (01380) 722872
Beer range varies H
The 'Gate has been revitalised by the landlord who took it on three years ago. Two ales from Hop Back are available alongside guests from Downton or other local breweries. Cosy and friendly, it has three small bar areas, plenty of stools and seats, unobtrusive background music and some nooks and crannies in which to enjoy an undisturbed pint or two. There is a large function room used for the annual beer festival and a drinking area outside with benches. P (2,49)

Vaults

28A St John's Street, SN10 1BN (opp town hall)
12-9 (6 Sun) ☎ (01380) 721443 thevaultsdevizes.com
Beer range varies H
A new micro pub and beer shop in town set up to feature the ales of the Kennet & Avon Brewery plus real ales from across the country. It stocks around 120 bottled beers from around the world as well as two cask-conditioned lagers and a draught cider. All the fittings and furniture are made from recycled materials and the huge cellar is available to see by appointment. No music, just friendly banter, great staff and something for everyone. P (2,49)

Dilton Marsh

Prince of Wales

94 High Street, BA13 4DZ
6-11 (midnight Fri); 12-11 Sat; 12-10.30 Sun
☎ (01373) 865487 powdiltonmarsh.co.uk
St Austell Trelawny, Tribute; guest beer H
A smart, friendly locals' pub, refurbished in 2013, with a bar area, separate dining space and a skittle alley doubling as a function room. Outside is a paved area to the side and the beer garden. Traditional pub food is served including Sunday lunches. The guest beer could be from St Austell (HSD or Proper Job) but quite often comes from elsewhere – London Pride, Bass, Courage Best and beers from local micros Moles and Cheddar Ales are among the favourites. P

East Knoyle

Fox & Hounds

Wise Lane, The Green, SP3 6BN ST87113135
11.30-3, 5.30-11 ☎ (01747) 830573
foxandhounds-eastknoyle.co.uk
Beer range varies H
Attractive old thatched black and white pub situated high on a hillside with extensive panoramic rural views. Comfortable and cosy inside, the warm welcome is enhanced in winter by a blazing log fire in a huge inglenook fireplace. Three ales are always available encompassing a wide range of strengths and varying continuously, with local beers given prominence. The real cider is Thatchers Cheddar Valley. Food is served at all sessions. An adjacent skittle alley doubles as a function room. Q P

Ebbesbourne Wake

Horseshoe

The Cross, SP5 5JF
12-3 (not Mon), 6.30-11; 12-4 Sun ☎ (01722) 780474
Bowman Swift One; Otter Bitter; Palmers Dorset Gold; guest beers G
Unspoilt 18th-century pub in a remote rural setting at the foot of an old ox drove. This friendly pub has

two small bars that display an impressive collection of old farm implements, tools and lamps, plus a restaurant, conservatory and pleasant garden. Good local food is available Tuesday to Sunday and five beers are served direct from casks stillaged behind the bar. Real cider is also usually available. The original serving hatch just inside the front door is still in use. Q🐴❀🛏◐◑♣🍎P🚌(29)

Edington

Three Daggers

Westbury Road, BA13 4PG

⏲ 8am-11; 9am-10.30 Sun ☎ (01380) 830940

🌐 threedaggers.co.uk

Three Daggers Daggers Ale; guest beers [H]

This refurbished village pub is now the brewery tap for the eponymous brewery situated in a new adjacent farm shop. The pub has a main bar with three distinct drinking areas, leading to a seating area and a dining room. Two mirrors hide TV screens that are occasionally used for sporting events. Dogs are welcomed with free biscuits, and accommodation is available. The cider is from Thatchers. Q🐴❀🛏◐◑♿♣🍎P🚌(87)🐾📶

Hamptworth

Cuckoo Inn ⓛ

SP5 2DU

⏲ 12-3, 5.30-11; 12-11 Fri & Sat; 12-10.30 Sun

☎ (01794) 390302

Bowman Elderado; Hop Back Golden Best, Summer Lightning; Ringwood Best Bitter; guest beers [G]

Friendly real ale pub situated in the Wiltshire countryside. All ales are served straight from the cask. The pub has a square-shaped main room and three further rooms for drinking and conversation. Food is simple fare – pasties in winter, ploughman's and barbecues in summer. Pizza is served on Wednesday and fish and chips on Friday. Live music features on Thursday evening. Beer festivals are held in May and September. Dogs are welcome in the large garden. Q🐴❀⛺♣🍎P🐾

Heytesbury

Red Lion

42a High Street, BA12 0EA

⏲ 11-11 ☎ (01985) 840315 🌐 redlionheytesbury.co.uk

Plain Arty Farty; Ringwood Best Bitter; guest beer [H]

A proper village inn with a strong local following as well as an ideal base for visitors with well-appointed guest rooms. The beers from Ringwood and Plain Ales are regulars, complemented by a guest ale. Traditional pub food ranges from sandwiches and snacks to more substantial main meals. The garden, running down to the River Wylye, has plenty of seating and a play area for children. Horses are welcome with their own 'parking' area at the rear of the pub. Q🐴❀🛏◐◑♿♣P🚌(55,265)🐾

Highworth

Saracen's Head ⓛ

High Street, SN6 7AG

⏲ 11-11 (midnight Fri & Sat) ☎ (01793) 762284

🌐 saracenshead.co.uk

Arkells 3B, Wiltshire Gold, Moonlight Ale [G]**, seasonal beer** [H]

This former coaching inn dates back to 1825 and is one of Highworth's oldest buildings. It has a snug bar popular with locals, a lounge bar mainly used for dining, and comfortable outside seating. Occasional themed food nights are offered. Owned by Arkells, the ales – three regulars plus a seasonal – are on gravity dispense. The car park is in Brewery Street, with disabled access. Accommodation is in 12 en-suite bedrooms. ❀🛏◐◑♿♣P🚌(7,64)📶

Hindon

Angel Inn

High Street, SP3 6DJ

⏲ 11-11 ☎ (01747) 820696 🌐 angel-inn-at-hindon.co.uk

Otter Bitter; Sharp's Doom Bar; Timothy Taylor Landlord; guest beer [H]

A beautifully restored 18th-century coaching inn, the Angel was originally known as the Grosvenor Arms. Prior to its construction in 1750, a medieval inn, the Angel, existed on the site. The pub retains many original features including the wooden floors, beams and a huge stone fireplace. It is set in an attractive village with a spired church close by. Q🐴❀🛏◐◑♿P🚌(25)🐾📶

Holt

Tollgate Inn

Ham Green, BA14 6PX (on B3105 between Bradford-on-Avon and Melksham)

⏲ closed Mon; 9am-11.30 (4 Sun) ☎ (01225) 782326

🌐 tollgateholt.co.uk

Box Steam Golden Bolt, Tunnel Vision; St Austell Tribute; guest beer [H]

A real gem, this old village pub has an upmarket atmosphere with a wood-burning stove, oak floors and comfy sofas to relax in. The range of four or five beers, which changes daily, includes a good selection of local brews – often including ales from Box Steam in the village – alongside many from smaller breweries further afield. A real cider is on handpump in the summer months. A deli farm shop is on the premises. Q🐴❀🛏◐◑🍎P🚌(237)📶

Idmiston

Earl of Normanton 🏆 ⓛ

Tidworth Road, SP4 0AG

⏲ 12-2.30, 6-11; 12-3, 7.45-10.30 Sun ☎ (01980) 610251

🌐 earlofnormanton.co.uk

Exmoor Gold; Flowerpots Bitter; Hop Back Summer Lightning; guest beers [H]

Popular roadside pub with a loyal village clientele and a welcoming atmosphere enhanced by two real fires in winter months. LocAle accredited, it offers two guest ales mostly from nearby breweries. Good-value home-cooked food is served (no food Sun eve). There is a small, pleasant garden on the steep hill behind the pub and a heated, covered smoking area. B&B is available. Local CAMRA Country Pub of the Year 2014. Q🐴❀🛏◐◑P🚌(66,67)📶

Kington St Michael

Jolly Huntsman

SN14 6JB

⏲ 11.30-2.30, 6-11 (midnight Fri & Sat); 12-3, 7-10.30 Sun

☎ (01249) 750305 🌐 jollyhuntsman.com

Moles Tap Bitter; Wadworth 6X; guest beers [H]

A former 18th-century brewery situated on the village high street, this free house offers a warm and friendly welcome to all. One of the old wells used in the brewing process is still in existence today. A range of locally brewed real ales and ciders is offered along with an excellent food menu available lunchtimes and evenings, featuring a range of traditional fare and chef's specials. Themed evenings with a buffet are hosted on occasion. Accommodation is en suite with free Wi-Fi. Q🐎🛏◑♿🍎P🚌(99)

Lacock

Bell Inn 𝕃

The Wharf, SN15 2JP (½ mile out of Lacock towards Bowden Hill)
⏲ 11-2.30, 5-11; 11.30-11 Sat; 12-10.30 Sun
☎ (01249) 730308 🌐 thebellatlacock.co.uk
Bath Ales Barnsey; Great Western Maiden Voyage; guest beers 🄷
On the edge of the National Trust village of Lacock, this popular free house has been run by the same family since 2000. Local CAMRA Pub of the Year for nine years in a row, it has an excellent reputation for quality food and ale. Five ales and a cider are usually available, and two beer festivals are held each year. Following refurbishment in 2014, the pub retains a traditional feel and offers a warm welcome to all. It is on National Cycle Route 403. Q🐎❀◑⛺♣🍎P🐾📶

George Inn 𝕃

4 West Street, SN15 2LH
⏲ 11-11 (10.30 Sun) ☎ (01249) 730263
Wadworth Henry's IPA, Horizon, 6X, Bishops Tipple; guest beers 🄷
Dating back to 1361, the George sits in the National Trust village of Lacock, famed for the Abbey and Fox Talbot Museum. The pub retains the old oak beams and a large inglenook fireplace with a dog-driven spit still in place. The full range of Wadworth beer is rotated along with a guest ale. Locally-sourced food is served by friendly staff. Real cider and perry is always available. Beer festivals are held every bank holiday weekend.
Q🐎❀◑⛺P🚌(234)🐾

Rising Sun 𝕃

Bowden Hill, SN15 2PP
⏲ 12-11 (9 Sun) ☎ (01249) 730363
🌐 therisingsunlacock.co.uk
Moles Best Bitter, Mole Catcher, seasonal beer 🄷
This friendly local pub was built in stone in the 17th century. It has flagstone floors, real fires and traditional furniture. There is a conservatory for dining and a large terraced garden with far-reaching views. The Riser is the tap for Moles Brewery, five miles away. The regular Moles beers are complemented by seasonal brews. A choice of home-cooked foods is available daily.
🐎❀◑♣🍎P🐾

Laverstock

Duck 𝕃

Duck Lane, SP1 1PU
⏲ 12-midnight ☎ (01722) 327678
🌐 theduckatlaverstock.com
Hop Back Golden Best, Crop Circle, Summer Lightning; guest beers 🄷
Large open-plan pub with ample car parking. A full menu is available lunchtimes and evenings, with a popular Sunday roast and a barbecue. Live music is hosted at weekends and a quiz on Tuesday. Music festivals and themed food nights also feature. There is full disabled access and facilities. Ideally located for walkers on the Clarendon Way.
Q🐎❀◑♿P🚌(66)🐾📶

Malmesbury

Whole Hog 𝕃

8 Market Cross, SN16 9AS
⏲ 11-11 (midnight Sat); 12-11 Sun ☎ (01666) 825845
Stonehenge Pigswill; Wadworth 6X; Young's Bitter; guest beers 🄷
Located between the 15th-century Market Cross and Abbey, this pub occupies a commanding position at the top of the High Street and offers a fine opportunity to watch the world go by when seated at the large front window. A good selection of home-made food complements the ever-changing range of guest beers, where the emphasis is on new, different and unusual ales. A pub central to the community and equally welcoming to visitors. Q◑♣🍎🚌

Melksham

Bear

3 Bath Road, SN12 6LL
⏲ 8am-midnight ☎ (01225) 792690
Greene King Abbot; Prescott Hill Climb; Ruddles Best Bitter; Wadworth 6X; guest beers 🄷
A clean and high specification Wetherspoon pub with a plethora of local history adorning the walls. Friendly and helpful staff serve a range of four regular ales and five or six guests, often including an American craft-style beer. A full range of food is always available, including popular steak and curry nights weekly. Outside is a large seating area for drinkers. Q🐎❀◑♿⇌🍎P🚌📶

Netherhampton

Victoria & Albert

SP2 8PU
⏲ 11-3, 5.30-11; 12-3, 7-10.30 Sun ☎ (01722) 743174
Beer range varies 🄷
This welcoming classic thatched inn dates from 1540. Inside, a log fire greets customers in the winter while outside a large garden and patio await. Three handpulls dispense an ever-changing range of real ales from far and wide, plus Black Rat cider. Quality food is prepared in the pub, ranging from light snacks to full meals. Local CAMRA and Wessex Region Pub of the Year 2012. Quintessential England – a gem. Q🐎❀◑🍎P🐾📶

Pewsey

Coopers Arms 𝕃

37-39 Ball Road, SN9 5BL
⏲ 5 (12 Sat)-11; 12-10.30 Sun ☎ (01672) 562495
Fuller's London Pride; Wadworth 6X; guest beers 🄷
Down-to-earth thatched pub on the eastern edge of Pewsey. Four real ales are served – one of the two guests is from Three Castles. A popular local, it runs a cricket team during the season and has connections with the local rugby team. Live music plays on Friday nights including bands from the US from time to time. Special entertainment is hosted

at Christmas – this could be opera or an orchestra performing at the pub. Holiday cottages are available. P (X5)

Crown Inn

60 Wilcot Road, SN9 5EL

4 (12 Wed & Thu)-11; 12-11.30 Fri; 12-midnight Sat; 12-10.30 Sun ☎ (01672) 562653

thecrowninnpewsey.com

Wadworth 6X; guest beers

The Crown Inn is home to World's End brewery and always offers four of its own brews, plus one each from Stonehenge and Hopback. Two ciders are also available. This traditional village local has a small bar with pool and darts and a lounge with an attractive stone and brick fireplace in the centre. There are chess and poetry nights, and live music twice a month. Food is served Friday evening and Sunday lunchtime only unless by prior arrangement. (X5)

Ramsbury

Crown & Anchor

1 Crowood Lane, SN8 2PT

12-3, 6.30-11; 12-10.30 Sun ☎ (01672) 520335

Wickwar BOB; guest beers

A quiet and welcoming 19th-century country pub with a small bar surrounded by three rooms, two with fireplaces. Interesting bric-a-brac adorns the low ceiling beams including 200-year-old blacksmith's fixings and a Victorian beer engine that was used behind the bar and is now on display. Thursday is acoustic music night and a quiz is held every Sunday evening. There is a garden area behind the pub. Two en-suite B&B rooms are available. Q P (46,48)

Royal Wootton Bassett

Five Bells

Wood Street, SN4 7BD

12-3, 5-11.30; 12-midnight Fri-Sun ☎ (01793) 849422

Black Sheep Best Bitter; Fuller's London Pride; guest beers

Dating back to before 1841, this cosy local has a thatched roof and beamed ceiling. The bar sports six handpumps for two regular and four guest ales, usually including a beer from Braydon Ales. Westons Old Rosie cider is on another pump. Food is served lunchtimes and evenings. Special events are celebrated throughout the year. Quiz night is the last Sunday of the month and there is a Tuesday book club and a summer beer festival. The pub has darts and crib teams. (55)

Salisbury

Duke of York

34 York Road, SP2 7AS

6 (3 Sat)-midnight; 4-11 Sun ☎ (01722) 503872

Beer range varies

Built in 1901 by Ushers and situated down a quiet side street, just a short walk from the station, this small, single-bar pub reopened in 2011 after a long closure. A genuine free house, it has five real ales from far and wide, normally including a selection of local beers. The two changing real ciders are from producers across the country. There is a strong community focus and conversation thrives. The pub hosts regular quizzes, summer events and beer festivals. (R1)

King's Head

Bridge Street, SP1 2ND

7am-midnight (1am Thu-Sat) ☎ (01722) 342050

Greene King Abbot; Ruddles Best Bitter; guest beers

Formerly the County Hotel, this fine stone building is a Wetherspoon Lloyds No.1 bar sitting alongside the River Avon in the city centre. Busy during the day with drinkers and diners, it attracts a younger crowd in the evenings, particularly on Friday and Saturday when the resident DJ spins the discs. Up to seven guest beer handpulls dispense a wide range of ales from far and wide, with dark beers often featuring. The standard Wetherspoon food fare and bottle range can be found.

Rai d'Or

69 Brown Street, SP1 2AS

5-11; closed Sun ☎ (01722) 327137 raidor.co.uk

Beer range varies

Characterful 13th-century free house with a fascinating history. An inglenook fireplace and low ceilings make for an appealing ambience. Excellent, reasonably priced Thai food is complemented by two ever-changing, usually local, beers. It can be busy at food times, but drinkers are always welcome. There is a discount on food before 6.30pm and on beer for CAMRA members. A former local CAMRA Pub of the Year.

Railway Inn/Dust Hole

59 Tollgate Road, SP1 2JG

12-3 (not Wed & Sat), 7-11; 12-3, 6-11 Sun ☎ (01722) 324537 thedusthole.vpweb.co.uk

Downton Honey Blonde; guest beer

Friendly local pub close to Salisbury College. This is the only public house in the country to be licensed under two official names – look at the sign hanging outside. The Railway refers to its proximity to the now-closed goods railway station and the Dust Hole to the coal dust that used to be blown into the bar. No danger of that now. The pub was bought by a local in 2013 and is now a free house.

Village Freehouse

33 Wilton Road, SP2 7EF

4 (11 Fri & Sat)-11; 12-11 Sun ☎ (01722) 329707

Downton Quadhop; guest beers

Friendly revitalised local close to the railway station. It offers four changing guest beers, with the focus on local microbreweries and beers unusual for the area —requests welcome. The only regular outlet in Salisbury for dark beers, a dark ale, mild, porter or stout are always on offer. Terrestrial TV and Sky Sports are screened. Popular with rail users, it features rail memorabilia and books. Fresh rolls are available but you are welcome to bring your own food. Salisbury CAMRA Pub of the Year 2014. (R3)

Winchester Gate

113-117 Rampart Road, SP1 1JA

3 (12 Thu-Sat)-11; 12-10 Sun ☎ (01722) 322834

winchestergate.co.uk

Hop Back Crop Circle; guest beers

An inn since the 17th century, this free house once provided for travellers at the city's east tollgate. Four handpumps offer ales from across the UK, and a real cider is often alongside. Three beer festivals feature each year, and cider festivals in the spring and autumn. The garden has a pétanque terrain and boules can be played. Live music plays every weekend, with an open mic night on the third Wednesday of the month. Filled rolls are sold. LocAle accredited and local CAMRA Pub of the Year 2013. ❀♣P🚌

Wyndham Arms

27 Estcourt Road, SP1 3AS

12-midnight Fri & Sat; 4.30-11.30; 12-11.30 Sun

☎ (01722) 328594

Hop Back Heracles, Golden Best, Citra, Crop Circle, Summer Lightning, seasonal beers H

The birthplace of Hop Back Brewery, the Wyndham celebrated 27 consecutive years in the Guide in 2014. A traditional ale house, it has a single bar with six handpumps serving a selection of Hop Back ales and occasionally one from Downton. There is also a fine selection of bottled beers and wines. This is a pub for conversation, good natured banter and fine ales. ♣🚌(R2,R7)

Semley

Benett Arms

Village Green, SP7 9AS (1 mile E of A350) ST891270

12-3, 5-11 ☎ (01747) 830221 benettarms.co.uk

Ringwood Best Bitter; guest beers H

A former Gibbs Mew country pub, this is now a genuine free house sitting by the village green and pond in a quiet village, with a single small bar and separate dining areas. The beer choice varies but there are usually three on offer, either on handpump or direct from the cellar. Excellent home-cooked food is available at all sessions. A warm welcome is extended to all, including families and dogs, in an area popular with walkers. Q❀P🚌(84,247)

Swindon

Blunsdon Arms

Lady Lane, SN25 2NA

11-midnight ☎ (01793) 729801

Beer range varies H

This large open-plan Ember Inns pub opened in 2006. The beer selection changes weekly, with ales from many different breweries, but always including either Wadworth 6X, Bath Ales Gem or Butcombe Bitter. Real cider is also on offer. CAMRA members receive a 20p discount per pint (not Mon). Daily food specials are pie night Monday, burger night Tuesday, sausage night Wednesday, grills on Thursday and roasts on Sunday. Food is served daily until 10pm. ❀P🚌(11A,15)

Glue Pot

5 Emlyn Square, SN1 5BP

12 (4.30 Mon)-11; 11.30-11 Fri & Sat; 12-10.30 Sun

☎ (01793) 497420

Downton New Forest Ale; Hop Back Crop Circle, Summer Lightning; guest beers H

The Glue Pot is part of the historic sandstone Railway Village built in the 1840s in Swindon. There are six Hop Back or Downton ales including some seasonals, two guest ales and five real ciders. Food is served Wednesday to Friday lunchtimes. This is usually a quiet pub but it gets quite busy at weekend evenings. There is a pub quiz on Thursday night. Note the one remaining window still with the Allsopp's logo. Well worth a visit. ❀♣🚌(8,14)

Hop Inn

7 Devizes Road, SN1 4BJ

12-11 (midnight Fri & Sat); 12-10.30 Sun

☎ (01793) 976833 hopinnswindon.co.uk

Beer range varies H

A converted former shop, this venue, opened in 2012, has an unusually open aspect to the front, making it very inviting. Inside it is furnished in an eclectic style with bright plastic chairs and tables made from reclaimed wood. A genuine free house, it has five handpumps, one dispensing the house beer brewed by Ramsbury and the others offering an ever-changing variety of guest ales sourced from smaller breweries. There are also two real ciders in boxes. 🚌(12,15)

Weighbridge Brewhouse

Penzance Drive, SN5 7JL

11 (12 Sun)-11 ☎ (01793) 881500

weighbridgebrewhouse.co.uk

Weighbridge Brewhouse Brinkworth Village, Weighbridge Best, Pooley's Golden, seasonal beers H

The Weighbridge Brewhouse is an upmarket brewpub and gastro-pub in the former home of Archers brewery. It features a long shiny bar with six handpumps dedicated to the real ales crafted on the premises. Three regular ales are joined by new and seasonal offerings. Seating in the bar is limited, although a terrace is opened in warmer weather. Live music features on Thursday, Friday and Saturday evenings. ❀P🚌(8,55)

Wheatsheaf

32 Newport Street, SN1 3DP

12-3, 5-11; 12-midnight Fri & Sat; 12-11 Sun

☎ (01793) 496396

Butcombe Bitter H**; Wadworth Henry's IPA, Horizon, 6X, Swordfish** A**; guest beer** H

The pub has a smart appearance following a major refurbishment. Two rows of three wooden casks are on racking behind the front bar, but the casks are decorative only – the beer is pumped up by air pressure from wooden casks in the cellar. There are also ales on handpump including a non-Wadworth guest plus a real cider from Westons. Q❀🚌(11,12)

Tisbury

Benett Arms

High Street, SP3 6HD

12-midnight ☎ (01747) 870428 benetttisbury.co.uk

Keystone Bedrock, Large One; guest beer H

A warm welcome and friendly conversation await you in Keystone Brewery's first pub, which reopened in 2012. The front bar is furnished with a range of tables and chairs, the rear bar has a pool table and there are tables outside to the front. The Large One is called Gordon Benett, the guest beer is frequently from a South-West brewery, and a real cider is often available. There are hot snacks, Sunday lunches, special food nights and Tuesday seniors' lunches. ❀♣🚌(25,26)

Boot Inn

High Street, SP3 6PS

11-2.30, 7-11; 12-3 Sun ☎ (01747) 870363

Beer range varies G

Fine village pub built of Chilmark stone, licensed since 1768, with a relaxed, friendly atmosphere appealing to locals and visitors alike. Run by the same landlord since 1976, it became a free house in 2009. It offers three or four ales sourced from local breweries, as well as from further afield, with a Sixpenny and a Bath Ales beer often available. Excellent food is served (pizzas only on Tue) and there is a spacious garden. A former local CAMRA Pub of the Year. Q❀◑⇌♣P🚌(25,26)

Trowbridge

Rose & Crown

36 Stallard Street, BA14 9AA

10-midnight ☎ (01225) 938936 roseandcrown.uk.com

Wadworth 6X; guest beers H

Conveniently close to Trowbridge station, this pub is part of the splendid Banwell House chain. Refurbished in 2011, a single bar serves two areas, both of which have a light and airy yet cosy feel. Open mic and comedy nights are hosted occasionally. One or two guest beers are available, mostly from micros around the South-West region including Cheddar, Prescott and Butcombe, but with an emphasis on more unusual beers. Blindman's Golden Crown is a semi-regular. Q❀◑♿⇌🍎🚌🐾

Upavon

Ship L

10 High Street, SN9 6EA

11-12.30am (1am Thu-Sat); 12-11 Sun ☎ (01980) 630313 theshipinnupavon.co.uk

Wadworth 6X; guest beers H

Parts of the Ship Inn date from the 15th century. Completely refurbished in recent years, it combines traditional wooden beams with a light, open interior. The decor, including a huge model of the Cutty Sark in the dining room, has a nautical or local theme. Tuesday is fish and chips night and home-made pizzas are cooked in a wood-fired pizza oven. The four guest ales are usually local and three real ciders and 40 malt whiskies are available. ❀◑♿🍎🚌(X5)🐾

Urchfont

Lamb Inn

The Green, SN10 4QU

6-11 Mon; 12-3, 6.30-11; 12-6 Sun ☎ (01380) 848848 lambinnurchfont.co.uk

Wadworth Henry's IPA, 6X, seasonal beer H

The Lamb is a comfortable and friendly pub at the heart of the village. Warm and cosy, it features Wadworth ales plus a varied and good-value restaurant menu. With plenty of wooden tables and chairs and a welcoming bar area, it is popular with locals and visitors alike. There is a large function room and, outside, the pleasant beer garden is a lovely spot to while away a summer's afternoon. ❀◑♣P🚌(271)🐾

Wanborough

Harrow

High Street, SN4 0AE

11-10; 9am-11 Fri & Sat; 10-9 Sun ☎ (01793) 791792 theharrowwanborough.co.uk

Otter Bitter; Sharp's Doom Bar; Timothy Taylor Landlord; guest beer H

Beautiful listed thatched building dating back to 1747 with huge fireplaces and a wealth of old exposed beams. It was reopened in 2011 following refurbishment, and boasts a new flagstone floor and bar top. The Harrow is thriving with a new landlady and now offers varied, interesting and good-quality food, made with local produce where possible. Coffee and breakfast are served from 9am Thursday to Sunday. Live music features on bank holidays. ❀🛏◑♿P🚌(46A,47)

Warminster

Fox & Hounds

6 Deverill Road, BA12 9QP

11-11 ☎ (01985) 216711

Wessex Warminster Warrior; guest beers H

This friendly two-bar pub was local CAMRA Pub of the Year 2012 and Rural Pub 2013. The main bar has a pool table and sports TV at the back; a snug bar is at the side. There is a large skittle alley and function room. Regular ciders are from Thatchers and Rich's, with up to five guests. Guest real ales are usually from local breweries. Closing time may be later than 11pm. Q❀♿♣🍎P🚌🐾

Organ Inn

49 High Street, BA12 9AQ

4 (12 Sat)-midnight; 4-11 Sun ☎ (01985) 211777 theorganinn.co.uk

Beer range varies H

An inn until 1913, the Organ then became a butcher's shop, and later a fishmonger's and greengrocer's, but reopened as a pub in 2006. The welcoming interior includes three rooms with a traditional feel, along with a snug games room and a skittle alley. The beer range constantly changes but will always include Organ Bitter (the brewery is a secret). Ciders are mainly from Westons plus guests. A beer festival is held in September. Bar snacks are interesting and there is an art gallery upstairs. Q❀♿⇌♣🍎🚌🐾

Whiteparish

Parish Lantern L

Romsey Road, SP5 2SA

11.30-3, 5-11; 11.30-11 Fri & Sat; 12-10.30 Sun ☎ (01794) 884392 theparishlantern.co.uk

Flack Manor Flack's Double Drop; Sharp's Doom Bar; guest beers H

A welcoming pub run by the same couple since 1991. The single bar has a central fireplace and areas for dining, pool and darts. Guest beers are from Hop Back, Downton or other local breweries. There are family events on bank holidays and occasional beer festivals. Food is served lunchtimes and evenings, including regular themed nights. A spacious garden with play equipment for children and a chicken coop leads to a camping area with space for five caravans. ❀◑♿♣P🚌(X7,34)

Wilton

Swan L

SN8 3SS

12-3, 6-11; 12-11 Sat; 12-10.30 Sun ☎ (01672) 870274 theswanwilton.co.uk

Beer range varies H/G

A pretty red-brick village pub near the Kennet & Avon Canal and Wiltshire's only working windmill, with an attractive interior. The emphasis is on dining, with good local food always popular (no eve meals Sun), and themed food nights. The five varying guest beers are mostly local, with the beer board displaying the distance to the brewery. Beer dispense is a mixture of handpump and gravity. Traditional draught ciders are also available. There is a quiz on the second Monday of the month. ❀◑ ●P🚌(21)🐾📶

Wroughton

Carters Rest L

57 High Street, SN4 9JU

⏲ 5-11 (midnight Fri); 12-midnight Sat; 12-11 Sun
☎ (01793) 812288

Cotswold Spring Stunner; Otter Amber; Ramsbury Flint Knapper; Sharp's Doom Bar; guest beers H

Traditional pub dating from 1904 with a separate lounge and bar. Run by the same licensees since 2006, the pub has built up a good reputation for real ale and has won several awards. It has 13 handpumps serving four regular and seven guest ales, plus two ciders or perries. An annual beer festival is hosted. Live music plays on the last Sunday of the month and quiz night is every Thursday. ❀♣●P🚌(49,72)

Zeals

Bell & Crown

New Road, BA12 6NJ

⏲ 11-3, 5-11; 11-11 Fri & Sat; 11-4 Sun ☎ (01747) 840404
🌐 bellandcrown.com

Beer range varies H

Refurbished in the past few years with comfortable furnishings, flagstone floors and an open fire, this is a fine-dining pub with a separate traditional bar and real ales. The beer choice changes regularly, with West Country breweries always well represented. The country pub attracts both locals and visitors to the area. The National Trust property of Stourhead is nearby. Q❀◑♿P🚌(158)

King's Head, Salisbury

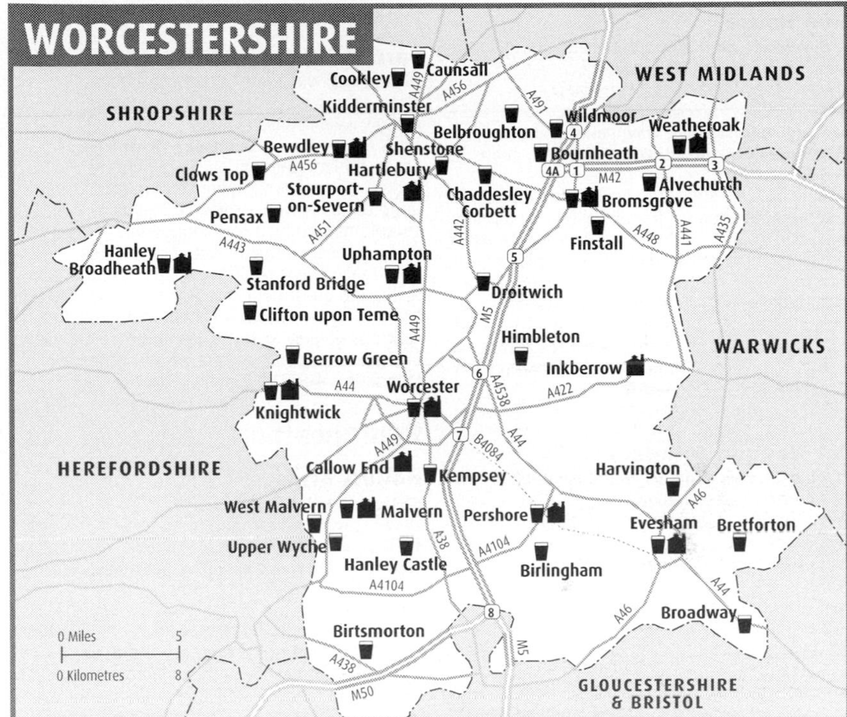

Alvechurch

Weighbridge 🏆 L

Scarfield Wharf, Scarfield Hill, B48 7SQ (follow signs to marina from village) SP022721
☉ 12-3, 7-11; 12-3, 7-10.30 Sun ☎ (0121) 445 5111
🌐 the-weighbridge.co.uk
Weatheroak Tillerman's Tipple; guest beers H
This cosy canalside pub is local CAMRA Pub of the Year. It has two small lounges, a public bar and a pleasant garden. Good-value home-cooked food is served lunchtimes and evenings (no food Tue or Wed eves) and it does excellent Sunday lunches. House beers are Weatheroak Tillerman's Tipple and Kinver Bargees Bitter, and changing guest beers include a mild. Real cider or perry is available. A covered area outside can be used for functions. Spring and autumn beer festivals are held.
Q❀◑≠●P🚌(146)

Belbroughton

Holly Bush

Stourbridge Road, DY9 9UG
☉ 11.30-11; 11.30-3, 6-11 Sat; 12-3, 7-10.30 Sun
☎ (01562) 730207
Hobsons Mild, Twisted Spire, Town Crier H
Originally a row of terraced cottages built to house agricultural workers, this has been a pub since 1845. Recently redecorated after a major flood, the building is full of character and has a single bar serving three separate areas. Excellent traditional home-made food is served in the dining room. Thatchers cider is on handpump. Located on a dual carriageway between Hagley and the M5 motorway, the pub is near the National Trust Clent Hills. Q❀◑♿●P🚌🐾

Berrow Green

Admiral Rodney L

WR6 6PL
☉ 12-3 (not Mon), 5-11; 12-11 Sat; 12-10.30 Sun
☎ (01886) 821375 🌐 admiral-rodney.co.uk
Wye Valley Bitter, HPA; guest beers H
A country pub on the Worcestershire Way. The bar has TV and the lounge is decorated with nautical scenes. There is a separate restaurant/function room. Guest ales are often from local microbreweries and meals are freshly prepared from locally grown ingredients (no food Mon, lunchtime only Sun). A disabled toilet and baby-changing facilities are available, and outside is a skittle alley, floodlit garden and covered and heated patio. Folk music plays on the third Wednesday of the month. En-suite accommodation is popular with walkers. Q❀🛏◑♿⛺♣P🐾📶

Bewdley

Little Pack Horse L

31 High Street, DY12 2DH (300yds from St Anne's Church)
☉ 12-3, 6-11; 12-3, 5-midnight Fri; 11-midnight Sat; 11-10.30 Sun ☎ (01299) 403762 🌐 littlepackhorse.co.uk
Bewdley Worcestershire Way; Hobsons Town Crier; guest beers H
Tucked away at the end of the High Street, the pub has a reputation for good beer and food. Dating from the 15th century, the cosy interior is an interesting mix of ancient walls and timbers. Four ales are available including one from nearby Bewdley Brewery. Home-cooked, seasonal food includes the famous Desperate Dan Pie in various sizes. Fish and vegetarian meals and daily specials are on the chalkboard. ❀◑🚌🐾📶

Mug House 𝕃

12 Severnside North, DY12 2EE (150yds along Severnside North from river bridge)
12-11 (11.30 Fri & Sat) ☎ (01299) 402543
mughousebewdley.co.uk
Bewdley Worcestershire Way; Purity Mad Goose; Timothy Taylor Landlord; Wye Valley HPA; guest beer Ⓗ
Located on the side of the Severn, the Mug House is not to be missed – a friendly pub that welcomes locals and visitors alike. It serves four regular beers, including one from Bewdley Brewery, plus a guest. The lounge bar has cosy settles and a log fire, and to the rear is a sun terrace with a glass-covered patio in lovely surroundings with grapevines and wisteria. Fine food is served in the restaurant and lunchtime meals throughout the pub and garden.
Q(SVR)

Old Waggon & Horses 𝕃

91 Kidderminster Road, DY12 1DG (on Bewdley-Kidderminster road, Catchems End)
12-11; 11.30-1am Fri & Sat ☎ (01299) 403170
waggonbewdley.co.uk
Banks's Mild, Bitter; Bathams Best Bitter; guest beer Ⓗ
Popular with locals and visitors, the pub has a central bar that serves three distinct areas. The small wooden-floored snug has settles, tables and a dartboard; the larger room has a roll-down screen for major sporting events, bench seating and a TV. An old kitchen range in the dining area adds to the cottage feel. Food is available Tuesday and Thursday evenings with a carvery on Sundays. The attractive terraced garden is on many levels. Guest ales come from local independents.
Q(SVR)P

Rising Sun 𝕃

139 Kidderminster Road, DY12 1JE (just off E end of bypass at Catchems End)
12-midnight ☎ (01299) 409440
Banks's Mild Ⓟ**, Bitter; Enville Ale; Wye Valley HPA** Ⓗ
This lively and welcoming terraced pub dating from 1845 brewed its own ales until 1923. It has a single large comfortable lounge bar and offers four regular beers. The cask mild is on electric dispense. Cobs and pork pies are available all day. Crib and darts are played, and a quiz night is held on Tuesday. On Saturday evenings and occasionally on Sunday afternoons there is live music. To the rear is a pleasant, quiet garden. Q

Birlingham

Swan 𝕃

Church Street, WR10 3AQ
12-3, 6.30-11 (10.30 Sun) ☎ (01386) 750485
theswaninn.co.uk
Wye Valley Bitter; guest beers Ⓗ
A classic wood-beamed thatched free house in a quiet village. Ever-changing guest beers are from around the country and two real ciders are usually available. The small bar displays old photos of the surrounding area and there is a separate area for games. Good-quality food is served in the conservatory. Two excellent beer festivals are held in the extensive garden in May and September. There is a large car park opposite.
QP(382)

Birtsmorton

Farmers Arms

Birts Street, WR13 6AP (off B4208) SO790363
11 (12 Sun)-4, 6-midnight ☎ (01684) 833308
farmersarmsbirtsmorton.co.uk
Hook Norton Hooky, Old Hooky; guest beers Ⓗ
Grade II black and white village pub, circa 1480, tucked away down a quiet country lane. It has a large bar area with a splendid inglenook fireplace, complemented by a cosy lounge with old settles and low beams. Good-value, home-made, traditional food is on offer lunchtimes and evenings daily, and guest beers are from local independent brewers. A beer festival is held in August. The spacious garden, with swings, provides fine views of the Malvern Hills. A caravan site is nearby.
QP(577)

Bournheath

Nailers Arms

62 Doctors Hill, B61 9JE
12-midnight (1am Fri & Sat); 12-11.30 Sun
☎ (01527) 873045 thenailersarms.co.uk
Wadworth 6X; Wye Valley HPA; guest beers Ⓗ
Dating from the late-18th century, this whitewashed three-gabled building was once a nailmaker's workshop-cum-brewery. The bar has a traditional quarry-tiled floor and a real fire. Two guest ales are usually on handpump. A reasonably priced food menu is available in the lounge/restaurant – the carvery is ever-popular. A beer festival in May has become a major attraction in the pub's calendar. The restaurant closes occasionally for functions. P

Bretforton

Fleece Inn ★ 𝕃

The Cross, WR11 7JE (near church)
11-11.30 (10.30 Sun) summer; 11-3, 6-11 Mon & Tue; 11-11.30; 12-10.30 Sun winter ☎ (01386) 831173
thefleeceinn.co.uk
Uley Pig's Ear Strong Beer; Wye Valley Bitter; guest beers Ⓗ
Renowned 15th-century timber-framed village pub owned by the National Trust on the edge of the Cotswolds. Recognised by CAMRA as having a nationally important historic pub interior, it houses a world-famous collection of 17th-century pewter. The pub has three main rooms, an orchard and

INDEPENDENT BREWERIES

Ambridge Inkberrow
Bewdley Bewdley
Bird's Bromsgrove
Brandy Cask Pershore
Cannon Royall Uphampton
Evesham Evesham
Firefly Worcester
Friday Beer Malvern
Joseph Herbert Smith Hanley Broadheath
Malvern Hills Malvern
Pope's Worcester
St George's Callow End
Teme Valley Knightwick
Weatheroak Hill Weatheroak
Winning Post Worcester (NEW)
Worcester Worcester (NEW)
Worcestershire Hartlebury

adjacent medieval barn. Food comes highly recommended. Entertainment includes local morris dancers and live music. Two regular beers are complemented by three guests from local micros and up to four ciders including one produced at the Fleece. Local CAMRA branch Pub of the Year 2013. Q ♿ ♣ (554) ☂

Broadway

Crown & Trumpet [L]

14 Church Street, WR12 7AE (just off Cotswolds Way)
11-2.30, 5-11; 11-11 Fri-Sun ☎ (01386) 853202
cotswoldholidays.co.uk
Butcombe Bitter; Cotswold Spring Codger; Stanway Morris A'Leaping; Stroud Tom Long; guest beer [H]
Picturesque 17th-century Cotswold stone inn on the road to Snowshill, complete with oak beams and log fires along with plenty of Flowers Brewery memorabilia. Stanway beers alternate throughout the seasons; other guest beers are from local microbreweries. Black Rat cider and perry are available. The food menu offers specials featuring locally grown produce, enjoyed by locals, tourists and walkers. The pub has an unusual range of pub games and hosts entertainment including live music. Local CAMRA Pub of the Year 2012. Q ♿ ♣ P (559) ☂

Bromsgrove

Golden Cross Hotel [L]

20 High Street, B61 8HH
8am-midnight (1am Fri & Sat) ☎ (01527) 870005
Greene King Abbot; Ruddles Best Bitter; guest beers [H]
This stylish, split-level Wetherspoon pub with 12 individual booths and interesting glasswork is located in Bromsgrove town centre – it was previously a hotel and coach house. The two permanent beers are complemented by seven varying guests, often from local breweries. Regular themed beer festivals are held showcasing guest breweries, with discounts for CAMRA members. There is a Pay & Display car park at the rear. Q ♿ P ☂

Ladybird [L]

2 Finstall Road, B60 2DZ (on B4184) SO969695
11-11; 12-10.30 Sun ☎ (01527) 878014
ladybirdinn.co.uk
Bathams Best Bitter; Bird's Amnesia; Wye Valley HPA [H]
This popular local is situated adjacent to the town's railway station. The light, airy lounge, with polished wooden floor, has historical railway photographs and a dartboard in an alcove, in contrast to the busy bar. Two function/meeting rooms of different sizes are available on the first floor. Pub grub is served every day; however, if your taste is for Italian cuisine try the adjoining privately run restaurant. The attached 45-room Travelodge offers accommodation with breakfast available at the Ladybird. ♿ ♣ P ☂

Caunsall

Anchor Inn [L]

DY11 5YL (off A449 Kidderminster-Wolverhampton road)
11-4, 7-11; 11-3, 7-10.30 Sun ☎ (01562) 850254
theanchorinncaunsall.co.uk
Hobsons Best Bitter, Town Crier; Wye Valley HPA, Butty Bach; guest beer [H]
Popular traditional village local run by the same family since 1927. A central doorway leads to the little-changed bar with its original 1920s furniture and horse-racing memorabilia. The pub is renowned for its six real ales, ciders and well-filled cobs. The friendly staff welcome an impressive mix of customers and the pub gets busy at lunchtimes. Easily reached from the nearby canal, this gem is well worth a visit. Local CAMRA Pub of the Year 2012. Q ♿ ♣ P ☂

Chaddesley Corbett

Swan [L]

The Village, DY10 4SD SO892737
11 (12 Sun)-11 ☎ (01562) 777302
Bathams Mild Ale, Best Bitter [H]
Dating from 1606, this village pub has a large lounge, snug and public bar. Rolls and pork pies are available daily at lunchtime; the restaurant serves evening meals Thursday to Saturday. A jazz night is held every Thursday evening. The large garden with children's play area overlooks beautiful countryside. Bathams XXX is served seasonally and the regular cider is Westons Old Rosie. The pub is well used by walkers and the Elizabethan Harvington Hall is a mile away. Q ♿ ♣ P

Clifton upon Teme

Lion Inn [L]

1 The Village, WR6 6DH
4-midnight Mon; 12-1am ☎ (01886) 812975
thelionclifton.co.uk
Otter Bitter; Wye Valley HPA; guest beers [H]
Imposing black and white building with a Georgian façade, originally the village court and manor house. Comfy seats and bar stools welcome drinkers. The timber-framed restaurant, separated from the main bar by a large woodburner, features themed evenings every week. A musical jam session is hosted every other Thursday. A separate games room with sports TV and a pool table is decorated with old road signs and pictures of nearby Shelsley Walsh Hill Climb. Q ♣ P ☂

Clows Top

Colliers Farm Shop & Café [L]

Tenbury Road, DY14 9HA (on main A456 Kidderminster-Tenbury road)
9am-6 (9 Fri) ☎ (01299) 832242 colliersfarmshop.co.uk
Hobsons Best Bitter [H]
Local community farm shop and café with a bar serving a local ale and real ciders from nearby producers. The café was previously the pub lounge and is somewhere to linger and enjoy good-value home-cooked meals and a beer. An extensive and unusual range of UK and foreign bottled beers is available in the shop. Food is served during the day until 5.30pm (8.30pm Fri). ♿ P ☂

Cookley

Eagle & Spur

176 Castle Road, DY10 3TB
12-11 ☎ (01562) 850184
Banks's Mild; Caledonian Golden XPA; guest beers [H]

Friendly and lively village local serving four real ales, real cider, food and cakes. The main lounge bar is usually busy with conversation; a separate dining room is to the front. Further inside is a cosy lounge and a large conservatory used by local groups for functions. Tables outside are popular for relaxing on warm summer days. On New Year's Day the pub hosts traditional displays of Border Morris and a mummers' play that draw a large crowd. P

Droitwich

Droitwich Legion Inn

Salwarpe Road, WR9 9BH (250yds NNE of rail station)
12-11 ☎ 07927 438047
Cannon Royall Fruiterers Mild; guest beers H
A short walk from the railway station, Cannon Royall Brewery now runs this former British Legion Club as a pub, offering up to five beers from the brewery including a mild. Regimental memorabilia still adorn the bar, and a large function room hosts a mixture of celebrations and community events. There is a skittle alley and snooker table. Live music features every third Friday of the month. Food from local takeaways can be ordered to eat in the pub. P(144)

Hop Pole

40 Friar Street, WR9 8ED
12-11 (10.30 Sun) ☎ (01905) 770155
Enville Ale; Malvern Hills Black Pear; Wye Valley HPA, Butty Bach; guest beers H
An 18th-century black and white timbered inn, popular with locals and visitors alike. Guest beers are mostly from local breweries. Good-value home-cooked food is served at lunchtimes. A separate pool room adjoins the bar and there is a heated patio area outside for smokers. Live music plays on some weekends. Close by is the Droitwich Barge Canal which offers secure moorings. A warm welcome is assured at this friendly pub.

Old Cock Inn

Friar Street, WR9 8EQ
12 (6 Mon)-11; 12-midnight Fri & Sat ☎ (01905) 770754
oldcockinn.co.uk
Marston's EPA; Wychwood Hobgoblin; guest beers H
Droitwich's oldest licensed premises, first permitted to sell alcohol in 1712, and located in the old part of the town. The central bar serves four open-plan rooms decorated with interesting old artefacts and local photographs. There is a function room and a patio garden. Guest beers are from the Marston's portfolio, and Thatchers Heritage cider is on handpump. CAMRA members receive a 10 per cent discount on real ale and cider.
(144)

Evesham

Olde Red Horse

17 Vine Street, WR11 4RE
10-11 (midnight Fri & Sat); 12-11 Sun ☎ (01386) 442784
M&B Brew XI; Wells Bombardier; guest beer H
Black and white 15th-century coaching inn in the heart of historic Evesham. This friendly two-room local attracts all ages and with five letting rooms is popular with visitors. The public bar has a TV, dartboard and jukebox, and the lounge has an area set aside for dining. Traditional home-cooked food is served including excellent-value steaks. The heated rear courtyard features an attractive fish pond. There is a mid-week happy hour with discounts on beers and Thatchers Cheddar Valley cider. (50)

Finstall

Cross Inn

34 Alcester Road, B60 1EW (on B4184)
12-11.30 (midnight Fri & Sat) ☎ (01527) 872911
Purity Mad Goose; Thwaites Lancaster Bomber; guest beer H
Friendly village pub popular with locals. It offers a guest beer, usually from a nearby brewery, and locally produced Tardebigge Cider sold from the tub. No hot food is available but fresh cobs, pickled eggs and locally made pickles, chutneys, jams and free range eggs are sold at the bar. A small meeting room next to the bar has historic interest. To the rear are a beer garden and large car park. Two fundraising events are held for a local charity each summer. P(142,143)

Hanley Broadheath

Fox Inn

WR15 8QS SO671652
5-11; 3-12.30am Fri; 12-12.30am Sat; 12-10 Sun
☎ (01886) 853189
Bathams Best Bitter; Joseph Herbert Smith Foxy Lady; guest beers H
The main bar of this 16th-century black and white timbered free house is decorated with hops and has a large fireplace with a wood-burning stove. The panelled dining area is separated from the bar by wood beams. The games room has a pool table, TV and darts. Home-made food, including Sunday lunch, is available, with bar snacks at any time. One guest beer is usually from the JHS brewery which is in an outbuilding. Lawnmower racing is held in the adjoining field in August.
Q P

Hanley Castle

Three Kings ★

Church End, WR8 0BL (signed off B4211) SO838420
12-3, 7-11 (10.30 Sun) ☎ (01684) 592686
Butcombe Bitter; Hobsons Best Bitter; guest beers H
On CAMRA's National Inventory of Historic Pub Interiors, this unspoilt 15th-century country inn on the village green near the church has been run by the Roberts family since 1911. The three-room interior comprises a small snug with large inglenook, serving hatch and settle wall, a small side room, and Nell's Lounge with another inglenook, beams and its own entrance. Three guest ales are on offer, often from local breweries, and Westons Old Rosie cider. Live music sessions feature regularly and a popular beer festival is held in November. Q P(363)

Harvington

Coach & Horses

Station Road, WR11 8NJ
5 (12 Sat)-midnight; 12-11.30 Sun ☎ (01386) 870249
Greene King IPA; guest beers H
Traditional village pub with a separate bar with a real fire and a lounge with a log-burning inglenook. Photos of old Harvington adorn the

walls. The pub's real ale drinkers select the guest beers from Finest Cask and SIBA lists. Good-value food is served. A local ukulele group plays on Tuesday and a fun quiz is hosted on Sunday night. The skittle alley doubles as a function room. Dogs and muddy boots are welcome in the bar. Local CAMRA branch Pub of the Year 2014.
(28)

Himbleton

Galton Arms

Harrow Lane, WR9 7LQ
12-2 (not Mon), 4.30-11; 11-11 Sun (01905) 391672
Banks's Bitter; Bathams Best Bitter; Wye Valley HPA; guest beer H
An interesting rural pub on the edge of the village with a friendly welcome. The original black-and-white beams divide up the interior, and open fires enhance the cosy ambience in winter. Good-value food is served in a separate dining area. The guest beer is usually from a local brewery.
QP

Kempsey

Walter de Cantelupe

34 Main Road, WR5 3NA (next to post office)
closed Mon; 12-2, 6-11; 12-9 Sun (01905) 820572
walterdecantelupe.co.uk
Timothy Taylor Landlord; guest beers H
Named after a 13th-century Bishop of Worcester, the pub features a cosy drinking area, a large settle from the 1700s and an imposing inglenook fireplace. Traditional but inventive food uses local ingredients, and snacks are often available outside restaurant hours. Events throughout the year include a paella party in June in the walled garden. Local beers are served in lined glasses, with third-of-a-pint glasses available, and CAMRA members receive a 10 per cent discount on ale. The pub may stay open all day on summer weekends and winter hours may vary.
QP(32,362)

Kidderminster

Olde Seven Stars

13-14 Coventry Street, DY10 2BG
11-11 (11.30 Fri & Sat); 12-11 Sun (01562) 755777
yeoldesevenstars.co.uk
Beer range varies H
With six ever-changing real ales and one draught cider, this historic town-centre family-friendly pub is well worth visiting. The front and rear bars retain many original features from previous ages. Cobs and pork pies are served, and customers can order in their own food (there are plenty of takeaways nearby) – tableware and condiments provided. A quiet rear garden is popular in summer. The friendly atmosphere and excellent ales have won the pub a number of CAMRA awards.

Station Inn

7 Farfield, DY10 1UG
12-11 (01562) 569621 stationkidderminster.co.uk
Enville Ale; Thwaites Wainwright; guest beers H
This friendly pub is only a short walk from both the main line and Severn Valley Railway stations. Two rooms are served from a central bar and there is a large beer garden to the rear. Up to four ales are usually available including beers from Enville. The pub has a reputation for good-value home-cooked food sourced from local suppliers – the traditional roasts on Sunday are always popular. Quiz night is Thursday and there is a warming fire in winter.
QP

Swan

Vicar Street, DY10 1DE
10-11 (1am Fri & Sat); 12-7 Sun (01562) 823008
Bewdley Worcestershire Sway; St Austell Tribute; guest beers H
This one-room pub opposite the town hall, dating from 1865, is a worthy survivor of town-centre redevelopment. It serves real ciders and up to six real ales, including one from Bewdley Brewery. The front bar area gets lively on rugby match days – there is an area with quieter tables for dining towards the back. Bar food is available Monday to Saturday, with breakfast from 10am. A beer festival is held over the August bank holiday.

Weavers Real Ale House

98 Comberton Hill, DY10 1QH
closed Mon; 12-11 (01562) 229413
Three Tuns XXX; Wye Valley HPA; guest beers H
The single-room lounge bar is reminiscent of a traditional pub, with old pictures and posters on the walls and a conversational atmosphere. Six real ales are served including a dark, a stout and a mild, plus two ciders and a perry. Inexpensive pub snacks such as pork pies and cobs are always available. Just a short walk from the railway station, this is a place to stop off for a quite pint and a chat on the way into town. Public parking is a short distance away. Q

Knightwick

Talbot

WR6 5PH (on B4197, 400yds from A44 jct)
10-11 (01886) 821235 the-talbot.co.uk
Hobsons Best Bitter; Teme Valley T'Other, This, That H
Dating back to the 14th century, this former coaching inn has been refurbished and extended. Now a spacious country pub, it has a taproom, lounge bar with a large fireplace and an attractive conservatory, especially fine in summer. The small wood-panelled restaurant serves an imaginative menu featuring local ingredients. Three or four beers from the Teme Valley Brewery behind the pub are usually available. There is a farmers' market outside on the second Sunday of the month. Beer festivals are held in April, June and early October (for green hop beers).
QP(420)

Malvern

Great Malvern Hotel

Graham Road, WR14 2HN
10-11; 11-10.30 Sun (01684) 563411
great-malvern-hotel.co.uk
Wye Valley HPA, Butty Bach H
Popular hotel public bar a short walk from the Malvern Theatres complex, ideal for pre- and post-performance refreshment. The beer range usually includes something from Malvern's two breweries. Meals are served in the bar and in the adjoining brasserie, including Sunday lunches. There is a comfortable lounge with lots of sofas, fresh coffee

and newspapers. Live music sessions are held throughout the week. The Great Shakes cellar bar features sports TV and is available to hire. On-site parking is limited but there is public parking nearby. ⇌(Great Malvern)P

Morgan

52 Clarence Road, WR14 3EQ

12-3.30, 5-11; 12-11 Fri & Sat; 12-10.30 Sun

☎ (01684) 578575

Wye Valley Bitter, HPA, Butty Bach; guest beer Ⓗ

Wye Valley Brewery has created a real ale magnet here, named after the town's Morgan car factory. The open-plan interior is divided into an area where darts can be played, a drinking area and a slightly raised seating area with comfy settees to relax in. The welcoming landscaped garden has plenty of seating, a fish pond and 'Them Organ' gates. Weekly activities include a book club, quizzes on Tuesday and an open-mic night on Wednesday. The guest beer is from the Wye Valley range. ♿⇌(Great Malvern)♣

Nag's Head

19-21 Bank Street, WR14 2JG (off Graham Rd at Link Top common)

11-11.15 (11.30 Fri & Sat); 12-11 Sun ☎ (01684) 574373

nagsheadmalvern.co.uk

Banks's Bitter; Bathams Best Bitter; St George's Friar Tuck, Charger, Dragons Blood; Wood Shropshire Lad; guest beers Ⓗ

A popular free house where the permanent beers, including those from the owner's brewery, St George's, are joined by up to eight guests, usually including one from Otter, plus two draught ciders. Mismatched furniture, nooks and crannies, newspapers and foliage create a homely environment, attracting visitors throughout the week. Outside is a large heated area to the front and a garden to the rear. A No Swearing rule is enforced. The car park is small but there is ample parking on the street. ♣P(44,44A)

Pensax

Bell

WR6 6AE (on B4202 Clows Top-Great Whitley road)

12-2.30 (not Mon), 5-11; 12-10.30 Sun ☎ (01299) 896677

Bewdley Worcestershire Way; Exmoor Gold; Hobsons Best Bitter; Wye Valley HPA; guest beers Ⓗ

Local CAMRA Pub of the Decade and previous West Midlands Pub of the Year. This family- and dog-friendly pub is not to be missed. Six constantly changing real ales are on offer, plus local cider and perry. There is a separate dining room and a snug where families are welcome. A good food menu features local seasonal ingredients. Wooden floors, hanging hops, open fires and pew seating give a true country feel. Well worth making a detour to visit. Q♿P

Pershore

Brandy Cask

25 Bridge Street, WR10 1AJ

11.30-2.30, 7-11 (11.30 Thu); 11.30-3, 7-11.30 Fri & Sat; 12-3, 7-11 Sun ☎ (01386) 552602

Brandy Cask Whistling Joe, Brandy Snapper, John Baker's Original; guest beers Ⓗ

At least three house ales are always available at this brewpub as well as a wide range of guest beers from around the country. Cheddar Valley cider is also normally stocked. Food is good and reasonably priced (no food Mon or Tue in winter). The beautifully kept rear garden runs down to the River Avon. This is a classic hostelry well worth a visit. Q

Shenstone

Plough

DY10 4DL (off A450/A448) SO865735

12.30-3.30, 6-11; 12-11 Fri & Sat; 12-10.30 Sun

☎ (01562) 777340

Bathams Mild Ale, Best Bitter Ⓗ

This traditional community pub has been at the heart of the village since 1840. A long single bar serves both the public room areas and the lounge, where there is a real fire. Cobs and pork pies are available at lunchtimes. Bathams XXX is added to the range in winter. A large enclosed courtyard serves as an overflow area, and children are welcome here. Local morris teams dance during the summer months. The Elizabethan Harvington Hall is two miles down the road. Q♿♣P

Stanford Bridge

Bridge

WR6 6RU (signed 100yds off B4203)

12-midnight (1am Fri & Sat) ☎ (01886) 812771

Hobsons Mild, Twisted Spire; Otter Bright; Wye Valley HPA; guest beers Ⓗ

Large ornate pub with a black and white exterior. Its many rooms provide space for socialising, games and dining. The games room has a pool table and sports TV, and the pub hosts cricket and rugby teams. There is also a TV on the large covered patio outside. A stout from Malvern Hills or Wye Valley features in winter. The cider is from Thatchers or Westons. Beer festivals are held at Easter, in July and October, and quiz nights and live music are hosted regularly. ♿♣P

Stourport-on-Severn

Hollybush

Mitton Street, DY13 9AA

12-11 (midnight Fri & Sat); 12-10.30 Sun

☎ (01299) 827435 hollybushrealalespub.co.uk

Black Country Pig on the Wall; guest beers Ⓗ

This welcoming pub offers six real ales from independent breweries and real cider. A single bar serves a split-level lounge with a snug, an upper function room where darts are played and a quiet beer garden at the back. Regular weekly events include live music, quizzes and TV sport, and beer festivals are held twice a year in the main lounge. The pub was awarded local CAMRA Gold Pub of the Year in 2013 in recognition of its outstanding ales and community events. Q♣

Rock Tavern

80 Wilden Lane, DY13 9LR

12-3, 6-11; 12-midnight Fri & Sat; 12-6 Sun

☎ (01299) 822962 rocktavern-stourport.co.uk

Greene King Abbot; St Austell Tribute; guest beers Ⓗ

This old pub with a lounge bar and restaurant has been refurbished in a comfortable modern style. It offers four beers including at least one from a local brewery. Home-made food is served most lunchtimes and evenings (not Mon), all made with locally sourced and free range ingredients. The smoking area outside is next to a cave cut into the rock, and the pub is handy for a country walk along the adjacent old railway line. Car parking is immediately opposite. ⛅❀◑♿P🐾📶

Uphampton

Fruiterer's Arms 𝕃

Uphampton Lane, WR9 0JW (down lane off A449 at Reindeer pub) SO838648
⏲ 12-11.30 (midnight Fri & Sat); 12-11 Sun
☎ (01905) 620305
Cannon Royall Fruiterers Mild, King's Shilling, Arrowhead Bitter; guest beer Ⓗ
The pub has been in the same family for 163 years, with Ted working here since 1951. The ales from the independent Cannon Royall Brewery behind the pub are reasonably priced in both the bar and the comfortable lounge. The guest beers are Cannon Royall seasonals and local perry and cider are also served. Filled rolls are available Friday to Sunday. Home-made pickles are sold at the bar. Children under 14 are welcome until 9pm.
Q♣●P🚌

Upper Wyche

Wyche Inn 𝕃

Wyche Road, WR14 4EQ (on B4218, follow signs from Malvern to Colwall)
⏲ 12 (11 Sat & Sun)-11 ☎ (01684) 575396
🌐 thewycheinn.co.uk
Wye Valley HPA; guest beers Ⓗ
Laying claim to being the highest pub in Worcestershire, this free house has panoramic views towards the Cotswolds. Ideally situated for hill walkers, it offers two bars – one with pool and darts, the other dedicated to drinking and dining. A range of up to five real ales is available, all sourced from small and micro breweries, including some locals. Home-cooked food is served lunchtimes and evenings, with a different theme every day. Steak nights on Tuesday and Saturday are especially popular. B&B and holiday cottage accommodation are AA 4-star rated. Q❀🛏◑♣P🚌🐾📶

Weatheroak

Coach & Horses 𝕃

Weatheroak Hill, B48 7EA (Alvechurch-Wythall road) SP057740
⏲ 11.30-11; 12-10.30 Sun ☎ (01564) 823386
🌐 coachandhorsesinn.co.uk
Hobsons Best Bitter; Holden's Black Country Bitter, Golden Glow; Weatheroak Hill Gold, Icknield Pale Ale; Wood Shropshire Lad; guest beers Ⓗ
Award-winning country free house with a traditional bar with real fire and quarry-tiled floor, a modern lounge bar and a restaurant. The former coach house has been in the same family for over 40 years. Meals are served lunchtimes and evenings (no food Sun eve), and fresh rolls are always available. Up to 10 real ales are sourced from breweries across the West Midlands, including the on-site Weatheroak Hill. Q⛅❀◑♿P🐾📶

West Malvern

Brewers Arms 𝕃

Lower Dingle, WR14 4BQ (S end of village, down track by pub sign on B4232)
⏲ 12-3, 6-midnight; 12-midnight Fri-Sun ☎ (01684) 568147
Malvern Hills Black Pear; Marston's Burton Bitter; Wye Valley HPA; guest beers Ⓗ
Welcoming traditional pub, the centre of the village community and an ideal refreshment stop for visitors to the Malvern Hills. Up to eight real ales and a draught cider, usually Westons, are available. Home-cooked food is served lunchtimes and evenings (except Sun eve). Be prepared for random musical performances by local bands and choirs. The cosy bar can get busy but extra space is available in the function room or in the garden, with views to the Black Mountains.
Q⛅❀◑●🚌(675)🐾📶

Wildmoor

Wildmoor Oak 𝕃

Top Road, B61 0RB SO963756
⏲ 5-10.30 Mon; 12-11 (midnight Fri & Sat); 12-10.30 Sun
☎ (0121) 453 2696 🌐 wildmooroak.com
Beer range varies Ⓗ
This rural inn offers a changing range of ales, often including Wye Valley HPA. Located near the M5, it has a reputation locally for its excellent Caribbean and British menu prepared by award-winning chef Lorenzo. Monthly Caribbean nights, music and quiz nights and an annual beer and cider festival provide the entertainment at this friendly community pub. CAMRA members receive a 10 per cent discount on food and drink. A former local branch Cider Pub of the Year. ⛅❀◑♣●P🚌🐾📶

Worcester

Bell 𝕃

35 St Johns, WR2 5AG (W side of Severn off A44)
⏲ 10-1am; 11-midnight Sun ☎ (01905) 424570
Fuller's London Pride; Thwaites Wainwright; guest beers Ⓗ
A community pub dating from the 17th century with two small rooms on one side and the main bar on the other, separated by a central corridor. At the rear is a second bar used at busy times, and a room available for functions. There is also a popular skittle alley. Guest beers always include one from Hobsons and two from local independent brewers. Live music often plays at weekends. ⛅❀♣🚌🐾📶

Cardinal's Hat

31 Friar Street, WR1 2NA
⏲ 12 (4 Mon)-11; 12-10.30 Sun ☎ (01905) 724006
🌐 the-cardinals-hat.co.uk
Beer range varies Ⓗ
A stone-flagged, panelled passageway leads through Worcester's oldest pub to the small rooms and outdoor patio at the rear. The main bar at the front with scrubbed wooden floor, beams and leaded windows is full of life. The atmospheric back room features wood panelling, a stone floor, serving hatch and impressive fireplace with woodburner and melting candles. The small snug has views of the bustling old street outside. Beers are local and ciders come from Westons, Hogan's and Orchard Pig. Q⛅❀◑⇌(Foregate St)♣●🐾

Chestnut

17 Lansdowne Road, WR1 1SS (off the Tything)
⏲ 3-11; 12-midnight Fri & Sat; 12-11 Sun ☎ 07598 393109
Thwaites Wainwright; Wye Valley HPA; guest beers Ⓗ
Friendly back-street local with two rooms decorated with an eclectic mix of art and interesting artefacts ranging from a vinyl music

ENGLAND

player to books and a pulpit. Live music is hosted every weekend, an open-mic night every other Thursday and a quiz night once a month. Steak night is Wednesday and curries feature mid-week. Breakfast is served on Saturday 10am-2pm and Sunday roasts 1pm-late. Barbecues are held in summer. ❀◑◐⇌(Foregate St)♣●ᯤ

Dragon Inn

51 The Tything, WR1 1JT (on A449, 300yds N of Foregate St station)

4.30 (12 Fri & Sat)-11; 1-4, 7-10.30 Sun ☎ (01905) 25845

dragoninn-worcester.com

Beer range varies Ⓗ

Georgian building on the edge of the city centre, offering an array of six pumps serving an ever-changing choice of beers biased towards Yorkshire, including the Little Ale Cart Brewery in Sheffield, and often something from Mighty Oak. The handpulled draught cider is Thatchers Cheddar Valley. Bottle-conditioned Belgian beers are also offered. There is a large covered seating area outside. Themed beer and food nights feature on Thursdays, and a monthly quiz night on Tuesdays. Good-value lunchtime meals are served Friday to Sunday. ❀◑⇌(Foregate St)♣●

King Charles II

29 New Street, WR1 2DP

11.30 (11 Sat)-11 ☎ (01905) 726100

thekingcharleshouse.com

Beer range varies Ⓗ

A recently opened pub which has made its home in a gorgeous listed Tudor black and white former restaurant. A range of eight beers – a varying mix from Sadler's, Craddock's and Bridgnorth – is on the pumps, alongside Barbourne ciders and occasionally a perry. Check out the rollercoaster ride on the first floor and the skeleton in the oubliette. King Charles II escaped from here after the battle of Worcester, but the beer range was not so good then. Q◑◐⇌(Foregate St)♣●ᯤ

Paul Pry ★

6 The Butts, WR1 3PA

12-8 (10 Fri & Sat); closed Sun ☎ (01905) 729290

Beer range varies Ⓗ

An old town-centre market tavern with a well-preserved listed interior. The main bar has a splendid ornate bar-back, with mahogany and etched glass to the fore. The back room is an airy homage to Victoriana. The tiled passageway has a couple of steps leading to the toilets and yet more tilework. Up to four guest ales are available on handpumps, with local Worcester breweries regularly featured. Close to the bus station and library complex. ◑⇌(Foregate St)●

Plough

23 Fish Street, WR1 2HN (on Deansway)

12 (4.30 Thu)-11; 12-11.30 Fri & Sat; 12-10.30 Sun

☎ (01905) 21381 theplough-worcester.com

Hobsons Best Bitter; Malvern Hills Black Pear; guest beers Ⓗ

This Grade II-listed pub near the cathedral has a short flight of steps leading to a tiny bar with rooms on either side. The beers come from breweries in Worcestershire and surrounding counties. Draught cider and perry are from Barbourne in the city. There is a patio area outside. Rolls are available at weekends and when cricket is on. ❀⇌(Foregate St)♣●

Wheatsheaf Inn

192 Henwick Road, WR2 5PF

12-midnight ☎ 07891 668030

Marston's Burton Bitter, Pedigree; guest beers Ⓗ

Small Grade II-listed 18th-century terraced local, attracting both young and old. A varied selection of guest ales is offered including one from St George's, and two draught ciders. The rear balcony has views of the River Severn to the cathedral. A footpath from the riverside provides alternative access via a flight of steps. The separate pool room is family-friendly, and sport on TV creates a lively atmosphere. Hot and cold pies and snacks are served all day and newspapers are available. ❀♣●ᯤ

Magpie & stump

This favoured tavern, sacred to the evening orgies of Mr Lowten and his companions, was what ordinary people would designate a public-house. That the landlord was a man of money-making turn was sufficiently testified by the fact of a small bulkhead beneath the tap-room window, in size and shape not unlike a sedan-chair, being underlet to a mender of shoes; and that he was a being of philanthropic mind was evident from the protection he afforded to a pieman, who vended his delicacies without fear of interruption on the very door-step.

In the lower windows, which were decorated with curtains of a saffron hue, dangled two or three printed cards bearing reference to Devonshire cider and Dantzig [sic] spruce, while a large blackboard announcing in white letters to an enlightened public, that there were 500,000 barrels of double stout in the cellars of the establishment, left the mind in a not unpleasing state of doubt and uncertainty as to the precise direction in the bowels of the earth, in which this mighty cavern might be supposed to extend.

Charles Dickens, The Pickwick Papers, 1837. The Magpie & Stump, London EC4, stands opposite the Old Bailey and featured in the TV series Rumpole. Danzig beer was flavoured with spruce cones and twigs.

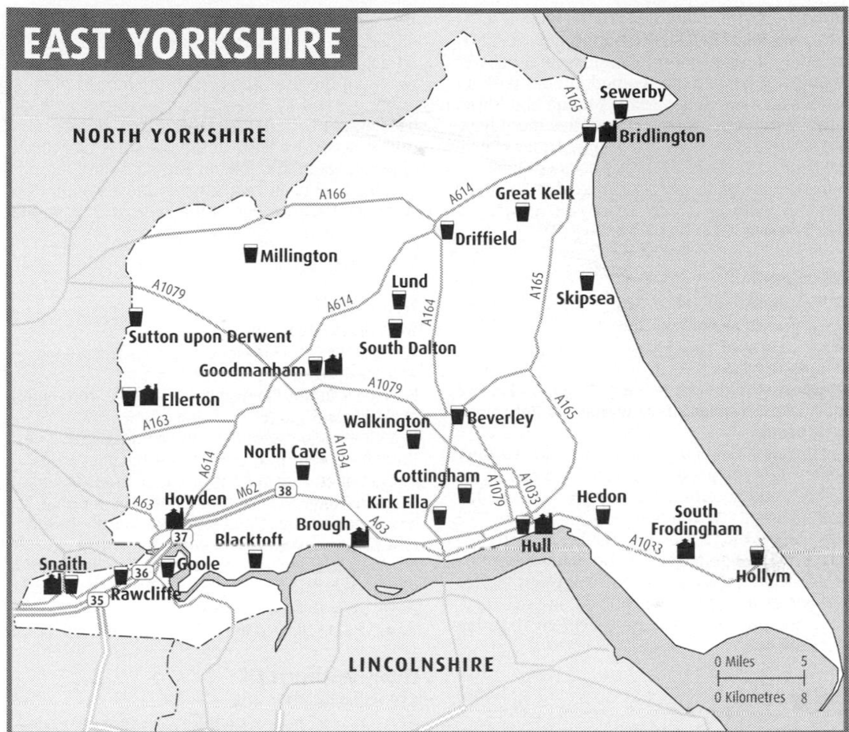

YORKSHIRE (EAST)

Beverley

Chequers Micropub

15 Swaby's Yard, Dyer Lane, HU17 9BZ (off Saturday Market)

closed Mon; 12-11; 12-10 Sun ☎ 07964 227906

chequersmicropub.co.uk

Beer range varies H

Yorkshire's first micropub, in a former baker's and near the bus station. Local microbreweries represented include Atom, Brass Castle, Great Newsome and Wold Top, plus micros from throughout the UK. Six ciders/perries are sold. The cellar and toilets are above the bar. Typically for a micropub, no lager, keg beer or spirits are sold, and there is no TV or loud music, making this a place for real conversation, like pubs used to be.

Q

Cornerhouse

2 Norwood, HU17 9ET

closed Mon; 5-midnight (1am Fri); 10-1am Sat; 10-11 Sun

☎ (01482) 882652

Abbeydale Deception; Black Sheep Best Bitter; Greene King IPA; Tetley Bitter; Timothy Taylor Landlord; guest beers H

The Cornerhouse looks like a gastro-pub, but the customers are mainly here for the real ale on 12 handpumps and the real cider on two handpumps. Yorkshire brewers feature prominently and a mild is sometimes available. A coal fire warms the far end of the room and there is unusual gallery seating off the bar. Curry night is Tuesday and quiz night Wednesday. Food is served weekday evenings and all day weekends – when you can get breakfast from 10am-1pm. P

Dog & Duck

33 Ladygate, HU17 8BH (off Saturday Market adjacent to Browns store)

11-4, 7-midnight; 11-midnight Fri & Sat; 11.30-3, 7-11 Sun

☎ (01482) 862419 bedandbreakfastbeverley.com

Black Sheep Best Bitter; Copper Dragon Golden Pippin; John Smith's Bitter; Timothy Taylor Golden Best; guest beers H

The pub was built in the 1930s and has been run by the same family for over 40 years. It comprises three areas: a bar with a period brick fireplace and bentwood seating, a front lounge, and a rear snug. The good-value, home-cooked lunches are popular. Guest accommodation is in six purpose-built self-contained rooms to the rear. Close to Beverley bus station. Lined glasses are used only for Black Sheep beer.

Tiger Inn

Lairgate, HU17 8JG (near memorial hall)

closed Mon; 11-11 (midnight Fri & Sat); 12-11 Sun

☎ (01482) 869040 tiger-inn-beverley.co.uk

Great Newsome Sleck Dust; Rooster's Yankee; Timothy Taylor Landlord; Wychwood Hobgoblin H

INDEPENDENT BREWERIES

All Hallows Goodmanham
Atom Hull (NEW)
Bird Brain Howden
Bridlington Bridlington (NEW)
Crystalbrew Brough (NEW)
Great Newsome South Frodingham
Half Moon Ellerton (NEW)
Old Mill Snaith
Whalebone Hull
Yorkshire Hull

Attractive 18th-century building re-fronted in 1930s brewers' Tudor style by the now defunct Darley & Co, which once owned several pubs in Beverley. It has a multi-roomed interior with a public bar, snug, dining room/lounge and function room. Many local clubs and societies meet here and folk music sessions are held on Friday evening. The large car park to the rear was once stables and outbuildings. Meals are served lunchtimes and evenings, with an all-day Sunday carvery. Q❀◑⇌♣●P🚌(X46,X47)🐾📶

Woolpack

37 Westwood Road, HU17 8EN (easily reached from town centre by walking up Newbegin off Lairgate)
4.30-10.30 Mon; 12-3, 4.30-11; 12-11 Sat & Sun
☎ (01482) 867095
Brakspear Oxford Gold; Jennings Bitter, Cocker Hoop, Sneck Lifter; Marston's EPA; Wychwood Hobgoblin; guest beer Ⓗ
In a Victorian residential street west of the town centre, the Woolpack started life as a pair of cottages and became a public house around 1831, later adding its own brewhouse and stables. It is now owned by Marston's. It retains a quarry-tiled snug from that period and an open fire burns in the winter; there is a more recent extension to the rear. Meals are served lunchtimes and evenings (12-7pm Sun). Quiz nights are held on Thursdays. Q🛋❀◑♣🐾

Blacktoft

Hope & Anchor

Blacktoft Lane, DN14 7YW (3½ miles S of Gilberdyke rail station; follow signs to Blacktoft)
12 (4 Mon)-11; 12-10.30 Sun ☎ (01430) 440441
Greene King Abbot; Jennings Dark Mild; Marston's Pedigree; guest beers Ⓗ
Thriving village local in a superb location on the bank of the River Ouse. The RSPB's Blacktoft Sands bird sanctuary is visible on the far bank. Humour, past and present, is a feature of the old pub – look for the Laurel and Hardy memorabilia. The conservatory offers fine river views and popular home-cooked meals, available lunchtimes and evenings during the week, all day at weekends. Two guest beers change regularly, with Hop Studio ales regularly on offer. 🛋❀◑⛺♣P📶

Bridlington

Marine Bar 𝕃

North Marine Drive, YO15 2LS (1 mile NE of centre)
11-11 (11.30 Sat) ☎ (01262) 675347 🌐 marinebar.net
John Smith's Bitter; Timothy Taylor Landlord; Wold Top Bitter; guest beers Ⓗ
Large open-plan bar, part of the Expanse Hotel on the seafront, with spectacular sea views from the outdoor seating. It attracts a good mix of regulars and is welcoming to the influx of summer visitors. Home-cooked food, including vegetarian options, is served daily. Ample car parking is available on the promenade. It is also on a land train route during the summer season. Twice-weekly quizzes and live music nights are popular. Runner-up local CAMRA Town Pub of the Year 2012. ❀🛏◑♿⛺♣P🚌

Telegraph Inn 🏆 𝕃

110 Quay Road, YO16 4JB (10 mins from rail station)
12-midnight (1am Fri & Sat) ☎ (01262) 674592
Wold Top Anglers Reward; guest beers Ⓗ
This welcoming, traditional, family-run inn houses Bridlington's only microbrewery. A free house, it offers four guest ales from across Yorkshire plus two from the brewery, served in an open plan room warmed by logburners. The spacious walled beer garden includes a covered area with a chiminea, with a view of the brewery. Live music plays on Saturdays, folk on Tuesdays, and the pub is home to pool and darts teams and a scooter club. Local CAMRA town Pub of the Year 2013. ❀⇌♣🚌

Cottingham

Blue Bell

West Green, HU16 4BH
closed Mon; 11-11 (midnight Fri & Sat); 12-10.30 Sun
☎ (01482) 847113
Brakspear Bitter; Ringwood Boondoggle, Fortyniner; guest beers Ⓗ
In a picturesque setting overlooking the green near the village centre, this attractive building is split into a bar and restaurant. The restaurant has a log fire and enjoys a high reputation. The modern bar has deep armchairs and low-level music. To the rear there is a secluded beer garden with a covered smoking area and heaters. Open mic music night is Wednesday and live jazz plays on Sunday evening. Dogs are welcome in the bar.
❀◑♿P🚌(110,115)🐾

King William IV

152 Hallgate, HU16 4DB
11-11 (midnight Fri & Sat); 12-11 Sun ☎ (01482) 875996
🌐 kingwilliamcottingham.co.uk
Banks's Sunbeam; Jennings Cumberland Ale; Marston's Pedigree; guest beers Ⓗ
Village-centre pub with a traditional bar and lounge, and free of music. At the rear a former brewery has been converted into a function room offering live music and special events. The pub also hosts weekly quiz nights and an annual music festival. The rear beer garden and side courtyard have covered smoking areas. Excellent-value meals are served in large and small portions. Up to four guest beers and a cider are on handpump. Local CAMRA branch runner-up Village Pub of the Year 2013. Q❀◑⇌♣●🚌

Railway

11 Thwaite Street, HU16 4QT
12-midnight (12.30am Fri & Sat) ☎ (01482) 622980
🌐 railwaycottingham.co.uk
Black Sheep Best Bitter; Theakston Old Peculier; Timothy Taylor Landlord; guest beers Ⓗ
Large detached pub that has benefited from a tasteful refurbishment. There are deep leather seats in the comfortable lounge, where bands play at weekends. The separate bar has live sport on TV and is a base for darts, pool and football teams. This is a child-friendly venue which is popular with diners. Four guest beers and two ciders are usually on offer. Local CAMRA Village Pub of the Year runner-up 2012. 🛋❀◑⇌♣●P🚌📶

Driffield

Mariners Arms

47 Eastgate South, YO25 6LR (on back street running parallel with Middle St)
3 (12 Sat & Sun)-midnight ☎ (01377) 253708
Banks's Sunbeam; Jennings Bitter; Ringwood Best Bitter; guest beer Ⓗ

A street-corner local well worth seeking out. The beer range is from the Marston's portfolio, as an alternative to the other breweries more commonly available in the town. Formerly part of the Hull Brewery estate, its four small rooms have now become two: a basic bar and a more comfortable lounge. Live sport is shown and the pub fields various sports teams. The long-standing licensees enjoy a loyal following among locals and offer a friendly welcome to all visitors. ❀⇌♣P🚌(121)

Ellerton

Boot & Shoe

Main Street, YO42 4PB

5.30 (12 Sat & Sun)-midnight ☎ (01757) 288346

bootandshoeinn.co.uk

Beer range varies H

A welcoming country village inn of character dating from the 17th century. The building wraps around a large tree and features low-beamed ceilings. There is a cosy bar area with exposed brick and an open fire, plus two intimate separate dining rooms. Four real ales are on offer in this free house, including Old Boot and Tom Tate especially brewed by the Dark Horse brewery. Food is served Friday and Saturday evenings and Sunday lunchtimes (booking advisable). Q◑◐♣P🐾

Goodmanham

Goodmanham Arms L

Main Street, YO43 3JA

11-midnight (11 Sun) ☎ (01430) 873849

goodmanhamarms.co.uk

All Hallows Mischief Maker, Peg Fyte Mild; Hambleton Stallion; Theakston Best Bitter, Old Peculier; guest beer H

Close to the Wolds Way footpath and an ideal resting place for walkers, this traditional village pub has a small beer garden at the front and a hidden garden to the rear. It serves up to seven real ales, usually including a mild, and Old Peculier is from the wood. A microbrewery on the site started brewing in 2012, producing All Hallows beers. Food is available lunchtimes plus Monday and Friday evenings. A former local CAMRA Village Pub of the Year. Q◑◐●P🐾

Goole

City & County L

Market Square, DN14 5DR

8am-midnight ☎ (01405) 722600

Greene King Abbot; Ruddles County; guest beers H

This town-centre Wetherspoon pub with a high ceiling is a converted Midland Bank – the bar is where the counter once stood. Smaller than many others of its type, it has a friendly and popular feel. The staff are adept at raising money for various charities, including local schools and disabled groups. The restaurant section is separated from the bar by the stairwell and kitchen. You can always get a real cider here. Q♉❀◑◐♿⇌●

Great Kelk

Chestnut Horse L

Main Street, YO25 8HN

closed Mon & Tue; 6 (5.30 Fri & Sat)-11; 12-10.30 Sun ☎ (01262) 488263 chestnuthorsekelk.co.uk

Wold Top Bitter; guest beers H

Built in 1793, this delightful Grade II-listed rural community pub nestles in the Yorkshire Wolds, with an open log fire in the winter and a walled beer garden for the summer. The traditional inn uses local produce to complement its special pie menu, available until 8.30pm (no meals 3-5pm Sun). Two guest beers are offered alongside a selection of Belgian bottled beers, all served in their own branded glasses. A games room doubles as a family room in the daytime. Q♉❀◑◐♣P

Hedon

Haven Arms L

Sheriff Highway, HU12 8HH

9am-11 (midnight Fri & Sat) ☎ (01482) 897695

havenarms.co.uk

Black Sheep Best Bitter; Timothy Taylor Landlord; guest beers H

The pub is situated in the historic Haven area of town, once the largest port on the Humber. It is licensed for weddings, and the large bar, dining room and permanent marquee can accommodate all customer requirements. Reasonably priced pub food, freshly prepared from local ingredients, is served all day from 9am. Three guest beers, one usually dark and one often from a local microbrewery, are on the bar. One real cider is always available, increasing to two or three from April to September. ♉❀◑◐♿⛺♣●P🚌🐾

Shakespeare Inn L

9 Baxtergate, HU12 8JN

12-11 (11.30 Fri & Sat); 12-10.30 Sun ☎ (01482) 898371

Tetley Bitter; Timothy Taylor Landlord; guest beers H

A 300-year-old pub in the centre of historic Hedon, largely unaltered for the past 50 years, featuring original Darley's wall sconces. It is popular with all ages, with a wide and varied clientele. Rugby League memorabilia, reflecting the landlord's previous career, adorns the walls, and a friendly atmosphere encourages the art of conversation. The food menu features freshly cooked local produce, alongside a popular changing specials menu. Three guest beers are available, one usually from a local brewery. Q♉❀◑◐♿♣P🚌

Hollym

Plough Inn 🏆 L

Northside Road, HU19 2RS

closed Mon; 6 (5 Thu; 3 Fri; 12 Sat)-midnight; 12-11 Sun ☎ (01964) 612049 theploughinnhollym.co.uk

Beer range varies H

Family-run 200-year-old free house of wattle and daub construction offering five real ales, one usually a Greene King beer. Primarily a locals' pub, a base for Withernsea rugby club and the local running club, it is also a haven for discerning holidaymakers in the summer. Photographs in the bar depict its role as an ARP station during World War II. Local CAMRA Village Pub of the Year 2013. ♉❀🛏◑◐⛺♣●P📺🚌🐾

Hull

Admiral of the Humber 🏆

1 Anlaby Road, HU1 2NT

8am-midnight (1am Fri & Sat) ☎ (01482) 381850

Greene King Abbot; Marston's Pedigree; Ruddles Best Bitter; guest beers H

A former paint and wallpaper shop – previously the site was well connected to Hull's seafaring past. Now a large single room, mostly on one level, the building is ideally suited to those finding steps or stairs a problem. This Wetherspoon pub prides itself on being part of the community as far as sport is concerned and is away-fan-friendly (exceptions may apply). A designated area is set aside for diners during the day, and children are welcome until 6pm. Local CAMRA Pub of the Year 2013.
♘◑♿⇄♣●🚌📶

Gardeners Arms

35 Cottingham Road, HU5 2PP
⏲ 11 (12 Sun & Mon)-midnight ☎ (01482) 342396
🌐 thegardenersarmshull.co.uk
Greene King IPA; Tetley Bitter; guest beers Ⓗ
Two miles north of the city centre, this is a friendly pub, appealing to drinkers and diners on a budget. The front bar features a matchwood ceiling while the back bar houses five pool tables. Sport TV is shown throughout the pub, which has four changing guest beers from the M&B list. Children are welcome until 7pm, with special offers on meals at half term. The pub supports a ladies' hockey team, local Rugby Union and Sunday league football teams.
♘❀◑♿♣●P🚌(105,X47)📶

Hop & Vine

24 Albion Street, HU1 3TG (250yds from Hull New Theatre)
⏲ 4-11 Tue; 11-11 (11.30 Fri & Sat); closed Sun & Mon ☎ 07500 543199 🌐 hopandvinehull.co.uk
Beer range varies Ⓗ
Atmospheric basement-bar free house serving three changing guest beers from independent breweries, plus rare farmhouse ciders and perry. Oversized lined glasses are used. A select range of Belgian bottled beers plus draught Budweiser Budvar and Pilsner Urquell are stocked. Freshly made food including home-baked bread is served until 9pm. Shove-ha'penny, cribbage and shut the box games are available. A former CAMRA National Cider Pub of the Year and four-times Yorkshire regional winner, including 2014. Closed between Christmas and New Year. ◑⇄♣●P🚆🚌🐾📶

Larkin's Bar

48-52 Newland Avenue, HU5 3AE (nr jct of De Grey St)
⏲ 11-11 ☎ (01482) 440991 🌐 larkinsbar.co.uk
Great Newsome Sleck Dust; Wold Top Wold Gold; guest beer Ⓗ
A one-roomed café-bar that was once two shops, named after poet Philip Larkin. Changing beers from Great Newsome and Wold Top breweries are usually offered, with a third often coming from Cottage brewery. A selection of continental bottled beers is also available. Food is served noon-8.30pm (until 8pm Fri and Sat). The interior can be partitioned for functions, and there are drinking areas outside at the front and rear. ♘❀◑♿🚌

New Adelphi Club

89 De Grey Street, HU5 2RU
⏲ 8pm-11 ☎ (01482) 348216 🌐 theadelphi.com
Oakham Citra; guest beers Ⓗ
Hull's justifiably famous music venue has been the launch pad to many an illustrious career and has hosted a veritable Who's Who of popular music since opening in 1984. The main music room is supplemented by a small front bar which accommodates a pool table and features a cut-off bus front as the counter. Access to the small bar is free at all times and no membership restrictions apply. Benefit from a £1 reduction on ale when no musicians are booked. ♣●P🚌

Olde Black Boy ★

150 High Street, Old Town, HU1 1PS
⏲ 12.30 (5 Mon-Wed)-11.30 ☎ (01482) 326516
🌐 yeoldeblackboy.weebly.com
Beer range varies Ⓗ
Historic pub, licensed since 1729 but which has also been, variously, a wine merchant and a tobacco dealer, traditionally represented by an Indian chief or black boy; note the carved boy's head above the fireplace. First Mondays of the month are for folk music; anyone is welcome to play. Guest beers vary widely and Westons Old Rosie cider is also on tap. Bar snacks are now served at all times and an upstairs room may also be available. Q♣●🚌

Olde White Harte ★

25 Silver Street, Old Town, HU1 1JG
⏲ 11-midnight (1am Fri & Sat); 12-midnight Sun
☎ (01482) 326363 🌐 yeoldewhiteharte.com
Caledonian Deuchars IPA, Flying Scotsman, Golden XPA; Theakston Best Bitter, Lightfoot, Old Peculier Ⓗ
Historic pub in a 17th-century merchant's house, with strong connections to the Civil War. The existing ground floor interior dates back to a major refurbishment in 1881, which was an idealised re-creation of an old English inn, complete with massive inglenook fireplaces and stained glass windows. The first floor has restaurant facilities and the Plotting Parlour is available for meetings and functions. There is also a courtyard with heating providing an all-weather outdoor drinking area.
❀◐♣●🚌

Pave

16-20 Princes Avenue, HU5 3QA (in the Avenues area)
⏲ 11-11 (11.30 Fri & Sat) ☎ (01482) 333181
🌐 pavebar.co.uk
Tetley Gold; Theakston Best Bitter; guest beers Ⓗ
A continental-style café bar with a diverse range of customers. As well as the regular real ales, there are three guests which are usually sourced locally, and a varied range of European draught and bottled beers. Food, including vegetarian choices, is served daily. Complementary live entertainment is provided on Tuesday evenings and Sunday afternoons, but the bar closes to the general public when comedy nights and world music nights are held. Westons cider is sold. ♘❀◑♿●🚌

St John's Hotel

10 Queens Road, HU5 2PY
⏲ 12-11 (11.30 Thu; midnight Fri & Sat) ☎ (01482) 341013
Marston's EPA, Old Empire; guest beers Ⓗ
A classic Grade II-listed street-corner local boasting one of the least-altered interiors in the city. The welcoming front-corner public bar complements a quiet back room, with original bench seating. A more basic larger room accommodates the pool table and is home to the beer festival bar three times a year. This is a genuine community local and is home to two dart teams, a pub football team and the Oddfellows cricket league. A popular open mic night is hosted on Tuesdays. Q❀♿♣P🚌🐾📶

Three John Scotts

Lowgate, Old Town, HU1 1AA
⏲ 8am-midnight (1am Fri & Sat) ☎ (01482) 381910

Greene King Abbot; Marston's Pedigree; Ruddles Best Bitter; guest beers Ⓗ
Originally an Edwardian post office, this open-plan Wetherspoon features modern decor and works of art. It is named after three past incumbents of the church opposite. The pub has established a broad customer base appealing to all types of clientele. Wetherspoon's club meal offers are served Tuesday, Thursday and Sunday throughout the year. Up to 10 real ales and additional real ciders are available. Children are welcome up to 7pm. Local CAMRA Hull Pub of the Year runner-up 2013.

Whalebone

165 Wincolmlee, HU2 0PA
11-midnight ☎ (01482) 226648
Copper Dragon Best Bitter; Timothy Taylor Landlord; Whalebone Neckoil Bitter; guest beers Ⓗ
Built in 1796, the pub is situated in a former industrial area – look for the illuminated M&R Ales sign. The comfortable saloon bar is adorned with photos of bygone Hull pubs, CAMRA awards and mementos of the city's sporting heritage. The adjacent Whalebone Brewery opened in 2003, and its beers are sold exclusively here. Broad Oak Kingston Black and Westons Old Rosie ciders are stocked, together with European draught and bottled beers.

Wm Hawkes

32 Scale Lane, HU1 1LF
12-11 (11.30 Fri-Sun) ☎ (01482) 224004
wmhawkes.co.uk
Beer range varies Ⓗ
Named after a gunsmith who occupied the premises in the 19th century, the pub opened in the summer of 2012, yet feels like it has been operating for decades. This is testament to the conversion carried out by the licensees – using fittings reclaimed from other pubs and decorating with antiques and bric-a-brac to create the right ambience. Nine real ales from a variety of national and local breweries and a changing real cider are available; there is no gas-assisted dispense. Q

Kirk Ella

Beech Tree

South Ella Way, HU10 7LY
11-11 (midnight Thu-Sat) ☎ (01482) 654350
Black Sheep Best Bitter; Kirkstall Three Swords; Tetley Bitter; guest beers Ⓗ
Open-plan establishment on the western outskirts of Hull, owned by a pub company committed to cask ale. Up to eight real ales are available, including at least one dark beer – try-before-you-buy is encouraged. Food is served 12-10pm every day. Monday and Wednesday are quiz nights. Families with children are welcome throughout. Buses stop close to the pub until early evening, and later stop only a 10-minute walk away. The usual Ember Inns CAMRA member discount is offered.
P (154,180)

Lund

Wellington Inn

19 The Green, YO25 9TE
12-3, 6.30 (7 Mon)-11; 12-11 Sun ☎ (01377) 217192
thewellingtoninn.co.uk
John Smith's Bitter; Theakston Best Bitter; Timothy Taylor Landlord; guest beer Ⓗ
Enjoying a prime location on the green in this award-winning Wolds village, most of the pub's trade comes from the local farming community. Renovated by the present licensee, it features stone-flagged floors, beamed ceilings and three real fires. The multi-roomed interior includes a games room and a candlelit restaurant serving evening meals Tuesday-Saturday. Good food can also be enjoyed at lunchtime from the bar menu and specials board. Guest beers are usually from local breweries. P

Millington

Gait

Main Street, YO42 1TX
closed Mon; 12-3 (not Tue-Thu), 6-11; 12-4, 6-11 Sat
☎ (01759) 302045 gait-inn-millington.co.uk
Black Sheep Best Bitter; Tetley Bitter; Theakston Best Bitter; guest beers Ⓗ
A pretty pub in the Yorkshire Wolds, three miles from Pocklington, which is popular with locals, farmers and walkers. It serves two guest beers, with at least one from a local microbrewery. The slightly quirky single bar has mismatched tables, knick-knacks on the walls and a wonderful old Yorkshire map on the ceiling. An annual beer festival is staged, with up to 35 beers. This no-nonsense community pub is well worth a visit.
P

North Cave

White Hart

20 Westgate, HU15 2NJ
4-11; 12-midnight Fri & Sat; 12-11 Sun ☎ (01430) 470940
whitehartnorthcave.co.uk
Beer range varies Ⓗ
This welcoming traditional village pub is a credit to the community it serves. It has three rooms, one now only used for Sunday lunches. The long bar to the side and rear is where the real ale is dispensed on three handpulls, while the quieter front bar has comfortable seating. Real fires are lit during the winter months, providing home-from-home comfort. Walkers and dogs are welcome. Local brewery Great Newsome supplies a house beer, White Hart 1776. P (155)

Rawcliffe

Jemmy Hirst at the Rose & Crown

26 Riverside, DN14 8RN (from village green turn N on Chapel Lane)
6 (5 Fri)-midnight; 12-midnight Sat & Sun
☎ (01405) 831038 jemmyhirst.freeservers.com
Timothy Taylor Landlord; guest beers Ⓗ
An outstanding free house that locals say is the heart of the village, well known regionally and winner of numerous CAMRA branch awards, including Pub of the Year seven times. There is always a warm, friendly welcome from the owners, locals and Bruno the dog. Book-lined walls and an open fire provide a haven on a cold winter's day. You can sample five real ales and a traditional cider here. The patio or riverbank beckon in warmer weather. QP (88,400)

Sewerby

Ship Inn
Cliff Road, YO15 1EW
11.30-11 ☎ (01262) 672374 shipinnsewerby.co.uk
Banks's Bitter; guest beers H
Village-centre pub, featuring a wood-panelled bar with beamed ceiling, serving both locals and holidaymakers; there is also a separate dining room and lounge. It is dog-friendly and has a beer garden with a children's play area. Food is on offer either as snacks or main meals; booking is recommended for the Sunday carvery. Nearby is a model village and Sewerby Hall, with clifftop walks. A land train terminates close to the pub. No food on Mondays. ❀◗▲♣P🚌🐾

Skipsea

Board Inn
Back Street, YO25 8SU (off B1242)
6-11; 12-midnight Sat; 12-11 Sun ☎ (01262) 468342
Beer range varies H
Situated a mile from the sea in the village conservation area, this homely pub dating from 1642 is popular with locals and a mecca for holidaymakers. Walkers and cyclists are made welcome. It has a traditional separate bar room and lounge, and serves three beers from the Marston's portfolio, reducing to two in winter. The large restaurant offers home-prepared food made with locally-sourced produce (booking is recommended for Sunday lunches). Functions can be catered for. Closed on Tuesdays in January and February. ◖◗▲P🚌(130)🐾

Snaith

Brewers Arms
10 Pontefract Road, DN14 9JS
12-midnight (11.30 Sun) ☎ (01405) 862404
Old Mill Traditional Bitter, Blonde Bombshell; guest beers H
A fine example of a large village pub, which has recently undergone refurbishment to its bedrooms and cosmetic changes to the bar. It is the brewery tap for the local Old Mill Brewery and is its flagship establishment. There are four themed bar areas which feature stuffed animals and birds, three fires, a well (containing a skeleton) and fishing rods. Four real ales are always on handpump, plus draught cider. Q❀◖◗♿♣P🚌

South Dalton

Pipe & Glass
West End, HU17 7PN
closed Mon; 12-11 (10.30 Sun) ☎ (01430) 810246
pipeandglass.co.uk
Black Sheep Best Bitter; guest beers H
Delightful hostelry that stands at the site of the original gatehouse to Dalton Hall, featuring exposed beams and custom-made furniture. The chef/owner holds a Michelin star for the fifth year running – quality meals are served lunchtimes and evenings. Three guest beers come from Yorkshire breweries, one from Wold Top, and real cider from Moorlands Farm. Two double rooms are available to let, and walkers are made welcome. The pub closes for the first two weeks in January.
Q❀◖◗♿P🚌(142)

Sutton upon Derwent

St Vincent Arms
Main Street, YO41 4BN
12-3, 6-11 (10.30 Sun) ☎ (01904) 608349
stvincentarms.co.uk
Fuller's Chiswick Bitter, London Pride, ESB; Timothy Taylor Golden Best, Landlord; York Yorkshire Terrier; guest beers H
Former winner of many York CAMRA awards, this pretty white-painted village hostelry on a bend in the road has been family-owned and well run for many years. A long-time supporter of Fuller's beers, this free house has a consistent but large beer range. The bar, featuring a large Fuller, Smith & Turner mirror, is popular with locals. Another small bar with a serving hatch leads to the dining rooms. It also serves excellent food, catering for a variety of tastes. Q❀◖◗P

Walkington

Barrel Inn
35 East End, HU17 8RX
4.30-midnight; 12-1am Sat & Sun ☎ 07550 078833
Beer range varies H
Friendly drinkers' local in a quiet three-pub village, and one of only two Thwaites' pubs in East Yorkshire. Inside, it has a front bar featuring a log fire and beamed ceiling, with a step leading to the connecting lounge, also with a log fire. There is subtle piped music throughout and a TV for sport. Live music is hosted occasionally. Families are welcome. Up to five real ales are sold, including one free of tie. A secluded cottage-style beer garden is at the rear. ❀♣🚌(61,180)

YORKSHIRE (NORTH)

Aldbrough St John

Stanwick
High Green, DL11 7SZ (1 mile from B6275)
12-3, 5.30 (6.30 Sat)-11; 12-10.30 Sun ☎ (01325) 374258
thestanwickinn.co.uk
Daleside Bitter; Jarrow Rivet Catcher; guest beers H
In a picturesque village on one of the country's largest village greens, this welcoming 19th-century inn has two bars: one for drinkers and one for the two excellent restaurants, where locally-sourced food is served seven days a week. The Stanwick is the brewery tap for the village's Mithril Ales, and one of its beers is always featured alongside another guest. Crickets, quoits and darts are supported by the pub. Look out for the take-away fish and chips baguette, available 2-5pm Wednesday and Sunday. Q◗♿🚌(29)🐾

Appletreewick

Craven Arms Inn
BD23 6DA
11-11; 12-10.30 Sun ☎ (01756) 720270
craven-cruckbarn.co.uk
Dark Horse Hetton Pale Ale; Moorhouse's Black Witch, Blond Witch; Theakston Old Peculier; Thwaites Original, Wainwright; guest beers H
Dating from 1548, this multi-roomed Dales free house has stone-flagged floors, oak beams and gas lighting. The main bar features an original Yorkshire range while the cosy taproom has ring the bull. A snug behind the bar leads to the cruck

barn, added in 2006 and built using traditional techniques. This can be hired for functions. The house beer, Cruck Barn Bitter, is brewed by Dark Horse. Guest ales are served in summer and usually include a dark beer. Q❀◑▲♣●P (74)

New Inn

BD23 6DA

12-11 ☎ (01756) 720252

the-new-inn-appletreewick.com

Black Sheep Best Bitter; Goose Eye Chinook Blonde; Theakston Old Peculier; guest beer Ⓗ

Solidly built whitewashed Dales pub offering a warm welcome, be it huddling round the real fire in winter or soaking up the sun in one of the two beer gardens overlooking the river in summer. Up to five cask beers are on offer alongside a range of foreign bottled beers and a real cider. Food is served all day. Well-behaved dogs are welcome and there is a nearby cycle livery.

❀◑▲♣●P (74)

Askrigg

King's Arms

Main Street, DL8 3HQ

11-11 (midnight Fri & Sat) ☎ (01969) 650113

kingsarmsaskrigg.co.uk

Black Sheep Best Bitter; Theakston Best Bitter; guest beers Ⓗ

This pub and village starred in All Creatures Great and Small and both retain great character. The bar of this historic free house serves two stone-flagged rooms, with two dining areas at the front and a vaulted games room to the rear, plus a small outdoor courtyard. A picture of the local Friendly Society dominates the bar above the huge open fireplace. Three house beers are from the local Yorkshire Dales brewery; no keg ales are sold.

❀◑● (156)

Aysgarth

George & Dragon

DL8 3AD (on main A684 between Hawes and Leyburn)

8am-midnight ☎ (01969) 663358

georgeanddragonaysgarth.co.uk

Black Sheep Best Bitter; John Smith's Bitter; guest beers Ⓗ

Less than a mile from the famous Aysgarth Falls on the River Ure, this 17th-century coaching inn is surrounded by stunning Dales countryside. It caters for drinkers in its cosy wood-panelled bar which serves up to five real ales, usually including two from the local Yorkshire Dales brewery. For diners there is a separate restaurant, and en-suite accommodation is also offered. An outside drinking area has thatched umbrellas and great views.

Q❀◑♣P (156)

Barkston Ash

Boot & Shoe

Main Street, LS24 9PR (on A162 4 miles S of Tadcaster)

closed Mon; 5-11 (midnight Fri & Sat); 12-10.30 Sun

☎ (01937) 557374 bootandshoe.info

Tetley Bitter; Theakston Black Bull Bitter; guest beers Ⓗ

Typical friendly family-run village pub with a cosy bar – although the rooms have been opened up, there is a separate dining area serving good hearty pub food and a great Sunday lunch. Pizza and fish and chips can be eaten in or taken away. Outside there is a pleasant decked area for summer drinking, where beer festivals are held on the second weekend in July and the second Saturday in December. Q❀◑♿♣P (492,493)

Beck Hole

Birch Hall Inn ★

YO22 5LE (750yds N of Goathland)

11-11 summer; 11-3, 7.30-11 (closed Mon eve & Tue) winter ☎ (01947) 896245 beckhole.info

Black Sheep Best Bitter; North Yorkshire Beckwatter; guest beer Ⓗ

Unspoilt, family-run rural gem, resting amid a hamlet of nine cottages, run by the same licensee for 34 years. A CAMRA multi award-winner, including branch Pub of the Year in 2014, it comprises a big bar and a small bar, sandwiching a sweet shop. Rural scenes, painted by the licensee, adorn the walls, while the pub sign, a painting of the Murk Esk, was donated by Algernon Newton RA in 1944. Sandwiches, pies, beer cake and traditional sweets are always on sale.

Q❀♿♣●

INDEPENDENT BREWERIES

BAD Dishforth (NEW)
Barkston Barkston Ash
Black Sheep Masham
Brass Castle Malton
Brown Cow Barlow
Captain Cook Stokesley
Copper Dragon Skipton
Daleside Harrogate
Dark Horse Hetton
Four Thorns Heslington
George Samuel Welbury (NEW)
Great Heck Great Heck
Great Yorkshire Cropton
Hambleton Melmerby
Harrogate (Spa Town Ales) Harrogate (NEW)
Hop Studio Elvington
John Smith's Tadcaster
Jolly Sailor Selby
Knaresborough Knaresborough
Little Brew York
Mithril Aldbrough St John
Naylor's Cross Hills
North Riding Scarborough
North Yorkshire Pinchinthorpe
Pennine Well
Redscar Redcar
Richmond Richmond
Rooster's Knaresborough
Rudgate Tockwith
Rydale York (NEW)
Samuel Smith Tadcaster
Scarborough Scarborough
Settle Settle
Theakston Masham
Three Peaks Settle
Treboom Shipton-by-Beningbrough
Truefitt Middlesbrough
Wainstones (Stokesley) Stokesley
Wall's Northallerton
Wensleydale Bellerby
Whitby Whitby
Wold Top Wold Newton
York York
Yorkshire Dales Askrigg
Yorkshire Heart Nun Monkton

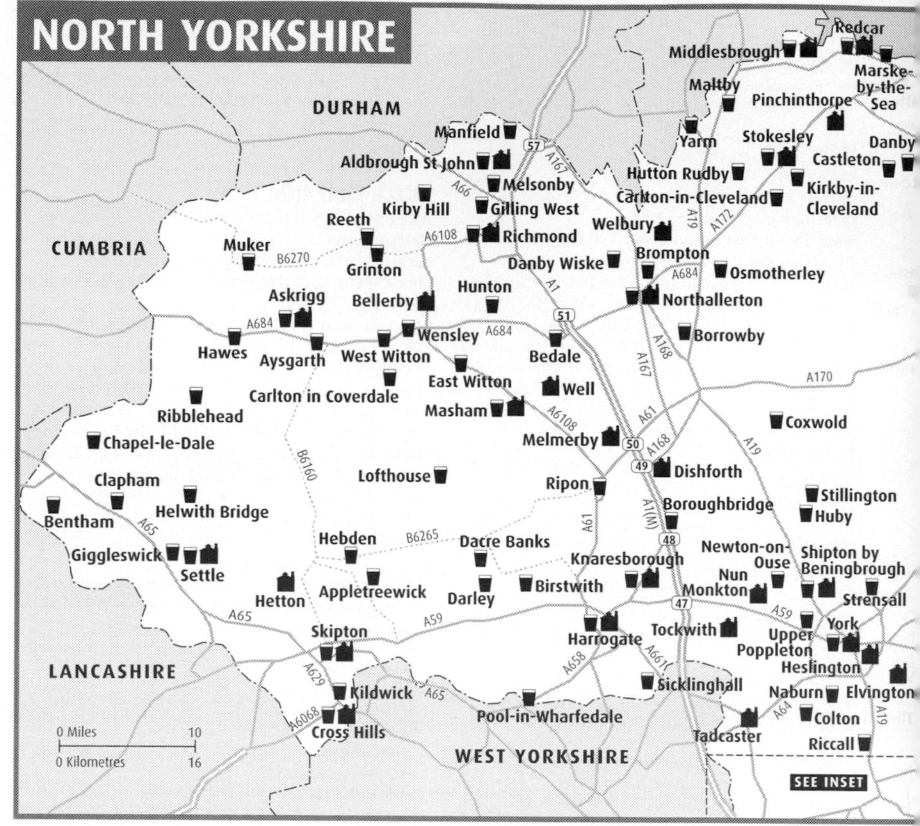

Bedale

Green Dragon

16 Market Place, DL8 1EQ

☼ 11.30-midnight (1am Fri & Sat); 11.30-11 Sun
☎ (01677) 425246

Ringwood Best Bitter, Boondoggle; Wychwood Hobgoblin Ⓗ

Comfortable 17th century inn with a single bar room, set on the picturesque high street of this market town, known as the gateway to the dales. Outside is a beer garden for warmer weather. Up to four ales from the Marston group are on handpump. Live music is often a feature at weekends. A few hundred yards away, the Wensleydale railway station offers regular heritage trains along the picturesque dale.

🐎❀🛏⇌♣🚌🐾📶

Bentham

Horse & Farrier

83 Main Street, LA2 7HR

☼ 12-2 (not Tue), 6-10.30; 12-2, 6-midnight Fri; 12-midnight Sat; 12-10.30 Sun ☎ (015242) 61381
🌐 horseandfarrierinn.co.uk

Copper Dragon Best Bitter; guest beer Ⓗ

This hostelry dates from 1661 and is at the western end of the village of High Bentham. It has a single low-beamed bar with cosy corners and an antique fireplace, mainly used by locals. Biker bite night is on Tuesdays in the summer, live music takes place on Saturday nights, a quiz on Wednesdays, and jamming on the first and third Thursdays of the month. Theakston's beers feature regularly.

Q❀◑Å⇌P🚌(80)🐾

Birstwith

Station Hotel

Station Road, HG3 3AG

☼ 10-11 (midnight Fri); 12-11 Sat; 12-9 Sun
☎ (01423) 770254 🌐 station-hotel.net

Tetley Bitter; guest beers Ⓗ

This former station hotel has undergone a high-quality refurbishment and is now a popular drinking and dining pub. It has three open-plan public bar spaces and a separate dining area at the rear. There is a large beer garden at the back. Four rooms and a holiday cottage are available. The pub is noted for its locally-sourced food, served all day. The guest beers are usually from local breweries such as Ilkley, Copper Dragon and Rudgate.

🐎❀🛏◑♿P🚌(24)📶

Boroughbridge

Black Bull Inn 𝕃

6 St James Square, YO51 9AR

☼ 11-midnight; 12-11 Sun ☎ (01423) 322413
🌐 blackbullboroughbridge.co.uk

John Smith's Bitter; Timothy Taylor Boltmaker; guest beer Ⓗ

Nestling in a corner of the market square, this 13th-century pub, immaculately kept and comfortably furnished, is popular with locals and

tourists alike. A Grade II listed gem, it has a resident ghost and is well worth a visit. Three drinking and dining areas include a small cosy snug and a larger distinctive bar with open fires, both serving good-value beers. A wide range of bar meals is available and there is a separate restaurant. Q⛺◑ ⛺♣P🚌(142,143)🐾📶

Borrowby

Wheatsheaf Inn

YO7 4QP (800yds from A19)

⏲ 5.30-11; 12-10.30 Sun ☎ (01845) 537274

Daleside Bitter; guest beers Ⓗ

A well-kept and welcoming free house in a rambling, attractive village a short hop from the busy A19 trunk route. The cosy public bar features a low-beamed ceiling and a splendid canopied fireplace, showing its 17th-century origins and giving a traditional feel, particularly in winter. There is a small dining room and a further drinking area to the rear. Two guest beers are generally on offer, usually from Yorkshire microbreweries. Q🐴❀◑♣P🐾📶

Brompton

Green Tree

Stokesley Road, DL6 2UA (on main A684)

⏲ 12-2, 6-11; closed Tue; 11-11 Sat & Sun ☎ (01609) 780251

Copper Dragon Best Bitter; Fuller's London Pride; guest beer Ⓗ

On the edge of the village on the main A684 Northallerton-Osmotherley road, this traditional single-room pub retains the feel of a community local. There are distinct bar and dining areas, the former retaining a tiled floor and open fire. To the rear, a sheltered beer garden is claimed to be sun-drenched, and includes a quoits pitch. Guest beers are often from Wall's of Northallerton or other Yorkshire microbreweries. 🐴❀◑♣P🚌🐾📶

Burn

Wheatsheaf 🏆 L

Main Road, YO8 8LJ

⏲ 12-midnight (11.30 Sun) ☎ (01757) 270614

🌐 wheatsheafburn.co.uk

John Smith's Bitter; Timothy Taylor Golden Best; guest beers Ⓗ

Comfortable pub on the A19 serving a varied range of guest beers, mainly from Yorkshire breweries. A narrow entrance leads to the bar, separate pool room and spacious lounge with a huge open fire. There is a collection of artefacts from bygone days and memorabilia of 578 Squadron stationed at Burn in World War II. Food is served lunchtimes, with traditional roast lunches on Sunday, and Wednesday to Saturday evenings. Regular beer festivals and a monthly jazz night take place. Q❀◑♣P🚌

Carlton in Coverdale

Foresters Arms L

DL8 4BB

⏲ 12-2, 6-11 (midnight Fri); 12-midnight Sat & Sun

☎ (01969) 640272 🌐 forestersarms-carlton.co.uk

Black Sheep Best Bitter; John Smith's Bitter; guest beers Ⓗ

In community ownership since 2011, this 250-year-old free house is well worth seeking out, and convenient for the Forbidden Corner fantasy maze a mile or so away. Beamed ceilings and an open fire contribute to its character, with wooden settles fashioned from pews from the former village church. Up to three guest ales from local and regional microbreweries are always on tap, and lunchtime and evening meals use locally-sourced produce. Q🐴❀⛺◑♿♣🍎P🐾📶

Carlton-in-Cleveland

Blackwell Ox Inn

TS9 7DJ (400yds E of A172)

⏲ 11.30-11 ☎ (01642) 712287 🌐 theblackwellox.co.uk

Beer range varies Ⓗ

In a beautiful area on the edge of the national park, this impressive, multi-roomed village inn is renowned for its good-value Thai cuisine as well as its fine beers. Winter Monday evening Thai buffets can easily become habit forming. Look out also for lunch and early doors year-round specials. But you do not have to eat, as drinkers are always made most welcome. Four handpumps provide an eclectic range of varying beer styles. The garden has an extensive children's play area. Q🐴❀◑P🚌(80)

Castleton

Downe Arms

3 High Street, YO21 2EE (500yds S of railway station)

⏲ 12-midnight (11.30 Sun) ☎ (01287) 660223
🌐 thedownearms.co.uk
Camerons IPA, Strongarm; Sharp's Doom Bar; guest beers Ⓗ
This superb family-run and recently refurbished country inn is under the stewardship of an enthusiastic CAMRA member, who gives a small reduction in the price of the five real beers to card-carrying members. Pleasant days are enhanced by the superb views over the North York Moors and the Esk Valley from the south-facing gardens. Lunchtime and early doors specials are available from the daily changing menu, which always features home-made pies, and even includes a takeaway service. There are four letting bedrooms.
Q🐴❀🛏◑♿⇌(Castleton Moor)P🚌(26,27)🐾📶

Eskdale Inn
Station Road, YO21 2EU (next to railway station)
NZ684085
⏲ 12-11 ☎ (01287) 660333
Black Sheep Best Bitter; Tetley Bitter; guest beers Ⓗ
Wedged between the Esk Valley railway and the River Esk, this picturesque former station hotel offers a friendly welcome. The casks sit in a cool cellar directly beneath the handpumps and well away from the roaring fire. The guest beers are often chosen by the locals themselves and are usually something interesting. Good-value food, served all day every day, includes a specials board and a children's menu. The pub supports darts and pool teams. Two letting bedrooms are available.
Q🐴❀🛏◑⇌(Castleton Moor)♣P🚏🚌(26,27)🐾

Chapel-le-Dale

Hill Inn
LA6 3AR (on B6255)
⏲ closed Mon; 12-3, 6-11; 12-11 Sat ☎ (015242) 41256
🌐 oldhillinn.co.uk
Black Sheep Best Bitter; Dent Golden Fleece, Aviator; Theakston Best Bitter; guest beer Ⓗ
The inn dates from 1615 and is beloved of generations of hikers and potholers. Well-worn paths run from here to both Whernside (Yorkshire's highest peak) and Ingleborough (its best known). Restored in 2001 with great care, soft furnishings are eschewed in favour of woodwork (in a variety of sorts) and some exposed limestone stonework. Run by a family of chefs, the pub is popular with diners – puddings are a speciality and there is a sugar sculpture exhibition in an adjoining room.
Q🛏◑P🚏🚌(831)🐾📶

Church Fenton

Fenton Flyer L
Main Street, LS24 9RF
⏲ 5-11 (midnight Fri); 12-midnight Sat; 12-10.30 Sun
☎ (01937) 558137
John Smith's Bitter; guest beers Ⓗ
A cosy, warm and welcoming village pub. The WWII memorabilia and name come from the recently closed nearby airbase. The five LocAles are well kept. Food is available on Friday and Saturday evenings. A Wednesday night quiz raises money for local charities, live music is on the first Friday of each month, and there is a monthly Saturday disco and karaoke. Sky Sports TV is shown.
🐴❀◗♿♣P🚌(492)🐾📶

Clapham

Old Manor House L
Church Avenue, LA2 8EQ
⏲ closed Tue; 10-6 (7 Fri & Sat) ☎ (015242) 51144
🌐 claphambunk.com
Bowland Hen Harrier; Copper Dragon Golden Pippin; guest beers Ⓗ
The old manor house, dating back to around 1620, has a bunkhouse, a café and a bar called the Reading Room. The café and the bar are in separate but connected rooms. A wood-burning stove is set in a huge fireplace (dated 1701), the floor is flagged, and art for sale hangs on the walls. Giant Jenga is played. Do not overlook the bottled beers and ciders. ❀🛏⛺🍎🚌(581)🐾📶

Cliffe

New Inn L
York Road, YO8 6NN
⏲ 2-11; 12-midnight Fri & Sat; 12-10.30 Sun
☎ (01757) 633888 🌐 newinncliffe.co.uk/cms
John Smith's Bitter; guest beers Ⓗ
This welcoming village inn has been transformed from an Enterprise no-hoper into a Yorkshire beer mecca by licensees Ian and Adele. Cosy, two-roomed and serving five guest beers, almost always local and certainly from Yorkshire, this is a key stop-off point from the nearby A63. With log fires in winter and a welcoming beer garden in summer, you will always feel at home. Watch out for the annual August bank holiday beer festival.
🐴❀♿⛺♣P🚌(4)📶

Cloughton

Hayburn Wyke Hotel
Newlands Road, YO13 0AU (off the Ravenscar Road, 1½ miles N of jct with A171)
⏲ 11-midnight; 11-3, 6-midnight Mon-Fri winter
☎ (01723) 870202 🌐 hayburnwykeinn.co.uk
Black Sheep Ale; Daleside Bitter; Theakston Old Peculier Ⓗ
An 18th-century coaching inn in woodland next to the disused Scarborough to Whitby railway and only minutes from the Cleveland Way coastal path and rocky beach. It is popular with cyclists and walkers. Home-made food is served every lunchtime and evening, with the Sunday carvery a local favourite. En-suite accommodation is available. Outside is a well-provisioned children's play space and a sizeable heated smoking area.
❀🛏◑⛺♣P🚌(115)

Colton

Old Sun Inn L
Main Street, LS24 8EP
⏲ 12-3, 6-11; 12-11 Sun ☎ (01904) 744261
🌐 yeoldsuninn.co.uk
Beer range varies Ⓗ
A 17th-century village pub with an award-winning restaurant featuring locally-sourced produce. There are four cosy dining areas together with a drinkers-only bar with five handpumps. It also has an extensive wine list. The interior features traditional low beamed ceilings, and in the winter there are two fires. For the summer there is a patio and a large picnic area. Functions are catered for. Next door is a B&B owned by the publican.
Q🐴❀🛏◑♿P🚌(21)📶

Coxwold

Fauconberg Arms 🄻
YO61 4AD
⏲ 10-midnight ☎ (01347) 868214 🌐 fauconbergarms.com
John Smith's Bitter; Theakston Best Bitter; guest beer Ⓗ
A 17th-century country inn, close to Shandy Hall and Newburgh Priory, with a cosy beamed front bar, a rear bar with dartboard and piano, and a separate dining room. Guest beers are normally LocAles. In summer Husthwaite cider, served from a handpump, is also available. Along with a good reputation for food, and accommodation, the pub is still a village local. Regular quizzes and other events are held. Q❀🛏◑●P🚌(31X)📶

Cropton

New Inn 🄻
YO18 8HH
⏲ 11-11 (midnight Fri & Sat) ☎ (01751) 417330
🌐 newinncropton.co.uk
Great Yorkshire Pale, Classic, Golden; guest beers Ⓗ
Great Yorkshire's brewery tap, this is a family-run pub on the edge of the North Yorkshire Moors National Park in an attractive stone building. It is an ideal base for walking and cycling, offering food in the bars, B&B accommodation and camping. Up to six of the brewery's ales are available. There is also a beer festival in November and a music festival in the summer. Q❀🛏◑♿⛺♣P🚌🐾📶

Cross Hills

Naylor's Beer Emporium 🄻
Midland Mills Station Road, BD20 7DT (in industrial estate on right over railway bridge from Cross Hills)
⏲ 3-11 Fri ☎ (01535) 637451 🌐 naylorsbrewery.co.uk
Beer range varies Ⓗ
Only open for one day per week, the Beer Emporium gets busy at times despite having moved to larger premises across the yard to cope with demand. In good weather customers spill out into the yard outside. The emphasis is on good company, friendly chatter and the appreciation of quality beer. Three cask ales from the Naylor's range are usually available alongside other Naylor's products and some foreign bottled beers. Brewery souvenir merchandise can also be purchased. ❀♿P🚌(66,66A)🐾📶

Old White Bear 🄻
6 Keighley Road, BD20 7RN (on A6068)
⏲ 11-11 ☎ (01535) 632115 🌐 oldwhitebear.co.uk
Naylor's Pinnacle Mild, Pinnacle Bitter, Velvet, Pinnacle Blonde; guest beers Ⓗ
Popular four-room village pub, with exposed timbers said to have come from a ship of the same name. Built in 1735, it had a chequered history as a hotel, brothel, council meeting room and dance hall before becoming a pub. The top room, with stone-flagged floor, is used mainly as an eatery, with good-value meals dished up. Children and dogs are welcome. The back room has darts and ring the bull. Guest beers are from Naylor's.
❀◑♣P🚌🐾📶

Dacre Banks

Royal Oak Inn
Oak Lane, HG3 4EN
⏲ 11.30-11; 12-10.30 Sun ☎ (01423) 780200
🌐 the-royaloak-dacre.co.uk
Beer range varies Ⓗ
A family-run Grade II-listed pub dating from 1752 and in the heart of Nidderdale. At the rear are views of the dale, while a cosy seating area at the front is complete with a real fire. Outside is an attractive garden and boules is played beside the car park. Up to five real ales from Rudgate and Greene King are on handpump. Food majors on local produce and is served in the bar and a separate restaurant. Q❀🛏◑♣P🚌(24)

Danby

Duke of Wellington
West Lane, YO21 2LY (300 yds N of railway station)
⏲ 12-2.30 (not Mon), 7-11; 12-11 Fri & Sat; 12-2.30, 7-10.30 Sun ☎ (01287) 660351 🌐 dukeofwellingtondanby.co.uk
Copper Dragon Scotts 1816; Daleside Bitter; guest beer Ⓗ
An 18th-century inn, and recent local CAMRA Pub of the Year, set in idyllic national park countryside, close to the visitor centre and equally famous bakery. It was used as a recruiting post during the Napoleonic Wars. A cast-iron plaque of the first Duke, unearthed during restorations, hangs above the fireplace. All the beers are local, while the menu offers traditional British home-cooked meals at their best, using locally-sourced produce. Cider and perry are served Easter-October.
Q🛏◑≠♣●🚌(27)🐾

Danby Wiske

White Swan 🄻
DL7 0NQ (approx 3 miles N of Northallerton off A167)
⏲ 12-11 Apr-Oct; 7 (6 Fri)-11 (closed Tue); 12-3, 6-11 Sat; 12-3, 7-10 Sun Nov-Mar ☎ (01609) 775131
🌐 thewhiteswandanbywiske.co.uk
Beer range varies Ⓗ
A haven for coast-to-coast walkers, this CAMRA award-winning pub offers B&B and camping facilities. The opened-out interior features an attractive stone floor and wood-burning stoves. It is the unofficial brewery tap for Wall's of Northallerton and up to five changing beers and a cider are available, depending on the time of year. Snacks are served on spring and summer lunchtimes, with locally-sourced evening meals to order from April to October. The local sword dancers meet here. Q❀🛏◑⛺♣●P🐾📶

Darley

Wellington Inn
Darley Carr, HG3 2QQ (on B6451 W of village)
⏲ 12-11 (midnight Fri & Sat); 12-10.30 Sun
☎ (01423) 780362 🌐 wellington-inn.co.uk
Black Sheep Ale; Copper Dragon Golden Pippin; Tetley Bitter; Timothy Taylor Landlord Ⓗ
Much-extended, popular stone-built inn on the edge of Nidderdale, food-led but with a range of well-kept ales. The original pub houses a comfortable bar with pool table, and the long extension provides more space, essentially for diners, in a baronial hall-styled room – the fireplace is especially magnificent. Behind is a dining room with spectacular views across Nidderdale.
❀🛏◑♣P🚌🐾📶

East Witton

Cover Bridge Inn 🄻

DL8 4SQ (½ mile N of village on A6108)
✪ 11-midnight; 12-11.30 Sun ☎ (01969) 623250
🌐 thecoverbridgeinn.co.uk
Black Sheep Best Bitter; John Smith's Bitter; Theakston Best Bitter, Old Peculier; Timothy Taylor Landlord; guest beers 🄷
Numerous CAMRA awards tell their own story about this ancient inn, half a mile north of the village. The River Cover runs alongside the attractive garden and play area, near its confluence with the River Ure. Fathom out the door latch and you will find a warm welcome in the unspoilt public bar, with its splendid hearth, and tiny lounge. Excellent home-cooked food is offered lunchtime and evening, along with locally brewed beers, two real ciders and a perry.
Q❀⇆◑♿♣●P⊟🚌(159)🐾ᯤ

Egton

Wheatsheaf Inn

YO21 1TZ
✪ closed Mon; 11.30-2.30, 5.30-11; 11.30-11 Sat & Sun
☎ (01947) 895271 🌐 wheatsheafegton.com
Black Sheep Best Bitter; Timothy Taylor Landlord 🄷
Winner of many CAMRA awards, this Grade I-listed 19th-century pub serves only Yorkshire beers. It is now in its 15th year in the Guide, and remains under the stewardship of a licensee with 28 years of continuous Guide recognition. Church pews, collectables and a roaring range add to the ambience. The grassy area to the front and boules pitch to the rear are ideal for summer drinking. The first-class restaurant menu features local meat, fish and game. Q❀⇆◑♿♣P⊟🚌(99)🐾

Filey

Bonhomme's Bar

Royal Crescent Court, The Crescent, YO14 9JH
✪ 11 (12 winter)-midnight; 11-1am Fri & Sat; 12-midnight Sun ☎ (01723) 515325
East Coast Bonhomme Richard; guest beers 🄷
Located just off the fine Victorian Royal Crescent Hotel complex, the bar's name celebrates John Paul Jones, father of the American Navy. His ship, the Bonhomme Richard, was involved in a battle off nearby Flamborough Head during the War of Independence. Five handpumps serve one East Coast beer plus four rotating guests. A fun quiz is on Saturday, and the main quiz is on Sunday.
≿⥱●🚌🐾

Imperial

20-22 Hope Street, YO14 9DL
✪ 12-midnight ☎ 07807 503741
Copper Dragon Golden Pippin; John Smith's Bitter; guest beers 🄷
Sympathetically restored two-roomed town-centre pub with traditional wood and stone floors, within easy reach of Filey beach and Filey Brigg, which ends the Cleveland and Wolds Way walks. It is popular with walkers, birdwatchers and campers. Guest ales are changed regularly and quizzes are staged on Sunday evenings during the winter months. Pub teams participate in local pool and darts leagues. Occasional live entertainment features at weekends. Of note are the numerous old photographs of Filey displayed in both bars.
≿♿⛺⥱♣🚌🐾ᯤ

Giggleswick

Hart's Head Hotel 🄻

Belle Hill, BD24 0BA (on B6480 1 mile N of Settle)
✪ 5.30 (12 Fri-Sun)-11 ☎ (01729) 822086
🌐 hartsheadinn.co.uk
Tetley Bitter; guest beers 🄷
Open-plan 18th-century coaching inn where the bar separates the comfortable lounge from the area where pub games are played and sport is shown on TV. Freshly prepared meals from a varied menu are served in the adjacent dining room. The pleasant sloping beer garden at the rear is a great place to soak up the summer sun. Three changing guest beers are on offer from smaller Yorkshire, Lancashire and Cumbrian breweries such as Dent, Kirkby Lonsdale and Lancaster.
≿❀⇆◑♿⛺♣P🚌(580,581)🐾ᯤ

Gilling West

White Swan 🄻

51 High Street, DL10 5JG (1 mile W of Scotch Corner, off A66)
✪ 10.30-11 ☎ (01748) 82512 🌐 thewhiteswan.co
Mithril White Swan Bitter; guest beers 🄷
A historic coaching inn with open fires, slate stone floors and a courtyard garden blending the modern with the traditional. Four real ales from local microbreweries, several craft beers and lagers, and over 40 bottled beers are here to tempt you. A flagship burger and steak menu showcases the best of the region's produce, featuring 35-day aged beef, local game, artisan bakers and cheese makers, and a house smokery. Quiz and live music nights are held fortnightly and monthly.
Q≿❀⇆◑⛺♣P🚌(29)🐾ᯤ

Great Heck

Bay Horse

Main Street, DN14 0BE (off A645 between Pontefract and Snaith)
✪ 5-10 (11 Thu; midnight Fri); 12-midnight Sat; 12-10 Sun
☎ (01977) 661125
Old Mill Traditional Bitter, Blonde Bombshell; guest beer 🄷
An Old Mill tied house, this cosy, inviting and traditional pub in a remote country hamlet serves well-kept ales from the brewery's range. The bar is divided into three distinct areas – a dining room at each end and a lounge in the middle – with comfortable seating warmed by a log-burning fire. There are many interesting artefacts and pictures decorating the walls. Oak beams add to the ambience. Food is served evenings and weekends.
Q≿◑♿Pᯤ

Grinton

Bridge Inn

DL11 6HH (on B6270, 1 mile E of Reeth)
✪ 12-midnight (11 Sun) ☎ (01748) 884224
🌐 bridgeinn-grinton.co.uk
Jennings Bitter, Cumberland Ale; guest beer 🄷
Friendly and well-run country inn close to the River Swale, set beneath the towering hills of Fremington Edge and Harkerside. Its lounge, wood-panelled bar and two restaurant rooms are a haven for walkers and cyclists on the Coast-to-Coast and Inn Way walks and the Dales Cycle Way. Fresh, home-made food is available all day along with

beers from the Marston's range. But do not even think about using a mobile phone.
Q (30)

Grosmont

Crossing Club

Co-operative Building, Front Street, YO22 5QE (opp NYMR car park)
8-11 07766 197744
Beer range varies H
Set amid beautiful scenery in the Esk Valley, this 2014 branch Club of the Year is directly opposite the NYMR/Esk Valley railway stations in what was the village Co-operative store's delivery bay. Converted by dedicated villagers into a railway-themed private members' club, a warm welcome is always extended to CAMRA members. For the railway enthusiast, both steam and diesel memorabilia adorn the walls. Five handpumps have served over 900 different beers during the club's 15-year existence. Q (99)

Harrogate

Blues Café Bar

4 Montpellier Parade, HG1 2TJ
10-1am; 12-12.30am Sun (01423) 566881
bluesbar.co.uk
Beer range varies H
A small single-room live music bar modelled on an Amsterdam café bar. There is live music seven evenings a week, with two sessions on a Sunday. Popular with music lovers, it can get busy. Four rotating guest beers are offered, sourced from far and wide. Food is served from 10am until early evening (2pm Sun) and upstairs there is an Egyptian restaurant open from Tuesday to Saturday. Children are welcome until 7pm.

Coach & Horses

16 West Park, HG1 1BJ
11-11; 12-10.30 Sun (01423) 561802
thecoachandhorses.net
Tetley Bitter; Timothy Taylor Landlord; guest beers H
The central bar is surrounded by snugs and alcoves, creating a cosy atmosphere, and outside there are tables and chairs for customers in summer. Window boxes provide a quite spectacular display. The guest beers usually include one from Rooster's, Daleside and Ilkley. Excellent meals are served at lunchtime and there are frequent themed food evenings. Many of these, together with a Sunday night quiz, have raised over £250,000 for a local children's hospice. Q

Hales Bar L

1-3 Crescent Road, HG1 2RS
12-midnight (1am Thu-Sat); 12-11.30 Sun
(01423) 725570 halesbar.co.uk
Daleside Old Leg Over; Timothy Taylor Landlord; guest beers H
Harrogate's oldest pub and identified by CAMRA as having a regionally important historic interior, the lounge here has a Victorian-style interior with original gas lighting over the bar. The separate snug is also used as a tea room. There are six handpumps, two serving an ever-changing range of guest beers. Karaoke and occasional party nights are held. The pub is a rare outlet for Draught Bass, and a house beer is supplied by Daleside. Food is served lunchtimes and evenings.

Harrogate Tap

Station Parade, HG1 1TE
10-11 (midnight Fri & Sat) (01423) 501644
harrogatetap.co.uk
Beer range varies H
The redundant Victorian station refreshment room, closed for over 30 years, has been given a new lease of life by the owners of the Tap group of station bars. Twelve handpumps serve a changing range of beers from brewers as diverse as Thornbridge, Rooster's and Black Sheep, and there is always a real cider from Thistley Cross. Wood panelling, tiled floors, leather and brass dominate the traditional decor in both the main bar and the small snug at one end. Q

Old Bell Tavern

6 Royal Parade, HG1 2SZ
12-11 (10.30 Sun) (01423) 507930
Hawkshead Windermere Pale; guest beers H
Housed in the former Farrar's toffee shop, the Old Bell became a pub in 1999 on the site of the Blue Bell Inn. There is a changing range of eight guest beers, usually including a Rooster's, a Taylor's, one from Okells from the Isle of Man, and a dark beer. A real cider and a range of UK and foreign bottled beers complete the choice. The side room has a collection of Farrar's memorabilia, and upstairs is a well-regarded restaurant. Q

Swan on the Stray

17 Devonshire Place, HG1 4AA
11-11; 12-10.30 Sun (01423) 524587
Ilkley Mary Jane; Okells Manx Pale Ale; guest beers H
Formerly known as the Black Swan, this pub was extensively refurbished in a modern style and reopened in early 2010. Eight real ales are on tap with four changing regularly, many from Yorkshire micros. A range of foreign beer is available on draught plus a real cider and an added selection in bottles. Allied to a good wine choice and excellent bar meals, the pub appeals to all age groups. There is a beer garden at the rear, and well-behaved children are welcome until 8pm.
P (104,111)

Winter Gardens

4 Royal Baths, HG1 2RR
7am-midnight (1am Thu; 2am Fri & Sat)
(01423) 877010
Greene King Abbot; Ruddles Best Bitter; guest beers H
An outstanding building sympathetically converted by Wetherspoon. The Parliament Street entrance leads from a Hollywood-style staircase into a large and magnificent room. The usual Wetherspoon mix of national standards and local guest beers is available across three sets of handpumps, spread out along the long L-shaped bar. The local Daleside Brewery sometimes provides a house beer. The pub can get busy due to its location near Harrogate's conference and exhibition centre.

Hawes

White Hart Country Inn

Main Street, DL8 3QL (on one-way system westbound)
11-11 (01969) 667259 whitehartcountryinn.co.uk
Theakston Best Bitter; guest beers H
Traditional pub located on this bustling Dales town's short one-way system. The decor reflects

Hawes' place as a centre for walking and outdoor activities, with photographs and paintings of local landmarks, as well as dried hop bines. Guest beers are usually from local brewers such as Wensleydale, Yorkshire Dales and Wall's of Northallerton. There is a separate dining room where food is served daily 12-9pm, including beef and lamb from the family farm nearby.
Q P (156)

Hebden

Clarendon Hotel

BD23 5DE

10.30-3, 5.30-11; 10.30-11 Sat & Sun ☎ (01756) 752446

theclarendonhotel.co.uk

Tetley Bitter; Timothy Taylor Boltmaker; guest beers [H]

Small, family-run hotel in a quiet Wharfedale village, near Grassington, ideally situated for exploring the surrounding countryside. The main lounge bar has a separate dining area and there is a cosy side area containing a real fire and dartboard. Accommodation is in two double en-suite bedrooms. Up to four guest beers are served, often from Black Sheep, Thwaites or Marston's. Parking is at the front or in the car park across the road. Bus 72 runs Monday to Saturday from Skipton. P (72)

Helwith Bridge

Helwith Bridge

BD24 0EH (off B6479 at Helwith Bridge)

12-midnight ☎ (01729) 860220 helwithbridgeinn.co.uk

Three Peaks Helwith Bridge Bitter, Whernside Pale Ale; Thwaites Original; guest beers [H]

Despite its relative isolation in the tiny hamlet of Helwith Bridge, this is a thriving, no-frills community local where the emphasis is on real ale. The pub has three separate rooms, all reached via the flagged main bar area. Close to Pen-y-Ghent, it is the starting point of the Three Peaks cycle race. The house beer, Helwith Bridge Bitter, is Three Peaks Pen-y-Ghent. Self-catering accommodation is available in the adjacent bunk-barn.
P (11)

Huby

Mended Drum

Tollerton Road, YO61 1HT

12-midnight (12.30am Fri & Sat) ☎ (01347) 810264

themendeddrumhuby.blogspot.co.uk

Black Sheep Best Bitter; guest beers [H]

This free house, an ex-Vaux pub, continues to evolve. With separate lobby, bar, restaurant and games area, a TV has, by request, been installed in the lobby area for major sporting events – rolling news programmes are kept muted unless customers ask for sound. The bar has one regular and up to two guest cask beers, plus one real cider in a box. It is a friendly village inn popular with cycling groups and hikers, and dogs are welcome.
(40)

Hunton

Countryman's Inn

DL8 1PY

6-11 (midnight Fri); 12-2.30, 6-midnight Sat; 12-11 Sun

☎ (01677) 450554 countrymansinn.co.uk

Black Sheep Best Bitter; Theakston Black Bull Bitter; guest beers [H]

A welcoming community free house, slightly off the beaten track but worth searching out. It survived a closure threat a few years ago thanks to a lively campaign by villagers and is now thriving. The comfortable one-room interior has a separate dining area and offers a wide-ranging food menu, along with guest beers, usually LocAles such as Wensleydale Semer Water. A third guest beer is on in the summer months.
Q P (155)

Hutton Rudby

King's Head

North Side, TS15 0DA (W end of village)

4-11.30; 12-midnight Fri-Sun ☎ (01642) 700342

Camerons Strongarm; Jennings Cocker Hoop, Cumberland Ale; guest beer [H]

Set in a beautiful village, this previous CAMRA award-winner is a traditional locals' pub where a friendly welcome is assured. It comprises a comfortable and always busy main bar, and a snug where children are welcome. Four handpumps include a guest from the Marston's range. Real fires, quiz night on Tuesday, steak nights on Wednesday and Friday, and live music on Saturday all add to the experience. Outside is a smokers' paradise, complete with TV. Winter opening hours may vary. Q (80,82)

Kildwick

White Lion

Priest Bank Road, BD20 9BH

12-11 (midnight Fri & Sat); 12-10.30 Sun

☎ (01535) 632265 thewhitelionkildwick.co.uk

Copper Dragon Silver Myst; Tetley Bitter; Timothy Taylor Landlord; guest beer [H]

Centuries-old but recently refurbished two-roomed pub in a quiet village just off the A629, opposite the medieval church. Look out for the original Tetley neon sign. The pleasant lawned beer garden is south-facing, affording views across the Aire Valley. The pub hosts the Keighley and Craven Athletic Club and makes a good base for walks over Kildwick moor or along the nearby Leeds and Liverpool Canal. One dark beer, usually a mild, is always served, with two further guest beers available in summer.
P (66,66A)

Kirby Hill

Shoulder of Mutton

DL11 7JH (2½ miles from A66, 4 miles NW of Richmond)

12-3 (not Mon-Fri), 6-11.30 (11 Sun) ☎ (01748) 822772

shoulderofmutton.net

Daleside Bitter; guest beers [H]

Ivy-fronted country inn in a beautiful hillside setting overlooking Lower Teesdale and the ruins of Ravensworth Castle. The pub has an open-front bar that links the lounge with a cosy restaurant to the rear. Three guest beers (four in summer) are chosen by the regulars. On the edge of the Yorkshire Dales, this is a popular venue for walkers. Excellent food is available Wednesday to Sunday, although the bar area remains for drinkers. There are five en-suite guest bedrooms. Q

Kirk Smeaton

Shoulder of Mutton

Main Street, WF8 3JY (follow signs from A1)
12-midnight (1am Fri & Sat); 11.30-midnight Sun
(01977) 620348
Black Sheep Best Bitter; guest beer H
Award-winning rural gem, situated conveniently for the Went Valley and Brockadale Nature Reserve. Popular with walkers and the local community, there is always a warm welcome from the friendly clientele in this attractive free house. The pub comprises a large lounge with open fires and a cosy dark-panelled snug. The spacious garden has a covered and heated shelter for smokers, and ample parking. The beer is always in superb condition. Quiz night is Tuesday.
P (409)

Kirkby-in-Cleveland

Black Swan

Busby Lane, TS9 7AW (½ mile W of B1257) NZ539060
12-midnight (01642) 712512
Bradfield Farmers Blonde; Copper Dragon Golden Pippin; Timothy Taylor Landlord; guest beer H
Nestling at the foot of the North York Moors, and at the crossroads of this ancient village, this warm and cosy free house, comprising a bar, lounge/restaurant and conservatory, affords a friendly and genuine welcome. Three regular beers and a guest ale, all usually from Yorkshire, are served in a convivial atmosphere, where making conversation seems a must. Bar snacks and a full menu, including daily specials, are good value. There is a pool table. Q P (89)

Knaresborough

Blind Jack's L

19 Market Place, HG5 8AL
4 (3 Fri; 12 Sat)-11; 12-10.30 Sun (01423) 869148
Black Sheep Best Bitter; Hop Studio Blonde; Kirkstall Pale Ale; guest beers H
A multi-roomed pub with bare brick walls, wooden floorboards and panelling. An award-winning ale house, it provides a focal point both for locals and the many visitors who appreciate the excellent selection of ales, cosy ambience and lively banter. The beer range usually includes at least one from the small brewery on the premises, which produces exciting, radical beers. Listed in this Guide since 1993. Q

Cross Keys

Cheapside, HG5 8AX
12 (4 Mon & Tue)-11; 12-midnight Fri & Sat
(01423) 863562
Fuller's London Pride; Ossett Yorkshire Blonde, Big Red Bitter, Silver King; guest beers H
Refurbished in Ossett Brewery's trademark style of stone-flagged floors, bare brick walls and stained glass, this traditional pub serves four regular beers and two guests; one usually a dark beer or stout, from either a microbrewery or from the Ossett company. Thursday is quiz night and a live band plays twice a month on Saturday nights.
(1)

Half Moon

1 Abbey Road, HG5 8HY
5 (12 Sat)-11; 12-10.30 Sun (01423) 313461
Beer range varies H
Small in size but big in atmosphere, this free house has been sympathetically restored to a high standard by its independent owners. Bare brick walls, reclaimed furniture and real fires give the pub a welcoming ambience. Four handpumps dispense a varying range of Yorkshire beers, usually including one from nearby Rooster's. A grazing menu of meat and cheese platters complements the beers. The pub hosts a team in the annual tug of war across the adjacent River Nidd. (56,57)

Mitre Hotel

4 Station Road, HG5 9AA (opp railway station)
12-11 (01423) 868948 themitreinn.co.uk
Black Sheep Ale; Okells Manx Pale Ale; guest beers H
Ideally placed for the railway station, this Market Town Tavern pub serves eight ales, with several from Yorkshire breweries and one pump dedicated to the town's own Rooster's brewery. There is a good range of speciality bottled beers too. Pumpclips adorn the walls of the modern split-level bar. There is a side room and a downstairs function room, and a beer garden with views of the local church. Food is served daily and live music plays on Sunday evenings.
(1)

Lastingham

Blacksmiths Arms

Anserdale Lane, YO62 6TN
11.30-11.30 (01751) 417247
blacksmithslastingham.co.uk
Theakston Best Bitter; guest beers H
Pretty stone inn in a conservation village opposite St Mary's Church, famous for its 11th-century crypt. The interior comprises a cosy bar with a York range lit in winter, a snug, and two dining rooms. Excellent-quality food including local game dishes is served alongside interesting guest beers. A secluded beer garden is to the rear. This remote pub is popular with locals, walkers and shooting parties. Q

Lealholm

Board Inn

Village Green, YO21 2AJ
9am-midnight (2am Fri & Sat) (01947) 897279
theboardinn.com
Beer range varies H
Overlooking the River Esk, this family-run 17th-century free house is at the centre of village life. Four beers, four real ciders and 60 whiskies are served. The place comprises a busy locals' bar, a lounge, a restaurant, and a riverside patio where an Easter beer festival is held. The superb menu is virtually all traceable to within 800 yards of the pub. The licensees air-cure their own hams, keep hens and ducks, own their own livestock, and have local salmon-fishing rights.
Q P (99)

Leavening

Jolly Farmers L

Main Street, YO17 9SA
5.30-midnight; 5-1am Fri; 12-1am Sat; 12-midnight Sun
(01653) 658276
Timothy Taylor Landlord; York Guzzler; guest beers H

A 17th-century pub on the edge of the Yorkshire Wolds between York and Malton and at the heart of the village community. Extended, but still cosy, it has two small bars divided by a real fire, as well as an adjoining family room and dining rooms. It is a former local CAMRA Pub of the Year. Guest beers from independent breweries and regular beer festivals make this a pub worth seeking out. The menu includes locally-caught game dishes in season. Q

Lofthouse

Crown Hotel

Thorpe Lane, HG3 5RZ
12-3, 6-11; 12-3, 7-10.30 Sun ☎ (01423) 755206
nidderdale.co.uk/crownlofthouse/crown-hotel-loft-house.htm
Black Sheep Best Bitter; Theakston Best Bitter; guest beer H

A handsome stone building in almost the last village in beautiful Nidderdale. An unusual panelled entrance corridor leads to a traditionally furnished, comfortable bar with a dining room beyond. Local pictures, maps and lots of brassware decorate the walls. An open fire in winter warms your bones following an exploration of the surrounding area of outstanding natural beauty, and walking sticks are for sale if needed. There is often a guest beer from Rudgate.

Loftus

Station Hotel

Station Road, TS13 4QB (100yds S of A174)
3-11; 12-11.30 Sat & Sun ☎ (01287) 640373
Beer range varies H

This once-bustling railway hotel is now a free house. The last passenger train left in 1953 – the overgrown platform is still in situ. The licensee, a keen musician and local independent councillor, has served best and premium bitters for 23 years, and anything under 4% ABV generally meets with the locals' disapproval. The pub comprises a cosy bar, a lounge and a function room where live music plays Thursday/Saturday. Fans of particularly eccentric railway memorabilia are especially well catered for. (4,5)

Maltby

Manor House

High Lane, TS8 0BN (at jct of A1044 and A1045, 2½ miles E of Yarm)
11-11; 12-10.30 Sun ☎ (01642) 764153
themanorhouseteesside.co.uk
Beer range varies H

This hostelry is on the western outskirts of the pretty village and close to one of Europe's largest private housing estates. Now in its sixth year of operation following extensive, careful and restrained renovations, the Sir John Fitzgerald house, and 2013 CAMRA branch award winner, is a busy establishment with a welcoming cosiness and warmth. Friendly, enthusiastic staff ensure that three, often four, guest beers provide an interesting mix of differing styles. Food is served all day every day. Quiz night is Monday.
QP (507)

Malton

Crown Hotel

12 Wheelgate, YO17 7HP
11-11 (11.30 Fri & Sat); 12-11 Sun ☎ (01653) 692038
suddabys.co.uk
Thwaites Original; guest beers H

This Grade II-listed market-town pub has been in the same family for 135 years and in the Guide for over 25. Double Chance, brewed by Four Thorns, is one of two regular beers offered. Beer festivals are held three times annually. The on-site shop stocks more than 200 beers, specialising in Belgian and British microbreweries. A covered smoking patio is at the rear. Accommodation is available (a discount is offered for CAMRA members staying two nights or more). QP

New Malton

4 Market Place, YO17 7LX
11.30-11; 12-10.30 Sun ☎ (01653) 693998
thenewmalton.co.uk
Beer range varies H

Situated in the busy market place, this Grade II-listed building, formerly tea rooms, has been sensitively renovated. The large single-room interior is divided into three distinct drinking and dining areas. Three handpumps serve varying beers from Yorkshire breweries including Great Yorkshire, Partners and Acorn. Meals are served midday-9pm every day, all locally sourced and prepared on site. There is small area at the front for alfresco drinking. Children and dogs are welcome. Q

Manfield

Crown Inn

Vicars Lane, DL2 2RF (500yds from B6275)
5 (12 Sat)-11.30; 12-11 Sun ☎ (01325) 374243
Village White Boar; guest beers H

Local CAMRA Country Pub of the Year 12 times, and previously Yorkshire Pub of the Year, this 18th-century inn is in a quiet village. It has two bars and a games room. A mix of locals and visitors creates a friendly atmosphere. Seven guest beers from microbreweries, plus two ciders or perries, are on offer. A 20-beer festival is held over the May Day weekend and a 14-cider festival in July. There is a monthly quiz on a Tuesday night.
QP (29)

Marske-by-the-Sea

Clarendon

88-90 High Street, TS11 7BA
11-11 (11.30 Fri-Sun) ☎ (01642) 490005
Black Sheep Best Bitter; Camerons Strongarm; Copper Dragon Golden Pippin; Theakston Best Bitter, Old Peculier; guest beer H

A 2013 branch award winner, the Middle House, as it is known, is a family-run one-room locals' pub, where the walls are adorned with photographs of yesteryear. Six beers are served from a mahogany island bar – a rarity on Teesside. There is no TV, jukebox or pool table, and no children and teenagers – just locals indulging in convivial conversation. There is no catering, but tea and coffee are available, together with excellent home-made scones at lunchtimes, while a buffet is provided free of charge on Tuesday evenings.
QP (3,4)

ENGLAND

Masham

White Bear

Wellgarth, HG4 4EN
🕐 11-midnight ☎ (01765) 689319
🌐 thewhitebearhotel.co.uk
Caledonian Deuchars IPA; Theakston Best Bitter, Black Bull Bitter, XB, Old Peculier 🅗
The de facto brewery tap for Theakston, the White Bear offers food, drink, accommodation and conference facilities. There is a large dining area to one side and a small cosy taproom to the other serving almost the full range of Theakston beers. The pub hosts a popular three-day beer festival in late June, with over 30 beers on offer. The building was a victim of wartime bombing and derelict for many years before being renovated to a high standard. ❀🛏◑♿♣P🚌(159,144)🐾📶

Melsonby

Black Bull

19 West Road, DL10 5ND (1 mile N of A66 and 1 mile from A1)
🕐 5.30-11; 4-midnight Fri & Sat; 5-11.45 Sun
☎ (01325) 718811
Beer range varies 🅗
Late 18th-century community pub with a long single room which has seating either end of the central bar. Upstairs there is a function/games room available for parties. Up to three beers from national and local micros are on handpump, often from Jarrow and local Mithril Ales. There are unusual pub games, including ring the bull, and the bar is home to men's and women's darts teams, dominoes on Mondays, and various club meetings. It will open earlier by prior arrangement for walking groups. ❀♣🍎▯🚌(29)🐾📶

Middlesbrough

Dr Phil's Real Ale House

10 Pilkington Buildings, Roman Road, TS5 6DY (100yds N of jct of Roman Rd and The Crescent)
🕐 closed Mon; 1-8 (9 Thu & Fri); 12-9 Sat; closed Sun ☎ 07525 337123
Beer range varies 🅗
Opened in 2013 by an enthusiastic CAMRA member, the first micropub in Middlesbrough is situated in the leafy suburbs of Linthorpe, tucked in among a terrace of shops. The five-yards-square drinking area manages to accommodate an eclectic mix of drinkers, who have a choice of four constantly changing guest ales, as well as a cider or perry. Since opening, over 300 different real ales have been served. Often, a cask does not even manage to last the day. Q♿♣🍎▯🚌(11,17)

Swatter's Carr

228-230 Linthorpe Road, TS1 3QW (W side of university, 750yds S of town centre)
🕐 8-midnight ☎ (01642) 239060
Adnams Broadside; Fuller's London Pride; Greene King Abbot; Ruddles Best Bitter; Sharp's Doom Bar; guest beers 🅗
A Wetherspoon conversion of the Empire and now named after the original 17th-century farmstead. During the last 300 years it has had a fascinating history as a hotel and an opera house among other incarnations. Set in the heart of student land, and a meeting place for the Teesside University Real Ale Society, the pub is popular. It has nine handpulls, and real cider is also served. Meet the Brewer sessions, beer festivals, a January sale, and celebrations of various saints' days are all hosted. 🐎❀◑♿⇌🍎🚌📶

Muker

Farmers Arms Ⓛ

DL11 6QG
🕐 11.30-midnight (11 Mon); 11.30-11 Sun
☎ (01748) 886297 🌐 farmersarmsmuker.co.uk
Black Sheep Best Bitter; Theakston Best Bitter, Old Peculier; Yorkshire Dales Muker Silver; guest beer 🅗
The bleak but beautiful Dales countryside attracts countless visitors to this former lead-mining village in the heart of Swaledale, near both the Coast-to-Coast and Pennine Way routes. This traditional inn, with its stone-flagged bar and open fire, is popular both with locals and walkers, cyclists and other visitors. As well as a range of local ales, home-prepared food is served every day and there is a guest beer in summer. Q🐎❀🛏◑⛺♣P🐾

Naburn

Blacksmiths Arms

Main Street, YO19 4PN
🕐 11.30-11.30 (12.30am Fri & Sat); 12-11.30 Sun
☎ (01904) 623464 🌐 blacksmithsarmsnaburn.co.uk
Marston's EPA; Wychwood Hobgoblin; guest beers 🅗
Set alongside the River Ouse in the heart of the village and within easy reach of nearby York, this is a bustling and thriving pub. It is the sort of place where customers arrive by foot, cycle, horse or even boat. Licensees Ian and Maria have been here for nine years serving top-quality beers and food. 🐎❀🛏◑♿⛺♣🚌(4,42)🐾📶

Newton-on-Ouse

Dawnay Arms Ⓛ

Moor Lane, YO30 2BR
🕐 closed Mon; 12-2.30, 6-11; 12-11 Sat; 12-10 Sun
☎ (01347) 848345 🌐 thedawnayatnewton.co.uk
Black Sheep Best Bitter; guest beers 🅗
Country gastro-pub with an emphasis on locally-sourced food and Yorkshire beer. The modern British menu often includes local game. The interior is a mix of rustic wooden and upholstered furniture. There are two open fires in winter, and a pleasant garden that leads down to the River Ouse. The pub is handily placed for the bus to and from York. Guest beers are from Yorkshire breweries. The Dawnay is in the Good Food Guide and often busy (booking is advisable).
Q🐎❀◑♿P🚌(29)🐾📶

Northallerton

Tickle Toby Inn Ⓛ

180 High Street, DL7 8JZ
🕐 11-11 ☎ (01609) 778760
Black Sheep Best Bitter; guest beers 🅗
Taking its name from a notorious local 18th-century highwayman and pickpocket, this town-centre pub has a narrow single bar with several drinking areas. Popular with all age groups, it offers a range of guest beers from local and regional breweries and can be busy during the weekly Wednesday and Saturday markets which take place outside, and on weekend evenings. Meals are served every lunchtime and Wednesday-Friday evenings.
🐎◑⇌♣🚌📶

Tithe Bar

2A Friarage Street, DL6 1DP (off High St near hospital)
12-11 (midnight Fri & Sat) (01609) 778482
Ilkley Mary Jane; Okells Manx Pale Ale; guest beers
This cosmopolitan town-centre bar is part of the small Market Town Taverns chain and shows a strong commitment to real ale as well as stocking numerous continental and speciality bottled beers. The decor is simple, with wooden floors throughout, and there is no music or other electronic entertainment, just conversation. Food is served lunchtimes and early evenings, with a brasserie open upstairs Tuesday-Saturday evenings. Children are welcome during the daytime. Q

Osgodby

Wadkin Arms

Cliffe Road, YO8 5HU
12-11 (midnight Fri & Sat) (01757) 702391
wadkinarms.co.uk/1.html
Brown Cow White Dragon; John Smith's Bitter; guest beers
At the heart of the village and the community, this is a welcoming and cosy pub where the licensee is most sympathetic to CAMRA's aims. There is an emphasis on local beers and you will find a couple of mini beer festivals through the summer months. The Wadkin has recently begun to serve meals, and look out for a discount for card-carrying CAMRA members. P(4)

Osmotherley

Golden Lion

6 West End, DL6 3AA (in village centre, 1 mile E of A19)
12-2.30 (not Mon & Tue), 6-11; 12-midnight Sat; 12-10.30 Sun (01609) 883526 goldenlionosmotherley.co.uk
Timothy Taylor Landlord; guest beers
Popular with visitors to the North York Moors, this village is at the start of the long-distance Lyke Wake Walk. Hikers and others can often be seen taking a well-earned rest at the outside drinking tables. Inside, there is an emphasis on food, but also a warm welcome for drinkers. The locally sourced fare has a fine reputation. Regularly changing beers are from local Yorkshire breweries and there is a beer festival each November.
Q(80,89)

Pickering

Sun Inn

136 Westgate, YO18 8BB (on A171 400yds W of traffic lights in town centre)
4-11; 12-midnight Fri & Sat; 12-11 Sun (01751) 473661
thesuninn-pickering.co.uk
Leeds Best; Tetley Bitter; guest beers
Friendly local CAMRA Rural Pub of the Year, close to the town and steam railway. Four guest ales are offered including three from Yorkshire micros. A cosy bar with a real fire leads to a separate room, ideal for families and for special events, which opens onto a large enclosed beer garden. Children, walkers and dogs (on leads) are welcome. Regular events include a bi-weekly acoustic music session, community choir, monthly charity quiz and a vinyl night every third Thursday.

Pool-in-Wharfedale

Hunters Inn

Harrogate Road, LS21 2PS
12-11 (10.30 Sun) (0113) 284 1090
Black Sheep Best Bitter; Thwaites Nutty Black; guest beers
The inn is situated in lower Wharfedale, on the main Harrogate to Bradford road. The large single-room interior incorporates a raised area with a warming real fire during the colder months. The windowed front wall gives views across to the southern ridge of Wharfedale. The three-sided bar has handpumps all round, with up to 11 cask ales from far and wide, but mainly from Yorkshire, listed on blackboards. P

Redcar

Turners Mill

Greenstones Road, TS10 2RA (off B1269, ½ mile S of town)
11.30-midnight (01642) 496021
Beer range varies
An increasingly popular M&B Ember Inn and CAMRA branch 2013 Pub of the Year, lying close to the town's racecourse. Recently refurbished, a cosy, relaxing and welcoming ambience prevails. The ever-enthusiastic staff serve up to eight beers, one of which is usually a stout/porter/old ale, and all on a try-before-you-buy basis. Reasonably priced food is served all day every day. Quiz nights are Wednesday and Sunday. An email newsletter details the venue's latest offers.
(East)P(22,64)

Reeth

Buck Hotel

DL11 6SW
12-midnight (01748) 884210 buckhotel.co.uk
Black Sheep Best Bitter; Copper Dragon Best Bitter; Timothy Taylor Landlord; guest beers
In the centre of Reeth, the Buck was originally a Swaledale coaching inn and retains its beamed ceilings, open fire and even an ice house. Also known as the Top House, it offers five cask ales and six real ciders along with home-cooked food. Regular music events include occasional visits from some surprisingly well-known names. A little quieter, quoits is popular in the summer, with three teams based here along with two darts teams. (30)

Ribblehead

Station

Ingleton, LA6 3AS (on B6255 near B6479 jct)
11-11; 12-10.30 Sun (015242) 41274
thestationinn.net
Beer range varies
Built at the same time as the nearby viaduct (1874), this inn is a welcome refuge in a bleak spot in the midst of superb walking country. During the day the main bar room is laid out for diners, while the smaller room has pub games and TV sport. A surprisingly large number of locals frequent the plainly furnished bar. There is a good train service but buses are rare. It has a bunk barn next door, and wild camping behind.
P(831)

Riccall

Greyhound

82 Main Street, YO19 6TE
12 (3 Mon-Fri winter)-midnight; 12-11.30 Sun
(01757) 249101 thegreyhoundriccall.co.uk
Tetley Mild, Bitter; Theakston Best Bitter; guest beers H
Busy village inn with seven real ales on at peak times. A member of the Ossett Beer Excellence Club, an Ossett ale can always be found alongside the regular Theakston and Tetley offerings, while three interesting guests complete the range. The pub boasts successful darts, dominoes and pool teams and is a fine stopping-off point on the York-Selby cycle trail. P(415,416)

Richmond

Bishop Blaize Hotel

Market Place, DL10 4QL
11-12.30am (1.30am Fri & Sat) (01748) 823065
Timothy Taylor Landlord; guest beers H
Town-centre pub on the historic cobbled marketplace and close to the walls of Richmond's spectacular Norman castle. There is a strong commitment to cask ale here, with three changing guest ales from national and regional brewers, which has earned the pub CAMRA commendations. Home-cooked traditional food is available daily. Music TV, pool and live TV sport are popular, and there are also regular folk nights. A 10 per cent discount on real ales is offered to CAMRA members.

Ralph Fitz Randall

6 Queens Road, DL10 4AE (on edge of town centre on main Scotch Corner road)
9am-midnight (1am Fri & Sat) (01748) 828080
Greene King Abbot; Ruddles Best Bitter; guest beers H
Converted from Richmond's former post office and telephone exchange, this large single-bar Wetherspoon house is set on three levels, with a large family dining area and a patio to the rear. It offers up to eight guest beers and has won numerous CAMRA awards. Locally brewed ales are always on offer and there are themed monthly beer festivals, usually featuring a particular brewery or beer style. Low-volume TVs cater for sports fans. Breakfast is available from 8am.
QP

Ripon

King William IV

10 Blossomgate, HG4 2AJ
4-11; 3-midnight Fri; 12-midnight Sat; 12-11 Sun
(01765) 608271
Hambleton Bitter; Theakston Best Bitter; Village Brewer White Boar; guest beers H
A community-led pub with a large sports following, where five screens show Sky and BT sports channels. The pub hosts many local teams and has regular quiz and music nights, including the ever-popular GlastonBilly in August when local musicians play for charity over a full day. The Victorian building has original West Riding Brewery stained glass windows, and there is a hidden beer garden for the summer and roaring log fires in winter. A drinking person's pub for sociable people.

One-Eyed Rat

51 Allhallowgate, HG4 1LQ
5 (12 Fri & Sat)-11; 12-10.30 Sun (01765) 607704
oneeyedrat.com
Beer range varies H
A Guide fixture set within a terrace of 200-year-old houses, the narrow frontage leading to a warm and welcoming family-run hostelry. Seven changing guest beers plus a real cider are served. There is always a pump dedicated to a mild, stout or porter and another for a stronger beer at around 5% ABV. The pub hosts regular live music and holds two beer festivals a year. A classic. Q

Royal Oak

36 Kirkgate, HG4 1PB
11-11 (midnight Fri & Sat) (01765) 602284
royaloakripon.co.uk
Timothy Taylor Dark Mild, Golden Best, Boltmaker, Landlord; guest beers H
Housed in an 18th-century coaching inn, in the centre of historic Ripon, the Royal Oak serves a top-quality range of Timothy Taylor beers alongside regular guests from other Yorkshire breweries. Beautifully renovated in a modern idiom, the pub is separated into relaxed dining areas with log-burning stoves and comfortable seating, and serves a first-class locally-sourced menu. Accommodation is available in six stylish and comfortable bedrooms and includes a hearty English breakfast.
P

Unicorn Hotel

Market Place East, HG4 1BP
7am-12.30am (11.30 Sun) (01765) 602202
Greene King Abbot; guest beers H
An old coaching inn renovated and modernised to a high standard by Wetherspoon in 2011 – its low ceilings and subdued lighting generate a different ambience to many Wetherspoon establishments. The rear bar offers the standard national beers and a carefully chosen selection of ales from smaller breweries in Yorkshire and beyond. The pictures on the walls celebrate local worthies such as Lewis Carroll, as well as the medieval splendours of Fountains Abbey. There are 32 letting rooms.
P(36)

Water Rat

24 Bondgate Green, HG4 1QW
11-11 (01765) 602251 thewaterrat.co.uk
Theakston Best Bitter; guest beers H
Located by the side of the River Skell with a fine view of Ripon cathedral from its riverside conservatory and terrace, this is Ripon's only riverside pub. An emphasis on affordable home-cooked traditional English pub food means it tends to get busy at times. There is a small snug at the front. Theakston ales are supplemented by other local ales, typically from Rudgate, Rooster's, Salamander or Copper Dragon.

Robin Hood's Bay

Dolphin

King Street, YO22 4SH (on steep pedestrian-only road, down towards bay from top car park)
11 (12 Sun)-11 (01947) 880337
Caledonian Deuchars IPA; Theakston Best Bitter, Old Peculier; guest beer H
Olde-worlde pub, full of memorabilia, popular with locals and visitors alike, and where dogs and

muddy boots are made equally welcome. It comprises an atmospheric public bar where a real fire burns for most of the year, and a large family/dining room. Three regular beers and a guest are served. Quizzes takes place on Sundays, with rhythm and blues on Mondays and a folk club on Fridays. Access to this part of the village is not that easy for the less able-bodied.
(93,X93)

Victoria Hotel

Station Road, YO22 4RL (at top of cliff by car park)
11.30 (12 Sun)-11.30 ☎ (01947) 880205
victoriarhb.com
Camerons Strongarm; North Yorkshire Robin Hood; Theakston Best Bitter, Lightfoot; guest beers [H]
A warm welcome awaits you at this 19th-century hotel, set in a superb location on the edge of the cliffs, overlooking the bay of this picturesque resort and providing stunning views from the tea rooms and gardens. The friendly bar serves six beers including two guests, usually from local breweries. Beer bats, holding six third-pints, are available. A good-value, highly regarded menu, including daily specials, is served lunchtimes and evenings. There is a separate family room. Q P (93,X93)

Saltburn-by-the-Sea

Saltburn Cricket, Bowls & Tennis Club

Marske Mill Lane, TS12 1HJ (next to leisure centre)
8-midnight (1am Fri & Sat); 11.30-3, 8-midnight Sun
☎ (01287) 622761
Beer range varies [H]
Visitors are made welcome at this local CAMRA branch multi-award winner. A private sports club, run by an enthusiastic steward, it is well supported by the local community. In addition to other sports, it is also the watering hole for the local diving club. The bar sits in a spacious, comfortable lounge, which can be subdivided for different functions. The balcony, ideal for lazy summer afternoons, overlooks the cricket field. Two changing beers are served, often not even lasting the night.
P (3,4)

Scarborough

Alma

1 Alma Parade, YO11 1SJ
11.30-11 (midnight Fri & Sat); 12-11 Sun
☎ (01723) 840068
Black Sheep Best Bitter; guest beers [H]
A town-centre local just off the main shopping precinct, with two rooms containing a large and varied collection of memorabilia. The cosy back snug bar retains an old-world character even though it now doubles as a games room. One regular beer and three rotating guests are offered, together with Old Rosie cider. There is a smoking/drinking area at the front of the pub. Children are welcome until early evening. Q

Angel

46 North Street, YO11 1DF
11 (12 Sun)-midnight ☎ (01723) 365504
Copper Dragon Golden Pippin; Tetley Bitter; Timothy Taylor Landlord; guest beer [H]
Friendly town-centre local close to the main shopping area, with a single-room horseshoe bar displaying an excellent collection of saucy seaside postcards. An interest in sport and games is reflected in the impressive array of trophies won by various pub teams as well as the large-screen TVs for viewing sporting events. Occasional guest beers are added in summer. It has a surprisingly spacious and well-appointed patio garden at the rear, with two boundary walls displaying superb graffiti wall art depicting angels.

Cellars

35-37 Valley Road, YO11 2LY
4-11 winter; 12-midnight Sat; 12-10.30 Sun
☎ (01723) 36715 scarborough-brialene.co.uk/cellars.htm
Camerons Strongarm; Jennings Sneck Lifter; guest beers [H]
A family-run pub converted from the cellars of a Victorian house, this is Scarborough's longest consecutive Guide entry (15 years). Six handpumps dispense guest beers from nationwide micros. Locally-sourced, home-cooked food is served lunchtimes and evenings – the Sunday lunches are popular. Quiz night is Tuesday, open mic night is Wednesday, local acoustic acts appear on Thursday, and Saturday is live music night. The patio fronting the pub is popular in summer. Children and dogs are welcome and accommodation is available.
P

Indigo Alley

4 North Marine Road, YO12 7PD
4 (12 Fri-Sun)-11 ☎ (01723) 350599
Wold Top Indigo Ale; guest beers [H]
Recently upgraded, this is a welcoming pub with an open-plan interior retaining a rustic feel, with bare floorboards and sporting a logburner. It has come back on the real ale and traditional cider trail after a few years in the wilderness and is now a true free house. Pool, darts, dominoes and chess can all be played. Locally brewed Indigo Ale and draught Thatchers cider complement specialist lagers. The pub is both dog and child friendly, with live entertainment offered every Friday.

North Riding Brew Pub

161-163 North Marine Road, YO12 7HU
12-midnight (1am Fri & Sat) ☎ (01723) 370004
northridingbrewpub.com
Timothy Taylor Landlord; York Guzzler; guest beers [H]
Scarborough's only brewpub and current local CAMRA Town Pub of the Year, it is situated just down from the cricket ground. It has now served over 2,000 guest ales in addition to its own North Riding beers. Two or more guests regularly come from Elland, Thornbridge and Yorkshire Dales, as well as other microbreweries far and wide. It has a public bar, quiet lounge and upstairs dining room serving home-cooked food, all with real fires. Quiz night is Thursday. Q

Scholars Bar

6 Somerset Terrace, YO11 2PA
4.30 (12 Fri & Sun)-midnight ☎ (01723) 449836
Copper Dragon Golden Pippin; Hambleton Nightmare; York Yorkshire Terrier; guest beers [H]
A warm and friendly atmosphere prevails at this town-centre pub at the rear of the main shopping centre. It has a large front bar and a games room. Seven handpumps serve a rotating range of beers from Ossett, Fernandes, Rat and other breweries – mainly from the Yorkshire region. Numerous screens show major sporting events. Twenty-eight pints are the grand prize at the Thursday evening

quiz, and more free beer can be won rolling dice on Monday, Tuesday, Wednesday and Sunday nights. ♿⇌♣🚌

Valley Bar

51 Valley Road, YO11 2LX
12-midnight (1am Thu-Sat) ☎ (01723) 372593
valleybar.co.uk
Dark Star Hophead; Theakston Best Bitter; guest beers H
A cellar bar with six handpumps offering mainly microbrewery beers, usually including one or more from Scarborough Brewery. Up to eight real ciders and perries are also sold, with Broadoak perry a regular, together with over 100 bottles of Belgian beers including Cantillon. Upstairs is a pool table, and further rooms offering additional seating which can be used for meetings.

Settle

Talbot Arms

High Street, BD24 9EX
11.30-11 ☎ (01729) 823924 talbotsettle.co.uk
Theakston Best Bitter; guest beers H
Just off the square, this family-run free house offers a welcoming and friendly atmosphere. A stove glows in the large stone feature fireplace to the left of the main entrance, with pool table, dartboard, and dominoes tables beyond providing a base for teams in local leagues. A pleasant, terraced beer garden is at the rear. The three to five guest beers and cider are usually from Cumbria, Lancashire or Yorkshire. Food is served 12-8pm all week.
P

Thirteen

13 Duke Street, BD24 9DU
4-8 Mon; 10.30-10 (8 Tue); 11-11 Fri & Sat; closed Sun
☎ (01729) 824356 thirteencafebar.co.uk
Dark Horse Best Bitter, Hetton Pale Ale; Goose Eye Chinook Blonde H
Situated on the main street between the square and the railway station, Thirteen's narrow frontage hides a long, thin room with a relaxed café-bar atmosphere and a modern feel, where you are as welcome in hiking boots as you are in high heels. The owners are very much hands on, and can usually be found behind the bar joining in the banter. Themed dining evenings include steak night and tapas. ♿

Shipton by Beningbrough

Dawnay Arms

Main Street, YO30 1AB
12-2.30 (not Mon & Tue), 5.30-midnight; 6-midnight Sat; 12-11 Sun ☎ (01904) 470334 thedawnayarms.co.uk
Tetley Bitter; guest beers H
Built in 1730, this is a traditional country inn. One of the three handpumps always serves a LocAle, often from Treboom Brewery. The wide-ranging pub food cooked on the premises includes gluten-free and vegetarian options. There is an open bar area with a real fire, a separate area for quiet drinking, and a family room. Old pictures and items of local history are on display. Regular quiz nights and community charity events are hosted, including occasional live music.
♿P🚌(31,31X)

Sicklinghall

Scotts Arms

Main Street, LS22 4BD (3 miles W of Wetherby)
11-11 (10 Sun) ☎ (01937) 582100 scottsarms.com
Black Sheep Best Bitter; Theakston Old Peculier; Thwaites Wainwright; Timothy Taylor Landlord H
Welcoming village inn with an excellent reputation for food, served in two large but intimate lounges. An upper-level bar caters for drinkers, while the lower-level one welcomes both diners and drinkers. The occasional guest beers tend to be from northern breweries. The garden area is popular with families and walkers in summer as this is good rambling territory. The village shop, with a visiting post office one day a week, is in the pub grounds. P

Skipton

Albion

27 Otley Street, BD23 1EL
11-11 (1am Wed, Fri & Sat); 12-11 Sun ☎ (01756) 794793
Butcombe Bitter; Caledonian Golden XPA; Theakston Best Bitter; guest beers H
Small and friendly, this stone-built Victorian pub is only just off the High Street but is a welcome refuge from the bustle of the town centre. Recently refurbished inside, it has a small beer garden to the side and retains a traditional atmosphere. Food is served lunchtime and evening Monday to Friday and all day at weekends. (Evening meals are not available January to March.) Handy for the central car and coach parks. Dogs are welcome outside food times. ♣🚌

Bistro des Amis

1 Jerry Croft, BD23 1DX (entrance is from Jerry Croft, next to town hall)
10-11; 11-9 Sun ☎ (01756) 797919
lebistrodesamis.co.uk
Ilkley Mary Jane; Timothy Taylor Landlord H
French-style bistro focusing on quality food and comfortable, relaxed dining. While the emphasis is on food, the drinker is made welcome in the small bar area. Ensconced in a comfortable chair with table service, the buzz of conversation and a little light jazz playing in the background, it can be difficult to leave. Food is served all day Sunday. The mezzanine area is suitable for private dining or meetings for up to 10 people. ♿🚌

Narrow Boat

38 Victoria Street, BD23 1JE (alleyway off Coach St near canal bridge)
12-11 ☎ (01756) 797922
Black Sheep Golden Sheep; Ilkley Mary Jane; Okells Bitter; Timothy Taylor Landlord; guest beers H
On a quiet back street between the High Street and the canal, this civilised beer drinkers' emporium is worth seeking out. Bare floorboards, old church pews and international breweriana create an atmosphere in which no piped music, jukebox or gaming machines disturb the conversation. Guest ales, usually including a dark beer, are complemented by continental bottled and draught beers and up to four ciders or perries. There is a quiz on Wednesdays. Q♿⇌🚌

Woolly Sheep

38 Sheep Street, BD23 1HY
10-11 (midnight Thu; 1am Fri & Sat); 12-11 Sun
☎ (01756) 700966 woollysheepinn.co.uk

Timothy Taylor Dark Mild, Golden Best, Boltmaker, Landlord, Ram Tam; guest beer H
This pub, managed by Timothy Taylor, is situated near the bottom of Skipton High Street. One long bar serves both the comfortable front room with its real fire and the larger flag-floored bar area behind. The area towards the rear is on two levels and priority here is given to diners. At the back, the traditional cobbled courtyard has decking with comfortable seating, a canopy and infra-red heaters. Food is served all day.

Staxton

Hare & Hounds
Main Street, YO12 4TA
12-midnight (01944) 710243
Theakston Old Peculier; Timothy Taylor Landlord; guest beers H
Imposing former coaching inn on the A64 – an excellent oasis when travelling to the east coast. The bar and lounge/dining area feature low beams and real fires. Guest beers are usually from the Enterprise/SIBA scheme, often from Wold Top and Great Yorkshire breweries. The three handpumps in winter rise to five in summer. Home-cooked meals are served every day, with seafood from Filey a speciality in summer. There are large grassed drinking areas outside.
Q P

Stillington

White Bear
Main Street, YO61 1JU
12-2.30 (not Mon), 5.30-11; 12-2.30, 5.30-midnight Sat; 12-11 Sun (01347) 810338 thewhitebearinn-york.co.uk
Marston's Burton Bitter; Samuel Smith Old Brewery Bitter; guest beers H
Bustling, traditional, village free house committed to a good turnover of local beers, so there is always something new to try. In the separate bar, appetising food is popular as an excellent beer accompaniment. Attracting visitors and locals alike, a warm Yorkshire welcome is assured. Well worth a visit. P (40)

Stokesley

Spread Eagle
39 High Street, TS9 5AD
11-11; 12-10.30 Sun (01642) 710278
Camerons Strongarm; Marston's Pedigree; guest beers H
A small, unspoilt market-town pub where friendly regulars drink at one end and an open fire welcomes diners at the other. Excellent and good-value home-cooked food, complete with details of where the produce has been sourced, is served all day. Two interesting and stronger guest beers are always on sale. Children are welcome. A rear garden leads down to the tranquil River Leven, where over-fed ducks amuse children and adults alike. Tuesday is live music night.
Q (29A,80)

White Swan
1 West End, TS9 5BL (at W end of town, well beyond the shops)
11.30 (12 Sun)-11 (01642) 710263
thewhiteswanstokesley.co.uk
Captain Cook Red Bay, Slipway, Endeavour, Black Porter, Discovery, Schooner Granville; guest beer H
A local CAMRA multi-award winner and home of Captain Cook Brewery, this superb and traditional one-room 18th-century local is in one of the prettiest areas of this friendly market town. An enthusiastic, hands-on licensee and proud brewery owner serves the brewery's beers together with a locally sourced guest. Quiz night is Wednesday and music nights are held monthly. Beer festivals take place at Easter and in October. Ploughman's lunches are served Wednesday-Saturday. Dogs are welcome, but children are not allowed.
Q (29A,80)

Strensall

Ship
23 The Village, YO32 5XS
12-11 (midnight Fri & Sat) (01904) 490302
theshipinn-strensall.co.uk
John Smith's Bitter; Timothy Taylor Landlord; guest beers H
Busy family-run village pub near the River Foss, offering four real ales, one real cider and restaurant food. Open all day and late at the weekend, it is popular with walkers, cyclists and caravanners in summer, and family and dog friendly, with outside seating and a children's play area at the rear. Regular events include music, quizzes and an annual spring beer festival. The bus stop from York is just across the road. P (5)

Thixendale

Cross Keys
YO17 9TG
12-3 (not Mon-Thu), 6-11; 12-3, 7-11 Sun
(01377) 288272
Jennings Bitter; Tetley Bitter; guest beer H
Dating back to at least 1851, this is a small award-winning single-roomed village pub, nestling in the dry valleys of the Yorkshire Wolds and popular with walkers, including those on the Wolds Way. Children are welcome in the beer garden. Good-value pub grub is served. Accommodation is in the adjoining converted stable. It will open weekday lunchtimes by appointment for parties of six or more (but needs three days' notice). Q

Thorganby

Ferry Boat Inn
YO19 6DD
closed Mon; 7-11.30; 12-11.30 Sat; 12-3, 7-11 Sun
(01904) 448224
Beer range varies H
Yorkshire CAMRA Pub of the Year runner-up in 2013, this gem has been in the same family since 1948. It is welcoming, comfortable and cosy. A large garden runs down to a willow tree on the bank of the River Derwent. The focus here is on providing a good choice of well-kept beers (the huge ceiling pumpclip collection reflects this). Robust sandwiches are served at weekend lunchtimes. Acoustic folk musicians get together on the third Sunday of each month.
Q P (35)

Thornton le Dale

Buck Hotel

Chestnut Avenue, YO18 7RW
12-11 (4-10.30 winter) Mon; 12-midnight
(01751) 474212
Tetley Bitter; guest beers H
A welcoming, traditional pub with two guest beers (three in summer) coming from Yorkshire and beyond. Copper Dragon and Ossett ales are often available. Home-made pub food is served daily until 8.30pm (3pm Sun). Pool and darts matches and quizzes are held weekly. The beer garden is a suntrap in summer – the perfect place to sit and soak up the beautiful village atmosphere or to relax after a day in Dalby Forest or on the moors.
P

Upper Poppleton

Lord Collingwood

The Green, YO26 6DP
closed Mon; 12-3, 5-midnight; 12-midnight Fri-Sun
(01904) 794388 thelordcollingwood.co.uk
Banks's Sunbeam; guest beer H
Situated on the village green, this pleasant hostelry dating back 300 years retains its character despite mid 20th-century attempts at making the building open plan. The main bar area is laid out for dining during meal service times. The side bar is kept for drinkers, pub games and the occasional TV. The pub always seems to cater seamlessly for diners, drinkers and village groups. P(10)

Wensley

Three Horseshoes

DL8 4HJ (on A684)
closed Mon; 12-3, 5.30-11; 12-11 Sat; 12-6 Sun
(01969) 622327
Theakston Best Bitter; Wall's County Town Gun Dog Bitter; guest beers H
This traditional old country pub is full of atmosphere, with its small bar and dining room both featuring low beams and real fires. Outside there is a terraced beer garden offering glorious views across Wensleydale, and a real suntrap on fine days. Wholesome and reasonably priced lunchtime and evening meals are served daily (no food Mon). Beers from Yorkshire Dales brewery are regularly available, as well as real cider and perry.
QP(156)

West Witton

Fox & Hounds L

DL8 4LP (on A684)
12-3, 6-midnight; 12-midnight Sat & Sun
(01969) 623650 foxwitton.com
Black Sheep Best Bitter; John Smith's Bitter; guest beers H
Friendly, family-run free house full of character, with a down-to-earth bar and games room popular with locals and visitors alike. Good-value meals are served all week, with a roast on Sunday. The pub was once a rest house for Jervaulx Abbey monks in the 1400s, and the dining room boasts an inglenook fireplace with a quaint oven. A pleasant patio at the rear leads onto the quoits pitch; beware the tight entry to the car park.
P(156)

Whitby

Black Horse

91 Church Street, YO22 4BH (E side of swing bridge on way to Abbey steps, close to old market square)
11-11; 12-10.30 Sun (01947) 602906
the-black-horse.com
Adnams Southwold Bitter; Black Dog Rhatas; Black Sheep Ale; guest beers H
A former local CAMRA branch award winner, this little multi-roomed gem dating from the 1600s offers a warm welcome. The frontage, with its frosted glass, together with one of Europe's oldest public serving bars, was built in the 1880s and remains largely unchanged. Beer is dispensed from five handpumps, and hot lunches are served during the winter months. Snuff, tapas, olives, Yorkshire cheeses and hot drinks are always available. The cider is Westons Rosie's Pig. Accommodation is available in four bedrooms.
Q(93,840)

Board Inn

125 Church Street, YO22 4DE (N end of Church St by abbey steps)
11.30 (11 Sun)-11 (01947) 602884
theboardinnwhitby.co.uk
Caledonian Deuchars IPA; Theakston Old Peculier, XB H
The last remaining Board of several that existed during the 1800s on Church Street – traditional shops that sold ale, among other produce, and displayed their wares on chalkboards. Today, three beers are served, allowing the drinker, from the front snug, to admire, or even contemplate climbing, the 199 steps up to the abbey. There are also fine harbour views to the rear from the refurbished lounge/restaurant, where reasonably priced meals are served. The famous Fortune's smokehouse can be found nearby.
(93,840)

Golden Lion

8 Golden Lion Bank, YO21 3BS (20yds W of swing bridge)
11-11 (01947) 602106
Black Sheep Best Bitter; Wells Bombardier; guest beers H
Just tucked away up Golden Lion Bank, a warm welcome is guaranteed at this traditional, small and friendly pub, where locals and visitors alike experience a great atmosphere and where nothing appears to have changed over the years. A varied mix of the more well-known national beers is served from four handpumps, though this selection may be reduced in the quieter winter months. For the numismatists among us, the tables in the lounge are adorned with old pennies.
(93,840)

Granby Hotel

34 Skinner Street, YO21 3AJ (West Cliff, between Flowergate and North Terrace)
11-midnight (01947) 601747
Camerons Strongarm; Jennings Sneck Lifter; Marston's Pedigree; Wychwood Hobgoblin H
Marvellous privately owned free house, attracting both locals and those staying in the West Cliff B&Bs. This busy two-room pub is just off the main tourist drag, and is well worth searching out. Though the pub is not tied, three of the regular beers are from Marston's, together with the Strongarm.
Particularly noted for its meals, both for value and

for size, the pub is also ideally placed for those requiring a visit to the famous Botham's Bakery. (93,840)

Little Angel Inn

18 Flowergate, YO21 3BA (200yds W of swing bridge, and 200yds N of railway/bus station)
11.30 (11 Sun)-11 ☎ (01947) 820475
littleangelwhitby.co.uk
Maxim Double Maxim; Tetley Bitter; guest beers H
Attracting locals and visitors alike, a genuine friendly welcome is assured at this recently refurbished pub where, it is rumoured, the remains of the castle form part of the structure. Pub food, large-screen TVs, live music, outside drinking and even a horse mount – for those who require this particular facility – complement the five beers served to three separate rooms from a central bar. (93,840)

Station Inn

New Quay Road, YO21 1DH (opp bus and railway stations)
10-midnight (11.30 Sun) ☎ (01947) 603937
stationinnwhitby.co.uk
Black Dog Whitby Abbey Ale; Camerons Strongarm; Copper Dragon Challenger IPA; Whitby Platform 3; guest beers H
Situated next to the harbour/marina, this convivial multi-roomed pub is a recent CAMRA branch Pub of the Year. The enthusiastic licensees ensure that the eight beers, including the house beer, Whitby Platform 3, always represent a superb range of styles, while cider and fruit wines mean there is something for everyone. Opposite the bus station and NYMR/Esk Valley railway, the pub has become the discerning traveller's waiting room. Live music is played three evenings a week.
(93,840)

Yarm

Black Bull

40-42 High Street, TS15 9BH (E side of High St, by town hall)
11.30-midnight (1am Fri & Sat) ☎ (01642) 791251
Draught Bass; guest beers H
Situated in the centre of a pleasant town, this popular M&B Nicholson's pub has the best and largest beer garden and heated patio in the area. It has been the favourite haunt, especially on Tuesdays, for Teesside's 30-somethings, and now much older, for decades. Much extended over the years, with two separate bars, there are now five handpumps, which are busy during the day, and extremely busy evenings and weekends. Good-value pub food is served all day every day.
Q (Eaglescliffe) (7,17)

York

Blue Bell ★

53 Fossgate, YO1 9TF
11-11; 12-10.30 Sun ☎ (01904) 654904
Bradfield Farmers Bitter, Farmers Blonde; Rudgate Ruby Mild; Timothy Taylor Landlord; guest beers H
Recognised by CAMRA as having a nationally important historic interior, this pub comprises a central bar serving two small rooms and, through a servery, the side corridor. This is a small place and can get busy. A strict no groups policy applies and entry to the pub may be restricted at busy times or on special occasions such as race days. Three guest beers supplement the four regulars. Sandwiches are served at lunchtimes. Q

Brigantes

114 Micklegate, YO1 6JX
12-11 ☎ (01904) 675355
Beer range varies H
Refurbished and expanded in 2013, this cheerful and welcoming pub is a real ale and real food haven. Run by a beer enthusiast, the 10 handpumps include regular beers from York, Leeds, Timothy Taylor, Okells, Great Heck and Black Sheep, plus four guests. Continental beers and real cider are also on offer. All ales come in a choice of one-third, half, two-third and pint measures. The regular menu is supplemented with daily specials and one room is set aside for diners until 9pm.
Q

Golden Ball ★

2 Cromwell Road, YO1 6DU
5 (4 Fri; 12 Sat)-11.30; 12-11 Sun ☎ (01904) 652211
goldenballyork.co.uk
Everards Tiger; Timothy Taylor Golden Best; Treboom Yorkshire Sparkle; guest beers H
Opened as York's first community co-operative pub in 2012, this warm and family-friendly pub has a nationally important historic interior and is Grade II-listed. It has three rooms, a snug and a beer garden. The bar offers seven handpumps serving regular Yorkshire beers and guests, and also sells fresh eggs and bread from local producers. The pub hosts traditional bar billiards games, community group meetings, open mic and quiz nights.
Q

Maltings

Tanners Moat, YO1 6HU
11-11; 12-10.30 Sun ☎ (01904) 655387 maltings.co.uk
Black Sheep Best Bitter; York Guzzler; guest beers H
A former Yorkshire CAMRA Pub of the Year, the Maltings has a lovely atmosphere, real-effect gas fire, a covered smoking area outside, live music every Monday and Tuesday, and bags of character. There are reclaimed doors covering the ceiling and even a reclaimed toilet acting as a seat in one of the corners. Friendly, knowledgable staff serve a changing mix of local beers and some from further afield, always including at least one from Rooster's in Knaresborough.

Minster Inn

24 Marygate, YO30 7BH
2-11; 12-midnight Fri; 11-midnight Sat; 12-10.30 Sun
☎ (01904) 624499
Banks's Sunbeam; Jennings Sneck Lifter; Marston's Burton Bitter; guest beers H
There is always a friendly (Sally) and colourful (Dave) welcome in this traditional pub. You are sure to get a great pint and strike up a conversation with the locals. Dating from 1903, the Edwardian interior is mostly unchanged, with two rooms off the corridor bar and the main bar in the third room. There are table puzzles and games for all. Guest beers come from the Marston's range.
Q

Phoenix

75 George Street, YO1 9PT
6-11; 4.30-11.30 Fri; 12.30-11.30 Sat; 2.30-11 Sun
☎ (01904) 656401 thephoenixinnyork.co.uk

Timothy Taylor Landlord; Wold Top Bitter; guest beers 🄷
An independently run CAMRA pub with a regionally important historic interior, where a friendly welcome awaits. Relax in the traditional pub atmosphere without the noise of gaming machines, TVs or jukebox. You can enjoy your beer while reading a newspaper and listening to the muted conversations of fellow drinkers. In the winter months a real log fire is lit in the front room. The rear room boasts a bar billiards table.
Q🐎❀☾♣🚌🐾

Pivni

6 Patrick Pool, YO1 8BB
⏲ 11.30-11.30 (11.45 Fri & Sat) ☎ (01904) 635464
🌐 pivni.co.uk
Buxton Moor Top; guest beers 🄷
Part of the expanding group of Pivovar UK craft beer houses, the bar has five cask ales from highly regarded breweries such as Thornbridge, Buxton, Hardknott, Marble, Dark Star and many more, changing regularly. These are complemented by a changing range of craft keg beers, mostly from Europe, the US and the UK. There is also an extensive selection of bottled beers. Formerly a travel agents, the 12th-century timber-framed building dates back to 1190. Snacks including pies and cheeseboards are served. ♿●🐾

Rook & Gaskill 𝕃

12 Lawrence Street, YO10 3WP
⏲ 3 (12 Fri-Sun)-midnight ☎ (01904) 655459
Beer range varies 🄷
Mere yards outside the city walls resides this beer haven. Refurbished in 2012, it is a simply furnished pub with a split-level bar that attracts beer lovers from near and far. The licensee is renowned for sourcing beers from throughout the UK, many of which will rarely be found elsewhere in the city. Up to six guests supplement a Castle Rock and a Wharfe Bank beer. ❀◗●🚌🐾ᯤ

Slip Inn 𝕃

Clementhorpe, YO23 1AN
⏲ 5-11.30; 4-midnight Fri; 12-midnight Sat; 12-11 Sun
☎ (01904) 621793 🌐 theslipinnyork.co.uk
Leeds Pale; Rudgate Ruby Mild; Timothy Taylor Boltmaker; Wold Top Wold Gold; guest beer 🄷
Just outside the walls and close to river, this independent free house is a thriving local community pub with two bars, a snug and a sheltered courtyard to the rear. Battle of the Brewery events feature regularly, as well as several beer festivals each year, including one held jointly with the Swan just up the road. Traditional pub games are played, with a darts team and regular dominoes and cribbage games.
❀♣●🚌(11)🐾ᯤ

Swan ★

16 Bishopgate Street, YO23 1JH
⏲ 4-11 (11.30 Thu); 1-midnight Fri; 12-midnight Sat; 12-10.30 Sun ☎ (01904) 634968
Saltaire Blonde; Tetley Bitter; Timothy Taylor Landlord; guest beers 🄷
A popular local pub with a traditional West Riding layout – it has a bar in a wide passageway and two rooms at either end of the bar. It has a nationally important historic pub interior and features on the cover of Yorkshire's Real Heritage Pubs. The beer garden to the rear has a covered and heated smoking area. The venue hosts an annual beer festival jointly with the Slip Inn down the road. Three guest beers come from around the country along with real ciders and perries. ❀♣●🚌(11)🐾

Volunteer Arms 𝕃

5 Watson Street, Holgate, YO24 4BH
⏲ 5-11 (midnight Fri); 12-midnight Sat; 12-11 Sun
☎ (01904) 541945 🌐 volunteerarmsyork.co.uk
Brown Cow Mrs Simpsons Thriller in Vanilla; Leeds Yorkshire Gold; Saltaire Pride; Timothy Taylor Landlord; Treboom Yorkshire Sparkle; guest beers 🄷
Cosy, welcoming street-corner local a short walk from the train station and near the iron bridge, with a strong community following. Saved from closure and much improved, it is a free house with a range of beer styles, featuring Yorkshire regulars, changing guests from across the country, and a changing real cider. A wide mix of music events (country/folk/blues/rock/open mic) takes place, and there is a Sunday night quiz. No hot food is served, but there is a nice range of pork pies and pickles. Q⇌●🚌(1,10)🐾ᯤ

York Tap

Railway Station, Station Road, YO24 1AB
⏲ 10-11 (11.45 Fri & Sat); 11-11 Sun ☎ (01904) 659009
🌐 yorktap.com
Beer range varies 🄷
Impressive conversion of the former railway station tea rooms into a stunning pub with a circular wooden bar and stained glass in the ceiling domes and windows. There are 20 handpumps selling 18 cask beers plus two ciders or perries. The beers are chosen from some of Britain's finest breweries, with all styles and strengths represented. There is an outdoor drinking area on the platform side. This bar is the first and last stop for many visitors to York. ♿⇌●🐾

YORKSHIRE (SOUTH)

Arksey

Plough Inn 𝕃

2 High Street, DN5 0SF (behind church)
⏲ 7 (6.30 Thu & Fri)-11; 12-2.30, 6.30-11 Sat; 12-3.30, 8-11 Sun ☎ (01302) 872472 🌐 arkseyplough.co.uk
Imperial Best Bitter; Old Mill Blonde Bombshell; guest beer 🄷
Welcoming multi-roomed community pub with attractive hanging baskets in summer. Brasses and old photographs of the village, some depicting the floods, adorn the lounge, which is heated by a log-burning fire. This friendly free house features beers from small independent local breweries. Reasonably priced bar meals are served Thursday, Friday, and Saturday evenings. The Sunday lunch is popular. Quiz nights are Thursday and Sunday.
Q🐎❀☾◗♿♣🚌(64,64a)ᯤ

Armthorpe

Wheatsheaf 𝕃

Church Street, DN3 3AE
⏲ 12 (5 Mon)-11; 12-11.30 Fri & Sat; 12.30-11 Sun
☎ (01302) 835868
Courage Directors; Sharp's Doom Bar; guest beers 🄷
Since the current management introduced real ale three years ago, this large village pub has established itself with CAMRA members thanks to the quality and variety of beers. With a strong emphasis on supporting the community, it provides

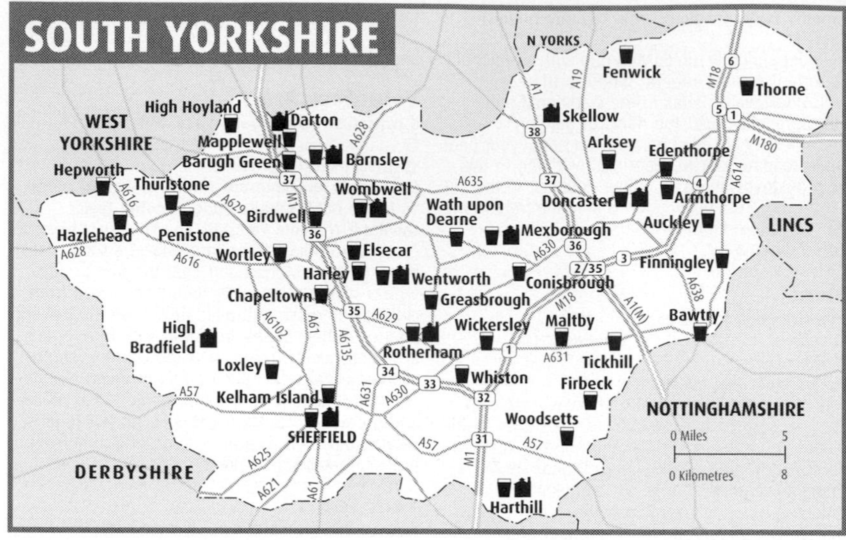

a number of events throughout the year. The pub has a 1920s design with separate bar and lounge areas. There is a conservatory area where meals are served. (81,82)

Auckley

Eagle & Child

24 Main Street, DN9 3HS

11.30-3, 5-11; 11.30-11 Fri & Sat; 12-10.30 Sun
(01302) 770406 eagleandchildauckley.co.uk

Black Sheep Best Bitter; John Smith's Bitter; Timothy Taylor Landlord; guest beers H

This gem of a village pub, recently refurbished while retaining its original character, has won several CAMRA awards over the years. It has a long tradition of offering a range of quality ales, with five cask beers always on handpump. A varied choice of freshly prepared meals is available at reasonable prices. Family-friendly, there is a pleasant outdoor children's area to the rear of the car park. Robin Hood Airport is nearby.
Q P (91)

Barnsley

Joseph Bramah

Market Hill, S70 2PX

8am-midnight (1am Wed, Fri & Sat) (01226) 320890

Greene King Abbot; Ruddles Best Bitter; guest beers H

Named after the famous local inventor who among other things invented a form of beer engine, this Lloyds No.1 bar provides the standard Wetherspoon core range of beers, plus up to four changing microbrewery guests, as well as value-for-money meals. Set over two floors, you can find some quieter areas, especially in the smaller upstairs bar. Outside is a sheltered and heated smoking courtyard. This popular watering hole in the heart of town caters for all.

Old No.7

7 Market Hill, S70 2PX

closed Mon; 12-midnight (01226) 244735
oldno7barnsley.co.uk

Acorn Barnsley Bitter, Blonde; guest beers H

The tap for Acorn Brewery, this pub is also handy for the new Experience Barnsley museum. Two bars offer eight real ales from Acorn and other microbreweries, real ciders and perry, plus a wide range of continental bottled beers and lagers. Numerous beer festivals are hosted throughout the year. There is live music on Friday nights and a monthly Celtic music session. CAMRA regional Pub of the Year 2013, regional Cider Pub of the Year 2013, and branch Cider Pub of the Year 2014.

Silkstone Inn

64 Market Street, S70 1SN

8am-midnight (01226) 320860

Greene King Abbot; Ruddles Best Bitter; guest beers H

In the main shopping area, the Silkstone Inn is named after a famous coal seam that stretched under Barnsley. The decor reflects this throughout –

INDEPENDENT BREWERIES

Abbeydale Sheffield
Acorn Wombwell
Blue Bee Sheffield
Bradfield High Bradfield
Brew Company Sheffield
Chantry Rotherham
Concertina Mexborough
Doncaster Doncaster
Geeves Barnsley
Glentworth Skellow
Harthill Village Harthill
Imperial Mexborough
Kelham Island Sheffield
Little Ale Cart Sheffield
On the Edge Sheffield
Sheffield Sheffield
Stancill Sheffield (NEW)
Tapped Sheffield
Toolmakers Sheffield
Two Roses Darton
Wentworth Wentworth
White Rose Sheffield
Wood Street Sheffield

including the coal-like droplets on the lights. A central modern fireplace creates a warming atmosphere. The pub offers two permanent beers and up to three guest ales, plus a real cider to satisfy the client mix. The pub is popular with families and older couples. Q

Barugh Green

Crown & Anchor

Barugh Lane, S75 1LL (on B6428)
11.30-11 (midnight Fri & Sat); 11-11 Sun
(01226) 387200 thecrownandanchor.com
Acorn Barnsley Bitter; guest beers
Known locally as the White House, the pub has been extensively redeveloped by its current owner and now has a spacious bar area and restaurant. The bar showcases a varied selection of real ales from local and national brewers and stocks a few unusual bottles not seen in the area. The pub has become a firm favourite with the local community for its food offerings and its ever-popular quiz nights. A real ale asset and well worth a visit. P

Bawtry

Ship

Gainsborough Road, DN10 6HT (on A631 near traffic lights)
12-11 (10.30 Sun) (01302) 710275
theship-bawtry.com
Beer range varies
One of the local CAMRA area's success stories – the current licensees took over this run-down roadside venue in 2007 and transformed it. Refurbished inside and out, the pub offers good-quality meals at reasonable prices. Four cask ales from the Marston's portfolio are always on offer and beer festivals are held twice a year. It was local CAMRA Pub of the Year in 2011 and, with several other accolades as well, the Ship should please just about anyone. P(21,25)

Birdwell

Cock Inn

Pilley Hill, off The Walk, S70 5UD
12-11 (11.30 Thu; midnight Fri & Sat); 12-11.30 Sun
(01226) 742155
Courage Best Bitter; guest beers
This small stone-built village pub is welcoming, with its roaring open coal fire. The main bar has a slate floor, beams, brassware and old village pictures. Five real ales are always on, with three changing guests including at least one from a local brewery. Home-cooked food is served daily – Sunday lunch is extremely popular and booking in advance is recommended. Q P(7A,67A)

Chapeltown

Commercial

107 Station Road, S35 2XF
12-11 (midnight Fri & Sat) (0114) 246 9066
thecommie.co.uk
Wentworth WPA, Best Bitter, Bumble Beer; guest beers
Built in 1890, this well-established free house is a regular outlet for Wentworth beers. As well as six guest beers, including a stout or porter, there is also at least one real cider. An island bar serves the lounge, games room and snug. Beer festivals are held in May and November. There is an outdoor area to the rear of the pub, and an upstairs function room which is home to regular live folk sessions. Children are welcome. No meals Sunday evening. P(265,31A)

Conisbrough

Hilltop

Sheffield Road, DN12 2AY (on A630 at jct of Sheffield Rd and Old Rd)
closed Mon; 5 (12 Sun)-midnight (01709) 868811
thehilltophotel.co.uk
Welbeck Abbey Red Feather; guest beers
A traditional free house serving up to four ales on the outskirts of Conisbrough, it offers a relaxed and friendly atmosphere. It is split into a public bar and lounge/dining area. The latter incorporates Bully's Steakhouse, serving locally-sourced, home-prepared food on weekend evenings. The pie shop is open Wednesday to Friday. Most beers are from local breweries, including Wentworth, Welbeck, Acorn, Pennine, Imperial and Concertina. Quiz night is Wednesday. Q P(X78)

Doncaster

Corner Pin

145 St Sepulchre Gate West, DN1 3AH (on W side of dual carriageway)
12-11.30 (10 Sun) (01302) 340670
York Guzzler; guest beers
Popular traditional pub situated conveniently for the town centre and travel interchange, comprising a smart lounge area and public bar, with a decked outside area to the rear. The beers, in a variety of styles, are from small independent breweries, and a discount is offered to CAMRA members. Beer festivals are held twice-yearly. Food is served all day Friday and Saturday, and booking is advised for the excellent Sunday lunches. Local CAMRA Pub of the Year 2014.

Gate House

Priory Walk, DN1 1TS (off High St, precinct is near Mansion House)
9am-midnight (1am Fri & Sat) (01302) 554540
Greene King Abbot; Ruddles Best Bitter; guest beers
A bistro-style Wetherspoon bar, unusual in that it was purpose built for this role rather than converted. It sits on the site of a gatehouse to a medieval priory and is an oasis for real ale drinkers in the middle of a number of non-real-ale outlets. Guest beers from Yorkshire breweries are featured as well as those from further afield. Do not overlook the bank of handpumps at the far end of the bar.

Plough ★

8 West Laith Gate, DN1 1SF (close to Frenchgate shopping centre)
11-11; 11-4, 7-11 Sun thelittleplough.co.uk
Acorn Barnsley Bitter; guest beers
The Little Plough, as the locals know it, is a friendly haven for anyone wishing to escape the town-centre bustle. CAMRA-friendly, the pub offers local guest ales and twice-yearly beer festivals. The interior dates from 1934 and features in CAMRA's National Inventory of Historic Pub Interiors. There is a public bar at the front and a comfortable lounge

to the rear, warmed by a real fire, with pictures of old agricultural scenes. A winner of many CAMRA awards. Q❀⇌🚌

Red Lion

37/38 Market Place, DN1 1NH (S corner of Market Place)

9am-11.30 (midnight Fri & Sat); 9am-11 Sun

☎ (01302) 732120

Greene King Abbot; Ruddles Best Bitter; guest beers Ⓗ

Large historic pub enjoying a renaissance as a Wetherspoon establishment. A strong commitment to real ale, particularly from microbreweries, has earned it several local CAMRA awards. Although much altered over the years, it was here in 1776 that the idea was first mooted for Doncaster's oldest horse race, the St Leger, an association commemorated by a wall display and a brass plate. ◑♿⇌♣🚌(76)

Salutation

14 South Parade, DN1 2DR

12-midnight (10.30 Mon; 11.30 Tue & Wed); 12-10.30 Sun

☎ (01302) 340705

Black Sheep Best Bitter; guest beers Ⓗ

The Salutation is a popular former coaching inn dating back to at least the 17th century. It is so steeped in Doncaster's history that there is a book written about it. Doncaster Rovers football club started out here, using the upstairs room as a changing room. The pub has seven handpumps offering a rotation of well-kept real ales and ciders. Hot food is served. ❀◑P🚌

White Swan

34 French Gate, DN1 1QQ (next to Church Way and Frenchgate shopping centre)

10-11 (midnight Fri & Sat); 11-10.30 Sun

☎ (01302) 366573

Black Sheep Best Bitter; guest beer Ⓗ

Traditional town-centre pub with a small front tap leading past the raised bar into a long narrow lounge. The Irish-themed decor reflects the previous licensee's heritage and is complemented by interesting photos of old Doncaster. Supportive of local micros, beers from Glentworth and Doncaster breweries are usually on offer. Live music features at weekends and there is a jazz session on the first Saturday afternoon of the month. Good-value meals are served until 6pm Monday-Saturday. ❀◑♿⇌🚌

Edenthorpe

Eden Arms

Eden Field Road, DN3 2QR (next to Tesco)

11-11; 11.30-11.30 Wed; 11.30-midnight Thu-Sat

☎ (01302) 888682

Abbeydale Moonshine Ⓗ; Leeds Best Ⓗ/Ⓐ, York Guzzler; guest beers Ⓗ

Fine, modern estate pub with a welcoming atmosphere. The large one-roomed interior is made cosy and warm by several fires and has many diverse areas to enjoy. As you enter you are immediately confronted by a billboard showing current and forthcoming real ales. Three well-kept regular beers are always on offer from less commonly found breweries. Popular and busy but rarely crowded, the customers and staff raise impressive amounts for charity.
Q❀◑♿P🚌(87)

Elsecar

Crown Inn

Fitzwilliam Street, S74 8EL

11-11 ☎ (01226) 743851

Beer range varies Ⓗ

In a picturesque village and near the Trans Pennine Trail, this traditional pub has two rooms, the front popular with locals and the rear used for more formal occasions. There is a large garden to the rear with a children's play area. The cask ales are from local breweries. The family owners are established licensees in the village, having previously run the nearby Fitzwilliam and the Market. ❀⇌P🚌(66)

Fitzwilliam Arms

42 Hill Street, S74 8EL

12-11 ☎ (01226) 740191

Beer range varies Ⓗ

Near the train station in a real ale haven, this pub is at the heart of the community, hosting regular events and music. The Fitzwilliam is a lovely stone-fronted pub that boasts a superb beer garden with an impressive children's play area. It has recently been extended to incorporate a new bar area and fantastic restaurant. Step inside and you are greeted with welcoming hospitality and a great range of up to four local cask ales. ❀⇌P🚌(66)

Fenwick

Baxter Arms

Fenwick Lane, DN6 0HA

5.30 (11.30 Sat & Sun)-midnight ☎ (01302) 702671

Theakston Best Bitter; guest beer Ⓗ

A rural gem well worth seeking out. This welcoming pub, converted from a farmhouse in 1973, comprises two rooms, both with open fires. The smaller room has a snooker table. Bar food is available all day Saturday and Sunday, and weekday evenings. Guest beers are from small independent breweries. Outside there is a large sheltered garden with swings, and a seating area at the front. Wednesday is quiz night.
Q❀◑♿▲♣P

Finningley

Harvey Arms

Old Bawtry Road, DN9 3BY

12-3 (not Mon), 5-11; 12-midnight Sat; 12-11 Sun

☎ (01302) 770200

Beer range varies Ⓗ

Popular village local set in an attractive location near the green. There has been a pub on the site since the 1840s. Recently refurbished, it has gained an excellent reputation for the quality of its food as well as its beer. Up to four cask ales are served, coming from a variety of breweries, local and national. Timothy Taylor Landlord and Sharp's Doom Bar are staples of the beer range.
Q❀◑♿P🚌(91,X91)

Firbeck

Black Lion

9 New Road, S81 8JY (opp village hall)

closed Mon; 12-3, 5.30-11; 12-5 Sun ☎ (01709) 812575

John Smith's Bitter; guest beers Ⓗ

Traditional village pub and restaurant, now a free house, which has returned to its former glory. It attracts diners, walkers and the local farming community. Four guest beers are offered, usually including ales from local microbreweries. Pictures of old Firbeck adorn the walls of the snug area. There are two letting rooms. Winner of local CAMRA branch Best Sunday Lunch award 2013. Q❀🛏◑♿♣P🐾

Greasbrough

Prince of Wales

9 Potter Hill, S61 4NU (1½ miles from Rotherham central)

🕐 11-4, 7-11; 12-3, 7-10.30 Sun ☎ (01709) 551358

Beer range varies Ⓗ

Do not be put off by the shabby exterior of this classic street-corner local – it continues to offer top-quality cask beer at a fair price from a variety of independent breweries and a warm welcome. The single guest beer can change up to three times a day, ensuring its quality, and is served in rare oversized glasses. The landlord, Dennis, has been here more than 35 years, and has many local CAMRA awards to his credit. Q❀♣🚉🚌(43A,227)

Harley

Horseshoe L

9 Harley Road, S62 7UD (off A6135 on B6090, 1 mile from Wentworth)

🕐 4-11 (10 Mon); 2-11 Sat; 12-10.30 Sun ☎ (01226) 742204

Bradfield Farmers Blonde; Copper Dragon Golden Pippin; guest beers Ⓗ

This street-corner local hosts regular events and is home to football and pool teams. Guest beers change frequently, so you know they are at their best, with ales often coming from local breweries. A carvery is held 12-3pm Sunday (book to avoid disappointment). The Horseshoe has been the hub of the local community for well over a century, and is handy for visitors to the Wentworth estate, the Needle's Eye and Elsecar Heritage Centre. ❀♣🚌(44)

Harthill

Beehive 🏆 L

16 Union Street, S26 7YH (opp village church)

🕐 closed Mon; 12-2.30, 6-11 (11.30 Fri); 12-3, 6-11.30 Sat; 12-11 Sun ☎ (01909) 770205

Tetley Bitter; Timothy Taylor Landlord; guest beers Ⓗ

The Beehive has been welcoming drinkers since 1833. Excellent home-cooked food and up to 10 real ales are offered. As the brewery tap, the full range of Harthill Village beers is always available. There is a full-size snooker table and function room with disabled access. A popular beer and music festival is held in the garden in July. Local CAMRA Pub of the Year 2013 and 2014. Q❀◑♿♣P🚌

Hazlehead

Dog & Partridge L

Bord Hill, Flouch, S36 4HH (on A628 Barnsley-Manchester road near Flouch roundabout)

🕐 12-11 ☎ (01226) 763173 🌐 dogandpartridgeinn.co.uk

Acorn Barnsley Bitter; guest beers Ⓗ

Set in the Dark Peak District high on the Woodhead Pass, this lively country pub with its wooden-beamed ceilings has always keenly supported CAMRA's aims. At least one of its real ales is brewed locally. The warm open fire provides a very welcome respite from the often wild weather outside. Enlarged over the years, the venue has grown to include modern accommodation and all-day quality food. This is the jewel in Barnsley's pub crown. Q🐴❀P

Hepworth

Fox House Inn L

Penistone Road, HD9 2TR

🕐 11.30-2 (not Mon), 6-11.30; 12-11.30 Sun

☎ (01226) 762536 🌐 thefoxhouseinn.co.uk

Beer range varies Ⓗ

High on the moors, this pub is famed for its food (diners are advised to book). The pub has been in the same family for over 25 years, originally founded by current chef Michael Millas' father, Leon. The pub prides itself on using fresh local produce from farms and businesses in the surrounding area. The five rotating cask ales come from local breweries such as Two Roses and Ossett. Food is served until around 9pm. 🐴❀P🚌(25)

High Hoyland

Cherry Tree L

Bank End Lane, S75 4BB

🕐 12-3, 5.30-midnight; 12-midnight Fri-Sun

☎ (01226) 382541

Acorn Barnsley Bitter; Black Sheep Best Bitter; Elland Best Bitter; guest beers Ⓗ

Near to Cannon Hall Country Park, the Cherry Tree has far-reaching views over open countryside and is well worth a visit. There is a long central bar with dining areas to both sides. The pub offers good-value quality food (booking advised). Outside, there is plenty of seating for patrons to enjoy the magnificent scenery. The pub is popular with locals and visitors alike, and walkers are more than welcome. ❀🍎P

Loxley

Nag's Head Inn L

Stacey Bank, S6 6SJ

🕐 11.30-11.30 ☎ (0114) 285 1202

Bradfield Farmers Bitter, Farmers Blonde, Farmers Brown Cow; guest beer Ⓗ

A two-roomed country pub on the main road out of Loxley towards High Bradfield. This is the nearby Bradfield Brewery's tap, with five beers from the range including seasonal beers and specials. Good home-cooked food is served lunchtimes and evenings (no food Sun eve or Mon). Excellent views overlooking the Loxley Valley can be enjoyed from the outside drinking area. The games room has a snooker table. 🐴❀◑♣P🚌(61,62)🐾

Maltby

Queen's Hotel

Tickhill Road, S66 7NQ

🕐 8am-midnight (1am Thu-Sat) ☎ (01709) 812494

Greene King Abbot; Ruddles Best Bitter; guest beers Ⓗ

Now firmly established, this spacious pub has an attractive family dining area offering typical Wetherspoon value-for-money food and drink. A 20p per pint discount for CAMRA members has contributed to a much-needed raising of the profile of real ale in Maltby. Local CAMRA Best Pub Refurbishment award 2013. 🐴❀◑♿🍎P🚌(1)📶

Mapplewell

Talbot Inn

Towngate, S75 6AS

2-11; 11.30-midnight Fri & Sat; 11.30-11 Sun
(01226) 385629

Two Roses Heron Porter; guest beers H

New owners took over this 18th-century pub in 2013, rescuing it from the clutches of developers. Since then they have transformed it by reintroducing the restaurant upstairs and bar meals downstairs. This is a friendly pub, the hub of the local community, welcoming customers of all ages. There is also a local-sourcing ethos, primarily to support other local businesses but also to minimise the environmental impact of delivery. This includes the guest beers, all from Two Roses. P (1,93A)

Mexborough

Concertina Band Club

9a Dolcliffe Road, S64 9AZ (off Bank St, halfway up hill)

2-4 (5 Fri & Sat), 7.45-11; 12-3, 7.45-10.30 Sun
(01709) 580841

Concertina Club Bitter, Old Dark Attic, Bengal Tiger; John Smith's Bitter; guest beer H

Long-established club and brewery with an interesting history, and a regular in this Guide. The Tina, as it is known locally, was originally home to a concertina band which was formed in 1887. Pictures and memorabilia as well as many CAMRA awards decorate the main room. The cellar brewery provides three regular ales including the award-winning Bengal Tiger and occasional guests. CAMRA members are very welcome – just show this Guide or your membership card.
Q

Imperial Brewery Tap

Arcadia Hall, Cliff Street, S64 9HU (opp bus station)

4.30-midnight; closed Tue; 12-midnight Sat & Sun 07428 422703

Imperial Best Bitter, Blonde; guest beers H

This friendly brewery tap has a large main bar with a cosy lounge area, plus a separate games room. Six handpumps dispense excellent-quality Imperial ales (which may include seasonal specials and one-off brews) as well as guest beers – all served in lined measured glasses. Two real ciders are also available. There is entertainment most evenings and a lunchtime carvery every Sunday. Two beer festivals are staged each year, the one in December featuring beers from new breweries.
P

Penistone

Royal British Legion Club

14 St Mary's Street, S36 6DT

11-3 (4.45 Thu), 7-11; 11-11.30 Sat; 12-11 Sun
(01226) 766911

Beer range varies H

A spacious, comfortable and well-appointed modern club with lounge/concert room and separate large games/TV room with two snooker tables. Two competitively priced real ales are sold, well-tended by the enthusiastic steward. The Trans Pennine Trail on former railway track runs at the rear of the club. Bingo takes place on Monday evenings and regular entertainment on other days. Non-members need to be officially signed in (CAMRA members should show their membership card). P

Rotherham

Bluecoat

The Crofts, S60 2JD (behind town hall, off Moorgate Road, A618)

8am-midnight (1am Fri & Sat) (01709) 580841

Greene King Abbot; Ruddles Best Bitter; guest beers H

Originally a charity school, opened in 1776, it became a Wetherspoon pub in 2001. The selection of up to 10 beers is listed on a screen at the end of the bar. Westons Old Rosie or Organic cider is served from a cask behind the bar. The pub commissions a specially brewed beer four times a year from a local brewery. Winner of local CAMRA Pub of the Year four times. P

Bridge Inn

1 Greasbrough Road, S60 1RB (alongside Chantry Bridge, between bus and rail stations)

12-midnight (1am Sat) (01709) 836818

Old Mill Traditional Bitter, Yorkshire Porter; guest beers H

The first home of Rotherham CAMRA, the pub reverted to its original name after a spell as Nellie Denes. It is an Old Mill tied house, built in 1930 using stone from the previous Bridge Inn, which dated back to the 1700s. Two guest beers are usually sourced from microbreweries, and the real cider changes. There is live music every Saturday evening, with folk and jazz once a month, and there are two function rooms upstairs.

New York Tavern

84 Westgate, S60 1BD

12-midnight (01709) 375596

Beer range varies H

Reopened by a team from Chantry Brewery, the pub has been fully refurbished as a real ale-led establishment. Five Chantry beers are on handpump plus four guest ales and real cider, all at competitive prices. A large selection of foreign bottled beers and, unusually, snuff, is stocked. The venue bears the old name of the area and of a pub demolished when the nearby ring road was built. Near the New York football stadium.

Woodlands

Doncaster Road, S65 1NN (access from Ridge Rd above)

7-11; 12-4, 7-midnight Fri; 2-midnight Sat; 12-11 Sun
(01709) 382777 thewoodlandsclub.co.uk

Beer range varies H

Set in beautiful grounds, this club offers two well-kept beers from local breweries, served in oversized glasses and at reasonable prices. Facilities include two snooker tables and TV sport, with live entertainment on Thursday, Friday and Saturday evenings. Sunday from 4pm is open mic, and music festivals are held outside in the summer. CAMRA members are welcome with this Guide or a membership card. Q P

Sheffield: Central

Bath Hotel ★

66-68 Victoria Street, S3 7QL

12-11 (12.30am Fri & Sat); 12-6 Sun (0114) 249 5151
beerinthebath.co.uk

Beer range varies H

A careful restoration of the 1930s interior gave this two-roomed pub a conservation award and acknowledgement by CAMRA as having a nationally important historic pub interior. The bar lies between the tiled lounge, a small corridor drinking area and the cosy well-upholstered snug. There are usually three Thornbridge beers and three guests on, plus a good choice of malt whiskies and continental beers. Regular live music is hosted and a weekly quiz on Thursdays.

Devonshire Cat

49 Wellington Street, S1 4HG

11.30-11 (1am Fri & Sat); 12-10.30 Sun
(0114) 279 6700 devonshirecat.co.uk

Abbeydale Moonshine; guest beers H

With 12 handpumps adorning the bar and over 100 beers from around the world, the Dev Cat is a great place for the discerning drinker. Now operated by Abbeydale Brewery, which provides the eponymous house beer, there is always a choice of its beers as well as a number of interesting guests. The menu ranges from light snacks through to hearty meals, served all day to 8pm (6pm Sun). An excellent stopping-off point for anyone on a brief visit to the city.

Henry's Café Bar

38 Cambridge Street, S1 4HP

9am-midnight (1am Fri & Sat) 0872 107 7077

Clark's Classic Blonde; guest beers H

Former café/bar reopened as a free house in 2010 after being derelict. Now thriving again following a thorough refurbishment, it offers one of the largest selections of cask ales in the city centre, with up to 11 guest beers. The ground floor is open plan, with seating at various levels around the long bar counter. Meals prepared from good locally-sourced produce are served daily 11am-7pm in the main bar area. The in-house Aardvark Brewery is being established on site.

Hop

West One Plaza, Fitzwilliam Street, S1 4JB

12-12.30am (0114) 278 1000 thehop-sheffield.com

Fuller's London Pride; Ossett Yorkshire Blonde, Big Red Bitter, Silver King, Excelsior; guest beers H

Unusually, this is a pub conversion by Ossett Brewery from former supermarket premises, set in a modern bar/restaurant/shopping complex near the lively West Street drinking circuit. From the entrance there is a small snug area, before the main bar with 10 handpumps featuring up to four guest beers and a real cider. This leads to a larger room used for regular live music sessions, which is overlooked by a balcony seating area. Food is served all day to 7pm.

Red Deer L

18 Pitt Street, S1 4DD

12-midnight (1am Fri & Sat); 12-11 Sun
(0114) 272 2890 red-deer-sheffield.co.uk

Copper Dragon Golden Pippin; Kelham Island Easy Rider; Moorhouse's Pride of Pendle; Timothy Taylor Landlord; guest beers H

A genuine, traditional local in the heart of the city. The small frontage of the original three-roomed pub hides an open-plan interior extended to the rear with a gallery seating area. As well as the impressive range of cask beers, including up to four guest ales, there is also a selection of continental bottled beers. Meals are served lunchtimes and evenings daily. The popular quiz is held on Tuesday night, and an upstairs function room is available for bookings. Q

Rutland Arms L

86 Brown Street, S1 2BS

12-11 (midnight Thu-Sat) (0114) 272 9003
rutlandarmspeople.co.uk

Blue Bee Bees Knees Bitter, Nectar Pale; guest beers H

Occupying a corner spot in the Cultural Industries Quarter and near Sheffield's main railway station, this pub reopened as a free house in 2009. The comfortable interior provides ample seating either side of the entrance, and the walls are decorated with changing displays of work from local artists, as well as photos of old Sheffield pubs. Most of the guest beers come from other local breweries, and separate beer and cider festivals are held annually. Food is served throughout the day.

Sheffield Tap ★ L

Platform 1b, Sheffield Station, Sheaf Street, S1 2BP

11-11; 10-midnight Fri & Sat (0114) 273 7558
sheffieldtap.com

Thornbridge Jaipur IPA; guest beers H

Opened in 2009, this was originally the First Class refreshment room for Sheffield Midland Station, built in 1904. After years of neglect the main bar area has been the subject of an award-winning restoration and retains many original features. Further seating has been provided in the entrance corridor and to the right of the bar. Usually at least two beers are from the on-site Tapped Brewery, which was opened in 2013 in the impressive former dining room, and can be viewed behind the glass screen. Q

Sheffield: Kelham Island

Fat Cat L

23 Alma Street, S3 8SA

12-11 (midnight Fri & Sat) (0114) 249 4801
thefatcat.co.uk

Kelham Island Best Bitter, Pale Rider; Timothy Taylor Landlord; guest beers H

Opened in 1981 and still ferociously independent, this is the pub that started the real ale revolution in the area. Beers from around the country are served alongside those from the adjacent Kelham Island Brewery. Vegetarian and gluten-free dishes feature heavily on the menu (evening food to 8pm, not Sun). The walls are covered with many awards presented to the pub and brewery. Beer festivals are held every August and at various other times. Monday is curry and quiz night.
QP

Harlequin L

108 Nursery Street, S3 8GG

12-11 (11.30 Thu & Fri; midnight Sat) (0114) 249 4181
theharlequinpub.co.uk

Brew Company Blonde; guest beers H

Operated by the Brew Company, the Harlequin takes its name from another former Ward's pub just round the corner, now demolished. The large open-plan interior features a central bar with seating on two levels. There are two regular and several other beers from The Brew Co, as well as guests from far and wide, with the emphasis on microbreweries. A range of boutique bottled beers is also available. Wednesday is quiz night and there is live music at weekends.

Kelham Island Tavern 🏆 L

62 Russell Street, S3 8RW
12-midnight ☎ (0114) 272 2482
Acorn Barnsley Bitter; Bradfield Farmers Bitter; Pictish Brewers Gold; Thwaites Nutty Black; guest beers H
Former CAMRA National Pub of the Year, this small gem was rescued from dereliction in 2002. Twelve handpumps dispense an impressive range of beers, always including a mild, a porter and a stout. In the warmer months you can relax in the pub's multi-award-winning beer garden. Regular folk music features on Sunday evening and quiz night is Monday. No meals Sunday. Q

Riverside

1 Mowbray Street, S3 8EN
12-11 (midnight Fri & Sat) ☎ (0114) 281 3621
riversidesheffield.co.uk
Brew Company Blonde; guest beers H
Set on the bank of the River Don, the pub has a pleasant terrace overlooking the river. The interior is largely open plan but with a separate room to the right of the main entrance. Furnishings include a mix of comfortable sofas and armchairs together with more spartan canteen-style tables and chairs. The two house beers from The Brew Co are complemented by a changing selection of guest ales, mostly from local breweries. Live music is featured at weekends.

Shakespeares Ale & Cider House L

146-148 Gibraltar Street, S3 8UB
12-midnight (1am Fri & Sat) ☎ (0114) 275 5959
shakespeares-sheffield.co.uk
Abbeydale Deception; guest beers H
Originally a coaching inn from 1821, the hostelry reopened as a free house in 2011, following a refurbishment including incorporation into the archway to the rear yard. The central bar serves three rooms including the extension, and there is a further room across the corridor. Up to eight changing guest beers are available, together with real cider and over 100 whiskies. There is regular live music in the upstairs Bard's Bar, a quiz is held on Thursdays, and several beers festivals are staged each year. Q

Wellington L

1 Henry Street, S3 7EQ
12-11; 12-3.30, 7-10.30 Sun ☎ (0114) 249 2295
Little Ale Cart Dog Standard Bitter; guest beers H
A popular two-roomed street-corner local that champions a range of beers from small independent breweries. The 10 handpumps always offer a stout or porter, a cider, and at least three beers from the in-house Little Ale Cart brewery. This has recently relocated to larger premises, having outgrown the old brewery next to the secluded beer garden. A range of continental bottled beers is also available. Q

Sheffield: North

Blake Hotel

53 Blake Street, Walkley, S6 3JQ
12-11.30 ☎ (0114) 233 9336
Acorn Blonde; guest beers H
At the top of a steep hill, this community pub reopened as a free house in 2010 after seven years of closure. Extensively restored, it has retained many traditional Victorian features, with original etched windows and mirrors from bygone breweries. A large decked garden has been developed to the rear. There are five guest beers, usually including a stout or porter, the majority from small independent breweries. The shelves behind the bar display possibly the most extensive range of whiskies in Sheffield. Q

Gardeners Rest L

Neepsend Lane, Neepsend, S3 8AT
3-11; 12-midnight Fri & Sat; 12-11 Sun ☎ (0114) 272 4978
Sheffield Crucible Best, Five Rivers, Blanco Blonde, Porter; guest beers H
The tap for the nearby Sheffield Brewery, reopened in 2009 after refurbishment following severe flood damage in 2007. The clean, bright interior has retained the cosy lounge. The main bar area features art exhibitions and live music at weekends, and has a restored bar billiards table. To the rear is a conservatory leading to the beer garden overlooking the River Don. In addition to at least four Sheffield Brewery beers, there are up to six guests, mostly from small independent breweries. Q (53)

Hillsborough L

54-58 Langsett Road, Hillfoot, S6 2UB
12-11 (midnight Fri & Sat) ☎ (0114) 232 2100
hillsborough-hotel.co.uk
Wood Street Pale Ale, Bitter, Ebony Stout; guest beers H
Privately owned hotel with six en-suite rooms. Home-cooked meals are served throughout the day and a function room is available for all occasions. The Wood Street beers are brewed in the cellar and at least four are always available on the bar, together with guest beers from local and other independent breweries. There are regular themed events, with folk music on Sunday evenings and a quiz on Tuesdays. Brewery tours can be arranged. Q

New Barrack Tavern L

601 Penistone Road, Hillsborough, S6 2GA
11-11 (midnight Fri & Sat); 12-11 Sun ☎ (0114) 234 9148
Acorn Barnsley Bitter; Bradfield Farmers Bitter; Castle Rock Harvest Pale, Screech Owl; guest beers H
Multi-roomed pub offering up to five guest beers, including seasonal ales from Castle Rock. Home-cooked food is available daily, with roasts on Sundays. The front bar has a local sports theme, while the main room features live bands weekends and a comedy club on the first Sunday of the month. Bottles from the Discover World Beers range are stocked. Outside is the award-winning heated, covered patio garden. Handy for Sheffield Eagles rugby games at the nearby Owlerton Stadium. Q (53)

Sheffield: South

Broadfield

452 Abbeydale Road, Nether Edge, S7 1FR
12-midnight (1am Fri & Sat); 12-11 Sun
☎ (0114) 255 0200 thebroadfield.co.uk
Abbeydale Moonshine; Bradfield Farmers Blonde; Saltaire Pride; guest beers H
The pub was built on Abbeydale's Broad Fields in 1896 by dairy farmer Albert Twigg, who became its first landlord. The Forum Café Bar Group took over in 2011 and significantly changed the style and atmosphere to create a more authentic Yorkshire pub. An extensive menu is offered, with hand-made pies and sausages a feature. Five guest beers

supplement the regulars, and a wide range of bottled and draught continental and world beers can also be sampled. Another attraction is the bi-monthly whisky club. ❀◑◗♿●P🚌🐾📶

Sheaf View

25 Gleadless Road, Heeley, S2 3AA

⏲ 11.30-11.30 (12.30am Fri & Sat) ☎ (0114) 249 6455

Acorn Blonde; Kelham Island Easy Rider; guest beers Ⓗ

A genuine free house since 2000 following major refurbishment, the Sheaf has won numerous awards. Lots of interesting breweriana adorn the walls and shelves. There are six changing guest ales and a good range of draught and bottled continental beers, with malt whisky lovers also well catered for. This is a thriving local which gets especially busy on Wednesday quiz night and before Sheffield United home games.
Q❀♿♣●P🚌🐾

White Lion 𝕃

615 London Road, Heeley, S2 4HT

⏲ 11.30-11.30 (12.30am Fri & Sat) ☎ (0114) 255 1500

🌐 whitelionsheffield.co.uk

Abbeydale Moonshine; Tetley Bitter; Thornbridge Jaipur IPA; Wychwood Hobgoblin; guest beers Ⓗ

This Grade II-listed pub has been respectfully refurbished over the years. A tiled central corridor links a number of delightful small rooms and leads to the larger rear concert room. There are four changing guest beers, and a good selection of malts. The pub hosts many community events and frequent beer festivals. The varied programme of live music caters for all tastes. A popular quiz on Wednesday is accompanied by a free buffet.
❀♣●🚌🐾📶

Sheffield: West

Closed Shop 𝕃

52-54 Commonside, S10 1GG

⏲ 12-11 (12.30am Fri & Sat) ☎ (0114) 266 0330

🌐 theclosedshopsheffield.co.uk

Blue Bee Bees Knees Bitter, Nectar Pale; guest beers Ⓗ

Between Crookes and Walkley, this is a historic pub that benefited from a refurbishment following a change of management in 2013. There are now eight handpumps, dispensing beers from Blue Bee and other local breweries as well as guests, and three real ciders and a perry are sold. There are three main areas and a beer garden with a pool table in the raised area at the rear, and ample comfortable seating at the front. Meals are served to 9pm. Q🐴❀◑◗♣●P🚏🚌(95)🐾📶

Francis Newton

7 Clarkehouse Road, Broomhall, S10 2LA

⏲ 8am-midnight (1am Fri & Sat) ☎ (0114) 267 3660

Adnams Broadside; Fuller's London Pride; Greene King Abbot; Ruddles Best Bitter; guest beers Ⓗ

Between the Botanical Gardens and the Hallamshire Hospital, this Wetherspoon pub was formerly Broombank House, once the home of Victorian steel magnate Francis Newton, who was Master Cutler in 1844. The open-plan interior is divided into several distinct areas, and the extensive grounds adjoin Lynwood Gardens, a community nature reserve. The pub is popular with families, and food is served all day till 11pm.
Q🐴❀◑◗♿●P🚌(70,120)📶

Greystones 𝕃

Greystones Road, S11 7BS

⏲ 12-11 (11.30 Fri & Sat) ☎ (0114) 266 5599

🌐 mygreystones.co.uk

Thornbridge Wild Swan, Lord Marples, Kipling, Jaipur IPA; guest beers Ⓗ

A spacious yet homely family-friendly pub, serving as the flagship for Thornbridge Brewery. It boasts eight handpulled real ales showcasing the Thornbridge range, including seasonals and specials. The Backroom hosts some of the finest in contemporary live folk/rock/blues and Americana in the country, along with comedy nights and community projects. Hot food is served up daily 12-6pm, along with a range of locally-sourced pies made using Thornbridge beer.
Q🐴❀◑♿♣P🚌(84)🐾📶

Porter Brook 𝕃

565 Ecclesall Road, Sharrow, S11 8PR

⏲ 11 (12 Sun)-11 ☎ (0114) 266 5765

Abbeydale Moonshine; Bradfield Farmers Blonde; Greene King IPA, Abbot; Morland Old Speckled Hen; guest beers Ⓗ

Opened in the 1990s following conversion from a house on the banks of the River Porter, this is still the leading outlet for real ale on Ecclesall Road. Although now owned by Greene King, the 10 handpumps usually feature several local beers in addition to the regulars from Abbeydale and Bradfield. The open-plan interior is comfortably furnished, and the pub attracts a varied clientele, including students from the nearby campus. Meals are served throughout the day to 9pm. ❀◑◗♿🚌📶

Ranmoor Inn 𝕃

330 Fulwood Road, Ranmoor, S10 3GD

⏲ 11.30-11; 12-10.30 Sun ☎ (0114) 230 1325

🌐 ranmoorinnsheffield.co.uk

Bradfield Farmers Bitter, Farmers Blonde; Timothy Taylor Landlord; guest beer Ⓗ

Renovated Victorian local with original etched windows, lying in the shadow of Ranmoor Church. Now open plan, the seating areas reflect the old room layout. A friendly, old-fashioned hostelry, it has a diverse clientele. Q❀◑🚌(120)🐾📶

Rising Sun

471 Fulwood Road, Nether Green, S10 3QA

⏲ 12-11 ☎ (0114) 230 3855

Abbeydale Daily Bread, Brimstone, Moonshine, Absolution; guest beers Ⓗ

Operated by local brewer Abbeydale, this is a large suburban roadhouse in the leafy western side of the city. The two rooms are comfortably furnished, with a raised area to the rear of the main bar. A range of Abbeydale beers is always served, with up to six guests - mainly from micros - dispensed from the impressive bank of 13 handpumps. There is live music on Monday, with quizzes on Sunday and Wednesday. The popular Sunfest beer festival is held every July. Q🐴❀◑◗♣●P🚌(120)🐾📶

University Arms

197 Brook Hill, Broomhall, S3 7HG

⏲ 12-11 (midnight Fri & Sat); closed Sun ☎ (0114) 222 8969

Beer range varies Ⓗ

Owned by the University of Sheffield, this former staff club became a pub in 2007. The open-plan lounge has a bar at one end adjacent to a small alcove seating area, and a conservatory leads to the large garden. Many of the guest beers are local and there are regular beer festivals. Entertainment includes a quiz on Tuesday and live blues or jazz some weekends. No food Saturday evening. Q❀◑⛾♣🚌(51,52)🐾

York 𝕃
243-247 Fulwood Road, Broomhill, S10 3BA
✪ 11.30-11.30 (12.30am Fri & Sat) ☎ (0114) 266 4624
🌐 theyorksheffield.co.uk
Bradfield Farmers Blonde; guest beers Ⓗ
Occupying a prominent site in the centre of Broomhill, the York was built in the 1830s and was originally a blackmith's and alehouse called the Travellers Inn. Extensively refurbished in 2010, with parquet flooring and wood-panelled walls, it now offers high-quality dining, with its own bakery and smokery. The house beer is complemented by a range of up to six, mainly local, guest ales and two real ciders. Beer and food events feature regularly throughout the year. Q❀◑♿●🚌🐾ᯤ

Thorne

Windmill
19 Queen Street, DN8 5AA
✪ 2-11 (11.30 Fri & Sat); 12-midnight Sun ☎ (01405) 812866
Greene King IPA; Timothy Taylor Landlord; guest beers Ⓗ
This friendly community pub close to the town centre comprises a smart cosy lounge linked by an archway to a larger public bar. Up to four well-kept real ales are on offer, with one of the guests usually from York Brewery. Unobtrusive big screens are in evidence but conversation and cheerful banter are the order of the day here. Outside is a large beer garden with play equipment and ample parking. Quiz night is Sunday.
❀⇌(North)♣P🚌(87,88)🐾ᯤ

Thurlstone

Huntsman 𝕃
136 Manchester Road, S36 9QW
✪ 6 (5 Fri & Sat)-11; 12-10.30 Sun ☎ (01226) 764892
🌐 thehuntsmanthurlstone.co.uk
Black Sheep Best Bitter; Tetley Bitter; Timothy Taylor Landlord; guest beers Ⓗ
On the East-West Pennine route (A628), this popular local community pub is a genuine and friendly meeting place, where drinking and talking are the modus operandi in the long and thin oak-beamed main bar area. Old-fashioned pub games, locally-sourced cask ales and a warm welcome for dogs help to make this a hostelry that should not be passed by. There is no jukebox or TV, Wednesday is live music night. Q♨❀🚌

Tickhill

Scarbrough Arms 𝕃
Sunderland Street, DN11 9QJ (on A631 near Buttercross)
✪ 12-11; 12-10.30 Sun ☎ (01302) 742977
Greene King Abbot; John Smith's Bitter; Morland Old Speckled Hen; Timothy Taylor Landlord; guest beer Ⓗ
A deserving Guide entry since 1990, this three-roomed stone-built pub has won several CAMRA awards over the years. Originally a farmhouse, the building dates back to the 16th century, although structural changes have taken place since. The snug is a delight, with its barrel-shaped furniture and real fire, while bar billiards can be played in the bar. An outbuilding doubles as a covered smoking area and an extension for beer festivals held in spring and autumn. Real cider is on in summer. Q♨❀🛏♿♣●P🚌(22,205)🐾ᯤ

Wath upon Dearne

Church House
Montgomery Square, S63 7RZ
✪ 8am-midnight ☎ (01709) 879518
Greene King Abbot; Ruddles Best Bitter; guest beers Ⓗ
Large pub with an impressive frontage set in a pedestrian square in the town centre, with excellent access to local bus services. It was built in 1810, consecrated by the nearby church in 1912, became a pub in the 1980s, and then a Wetherspoon in 2000. Handy for exploring the RSPB Old Moor Wetlands Centre and for Manvers, it serves a wide variety of beers from both national and local brewers. Westons ciders are on handpull.
❀◑♿●P🚌ᯤ

Wentworth

George & Dragon
85 Main Street, S62 7TN (set back from road on B6090)
✪ 10-11 (10.30 Sun) ☎ (01226) 742440
🌐 georgeanddragonwentworth.co.uk
Beer range varies Ⓗ
In a picturesque village, this free house offers up to six ales from local and national brewers. The pub has a car park and patio, and a grassed area at the rear with a children's adventure playground and a craft shop. Home-cooked food is popular here. This local is handy for historic Wentworth Woodhouse and Hoober Stand, and has been licensed since 1804. Q❀◑P🚌(44,227)🐾

Rockingham Arms
8 Main Street, S62 7TL
✪ 11-11; 12-10.30 Sun ☎ (01226) 742075
Beer range varies Ⓗ
Country pub situated in the grounds of the Wentworth estate near the Wentworth Brewery. An ideal stop-off point for walkers, the pub offers accommodation, local entertainment and a range of home-cooked meals. A crown green bowling green is attached. The pub is welcoming, warmed by real fires in winter and with a patio and garden for summer drinking. ♨❀🛏◑P🚌(227)🐾

Whiston

Chequers Inn
Pleasley Road, S60 4HB (on A618, 1½ miles from M1 jct 33)
✪ 12 (4 Mon & Tue)-11; 12-11.30 Fri & Sat
☎ (01709) 829168
Jennings Cumberland Ale; Tetley Bitter Ⓗ
Next to a 13th-century thatched barn, this friendly local replaced an old coaching inn when the road was widened in 1933. One side of the bar acts as a taproom, with a split-level lounge to the right. The large garden features a barbecue area. Situated in the heart of Whiston, the pub is a regular local CAMRA award winner. The food is home-cooked by chefs. Features include quiz nights, discos, regular live music and scooter club meets. ❀◑♿♣P🚌

Hind
285 East Bawtry Road, S60 4ET (on A631 link road between M1 and M18)

⏲ 12-11 (midnight Thu-Sat) ☎ (01709) 704351
Tetley Bitter; Timothy Taylor Landlord; guest beers Ⓗ
Large pub, built for Mappins Brewery of Rotherham in 1936. Originally known as King Edward VIII, it was renamed when the king abdicated. Since refurbishment by Ember Inns, the interior has been opened out, creating good disabled access. There are extensive gardens and a patio to the rear, with a snooker table upstairs (membership required to play). Daytime, evening and, now, takeaway food, is popular, and third-of-a-pint tasting racks are available. CAMRA members get 20p a pint discount – show your membership card. Q❀◑◐♿P🚌

Wickersley

Wickersley Old Village Cricket Club

Northfield Lane, S66 2HL
⏲ 5-10 (11 Wed, Fri & Sat); 12-10 Sun ☎ (01709) 700536
Beer range varies Ⓗ
Since the club started selling Chantry Brewery ales, demand for real ale has increased and there are now three handpumps on the go in this comfortably appointed and friendly venue. The large lounge offers a more peaceful location for a quality beer than the nearby pubs. CAMRA members are more than welcome for a good-value and well-kept pint, and of course you could always watch the cricket. ❀♣P🚌

Wombwell

Anglers Rest 𝕃

66 Park Street, S73 0HS
⏲ 5-midnight; 12-1am Sat; 12-midnight Sun
☎ (01226) 345747 🌐 anglersrestwombwell.co.uk
Geeves No.1, Gunwale Dance; guest beers Ⓗ
Situated on the edge of the town centre, close to the shopping area, this popular local is the brewery tap for Barnsley's Geeves Brewery. It is a multi-roomed local with separate TV, meeting and games rooms. The covered outside seating area has a wood-burning stove for winter nights but is a sun-worshippers' paradise in the warmer months. Guest beers come from other local breweries. The pub hosts a popular quiz night on a Tuesday. Q❀⇌●P▯🚌

Woodsetts

Butchers Arms

2 Gildingswell Road, S81 8QA
⏲ 12-11 (midnight Fri & Sat) ☎ (01909) 567700
Courage Best Bitter; guest beers Ⓗ
A joint venture between Raw Pub Co and Enterprise, the Butchers had a complete refurbishment in a contemporary style and reopened in 2013. Raw ales are prominently featured alongside the guest beers, and there is an interesting range of foreign specialist small batch bottled beers to try. Quality home-cooked food is another major attraction at this friendly community pub. Beer festivals and live music are also on the menu. Q❀◑◐P🚌📶

Wortley

Wortley Men's Club 𝕃

Reading Room Lane, S35 7DB (at back of Wortley Arms public house)
⏲ 2 (12 Sat & Sun)-11 ☎ (0114) 288 2066
Timothy Taylor Landlord; guest beers Ⓗ
In the heart of this pretty village, surrounded by open countryside, the outside of the building is impressive, with traditional timber framing and a small beer garden. The opulent interior has ornate ceilings, a small bar area, a plush lounge and a large games room. The guest ale comes from a local brewery and a guest draught cider is always kept. Show your CAMRA membership card or a copy of this Guide on entry. CAMRA branch Club of the Year 2013. Q❀●P🚌(23,29)

YORKSHIRE (WEST)

Addingham

Swan Inn 𝕃

106 Main Street, LS29 0NS
⏲ 5.30-11; 12-midnight Sat; 12-10.30 Sun
☎ (01943) 831999 🌐 swan-addingham.co.uk
Ilkley Mary Jane, Black; Timothy Taylor Golden Best; guest beers Ⓗ
This friendly village local retains a four-room layout arranged around a small central bar. The stone-flagged bar, snug and taproom are all warmed by real fires in winter. Live bands perform on Saturday evenings, folk and acoustic nights are hosted monthly and there is a quiz each Wednesday. Food is served Wednesday, Friday and Saturday evenings, and Saturday and Sunday lunchtimes. Guest beers come from the SIBA and Enterprise lists. Well-behaved dogs are welcome.
♨❀◑◐♣P🚌🐾

Alverthorpe

Alverthorpe Working Men's Club 𝕃

111 Flanshaw Lane, WF2 9JG (on road from Alverthorpe to Flanshaw)
⏲ 2-11; 11.30-11 Fri & Sat; 12-11 Sun ☎ (01924) 374179
Bob's White Lion; Tetley Bitter; guest beers Ⓗ
Multi-roomed working men's club with a cosy interior and unusual stained glass features. A wide selection of guest ales is featured, mainly from local micros. The club is a regular winner of local CAMRA awards. Live entertainment takes place on Saturday and Sunday. Snooker and darts are among the traditional games, with wide-screen TV for the armchair enthusiasts. The club is home to sporting teams and there is a floodlit bowling green.
♨❀♿♣P🚌(103,114)

Baildon

Bull's Head Inn 𝕃

6 Westgate, BD17 5ES
⏲ 12-11.30 (midnight Fri & Sat) ☎ (01274) 976416
Saltaire Blonde; Sharp's Doom Bar; Tetley Bitter; guest beers Ⓗ
Two-roomed establishment with log fires and a warming atmosphere. Although it is very much a locals' pub, visitors are always welcome. There are up to three regularly available real ales and three guests. Pictures of the local area in olden days adorn the walls. There is a quiz on Tuesday nights. Occasional music nights are held and piped background music is often played. The pub is very welcoming to dogs. ❀♣P🚌🐾📶

Junction 𝕃

1 Baildon Road, BD17 6AB (on A6038)
⏲ 12-midnight (1am Fri & Sat) ☎ (01274) 582009

WEST YORKSHIRE

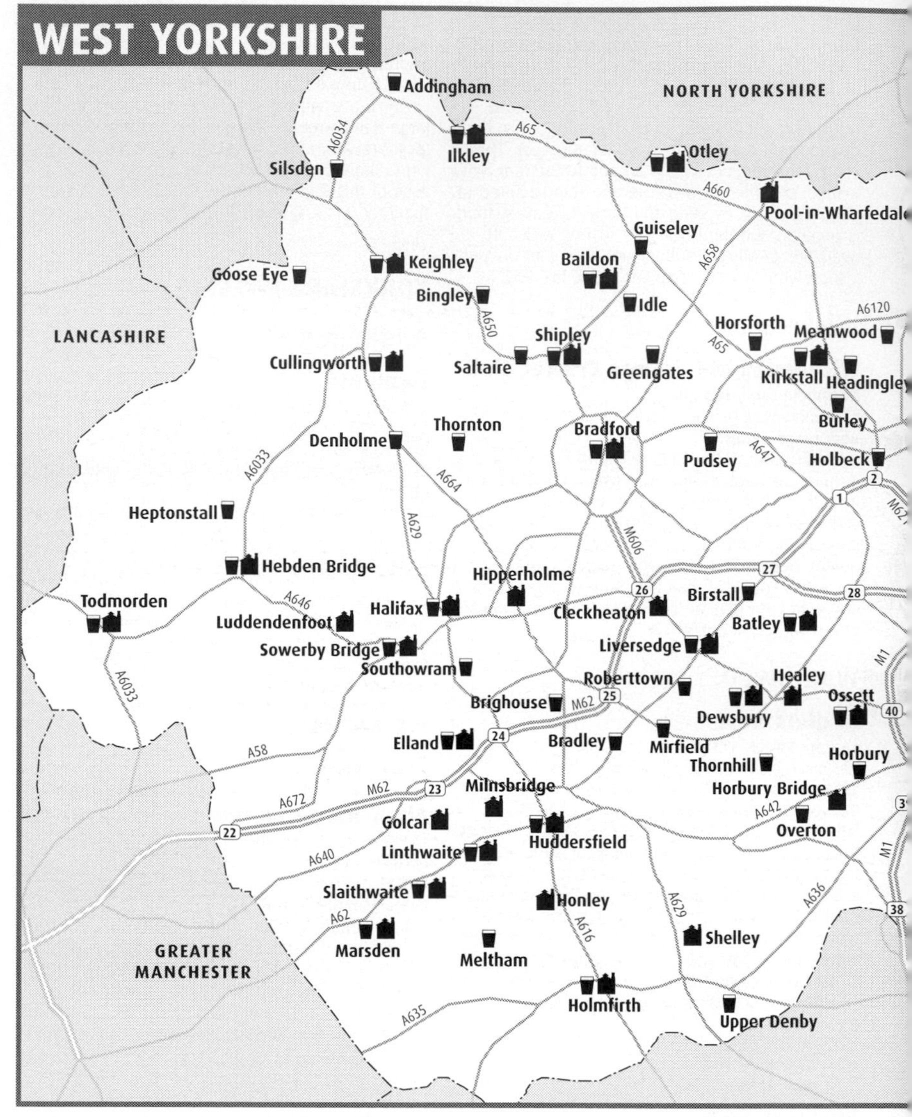

Fuller's ESB; Oakham JHB; Saltaire Blonde; Tetley Bitter; guest beers H

A popular three-roomed local comprising a lounge, public bar and a games area. The four regularly available beers are complemented by three guest ales. Beers from the in-house Junction Brewery usually feature. Real cider and foreign bottled beers are also sold. Food is served weekday lunchtimes and other times by arrangement. A quiz night is held on Thursdays, a jamming session on Sunday nights, and pub games on other evenings. A regular beer festival features at the end of July. ❀◐♣●🚌🐾

Batley

Taproom

4 Commercial Street, WF17 5HH

⏲ 4-11; 2-midnight Fri; 12-midnight Sat & Sun

☎ (01924) 440539 🌐 taproombatley.com

Ossett Yorkshire Blonde; Theakston Old Peculier; guest beers H

Vibrant town-centre pub and popular live music venue. It has two rooms – local bands and musicians perform in the room on the left every Friday and Saturday night (entry is free). Quiz night is Wednesday. Barstow's Snug function room can be hired for parties and events. Real ales include four rotating guests, with at least one dark, golden and light ale usually available. A 20p per pint discount is offered to CAMRA members. There is also a fine wine list. ❀⇌●P🚌(212,281)🐾 ᯤ

Bingley

Foundry Hill L

Wellington Street, BD16 2NB (opp railway station)

⏲ closed Mon & Tue; 12-midnight; 12-9 Sun

☎ (01274) 566144 🌐 foundryhillbar.co.uk

Beer range varies H

Modern basement venue comprising a small bar area and an adjacent larger lounge. A varying range of real ales ales is sold, often from local breweries as well as from further afield. A cider is also usually available. Good home-made food is freshly cooked to order. The pub can get quite busy, especially at weekends. The whole of the pub, or part of it, can be hired for functions. A mobile bar and outside catering are also offered.

Off the Tap

Burrage Street, off Chapel Lane, BD16 1GH (close to railway station)
closed Mon; 12 (4 Tue)-11.30; 2-11.30 Sun ☎ 07960 995267 offthetap.co.uk
Beer range varies H/G
A single-room café-style pub offering up to six real ales, with the majority served direct from the cask. A range of beer styles and ales from local breweries are featured. At least one real cider and perry are also sold, as are bottled beers and wines. Live bands often play and there are regular open mic nights mid-week. The pub is closed on Mondays (except bank holidays) and is usually closed for the first few weeks in January.

Birstall

Horse & Jockey

97 Low Lane, WF17 9HB (on A643 near village centre)
12 (4 Wed)-midnight; 12-1am Fri & Sat ☎ (01924) 472559
John Smith's Bitter; Ossett Silver King; guest beers H
A country-style pub first licensed in the 1750s, which lies west of the village centre. The open-plan bar is divided into four areas, with half-panelled walls and beamed ceilings. Photos show it was once a Kirkstall Brewery house. Darts, dominoes and pool are played, on Thursdays there is a music and knowledge quiz, and on Saturdays karaoke. Sandwiches and burgers are served. Guest beers come from independent breweries. Outside is a paved drinking and smoking patio. Pub policy says no hats, no tracksuit bottoms. A 20p per pint CAMRA discount is offered. ♣P(220,283)

Bradford

Castle

20 Grattan Road, BD1 2LU
12 (1 Sun)-11 ☎ (01274) 393166
castle-hotel-bradford.co.uk
Jennings Cumberland Ale; guest beers H
On the edge of the city centre, this imposing stone pub, built in 1898, comprises a large open-plan room with a wraparound bar to one side. Formerly a Webster's house, it now sells a variety of beers in a relaxing atmosphere. It often stocks at least one ale from a local brewery. Good city-centre accommodation is available. There is a dartboard and TV to one end of the room, and live folk music is hosted on a Friday night.
(Forster Square)♣

Corn Dolly

110 Bolton Road, BD1 4DE
11.30-11; 12-10.30 Sun ☎ (01274) 720219
Everards Tiger; Moorhouse's Pride of Pendle, Blond Witch; guest beers H
Multi-award-winning pub that is a short distance from the city centre and Forster Square railway station. Previously called the Wharf due to its location near the former Bradford canal, it first opened its doors in 1834. An open-plan layout incorporates a games area to one end. Good-value food is served weekday lunchtimes. It has a friendly atmosphere and is popular before Bradford City matches. A collection of pumpclips adorns the beams. (Forster Square)♣P

Fighting Cock

23 Preston Street, Listerhills, BD7 1JE (close to Grattans, off Thornton Rd)
11.30-11; 12-10.30 Sun ☎ (01274) 726907
Copper Dragon Golden Pippin; Greene King Abbot; Theakston Old Peculier; Timothy Taylor Boltmaker, Landlord; guest beers H
A drinkers' paradise in an industrial area, this award-winning pub is 20 minutes' walk from the city centre and close to the bus routes along Thornton Road. It is a popular, unpretentious pub

that appeals to a wide variety of people, from loyal locals to well-travelled real ale enthusiasts. Twelve real ales are usually on sale, including at least one dark beer. Real ciders, foreign bottled beers and fruit wines are also stocked. Good-value lunches are served Monday to Saturday. ◐♣●🚌

Haigy's 𝕃

31 Lumb Lane, Manningham, BD8 7QU

5-1am (2am Sat); 2-10.30 Sun ☎ (01274) 731644

Tetley Mild, Bitter; guest beers Ⓗ

Friendly locals' pub on the edge of the city centre. The guest ales are often of the blonde and golden variety, and mainly from local microbreweries. A fine collection of porcelain teapots and an extensive range of pictures is on display in the comfortable lounge. There is a heated smoking area to the rear and a large-screen TV for sport. On Saturdays, when Bradford City football club are playing at home, the pub opens at midday. ❀⇌(Forster Square)♣P🚌(620,621)🐾

Jacobs Beer House 𝕃

14 Kent Street, BD1 5RL

closed Sun & Mon; 12-11 (midnight Fri & Sat) ☎ (01274) 394479

Saltaire Blonde; guest beers Ⓗ

Refurbished and reopened in 2013, this historic pub was formerly known as Jacobs Well, and is the only building, dating from about 1830, on what is left of Kent Street. It comprises a single open-plan room but with a rustic, multi-room feel. Nine handpulls offer a varying range and style of real ales. Real cider and bottled beers are also sold. The nearby council office car park can be used at nights and weekends. ❀⇌(Interchange)●🚌🐾

Monkey 𝕃

931 Great Horton Road, Great Horton, BD7 4AQ

3-midnight (1am Fri); 1-1am Sat; 1-midnight Sun ☎ 07957 856180

Beer range varies Ⓗ

Located between Bradford and Queensbury, this free house was originally two 17th-century cottages and comprises a lounge and games room. There are real fires during colder periods. The real ales are from the nearby Junction Brewery plus other local microbreweries. Bottled, imported beers are also stocked. One of the outdoor areas has a barbecue and a covered, seated smoking area. The other is elevated and offers magnificent views over and beyond Bradford. The pool table, jukebox and Wi-Fi are all free. ❀♣🚌🐾

New Beehive Inn ★ 𝕃

171 Westgate, BD1 3AA (on B6144)

1-11 (1am Fri & Sat); 6-11 Sun ☎ (01274) 721784

Beer range varies Ⓗ

Multi-roomed, Edwardian, gas-lit free house, built in 1901 and remodelled by William Whitaker & Co in 1936. It has been identified by CAMRA as having a nationally important historic pub interior. The interior comprises a drinking hallway and three rooms with wood panelling. The front room still has fittings from the original construction. Beers are almost exclusively from local microbreweries. Open mic nights and monthly acoustic sessions take place. Look at the impressive paintings in the back bar and spot the celebrities. ❀◐◑⇌(Forster Square)♣●P🚌🐾

Sir Titus Salt 𝕃

Unit B, Windsor Baths, Morley Street, BD7 1AQ (behind Alhambra theatre)

9am-midnight (1am Fri & Sat) ☎ (01274) 732853

Greene King Abbot; Ruddles Best Bitter; guest beers Ⓗ

Excellent conversion of a former public baths by Wetherspoon, consisting of a large open-plan main room with an additional room to one side and an upper mezzanine area. Ten handpumps serve a

INDEPENDENT BREWERIES

Baildon Baildon (NEW)
Barearts Todmorden
Barge & Barrel Elland
Ben Rhydding Ilkley (NEW)
Bob's Healey
Bosun's Horbury Bridge (NEW)
Bridestones Hebden Bridge
Bridgehouse Keighley
Briscoe's Otley
Burley Street Leeds
Cap House Batley
Clark's Wakefield
Collingham Collingham
Elland Elland
Empire Slaithwaite
Fernandes Wakefield
Five Towns Wakefield
Golcar Golcar
Goose Eye Keighley
Halifax Steam Hipperholme
Hamelsworde Hemsworth
Hand Drawn Monkey Huddersfield
Haworth Steam Cleckheaton
Ilkley Ilkley
James & Kirkman Pontefract
Junction Baildon
Kirkstall Leeds: Kirkstall
Landlord's Friend Luddendenfoot
Leeds Leeds
Linfit Linthwaite
Little Valley Hebden Bridge
Magic Rock Huddersfield
Mallinson's Huddersfield
Milltown Milnsbridge
New Inn Liversedge
Nook Holmfirth
Oates Halifax
Old Spot Cullingworth
Ossett Ossett
Owenshaw Mills Sowerby Bridge
Partners Dewsbury
Rat Huddersfield
Revolutions Whitwood
Ridgeside Leeds
Riverhead Marsden
Salamander Bradford
Saltaire Shipley
Slightly Foxed Sowerby Bridge
Small World Shelley (NEW)
Sportsman Huddersfield
Stod Fold Halifax (NEW)
Summer Wine Honley
Sunbeam Leeds
Tapped Leeds (NEW)
Thirstin Honley (NEW)
Tigertops Wakefield
Timothy Taylor Keighley
Wharfe Bank Pool-in-Wharfedale
Wharfedale Ilkley

variety of real ales. Named in honour of a local industrial philanthropist, the interior decoration includes photographs and other artefacts relating to his life. Located within Bradford's cultural quarter, the National Media Museum and Alhambra theatre are nearby. Many of the city's famous curry houses are also close by.
Q(Interchange)

Sparrow Bier Café

32 North Parade, BD1 3HZ
11-11 (midnight Thu-Sat); 12-11 Sun (01274) 270772
thesparrowbradford.co.uk
Beer range varies H
Opened in 2011 by local enthusiasts, this simply furnished café-style pub was the local CAMRA branch's Pub of the Year 2012. It has a main bar area with additional seating in the basement. Four varying cask ales cover a range of styles and strengths. Craft ales and imported Pilsners are available on draught, and at least two real ciders. The pub does not do meals but deli sandwiches and platters are provided.
(Forster Square)

Bradley

White Cross

2 Bradley Road, HD2 1XD (on A62, 3 miles from Huddersfield centre, at Leeds Rd/Bradley Rd crossroads)
11.45-11 (midnight Fri & Sat); 12-10.30 Sun
(01484) 425728
John Smith's Bitter; Thwaites Wainwright; guest beers H
Standing at a busy crossroads and close to the canal, this award-winning local has featured for over 10 years in the Guide. Its historic roots date from 1806 and the pub still retains its Bentley's Yorkshire Breweries green tiled entrance and windows. The dining area and lounge sit either side of the central bar, where two regular beers are supported by up to four varied guests. Home-cooked food is served lunchtimes (but not Sat). A beer festival is held each February. P

Brighouse

Red Rooster

123 Elland Road, Brookfoot, HD6 2QR (on A6025 towards Elland)
4-11; 12-midnight Fri & Sat; 12-10.30 Sun
(01484) 713737
Abbeydale Moonshine; Moorhouse's Blond Witch; Saltaire Blonde; Timothy Taylor Boltmaker, Landlord; guest beers H
Half a mile from Brighouse town centre, it is well worth the walk to this excellent free house. Formerly known as The Wharf, the Rooster was purpose-built around 1900 for the adjacent coal wharf which served much of western Yorkshire. Three wharfmen's cottages still stand alongside the pub by the red beck. About 400 yards further on is the Cromwell Bottom nature reserve, from where you can walk along the canal to Elland or Brighouse. Dark beers are always on tap.
P(571,E7)

Richard Oastler

Bethell Street, HD6 1JN
8am-midnight (01484) 401756
Greene King Abbot; Ruddles Best Bitter; guest beers H
A Grade II-listed former Methodist chapel converted to a successful Wetherspoon pub. It has a magnificent but inaccessible upper floor with original chapel pews, and the impressive ceiling has been retained. Eight guest ales are served, always including a dark beer, and local microbreweries are regularly featured. Two traditional ciders from the Westons range are also on the bar. The usual good-value Wetherspoon food menu is available all day.

Castleford

Glass Blower

15 Bank Street, WF10 1JD (rear also accessible from Aire St car parks off road by Allinson flour mill)
8am-midnight (1am Fri & Sat) (01977) 520390
Greene King Abbot; Ruddles Best Bitter; guest beers H
Characterful former post office converted by Wetherspoon. Four guest beers are available, usually including one dark and one special from microbrewers. The name refers to the town's history of glass bottle making, with some examples on display. Locally born sculptor Henry Moore is represented via reproductions adorning the walls. It is a popular venue for families and rugby fans on match days. Regular Meet the Brewer events and brewery visits are arranged. Children are welcome in the family area.
P

Junction

Carlton Street, WF10 1EE (enter Castleford on A655; pub is on corner with Carlton St at top of town centre)
2-8.30 (11 Wed & Thu); 12-11 Fri-Sun (01977) 278867
thejunctionpubcastleford.com
Beer range varies H
Rejuvenated pub handy for bus and train stations and specialising in beers from the wood. Regular Ridgeside and up to five guest beers are served, mostly drawn from the pub's own wooden casks which are loaned to enterprising local brewers including Elland and Walls. It has an annual Easter Wood Beer Festival. The large horseshoe-shaped bar is kept warm with open fires; a stove-heated snug is available for functions. Folk night is on the last Sunday of each month, and quiz night is Wednesday. Q

Cullingworth

George Hotel

Station Road, BD13 5HN
12-11 (midnight Fri & Sat) (01535) 275566
thegeorgecullingworth.co.uk
Old Spot Light But Dark, Spot Light, Inn-Spired, OSB, Spot o' Bother; guest beers H
Rescued from oblivion in 2011 by local brewery owners, this lovely old-fashioned village pub has a pleasant setting near the church. The emphasis is primarily on food although there is also a pleasant drinking area. Substantial meals are available from the extensive and imaginative menu, and meal deals are offered Mondays and Wednesdays from 5pm. It is the tap for Old Spot Brewery, and a large range of its beers is sold as well as guest ales. Children are welcome until 9pm. P

Darrington

Spread Eagle

Estcourt Road, WF8 3AP (in centre of village on road linking A1 Darrington exit with Pontefract)
12-3 (not Mon), 5-11; 12-3, 5-midnight Sat; 12-10.30 Sun
(01977) 699698
Copper Dragon Golden Pippin; guest beers H
Friendly and welcoming community pub in the heart of the village. Two guest ales, usually from Yorkshire breweries, complement the regular beer. Good-quality food is served both in the bar and in a small dining area (no food Sun eve or all day Mon). Monday is quiz night. There is a pleasant function room for hire and a patio outside. It is said that there have been sightings here of the ghost of a boy who was shot for horse rustling in 1685. QP (408,409)

Denholme

New Inn L

Denholme Gate, BD13 4JT (on A629)
5 (2 Sat & Sun)-11 (01274) 833871
Tetley Bitter; guest beers H
Friendly locals' pub alongside the Keighley to Halifax road. It supports local microbreweries as well as offering guest ales from further afield. All beers are keenly priced. The premises have an open-plan layout but still retain a multi-room feel. The conservatory houses a pool table and matches are played on Monday nights. Tuesday nights host a jam session. The pub sits high on the hillside with stunning views. For the energetic, the Great Northern walking/cycling trail is nearby.
P

Dewsbury

Leggers L

Calder Valley Marina, Mill Street East, WF12 9BD (off B6409, follow brown signs to canal basin)
10.30-11 (midnight Fri & Sat); 11-10.30 Sun
(01924) 502846
Abbeydale Moonshine; Everards Tiger; guest beers H
Once the hayloft above stables by the canal basin, the low beams here, a powerful stove, deep seating and quirky items on display make for a unique atmosphere. Six beers listed on the school blackboard include ale from Rooster's and Moorhouse's, plus a real cider. Outside, a large decked area is excellent in summer. Light meals are served all day until 8pm and there is a pool table and a function room. Bus and rail stations are just within a mile. P

West Riding Refreshment Rooms L

Dewsbury Railway Station, Wellington Road, WF13 1HF
12-11 Mon; 11-11 (midnight Thu & Fri); 10-midnight Sat
(01924) 459193 imissedthetrain.com
Black Sheep Best Bitter; Timothy Taylor Landlord; guest beers H
In a listed railway station building, the West has been in the Guide since opening more than 20 years ago, and has been local CAMRA Pub of the Year numerous times. Eight handpumps offer an excellent range of guest beers including some from its own Sportsman Brewery. Two real ciders and a perry are also available plus a range of speciality bottled beers. Live music plays in summer in the decked beer garden. Good-value lunches are served daily, with early evening meals from Tuesday to Thursday. P

Elland

Barge & Barrel

10-20 Park Road, HX5 9HP (on A6025 NE of town centre)
12-11.30 (01422) 371770
Abbeydale Moonshine; Black Sheep Best Bitter; Milltown Platinum Blonde; Phoenix Wobbly Bob; Timothy Taylor Landlord; guest beers H
A large roadside pub built to serve the former Elland station. A three-sided bar serves the comfortable lounge, with views over the canal and river to Elland town. Opposite, a games area and a snug with an open fire are separated from the bar by partitions of modern stained glass. Guest beers are mainly from microbreweries. The in-house brewery reopened in 2013, with three main beers. The smoking shelter is heated. Thursday is quiz night. QP

Drop Inn

12 Elland Lane, HX5 9DU (off link road from A629 to town centre)
4-11; 12-midnight Fri & Sat; 12-11 Sun (01422) 387484
Ossett Pale Gold, Yorkshire Blonde, Silver King; guest beers H
Stone flags and floorboards, and a brick arch between rooms, are typical of the Ossett Brewery pub style. French Renaissance pictures add to the decor along with cigar containers, stone jars and tankards. A stove occupies a large cottage fireplace in the side room. A quiz is held every Thursday. Seven beers in total are served, with four guest beers from Fuller's, other Ossett group breweries and microbreweries. Outside is a heated smoking shelter. Q (278,503)

Goose Eye

Turkey Inn L

BD22 0PD
12-11 (midnight Fri & Sat) (01535) 681339
theturkeyinn.com
Goose Eye Bitter, Chinook Blonde; Timothy Taylor Golden Best, Landlord; guest beers H
Friendly historic pub in a tiny hamlet approached by steep roads or a riverside footpath. It has three snugs, each with a real fire to keep out the winter chill, and is a good base for exploring the surrounding countryside. The stained glass windows facing the road date from when it was an Aaron King pub. It has a pool table, holds a quiz night on Wednesdays, and hosts occasional live music. Food is served all day. Two guest beers are usually served, one from Goose Eye.
P

Greengates

Albion

25 New Line, BD10 9AS
12-11 (01274) 613211
Acorn Barnsley Bitter; Tetley Bitter; guest beers H
Comfortable, traditional, neighbourhood pub with an L-shaped lounge and a separate public bar where pub games can be played. Previously pubco-owned, this establishment became a free house in 2014. Consistently good beer and real cider are

served here by dedicated staff. The venue is popular with the local community and is home to a thriving social club. The pub is alongside the main Leeds-Keighley (A657) road and served by a regular bus service. ♣♦P⊡🚌(760)

Guiseley

Coopers 𝕃

4-6 Otley Road, LS20 8AH

12-11 (midnight Fri & Sat) ☎ (01943) 878835

Okells Manx Pale Ale; Rooster's Wild Mule; Timothy Taylor Landlord; guest beers Ⓗ

Light, modern, airy bar/diner converted from a former Co-operative store and extended in 2014. Eight ales are served, generally from Yorkshire or northern micros, with a dedicated dark beer pump and a large selection of continental bottled beers. A diverse range of meals is available until 9pm. The outdoor drinking area is a raised veranda. The large upstairs function room hosts regular music events and a monthly comedy club, and also serves as extra dining space. Q❀◑♿⇌♦🚌🐾📶

Guiseley Factory Workers Club 𝕃

6 Town Street, LS20 9DT

1-11 (midnight Fri); 11.30-midnight Sat; 11-11 Sun ☎ (01943) 874793 🌐 guiseleyfactoryworkersclub.co.uk

Tetley Bitter; guest beers Ⓗ

This friendly club was founded over 100 years ago by the Yeadon and Guiseley Factory Workers Union. It serves three rapidly changing guest ales from micros and independents from anywhere in the UK, usually including a dark beer. The interior is three-roomed, with a small lounge, concert room and snooker room. The venue hosts many other local clubs and organisations. An annual beer festival is held in April. CAMRA members are welcome with this Guide or a membership card. ❀⇌♣P🚌🐾📶

Halifax

Barum Top 𝕃

17 Rawson Street, HX1 1NX

8am-midnight (1am Fri & Sat) ☎ (01422) 300488

Greene King Abbot; Marston's Pedigree; Ruddles Best Bitter; guest beers Ⓗ

A popular Wetherspoon pub in the heart of Halifax. Formerly a garage, it is in the area once known as Barum Top, so named from the Yorkshire word bouram, meaning a natural watercourse. Before the advent of purpose-built drainage systems, this watercourse descended from Barum Top into Hebble Brook. This is a large, open pub with an upper balcony and a separate area for food or families. Food is served daily until 10pm, with breakfast 8am-noon. ☕◑♿⇌♦🚌📶

Big Six

10 Horsfall Street, King Cross, HX1 3HG (off A646 Skircoat Moor road at King Cross)

4 (3.30 Fri)-11; 12-midnight Sat & Sun ☎ (01422) 350169 🌐 thebig6inn.co.uk

Old Mill Traditional Bitter; guest beers Ⓗ

A hidden gem in a row of terraces, next to the Free School Lane recreation ground, with a rear beer garden. The emphasis at this friendly venue is on good beer and conversation. A through corridor separates the bar and games room from the two lounges. The pub's name derives from the mineral water company that operated here a century ago, whose memorabilia adorn the walls. Four rotating beers from regional or microbreweries are served, plus a house beer. The weekly quiz is hosted on a Monday evening. Q❀♣♦🚌(577,832)🐾

Cock o' the North

The Conclave, South Edge Works, Hipperholme, HX3 8EF (on A644)

5 (4 Fri)-11; 12-11 Sat & Sun ☎ 07974 544980

🌐 halifax-steam.co.uk

Halifax Steam Aussie Kiss, Jamaican Ginger, Uncle Jon, Cock o' the North; guest beers Ⓗ

The bar has recently taken over the entire sectional building, the brewery having been moved into a unit in the adjoining red-brick Vulcan works. Despite being slightly over-chilled, the 10 handpulls showcase Halifax Steam beers. The atmosphere is relaxed, with a friendly, varied clientele. Five rotating ciders are available. Wednesday is quiz night and live acoustic music plays from 4pm on the first Sunday of the month. Q❀⋀P🚌(548,549)

Cross Keys 🏆

3 Whitegate, Siddal, HX3 9AE

3 (12 Fri-Sun)-11 ☎ (01422) 300348

Beer range varies Ⓗ

After it was run down in the hands of a pub company, this pub reopened with new owners as a true free house at the end of 2012. The cosy, three-roomed interior with a real fire is set around a 17th-century core. Ten handpulls serve nine beers from microbreweries, always including a dark beer, and a changing real cider. The pub offers pork pies, darts, dominoes and a bull ring, plus live music on Sunday afternoons. Walkers and cyclists are welcome, and two letting rooms are available. ❀🛏♣P🚌(542,555)🐾📶

Dirty Dick's Food & Ale Emporium 𝕃

1 Clare Road, HX1 2HX

12-11 ☎ 07887 510354

Empire Dirty Dick's Ale; guest beers Ⓗ

Impressive Grade II-listed building constructed in 1931 from timbers from HMS Newcastle. The interior comprises three discernible areas: a main bar, semi-divided into two, and a separate side room. There is also a large function room upstairs. Generally there are nine real ales available, eight from a changing range from microbreweries, and the pub's own-branded Dirty Dick's. Located close to the theatre quarter, this is an ideal place for pre-show drinks. Q◐⇌♦P🚌

Golden Fleece

1 Bradshaw Lane, Bradshaw, HX2 9UZ

4 (12 Sat)-midnight; 12-10.30 Sun ☎ 07522 190990

Saltaire Blonde; guest beers Ⓗ

Situated at the heart of Bradshaw, this busy village pub provides the focus for a variety of sports enthusiasts including pool teams, Sunday footballers and a Sky TV dominoes team. Popular with quiz teams two nights a week, there is also a Saturday disco night, as well as 1960s and '70s theme nights. Barbecues feature in the summer to take advantage of the beer garden which enjoys excellent views across nearby countryside. ❀♿♣P🚌📶

Sportsman Inn

Bradford Old Road, Swalesmoor, HX3 6UG (off A647, 1 mile N of centre)

12-2.30 (not Mon), 6-11; 12-2.30, 6-midnight Fri; 12-midnight Sat; 12-11 Sun ☎ (01422) 367000
sportsmaninnandleisure.co.uk
Copper Dragon Golden Pippin; guest beers H
This countryside pub with stunning views is a popular stop-off point for walkers. Guest beers are from microbreweries near and far, and two-pint containers are available for takeaways. A quiz night is staged every Friday. There is an adjoining dry ski slope and children's adventure play centre, and free room hire for events. Q (576)

Three Pigeons ★
1 Sun Fold, HX1 2LX
4 (12 Fri-Sun)-11.30 ☎ (01422) 347001
Ossett Pale Gold, Big Red Bitter, Excelsior; guest beers H
A striking octagonal drinking lobby forms the hub from which several distinctive rooms radiate in this Art Deco pub built in 1932 by Webster's Brewery. Sensitively refurbished and maintained by Ossett Brewery, the Three Pigeons attracts a variety of local groups and societies, together with football and Rugby League enthusiasts. Up to five guest beers come from local and regional microbrewers, Fuller's, and from Ossett's own stable of pub-based microbreweries.

Travellers Inn
53 Tanhouse Hill, Hipperholme, HX3 8HN
12-midnight (11 Mon; 11.30 Tue & Wed); 12-11 Sun ☎ (01422) 202494
Ossett Pale Gold, Silver King, Premium Yorkshire Blonde, Excelsior; guest beers H
Opposite the former railway station, this traditional, 18th-century, stone-built local has taken in adjoining cottages to create a series of distinct spaces. Well-behaved children and dogs on leads are welcome until 7pm. A covered yard with heating is provided for smokers. Monthly curry nights and special events are arranged. Four guest beers are from Ossett group breweries, and microbreweries, and always include a dark brew.

Heath

King's Arms ★ L
Heath Common, WF1 5SL (at edge of Heath village on common, off A655 Wakefield-Normanton road)
12-11 (midnight Fri & Sat) ☎ (01924) 377527
thekingsarmsheath.co.uk
Ossett Yorkshire Blonde, Silver King; Tetley Bitter; guest beers H
This hostelry, acquired by Clark's Brewery in 1989, is now leased to Ossett Brewery. Built in the early 1700s and converted into a public house in 1841, it has three oak-panelled rooms with gas lighting, plus a conservatory and gardens to the rear. In the summer months you can sit outside and relax peacefully amid the acres of common grassland surrounding the area. A quiz is staged on Tuesdays. Time may be called earlier on quiet evenings.
QP (188)

Hebden Bridge

Hinchliffe Arms
Church Lane, Cragg Vale, HX7 5TA (300yds down hill off B6138, 2 miles S of Mytholmroyd) SD999232
closed Mon; 12-3 (not Tue), 5-11; 4.30-11 Fri; 12-11 Sat; 12-9 Sun ☎ (01422) 883256
hinchliffearmscraggvale.co.uk
Beer range varies H
Elegant country house-style pub and restaurant in an idyllic riverside setting in a beautiful, deep wooded valley. A magnet for walkers, cyclists and day trippers, as well as locals, the pub is noted not only for fine dining but also for the changing range of beers on its four handpumps. These are often from breweries rarely seen in Yorkshire, such as Bespoke and Derventio. Dogs are welcome in the bar. Reservation for dining is advisable, essential at weekends. QP (900,901)

Old Gate Bar & Restaurant
1-5 Old Gate, HX7 8JP
10-midnight (11 Sun) ☎ (01422) 843993
oldgatehebden.co.uk
Magic Rock Ringmaster; Moorhouse's Pride of Pendle; guest beers H
Smart, modern, town-centre bar and restaurant spread over two floors. The impressively long copper-topped downstairs bar has nine handpumps serving guest beers and a rotating cider, as well as the two regular ales. The guest beers are from a wide variety of independents up and down the country, with Yorkshire and Midlands microbreweries featuring regularly. A range of foreign bottle beers is stocked, and good-quality food is served all day.

Robin Hood
Cragg Road, Cragg Vale, HX7 5SQ (on B6138 1½ miles S of Mytholmroyd)
3 (12 Fri-Sun)-midnight ☎ (01422) 885899
Timothy Taylor Golden Best, Landlord; guest beers H
Friendly two-roomed split-level local in a beautiful wooded valley popular with walkers and cyclists. On entering, the cosy bar, with a real fire in winter, is to the right, while the larger dining room is to the left. The pub has a strong community feel and several local organisations meet here. The two guest beers are usually from Yorkshire microbreweries such as Abbeydale and Bob's. A Westons cider is normally available. Food is served Friday to Sunday. Q (900,901)

Heptonstall

White Lion
58 Towngate, HX7 7NB
12-midnight ☎ (01422) 842027
Thwaites Wainwright; guest beers H
Friendly local in the cobbled main street of a historic conservation village. The single bar serves two distinct drinking areas – the smaller one, on the left as you enter, has a real fire in winter, and the larger area to the right has a piano. The licensee also runs a beer and cider wholesale business, and the three guest beers and three ciders come from far and wide. There is a pretty suntrap beer garden to the rear. QP (596)

Holmfirth

Nook (Rose & Crown) L
7 Victoria Square, HD9 2DN (down alley behind Barclays bank)
11.30-midnight ☎ (01484) 682373
thenookbrewhouse.uk
Nook Yorks, Best, Blond; guest beers H

The Nook (properly, the Rose & Crown) dates from 1754, and is a real ale institution. It has appeared more than 30 times in this Guide, and continues to evolve. It serves home-cooked food all day, and has been dispensing beers from its own brewhouse since 2009. Guest beers are also stocked, and Pure North ciders. There is a popular folk club every Sunday evening, and real ale festivals on the weekend before Easter and over the August bank holiday.

Horbury

Boons Horbury

6 Queen Street, WF4 6LP (in town centre off B6128 Horbury-Ossett road, opp Co-Op)

11-11; 12-10.30 Sun (01924) 280442

Black Sheep Best Bitter; Clark's Classic Blonde; Timothy Taylor Landlord; guest beers

One of the small number of tied houses owned by Clark's Brewery of Wakefield, this popular community pub is located in the centre of the town, just off the High Street, and attracts people of all ages. The interior is based on a traditional layout around a central bar. The pub has a sizeable outdoor drinking area which is well used in summer.

Cricketers Arms

22 Cluntergate, WF4 5AG (right fork off High St at its lower end)

2-11; 11-midnight Fri & Sat; 12-11 Sun (01924) 267032

thecricketershorbury.co.uk

Castle Rock Harvest Pale; Timothy Taylor Landlord; guest beers

Located on the edge of the town centre, this former Tetley's house has now reopened as a genuine free house. The pub has had a tasteful refurbishment which has extended the length of the bar. Cheese and meze boards are available at any time. There is a bus stop close by with a frequent service to Wakefield, Ossett and Dewsbury. P

Horsforth

Town Street Tavern

16-18 Town Street, LS18 4RJ

12-11 (10.30 Sun) (0113) 281 9996

Ilkley Mary Jane; Leeds Best; Okells Manx Pale Ale; Timothy Taylor Golden Best; guest beers

Eight ales are served in this modern café-style bar on the main shopping street in Horsforth, alongside draught and bottled imported beers. Large windows, wooden floors and no piped music help to create a pleasant ambience. A small patio to the right of the bar area allows some space for outdoor drinking. The upstairs brasserie serves meals from 6pm, while a bar menu operates at lunchtimes and until 6pm at weekends. Accompanied children are allowed in the main bar until 6pm.

Q (50,50A)

Huddersfield

Cherry Tree

14-18 John William Street, HD1 1BG

7am-midnight (1am Fri & Sat) (01484) 448190

Elland 1872 Porter; Exmoor Gold; Greene King Abbot; Ruddles Best Bitter; guest beers

A modern town-centre Wetherspoon outlet, on two levels. Converted in 2001 from a former bed shop, it has featured several times in the Guide. Alongside the permanent beers are six rotating guest beers, regularly from Saltaire, Leeds, Phoenix, Naylor's, Acorn and Moorhouse's breweries. American craft beers in cask may feature occasionally. Three real ciders and one perry are always stocked. Food is served 7am-11pm and alcohol from 9am.

Grove

2 Spring Grove Street, HD1 4BP

12-11 (midnight Thu-Sat) (01484) 430113

groveinn.co.uk

Magic Rock Ringmaster; Thornbridge Jaipur IPA; Timothy Taylor Landlord; guest beers

This inn serves a stunning list of 18 cask ales all year round. Magic Rock Ringmaster, Taylor Landlord and Thornbridge Jaipur are on permanently, with eight rotating pumps featuring beers from Magic Rock, Dark Star, Oakham, Gadds', Buxton, Fuller's, Thornbridge and Durham. The remaining seven ales are chosen from breweries across the UK. Stouts, porters and strong ales are regularly on the bar. In addition, there are over 250 foreign bottled beers from across Europe and the US. Real cider is also sold. Q

HDM Beer Shop

27 Wood Street, HD1 1DU

11-11 (1am Thu-Sat); 12-8 Sun hdmbeershop.co.uk

Beer range varies

This real ale bar and off-licence is a real gem, about a three-minute walk from the train station, and the tap for Hand Drawn Monkey Brewing. It sells an eclectic mix of beers, normally two cask beers from HDM and two other guests, as well as five real ciders and one perry. There is also a huge choice of bottled ales from across Europe and the US.

Q

King's Head

St George's Square, HD1 1JF (in station buildings, on left when exiting station)

11 (11.30 Mon)-11; 12-11 Sun (01484) 511058

Bradfield Farmers Blonde; Magic Rock Ringmaster; Timothy Taylor Golden Best, Landlord; guest beers

A popular fixture in Huddersfield's real ale scene, conveniently situated at the listed railway station. A warm and friendly atmosphere makes it a necessary stop for the weary traveller. Ten beers are stocked (four regular, six guest), all top quality and sold at competitive prices. There are always two dark ales, as well as real cider on handpull. Live bands play on Sunday afternoons. It can get busy at weekends, but is a real local gem to appreciate.

Rat & Ratchet

40 Chapel Hill, HD1 3EB (on A616 below ring road)

3-11 Mon; 12 (3 Tue)-midnight; 12-11 Sun

(01484) 542400

Fuller's London Pride; Ossett Pale Gold, Silver King, Excelsior; Rat White Rat; guest beers

The Rat and Ratchet has been part of Huddersfield's real ale scene for many years, regularly winning awards from CAMRA and others. This friendly pub offers 13 handpumps: three Rat beers (from the on-site Rat brewery), three Ossett, a Fuller's, and five guest beers including a mild and a stout or porter, as well as a draught cider. A range of six ciders and two perries is also available. The pub quiz is on Wednesdays, and regular beer festivals are held. P

Sportsman

1 St John's Road, HD1 5AY

12-11; 11-midnight Fri & Sat ☎ (01484) 421929

underthevíaduct.com

Timothy Taylor Boltmaker; guest beers H

This restored 1930s pub has won a CAMRA English Heritage Conservation Pub Design award. Eight handpumps include a dedicated pump for a Mallinsons beer. Guest ales often come from local breweries Empire, Golcar and Magic Rock. A stout/porter is usually served, along with two ciders, often from Pure North. This pub has established itself as a favourite of the Huddersfield drinking scene, and was local CAMRA Pub of the Year in 2013. Food times vary – phone to check.

Star

7 Albert Street, HD1 3PJ (off A616)

closed Mon; 5 (12 Sat)-11; 12-10.30 Sun

☎ (01484) 545443 thestarinn.info

Pictish Brewers Gold; guest beers H

This multi-award-winning back-street local has featured in the Guide for over 10 years. It is a showcase for new breweries, with guest ales sourced both nationally and locally, and has dedicated pumps for dark beer, as well as Taylor's and Mallinsons breweries. With no jukebox, pool table or games machine, lively conversation around the bar and a real fire during the winter months, there is always a great atmosphere. Three seasonal beer festivals are held every year in its marquee, featuring only handpulled beers.

Q

Vulcan

32 St Peters Street, HD1 1RA

9am-1am (2am Fri & Sat) ☎ (01484) 302040

Copper Dragon Golden Pippin; Thwaites Wainwright; guest beers H

A traditional town-centre pub with a long-standing licensee and generous opening hours. It has six handpumps, with four guest beers most commonly from Yorkshire and Lancashire, where Mallinsons and Moorhouse's feature regularly. Bargain-priced lunches are available every day, and free food is served for regulars Friday teatime. There is a daily happy hour, extended on Wednesday evenings. The pub attracts all age groups, catering for enthusiasts of pool, karaoke and televised horse racing on Racing UK. Live bands are on stage every Sunday evening.

Idle

Symposium Ale & Wine Bar

7 Albion Road, BD10 9PY (near village green)

12-2.30 (not Mon-Wed), 5.30-11; 12-11 Fri & Sat; 12-10.30 Sun ☎ (01274) 616587

Beer range varies H

This venue is a popular bar/restaurant in the heart of the village, housed in a Victorian building which was formerly a general grocer's and wine merchant's. There are always six real ales on sale, and it also hosts a beer festival. Beers from around the world, both draught and bottled, are offered. Excellent meals are served from an inventive menu, with regular themes. The rear snug can be used as a small function room and leads to an elevated terrace outside. Q

Ilkley

Bar t'at

7 Cunliffe Road, LS29 9DZ

12-11; 12-10.30 Sun ☎ (01943) 608888

Black Sheep Best Bitter; Ilkley Mary Jane; Rooster's Wild Mule; Timothy Taylor Landlord; guest beers H

Popular side-street pub in the Market Town Taverns group which opened in 1999, having been converted from a former china shop. It has a music-free bar area, a basement restaurant and outdoor seating. The pub is renowned for the quality of its beer and food. The guest real ales come in a good, often eclectic, variety of beer styles, many from Yorkshire breweries. A wide range of quality foreign beers is also offered, and fresh home-cooked food is on the menu every day.

Q

Crescent Inn

Brook Street, LS29 8DG (within Crescent Hotel)

12-11 (midnight Thu-Sat) ☎ (01943) 600012

Black Sheep Ale; Leeds Best; Saltaire Blonde; guest beers H

Refurbished in 2011, the pub is on the ground floor of a town-centre building that has been a hotel since 1861. Eight real ales are always on offer. The house ale is produced by Ilkley Brewery and the guests are usually from other local breweries. The interior retains the original plasterwork and decorations, and is smartly furnished. Bar meals are served, with meal deals during the week. There is also a restaurant adjacent. The pub has full disabled facilities but the rear door provides the best access.

Keighley

Boltmakers Arms

117 East Parade, BD21 5HX

11-midnight (11 Mon); 12-11 Sun ☎ (01535) 661936

boltmakers.com

Timothy Taylor Dark Mild, Golden Best, Boltmaker, Landlord, Ram Tam; guest beers H

Unchanging classic Keighley town-centre pub, the de facto Timothy Taylor brewery tap. Brewery, whisky and music memorabilia adorn the walls of the small, single, split-level room. The guest beers and handpulled cider are from various sources at the licensee's whim, and there is also a fine selection of single malts. A quiz is hosted every Tuesday night and occasional live music on Wednesdays.

Brown Cow

5 Cross Leeds Street, BD21 2LQ

4-11; 12-10.30 Sun

Timothy Taylor Golden Best, Boltmaker, Landlord; guest beers H

Family-run community local bought from Timothy Taylor in 2013. The ethos of this award-winning free house remains the same, with quality, beer choice and customer comfort the priorities. A no-bad-language policy is in force. The pub is adorned with local breweriana, including the original sign from the entrance to Bradford's now-defunct Trough Brewery. The back room can be booked for meetings. A discounted beer on Super Saver Sunday is always popular. The four guest beers are mainly from local microbreweries.

Q P

Cricketers Arms

Coney Lane, BD21 5JE

4-11; 12-midnight Fri; 11.30-midnight Sat; 12-11 Sun (01535) 669912 cricketersarmskeighley.co.uk

Yates Bitter, Golden Ale; guest beers Ⓗ

Serving four guest beers from far and wide and a range of bottled beers alongside the regular ales, the Cricketers is a family-owned free house on the edge of the town centre. Live bands play Friday and Saturday evenings, when the additional downstairs bar is open from 7.30pm offering another real ale. Quiz night is Wednesday and the last Thursday of the month is comedy night, when entry to the pub is by advance ticket only.

Ledsham

Chequers

Claypit Lane, LS25 5LP

11-11; 12-6 Sun (01977) 683135

thechequersinn.com

Brown Cow Sessions; Leeds Best; Theakston Best Bitter; Timothy Taylor Landlord; guest beer Ⓗ

Picture-postcard stone-built village pub with a well-kept garden area for the summer months and open fires inside for the winter. This is a historic pub that can be traced back to 1540 and still retains many original features. It is situated in picturesque countryside and is well used by walkers and their furry friends, who are warmly welcomed, boots and all. The guest beer is normally from Abbeydale Brewery. QP(175,405)

Leeds: Burley

Fox & Newt

7-9 Burley Street, LS3 1LD

12-11 (1am Fri; midnight Sat) (0113) 245 4527

Burley Street Laguna Seca; guest beers Ⓗ

A short walk from the city centre, this is the home of Burley Street Brewhouse. Downstairs is wood-floored, with a raised section at one end. The upstairs rooms are reserved for live music and entertainment. On the bar are six handpumps, three dispensing Burley Street beers and three dispensing guest beers, mainly sourced from local microbreweries. There is a small outdoor seating area which is pleasant during the summer months.

Q

Leeds: Chapel Allerton

Regent

15-17 Regent Street, LS7 4PE

12-11 (midnight Thu-Sat); 11-11 Sun (0113) 293 9395

Kirkstall Three Swords; Leeds Pale; Tetley Bitter; guest beers Ⓗ

Welcoming and well-managed two-roomed Victorian pub in the heart of Chapel Allerton. Three regular and five changing guest beers are offered, with a dark beer always available. Beers are chosen from the SIBA list and customer suggestions. A Monday night discount to is offered on cask beers. Food is served until late. Regular quizzes and entertainment take place and the pub holds beer festivals in April, June and October.

P

Three Hulats

13 Harrogate Road, LS7 3NB

8am-midnight (1am Fri & Sat) (0113) 262 0524

Greene King Abbot; Ruddles Best Bitter; guest beers Ⓗ

Large Wetherspoon pub in a building that dates from the 1930s. Inside there is a variety of seating areas. On the bar, one pump always has an Ossett beer on and there are five changing guest beers. The pub hosts various local community groups, there is a weekly quiz, regular beer festivals, and a farmers' market is held outside every last Sunday of the month. Families are welcome until 9pm, and food is served until 11pm. P

Leeds: City Centre

Crowd of Favours

4-12 Harper Street, LS2 7EA

12-11; 11-midnight Sat; 11-10.30 Sun (0113) 246 9405

crowdoffavours.co.uk

Leeds Pale, Yorkshire Gold, Best, Midnight Bell; guest beers Ⓗ

Former fish and chip shop brilliantly converted by Leeds Brewery and opened in 2013. At ground level there are three distinct areas and downstairs is a large basement area used for live music, film nights and private functions. A large number of different guest ales have been served since opening and an extensive range of international bottled beers is also stocked. The food is made using local produce whenever possible and is served until one hour before closing.

Friends of Ham

4 New Station Street, LS1 5DL

12-11 (midnight Thu-Sat); 1-10 Sun (0113) 242 0275

friendsofham.com

Beer range varies Ⓗ

Cafe bar and charcuterie serving real ales, the upstairs bar has three handpumps serving beers that are mainly from microbreweries, often local ones. An extensive range of bottled beers from around the world is also available. The food counter serves meat and cheese platters. Downstairs is a larger room with bench seating, tables and comfy sofas. There is also a shuffleboard table and a selection of board games to keep the customers entertained. Live music features occasionally.

Hop

Granary Wharf, Dark Neville Street, LS1 4BR

12-midnight (0113) 243 9854 thehop-leeds.co.uk

Ossett Pale Gold, Yorkshire Blonde, Big Red Bitter, Silver King, Excelsior; guest beers Ⓗ

Owned by Ossett Brewery, the pub opened in 2010 and is built into the railway arches under the platforms of Leeds station. Ten handpumps dispense the Ossett range along with guest ales. As well as real cider, a perry is normally available. There is a programme of regular events including quizzes and live music, and a beer festival is held twice a year. Award-winning pies are available at lunchtime from Andrew Jones of Huddersfield.

North

24 New Briggate, LS1 6NU

11-1am (2am Wed-Sat); 12-midnight Sun

(0113) 242 4540 northbar.com

Beer range varies Ⓗ

Small bar offering both real ales and a huge range of beers from around the world. The bar is along one wall and has five handpumps on it. One of the real ales will always be from a local brewery and there will normally be a dark beer available. Pictures from local artists are often displayed. Regular beer-related events are held. Bar food such as pork pies and cheese platters can be ordered.

Palace

Kirkgate, LS2 7DJ

10-11.30 (midnight Fri & Sat); 10-11 Sun

(0113) 244 5882

St Austell Nicholson's Pale Ale; Tetley Bitter; guest beers H

Former Melbourne Brewery house in the shadow of the Leeds Minster. The central bar area links two drinking areas to either end of the premises, with plenty of tables available. A good variety of guest beers includes at least one local ale and usually at least one dark beer. There is a heated courtyard bedecked with fairy lights to the rear of the building. Food is served all day including a wide range of sausages.

Scarbrough Hotel

Bishopgate Street, LS1 5DY

10-midnight (1am Fri & Sat); 10-10.30 Sun

(0113) 243 4590

Tetley Bitter; guest beers H

Busy ale house which was refurbished in 2013 and the bar moved further back. The building dates from 1765 and became a pub in 1826. It is named after Henry Scarbrough, the first owner, though it was then known as the King's Arms. At either end of the long bar are comfortable seating areas. The selection of guest ales is from both local breweries and further afield. A good range of pies is on the food menu.

Stick or Twist

Podium Buildings, Merrion Way, LS2 8PD

8am-midnight (1am Fri & Sat) (0113) 234 9748

Greene King IPA, Abbot; guest beers H

The oldest Wetherspoon in Leeds and the closest pub to Leeds Arena, it is of large open-plan design and the long bar has 12 handpumps serving an extensive selection of mainly local real ales. A real cider or perry is dispensed from a 20-litre box in one of the fridges. The outside seating area makes a pleasant suntrap during the summer months. Food is served from 8am to 11pm every day.

Q

Templar

2 Templar Street, LS2 7NU

11-11; 12-10.30 Sun (0113) 243 0318

Ridgeside Templar; Tetley Bitter; guest beers H

Community local in the city centre which is under possible long-term threat from the development of the Eastgate quarter. Once a Melbourne Brewery house, it retains the exterior glazed Burmantoft tiles and bowing courtier logo in the leaded window panes. Wooden panelling service bells reflect its illustrious past, updated by large-screen TVs showing a range of sport. This pub is one of the few remaining stockists of Tetley Bitter in the city centre since it stopped being brewed in Leeds.

Veritas Ale & Wine Bar

43 Great George Street, LS1 3BB

11-11; 12-10.30 Sun (0113) 242 8094

Black Sheep Best Bitter; Ilkley Mary Jane; Thwaites Wainwright; Timothy Taylor Landlord; guest beers H

This modern bar, attracting a broad clientele, is an L-shaped open-plan room divided into four separate areas. It is well known for the quality of its food, and the deli bar features a range of meals made with local produce, available to eat in or take away. Guest beers are mainly from local microbreweries. A wide selection of wines is also available along with draught and bottled foreign beers and real cider. Q

Victoria Family & Commercial Hotel

28 Great George Street, LS1 3DL (behind town hall)

10-11 (midnight Thu-Sat); 12-10.30 Sun

(0113) 245 1386

St Austell Nicholson's Pale Ale; Tetley Bitter; guest beers H

Built in 1865 as a 28-room hotel to accommodate visitors to the assizes court in Leeds town hall, the building has an impressive Victorian exterior and ornate interior with high ceilings. There is a long main bar area and two separate rooms, all of which feature a deal of polished wood and shiny brass. The guest beers are a selection of local ales and quality beers from around the country. Food is served all day including a wide range of sausages.

Whitelock's First City Luncheon Bar ★

Turks Head Yard, LS1 6HB (off Briggate)

11-11 (1am Fri & Sat); 12-6 Sun (0113) 245 3950

whitelocksleeds.com

Leeds Pale; Theakston Best Bitter; guest beers H

Whitelock's is an iconic Leeds pub, described by John Betjeman as 'the very heart of Leeds'. First licensed in 1715, the long, narrow interior dates from 1895 and is a showcase of Victorian brass and glass. The unusual bar, with the serving staff on a higher level than the customers, offers a good range of both local and national beers. Seating outside in the yard is often in demand, even during the winter months. Q

Leeds: Headingley

Arcadia Ale & Wine Bar

34 Arndale Centre, Otley Road, LS6 2UE (corner of Alma Rd)

12-11 (0113) 274 5599

Black Sheep Best Bitter; Timothy Taylor Landlord; guest beers H

A small, well-established and multi-award-winning pub which has been cleverly converted from a former bank. The bar has ground floor rooms plus an upstairs mezzanine level. Eight beers are offered, often from breweries such as Rooster's, Elland and Ilkley, plus guest ales from around the region. Draught and bottled foreign beers, together with a range of wines, also feature. Food is served Thursday to Sunday (all day Sat). Children and anyone wearing fancy dress are not permitted.

Q

Leeds: Holbeck

Grove Inn

Back Row, LS11 5PL

12-11 (midnight Fri & Sat) (0113) 243 9254

thegroveinn.com

Daleside Blonde; guest beers H

Tucked away in the shadow of much larger modern buildings, the Grove is a traditional West Riding pub, with four rooms off a corridor. To the front is a public bar and two small side rooms. Live music takes place in the concert room to the rear of the pub. On the compact bar are eight handpumps serving a good range of real ales which are mostly from local breweries. Outside is a heated drinking area. ❀⇌♣🍎🚌🐾📶

Midnight Bell 🄻
101 Water Lane, LS11 5QN
11.30-11 (midnight Fri & Sat); 12-11 Sun
☎ (0113) 244 5044 🌐 midnightbell.co.uk
Leeds Pale, Yorkshire Gold, Best, Midnight Bell; guest beers 🄷
A thriving modern pub in the heart of Holbeck urban village that mixes old and new perfectly. Making best use of the old fabric, the Midnight Bell is open plan, with exposed brick and beams sitting neatly alongside the concrete bar and new chunky furniture. Cosy in the winter when dimly lit and log-fire warmed, it is bright and airy in the summer when you do not even have to go inside to order a beer. ❀◖◗♿⇌🍎🚌

Leeds: Kirkstall

Kirkstall Bridge Inn 🄻
Bridge Road, LS5 3BW
12-11.30 (12.30am Fri & Sat) ☎ (0113) 278 4044
🌐 kirkstallbridge.co.uk
Kirkstall Pale Ale, Three Swords, Black Band Porter; guest beers 🄷
The tap for Kirkstall Brewery, the interior is decorated with an array of pub and brewery memorabilia along with old photographs. The upstairs bar has eight handpumps, normally four Kirkstall beers and four guests. Also available is a good range of bottled beers. There is a second bar area downstairs where dogs are welcome. Deli platters are available every day from 12-8pm and roast dinners on Sundays. Street food pop-ups are a regular feature outside. ❀◖◗P🚌🐾

West End House 🄻
26 Abbey Road, LS5 3HS
11.30-11 (11.30 Thu; midnight Fri & Sat); 12-11.30 Sun
☎ (0113) 278 6332 🌐 westendleeds.co.uk
Beer range varies 🄷
Traditional stone-built pub with a central bar surrounded by comfortable seating and a dining area towards the back of the building. On the bar four handpumps dispense regularly changing beers, mainly from local breweries. There are also handpumps for cider and perry. Food is served lunchtimes and early evenings during the week, and all day until 7.30pm on Saturday, 6pm on Sunday. The ingredients are sourced locally whenever possible. Quiz nights are held on Tuesdays and Thursdays.
❀◖◗♿⇌(Headingley)🍎🚌

Leeds: Meanwood

East of Arcadia 🄻
607 Meanwood Road, LS6 4HQ
11-11 (11.30 Fri & Sat); 12-11 Sun ☎ (0113) 275 5488
Black Sheep Best Bitter; Ilkley Mary Jane; Leeds Pale; guest beers 🄷
A modern bar that occupies a prominent corner position in the heart of Meanwood. Open plan and on one level, it has a carpeted area that follows the sweep of tall windows curving around the pub. Closer to the bar there is a bare-boarded area with large casks that have been converted to small tables complete with foot rails. The light-coloured walls display international breweriana. Beers from both Ridgeside and Timothy Taylor breweries are always available. Quiz night is Wednesday.
♉◖◗♿🚌🐾📶

Linthwaite

Sair 🄻
139 Lane Top, HD7 5SG (top of Hoyle Ing, off A62)
5 (12 Fri & Sat)-11; 12-10.30 Sun ☎ (01484) 842370
Linfit Bitter, Gold Medal, Special, Swift, Autumn Gold, Old Eli 🄷
High on the edge of the Colne Valley, the Sair Inn is home to the famous Linfit Brewery, which recently celebrated over 30 years of brewing. The brewpub, steeped in local history, is a traditional multi-roomed stone building with a central bar, real fires and a long-suffering landlord. The beer range is as LocAle as it gets, with eight beers unique to the pub, and real cider from Pure North. It is a welcome refuge for walkers, musicians and visitors alike. Q❀♣🍎🚌🐾

Liversedge

Black Bull 🄻
37 Halifax Road, WF15 6JR (on A649, 400yds from A62 towards Halifax)
12-midnight (1am Fri & Sat) ☎ (01924) 403779
Fuller's London Pride; Ossett Pale Gold, Yorkshire Blonde, Silver King, Excelsior; guest beers 🄷
In the Guide for the 11th year running, this is an excellent, sociable, community local with a warm welcome. The first of Ossett Brewery's chain of lovingly restored pubs, it offers a blend of cosy corners and open spaces where groups can mix, including the Chapel, with its high roof, stained glass and woodwork. Nine pumps dispense a range of beer styles including a mild or dark ale. The pub hosts a popular quiz night on Tuesday, and darts and dominoes night on Monday.
♉❀♣P🚌(220,252)🐾

Marsden

Riverhead Brewery Tap 🄻
Peel Street, HD7 6BR
12-midnight (1am Fri); 11-1am Sat ☎ (01484) 844324
🌐 theriverheadmarsden.co.uk
Ossett Yorkshire Blonde, Silver King; Riverhead Butterley Bitter, March Haigh, Redbrook Premium; guest beers 🄷
Up to 10 beers are on the bar at this Ossett Brewery pub. Alongside the permanent beers are others from Ossett, Riverhead, Fuller's and guests. A pub since 1995, it provides a friendly welcome to all. The upstairs restaurant serves great food and the microbrewery is visible from the bar. A popular stop on the real ale rail trail, the pub gets busy with ale trailers on Saturdays. Walkers and dogs are welcome. A riverside terrace is also used for alfresco drinking. Q❀◖◗♿⇌🍎🚌(185)

Meltham

Wills o' Nats
Blackmoorfoot Road, HD9 5PS

12-3, 5-11; 11.30-midnight Sat; 11.30-11 Sun
(01484) 850078 willsonats.com
Black Sheep Best Bitter; Greene King IPA; Timothy Taylor Landlord; guest beers H
In 1890 William, son of Nathaniel, took over the Spotted Cow, which gradually became Wills o' Nats. Today it is renowned for locally-sourced home-cooked food and six or more ales. Live music events are held on the first Saturday of each summer month, when you can camp behind the pub. The building is close to the Peak District and is surrounded by stunning views. A welcome stop for families, walkers and their dogs, and a regular in our Guide. P (388)

Mirfield

Flowerpot

65 Calder Road, WF14 8NN (over river, 400yds S of railway station)
12-11.30 (12.30am Fri & Sat) (01924) 496939
Fuller's London Pride; Ossett Yorkshire Blonde, Big Red Bitter, Silver King, Excelsior; guest beers H
Following a major yet typically sensitive refurbishment by Ossett Brewery, including an impressive tiled flowerpot set in the floor and real fires in each of the three rooms, the pub has gone from strength to strength. In summer the riverside terrace is popular. Eight ales come from Ossett, Fernandes, Rat, Riverhead plus other independents, with a mild or stout normally on offer as well. Haigh's local farm supplies five different pies, served with peas, Monday to Friday lunchtimes. P (262)

Navigation Tavern

6 Station Road, WF14 8NL (next to railway station)
11.30 (12 Sun)-11 (01924) 492476
Caledonian Deuchars IPA; John Smith's Bitter; Theakston Best Bitter, Black Bull Bitter, XB, Old Peculier; guest beers H
Popular canalside free house serving up to eight regulars, plus up to four guests at weekends, and a registered ambassador for Theakston beers at keen prices. The pub features on the Transpennine Rail Ale Trail and holds renowned beer festivals three times a year. It hosts Saturday night entertainment and is home to active sports and pool teams. A large function room/restaurant and en-suite B&B with stairlift are available. At least two real cider/perry choices are offered.
P (203,253)

Old Colonial

Dunbottle Lane, WF14 9JJ (off A644 up Church Lane, 1 mile NE of station)
5-11; 12-midnight Fri & Sat; 12-11 Sun (01924) 496920
theoldcolonial.webplus.net
Copper Dragon Best Bitter; guest beers H
National Pubs in Bloom champion twice, this former club with fascinating memorabilia offers a cosy area with sofas around the fire. There is a Royal British Legion memorial in the garden and local charities are well supported. The spacious conservatory is popular for functions and meetings. Up to six ales from the likes of Thwaites, Lees, the Marston's portfolio and small brewers are on the bar. Lunches and evening meals are served Thursday to Saturday and the excellent-value Sunday lunch is recommended.
P (202,205)

North Featherstone

Bradley Arms

98 Willow Lane, WF7 6BJ (on B6128 Castleford-Featherstone road, opp St Wilfrid's high school)
2 (12 Thu)-11; 12-midnight Fri & Sat; 12-11 Sun
(01977) 794346 bradleyarmsfeatherstone.com
Black Sheep Best Bitter; Leeds Best; guest beer H
A lovely old ex-farm building set on several levels offering a choice of rooms. It has an open fire for winter months and a large beer garden to the rear with a children's play area during the summer. This inn was a key location in the infamous Featherstone Massacre of 12 September 1893, the last occasion on which British troops shot and killed British citizens on English soil. The first ever speech on workers' rights was made here by Robert Bontine Cunninghame Graham, co-founder of the Scottish Labour Party, who also spoke here at the time of the Massacre (see memorabilia). The taproom is dedicated to Rugby League.
Q P

Ossett

Brewers Pride

Low Mill Road, Healey Road, WF5 8ND (in Healey Mills industrial area beside River Calder; Healey Rd runs straight down from The Green, by Dimplewell Lodge Hotel, then left at Matthews Foods)
12-11; 12-10.30 Sun (01924) 273865
brewers-pride.co.uk
Bob's White Lion; Rudgate Ruby Mild; guest beers H
An independent free house on the outskirts of Ossett and close to the Calder and Hebble canal. Three regular beers are sold plus seven guest ales from microbreweries. Food is served lunchtimes and there are themed food evenings (pies, tapas, Brewer's Madness and specials). Monday is quiz night and there is live music on the first Sunday of each month. Dogs are welcome, and well-behaved children until 8pm. Bus 102 (daytime only) stops 150 yards away. Q (102)

Old Vic

47 Manor Road, WF5 0AU (left turn from B6128 at S end of Ossett, or right turn from the Green nr Ossett school)
4-11; 12-midnight Fri & Sat; 12-11 Sun (01924) 273516
Fuller's Bengal Lancer; Ossett Pale Gold, Yorkshire Blonde, Silver King, Excelsior; guest beers H
Friendly local pub a 10-minute walk from Ossett town centre. Fresh home-cooked food is served. Two varying guest beers and an alternating stout or porter complement the regular well-kept beers. Taken over a couple of years ago by Ossett Brewery, this pub has undergone a renaissance.
P

Otley

Fleece

Westgate, LS21 3DT
11.30 (12 Sun)-11.30 (01943) 465034
fleece-otley.co.uk
Wharfe Bank Printers Ink, Washburn Best, Tether Blond, Othelia Gold; guest beers H
A Grade II-listed building retaining many original features, with a main room divided into three areas. To the left of the entrance is a public bar with its own real fire, where dogs are welcome. An extensive food menu is offered, with locally-sourced produce used whenever possible. An attractive terraced garden with seating and tables

stretches down to the River Wharfe. The handpumps on the bar offer at least four beers from the Wharfe Bank range, plus guest ales.
❀◑♿♣●P🚌(X84,33A)🐾📶

Horse & Farrier 🄻

7 Bridge Street, LS21 1BQ
⏲ 11-11 (midnight Fri); 12-midnight Sat; 12-11 Sun
☎ (01943) 468400
Black Sheep Best Bitter; Ilkley Mary Jane; guest beers Ⓗ
Part of the Market Town Taverns chain, this pub is open plan with one large room divided into three wood-floored drinking areas, and a carpeted area for diners. Upstairs is a function room. On the bar are eight handpumps serving a variety of ales from around the country, normally including beers from Timothy Taylor and Rooster's breweries. This venue also has a good selection of bottled foreign beers. Children may accompany diners until 8pm.
Q❀🛏◑♿●P🚌🐾

Junction Inn 🄻

44 Bondgate, LS21 1AD
⏲ 11 (11.30 Thu)-11; 11-midnight Fri & Sat; 12-10.30 Sun
☎ (01943) 463233
St Austell Tribute; Theakston Best Bitter, Old Peculier; Timothy Taylor Boltmaker, Landlord; guest beers Ⓗ
A solid-looking stone-built pub on a prominent street-corner site on the approach from Leeds. Up to 11 ales from around the country are dispensed, along with a real cider and a wide range of malt whiskies. There is a central fireplace, and a collection of leather harnesses and saddles hangs from the ceiling. Pictures of old Otley and some interesting metal beer advertisements and mirrors complete the decor. To the front, roadside tables allow for outdoor drinking. ❀♣●🚌🐾

Old Cock 🄻

11-13 Crossgate, LS21 1AA
⏲ 11-11 ☎ (01943) 464424 🌐 theoldcockotley.co.uk
Ilkley Mary Jane; Theakston Best Bitter; guest beers Ⓗ
Compact and welcoming, this pub opened in 2010 after it was converted from a café, and has quickly established a traditional pub feel, winning the local CAMRA Pub of the Year award for the past three years. There are two rooms downstairs with stone-flagged floors, and a further room upstairs. A genuine free house, the guest ales are mostly from local breweries. At least two real ciders are also served, plus a range of foreign beers. No admittance to under-18s. Q♿●🚌🐾📶

Overton

Reindeer Inn 🄻

204 Old Road, WF4 4RL (signed off A642 near National Coal Mining Museum)
⏲ 12 (4 Mon)-midnight; 12-11 Sun ☎ (01924) 848374
Beer range varies Ⓗ
This traditional, independent free house was once a coaching inn. It is the tap for Cap House Brewery, and also sells locally-sourced guest beers. Home-cooked food is served in the restaurant or conservatory which leads out into the beer garden overlooking the National Coal Mining Museum. Quiz night is Wednesday. The games room has a pool table, dartboard, dominoes and games machines. The restaurant is open Tuesday-Sunday lunchtimes and Wednesday-Saturday evenings.
🐮❀◑♣●P🚌(232,128)

Pontefract

Broken Bridge 🄻

5 Horsefair, WF8 1PE (near bus station)
⏲ 12-midnight ☎ (01977) 781640
Greene King IPA; Ruddles Best Bitter; Wychwood Hobgoblin; guest beers Ⓗ
This former charity shop's name is a translation of the original Roman name of the town. There are numerous pictures depicting the history of Pontefract adorning the walls. It is popular at weekends, the small entrance belying the large one-room interior, which leads eventually to a rear courtyard. Unusually for a Wetherspoon outlet, the pub has a dartboard. The beer range regularly features Acorn, Saltaire and WharfeBank breweries. There are regular Meet the Brewer evenings. Children are welcome.
❀◑♿⇌(Monkhill/Baghill/Tanshelf)♣●🚌📶

Robin Hood 🄻

4 Wakefield Road, WF8 4HN (at Town End, jct of A645 Wakefield Rd with roads to Barnsley, Doncaster and A1, opp major set of traffic lights)
⏲ 5-11; 12-1am Fri & Sat; 12-midnight Sun
☎ (01977) 702231
Beer range varies Ⓗ
Busy establishment on the notorious Town End traffic lights, which are due to be replaced by two roundabouts. There are four separate drinking areas including a public bar. Quizzes are held on Tuesday and Sunday evenings and darts and dominoes teams play in the local leagues. The pub has its own on-site brewery.
Q❀♿⇌(Tanshelf)♣●🚌🐾

Pudsey

Fleece 🄻

100 Fartown, LS28 8LU
⏲ 12-11 (10.30 Sun) ☎ (0113) 236 2748
🌐 fleecefartown.co.uk
Leeds Pale; Tetley Bitter; Timothy Taylor Boltmaker, Landlord; guest beer Ⓗ
Popular and welcoming, this well-established pub just on the edge of Pudsey caters for locals and visitors alike. The central bar serves a plush lounge, featuring film-related prints and bits and pieces, and a proper taproom where sport and banter rule. Quiz nights and charity events are well attended, but the secret of the Fleece's success is old-fashioned good quality and friendly service. The guest beer is usually pale and from a local brewery.
❀♣P🚌

Roberttown

New Inn

Roberttown Lane, WF15 7NP
⏲ 3-11; 12-11.30 Fri & Sat; 12-10.30 Sun ☎ (01924) 402069
🌐 thenewinnroberttown.com
Abbeydale Moonshine; Leeds Best; guest beers Ⓗ
A fine example of an old Webster's house, rescued from the clutches of a major pub company. The central part of the property has been a pub since at least 1870. One of the New Inn's own cellar-brewed ales is always on the bar, together with a dark beer and Bobtown Blonde, brewed exclusively by Mallinsons. There is a snug with comfy chairs, and a function room used for occasional live music and events. The Wednesday quiz is recommended. Food is served 12-9pm Friday-Sunday.
🐮❀◑♣P🚌(220,221)

Saltaire

Fanny's Ale & Cider House

63 Saltaire Road, BD18 3JN (on A657 opp fire station)
11.30 (5 Mon)-11; 11.30-midnight Fri & Sat; 12-10.30 Sun
(01274) 591419
Ossett Treacle Stout; Timothy Taylor Golden Best, Landlord; guest beers H
Near the World Heritage Site of Saltaire and the historic Salts Mill, this cosy pub was formerly a beer shop. It is now a free house and stocks three regular ales, up to five guests, a craft keg beer, and draught ciders as well. An extension has increased seating capacity downstairs and added disabled access. Upstairs there is a room with comfortable seating. The gas-lit lounge is adorned with breweriana, and real fires add nicely to the welcome. Q

Shipley

Ring o' Bells

3 Bradford Road, BD18 3PR (on A650)
11-midnight (1am Fri & Sat); 12-11 Sun
(01274) 584386 theringobellsshipley.co.uk
Leeds Pale; Tetley Bitter; Timothy Taylor Boltmaker, Landlord; guest beers H
Traditional roadhouse-type pub with an impressive frontage, located close to the historic village of Saltaire. It has a comfortable, homely feel. Sports matches are shown on several TV screens. Bands occasionally perform at the pub. Popular poker games and weekly quizzes are held. The small Edwardian smoke room merits a place in CAMRA's book, Yorkshire's Real Heritage Pubs, and is where activity groups, including writers and anglers, meet up. (Saltaire)P

Sir Norman Rae

Victoria House, Market Place, BD18 3QB
8am-11 (midnight Fri & Sat) (01274) 535290
Greene King Abbot; Ruddles Best Bitter; guest beers H
A typical conversion by Wetherspoon from a previous use. Formerly a Co-op department store, this example opened originally as a Lloyds No.1 bar but was converted to the standard Wetherspoon format. There are 10 handpumps dispensing real ale, usually focusing on local breweries, with Greene King beers also present on the bar. Real cider is served as well. Regular Meet the Brewer nights are held. The pub is conveniently located next to Shipley bus station and close to the railway station.

Silsden

King's Arms

Bolton Road, BD20 0JY
12-midnight (01535) 653216
Saltaire Blonde; Theakston Best Bitter; guest beers H
A great place to visit, this award-winning, bustling, community pub hosts music nights on Tuesday and Thursday, a quiz night on Wednesday, and regular beer festivals. Partitions divide the main bar into three distinct areas, each with its own feel, one with a pool table. Westons cider or perry and at least three guest beers from near and far, often including a darker beer, provide something for all tastes. Regular buses between Keighley and Ilkley stop outside. Dogs and well-behaved children are allowed. P

Slaithwaite

Commercial

1 Carr Lane, HD7 5AN (off A62)
12-midnight (1am Fri & Sat) (01484) 846258
commercial-slaithwaite.co.uk
Beer range varies H
Since reopening in 2009, this village-centre free house, a true community pub, has enjoyed great success. Nine handpumps provide ample variety, with the keenly priced house beers Commerciale and Moonraker Mild (supplied by Empire Brewery), six rotating guests, and Cornish Orchards farmhouse cider permanently on tap. The Commercial is a not-to-be-missed stop for Transpennine Rail Ale Trailers and welcomes ramblers and their dogs. Light snacks and beverages are served Friday-Sunday. An upstairs function room can be used free of charge. Q

Southowram

Shoulder of Mutton

14 Cain Lane, HX3 9SB
2-11; 12-midnight Fri & Sat; 12-10.30 Sun 07707 358697
Saltaire Blonde; guest beers H
A popular local built in the 18th century in a hilltop village important for its stone quarries. It has won awards for the summer floral displays on its frontage. The L-shaped lounge incorporates exposed stonework behind the bar, and an open fire ensures customers are warm in the winter. A separate room has a pool table. Regular changing guest beers are dispensed. Charity events are held during the year and there is a Thursday evening quiz. (571,572)

Sowerby Bridge

Firehouse

1 Town Hall Street, HX6 2QD
4 (12 Fri-Sun)-11.30 (01422) 832586
firehouserestaurant.co.uk
Moorhouse's Blond Witch; Timothy Taylor Landlord H
Close to the bridge crossing the River Calder in the centre of Sowerby Bridge, this prominent building, dating from 1874, is a popular venue for those who like to eat out with the option of a traditional pint. It is a family-run outlet that has built a popular reputation for food and real ale, in particular for the authentic Italian pizzas cooked in an open pizza oven. There is always a guest beer from a local or regional brewer.

Puzzle Hall

21 Hollins Mill Lane, HX6 2RF (400yds from A58)
3-midnight (1am Fri); 1-1am Sat; 1-11.30 Sun
(01422) 835547 puzzlehall.com
Beer range varies H
The Puzzle Hall can be found nestling between the canal and the river. The 17th-century building once included a brewery; it now provides a welcoming atmosphere, six varying ales and a venue for live bands. Music features on Thursday and Saturday nights, and poetry recitals on the first Monday of the month. Thai food is served from Wednesday to Sunday 5-9pm.

Shepherd's Rest

125 Bolton Brow, HX6 2BD (on A58 towards Halifax)
3 (12 Fri & Sat)-midnight (01422) 831937

Ossett Pale Gold, Shepherd's Rest, Excelsior; Timothy Taylor Landlord; guest beers 🄷
Built in 1877, this establishment took the name of a previous pub on the other side of the busy main road. It was purchased by Ossett Brewery in 2005 and the available space has been used to good effect. From the entrance steps, a triangular area leads to the bar, which faces a cosy and compact lounge with a large brick-arched fireplace, comfortable seating and a flagged floor, which in turn leads to an enclosed outside area. Monday is quiz night. Q❀⇌♣🚌🐾

Thornhill

Savile Arms

12 Church Lane, WF12 0JZ (on B6117, 2½ miles S of Dewsbury)
⏲ 5 (4 Fri)-11; 12-4.30, 7-11 Sat & Sun ☎ (01924) 463738
Black Sheep Best Bitter; guest beers 🄷
Known as the Church House, this village and community pub dates from 1777. Four handpumps in the beamed bar area frequently offer beer from breweries in the Heavy Woollen district. A colourful mural depicting Thornhill's history illuminates the lounge. Traditional bar billiards is played in the taproom which stands on the consecrated ground of the parish church. A steep staircase leads to a secret garden with picnic tables for barbecues. Saturdays are popular, with themed home-made meal evenings. ❀♣P🚌(128,281)🐾

Thornton

New Inn

363 Thornton Road, BD13 3JX (on B6145)
⏲ 11-midnight ☎ (01274) 921505
Beer range varies 🄷
Located alongside the main road through Thornton, this large pub has an open-plan format but still retains a multi-room feel. Six handpumps on the bar serve a varying range of real ales, while real ciders and perries are also on sale. Good-value home-cooked food is offered. Music is a key feature of the pub and a jamming session takes place on a Monday night. Friday hosts an open mic night and live bands perform on a Saturday.
❀◐◑●P🚌

Todmorden

Masons Arms

1 Bacup Road, OL14 7PN (on A681 near jct with A6033)
⏲ 3 (12 Fri-Sun)-midnight ☎ (01706) 812180
Beer range varies 🄷
Sandwiched between the railway viaduct and the canal, this welcoming local was once a mortuary. The tables, formerly used for laying out bodies, are still in use for drinking and dining. Five rotating competitively priced ales from local Lancashire and Yorkshire microbreweries are complemented by good-value traditional pub grub. The room to the right of the entrance has a real fire in winter, and you will likely be drawn into good conversation with the regulars.
Q🐎❀◐◑⇌(Walsden)🚌(589,590)

Staff of Life

550 Burnley Road, Lydgate, OL14 8JF
⏲ 12-3, 5.30-11; 12-midnight Fri-Sun ☎ (01706) 819033
🌐 staffoflifeinn.org.uk
Timothy Taylor Golden Best, Landlord; guest beers 🄷
Comfortable roadside inn nestling in a deep, narrow valley beneath the local landmark of Eagle's Crag. The three guest ales come from a variety of northern independents, and the pub has a good reputation for its food, which can be enjoyed at a table in one of the several cosy nooks and crannies, or on the balcony. Admire the unusual artwork on the walls and then ask the landlord about the legend of the White Doe.
Q🐎❀🛏◐◑Ⓐ♣P🚌(589,592)🐾📶

Upper Denby

George Inn

114 Denby Lane, HD8 8UE
⏲ 5-10.30 (11.30 Fri); 1-11.30 Sat; 11.30-10.30 Sun
☎ (01484) 861347 🌐 thegeorgeinn-upperdenby.co.uk
Tetley Bitter; Timothy Taylor Landlord; guest beer 🄷
Family-run village local going from strength to strength since becoming a free house in late 2012. Ramblers are welcome here and the pub runs pie and peas walks (a countryside walk followed by food back at the George) and other function days. Occasional live music and traditional singalongs also take place. Home-made pies are available, and families are welcome until 8.30pm.
🐎❀Ⓐ♣P🚌🐾📶

Wakefield

Black Rock

19 Cross Square, WF1 1PQ (between Bull Ring and top of Westgate)
⏲ 11-11 (midnight Sat); 12-10.30 Sun ☎ (01924) 375550
Tetley Bitter; guest beers 🄷
A famous and largely unspoilt old Melbourne house opened in 1842. There is a blue plaque for Archbishop John Potter. An arched, tiled façade leads into this compact city-centre local, where there is a warm welcome and a comfy interior, with many photographs of old Wakefield adding to the proper pub feel. The Rock has been a bastion for the ale drinkers of Wakefield and now offers three guest beers. Drinkers are encouraged to suggest beers they would like to try.
Q⇌(Westgate)🚌

Bull & Fairhouse 🄻

60 George Street, WF1 1DL (turn right out of Westgate Station, left at Westgate, right at lights, bear left at bottom of hill, pub is on left after 200yds)
⏲ 4-11; 12-midnight Fri & Sat; 12-11 Sun ☎ (01924) 362930
Bob's White Lion; guest beers 🄷
Formerly the Bull, the pub has reverted to an earlier name alluding to the cattle market and fairground in the area. The comfortable multi-roomed premises now enjoy a lighter feel, with a new lounge at the front and the toilets relocated to the rear, improving disabled access via a passageway. Play Your Cards Right is held on Thursdays with live music at weekends. The brewery tap for Great Heck, it also offers a changing real cider/perry on gravity.
Q⇌(Westgate)♣●🚌(443,444)🐾

Fernandes Brewery Tap & Bier Keller 🄻

5 Avison Yard, Kirkgate, WF1 1UA (turn right approx 100yds S of George St/Kirkgate jct)
⏲ 4-11 (11.30 Thu); 12-midnight Fri & Sat; 12-11 Sun
☎ (01924) 386348
Ossett Big Red Bitter; guest beers 🄷

Owned by Ossett Brewery, Fernandes Brewery operates in the cellar here. It has 11 handpulls – two dedicated to dark beers, five offering ales from Fernandes, Ossett and Fuller's, three for guest beers, and one for a draught cider. The Bier Keller, which opens 6pm-midnight Friday and Saturday, serves premier foreign beers on draught plus an Ossett beer and a cider on handpump. There is a quiz on Wednesday evenings, folk music on the first Sunday of each month and open mic on the third Sunday. ◑⇌(Kirkgate)●⊟🐾

Harry's Bar

107B Westgate, WF1 1EL

⏲ 5 (4 Fri & Sat)-1am; 12-midnight Sun ☎ (01924) 373773

Bob's White Lion; Moorhouse's Pride of Pendle; guest beers Ⓗ

Small one-roomed pub set in an alleyway just off Westgate. A real fire and a bare brick and wood interior plus vintage sporting pictures enhance this small, cosy venue. There is also a fantastic view of Wakefield's famous 99-arch viaduct – if only steam trains were a regular feature. A selection of bottled Belgian beers complements the real ales. The hours permitted by the pub's licence are greater. Local CAMRA Pub of the Year 2013.
❀⇌(Westgate)●P⊟

Henry Boons

130 Westgate, WF2 9SR (200yds below railway bridge on Westgate)

⏲ 11-11 (1am Fri & Sat) ☎ (01924) 378126

Clark's Classic Blonde, Westgate Gold; Timothy Taylor Landlord; guest beers Ⓗ

Quiet in the daytime, the pub gets busy in the evenings as it is on the Westgate Run. It is the brewery tap for Clark's, which is behind the pub. Hogsheads are in use as tables and there are many items of breweriana, plus a thatched bar. This pub caters for drinkers of all ages and features live music. Two function rooms are available for hire. Most bus routes to the west of the city pass the door. ◐♿⇌(Westgate)♣⊟🐾

Hop

19 Bank Street, WF1 1EH (in cobbled street off Westgate almost opp Theatre Royal)

⏲ 4-midnight (2am Fri); 12-2am Sat; 4-11 Sun
☎ (01924) 367111 🌐 thehopwakefield.co.uk

Fuller's London Pride; Ossett Yorkshire Blonde, Silver King, Excelsior; guest beers Ⓗ

Converted into a venue for music, comedy and conversation, this Georgian building retains bare brick walls, fireplaces and other original features, along with new additions including a VW camper van turned into a bar. There are nine handpumps, one reserved for a dark beer and one for a Fernandes or Riverhead beer. A selection of bottled Belgian beers is also kept. Open mic night is Monday, quiz night Tuesday, and live music plays on Thursday, Friday and Saturday. Rooms are available for private hire. ❀♿⇌(Westgate)●⊟

Wakefield Labour Club

18 Vicarage Street, WF1 1QX (at top of Kirkgate, round corner from Wakey Tavern)

⏲ 11-4 (Sat only), 7-11 ☎ (01924) 215626
🌐 theredshed.org.uk

Beer range varies Ⓗ

Known as the Red Shed, this is a second-hand army hut which has been extensively refurbished, and is home to many union, community and charity groups. It has three rooms, two of which can be hired for functions. There is an extensive collection of union plates and badges over the bar as well as numerous CAMRA awards adorning the walls. Quiz night is Wednesday, live music plays on the second Saturday, and open mic folk music night is the last Saturday of each month.
Q⛾♿⇌(Kirkgate/Westgate)♣●P⊟🐾

Wetherby

Muse Ale & Wine Bar

16 Bank Street, LS22 6NQ

⏲ 11-11; 12-10.30 Sun ☎ (01937) 580201

Black Sheep Ale; Okells Manx Pale Ale; guest beers Ⓗ

Modern single-storey venue with separate bar and dining areas. Part of the Market Town Taverns chain of pubs, it prides itself on its gastronomic dishes and fine range of beers and wines. The four guest beers change regularly, always including at least one from a local brewery. Outside there is a seating area and a small car park. In summer a special window is opened allowing access to the bar from outside. Q❀◑♿P⊟🐾📶

Wintersett

Anglers Retreat

Ferrytop Lane, WF4 2EB (between villages of Crofton and Ryhill; follow local signs for nearby Anglers Country Park)

⏲ 12-3, 7-11 (not Tue); 12-11 Sat; 12-3.30, 7-11 Sun
☎ (01924) 862370

Acorn Barnsley Bitter; Morland Old Golden Hen, Old Speckled Hen; Samuel Smith Old Brewery Bitter Ⓗ

This cosy old-fashioned locals' pub is a rare example of a no-frills rural alehouse. The owner has just celebrated 20 years in charge. Close to the Angler's Country Park, Haw Wood and the Trans Pennine Trail, it is frequented by twitchers, cyclists, walkers and bikers. There is a beer garden to the side and seats at the front for fine weather drinking. A large car park is across the road and a frequent bus service passes within three minutes' walk. Q❀♿▲♣P⊟🐾

Pub opening hours

The Licensing Act of November 2005 for England and Wales gave pub owners the ability to apply for more flexible and extended opening hours from the licensing authorities. The most obvious change has been that many pubs now stay open until midnight or later at weekends. The experience of the first year of the law was that some pubs scaled down their opening hours where they found there was insufficient demand to remain open until midnight or later. The opening hours for pubs listed in the Guide have been checked before going to press, but readers planning to make journeys to pubs are advised to phone and check current hours.

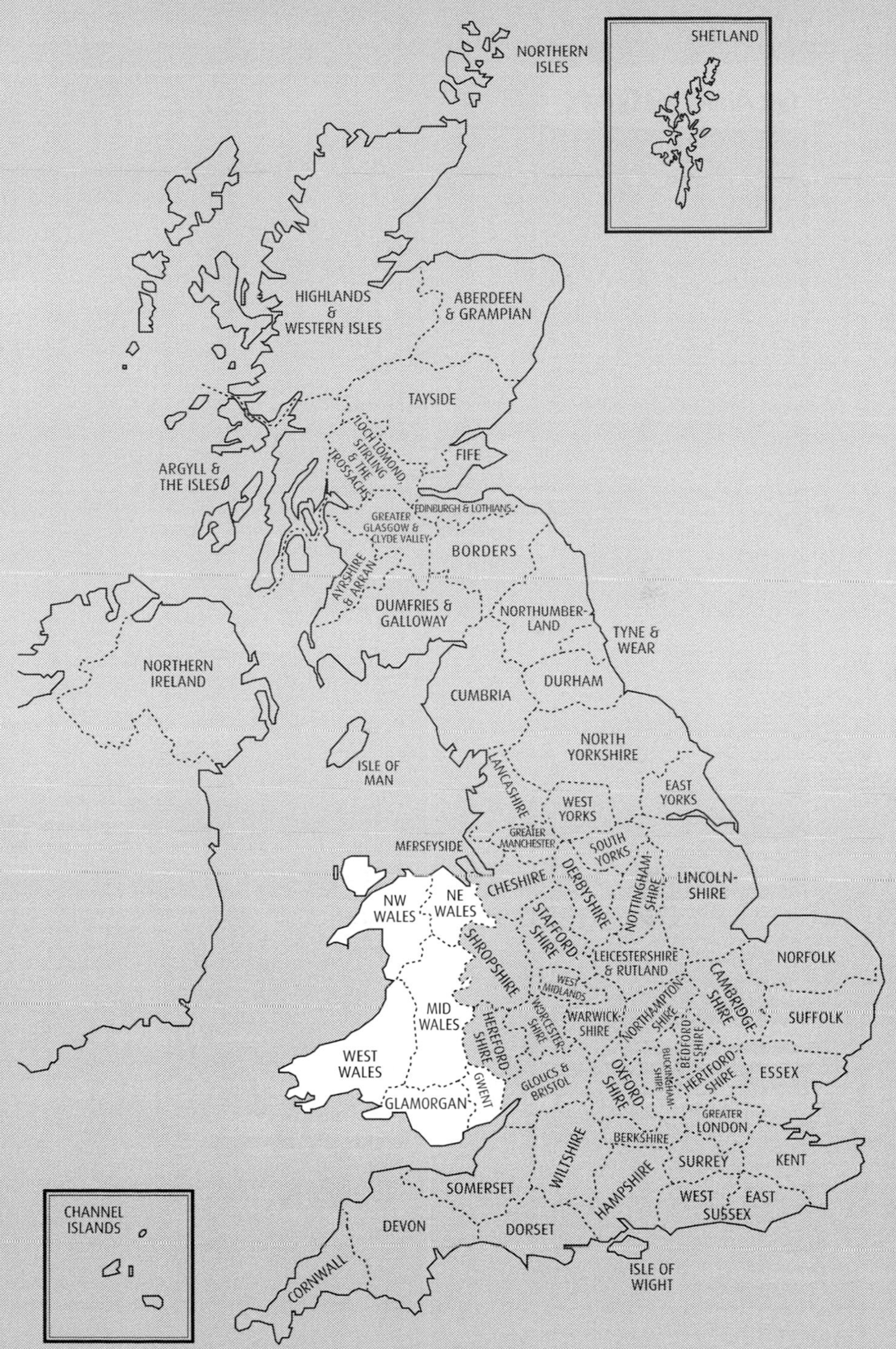
NORTHERN ISLES
SHETLAND
HIGHLANDS & WESTERN ISLES
ABERDEEN & GRAMPIAN
TAYSIDE
LOCH LOMOND, STIRLING & THE TROSSACHS
FIFE
ARGYLL & THE ISLES
EDINBURGH & LOTHIANS
GREATER GLASGOW & CLYDE VALLEY
BORDERS
AYRSHIRE & ARRAN
DUMFRIES & GALLOWAY
NORTHUMBER-LAND
TYNE & WEAR
NORTHERN IRELAND
DURHAM
CUMBRIA
NORTH YORKSHIRE
ISLE OF MAN
LANCASHIRE
EAST YORKS
WEST YORKS
GREATER MANCHESTER
SOUTH YORKS
MERSEYSIDE
CHESHIRE
DERBYSHIRE
NOTTINGHAM-SHIRE
LINCOLN-SHIRE
NW WALES
NE WALES
STAFFORD SHIRE
SHROPSHIRE
LEICESTERSHIRE & RUTLAND
NORFOLK
WEST MIDLANDS
CAMBRIDGE-SHIRE
MID WALES
HEREFORD-SHIRE
WORCESTER-SHIRE
WARWICK-SHIRE
NORTHAMPTON-SHIRE
BEDFORD-SHIRE
SUFFOLK
WEST WALES
BUCKINGHAM-SHIRE
HERTFORD-SHIRE
ESSEX
GWENT
GLOUCS & BRISTOL
OXFORD-SHIRE
GLAMORGAN
GREATER LONDON
BERKSHIRE
WILTSHIRE
SURREY
KENT
SOMERSET
HAMPSHIRE
WEST SUSSEX
EAST SUSSEX
CHANNEL ISLANDS
DEVON
DORSET
CORNWALL
ISLE OF WIGHT

Wales

GLAMORGAN

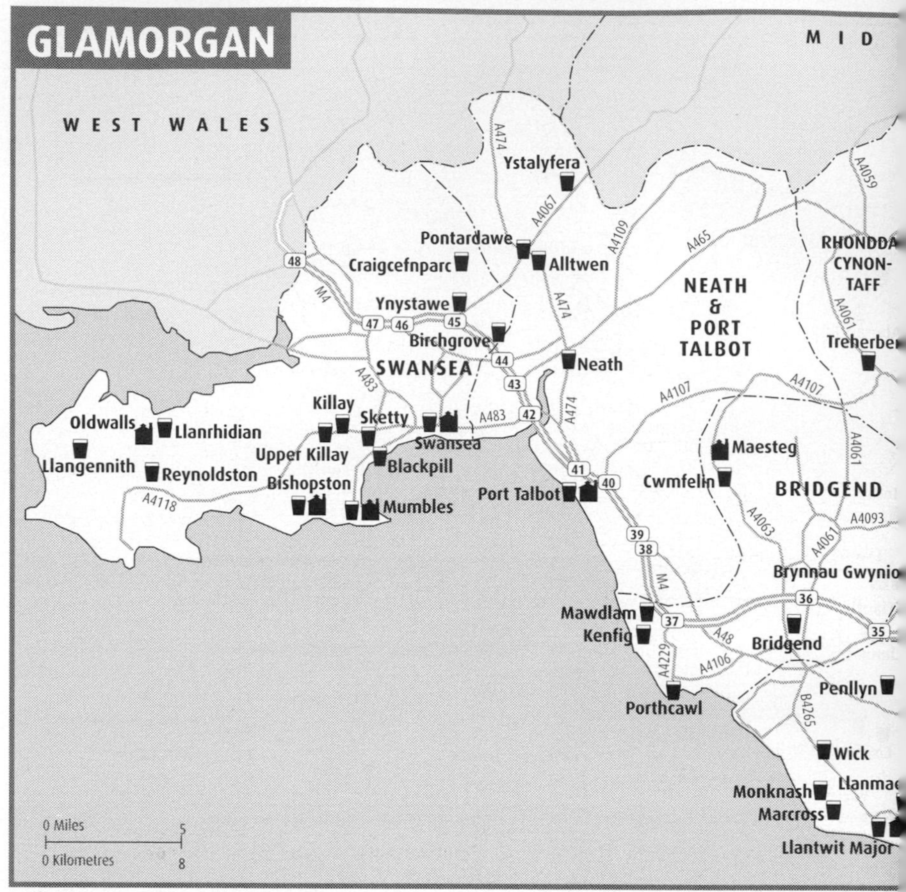

Authority areas covered: Bridgend UA, Caerphilly UA (part), Cardiff UA, Merthyr Tydfil UA, Neath & Port Talbot UA, Rhondda, Cynon & Taff UA, Swansea UA, Vale of Glamorgan UA

Aberdare

Whitcombe Inn

Whitcombe Street, CF44 7DA

✪ 12-11.15 ☎ (01685) 875106

Grey Trees Caradogs, Diggers Gold; guest beers Ⓗ

Welcoming and friendly traditional street-corner local, close to the town centre, in a valleys terrace. Local brewery Grey Trees features prominently on the bar, and other beers from its range may substitute. The large front bar backs onto a pool room at the rear. Sport is sometimes on TV, but is rarely intrusive. Live music is hosted occasionally. ≈♣🚌

Aberthin

Hare & Hounds

Aberthin Road, CF71 7LG

✪ 12-midnight (1am Fri & Sat) ☎ (01446) 774892

Draught Bass Ⓖ**; Hancocks HB; Kite Cwrw Gorslas; Wye Valley HPA; guest beer** Ⓗ

Friendly village pub with stone walls, wooden beams and a log fire providing plenty of character. The cosy bar to the left of the entrance tends to be where the locals gather, while a second bar has been added in the dining area to the right. Good, basic food is served and occasional beer festivals are held. The south-facing beer garden is a summer suntrap. Winner of local CAMRA Most Improved Pub of the Year 2014. Q❀◑♿♣●P🐾 Wi-Fi

Alltwen

Butchers at Alltwen

Alltwen Hill, SA8 3BP (off A474)

✪ 12-2, 6-11; 12-midnight Fri & Sat; 12-10 Sun

☎ (01792) 863100 🌐 thebutchersarmsalltwen.co.uk

Beer range varies Ⓗ

This free house, no longer tied, offers two well-kept ales, often from Wye Valley and Marston's. Other local and national beers also feature, and where possible ales requested by the regulars are made available. Essentially a destination pub for diners, a wide range of good fresh food is served. The attractive deck area gives views down the Swansea Valley, providing a pleasant spot for summer evening drinking. Q❀◑♿P🚌(122)

Gwyn Arms

Gwyn's Place, SA8 3AJ

✪ 4 (12 Sat & Sun)-midnight ☎ (01792) 896746

Beer range varies Ⓗ

Recently refurbished, this traditional village free house has retained its old wooden fittings. A warm welcome is assured from friendly staff and locals.

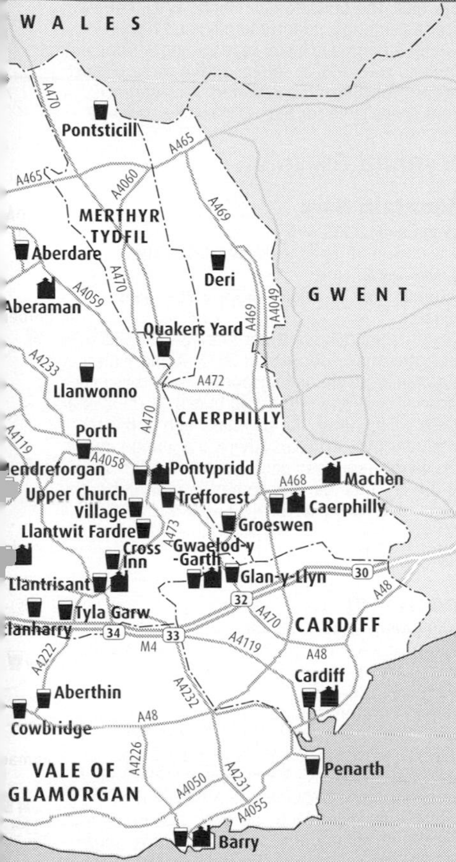

Local brews are regularly included among the beers. Live music plays at weekends and an open guitar jam session on Wednesdays. Situated in the picturesque Swansea Valley, the National Cycle Path 43 and footpaths for walkers are not far away. Q (122)

Barry

Barry West End Club

54 St Nicholas Road, CF62 6QY
1-midnight; 11-11 Sun (01446) 735739
Morland Old Speckled Hen; Rhymney Dark; Wye Valley Bitter; guest beers H
The new steward has upheld the fine traditions of this multiple CAMRA branch Club of the Year winner. Featuring a bar, lounge, function room and snooker room, the club is a hub of local activity, fielding eight skittles teams, two adult and two junior football teams and two snooker teams. It is also home to fishing and scuba clubs. Meals are a recent addition and with two beer festivals a year this establishment is well worth a visit. Q (Barry)

Sir Samuel Romilly

Romilly Buildings, CF62 7AU
8am-midnight (1am Fri & Sat) (01446) 724900
Greene King Abbot; Ruddles Best Bitter; guest beers H
This spacious Wetherspoon pub is named after a landowner and legal reformer from the 1800s. It opened in 2009 in a building that was previously a market hall, theatre and bank, the vault of which remains and is used as a seating area. A large mural above the side entrance depicts life in old Barry, with many more pictures of the town inside. A typical range of guest ales includes beers from local breweries such as Vale of Glamorgan. Q

Birchgrove

Bowen Arms

Birchgrove Road, SA7 9JR (just off M4 jct 44)
12-11 (midnight Fri & Sat) (01792) 324712
Felinfoel Best Bitter, Double Dragon; guest beer H
Comfortable pub with a single bar and separate function room. A games room adjoins the main bar, with a pool table, dartboard and TV sport. Outside, there is a play area for children and extensive seating. Live music plays occasionally during holiday periods and some weekends. Popular with diners, meals are available lunchtimes and evenings Monday-Thursday, all day until 8pm Friday and Saturday, and until 4pm Sunday. P (30,59)

Bishopston

Joiners Arms

50 Bishopston Road, SA3 3EJ
3-10.30 Mon & Tue; 11.30-11; 12-10.30 Sun
(01792) 232658
Courage Best Bitter; Marston's Pedigree; Swansea Bishopswood Bitter, Three Cliffs Gold, Original Wood; guest beers H
Situated in the heart of the village, this 1860s free house is popular with locals and visitors. Home of the Swansea Brewing Company, the pub has two bars and holds beer festivals and occasional music events, usually around public holidays. Good-value food is served lunchtimes and evenings (no food Mon and eve Sun). There is a small car park. A former winner of several local CAMRA awards. P (14)

INDEPENDENT BREWERIES

Artisan Cardiff
Brains Cardiff
Bullmastiff Cardiff
Carters Machen
Celt Experience Caerphilly
Cerddin Maesteg
Crafty Devil Cardiff (NEW)
Gower Oldwalls
Grey Trees Aberaman
Kite Llantrisant
Mountain Hare Brynnau Gwynion (NEW)
Mumbles Mumbles
Neath Port Talbot
Otley Pontypridd
Pixie Spring/Hopcraft Pontyclun
Swansea Bishopston
Tomos & Lilford Llantwit Major (NEW)
Tomos Watkin Swansea
Vale of Glamorgan Barry
Violet Cottage Gwaelod-y-Garth
Zerodegrees Cardiff

Valley

41 Bishopston Road, SA3 3EJ

12-11 (11.45 Fri & Sat) ☎ (01792) 234820

Brains Rev James; Courage Best Bitter; guest beers Ⓗ

Traditional country pub set in the heart of this Gower village. A large porch area leads to a split-level bar and dining area, with exposed beams, an open fire and hearth helping to create a cosy atmosphere. Live music and quiz nights feature occasionally. A wide variety of value-for-money home-cooked meals using local ingredients is served daily. ❀◐◑♿♣●P🚌(14)

Blackpill

Woodman

120 Mumbles Road, SA3 5AS (near turn off for B4436)

12-11 (10.30 Sun) ☎ (01792) 402700

Beer range varies Ⓗ

Local scenes of yesteryear decorate the various nooks and rooms of this spacious establishment situated between the seafront of Swansea Bay and the entrance to the beautiful Clyne Gardens. Popular with both families and diners, the pub is also welcoming to those seeking liquid refreshment only. A constantly changing range of guest ales is offered. There are three seating areas outside including a small beer garden. Meals are served until 10pm (9.30pm Sun).

Q❀◐◑♿P🚌

Bridgend

Cabo Roche

Five Bells Road, CF31 3HW

11 (12 Sat)-11.30; 12-10.30 Sun ☎ (01656) 663555

Sharp's Doom Bar; guest beer Ⓗ

Situated at the southern end of the town centre and close to the college, this establishment has continued to thrive since its conversion from a bathroom showroom to a bar in 2007. A mixed clientele uses the three distinct areas: a café, bar and lounge with comfortable settees. TV sport is available throughout, and real ale on two handpumps, one often an interesting and well-chosen guest beer. Lunches are served Monday to Friday. ❀◐♿⇌P🚌(303,X2)

Coach Inn

37 Cowbridge Road, CF31 3DH

11.30-11; 12-10.30 Sun

Wye Valley Butty Bach Ⓗ**; guest beers** Ⓗ/Ⓖ

Basically furnished free house serving up real ale and cider from Wales and beyond. Three guest beers on handpull and two served straight from the cask complement the house ale Butty Bach. Continental beers are available including takeaway bottles. Customers enjoy open mic nights, special themed nights, brewery trips, a spring beer festival every Easter weekend and a stout and porter festival in November. The pub has an art wall to display the work of local artists.

❀⇌♣●🚌(303,X2)

Wyndham Arms

Dunraven Place, CF31 1JE

9am-midnight (1am Fri & Sat) ☎ (01656) 673571

Greene King Abbot; Ruddles Best Bitter; guest beers Ⓗ

Beers from South Wales breweries feature strongly in this town-centre Wetherspoon hotel which hosts regular Meet the Brewer nights to promote local cask ales. The building dates from 1792, named after a centuries-old local family, and has 25 en-suite bedrooms available. Seating ranges from high stools to comfortable settees in the three distinct sections for drinking and dining. A conference room is available for hire. Q◐◑♿⇌●🚌

Brynnau Gwynion

Mountain Hare

Brynna Road, CF35 6PG

12 (5 Mon)-11; 12-10.30 Sun ☎ (01656) 860453

mountainhare.co.uk

Mountain Hare First Gold; Wickwar BOB; guest beers Ⓗ

A community pub which resumed brewing its own beer after many decades in 2013. Along with a Mountain Hare ale on handpump, there is usually a Wickwar beer and interesting guests. A traditional Welsh village local, the pub has been in the same family for over 40 years. There is a lounge, public bar, games room and garden. Sport is often shown on the TV in the bar and games room in this rugby lovers' pub. ❀♿♣●P🚌(44,244)

Caerphilly

Green Lady

Pontygwindy Road, CF83 3HF

10-11 (midnight Fri); 9am-midnight Sat; 9am-11 Sun

☎ (029) 2085 1510

Beer range varies Ⓗ

Modern Marston's pub alongside the old main road, north of the town centre. Comfortable and spacious, it has a separate restaurant. Three handpumps dispense beers from the Marston's group, including seasonals. Good-value meals are available daily (no food Sun eve). Live music features on most Friday and Saturday evenings. ❀◐◑♿⇌(Energlyn & Churchill Park)P🚌(26,50)

Malcolm Uphill

89-91 Cardiff Road, CF83 1FQ

8am-midnight ☎ (029) 2076 0720

Greene King Abbot; Ruddles Best Bitter; guest beers Ⓗ

Popular Wetherspoon pub, situated at the top of the town, handy for the rail and bus interchange. The name recalls a local motorbike champion. Two or three guest beers are usually on sale, plus two guest ciders. The usual Wetherspoon deals and promotions are offered. Ask staff if the separate accessible entrance is needed. The pub can be busy at weekends. Q❀◐◑♿⇌●🚌

Cardiff

Albany

105 Donald Street, Roath, CF24 4TL

12-11 (11.30 Fri & Sat); 12-10.30 Sun ☎ (029) 2031 1075

Brains Dark, Bitter, SA, SA Gold, Rev James; guest beers Ⓗ

A friendly pub in a residential area catering for a wide range of customers from locals to students. A range of Brain's beers is available, often including one from the Brain's craft brewery. One area is lively with pub games, TV showing live sport and a skittle alley. The lounge is quieter and offers a reasonably priced food menu. A quiz is held weekly. There is a covered, heated smoking area, and the large beer garden is popular in summer. ❀◐◑♣🚌(57,58)

Andrew Buchan

29 Albany Road, Roath, CF24 3LH

11-11

Rhymney Best, Hobby Horse, Dark, Bevan's Bitter, Bitter, Export Ale; guest beer H

This recently converted shop is the only regular outlet for the full range of Rhymney beers. It features an open fireplace with the brewery moose head hanging above. There is an upstairs meeting room, available free of charge for community groups. The pub has developed a good reputation for live music with bands playing several times a week. Happy hour is 5-7pm. (Cathays)

Chapter Arts Centre

Market Road, Canton, CF5 1QE (off Cowbridge Road East behind police station)

12-11 (12.30am Fri; midnight Sat); 12-10.30 Sun

(029) 2030 4400 chapter.org

Ringwood Best Bitter; guest beers H

Located west of the city centre, Chapter is a multi-purpose venue offering two cinemas, performance spaces and an art gallery. The contemporary café-bar serves a choice of up to five guest ales, some from the Marston's range and others from across the country including microbreweries. A guest cider together with an inspiring range of continental bottled beers are also available. Regular beer festivals are held throughout the year. Food is reasonably priced and of good quality.

P(17,18)

City Arms

10-12 Quay Street, CF10 1EA

12-11 (midnight Thu; 2am Fri & Sat); 12-10 Sun

(029) 2064 1913 thecityarmscardiff.com

Brains Dark, Bitter, SA, Rev James H**; guest beers** H/G

Attractive 1880s pub in the heart of Cardiff's beer quarter. It has two rooms served by a central bar that features gravity stillage as well as many handpumps. Decor is basic and the pub has a Dutch bier huis feel to it. A Brain's house, it serves a good selection of Brain's beers, including ones from its craft brewery, alongside many guest beers from a wide range of breweries around the UK. Beer-related events and live music nights are hosted.

(Central)

Cricketers

66 Cathedral Road, Pontcanna, CF11 9LL

11.30-11 (029) 2034 5102 cricketerscardiff.co.uk

Evan Evans Best Bitter, Cwrw, Warrior; guest beer H

Set in a substantial Victorian house on a main road, this pub is within easy walking distance from Cardiff Castle and the city centre. It is the only regular outlet in Cardiff for the full range of Evan Evans beers, as well as occasional ones under the Archers and WH Buckley brands. Quality food is available, with a daily menu and chalkboard specials. There is an upstairs meeting room. Popular on cricket and rugby international days.

Halfway

247 Cathedral Road, Pontcanna, CF11 9PP

12-11.30; 11-midnight Fri & Sat; 11-11 Sun

(029) 2066 7135

Brains Dark, Bitter, SA, SA Gold, Rev James; guest beers H

Bustling Victorian pub with a varied clientele in the urban village of Pontcanna. The large open-plan interior offers a number of comfortable areas for drinking and dining – food is served all day. Sporting events are shown on multiple screens. Beers from Brain's craft brewery often feature and the keen licensee holds a beer festival over the August bank holiday. The skittle alley is available to hire. Nearby is a rare example of a trolleybus turning circle.

Lansdowne

71 Beda Road, Canton, CF5 1LX

12-11 (11.30 Fri & Sat); 12-10.30 Sun (029) 2022 1312

thelansdownecardiff.co.uk

Beer range varies H

Recently restored on the ground floor of a previously substantial hotel, this is an excellent example of a friendly community pub. Beers are sourced by an enthusiastic manager, mainly from smaller local independent breweries supplemented by quality UK brews. Real cider is occasionally available. An ever-changing menu of good home-made pub food is offered, made with local ingredients. There are themed activities on some evenings, and a beer festival in the summer. Local CAMRA Pub of the Year 2014.

(Ninian Park)(12,13)

Mochyn Du

Sophia Close, Pontcanna, CF11 9HW

12-11 (midnight Fri & Sat); 12-10.30 Sun

(029) 2037 1599 ymochyndu.com

Beer range varies H

Located a short walk from the city centre, off Cathedral Road near the Glamorgan County Cricket Club, this large, attractive free house offers a choice of up to four real ales. It hosts regular Welsh themed events and is a popular meeting place for its Welsh-speaking clientele. The conservatory provides a smart and comfortable atmosphere in which to enjoy good home-cooked food. The large decked areas outside are pleasant in fine weather.

QP

Mount Stuart

Landsea House, Stuart Place, Cardiff Bay, CF10 5BU

9am-11.30 (12.30am Fri & Sat) (029) 2044 8000

Greene King Abbot; Ruddles Best Bitter; guest beers H

In the heart of Cardiff Bay, the Mount Stuart is a contemporary Wetherspoon pub constructed largely of glass, giving fine views in all directions. It has two storeys, with outdoor drinking areas on both levels – the upper one in particular is a lovely place to be on a good day with views across the Bay to Penarth Head and on to Somerset. There are bars on both levels and several contrasting seating areas. Q(Bay)

Pen & Wig

1 Park Grove, CF10 3BJ

11.30-midnight (1am Fri & Sat); 11.30-11.30 Sun

(029) 2037 1217 penandwigcardiff.co.uk

Beer range varies H

A short stroll from the city centre, this lively Victorian pub has recently been refurbished and attracts a mixed clientele of students, professional people and other folk. It offers a varied beer range featuring ales from large, micro and local breweries. Board games are available. An extensive garden including a covered area for smokers is at the rear of the bar.

(Cathays)

Rummer Tavern

14 Duke Street, CF10 1AY
11.30-midnight; 12-11 Sun ☎ (029) 2023 5091
therummertaverncardiff.co.uk
Hancocks HB; Wye Valley HPA; guest beers Ⓗ
Opposite Cardiff Castle, this is Cardiff's oldest trading pub. The interior is narrow but long, with dark wood panelling throughout and leaded windows, divided into a series of simply furnished areas. Real cider complements the beer range, and pub food is served until early evening. An upstairs room is available for hire.
(Queen St/Central)

Urban Tap House

26 Westgate Street, CF10 1DD
12-2am ☎ (029) 2039 9557 urbantaphouse.co.uk
Tiny Rebel Fubar, Dirty Stop Out; guest beers Ⓗ
A real ale mecca a drop kick away from the Millennium Stadium. This prominent, red-brick building has an interior dominated by Tiny Rebel Brewery's quirky, punky artwork. There is a variety of rooms spread over two floors, some available for hire. Real ales are from craft breweries and a wide range of real ciders and craft keg and bottled beers is served. A gravity beer bar operates on rugby international days. A homebrew club meets once a month. (Central)

Zerodegrees

27 Westgate Street, CF10 1DD
12-midnight (11 Sun) ☎ (029) 2022 9494
zerodegrees.co.uk/cardiff
Zerodegrees Mango Wheat Pils, Wheat Ale, Black Lager, Pale Ale, Pilsner; guest beer Ⓐ
Set in a listed former bus garage, the on-site brewery is the first thing you notice from the street, forming a backdrop to the well-stocked bar, with the beer storage tanks to one side. The decor is contemporary and there are two upstairs areas for diners, one opening onto a small balcony. A large wood-fired oven is used for excellent pizzas, available alongside other tasty food. Happy hour is 4-7pm Monday-Friday, but halfs cost more than pints at all times. (Central)

Cowbridge

Vale of Glamorgan Inn

51 High Street, CF71 7AE
11.30-11 (midnight Fri & Sat); 12-11 Sun
☎ (01446) 772252
Adnams Broadside; Hancocks HB; Wye Valley HPA, Butty Bach; guest beer Ⓗ
Popular single-roomed pub in the centre of town. The bar area has wood floors and a warming fire, with more seating in the lounge section. Pumpclips hanging over the bar showcase the many guest beers sold. Outside there is an attractive enclosed beer garden with a separate covered and heated smoking area. The annual beer festival coincides with the town's food and drink festival. Good-value home-made food is served at lunchtime (no food Sun). A former CAMRA branch Pub of the Year.
Q (X2)

Craigcefnparc

Rock & Fountain

Rhyddwen Road, SA6 5RA
5 (4 Fri; 3 Sat)-11; 12-10.30 Sun ☎ (01792) 843347
Felinfoel Stout, Celtic Pride; guest beer Ⓗ
Friendly local situated on the side of a steep hill close to the RSPB Cwm Clydach bird sanctuary. There is an outside patio area with seating where you can enjoy the view across the valley. The pub has a comfortable lounge featuring pictures of local interest and pub memorabilia, with a separate games bar for pool, darts, dominoes and sport on TV. P(121)

Cross Inn

Cross Inn Hotel

Main Road, CF72 8AZ
12-11 ☎ (01443) 223431
Hancocks HB; Sharp's Doom Bar; Wye Valley HPA; guest beer Ⓗ
A warm, welcoming, part stone-flagged traditional pub, popular with locals and visitors. The large single room is subdivided into a bar area and larger lounge section. The landlord and landlady keep both the pub and beers in immaculate condition. Poker nights and curry nights feature regularly, and Sunday lunches are recommended (booking advised). QP

Cwmfelin

Cross Inn

Maesteg Road, CF34 9LB
11.45-midnight (1am Fri & Sat); 11-midnight Sun
☎ (01656) 732476 cerddinbrewery.co.uk
Cerddin Solar, Cascade; Wye Valley Butty Bach; guest beers Ⓗ
In an area where good real ales are hard to find, this friendly multi-room pub with its own green-energy-run Cerddin Brewery is a breath of fresh air. Cerddin is Welsh for rowan tree which, in mythology, has magical properties. The pub is situated between Maesteg and Bridgend, with buses stopping at the front door and the railway station within walking distance. Local CAMRA branch Pub of the Year in 2013.
Q(Garth)(32)

Deri

Old Club

93 Bailey Street, CF81 9HX
5 (12 Sat & Sun)-midnight ☎ (01443) 830278
Beer range varies Ⓗ
Proudly independent public house offering a commendably diverse and innovative beer range. Two beers are always available, rising to three at weekends – national brands are rarely seen here. The nearest transport hub is Bargoed, where a bus or taxi to Deri can be found. Alternatively, the former railway path to Deri is a pleasant 45-minute stroll. Cwm Darran Country Park is nearby.
(1)

Glan-y-Llyn

Fagin's Ale & Chop House

9 Cardiff Road, CF15 7QD
11-11 (midnight Thu & Fri); 12-midnight Sat; 12-10.30 Sun
☎ (029) 2081 1800 faginsalehouse.co.uk
Dark Star Hophead Ⓗ**; guest beers** Ⓖ
This one-bar free house is popular with all ages. Three gravity-dispensed guest ales change continually, regularly featuring modern hoppy brews. Two changing ciders, usually from Gwynt y Ddraig, are on handpump. The bar and a separate

restaurant offer good-value meals from the same menu. Live music features most Thursday evenings and sometimes on Saturdays. The pub is well served by public transport. CAMRA branch Pub of the Year 2014. (26,132)

Groeswen

White Cross Inn

CF15 7UT (overlooking Groeswen Chapel)

4 (12 Fri-Sun)-midnight ☎ (029) 2085 1332

thewhitecrossinn.co.uk

Beer range varies H

A little off the beaten track, this traditional gem is well worth seeking out. Three changing beers are available, always including a dark ale, and a real cider is sometimes stocked. Prices are keen and beer festivals are hosted on occasion. A pub for the community, entertainment includes spiritualist evenings, beerbellies evenings, karaoke and live music evenings. Road access is narrow, though the pub is not far from main roads, and local buses stop a mile away. P

Gwaelod-y-Garth

Gwaelod-y-Garth Inn

Main Road, CF15 9HH

10-11; 12-10.30 Sun ☎ (029) 2081 0408

gwaelodinn.co.uk

Wye Valley Bitter; guest beers H

Situated in the centre of the village, this is a stone-built multi award-winning village local. The location, on the foothills of the Garth Mountain, from where its Welsh language name is derived, offers splendid views across the valley. Expect to find at least one beer from the on-site Violet Cottage Brewery, complementing a varying range of real ales from other brewers. There is an upstairs restaurant but diners are equally welcome to take meals in the bar area. QP(26B)

Hendreforgan

Griffin Inn L

Gilfach Goch, CF39 8YL (from Tonyrefail on A4093, turn down lane after Gilfach Goch sign)

7 (6 Fri)-11; 12-11 Sat & Sun ☎ (01443) 670379

Brains SA H

Although just one cask ale is served, this pub at the bottom of a country lane is well worth a visit. Listed in CAMRA's Real Heritage Pubs of Wales, the Griffin (known locally as the Bog) has been in the same family for over 50 years. The oldest building in the village, period features in the back bar include a splendid Victorian counter with an 1870 till, still in use, and gleaming brasses.
QP(150,172)

Kenfig

Prince of Wales

CF33 4PR

12-11 (8 Mon); 12-1am Fri & Sat ☎ (01656) 740356

princekenfig.co.uk

Draught Bass; guest beers G

Steeped in local history, this inn dates from around the 15th century, and the current landlord is only the 11th since 1816. Visitors can expect three or four quality ales on gravity, good food and a warm welcome. Family- and dog-friendly, the interior is comfortable and cosy, and outside is a stunning view over Kenfig Nature Reserve. The Draught Bass is renowned throughout the local area, outselling the pub's lagers by three-to-one.
QP(63B)

Killay

Village Inn

5-6 Swan Court, The Precinct, SA2 7BA

10.30-11.30; 12-11.30 Sun ☎ (01792) 203311

Evan Evans Warrior; Fuller's London Pride; Timothy Taylor Landlord; guest beer H

Cosy pub with an L-shaped bar and wood panelling, situated in a small shopping precinct. Home-made food is served until 8pm daily from a wide-ranging, daily-changing menu, both in the bar and separate restaurant (booking essential). The pub shows selected sport on TV, holds a quiz on Sunday and Tuesday evenings and hosts monthly gatherings of a Song Writers' Guild. An annual beer festival features in April. Local CAMRA Pub of the Year 2012. P(20,21)

Llangennith

King's Head L

SA3 1HX

11-11; 12-10.30 Sun ☎ (01792) 386212

kingsheadgower.co.uk

Gower Brew One, Sampson's Jack, Best Bitter, Gold; guest beer H

A row of three 16th-century stone-built cottages, the pub has been owned and run by the same family for many years. The full range of ales from nearby Gower Brewery is available plus a cask cider. An impressive variety of home-made food is served all day, with dishes inspired by fresh local produce. Situated at the Western end of the Gower Peninsula, a short distance from the sandy stretches of Llangennith Beach, the pub offers quality 4-star accommodation.
P(116)

Llanharry

Fox & Hounds

Llanharan Road, CF72 9LL

12-11 (midnight Fri & Sat) ☎ (01443) 222124

fox-and-hounds-inn-llanhari.co.uk

Beer range varies H

Family owned and independent since 2011, this delightful stone inn has rapidly established a reputation for being one of the best pubs in the area. Sassy modern styling in traditional materials creates a relaxing and comfortable ambience. Up to four guest beers are available, offering a range of flavours to suit all tastes, sourced from micro and smaller breweries. A selection of bottled real ciders is available. P(44,244)

Llanmaes

Blacksmiths Arms

CF61 2XR

12-11.30 (10.30 Sun) ☎ (01446) 795996

blacksmithsarmsllanmaes.co.uk

Brains Rev James; Hancocks HB; guest beers H

Deservedly popular inn opposite the village green, which hosts a beer festival each summer as part of the village fair. Highly regarded food includes traditional home-cooked Sunday lunches and steaks on a Tuesday night. Charity quiz nights are on Wednesday and Sunday. There is disabled access throughout, and a heated and canopied smoking area. Q🐴❀◐◑♿P🐾📶

Llanrhidian

Dolphin Inn

SA3 1EH (just off B4295 N Gower Road)

⏲ 1 (4.30 Mon)-11 summer; 4.30 (1 Fri & Sat)-11 winter; 12-11 Sun ☎ (01792) 391069 🌐 thedolphininngower.co.uk

Brains Rev James; Fuller's London Pride; guest beer 🄷

Cosy village pub dating from the 18th century on the north side of Gower (look for the yellow dolphin signs), situated next to a 13th-century church, with stunning views of the estuary from the lovely beer gardens. The characterful single-room interior is warmed by a solid fuel stove. There is a children's play area at the rear with a fenced area for rabbits and poultry to roam. Cold snacks are available until 8pm. Afternoon opening times may vary. 🐴❀P🚌(115,116)🐾

Greyhound Inn 🄻

Oldwalls, SA3 1HA (1 mile W of Llanrhidian on B4295)

⏲ 11-11 ☎ (01792) 391027

🌐 thegreyhoundinnoldwalls.co.uk

Gower Brew One, Sampson Jack, Best Bitter, Gold, seasonal beer; guest beers 🄷

Traditional 19th-century inn with a welcoming atmosphere, offering a range of ales from the pub's on-site Gower microbrewery. An extensive home-cooked bar menu is available until 9pm every day. Outside at the rear is a large beer garden with a children's play area and wonderful views over the Gower countryside. Home of the Halfpenny Folk Club on a Sunday evening, and the venue for the Gower Folk Festival in June. Local CAMRA Branch Pub of the Year 2013.
Q🐴❀◐◑♿♣P🚌(116)🐾

Llantrisant

Cross Keys Hotel

High Street, CF72 8BR

⏲ 4-midnight (12.30am Fri); 12-midnight Sat & Sun

☎ (01443) 222155

Greene King IPA; guest beers 🄷

Large open-plan pub on the main road through Llantrisant old town. The Greene King IPA may be replaced for another beer; the two guest beer pumps serve ales from local brewery Pixie Spring/ Hopcraft. Among the diverse entertainment on offer are free cheeses on Monday nights, live music on Friday and Saturday nights, and Sunday night darts, with beer as the prize. Children are admitted until 9pm. ❀🛏♣🚌(100,400)🐾📶

Llantwit Fardre

Crown Inn

Main Road, CF38 2HL

⏲ 1 (3 Mon & Tue)-midnight; 12-midnight Sat & Sun

☎ (01443) 218277 🌐 freewebs.com/crowninn

Beer range varies 🄷

Friendly pub with a large bar and an interesting mix of spaces including a function room and separate games area. Two ever-changing guest beers are served. Live music features on Fridays and a quiz on Sundays, and various other events are hosted throughout the year in aid of the local community and charities. Well served by local buses. 🐴❀◐◑P🚌(100,400)🐾📶

Llantwit Major

King's Head

East Street, CF61 1XY

⏲ 11.30-11.30 (midnight Fri & Sat); 11.30-11 Sun

☎ (01446) 792697 🌐 sabrain.com/kings-head

Brains Bitter; guest beers 🄷

This family-run town-centre local is a fine example of a community pub. It has a traditional two-bar interior, with a long stone-floored public bar well used by darts and pool teams, and a comfortable lounge with a carpeted floor and wood panelling, leading to the beer garden. Both bars have large-screen TVs for sport. Ales are generally from Brains including one of its speciality craft beers.
Q🐴❀⇌♣🚌🐾📶

Old Swan Inn

Church Street, CF61 1SB

⏲ 12-11 (10.30 Sun) ☎ (01446) 792230

🌐 knifeandforkfood.co.uk/swan

Beer range varies 🄷

The oldest pub in town overlooks St Illtyd's Church to the side and the town hall at the front in this historic old part of Llantwit Major. An ever-changing range of ales often showcases Welsh beers. The front bar is popular with drinkers and diners – excellent food is a feature of this attractive and comfortable hostelry – while the popular back bar is somewhat livelier. Beer festivals are hosted in spring and summer. There is free public parking behind the town hall.
Q🐴❀◐◑⇌♣🍎🚌(95,303)🐾📶

Llanwonno

Brynffynon Hotel

CF37 3PH (opp church) ST030955

⏲ closed Mon; 12-11 (10.30 Sun) ☎ (01443) 790272

🌐 brynffynonhotel.com

Beer range varies 🄷

Set on top of the ridge between the Cynon and Rhondda Fach valleys, this tranquil country inn is well-worth the effort to seek out. The lounge has a timeless atmosphere with relaxing leather couches and log-burning fire. The dining room serves food of an excellent standard (booking recommended). Two guest beers are available, and regular beer festivals are held throughout the year. A patio offers views of the forest and ancient churchyard.
🐴❀🛏◐◑⛺P

Marcross

Horsehoe Inn

CF61 1ZG

⏲ 12-2.30 (not Mon), 6-11; 12-11 Sat; 12-10.30 Sun

☎ (01656) 890568 🌐 theshoesmarcross.co.uk

Wye Valley Butty Bach; guest beers 🄷

A beautiful 19th-century pub in the tiny village of Marcross. Good food is offered along with regularly changing guest ales often from Welsh breweries. The small interior is cosy on a winter's evening, and on a sunny day the beer garden is a delight. Conveniently situated near the Nash Point car park – from here you can walk along the coastal path or just enjoy the views across the channel.
Q🐴❀◐◑P🚌(303)

Mawdlam

Angel Inn

Marlas Road, CF33 4PG
12-11 (10.30 Sun) ☎ (01656) 740456
Draught Bass; guest beers G
Although the majority of the pub's trade is food service – the large car park can fill up at peak times – there is a comfortable bar for drinkers to the left, which has a TV for sport. The four ales are all served straight from the cask, kept at a perfect temperature out the back. Close to the M4 motorway and the Kenfig Nature Reserve.
Q P (63B)

Monknash

Plough & Harrow

CF71 7QQ
12-midnight ☎ (01656) 890209 ploughandharrow.org
Wye Valley HPA; guest beers H
Renowned, welcoming, 14th-century pub, originally a monastic farmhouse for Neath Abbey, with many original features remaining. Up to eight real ales are offered, four on handpump, the others served direct from casks, with local breweries well supported, along with real cider and perry. Good home-cooked food is available, and the large log fires add warmth in winter. The spacious garden is popular and hosts beer festivals in summer. Local CAMRA Cider Pub of the Year winner.
Q P (303)

Mumbles

Park Inn

23 Park Street, SA3 4DA
4 (12 Fri-Sun)-midnight ☎ (01792) 366738
Beer range varies H
The convivial atmosphere in this small establishment attracts discerning drinkers of all ages, though the games room is particularly popular with younger people. Five handpumps dispense an ever-changing range of beers, with particular emphasis on independent breweries from Wales and the west of England. Alongside a fine display of pumpclips are pictures of old Mumbles and its pioneering railway. A popular quiz is held on Thursdays, with occasional music at weekends. (2,3)

Pilot Inn

726 Mumbles Road, SA3 4EL
12-11 (midnight Fri & Sat) ☎ (01792) 366643
thepilotofmumbles.co.uk
Draught Bass; Sharp's Doom Bar; guest beers H
Welcoming and friendly local on the seafront at Mumbles and home to the Mumbles Brewing Company. Six ales are always available, including three or four from the pub brewery. A wide range of bottled ciders is also stocked and hot drinks are served too. This historic pub, built in 1849, is next to the coastal path and is popular with lifeboatmen, locals, real ale fans, walkers and cyclists. Local CAMRA Pub of the Year 2014.
Q (2b)

Neath

Borough Arms

2 New Henry Street, SA11 1PH (off Briton Ferry road)
4-11 (8 Mon); 12-11 Sat; 12-8 Sun ☎ (01639) 644902
Draught Bass H/G**; guest beers** H
This cosy, traditional little gem is well worth the walk from Neath town centre. The horseshoe-shaped bar has four to six ever-changing beers from local and national breweries and a selection of bottled ciders. A friendly locals' pub, it shows a variety of sports events on TV. Winner of local CAMRA Pub of the Year title three times, this is probably the best back-street pub in Wales.
Q

David Prothero

7 Windsor Road, SA11 1LS
8am-midnight (1am Fri) ☎ (01639) 622130
Greene King Abbot; Ruddles County; guest beers H
Situated opposite Neath railway station, this popular Wetherspoon outlet was the former Neath Police Station. It is named after the first policeman to be appointed in 1836 – the four alcoves were once the lock-ups for the town. Wall-mounted TVs show news bulletins with teletext. Two real ciders are also available.

Penarth

Bear's Head

37-39 Windsor Road, CF64 1JD
8am-11.30 ☎ (029) 2070 6424
Bullmastiff Son of a Bitch; Greene King Abbot; Ruddles Best Bitter; guest beers H
A Wetherspoon outlet right in the town centre with an extensive open-plan interior including a small comfortable family area upstairs. A clientele of all ages enjoys a variety of up to eight ales, with locally brewed Vale of Glamorgan, Bullmastiff, Celt and other Welsh beers making regular appearances. There is a steady trade most of the week, but it can be busy on Friday and Saturday evenings. The pub's name is a rough translation of Penarth – pen meaning head and arth meaning bear. Q (Dingle Rd)

Golden Lion

69 Glebe Street, CF64 1EF
10-11; 11-midnight Fri & Sat; 12-10.30 Sun
☎ (029) 2070 1574
Felinfoel Double Dragon; guest beers H
A JW Bassett pub situated a short walk from the town centre. Recently refurbished to a high standard, and resembling a London-style bar, the pub offers good-value food including a Sunday carvery, and two or three real ales usually from Welsh breweries. TV sport is available throughout, even in the small beer garden, and the jukebox has an impressive 20,000 tracks – it can be lively. Regulars include local sports teams, including football and darts. (Dingle Rd)

Pilot

67 Queen's Road, CF64 1DJ
12-11 (midnight Fri & Sat); 12-10.30 Sun
☎ (029) 2071 0615 knifeandforkfood.co.uk/pilot
Beer range varies H
For many years a Brain's pub, the Pilot was refurbished in 2012 and is now operated by Knife and Fork Food, with the emphasis on high-quality food and drink. Ales are sourced from all over the country, and quality Welsh breweries often feature, especially Otley. Three of the four handpumps are usually used for beer, the fourth serving real cider. There is seating outside at the front for warm weather, and a view across Cardiff Bay at the rear.
Q (Dingle Rd)

WALES

Penllyn

Red Fox

CF71 7RQ

12-11 (10 Sun) ☎ (01446) 772352 redfoxinn.co.uk

Hancocks HB; Tomos Watkin OSB; guest beers H

This pub was almost closed and turned into accommodation but was saved by the village residents. It has gone from strength to strength over the past eight years and is now a popular and friendly local. The bar area and separate restaurant have flagstone floors and little nooks and crannies, and outside there are patio areas front and back. A warm welcome is offered to regulars and newcomers alike. Local CAMRA Pub of the Year 2014. QP

Pontardawe

Dillwyn Arms Hotel

The Cross, SA8 4EB

12-midnight ☎ (01792) 863310

Young's Special; guest beer H

Prominently situated in the centre of Pontardawe, the pub has benefited from many improvements of late. There is a separate restaurant and a comfortable lounge bar on the ground floor served by a central bar, and 3-star accommodation on the first floor. Two real ales of consistent quality are always available. Live music is a popular attraction on Sunday evenings. A decked terrace at the rear overlooks the river and caters for both smokers and drinkers. P(120,132)

Pontardawe Inn

123 Herbert Street, SA8 4ED

12-midnight ☎ (01792) 447562

Banks's Bitter; Marston's Pedigree; guest beers H

Now back to its best, the Gwachel, as it is known locally, is a focal point for the community. Live music features regularly in the rear bar on Friday and Saturday evenings, with Welsh language bands playing once a month. The guest ales are usually from the Marston's range and the pub puts on three beer festivals in May, August and November. The new landscaped garden is popular with drinkers and diners. QP

Travellers Well

76 Commercial Road, Rhydyfro, SA8 4SS

3-11; 12-midnight Fri & Sat; 12-11 Sun ☎ 07757 561568

thetravellerswell.info

Beer range varies H

Known as The Travs, it has a public bar, lounge and games area. Two guest beers are available, usually from Welsh microbreweries, and hot and cold snacks are served. The pub is situated in a good area for walkers between the Baran and Gwrhyd mountains. Carn Llechart stone circle and the 1,500-year-old Llangiwg Church are worth visiting while in the area. P

Pontsticill

Red Cow

CF48 2UN (follow signs for Brecon Mountain Railway)

10.30-midnight ☎ (01685) 384828

Wye Valley Bitter; guest beers H

Set within the Brecon Beacons National Park, this traditional inn has flagstone floors and a real ale enthusiast landlord. A popular locals' pub, it also attracts walkers and visitors to the beautiful Pontsticill Reservoir. The Brecon Mountain Railway is a modest but steep walk away. Hearty good-value lunches are served 12-4pm Tuesday-Sunday. P(24)

Pontypridd

Bunch of Grapes

Ynysangharad Road, CF37 4DA (off A4054)

11-1am (midnight Sun) ☎ (01443) 402934

bunchofgrapes.org.uk

Otley 01, 02 Croeso; guest beers H

A short stroll from the town centre, this popular pub has distinct areas around a central bar. Six guest beers accompany four from Otley Brewery, plus two cider or perries. Guest ales are varied and wide ranging. A separate and acclaimed restaurant serves locally-sourced food and hosts popular themed nights - booking is advised, especially at weekends. Beer, cider and cheese festivals, and much more, all feature. A winner of many CAMRA and other awards. QP

Llanover Arms

Bridge Street, CF37 4PE (opp N entrance to Ynysangharad Park, off A470)

11-midnight (11 Sun) ☎ (01443) 403215

Brains Bitter; guest beers H

Historic free house in the same family for over a century, built around 1794 to serve thirsty boatmen working the newly opened Glamorganshire Canal. Three rooms are linked by a central passageway, each room with its own regulars. Nearby is Ynysangharad Park and the famous town bridge and museum. The Taff Trail passes close by. QP

Patriot Bar

25B Taff Street, CF37 4UA (at N end of main shopping street)

10 (12 Sun)-midnight ☎ (01443) 407915

Rhymney Hobby Horse, Dark, Bevans Bitter, Bitter, Export Ale H

Owned by Rhymney Brewery, this no-frills bar serves keenly priced beers to a varied clientele. Formerly a travel agents, it has a functional and basic interior and is known locally as the Wonky Bar. Convenient for the bus and railway stations, it is located on the main shopping street close to the Muni Arts Centre. The bar offers a 'husband minding service'.

Port Talbot

Lord Caradoc

69-73 Station Road, SA13 1NW

8am-midnight (1.30am Fri & Sat) ☎ (01639) 896007

Brains Rev James; Greene King Abbot; Ruddles County; guest beers H

A Wetherspoon Lloyd's Bar in the centre of Port Talbot, close to both bus and railway stations. It has a good atmosphere attracting a varied clientele from shoppers to regulars. Three regular ales are on offer and usually two or three guest ales, often from South Wales regional and microbreweries.

Porth

Rheola

Rheola Road, CF39 0LF

2-midnight; 1-1am Fri; 12-1am Sat; 12-midnight Sun

☎ (01443) 682633

Draught Bass; Jennings Cumberland Ale; guest beer Ⓗ
This free house is situated where the Rhondda Valley divides and is well-served by bus and train. A central bar separates the games room, which can sometimes be loud, and the comfortable lounge. Quiz nights, whist nights and live music nights all feature. An extra guest beer is added at weekends and all the beers are competitively priced. The outdoor smoking area is sheltered. ❀⇌♣P🚌

Porthcawl

Lorelei Hotel

36-38 Esplanade Avenue, CF36 3YU
5 (12 Fri-Sun)-11 ☎ (01656) 788342 🌐 loreleihotel.co.uk
Rhymney Export Ale Ⓗ**; Worthington's Bitter** Ⓖ**; guest beers** Ⓗ
Close to the seafront and the Grand Pavilion, this seaside hotel has featured in the Guide for the past 16 years. It serves four draught beers and five continental beers, plus cider during the summer months, and hosts beer festivals twice a year. The building, dating from around the end of the last century, was originally two separate buildings. During the First World War one was used as a hospice for injured soldiers. Q❀♣🚌

Quakers Yard

Glantaff Inn

Cardiff Road, CF46 5AH
11-4, 6-1am; 11-1am Fri & Sat; 11-midnight Sun
☎ (01443) 410822
Beer range varies Ⓗ
Set above the river, this pub is popular with walkers and cyclists on the nearby Taff Trail. Its comfortable bar recalls local history in early photographs and artefacts. Three beers are usually available – two tend to change regularly, the third is often a guest beer back by popular demand. Styles and breweries vary, with a local beer frequently among the range. Good-value, quality food is served. 🚌(7,78)

Reynoldston

King Arthur Hotel

Higher Green, SA3 1AD (on village green)
10-11 ☎ (01792) 390775 🌐 kingarthurhotel.co.uk
Draught Bass; Felinfoel Double Dragon; guest beers Ⓗ
Traditional family-owned hotel with efficient and friendly staff. Situated at the foot of Cefn Bryn in beautiful Gower, it overlooks the village green and has a covered seating area outside. The cosy, atmospheric main bar is open to drinkers and diners, offering home-cooked food with a difference, made with local produce. Main meals are served lunchtimes and evenings, snacks are available all day. Beer can be bought to take out. The hotel is an acclaimed wedding venue.
❀♿P🚌(118,116)

Sketty

Vivian Arms

104 Gower Road, SA2 9BZ (Sketty Cross, jct of A4118 and A4216)
12-11 (midnight Fri & Sat) ☎ (01792) 516194
🌐 sabrain.com/vivianarms
Brains Bitter, SA, Rev James; guest beers Ⓗ
Situated on the main crossroads in Sketty, the Vivs is a spacious pub which attracts a wide range of customers young and old. It has a mixture of seating areas including comfortable sofas, and plenty of TV screens throughout the pub show live sport. Two frequently changing guest beers are available alongside the Brain's standards. The pub has a small meeting room and is suitable for family dining. Meals are served until 9pm Monday to Saturday and 6pm on Sunday.
❀♿🚌(20,21)

Swansea

Bank Statement

57/58 Wind Street, SA1 1EP
8am-1am (2am Sat; midnight Sun-Tue) ☎ (01792) 455477
Greene King Abbot; Ruddles Best Bitter; guest beers Ⓗ
A former Midland Bank, sympathetically transformed by Wetherspoon and retaining its original ornate interior. Trading as a Lloyds No.1, the bar is at the heart of the city's popular pub quarter and has a large ground floor with plenty of seating. Popular with all ages, it is busy throughout the week as well as at the weekend. An increased commitment to real ale has resulted in the availability of four guest beers and a cask cider.
♿⇌🚌(500)

Brunswick Arms

3 Duke Street, SA1 4HS (between St Helens Rd and Walter Rd)
11.30-11; 12-10.30 Sun ☎ (01792) 465676
🌐 brunswickswansea.com
Caledonian Golden XPA; Courage Best Bitter; Greene King Abbot; Morland Old Speckled Hen Ⓗ**; guest beers** Ⓗ/Ⓖ
Side-street pub with the air of a country inn in the city. Wooden beams and comfortable seating create a traditional, relaxing atmosphere. The walls are adorned with interesting, ever-changing displays of artwork, with pictures for sale. Home made specialities are available from the food menu, including curry and pie of the week. A quiz is held on Monday evening and live acoustic music plays on Sunday, Tuesday and Thursday. A guest beer, often from a local microbrewery, is on gravity dispense. ♿🚌(200)

No Sign Bar

56 Wind Street, SA1 1EG
11-11 (midnight Wed & Thu; 1am Fri & Sat); 12-11 Sun
☎ (01792) 465300 🌐 nosignwinebar.com
Beer range varies Ⓗ
Historic narrow bar established in 1690, formerly known as Mundays Wine Bar and reputedly a regular haunt of Dylan Thomas. Architectural signs from various periods of the pub's past remain, some dividing the interior into separate bar areas (including one above the main bar). Quality food and wine are available and there are usually four cask ales on sale. Live acoustic music features on Sunday and local bands play in the extensive Vault basement at weekends. ❀⇌🚌(500)

Potters Wheel

85-86 The Kingsway, SA1 5JE
8am-midnight (1am Thu-Sat) ☎ (01792) 465113
Brains SA; Greene King Abbot; Ruddles Best Bitter; guest beers Ⓗ
A city-centre Wetherspoon outlet named after the old pottery industry. The long sprawling bar area has various seating layouts and attracts customers of all ages and backgrounds. A strong connection to

the local CAMRA branch is evident from the real ale information board. An interesting selection of guest beers and a commitment to local microbreweries, enhanced by the introduction of casks on a back bar stillage, has boosted the pub's sale of real ales. Cask cider is always available. Q

Queen's Hotel

Gloucester Place, SA1 1TY (near Waterfront Museum)
11-11 (midnight Sat); 12-10.30 Sun (01792) 521531
Theakston Best Bitter, Old Peculier; guest beers H
This vibrant free house is near the Dylan Thomas Theatre, City Museum, National Waterfront Museum and marina. The walls display photographs depicting Swansea's rich maritime heritage. The pub enjoys strong local support and home-cooked lunches are popular. Evening entertainment includes a Sunday quiz and live music on Saturday. This is a rare local outlet for Theakston Old Peculier in addition to a seasonal guest beer, often from a local microbrewery.

Uplands Tavern

42 Uplands Crescent, Uplands, SA2 0PG
11-11 (midnight Fri & Sat) (01792) 458242
Greene King IPA, Abbot; guest beers H
In the heart of Swansea's student quarter, the Tav is a large single-room pub, popular with regulars from all walks of life. It is another former haunt of Dylan Thomas, commemorated in a separate snug area. The pub now has a deserved reputation for the quality and variety of its live music at weekends. There is a large heated drinking area outside at the front. Quiz night is Wednesday. (20,21)

Westbourne

1 Brynymor Road, SA1 4JQ
11-11.30 (11 Mon; 12.30am Fri & Sat); 11-11 Sun
(01792) 476637 westbourneswansea.com
Greene King Abbot; Sharp's Doom Bar; guest beers H
Located on the western fringe of the city centre, this street-corner pub has a single split-level bar and a heated terrace outside. Renowned in the area, it is now the place to go for young and old alike. Five or six ales are always available – customers are able to request a particular beer on the pub's website. A popular quiz is held on Tuesday evening. (2,3)

Trefforest

Otley Arms

Forest Road, CF37 1SY (on gyratory system)
11-midnight (1am Sat); 12-midnight Sun
(01443) 402033 otleyltd.co.uk
Otley 01, 02 Croeso; guest beers H
The original Otley family street-corner pub, gradually expanding its way along the terrace. Inside is a multitude of drinking areas and outside a heated and covered smoking area. Popular with university students and locals, this establishment is well-served by public transport and easily accessible from Cardiff and many valley towns. The four guest beers include one from the Otley range. A beer festival is held annually in October. (100,244)

Rickards Arms

61 Park Street, CF37 1SN
10-midnight (1am Fri & Sat); 12-11 Sun
(01443) 402305 otleyltd.co.uk
Otley 01; guest beers H
A firm favourite with students from the nearby university campus and equally popular with locals. The cosy atmosphere is enhanced by separate drinking spaces, including a vaulted cellar and upstairs dining area. Famed for its good-value bar food, the breakfasts are a notable feast. Entertainment includes regular quiz nights and music events. Two guest beers are often from the Otley range. (100,244)

Treherbert

Baglan Hotel

30 Baglan Street, CF42 5AW
11-11 (01443) 776111
Brains SA; guest beers H
This free house has been in the same family for over 60 years and the current landlord was born in the pub. Pictures of celebrities who have stayed here and old brewery memorabilia adorn the walls. A large flatscreen TV and dartboard are provided but it is conversation that dominates. Four guest beers from local breweries are usually available. A comfortably furnished lounge is used mainly for dining. (120,130)

Tyla Garw

Boar's Head

Coedcae Lane, CF72 9EZ (600yds from A473 over level crossing)
4-10 Mon; 12-11; 12-10 Sun (01443) 225400
Beer range varies H
The pub has four separate rooms, two set aside for dining, served by a single bar. Up to eight ever-changing beers are available, covering all styles from golden ales to dark milds and porters. Staff and locals are always happy to advise on choices. One or two beer festivals are held every year, with some beers served from the cask. Sunday lunches are busy and booking is advised. The direct walking route to Pontyclun station cuts through a small industrial area. Q (Pontyclun)P

Upper Church Village

Farmers Arms

St Illtyd Road, CF38 1EB
3-11 Mon-Wed; 12-midnight; 12-10.30 Sun
(01443) 205766
Brains Rev James; guest beer H
Single-bar village local with pleasant garden areas. The guest beer is often an unusual one for the area, generally from a smaller brewer. There is a popular quiz on Tuesdays and live music on alternate Thursdays. Beer and conversation are the main attractions, unless there is rugby on TV. No food available on Mondays. P (90)

Upper Killay

Railway Inn

553 Gower Road, SA2 7DS
12-11 (10.30 Sun) (01792) 203946
Swansea Deep Slade Dark, Bishopswood Bitter, Three Cliffs Gold, Original Wood; guest beer H
A classic locals' pub set in woodlands at the top end of Clyne Valley. The adjacent former railway line now forms part of route 4 of the National Cycle Network. In the winter the real fire in the lounge provides welcome warmth and cheer. Traditional

cider and at least one guest beer are kept alongside the Swansea Brewing Company beers. A large area outside hosts occasional barbecues, music events and boules tournaments in summer. Q❀♣🍎P🚌

Wick

Star Inn

Ewenny Road, CF71 7QA

⏲ 12 (5 Mon)-11.30; 12-10.30 Sun ☎ (01656) 890080
🌐 thestarinnwick.co.uk

Sharp's Doom Bar; guest beer Ⓗ

After a period of closure, the Star was totally refurbished by new owners late in 2012, returning it to its former glories when it was a Guide regular. Originally three farm cottages, the interior has a traditional bar and a lounge/diner and is flagstoned throughout. The friendly staff serve excellent home-cooked meals – the choice of Sunday roasts is particularly inspiring. Well-behaved dogs on leads are welcome in the bar. Q🛏❀◐◑♿P🚌(303)🐾

Ynystawe

Millers Arms

634 Clydach Road, SA6 5AY (on B4603, ½ mile N of M4 jct 45)

⏲ 11.30-3, 6 (5 Sat)-11; 12-3, 7-10.30 Sun
☎ (01792) 842614 🌐 millers-arms.co.uk

Greene King Abbot; Rhymney Hobby Horse; guest beer Ⓗ

Friendly community pub with a highly decorative interior including an extensive teapot collection, celebrity photo of the landlord with Tom Jones, and artwork by Katherine Jenkins. Busy periods require booking for meals, which are good value and home cooked, served in the pub and separate restaurant. In the spring a garden nesting box is on CCTV for twitchers. The pub is on the main bus routes to/from Swansea Valley and on route 43 of the National Cycle Network. 🛏❀◐◑♿P🚌(145,212)

Ystalyfera

Wern Fawr 𝕃

47 Wern Road, SA9 2LX

⏲ 2-5 (not Mon & Sat), 7-11; 12-11 Sun ☎ (01639) 843625

Bryncelyn Holly Hop, Buddy Marvellous, Oh Boy; guest beer Ⓗ

The Wern Fawr's cask beers are all from the Bryncelyn Brewery which started in the cellar of the pub in 1999. There are three regular beers plus a seasonal ale which changes frequently, all with Buddy Holly-themed names. The bar is home to a large collection of artefacts from the locality and is firmly on the must-visit list for real ale and historic pub enthusiasts. Q❀♣🚌(125)🐾

City Arms, Cardiff

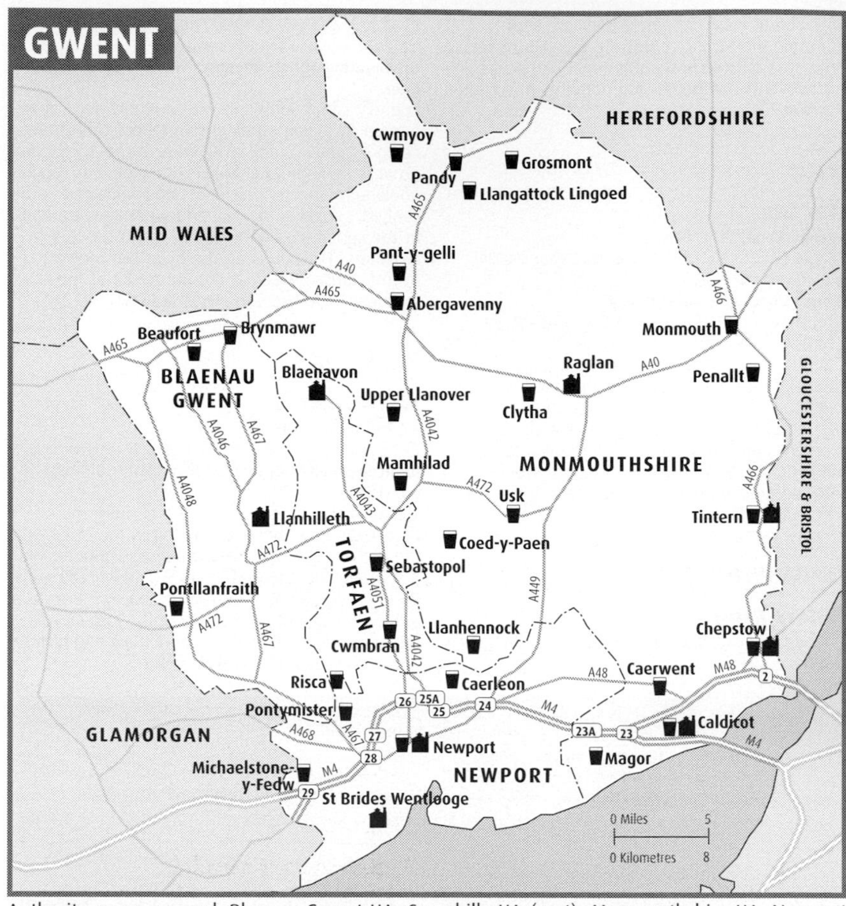

Authority areas covered: Blaenau Gwent UA, Caerphilly UA (part), Monmouthshire UA, Newport UA, Torfaen UA

Abergavenny

Angel Hotel

15 Cross Street, NP7 5EW

10-2.30, 6-11 (11.30 Fri & Sat); 12-2.30, 6-10.30 Sun

☎ (01873) 857121 🌐 angelhotelabergavenny.com

Rhymney Bitter; Wye Valley Bitter, HPA; guest beer Ⓗ

Established in 1829, this former coaching inn remains a focal point for the community. The main Foxhunter bar, named after a champion show-jumping horse, has an open fire, large tables and leather settees, and there are other smaller rooms, marked by high-quality fittings and artworks. There is a strong commitment to real ale, together with high-quality food and accommodation.

Q ❀ ◑ ♿ ≠ P 🚌 (X3,X4)

Grofield

Baker Street, NP7 5BB

5-11 Mon; 11-11.30 ☎ (01873) 858939

Rhymney Bitter; Sharp's Doom Bar; guest beer Ⓗ

Climbing a few steps takes you into this smart lounge bar which is popular with shoppers, cinemagoers and a loyal regular clientele. The decor is stylishly modern with attractive artwork on the walls, comfortable seating and smart leather cladding around the bar counter. Good-quality bar meals are available at lunchtimes. To the rear is a beer garden for alfresco drinking and dining. The regular ales are firmly established and are usually joined by an interesting guest.

Q ❀ ♣ 🚌 (X4,X43)

Station Hotel

37 Brecon Road, NP7 5UH

5 (2 Wed; 1 Thu)-11; 1-11.30 Fri; 12-11.30 Sat; 11.30-11 Sun ☎ (01875) 854759

Butcombe Bitter; Draught Bass; Wye Valley HPA; guest beer Ⓗ

Just outside the town centre, this is one of the few remaining traditional pubs left in the area, with a separate bar and lounge. Featuring among CAMRA's Real Heritage Pubs of Wales, its almost legendary status as a mecca for real ale drinkers does not prevent it from being a real local for the

INDEPENDENT BREWERIES

Castles Caldicot (NEW)
Coach & Horses Chepstow (NEW)
Kingstone Tintern
Rhymney Blaenavon
Tiny Rebel Newport
Tudor Llanhilleth
Untapped Raglan
Warcop St Brides Wentlooge (brewing suspended)

neighbourhood. Don't be confused by the name and the railway memorabilia – Brecon Road station and the line closed years ago. ♣P🚌(X4,X43)🐾

Beaufort

Cendl Inn 🄻

Beaufort Hill, NP23 5QN
🕐2 (12 Sat)-midnight; 12-10.30 Sun ☎(01495) 308627
Rhymney Export Ale 🄷
Taking its name from what is believed to be the old Welsh name for the village, this is a traditional drinkers' pub on the main road through Beaufort. It has a lively but friendly public bar and a separate quieter lounge where you will find the single handpump. Rhymney Export is occasionally replaced by a guest beer. There is a pleasant garden at the rear for finer weather. Closing time can vary according to trade. Q❀♣P🚌(X4)🐾

Brynmawr

Hobby Horse

30 Greenland Road, NP23 4DT
🕐11.45-3, 7-11; 11.30-midnight Sat; 11.45-10.30 Sun
☎(01495) 310996
Beer range varies 🄷
In August 2014 this fine example of a traditional community pub celebrated 25 years ownership in the same family and in September it made its 10th consecutive Guide appearance. On entering, to the left is a lounge and dining area that merges into a small bar area; a separate restaurant is to the right. The two ales are ever changing and mainly sourced from a core list of 10 or so breweries.
❀♣P🚌🐾

Caerleon

Bell Inn

Bulmore Road, NP18 1QQ
🕐12-11; 12-10.30 Sun ☎(01633) 420613
🌐 thebellatcaerleon.co.uk
Wye Valley HPA; guest beers 🄷
Award-winning pub where customers enjoy superb food washed down with a choice from a wide drinks range. While the emphasis is on dining during peak times, there is usually space for those just wanting to enjoy a relaxing drink in a pub that is rightly proud of its choice of ales and extensive range of ciders and perries. Expect to see a mix of popular nationally listed ales sitting alongside a more rare visitor. A former Welsh Cider Pub of the Year. ❀♣P🚌(27,60)🐾

Hanbury Arms 🄻

High Street, Uskside, NP18 1AA
🕐11.30-11; 12-midnight Fri & Sat; 12-11 Sun
☎(01633) 420361 🌐 sabrain.com/hanbury
Brains Bitter, SA, Rev James; guest beers 🄷
Caerleon's oldest inhabited building has a Norman tower forming part of its fabric. The spacious interior offers a choice of connected drinking and dining areas, some with riverside views. Alfred, Lord Tennyson wrote his Idylls of the King here and there is a wall plaque to commemorate the event. Reasonably priced food is available all day. The range of Brain's beers is supplemented by a guest often from the Brain's craft brewery. Quiz nights are Sunday and Tuesday. Q❀P🚌🐾

Caerwent

Coach & Horses

Green Lane, NP26 5AX
🕐11-11 ☎(01291) 420352
🌐 caerwent-coachandhorses.co.uk
Brains Rev James; Wye Valley HPA, Dorothy Goodbody's Golden Ale, Butty Bach; guest beer 🄷
Surrounded by a village steeped in Roman history with many significant remains, this pub is an ideal base from which to explore the locality. A Roman defensive wall forms one boundary of the extensive pub garden and play area. The roadside entrance leads into the public bar where sporting memorabilia and trophies are displayed. At the rear is an intimate lounge which gives access to the pleasant dining room. Food is popular here with dishes using mainly locally-sourced produce.
❀♣P🚌(73)🐾

Caldicot

Cross Inn

1 Newport Road, NP26 4BG
🕐11-11 (12.30am Thu-Sat); 12-11 Sun ☎(01291) 420692
Greene King IPA; Sharp's Doom Bar; guest beer 🄷
A lively hostelry at the centre of this small town and handily placed by the main bus stops and shopping area. It is clearly a locals' pub with a loyal following but there is a warm welcome for those passing through. The regular ales are popular and the guest ale, usually from a local brewery, provides an interesting alternative. A draught cider is also often on offer. At weekends live music is a big attraction. ❀♣P🚌(74,X74)🐾

Chepstow

Chepstow Athletic Club 🄻

Mathern Road, Bulwark, NP16 5JJ (off Bulwark Rd)
🕐7-11 (11.30 Fri); 12.30-11.30 (midnight summer) Sat; 12-4.30, 7-11 Sun ☎(01291) 622126
Brains SA; guest beers 🄷
CAMRA members and visitors (whether sporty or not) get a warm welcome at the Athy, where fans and players from a wide variety of sports create strong demand and rapid turnover for the four or five cask ales on offer. A comfortable lounge gives access to a raised fine-weather patio within hitting distance of well-struck cricket balls. This consistently popular community venue also hosts a range of local groups and organisations including the famously thirsty Chepstow Male Voice Choir.
❀♣P🚌(74,X74)

Clytha

Clytha Arms 🏆 🄻

Groesonen Road, NP7 9BW (on B4598 old road between Abergavenny and Raglan)
🕐12-3 (not Mon), 6-midnight; 12-midnight Fri-Sun
☎(01873) 840206 🌐 clytha-arms.com
Wye Valley Bitter; guest beers 🄷
Gwent CAMRA Cider & Country Pub of the Year 2014 has a landlord dedicated to the art of hospitality. Offering up to seven real ales, always including a beer from Kite, and a variety of local ciders and perries, and serving locally-sourced innovative food, this is understandably a very popular venue. High-class accommodation and camping facilities make this former dower house an excellent base for the many festivals held

throughout the year. Whether you prefer cider, beer, dumplings or traditional pub games, there is a festival for you. Q🐴❀🛏◐◑♣🍎P🚌(83)🐾

Coed-y-Paen

Carpenters Arms

NP4 0TH (aim for Llandegfedd Reservoir, cross the dam, the pub is ½ mile further on left) SO986334

🕓 closed Mon; 12-3, 6-11; 12-11 Sat; 12-5 Sun

☎ (01291) 672621 🌐 thecarpenterscoedypaen.co.uk

Wye Valley Butty Bach; guest beers [H]

To the right of the small flagstone bar is an intimate restaurant while to the left is a larger restaurant and function rooms. A licence to perform weddings can make Saturday afternoons extremely busy. The guest ales are usually well-known brands while the regular Wye Valley ale is subject to change. The owner is a chef and food is mainly sourced locally. The pub is half a mile from Llandegfedd Reservoir, for sailing, windsurfing and fishing. 🐴❀◐◑♿⛺P🐾

Cwmbran

Bush Inn

Graig Road, Upper Cwmbran, NP44 5AN

🕓 12 (4 Mon-Wed)-11.30 ☎ (01633) 483764

🌐 thebushuppercwmbran.co.uk

Beer range varies [H]

In fine weather, this mountainside pub gives superb views over Cwmbran towards the Bristol Channel. There is comfy sofa seating, a jukebox and a choice of tabletop games. Musical instruments are dotted around while one wall features old pictures of the pub and snapshots of local industrial history. The mainly local real ales are constantly changing and up to five real ciders are also on offer. Live music and home-made food (book for curry night on Wednesday) add to the attractions. 🐴❀◐◑♣🍎P🚌(1,8)🐾

Queen Inn

Upper Cwmbran Road, Upper Cwmbran, NP44 5AX

🕓 12-11.30 (11 Sun) ☎ (01633) 484252

🌐 thequeeninn.co.uk

Beer range varies [H]

With the pub's own wildfowl swimming in the stream out front, and a steep tree-covered hill behind, this pub has a distinct country feel. Inside, there is a lounge-cum-dining room and linked bar area, leading to another cosy dining room, separated from the bar by a fireplace with a log burner. Two of the three ales are sourced from Enterprise while the third can come from anywhere but is often from a local brewery.
🐴❀◐◑♣🍎P🚌(1,8)🐾

Cwmyoy

Queen's Head

NP7 7NY (in village, take lane signed to Llanthony, pub is 1 mile on right) SO311221

🕓 10.30-2 Mon & Thu, 6-11; closed Wed; 10.30-3, 6-11 Sat; 12-4 Sun ☎ (01873) 890241

Beer range varies [H]

Exploring the scenic Llanthony Valley on foot is thirsty work, and while en route back from the famous old priory you could do a lot worse than call in at this fine old country inn for some well-earned refreshment. The Queen's is typical of what you would imagine a traditional country pub should be – all wooden beams and flagstone floors, plus a warming fire on cold days. One or two ales are sourced from the excellent Celt Experience/Newsman's range. Q❀◐P

Grosmont

Angel Inn

NP7 8EP

🕓 12 (6 Mon & Wed winter)-11 ☎ (01981) 240646

🌐 grosmont.org/group/the-angel-inn

Castle Rock Harvest Pale; Wye Valley Butty Bach; guest beer [H]

Perched high, almost on England's border, this pub really is the village hub. The traditional bar, to the left as you walk in, has a rustic charm, with a selection of wooden tables, attractive benches and settles, as well as hop-decorated beams. Guitars on the bar wall reflect the importance of music on pub life – live bands play here on a regular basis. Beer and cider festivals take place in summer and autumn respectively. 🐴❀◐◑♣🍎P🐾

Llangattock Lingoed

Hunter's Moon Inn

NP7 8RR (2 miles off B4521 Abergavenny-Ross old road at Llanvetherine at road bridge at end of village) SO363201

🕓 12-11 ☎ (01873) 821499 🌐 hunters-moon-inn.co.uk

Wye Valley HPA [H]**, Butty Bach; guest beer** [H]/[G]

Charming 13th-century pub lying on the long-distance Offa's Dyke Path and next to a village church. Now run by three generations of the same family, the atmosphere is often lively. Within the thick, historic walls is an attractive, flagstone-floored bar where an owl gazes down at you from under a hunter's moon. A woodburner provides heat when needed. In summer, walkers can enjoy food and drink outside at any time of day.
Q🐴❀🛏◐◑♿♣P🐾📶

Llanhennock

Wheatsheaf

Caerleon, NP18 1LT (turn right 1 mile along Usk Rd heading N from Caerleon, then bear left at fork) ST353927

🕓 11 (12 summer)-11; 12-4, 8-11 Sun ☎ (01633) 420468

🌐 thewheatsheafatllanhennock.webs.com

Fuller's London Pride; guest beers [H]

One of Gwent's most consistent pubs, the Wheatsheaf has made 29 consecutive appearances in this Guide. There are bars to the left and right on entering, both full of bric-a-brac, memorabilia and old photographs. Two guest beers are usually available, at least one from a local brewery. A lovely garden with attractions for children is adjacent to the entrance and boules is played in the car park, which has fine surrounding views. Darts is popular throughout the year.
🐴❀◐⛺♣P🐾

Magor

Wheatsheaf [L]

The Square, NP26 3HN

🕓 10-11 (midnight Fri & Sat); 12-11 Sun ☎ (01633) 880608

Beer range varies [H]

Attractive and well-run pub that epitomises a 21st-century village local, maintaining a traditional layout and decor, while bowing a little to modernity. While there are some restrictions with the beer range, there is nearly always something to tempt visitors and regulars alike. Marinello's coffee shop offers good breakfast options from 10am before the main lunchtime trade. Worth seeking out for good ale and food with an ambience to match. (62,74)

Mamhilad

Horseshoe Inn

Old Abergavenny Road, NP4 8QZ

closed Mon; 11.30-3, 5.45-midnight; 11.30-midnight Fri-Sun (01873) 880542 thehorseshoeinn.org

Sharp's Doom Bar; guest beer H

A tastefully refurbished country pub with a modern slate-floored bar. This welcoming inn, enjoying a new lease of life, serves a locally produced ale and real cider alongside the locals' favourite, Doom Bar. An interesting à la carte menu as well as hearty traditional fare are ample provision for walkers, canal boaters and tourists alike. Nearby are the Monmouthshire and Brecon Canal and the 200-year-old Goytre Wharf industrial heritage site and canal boat marina. P

Michaelstone-y-Fedw

Cefn Mably Arms

CF3 6XS

12-2.30, 5.30-11 Mon; 12-3.30, 5.30-11.30 (midnight Fri & Sat); 12-8.30 Sun (01633) 680347

thecefnmablyarms.co.uk

Brains Bitter; Butcombe Gold; guest beers H

Popular country pub, off the beaten track and with no access by public transport, but worth seeking out. The interior divides into two separate areas, and is mainly set out for diners. A recent addition is an annexe to one of the rooms, with access to the garden. St Michael's Church is next to the pub, in the traditional rural manner. It is rumoured that witches were once hung from the 800-year-old oak tree – the oldest in South Wales – in the car park. QP

Monmouth

Old Nag's Head

Granville Street, NP25 3DR

12-midnight (01600) 712220

Brains Rev James, IPA H

This ancient pub seems to whisk you back in time as soon as you cross its threshold. Part of its structure is a medieval tower which once formed part of the town's Dixton Gate. Within this fascinating interior, a central bar dispenses the regular ales which are sometimes joined by a guest at busy times. Music nights are popular here and on the walls, behind various instruments, are black and white pictures of stars of the past. (Bus station)

Newport

Godfrey Morgan L

158 Chepstow Road, Maindee, NP19 8EG

8am-midnight (1am Fri & Sat) (01633) 221928

Brains SA; Greene King Abbot; Ruddles Best Bitter; guest beers H

This popular Wetherspoon pub was once a cinema, and numerous photos of erstwhile stars of stage and screen with local connections are dotted around the walls. As many as nine ales are on handpull, plus cider on gravity dispense. Godfrey Morgan was a lucky survivor of the ill-fated charge of the Light Brigade. The main entrance is on the busy Chepstow Road, and there is limited parking at the rear. QP

Lamb

6 Bridge Street, NP20 4AL

9am-9 (11 Wed & Thu; 2am Fri & Sat); 12-8 Sun

(01633) 266801

Hook Norton Hooky; Wye Valley HPA; guest beers H

Take a few moments to admire the highly attractive dark-tiled exterior before stepping into this rejuvenated pub. One area has a decorative fireplace with a large TV screen above for sport and music channels. Plenty of high stools provide seating near the bar while old prints of yesteryear in Newport are displayed. A Tiny Rebel Brewery ale joins the house beers. What is described as Welsh comfort food is becoming increasingly popular. Quiz night is Wednesday, live music plays on Friday.

St Julian Inn

Caerleon Road, NP18 1QA

11.30-11.30 (midnight Fri & Sat); 12-11 Sun

(01633) 243548 stjulian.co.uk

Wells Bombardier; Young's Bitter; guest beers H

A busy pub, a model of consistency, on the bank of the River Usk, within sight of historic Caerleon. There is a balcony at the rear overlooking the river, with fine countryside views. A central bar serves four ales including two guests, often from Welsh and West Country brewers. The pub is clearly divided between various sections, some catering for diners, with the original roadside tavern occupied mainly by drinkers. There is also a function room and skittles alley. P

Pandy

Rising Sun

Old Hereford Road, NP7 8DL (just off A465 at S end of village)

closed Mon; 12-3 (not Tue-Fri), 7-11; 12-11 Sat & Sun summer (01873) 890254 therisingsunpandy.com

Wye Valley Butty Bach; guest beer H

Fully refurbished en-suite guest accommodation is available at this well-established roadside inn. With camping/caravan facilities open from March to October, the pub caters for tourists to the Brecon Beacons National Park, walkers on the Offa's Dyke Path and motorists on the busy A465 Abergavenny/Hereford road. Darts and pool are played weekly, plus skittles on portable lanes (book ahead). Wye Valley Butty Bach is always on offer alongside a varying second ale.
P (X33)

Pant-y-gelli

Crown Inn

Old Hereford Road, NP7 7HR

12-2.30 (not Mon), 6-11; 12-3, 6-11 Sat; 12-3, 6-10.30 Sun

(01873) 853314 thecrownatpantygelli.com

Draught Bass; Rhymney Best; Wye Valley HPA; guest beer H

Three regular beers, each of a different character, are joined by a weekly changing guest from one of the South Wales independent breweries. In recent years the Crown has built up a well-deserved reputation as a gastro-pub, making it a popular venue for foodies, but its commitment to remaining a local for the community remains as strong as ever. Situated at the foot of the Sugar Loaf mountain, it is a popular stop-off for walkers and the patio has wonderful views. ᘐ❀◐◑P

Penallt

Boat Inn

Lone Lane, NP25 4AJ

✪ closed Tue; 12-3, 5-midnight (9 Mon); 12-11 Sat; 12-9 Sun ☎ (01600) 712615 🌐 theboatpenallt.co.uk

Wye Valley Butty Bach; guest beers [G]

Located impressively close to the River Wye and accessed from England by footway along an antique former rail bridge, the Boat features a cosy main bar and side room. The cool stillage behind the bar has three cask ales, often alongside two or more ciders (several bottled ciders are available, too). Walkers who explore this beautiful valley stop here for the pub's generous meals and snacks. Riverside tables and a hillside garden are popular in fine weather. ᘐ❀◐◑♣●P🚌(69)🐾

Pontllanfraith

Crown Inn

The Bryn, NP12 2HE

✪ 4 (2 Fri)-1am; 12-1am Sat & Sun ☎ (01495) 223404

Brains Rev James; guest beers [H]

This friendly pub has a traditional public bar with a pool table, assorted settles and tables, plus a jukebox. The handpumps can be found in the spacious lounge-cum-dining room. Up to four ales may be on at peak times including Brains Rev James and often an ale from Butcombe Brewery. The attractive coalburner is a welcoming sight on cold days. The food menu offers a choice of popular dishes and tempting desserts.
ᘐ❀◐◑♿♣P🚌(7,26)

Pontymister

Commercial

Commercial Street, NP11 6BA

✪ 11 (10 Sat)-11.30; 12-11.30 Sun ☎ (01633) 612608
🌐 thecommercialpontymister.com

Beer range varies [H]

Thriving pub on the busy main road through town, winner of numerous awards, and succeeding in an area that has seen several pubs fall by the wayside. Good-value locally-sourced food is available. The four handpumps frequently serve beers from Newport's acclaimed Tiny Rebel Brewery, or sometimes other breweries with whom they operate a reciprocal trading arrangement. There is a popular high-quality jukebox plus several large TV screens often showing racing, though these are usually muted.
ᘐ❀◐◑♿⇌(Risca & Pontymister)♣●🚌

Risca

Fox & Hounds

Park Road, NP11 6PW

✪ 12-midnight (10.30 Sun) ☎ (01633) 612937

Beer range varies [H]

Busy and basic local overlooking a park, with views across the main road to the hills beyond. One ale is served, most often from Wye Valley's Dorothy Goodbody's range. This is very much a community pub, with events on most nights of the week. The interior is broadly divided into two areas, with comfortable seating in one and a pool table in the other. There are spacious drinking and smoking areas outside. A local cider is available during the summer months. ❀⇌♣●P🚌🐾

Sebastopol

Open Hearth

Wern Road, NP4 5DR

✪ 11.30-midnight; 12-11.30 Sun ☎ (01495) 763752

Wye Valley HPA; guest beers [H]

Nestling beside the Monmouthshire and Brecon Canal, this friendly family-run pub exudes tranquility although it has its livelier moments, especially when international rugby is on TV and live music is hosted. Popular cask ales appear on rotation and sometimes a local guest ale is added to bring an interesting variety to the bar. The menu lists a good choice of established pub favourites. Outside, towpath seating and a large garden are popular in good weather. Last entry is 11pm.
ᘐ❀◐◑♣P🚌(23,X24)🐾

Sebastopol Social Club [L]

Wern Road, NP4 5DU (on corner of Wern Rd with Austin Rd)

✪ 12-11 (midnight Fri & Sat); 12-10.30 Sun
☎ (01495) 763808 🌐 sebastopolsocial.org.uk

Wye Valley HPA; guest beers [H]

Serial CAMRA award winner offering a range of up to seven cask ales of different styles and strengths plus a draught cider at keen prices. A go-ahead committee and enthusiastic stewardess have seen this club thrive as a community hub. Entertainment comes in the form of darts, pool, skittles, bingo, live sport and music channels on TV, and live music on Saturdays. A popular annual beer festival is held. All are welcome but entry rules may apply on busy occasions. ❀♣●P🚌(23,X24)🐾📶

Tintern

Anchor Inn

NP16 6TE (off A466 at Tintern Abbey)

✪ 9am-11; 12-10.30 Sun ☎ (01291) 689582
🌐 theanchortintern.com

Otter Ale; Wye Valley Bitter; guest beers [H]

Reputedly the devil himself used to shout down from his rock pulpit high on the hillside above at Cistercian monks as they toiled in their abbey and its cider mill (now the main bar of this pub), urging them to abandon their labours. These days the glorious abbey attracts visitors from around the world, many of whom gravitate towards this family-run riverside hostelry with its large grounds, garden room and restaurant area with a delightful tiny side room. ᘐ❀◐◑●P🚌(69)📶

Wye Valley Hotel

Monmouth Road, NP16 6SQ

✪ 11-3, 6-11; 12-3, 6.30-10.30 Sun ☎ (01291) 689441
🌐 thewyevalleyhotel.co.uk

Wye Valley Bitter; guest beer [H]

This attractive hotel stands at the north of the village, a short stroll from the old Tintern railway station. Comfortable and well run, the building looks at its best in summer when the flower displays make it hard to miss. The landlord is a long-time supporter of Wye Valley Brewery – there are usually one or two of its ales on sale and occasionally another from locally based Kingstone Brewery. An impressive array of beer bottles is on display. P (69)

Upper Llanover

Goose & Cuckoo

NP7 9ER (turn off A4042 at the sign to Upper Llanover, then follow hand-written signs to the Goose) SO292073
closed Mon; 11.30-3, 7-11 Tue-Thu; 11.30-11 Fri & Sat; 12-10.30 Sun ☎ (01873) 880277 gooseandcuckoo.com
Celt Experience Iron Age; Rhymney Bitter; guest beer
Situated high above the picturesque village of Llanover, this charming one-room pub offers fine views across the Usk Valley. It owes its existence to the fact that it lay just outside the jurisdiction of Lady Llanover, a strict teetotaller, who allowed no alcohol on her land. Enjoy a warm welcome and a bowl of hearty bean soup while perusing the pictures and cuttings on the walls which open a window onto the social history of the area.
Q P

Usk

King's Head Hotel

18 Old Market Street, NP15 1AL
11-11 (10.30 Sun) ☎ (01291) 672963
Fuller's London Pride; Greene King Abbot; Timothy Taylor Landlord
This cosy nook maintains high standards with carefully selected quality ales and appetising meal choices. Settle into the delightful lounge bar and enjoy its old-world charm with its low-beamed ceilings and warming dark decor. At one end a great log fire gives welcoming warmth in cold weather, and the walls and shelves are covered in all sorts of memorabilia. Can you spot the TV? A mix of en-suite and budget accommodation is available. Q P (60,63)

New Court Hotel

62 Maryport Street, NP15 1AD
12-11 (10.30 Sun) ☎ (01291) 671319
thenewcourthotel.co.uk
Sharp's Doom Bar; Wye Valley HPA; guest beers
Bold new ownership and an impressive makeover have seen this establishment emerge as a popular dining and drinking destination. The interior has been tastefully redecorated making use of existing features such as low beams, wooden floors and flagstones. Stylish period furniture adds to the ambience. Taking centre stage on the bar are handpumps dispensing up to five real ales and two local ciders. For diners there is a tempting range of appetisers, main courses and desserts to savour.
Q (60,63)

Station Hotel, Abergavenny (Photo: Chris Gillette)

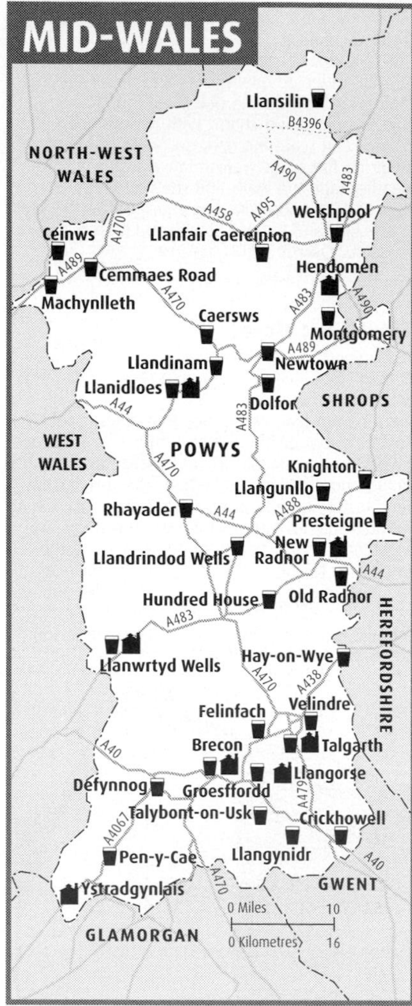

Authority area covered: Powys UA

Brecon

Brecon Rugby Club

63 The Watton, LD3 7EL
⏲ 5 (11 Sat & Sun)-11 ☎ (01874) 624848 🌐 breconrfc.co.uk
Beer range varies 🄷
A founder member of the Welsh Rugby Union, this friendly and welcoming club is open to all. A large main bar with a separate lounge is towards the front, and a large function room with a big screen behind. Outside is a spacious patio garden and the Brecon Pétanque Club. Beers from Brecon Brewing and Wye Valley are frequently available plus bottled ciders from Gwynt y Ddraig. The club is often busy during the rugby season, particularly when Wales are playing. Local CAMRA Club of the Year 2014. ⛴❀◐♣P🚌🐾

Clarence

25 The Watton, LD3 7ED
⏲ 12-midnight (2am Fri & Sat) ☎ (01874) 622810
Wye Valley Bitter, Butty Bach; guest beer 🄷
Two-roomed town-centre community pub with a contemporary, welcoming, relaxed atmosphere. The newly extended front bar tends to be frequented by locals, while the larger back bar is more popular with diners. A large screen draws a crowd for big sporting events. The spacious garden is a major attraction, especially during the jazz festival. Guest beers are generally sourced from local breweries. ❀◑♣●🚌🐾

Caersws

Red Lion

3 Main Street, SY17 5EL (on B4569)
⏲ 3-11.30 (midnight Fri); 12-midnight Sat; 12-11.30 Sun
☎ (01686) 689378 🌐 hophouseinns.co.uk/The-Red-Lion
Monty's MPA; guest beers 🄷
Wood-beamed village locals' pub with two bars, attracting a varied clientele of all ages. Early evenings can be boisterous with the after-work crowd calling in on their way home. The pub is part of Monty's Hophouse Inns and locally produced beer from Monty's Brewery is always on offer. Good-value meals are served. A beer festival is held on the August bank holiday weekend. A patio area is available at the rear of the pub for outside drinking. ❀◑♿⇌♣●P🚌(X75,X85)🐾📶

Ceinws

Tafarn Dwynant

SY20 9HA (off A487 3 miles N of Machynlleth)
⏲ closed Mon & winter Sun; 5.30 (3 Sat & Sun)-11
☎ (01654) 761660 🌐 tafarndwynant.co.uk
Purple Moose Cwrw Eryri/Snowdonia Ale; guest beers 🄷
Set in a quiet village, this friendly community free house is handy for attractions such as the Centre for Alternative Technology. Guest beers vary in number and come from Welsh breweries such as Brecon, Cwrw Cader and Purple Moose; mini beer fests extend the range. The landlord's own artwork is on display. Occasional live acoustic music is hosted. The front patio is used for alfresco drinking, with stunning views across the wooded Dulas Valley. Local bus 34 stops outside, longer-distance buses ply the A487 across the bridge.
Q⛴❀◑⛺🚌(34)🐾

Cemmaes Road

Dovey Valley Hotel ★

SY20 8JZ
⏲ 6-11 (10.30 Sun) ☎ (01650) 511335
Beer range varies 🄷
Serving real ale for the first time in three decades, this gem is a true survivor and has been identified by CAMRA as having a nationally important historic pub interior comprising of one main bar plus a recently opened snug room. Enhanced under new ownership, carpet tiles have been removed to reveal the original slate floor and fascinating photographs and posters (some rescued from the

INDEPENDENT BREWERIES

Brecon Brecon
Bryncelyn Ystradgynlais
Heart of Wales Llanwrtyd Wells
Monty's Hendomen
Radnorshire New Radnor
Redstone Llangorse
Rotters Talgarth
Waen Llanidloes

attic) now adorn the walls. Beer is sourced from local microbreweries, usually Monty's or Cwrw Cader, and Gwynt y Ddraig cider is often available. Q❀P

Crickhowell

Bear Hotel

High Street, NP8 1BW

11-3, 6 (7 Sun)-11 ☎ (01873) 810408 bearhotel.co.uk

Brains Rev James; guest beers H

Originally a 15th-century coaching inn, this is now an award-winning hotel. The multi-roomed bar enjoys grand surroundings with exposed beams, wood panelling, fine settles and an eclectic selection of furnishings and decorations. The two bar rooms have open fireplaces, as does one of the side rooms. Food is excellent, the varying menu featuring much local produce. The Bear is an excellent base for exploring the surrounding Black Mountains and Brecon Beacons National Park. Q❀P

Defynnog

Tanners Arms L

LD3 8SF

5 (12 Fri-Sun)-midnight ☎ (01874) 638032

tannersarmspub.com

Beer range varies H

Family-run country pub famous for the warm welcome it offers to locals and tourists alike, set in the delightful village of Defynnog in the Brecon Beacons National Park. The pub has traded continuously since 1870 but the original buildings (cottages for the workers at the nearby tannery) date to circa 1806. Home-cooked food is well worth stopping by for and a selection of real ciders is usually on offer. Local CAMRA branch award winner. ❀♣P

Dolfor

Dolfor Inn

SY16 4AA

12-11 (10.30 Sun) ☎ (01686) 626531

thedolforinn.co.uk

Brains Bitter; Wye Valley Butty Bach H

This former drovers' inn reopened in 2012. The bar area has settles, a low ceiling and a cosy atmosphere, and there is a popular games area adjacent. The stone-walled, wood-beamed restaurant has an inglenook fireplace. For larger parties there is a room converted from the old stable block. The pub is gaining a good reputation for its food and is handy for walkers on the Kerry Ridgeway path. ❀♣P

Felinfach

Griffin L

LD3 0UB (just off A470 3 miles NE of Brecon)

12-11.30 ☎ (01874) 620111 eatdrinksleep.ltd.uk

Beer range varies H

The Griffin's ethos – the simple things in life done well – says it all. A welcoming country pub, restaurant and hotel, the emphasis here is on good beer and excellent food. The multi-roomed layout allows for discrete areas for drinking and dining. A huge fireplace between the bar and the main dining area dominates during winter, while an Aga lurks in a side room, providing warmth throughout the building. The large beer garden affords superb views of the surrounding mountains. Q❀P

Groesffordd

Three Horseshoes

LD3 7SN

12-3 (not Mon), 5-11; 12-11 Fri-Sun ☎ (01874) 665672

threehorseshoesgroesffordd.co.uk

St Austell Tribute; guest beers H

Busy village-centre pub in the heart of the Brecon Beacons, boasting superb views from both the front and rear outdoor seating areas. The pub is only a 10-minute walk from the Brynich Lock on the Monmouthshire and Brecon Canal. Excellent food is on offer and it is worth booking ahead to avoid disappointment. Various events are held throughout the year. ❀♣P

Hay-on-Wye

Blue Boar

Oxford Road, HR3 5DF

9am-11 ☎ (01497) 820884

Hook Norton Hooky; Timothy Taylor Landlord; guest beers H

Comfortable and friendly town-centre pub, owned and run by the same family for many years. A large central bar dominates, with two separate seating areas on either side, each with its own log fire. Two regular beers are usually supplemented by one or two guests. Food is available all day in the bar or in the separate dining area. Q

Hundred House

Hundred House

LD1 5RY (on A481, near Builth Wells)

12-2, 5.30-11; 11-11 Sat & Sun ☎ (01982) 570231

Greene King Abbot; Wye Valley Butty Bach; guest beer H

Located among rolling Welsh hills, the Hundred House Inn takes its name from the Saxon 'hundred' which was an administrative area. At one time a drovers' inn, it is now a traditional, welcoming and friendly local, well patronised by the farming community. There is a lounge, locals' bar, pool room with TV (for rugby), restaurant area and beer garden. Afternoon closing times are flexible – the pub usually stays open if there are customers. Q❀♣P

Knighton

Horse & Jockey

Wylcwm Place, LD7 1AE

11-11 ☎ (01547) 520062 thehorseandjockeyinn.co.uk

Beer range varies H

The pub is of late medieval origins, set around a courtyard, and has a large restaurant converted from the original stables. It has been owned by the same family since 1989. The building is a pleasing mixture of old and new, with a variety of rooms and seating outside in the courtyard. It offers an extensive food menu featuring fresh local produce plus a pizza menu. There are three cask beers, usually from Welsh and border breweries. Q❀

Llandinam

Lion Hotel

SY17 5BY (on A470)
closed Mon; 12-3, 6-11; 12-11 Sat; 12-10.30 Sun
(01686) 688233 lionllandinam.com
Three Tuns XXX; Wood Special Bitter; guest beer H
Comfortable village hotel with a bar dominated by a large wooden beam and an open stone fire. Owned by an award-winning chef and his wife, it has been resurrected after lying dormant for 18 months. The venue is popular and a large selection of bar and restaurant meals is available (booking advised). There is a spacious garden and benches at the rear for outside drinking. The hotel is fast becoming the hub of the village, with a warm welcome for families. P (X75)

Llandrindod Wells

Conservative Club

South Crescent, LD1 5DH (opp bandstand)
11-2, 5.30-11; 11-11.30 Fri & Sat; 11.30-10.30 Sun
(01597) 822126
Banks's Bitter; Marston's Pedigree; guest beer H
Located in the centre of this historic spa town, the Con Club is a regular in the Guide. It has a large lounge, TV room, games bar, snooker and pool tables, and a small front patio/smoking area. Until the early 1970s the building was the Lansdown Hotel. Good-value lunches are served Wednesday to Friday and Sundays. CAMRA members are welcome but visitors must be signed in.
Q

Llanerch Inn

Llanerch Lane, LD1 6BZ (close to railway station)
11-11 (01597) 822234 thellanerchinn.co.uk
Hancocks HB; Rhymney Export Ale; guest beers H
This 16th-century former coaching inn pre-dates the Victorian town. The pub is much extended with rooms on several levels but retains original features. Outside, there are tables in an old orchard at the front, plus a covered rear patio. A wide selection of meals is available, including home-made specials. Three guest beers, often from Brains or St Austell, are on offer alongside Gwynt y Ddraig Dog Dancer cider. Live music acts feature on Friday or Saturday nights. There is a games room with darts, pool and TV. Q P

Llanfair Caereinion

Goat Hotel

High Street, SY21 0QS (off A485)
11-11 (midnight Fri & Sat) (01938) 810428
thegoathotel.co.uk
Beer range varies H
Excellent 300-year-old beamed coaching inn with a welcoming atmosphere which attracts both locals and tourists. The plush lounge, dominated by a large inglenook and open fire, has comfortable leather armchairs and sofas. There is a dining room serving home-cooked food and a games room to the rear. The choice of real ale always includes one from the ever-popular Wood Brewery.
Q P

Llangunllo

Greyhound

LD7 1SP (on B4356, off A488)
closed Mon & Tue; 4.30-11 (2am Fri); 2-2am Sat; 2-11 Sun
(01547) 550400
Beer range varies H
This cosy, former 16th-century cottage is a lovely old-fashioned hostelry in a beautiful mid-Wales setting. The beers are mainly from the Welsh borders and the Midlands. The present owners are lovingly restoring the pub and bringing it back to life as a community venue. Open mic nights are held on the first and third Saturdays of every month. Opening times are approximate – ring the doorbell any time after mid-day and with luck you will be served. P

Llangynidr

Red Lion

Duffryn Road, NP8 1NT (off B4558)
12-11 (01874) 730223 theredlionpowys.co.uk
Rhymney Best; guest beers H
Popular village local, off the beaten track, which offers a warm welcome to walkers, boaters, families and dogs. The beer range changes regularly and good-value home-cooked food is served in the bar. A separate games area, outside seating and children's play area make this a pub for all. P

Llanidloes

Angel Hotel

High Street, SY18 6BY (off A470)
12-2.30 (not Wed), 5-11.30; 12-3, 7-11.30 Sun
(01686) 412381
Everards Tiger; Greene King Abbot; Shepherd Neame Bishops Finger; guest beer H
Attractive and friendly edge-of-town pub with two comfortable bars. The larger of the two rooms has a stone fireplace and old photographs on the walls. The smaller room has an interesting bar inlaid with old pennies. There is a restaurant to the rear. The building was built in 1748 and Chartists held meetings here between 1838 and 1839. Outside seating is available at the front of the pub.
Q (X75,525)

Stag Inn

15 Great Oak Street, SY18 6BU (off A470)
12-11 (1.30am Fri); 11-1.30am Sat (01686) 414824
staginnllanidloes.co.uk
Purple Moose Cwrw Eryri/Snowdonia Ale; Shepherd Neame Bishops Finger H
Friendly town-centre pub offering two real ales and a real cider. The long premises is divided in two – the wooden-floored front area has wall seating and a wood-burning stove, the rear area through an archway has comfortable sofas, a pool table and a piano. There is an outside drinking space to the rear. The pub hosts live music at weekends. Reasonably priced bar snacks are served and take-away tea and coffee are available.
(X75,525)

Llansilin

Wynnstay Inn

SY10 7QB
5.30-10.30 (11 Thu); 1.30-11 Fri; 12-11 Sat & Sun
(01691) 791355 thewynnstayinn.weebly.com
Greene King IPA; Young's Bitter; guest beer H
Built in 1784, the Grade II-listed Wynnstay is the last of five inns the village once supported. It has a

public bar, lounge, pool room and a separate dining room which can be used for small functions. The inn is close to attractions including Pistyll Rhaeadr waterfall, Offa's Dyke Path and the Tanat Valley. The hub of the local community, it is home to various pub teams and hosts regular music nights. Q

Llanwrtyd Wells

Neuadd Arms Hotel

The Square, LD5 4RB
11-midnight (2am Fri & Sat) (01591) 610236
neuaddarmshotel.co.uk
Felinfoel Double Dragon; Heart of Wales Aur Cymru, Welsh Black; guest beers H
This large Victorian hotel serves as the tap for the Heart of Wales Brewery. The Bells Bar features a large fireplace and an eclectic mix of furniture. The bells formerly used to summon servants remain on one wall, along with the winners' boards from some of the town's more unusual competitions. The lounge bar is a little more formal. The hotel takes part in the town's annual events including a major beer festival in November. A good range of real ciders is kept. Q

Machynlleth

Dyfi Forester

4 Heol y Doll, SY20 8BQ
11.45 (11 Sat & Sun)-1am 07581 025224
Wye Valley Butty Bach; guest beer H
Halfway between the railway station and town centre, this basic down-to-earth drinkers' local is showing a renewed commitment to real ale (ignore the large Carling sign outside!). A quirky exterior with some original stained glass leads to the welcoming single bar. The beer turnover is rapid – the guest may be another from the Wye Valley range. Machynlleth, surprisingly bustling given its small size, is a splendid touring centre with good transport links. Enter as a stranger, leave as a friend.

Montgomery

Crown Inn

Castle Street, SY15 6PW
11-11 (01686) 668533
Brains Barry Island; Wye Valley Butty Bach; guest beer H
The Crown is the last traditional local in a town that once supported a multitude of hostelries, and is home to a large number of local sports teams. The public bar is long and quite narrow with a pool and games area at the rear. A small snug sits opposite the public bar, with a large array of trophies in it. There are benches for outside drinking. Beware of the low beams in the bar area.

New Radnor

Radnor Arms

Broad Street, LD8 2SP
12-2.30 (not Wed), 5-10.30; 12-11 Sat; 12-10.30 Sun
(01544) 350232
Beer range varies H
A traditional village pub with two bars in a building that dates from around 1700. During World War II it was popular with the troops from a nearby army camp and American servicemen from Kington. There are two rotating guest beers, usually from local breweries, and a range of real cider. The nearby Radnorshire Brewery is the county's only brewery, situated just down the road at Brookside Farm, and its beers feature regularly on the bar. Opening hours can vary. P

Newtown

Bell Hotel

30 Commercial Street, SY16 2DE (on B4568)
4 (12 Sat & Sun)-11 (01686) 625540
Brains Rev James; Monty's MPA H
Locals' bar in a hotel about five minutes' walk from the town centre. The public bar has a pool table, darts and a live entertainment area, and to the right of the main entrance is a comfortable lounge area. A local beer from Monty's is usually available alongside a real cider. The hotel offers reasonably priced rooms and is usually fully booked during the week. P

Railway Tavern

Old Kerry Road, SY16 1BH (off A483)
11-2, 7-midnight; 11-midnight Tue (1am Fri & Sat); 11-midnight Sun (01686) 626156
Worthington's Bitter; guest beers H
The 20th consecutive appearance in the Guide for Dave and Eileen's one-bar local near the station. Two guest beers from regional or small breweries are always on offer. The Railway hosts a number of darts and dominoes teams and can get crowded on match nights. The pub is essentially divided in two – a lower bar area and a rear area with wall benches and tables. Note the poster listing over 50 pubs that once operated in Newtown.
Q (X75)

Sportsman

17 Severn Street, SY16 2AQ (off A483)
closed Mon; 12-11 (11.30 Fri & Sat); 12-10 Sun
(01686) 623978 sportsmannewtown.co.uk
Monty's Old Jailhouse, MPA, Sunshine, Mischief; guest beers H
The Monty's Brewery tap is Montgomeryshire CAMRA 2014 Pub and Cider Pub of the Year. Five Monty's beers are available plus three guest ales and six ciders. The pub is divided into three areas – a snug with comfortable wall seating, a main bar area and a rear tiled games area with pool table, TV and darts. The bar has a muted TV showing silent movies and classic cartoons. There is a patio at the rear for alfresco drinking. Q (X75)

Old Radnor

Harp Inn

LD8 2RH (signed from Walton on A44)
closed Mon; 12-3 (not Tue-Fri), 6-11 (10.30 Sun)
(01544) 350655 harpinnradnor.co.uk
Beer range varies H
This early 15th-century Welsh longhouse commands a fine view over the Radnor Valley. The building was rescued and restored by the Landmark Trust in 1972 and then sold on in 1983. The interior is a tasteful mix of old and new, including a modern restaurant serving good food made with locally-sourced seasonal ingredients. There are occasional steak nights and seasonal tastings. Ales mainly come from local microbreweries and beer festivals are hosted from time to time. QP

Pen-y-Cae

Ancient Briton

Brecon Road, SA9 1YY (on A4067 just S of village)
12-midnight (01639) 730273 ancientbriton.co.uk
Wye Valley HPA, Butty Bach; guest beers H
Lovely country pub situated on the A4067 in the Brecon Beacons National Park and Fforest Fawr Geopark. On entering you are greeted by a welcoming array of 14 handpumps dispensing up to 10 real ales, two ciders and a perry. The bar is open plan with a real fire in winter. Camping and caravanning facilities are available at the rear of the building. The Ancient, as it is locally known, has often won local CAMRA Pub of the Year in recent years as well as other well-deserved awards.
P (63)

Presteigne

Duke's Arms

Broad Street, LD8 2AD
11-11 (01544) 267318
Beer range varies H
This is one of the oldest pubs in Radnorshire, dating from about 1480. At one time most of the town's major functions were held here, including the sheriff's lunches, public dinners, political meetings, concerts and balls. There are open fires in winter and live music some Wednesdays and weekends. Two handpumps serve beers from local breweries. Newspapers are available behind the bar. The pub has a separate pool room.

Radnorshire Arms Hotel

High Street, LD8 2BE
11-11 (01544) 267406 radnorshirearmshotel.com
Sharp's Doom Bar; guest beers H
The building was originally the country home of Sir Christopher Hatton, a favourite of Queen Elizabeth I. It became a busy posting house, where coaches changed horses on the London to Aberystwyth route. The pub retains many original features including floorboards and beams, oak panelling and a priest hole. There are three or four handpumps serving beers from Wales and the Marches. Live music includes Monday evening jam sessions. A beer festival is held in October.
P

Rhayader

Cornhill Inn

West Street, LD6 5AB (400yds W of clock tower on A470)
4 (12 Sat & Sun)-midnight (01597) 810029
Beer range varies H
Sixteenth-century inn providing a pub experience sometimes lost in this modern world. It has two separate rooms either side of the entrance, one with a log fire in winter, and a lively, friendly atmosphere is assured. The beers are from the Marston's range plus one local Welsh brew. Outside are a beer garden and covered smoking area. For many years there was a blacksmith's forge at the rear, now converted into a holiday cottage.
Q

Talgarth

Tower Hotel L

The Square, LD3 0BW
4 (11 Fri-Sun)-11 (01874) 711253
towerhoteltalgarth.co.uk
Rotters Utter Rotter, Black Route; guest beers H
Bright yet cosy modern bar in a small traditional hotel, with a separate restaurant area. Sky Sports is popular for major rugby and football matches. The on-site Rotters microbrewery provides many of the ales, but the enthusiastic landlord regularly sources up to four guest beers and a range of real ciders. A spring beer festival is hosted alongside a bike festival, and smaller festivals are staged at other times. A multiple local winner of CAMRA awards for beer and cider. P

Talybont-on-Usk

Star Inn L

LD3 7YX (on B4558 between Brecon and Crickhowell)
11.30-3, 5-11.30; 11-11 Fri-Sun (01874) 676635
starinntalybont.co.uk
Beer range varies H
Large and lively pub alongside the Monmouthshire and Brecon Canal, with a spacious garden that is extremely popular in summer. The beer range varies constantly, with local ales well represented, served alongside a choice of real ciders. Live music evenings are held regularly, and quiz nights are popular. Excellent food makes good use of local produce. Twice-yearly beer festivals are proving popular. Local CAMRA Pub of the Year 2009-14 and South Wales CAMRA Pub of the Year 2013.

Velindre

Three Horseshoes

LD3 0SU
closed Mon; 12-3, 6-11 (midnight Fri); 12-midnight Sat & Sun (01497) 847304
Beer range varies H
A warm and friendly free house, off the beaten track in a quiet village location between Talgarth and Hay-on-Wye. Two or three guest ales are usually on offer, plus local cider, all at reasonable prices. Good-value snacks and traditional pub food are served, including popular Sunday roasts.
P

Welshpool

Bistro 7

7 Hall Street, SY21 7RY (off A483)
12-11; closed Sun (01938) 552879 bistroseven.co.uk
Beer range varies H
Formerly the Crown, this friendly town-centre bar and restaurant has a continental feel. Drinkers are welcome and the three changing ales are promoted enthusiastically by the landlord. The recently expanded family-run premises offers an excellent range of simple home-cooked food. There is plenty of outside seating at the front and in the beer garden to the rear. A public car park is opposite. (X75)

I never drink water. I'm afraid it will become habit-forming. **W C Fields**

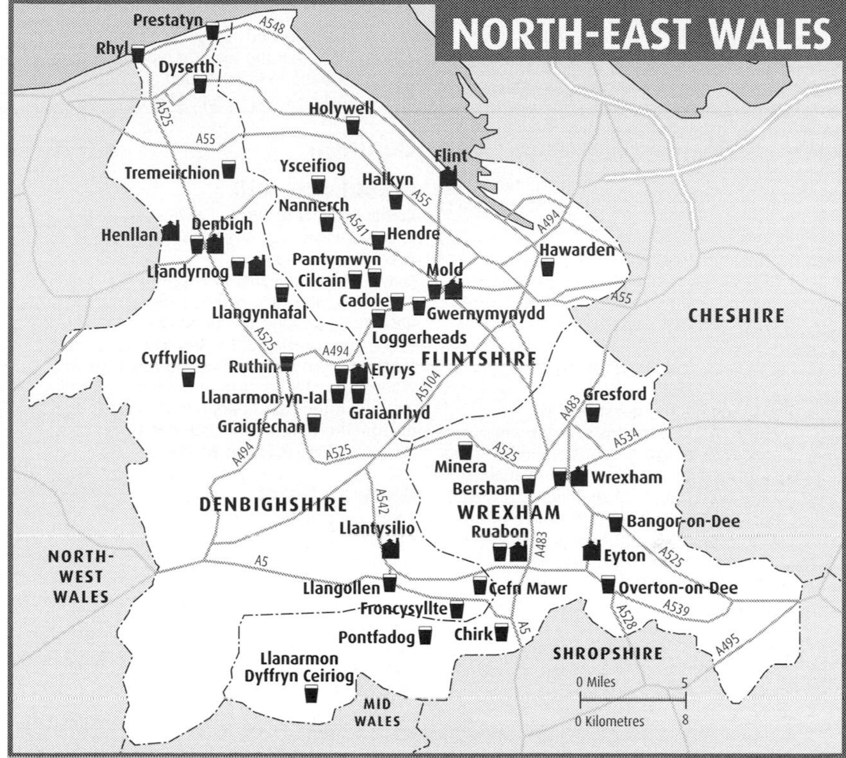

Authority areas covered: Denbighshire UA, Flintshire UA, Wrexham UA

Bangor-on-Dee

Buck House Hotel L

High Street, LL13 0BU (just off A525 Wrexham-Whitchurch road, opp church)

11.30 (12 Sun)-midnight ☎ (01978) 780336

buckhousehotel.co.uk

Beer range varies H

This traditional family-run village inn is the hub of the community and local groups meet here on a regular basis. Warm, friendly and full of character, it serves good, reasonably priced food and there is a separate à la carte restaurant which can be expanded with a marquee for private functions. Q❀♣P(146)

Bersham

Black Lion

Y Ddol, LL14 4HN (off B5099 near Bersham Heritage Centre)

11.30-12.30am (1am Fri & Sat); 11.30-midnight Sun ☎ (01978) 365588 blacklioninnbersham.com

Hydes Original Bitter H

Known locally as the Hole in the Wall, this friendly pub overlooks the delightful Clywedog River and is adjacent to the Clywedog Industrial Trail. It is popular with locals, walkers and visitors to the nearly Bersham Heritage Centre. The wood-panelled bar serves two rooms, both with real fires in winter, and a games room. Basic hot bar food is available all day. There is a play area in the garden. Beer and music festivals are usually in July and October. ❀♣P(6)

Cadole

Colomendy Arms

Village Road, CH7 5LL (off A494 Mold-Ruthin road)

7 (6 Thu, 4 Fri)-11; 2-11 Sat & Sun ☎ (01352) 810217

Beer range varies H

A regular in this Guide, the Colomendy is close to Loggerheads Country Park and is a typical two-room local. The walls tell the story of this ancient historic village originally named Cat Hole. An ever-changing selection of six beers from near and far keeps the clientele guessing. Two coal fires help make this unspoilt old-fashioned pub homely. Q❀♣P

Cefn Mawr

Mill L

Mill Lane, LL14 3NL

12-midnight (1am Fri & Sat) ☎ (01978) 821799

INDEPENDENT BREWERIES

Axiom Wrexham (NEW)
Big Hand Wrexham
Buzzard Llandyrnog
Denbigh Denbigh
Facer's Flint
Hafod Mold
Heavy Industry Henllan
Ial Eryrys (NEW)
Llangollen Llantysilio
McGivern Ruabon
New Plassey Eyton
Sandstone Wrexham

Beer range varies Ⓗ
Small and basic locals' free house within easy walking distance of the Llangollen Canal, Trevor Basin and the world famous Pontcysyllte Aqueduct. Situated down a narrow one-way lane in the lower part of an old industrial village, the smoking area backs onto the original mill stream. A large-screen TV shows sport in the main bar. A Facer's or Offa's Dyke beer is usually available, and depending on the time of year there may be an additional guest ale. No food is served. ❀♣ (2,5)

Chirk

Boathouse

Chirk Marina, LL14 5AD
closed Mon; 11-11; 12-7 Sun ☎ (01691) 772493
theboathouseatchirk.co.uk
Stonehouse Station Bitter; guest beer Ⓗ
Formerly a golf clubhouse, this café-bar and restaurant sits in 4½ acre grounds at Chirk Marina. There are fine views of the Llangollen Canal from the terrace. Up to three local real ales are served and real cider from Llandegla is available in the summer. Many activities and events take place here, and there are also regular themed food nights. Q❀◐♿P

Hand Hotel

Church Street, LL14 5EY
10.30-11 (midnight Thu-Sat); 12-10.30 Sun
☎ (01691) 773472 thehandhotelchirk.co.uk
Stonehouse Station Bitter, Cambrian Gold; guest beer Ⓗ
This old coaching inn was built to supply the needs of travellers from London to Ireland, and was also a stopping place for the mail coaches. There is a public bar, a lounge bar where food is served and which also caters for guests staying at the hotel, plus a separate restaurant. The lounge is dominated by a large red wooden sculpture of a Welsh dragon. The old brewery building behind the hotel is now converted for functions.
❀◐P

Cilcain

White Horse

Ffordd Y Llan, CH7 5NN (signed from A451 Mold-Denbigh road)
12-3, 6-11; 12-11 Sat; 12-10.30 Sun ☎ (01352) 740142
Banks's Bitter; guest beer Ⓗ
Traditional whitewashed village pub beside the Clwydian Range, popular with both locals and visitors. The central bar serves two separate areas – a cosy multi-roomed area with exposed beams, suitable for dining, and a quarry-tiled public bar where walkers and dogs are welcome. The pub offers two beers, one a regularly changing guest, and food is served lunchtimes and evenings throughout the week.
Q❀◐♿♣P (14C)

Cyffylliog

Red Lion Hotel

LL15 2DN (4 miles W of Ruthin, off B5105 at Llanfwrog)
5 (12 Fri)-11; 12-midnight Sat; 12-4 Sun
☎ (01824) 710351 redlionhotel.biz
Marston's Burton Bitter, Pedigree; guest beer Ⓗ
At the village centre, with parts dating back to 1640s, this inn has a public bar with pool table and TV, a lounge bar with an open fire and adjoining rooms for dining, and a larger dining room. Plaques are embedded in the walls in wood and ceramics, and many windows are stained glass. There is also a well-stocked village shop. ◐♣P

Denbigh

Brookhouse Mill

Ruthin Road, LL16 4RD (off A525 south of Denbigh)
12-3, 6-11.30; 12-11 Sun ☎ (01745) 813377
brookhousemill.co.uk
Conwy Welsh Pride/Balchder Cymru; guest beers Ⓗ
A former water mill by the River Ystrad, the venue has a main bar and several smaller rooms. There is also a smart restaurant with a conservatory and function room upstairs. The old mill cogs and wheels can still be seen in the low-beamed interior. Three cask beers are from North Wales micros. The outside drinking area is particularly attractive. Q❀◐♿♣P (X5,X50)

Railway Hotel

2 Ruthin Road, LL16 3EL
12-midnight (1am Fri & Sat) ☎ (01745) 812376
Purple Moose Cwrw Eryri/Snowdonia Ale; guest beer Ⓗ
The Railway is situated in the lower part of Denbigh, half a mile from the historic castle. It has five rooms off the basic public bar including a games room with pool table and sport TV room. All display memorabilia are from the now demolished Rhyl to Corwen, Vale of Clwyd railway. Two ales are available, usually from Welsh microbreweries.
Q♿♣P

Dyserth

New Inn

Waterfall Road, LL18 6ET (on B5119 close to waterfall)
11.30 (12 Sun)-11 ☎ (01745) 570482
thenewinndyserth.co.uk
Banks's Mild; Marston's Burton Bitter; guest beer Ⓗ
A 400-year-old pub, which has been modernised and extended. Many pictures of old Dyserth adorn the walls. There are three areas inside, with a focus on food, but there is space for drinkers and four real ales are available including a cask-conditioned mild. The good-sized garden has plenty of tables for warmer weather. Q❀◐♿P

Eryrys

Sun Inn

Village Road, CH7 4BX
3.30-11; 1-10.30 Sun ☎ (01824) 780402
Theakston Best Bitter; guest beers Ⓗ
This country pub, close to the village church and located within the Clwydian Range, is also reputedly one of the highest pubs in Wales, set 1148ft above sea level. It has a separate area for diners, with meals served Tuesday to Saturday 5.30-9pm and Sunday 1-4.30pm. One or two guest ales are available, usually sourced from local microbreweries. Accommodation is offered in a well-appointed two-bedroom apartment above the pub. ❀◐P

Froncysyllte

Aqueduct Inn

Holyhead Road, LL20 7PY (beside A5)

⏲ 5 (12 Fri-Sun)-11 ☎ (01691) 777118
🌐 theaqueductinn.co.uk
Stonehouse Station Bitter, Cambrian Gold Ⓗ
Unmissable in canary yellow, this former Admirals Tavern reopened in 2013 as a free house and has been revitalised as a result. It is a simple three-roomed affair with a small central bar, games room and comfortable lounge with woodburner. Rear veranda decking offers panoramic views, not least of the Llangollen Canal as it approaches the world-famous aqueduct. Two regular and one varying beer from Stonehouse are available. There is additional parking down the lane.
❀◐◑♣P🚌(5A,64)🐾

Graianrhyd

Rose & Crown

Llanarmon Road, CH7 4QW (on B5430 off A5104)
⏲ 4-11 (midnight Fri & Sat); 12-10.30 Sun
☎ (01824) 780727 🌐 theroseandcrownpub.co.uk
Beer range varies Ⓗ
Popular 200-year-old village pub, welcoming locals and visitors alike. The main bar area has an open fire and traditional copper-topped tables. The smaller side bar has a log-burning stove. Lunchtime bar snacks and full evening meals are served (no eve meals Mon). The range of beers is a mix of local and national – pumpclips on and around the bar are testimony to the wide variety on offer. Real cider is available from time to time. Q❀◐◑♣P🐾

Graigfechan

Three Pigeons Inn

LL15 2EU (on B5429 about 3 miles from Ruthin)
⏲ 5-8 Mon; 12-3, 5.30-11; 12-11 Sat; 12-10.30 Sun
☎ (01824) 703178 🌐 threepigeonsinn.co.uk
Sharp's Doom Bar; guest beers Ⓗ
A historic drovers' tavern close to Offa's Dyke and overlooking the Vale of Clwyd. The bar is used by locals and walkers, with dogs welcome. Other areas are mainly for diners. Four beers are on offer and these can be enjoyed on the extensive beer terrace with views over Clocaenog Forest. There are two self-catering apartments and camping facilities on the pub grounds.
❀🛏◐◑⛺♣🍎P🚌(76)🐾📶

Gresford

Griffin Inn

Church Green, LL12 8RG
⏲ 4 (7.30 Wed)-11.30; 4-11 Sun ☎ (01978) 852231
Adnams Southwold Bitter; Courage Best Bitter; guest beer Ⓗ
Friendly community pub next to the 15th-century All Saints Church, whose bells are one of the Seven Wonders of Wales, the irregular, open-plan, single room is adorned with a variety of interesting pictures. The bar is the centre of lively conversation but there are quieter corners. Outside, there is a lawned area to the side with seating. Children are welcome in some areas until 8pm.
Q❀♣P🚌(1)📶

Pant-yr-Ochain 𝕃

Old Wrexham Road, LL12 8TY (off A5156, E from A483, follow signs to The Flash)
⏲ 11.30-11 (10.30 Sun) ☎ (01978) 853525
🌐 pantyrochain-gresford.co.uk
Phoenix Brunning & Price Original; Purple Moose Cwrw Eryri/Snowdonia Ale; guest beers Ⓗ
Lovingly restored 16th-century dower house beside a small lake within extensive gardens. Hugely popular but still quiet, the central room, dominated by a large double-fronted bar, leads to a variety of seating areas including a garden room, a small snug behind the period inglenook fireplace, and the patio and lawn outside. Food is served all day alongside three regular beers and three guests, often local, and draught cider is usually available too. Q❀◐◑♿♣🍎P🐾📶

Gwernymynydd

Owain Glyndwr

Glyndwr Road, CH7 5LP (signed 1 mile S of Gwernymynydd off A494)
⏲ 5-11; 12-10 Sun ☎ (01352) 752913
Thwaites Wainwright; guest beer Ⓗ
Traditional single-room pub in an elevated position with panoramic views over a great distance. Named after a famous Welsh freedom fighter, the interior is decorated with items dedicated to his memory. The guest beer is often from a local micro such as Hafod or Buzzard. Sunday lunch is served and evening meals Thursday to Saturday. Car parking can be limited at times. ❀◐◑♿♣P📶

Halkyn

Blue Bell Inn 𝕃

Rhosesmor Road, CH8 8DL (on B5123)
⏲ 3 (5 Wed)-11; closed Tue; 5-midnight Fri; 12-midnight Sat; 12-11 Sun ☎ (01352) 780309 🌐 bluebell.uk.eu.org
Facer's Clwyd Gold, North Star Porter; guest beers Ⓗ
Situated on Halkyn Mountain with spectacular views across the Dee Estuary and local countryside, the Blue Bell is a winner of many awards. The landlords are enthusiastic supporters of real ale and cider. The pub is a focal point for the local community, with regular walks, music including Sunday jazz, and a class in conversational Welsh. CAMRA members receive a discount. The pub is now also the post office. Q⛺♣🍎P🚌(126)📶

Hawarden

Glynne Arms 𝕃

3 Glynne Way, CH5 3NS
⏲ 11-11 ☎ (01244) 569988 🌐 theglynnearms.co.uk
Beer range varies Ⓗ
This 200-year-old coaching inn at the heart of the village reopened in 2013 following extensive refurbishment. Owned by the Gladstone family, it is filled with books, pictures and curios relating to the former prime minister. It has a simply furnished bar with an unusual bar with a curved top, and a larger back room with a parquet floor. There is a separate dining room serving unpretentious locally-sourced food. A free house, it provides a choice of beers from local breweries in Wales, Cheshire and Shropshire.
❀◐◑♿⇌P🚌(4,11)🐾📶

Hendre

Dderwen (Oak) 𝕃

Denbigh Road, CH7 5QE (on A541)
⏲ 7-midnight ☎ (01352) 741466
Beer range varies Ⓗ

WALES

A roadside pub with a central bar serving two rooms, each with an impressive pottery collection. Two cask ales are offered from local Welsh microbreweries, often the nearby Hafod Brewery. The pub has a strong community focus, hosting a range of social and community activities, and is popular with walkers and visitors to the nearby Clwydian hills. The smaller bar features photographs and mementoes of past mining works. Local CAMRA branch Pub of the Year 2012. Q♣P

Holywell

Market Cross

9-11 High Street, CH8 7LA

8am-midnight (1am Fri & Sat) (01352) 717800

Greene King Abbot; Ruddles Best Bitter; guest beers H

Converted from an old Woolworth's store, this is a warm, welcoming pub, with helpful and friendly staff. It has a log-burning open fire with sofas around it, providing a cosy area. The walls feature photographs and illustrations of local historic sites and celebrities, as well as paintings by a local artist. Although usually silent, the TV volume may be turned up for big rugby or football matches. Beers from Brains, Purple Moose and Peerless appear regularly. Q (X11,11)

Llanarmon Dyffryn Ceiriog

Hand at Llanarmon

LL20 7LD (end of B4500 from Chirk)

11-11 (12.30am Fri & Sat); 12-11 Sun (01691) 600666

thehandhotel.co.uk

Beer range varies H

Cosy, family-run free house in a scenic location at the head of the delightful Ceiriog Valley and marked by a giant hand sculpture. There are always two real ales available, usually one each from Conwy and Weetwood breweries. Food and accommodation are both of a high standard and it is advisable to book meals at busy times. This dog-friendly pub is popular with cyclists, walkers and tourists. The enthusiastic owners have published a book of local walks. Q♣P

Llanarmon-yn-Ial

Raven Inn L

Ffordd-Rhew-Ial, CH7 4QE (signed 500yds west of B5430)

closed Mon; 5-10.30 (11 Fri); 12-11 Sat; 12-9 Sun

(01824) 780833 raveninn.co.uk

Beer range varies H

Threatened with closure, the Raven was rescued by locals and is run almost entirely by the village community. Drinkers can choose from three micro-brewed cask ales usually from local breweries, including a house beer from Purple Moose, three real ciders and often a perry. The cider is served direct from taps behind the bar. Good locally-sourced home-cooked food is available at reasonable prices. Accommodation is offered in three self-catering rooms.

Q♣P(2)

Llandyrnog

Kinmel Arms

Waen, LL16 4HN

12-3, 5-11; 12-midnight Sat; 12-11 Sun

(01824) 790291 kinmelarms.com

Thwaites Original, Lancaster Bomber; guest beers H

Traditional, warm and friendly pub handy for Offa's Dyke Path and Moel Arthur iron age hill fort. The front bar area features a large fireplace, to the rear there are cask ends from the long defunct Chester Northgate brewery on display, and to the right a large separate dining room. The guest beer is usually from the local Buzzard or Heavy Industry microbreweries. Q P(50)

Llangollen

Ponsonby Arms L

Mill Street, LL20 8RY (near steam railway)

11-11 (midnight Fri & Sat) (01978) 447985

ponsonbyarms.com

Purple Moose Cwrw Eryri/Snowdonia Ale; Salopian Shropshire Gold; guest beers H

Welcoming free house rescued from near dereliction by the owners of the nearby Sun Inn. Regular breweries featured here include Purple Moose, Ulverston and Salopian, supplemented by up to 10 beers from other micros. Situated close to Llangollen railway station, the pub has use of the adjacent council car park (ask at the bar for a free ticket). The beer garden overlooks the river. Quiz night is Tuesday and cask ale promotion is Friday night 6-7pm. Q P(5,X94)

Sun Inn

49 Regent Street, LL20 8HN (400yds E of town centre on A5)

5-1am (2am Fri & Sat) (01978) 860079

Purple Moose Cwrw Eryri/Snowdonia Ale; Salopian Shropshire Gold; guest beers H

This characterful free house is a sister pub to the nearby Ponsonby Arms but offers late night drinking and live music Wednesday to Saturday. The traditional stone-flagged bar room has two open fires and the small raised games area has a pool table and table football. A smaller cosy room can be reached via the walled, covered seating area outside. Up to six guest ales are on offer in summer, dropping to four in winter. ♣(64)

Llangynhafal

Golden Lion Inn

LL16 4LN (at village crossroads)

closed Mon; 6 (4 Fri)-11; 12-11 Sat; 12-10.30 Sun

(01824) 790451 thegoldenlioninn.com

Holt Bitter; guest beers H

Situated at the village crossroads, this welcoming inn has a public bar with TV and pool table, and a lounge bar with a dining area. Regularly changing guest beers are often from Purple Moose or Facer's. The licensees are enthusiastic supporters of the inter-pub Route 76 beer festival, held each July. The Golden Lion has twice been awarded local CAMRA Pub of the Year. ♣P(76)

Loggerheads

We Three Loggerheads

Ruthin Road, CH7 5LH (on A494)

12-10.30 (11 Fri & Sat) (01352) 810337

we-three-loggerheads.co.uk

Black Sheep Best Bitter; Hafod Hopper; guest beer H

The pub is separated from Loggerheads Country Park by the A494 and a footbridge over the River

Alyn. A comfortable bar/lounge and an elevated restaurant make this a pleasant place to take a break. A painting of The Three Loggerheads, reputedly painted by 18th-century artist Richard Wilson to pay his bar bills, hangs at the foot of the stairs. At least one beer is from the local brewery Hafod.

Minera

Tyn-Y-Capel

Church Road, LL11 3DA

closed Mon & Tue; 6-10.30 Wed; 12-11 Thu-Sat; 12-10.30 Sun (01978) 269347 tyn-y-capel.com

Beer range varies

Much-modernised coaching inn originally dating from 1250AD. After a long period of closure it was reopened in 2013 as a not-for-profit community venture staffed mainly by local volunteers. A warm welcome awaits any visitor, with a choice of rooms in the large, airy interior. Impressive outside seating areas make the most of its glorious elevated setting opposite Esclusham Mountains. It has a permanent house ale by Big Hand, four rotating guest ales from local microbreweries, plus real cider.

Q P (9,10)

Mold

Gold Cape

8-8A Wrexham Street, CH7 1ES (next to Market Square crossroads)

8am-midnight (1am Fri & Sat) (01352) 705920

Greene King Abbot; Ruddles Best Bitter; guest beers

The Gold Cape is named after a 4,000-year-old gold peytrel found nearby in 1831 - an impression of the ceremonial cape stands in the entrance to this former shop. This medium-sized Wetherspoon pub has a bar staff with a keen passion for cask beer. The walls display pictures of Mold's past, including local poet Daniel Owen. The pub takes part in a twice-yearly bus-driven beer festival involving up to 10 pubs in the area. Q

Nannerch

Cross Foxes

Village Road, CH7 5RD

closed Mon; 6-11; 12-2.30, 4-11 Sun (01352) 741293

Buzzard Pale of Clwyd; guest beers

Set in a charming village close to the church, the Cross Foxes was built by the 18th-century Williams family of Penbedw Estate. It was at one time also a butcher's – the hooks still remain over the bar. The interior has altered very little and divides into four areas – the bar with a large fireplace, where dogs are allowed, a reception bar, lounge and function room. The regular beer is from local brewery Buzzard. Tuesday is curry and a pint night.

P (14)

Overton-on-Dee

White Horse Inn

21 High Street, LL13 0DT

closed Mon; 5.30-10.30 Tue; 12-2.30, 5.30-midnight; 12-midnight Sat; 12-9 Sun (01978) 710111

thewhitehorseoverton.co.uk

Joule's Blonde, Pale Ale, Slumbering Monk

Attractive red-brick mock-Tudor building situated in the heart of the village, part of the small but impressive Joule's Brewery estate. A CAMRA pub design winner, it features frosted and latticed windows, pristine wood partitioning and restored fireplaces, two with wood-burning stoves. A former pantry, coal shed and wash house to the rear have been converted into dining spaces. Three Joule's regulars feature on the bar plus a seasonal ale. Excellent food is served lunchtimes (no food Tue lunch) and evenings. Ample street parking is usually available.

Q (146)

Pantymwyn

Crown Inn

Cilcain Road, CH7 5EH

5-11 Mon-Wed; 12.30-midnight; 12.30-11 Sun

(01352) 740462

Brains Rev James; Facer's This Splendid Ale; guest beers

A popular and friendly village local with a good reputation for Welsh beers and locally-sourced food. Three regular ales are complemented by a changing guest beer. Bay windows overlook the front terrace, and at the rear is a beer garden and extensive children's play area. Excellent food is served including ever-popular steaks and generous portions of fish and chips. A favourite with walkers in the area, the pub can get busy, especially at weekends. There is a regular Sunday night quiz.

P (6)

Pontfadog

Swan Inn (Graig)

Llanarmon Road, LL20 7AR (on B4500 next to post office)

12-2, 4.30-11; 6-11 Sat; 7.30-10.30 Sun

(01691) 718273 theswaninnpontfadog.co.uk

Beer range varies

Welcoming traditional village free house in the scenic Ceiriog Valley. The cosy red-tiled bar features a central fireplace which separates the TV and darts area from the servery, favoured by the locals. The garden is accessed via the dining room to the side. Cask beer can be from any origin, from nationals through to locals such as Stonehouse Brewery. Themed food nights are popular. Note that hours may vary; ring first to check.

P (64,65)

Prestatyn

Archies

151 High Street, LL19 9AS

closed Mon; 5-11; 12-1.30am Fri & Sat; 12-11 Sun 07592 860563

Facer's Flintshire Bitter; guest beers

Modern open-plan pub with floorboards throughout. Bifold doors along the frontage open onto a raised decking area facing the high street. An all-round friendly venue catering for a varied clientele, it offers Sky Sports, regular live music and a weekly quiz. Afternoons can be quiet. The standard beer is Facer's Flintshire Bitter, with many guests, usually from local breweries. It's a rare outlet for Joule's beers in North Wales.

WALES

Halcyon Quest Hotel 🏆 L

17 Gronant Road, LL19 9DT (on A547 E of town centre)
3-11.30 (12.30am Fri & Sat); 12-11.30 Sun
☎ (01745) 852442 halcyonquest-hotel.com
Facer's Flintshire Bitter; guest beers H

The Halcyon Quest, or HQ as it is known locally, is located on the southern edge of the town. The single bar has much sporting memorabilia and even a rowing boat hanging from the ceiling. Five beers are usually available, including one from local brewery Facer's. There is a pleasant garden at the rear. The northern end of Offa's Dyke footpath is close by. Accommodation is in eight double rooms and one single. P (35,36)

Rhyl

Cob & Pen

153 High Street, LL18 1UF
11-11 (midnight Fri & Sat); 12-11 Sun ☎ (01745) 350446
Banks's Mild; Marston's Burton Bitter, Pedigree; guest beer H

Close to the railway station, this pub was totally refurbished in 2013. It is multi-roomed with a snug to the right of the entrance and another at the rear. There is also a dedicated sports lounge with pool, darts and large-screen TV. Many pictures of old Rhyl adorn the walls.

Sussex

20-26 Sussex Street, LL18 1SG
8am-midnight (1am Fri & Sat); 8am-10.30 Sun
☎ (01745) 362910
Greene King Abbot; Ruddles Best Bitter; guest beers H

Wetherspoon pub in a pedestrian part of town, divided into three areas and decorated with pictures of old Rhyl alongside modern art. In the past the building has been a Welsh Wesleyan chapel. It is a popular place for locals and holidaymakers. Meet the Brewer events are held monthly. Q P

Ruabon

Bridge End Inn 🏆 L

5 Bridge Street, LL14 6DA
5 (4 Fri)-11; 12-11 Sat & Sun ☎ (01978) 810881
mcgivernales.co.uk
Beer range varies H

Once a coaching inn and close to the railway station, it has won numerous awards since being taken over and completely revitalised by the McGivern family in 2009, and is a former CAMRA National Pub of the Year. Eight changing cask ales are available with at least one from the on-site McGivern Ales. Real cider is also served. Families are welcome in the lounge. A beer festival is held over the August bank holiday weekend.
Q (Ruabon) P (2,5)

Ruthin

Castle Hotel

St Peter's Square, LL15 1AA
7am-midnight (1am Fri & Sat) ☎ (01824) 709960
Greene King Abbot; Ruddles Best Bitter; guest beers H

The Castle Hotel stands in St Peter's Square at the highest point in Ruthin. Now a Wetherspoon hotel with 17 rooms, its multi-area interior has different historic themes – Owain Glyndwr, the Myddelton family and Ruthin Castle feature alongside a mention of a long-defunct brewery on the premises. The hotel car park is for residents only. The town itself has many attractions such as the old gaol. P

Tremeirchion

Salusbury L

LL17 0UN (1 mile S of A55 from jct 30)
closed Mon; 12 (6 Tue)-11 (11.30 Fri & Sat); 12-10.30 Sun
☎ (01745) 710262
Marston's Burton Bitter; guest beer H

Popular village inn with a lounge and a separate walkers bar, where dogs are allowed, plus two dining rooms and a snug to the right of the entrance. Note the beam over the fireplace, dated 1554. The games room has sport TV and outside there's a large garden with children's play equipment. The menu consists of mostly locally-sourced food (booking advisable for Sun lunchtime). The house beer, Summer Ale, is brewed by Facer's of Flint. P

Wrexham

Elihu Yale

44-46 Regent Street, LL11 1RR
8am-midnight (1am Fri & Sat) ☎ (01978) 366646
Greene King Abbot; Ruddles Best Bitter; guest beers H

Formerly a cinema, this is a popular Wetherspoon town-centre pub. Both railway stations and the bus station are within walking distance. As well as the two regular beers there are at least six guests including one from a North Wales brewery, and no fewer than two real ciders. The large single room has various seating areas, with a quieter area near the front of the pub. Families are welcome until 9pm. Q (Central)

Royal Oak

35 High Street, LL13 8HY
12-midnight ☎ (01978) 358547 joulesbrewery.co.uk
Joule's Blonde, Pale Ale, Slumbering Monk; guest beer H

A Grade II-listed building with a long, narrow interior. The real fire, wood panelling and etched brewery mirrors around the bar create a comfortable ambience. Three beers from Joule's are always available plus a changing guest. Real cider is dispensed from a fifth handpump. The small beer garden on the roof is open April to September. No food is available but you are welcome to bring your own. Darts and traditional pub board games are played.

Ysceifiog

Fox ★ L

Ysceifiog Village Road, CH8 8NJ (signed from B5121)
4 (3 Fri)-11; 1-11 Sat & Sun ☎ (01352) 720241
Thwaites Original, Lancaster Bomber; guest beer H

Identified by CAMRA as having a nationally important historic pub interior, this classic village inn has a four rooms, unchanged from the 1930s. A sliding door leads to the tiny front bar with an old counter, panelling on the window side, a tiled fireplace with a coal fire and bare bench seating, including some attached to the front of the counter. Four beers are served with two regularly changing guests from local micros. Q

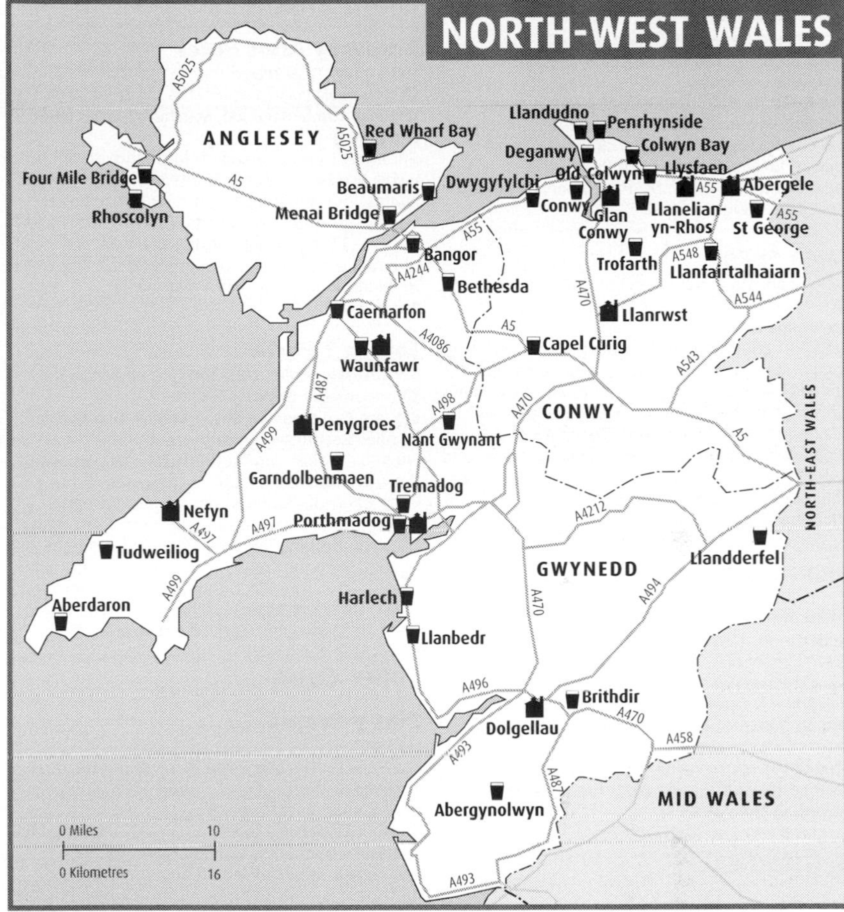

Authority areas covered: Anglesey UA, Conwy UA, Gwynedd UA

Aberdaron

Ty Newydd

LL53 8BE

11-midnight (10.30 Sun) ☎ (01758) 760207

gwesty-tynewydd.co.uk

Cwrw Llŷn Brenin Enlli; guest beer H

The hotel is situated at the centre of a historic village at the end of the Lleyn Peninsula. Freshly caught Bardsey lobster and crab are on the menu, as well as afternoon teas. Beers are from two local breweries. Eleven en-suite bedrooms are available, with stunning sea views. The Wales coastal footpath passes through the village. Bus services run from Pwllheli. Q

Abergynolwyn

Railway Inn

LL36 9YN (on B4405)

12-midnight (11 Sun) ☎ (01654) 782279

Beer range varies H

Hospitable community local in the centre of the village not far from the Talyllyn Railway. Excellent food is served and, following a refit, the range of beers is set to increase. The pub has stunning views of the nearby hills and there is wonderful walking nearby. Q P

Bangor

Boatyard

Garth Road, LL57 2SF (off old A5, follow pier signs)

11 (12 Sun)-11 ☎ (01248) 362462

Marston's Burton Bitter, Pedigree; guest beers H

Formerly the Union Garth, this large multi-roomed pub is in lower Bangor. It has been refurbished and now has a well-appointed restaurant and pleasant seating areas. The garden area overlooks the sea and Penrhyn Harbour. Guest beers are usually from the Marston's range. The Boatyard is popular with clubs, students and locals. Q

INDEPENDENT BREWERIES

Big Bog Waunfawr
Cader Dolgellau
Conwy Llysfaen
Great Orme Glan Conwy
Llŷn Nefyn
Lleu Penygroes (NEW)
Nant Llanrwst
North Wales Abergele
Purple Moose Porthmadog
Snowdonia Waunfawr

Mostyn Arms

27 Ambrose Street, LL57 1BH (off Beach Rd)
3 (1 Sat & Sun)-midnight ☎ (01248) 364572
Beer range varies Ⓗ
This small, friendly back-street pub has been completely refurbished with a pool area, lounge space with Sky Sports and a small bar. Beers are sourced locally, usually from Purple Moose and Great Orme breweries. No food is served. Note the limited opening hours.

Tap & Spile

Garth Road, LL57 2SW (off old A5, follow pier signs)
12-11 (11.30 Tue, Fri & Sat) ☎ (01248) 370835
Beer range varies Ⓗ
Busy pub attracting locals, students and visitors to Bangor, with a changing range of up to six real ales from different breweries. It enjoys excellent views of the magnificent pier, Menai Straits and over to Beaumaris. Good wholesome food including vegetarian options is served at sensible prices, and seven letting rooms are available. A former winner of local CAMRA branch Pub of the Year.
Q

Beaumaris

Olde Bull's Head Inn

Castle Street, LL58 8AA
11-11 ☎ (01248) 810329 bullsheadinn.co.uk
Draught Bass; Hancocks HB; guest beer Ⓗ
This Grade II-listed building was the original posting house of the borough. Dr Johnson and Charles Dickens were famous guests and each bedroom is named after a Dickens character. The beamed bar has a large open fire. Parking is limited. Q P

Bethesda

Douglas Arms Hotel ★

High Street, LL57 3AY
6-11; 3.30-midnight Sat; 1-3, 7-11 Sun ☎ (01248) 600219
Marston's Burton Bitter, Pedigree; guest beers Ⓗ
Built in 1820, this was an important coaching inn on the historic Telford post route from London to Holyhead. The Grade II-listed building is recognised by CAMRA as having a nationally important historic pub interior. The four-room interior has not changed since the 1930s and includes a snug, lounges and a large tap room with a full-size snooker table. Bethesda is convenient for buses to the Ogwen Valley and the surrounding mountains.
Q

Brithdir

Cross Foxes

Dolgellau, LL40 2SG (A470 and A487 jct)
11-midnight ☎ (01341) 421001
Cwrw Cader Cader Gold; guest beers Ⓖ
A newly refurbished Grade II-listed building situated near the foot of Cader Idris mountain and four miles from the historic town of Dolgellau. Beers are usually from Cader Ales and other local microbreweries. Breakfast is served from 8am and meals are available throughout the day until 9pm. Dogs are welcome in the bar area. The hotel has Welsh Tourist Board 5-star grading. Bus service T2 passes by, but please check times.
Q P (T2)

Caernarfon

Anglesey Arms Hotel

Slate Quay, LL55 2PB
12-midnight (1am Fri & Sat); 12-11 Sun ☎ (01286) 672158
Jennings Cumberland Ale; Marston's Burton Bitter, Pedigree Ⓗ
An ancient pub in a superb location with amazing vistas across the Menai Straits to Anglesey. Built against the town walls and next to Caernarfon Castle, the Anglesey attracts a mix of locals and visitors. Sitting outside on the sea wall, the views of bird life and sunsets are breathtaking. The Welsh Highland Railway is half a mile away.
P

Tafarn Y Porth

5-9 Eastgate Street, LL55 1AG (just off Bangor Rd)
9am-midnight ☎ (01268) 662920
Big Bog Bog Standard Bitter; Greene King Abbot; Ruddles Best Bitter; guest beers Ⓗ
Friendly, welcoming Wetherspoon pub opposite the town walls and close to the castle. It has a large open-plan interior and a spacious partly-covered courtyard outside with plenty of seating. The real ale range often includes a beer from the Big Bog Brewing Company in Waunfawr, just a few miles away. The pub's location is handy for the Welsh Highland Railway, which takes you to the heart of Snowdonia. Q

Capel Curig

Plas y Brenin

LL24 0ET
12-2, 6-11; 11-11 Sat; 12-10.30 Sun ☎ (01690) 720214
pyb.co.uk
Nant Brenin; guest beers Ⓗ
Outdoor centre in a lovely rural area. The raised bar overlooks twin lakes Llŷnnau Mymbyr, with spectacular views of Mount Snowdon. The furnishing is basic but modern with wooden floors, tables and chairs. Excellent, hearty and reasonably priced meals are available while outdoor drinking is the best way to enjoy the views. There is also a TV and large dining area. Three handpumps dispense local beers from Conwy, Great Orme, Nant and Purple Moose breweries. Q P

Colwyn Bay

Pen-y-Bryn

Pen-y-Bryn Road, LL29 6DD
11.30-11; 12-10.30 Sun ☎ (01492) 533360
penybryn-colwynbay.co.uk
Phoenix Brunning & Price Original; Purple Moose Cwrw Eryri/Snowdonia Ale; guest beers Ⓗ
Open-plan pub popular with all ages, with large bookcases, old furniture and real fires in the winter months. Panoramic views of Colwyn Bay and the Great Orme can be admired from the terrace and garden. Excellent, imaginative bar food is served – the menu is updated daily. There are four guest beers, mainly from local and independent breweries. Q P

Picture House

24-26 Prince's Drive, LL29 8LA
8am-midnight (1am Fri & Sat) ☎ (01492) 535286
Greene King Abbot; Ruddles Best Bitter; guest beers Ⓗ
Wetherspoon pub in the former Princess Cinema, now a Grade II-listed building. The walls of the

three-level building, which also has an upper balcony, are adorned with theatre memorabilia. There are eight handpumps featuring at least one beer from a local brewery such as Conwy, Purple Moose or Big Bog, plus guest ciders. Local beer festivals, in addition to Wetherspoon's national events, are held throughout the year. A former local CAMRA Pub of the Year.

Conwy

Albion Ale House

Uppergate Street, LL32 8RF

12-11 (midnight Fri & Sat) (01492) 582484
albionalehouse.weebly.com

Beer range varies H

Multi-roomed pub with a nationally important historic interior superbly refurbished by the current owners. There is no music or TV, just pleasant conversation. The pub is managed by four local brewers – Conwy, Great Orme, Nant and Purple Moose – and showcases their beers as well as guest ales. There are two guest Welsh ciders. A good selection of wines and malt whiskies is also available. CAMRA awards include branch and Welsh Pub of the Year. Q (5,19)

Castle Hotel

High Street, LL32 8DB

10.30-11 (10.30 Sun) (01492) 582800
castlewales.co.uk

Conwy Clogwyn Gold, Welsh Pride/Balchder Cymru, Dawson's Dark H

An old coaching inn dating back to the 15th century, this privately owned hotel is now an upmarket meeting place. Winner of the CAMRA branch Food Pub of the Year 2013, one of the partners is Graham Tinsley, head of the Welsh Culinary Team, and excellent food, made from the finest local produce, is served in the bar and restaurant. A local beer from Conwy Brewery, Dawson's Dark, is only available here, the cider is from Gwynt y Ddraig.
QP (5,19)

Old White House

Bangor Road, LL32 8DP

4 (12 summer)-11; 12-midnight Thu-Sun
(01492) 573133 oldwhitehouseconwy.com

Conwy Welsh Pride/Balchder Cymru; Tetley Bitter; guest beer H

This 17th-century building was once a coach house. The long central bar, featuring a large log-burning stove and a high-beamed roof space, serves the open-plan front lounge and a small rear dining area. The pub hosts a general knowledge quiz on Tuesday, a music quiz on Friday night and live entertainment on Saturday night. Live football is screened on big TVs. Food is available Tuesday to Sunday evenings and all day every day in summer.
P (5,X5)

Deganwy

Castle View

Pentywyn Road, LL31 9TH

12-11 (10 Sun) (01492) 583777 castleviewpub.com

Sharp's Doom Bar; Tetley Bitter; guest beers H

Nicely spruced-up pub divided into various wood-panelled rooms and alcoves with comfortable seating and many depictions of old local scenes. Big picture windows and a raised terrace afford breathtaking views across the Conwy Estuary toward the famous medieval castle and bridges. A heated patio is to the rear. Guest beers always include one light brew such as Robinsons Dizzy Blonde. An extensive food menu features locally-sourced products. The Monday night quiz is popular. P (13,19)

Dwygyfylchi

Gladstone

Ysgubor Wen Road, LL34 6PS

closed Mon & Tue winter; 12-11 (midnight Fri & Sat); 12-9 winter Sun (01492) 623231 thegladstone.co.uk

Black Sheep Best Bitter; guest beers H

Renowned for its magnificent sea views, this pub has been well refurbished but retains many original features including the alcoves and traditional decor with wood panelling and old photographs. A central bar serves both dining and drinking areas. Comfortable sofas surround a wood-burning stove and a galleried balcony with tables and booths overlooks the bar. The restaurant offers imaginative food sourced locally. There is a function room, accommodation in six luxury rooms, and the pub has a wedding licence.
P (5,X5)

Penmaenmawr Golf Club

Conwy Old Road, LL34 6RD

11-11 (10 Sun) (01492) 623330 pengolf.co.uk

Beer range varies H

Plush one-room clubhouse with stunning sea and mountain views from the outdoor drinking area that overlooks the golf course. Inside there is a pool table and a TV for sporting fixtures, and regular events are hosted in the evenings. Good-value hearty meals are served from the kitchen. Up to two guest beers are available from local and independent breweries. Visitors are welcome at this friendly venue. P

Four Mile Bridge

Anchorage Hotel

LL65 2EZ (on B4545, just past bridge to Holy Island)

11 (12 Sun)-11 (01407) 740168

Draught Bass; Theakston XB; Timothy Taylor Landlord; guest beers H

Family-run hotel situated on Holy Island close to Trearddur Bay. It has a large, comfortable lounge bar and a dining area serving a wide selection of meals. The hotel is near some fine sandy beaches and coastal walks. Its proximity to the A55 makes it a useful stopping-off point for Holyhead Port.
Q

Garndolbenmaen

Cross Foxes

LL51 9TX (between Caernarfon and Porthmadog off A487)

6-11; 12.30-2.30, 6.30-11 Sun (01766) 530246
crossfoxesinn.co.uk

Beer range varies H

Two-roomed village inn dating from the 19th century with a central bar. The pub is popular with locals and visitors for its ever-changing range of beer and good home-cooked food. Meals are served Sunday lunchtime and every evening. The dining area converts into a popular skittle alley in winter. The local bus stops close by. Q

WALES

Harlech

Branwen Hotel

Ffordd Newydd, LL46 2UB (on A462 below castle)
11-11 (01766) 780477 branwenhotel.co.uk
Beer range varies H
Warm and welcoming family-run hotel and bar overlooked by Harlech Castle. The popular and stylish bar offers a wide range of cask ales as well as foreign beers. A large selection of wines and malt whiskies is also stocked. Ask for your favourite malt – they are sure to have it. A former local CAMRA award winner. Q

Llanbedr

Ty Mawr Hotel

LL45 2HH
11-11 (01341) 241440 tymawrhotel.com
Beer range varies H
Small country hotel set in its own grounds. The modern lounge bar has a slate-flagged floor and cosy wood-burning stove. Unusual flying memorabilia reflect connections with the local airfield. French windows open out onto a veranda and landscaped terrace with seating. A beer festival is held in a marquee on the lawn each year. Popular with locals and walkers, dogs and children are welcome. Meals are served all day. Q

Llandderfel

Bryntirion Inn

LL23 7RA (on B4401 4 miles E of Bala)
11 (12 Sun)-11 (01678) 530205 bryntirioninn.co.uk
Purple Moose Cwrw Eryri/Snowdonia Ale; guest beer H
Former hunting lodge and coaching inn dating back to 1695 and overlooking the River Dee. The single bar services a number of rooms to accommodate diners and families in addition to the cosy and comfortable bar area with a log fire. There is a small covered courtyard at the rear. The regular beer is from the Purple Moose Brewery range and a second guest beer is sourced from other local or national brewers. Good-value accommodation is available. Q P (X94)

Llandudno

Albert

56 Madoc Street, LL30 2TW
11-11; 12-10.30 Sun (01492) 877188
albertllandudno.co.uk
Theakston Best Bitter; guest beers H
Just off the town centre and close to the railway station, this popular pub restaurant offers five handpulled ales from local and independent breweries. The beers on offer are clearly displayed on blackboards above and beside the L-shaped bar. Third-of-a-pint glasses are available as well as CAMRA discounts. A range of tasty meals is served throughout the day. The decor is modern, with interesting photographs and pictures on display. Q

Cottage Loaf

Market Street, LL30 2SR
11-11 (01492) 870762 the-cottageloaf.co.uk
Conwy Welsh Pride/Balchder Cymru; Courage Directors; guest beers H
The building was previously a bakery, hence the name. The interior features stone-flagged floors, an impressive fireplace and a raised timber-floored area – much of the wood came from the Flying Foam, a schooner shipwrecked at Llandudno's West Shore. The Loaf is a popular meeting place for people of all ages, with excellent home-cooked food served all day every day. A major refurbishment took place early in 2014. The guest cider often comes from Gwynt y Ddraig. (5,12)

Palladium

7 Glodaeth Street, LL30 2DD
8am-midnight (1am Fri & Sat) (01492) 863920
Greene King Abbot; Ruddles Best Bitter; guest beers H
A huge Wetherspoon pub, converted from a theatre originally built in 1920 on the site of the Market Hall. The pub opened in 2001 and was the largest pub in the UK at the time. The boxes and upper seating can still be seen, although not used, and the walls are adorned with theatrical memorabilia including original programmes bearing the names of the stars of the day. There are spacious areas on split levels, including a family dining room. A lift is available. (5,12)

Snowdon

11 Tudno Street, LL30 2HB
12-11 (11.30 Fri & Sat); 12-10.30 Sun (01492) 872166
the-snowdonhotel.co.uk
Draught Bass; guest beers H
Just off the town centre near the tram station is one of the oldest pubs in Llandudno. Up to four real ales are served – with three thirds available for the price of a pint. The pub has a large drinking area with a small side snug. Look for the Snowdon mirror above the fireplace. Outside, the drinking area by the road has a fine view of the Great Orme and the goats if you are lucky. The garden won Llandudno in Bloom for its floral displays. (5,12)

Llanelian-yn-Rhos

White Lion

LL29 8YA
closed Mon; 11.30-3, 6-midnight; 12-11 Sun
(01492) 515807 whitelioninn.co.uk
Marston's Burton Bitter, Pedigree; guest beer H
A regular in the Guide for more than 20 years, this 16th-century inn situated in the hills above Old Colwyn, next to St Elian's Church, offers a warm welcome. Gracing the entrance are two white stone lions, leading into the bar area with slate-flagged flooring and large comfortable chairs around the log fires. Decorative stained glass is mounted above the bar in the tiny snug. The restaurant serves delicious home-cooked food. Jazz night is Tuesday, quiz night Thursday. Q P

Llanfairtalhaiarn

Black Lion Hotel

Swan Square, LL22 8RY
closed Mon; 12-11 (01745) 720205
theblacklionnorthwales.co.uk
Robinsons 1892 Dark, Trooper, Double Hop H
Delicious food, tasty real ales and a warm welcome. On the banks of the River Elwy in an area

of outstanding natural beauty, the Black Lion is one of North Wales' leading destination pubs. So drop in for a pint, try some of the famous locally-sourced home-cooked food, or even stop over in the luxury accommodation. (43,43a)

Menai Bridge

Anglesey Arms

Mona Road, LL59 5EA (by Menai Suspension Bridge)

11-11 (midnight Thu-Sat); 12-11 Sun (01248) 712305

anglesey-arms.co.uk

Lees Manchester Pale Ale, The Governor, Bitter; guest beers H

Dating back more than 200 years, this old coaching house has recently been completely refurbished. It is on the main route to Holyhead and ideally situated for Snowdonia, the Lleyn Peninsula, the resorts of Anglesey and the Irish Ferries. Guest beers and seasonal ales are from the JW Lees list and local produce is used in most meals. The large rear rooms are available for functions.

Liverpool Arms

St George's Pier, LL59 5EY

12-2, 5-11.30; 12-11.30 Fri-Sun (01248) 712453

Facer's Flintshire Bitter; Purple Moose Cwrw Eryri/ Snowdonia Ale H/G**, Ochr Tywyll y Mws/Dark Side of the Moose; guest beer** H

Recently refurbished, the Livvy now has four cask ales on offer and serves good-quality home-cooked food. This nautically themed pub is frequented by locals, students in term time and the local sailing fraternity. A short walk takes you beneath the famous suspension bridge.

Nant Gwynant

Pen-y-Gwryd

LL55 4NT (at jct of A486 and A4086)

11-11 (winter hours limited) (01286) 870211

pyg.co.uk

Purple Moose Cwrw Eryri/Snowdonia Ale, Cwrw Madog/Madog's Ale H

Built in 1810 and Grade II-listed, this famous hotel is situated in the heart of Snowdonia. It was used by the team who made the first ascent of Everest, and the Everest Room has famous signatures on the ceiling; there are two other small rooms plus a dining room. The hotel features in CAMRA's Real Heritage Pubs of Wales and Great British Pubs. Winter opening is restricted but the bar opens for festivities over the New Year.

Old Colwyn

Red Lion

385 Abergele Road, LL29 9PL

5-11; 4-midnight Fri; 12-midnight Sat; 12-11 Sun

(01492) 515042

Holden's Black Country Mild; Marston's Burton Bitter; guest beers H

This free house serves up to five guest ales from independent and local brewers. It has a cosy L-shaped lounge featuring a real coal fire, antique brewery mirrors and other memorabilia, and a traditional public bar with a pool table, darts and TVs. To the rear is a Victorian-style covered and heated smoking conservatory. The Real Ale Club every Thursday offers nine beers at reduced prices. Guest ciders add to the attractions.

Penrhynside

Cross Keys Inn

Pendre Road, LL30 3DD

closed Mon; 5 (12 Sat)-midnight; 12-11.30 Sun

(01492) 547070

Facer's Flintshire Bitter; guest beer H

This 19th-century free house is a winner of local CAMRA awards and offers a warm and friendly welcome. It has a cosy front room with a central bar, rear pool room and side lounge boasting unrivalled views of the surrounding area towards Penrhyn Bay and Rhos-on-Sea. Occasional karaoke and live music nights are hosted.

Penrhyn Arms

Pendre Road, LL30 3BY

5 (4.30 Thu; 4 Fri; 12 Sat)-11.45; 12-11 Sun 07780 678927 penrhynarms.com

Banks's Bitter; Marston's Pedigree; guest beers H

This welcoming local has up to four guest beers, concentrating on new breweries and new beers, plus a winter ale on gravity at Christmas. The spacious L-shaped bar has pool, darts and a wide-screen TV. Thursday is cheese night. Accommodation is available in a self-contained flatlet. A winner of many awards including local CAMRA Pub of the Year as well as regional, Welsh and national cider awards and National Cider Pub of the Year finalist 2012.

Porthmadog

Ship Inn

14 Lombard Street, LL49 9AP

12-2.30, 5.30-11 (11.30 Thu-Sat) (01766) 512990

Beer range varies H

Traditional pub in a picturesque location behind the park in the centre of this harbour town. Friendly and efficient staff dispense frequently changing ales and serve quality food, including pub favourites steak and ale pie, lasagne and barbecue ribs. The pub has a separate bar and lounge, and a room available for private events, and is popular with locals and tourists. A quiz is hosted on Thursday night. A former local CAMRA Pub of the Year award winner.

Spooner's Bar

Harbour Station, LL49 9NF

9-11; 12-10.30 Sun (01766) 516032

Beer range varies H

Spooner's beer range varies, but there are always at least two ales from the local Purple Moose Brewery. Situated in the terminus of the world-famous Ffestiniog Railway and Wesh Highland Railway, steam trains are outside the door most of the year. Food is served every lunchtime, evening meals Tuesday to Saturday, but check first out of season. A former local CAMRA Pub of the Year award winner. (Ffestiniog Railway)

Station Inn

LL49 9HT (on mainline station platform)

11-11 (midnight Thu-Sat); 12-11 Sun (01766) 512629

Brains Bitter; Purple Moose Cwrw Eryri/Snowdonia Ale; guest beer H

On the Cambrian Coast railway platform, this pub is popular with locals and visitors alike. It has a large lounge and a smaller public bar, and can get busy at the weekend and on nights when live football is shown on TV. A range of pies and sandwiches is available all day.

Red Wharf Bay

Ship Inn

LL75 8RJ (off A5025 between Pentraeth and Benllech)
11-11 (10.30 Sun) ☎ (01248) 852568
shipinnredwharfbay.co.uk
Adnams Broadside; Brains SA; guest beers H
Previously known as the Quay, the Ship enjoys an excellent reputation for its bar and restaurant, with meals served lunchtimes and evenings. It gets busy with locals and visitors in summer. The garden has panoramic views across the bay to south-east Anglesey. The resort town of Benllech is two miles away and the coastal path passes the front door. Beers can be expensive. **Q**

Rhoscolyn

White Eagle

LL65 2NJ (off B4545 signed Traeth Beach)
12-3, 6-11; 12-11 Sat; 12-10.30 Sun ☎ (01407) 860267
white-eagle.co.uk
Marston's Burton Bitter, Pedigree; Weetwood Eastgate Ale; guest beers H
Saved from closure by new owners, this pub has been renovated and rebuilt with an airy, brasserie-style ambience. It has a fine patio enjoying superb views over Caernarfon Bay and the Lleyn Peninsula to Bardsey Island. The nearby beach offers safe swimming with a warden on duty in the summer months. The pub is also close to the coastal footpath. Excellent food is available lunchtimes and evenings, all day during the school holidays.
Q

St George

Kinmel Arms

LL22 9BP
closed Sun & Mon; 12-3, 6-11 (11.30 Fri & Sat)
☎ (01745) 832207 thekinmelarms.co.uk
Facer's Flintshire Bitter; guest beers H
This former 17th-century coaching inn is set on the hillside overlooking the sea. A central bar serves a large combined dining and drinking area with a real log fire in one corner and a spacious conservatory at the rear. Two guest beers come from independent breweries, plus a Welsh cider or perry and a selection of Belgian and continental beers. The pub has a reputation for good food. Luxury accommodation is available in four comfortable suites. **Q P**

Tremadog

Union Inn

7 Market Square, LL49 9RB
12-2, 5.30-12.30am (11 Sun) ☎ (01766) 512748
union-inn.com
Big Bog Bog Standard Bitter; Great Orme Cambria; Purple Moose Cwrw Eryri/Snowdonia Ale H
Friendly village local situated in the village square, with two separate cosy bars and a restaurant at the rear. The pub has a policy of using locally-sourced produce, and the ale range features mainly local beers. Excellent food is served in the bar and restaurant. Children are welcome and there are board games available. Frequent bus services pass the building. Tremadog was the birthplace of Lawrence of Arabia. **Q** (1A,T2)

Trofarth

Holland Arms

Llanrwst Road, LL22 8BG
12-3, 7-11 Mon & Tue; closed Wed & Thu; 12-3, 6-11 Fri & Sat; 12-10.30 Sun ☎ (01492) 650777
thehollandarms.co.uk
Beer range varies H
Eighteenth-century coaching house set in a country landscape within sight of Snowdonia. It has a pleasantly furnished bar, lounge and restaurant areas. Excellent meals are available daily, with a special themed menu on Monday. Beers are all local, from Conwy, Great Orme and Nant breweries. Live music features occasionally. **Q P**

Tudweiliog

Lion Hotel

LL53 8ND (on B4417)
11-11 (12-2, 6-11 winter); 11.30-11 Sat; 11-10.30 (12-3 winter) Sun ☎ (01758) 770244
Beer range varies H
The origins of this free house go back more than 300 years. A village inn set on the glorious, quiet north coast of the Lleyn Peninsula, cliffs and beaches are a mile away by footpath, a little further by road. Up to three beers are served depending on the season, with Purple Moose a firm favourite. The pub is accessible by bus from Pwllheli during the day only. Closed Monday lunchtimes in winter. **Q** (8)

Waunfawr

Snowdonia Park

Beddgelert Road, LL55 4AQ
11-11 (10.30 Sun) ☎ (01286) 650409
snowdonia-park.co.uk
Snowdonia Gold, Carmen Sutra, Dark & Delicious; guest beers H
Home of the Snowdonia and Big Bog Breweries, this is a popular pub for walkers, climbers and families, with children's play areas inside and out. Meals are served all day. The pub adjoins Waunfawr station on the Welsh Highland Railway – stop off here before continuing on one of the most scenic sections of narrow gauge railway in Britain. There is a large campsite adjacent on the riverside. Local CAMRA Pub of the Year 2014.
Q P

Sailors Arms

Up the street, in the Sailors Arms, Sinbad Sailors, grandson of Mary Ann Sailors, drew a pint in the sunlit bar. The ship's clock in the bar says half past eleven. Half past eleven is opening time. The hands of the clock have stayed still at half past eleven for fifty years. It is always opening time in the Sailors Arms.
Dylan Thomas, Under Milk Wood

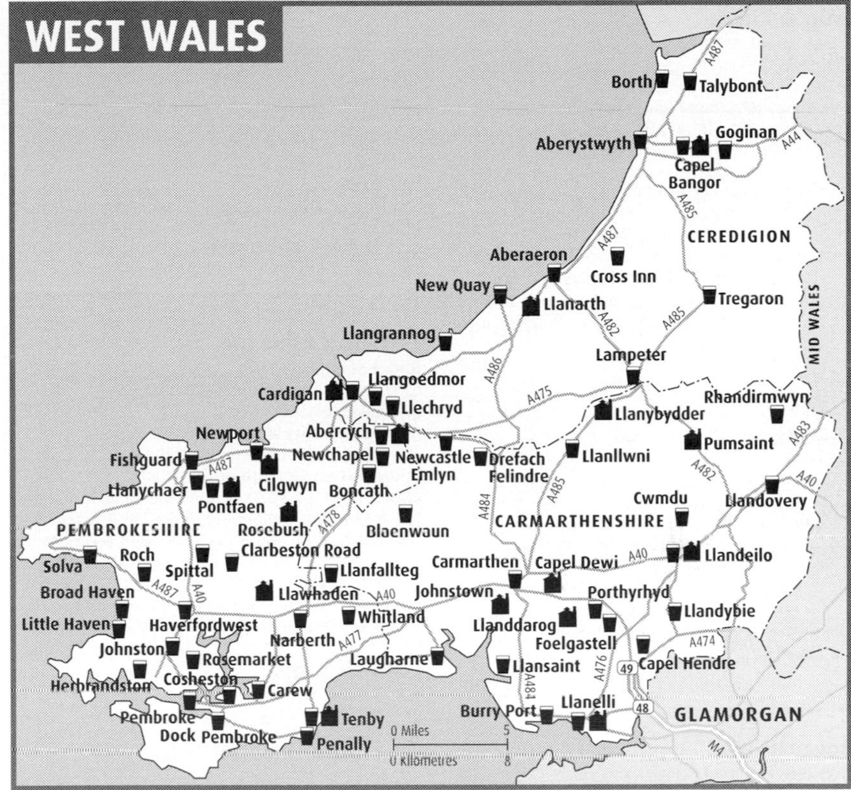

Authority areas covered: Carmarthenshire UA, Ceredigion UA, Pembrokeshire UA

Aberaeron

Cadwgan Inn

10 Market Street, SA46 0AU (off A487, overlooking harbour)
12-11 (midnight Fri & Sat); 12-5 Sun ☎ (01545) 570149
Hancock's HB; guest beer H
Named for the last ship to be built at Aberaeron, this welcoming single-bar pub, the best traditional drinking house in an attractive Regency planned town, is a cosy spot to relax, chat, or watch rugby or racing on TV. The guest beer is chosen from a wide range of micro and regional breweries. Outside, the small pavement drinking area is a suntrap, and there is a smoking area at the rear. The free public car park opposite fills up quickly, especially in summer. (T1,X50)

Abercych

Nag's Head

SA37 0HJ (on B4332 between Cenarth and Eglwyswrw)
11-3 (not Mon), 6-11; 12-10.30 Sun ☎ (01239) 841200
Beer range varies H
This well-restored old smithy boasts a beamed bar and riverside garden. The bar area is furnished with collections of old medical instruments, railway memorabilia and timepieces showing the time in various parts of the world. Space is also found for an extensive display of beer bottles. The pub showcases the products of the on-site Cych Valley Brewery, reopened in 2012 after a decade of inactivity, with at least three beers generally available. QP

Aberystwyth

Glengower Hotel

3 Victoria Terrace, SY23 2DH (N end of promenade)
12-11 ☎ (01970) 626191 glengower.co.uk
Wye Valley Butty Bach; guest beers H
Excellent coastal views can be enjoyed from the suntrap front terrace at this seafront hotel. Inside are a light, airy front bar, quieter dining area, and a large back room with pool and electronic games. Two guest beers (three at busy times), often from Welsh micros, are perhaps rather expensive by local standards. The cider is from Gwynt y Ddraig. Good-value food is served until 8pm (6pm Sun). The hotel closes for a fortnight over Christmas/New Year. (03)

Hen Orsaf

26 Alexandra Road, SY23 1LN
9am-midnight (1am Fri & Sat) ☎ (01970) 636080
Greene King Abbot; Ruddles Best Bitter; guest beers H
An award-winning conversion of Aberystwyth's 1924-built ex-GWR railway station, this much-improved Wetherspoon pub offers up to six guest beers with a good balance of golden, copper and dark ales, frequently featuring Welsh microbreweries such as Mantle and Waen. The usual Wetherspoon policies and promotions apply. Trains, buses and taxis are all adjacent. Outdoor drinking is available on the old station concourse.

Ship & Castle

1 High Street, SY23 1JG

2-midnight (1am Fri); 12-1am Sat ☎ 07773 778785

shipandcastle.co.uk

Wye Valley HPA, Butty Bach; guest beers H

Real ale mecca offering three eclectically sourced and rapidly changing microbrewery guests, real cider and perry from Gwynt y Ddraig, a couple of craft kegs, and one or two classy bottled beers from Tiny Rebel or Kernel. You can sample the range with a 'five pump platter' of five third-pint measures. The decor in the lower seating area reflects the pub's name. Beer festivals feature in the spring and autumn. A popular venue to watch Six Nations rugby – all supporters are made most welcome.

Blaenwaun

Lamb Inn

SA34 0JD

4.30-midnight (2am Fri & Sat) ☎ (01994) 448899

Beer range varies H

The Lamb is set in an idyllic area and has an original old local ambience with a relaxing atmosphere and welcoming and friendly staff. It offers a range of three to four real ales. A small, quaint pub, darts and pool are played here. There is plenty of parking and a campsite half a mile away. QP

Boncath

Boncath Inn

SA37 0JN (on B4332 between Cenarth and Eglwyswrw)

11-11; 12-10.30 Sun ☎ (01239) 841241

Worthington's Bitter; guest beer H

This friendly and welcoming pub dates back to the 18th century and is the hub of this attractive village. The interior is divided into several seating areas creating an intimate atmosphere, and the walls display items of local historic interest. Home-cooked meals are recommended. A beer festival is held each August bank holiday weekend. Up to four guest beers are offered, including some from the increasing number of small breweries hereabouts. P(430)

Borth

Victoria Inn

High Street, SY24 5HZ

11-2am ☎ (01970) 871417

Sharp's Doom Bar; Wye Valley HPA, Butty Bach; guest beer H

This well-refurbished family-friendly beachside pub has two bars downstairs complemented by an outside decking area, with another bar and restaurant upstairs leading to a terrace with stunning sea views. Live music plays most weekends. Popular with locals and holidaymakers alike, log-burning fires add a cosy feel all year round. Buses from Aberystwyth stop outside (but no Sunday and limited evening services); trains run until late seven days a week.
(512)

Broad Haven

Galleon

35A Enfield Road, SA62 3JW (at seaward end of B4341)

11 (12 Sun)-11 ☎ (01437) 781974

Beer range varies H

With a hospitable and welcoming landlady and a cosy, homely atmosphere, this friendly hostelry offers breathtaking views over St Brides Bay. Converted from a tea room in the 1980s, the pub has now become a widely appreciated feature of the Havens community, serving well-reputed food and a range of Brain's beers. With a delightful sandy beach, Broad Haven remains popular as a holiday resort for day trips and longer stays.
QP(311)

Burry Port

Coasting Pilot Inn

Bridge Street, SA16 0NR

11-11 (10.30 Sun) ☎ (01554) 833520

coastingpilothotel.co.uk

Beer range varies H

The Coasting Pilot is situated in the harbour town of Burry Port on Carmarthen Bay. Dating from the 1820s, it is reputed to be the oldest pub in town. It has a spacious lounge and dining area where live music is hosted, and a large bar with a pool table, state of the art jukebox, darts and big-screen TVs. The pub is known locally for good beer, quality food and a wonderful friendly atmosphere.
(Pembrey & Burry Port)

Cornish Arms

1 Gors Road, SA16 0EL

12-11 (10.30 Sun) ☎ (01554) 833224

Beer range varies H

Centrally located in a coastal town and conveniently situated within 100 yards of rail and bus stations, this friendly pub restaurant is popular with locals and visitors to the area. The bar offers a choice of four real ales, while the restaurant is renowned for its good-quality food, with fish dishes a speciality. Outside, there is a beer garden and smoking area.
Q(Pembrey & Burry Port)

Capel Bangor

Tynllidiart Arms

SY23 3LR

12-3 (not Mon), 5-midnight; 12-midnight Sun

☎ (01970) 880248 tynllidiartarms.com

Hancock's HB; Wye Valley Butty Bach; guest beer H

Renowned for its food, this village pub also welcomes drinkers and plans to reopen its brewery

INDEPENDENT BREWERIES

Bluestone Cilgwyn (NEW)
Caffle Llawhaden (NEW)
Coles Llanddarog
Cych Valley Abercych
Evan Evans Llandeilo
Felinfoel Llanelli
Friends Arms Johnstown
Gwaun Valley Pontfaen
Gwynant Capel Bangor (brewing suspended)
Handmade Capel Dewi (NEW)
Jacobi Pumsaint
Mantle Cardigan (NEW)
Mercian Llanybydder
Penlon Cottage Llanarth
Preseli Tenby
Seren Rosebush (NEW)

– officially the world's smallest commercial brewery, housed in a disused toilet at the front – in the near future. The restaurant is upstairs, but food is also served in the downstairs bar (no evening meals Sun or Mon). Open fires add to the cosy ambience in winter. Monday is ladies' darts night, Tuesday is pie night. The bus service is daytime only. Q (525,X47)

Capel Hendre

King's Head Hotel

Waterloo Road, SA18 3SF

4-midnight; 1-10 Sun (01269) 842377

Sharp's Doom Bar; guest beers

Local village pub tucked away just a couple of miles from the former mining town of Ammanford. The main bar has pool and darts, with a sliding door leading to a separate snug. Sharp's Doom Bar is usually on offer alongside a varied choice of guest beers from brewers including Tomos Watkin and Kite. No food is available. There is a large car park. P (128,129)

Cardigan

Eagle Inn

Castle Street, SA43 3AA

12-11 (01239) 612046 theeagleinncardigan.co.uk

Beer range varies

A sympathetically refurbished, traditional Welsh pub on the outskirts of Cardigan town. Real ale and good food are served by friendly and attentive staff. Live bands play regularly and open mic nights are hosted. Live Sky Sports is shown on TV. Quiz nights are popular and the pub has its own teams. Well worth venturing over the bridge for.

Grosvenor

Bridge Street, SA43 1HY

11-11 (01239) 613792

Beer range varies

Situated on the edge of the town centre next to Cardigan Castle and the River Teifi, this large pub offers a good choice of ales, including a selection of bottled beers. The spacious open-plan bar/lounge provides various areas for relaxing, drinking and eating, while an extra room upstairs is also used for dining as well as functions. Good-value food is served lunchtimes and evenings every day.

Carew

Carew Inn

SA70 8SL (off A477 before Pembroke Dock)

11 (11.30 Sun)-11 (01646) 651267 carewinn.co.uk

Brains Rev James; Evan Evans Cwrw

Situated close to Carew's historic Celtic Cross, castle and tidal mill, this is the former estate pub of the Trollope-Bellew family. Its village location is convenient for many nearby attractions including Oakwood theme park. A pine-boarded bar features photographs of the local area from the past. Outside there is a marquee and a large grassed garden with a children's play area.
Q P (361)

Carmarthen

Friends Arms

Old St Clears Road, Johnstown, SA31 3HH

12-11 (midnight Fri); 11-midnight Sat; 11-11 Sun (01267) 234073 thefriendsarms.co.uk

Banks's Bitter; Evan Evans Cwrw; guest beers

Excellent local hostelry half a mile from the town centre, with a cosy and friendly atmosphere and a warm welcome, enhanced by two open fires. Popular with sports fans, it has Sky Sports and ESPN, plus pool and darts. A quiz and bingo are held on alternate Wednesdays during the summer. Three real ales are usually offered, with a 10 per cent discount for CAMRA members. A former local CAMRA Pub of the Year, it has its own microbrewery producing a selection of ales.
(222,322)

Hen Dderwen

47-48 King Street, SA31 1BH

8am-midnight (1am Sat) (01267) 242050

Greene King Abbot; Ruddles Best Bitter; guest beers

This Wetherspoon pub opened in 2002 and is named after the Carmarthen legend of Merlin and the Old Oak – the story is told in pictures and plaques on the walls. The interior is divided into two distinct spaces – the principal drinking area is at the front while the area to the rear tends to be mainly used by diners. A good selection of real ales is offered. Food is served all day including the chain's standard meal deals. Q P

Queen's Hotel

10 Queen Street, SA31 1JR

10-midnight; 11-8 Sun (01267) 231800

Beer range varies

Town-centre pub near Carmarthenshire county hall with a bar, lounge and small function room. The public bar is used by locals and has TV for sporting events. Locally sourced ales are always available from the likes of Evan Evans Brewery. The patio nestles beneath the castle walls and is a suntrap during the summer months. Upstairs function rooms are available, and the local CAMRA branch meets here.

Stag & Pheasant

34 Spilman Street, SA31 1LQ

12-midnight (11 Sun) (01267) 232040

Jennings Cocker Hoop; Ringwood Fortyniner

A busy locals' pub with a warm and friendly atmosphere on the main thoroughfare in Carmarthen, making it a popular venue for tourists and locals, including fishermen and golfers. The pub boasts an excellent beer garden with outdoor heaters at the rear. Fortyniner is joined by another beer from the Marston's group during busy periods. Historically, the building was a stable block serving the hotel opposite. It is within walking distance of the bus and railway stations.

Clarbeston Road

Cross Inn

SA63 4UL (N of railway station on road to Llysyfran reservoir) SN019211

11.30 (11 Sun)-11 (01437) 731506

Courage Directors; Greene King Abbot; guest beer

Multi-roomed village inn, well worth seeking out, with stone and wood floors and original oak beams in abundance. The large bar area with a pool table,

TV for sport and a jukebox is complemented by two small snugs and a dining room. Reasonably priced home-cooked food is served Thursday to Saturday evenings and Sunday lunchtime. Outside there are more spacious drinking areas. A beer festival is held in summer. Q P (313)

Cosheston

Brewery Inn

SA72 4UD (off A477)

closed Mon; 12-3, 6-11; 12-4, 5-11 Sun (01646) 686678

Courage Directors; guest beer H

Set between Cosheston Pill and the Carew Estuary just north-east of Pembroke, this light and airy stone-built inn boasts a traditional slate floor and bar, roof beams and comfortable seating. Paintings, drawings and photographs by local artists adorn the walls. Despite the name, there has been no brewery here since 1889. QP

Cross Inn (Llanon)

Rhos yr Hafod Inn

SY23 5NB (at B4337/B4577 crossroads)

5-11; closed Sun (01974) 272644

rhos-yr-hafod-inn.co.uk

Evan Evans Best Bitter; guest beer H

Cosy drinking areas cluster around the small central bar at this quiet, friendly pub. The back room has old photographs of local scenes; a roadside drinking area at the front catches the evening sun, and there is an attractive garden at the rear. The guest beer is often from a Welsh brewery. Situated at a prominent crossroads and with ample parking, it is a haven for local real ale drinkers and visitors alike. Dogs are welcome, but please check on arrival – the pub has its own dogs. QP

Cwmdu

Tafarn Cwmdu L

SA19 7DY (off B4302 at Halfway)

7-11; closed Sun-Tue (01558) 685088 cwmdu.com

Beer range varies G

Owned by the National Trust and run by the local community, it is featured in CAMRA's Real Heritage Pubs of Wales. The pub is the centre of activities for the village. A folk night features on the first Friday of the month. The pub will open at the request of visitors for a special occasion and can also be hired for private parties. There is a sitting room upstairs with free access to a computer. P

Drefach Felindre

Tafarn John Y Gwas

SA44 5XG

5-11; 4-midnight Fri; 12-midnight Sat; 12-11 Sun (01559) 370469 johnygwas.co.uk

Beer range varies H

This early 19th-century village tavern with its striking yellow and black livery attracts locals and tourists alike with snugs, wood-burning stoves, quality beer and cider and a warm welcome. At least two ales are generally offered with a nationally recognised name flanked by local and/or microbrewery beers. A wide variety of bottled beers and ciders is also available. Bar meals (Fri & Sat eve), include home-made stone-baked pizzas. P (460)

Fishguard

Pendre Inn

High Street, SA65 9AT (200yds from A40 roundabout next to petrol station)

4-midnight Mon; 11-midnight (1am Fri & Sat); 12-11.30 Sun (01348) 874128 thependreinn.co.uk

Hancock's HB; guest beers H

Friendly traditional pub on the main road south out of town with a good local following and an established reputation for its beer. Two guest ales change regularly. Built around 1790, close to the tollgate on the turnpike road to Haverfordwest, the pub offers pool and darts in the large back bar, while the front bar boasts an inglenook fireplace. Meals, served lunchtimes and evenings (not Mon), include home-made steak and ale pie, curries and desserts. QP (412)

Foelgastell

Smiths Arms

Heol y Foel, SA14 7EL

12-11 (11.30 Fri & Sat) (01269) 842213

thesmithsarms.co.uk

Beer range varies G

This friendly local pub, signposted from the A48 dual carriageway, is a handy stopping-off point for travellers. Open all day from noon, food is available at all times except Sunday evening, with a choice of bar or restaurant menus. Typically one or two real ales from local and national breweries are on sale while real cider is usually also available. Ideal for the nearby National Botanic Garden of Wales. P (166)

Goginan

Druid Inn

SY23 3NT (on A44 6 miles E of Aberystwyth)

12-midnight (1am Fri & Sat) (01970) 880650

goginan.com/druid-inn

Wye Valley Bitter, HPA, Butty Bach; guest beer H

This comfortable, good-humoured village pub, local CAMRA Pub of the Year 2013 and 2014, is the beating heart of this historic former lead-mining community. A dining room and pool room flank the L-shaped main bar where dogs are welcome. The licensee's beer wholesaling business sources the guest beer (occasionally two), plus real cider in summer. Music nights and themed food evenings take place occasionally. Food is popular and high-quality (no meals Tues). Buses are daytime only, Monday-Saturday. P (525,X47)

Haverfordwest

Bristol Trader

Quay Street, SA61 1BE

11-11 (1am Sat); 12-10.30 Sun (01437) 762122

Worthington's Bitter; guest beers H

Dating back to Haverfordwest's days as a port, this pub retains some character despite modernisation. A quiet venue in the daytime, popular for dining, food is served until 7pm in a large dining area or at outside tables overlooking the river. It gets lively with a younger age group in the evening. In the late 1950s this was the first pub in town to have carpet on the floor. Two guest ales are served.

Herbrandston

Taberna Inn

SA73 3TD (3 miles W of Milford Haven)

12-3 (2 Sun), 6-11 ☎ (01646) 693498

Beer range varies H

Designed and built in 1963 by a local carpenter and builder with an eye to the area's then rapidly developing oil and petrochemical industry, this pub has a pleasant atmosphere and welcoming locals. Two guest beers and two real ciders are served – the pub issues a list of all guest beers sold throughout the year. Local CAMRA Pub of the Year 2012 and 2013. Buses are infrequent.
Q❀⇆ (315)

Johnston

Vine Inn

Vine Road, SA62 3NY (on A4076 N of railway station)

closed Mon; 11-2, 6-11; 12-11 Sat & Sun

☎ (01437) 890611

Beer range varies H

This notably friendly pub, its exposed beams adorned with pumpclips, offers three changing guest beers. It has a separate dining room and a small area for private functions. The warm welcome and helpful staff, along with great beer, have seen it crowned Pembrokeshire CAMRA Pub of the Year for 2014. Once the junction for Brunel's port of Neyland, Johnston is now a request stop on the railway line to Milford Haven. No meals Sunday evening. ❀&≠P (302,349)

Lampeter

King's Head

14 Bridge Street, SA48 7HG

3-12.30am (1.30am Sun) ☎ (01570) 421498

Beer range varies H

This town-centre pub has two bars and a large function room, with a good mix of customers – locals, students and tourists – in this university town, which is home to the oldest established rugby club in Wales. Good food is served all day, with dishes such as rabbit stew on the menu. Two beers from the Marston's group are served.
Å♣ (585,T1)

Laugharne

New Three Mariners Inn L

Victoria Street, SA33 4SE

12 (4 winter)-11 ☎ (01994) 427426

Greene King Abbot; guest beers H

The building is located in the centre of the historic township of Laugharne and only yards from its early 11th-century castle. Dylan Thomas lived in the town for a number of years and he and his wife Caitlin are laid to rest in the graveyard of St Martin's Church. The pub moved to its current site when the original ale house opposite was converted to a shop. Popular with locals, it hosts a weekly quiz night. ❀⇆&Å♣P

Little Haven

Castle

1 Grove Place, SA62 3UG (opp beach)

10-11 (1am Fri) ☎ (01437) 781445

Jennings Cocker Hoop; Mansfield Cask Ale; Marston's Pedigree; guest beer H

The main bar of this tastefully modernised pub is split into separate areas by pillars and low dividers. A separate games area has darts and pool. Steeped in local history, the Castle opened in 1871 and is reputedly haunted. The guest beer is generally from the Marston's group. The bus service is the infrequent but scenic Puffin Shuttle (not every day in winter); nearby Broad Haven has a somewhat better service. Q&Å≠♣ (400)

Llandeilo

Angel Hotel

62 Rhosmaen Street, SA19 6EN

11.30-3, 6-11; closed Sun ☎ (01558) 822765

angelbistro.co.uk

Beer range varies H

Ideally located in the centre of this picturesque Tywi Valley town, the Angel ministers to all needs. The main bar is a U-shaped room providing three real ales, mainly from local breweries, and bar meals. At the back is a bistro dating back to the 1700s, while the first floor offers a beer garden to the rear and a function room boasting a Michelangelo-inspired hand-painted mural. Themed meal nights and music nights are held regularly. ❀⇆≠

Cottage Inn

SA19 6SD (on A40, 2 miles W of town centre)

12-11 ☎ (01558) 613371 thecottageinnllandeilo.com

Gower Gold; Sharp's Doom Bar; guest beer H

A popular family-run local community pub on the A40. Dating back to the 1850s, it was formerly a coaching inn and a drovers' hostelry. Sky TV is available and the pub gets busy when major sporting events are screened. There is a separate restaurant/function room area, and at the rear is a covered smoking area and a large car park with caravanning and camping space. Two or three guest ales are available. Q❀⇆&P

White Horse

Rhosmaen Street, SA19 6EN

11-11; 12-10.30 Sun ☎ (01558) 822424

Evan Evans Archers ASB, Cwrw, Warrior; guest beers H

Grade II-listed coaching inn dating from the 16th century. The tap for the local Evan Evans Brewery, this multi-roomed pub is popular with all ages. There is a small outdoor drinking area to the front and a large council car park to the rear with access to the pub down a short flight of steps. The covered area for smokers has its own TV showing sport. Carmarthenshire CAMRA Pub of the Year 2014.
≠ (103,X13)

Llandovery

King's Head L

1 Market Square, SA20 0AB

10-11 ☎ (01550) 720393 kingsheadcoachinginn.co.uk

Evan Evans Cwrw; guest beers H

Former coaching inn dating from the 1700s in a historic town on the edge of the Brecon Beacons. Newly refurbished yet still traditional, it is a popular base for many organisations including the Rotary Club and cattle breeders. Good food ranges from bar meals to à la carte. Guest beers usually include local Welsh ales.
Q⇆Å≠♣ (280,281)

Llandybie

Ivy Bush

18 Church Street, SA18 3HZ (100yds from church)
12-midnight (11 Mon); 11-midnight Sat & Sun
☎ (01269) 850272
Timothy Taylor Landlord; guest beer H
The oldest pub in the village, this friendly local dates back nearly 300 years. The single-bar room has two comfortable seating areas. Pub games and quizzes are run weekly and a large-screen TV shows sport. The guest beer changes regularly. The railway station nearby is on the scenic Heart of Wales line. At least one guest ale is usually available alongside Landlord. P (103,X13)

Llanelli

Harry Watkins

2 Millfield Road, Felinfoel, SA14 8HY (on A476)
closed Mon; 12-11 ☎ (01554) 776644
Banks's Bitter; Ringwood Fortyniner; guest beers H
Renamed after a local rugby hero of yesteryear who features on the pub walls, the pub was originally called the Bear. The open-plan, split-level, family-friendly hostelry has defined dining spaces and a function room. There are covered and open drinking areas outside. Although there is no car park, there is usually ample room to park on the road. National cycle and walking paths to the Swiss Valley and beyond are nearby.

York Palace

51 Stepney Street, SA15 3YA (opp Town Hall Square Gardens)
9am-midnight (1am Fri & Sat) ☎ (01554) 758609
Greene King Abbot; Ruddles Best Bitter; guest beers H
This former cinema in the town centre is a typical Wetherspoon conversion arranged over two levels. The walls are adorned with photographs of local industrial history including Llanelli's famous tin-plate industry. Guest beers are often sourced locally and are discounted on Wednesday and Sunday (CAMRA members receive a discount at all times). There is easy access to the bus station and the railway station is a 10-minute walk.
Q

Llanfallteg

Plash

SA34 0UN (off A40 at Llanddewi Velfrey)
12 (5 Mon & Tue)-11 ☎ (01437) 563472
Wye Valley Butty Bach; guest beers H
A terrace-style cottage pub with a garden, the Plash is the centre of village life, with welcoming locals. An inn for more than 180 years, it has had four different names in that time. The guest beers are usually from small independent breweries. Home-made food, using locally-sourced ingredients, is available, with specials on Tuesday, Wednesday, Friday and Saturday. The disabled entrance is to the rear. A small cottage is available to let. Local CAMRA Pub of the Year 2012.
Q

Llangoedmor

Penllwyndu

SA43 2LY (on B4570)
11 (3 Mon)-11 ☎ (01239) 682533
Courage Directors; guest beers H
Old-fashioned ale house standing at an isolated crossroads where Cardigan's evil-doers were once hanged – the pub sign is worthy of close inspection. The cheerful and welcoming public bar retains its quaint appeal with a slate floor and inglenook with wood-burning stove. Good home-cooked food including traditional favourites is available all day, served in the bar and separate restaurant. Free live music plays on the third Thursday evening of the month. P

Llangrannog

Pentre Arms Hotel

SA44 6SP (at seaward end of B4321/B4334)
12-midnight ☎ (01239) 654345 pentrearms.co.uk
Gales Seafarers Ale; St Austell Tribute; guest beer H
Set on the Wales Coast Path in a former seafaring village, this pub commands tremendous sea views (also viewable via beach webcam on the website). The main bar is flanked by a games room – with poker on winter Wednesdays – and dining room. The guest beer, available in summer, is usually from a Welsh brewery. Live music features at weekends. The Cardi Bach coastal bus runs all year (not Wed) and in summer there is a park-and-ride from the top of the village. Dogs welcome in bar only. (600)

Llanllwni

Talardd Arms

SA39 9DX (on A485)
12-2.30, 6-11 ☎ (01559) 395633 talardd.com
Evan Evans Warrior H
There are records of this old drovers' inn dating back to 1626 – drovers would stop for refreshments for man and beast before driving their livestock over Llanllwni Mountain on their way to markets over the border. Though modernised these days, Tafarn y Talardd still offers that old warm and friendly welcome. Live music, quizzes and film nights are organised most Mondays. One well-kept ale is available on the bar. P (T1)

Llansaint

King's Arms

13 Maes yr Eglwys, SA17 5JE
closed Mon & Tue; 6-11 Wed-Fri; 12-11 Sat; 12-2.30, 6.30-10.30 Sun ☎ (01267) 267487
Young's Special; guest beers H
A former local CAMRA Pub of the Year, this friendly village local has been a pub for over 200 years. Situated near an 11th-century church, it is reputedly built from stone recovered from the lost village of St Ishmaels. Music and poetry nights are held on the third Friday of the month. Two guest beers from smaller breweries are usually offered. Good-value home-cooked food is served. Carmarthen Bay Holiday Park is a few miles away.
Q (198)

Llanychaer

Bridge End Inn L

SA65 9TB (on B4313, 2 miles SW of Fishguard)
12-11 (midnight Sat) ☎ (01348) 872545
Draught Bass; guest beers G
Known locally as the Bont, this friendly country pub, over 150 years old, nestles in the beautiful

Gwaun valley at a bridging point across the river. The comfortable lounge-style bar serves beer straight from the cask; one of the two guest beers is usually from the local Bluestone brewery. The dining room is housed in the smithy, once run as a complementary business to the pub, and features many reminders of its former use including an external waterwheel. Home-made food is served seven days a week, with Sunday lunch being particularly popular. Q ❀◐◑♿▲♣P

Llechryd

Seven Stars

SA43 2NR (on A484)
12-midnight ☎ (01239) 682115
seven-stars-cardigan.co.uk
Wadworth 6X; guest beer Ⓗ
This sympathetically modernised inn is situated in the quaint village of Llechryd, just a short walk from the Grade II-listed bridge that spans the River Teifi at its highest tidal point. The pub itself offers a separate bar and restaurant as well as accommodation. The hosts cannot seem to do enough for you, with everything offered from packed lunches to fishing gear. Good real ale is obviously a bonus. ❀🛏◐◑P🚌(460)🐾

Narberth

Dingle Inn

Jesse Road, SA67 7DP (on A478 northern approach to town)
11 (12 Sun)-11 ☎ (01834) 861806
Beer range varies Ⓗ
Formerly a caravan-site bar, there is still space for tourers and campers here. The inn is now a friendly local offering a range of beers, chosen by the regulars, from near and far. Narberth's distinctive community spirit has brought the town a range of specialist shops including food and drink retailers, and facilities such as the award-winning museum, that would be the envy of many larger places. The railway station is a mile from the town.
❀🛏◐◑♿▲⇌🚌

New Quay

Sea Horse Inn

Uplands Square, SA45 9QH
11-11 ☎ (01545) 560736
Beer range varies Ⓗ
This welcoming one-roomer, decorated with fascinating old photographs and cartoons, offers one real ale in winter, two or more (plus Westons Old Rosie cider) in summer, largely from national brewers or Welsh regionals such as Kite, and runs a beer festival around the August bank holiday. Quiz night is Thursday, and a singer performs most Fridays. A small patio with bench seating can catch the sun. Generously filled crusty rolls are available while stocks last. Closing time may vary.
❀▲♣🚌(X50)🐾

Newcastle Emlyn

Ivy Bush

Emlyn Square, SA38 9BG
10-11; 10.30-8 Sun ☎ (01239) 710542
Draught Bass; guest beer Ⓗ
Very much a local pub with a traditional separate bar area and plenty of small, intimate nooks. Located at the top end of this market town, it has lots of local parking, shopping and public transport links. Pool and darts are available in an area to the rear of the pub. No food is served but there is a chip shop/cafe next door. ❀♣P🚌(460)🐾

Newchapel

Ffynone Arms

SA37 0EH (on B4332 between Cenarth and Eglwyswrw)
5-11 (1am Fri); 1-1am Sat; 12-11 Sun ☎ (01239) 841800
ffynnonearms.co.uk
Evan Evans BB/Best Bitter; guest beers Ⓗ
Once a famously simple, even spartan, establishment, this stone-built pub has been thoroughly modernised, the interior now featuring much exposed oak. The food is home-made, and a wide range of dietary requirements can be catered for. Sunday lunch is a carvery, and a takeaway menu is available on Wednesday evening. Guest beers are usually sourced from Welsh breweries. The peaceful garden has a pond and waterfall.
❀◐◑♿🍎P

Newport

Castle Inn

Bridge Street, SA42 0TB
11-midnight (1am Fri & Sat) ☎ (01239) 820742
Felinfoel Double Dragon; Wye Valley Butty Bach; guest beer Ⓗ
Friendly, popular local in a characterful small town, with an attractive bar featuring some impressive wood panelling. Food is served lunchtimes and evenings in an extensive dining area. Beer and cider festivals are held during the early May and August bank holiday weekends. The guest beer is from Cardigan's highly regarded Mantle Brewery – usually either Cwrw Teifi or Dark Heart. A wealth of prehistoric remains, and the Wales Coastal Path, make this a popular walking centre.
Q❀🛏◐◑♿▲⇌♣🍎P🚌(412)

Golden Lion

East Street, SA42 0SY (on A487)
12-midnight (11 Sun) ☎ (01239) 820321
Brains Rev James; Draught Bass; guest beer Ⓗ
Another of the town's sociable locals, this one is reputed to have its own resident ghost. A number of internal walls have been removed to form a spacious open-plan bar area, with distinct sections helping to retain a cosy atmosphere. Car parking space is available on the opposite side of the road.
Q❀◐◑▲♣P🚌(412)

Pembroke

Royal Oak

138-140 Main Street, SA71 4HN
2 (12 Sat & Sun)-midnight ☎ (01646) 682537
Hancock's HB; guest beer Ⓗ
Situated at the east end of this historic town, this well-established pub with coach arch and stable yard – now used as beer garden – offers a warm and friendly welcome from an enthusiastic licensee. The traditional interior features exposed oak beams in the bar. Pub games include shove-ha'penny. Two guest beers are usually offered; one is either Sharp's Doom Bar or Brains Rev James.
❀◐♿▲⇌♣🍎🚌(349, 356)

Pembroke Dock

First & Last

London Road, Waterloo, SA72 6TX (on A477)
10-1am (1.30am Thu-Sat) (01646) 682687
Brains Rev James; Worthington's Bitter; guest beer H
Small, friendly, single-bar local in the same family for the past 50 years. The walls display an eclectic mix of photos and prints. Food is standard pub fare. Formerly the Commercial, the pub acquired its current more distinctive name in 1991 to reflect its edge-of-town location. It is handy for the Cleddau Bridge, giving easy access to Haverfordwest and the beaches and other attractions of west and north Pembrokeshire. QP (349,356)

Station Inn

Hawkestone Road, SA72 6JL (in station building)
12-3, 6-midnight (12.30am Fri & Sat); 12-3, 7-10.30 Sun
(01646) 621255
Beer range varies H
Housed in the town's railway station where trains still depart for Carmarthen and Swansea (and, on summer Saturdays, far-off Paddington), this town-centre pub, long a staple of the Pembrokeshire real ale scene, is close to both the ferry terminal and Wales Coast Path. Three eclectically sourced real ales are generally on sale, with Young's Bitter a frequent visitor along with many Welsh beers.
QP

Penally

Cross Inn

SA70 7PU
12-11 (12.30am Fri & Sat) (01834) 844665
crossinnpenally.co.uk
Hancock's HB; guest beer H
Situated in a picturesque village with some well-preserved Georgian and Victorian houses, this Grade II-listed pub has a wood and brick bar leading to the restaurant. Pictures and shields of locally stationed regiments adorn the walls. The sporting prowess of the locals is evident from the cups and shields on the trophy shelf. A signed photo and a set of darts used by Phil 'The Power' Taylor is framed in an alcove.
Q (349)

Pontfaen

Dyffryn Arms ★

SA65 9SG (off B4313)
11-midnight; 12-10.30 Sun (01348) 881305
Draught Bass G
This much-loved inn, a reminder of how all country pubs must once have looked, is the hub of life in a secluded valley whose distinctive cultural traditions include a long history of farmhouse brewing. There is no bar counter – beer is served by the jug through a serving hatch. Conversation is the main form of entertainment, and the pub's relaxed atmosphere is captivating. A timeless gem to be treated with respect. It may close early, or during the daytime, if there are no customers.
Q

Gwaun Valley Brewery

Kilkiffeth Farm, SA65 9TP (on B4313 between Fishguard and Maenclochog)
11-6; 11-5.45, 7-midnight Fri & Sat (01348) 881304
gwaunvalleybrewery.co.uk
Beer range varies H
Family-run brewery, pioneer of the new wave of Pembrokeshire brewing, set in the north Pembrokeshire countryside, with views to the Gwaun Valley and the Preseli Hills. Half the converted farm building that houses the brewery is used as a tasting area, function room and bar, with live acoustic music on Saturday night. A selection from the brewery's range of draught and bottle-conditioned beers is on offer at this relaxed and welcoming venue. QP

Porthyrhyd

Mansel Arms

Banc y Mansel, SA32 8BS (on B4310 between Porthyrhyd and Drefach)
5-11; 3-midnight Sat; 12-6 Sun (01267) 275305
Beer range varies H
Friendly 18th-century former coaching inn with wood fires in each room. The original limestone flags have been broken up and used in the fireplace, and low beams have been added to create atmosphere, with numerous jugs hanging from them in the bar. Pool and darts are played in a room to the rear, which was originally used for slaughtering pigs. Beers are varied with the Young's range always popular as well as local ales.
QP (129)

Rhandirmwyn

Royal Oak L

SA20 0NY SN80744884
12-2, 6-11 (10.30 Sun) (01550) 760201
theroyaloakinn.co.uk
Beer range varies H
Remote, stone-flagged inn with excellent views of the Tywi Valley and close to an RSPB bird sanctuary. Originally built as a hunting lodge for the local landowner, it is now a focal point for community activities and popular with fans of outdoor pursuits. Two or three guest beers are offered and the good wholesome food is recommended. There are panoramic views from the beer garden at the side of the pub. Four times local CAMRA Pub of the Year. QP

Roch

Victoria Inn

SA62 6AW (on A487)
12-2, 5-11 Mon & Tue; 12-11; 12-10.30 Sun
(01437) 710426
Black Sheep Best Bitter; guest beers H
A little gem with views across St Brides Bay, this locals' pub offers a warm welcome. The inn was established in 1851 although parts are older, and it has retained much of its old-world charm, with beamed ceilings and low doorways. The menu features home-made Welsh dishes made with local produce where possible. Curry and a pint night is Friday. Guest beers include a house ale sourced from a local brewery. Live music plays occasionally.
QP (411)

Rosemarket

Huntsman

3 West Street, SA73 1JH
4-11; 12-midnight Sat; 12-11 Sun (01646) 600514
Courage Directors; guest beers H

This friendly pub offers two guest beers throughout the year. While it is known for its food, the warm welcome from the locals and the helpfulness of the licensees also make it a great place to while away an evening over a pint or two. Accommodation is provided in nearby holiday cottages. A late medieval dovecote is a noteworthy feature of the village. Buses are infrequent.
P (308)

Solva

Harbour Inn

SA62 6AW (on A487 next to harbour)
11-11 ☎ (01437) 720013
Beer range varies H
Delightful seaside inn next to the tiny harbour, now the haunt of leisure sailors but once a port of embarkation for North America. It offers a range of Brain's beers including seasonals and sometimes guests from other breweries. A community pub with a traditional atmosphere, it serves as a base for many village activities and is popular with locals who come to enjoy a quiet, relaxing pint. Nearby camping facilities cater for both caravans and tents.
Q P (411)

Spittal

Pump on the Green

SA62 5QT
closed Mon; 11-11 (1am Sat); 11-10 Sun
☎ (01437) 741881
Sharp's Doom Bar; guest beer H
Set on the village green, this community pub comprises a U-shaped bar with satellite TV for sport, a games area with pool and darts, and a separate dining area (food can also be served in the main bar). The changing guest beer is sourced from a local brewery. Nearby Scolton Manor, with its country park and museum, offers an insight into Pembrokeshire life. P

Talybont

White Lion (Llew Gwyn)

SY24 5ER
12-midnight ☎ (01970) 832245
Banks's Mild, Bitter; guest beer H
Following vicissitudes including a major flood, this friendly community pub has now re-established itself as the hub of village life. The main bar with its old slate floor, heated by a small solid-fuel stove, is complemented by a games room and dining room; outside, there is a beer garden to the rear, and tables at the front facing the village green. Up to four guest beers are from the Marston's group. Evening and Sunday bus services are limited. P (T2,X28)

Tenby

Hope & Anchor

St Julian Street, SA70 7AS
11-11; 12-10.30 Sun ☎ (01834) 842131
Brains Rev James; guest beers H
Set at the fringe of the Old Town on the way down to the harbour, this welcoming pub offers three guest beers. While food is important here, with numerous specials supplementing the standard menu, the well-judged layout, convivial atmosphere and interesting locally themed decor make it an excellent place to relax over a beer while visiting this attractive town.

Tregaron

Talbot

The Square, SY25 6JL
9am-11 ☎ (01974) 298208 ytalbot.com
Mantle Cwrw Teifi; guest beers H
This heritage pub of immense character offers a choice of rooms – a main bar with TV, small front lounge, and beamed and flagstoned snug with inglenook fireplace. Up to four guest beers are mainly from Welsh breweries including Evan Evans, Mantle and Purple Moose, while Wye Valley sometimes sneaks in from over the border. A choice of ciders comes from Gwynt y Ddraig. The locally-sourced food is excellent – pie of the day and cawl (lamb broth served with local cheese) are particularly recommended. Ask about the elephant.
Q P (585,588)

Whitland

Station House Hotel

St Johns Street, SA34 0AP
9am-1am (2am Fri & Sat) ☎ (01994) 240556
stationhousewhitland.co.uk
Worthington's Bitter; guest beers H
A smile and a warm welcome are always on tap at this friendly hostelry. Very much a locals' pub, the regulars range in age from 18 to 80. There is something for everyone here, with pool and darts teams and bingo on Sunday evenings. A small separate room is available for people looking for a quiet corner. The pub is only 20 yards from the railway station. The outside drinking area is partly under cover. P

Wer Kein Bier hat,
Hat nichts zu trinken.
Martin Luther

When you have no beer,
You have nothing to drink.

Luther (1483-1546), was an Augustinian friar who rebelled against the excesses of the Papacy and sparked the Protestant reformation. When he was put on trial for heresy at the Diet of Worms in 1521, he was refreshed with supplies of beer from Einbeck in Lower Saxony. Einbeck gave its name to the strong German beer style known as Bock.

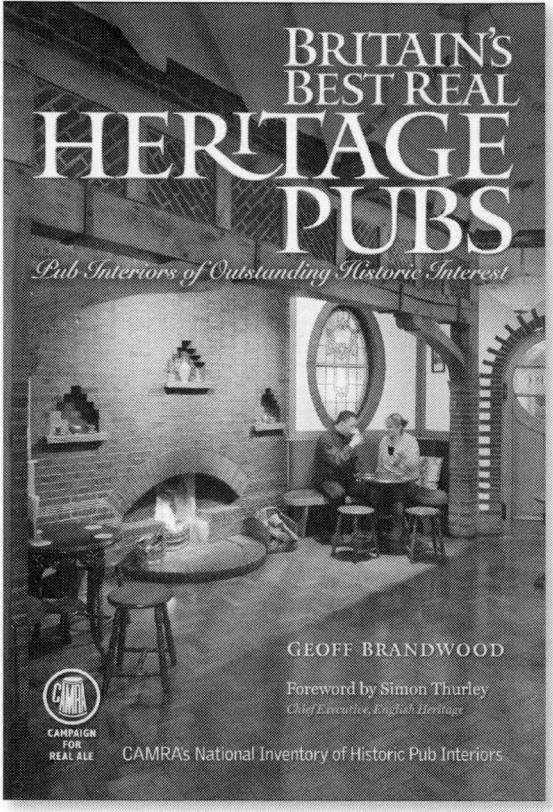

NORTHERN ISLES
SHETLAND
HIGHLANDS & WESTERN ISLES
ABERDEEN & GRAMPIAN
TAYSIDE
LOCH LOMOND, STIRLING & THE TROSSACHS
FIFE
ARGYLL & THE ISLES
EDINBURGH & LOTHIANS
GREATER GLASGOW & CLYDE VALLEY
BORDERS
AYRSHIRE & ARRAN
DUMFRIES & GALLOWAY
NORTHUMBERLAND
TYNE & WEAR
NORTHERN IRELAND
DURHAM
CUMBRIA
NORTH YORKSHIRE
ISLE OF MAN
LANCASHIRE
WEST YORKS
EAST YORKS
GREATER MANCHESTER
MERSEYSIDE
SOUTH YORKS
CHESHIRE
DERBYSHIRE
NOTTINGHAMSHIRE
LINCOLNSHIRE
NW WALES
NE WALES
STAFFORD SHIRE
SHROPSHIRE
LEICESTERSHIRE & RUTLAND
NORFOLK
WEST MIDLANDS
CAMBRIDGESHIRE
MID WALES
HEREFORDSHIRE
WORCESTERSHIRE
WARWICKSHIRE
NORTHAMPTONSHIRE
BEDFORDSHIRE
SUFFOLK
BUCKINGHAMSHIRE
WEST WALES
GWENT
GLOUCS & BRISTOL
OXFORDSHIRE
HERTFORDSHIRE
ESSEX
GLAMORGAN
GREATER LONDON
BERKSHIRE
WILTSHIRE
SURREY
KENT
SOMERSET
HAMPSHIRE
WEST SUSSEX
EAST SUSSEX
CHANNEL ISLANDS
DEVON
DORSET
ISLE OF WIGHT
CORNWALL

Scotland

ABERDEEN & GRAMPIAN

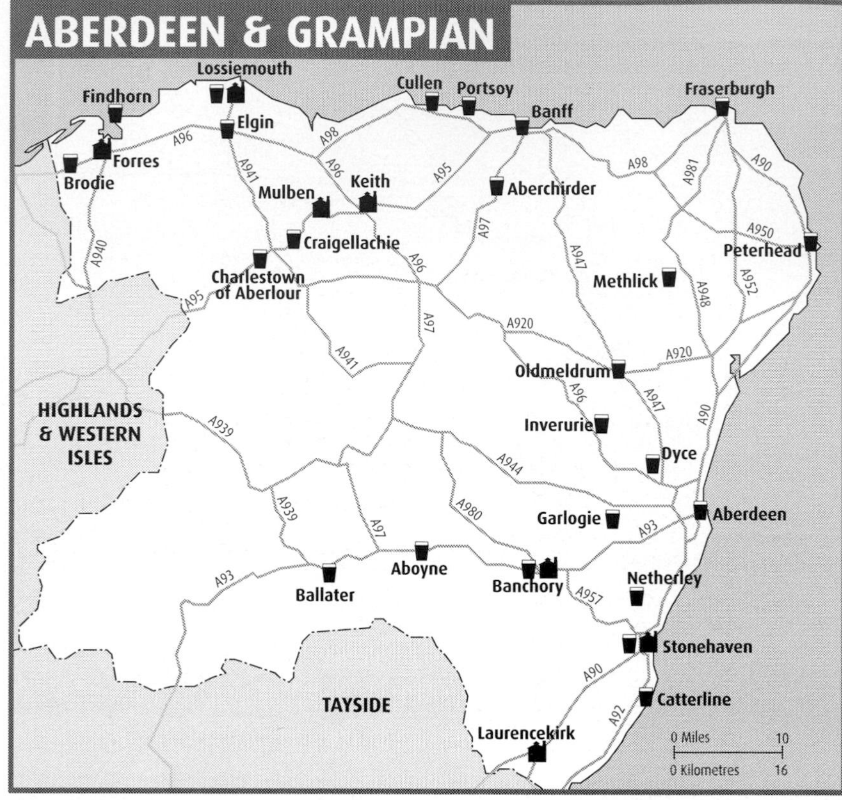

Authority areas covered: Aberdeenshire UA, City of Aberdeen UA, Moray UA

Aberchirder

New Inn

79 Main Street, AB54 7TB

12 (5 Mon)-12.30am; 12-11 Sun (01466) 780633

newinnaberchirder.co.uk

Beer range varies H

The owner of this comfortable inn took over in 2011 and the pub has since gained a reputation for offering a changing selection of quality ales from a variety of breweries, mainly local Scottish but also from Yorkshire. The cosy bar has different seating areas and there is a separate restaurant and a large function room at the rear. Children are welcome in the lounge until 9pm. Food is served lunchtimes and evenings except Monday. (Limited bus service from Huntly/Macduff, with no Sunday service.) (301)

Aberdeen

Archibald Simpson

5 Castle Street, AB11 5BQ (E end of Union Street)

8am-midnight (1am Fri & Sat); 8-11 Sun

(01224) 621365

Caledonian Deuchars IPA; Greene King Abbot; guest beers H

This Wetherspoon pub is in one of many monumental granite buildings in central Aberdeen designed by local architect Archibald Simpson. The former local headquarters of Clydesdale Bank, it retains many original architectural features. The main room is the high-ceilinged central hall, and there are additional seating areas to the side. The long bar features 12 handpumps offering a variety of beers, from mostly Scottish breweries. A former local CAMRA Pub of the Year.

Carriages

101 Crown Street, AB11 6HH

11-2.30, 4.30-midnight; 11-midnight Fri & Sat; 5.30-11 Sun

(01224) 595440

Caledonian Deuchars IPA; guest beers H

Mirrored bar in the basement of the modernised Brentwood Hotel, fitted out with plenty of comfortable seating. A winner of numerous local CAMRA awards, it offers eight changing beers, usually sourced from a mix of national brands and Scottish micros including Houston, Highland and Kelburn. Lunches are available in the bar and the adjoining restaurant is open in the evening. Railway and bus stations are easily reached by descending the stairs from nearby Crown Terrace to Bridge Street. P

INDEPENDENT BREWERIES

Brewmeister Keith
Burnside Laurencekirk
Deeside Banchory
six°north Stonehaven
Spey Valley Mulben
Speyside Craft Forres
Windswept Lossiemouth

Grill ★

213 Union Street, AB11 6BA
10-midnight (1am Fri & Sat); 12.30-midnight Sun
(01224) 573530 thegrillaberdeen.co.uk
Caledonian 80; Harviestoun Bitter & Twisted; guest beers H
With an exquisite interior redesigned in 1926 and remaining largely unchanged since, this is the only pub listed on CAMRA's National Inventory of Historic Pub Interiors in the area. For men only until 1975, ladies' toilets were eventually provided in 1998. Situated across from the Music Hall, musicians often visit during concert breaks. Guest ales are frequently from Scottish micros and a large selection of malts is stocked. Bar snacks are available. CAMRA branch Pub of the Year 2012.

Justice Mill

423 Union Street, AB11 6DA
8am-midnight (1am Fri & Sat); 9am-11 Sun
(01224) 252410
Caledonian Deuchars IPA; Greene King Abbot; guest beers H
Long, narrow and dark Wetherspoon outlet with some raised seating near the bar and booths at both the main entrance and the rear entrance on Justice Mill Lane (hence the name of the pub). The quieter family-friendly atmosphere changes to a loud maelstrom favoured by a younger clientele in the evenings, with DJs at weekends. Alcohol is served from 11am (12.30pm Sunday). The pub has two statement art pieces – a statue of an upside down man and a fire behind glass.

Moorings

2 Trinity Quay, AB11 5AA (facing quayside at bottom of Market St)
12-midnight; 1-3am Fri & Sat; 1-midnight Sun
(01224) 587602
Beer range varies A
Historic harbourside bar that changes character from friendly laid-back local to raucous rock bar on weekend evenings, when there may be a cover charge after 8.45pm. The eclectic jukebox is in regular use by a varied clientele. A wide selection of beers, mainly from Scottish micros, is now served on American-style fonts with electronic display to differentiate them from other beer types. Four times CAMRA City Pub of the Year and current branch winner. CAMRA members receive a discount.

Old Blackfriars

52 Castle Street, AB11 5BB
10-11 (1am Fri & Sat) (01224) 581922
Belhaven 80/- Ale; guest beers H
On the Castlegate in the historic centre of the city, this Belhaven pub with lots of exposed stonework and ancient wood now has just one bar on the lower level, but ales may be ordered from the upper section of the bar. Three guest beers are on offer, usually Inveralmond Ossian and Cairngorm Trade Winds, as well as beers from the Greene King range and house ale. Good food is served daily until 9pm. Quiz night is Tuesday, with acoustic music on Thursday and Friday.

Prince of Wales

7 St Nicholas Lane, AB10 1HF (lane opp Marks & Spencer)
10-midnight (1am Fri & Sat) (01224) 640597
princeofwales-aberdeen.co.uk
Beer range varies H
Among the oldest bars in Aberdeen with possibly the longest bar counter in the city, the Prince has a friendly atmosphere and a large following of regulars. Featured in Scotland's True Heritage Pubs, it offers up to eight ales – a selection of Scottish and English plus the usual Greene King/Belhaven brands and two house ales, one brewed by Inveralmond. Folk night is Sunday and quiz night Monday. Good-value food is served daily until 9pm. Q

Six Degrees North

6 Littlejohn Street, AB10 1FF
11-midnight (1am Fri & Sat); 12.30-midnight Sun
(01224) 379192 sixdnorth.co.uk
Beer range varies H
A conversion of part of former college premises, this establishment features an industrial-style décor with exposed granite, stone floors and plenty of steelwork, furnished with basic wooden benches. A balcony forms an upper drinking area. A large blackboard displays the changing range of around 20 Belgian craft ales, up to four craft ales brewed in Stonehaven by the pub owner, plus a variety of cask beers. A vast range of Belgian bottled beers is also stocked. Hearty bar snacks are available. Q (20)

St Machar Bar

97 High Street, Old Aberdeen, AB24 3EN
11-11 (midnight Fri); 12.30-11 Sun (01224) 483079
themachar.com
Caledonian Deuchars IPA; guest beers H
Located in the photogenic and historic Old Aberdeen conservation area amid the university buildings and close to Kings College, the pub is frequented by academia and locals alike. Up to four guest beers, frequently from Scottish micros and including a house beer from Brains, are available alongside a comprehensive selection of whiskies. A splendid mirror from the long-gone Thomson Marshall Aulton Brewery just down the street adorns the wall just inside the front door, and one from the Devanha Brewery is outside the toilets. CAMRA members, students and OAPs receive a discount. (20)

Under the Hammer

11 North Silver Street, AB10 1RJ (off Golden Square)
5-midnight (1am Thu); 4-1am Fri; 2-1am Sat; 6-midnight Sun (01224) 640253
Caledonian Deuchars IPA; Inveralmond Ossian; guest beer H
Located in a quiet street just minutes off Union Street, this popular pub is in a basement next to an auction house - hence the name - and is convenient for the Music Hall and His Majesty's Theatre. Works by local artists on the walls are for sale if they take your fancy and one wall has posters advertising forthcoming and past events in town. Guest beers usually come from a wide variety of Scottish breweries including locals. Unobtrusive background music plays.

Aboyne

Boat Inn

Charleston Road, AB34 5EL (N bank of River Dee next to Aboyne Bridge)
11-11 (midnight Fri & Sat) (01339) 886137
theboatinnaboyne.co.uk
Beer range varies H

SCOTLAND

Popular riverside inn with a food-oriented lounge featuring an upper dining area. The public bar has been extended and refurbished with a recess at the back used on live music nights. Junior diners (and adults) may request to see the model train, complete with sound effects, traverse the entire pub at picture-rail height upon completion of their meal. The local Rotary Club regularly meets here. Three ales are served, all usually from Scottish micros. Quiz night is monthly.
Q

Ballater

Alexandra Hotel

12 Bridge Square, AB35 5QJ
11-2.30, 5-midnight; 11-midnight Fri-Sun
(01339) 755376 alexandrahotelballater.co.uk
Cairngorm Trade Winds; guest beers
Originally built as a private home in 1800 and becoming the Alexandra Hotel in 1915, this smart refurbished lounge bar is popular with locals for bar suppers and regular bar drinkers too. Ales are supplied from Cairngorm, Inveralmond and Orkney. Handy for a stop-off on your way to Braemar for the Highland Games or for a visit with the royals at Balmoral. P

Glenaden Hotel

6 Church Square, AB35 5NE
11-midnight (1am Thu-Sun) (01339) 755488
Beer range varies
Situated on the far side of the town square, this small hotel displays a prominent external sign for its Barrel Lounge. An annual beer festival is held in the lounge area to the rear in autumn. The hotel is next door to what used to be the only ale outlet in the village, the Prince of Wales, now a tandoori restaurant. Two beers are available in summer, usually Scottish, from Windswept and others, but often just one in winter. QP

Banchory

Douglas Arms Hotel

22 High Street, AB31 5SR
11-midnight (1am Fri & Sat); 12-11 Sun
(01330) 822547 douglasarms.co.uk
Cairngorm Trade Winds; guest beers
Small hotel offering relatively inexpensive accommodation with three separate bars and rooms with plasma TVs where different sports can be watched. The public bar is a classic Scottish long bar with etched windows and vintage mirrors and is featured in Scotland's True Heritage Pubs. Adjacent is a snug area and a separate lounge in three parts, divided by former exterior and internal walls, primarily used for bar suppers. To the rear is a large south-facing exterior decking area. The public bar does not usually open until 3pm.
Q

Ravenswood Club (Royal British Legion)

25 Ramsay Road, AB31 5TS (2nd right up Mount St)
11-11 (midnight Fri & Sat) (01330) 822347
banchorylegion.com
Beer range varies
Large British Legion club with a comfortable lounge adjoining the pool and TV room and a spacious function room well-used by local clubs and societies as well as members. Darts and snooker are popular and played most evenings. The two handpumps offer excellent value and the beer choice is constantly changing, with ales consistently the best quality in the village. An elevated terrace has fine views of the Deeside hills. Show a copy of this Guide or your CAMRA membership card for entry. P

Banff

Ship Inn

8 Deveronside, AB45 1HP (on seafront near harbour)
12-midnight (1am Fri & Sat) (01261) 812620
Theakston XB; guest beer
The interior of this historic nautical-themed inn featured in the film Local Hero. It has a wood-panelled bar and lounge with sea views through the small windows and a fine view across the Deveron mouth to Macduff. A blocked carriage arch hints at the earlier history of the building. Banff Marina, Duff House Gallery (National Gallery of Scotland) and Macduff Aquarium are close by, as are several golf courses. Karaoke and live music feature at weekends. The guest ale is selected by regulars.

Brodie

Old Mill Inn

IV36 2TD (on main A96 between Forres and Nairn)
11.30-11; 11.45-11 Sun (01309) 641605
oldmillinnbrodie.com
Beer range varies
This gem is a spacious, family-friendly inn with a cosy fireside area, smart restaurant, function room and a charming conservatory with views of the old watermill and garden. Up to five ales are available, mainly from Scottish micros, and an excellent range of meals is offered with specials changing on a daily basis. Live Scottish/Irish instrumental music plays on Sunday evening. Brodie Castle is nearby and the popular Brodie Country Fare is opposite. A beer festival is held in June. Local CAMRA Country Pub of the Year 2012.
QP(10,11)

Catterline

Creel Inn

AB39 2UL (on coast off A92, 5 miles S of Stonehaven)
closed Mon & Tue; 12-2, 5.30-midnight (1am Fri & Sat); 12-midnight Sun (01569) 750254 thecreelinn.co.uk
Beer range varies
Set in a scenic cliff-top location, the view from the rear garden of this small village inn is not to be missed. Catterline is known as an artists' village, the most famous being Joan Eardley – one of her paintings is on display in the pub along with other artists' work. The Creel is primarily a food venue but the bar area serves as the village local with up to four beers on offer, usually from Scottish micros. Todhead Lighthouse, Crawton Bird Sanctuary and Kinneff Old Church are nearby. QP

Charlestown of Aberlour

Mash Tun

8 Broomfield Square, AB38 9QP (signed from village square)
12-12.30am (1am Fri & Sat); 12.30-12.30am Sun
(01340) 881771 mashtun-aberlour.com
Beer range varies

A traditional hostelry promoted as a whisky bar – especially busy during whisky festivals and the Aberlour Games weekend. It stocks the only full collection of Glenfarclas whisky in the world alongside more than 100 other malts. The Speyside Way and Alice Little Park are just outside the door and the bar is on the bank of the River Spey, making it popular with fishermen. One beer from Cairngorm and sometimes one from Spey Valley are available, but just the one in winter. Food is served all day Saturday and Sunday.
(36)

Craigellachie

Highlander Inn

10 Victoria Street, AB38 9SR (opp post office)
12-11 (12.30am Fri & Sat) (01340) 881446
whiskyinn.com
Cairngorm Trade Winds; guest beers H
Picturesque whisky and cask ale bar on Speyside's Whisky Trail, close to the Speyside Way which runs along the car park, with the river itself just beyond. Popular with tourists, walkers and fishermen, it is busy during whisky festivals. It offers a fine selection of malt whiskies and good-value tasting sessions. Craigellachie Real Ale Club meets on the first Wednesday of the month, and its members help to choose the pub's guest ales. Two ales are on in winter, increasing to three in summer.
Q P (36)

Cullen

Three Kings

17-21 North Castle Street, AB56 4SA
12-2, 5-11 (12.30am Thu-Sat) (01542) 840031
Beer range varies H
Situated close to impressive but now defunct railway viaducts, this small, family-run pub was converted over 40 years ago from 150-year-old railway workers' cottages. A low-beamed roof and real fire help to create a cosy atmosphere on colder days. There is a separate restaurant to the rear and a large outdoor drinking area complete with pétanque courts. Up to three beers are served, mainly from Scottish micros including Windswept, Cairngorm and Orkney. (305)

Dyce

Granite City

Main Terminal, Aberdeen Airport, AB21 7DU
6am (8am Sat)-10; 8am-9 Sun (01224) 725711
Sharp's Doom Bar; guest beers H
In the main terminal of Aberdeen Airport, close to the entrance, this Wetherspoon bar is popular with airport staff, travellers and offshore workers. The walls display informative framed photographs of local personalities including 'The Scottish Samurai' Thomas Blake Glover – one of the prime movers of Japan's industrialisation in the late 19th century. An extensive outdoor area features the Baby Boar, a sculpture carved from a one-ton boulder of local Kemnay granite. (727)

Elgin

Drouthy Cobbler

Shepherd's Close, 48a High Street, IV30 1BU
8am-12.30am (1.30am Fri & Sat) (01343) 553933
thedrouthycobbler.co.uk
Beer range varies H
Smart, long and narrow bar opened after extensive refurbishment in 2013. The venue is named after John Shanks who was a shoemaker and an important figure in the conservation of Elgin Cathedral. Sponsored by local gentleman Isaac Forsyth, Shanks was officially appointed Keeper and Watchman in 1826. Food will be served when the kitchen refurbishment is completed. An upstairs function room will also be available. A large and constantly increasing whisky collection is stocked. Three ales come from Scottish micros.
Q

Muckle Cross

34 High Street, IV30 1BU
8am-midnight (1am Fri & Sat); 9am-11.45 Sun
(01343) 559030
Greene King Abbot; guest beers H
A small, deservedly popular Wetherspoon pub in a former bicycle repair shop with friendly, efficient staff, where alcohol is served from 11am daily. The long, pleasant room has ample seating, including a family area. Eight handpumps offer a wide range of beers from national and Scottish micros. The pub also stocks a good choice of malt whiskies from more than 20 local distilleries. An extensive menu features healthy options as well as pub grub.

Findhorn

Kimberley Inn

94 Findhorn, IV36 3YG
12-midnight (01309) 690492 kimberleyinn.com
Beer range varies H
Self-styled as 'Moray's Seafood Pub', the Kimberley is situated right on the shore of Findhorn Bay in a charming seaside village with a fine stretch of beach. The three-section interior includes a family room with wood-panelled walls, a snug with splendid views of the hills across the Moray Firth, and the bar with an excellent open log fire. Two ales (one in winter) are mainly from Scottish micros. The extensive menu features home-cooked food, especially local seafood, and local ice cream.
Q P

Fraserburgh

Elizabethan Bar & Lounge

36 Union Grove, AB43 9PH
9.30am (11 Sun)-1am (01346) 515148
Fuller's London Pride; guest beers H
Set in the middle of a housing estate and near the local Academy, with a mock-Tudor exterior, the large bar and lounge have three distinct sections, with sport on TV in two of them. The bar has featured more than 600 different ales over the past few years, as well as over 200 malts – the largest collection in the area. A recent winner of the SLTN Beer Quality Award. P

Garlogie

Garlogie Inn

AB32 6RX
closed Mon winter; 11-2.30, 5-10.30 (11.30 Fri & Sat); 12.30-9 Sun (01224) 743212 garlogieinn.com
Beer range varies H
This roadside inn dating from the early 19th century has been run by the Quinn family for nearly

SCOTLAND

30 years. Numerous extensions have been added to the original building, including a large restaurant area, and the pub has a reputation for excellent food (booking advised). Drinkers are welcome in the small bar area, with a single pump dispensing a beer usually from a Scottish brewery, often the local Deeside, or occasionally an English one. Drum Castle and Cullerlie stone circle are close at hand. Q❀◑♿P🚌(210)📶

Inverurie

Black Bull

50 North Street, AB51 4RS (on B9001 heading N)
⏲ 12-3, 5-midnight; 11-12.30am Sat; 11-11 Sun
☎ (01467) 621242 🌐 blackbullinninverurie.com
Inveralmond Ossian; guest beers Ⓗ
This old staging inn is now a friendly family-run small hotel and local pub with a separate pool room. There is live music each Saturday and a quiz night on Thursday, and the pub is home to four darts teams. One Inveralmond beer is usally served with up to two guests often from Scottish micros but sometimes from further afield. The pub stages an annual festival featuring UK-wide ales and ciders. Bar snacks are served.
❀🛏◑♿≋♣P🚌🐾📶

Gordon Highlander

West High Street, AB51 3QQ
⏲ 8am-11.30; 9am-1am Fri & Sat; 9am-11.30 Sun
☎ (01462) 626780
Caledonian Deuchars IPA; Greene King Abbot; guest beers Ⓗ
A Wetherspoon pub in a splendid Art Deco building which used to be the Victoria Cinema. The name refers to the famous local regiment, and also to a preserved steam engine named after the regiment, which was based at the now defunct Inverurie Locomotive Works nearby. Both historical references are documented in various displays. The books on the shelves are free to read and take home, with donations welcome. There are at least three guest ales. The usual Wetherspoon beer festivals feature. 🐴◑♿≋🚌📶

Lossiemouth

Skerry Brae Hotel

Stotfield Road, IV31 6QS
⏲ 12-11 (midnight Fri & Sat) ☎ (01343) 812040
🌐 skerrybrae.co.uk
Beer range varies Ⓗ
Hotel and restaurant with a modern lounge bar, refurbished in 2012, with commanding views across the championship golf course, West Beach and the Moray Firth – ideal for sunny days at the coast which can be viewed from the deck and large conservatory. The bar usually offers at least two ales from the local Windswept Brewing and has a decent selection of malt whiskies. Hearty food is served all day, every day.
Q🐴❀🛏◑♿⛺♣P🚌🐾📶

Methlick

Ythanview Hotel

Main Street, AB41 7DT
⏲ 11-2.30, 5-11 (1am Fri); 11-12.30am Sat; 12-11 Sun
☎ (01651) 806235 🌐 ythanviewhotel.co.uk
Beer range varies Ⓗ
Traditional inn in the village centre, home to the Methlick Cricket Club. Log fires warm both the lounge and the friendly public bar at the rear, which is heavily sports themed. The pub is renowned for the owner's special whole chilli curry, and steak night on Thursday is also popular. Bands play on some Saturdays and quiz nights are hosted. Beers are exclusively from Scottish micros. Haddo House, Tolquhon Castle and Pitmedden Garden are nearby. ❀🛏◑♣P🚌

Netherley

Lairhillock Inn

AB39 3QS (signed off B979, 3 miles S of B9077)
⏲ 11-11 (midnight Fri & Sat) ☎ (01569) 730001
🌐 lairhillock.co.uk
Timothy Taylor Landlord; guest beers Ⓗ
The 'INN' sign on the roof of this rambling building in attractive open countryside makes it easy to spot from the road. It has a traditional wood-panelled bar warmed by a large log fire in winter, and a lounge with an open fireplace and a large conservatory area, popular for dining. A separate function room, the Crynoch, is also available. Three guest beers (two in winter) are frequently sourced from Scottish breweries. Convenient for the attractions of Stonehaven and Royal Deeside.
Q🐴❀◑♿♣P🐾

Oldmeldrum

Redgarth Hotel

Kirk Brae, AB51 0DJ (outskirts of village, signed off A947 road)
⏲ 11-3, 5-11 (midnight Fri & Sat); 12-3, 5-11 Sun
☎ (01651) 872353 🌐 redgarth.com
Beer range varies Ⓗ/Ⓖ
This renowned local hotel and pub has imposing views over the eastern Grampian mountains. A winner of many local CAMRA awards, it retains a strong reputation for its imaginative choice of beers, sourced from, among others, Timothy Taylor and many Scottish micros. A successful blend of popular family restaurant and marvellous real ale pub, it is appreciated by a dedicated core of regulars. During occasional Brewers in Residence evenings, three handpumped ales may be supplemented by many more on gravity.
Q🐴❀🛏◑⛺♣P📶

Peterhead

Cross Keys

23-27 Chapel Street, AB42 1TH
⏲ 8am-11 (1am Fri & Sat); 9am-11 Sun ☎ (01779) 483500
Caledonian Deuchars IPA; Greene King Abbot; guest beers Ⓗ
A typical Wetherspoon outlet located in the centre of a bustling port, close to the local museum, where you can learn about the town's maritime history. The pub is named after the chapel dedicated to St Peter that previously stood on the site. The long single-room interior has the bar towards the front and a large seating area to the rear. A sheltered and heated area outside caters for hardy souls and smokers. Children are welcome until 8pm if dining. 🐴❀◑♿🍎🚌(260,263)📶

Portsoy

Shore Inn

Church Street, AB45 2QR (overlooking harbour)
11-11 (midnight Thu; 1am Fri & Sat) ☎ (01261) 842831
Beer range varies H
This ancient 18th-century coastal inn situated on the oldest harbour on the Moray coast exudes an old-time atmosphere with its low ceilings and dark wooden bar fittings. Up to two ales are stocked (only one off-season), often from Orkney or Windswept breweries. The village hosts an annual boat festival in early July with an outside bar and additional beers on offer. Meal service times vary according to the season – phone ahead to check.

Stonehaven

Marine Hotel

9-10 Shorehead, AB39 2JY (overlooking harbour)
11-midnight (1am Fri & Sat) summer; 11-11 Sun winter
☎ (01569) 762155 marinehotelstonehaven.co.uk
Caledonian Deuchars IPA; Timothy Taylor Landlord; guest beers H
This small harbourside hotel features a bar with simple wood panelling, a rustic lounge with an open fireplace and an upstairs restaurant. Seating outside offers a splendid view of the harbour. Guest ales are mostly sourced from local and regional breweries, with something from sister brewery Six Degrees North. Also on sale are several draught Belgian beers and a massive choice of bottled Belgian beers. Historic Dunnottar Castle is one mile south. Multiple winner of CAMRA branch Pub of the Year and country winner in 2014.

Ship Inn

5 Shorehead, AB39 2JY (on harbour front)
11-midnight (1am Fri & Sat) ☎ (01569) 762617
shipinnstonehaven.com
Beer range varies H
Built in 1771, this harbour-front hotel has a maritime themed, wood-panelled bar and a seating area outside overlooking the water. The bar boasts a mirror from the defunct Devanha Brewery as a prominent feature. Two beers are offered, one from the Inveralmond Brewery. An extensive range of malt whiskies is stocked. A modern restaurant with panoramic harbour views is adjacent to the bar, with food served all day at the weekend. Accommodation is available in 11 guest rooms.

Six Degrees North, Aberdeen

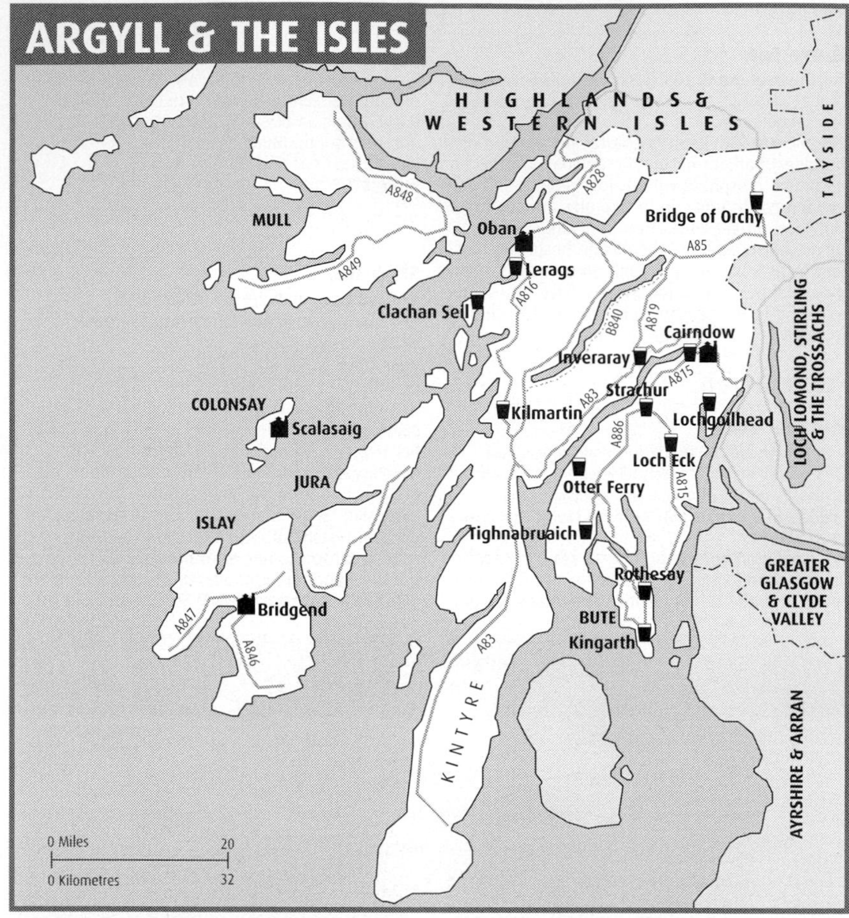

Authority area covered: Argyll & Bute UA

Bridge of Orchy

Bridge of Orchy Hotel

PA36 4AD

11-10.45 (11.45 Fri & Sat) (01838) 400208

Harviestoun Bitter & Twisted; guest beers H

Situated on the A82 road to Glencoe and Fort William, and with a nearby rail station, this remote hotel is surprisingly accessible. The comfortably furnished bar has three handpumps and the terrace offers impressive views of Glen Orchy and the surrounding mountain scenery. Food and accommodation are high quality. The hotel is close to the West Highland Way which makes it a convenient resting place for walkers. Many other outdoor activities can be found nearby.

P (914)

Cairndow

Fyne Ales Brewery Tap

PA26 8BJ (up side road at head of Loch Fyne)

10-6 (01499) 600120 fyneales.com/brewery-tap

Fyne Ales Jarl; guest beers H

The brewery tap and shop opened in 2012 in what was originally a farm building. The bar with its fine polished granite front has five handpumps selling a range of Fyne Ales beers along with a full selection of bottled beers. Meat from the farm is available for sale and is also used to make excellent snacks such as steak pies and venison sausage rolls. A courtyard looking across to the brewery is pleasant in fine weather. **Q P**

Stagecoach Inn L

PA26 8BN (on slip road off A83)

11-11 (1am Fri & Sat); 11-midnight Sun

(01499) 600286 cairndowinn.com

Beer range varies H

Down a loop road, formerly the main road and signed on the current A83 section, this former coaching inn offers a pleasant spot to break a journey through Argyll. The bar has up to two handpumps dispensing mainly beers from nearby Fyne Ales and occasionally other Scottish microbreweries. Archways lead to the dining room and comfortable lounge with a log fire. In summer the attractive views over Loch Fyne can also be enjoyed from the lochside garden. Winter hours

INDEPENDENT BREWERIES

Argyll Oban
Colonsay Scalasaig: Isle of Colonsay
Fyne Cairndow
Islay Bridgend: Isle of Islay

may vary. B&B accommodation is available in 19 en-suite rooms.
🐴❀🛏◑◗♿▲♣P🚌(926,976)🐾📶

Clachan Seil

Tigh an Truish Inn 🄻

PA34 4QZ

⏲ 11-11; 12-11 Sun summer; 12-2.30, 5-8; 11-2.30, 5-midnight Thu; 12-2.30, 5-midnight Fri; 12-midnight Sat; 12-8 Sun winter ☎ (01852) 300242 🌐 tigh-an-truish.co.uk

Beer range varies 🄷

This attractive rural inn is worth leaving the A816 for en route to visit Seil Island. Twice winner of local CAMRA Argyll Pub of the Year, it has three handpumps serving Scottish beers, often from local Fyne Ales. In summer, the sheltered, sunny garden and front patio offer pleasant settings and views of Telford's famous Clachan Bridge. The bar room has rustic wooden furniture and an iron stove. Meals, available only in the summer, are served in the bar and separate dining room. Q🐴❀🛏◑◗P🚌(418)🐾

Inveraray

George Hotel

Main Street East, PA32 8TT

⏲ 11 (12 Sun)-midnight ☎ (01499) 302111

Beer range varies 🄷

Located in the charming planned town of Inveraray, the George has been owned by the same family for six generations. Two beers come mostly from Fyne Ales, but also from the new Thorn Dhu Brewery near Lochgair. Visitors tend to drink in the main lounge, while locals prefer the rear public bar. Live blues, folk and rock feature on Friday and Saturday evenings. High-quality bar food and a tempting whisky list are also on offer at this great traditional pub.
Q🐴❀🛏◑◗♿▲🚌(926,976)📶

Kilmartin

Kilmartin Hotel 🄻

PA31 8RQ (on A816 10 miles N of Lochgilphead)

⏲ 12 (5 Mon-Thu winter)-11; 12-midnight Fri; 12-1am Sat; 12-11 Sun ☎ (01546) 510250 🌐 kilmartin-hotel.com

Beer range varies 🄷

It is easy to spot this white hotel on the A816, perched on a hilltop overlooking a historic glen, and its location halfway to Oban makes it an ideal place to break a journey, for food or overnight. Up to three ales are served in the long, narrow bar room, often from Fyne Ales and other Scottish breweries. Good home-made food is served evenings and some lunchtimes (check ahead). Children are welcome in the dining room, rear rooms and in the garden.
🐴❀🛏◑◗♿P🚌(423)🐾📶

Kingarth: Isle of Bute

Kingarth Hotel

PA20 9LU (on A844 at jct for turn-off to Kilchattan)

> She drank good ale,
> good punch and wine
> And lived to the age of ninety-nine.
> **Epitaph to Rebecca Freeland (1741) at Edwalton, Nottinghamshire**

⏲ 12-midnight ☎ (01700) 831662 🌐 kingarthhotel.co.uk

Beer range varies 🄷

A friendly welcome awaits at this rare gem of a pub set in a secluded yet accessible location on the south of the Isle of Bute. Two handpumps supply an ever-changing range of beers from all over Britain. A popular destination for diners, it is the perfect place to return to after a stroll to Kilchattan Bay, for a few beers, a game of pool and an alfresco meal under cover on the rear veranda or the front patio. 🐴❀🛏◑◗P🚌(490)🐾📶

Lerags

Barn

PA34 4SE

⏲ 12-11 Sun & summer; closed Mon-Thu; 5-11 Fri & Sat winter ☎ (01631) 564618 🌐 cologin.co.uk/country-inn

Fyne Ales Highlander; guest beer 🄷

Well worth a detour from the A816 Oban road, Lerags Glen offers an escape from the beaten track, with attractive hill walks, fishing and coastal scenery. The child-friendly Barn is an ideal place to stop for refreshments, with a Fyne Ale, usually Highlander, available, and food served all day from a varied menu in the bar/restaurant. There are outside areas for drinking and for children to play. Telephone ahead to check opening and dining hours in winter. Q🐴❀🛏◑◗▲P🐾📶

Loch Eck

Coylet Inn

PA23 8SG (on A815 6 miles N of Dunoon)

⏲ 12-11 ☎ (01369) 840426 🌐 thecoyletinn.co.uk

Fyne Ales Highlander; guest beers 🄷

Attractive 17th-century coaching inn set amid scenic surroundings with views over Loch Eck, a mirror to the hills on windless days. The log fire in the bar is a welcome sight at the end of the day for hill walkers and anglers. Up to three beers come from Fyne Ales, Orkney and Thorn Dhu breweries. Excellent meals from a varied menu featuring local produce are available in the bar and the popular restaurant (book ahead if dining).
🐴❀🛏◑◗▲P🚌(484,486)🐾📶

Lochgoilhead

Shore House Inn 🄻

PA24 8AA

⏲ closed Mon & Tue; 12-11 ☎ (01301) 703340 🌐 theshorehouse.net

Fyne Ales Highlander; guest beer 🄷

The Shore House was originally built in the 1850s as the village manse and stands on the waterfront with an uninterrupted vista down the loch. The refurbished bar is bright and comfortable, offering two beers in the summer including a guest from the Fyne Ales range and one in winter. The newly built restaurant with lovely views and an outside terrace features local produce and a wood-fired pizza oven. The pub is closed from early January until early February. Q🐴❀🛏◑◗♿P🚌(302,484)📶

Otter Ferry

Oyster Catcher 🄻

PA21 2DH (on B8000 E coast of Loch Fyne)

⏲ 11-11 ☎ (01700) 821229 🌐 theoystercatcher.co.uk

Fyne Ales Jarl; guest beer 🄷

Large windows in this attractive building provide views over Loch Fyne to the Kintyre Peninsula. Reached by a scenic trip along a single track road, the pub offers a break on a tour of west Cowal. Beers are from Fyne Ales with occasional summer guests from other breweries. In summer the beer garden and lochside lawn are pleasant. The menu is diverse with local seafood a speciality. Winter hours may vary. P

Rothesay: Isle of Bute

Black Bull Inn

West Princes Street, PA20 9AF (opp harbour)
11-11 (midnight Fri & Sat); 12.30-11 Sun
(01700) 502366
Caledonian Deuchars IPA; Inveralmond Lia Fail
Enjoy the pleasant train ride from Glasgow and embark on the ferry from the splendour of Wemyss Bay. Perhaps visit the Victorian toilets on Rothesay Pier and look at the rare Victorian postbox by the Discovery Centre, before sampling the beers in this two-bar pub. Meals are also available in a separate dining area. A visit to Mount Stuart House could be taken before a final beer and the ferry home. Popular with locals and yachtsmen.

Strachur

Creggans Inn

PA27 8BX (on A815 at N end of village)
11 (12 Sun)-11 (01369) 860279 creggans-inn.co.uk
Beer range varies
This historic inn sits on the shores of Loch Fyne looking across to Inverary. The cosy MacPhunn's bar is warmed by a log fire and is home to the local shinty team. An extension behind the fireplace offers extra seating and a pool table. Meals can be taken in the bistro dining room off the bar or in a separate restaurant with a more extensive menu, both featuring local produce. The two real ales usually come from Fyne Ales.
Q P (484,486)

Tighnabruaich

Kames Hotel

PA21 2AF
12-midnight (1am Fri & Sat) (01700) 811489
kames-hotel.com
Fyne Ales Highlander; guest beer
Perched on a hillside above a rocky beach, this hotel provides stunning views of its moorings and the Kyles of Bute. Two handpumps in the central bar serve Highlander and another ale from Fyne Ales. The bar extends into the lounge, with comfortable chairs, pool, darts, TV and a wood-burning stove. Pictures of old sailing ships and historic characters adorn the walls. The bar is a favourite among locals and visitors from land and sea. P (477,478)

Reading the runes

There are terms and expressions used in the pub trade that need to be translated in to a language understood by consumers.

'Wet pub' doesn't mean the roof leaks but indicates that beer and other alcohols are the main feature, rather than food.

Stillage is a cradle or platform in the pub cellar where casks of beer are stored horizontally while a secondary fermentation takes place.

'Barrel behind the bar' is a widely-used description but usually inappropriate as a barrel is a large 36-gallon container, too big to store at bar level. The correct term for a container for real ale is cask and casks come in several sizes: 4½ gallon pins; nine-gallon firkin; 18-gallon kilderkin; 36-gallon barrels; and 54-gallon hogshead. Hogsheads are rare, though Joseph Holt's brewery in Manchester still uses them. Most pubs use firkins and kilderkins these days. If a cask is used at bar level to serve a seasonal beer such as winter ale, it's likely to be a pin.

Beer 'served by gravity' means it comes straight from the cask and is not drawn by a beer engine and handpump.

'Tight sparkler' is a small device containing a mesh that's screwed to the nozzle of a beer engine operated by a handpump on the bar. The sparkler agitates the beer as it enters the glass and creates the tight, thick head of foam preferred by northern drinkers. As we make clear in the Wetherspoon entries in Greater London, if you don't like beer with a northern head, ask the bar staff to remove the sparkler.

'Cask breather' is a system used by a few brewers to prolong the life of cask beer – and it's not acceptable to CAMRA and the Good Beer Guide. Casks are connected to cylinders of carbon dioxide and a demand valve injects gas in to the cask as beer is drawn off. If the gas is absorbed in to the beer, it can become unnaturally gassy.

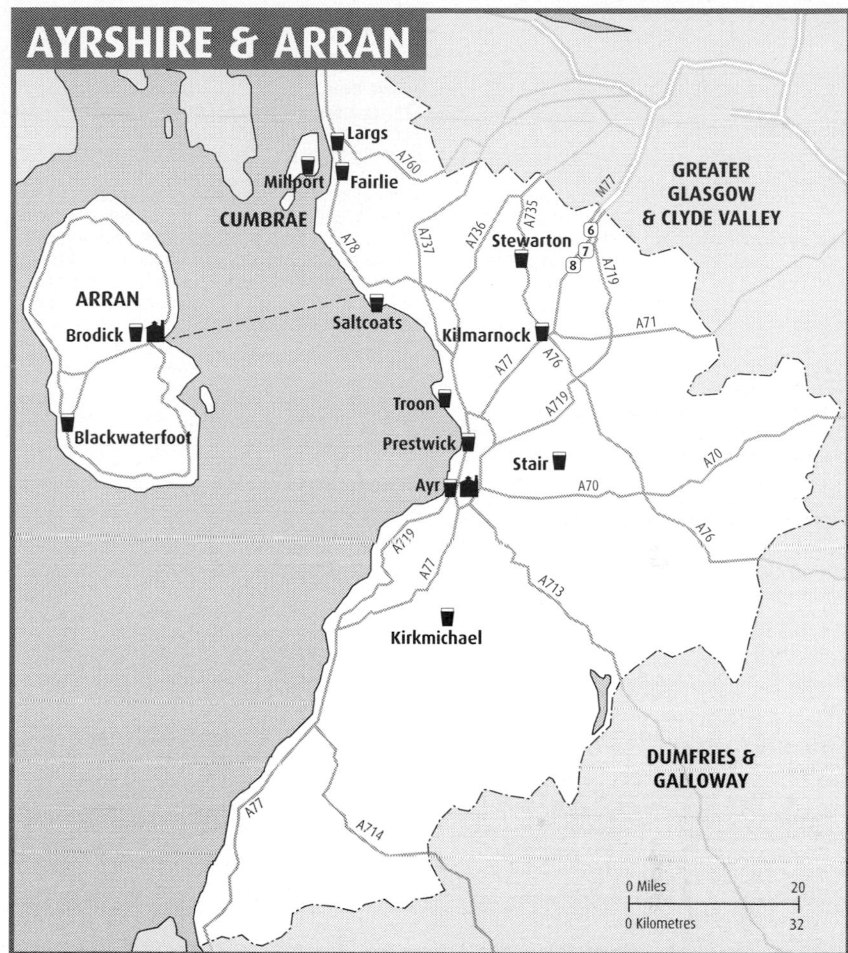

Authority areas covered: East Ayrshire UA, North Ayrshire UA, South Ayrshire UA

Ayr

Abbotsford Hotel

14 Corsehill Rd, KA7 2ST

10-12.30am; 12-midnight Sun ☎ (01292) 261506

abbotsfordhotel.co.uk

Caledonian Deuchars IPA; Marston's Pedigree; guest beer H

This family-run hotel, in a residential area south of the town centre, is convenient for the seafront, local golf courses, Burns-related attractions and other delights of the area. Three handpumps dispense the real ales in the aptly named Copper Bar. The guest beer is usually from a larger English brewery. Meals, for which booking is advised, are served in both the bar and in a separate restaurant area. There is also a pool/TV room and a function room/conservatory.

P (57,361)

Chestnuts Hotel

52 Racecourse Road, KA7 2UZ (A719, 1 Mile S of centre)

10-11 (12.30am Fri & Sat) ☎ (01292) 264393

chestnutshotel.com

Beer range varies H

Three changing real ales from both local and larger regional breweries are on offer in The 19th Hole at this well-appointed family-run hotel. The bar itself is a focal point for locals and tourists and features golfing prints and memorabilia, discreet seating around a cosy log fire and a vaulted ceiling that holds a record-breaking collection of whisky water jugs. High-quality meals are served in the bar and the separate restaurant. There is plenty of seating in the garden. P (9)

Geordie's Byre

103 Main Street, KA8 8BU (N of centre, over river towards Prestwick)

11-11 (midnight Thu-Sat); 12.30-11 Sun

☎ (01292) 264925

Beer range varies A

This CAMRA award-winning 18th-century pub, located in the Newton area of Ayr, serves up to four guest ales, sourced from far and wide. It is one of the few Scottish pubs still using traditional

INDEPENDENT BREWERIES

Arran Brodick: Isle of Arran

Ayr Ayr

Scottish tall founts. Both the public bar and the lounge feature a wealth of memorabilia. A wide selection of malt whiskies and rums is available. Handy for several local bus routes. Q♿🚌🐾📶

Glen Park Hotel 𝕃

5 Racecourse Road, KA7 2DG

10 (12 Sun)-midnight ☎ (01292) 263891

Ayr Leezie Lundie, Jolly Beggars; guest beers Ⓗ

This comfortable lounge bar, in an attractive 1860s B-Listed Victorian building, is the brewery tap for Ayr Brewing Company which brews in the rear of the building. The guest beers are from Ayr Brewing and usually include a seasonal. Plans are in place to make food available during the summer months. ❀🛏♿⇌P🚌(9)🐾📶

Newton Arms

111-113 Main Street, KA8 8BX

11-12.30am ☎ (01292) 262515 🌐 thenewtonarms.co.uk

Beer range varies Ⓗ

Recently refurbished family pub on the main road in Newton-on-Ayr, handy for a selection of bus routes. Timothy Taylor Landlord is often available and there is always an ale from a local brewery. Reasonably priced meals are served noon-8pm. Close to Somerset Park, home of Ayr Utd FC. ❀◐⇌(Newton-on-Ayr)🚌(2,4,14)📶

Wellingtons Bar

17 Wellington Square, KA7 1EZ

11-12.30am; 12-midnight Sun ☎ (01292) 262794

🌐 welliesbar.weebly.com

Beer range varies Ⓗ

A large Wellington boot advertises the location of this basement bar. Close to the seafront, bus station and local government offices, it attracts tourists and office workers alike. The Wednesday evening quiz is popular and weekend music includes live music or a DJ on Saturday and an acoustic session on Sunday evening. The two changing ales usually include at least one from either Kelburn or Fyne Ales. ◐⇌🚌🐾📶

West Kirk 𝕃

58A Sandgate, KA7 1BX (close to bus station)

8am-midnight (12.30am Fri & Sat) ☎ (01292) 880416

Caledonian Deuchars IPA; Greene King Abbot; guest beers Ⓗ

This Wetherspoon conversion of a former church retains many original features – access to the toilets is via the pulpit. Up to eight changing guest ales are offered and local micros are usually well represented. Licensed from 10am, meals are available all day, with breakfast from 8am. Outside, the front drinking area has a shelter for smokers. Handy for Ayr bus station. ❀◐♿⇌🍎🚌📶

Blackwaterfoot: Isle of Arran

Kinloch Hotel

KA27 8ET

12-midnight ☎ (01770) 860444 🌐 bw-kinlochhotel.co.uk

Beer range varies Ⓗ

This family hotel is a hidden gem on the west coast of the Isle of Arran. Sitting in a quiet rural village, it offers coastal comfort and spectacular scenery. The Kinloch serves fabulous local produce including fish and seafood. It has 37 bedrooms, a restaurant and three bars. Facilities include a heated indoor swimming pool, children's pool, squash court, snooker room, fitness room and a sauna. ❀🛏◐♿⛺♣🍎P🚌🐾📶

Brodick: Isle of Arran

Ormidale Hotel

Knowe Road, KA27 8BY (off A841 at W end of village)

12.30-2.30 (summer only), 4-midnight; 12-1am Sat; 12-midnight Sun ☎ (01770) 302293 🌐 ormidale-hotel.co.uk

Arran Guid Ale; guest beers Ⓐ

Large red sandstone hotel with a small bar and spacious conservatory set in seven acres of grounds. Beers are served from traditional Scottish tall founts on the boat-shaped bar, with Arran Blonde a regular in summer. Home-cooked meals are recommended. Discos and folk nights are held, and the attractive beer garden has views across Brodick Bay. Accommodation is now available all year round. ❀🛏◐♣P🚌(324)🐾📶

Fairlie

Village Inn 𝕃

46 Bay Street, KA29 0AL

11-midnight (1am Fri & Sat); 12.30-midnight Sun ☎ (01475) 568432 🌐 villageinnfairlie.co.uk

Beer range varies Ⓗ

This is the only licensed establishment in the seaside village of Fairlie, once famous for classic yacht building. Up to three regularly changing ales are available, often from local breweries, and an annual real ale festival is hosted. Good-quality and reasonably priced food is served in the bar and restaurant. Weekly quiz nights and occasional live music nights are held. Children are welcome until 10pm but not in the public bar which is a child-free oasis. Q❀◐♿P🚌(585)🐾📶

Kilmarnock

Wheatsheaf Inn

70 Portland Street, KA1 1JG (near bus and rail stations)

8am-midnight (1am Fri & Sat) ☎ (01563) 572483

Caledonian Deuchars IPA; Greene King Abbot; guest beers Ⓗ

Sizeable town centre Lloyds No.1 bar, originally the historic Wheatsheaf Hotel, famous for its links to Robert Burns, who was first published in Kilmarnock. Licensed from 10am, the bar is divided into various seating areas, with booths, sofas and a raised dining space. DJs entertain on a Friday and Saturday, with karaoke early on Friday evening, but otherwise conversation holds sway. Food is standard Wetherspoon fare and nine handpumps dispense a range of ales plus real cider. ❀◐♿⇌🍎🚌📶

Kirkmichael

Kirkmichael Arms

3-5 Straiton Road, KA19 7PH

12-midnight (12.30am Fri & Sat) ☎ (01655) 750200

🌐 kirkmichaelarms.co.uk

Beer range varies Ⓗ

A friendly country pub at the heart of the community with a lounge bar and separate dining room. Two handpumps serve an Ayr Brewing beer plus a guest. Excellent meals are available, with food sourced locally where possible. Walkers and dogs are made welcome, and small functions are catered for. Q❀◐♿♣🚌(361)🐾📶

Largs

JG Sharps Bar

34-36 Nelson Street, KA30 8LW (off seafront at Nardini's)
⏲ 11-midnight (1am Fri & Sat); 12.30-midnight Sun
☎ (01475) 675515 🌐 jgsharps.co.uk
Caledonian Deuchars IPA; guest beer [H]
Set back from the seafront and Main Street on the corner of Nelson Street and Boyd Street, this is a large traditional pub with many different drinking areas. An open fire warms the bar area and there is space for smokers in the beer garden outside. Good-quality pub meals are served at lunchtime and Friday-Sunday evenings. Games and TV are in evidence and there is occasional live music.
Q🐴❀◑♿⇌♣🚌🐾📶

Millport: Isle of Cumbrae

Frasers Bar 𝕃

7 Cardiff Street, KA28 0AS
⏲ 11-midnight (1am Thu-Sat) ☎ (01475) 530518
🌐 frasersbar.co.uk
Beer range varies [H]
Recently refurbished, this is a welcoming town-centre pub close to the pier. Millport is a popular destination for day trippers from Largs. Cycling round the island is popular and bike hire is available nearby. The bar is decorated with an extensive collection of pictures of Clyde steamers. Two handpumps usually serve beers from Kelburn and Houston breweries. Children are welcome in the rear lounge until 8pm. Buses meet every ferry from Largs and stop across the road.
Q🐴❀◑♿⛺♣🚌(320)🐾📶

Prestwick

Prestwick Pioneer

87 Main Street, KA9 1JS
⏲ 8am-midnight (12.30am Fri & Sat) ☎ (01292) 473210
Caledonian Deuchars IPA; Greene King Abbot; guest beers [H]
Modern Wetherspoon outlet in a former Woolworth's store, named after the first Scottish Aviation Pioneer built in 1947 at the nearby international airport. It has an airy feel with light wood decor, and features photos of early Open Golf Championships at Prestwick and of Elvis at the nearby airport – the only place in the UK on which he stepped foot. Licensed from 10am, 10 handpumps serve local and national ales and food is available all day. 🐴◑♿⇌●🚌📶

Saltcoats

Salt Cot 𝕃

7 Hamilton Street, KA21 5DS
⏲ 8am-midnight (1am Fri & Sat) ☎ (01294) 465924
Caledonian Deuchars IPA; Greene King Abbot; guest beers [H]
A good Wetherspoon conversion of a former cinema, the pub gets its name from the original cottages at the salt pans. Licensed from 10am, it has an area where children are permitted and there is a family menu. At least one of the guest beers is locally sourced, often from Arran Brewery. There are TVs in the bar area but the sound is only turned on a few times a year for rugby internationals. Food is available daily until 11pm.
Q🐴◑♿⇌●🚌(11,585)📶

Stair

Stair Inn

KA5 5HW (on B730 7 miles E of Ayr)
⏲ 12-11 (1am Fri & Sat) ☎ (01292) 591650 🌐 stairinn.co.uk
Beer range varies [H]
This family-run hotel on the banks of the River Ayr is well-worth seeking out. The comfortable bar and adjacent restaurant feature bespoke hand-made furniture and the bedrooms are furnished in a similar style. One or two guest ales are available. The food menu relies heavily on local produce and fish from the inn's own smokehouse is a speciality (booking advised at weekends). Q❀🛏◑♿P📶

Stewarton

Millhouse Hotel

6-8 Dean Street, KA3 5EQ
⏲ 11-midnight (1am Fri & Sat); 12-midnight Sun
☎ (01560) 482255
Beer range varies [H]
This friendly hotel bar always has up to three real ales available, often from the Orkney range or from more local brewers such as Arran, Houston, Kelburn or Strathaven. First-class food is served in the restaurant or bar (booking advised at weekends). En-suite overnight accommodation is available.
🐴❀🛏◑♿⇌P🚌🐾📶

Troon

Bruce's Well

91 Portland Street, KA10 6QN
⏲ 11-midnight (1am Fri & Sat); 12-midnight Sun
☎ (01292) 311429
Caledonian Deuchars IPA; guest beer [H]
A friendly, spacious and comfortable lounge bar, close to Troon town centre and a short walk from the station. All major sporting events are screened on a number of TVs but the volume is kept down. The bar may open earlier than advertised if there is a big sporting event on. A guest ale comes from the Belhaven list and changes regularly. Unusually, the cellar is situated in a temperature-controlled room off the main bar area. ⇌🚌📶

Harbour Bar

169 Templehill, KA10 6BH (opp P&O ferry terminal)
⏲ 11-1am ☎ (01292) 312668
Beer range varies [H]
Overlooking Troon's North Bay, one bar serves both public and lounge areas. One real ale is always available, two over the summer, usually from Scottish breweries. A good range of malt whiskies and rums is stocked. Popular meals are served throughout the day. A 'smart' quiz is hosted on Thursday night, an open mic session on Sunday, and other events are regularly scheduled. There is a pool table and jukebox. ◑♿♣P🚌(10,110)📶

McKay's

69 Portland Street, KA10 6QU
⏲ 10-12.30am (midnight Sun) ☎ (01292) 737372
Cairngorm Wildcat; Caledonian Deuchars IPA; guest beer [H]
This town-centre pub was remodelled in 2008 and an extension added to the beer garden in 2010, making it popular in summer. The guest beer is usually Inveralmond Ossian or Cairngorm Trade Winds. Food is served lunchtimes Monday-Thursday and until 8pm Friday-Sunday. A quiz features on Wednesday evening. 🐴❀◑♿⇌🚌

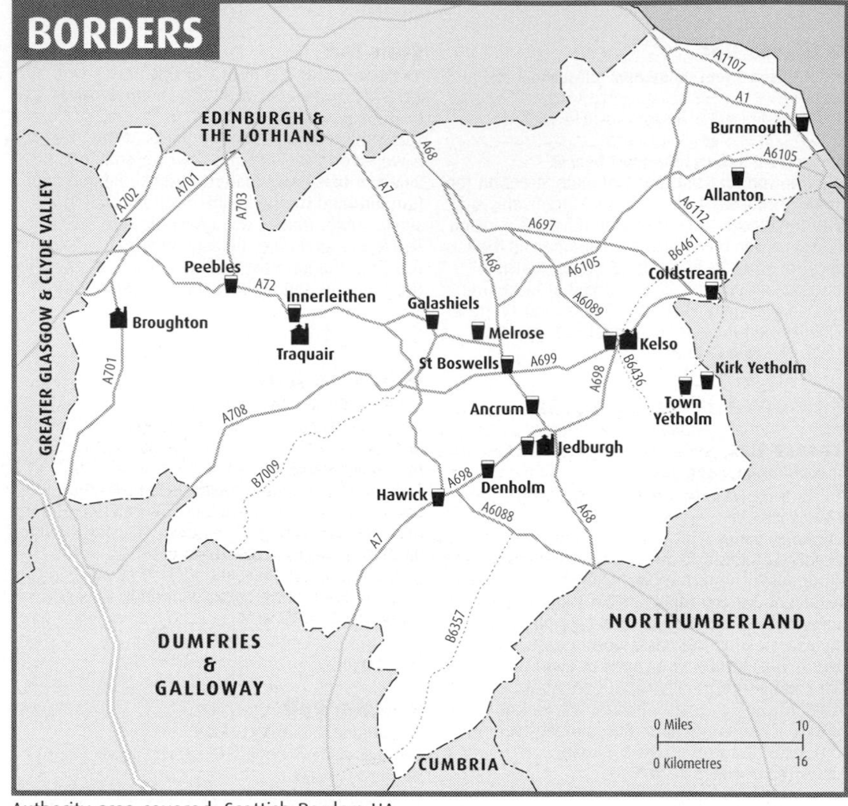

Authority area covered: Scottish Borders UA

Allanton

Allanton Inn

TD11 3JZ

✪ 12-11 ☎ (01890) 818260 🌐 allantoninn.co.uk

Beer range varies Ⓗ

Dating back to the 18th century, this old coaching inn has a bright, airy feel. Quality food is served in the front dining rooms. The rear bar area, which looks out over a superb beer garden to the countryside beyond, can also be used by diners at busy times. Two real ales are available, often from Scottish Borders Brewery and other Scottish micros such as Fyne. With six en-suite rooms, this is an ideal base for exploring Berwickshire and north Northumberland. (260)

Ancrum

Cross Keys Inn

The Green, TD8 6XH (on B6400, off A68)

✪ 6-11; 5-midnight Fri; 12-midnight Sat; 12-11 Sun

☎ (01835) 830242 🌐 ancrumcrosskeys.com

Scottish Borders Game Bird; guest beer Ⓗ

Perched on the Ale Water (yes really!), and soon celebrating its 200th birthday, this village local's front bar has remained largely untouched since 1906, retaining pine panelling throughout. There is also a comfortable drinking and dining area, and there are plans to create an additional snug. Owned by Scottish Borders Brewery, food is an intrinsic part of the operation. Local produce (sometimes foraged) is available in line with a 'plough to platter' ethos matching the brewery's 'plough to pint' philosophy.

P (25,68)

Burnmouth

First & Last

Upper Burnmouth, TD14 5SL

✪ 12 (11 summer)-midnight; 12-1am Fri & Sat

☎ (01890) 781306 🌐 firstandlast.co

Beer range varies Ⓗ

Frequented by locals and travellers on the adjacent A1, the pub, with bar, dining room and pool room, has a good following for real ale. Beers are usually from the Tempest Brewery in Kelso. The bar area is decorated with old photographs and nautical artefacts which, along with a real fire, help to create a warm and welcoming feel. Meals are served all day. Live music plays on some weekends. P (253)

Coldstream

Besom

75-77 High Street, TD12 4AE

INDEPENDENT BREWERIES

Broughton Broughton
Scottish Borders Jedburgh
Tempest Kelso
Traquair House Traquair

⌚ 11-midnight (1am Fri & Sat); 12.30-midnight Sun
☎ (01890) 882391 🌐 besom-inn.co.uk
Stewart Edinburgh Gold; guest beer Ⓗ
One of the first and last pubs in Scotland, this three-roomed gem has remained relatively unchanged since it was built in the 1890s and revamped circa 1910. The cosy bar retains its original counter and gantry, while the diverse range of memorabilia, bookshelves and sofa seating gives the feel more of a living room than a pub. The lounge (where families are welcome) leads to a room dedicated entirely to the memory of Coldstream Guards. Q♣(67,904)

Denholm

Auld Cross Keys Inn

Main Street, TD9 8NU
⌚ 12-11 (midnight Thu; 1am Fri & Sat); 12.30-midnight Sun
☎ (01450) 870305 🌐 crosskeysdenholm.co.uk
Northumberland Fog On The Tyne; Scottish Borders Game Bird Ⓗ
The public bar of this village hotel tends to be favoured by drinkers and those who enjoy sport on TV or a game of pool. Others may prefer the additional comfort of the lounge or restaurant. Folk music sessions are hosted on alternate Thursdays and there are occasional concerts. Food is served lunchtimes and evenings, all day on Sunday, and the hotel has been awarded several accolades. An annual beer festival is usually in March.
Q♣P(20)

Galashiels

Hunter's Hall

56 High Street, TD1 1SE
⌚ 8am-midnight (1am Thu-Sat) ☎ (01896) 759795
Caledonian Deuchars IPA; Greene King Abbot; guest beers Ⓗ
Originally built as a church, sadly the conversion by Wetherspoon saw a false ceiling installed, hiding some of the original features. The bar is set on two levels, with areas for families. The main area has bare stone walls with some booth seating and there are several displays by local artists, mainly depicting the Gala area. Food is served all day; alcohol is not served until 11am. The real cider is usually from Westons. Q

Hawick

Bourtree

22 Bourtree Place, TD9 9HL (NE edge of town centre)
⌚ 8am-midnight (1am Fri & Sat) ☎ (01450) 360450
Caledonian Deuchars IPA; Greene King Abbot; guest beers Ⓗ
Built as Hawick Conservative Club in 1897, this listed building has been stunningly transformed into a Wetherspoon pub. The former snooker hall forms the main area, while there are three further areas for quieter or private use. Pictures show a history of Hawick life, including mills, railways, common riding and motorbiking. Regular cask ale and cider promotions and festivals are held. Food is served all day; alcohol is not served until 11am (12.30pm Sunday). QP(20,95)

Exchange Bar (Dalton's)

1 Silver Street, TD9 0AD (off SW end of High St)
⌚ 11-11 (1am Fri & Sat); 12.30-11 Sun ☎ (01450) 376067
Beer range varies Ⓗ
Hidden away between the imposing St Mary's Kirk with its winkie bells and the Hawick Heritage Hub and Heart of Hawick centre, this pub was once Hawick Corn Exchange. It is a Victorian gem with dark-wood panelling and ornate cornice work. A previous owner was named Dalton and the name has stuck. The bar is popular with knowledgable locals and there is a comfy lounge used for parties, Friday karaoke and Sunday folk sessions. Children are not admitted. ♣(20,95)

Innerleithen

Traquair Arms Hotel

Traquair Road, EH44 6PD (B709, off A72)
⌚ 11-11 (midnight Fri & Sat); 12-11.30 Sun
☎ (01896) 830229 🌐 traquairarmshotel.co.uk
Caledonian Deuchars IPA; Timothy Taylor Landlord; Traquair House Stuart Ale Ⓗ
Elegant 18th-century hotel in the scenic Tweed Valley. The comfortable lounge bar features a welcoming real fire in winter. A bistro area and separate restaurant provide plenty of room for diners, with meals served all day at weekends. Visitors including walkers, shooters, anglers and cyclists are all welcome, along with the locals. It is one of the few outlets for draught ales from Traquair House. Bear Ale may replace Stuart Ale at times. P(62)

Jedburgh

Canon (Exchange Inn)

8 Exchange Street, TD8 6BH
⌚ 11 (3 winter)-midnight; 11-1am Fri & Sat; 12.30-11 Sun
☎ (01835) 863243
Beer range varies Ⓗ
Compact town-centre local with a traditional atmosphere, featuring a welcoming real fire, original stone wall and dark-wood beams. The long bar has a small alcove-like area at the end. Popular with sports fans, the walls are adorned with rugby memorabilia and local history material. Time can easily be whiled away reading the walls or catching up with sporting events on TV. Please leave the kids at home. ♣(20,68)

Kelso

Cobbles 🏆

7 Bowmont Street, TD5 7JH (off NE side of town square)
⌚ 11.30-11 (1am Fri & Sat); 12-11 Sun ☎ (01573) 223548
🌐 thecobbleskelso.co.uk
Beer range varies Ⓗ
An award-winning gastro-pub offering an eclectic mix of British classics, Pacific Rim and modern European cuisine, using the finest locally-sourced and seasonal ingredients. To the right of the main dining area is a lounge bar where beers from Tempest, the pub's own microbrewery, are featured. Though the focus is on food, drinkers are welcome here. Private functions are catered for upstairs. Local CAMRA Pub of the Year 2014 and Scottish Pub of the Year 2013.

Kirk Yetholm

Border

The Green, TD5 8PQ
⌚ 11 (12 Sun)-midnight; 11-1am Fri & Sat; 12-11 winter
☎ (01573) 420237 🌐 theborderhotel.com
Beer range varies Ⓗ

An attractive 260-year-old coaching inn with bar areas and a conservatory restaurant. Popular with walkers, it is at the start of the new Scottish National Trail, on St Cuthbert's Way, and marks the official end of the Pennine Way. Those completing the Pennine Way are entitled to a free pint, a tradition from Wainwright's time. The inn is noted for its hearty food and quality real ales from independent breweries on both sides of the border. ❀ ⛺ ♣ P 🚌 (81) 🐾 📶

Melrose

George & Abbotsford Hotel

High Street, TD6 9PD

11-11 (1am Fri & Sat); 12-11 Sun ☎ (01896) 822308

georgeandabbotsford.co.uk

Beer range varies Ⓗ

A spacious hotel overlooking the main street with a comfortable bar and lounges. Four interesting real ales from both sides of the border are on offer, often including a Tempest beer. Meals are served all day on Saturday and Sunday in summer, in the courtyard garden if weather permits. New owners have refurbished the pub and there are plans to restore the real fire and extend the ground floor accommodation. Q ❀ ⛺ ♣ P 🚌 (62,68) 🐾 📶

King's Arms Hotel

High Street, TD6 9PB

11-11 (midnight Fri & Sat); 12-11 Sun ☎ (01896) 822143

kingsarms-melrose.co.uk

Caledonian Deuchars IPA; guest beers Ⓗ

An old coaching inn dating from 1793, the bar has a wooden floor and church pew seating, and is decorated with rugby memorabilia and old local photographs. There is a large-screen TV for sports events. The quieter lounge is comfortably furnished and has a lovely old carved door set into the ceiling. There are also dining rooms upstairs. Food is served all day on Saturday and Sunday. National Cycle Route 1 passes the door.
Q ❀ ⛺ ♣ P 🚌 (62,68) 🐾 📶

Peebles

Bridge Inn (Trust)

Portbrae, EH45 8AW

11-midnight (1am Thu-Sat); 12-midnight Sun
☎ (01721) 720589

Caledonian Deuchars IPA; guest beers Ⓗ

Cheerful, welcoming single-roomed town-centre local, also known as the Trust. The mosaic entrance floor shows it was once the Tweedside Inn. The bright, comfortable bar is decorated with jugs, bottles, memorabilia of outdoor pursuits and photos of old Peebles. An outdoor heated patio area overlooks the river. The Gents is superb, with well-maintained original Twyford Adamant urinals. There is sports TV and live music on Sunday evening. Children are not admitted. CAMRA Borders Pub of the Year runner-up 2014. ❀ ⛺ ♣ 🚌 (62) 🐾

Crown Hotel

54 High Street, EH45 8SW

11-midnight (1am Thu-Sat) ☎ (01721) 720239

crownhotelpeebles.com

Beer range varies Ⓗ

The Crown dates back to the early 1600s and has a basic narrow bar that opens out to a seating area with a leather settee and banquettes. There are wooden floors and half-panelled walls throughout. At the back of the bar, down a flight of steps, is a lovely restaurant area with a conservatory. Meals are served all day. The bar is popular with the locals, who make visitors welcome. Live music is hosted occasionally. ❀ ♿ ⛺ ♣ 🚌 (62) 🐾 📶

St Boswells

Buccleuch Arms

TD6 0EW (on A68)

11 (12 Sun)-11 ☎ (01835) 822243

buccleucharmshotel.com

Beer range varies Ⓗ

The only hostelry in the village, this well-appointed roadside hotel sits adjacent to the cricket ground and village green. The lounge bar, with its half-panelled walls and large real fire, attracts a mixed clientele including hunters, fishers and shooters, and can be busy at peak times. A new bistro with a more extensive menu has recently been added. A real ale from Scottish Borders Brewery is usually available. Meals are served all day.
❀ ♿ P 🚌 🐾 📶

Town Yetholm

Plough Hotel

High Street, TD5 8RF

11-midnight (1am Fri & Sat) ☎ (01573) 420215

ploughhotelyetholm.co.uk

Beer range varies Ⓗ

A friendly village inn dating from 1710 set in a rural village, with the Pennine Way, St Cuthbert's Way and the new Scottish National Trail nearby. A large wood-burning stove sitting beneath two stags' heads dominates the bar, where the locals are happy to chat with visitors. Sport is often shown on TV. Food is served in the bar and the attractive little dining room. ❀ ⛺ ♣ P 🚌 (81) 🐾 📶

One hundred years old

I met the other day an old man, who asked me to drink. 'I am not thirsty,' said I, 'and I will not drink with you.' 'Yes, you will,' said the old man, 'for I am this day one hundred years old; and you will never again have the opportunity of drinking the health of a man on his hundredth birthday.' So I broke my word and drank. 'How have you passed your time?' said I. 'As well as I could,' said the old man, 'always enjoying a good thing when it came honestly within my reach; not forgetting to praise God for putting it there.' 'I suppose you were fond of a glass of good ale when you were young.' 'Yes,' said the old man, 'I was, and so, thank God, I am still.' And he drank off a glass of ale.

George Barrow, 1857

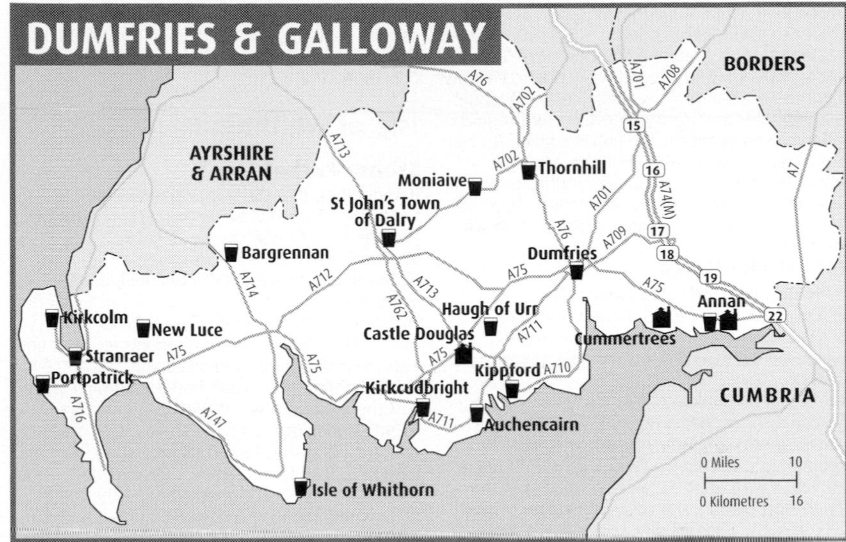

Authority area covered: Dumfries & Galloway UA

Annan

Blue Bell Inn

10 High Street, DG12 6AG
11-11 (midnight Thu-Sat); 12.30-11 Sun
(01461) 202385
Caledonian Deuchars IPA; guest beers H
A former coaching inn at the entrance to the town from the west, this is a busy, friendly pub which offers a selection of beers drawn from throughout the UK. A courtyard to the rear of the building offers a pleasant seated area in summer, and also acts as a focus for the pub's annual beer festival in August. P

Auchencairn

Old Smugglers Inn

11-13 Main Street, DG7 1QU
12 (5 Mon)-11; 12-midnight Fri & Sat (01556) 640331
solwaysmugglers.co.uk
Beer range varies H
Set in a quiet village on the Solway coast, this inn has been a popular pub with villagers and visitors for many years. Managed by a CAMRA member with experience in the brewing industry, two cask ales are served in the hotel bar. The hotel serves good freshly cooked, locally-sourced food in the restaurant and in the welcoming public bar.
Q P

Bargrennan

House o' Hill Hotel

DG8 6RN (just off A714 on Glentrool road)
12-11 (closed Mon Nov-Mar) (01671) 840243
houseohill.co.uk
Beer range varies H
Situated in Galloway Forest Park, this small hotel is popular with walkers, climbers, anglers and cyclists. Fully refurbished, it has an attractive interior including a small function room. Two beers are offered, mainly from Scottish microbreweries, and three-day beer festivals with food and live music are held twice a year. The pub specialises in good-value home cooking, using locally-sourced supplies and home-grown produce. Regular music events featuring local artists are held throughout the year. Closed most of January.
P (359)

Dumfries

Cavens Arms

20 Buccleuch Street, DG1 2AH
11-11 (midnight Thu-Sat); 12.30-11 Sun
(01387) 252896
Beer range varies H
A busy town-centre pub with a reputation built on the quality of its ales, excellent pub grub and friendly customer service. Three house beers and four guests – and occasionally up to 10 ales – are usually on offer, drawn from a varying range of UK breweries. Regular charity quizzes and other themed nights are hosted. Frequent local CAMRA Pub of the Year including 2014.

Coach & Horses

66 Whitesands, DG1 2RS
11 (12.30 Sun)-11 (01387) 279754
Draught Bass H
This former coaching inn on the Whitesands was extensively renovated to provide a pleasant bar area with a flagstone floor and warming open fire. Regular live music sessions are hosted at weekends – the venue is a favourite with local blues fans. Just one cask ale is available – Bass Red Triangle. Handy for local tourist attractions and car parking.

New Bazaar

38-39 Whitesands, DG1 2RS
11-11 (midnight Thu-Sat); 12.30-11 Sun
(01387) 268776

INDEPENDENT BREWERIES

Andrews Cummertrees
Madcap Annan
Sulwath Castle Douglas

SCOTLAND

Greene King Abbot; Theakston XB; guest beers Ⓗ
Former coaching inn beside the River Nith with a pleasant airy bar featuring an impressive Victorian gantry and a cosy lounge with a warming coal fire in winter. A small room is available for meetings. Four cask ales are usually on offer – two regulars and two varying guests. The pub is a favourite with football supporters before and after matches at nearby Palmerston Park, and is ideally situated for car parking and local tourist attractions. There are areas for smoking and seating outside.

Robert the Bruce

81/83 Buccleuch Street, DG1 2AB
11-midnight (1am Fri & Sat); 12.30-midnight Sun
(01387) 270320
Caledonian Deuchars IPA; Greene King Abbot; guest beers Ⓗ
This former Methodist church, sensitively converted by Wetherspoon, has a relaxed atmosphere. A popular meeting place in the town centre, it regularly features seven cask ales, and 10 during festivals – with up to 50 ales on offer over the period. The menu is varied with a range of good-value meals served all day, every day. There is a good outside smoking area. Q

Ship Inn

97 St Michael Street, DG1 2PY
11 (12.30 Sun)-11 (01387) 255189
Caledonian Deuchars IPA; Morland Old Speckled Hen; guest beers Ⓗ
A small, traditional, uncomplicated pub, popular with locals and offering a friendly welcome to visitors. It has a front bar featuring stained glass panels in the two front windows and a small rear lounge. Up to five ales are available. The pub is situated directly opposite the historic St Michael's Kirkyard where Robert Burns is buried and within 300 yards of Burns House where the poet spent the last few years of his life. Q

Tam o' Shanter

113/117 Queensberry Street, DG1 1BH
11-midnight (11 Mon & Tue); 12.30-7.30 Sun 07855 473933
Broughton Bramling Cross; guest beers Ⓗ
A long-established ale pub in Dumfries, this old coaching inn dating back to 1630 has been held in high regard on the Dumfries beer scene for many years. The small, traditional interior includes a main bar, two quiet rooms behind and an upstairs room which hosts live music and other functions. A rotating range of five ales includes at least three from Broughton Brewery. Comfortable and cosy, with a warming gas fire in the bar, it is well positioned just off the High Street. QP

Haugh of Urr

Laurie Arms Hotel

11-13 Main Street, DG7 3YA
12 (12.30 Sun)-3, 5.30-midnight (01556) 660246
haugh-of-urr.com
Beer range varies Ⓗ
Welcoming family-run pub and restaurant in a charming, quiet village, popular with locals and visitors for its range of ales and good food, freshly cooked and featuring local produce. The bar has a genuine village-inn atmosphere, enhanced on cold winter nights by a warming log fire. Up to four beers are available depending on the season, mainly from small independent breweries. The toilets feature an interesting selection of saucy seaside postcards. Former CAMRA Scottish Pub of the Year and joint branch winner in 2012.
QP

Isle of Whithorn

Steam Packet Inn

Harbour Row, DG8 8LL (B7004 from Whithorn)
11-11 (12.30am Fri & Sat) summer; 11-3, 6-11 Tue-Thu; 11-11 (midnight Fri & Sat) winter; 12-11 Sun
(01988) 500334 steampacketinn.biz
Belhaven IPA; Timothy Taylor Landlord; guest beers Ⓗ
Traditional and historic family-run hotel overlooking the harbour, welcoming to locals and visitors alike, including families and pets. The public bar has stone walls and a multi-fuel stove, and there are pictures of the village and maritime events throughout. Four guest ales from a wide variety of breweries are available in both bars. The extensive food menu features local produce – the Sunday hot buffet is a speciality and there are various themed food nights. Discounted B&B is available for CAMRA members.
Q(415)

Kippford

Anchor Hotel

DG5 4LN
11-3, 6-11; 12.30-11 Sun (01556) 620205
anchorhotelkippford.co.uk
Sulwath Criffel; guest beers Ⓗ
On the main street in the heart of a popular sailing centre, this friendly inn has fine views over the Urr estuary. The small cosy bar is warmed by an open log fire in winter. Seasonal food includes fish specials and traditional pub favourites. When the weather is warm and sunny there can be no greater pleasure in life than sitting at a table outside the Anchor watching the world go by.
P

Kirkcolm

Blue Peter Hotel

23 Main Street, DG9 0NL (A718 5 miles N of Stranraer)
6 (4 Fri)-11.30; 12-midnight Sat; 12.30-11.30 Sun
(01776) 853221 thebluepeterhotel.co.uk
Beer range varies Ⓗ
A small family-run hotel, now under new ownership, with two bars packed with memorabilia and, outside, a decked patio for viewing the abundant wildlife, including red squirrels. Two handpumps in each bar dispense a constantly changing range of ales. Home-cooked food is made with fresh local produce, also available to take away. Good value B&B is offered, with a discount for CAMRA members. Popular with walkers, bird and wildlife watchers and real ale enthusiasts. Q(408)

Kirkcudbright

Masonic Arms

19 Castle Street, DG6 4JA
11.30 (11 Sun)-11 (01557) 330517
Beer range varies Ⓗ
The Masonic has been a firm favourite in the town with real ale enthusiasts over a period of many years. It has a sociable main bar with a relaxed

ambience, welcoming to both locals and visitors. The tables and bar fronts are made from old malt whisky casks from Bowmore Distillers. There is a smaller back bar and a pleasant garden with a smoking area. ❀♿⛺🚌🐾

Moniaive

Craigdarroch Arms Hotel

High Street, DG3 4HN

12-midnight ☎ (01848) 200205 craigdarrocharms.co.uk

Beer range varies H

The Craigdarroch Hotel has been at the heart of Moniaive's community for over a century. Two ales are usually served. It attracts many outdoor enthusiasts, including cyclists, anglers and shooters. The village hosts regular music festivals – with major artists performing to audiences in the Marquee Club in the hotel garden. The hotel also holds an annual beer festival. The restaurant serves excellent, freshly prepared meals. Children are welcome. Q❀P🚌🐾

New Luce

Kenmuir Arms Hotel

31 Main Street, DG8 0AJ (8 miles N of Glenluce along old military road)

12 (5 winter)-11 ☎ (01581) 600218

kenmuirarmsnewluce.com

Beer range varies H

Situated in a beautiful village on the banks of the River Luce, this picturesque hotel has well-kept gardens by the river. The public bar offers one real ale, two in summer, sourced from all over the UK. Home-cooked, freshly prepared food is served at lunchtimes and in the evenings. This is a popular stopping-off point for walkers on the Southern Upland Way and the hotel offers a luggage transfer service. Q❀♿⛺♣P

Portpatrick

Crown Hotel

9 North Crescent, DG9 8SX (overlooking harbour)

11-midnight (1am Fri & Sat); 12-midnight Sun

☎ (01776) 810261 crownportpatrick.com

Beer range varies H

This hotel overlooks the picturesque and historic Portpatrick harbour with views on a clear day across to Ireland. The large comfortable bar area at the front of the building is adorned with fine pictures and ornaments and warmed by an open fire. Two regularly changing ales are available from across the UK. Live music plays on Friday and Saturday nights, featuring both local and visiting musicians and groups.

❀♿⛺♣🚌 (367)🐾

St John's Town of Dalry

Clachan Inn

8-10 Main Street, DG7 3UW

11 (12 Sun)-11 ☎ (01644) 430241 theclachaninn.co.uk

Beer range varies H

In a picturesque village, this inn has established a reputation for quality food, cosy, well-appointed bedrooms and a welcoming atmosphere. It features an attractive, traditional main bar and a separate restaurant. Two cask ales are always available. The Clachan prides itself on using local produce including organic lamb and venison, and offers a varied menu including excellent daily specials. The inn suits the needs of all those who enjoy country life, and is a handy stop for walkers on the Southern Upland Way.

Q❀♿⛺P🚌🐾

Stranraer

Grapes

4-6 Bridge Street, DG9 7HY

11-11.30 (midnight Thu-Sat); 12.30-11.30 Sun

☎ (01776) 703386 thegrapesbar.co.uk

Beer range varies H

This popular historic public bar, with impressive mirror and gantry, has altered little in over 50 years. It has a separate refurbished snug bar, an upstairs function room with 1930s Art Deco gantry and counter, and a small courtyard with tables and chairs. Regular live music features in the bar on Friday evenings, and occasional music nights in the function room. Two ales are usually on offer, sourced from all over Britain, although there may be just one in winter. ❀♣🚌🐾

Thornhill

Buccleuch & Queensberry Arms Hotel

112 Drumlanrig Street, DG3 5LU

11 (12.30 Sun)-11 ☎ (01848) 330215

buccleuchhotel.co.uk

Beer range varies H

Built by the Duke of Buccleuch in 1855 to replace the original coach house which dated from 1714, it is set in the heart of this market town. Recently renovated, the hotel caters for anglers and shooters and is an ideal base for exploring the beautiful countryside of Dumfries and Galloway. The main lounge and bar facilities give hotel guests the opportunity to mix with anglers and village worthies, who meet in the evening to enjoy a choice of cask ales or a wee dram.

Q❀♿P🚌🐾

Recipe for buttered beer

Take a quart or more of Double Beere and put to it a good piece of fresh butter, sugar candie an ounce, or liquerise in powder, or ginger grated, of each a dramme, and if you would have it strong, put in as much long pepper and Greynes, let it boyle in the quart in the maner as you burne wine, and who so will drink it, let him drinke it hot as he may suffer. Some put in the yolke of an egge or two towards the latter end, and so they make it more strength-full.

Thomas Cogan, The Haven of Health, 1584

SCOTLAND

EDINBURGH & THE LOTHIANS

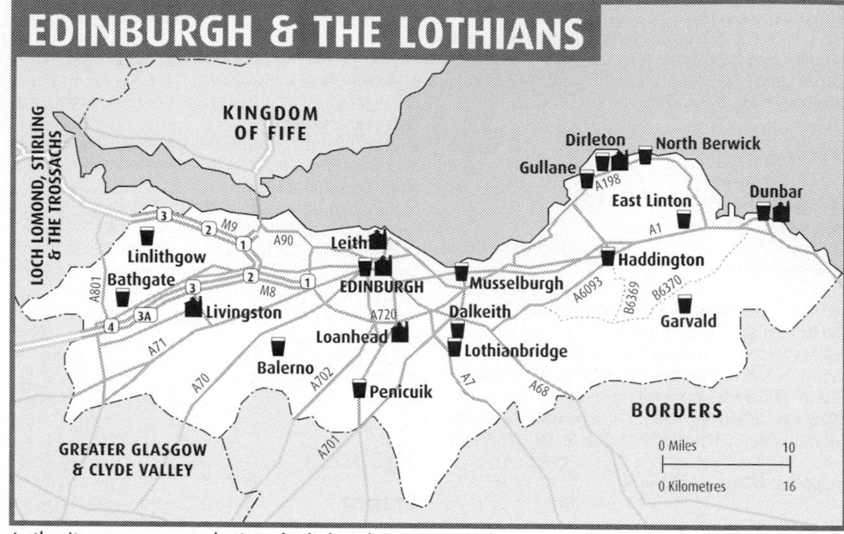

Authority areas covered: City of Edinburgh UA, East Lothian UA, Midlothian UA, West Lothian UA

Balerno

Grey Horse

20 Main Street, EH14 7EH (off A70, in pedestrian area)
10 (11 Sun)-1am ☎ (0131) 449 2888
greyhorsebalerno.com
Beer range varies Ⓗ
Traditional stone-built village-centre pub dating from the 18th century. The public bar retains some original features, with wood panelling and a fine Bernard's mirror, and the pleasant lounge has green banquette seating. The restaurant next door is part of the pub so you can have a beer with your meal in the evening. One folk and one jazz night are held each month. CAMRA Lothian Pub of the Year runner-up 2014. Q ♣ (44)

Bathgate

James Young

36-44 Hopetoun Street, EH48 4EU
8am-midnight (1am Fri & Sat) ☎ (01506) 651600
Caledonian Deuchars IPA; Greene King Abbot; guest beers Ⓗ
Wetherspoon pub on two levels named after James Young Simpson, Scottish obstetrician and an important figure in the history of medicine. He was credited with discovering the anaesthetic properties of chloroform and successfully introducing it for general medical use. Licensed from 11am (12.30pm Sunday). Major sport is shown on TV, with subtitled news at other times. Music plays on Fridays and Saturdays from 7pm. Children are welcome until 8pm.

Dalkeith

Blacksmith's Forge

Newmills Road, EH22 1DU
8am-midnight (1am Fri & Sat) ☎ (0131) 561 5100
Caledonian Deuchars IPA; Greene King Abbot; guest beers Ⓗ
Large open-plan Wetherspoon pub divided into several areas with a mix of tables and chairs, high tables and booths with bench seating. The decor includes images of a forge and a large model anvil. Licensed from 11am (12.30pm Sunday). Six guest beers are on offer, often from local Scottish breweries. Background music plays on Friday and Saturday evenings; the pub is quiet at other times. Families are welcome for meals, which are served all day. Q

Dirleton

Castle Inn

Manse Road, EH39 5EP (off A198)
11-11 (1am Fri & Sat) ☎ (01620) 850221
castleinndirleton.com
Caledonian Deuchars IPA, Flying Scotsman; guest beer Ⓗ
Attractive 19th-century coaching inn overlooking the village green and opposite the castle ruins and garden. To the right of the front door is the bar, with a small dining area to the rear. To the left is a comfortable bistro area where meals are served all day. There is also a separate restaurant. The food menu is comprehensive, featuring local produce and daily specials. A TV in the bar area is not intrusive. ♣P (X24,X124)

Dunbar

Volunteer Arms

17 Victoria Street, EH42 1HP
12-11 (midnight Thu; 1am Fri & Sat); 12.30-midnight Sun
☎ (01368) 862278 volunteerarmsdunbar.co.uk

INDEPENDENT BREWERIES

Alechemy Livingston
Barney's Edinburgh
Belhaven (Greene King) Dunbar
Caledonian Edinburgh
Elixir Livingston
Knops Dirleton
Pilot Leith (NEW)
Stewart Loanhead
Top Out Loanhead (NEW)

Beer range varies Ⓗ
Close to Dunbar harbour, this is a friendly, traditional locals' pub. The cosy panelled bar is decorated with lots of fishing and lifeboat-oriented memorabilia. Two real ales are available, often from smaller breweries. Upstairs is a restaurant serving an excellent good-value menu with an emphasis on seafood. In summer, meals are served all day until 9.30pm. Dogs are permitted after 9pm.

East Linton

Crown & Kitchen

25-27 Bridge Street, EH40 3AG
11 (5 Mon)-11; 11-1am Thu & Fri; 11-midnight Sun
(01620) 860098 crownandkitchen.com
Caledonian Deuchars IPA; guest beers Ⓗ
A long-established red sandstone pub and restaurant in the centre of a conservation village. The recently transformed interior is now contemporary and classy with unusual 1940s engraved window screens featuring pub scenes and old Belhaven adverts. A real wood fire warms the main bar area. Good-quality fresh food is served (all day on Sunday) in both the bar and the restaurant to the rear. By catering for all tastes the Crown attracts a wide clientele.
(X6,120)

Linton

3 Bridge End, EH40 3AF
12-11 (midnight Fri & Sat) (01620) 860202
Beer range varies Ⓗ
Small, welcoming, traditional hotel by the historic brig over the Tyne in a pretty conservation village. There is a quiet, comfortably furnished public bar and a popular restaurant to the rear. Three handpumps usually serve at least one beer from a Scottish microbrewery. The restaurant features good-quality, award-winning, locally-sourced Scottish cuisine. Stained glass windows and a rooftop statue reflect the hotel's former name — the Red Lion. Q (120,X6)

Edinburgh: Central

Abbotsford Bar & Restaurant ★

3-5 Rose Street, EH2 2PR (city centre)
11-11 (midnight Fri & Sat); 12.30-11 Sun
(0131) 225 5276 theabbotsford.com
Beer range varies Ⓗ/Ⓐ
A traditional Scottish bar listed on CAMRA's National Inventory of historic pub interiors. The magnificent island bar and gantry in dark mahogany have been a fixture since 1902. The ornate plasterwork and corniced ceiling are outstanding and highlighted by concealed lighting. Six real ales are available, usually from Scottish microbreweries. There is an extensive food menu, served all day in the bar. Diners in the restaurant upstairs can order real ale from downstairs.
Q (Waverley)

Blue Blazer

2 Spittal Street, EH3 9DX
11 (12 Sun)-1am (0131) 229 5030
Cairngorm Trade Winds Ⓐ**; Caledonian Deuchars IPA; Orkney Dark Island; Stewart 80/-** Ⓗ**; guest beers** Ⓗ/Ⓐ
Two-roomed pub nestling in the shadow of Edinburgh Castle, with wooden floors, high ceilings and old brewery window panels; candles in the evening add to the traditional feel. Named after a local school uniform, a tile blue blazer is inlaid on the floor. The pub specialises in beers from Scottish micros. Close to theatres and cinemas, closing time is later during August and December. Toasties are available all day. Children are not admitted.

Bow Bar

80 West Bow, EH1 2HH (in Old Town, off Grassmarket)
12-midnight; 12.30-11.30 Sun (0131) 226 7667
Alechemy Bowhemia; Fyne Hurricane Jack; Stewart Edinburgh No.3; guest beers Ⓐ
One of the first re-creations of a classic Scottish one-roomed ale house, dedicated to traditional Scottish air pressure dispense and upright drinking. The five guest beers can be from anywhere in the UK, and regular beer festivals are held. The walls are festooned with original brewery mirrors and the superb gantry does justice to an award-winning selection of around 200 single malt whiskies and international bottled beers. Pies, soup and bridies are available at lunchtime. Children are not admitted. Q (Waverley) (2)

Cafe Royal ★

19 West Register Street, EH2 2AA (off E end of Princes St)
11-11 (midnight Thu; 1am Fri & Sat); 12.30-11 Sun
(0131) 556 1884 caferoyaledinburgh.co.uk
Broughton Coulsons EPA; guest beers Ⓗ
One of the finest Victorian pub interiors in Scotland, dominated by an impressive oval island bar with ornate brass light fittings and magnificent ceramic tiled murals of innovators made by Doulton from pictures by John Eyre. The sporting windows of the Oyster Bar were made by the same firm that supplied windows for the House of Lords. Six guest beers are available from regional breweries such as Fyne, Harviestoun and Kelburn. Meals are served all day. (Waverley)

Guildford Arms

1 West Register Street, EH2 2AA (off E end of Princes Street)
11-11 (midnight Fri & Sat) (0131) 556 4312
guildfordarms.com
Beer range varies Ⓗ
A large pub built in the golden age of Victorian pub design. The high ceiling, cornices and friezes are spectacular, as are the window arches and screens. The restaurant is upstairs in a noteworthy gallery. There is a large standing area around the canopied bar plus seating areas to the rear. The diverse range of 10 real ales includes many from Scottish micros. A single but varying real cider is sold. Bar snacks are available all day. (Waverley)

Jolly Judge

7a James Court, Lawnmarket, EH1 2PB (in Old Town)
12-11 (midnight Fri & Sat); 12.30-11 Sun
(0131) 225 2669 jollyjudge.co.uk
Beer range varies Ⓗ
Steps lead down to the entrance of this comfortable bar hidden down an Old Town close just off the Royal Mile. A welcome spot for refreshment after visiting the Castle, it offers low beams, an attractive painted ceiling, a log fire and a tranquil atmosphere. The real ales are often from Scottish or Northumbrian micros and a single but varying real cider is sold. Dogs are permitted after 3pm. CAMRA Scotland Cider Pub of the Year 2013.
(Waverley)

SCOTLAND

Lock 25

85-87 Fountainbridge, EH3 9PU
12-midnight; closed Sun ☎ (0131) 228 8831
lock25.co.uk
Caledonian Deuchars IPA; guest beers H
Remodelled pub that combines a traditional atmosphere with a modern edge, to appeal to the wide clientele now working and living nearby. The inside is deceptively spacious, with an L-shaped bar and seating ranging from high stools to comfortable armchairs. The guest beers are from Caledonian and local microbreweries such as Stewart, and a varying real cider is sold. Home-made meals are served all day including a steak and guest ale pie.

Oxford Bar ★

8 Young Street, EH2 4JB (in New Town, off Charlotte Sq)
11-midnight (1am Fri & Sat); 12.30-11 Sun
☎ (0131) 539 7119 oxfordbar.co.uk
Caledonian Deuchars IPA; guest beers H
Small, basic, vibrant drinking shop mostly unaltered since the late-19th century. The bar counter nearly fills the small front room but there is more space in the side room. It is renowned as one of the favourite pubs of Rebus and his creator Ian Rankin, and a haunt of many other famous and infamous characters over the years. The three guest beers are usually from Scottish breweries. Children are not admitted. A real taste of New Town past. Q

Thomson's Bar

182-184 Morrison Street, EH3 8EB
12-11.30 (midnight Thu & Sat; 1am Fri); 4-11.30 Sun
☎ (0131) 228 5700 thomsonsbaredinburgh.co.uk
Beer range varies H/A
Superb single-roomed bar modelled on the style of Glasgow architect Alexander 'Greek' Thomson. The hand-made gantry and room panelling are inlaid with scenes from Greek mythology, and the walls are decorated with rare mirrors, adverts and point of sale material from long-forgotten breweries. Up to six, often hoppy, real ales are served from a variety of breweries including Oakham Ales. No food is served on Sunday and pies only on Saturday. Children are not admitted.
Q (Haymarket)

Edinburgh: East

Regent

2 Montrose Terrace, EH7 5DL
12 (12.30 Sun)-1am ☎ (0131) 661 8198
theregentbar.co.uk
Caledonian Deuchars IPA; guest beers H
Large tenement bar with two rooms, one music free. Popular with gay and lesbian real ale drinkers, it offers two guest beers from a variety of breweries, along with Westons Old Rosie. Bar snacks and simple meals, including good vegetarian and vegan options, are served all day. Comfortable seating ranges from banquettes to leather sofas and armchairs. A novel slant on pub games is the pommel horse by the toilets.

Edinburgh: North

Cumberland Bar

1-3 Cumberland Street, EH3 6RT (in New Town)
12-midnight (1am Thu-Sat); 11-midnight Sun
☎ (0131) 558 3134 cumberlandbar.co.uk
Caledonian Deuchars IPA; guest beers H
Elegant, traditional New Town pub with half-wood panelling complemented by dark green leather seating. Exquisite brewery mirrors hang beside framed, decorative and illustrative posters. The corridor between the front drinking area and another cosy drinking area at the back is flanked by a small snug and a side room. Seven guest beers are generally from smaller breweries such as Alechemy, Fyne and Highland. Meals are served all day (until 6pm Sun). Q

Kay's Bar

39 Jamaica Street West, EH3 6HF (in New Town, off India St)
11-midnight (1am Fri & Sat); 12.30-11 Sun
☎ (0131) 225 1858 kaysbar.co.uk
Caledonian Deuchars IPA; Theakston Best Bitter; guest beers H
A cosy and convivial pub that retains many features from its days as a Victorian wine merchant, including the old whisky barrels. Considering its size, it offers an impressive range of real ales, with two regulars and five guests. There is also a good whisky selection behind the bar. If the front bar is busy, try the small room at the back. Lunches are mainly traditional Scottish fare. Children are not admitted, dogs permitted after 2.30pm.
Q

Smithies Ale House

49-51 Eyre Place, EH3 5EY (½ mile N of centre)
11-midnight (1am Fri & Sat); 12-midnight Sun
☎ (0131) 556 9805
Caledonian Deuchars IPA; Fyne Ales Jarl; Stewart Brewing Edinburgh Gold H
A single-roomed pub with a central bar, tucked away up a side street. A set of 19 beautifully handpainted mirrors depict flora and fauna and the national emblems and flags of Scotland, Wales, Ireland and England. A comfortable place for a quiet drink, with newspapers provided. Major sport events are shown on the TV. Meals are served all day. (8,23)

Stockbridge Tap 🏆

2-4 Raeburn Place, Stockbridge, EH4 1HN
12-midnight (1am Fri & Sat); 12.30-midnight Sun
☎ (0131) 343 3000
Alechemy Ritual; Stewart Pentland IPA, 80/-; guest beers H
Very much a specialist real ale house, offering unusual and interesting beers from all over the UK and holding occasional beer festivals. The L-shaped room, with bright bar area, boasts mirrors from lost breweries including Murray's and Campbell's. There is plenty of seating and also ample space for vertical drinking. Good pub food is served (no meals all day Mon or Fri-Sun eves). Children are not admitted. CAMRA Edinburgh Pub of the Year 2014.

Teuchters Landing

1c Dock Place, Leith, EH6 6LU
11 (12.30 Sun)-1am ☎ (0131) 554 7427
aroomin.co.uk/teuchters-landing
Caledonian Deuchars IPA; Fyne Jarl; Highland Sneaky Wee Orkney Stout; Inveralmond Ossian; guest beer H
Converted from the former waiting room for the Leith to Aberdeen ferry, the attractive bar has a wood-panelled ceiling shaped like an upturned

boat and edged with tiles featuring random Scottish place names. There are also some smaller rooms and a large conservatory extension that opens out onto a pontoon floating on the Water of Leith. The menu includes meals served in small or large mugs. An excellent selection of malt whiskies is available.

Windsor

45 Elm Row, EH7 4AH

11 (12 winter)-1am; 12.30-1am Sun ☎ (0131) 556 4558

Caledonian Deuchars IPA; guest beers Ⓗ

This late-Victorian locals' bar has been opened out but retains a traditional look with fine ceiling cornices and nooks and crannies. Comfortable green leather armchairs and bench seating complement the extensive wood panelling. A raised area at the back features a mirror and window with the pub logo. The three guest ales come from a range of Scottish breweries. Simple bar snacks are served. Children are not admitted.

Edinburgh: South

Auld Hoose

23-25 St Leonards Street, EH8 9QN

12 (12.30 Sun)-12.45am ☎ (0131) 668 2934

theauldhoose.co.uk

Harviestoun Bitter & Twisted; Wychwood Hobgoblin; guest beer Ⓗ

Traditional pub dating back to the 1860s with a large central horseshoe-shaped bar and lots of pictures of old Edinburgh. This is a friendly pub with a broad clientele, including students. The jukebox features metal and punk. A pub quiz is held every Tuesday. Good food is served all day including vegetarian and vegan options (CAMRA members and students receive a 10 per cent discount). The guest beer is usually from a smaller brewery. Newspapers are provided. Children are not admitted. (14)

Bennets of Morningside

1 Maxwell Street, Morningside, EH10 5HT

11-midnight (1am Wed-Sat) ☎ (0131) 447 1903

bennetsofmorningside.co.uk

Caledonian Deuchars IPA; Hadrian Border Tyneside Blonde; Timothy Taylor Landlord; guest beers Ⓗ

A cosy, traditional single-room tenement bar in the Morningside area of the city. Sympathetically refurbished, photographs of old Edinburgh adorn the walls along with some interesting brewery mirrors. The guest ales tend to be from Scotland and north-east England, and one beer is always offered at a competitive price. Simple bar snacks are served all day. There is a paved outdoor drinking area to the front. Children are not admitted.

Cask & Barrel (Southside)

24-26 West Preston Street, EH8 9PZ

12-midnight (1am Fri); 11-1am Sat; 12.30-midnight Sun

☎ (0131) 667 0856

Caledonian Deuchars IPA; Highland Orkney Best; Stewart 80/-; guest beers Ⓗ

Modern re-creation of a Scottish city or tenement bar. The single room, with windows front and back, is divided by a horseshoe bar with a dark-wood gantry adorned with decorative wooden casks. The walls support a fine range of old photos, framed advertisements and historic brewery and distillery mirrors. A good place to try beers from Scottish breweries, along with some from 'down south'. Children are not admitted. CAMRA Edinburgh Pub of the Year runner-up in 2014.

Cloisters Bar

26 Brougham Street, EH3 9JH

12-midnight (1am Fri & Sat); 12.30-midnight Sun

☎ (0131) 221 9997 cloistersbar.com

Stewart Pentland IPA, Holy Grale; guest beers Ⓗ

Set in the former All Saints parsonage, this bare-boarded ale house is popular with a broad cross-section of drinkers. Old pews give it a traditional, friendly feel. A fine selection of brewery mirrors adorns the walls and the wide range of single malt whiskies does justice to the outstanding gantry. Seven guest beers are from breweries UK-wide. Bar meals are freshly prepared from local ingredients (no food Mon or Sun eve). Children are admitted at lunchtimes if dining.

Q (24)

Dagda Bar

93-95 Buccleuch Street, EH8 9NG

12.30 (1 Sun)-1am ☎ (0131) 667 9773

Beer range varies Ⓗ

A really cosy howff situated in the heart of the university area attracting a wide-ranging clientele. The small single room has banquette seating on three sides and a welcoming U-shaped bar. The staff are knowledgable about their beers, which are usually from local breweries, including their own Dagda Ale of secret origin. There is also a good range of whiskies and bottled beers. Children are not admitted. An essential stop on any Southside pub walk.

Leslie's (John Leslie) Bar ★

45-47 Ratcliffe Terrace, EH9 1SU

11-midnight (1am Fri & Sat) ☎ (0131) 667 7205

lesliesbar.com

Caledonian Deuchars IPA; Timothy Taylor Landlord; guest beers Ⓗ

This outstanding Victorian inn retains the original fine ceiling, cornice, leaded glasswork and half-wood panelling. The island bar has a spectacular snob screen which divides the interior. Small 'ticket window' hatches allow customers to order drinks without being seen. A plaque near the fireplace details the history of this superb pub. The three guest beers are usually from smaller breweries. Straightforward bar meals are served all day.

(42,67)

Edinburgh: West

Athletic Arms (Diggers)

1-3 Angle Park Terrace, EH11 2JX

11 (12.30 Sun)-1am ☎ (0131) 337 3822

Caledonian Deuchars IPA, Flying Scotsman; Stewart Diggers 80/- Ⓐ**; guest beers** Ⓗ

Situated between two graveyards, the name Diggers became synonymous with this Edinburgh pub legend, which opened in 1897. Banquette seating lines the walls, and a compass drawing in the floor aids the geographically challenged. A smaller back room has a dartboard and further seating. Quieter now than in its heyday, though packed when Hearts are at home, it continues to extend a warm welcome to locals and visitors alike, along with their dogs. However, children are not admitted. The pies are outstanding.

SCOTLAND

Caley Sample Room

56 Angle Park Terrace, EH11 2JR
12-midnight (1am Fri); 11-1am Sat; 11-midnight Sun
(0131) 337 7204 thecaleysampleroom.co.uk
Caledonian Deuchars IPA; guest beers H
Large one-roomed bar with iron pillars and bare brick walls, which resembles the sample cellar at the nearby Caledonian brewery. There are seven guest beers, usually from micros, and an interesting range of bottled beers. The real cider is often Westons Old Rosie. Popular high-quality food is served all day. The atmosphere is usually relaxed but hots up when Hearts are at home. Dogs are permitted outwith the food area.

Fountain

127-131 Dundee Street, EH11 1AX
10-midnight (1am Thu-Sat); 11-midnight Sun
(0131) 229 1899 thefountainbar.co.uk
Beer range varies H
Modern open-plan lounge bar with separate bar and dining areas. Quality food is served all day with daily specials and meal deals. The real ales are often from Harviestoun, Orkney and Stewart. Children are welcome and a box of toys and games is provided to keep them amused. Dogs are permitted in the bar area.

Garvald

Garvald Inn

EH41 4LN
closed Mon; 12-11 (midnight Fri & Sat); 12.30-7 Sun
(01620) 830311 thegarvaldinn.co.uk
Beer range varies H
A family-run 18th-century pub in a pretty village by the Lammermuir Hills. The bar is cosy and welcoming, with half-panelled walls, a crimson colour scheme and an exposed stone wall with a large wood-burning stove. The single real ale is often from Stewart Brewing. The inn is popular for food, served in both the bar and tiny dining room — the dinner menu being particularly impressive. Live music and open mic sessions feature occasionally.
Q P

Gullane

Old Clubhouse

East Links Road, EH31 2AF (W end of village, off A198)
11-11 (midnight Thu-Sat); 12-11 Sun (01620) 842008
oldclubhouse.com
Caledonian Deuchars IPA; Timothy Taylor Landlord; guest beer P
There is a colonial touch to this pub, with views over the golf links to the Lammermuir Hills. The half-panelled walls are adorned with historic memorabilia and stuffed animals. Caricature statuettes of the Marx Brothers and Laurel and Hardy look down from the gantry. Food features highly and is served all day – the extensive menu includes seafood, pasta, barbecue, curries, salads and burgers. (X24,124)

Haddington

Tyneside Tavern

10 Poldrate, EH41 4DA (on B6368)
11-11 (midnight Thu; 1am Fri & Sat); 12.30-11 Sun
(01620) 822221 tynesidetavern.com
Caledonian Deuchars IPA; guest beers H
An unusual twin-gable-ended building dating from the 18th century, next to an old watermill by the River Tyne. The bar of this community pub, with its open fire in winter and sport on TV, is popular with locals. In the more spacious lounge the focus is on food, which is available all day. The pub offers an excellent range of guest beers, including some little-known ones from south of the border.

Victoria Inn & Avenue Restaurant

9 Court Street, EH41 3JD
11-11 (midnight Fri & Sat) (01620) 823332
theavenuerestaurant.co.uk
Beer range varies H
A stylish inn overlooking the town square. The focus is on quality food (served all day Sun until 5pm); however, drinkers are made most welcome. The cosy bar with its horseshoe counter has bar chairs and two tall tables backing on to the dining area. In summer the front pavement area is a popular suntrap where visitors can sit and watch the world go by. Real ales are from the Belhaven/ Greene King list. There are five attractive en-suite bedrooms. Q

Linlithgow

Four Marys

65-67 High Street, EH49 7ED
12-11 (midnight Wed & Thu; 12.30am Fri & Sat); 12.30-11 Sun (01506) 842147 thefourmarys.co.uk
Belhaven 80/- Ale, St Andrew's Ale; Caledonian Deuchars IPA; guest beers H
A stone's throw from Linlithgow Palace, birthplace of Mary Queen of Scots, the building dates back to around 1500. The pub is named after the Queen's ladies-in-waiting. Initially a dwelling house, the building has had several changes of use over the years – at one time it was a chemist's run by the Waldie family whose most famous member, David, jointly helped establish the anaesthetic properties of chloroform in 1847. Beer festivals are held in May and October. Local CAMRA Pub of the Year 2013. Q

Platform 3 L

1a High Street, EH49 7AB
10.30-midnight (1am Fri & Sat); 12.30-midnight Sun
(01506) 847405 platform3.co.uk
Caledonian Deuchars IPA; guest beers H
Small, friendly hostelry on the railway station approach, originally the public bar of the hotel next door, then in 1998 renovated as a pub in its own right. Look out for the goods train that journeys from the station above the bar with ducks waiting on a train that never comes. Licensed from 11am (12.30pm Sunday), three beers are available including one from Stewart and one from another Scottish brewery. Dogs are welcome, with biscuits 'on tap'.

Lothianbridge

Sun Inn

EH22 4TR (on A7, near Newtongrange)
11-11 (midnight Fri & Sat) (0131) 663 2456
thesuninnedinburgh.co.uk
Stewart Pentland IPA; guest beer H
Built circa 1870, the Sun is situated by the impressive, soon to be reopened, 23-span Waverley line viaduct. Now a well-appointed,

award-winning gastro-pub, meals (served all day until 7pm Sun) are made from high-quality local ingredients. At busy times space is limited for drinkers, with tables set out for diners. The building has a contemporary feel, with a mix of exposed stone, wooden floors and carpets. A part-covered courtyard overlooking the garden is also used for dining in the summer. The guest beer is usually from a local brewery. The bar may close earlier if quiet. ❀🛏◑♿⛺P🚌(29,39)📶

Musselburgh

David Macbeth Moir

Bridge Street, EH21 6AG (opp Brunton Theatre)
8am-11 (midnight Fri & Sat) ☎ (0131) 653 1060
Caledonian Deuchars IPA; Greene King Abbot; guest beers H
Wetherspoon pub named after a local physician and writer, set in a converted cinema dating back to 1935. The main door and original features have been beautifully restored, and the vast single-room bar is filled with cinema-related Art Deco artefacts. The long bar counter has 10 handpumps offering a good mix of guest ales, plus Westons Old Rosie cider. Licensed from 11am (12.30pm Sunday). Food is served all day. ❀◑♿🍎🚌(26,44)📶

Levenhall Arms

10 Ravensheugh Road, EH21 7PP (on B1348)
12-11 (midnight Thu; 1am Fri & Sat); 12.30-midnight Sun
☎ (0131) 665 3220
Inveralmond Ossian A**; guest beers** H/A
A three-roomed hostelry dating from 1830 and close to the racecourse. The lively, cheerfully decorated public bar is half timber-panelled. A smaller area leads off, with a dartboard and pictures of old local industries. Expect some interesting guest beers from smaller breweries. The lounge has been franchised as an Indian restaurant and has comfortable seating. Lunches served only in summer. ❀◑⛺♣P🚌🐾📶

Volunteer Arms (Staggs) 🏆

81 North High Street, EH21 6JE (behind Brunton Hall)
12-11 (11.30 Thu; midnight Fri); 11-midnight Sat; 12.30-11 Sun ☎ (0131) 665 9654 🌐 staggsbar.com
Beer range varies H
Superb pub run by the same family since 1858. The bar and snug are traditional, with a wooden floor, wood panelling and mirrors from defunct local breweries. The attractive gantry is topped with old casks. The more modern lounge opens at the weekend. Up to eight guest beers, mostly pale and hoppy but often one darker, change regularly. Local CAMRA Pub of the Year 2014 and winner of many previous awards (see the bar wall). ❀♣🚌🐾📶

North Berwick

Nether Abbey Hotel

20 Dirleton Avenue, EH39 4BQ (on A198)
11-11 (midnight Thu; 1am Fri & Sat) ☎ (01620) 892802
🌐 netherabbey.co.uk
Beer range varies H
Busy, family-run and award-winning hotel in a stone-built villa, offering a bright, contemporary interior comprising open-plan, split-level rooms. The lower area is the recently expanded Fly Half Bar and the upper area is a restaurant. Real ales are often from Scottish micros and are now dispensed by handpump – sparklers can be removed on request. The Nethers is famous for its good, freshly cooked and locally-sourced cuisine as well as its ale. Food is served all day Friday to Sunday. ❀🛏◑♿⛺⇌P🚌(X24,124)🐾📶

Ship Inn

7-9 Quality Street, EH39 4HJ
11-11 (1am Thu-Sat) ☎ (01620) 890676
Beer range varies H
Spacious, open-plan bar located beneath a tenement block at the leafy east end of town. The bar area has pine floorboards, a mahogany counter and a dark-stained wood gantry. A quieter carpeted area is to the rear. The various guest beers tend to have higher ABVs. The pub is popular for food, with good vegetarian options, served all day until 8pm – the menu recommends a beer to complement each dish. Regular live music plays on weekend evenings. ❀◑⛺♣🚌🐾📶

Penicuik

Navaar House Hotel

23 Bog Road, EH26 9BY
12-1am (midnight Sun) ☎ (01968) 672683
🌐 navaarhouse.co.uk
Beer range varies H
A lively pub with a strong community spirit, situated in an old private house, built circa 1895 for Professor James Cossar Ewart and where he conducted his world-famous work on animal hybrids, known as the Pennycuik Experiments. The large bar is open plan, with a log and coal fire and TV screens for sport. The real ale is usually from Stewart or another Scottish micro. The restaurant serves good locally-sourced food (all day Sat & Sun), and a large patio and decked area is popular in summer. ❀🛏◑♣P🚌(37)🐾📶

Johnnie Dowie was the sleekest and kindest of landlords. Nothing could equal the benignity of his smile when he bought in a bottle of ale to a company of well-known and friendly customers. It was a perfect treat to see his formality in drawing the cork, his precision in filling the glasses, his regularity in drinking the health of all present in the first glass (which he always did, and at every successive bottle) and then his douce civility in withdrawing. Johnnie lived till within the last few years and with laudable attachment to the old costume, always wore a cocked hat, and buckles at knee and shoes, as well as a cane with a cross top, somewhat like an implement called by Scottish gardeners 'a dibble'.

William Hone, The Year Book, 1839. Dowie died in 1817. His Edinburgh tavern was frequented by Robert Burns and Adam Smith.

SCOTLAND

GREATER GLASGOW & CLYDE VALLEY

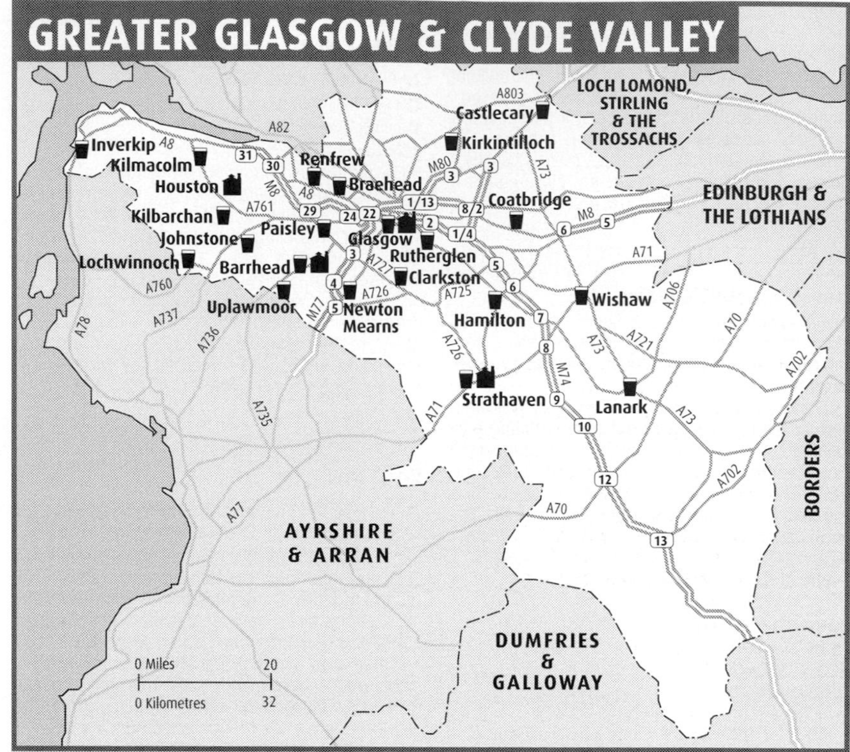

Authority areas covered: City of Glasgow UA, Dunbartonshire UAs, Inverclyde UA, Lanarkshire UAs, Renfrewshire UAs

Barrhead

Cross Stobs Inn

2-6 Grahamston Road, G78 1NS (on B7712)
11-11 (midnight Thu & Sat; 1am Fri); 12.30-11 Sun
(0141) 881 1581
Beer range varies H
Eighteenth-century coaching inn on the road to Paisley. The public bar has a real coal fire and retains much of its original charm with antique furniture and service bells. The lounge is spacious and leads out to an enclosed garden to the rear. There is also an outside drinking area at the front of the pub. The public bar leads to a pool room and a function suite. P (51,101)

Waterside Inn

The Hurlet, Glasgow Road, G53 7TH (A736, near Hurlet)
11-11 (midnight Fri & Sat); 12.30-11 Sun
(0141) 881 2822 thewatersideinn.net
Beer range varies H
Comfortable, welcoming and friendly bar and restaurant on the outskirts of town, near Levern Water. Food is the main focus here, but there is a cosy area with a real fire for those just wanting a relaxing drink. The decor is clean and traditional, and features old local photographs. Various theme nights are held fairly regularly. There is also a spacious function suite to the rear of the building. The beer is always from the local Kelburn Brewery. QP (103,X44B)

Braehead

Steam Wheeler

1 Row Avenue, G51 4SY
11-11 (0141) 886 3995
steamwheelerpubbraehead.co.uk
Beer range varies H
Modern Marston's family-friendly pub restaurant, situated close to Braehead shopping centre and the King George V Dock. The focus is on dining, with carvery meals served all day, but real ale is not forgotten, with three handpumps serving a selection of English ales primarily from the Marston's range. P

Castlecary

Castlecary House Hotel

Castlecary Road, G68 0HD (just off A80 nr M80 jct 4)
11 (12.30 Sun)-11.30 (01324) 840233
castlecaryhotel.com
Beer range varies H
A secluded hotel worth seeking out – look for the railway viaduct near the A80/B816 junction. The main bar is the Poacher's Lounge, but the handpumps are to be found in a smaller bar to the side. Up to four ales come from An Teallach and other Scottish breweries. The Forth & Clyde Canal, Antonine Way and remains of the Roman Antonine Wall are close by, making it a handy stop-off for visitors to the area. QP (X37,X39)

Clarkston

White Cart

61 East Kilbride Road, G76 8HX
11.30 (12 Sun)-11 ☎ (0141) 644 2711
Beer range varies H
A friendly welcome awaits you at this large Chef & Brewer pub. The emphasis here is on food service but there are four handpumps dispensing a changing choice of beers, one always from the Kelburn brewery. A patio area at the front is popular in the summer and there is an area for families inside. (Busby)P

Coatbridge

Vulcan

181 Main Street, ML5 3HH (Jct with Dunbeth Rd)
11-midnight (1am Fri & Sat) ☎ (01236) 437972
Caledonian Deuchars IPA; Greene King Abbot; guest beers H
Fairly modern town centre hostelry at the end of the main street. Unusually for Wetherspoon, the building was already a pub before it was adopted by the chain, and it is more modest in size than most. As a result, it has a cosy, homely feel and is popular with locals. It is named after the first iron boat on the nearby Monkland Canal. Up to four guest beers augment the two regulars. A raised area is handy for groups.
(Sunnyside)

Glasgow

Babbity Bowster

16-18 Blackfriars Street, Merchant City, G1 1PE
11 (12.30 Sun)-midnight ☎ (0141) 552 5055
babbitybowster.com
Caledonian Deuchars IPA; Fyne Jarl; guest beer H
A unique establishment with its own decor and ambience, named after a Scottish dance. Located down a small pedestrianised street, it offers a convenient retreat from the Merchant City bustle for a drink or a meal. The café-style bar room has three beers, usually Scottish. Good food served in both the bar and upstairs restaurant features Scottish ingredients but often with French influences. There are a pleasant patio and garden where boules is played in summer.
Q (High St)

Blackfriars L

36 Bell Street, Merchant City, G1 1LG
11 (12.30 Sun)-midnight ☎ (0141) 552 5924
blackfriarsglasgow.com
Beer range varies H
Cosmopolitan corner pub in the heart of Glasgow's Merchant City. Friendly staff serve five changing beers from around the UK, including many Scottish ales and always one from Kelburn Brewing. Interesting bottled beers from the UK, Europe and US are also stocked. Good food helps to keep the pub popular and it can be busy, especially at weekends. A café-style raised corner overlooks two streets, while a quieter rear area offers diners a retreat from the bar room. Live music plays on Tuesday and Sunday nights.
(Argyle St)

Bon Accord

153 North Street, Charing Cross, G3 7DA
11 (12.30 Sun)-midnight ☎ (0141) 248 4427
bonaccordweb.co.uk
Caledonian Deuchars IPA; Marston's Pedigree; guest beers H
Glasgow's first real ale pub, now an institution, has won numerous awards for its ale and cider over the years and has also established a reputation for its malt whiskies – around 400 are currently available, with regular tastings. The long bar hosts 10 beers from Scotland and all over the UK, with several beer festivals a year, often themed, showcasing particular areas. Good home-made food is served until 8pm. Live music is hosted on Saturday night.
(Charing Cross) (2)

Camperdown Place

4-5 West George Street, G2 1DR
11-midnight ☎ (0141) 331 6600
Adnams Broadside; Caledonian Deuchars IPA; Greene King Abbot; guest beers H
Friendly below-street-level pub, situated outside Queen Street station and always busy with travellers. City workers come for lunch or an after-work drink, while locals arrive later in the evening. Eight handpumps offer well-kept beers with ever-changing guests. Smaller than most Wetherspoon pubs, upholstered furniture and Tiffany lamps create a comfortable setting. Upstairs, the covered patio provides views of activities in busy George Square. (Queen St)

Curlers Rest

256-260 Byres Road, Hillhead, G12 8SH
12-midnight ☎ (0141) 341 0737
thecurlersrestglasgow.co.uk
Caledonian Deuchars IPA; Sharp's Doom Bar; Stewart 80/-; guest beers H
The Curlers Rest occupies an 18th-century building on a site where a tavern is reputed to have once existed alongside a curling pond, though little remains of the original building. The large bar downstairs, furnished with a mix of rustic seating and comfortable sofas, offers the full range of cask ales including two guests and world beers. The bar upstairs provides more seating and open fires, though with a smaller range of beers.

Drum & Monkey

91-93 St Vincent Street, G2 5TF
11-midnight; 12.30-11 Sun ☎ (0141) 221 6636
St Austell Nicholson's Pale Ale; guest beers H
City-centre corner pub, previously a bank, handy for both main railway stations. A narrow horseshoe bar sits in the centre of the main room, and two raised areas offer views onto St Vincent and Renfield Street. There is a rear dining room. Good-quality pub food is served throughout. Four guest beers from all over Britain accompany the regular Nicholson's Pale Ale. Beer festivals feature occasionally, with ales on gravity dispense.
(Central)

Edward Wylie

Bothwell Street, G2 6TS
7am-11.30 (midnight Fri & Sat); 8am-11.30 Sun
☎ (0141) 229 5480

INDEPENDENT BREWERIES

Clockwork Glasgow
Drygate Glasgow (NEW)
Houston Houston
Kelburn Barrhead
Strathaven Strathaven

SCOTLAND

Caledonian Deuchars IPA; Greene King Abbot; guest beers [H]
This vibrant city-centre pub, named after the architect who designed the building, is located in the middle of the financial services district. Popular with office workers and shoppers alike, it offers a range of ever-changing beers. The pub hosts a series of beer festivals and Meet the Brewer events across the year, featuring leading breweries and the best of the newcomers, served on 10 handpumps. (Central)

Granary

10 Kilmarnock Road, Shawlands, G41 3NH
12-11; 11-midnight Fri; 10-midnight Sat; 10-11 Sun
(0141) 649 0594
St Austell Nicholson's Pale Ale; guest beer [H]
Two-roomed Nicholson's house in a prominent tenement building at Shawlands Cross. Ales are in the back bar, with one ever-changing guest – usually a pale Scottish beer. The front room is open at weekends and when busy, though it is mostly reserved for diners. TV sport is popular in both rooms. Beer festivals are held twice a year with ales on gravity, dispensed directly from the cask. The pub is well served by public transport.
(Crossmyloof)

Hengler's Circus

351-363 Sauchiehall Street, Charing Cross, G2 3HU
11-midnight (0141) 331 9810
Caledonian Deuchars IPA; Greene King Abbot; guest beers [H]
A spacious Wetherspoon pub with a large number of handpumps providing a wide range of ales from across the UK. It hosts a number of events of interest to real ale drinkers including Meet the Brewer evenings and tap takeovers. An eclectic range of patrons is catered for, including shoppers, theatregoers, students and beer enthusiasts. Well served by public transport, with bus stops and a taxi rank adjacent.
Q (Charing Cross)

Horse Shoe ★

17-19 Drury Street, G2 5AE
11-midnight (01546) 606369
Caledonian Deuchars IPA [H]**; Harviestoun Bitter & Twisted** [P]**; guest beers** [H]
Down a side street near Central Station, the pub has been identified by CAMRA as having a nationally important historic interior. It claims to have the longest continuous bar in Britain at 104ft 3in. Note the embossed mirrors, mosaic floor and stained glass ceiling. Three beers from the Mitchells & Butlers range plus Thwaites and Stewart ales augment the regulars. Good-value meals are served in the bar and upstairs lounge and the pub can be busy lunchtimes and evenings.
Q (Central)

Inn Deep

445 Great Western Road, Hillhead, G12 8HH
12-midnight (11 Sun) (0141) 357 1075 inndeep.com
Beer range varies [P]
Described as a Riverside Craft Beer and BBQ, Inn Deep is situated in arches beside the River Kelvin adjacent to Kelvin Bridge. Its position on the walkway makes it an ideal place for a pint after a walk along the river bank; there is also an entrance on the main road. The pub has strong links with Williams Bros and the three beers on offer often include one of its range along with ales from other more experimental breweries across the country. Popular with young real ale fans.
(6,20)

Laurieston Bar ★

58 Bridge Street, Laurieston, G5 9HU
11-midnight; 12.30-11 Sun (0141) 429 4528
thelauriestonbar.com
Beer range varies [H]
Identified by CAMRA as having a historic interior of national importance, there are few such time capsules remaining. Against all the odds, the original 1960s decor has been retained, down to the formica-topped mini tables and horseshoe bar, all in splendid condition. A selection of Fyne Ales is available in the bar and rear lounge, helping to put the Laurieston firmly on Glasgow's real ale map. Owned and run by two brothers from a publican family, the staff are friendly and welcoming.
(Central)

Mulberry St

778 Pollokshaws Road, Strathbungo, G41 2AE
11-11 (midnight Fri & Sat); 12.30-11 Sun
(0141) 424 0858 mulberrystbarbistro.com
Harviestoun Bitter & Twisted; guest beers [H]
Small community pub in the Strathbungo conservation area, run by an Italian family and named after a street in New York's Little Italy. However, the beers are Scottish, with up to three available from Fyne Ales and Harviestoun, plus continental beers on draught and in bottle and St Mungo lager from German-beer influenced West Brewery. Good food is served in both the bar and bistro. Popular with locals, in summer the seating area outside quickly fills.
(Queen's Park)

Pot Still

154 Hope Street, G2 2TH
11-midnight (0141) 333 0980 thepotstill.co.uk
Beer range varies [H]
Cosy, family-run city bar on a major bus route and not far from both main rail stations. The interior is arranged to seat a surprising number, but it can get busy at times. A mezzanine corner overlooks the bar. Four handpumps serve ever-changing local ales, often including an IPA and a Caledonian seasonal ale. Renowned for stocking over 300 whiskies, enthusiasts come from afar to sample rare bottles. Food includes good-value pies and other pub favourites. (Queen St)

Sir John Stirling Maxwell

136-140 Kilmarnock Road, Shawlands, G41 3NN
11-midnight (0141) 636 9024
Caledonian Deuchars IPA; Greene King Abbot; guest beers [H]
Open-plan Wetherspoon conversion of a supermarket at the south end of Shawlands shopping centre. Ten handpumps dispense mainly higher-strength local and national ales plus one cider. Popular with locals and shoppers, it tends to attract a more mature clientele as well as families dining in a raised area at the rear. A well-run community pub, it hosts regular Meet the Brewer events and occasional brewery trips, plus a monthly quiz. (Pollokshaws East)

Society Room

151 West George Street, G2 2JJ
11-midnight (0141) 229 7560
Greene King Abbot; guest beers [H]

Part obscured by large concrete buttresses, this Wetherspoon Lloyds No.1 bar can be hard to spot at first. Inside it is more conventional, with large windows overlooking the street and a spacious interior extending beyond the long counter to a rear area, used for dining. Popular with locals during the day for the higher-strength beers, in the evening it attracts a pre-club crowd. Music plays and this can be loud until late, especially at the weekend. ◐◑♿⇌(Central)🚇🚌📶

State Bar

148 Holland Street, Charing Cross, G2 4NG (off Sauchiehall St)

🕘 11 (12.30 Sun)-midnight ☎ (0141) 332 2159

Houston Killellan Bitter; Stewart Edinburgh No.3 Premium Scotch Ale; guest beers Ⓗ

Glasgow CAMRA Pub of the Year in 2012, this popular and welcoming bar in the Charing Cross area is handy for restaurants and entertainment venues. As well as the four regular beers there are three guests, often from Scottish breweries including Fyne Ales and Williams Bros, but also from anywhere in Britain. Food is available at lunchtimes only. Live blues features in the public bar on a Tuesday night and comedy in the downstairs room on a Saturday. ◐⇌(Charing Cross)🚇🚌(3,4)

Tennent's

191 Byres Road, Hillhead, G12 8TN

🕘 11 11 (midnight Thu-Sat); 12.30-11 Sun ☎ (0141) 339 7203 🌐 thetennentsbarglasgow.co.uk

Brains Rev James; Caledonian 80; Fuller's London Pride; Harviestoun Natural Blonde; Marston's EPA; St Austell Tribute; guest beers Ⓗ

Tennent's has been at the heart of the community since opening in the 1880s, and although it has undergone many refurbishments it has kept its traditional character. The large open bar with a small lounge to one side is frequented by locals as well as staff and students from the neighbouring university. Several TV screens show mainly sport. The pub offers nine regular beers plus three guests and serves good-value food at all times. ◐◑♿🚇🚌🐾📶

Three Judges

141 Dumbarton Road, Partick, G11 6PR

🕘 11-midnight; 12.30-midnight Sun ☎ (0141) 337 3055 🌐 threejudges.co.uk

Caledonian Deuchars IPA; guest beers Ⓗ

A must-visit for real ale enthusiasts, this is a traditional corner pub. Nine handpumps serve an ever-changing selection of beers, often new ones, from all over Britain, plus a cider. It is all about the beer and the buzz of conversation here, and it can be loud when the pub is busy. Live jazz features every Sunday afternoon. No food is available but it may be brought in. A winner of many CAMRA awards, members receive a 30p per pint discount on ale. Conveniently sited for rail, subway and bus routes. Q⇌(Partick)🚇🍎🚌🐾📶

Ubiquitous Chip

12 Ashton Lane, Hillhead, G12 8SJ

🕘 11-1am ☎ (0141) 334 5007 🌐 ubiquitouschip.co.uk

Caledonian Deuchars IPA; Fyne Chip 71 Ⓟ**; guest beer** Ⓗ

The Chip opened in 1971 as a restaurant in converted stables buildings in a busy lane off Byres Road, and quickly gained a reputation for quality Scottish cuisine. The cosy wine bar upstairs with stained glass panels and an open fire offers a fine selection of wines and whiskies as well as real ales. The small bar downstairs sells the specially brewed Chip 71 and affords easy access to the tables and chairs on the lane. Q◐◑🚇🚌📶

Hamilton

George Bar

18 Campbell Street, ML3 6AS

🕘 12-11.45 (1am Fri); 12.30-11.45 Sun ☎ (01698) 424225

Beer range varies Ⓗ

Traditional family-run pub in a pedestrianised area just off the inner ring road in the town. It has been gradually renovated over the years and café-style seating added outside, but it has always retained its character. Three ever-changing beers frequently include guests from the nearby Strathaven Ales, attracting locals and visitors. Two beer festivals are held each year. Meals are served until 6pm (no food Sun). ◐♿⇌(Central)🚌

Inverkip

Inverkip Hotel

Main Street, PA16 0AS

🕘 11 (12.30 Sun)-11.30 ☎ (01475) 521478 🌐 inverkip.co.uk

Arran Red Squirrel; guest beer Ⓗ

Small family-run hotel just a short walk from the large Inverkip Marina, making it an ideal staging post for those just messing about on the river or passing through on the way to Largs and the Ayrshire coast. This is the only outlet in the area that regularly sells beer from the Isle of Arran Brewery, with a guest usually from another local brewery. ❀🛏◐◑⇌P🚌(578,580)

Johnstone

Callum's

26 High Street, PA5 8AH

🕘 11-11.30 (1am Fri & Sat); 12.30-midnight Sun ☎ (01505) 322925 🌐 callums-bar.com

Caledonian Deuchars IPA; Kelburn Pivo Estivo; Orkney Dark Island; guest beers Ⓗ

Popular town-centre pub offering a friendly welcome and a comfortable atmosphere. A large but unobtrusive TV screen features major sporting events. The lounge has an area for formal dining with themed nights. There is a function room for private parties. Quiz night is Thursday, live music plays on Saturday and open mic night is Sunday. Six real ales are available, mainly from local Kelburn and Houston breweries. ◐◑♿⇌🚌(36,38)

Kilbarchan

Glen Leven Inn

25 New Street, PA10 2LN

🕘 11.45-11 (midnight Thu; 1am Fri & Sat); 12.30-midnight Sun ☎ (01505) 702481

Beer range varies Ⓗ

Busy local pub within a conservation village and 100 yards from the famous Weaver's Cottage owned by the National Trust. Ales are from the Punch Taverns list. The pool table and TV screens attract the locals. Look for 'Piper Habbie' above the fireplace. Live music is hosted most Saturday and Sunday nights plus a quiz on Tuesday evenings. The beer garden is popular in summer. Food is served in the separate Weavers Restaurant. ❀◐◑♿P🚌(36)🐾

Kilmacolm

Pullman Tavern

Elthinstone Court, Lochwinnoch Road, PA13 4LG

⚙ 11-11 (midnight Wed; 1am Fri & Sat); 12.30-11 Sun
☎ (01505) 874501

Beer range varies Ⓗ

This Mitchells & Butlers establishment is the only pub in a small conservation village and was converted from a railway station that once served this area of the countryside. There is a large seating area outside which is particularly popular in the summer months with families, walkers and cyclists. A Sustrans cycle path from Paisley to Gourock passes by the building.
❀◑♿P🚌 (X7)🐾📶

Kirkintilloch

Kirky Puffer

1-11 Townhead, G66 1NG (by canal)

⚙ 11-midnight (1am Fri) ☎ (0141) 775 4140

Caledonian Deuchars IPA; Greene King Abbot; guest beers Ⓗ

Named after the small steamboats that were built nearby, this large Wetherspoon pub has a spacious feel with various nooks and crannies offering different environments in which to enjoy a drink and a meal. Guest beers constantly change and have a Scottish flavour, although American-style and English IPAs make regular appearances. A family-friendly pub holding various community events, it is also popular with travellers on the canal and Antonine Way. Served by regular buses to Glasgow. Q🛋◑♿🚌 (X85,88)📶

Lanark

Clydesdale Inn

15 Bloomgate, ML11 9ET

⚙ 11-1am; 12.30-11.30 Sun ☎ (01555) 678740

Caledonian Deuchars IPA; Greene King Abbot; guest beers Ⓗ

A Wetherspoon conversion of a former coaching inn that can name Wordsworth and Dickens as former visitors. Today it is a community-friendly pub, popular with locals, but also a convenient hostelry for visitors to New Lanark Village and Falls of Clyde. The central bar hosts eight handpumps serving a selection of beers from all over the UK. There are two rooms to the side and another to the rear which is used at busy times and for functions.
Q🛋◑♿⛺≷P🚌📶

> There is not a brewer who doesn't doctor his beer with something or other. Really something is in it.
> Four glasses made a Brooklyn man shoot down Dr Duggan in cold blood. Beer made a New York husband put a hole through his wife with a 22-calibre defender. Murder is in it. Who drinks lager beer is too apt to swallow the murder with it.
> **Elisha Chenery MD, 1889**

Lochwinnoch

Brown Bull

32 Main Street, PA12 4AH

⚙ 12-11 (midnight Fri; 11.45 Sat); 12.30-11 Sun
☎ (01505) 843250

Caledonian Deuchars IPA; guest beers Ⓗ

A family-run free house, this village pub is more than 200 years old. Popular with locals and visitors alike, it offers an ever-changing choice of three guest ales. Quiz night is Tuesday and live music features every second Sunday. Meals are available in the bar and in the restaurant upstairs, made with local produce. ❀◑♿🍎🚌🐾📶

Newton Mearns

Osprey

Stewarton Road, G77 6NP

⚙ 12-11; 12.30-10.30 Sun ☎ (0141) 639 7453

Caledonian Deuchars IPA; guest beer Ⓗ

This refurbished pub retains an olde-worlde theme with oak beams and stone floors. It has four rooms off a main bar area. Opposite the bar, the snugs are adorned with various tiles and artwork. The restaurant area to the right has pictures with a golf theme, while the area on the left is more mix and match. It's an ideal refreshment stop for visitors to the nearby Pollok House and Burrell Collection of artworks. 🛋❀◑♿♣P🚌 (44A)🐾📶

Paisley

Bull Inn ★ L

7 New Street, PA1 1XU

⚙ 11-midnight (1am Fri & Sat); 12.30-midnight Sun
☎ (0141) 849 0472 🌐 bullinnpaisley.co.uk

Caledonian Deuchars IPA; guest beers Ⓗ

Established in 1901 and identified by CAMRA as having a nationally important historic interior, this is the oldest inn in Paisley. The pub retains many original features including stained-glass windows, three small snugs and a spirit cask gantry, and boasts the only original set of spirit cocks left in Scotland. Guest ales are usually Scottish, with an emphasis on the local Houston and Kelburn breweries. ◑≷(Gilmour St)🚌🐾📶

Corkers Bar 🏆 L

51 Causeyside Street, PA1 1YN

⚙ 11-11 (midnight Thu; 1am Fri); 12.30-midnight Sun
☎ (0141) 889 5333

Kelburn Pivo Estivo, Red Smiddy, Jaguar Ⓗ

A Paisley institution – this pub was closed for several years before making its long-overdue return in 2013. The open-plan bar has six large TV screens showing sport or news. Live music or a DJ play occasionally. Excellent home-cooked food is served daily. There are three handpumps dispensing beer from the local Kelburn Brewing. A welcome addition to Paisley's small real ale portfolio. 🛋◑≷(Canal)🚌📶

Harvies Bar L

86 Glasgow Road, PA1 3NU

⚙ 11-midnight (1am Fri & Sat); 12.30-midnight Sun
☎ (0141) 889 0911

Kelburn Goldihops; Theakston XB Ⓗ

Popular tenement-style local situated on the main Paisley to Glasgow road. The spacious open-plan bar, with raised seating, has three large TV screens showing sport and music videos with the volume turned down low. The pub can get busy during major football matches. Sunday features a quiz night and Monday is poker night. Live music or a DJ play occasionally. The guest beer is from the local Kelburn Brewing. ◐♿⇌(Hawkhead)🚌(9,36)📶

Last Post

2 County Square, PA1 1BN
8am-midnight ☎ (0141) 849 6911
Caledonian Deuchars IPA; Greene King Abbot; Ruddles Best Bitter; guest beers
Large Wetherspoon pub converted from the town's main post office. Open plan in design, there is plenty of seating. The standard food menu is available. Next to Gilmour Street railway station and close to the bus station, it is handy for a pint between trains or buses. It was the first Wetherspoon pub to hold a Battle of the Brewers competition and continues to run them regularly throughout the year. Six guest ales are usually available. ◐♿⇌(Gilmour St)🚌(9,36)📶

Renfrew

Lord of the Isles

Unit 21 Xscape, Kings Inch Road, PA4 8XQ
8am-midnight (1am Fri & Sat) ☎ (0141) 886 8930
Greene King Abbot; guest beers
Large, purpose-built Wetherspoon establishment attached to the Xscape Leisure Complex with its cinema, ski slope and rock climbing. A short stroll allows you to watch the ships docked at Yarrows Shipyard. Throughout the pub the walls display photographs depicting the history of industry on the River Clyde. The outside seating area is south facing and a suntrap on warm summer days. Food is available all day and three ever-changing guest ales are on handpump. ❀◐♿P🚌📶

Rutherglen

An Ruadh Ghlean

40-44 Main Street, G73 2HY
11-11.45; 8am-midnight Fri & Sat ☎ (0141) 613 2370
Caledonian Deuchars IPA; Greene King Abbot; guest beers
A recent opening by Wetherspoon in the former real ale desert of Rutherglen, one of the oldest royal burghs in Scotland. An Ruadh Ghlean is the Gaelic name for the burgh, meaning 'the red valley'. The long, narrow pub has three distinct seating areas, with views of the pub's cellar from the windows at the rear. Outside is a smoking area and multi-level garden. Q❀◐♿⇌🚌📶

Strathaven

Weavers

1-3 Green Street, ML10 6LT
5.30 (11.30 Mon)-midnight; 5.30-1am Thu; 11.30-1am Fri & Sat; 2-1am Sun ☎ 07749 332914
Beer range varies
Local CAMRA Pub of the Year for 2013, this family-run pub takes its name from the town's historic industry. A community hub and meeting place, the single room has a modern feel and is decorated with black and white photographs of pop singers and movie stars of yesteryear. Four handpumps offer an ever-changing range of beers, the fourth coming exclusively from the nearby Strathaven Ales. ♿🚌(13)📶

Uplawmoor

Uplawmoor Hotel

66 Neilston Road, G78 4AF (off A736)
11-11 (midnight Sat); 12.30-11 Sun ☎ (01505) 850565
uplawmoor.co.uk
Houston Killellan Bitter; Kelburn Red Smiddy
Situated in a tranquil village setting just over 10 miles from Glasgow, the building dates back to the 18th century. It was originally a coaching inn used by travellers and customs officers chasing smugglers en-route between Glasgow and the south-west coast of Scotland. Today the hotel continues to offer travellers the opportunity to relax and explore. The interior is rustic and cosy with a public bar, pool room and lounge bar. Bar meals are served until 9.30pm.
❀◐♿P🚌(395,X44B)📶

Wishaw

Wishaw Malt

62-66 Kirk Road, ML2 7BL
8am-midnight (1am Fri & Sat) ☎ (01360) 660245
Greene King Abbot; Ruddles Best Bitter; guest beers
Former furniture store converted into a pub a decade ago, taking the name of a Wishaw distillery of the 19th century. In many ways a typical small-town Wetherspoon pub, it buzzes with the sound of conversation, and TVs show racing in the background. Beers come from all over, with a preference for pale and blonde ales. To the side is a narrow patio beer garden. Breakfast is available from 8am every day. ❀◐♿⇌🚌(240,267)📶

SCOTLAND

The ale diet

Boniface: Sir, I have now in my cellar ten tun of the best ale in Staffordshire; 'tis smooth as oil, sweet as milk, clear as amber, and strong as brandy; and will be just 14 years old the fifth day of next March, old style.
Aimwell: You're very exact, I find, in the age of your ale.
Boniface: As punctual, sir, as I am in the age of my children. I'll show you such ale: I have lived in Lichfield, man and boy, about eight-and-fifty years, and, I believe, have not consumed eight-and-fifty ounces of meat.
Aimwell: At a meal, you mean, if one may guess your sense by your bulk.
Boniface: Not in my life, sir, I have fed purely upon ale; I have eat my ale, drank my ale, and I always sleep upon ale.
George Farquhar, The Beaux-Stratagem, 1701

HIGHLANDS & WESTERN ISLES

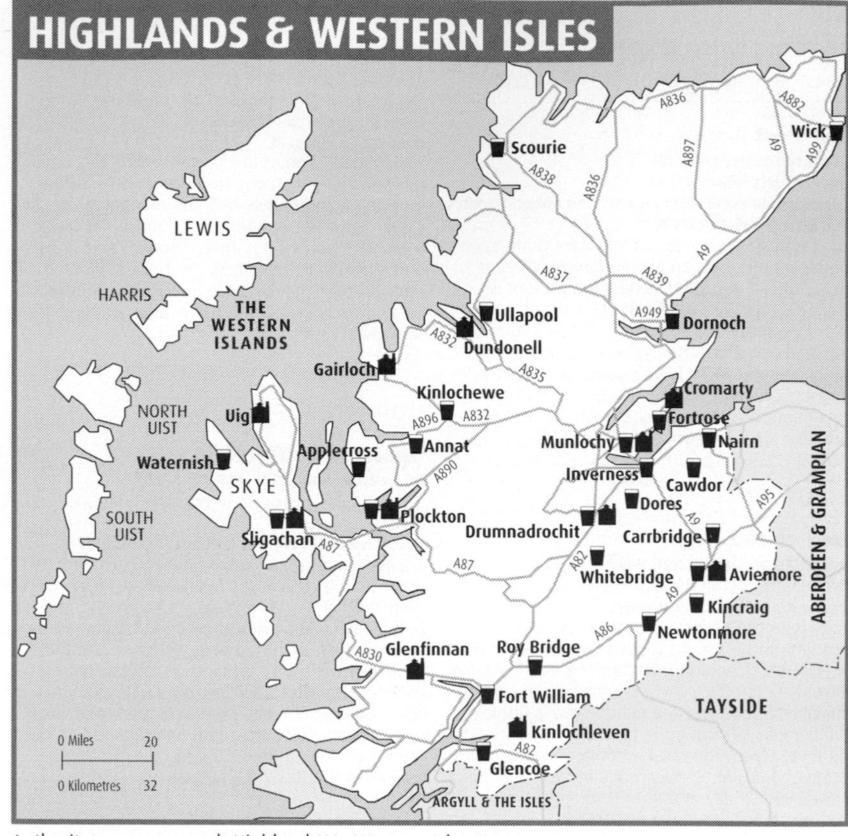

Authority areas covered: Highland UA, Western Isles UA

Annat

Torridon Inn

IV22 2EY (just off A896, at head of Loch Torridon)
NG889541
11-11 (Thu-Sat only Nov-Mar); 12 (5 Nov-Mar)-11 Sun
(01445) 791242 thetorridon.com/inn
Beer range varies H

One or two ales are served in the winter with up to six in summer. Real cider is also sometimes available in the summer months. An excellent base for outdoor enthusiasts and families alike, it opens early for breakfast at 8am and serves good food all day in generous portions. Traditional music features weekly in the summer and there is a beer festival in October. The inn is closed from early December to mid-February.

Applecross

Applecross Inn

Shore Street, IV54 8LR NG710444
11-11.30 (midnight Fri); 12.30-11.30 Sun
(01520) 744062 applecross.uk.com/inn
Beer range varies H

On the shore of the Applecross Peninsula, enjoying views of the Isle of Skye and Raasay, the inn is reached by a single track road over the highest vehicular ascent in Britain, or by a longer scenic coastal route, but is well worth seeking out. Isle of Skye and An Teallach beers are served alongside a large malt whisky selection. This small family-run inn is renowned for its award-winning local seafood and venison.

Aviemore

Cairngorm Hotel

Grampian Road, PH22 1PE (opp railway station)
11-midnight (1am Fri & Sat); 11.30-midnight Sun
(01479) 810233
Cairngorm Stag, Gold H

The lounge bar of this privately owned hotel, though large, has a cosy feel. Although the trade is mainly holidaymakers, the bar is popular with locals, with a large-screen TV showing sport. Decorated with tartan wall coverings, there is a Scottish theme throughout the hotel, and Scottish entertainment features on many afternoons and evenings.

Old Bridge Inn

Dalfaber Road, PH22 1PU
12-midnight (1am Fri & Sat); 12.30-midnight Sun
(01479) 811137 oldbridgeinn.co.uk
Cairngorm Trade Winds; Caledonian Deuchars IPA; guest beer H

Busy pub, popular with outdoor enthusiasts, serving good-quality food made with locally-sourced ingredients. Originally a cottage and now greatly enlarged, it lies on the road to the Strathspey Steam Railway overlooking the River Spey. The two guest handpumps dispense the seasonal offering from the local Cairngorm Brewery plus another Scottish ale. Live entertainment is hosted twice weekly, including traditional and modern Scottish music and bands. Children are welcome and there is a bunkhouse attached. P (15,15X)

Carrbridge

Cairn Hotel (Rowanlea Bar)

Main Road, PH23 3AS (just off A9 on B9153 to N of Carrbridge)
11-midnight (1am Fri & Sat); 12.30-11 Sun
(01479) 841212 cairnhotel.co.uk
Beer range varies H
Along the road from the Landmark Adventure Park, the Cairn is a traditional Highland inn with seven guest rooms. It is in the Cairngorm National Park and is popular with both locals and visitors. Freshly cooked, seasonal bar meals are available alongside three real ales. Local beers from the Black Isle and Cairngorm breweries are favourites, and the third pump features a different Scottish guest ale with every cask. P

Cawdor

Cawdor Tavern

The Lane, IV12 5XP (from A96 take B9090) NH845500
11-11 (midnight Fri & Sat) summer; 11-3 (midnight Fri & Sat) winter; 12.30-11 Sun (01667) 404777
cawdortavern.com
Beer range varies H
Owned by the same family for nearly 20 years, the pub is at the heart of this conservation village, a short walk from the famous castle and within easy reach of local historic attractions. It has a spacious lounge and cosy public bar, both wood panelled and with log fires, and a large restaurant. Up to five handpumps offer Orkney and Atlas ales – the family also owns the Orkney Brewery at Quoyloo. The Cawdor has a reputation for good food.
QP

Dores

Dores Inn

IV2 6TR (on B862 from Inverness at B852 jct)
11-11 (midnight Fri & Sat); 12.30-11 Sun
(01463) 751203 thedoresinn.co.uk
Beer range varies H
On the south side of Loch Ness, just eight miles from Inverness, this inn enjoys spectacular views and is ideal for Nessie spotting. The cosy wood-finished bar serves up to four ales, nearly always from Scottish independent breweries, with an occasional English ale featured. The welcoming, extended dining room serves good food made with locally-sourced ingredients and can get busy at times. Home baking is available and the inn opens at 10am for coffee. QP (302,303)

Dornoch

Dornoch Castle Hotel

Castle Street, IV25 3SD
11-11 (1am Fri; 11.45 Sat); 12.30-11 Sun
(01862) 810216 dornochcastlehotel.com
Cromarty Happy Chappy; guest beers H
It is worth diverting off the A9 to Dornoch Castle Hotel just to marvel at the interior of the building, parts of which date back to 1577; it has been refurbished while retaining its original character. Up to three ales from Cairngorm, Cromarty and Orkney breweries are usually available, alongside a massive collection of 300 single malt whiskies. Local attractions include the 13th-century cathedral opposite, golf course and beaches.
QP (25X,X99)

Drumnadrochit

Benleva Hotel

Kilmore Road, IV63 6UH (signed 800yds from A82)
12-midnight (1am Fri); 12.30-11 Sun (01456) 450080
benleva.co.uk
Beer range varies H
Popular, friendly village inn near Loch Ness, catering for locals and visitors. A 400-year-old former manse, the sweet chestnut outside was once a hanging tree. Six handpumps dispense Loch Ness Brewery ales accompanied by other Scottish offerings and real cider. Lunches, evening meals and Sunday roasts are available. Entertainment includes poker nights, occasional quiz nights and traditional music. Home of the famous Loch Ness Beer Festival in September and local CAMRA Pub of the Year in 2013. P

SCOTLAND

Fort William

Ben Nevis Inn

Achintee Road, Claggan, PH33 6TE NN125729
12-11 (closed Mon-Wed Nov-Mar) (01397) 701227
ben-nevis-inn.co.uk
Beer range varies H
The inn is housed in a characterful 200-year-old building in beautiful Glen Nevis at the start of the Ben Nevis mountain path, close to the end of the West Highland Way. The bar, with long beer hall-style tables, is an ideal setting for live music, hosted every Tuesday in summer. The daily-changing menu offers a mix of traditional favourites and innovative international dishes made with fresh local produce, to accompany a choice of three ales sourced from local breweries. Bunkhouse accommodation sleeps up to 20 people. QP

Cobbs at Nevisport

Airds Crossing, PH33 6EU (beneath Nevisport shop)
11-midnight (1am Fri & Sat); 12.30-midnight Sun
(01397) 704790 cobbs-at-nevisport.co.uk
Beer range varies H
At the West Highland Way finish and Great Glen Way start, convenient for the Ben Nevis range, this is a favourite meeting place for outdoor enthusiasts. A large open fire warms the bar which is adorned with classic mountaineering photographs and historic skiing gear. Four

INDEPENDENT BREWERIES

An Teallach Dundonell
Black Isle Munlochy
Cairngorm Aviemore
Cromarty Cromarty
Cuillin Sligachan: Isle of Skye
Glenfinnan Glenfinnan
Isle of Skye Uig: Isle of Skye
Loch Ness Drumnadrochit
Old Inn Gairloch
Plockton Plockton
River Leven Kinlochleven

handpumps dispense a regularly changing range of real ales from various Highlands and Islands breweries. Bar meals are served all day and children are welcome in the upstairs restaurant. Regular music nights feature local bands.
P

Grog & Gruel

66 High Street, PH33 6AE
12-11.30 (12.30am Thu-Sat); 12.30 (5 winter)-11.30 Sun
(01397) 705078 grogandgruel.co.uk
Beer range varies H
Award-winning traditional ale house located halfway along the pedestrianised high street, just a few steps from the end of the West Highland Way. Up to six predominantly Scottish beers are served, fewer in winter. Light bar meals and snacks are available all day, and evening meals in the upstairs restaurant. Popular with locals, tourists and outdoor enthusiasts, regular events include live music, open mic nights and beer festivals.

Fortrose

Anderson

Union Street, IV10 8TD
4 (3 Sun)-11.30 (01381) 620236 theanderson.co.uk
Beer range varies H
A huge selection of ales, malt whiskies and Belgian beers has been served here over the years. The food menu offers must-try global cuisine featuring local ingredients. Wood-burning stoves keep the rooms cosy and warm. Quiz and music nights are hosted weekly. During the winter months CAMRA members can book a two-night stay with the second night free. The pub closes for four weeks in November. Q P (26)

Glencoe

Clachaig Inn

PH49 4HX (on slip road off A82)
11-11 (midnight Fri; 11.30 Sat); 12.30-11 Sun
(01855) 811252 clachaig.com
Beer range varies H
Nestling among spectacular mountains, the Clachaig is frequented by climbers, walkers and tourists who come for the stunning scenery. The main bar, furnished with wooden benches and upholstered seating around the walls, has up to 15 handpumps serving beers from a wide range of Scottish breweries. Even the lagers are brewed by Scottish micros. A hearty food menu is on offer throughout the day. Live music often plays at weekends. P (916)

Inverness

Blackfriars

93-95 Academy Street, IV1 1LU
11 (4.30 Mon)-11.30; 11-1am Fri; 11-12.30am Sat; 2-9 Sun
(01463) 233881 blackfriarshighlandpub.co.uk
Caledonian Golden XPA; guest beers H
This popular traditional pub has a spacious single-room interior with a large standing area by the bar and ample seating in comfortable alcoves. The five handpumps deliver a combination of Scottish and English ales, with Scottish beers often from Orkney and Highland breweries and local ales from Loch Ness, Cairngorm and Cromarty. Good-value home-cooked Scottish fare is served with daily specials including a home-made soup. A welcoming music-oriented venue, bands perform at weekends.

Castle Tavern

1 View Place, IV2 4SA (top of Castle St)
11-1am (12.30am Sat); 12-midnight Sun
(01463) 718178 castletavern.net
Beer range varies H
A 73-mile hike along the Great Glen Way or a five-minute stroll from the city centre brings you to this friendly hostelry in a listed building facing the Castle and boasting fine views across the River Ness towards the Cathedral. Six handpumps dispense a changing range of beers and beer styles, often featuring Scottish independents and LocAle breweries. Bar meals are served all day, and there is a separate first-floor restaurant. A Victorian-style canopy covers the large beer patio.

Clachnaharry Inn

17-19 High Street, Clachnaharry, IV3 8RB (on A862 Beauly road)
11-11 (midnight Thu; 1am Fri & Sat); 12-11 Sun
(01463) 239806 clachnaharryinn.co.uk
Beer range varies H
Popular with locals and visitors, this friendly 17th-century coaching inn offers high-quality food made with locally-sourced ingredients lunchtimes and evenings, and families are welcome. Four handpumps dispense Scottish beers from Inveralmond, Orkney, Atlas and Cairngorm as well as some from Greene King breweries. The large patio area affords fine views over the Caledonian Canal sea lock and Beauly Firth toward the Munro Ben Wyvis. Quiz night is Wednesday and a Scottish music jamming session is hosted every Thursday evening. Q P (28A)

Corriegarth

5-7 Heathmount Road, IV2 3JU
11-midnight (1am Fri & Sat); 12-midnight Sun
(01463) 242730 corriegarth.com
Caledonian Deuchars IPA; Cromarty Happy Chappy; guest beers H
The Corriegarth is one of Inverness's oldest private hotels, constructed around 1840. It is situated in the Crown area of Inverness, a two-minute walk from the city centre, and has six en-suite bedrooms. It has recently been refurbished to a high standard and is a comfortable, friendly place. In addition to the regular beers, there is a Punch house ale and an occasional guest beer.
Q P

King's Highway

72-74 Church Street, IV1 1EN
7am-midnight (1am Thu & Fri); 7am-midnight Sun
(01463) 251830
Adnams Broadside; Caledonian Deuchars IPA; Fuller's London Pride; Greene King Abbot; Sharp's Doom Bar; guest beers H
This former hotel is now a Wetherspoon pub with a 27-room lodge attached which was refurbished in 2013. The vast single-roomed bar is broken up by several pillars and plenty of comfortable seating in alcoves. Up to 10 handpumps serve the regular ales alongside a good mix of guests, including beers from Houston, Cairngorm and An Teallach. Food is standard Wetherspoon fare. Customers are the typical eclectic mix and the pub gets busy at weekends. P

Number 27

27 Castle Street, IV2 3DU
11-11 (12.30am Fri & Sat); 12.30-11 Sun
(01463) 241999
Beer range varies H
Alongside the four handpumps, this popular city-centre bar/restaurant offers a large bottled range including continental brews. There is usually an ale from Windswept and Loch Ness breweries, accompanied by one or two from other Scottish micros. A wide selection of malt whiskies is also stocked. The venue has a reputation for good food – lunches range from sandwiches to light bites while the comprehensive evening menu features traditional main courses made with locally-sourced ingredients including venison and steak.

Kincraig

Suie Hotel

PH21 1NA (at head of Loch Insh on B9152) NH829057
5-11 (1am Fri & Sat) (01540) 651344 suiehotel.com
Cairngorm Trade Winds; guest beer H
Victorian character hotel located at the south end of the village, run by only the second owner in 108 years. The wooden-floored bar features a large wood-burning stove plus a pool table and jukebox. Three pumps dispense a selection from the local Cairngorm Brewery plus another Scottish guest. Close to the River Spey and Loch Insh, the bar is popular with locals, hillwalkers, skiers and cyclists. Traditional Scottish music is hosted regularly and good food is served. P (209)

Kinlochewe

Kinlochewe Hotel

IV22 2PA (beside A832 on Gairloch Road) NH028619
11 (12.30 Sun)-midnight (01445) 760253
kinlochewehotel.co.uk
Beer range varies H
Friendly, family-run 1800s coaching inn. Set in the heart of the magnificent Torridon mountains at the foot of Beinn Eighe, this is an ideal base for exploring the wild scenery of the north-western Highlands. Freshly cooked seasonal dishes are made with high-quality local produce including seafood, game and beef, with an emphasis on simplicity and flavour. Up to five handpumps serve ales from An Teallach and Orkney with a guest in summer. The cider is Westons Family Reserve. A 12-bed bunkhouse is attached.
Q P

Munlochy

Allangrange Arms

58 Millbank Road, IV8 8NL
11-11 (1am Fri & Sat) (01463) 819862
allangrangearms.com
Cromarty Happy Chappy; guest beer H
Popular and modern family-friendly pub in the highland village of Munlochy. Two Scottish real ales are on handpump, three in the summer. Quality food made with local produce is served every day and a children's menu is available. The bar area has cosy booth seating, the small open-plan lounge has sofas and big-screen TV for sport. There is a separate restaurant area and a private function room. Live music features regularly. Seating outside is pleasant on warmer days.
Q P (26)

Nairn

Braeval Hotel

Crescent Road, IV12 4NB
12-midnight (12.30am Thu-Sat) (01667) 452341
braevalhotel.co.uk
Beer range varies H
The family-run Bandstand Bar in the Braeval Hotel has nine handpumps (fewer in winter) offering a good selection of English and Scottish ales. Real cider is available in the summer. A week-long beer festival is hosted every spring with at least 100 ales and live music throughout the event. The hotel has a popular sea-view restaurant and 10 en-suite rooms. CAMRA members receive a 10 per cent discount on accommodation. Highlands & Western Isles Pub of the Year 2014.
Q P

Newtonmore

Glen Hotel

Main Street, PH20 1DD
11 (12.30 Sun)-midnight (01540) 673203
theglenhotel.co.uk
Beer range varies H
Small, welcoming, family-run Edwardian hotel with the Monadhliath and Cairngorm mountain ranges on its doorstep. It has a good local trade and is also popular with outdoor enthusiasts and tourists. There is a large bar room and separate games and dining rooms, with regular quiz and games nights. Up to three handpumps dispense mainly Scottish beers, usually including one from Cairngorm and Caledonian breweries, plus a Westons cider or perry in the summer. An extensive menu includes a good selection of vegetarian dishes.
P

Plockton

Plockton Hotel

41 Harbour Street, IV52 8TN NG803334
11-midnight; 12.30-11 Sun (01599) 544274
plocktonhotel.co.uk
Beer range varies H
Sheltered by mountains and fanned by the warm air of the Gulf Stream, the hotel is at the edge of Loch Carron and boasts breathtaking views across the bay. Seafood is the speciality on an excellent menu that also features locally reared beef and venison. The village has much to offer and is a regular haunt for outdoor enthusiasts. Brews from a variety of Highlands and other Scottish micros are regularly on handpump including a house ale from Inveralmond. Closed throughout January.
Q P

Plockton Inn

Innes Street, IV52 8TW NG802333
11-1am (12.30am Sat); 11-11 Sun (01599) 544222
plocktoninn.co.uk
Beer range varies H
Located in a picture-postcard Highland village, this popular inn has been owned and run by a local family for many years. Locally caught fish and shellfish take pride of place on the menu – the seafood platter includes fish smoked on the premises. Every Tuesday and Thursday there are live music sessions in the public bar and all are welcome to join in. The real ales include locally brewed Plockton Brewery beers.
Q P

SCOTLAND

Roy Bridge

Stronlossit Inn

Main Street, PH31 4AG NN272812
11-11.45 (1am Thu-Sat); 12.30-11.45 Sun
☎ (01397) 712253 stronlossit.co.uk
Beer range varies H
Privately owned Scottish country inn and hotel in the heart of Lochaber, an ideal base for exploring the Ben Nevis range, the Great Glen and the Parallel Roads of Glen Roy. Three handpumps dispense a selection of Scottish beers, often from Highlands and Islands breweries, plus an occasional cider. Freshly prepared food made with ingredients sourced from local suppliers is served all day. High-quality budget rooms, adjacent to the main hotel, are designed to meet the needs of outdoor enthusiasts. Q❀🛏◑♿▲⇌🍎P🚌

Scourie

Scourie Hotel

IV27 4SX (on A894 between Laxford Bridge and Kylesku) NC156447
11-11 summer; 5-8.30; 12-2.30, 5-11 Sat, 6-9 Sun winter
☎ (01971) 502396 scourie-hotel.co.uk
Beer range varies H
Converted 1640 coaching inn in the heart of the wonderland wilderness of north-west Sutherland. Close to the Handa Island ferry, and a short drive to the peaks of Arkle and Foinavon, this is an ideal base for exploring. It is also popular with fishermen who enjoy access to around 300 lochs with 46 hotel-controlled beats. In addition to a fixed bar menu, the dining room offers high quality meals featuring seafood. Four handpumps serve mainly Scottish beers and a cider. Closed weekday lunchtimes in winter. Q❀🛏◑▲♣🍎P

Sligachan: Isle of Skye

Sligachan Hotel

IV47 8SW NG485298
10-11.30 ☎ (01478) 650204 sligachan.co.uk
Beer range varies H
Home to the Cuillin Brewery, the Sligachan Hotel has served mountaineers, walkers and lovers of the wild Highlands scenery for nearly 180 years, and has been in the same family for the last 100. Open from March to the end of October, with the larger Seumas Bar open from May to September, up to to four ales are available in season, usually from Cuillin but sometimes a guest. Seumas Bar also stocks over 370 Scottish malts, 90 of them on optics. ❀🛏◑♿▲P🚌🐾

Ullapool

Argyll Hotel

18 Argyll Street, IV26 2UB
11-1am; 12-midnight Sun ☎ (01854) 612422
theargyllullapool.com
Beer range varies H
Busy, small hotel offering breakfast, lunch and dinner all made with locally-sourced produce, with good vegetarian and coeliac choices. The beer range includes three changing guest ales plus another from the local An Teallach brewery. Live music features on Monday and live bands play on Tuesday and weekends March-October. There are regular beer festivals including a cider and blues music festival in September. A weekly curry night, quiz and poker keep the bar busy. Ideally located for the ferry to the Hebrides.
❀🛏◑♿▲♣🍎P🚌🐾

Morefield Motel

North Road, IV26 2TQ (off A835)
12 (12.30 Sun)-11 ☎ (01854) 612161
morefieldmotel.co.uk
Beer range varies H
Locally caught seafood is the speciality on the menu at this family-run, friendly motel. Three ales are predominantly from local Highlands breweries and include at least one from Cairngorm. The annual Ullapool beer festival is held here in October. The Western Isles ferry terminal in the centre of Ullapool is a short distance away. Winter opening hours vary. Q❀🛏◑♿▲P🚌🐾

Waternish: Isle of Skye

Stein Inn

MacLeod's Terrace, IV55 8GA (N of Dunvegan, on B886) NG263564
11-midnight (1am Fri; 12.30am Sat); 11.30-11 Sun summer; 12-11 (midnight Fri & Sat) winter
☎ (01470) 592362 steininn.co.uk
Beer range varies H
Dating back to the 18th century, this is the oldest inn on the Isle of Skye, nestling in a row of whitewashed cottages on the shores of Loch Bay, owned and run by the same family for 20 years. A large stove warms the cosy low-beamed bar which has fine views over the sea loch to Rubha Maol. Locally caught seafood, landed at the nearby jetty, is served Easter to October in the bar and restaurant. Guest ales are from Cairngorm, Highland and Loch Ness. For seafarers there are four council moorings. Q❀🛏◑♿♣P🐾

Whitebridge

Whitebridge Hotel

IV2 6UN (on B862, SW side of Loch Ness) NH487152
11 (12 Sun)-11 summer; 11-2.30, 5-11; 11-11 Sat; 12-11 Sun winter ☎ (01456) 486226 whitebridgehotel.co.uk
Beer range varies H
Built in 1899 and located on the quiet side of Loch Ness, this hotel has fishing rights on two local lochs. Inside, the attractive pitch pine-panelled bar, with a welcoming wood-burning stove, has an alcove with a pool table and a separate area used for dining. Most of the traditional pub food is home cooked. One or two ales are stocked, usually from Cairngorm and Cromarty. The hotel has a green tourism policy. Q❀🛏◑♿♣P🚌(301)🐾

Wick

Alexander Bain

Market Place, KW1 4LP (in pedestrianised area)
8am-11 ☎ (01955) 609920
Caledonian Deuchars IPA; guest beers H
Currently the most northerly Wetherspoon pub in the UK and once the Wick post office, it is named after the locally born inventor. The large one-room bar has many comfortable alcoves. Three handpumps (two in winter) serve slightly fewer ales than the usual Wetherspoon offering, but the standard reasonably priced meals are available. Always busy with locals, music groups play regularly. Q❀◑♿▲⇌P🚌(X97,X99)

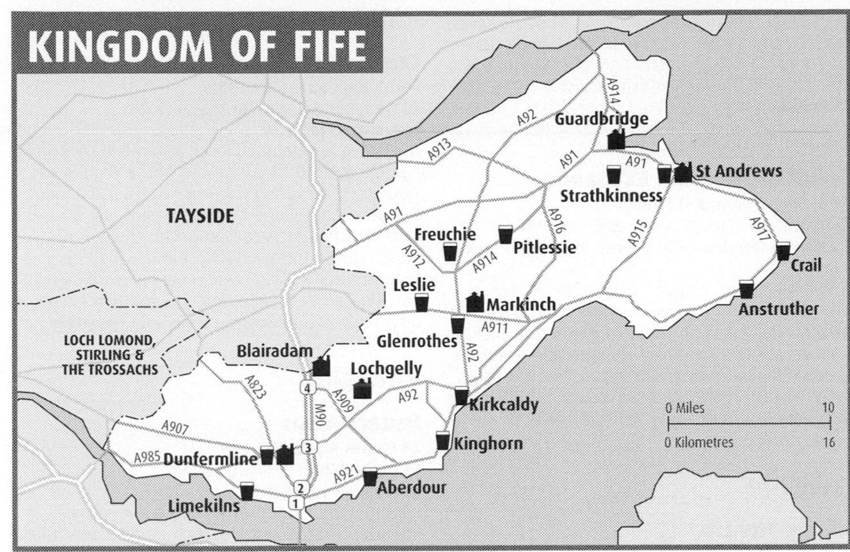

Authority area covered: Fife UA

Aberdour

Cedar Inn

20 Shore Street, KY3 0TR

11 (12.30 Sun)-11.45 ☎ (01383) 860310
thecedarinn.co.uk

Beer range varies Ⓗ

A lovely white building just off the Fife coastal path. Enter through the front door and to your left is a lounge restaurant, to the right is a small bar counter with three handpulls and an extensive whisky range. Enjoy a quiet drink in the conservatory or continue through to the main bar, where you can enjoy a wide range of TV sport.

Foresters Arms

35 High Street, KY3 0SJ

11 (12.30 Sun)-midnight ☎ (01383) 860544
forries.co.uk

Caledonian Deuchars IPA; guest beers Ⓗ

A pub at the centre of the community, right in the middle of the village, only minutes away from the railway station. An ideal stop-off for walkers on the Fife coastal path, this family-run inn offers a friendly welcome to all. Live music, quizzes and theme nights are held regularly. Warm yourself by the real coal fire, and enjoy a good pub lunch.

Anstruther

Boathouse (Salutation)

28 Shore Street, KY10 3AQ

12-11 (midnight Fri & Sat) ☎ (01333) 312105
at-the-shore.co.uk

Beer range varies Ⓗ

The Boathouse is right in the middle of town, by the harbour. It has two handpulls, which offer a variety of beers from local and national breweries. Enjoy a snack in the main bar, or pop into the main restaurant and enjoy fresh, locally prepared meals, while taking in the views of the harbour. At the back of the bar is a games area, featuring a pool table.

Ship Tavern

49 Shore Street, KY10 3AQ

11-midnight (1am Fri & Sat); 12.30-midnight Sun
☎ (01333) 310347

Beer range varies Ⓗ

This traditional pub on the harbour front is a popular meeting place for fishermen, locals and visitors to the museum. Next door to the famous Anstruther Fish Bar & Restaurant, the bar has all the character you would expect from a historic fishing village inn. Two ever-changing ales are sourced from breweries all over the UK, as well as the local Beeches and Eden (St Andrews) breweries. Take in the views of the harbour or relax in the comfort of the back room.

Crail

Golf Hotel

4 High Street, KY10 3TD

11-midnight (1am Thu-Sat); 12.30-midnight Sun
☎ (01333) 450206 thegolfhotelcrail.com

Beer range varies Ⓗ

The Golf Hotel is a listed 16th-century coaching inn in a picturesque village in the East Neuk of Fife. The historic bar dates back to 1721, making it one of the oldest in Scotland. The room retains the original low-beamed ceiling, wooden floor and a 16th-century fireplace with a marriage lintel over it bearing the initials of the original owners. Relax with a beer in the garden or enjoy a meal in the restaurant after walking the coastal path.

Dunfermline

Commercial Inn 🏆

13 Douglas Street, KY12 7EB

10-11 (midnight Fri & Sat) ☎ (01383) 733876

Caledonian Deuchars IPA, 80; Courage Best Bitter; Theakston Old Peculier; guest beers Ⓗ

This cosy town-centre establishment can be found just off the High Street adjacent to the main post office, situated in a historic building dating back to the 1820s. A renowned ale house, it offers seven real ales and a cider. Good food and friendly service attract an eclectic clientele. CAMRA Kingdom of Fife Pub of the Year and Scottish finalist in 2014.

Guildhall & Linen Exchange

79-83 High Street, KY12 7DR

8am-midnight (1am Fri & Sat) ☎ (01383) 749800

Caledonian Deuchars IPA; Greene King Abbot; guest beers Ⓗ

A split-level Wetherspoon pub set in a category A listed building, decorated throughout with a mix of modern and Art Deco features. Numerous pictures from years gone by depict Dunfermline's and the Guildhall's past. Among the guest ales are beers from the historic Abbot Brew House, which brews less that 400 yards away.

Freuchie

Albert Tavern

2 High Street, KY15 7EX

5 (12 Fri & Sat)-midnight; 12.30-midnight Sun ☎ 07876 178 863

Beer range varies Ⓗ

A multi-award-winner, including former Scottish and national CAMRA Pub of the Year, Kingdom of Fife Pub of the Year, and a finalist in 2014. A friendly village local, the Albert was reputedly a coaching inn when nearby Falkland Palace was a royal residence. Wainscot panelling and two old brewery mirrors decorate the walls of the bar. A TV in the lounge screens sport. Five handpumps offer beers that change weekly. Q

Lomond Hills Hotel

High Street, KY15 7EY

11-2, 5-midnight; 11-midnight Fri & Sat; 12.30-midnight Sun ☎ (01337) 857329 lomondhillshotel.com

Beer range varies Ⓗ

Comfortable country hotel, originally a coaching inn established in 1733, with a marvellous view of the Lomond Hills and handy for visiting Falkland Palace. The small, welcoming public bar sports a carved bar top and wood panelling on the walls. A plasma screen shows sport. Two beers are always available. Meals are served in the family lounge and in a separate dining room. Outside there is a smoking area and beer garden. P

Glenrothes

Golden Acorn

1 North Street, KY7 5NA

7am-midnight (1am Fri) ☎ (01592) 751175

Caledonian Deuchars IPA; Greene King Abbot; guest beers Ⓗ

Wetherspoon establishment with a bar and hotel, located near the town centre with the bus station only two minutes' walk away. Real ale is offered on seven handpumps alongside a regular cider. The standard Wetherspoon beer festivals and special deals are available. The walls are decorated with scenes of the local area in days gone by and plasma screens show a number of sporting events. CAMRA Kingdom of Fife Pub of the Year runner-up 2014. P

Kinghorn

Crown Tavern

55-57 High Street, KY3 9UW

11 (12.30 Sun)-11.45 ☎ (01592) 890340

Beer range varies Ⓗ

A bustling two-roomed local, also called the Middle Bar, situated to the west end of the High Street. Two guest ales from microbreweries throughout the UK can be found here, as well as ale from the local Beeches brewery. Attractive stained-glass panels adorn the windows, and the high ceilings feature ornate plaster work. Mainly a sports bar, two TVs screen a wide range of sporting events. A pool table can be found to the side.

Kirkcaldy

Feuars Arms ★

28 Bogies Wynd, KY1 2PH

11.30-midnight ☎ (01592) 205577

Beer range varies Ⓗ

Identified by CAMRA as having a nationally important historic interior with original Edwardian fittings and displays of ceramics. A 59ft-long bar counter is fronted with brown Art Nouveau-style tiles. The large bar area has a mosaic floor, mahogany gantry and long-case clock. Features include stained glass windows with the arms of Scotland, England and Ireland, lots of etched glass and two mosaic porch floors. The Gents is also worth a visit to view the original features. Q

Harbour Bar

471-475 High Street, KY1 2SN

11-3, 5-midnight; 11-midnight Thu-Sat; 12.30-midnight Sun ☎ (01592) 264270

Beer range varies Ⓗ

The building dates from around 1870 and was a ship chandlers before it became a pub in 1924. It is one of just a few pubs to still have the historic jug bar. The lounge is light and airy with ornate cornices. Six handpumps sell up to 20 different beers a week from micros all over Britain. Kingdom of Fife CAMRA Pub of the Year on numerous occasions, a finalist in 2014 and a previous Scottish Pub of the Year winner. Q

Robert Nairn

2-6 Kirk Wynd, KY1 1EH

8am-midnight (1am Fri & Sat); 8am-11 Sun ☎ (01592) 205249

Caledonian Deuchars IPA; Greene King Abbot; guest beers Ⓗ

A Wetherspoon Lloyd's No.1 with a split-level lounge and pictures of old Kirkcaldy on the walls. Six handpulls dispense a variety of beers and regular Meet the Brewer evenings are hosted. Set in the city centre, this lively pub attracts a mixed clientele, young and old, who all enjoy the real ales. Big TVs show a range of sporting events and rolling news stories.

INDEPENDENT BREWERIES

Abbot Dunfermline (NEW)
Beeches Lochgelly
Eden St Andrews Guardbridge
Loch Leven Blairadam
Luckie Markinch
St Andrews St Andrews

Leslie

Burns Tavern

184 High Street, KY6 3DB

12 (11 Fri & Sat)-midnight; 12.30-midnight Sun

☎ (01592) 741345

Timothy Taylor Landlord; guest beer H

Typical Scottish two-room, main-street local in a town once famous for papermaking. The public bar is on two levels, the lower lively and friendly, the upper with a large-screen TV, pool table and football memorabilia on the walls. The lounge bar is quieter and more spacious. Competitions and quizzes are held weekly, and karaoke on Saturday. Leslie Folk Club plays here on a Sunday. Two beers are usually available in this honest local. ♣P

Limekilns

Ship Inn

Halketts Hall, KY11 3HJ

11-11 (midnight Fri & Sat); 12.30-11 Sun

☎ (01383) 872247

Beer range varies H

Set on the waterfront in a small rural village, this establishment has excellent views across the River Forth. Three guest ales are available, mostly from microbreweries throughout the UK. The bar has a cosy alcove to the left, and a maritime theme features throughout the building. Meals are served lunchtimes with fish and seafood the speciality (booking is essential). QP

Pitlessie

Village Inn

Cupar Road, KY15 7SU

11.30-2.30, 5-midnight; 11.30-midnight Fri-Sun

☎ (01337) 830595

Beer range varies H

Old coaching inn decorated with pictures of the maltings that were once opposite. A lovely real fire helps create a cosy atmosphere in the wood-panelled, stone and plaster-walled interior. The room has a corner bar with bar stools and a separate seating area for bar meals or drinks. Two ever-changing ales are offered. There is also a large restaurant and separate pool room. High teas are served on Sunday afternoon. P

St Andrews

Central Bar

77 Market Street, KY16 9NU

11-11.45 (midnight Fri & Sat); 12.30-11.45 Sun

☎ (01334) 478296

Courage Best Bitter; Fuller's London Pride; Inveralmond Lia Fail; Theakston Old Peculier; guest beers H

A busy city-centre pub on one of St Andrews' main streets, attracting a good mix of students, tourists and locals. The pub has a Victorian-style island bar, large windows and ornate mirrors, creating a late-19th-century feel. Seating outside on the pavement is popular in summer. Local CAMRA Pub of the Year winner in 2012-13, and a 2014 finalist. Q

Criterion

99 South Street, KY16 9QW

11-midnight (1am Fri & Sat); 12.30-midnight Sun

☎ (01334) 474543

Caledonian Deuchars IPA; guest beers H

Lovely local with a big picture window and oak-panelled walls adorned with photographs of St Andrews in days gone by. The pub is renowned for its home-made meals, served until 5pm. Background music plays and a plasma screen shows sport. Open music night on Monday is popular with local artists, and a regular quiz night is hosted during the week. There is seating outdoors on the pavement.

Whey Pat Tavern

1 Bridge Street, KY16 9EX

11-midnight (1am Thu-Sat); 12-midnight Sun

☎ (01334) 477740 wheypat-standrews.co.uk

Belhaven IPA; Greene King IPA; guest beers H

A town-centre pub on a busy road junction just outside the old West Port Gate. This is the bar with the longest history in St Andrews – the current building dates from 1902 but there has been a hostelry here since 1580. The front bar is L-shaped with a dartboard and TV, and there is an airy lounge to the rear. Theme nights and activities are held during the week. A mixed clientele of all ages frequents this usually busy venue. ♣

Strathkinness

Tavern

4 High Road, KY16 9RS

5-11 (midnight Sat & Sun) ☎ (01334) 850085

strathkinnesstavern.co.uk

Beer range varies H

Public bar with seating and a comfortable lounge at one end. There is a separate room with a dartboard, pool table and Sky TV. Three handpulls offer a choice of changing guest ales. Lunches and evening meals are served in the bar and restaurant. Quiz nights are the first and third Tuesday of each month and ceilidh evenings are on Monday. There is a beer garden to the rear and lovely views over the river estuary to the front. Q♣P

SCOTLAND

Store of good ale

Though it was but about the middle of August, and in some places the harvest hardly got in, we saw the mountains covered with snow, and felt the cold very acute and piercing but we found, as in all these northern counties, the people had a happy way of mixing the warm and the cold together; for store of good ale which flows plentifully in the most mountainous parts of this country seem abundantly to make up for all the inclemencies of the season, or difficulties of travelling.

Daniel Defoe, A Tour Through the Whole Island of Great Britain, 1726

LOCH LOMOND, STIRLING & THE TROSSACHS

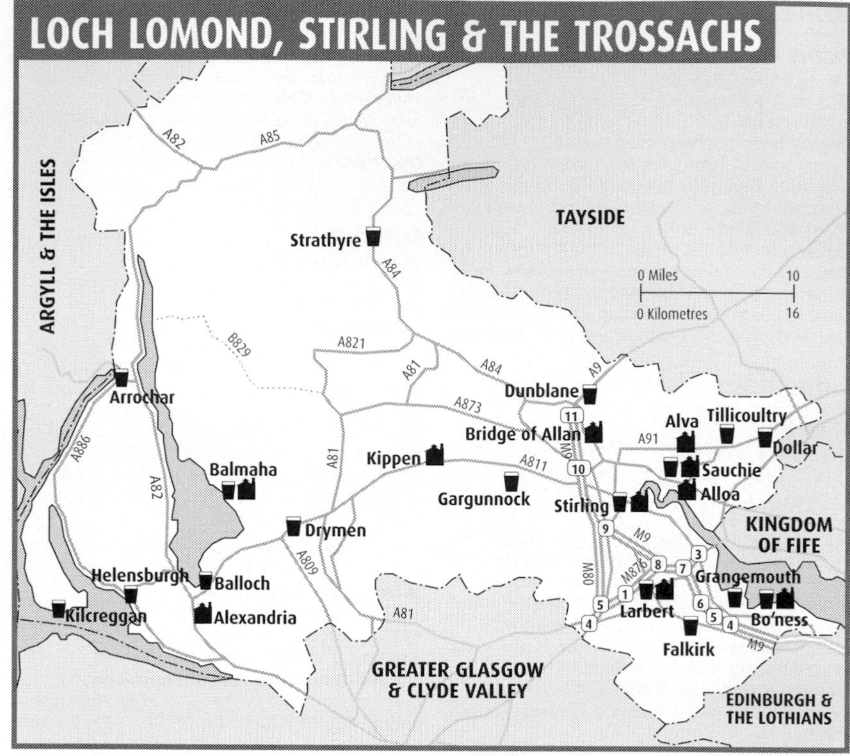

Authority areas covered: Argyll & Bute UA (part), Clackmannanshire UA, Falkirk UA, Stirling UA, West Dumbartonshire UA

Arrochar

Village Inn

Shore Road, G83 7AX

11-12.30am (1.30am Fri & Sat); 12-midnight Sun
(01301) 702279 villageinnarrochar.co.uk

Beer range varies H

Spectacular views across Loch Long can be enjoyed from the front patio and beer garden. In the bar, four handpumps dispense an ever-changing selection of the best local ales, with Houston Brewery a regular contributor. Ale festivals feature regularly and live music is hosted on occasion. The restaurant is popular with locals, day-trippers and hillwalkers. Dominoes is played here.

Balloch

Balloch House Hotel

Balloch Road, G83 8LQ

12-11; 12.30-10.30 Sun (01389) 752579

Caledonian Deuchars IPA; guest beers H

Set in a prime location on the River Leven by Loch Lomond, sylvan views can be enjoyed from the garden. The well-appointed interior offers a choice of seating and dining areas, with many exposed beams. Friendly staff serve ales from the Vintage Inns list through three handpumps. A great spot from which to explore the National Park or just to spend some time on the Bonnie Banks.

Balmaha

Oak Tree

Main Street, G63 0JQ

11-midnight (01360) 870357 oak-tree-inn.co.uk

Balmaha Blonde; guest beers H

An award-winning pub restaurant, the Oak Tree now boasts its own Balmaha microbrewery on site and offers its own ales on three handpumps in the bar. When demand is high, other Scottish ales, usually from Orkney, will also be available. Meals are served all day and there is a large drinking area outside under the eponymous tree.

Bo'ness

Corbie Inn

84 Corbiehall, EH51 0AS

12-11; 12.30-11 Sun (01506) 825307 corbieinn.co.uk

Beer range varies H

INDEPENDENT BREWERIES

Balmaha Balmaha
Black Wolf Stirling
Devon Sauchie
Fallen Kippen (NEW)
Harviestoun Alva
Kinneil Bo'ness
Loch Lomond Alexandria
TinPot Bridge of Allan
Tryst Larbert
Williams Alloa

Six ales are usually to be found on handpump, including one from the Kinneil Brew Hoose at the back of the premises. An ideal refreshment stop after a visit to the Bo'ness and Kinneil Railway or the Bo'ness Motor Museum, and also handy for the Hippodrome, Scotland's oldest purpose-built picture house. Q◑P

Dollar

King's Seat

23 Bridge Street, FK14 7DE

12-midnight (1am Fri & Sat); 12.30-midnight Sun
(01259) 742515 kingsseat.com

Harviestoun Bitter & Twisted; guest beers

Cosy, welcoming bar and restaurant situated in the quaint village of Dollar. Up to six ales and real cider are on offer during the summer, along with bar snacks and restaurant food. Dogs and children are welcome and there are tables and chairs outside for warmer weather. Occasional barbecues and live folk music are hosted. There are many great walks and attractions nearby. Q(23,65)

Drymen

Clachan

2 Main Street, G63 0BG

11-midnight (1am Fri & Sat); 12.30-midnight Sun
(01360) 660824 clachaninndrymen.co.uk

Beer range varies

The oldest licensed premises in Scotland, dating from 1734. There are two handpumps dispensing an ever-changing selection of excellent local and Scottish beers. Visitors can be sure of a warm welcome, and the pub is a popular stop-off for walkers on the West Highland Way and tourists exploring Loch Lomond National Park. Quality food is served all day in the bar and restaurant of this busy pub. P

Dunblane

Tappit Hen

Kirk Street, FK15 0AL

11 midnight (1am Fri & Sat) (01786) 825226
thetappithen-dunblane.co.uk

Belhaven IPA; guest beers

Facing the picturesque cathedral, this is a traditional single-room establishment with the interior split into different areas by wooden dividers. The pub is a cosy meeting point for the local community and a delightful discovery for visitors. It hosts a weekly folk music night on a Tuesday and a real ale festival once or twice a year. The locals regularly get together to hold fund-raising events in support of local charities.

Falkirk

Behind the Wall

14 Melville Street, FK1 1HZ

5-9 (11 summer); 5-1am Fri & Sat; 12.30-midnight Sun
(01324) 633338 behindthewall.co.uk

Beer range varies

Popular for watching live sports events, this spacious venue was once a bra factory. It has plenty of seating and several wide screens. The large room doubles as a live music and comedy venue, hosting bands both local and from many parts of the UK. Eglesbrech is the real ale and a whisky bar upstairs is divided into two rooms, with timber furnishings and a wood-burning stove.
(Grahamston)

Carron Works

Bank Street, FK1 1NB

8am-midnight (1am Fri & Sat) (01324) 673020

Caledonian Deuchars IPA; Greene King Abbot; guest beers

In a converted cinema, this is an excellent Wetherspoon venue with helpful staff dispensing the chain's guest beers. Centrally situated, with a spacious interior, the pub is popular with locals and CAMRA members. It is keen to promote real ale and holds frequent festivals. The standard Wetherspoon menu is available all day.
(Grahamston)

Wheatsheaf Inn

16 Baxters Wynd, FK1 1PF

11-midnight (1am Fri & Sat); 12.30-midnight Sun
(01324) 638282

Caledonian Deuchars IPA; guest beers

This public house, dating from the late-18th century and retaining much of its original character, can be found off the High Street via one of the vennels. The wood-panelled bar is furnished in traditional style with plenty of interesting features from the past. Guest beers come from microbreweries in Scotland and England, with two on offer mid-week and three at the weekend. A must-visit venue. (Grahamston)

Gargunnock

Gargunnock Inn

Main Street, FK8 3BW

12-midnight (1am Fri & Sat); 12.30-midnight Sun
(01786) 860333 gargunnockinn.co.uk

Beer range varies

Dating from the 1700s, the inn is now a roomy yet cosy pub and restaurant. The bar has two handpumps offering at least one Scottish ale. There are numerous restaurant rooms and seating areas, two wood-burning stoves, exposed beams and original features. An extensive food menu is served throughout – chicken with haggis and Aberdeen Angus steaks are notable. Close by, popular local walks abound. The annual beer festival is the second Sunday in August. QP(12)

Grangemouth

Earl of Zetland

Bo'ness Road, FK3 8AN

8am-midnight (1am Fri & Sat) (01324) 499940

Caledonian Deuchars IPA; Greene King Abbot; guest beers

An excellent Wetherspoon conversion of a town-centre church, retaining ecclesiastical features such as the organ pipes above the bar and stained-glass windows. Ample seating is available at tables or in pew booths. The permanent beers are supplemented by two guests mid-week and up to four at the weekend. TVs screen show sporting events with news channels on silent at other times.

Helensburgh

Commodore

112-117 West Clyde Street, G84 8ES

SCOTLAND

11-11; 12.30-10.30 Sun ☎ (01436) 676924
Caledonian Deuchars IPA; guest beers 🄷
Situated on the shores of the Gareloch, the pub has views of the Clyde and passing submarines. A bar area with a variety of seating adjoins the restaurant area. Deuchars IPA and two other ales from the Innkeeper's Lodge range are available. The pub is less than 10 minutes from Helensburgh Central and the Glasgow bus service terminates outside. ❀🛏◐♿P🚌

Henry Bell
19-29 James Street, G84 8AS
8am-midnight ☎ (01436) 863060
Caledonian Deuchars IPA; Greene King Abbot; guest beers 🄷
A tasteful renovation of a former furniture store, the decor is much influenced by the great Scottish designer Charles Rennie Mackintosh. Other decoration celebrates John Logie Baird, the inventor of TV, and Henry Bell, who designed the first commercial steamship. The pub is divided into three distinct areas to provide for a wide clientele. This smaller-scale Wetherspoon makes a pleasant change. Q♞❀◐♿≋(Central)🚌📶

Kilcreggan

Kilcreggan Hotel 🄻
Argyll Road, G84 0JP (turn off Shore Rd at Donaldson's Brae)
12-midnight (1am Fri & Sat) ☎ (01436) 842243
kilcregganhotel.com
Beer range varies 🄷
This pub affords the best view of the Clyde from its lofty position on the Rosneath Peninsula. Set in verdant grounds, it can be approached via the ferry from Gourock or the bus from Helensburgh. Up to four pumps dispense a range of beers from Scottish micros plus surprises from throughout Britain – Bass is a frequent guest. Good food is available and the sun-catching patio garden is the perfect place to relax. Check ahead for winter hours.
♞❀🛏◐P🚌(316)📶

Larbert

Station Hotel
2 Foundry Loan, FK5 4AW
12-11 (midnight Thu; 1am Fri & Sat); 12.30-11 Sun
☎ (01324) 557186 thestationhotellarbert.co.uk
Beer range varies 🄷
Situated next to the railway station and on a regular bus route, this hotel attracts both visitors and locals. Up to five cask ales are on offer in the traditional public bar and in the adjacent lounge bar. The pub supports a number of local groups and is popular with the community. Large-screen TVs show major sporting events and it has a games room. ❀🛏≋P🚌(6,7)

Sauchie

Mansfield Arms
7 Main Street, FK10 3JR
11-midnight ☎ (01259) 722020 devonales.com
Devon Original (70/-), Thick Black, Pride; guest beer 🄷
The oldest operating microbrewery in the county, this traditional two-bar pub brews four Devon ales which are dispensed via T-bar fonts. Family-owned and run, and situated within an ex-mining community, the bar is popular with the locals who enjoy the lively banter. Good food is served in the lounge, and both beer and food are excellent value for money. The pub is on the Stirling via Alloa circular bus route. ♞◐♿P▯🚌(62,63)🐾

Stirling

Inn at Torbrex
Torbrex Lane, FK7 9HD
11-midnight (1am Fri & Sat) ☎ (01786) 461832
torbrexinn.co.uk
Caledonian Deuchars IPA; guest beers 🄷
The Inn was originally built in 1721 as a grand laird's house in the village of Torbrex. The design of the front of the building retains all the window and door openings of the original house, along with some of the original beams and the date plaque at the front door. Inside, hardwood and stone slabbed flooring and lots of natural wood on the walls creates the feel of a country pub. The guest beers change regularly. ♞◐♿P🚌🐾

Portcullis Hotel
Castle Wynd, FK8 1EG (adjacent to castle esplanade)
11-11; 11.30-midnight Wed-Sat; 11.30-11 Sun
☎ (01786) 472290 theportcullishotel.com
Beer range varies 🄷
Popular pub at the top of the town, originally the old grammar school building. Exposed stone walls and an open fireplace with ornate surround create a warm welcome in the heart of old Stirling. Frequented by tourists and supported by locals, the pub is renowned for its food and regularly changing selection of Scottish ales from the far north and west. Always busy, diners are advised to reserve a table. Q♞❀🛏◐♿≋P🚌📶

Strathyre

Inn & Bistro 🏆
Main Street, FK18 8NA
12-midnight (1am Fri & Sat); 12.30-midnight Sun
☎ (01877) 384224 innatstrathyre.co.uk
Beer range varies 🄷
Cosy, popular pub, serving meals in the bar and bistro, all made with local produce. The beers are mainly Scottish during the summer tourist season and from south of the border off season. The beer garden in a raised position enjoys panoramic views. Hill walking, fishing, golf and watersports are all close at hand. Stirling, Callander and the Trossachs are within easy travelling distance. Accommodation is available, and dogs and children are permitted in the bar.
Q♞❀🛏◐♣P🚌(C60)🐾📶

Tillicoultry

Woolpack Inn
1-3 Glassford Square, FK13 6AU
11-midnight (1am Fri & Sat) ☎ (01259) 750109
woolpack.jimdo.com
Beer range varies 🄷
Originally a drovers' inn, this pub is well used by friendly locals and holidaying visitors, with a comfortable feel, log stove and low ceilings, and no intrusive TV or music. Ales on four handpumps are selected from the Belhaven list and change regularly. A good selection of malt whiskies is also available. Home-cooked meals are served at the weekend. Q♞◐♣🐾

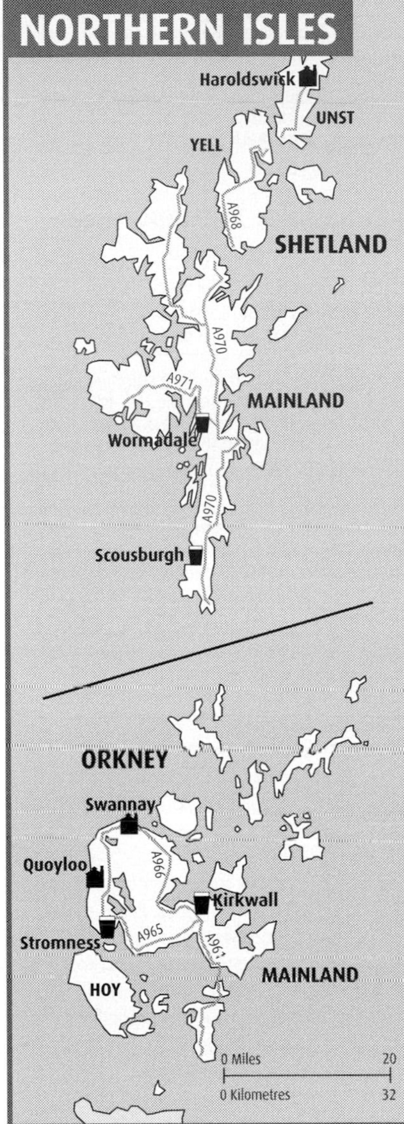

Authority area covered: Highland UA

Kirkwall: Orkney

Ayre Hotel

Ayre Road, KW15 1QX

11-11 (1am Thu & Fri); 12-midnight Sun
(01856) 873001 ayrehotel.co.uk

Highland Scapa Special H

Overlooking Kirkwall harbour, with buses and ferries nearby to and from Aberdeen, Lerwick and most of the outlying Orkney islands, this large, friendly and family-run hotel is well placed for exploring. The cosy lounge bar has comfortable seating and is popular with locals and visitors alike. There is a hostel next door and a campsite a short walk away. Meals are served lunchtimes (12-2pm) and evenings (6-9pm) and feature Orkney beef, fish and other locally-sourced produce.

Bothy Bar (Albert Hotel)

Mounthoolie Lane, KW15 1HW (100yds from harbour along Junction Rd)

11-11.30 (1am Thu-Sat); 12-11.30 Sun (01856) 876000
alberthotel.co.uk

Highland Scapa Special; Orkney Red MacGregor; guest beers H

After reconstruction following a fire a few years ago, the Bothy has more space than previously and it has maintained its position as a popular bar in the town centre. Frequented by locals, after-work drinkers and as part of the weekend circuit, TVs cater for sports fans and there are alcoves for more intimate gatherings. Guest beers are from Orkney and Highland breweries. Handy for buses, ferries and the main shopping area, it is also close to tourist attractions.

Helgi's Bar

14 Harbour Street, KW15 1LE (by harbour)

11-11 (1am Sat); 12.30-11 Sun (01856) 879293
helgis.co.uk

Highland Scapa Special, Orkney IPA; guest beer H

Named in honour of the warrior Helgi who had a tavern on the harbour front, this pub is traditional in style with a local stone floor and wood panelling. It hosts regular music sessions and special food nights where food is matched with the ales currently on handpump. A quiz night is held every Thursday. Guest ales are from Highland, including hard-to-find brews. Seafood is landed daily on the harbour. Q

Shore

Shore Street, KW15 1LG (on harbour road)

11.30-midnight (1am Fri); 9am-1am Sat; 9am-midnight Sun (01856) 872200 theshore.co.uk

Highland Scapa Special H

This smart, modern venue at the pier head may sometimes be the first experience of a Scottish bar for passengers disembarking from cruise ships. Welcoming staff and friendly locals help create the right atmosphere for enjoying the local ale on offer. The main street is just around the corner. The ferries for trips to Westray, Sanday and other Northern Isles leave just across the road.

Scousburgh: Shetland

Spiggie Hotel

ZE2 9JE (signed from A970 off B9122)

12-2, 5.30-11; closed Tue; 12-11 Sat; 12-10 Sun
(01950) 460409 thespiggiehotel.co.uk

Beer range varies H

Small family-run hotel built as the original terminus of the Northern Isles ferries on an elevated site, with wonderful scenic views. The gleaming white Scousburgh Sands are within five minutes' walk, with Sumburgh Head, Jarlshof and Old Scatness a short drive away. Birdwatching and trout fishing on the loch may be arranged. The hotel has a small stone-floored bar and adjacent restaurant – phone to check food availability and opening hours in winter. Beers come from Valhalla and Highland breweries, with only one in winter. P

INDEPENDENT BREWERIES

Highland Swannay: Orkney
Orkney Quoyloo: Orkney
Valhalla Haroldswick: Unst

Stromness: Orkney

Ferry Inn

10 John Street, KW16 3AD (opp ferry terminal)
10-11 (midnight Fri & Sat); 9.30am-11 Sun
(01856) 850280 ferryinn.com
Highland Scapa Special, Orkney IPA; Orkney Corncrake; guest beer H
Reopened after a facelift in 2013, the Ferry is handy for buses and the ferry from Scrabster. The bar is well used by locals and visitors including divers who come to Orkney to explore the sunken German fleet at Scapa Flow. Other attractions include the Ring of Brodgar and Skara Brae village. It is busy during the annual folk and blues festivals and the famous Stromness Shopping Week. Guest beers come from both local Orkney and Highland breweries. Winter hours vary, with the bar not opening till 4pm.

Stromness Hotel

15 Victoria Street, KW16 3AA (opp pier head)
11-11 (1am Fri & Sat); 12-11 Sun (01856) 850298
stromnesshotel.com
Highland Scapa Special, Orkney IPA; Orkney Northern Light, Dark Island; guest beer H
The main bar is the Hamnavoe lounge on the first floor, with a commanding view of the harbour. To complement the beer, there are over 100 whiskies available in the adjoining whisky bar. Rock, jazz and blues festivals are hosted in the spacious function room. The hotel is normally closed in January and February, but a single ale can always be found in the ground floor Flattie Bar. There are good transport links to Scara Brae and the Ring of Brodgar. P

Wormadale: Shetland

Westings Inn

ZE2 9LJ (8 miles N of Lerwick on A971)
12.30-2.30, 5.30-10.30; 6.30-10.30 Sun
(01595) 840242 westings.shetland.co.uk
Beer range varies H
Isolated white-painted inn in a stunning location near the summit of Wormadale Hill, two miles west of Tingwall airstrip. There are marvellous sea views from the comfortable lounge area and adjacent games area of Whiteness Voe, Western Shetland and the outlying islands. Three ales are usually available in summer, one in winter, often from Fuller's or Timothy Taylor. Evening meals are served 7-8pm Monday-Friday by arrangement. The bar may stay open until 1am if busy. Caravans are welcome and camping is available in the pub grounds. P

All hands to the pumps

British beer is unique and so are the methods used for serving it. The best-known English system, the beer engine operated by a handpump on the pub bar, arrived early in the 19th century. It coincided with and was prompted by the decline of the publican brewer and the rise of commercial companies that began to dominate the supply of beer to public houses. In order to sell more beer, commercial brewers and publicans looked for faster and less labour-intensive methods of serving beer.

In The Brewing Industry in England, 1700-1830, Peter Mathias records that 'most beer had to be stored in butts in the publicans' cellars for the technical reason that it needed an even and fairly low temperature, even where convenience and restricted space behind the bar did not enforce it. This meant, equally inevitably, continuous journeying to and from the cellars by the potboys to fill up jugs from the spigots: 'a waste of time for the customer and of labour and trade for the publican. Drawing up beer from the cellar at the pull of a handle at the bar at once increased the speed of sale and cut the wage bill.'

The first attempt at a system for raising beer from cellar to bar was patented by Joseph Bramah in 1797. But his system – using boxes of sand that pressed down on storage vessels holding the beer – was so elaborate it was never used. But his idea encouraged others to develop simpler systems. Mathias writes: 'One of the few technical devices of importance to come into the public house since the publican stopped brewing his own beer was the beer engine. It was, from the first, a simple manually operated pump, incorporating no advances in hydraulic knowledge or engineering skill, similar in design to many pumps used at sea, yet perfectly adapted to its function in the public house.'

By 1801, John Chadwell of Blackfriars, London, was registered as a 'beer-engine maker' and soon afterwards Thomas Rowntree in the same area described himself as a 'maker of a double-acting beer-machine'. By the 1820s, beer engine services had become standard throughout most of urban England and Gaskell & Chambers in the Midlands had become the leading manufacturer, employing more than 700 people in their Birmingham works alone.

Until recent times, cask-conditioned beer in Scotland was served by air pressure. In the pub cellar a water engine, which looks exactly the same as a lavatory cistern but works in reverse, used water to produce air pressure that drove the beer to the bar. Sadly, these wonderful Victorian devices are rarely seen, and the Sassenach handpump and beer engine dominate the pub scene.

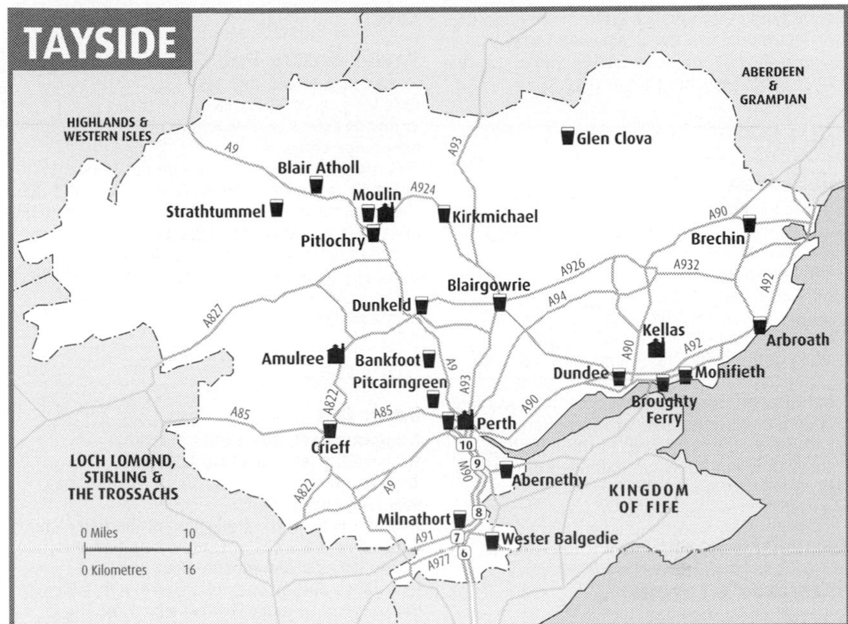

Authority areas covered: Angus UA, City of Dundee UA, Perth & Kinross UA

Abernethy

Crees Inn

Main Sreet, PH2 9LA

11-2, 5-11; 11-11 Sat & Sun ☎ (01738) 850714

creesinn.co.uk

Beer range varies H

A picturesque former farmhouse lying in the shadow of the imposing Abernethy Tower – one of only two Pictish watchtowers in Scotland. Up to six ales are available, mostly from English breweries. A good selection of meals is served lunchtimes and evenings, made with fresh local produce. Hops adorn the beams in the lounge seating area.

Arbroath

Corn Exchange

14 Olympic Centre, Market Place, DD11 1HR

11-midnight (1am Sat & Sun) ☎ (01241) 432430

Caledonian Deuchars IPA; Greene King Abbot; guest beers H

Located just off the High Street, this Wetherspoon pub occupies a 19th-century former corn exchange. Two guest beers are usually available in addition to the two regulars. Although largely open plan, there are a number of booths offering some privacy. Food is served daily from 8am or you could try the famous Arbroath Smokies from one of the local producers. Boat trips offering fishing or a visit to the 200-year-old Bell Rock lighthouse can be found at the nearby harbour.

Bankfoot

Bankfoot Inn

Main Street, PH1 4AB

12-2 (not Mon & Tue), 6-11; 12-2, 4.30-12.30am Fri; 12-12.30am Sat; 12-midnight Sun ☎ (01738) 787243

bankfootinn.co.uk

Beer range varies H

Traditional 18th-century coaching inn on the main street. Extensively refurbished in recent years, it has a small public bar, a lounge with a fine oak bar and an adjoining restaurant. Two real fires in winter make it a cosy howff. The owners are real ale enthusiasts and strongly committed to local breweries. Two ale fests are held each year. Live music nights feature regularly. All interests are catered for here – golf, fishing, shooting, hiking and cycling.

Blair Atholl

Atholl Arms Hotel

PH18 5SG

12 (3 Nov-Feb)-11; 12-11.45 Fri & Sat ☎ (01796) 481205

athollarmshotel.co.uk

Moulin Light, Braveheart, Ale of Atholl, Old Remedial H

Built in 1832, the Atholl Arms has a grand, imposing façade in a traditional Victorian Highland style. The characterful Highland Bothy Bar offers four ales produced by the local Moulin Brewery, and serves freshly cooked food all day. Blair Atholl and the surrounding area is a popular destination for walking, climbing, biking and sightseeing.

Blairgowrie

Ericht Alehouse

13 Wellmeadow, PH10 6ND

1-11 ☎ (01250) 872469

Beer range varies H

Classic town-centre pub with a friendly atmosphere. There are two seating areas separated by a well-stocked bar, with an open log fire in the lounge. Up to six handpumps serve a wide range of ever-changing ales and a cider, and a selection of bottled continental beers is also available. No food is served but customers are welcome to bring their own. Occasional live music plays on Friday evenings. A winner of local CAMRA Pub of the Year several times over the past decade.

Brechin

Caledonian

43 South Street, DD9 6DZ

closed Mon & Tue; 5-10 Wed & Thu; 4.30-11.30 Fri; 3-11.30 Sat; 3-11 Sun ☎ (01356) 624345

Beer range varies H

Named after the privately run railway whose terminus is opposite, the Caledonian features a large bar and dining area. Houston and Inveralmond provide the regular ales although guest beers sourced by the landlord on trips to Hampshire are frequently available. A wide range of continental bottled beers is also offered. Live folk music on the last Friday of the month is popular. Opening hours are extended in summer.

Broughty Ferry

Fisherman's Tavern

10-16 Fort Street, DD5 2AD

11-midnight (1am Thu-Sat) ☎ (01382) 775941

Beer range varies H

Licensed since 1857, this famous hostelry was originally three fishermen's cottages, later converted into a small hotel. The bar is to the right of the entrance, and a snug is to the left, leading to the dining room/lounge. The lounge to the rear has disabled access from Bell's Lane. Entertainment includes traditional music on Thursday night, a monthly quiz, and an annual beer festival in late May. Up to six real ales come from Scottish and English breweries.

Royal Arch

285 Brook Street, DD5 2DS

11-midnight (1am Fri & Sat); 12.30-midnight Sun ☎ (01382) 779741

Caledonian Deuchars IPA; guest beers H

A popular locally-owned pub in the centre of 'the Ferry'. There are three TVs in the public bar for the many sports fans, and good-quality meals are served in the Art Deco lounge. Three handpulls dispense ales from local brewers as well as from all over Britain. The gantry in the public bar was rescued long ago from the demolished Craigour Bar in Dens Road, and the exterior was refurbished in 2014. Pavement tables are popular in good weather.

Ship Inn

121 Fisher Street, DD5 2BR

11 (12.30 Sun)-11 ☎ (01382) 214235

theshipinn-broughtyferry.co.uk

Timothy Taylor Landlord; guest beers H

Traditional free house on the waterfront at Broughty Ferry, with views over the Tay towards Fife. Dating back to 1847, this cosy retreat has some nautical features and is interesting and atmospheric. Three real ales are usually available. A range of tasty bar meals is on offer and there is a quality restaurant upstairs. Pavement seating just outside is ideal for watching the activity on the river.

Crieff

Tower Gastro Pub

81 East High Street, PH7 3JA

12.30-11; 11-12.30am Fri & Sat; 11-11 Sun

☎ (01738) 650050 thetowercrieff.com

Beer range varies H

This small family-run gastro-pub has been tastefully refurbished by licensees Annie and Bob. There is a comfortable seating area overlooking the beer garden and south to the Ochil Hills. Two handpumps serve ales from local breweries, especially Inveralmond and StrathBraan. Attached to the pub are three self-catering apartments. Q (15,47)

Dundee

Bank Bar

7-9 Union Street, DD1 4BN

11-midnight (10 Mon & Tue); 12.30-7 Sun

☎ (01382) 205037

Beer range varies H

A former bank with a collection of themed pictures decorating the walls, it is now a no-nonsense ale house. It has a bare-boards floor, wooden furnishings and a series of alcoves with tables in the tradition of older Scottish city pubs. The management is enthusiastic about supporting small brewers and, while beers from many parts are available on up to three handpumps, Inveralmond ales feature regularly. Food is served until 7pm. Live music plays on Friday and Saturday nights.

Capitol

7-9 Seagate, DD1 2EG

8am-11 ☎ (01382) 205950

Greene King Abbot; guest beers H

Formerly the Capitol cinema, built in 1945, but converted into a Wetherspoon Lloyd's in 2003. The foyer is now a family area, with steps leading to the main area and a staircase rising to a large balcony. The long bar has nine handpulls with six in use at most times. The venue is popular with shoppers during the day and lively on Friday and Saturday evenings. It is a great place to enjoy the annual Dundee Blues Bonanza when the balcony fills with younger drinkers.

Counting House

67-71 Reform Street, DD1 1SP

8am-midnight ☎ (01382) 225251

Caledonian Deuchars IPA; Greene King Abbot; guest beers H

This Wetherspoon conversion of a former bank in the heart of Dundee, refurbished in 2013, has become a popular local for many city ale drinkers. Halfway between the Overgate and Wellgate shopping centres, on the corner of Albert Square, it is also a handy watering hole for visitors to the McManus Galleries. It has 10 handpulls, most usually in use, with one for Thatchers cider and additions during beer festivals. Food is available until 10pm.

INDEPENDENT BREWERIES

Inveralmond Perth
MòR Kellas
Moulin Moulin
Strathbraan Amulree

Drouthy's

142 Perth Road, DD1 4JW

11-midnight ☎ (01382) 202187 drouthysdundee.co.uk

Beer range varies P

Owned by local pub company Fuller Thomson, this is a comfortable venue with a smallish upstairs area with a bar and neat seating, and a large chalkboard listing the day's food and drink options. Quiet music creates a pleasant atmosphere. There are four cask ales, with a good variation on the guest beer front, and lots of craft keg beers also. A tricky spiral staircase takes you down to the toilets and a further seating area, which can be booked for small functions.

Phoenix

103 Nethergate, DD1 4DH

11-midnight ☎ (01382) 200014

Caledonian Deuchars IPA; Timothy Taylor Landlord; guest beers H

This splendidly re-created traditional local – only the ceiling and pillars are original – has proved to be one of the city's most popular real ale outlets down the years. Eccentric in decor, it has sturdy wooden seats and tables and green leather benches, plus intimate nooks for a quiet drink. It is handy for the Rep Theatre, Dundee Contemporary Arts and Bonar Hall.

Speedwell (Mennie's) ★

165-167 Perth Road, DD2 1AS

11 (12.30 Sun)-11 ☎ (01382) 667783

Caledonian Deuchars IPA; guest beers H

One of the finest examples of an Edwardian pub interior in the country, the building features in CAMRA's Scotland's True Heritage Pubs. Built in 1903 for James Speed, it is known as Mennie's after the family who ran it for more than 50 years. The L-shaped bar is divided by a part glazed screen and has a magnificent mahogany gantry and counter, dado panelled walls and an anaglypta Jacobean ceiling. There are two sitting rooms, separated by a glass screen. Three real ales are on handpull. Q

Dunkeld

Royal Dunkeld Hotel

Atholl Street, PH8 0AR

11-11 (12.15am Fri & Sat); 12-11 Sun ☎ (01350) 727322 royaldunkeld.co.uk

Cairngorm Trade Winds; Stewart 80/-; guest beer H

Located on the main street near the cathedral, this former coaching inn is now a comfortable hotel. It has a restaurant, lounge bar and public bar with an open fire. A pool room with dartboard is adjacent. Outside, the large beer garden is a suntrap in summer. Three handpulls serve real ale. Good food is available in the bar and restaurant. An ideal base for a variety of outdoor activities including walking, fishing and golf.

Taybank Hotel

Tay Terrace, PH8 0AQ

11-11 ☎ (01350) 727340 thetaybank.co.uk

Strathbraan Due South, Head East; guest beer H

'Scotland's musical meeting place' hosts regular organised and impromptu music sessions in an intimate room with an L-shaped bar, attracting locals and tourists. It dispenses the range of Strathbraan ales on four handpulls. Excellent meals, including the Taybank stovies, are highly recommended. Friendly staff offer a warm welcome to all visitors, including dogs and children. The car park and beer garden are opposite, beside the mighty River Tay, and there is a patio for those not nimble enough to cross the road. P

Glen Clova

Glen Clova Hotel

DD8 4QS

11-11 (1am Fri & Sat); 12-11 Sun ☎ (01575) 550350 clova.com

Beer range varies H

Situated near the head of one of Scotland's most beautiful glens, the hotel is popular with walkers after a day on the hills. The bar has a large log-fired stove and plenty of character. Two handpumps supply the ales, usually from Scottish breweries. Local food, including lamb and venison, is served in both the bar and adjoining restaurant. The hotel offers a range of accommodation. A summer beer festival is held in the field opposite. P

Kirkmichael

Strathardle Inn

PH10 7NS (on A924)

12-2 (not Mon summer; not Mon-Fri winter), 5-11 ☎ (01250) 881224 strathardleinn.co.uk

Beer range varies H

Small, friendly hotel with a bar room with a coal fire and horse brasses around the mantelpiece. The historic coaching inn, dating back to the late 1700s, has a 700-yard fishing beat on the River Ardle which passes in front of the building. The Cateran Trail is also nearby and the Southern Highlands, Glenshee ski slopes, Deeside and Angus Glens are all within reach. Up to three ales are available from Scottish micros, and good lunches and evening meals are served.

Milnathort

Village Inn

36 Wester Loan, KY13 9YH

2-11 (midnight Fri); 12-midnight Sat; 12.30-11 Sun ☎ (01577) 863293

Beer range varies H

This friendly local has a semi open-plan interior featuring classic brewery mirrors and local historic photographs. The comfortable lounge area has low ceilings, exposed joists and stone walls, and the bar area is warmed by a log fire. At the rear is a games room with a pool table. This pub has been family owned since 1985 and serves various beers, often locally sourced. Milnathort links some great cycling routes through the Ochils, via Burleigh Castle, to the more leisurely Loch Leven Heritage Trail.

Monifieth

Milton Inn

Grange Road, DD5 4LU

closed Mon; 12-2.30, 5-11; 12-midnight Fri & Sat; 12-11 Sun ☎ (01382) 532620 themiltoninn.co.uk

Beer range varies H

Set back from the road with large gardens and a sunny deck area to the rear, this family-run inn offers a genuinely warm and friendly welcome. The well-kept ales change frequently, with three

SCOTLAND

usually available. These are complemented by excellent food and an impressive selection of single malt whiskies, all served by pleasant, enthusiastic and knowledgable staff. (Balmossie)

Moulin

Moulin Inn

11-13 Kirkmichael Road, PH16 5EH

11 (12 Nov-Apr)-11; 11-11.45 Fri & Sat; 12-11 Sun (01796) 472196 moulininn.co.uk

Moulin Light, Braveheart, Ale of Atholl, Old Remedial

First opened in 1695, the inn is the oldest part of the Moulin Hotel, situated within the village square of Moulin, an ancient crossroads, just east of Pitlochry. Full of character and charm, it is traditionally furnished and has two log fires. A good choice of home-prepared local fare is available, along with the Moulin's own beer, brewed in the old coach house behind the hotel. Outside is an area for dining and drinking in good weather. An ideal base for exploring and outdoor pursuits, there are several marked walks nearby. QP

Perth

Capital Asset

26 Tay Street, PH1 5LQ

11-11.30 (12.30am Thu-Sat) (01738) 580457

Caledonian Deuchars IPA; Greene King Abbot; guest beers

Formerly a savings bank, this Wetherspoon venue retains the original high ceilings and ornate cornices. The large safe from its banking days can be found in the family area. Pictures of old Perth adorn the walls of the open-plan lounge which overlooks the River Tay. A variety of five ales is dispensed, and food is available all day. Twice-yearly beer festivals are popular with local ale drinkers. Q

Cherrybank Inn

210 Glasgow Road, PH2 0NA

11-11 (12.30am Thu-Sat); 12-midnight Sun (01738) 624349 cherrybankinn.co.uk

Inveralmond Independence, Ossian; guest beers

This 250-year-old former drovers' inn is a popular watering hole and stopover for travellers. Six ales from Inveralmond and other Scottish independents are available, alongside good bar lunches and evening meals. The inn has a multi-roomed public bar, a larger L-shaped lounge with views up to a woodland walk, and seven well-appointed en-suite rooms. Golf can be arranged for residents. Tayside CAMRA Pub of the Year 2011. QP

Greyfriars

15 South Street, PH2 8PG

11-11 (11.45 Fri & Sat); 3-11 Sun (01738) 633036 greyfriarsbar.com

Beer range varies

City-centre lounge bar serving up to four ales, often including an Inveralmond beer. Good-value lunches are available in the bar and in a small upstairs area. The pub takes its name from the former Greyfriars monastery. Nearby attractions include a Victorian theatre, art gallery, museum and concert hall. This may well be the smallest lounge bar in the Fair City but it has an enviable reputation among locals and visitors as one of the friendliest.

Pitcairngreen

Pitcairngreen Inn

PH1 3LP

11-11 (midnight Fri & Sat); 12-11 Sun (01738) 583022 pitcairngreeninn.co.uk

Beer range varies

Steeped in local history, this former coaching inn is a fairly large establishment in a small village, divided into several different areas, with a large open log fire in the snug. Locally sourced real ale is served through three handpulls, with two or three real ciders also available. Good seasonal food using local ingredients is cooked to order. Outside is a spacious seating area and the car park is just across the road. P(14,15)

Pitlochry

Old Mill Inn

Mill Lane, PH16 5BH (in town centre)

11-11 (midnight Sat & Sun) (01796) 474020 theoldmillpitlochry.co.uk

Strathbraan Due South, Head East; guest beers

Built in the 19th century as a mill, with the old mill wheel still in place. The bar, which has a real fire, offers a varied selection of guest ales, usually from Scottish microbreweries. The restaurant serves good food with an emphasis on fresh local produce from 8am to 8.45pm daily. Live music features at the weekend and there is a pleasant area outside for warmer days. P

Strathtummel

Loch Tummel Inn

PH16 5RP

11-11 (closed Mon & Tue winter) (01882) 634272 lochtummelinn.co.uk

Beer range varies

Located on a hillside with spectacular views across Loch Tummel, this 200-year-old former coaching inn is an ideal place to stop off and enjoy friendly Highland hospitality. The bar area comprises the former coach house and stables, with pews and a wood-burning stove adding to the traditional ambience. The outside drinking area overlooking the loch is a superb spot to linger on a summer's day. Two ales are usually available, often from Inveralmond, and good food is served daily. QP

Wester Balgedie

Balgedie Toll Tavern

KY13 9HE (2 miles E of M90 at jct of A911 and B919)

11-11 (11.30 Thu; 12.30am Fri & Sat); 12.30-11.30 Sun (01592) 840212

Harviestoun Bitter & Twisted; guest beer

Welcoming and comfortable rural tavern dating from 1534. Now much extended, the oldest part of the building, the toll house, is at the southern end. It has three seating areas plus a small bar with low ceilings, oak beams, horse brasses, wooden settles and works of art by a local painter. A good selection of meals and bar snacks is available. Guest beers are rotated, mainly sourced from Scottish independent breweries. P

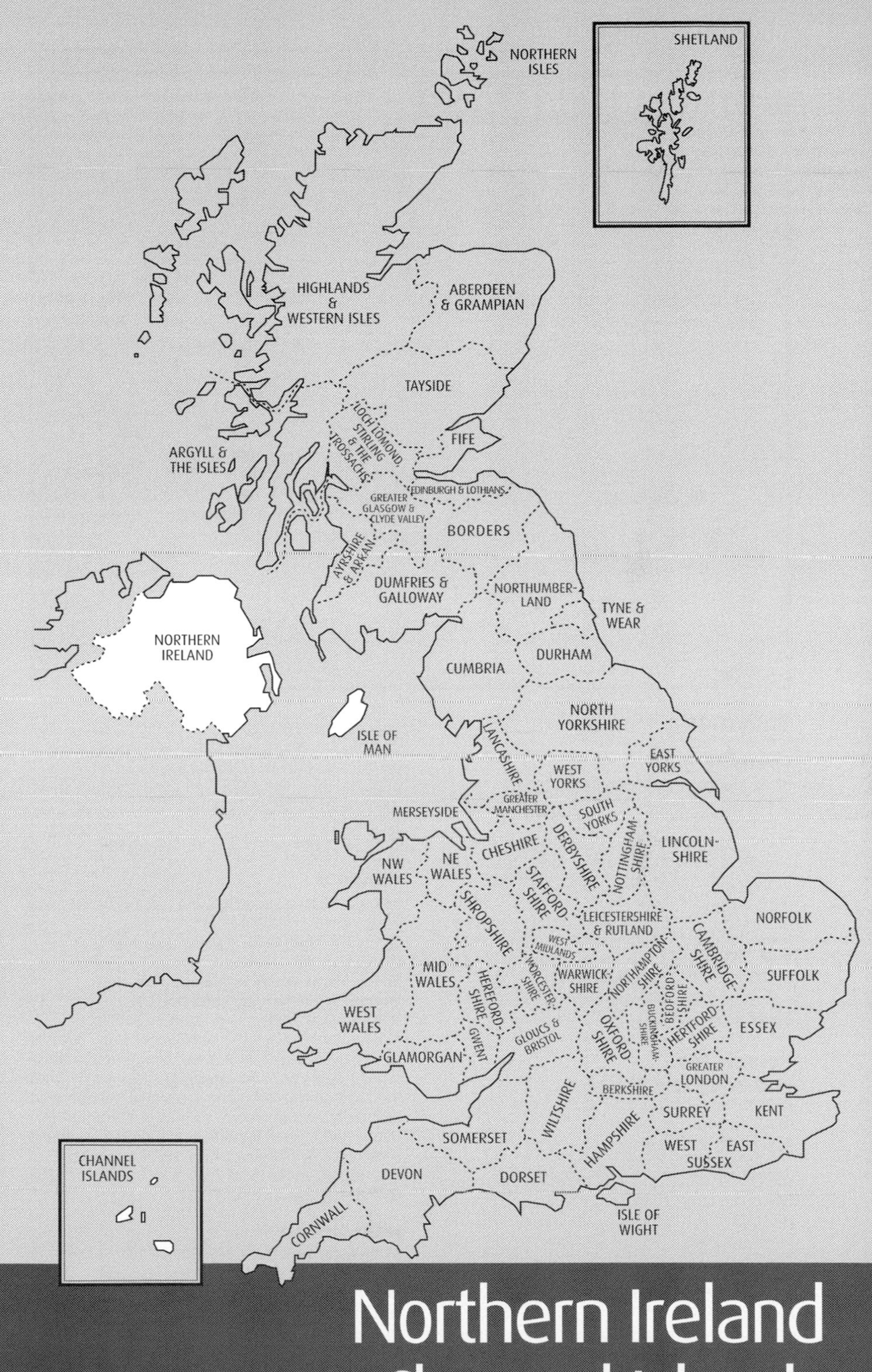
SHETLAND
NORTHERN ISLES
HIGHLANDS & WESTERN ISLES
ABERDEEN & GRAMPIAN
TAYSIDE
LOCH LOMOND, STIRLING & THE TROSSACHS
FIFE
ARGYLL & THE ISLES
EDINBURGH & LOTHIANS
GREATER GLASGOW & CLYDE VALLEY
BORDERS
AYRSHIRE & ARRAN
DUMFRIES & GALLOWAY
NORTHUMBERLAND
TYNE & WEAR
NORTHERN IRELAND
DURHAM
CUMBRIA
NORTH YORKSHIRE
ISLE OF MAN
LANCASHIRE
WEST YORKS
EAST YORKS
GREATER MANCHESTER
MERSEYSIDE
SOUTH YORKS
CHESHIRE
DERBYSHIRE
NOTTINGHAMSHIRE
LINCOLNSHIRE
NW WALES
NE WALES
STAFFORDSHIRE
SHROPSHIRE
LEICESTERSHIRE & RUTLAND
NORFOLK
WEST MIDLANDS
CAMBRIDGESHIRE
MID WALES
HEREFORDSHIRE
WORCESTERSHIRE
WARWICKSHIRE
NORTHAMPTONSHIRE
SUFFOLK
BEDFORDSHIRE
BUCKINGHAMSHIRE
WEST WALES
HERTFORDSHIRE
ESSEX
OXFORDSHIRE
GWENT
GLOUCS & BRISTOL
GLAMORGAN
GREATER LONDON
BERKSHIRE
WILTSHIRE
SURREY
KENT
SOMERSET
HAMPSHIRE
WEST SUSSEX
EAST SUSSEX
CHANNEL ISLANDS
DEVON
DORSET
ISLE OF WIGHT
CORNWALL

Northern Ireland
Channel Islands
Isle of Man

NORTHERN IRELAND

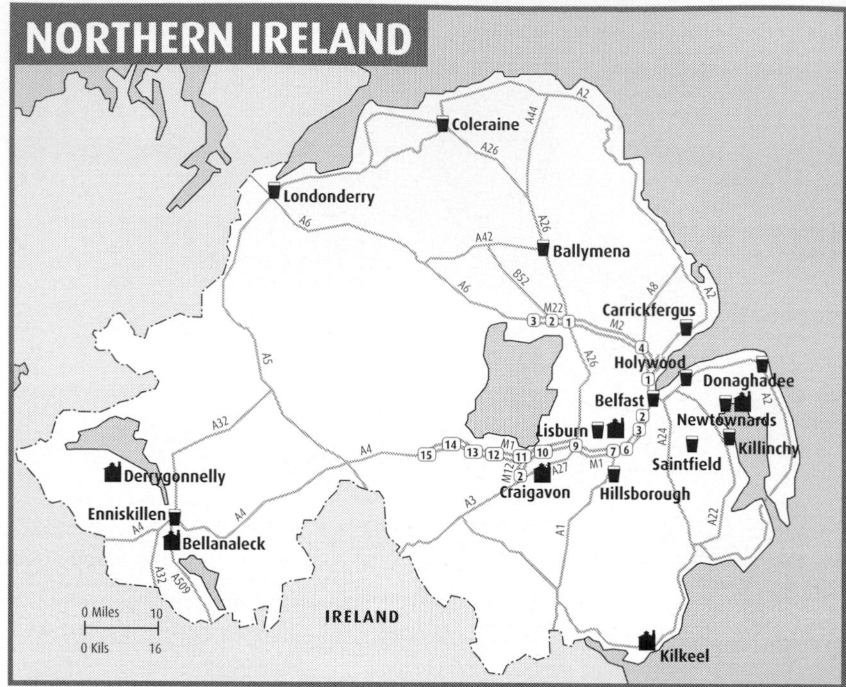

Ballymena

Spinning Mill

17-21 Broughshane Street, BT43 6EB

8am-midnight (1am Fri & Sat) (028) 2563 8985

Greene King Abbot; guest beers H

Wetherspoon's first pub in Northern Ireland brought real ale to a keg-only town. It is a busy town-centre venue with bars upstairs and downstairs. There are plenty of nooks to sit in and up to eight handpumps are in action. The pub opens for breakfast from 8am, alcohol is served from 11.30am (12.30pm Sun). Local CAMRA Pub of the Year in 2012. Q P

Belfast

Botanic Inn

23-27 Malone Road, BT9 6RU

11.30-1am; 12-midnight Sun (028) 9050 9740

thebotanicinn.com

Whitewater Belfast Ale H

The Bot could be characterised as a students and sports pub, although locals make up the regulars too. It is a large venue and offers three busy bars. Downstairs is the main bar and beside it is the public bar where the real ale, always Whitewater's Belfast, is a little cheaper. Sports memorabilia and numerous TV screens adorn the walls. DJs, live music, good food and a nightclub also feature. Q (8B)

Bridge House

37-43 Bedford Street, BT2 7EJ

8am-midnight (1am Fri & Sat); 12-midnight Sun (028) 9072 7890

Greene King IPA, Abbot; guest beers H

Large Wetherspoon pub on two floors, with the main bar downstairs and the family area and toilets upstairs. Eight handpumps dispense two regular beers and up to six constantly changing guests. The bi-annual Wetherspoon beer festivals, and occasional festivals featuring local ales, are very popular. The chain's standard good-value food menu is available. A busy pub, especially at weekends, with friendly, helpful, knowledgable staff. Q (Great Victoria St)

Crown ★

46 Great Victoria Street, BT2 7BA (opp Europa Hotel and Great Victoria St station)

11.30-midnight; 12.30-11 Sun (028) 9024 3187

crownbar.com

Hilden Ale; St Austell Nicholson's Pale Ale; Whitewater Belfast Ale; guest beers H

The Crown is well known as an architectural masterpiece, owned by the National Trust, but less so as a great outlet for real ale. Alongside the three regular beers are two varying guests, usually from the M&B portfolio, with an occasional beer brewed especially for the Crown, such as Winter Stout by Harviestoun. Good traditional pub food is available both upstairs and downstairs. CAMRA Northern Ireland Pub of the Year 2013.

Q (Great Victoria St)

John Hewitt

51 Donegal Street, BT1 2FH (100yds from St Anne's Cathedral)

11.30 (12 Sat)-1am; 7-midnight Sun (028) 9023 3768

thejohnhewitt.com

INDEPENDENT BREWERIES

Ards Newtonards
Clanconnel Craigavon
Hilden Lisburn
Inishmacsaint Derrygonnelly
Sheelin Bellanaleck
Whitewater Kilkeel

Shepherd Neame Master Brew; guest beer Ⓗ
Named after the poet, the John Hewitt offers something a little different. It is run by the Belfast Unemployed Resource Centre, and profits go to fund the centre's work. It is also a focal point for live music, charity events, art exhibitions and beer events such as festivals and tasting sessions. Occasional guests are often from breweries in the Republic of Ireland. Q

Molly's Yard

1 College Green Mews, BT7 1LN
12-9 (9.30 Fri & Sat); closed Sun ☎ (028) 9032 2600
mollysyard.co.uk
Hilden Ale Ⓗ
Situated near Queen's University, this is a highly regarded restaurant where you can enjoy handpulled real ale with your meal. It has a cosy bistro downstairs with a larger room upstairs. The bistro is half wood-lined, and the WC is partly papered with music scores. Part of the Hilden Brewing organisation, good locally-sourced food and beer are served, with a variety of Hilden's output available on two handpumps.
Q (Botanic) (7A)

Sunflower

65 Union Street, BT1 2JG
11.30-midnight (1am Thu-Sat); 5-11 Sun
☎ (028) 9023 2474 sunflowerbelfast.com
Hilden Twisted Hop Ⓗ
This is a traditional corner pub, recently converted to real ale. It is situated north of the city centre, behind Belfast Central Library. The bar downstairs is cosy and has one handpump, usually serving an ale from Hilden Brewery. The owner has a pedigree in real ale, having managed the nearby John Hewitt. The Sunflower has become known as a live music venue with acts in the bar and in the lounge upstairs. Q

Carrickfergus

Central Bar

13-15 High Street, BT38 7AN (opp castle)
8am-midnight (1am Fri & Sat) ☎ (028) 9335 7840
Greene King IPA, Abbot; guest beers Ⓗ
Busy town-centre Wetherspoon with a lively downstairs bar and a quieter family dining space upstairs. The dining area enjoys a fantastic view which includes Belfast Lough and Carrickfergus Castle. Handpumps on both levels dispense the two house beers plus up to three guests. Like other outlets in the chain, alcohol is served from 11.30am (12.30pm Sun). Easy to get to by bus and rail. Q (563)

Coleraine

Old Courthouse

Castlerock Road, BT51 3HP
8am-midnight (1am Fri & Sat) ☎ (028) 7032 5820
Greene King IPA, Abbot; guest beers Ⓗ
One of those Wetherspoon venues that does not look like a pub at first. It was a courthouse from 1852 to 1985, but now people are called to a different type of bar. There are five handpumps with up to three guest ales plus the regulars. Food can be served downstairs or on the imposing balcony accessed by a grand staircase. Alcohol is served from 11.30am (12.30pm Sun). Q

Donaghadee

Moat Inn

102 Moat Street, BT21 0ED
11.30-11.30; 12.30-10 Sun ☎ (028) 9188 3297
moatinn.co.uk
Whitewater Belfast Ale; guest beer Ⓗ
On the main road into Donaghadee, the Moat has a public bar, lounge, upstairs restaurant and garden area for summer days. There are two handpumps in the public bar supplying beers mainly from Whitewater Brewery, often Belfast Ale and Copperhead, with occasional guests. The seaside town is known for the lighthouse and the picturesque harbour just a few hundred yards away. The pub and locality are well worth a visit.
Q

Enniskillen

Linen Hall

11-13 Townhall Street, BT74 7BD
8am-midnight (11 Sun-Tue; 1am Sat) ☎ (028) 6634 0910
Adnams Broadside; Greene King Abbot; guest beers Ⓗ
The former Vintage Pub has become a busy Wetherspoon outlet. It has one bar with several drinking areas on different levels. There are five handpumps dispensing the house beers and guests, and real cider is available on gravity. The area, some 80 miles from Belfast, is well worth a visit. Alcohol is served from 11.30am (12.30pm Sun). Q P (261)

Hillsborough

Hillside

21 Main Street, BT26 6AE
12-11.30 (1am Fri & Sat); 12-11 Sun ☎ (028) 9268 9233
hillsidehillsborough.co.uk
Hilden Ale, Scullion's Irish, Twisted Hop Ⓗ
An outlet for the Hilden Brewery from the neighbouring city of Lisburn, with three handpumps serving Hilden beers and an occasional guest. The interior has been opened up to make three drinking areas, in addition to a restaurant at the back. Food is served throughout the pub. The walls are adorned with pictures of hunting and old Hillsborough. Live music acts play at the weekend and there is a summer beer festival. Outside is a pretty cobblestone beer garden.
Q (38,238)

Holywood

Dirty Duck Ale House

3 Kinnegar Road, BT18 9JN
12-1am (11 Mon & Wed; midnight Tue); 12.30-11 Sun
☎ (028) 9059 6666 thedirtyduckalehouse.co.uk
Inveralmond Thrappledouser; Shepherd Neame Master Brew; guest beer Ⓗ
A compact real ale pub, yards from Belfast Lough. The Duck has sold ale for many years and is a previous CAMRA Northern Ireland Pub of the Year. Three ales are usually available, often from Inveralmond, Hilden and Shepherd Neame. The house beer, Dirty Duck Ale, is brewed by Hilden. Great food is available in the bar downstairs and in the restaurant upstairs. The view is impressive and there is a corner celebrating locally born golfing hero Rory McIlroy. Q

Killinchy

Daft Eddy's

Sketrick Island, BT23 6QH (2 miles N of Killinchey at Whiterock Bay)

11.30-11.30 (1am Fri); 12-10.30 Sun (028) 9754 1615

dafteddys.co.uk

Whitewater Bee's Endeavour H

Set in glorious surroundings, this old favourite has been renovated in recent times. A new log cabin-style public bar, the Lodge, has been built inside the restaurant, and the old public bar has been replaced with the Islands, a pleasant coffee bar. The restaurant continues to serve quality local food, with oysters and lobster among the specialities. An alfresco dining area has also been added. One ale is available from Whitewater, often Belfast Ale, Copperhead or Bee's Endeavour. **Q**

Lisburn

Tap Room

Hilden Brewery, BT27 4TY (5 mins walk from Hilden railway halt)

closed Mon; 12-2.30, 5.30-9; 12-3 Sun (028) 9266 3863

taproomhilden.com

Hilden Ale H

The Tap Room Restaurant sits beside Hilden Brewery in the U-shaped courtyard of the Scullion family's Georgian mansion. It is a long building with dining, bar and seating areas. Diners can enjoy a choice of two ales from the brewery next door along with high-quality, locally-sourced seasonal food. The venue often hosts functions, including an annual beer festival, and brewery tours can be arranged. **Q** (325H)

Tuesday Bell

4 Lisburn Square, BT28 1TS (near bus station)

8am-11 (028) 9262 7390

Adnams Broadside; Greene King Abbot; guest beers H

A large two-floor Wetherspoon pub, part of the Lisburn Square shopping precinct. There are a total of eight handpumps, five downstairs and three upstairs. Local ales from Hilden Brewery occasionally appear along with the house beers and guests. There are TV screens showing BBC news and occasional sporting events. Background music plays in the upstairs bar at the weekend. Alcohol is served from 11.30am (12.30pm Sun). **Q P**

Londonderry

Diamond

23-24 The Diamond, BT48 6HP (centre of walled city)

8am-midnight (11 Mon & Tue; 1am Fri & Sat)

(028) 7127 2880

Greene King IPA, Abbot; guest beers H

In the heart of the main shopping district is the Diamond, one of the city's two Wetherspoon establishments. In an elevated location inside the city walls, this two-storey pub has good views from the upper floor. There are large bars on both floors with a total of 10 handpumps. A varied range of guest ales is usually on offer alongside the regular beers. Real cider is available on gravity. Alcohol is served from 11.30am (12.30pm Sun). **Q**

Ice Wharf

Strand Road, BT48 7AB

8am-midnight (1am Thu-Sat) (028) 7127 6610

Greene King Abbot; guest beers H

A wide, spacious hostelry not far from the city's Guildhall Square on the Strand Road. A former hotel, it was Wetherspoon's first Lloyds No.1 bar in Northern Ireland. The large single-room interior has screens dividing the bar from the seating area. As well as the regular and guest ales, cider is available on gravity. Alcohol is served from 11.30am (12.30pm Sun). **Q**

Newtownards

Spirit Merchant

54-56 Regent Street, BT23 4LP (next to bus station)

8am-midnight (028) 9182 4270

Greene King IPA, Abbot; guest beers H

Wetherspoon pub near the bus station. Warm and welcoming, it has the feel of a local, with knowledgable, friendly and helpful staff. Five handpumps dispense the regular beers plus up to two changing guests. There are three TV screens and a smoking area in the heated courtyard to the side. The standard good-value Wetherspoon food menu is served, with breakfast from 8am. Alcohol is available from 11.30am (12.30pm Sun). **Q** (6,10)

Saintfield

White Horse

49-53 Main Street, BT24 7AB

11.30-11.30; 12-10.30 Sun (028) 9751 1143

whitehorsesaintfield.com

Whitewater Copperhead, Belfast Ale, Bee's Endeavour; guest beer H

Situated in the main street of the historic town of Saintfield, 10 miles from Belfast, this former coaching inn is now a modern pub with bar, lounge and bistro areas. Despite the modernisation, part of the old walls can be still seen. Effectively the brewery tap for Whitewater Brewery, three or more of its ales are always on handpump. **Q** (15,215)

SIBA Direct Delivery Scheme

In 2003 the Society of Independent Brewers (SIBA) launched a Direct Delivery Scheme (DDS) that enables its members to deliver beer to individual pubs rather than to the warehouses of pub companies. Before the scheme came into operation, small craft brewers could only sell beer to the national pubcos if they delivered beer to their depots. Now SIBA has struck agreements with Admiral Taverns, Edinburgh Woollen Mills, Enterprise Inns, New Century Inns, Orchard Pubs, and Punch, as well as off-licence chains Asda and Thresher to deliver direct to their pubs or shops. The scheme has been such a success that DDS is now a separate subsidiary of SIBA. See **www.siba.co.uk/dds_site**

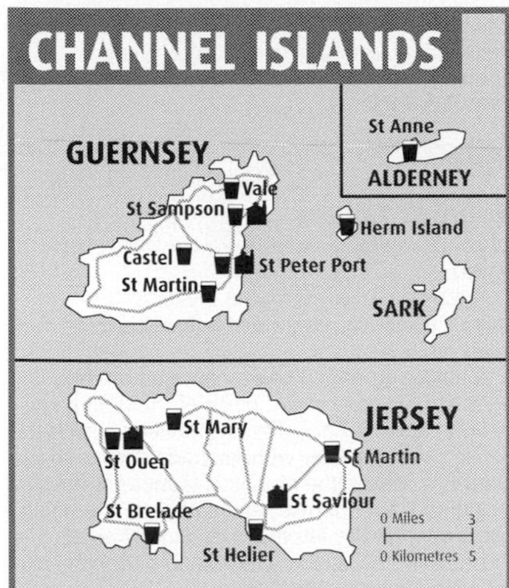

ALDERNEY

St Anne

Georgian House Hotel

Victoria Street, GY9 3UF
10-midnight (12.30am summer) ☎ (01481) 822471
georgianalderney.com
Jennings Sneck Lifter; Wychwood Hobgoblin; guest beers H
Just up from the town church, the hotel extends a warm welcome to all. The pleasant garden has an outside bar and extra casks during the summer months, and sometimes hosts live music. Meals are served all day and real cider may be available in summer. During the winter there are two fires to add to the warm and cosy atmosphere.
P

GUERNSEY

Castel

Fleur du Jardin

Kings Mills, GY5 7JT
10.30-11.45 ☎ (01481) 257996 fleurdujardin.com
Sharp's Doom Bar; White Rock Wonky Donkey; guest beer H
A building of unique charm with two bars – one traditional, small and cosy, attached to the restaurant, the other recently renovated in a more contemporary style to create a comfortable, relaxing area to enjoy a beer. A door from this area leads to a large covered patio and out to the garden. Menus in both the bar and restaurant feature fresh local produce. QP

Grand Mare Hotel & Golf Club

Vazon Bay, GY5 7LL (on Vazon coast road)
10 (11 Sun)-11.45 ☎ (01481) 256576
lagrandemare.com
Black Sheep Ale; Sharp's Doom Bar; guest beers H
The hotel is open all year and welcomes guests and locals alike. It is situated opposite the beach at Vazon, one of the popular west-coast bays. The Club bar has a large-screen TV showing sport and a fire in the winter months. There is also a separate bar with comfy seating attached to the large restaurant. Children are welcome. P

Herm Island

Mermaid Tavern

GY1 3HR (travel Trident ferry from St Peter Port to Herm, then follow signposts)
11 (12 Sun)-10.45; winter hours vary ☎ (01481) 750050
herm.com/mermaid
Beer range varies H
A short trip by ferry from Guernsey takes you to Herm. Originally a fishermen's pub, the Mermaid is the social centre of the island. A large courtyard acts as a suntrap in the summer while in winter an open fire creates a cosy atmosphere. Real ale and cider festivals are held twice a year. The house beer is 4.2% ABV Herm Island Gold. A trip to Herm to discover the island's peace, tranquility and outstanding natural beauty is a must for any visitor to Guernsey.

St Martin

Captain's Hotel

La Fosse, GY4 6EF
11-11 (midnight Fri & Sat); 12-4 Sun ☎ (01481) 238990
thecaptainshotel.co.uk
Black Sheep Best Bitter; Fuller's London Pride H
In a secluded location down a country lane, this is a popular locals' pub with a lively, friendly atmosphere. It has a small comfortable area in front of the bar furnished with a sofa. Quality meals can be enjoyed in the bar or bistro area, or you can take away a pizza. A meat draw is held on Friday. The car park to the rear fills up quickly. P

Douvres Hotel

La Fosse, GY4 6ER
10.30-12.30am ☎ (01481) 238731
lesdouvreshotel.co.uk
Beer range varies H
Former 18th-century manor house set 2½ miles from St Peter Port in private gardens in St Martins, near the south coast, cliff walks and the tiny fishing harbour. A changing range of beers is available on two handpumps. Excellent meals are served in the bar and separate restaurant. Live music features on Friday nights and occasional Wednesdays. The pub is popular with locals and visitors. P

St Peter Port

Cock & Bull

Lower Hauteville, GY1 1LL
11-2.30, 4-12.45am; 11-12.45am Fri & Sat; closed Sun
☎ (01481) 722660
Beer range varies H
Popular pub, just up the hill from the town church, with five handpumps providing a changing range of beer and cider. Live music features throughout the week, with salsa, baroque or jazz on Monday, open mic on Tuesday, jazz on Wednesday, Irish on Thursday and on Saturday a silent set – gentle music that won't hinder good conversation. A meat draw is held on Friday. Seating is on three levels. The pub only opens on Sunday for live rugby.

INDEPENDENT BREWERIES

Liberation St Saviour: Jersey
Pocket St Ouen: Jersey
Randall St Peter Port: Guernsey
White Rock St Sampson: Guernsey (NEW)

ISLANDS

Cornerstone Café Bar

2 La Tour Beauregard, GY1 1LQ

11-11.30; 10-12.30am Fri; 11-12.30am Sat; 12-7 Sun
(01481) 713832 cornerstoneguernsey.co.uk

Beer range varies [H]

This café has a small bar area to the front and further seating to the rear, and was local CAMRA Pub of the Year 2013. Regular quiz evenings are held and there is a large screen for sporting events. The menu offers a wide range of meals plus daily specials (no food Sun, unless advertised). Ales from Randalls, Liberation and White Rock are among the beers available on four handpumps – check the website for what is on and what is coming.

Ship & Crown

North Esplanade, GY1 2NB (opp Crown Pier car park on sea front)

10 (12 Sun)-12.45am (01481) 728994

Liberation Ale; guest beers [H]

Traditional local located in the heart of the town, with fantastic views of the harbour, neighbouring islands and Castle Cornet. The walls are decorated with photos of local shipwrecks, Guernsey and the pub under German occupation. Friendly and welcoming staff make it popular with locals, yachtsmen and tourists. All major sports events are shown in a friendly and lively atmosphere. An ideal place to enjoy a pint and a good-value meal, the pub has been in the same family for 34 years.

St Sampson

La Fontaine

Vale Road, GY2 4DS

11 (10 Sat)-midnight; 12-6 Sun (01481) 247644

Randalls Patois, Hanois Island Stout [H]

The Fontaine is situated on the main road from the Halfway towards L'Ancresse Common and Pembroke Bay. There is a public bar on the road frontage and a large back bar with a serving hatch through to the front. Occasional live music and various social events are hosted, and euchre teams meet once a week. Traditional pub games such as shove-ha'penny, bar billiards and darts are played. With a welcoming host, the pub is popular with locals, particularly for the meat draw on Fridays and Saturdays. P

Pony Inn

Les Capelles, GY2 4GX (on main road between Guernsey Candles and Oatlands Centre)

11 (3 Mon)-11; 10-11 Sat; 12-6.30 Sun (01481) 244374

Beer range varies [H]

A good pub with well-maintained beer and generous portions of excellent food served in the main bar, conservatory area and separate family dining room (booking advisable, particularly at weekends). The public bar at the side shows televised sports and has a pool table. The staff are friendly and families are welcome. There is disabled access for wheelchair users. P

> 'What is your best – your very best – ale a glass?' 'Twopence-halfpenny,' says the landlord, 'is the price of the genuine Stunning Ale.' 'Then,' says I, producing the money, 'Just draw me a glass of the Genuine Stunning, if you please, with a good head to it.'
> **Charles Dickens, David Copperfield**

Vale

Houmet Tavern

Rousse, GY6 8AR (between Vale Church and Rousse Tower)

10-12.45am (6 Sun) (01481) 242214

Sharp's Doom Bar; Wychwood Hobgoblin; guest beers [H]

A popular pub with a coastal position offering picturesque views of the north of the Island. The Houmet has two bars – the Anchor Bar, which is the public bar at the rear with pool and darts, and the Front Bar, where the emphasis is more on food, including fresh Guernsey seafood. Only the public bar is open in the afternoon during the week. The same choice of beer is available in both bars, plus occasional guests. P

JERSEY

St Brelade

Old Smugglers Inn

Le Mont du Ouaisne, JE3 8AW

11-11 (01534) 741510 oldsmugglersinn.com

Draught Bass [H]**; Greene King Abbot** [G]**; guest beer** [H]

Perched on the edge of Ouaisne Bay, set within former granite-built fishermen's cottages, the Smugglers has been the jewel of the Jersey real ale scene for many years. Steeped in history, dating back to when pirates were known to enjoy an ale or two here, its foundations are reputedly from the 13th century. Up to four ales are available including one from Skinner's, and mini beer festivals are regularly held. The pub is renowned for good food including fresh daily specials.
Q P (12,15)

St Helier

Forum

13 Grenville Street, JE2 4UF

11-11 (01534) 768105

Liberation Ale; guest beers [H]

On the outskirts of town, the pub is named after the cinema that once stood opposite. It has a modern interior but with a classic feel and includes a number of brass plaques that were taken from the old Royal Court building. Live sport and background music often feature. Three real ales are always available, and a large range of real ciders. Food is served in the bar from the Indian restaurant above. (3)

Lamplighter

9 Mulcaster Street, JE2 3NJ

11-11 (01534) 723119

Ringwood Best Bitter, Fortyniner; Wells Eagle IPA, Bombardier [H]**; guest beer** [G]

A traditional pub with a modern feel. The gas lamps that gave the pub its name remain, as does the original antique pewter bar top. An excellent range of up to eight real ales is available including one from Skinner's – recent refurbishment means all are now served direct from the cellar. A real cider is also sometimes on offer. Local CAMRA Pub of the Year 2012.

Peirson

17 Royal Square, JE2 4WA
10 (11 Sun)-11 (01534) 722726
Draught Bass; Liberation Ale H; guest beer G
Nestled in the corner of the Royal Square in the centre of St Helier, the pub is named after British army officer Major Francis Peirson, and contains historic reminders of the Battle of Jersey in 1781. Two ales are always on handpump plus an occasional additional beer on gravity. Excellent food is served at lunchtime throughout the year, with evening meals also on offer in summer. The pub has a good reputation with locals and visitors alike. Outside seating is extremely popular in the summer months. Q

Post Horn

Hue Street, JE2 3RE
10 (11 Sun)-11 (01534) 872853
Liberation Ale; guest beer H
Busy, friendly pub adjacent to the precinct and five minutes' walk from the Royal Square. Popular at lunchtimes with its own nucleus of regulars, it offers up to four draught ales. The large L-shaped public bar extends into the lounge area where there is an open fire and TV showing sport. A good selection of freshly cooked food is served. There is a large function room on the first floor, a drinking area outside and a public car park nearby.

St Martin

Royal

La Grande Route de Faldouet, JE3 6UG
10 (11 Sun)-11 (01534) 856289
Draught Bass; Ringwood Best Bitter H; guest beer G
Large, traditional, country-style inn at the centre of St Martin with sizeable public and lounge bars and restaurant area. Owned by Randalls, it has been under the same management for more than 25 years. The interior features traditional furnishings, cosy corners and a real fire in colder months. Guest ales are from the Marston's, Sharp's and Skinner's stables. Good food is popular with locals and visitors alike, with a quality menu served lunchtimes and evenings until 8.30pm (no food Sun eve). P (3)

Rozel Bar & Restaurant

La Valle de Rozel, JE3 6AJ
10 (11 Sun)-11 (01534) 863478 liberationgroup.com
Draught Bass; Liberation Ale; guest beer H
A charming hostelry tucked away in the north-east corner of the island, under new management as a Liberation Group partner pub. It has a delightful beer garden and an excellent restaurant upstairs. Bar meals are served in the public bar and snug, where there is a real fire in the winter. Guest beers from Skinner's and Ringwood are often available. Locals are friendly if sometimes a little rumbustious. (3,13)

St Mary

St Mary's Country Inn

La Rue des Buttes, JE3 3DS
10 (11 Sun)-11 (01534) 482897
Liberation Ale; guest beer H
An archetypal country inn from the outside, this 17th-century farmhouse is opposite the Norman parish church. Following refurbishment in 2009, the interior is contemporary with a main bar and an extensive dining area. The four handpumps serve Liberation and three guest beers, and reasonably priced good food is available daily from an extensive menu. The inn has a comfortable and relaxed atmosphere with seating outside front and rear for when the sun shines. A reasonable walk from the north coast. P (25,27)

St Ouen

Farmers Inn

La Grande Route de St Ouen, JE3 2HY
10 (11 Sun)-11 (01534) 485311
Draught Bass; Liberation Ale; guest beers H
Situated in the hub of St Ouen, the rustic Farmers Inn is a typical country pub offering up to three ales as well as a locally made cider when available (usually April-July). Traditional pub food is served in generous portions. Best described as a friendly community local, there is a good chance of hearing Jersey French (Jerriais) spoken at the bar. P (8,9)

Moulin de Lecq

Le Mont de la Greve de Lecq, JE3 2DT
11-11 (01534) 482818 moulindelecq.com
Greene King Abbot G; Wells Bombardier H; guest beer G
Another free house on the island offering a range of real ales, the Moulin is a converted 12th-century watermill situated in the valley above the beach at Greve de Lecq. The waterwheel is still in place and the turning mechanism can be seen behind the bar. A restaurant adjoins the mill. There is a children's play space and a barbecue area used extensively in the summer. Q P (9)

The importance of the pub

Perhaps the workman spends, night after night, more than he should on beer. Let us remember, if he needs excuse, that his employers have found him no better place and no better amusement than to sit in a tavern, drink beer (generally in moderation), and talk and smoke tobacco. Why not? A respectable tavern is a very harmless place; the society which meets there is the society of the workman; it's his life; without it he might as well have been a factory hand of the good old time – such as hands were 40 years ago; and then he should have but two journeys a day – one from bed to mill, and the other from mill to bed.

Walter Besant, As We Are and As We May Be, 1903

ISLANDS

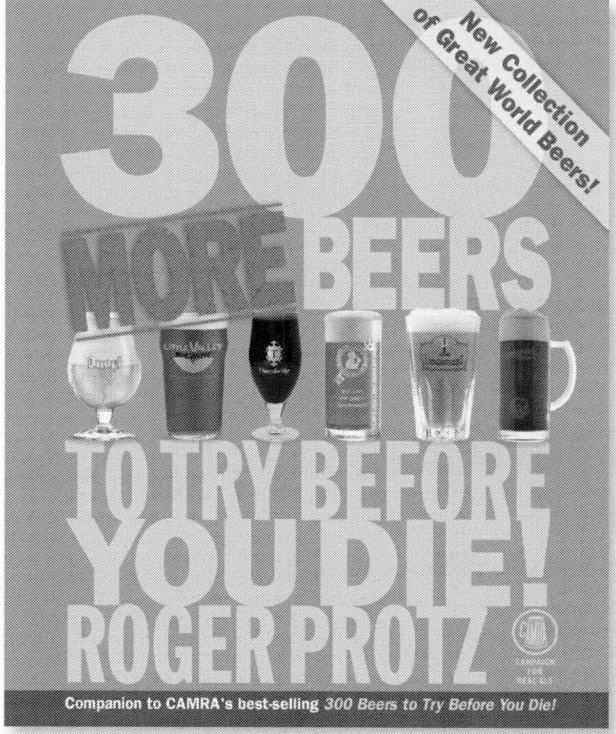

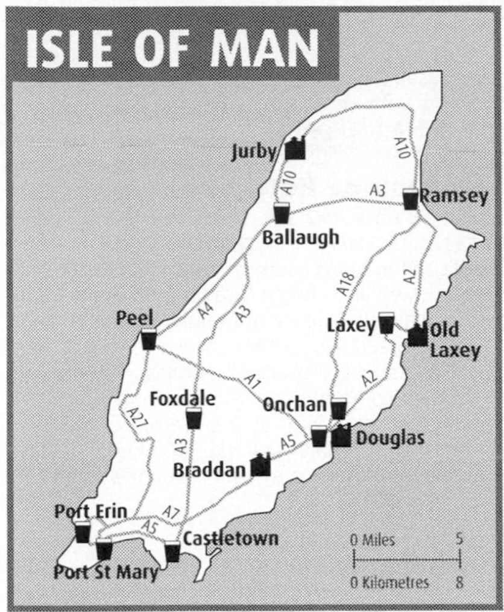

Ballaugh

Raven

The Main Road, IM7 5EG

☉ 12-midnight ☎ (01624) 896128

Okell's Bitter; guest beers Ⓗ

Village-centre hostelry on the TT course adjacent to Ballaugh Bridge. A family-friendly locals' pub with good quality food and ale, the house brew is Raven's Claw, brewed by Okell's. The pub has a comfortable main bar with three areas, one mainly for dining, and a separate games room with pool and darts. The paved patio adjacent to the car park is ideal for watching the TT and Manx Grand Prix races. Q❀◐◑♿♣P🚌(5,6)

Castletown

Castle Arms

The Quay, IM9 1LD

☉ 12-11 (midnight Fri & Sat) ☎ (01624) 824673

Okell's Bitter; guest beers Ⓗ

An attractive and historic pub, the Castle Arms is also know as the Glue Pot – presumably due to the difficulty its clientele have in extricating themselves. It is next to Castletown harbour beneath the walls of Castle Rushen and handy for other heritage attractions. Two small ground-floor rooms have nautical and Manx motor racing themes. The patio is ideal for watching quayside vessels and waterfront wildlife. The only pub in the British Isles to feature on a banknote (Manx £5). ❀◐▲⇌♣🚌(1,2)

Sidings

Victoria Road, IM9 1EF

☉ 11.30-11.30 (12.30am Fri & Sat) ☎ (01624) 823282

Bushy's Castletown Bitter, Ruby 1874 Mild, Bitter; Okell's Bitter; guest beers Ⓗ

The Sidings is a favourite with locals and visitors, comprising two large lounges, a pool room and large beer garden at the rear. On entering, the 10 handpumps stretching the length of the bar are a welcome sight. Only a Heineken font slap bang in the middle mars this pleasant vista. The pub is a popular stop-off for bus and train travellers calling in to enjoy the range of guests and local beers on offer. ❀◐⇌♣P🚌📶

Douglas

Albert Hotel

3 Chapel Row, IM1 2BJ

☉ 10-11 (11.45 Fri & Sat); 12-11 Sun ☎ (01624) 673632

Bushy's Castletown Bitter; guest beer Ⓗ

The nearest real ale pub to the sea terminal, the Albert is an unspoilt local with many regulars. It has a traditionally laid-out central bar and dark-wood panelling, with a pool table in one room and interesting pictures of Steampacket boats in the other. Sport on TV is a frequent feature but never loud enough to spoil conversation. Drinks are reasonably priced, with three local beers from Okell's, Bushy's, Dog House and Hooded Ram as well as an occasional guest. Q♣🚌

Cat With No Tail

Hailwood Court, Governors Hill, IM2 7EA

☉ 12-11 (midnight Fri & Sat) ☎ (01624) 616364

Okell's Bitter; guest beer Ⓗ

A modern pub serving Governors Hill housing estate, situated two miles from central Douglas. The Cat has a public bar with large-screen Sky Sports, pool and darts. Karaoke night is the last Friday of each month. The large lounge has a conservatory which leads to a spacious outside seating area with patio and play area. The main beer is Okell's Bitter with a seasonal or guest beer usually also on offer. ⛹❀◐◑♿P🚌(12,22)

Horse & Plough

Isle of Man Business Park, Bradden, IM2 2QZ

☉ 12-3, 5-11 (midnight Fri); 12-midnight Sat; 12-11 Sun ☎ (01624) 626060

Okell's Bitter; guest beers Ⓗ

Modern Heron & Brearley pub, serving the IoM Business Park and nearby housing estate. There is ample space for diners, families and drinkers to relax in an informal atmosphere, with a good design of offshoot rooms. The large conservatory is popular for functions, and leads to an outside seating area at the rear. There is a pool table and TV sport. An interesting food menu accompanies up to four real ales. The pub is very busy following an excellent refurb. ⛹❀◐◑♿♣P🚌

Old Market Inn

Chapel Row, IM1 2BJ

☉ 9am-midnight (11.30 Sun)

Bushy's Old Bushy Tail; guest beer Ⓗ

The Old Market Inn – probably the smallest pub on the island – has a big heart, handy as a waiting room for the nearby bus station, the Steam Packet ferry, horse trams during the summer, and even the steam railway just along the quay. Keep an eye on the time though, as you are bound to end up in conversation with fellow drinkers and may miss your chosen mode of transport. ⇌🚌📶

Prospect Hotel

Prospect Hill, IM1 1ET

☉ 12-11 (midnight Fri & Sat); closed Sun ☎ (01624) 616773

Okell's Bitter; guest beers Ⓗ

INDEPENDENT BREWERIES

Bushy's Braddan
Doghouse Jurby
Hooded Ram Douglas (NEW)
Okells Douglas
Old Laxey Old Laxey

Opened in 1857, the pub is in the finance sector of the island's capital. The law courts are in close proximity and the walls feature many pictures relating to the law profession. A library area is for those wanting a quiet drink. The bar is busy and popular, especially among office workers. Up to six real ales may be on, often chosen by customers. Wednesday is quiz night.

Queen's Hotel

Queens Promenade, IM2 4NL

12-midnight (1am Fri & Sat) ☎ (01624) 674438

Okell's Bitter; guest beers H

One of just a few remaining pubs on Douglas promenade, the refurbished Queens is popular with visitors and locals alike. There is a great view of Douglas bay, ferries and trams from the outside drinking terrace, which has plenty of seating under heated awnings. Inside there are three distinct areas, one with a pool table, two with low-volume TVs featuring sport. Pub grub is served seven days a week and there is live music at weekends.
Q (Derby Castle)

Railway Hotel

North Quay, IM1 5AB

12-11 (midnight Fri & Sat) ☎ (01624) 670773

Okell's Bitter; guest beer H

A popular harbourside pub, with the guest beers served alongside several world beers, both on draught and in bottles. The Railway has recently undergone a major refurbishment and has an ultra-modern, comfortable lounge divided into three areas – one with impressive views of the quayside. As the name suggests it is convenient for the steam railway.

Rovers Return

11 Church Street, IM1 2AG

12-11 (midnight Fri & Sat) ☎ (01624) 676459

Bushy's Ruby 1874 Mild, Bitter; guest beers H

The Rovers is an interesting pub to say the least – handpumps fashioned from fire hoses, a real fire beneath the dartboard and a shrine to Blackburn Rovers FC are just some of its quirks. Then there is its truly eclectic and enthusiastic clientele. Desperate Dan-size portions of food are served at lunchtimes. The building would be a famous landmark if it was not tucked away behind the town hall.

Sir Norman's (Sefton)

Harris Promenade, IM1 2RW (on seafront)

10-midnight ☎ (01624) 645500 seftonhotel.co.im

Bushy's Bitter; Okell's Bitter; guest beers H

Sir Norman's bar is named after the actor Sir Norman Wisdom who lived on the island for several years. It is becoming renowned as the place to drink a real ale before or after visiting the Victorian Gaiety Theatre. The performers also use the bar as a green room, unwinding in the peaceful atmosphere and enjoying the excellent service.
Q

Terminus Tavern

Strathallan Crescent, IM2 4NR

12-11 (midnight Fri & Sat) ☎ (01624) 624312

Okell's Bitter; guest beers H

Refurbished a couple of years ago, the Terminus offers one or two guest beers alongside Okell's Bitter. The spacious front bar is comfortable, with alcoves around the front windows. Popular for dining, the pub can get busy during food hours. There is also a back bar/games room. The large seating area outside is next to the starting point for the seasonal horse trams and Manx Electric Railway, with views across Douglas Bay.
(MER) P

Woodbourne Hotel

Alexander Drive, IM2 3QF

3 (12 Sat & Sun)-midnight ☎ (01624) 676754

Okell's Bitter; guest beers H

Large three-bar Victorian local in a residential area within walking distance of Douglas centre. A range of Okell's beers is available alongside four or five guest beers. The Woody is a popular, friendly pub with a varied clientele, and boasts a genuine community spirit, with a proud record of charity fundraising. A regular pub quiz is held on Sunday evening, and there is a separate games room for pool.

Foxdale

Baltic Inn

1 Glentramman Terrace, IM4 3EE

4 (2 Fri & Sat)-midnight ☎ (01624) 801305

Okell's Bitter H

Quiet, cosy local, with a roaring real fire in winter. It now has real ale on handpump as well as the bottled Okell's IPA. There are some very interesting photos on the walls of Foxdale during the mining boom. Well worth a visit. Q

Laxey

Bridge Inn

6 New Road, IM4 7BE

11.30-11 (midnight Fri & Sat) ☎ (01624) 862414

Bushy's Ruby 1874 Mild, Bitter H

Popular and lively local pub in the centre of the village. The Bridge has been refurbished but retains its friendly atmosphere and continues to serve an excellent pint. It offers occasional live music, a wide-screen TV and pool table. In 1897, after the Snaefell mining disaster in which 20 men perished, the cellar area was used as a temporary morgue. There are rumours of a resident ghost.

Onchan

Manx Arms

Main Road, IM3 1BE

3-11; 12-midnight Fri-Sun ☎ (01624) 675484

Okell's Bitter; guest beer H

Traditional village pub on the main road with a lounge and bar with pub games including pool, darts and dominoes, and a large-screen TV for sport. Live music features most Saturday evenings as well as an occasional karaoke night. There is an attractive heated patio at the front for smokers and another at the rear next to the large car park. The regular beer is from Okell's with a seasonal or guest ale also usually on offer. A lively and friendly pub. P (3,23)

Peel

Creek Inn

Station Place, IM5 1AT

10-11 (midnight Fri & Sat) ☎ (01624) 842216

Okell's Bitter; guest beers H

Traditional harbourside pub popular with locals and tourists, with ample outdoor seating on the edge of the picturesque harbour. The lounge bar has a nautical theme with etched glass screens featuring sailing ships separating the cosy seating areas. A good selection of ales is on offer to complement the comprehensive food menu. Locally caught Manx queenies (queen scallops) are a speciality, together with locally-cured kippers. The pub hosts live music at weekends. (5,6)

Marine Hotel

Shore Road, IM5 1AH

12-midnight ☎ (01624) 842337

Bushy's Bitter; Okell's Bitter; guest beers H

Popular with all ages, the Marine Hotel overlooks the beach and historic Peel Castle. It has two bar areas and a large bar restaurant accessed via a separate entrance, serving excellent meals seven days a week. A much-improved pub in recent years, it offers locally brewed beers plus guests. (5,6)

White House Hotel

2 Tynwald Road, IM5 1LA

11-midnight ☎ (01624) 842252

thewhitehousepeel.com

Bushy's Ruby 1874 Mild, Bitter; Moorhouse's Pride of Pendle; Okell's Bitter; guest beers H

This is a truly classic establishment – cosy, friendly and welcoming. It has a snug, public bar, separate pool room and a larger room for TV sport and live music at the weekends. One of the few pubs on the island to sell real cider, usually Westons, it was local CAMRA Pub of the Year in 2013 and again in 2014. QP (5,6)

Port Erin

Bay Hotel

Shore Road, IM9 6HL

12 (4 winter)-midnight; 12-1am Fri & Sat

☎ (01624) 832084

Bushy's Castletown Bitter, Ruby 1874 Mild, Bitter, Old Bushy Tail; guest beers H

Bushy's flagship pub is on one of the best beaches on the island. Beach concerts and and a promenade patio make the Bay a great summertime venue, with local bands playing in the winter. The full range of Bushy's brews is available, and can be sampled with a special tasting tray. The interior comprises four traditional rooms – public bar, quiet room, dining room and band area. Q

Falcon's Nest Hotel

Station Road, IM9 6AF

10.30-midnight (1am Fri & Sat); 10.30-11 Sun

☎ (01624) 834077

Bushy's Bitter; Okell's Dr Okell's IPA; guest beers H

The Falcon's Nest Hotel on the south-west coast, overlooking the beautiful crescent-shaped bay, is a free house with two bars. The residents' lounge bar is also open to the public, in the true tradition of a public house, where visitors can enjoy an ever-changing range of guest beers and local ales relaxing in front of an open fire. The Victorian-style Gladstone restaurant offers an extensive à la carte menu and an ever-popular Sunday lunchtime carvery. Q

Port St Mary

Albert Hotel

Athol Street, IM9 5DS

11-midnight; 12-1am Fri & Sat; 12-midnight Sun

☎ (01624) 832118

Bushy's Bitter, Old Bushy Tail; Okell's Bitter; guest beer H

Traditional pub in the heart of the village boasting impressive views over the picturesque harbour. It has three rooms – a large public bar with a games area and a smaller lounge bar, both warmed by real fires, and a seating area with tables used during busier times. Well decorated and comfortably furnished, with Manx Gaelic language quotations adorning the walls, this is an ideal pub to relax in following a sea fishing trip. Beware the low doorway to the Gents. QP (1,2)

Railway Station Hotel

Station Road, IM9 5LF

11-11 (midnight Fri & Sat) ☎ (01624) 830138

Bushy's Bitter, Old Bushy Tail; Okell's Bitter; guest beer H

A welcoming place for drinkers and diners, almost on the station platform, convenient for rail and bus travellers. The beer garden is now complete, along with a secure and safe children's playground. The pub has a restaurant for finer dining and also serves pub lunches/snacks in the lounge area. There are band nights in the Sports Bar most weekends. You can book one of the four guest bedrooms if you fancy a longer stay. Q

Shore Hotel

Shore Road, IM9 5LZ

12-11.30 (midnight Fri & Sat); 12-11 Sun

☎ (01624) 832269

Bushy's Old Bushy Tail; Okell's Bitter H

Large sturdy building with stunning views over Gansey Bay. There is a bar with a pool table and a popular restaurant, also available for private functions. The outdoor seating area is sheltered from what can be biting winds. A quiz is held on Tuesday night. This is one of the few outlets that regularly sells Old Bushy Tail. P

Ramsey

Mitre

16 Parliament Street, IM8 1AP

11-11 ☎ (01624) 813257

Okell's Bitter; guest beers H

Large building with views of the quayside. There are distinct and separate bars on three levels; the basement bar is popular with young revellers at the weekend, while live music is hosted in the upstairs bar. Lunchtime food is available including the popular Sunday carvery. Okell's Jough is often available alongside two beers from other local breweries.

Plough

46 Parliament Street, IM8 1AN

4.30-11 (midnight Fri); 12-midnight Sat; 12-11 Sun

☎ (01624) 813323

Okell's Bitter; guest beer H

Busy pub on Ramsey's main street where during the day shoppers taking a break mingle with football fans. In the evening a mixed clientele vies for space in the two small bar areas. This free house has sold Okell's Bitter for several years and more recently has added an ever-changing guest

ISLANDS

beer. The Plough is a proud sponsor of Shennaghys Jiu, a Manx music festival held in Ramsey in March/April. ◐ ⇌(MER)♣

Trafalgar Hotel

West Quay, IM8 1DW

11-11 (12.15am Fri & Sat); 11.30-11 Sun

☎ (01624) 814601

Bushy's Bitter; Moorhouse's Black Cat; Okell's Bitter; guest beer Ⓗ

Traditional single-room pub on the harbour behind the main shopping street. A CAMRA Isle of Man branch Pub of the Year finalist for many years, the real ales including guests are sourced from all over the UK. Popular during TT week, it is just around the corner from spectacular views of the racecourse. A function room is available upstairs for meetings. Always busy but friendly and welcoming, it has been under the same ownership for the past 21 years. **Q**⛺⇌(MER)♣🚌

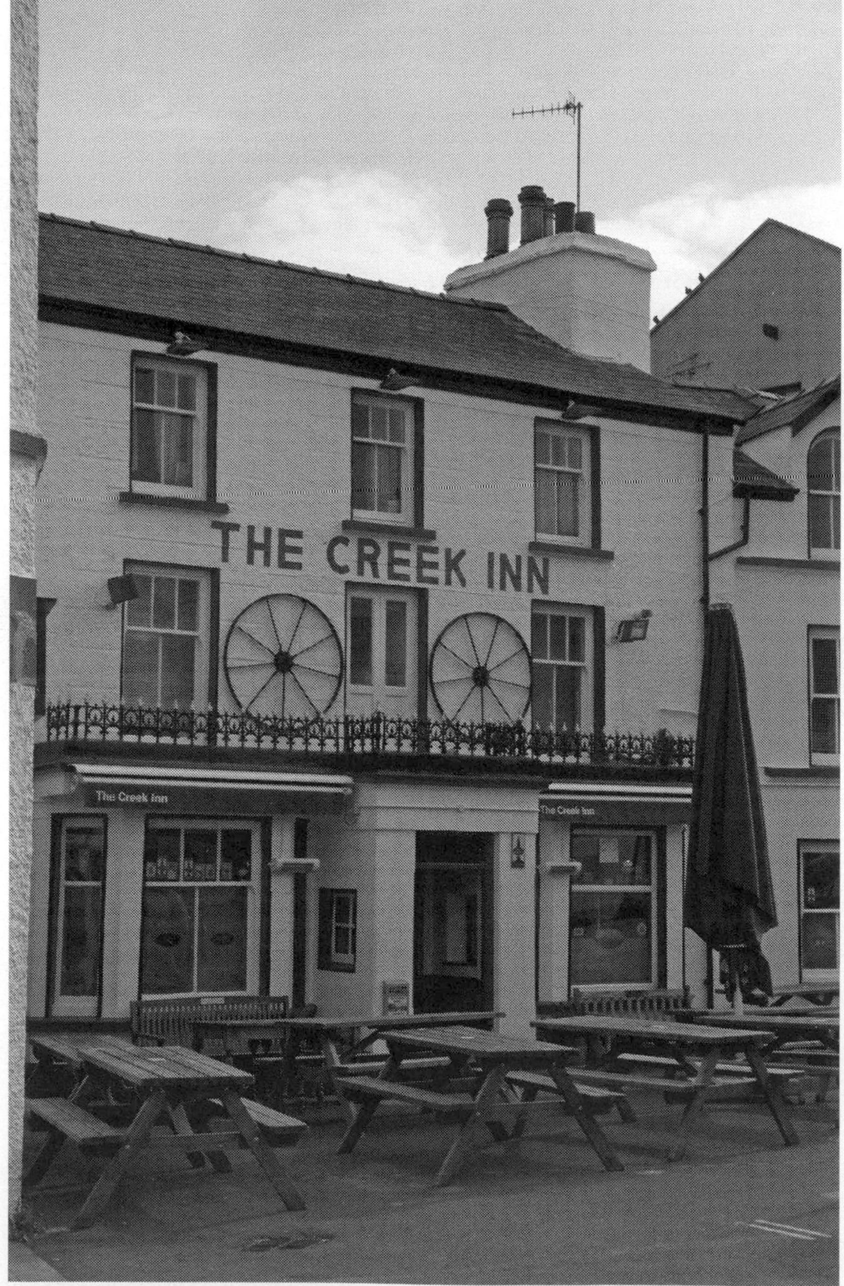

Creek Inn, Peel (Photo: Tom Stainer)

Partridge, Partridge Green (p461)

Dark Star, Partridge Green (p741)

The Breweries

A Future for British Beer

History in the making

SIBA
local beer
Society of Independent Brewers

"Beer is having a moment," says the Let There Be Beer feature in this edition of CAMRA's *Good Beer Guide*. And here in the **Society of Independent Brewers** we couldn't agree more. As we push towards 800 brewing members, we occasionally have to pinch ourselves to remember where we began, with just 20 pioneering microbrewers, in 1980.

During the previous decade the UK had seen its roll call of independent brewing companies fall to below 100. What is astonishing today is that this rather less-than-grand total in the mid 1970s is not dissimilar to the current augmentation every year of the brewing ranks reported in successive Good Beer Guides. For those who regularly chant the mantra that "history is boring", you really haven't been paying much attention to 21st century British brewing, have you?

Even more than with most time lines from there to here, there is a fascinating and complex story to be told: 40 years that have seen consumer revolt and campaigning success; brewing revival and innovation; far-sighted and judicious political and fiscal support; and a growing popular awareness and appreciation of today's explosion in beer diversity and choice. Together these factors have combined to generate a fertile breeding ground for the growth of the British beer industry. Furthermore, they have countered the sometime negativity of punitive duty policies, of loss-leading supermarket booze, changes in leisure habits and consequent pub closures, and of the sledgehammer attacks of an undiscerning harm reduction lobby that cannot tell the difference between good beer in good company and an alcohol hit for the alcohol's own sake.

The culture of beer-drinking has changed, of that there is no doubt. Indiscriminate "swilling" is not quite a thing of the past, but if that's your die-hard habit you're unlikely to be buying this book. The pages that follow bear witness to the evolution of beer and brewing – at a near revolutionary rate – to give us more breweries than virtually all of us have known in our lifetimes; more beer styles and more breadth of flavours than any of us have ever experienced; and more permanent, regular, seasonal, special and one-off brands, available across the country, than we could ever have dreamt of.

From moment to momentum

Of course, although absorbing in itself in the way it can paint a vivid and exciting picture of times past, history's enduring value lies in the lessons it teaches as we get to grips with our

SIBA's BeerX is now a major annual event, combining a trade exhibition, conference, seminars, beer competition and a beer festival open to the public.

own present and seek to take charge of our future. This is not to deny the "runaway roller-coaster" effect – life is indeed what happens while you're making other plans and, when a movement gathers speed and becomes bigger than the sum of its parts, it can be an over-analytical and essentially academic exercise to try and articulate neat and sequential explanations for how and why we are going where we are. Which all sounds too dry for beer and brewing – let's just enjoy the ride!

But in spite of both fortuitous and challenging social, economic and political circumstances, there has been and continues to be enough method in the madness of the modern British brewing industry to make us masters of our own destiny. The various consumer and industry pressure groups and trade associations – including CAMRA and SIBA at the forefront – have worked together and with their parliamentary champions over the last couple of years to turn the tide in beer's favour and to generate a mood of great positivity and optimism going forward. The natural environment for our national drink's sociable enjoyment – the Great British Pub – still perhaps needs to complete its redesign and regeneration, and rediscover its traditional confidence as the hub of the community, but that's a work-in-progress being undertaken with passion and dedication and sheer hard work by landlords and landladies up and down and across the country.

SIBA is a coherent and organised force with a vision and strategic mission to build the future of British beer. We combine the commercial imperatives of our members' businesses with their community foundations and their commitment to a responsible and sustainable future; we strive to ensure their individual voices are heard within their representative body, and their united voice carries weight and commands attention in the corridors of power; and we keep top quality British beer at the very heart of all that we do.

It is ironic that the peculiarities of the English language give power and purpose to beer's "moment" by adding a little "...um" – for there is certainly no indecision or procrastination about the way SIBA and CAMRA stand up for the very best times ahead for beer, brewers, pubs and drinkers. But it is thus that a moment gathers impetus and becomes momentum!

So without further hesitation we ask you to raise your glasses and toast the very best of futures for British beer. Cheers!

Cyclops Beer – the key to beer tasting

There are thousands of real ales in this copy of the *Good Beer Guide*, probably more than ever given the increasing number of British breweries. This is a welcome development but how do you know which ones you're going to enjoy the most?

You don't often know what a beer will taste like from its name alone or from the pump clip, so do you take a risk and hope for the best, or stick to those beers and breweries that you know and trust?

A beer tasting scheme, called Cyclops, was set up to help beer drinkers find their way through the myriad tastes and flavours that we find in real ale. Run by members of the beer industry, including CAMRA and SIBA, Cyclops can help inform your decision with its simple tasting notes which are available for almost two thousand British beers. Hundreds of brewers have signed up to be accredited by Cyclops since its inception in 2006. Cyclops tasting notes tell you how a beer will look, smell and taste, and how bitter and sweet it is. You can also see at a glance its beer style, colour and ABV.

Cyclops tasting notes are increasingly used in pubs around the UK. You can find them on beer mats, chalkboards, glasses as well as brewery websites and even in some supermarkets. Many pubs and breweries also use them to train staff as they take the jargon out of beer descriptions. If you use our tasting notes you will develop an understand of your favourite tastes and flavours in real ale; you may discover that you're a Hop Head if your bitter rating is always 5/5, or a Sweet Tooth, or you may prefer a well-balanced beer if you enjoy a real ale with both bitter and sweet, malty flavours. You can then find more beers with similar profiles and develop an awareness of what, to you, makes a great beer.

You can find the ever-growing number of Cyclops tasting notes at **www.cyclopsbeer.co.uk** and also on the CaskFinder App which is free to download. We hope you enjoy your voyage of discovery using Cyclops Beer.

The Good, the Bad and the Bubbly

Who is brewing fine beer... and who to avoid

The Breweries section proves why the *Good Beer Guide* is more – far more – than just a pub guide. CAMRA has a nationwide team of volunteers called Brewery Liaison Officers attached to every brewery, large and small. They report on a regular basis on the activities of their breweries, which enables the Campaign to compile and constantly update a vast database of information about all the breweries based in the UK and, most importantly, on the range of beers produced.

Beer drinking in general is in decline in Britain, but this does not deter new small breweries opening for business. As any economist knows, it's possible to grow one sector within an overall declining market and that certainly holds true for British brewing. Since the last edition of the Guide was published, 170 new breweries have come on stream. Real ale is a success story. Cask Marque is an independent organisation that monitors beer quality in pubs and awards certificates to publicans who meet its strict standards. It reports that it is pubs with a good range of real ales that are bucking the trend of decline and closure, and growing their business.

The evidence shows that beer drinkers and pub goers – including a growing number of younger drinkers – are switching to cask beer. They appreciate the range of styles on offer and the full-bodied flavours they deliver. Curiously, this message hasn't reached the boardrooms and marketing departments of the giant breweries that dominate production in this country. Sales of their global lagers and 'cream-flow' keg ales are in decline or in some cases free-fall, yet in most cases they are unable to respond to consumer demand for beers with taste.

With so many beer brands now available and many of them owned by the big players in the market, it will be helpful for users of the Guide to give an over-view of the current brewing scene.

The globals

Heineken UK is Britain's biggest brewer as a result of buying the Scottish & Newcastle group in 2008. S&N defied the logic of its name and history by no longer brewing in either Scotland or Newcastle, though shortly before its takeover it acquired the Caledonian Brewery, the Edinburgh independent best-known for Deuchars IPA cask beer. The Dutch group has maintained production at Caledonian and makes cask beers from other breweries available in the former S&N pub estate. But in 2014, Heineken announced it was disposing of around 10 per cent of its 1,250 pubs so its contribution to the real ale sector will decline. It concentrates production at two giant beer factories, Royal in Manchester – which produces 'Australian' Foster's and 'French' Kronenbourg – and John Smith's in Tadcaster. Smith's produces only processed beers: the cask version of John Smith's Bitter has been out-sourced to Cameron's in Hartlepool. The famous bottled beer, Newcastle Brown Ale, has lost its EU guarantee of authenticity by being moved from Tyneside to Yorkshire. Heineken has sold its interest in the Courage, McEwan's and Younger's brands to Charles Wells.

Carlsberg, based in the famous Danish city of Northampton, was originally called Carlsberg-Tetley. Its lack of interest in ale was underscored when it dropped both Tetley from its name and closed the historic brewery in Leeds. The Tetley cask beers are now brewed for Carlsberg by Banks's in Wolverhampton, which has led to a wholly-predictable decline in sales in God's Own Country.

Molson Coors, a Canadian-American conglomerate based in the former Bass breweries in Burton-on-Trent, is the only global brewer to show some interest in the cask sector. In 2011 it bought Sharp's in Cornwall and has busily expanded sales of its leading brand, Doom Bar. It owns a number of other cask brands but cannot brew them in Burton as the equipment needed, such as cask racking, was stripped out years ago. Its cask ales are brewed under licence by several regional brewers.

The British end of AB InBev, the world's biggest brewing group, shows no interest in cask beer whatsoever. It's best known for Stella Artois – the British version is brewed in South Wales – and American Budweiser – not be confused with Czech Budweiser Budvar. The group owns such once-legendary ales as Draught Bass, Boddington's and Flower's. The Flower's beers have been discontinued and Boddington's is now keg-only. Draught Bass, brewed for the group by Marston's, is showing signs of recovery, with many more pubs in the Guide this year stocking what was once Britain's premium cask ale. Will the dollar/euro/real drop at AB InBev? Don't hold your breath.

Big regionals

In spite of the continuing and dynamic growth of the small independent sector, real ale production is dominated by three major regional groups – Greene King, Marston's and Charles Wells – with Fuller's coming up fast on the rails.

As well as its own brands, Greene King also brews the Hardy & Hanson, Morland and Ruddles beers it has acquired as a result of takeovers. Production is centred at its brewery in Bury St Edmunds. It has responded to criticism that its flagship IPA is not a true India Pale Ale at 3.6 per cent by adding an IPA Reserve that's closer to the mark at 5.4 per cent. At a cost of £750,000, it has added a smaller plant within the main brewery that produces a big range of short-run beers. A bottled beer led the field – Double Hop Monster IPA at 7.2 per cent shows the group is listening to consumers and responding to a changing beer market.

A Greene King TV advertisement shows cask beer being stillaged, tapped and spiled in a pub cellar, followed by the beer being pulled to the bar by a traditional handpump. This can only raise the awareness of the skill that goes into real ale brewing – an awareness aimed at younger drinkers, as the ads are shown predominantly on 'youth' channels.

Charles Wells has also promoted its Bombardier premium cask ale on TV with a series of ads featuring the comedy actor Rik Mayall. The promotion came to a sudden end with the death of Mayall in 2014 but will be resumed in a different form. The Bedford-based company became Wells & Young's in 2006 following the closure of Young's London brewery. But they have de-coupled: Young's is a stand-alone pub company taking the Young's beers from Bedford, while Wells has bought from S&N/Heineken the Courage, McEwan's and Younger's brands.

Marston's has followed a different course to Greene King's, maintaining production at breweries it has acquired. Banks's, Brakspear, Jennings, Ringwood and Wychwood continue to brew independently of the Burton head quarters. The Hobgoblin brands in particular have seen spectacular growth. Marston's in 2014 unveiled a new bottling plant in Burton with facilities to produce more bottle-conditioned beers and it's hoped that Old Empire, Owd Rodger and Sneck Lifter may be produced in this form.

Fuller's has invested £5 million in extending capacity at its West London brewery. While London Pride remains one of the country's leading cask ales, the company is not resting on its laurels. Bengal Lancer is one of the finest of the new IPAs while drinkers are regaled with recreations of beers from the 19th and early 20th centuries along with strong ales matured in oak casks.

The independents

The independent sector not only flourishes but is often the pacesetter where new development is concerned. Golden Ale, now a major feature of today's drinking, owes its origins to microbrewers back in the 1980s. Small brewers, with their flexible plants, are able to move swiftly to innovate and meet the restless demands of modern drinkers. Fruit beers, sour beers, chocolate and coffee beers, Belgian-style abbey beers, and beers aged in whisky casks now feature prominently on independent brewers' lists.

Many brewers are 'putting something back' by recycling grain, hops and water and developing reed beds to absorb waste material. Adnams in Suffolk, which now has a national presence, has been the pacesetter in this regard. The ethos of many small brewers is to stay determinedly small, while the likes of Hogs Back, Moorhouse's, Skinner's and Thornbridge have grown to the size of longer-established family brewers.

In Scotland, the success and growth of the likes of Fyne, Highland, Orkney and Stewart's, among others, has brought brewing pride back to a country that for decades was a wasteland thanks to a giant duopoly. Wales has also seen a similar spirited growth in the number of new breweries, while the major independent, Brain's of Cardiff, has added to drinkers' choice with a range of new beers from a pilot plant.

At the minnow end of the industry, there are now a number of 'cuckoo' or 'gypsy' breweries. These are nano-brewers who rent space on other brewers' plants to produce their short-run beers. Some people disapprove of this practice but it adds to choice and diversity and in some cases the cuckoos will move on and build their own nests.

The independent sector is vibrant, dynamic and, above all, growing. There is a beer for all seasons and all tastes. It's a good time to be drinking in Great Britain.

Thornbridge in Bakewell... fast-growing independently

How to use the Breweries section

This section lists breweries operating in the United Kingdom, the Isle of Man and the Channel Islands. Breweries are listed in alphabetical order. They include independent companies (regional, family, micro-brewers and brewpubs), national brewers and global groups. If a brewery owns more than one site, these are cross-referenced. Within each brewery entry, regular beers are listed in increasing order of strength. Websites should be consulted when breweries produce occasional or seasonal beers that are available for less than six months of the year. We mention when breweries produce bottle-conditioned beers but do not list or evaluate them: for further information, see the Guide's sister publication, the *Good Bottled Beer Guide*.

KEY TO SYMBOLS

A brew-pub: a pub that brews beer on the premises.

The brewery is affiliated with the Cyclops system for describing beers to consumers.

CAMRA tasting notes, supplied by a trained CAMRA tasting panel. Beer descriptions that do not carry this symbol are based on more limited tastings or have been obtained from other sources.

A CAMRA Beer of the Year in 2013.

One of the 2014 CAMRA Beers of the Year: a finalist in the Champion Beer of Britain competition held during the Great British Beer Festival in London in August 2014, or the Champion Winter Beer of Britain competition held earlier in the year.

The brewery's beers can be acceptably served through a 'tight sparkler' attached to the nozzle of the beer pump, designed to give a thick collar of foam on the beer.

The brewery's beers should NOT be served through a tight sparkler. CAMRA is opposed to the growing tendency to serve southern-brewed beers with the aid of sparklers, which aerate the beer and tend to drive hop aroma and flavour into the head, altering the balance of the beer achieved in the brewery. When neither symbol is used it means the brewery in question has not stated a preference.

ABBREVIATIONS

OG Stands for Original Gravity, the measure taken before fermentation of the level of 'fermentable material' (malt sugars and added sugars) in the brew. It is only a rough indication of strength and is no longer used for duty purposes.

ABV Stands for Alcohol by Volume, which is a more reliable measure of the percentage of alcohol in finished beer. Many breweries now only disclose ABVs but the Guide lists OGs where available. Often the OG and the ABV of a beer are identical, i.e. 1035 and 3.5 per cent. If the ABV is higher than the OG, i.e. OG 1035, ABV 3.8, this indicates that the beer has been 'well attenuated' with most of the malt sugars turned into alcohol. If the ABV is lower than the OG, this means residual sugars have been left in the beer for fullness of body and flavour: this is rare but can apply to some milds or strong old ales, barley wines and winter beers.

SIBA Indicates a member of the Society of Independent Brewers.

IFBB Indicates a member of the Independent Family Brewers of Britain.

NOTE: The Breweries section was correct at the time of going to press and every effort has been made to ensure that all regularly-available cask-conditioned beers are included.

The Breweries

The breweries listed in this section include micro, small, family, regional, national and global companies. Please use the Beer index (p935) to help locate beers.

1648 SIBA

Old Stables Brewery, Mill Lane, East Hoathly, East Sussex, BN8 6QB
(01825) 840830 1648brewing.co.uk
Tours by arrangement

The 1648 brewery, set up in the old stable block at the King's Head pub in 2003, derives its name from the year of the deposition of King Charles I. One pub is owned and more than 40 outlets are supplied. Seasonal beers: see website. Bottle-conditioned beers are also available.

Triple Champion (OG 1041, ABV 4%)
A chestnut-coloured traditional English ale, deep-flavoured and full-bodied.

Royal Britannia (OG 1041, ABV 4.1%)
Gold-coloured ale with a malty flavour. Lightly hopped with a citrus aroma.

Signature (OG 1044, ABV 4.4%)
Pale, light and crisp refreshing ale with a bitter aftertaste.

Laughing Frog (OG 1052, ABV 5.2%)
A full-bodied, gold-coloured ale. Lightly hopped with a malty flavour.

2 & Nine (NEW)

Tavern, 29 Church Street, Warrington, Cheshire, WA1 2SS 07917 730184

Office: 72 Rydal Avenue, Warrington, Cheshire, WA4 6AT johnwilkinson530@yahoo.co.uk

2 & Nine first brewed in 2014 using the 0.5-barrel plant that was initially used by sister brewery 4Ts (qv). The plant is situated in the kitchen of the Tavern in Warrington and brewing takes place once or twice a week, carried out by the 4Ts brewer. The brewery offers 'brew days' for anyone wanting to brew their own beer.

3 Brewers SIBA

The Potato Shed, Symonds Hyde Farm, Symonds Hyde Lane, Hatfield, Hertfordshire, AL10 9BB
(01707) 271636 3brewers.co.uk
Shop Tue-Fri 12-7pm, Sat 11am-7pm
Tours by arrangement

Launched in 2013 by three enthusiastic brewers from St Albans who transformed a former potato shed into an eight-barrel brewery. It is located on a working farm and sources fresh water from the farm borehole. The brewery supplies two permanent beers to pubs in and around St Albans and also local beer festivals. Spent malt is turned into compost for the farm.

Golden (OG 1038, ABV 3.8%)
Gold-coloured beer with a subtle citrus flavour and a hint of sweetness.

Classic English Ale (OG 1040, ABV 4%)
Deep amber-coloured with a light, hoppy aroma and a rich, rounded malty taste balanced by subtle hoppiness to give a clean, smooth and refreshing ale.

Special English Ale (ABV 4.7%)
A copper-coloured, robust and full-bodied ale with a hint of berries. Well-balanced, smooth and moreish.

360° (NEW) SIBA

Unit 22, Bluebell Business Estate, Sheffield Park, East Sussex, TN22 3HQ
(01825) 722375 360degreebrewing.com

Brewing began in 2013 using a six-barrel plant. Seasonal beers are also available.

Pale #39 (ABV 3.9%)
A light but full-flavoured zesty golden ale.

Sussex #42 (ABV 4.2%)
A traditional, copper-coloured best bitter. Aromatic with a clean bitterness.

Pacific Pale #49 (ABV 4.9%)
A chestnut-coloured pale ale with fruit and floral flavours and crisp bitterness.

West Coast IPA #56 (ABV 5.6%)
Intense tropical fruit flavours and a long, bitter finish.

4Ts

Unit 15, EBL Centre, Picow Farm Road, Runcorn, Cheshire, WA7 4UA

Office: 72 Rydal Avenue, Warrington, Cheshire, WA4 6AT 4tsbrewery.co.uk

4Ts began brewing in 2010 in Warrington but moved to larger premises in Runcorn using a five-barrel plant in 2012. Beers are usually available in the Tavern, Warrington.

Keep Calm (OG 1037, ABV 3.7%)
A pale, refreshing, smooth-tasting beer.

Wise (OG 1040, ABV 4%)
A refreshing beer with aromas of grapefruit and citrus.

Stack (OG 1042, ABV 4.2%)
A well-balanced, easy-drinking pale and hoppy beer.

Side (OG 1048, ABV 4.8%)
A dark tawny-coloured bitter with complex flavours. Full-bodied with a hoppy aftertaste.

Loaded (OG 1050, ABV 5%)
A full strength pale beer with a big hop finish. Tropical fruits, grapefruit and passion fruit aromas come through in the mouth.

Master (OG 1059, ABV 5.9%)
A classic, well-balanced strong beer.

8 Sail SIBA

Heckington Windmill, Hale Road, Heckington, Lincolnshire, NG34 9JW
(01529) 469308 8sailbrewery.co.uk
Shop Thu-Sun 12-5pm

8 Sail Brewery was established in 2010 and operates on a six-barrel brew plant. The brewery

nestles in the shadow of Heckington Windmill, Britain's only eight sailed windmill, from where the brewery takes its name. The brewery shop stocks Lincolnshire bottle-conditioned beers alongside local ciders. Plans are ongoing to install a Victorian bar and display of pub drinking vessels. All beers are also available bottle conditioned.

Millwright Mild (OG 1035, ABV 3.5%)
A mild with rich, dark flavours balanced lightly with hops. The aroma is chocolate with a dry roast and liquorice flavour.

Ale (OG 1038, ABV 3.8%)
A refreshing traditional English pale ale.

Windmill Bitter (OG 1038, ABV 3.8%)
An amber-coloured session bitter with a good blend of malt and hops.

Windy Miller (OG 1038, ABV 3.8%)
A dark and fruity session ale. A selection of malts combine with continental hops to give a pleasant, easy-drinking beer.

Blonde (OG 1040, ABV 4%)
A blonde beer, gently hopped to create a refreshing taste.

Merry Miller (OG 1041, ABV 4.1%)
A traditional bitter. Mid brown in colour with a nutty, malty flavour.

Flour Power (OG 1042, ABV 4.2%)
A refreshing, hoppy beer with an orange citrus and floral aroma and taste.

Golden Ale (OG 1044, ABV 4.4%)
A well-balanced pale beer boasting a citrus and peach aroma with a grassy touch and a dry and slightly tart, citrus-dominated flavour.

Millstone (OG 1045, ABV 4.5%)
A traditional premium bitter with a good balance of malt and hops.

Oat Malt Stout (OG 1046, ABV 4.6%)
A rich, dark, smooth stout brewed with a generous amount of oat malt.

Damson Porter (OG 1050, ABV 5%)
Damsons have been added to give a full-bodied fruitiness to the rich, complex flavours. The aroma is bitter with caramel tones with a malty and slightly fruity flavour with a bitter finish.

Sail Away (OG 1050, ABV 5%)
Brewed in the style of a German Kölsch beer with a good balance of malt and hops.

Victorian Porter (OG 1050, ABV 5%)
A true porter brewed to a classic Victorian recipe. An aroma of berries, sour fruits and roasted malts and deep, intense, chocolate flavours give this dark beer a rich and full-bodied flavour.

Old Colony (OG 1053, ABV 5.3%)
An American-style pale ale.

Black Widow (OG 1055, ABV 5.5%)
A strong, dark ruby mild. Dark malt and liquorice flavours dominate.

John Barleycorn IPA (OG 1055, ABV 5.5%)
Brewed to recreate the taste of an original English IPA.

Imperial Oat Malt Stout (OG 1067, ABV 6.8%)
A black beer brewed with a generous amount of black and oat malt. Liquorice and linseed have been added to complement the dark malts.

A-B InBev

Porter Tun House, 500 Capability Green, Luton, Bedfordshire, LU1 3LS
☎ (01582) 391166 🌐 inbev.com

No real ale. The biggest merger in brewing history in 2008 created AB InBev, when InBev of Belgium and AmBev of Brazil bought American giant Anheuser-Busch, best-known for the world's biggest (but not best) beer brand, Budweiser. The giant is a major player in the European market with such lager brands as Stella Artois and Jupiler. It has a slight interest in ale brewing with the cask- and bottle-conditioned wheat beer, Hoegaarden, and the Abbey beer Leffe. It has a ruthless track record of closing plants and disposing of brands: it has already announced the closure of the historic Stag Brewery in Mortlake, London, formerly Watney's, where the British version of Budweiser is brewed. It's not known where the brand will be produced following the closure of the Mortlake plant but it's unlikely that many readers of the Good Beer Guide will care. In 2000 Interbrew, as it was then known, bought both Bass's and Whitbread's brewing operations, giving it a 32 per cent market share. The British government told Interbrew to dispose of parts of the Bass brewing group, which were bought by Coors, now Molson Coors (qv). Draught Bass has declined to around 37,000 barrels a year: it once sold close to one million barrels a year, but was sidelined by the Bass empire. It is now brewed under licence by Marston's (qv). Cask conditioned Boddingtons was brewed for AB InBev by Hydes but the contract expired in 2012 and the beer is currently not being brewed. AB InBev has put Draught Bass, Boddingtons and Flowers cask beers up for sale for £15 million.

Abbey SIBA

Abbey Brewery, Camden Row, Bath, BA1 5LB
☎ (01225) 444437 🌐 abbeyales.co.uk
Tours by arrangement

Founded in 1997, Abbey Ales was the first brewery in Bath for over 50 years. It supplies more than 80 regular outlets within a 20-mile radius of Bath, while selected wholesalers deliver beer nationally. It has four tied houses. Seasonal beers: see website.

Bellringer (OG 1042, ABV 4.2%)
A notably hoppy ale, light to medium-bodied, clean-tasting, refreshingly dry, with a balancing sweetness. Citrus, pale malt aroma and dry, bitter finish.

Abbey Ford (NEW)

c/o 6 Ford Road, Chertsey, Surrey, KT16 8HD
🌐 abbeyfordbrewery.co.uk

Abbey Ford began brewing in 2013. Beers can be found around the Chertsey area.

Knight on the Tiles (ABV 4%)
A well-balanced best bitter. Dark amber in colour it is refreshing sweet to start with a subtle hop finish.

AD 666 Special (ABV 4.8%)
A full-bodied special bitter. Sweet malt up front transitions to a slightly bitter finish.

Abbey Grange

See Llangollen

Abbeydale SIBA

Unit 8, Aizlewood Road, Sheffield, South Yorkshire, S8 0YX
☎ (0114) 281 2712 abbeydalebrewery.co.uk

Since starting in 1996, Abbeydale Brewery has grown steadily; it now produces upwards of 130 barrels a week, and recent investment has enabled further growth. The regular range is complemented by ever-changing seasonals – see website.

Matins (OG 1034.9, ABV 3.6%)
Pale and full flavoured; a hoppy session beer.

Brimstone (OG 1039, ABV 3.9%)
A russet-coloured bitter beer with a distinctive hop aroma.

Moonshine (OG 1041.2, ABV 4.3%)
A well-balanced pale ale with a full hop aroma. Pleasant grapefruit traces may be detected.

Absolution (OG 1050, ABV 5.3%)
A fruity pale ale, deceptively drinkable for its strength. Sweetish but not cloying.

Black Mass (OG 1065, ABV 6.7%)
A strong black stout with complex roast flavours and a lasting bitter finish.

Abbot (NEW)

Maygate, Dunfermilne, KY12 7NE
☎ (01383) 733266 abbothouse.co.uk
Shop 10am-5pm daily
Tours by arrangement

Brewing began in 2013 in an outbuilding adjoining the historic Abbot House Heritage Centre and Dunfermline Abbey. The layout of the brewhouse and brewing methods used replicate pre-industrial 17th century brewing of the time. A wide range of beers is produced, many of which utilise historic recipes adapted to suit modern tastes. There is a public viewing area with accompanying storyboards for visitors detailing the historic role of ale in Dunfermline.

Pilgrim (OG 1030, ABV 3%)
A light session ale with hoppy undertones.

Pot Stirrer (OG 1040, ABV 4.2%)
A classic red-coloured Scottish beer with a balance of slightly peppered malt and refreshing hops.

Dunfermline Nut Brown (OG 1045, ABV 4.4%)
A dark premium beer using a blend of six different malts balanced by traditional English hops.

Adventuress (OG 1046, ABV 4.5%)
A well-balanced golden ale.

Scottish Blossom Honey Beer (OG 1047, ABV 4.8%)
A lightly hopped and malted honey beer made with the honey gathered from Perthshire fruit fields.

Scottish Heather Honey Beer (OG 1047, ABV 4.8%)
A lightly hopped and malted honey beer made with heather honey ensuring the subtle aroma and taste predominates.

Ale Wand (OG 1048, ABV 5%)
A dark malty brew with liquorice and dark chocolate overtones.

Benedictus (OG 1068, ABV 7%)
A highly aromatic strong beer, rich in flavour.

Acorn SIBA

Unit 3, Aldham Industrial Estate, Mitchell Road, Wombwell, Barnsley, South Yorkshire, S73 8HA
☎ (01226) 270734 acorn-brewery.co.uk
Shop Mon-Fri 9am-5pm
Tours by arrangement

Acorn was set up in 2003 with a 10-barrel plant expanding to 20-barrels when the brewery moved to larger premises. All beers are produced using the Barnsley Bitter yeast strain, dating back to the 1850s. Seasonal and bottle-conditioned beers are available: see website.

Yorkshire Pride (OG 1037, ABV 3.7%)
A session beer that's golden in colour with pleasing fruit notes. A mouthwatering blend of malt and hops create a fruity taste which leads to a clean, bitter finish.

Barnsley Bitter (OG 1038, ABV 3.8%)
A brown bitter with a smooth malty bitterness throughout with notes of chocolate and caramel. Fruity bitter finish.

Barnsley Gold (OG 1041.5, ABV 4%)
A golden ale with fruit in the aroma with a hoppy and fruity flavour throughout. A well-hopped, clean, dry finish.

Blonde (OG 1040.5, ABV 4%)
A clean tasting golden-coloured hoppy beer with a refreshing bitter and fruity aftertaste.

1887 Red (OG 1044, ABV 4.4%)

Old Moor Porter (OG 1045, ABV 4.4%)
A rich tasting porter, smooth throughout with a hint of chocolate and liquorice.

Sovereign (OG 1044, ABV 4.4%)
Brown in colour with malt and fruit aromas, a roast maltiness and fruitiness carry throughout including the aftertaste.

Gorlovka Imperial Stout (OG 1058, ABV 6%)
This black stout is rich and smooth and full of chocolate and liquorice flavours with a fruity, creamy finish.

Acton

Unit 2, 13B Castle Island Way, North Seaton, Northumberland, NE63 0XL ☎ 07707 703182
actonales1@outlook.com

Formerly known as Gundog, brewing began in 2011 using a 10-barrel plant. Regular beers are produced on a rotating schedule, along with monthly ales and specials.

Adkin

Correspondence only: c/o 52 Adkin Way, Wantage, Oxfordshire, OX12 9HW ☎ 07709 86149
adkinbrewery.co.uk
Tours by arrangement (limited to four persons)

Adkin was established on a 0.5-barrel plant in 2007. A new similar-sized plant was installed in 2013. Twelve brews are produced by prior order. The beers are most easily found at regional beer festivals, but are starting to appear in the local free trade. Bottle-conditioned beers are available.

Adnams SIBA

Sole Bay Brewery, East Green, Southwold, Suffolk, IP18 6JW
☎ (01502) 727200 adnams.co.uk
Shop 10am-6pm daily
Tours by arrangement

The company was founded by George and Ernest Adnams in 1872. About 70 pubs are owned and there is national distribution. Beers are from a new 300 barrel plant within the confines of the present site. Seasonal beers: see website.

Lighthouse (OG 1037, ABV 3.4%)
A quaffable beer with bitterness predominating.

Southwold Bitter (OG 1037, ABV 3.7%)
Aromas of toffee apple, caramel and sulphur. Taste is a complex mix of malt toffee and roast bitterness with hops. Malty bitter and apple flavours linger into the aftertaste.

Explorer (OG 1042, ABV 4.3%)
Fruity bitter taste with very delicate sweet aftertaste.

Ghost Ship (OG 1046, ABV 4.5%)

Broadside (OG 1049, ABV 4.7%)
Rich, malty aroma with blackberries and dried fruit. Rich and full flavours of malt and fruit, with roast and caramel notes and subtle hops. Well-balanced, long-lasting aftertaste.

Adur

Brick Barn, Charlton Court, Mouse Lane, Steyning, West Sussex, BN44 3DG
☎ (01903) 867614 adurvalleycoop.com
Tours by arrangement

Adur Brewery was launched in 2008 on a 5.5-barrel plant, marking the return of brewing to the Adur Valley after an interval of nearly 100 years. A large part of the output is sold as bottle-conditioned beer. The brewery is in the course of a transition to a co-op. See the website for the latest information.

Ropetackle Golden Ale (OG 1036, ABV 3.4%)
A light, golden ale with an initial sweetness and delicate aroma balanced by a dry finish.

Hop Token: Amarillo (OG 1040, ABV 4%)
An amber bitter giving notes of peach and grapefruit in both aroma and taste, a good bitterness and a long, dry finish.

Hop Token: Summit (OG 1040, ABV 4%)

Velocity (OG 1044, ABV 4.4%)
Traditional best bitter with a hoppy aroma and a hint of marmalade in the taste.

Black William (OG 1055, ABV 5%)
A rich, black stout with dark chocolate aromas and roasted flavours.

Robbie's Red (OG 1050, ABV 5.2%)
A strong red-brown ale with an aroma of malt and hops. Slight initial sweetness leads into complex flavours including smoky orange peel and a satisfying bitterness which persists into the long finish.

Alcazar

Alcazar Brewery, Church Street, Old Basford, Nottingham, NG6 0GA
☎ (0115) 978 2282

Office: Turnstone Taverns, c/o Railway Tavern, 188 Station Road, Langley Mill, Nottinghamshire, NG16 4AE turnstonetaverns.co.uk
Tours by arrangement

Alcazar was established in 1999 and is located behind its brewery tap, the Fox & Crown. The brewery is full mash with a 10-barrel brew length. Seasonal beers are available.

Sheriffs Gold (OG 1036, ABV 3.6%)
Slightly sweet yellow session bitter made with First Gold and Goldings hops.

Ale (OG 1040, ABV 4%)
Flagship golden ale, full of citrus hops with a dry, bitter aftertaste.

New Dawn (OG 1045, ABV 4.5%)
Full-bodied golden ale, brewed with Cascade hops.

Foxtail (OG 1049, ABV 4.9%)
A strong malty and bitter brown ale. Named Brush Bitter in the brewery tap.

Vixen's Vice (OG 1052, ABV 5.2%)
A premium strength hoppy pale ale.

Alchemist

See Golden Duck

Alechemy SIBA

Unit 2c, Young Square, Brucefield Industry Park, Livingston, EH54 9BX ☎ 07748 156973
alechemybrewing.com

Dr James Davies, a keen craft brewer and chemist, started brewing using a 12-barrel plant in 2012. Seasonal beers, often interestingly hoppy, are available and new beers are regularly produced: see website for details.

Rhapsody (OG 1038, ABV 3.8%)

Ritual (OG 1042, ABV 4.1%)
Well balanced golden ale. A strong hop character, balanced by malt and fruit with a long, dry finish.

Five Sisters (OG 1045, ABV 4.3%)
Flavoursome tawny beer with excellent balance of malt, hops and fruit plus hints of roast and caramel. Lingering distinctive finish.

Black Aye PA (OG 1047, ABV 4.6%)
A dark robust beer with substantial malt and a significant hop character. Roast, caramel and fruit add to the complexity.

Citra Burst (OG 1056, ABV 5.4%)

Rye O' Rye (OG 1056, ABV 5.6%)
Rich amber beer with a light floral and citrus aroma and distinct rye spiciness.

AleCraft

c/o Farmers Boy, 134 London Road, St Albans, Hertfordshire, AL1 1PQ ☎ 07939 634677

Office: 17 Springhill, Nuneaton, Warwickshire, CV10 0NP alecraftmanagement.co.uk

AleCraft began brewing in 2012 utilising the equipment at the Verulam brewery in St Albans. Beers are delivered direct to Yorkshire, the Midlands and the south east. All beers are also available bottle conditioned.

Simplicity (OG 1038, ABV 3.6%)
A hoppy, straw-coloured session bitter with a hop nose and flavour.

Sauvin so Good (OG 1039, ABV 4%)
Straw-coloured ale with a massive citrus and gooseberry nose and flavour that lingers through to the long, bitter finish.

Night on the Tiles (OG 1044, ABV 4.7%)
American pale ale with a big hop character.

Bartholomew Porter (OG 1048, ABV 4.8%)
An almost pure black ale overrun with massive chocolate, burnt and roast malt flavours.

Fudgey Porter (OG 1048, ABV 4.8%)
A version of Bartholomew Porter with vanilla fudge added.

Sonoma (OG 1070, ABV 8%)
An American-style double IPA. Deep golden in colour with a big hop character.

Ales of Scilly SIBA

2b Porthmellon Industrial Estate, St Mary's, Isles of Scilly, Cornwall, TR21 0JY
☎ (01720) 423233 ☎ 07810 816681
✉ mark@alesofscilly.co.uk
Shop by arrangement with the brewer – call first
Tours by arrangement

Opened in 2001, Ales of Scilly is the most south-westerly brewery in Britain. Several local pubs are supplied, with regular exports to mainland beer festivals. One or two seasonal beers appear throughout the summer, from March to September.

Scuppered (OG 1041, ABV 4.2%)
Faint aroma of malt and apples giving sweet maltiness balanced by bitterness and fruit esters. Malt and sweet fruit finish.

Alfred's SIBA

Unit 5B, Scylla Industrial Estate, Winnall Valley Road, Winchester, Hampshire, SO23 0LD
☎ (01962) 859999 alfredsbrewery.co.uk
Shop Fri 3-7pm, Sat 9.30am-12.30pm
Tours by arrangement

A 3.5-barrel brewhouse opened by Steve and Isabelle Haigh in 2012. Steve previously brewed for three other renowned Hampshire breweries. Fermentation capacity has since increased from one to three vessels, making room for experimentation which usually results in a new recipe each quarter. Deliveries are made to pubs within 15 miles of Winchester. Seasonal, one-off and bottle-conditioned beers are available.

Saxon Bronze (OG 1038, ABV 3.8%)
A distinct, bronze-coloured brew. Tangerine and citrus fruit from the hops lead to a clean finish.

Winchester Pale Ale (OG 1045, ABV 4.5%)
A crisp, clean and hoppy golden beer.

All Hallows

Goodmanham Arms, Main Street, Goodmanham, East Yorkshire, YO43 3JA
☎ (01430) 873849 goodmanhamarms.co.uk

Abbie Logozzi started brewing in 2012 in outbuildings behind the Goodmanham Arms using a five-barrel plant. The brewery name comes from the adjacent 12th-century All Hallows Church. Local legendary characters are used in the naming of some of the beers. Brews are supplied to the pub, beer festivals when requested, and to the local free trade. Seasonal and occasional brews supplement the core range.

Peg Fyfe Dark Mild (OG 1032, ABV 3.2%)

Mischief Maker (OG 1038, ABV 3.8%)
A copper-coloured session bitter.

Ragged Robyn (OG 1050, ABV 5%)
A traditional ruby-coloured heritage ale.

Allendale SIBA

Allen Mills, Allendale, Northumberland, NE47 9EQ
☎ (01434) 618686 allendalebrewery.com
Shop Mon-Fri 9am-5pm
Tours by arrangement

Brewing returned to Allendale in 2006 and the business now supplies over 300 pubs, shops and restaurants across the North of England from its 10-barrel plant. Seasonal beers: see website.

North Sheep (OG 1036, ABV 3.6%)
A light summery ale, golden amber in colour.

Wagtail Best Bitter (OG 1037, ABV 3.8%)
Amber bitter with spicy aromas and a long, bitter finish.

Golden Plover (OG 1039, ABV 4%)
Light, refreshing, easy-drinking blonde beer with a clean finish.

Pennine Pale (OG 1040, ABV 4%)
A light golden ale, brewed with a trio of American hops for a full citrus fruit flavour and a refreshing finish

Swift (OG 1045, ABV 4.5%)
A golden amber-coloured ale with a grapefruit bite. Full-bodied with a hoppy finish.

Adder Lager (OG 1050, ABV 5%)
A crisp, refreshing Pilsner-style lager.

APA (OG 1056, ABV 5.5%)
A full bodied IPA with citrus and tropical aromas, full of flavour and refreshing bitterness.

Wolf (OG 1053, ABV 5.5%)
Full-bodied red ale with bitterness in the taste giving way to a fruity finish.

AllGates SIBA

The Old Brewery, Brewery Yard, off Wallgate, Wigan, WN1 1JU
☎ (01942) 234976 allgatesbrewery.com
Tours by arrangement

AllGates commenced brewing in 2006 in a fully restored Grade II-listed tower brewery at rear of Wigan's General Post Office as a modern five-barrel plant. Beers are principally delivered to its own eight-pub estate. Seasonal beers and monthly specials: see website.

All Black (OG 1036, ABV 3.6%)
Dark brown beer with a malty, fruity aroma. Creamy and malty in taste, with blackberry fruits and a satisfying aftertaste.

Ostara (OG 1036, ABV 3.6%)
Pale blonde, easy-drinking ale.

California (OG 1037, ABV 3.8%) ◆
A pale yellow beer with a restrained hoppy and fruity aroma. It is clean and fresh tasting, with hops and fruit in the mouth and a bitter, hoppy finish.

Napoleon's Retreat (OG 1038, ABV 3.9%)
A deep copper-coloured traditional session bitter.

Pretoria (OG 1039, ABV 3.9%)
Refreshing golden session ale with distinctive citrus aromas.

Citra (OG 1042, ABV 4.2%)
Single hopped pale ale with citrus aromas.

Allsaints

c/o Coastal Brewery, Unit 10B, Cardrew Industrial Estate, Redruth, Cornwall, TR15 1SS

Formerly known as Doghouse Brewery, which closed in 2007, Allsaints recommenced production in 2008 and currently use spare capacity at Coastal Brewery in Redruth. Four regular beers are produced and changing seasonal beers.

St Piran Cornish Best Bitter (OG 1040, ABV 4%)

St Arnold (OG 1046, ABV 4.6%)

Alnwick

Alnwick, Northumberland
✉ **info@spiritofnorthumberland.com**

Beers are contract brewed by three unnamed northern breweries.

Canny Bevvy (ABV 2.8%)

Scotch Ale (ABV 3.6%)

Amber Ale (ABV 3.8%)

Gold (ABV 4.2%)

IPA (ABV 4.5%)

Stout (ABV 4.5%)

Brown Ale (ABV 4.7%)

Amber SIBA

Unit A, Asher Lane Business Park, Pentrich, Ripley, Derbyshire, DE5 3SW
☎ **(01773) 512864** 🌐 **amberales.co.uk**
Tours by arrangement

Amber Ales began production in 2006 on a five-barrel plant. Five core beers and a range of experimental and seasonal ales are all available at the brewery tap, the Talbot Taphouse in Ripley. Around 50 outlets are supplied direct, further afield via distributors. Bottle-conditioned beers are available and are suitable for vegetarians and vegans.

Chocolate Orange Stout (OG 1040, ABV 4%)

Derbyshire Gold (OG 1039, ABV 4%)
A well-hopped golden ale.

Original Black Stout (OG 1040, ABV 4%)
Traditional stout made with a complex blend of five malts to give a full-flavoured yet smooth and easy-drinking base with a subtle hop aroma.

Barnes Wallis (OG 1040, ABV 4.1%)
An easy-drinking IPA-style bitter, copper-coloured with a full malt flavour.

Revolution (OG 1047, ABV 4.5%)

Dambuster (OG 1051, ABV 5.5%)

Imperial IPA (OG 1058, ABV 6.5%)
Traditional IPA with a substantial malty base and big hop profile.

Ambridge SIBA 👁

Unit 2A, Priory Piece Business Park, Priory Farm Lane, Inkberrow, Worcestershire, WR7 4HT
☎ **(01386) 792233** 🌐 **ambridgebrewery.co.uk**
Tours by arrangement

Ambridge began brewing in 2013, initially for the family pub, the Bulls Head in Inkberrow. Later that year they acquired the Wyre Piddle Brewery. The beers from both breweries continue to be brewed but during 2013 relocated to a single brew house on the outskirts of the village. Further regular and seasonal beers are planned.

Shires Bitter (OG 1039, ABV 3.8%)
A premium bitter with a good balance of hops and malt. Hops carry on from the taste to a bittersweet finish.

Just Jane (OG 1040, ABV 3.9%)
Refreshing golden session beer. Hops are balanced by malt throughout.

WPA (Worcestershire Pale Ale) (OG 1043, ABV 4.2%)
A premium pale ale with a good balance of hops and malt. Hops carry on from the taste to a bittersweet finish

Red Zeppelin (OG 1046, ABV 4.5%)
Deep amber red-coloured ale, with a distinctive hop aroma and palate.

Brewed under the Wyre Piddle name:

Piddle in the Hole (OG 1040, ABV 3.9%) ◆
Copper-coloured and quite dry, with lots of hops and fruitiness throughout.

Piddle in the Dark (OG 1046, ABV 4.5%)
A rich ruby-coloured bitter with a smooth flavour.

Piddle in the Wind (OG 1046, ABV 4.5%) ◆
A superb mix of flavours. A hoppy nose continues through to a lasting aftertaste, making it a good, all-round beer.

An Teallach SIBA

Camusnagaul, Dundonnell, Garve, IV23 2QT
☎ **(01854) 633306** ✉ **ataleco1@yahoo.co.uk**
Tours by arrangement

An Teallach was formed in 2001 by husband and wife team David and Wilma Orr on Wilma's family croft on the shores of Little Loch Broom, Wester Ross. 60 pubs are supplied.

Ale (OG 1042, ABV 4.2%) ◆
A classic pint in the Scottish 80/- tradition. Plenty of malt in the nicely-balanced bittersweet taste.

Crofters Pale Ale (OG 1042, ABV 4.2%) ◆
A good quaffing, lightly-flavoured golden ale. Citrus hops in the taste and with a slight astringency in the finish.

Suilven (OG 1043, ABV 4.3%) ◆
A refreshing yellow brew with plenty of citrus fruits and hops throughout.

Beinn Dearg Ale (OG 1044, ABV 4.4%) ◆

A well-balanced malty, hoppy, sweetish beer with a long, malty bitter aftertaste.

Kildonan (OG 1044, ABV 4.4%) ◆
Plenty of fruit and a good smack of bitterness in this golden ale.

Anarchy SIBA

Unit 5, Whitehouse Farm Centre, Stannington, Northumberland, NE61 6AW
☎ (01670) 789755 ☎ 07702 810111
anarchybrewco.com
Shop 12-5.30pm first Sat of the month
Tours by arrangement

Anarchy began brewing in 2012 using a 10-barrel plant producing a range of hand-crafted beers and lagers. All regular beers are available in bottle-conditioned form. Some beers are produced in collaboration with local bands.

Smoke Bomb (OG 1043, ABV 3.9%)
A bitter with a light smoky nose and citrus flavours matched with dark, smooth toffee malts.

Blonde Star (OG 1041, ABV 4.1%)
Lemon, grapefruit and passion fruit flavours from the hops combine with pale malts to give a crisp and fresh, light-bodied session blonde.

Citra Star (OG 1041, ABV 4.1%)
Citrus, grapefruit, lemon, lime and passion fruit flavours come from the hops to give a clean, crisp, light-bodied blonde beer.

Rough Justice (OG 1046, ABV 4.5%)
Resinous pine and orange flavours create a dry and bitter dark red rye beer.

Grin & Bare It (OG 1050, ABV 5%)
Pale wheat beer made with South Pacific hops.

Urban Assault (OG 1050, ABV 5%)
Medium-bodied light red pale ale with heavy notes of lemon, orange and passion fruit in the flavour, followed by a bitter finish.

Crime Scene (OG 1056, ABV 5.5%)
Fruit-flavoured medium-bodied amber beer made using caramel malts that meld into a long-lasting bitter aftertaste.

Quiet Riot (OG 1063, ABV 6.6%)
Kiwi fruit, lime and orange zest flavours combine to give a big bitterness that is balanced with sweet malts.

Sublime Chaos (OG 1075, ABV 7%)
Liquorice, chocolate and caramel-flavoured breakfast stout infused with Ethiopian Guji natural coffee beans backed with dark malts.

Anchor Springs SIBA

Lineside Way, Wick, West Sussex, BN17 7EH
debbie@jenkinslittlehampton.co.uk

Kevin Jenkins, owner of the Crown, Littlehampton, established the brewery in 2010 using the five-barrel plant previously used at the Dark Star brewery. Main outlets are its brewery tap, the Crown in Littlehampton, and the Spy Glass in Worthing.

LA Gold (OG 1039.5, ABV 3.7%)
A golden session ale. Initial sweetness leads to a citrus kick and lingering crisp, clean finish.

Mild (OG 1045.5, ABV 3.8%)

Worthing Best (OG 1045, ABV 4%)
Blackberry fruit aroma. Sweet initial taste followed by bitter sharpness. A good malty mouthfeel with more dark berry fruit leads to a lingering, rising bitter finish.

Riptide (OG 1045, ABV 4.1%)
A copper-coloured ale, lightly hopped with a malted caramel nose and initial sweetness of milk chocolate leading to a complex palate and lingering bitter finish.

Hornblower (OG 1045, ABV 4.5%)

Mothers Ruin (OG 1063, ABV 6%)
A copper red-coloured ale, malty with spices and orange zest and a complex flavour with a balance of sweetness and a bitter finish.

Andrews

1 Railway Cottages, Cummertrees, Dumfriesshire, DG12 5QG
☎ (01461) 700387
aemmerson999@googlemail.com

Andrews Ales began brewing in 2011 in the garage of the family home. After some initial success brewing capacity expanded to three barrels. Beers are supplied direct to pubs and independent shops. The core range of beers is supplied on demand. Seasonal and bottle-conditioned beers are also available.

Andwells SIBA

Andwell Lane, Andwell, Hampshire, RG27 9PA
☎ (01256) 761044 andwells.com
Shop Mon-Fri 10am-6pm, Sat 10.30am-1pm
Tours by arrangement

Andwell commenced brewing in 2008 on a 10-barrel plant. It relocated and expanded in 2011 to an idyllic riverside location with a new bespoke 20-barrel plant and now offers tours and direct sales from its brewery shop. Beer is distributed within a 40-mile radius to Hampshire, Surrey, Wiltshire, Berkshire, Greater London and the Isle of Wight. More than 200 outlets are supplied. Seasonal beers are available.

Resolute Bitter (OG 1038, ABV 3.8%) ◆
An easy-drinking session bitter. A malty aroma leads into an initially malty flavour with some bitterness and sweetish finish.

Gold Muddler (OG 1039, ABV 3.9%) ◆
Light golden-coloured standard bitter. The aroma of hops and malt is carried into the flavour with solid bitterness and a dry, biscuity finish.

King John (OG 1042, ABV 4.2%) ◆
Malty best bitter, low in hops with short initial bitterness and underlying sweetness, leading to some dryness in the finish.

Rudy Darter (OG 1047, ABV 4.6%)
A ruby chestnut-coloured ale with a hoppy, spicy aroma and a full-bodied and fruity taste with a dry finish.

Angel SIBA

62a Furlong Lane, Halesowen, West Midlands, B63 2TA ☎ 07847 300350 angelales.co.uk

Angel Ales began brewing commercially in 2011. The brewery building has been a Chapel of Rest, a coffin makers' workshop and a pattern makers before becoming a brewhouse. All beers are produced using organic ingredients where possible, and all stouts are vegan-friendly. Seasonal beers: see website.

Ale (OG 1042, ABV 4.1%)
Pale and intensely hopped bitter with a citrus nose and lingering bitter finish.

Animal

See XT

Anspach & Hobday (NEW)

118 Druid Street, Southwark, London, SE1 2HH
☎ (020) 8617 9510 🌐 anspachandhobday.com

Anspach & Hobday began commercial brewing in 2014 using a one-barrel plant based in an archway at the start of the Bermondsey Beer Mile. There are plans for expansion. Beer is mostly bottled or kegged with some available cask-conditioned. The brewery shares premises with Bullfinch Brewery (qv).

The Smoked Brown (ABV 6%)

The Porter (ABV 6.7%)

Appleford SIBA

Unit 14, Highlands Farm, High Road, Brightwell-cum-Sotwell, Oxfordshire, OX10 0QX
☎ (01235) 848055 🌐 applefordbrewery.co.uk

Appleford Brewery opened in 2006 when two farm units were converted to house an eight-barrel plant. Deliveries are made to a number of local outlets as well as nationally, via the brewery or wholesalers. Occasional and bottle-conditioned beers are available.

Brightwell Gold (OG 1041, ABV 4%)

Power Station (OG 1043, ABV 4.2%)
A copper-coloured, slightly malty bitter.

Arbor SIBA

Unit 4, Lawrence Hill Industrial Estate, Croydon Street, Bristol, BS5 0EB
☎ (0117) 329 2711 🌐 arborales.co.uk

Arbor Ales opened in 2007 in the back of the Old Tavern pub. In 2012 it moved and expanded to a new 12-barrel plant. Two pubs are owned and a wide range of beers brewed, with particular pride taken in darker ales.

Brigstow Bitter (OG 1042, ABV 4.3%)
Mid-brown best bitter with plenty of malt and fruit on the tongue. Bitter balancing hop with a long and fruity finish.

Oyster Stout (OG 1046.5, ABV 4.6%)
A rich stout with chocolate undertones. Real oysters are added in the copper. Fruity and roast flavours with a creamy mouthfeel.

Yakima Valley (OG 1067, ABV 7%)
A full-bodied American IPA featuring powerful hops. Citrus fruit aromas with a smooth mouthfeel lead to a lasting, soft bitter aftertaste.

Archerfield

See Knops

Archers

See Evan Evans

Ards

34b Carrowdore Road, Newtonards, Co Down, BT22 2LX ☎ 07515 558406
✉ ardsbrewing@blackwood34.plus.com

Ards began brewing in 2011 using a 100-litre plant. Plans are in hand to increase this considerably, allowing cask production in addition to the increasing range of bottle-conditioned beers.

Argyll SIBA

Cuan Mor, 60 George Street, Oban, Argyll, PA34 5DS
☎ (01631) 565078 🌐 obanbaybrewery.co.uk
Tours by arrangement

Argyll Breweries was formed in 2010 following the merger of Oban Bay and Isle of Mull breweries, continuing to trade under those names. Cask production is only at the Oban site.

Kilt Lifter (OG 1039, ABV 3.9%)

Skinny Blonde (OG 1041, ABV 4.1%)

Ginger Jakey (OG 1042, ABV 4.2%)

Skelpt Lug (OG 1042, ABV 4.2%)

Fair Puggled (OG 1045, ABV 4.5%)

Arkell's SIBA IFBB

Kingsdown, Swindon, Wiltshire, SN2 7RU
☎ (01793) 823026 🌐 arkells.com
Brewery merchandise can be purchased at reception
Tours by arrangement

Arkells Brewery was established in 1843 by John Arkell and the Arkell family still brew beer in the original Victorian Brewhouse. The brewery owns 99 pubs in Berkshire, Gloucestershire, Oxfordshire and Wiltshire. Seasonal beers: see website.

2B (OG 1032, ABV 3.2%)
Light brown in colour, malty but with a smack of hops and an astringent aftertaste. It has good body for its strength.

3B (OG 1040, ABV 4%)
A medium brown beer with a strong, sweetish malt/caramel flavour. The hops come through strongly in the aftertaste, which is lingering and dry.

Wiltshire Gold (OG 1040, ABV 4%)
A light golden-coloured ale with a satisfyingly sweet malty flavour and a mellow floral hop aroma followed by a distinctive hoppy taste.

Bee's Organic (OG 1045, ABV 4.5%)
A golden ale with a light, fresh taste. Organic honey adds a hint of honey to the beer.

Moonlight (OG 1046, ABV 4.5%)
An auburn-coloured beer with a warm toasty aroma and distinctive citrus hoppy flavour.

Kingsdown (OG 1051, ABV 5%)

A rich, deep russet-coloured beer, a stronger version of 3B. The malty/fruity aroma continues in the taste, which has a hint of pears. Hops come through in the aftertaste.

Arkwright's

c/o The Real Ale Shop, 47 Lovat Road, Preston, Lancashire, PR1 6DQ ☎ 07944 912326
arkwrightsbrewery.com

Arkwright's began brewing at the rear of the Real Ale Shop in 2010 using a 2.5-barrel plant.

Arran SIBA

Cladach, Brodick, Isle of Arran, North Ayrshire, KA27 8DE
☎ (01770) 302353

Office: 100 Wellington Street, Glasgow, G2 6DH
arranbrewery.com
Shop summer Mon-Sat 10am-5pm, Sun 12.30-4.30pm; winter Tue-Sat 10.30am-4.30pm, Sun-Mon closed
Tours by arrangement

The brewery opened in 2000 using a 20-barrel plant. 300 outlets are supplied direct. Seasonal and bottle-conditioned beers are also available.

Guid Ale (OG 1038, ABV 3.8%)

Red Squirrel (OG 1038, ABV 3.9%)
Session beer with a balanced malty, hop blend containing hints of liquorice and burnt toffee with a characteristic nutty aroma.

Dark (OG 1042, ABV 4.3%)
A well balanced malty beer with plenty of roast and hop in the taste and a dry, bitter finish.

Sunset (OG 1042, ABV 4.4%)
A mid-amber summer ale, light perfumed aroma, good balance of malt, fruit and hops with a pleasant dry finish.

Clyde Puffer (OG 1045, ABV 4.5%)
A stout with a deep, dark colour. Sweet and mellow with a low hop taster.

Fireside (OG 1044, ABV 4.7%)
A smooth malty brew with a pleasant hop character. Fireside has a bittersweet finish with a hint of ginger.

Blonde (OG 1048, ABV 5%)
A hoppy beer with substantial fruit balance. The taste is balanced and the finish increasingly bitter. An aromatic strong bitter that drinks below its weight.

Brewery Dug (OG 1055, ABV 5.5%)
An American-style IPA with a strong aroma. Dry hopped for extra flavour.

Arrow

c/o Wine Vaults, 37 High Street, Kington, Herefordshire, HR5 3BJ
☎ (01544) 230685 deanewright@yahoo.co.uk

Brewer Deane Wright built this five-barrel brewery at the rear of The Wine Vaults and started brewing in 2005. The Wine Vaults is the only pub outlet for Arrow Bitter.

Bitter (OG 1042, ABV 4%)

Art Brew SIBA

Dorset ☎ 07881 783626
artbrewdorset@googlemail.com

Brewing started in 2008 on a five-barrel plant near the Jurassic Coast. The brewery is in the process of moving so beers are currently produced by Sherfield Village Brewery (qv) in Hampshire. Bottle-conditioned beers are available.

Artisan

183a Kings Road, Cardiff, Glamorgan, CF11 9DF
☎ 07505 401939 artisanbeer.co.uk
Tours by arrangement (small groups only)

Artisan was established in 2008. All beers are unfiltered, without additives or preservatives and suitable for vegans. The main output is bottled and keg beers, although cask-conditioned versions can be produced on request. The trade name Pipes is used for some of the output.

Arundel SIBA

Unit C7, Ford Airfield Industrial Estate, Ford, Arundel, West Sussex, BN18 0HY
☎ (01903) 733111 arundelbrewery.co.uk
Shop 10am-7pm daily (1 Quay House, River Road, Arundel)
Tours by arrangement

Founded in 1992, Arundel Brewery is the historic town's first brewery in 70 years. A range of occasional brands is available in selected months. Seasonal beers: see website.

Black Stallion (OG 1037, ABV 3.7%)
A dark mild. Strong chocolate and roast aromas, which lead to a bitter taste. The aftertaste is not powerful but the initial flavours remain in the dry and clean finish.

Castle (OG 1038, ABV 3.8%)
A pale tawny beer with fruit and malt noticeable in the aroma. The flavour has a good balance of malt, fruit and hops, with a dry, hoppy finish.

Sussex Gold (OG 1042, ABV 4.2%)
A golden-coloured best bitter with a strong floral hop aroma. The ale is clean-tasting and bitter for its strength, with a tangy citrus flavour. The initial hop and fruit die to a dry and bitter finish.

Sussex IPA (OG 1045, ABV 4.5%)
Formerly known as Heritage IPA. A special bitter with a complex roast malt flavour leading to a fruity, hoppy, bittersweet finish.

Stronghold (OG 1047, ABV 4.7%)
A smooth, full-flavoured premium bitter. A good balance of malt, fruit and hops comes through in this rich, chestnut-coloured beer.

Trident (OG 1050, ABV 5%)
An amber-coloured strong beer with a citrus, fruity aroma. The taste is clean and refreshing with a hoppy, fruity flavour and a pleasant dry, bitter finish.

Ascot SIBA

Unit 5, Compton Place Business Centre, Surrey Avenue, Camberley, Surrey, GU15 3DX
☎ (01276) 686696 ascot-ales.co.uk
Shop Mon-Fri 10am-3pm
Tours by arrangement

⊗ Ascot Ales began production in 2007 on a four-barrel plant. The brewery has successfully expanded over the years and is now brewing six regular beers and many seasonals including a single hop series: see website. Bottle-conditioned beers are available and suitable for vegans.

Aureole Ale (OG 1032, ABV 3.3%)
A golden ale with citrus flavours.

Alley Cat Ale (OG 1038, ABV 3.8%) ◆
A pale brown session bitter with malt flavours present throughout. Dry with a lasting sharp and bitter finish.

On the Rails (OG 1039, ABV 3.8%) ◆
Chocolatey mild with a notable hop character throughout, bittersweet in the taste and aftertaste, with a dry finish.

Posh Pooch (OG 1042, ABV 4.2%) ◆
A best bitter with balancing biscuity malt sweetness. Some citrus fruitiness and a clean hoppy aftertaste.

Penguin Porter (OG 1045, ABV 4.5%)

Alligator Ale (OG 1047, ABV 4.6%) ◆
Some grapefruit in the aroma, with hop and bitterness in the taste and plenty of balancing biscuit in the aroma and aftertaste.

Single Hop (OG 1045, ABV 4.6%)
Copper IPA brewed each month showcasing a single hop variety

Anastasia's Exile Stout (OG 1049, ABV 5%) ◆
Burnt coffee aromas lead to a roast malt flavour in this black beer. Notably fruity throughout, with a bittersweet aftertaste.

Rhino Rye (OG 1049, ABV 5%)

Red IPA (OG 1054, ABV 5.5%)
An intensely hopped IPA with a citrus, grapefruit taste

Ashley Down

Unit 2, 6-8 York Street, St Werburghs, Bristol, BS2 9XT
☎ (0117) 983 6567 ☎ 07563 751200
✉ ashleydownbrewery@gmail.com

⊗ Ashley Down began brewing in 2011 using an 8.5-barrel plant in the owner's garage. In 2014 the brewery relocated to an industrial unit, with room for expansion.

York Street (OG 1034, ABV 3.5%)
A rich amber beer with a dry spiced aroma and caramel/black pepper taste.

Sideways (OG 1036, ABV 3.7%)
A straw-coloured beer with an aroma of tropical fruits and hoppy bitterness.

Vanguard (OG 1042, ABV 3.9%) ◆
A dark mild style with strong roast on the nose. Fruit and malt flavours combine with astringency, leaving a dry finish.

Remedy (OG 1037.5, ABV 4%)
A chestnut-coloured beer with good malt up front followed by spicy flavours and bitterness.

Landlords Best (OG 1040, ABV 4.2%) ◆
Best bitter with hints of toffee and fruit. A malty aroma with well-balanced flavours and astringent aftertaste.

Pale Ale (OG 1040, ABV 4.3%) ◆
A good balance between malt and hoppy bitterness with a mildly astringent finish.

Ashover SIBA

1 Butts Road, Ashover, Derbyshire, S45 0EW
☎ 07803 708526 🌐 ashoverbrewery.com
Tours by arrangement

Ashover Brewery first brewed in 2007 on a 3.5-barrel plant in the garage of the cottage next to the Old Poets' Corner pub. The brewery caters mainly for this and its sister pub, the Poet & Castle in Codnor. Other local free houses and festivals are also supplied.

Light Rail (OG 1038, ABV 3.7%) ◆
Light in colour and taste, with initial sweet and malt flavours, leading to a bitter finish and aftertaste.

Poets Tipple (OG 1041, ABV 4%) ◆
Complex, tawny-coloured beer that drinks above its strength. Predominantly malty in flavour, with increasing bitterness towards the end.

Hydro (OG 1043, ABV 4.2%) ◆
Easy to drink golden beer with a predominantly hoppy aroma. Hop and fruit flavours and an initial sweetness lead to a dry, clean finish and aftertaste.

Rainbows End (OG 1045, ABV 4.5%) ◆
Slightly smooth, bitter golden beer with an initial sweetness. Grapefruit and lemon hop flavours come through strongly as the beer gets increasingly dry towards the finish, ending with a bitter, dry aftertaste.

Coffin Lane Stout (OG 1050, ABV 5%) ◆
Excellent example of the style, with a chocolate and coffee flavour, balanced by a little sweetness. Finish is long and quite dry.

Butts Pale Ale (OG 1055, ABV 5.5%) ◆
Pale and strong yet easy to drink golden bitter. Combination of bitter and sweet flavours mingle with an alcoholic kick, leading to a warming yet bitter finish and aftertaste.

Atlantic

Treisaac Farm, Treisaac, Newquay, Cornwall, TR8 4DX
☎ (01637) 880326 🌐 atlanticbrewery.com

⊗ Atlantic is a specialist micro-brewery producing organic and vegan ales. All ales are unfiltered and finings-free. There are nine core brews including four food-matched Dining Ales developed with Michelin chef Nathan Outlaw. Casks are supplied locally and to London, with bottles available nationally.

Ale (OG 1038, ABV 4%) ◆
A pale amber ale, with good body, sweet malt and hints of vanilla. Well hopped yet balanced, including Cornish Fuggles.

Gold (OG 1043, ABV 4.6%) ◆
Refreshing, crisp golden ale lightly spiced with zingy ginger. Dry finish with the lingering light marmalade of First Gold hops.

Pilgrim (OG 1046, ABV 4.6%) ◆
A ruby-brown beer with a malty nose. Malt dominates the creamy taste and finish balanced by bitter and fruity hops.

Blue (OG 1045, ABV 4.8%) ◆
This dark ruby porter floods the palate with sweet malt, roast coffee, dark chocolate, a soft smokiness and orangey nose.

Red (OG 1047, ABV 5%) ◆

Malty, smooth red ale with nutty flavours and natural cloudiness. Dryness of the hop finish is balanced by sweet malt.

Fistral (OG 1048, ABV 5.2%) ◆
A creamy, crisp golden beer using extra pale and wheat malt. Refreshing citrus tangs and floral hop notes with sweetness.

Discovery – Easterly (OG 1050, ABV 5.5%) ◆
A golden pale ale with crisp distinct flavours of lime, chilli and ginger. Sweet malt balances the citrus aroma.

Discovery – Northerly (OG 1050, ABV 5.5%) ◆
Rich Cornish porter with blackcurrant and molasses. Full-bodied dark roasted malts, hints of chocolate, ripe blackcurrants and black cherries.

Discovery – Southerly (OG 1050, ABV 5.5%) ◆
Smooth blonde ale with elderflower and lemon. Gentle hops, sweet malt with a floral and citrus zest finish.

Discovery – Westerly (OG 1050, ABV 5.5%) ◆
Red Celtic ale with cinnamon and orange. Full-bodied bitter with gentle citrus marmalade and mild nutty spice flavours.

Atlas

See Orkney

Atom (NEW) SIBA

Unit 4 Food & Tech Park, Malmo Road, Sutton Fields Industrial Estate, Hull, East Yorkshire, HU7 0FY
☎ 07908 737769 🌐 atombeers.com

Atom is a collaboration between Allan Rice and Sarah Thackray, established in 2013 in a modern industrial unit in Hull. The 10-barrel plant, which came from Oban Ales, is supplemented by a fermentation capacity of 40 barrels and a conditioning capacity of 60 barrels.

Blonde Ale (ABV 4%)
A fresh, smooth, easy-drinking pale beer with citrus notes.

Pale Ale (ABV 4.5%)
A malty and hoppy pale ale with a full flavour.

Dark Alchemy (ABV 4.9%)
A rich, complex malty beer with the bitterness and aroma from cardamom and coriander but no hops creating a porter rich in body, smooth and characterful.

India Pale Ale (ABV 5.6%)
An IPA with plenty of malt and juicy hops.

Atomic

c/o Alexandra Arms, 72-73 St James Street, Rugby, Warwickshire, CV21 2SL
☎ (01788) 576194

Correspondence: 1 Lower Hillmorton Road, Rugby, Warwickshire, CV21 3ST 🌐 atomicbrewery.com
Tours by arrangement

Atomic Brewery started production in 2006 and is run by CAMRA members Keith Abbis and Nick Pugh. Two pubs are owned, the Victoria Inn and the Alexandra Arms in Rugby, the latter being where the brew plant resides.

Strike (OG 1039, ABV 3.7%)
A pale golden ale with a sharp, fruity, aromatic aroma and a good sharp bitter finish.

Fission (OG 1040, ABV 3.9%)
An amber-coloured session ale.

Spectrum (ABV 4%)
Pale golden with a huge grapefruit aroma.

Dark Matter (ABV 4.1%)
A dark, well-hopped ale with hints of chocolate and a bitter finish.

Fusion (OG 1042, ABV 4.1%)
A golden-coloured ale with a citrus, well-hopped aroma and a good bitter finish.

Half Life (OG 1051, ABV 5%)
A premium IPA, golden-coloured with a citrus nose to finish.

Attwood

See Worcestershire

Austendyke

The Beeches, Austendyke Road, Weston Hills, Spalding, Lincolnshire, PE12 6BZ ☎ 07866 045778

Austendyke started brewing in 2012 on a seven-barrel plant. The brewery is operated on a part-time basis by brewer Charlie Rawlings and business partner Nathan Marshall, who handles sales.

Long Lane (OG 1039, ABV 4%)
A traditional copper-coloured bitter.

Holbeach High Street (OG 1045, ABV 4.5%)
An old-fashioned dark best bitter.

Axholme SIBA

7 Lakes County Park, Wharf Road, Crowle, Lincolnshire, DN17 4JS ☎ 07551 910040

Office: 2 Garthorpe Road, Luddington, Lincolnshire, DN17 4QT 🌐 axholmebrewing.co.uk

Former Thorne brewer Mike Richards commissioned Scunthorpe's first-ever microbrewery in 2012 using a 2.5-barrel plant from Brupaks. In 2013 the company relocated to a brand new four-barrel brewery in Crowle. Seasonal and one-off brews are available.

Best Bitter (OG 1037.4, ABV 3.8%)
Traditional English session bitter. Malty fruit cake flavours dominate with a peppery hop finish.

Darleys Ghost (OG 1042.6, ABV 4.2%)
Spiced red ale with fruity hop flavours and a delicate hop finish balanced with warming cinnamon.

Clearwater Pale Ale (OG 1041.3, ABV 4.3%)
A fresh and spicy take on the pale ale style, with grassy and herbal flavours dominating. Crisp flavours with a rounded bitter finish.

Special Reserve (OG 1072, ABV 7.2%)
Chocolately throughout and gently bittersweet with a strong toasty roast malt character and underlying caramel.

Axiom (NEW)

Unit 4a, Wrexham Enterprise Park, Ash Road North, Wrexham Industrial Estate, Wrexham, LL13 9JT
☎ 07544 280353 🌐 axiombrewing.co.uk

Axiom began brewing in 2014 using a self-built four-barrel plant.

New Dawn (ABV 4.2%)
A golden session beer. Light with a fresh hoppiness.

Red Mist (ABV 4.5%)
An American-style red rye ale. A subtle spiciness from the rye combines with pine and grapefruit from the hops.

Dusk (ABV 4.9%)
A rich, dark beer with notes of figs, raisins and dark chocolate. Bitter, yet sweet.

Aylesbury

Hop Pole, 83 Bicester Road, Aylesbury, Buckinghamshire, HP19 9AZ
☎ (01844) 239237 aylesburybrewhouse.co.uk
Shop Wed-Sat 12-6pm
Tours by arrangement

Established in 2011 at the Hop Pole as a sister brewery to Vale in Brill. Limited edition, one-off beers are brewed on a weekly basis.

Pure Gold (OG 1040, ABV 3.8%)
Deep golden-coloured beer with a fruity citrus aroma, a hoppy bite and dry, zesty finish.

Ayr SIBA

5 Racecourse Road, Ayr, KA7 2DG
☎ (01292) 263891
anthony.valenti@btinternet.com
Tours by arrangement

Ayr began brewing in 2009 on a five-barrel plant and is located at the Glenpark Hotel. As well as the hotel, around 50 other outlets are supplied throughout Scotland and the north of England. Seasonal Beers are available.

Leezie Lundie (OG 1037.5, ABV 3.8%)
A pale golden session ale with hints of grapefruit and a dry lingering finish.

Jolly Beggars (OG 1041, ABV 4.2%)
A complex best bitter with plenty of character and lingering malty aftertaste.

Rabbie's Porter (OG 1042.5, ABV 4.3%)
A robust full-bodied porter with well-balanced toffee, fruity malt and a slightly smoky finish.

Towzie Tyke (OG 1044.5, ABV 4.6%)
An amber-coloured ale with a dry, long, bitter finish.

B&T SIBA

The Brewery, Shefford, Bedfordshire, SG17 5DZ
☎ (01462) 815080 banksandtaylor.com
Tours by arrangement (CAMRA branches only)

Banks & Taylor – now just B&T – was founded in 1982. It produces twelve regular beers, plus monthly specials and occasional beers: see website for details. There are seven tied houses, all sell B&T beers plus guest beers and real cider.

Two Brewers Bitter (OG 1036, ABV 3.6%)
Bronze-coloured bitter with citrus hop aroma and taste and a dry finish.

Shefford Bitter (OG 1038, ABV 3.8%)
A pale brown beer with a light hop aroma and a hoppy taste leading to a bitter finish.

Shefford Dark Mild (OG 1038, ABV 3.8%)
A dark beer with a well-balanced taste. Sweetish, roast malt aftertaste.

Golden Fox (OG 1041, ABV 4.1%)
A golden hoppy ale, dry tasting with a fruity aroma and citrus finish.

Fruit Bat (OG 1045, ABV 4.2%)
A warming straw-coloured beer with a generous taste of raspberries and a bitter finish.

Black Dragon Mild (OG 1043, ABV 4.3%)
Black in colour with a toffee and roast malt flavour and a smoky finish.

Dunstable Giant (OG 1044, ABV 4.4%)
Dark tawny bitter with a subtle blend of malt and hops.

Dragon Slayer (OG 1045, ABV 4.5%)
A golden beer with a malt and hop flavour and a bitter finish. More malty and less hoppy than is usual for a beer of this style.

Edwin Taylor's Extra Stout (OG 1045, ABV 4.5%)
A complex black beer with a bitter coffee and roast malt flavour and a dry bitter finish.

Shefford Pale Ale (SPA) (OG 1045, ABV 4.5%)
A well-balanced beer with hop, fruit and malt flavours. Dry, bitter aftertaste.

SOD (OG 1050, ABV 5%)
SOS with caramel added for colour.

SOS (OG 1050, ABV 5%)
A rich mixture of fruit, hops and malt is present in the taste and aftertaste of this beer. Predominantly hoppy aroma.

Baby Ox

See Oxfordshire

Bacchus

Bacchus Hotel, 17 High Street, Sutton-on-Sea, Lincolnshire, LN12 2EY
☎ (01507) 441204 bacchushotel.co.uk
Tours by arrangement

Bacchus began brewing in 2010. A two-barrel plant is used to supply the Bacchus Hotel. New equipment and a bottling line were installed in 2013.

Best Bitter (OG 1043, ABV 4.3%)

Blonde (OG 1045, ABV 4.5%)

Sutton Pride (OG 1045, ABV 4.5%)

Backyard SIBA

Unit 8a, Gatehouse Trading Estate, Lichfield Road, Brownhills, Walsall, West Midlands, WS8 6JZ ☎ 07591 923370 thebackyardbrewhouse.com
Shop: ring brewery for details
Tours by arrangement

Backyard began brewing in 2008 and expanded in 2012 to a 12-barrel plant brewing up to 50 barrels a week. Seasonal and monthly specials are available: see website. One pub is owned, the Fountain in Walsall. A one-barrel plant for experimental beers is planned.

Bitter (OG 1040, ABV 3.8%)

A blonde-style beer, slightly sweet with hints of tangerine and fruit salad.

The Hoard (OG 1040, ABV 3.9%)

Blonde (OG 1041, ABV 4.1%)

Gold (OG 1044, ABV 4.4%)
A dark, rich brew, full of bitter chocolate and fruit malt character and a rounded bitter finish.

Premium (OG 1047, ABV 4.5%)

Oatmeal Stout (OG 1049, ABV 4.8%)

IPA (OG 1049, ABV 5%)

East India (OG 1061, ABV 6.3%)
An authentic old English IPA.

BAD (NEW)

Unit 3, North Hill Road, Dishforth, North Yorkshire, YO7 3DH
☎ (01423) 324005 🌐 wearebad.co

Brewing commenced in 2014 using a new 13-barrel plant. A 2.5-barrel plant is used for monthly specials and for more experimental and radical brews. A distillery is planned, hence the name is an acronym for the Brewing and Distilling Company.

Comfortably Numb (ABV 3.8%)
A golden pale ale with notes of tangerine, mango, grapefruit and pineapple. Fruity with a little bitterness.

Love Over Gold (ABV 4.1%)
A hoppy and easy drinking New World pale ale with grapefruit and grassy notes.

Wild Gravity (ABV 5.2%)
A bold IPA with a rich, malty backbone.

Dazed & Confused (ABV 5.5%)
A dark, rich and modern milk stout with hints of cherries, chocolate, coffee and almonds.

Bad Seed (NEW) SIBA

Unit 6, 6 Rye Close, York Way Industrial Estate, Malton, North Yorkshire, YO17 6YD
🌐 badseedbrewery.com

Bad Seed was established in 2013 by James Broad and Chris Waplington using a four-barrel plant that produces a core range of bottled beers supplemented by a few specials.

Badger

See Hall & Woodhouse

Baildon (NEW)

Unit D, Tong Park Business Centre, Otley Road, Baildon, West Yorkshire, BD17 7QD ☎ 07914 025148
🌐 baildonbrewing.co.uk

Brewing began in 2014 using a six-barrel plant. Seasonal beer is available.

Blonde (ABV 3.6%)

Brunette (ABV 3.9%)

Ballard's SIBA

The Old Sawmill, Nyewood, Petersfield, GU31 5HA
☎ (01730) 821362 🌐 ballards-brewery.org.uk
Shop Mon-Fri 8am-4pm
Tours by arrangement

Launched in 1980 by Mike and Carola Brown at Cumbers Farm, Trotton, Ballard's has been trading at Nyewood since 1988 and now supplies 70-80 outlets. Seasonal beers: see website. Bottle-conditioned beers are also available.

Midhurst Mild (OG 1034, ABV 3.4%)
Traditional dark mild, well-balanced and refreshing with a biscuity flavour.

Golden Bine (OG 1038, ABV 3.8%)
Amber, clean-tasting bitter. A roast malt aroma leads to a fruity, slightly sweet taste and a dry finish.

Best Bitter (OG 1042, ABV 4.2%)
A copper-coloured beer with a malty aroma. A good balance of fruit and malt in the flavour gives way to a dry, hoppy aftertaste.

Wild (OG 1047, ABV 4.7%)
A blend of Mild and Wassail.

Nyewood Gold (OG 1050, ABV 5%)

Wassail (OG 1060, ABV 6%)
A strong, full-bodied, tawny-red, fruity beer with a predominance of malt throughout, but also an underlying hoppiness.

Balmaha Brewery

Oak Tree Inn, Balmaha, Loch Lomond, G63 0JQ
🌐 oak-tree-inn.co.uk
Tours by arrangement (CAMRA members only, max 12)

Balmaha began brewing in 2012 using a one-barrel plant.

Blonde (ABV 4%)

Best (ABV 4.5%)

70/- (ABV 5%)

Bank Top SIBA

The Pavilion, Ashworth Lane, Bolton, Lancashire, BL1 8RA
☎ (01204) 595800 🌐 banktopbrewery.com
Tours by arrangement

Bank Top was established in 1995. Since 2002 the brewery has occupied a Grade II-listed tennis pavilion. In 2007 the brewing capacity was doubled with the installation of a new 10-barrel plant and in 2008 David Sweeney became the sole proprietor.

Barley to Beer (OG 1036, ABV 3.6%)
A pale bitter with a citrus lemon and herbal finish.

Sweeneys (OG 1038, ABV 3.8%)
An amber bitter with a bold, crisp flavour and a delicate, slightly spicy aroma.

Bad to the Bone (OG 1040, ABV 4%)
A tan-coloured beer with floral qualities and delicate citrus notes.

Dark Mild (OG 1040, ABV 4%)
Dark brown beer with a malt and roast aroma. Smooth mouthfeel, with malt, roast malt and hops prominent throughout.

Flat Cap (OG 1040, ABV 4%)
Amber ale with a modest fruit aroma leading to a beer with citrus fruit, malt and hops. Good finish of fruit, malt and bitterness.

THE BREWERIES

Gold Digger (OG 1040, ABV 4%) ◆
Gold-coloured, with a citrus aroma, grapefruit and a touch of spiciness on the palate; a fresh, hoppy citrus finish.

Old Slapper (OG 1042, ABV 4%)
A quaffable golden-amber beer with citrus, floral and peach notes on the nose. Lightly hopped with a soft fruity taste.

Pavilion Pale Ale (OG 1045, ABV 4%) ◆
A yellow beer with a citrus and hop aroma. Big fruity flavour with a peppery hoppiness; dry, bitter yet fruity finish.

Blonde (OG 1050, ABV 5%)
A pale ale with a pleasant woody flavour and distinct berry aroma.

Port O Call (OG 1050, ABV 5%) ◆
Dark brown beer with a malty, fruity aroma. Malt, roast and dark fruits in the bittersweet taste and finish.

Leprechaun Stout (OG 1060, ABV 6%)
A sweet mahogany coloured beer with a roasted coffee smell and a hint of chocolate and treacle in the taste.

Banks's

Park Brewery, Wolverhampton, West Midlands, WV1 4NY
☎ (01922) 711811 🌐 bankssbeer.co.uk
Shop Mon-Fri 10am-5pm, Sat 9.30am-12pm (excluding Bank Holidays)
Tours by arrangement

Banks's was formed in 1890 by the amalgamation of three local companies. Hanson's was acquired in 1943 but its Dudley brewery was closed in 1991. Hanson's beers are now brewed in Wolverhampton, though a few of its pubs retain the Hanson's livery. Banks's Mild is a fine example of West Midlands mild ale and in 2010 the group decided to return to the traditional name of Mild, rather than Original, to keep pace with growing demand for the style. Part of Marston's PLC.

Mild (OG 1036, ABV 3.5%) ◆
An amber-coloured, well-balanced, refreshing session beer.

Bitter (OG 1038, ABV 3.8%) ◆
A pale brown bitter with a pleasant balance of hops and malt. Hops continue from the taste through to a bittersweet aftertaste.

Mansfield Cask Ale (OG 1038, ABV 3.9%)

Sunbeam (OG 1042, ABV 4.2%)
Zesty golden blond ale, with citrus and grapefruit overtones. A vibrant hop aroma leads to a long finish.

Brewed for Carlsberg Tetley:

Tetley Mild (OG 1034, ABV 3.3%)

Tetley Bitter (OG 1035, ABV 3.7%)

Brewed for Marston's:

EPA (OG 1036, ABV 3.6%)

Barearts

Studio Bar and Gallery, 108-110 Rochdale Road, Todmorden, West Yorkshire, OL14 7LP
☎ (01706) 839305 🌐 barearts.com
Shop Wed-Fri 4-9.45pm, Sat 12-9.45pm, Sun 12-8.45pm

A four-barrel brewery that began production in 2005 and is named after an art gallery dedicated to nude artwork. Beer is available only from the beer shop and studio bar or by mail order. All beers are sold in bottles or five-litre mini casks and are all conditioned by secondary fermentation.

Barge & Barrel

Barge & Barrel, 10-12 Park Road, Elland, West Yorkshire, HX5 9HP
☎ (01422) 371770
✉ bargeandbarrelbrewery@hotmail.co.uk

The brewery was founded by John Eastwood at the Barge & Barrel pub in 1993. Andrew Firth took over as head brewer in 2013. Beers are mainly produced for the pub but can increasingly be found locally.

Paige 3 Blonde (ABV 3.9%)

One For The Road (ABV 4.4%)

Aye Ayrton (ABV 5%)

Barkston

Orchard House, Saw Wells Court, Barkston Ash, North Yorkshire, LS24 9UJ
☎ (0845) 224 6324 ☎ 07764 750959
🌐 barkstonbrewery.com

Barkston Brewery is situated in the picturesque village of Barkston Ash, four miles south of Tadcaster. Production started in 2011 experimenting with different malt and hop combinations before settling on the current range of four beers. New equipment to increase capacity was installed in 2013.

3B (OG 1040, ABV 4%)
A session beer with a creamy head and smooth taste.

Blonde (OG 1040, ABV 4%)
A light golden beer with an intense hoppy flavour and a light citrus aroma.

Gold (OG 1040, ABV 4%)
A golden summer ale with a mix of subtle and refreshing hop flavours and aromas.

Belle (OG 1047, ABV 4.7%)
A dark ruby-coloured beer from with a biscuit flavour from heavily roasted malt combinations.

Barlick

Greyhound, 61 Manchester Road, Barnoldswick, Lancashire, BB18 5PW
☎ (01282) 850670 🌐 barlick-brewery.co.uk

Barlick began brewing in 2012 at the Greyhound in Barnoldswick, where a beer is always available. A four-barrel plant is used. Barlick is the colloquial name for the town.

Barlicker Bitter (ABV 3.6%)

Golden Blonde (ABV 3.8%)

Hare of the Dog (ABV 4.1%)

Barlow SIBA

Units 5 & 6, Shippen Rural Business Centre, Church Farm, Barlow, Derbyshire, S18 7TR
☎ (0114) 289 1767 🌐 barlowbrewery.co.uk
Ring for shop opening times

Brewing started in 2009 on a self-built 2.5 barrel plant. Expansion to five-barrel capacity was completed in 2014. Beers are supplied to the Hare & Hounds in Barlow and other local outlets. The brewery acquired its first pub, the Tap House, in 2014. All beers are bottle-conditioned and are available from the brewery shop and local off licences.

Heath Robinson (OG 1039, ABV 3.8%)
A traditional dark bitter with a malty background and a balanced, bitter finish.

Betty's Blonde (OG 1042, ABV 4%)
Brewed with a blend of pale malts to give a light golden colour, hopped for subtle citrus and passionfruit flavours with a clean, crisp finish.

Carnival Ale (OG 1042, ABV 4%)
A light, golden pale ale with a citrus finish.

Dark Horse (OG 1043, ABV 4.2%)
A dark bitter with a coffee aroma. Well-hopped for a balanced finish.

Three Valleys IPA (OG 1052, ABV 5%)
An American-style IPA bursting with tropical fruit and citrus flavours with a clean bitter finish.

Full Monty (OG 1067, ABV 6.5%)
A strong, full-flavoured IPA. Gold-coloured with complex passionfruit, citrus and mandarin orange flavours with a warming alcoholic finish.

Anastasia (OG 1076, ABV 7.5%)
Strong, dark and smooth with complex malt flavours, chocolate, coffee and a hint of fruit.

Barnet

Black Horse, Wood Street, High Barnet, EN5 4BW
☎ (020) 8449 2230 🌐 blackhorsebarnet.co.uk/brewery

Brewing began in 2013. One beer is regularly available with additional different brews produced each week.

Palomino (ABV 4%)

Barney's SIBA

Summerhall Brewery, 1 Summerhall, Edinburgh, EH9 1PL 🌐 barneysbeer.com
Tours by arrangement

The only microbrewery in Edinburgh's city centre, Barney's Beer was founded in 2010 and now brews on the site of the original 1800s Summerhall brewery. Summerhall is Edinburgh's centre for the arts and science.

Good Ordinary Pale Ale (OG 1038, ABV 3.8%)
An English-style bitter; gold-coloured and full-bodied.

Extra Pale (OG 1040, ABV 4%)
A light and refreshing beer.

Red Rye (OG 1044, ABV 4.5%)
Copper-coloured beer with a clean, crisp, dry and fruity taste.

Volcano IPA (OG 1049, ABV 5%)
A light-coloured, American-style pale ale, erupting with hops.

Barngates SIBA

Barngates, Cumbria, LA22 0NG
☎ (01539) 436575 🌐 barngatesbrewery.co.uk
Tours by arrangement

Barngates was established in 1997 to supply only the Drunken Duck Inn. Expansion over the years plus a new purpose-built 10-barrel plant in 2008 means it now supplies more than 150 outlets throughout Cumbria, Lancashire, Yorkshire and Northumberland. Occasional beers are produced.

Cat Nap (OG 1037, ABV 3.6%)
Pale beer, unapologetically bitter, with a dry, astringent finish.

Pale (OG 1036, ABV 3.6%)
A well-balanced, fruity, hoppy bitter with plenty of flavour for its strength.

Cracker (OG 1038, ABV 3.9%)
A flavoursome malty bitter, fruity but not sweet. Dry in taste rather than finish.

Brathay Gold (OG 1042, ABV 4%)
Attractive sweet and rich aroma is followed by plenty of fruit and hops then a long, bitter finish.

Goodhew's Dry Stout (OG 1045, ABV 4.3%)
The inviting roast aroma leads to and easy-drinking, full-bodied and well-balanced roasty stout.

Tag Lag (OG 1044, ABV 4.4%)
A pale amber beer, smooth and sweetly malty to begin but a lasting, bitter finish.

Red Bull Terrier (OG 1048, ABV 4.8%)
Red beer with full mouthfeel and roast bitterness lingering through to the long finish.

Barnsley

See Wentworth

Barrowden

c/o Exeter Arms, 28 Main Street, Barrowden, Rutland, LE15 8EQ
☎ (01572) 747247 🌐 exeterarmsrutland.co.uk
Shop 12-2.30pm (3.30pm Sat), 6-11, 12-5pm Sun

The brewery was established in 1998. Martin Allsopp bought the pub and brewery in 2005, which is situated in a barn at the back of the Exeter Arms.

Pilot (OG 1028, ABV 2.6%)

Seventy Lambs (OG 1038, ABV 3.6%)

Beech (OG 1040, ABV 3.8%)

Own Gear (OG 1040, ABV 4%)

Hop Gear (OG 1046, ABV 4.4%)

Bartrams

Rougham Estate, Ipswich Road (A14), Rougham, Suffolk, IP30 9LZ
☎ (01449) 737655 🌐 bartramsbrewery.co.uk
Shop Tue & Sat 12-6pm
Tours by arrangement

The brewery was set up in 1999. In 2005 the plant was moved to a building on Rougham Airfield, the site of Bartram's Brewery between 1894 and 1902 run by Captain Bill Bartram. His image graces the pump clips. Beers are available in a selection of local pubs and there is a large amount of trade through local farmers' markets. Marld, Beltane Braces and all porters and stouts are suitable for vegetarians and vegans. Seasonal beers: see website.

Marld (OG 1033, ABV 3.4%)
A traditional mild. Spicy hops and malt with a hint of chocolate, slightly smoky with a light, roasted finish.

Premier Bitter (OG 1038, ABV 3.7%)
A traditional quaffing ale, full-flavoured but light, dry and hoppy.

Rougham Ready (OG 1038, ABV 3.8%)
A light, crisp bitter, surprisingly full bodied for its strength.

Red Queen (OG 1039, ABV 3.9%)
Typical IPA style, chocolate malt in the foreground while the resiny hop flavour lingers.

Cat's Whiskers (OG 1040, ABV 4%)
A straw-coloured beer with ginger and lemons added; a unique flavour experience.

Grozet (OG 1040, ABV 4%)
Gooseberries are added to give an appealing extra dimension.

Bee's Knees (OG 1042, ABV 4.2%)
An amber beer with a floral aroma; honey softness on the palate leads to a crisp, bitter finish.

Catherine Bartram's IPA (OG 1043, ABV 4.3%)
A full-bodied malty IPA style; tangy hops lead the malt throughout and dominate the dry, hoppy aftertaste.

Jester Quick One (OG 1044, ABV 4.4%)
A sweet reddish bitter using fruity hops.

Beltane Braces (OG 1046, ABV 4.5%)
Smooth and dark.

Stingo (OG 1045, ABV 4.5%)
A sweetish, fruity bitter with a hoppy nose. Light honey softens the bitter finish.

Beer Elsie Bub (OG 1048, ABV 4.8%)
Originally brewed for a Pagan wedding, this strong honey ale is now brewed all year round.

Captain Bill Bartram's Best Bitter (OG 1048, ABV 4.8%)
Modified from a 100-year old recipe, using full malt and traditional Kentish hops.

Captain's Stout (OG 1049, ABV 4.8%)
Biscuity dark malt leads to a lightly smoked aroma, plenty of roasted malt character, coffee notes and a whiff of smoke.

Cherry Stout (OG 1048, ABV 4.8%)
Sensuous hints of chocolate lead to a subtle suggestion of cherries.

Suffolk 'n' Strong (OG 1050, ABV 5%)
A light, smooth and dangerously potable strong bitter, well-balanced malt and hops with an easy finish.

Comrade Bill Bartram's Egalitarian Anti Imperialist Soviet Stout (OG 1070, ABV 6.9%)
A Russian stout by any other name, a luscious easy-drinking example of the style.

Barum SIBA

c/o Reform Inn, Pilton, Barnstaple, Devon, EX31 1PD
☎ (01271) 329994 barumbrewery.co.uk
Tours by arrangement

Barum was formed in 1996 by Tim Webster and is housed in a conversion attached to the Reform Inn that acts as the brewery tap and main outlet. Distribution is exclusively within Devon. Seasonal beers are brewed.

Original (OG 1044, ABV 4.4%)

EPA (OG 1046, ABV 4.6%)

Breakfast (OG 1048, ABV 5%)

Baseline

Golding Barn Industrial Estate, Henfield Road, Small Dole, West Sussex, BN5 9XH
☎ (01903) 879111 baselinebrewing.co.uk

Brewing started in 2012 on a five-barrel plant nestling in the South Downs. A batch sparge mash process is used. The beer is unfined with no Isinglass, making it suitable for vegetarians.

Thunderbolt Bitter (OG 1040, ABV 4%)
A full-flavoured, copper-coloured session bitter.

Dark Matter (OG 1055, ABV 5.5%)
A dark, full-bodied ale. The initial flavour is roasted malt with spicy hops and a fruity but dry bitter finish.

English Electric Lightning (OG 1060, ABV 6%)
A classic English special bitter, burnished orange-coloured.

Batemans SIBA IFBB

Salem Bridge Brewery, Mill Lane, Wainfleet, Lincolnshire, PE24 4JE
☎ (01754) 880317 bateman.co.uk
Visitor centre & shop: see website for times
Tours by arrangement

Bateman's Brewery is one of Britain's few remaining independent family-owned and managed brewers. Established in 1874 it has been brewing award-winning beers for four generations. All 62 tied houses serve cask-conditioned beer. See website for seasonal and speciality beers. Beers are sometimes marketed as the Salem Bridge Brewery range.

Black & White (OG 1036, ABV 3.6%)
Gentle roast fruity airs preface this red-brown, caramel-infused brew. Malt and a stewed plummy sweetness initially give depth. Caramel dominates the short simple finish.

XB (OG 1037, ABV 3.7%)
A well-rounded, smooth malty beer with a blackcurrant fruity background. Hops flourish initially before giving way to a bittersweet dryness that enhances the mellow malty ending.

Yella Belly Gold (OG 1039, ABV 3.9%)
A gold-coloured, refreshing beer with a citrus flavour and aroma, which is quite dry.

XXXB (OG 1048, ABV 4.5%)
A brilliant blend of malt, hops and fruit on the nose with a bitter bite over the top of a faintly banana maltiness that stays the course. A russet-tan brown classic.

Salem Porter (OG 1048, ABV 4.7%)
A black and complex mix of chocolate, liquorice and cough elixir.

Bath Ales SIBA

Hare House, Southway Drive, Warmley, Bristol, BS30 5LW
☎ (0117) 947 4797 bathales.com
Shop Mon-Fri 9am-5pm, Sat 9am-12pm
Tours by arrangement

Established in 1995, Bath Ales use traditional brewing techniques with cutting-edge technology. An experimental brewery produces short runs of unusual brews under the Beerd brand. More than 400 regional outlets are supplied. Twelve pubs and sites are operated across the south west, all serving cask ale, one of which brews its own IPA. Seasonal and bottle-conditioned beers: see website.

Special Pale Ale (OG 1039, ABV 3.7%)
Hoppy, pale golden session bitter. Light citrus aroma with bitter flavours, a hint of caramel and a bitter aftertaste.

Gem (OG 1042, ABV 4.1%)
Pale brown best bitter with sweet fruit and malt flavours. Little aroma but a balanced taste with a slight bitter finish.

Barnsey (OG 1045, ABV 4.5%)
Dark brown with a grainy mouthfeel and caramel nose. Malt, dark fruit and bonfire toffee taste leading to a lingering bitter finish.

Platform 3 (OG 1055, ABV 5.7%)
A refreshing IPA with tropical fruit aromas, hints of citrus honey flavours, and a long, bitter finish.

Bathams IFBB

Delph Brewery, Delph Road, Brierley Hill, West Midlands, DY5 2TN
☎ (01384) 77229 bathams.com

A classic Black Country small brewery established in 1877. Tim and Matthew Batham represent the fifth generation to run the company. The Vine, one of the Black Country's most famous pubs, is also the site of the brewery. The company has 11 tied houses and supplies around 30 other outlets. Batham's Bitter is delivered in 54-gallon hogsheads to meet demand. Seasonal beer is also brewed.

Mild Ale (OG 1036.5, ABV 3.5%)
A fruity, dark brown mild with malty sweetness and a roast malt finish.

Best Bitter (OG 1043.5, ABV 4.3%)
A pale yellow, fruity, sweetish bitter, with a dry, hoppy finish. A good, light, refreshing beer.

Battledown SIBA

Keynsham Works, Keynsham Street, Cheltenham, Gloucestershire, GL52 6EJ
☎ (01242) 693409 battledownbrewery.com
Shop open Wed-Sat am – see website for times
Tours by arrangement

Established in 2005 by Roland and Stephanie Elliott-Berry, and joined in 2006 by Ben Jennison-Phillips (ex-Whittingtons), Battledown operates an eight-barrel plant from an old engineering works and supplies more than 250 outlets. Visitors are always welcome. There is an online shop for mail order purposes. Seasonal beers are also brewed.

Sunbeam (OG 1037, ABV 3.8%)
A golden pale ale with a refreshing aroma and sharp but smooth taste, leaving a dry, hoppy aftertaste which lingers on the palate.

Natural Selection (OG 1041, ABV 4.2%)
A deep golden beer, the malts evident but giving way to the triple hop addition giving a spicy and slightly citrus finish.

Premium (OG 1046, ABV 4.6%)
A rich amber ale. A malty aroma and taste with a deep, satisfying, full-bodied fruit and malt texture leaving a well-rounded, mellow aftertaste.

Special (OG 1050, ABV 5.2%)
A well-balanced and crisp pale ale.

Battlefield

See Tunnel

Bays SIBA

Aspen Way, Paignton, Devon, TQ4 7QR
☎ (01803) 555004 baysbrewery.co.uk
Shop Mon-Fri 8am-5pm
Tours by arrangement

Bays Brewery opened in 2007 in an old steel fabrication unit in Paignton using a 20-barrel plant. The brewery delivers to many pubs, hotels and restaurants in the south-west and further afield. Seasonal beers: see website.

Topsail (OG 1040, ABV 4%)

Gold (OG 1042, ABV 4.3%)

Devon Dumpling (OG 1048, ABV 5.1%)

Beachy Head SIBA

Seven Sisters Sheep Centre, Birling Manor Farm, Gilberts Drive, East Dean, East Sussex, BN20 0AA
☎ (01323) 423313

Estates Office: The Green, East Dean, East Sussex, BN20 0BS beachyhead.org.uk
Tours by arrangement

The 2.5-barrel brew plant was installed at the rear of the sheep centre in late 2006. Beachy Head Brewery produces both cask and bottle-conditioned ales, supplied regularly to around 25 outlets, three of which are local pubs. The brewery tap is the Tiger Inn in East Dean village.

Lighthouse Ale (OG 1038, ABV 3.6%)

Southdowns Ale (OG 1047, ABV 4.4%)

Beachy Original (OG 1047, ABV 4.5%)

Legless Rambler (OG 1053, ABV 5%)

Bear Claw

Unit 3 Meantime Workshops, Spittal, Northumberland, TD15 1RG ☎ 07919 276715
enderkue@netscape.net

Bear Claw began brewing in 2012 on a two-barrel plant, producing an ever-changing range of mainly highly-hopped cask-conditioned ales, including continental styles. Beers are regularly available at

THE BREWERIES

the Barrels Alehouse in Berwick upon Tweed. Expansion is planned as demand is high.

Beartown SIBA

Bromley House, Spindle Street, Congleton, Cheshire, CW12 1QN
☎ (01260) 299964 beartownbrewery.co.uk
Shop Mon-Fri 9am-5pm, Sat 9am-4pm
Tours by arrangement

Congleton's links with brewing can be traced back to 1272. Two of its most senior officers at the time were Ale Taster and Bear Warden, hence the name of the brewery. Beartown began brewing in 1994, a 25-barrel plant is used. Both the brewery's Navigation in Stockport and the Beartown Tap have been named CAMRA regional pubs of the year. More than 250 outlets are supplied. Seasonal beers are available.

Best Bitter (OG 1037, ABV 3.7%)
A copper-coloured session beer with a full palate of malt and crisp hops.

Bear Ass (OG 1040, ABV 4%)
Dark ruby-red, malty bitter with a good hop nose and fruity flavour with a dry, bitter, astringent aftertaste.

Ginger Bear (OG 1040, ABV 4%)
The flavours from the malt and hops blend with the added bite from the root ginger to produce a quenching blonde ale.

Kodiak Gold (OG 1040, ABV 4%)
Hops and fruit dominate the taste of this crisp yellow bitter and these follow through to the dryish aftertaste. Biscuity malt also comes through on the aroma and taste.

Bearskinful (OG 1042, ABV 4.2%)
Biscuity malt dominates the flavour of this amber best bitter. There are hops and a hint of sulphur on the aroma. A balance of malt and bitterness follow through to the aftertaste.

Bearly Literate (OG 1045, ABV 4.5%)
Golden pale ale. Floral scented and packed with the flavours of summer fruits and lemon, ending with a smooth dryness.

Polar Eclipse (OG 1048, ABV 4.8%)
Classic black, dry and bitter stout, with roast flavours to the fore. Good hop on the nose follow through the taste into a long, dry finish.

Blackbear (OG 1050, ABV 5%)
Dark ruby-coloured strong mild ale. Subtle roast and malt flavours fill the taste, complemented by a mellow sweetness.

Bruins Ruin (OG 1050, ABV 5%)
Deep copper-coloured premium ale. Full of malty character and a palate of sweet, smooth, fruity flavours.

Beavertown SIBA

Units 17-18, Lockwood Industrial Estate, Mill Mead Road, Tottenham Hale, London, N17 9QP
☎ (020) 8525 9884 beavertownbrewery.co.uk

Beavertown began brewing in 2012 using a four-barrel plant next door to its brewery tap, Duke's Brew & Que, N1. In 2013 the brewery relocated to bigger premises, and in 2014 relocated again to Tottenham Hale using a new 30-barrel plant. The four-barrel plant in N1 is still used for specials and experimental beers. There is little cask-conditioned production but bottle-conditioned beers are available.

Beckstones

Upper Beckstones Mill, The Green, Millom, Cumbria, LA18 5HL
☎ (01229) 775294 beckstonesbrewery.co.uk

On the site of an 18th-century mill, with its own water supply, this five-barrel, one-man operation continues to win awards. Beer names have connections to the long-closed Millom Iron Works or local characters; the brewer designs the distinctive pump clips.

Barley Juice (OG 1033, ABV 3.4%)
Full-flavoured, beautifully balanced, emphatically fruity, hoppy beer.

Beer O'Clock (OG 1036, ABV 3.5%)
A fascinating blend of flavours delivering ever-changing mouthfuls of sweet, fruity and hoppy bitterness.

Black Gun Dog Freddy Mild (OG 1038, ABV 3.8%)
A full-bodied, beautifully balanced ruby dark mild, replete with fruit and roast malt.

Iron Town (OG 1038, ABV 3.8%)
Creamy sweet brown ale full of well-balanced fruit and hop.

Border Steeans (OG 1040, ABV 4.1%)
An old-fashioned style tawny bitter with a sweet start, some bitter notes and plenty of aftertaste.

Rev Rob (OG 1044, ABV 4.6%)
A golden beer with a pronounced grapefruit aroma and taste. The hoppy bitterness lasts through to the aftertaste.

Bedlam SIBA

Albourne Farm, Shaves Wood Lane, Albourne, West Sussex, BN6 9DX bedlambrewery.co.uk

Bedlam began brewing in 2012. Brewing takes place on part time basis in a converted barn at Albourne Manor House. Beer is supplied to outlets in Sussex and Surrey and local beer festivals. Bottle-conditioned beer is sometimes available.

Best Bitter (ABV 4%)

Hoppy Golden Ale (ABV 4.2%)
A traditional English session bitter.

Porter (ABV 5%)

Beeches

39 The Beeches, Lochgelly, KY5 9QB
☎ (01592) 782474
thebeechesbrewery@gmail.com

Beeches Brewery started production in 2012 using a 10-gallon plant in a small outbuilding at the rear of a family home. It came in to existence from the love of small batch home brewing.

Amazing Ale (OG 1040, ABV 3.6%)
A blonde pale ale, with a sweetness on the palate and a floral aftertaste.

Amazing Citra (OG 1038, ABV 3.8%)
A light, easy-drinking session ale with a grapefruit character from the hop.

Cats IPA (OG 1039, ABV 3.9%)
A pale ale with a floral aroma. Slightly spicy with a citrus aftertaste.

Cats Whiskers (OG 1042, ABV 3.9%)
A golden pale ale, light and crisp with a citrus aftertaste.

Meedies Mash (OG 1046, ABV 3.9%)
Amber in colour, with a malty nose, bitter finish and a slightly spicy aftertaste.

Beech Nut Ale (OG 1041, ABV 4.1%)
Malt on the nose and smooth drinking with chocolate notes and a slight malty taste.

Hop Trial (OG 1046, ABV 4.2%)

Sleeping Giant (OG 1042, ABV 4.2%)

Cats Capers (OG 1046, ABV 4.4%)

Meedies Magic (OG 1040, ABV 4.4%)

Blonde Bi'ere (OG 1052, ABV 4.8%)

Lo'Gelly Happylands (OG 1056, ABV 5.5%)

Beer Engine SIBA

Newton St Cyres, Devon, EX5 5AX
☎ (01392) 851282 ⊕ thebeerengine.co.uk
Tours by arrangement

Beer Engine was developed in 1983 and is the oldest continuously-working microbrewery in Devon. The brewery is visible behind glass downstairs in the pub. Several outlets are supplied, as well as local beer festivals. Seasonal beer is also available.

Rail Ale (OG 1037, ABV 3.8%) ◆
A straw-coloured beer with a fruity aroma and a sweet, fruity finish.

Silver Bullet (OG 1040, ABV 4%)
A light, medium-strength summer beer with a bitter aftertaste.

Piston Bitter (OG 1043, ABV 4.3%) ◆
A mid-brown, sweet-tasting beer with a pleasant, bittersweet aftertaste.

Sleeper Heavy (OG 1052, ABV 5.4%) ◆
A red-coloured beer with a fruity, sweet taste and a bitter finish.

Beer Geek

Unit D3, Aston Seedbed Centre, Aston, Birmingham, B7 4NT ☎ 0844 272 7207 ⊕ beergeekbrewery.com

⊗ Beer Geek began brewing in 2012 using a 15-barrel plant. A change of ownership in 2013 has seen investment in improving the core range of beers.

Geek Unique (OG 1043, ABV 4.3%)
A dark bitter with sweet, malty flavours creating a fruity, bold aftertaste.

Great White Geek (OG 1045, ABV 4.5%)
A light yet full-flavoured ale with a hint of floral aromas and a lingering, hoppy finish.

Dark Side of the Geek (OG 1055, ABV 5.5%)
A malty dark ale with soft, fruity aromas. Smooth and tasty.

Beer Studio

See Hydes

Beerd

See Bath Ales

Beeston SIBA

Fransham Road Farm, Beeston, Norfolk, PE32 2LZ
☎ (01328) 700844 ⊕ beestonbrewery.co.uk
Tours by arrangement

⊗ The brewery was established in 2006 in an old farm building using a five-barrel plant. Brewing water comes from a dedicated borehole and raw ingredients are sourced locally whenever possible. All beers are also available bottle conditioned and in five-litre mini casks.

The Squirrels Nuts (OG 1035, ABV 3.5%)

Bloomers (OG 1039, ABV 4%)

Worth the Wait (OG 1041, ABV 4.2%) ◆
Hoppy throughout with a growing dryness. Complex and grainy with fruit notes, malt and understated bitterness.

Stirling (OG 1045, ABV 4.5%)
A rich, malty red bitter with toffee notes.

The Dry Road (OG 1048, ABV 4.8%)

Village Life (OG 1047, ABV 4.8%) ◆
Copper-coloured with a nutty character. Malty throughout, a bittersweet background gives depth. Strong toffee apple finish.

On the Huh (OG 1048, ABV 5%) ◆
A fruity raisin aroma. A bittersweet maltiness jousts with caramel and roast. A dry hoppiness adds to a strong finale.

Old Stoatwobbler (OG 1065, ABV 6%)

Brewed for Brancaster Brewery:

Best (OG 1038, ABV 3.8%)
Refreshing session pale ale with a touch of citrus on the finish.

Sharpie K-12 (ABV 4.3%)
A hoppy, copper-coloured bitter with a refreshing tang.

Malthouse Bitter (OG 1044, ABV 4.4%)
A malty character with distinct bitterness on the finish.

Oyster Catcher (ABV 4.4%)
A golden ale, refreshing and moreish.

The Wreck SS Vina (ABV 4.8%)
Flavours of sweet coffee and malt with an aromatic finish.

Belhaven

Brewery Lane, Dunbar, EH42 1PE
☎ (01368) 862734

Office: Spott Road, Dunbar, EH42 1RS
⊕ belhaven.co.uk
Shop open during tours
Tours by arrangement

Belhaven brewery is one of the oldest brewing sites in Scotland. Established in Dunbar in 1719, it brews beers made with water from its own well and local Scottish barley. Part of Greene King PLC.

60/- Ale (OG 1030, ABV 2.9%) ◆
A fine example of a Scottish light. This bittersweet, reddish-brown beer is dominated by fruit and malt

with a hint of roast and caramel, and increasing bitterness in the aftertaste.

IPA (OG 1038, ABV 3.8%)
A golden ale with refreshing floral and citrus tones produced by a well-balanced fusion of malt and hops giving a clean, crisp flavour.

80/- Ale (OG 1040, ABV 4.2%) ◆
One of the last remaining original Scottish 80 Shillings. Malt is the predominant flavour characteristic, though it is balanced by fruit and a little hop. A complex ale, true to the 80/- style.

Black (OG 1041, ABV 4.2%)
A smooth, balanced stout with malty body and roast notes of dark chocolate and coffee.

St Andrew's Ale (OG 1046, ABV 4.9%)
A bittersweet beer with lots of body. The malt, fruit and roast mingle throughout with hints of hop and caramel.

Bell Street

57-59 Bell Street, Henley-on-Thames, Oxfordshire, RG9 2BA
☎ (01491) 576554 🌐 bellstreetbrewery.co.uk

Bell Street was established in 2013 using a 2.5-barrel plant. It is situated at the rear of Brakspear Pub Co's refurbished Bull on Bell St. The beers are sold at the pub and through the Brakspear Pub Co estate. Seasonal and special beers are available.

Brakspear Special (OG 1043, ABV 4.3%)
Tawny/amber beer with a well-balanced aroma and a hint of sweetness. Full bodied, the initial sweetness gives way to a dry hop bitterness. Also brewed by Brakspear Brewing Co as a late winter seasonal beer.

Belleville SIBA

Unit 36, Jaggard Way, Wandsworth Common, London, SW12 8SG ☎ 07712 298273
🌐 bellevillebrewing.co.uk
Tours by arrangement

Belleville began brewing in 2012. It was formed by a group of parents who met in the playground of a local primary school and specialises in American-style beers.

Northcote Blonde (OG 1042, ABV 4.2%) ◆
Smooth dark golden ale with biscuity character and a trace of hoppy bitterness. Fruit is pineapple, orange and mixed citrus.

Battersea Brownstone (OG 1048, ABV 4.8%) ◆
Complex beer with chocolate and blackcurrant notes on the nose and palate coupled with a little malty sweetness. Hoppy, bitter finish.

Chestnut Porter (OG 1049, ABV 4.9%) ◆
Brown creamy beer with roast and nutty notes throughout and a little hoppiness and fruit. Faintly bitter. Short dry finish.

Commonside Pale Ale (OG 1050, ABV 5%) ◆
A full-flavoured golden beer with hops and fruit throughout. The initial palate is sweet but then bitterness develops.

Thames Surfer (OG 1057, ABV 5.7%) ◆
Strong pale brown IPA with citrus, hops, honey and spicy notes. There is a long lasting faintly hoppy, bitter finish.

Tie-Dye Rye (ABV 5.8%)

Bellinger's SIBA

Station Road, Grove, Oxfordshire, OX12 0DH
☎ (01235) 772255 🌐 bellingersbrewery.co.uk
Shop Mon-Sat 6am-9pm, Sun 7am-8pm
Tours by arrangement

⊗ The late Mike Bellinger established the brewery as a family partnership in 2011. The five-barrel plant produces four core beers plus seasonals. As well as supplying beer in casks, bottles and polypins are sold in the garage forecourt shop.

Blenheim (OG 1037, ABV 3.9%)
A light, malty session bitter.

Original Bitter (OG 1040, ABV 4.1%)
A light and refreshing, easy-drinking beer.

Best Bitter (OG 1046, ABV 4.9%)
Rich tasting with a complex flavour.

IPA (OG 1050, ABV 5%)

Belvoir SIBA

Crown Park, Station Road, Old Dalby, Leicestershire, LE14 3NQ
☎ (01664) 823455 🌐 belvoirbrewery.co.uk
Tours by arrangement

Belvoir (pronounced 'beaver') Brewery was set up in 1995 by former Shipstone's and Theakston's brewer Colin Brown. Long-term expansion has seen the introduction of a 20-barrel plant that can produce 50 barrels a week. There is also a visitor centre incorporating brewery memorabilia, a bar, restaurant and shop (open seven days a week). Around 150 outlets are supplied direct. Seasonal and bottle-conditioned beers are also available.

Dark Horse (OG 1034, ABV 3.4%)

Whippling (OG 1037, ABV 3.6%)

Star Bitter (OG 1039, ABV 3.9%) ◆
Reminiscent of the long-extinct Shipstone's Bitter, this mid-brown bitter lives up to its name as it is bitter in taste but not unpleasantly so.

Gordon Bennett (OG 1041, ABV 4.1%)
Light chestnut beer with a biscuity character and a pleasant hop finish.

Beaver Bitter (OG 1043, ABV 4.3%) ◆
A light brown bitter that starts malty in both aroma and taste, but soon develops a hoppy bitterness. Appreciably fruity.

Oatmeal Stout (OG 1044, ABV 4.3%)

Peacock's Glory (OG 1048, ABV 4.7%)
Premium full-bodied golden beer.

Old Dalby (OG 1050, ABV 5.1%)
A rich, smooth ruby red strong ale with a pleasant hop character.

Contract brewed for Hoskins Brothers:

Hob Bitter (OG 1040, ABV 4%)

IPA (OG 1040, ABV 4%)

White Dolphin (OG 1040, ABV 4%)

Contract brewed for Shipstone's Beer Co Ltd:

Bitter (OG 1036, ABV 3.8%)
Golden amber-coloured, dry, classic Nottingham-style bitter.

Contract brewed for Steamin' Billy Brewing Co:

Tipsy Fisherman (OG 1036, ABV 3.6%)

A traditional light amber-coloured bitter with a mellow, crisp flavour and hoppy aftertaste.

Bitter (OG 1043, ABV 4.3%)
A golden bitter with a pronounced floral flavour and aroma followed by a lingering hoppy aftertaste.

1485 (OG 1050, ABV 5%)

Skydiver (OG 1050, ABV 5%)
A mahogany coloured beer with a fine balance of malty sweetness and hop bitterness. Deceivingly drinkable.

Ben Rhydding (NEW)

Margerison Crescent, Ben Rhydding, Ilkley, West Yorkshire, LS29 8QZ ⊕ benrhyddingbrewery.com

Ben Rhydding began brewing in 2013 specialising in bottle-conditioned beers made in small batches. Occasional casks are produced for local beer festivals or other local events. Seasonal beers are available.

Beowulf SIBA

Forest of Mercia, Chasewater Country Park, Pool Lane, Brownhills, Staffordshire, WS8 7NL
☎ (01543) 454067 ⊕ beowulfbrewery.com
Tours by arrangement

Beowulf Brewing Company is based at the beers appear as guest ales predominantly in the central region, but also across the country. The brewery's dark beers have a particular reputation for excellence. Seasonal and bottle-conditioned beers are available.

Beorma (OG 1038, ABV 3.9%)
A well-balanced session ale with a malty hint of fruit giving way to a lingering bitterness. Background spice excites the palate.

Chasewater Bitter (OG 1043, ABV 4.4%)
Golden bitter, hoppy throughout with citrus and hints of malt. Long mouth-watering, bitter finish.

Dark Raven (OG 1048, ABV 4.5%)
Dark with apple and bonfire in the aroma; sweet and smooth like liquid toffee apples with a sudden bitter finish.

Swordsman (OG 1045, ABV 4.5%)
Pale gold, light fruity aroma, tangy hoppy flavour. Faintly hoppy finish.

Folden Cross (OG 1045, ABV 4.6%)
Malt and caramel aromas and tastes with hints of fruity biscuits are nudged aside by the robust hops which give a lingering bitter edge.

Hurricane (OG 1041, ABV 4.6%)

Dragon Smoke Stout (OG 1048, ABV 4.7%)
Black with a light brown creamy head. Tobacco, chocolate, liquorice and mixed fruity hints on the aroma. Bitterness fights through the sweet and roast flavours and eventually dominates. Hints of a good port emerge.

Finn's Hall Porter (OG 1049, ABV 4.7%)
Dark chocolate aroma, after dinner mints, coffee and fresh tobacco. Good bitterness with woodland hints of autumn. Long late bitterness with lip-drying moreishness.

Mercian Shine (OG 1048, ABV 5%)
Amber to pale gold with a good bitter and hoppy start. Plenty of caramel and hops with background malt leading to a good bitter finish with caramel and hops lingering in the aftertaste.

IPA (OG 1074, ABV 7.2%)
Malty aroma with plenty of hops. Sweet malty start, malty middle and hoppy finish. Complex tastes abound with fruit, sweetness and hops all combining to produce a terrific taste, strong and warming.

Berrow

See Towles'

Bespoke SIBA

Unit 5, The Mews, Mitcheldean, Gloucestershire, GL17 0SL
☎ (01594) 546557 ⊕ bespokebrewery.co.uk
Shop Mon-Fri 9am-5pm
Tours by arrangement

Brewing commenced in 2012 on a 5.5-barrel plant on the site of the former Wintles Brewery. In 2014 capacity was increased to 12 barrels. The brewery offers speciality labelled bottles for celebratory occasions. An on-site brewery tap opens on Fridays 2-11pm.

Leading Light (OG 1035, ABV 3.5%)
A light blonde ale with a refreshing citrus hop finish.

Saved by the Bell (OG 1038, ABV 3.8%)
A light refreshing session bitter with a spicy hop bite and a light floral aroma from the late hop addition.

Running the Gauntlet (OG 1046, ABV 4.4%)
Full-flavoured malty bitter with rich roasted undertones balanced with good hop bitterness and spicy blackcurrant aromas from late hopping.

Going Off Half-Cocked (OG 1045, ABV 4.6%)
A spicily-hopped golden pale ale.

Money for Old Rope (OG 1049, ABV 4.8%)
Classic stout with rich dry flavours of malt and grain with deep hop bitterness.

Over a Barrel (OG 1052, ABV 5%)
A richly-coloured fruity strong ale with generous peppery finish.

Betjeman

Shoulder of Mutton, 38 Wallingford Street, Wantage, Oxfordshire, OX12 8AX ⊕ themutton.co.uk

Betjeman Brewery was established in 2011 by the former Pitstop Brewery owner, and is based in the Shoulder of Mutton in Wantage. Brewing is currently undertaken at other breweries' premises while plans to build a new brewery plant are continuing. Beers are available in the Shoulder of Mutton and at local festivals. Seasonal and occasional beers are available.

Bit O' Blonde (OG 1038, ABV 4%)
A good balance of a malt background and a strong hop presence.

Wantage Bells (OG 1054, ABV 5%)
An easy-drinking, strong bitter with an initial malty flavour followed by a refreshing hoppy dryness.

Poetry In Motion (OG 1059, ABV 5.5%)
A robust and full flavoured red IPA bursting with hops.

THE BREWERIES

Bewdley SIBA

Unit 7, Bewdley Craft Centre, Lax Lane, Bewdley, Worcestershire, DY12 2DZ
☎ (01299) 405148 🌐 bewdleybrewery.co.uk
Tours by arrangement

Bewdley began brewing in 2008 on a six-barrel plant in an old school, upgrading to a 10-barrel plant in 2014. Brewing experience days are offered, ring for details. Beers are brewed with a railway theme for the nearby Severn Valley Railway. Seasonal beers: see website. Bottle-conditioned beers are also available.

Worcestershire Way (OG 1036, ABV 3.6%)
A light beer with citrus notes.

Old School Bitter (OG 1038, ABV 3.8%)
A session bitter with a hoppy finish.

Severn Way (OG 1040, ABV 4%)

Worcestershire Sway (OG 1049, ABV 5%)
A stronger version of Worcestershire Way, slightly sweeter with more body.

William Mucklows Dark Mild (OG 1060, ABV 6%)

Bexar County

8 Belgic Square, Padholme Road, Peterborough, Cambridgeshire, PE1 5XF ☎ 07934 722584
🌐 bexarcountybrewery.com

Bexar was established in 2013, brewing American-style beers. There is no regular beer list, as the brewer is constantly innovating new recipes.

Big Bog

c/o Snowdonia Park Free House, Waunfawr, Gwynedd, LL55 4AQ ☎ 07769 110791
🌐 bigbog.co.uk

Big Bog was established in 2011 by Paul Jefferies of Hydes Brewery. The brewery, which shares its site with the Snowdonia Parc brewpub, underwent rapid expansion in 2013 and now supplies 85 outlets direct. Seasonal beers are available.

Bog Standard Bitter (OG 1036, ABV 3.6%)

Welsh Pale Ale (OG 1042, ABV 4.2%)

Swampy (OG 1044, ABV 4.7%)

Quagmire (OG 1058, ABV 6%)

Bog Super IPA (OG 1068, ABV 7%)

Big Clock (NEW)

Grants, 1 Manchester Road, Accrington, Lancashire, BB5 2BQ
☎ (01254) 393938 🌐 thebigclockbrewery.co.uk

Brewing commenced in 2014 using a 6.5-barrel plant.

Sunny Boy (ABV 3.8%)

Pals (ABV 4%)

Dirty Blonde (ABV 4.2%)

Dark Knight (ABV 4.5%)

100 (ABV 5.3%)

Big Ears (NEW)

Prince of Wales, Green Tye, Hertfordshire, SG10 6JP
☎ (01279) 842139 🌐 thepow.co.uk/the-brewery

Brewing began in 2014 on a plant housed at the rear of the pub.

Big Hand SIBA

Unit A1, Abbey Close, Redwither Business Park, Wrexham, LL13 9XG
☎ (01978) 660709 ✉ dave@bighandbrewing.co.uk
Tours by arrangement

Big Hand began brewing in 2013 using a 10-barrel plant. The brewer continually tries innovative brews, such as producing a green hop ale, with many becoming regulars.

Zeta Two (OG 1035, ABV 3.6%)
A crisp, clean American pale ale with a citrus hop flavour and aroma.

Delta (OG 1036, ABV 3.7%)

King's Bane (OG 1038, ABV 3.9%)
A dry, crisp bitter. Toffee flavours with a subtle blackberry hop aroma.

Little Monkey (OG 1039, ABV 4%)
A dark mild. Toffee and caramel carried along in a complex malty sweetness.

First Hand (OG 1041, ABV 4.2%)
A classic amber-coloured best bitter; biscuity and light.

Melyn (OG 1045, ABV 4.6%) ◆
A malty, hoppy beer with a faint fruit aroma and bittersweet taste. The initial sweet malt flavours combine with hoppy bitterness in the aftertaste.

Epsilon (OG 1050, ABV 5.2%)

Big Lamp

Grange Road, Newburn, Newcastle upon Tyne, NE15 8NL
☎ (0191) 267 1689 🌐 biglampbrewers.co.uk
Tours by arrangement

Big Lamp started in 1982 and relocated in 1997 to a 55-barrel plant in a former water pumping station. It is the oldest microbrewery in the north-east of England. Around 160 outlets are supplied and two pubs are owned, one of which (the Keelman) is attached to the brewery. Seasonal and bottle-conditioned beers are available.

Sunny Daze (OG 1036, ABV 3.6%) ◆
Golden, hoppy session bitter with a clean taste and finish.

Bitter (OG 1039, ABV 3.9%) ◆
A clean-tasting bitter, full of hops and malt. A hint of fruit with a good, hoppy finish.

Summerhill Stout (OG 1044, ABV 4.4%) ◆
A rich, tasty stout, dark in colour with a lasting rich roast character. Malty mouthfeel with a lingering finish.

Prince Bishop Ale (OG 1048, ABV 4.8%) ◆
A refreshing, easy-drinking bitter. Golden in colour, full of fruit and hops. Strong bitterness with a spicy, dry finish.

Premium (OG 1052, ABV 5.2%) ◆
Hoppy ale with a good bitter finish.

Keelman Brown (OG 1057, ABV 5.7%)
A full-bodied ale with a hint of toffee.

Binghams SIBA

Unit 10, Tavistock Industrial Estate, Ruscombe, Berkshire, RG10 9NJ
☎ (0118) 934 4376 🌐 binghams.co.uk
Shop Mon-Thu 10am-6pm (7pm Fri), Sat 12-6pm, closed Sun
Tours by arrangement

Binghams began brewing in 2010, producing 40 firkins in each batch. Head brewer, Chris Bingham, is a member of the local branch of CAMRA and had extensive experience in home-brewing and a local brewery prior to starting up.

Twyford Tipple (ABV 3.7%)
Tawny-coloured bitter with a good balance of malt and hops in the flavour and a citrus hop finish.

Brickworks Bitter (ABV 4.2%)
Chestnut-coloured with a slightly nutty hint. The hops balance the maltiness to provide a well-rounded best bitter.

Coffee Stout (ABV 5%)
A mellow beer with darks malts that complement the coffee flavour.

Doodle Stout (ABV 5%)
A blend of dark malts provide a complex character. Named after the brewery dog called Stout that happens to be a Labradoodle.

Ginger Doodle Stout (ABV 5%)
A dark stout with a subtle hint of ginger which rounds off the bitterness.

Hot Dog Chilli Stout (ABV 5%)
Doodle Stout with a hint of chilli to provide a warm glow on the aftertaste.

Space Hoppy IPA (ABV 5%)
A classic example of the style. Pale golden and packed with hops to create a complex flavour and a long citrus finish.

Vanilla Stout (ABV 5%)
Infused with vanilla pods that complement the dark malts to create a smooth-drinking, dark stout.

Bird Brain SIBA

30 Hailgate, Howden, East Yorkshire, DN14 7SL
☎ (01430) 432166
✉ birdbrainbrewery@tiscali.co.uk

Bird Brain began brewing in 2009 on a two barrel plant expanded to four-barrel capacity in 2012. Brewing twice a month, the brewery supplies local pubs and beer festivals. Seasonal beers are available.

Shiny (OG 1038, ABV 3.9%)

Howden Bittern (OG 1039, ABV 4%)

Bird's SIBA

Ladybird Barn, Old Burcot Lane, Bromsgrove, Worcestershire, B60 1PH
☎ (01527) 889870 🌐 birdsbrewery.co.uk
Shop Mon-Fri 9am-5pm, Sat 10am-4pm
Tours by arrangement

Bird's began brewing in 2009, supplying its beers to pubs across the West Midlands. One-off brews are produced for special events. Bottle-conditioned beer is also available.

Eureka (OG 1036, ABV 3.6%)
A malty beer with a hint of sweetness and a distinctive nutty finish.

Mild High Club (OG 1037, ABV 3.7%)
A traditional mild. A full malty flavour give way to a dry finish with a creamy nutty aftertaste with just a hint of dark chocolate.

Natural Blonde? (OG 1040, ABV 4%)
A refreshing pale blonde beer. Floral on the nose, plenty of fruit and hops in the mouth with just the right amount of malt to balance. A pleasantly hoppy aftertaste with a gently crisp bitter finish.

Amnesia (OG 1045, ABV 4.5%)
A pale straw ale with a fruity zest, a slight orange citrus undertone combining with a mixture of hops to provide a dryish hoppy finish.

Black Widow Stout (OG 1045, ABV 4.5%)
A traditional smooth and satisfying stout. A roasted malt flavour with a bitter edge and overtones of blackcurrant, raisins and liquorice.

Skullduggery (OG 1052, ABV 5.2%)
A strong tawny ale, well-rounded with an initial sweetness followed by hoppiness with hidden tones of molasses.

Bishop Nick SIBA

33 East Street, Braintree, Essex, CM7 3JJ
☎ (01376) 349605

Office: The Chestnuts, Chelmsford Road, Felsted, Essex, CM6 3ET 🌐 bishopnick.com

Bishop Nick was launched in 2011 by Nelion Ridley, sixth generation of the brewing family that started Ridley's Brewery near Chelmsford in 1842. Beers were initially brewed using spare capacity at Felstar, but in 2013 the brewery moved to Braintree using a 20-barrel plant. Three regular beers are brewed as well as a limited edition range. All beers are also available bottle conditioned.

Ridley's Rite (OG 1036, ABV 3.6%)

Heresy (OG 1040, ABV 4%)

1555 (OG 1043, ABV 4.3%)

Bishop's Crook (NEW)

51 Woodford Close, Penwortham, Lancashire, PR1 9BX ☎ 07516 478003
🌐 bishopscrookbrewery.com

Bishop's Crook is a small brewery based at the home of one of the owners. It started brewing commercially in 2013 and currently has just a handful of regular outlets.

The Withy Way (OG 1038, ABV 3.8%)
A light and refreshing pale ale.

Initiate (OG 1040, ABV 4%)
A triple-hopped pale ale with an initial bitterness and a refreshing citrus aftertaste.

Brown Edge (OG 1041, ABV 4.1%)
A chestnut-coloured ale with slight malty tones and a hoppy finish.

Bishop's Stortford

Correspondence: 24 Trinity Street, Bishop's Stortford, CM23 3TJ

☎ (01279) 850923 ☎ 07981 856404
✉ bishopstortfordbrewery@hotmail.co.uk

Established in 2012, the brewery rapidly encountered demand that exceeded capacity. Brewer Darren Lawrence has therefore contracted use of the plant a neighbouring brewery, retaining his own techniques for the ales listed below together with occasional seasonal beers including milds and porters. The customer base is local, comprised of approximately 20 pubs and clubs.

Stortford Sunrise (ABV 4%)
A refreshing golden ale with a subtle hint of Belgian Witbier.

Stortford Sunset (ABV 4.2%)
A complex beer with a golden hue.

Black Cat SIBA

Eridge Road, Groombridge, Kent, TN3 9NJ ☎ 07948 387718 🌐 blackcat-brewery.com
Tours by arrangement

Black Cat began brewing in 2011 using a 2.5-barrel plant supplying three to four local pubs. It is owned and run by an airline pilot. Seasonal and bottle-conditioned beers are available.

Original (OG 1042, ABV 4.2%)
A hoppy, bitter, amber-coloured beer balanced with malt.

Black Country SIBA

Rear of Old Bulls Head, 1 Redhall Road, Lower Gornal, West Midlands, DY3 2NU
☎ (01384) 480156

Office: Unit 4, Tansey Green Road, Pensnett, West Midlands, DY5 4TL 🌐 blackcountryinns.co.uk
Tours by arrangement

Brewing started on the site in the 1830s and continued until 1934. Brewing recommenced in 2004. In 2012 much of the equipment was replaced or refurbished. Seasonal beers: see website. Beers are also brewed under the Thomas Guest Brewing Company name.

Bradley's Finest Golden (OG 1040, ABV 4.2%)
A straw-coloured quaffing beer with a bold citrus hop aroma, fruity balanced sweetness and a lingering, refreshing aftertaste.

Pig on the Wall (OG 1042, ABV 4.3%)
A refreshing chestnut brown beer with a complex flavour of light hops giving way to a bittersweet blend of roasted malt. Suggestions of chocolate and coffee undertones.

Fireside (OG 1047, ABV 5%)
A well-rounded premium bitter, amber in colour, clean in taste leading to a pleasant, dry finish.

Black Dog

See Hambleton

Black Flag (NEW)

Unit 4D, Bridge Road Industrial Estate, Goonhavern, Cornwall, TR4 9QL
☎ (01872) 858004 🌐 blackflagbrewery.com

Black Flag began brewing in 2013 using an eight-barrel plant. Seasonal beers are available.

Fang (OG 1040, ABV 4%)
A balanced pale ale with seasonal dry hop addition.

Naughty Pilchard (OG 1040, ABV 4%)
Pale brown light bitter with some hop aroma. Sweet malt and hops dominating the taste. Long, refreshing hop-bitter finish.

Blonde (OG 1042, ABV 4.2%)
A light and fruity golden ale, full bodied and powerfully-hopped giving a citrus zing.

White Cross IPA (OG 1057, ABV 5.7%)
A fruity, heavily-hopped IPA.

Black Hole SIBA

Unit 63GF, IMEX Business Park, Shobnall Road, Burton upon Trent, Staffordshire, DE14 2AU
☎ (01283) 619943 ☎ 07864 966452
🌐 blackholebrewery.co.uk
Tours by arrangement

Black Hole was established in 2007 with a purpose-built 10-barrel plant in the former Ind Coope bottling stores. Fermenting capacity was increased in 2012 to enable the production of up to four brews per week. More than 400 outlets are supplied directly, and many more via wholesalers. Seasonal and special beers are available. The brewery was bought by the owners of Mr Grundy's Brewery (qv) in 2014.

Bitter (OG 1040, ABV 3.8%)
Amber glow and malt and spicy hop aroma. Fresh lively session beer hopped to give a clean crisp finish of hoppy dryness and touch of astringency.

Cosmic (OG 1044, ABV 4.2%)
Almost golden with an initial malt aroma. The complex balance of malt and English hops give lingering tastes of nuts, fruit and a dry hoppy bitterness.

Red Dwarf (OG 1045, ABV 4.5%)
Red as named with a sweetshop start of sweet fruits with citrus centres. Malt is elbowed aside by the hops which dominate the tongue-tickling bitter end.

Supernova (OG 1048, ABV 4.8%)
Pure gold. Like marmalade made from Seville oranges and grapefruit, the aroma mimics the sweet start but gives way to the hops which deliver a dry, lingering bitter finish.

Cyborg (OG 1055, ABV 5.5%)
A rich golden ale, with a combination of hops that provide a citrus aroma with a bitter taste.

Milky Way (OG 1059, ABV 6%)
Honey and banana nose advises the sweet taste but not the sweet, dry spicy finish from this wheat beer.

Black Horse SIBA

26 Nottingham Court, Nottingham Road, Louth, Lincolnshire, LN11 0WB
☎ (01507) 311109

Office: Freshwater Cottage, 2 Chapel Brow, Charlesworth, Derbyshire, SK13 5HH
🌐 blackhorsebrewing.co.uk

Tony Howkins began brewing in 2012 using a 0.5-barrel plant located in former stables at the Black Horse pub in Grainthorpe. In 2013 the brewery relocated and upgraded to a five-barrel plant. 15-20 outlets are supplied direct.

Mild Midlander (OG 1036, ABV 3.6%)

Wheres My Fiorucci? (OG 1038, ABV 3.8%)

Queens (OG 1040, ABV 4%)

Pleasant Blonde (OG 1042, ABV 4.2%)

Saturdays Blonde (OG 1042, ABV 4.2%)

Black Frog (OG 1044, ABV 4.6%)

Black IPA (OG 1044, ABV 4.6%)

Nicholas de Luda (OG 1050, ABV 5.4%)

Black Iris SIBA

Unit 1, Shipstone Street, New Basford, Nottingham, NG7 6GJ ☎ 07816 148913 🌐 blackirisbrewery.co.uk

Black Iris began brewing in 2011 in Derby and relocated to a new site in Nottingham with a larger 10-barrel brewhouse in 2014. Seasonal and occasional beers are available.

Snake Eyes (OG 1038, ABV 3.8%)

Bleeding Heart (OG 1044, ABV 4.5%)

Stab in the Dark (OG 1050, ABV 5%)

Better The Devil You Know (OG 1053, ABV 5.5%)

Black Isle

Old Allengrange, Munlochy, Ross-shire, IV8 8NZ
☎ (01463) 811871 🌐 blackislebrewery.com
Shop Mon-Sat 10am-6pm, Sun 11am-5pm (Apr-Sep)
Tours by arrangement

Black Isle Brewery was set up in 1998 in the heart of the Scottish Highlands. All beers are organic with Soil Association certification. Bottled beers are available by mail order and suitable for vegetarians and vegans. Seasonal beer: see website.

Yellowhammer (OG 1038, ABV 3.9%) ◆
A refreshing, hoppy golden ale with light hop and passion fruit throughout. A short bitter finish.

Red Kite (OG 1042, ABV 4.2%) ◆
Tawny ale with light malt on the nose and some fruit on the palate. Slight sweetness in the taste and a short, bitter finish.

Porter (OG 1046, ABV 4.6%) ◆
A hint of liquorice and burnt chocolate on the nose and a creamy mix of malt and fruit in the taste.

Black Paw SIBA

Unit 4, Westgate Road, Bishop Auckland, County Durham, DL14 7AX
☎ (01388) 602144 🌐 blackpawbrewery.co.uk

Black Paw began brewing in 2011 using a 12-barrel plant. Pubs are supplied across the north east of England. Seasonal beers: see website.

Bishop's Best (OG 1038, ABV 3.8%)
Tasty session bitter with a slight hint of chocolate.

Paw's Gold (OG 1040, ABV 4%)
A rich golden bitter with the malt and hop taste coming through.

Archbishop's Ale (OG 1041, ABV 4.1%)
Full-flavoured and smooth.

Polar Paw (OG 1044, ABV 4.4%)
Bittersweet dark ale with a pleasant hoppy aroma and aftertaste.

Dark Knights (ABV 5%)

Dark Seam (OG 1050, ABV 5%)
A dark and full-flavoured beer with definite chocolate taste and a hint of coffee.

Black Rock (NEW) SIBA

Unit 6C, Empire Way, Tregoniggie Industrial Estate, Falmouth, Cornwall, TR11 4SN
☎ (01326) 379477 🌐 blackrockbrewing.com

Black Rock began brewing in 2013. Beers are available in Five Degrees West in Falmouth and a number of other local outlets. Further beers are planned plus a bottling line.

Pale Ale (OG 1042, ABV 4.2%)
Honey-coloured, well-balanced bitter with a hint of citrus and a long-lasting flavour.

Black Sheep SIBA

Wellgarth, Masham, Ripon, North Yorkshire, HG4 4EN
☎ (01765) 689227 🌐 blacksheepbrewery.co.uk
Shop and Bistro 10am-5pm daily
Tours by arrangement

Black Sheep was established in 1992 by Paul Theakston, a member of Masham's famous brewing family, in the former Wellgarth Maltings using the traditional Yorkshire Square fermenting system. The company now supplies around 600 free trade outlets, with national exposure through pubcos and wholesale channels, but owns no pubs. Production is 75% cask-conditioned with the remainder bottled. Paul has now handed over operations to his sons.

Best Bitter (OG 1038, ABV 3.8%) ◆
A hoppy and fruity beer with strong bitter overtones, leading to a long, dry, bitter finish.

Golden Sheep (OG 1039, ABV 3.9%)
A balanced blonde beer with a dry and refreshing bitterness. Light golden in colour with fresh citrus fruit flavours and a clean, crisp finish.

Ale (OG 1044, ABV 4.4%)
A premium bitter with robust fruit, malt and hops.

Riggwelter (OG 1059, ABV 5.9%) ◆
A fruity bitter, with complex underlying tastes and hints of liquorice and pear drops leading to a long, dry, bitter finish.

Black Tor (NEW) SIBA

5 Gidleys Meadow, Christow, Exeter, Devon, EX6 7QB
☎ (01647) 252120 🌐 blacktorbrewery.co.uk

Black Tor began brewing in 2013 after taking over the former Gidley's Brewery.

Pride of Dartmoor (ABV 4%)
A malty best bitter.

Dartmoor Pale Ale (ABV 4.5%)
A straw-coloured beer; hoppy and aromatic.

Honour (ABV 5.2%)
A stronger version of Pride of Dartmoor.

Templar's IPA (ABV 5.8%)
Classic IPA flavours with a gentle dark fruit twist.

Black Wolf SIBA

Unit 7c, Bandeath Industrial Estate, Throsk, Stirling, FK7 7NP
☎ (01786) 817000 🌐 blackwolfbrewery.com

Established in 2005, and now owned by VC2 Brands, the brewery is located in a former torpedo factory on the shores of the River Forth. A large range of award-winning cask and bottled beers are available, including many seasonal beers. In 2014 the brewery changed its name from Traditional Scottish Ales to Black Wolf Brewery and rebranded its range of beers.

Big Red (ABV 3.8%)
A ruby ale with hints of tropical fruit and sweet treacle balanced by a bitter, hoppy finish.

Nevis (OG 1041, ABV 4%)
A traditional Scottish 80/-, with a distinctive roast and caramel character. Bittersweet fruit throughout provides the sweetness typical of a Scottish Heavy.

Rok IPA (ABV 4%)
A well-rounded modern IPA with fruity flavours.

Gold Digger (ABV 4.2%)
A blonde beer bursting with grapefruit and peach flavours.

Florida Black (OG 1050, ABV 4.5%)
A sweetish stout, surprisingly not dark in colour. Plenty of malt and roast balanced by fruit and finished with a hint of hop.

William Wallace (OG 1048, ABV 4.5%)
A Scottish 80/- export with a slightly sweet and malty taste with a hint of toffee.

Lomond Gold (OG 1052, ABV 5%)
A malty, bittersweet golden ale with plenty of fruity hop character.

BlackBar

Unit B3, Button End Industrial Estate, Harston, Cambridgeshire, CB22 7GX
☎ (1223) 872131 🌐 blackbar.co.uk

BlackBar Brewery was established in 2011. 10 outlets are supplied direct.

Bitter (ABV 3.6%)
A malty tawny-coloured bitter with a noble hop finish.

Blacklight (ABV 4%)

Black Economy (ABV 4.6%)

Blackbeck

Blackbeck Inn, Egremont, Cumbria, CA22 2NY
☎ (01946) 841661 🌐 blackbeckbrewery.co.uk

A five-barrel brewery, established in 2009 and owned by a father and daughter team, producing hand-crafted ales using English malts and hops. Beers have fairground themed names and are also available in bottles and mini casks.

Belle (OG 1038, ABV 3.8%)
A sweet, tasty, dark mild.

Trial Run (OG 1037, ABV 3.8%)
A fresh and fruity yellow beer with a lasting hoppy finish.

Blackedge SIBA

Shuttle House, Hampson Street, Horwich, BL6 7JH
☎ (01204) 692976 🌐 blackedgebrewery.co.uk
Shop Wed-Sat 10am-5pm
Tours by arrangement

Blackedge, established in 2011, is a traditional five-barrel brewery, producing hand-crafted ales using only natural ingredients. In addition to the core range special seasonal beers are brewed monthly. The brewery houses a shop selling hand-bottled beers and various branded gifts.

Session (OG 1038, ABV 3.5%)
A golden session bitter, surprisingly full bodied with a grapefruit flavour and aroma.

HoP (OG 1039, ABV 3.8%)
Generously hopped to give a clean, dry, refreshing and hoppy citrus, floral-flavoured session beer.

Black (OG 1047, ABV 4%)
A velvety stout with intense roasted barley flavours and rich undertones of chocolate and coffee with a liquorice finish.

Pike (OG 1042, ABV 4%)
A pale ale with plenty of sweet citrus hop flavour

American Pale Ale (OG 1043, ABV 4.2%)
Light hoppy beer made using American hops giving intense citrus aromas.

Platinum (OG 1046, ABV 4.4%)
Blonde ale, light in colour, lightly hopped to give a clean, citrus flavour and aroma.

BLONDe (OG 1046, ABV 4.5%)
Full-flavoured, full-bodied blonde ale, well-hopped to give clean, crisp fruity flavour and aroma.

Dark Rum (OG 1045, ABV 4.6%)
Dark, rich porter with roasted coffee and chocolate flavours, hints of liquorice and finished with sweetness from dark rum.

IPA (OG 1047, ABV 4.7%)
Full-bodied, full-flavoured and well-balanced hoppy and intensely citrus with grapefruit aroma.

Black Port (OG 1045, ABV 4.9%)
Black beer with malty, fruity aroma. Rich, with chocolate and dark fruits to taste with a slightly drier finish.

Blackhill SIBA

Pontop Business Park, Harelaw Industrial Estate, Stanley, County Durham, DH9 8HN ☎ 07905 778286
🌐 blackhillbrewery.com

Blackhill began brewing in 2012 using spare capacity at Geltsdale Brewery. In 2013 it moved to its own premises using a 10-barrel plant. Beers are named after Durham coal mining seams. One-off and seasonal beers are available.

Top Busty (ABV 3.7%)

Bottom Busty (ABV 3.9%)

Tilley (ABV 3.9%)

70 Fathom (ABV 4%)

Blackjack SIBA

36 Gould Street, Manchester, M4 4RN
☎ (0161) 819 2767 🌐 blackjackbeersltd.co.uk

Blackjack started brewing in 2012 using a 4.5-barrel plant. Beers are named with a playing card theme, and are widely available in the local free trade as well as further afield. House beers and one-off specials are available.

Shuffled Deck (OG 1039, ABV 3.9%)
Aromas are marmalade with pine and grapefruit. Flavours are woody with sweet citrus and bitter grapefruit with a dry finish.

New Deck (OG 1042, ABV 4.2%)
A crisp hoppy ale with a satisfying finish.

First Deal (OG 1044, ABV 4.4%)
A ruby ale with a dried fruit aroma with berry flavours, earthy malts and a spicy, bitter finish.

Stout (OG 1050, ABV 5%)
Aroma is roasted malts and chocolate syrup. Flavour is similar with a hint of maple syrup and light bitter hops. Finish is slightly fruity.

Aces High (OG 1055, ABV 5.5%)
Aroma has some ripe citrus notes of melon and orange. Flavour is sweet, with mild grass and pine, along with more ripe tangerine and melon.

Blackmore

Trooper Inn, Golden Hill, Stourton Caundle, Dorset, DT10 2JW
☎ (01963) 362405 ✉ kevinstaunton@aol.com

This small 0.5-barrel brewpub began brewing in 2011. One beer from the range of two is produced per week.

Ale (OG 1038, ABV 3.8%)

Pale (OG 1042, ABV 4.2%)

Blackwater

See Salopian

Blakemere SIBA

Blakemere Craft Centre, Chester Road, Sandiway, Northwich, Cheshire, CW8 2EB
☎ (01606) 301000 ☎ 07552 766355
blakemerebrewery.co.uk
Shop Mon-Fri 10am-4pm, Sat & Sun 12-4pm

Formerly known as Northern, brewing began in 2003 on a five-barrel plant in Runcorn. In 2005 the brewery was renamed and relocated to a larger unit at Blakemere Craft Centre. Bottle-conditioned beers are available from the on-site shop.

Freshly Squeezed (OG 1039, ABV 3.8%)

Bobby Dazzler (OG 1040, ABV 3.9%)

Navajo (OG 1039, ABV 3.9%)

Soul Rider (OG 1042, ABV 4%)

Bronze (OG 1043, ABV 4.1%)

Cherry Baby Mild (OG 1040, ABV 4.1%)

Gold (OG 1046, ABV 4.3%)

Pinnacle (ABV 4.4%)

Hit & Run (OG 1044, ABV 4.5%)

Jewel IPA (OG 1046, ABV 4.6%)

Chilli Chocolate Stout (OG 1045, ABV 5%)

Fruit Stout (ABV 5%)

Soul Time (OG 1049, ABV 5%)
A rich, ruby-coloured bitter.

Summit Special (OG 1049, ABV 5%)
A fruity premium bitter made from a single hop variety.

Two Tone Special (OG 1049, ABV 5%)

Deep Dark Secret (OG 1050, ABV 5.2%)

Cosmic IPA (OG 1057, ABV 6%)
A highly-hopped, strong IPA.

Blindmans SIBA

Talbot Farm, Leighton, Frome, Somerset, BA11 4PN
☎ (01749) 880038 blindmansbrewery.co.uk
Tours by arrangement

Established in 2002 in a converted milking parlour and purchased by its current owners in 2004, this five-barrel brewery has its own water spring. The range of ales is regularly on tap at the Cornerhouse in Frome. Seasonal beers: see website.

Buff (OG 1036, ABV 3.6%)
An amber-coloured, smooth session beer.

Golden Spring (OG 1040, ABV 4%)
Fresh and aromatic straw-coloured beer, brewed using selected lager malt.

Mine Beer (OG 1042, ABV 4.2%)
A full-bodied, copper-coloured, blended malt ale.

Icarus (OG 1045, ABV 4.5%)
A fruity, rich ruby ale.

Blue Anchor SIBA

50 Coinagehall Street, Helston, Cornwall, TR13 8EL
☎ (01326) 562821 spingoales.com
Tours by arrangement

The Blue Anchor is a 15th-century thatched brewpub, the oldest continuously brewing plant in the country. It's home to the famous Spingo ales, which are produced from the well water beneath the establishment. All regular brews are available bottle-conditioned.

Flora Daze/ Spingo Original (OG 1040, ABV 4%)
A well-hopped, light tanned bitter with a strong floral/citrus aroma from a late addition of hops. A good hop character flavour with a smooth, delicate, dry finish.

Diamond Jubilee/IPA (OG 1045, ABV 4.6%)
Bittersweet hops and fruit dominate this golden beer, enhanced by a unique nutty, earthy character. Powerful whiff of esters and alcohol on the nose, and a long, dry, fruity finish.

Ben's Stout (OG 1048, ABV 4.8%)
A classic stout complemented by the brewery's sweet spring water.

Spingo Middle (OG 1050, ABV 5.1%)
Tawny in appearance, aromatic malt and esters lead into a sweet, malty and bitter taste with hints of green apple and grapefruit. The finish is lingering malt and dry bitterness.

Spingo Special (OG 1066, ABV 6.7%)
Darker than Middle with a pronounced earthy character on the nose balanced by rich fruit. Fruit and peppery hops dominate the mouth, followed by a long finish with malt, fruit and hops.

THE BREWERIES

Blue Bee SIBA

Unit 29-30, Hoyland Road Industrial Estate, Sheffield, South Yorkshire, S3 8AB ☎ 07787 566326
bluebeebrewery.co.uk
Tours by arrangement

Blue Bee was set up in 2010 by award-winning brewer Richard Hough. The beers are available to the free trade across Yorkshire, the Midlands and north west England with the core range complemented by monthly specials: see website.

Bees Knees Bitter (OG 1040, ABV 4%)
A dark bitter, deep chestnut in colour. A distinctive hop character leads to a lasting bitter finish.

Nectar Pale (OG 1040, ABV 4%)
A refreshing, zesty pale ale.

Lustin for Stout (OG 1048, ABV 4.8%)
A rich, complex stout, full-bodied and black in colour. Plenty of roast malt flavours.

Porter (OG 1048, ABV 5%)
A classic porter with a hoppy twist.

Tangled Up IPA (OG 1060, ABV 6%)
A pale beer with floral hoppy aromas, citrus flavours and a hoppy, bitter finish.

Blue Bell

Cranesgate South, Whaplode St Catherine, Lincolnshire, PE12 6SN
☎ (01406) 701000 ☎ 07813 819746

Office: Sycamore House, Lapwater Lane, Holbeach St Marks, Lincolnshire, PE12 8EX
bluebellbrewery.co.uk
Tours by arrangement

The Blue Bell Brewery was founded in 1998 in a former potato shed located behind the Blue Bell pub, Whaplode St Catherine. The brewery operates as a separate business from the Blue Bell pub but the pub does act as the brewery tap. Bottle-conditioned beers are available. Ingledingle Ale is only available in the Blue Bell pub.

Frightened Pheasant (OG 1037, ABV 3.7%)

Old Honesty (OG 1040, ABV 4.1%)

Ingledingle Ale (OG 1054, ABV 5.1%)

Blue Bell Brewhouse (NEW)

Blue Bell Cider House, Warings Green Road, Warings Green, West Midlands, B94 6BP ☎ 07922 554181

A one-barrel plant set up in 2013 to resurrect on-site brewing at the Blue Bell Cider House (brewing ceased in 1968), expanding to a 2.5-barrel plant in 2014. Operated by the ex-head brewer at Weatheroak Hill and the Old Pie Factory, it brews solely for the Blue Bell and local festivals. Initially brewing an ever-changing range, a regular beer is now available.

Harley Barley (ABV 4.2%)

Blue Cow

High Street, South Witham, Lincolnshire, NG33 5QB
☎ (01572) 768432 bluecowinn.co.uk
Tours by arrangement

Blue Cow is a traditional 13th-century pub with a brewery. The beer is only available in the pub or at CAMRA beer festivals.

Best Bitter (OG 1038, ABV 3.8%)
A hoppy golden ale with a fresh initial taste.

Witham Wobbler (OG 1046, ABV 4.5%)
Dark amber in colour with a rich malty aromatic nose leading to an impressive bitterness.

Blue Monkey SIBA

10 Pentrich Road, Giltbrook Industrial Park, Giltbrook, Nottinghamshire, NG16 2UZ
☎ (0800) 028 0329 bluemonkeybrewery.com
Shop Mon-Sat 9.30am-4.30pm

Blue Monkey was established in 2008 as a 10-barrel plant but moved in 2010 to a bigger site to meet increasing demand. It now brews around 15,000 pints a week to supply more than 200 local outlets and selected national distributors. The name stems from a nickname for the blue flames that used to rise from the chimneys of Stanton Ironworks, a prominent local foundry.

Marmoset (OG 1038, ABV 3.6%)
Highly hopped citrus golden beer with a dry bitter finish.

BG Sips (OG 1041, ABV 4%)
Pale golden hoppy beer, brewed mainly with Brewers Gold hops. Fruity and bitter.

Sanctuary (OG 1041.8, ABV 4.1%)
Copper-coloured malty beer with German and American hops.

99 Red Baboons (OG 1042, ABV 4.2%)
Red in colour with a malty fruitiness. Not overly hoppy.

Infinity (OG 1045.7, ABV 4.6%)
Golden ale packed with Citra hops.

Guerrilla (OG 1052, ABV 4.9%)
A creamy stout, full of roast malt flavour and a slightly sweet finish.

Ape Ale (OG 1052, ABV 5.4%)
Intensely hopped strong golden ale with dry bitter finish.

Blueball

Kash 22, Frodsham, Cheshire, WA6 6QW
☎ (01928) 732290

Blueball originally started brewing as Bridgewater Brewery in 2010 behind a homebrew shop in Frodsham. The business relocated and expanded later the same year using a five-barrel plant. A bar and restaurant, Kash, opened in Chester in 2011. In 2013 the brewery relocated to a newly opened second bar, Kash 22, in Frodsham.

Mild Mannered Mae (OG 1033, ABV 3.5%)
A black/brown mild with an aroma which is sweet, malty and shows fruit. The taste is sweet but is kept in check by a light bitterness from the hops and subtle coffee notes from the roasted malt.

Indie Girl (OG 1036, ABV 3.8%)
A golden beer with an aroma of citrus and tropical fruits. The finish is clean and dry with a long, hoppy aftertaste.

Laid Back Lucille (OG 1036, ABV 3.8%)
An auburn-coloured bitter with a light malt profile showing some caramel notes and a floral and citrus

fruit aroma. The finish is bitter and full but not overpowering.

Gold Digger (OG 1038, ABV 4%)
A gold-coloured beer with a subtle malt profile making way for a tropical fruit explosion. The nose is sweet and fruity giving hints of passion fruit. The taste is crisp and bitter with a refreshing, dry finish.

Zeppelin (OG 1053, ABV 5.5%)

Spank (Industrial IPA) (OG 1059, ABV 6%)
A sweetish strong ale.

Bluestone (Lancashire) SIBA

Unit 6, Daniel Street Industrial Estate, Whitworth, Lancashire, OL12 8BX ☎ 07802 792536
bluestonebrewery.co.uk

Bluestone is a small one-barrel brewery using traditional methods including 'double dropping'. Brewing only takes place at weekends, operating from the back of the owner's industrial unit. There are plans for relocation and expansion to a 2.5-barrel plant.

Quarrymans Stout (OG 1041, ABV 4%)
A traditional black stout.

EPA (English Pale Ale) (OG 1042, ABV 4.2%)
A traditional dry pale ale with strong malt and hop flavours.

AKA (Amber Kitchen Ale) (OG 1043, ABV 4.4%)
Based on an old recipe, this is a mild/brown ale, lightly-hopped with a caramel and liquorice malty flavour.

Bluestone (Wales) (NEW) SIBA

Tiriet, Cilgwyn, Pembrokeshire, SA42 0QW
☎ (01239) 820833 bluestonebrewing.co.uk
Tours by arrangement

Bluestone Brewing is a family-run business established in 2013 on a working organic hill farm in the Preseli Hills within the Pembrokeshire Coast National Park. The 10-barrel brewery has been installed in a renovated 200-year-old stone barn, which also doubles as a cold store and office. Water is used from a private supply that filters down through the Preseli Hills. 40 local outlets are supplied.

Rockhopper (OG 1039, ABV 3.9%)
A classic amber-coloured bitter with a light malt base and spicy fruitiness.

Bedrock Blonde (ABV 4%)
A delicately-hopped, straw-coloured blonde ale with creamy soft and malt flavours.

Rocketeer (OG 1046, ABV 4.6%)
A traditional full-bodied bitter with a rich, malty base.

Blythe SIBA

Blythe House Farm, Lichfield Road, Hamstall Ridware, Staffordshire, WS15 3QQ ☎ 07773 747724
blythebrewery.co.uk
Tours by arrangement

Blythe began brewing in 2003 using a 2.5-barrel plant in a converted barn. As well as specials, seasonal beers are produced on a quarterly basis. 15 outlets are supplied. Bottle-conditioned beers are also available.

Ridware Pale (OG 1042, ABV 4.3%) ◆
Bright and golden with a bitter floral hop aroma and citrus taste. Good and hop-sharp, bitter and refreshing. Long, lingering bite with ripples of citrus across the tongue.

Chase Bitter (OG 1044, ABV 4.4%) ◆
Fresh fruity aroma touched by malt from this amber beer. Sweet biscuity start with caramel support and fruit hints. Hops emerge and intensify to give a satisfyingly bitter finish.

Staffie (OG 1044, ABV 4.4%) ◆
Hoppy and grassy aroma with hints of sweetness from this amber beer. A touch of malt at the start is soon overwhelmed by hops. A full hoppy, mouth-watering finish.

Palmers Poison (OG 1045, ABV 4.5%) ◆
Refreshing darkish beer. Tawny but light headed. Coffee truffle aroma, pleasingly sweet to start but with a good hop mouthfeel.

Johnsons (OG 1056, ABV 5.2%) ◆
Black with a thick head. Refreshingly hoppy and full bodied with lingering bitterness of chocolate, dates, coal smoke and liquorice.

Bob's SIBA

Healey Brewery, Brewers Pride, Low Mill Road, Healey, West Yorkshire, WF5 8ND ☎ 07789 693597
Tours by arrangement

The brewery was founded in 2002 by Bob Hunter in outbuildings behind the Red Lion pub and moved to a new 10-barrel plant, part of the original Ossett brewhouse, in 2009. Production is up to 650 gallons a week and the beers appear regularly in more than 25 freehouses across West Yorkshire and in the West Midlands via wholesalers.

White Lion (OG 1043, ABV 4.3%)
Pale, flowery, lager-style beer.

Chardonnayle (OG 1051.5, ABV 5.1%)
Complex, strong pale ale with hints of lemongrass and fruits, aroma hops dominating the flavour.

Boggart Hole Clough SIBA

Building 7, Wilsons Park, Monsall Road, Newton Heath, Manchester, M40 8WN
☎ (0161) 277 9666 boggart-brewery.co.uk

A continually growing brewery, now an eight-barrel plant in its third home, with its own distribution arm, working extensively with north-west breweries and outlets. Monthly specials and unique commissions are available: see website.

Cascade (OG 1040, ABV 4%)
A bitter, hoppy session ale.

Dark Mild (OG 1040, ABV 4%)
A classic dark mild.

I AM BEER (OG 1042, ABV 4.2%)
A light coloured beer with a fresh fruit flavour.

Mud Brawler (ABV 4.5%)
A robust porter complemented with fresh vanilla.

Rum Porter (OG 1046, ABV 4.6%)
A classic porter with a smooth roast finish, enhanced by a sweet spicy hop taste, complemented with a hint of dark rum.

Bollington SIBA

Adlington Road, Bollington, Cheshire, SK10 5JT
☎ (01625) 575380 🌐 bollingtonbrewing.co.uk
Tours by arrangement

⊗ Bollington began brewing in 2008 with the Vale Inn, Bollington as the brewery tap. Around 40 outlets are supplied direct. The Park Tavern in Macclesfield and the Cask Tavern in Poynton are also owned. All three pubs serve mainly Bollington beers.

Light Nancy (OG 1035, ABV 3.4%)
A light pale beer with good body and grapefruit and lemon hop flavours.

Long Hop (OG 1039, ABV 3.9%)
Pale lager-style bitter with fruity, refreshing hops.

Nights (OG 1038, ABV 3.9%)
A smooth traditional dark ale with a light flavour and aroma, but a definite bitterness.

Park Life (OG 1041, ABV 4.1%)
A light golden bitter with a slightly spicy aroma and hoppy aftertaste.

White Nancy (OG 1040, ABV 4.1%)
Pale bitter with good hoppiness and light body.

Best (OG 1041, ABV 4.2%)
A hoppy bitter. Clean and crisp with a light golden colour and a refreshing bitter aftertaste.

Dinner Ale (OG 1042, ABV 4.3%)
Deep copper-coloured beer with a fresh, slightly fruity nose. A traditional bitter with a dry, hoppy finish.

Winter Reserve (OG 1044, ABV 4.5%)

Oat Mill Stout (OG 1049, ABV 5%)
An oatmeal stout with a twist. A hoppy bitter taste keeps the sweetness in check.

Eastern Nights (OG 1056, ABV 5.6%)
A pale gold-coloured, well-balanced IPA with a modest hop content.

Goldenthal (OG 1068, ABV 7.4%)
A gold-coloured, hoppy barley wine.

Bondgate (NEW)

30 Bondgate Close, Hexham, Northumberland, NE46 1DG ☎ 07500 018209
🌐 bondgatebrewery.moonfruit.com

Bondgate began brewing in 2013 using a three-barrel plant built from salvaged equipment. Limited edition ales: see website.

Ghost Empire Pale Ale (ABV 4.3%)

Tigerfish IPA (ABV 5.3%)

Storm Crow Black Ale (ABV 5.5%)

Bootleg IFBB

Horse & Jockey, 9 The Green, Chorlton-cum-Hardy, M21 9HS
☎ (0161) 860 7794 🌐 horseandjockeychorlton.com
Tours by arrangement

⊗ Situated in the Horse & Jockey Inn on the Green, the brewery is in a tiny space above the dining room where evidence remains of a historic brewery. The regular beers are complemented by seasonal ales.

Chorlton Pale Ale (OG 1040, ABV 4%)
A refreshing blonde beer with a hint of citrus and a long, dry finish.

Black Widow (OG 1041.3, ABV 4.4%)
A smooth, easy-drinking stout with subtle hints of coffee and chocolate and a long, dry finish.

Contraband (OG 1037.2, ABV 4.5%)
A crisp, dry pale ale, hoppy with a hint of grapefruit.

Lawless (OG 1042.6, ABV 4.7%)
A somewhat dry taste, this copper-coloured ale has a hint of spice in the nose and a slight presence of caramel in the aftertaste.

Borough (NEW) SIBA

3 Dalton Square, Lancaster, LA1 1PP
🌐 theboroughbrewery.co.uk

Borough Brewery is located in the cellar of the Borough pub in Lancaster town centre. A 2.5-barrel plant is used to produce vegetarian and vegan beers.

Pale (OG 1041, ABV 3.7%)

Bitter (OG 1043, ABV 4%)
A well-balanced malty ale with a delicate floral aroma.

Wintertime Dark (OG 1051, ABV 5%)
A substantial, full-bodied stout.

Borough Arms (Crewe)

33 Earle Street, Crewe, Cheshire, CW1 2BG
☎ (01270) 254999 🌐 borougharmscrewe.co.uk
Tours by arrangement

A two-barrel brewery opened in 2005 to supply the pub. The beers are available at the pub and beer festivals. Seasonal and one-off brews are available.

Sailor Moon (OG 1041, ABV 4.1%)
Pale golden beer; bittersweet with spicy notes.

White Rabbit (OG 1043, ABV 4.3%)
A blonde ale with citrus hoppiness.

Flathead APA (OG 1051, ABV 5.1%)
Full-bodied American pale ale.

Bosun's (NEW) SIBA

Unit 20, Wakefield Commercial Park, 97 Bridge Road, Horbury Bridge, West Yorkshire, WF4 5NW ☎ 07703 535735 🌐 bosunsbrewery.co.uk
Tours by arrangement

The first brew was produced in 2013 by a father and son team who have both served in the armed forces. The regular beers are produced on a 10-barrel plant with some given military themed names. Seasonal beers: see website.

Golden Rivet (OG 1037, ABV 3.7%)
A smooth malty golden beer named after the mythical last rivet fixed when a ship is built.

Maiden Voyage (OG 1039, ABV 3.9%)
Chestnut-coloured traditional English ale.

Bermuda Triangle (OG 1041, ABV 4.1%)
Fruity blonde ale with a soft citrus aroma and flavour.

Whistle (OG 1043, ABV 4.3%)
Well-rounded golden best bitter.

Botley SIBA

Botley Mills, Mill Hill, Botley, Hampshire, SO30 2GB
☎ (01489) 784867 ⊕ botley-brewery.co.uk

⊗ Botley was established in 2010 and uses a five-barrel plant. As well as the core range of three beers, seasonal and bottle-conditioned beers are also available.

Mill (OG 1038, ABV 3.8%)
A light session bitter, copper in colour, with a fresh aftertaste.

Bottas (OG 1042, ABV 4.2%)
An amber-coloured best bitter with a hoppy aroma and a good depth of flavour.

Cobbett's (OG 1045, ABV 4.5%)
A light, fruity golden ale with a clean, bitter finish.

Bottle Brook

Church Street, Kilburn, Belper, Derbyshire, DE56 0LU
☎ (01332) 880051

⊗ A sister brewery to Leadmill (qv), Bottle Brook was established in 2005 using a 2.5-barrel plant on a tower gravity system. New world hops are predominantly used. The core range of beers is supplemented by one-off brews.

Columbus (OG 1040, ABV 4%)

Heanor Pale Ale (OG 1041, ABV 4.2%)

Roadrunner (OG 1047, ABV 4.8%)

Mellow Yellow (OG 1054, ABV 5.7%)

Rapture (OG 1058, ABV 5.9%)

Sand in the Wind (OG 1060, ABV 6.1%)

Bournemouth (NEW)

Unit 12, 4-6 Abingdon Road, Nuffield Industrial Estate, Poole, Dorset, BH17 0UG
☎ (01202) 280405 ⊕ bournemouthbrewery.co.uk
Shop Wed-Fri 12-7pm, Sat & Sun 10am-4pm (ring first)
Tours by arrangement

Bournemouth began brewing in 2013 using a one-barrel plant but has since increased capacity to seven barrels. Most of the beer is sold directly from the brewery itself and is brewed on demand. A small proportion goes to local pubs and beer festivals, which is increasing as production grows.

Best (OG 1039, ABV 3.9%)
A session bitter with a slightly malty taste.

Wessex Wobble (OG 1043, ABV 4.4%)
Best bitter with a mildly hoppy taste.

Battleaxe (OG 1057, ABV 5.5%)
Lots of dark malt rounded off with powerful hops.

Bowland SIBA

Bashall Town, Clitheroe, Lancashire, BB7 3LQ
☎ (01200) 443592 ⊕ bowlandbrewery.com
Shop Mon-Sun 10.30am-5pm
Tours by arrangement

Bowland Brewery opened in 2003 and now serves 100 outlets throughout the north west of England. Seasonal beers: see website.

Pheasant Plucker (OG 1036, ABV 3.6%)
Light and refreshing with citrus notes.

Sawley Tempted (OG 1038, ABV 3.7%)
A copper-coloured fruity session bitter with toffee in the mouth and a spicy finish.

Gold (OG 1039, ABV 3.8%)
A hoppy golden bitter with intense grapefruit flavours.

Hen Harrier (OG 1040, ABV 4%)
The malty start belies what comes next: fruity, sweet, hoppy bitter with a long-lasting finish comprising of all the previous elements.

Dragon (OG 1043, ABV 4.2%)
A golden bitter with rounded fruit in the mouth and a refreshing finish.

Admiral of the Blues (OG 1046, ABV 4.4%)
Luscious tropical fruit flavours and generously hopped.

Bowman

Wallops Wood, Sheardley Lane, Droxford, Hampshire, SO32 3QY
☎ (01489) 878110 ⊕ bowman-ales.com
Tours by arrangement

⊗ Brewing started in 2006 in converted farm buildings. The brewery supplies more than 100 outlets. A new 40-barrel plant came on line in 2013, working alongside the original 20-barrel plant. In addition to the standard beers a range of celebratory and seasonal brews is produced. Bottle-conditioned beers are also available.

Elderado (OG 1036, ABV 3.5%)
Straw-coloured beer flavoured with elderflower. Citrus aroma with fruity, bitter taste. Good hoppiness and background sweetness. Dry, bitter finish.

Swift One (OG 1038, ABV 3.8%)
Easy-drinking bitter, well-balanced with sweet maltiness leading to a bittersweet finish and slightly dry hoppy aftertaste.

Yumi (OG 1039, ABV 3.9%)
A fairly bitter beer, rich amber in colour, brewed using only English hops. Yumi is a type of Japanese longbow.

Wallops Wood (OG 1040, ABV 4%)
No particular flavour dominates this well-crafted beer. Malt flavours throughout balanced by toffee notes, sweetness and a slightly dry finish.

Quiver Bitter (OG 1043, ABV 4.5%)
Fruity best bitter, golden in colour with a hoppy aroma leading through to a balanced, bittersweet taste and refreshing hoppy finish.

Bowness Bay

Green Lane, Winster, Cumbria, LA23 3NL ☎ 07768 116794 ⊕ bownessbaybrewing.co.uk

Bowness Bay began brewing in 2012 using a four-barrel plant from the closed Northcote Brewery in Norwich.

Mere Gold (OG 1038, ABV 3.8%)
A smooth, rich, hoppy golden ale with light tropical fruit flavours.

Swan Blonde (OG 1039, ABV 4%)
Pale and fresh, with a crisp, dry hoppiness.

Swift Bitter (OG 1044, ABV 4.5%)
Full and rounded with a creamy caramel undercurrent.

Teal Tipple (OG 1045, ABV 4.5%)
A copper-coloured session ale, light and refreshing.

Swan Black (OG 1046, ABV 4.6%)
A black IPA. Chocolate sweetness and subtle citrus flavours.

Box Steam SIBA

The Midlands, Holt, Wiltshire, BA14 6RU
☎ (01225) 782700 boxsteambrewery.com
Shop Mon-Thu 10am-5pm, Fri 10am-6pm
Tours by arrangement

The brewery was founded in 2004 and boasts a Fulton steam-fired copper, hence the name. New ownership since 2006 meant expansion and increased capacity with the brewery moving to larger premises in Holt in 2011. Two pubs are owned and more than 100 outlets supplied. Seasonal beers are brewed.

Golden Bolt (OG 1037.5, ABV 3.8%)
A straw-coloured bitter, well flavoured with a slightly dry, hoppy aftertaste.

Chuffin Ale (OG 1040, ABV 4%)
A full-flavoured bitter, chestnut brown in colour with a fruity aroma and a smooth, rich taste.

Tunnel Vision (OG 1040.5, ABV 4.2%)
A well-rounded light amber bitter. Clean tasting, with a slight bitterness on the finish.

Steam Porter (OG 1045, ABV 4.4%)
A smooth-drinking, well-rounded porter with a slightly smoky aroma. Roasted malts give way to chocolate undertones on the palate.

Funnel Blower (OG 1045, ABV 4.5%)
Dark brown in colour, with a subtle vanilla aroma. Vanilla sweetness contrasts with the slight bitterness from roasted barley and chocolate malts.

Piston Broke (OG 1045, ABV 4.5%)
A fine, full-bodied deep golden ale with a refreshing hoppy, citrus palate and a subtle fruit-hop aroma.

Derail Ale (OG 1049, ABV 5.2%)
Hoppy, traditional India Pale Ale. Full-flavoured with an intense floral aroma, finished with well-balanced bitterness.

Bradfield SIBA

Watt House Farm, High Bradfield, Sheffield, South Yorkshire, S6 6LG
☎ (0114) 285 1118 bradfieldbrewery.co.uk
Shop Mon-Sat 10am-4pm

Established in 2005, Bradfield is a family-run business, based on a working farm in the Peak District using pure Milstone Grit springwater. In 2009 the brewery bought its first brewery tap, the Nags Head in Loxley. Seasonal beers: see website. Bottle-conditioned beers and five-litre mini casks are also available.

Farmers Bitter (OG 1039, ABV 3.9%)
A traditional copper-coloured malt ale with a floral aroma.

Farmers Blonde (OG 1041, ABV 4%)
Pale, blonde beer with citrus and summer fruits aromas.

Farmers Stout (OG 1045, ABV 4.5%)
A dark stout with roasted malts and flaked oats and a subtle, bitter hop character.

Brains IFBB

Crawshay Street, Cardiff, CF10 1SP
☎ (029) 2040 2060 sabrain.com

Brains was established in 1882 at the Old Brewery moving to the former Hancock's brewery site in 1999. The company has remained in family ownership and runs over 270 pubs throughout Wales, the Midlands and the West Country and is heavily involved in sponsoring Welsh sport. A new microbrewery within the existing brewery has produced an ever-increasing range of new beers which have proved popular within the Brains estate. Seasonal beer: see website.

Dark (OG 1035.5, ABV 3.5%)
A classic dark brown mild, a mix of malt, roast, caramel with a background of hops. Bittersweet, mellow and with a lasting finish of malt and roast.

Bitter (OG 1036, ABV 3.7%)
Amber-coloured with a gentle aroma of malt and hops. Malt, hops and bitterness combine in an easy-drinking beer with a bitter finish.

SA (OG 1042, ABV 4.2%)
A mellow, full-bodied beer. Gentle malt and hop aroma leads to a malty, hop and fruit mix with a balancing bitterness.

SA Gold (OG 1042, ABV 4.2%)
A golden beer with a hoppy aroma. Well balanced with a zesty hop, malt, fruit and balancing bitterness; a similar satisfying finish.

Rev James (OG 1045.5, ABV 4.5%)
A faint malt and fruit aroma with malt and fruit flavours in the taste, initially bittersweet. Bitterness balances the flavour and makes this an easy-drinking beer.

Contract brewed for AB InBev:

Flowers IPA (OG 1036, ABV 3.6%)

Flowers Original (OG 1042, ABV 4.2%)

Contract brewed for Molson Coors:

M&B Brew XI (OG 1036, ABV 3.6%)

Hancock's HB (OG 1037, ABV 3.7%)

Worthingon's (OG 1037, ABV 3.7%)

Brakspear

Eagle Maltings, The Crofts, Witney, Oxfordshire, OX28 4DP
☎ (01993) 890800 brakspear-beers.co.uk
Shop Mon-Sat 10am-5pm (excluding Bank Holidays)
Tours by arrangement

Brakspear beers have been brewed in Oxfordshire since 1779. They continue to be traditionally crafted at the Wychwood Brewery (qv) in the historic market town of Witney using the original Victorian square fermenters and the renowned 'double drop' fermenting system. Part of Marston's PLC.

Bitter (OG 1035, ABV 3.4%)
A classic copper-coloured pale ale with big hop resins, juicy malt and orange fruit aroma, intense hop bitterness in the mouth and finish, and a firm maltiness and tangy fruitiness throughout.

Oxford Gold (OG 1040, ABV 4%)
A fruit-flavoured golden beer with a zesty aroma.

Brampton SIBA

Unit 5, Chatsworth Business Park, Chatsworth Road, Chesterfield, Derbyshire, S40 2AR
☎ (01246) 221680 🌐 bramptonbrewery.co.uk
Shop via website
Tours by arrangement

The original Brampton Brewery closed in 1955. In 2007 a new brewery was established, and brewing commenced on an eight-barrel plant. Two tied houses are situated close to the brewery. Seasonal beers and bottle-conditioned beers are available.

Golden Bud (OG 1037, ABV 3.8%)
Crisp and refreshing golden bitter with a pleasant balance of citrus, sweetness and bitter flavours. Light and easy to drink.

1302 (OG 1039, ABV 4%)
A sweet pale ale.

Griffin (OG 1040, ABV 4.1%)
A pale, slightly-sweet summer ale.

Best (OG 1041, ABV 4.2%)
Classic, drinkable bitter with a predominantly malty taste, balanced by caramel sweetness and a developing bitterness in the aftertaste.

Impy Dark (OG 1047, ABV 4.3%)
Strong roasted coffee aroma and a rich flavour of vine fruit and chocolate combine to make this a tasty mild ale.

Jerusalem (OG 1046, ABV 4.6%)
The rich and roasted malt notes defy the pale colour in this special bitter.

Tudor Rose (OG 1045, ABV 4.6%)
A well-balanced and creamy pale ale with big hop nose.

Wasp Nest (OG 1049, ABV 5%)
Strong and complex with malt and hop flavours and a caramel sweetness.

Speciale (OG 1056, ABV 5.8%)
An IPA-style ale, the fruity hoppiness is balanced by the residual sweetness of such a strong ale.

Brancaster

See Beeston

Brandon

76 High Street, Brandon, Suffolk, IP27 0AU
☎ (01842) 878496 🌐 brandonbrewery.co.uk
Shop Mon-Sat 9am-5pm (please ring before visiting), closed Thu
Tours by arrangement

Brandon started brewing in 2005 on the site of an old dairy. Beers are based on traditional styles which include unique recipes and incorporate locally-sourced ingredients. All beers are also available bottle conditioned.

Breckland Gold (OG 1038, ABV 3.8%)
A combination of hops give a delicate, smooth, slightly spicy taste and a dry, lingering, malty finish.

Old Rodney (OG 1040, ABV 4%)
Damson jam aroma precedes a flavoursome balance of malt, fruit and hops in this tawny best bitter. Gently fading finish.

Paddys Pride (OG 1040, ABV 4%)
A dark ruby mild, smooth malt flavours ending with a little roast bitterness.

Saxon Gold (OG 1040, ABV 4%)
A pale, golden beer with a subtle aroma of hops. The taste is a clean, crisp mix of spice and bitter fruits with a dry, hoppy finish.

Strawberry Wheat (OG 1040, ABV 4%)
A pale ale, includes torrified wheat and pulped strawberrys.

Waxies Dargle (OG 1040, ABV 4%)
This copper-coloured brew has rich malt flavours and a rich hoppiness.

Molly's Secret (OG 1041, ABV 4.1%)
A pale ale based on an old recipe.

Norfolk Poacher (OG 1041, ABV 4.1%)
A rich malty roast aroma that follows through to flavours of malt, hops, fruit and sweetness. Upstanding sweetness in a long complex finish.

Royal Ginger (OG 1041, ABV 4.1%)
A refreshing summer ale with a distinctive mix of malt and hoppy spice, balanced with a gentle ginger flavour and finish.

Gun Flint (OG 1042, ABV 4.2%)
Roasted malts are used to produce a malty, chocolate flavour. This combines well with spicy, citrus hops to give a dry, bittersweet, roasted malt finish.

Wee Drop of Mischief (OG 1042, ABV 4.2%)
An amber-coloured premium bitter. Gentle malt flavours give way to a delightful hop character and a dry, increasingly bitter aftertaste.

Rusty Bucket (OG 1044, ABV 4.4%)
Aromas of figs and malt with dried fruit, and flavours of malt and hops, leading to a bitter, biscuity aftertaste. A well-balanced traditional best bitter.

Grumpy Bastard (OG 1045, ABV 4.5%)

Slippery Jack (OG 1045, ABV 4.5%)
A dark brown stout. Complex but well-balanced flavours of roasted grain and hop bitterness. Dry with a lingering, pleasantly bitter finish.

'Old On To Your 'At (OG 1047, ABV 4.7%)
Dark amber in colour, big malt flavours overlaid with a tangy fruit bitterness.

Napper Tandy (OG 1050, ABV 5%)
A reddish amber beer, full-bodied with a malty aroma. Crisp and spicy with an underlying citrus flavour and a dry, malty, bitter fruit finish.

Brandy Cask

Brandy Cask, 25 Bridge Street, Pershore, Worcestershire, WR10 1AJ
☎ (01386) 552602
Tours by arrangement

Brewing started in 1995 in a refurbished bottle store in the garden of the pub. Brewery and pub now operate under one umbrella, with brewing carried out by the owner/landlord.

Branscombe Vale SIBA

Branscombe, Devon, EX12 3DP
☎ (01297) 680511 🌐 branscombevalebrewery.co.uk

⊗ The brewery was set up in 1992 in cowsheds overlooking the sea owned by the National Trust, the two partners converting the sheds and digging their own well. In 2008 a new 25-barrel plant was shoehorned in through the roof.

Mild (OG 1036, ABV 3.7%)

Branoc (OG 1038, ABV 3.8%)
Pale brown brew with a malt and fruit aroma and a hint of caramel. Malt and bitter taste with a dry, hoppy finish.

Draymans Best Bitter (OG 1042, ABV 4.2%)

BVB Best Bitter (OG 1045, ABV 4.6%)
Reddy/brown-coloured beer with a fruity aroma and taste, and bitter/astringent finish.

Summa That (OG 1049, ABV 5%)
Light golden beer with a clean and refreshing taste and a long, hoppy finish.

Brass Castle SIBA

10 Yorkersgate, Malton, North Yorkshire, YO17 7AB
☎ 07563 579723 brasscastlebrewery.co.uk
Tours by arrangement

The original brewery was in the owner's garage in Pocklington with further production at the Brew House on the Garrowby Estate courtesy of the Earl of Halifax before moving to Malton towards the end 2013. All beers are unfined and so are suitable for vegetarians and vegans.

Cliffhanger (OG 1040, ABV 3.8%)
A refreshing hop-laden golden ale infused with citrus notes.

Tail Gunner (OG 1042, ABV 4%)
A dry-hopped rye session ale with a reddish hue. Originally brewed for the Jubilee celebrations.

Best Bitter (OG 1046, ABV 4.5%)
A brass-coloured traditional special bitter.

Brass Lager (OG 1058, ABV 5.3%)
A malt forward Vienna lager.

Bad Kitty (OG 1060, ABV 5.5%)
A chewy chocolate and vanilla porter.

Sunshine (OG 1061, ABV 5.7%)
A full-bodied IPA.

Braydon Ales SIBA

The Brewhouse, Preston West Farm, Preston, Chippenham, Wiltshire, SN15 4DX
☎ (01249) 892900 braydonales.co.uk
Tours by arrangement

⊗ In 2009 three friends bought the Burford Brewery and relocated it to a farm building in Wiltshire. A five-barrel plant is used to supply pubs and clubs in the area as well as direct sales from the brewery.

Thrudger (OG 1038, ABV 3.8%)
A pale single malt/single hop easy-drinking beer with a citrus taste.

RWB (OG 1041, ABV 4%)
Light copper-coloured ale with a gentle bitter taste.

Yer Tiz (OG 1042, ABV 4.1%)
Triple-hopped but well-balanced bitter.

Brecon Brewing Ltd SIBA

8a Brecon Enterprise Park, Brecon, Powys, LD3 8BT
☎ (01874) 620800 breconbrewing.co.uk
Shop Mon-Fri 9am-5pm
Tours by arrangement

Brecon was established in 2011 by Buster Grant. Seasonal and special beers are also available including beers from the Genesis Project: see website.

Three Beacons (OG 1030, ABV 3%)
A low ABV American Pale Ale; golden-hued, full-bodied and extensively hopped.

Welsh Beacons (OG 1037, ABV 3.7%)
Brewed in the style of a Welsh pale ale, this is a golden bitter with a gentle floral bitterness and a full flavour.

Copper Beacons (OG 1041, ABV 4.1%)
A copper-coloured best bitter; smooth with well-balanced fruit and hop flavours.

Gold Beacons (OG 1042, ABV 4.2%)
A deep golden ale, with soft, well-defined bitterness which balances a blend of malts.

Red Beacons (OG 1050, ABV 5%)
A premium red-coloured, complex IPA; smooth and well-hopped.

Brentwood SIBA

Calcott Hall Farm, Ongar Road, Brentwood, Essex, CM14 5RE
☎ (01277) 375577 brentwoodbrewing.co.uk
Shop Mon-Fri 9am-5pm
Tours by arrangement

⊗ Since its launch in 2006 Brentwood has steadily increased its capacity and distribution, relocating to a new purpose-built brewery unit in 2013 with a visitor centre. Seasonal and special beers are also available including more unusual beer styles under the Elephant School brand name.

BBC2 (OG 1030, ABV 2.5%)
Full-bodied mid-brown bitter with a dry tropical citrus flavour.

IPA (OG 1039, ABV 3.7%)
A lightly-hopped, pale session beer.

Marvellous Maple Mild (OG 1038, ABV 3.7%)
Dark brown mild with a hint of maple syrup.

Best (OG 1042, ABV 4.2%)
A traditional, light-coloured best bitter with a well-rounded flavour and aroma.

Gold (OG 1043, ABV 4.3%)
A heavily-hopped golden beer with a fruity taste and bitter finish.

Chockwork Orange (OG 1067, ABV 6.5%)
A deep chocolate malty beer brewed with oranges and matured to provide a classic old ale.

Brew By Numbers

79 Enid Street, London, SE16 3RA ☎ 07528 684105
brewbynumbers.com

Brew By Numbers is a small brewery established in 2012 with plans to move to larger premises. The vegan-friendly beers are bottled on site, with primary fermentation yeast carried over. Each beer is also sold by number, the first part relating to the style of beer and the second to the recipe within that style.

Brew Company SIBA

Unit 7, 106 Fitzwater Road, Sheffield, South Yorkshire, S2 2SP
☎ (0114) 270 9991 ✉ thebrewcompany@gmail.com

Brewer Pete Roberts set up this eight-barrel plant in part of a former factory in Sheffield's industrial east end in 2008. It relocated in 2014. House beers are brewed for the nearby Harlequin and Riverside pubs along with regular seasonal brews.

Simcoe (OG 1037, ABV 3.8%)
A pale session bitter with a passion fruit, apricot and pine aroma from the hops and sharp juicy flavour.

Blonde (OG 1039, ABV 4%)
A light-coloured, easy-drinking session beer brewed with German hops.

Liquid Gold (OG 1039, ABV 4%)
A deep golden orange beer with sweet malt overtones balanced by refreshing fruity and spicy hop characteristics.

Blonde Ambition (OG 1041, ABV 4.2%)
Blonde ale with a malty taste combining with a zesty character and fruity bite, a gentle bitter taste and clean, refreshing finish.

New England Best (OG 1041, ABV 4.2%)
Rich, smooth beer with a distinctive malty base, a rich flavour and dark colouring.

Hop Ripper IPA (OG 1041.7, ABV 4.3%)
A pale IPA, bitter and hoppy.

Oat Stout (OG 1042, ABV 4.3%)
Dark, full-bodied traditional stout.

Hop Monster (OG 1043.6, ABV 4.5%)
Golden ale with resinous pink grapefruit, biting citrus and soft floral characters and a long, bitter finish. Very hoppy.

Yellow Rose (OG 1044, ABV 4.5%)
Golden ale combining quality malts hopped with Amarillo giving a floral and fruity character.

Kiwi Pale Ale (OG 1045, ABV 4.6%)
New Zealand style pale ale with floral characters of pine needles, tropical fruits and citrus notes.

Frontier IPA (OG 1045.5, ABV 4.7%)
Straw-coloured, crisp and dry with a bitter aftertaste.

Crazy Horse IPA (OG 1049, ABV 5.1%)
Full-flavoured IPA with a clean, sharp pine-like aroma complemented by a hint of citrus and tropical fruit characters.

BrewDog SIBA

Unit 1, Kessock Workshops, Kessock Road, Fraserburgh, AB43 8UE
☎ (01346) 519009 🌐 brewdog.com
Tours by arrangement

BrewDog was established in 2007 by James Watt and Martin Dickie. Seven bars are owned. Most of the production goes into bottles with some keg production. No cask beers are produced at the moment.

Brewhouse & Kitchen (Dorchester) (NEW)

17 Weymouth Avenue, Dorchester, DT1 1QY
☎ (01305) 265551 🌐 brewhouseandkitchen.com
Tours by arrangement

Opened in 2014 this brewpub is a sister to the Brewhouse & Kitchen in Portsmouth. The five-barrel copper clad plant is on full public display in the main bar area. Apart from the main beer portfolio there will be many seasonal and specials created. Carry-outs are available in pins and mini-kegs and a 'brewery experience' is planned.

Station Masters Ale (OG 1035, ABV 3.2%)
A golden session ale with a dry mouthfeel.

Crickmay (OG 1044, ABV 4.2%)
Traditional copper-coloured ale with a good bitter bite and fruitcake sweetness.

Durnovaria Dark (OG 1046, ABV 4.7%)
A hoppy black ale with a rich taste.

Cerne Abbas Giant (OG 1052, ABV 5.5%)
An American-style IPA, golden in colour with a citrus/pine aroma and a biscuity backbone.

Brewhouse & Kitchen (Portsmouth) (NEW)

26 Guildhall Walk, Portsmouth, Hampshire, PO1 2DD
☎ (023) 9289 1340 🌐 brewhouseandkitchen.com

A 2.5-barrel plant sited within a pub and restaurant which opened in 2013. The beers are mostly cask-conditioned, but are also available in one-gallon mini kegs for takeaway.

Little Bricky (OG 1035, ABV 3.4%)
A dark brown mild, the flavour focusing more on a blend of malts than hops. The name pays homage to a former Brickwoods beer, a Portsmouth brewery that closed in 1983.

Mucky Duck (OG 1035, ABV 3.4%)
A light copper-coloured session bitter with a good balance of malt and hops in both flavour and aroma.

Sexton (OG 1040, ABV 4%)
Pale gold-coloured beer with a soft bitterness and a fruity hop flavour and aroma.

Troubleshooter (OG 1040, ABV 4%)
A deep copper-coloured traditional bitter with caramel malt being balanced by bitterness from English hops.

Black Swan (OG 1056, ABV 5.7%)
A big, bold, hoppy American-style black ale. A firm bitterness supports a pronounced hop flavour and aroma.

Brewmeister SIBA

Unit R, Isla Bank Mills, Keith, AB55 5DD
☎ (01542) 488006 ☎ 07827 333646
🌐 brewmeister.co.uk

Brewmeister began brewing in 2012 at Kincardine O'Neil, Aberdeenshire, but moved in 2013 to an industrial unit in Keith in Moray and again in 2014 to a bigger unit on the same estate. Beer is mainly available in bottles in selected specialist off-licenses although cask is becoming available in a few outlets. There are plans to open a pub in Aberdeen. Bottle-conditioned Snake Venom, at 67.5% ABV, is allegedly the strongest beer in the world.

Blonde (OG 1050, ABV 4%)

Light and refreshing with a light, hoppy profile.

Kaiser (OG 1042, ABV 4.5%)
A wheat beer with honey notes.

Supersonic IPA (OG 1048, ABV 5%)
Extremely hoppy with hints of pineapple and banana.

The Black Hawk (OG 1051, ABV 5%)
A coffee stout made with chocolate and coffee beans.

Ten (OG 1098, ABV 10.1%)
Slightly sweet but hoppy with a fruity aroma and complex malty character.

Brewshed

1 Tayfen Road, Bury St Edmunds, Suffolk, IP32 6BH
☎ (01284) 848066 🌐 brewshedbrewery.co.uk

⊗ Brewshed began brewing in 2011 using a five barrel plant in the buildings located behind the Beerhouse, one of its pub outlets.

Pale Ale (OG 1040, ABV 3.9%)

Best Bitter (OG 1044, ABV 4.3%)

Rioja Porter (OG 1048, ABV 4.8%)

American Blonde (OG 1055, ABV 5.5%)

Brewshine (NEW)

4 Littledale, Kendal, Cumbria, LA9 7SG
🌐 brewshine.co.uk

Brewing began in 2014 using a nine-gallon plant situated in a garage in Kendal. There are plans for expansion.

Silly Billy (OG 1038, ABV 3.8%)
A smooth, copper-coloured bitter with balanced flavours and a caramel finish.

Billonde (OG 1040, ABV 4%)
Refreshing with a light citrus, fruity flavour.

Billy Goat Ale (OG 1040, ABV 4%)
A dark-amber coloured ale with a rich, malty taste. Well-balanced with hops to leave a dry caramel/chocolate finish.

Billyonaires Gold (OG 1040, ABV 4%)
A light beer with a citrus, fruity flavour.

Brewster's SIBA

Unit 5, Burnside, Turnpike Close, Grantham, Lincolnshire, NG31 7XU
☎ (01476) 566000 🌐 brewsters.co.uk
Tours by arrangement

⊗ Brewster is the old English term for a female brewer and Sara Barton is a modern example. Originally established in the Vale of Belvoir in 1998 and moving to Grantham in 2006, Brewsters produces a range of traditional and innovative beers with two regularly changing ranges; Wicked Women (4.8%) and WhimsicAles (4.0%).

Hophead (OG 1036, ABV 3.6%)
This amber beer has a floral/hoppy character; hops predominate throughout before finally yielding to grapefruit in the lasting dry finish.

Marquis (OG 1038, ABV 3.8%)
A well-balanced and refreshing session bitter with maltiness and a dry, hoppy finish.

Hopticale Illusion (OG 1040, ABV 4%)
A deep red-coloured session beer with a big hop flavour balanced with roast malts.

Aromantica (OG 1042, ABV 4.2%)
A light amber-coloured brew with a slightly sweet, nutty flavour. Citra hops to the fore give tropical hop notes and aromas of lime and passion fruit with a refreshingly long, aromatic finish.

Hop A Doodle Doo (OG 1043, ABV 4.3%)
A copper-coloured ale with a rich, full-bodied feel and fruity hop character.

Decadence (OG 1044, ABV 4.4%)
A golden ale with a hint of malt sweetness with passion fruit and grapefruit aromas on the nose. First taste gives a complex zesty hop palate leading on to a fresh herby finish.

Aromatic Porter (OG 1045, ABV 4.5%)
A rich, dark porter brewed with rich roast and caramel flavours from a blend of dark malts. A big hop taste of citrus and tropical fruit flavours balance the malts.

Stilton Porter (OG 1049, ABV 4.9%)
A rich, roast-flavoured porter brewed with four types of malt and balanced with spicy rich hop flavours from English varieties.

Briarbank (NEW) SIBA

70 Fore Street, Ipswich, Suffolk, IP4 1LB
☎ (01473) 284000 🌐 briarbank.org
Tours by arrangement

Briarbank began brewing in 2013 and is housed in a converted bank to the rear of the Isaac's complex, which is mostly a conversion of old Isaac Lord's Warehouse, previously a maltings. Tours are run of the restored malting machinery room and the brewery, finishing in the tasting room where the beers are available. Other local outlets are also supplied. Seasonal beers: see website.

IPA (Ipswich Pale Ale) (ABV 3.6%)
A hoppy, chestnut-coloured ale with a citrus aroma.

Briar Bitter (ABV 3.7%)
A traditional, copper-coloured English bitter.

Samuel Harvey VC (ABV 3.7%)
A light, hoppy ale. Full-flavoured with hints of grapefruit and orange.

Dark Knight (ABV 3.8%)
A smooth session mild. Easy-drinking with a deep ruby colour.

Cardinale Wolsey (ABV 4%)
A dark traditional beer, made in the style of a 14th century old ale.

Briar Cobnut (ABV 4.2%)
Full-bodied with a sweet finish.

Hawksmoor Stone Brew (ABV 4.3%)
A complex and fruity ale. Hot granite is used to assist the boil.

Perpendicular (ABV 4.4%)
A golden yellow-coloured ale with a floral flavour.

Old Spiteful (ABV 4.8%)
A golden ale, well-balanced with a malty body.

Suffolk Pride (ABV 4.8%)
A malty, copper-coloured beer with a slight toasty flavour.

Tipple Tattle (ABV 5%)
A rich golden ale with hints of orange.

Brick (NEW) SIBA

Arch 209, Blenheim Grove, Peckham, London, SE15 4QL ☎ 07747 787636 🌐 brickbrewery.co.uk

Brick began brewing in 2013. A brewery tap room is open on Saturdays from 12-6pm. The beers brewed vary from week to week. Local pubs, bars and restaurants are also supplied.

Kinsale Bitter (ABV 4%)

Bridestones SIBA

Smithy Farm, Long Causeway, Blackshaw Head, Hebden Bridge, West Yorkshire, HX7 7JB
☎ (01422) 847104 🌐 bridestonesbrewing.co.uk

Bridestones, situated close to a rock outcrop from which it takes its name, started brewing in 2006 and currently supplies more than 60 outlets. Its brewery tap is the New Delight Inn in Blackshaw. Seasonal and bottle-conditioned beers are available.

Indians Head (OG 1037, ABV 3.7%)
Light amber session bitter with a citrus hop finish.

Sandstone (OG 1039, ABV 3.9%)
A pale session ale with a smooth, clean taste.

Pennine Gold (OG 1043, ABV 4.3%)
Good hop aroma and flavour; fruity, refreshing and easy to drink best bitter.

Dark Mild (OG 1045, ABV 4.5%)
Dark brown strong mild with a complex nose of caramel and roasted malt. Good balance of sweetness and bitterness on the palate. Upfront bitterness in the finish.

American Pale Ale (OG 1050, ABV 5%)
A strong but easy-drinking pale ale.

Bridgehouse SIBA

Unit 1, Aireworth Mills, Aireworth Road, Keighley, West Yorkshire, BD21 4DH
🌐 bridgehousebrewery.co.uk

Bridgehouse began brewing in 2010 using a 10-barrel plant. The brewery purchased the recipes and branding of Old Bear Brewery in 2014 and moved into its premises in Keighley.

Blonde (OG 1040, ABV 4%)

Porter (OG 1045, ABV 4.5%)

Moorland Bitter (OG 1052, ABV 5.2%)

Brewed under the Old Bear Brewery name:

Estivator (OG 1037, ABV 3.8%)
This straw-coloured bitter has a grassy hop character in the aroma and taste with marmalade fruitiness. The finish is dry and bitter.

Great Bear (OG 1039, ABV 3.9%)

Black Mari'a (OG 1043, ABV 4.2%)
A black stout, smooth on the palate with a strong roast malt flavour and fruity finish.

Yorkshire Ale (OG 1042, ABV 4.2%)

Honeypot (OG 1044, ABV 4.4%)
Straw-coloured beer enhanced with golden honey.

Goldilocks (OG 1047, ABV 4.5%)
A fruity, straw-coloured golden ale, well-hopped and assertively bitter through to the finish.

Hibernator (OG 1055, ABV 5%)
A complex rich dark ale dominated by roast and bitter flavours against a background sweetness. Look for roast coffee, hints of caramel and dark vine fruit on the nose. The finish is distinctly bitter and quite astringent.

Bridgetown

Albert Inn, Bridgetown Close, Totnes, Devon, TQ9 5AD
☎ (01803) 863214 🌐 albertinntotnes.com/bridgetown-brewery

Bridgetown started brewing in 2008 on a 2.5-barrel plant. Seasonal beers are available.

Albert Ale (OG 1036, ABV 3.8%)

Bridlington (NEW)

110 Quay Road, Bridlington, East Yorkshire, YO16 4JB
☎ (01262) 674592

Bridlington was founded in 2014 and is based in an outhouse in the beer garden of the Telegraph Inn. One regular ale is produced with further beers planned.

Jackdaw (ABV 4.3%)
A porter produced from an old English recipe.

Briggs (NEW)

c/o Unit 1, Waterhouse Mill, 65-71 Lockwood Road, Huddersfield, West Yorkshire, HD1 5QU ☎ 07427 668004 🌐 briggssignatureales.weebly.com

Nick Briggs, a former member of the brewing team at Mallinson's and assistant head brewer at Elland, has branched out on his own producing his first brew on the Mallinson's plant.

Northern Soul (OG 1038, ABV 3.8%)
Pale bitter with a citrus and zesty aroma from an abundance of American hops.

Brightlingsea

Rosebud, 66-67 Hurst Green, Brightlingsea, Essex, CO7 0EH
☎ (01206) 304571 🌐 rosebudpub.co.uk

Brightlingsea operates from a 3.5-barrel plant within the Rosebud pub. Beers are brewed on demand and the pub aims to have at least one on sale at any time.

Brighton Bier

Hand in Hand Pub, 33 Upper St James Street, Kemptown, Brighton, East Sussex, BN2 1JN ☎ 07515 956976 🌐 brightonbier.com

Brighton Bier was established in 2013 and is based at the Hand in Hand pub in Brighton (Kemptown Brewery). Beers are available in the pub and at other outlets in the South East. One pub is owned, in collaboration with Late Knights Brewery (qv), the Brighton Beer Dispensary in Brighton. Monthly seasonal beers are available.

Thirty Three (OG 1035, ABV 3.3%)
A pale ale brewed with three different malts, three different yeasts and three different hops.

West Pier Pale Ale (ABV 4%)
A classic, hop forward pale ale.

Underdog Best Bitter (ABV 4.2%)
A crisp hop bitterness and a rich, satisfying malt flavour.

No Name Stout (ABV 5%)
A rich, satisfying stout with generous amounts of oatmeal giving it a silky mouthfeel.

South Coast IPA (ABV 5%)
A clean-tasting IPA.

The Grand Porter (ABV 5.2%)
A rich, satisfying, robust porter packed with flavours of dark chocolate and a hint of coffee.

Brightside SIBA

Unit 10, Dale Industrial Estate, Radcliffe, M26 1AD
☎ (0161) 725 9644 ☎ 07870 207442
🌐 brightsidebrewing.co.uk

Brightside began commercial production in 2011 using a 2.5-barrel plant. It started life in the back room of the family's bakery but expanded into a dedicated industrial unit in 2013 and upgraded to a 15-barrel plant in 2014.

Odin (OG 1038, ABV 3.8%)
A fresh, light-bodied blonde ale brewed with a fruity, citrus flavour and moderately bitter finish.

The Beast (OG 1039, ABV 3.8%)
A dark amber-coloured, malty bitter with more flavour than its strength suggests.

The Inn Crowd (OG 1040, ABV 3.8%)
A dark mild, full-bodied and rich with caramel notes but not heavy.

Our Town (OG 1040, ABV 4%)
A copper-coloured beer with tropical fruit flavours.

Best Bitter (OG 1044, ABV 4.3%)
A dark amber-coloured traditional English best bitter showing a great depth of flavour.

Underworld (OG 1049, ABV 4.4%)
A dry, medium-bodied porter. A little more bitter than you might expect from a traditional porter. Aromas of coffee and dried fruit.

Solstice Golden Ale (OG 1043, ABV 4.5%)
A refreshing, light golden-coloured ale with a mild spicy hop character and a hint of fruit.

Darkside Stout (OG 1052, ABV 4.6%)
This jet black stout has flavours reminiscent of espresso coffee and dark chocolate, with more than a touch of smoke on the finish. More hops than are usual for a stout enhance the roast malt bitterness.

Manchester Skyline (OG 1044, ABV 4.6%)
Lager malt, wheat and four speciality malts give a deep golden colour and complex flavour.

Maverick IPA (OG 1047, ABV 4.8%)
A light amber-coloured IPA but with a weighty rich, malty base and punchy citrus hop character. Refreshingly bitter but not overpowering.

Amarillo (OG 1048, ABV 5%)
A broad blend of malts create a complex malt profile to complement a single hop variety. A dry, light amber-coloured beer, liberally hopped without being overwhelmingly bitter.

Brightwater Brewery SIBA

9 Beaconsfield Road, Claygate, Surrey, KT10 0PN
☎ (01372) 462334 🌐 brightbrew.co.uk

⊗ Brightwater is an eco-friendly five-barrel brewery with two six-barrel fermenters, situated at the rear of a domestic property. Established in 2013, it currently supplies two outlets on a regular basis.

Little Nipper (OG 1033, ABV 3.3%)

Top Notch (OG 1035, ABV 3.5%)
Balanced amber ale, with floral hop notes providing a clean, bitter finish.

Daisy Gold (OG 1040, ABV 4%) ◆
Golden-coloured ale with a moderate tropical fruit hoppy character and some balancing malt leading to a bittersweet finish.

Wild Orchid (OG 1040, ABV 4%)
Dark oatmeal porter enhanced with a Madagascan vanilla pod in each cask giving the beer fragrant vanilla undertones.

All Citra (OG 1043, ABV 4.3%)
Bitter with bite and a distinctly citrus flavour.

Brigstock Brewhouse

7 Park Walk, Brigstock, Kettering, Northamptonshire, NN14 3HH
☎ (01536) 373428 🌐 brigstockbrewhouse.co.uk

Philip Wilks began brewing in 2012 on a small 52-litre plant using natural spring water from a local limestone aquifer. Six regular beers are brewed, and are also available bottle-conditioned.

Autumn Harvest (OG 1049, ABV 4.2%)
A mellow autumnal beer with a citrus aroma and lingering hoppy taste.

Gold (OG 1049, ABV 4.2%)
A golden summer ale with a zesty aroma and refreshing citrus taste.

Liberator (OG 1049, ABV 4.2%)
A refreshing ale; bitter with subtle flavours of toffee, honey and mead.

Old Nick's Favourite (OG 1053, ABV 4.8%)
A dark, rich beer with a distinctive flavour of liquorice and toffee, gained through a union of black strap molasses with black and chocolate malts.

Potter's Ruin (OG 1053, ABV 4.8%)
A distinctive fruity taste, rounded with a toffee flavour and a hoppy finish.

Brimstage SIBA

Home Farm, Brimstage, CH63 6HY
☎ (0151) 342 1181 🌐 brimstagebrewery.com
Tours by arrangement

Brewing started in 2006 on a 10-barrel plant in a redundant farm dairy in the heart of the Wirral countryside. This is Wirral's first brewery since the closure of the Birkenhead Brewery in the late 1960s. Around 60 outlets are supplied.

Sandpiper Light Ale (OG 1036.5, ABV 3.6%)
A session beer, well-balanced, light and refreshing with tropical fruit flavours.

Trappers Hat Bitter (OG 1037.5, ABV 3.8%)
Gold-coloured with a complex bouquet, it provides a mouthful of fruit zest, with hints of orange and grapefruit. A refreshingly hoppy session brew.

Rhode Island Red Bitter (OG 1039, ABV 4%) ◆

Red, smooth and well-balanced malty beer with a good dry aftertaste. Some fruitiness in the taste.

Scarecrow Bitter (OG 1041, ABV 4.2%)
Orange marmalade in colour, this well-balanced session brew has a distinct citrus fruit bouquet and a bitter finish.

Briscoe's

16 Ash Grove, Otley, West Yorkshire, LS21 3EL
☎ (01943) 466515 ✉ briscoe.brewery@virgin.net

The brewery was launched in 1998 by microbiologist/chemist Dr Paul Briscoe in the cellar of his house with a one-barrel brew length. Dr Briscoe is currently producing one brew per week on his original plant; several beers are produced on an irregular basis.

Chevin Bitter (OG 1039, ABV 3.8%)
A golden, hoppy bitter.

Lighter Shade of Pale (OG 1040, ABV 4%)

Burnsall Classic (OG 1041, ABV 4.1%)

Bristol Beer Factory SIBA

Unit A, The Old Brewery, Durnford Street, Ashton, Bristol, BS3 2AW
☎ (0117) 902 6317

Office: c/o Tobacco Factory, Raleigh Road, Southville, Bristol, BS3 1TF 🌐 bristolbeerfactory.co.uk
Shop Mon-Fri 9am-5pm
Tours by arrangement

A 30-barrel microbrewery in a part of the former Ashton Gate Brewing Co, which closed in 1933. 50 outlets are supplied and output and brewing capacity are steadily increasing. Seasonal beers are also available.

Nova (OG 1040, ABV 3.8%)
Citrus hop aroma to this straw-coloured, light bodied and bitter session ale. Hop led taste with lemon fruit and pale malt following into a bitter hop aftertaste.

Seven (OG 1043, ABV 4.2%)
Mid-brown best bitter with a malty aroma. Balanced malt and hops with fruit flavours. Malt and bitter remain on the aftertaste.

Sunrise (OG 1044, ABV 4.4%)
Refreshing golden ale with grassy hops giving bitter citrus fruit flavours leading to a bitter finish.

Milk Stout (OG 1049, ABV 4.5%)
Distinctive full-bodied black stout with strong black treacle aroma and flavour and lactose sugar creaminess. Well-balanced with malt and roast and a bitter background.

Britannia SIBA

Royal Standard of England, Forty Green, Buckinghamshire, HP9 1XS
☎ (01494) 673382 🌐 rsoe.co.uk

Britannia began brewing in 2012. The brewery is located in one of the outbuildings at the Royal Standard of England pub in Forty Green, Buckinghamshire. Brewing is currently suspended.

Pale Ale (OG 1042, ABV 4%)

Golden Ale (OG 1044, ABV 4.2%)

Britman (NEW)

The Stables, Burton Manor, Burton, Cheshire, CH64 5SJ ☎ 07925 875836
✉ britmanbrewerburtonmanor@gmail.com

Britman began brewing in 2014 in the converted stables of an old manor house. The owner, who has retired from the motor industry, built the 100-litre brewery himself. Beers are available in selected local pubs.

Best Bitter (ABV 4%)

Porter (ABV 4%)

Golden Ale (ABV 4.5%)

Brixton (NEW)

Arch 547, Brixton Station Road, Brixton, London, SW9 8PF ☎ 07761 436757 🌐 brixtonbrewery.com
Shop Sat 12-4pm or by appt

Located in a railway arch in central Brixton, the brewery opened in 2013 using a 2.5-barrel plant. The bulk of its production is currently bottled, but cask ales feature as occasional guests in several Brixton pubs. All beers are named after places in Brixton.

Reliance Pale Ale (OG 1042, ABV 4.2%)

Effra Ale (OG 1045, ABV 4.5%)
A session bitter. A smooth, amber ale that balances pine, lime and grassy hops.

Atlantic APA (OG 1054, ABV 5.4%)

Electric IPA (OG 1065, ABV 6.5%)
A full-bodied IPA balancing malty sweetness and hoppy bitterness with a floral, citrus and tropical fruit hit.

Brockley SIBA

31 Harcourt Road, Brockley, London, SE4 2AJ
☎ 07814 584338 🌐 brockleybrewery.co.uk

Brockley began brewing in 2013 using a five-barrel plant. It was set up in a disused builder's workshop by a group of locals passionate about real ale.

Golden Ale (OG 1038, ABV 3.8%)
A hoppy golden ale with some citrus throughout and a bitter finish. Trace of caramelised malt.

Pale Ale (OG 1041, ABV 4.1%)

Red Ale (OG 1048, ABV 4.8%)

Brodie's SIBA

816a High Road, Leyton, London, E10 6AE ☎ 07828 498733 🌐 brodiesbeers.com
Tours by arrangement

Siblings James and Lizzie began commercial brewing in 2008 on a five-barrel plant at the back of the William IV pub in East London. Beers are available at the William IV and their small chain of family-owned pubs as well as other local outlets. All cask ales are available bottle conditioned. Seasonal ales and festival specials are also brewed regularly: see website.

Citra (OG 1031, ABV 3.1%)
Citrus and tropical fruit in aroma and flavour, which is dry and bitter and faintly sweet. Bitterness grows on drinking.

Kiwi (ABV 3.8%)

THE BREWERIES

A smooth-drinking yellow beer. Flavour is malty sweet overlaid by green fruit, a little hops and a bitter character.

Bethnal Green Bitter (OG 1040, ABV 4%) ◆
A brown, refreshing but full-bodied bitter with a malty sweetness. Finish is dry with an increasing bitterness.

Old Street Pale Ale (OG 1050, ABV 5%) ◆
Hops and citrus fruit are balanced in this golden beer by the bitterness, a biscuity sweetness and a creamy mouthfeel.

California (OG 1053, ABV 5.3%) ◆
Smooth yellow beer with a citrus fruit aroma. Sweet citrus fruit is balanced with bitterness on the palate and aftertaste.

Broughs

Springfield Brewery, Grimstone Street, Wolverhampton, West Midlands, WV10 0JP ☎ 07814 158292

Office: 192 Staveley Rd, Wolverhampton, West Midlands, WV1 4RL ✉ broughsltd@yahoo.co.uk
Tours by arrangement

Broughs is a family-run brewery which began trading in 2008 using spare capacity at several breweries around the West Midlands region. In 2011 it moved into rented premises at the former Butlers Springfield brewery (1873-1991) and now brews three times a week on its own four-barrel plant. No pubs are owned, but the brewery has a visitor's bar and more than 30 outlets across the West Midlands, Staffordshire and Shropshire are regularly supplied direct. Seasonal and bottle conditioned beers are available.

Original (OG 1036, ABV 3.6%)
A pale, easy-drinking session bitter, well-balanced with refreshing English hops.

Springfield (OG 1040, ABV 4%)
A light golden session ale with a subtle clean taste created by an unusual blend of hops.

Bitter (OG 1043, ABV 4.3%)
A typical Black Country style golden bitter, well-balanced with a sweet aftertaste.

Blonde (OG 1046, ABV 4.6%)
A contemporary hoppy and fruity pale yellow ale. Refreshing and easy drinking.

Pale Ale (OG 1048, ABV 4.8%)
A traditional strong, pale ale bursting with a sweet, even-hopped flavour and a pleasant bitter finish.

Superior (OG 1050, ABV 5%)
A strong, dark mild with a sweet, malty finish. Mainly brewed throughout autumn/winter.

Broughton SIBA

Broughton, ML12 6HQ
☎ (01899) 830345 🌐 broughtonales.co.uk
Shop Mon-Fri 8am-4pm
Tours by arrangement

Founded in 1979, Broughton Ales was then one of the very first microbreweries. Broughton has developed since then and though more than 60% of production goes into bottle for sale in Britain and abroad, it retains a sizeable range of cask ales. Seasonal beers: see website. All beers are suitable for vegetarians.

The Reiver (OG 1038, ABV 3.6%)
A light-coloured session ale with a predominantly hoppy flavour and aroma on a background of fruity malt. The aftertaste is crisp and clean.

Willacade (OG 1036, ABV 3.6%)
A crisp and easy-drinking session beer with floral and citrus on the nose.

Bramling Cross (OG 1041, ABV 4.2%)
A golden ale with a blend of malt and hop flavours followed by a hoppy aftertaste.

Clipper IPA (OG 1042, ABV 4.2%)
A light-coloured, crisp, hoppy beer with a clean aftertaste.

Merlin's Ale (OG 1042, ABV 4.2%) ◆
A well-hopped, fruity flavour is balanced by malt in the taste. The finish is bittersweet, light but dry.

Exciseman's 80/- (OG 1046, ABV 4.6%)
A traditional 80/- cask ale. A dark, malty brew. Full drinking with a good hop aftertaste.

Dark Dunter (OG 1050, ABV 4.8%)
Bursting with oatmeal and chocolate aromas complemented by dark roasted malts and a rich aftertaste.

6.2 IPA (OG 1060, ABV 6%)
With quadruple the hops of a typical IPA, this dark chestnut brown example has a bold citrus aroma and a biscuit bitter aftertaste.

Old Jock (OG 1070, ABV 6.7%)
Strong, sweetish and fruity in the finish.

Brown (NEW) SIBA

Unit 1, Derby Road, Clay Cross, Derbyshire, S40 9AG
☎ (01246) 251859 🌐 brownalesbrewery.co.uk

Brown Ales is a family-run business that began brewing in 2013 using a 10-barrel plant.

Inception (OG 1038, ABV 3.8%)
A malty amber ale.

The Shining (OG 1039, ABV 4%)
An easy-drinking blonde beer.

Twilight (ABV 4.4%)
A rich, dry stout.

Gravity (ABV 4.8%)
A powerfully-hopped American pale ale.

Brown Cow

Brown Cow Road, Barlow, Selby, North Yorkshire, YO8 8EH
☎ (01757) 618947 🌐 browncowbrewery.co.uk

Brewing since 1997, Keith and Sue Simpson are operating the six-barrel plant at its maximum capacity of 17 barrels per week. In addition to the five regular beers a range of seasonal, occasional and one-off brews is also available. Bottled beers are also brewed for Suddaby's.

Sessions (OG 1033, ABV 3.6%)
A pale, hoppy session beer with a refreshing finish and citrus notes in the aftertaste.

Bitter (OG 1038, ABV 3.8%)
Copper-coloured classic bitter brewed with English hops. Round and full in flavour with a smooth finish.

White Dragon (OG 1039, ABV 4%)

A pale, aromatic beer with a good level of bitterness, citrus undertones and a clean finish.

Captain Oates Mild (OG 1044, ABV 4.5%)
A dark mild with complex mix of malts and oats. Well-balanced with undertones of coffee and chocolate.

Mrs Simpsons Thriller in Vanilla (OG 1049, ABV 5.1%)
A rich porter brewed with fresh vanilla pods complementing the dark malts.

Broxbourne

Unit 17, Hoddesdon Industrial Estate, Pindar Road, Hoddesdon, Hertfordshire, EN11 0DD
☎ (01438) 940937 broxbournebrewery.co.uk

Broxbourne began brewing in 2013 using a two-barrel plant. Bottle-conditioned beers are also produced under the Fallen Angel brewery name.

Cowgirl Gold (ABV 4.2%)

Angry Ox Bitter (ABV 4.8%)

Brunswick SIBA

1 Railway Terrace, Derby, DE1 2RU
☎ (01332) 410055
brunswickbrewingcompany.co.uk
Tours by arrangement

Currently Derby's oldest brewery, it is a 10-barrel tower brewery built as an extension to the Brunswick Inn in 1991. Bought by Everards in 2002, it is now run separately yet in conjunction with the pub. Everards, wholesalers, regional outlets and the Brunswick Inn are supplied. Seasonal beers are available.

White Feather (OG 1038, ABV 3.6%)
A pale, easy-drinking yet full-bodied session beer.

Triple Hop (OG 1040, ABV 4%)
Straw-coloured beer with a distinctive bitterness.

The Usual (OG 1042, ABV 4.2%)
A traditional English malty best bitter, smooth with hints of toffee.

Railway Porter (OG 1045, ABV 4.3%)
A classic English black porter. Lightly hopped and smooth on the palate with roasted coffee flavours.

Rocket (OG 1047, ABV 4.7%)
A 'New World' IPA with citrus, apricot and mango flavours.

Black Sabbath (OG 1058, ABV 6%)
A strong dark ale with finely balanced flavours of liquorice, coffee and chocolate.

Bryncelyn

Unit 303, Ystradgynlais Workshops, Trawsffordd Road, Ystradgynlais, SA9 1BS
☎ (01639) 841900
bryncelynbrewery@hotmail.co.uk
Tours by arrangement

Opened in 1999, the brewery relocated to its present premises in 2008 with a six-barrel plant acquired from Webbs Brewery of Ebbw Vale. The owner is fond of Buddy Holly and this is reflected in the beer names. Seasonal beers are available.

Holly Hop (OG 1039, ABV 3.9%)
Pale amber with a hoppy aroma. A refreshing hoppy, fruity flavour with balancing bitterness; a similar lasting finish. A beer full of flavour for its gravity.

Buddy Marvellous (OG 1040, ABV 4%)
Dark brown with an inviting aroma of malt, roast and fruit. A gentle bitterness mixes roast with malt, hops and fruit, giving a complex, satisfying and lasting finish.

Sleeping Giant (OG 1043, ABV 4.3%)
Hoppy bitter with a balance of malt.

Oh Boy (OG 1045, ABV 4.5%)
An inviting aroma of hops, fruit and malt, and a golden colour. The tasty mix of hops, fruit, bitterness and background malt ends with a long, hoppy, bitter aftertaste.

Buckingham SIBA

Unit 3, Hillcrest Rise, Buckingham, MK18 1SL
☎ (01280) 422830 buckingham-brewery.co.uk

Owned by the Hynes family, Buckingham began brewing in 2011 using a 2.5-barrel plant and is the only microbrewery in Buckingham; the first to brew in the historic market town since 1897. In 2013 the brewery moved from a domestic garage into an industrial unit, still using the original kit. All beers are also available bottle-conditioned.

Golden (OG 1040, ABV 3.8%)

Bitter (OG 1042, ABV 4%)

Mild (OG 1040, ABV 4%)

Best Bitter (OG 1045, ABV 4.3%)

Old English Ale (OG 1060, ABV 6%)

Bude (NEW) SIBA

Unit 1, Kings Hill Industrial Estate, Bude, Cornwall, EX23 8QN
☎ (01288) 359937 budebrewery.co.uk

Originally established in 2011 near Launceston as Fry's Brewery, and now relocated to Bude, it started beer production under the Bude Brewery name in 2014. The beer range has also been revamped, with a core range of four brews currently in production.

Neet (OG 1037, ABV 3.7%)

Haven (OG 1042, ABV 4.2%)

Summerleaze (OG 1047, ABV 4.7%)

Black Rock (OG 1051, ABV 5.1%)

Buffy's SIBA

Rectory Road, Tivetshall St Mary, Norfolk, NR15 2DD
☎ (01379) 676523 buffys.co.uk

Established in 1993, Buffy's brewing capacity is 20 barrels. The brewery owns two pubs, the Wicklewood Cherry Tree and the Foulden White Hart. Barley for all brewing is grown in Norfolk. Around 100 outlets are supplied. Seasonal and bottle-conditioned beers are available.

Norwich Terrier (OG 1036, ABV 3.6%)
A peachy aroma introduces this refreshing, gold-coloured bitter. Strong bitter notes, hops and grapefruit produce a long, dry finish.

Bitter (OG 1039, ABV 3.9%)

A strong plummy aroma leads into a sweet malty beginning. Caramel notes add depth to a long, fruity finish.

Mild (OG 1042, ABV 4.2%) ◆
Complex with a smooth but grainy feel. Caramel and blackcurrant initially bolster the heavy malt influence. Short, malty finish.

Polly's Folly (OG 1043, ABV 4.3%) ◆
Well-balanced with a definitive malty spine. Elderberry notes and a long, dry, bittersweet finale.

Hopleaf (OG 1044.5, ABV 4.5%) ◆
A gentle hop nose. Strawberries mingle with the hops as the malt gently subsides to leave a bittersweet, dry finish.

Mucky Duck (OG 1044, ABV 4.5%) ◆
Roasted malt throughout with a sweet fruitiness giving depth without becoming dominant. Chewy mouthfeel and lingering finish.

Norwegian Blue (OG 1049, ABV 4.9%) ◆
Nutty caramel aroma. A well-balanced mix of malt and bitterness with caramel, hops, and sweetness. Strong, increasingly bitter finish.

Ale (OG 1055, ABV 5.5%)

Bull Lane

See Stables

Bullfinch (NEW)

118 Druid Street, Southwark, London, SE1 2HH
☎ 07899 795823 ⊕ thebullfinchbrewery.co.uk

Bullfinch began brewing in 2014 using a 2.5-barrel plant. Production is mainly keg but bottle-conditioned beers are available. The brewery shares premises with Anspach & Hobday (qv).

Bullmastiff SIBA

14 Bessemer Close, Leckwith, Cardiff, CF11 8DL
☎ (029) 2066 5292 ✉ bob.bullmastiff@live.co.uk

An award-winning small brewery run by brothers Bob and Paul Jenkins since 1987. The name stems from their love of the bullmastiff breed. 50 outlets are supplied.

Jack the Lad (OG 1041, ABV 4.1%)

Welsh Black (OG 1050, ABV 4.8%)

Welsh Red (OG 1048, ABV 4.8%)

Son of a Bitch (OG 1062, ABV 6%) ◆
A complex, warming amber ale with a tasty blend of hops, malt and fruit flavours, with increasing bitterness.

Bumpmill

The Cottage, Hallfieldgate, Shirland, Derbyshire, DE55 6AG
☎ (01773) 830431 ⊕ bumpmillbrewery.co.uk

A four-barrel family brewery located in a converted building overlooking the beautiful Amber Valley. The name comes from the site of an old Bump Mill close by – bump was coarse cotton used to make wicks for candles.

Moonraker (OG 1038, ABV 3.8%)
A quaffable blonde ale.

Drops of Jupiter (OG 1040, ABV 4%)
A blonde pale ale with grapefruit notes leading to a slightly bitter finish.

Heart of Gold (OG 1042, ABV 4.2%)
A golden pale ale.

Thunder Road (OG 1044, ABV 4.4%)
A copper-coloured premium bitter. Full-bodied chocolate and roast malt with a smooth finish.

Glory Daze (OG 1045, ABV 4.5%)
A traditional amber-coloured bitter.

Buntingford SIBA

Greys Brewhouse, Therfield Road, Royston, Hertfordshire, SG8 9NW
☎ (01763) 250749 ⊕ buntingford-brewery.co.uk
Tours by arrangement

Brewing commenced on the current site in 2005 and has expanded to a capacity of around 60 barrels per week. Two regular beers are brewed year round alongside seasonal and occasional brews and various themed specials. The beers are brewed using water from an on-site well and all liquid waste is treated in a reed bed. The brewery is located on a conservation farm and there is a wide variety of bird life visible from the doors of the brewhouse, often including rare and endangered species.

Highwayman (OG 1036, ABV 3.6%)

Twitchell (OG 1038, ABV 3.8%)

Burley Street SIBA

Fox & Newt, 7-9 Burley Street, Leeds, LS3 1LD
☎ (0113) 245 4505 ✉ i_bennett.fox@hotmail.co.uk

Burley Street Brewhouse is in the cellar of the Fox & Newt pub where the first brewery was installed by Whitbread in the 1980s. The freehold was purchased by the current owners and brewing recommenced in 2010. 12 outlets are supplied direct.

The Brickyard (OG 1038.5, ABV 3.7%) ◆
Drinkable session bitter with a good mix of malt and hops, amber-coloured with an increasingly bitter finish.

SPA Francorchamps (OG 1039.5, ABV 3.8%) ◆
Light-coloured beer with a lemony, bittersweet citrus flavour, the bitterness from the hops is present throughout the taste.

Laguna Seca (OG 1041, ABV 4%) ◆
A smooth golden beer, the exotic fruit hop flavours and aromas are balanced by sweetness, the finish is quite bitter.

Burning Sky (NEW)

Place Barn, The Street, Firle, East Sussex, BN8 6LP
☎ (01273) 858080 ⊕ burningskybeer.com

Burning Sky started brewing in 2013 using a 15-barrel plant, based on the Firle Estate in the South Downs. It is owned and run by Mark Tranter (ex-Dark Star head brewer). Brewing takes place four days a week. The brewery has its own yeast strains suited to the beer styles. They specialise in pale ales and Belgium inspired farmhouse beers and have an extensive barrel aging programme. Bottle-conditioned beers are available.

Plateau (OG 1035, ABV 3.5%)
Pale gold in colour, with a crisp malt edge and sharp bitterness. Full in flavour, zesty and refreshing.

Aurora (OG 1056, ABV 5.6%)
A premium strength pale ale, with a blend of malts to provide a juicy backbone and a pale amber colour. Hops give a resinous mouthfeel and big citrus and tropical fruit flavours, which are prominent, yet well-balanced.

Devils Nest IPA (OG 1070, ABV 7%)
A full-strength IPA named after a nook on the South Downs near the brewery. It has a burnt orange colour and full flavour.

Burnside SIBA

Laurencekirk Business Park,, Laurencekirk, Aberdeenshire, AB30 1EY
☎ (01561) 377316 🌐 burnsidebrewery.co.uk

Burnside began brewing in 2010 using a 2.5-barrel plant. There are plans for an upgrade to a 6.5-barrel plant. Bottle conditioned beers are available.

Burscough SIBA

c/o Hop Vine, Liverpool Road North, Burscough, Lancashire, L40 4BY
☎ (01704) 893799 🌐 burscoughbrewery.co.uk

Burscough commenced brewing in 2010 in old stable buildings in the courtyard to the rear of the Hop Vine. Currently brewing on a four-barrel plant but plans are underway to relocate and expand.

Flat Rib Mild (OG 1036, ABV 3.6%)
A classic mild; dark and satisfying.

Priory Gold (OG 1038, ABV 3.8%)
A sweet and fruity, lightly-bittered, easy-drinking session beer.

Duke of Lancaster (OG 1040, ABV 4%)
A traditional amber-coloured best bitter. Full-flavoured with a noticeable blackcurrant finish.

Mere Blonde (OG 1040, ABV 4%)
A pale, full-flavoured golden ale with a light bitterness and a prominent citrus hop aroma. The malt undertones in the body are complemented by a full hop flavour which gives way to a massive almost grapefruit-like finish.

Ringtail (OG 1042, ABV 4.2%)
A ruby red ale. Full-bodied with a prominent bitterness and a malt character. A noticeable grassy aroma with hints of marmalade and molasses.

Black Canon Stout (OG 1045, ABV 4.5%)
A dark stout, full-flavoured with hints of coffee and liquorice in the finish, named after the Augustine Friars who inhabited Burscough Priory in the 12th century.

Mug Billy (OG 1045, ABV 4.5%)
A traditional best bitter. Light amber in colour and easy-drinking with a noticeable bitterness.

Wailing Willy (OG 1050, ABV 5%)
A premium pale beer with a slightly fruity taste.

Thorougood (OG 1051, ABV 5.1%)
A dangerously drinkable ale. Golden in colour with a citrus finish.

Sutler's IPA (OG 1055, ABV 5.5%)
A powerful amber-coloured, heavily-hopped ale. A sharp lip-smacking prominent bitterness gives way to a massive aroma with hints of grapefruit and other citrus fruits.

Burton Bridge SIBA

24 Bridge Street, Burton upon Trent, Staffordshire, DE14 1SY
☎ (01283) 510573 🌐 burtonbridgebrewery.co.uk
Shop 12-2.15, 5-11pm daily
Tours by arrangement

The brewery was established in 1982 by Bruce Wilkinson and Geoff Mumford and owns five pubs in the local area, including its CAMRA award-winning brewery tap. More than 300 outlets are supplied direct. There is an ever-changing range of monthly beers. Bottle-conditioned beers are also available.

Golden Delicious (OG 1037, ABV 3.8%)
A Burton classic with sulphurous aroma and well-balanced hops and fruit. An apple fruitiness, sharp and refreshing start leads to a lingering, mouth-watering bitter finish with a hint of astringency. Light, crisp and refreshing.

Sovereign Gold (OG 1040, ABV 4%)
Sweet caramel aroma with a grassy hop start with malt overtones. Fresh and fruity with a bitterness that emerges and continues to develop.

XL Bitter (OG 1039, ABV 4%)
Another Burton classic with sulphurous aroma. Golden with fruit and hops and a characteristic lingering aftertaste hinting of toffee apple sweetness.

Bridge Bitter (OG 1041, ABV 4.2%)
Gentle aroma of malt and fruit. Good balanced start finishing with a robust hop mouthfeel.

Burton Porter (OG 1044, ABV 4.5%)
Chocolate aromas and smooth taste of smoky roasted grain and coffee.

Damson Porter (OG 1044, ABV 4.5%)

Stairway to Heaven (OG 1049, ABV 5%)
Golden bitter. A perfectly balanced beer. The malty and hoppy start leads to a hoppy body with a mouthwatering finish.

Top Dog Stout (OG 1049, ABV 5%)
Black and rich with a roast and malty start. Fruity and abundant hops give a fruity, bitter finish with a mouth-watering edge. Also available as Bramble Stout.

Festival Ale (OG 1054, ABV 5.5%)
Caramel aroma with plenty of hop taste balanced by malty sweetness.

Thomas Sykes (OG 1095, ABV 10%)
Kid in a sweetshop aroma. Rich fruity spirited tastes – warming and dangerously drinkable.

Burton Old Cottage

Unit 10, Eccleshall Business Park, Hawkins Lane, Burton upon Trent, Staffordshire, DE14 1PT ☎ 07909 931250 🌐 oldcottagebeer.co.uk
Tours by arrangement

The brewery was originally installed in the old Heritage Brewery. When the site was taken over, it moved to a modern industrial unit. The brewery was sold in 2005, the following year saw heavy investment in new production and storage facilities by the new owners.

Oak Ale (OG 1044, ABV 4%)
Tawny, full-bodied bitter. A sweet start with balanced fruit gives way to a slight roast taste with some caramel for interest. A dry, hoppy finish satisfies the palate.

Chestnut (OG 1042, ABV 4.2%)
A dark session ale with a touch of bitterness and a pleasant, full aftertaste.

Stout (OG 1047, ABV 4.7%)
Roast aroma with background fruit, roast tastes with gentle sweetness. Bitterness develops surprisingly from the sweet start to leave a sharp edged mouthfeel. Roast throughout with a malt background.

Pastiche (OG 1050, ABV 5.2%)
A smooth, balanced ale with a complex taste and aroma.

Halcyon Daze (OG 1050, ABV 5.3%)
Tawny and creamy with touches of hop, fruit and malt aroma. Fruity taste and finish.

Burtonwood

Bold Lane, Burtonwood, Warrington, Cheshire, WA5 4TH
☎ (01925) 220022 thomashardybrewery.co.uk

Thomas Hardy's only brewery, run by Peter Ward as a contract operation mainly for Heineken/John Smiths. Currently producing no real ale.

Bushy's SIBA

Mount Murray Brewery, Mount Murray, Braddan, Isle of Man, IM4 1JE
☎ (01624) 661244 bushys.com
Tours by arrangement

Launched in 1986 as a brewpub, Bushys relocated in 1990 when demand outgrew capacity. Bushys goes one step further than the Manx Pure Beer Law preferring the German Reinheitsgebot (Pure Beer Law) that excludes sugar. Seasonal beers are numerous: see website.

Castletown Bitter (OG 1035, ABV 3.5%)
A light, golden beer full of floral and citrus hints. A refreshing session beer.

Ruby (1874) Mild (OG 1035, ABV 3.5%)
Classic full-bodied malty ruby mild with sweet caramel flavours throughout, and well-balanced hops.

Bitter (OG 1038, ABV 3.8%)
A traditional malty and hoppy beer with good balnace. The fruit lasts through to the bitter finish.

Old Bushy Tail (OG 1045, ABV 4.5%)
A reddish-brown beer with a pronounced hop and malt aroma, the malt tending towards treacle. Slightly sweet and malty on the palate with distinct orange tones. The full finish is malty and hoppy with a hint of toffee.

Butcombe SIBA

Cox's Green, Wrington, Somerset, BS40 5PA
☎ (01934) 863963 butcombe.com
Shop Mon-Fri 9am-5pm, Sat 9am-12pm
Tours by arrangement

Established in 1978 by Simon Whitmore and sold to Guy Newell and friends in 2003, Butcombe moved to a new purpose-built brewery with a 150-barrel plant in 2005. It supplies about 500 outlets directly and similar numbers via wholesalers and pub companies. The brewery has an estate of 18 freehouses. Seasonal beers: see website.

Adam Henson's Rare Breed (ABV 3.8%)
Sulphurous aroma with undertones of unripe fruit which are confirmed in the thin-bodied flavour. Bitterness and astringency dominate and continue into the finish.

Bitter (OG 1039, ABV 4%)
Notably bitter tawny ale. Malt with hops and ripe fruit contribute to a well-balanced flavour. Long, refreshing, bitter aftertaste.

Gold (OG 1045, ABV 4.4%)
Amber golden ale with light aroma of fruit and hops, leading to well-balanced flavours of malt, pale fruit and hops. Bitter aftertaste.

Haka (OG 1045, ABV 4.5%)
Light gold in colour with aromas of tropical fruits giving way to a unique grapefruit sharpness in the taste offset by hints of grape, gooseberries, peach, mango, citrus, pineapple and passion fruit.

Butts SIBA

Northfield Farm, Wantage Road, Great Shefford, Berkshire, RG17 7BY
☎ (01488) 648133 buttsbrewery.com
Shop 10am-4pm daily

The brewery was set up in a converted barn in 1994. In 2002 the brewery took the decision to become dedicated to organic production; all the beers brewed use organic malted barley and organic hops and are certified by the Soil Association. Occasional, seasonal and bottle-conditioned beers are also available: see website.

Jester (OG 1036, ABV 3.5%)
A pale brown session bitter with a hoppy aroma and a hint of fruit. The taste balances malt, hops, fruit and bitterness with a hoppy aftertaste.

Traditional (OG 1040, ABV 4%)
A pale brown bitter that is quite soft on the tongue with hoppy citrus flavours accompanying a gentle bittersweetness. A long, dry aftertaste is dominated by fruity hops.

Barbus Barbus (OG 1046, ABV 4.6%)
Golden ale with a fruity hoppy aroma and a hint of malt. Hops dominate taste and aftertaste, accompanied by fruitiness and bitterness, with a hint of balancing sweetness.

Buxton SIBA

Unit 4, Staden Business Park, Staden Lane, Buxton, Derbyshire, SK17 9RZ
☎ (01298) 24420 buxtonbrewery.co.uk

Buxton Brewery was set up in 2009 as a five-barrel plant. It currently operates on a 24-barrel plant. Water is drawn from its own borehole. Its brewery tap is in Buxton and it exports to 25 countries. Special edition and bottle-conditioned beers are available.

Jacob's Ladder (OG 1027, ABV 2.7%)

Moor Top (OG 1037, ABV 3.6%)
Dry-hopped blonde ale with a citrus flavour and aroma. It has a sweetness balanced with a lingering bitter finish backed up with a late grapefruit hit.

Rednik Stout (OG 1041, ABV 4.1%)

Special Pale Ale (OG 1041, ABV 4.1%)
Light and refreshing, delicately hopped ale with a clean taste, a creamy mouthfeel and nutty notes.

American Rye (OG 1043, ABV 4.3%)
Hoppy amber ale, brewed with some rye.

Black Rocks (OG 1055, ABV 5.5%)
A black IPA.

Wild Boar (OG 1057, ABV 5.7%)

Buzzard

Speddyd Farm, Llandyrnog, Denbighshire, LL16 4LE
☎ 07972 202880 🌐 buzzardbrewery.co.uk

Brewing commenced in 2013 on a 2.5-barrel plant in a former farm building. 15-20 pubs are supplied locally.

Village Bitter (OG 1039, ABV 3.9%)

Pale of Clwyd (OG 1042, ABV 4.2%)
A light and fruity best bitter with a sweetish initial taste and a hoppy, dry finish.

Vale Ale (OG 1045, ABV 4.5%)

By the Horns SIBA

Unit 25, Summerstown, London, SW17 0BQ
☎ (020) 3417 7338 🌐 bythehorns.co.uk

By the Horns began brewing in 2012 using a 5.5-barrel plant. It is located in industrial units near Wimbledon Stadium. The brewery has a licence for off sales, and hold regular (monthly) open days.

Stiff Upper Lip Pale Ale (OG 1038, ABV 3.8%)
A classic amber-coloured bitter, well-balanced with hops to the fore and a hint of citrus. Dry, bitter finish.

Bobby on the Wheat (OG 1047, ABV 4.7%)
Citrus fruit is present throughout this wheat beer with some spice on the nose and banana on the palate.

Diamond Geezer (OG 1049, ABV 4.9%)
Malty hoppy red ale with blackcurrant, citrus and faint roast notes. Bitterness develops and builds in the aftertaste.

Byatt's SIBA

Unit 10 Lythalls Lane Industrial Estate, Lythalls Lane, Coventry, CV6 6FL
☎ (024) 7663 7996 🌐 byattsbrewery.co.uk

Established in 2011 and located on the north side of Coventry, now supplying the local West Midlands area and expanding into other regions, this was the first commercial brewery in the city for over 80 years. Bottle-conditioned beers are also available.

XK Dark (OG 1038, ABV 3.5%)
Big malt aroma and flavours. Bitter chocolate and blackberries and a soft, lingering bitterness.

Coventry Bitter (OG 1039, ABV 3.8%)
A smooth, refreshing session beer. Earthy and grassy with hints of citrus fruits and a lingering bitterness.

Big Cat (OG 1042, ABV 4%)
A pale bronze-coloured ale with a biscuity sweetness. Refreshing with light fruit and spice notes.

Phoenix Gold (OG 1043, ABV 4.2%)
A pale ale with an initial sweetness. Crisp and refreshing with a rounded bitterness.

Urban Red (OG 1047, ABV 4.5%)
A ruby red ale with rich malt flavours and a floral aroma, fruit and spice notes and a well-balanced finish.

Regal Blond (OG 1053, ABV 5.2%)
A strong, zesty golden ale with pine, citrus lemon and grassy notes. Smooth and easy-drinking.

C&C Wellpark

Wellpark Brewery, 161 Duke Street, Glasgow, G31 1JD

No real ale.

Cader SIBA

Unit 4, Marian Mawr Enterprise Park, Dolgellau, Gwynedd, LL40 1UU ☎ 07931 734655
🌐 caderales.com
Tours by arrangement

Cader Ales was founded in 2012 by a husband and wife team. It was expanded in 2013 to its present 5-barrel capacity.

Gold (OG 1038, ABV 3.8%)

Idris Bitter (OG 1041, ABV 4.1%)

Tallyllyn Pale Ale (OG 1044, ABV 4.4%)
An IPA-style bitter.

Red Bandit (OG 1050, ABV 5%)

Caffle (NEW) SIBA

The Old School, Llawhaden, Pembrokeshire, SA67 8DS
☎ (01437) 541502 🌐 cafflebrewery.co.uk
Tours by arrangement

Caffle began brewing in 2013 using a four-barrel plant producing ale in small batches, mainly for the local market.

Sholly Amber (OG 1043, ABV 4.1%)

Kift Blonde (OG 1044, ABV 4.3%)

Darker Side of Pale (OG 1044.5, ABV 4.4%)

In The Grip (OG 1052, ABV 4.7%)

Drop Squint (OG 1052, ABV 5.2%)

Cairngorm SIBA

Unit 12, Dalfaber Industrial Estate, Aviemore, Highlands, PH22 1ST
☎ (01479) 812222 🌐 cairngormbrewery.com
Shop Mon-Sat 10am-5.30pm (online shop also available)
Tours by arrangement

Cairngorm produces seven regular cask beers along with seasonal ales. Now with its own bottling line and a capacity of 140 barrels, the free trade is supplied as far as the central belt, nationaly via wholesalers. Seasonal beers: see website.

Caille (OG 1039, ABV 3.8%)
Pale golden ale with a subtle malt background and long-lasting citrus hop bitterness.

Nessies Monster Mash (OG 1040, ABV 4.1%)
A good traditional English-type bitter with plenty of bitterness and strong malt flavour and a fruity

background. Lingering bitterness in the aftertaste with diminishing sweetness.

Stag (OG 1040, ABV 4.1%)
A fine best bitter with plenty of roast and hop throughout. This tawny brew also has plenty of malt in the lingering bittersweet aftertaste.

Trade Winds (OG 1043, ABV 4.3%)
A massive citrus fruit, hop and elderflower nose leads to hints of grapefruit in the mouth. The exceptional bittersweetness in the taste lasts through the long, lingering aftertaste.

Black Gold (OG 1044, ABV 4.4%)
Roast malt dominates throughout, slight smokyness in aroma leading to a liquorice and blackcurrant background taste giving it a background sweetness. Long, dry bitter finish.

Cairngorm (OG 1044, ABV 4.5%)
Fruit and hops to the fore with a hint of caramel in this sweetish brew. Also known as Sheepshaggers Gold.

White Lady (OG 1048, ABV 4.7%)
Bavarian style wheat beer with additional hints of roast malt for colour. Brewed with orange peel and coriander giving fruit flavours and a hint of spice.

Wildcat (OG 1049.5, ABV 5.1%)
A full-bodied warming strong bitter. Malt predominates but there is an underlying hop character through to the well-balanced aftertaste. Drinks dangerously less than its strength.

Caledonian SIBA

42 Slateford Road, Edinburgh, EH11 1PH
(0131) 337 1286 caledonianbeer.com
Tours by arrangement

The brewery was founded by Lorimer & Clark in 1869 and was sold to Vaux of Sunderland in 1919. In 1987 the brewery was saved from closure by a management buy-out and became independent. The brewery was purchased by S&N in 2004 and became part of Heineken in 2008. Monthly guest beers are produced which are sometimes of an unusual style, as well as a rolling programme of special beers covering each of the seasons.

Deuchars IPA (OG 1039.5, ABV 3.8%)
Golden session ale with hop aroma and dry bitter finish. Balanced, with malt adding body and fruit a balancing sweetness.

Flying Scotsman (OG 1045.5, ABV 4%)
Well balanced, malty beer with bittersweet character. Similar to a Scottish 80/-, but dryer and with more hop bitterness.

80 (OG 1042.4, ABV 4.1%)
A predominantly malty, brown beer with soft roast and caramel throughout. Fruit gives sweetness, typical of a Scottish 80/-.

Golden XPA (OG 1044, ABV 4.3%)
Well-balanced golden ale with malt and fruit throughout, Hops come to the fore in the increasingly dry, bitter aftertaste.

Calverley's (NEW)

23a Hooper Street, Cambridge, CB1 2NZ
(01223) 312370 calverleys.com

Sam Calverley and his brother began brewing in 2013 after many years as home brewers. Currently supplying local pubs, the first brew was also available at Cambridge Beer Festival.

Citra Bitter (ABV 3.6%)
A classic bitter with a modern hop.

Best Bitter (ABV 4.8%)
A smooth amber ale, with a good balance of malt and subtle bittering hops.

IPA (ABV 5%)

Calvors

Home Farm, Coddenham Green, Suffolk, IP6 9UN
(01449) 711055 calvors.co.uk

Calvors Brewery was established in 2008. Originally brewing keg lagers, cask-conditioned beer is now available. One pub is owned, the Rampant Horse Inn in Needham Market.

Lodestar Festival Ale (OG 1038, ABV 3.8%)
A straw-coloured ale with a gentle sweetness and honey aroma. Lightly-hopped and well-balanced.

Smooth Hoperator (OG 1040, ABV 4%)
A pale ale combining four different malts to give a background sweetness. Well-rounded and easy-drinking.

Cambridge (NEW)

1 King Street, Cambridge, CB1 1LH
(01223) 858155 thecambridgebrewhouse.com

Brewing began in 2013. Seasonal beers are available.

King's Parade (ABV 3.8%)
A good traditional English bitter with moderate biscuity malt and resiny hop throughout and a hint of caramel. Dry finish.

Misty River (ABV 4.2%)
Golden beer dominated by grapefruit on the nose, palate and a lingering dry aftertaste.

Night Porter (ABV 4.4%)
A creamy black/red beer luxuriating in a blend of dark chocolate and coffee, softened by raisins.

Cambrinus

See Liverpool Organic

Camden Town SIBA

55-59 Wilkin Street Mews, Kentish Town, London, NW5 3NN
(020) 7485 1671 camdentownbrewery.com
Tours by arrangement

No real ale.

Camerons

Lion Brewery, Stranton, Hartlepool, County Durham, TS24 7QS
(01429) 852000 cameronsbrewery.com
Shop Mon-Sat 12-4pm
Tours by arrangement

Founded 1865, Camerons was bought 2002 by Castle Eden and production moved to Hartlepool. In 2003 the Lions Den, a 10-barrel microbrewery, was set up to produce and bottle small batches of guest ales and undertake contract brewing and bottling. Monthly specials beers: see website.

Best Bitter (OG 1036, ABV 3.6%)
A light bitter but well-balanced, with hops and malt.

Camerons IPA (OG 1038, ABV 3.8%)
A straw-coloured, light IPA.

Strongarm (OG 1041, ABV 4%)
A well-rounded, ruby-red ale with a distinctive, tight creamy head; initially fruity, but with a good balance of malt, hops and moderate bitterness.

Trophy Special (OG 1040, ABV 4%)
An amber ale, slightly sweet and malty, fruity and hoppy.

Gold Bullion (OG 1043, ABV 4.3%)
Gold-coloured, full-bodied ale with a good hop flavour.

For John Smith's (Heineken Tadcaster):

Bitter (OG 1035, ABV 3.8%)

Cannon Royall SIBA IFBB

Fruiterer's Arms, Uphampton Lane, Uphampton, Worcestershire, WR9 0JW
☎ (01905) 621161 cannonroyall.co.uk
Tours by arrangement (CAMRA only)

Cannon Royall's first brew was in 1993 in a converted cider house behind the Fruiterer's Arms. The brewery supplies a number of mainly local outlets. Seasonal beers are regularly produced. Bottle-conditioned beers are also available.

Fruiterers Mild (OG 1037, ABV 3.7%)
This black-hued brew has rich malty aromas that lead to a fruity mix of bitter hops and sweetness, and a short, balanced aftertaste.

Hunny Bear (OG 1038, ABV 3.8%)

King's Shilling (OG 1038, ABV 3.8%)
A golden bitter that packs a citrus hoppy punch throughout.

Arrowhead Bitter (OG 1039, ABV 3.9%)
A powerful punch of hops attacks the nose before the feast of bitterness. The memory of this golden brew fades too soon.

Arrowhead Extra (OG 1043, ABV 4.3%)
A Fuggles hop punch leads to a smooth palate and pleasant finish with a good malt balance.

Blond Bombshell (OG 1043, ABV 4.3%)

Grapeshot (OG 1043, ABV 4.3%)
Gold with a citrus bite.

Hood (OG 1043, ABV 4.3%)

Old Gusty (OG 1043, ABV 4.3%)
Pale bitter with a dry aftertaste

Slap Ale (OG 1043, ABV 4.3%)
Pale with a hoppy palate that is not overpowering.

Teddy Bear (OG 1043, ABV 4.3%)
Pale, easy-drinking bitter.

Canterbury Ales SIBA

Unit 7, Stour Valley Business Park, Ashford Road, Chartham, Kent, CT4 7HF
☎ (01227) 732541 canterbury-ales.co.uk
Tours by arrangement

Brewing commenced in 2010. The eight-barrel plant was supplied by PBC Brewery Installations.

The Wife of Bath's Ale (OG 1038, ABV 3.9%)
A golden beer with strong bitterness and grapefruit hop character, leading to a long, dry finish.

The Reeve's Ale (OG 1040, ABV 4.1%)

The Miller's Ale (OG 1044, ABV 4.5%)

Canterbury Brewers

Foundry Brew Pub, White Horse Lane, Canterbury, Kent, CT1 2RU
☎ (01227) 455899 thefoundrycanterbury.co.uk

The Foundry is a brewery, restaurant and bar occupying an industrial two storey building, originally a Victorian foundry, tucked away in the heart of Canterbury.

Loco IPA (OG 1038, ABV 3.9%)

Foundryman's Gold (OG 1040, ABV 4%)

GB (OG 1040, ABV 4.1%)

Foundry Torpedo (OG 1044, ABV 4.5%)

Foundry Red Rye (OG 1058, ABV 5.6%)

Streetlight Porter (OG 1059, ABV 5.8%)

Cap House

444-446 Bradford Road, Batley, West Yorkshire, WF17 5LW
☎ (01924) 479909 caphousebrewery.co.uk

Cap House began in 2011 using a 2.5-barrel brew plant as a joint venture between Peter Lister, who has a plastics business at the location, and Gary Wardman of the Reindeer Inn, Overton, which is the brewery tap. Seasonal/special beer: see website.

Miners A Pint (OG 1038, ABV 3.8%)
A tangy session bitter with a smooth mouthfeel and toffee undertones. A deep, dry finish with lingering fruit notes.

Blonde & Beyond (OG 1040, ABV 4%)
A light hoppy beer with a well-balanced fruity taste. Refreshing citrus and grapefruit flavours for a bittersweet finish.

Fox Hunter (OG 1040, ABV 4%)
An easy-drinking, full-bodied ale with a thick creamy head. A subtle balance of hoppy, fruity, bittersweet flavours of caramel and a hint of liquorice with a malty fruit aroma.

Hay Blondie (ABV 4.2%)
A light, golden ale.

Miners a Light (OG 1042, ABV 4.2%)
A smooth, blonde ale brewed with lager malts and specially selected hops releasing light fruity notes with a hint of citrus.

Ruby (OG 1054, ABV 5.6%)
A rich ruby ale with a smooth finish, fruity nut/toffee aroma and tangy palate.

Captain Cook SIBA

White Swan, 1 West End, Stokesley, North Yorkshire, TS9 5BL
☎ (01642) 710263 captaincookbrewery.com
Tours by arrangement

THE BREWERIES

The Captain Cook Brewery is located within the 18th-century White Swan pub. The brewery, which started in 1999, has a six barrel plant. Seasonal beers are also available.

Resolution (OG 1037, ABV 3.7%)

Botany Bay (OG 1040, ABV 4%)
A light ale with a hint of grapefruit.

Red Bay (OG 1040, ABV 4%)
An Irish-style, red, hoppy ale.

Sunset (OG 1040, ABV 4%)
A smooth, light ale with hint of citrus flavours.

Slipway (OG 1042, ABV 4.2%)
A light-coloured, full-flavoured, hoppy ale with a smooth malt aftertaste.

Endeavour (OG 1043, ABV 4.3%)
A brown ale with a bitter finish.

Black Porter (OG 1044, ABV 4.4%)
Chocolate notes and dominant roast flavours lead to a dry, bitter finish.

Discovery (OG 1044, ABV 4.4%)
Mid brown-coloured malted ale with a bitter finish.

Carlisle (NEW) SIBA

Spinners Arms, Cummersdale, Carlisle, Cumbria, CA2 6BD
(01228) 532928 thespinnersarms.org.uk
Tours by arrangement

Carlisle is a family-run brewery established in 2013 using a 2.5-barrel plant. Situated behind the owner's freehouse, beer is available in the pub and other local outlets.

Maiden (OG 1038, ABV 3.8%)
Toffee flavours with honey and almond tones.

Spun Gold (OG 1044, ABV 4.2%)
A crisp, hoppy beer.

Oatmeal Stout (OG 1047, ABV 4.4%)
Chocolate and liquorice flavours.

Flaxen (OG 1045, ABV 4.5%)
Hoppy blonde session beer.

Magic Number (OG 1045, ABV 4.5%)
Smooth with caramel undertones.

Carlsberg-Tetley

Jacobson House, 140 Bridge Street, Northampton, NN1 1PZ
(01604) 668866 carlsberg.co.uk

No real ale.

Carters

White Hart Inn, White Hart Lane, Machen, CF83 8QQ
(01633) 441005

The one-barrel plant is located at the rear of the pub. Brewing is undertaken by licensee Alan Carter on an occasional basis, infrequently, and usually for special occasions. No regular beers, brews tend to trial new recipes.

Castle SIBA

Unit 9a-7, Restormel Industrial Estate, Liddicoat Road, Lostwithiel, Cornwall, PL22 0HG
(01726) 871133 castlebrewery@aol.com

Brewing started in 2008 on a two-barrel plant. Only bottle-conditioned ales are produced.

Castle Rock SIBA

Queensbridge Road, Nottingham, NG2 1NB
(0115) 985 1615 castlerockbrewery.co.uk
Tours by arrangement

Castle Rock was established in 1998. Since then capacity has steadily increased with the largest expansion taking place in 2010 which gave a total capacity of 360 barrels per week. Beers are distributed through its estate of 18 pubs and further afield through wholesalers. A different beer is brewed monthly to support the Nottinghamshire Wildlife Trust and a unique Nottinghamian Celebration beer is brewed quarterly. A visitors' centre opened in 2011.

Sheriff's Tipple (OG 1034, ABV 3.4%)
Tawny-coloured malty beer with Goldings hops.

Black Gold (OG 1037, ABV 3.8%)
A dark ruby mild. Full-bodied and fairly bitter.

Harvest Pale (OG 1037, ABV 3.8%)
Pale yellow beer, full of hop aroma and flavour. Refreshing with a mellowing aftertaste.

Preservation Fine Ale (OG 1044, ABV 4.4%)
A traditional copper-coloured English best bitter with malt predominant. Fairly bitter with a residual sweetness.

Elsie Mo (OG 1045, ABV 4.7%)
A strong golden ale with floral hops evident in the aroma. Citrus hops are mellowed by a slight sweetness.

Midnight Owl (OG 1055, ABV 5.5%)
A rich, warming winter ale with a distinctive hop and caramel finish.

Screech Owl (OG 1055, ABV 5.5%)
A classic golden IPA with an intensely hoppy aroma and bitter taste with a little balancing sweetness.

Castles (NEW) SIBA

Symondscliffe Way, Caldicot, NP26 5PW
(01291) 422032 castlesbrewery.co.uk

Castles began brewing in 2014, producing both bottled and cask-conditioned beers.

Court Jester (OG 1038, ABV 3.8%)

White Knight (OG 1041, ABV 4.1%)
An American-style pale ale, with a peach aroma and vibrant taste.

Portcullis (OG 1042, ABV 4.2%)
A russet brown-coloured ale with a tropical fruit aroma. Full-bodied with a malty, rounded taste.

Kings Reserve (OG 1043, ABV 4.3%)
An amber-coloured ale with an orange, dry taste.

Castor SIBA

30 Peterborough Road, Castor, Cambridgeshire, PE5 7AX
(01733) 380337 castorales.co.uk
Tours by arrangement

This three-barrel brewery, established in 2009, is located in a specially converted outhouse in the garden of the founder brewer. The Prince of Wales Feathers in Castor village features the beers, as well as the Beehive in Peterborough and other local outlets.

Roman Gold (OG 1037, ABV 3.7%)
A gold-coloured session bitter full of floral and citrus hints.

Hopping Toad (OG 1040, ABV 4.1%)
A light golden bitter, the pale malt balanced by bittering and aroma hops giving a refreshing citrus flowery finish and a fruity aftertaste.

12th Man (OG 1044, ABV 4.5%)
A triple-hopped beer with spicy citrus and floral aromas and taste and an orange finish.

Imperial Palace Ale (OG 1045, ABV 4.6%)
An IPA-style, heavily hopped bitter giving way to a grapefruit and floral finish.

Old Scarlet (OG 1045, ABV 4.6%)
A complex grain bill produces a ruby-coloured malty beer balanced by subtle hops with a fine aroma and citrus finish. A premium bitter.

Cathedral Heights SIBA

Unit 12, Churchill Business Park, Bracebridge Heath, Lincoln, LN4 2HD ☎ 07545 090318
chbrewery.co.uk

Cathedral Heights was created by Steve Marston in 2011, after previous experiences of brewing at Milestone and after Cathedral Ales of Lincoln ceased to exist. It moved to its present location in 2013 after a year out of production.

Just Married (OG 1037, ABV 3.8%)
A light and refreshing pale ale with a hoppy finish.

Churchills Pride (OG 1038, ABV 3.9%)
A copper-coloured ale.

BBH Bitter (OG 1042, ABV 4.3%)
A complex and refreshing golden bitter.

Devils Nightmare (OG 1042, ABV 4.3%)
A smooth, dark mild; sweet and malty.

Steep Hill (OG 1041, ABV 4.3%)
A dark copper-coloured ale with malty tones and a fruity finish.

Castle Dungeon (OG 1050, ABV 5.4%)
A full-bodied oyster stout.

Cats (NEW) SIBA

Unit 22, Sugarswell Business Park, Shenington, Oxfordshire, OX15 6HW ☎ 07557 527789
catsbrewingco.com

Chris and Tom's brewery (hence Cats), was set up in 2013 using a six-barrel plant.

Tabby (ABV 4.1%)
A fruity amber ale.

Mog (ABV 4.5%)
A light, crisp pale ale.

Clouder (ABV 5%)
A yellow-coloured, mellow wheat beer.

Caveman

The Cave (below George & Dragon), 1 London Road, Swanscombe, Kent, DA10 0LQ ☎ 07900 234644
cavemanbrewery.co.uk

Caveman began brewing in 2012 and moved to its current site beneath the George & Dragon pub in 2013 with a four-barrel plant originally from the Devilfish Brewery. It is named for the local discovery in the 1930s of skull fragments from a Paleolithic human, then the oldest remains found in the UK. Beers can be found nationwide through various wholesalers with direct supply to London, Kent and parts of Sussex. Seasonal and bottle-conditioned beers: see website.

Palaeolithic (OG 1037, ABV 3.8%)
A pale ale with Cascade hops and some slight malt sweetness.

Citra (OG 1041, ABV 4.1%)

Mesolithic (OG 1044, ABV 4.5%)
A dry-hopped pale ale with a summer fruit aroma.

Prehistoric Amber (OG 1044, ABV 4.5%)
An IPA with a roast malt flavour.

Clovis Point Brown (OG 1051, ABV 5.2%)
A US-style brown ale with a roast caramel and fruity hop character.

Cavedweller Porter (OG 1060, ABV 5.8%)
A porter with a coffee, chocolate and roast malt flavour set against subtle refreshing hops.

Megalithic IPA (OG 1057, ABV 5.9%)
An IPA with a biscuit malt body balanced against a heavy hit of fruit.

Caythorpe SIBA

c/o Black Horse, 29 Main Street, Caythorpe, Nottinghamshire, NG14 7ED
☎ (0115) 966 4933 caythorpebrewery.co.uk
Tours by arrangement

Established in 1996 using a 2.5-barrel plant in a building at the rear of the Black Horse pub, the brewery upgraded to a six-barrel plant in 2010.

Dark Gem (OG 1033.3, ABV 3.5%)
A subtly-hopped dark mild with a hint of chocolate.

One Swallow (OG 1034, ABV 3.6%)
A golden session bitter, crisp and well hopped.

Cocker Beck (OG 1034.7, ABV 3.7%)
A copper-coloured, light-flavoured bitter.

Dover Beck (OG 1037, ABV 4%)
Pale brown well-balanced session bitter. Initial malt is offset by a slight hoppy bitterness.

Outlaw (ABV 4%)

Stout Fellow (OG 1040, ABV 4.2%)
A dark stout, brewed with roasted barley to give a roast character.

Classic (OG 1042, ABV 4.6%)
Traditional copper-coloured premium bitter, malty and well hopped.

Celt Experience SIBA

Unit 2E, Pontygwindy Industrial Estate, Pontygwindy Road, Caerphilly, CF83 3HU
☎ (029) 2086 7707 theceltexperience.co.uk
Shop Mon-Fri 10am-4.30pm
Tours by arrangement

Established in 2007 as successor to Newmans of Somerset and expanded in 2014, Celt Experience produces a permanent range of beers and the seasonal Shape Shifter range. There are also occasional collaborative brews in conjunction with guest brewers and beer writers. Beers are distributed widely.

La Tene (OG 1033, ABV 3.3%)

Iron Age (OG 1035, ABV 3.5%)

Dark Age (OG 1040, ABV 4%)

Golden (OG 1045, ABV 4.2%)

Native Storm (OG 1044, ABV 4.4%)

Silures (OG 1046, ABV 4.6%)

Castell Coch (OG 1047, ABV 4.7%)

Bleddyn (OG 1056, ABV 5.6%)

Cerddin SIBA

c/o Cross Inn, Maesteg Road, Maesteg, CF34 9LB
☎ (01656) 732476 cerddinbrewery.co.uk
Tours by arrangement

Established in 2010 using a 2.5-barrel plant with conditioning and malting rooms in a converted garage. Beer is usually only available from the owner's pub, the Cross Inn in Maesteg. Seasonal and bottle-conditioned beers are available.

Solar (OG 1040, ABV 4%)

Cascade (OG 1047, ABV 4.8%)

Chalk Hill

Rosary Road, Norwich, NR1 4DA
☎ (01603) 477078 thecoachthorperoad.co.uk
Tours by arrangement

Chalk Hill began production in 1993 on a 15-barrel plant. It supplies local pubs and festivals.

Tap Bitter (OG 1036, ABV 3.6%)
Easy-drinking, well-balanced bitter with a light, hoppy character in both aroma and taste. Initially malt provides some contrast but fades rapidly in a quick, increasingly dry and bitter finish.

CHB (OG 1042, ABV 4.2%)
Malt comes to the fore as a fruity cooking apple beginning melds into the hoppy bittersweet background. A gentle malt aroma and sticky mouthfeel. Long finish.

Gold (OG 1043, ABV 4.3%)
Light hoppy airs introduce this yellow-gold ale. Grapefruit, banana and hops mingle in a well balanced beginning. The finish develops a growing bitterness as it slowly subsides.

Dreadnought (OG 1049, ABV 4.9%)
A rich, resinous aroma fittingly introduces a heavily malt-influenced brew. Raisin and plum vie with each other to match the sweet malty backbone. Malt remains in a decidedly singular and abrupt ending.

Chantry SIBA

Unit 1, Callum Court, Gateway Industrial Estate, Parkgate, Rotherham, South Yorkshire, S62 6NR
☎ (01709) 711866 chantrybrewery.co.uk

Brewing returned to Rotherham with the opening of Chantry in 2012 using the latest brewing technology in a 20-barrel state of the art plant built by Sheffield-based Moeschle UK.

New York Pale (OG 1039, ABV 3.9%)
A pale session bitter with a refreshing citrus taste and a crisp bitter finish.

Iron & Steel Bitter (OG 1040, ABV 4%)
Chestnut-coloured beer with complex spicy flavours of dark fruits and a clean finish. An easy-drinking Yorkshire session bitter.

Diamond Black Stout (OG 1045, ABV 4.5%)
Full-bodied dry stout with a bitter finish, spicy with hints of liquorice and dark berries.

Chapel (NEW)

Dinesfield, Chapel Lane, Criftins, Shropshire, SY12 9LZ
☎ (01691) 690412 ☎ 07928 682174
chapelbrewery.co.uk

Chapel began brewing in 2013 using a one-barrel plant behind the brewer's bungalow. Occasional specials are brewed for festivals.

Angel's Share (OG 1040, ABV 4%)
A blonde session beer with a delicate, floral nose and herbal spicy taste.

Miracle (OG 1044, ABV 4.4%)
A full-flavoured blonde beer. Floral, grapefruit, lychees and pine.

Babylon (OG 1048, ABV 5%)
A traditional English ale with a malty flavour.

Chapel Street (NEW)

Thatched House, Ball Street, Poulton-le-Fylde, Lancashire, FY6 7BG
☎ (01253) 891063 thatchedhousepoulton.co.uk

Brewing started in 2014 using a four-barrel plant.

Blonde (ABV 3.8%)

Gold (ABV 4.1%)

Cheddar SIBA

Winchester Farm, Draycott Road, Cheddar, Somerset, BS27 3RP
☎ (01934) 744193 cheddarales.co.uk
Shop Mon-Fri 8am-4pm, Sat-Sun by appointment
Tours by arrangement

Established in 2006 in Cheddar, this 100-barrel brewery has a production split of approximately 85% cask-conditioned beer with the remainder bottle conditioned. The new bottling plant produces around 75,000 bottles annually. Around 450 outlets and 80 pubs are supplied. Seasonal beers: see website.

Bitter Bully (OG 1038.5, ABV 3.8%)
A light, refreshing, hoppy bitter. Gentle maltiness leads to a bitter finish.

Gorge Best (OG 1040, ABV 4%)
Initial light aroma which belies the complex flavours of malts and pale fruit. The faint sweetness progresses to a dry bitter finish.

Potholer (OG 1043.5, ABV 4.3%)
Pale bitter with fruity hop aroma. Fruity sweetness on the palate, ending with a bitter finish with slight astringency.

Totty Pot (OG 1044.5, ABV 4.5%)
This porter has roast and malt throughout, along with coffee and dark fruit flavours. Roast flavours remain in the smooth aftertaste.

Cheshire Brew Brothers (NEW) SIBA

Unit 6, Stanney Mill Industrial Estate, Dutton Green, Ellesmere Port, Cheshire, CH2 4SA ☎ 07890 567582 🌐 cheshirebrewbrothers.co.uk

Brewing began in 2014. The brewery is run by two friends who call themselves the Brew Bros after being inspired by a beer trip to Belgium.

Gold (ABV 3.6%)
Deep gold-coloured beer with soft, citrus, honey taste and floral, honey aroma.

Amber (ABV 3.8%)
Dry, hoppy and fruity amber ale with a spicy, malty aroma.

Tawny (ABV 3.8%)
A pale copper-coloured bitter. Spicy, malty and dry with a hoppy aroma.

Dark (ABV 4%)
Deep red porter with a hoppy, dry, coffee taste and roasted, malty aroma.

Cheshire Brewhouse SIBA

Unit 5, Daneside Business Park, Riverdane Road, Congleton, Cheshire, CW12 1UN ☎ 07830 304929 🌐 cheshirebrewhouse.co.uk

Cheshire Brewhouse was established in 2012 using a five-barrel plant, expanding in 2014 to a 10-barrel one. The business has taken over adjacent premises and the brewery is now capable of producing 120 nine-gallon casks per week. Bottling is carried out on site.

Cheshire Gap (ABV 3.7%)

A Little Lupy (ABV 3.8%)
A pale, hoppy session ale.

Engine Vein (ABV 4.2%)
A copper-coloured session bitter named after the Alderley Copper Mine.

Lindow 'The Black Lake' (ABV 4.5%)
A light stout.

DBA (ABV 4.6%)
A Burton-style bitter.

Lupy as a Toucan (ABV 5%)
A well-hopped pale ale.

Chiltern SIBA

Nash Lee Road, Terrick, Aylesbury, Buckinghamshire, HP17 0TQ
☎ (01296) 613647 🌐 chilternbrewery.co.uk
Shop Mon-Thu & Sat 9am-5pm, Fri 9am-7pm
Tours by arrangement

Founded in 1980, Chiltern was one of the first microbreweries in the country and is the oldest independent brewery in Buckinghamshire and the Chiltern Hills, growing from a capacity of five to its present 15-barrel plant. Now run by the second generation of the Jenkinson family, George and Tom, it supplies around 100 outlets including its own brewery tap, The Farmers' Bar, at the historic King's Head in Aylesbury. Seasonal beers: see website. Bottle-conditioned beers are also available.

Chiltern Ale (OG 1037, ABV 3.7%)
An amber, refreshing beer with a slight fruit aroma, leading to a good malt/bitter balance in the mouth. The aftertaste is bitter and dry.

Beechwood Bitter (OG 1043, ABV 4.3%)
This pale brown beer has a balanced butterscotch/toffee aroma, with a slight hop note. The taste balances bitterness and sweetness, leading to a long, bitter finish.

Julian Church

Old Dairy, Whitehill Farm, Loddington Road, Cransley, Northamptonshire, NN14 1PY ☎ 07794 289559 🌐 jchurchbrewery.co.uk
Tours by arrangement

Julian Church started brewing in 2009 at the Alexandra Arms in Kettering on Nobby's Brewery's old five-barrel plant when Nobby's expanded and moved. In 2014 the brewery moved to bigger premises in an old dairy at Cransley near Kettering.

More Tea Vicar (OG 1037, ABV 3.7%)

Gold Testament (OG 1036, ABV 3.9%)

Parson's Nose (OG 1037, ABV 3.9%)
Mahogany-coloured beer with a nutty taste and a warm, spicy finish.

Lion's Den (OG 1040, ABV 4%)
A red/brown-coloured bitter.

Martyr (OG 1040, ABV 4.1%)
An amber-coloured beer with a caramel flavour and a light, bitter finish.

Cannon Crisparkle (OG 1045, ABV 4.5%)

Church End SIBA

Ridge Lane, Nuneaton, Warwickshire, CV10 0RD ☎ (01827) 713080 🌐 churchendbrewery.co.uk
Shop open during tap opening hours
Tours by arrangement

The brewery started in 1994 in an old coffin shop in Shustoke. It moved to the present site and upgraded to a 10-barrel plant in 2001 with further expansion to a 20-barrel plant in 2008. Bottle-conditioned beers are also available. Many one off specials and old recipe beers are produced.

Poachers Pocket (OG 1036, ABV 3.5%)

Cuthberts (OG 1038, ABV 3.8%)
A refreshing, hoppy beer, with hints of malt, fruit and caramel taste. Lingering bitter aftertaste.

Goats Milk (OG 1038, ABV 3.8%)

Gravediggers Ale (OG 1038, ABV 3.8%)

What the Fox's Hat (OG 1044, ABV 4.2%)
A beer with a malty aroma, and a hoppy and malty taste with some caramel flavour.

Vicar's Ruin (OG 1044, ABV 4.4%)
A straw-coloured best bitter with an initially hoppy, bitter flavour, softening to a delicate malt finish.

Stout Coffin (OG 1046, ABV 4.6%)

Fallen Angel (OG 1050, ABV 5%)

Church Farm SIBA

Church Farm, Budbrooke, Warwickshire, CV35 8QL ☎ (01926) 411569 🌐 churchfarmbrewery.co.uk

Church Farm was established in 2012 in the farm's former dairy. The plant was converted from the old milk processing equipment and has now expanded to seven-barrel capacity to meet demand. Beers are brewed from local ingredients and the water comes from the farm's own well. Bottle-conditioned beers: see website.

Old Pal (OG 1038, ABV 3.6%)
A pale, golden ale. Slight flowery hop aroma and mouthfeel, with a smooth mellow taste and long-lasting finish.

Ren's Pride (OG 1044, ABV 4%)
An amber-coloured best bitter with a slightly sweet taste. The distinctive initial flavour comes from a complex array of malts.

Brown's Porter (OG 1042, ABV 4.2%)
A porter with a smooth coffee taste and a long-lasting, creamy aftertaste.

Harry's Heifer (OG 1044, ABV 4.2%)
A light amber-coloured best bitter with slight floral notes.

Ciren

Twelve Bells, 12 Lewis Lane, Cirencester, Gloucestershire, GL7 1EA
☎ (01285) 652230 twelvebellscirencester.com/cirencester-ales-brewery.html
Tours by arrangement

Ciren Ales is a small microbrewery at the rear of the Twelve Bells pub in Cirencester established in 2012. The brewer is the owner Steve.

Bells Bitter (OG 1040, ABV 3.8%)
Light brown-coloured bitter with a hoppy taste.

Bellend Blonde (OG 1044, ABV 4.2%)
A light, citrus, fruity beer.

Bells Best Mate (OG 1044, ABV 4.2%)
A dark full-flavoured beer.

City of Cambridge

See Wolf

Clanconnel

PO Box 316, Craigavon, Co Armagh, BT65 9AZ
☎ 07711 626770 clanconnelbrewing.com

Clanconnel started producing bottled beer in 2008. Cask-conditioned beer is occasionally available.

Clarence & Fredericks SIBA

35a Neville Road, Croydon, CR0 2DS
cfbrewing.co.uk
Shop: ring for times

Clarence & Fredericks began brewing in 2012 using a 10-barrel plant on an industrial estate in Croydon. Seasonal beers are available.

Golden Ale (OG 1038, ABV 3.8%)
Refreshing yellow beer with a citrus character. Bitterness grows on drinking with hints of dryness balanced by a little malt.

Best Bitter (OG 1041, ABV 4.1%)
Traditional best bitter with marmalade, spiced hops and a little dried apricot fading in the finish as the bitterness develops.

American Pale Ale (OG 1045, ABV 4.5%)
Strongly hoppy grapefruit beer with a tangy mouthfeel. Finish is a balance of malt and fruit and a dry bitterness.

Clark's SIBA

Westgate Brewery, Wakefield, West Yorkshire, WF2 9SW
☎ (01924) 373328 hbclark.co.uk
Tours by arrangement

Founded in 1906, Clark's ceased brewing during the 1960s/70s but resumed cask ale production in 1982 and now delivers to around 220 outlets. Monthly specials complement the regular beer range and its three pubs all serve cask ale.

Traditional (OG 1038, ABV 3.8%)
Copper brown-coloured beer with a hoppy aroma and lasting bitter taste.

Classic Blonde (OG 1039, ABV 3.9%)
Pale straw-coloured beer with a fruity aroma and light spicy taste.

Westgate Gold (OG 1042, ABV 4.2%)
Golden beer with creamy malt aroma and a sharp, dry finish.

Clarkshaws (NEW) SIBA

Tyrell Trading estate, Tyrrell Road, East Dulwich, London, SE22 9NA clarkshaws.co.uk

Clarkshaws is a small brewery established in 2013 focusing on using ingredients sourced in the UK and on reducing beer miles. The beers are vegetarian and are accredited by the Vegetarian Society.

Gorgon's Alive! (ABV 4%)
Honey and spice with a pleasant bitter finish.

Phoenix Rising (ABV 4%)
Hints of chocolate with well-balanced malt in the mouth.

Hellhound IPA (ABV 5.5%)
Spicy and citrus notes in this amber-coloured beer with a bitterness in the flavour and finish, which is dry.

Clearwater SIBA

Unit 1, Little Court, Manteo Way, Gammaton Road, Bideford, Devon, EX39 4FG
☎ (01237) 420492 clearwaterbrewery.co.uk
Tours by arrangement

Clearwater began brewing in 1999 using a 10-barrel brewery, relocating from Great Torrington to Bideford in 2014. It regularly supplies more than 250 outlets across the south west and increasingly supplies national wholesalers with its 'Devon's Own' labelled beers.

Best Bitter (OG 1037.3, ABV 3.4%)

True Delight (OG 1033, ABV 3.4%)

Real Smiler (OG 1037, ABV 3.7%)
Crisp, fresh cut apples and melon on the nose accompanies a honeyed tone. A light biscuit taste, with the most delicate of tannins.

Devon Dympsy (OG 1039, ABV 4%)

Proper Ansome (OG 1041, ABV 4.2%)
Fresh, immediate hoppy aromas and caramel colour. Eddying honeyed sweetness and lightly earthy scent reveal a herbal edge.

Devon Darter (OG 1043, ABV 4.5%)

Dark Night (OG 1050, ABV 5.2%)

Cliff Quay

Unit 1, Meadow Works, Kenton Road, Debenham, Suffolk, IP14 6RP
☎ (01728) 684097 🌐 cliffquay.co.uk
Shop Mon-Fri 10am-5pm, Sat 10am-1pm

Cliff Quay was established in 2008 by former Wychwood brewer Jeremy Moss and John Bjornson (owner of the Earl Soham Brewery) in part of the historic Tolly Cobbold brewery in Ipswich. In 2012 the brewery relocated to Debenham, a small, picturesque market town, due to redevelopment of the former brewery site.

Classic Bitter (OG 1034, ABV 3.4%) ◆
Pleasantly drinkable, well-balanced malty sweet bitter with a hint of caramel, followed by a sweet/malty aftertaste. A good flavour for such a low gravity beer.

Anchor Bitter (OG 1040, ABV 4%)

Black Jack Porter (OG 1042, ABV 4.2%) ◆
Unusual dark porter with a strong aniseed aroma and rich liquorice and aniseed flavours, reminiscent of old-fashioned sweets. The aftertaste is long and increasingly sweet.

Tolly Roger (OG 1042, ABV 4.2%) ◆
Well-balanced, highly drinkable, mid-gold summer beer with a bittersweet hoppiness, some biscuity flavours and hints of summer fruit.

Tumblehome (OG 1047, ABV 4.7%)

Sea Dog (OG 1053, ABV 5.3%)
A strong, hoppy beer bursting with the flavours of lemon and grapefruit with a full maltiness in contrast.

Clipper (NEW)

Bell & Talbot, 2 Salop Street, Bridgnorth, Shropshire, WV16 4QU
🌐 bellandtalbotbridgnorth.co.uk

Clipper began brewing in 2014 using a two-barrel plant in an old two-storey brewhouse at the rear of the Bell & Talbot in Bridgnorth. Two beers are produced and are only available in the pub.

Special Bitter (OG 1038, ABV 3.8%)

Pale Ale (ABV 4.1%)

Clockwork

Maclay Inns PLC, 1153-1155 Cathcart Road, Glasgow, G42 9HB
☎ (0141) 649 0184 🌐 clockworkbeercompany.co.uk
Tours by arrangement

Established in 1997, Clockwork is now owned by Maclay Inns. The beers are stored in cellar tanks where fermentation gases from the conditioning vessel blanket the beers (but not under pressure). A wide range of ales, lagers and specials are produced. Most beers are naturally gassed while the Original Lager and Hazy Daze Ginger are pressurised. Some updated Maclay's recipes have been introduced as guest ales.

Amber IPA (OG 1038, ABV 3.8%)

Red Alt (OG 1044, ABV 4.4%)

Lager (OG 1048, ABV 4.8%)

Seriously Ginger (OG 1050, ABV 5%)

Clouded Minds (NEW)

c/o School House Farm, Lodge Lane, Shottle, Derbyshire, DE56 2DS ☎ 07530 998149

Office: 78a Turnpike Lane, London, N8 0PR
🌐 cloudedminds.co.uk

Originally brewing in London, Clouded Minds relocated their brewing operations in 2014 to use spare capacity at Shottle Farm Brewery (qv). Now four days of the week head brewer Riccardo Pulcinelli leaves his home of north London to live and work at the brewery in Derbyshire.

Catholic's Choice (ABV 2.8%)

Luppol (ABV 4.2%)

Clout Stout (ABV 4.5%)

Single Hop Nugget (ABV 4.8%)

Hazelnutter (ABV 5%)

Black Pike (ABV 6.1%)

Dolce Vita (ABV 6.2%)

Double Clout Stout (ABV 6.6%)

Clun SIBA

White Horse Inn, The Square, Clun, Shropshire, SY7 8JA
☎ (01588) 640305 🌐 whi-clun.co.uk/the-clun-brewery

Formerly a tiny brewery, capacity was increased to 2.5 barrels in 2010. Established behind the White Horse in Clun, beers are produced for the pub and increasingly the local trade. Seasonal specials are available.

Loophole (OG 1035, ABV 3.5%)
A dry, hoppy, light-coloured beer.

Pale (OG 1040, ABV 4.1%)
A pale, clean-tasting bitter.

Citadel (OG 1065, ABV 5.9%)
A strong ale. Golden in colour, the rich and fruity malt flavours are met head on by intense hop bitterness and aroma which give rise to a long-lasting, dry finish.

Coach & Horses (NEW)

Welsh Street, Chepstow, Gwent, NP16 5LN
☎ (01291) 622626

Pub brewery that presently only brews for special events.

Coach House SIBA

Wharf Street, Howley, Warrington, Cheshire, WA1 2DQ
☎ (01925) 232800 🌐 coach-house-brewing.co.uk

Coach House started in 1991 following the closure of Greenall Whitley Brewery, which had a presence in Warrington since 1762. With a fermentation capacity of 240 barrels, the brewery produces permanent and seasonal brews plus a range of speciality beers.

Coachman's Best Bitter (OG 1037, ABV 3.7%) ◆
A well-hopped, malty bitter, moderately fruity with a hint of sweetness and a peppery nose.

Gunpowder Mild (OG 1037, ABV 3.8%) ◆

Biscuity dark mild with a blackcurrant sweetness. Bitterness and fruit dominate with some hints of caramel and a slightly stronger roast flavour.

Honeypot Bitter (OG 1037, ABV 3.8%)
A medium-bodied golden bitter, lightly hopped. Brewed with Cheshire honey.

Farrier's Best Bitter (OG 1038, ABV 3.9%)
A smooth tawny-coloured beer, slightly sweet but with rich hop flavours developed in the mouth.

Cromwells Best Bitter (OG 1040, ABV 4%)
Amber-coloured, well-balanced beer with a smooth, clean-hopped finish.

Cheshire Gold (OG 1042, ABV 4.1%)
A pale golden beer with a pine and lemon crispness.

Dick Turpin (OG 1042, ABV 4.2%) ◆
Malty, hoppy pale brown beer with some initial sweetish flavours leading to a short, bitter aftertaste. Sold under other names as a pub house beer.

Flintlock Pale Ale (OG 1044, ABV 4.4%)
A pale golden beer, light on the palate with a touch of sweetness in the finish.

Innkeeper's Special Reserve (OG 1045, ABV 4.5%) ◆
A dark, full-flavoured bitter. Fruity with a strong, bitter aftertaste.

Postlethwaite (OG 1045, ABV 4.6%)

Posthorn Premium (OG 1050, ABV 5%)

Coastal SIBA

Unit 10B, Cardrew Industrial Estate, Redruth, Cornwall, TR15 1SS
☎ (01209) 212613 ⊕ coastalbrewery.co.uk

Coastal was set up in 2006 on a five-barrel plant by the former brewer and owner of the Borough Arms in Crewe, Cheshire. Seasonal beers and two monthly specials are produced as well as bottle-conditioned beers.

Cornish Bronze (OG 1037, ABV 3.7%)

Hop Monster (OG 1038, ABV 3.7%)

Handliner (OG 1040, ABV 4%)

Merry Maidens Mild (OG 1040, ABV 4%) ◆
Dark red mild with roast malt aroma. Sweet malt, toffee, hop bitterness and roast notes, finishing dry with bitter coffee.

Poseidon (OG 1040, ABV 4%)

Angelina (OG 1042, ABV 4.1%)

Golden Hinde (OG 1044, ABV 4.3%)

Pier Porter (OG 1043, ABV 4.3%)

Winnies Honey Heaven (OG 1044, ABV 4.4%)

Cornish Cascade (OG 1050, ABV 5%)

Sea King (OG 1056, ABV 5.5%)

Golden Gorse (OG 1056, ABV 5.6%)

St Pirans Porter (OG 1060, ABV 6%)

West Coast IPA (OG 1075, ABV 7.5%)

Erosion (OG 1080, ABV 8%) ◆
After an aroma promising roast caramel this powerful, warming dark old ale bursts with molasses and roast malt. Liquorice adds to the finish.

Kernow Imperial Stout (OG 1090, ABV 9%)

Colchester SIBA

Viaduct Brewhouse, Unit 16, Wakes Hall Business Centre, Wakes Colne, Essex, CO6 2DY
☎ (01787) 829422 ⊕ colchesterbrewery.com
Shop Mon-Fri 9am-5pm
Tours by arrangement

⊗ Set up in 2012 by three friends, Tom Knox, Roger Clark and Andy Bone, using the 'double drop' process. Popular during the early 20th century this process requires additional brewing vessels in a two-tier system resulting in clean beer with pronounced flavours.

Diesel (OG 1037, ABV 3.6%)
An amber-coloured session bitter.

AK Pale (OG 1038, ABV 3.7%)
A mildy-hopped pale ale. Fresh and fruity.

Metropolis (OG 1039, ABV 3.9%)
A golden-coloured hoppy beer with a long, spicy finish.

Braggot (ABV 4%)
An easy-drinking honey beer.

No. 88 (ABV 4%)
A dark amber-coloured malty bitter.

Colchester No 1 (OG 1042, ABV 4.1%)
A classic English copper-coloured best bitter.

Drizzle (ABV 4.2%)

Red Diesel (OG 1042, ABV 4.2%)
Red-coloured best bitter, well-balanced with a long, rich finish.

Romani ite Domum (ABV 4.3%)
A hoppy golden ale.

Trinovantes Gold (OG 1044, ABV 4.3%)
A very hoppy beer.

Anne Downes (OG 1045, ABV 4.4%)
Dark brown-coloured bitter, full and fruity with a lingering hoppy finish.

Mild Ale (OG 1047, ABV 4.5%)
A dark ruby mild. Sweet and fruity.

Brazilian Coffee & Vanilla Porter (ABV 4.6%)

Double Brown Ale (OG 1047.5, ABV 4.6%)
Dark brown-coloured, malty, sweetish and balanced.

Old King Coel London Porter (OG 1052.5, ABV 5%)

Coles Family

White Hart Thatched Inn & Brewery, Llanddarog, Carmarthen, SA32 8NT
☎ (01267) 275395 ⊕ thebestpubinwales.co.uk

The brewery is based at the ancient White Hart Inn, built in 1371, which historically had a brewery on site. Brewing started again in 1999 on a nine-gallon plant. A one-barrel plant was fitted in 2000 and in 2012 the brewery was opened to the public. Many unique ales are brewed throughout the year with cider also produced.

Merlins (OG 1040, ABV 4%)
A rich, creamy stout.

Swn y Dail (OG 1040, ABV 4%)

Golden Ale (OG 1042, ABV 4.2%)

Llanddarog (OG 1042, ABV 4.2%)

Cwrw Blasus (OG 1044, ABV 4.4%)

Collingham SIBA

Brooklands, Leeds Road, Collingham, Leeds, West Yorkshire, LS22 5AA
☎ (01937) 573096 🌐 collinghamales.co.uk

Microbrewery based in the village of Collingham, brewing handcrafted ales for the local community. The owner was formerly head brewer at one of Yorkshire's most prestigious, regional family breweries. Seasonal beers are available.

Blonde (OG 1038, ABV 3.8%)

Journeyman (OG 1039, ABV 3.9%)
A best bitter with a full measure of maltiness and a hoppy flavour.

Artisan's Choice (OG 1043, ABV 4.4%)
A fruity, well-balanced beer with sweetness and bitterness in unison and plenty of hop character.

Colonsay SIBA

The Brewery, Scalasaig, Isle of Colonsay, PA61 7YT
☎ (01951) 200190 🌐 colonsaybrewery.co.uk

Colonsay began brewing in 2007 on a five-barrel plant. Beer is mainly bottled or brewery conditioned for the local trade.

Combe Martin

4 Springfield Terrace, High Street, Combe Martin, Devon, EX34 0EE
☎ (01271) 883507

Combe Martin began brewing in 2005 producing bottled beers on an occasional basis.

Compass SIBA

7 Clare Terrace, Carterton, Oxfordshire, OX18 3ES
☎ (01993) 846846 🌐 compassbrewery.com

Compass began brewing in 2009 using spare capacity at other breweries, but moved to its own plant in Carterton in 2012. It is run by Matthias Sjoberg, who takes brewing ideas from around the world to create experimental and interesting recipes.

Isis Pale Ale (OG 1041, ABV 4.1%)
Malty aromas on a backdrop of hops. Sweet malt with some fruity esters and a gentle bitterness that lingers.

Baltic Night Stout (OG 1048, ABV 4.8%)
Well-balanced roasted bitterness with a hoppy, floral aroma. Roasted barley gives it a hint of coffee and a long, dry cocoa finish.

King's Shipment IPA (OG 1060, ABV 6%)
A strong IPA with hoppy bitterness balanced with malty sweetness. Dry hopped with oak chips. Based on East London Bow Brewery's IPA brewed in the 1790s for shipment to India.

Concertina SIBA

9a Dolcliffe Road, Mexborough, South Yorkshire, S64 9AZ
☎ (01709) 580841 ✉ concertina@btconnect.com
Tours by arrangement

Concertina started in 1992 in the cellar of a club once famous as the home of a long-gone concertina band. The plant produces up to eight barrels a week for the club and other occasional direct outlets and the wider trade via beer wholesalers. Seasonal beers and specials: see website.

Concrete Cow SIBA

59 Alston Drive, Bradwell Abbey, Milton Keynes, Buckinghamshire, MK13 9HB
☎ (01908) 316794 🌐 concretecowbrewery.co.uk
Shop Sat 12-2pm
Tours by arrangement

Concrete Cow opened in 2007 on a 5.5-barrel plant. The beers are named after aspects of local history. The brewery supplies pubs, farmers' markets, local shops and restaurants. Seasonal and bottle-conditioned beers: see website.

Bit o' Bully (OG 1035, ABV 3.5%)
A golden bitter full of biscuit, malt, grain and toast flavours.

Pail Ale (OG 1036, ABV 3.7%)
A light-coloured ale brewed using lager malt.

Fenny Popper (OG 1039, ABV 4%)
A light-coloured, zesty ale.

Cock 'n' Bull Story (OG 1041, ABV 4.1%)
A dark amber-coloured malty beer.

Cloven Hoof (OG 1045, ABV 4.5%)
A dark vanilla stout flavoured with natural vanilla pods.

Coniston SIBA

Coppermines Road, Coniston, Cumbria, LA21 8HL
☎ (01539) 441133 🌐 conistonbrewery.com
Shop (in Black Bull Inn) 11am-11pm
Tours by arrangement

A 10-barrel plant started in 1995 behind the Black Bull Inn in Coniston, it now brews 40 barrels a week and supplies numerous outlets locally and nationally. Some bottle-conditioned Coniston beers are brewed using Hepworth's Horsham plant, others are bottled on site.

Oliver's Light Ale (OG 1035, ABV 3.4%)
A fruity, hoppy, straw-coloured bitter with plenty of flavour for its strength.

Bluebird Bitter (OG 1036, ABV 3.6%)
A yellow-gold, predominantly hoppy and fruity beer, well-balanced with some sweetness and a rising bitter finish.

Bluebird Premium XB (OG 1040.5, ABV 4.2%)
Well-balanced, hoppy and fruity golden bitter. Bittersweet in the mouth with dryness building.

Old Man Ale (OG 1040.5, ABV 4.2%)
Fruity, winey beer with a complex, well-balanced richness.

Special Oatmeal Stout (OG 1045, ABV 4.5%)
A well-balanced, easy-drinking stout, fruity with a balanced ratio of malt to hop bitterness.

Coniston K7 (OG 1045, ABV 4.7%)

Thurstein Pilsner (OG 1044.5, ABV 4.8%)
True to style; mild but unusually sweet, with a hoppy fruitiness.

Blacksmiths Ale (OG 1047.5, ABV 5%)

A well-balanced strong bitter with hints of Christmas pudding.

Infinity IPA (OG 1055, ABV 6%)
High impact strong bitter. Fruity aromas persist in the powerful but well-balanced hoppiness and sweetness with nothing being lost in the finish.

No. 9 Barley Wine (OG 1087.5, ABV 8.5%)
Hops and alcohol dominate with appropriate sweetness and fruit on the tongue. A full-bodied and beautifully balanced beer.

Conquest

See Whitby

Consett Ale Works SIBA

Grey Horse Inn, 115 Sherburn Terrace, Consett, Co Durham, DH8 6NE
☎ (01207) 591540 consettaleworks.co.uk
Tours by arrangement

The brewery opened in 2006 in the stables of a former coaching inn at the rear of the Grey Horse, Consett's oldest pub. The name commemorates the historic Consett Steel Works that closed in 1980. The brewery expanded in 2007 to cope with demand. More than 100 outlets are supplied direct. Seasonal beers are sometimes available.

Steel Town Bitter (OG 1039, ABV 3.8%)

White Hot (OG 1040, ABV 4%)

Cast Iron (OG 1040, ABV 4.1%)

Consett Stout (OG 1045, ABV 4.3%)

Men of Steel (OG 1045, ABV 4.3%)

Red Dust (OG 1045, ABV 4.5%)

Conwy SIBA

Unit 2, Ty Mawr Enterprise Park, Tan y Graig Road, Llysfaen, LL29 8UE
☎ (01492) 514305 conwybrewery.co.uk
Shop Mon-Fri 9am-5pm (please ring if making special trip)
Tours by arrangement

Conwy started brewing in 2003, relocating to its present address in 2013. Around 50 outlets are supplied. Seasonal beers: see website. Bottle-conditioned beers are also available.

Clogwyn Gold (OG 1036, ABV 3.6%)
A full-flavoured golden ale featuring strong citrus fruit flavours throughout. Hoppy bitterness dominates the full mouthfeel and lasting finish.

Infusion (OG 1040, ABV 3.9%)
Light, refreshing pale ale with a long, hoppy finish.

Minera Mountain Ale (OG 1040, ABV 4%)
Copper-coloured, light and crisp ale with a hint of heather.

Welsh Pride/Balchder Cymru (OG 1041, ABV 4%)
A clean-tasting malty bitter. Fruit in aroma and taste with a crisp, grainy mouthfeel and a lingering, hoppy, bitter aftertaste.

Honey Fayre/Cwrw Mel (OG 1045, ABV 4.5%)
Golden best bitter with a hint of honey sweetness balanced by an increasingly hoppy, bitter finish. Slightly thin mouthfeel for a beer of this strength.

Rampart (OG 1046, ABV 4.5%)
A dark, fruity beer with a sweetish initial taste. Fruit flavours accompanied by the underlying hoppiness continue into the bittersweet aftertaste.

Copper Dragon SIBA IFBB

Snaygill Industrial Estate, Keighley Road, Skipton, North Yorkshire, BD23 2QR
☎ (01756) 702130 copperdragon.uk.com
Bistro/Bar/Shop: see website for opening times
Tours by arrangement

Copper Dragon began brewing in 2003 and a technologically advanced, purpose-built 'double 60' brewhouse was commissioned in 2008 and produces six core beers supplemented by limited edition ales. The site has a visitor centre, shop, conference facilities and a bar/bistro.

Black Gold (OG 1036, ABV 3.7%)
This smooth dark ale has a malty, roast character throughout with dark vine fruit notes and a bitter roast finish.

Best Bitter (OG 1036, ABV 3.8%)
A traditional Yorkshire bitter with a malty aroma, a hoppy bitter taste with hints of fruit and a bitter finish.

Golden Pippin (OG 1037, ABV 3.9%)
This golden ale has a citrus aroma and flavour. The dry, bitter astringency increases in the aftertaste.

Cobbler's Cask (OG 1040, ABV 4%)
An amber-coloured bitter with a refreshing hoppy aftertaste.

Silver Myst (OG 1040, ABV 4%)
A cask-conditioned Pilsner.

Scotts 1816 (OG 1041, ABV 4.1%)
This best bitter is fruity and malty with a bitter finish. Look for hints of nuts, tropical fruits and vanilla in the aroma and taste.

Copper Kettle

Bencroft Grange, Bedford Road, Rushden, Northamptonshire, NN10 0SE ☎ 07883 833687 ckcb.webs.com

Established in 2012 by three former soldiers turned brewers who set up a 3.5-barrel plant on a historic farm and former site of an alehouse. The beers can be found at a number of local pubs, clubs and at beer festivals. Bottle-conditioned beer is available direct from the brewery and at local farmers' markets.

UXB (OG 1037, ABV 3.6%)
Chestnut-coloured beer with a full body for its strength.

Vann's Cross (OG 1039, ABV 3.8%)
A copper-coloured ale.

Cornucopia (OG 1041, ABV 4%)
A dark gold-coloured session ale.

Bencroft Best Bitter (OG 1042, ABV 4.1%)
A mid amber bitter with a citrus and spice aroma and flavour.

Coppice Side

Unit 3, Heanor Small Business Centre, Adams Close, Heanor, Derbyshire, DE75 7FW ☎ 07790 305682

A five-barrel plant, Coppice Side was established in 2010. The site is shared with Leadmill Brewery (qv), although the two breweries are separate enterprises. Traditional English hops are used wherever possible. The brewery tap is the Butchers Arms in Langley.

Nottingham Blonde (OG 1040, ABV 4%)
Crisp and hoppy with a fruity aroma.

Owd Miner (OG 1040, ABV 4%)
Traditional copper-coloured ale with good hop characteristics.

Unit 3 IPA (OG 1041, ABV 4.2%)

XOB (OG 1043, ABV 4.4%)

Coppice Light (OG 1044, ABV 4.5%)

Ninkasi (OG 1045, ABV 4.6%)

Scary Crow (OG 1052, ABV 5%)
Flagship premium pale ale. Full mellow flavour with citrus and floral notes.

Copthorne

Majors Farm, Woodcotes Lane, Darlton, Nottinghamshire, NG22 0TL ☎ 07523 340989
✉ copthornebrewery@gmail.com

Former Milestones brewer Dean Penney started production in 2010 in converted outbuildings at the Nags Head in Sutton-on-Trent. The 3.5-barrel plant was previously installed at the former Cathedral Brewery in Lincoln. The brewery relocated to larger premises in 2011.

Gold (OG 1037, ABV 3.6%)
A hoppy golden ale with a bitter finish.

Classic (OG 1038.2, ABV 3.8%)
A light, hoppy session ale.

Comanchie (OG 1040, ABV 4%)
Copper-coloured with caramel overtones.

Cossack (OG 1042.6, ABV 4.3%)
A bronze-coloured ale with a hint of toffee.

Coquetdale

Unit 4c, Rothbury Industrial Estate, Rothbury, Northumberland, NE65 7QJ
☎ (01669) 621411 ✉ owen.jackson@btconnect.com

Coquetdale brews on a five-barrel plant, originally from Geltsdale brewery, where the owner/brewer also received brewing training. The brewery has an expanding portfolio of locally named beers.

Snitter (OG 1038, ABV 3.8%)
A malty traditional bitter.

Coquet Ale (OG 1041, ABV 4.1%)
A refreshing pale ale.

Thrum (OG 1043, ABV 4.3%)
A fruity and spicy pale ale.

Corfe Castle

Bucknowle Farm, Corfe Castle, Dorset, BH20 9BP
☎ (01929) 480730 🌐 corfecastlebrewery.co.uk

Corfe Castle is a family-owned brewery established in 2012, brewing in the beautiful Corfe Valley in Dorset. The range of four cask ales is brewed in limited quantities, being supplied to local pubs and festivals in and around Dorset.

Castle Ale (OG 1044.8, ABV 4.2%)
Light golden ale, with a malty taste, and a crisp, dry hop finish.

Raven (OG 1044.8, ABV 4.2%)
A porter with a smooth and rich mix of roasted malt and traditional English hops.

Gloriette (OG 1047.2, ABV 4.5%)
Traditional English best bitter. Named after the great banqueting hall in Corfe Castle.

Sovereign (OG 1047.2, ABV 4.5%)
A full-flavoured golden ale.

Corinium

Cirencester, Gloucestershire, GL7 2HB ☎ 07716 826467 🌐 coriniumales.co.uk

⊗ Corinium Ales was launched in 2012. Brewing takes place on a 0.5-barrel plant in a converted garage. Three award-winning beers are mainly available bottle-conditioned and make up the brewer's 'Roman Collection' but cask-conditioned production of the beers is increasing.

Gold (OG 1043, ABV 4.2%)
An easy-drinking, fruity ale with a mellow blend of malt and hops and a soft bitter finish.

Centurion (OG 1051, ABV 4.7%)
A rich, malty stout with toasty chocolate undertones. Lightly hopped leaving a well-rounded aftertaste.

Ale Ceasar (OG 1050, ABV 5%)
A stimulating and well-hopped IPA with a tropical fruit aroma balanced with a pleasing bitterness.

Cornish Chough SIBA

Trethvas Farm, Lizard, Cornwall, TR12 7AR
☎ (01326) 290908
Tours by arrangement

⊗ Cornish Chough, the most southerly brewery on the UK mainland, commenced brewing in 2011 at its present location on Trethvas Farm, Lizard village. The brewery has its own borehole and draws water from between two seams of serpentine rock.

Serpentine (OG 1042, ABV 4%) ◆
Light-bodied tawny best bitter with gentle malt and ripe fruit aroma. Strongly malty in taste with sweetness and a delicious bitterness plus a hint of grapefruit that lingers into a dry finish.

Kynance Blonde (OG 1039, ABV 4.2%) ◆
Refreshing amber ale. Sweetness throughout with oranges, pears and mango fruits in the mouth. Dry bitterness rises towards the finish.

Cadgwith Crabber (OG 1043, ABV 4.3%)

Fire Raven (OG 1047, ABV 4.7%)

Lizard Storm (OG 1048, ABV 4.8%) ◆
Malt aroma leads into a sweet, full-bodied brown beer. Malt and stone fruits dominate, finishing with rising bitterness and dryness.

Cornish Crown SIBA

End Unit, Badger's Cross Farm, Badger's Cross, Penzance, Cornwall, TR20 8XE
☎ (01736) 449029 🌐 cornishcrown.co.uk

⊗ Cornish Crown began brewing in 2012 on a six-barrel plant and is based on a farm high above Mounts Bay. It was established by the brewer and landlord of the Crown Inn in Penzance, which acts as the brewery tap. Beer is available in local outlets and can be found as far away as the Southampton Arms in London.

Mousehole (OG 1039, ABV 3.9%)
A mid brown beer with a light bitterness and light hop finish.

St Michaels (OG 1040, ABV 4%) ◆
Tawny-coloured beer with malt and hop aroma. Bitter and malty throughout with roast notes initially and dryness in the finish.

Causeway (OG 1041, ABV 4.1%)

One Hop One Grain (OG 1041, ABV 4.1%)

Honeyfuggle (ABV 4.5%)

SPA (OG 1048, ABV 4.8%) ◆
Heavily-hopped, refreshing golden beer with biscuit malt and stone fruits in the mouth. Finish is bitter, hoppy and dry.

Porter (ABV 5.2%)
A light-coloured porter made with Madagascan vanilla.

IPA (OG 1055, ABV 5.5%)

Red IPA (ABV 5.9%)
A hoppy, citrus IPA with a distinctive red hue.

Corvedale SIBA

Sun Inn, Corfton, Craven Arms, Shropshire, SY7 9DF
☎ (01584) 861239 ⊕ corvedalebrewery.co.uk
Tours by arrangement

Brewing started in 1999 behind the pub. Landlord Norman Pearce is also the brewer and uses only British malt and hops, with water from a local borehole. Seasonal beers are also brewed. Bottle-conditioned beers are suitable for vegetarians and vegans.

Dale Ale (OG 1040, ABV 4%)
Aromas of smoky molasses and dates with fruity, nutty, toffee tastes.

Fuggles Gold (OG 1042, ABV 4.2%)

Golden Dale (OG 1043, ABV 4.2%)

Katie's Pride (OG 1040, ABV 4.3%)

Norman's Pride (OG 1043, ABV 4.3%)
A golden amber-coloured beer with a refreshing, slightly hoppy taste and a bitter finish.

Farmer Rays Ale (OG 1045, ABV 4.5%)
A clear, ruby-coloured bitter with a smooth malty taste.

Oatmeal Stout (OG 1045, ABV 4.5%)

St George's Stout (OG 1045, ABV 4.5%)

Dark & Delicious (OG 1045, ABV 4.6%)
A dark ruby-coloured beer with hops on the aroma and palate, and a sweet aftertaste.

Cotleigh SIBA

Ford Road, Wiveliscombe, Somerset, TA4 2RE
☎ (01984) 624086 ⊕ cotleighbrewery.com
Shop Mon-Sat 10am-4pm
Tours by arrangement

Established in 1979, Cotleigh is based in the historic brewing town of Wiveliscombe. It supplies direct to 750 pubs, 200 retailers and selected wholesalers. Seasonal and bottle-conditioned beers: see website.

Harrier (OG 1035, ABV 3.5%)
A light, golden-coloured low alcohol beer with a delicate floral and fruity aroma and a refreshing sweet and slightly hoppy finish.

Tawny Owl (OG 1038, ABV 3.8%) ◆
Well-balanced, tawny-coloured bitter with plenty of malt and fruitiness on the nose, and malt to the fore in the taste, followed by hop fruit, developing to a satisfying bitter finish.

Commando Hoofing (OG 1040, ABV 4%)
A pale golden beer, refreshing and slightly sparkling.

Cotleigh 25 (OG 1040, ABV 4%)
American Cascade hops gives this pale golden beer a fresh aroma and fruit-filled finish.

Golden Seahawk (OG 1042, ABV 4.2%) ◆
A gold, well-hopped premium bitter with a flowery hop aroma and fruity hop flavour, clean mouthfeel, leading to a dry, hoppy finish.

Barn Owl (OG 1045, ABV 4.5%) ◆
A pale to mid-brown beer with a good balance of malt and hops on the nose; a smooth, full-bodied taste where hops dominate, but balanced by malt, following through to the finish.

Honey Buzzard (OG 1045, ABV 4.5%)
Honey is infused with the brew during fermentation to give a smooth creamy and chocolate palate offering a subtle bittersweet finish.

Old Buzzard (OG 1048, ABV 4.8%)
A traditional dark ale, deep copper red in colour with roasted chocolate malt giving a dry nutty flavour with hints of Amarone biscuit. The finish in the mouth is dry, smoky and smooth.

Cotswold SIBA

College Farm, Stow Road, Bourton-on-the-Water, Gloucestershire, GL54 2HN
☎ (01451) 824488 ⊕ cotswoldlager.com
Tours by arrangement

An independent producer of lager and speciality beers. The brewery was established in 2005 and moved to its current location in 2010. More than 60 outlets are supplied. Seasonal and bottle-conditioned beers are also available.

Cask (ABV 4%)
A copper-coloured, well-hopped, easy-drinking ale.

Cotswold Lion SIBA

Grain Store 5, Dowmans Farm, Coberley, Gloucestershire, GL53 9QY
☎ (01242) 870164 ⊕ cotswoldlionbrewery.co.uk

Brewing began in 2012 using a 10-barrel plant located in a grain store on a farm in the Cotswolds. It's a new venture for John Kemp, former head brewer of Nailsworth Brewery, and Andy Forbes, formerly of Festival Brewery.

Shepherd's Delight (OG 1036, ABV 3.6%)
A light session ale, crisp and full of citrus flavours.

Best in Show (OG 1042, ABV 4.2%)
Plenty of blackberry fruit with a hint of honey.

Golden Fleece (OG 1044, ABV 4.4%)
An IPA, filled with Jamaican fruit.

Cotswold Spring SIBA

Dodington Spring, Dodington Ash, Chipping Sodbury, Gloucestershire, BS37 6RX
☎ (01454) 323088 springbrewing.com
Shop Mon-Fri 9am-5pm, Sat 10am-1pm
Tours by arrangement

Cotswold Spring opened in 2005 with a 10-barrel plant. All the beers are produced using spring water sourced from a borehole on site. Seasonal and bottle-conditioned beers: see website.

Ambler (OG 1040, ABV 3.8%)
Malty aromas and taste give way to dried fruit and hop flavours. Finishes with slight astringency.

Stunner (OG 1041, ABV 4%)
Spicy biscuit aromas blend into hoppy and pale fruit flavours. Refreshing, hoppy and slightly astringent finish.

Codger (OG 1042, ABV 4.2%)
Quite bitter with a slightly malty background. Hops throughout give lasting bitterness which complements the hints of fruit flavour.

Cottage SIBA

The Old Cheese Dairy, Hornblotton Road, Lovington, Somerset, BA7 7PS
☎ (01963) 240551 cottagebrewing.co.uk
Tours by arrangement

The brewery was established in 1993 with the beer names mostly following a transport theme. A new brewing plant is in use and a visitor centre and bar are now open. 1,500 outlets are supplied direct. Seasonal and special beers: see website.

Southern Bitter (OG 1039, ABV 3.7%)
Gold-coloured beer with malt and fruity hops on the nose. Malt and hops in the mouth with a long, fruity bitter finish.

Pacific (OG 1040, ABV 4%)
A gold-coloured ale with a vibrant hop aroma and finish.

Duchess (OG 1042, ABV 4.2%)
A tawny-coloured ale with a balanced bitter finish and distinctive spicy aroma.

Somerset & Dorset (S&D) (OG 1045, ABV 4.4%)
A traditional best bitter with a deep red colour. Well-hopped with a rich, malty flavour.

Golden Arrow (OG 1045, ABV 4.5%)
A hoppy golden bitter with a powerful floral bouquet, a fruity, full-bodied taste and a lingering dry, bitter finish.

Goldrush (OG 1051, ABV 5%)
A deep golden premium ale. Well-balanced with a distinctive and vibrant aroma.

Norman's Conquest MM (OG 1050, ABV 5%)
A dark, mature, smooth ale. Full-bodied with hints of chocolate, bitter orange and vine fruits.

Country Life SIBA

The Big Sheep, Abbotsham, Bideford, Devon, EX39 5AP
☎ (01237) 420808 countrylifebrewery.co.uk
Shop 1-5pm daily (Apr-Oct), winter hours vary – call to confirm
Tours by arrangement

Country Life is based at the Big Sheep tourist attraction. The brewery offers a beer show and free samples in the shop during the peak season (Apr-Oct). A 15.5-barrel plant was installed in 2005, making Country Life the biggest brewery in north Devon. Around 100 outlets are supplied. Seasonal and bottle-conditioned beers are available.

Old Appledore (OG 1037, ABV 3.7%)
A classic session beer with a depth of taste.

Reef Break (OG 1040, ABV 4%)
A beer with a gentle, sweet malty taste.

Pot Wallop (OG 1044, ABV 4.4%)
A light straw-coloured beer, easy-drinking and refreshing.

Shore Break (OG 1043, ABV 4.4%)
A light, easy-drinking, refreshing ale.

Black Boar/Board Break (OG 1045, ABV 4.5%)
An easy-drinking porter. Smoky and rich on the nose with coffee and toffee notes.

Golden Pig (OG 1046, ABV 4.7%)
A full-bodied, smooth premium ale.

Country Bumpkin (OG 1058, ABV 6%)
A malty, full-flavoured, smooth tasting beer.

Contract brewed for Heddon Valley Ales:

Dr Heale (ABV 3.8%)

Miss Loosemore (ABV 4.5%)

Cox & Holbrook

Manor Farm, Brettenham Road, Buxhall, Suffolk, IP14 3DY
☎ (01449) 736323
Tours by arrangement

First opened in 1997, the brewery concentrates on producing a range of bitters, four of which are available at any one time, along with more specialised medium strength beers and milds. There is also a strong emphasis on the preservation and resurrection of rare and traditional styles. Bottle-conditioned versions of draught beers are available at varying times of the year.

Crown Dark Mild (OG 1037, ABV 3.6%)
Thin tasting at first but plenty of malt, caramel and roast flavours burst through to give a thoroughly satisfying beer.

Shelley Dark (OG 1036, ABV 3.6%)
Full-flavoured and satisfying.

Beyton Bitter (OG 1038, ABV 3.8%)
A traditional bitter, pale tawny in colour, malty with Fuggles and Goldings hops.

Old Mill Bitter (OG 1038, ABV 3.8%)
Pale, hoppy and thirst quenching.

Rattlesden Best Bitter (OG 1043, ABV 4%)
A full-bodied and malty best bitter.

Albion Pale Ale (OG 1042, ABV 4.2%)
Refreshingly clean, hoppy ale.

Remus (OG 1045, ABV 4.5%)
An amber-coloured ale, soft on the palate with full hop flavours but subdued bitterness.

Goodcock's Winner (OG 1050, ABV 5%)
An amber-coloured ale, malty but not heavy, with a sharp hop finish.

Ironoak Single Stout (OG 1051, ABV 5%)

Full-bodied with strong roast grain flavours and plenty of hop bitterness plus a distinct hint of oak.

Stormwatch (OG 1052, ABV 5%)
An unusual premium pale ale with a full, slightly fruity flavour.

Stowmarket Porter (OG 1056, ABV 5%) ◆
Strong caramel flavour and lingering caramel aftertaste, balanced by full malt and roast flavours. The overall impression is of a very sweet beer.

East Anglian Pale Ale (OG 1059, ABV 6%)
Well-matured, pale beer with a strong Goldings hops character.

CrackleRock (NEW)

The Old Cooperage, High Street, Botley, Hampshire, SO30 2EA ☎ 07733 232806 🌐 cracklerock.co.uk

⊗ Experienced head brewer Andy Ingram began brewing in 2014 at the Old Cooperage in the centre of Botley using refurbished equipment. Further beers are planned, with both on and off sales expected to be available.

Crackerjack (OG 1039, ABV 3.8%)
Clean-tasting, light hoppy ale.

Barleycorn (OG 1043, ABV 4.2%)
Well-balanced traditional English bitter.

Gold Rush (OG 1046, ABV 4.5%)
A golden ale with a malty, hoppy flavour.

Craddock's SIBA

Duke William, 25 Coventry Street, Stourbridge, West Midlands, DY8 1EP
☎ (01384) 440202 🌐 craddocksbrewery.com
Tours by arrangement

Craddock's began production using a four-barrel plant at the Duke William in Stourbridge, originally to provide beer festivals and the other family-owned pub, where the deliveries are made by dray horse. Bottle conditioned beer is also available at the local farmers' market.

Honey Ewe (ABV 3.8%)

Saxon Gold (OG 1038, ABV 4%)

Crazy Sheep (ABV 4.5%)

Goat Herder Stout (ABV 4.5%)

Lion's Pride (ABV 4.5%)

Capra (ABV 5%)
A pale, lightly-hopped, fruity premium bitter. A sweet start leading to dry finish, with grapefruit and pineapple undertones.

Troll (OG 1052, ABV 5.4%)
A deceptively strong golden ale, with a bittersweet taste, and dry hop finish.

Craftsman (NEW)

Old Abbey Inn, 61 Pencroft Way, Manchester Science Park, Manchester, M15 6AY ☎ 07908 108860
🌐 craftsmanbrewery.com

Craftsman began brewing in 2014 using a 100-litre plant in the cellar of the Old Abbey Inn on the Science Park in Manchester. Capacity is expected to increase to 300 litres using a larger plant. Beers are brewed on demand.

Crafty

Carpenters Arms, 10 High Street, Great Wilbraham, Cambridgeshire, CB21 5JD
☎ (01223) 813938 🌐 craftybeers.co.uk

⊗ Crafty Beers are brewed by Robert Beardsmore in the old stables at the Carpenters Arms in Great Wilbraham. This small 1.5-barrel brewpub started production in 2012. Beer is available in the Carpenter Arms and can also be found at a number of local beer festivals. Further beers are planned. Bottle-conditioned beers are also available.

Sixteen Strides (OG 1037, ABV 3.8%)
A well-hopped pale ale with plenty of citrus aroma.

Carpenter's Cask (OG 1042, ABV 4.2%) ◆
A well-balanced amber-coloured brew with biscuit malt character giving way to hops on the palate and a long finish.

Sauvignon Blonde (OG 1044, ABV 4.4%)
An aromatic golden ale.

Crafty Devil (NEW)

27 Loftus St, Cardiff, CF5 1HL

Brewing commenced in 2014 initially producing keg and bottle-conditioned beers.

Crafty Pint (NEW)

Half Moon, 130 Northgate, Darlington, County Durham, DL1 1QS
☎ (01325) 469965 🌐 thecraftypint.co.uk

The Crafty Pint Brewery was established in 2013 in the cellar of the Half Moon in Darlington, bringing commercial brewing brewing back to Darlington for the first time since 1934. The brew length is only 10 gallons making it a nano brewery.

School's Out (OG 1040, ABV 4%)

Tawny Mild (OG 1040, ABV 4%)

Elder Ale (OG 1044, ABV 4.4%)
A golden ale with hints of elderflower.

Porter (OG 1045, ABV 4.5%)

Crate

Unit 7, White Building, Queens Yard, Hackney Wick, London, E9 5EN ☎ 07834 275687
🌐 cratebrewery.com

Crate is a brewery and pizzeria opened in 2012 and situated in a canalside former print factory.

Best Bitter (OG 1045, ABV 4.3%) ◆
Easy-drinking brown malty beer with honey, a dry bitterness and some nutty notes. The hops are peppery in character.

Stout (OG 1057, ABV 5.7%) ◆
Slightly smoky nose with blackcurrant fruit. Caramelised toffee and liquorice flavour that lingers. A little black roast notes throughout.

Cromarty

Davidston, Cromarty, IV11 8XD
☎ (01381) 600440 🌐 cromartybrewing.co.uk
Shop Mon- Fri 10am-5pm
Tours by arrangement

Cromarty began brewing in 2011 in a purpose-built brewhouse. Additional fermenters were installed in 2013 to meet demand. The brewery continues to experiment with beers including collaborations with other craft breweries.

Happy Chappy (OG 1040, ABV 4.1%) ◆
A golden ale with plenty of hop character. Floral citrus hop aroma with a good bitter taste which increases in aftertaste.

Brewed Awakening (OG 1048, ABV 4.7%) ◆
A roasted malty brew with added coffee making for a dry, bitter finish.

Red Rocker (OG 1048.5, ABV 5%) ◆
Red-coloured bitter using rye.

Cronx SIBA

Unit 6, Vulcan Business Centre, Vulcan Way, New Addington, Croydon, CR0 9UG
☎ (01689) 809093 🌐 thecronx.com

⊗ Cronx began brewing in 2012 and is the first commercial brewery in the area since 1954. Seasonal and one-off beers are also available.

Standard (ABV 3.8%) ◆
Easy-drinking brown bitter with sweetish fudge and spicy hoppiness notes throughout. A malty bitter finish with a dryness that remains.

Kotchin (ABV 3.9%) ◆
Grapefruit beer with pleasant hoppy notes. A little sweetness is balanced by a crisp bitter finish that grows on drinking.

Entire (ABV 5.2%) ◆
Dark brown porter with chocolate roast notes in the aroma, flavour and finish. The fruit character is of caramelised raisins.

Cropton

See Great Yorkshire

Cross Bay SIBA ◉

White Lund Industrial Estate, Morecambe, Lancashire, LA3 3PT
☎ (01524) 39481 🌐 crossbaybrewery.co.uk
Shop Mon-Fri 9am-4pm, Sat 9.30-11.30am, Sun 10-11am
Tours by arrangement

◎Cross Bay commenced brewing in 2011 on a 28-barrel brew plant and has a brewing capacity of 168 barrels per week. An expansion is planned in the near future to meet demand.

Halo (OG 1037, ABV 3.6%) ◆
Initial sweetness leads to a fruity, delicate hoppy bitterness, ending with a light finish.

Nightfall Pale Bitter (OG 1038, ABV 3.8%) ◆
A sweet, malty, gently-hopped bitter with some fruit.

Dusk Ruby Ale (OG 1040, ABV 4%)
A ruby ale, kicking in with a strong fruity nose, bursting onto the palate with a roasted but fruity bitter body with hints of cocoa.

Sunset Blonde Bitter (OG 1043, ABV 4.2%) ◆
Sweet and fruity bitter.

Zenith (OG 1050, ABV 5%)
Light and refreshing in colour with a distinct tropical aroma, this IPA has a citrus/fruity body followed by a hefty kick from the triple blend of hops.

Crouch Vale SIBA ◉

23 Haltwhistle Road, South Woodham Ferrers, Essex, CM3 5ZA
☎ (01245) 322744 🌐 crouchvale.co.uk
Shop Mon-Fri 8.30am-5pm
Tours by arrangement

⊗ Founded in 1981 by two CAMRA enthusiasts, Crouch Vale is now well established as a major player in Essex brewing, having moved to larger premises in 2006. The company is also a major wholesaler of cask ale from other independent breweries, which it supplies to more than 100 outlets as well as beer festivals throughout the region. One tied house, the Queen's Head in Chelmsford, is owned. Seasonal beers: see website.

Blackwater Mild (OG 1037, ABV 3.7%) ◆
A dark bitter rather than a true mild. Roasty and very bitter towards the end.

Essex Boys Best Bitter (OG 1038, ABV 3.8%)
Full-bodied and malty with hops shining through; a classic session beer.

Brewers Gold (OG 1040, ABV 4%) ◆
Pale golden ale with a striking citrus nose. Sweet fruit and bitter hops are well matched throughout.

Yakima Gold (OG 1042, ABV 4.2%)
Pale and earthily aromatic.

Amarillo (OG 1050, ABV 5%)
A strong golden ale with a spicy aroma, juicy malt mouthfeel and an extremely long and bitter hop finish.

Crown

See Wood Street

Crystalbrew (NEW)

Building 40, British Aerospace Business Park, Saltgrounds Road, Brough, East Yorkshire, HU15 1EQ
☎ 07773 958380 🌐 crystalbrew.co.uk

Brewing began in 2014. The brewery is named in honour of Hull University's world famous Crystal Group in Chemistry, the first group to successfully make the liquid crystals that are an essential part of modern life.

Crystal Limonite Bitter (ABV 3.8%)

Crystal Jade (ABV 4%)

Crystal Blonde (ABV 4.5%)

Cuillin

▤ Sligachan Hotel, Sligachan, Carbost, Isle of Skye, IV47 8SW
☎ (01478) 650204 🌐 sligachan.co.uk
Tours by arrangement

◎The five-barrel brewery opened in 2004 and is situated in central Skye at the foot of the Cuillin mountains. The water from the Cuillins provides a distinctive colour and taste to the ales. Specials and seasonal ales are available throughout the year. The brewery is closed in winter.

Cullercoats SIBA

Westfield Court, Maurice Road Industrial Estate, Wallsend, Tyne & Wear, NE28 6BY
☎ (0191) 252 8765

Office: 17 St Oswins Avenue, Cullercoats, Tyne & Wear, NE30 4PH cullercoatsbrewery.co.uk

Ex-solicitor Bill Scantlebury established Cullercoats in 2011 and brews at least once a week producing about 18 barrels with the help of brewer's mate Doug. Wife Anna keeps the paperwork at bay.

Shuggy Boat Blonde (OG 1039, ABV 3.8%)
A refreshing, smooth blonde beer.

Lovely Nelly (OG 1039, ABV 3.9%)
A full-bodied amber-coloured session beer with a biscuit malt flavour balanced with a smooth hoppy bitterness.

Jack the Devil (OG 1045, ABV 4.5%)
A rich, dark chestnut-coloured ale. Well-balanced with a malty nuttiness and a fresh hoppy aroma.

Watch House Winter Warmer (OG 1050, ABV 5%)
Warming dark English ale, malty with spicy/berry flavours.

Cumberland

The Forge, Great Corby, Carlisle, Cumbria, CA4 8LR
☎ (01228) 560899 cumberlandbreweries.co.uk

Cumberland was established in 2009 with a bespoke 10-barrel brewing plant and situated in a building at the heart of the village, previously the farriers shop from 1833. A new building has been prepared for an expansion to increase capacity six fold.

Corby Ale (OG 1038, ABV 3.8%)
A fruity session beer with sweetness leading to gentle bitterness in the aftertaste.

Corby Blonde (OG 1042, ABV 4.2%)
Melon fruity hoppiness gives a light refreshing drink.

Cumbrian Legendary SIBA

Old Hall Brewery, Esthwaite Water, Hawkshead, Cumbria, LA22 0QF
☎ (01539) 436436 cumbrianlegendaryales.com
Tours by arrangement

First established in 2003, the brewery is located in an idyllic position in a renovated barn on the shores of Esthwaite Water. The success of Loweswater Gold has meant the brewery is thriving.

Esthwaite Bitter (OG 1038.5, ABV 3.8%)
Amber-coloured session ale with sweetness, fruit and hoppiness in fine balance. (Formerly Dickie Doodle).

Langdale (OG 1040, ABV 4%)
Fresh grapefruit aromas with hoppy fruity flavours and crisp long hop finish, make for a well-balanced beer.

Grasmoor Dark Ale (OG 1043, ABV 4.3%)
Dark fruity beer with complex character and roast nutty tones leading to a short refreshing finish.

Loweswater Gold (OG 1041, ABV 4.3%)
A dominant fruity body develops into a light bitter finish. A beer that belies its strength.

Cych Valley

Abercych, Pembrokeshire, SA37 0HJ
☎ (01239) 841200 info@nagsheadabercych.co.uk

Brewing began in 2012 on a five-barrel plant in a brewhouse on the same site as the Nag's Head Inn. Bottle-conditioned beers are available.

Daleside SIBA

Camwal Road, Starbeck, Harrogate, North Yorkshire, HG1 4PT
☎ (01423) 880022 dalesidebrewery.com
Shop Mon-Fri 9am-4pm (Off sales only)

Opened in 1991 in Harrogate with a 20-barrel plant, the brewery delivers direct to a range of outlets including pubs, restaurants and farm shops from Newcastle to Chesterfield as well as nationally via wholesalers. Seasonal beers: see website.

Bitter (OG 1039, ABV 3.7%)
Pale brown in colour, this well-balanced, hoppy beer is complemented by fruity bitterness and a hint of sweetness, leading to a long, bitter finish.

Blonde (OG 1040, ABV 3.9%)
A pale golden beer with a predominantly hoppy aroma and taste, leading to a refreshing hoppy, bitter but short finish.

Old Leg Over (OG 1043, ABV 4.1%)
Well-balanced mid brown refreshing beer that leads to an equally well-balanced fruity, bitter aftertaste.

Special Bitter (OG 1043, ABV 4.1%)
An amber-coloured beer with a malty nose and a hint of fruitiness. Hops and malt carry over to leave a clean, hoppy aftertaste.

Monkey Wrench (OG 1055, ABV 5.3%)
Premium deep chestnut red-coloured beer with a spicy fruit aroma and warming spicy flavour.

Morocco Ale (OG 1057, ABV 5.5%)
A rich, dark spiced ale

Dancing Duck SIBA

1 John Cooper Buildings, Payne Street, Derby, DE22 3AZ
☎ (01332) 205582 dancingduckbrewery.com

Dancing Duck was established in 2010 by Rachel Mathews using a 10-barrel brew plant. Its name comes from the local greeting 'ay up me duck'. The brewery operates two local pubs, the Exeter Arms and the New Zealand Arms in Derby.

Ay Up (OG 1040.5, ABV 3.9%)
A pale session bitter. Subtle malt and floral notes are matched with citrus hop, rounded off with a slightly dry finish.

Nice Weather (OG 1042, ABV 4.1%)
Copper-coloured fruity ale packed full of flavour. Blackberry, strawberry and floral rose notes in perfect balance with just the right amount of malt character.

22 (OG 1044.1, ABV 4.3%)

A well-balanced best bitter with a malty flavour and dark fruit notes offset by a strong hop with a very clean finish.

DCUK (OG 1042, ABV 4.3%)
A pale ale with a fruity aroma. A juicy citrus flavour with hints of orange, mango, lemon and pine.

Dark Drake (OG 1051, ABV 4.5%)
Malty caramel liquorice flavours combine in a smooth-drinking velvety oatmeal stout with a freshly roasted coffee and tea finish.

Gold (OG 1046.5, ABV 4.7%)
A modern IPA with powerful hoppy bitterness and aroma balanced with strong malt notes. The hops give peppery, plum-like and orange zesty flavours.

Amberillo (OG 1047.2, ABV 4.8%)
An easy-drinking amber-coloured ale. Earthy aromatic hops are balanced with biscuit malt flavours leading to a spicy, peppery finish.

Duck's Courage (OG 1048.8, ABV 5%)

Abduction (OG 1053, ABV 5.5%)
An IPA with a myriad of tropical flavours in balance with an enjoyable level of hoppy bitterness, a good malt character and very clean finish.

Dancing Man

Platform Tavern, Town Quay, Southampton, SO14 2NY
☎ (023) 8033 7232 dancingmanbrewery.co.uk

Dancing Man began brewing in 2011 at the Platform Tavern. A move is planned in the near future to the historic Wool House in order to expand the brewery and include an onsite bar and restaurant. One-off and rare brews are available throughout the year.

Pilgrim's Pale Ale (OG 1039, ABV 3.9%)
A pale golden ale with tropical fruit aromas, a smooth bitter flavour and a clean and crisp finish.

Old Troubadour (OG 1041, ABV 4.1%)
A copper-coloured session beer with orange peel and floral notes.

Fiddler's Jig (OG 1047, ABV 4.8%)
A rich malt body, with fruity hop flavours.

Big Casino (OG 1049, ABV 5%)
Pine and citrus fruit aroma with a warming malt body and a smooth bitterness with juicy hop flavours.

Last Waltz (OG 1052, ABV 5.3%)
A Black IPA with an intense hoppy nose with tropical fruit notes, a smoky roasted malt flavour and a dry bitter finish.

Dark Horse SIBA

Coonlands Laithe, Hetton, North Yorkshire, BD23 6LY
☎ (01756) 730555
Tours by arrangement

Formerly the Wharfedale Brewery, Dark Horse opened in 2008 with new owners. The brewery is based in an old hay barn within the Yorkshire Dales National Park. More than 15 outlets are supplied direct.

Best Bitter (OG 1038, ABV 3.8%)
Well-balanced bitter with biscuity malt and fruit on the nose continuing into the taste. Bitterness increases in the finish.

Hetton Pale Ale (OG 1041, ABV 4.2%)
Golden, well-balanced, full-bodied, with hoppy bitterness on the palate overlaying a malty base and a spicy citrus character.

Dark Star SIBA

22 Star Road, Partridge Green, West Sussex, RH13 8RA
☎ (01403) 713085 darkstarbrewing.co.uk
Shop closed Tue & Sun, Mon & Wed-Fri 10am-5.30pm, Sat 9am-4.30pm
Tours by arrangement

Dark Star started in the cellar of the Evening Star in Brighton and in 2010 moved to its current premises using a 45-barrel plant. Copies of classic European, American or old English beer styles are regularly produced. The range of beer is divided between permanent, seasonal and monthly specials: see website. Bottle-conditioned beer is also available.

The Art of Darkness (OG 1040, ABV 3.5%)
Classic roast flavours along with a hint of sweetness with well-balanced fruit and spicy notes.

Hophead (OG 1040, ABV 3.8%)
A golden-coloured bitter with a fruity/hoppy aroma and a citrus/bitter taste and aftertaste. Flavours remain strong to the end.

Partridge Best Bitter (OG 1041, ABV 4%)
Traditional Sussex-style best bitter.

Espresso (OG 1043, ABV 4.2%)
Freshly ground Arabica coffee beans are added to the copper for a few minutes after the boil of this rich black beer.

American Pale Ale (OG 1048, ABV 4.7%)
American-style pale ale full of the aroma of hops.

Festival (OG 1051, ABV 5%)
A chestnut, bronze-coloured bitter with a smooth mouthfeel and freshness.

Original (OG 1051, ABV 5%)
A dark strong and bitter beer that defies classification.

Winter Meltdown (OG 1051, ABV 5%)
A deep bronze-coloured beer which is cask conditioned with Chinese stem ginger and other spices to produce an aromatic warmth.

Revelation (OG 1056, ABV 5.7%)

DarkTribe

Dog & Gun, High Street, East Butterwick, Lincolnshire, DN17 3AJ
☎ (01724) 782324 darktribe.co.uk
Tours by arrangement

A small brewery was built during the summer of 1996 in a workshop at the bottom of his garden by Dave 'Dixie' Dean. In 2005 Dixie bought the Dog & Gun pub and moved the 2.5-barrel brewing equipment there. The beers generally follow a marine theme, recalling Dixie's days as an engineer in the Merchant Navy and his enthusiasm for sailing. Local outlets are supplied. Seasonal beers are also produced.

Dixie's Mild (OG 1034, ABV 3.6%)

Honey Mild (OG 1032, ABV 3.6%)

Three Point Six (OG 1033, ABV 3.6%)

THE BREWERIES

Full Ahead (OG 1034, ABV 3.8%) ◆
A malty smoothness is backed by a slightly fruity hop that gives a good bitterness to this amber-brown bitter.

Captain Floyd (OG 1035, ABV 3.9%)

Ruddy L (OG 1035, ABV 3.9%)

Albacore (OG 1036, ABV 4%)

Sternwheeler (OG 1037, ABV 4.2%)

Old Gaffer (OG 1038, ABV 4.5%)

Dartmoor SIBA

The Brewery, Station Road, Princetown, Devon, PL20 6QX
☎ (01822) 890789 ⊕ dartmoorbrewery.co.uk
Tours by arrangement

Established in 1994, it is the highest brewery in England at 1,400 feet above sea level. In 2012 the capacity was increased to 360 barrels per week by the addition of another 60-barrel fermenter. Formerly named Princetown Brewery.

Dartmoor IPA (OG 1039.5, ABV 4%) ◆
There is a flowery hop aroma and taste with a bitter aftertaste to this full-bodied, amber-coloured beer.

Dragon's Breath (OG 1044, ABV 4.4%)
A unique winter warmer flavoured with black treacle. Deep ruby brown-coloured, rich and full-bodied with an aftertaste of Morello cherries.

Legend (OG 1043.5, ABV 4.4%)
Smooth, full-flavoured and balanced with a crispy malt fruit finish. Golden brown in colour and an aroma of fresh baked bread with a hint of spice.

Jail Ale (OG 1047.5, ABV 4.8%) ◆
Hops and fruit predominate in the flavour of this mid-brown beer, which has a slightly sweet aftertaste.

Darwin SIBA

1, West Quay Court, Sunderland Enterprise Park, Sunderland, Tyne & Wear, SR5 2TE
☎ (0191) 549 9450 ⊕ darwinbrewery.com
Tours by arrangement

Established in 1994, Darwin Brewery is now based in purpose-built premises in Sunderland with a 3.5-barrel brew plant. The brewery supports students on Brewlab brewing courses, who produce many unique specialist and international beers, often available locally. A range of established Darwin beers are also produced, some based on historical analysis or student initiatives.

Ghost Ale (OG 1041, ABV 4.1%)

Killer Bee (OG 1065, ABV 6%)
A strong but light ale matured with honey.

Extinction Ale (OG 1084, ABV 8.3%)

Dawkins SIBA

The Now Thus Brewery, Unit 7, Timsbury Workshop Estate, Hayeswood Road, Timsbury, Bath, BA2 0HQ
☎ (01761) 472242 ⊕ dawkins-ales.co.uk
Tours by arrangement

The established Dawkins Taverns group of independent Bristol pubs bought the former Matthews Brewery in 2009. Five pubs are owned and around 80 outlets are supplied direct. A core range of four ales are produced plus around 12 specials per year: see website.

Bristol Blonde (ABV 3.8%)
A pale gold-coloured beer with citrus aroma and flavour with tones of vanilla.

Bristol Best (OG 1041, ABV 4%)
Copper-coloured with a malty aroma. Malt flavour with biscuity tones and a bitter finish.

Miners Gold (OG 1040, ABV 4%)
Golden ale with a slightly spicy fruit aroma and flavour.

Green Barrel (ABV 4.2%)

Resolution IPA (OG 1053, ABV 5.3%)
An amber gold-coloured IPA with a mango/grapefuit flavour.

Deeply Vale SIBA

Unit 24, Peel Industrial Estate, Chamberhall Street, Bury, BL9 0LU
☎ (0161) 761 7334 ⊕ deeplyvalebrewery.com

Deeply Vale is a family-run business established in 2012 using a 2.5-barrel plant. The brewery's name immortalises the Deeply Vale area near Bury, famed for legendary 1970s music festivals.

Still Walking (OG 1036, ABV 3.8%)
A light, well-balanced, easy-drinking session ale with a fruity aroma and a velvety smooth feel.

Golden Vale (OG 1041, ABV 4.2%)
A deep golden ale. The flavour is refreshing, robust and satisfyingly malty. A complex bitterness with a smooth, caramel finish.

DV8 (OG 1050, ABV 4.8%)
A breakfast stout. Thick and creamy.

Deeside SIBA

Lochton of Leys, Banchory, AB31 5QB
☎ (01330) 825598

Office: Escape Business Technologies, 5 Carden Place, Aberdeen, AB10 1UT ⊕ deesidebrewery.co.uk

Originally established as Hillside Brewery in 2005, it quickly expanded and was renamed Deeside Brewery in 2006. The company was sold in 2012 and moved to new premises in 2013.

Swift (OG 1038, ABV 3.8%)
A light session pale ale.

Macbeth (OG 1042, ABV 4.1%)
Soft bitterness, melon and floral notes. A dry finish with tropical fruit.

Delavals

26 Windsor Gardens, Whitley Bay, NE26 3BG ☎ 0844 504 2214 ⊕ delavals.com

Delavals started brewing in 2010, reviving an 18th century ale for Seaton Delaval Hall in partnership with the National Trust. They continue to work closely to create a range of fine ales that help to promote and preserve regional landmarks. Currently brewing on a two-barrel plant and directly supplying 50 outlets. Brewing is currently suspended.

Souter Lighthouse Best Bitter (OG 1037.5, ABV 3.8%)

A traditional copper-coloured English bitter. Well-rounded and bittersweet with a little malt and rich fruity aromas.

Lindisfarne Castle Dark Ale (OG 1039, ABV 4%)
An old Scottish ale with a twist, an amber/stout fusion. Light and easy-drinking for a dark ale. Sweet and malty, made with Hyssop to give a silky finish.

Seaton Delaval Hall Pale Ale (OG 1040.6, ABV 4.2%)
A golden-coloured classic English pale ale, crisp and refreshing with a hoppy aroma and a dry finish.

Washington Old Hall Honey Beer (OG 1045.4, ABV 4.6%)
A golden ale with honey, not sweet as you might expect, but a blend of biscuity malt, light floral aromas and warming honey.

Dem Bones (NEW)

Marlow Road, Leicester, LE3 2BQ

Dem Bones was established in 2013 using a 0.5-barrel plant producing one or two brews a week and concentrating on classic British and European styles. Bread is also baked, strongly influenced by Italian and French traditions.

DemonBrew

c/o Tryst Brewery, Lorne Road, Larbert, Stirlingshire, FK5 4AT ☎ 07974 107453 🌐 demonbrew.com

DemonBrew began brewing in 2011 and currently use spare capacity at Tryst Brewery (qv). Seasonal and bottle-conditioned beers are available.

Firehead (ABV 3.9%)

Redline (ABV 4.3%)

Demon Black (ABV 4.4%)

Pacific Kick (ABV 5.4%)

Denbigh

c/o Hope & Anchor Inn, 94 Vale Street, Denbigh, LL16 3BW
☎ (01745) 817021 ✉ bragdy@shworth.com

Brewing commenced in 2012 at the rear of the Hope & Anchor pub. The brewery re-located in 2014 to a dedicated brewhouse in the town. Beers are mainly bottle-conditioned for markets and fairs but also supplied cask-conditioned to the pub.

Cadlas Ceiliogod (Cock Pit) (OG 1035, ABV 3.5%)
A tawny-coloured bitter. Well-hopped with caramel and malt highlights.

Earls Folly (OG 1045, ABV 4.5%)

Cwrw Du'nbych (Denbigh Black) (OG 1050, ABV 5%)
A traditional Celtic black porter. Brewed with patent black malt for a rich, roasted flavour and hints of muscovado.

No X (OG 1047, ABV 5.3%)
A cask-conditioned lager.

Dent SIBA

Hollins, Cowgill, Dent, Cumbria, LA10 5TQ
☎ (01539) 625326 🌐 dentbrewery.co.uk
Merchandise available from George & Dragon, Dent
Tours by arrangement

Dent was set up in 1990 in a converted barn next to a former farmhouse in the Yorkshire Dales National Park. In 2005 the brewery was completely refurbished and capacity expanded. One pub is owned. More than 150 outlets are supplied direct.

Golden Fleece (OG 1035, ABV 3.7%) ◆
Light, hoppy and fruity easy-drinking summer bitter with a lingering bitter aftertaste

Station Porter (OG 1042, ABV 3.8%)
A dark traditional porter with delicate tones of five different malts, a rich, smooth head and lingering, light bitter aftertaste.

Aviator (OG 1039, ABV 4%) ◆
This medium-bodied amber ale is characterised by strong citrus and hoppy flavours that develop into a long bitter finish.

Ramsbottom Strong Ale (OG 1042, ABV 4.5%) ◆
This complex, mid-brown beer has a warming, dry, bitter finish to follow its unusual combination of roast, bitter, fruity and sweet flavours.

Kamikaze (OG 1047, ABV 5%) ◆
Hops and fruit dominate this full-bodied, golden, strong bitter, with a dry bitterness growing in the aftertaste.

T'owd Tup (OG 1056, ABV 6%) ◆
A rich, full-flavoured, strong stout with a coffee aroma. The dominant roast character is balanced by a warming sweetness and a raisiny, fruitcake taste that linger on into the finish.

Derby SIBA

Masons Place Business Park, Nottingham Road, Derby, DE21 6AQ
☎ (01332) 242888 🌐 derbybrewing.co.uk
Tours by arrangement

A family-run microbrewery, established in 2004 in the old Masons Paintworks Varnish Shed by head brewer Trevor Harris, founder and former brewer at the Brunswick Inn, Derby (qv). The business has grown over the years and three pubs are now owned around Derby. More than 400 outlets are supplied including major retailers. In addition to the core range there are at least four new beers each month which includes the bi-monthly 'Brewers Choice' range of beers.

Hop Till You Drop (OG 1039, ABV 3.9%)
A blonde brew with fruity overtones and a dry finish.

Triple Hop (OG 1041, ABV 4.1%)
A classic pale ale, well-balanced with a combination of triple hop varieties.

Business As Usual (OG 1044, ABV 4.4%)
An easy-drinking, flavoursome copper-coloured beer, well-balanced, smooth and malty with a satisfying finish.

Double Mash (OG 1046, ABV 4.6%)
A balanced ruby brew, crafted using the double mash brewing process.

Penny's Porter (OG 1046, ABV 4.6%)
A rich, dark, robust brew with a fine hop balance.

Old Friend (OG 1047, ABV 4.7%)
A classic well-rounded brew, balanced and full-bodied.

Dashingly Dark (OG 1048, ABV 4.8%)

THE BREWERIES

A smooth dark brew with complex flavours and a chocolate roasted finish.

Mercia IPA (OG 1050, ABV 5%)
An IPA created with a modern twist.

Old Intentional (OG 1050, ABV 5%)
A full-bodied, malty premium beer rich chestnut in colour and well-balanced with a delicate sweet aroma and a smooth finish.

Quintessential (OG 1058, ABV 5.8%)
Complex and well-rounded with fruit and citrus flavours.

Derventio SIBA

Long Mill, Darley Abbey Mills, Darley Abbey, Derbyshire, DE22 1DZ
☎ (01332) 380199 ⊕ derventiobrewery.co.uk
Tours by arrangement

Derventio Brewery was established in 2005 and first brewed in 2006 at Trusley Brook Farm. In 2011 the six-barrel brewery relocated to the Grade I-listed Long Mill, which is part of the Derwent Valley Mills World Heritage Site. The brewery tap can be hired for private parties. A popular 'Day with the Brewer' is available, by prior arrangement, for up to three people on Saturday mornings. The brewery is one of the founding members of the Derbyshire Brewers Collective. Seasonal beers and monthly specials are also brewed.

Cleopatra (OG 1048.4, ABV 5%)
A complex beer rounded off with a hint of apricot.

Derwent SIBA

Units 2a-2c, Station Road Industrial Estate, Silloth, Cumbria, CA7 4AG
☎ (01697) 331522 ⊕ derwentbrewery.co.uk

Derwent was set up in 1996 in Cockermouth and moved to Silloth in 1998. A large range of ales is produced, available throughout the north of England.

Carlisle State Bitter (OG 1036, ABV 3.7%)
Malty, biscuity, hoppy beer with a gold colour.

W&M Mild (OG 1036, ABV 3.7%)

Parsons Pledge (OG 1039, ABV 4%)
Amber ale with a biscuity tang and a slightly fruity finish.

Reaper (OG 1042, ABV 4.3%)

Mutineer (OG 1043, ABV 4.4%)

W&M Pale Ale (OG 1042, ABV 4.4%)
A sweet, fruity, hoppy beer with a bitter finish.

Deverell's SIBA

Unit 16, Globe Industrial Estate, Grays, Essex, RM17 6ST ☎ 07843 627791 ⊕ deverellsbrewery.com

Established in 2012 using a 2.5-barrel plant, Deverell's was the first commercial brewer in Thurrock since Charringtons acquired and closed Seabrooks Brewery more than 80 years ago. The brewery now operates its own pub, the Traitors Gate, in Grays. Special monthly brews are available exclusively for the pub.

Rock n Rolla (OG 1040, ABV 4%)

Redemption (ABV 4.5%)
Full-flavoured, amber-coloured ale. Sweet with caramel and a well-balanced hop profile.

Devon

Mansfield Arms, 7 Main Street, Sauchie, Clackmannanshire, FK10 3JR
☎ (01259) 722020 ⊕ devonales.com
Tours by arrangement (small groups preferred)

Established in 1992 to produce high quality cask ales for the Mansfield Arms, Sauchie, Devon is the oldest operating brewery in the county. A second pub, the Inn at Muckhart, was purchased in 1994 and the only beers sold there are from the Devon Ales brewery. The brewery is now selling beer to the open market.

Original (70/-) (OG 1038, ABV 3.8%)
A full-bodied session ale with a prominent malty flavour and a distinct hoppiness.

Thick Black (OG 1042, ABV 4.2%)

Pride (OG 1046, ABV 4.8%)
A flavourful, full-bodied beer.

Devon Earth SIBA

Buckfastleigh, Devon ☎ 07927 397871

Office: 7 Fernham Terrace, Torquay Road, Paignton, Devon, TQ3 2AQ ✉ info@devonearthbrewery.co.uk

Devon Earth was launched in 2008 on a 2.5-barrel plant located on the banks of the River Dart on the edge of Dartmoor and is run on a part-time basis. It supplies beer festivals and pubs mainly in the Torbay area. As well as three regular ales, seasonal specials are also produced.

Dickensian SIBA

Roden Nurseries, Roden Lane, Roden, Shropshire, TF6 6BP ☎ 07752 331633
⊕ dickensianbrewery.co.uk

Now using a 12-barrel brewing kit in an old vehicle storage shed, its smaller kettle being unable to keep up with demand; the beers are named around Dickens' novels and characters, and are given volume numbers.

Ale of Two Cities (ABV 3.8%)
Light amber-coloured session bitter, triple hopped.

David Hopperfield (ABV 4%)
A hoppy pale ale, dry and refreshing.

Martin Guzzle Wit (ABV 4.2%)
A blonde ale with a light, crisp finish.

Nicholas Nicklebeer (ABV 4.4%)

Great Fermentations (ABV 4.6%)
A cloudy wheat beer from a traditional Belgian recipe. Sweet and deceptively strong.

Digfield SIBA

Lilford Lodge Farm, Barnwell, Northamptonshire, PE8 5SA
☎ (01832) 273954 ⊕ digfield-ales.co.uk

Digfield Ales started brewing in 2005 on a five-barrel plant, which was later expanded to seven barrels. Increased demand led to a move to larger premises in 2012, still in the Barnwell area. A reed bed effluent system has been installed and brewing capacity increased to 15 barrels with new equipment. More than 40 free houses are supplied. Seasonal beers: see website.

Fools Nook (OG 1037, ABV 3.8%) ◆
The floral aroma, dominated by lavender and honey, belies the hoppy bitterness that comes through in the taste of this golden ale. A fruity balance lasts.

Barnwell Bitter (OG 1039, ABV 4%) ◆
A fruity, sulphurous aroma introduces a beer in which sharp bitterness is balanced by dry, biscuity malt.

Shacklebush (OG 1044, ABV 4.5%) ◆
This amber brew begins with a balance of malt and sulphury hop on the nose which develops on the palate, complemented by a mounting bitterness. Good dry finish with lingering malt notes.

Mad Monk (OG 1047, ABV 4.8%) ◆
Fruity beer with bitter earthy hops in evidence.

Doghouse SIBA

Unit 7, The Paddocks, Jurby Industrial Estate, Jurby, Isle of Man, IM7 3BD ☎ 07624 233052
🌐 doghousebrewery.im

Doghouse began brewing in 2012 using equipment manufactured in Germany by Biering.

Mild (OG 1034, ABV 3.5%)
A dark brown mild with a malty, chocolate aroma and malty, toffee taste.

Bitter (OG 1036, ABV 3.7%)
A straw-coloured bitter with a fruity, hoppy, earthy aroma, and a dry hoppy bitterness.

Best Bitter (OG 1041, ABV 4.2%)
Brown bitter with a malty, fruity aroma, and a dry fruity bitterness.

Gold (OG 1043, ABV 4.4%)
Straw-coloured beer with a citrus, hoppy, floral aroma, and a citrus, lemon, zesty taste.

Pale Ale (OG 1045, ABV 4.6%)
A light gold-coloured ale with floral, citrus, hoppy aromas and citrus and soft fruit taste.

Dark IPA (OG 1048, ABV 5%)
Chestnut brown in colour with spicy, fruity and citrus aromas and fruit and crisp bitterness in the taste.

Dominion SIBA

Unit Z, New House Farm, Little Laver Road, Moreton, Essex, CM5 0JE
☎ (01277) 890580
🌐 dominionbrewerycompany.com
Tours by arrangement

⊗ Dominion was established in 2012 by Andy Skene, renting the premises and Pitfield brand names from the founder of Pitfield, Martin Kemp.

Dark Mild (OG 1036, ABV 3.4%)

Pure Gold (OG 1039, ABV 3.9%)
Gold-coloured beer, initially malty with a complex bitter finish.

Sovereign IPA (OG 1066, ABV 7%)
IPA aged in cognac casks.

Yukon Gold (OG 1090, ABV 9.7%)

Brewed for the Woodbine Inn, Waltham Abbey:

Woodbine Racer (OG 1042, ABV 4.2%)

Under the Epping Brewery brand name:

Forest Bitter (OG 1036, ABV 3.7%)
A traditional amber-coloured bitter.

Under the Pitfield Brewery brand name:

Bitter (OG 1036, ABV 3.7%)
A session beer. Amber-coloured, malty and nutty with a dry bitter finish.

Lager (OG 1037, ABV 3.7%)
Cask-conditioned lager.

Chococino Dark Beer (OG 1038, ABV 4%)

Shoreditch Stout (OG 1040, ABV 4%) ◆
Chocolate and a raisin fruitiness on the nose lead to a fruity roast flavour and a sweetish finish with a little bitterness.

Eco Warrior (OG 1043, ABV 4.5%) ◆
Golden ale with a vivid, citrus hop aroma. The hop character is balanced with a delicate sweetness in the taste, followed by an increasingly bitter finish.

Red Ale (OG 1046, ABV 4.8%) ◆
Complex beer with a full, malty body and strong hop character.

1850 London Porter (OG 1048, ABV 5%) ◆
Big-tasting dark ale dominated by coffee and forest fruits. The finish is dry but not acrid.

N1 Wheat Beer (OG 1048, ABV 5%)
Brewed with a high percentage of malted wheat with classic Belgian wheat beer flavours.

1837 India Pale Ale (OG 1065, ABV 7%) ◆
A true IPA, strong in alcohol, with lots of hops, a light copper-coloured beer with floral aroma.

1792 Imperial Chocolate Stout (OG 1070, ABV 7.3%)
A traditional stout with overtones of chocolate.

Doncaster

Unit 4a, Coopers Mill Business Park, Clay Lane West, Doncaster, South Yorkshire, DN2 4QR ☎ 07770 958394 🌐 doncasterbrewery.co.uk

The brewery was launched in 2012 to coincide with the Ledger Festival, promoting all things Doncaster to help put the town firmly back on the map. All of the beers, produced on the 15-barrel plant, built from scratch by husband and wife team Ian and Alison Blaylock, are Doncaster themed. Seasonal beers: see website.

Sand House (OG 1038, ABV 3.8%)

Cheswold (OG 1042, ABV 4.2%)

First Aviation (OG 1050, ABV 5%)
A strong pale ale.

Donnington

Upper Swell, Stow-on-the-Wold, Gloucestershire, GL54 1EP
☎ (01451) 830603 🌐 donnington-brewery.com

Thomas Arkell bought a 13th-century watermill in 1827 and began brewing on the site in 1865; the waterwheel is still in use. Thomas's descendant Claude owned and ran the brewery until his death in 2007, supplying 20 outlets direct. It has now passed to Claude's cousin, James Arkell, also of Arkells Brewery, Swindon (qv). Bottle-conditioned beer is available.

BB (OG 1035, ABV 3.6%) ◆

A pleasant amber bitter with a slight hop aroma, a good balance of malt and hops in the mouth and a bitter aftertaste.

Gold (ABV 4%)
A golden ale with a citrus flavour followed by a rounded malt finish.

SBA (OG 1045, ABV 4.4%) ◆
Malt dominates over bitterness in the subtle flavour of this premium bitter, which has a hint of fruit and a dry, malty finish.

Dorking SIBA

Engine Shed, Dorking West Station Yard, Station Road, Dorking, Surrey, RH4 1HF
☎ (01306) 877988 ⊕ dorkingbrewery.com
Tours by arrangement

⊗ Dorking started brewing in 2008 and supplies an increasing number of local pubs and clubs. New fermenters were purchased in 2013 and brewing takes place at least twice a week. Seasonal beers are available.

Gold (OG 1042, ABV 3.8%)

DB Number One (OG 1045, ABV 4.2%) ◆
Hoppy best bitter with underlying orange fruit notes. Some balancing malt sweetness in the taste leads to a dry bitter finish.

Red India Ale (OG 1051, ABV 5%)

Dorset SIBA

Unit 7, Hybris Business Park, Warmwell Road, Crossways, Dorset, DT2 8BF
☎ (01305) 777515 ⊕ dbcales.com
Tours by arrangement

⊗ Founded in 1996, Dorset Brewing Company relocated from Brewers Quay, Weymouth, once the old Devenish and Groves breweries site, to new purpose-built premises in 2010. In 2008 it took over the running of Dorchester's brewpub, Tom Brown's (Goldfinch Brewery). Beers are available in local pubs and selected outlets throughout the south west. Monthly specials are brewed: see website.

Dorset Knob (OG 1039, ABV 3.9%) ◆
Complex bitter ale with strong malt and fruit flavours despite its light gravity.

Tom Brown's (OG 1039, ABV 4%)
A pale bitter with a fruity nose. The taste is bittersweet with malt, fruit and some hop. Complex aftertaste.

Jurassic (OG 1040, ABV 4.2%) ◆
Clean-tasting, easy-drinking bitter. Well balanced with lingering bitterness after moderate sweetness.

Yachtsman (OG 1048, ABV 4.7%)
A pale golden bitter-tasting beer with hints of vanilla and honey in the aroma and aftertaste.

Durdle Door (OG 1046, ABV 5%) ◆
A tawny hue and fruity aroma with a hint of pear drops and good malty undertone, joined by hops and a little roast malt in the taste. Lingering bittersweet finish.

Brewed under the Goldfinch Brewery name:

Flashman's Clout (OG 1045, ABV 4.5%)

Dorset Piddle

See Piddle

Double Top SIBA

Unit 4, Kilton Terrace, Worksop, Nottinghamshire, S80 2DQ ☎ 07973 521824
Office: the Mallard, Station Approach, Carlton Road, Worksop, Nottinghamshire, S81 7AG
Tours by arrangement

Double Top began brewing in 2011 and now uses a 2.5-barrel plant with fermenting capacity for 7.5-barrels per week. It caters for its brewery tap, the Mallard on Platform 1 of Worksop railway station, and for regional beer festivals and free houses.

Golden Arrow (OG 1038, ABV 3.9%)
A golden ale with citrus notes.

Shanghai Bitter (OG 1041, ABV 4.2%)
A light, hoppy session ale.

Adonis (OG 1042, ABV 4.3%)
A pale bitter with a dry, biscuity finish.

Treble 20 (OG 1043, ABV 4.5%)
A straw-coloured beer, hoppy and bitter.

Madhouse (OG 1055, ABV 5.2%)
A modern-style porter.

IPA (OG 1055, ABV 5.5%)
A deep golden-coloured, strong traditional IPA.

Dove Street SIBA

82 St Helens Street, Ipswich, Suffolk, IP4 2LB
☎ (01473) 211270 ⊕ dovestreetbrewery.co.uk
Shop 12-10pm daily (ask at Dove Street Inn bar)
Tours by arrangement

⊗ Dove Street began brewing in 2011 using a 2.5-barrel plant in a garage opposite the Dove Street Inn. The pub and beer festivals are supplied.

Underwood Mild (OG 1033, ABV 3.2%)
A dark, traditional mild, packed with flavour and aroma, with freshness and spice.

Bitter (OG 1038, ABV 3.7%)
A traditional bitter with a dry finish.

Incredible Taste Fantastic Clarity (OG 1041, ABV 4%)
A golden, hoppy session beer; clean, clear and crisp.

Dove Elder (OG 1042, ABV 4.1%)
Traditionally brewed speciality beer. Late hopped with Brewers Gold and the wort percolated over dried elderflower.

Thirsty Walker (OG 1047, ABV 4.6%)
A strong, well-balanced beer.

Summer Light Evening (OG 1051, ABV 5%)
Light with a bitter finish and an underlying flavour of caramel.

Old Ipswich Liquor (OG 1055, ABV 5.5%)
Aged for deep complex flavours, chocolate and liquorice notes with an in-depth long, well-rounded finish.

Dow Bridge SIBA

2-3 Rugby Road, Catthorpe, Leicestershire, LE17 6DA

☎ (01788) 869121 🌐 dowbridgebrewery.co.uk
Tours by arrangement

Dow Bridge commenced brewing in 2001 and takes its name from a local bridge where Watling Street spans the River Avon. The brewery uses English whole hops and malt with no adjuncts or additives. More than 50 outlets are supplied direct. Seasonal and bottle-conditioned beers are available: see website.

Bonum Mild (OG 1035, ABV 3.5%)
Complex dark brown, full-flavoured mild, with strong malt and roast flavours to the fore and continuing into the aftertaste, leading to a long, satisfying finish.

Acris (OG 1037, ABV 3.8%)
Classic session bitter, packed with flavour.

Centurion (OG 1039, ABV 4%)
Copper-coloured, well-rounded best bitter. Good balance of malt and hops in the flavour.

Legion (OG 1041, ABV 4.1%)
Golden hoppy ale. A good balance of malt and fruity hop on the nose and palate.

Ratae'd (OG 1041, ABV 4.3%)
Tawny-coloured, full-bodied beer with bitter hop flavours against a grainy background, leading to a long, bitter and dry aftertaste.

Dark (OG 1042, ABV 4.4%)
A strong, dark, full-bodied ale with roast malt giving hints of chocolate.

Gladiator (OG 1046, ABV 4.5%)
Ruby chestnut-coloured, well-balanced beer. Smooth and malty, but with a bitter, dry finish. Some fruit aroma and slight toffee sweetness.

Fosse Ale (OG 1046, ABV 4.8%)
Well-balanced, premium beer with caramel and burnt toffee flavours leading to a hoppy, dry finish.

Praetorian Porter (OG 1048, ABV 5%)
Dark, rich, full-bodied porter. Slightly sweet with hoppy undertones.

Onslaught (OG 1049, ABV 5.2%)
A deep ruby-coloured strong ale. A good balance of fruit and hops with rich flavours and aroma.

Downlands SIBA

Unit Z (2a), Mackley Industrial Estate, Small Dole, West Sussex, BN5 9XE
☎ (01273) 495596 🌐 downlandsbrewery.com

Previously known as SouthDowns Brewery, Downlands began brewing in 2012 using a 10-barrel plant. Beers are distributed along the south coast and to CAMRA beer festivals. Seasonal and special beers are available.

Truleigh Gold (OG 1035, ABV 3.7%)
Crisp, clean, refreshing pale golden ale with apricot, orange and citrus aromas and a dab of sweetness.

Ruskin's Ram (OG 1041, ABV 4%)
Traditional English ale with a sharp, clean, malty taste complemented by a subtle aroma with hints of vanilla and elderflower.

Pale (OG 1040, ABV 4.1%)
Each gyle is brewed with a unique hop build.

APA (Anglo Pale Ale) (OG 1045.5, ABV 4.7%)
An American-style pale ale made entirely with British ingredients.

Devils Dyke Honey Porter (OG 1050, ABV 5%)

Devils Dyke Porter (OG 1050, ABV 5%)
Well-balanced with toffee, chocolate and smoky flavours complemented by a subtle hint of marmalade.

Downton SIBA

Unit 11, Batten Road, Downton Industrial Estate, Downton, Wiltshire, SP5 3HU
☎ (01725) 513313 🌐 downtonbrewery.com
Shop Mon-Fri 9am-5pm

Downton was set up in 2003. The brewery has a 20-barrel brew length and produces around 1,500 barrels a year. Eight regular beers are produced together with speciality and experimental beers. Around 100 outlets are supplied direct. Bottle conditioned beers are available.

New Forest Ale (OG 1037, ABV 3.8%)
An amber-coloured bitter with subtle aromas leading to good hopping on the palate. Some fruit and predominant hoppiness in the aftertaste.

Quadhop (OG 1038, ABV 3.9%)
Pale golden session beer, initially hoppy on the palate with some fruit and a strong hoppiness in the aftertaste.

Elderquad (OG 1039, ABV 4%)
A pale, hoppy session beer with hints of sweetness. A subtle elderflower aroma balances the hops.

Honey Blonde (OG 1041, ABV 4.3%)
Straw-coloured golden ale, easy-drinking with initial bitterness giving way to slight sweetness and a lingering balanced aftertaste.

Nelson's Delight (ABV 4.5%)
An amber-coloured bitter full of hoppy character and a rich resinous aroma. Underlying sweetness and strength provided by the addition of navy rum.

Dark Delight (OG 1053, ABV 5.5%)
A strong dark brown best bitter, malt and roast in the aroma and on the palate initially, giving way to a balanced lingering aftertaste with noticeable hoppiness.

Chocolate Orange Delight (ABV 5.8%)
A speciality old ale with pronounced chocolate flavours. A pleasant orange addition combines perfectly.

IPA (OG 1063, ABV 6.8%)
A traditional IPA with intense floral aromas and a powerful bitterness.

Dragonfly (NEW) SIBA

George & Dragon, 183 High Street, Acton, London, W3 9DJ
☎ (020) 8992 3712 🌐 dragonflybrewery.co.uk

Brewing began in 2014 using a 10-barrel plant. The chinese-built brewing kit can produce 1,000 litres per brew. The George & Dragon is supplied along with other local outlets.

2 O'Clock Ordinary (ABV 4%)
A full-flavoured best bitter with notes of caramel and nuts.

Dark Matter (ABV 4.3%)
A rich stout with a smooth mouthfeel and dark malt flavours.

Early Doors (ABV 4.3%)

THE BREWERIES

A golden, hoppy pale ale with a crisp bitterness.

Draycott

Low Farm, 30 Mill Road, Buckden, Cambridgeshire, PE19 5SS
☎ (01480) 812404 🌐 draycottbrewery.co.uk

The brewery is located in an old farm complex and was set up by Jon and Jane Draycott in 2009. Only one-pint bottle-conditioned beers are produced.

Driftwood

Driftwood Spars Hotel, Trevaunance Cove, St Agnes, Cornwall, TR5 0RT
☎ (01872) 552428 🌐 driftwoodsparsbrewery.co.uk
Shop Mon-Fri 11am-5pm
Tours by arrangement

Brewing since 2000 on a custom-built five-barrel plant, the brewery has since expanded to incorporate additional fermentation and conditioning capacity plus a brewery shop and visitor centre with annual production now standing at 1,300 barrels. Monthly specials are produced for selected circulation only. A limited range of bottle-conditioned beers is also available.

Dek (OG 1038, ABV 3.8%)
Fruity, grassy hops on the nose lead to bitter, resinous, citrus hops and pronounced dryness in the mouth all the way through. Amber beer in the golden ale style.

Trouble & Strife (OG 1037, ABV 3.8%)
Light-drinking amber session bitter with aroma of hop fruit. Goldings and Fuggles hops provide a dominant bitter flavour balanced by gentle sweetness, hop fruit, malt and astringency.

Blue Hills Bitter (OG 1039, ABV 4%)
Medium-bodied refreshing bitter with a hoppy aroma. Flowery, grassy hops dominate the flavour to the end with gentle biscuity malt.

Red Mission (OG 1040, ABV 4%)
Tawny best bitter with fruity hops and light malt on the nose. Malt and hops create a balanced taste with bitterness running through to a dry, hoppy finish.

Montol (OG 1040, ABV 4.1%)
Grapefruit from citrus hops plus vine fruit aroma. Pronounced hop bitterness and sweet malt flavour lasting into a long finish.

Badlands Bitter (OG 1047, ABV 4.8%)
Red winter warmer, rich in sweet malt, figs and raisins balanced by hoppiness, finishing with fruit esters, bitterness and dryness.

Lou's Brew (OG 1049, ABV 5%)
Heavily-hopped golden ale with a dry and bitter finish. Light citrus, apple and pear in the aroma and flavour with some malt.

Alfie's Revenge (OG 1060, ABV 6.5%)
Rich, smooth old ale. Smoky malt, coffee and fudge flavours with fruit esters and bitter hops through to the finish.

Dronfield

c/o Wood Street Brewery, Hillsborough Hotel, Wood Street, Sheffield, South Yorkshire, S6 2UB ☎ 07966 143420

Dronfield began brewing in 2013 using spare capacity at Wood Street Brewery (qv). Different beers are brewed each month. Local pubs and beer festivals are supplied.

Citra (OG 1038, ABV 3.8%)

Amber (OG 1042, ABV 4.2%)

Topaz Pale (OG 1043, ABV 4.3%)

Drygate (NEW)

85 Drygate, Glasgow, G4 0UT
☎ (0141) 212 8810 🌐 drygate.com

Restaurant, bar and microbrewery, Drygate is a joint venture of Tennent's and Williams Bros, though operationally independent. The on-site brewery began production in 2014. A core range of keg and bottled beers has been launched. The brewery is also committed to cask-conditioned ale, but permanent cask beers have not been developed yet.

DT

Royal Standard Inn, 700 Dorchester Road, Upwey, Dorset, DT3 5LA
☎ (01305) 812558 🌐 theroyalstandardupwey.co.uk

DT Ales began brewing in 2010 to supply the pub using a one-barrel plant. No other outlets are supplied.

dt3 (ABV 3.5%)
A light, pale session ale with hoppy notes.

dt4 (ABV 4.5%)
A robust, smoky and hoppy ale.

Dukeries SIBA

Carlton Forest Distribution Centre, Unit 6, Blyth Road, Worksop, Nottinghamshire, S81 0TP ☎ 07584 305207 ✉ phil.owen@dukeriesbrewery.co.uk

Founded in 2012 and located in the heart of the Dukeries in Nottinghamshire this five-barrel plant produces six permanent ales and several seasonal beers throughout the year. The brewery tap is the Anchor Inn, Worksop.

Blonde (OG 1040, ABV 3.8%)
A strong amber session ale with a blend of tropical fruit flavours.

Baronet (OG 1039, ABV 3.9%)
Traditional chestnut-coloured bitter with good hops on the nose and bags of fruity flavours, bitter finish.

A Ray of Sunshine (OG 1041, ABV 4.2%)
A fruity beer, full of character and flavour. Tropical fruits throughout with a clean, fresh feel on the palate.

De Lovetot (OG 1041, ABV 4.2%)
A golden pale ale. Well-balanced and drinkable, with citrus fruit and hops aroma, leading to a clean, smooth, hoppy finish.

Lime Tree (OG 1043, ABV 4.4%)
A rich black porter.

Mining (OG 1043, ABV 4.5%)
A dark beer with robust, rich flavours leading to a well-balanced, dry finish.

IPA (OG 1046, ABV 4.9%)
A traditional English IPA, full of complex character.

Dunham Massey

100 Oldfield Lane, Dunham Massey, WA14 4PE
☎ (0161) 929 0663 🌐 dunhammasseybrewing.co.uk
Shop Mon-Fri 10am-5pm, Sat-Sun 11am-4pm

Opened in 2007, Dunham Massey brews traditional north-western ales using only English ingredients. The beer range is also available bottle conditioned. Around 30 outlets are supplied direct, along with the brewery tap, Costello's Bar, Altrincham. A sister brewery, Lymm (qv), opened in 2013 with Costello's Bar in Stockton Heath tied to both breweries.

Little Bollington Bitter (OG 1037, ABV 3.7%)
Straw-coloured light ale with malt and citrus fruit taste and a dry, bitter finish.

Chocolate Cherry Mild (OG 1040, ABV 3.8%)
A speciality beer with the dark chocolate, coffee and liquorice flavours of a dark mild blended with a dry, bittersweet cherry flavour.

Dunham Dark (OG 1040, ABV 3.8%)
Dark brown beer with malty aroma. Fairly sweet, with malt, some roast, hop and fruit in the taste and finish.

Dunham Light (OG 1040, ABV 3.8%)
A creamy, malty, easy-drinking, light mild.

Mildly Ginger (OG 1040, ABV 3.8%)

Big Tree Bitter (OG 1041, ABV 3.9%)
The brewery's flagship session bitter, golden in colour and full-bodied with a good balance of hops and malt.

Obelisk (OG 1040, ABV 3.9%)
Light and hoppy but not too bitter, with hints of citrus and grapefruit.

Dunham Milk Stout (OG 1051, ABV 4%)
A classic, full-bodied, sweet stout with a creamy, roast malt character. Brewed with lactose (milk sugar) because this type of sugar is not fermented into alcohol which leaves a sweet flavour in the beer.

Landlady (OG 1040, ABV 4%)
A light, refreshing, biscuity, dry ale, with a spicy hop finish.

Dunham Stout (OG 1046, ABV 4.2%)
A creamy, full-bodied dry stout, with a classic bitter, burnt, dark roast flavour.

Stamford Bitter (OG 1045, ABV 4.2%)
A golden, full-bodied bitter with a complex blend of hops giving a slightly dry finish.

Deer Beer (OG 1047, ABV 4.5%)
A clean, full-bodied, malty English ale, with a hint of toffee, and a distinct hop finish.

Cheshire IPA (OG 1047, ABV 4.7%)
A fairly strong, pale, hoppy and bitter, based on the IPAs of old.

Altrincham Pilsner (OG 1048, ABV 4.8%)
A cask-conditioned lager, light, refreshing and full of flavour.

Dunham Porter (OG 1056, ABV 5.2%)
A classic old-style English porter, creamy and full bodied.

East India Pale Ale (OG 1062, ABV 6%)
Light and hoppy.

Dunham Gold (OG 1070, ABV 7.2%)
A Belgian-style English ale. Strong, light and fruity, with a hoppy finish.

Dunscar Bridge SIBA

Dunscar Business Park, Blackburn Road, Bolton, BL7 9PQ
☎ (01204) 600713 🌐 dunscarbridge.co.uk
Tours by arrangement

Dunscar Bridge began brewing in 2009 on a 4.5-barrel plant in the Brewhouse pub in Eagley. An additional 25-barrel plant was added in 2012 in the former Dunscar bleach works, a stone's throw from the Brewhouse.

Steeplejack (OG 1039, ABV 3.8%)
A light gold-coloured beer with an aroma of hops and mature fruit and a sweet, hoppy and fruity taste.

Rialto 47 (OG 1040, ABV 3.9%)
A golden, fruity, beer with a full-bodied, hoppy taste.

Wicketkeeper (OG 1040, ABV 4%)
Amber-coloured, well-balanced and moreish best bitter.

DBB (Dunscar Best Bitter) (OG 1040, ABV 4.1%)
Dry-hopped for intensity of flavour and aroma.

Porters Black (OG 1048, ABV 5%)
Silky smooth on the palate with plummy fruit flavours.

Durham SIBA

Unit 6a, Bowburn North Industrial Estate, Bowburn, County Durham, DH6 5PF
☎ (0191) 377 1991 🌐 durhambrewery.co.uk
Shop Mon-Fri 8am-4pm, Sat 10am-2pm
Tours by arrangement

Established in 1994, Durham has a portfolio of around 40 beers, some permanent, some on rotation with new beers appearing regularly. Five litre mini-casks can be purchased in the shop or online. Bottle-conditioned beers are available and suitable for vegans.

Magus (OG 1036, ABV 3.8%)
Pale malt gives this brew its straw colour but the hops define its character, with a fruity aroma, a clean bitter mouthfeel, and a lingering dry, citrus-like finish.

John Duck (ABV 3.9%)

Apollo (OG 1040, ABV 4%)

Black Velvet (OG 1040, ABV 4%)

White Gold (OG 1040, ABV 4%)

White Amarillo (OG 1041, ABV 4.1%)

Evensong (OG 1050, ABV 5%)

Earl Soham SIBA

Meadow Works, Cross Green, Debenham, Suffolk, IP14 6RP
☎ (01728) 861213 🌐 earlsohambrewery.co.uk
Tours by arrangement

Earl Soham was set up behind the Victoria pub in 1984 and continued there until 2001 when the brewery relocated, moving again in 2013 to Debenham. The Victoria and the Station in Framlingham both sell the beers on a regular basis, as does the Brewery Tap in Ipswich. When there is spare stock, beer is supplied to local free houses and as many beer festivals as possible. 30 outlets are supplied and three pubs are owned. Seasonal and bottle-conditioned beer is available.

Gannet Mild (OG 1034, ABV 3.3%) ◆
A well-balanced mild, sweet and fruity flavour with a lingering, coffee aftertaste.

Victoria Bitter (OG 1037, ABV 3.6%) ◆
A light, fruity, amber session beer with a clean taste and a long, lingering hoppy aftertaste.

Sir Roger's Porter (OG 1042, ABV 4.2%) ◆
Roast/coffee aroma and berry fruit introduce a full-bodied porter with roast/coffee flavours. Dry roast finish.

Albert Ale (OG 1045, ABV 4.4%)
Hops dominate every aspect of this beer, but especially the finish. A fruity, astringent beer.

Brandeston Gold (OG 1045, ABV 4.5%) ◆
Popular beer brewed with local ingredients. A sharp clean flavour, malty/hoppy and heavily laden with citrus fruit. Malty finish.

Earls

Earl of Essex, 25 Danbury Street, Islington, London, N1 8LE
☎ (020) 7424 5828 🌐 earlofessex.net

Brewing began in 2013 using a four-barrel plant.

Earl (ABV 3.8%) ◆
Light-drinking bitter with a little citrus character and a malty sweetness balanced by a trace of bitterness.

East London SIBA

Unit 45, Fairways Business Centre, Lammas Road, London, E10 7QB ☎ 07900 288873
🌐 eastlondonbrewing.com

⊗ The East London Brewing Company is a 10-barrel microbrewery run by a husband-and-wife team. It has been producing ales for pubs, bars, restaurants and off-licences since 2011.

Orchid (OG 1040, ABV 3.6%) ◆
Black mild with traces of vanilla in the aroma and flavour with dark roast notes and a little fruitiness.

ELB Pale Ale (OG 1042, ABV 4%) ◆
Dark gold beer with a fruity aroma and a slightly citrus marmalade character in the flavour. Lingering bitter finish.

Foundation Bitter (OG 1044, ABV 4.2%) ◆
Hoppy brown best bitter with pronounced bitterness. It is balanced by a little fudgy maltiness and a touch of blackcurrant.

Nightwatchman (OG 1046, ABV 4.5%) ◆
Sweet caramelised fruit diminishes in this brown beer's aftertaste, which is complex with a hint of treacle and some dryness.

Jamboree (OG 1048, ABV 4.8%) ◆
Golden beer with lychee and caramelised orange and some peppery hop in the flavour. Finish is bitter and slightly dry.

Quadrant Oatmeal Stout (OG 1063, ABV 5.8%)
A smooth stout with a silky mouthfeel, rich dark fruit flavour and hints of coffee.

Eastwood

See Barge & Barrel

Eccleshall

See Slater's

Eden SIBA

Brougham Hall, Brougham, Cumbria, CA10 2DE
☎ (01768) 210565 🌐 edenbrewery.com

Set up in 2011, Eden Brewery is run by Jason Hill and Stephen Mitchell. The five-barrel brewery is located in the Old Brewery at historic Brougham Hall and has the capacity to brew 45 barrels per week.

Best (OG 1039, ABV 3.8%)
A well-balanced traditional ale. Light chestnut in colour with subtle character and flavour.

Fuggle (OG 1039, ABV 3.8%)
A single malt, single hop pale ale.

Dark Knight (OG 1040, ABV 4%) ◆
Traditional north western dark mild; good balance of fruit and gentle roast flavours, lasting through to the finish.

Gold (OG 1042, ABV 4.2%) ◆
Gentle fruity and honey aromas to start, leading to a well-balanced sweet beer with a lasting hoppy finish.

First Emperor (OG 1046, ABV 4.6%) ◆
Fruity beer with balanced malt and hops and a hint of butterscotch combining to a rich bitter finish.

Eden St Andrews SIBA

Main Street, Guardbridge, KY16 0UU
🌐 edenbrewerystandrews.com
Shop Mon-Fri 10am-9pm, Sat 10am-4pm
Tours by arrangement

◎Established in 2012 using a five-barrel plant in part of the former Guardbridge paper mills. Bottle-conditioned beer is available.

St Andrews Blonde (OG 1040, ABV 3.8%)

19th (OG 1041, ABV 3.9%)

Clock Brew (OG 1045, ABV 4.3%)

1882 Lager (OG 1048, ABV 4.5%)

Seggie Porter (OG 1053, ABV 5.5%)

Elephant School

See Brentwood

Elgood's SIBA IFBB

North Brink Brewery, Wisbech, Cambridgeshire, PE13 1LW
☎ (01945) 583160 🌐 elgoods-brewery.co.uk
Shop Tue-Thu 11.30am-4.30pm (May-Sep)
Tours by arrangement

⊗ The North Brink brewery was established in 1795. Owned by the Elgood family since 1878, the fifth generation are now involved in running the business. The brewery has approximately 30 tied pubs within a 50-mile radius of Wisbech. Seasonal beers: see website.

Black Dog (OG 1036.8, ABV 3.6%) ◆
Black red mild with liquorice and chocolate. Dry roasty finish.

Cambridge Bitter (OG 1037.8, ABV 3.8%) ◆
Fruit and malt on the nose with increasing hops and balancing malt on the palate. Dry finish.

Golden Newt (OG 1041.5, ABV 4.1%) ◆
Golden ale with floral hops and sulphur aroma. Floral hops and a fruity presence on a bittersweet background lead to a short, muted hoppy and fruity finish.

EP (OG 1043.8, ABV 4.3%)
A premium robust ale with an aroma of hops and malt.

Black Eagle Imperial Stout (OG 1087, ABV 8.7%) ◆
Raisins and soft fruit complement roast malt in this warming dark ruby stout. Bittersweet conclusion.

Elixir

c/o Alechemy Brewing Ltd, Unit 2c, Young Square, Brucefield Industrial Estate, Livingston, West Lothian, EH54 9BX ☎ 07760 330122 🌐 elixirbrew.com

Since 2012 avid Aussie home brewer Ben Bullen has brewed his Elixir beers at the Alechemy brewery using large quantities of New World hops with a focus on the best of Australian and New Zealand varieties. Ben strives to produce unique beers often with the addition of unusual ingredients.

Elland SIBA

Units 3-5, Heathfield Industrial Estate, Heathfield Street, Elland, West Yorkshire, HX5 9AE ☎ (01422) 377677 🌐 ellandbrewery.co.uk
Tours by arrangement

Originally formed in 2002 as Eastwood & Sanders by the amalgamation of the Barge & Barrel and West Yorkshire Breweries, the company was renamed Elland in 2006 to reinforce its links with the town. The brewery has a capacity of 50 barrels per week. Seasonal and special beers: see website.

Bargee (OG 1038, ABV 3.8%) ◆
Amber, creamy session bitter. Fruity, hoppy aroma and taste complemented by a bitter edge in the finish.

Best Bitter (OG 1041, ABV 4%) ◆
Creamy, yellow, hoppy ale with hints of citrus fruits. Pleasantly strong bitter aftertaste.

Beyond the Pale (OG 1042, ABV 4.2%) ◆
Gold-coloured, robust, creamy beer with ripe aromas of hops and fruit. Bitterness predominates in the mouth and leads to a dry, fruity and hoppy aftertaste.

Eden (OG 1042, ABV 4.2%) ◆
A yellow, fruity, hoppy, creamy bitter. Citrus fruit with assertively bitter taste to finish.

Nettlethrasher (OG 1044, ABV 4.4%) ◆
Grainy amber-coloured beer. A rounded nose with some fragrant hop notes followed by a mellow nutty and fruity taste and a dry finish.

1872 Porter (OG 1065, ABV 6.5%) ◆
Creamy, full-flavoured porter. Rich liquorice flavours with a hint of chocolate from roast malt. A soft but satisfying aftertaste of bittersweet roast and malt.

Elliswood SIBA

Unit 3, Southways Industrial Estate, Coventry Road, Hinckley, Leicestershire, LE10 0NJ ☎ 07717 662139 🌐 theelliswoodbrewery.co.uk

Tracy Ellis and Phil Woodward began brewing in 2013 using a David Porter 5.5-barrel system with a capacity to brew twice weekly.

Conny Quaffer (OG 1041, ABV 4.1%)
A golden-coloured beer with a crisp, clean biscuit taste and a fine blend of three hops.

Barrel of Laughs (OG 1042, ABV 4.2%)
A copper-coloured beer with a fine balance of hops, giving a spicy vanilla undertone. Slight bitterness all the way through with a sweet, pleasant aftertaste.

Just One More (OG 1042, ABV 4.2%)
A citrus beer with blackberry and grapefruit undertones.

Nelsons Right Arm (OG 1044, ABV 4.5%)
A deep dark red-coloured beer with heavy hints of autumn fruits.

Legless (OG 1048, ABV 4.9%)
Gold-coloured, easy-drinking but full-bodied beer with undertones of blackberry and spice.

Last Porter Call (OG 1051, ABV 5.1%)
A modern robust porter with depth and complexity. A malty palate and spicy, earthy aroma give a subtle almond taste.

Shipwrecked (OG 1054, ABV 5.4%)
A bronze-coloured beer, crisp and dry with a smooth, clean hoppy taste and a slight lemon aroma.

Elmtree SIBA

Snetterton Brewery, Unit 10, Oakwood Industrial Estate, Harling Road, Snetterton, Norfolk, NR16 2JU ☎ (01953) 887065 🌐 elmtreebeers.co.uk
Shop Mon-Wed & Sat 11am-4pm
Tours by arrangement

Elmtree was established in 2007 using a five-barrel plant and moved in 2008 to new premises. 120 outlets are supplied direct. All beers are available in (vegan) bottle-conditioned form.

Burston's Cuckoo (OG 1038, ABV 3.8%)
A feast of floral hops with a hint of citrus, rounding off into a refreshingly long, dry finish.

Bitter (OG 1041, ABV 4.2%)
A well-balanced, copper-coloured crisp beer, the early malt notes give way to a distinctively complex hop finish.

Mad Maudie (OG 1044, ABV 4.5%)
A clear fresh ale. The unusual hop combination imparts a light hint of white wine.

Norfolk's 80 Shilling Ale (OG 1044, ABV 4.5%)
A Norfolk take on the tradition Scottish style of malty best bitters.

Dark Horse (OG 1050, ABV 5%) ◆
A roast, slightly salty aroma and matching initial taste introduce this coal black stout. The roast notes are aided by a fruity, prune-like background. Increasingly malty finish.

Golden Pale Ale (OG 1048, ABV 5%)
A pale ale in the traditional style that is initially malty and delicately bittered. The long dry biscuit finish is enhanced by the subtle citrus aromas.

THE BREWERIES

Nightlight Mild (OG 1057, ABV 5.7%) ♦
A heavy mix of liquorice, roast and malt infuses aroma and taste. The heavy character is lightened by a sweet, spicy, slowly-developing aftertaste.

Elveden

The Courtyard, Elveden Estate, Elveden, Thetford, Norfolk, IP24 3TA
☎ (01842) 878922

Elveden is a five-barrel brewery based on the estate of Lord Iveagh, a member of the ennobled branch of the Guinness family. The brewery is run by Frances Moore, daughter of Brendan Moore at Iceni Brewery (qv) and produces three ales: Elveden Stout (ABV 5%) and Elveden Ale (ABV 5.2%), which are mainly bottled in stoneware bottles. The third is Charter Ale (ABV 10%) to mark the celebrations for the award of a Royal Charter for Harwich in 1604. The beer is available in cask and bottle-conditioned versions. The phone number listed is shared with Iceni. The majority of sales take place through the farm shop, adjacent to the brewery.

Empire SIBA

The Old Boiler House, Unit 33, Upper Mills, Slaithwaite, Huddersfield, West Yorkshire, HD7 5HA
☎ (01484) 847343 🌐 empirebrewing.com
Tours by arrangement

Empire Brewing was set up 2006 in a mill on the bank of the scenic Huddersfield Narrow Canal, close to the centre of Slaithwaite. In 2011 the brewery upgraded from a five-barrel to a 10-barrel plant. Beers are supplied to local free houses and through independent specialist beer agencies and wholesalers. Seasonal and bottle-conditioned beers are also available.

Golden Warrior (OG 1039.5, ABV 3.8%)
Pale bitter, quite fruity with a sherbet aftertaste, moderate bitterness.

Strikes Back (OG 1041, ABV 4%)
Pale golden session bitter with a hoppy aroma and good hop and malt balance with a citrus flavour, light on the palate.

Valour (OG 1042.5, ABV 4.2%)

Longbow (OG 1043, ABV 4.3%)

Imperium (OG 1050, ABV 5.1%)

Emsworth

Rear of 16 West Street, Emsworth, Hampshire, PO10 7DY ☎ 07717 510294
🌐 theemsworthbrewery.co.uk

Michael and Hilary Bolt began brewing in 2012 on a 2.5-barrel plant, obtained from Oban Ales, in a shed behind an antiques shop in Emsworth. Seasonal beer is also available.

Slipper (OG 1039, ABV 3.9%)

Fairfield (OG 1041, ABV 4.1%)

Wayfarer (OG 1041, ABV 4.1%)

Ennerdale SIBA

Croasdale Farm Barn, Ennerdale, Cumbria, CA23 3AT
☎ (01946) 861755 🌐 ennerdalebrewery.co.uk
Tours by arrangement

Ennerdale began brewing in 2010. This 10-barrel brewery is situated in a converted barn in the village of Croasdale overlooking the Ennerdale Valley. All the beers are produced using the brewery's own source of spring water. Beers are distributed largely in West Cumbria but also into the Lake District more widely.

Blonde (OG 1039, ABV 3.8%) ♦
A sweet, fruity, light-coloured beer with gentle bitterness.

Black Sail Bitter (OG 1040, ABV 3.9%) ♦
The roasted malt underpins this tawny, drying, hoppy bitter.

Darkest (OG 1044, ABV 4.2%) ♦
Sweet, roasty, black mild with a fruity hoppy flavour.

Wild Ennerdale (OG 1043, ABV 4.2%)
Golden amber in colour, with a good hop aroma and well-rounded bitterness.

Enville SIBA

Coxgreen, Hollies Lane, Enville, DY7 5LG
☎ (01384) 873728 🌐 envilleales.com
Tours by arrangement

Enville Brewery is sited on a picturesque Victorian, Grade II-listed farm complex, using natural well water, traditional steam brewing and a reed and willow effluent plant. Enville Ale is infused with honey and is from a 19th-century recipe for beekeeper's ale passed down from the former proprietor's great-great aunt. Seasonal beers: see website.

LPA (Light Pale Ale) (OG 1039, ABV 4%)
Traditional session bitter; dry and golden with a mellow, hoppy flavour.

Nailmaker Mild (OG 1041, ABV 4%)
A well-defined hop aroma and underlying sweetness give way to a dry finish.

Simpkiss (OG 1039, ABV 4%)

Cherry Blonde (OG 1042, ABV 4.2%)
A light blonde bitter, delicately infused with essence of cherry to produce a Belgian-style fruit beer, which has a bitter finish and is dry, hoppy and refreshing.

Saaz (OG 1042, ABV 4.2%) ♦
Golden lager-style beer. Lager bite but with more taste and lasting bitterness. The malty aroma is late arriving but the bitter finish, balanced by fruit and hops, compensates.

White (OG 1041, ABV 4.2%) ♦
Yellow-coloured with a malt, hops and fruit aroma. Hoppy but sweet finish.

Ale (OG 1044, ABV 4.5%) ♦
Sweet malty aroma and taste, honey becomes apparent before bitterness finally dominates.

Old Porter (OG 1044, ABV 4.5%) ♦
Black with a creamy head and sulphurous aroma. Sweet and fruity start with touches of spice. Good balance between sweet and bitter, but hops dominate the finish.

Ginger Beer (OG 1045, ABV 4.6%) ♦
Golden bright with gently gingered tangs. A drinkable beer with no acute flavours but a satisfying aftertaste of sweet hoppiness.

Epping

See Dominion

Evan Evans SIBA

The New Brewery, 1 Rhosmaen Street, Llandeilo, Carmarthenshire, SA19 6LU
☎ (01558) 824455 🌐 evan-evans.com
Shop Mon-Fri 10am-4pm
Tours by arrangement

Evan Evans opened in 2004. Brewing capacity is now 8,000 barrels per annum. Eight pubs are owned. It is Wales' first Soil Association organic-approved brewery. In 2009 the brewery bought Archers Brewery of Swindon's brands and now brew all of Archer's regular and seasonal ales.

BB (OG 1036, ABV 3.6%)
An easy-drinking best bitter. Malty with a clean hop palate.

Cwrw (OG 1043, ABV 4.2%)

Warrior (OG 1046, ABV 4.6%)

Under the Archer's Brewery name:

Golden Ale (OG 1040, ABV 4%)

ASB (OG 1041, ABV 4.1%)

Empire (OG 1047, ABV 4.7%)

Evening Star

Olde England Pub, 113 Corporation Street, St Helens, Merseyside, WA10 1SX ☎ 07754 730589 🌐 1854pub.com

Set up in a room at the rear of the Olde England pub in St Helens, the brewery is named after the last steam locomotive to be built for British Railways. Four core beers are brewed for the pub plus one changing 'novelty' beer.

Evening Star (OG 1037, ABV 3.7%)
A hoppy session bitter.

Sans Pareil (OG 1045, ABV 4.5%)

George Stephenson IPA (OG 1058, ABV 5.8%)

The Rocket (OG 1058, ABV 6.5%)

Everards SIBA IFBB

Castle Acres, Narborough, Leicestershire, LE19 1BY
☎ (0116) 201 4100 🌐 everards.co.uk
Shop Mon-Fri 10am-5pm, Sat 10am-2pm
Tours by arrangement

Established by William Everard in 1849, Everards brewery remains an independent family-owned company. Four core ales are brewed as well as a range of seasonal beers – see website for more details. Everards owns a pub estate of more than 170 tenanted houses throughout the Midlands.

Beacon Bitter (OG 1036, ABV 3.8%) ◆
Light, refreshing, well-balanced pale amber bitter in the Burton style.

Sunchaser Blonde (OG 1038, ABV 4%) ◆
A golden brew with a sweet, lightly-hopped character. Some citrus notes to the fore in a quick finish that becomes increasingly bitter.

Tiger (OG 1041, ABV 4.2%) ◆
A mid-brown, well-balanced best bitter crafted for broad appeal, benefiting from a long, bittersweet finish.

Original (OG 1050, ABV 5.2%) ◆
Full-bodied, mid-brown strong bitter with a pleasant rich, grainy mouthfeel. Well-balanced flavours, with malt slightly to the fore, merging into a long, satisfying finish.

Evesham SIBA

17 Oat Street, Evesham, Worcestershire, WR11 4PJ
☎ (01386) 443628 ✉ eveshambrewery@aol.com

Evesham Brewery is located in the former Green Dragon pub. Beer is produced as required by demand from the brewery's own pub. Other local outlets are supplied.

Exe Valley SIBA

Land Farm, Silverton, Exeter, Devon, EX5 4HF
☎ (01392) 860406 🌐 exevalleybrewery.co.uk

Exe Valley was established as Barron's Brewery in 1984. The brewery is located in a converted barn overlooking the Exe Valley and Dartmoor hills. Locally-sourced malt and English hops are used, along with the brewery's own spring water. Around 100 outlets are supplied within a 45-mile radius of the brewery. Beers are also available nationally via wholesalers. Seasonal beers: see website.

Bitter (OG 1036, ABV 3.7%) ◆
Mid-brown bitter, pleasantly fruity with underlying malt through the aroma, taste and finish.

Barron's Hopsit (OG 1040, ABV 4.1%) ◆
Straw-coloured beer with strong hop aroma, hop and fruit flavour and a bitter hop finish.

Dob's Best Bitter (OG 1040, ABV 4.1%) ◆
Light brown bitter. Malt and fruit predominate in the aroma and taste with a dry, bitter, fruity finish.

Devon Glory (OG 1046, ABV 4.7%)
Mid-brown, fruity-tasting beer with a sweet, fruity finish.

Mr Sheppard's Crook (OG 1046, ABV 4.7%) ◆
Smooth, full-bodied, mid-brown beer with a malty-fruit nose and a sweetish palate leading to a bitter, dry finish.

Exeter Old Bitter (OG 1046, ABV 4.8%) ◆
Mid-brown old ale with a rich fruity taste and slightly earthy aroma and bitter finish.

It's Phil's Ale (OG 1046, ABV 4.8%)
A deep golden beer with a big hop flavour.

Winter Glow (OG 1056, ABV 6%)

Exeter SIBA

Unit 1, Cowley Bridge Road, Exeter, Devon, EX4 4NX
☎ (01392) 823013 🌐 exeterbrewery.co.uk

Exeter Brewery, formerly Topsham & Exminster, began brewing in 2003. In 2012 the brewery moved to a larger site in Exeter.

Lighterman (OG 1036, ABV 3.6%)
A light copper-coloured ale with a fruity malt flavour and a traditional bitter finish.

Avocet (OG 1038.5, ABV 3.9%)

THE BREWERIES

A straw-coloured organic beer with a refreshing, slightly citrus taste and hoppy aroma.

Fraid Not (OG 1040, ABV 4%)
A golden hoppy beer. A distinct clean citrus bitterness and lasting dry finish.

Ferryman (OG 1041, ABV 4.2%)
Classic copper-coloured session ale. Well-balanced, sweet, warm malt flavour. Crisp, bitter finish.

County Best (OG 1045, ABV 4.6%)
Premium strength best bitter with a rich malt, fruity flavour and a smooth bittersweet finish.

Darkness (OG 1050, ABV 5.1%)
Well-balanced stout with complex chocolate and coffee flavours.

Exmoor SIBA

Golden Hill Brewery, Wiveliscombe, Somerset, TA4 2NY
(01984) 623798 exmoorales.co.uk
Tours by arrangement

Somerset's largest brewery was founded in 1980 in the old Hancock's brewery, which closed in 1959. Around 250 outlets in the south west are supplied and others nationwide via wholesalers and pub chains. Seasonal beers: see website. Exmoor are due to move to new and larger premises in Old Brewery Road, Wiveliscombe, only 50 yards or so from their current location.

Ale (OG 1039, ABV 3.8%)
A pale to mid-brown, medium-bodied session bitter. A mixture of malt and hops in the aroma and taste lead to a hoppy, bitter aftertaste.

Fox (OG 1043, ABV 4.2%)
A mid brown-coloured beer. A slight maltiness on the tongue is followed by a burst of hops with a lingering bittersweet aftertaste.

Gold (OG 1045, ABV 4.5%)
A yellow/golden best bitter with a good balance of malt and fruity hop on the nose and palate. The sweetness follows through an ultimately more bitter finish.

Stag (OG 1050, ABV 5.2%)
A pale brown beer, with a malty taste and aroma, and a bitter finish.

Beast (OG 1066, ABV 6.6%)
A dark brew with the characteristics of a strong porter. A blend of malt and hops with a complex, long aftertaste.

Facer's

A8-9, Ashmount Enterprise Park, Aber Road, Flint, CH6 5QT 07713 566370 facers.co.uk
Tours by arrangement

Facer's is the oldest existing brewery in Flintshire. Ex-Boddington head brewer Dave Facer ran the brewery single handed from its launch in 2003 until he took on his first employee in 2008 and expanded to twice the floor space. Around 80 outlets are supplied.

Mountain Mild (OG 1035, ABV 3.3%)

Clwyd Gold (OG 1034, ABV 3.5%)
Clean tasting session bitter, mid-brown in colour with a full mouthfeel. The malty flavours are accompanied by increasing hoppiness in the bitter finish.

Flintshire Bitter (OG 1036, ABV 3.7%)
Well-balanced session bitter with a full mouthfeel. Some fruitiness in aroma and taste with increasing hoppy bitterness in the dry finish.

Abbey Original (OG 1038, ABV 4%)

Abbey Red (OG 1038, ABV 4%)

North Star Porter (OG 1040, ABV 4%)
Dark, smooth, porter-style beer with good roast notes and hints of coffee and chocolate. Some initial sweetness and caramel flavours followed by a hoppy bitter aftertaste.

Sunny Bitter (OG 1040, ABV 4.2%)
An amber beer with a dry taste. The hop aroma continues into the taste where some faint fruit notes are also present. Lasting dry finish.

DHB (Dave's Hoppy Beer) (OG 1041, ABV 4.3%)
A dry-hopped version of Splendid Ale with some sweet flavours also coming through in the mainly hoppy, bitter taste.

This Splendid Ale (OG 1041, ABV 4.3%)
Refreshing tangy best bitter, yellow in colour with a sharp hoppy, bitter taste. Good citrus fruit undertones with hints of grapefruit throughout.

Landslide (OG 1047, ABV 4.9%)
Full-flavoured, complex premium bitter with tangy orange marmalade fruitiness in aroma and taste. Long-lasting hoppy flavours throughout.

Fakir

c/o 30 Harford Street, Norwich, NR1 3AY 07713 789085 fakirbrewery.com

Fakir began brewing in 2010 using spare capacity at several breweries based in Norfolk. Cask-conditioned beer is supplied to local pubs and Indian restaurants, bottle-conditioned beer is also available. Further beers are planned.

Old Fakir's Gold (OG 1048, ABV 5.1%)
A golden ale with a delicate citrus grapefruit aroma and a lasting bitterness.

Fallen (NEW)

Station House, Kippen, Stirlingshire, FK8 3JA 07507 862167 fallenbrewing.co.uk

Fallen began brewing in 2014 using a 10-barrel plant. Seasonal and bottle-conditioned beers are available.

1703 (ABV 3.9%)
A classic amber-coloured session beer with a citrus bite and warming caramel toffee backbone.

Odyssey (ABV 4.1%)
An easy-drinking blonde ale with a fruity aroma and slightly spicy, citrus flavour.

Dragonfly (ABV 4.6%)
An amber-coloured ale with a floral/citrus hop aroma. The initial flavour hit is resinous, citrus and pine followed by a rich biscuit and caramel maltiness, finishing with a lingering bitterness.

Blackhouse (ABV 5%)
A complex, deep brown, smoky porter with a subtle fruity hop flavour.

Grapevine (ABV 5.4%)
A pale ale with an almost vinous flavour and aroma. Dominant flavours are floral, citrus, tropical, fruity and bitter.

Fallen Angel

See Broxbourne

Falstaff

24 Society Place, Normanton, Derby, DE23 6UH
07947 242710 falstaffbrewery.co.uk

Attached to the Falstaff freehouse, the brewery dates from 1999 but was refurbished and re-opened in 2003 under new management. Themed special beers are produced all year round, including exclusive specials for the Babington Arms, Derby.

3 Faze (OG 1040, ABV 3.8%)
Light gold in colour with a malt and honey nose. Smooth malt flavours lead to a clean, balanced malt and hop finish.

Fist Full of Hops (OG 1044, ABV 4.5%)
An amber ale with lots of hop.

Phoenix (OG 1045, ABV 4.7%)
A smooth, tawny ale with fruit and hop, joined by plenty of malt in the mouth. A subtle sweetness produces a drinkable ale.

Smiling Assassin (OG 1050, ABV 5.2%)
A copper-coloured beer with sweet malt flavours.

Faringdon

1 Park Road, Faringdon, Oxfordshire, SN7 7BP
(01367) 241480 swanfaringdon@yahoo.co.uk
Tours by arrangement

Faringdon opened in 2010 using a one-barrel plant; brewing on a larger-scale began in 2011. The beers are brewed by Stuart Bruton and supplied to the brewery tap, the Swan. Occasional and bottle-conditioned ales are available.

Folly Ale (OG 1039.5, ABV 4%)
A traditional English bitter. Burnt gold in colour with a sweet aroma but no lingering aftertaste.

Farmer's

See Maldon

Farriers Arms

The Forstal, Mersham, Kent, TN25 6NU
(01233) 720444 thefarriersarms.com
Tours by arrangement

Brewing commenced in 2010 in this brewpub owned by a consortium of villagers.

Farriers 1606 (OG 1038, ABV 3.7%)

Fat Cat

Fat Cat Brewery Tap, 98-100 Lawson Road, Norwich, NR3 4LF
(01603) 788508 fatcatbrewery.co.uk
Tours by arrangement

Fat Cat Brewery was founded by the owner of the Fat Cat free house in Norwich. Brewing started in 2005 at the Fat Cat's sister pub, the Fat Cat Brewery Tap, under the supervision of former Woodforde's owner Ray Ashworth. Seasonal beers, bottle-conditioned beers and occasional one-off brews are also available.

Bitter (OG 1038, ABV 3.8%)
Gold-coloured with a grapefruit and sulphur aroma. A mix of malt, citrus and hop with a dry bitter ending.

Hell Cat (OG 1040, ABV 4.1%)
Clementines and hops anchor this lively but full-bodied brew. A strong bittersweet but satisfying finale.

Top Cat (OG 1047, ABV 4.7%)
A complex malt, caramel, and blackberry aroma leads into a similarly creamy beginning which continues to a richly satisfying finish.

Marmalade Cat (OG 1055, ABV 5.5%)
Rich and complex with malt and marmalade dominating every corner. Copper-coloured and grainy with a solid bitter finale.

Fat Pig (NEW)

2 John Street, Exeter, EX1 1BL
(01392) 437217 fatpig-exeter.co.uk

Brewing commenced in 2013 using a 2.5-barrel plant to supply the Fat Pig and its sister pub the Rusty Bike in Exeter. Seasonal beers are available.

Pigasus Brown Ale (OG 1039, ABV 3.9%)

Pigmalion Bitter (OG 1042, ABV 4.2%)

John Street Ale (OG 1043, ABV 4.3%)

Long Pig Weissbeer (ABV 4.3%)

Ham 69 ESB (OG 1048, ABV 4.8%)

Phat Nancys IPA (OG 1051, ABV 4.8%)

Steam Hammer American IPA (ABV 4.8%)

Felinfoel SIBA

Farmers Row, Felinfoel, Llanelli, Carmarthenshire, SA14 8LB
(01554) 773357 felinfoel-brewery.com
Shop 9am-4pm daily
Tours by arrangement

Founded in the 1830s, the company is still family-owned and is now the oldest brewery in Wales. The present buildings are Grade II*-listed and were built in the 1870s. It supplies cask ale to half its 84 houses, though some use top pressure dispense, and to approximately 350 free trade outlets.

Best Bitter (OG 1038, ABV 3.8%)
A well-balanced beer, with a low aroma. Bittersweet initially with an increasing moderate bitterness.

Double Dragon (OG 1042, ABV 4.2%)
This pale brown beer has a malty, fruity aroma. The taste is also malt and fruit with a background hop presence throughout. A malty and fruity finish.

Fell

Unit 27, Moor Lane Business Park, Flookburgh, Cumbria, LA11 7NG
(01539) 558980 fellbrewery.co.uk

Fell Brewery was founded in 2012 by homebrewer Tim Bloomer and friend Andrew Carter, brewing beers inspired by their travels in the USA and Belgium.

Patriot Wheat (OG 1043, ABV 4.5%)

Robust Porter (OG 1051, ABV 4.8%)

Progressive Pale (OG 1051, ABV 5.1%)

Tinder Box IPA (OG 1059, ABV 6.3%)

Fellows

2 Leopold Walk, Cottenham, Cambrideshire, CB24 8XS
☎ (01954) 250262 🌐 fellowsbrewery.co.uk

⊗ Fellows began production in 2010 though brewer Mark Burton had been developing recipes for a year or so before. Five regular beers are available with plans for a series of special ales. Beers are increasingly visible in the local free trade.

Cambridge Fellow (OG 1038, ABV 3.8%)
A golden session ale, light and clean-tasting.

Gulping Fellow (OG 1042, ABV 4.2%)
A dry bitter finish complements the spicy hop character of this well-balanced best bitter.

Burton Snatch (OG 1048, ABV 4.8%)
Blonde ale with a citrus aroma and refreshing mouthfeel. A hint of wet leather completes the finish.

Jolly Fellows (OG 1050, ABV 5%)
Full-bodied, clean-tasting premium bitter.

Clever Fellow (OG 1052, ABV 5.2%)
Malt loaf and toffee flavours combine with back of the tongue bitterness to achieve a balanced richness.

Felstar

Felsted Vineyards, Crix Green, Felsted, Essex, CM6 3JT
☎ (01245) 361504 🌐 felstarbrewery.co.uk
Shop 10am-dusk daily
Tours by arrangement

⊗ Felstar Brewery opened in 2001 with a five-barrel plant based in the old bonded warehouse of the Felsted Vineyard. A small number of outlets are supplied. Seasonal and bottle-conditioned beers are available.

Felstar (OG 1036, ABV 3.6%)
Amber-coloured session bitter with an aroma of traditional English hops and a long bitter finish.

Summer Light (OG 1038, ABV 3.8%)

Old Essex (OG 1039, ABV 3.9%)

Crix Forest (OG 1040, ABV 4%)
A toasty dark mild with hints of berries, a hoppy nose and a bitter finish.

Lightburst (OG 1040, ABV 4%)

Witchcraft (OG 1044, ABV 4.4%)

Good Knight (OG 1050, ABV 5%)
A dark porter with gentle smoky and spicy flavours balancing the bitter hoppiness.

Hoppy Hen (OG 1050, ABV 5%)
An old ale with rich malty and spicy flavours and strong hoppy nose and bitter finish from American hops.

Fernandes

5 Avison Yard, Kirkgate, Wakefield, West Yorkshire, WF1 1UA
☎ (01924) 291709 🌐 ossett-brewery.co.uk
Tours by arrangement

Opened in 1997 housed in a 19th-century malthouse, Ossett Brewing Company purchased the brewery and tap in 2007 but independent brewing continues. The tap sells Fernandes and Ossett beers as well as guest ales; the former are more widely available through Ossett's supply chain.

Malt Shovel Mild (OG 1038, ABV 3.8%)
A dark, full-bodied, malty mild with roast malt and chocolate flavours, leading to a lingering, dry, malty finish.

Strawdog (ABV 3.8%)
A well-hopped session ale.

Triple O (OG 1041, ABV 3.9%)
A light, refreshing, hoppy session beer with a lingering fruity finish.

Ale to the Tsar (OG 1042, ABV 4.1%)
A pale, smooth, well-balanced beer with some sweetness leading to a nutty, malty and satisfying aftertaste.

Centennial (OG 1043, ABV 4.1%)
Light-coloured extremely hoppy beer with a long, lingering aftertaste.

Cascade Torrent (ABV 4.6%)

Black Voodoo (ABV 5.1%)

FILO Brewery SIBA

The Old Town Brewery, Torfield Cottage, 8 Old London Road, Hastings, East Sussex, TN34 3HA
☎ (01424) 420212 🌐 filobrewing.co.uk
Tours by arrangement

⊗ The brewery at the First In Last Out public house was established in 1985, with the current owners taking over in 1988. In 2011 the brewery relocated two minutes' walk away, remaining in the Old Town. The First In Last Out (FILO) is still supplied direct together with pubs throughout Sussex and Kent.

Mike's Mild (OG 1035, ABV 3.4%)

Crofters (OG 1037, ABV 3.8%)

Churches Pale Ale (OG 1042, ABV 4.2%)

Old Town Tom (OG 1044, ABV 4.5%)

Gold (OG 1050, ABV 4.8%)

Firebird (NEW) SIBA

Old Rudgwick Brickworks, Lynwick Street, Rudgwick, West Sussex, RH12 3DH
☎ (01403) 823180 🌐 firebirdbrewing.co.uk
Shop Mon-Fri 8am-5pm (7pm Fri), Sat 10am-3pm

Firebird began commercial brewing in 2013 using a 10-barrel plant. Seasonal beers are brewed as are various continental beer styles.

Heritage XX (ABV 4%)
A fresh, hoppy, full-bodied best bitter.

Paleface APA (ABV 5.2%)
A zesty, aromatic American pale ale.

Firebrick SIBA

Unit 10, Blaydon Business Centre, Cowen Road, Blaydon, NE21 5TX 🌐 firebrickbrewery.com

Firebrick began brewing in 2013 on a 2.5-barrel plant from the former Bull Lane Brewery in Sunderland. Expansion is planned. Beers are available at selected pubs in Tyne & Wear.

Blaydon Brick (OG 1038, ABV 3.8%)

Coalface (OG 1039, ABV 3.9%)

Elder Statesman (OG 1043, ABV 3.9%)

Firefly

Firefly, 54 Lowesmoor, Worcester, WR1 2SE
(01905) 616996 thefirefly@hotmail.co.uk

Firefly Brewing was established in 2012 using a 0.5-barrel plant. At present only the pub is supplied.

Pale Ale (OG 1042, ABV 4.2%)
An American-style IPA.

Black Colt (OG 1062, ABV 6.5%)
A hoppy black ale with citrus aromas and a lingering bitter finish with a hint of chocolate.

Firehouse (NEW)

Unit 8a, Harrison Way, Dowland Business Park, Manby, Lincolnshire, LN11 8UX 07956 405089
firehouse-brewery.co.uk

Firehouse began brewing in 2014 using a 0.5-barrel plant. It was founded by Jason Allen, a former home brewer. Further beers are planned.

Wobbly Weasel (ABV 4.9%)

Tetford Country Bitter (ABV 5.1%)

Firestorm

See Wharfe Bank

First Chop SIBA

Unit 3, Trinity Row, Trinity Way, Salford, M3 5EN
07970 241398 firstchopbrewingarm.com

First Chop Brewing Arm began brewing in 2012 at the Outstanding Brewery in Bury. Production was transferred to Salford in 2013 and the brewery now uses an eight-barrel plant situated in a railway arch, which also contains a secret garden and reggae sound system.

AVA (OG 1034, ABV 3.5%)
A fruity, hoppy session blonde ale.

MIA (OG 1035, ABV 3.5%)
A session beer with more malt and hop character than usual from a beer of this strength.

DOC (OG 1038, ABV 4.1%)
A generously-hopped pale ale with a pleasant, lingering bitterness.

HOP (OG 1038, ABV 4.1%)
A thirst-quenching session beer with massive hop flavours.

TEA (OG 1048, ABV 5%)
A full-bodied pale ale.

SIP (OG 1052, ABV 5.4%)
A full-bodied strong pale ale with tropical fruit flavours.

SYL (OG 1064, ABV 6.4%)
A black IPA.

Fisher SIBA

Lower Farm, Noke, Oxfordshire, OX3 9TX
(01865) 246611

Brewing commenced in 2012 on a five-barrel plant. Limited production of the four core beers is available at the James Street Tavern in Oxford, the Rock of Gibraltar in Bletchington and beer festivals. An increase in production and a bottling line are planned.

Vicar's Daughter (OG 1036, ABV 3.7%)
Light and hoppy session bitter.

Piper at the Gates of Dawn (OG 1038, ABV 3.9%)
A light bitter with malty overtones.

Solicitors (OG 1042, ABV 4.2%)
Dark, full-bodied, smoky bitter.

Confessor (OG 1043, ABV 4.4%)
A well-hopped spicy golden beer.

Five Points SIBA

3 Institute Place, Hackney Downs, London, E8 1JE
(020) 8533 7746 fivepointsbrewing.co.uk

Five Points commenced brewing in 2013 on a 10-barrel plant in the heart of Hackney. Based in a railway arch under Hackney Downs Railway Station, the brewery takes its name from the five-way junction where Dalston Lane, Amhurst Road and Pembury Road meet, the Five Points. Beers are available unfiltered in bottles.

Five Towns

651 Leeds Road, Outwood, Wakefield, West Yorkshire, WF1 2LU
(01924) 781887
malcolmbastow@googlemail.com

Five Towns began production on a 2.5-barrel plant in 2008 and mostly supplies outlets in Yorkshire. Seasonal and bottle-conditioned beers are also available.

Outwood Bound (OG 1040, ABV 4.2%)
A chestnut-coloured beer with a toffee nose and strong, dry, bitter finish.

Callum's Best (OG 1041, ABV 4.6%)
A dark-coloured bitter with a full flavour and bitter finish.

Ponte Carlo Stout (OG 1048.7, ABV 4.6%)
Bitter chocolate and malt aromas, smooth malt and chocolate with a hint of liquorice in the mouth and a dry, bittersweet finish.

Niamh's Nemesis (OG 1053, ABV 5.7%)
A full-bodied IPA with hints of grapefruit before a dry finish.

Flack Manor SIBA

8 Romsey Industrial Estate, Greatbridge Road, Romsey, Hampshire, SO51 0HR
(01794) 518520 flackmanor.co.uk
Shop Mon-Fri 9.30am-5pm, Sat 9.30am-12pm
Tours by arrangement

Flack Manor commenced brewing in 2010 using a 20-barrel plant purchased from Canada. The brewery employs the 'double drop' method of brewing. Beers are supplied to local outlets within approximately 30 miles of Romsey. Seasonal beers are available.

Flack's Double Drop (OG 1037, ABV 3.7%)

Brown session bitter. Hops and some bitterness in the taste with more hoppiness and some malt in a long finish.

Flack Catcher (OG 1045, ABV 4.4%)
Well-balanced best bitter with malty nose and citrus hints. Hoppy taste balanced with fruity sweetness and a lingering finish.

Flash

Moss Top Farm, Moss Top Lane, Flash, Staffordshire, SK17 0TA ✉ flashbrewery@hotmail.com

The brewery is located high in the Peak District and was founded by two friends who brew on a part-time basis. All natural ingredients are used including spring water and seaweed finings, which make the beer suitable for vegans. Due to the altitude a brick boiler was found and is used in the brewing process rather than electrical equipment. Three bottle-conditioned beers are produced and are sold at Leek market, which is the only sales outlet.

Flipside SIBA

The Brewhouse, East Link Trade Estate, Private Road No. 2, Colwick, Nottinghamshire, NG4 2JR
☎ (0115) 987 7500 🌐 flipsidebrewery.co.uk
Shop Mon-Fri 8am-6pm, Sat 10am-4pm, closed Sun
Tours by arrangement

Andrew and Maggie Dunkin established their six-barrel brewery in an industrial unit in Colwick in 2010. With production at full capacity the brewery expanded to 12 barrels in 2013 and relocated to a larger adjacent unit. In 2012 the Flipping Good Beer Shop opened, which also operates online. In 2014 Flipside's brewery tap opened, the Volunteer in nearby Carlton.

Sterling Pale (OG 1039, ABV 3.9%)
A hoppy pale ale. Easy-drinking with a bitter, spicy hop flavour.

Dark Denomination (OG 1041, ABV 4%)
Well-rounded, mildly-hopped beer. Chocolate and caramel malt combine delicately with blackcurrant flavours.

Copper Penny (OG 1043, ABV 4.2%)
An easy-drinking session bitter. Light brown, moderately bitter but with good hop flavours, ending with a hint of tangerine.

Golden Sovereign (OG 1043, ABV 4.2%)
A golden session ale. Refreshingly bitter with dry biscuit flavours. American hops are added to produce a citrus and grapefruit flavour in the finish.

Franc in Stein (ABV 4.3%)
A golden ale.

Random Toss (OG 1044, ABV 4.4%)
A refreshing pale ale with lemon and lime tropical fruit flavours.

Flipping Best (OG 1045, ABV 4.6%)
A traditional dark brown best bitter. Strong malt flavours complemented with good bitterness and gentle hop flavours.

Clippings IPA (OG 1062, ABV 6.5%)
A traditional IPA, golden in colour with crushed gooseberry and bitter white wine hop flavours.

Russian Rouble (ABV 7.3%)
A strong dark Imperial stout with rich chocolate and malt flavours.

Florence

Capital Pub Co PLC, 131-133 Dulwich Road, Herne Hill, London, SE24 0NG
☎ (020) 7326 4987 🌐 florencehernehill.com

The Florence has been brewing since opening in 2007. Purchased by beer historian Peter Haydon from Greene King following the acquisition of Capital Pubs, the Florence brews for Capital Pub Co pubs and produces 'A Head in a Hat' beers, specialising in London beer recipes, for the London free trade.

Flowerpots SIBA

Brandy Mount, Cheriton, Hampshire, SO24 0QQ
☎ (01962) 771534 🌐 flowerpots-inn.co.uk

Flowerpots began production in 2006. Catherine Bate and David Mackie are the brewers, alongside the brewery owner, Paul Tickner. Many local outlets are supplied direct. Seasonal beers: see website.

Perridge Pale (OG 1035.5, ABV 3.6%)
Pale, easy-drinking golden ale. Honey-scented with high hops, grapefruit and bitterness throughout. Crisp with some citrus notes.

Bitter (OG 1038, ABV 3.8%)
Dry, earthy hop flavours balanced by malt. Good bitterness with some hop in the aroma and a sharp, bitter finish. A refreshing bitter.

Goodens Gold (OG 1046, ABV 4.8%)
Complex full-bodied golden ale, bursting with hops and citrus fruit with a snatch of sweetness, leading to a long, dry finish.

Flying Monk (NEW)

Bradfield Manor Farm, Hullavington, Wiltshire, SN14 6EU
☎ (01666) 838415

Flying Monk was founded in 2014 by four friends who used to play at Minety Rugby Club, but who have access to significant brewing expertise.

Elmers (ABV 3.8%)

Fool Hardy SIBA

Hope Inn, 118 Wellington Road North, Heaton Norris, SK4 2LL
☎ (0161) 637 6191 🌐 foolhardyales.co.uk
Tours by arrangement

Martin Wood and Samantha Halfyard bought the Hope Inn in 2012 and installed a 2.5-barrel brewery in the cellar. The first beers went on sale in 2013. The brewery currently supplies the pub, local festivals and the free trade via distributors.

Rash Dash (OG 1038, ABV 3.8%)
A rich amber-coloured beer with a light floral aroma. Initial toffee flavour immediately gives way to hops that linger for a long finish.

Rou Shou (OG 1042.4, ABV 4.3%)

Risky Blond (OG 1042, ABV 4.4%)
An easy-drinking golden ale with a good balance of hops, subtle hints of citrus and a well-rounded finish.

Reckless Danger (OG 1054, ABV 5%)

An sweet tasting beer with bitterness poking through. A clean hoppy finish and moderate aftertaste.

Rogue Santa/Rata-tat-tat (ABV 5%)
A rich, dark beer, soft and creamy, having a moderate hop balance with mild hints of chocolate and orange.

Force (NEW)

Unit 2, Global Business Park, Wilkinson Road, Cirencester, Gloucestershire, GL7 1YZ ☎ 07532 097050 🌐 forcebrewery.com
Tours by arrangement

Force Brewery was established in 2014 using a four-barrel gravity-fed brew plant.

Yankee Zulu (OG 1039, ABV 4%)
A golden bitter with a subtle, spicy bitterness and mellow, floral aromas.

Thunderball (OG 1051, ABV 5%)
A robust stout. Deep, roasty flavours are met with a gentle smoothness and hop aroma.

Forge SIBA

Ford Hill Forge, Hartland, Devon, EX39 6EE ☎ (01237) 440015 🌐 forgebrewery.co.uk

Forge Brewery was established in 2008 using a five-barrel plant. Bottle-conditioned and seasonal beer is available.

Discovery (OG 1039, ABV 3.8%)
A golden, hoppy ale.

Devon Maid (OG 1040, ABV 4%)

Hartland Blonde (OG 1040, ABV 4%)
A light, hoppy beer with citrus notes.

Lite House (OG 1042, ABV 4.3%)
A gold-coloured beer with hints of elderflower and a citrus bite.

IPA (OG 1044, ABV 4.5%)
A light, hoppy beer with grapefruit and citrus notes.

Ascension (OG 1046, ABV 4.6%)
An amber-coloured beer with complex hops.

Rev Hawker (OG 1046, ABV 4.6%)

Dreckly (OG 1046, ABV 4.8%)
A warm, ruby-coloured strong premium ale fortified with gorse and heather, rich in malt with a spicy aroma and a malty aftertaste.

Handsome (OG 1048, ABV 5.1%)
A light brown, well-balanced, hoppy beer.

Foundry

See Canterbury Brewers

Four Alls

Ovington, North Yorkshire, DL11 7BP ☎ (01833) 627302 🌐 thefouralls-teesdale.co.uk
Tours by arrangement

The one-barrel brewery was launched in 2003 by John Stroud, one of the founders of Ales of Kent, using that name. In 2004 it became Four Alls, named after the pub where it is based, the only outlet for the beers.

Four Thorns

Deramore Arms, Main Street, Heslington, York, North Yorkshire, YO10 5EA ☎ 07815 153376 ✉ fourthorns@mail.com

Rob Franklin has been operating this one-barrel plant in an outbuilding at the back of the Deramore Arms since 2012. The beer range is supplied to the Deramore Arms and as guest beers to Whitelocks, Leeds. Beer is also contract brewed for Suddaby's.

Bitter (OG 1038, ABV 3.8%)
A traditional Yorkshire amber session bitter.

Pale (OG 1044, ABV 4.3%)
A fruity, well-balanced pale ale with hoppy tones in the finish.

Red Eye IPA (OG 1052, ABV 5.2%)
American-style IPA, ruby in colour, well-hopped.

Fourpure (NEW) SIBA

22 Bermondsey Trading Estate, Rotherhithe New Road, London, SE16 3LL 🌐 fourpure.com

Fourpure began brewing in 2013 producing bottle-conditioned beers. Beer is also available in cans and kegs.

Fownes Brewing

25 Clarence Street, Upper Gornal, West Midlands, DY3 1UL

Office: 42 The Ridgeway, Sedgley, West Midlands, DY3 3UR 🌐 fownesbrewing.co.uk

The brewery was established in 2012 by James and Tom Fownes in premises to the rear of the Jolly Crispin in Upper Gornal. It expanded to a three-barrel plant in 2014. Beers are available in the Jolly Crispin and local free houses.

Gunhild (OG 1041, ABV 4%)

Crispin's Ommer (OG 1038, ABV 4.1%)

Frost Hammer (OG 1047, ABV 4.6%)

Ulfsberg Cross (OG 1045, ABV 4.8%)

Firebeard's Old Favourite No. 5 Ruby Ale (OG 1051, ABV 5%)

King Korvaks Saga (OG 1058, ABV 5.4%)

Fox

22 Station Road, Heacham, Norfolk, PE31 7EX ☎ (01485) 570345 🌐 foxbrewery.co.uk
Tours by arrangement

Based in an old cottage adjacent to the Fox & Hounds pub, Fox Brewery was established in 2002 and now supplies around 50 outlets as well as the pub. All the Branthill beers are brewed from barley grown on Branthill Farm and malted at Crisps in Great Ryburgh. A hop garden next to the brewery, trialled during 2009, has been enlarged. Seasonal and bottle-conditioned beers are available.

Branthill Best (OG 1037, ABV 3.9%)

Heacham Gold (OG 1037, ABV 3.9%) ◆
A gentle beer with light citrus airs. A low but increasing bitterness is the major flavour as some initial sweet hoppiness quickly declines.

Red Knocker (OG 1037, ABV 3.9%)

LJB (OG 1040, ABV 4%) ◆

THE BREWERIES

A well-balanced malty brew with a hoppy, bitter background. The long finish holds up well, as a sultana-like fruitiness develops. Mid-brown with a slightly thin mouthfeel.

Nelson's Blood (OG 1049, ABV 4.1%)
A red-coloured, full-bodied beer, made with Nelson's Blood rum.

Warrior (OG 1043, ABV 4.4%)

Grizzly Beer (OG 1048, ABV 4.8%)
Honey wheat beer brewed from an American recipe.

IPA (OG 1051, ABV 5.2%)
Based on a 19th-century recipe. Easy drinking for its strength.

Foxfield SIBA

Prince of Wales, Foxfield, Broughton in Furness, Cumbria, LA20 6BX
☎ (01229) 716238 🌐 princeofwalesfoxfield.co.uk
Tours by arrangement

Foxfield is a 4.5-barrel plant in old stables attached to the Prince of Wales. Several other outlets are supplied. Tiger Tops in Wakefield is also owned. The beer range constantly changes with many occasional and seasonal beers. Dark Mild is suitable for vegans.

Dark Mild (OG 1040, ABV 3.7%)

Franklins SIBA

1066 Country Brewery, Pebsham Farm Industrial Estate, Pebsham Lane, Bexhill-on-Sea, East Sussex, TN40 2RZ
☎ (01424) 731066 🌐 franklinsbrewery.co.uk
Tours by arrangement

Formerly White Brewery, in 2011 the Franklins name was purchased from Sean Franklin of Roosters, who originally set up the brewery in 1980. Steve Medniuk (ex Dark Star) joined the brewery in 2012 as head brewer. There are plans for relocation and expansion.

English Garden (OG 1042, ABV 3.8%)

Mumma Knows Best (OG 1043, ABV 4.1%)

Pudding Stout (OG 1046, ABV 4.2%)

Grumpy Guvnor (OG 1047, ABV 4.5%)

Citra IPA (OG 1056, ABV 5.5%)

Freedom SIBA

1 Park Lodge House, Bagots Park, Abbots Bromley, Staffordshire, WS15 3ES
☎ (01283) 840721 🌐 freedomlager.com
Shop Mon-Fri 8.30am-5pm
Tours by arrangement

No real ale. Freedom specialises in producing hand-crafted English lagers, all brewed in accordance with the German Reinheitsgebot purity law. Six beers are currently produced.

Freeminer SIBA

Whimsey Road, Steam Mills, Cinderford, Gloucestershire, GL14 3JA
☎ (01594) 827989 ✉ sales@freeminer.co.uk

Founded by Don Burgess in 1992, Freeminer – previously Freeminer Brewery – changed hands in 2006 but Don Burgess remained in post. Bottle-conditioned beers are available (brewed for the Co-op). Co-op beers are now brewed with barley grown on Co-op farms and malted at Warminster. Fairtrade and organic beers are also produced, with limited edition cask versions available for Fairtrade fortnight.

Freeminer (ABV 4%)
A light brown, hoppy, distinctive beer.

Slaughter Porter (OG 1047, ABV 4.8%)
A porter with a well-defined aroma of Fuggles hops.

Speculation Ale (ABV 4.8%)
A premium strength ale with plenty of hops in the nose and rich malt flavours in the mouth. An initial sweetness is replaced by hops, leaving a complex but balanced hop and malt aftertaste.

Frensham (NEW)

The Old Dairy, Pierrepont Home Farm, The Reeds, Frensham, Surrey, GU10 3BS ☎ 07505 798380
🌐 frenshambrewery.co.uk

Set in the Surrey countryside, Frensham is a microbrewery situated in a 17th-century restored barn on a working dairy farm. Regular open days are held.

Forager (OG 1042, ABV 4.2%)

Friday Beer

Unit 4, Link Business Centre, Malvern, Worcestershire, WR14 1UQ
☎ (01684) 572648 🌐 thefridaybeer.com
Tours by arrangement

Founded in 2011, the Friday Beer Company primarily produces bottle-conditioned ales, selling across the Three Counties. Available cask-conditioned in a small number of local pubs.

Jubilee (OG 1034, ABV 3.1%)
Full-flavoured, easy-drinking session ale.

Friday Light (OG 1037, ABV 4.2%)
A straw-coloured ale, with generous malt flavours.

Pinnacle (OG 1046, ABV 4.5%)
Based on a traditional British bitter combining a variety of hops with grain and a touch of rye.

Black Hill Stout (OG 1052, ABV 4.7%)
A smooth, sweet stout full of complex malty flavours.

Friday Gold (OG 1054, ABV 5.6%)
A refreshing golden ale with a smooth texture and flavour with a slight taste of citrus.

Friends Arms

Old St Clears Road, Johnstown, SA31 3HH
☎ (01267) 234073 🌐 thefriendsarms.co.uk

Friends Arms Brewery opened in 2011 on the premises of the Friends Arms, a traditional local community pub, which acts as the brewery tap.

Frodsham SIBA

Lady Heyes Craft Centre, Kingsley Road, Frodsham, Cheshire, WA6 6SU

☎ (01928) 787917 🌐 frodshambrewery.co.uk
Shop 10am-4pm daily
Tours by arrangement

Frodsham has been brewing since 2005 (initially as Stationhouse Brewery in Ellesmere Port). Seasonal/occasional beers: see website. Most beers are available bottle conditioned and are suitable for vegans. A labelling service is provided for bottles to enable them to be personalised for commemorative occasions or as gifts.

Flaxen Jade (OG 1037, ABV 3.7%)
Blonde ale with citrus notes and a black pepper kick.

Devil's Garden (OG 1037, ABV 3.9%)
An amber beer with traditional biscuit flavour and raisin aftertaste.

Splash! (OG 1038, ABV 3.9%)
A blonde, refreshing, summer beer. Crisp and citrus with hoppy flavours.

Danny (OG 1038, ABV 4%)
Golden floral hoppy ale specially brewed to help restore the Daniel Adamson steamer.

Dark Ark Ale (OG 1039.6, ABV 4%)
A dark malty beer with rich raisin and fruit flavours.

Gold (OG 1037.9, ABV 4.1%)
Gold-coloured ale with rich hoppy flavours and a spicy tang.

Froda's Ale (OG 1040, ABV 4.2%)
A traditional tawny bitter with a hoppy and slight liquorice taste. Named after Froda, Saxon leader of Frodsham.

Buzzin' (OG 1042, ABV 4.3%) ◆
Golden fruity bitter dominated by a honey sweetness. Good hop flavours in the initial taste and a long, lasting dry finish.

Iron Man (OG 1043, ABV 4.5%)
Chestnut brown ale, nutty with a full hop flavour.

800 Ale (OG 1045.5, ABV 4.7%)
A golden bitter beer. Floral with late wine flavours.

Aonach (OG 1049, ABV 4.9%)
A typical Scottish-style 80/- beer. Dark amber in colour.

Lammastide (OG 1052, ABV 5%)
An English wheat beer with distinct elderflower aromas.

Titan's Bolt (OG 1085, ABV 8.5%)
A strong IPA. Chestnut-coloured with spicy hop notes and Madeira overtones.

Frog Island SIBA

The Maltings, Westbridge, St James Road, Northampton, NN5 5HS
☎ (01604) 587772 🌐 frogislandbrewery.co.uk
Tours by arrangement to licensed trade only

Established in 1994, Frog Island specialises in beers with personalised bottle labels, available by mail order. Some 40 free trade outlets are supplied. The brewery changed hands in 2013 and is now run by husband and wife team Paul Burchell and Zoe Cushnie. Seasonal and bottle-conditioned beers are available.

Best Bitter (OG 1038, ABV 3.8%) ◆
Blackcurrant and gooseberry enhance the full malty aroma with pineapple and papaya joining on the tongue. Bitterness develops in the fairly long Target/Fuggles finish.

Lock, Stock & Barrel (OG 1040, ABV 4%)
A rounded bittersweet malt taste is complemented by the late hopping, leading to a refreshing bitter finish.

Shoemaker (OG 1043, ABV 4.2%) ◆
An orangey aroma of fruity Cascade hops is balanced by malt. Citrus and hoppy bitterness last into a long, dry finish. Amber colour.

That Old Chestnut (OG 1044, ABV 4.4%)
A smooth, easy-drinking beer with subtle roasted notes. Cascade hops bring a sweet spiciness to the beer while Target hops contribute bitterness to the dry, malty finish.

Natterjack (OG 1048, ABV 4.8%) ◆
Deceptively robust, golden and smooth. Fruit and hop aromas fight for dominance before the grainy astringency and floral palate give way to a long, dry aftertaste.

Fire Bellied Toad (OG 1048, ABV 5%) ◆
Amber-gold brew with an extraordinary long bitter/fruity finish. Huge malt and hop flavours have a hint of apples.

Croak & Stagger (OG 1054, ABV 5.6%) ◆
The initial honey/fruit aroma is quickly overpowered by roast malt then bitter chocolate and pale malt sweetness on the tongue. Gentle, bittersweet finish.

Front Row SIBA

Unit 1, Hopkins Close, Greenfield Farm Industrial Estate, Congleton, Cheshire, CW12 4TR ☎ 07861 718673 🌐 frontrowbrewing.co.uk
Tours by arrangement (max. 10)

After starting operations on a 2.5-barrel plant in 2012, Front Row expanded to an eight-barrel plant at the beginning of 2014 to meet demand. Consolidation of the core and seasonal ranges is ongoing.

Crouch (OG 1039, ABV 3.8%)

Touch (OG 1038, ABV 4%)

Pause (OG 1049, ABV 4.5%)

Engage (OG 1047, ABV 4.8%)

Collapsed (OG 1052, ABV 5.6%)

Frothblowers (NEW) SIBA

Unit W34, Hastingwood Industrial Park, Wood Lane, Erdington, West Midlands, B24 9QR ☎ 07599 084605 🌐 frothblowers.co.uk/fbbc

Frothblowers began brewing in 2013 using a six-barrel plant. Seasonal beers: see website.

Piffle Snonker (ABV 3.8%)
A blonde beer with a floral nose and sweet start but bitter finish.

Monsoon Mild (ABV 4%)
A dark red, malty, well-balanced mild.

Gollop With Zest (ABV 4.5%)
A blonde beer with a floral start and citrus finish.

Hornswoggle (ABV 5%)
A full-bodied blonde beer with a floral nose and sweetish start, replaced by a dry and satisfying bitterness.

Fugelestou

See Fulstow

Fulflood Arms

28 Cheriton Road, Winchester, Hampshire, SO22 5EF
(01962) 842996
thefulfloodarms@hotmail.co.uk

The brewery was established in 2012 using a one-barrel plant supplying the pub and other local outlets. Brewing is currently suspended.

Full Mash SIBA

17 Lower Park Street, Stapleford, Nottinghamshire, NG9 8EW
(0115) 949 9262 fullmash.net

Brewing commenced in 2003, growing steadily with expansion in both capacity and outlets supplied. The core range is complemented by regular seasonal and one-off brews.

Whistlin' Dixie (OG 1040, ABV 3.9%)
A best bitter.

Seance (OG 1041, ABV 4%)
Predominantly hoppy golden beer, with a refreshing bitter finish.

Illuminati (OG 1043, ABV 4.2%)
Well-balanced pale ale with a full-bodied hop flavour and refreshing zesty finish.

Wheat Ear (OG 1043, ABV 4.2%)
Pale, clear wheat beer, fruity and aromatic.

Warlord (OG 1045, ABV 4.4%)
Amber-coloured beer with an initial malt taste leading to a dry, bitter finish.

Apparition (OG 1046, ABV 4.5%)
A pale hoppy bitter brewed with Brewers Gold hops.

Brewed for the Horse & Jockey, Stapleford:

Horse & Jockey (OG 1039, ABV 3.8%)

Fuller's SIBA IFBB

Griffin Brewery, Chiswick Lane South, London, W4 2QB
(020) 8996 2000 fullers.co.uk
Shop Mon-Fri 10am-8pm, Sat 10am-6pm
Tours by arrangement

Fuller, Smith and Turner's Griffin Brewery has stood on the same site in Chiswick for more than 350 years. The partnership from which the company now takes its name was formed in 1845 and members of the founding families are still involved in running the company today. Three different Fuller's beers have won the Champion Beer of Britain title, Chiswick Bitter, London Pride and ESB. At the end of 2005 Fuller's announced an agreed acquisition of Hampshire brewer George Gale. The company now operates 362 pubs and hotels. Fuller's stopped brewing at the Gale';s Horndean site in 2006 and all of the brands, including some seasonals, are now brewed at Chiswick. Seasonal beers: see website. Bottle-conditioned beers are available. In July 2014 Fuller's announced it planned to invest £5m in the brewery to double capacity.

Chiswick Bitter (OG 1034.5, ABV 3.5%)
Refreshing pale brown bitter with some citrus notes on the palate fading in the aftertaste, which is hoppy and slightly dry. Aroma is of hops with a trace of biscuit.

London Pride (OG 1040.5, ABV 4.1%)
Well-balanced smooth best bitter with orange citrus fruit, malt and hops in aroma and flavour, which linger into a slightly bitter aftertaste. Honey and toffee develop as the beer matures.

Bengal Lancer (OG 1049.5, ABV 5%)
Rich, creamy and well-balanced pale brown IPA with a gold hue. Hops with a dryish bitterness harmonise with the fruit and malty sweetness that linger into the aftertaste.

London Porter (OG 1056.8, ABV 5.4%)

ESB (OG 1054, ABV 5.5%)
Bitter orange marmalade with hops, creamy toffee and some raisins are all present in this multifaceted strong brown bitter. A satisfying long, bitter, dry finish balanced by a malty sweetness.

Under the Gale's brand name:

Seafarers Ale (OG 1036.8, ABV 3.6%)
A pale brown bitter, predominantly malty, with a refreshing balance of fruit and hops that lingers into the aftertaste where a dry bitterness unfolds.

HSB (OG 1050, ABV 4.8%)
Dates and dried fruit with some spicy hops in the nose adding to the caramelised orange and treacle in the flavour of this smooth brown beer. Malty throughout with a bittersweet finish.

Fulstow

13 Thames Street, Louth, Lincolnshire, LN11 7AD
(01507) 608202 fulstowbrewery.com
Shop 7-11pm (at brewery tap)
Tours by arrangement

Fulstow operates on a 2.5-barrel plant and started brewing in Fulstow in 2004. The brewery moved to Louth in 2006. 'Fugelestou Ales' are one-off beers produced along with the regular range, all only available at the brewery tap, the Gas Lamp Lounge, Louth.

Common (OG 1038, ABV 3.8%)
A copper-coloured, medium-bodied beer with a strong hop character and malt discernible in the taste.

Marsh Mild (OG 1039, ABV 3.8%)
Traditional mild with a malty aroma. Chocolate malt on the palate with toffee and caramel overtones.

Northway IPA (OG 1042, ABV 4.2%)
A clean, crisp ale with a citrus aroma; very hoppy with a dry finish.

Pride of Fulstow (OG 1045, ABV 4.5%)
Copper-coloured bitter with a ripe malt taste in the mouth and a good hop balance. A dry finish with blackcurrant fruit notes.

Sledgehammer Stout (OG 1077, ABV 8%)
A strong, dark stout with raisin, liquorice and roast barley notes balanced by a strong hop flavour.

Funfair SIBA

Chequers Inn, Toad Lane, Elston, Nottinghamshire, NG23 5NS

☎ (01636) 525257 🌐 funfairbrewingcompany.co.uk
Tours by arrangement

Funfair was launched in 2004 in Holbrook and is now situated at the Chequers Inn in Elston, where a new 10-barrel plant is used. The Chequers also serves as the brewery tap. More than 40 outlets are supplied. Seasonal beers: see website. Bottle-conditioned beers are available.

Gallopers (OG 1037, ABV 3.8%)
A well-hopped, pale session bitter.

Teacups (OG 1040, ABV 4%)
A traditional ginger beer.

Waltzer (OG 1044, ABV 4.5%)
Copper-coloured, easy-drinking bitter.

Brandy Snap (OG 1046, ABV 4.7%)
Golden ale containing root ginger.

Dive Bomber (OG 1047, ABV 4.7%)
Refreshing, straw-coloured premium ale.

Dodgem (OG 1047, ABV 4.7%)
Golden premium pale ale with a unique blend of hops.

Fuzzy Duck SIBA

18 Wood Street, Poulton Industrial Estate, Poulton-le-Fylde, Lancashire, FY6 8JY ☎ 07904 343729
🌐 fuzzyduckbrewery.co.uk
Tours by arrangement

Fuzzy Duck was established in 2006 as a commercial home-based brewery. It relocated to Poulton-le-Fylde later that year, expanding capacity to an eight-barrel plant. The brewery delivers over a wide area of the north west. Seasonal beers: see website.

Golden Cascade (OG 1038, ABV 3.8%)
Golden-coloured ale brewed with Cascade hops for a citrus flavour and a floral aroma.

Mucky Duck (OG 1042, ABV 4%)
Dark stout, slightly sweet with chocolate and coffee notes from the roasted malt.

Cunning Stunt (OG 1044, ABV 4.3%)
Amber-coloured beer with a blackcurrant and herbal aroma.

Pheasant Plucker (OG 1044, ABV 4.3%)

Ruby Duck (OG 1053, ABV 5.3%)
Dark ruby-coloured beer with a rich, full body and complex fruit flavours.

Fyne SIBA

Achadunan, Cairndow, Argyll, PA26 8BJ
☎ (01499) 600120 🌐 fyneales.com
Shop Mon-Sat 10am-5pm, Sun 12.30-5pm
Tours by arrangement

Fyne Ales has been brewing since 2001 and is situated at the head of Loch Fyne. In 2012 an on-site brewery tap was added. Seasonal beers are available.

Jarl (OG 1038, ABV 3.8%)
A light, golden ale with strong citrus notes.

Piper's Gold (OG 1037.5, ABV 3.8%)
Fresh, golden session ale. Well bittered but balanced with fruit and malt. Long, dry, bitter finish.

Maverick (OG 1040.5, ABV 4.2%)
Full-bodied, roasty, tawny best bitter. It is balanced, fruity and well-hopped.

Hurricane Jack (OG 1042.5, ABV 4.4%)
Smooth golden ale with deep citrus flavours that mellow to a lingering citrus bitter finish.

Vital Spark (OG 1042.5, ABV 4.4%)
A rich, dark beer that shows glints of red. The taste is clean and slightly sharp with a hint of blackcurrant.

Avalanche (OG 1043.5, ABV 4.5%)
This true golden ale starts with stunning citrus hops on the nose. Well-balanced with good body and fruit balancing a refreshing hoppy taste, it finishes with a long, bittersweet aftertaste.

Highlander (OG 1046, ABV 4.8%)
Full-bodied, bittersweet ale with a good dry hop finish. In the style of a Heavy although the malt is less pronounced and the sweetness ebbs away to leave a bitter, hoppy finish.

Black IPA (OG 1056, ABV 5.9%)

Sublime Stout (OG 1067, ABV 6.8%)
A hint of liquorice on the aftertaste.

Superior IPA (OG 1070, ABV 7.1%)
The aroma of apricot and pine resin is present giving a dusty, hoppy bitterness with a dry, fruity and hoppy aftertaste.

Gadds

See Ramsgate

Gale's

See Fuller's

Gambling Man

61 Low Willington, Willington, County Durham, DL15 9AB ☎ 07977 154675
🌐 gamblingmanbrewco.com

Gambling Man was established in 2011 by avid home brewers Paul Armstrong and Dave Walls. The brewery name was devised by the brewers during a game of five card draw and all of the regular ales have gambling/casino related names. Bi-monthly specials are available.

Croupier (ABV 3.4%)

Pit Boss (ABV 4.4%)

Jack of Clubs (ABV 4.7%)

Garage

c/o London Inn, 8 Church Road, Plympton St Maurice, Devon, PL7 1NH
☎ (01752) 657045 🌐 garagebrewery.co.uk
Tours by arrangement

Garage was established in 2011 by Russ Gibbs, a keen home brewer, in an outbuilding of the London Inn. It uses a one-barrel, self-constructed brew plant. The brewery is separate to the pub. All beers are full mash with no extract used. Seasonal and occasional ales are available. Brewing is currently suspended.

Stout Sam (OG 1040, ABV 3.9%)
Full-flavoured with a hint of toasted malt.

THE BREWERIES

Firkin Folly (OG 1044, ABV 4.4%)
Amber in colour. Refreshing and clean to the palate with a dry hoppy finish.

Radiator Spring (OG 1046, ABV 4.5%)
Ruby red in colour. Complex flavours, with a long-lasting finish.

Young Bob (OG 1064, ABV 6.2%)
Named after the Brewer's terrier dog. It is strong tasting, malty and ruby red in colour, with a hoppy finish.

Gargoyles

See Isca

Gas Dog

Noel's Arms, 31 Burton Street, Melton Mowbray, Leicestershire, LE13 1AE ☎ 07921 260063

Office: 9 Westview, Somerby, Leicestershire, LE14 2QH 🌐 gasdogbrewery.co.uk

Gas Dog began brewing in 2013 at the same premises as Parish Brewery, but using a separate 0.5-barrel plant. In 2014 it relocated to an outbuilding at the rear of the Noel's Arms in Melton Mowbray and a bottling plant was added. Two regular beers are produced along with special brews under the title 'Leicester Legends'.

Bitter (OG 1040, ABV 4%)
Hoppy, golden ale.

Dark Ale (OG 1040, ABV 4%)
Chocolate, dark malty brew.

Gates Burton

Reservoir Road, Burton upon Trent, Staffordshire, DE14 2BP
☎ (01283) 532567
✉ gatesburtonbrewery@talktalk.net
Tours by arrangement

The Gates Burton Brewery was established in 2011 using a one-barrel plant. Further beers are planned.

Reservoir Premium (OG 1046, ABV 4.6%)
Full-bodied and amber in colour with a well-balanced malt and hop character giving a smooth finish.

Damn (OG 1050, ABV 5%)
Smooth-drinking with chocolate malt tones and delicately hopped with a subtle, sweet finish.

Geeves SIBA

Unit 12, Grange Lane Industrial Estate, Carrwood Road, Stairfoot, Barnsley, South Yorkshire, S71 5AS
☎ 07859 039259 🌐 geevesbrewery.co.uk
Tours by arrangement

Geeves began brewing in 2011 using a 5.5-barrel plant with recipes developed when the owners lived on a narrow boat where they had to use rather ingenious brewing methods. This unusual heritage is reflected in the names of the regular and seasonal beers.

Navigation (OG 1038, ABV 3.8%)
A blonde session ale with a soft bitterness and light citrus, lemon and floral notes.

No 1 (OG 1038, ABV 3.8%)
Traditional bitter, well-rounded malty base with a hoppy finish.

Red Diesel (OG 1040, ABV 4.1%)

Gunwale Dance (OG 1043, ABV 4.2%)
A pale ale with a dry, citrus bitterness coupled by a zingy aftertaste and aroma.

Captain Gingerbread (OG 1043, ABV 4.3%)
A naturally hazy wheat beer infused with ginger. Spicy and refreshing with a hint of citrus.

Clear Cut (OG 1044, ABV 4.4%)
An pale ale with bags of American hops for a real citrus kick.

Smokey Joe Stout (OG 1050, ABV 5%)
A strong stout made with several different malts. Rich and robust.

Fully Laden (OG 1060, ABV 6%)
A strong IPA with a juicy, citrus, sweet floral taste and aroma with a satisfying bitterness.

Geipel (NEW) SIBA

Pantglas Llangwm, Corwen, LL21 0RN
☎ (01490) 420838 🌐 geipel.co.uk

Geipel commenced brewing in 2013 producing four unpasteurised and unfiltered beers in keg and bottle form only, mainly supplying bars and off-licenses in North Wales and Greater Manchester.

Geltsdale SIBA

Unit 1b, Townfoot Industrial Estate, Brampton, Cumbria, CA8 1SW
☎ (01697) 741541 🌐 geltsdalebrewery.com
Shop Mon-Sat 9am-5pm
Tours by arrangement

Geltsdale Brewery, established in 2006 by Fiona Deal, initially operated from a small unit in Bramptons Old Brewery which dated back to 1785. In 2013 production moved to Townfoot Industrial Estate. Beers are named after local landmarks within Geltsdale.

Black Dub (OG 1036, ABV 3.6%)
Treacle toffee, dark toast and molasses on the palate with loads of malt and sweet raisins.

King's Forest (OG 1039, ABV 3.8%)
A citrus, almost peppery aroma. Malt, caramel, digestive biscuits and hazelnuts on the palate.

Cold Fell (OG 1038, ABV 3.9%)
A sharp, fresh beer with a sweet, malty aftertaste. Zesty and hoppy with a hint of pine on the nose.

Bewcastle Brown Ale (OG 1039, ABV 4%)
A warm and nutty beer, delicately bittered and full-bodied.

Brampton Bitter (OG 1039, ABV 4%) ◆
Sweet, fruity, well-balanced hoppy bitter with a clean bitter aftertaste.

Tarn (OG 1039, ABV 4%)
A well-balanced beer, warm and smooth with subtle whisky notes and a soft bitterness.

Hell Beck (OG 1042, ABV 4.2%)
A soft, smooth start with espresso, toast and chocolate on the palate. Faint hints of liquorice on the nose.

Brewed for Independent Lakeland Breweries:

Aurora (OG 1039, ABV 3.9%) ◆

Malty and fruity, a gentle bitter with a sweet middle and finish.

George N Porter

See under Porter

George Samuel (NEW)

Duke of Wellington, Welbury, North Yorkshire, DL6 2SG
☎ (01609) 882464
georgesamuelbrewingcompany.co.uk

A small two-barrel brewery set up in a converted garage at the Duke of Wellington pub in the small village of Welbury near Northallerton, named after the two sons of the brewer.

By George She's Got It (OG 1036, ABV 3.6%)
A blonde session ale with a hoppy punch.

Brew It Again Sam (OG 1042, ABV 4.2%)

Golden Wellingtons (OG 1050, ABV 5%)
A golden premium ale with a bittersweet character.

George Wright

See under Wright

George's SIBA

Common Road, Great Wakering, Essex, SS3 0AG
☎ (01702) 826755 hopmonster.co.uk
Tours by arrangement

⊗ George's Brewery and Hop Monster Brewing Company are owned by the same brewer, brewing on the same plant. George's concentrates on traditional styles and Hop Monster on the more unusual. Special brews are available every month.

Wallasea Wench (OG 1037.5, ABV 3.6%)
A pale copper-coloured, easy-drinking beer with low bitterness and a smooth mouthfeel.

Wakering Gold (OG 1039.5, ABV 3.8%)
Bursting with fresh hop aroma.

Best (OG 1041, ABV 4%)
Copper-coloured session bitter.

Cockleboats (OG 1039, ABV 4%)
Deep copper-coloured beer brewed using five malts.

Broadsword (OG 1046, ABV 4.7%)
Ruby/copper-coloured with a malty smooth start and a well-balanced, dry finish.

Excalibur (OG 1051.5, ABV 5.4%)
Brewed in collaboration with Russ Barnes of Red Fox Brewery.

Merry Gentlemen (OG 1058, ABV 6%)
A warming winter ale. Dark chocolate, black cherries and old port flavours dominate this velvety old ale.

Excalibur Reserve (OG 1067, ABV 7.2%)
Full on citrus rush with fruit overtones and the warmth of ancient Armagnac.

Brewed for the Trout Tavern, Southend:

Trout Ale (OG 1037.5, ABV 3.6%)

Under the Hop Monster Brewery name:

Freak Show (OG 1042.5, ABV 4.2%)
Burnished copper-coloured beer full of malt and complex hop flavour. Permanent hop trial: different hops for each brew.

Banshee Porter (OG 1044, ABV 4.4%)
A complex porter made with 30% smoked malt.

Warlock Black IPA (OG 1044, ABV 4.4%)
Classic IPA flavour with a dark twist.

Gertie Sweet

See New Plassey

Gipsy Hill (NEW)

Unit 11, Hamilton Road Industrial Estate, 160 Hamilton Road, West Norwood, London, SE27 9SF
☎ (020) 8761 9061 gipsyhillbrewing.com

Gipsy Hill began brewing in 2014 using a 15-barrel plant, specialising in producing beers under 4.5% ABV. Further beers are planned. Seasonal beers: see website.

Southpaw (ABV 4.2%)

Glastonbury SIBA

Unit 11, Wessex Park, Somerton Business Park, Somerton, Somerset, TA11 6SB
☎ (01458) 272244 glastonburyales.com
Shop Mon-Fri 10am-4pm, Sat 10am-12.30pm
Tours by arrangement

Glastonbury Ales was established in 2002 on a five-barrel plant. In 2006 the brewery changed ownership and has now expanded to a 20-barrel plant. A shop opened in 2009. Seasonal beers: see website.

Mystery Tor (OG 1040, ABV 3.8%) ◆
A golden bitter with plenty of floral hop and fruit on the nose and palate, the sweetness giving way to a bitter hop finish. Full-bodied for a session bitter.

Lady of the Lake (OG 1042, ABV 4.2%) ◆
A full-bodied amber best bitter with plenty of hops to the fore balanced by a fruity malt flavour and a subtle hint of vanilla, leading to a clean, bitter hop aftertaste.

Love Monkey (OG 1042, ABV 4.2%)
Golden ale loaded with zesty fruity hops and a variety of malts. Refreshing fruity notes finally succumb to a robust, full body.

Black As Yer 'At (OG 1043, ABV 4.3%)

Hedge Monkey (OG 1048, ABV 4.6%)
A well-rounded deep amber-coloured bitter. Malty, rich and hoppy.

Golden Chalice (OG 1048, ABV 4.8%)
Light and golden best bitter with a robust malt character.

Thriller Cappuccino Porter (OG 1050, ABV 5%)

Glenfinnan

Sruth A Mhuilinn, Glenfinnan, PH37 4LT
☎ (01397) 704309 glenfinnanbrewery.co.uk

Glenfinnan opened in 2007 and operates on a four-barrel plant. It produces around 600 litres per

THE BREWERIES

week during the tourist season. Further expansion is planned. Seasonal beer is available.

Gold Ale (OG 1040, ABV 3.8%)

Standard Ale (OG 1044, ABV 4.2%)

Glentworth

Glentworth House, Crossfield Lane, Skellow, Doncaster, South Yorkshire, DN6 8PL
☎ (01302) 725555

The brewery was founded in 1996 and is housed in former dairy buildings. The five-barrel plant supplies more than 80 pubs. Production is concentrated on mainly light-coloured, hoppy ales. Seasonal beers are available and brewed to order.

Globe

144 High Street West, Glossop, Derbyshire, SK13 8HJ
☎ (01457) 852417 globepub.co.uk

Globe was established in 2006 by Ron Brookes on a 2.5-barrel plant in an old stable behind the Globe pub. Grandson Toby now has a major role in the brewery under the watchful eye of Ron. The beers are mainly for the pub but special one-off brews are produced for beer festivals.

Amber (OG 1040, ABV 3.9%)

Blondie (OG 1039, ABV 3.9%)

Stout (OG 1040, ABV 3.9%)

Comet (OG 1043, ABV 4.3%)

Gloucester SIBA

12-14 Llanthony Road, The Docks, Gloucester, GL1 2EH
☎ (01452) 690541 gloucesterbrewery.co.uk
Tours by arrangement

Situated in historic converted stables in the iconic Gloucester Docks, brewing began in 2011. The full range of beers is regularly found in pubs throughout Gloucestershire and further afield, notably Bristol. A new beer is brewed on a bi-monthly basis as part of a craft ale range. Bottle-conditioned beers are available.

Priory Pale (OG 1037, ABV 3.7%)
A refreshing hoppy ale with citrus and tropical notes.

Gold (OG 1040, ABV 3.9%)
A crisp, hoppy golden ale

Mariner (OG 1042, ABV 4.2%)
A smooth malty and hoppy copper-coloured ale.

Galaxy (ABV 5.2%)
A golden ale bursting with hop character.

Goacher's

Unit 8, Tovil Green Business Park, Burial Ground Lane, Tovil, Maidstone, Kent, ME15 6TA
☎ (01622) 682112 goachers.com
Tours by arrangement

A traditional brewery that uses only malt and Kentish hops for all its beers. Phil and Debbie Goacher have concentrated on brewing good wholesome beers without gimmicks. Two tied houses and around 30 free trade outlets in the mid-Kent area are supplied. Special is brewed for sale under house names. Seasonal beers: Silver Star (ABV 4.2%), Old 1066 Ale (ABV 6.7%).

Real Mild Ale (OG 1033, ABV 3.4%)
A rich, flavourful mild with moderate roast barley and a generous helping of chocolate malt

Fine Light Ale (OG 1036, ABV 3.7%)
A pale, golden brown bitter with a strong, floral, hoppy aroma and aftertaste. A hoppy and moderately malty session beer.

Special/House Ale (OG 1037, ABV 3.8%)

Best Dark Ale (OG 1040, ABV 4.1%)
Dark in colour but light and quaffable in body, this ale features hints of caramel and chocolate malt throughout.

Crown Imperial Stout (OG 1044, ABV 4.5%)
A good, well-balanced roasty stout, dark and bitter with just a hint of caramel and a lingering creamy head.

Gold Star Strong Ale (OG 1050, ABV 5.1%)
A strong pale ale brewed from Maris Otter malt and East Kent Goldings hops.

Goddards SIBA

Barnsley Farm, Bullen Road, Ryde, Isle of Wight, PO33 1QF
☎ (01983) 611011 goddardsbrewery.com

Anthony Goddard established what is now the oldest active brewery on the Isle of Wight in 1993. Originally occupying an 18th-century barn, a new brewery was built in 2008, quadrupling its capacity, which has since been further increased. Goddard's remain a locally-focused business distributing ales on the Isle of Wight and the easily accessible counties of southern England. Seasonal beers: see website.

Ale of Wight (OG 1037, ABV 3.7%)
An aromatic, fresh and zesty pale beer.

Scrumdiggity (OG 1039, ABV 4%)
Well-balanced session beer that maintains its flavour and bite with compelling drinkability.

Wight Squirrel (OG 1042.5, ABV 4.3%)
A russet-coloured best bitter with an initial dry taste on the palate.

Fuggle-Dee-Dum (OG 1047, ABV 4.8%)
Brown-coloured strong ale with plenty of malt and hops.

Goff's SIBA

9 Isbourne Way, Winchcombe, Gloucestershire, GL54 5NS
☎ (01242) 603383 goffsbrewery.com

Goff's is a family concern that has been brewing cask-conditioned ales since 1994. The ales are available regionally in more than 200 outlets and nationally through wholesalers. The addition of the seasonal Ales of the Round Table provides a range of 12 beers of which four or five are always available: see website for details.

Golcar

60a Swallow Lane, Golcar, West Yorkshire, HD7 4NB
☎ (01484) 644241 golcarbrewery.co.uk
Tours by arrangement

Golcar started brewing in 2001 and production has increased from 2.5 barrels to five barrels a week. The brewery owns one pub, the Rose & Crown at Golcar, and supplies other outlets in the local area.

Dark Mild (OG 1034, ABV 3.4%)
Dark mild with a light roasted malt and liquorice taste. Smooth and satisfying.

Pennine Gold (OG 1038, ABV 4%)
A hoppy and fruity session beer.

Guthlac's Porter (OG 1047, ABV 5%)
A robust all grain and malty working man's porter.

Golden Duck SIBA

Unit 2, Redhill Farm, Top Street, Appleby Magna, Leicestershire, DE12 7AH goldenduckbrewery.com

Golden Duck began brewing in 2012 using a five-barrel plant. It is run by the father and son team of Andrew and Harry Lunn. Beers have a cricket-related theme. Beer is always available in Mushroom Hall, Albert Village.

LFB (Lunns First Brew) (OG 1043, ABV 4.3%)
Traditional golden, hoppy session ale with citrus overtones.

Lunnys No. 8 (OG 1048, ABV 4.8%)

Nosey Parker (OG 1050, ABV 5%)
Premium golden ale, hoppy with a hint of citrus.

Reverend Green (OG 1055, ABV 5.5%)
Strong IPA with deep hoppy and fruity flavours.

Brewed for Alchemist Brewery:

Fire Starter (ABV 3.9%)
A golden, hoppy, light beer.

Golden Triangle SIBA

Unit 9, Watton Road, Norwich, NR9 4BG
☎ (01603) 757763 goldentrianglebrewery.co.uk

Golden Triangle, named after an area of Norwich, has been brewing modern, hop-forward ales on a 10-barrel plant since 2011. The brewery moved to the current premises in 2012, and continue to add new beers to their range. Beers are mainly found in pubs across Norwich.

City Gold (OG 1038, ABV 3.8%)
A lemon hop aroma introduces a smoky mix of citrus, hop, and bitterness. The finish develops a dry astringency.

Citropolis (OG 1039, ABV 3.9%)
A blonde ale. Light, refreshing and zesty with citrus hop notes and a fruity aroma.

Bonny's Gold (OG 1040, ABV 4%)
A golden citrus hoppy beer with a definite American hop profile. The two hops work well with a good malt backbone.

City Pale (OG 1042, ABV 4.2%)
A pale beer, grapefruit, lemon and marmalade citrus hop aromas. Crisp, dry, citrus hop and solid pale malty sweet body with floral hints on the palate.

Black Hops IBA (OG 1047, ABV 4.6%)
Intense hop and cherry aroma. Complex mix of malt, cherry and bitterness dominated by hops. Challenging, increasingly bitter ending.

Red Square (OG 1046, ABV 4.6%)

Hop Lobster (OG 1051, ABV 5.5%)

Goldmark SIBA

Unit 23, The Vinery, Arundel Road, Poling, West Sussex, BN18 9PY
☎ (01903) 297838 ☎ 07900 555415
goldmarks.co.uk

Ex-biochemist and home brewer Mark Lehmann began commercial brewing in 2013 using an 11-barrel plant. Beers are available in many outlets nationwide.

Ebony Mild (ABV 3.5%)
Black mild with hints of spice and a light, clean taste.

Liquid Gold (ABV 4%)
A refreshing golden ale with bursts of citrus and wild berries.

Phoenix (ABV 4.1%)
A brown bitter with hints of toffee, caramel and a smooth bitter finish.

American Hop Idol (ABV 4.4%)
A blonde American ale with tropical fruit, citrus and floral notes.

Warrior (ABV 4.6%)
A rich brown ale with hints of toffee, caramel and honey.

Hercules IPA (ABV 5.6%)
A golden hop celebration, with citrus and tropical fruit hints.

Goldstone (NEW) SIBA

The Forge, Ditchling Common Industrial Estate, Streat Lane, Ditchling, East Sussex, BN6 8SG
☎ (01444) 257053

Office: 257 Dyke Road, Hove, East Sussex, BN3 6PA
goldstonebrewery.co.uk

Located in an old forge in the South Downs, this is the brainchild of Mark Francis, who while running a bar in Brussels fell in love with the vast selection of Belgian beers. The team consists of Mark, his wife Alison and award-winning consultant brewer Richard Venour. The brewery is named after a 20-ton rock found in Sussex, believed to have been used by druids for worship.

Old Charmer (OG 1041, ABV 4.1%)
A light, thirst-quenching ale with an assertive bitterness and tropical fruit and spicy aroma.

Ruddy Duck (OG 1041, ABV 4.1%)
Medium-bodied dark ale with notes of caramel, chocolate and coffee and a dry finish.

Beacon Best Bitter (OG 1042, ABV 4.2%)
A well-balanced amber ale in the style of a traditional best bitter; there is maltiness on the palate with a pleasant dry, bitter finish.

Amarillo (OG 1044, ABV 4.4%)
Golden-coloured, single-hopped American-style ale with strong aromas of grapefruit and gooseberry and a dry bitter finish.

Cascade (OG 1044, ABV 4.4%)
An American-style, single-hopped ale with strong aromas of citrus fruit.

Goodall's

The Lodge, 88 Crewe Road, Alsager, Staffordshire, ST7 2JA
☎ (01270) 873669
✉ goodalls.brewery@hotmail.co.uk

Goodall's began brewing in 2010 at the Lodge in Alsager using a 2.5-barrel plant.

Goody Ales SIBA

Bleangate Brewery, Braggs Lane, Herne, Kent, CT6 7NP
☎ (01227) 361555 goodyales.co.uk

Goody began brewing in 2012 using a 10-barrel plant. A wood-burning boiler is used to heat the water for the brews using wood from its copse thereby minimising the use of non-renewable fuel.

Genesis (OG 1035, ABV 3.5%)

Good Health (OG 1038, ABV 3.6%)
A honey-coloured ale with a fresh hoppy finish and undertone of zesty orange.

Good Life (OG 1040, ABV 3.9%)

Good Heavens (OG 1042, ABV 4.1%)
Amber-coloured, hoppy bitter.

Good Sheppard (OG 1045, ABV 4.5%)
Deep amber-coloured ale with a vanilla twist on the palate and a soft feel on the tongue.

Goose Eye SIBA

Ingrow Bridge, South Street, Keighley, West Yorkshire, BD21 5AX
☎ (01535) 605807 goose-eye-brewery.co.uk
Tours by arrangement

Goose Eye is a family-run brewery supplying 60-70 regular outlets, mainly in Yorkshire and Lancashire. The beers are available through national wholesalers and pub chains. It produces monthly occasional and seasonal beers with entertaining names.

Springwell (OG 1036, ABV 3.6%)

Barm Pot Bitter (OG 1038, ABV 3.8%)
Bitter, hop and fruit flavours dominate this golden session bitter over a malty base. Increasingly dry and bitter finish.

Bitter (OG 1038, ABV 3.9%)
Traditional Yorkshire brown session bitter, well-balanced malt and hops with a pleasingly bitter finish.

Blackmoor (OG 1040, ABV 4%)
A dark session beer.

Bronte Bitter (OG 1040, ABV 4%)
A brown, malty and hoppy best bitter. Bitterness increases to give a lingering, dry finish.

No-Eye Deer (OG 1040, ABV 4%)
A faint fruity and malty aroma. Strong hoppy flavours and an intense, bitter finish characterise this pale brown bitter.

Chinook Blonde (OG 1042, ABV 4.2%)
An increasingly tart, bitter finish follows assertive grapefruit hoppiness in the aroma and tropical fruit flavours in this satisfying brew.

Golden Goose (OG 1045, ABV 4.5%)
A straw-coloured beer light on the palate with a smooth and refreshing hoppy finish.

Over and Stout (OG 1052, ABV 5.2%)
A full-bodied stout with roast and malt flavours mingling with hops, dark fruit and liquorice on the palate. Look also for tart fruit on the nose and a growing bitter finish.

Pommies Revenge (OG 1052, ABV 5.2%)
Golden strong bitter combining grassy hops, a cocktail of fruit flavours, a peppery hint and a hoppy, bitter finish.

Goosnargh SIBA

Horns Inn, Horns Lane, Goosnargh, Lancashire, PR3 2FJ
☎ (01772) 864382 yehornsinn.co.uk
Tours by arrangement (small groups preferred)

Brewing began in 2013 using a five-barrel plant in a tiny outbuilding at Ye Horns Inn. Most of the equipment came from the Grindleton Brewery, which closed in 2010. The beer is served at the pub and in local free houses. Seasonal and speciality beers are also brewed.

Truckle (OG 1035, ABV 3.7%)
A dark malty beer with a slight nutty taste and a hint of sweetness.

Bit o'Blonde (OG 1038, ABV 4%)
A light ale, crisp and clean.

Gold (OG 1037, ABV 4%)
A golden beer, light but hoppy with a zesty finish.

RGB (Real Goosnargh Bitter) (OG 1040, ABV 4.3%)
A copper-coloured beer with an earthy, fruity flavour. Nicknamed Reet Gradley Bitter.

Gower SIBA

Greyhound Inn, Oldwalls, LLanrhidian, SA3 1HA
☎ 07967 484356 gowerbrewery.com

Established in 2011 by master brewer Dave Campbell who has more than 24 years of brewing knowledge and experience. Seasonal and speciality ales are brewed alongside established beers.

Brew 1 (OG 1039, ABV 3.8%)
Honey-coloured ale with a pronounced floral aroma.

Black Diamond (OG 1042, ABV 4.2%)
A full-bodied Welsh porter, smoky, chocolate and liquorice flavours, with subtle spicy, bittering hops.

Sampson's Jack (OG 1042, ABV 4.2%)
A classic copper-coloured traditional British ale.

Best Bitter (OG 1045, ABV 4.5%)
A traditional honey-coloured ale with a full-bodied, balanced malty flavour and crisp lingering bite of hop.

Gold (OG 1045, ABV 4.5%)
Thirst quenching golden ale, refreshing citrus flavours and the aroma of Cascade hops.

Lighthouse (OG 1046, ABV 4.5%)
A light, thirst quenching continental-style lager.

Rumour (OG 1050, ABV 5%)
Strong ruby red ale, with complex tastes and aromas, produced from a delicate mix of malts and hops.

Power (OG 1052, ABV 5.5%)
A powerful IPA.

Grafters SIBA

Half Moon, 23 High Street, Willingham by Stow, Lincolnshire, DN21 5JZ
☎ (01427) 788340 ⊕ graftersbrewery.com
Tours by arrangement

Brewing started on a 2.5-barrel plant in 2007 in a converted garage adjacent to the owner's freehouse, the Half Moon. 2013 saw an upgrade to a 10-barrel plant. Six core beers and eight seasonals are brewed.

Moonlight (OG 1038, ABV 3.6%)
A light, citrus beer.

Traditional Bitter (OG 1040, ABV 3.8%)
A traditional beer, fairly light in colour but with a light, hoppy finish.

Over The Moon (OG 1041.5, ABV 4%)

Darker Side of the Moon (OG 1043, ABV 4.2%)
A dark, strong mild with a chocolate taste.

Luvly Jubblies (OG 1045, ABV 4.2%)
A golden brew with tropical hoppiness tracking the bitters through to its refreshing end.

Wobble Gob (OG 1050, ABV 4.9%)
A deep ruby-coloured beer. A blend of hops gives this beer a slightly floral and roasted taste.

Grafton SIBA

Walters Yard, Unit 4, Claylands Industrial Estate, Worksop, Nottinghamshire, S81 7DW
☎ (01909) 476121

Office: 8 Oak Close, Crabtree Park Estate, Worksop, Nottinghamshire, S80 1BH
✉ susanhale1865@gmail.com
Tours by arrangement

Grafton is a 12-barrel brewery established in 2007. The brewery tap is the Grafton Hotel, Worksop. A new brewery, visitors centre and shop opened in 2014.

Framboise (OG 1038, ABV 4%)
A pale yellow-coloured ale with a pleasant raspberry aroma leading to raspberry sweetness coming through on the palate and a smooth bitter finish.

Lasamboo (OG 1038, ABV 4%)
The addition of stem and fresh ginger gives warming ginger and lemon flavours.

Silhouette (OG 1038, ABV 4%)
A pale beer, the addition of vanilla pods gives a unique vanilla flavour.

Lady Julia (OG 1041, ABV 4.3%)
A golden ale. Wheat and barley produce a crisp beer with a floral hop aroma

Bananalicious (OG 1043, ABV 4.5%)
Mid brown ale with a banana and toffee aftertaste.

Lady Ruby (OG 1043, ABV 4.5%)
A dark ruby-coloured ale made with cherries. Hint of cherries on the nose, on the palate a bitter start which then finishes with a cherry bomb on the back of the tongue. An easy-drinking beer.

Apricot Jungle (OG 1046, ABV 4.8%)
A fruity, golden beer with honey, apricot and almond notes. The sweetness is balanced by hop bitterness.

Blondie (OG 1046, ABV 4.8%)
A strong golden-coloured beer whose aroma is dominated by characteristic citrus notes. Hops and fruit on the palate are balanced by malt, leading to a hoppy finish with soft fruit flavours.

Coco Loco (OG 1048, ABV 5%)
This dark/black-coloured beer is rich with caramel flavours. Full-bodied and well-balanced, coconut oil is added giving sweetness on the palate. An enjoyable, quirky beer.

Charioteer (OG 1063, ABV 6.5%)
An easy-drinking, strong beer. Subtle, with citrus flavours giving a fruity berry aroma and fruity flavour with a hint of malty sweetness, leading to a smooth, long finish.

Grain SIBA

South Farm, Tunbeck Road, Alburgh, Harleston, Norfolk, IP20 0BS
☎ (01986) 788884 ⊕ grainbrewery.co.uk
Shop Mon-Fri 10am-4pm, Sat 11am-3pm
Tours by arrangement

Grain Brewery was launched in 2006 by Geoff Wright and Phil Halls in a converted dairy in the Waveney Valley. It upgraded to a 15-barrel plant in 2012. Two bars are owned, the Plough, Norwich and the Corn Hall Bar, Diss.

Oak (OG 1038, ABV 3.8%)
A balanced mix of malt and hops with marmalade overtones. A hint of molasses in the short, sharp ending.

3.1.6. (OG 1039, ABV 3.9%)
Hops mingle with a citrus marmalade bite in both aroma and taste. Long strong finish with growing malty bitterness.

Blonde Ash Wheat Beer (OG 1040, ABV 4%)
Banana notes flow through this sweet smoky brew. Yellow hued with a grainy mouthfeel and a quick fruity finale.

Best Bitter (OG 1042, ABV 4.2%)
A well-balanced, complex bitter. A complex mix of flavours with malt and hops ably supported by caramel and bitterness.

Redwood (OG 1049, ABV 4.8%)
Heavy blackcurrant airs give way to a rich fruity bitterness with malt overtones. Copper-coloured, crisp and satisfying.

Blackwood Stout (OG 1050, ABV 5%)
Roast dominates from the initial aroma to the long lingering ending. A bittersweet chocolate undercurrent adds depth.

Porter (OG 1052, ABV 5%)
A creamy dark chocolate and roast character prevades throughout. A bittersweet edge grows in intensity. Black and brooding.

India Pale Ale (OG 1062, ABV 6.5%)
Powerful, complex and rich throughout. Malt and hops vie with tropical fruit and bitterness for dominance. Challenging and rewarding.

Grainstore SIBA

Station Approach, Oakham, Rutland, LE15 6RE
☎ (01572) 770065 ⊕ grainstorebrewery.com
Tours by arrangement

Grainstore, the smallest county's largest brewery, has been in production since 1995, founded by Tony Davis and Mike Davies. After 30 years in the

THE BREWERIES

industry Tony decided to set up his own business after finding a derelict Victorian railway grainstore building. 80 outlets are supplied.

Rutland Bitter (OG 1032, ABV 3.4%)
A light, well-balanced session beer. It is one of the few beers that is registered PGI (Protected Geographical Indication).

Rutland Panther (OG 1034, ABV 3.4%) ◆
This reddish-black mild punches above its weight with malt and roast flavours combining to deliver a brew that can match the average stout for intensity of flavour.

Cooking (OG 1036, ABV 3.6%) ◆
Tawny-coloured beer with malt and hops on the nose and a pleasant grainy mouthfeel. Hops and fruit flavours combine to give a bitterness that continues into a long finish.

Triple B (OG 1042, ABV 4.2%) ◆
Initially hops dominate over malt in both the aroma and taste, but fruit is there, too. All three linger in varying degrees in the sweetish aftertaste of this brown brew.

GB Best (OG 1043, ABV 4.3%)
A pronounced floral aroma and flavour.

Ratliffe's Stout (OG 1043, ABV 4.3%)

Gold (OG 1045, ABV 4.5%)
A refreshing light golden brew, with a mellow malt sweetness finely balanced by the smooth bitterness, subtle flavours and floral hop aromas.

Ten Fifty (OG 1050, ABV 5%) ◆
Pungent banana and malt notes on the nose. On the palate, rich malt and fruit is joined by subtle hop on a bittersweet base. Dry malt aftertaste with some fruit.

Rutland Beast (OG 1053, ABV 5.3%)
A unique strong mild ale. Complex flavours with chocolate and coffee notes as well as raisins and autumn fruits.

Nip (OG 1073, ABV 7.3%)
A well-balanced barley wine with a blend of sweetness and hop bitterness that. Smooth and warming with raisins and winter fruit as the dominant flavour notes.

Granite Rock (NEW)

Unit 19, Kernick Road Industrial Estate, Penryn, Cornwall, TR10 9EP
☎ **(01326) 379251** 🌐 **graniterockbrewery.co.uk**
Shop Mon-Fri 9am-5pm, Sat 10am-5pm
Tours by arrangement

Granite Rock was established in 2013 as a brewery and home brew shop. Located on an industrial estate in Penryn, the two-barrel plant produces three core beers, supplying the free trade in west Cornwall. Seasonal beer is available.

Penryn Company Pale Ale (OG 1040, ABV 4%)
A light, hoppy session beer.

Bronescombe's Vision (OG 1048, ABV 5.2%)
Deep hearty bitter with a malty, fruity aroma and a dry, bitter finish.

Glasney College Porter (OG 1050, ABV 5.4%)
Ruby-black porter with intense lingering burnt malt and earthy aromas and a smooth, smoky and gently bittersweet finish.

Great Heck SIBA

Harwinn House, Main Street, Great Heck, North Yorkshire, DN14 0BQ
☎ **(01977) 661430** 🌐 **greatheckbrewery.co.uk**
Tours by arrangement

Great Heck began production in 2008 in a converted slaughterhouse. The brewery moved across the road to a converted cottage in 2012 and now produces its regular beers on a 15-barrel plant with capacity for 45 barrels per week. Seasonal beers are available.

Powermouse (OG 1035, ABV 3.6%)
Pale session beer brewed with a unique blend of seven hop varieties.

Angel (OG 1037, ABV 3.9%)
A clean, dry, moderately bittered pale ale.

Dave (OG 1038, ABV 3.9%)
A dark session bitter with a satisfying roasty taste.

Andromeda IPA (OG 1041, ABV 4.1%)

Blonde (OG 1043, ABV 4.3%)
A well-balanced blonde beer with a zesty finish.

Voodoo Mild (OG 1043, ABV 4.3%)
Rich, black mild bursting with flavour from the roasted malts.

Yorkshire Pale Ale (OG 1043, ABV 4.3%)
A premium pale ale with a complex malt character and zesty finish.

Slaughterhouse Porter (OG 1045, ABV 4.5%)
A rich, dark, smooth-drinking porter with a tight, creamy white head.

Hopfweizen (OG 1045, ABV 4.7%)
Unusual German-style Weizen with American IPA-style flavour and aroma hops.

Treason Stout (OG 1054, ABV 5.4%)
An unfined wheat stout.

Yakima IPA (OG 1070, ABV 7.4%)
Deep golden in colour, low in bitterness. The alcohol balances the fruity hop flavours and aromas perfectly.

Great Newsome SIBA

Great Newsome Farm, South Frodingham, East Yorkshire, HU12 0NR
☎ **(01964) 612201** 🌐 **greatnewsomebrewery.co.uk**
Shop Mon-Fri 9am-4.30pm

Nestled in the Holderness countryside, Great Newsome began brewing in 2007 in renovated farm buildings. A range of beers are now brewed using barley from the farm and brewing can be seen from a newly-built viewing area. Beer is distributed throughout the UK and overseas. Seasonal beers: see website.

Sleck Dust (OG 1037, ABV 3.8%)
Straw-coloured, refreshingly bitter session beer with a floral aroma and subtle dry finish.

Pricky Back Otchan (OG 1042, ABV 4.2%)
Hoppy golden bitter with a fresh citrus aroma.

Frothingham Best (OG 1042, ABV 4.3%)
Dark amber best bitter with a subtle dry finish.

Jem's Stout (OG 1044, ABV 4.3%)
Dark, smooth beer with smoky, roasted malt flavours and aroma.

Great Oakley SIBA

Ark Farm, High Street South, Tiffield, Northamptonshire, NN12 8AB
☎ (01327) 351759 🌐 greatoakleybrewery.co.uk
Tours by arrangement

The brewery commenced production in 2005 in Great Oakley and relocated to Tiffield in 2012. It is run by husband and wife team Phil and Hazel Greenway. More than 60 outlets are supplied, including the George, Tiffield, which is the brewery tap. Seasonal beers: see website. Bottle-conditioned beers are available.

Welland Valley Mild (OG 1037, ABV 3.6%)
A dark, traditional mild. Full of flavour.

Eleanor Cross (OG 1039, ABV 3.8%)
An amber/gold-coloured ale.

Wagtail (OG 1040, ABV 3.9%)
Light-coloured with a unique bitterness derived from New Zealand hops.

Wot's Occurring (OG 1040, ABV 3.9%)
A mid-golden session bitter with a subtle hop finish.

Oakley Blonde (OG 1040, ABV 4%)
A blonde ale brewed with lager malt and German Hersbrucker hops.

Marching In (OG 1041, ABV 4.1%)
A golden, clean-tasting beer.

Harpers (OG 1044, ABV 4.3%)
Traditional mid-brown bitter with a malty taste and slight hints of chocolate and citrus in the finish.

Gobble (OG 1045, ABV 4.5%)
Straw-coloured with a pleasant hop aftertaste.

Delapre Dark (OG 1047, ABV 4.6%)
A dark, full-bodied ale made from five different malts.

Newport Delta (OG 1047, ABV 4.6%)
A blonde beer brewed with American Newport and Delta hops.

Abbey Stout (OG 1051, ABV 5%)
A dark rich stout.

Tailshaker (OG 1051, ABV 5%)
A complex golden ale with a great depth of flavour.

Great Orme SIBA

Nant y Cywarch, Glan Conwy, LL28 5PP
☎ (01492) 580548 🌐 greatormebrewery.co.uk

Great Orme is a five-barrel microbrewery situated on a hillside in the Conwy Valley between Llandudno and Betws-y-Coed, with views of the Conwy Estuary and the Great Orme. Established in 2005, it is housed in a number of converted farm buildings. Around 50 outlets are supplied.

Cambria (OG 1038, ABV 3.8%)
A pale brown malty session bitter with a dry taste. Some hoppy flavours develop in the bitter aftertaste.

Welsh Black (OG 1042, ABV 4%)
Smooth-tasting dark beer with roast coffee notes in aroma and taste. Sweetish in flavour and having some characteristics of a mild ale with hoppiness also present in the aftertaste.

Great Welsh (OG 1041, ABV 4.1%)
Sweetish best bitter with a smooth taste and a juicy mouth feel. Hoppy bitterness comes through in the finish.

Orme (OG 1042, ABV 4.2%)
Malty best bitter with a dry finish. Faint hop and fruit notes in aroma and taste, but malt dominates throughout.

Celtica (OG 1045, ABV 4.5%)
Yellow in colour with a zesty taste full of citrus fruit flavours. Some initial sweetness followed by peppery hops and a bitter finish.

Red Dragon (OG 1045, ABV 4.5%)
A red hued ale with complex character.

Ynys Mon (OG 1046, ABV 4.6%)
Deep copper-coloured with chocolate malts. Sweet aftertaste.

Merlyn (OG 1049, ABV 4.9%)
A strong ale with balanced hop bitterness and sweet malt.

Atlantis (OG 1050, ABV 5%)
Mid way between an American IPA and a traditional British ale.

Great Western SIBA

Stream Bakery, Bristol Road, Hambrook, Bristol, BS16 1RF
☎ (0117) 957 2842
🌐 greatwesternbrewingcompany.co.uk
Shop Mon, Wed-Thu 10am-5pm, Fri 10am-5pm, Sat 10am-2pm
Tours by arrangement

Great Western is a 12-barrel brewery set up in 2008 by Kevin Stone in a former bakery. The property has been renovated resulting in a bespoke showpiece brewery retaining many of the building's original features. 200 outlets are supplied and one pub is owned. Seasonal beers are available.

HPA (OG 1040, ABV 3.9%)
Hoppy yellow bitter with fresh fruit and pale malt aromas. Clean bitter citrus flavours with a lingering astringent finish.

Maiden Voyage (OG 1040, ABV 4%)
An amber bitter with a light aroma of malt and fruit. The complex taste is initially sweet and fruity (damson notes) and the slightly astringent finish is dry and biscuity.

The Shires (OG 1043, ABV 4.4%)
Tawny best bitter with fruit on the nose. Well-balanced flavours, long astringency in the aftertaste.

Classic Gold (OG 1044, ABV 4.6%)
Golden ale with subtle aromas of pale malt and fruits. Citrus fruits with balanced hop and malt character with a lingering bitter finish.

Old Higby (OG 1045, ABV 4.8%)
Full-bodied malty bitter with roast notes on the nose. Hints of fruit flavour give way to a bitter hop finish with some astringency throughout.

Great Yorkshire SIBA

Cropton, North Yorkshire, YO18 8HH
☎ (01751) 417330
🌐 thegreatyorkshirebrewery.co.uk
Tours by arrangement

THE BREWERIES

Great Yorkshire took over the Cropton Brewery in 2012 concentrating on the production of keg beers. The cask beer range is limited but includes seasonal and special beers: see website.

Yorkshire Pale (OG 1038, ABV 3.8%)
A pale ale, light and smooth with the flavours of mango and pineapple.

Yorkshire Classic (OG 1043.5, ABV 4%)
Light chestnut-coloured beer with a smooth, malty taste balanced with complex biscuit flavours.

Yorkshire Golden (OG 1045, ABV 4.2%)
A refreshing golden beer with hints of caramel and a honey-like sweetness.

Yorkshire Blackout (OG 1051, ABV 5%)

Green Dragon

Green Dragon, 29 Broad Street, Bungay, Suffolk, NR35 1EF
☎ (01986) 892681
Tours by arrangement

The Green Dragon pub was purchased in 1991 and the buildings at the rear converted to a brewery. In 1994 the plant was expanded and moved into a converted barn. The doubling of capacity allowed the production of a larger range of ales, including seasonal and occasional brews. The beers are available at the pub and beer festivals.

Chaucer Ale (OG 1037, ABV 3.8%)

Gold (OG 1045, ABV 4.4%)

Bridge Street Bitter (OG 1045, ABV 4.5%)

Green Duck

Unit 13, Gainsborough Trading Estate, Rufford Road, Stourbridge, West Midlands, DY9 7ND
greenduckbrewery.co.uk

Green Duck began brewing in 2012 via Grafton Brewery while acquiring equipment and premises. In 2013 brewing moved to Stourbridge with a tap room overlooking the brew plant. Beer festivals, quiz nights, charity and local CAMRA events take place at the brewery.

Green Jack SIBA

Argyle Place, Love Road, Lowestoft, Suffolk, NR32 2NZ
☎ (01502) 562863 green-jack.com
Tours by arrangement

After 10 years at Oulton Broad, Green Jack moved to the Triangle Tavern, Lowestoft in 2003 and then to a nearby 35-barrel plant in 2009. Three pubs are owned and more than 150 outlets supplied. Bottle-conditioned beers: see website.

Golden Best (OG 1038, ABV 3.8%)
Cut grass hop aroma deepens on the palate of this golden bitter. Initially bitter, the aftertaste is fairly short and hoppy.

Orange Wheat Beer (OG 1041, ABV 4.2%)
Marmalade aroma with a hint of hops, leading to a well-balanced blend of sweetness, hops and citrus with a malt background. Mixed fruit flavours in the aftertaste.

Trawlerboys Best Bitter (OG 1045, ABV 4.6%)
Tawny beer with an aroma of apple, sultana and malt plus hints of caramel and hops. Rich fig and plum base with malt and roast overtones. Strong finish with a sticky mouthfeel.

Lurcher Stout (OG 1046, ABV 4.8%)
Pleasant malt, roast and fruit aromas. Blackberry, raisin and port flavours. Long, dry bitter, roast finish.

Mahseer IPA (OG 1048, ABV 5%)

Rising Sun (OG 1048, ABV 5%)

Red Herring (OG 1048, ABV 5.1%)

Gone Fishing ESB (OG 1052, ABV 5.5%)

Ripper (OG 1074, ABV 8.5%)

Baltic Trader Export Stout (OG 1092, ABV 10.5%)

Green Mill SIBA

Harewood Arms, 2 Market Street, Broadbottom, SK14 6AX ☎ 07967 656887
greenmillbrewery.co.uk

Green Mill started brewing in 2007 on a 2.5-barrel plant and moved in 2010 to the Cask & Feather in Rochdale. The brewery relocated again in 2013 to the Harewood Arms in Broadbottom. A number of occasional beers are brewed. Around 40 outlets are supplied.

Gold (OG 1035, ABV 3.6%)
A quaffable golden session bitter.

Chief (OG 1041, ABV 4.2%)
A smooth, pale bitter with American hop varieties.

Citrus Snap (OG 1040, ABV 4.2%)
A copper-coloured bitter with citrus notes.

Old Git (OG 1040, ABV 4.2%)
A refreshing golden ale; complex and well-hopped.

Talisman (OG 1040, ABV 4.2%)
A straw-coloured golden ale with tropical fruit notes.

Flavia (OG 1042, ABV 4.5%)
A blonde beer with a fresh hop aroma brewed with lager malt, leading to a clean, dry finish.

Northern Lights (OG 1045, ABV 4.5%)
A pale premium bitter, well-hopped.

Big Chief (OG 1052, ABV 5.5%)
A hoppy premium bitter.

Greene King

Westgate Brewery, Westgate Street, Bury St Edmunds, Suffolk, IP33 1QT
☎ (01284) 763222 greeneking.co.uk
Shop Mon-Fri 10.30am-4.30pm; Sat 10.30am-5.30pm
Tours by arrangement

Greene King has been brewing in the market town of Bury St Edmunds since 1799. It brews its beers using water drawn from artesian chalk wells below its brew house as well as local East Anglia malt. Part of Greene King PLC.

XX Mild (OG 1035, ABV 3%)
A dark mild with a sweet and roast flavour.

IPA (OG 1036, ABV 3.6%)
Hop-infused fruit cake aromas. Complex flavours of malt, caramel and hop with both sweetness and

bitterness. A lingering mellow aftertaste with blackberries.

London Glory (OG 1041.1, ABV 4%)
Rich, fruity and full of flavour.

IPA Gold (OG 1041, ABV 4.1%)
A deep golden ale with a blend of tropical fruits, mango and spicy notes.

Abbot (OG 1049, ABV 5%)
Strong malt, toffee and caramel aromas. Rich malty caramel flavours with vine fruit and a little hop bite. Heavy sweet finish with a subtle hint of bitterness in the aftertaste.

IPA Reserve (OG 1055.5, ABV 5.4%)
A full-bodied amber ale. Grapefruit and orange citrus tones combine with the floral and herbal notes from the hops and lead to a dry bitter finish.

Brewed under the Hardys & Hansons brand name:

Bitter (OG 1038, ABV 3.9%)
A balance of sweetness and bitterness that combines with a subtle hop character. A distinctive beer with a full finish.

Olde Trip (OG 1043, ABV 4.3%)
A rich toffee flavoured beer with a fruity character and a clean, bitter finish.

Brewed under the Morland brand name:

Original Bitter (OG 1039, ABV 4%)
A subtle malt and fruit character and a pronounced bitter finish.

Old Golden Hen (OG 1038.6, ABV 4.1%)
Light golden beer with tropical fruit notes.

Old Speckled Hen (OG 1045, ABV 4.5%)
Smooth, malty and fruity, with a short finish.

Brewed under the Ruddles brand name:

Best Bitter (OG 1037, ABV 3.7%)
An amber/brown beer, strong on bitterness but with some initial sweetness, fruit and subtle, distinctive Bramling Cross hop. Dryness lingers in the aftertaste.

County (OG 1043, ABV 4.3%)
Sweet, malty and bitter, with a dry and bitter aftertaste.

Brewed under the Tolly Cobbold brand name:

English Ale (OG 1033.6, ABV 2.8%)
Amber ale brewed using a complex mix of hops to offer balanced bitterness with strong tropical notes.

Greenfield SIBA

Unit 8, Waterside Mills, Greenfield, Saddleworth, OL3 7NH
☎ (01457) 879789 greenfieldbrewery.co.uk
Shop 9am-5pm daily
Tours by arrangement

Greenfield was launched in 2002 and is situated in an old spinning mill next to the River Chew on the edge of the Peak District National Park. Spring water from the National Park is used for brewing. It is open to the public and supplies beer to them and to more than 200 outlets. Seasonal beers are available.

Silver Owl (OG 1042, ABV 4%)
A golden-amber beer with an aroma of citrus fruits and hints of vanilla – oranges, dryness and lightly-hopped taste.

Thirst Born (OG 1041, ABV 4.1%)
Floral citrus aroma with malt and hops. Taste of citrus, peach, floral malt.

Dobcross Bitter (OG 1041, ABV 4.2%)
An amber beer with lemon flavours and a dry finish.

Copper Caskade (OG 1042, ABV 4.3%)
A full-bodied, copper-coloured beer made with Cascade hops. A medium bitterness with a hoppy finish revealing both citrus and fruit tones.

Vanilla Stout (OG 1048, ABV 5.2%)
A true black stout. Initial flavours of both chocolate and coffee are revealed before the roasted malts give way to a natural vanilla finish, created by the use of real vanilla pods during the cask maturation stage.

Greenodd

Ship Inn, Main Street, Greenodd, Cumbria, LA12 7QZ ☎ 07782 655294
greenoddbrewery@yahoo.co.uk
Tours by arrangement

Greenodd was established in 2010 at the Ship Inn using a two-barrel plant. The majority of production goes to the Ship with the remainder going to local free trade.

Blonde (OG 1040, ABV 4%)

Best Bitter (OG 1041, ABV 4.1%)

Roundabout (OG 1043, ABV 4.3%)

Brunette (OG 1045, ABV 4.5%)

Greg's (NEW)

Dambusters Inn, 23 High Street, Scampton, Lincolnshire, LN1 2SD
☎ (01522) 731333 gregsbrewery.com

Greg's is a microbrewery launched in 2013 on the premises of the Dambusters Inn. The beer is brewed by Greg Algar, the landlord of the pub.

Aviator (ABV 3.8%)
A golden bitter with moderate bitterness and floral and citrus characteristics.

Just Bomber (ABV 4.2%)
A well-balanced session beer with a fresh, clean taste.

Grey Trees SIBA

Unit 5-6, Gasworks Road, Aberaman, CF44 6RS
☎ (01685) 267077 greytreesbrewery.com

Grey Trees began brewing at the Red Cow Inn in 2011 on the outskirts of Aberdare and relocated to its present location in 2013. The 10-barrel plant was originally used by Breconshire Brewery. It supplies an increasing number of local outlets.

Caradog's Bitter (OG 1038, ABV 3.9%)
A copper-coloured bitter with a crisp flavour and dry finish.

Black Road Stout (OG 1040, ABV 4%)
A dark, smooth stout with delicate roasted flavours and a bittersweet aftertaste.

Digger's Gold Ale (OG 1040, ABV 4%)
A golden ale with fresh citrus aromas and a subtle bitterness.

Drummer Boy Bitter (OG 1042, ABV 4.2%)

THE BREWERIES

JPR Pale Ale (OG 1046, ABV 4.7%)
A traditional British pale ale, well-balanced with both a citrus aroma and taste.

Gribble

Gribble Inn, Oving, West Sussex, PO20 2BP
☎ (01243) 786893 🌐 gribbleinn.co.uk

Established in 1980 using a five-barrel plant, the Gribble Brewery is the longest serving brewpub in the Sussex area. Independently owned and run by the licensees. A number of local outlets are supplied. Seasonal beers are available.

CHI P A (ABV 3.8%)

Ale (ABV 4.1%)

Fuzzy Duck (ABV 4.3%)

Reg's Tipple (ABV 4.8%)
Named after a customer from the early days of the brewery. It has a smooth, nutty flavour with a pleasant afterbite.

Plucking Pheasant (ABV 5%)

Pig's Ear (ABV 6%)

Wobbler (ABV 7.2%)

Griffin

Church Road, Shustoke, Warwickshire, B46 2LB
☎ (01675) 481205 🌐 griffininnshustoke.co.uk
Tours by arrangement

Brewing started in 2008 in the old coffin shop premises adjacent to the Griffin Inn. The five-barrel brewery is a venture between Griffin licensee Mick Pugh and his son Oliver. Most output goes to the pub, but free trade presence is increasing. Seasonal ales and occasional experimental brews are produced.

Pain in the Arse (OG 1037, ABV 3.7%)
Classic bitter, well-hopped with a malty aftertaste.

Gold (OG 1042, ABV 4.2%)
A light golden ale. Soft but with a full-bodied taste and citrus aroma.

Yeti (OG 1047, ABV 4.7%)
A light-coloured pale ale with a grapefruit aftertaste.

Thomas Guest

See Black Country

Gun Dog SIBA

Unit 5b, Great Central Way, Woodford Halse, Northamptonshire, NN11 3PZ
☎ (01327) 264095 🌐 gundogales.co.uk
Shop Mon-Fri 9am-5pm, Sat 10am-1.30pm
Tours by arrangement

Gun Dog began brewing in 2012 using a six-barrel plant. Seasonal beers are brewed. All beers are also available bottle conditioned.

Jack's Spaniels (OG 1038, ABV 3.8%)
A floral, refreshing blonde ale.

Booze Hound (OG 1042, ABV 4.2%)
A copper-coloured, easy-drinking, malty pale ale.

Lord Barker (OG 1042, ABV 4.2%)
A rich, dark, smooth and well-balanced stout with a chocolate nose, rounded taste in the mouth and a clean finish.

Bad to the Bone (OG 1045, ABV 4.5%)
A light brown English bitter. Biscuit undertones are balanced with a fruity hop finish.

Gundog

See Acton

Gwaun Valley

Kilkiffeth Farm, Pontfaen, SA65 9TP
☎ (01348) 881304 🌐 gwaunvalleybrewery.co.uk
Shop & Vistor Centre 10am-6pm daily
Tours by arrangement

Gwaun Valley began brewing in 2009 on a four-barrel plant in a converted granary. The brewery offers views of the Presel Hills and has a camp site, a holiday cottage and pitches for five caravans.

Golden Bitter (OG 1040, ABV 4%)
A smooth bitter ale with a strong hoppy flavour and a crisp finish.

Blodwen (OG 1041, ABV 4.1%)
Creamy full-bodied bitter, ruby red in colour with a hint of caramel.

Valley Brew (OG 1041, ABV 4.1%)
A double hopped bitter ale with a fine mellow taste and a balanced sweetness.

King of the Road (OG 1045, ABV 4.5%)
A full-bodied, smooth, classic light chestnut ale with a well-balanced finish.

Pembrokeshire Best (OG 1045, ABV 4.5%)
A full-flavoured, malty bitter ale with a hoppy finish.

Calon Lan (OG 1048, ABV 4.8%)
Malty with a medium body and a bittersweet aftertaste.

Gwynant

Tynllidiart Arms, Capel Bangor, Ceredigion, SY23 3LR
☎ (01970) 880248 🌐 tynllidiartarms.com
Tours by arrangement

Brewing started in 2004 in a former men's toilet at the front of the Tynllidiart Arms. Its 9-gallon brew length is recognised as the world's smallest commercial brewery by the Guinness Book of Records. Brewing is currently suspended, but may recommence. Meanwhile, brewing the one beer, which is occasionally available, has been contracted out.

Cwrw Gwynant (OG 1045, ABV 4.5%)

Gyle 59 (NEW) SIBA

The Brewery, Sadborow Estate Yard, Thorncombe, Dorset, TA20 4PW
☎ (01297) 678990 🌐 gyle59.co.uk

Gyle 59 is a 10-barrel brewery that began commercial production in 2014. All beers are unfined and available cask and bottle-conditioned. Bottling takes place on site with bottles being available by mail order. Beer can be bought at the brewery and a shop is planned.

Toujours (OG 1042, ABV 4%)
A saison-style beer.

Pale & Bitter (OG 1046, ABV 5%)
A strong pale ale.

IPA (OG 1050, ABV 5.3%)

Dorset Gipa (OG 1050, ABV 5.4%)
A ginger infused IPA.

Starstruck (OG 1060, ABV 6.6%)
A fruity porter enhanced by the addition of star anise.

The Favourite (OG 1060, ABV 6.6%)
A smooth, rich porter.

Hackney SIBA

Arch 358, Laburnum Street, London, E2 8BB
☎ (020) 3489 9595 🌐 hackneybrewery.co.uk

⊗ Having met eight years ago while working at the Eagle on Farringdon Road, home brewers and good friends Jon Swain and Peter Hills decided to turn their pastime in to a profession and brew beer in the heart of Hackney. They are committed to giving a penny from every pint sold to local community charities. Bottle-conditioned beers are also available.

Golden Ale (OG 1041, ABV 4%) ◆
A light fruity ale with a malty biscuit quality. A touch of dryness and a pleasant bitterness in the finish.

Best Bitter (OG 1044, ABV 4.4%) ◆
Malty sweetness is present with trace of toffee. Hop notes and a fruit cocktail flavour diminish in the dry aftertaste.

American Pale Ale (OG 1045, ABV 4.5%) ◆
Copper brown beer with a sweet citrus aroma and full smooth mouthfeel. Citrus and floral hops on the palate.

New Zealand Pale Ale (OG 1045, ABV 4.5%)
A pale ale with a tropical nose with a fruity hop flavour. Residual sweetness from the malts and a long, fruity aftertaste.

Hadrian Border SIBA

Unit 5 The Preserving Works, Newburn Industrial Estate, Shelley Road, Newburn, Newcastle upon Tyne, NE15 9RT
☎ (0191) 264 9000 🌐 hadrian-border-brewery.co.uk
Tours by arrangement

Originally based at the Four Rivers site in Newcastle, the brewery relocated to Newburn in 2011 with a new 30-barrel brew plant to meet increased demand. The company's products are popular on Tyneside and its customer base extends through Northumberland to Edinburgh and Glasgow and down to Yorkshire. The brands are also available nationally via wholesalers. Seasonal beers: see website.

Tyneside Blonde (OG 1037, ABV 3.9%) ◆
Refreshing blonde ale with zesty notes and a clean, fruity finish.

Farne Island Pale Ale (OG 1038, ABV 4%) ◆
A copper-coloured bitter with a refreshing malt/hop balance.

Flotsam (OG 1038, ABV 4%)
Bronze-coloured with a citrus bitterness and a distinctive floral aroma.

Needles & Pins (OG 1041.5, ABV 4.2%)
Dark amber-coloured beer, fruity and well-bodied.

Secret Kingdom (OG 1042, ABV 4.3%)
Dark, rich and full-bodied, slightly roasted with a malty palate ending with a pleasant bitterness.

Coast to Coast (OG 1041.5, ABV 4.4%)
Light amber-coloured, hoppy beer with a good malt balance.

Reiver's IPA (OG 1042, ABV 4.4%)
Golden bitter with a clean citrus palate and aroma with subtle malt flavours breaking through at the end.

Jetsam (OG 1043, ABV 4.5%)

Northumbrian Gold (OG 1044, ABV 4.5%)

Grainger Ale (OG 1045, ABV 4.6%)
A pale ale with a well-balanced, refreshingly bitter finish.

Hafod SIBA

Old Gas Works, Gas Lane, Mold, CH7 1UR ☎ 07901 386638 🌐 welshbeer.com

◎Hafod began brewing in 2011 on a small scale and moved to new premises in 2014 to provide additional capacity. A number of speciality beers are produced on a limited basis using ingredients from the local upland areas and heathlands. All beers are available bottle conditioned.

Taverns Tipple (OG 1034.5, ABV 3.5%)

Classic (OG 1036.5, ABV 3.8%) ◆
Copper coloured, smooth and full-bodied. Juicy malt taste with some initial toffee flavours and hops developing in the aftertaste.

Hopper (OG 1037, ABV 3.8%) ◆
A full-flavoured session bitter with a mouthwatering taste of peppery hops and a lasting dry finish.

Moel Famau Ale (OG 1039, ABV 4.1%) ◆
A speciality dark ale brewed using local heather giving a dry, roasty taste with underlying sweet malt flavours.

HE (OG 1040.5, ABV 4.3%)

Fenlli Honey Ale (OG 1044, ABV 4.4%)

Light (OG 1043, ABV 4.6%) ◆
Amber beer with a citrus fruit nose, sweetish taste with hints of vanilla, and a clean bittersweet finish.

Hammer (OG 1059, ABV 6.6%) ◆
A sweet, strong bitter full of tropical fruits in aroma and taste, balanced by a powerful hoppy finish.

Half Moon (NEW) SIBA

Forge House, Main Street, Ellerton, East Yorkshire, YO42 4PB
☎ (01757) 288977 🌐 halfmoonbrewery.co.uk

Established in 2013 by Tony and Jackie Rogers, the brewery is based in the original blacksmith's forge next to their house. A five-barrel plant produces three core beers and a special once a month. Ales are available locally.

Winter's Mild (OG 1033, ABV 3.3%)
A classic, easy-drinking mild.

F'Hops Sake (OG 1039, ABV 3.9%)
Pale session bitter with a fruity and hoppy aftertaste.

Gyle One (OG 1045, ABV 4.5%)
A bright golden ale with a refreshing hit of grapefruit and a hoppy finish.

Halfpenny

Crown Inn, High Street, Lechlade, Gloucestershire, GL7 3AE
☎ (01367) 252198 🌐 halfpennybrewery.co.uk
Shop at pub
Tours by arrangement

Halfpenny was established in 2008 on a four-barrel plant at the Crown at Lechlade, visible in an outbuilding, and has since expanded to a third fermentation vessel. 15-20 local outlets are supplied direct. Bottle-conditioned beers are available.

Ha'penny Ale (OG 1039, ABV 4%)

Thames Tickler (OG 1040, ABV 4%)

Anniversary Ale (OG 1042, ABV 4.2%)

Four Seasons' Ale (OG 1042, ABV 4.3%)

Old Lech (OG 1045, ABV 4.5%)

Halifax Steam

The Conclave, Southedge Works, Brighouse Road, Hipperholme, West Yorkshire, HX3 8EF ☎ 07974 544980 🌐 halifax-steam.co.uk

Halifax Steam was established in 2001 on a five-barrel plant and supplies only its brewery tap, the Cock o' the North, which is adjacent to the brewery. Approximately 150 different rotating beers are produced, three of which are permanent. 10-12 Halifax Steam beers are available at any one time, plus occasional guests on a fair trade basis.

Aussie Kiss (OG 1038, ABV 3.8%)
A light beer with a hoppy flavour and finish.

Uncle Jon (OG 1043, ABV 4.3%)
Roast predominates in this creamy, dark brown stout. The finish is smooth with no harsh edges.

Childcatcher (OG 1048, ABV 4.8%)
Pale, smooth-drinking beer with a citrus hop aroma and flavour.

Hall & Woodhouse (Badger) IFBB

Bournemouth Road, Blandford St Mary, Blandford Forum, Dorset, DT11 9LS
☎ (01258) 452141 🌐 hall-woodhouse.co.uk
Shop Mon-Sat 9am-6pm, Sun 11am-3pm (Easter-Oct)
Tours by arrangement

Founded by Charles Hall in 1777, Hall & Woodhouse is a major independent family brewer, run by the seventh generation of the founders. The Badger logo was adopted in 1875. The company moved from Ansty to its present site in 1899 and a new brewery was built on part of the existing site, taking over full production from the 1899 brewery in 2012. Cask-conditioned beer is sold in all 210 tied houses. Seasonal beers are available.

K&B Sussex Bitter (OG 1036, ABV 3.5%)
Traditional, lightly-hopped, easy-drinking session bitter with hints of malt and caramel and the traditional Badger fruit flavour predominating in the lingering bitter aftertaste.

Badger First Call (OG 1041, ABV 4%)
Good example of a best bitter with strong, but not over-powering, hop aromas and flavours and a good bittersweet aftertaste.

Tanglefoot (OG 1047, ABV 4.9%)
Relatively sweet-tasting and deceptive, given its strength. Pale malt provides caramel overtones and bittersweet finish.

Hambleton SIBA

Melmerby Green Road, Melmerby, North Yorkshire, HG4 5NB
☎ (01765) 640108 🌐 hambletonales.co.uk
Tours by arrangement

Established in 1991 on the banks of the River Swale in the Vale of York, expansion over the years has resulted in relocation to larger premises on several occasions, the last being in 2007. Capacity in the custom-built brewery is 100 barrels a week with a bottling line also catering for other micros and larger brewers, handling more than 50 brands. The core range is supplemented by a monthly special beer. The company contract brews for the Village Brewer, Black Dog Brewery and Northern Monk.

Bitter (OG 1038.5, ABV 3.8%)
A golden bitter with a good balance of malty and refreshing citrus notes leading to a mellow, tangy finish.

Stallion (OG 1041, ABV 4.2%)
A premium bitter, moderately hoppy throughout and richly balanced in malt and fruit, developing a sound and robust bitterness, with earthy hops drying the aftertaste.

Stud (OG 1042.5, ABV 4.3%)
A strongly bitter beer, with rich hop and fruit. It ends dry and spicy.

Nightmare (OG 1050, ABV 5%)
This impressively flavoured beer satisfies all parts of the palate. Strong roast malts dominate, but hoppiness rears out of this complex blend.

Contract brewed for Black Dog Brewery, Whitby:

Whitby Abbey Ale (OG 1037.5, ABV 3.8%)

Schooner (OG 1041.5, ABV 4.2%)

Rhatas (OG 1045, ABV 4.6%)

Contract brewed for Village Brewer:

White Boar (OG 1037.5, ABV 3.8%)

Bull (OG 1039, ABV 4%)

Hamelsworde

16 Longworth Road, Hemsworth, West Yorkshire, WF9 4SZ ☎ 07530 669332 🌐 hamelsworde.co.uk

The brainchild of enthusiastic home brewer Dan Jones, his beers were originally brewed using a 50-litre boiler in a converted garage. A one-barrel plant was installed in 2013.

Spanish Stout (OG 1045, ABV 4.2%)
A traditional stout with strong roasted flavours and a sweet liquorice taste complemented by aniseed.

Haley's Comet (OG 1047, ABV 4.5%)
A fresh, light summer ale with a citrus aroma and taste.

Jumping Pirate (OG 1051, ABV 4.9%)

A light but complex golden ale with floral, pine and citrus notes. Smooth on the finish.

Colin Brown Ale (OG 1054, ABV 5.2%)
A deep amber-red in colour. A fruity hop aroma leads on to a malty, nutty, bittersweet flavour with a long, dry aftertaste. The late hop addition creates a citrus burst.

Scalded Shoulder (OG 1054, ABV 5.2%)
A refreshing wheat beer, single-hopped and finished with coriander and orange.

Cherokee America IPA (OG 1063, ABV 6%)
A copper-coloured IPA with a strong, fruity hop aroma.

Hammerpot SIBA

Unit 30, The Vinery, Arundel Road, Poling, West Sussex, BN18 9PY
☎ (01903) 883338 🌐 hammerpot-brewery.co.uk

⊗ Hammerpot started brewing in 2005 using a five-barrel plant, which was upgraded to 10 barrels in 2011. The brewery supplies as far as London and Southampton. Seasonal, special and occasional beers: see website. Bottle-conditioned beers are also available.

Shooting Star (OG 1038, ABV 3.8%)

HPA (OG 1044, ABV 4.1%)
A light, golden tangy pale ale with a full, fresh hop flavour

Red Hunter (OG 1046, ABV 4.3%)
A ruby red bitter with a full-bodied, rich character. A premium bitter that drinks smoothly, leaving a fine lace in the glass.

Woodcote (OG 1047, ABV 4.5%)
A tangy amber-coloured bitter with a pleasant dry finish.

Brighton Belle (ABV 4.6%)
A pale amber-coloured bitter. Fresh floral hop notes, spicy orange, crisp grapefruit and a hint of caramel.

Bottle Wreck Porter (OG 1047, ABV 4.7%)
A traditional pitch black porter with coffee, chocolate and rich roast malt flavours.

Madgwick Gold (OG 1050, ABV 5%)
A golden ale with a fresh citrus spice hop aroma and a refreshing, thirst-quenching finish.

Hammerton (NEW)

Unit 8 & 9, Roman Way Industrial Estate, 149 Roman Way, Barnsbury, London, N7 8XH
☎ (020) 3302 5880 🌐 hammertonbrewery.co.uk

Hammerton Brewery originally began brewing in London in 1868. It ceased to brew in the late 1950s and was later demolished. In 2014, a member of the Hammerton family decided to resurrect the family name in brewing. A 15-barrel plant is used. Bottle-conditioned beers are available and seasonal beers are planned.

N1 (ABV 4.1%)

N7 (ABV 5.2%)

Pentonville (ABV 5.3%)

Hand Drawn Monkey

Plover Road Garage, Plover Road, Lindley, Huddersfield, West Yorkshire, HD3 3HS
☎ (01484) 655262 ☎ 07739 754816
🌐 hdmbeer.com

Hand Drawn Monkey commenced brewing on the Mallinson's Brewery plant during 2012 and took over the plant after Mallinson's moved premises.

Malpa (OG 1039, ABV 3.9%)

Pale Ale (OG 1040, ABV 4%)

Monkeys Love Hops (OG 1042, ABV 4.2%)

What Would Jephers Do? (OG 1045, ABV 4.5%)

Porter (OG 1048, ABV 4.8%)

IPA (OG 1050, ABV 5%)

Double Belgium (OG 1060, ABV 6%)

Handley's

Two Drinks Ltd, Willow Tree, Front Street, Barnby in the Willows, Nottinghamshire, NG24 2SA
☎ (01636) 629003 🌐 willowtreebarnby.co.uk

Handley's began brewing in 2011 on a 0.5-barrel plant installed behind the Willow Tree pub by owner Brett Handley. Beer is mostly sold in the pub but can be found at beer festivals and in other outlets if stocks permit.

Handmade (NEW)

Ffos Y Ffin Fawr, Capel Dewi, Carmarthenshire, SA32 8AG
☎ (01559) 371784 ☎ 07896 690020
🌐 handmadebeer.co.uk

Brewing began in 2013, the brewery is situated in a farm shed off the beaten track. The plant and site were previously used by the Ffos y Ffin Brewery. Bottle-conditioned beer is available.

Pale Ale (OG 1042, ABV 4.2%)

Special Bitter (OG 1045, ABV 4.5%)

Hanlons SIBA

Hill Farm, Half Moon Village, Newton St Cyres, Devon, EX5 5AE ☎ 07725 715155 🌐 hanlonsbrewery.com
Tours by arrangement

O'Hanlons is under new ownership and moved to Half Moon, near Exeter, in 2014. Renamed Hanlons, the company is producing the same range of ales and has added two more.

Yellowhammer (OG 1041, ABV 4%)
A well-balanced, smooth pale yellow beer with a predominant hop and fruit nose and taste, leading to a dry, bitter finish.

Dry Stout (OG 1043, ABV 4.2%)
A dark malty, well-balanced stout with a dry, bitter finish and plenty of roast and fruit flavours up front.

Port Stout (OG 1041, ABV 4.8%)
A black beer with roast malt in the aroma that remains in the taste but gives way to hoppy bitterness in the aftertaste.

Ha'penny SIBA

Cuckoo Hall Brewery, Unit 8, Aldborough Hall Farm, Aldborough Hatch, Ilford, Essex, IG2 7TD

☎ (020) 8599 1338 🌐 hapenny-brewing.co.uk
Tours by arrangement

⊗ Ha'penny was established in 2009 by two CAMRA members in a disused stable block that had a former life as a pub and beer house for the Aldborough Hall estate workers.

London Particular Ruby Ale (OG 1040, ABV 4%) ◆
Some spicy hops are present in this ruby brown beer with a little fruit character. Finish is slightly dry.

London Stone Bitter (OG 1045, ABV 4.5%) ◆
A traditional brown best bitter with a hoppy aroma. The bitter character on the palate fades in the dry aftertaste.

Happy Valley

8 Hazelhurst Drive, Bollington, Cheshire, SK10 5QT
☎ **07758 512080** 🌐 **happyvalleybrewery.co.uk**
Tours by arrangement

⊗ Happy Valley was established in 2010 by David and Nicola Hughes using a 2.5-barrel plant. Pubs are supplied in Cheshire, Derbyshire, Greater Manchester and Staffordshire.

Small & Mighty (OG 1036, ABV 3.6%)
A clean, crisp and refreshing ale with a lasting, floral citrus aroma with a hint of lemon.

Sworn Secret (OG 1038, ABV 3.8%)
Pale straw-coloured ale with a strong hop character. It has a pleasant hoppy nose with a citrus aftertaste.

Little Rascal (OG 1039, ABV 3.9%)
A light golden session ale, well-balanced with a lingering citrus and grapefruit aftertaste.

Five Rings (OG 1040, ABV 4%)
Crisp, clean-tasting ale.

Lazy Daze (OG 1042, ABV 4.2%)
Golden-coloured beer with a hoppy finish.

Black Magic (OG 1046, ABV 4.6%)
A full-bodied, hearty stout.

Tie the Knot (OG 1050, ABV 5%)
A straw-coloured strong bitter brewed in an IPA style. The beer has malt tastes and a big hop character.

Dangerously Dark (OG 1056, ABV 5.6%)
A black IPA.

Bollywood IPA (OG 1056, ABV 5.9%)
A full-bodied, straw-coloured strong beer. Rounded malt flavours blend with bitterness and a big hop character. Deep and intensely rich taste.

Harbour SIBA

Trekillick Farm, Kirland, Bodmin, Cornwall, PL30 5BB
☎ **(01208) 832131** 🌐 **harbourbrewing.com**

⊗ Harbour is an innovative 10-barrel brewery founded on the outskirts of Bodmin in 2011. Brewed using local spring water, the four regular beers are established in an increasing number of outlets.

Light (OG 1037, ABV 3.7%) ◆
Refreshing, light golden ale packed full of citrus hops all the way through. Some bitterness and dryness in the finish.

Amber (OG 1037.5, ABV 4%) ◆
Apple, citrus, tropical fruits and hints of toffee. Some malt and hops on the nose, finishing lightly bitter, malty and dry.

IPA (OG 1048.5, ABV 5%) ◆
Citrus hop and malt on the nose. Bitter with Seville orange hop balanced by malt and butterscotch. Bitter, dry finish.

Porter (OG 1055, ABV 5.5%) ◆
Smooth black porter with malt aroma. Roast malt, chocolate and smoky fruit flavours with sweetness and bitterness coming in.

Pale (OG 1059, ABV 6%)

Hardhead (NEW)

Unit 26, Pensilva Industrial Estate, Pensilva, Cornwall, PL14 5RE
☎ **(01208) 590707** 🌐 **hardheadbrewery.co.uk**

Hardhead is a three-barrel brewery situated on the southern edge of Bodmin Moor, established in 2014. Seasonal beers are available.

Best Bitter (OG 1040, ABV 4%)
An amber-coloured, malty and fruity brew with a clean finish.

India Pale Ale (OG 1055, ABV 5.5%)
An IPA with a crisp sharpness brewed with a mix of traditional and new hop varieties.

Hardknott SIBA

Unit 10, Devonshire Road Industrial Estate, Millom, Cumbria, LA18 4JS
☎ **(01229) 779309** 🌐 **hardknott.com**
Tours by arrangement

⊛ Hardknott began brewing in 2005 at the Woolpack Inn in Boot. The brewery relocated to Millom and expanded in 2010. It specialises in limited edition bottle-conditioned and regular cask-conditioned beers. All bottled beers are suitable for vegans.

Katalyst (OG 1040, ABV 3.8%) ◆
An assertively hoppy, bitter beer, with a sweet fruity taste which diminishes in the finish.

Lux Borealis (OG 1038, ABV 3.8%) ◆
Fruity, hoppy aromas lead to a well-balanced middle with hops increasing in the finish.

Continuum (OG 1042, ABV 4%) ◆
An amber-coloured beer with pronounced hops and bitterness right through to the aftertaste. Some maltiness in the aroma and taste.

Cold Fusion (OG 1044, ABV 4.4%) ◆
A well-balanced, mild sweet beer with ginger. The ginger bite builds in the finish.

Duality (OG 1044, ABV 4.5%)

Dark Energy (OG 1052, ABV 4.9%) ◆
A hoppy aroma leads to a dry hoppy beer with plenty of roast.

Code Black (OG 1056, ABV 5.6%) ◆
High impact hops and roast malt leave a lasting impression. A memorable beer.

Azimuth (OG 1057, ABV 5.8%) ◆
Floral and fruity esters and lots of interesting hops and some complex bitterness create a fascinating tasting experience.

Infra Red (OG 1065, ABV 6.2%)
Hints of toffee and popcorn. Citrus fruits dominate.

Hardys & Hansons

See Greene King

Haresfoot (NEW)

2 River Park Industrial Estate, Billet Lane, Berkhamsted, Hertfordshire, HP4 1HL
☎ (01442) 862878 🌐 haresfoot.com
Shop Thu & Fri 4-7pm, Sat 10am-6pm (excluding Bank Holidays)

Brewing returned to the heart of Berkhamsted in 2014 after an absence of 100 years. The brewery, established by a consortium of eight local businessmen, is situated in an industrial unit close to the Grand Union Canal and consists of a dual channel 12 and 2.5-barrel plant.

Lock Keeper's Launch Ale (OG 1039, ABV 3.9%)
A complex blend of malts with a hoppy edge and delicate fruit notes, leading to a long, bittersweet aftertaste.

Harrogate (NEW)

The Coach House, 31-35 West Lea Avenue, Harrogate, North Yorkshire, HG2 0AT 🌐 harrogatebrewery.co.uk

Started in 2013, the brewery also uses the name Spa Town Ales on the pumpclips for the five ales that are brewed.

Tewit Well Ale (OG 1041, ABV 4.1%)
Copper-coloured traditional Yorkshire bitter tasting of malt, spices and orange peel.

Stray Ale (OG 1042, ABV 4.2%)
Golden ale with a spicy flavour and lingering hop finish.

Pinewoods Pale Ale (OG 1044, ABV 4.4%)
Pale beer with the citrus flavours from American hops balanced by Kent Goldings.

Kursaal Porter (OG 1054, ABV 5.4%)
A rich, bittersweet porter tasting of espresso, liquorice and chocolate.

The Pump Room (OG 1054, ABV 5.4%)
Ruby brown-coloured, rich, dark and fruity beer.

Hart Family SIBA

The 1833 Brewery, 21 Nene Court, The Embankment, Wellingborough, Northamptonshire, NN8 1LD
🌐 hartfamilybrewers.com
Shop Sat 9am-5pm (other times by appt)
Tours by arrangement

Hart Family Brewers was established in 2012 using an eight-barrel plant. It is owned and operated by Rob and Sarah Hart, who are indulging their passion after a combined 25 years in the drinks industry. Recent expansion gives weekly production of up to 30 barrels per week. Bottle-conditioned beer is available.

House Beer (OG 1036, ABV 3.6%)
A classic country bitter with straightforward flavours of British malt and English hops.

No. 1 (OG 1043, ABV 4.1%)
A tawny beer with fruity, malty aromas and grassy, citrus notes. Fresh and fruity on the palate with spicy bitterness.

No. 9 (OG 1044, ABV 4.3%)
A golden beer, light and refreshing. Spicy grapefruit aromas and flavours supported by biscuity malt.

No. 3 (OG 1050, ABV 4.7%)
A fruity, ruby-coloured beer with malty and spicy aromas. Rounded, rich, malty flavours are supported by gentle spicy hoppiness.

No. 8 (OG 1055, ABV 5%)
A dark beer with toasted fruit aromas and hints of espresso. Warming roasted fruit and molasses flavours balanced by bitter coffee, chocolate and spice aromas over a long finish.

Hart of Preston SIBA

Unit 5, Oxhey Trading Estate, Greenbank Street, Preston, Lancashire, PR1 7PH
☎ (01772) 437651 🌐 hartbreweryltd.co.uk
Tours by arrangement

Hart opened in 1995 behind the Cartford Hotel in Little Eccleston. In 2010 the brewery relocated to Preston. It supplies a number of local outlets and arranges exchanges with other microbreweries.

Lancashire Best Bitter (OG 1039, ABV 3.9%)

Dishy Debbie (OG 1040, ABV 4%)

Ice Maiden (OG 1040, ABV 4%)
Hoppy, crisp, straw-coloured bitter with floral notes and a dry finish.

Nemesis (OG 1041, ABV 4.1%)

Ayson (OG 1042, ABV 4.2%)

Hart of Stebbing

White Hart, High Street, Stebbing, Essex, CM6 3SQ
☎ (01371) 856383 🌐 hartofstebbingbrewery.co.uk

The brewery was established in 2007 by Bob Dovey and Nick Eldred, who is also the owner of the White Hart pub where the brewery is based. At present only the White Hart and local beer festivals are supplied. Occasional specials are also brewed.

Hart IPA (OG 1035, ABV 3.5%)

Harthill Village SIBA

The Paddocks, 6 Union Street, Harthill, South Yorkshire, S26 7YH
☎ (01909) 774954 ☎ 07736 246474
🌐 harthillbrewery.co.uk

Brewing began in 2013 using a five-barrel plant supplying local pubs, clubs and shops. Seasonal beers are available.

Ace of Harts (OG 1039, ABV 3.9%)
A traditional, well-balanced amber bitter with a subtle malty sweetness and spicy, fruity aroma.

Hart Stopper (OG 1040, ABV 4%)
Hoppy blonde ale with a fresh aroma of citrus and berry fruits with hints of zest and spice

Hart's Desire (OG 1044, ABV 4.4%)
An amber premium ale with a fresh aroma of citrus with floral and spicy notes balanced with biscuity,malty, sweet flavours

Dark Hart (OG 1048, ABV 4.8%)
A rich, smooth, full-bodied dark ale with a toffee, malty sweetness and a dry, biscuity fullness complemented by the spicy, blackcurrant aroma.

Dark Hart Festival Reserve (OG 1065, ABV 6.5%)

THE BREWERIES

Premium version of Dark Hart with an increased intensity of flavour and hoppy finish.

Hartshorns

Unit 4, Tomlinsons industrial estate, Alfreton Road, Derby, DE21 4ED ☎ 07830 367125
hartshornsbrewery.com

Hartshorns began brewing in 2012 using a six-barrel plant installed by brothers Darren and Lindsey Hartshorn.

Highgate (OG 1044, ABV 4.3%)
Smooth, easy-drinking pale copper-coloured ale. Well-balanced malt sweetness with a fruity hop flavour and a well-rounded bitterness.

Stormin Auburn (OG 1045, ABV 4.5%)
A mild bitterness and crystal malt flavour characterise this amber ale, complemented by distinctive American hop flavour and aroma.

Floss the Boss (OG 1046, ABV 4.6%)
A thirst-quenching pale golden ale has three separate hop additions during the brewing process to give a distinct flavour, balanced with a rich, malty sweetness.

Brooklyn Nights (OG 1052, ABV 5.4%)
A punchy American brown ale with a complex malt base. A blend of all American hops provide abundant flavour and aroma, with an assertive bitterness and a clean, dry finish.

Shakademus (OG 1052, ABV 5.4%)
Full-bodied with a citrus hop bite, a satisfying premium golden ale.

Apocalypse (OG 1055, ABV 6.2%)
Easy-drinking golden ale with a clean bitter finish. Refreshingly crisp and packed with hop character.

Harveys IFBB

Bridge Wharf Brewery, 6 Cliffe High Street, Lewes, East Sussex, BN7 2AH
☎ (01273) 480209 harveys.org.uk
Shop Mon-Sat 9.30am-5.30pm
Tours by arrangement

Established in 1790, this independent family brewery operates from the banks of the River Ouse in Lewes. A major development in 1985 doubled the brewhouse capacity and subsequent additional fermenting capacity has seen production rise to more than 38,000 barrels a year. There is also a microbrewery on site used to brew special beers including replicating old Lewes Brewery recipes using the County Town Beers name. Harveys supplies real ale to all its 48 pubs and 550 free trade outlets in the south-east. Seasonal beers: see website. Bottle-conditioned beer is available.

Sussex Dark Mild (OG 1030, ABV 3%)
A dark copper-brown colour. Roast malt dominates the aroma and palate leading to a sweet, caramel finish.

Hadlow Bitter (OG 1033, ABV 3.5%)
Formerly Sussex Pale Ale.

Sussex Wild Hop (OG 1037, ABV 3.7%)

Sussex Best Bitter (OG 1040, ABV 4%)
Full-bodied brown bitter. A hoppy aroma leads to a good malt and hop balance, and a dry aftertaste.

Old Ale (OG 1043, ABV 4.3%)

Olympia (OG 1042, ABV 4.3%)

Armada Ale (OG 1045, ABV 4.5%)
Hoppy amber best bitter. Well-balanced fruit and hops dominate throughout with a fruity palate.

Harviestoun SIBA

Alva Industrial Estate, Alva, Clackmannanshire, FK12 5DQ
☎ (01259) 769100 harviestoun.com
Shop Mon-Fri 9am-5pm
Tours by arrangement

Based in Scotland, Harviestoun has grown from one man brewing in a bucket in his shed in 1983 to a 60-barrel, multi-award-winning brewery today. With a reputation for experimentation, it adds around eight seasonal specials to its core range, many also bottle conditioned. Seasonal beers: see website.

Bitter & Twisted (OG 1036, ABV 3.8%)
Refreshingly hoppy beer with fruit throughout. A bittersweet taste with a long bitter finish. A golden session beer.

Natural Blonde (OG 1040, ABV 4%)

Schiehallion (OG 1048, ABV 4.8%)
A Scottish cask-conditioned lager, brewed using a lager yeast and Hersbrucker hops. A hoppy aroma, with fruit and malt, leads to a malty, bitter taste with floral hoppiness and a bitter finish.

Harwich Town

Station Approach, Harwich, Essex, CO12 3NA
☎ (01255) 551155 harwichtown.co.uk
Tours by arrangement

Brewing started in 2007 on a five-barrel plant next to Harwich Town railway station. The brewer is a CAMRA member and former customs officer. Beers are named after local landmarks, characters or events. 50 outlets are supplied. The brewery holds a beer festival in July and a festival special is brewed for the Harwich & Dovercourt Bay Winter Ale Festival in December. Seasonal and bottle-conditioned beers are available.

Bay Bitter (OG 1036, ABV 3.6%)

Ha'penny Mild (OG 1036, ABV 3.6%)

EPA 100 (OG 1038, ABV 3.8%)

Leading Lights (OG 1038, ABV 3.8%)

Ganges (OG 1040, ABV 4%)

Misleading Lights (OG 1040, ABV 4%)

Bathside Battery Bitter (OG 1042, ABV 4.2%)

Redoubt Stout (OG 1042, ABV 4.2%)

Parkeston Porter (OG 1045, ABV 4.5%)

Lighthouse Bitter (OG 1048, ABV 4.8%)

Phoenix APA (OG 1052, ABV 5%)

Hastings SIBA

Unit 12, Conqueror Industrial Estate, Moorhurst Road, St Leonards on Sea, East Sussex, TN38 9NB
☎ (01424) 572050 hastingsbrewery.co.uk

Hastings is a small brewery established in 2010, exclusively producing unfined beers suitable for vegetarians and vegans. It currently operates on a five-barrel plant. Beers are available to the trade in cask and bottle and online in polypins and bottles.

Blonde (OG 1040, ABV 3.9%)

Best (OG 1042, ABV 4.1%)

Porter (OG 1050.5, ABV 4.5%)

Handmade No. 5 (OG 1050, ABV 4.8%)
A hoppy pale ale.

Havant SIBA

Unit 25, The Tanneries, Brockhampton Lane, Havant, Hampshire, PO9 1JB
☎ (023) 9247 6067 thehavantbrewery.co.uk
Shop Thu-Fri 2-5pm, Sat 11am-2pm
Tours by arrangement

Havant began brewing in 2009 on a one-barrel plant, upgraded in 2011 and moved to new premises in 2013, where it increased capacity to five barrels. Seasonal and specials beers: see website.

Decided (OG 1035, ABV 3.8%)

Started (OG 1039, ABV 4%)

Herd (OG 1045, ABV 4.2%)

Finished (OG 1049, ABV 5%)

Hawkshead SIBA

Mill Yard, Staveley, Cumbria, LA8 9LR
☎ (01539) 822644 hawksheadbrewery.co.uk
Shop & Bar Mon 12-5pm, Tue-Thu 12-6pm, Fri & Sat 12-11pm, Sun 12-8pm
Tours by arrangement

Hawkshead Brewery was established in 2002 by former BBC journalist Alex Brodie. The brewery outgrew its original premises (a barn at Hawkshead) and moved to its present site at Staveley in 2006 where a purpose built 20-barrel plant was installed. Further expansion in 2010 added a second bar to the Beer Hall, which is the visitor centre and brewery tap. A kitchen serves 'beer tapas' to complement the beer and the open-plan layout means visitors can see the brewery at work. Pubs are supplied throughout the north west. Seasonal and bottle-conditioned beers: see website.

Windermere Pale (OG 1036, ABV 3.5%)
Crisp and fruity yellow beer with hints of melon and grapefruit and a strong bitter aftertaste.

Bitter (OG 1037, ABV 3.7%)
Well-balanced, thirst-quenching beer with fruit and hops aroma, leading to a lasting bitter finish.

Red (OG 1042, ABV 4.2%)
An impressive colour for this richly flavoured beer; lots of fruitiness and good hop flavour with a lingering aftertaste.

Lakeland Gold (OG 1043, ABV 4.4%)
Fresh, well-balanced fruity, hoppy beer with a clean bitter aftertaste.

Dry Stone Stout (OG 1044, ABV 4.5%)
Black, dry, bitter stout with an astringent, roast finish.

Great White (OG 1048, ABV 4.8%)
A cloudy, spiced wheat beer brewed with coriander seeds and Seville orange peel.

Brodie's Prime (OG 1048, ABV 4.9%)
Complex, dark brown beer with plenty of malt, fruit and roast taste. Satisfying full body with clean finish.

Cumbrian Five Hop (OG 1050, ABV 5%)
A robust hoppy bitter with citrus hops and fruity middle.

Lakeland Lager (OG 1045, ABV 5%)
A cask-conditioned lager.

NZPA (OG 1056, ABV 6%)
A hoppy bitter with a sweet, fruity taste and a resounding dry bitter finish.

IPA (OG 1065, ABV 7%)
A modern IPA, amber in colour, with huge hop flavours.

Haworth Steam

Rose & Crown, 2 Westgate, Cleckheaton, West Yorkshire, BD19 5ET
☎ (01535) 646059 haworthsteambrewery.co.uk
Shop Mon-Thu & Sun 10am-6pm; Fri & Sat 10am-9pm

Established in 2011 using a five-barrel plant, the brewery now has online sales and a café, bar and bistro in Haworth acting as the brewery tap. There are plans to increase both beer range and production.

True Tyke (OG 1038, ABV 3.8%)
Amber-coloured Yorkshire bitter with creamy biscuit notes and a distinctive breadiness.

WD Austerity (OG 1038, ABV 3.8%)
Blonde ale with plenty of cereal and digestive biscuit on the nose. Creamy malt body gives a floral finish.

Ironclad 957 (OG 1043, ABV 4.3%)
Stout with caramel and raisin to the nose and a little drying smoke on the finish.

Fallwood XXXX (OG 1052, ABV 5.2%)
Full-bodied ale full of roasted barley and First Gold hops giving a toffee apple flavour with a hint of cider.

Hay Rake

Blackstone Edge Old Road, Littleborough, OL15 0JX
☎ (01706) 379689 hayrakebrewery.info

Mark Wickham, the landlord of the Rake Tapas Restaurant, resurrected the Hay Rake microbrewery in 2013. The Rake brewed its own beer during the reign of Queen Victoria but stopped in 1901. Mark is keen to revive the tradition of locally-brewed ale.

Dawn's Hopping Mad (OG 1038, ABV 3.8%)
A blend of five hops with a hint of chilli and ginger.

Dawn's Called Thyme (OG 1040, ABV 4%)
Citrus with a blend of thyme and fresh peaches.

Early Dawn (OG 1041, ABV 4.1%)
An IPA using a blend of four hops with a hint of honey and lemongrass.

Dawn's Dark Side (OG 1044, ABV 4.4%)
A blend of four hops with molasses and coriander.

Dawn's Autumn Gold (OG 1045, ABV 4.5%)
A blend of four hops with a hint of liquorice and golden syrup

Haywood Bad Ram SIBA

Callow Top Holiday Park, Buxton Road, Sandybrook, Ashbourne, Derbyshire, DE6 2AQ

☎ (01335) 344020 🌐 callowtop.co.uk/callow-top-brewery
Shop 9am-5pm (seasonal)
Tours by arrangement

Established in 2003, the brewery was based in a converted barn but a new brewery and bottling plant became operational in 2012. One pub is owned (on site) and several other outlets are supplied. Bottle-conditioned beers are available.

Thoroughbred Bad Ram (OG 1038, ABV 3.8%)
A refreshing straw-coloured ale with a crisp bite and spice and flowery notes.

Dr Samuel Johnson (OG 1044, ABV 4.5%)
A slightly fruity and refined spicy flavour.

Callow Top Imperial IPA (OG 1050, ABV 5.2%)
A full-bodied, rich ale with a fruity and slightly citrus aftertaste.

Head in a Hat

See Florence

Healey's

Wellington Inn, Main Street, Loppergarth, Cumbria, LA12 0JL
☎ (01229) 582388

Healey's began brewing in the Wellington in 2012 using a custom-made 2.5-barrel stainless steel plant, which can be viewed through full-length windows in the pub.

Golden (OG 1037, ABV 3.6%)

Dark Mild (OG 1038, ABV 3.7%)

Blonde (OG 1040, ABV 4%)
Aromatic bitter, sweet and tasty from the start with increasing hops and a dry bitter finish.

Best Bitter (OG 1042, ABV 4.2%)

Hearsall

c/o Hearsall Inn, 45 Craven Street, Coventry, West Midlands, CV5 8DS
☎ (024) 7671 5729

Hearsall began brewing in 2012 using a one-barrel plant, producing beer for the pub. The brewery upgraded to a 1.5-barrel plant in 2014.

Chapelfields Best (ABV 4%)

Heart of Wales

Stables Yard, Zion Street, Llanwrtyd Wells, Powys, LD5 4RD
☎ (01591) 610236 🌐 heartofwalesbrewery.co.uk
Shop 9am-10pm daily
Tours by arrangement

The brewery was set up with a six-barrel plant in 2006 in old stables at the rear of the Neuadd Arms Hotel. Beers are brewed using water from the brewery's own borehole. Seasonal brews celebrate local events such as the World Bogsnorkelling Championships. Seasonal and bottle-conditioned beers are available. All bottle-conditioned beers are suitable for vegetarians and vegans. Cambrian Heart Ale was commissioned by and is brewed for the Cambrian Mountains Initiative, inspired by the Prince of Wales, which aims to promote and support rural producers and communities in the region.

Irfon Valley Bitter (OG 1038, ABV 3.6%)

Aur Cymru (OG 1040, ABV 3.8%)

Bitter (OG 1042, ABV 4.1%)
A light chestnut-coloured bitter in the Northern style, it has a fine, smooth balance between malt and hop.

Big Red Chopper (OG 1043, ABV 4.3%)

Welsh Black (OG 1045, ABV 4.4%)
A full-flavoured, complex and smooth stout.

Cambrian Heart Ale (OG 1045, ABV 4.5%)
Light golden brown ale with a refreshing fruity body and lots of hops in the finish.

Noble Eden Ale (OG 1046, ABV 4.6%)
A dark brown premium ale bursting with fruit and malt, with a hint of chocolate. A full-bodied, flavoursome, satisfying pint.

Inn-stable (OG 1065, ABV 6.8%)
A powerful ale with a warming malty body and a smooth finish.

High as a Kite (OG 1095, ABV 10.5%)

Heath Village (NEW)

Owlcotes Farm, Shire Lane, Heath, Derbyshire, S44 5SQ ☎ 07530 211571

Small 100-litre plant established in 2014 on a farm in Heath Village. The brewery is run by a consortium of six people from the village. It is intended to expand the capacity in the future.

Heathton (NEW)

c/o Old Gate, Heathton, Shropshire, WV5 7EB
☎ (01746) 710431

This brewery is intended to be resurrected at the Old Gate pub, but until it is three beers are produced elsewhere. Each of the beers is being produced to a defined recipe in three different breweries, and are served only in the Old Gate.

Heavy Industry SIBA

The Old Slaughterhouse, Denbigh Street, Henllan, LL16 5AR
☎ (01745) 816316 🌐 heavyindustrybrewing.com

Established in 2012, Heavy Industry brews with a 10-barrel plant situated in an old slaughterhouse in the village of Henllan.

Electric Mountain (OG 1038, ABV 3.8%)
A copper-coloured beer with up-front bitterness, citrus notes and a refreshing finish.

High Voltage (OG 1045, ABV 4.5%)
A dry, bitter beer full of citrus fruit, hoppy flavours which dominate the taste and lasting bitter finish.

Nelsons Eye (OG 1045, ABV 4.5%)
Heavily-hopped with a strong, sharp bitter taste. Citrus fruit notes, mainly grapefruit, in the aroma and palate continue into the hoppy, bitter aftertaste.

Collaborator (OG 1050, ABV 5%)
A smooth and satisfying dark, hoppy beer. The juicy malty taste is roasty and leads to a dry, hoppy aftertaste.

Heddon Valley

See Country Life

Heineken Royal Trafford

Royal Brewery, 201 Denmark Road, Manchester, M15 6LD

No real ale.

Hektor's

The Office, Henham Park, Southwold, Suffolk, NR34 8AN ☎ 07900 553426 🌐 hektorsbrewery.com

Beers are brewed by the owner on the equipment of other breweries, including Green Jack and Oakham. However, there are plans to install a brewery in a converted barn at Henham Park in the future. Hektor's beers are provided to Henham Park's 65,000 annual visitors in addition to five other outlets and local events.

Pure (OG 1038, ABV 3.8%)

House (OG 1042, ABV 4.2%)

Scarecrow (OG 1050, ABV 5%)

Hellhound

6 Seager Court, Crockatt Road, Hadleigh, Suffolk, IP7 6RL ☎ 07850 076202 🌐 hellhound.co.uk

Hellhound began brewing in 2010 using a six-barrel plant. Seasonal beer is available.

Hen House

The Old Dairy, Walliscote Farm, High Street, Whitchurch-on-Thames, Oxfordshire, RG8 7EP
🌐 henhousebrewery.co.uk
Shop Sat 2-4pm

Hen House began brewing in 2012 on a 30-litre plant. Only bottle-conditioned beers are produced, available from the brewery shop. Seasonal and special beers: see website.

Henley

38 Market Place, Henley-on-Thames, Oxfordshire, RG9 2AH
☎ (01491) 576561 🌐 thehenleybrewhouse.co.uk

Henley began brewing in 2012 using a five-barrel plant situated in an old police station. Brewing takes place in the centre of the pub, with the plant visible through a glass wall. Seasonal beers are available.

Jail House (OG 1040, ABV 3.9%)
A copper-coloured beer with a light, refreshing bitterness.

Temple Island (OG 1046, ABV 4.5%)
A hoppy pale ale with a floral and citrus aroma and hints of grapefruit and spice in the taste.

Scull Duggery (OG 1048, ABV 4.8%)
A dark brown/ruby-coloured old ale full of malt character.

Blades of Glory (OG 1049, ABV 4.9%)
A Chinook-hopped American pale ale.

Hepworth SIBA

Beer Station, Railway Yard, Horsham, West Sussex, RH12 2NW
☎ (01403) 269696 🌐 hepworthbrewery.co.uk
Sales 9am-6pm daily
Tours by arrangement

Hepworth's was established in 2001, initially bottling beer only. In 2003 draught beer brewing was started with Sussex malt and hops. Around 270 outlets are supplied. Seasonal beers are available.

Traditional Sussex Bitter (OG 1035, ABV 3.5%)
A fine, clean-tasting amber session beer. A bitter beer with a pleasant fruity and hoppy aroma that leads to a crisp, tangy taste. A long, dry finish.

Dark Horse (OG 1038, ABV 3.8%)

Summer Ale (OG 1038, ABV 3.8%)

Pullman First Class Ale (OG 1041, ABV 4.2%)
A sweet, nutty maltiness and fruitiness are balanced by hops and bitterness in this easy-drinking, pale brown best bitter. A subtle bitter aftertaste.

Prospect Organic (OG 1045, ABV 4.5%)
A well-balanced and traditional brew.

Classic Old Ale (OG 1046, ABV 4.8%)
A traditional winter brew, rich with a variety of roasted malts balanced with sweetness and the bitterness of Admiral hops.

Iron Horse (OG 1048, ABV 4.8%)
There's a fruity, toffee aroma to this light brown, full-bodied bitter. A citrus flavour balanced by caramel and malt leads to a clean, dry finish.

Hereford SIBA

88 St Owen Street, Hereford, HR1 2QD
☎ (01432) 342125 ✉ jfkenyon@aol.com
Tours by arrangement

From its inception in 2000, the brewery has steadily increased production. In 2010 its name changed from the Spinning Dog to the Hereford Brewery. Around 50 outlets are supplied. Seasonal and bottle-conditioned beers are available.

Herefordshire Owd Bull (OG 1039, ABV 3.9%)
A session beer with an abundance of hops and bitterness. Dry with a citrus aftertaste.

Dark (OG 1040, ABV 4%)
A dark, malty mild with a hint of bitterness and a touch of roast caramel. A smooth, drinkable ale.

Herefordshire Light Ale (HLA) (OG 1040, ABV 4%)
A crisp, light, refreshing ale made with Herefordshire hops.

Best Bitter (OG 1042, ABV 4.2%)

Gamekeepers Bitter (OG 1042, ABV 4.2%)

Celtic Gold (OG 1045, ABV 4.5%)
A bright gold-coloured best bitter, full of fruit and blackcurrant flavours.

Mutley's Revenge (OG 1048, ABV 4.8%)
A strong, smooth, hoppy beer, amber in colour. Full-bodied with a dry, citrus aftertaste.

Mutts Nuts (OG 1050, ABV 5%)
A dark, strong ale, full-bodied with a hint of a chocolate aftertaste.

Hermitage (NEW)

Heathwaite, Slanting Hill, Hermitage, Berkshire, RG18 9QG
☎ (01635) 200907 ☎ 07980 019484
hermitagebrewery.co.uk

Brewing began in 2013 in the village of Hermitage, West Berkshire, using a 0.5-barrel plant. The owner, Richard Marshall, taught Food Science at degree level and has been brewing his own beers for more than 40 years. Bottle-conditioned beers are sold in local shops and post offices. Cask-conditioned beer is planned.

Hesket Newmarket SIBA

Old Crown Barn, Back Green, Hesket Newmarket, Cumbria, CA7 8JG
☎ (01697) 478066 hesketbrewery.co.uk
Shop Mon-Fri 8.30am-5pm, Sat 10am-2pm (summer)
Tours by arrangement

Founded in 1988, and bought by a co-operative in 1999 to preserve a community feel. All the beers are named after local fells, except for Doris' 90th Birthday Ale. Bottle-conditioned beers and take home pins are available.

Blencathra Bitter (OG 1035, ABV 3.2%) ◆
A malty, tawny ale, mild and mellow for a bitter, with a dominant caramel flavour.

Haystacks (OG 1037, ABV 3.7%) ◆
Light, easy-drinking, thirst-quenching blond beer; very pleasant for its strength.

Skiddaw Special Bitter (OG 1037, ABV 3.7%)
An amber session beer, malty throughout, well-balanced with a dryish finish.

Black Sail (OG 1042.1, ABV 4%) ◆
A sweet stout with roast flavours.

Helvellyn Gold (OG 1039, ABV 4%) ◆
Complex hoppy and fruity beer with malt presence and refreshing finish.

High Pike (OG 1042, ABV 4.2%) ◆
A traditional style bitter; fruity with a dry finish.

Doris' 90th Birthday Ale (OG 1045, ABV 4.3%)
A fruity premium beer.

Scafell Blonde (OG 1043, ABV 4.4%) ◆
A hoppy, sweet, fruity, pale-coloured bitter.

Brim Fell (OG 1047, ABV 4.5%)
A light, copper-coloured IPA. Enough body to back up the hop bitterness, and a little residual sweetness from the malt balances the beer well. A light malt giving way to floral and citrus hops.

Catbells Pale Ale (OG 1050, ABV 5%) ◆
Golden ale with a nice balance of fruity sweetness and bitterness, almost syrupy but with an unexpectedly dry finish.

Old Carrock Strong Ale (OG 1060, ABV 6%) ◆
Reddy brown strong ale, vine-fruity in flavour with slightly astringent finish.

Hewitt's

c/o Brentwood Brewery, Calcott Hall Farm, Ongar Road, Brentwood, Essex, CM15 9HS ☎ 07949 565424

Correspondence: 40 Marconi Road, Chelmsford, Essex, CM1 1QD hewittsbrewery.co.uk

Founded in 2010, Hewitt's use spare capacity at Brentwood Brewery (qv). Seasonal beers are available.

Dan's Hands (ABV 5%)
A dry-hopped blonde beer.

UnHung Hero (ABV 5%)
A gold-coloured beer, bitter with a long bitter aftertaste. Citrus notes, particularly bitter orange, with a hint of grapefruit.

Hexhamshire SIBA

Leafields, Ordley, Hexham, Northumberland, NE46 1SX
☎ (01434) 606577 hexhamshire.co.uk

Hexhamshire was founded in 1993 and is run by one of the founding partners and his family. 30 outlets are supplied direct and many others through the SIBA direct delivery scheme.

Devil's Elbow (OG 1036, ABV 3.6%) ◆
Amber brew full of hops and fruit, leading to a bitter finish.

Shire Bitter (OG 1037, ABV 3.8%) ◆
A good balance of hops with fruity overtones, this amber beer makes an easy-drinking session bitter.

Blackhall English Stout (OG 1040, ABV 4%)
A pleasant bitter beer with a strong roast malt flavour.

Devil's Water (OG 1041, ABV 4.1%) ◆
Copper-coloured best bitter, well-balanced with a slightly fruity, hoppy finish.

Whapweasel (OG 1048, ABV 4.8%) ◆
A smooth, hoppy beer with a fruity flavour. Amber in colour, the bitter finish brings out the fruit and hops.

Old Humbug (OG 1055, ABV 5.5%)

High House Farm SIBA

Matfen, Newcastle upon Tyne, NE20 0RG
☎ (01661) 886192/886769 (sales line)
highhousefarmbrewery.co.uk
Shop Sun-Tue 10.30am-5pm, Thu-Sat 10.30am-9pm, closed Wed
Tours by arrangement

The brewery was founded in 2003 by a Brewlab graduate on a working farm with a visitor centre, brewery shop and function room. This has now expanded to include a successful restaurant and wedding venue. More than 350 regional outlets are supplied with beers made using many ingredients from the farm.

Sundancer (OG 1036, ABV 3.6%)

Pullet Please (OG 1037, ABV 3.7%)
A pale gold-coloured refreshing ale with a delicate grapefruit nose and a crisp, dry finish. An easy-drinking bitter.

Auld Hemp (OG 1038, ABV 3.8%) ◆
Tawny-coloured ale with hop, malt and fruit flavours and a good bitter finish.

Nel's Best (OG 1041, ABV 4.2%) ◆
Golden hoppy ale full of flavour with a clean, bitter finish.

Matfen Magic (OG 1046.5, ABV 4.8%) ◆
Well-hopped brown ale with a fruity aroma. Malt and chocolate overtones with a rich, bitter finish.

High Weald SIBA

Unit 8, Bulrushes Business Park, Coombe Hill Road, East Grinstead, West Sussex, RH19 4LZ ☎ 07836 291430

Office: 23 Hermitage Road, East Grinstead, West Sussex, RH19 2BP 🌐 highwealdbrewery.co.uk

Tours by arrangement

Established in 2013 by a keen home brewer, High Weald has grown to a four-barrel plant size. The brewery produces both cask and bottle-conditioned ales, supplying local free houses, shops and festivals. Further expansion of both the beer range and brewing capacity is planned to satisfy demand.

Best (OG 1038, ABV 3.8%)

Greenstede Gold (OG 1040, ABV 4%)
A refreshing golden ale.

Wealden Pale Ale (OG 1041, ABV 4.1%)
A copper-coloured ale with good hop character and a long, malty finish.

Charcoal Burner (OG 1043, ABV 4.3%)
A traditional English stout. Roasted malts bring a rich, satisfying flavour, combined with velvety smoothness from generous quantities of oats.

Highland SIBA

Swannay Brewery, Swannay by Evie, Birsay, Orkney, KW17 2NP
☎ (01856) 721700
🌐 highlandbrewingcompany.co.uk

Tours by arrangement

Brewing began in 2006 at the redundant Swannay dairy. A bigger plant was soon required and installed to meet demand. Around 300 outlets are supplied throughout Scotland and the north of England. Seasonal beers are available.

Orkney Best (OG 1038, ABV 3.6%)
A refreshing, light-bodied, low gravity golden beer bursting with hop, peach and sweet malt flavours. The long, hoppy finish leaves a dry bitterness.

Island Hopping (OG 1039, ABV 3.9%)
Fruity hoppiness with some caramel with a lasting bitter aftertaste.

Dark Munro (OG 1040, ABV 4%)
The nose presents an intense roast hit which is followed by summer fruits in the mouth. The strong roast malt continues into the aftertaste.

Scapa Special (OG 1042, ABV 4.2%)
A good copy of a typical Lancashire bitter, full of bitterness and background hops, leaving your mouth tingling in the lingering aftertaste.

Pale Ale (ABV 4.7%)
Copper-coloured ale with resinous citrus hops on the nose with a generous floral note. Hops lead on the palate against a malty background with a long, lingering aftertaste.

Orkney IPA (OG 1048, ABV 4.8%)
A traditional bitter, with light hop and fruit flavour throughout.

St Magnus Ale (OG 1049, ABV 5.2%)
A complex, tawny bitter with a stunning balance of malt and hop and some soft roast. Full-bodied.

The Duke (ABV 5.3%)
Pale with fresh resiny hops right through to the finish.

Orkney Blast (OG 1058, ABV 6%)
Plenty of alcohol in this warming strong bitter/barley wine. A mushroom and woody aroma blossoms into a well-balanced smack of malt and hop in the taste.

Orkney Porter (OG 1082, ABV 9%)

Highwood

See Tom Wood (under W)

Highwood (Cann Do Beers) SIBA

12 Pooles Lane, Highwood, Essex, CM1 3QL
☎ (01245) 249300 🌐 canndobeers.com

Brewing began in 2010 using a 10-barrel plant.

Cannon's Gold (ABV 3.6%)

Cannon's IPA (ABV 3.6%)

Hilden SIBA

Hilden House, Hilden, Lisburn, Co Antrim, BT27 4TY
☎ (028) 9266 0800 🌐 hildenbrewery.co.uk

Shop Tue-Sun 12-2.30pm (3pm Sun) – Taproom Restaurant
Tours by arrangement

Established in 1981, Hilden is Ireland's oldest independent brewery. Now in the second generation of family ownership, the beers are widely distributed across the UK. Occasional brews plus seasonals are also produced. The beers are regularly available in Wetherspoons in Northern Ireland.

Ale (OG 1038, ABV 3.7%)
An amber-coloured beer with an aroma of malt, hops and fruit. The balanced taste is slightly slanted towards hops, and hops are also prominent in the full, malty finish.

Headless Dog (OG 1042, ABV 4.2%)
A well-hopped bright amber ale.

Irish Stout (ABV 4.3%)

Scullion's Irish (OG 1045, ABV 4.6%)
A bright amber ale, initially smooth with a slight taste of honey that is balanced by a long, dry aftertaste that lingers on the palate.

Twisted Hop (ABV 4.7%)

Barney's Brew (ABV 5%)

Halt (OG 1058, ABV 6.1%)
A premium traditional Irish red ale with a malty, mild hop flavour. This special reserve derives its name from the local train stop, which was used to service the local linen mill.

Hill Island SIBA

Unit 7, Fowlers Yard, Back Silver Street, Durham, DH1 3RA ☎ 07740 932584
✉ mike@hillisland.freeserve.co.uk

Shop Sat 10am-4pm
Tours by arrangement

Established in 2002, the brewery name is a literal translation of Dunholme from which Durham is derived. It is situated in the Fowlers Yard complex by the banks of the Wear in the heart of Durham City. Seasonal beers are available and brews can be crafted exclusively for individual pubs.

Peninsula Pint (OG 1036.5, ABV 3.7%)
Blonde and hoppy with a zesty aroma.

Dun Cow Bitter (OG 1041, ABV 4.2%)
Golden ale with hints of caramel and citrus hop flavours.

Cathedral Ale (OG 1042, ABV 4.3%)
Ruby red with hints of roast malts and crisp bitterness.

ThaI.P.A. (OG 1043, ABV 4.3%)

Griffin's Irish Stout (OG 1045, ABV 4.5%)
Black and bitter. Traditional Irish-style stout.

Hillside SIBA

Holly Bush Farm, Ross Road, Longhope, Gloucestershire, GL17 0NG
☎ (01452) 830222 ☎ 07905 246189
hillsidebrewery.com
Shop Mon-Fri 9am-5pm, Sat 10am-2pm
Tours by arrangement

Formerly known as May Hill, brewing commenced in 2011 using a six-barrel plant housed in a reconstructed farm dairy. A 200-foot bore hole gives the brewery its water supply. The regular beers are supplemented by limited-run craft specials that explore different styles and flavours.

Over the Hill (OG 1035, ABV 3.5%)
A full-bodied, single-hop, malty dark mild.

Pinnacle (OG 1042, ABV 3.8%)
A full-flavoured pale ale with a fresh fruity finish.

Legless Cow (OG 1043, ABV 4.2%)
A distinctive bitter with a rich caramel flavour and smooth, citrus hop finish.

Legend of Hillside (OG 1049, ABV 4.7%)
A traditional English IPA with subtle honey flavours and a strong hop finish.

Hobsons SIBA

Newhouse Farm, Tenbury Road, Cleobury Mortimer, Shropshire, DY14 8RD
☎ (01299) 270837 hobsons-brewery.co.uk
Shop Mon-Fri 9am-5pm
Tours by arrangement

Established in 1993 in a former sawmill, Hobsons relocated to a farm site with more space in 1995. A second brewery, bottling plant and a warehouse have been added along with significant expansion to the first brewery. Beers are supplied within a 50-mile radius. The brewery has an onsite wind turbine and utilises environmental sustainable technologies where possible. Seasonal beer is available.

Mild (OG 1034, ABV 3.2%)
A classic mild. Complex layers of taste come from roasted malts that predominate and give lots of flavour.

Twisted Spire (OG 1036, ABV 3.6%)
Vibrant blond beer with a light fizz and sweet floral aroma bringing bursts of refreshing flavour and a crisp dry finish.

Best Bitter (OG 1038.5, ABV 3.8%)
A pale brown to amber, medium-bodied beer with strong hop character throughout. It is consequently bitter, but with malt discernible in the taste.

Old Prickly (OG 1042, ABV 4.2%)
Pale ale with a complex hop flavour of floral and citrus notes with a lingering but subtle bitterness.

Town Crier (OG 1044, ABV 4.5%)
A full-flavoured crisp golden ale, straw-coloured with a hint of sweetness complemented by subtle hop flavours, leading to a dry finish.

Hoggleys

See Phipps

Hogs Back SIBA

Manor Farm, The Street, Tongham, Surrey, GU10 1DE
☎ (01252) 783000 hogsback.co.uk
Shop: see website
Tours by arrangement

This traditionally-styled brewery, established in 1992, boasts an extensive range of award-winning ales, brewed from the finest malted barley and whole English hops. The shop sells all the brewery's beers and related merchandise plus over 400 beers and ciders from around the world. Fully guided tours with tastings are available. In 2014 the brewery planted hops on neighbouring farmland, restoring the ancient Farnham White Bine variety. Seasonal beers: see website.

HBB (OG 1039, ABV 3.7%)
Biscuity aroma with some hops and lemon notes. Well-balanced, plenty of hop in the mouth with a long-lasting, dry bitter aftertaste.

TEA (OG 1044, ABV 4.2%)
A tawny-coloured best bitter with toffee and malt present in the nose. A well-rounded flavour with malt and a fruity sweetness.

Hop Garden Gold (OG 1048, ABV 4.4%)
Full-bodied with an aroma of malt, hops and fruit. Hoppy bitterness grows in an increasingly dry aftertaste with a hint of sweetness.

A over T (OG 1094, ABV 9%)

Holden's SIBA IFBB

George Street, Woodsetton, Dudley, West Midlands, DY1 4LW
☎ (01902) 880051 holdensbrewery.co.uk
Shop Mon-Fri 9am-5pm
Tours by arrangement

A family brewery spanning four generations, Holden's began life as a brewpub in the 1920s. Continued recent expansion sees 20 tied pubs, a new brewhouse and a shop. Seasonal beers: see website.

Black Country Mild (OG 1037, ABV 3.7%)
A good, red/brown mild; a refreshing, light blend of roast malt, hops and fruit, dominated by malt throughout.

Black Country Bitter (OG 1039, ABV 3.9%)
A medium-bodied, golden ale; a light, well-balanced bitter with a subtle, dry, hoppy finish.

Golden Glow (OG 1045, ABV 4.4%)
A pale golden beer with a subtle hop aroma plus gentle sweetness and a light hoppiness.

Special (OG 1052, ABV 5.1%) ◈
A sweet, malty, full-bodied amber ale with hops to balance in the taste and in the good, bittersweet finish.

Holsworthy

Unit 5, Circuit Business Park, Clawton, Devon, EX22 6RR
☎ (01566) 783678 🌐 holsworthyales.co.uk
Shop open Sat pm
Tours by arrangement

Holsworthy began brewing in 2011 using a six-barrel plant, serving the surrounding rural community.

Mine's a Mild (OG 1035, ABV 3.5%)
A traditional English mild with a rich, malty taste. Lightly hopped to give a good balance and finish.

Muck 'n' Straw (OG 1044, ABV 4.4%)

Make Me Hoppy (OG 1046, ABV 4.7%)

Tamar Black (OG 1048, ABV 4.8%)

Holt SIBA IFBB

The Brewery, Empire Street, Cheetham, Manchester, M3 1JD
☎ (0161) 834 3285 🌐 joseph-holt.com
Shop Mon-Fri 9am-4pm

The brewery, established in 1849 by Joseph and Catherine Holt, is still a family-run business and is now in the hands of the great, great-grandson of the founder. It supplies approximately 130 outlets as well as its own estate of 130 tied pubs.

Mild (OG 1033, ABV 3.2%) ◈
A dark brown/red beer with a fruity, malty nose. Roast, malt, fruit and hops in the taste, with strong bitterness for a mild, and a dry malt and hops finish.

IPA (OG 1038, ABV 3.8%) ◈
Golden bitter with biscuity malt, hops and restrained lemony notes. Dry, bitter finish.

Bitter (OG 1040, ABV 4%) ◈
Copper-coloured beer with malt and hops in the aroma. Malt, hops and fruit in the taste with a bitter and hoppy finish.

Honest Brew (NEW)

c/o Late Knights Brewery, 21 Southey Street, Penge, London, SE20 7JD
☎ (020) 3239 4553 🌐 honestbrew.co.uk

Honest Brew, a beer retailer, began brewing in 2013. Production is mostly bottled with occasional small runs of bottle-conditioned beer. A pilot kit is used at Late Knights Brewery (qv) plus spare capacity at other breweries around the UK.

Hooded Ram (NEW) SIBA

Hills Meadow, Douglas, Isle of Man, IM3 1LE
☎ (01624) 612464 🌐 hoodedram.com
Shop Sat 12-6pm
Tours by arrangement

Brewing began in 2013 on a 2.5-barrel Oban Ales plant purchased from Three Kings Brewery in North Shields. Beers are available cask-conditioned throughout the island and bottle-conditioned beers are sold directly through the brewery shop and in some local off-licences and restaurants/bars.

Rams Head Bitter (OG 1037, ABV 3.7%)

Sovereign Ram Single Hop (OG 1037, ABV 4.1%)

Amber Ram (OG 1038, ABV 4.3%)

Fat Ram Colonial Not So Pale Ale (OG 1044, ABV 4.5%)

Jack the Ram Stout (OG 1044, ABV 4.7%)

Little King Louis IPA (OG 1054, ABV 6%)

Hook Norton SIBA IFBB

The Brewery, Brewery Lane, Scotland End, Hook Norton, Oxfordshire, OX15 5NY
☎ (01608) 737210 🌐 hooky.co.uk
Visitor Centre & Shop Mon-Sat 9.30am-4.30pm
Tours by arrangement

Hook Norton was founded in 1849 by John Harris, a farmer and maltster. The current premises were built in 1900 and Hook Norton is one of the finest examples of a Victorian tower brewery. It is the oldest independent brewery in Oxfordshire, still housing much of the original machinery including a 25hp steam engine, which operates occasionally. Seasonal beers: see website.

Hooky Mild (OG 1033, ABV 2.8%) ◈
A chestnut brown, easy-drinking mild. A complex malt and hop aroma give way to a well-balanced taste, leading to a long, hoppy finish that is unusual for a mild.

Hooky (OG 1036, ABV 3.5%) ◈
A classic golden session bitter. Hoppy and fruity aroma followed by a malt and hops taste and a continuing hoppy finish.

Lion (OG 1043, ABV 4%)
Brewed with a blend of four malts and four varieties of hops to give a complex fruity nose and bittersweet finish.

Old Hooky (OG 1048, ABV 4.6%) ◈
A strong bitter, tawny in colour. A well-rounded fruity taste with a balanced bitter finish.

Hop Back SIBA

Units 22-24, Batten Road Industrial Estate, Downton, Salisbury, Wiltshire, SP5 3HU
☎ (01725) 510986 🌐 hopback.co.uk
Shop 9am-4.30pm daily (online orders can be collected from the brewery)
Tours by arrangement

Founded in 1987, Hop Back owns 10 pubs and distributes nationally. Monthly seasonal and bottle-conditioned beers are available. Bottled Crop Circle is accredited gluten-free and Entire Stout is suitable for vegans.

Heracles (OG 1028, ABV 2.8%) ◈
A refreshing pale yellow lower alcohol bitter, good hop taste right through and lasting bitterness.

Golden Best (OG 1035, ABV 3.5%) ◈
A light gold refreshing session bitter. The hoppy aroma leads to bitterness initially, lasting through to the finish with some fruit.

Redsells EKG (OG 1039, ABV 3.9%)
A classic, well-balanced English bitter.

Citra (OG 1044, ABV 4%) ◈

THE BREWERIES

Straw-coloured bitter with strong aromatic notes. Initially bitter, with stringent bitter and citrus fruit in the balanced aftertaste.

Crop Circle (OG 1041, ABV 4.2%)
A pale yellow best bitter with a fragrant hop aroma, complex hop, fruit and citrus flavours with a balanced hoppy, bittersweet aftertaste.

Spring Zing (OG 1041, ABV 4.2%)
A pale, aromatic and hoppy beer.

Taiphoon (OG 1041, ABV 4.2%)
A light gold speciality beer flavoured with lemongrass.

Entire Stout (OG 1044, ABV 4.5%)
A smooth, rich, ruby-black stout with strong roast and malt aromas and flavours, with a long bittersweet and malty aftertaste.

Summer Lightning (OG 1048, ABV 5%)
Golden-coloured strong bitter with a hoppy aroma and slightly astringent bitterness in the taste, balanced with some fruit sweetness, in the dry finish.

Hop Fuzz SIBA

Unit 8, Riverside Industrial Estate, West Hythe, Kent, CT21 4NB
☎ (01303) 230304 hopfuzz.co.uk

Hop Fuzz was started by two friends in 2011 and is situated on an industrial estate next to the Royal Military Canal (and a major cycle route) at West Hythe. The brewery is environmentally friendly, using solar power, recovering and re-using heat, and supplying feed to the local animal park. Major expansion took place in 2014.

Yellow Zinger (OG 1038, ABV 3.7%)

Martello (OG 1038, ABV 3.8%)

English (OG 1044, ABV 4%)
A malty, biscuity beer.

Goldsmith's (OG 1042, ABV 4.2%)
A classic golden ale.

Old American Pale (OG 1042, ABV 4.2%)

Northern Star (OG 1044, ABV 4.4%)
An amber-coloured ale with honey notes.

Steam Beer (OG 1044, ABV 4.4%)

Triumph (OG 1050, ABV 4.8%)
A stout with a coffee back taste.

Hop Kettle SIBA

Red Lion, 74 High Street, Cricklade, Wiltshire, SN6 6DD
☎ (01793) 750776 hopkettlebrewery.co.uk

Brewing began in 2012 using a four-barrel plant. The brewery is situated in a stone barn behind the Red Lion Inn, Cricklade. Many beer styles are brewed with some being barrel-aged in whisky and rum casks on site. There are plans to introduce an area that will allow people to dine among the brewing equipment.

Tricerahops (OG 1042, ABV 4.1%)

North Wall (OG 1043, ABV 4.2%)

Hop Monster

See George's

Hop & Stagger

3 West Castle Street, Bridgnorth, Shropshire, WV16 4AB
☎ (01746) 763962 hopandstaggerbrewery.co.uk

Hop & Stagger began brewing in 2012 having set up a 2.5-barrel plant at the White Lion Inn, Bridgnorth. Initially brewing a range of bitters and occasional seasonal ales exclusively for the pub.

Simpson's Original (OG 1038, ABV 3.6%)
A light mild.

Golden Wander (OG 1042, ABV 4.1%)
A crisp, pale golden ale with fruity notes and a light hopped finish.

Pure Amber (OG 1045, ABV 4.5%)
Zesty, light-coloured ale.

Hop Studio SIBA

3 Handley Park, Elvington Industrial Estate, York Road, Elvington, North Yorkshire, YO41 4AR
☎ (01904) 608029 thehopstudio.co.uk

Brewing began in 2012 using a 10-barrel plant situated just outside York. Freehouses in Yorkshire and Humberside are supplied direct and the beers are available further afield by arrangement or via wholesalers.

Blonde (OG 1037, ABV 3.5%)

XP – Extra Pale (OG 1043, ABV 4%)

Gold (OG 1048, ABV 4.5%)

Obsidian (OG 1052, ABV 5%)

XS – Extra Special (OG 1061, ABV 5.5%)

Vindhya (OG 1058, ABV 6%)

Hop Stuff (NEW) SIBA

Unit 7, Gunnery Terrace, Cornwallis Road, Woolwich, London, SE18 6SW ☎ 07850 086461
hopstuffbrewery.com

Hop Stuff began brewing in 2013. Seasonal beers: see website.

Fusilier (ABV 4.3%)

Pale Ale (ABV 4.5%)

Renegade IPA (ABV 5.6%)

Hopcraft

See Pixie Spring

Hopdaemon SIBA

Unit 1, Parsonage Farm, Seed Road, Newnham, Kent, ME9 0NA
☎ (01795) 892078 hopdaemon.com
Tours by arrangement

Tonie Prins originally started brewing in Tyler Hill near Canterbury in 2000 and moved to a new site in Newnham in 2005. The brewery currently supplies more than 100 outlets and is working at full capacity.

Golden Braid (OG 1039, ABV 3.7%)
A refreshing golden session bitter with a good blend of bittering and aroma hops underpinned by pale malt.

Incubus (OG 1041, ABV 4%)
A well-balanced, copper-hued best bitter. Pale malt and a hint of crystal malt are blended with bitter and slightly floral hops to give a lingering hoppy finish.

Skrimshander IPA (OG 1045, ABV 4.5%)
An aromatic copper-coloured pale ale with a refreshing taste and fruity finish.

Green Daemon (OG 1048, ABV 5%)
A golden beer with tropical fruit aromas and a crisp, clean finish. Brewed in the style of a Bavarian Helles (light lager).

Leviathan (OG 1057, ABV 6%)
A strong ruby ale with spicy hop aromas and a rich, malty finish.

Hope (NEW)

Corringham Road, Stanford-le-Hope, Essex, SS17 0AE
☎ 07903 793223 ✉ hopebrewery@gmail.com

Hope was founded in 2013 using a 0.25-barrel plant. There are plans for expansion. Occasional beers are available.

IPA (ABV 3.9%)

EPA (ABV 4%)

Strangely Brown (ABV 4%)

Citra (ABV 4.2%)

SX Dark (ABV 4.2%)

SX Gold (ABV 4.2%)

Dark Demon (ABV 4.4%)

Devil's Delight (ABV 4.4%)

Porter (ABV 4.6%)

White Dragon (ABV 5%)

Hope Valley

Castleton Losehill Hall YHA, Castleton, Derbyshire, S33 8WB ☎ 0845 371 9628

Brewing started in 2009 in the former Castleton Youth Hostel but moved to its present location in 2012 when this closed. The two-barrel plant was formerly used by Edale. All the profit from beer sales goes to support YHA's Breaks for Kids fund, which provides holidays based in hostels for children.

Hopshackle SIBA

Unit F, Bentley Business Park, Blenheim Way, Northfields Industrial Estate, Market Deeping, Lincolnshire, PE6 8LD
☎ (01778) 348542 🌐 hopshacklebrewery.co.uk
Tours by arrangement

Hopshackle was established in 2006 using a five-barrel plant. Monthly seasonals are brewed providing variety in styles and ABVs. More than 40 outlets are supplied direct. Bottle-conditioned beers are available.

Simarillo (OG 1037, ABV 3.8%)
Burnished gold-coloured with an aroma of citrus and soft fruits. The taste is tangy fruit with blackberry, plum and pineapple.

Hopstar SIBA

Unit 9, Rinus Business Park, Grimshaw Street, Darwen, Lancashire, BB3 2QX ☎ 07933 590159
🌐 hopstarbrewery.co.uk
Tours by arrangement

Hopstar first brewed in 2004 on a 2.5-barrel plant and expanded in 2010 to a new unit with a six-barrel plant. More than 100 outlets are supplied around Lancashire and the Greater Manchester area. Its brewery tap is Number 39, Darwen.

Chilli (OG 1039, ABV 3.8%)

Dizzy Danny Ale (OG 1039, ABV 3.8%)

Dark Knight (OG 1041, ABV 4%)

JC (OG 1041, ABV 4%)

Lancashire Gold (OG 1041, ABV 4%)

Lush (OG 1041, ABV 4%)

Smokey Joe's Black Beer (OG 1041, ABV 4%)

Hoptimists (NEW)

Unit 6, Ground Floor, Coopers Place, Combe Lane, Wormley, Surrey, GU8 5SZ
☎ (01428) 684121 🌐 hoptimists.co.uk

Hoptimists began brewing in 2013 using a six-barrel plant.

Golden Dawn (ABV 3.8%)

Glass Half Full (ABV 4%)

Hornbeam SIBA

1-1c Grey Street, Denton, Manchester, M34 3RU
☎ (0161) 320 5627 🌐 hornbeambrewery.com
Tours by arrangement

Hornbeam began brewing in 2007 on an eight-barrel plant. Regular monthly special beers are brewed. Seasonal beers: see website. Bottle-conditioned beers are also available.

Lemon Blossom (OG 1037, ABV 3.7%)
Golden, citrus and light in colour.

Mary Rose (OG 1037, ABV 3.8%)
Chestnut-coloured bitter with an initial citrus taste and floral, grassy notes in the finish.

Orange Blossom (OG 1038, ABV 3.8%)
Zesty golden-coloured pale ale.

Top Hop Best Bitter (OG 1041, ABV 4.2%)
Full-bodied with malt appeal and ample bitterness.

Black Coral Stout (OG 1043, ABV 4.5%)
A smooth, dry roast malt. Dark and full-bodied with a rich, creamy head. Satisfying with a subtle bitterness.

Hoskins Brothers

See Belvoir

Houston SIBA

South Street, Houston, Renfrewshire, PA6 7EN
☎ (01505) 612620 🌐 houston-brewing.co.uk
Shop open pub hours, daily
Tours by arrangement

Established by Carl Wengel in 1997, the brewery is attached to the Fox & Hounds pub and restaurant.

Houston deliver throughout Britain either direct or via a network of distributors. Seasonal and monthly beers: see website.

Killellan Bitter (OG 1037, ABV 3.7%) ◆
A light session ale, with a floral hop and fruity taste. The finish of this amber beer is dry and quenching.

APA (OG 1039, ABV 3.9%)
A pale, refreshing citrus ale. Zingy and fresh with an intense fruit taste.

Blonde Bombshell (OG 1040, ABV 4%)
A gold-coloured ale with a fresh hop aroma and rounded maltiness.

Peter's Well (OG 1042, ABV 4.2%) ◆
Well-balanced fruity taste with sweet hop, leading to an increasingly bittersweet finish.

Slainte (OG 1043, ABV 4.3%)
Hops explode on the nose leaving an aroma of malt and hops. The taste is long and deep with mature fruit notes that linger.

Tartan Terror (OG 1045, ABV 4.5%)

Howard Town SIBA

Hawkshead Mill, Hope Street, Glossop, Derbyshire, SK13 7SS
☎ (01457) 869800 🌐 howardtownbrewery.co.uk
Tours by arrangement

Howard Town was established in 2005 and is the Midlands most northerly brewery. More than 100 outlets are supplied – mainly as guest beers in the free trade. Seasonal and bottle-conditioned beers are available.

Mill Town Mild (OG 1038, ABV 3.5%)
A dark mild, slightly sweet with a hint of liquorice.

Bleaklow (OG 1038, ABV 3.8%)
A session beer with a light citrus flavour.

Longdendale Lights (OG 1039, ABV 3.9%)
A pale, light, easy-drinking beer.

Monk's Gold (OG 1040, ABV 4%)
Light and hoppy.

Wren's Nest (OG 1042, ABV 4.2%)
A light, hoppy beer.

Dinting Arches (OG 1045, ABV 4.5%)
A copper-coloured, medium strength beer. Hoppy with a malty flavour with a hint of blackcurrant.

Glott's Hop (OG 1049, ABV 5%)
A strong, hoppy bitter.

Dark Peak (OG 1062, ABV 6.4%)
A strong, dark porter, made with a blend of five malts.

Howling Hops

Cock Tavern, 315 Mare Street, Hackney, London, E8 1EJ 🌐 thecocktavern.co.uk

Brewing began in 2012. A wide range of cask and bottle-conditioned beers are produced. Four cask beers are usually available at any one time. One-off speciality beers and beers using new hop varieties are also brewed.

Mild (ABV 3.3%)

Pale Ale (ABV 3.8%)

Light Ale (ABV 4.2%)

Pale XX (ABV 5%)

Ruby Red (ABV 5%)

Smoked Porter (ABV 5.2%)

IPA (ABV 6%)

Old London Stout (ABV 6%)

Hoxne SIBA

Larch Barn, Heckfield Green, Suffolk, IP21 5AA
☎ 07515 003503 🌐 hoxnebrewery.co.uk

Hoxne Brewery was an idea conceived in 2013 with brewing commencing in 2014. It is a member of the East Anglian Brewers Co-operative and the Barley to Beer Project. Bottle-conditioned and seasonal beers are available.

Suffolk Punch (ABV 4.5%)

Brakey Wood (ABV 5.4%)

Heritage (ABV 6%)

Sarah Hughes

Beacon Hotel, 129 Bilston Street, Sedgley, Dudley, West Midlands, DY3 1JE
☎ (01902) 883381 🌐 sarahhughesbrewery.co.uk
Tours by arrangement

Traditional Black Country Victorian tower brewery, taken over by Sarah Hughes in 1921. Brewing ceased in the 1950s and recommenced in 1987. The original grist case and rare open-topped copper give a unique character to the brews. The Beacon Hotel is the brewery tap. A seasonal winter beer is brewed.

Pale Amber (OG 1038, ABV 4%)
A well-balanced beer, initially slightly sweet but with hops close behind.

Sedgley Surprise (OG 1048, ABV 5%) ◆
A bittersweet, medium-bodied, hoppy ale with some malt.

Dark Ruby Mild (OG 1058, ABV 6%) ◆
A dark ruby strong ale with a good balance of fruit and hops, leading to a pleasant, lingering hops and malt finish.

Humpty Dumpty SIBA

Church Road, Reedham, Norfolk, NR13 3TZ
☎ (01493) 701818 🌐 humptydumptybrewery.co.uk
Shop 12-5pm daily (Easter-end Oct), Sat 12.30-4pm (Nov-Xmas), closed Jan-Easter
Tours by arrangement

Established in 1998, this 11-barrel, award-winning brewery continues to grow and expand its range of beers. The on-site shop sells bottled beer from the brewery and local cider. Seasonal beers: see website.

Nord Atlantic (OG 1039, ABV 3.7%) ◆
Copper-coloured, full-bodied, with a grainy character, this lively mix of malt, caramel and apple fruitiness provides something for all. Hops and a liquorice bitterness appear at the end.

Little Sharpie (OG 1040, ABV 3.8%) ◆
Pronounced malty aroma gives way to a swirling biscuity mix of malt and hop. Growing bitterness in a long finish.

Lemon and Ginger (OG 1041, ABV 4%)
An amber, crisp ale with a ginger and lemon tang.

Swallowtail (OG 1041, ABV 4%) ◆
Easy drinking with a malty bittersweet character following from a strong hop aroma. An amber-hued, crisp finishing beer.

Ale (OG 1043, ABV 4.1%) ◆
A hoppy vanilla fudge bouquet develops through the initial taste to become the signature flavour. Malt provides balance as a gentle bitterness quickly recedes. Long, sweet, sticky finish.

Broadland Sunrise (OG 1044, ABV 4.2%) ◆
Hoppy throughout with a strong malt and bitter background. A grainy mouthfeel, hoppy aroma and long, strong finale.

Red Mill (OG 1045, ABV 4.3%)
A crisp, hoppy bitterness on top of a caramel and fruity malt backbone.

Reedcutter (OG 1045, ABV 4.4%) ◆
A sweet, malty beer, golden-hued with a gentle malt background. Smooth and full-bodied with a quick, gentle finish.

Cheltenham Flyer (OG 1048, ABV 4.6%) ◆
A full-flavoured golden, earthy bitter with a long, grainy finish. A strong hop bitterness dominates throughout. Little evidence of malt.

East Anglian Pale Ale (OG 1046, ABV 4.6%) ◆
A heavy sulphurous nose is lightened by hints of rhubarb. This carries into the flavour where a fruity sweetness contrasts with a grainy hoppiness. A long finish.

Norfolk Nectar (OG 1048, ABV 4.6%) ◆
A sweet honeyed note wraps around other flavours and aromas. Hops and caramel maintain a presence throughout to give a counterpoint to the rich, sweet base.

Railway Sleeper (OG 1049, ABV 5%) ◆
A rich Christmas pudding aroma leads into a delightfully fruity brew. Malt mingles with sultanas and raisins against a bittersweet backdrop. A full-bodied, smooth finish.

Hunsbury Craft

23 Limefields Way, East Hunsbury, Northamptonshire, NN4 0SA
☎ **(01604) 766228**
✉ **johngeorgemargetts@tiscali.co.uk**

Hunsbury Craft was established in 2010 using a 0.5-barrel plant, increasing to 2.25-barrel plant to meet demand.

Best Bitter (OG 1040, ABV 3.9%)

Copper (OG 1041, ABV 4.2%)

JD's Robust Porter (OG 1051, ABV 5.4%)

Mel's Mild (OG 1054, ABV 5.4%)

Magic (OG 1058, ABV 5.6%)

Young Chick (OG 1060, ABV 6%)

Old Rooster (ABV 7.1%)

Hunters SIBA

Bulleigh Barton Farm, Ipplepen, Devon, TQ12 5UE
☎ **(01803) 814399** 🌐 **thehuntersbrewery.co.uk**
Shop Mon-Fri 9am-5pm
Tours by arrangement

Hunters began brewing in 2008. The award-winning brewery has a 60-barrel brew length and 4,000 gallon fermenting capacity. A bottling, labelling and packing plant means it can turn out 3,000 bottle-conditioned beers per hour; this coupled with a dedicated conditioning room is enabling Hunters to bottle for others as well as itself. Seasonal beers are available.

Crack Shot (OG 1038, ABV 3.8%)
Good malt feel in the mouth, dry, tangy bitter finish.

Best (OG 1040, ABV 4%)
Three types of hop help produce a smooth, amber-coloured pint.

Crispy Pig (OG 1042, ABV 4%)
Speciality beer with a hint of apples.

Half Bore (OG 1040, ABV 4%)
Brewed with Devon honey for a full malty flavour.

Devon Dreamer (OG 1042, ABV 4.1%)
Delicious, smooth, refreshing session ale.

Pheasant Plucker (OG 1044, ABV 4.3%)
Full-flavoured with a bittersweet finish.

Royal Hunt (OG 1055, ABV 5.5%)

Black Jack (OG 1062, ABV 6%)
Strong but light triple-hopped stout made with Devon honey.

Full Bore (OG 1070, ABV 6.8%)
Malt flavours, made with Devon honey.

Hurns

See Tomos Watkin (under W)

Hurst SIBA

Western Road, Hurstpierpoint, West Sussex, BN6 9FH ☎ **07866 438953**
✉ **hurstbrewery@hotmail.co.uk**
Tours by arrangement

Hurst is a four-barrel microbrewery based at the White Horse, Hurstpierpoint, founded in 2012 but reviving a name dating back to 1862. Beers are available at the White Horse and other local outlets. Seasonal beer is available.

Founders Best Bitter (ABV 4.2%)
A nutty brown in colour, with a rounded malty taste suffused with subtle caramel.

Hydes IFBB

The Beer Studio, 30 Kansas Avenue, Salford, M50 2GL
☎ **(0161) 226 1317** 🌐 **hydesbrewery.com**

Hydes is a family-owned brewery dating from 1863. It had been on the same site for more than 120 years but moved to a new site in Salford in 2012. The brewery currently focuses entirely on the production of cask ales to be supplied to its own tied estate of more than 70 pubs and the wholesale market. Hydes also produce a range of cask-conditioned beers using rare and unusual hops and malts separately marketed as the Beer Studio and a bi-monthly changing beer marketed as the Lowry Collection celebrating Salford artist L.S. Lowry.

Light Mild/1863 (OG 1033.5, ABV 3.5%) ◆
Lightly-hopped, pale brown session beer with some hops, malt and fruit in the taste and a short, dry finish.

Owd Oak (OG 1033.5, ABV 3.5%) ◆
Dark brown/red in colour, with a fruit and malt nose. Taste includes biscuity malt and green fruits, with a satisfying aftertaste.

Original Bitter (OG 1036.5, ABV 3.8%) ◆
Pale brown beer with a malty nose, malt and an earthy hoppiness in the taste, and a good bitterness through to the finish.

Finest (OG 1044, ABV 4.5%)
Full-bodied and slightly sweet.

Ial (NEW)

Pant Du Rd, Eryrys, CH7 4DD ☎ 07956 440402
cwrwial.com

Cwrw Ial Community Brewery is run as a social enterprise assisted by EU funding with all profits used for local community projects. The 10-barrel plant is situated in a former truck maintenance workshop and first brewed in 2014.

The Volunteer (ABV 3.7%)

Iceni SIBA

Foulden Road, Ickburgh, Norfolk, IP26 5HB
☎ (01842) 878922 icenibrewery.co.uk/ extraordinaryales.co.uk
Shop Mon-Fri 8.30am-5pm, Sat 9am-3pm
Tours by arrangement

Iceni was launched in 1995 by Brendan Moore. The brewery is also the headquarters of the East Anglian Brewers Co-op (EAB). A new project has recently been launched titled Extraordinary Ales, whereby East Anglian brewers produce one-off brews using unusual and interesting ingredients and methods: see website for further details.

Fine Soft Day (OG 1038, ABV 4%) ◆
Toffee tickles both the nostrils and tastebuds as it hovers over a creamy, lightly-hopped backdrop in this golden brew. A gentle mix of flavours softly sinks into a pleasant sweetness.

Idle

White Hart Inn, Main Street, West Stockwith, DN10 4EY
☎ (01427) 753226
theidlebrewery@btinternet.com
Tours by arrangement

The brewery began production in 2007 and is situated in a converted stable at the back of the White Hart Inn, which Brian Cooper the brewer now owns, alongside the River Idle. Seasonal beers are available.

Golden Crown (OG 1038, ABV 3.8%)

Dog (OG 1041, ABV 4.2%)
A copper-coloured ale, moderately hoppy with a good balance of malt and hops leading to a bitter finish.

Sod (OG 1041, ABV 4.2%)

Tongue (OG 1041, ABV 4.2%)

Black & Tan (OG 1042, ABV 4.3%)

Black Abbot (OG 1044, ABV 4.6%)

Idle Landlord (OG 1044, ABV 4.6%)
A dark brown ale with plenty of body, a malty flavour and a caramel/coffee finish.

Ilkley SIBA

The New Brewery, Ashlands Road, Ilkley, West Yorkshire, LS29 8JT
☎ (01943) 604604 ilkleybrewery.co.uk
Tours by arrangement

After a gap of 80 years production started at a new site in 2009 using an eight-barrel plant, bringing brewing back to Ilkley. The brewery moved to larger premises in 2011 and has since upgraded to a 20-barrel plant brewing up to 160 barrels per week. Seasonal and bottle-conditioned beers: see website.

Dinner Ale (OG 1034, ABV 3.3%)
Light and crisp Victorian pale ale.

Mary Jane (OG 1036, ABV 3.5%)
A crisp, pale ale with citrus aromas.

Black (OG 1040, ABV 3.7%)
Dark mild with a blend of five malts to give a smooth, mellow, easy-to-drink malt flavour with a hint of liquorice in the finish.

Joshua Jane (OG 1038, ABV 3.7%)
A highly-hopped golden ale with a strong, bitter finish.

Gold (OG 1040, ABV 3.9%) ◆
An easy-drinking, golden-coloured ale with a light floral aroma leading to a soft citrus fruit flavour and a gentle bitter aftertaste.

Fireside Porter (OG 1042, ABV 4.2%)
A smoky and spicy porter balanced by rich fruit flavours.

Pale (OG 1042, ABV 4.2%)
A dry, crisp pale ale strongly hopped with floral hops to give a strong but mellow citrus finish.

Lotus IPA (OG 1055, ABV 5.6%)
Golden-coloured IPA with strong aromas and flavours of mango, grapefruit and all round citrus.

Siberia (OG 1052, ABV 5.9%)
A naturally cloudy saison using Yorkshire rhubarb with spice and vanilla flavours.

Imperial

Arcadia Hall, Cliff Street, Mexborough, South Yorkshire, S64 9HU ☎ 07428 422703
imperialclub@hotmail.co.uk

Five regular beers are produced on a six-barrel tower brewery system located in the basement of the Imperial Club, Mexborough. Beer is available in the club as well as local outlets.

Best Bitter (OG 1040, ABV 3.9%)

Blonde (OG 1042, ABV 4%)

Hop Bomb (OG 1042, ABV 4%)

Bees Knees (OG 1043, ABV 4.2%)

Darkness (OG 1042, ABV 4.2%)

Stout (OG 1047, ABV 4.6%)

Independent Lakeland Breweries

See Geltsdale and Strands

Indian Summer SIBA

Unit 3, Ashdon Road Commercial Centre, Saffron Walden, Essex, CB10 2NH ☎ 07896 637826
bombayblonde.co.uk

Indian Summer began brewing in 2012. Beers are branded as the Hop & Soul range. A bottled ale is also produced for Indian restaurants.

Hop & Soul Mild (OG 1038, ABV 3.7%)

Hop & Soul Amber (OG 1038, ABV 3.8%)
A light amber in colour with gentle bitterness and a warm, nutty finish.

Hop & Soul Blonde (OG 1045, ABV 4.5%)
Well-balanced, light and refreshing with a pleasant mouthfeel.

Hop & Soul Porter (OG 1047, ABV 4.6%)

Inishmacsaint

7 Drumadown Road, Drumskimly, Derrygonnelly, Co Fermanagh, BT93 6DN
☎ (028) 6864 1031 gordyfallis@hotmail.com

Inishmacsaint is a small-scale brewery that has been in production since 2009 brewing mainly bottle-conditioned beers. A larger brew plant has now come on stream.

Innis & Gunn

Canning Street, Edinburgh, EH3 8EG
☎ (0131) 272 2782 innisandgunn.com

Innis & Gunn does not brew but Tennents produces one regular bottled (not bottle-conditioned) beer for the company, Oak Aged Beer (ABV 6.6%). There are three further beers in the permanent range: Original (ABV 6.6%), Blonde (ABV 6%) and Rum Cask (ABV 7.4%). A range of limited edition beers is also produced each year.

Instant Karma (NEW)

4 John St, Clay Cross, Derbyshire, S45 9NQ
☎ (01246) 250366 instantkarmabrewery.co.uk

Instant Karma began brewing in 2012 using a five-barrel plant. The brewery is part of the Rykneld Turnpyke brewpub.

Test Brew Number One! (OG 1039, ABV 3.9%)

Test Brew Number Two! (OG 1045, ABV 4.5%)

Interbrew Magor

Magor Brewery, Magor, NP26 3DA

UK subsidiary of AB InBev. No real ale.

Interbrew Samlesbury

Cuerdale Lane, Samlesbury, Lancashire, PR5 0XD

UK subsidiary of AB InBev. No real ale.

Interbrew UK

Porter Tun House, Capability Green, Luton, Bedfordshire, LU1 3LS
☎ (01582) 391166

No real ale.

Inveralmond SIBA

22 Inveralmond Place, Inveralmond, Perth, PH1 3TS
☎ (01738) 449448 inveralmond-brewery.co.uk
Shop Mon-Fri 10am-5pm
Tours by arrangement

Established in 1997, Inveralmond was the first brewery in Perth for more than 30 years. The brewery has expanded from a 10-barrel to a 30-barrel plant and there are plans for further growth. Around 250 outlets are supplied. Seasonal beers: see website.

Independence (OG 1040, ABV 3.8%)
A well-balanced Scottish ale with fruit and malt tones. Hop provides an increasing bitterness in the finish.

Ossian (OG 1042, ABV 4.1%)
Well-balanced best bitter with a dry finish. This full-bodied amber ale is dominated by fruit and hop with a bittersweet character although excessive caramel can distract from this.

Thrappledouser (OG 1043, ABV 4.3%)
A refreshing amber beer with reddish hues. The crisp, hoppy aroma is finely balanced with a tangy but quenching taste.

Lia Fail (OG 1048, ABV 4.7%)
The Gaelic name means Stone of Destiny. A dark, robust, full-bodied beer with a deep malty taste. Smooth texture and balanced finish.

Ironbridge

See Wrekin

Irving SIBA

Unit G1, Railway Triangle, Walton Road, Portsmouth, Hampshire, PO6 1TQ
☎ (023) 9238 9988 irvingbrewers.co.uk
Shop Thu & Fri 3-6pm
Tours by arrangement

Established in 2007 by former Gale's brewer Malcolm Irving using a 15-barrel plant. Around 120 outlets are supplied in Hampshire, Sussex and Surrey with beers available further afield through beer swaps with other breweries. Seasonal beers: see website.

Frigate (OG 1039, ABV 3.8%)
Golden bitter with a citrus hop flavour complemented by a background sweetness.

Type 42 (OG 1042, ABV 4.2%)
A robust best bitter with a deep ruby red hue balancing sweet hedgerow berry notes with a long, roasted malt finish and a deep bitterness.

Admiral Stout (OG 1042.5, ABV 4.3%)
A classic dark oatmeal stout, deep black in colour with a smooth, rounded malt flavour balanced with a strong bitterness.

Invincible (OG 1048, ABV 4.6%)
Tawny-coloured strong bitter. Sweet and fruity with underlying maltiness throughout and gradually increasing dryness, contrasting with the sweet finish.

Iron Duke (OG 1053, ABV 5.3%)
A refreshing, well-balanced strong IPA. Hoppy – but not overly so.

THE BREWERIES

Irwell Works SIBA

Irwell Street, Ramsbottom, Lancashire, BL0 9YQ
☎ (01706) 825019 🌐 irwellworksbrewery.co.uk
Tours by arrangement

Irwell Works started brewing in 2010 in a building dating from 1888 that once housed the Irwell Works Steam, Tin, Copper & Iron Works. It now houses a six-barrel plant. A bar opened on the first floor in 2011.

Lightweights & Gentlemen (OG 1031, ABV 3.2%) ◆
Light, refreshing pale ale with some fruitiness and a hoppy, bitter finish.

Tin Plate (OG 1033, ABV 3.6%)
Brewed as a traditional dark mild, low in strength and a rich, creamy flavour but with a slight bitterness to contrast.

Copper Plate (OG 1036, ABV 3.8%) ◆
Traditional northern bitter. Copper-coloured with a satisfying blend of malt and hops and good bitterness.

Richard Mason 1888 (OG 1039, ABV 4%)
Richard Mason built Irwell Works in 1888. A mid-strength, single-hopped beer with a mild bitterness and pleasant, mildly-hopped aftertaste.

Costa Del Salford (OG 1039, ABV 4.1%)
A hoppy summer ale, this beer is light in colour with bags of flavour.

Steam Plate (OG 1042, ABV 4.3%)
A golden best bitter with medium bitterness balanced with a slight sweetness and a slightly nutty flavour.

Iron Plate (OG 1043, ABV 4.4%) ◆
Roast malt in the aroma is joined by hop and a toasty bitterness in the taste and finish.

Mad Dogs & Englishmen (OG 1052, ABV 5.5%)
Export style pale ale hopped in the style of an IPA. Little sweetness for its strength and a strong hop character make this a smooth, easy-drinking beer.

Isca SIBA

The Brewery, Court Farm, Holcombe Village, Dawlish, Devon, EX7 0JT ☎ 07773 444501
✉ iscaales@yahoo.co.uk

Two CAMRA members took over Gargoyles Brewery in 2009 under the name Isca Ales. The brewery has developed a market by bottling a lot of production and supplying beer festivals outside the region.

Citra (OG 1038, ABV 3.8%)
Light refreshing beer with a grapefruit aroma leading to a dry bitter finish.

Dawlish Summer (OG 1038, ABV 3.8%)
Light beer with a hoppy aroma.

Golden Ale (OG 1038, ABV 3.8%)
A golden bitter with a hoppy aroma.

Dawlish Bittter (OG 1042, ABV 4.2%)
Classic English bitter full of English hops and west country malt.

Glorious Devon (OG 1044, ABV 4.4%)
The combination of three hops gives a grassy hop aroma with hoppy aftertaste.

Holcombe Gold (OG 1045, ABV 4.5%)
Golden beer full of English and American hops leading to a dry bitter finish.

Dawlish Pale (OG 1050, ABV 5%)
Grassy hop aroma with intense hoppy aftertaste.

Achilles Ale (OG 1054, ABV 5.4%)
Dark, strong, malty ale.

Isfield SIBA

Unit 16, New Place Farm, Framfield, East Sussex, TN22 5RH
☎ (01825) 750633

Office: Imperial Cottage, Station Road, Isfield, East Sussex, TN22 5UJ ✉ enquiries@isfieldbrewing.co.uk

Isfield began brewing in 2012 using a five-barrel plant. Seasonal beer is available.

Bitter (OG 1039, ABV 3.7%)
A chestnut-coloured session bitter with a fruity and malty aroma and a biscuity sweet taste.

Straw Blond (OG 1042, ABV 4.1%)

Imperial Pale Ale (OG 1043, ABV 4.2%)

Toad in the Ale (OG 1050, ABV 4.8%)

Flapjack (OG 1055, ABV 5.3%)

Island SIBA

Dinglers Farm, Yarmouth Road, Newport, Isle of Wight, PO30 4LZ
☎ (01983) 821731 🌐 isleofwightbrewery.com
Tours by arrangement

Island Brewery is the realisation of Tom Minshull's ambition to brew real ales to complement the existing family-owned drinks distribution business. Brewing commenced in 2010 using a 12-barrel brewery. More than 100 outlets are supplied direct.

Nipper Bitter (OG 1038, ABV 3.8%)
Straw-coloured, light and refreshing with a distinguishable balance of malt and hops and a satisfying afterbite.

Wight Gold (OG 1040, ABV 4%)
Golden brown in colour with rounded malt and hops throughout.

Yachtsmans Ale (OG 1042, ABV 4.2%)
Chestnut-coloured ale with a rich, malty mouthfeel and hop aroma.

Wight Diamond (OG 1046, ABV 4.4%)

Wight Knight (OG 1045, ABV 4.5%)
Strong, full-bodied beer.

Vectis Venom (OG 1048, ABV 4.8%)
Easy-drinking with an underlying smoothness.

Earls RDA (OG 1052, ABV 5%)
Rich yet understated stout, with strong espresso aftertaste.

Islay SIBA

The Brewery, Islay House Square, Bridgend, Isle of Islay, PA44 7NZ
☎ (01496) 810014 🌐 islayales.com
Shop Mon-Sat 10.30am-5pm
Tours by arrangement

Brewing started on a four-barrel plant in a converted tractor shed in 2004. The brewery shop is next door. The island is more famous for its whisky, but the brewery has established itself as a must-see place for those visiting the eight working distilleries. Bottle-conditioned beers are available. Special beers are also brewed.

Isle of Avalon

See Wessex

Isle of Mull

See Argyll

Isle of Purbeck SIBA

Manor Road, Studland, Dorset, BH19 3AU
☎ (01929) 450227 isleofpurbeckbrewery.com
Tours by arrangement

Founded in 2003, the brewery is situated in the grounds of the Bankes Arms Hotel, overlooking Studland Bay on the Jurassic Coast. The 10-barrel plant produces six core beers plus seasonals and an annually-brewed cold filtered Pilsner lager called Purbex. The core beers are available nationwide via exchange swaps with other microbrewers. Bottle-conditioned beer is available direct from the brewery and from retailers throughout Hampshire and Dorset.

Purbeck Best Bitter (OG 1036, ABV 3.6%)
A classic malty best bitter with rich malt aroma and taste and smooth, malty bitter finish.

Harry's Best (OG 1040, ABV 4%)
A well balanced beer with sweet and malty flavours and a hint of spicy hops.

Fossil Fuel (OG 1040, ABV 4.1%)
Amber bitter with complex aroma with a hint of pepper; rich malt dominates the taste, leading to a smooth, dry finish.

Solar Power (OG 1043, ABV 4.3%)
Tawny-coloured ale with well-balanced flavours providing a strong bitter taste but short, dry finish.

Studland Bay Wrecked (OG 1044, ABV 4.5%)
Deep red ale with slightly sweet aroma reflecting a mixture of caramel, malt and hops that lead to a dry, malty finish.

Purbeck IPA (OG 1047, ABV 4.8%)
Mid-brown beer with hop/malt balance in the flavour and a long dry aftertaste.

Isle of Skye SIBA

The Pier, Uig, Isle of Skye, IV51 9XP
☎ (01470) 542477 skyebrewery.co.uk
Shop Mon-Sat 10am-6pm, Sun 12.30-4.30pm (Apr-Oct)

The Isle of Skye Brewery was established in 1995. Originally a 10-barrel plant, it was upgraded to 20-barrels in 2004. Angus MacRuary has sold the majority share holding to IOSB Holdings Ltd, but will continue to run the brewery side. Further expansion is planned. The new owner is planning to re-brand the brewery. Seasonal beers: see website.

Skye Otter Ale (OG 1041, ABV 4%)

Tarasgeir (OG 1040, ABV 4%)
The peat roasted barley dominates giving a mellow peaty whisky taste.

The Thistle and The Fern (OG 1041, ABV 4%)

Young Pretender (OG 1039, ABV 4%)
A fruity, full-bodied golden ale, predominantly hoppy and fruity. The bitterness in the mouth is also balanced by summer fruits and hops, continuing into the lingering bitter finish.

Red Cuillin (OG 1041, ABV 4.2%)
A light, fruity nose with a hint of caramel leads to a hoppy, malty, fruity flavour and a dry, bittersweet finish.

Hebridean Gold (OG 1041.5, ABV 4.3%)
Porridge oats are used to produce this speciality beer. Nicely balanced. it has a refreshingly soft fruity, bitter flavour with an oaty background.

Black Cuillin (OG 1044, ABV 4.5%)
A complex, tasty brew worthy of its many awards. Full-bodied with a malty richness. Malt holds sway but there are plenty of hops and fruit to be discovered in its varied character. A delicious Scottish old ale.

Blaven (OG 1047, ABV 5%)
A well-balanced strong amber bitter with kiwi fruit and caramel in the nose and a lingering sharp bitterness.

Cuillin Beast (OG 1066, ABV 7%)
A winter warmer; sweet and fruity, and much more drinkable than the strength would suggest. Plenty of caramel throughout with a variety of fruit on the nose.

Itchen Valley SIBA

Unit 4, Prospect Commercial Park, Prospect Road, New Alresford, Hampshire, SO24 9QF
☎ (01962) 735111/73642 itchenvalley.com
Shop Mon-Fri 9am-5pm
Tours by arrangement

Established in 1997, Itchen Valley moved to new premises in 2006 with a 20-barrel plant. The brewery has a gift shop and offers brewery tours and mini conferencing facilities. More than 350 pubs are supplied, with wholesalers used for further distribution. Seasonal and bottle-conditioned beers as well as monthly specials are available.

Godfathers (OG 1038, ABV 3.8%)
A pale brown bitter, with a malty aroma and taste and a light body, leading to a bittersweet finish.

Belgarum (ABV 3.9%)
A hoppy bitter sweetened with Hampshire honey and offset by the addition of elderflower.

Fagin's (OG 1041, ABV 4.1%)
Copper-coloured best bitter with a hint of crystal malt and a pleasant bitter aftertaste.

Hampshire Rose (OG 1042, ABV 4.2%)
A golden amber ale. Fruit and hops dominate the taste throughout, with a good mouthfeel.

Winchester Ale (OG 1042, ABV 4.5%)
Traditional English bitter, nut brown with a sweet, malty flavour and a good hoppy nose.

Pure Gold (OG 1046, ABV 4.8%)
Aromatic hoppy, strong bitter. Golden-coloured, with initial maltiness and grapefruit counter-balanced with some sweetness, leading to dry finish.

Jacobi SIBA

Penlanwen Farm, Pumsaint, Carmarthenshire, SA19 8RR
☎ (01558) 650605 jacobibrewery.co.uk

Brewing started in 2006 in a converted barn. Brewer Justin Jacobi is also the owner of the Brunant Arms in Caio, which is a regular outlet for the beers. The brewery is located 50 yards from the Dolaucothi mines where the Romans dug for gold. Further beers are planned including seasonals.

Light Ale (OG 1038, ABV 3.8%)

Red Squirrel (OG 1040, ABV 4%)
Auburn-coloured beer with fruit undertones and a dry bitter finish.

Dark Ale (OG 1052, ABV 5%)

James & Kirkman

4 Wakefield Road, Pontefract, West Yorkshire, WF8 4HN
☎ (01977) 702231
eastcoastbrewing@hotmail.co.uk

Brewing began in 2013 behind the Robin Hood pub using a 2.5-barrel plant. Beers were previously brewed at East Coast Brewing (qv), owned by the same brewers.

Star Light (OG 1032, ABV 3.2%)
A light, fruity session bitter.

James Street (NEW)

City Pub Company, 14 James Street West, Bath, BA1 2BX
☎ (01225) 805609 thebathbrewhouse.com
Tours by arrangement

The James Street Brewery opened in 2013 and is owned by the Henley Brewing Company, which owns several other pubs, including brewpubs, in Henley and Cambridge. The compact plant is on the ground floor of the Bath Brewhouse with the conditioning tanks on the first floor. Occasional special ales are brewed. The company's other pub, the Cork in Bath, is also supplied.

Gladiator (OG 1040, ABV 3.8%)

Emperor (OG 1044, ABV 4.4%)

Jarrow SIBA

54 Aidan Court, Jarrow, Tyne & Wear, NE32 3EF
☎ (0191) 483 6792 jarrowbrewery.co.uk
Tours by arrangement

Brewing commenced at the Robin Hood, Jarrow in 2002, moving to South Shields in 2008. In 2013 brewing returned to Jarrow using a 40-barrel plant. Brewing continues at South Shields. Seasonal beers are also available.

Bitter (OG 1037.5, ABV 3.8%)
A light, smooth, satisfying gold bitter. Subtle fruity hops give the taste profile on tongue and nose.

Rivet Catcher (OG 1039, ABV 4%)
A light, smooth, satisfying gold bitter. Subtle fruity hops give the taste profile on the tongue and nose.

Joblings Swinging Gibbet (OG 1041, ABV 4.1%)
A copper-coloured, evenly-balanced beer with a good hop aroma and a fruity finish.

Caulker (OG 1040.5, ABV 4.2%)
A light, smooth, satisfying golden hoppy ale with a lingering grapefruit zest finish.

Red Ellen (OG 1042.5, ABV 4.4%)
A rich ruby red, full-bodied ale with a citrus hop aroma.

McConnell's Irish Stout (OG 1045, ABV 4.6%)
A rich, creamy stout with a long, lingering liquorice and pale chocolate finish.

Westoe IPA (OG 1044.5, ABV 4.6%)
A pale gold ale with a soft malt character and refreshingly complex hop aroma – easy-drinking premium ale.

Isis (OG 1049, ABV 5%)
A well-balanced golden premium ale with a full hop aroma and grapefruit presence on the palate.

American IPA (OG 1051, ABV 5.5%)
A full-bodied golden IPA with orange and pink grapefruit hop flavours.

Jennings

Castle Brewery, Cockermouth, Cumbria, CA13 9NE
☎ 0845 129 7190 jenningsbrewery.co.uk
Shop Mon-Sat 10am-4pm
Tours by arrangement

Jennings Brewery was established as a family concern in 1828 in the village of Lorton. The company moved to its present location in 1874. Pure Lakeland water is still used for brewing, drawn from the brewery's own well. Monthly seasonal beers are available. Part of Marston's PLC.

Dark Mild (OG 1031, ABV 3.1%)
A well-balanced, dark brown mild with a malty aroma, strong roast taste, not over-sweet, with some hops and a slightly bitter finish.

Bitter (OG 1035, ABV 3.5%)
A malty beer with a good mouthfeel that combines with roast flavour and a hoppy finish.

Cumberland Ale (OG 1039, ABV 4%)
A tawny, hoppy beer with a dry aftertaste.

Cocker Hoop (OG 1044, ABV 4.6%)
Full-bodied complex bitter beer with plenty of hops and a rising bitter finish.

Sneck Lifter (OG 1051, ABV 5.1%)
A strong, dark brown ale with a complex balance of fruit, malt, sweet and roast flavours through to the finish.

Jo C's SIBA

The Old Store, Walsingham Road, West Barsham, Norfolk, NR21 9NP
☎ (01328) 863854 jocsnorfolkale.co.uk
Tours by arrangement

Starting in 2010, Jo Coubrough (the county's only brewster) established a 10-barrel brewery in a former farm building in Norfolk. The beers are available in Flying Kiwi Inns, other free trade outlets, and at the brewery. Mini-casks are available.

Norfolk Kiwi (OG 1038.5, ABV 3.8%)
Yellow, hop dominated bitter. Citrus notes vie with bitterness to add depth. Quick, slightly astringent finish.

Bitter Old Bustard (OG 1045, ABV 4.3%)

A mixture of malt and caramel on the nose is joined by a dark fruitiness in the flavour. Quick finish.

Knot Just Another IPA (OG 1052, ABV 5%)
A light amber, well-balanced, strong bitter. Well-hopped.

Jolly Sailor SIBA

Olympia Hotel, 77 Barlby Road, Selby, North Yorkshire, YO8 5AB
☎ (01757) 268918
jolly-sailor-brewery.webplus.net

Jolly Sailor began brewing in 2012 at Ricall Business Park, a former mine site near York. Production was moved to the Olympia Hotel, Selby, in 2013, where the regular beers are always available and increasingly in other local pubs. Seasonal beers: see website.

Bullseye Bitter (OG 1039, ABV 3.8%)

Jolly Blonde (OG 1036.5, ABV 3.8%)

Jolly Scotsman's Bitter (OG 1038, ABV 3.8%)
A fruity amber ale with citrus notes.

Yellow Jersey (OG 1036, ABV 3.8%)
A pale ale brewed with English hops.

Cue Brew (OG 1040, ABV 4%)
A dark mild.

Jollyboat SIBA

Coach House, Buttgarden Street, Bideford, Devon, EX39 2AU
☎ (01237) 424343
Tours by arrangement

Established in 1995, the brewery is named after a sailor's leave vessel and all the beers have a nautical theme. Most outlets supplied are in Devon.

Mainbrace (OG 1042, ABV 4.2%)
Pale brown brew with a rich fruity aroma and a bitter taste and aftertaste.

Plunder (OG 1049, ABV 4.8%)
Red/brown beer with an aromatic nose, a good balance of malt, hops and fruit present throughout leading to a bitter finish.

Jones The Brewer (NEW)

Unit 2, The Old Garage, Whitney-on-Wye, Herefordshire, HR3 6ER
☎ (01497) 831220 ☎ 07010 717232
jonesthebrewer.co.uk

Damian Jones started this four-barrel brewery in 2013. The regular beers are supplied to more than a dozen local outlets and are also available direct from the brewery: see website. Further beers are planned.

Abigail's Party (OG 1036, ABV 3.8%)
A light golden-coloured, easy-drinking pale ale. A zesty aroma leads to small fruit/malt sweetness, overlaid with dominant grapefruit and lemon citrus flavours building into a powerful but not excessive bitterness that lasts long into the finish.

Malty Python (OG 1049, ABV 4.2%)
A full-bodied, dark copper-coloured malty ale with toffee and caramel undertones.

Dennis Hopper (OG 1045, ABV 4.7%)
An American-style pale ale with a full but crisp malt body that is complemented by a refined bitterness and a full hop flavour.

Wheat Stone Bridge (OG 1052, ABV 5.7%)
A Belgian-style wheat beer with coriander and citrus zests backed by hop bitterness to complement the sweet banana undertones.

Joule's SIBA

The Brewery, Great Hales Street, Market Drayton, Shropshire, TF9 1JP
☎ (01630) 654400 joulesbrewery.co.uk
Tours by arrangement

Re-established in 2010, following a break of 40 years, Joule's is situated in Market Drayton and uses its own mineral water. It concentrates on three core beers and in 2013 launched a seasonal ale portfolio, experimenting with unusual beer styles.

Blonde (OG 1038, ABV 3.8%)
Light, refreshing and subtle, a well-balanced blonde beer with a citrus and hoppy aroma.

Pale Ale (OG 1042, ABV 4.1%)
Made from the original Joule's recipe from 1779. Fresh and clean, a crisp beer with an initial impact, giving way to a pleasant bitter finish.

Slumbering Monk (OG 1045, ABV 4.5%)
Full-bodied with deep, malty and nutty fullness. Hints of caramel give a round, soft, satisfying smoothness in this bright copper-coloured ale, cut with light hoppy bitterness.

Jubilee Tower

Unit 9, Rinus Business Park, Grimshaw Street, Darwen, Lancashire, BB3 2QX ☎ 07966 368339

Office: 4 Moor Close, Darwen, Lancashire, BB3 3LG
simonmara1@gmail.com

Brewing began in 2012 using spare capacity at Hopstar Brewery; Hopstar distributes the beer. Brewing is currently suspended.

Paper Chain (OG 1038, ABV 3.8%)
A copper-coloured session beer.

Junction

1 Baildon Road, Baildon, Shipley, West Yorkshire, BD16 6AB
☎ (01274) 582009

Junction is a small microbrewery established in 2012 in the cellar of the Junction pub in Baildon, brewing about 300 gallons a week. Beer is sold in the pub and other local outlets. Bottle-conditioned beer is available.

Tommy's Tipple (OG 1037, ABV 3.7%)
A chestnut-coloured session bitter; smooth tasting with a hoppy finish.

Blonde (OG 1040, ABV 4%)
A blonde session bitter, offering a big flavour and a dry finish.

Dark Thoughts (OG 1046, ABV 4.6%)
Porter with roasted, nutty flavours and hops which give a bitter edge.

Just A Minute

c/o Deerness Rubber Co Ltd, Coulson Street, Spennymoor, County Durham, DL16 7RS ☎ 07586 896091 🌐 justaminutebrewery.co.uk

Established by two friends in 2010, a 2.5-barrel plant was commissioned in 2011. Sales of bottled beers continue in local outlets. Seasonal beers are available.

Ruby Tuesday (OG 1039, ABV 3.9%)

Tyme Tunnel (OG 1041, ABV 4.1%)

Golden Dawn (OG 1043, ABV 4.3%)

IPA (OG 1046, ABV 4.6%)

Time 'n' 'Arf (OG 1050, ABV 5%)

Kelburn SIBA

10 Muriel Lane, Barrhead, East Renfrewshire, G78 1QB
☎ (0141) 881 2138 🌐 kelburnbrewery.com
Tours by arrangement

Kelburn is an award-winning family business established in 2002. Beers are available bottled and in take-away polypins. Seasonal beers: see website.

Goldihops (OG 1038, ABV 3.8%)
Well-hopped session ale with a fruity taste and a bitter finish.

Pivo Estivo (OG 1038, ABV 3.9%)

Misty Law (OG 1040, ABV 4%)
A dry, hoppy amber ale with a long-lasting bitter finish.

Red Smiddy (OG 1040, ABV 4.1%)
This bittersweet ale predominantly features an intense citrus hop character that assaults the nose and continues into the flavour, balanced perfectly with fruity malt.

Dark Moor (OG 1044, ABV 4.5%)
A dark, fruity ale with undertones of liquorice and blackcurrant.

Jaguar (OG 1043, ABV 4.5%)

Cart Noir (OG 1046, ABV 4.8%)

Cart Blanche (OG 1048, ABV 5%)
A golden, full-bodied ale. The assault of fruit and hop camouflages the strength of this easy-drinking ale.

Kelham Island SIBA

23 Alma Street, Sheffield, South Yorkshire, S3 8SA
☎ (0114) 249 4804

Office: Prospect House, 17 Alma Street, Sheffield, South Yorkshire, S3 8RY 🌐 kelhambrewery.co.uk
Shop Mon-Fri 9am-4pm (some weekends)
Tours by arrangement

Opened in 1990 behind the Fat Cat pub, the brewery moved to new purpose-built premises in 1999. The old building is used as a visitor centre. A brewery shop opened recently, together with new offices in nearby Prospect House. Monthly specials and bottle-conditioned beers are available.

Best Bitter (OG 1038, ABV 3.8%)
Classic amber Yorkshire bitter with spicy, earthy aromas and a sweet, refreshing, malty finish.

Pride of Sheffield (OG 1040.5, ABV 4%)
A full-flavoured amber-coloured bitter.

Easy Rider (OG 1041.8, ABV 4.3%)
A pale, straw-coloured beer with a sweetish flavour and delicate hints of citrus fruits. A beer with hints of flavour rather than full-bodied.

Riders on the Storm (OG 1045, ABV 4.5%)
A robust golden pale ale with berry notes and slight roasted notes.

Pale Rider (OG 1050, ABV 5.2%)
A full-bodied, straw-coloured pale ale, with a good fruity aroma and a strong fruit and hop taste. Its well-balanced sweetness and bitterness continue in the finish.

Keltek SIBA

Candela House, Cardrew Way, Redruth, Cornwall, TR15 1SS
☎ (01209) 313620 🌐 keltekbrewery.co.uk
Shop Mon-Fri 9am-5pm

Keltek has undergone a number of expansions in recent years and is now a major force in Cornwall and further afield. Natural Magik is the only bottle-conditioned beer available; bottling is also carried out for several other Cornish breweries.

Even Keel (OG 1034, ABV 3.4%)
Easy-drinking tawny bitter. Smooth malt and citrus fruit flavour and aroma, fading to a bitter, dry and nutty finish.

Golden Lance (OG 1038, ABV 4%)
Amber bitter promising fruit and hops. Assertive malt characteristic balanced by rising dry hop-bitterness and some citrus and elderflower fruit.

Magik (OG 1040, ABV 4.2%)
Tawny best bitter with a light malt aroma. Malt, caramel and bitterness in the mouth with a bitter, dry finish.

King (OG 1049, ABV 5.1%)
Copper-coloured strong ale. Biscuit malt throughout with sweet fruit, becoming bitter. Hops in the finish with citrus and pear fruits.

Kemptown SIBA

33 Upper St James's Street, Kemptown, Brighton, East Sussex, BN2 1JN
☎ (01273) 699595 ☎ 07967 681203
Tours by arrangement

Founded in 1989, the brewery is the smallest commercially operating tower brewery in the world. The beers are exclusively available on site at the Hand in Hand brewpub and are brewed by the team behind Brighton Bier.

Kemptown (OG 1040, ABV 4%)
A light session ale. Crisp and hoppy.

Ye Olde Trout (OG 1045, ABV 4.5%)
A golden brown beer with fruity aromas and a dry finish.

Kendal

Brewhouse at Burgundy's, 19 Lowther Street, Kendal, Cumbria, LA9 4DH
☎ (01539) 733803 🌐 burgundyswinebar.co.uk
Tours by arrangement

Kendal began brewing in 2011. Beer is now produced every week and the brewery is at full production.

Helga's Dunkel Bier (OG 1037, ABV 3.7%)
Brewed to the style of a traditional German dunkel bier (dark lager) with a smooth and malty taste.

Eleven Bells (OG 1039, ABV 3.9%)
A light, well-hopped beer with a citrus finish.

Pale Ale (OG 1042, ABV 4.2%)

Gold (OG 1043, ABV 4.3%)
A golden beer with a strong bitter finish.

Silver Tanner (OG 1044, ABV 4.4%)
Tan-coloured ale with malt flavour, citrus aroma and crisp hop bitterness.

Grisley Mires (OG 1048, ABV 4.8%)

Kennet & Avon (NEW)

Sells Green, Melksham, Wiltshire, SN12 6RW ☎ 07917 272482 kennetandavonbrewery.co.uk

Kennet & Avon began brewing in 2014, with the beers originally being brewed by Wessex Brewery (qv) while the plant was under construction. Beers are available at the owner's micropub, the Vaults in Devizes, and in outlets throughout the West Country.

Pillbox (OG 1039, ABV 4%)
A light refreshing ale with a hoppy bite.

Dundas (OG 1041, ABV 4.2%)
A copper-coloured best bitter with a pleasant bitterness and citrus hoppy aroma.

Rusty Lane (OG 1044, ABV 4.4%)
A rusty-coloured Irish-style red ale with rounded toffee malt flavour and floral hop finish.

Caen Hill Hop (OG 1050, ABV 5%)
A strong golden ale with a powerful floral hop flavour; American IPA-style.

Kent SIBA

The Long Barn, Birling Place Farm, Stangate Road, Birling, Kent, ME19 5JN
☎ (01634) 780037 kentbrewery.com

Kent Brewery was founded in 2010 by Toby Simmonds (ex-brewer from Dark Star) and Paul Herbert. Originally brewed at Larkins, a 10-barrel plant has been in operation at the Birling site since 2011. More than 150 outlets are supplied direct, mainly throughout Kent, Sussex and London. Seasonal and bottle-conditioned beers are available.

Session Pale (OG 1037, ABV 3.7%)

Black Gold (OG 1040, ABV 4%)

Pale (OG 1040, ABV 4%)

Cobnut (OG 1041, ABV 4.1%)

KGB (Kent Golding Bitter) (OG 1041, ABV 4.1%)

Zingiber (OG 1041, ABV 4.1%)

Brewers Reserve (OG 1050, ABV 5%)

Beyond The Pale (OG 1054, ABV 5.4%)

Enigma (OG 1055, ABV 5.5%)

Kernel SIBA

Arch 11, Dockley Road Industrial Estate, London, SE16 3SF
☎ (020) 7231 4516
Office: 01 Spa Terminus, Spa Road, London, SE16 4QT
thekernelbrewery.com
Shop and bar: Sat 9am-3pm

Kernel was established in 2010 by Evin O'Riordain and moved to larger premises in 2012 to keep up with demand. The brewery produces bottle-conditioned beers, as well as the occasional cask, and has won many awards for its wide, ever-changing range of pale and dark beers. Beers are available from the brewery on a Saturday as well as an exclusive selection of pubs around the country.

Table Beer (ABV 3%)

Keswick SIBA

The Old Brewery, Brewery Lane, Keswick, Cumbria, CA12 5BY
☎ (01768) 780700 keswickbrewery.co.uk
Shop – call for details (usually Mon-Fri 9am-5pm)
Tours by arrangement

Keswick, run by Sue Harrison, began brewing in 2006 using a 10-barrel plant. It is located on the site of a brewery that closed in 1897. Outlets include Middle Ruddings Hotel, Braithwaite and Dog & Gun, Keswick, with many other Lakeland pubs supplied. Seasonal beers: see website.

Thirst Gold (OG 1035, ABV 3.6%)
Golden in colour and full of flavour.

Thirst Session (OG 1036, ABV 3.7%)
A sweet start with a hint of roast gives way to a dry bitter finish.

Thirst Run (OG 1041, ABV 4.2%)
A well-balanced golden beer that maintains its fruitiness from start to finish.

Thirst Fall (OG 1047, ABV 4.8%)

Keystone SIBA

Old Carpenters Workshop, Berwick St Leonard, Wiltshire, SP3 5SN
☎ (01747) 820426 keystonebrewery.co.uk
Shop Mon, Tue & Fri 10am-5pm
Tours by arrangement

Set up in 2006 with a 10-barrel plant, the brewery uses a solar heating system to reduce carbon emissions. The brewer aims to be as sustainable and efficient as possible. Around 150 outlets are supplied. Seasonal beers: see website.

Bedrock (OG 1035, ABV 3.6%)
Copper-coloured bitter, hops and malt in the aroma, followed by fruit and bitterness in the taste. Long, lingering aftertaste.

Gold Hill (OG 1039, ABV 4%)
Amber-coloured bitter with floral/citrus aroma, clean tasting with balanced bittersweet taste right through to the aftertaste, which has a slightly hoppy astringency.

Gold Spice (OG 1039, ABV 4%)
A light-coloured, well-hopped beer with stem ginger added to the cask.

Large One (OG 1041, ABV 4.2%)

Copper-coloured malty best bitter, fruit and bitterness to the fore initially, long fruit and bitter hop flavours to the finish.

Cornerstone (OG 1047, ABV 4.8%)
A dark, strong beer with plenty of hops, well-balanced with a long, satisfying finish.

King Alfred (NEW)

11 Mill Rise, Bourton, Dorset, SP8 5DH
☎ (01747) 840967 ✉ kingalfredales@aol.com

⊗ King Alfred is a 0.5-barrel garage brewery that started production in 2012. It currently brews about once a month. A few local pubs and beer festivals are supplied.

871 (OG 1043, ABV 4.3%)
A malty bitter with balanced hop flavours.

Saxon Gold (OG 1048, ABV 4.8%)
A gold-coloured bitter with prominent hop flavours and aroma.

King Beer SIBA

3-5 Jubilee Estate, Foundry Lane, Horsham, West Sussex, RH13 5UE
☎ (01403) 272102 ⊕ kingbeer.co.uk
Shop Mon-Fri 9am-5pm, Sat 10am-2pm
Tours by arrangement

⊗ Launched in 2001, the brewery was purchased by Niki and Justin Deighton in 2013, along with existing head brewer Ian Burgess. Now brewing up to 110 barrels a week under the Kings Heritage and Kings Evolution brands. Seasonal and monthly beers: see website.

Horsham Best Bitter (OG 1038, ABV 3.8%)
A predominantly malty best bitter, brown in colour. The nutty flavours have some sweetness with a little bitterness that grows in the aftertaste.

Brighton Blonde (OG 1039, ABV 3.9%)
A crisp, refreshing, hoppy beer with a hint of malt to complement the hops. This golden, pale blonde ale has a distinctive hoppy aroma. An increasing dryness and straw bitterness to finish.

Kings Best (OG 1040, ABV 4%)
A light amber-coloured beer with a complex floral hop aroma. The palate feels clean and well-balanced with a lingering aftertaste. The subtle fresh hop remains into the finish.

Poachers Moon (OG 1040, ABV 4.1%)

Northern Lights (OG 1042, ABV 4.2%)

Lost Kingdom (OG 1052, ABV 5.2%)

King's Cliffe (NEW)

Unit 10, Kingsmead, Station Road, King?s Cliffe, Northamptonshire, PE8 6YH ☎ 07843 288088
⊕ kcbales.co.uk

In 2014, exactly 100 years after the last brewery in King's Cliffe ceased brewing, village resident Jeremy O'Neill set up this new venture.

5C (ABV 3.8%)

No. 10 (ABV 4%)

OBT (ABV 4.8%)

K2 (ABV 5.5%)

Kings Clipstone

Keepers Bothy, Kings Clipstone, Nottinghamshire, NG21 9BT
☎ (01623) 823589 ⊕ kingsclipstonebrewery.co.uk

Located in the heart of Sherwood Forest, Kings Clipstone began brewing in 2012 using a five-barrel plant. Further beers plus seasonals are planned. Beers are available nationwide to freehouses, festivals and wholesale markets.

Hop On (OG 1039, ABV 3.8%)
A pale and refreshing session beer with a fruity aroma.

Sire (OG 1043, ABV 4.2%)
A beer which is well-rounded with a clean, bitter finish.

Kings Head

Kings Head, 132 High Street, Bildeston, Ipswich, Suffolk, IP7 7ED
☎ (01449) 741434 ⊕ bildestonkingshead.co.uk
Tours by arrangement

⊗ Kings Head has been brewing since 1996 in an old cart lodge at the back of the pub. Under new ownership since 2008, the three-barrel plant brews fortnightly. Seasonal beers are available.

Bildeston Best (OG 1036, ABV 3.6%)
Traditional best bitter. Well-hopped with a malty sweetness and dry finish.

Brettvale Gold (ABV 3.6%)

Kingstone SIBA

Meadow Farm, Tintern, Monmouthshire, NP16 7NX
☎ (01291) 680111 ⊕ kingstonebrewery.co.uk
Shop Tue & Wed, Fri & Sat 10am-4pm
Tours by arrangement

Kingstone Brewery is located in the Wye Valley close to the famous Tintern Abbey. Brewing began on a four-barrel plant in 2005. All cask-conditioned ales are also available bottle conditioned. Special brews are marketed under the Hapax Brewing Co label.

Tewdric's Tipple (OG 1038, ABV 3.8%)
An ale with a dry, bitter character and tangy core.

Challenger (OG 1040, ABV 4%)
A smooth, richly-hopped, well-balanced ale with a malted nose and toffee undertones.

Gold (OG 1040, ABV 4%)
A straw-coloured, smooth ale with citrus notes and a balanced, hoppy finish.

Premium Stout (OG 1044, ABV 4.4%)
A smooth, rich stout with a bitter finish.

Classic (OG 1045, ABV 4.5%)
A balanced, distinctively hoppy, dry ale with a floral nose and smooth, well-balanced finish.

1503 (OG 1048, ABV 4.8%)
A deep chestnut red, lightly-hopped ale bursting with complex rich flavours.

Abbey Ale (OG 1051, ABV 5.1%)
An amber-coloured, full-flavoured ale. The hoppy edge is balanced by a smooth, malty richness.

Humpty (OG 1058, ABV 5.8%)

An IPA with a slightly sweet, floral nose, a balanced level of malt supporting the hops and finally a subtle but slightly citrus finish.

Kinneil

84 Corbiehall, Bo'ness, West Lothian, EH51 9QD
☎ (01506) 824574 🌐 kinneilbrew.co.uk

Kinneil began brewing in 2011 using a 2.5-barrel plant. The brewery is adjacent to the Corbie Inn but separately owned.

Katie Wearie's (OG 1039, ABV 3.8%)

Pennvael Amber (OG 1042, ABV 4%)

Kincardine Sunset (OG 1042, ABV 4.1%)

Caer Edin Dark (OG 1044, ABV 4.2%)

Kinver SIBA

Unit 1, Britch Farm, Rocky Wall, Kinver, Staffordshire, DY7 5NW 🌐 kinverbrewery.co.uk
Tours by arrangement

Established in 2004, Kinver produces a wide range of different beer styles including one-off specials. The brewery relocated in 2012 to a new 10-barrel plant on the edge of Kinver due to increased demand and has now added bottle-conditioned beers to its range. Around 30 outlets are supplied direct including several in Kinver.

Light Railway (OG 1038, ABV 3.8%)
Straw-coloured session beer. A fruity and malty start quickly gives way to well-hopped bitterness and lingering hoppy aftertaste.

Edge (OG 1041, ABV 4.2%)
Amber with a malty aroma. Sweet fruity start with a hint of citrus marmalade in the spicy malt; lasting hoppy finish that is satisfyingly bitter.

Crystal (OG 1043, ABV 4.5%)
Pale hoppy bitter with a citrus finish.

Noble 600 (OG 1043, ABV 4.5%)
Fruity hop aroma. Fruity start then the grassy hops give a sharp bitter finish with malt support.

Maybug (OG 1045, ABV 4.8%)
German-style cask-conditioned lager-style beer.

Half Centurion (OG 1047, ABV 5%)
A golden best bitter; malty before the American Chinook hop takes command to give a balanced hoppy finish and provide the great aftertaste.

Khyber (OG 1054, ABV 5.8%)
Golden strong bitter with a Centennial hop bite that overwhelms the fleeting malty sweetness and drives through to the long, dry finish.

Over the Edge (OG 1074, ABV 6.8%)

Kirkby Lonsdale SIBA

Unit 2F, Old Station Yard, Kirkby Lonsdale, Lancashire, LA6 2HP
☎ (01524) 272221 🌐 kirkbylonsdalebrewery.com

Kirkby Lonsdale is a family-run business established in 2009 on a six-barrel plant. Seasonal beers are available.

Tiffin Gold (OG 1036, ABV 3.6%)
A full-flavoured grapefruit, hoppy and bitter beer with a dry finish.

Stanley's Pale Ale (OG 1038, ABV 3.8%)
Hops dominate this sweet and fruity, well-balanced beer.

Ruskins Bitter (OG 1039, ABV 3.9%)
A tawny bitter with a distinctive aroma of fruit and malt. The clean, hoppy flavour is well-balanced with fruity sweetness leading to a sustained bittersweet finish.

Singletrack (OG 1040, ABV 4%)
Light ale with citrus aromas and a pleasant hoppy taste.

Radical Red (OG 1042, ABV 4.2%)
Malty beer with a caramel sweetness that is balanced by a bitter finish.

Monumental Blonde (OG 1045, ABV 4.5%)
Distinctly hoppy, a fruity, sweet, pale-coloured, full-bodied bitter.

Jubilee Stout (OG 1055, ABV 5.5%)
Rich, well-balanced stout with powerful malt character. A long aftertaste retains this complexity and is surprisingly refreshing.

Kirkstall SIBA

Unit 6, Canal Wharf, Wyther Lane, Kirkstall, Leeds, West Yorkshire, LS5 3BT
☎ (0113) 345 8835 🌐 kirkstallbrewerycompany.com
Tours by arrangement

Brewing began in 2011 at a site within yards of the original Kirkstall Brewery beside the Leeds-Liverpool canal with nearby Kirkstall Abbey and lost local industries providing inspiration for the beer names. The beer range can always be found at the recently refurbished Kirkstall Bridge Inn nearby. Seasonal beers and specials: see website.

BYB (Best Yorkshire Bitter) (OG 1036, ABV 3.5%)

Pale Ale (OG 1040, ABV 4%)
A refreshing golden-coloured bitter beer with citrus hop flavours and zesty bitterness, especially in the finish, which is lingering.

Three Swords (OG 1045, ABV 4.5%)
Good quantities of hops and juicy fruit define this yellow beer, a bittersweet taste and a tenacious pithy marmalade finish.

Dissolution IPA (OG 1050, ABV 5%)
Hops define this amber beer from the massive aroma, through the citrus fruit taste and finishing with yet more hops.

Black Band Porter (OG 1055, ABV 5.5%)
Dark, smooth and rich with a full aroma and even bigger flavour. Generous fruity taste, hints of chocolate and liquorice.

Kissingate

Pole Barn, Church Lane Farm Estate, Church Lane, Lower Beeding, West Sussex, RH13 6LU
☎ (01403) 891335 🌐 kissingate.co.uk
Tours by arrangement

Kissingate was founded in 2010 by husband and wife team Gary and Bunny Lucas. In 2012 the brewery moved into a new purpose-built barn conversion. Local outlets and beer festivals are supplied.

Storyteller (OG 1035, ABV 3.5%)
Light-coloured beer with a simple, crisp, lemon/pine finish.

Best (OG 1040, ABV 4%)

THE BREWERIES

Old Tale Porter (OG 1052, ABV 4.5%)
A classic, full-flavoured London porter.

Mandarina Red (OG 1048, ABV 4.8%)
A complex red IPA with multiple flavour layers of malt and prominent citrus fruits. Pine and citrus bitter finish.

Moon (OG 1050, ABV 4.8%)
A golden beer with a taste of lightly roasted malts, late autumn apples and a lingering hoppy bitterness.

Ruby Plum Porter (ABV 4.8%)
A deep ruby-coloured beer with roasted malt, cinnamon and sweet plum on the nose. Pleasant fruit and bitterness from the hops.

Micro Lot Coffee Porter (ABV 5%)
Brewed using specially imported coffee beans with aromas of dark malt and medium roasted coffee. Notes of chocolate, vanilla and roast chestnuts. A gentle balancing bitterness from the hops.

Smelter's Stout (OG 1052, ABV 5.2%)

Mary's Ruby Mild (OG 1072, ABV 6.5%)
Deep ruby in colour. Gentle aromas of well-aged Port, intense and rounded malt flavours and a light and floral hop aftertaste.

6 Crows (OG 1066, ABV 6.6%)

Kitchen Garden

Old Walled Garden, Sheffield Park, East Sussex, TN22 3QX
☎ (01825) 790775 ⊕ kitchengardenbrewery.co.uk
Shop Mon 1-5pm, Tue-Sun 10am-5pm

Kitchen Garden is a small one-barrel plant producing only bottle-conditioned ales, all suitable for vegetarians. It is situated in a Victorian walled kitchen garden at Sheffield Park. Occasional seasonal beers are produced. The beers are available from the brewery shop and at several outlets in Sussex including Middle Farm, Firle. Brewing is currently suspended.

Kite SIBA

Unit J, Llantrisant Business Park, Llantrisant, CF72 8LF
☎ (01443) 406080 ⊕ thekitebrewery.com

Kite Brewery was established in 2011 in Carmarthenshire using a 10-barrel plant. To keep pace with demand 2013 saw a move to an all new, state-of-the-art 30-barrel plant, allowing a brewing capacity of 150 barrels per week. The plant is specially designed to use only whole hops and not hop pellets. Monthly seasonal beers are available.

Billy Wynt Very Pale Ale (OG 1041, ABV 4%)

Cwrw Gorslas (OG 1041, ABV 4%)

Welsh Pale Ale (OG 1042, ABV 4.1%)

Thunderbird (OG 1046, ABV 4.5%)

Bull Ring Porter (OG 1047, ABV 4.7%)

Uncle Sam's APA (OG 1052, ABV 5.1%)

Knaresborough

19 Market Place, Knaresborough, North Yorkshire, HG5 8AL
☎ (01423) 869148

Established in 2012 above Blind Jacks pub in Knaresborough, the 0.5-barrel brewery specialises in stronger, sometimes experimental beers inspired by US craft brewing. There are few regular beers so expect the unexpected. Beers are usually only available at Blind Jacks.

Triple C (OG 1039, ABV 3.5%)

Mea Culpa Pale Ale (OG 1066, ABV 6.3%)

Expresso Stout (OG 1072, ABV 6.5%)

American Style Milk Stout (OG 1074, ABV 6.9%)

Blind Faith (OG 1077, ABV 7%)

Knops SIBA

The Walled Garden, Archerfield Estate, Dirleton, North Berwick, EH39 5HQ ☎ 07949 879147
⊕ knopsbeer.co.uk
Tours by arrangement

Knops began brewing in 2010 under contract. In 2013 it moved to new premises on the Archerfield Estate at Dirleton on the East Lothian coastline with an 11-barrel plant. Beers are based on modern interpretations of traditional styles and are bottled in-house. Cask-conditioned beers are available widely in Eastern Scotland and the Glasgow area.

East Coast Pale (OG 1039, ABV 3.8%)
A light aromatic session beer with malt and hops on the nose and some citrus notes.

Musselburgh Broke (OG 1045, ABV 4.5%)
Modern interpretation of a 19th century style. Has a chestnut colour and a malty sweetness, with some hops for balance.

California Common (OG 1048, ABV 4.6%)
A deep golden ale with a clean hop finish and light toffee notes followed by a lingering bitterness.

India Pale Ale (OG 1047, ABV 5%)
Light golden ale with a citrus and apricot aroma. Well balanced by a smooth honeyed malt backbone.

Black Cork (OG 1066, ABV 6.5%)
An intensely dark beer with a prominent chocolate/coffee bitterness and hop aroma.

Contract brewed for Archerfield Fine Ales:

Golden Ale (OG 1039, ABV 3.8%)

Dark Ale (OG 1046, ABV 4.7%)

India Pale Ale (OG 1047, ABV 5%)

Kubla

The Source Building, Tower Farm, Dean's Cross, Lydeard St Lawrence, Somerset, TA4 3QN ☎ 07855 342208 ⊕ kubla.co.uk

The five-barrel plant was formed in 2012 on Tower Farm in the Brendon Hills, Exmoor. Part of the farm was a former cheese factory. Beers are available in local pubs and clubs. Bottle-conditioned beer is also available.

Rise: Pale Ale (OG 1042, ABV 4.2%)

Rock: Saison (OG 1042, ABV 4.2%)

Paradise: Stout (OG 1048, ABV 4.8%)

Lacons SIBA

The Courtyard, Main Cross Road, Great Yarmouth, Norfolk, NR30 3NZ
☎ (01493) 850578 ⊕ lacons.co.uk

Tours by arrangement

Lacons has a rich history dating back to 1760. The brewery was closed by Whitbread in the 1960s. In 2010 a beer distributor, J.V. Trading, looked into the possibility of reopening the brewery, and acquired its trading name and yeast strains. The new brewery opened in 2013.

Encore (ABV 3.8%)

Legacy (ABV 4.4%)

Laine (Brighton)

North Laine Bar & Brewhouse, 27 Gloucester Place, Brighton, East Sussex, BN1 4AA
☎ (01273) 683666
✉ northlainepub@drinkinbrighton.co.uk
Tours by arrangement

The brewery is a five-barrel plant launched in 2012. It is based within the North Laine pub in Brighton, which is owned by the drinkinbrighton pub group. The brewing equipment and process can be viewed from the bar. Seasonal beers are available. A sister brewery to Laine in Hackney and Acton, London.

Oatmeal Stout (OG 1045, ABV 4.5%)

IPA (OG 1050, ABV 5%)

Porter (OG 1053, ABV 5.3%)

Laine (London) (NEW)

Acton: 264 Acton High Street, Acton, London, W3 9BH
☎ (020) 8993 4242

Hackney: People's Park Tavern, 360 Victoria Park Road, Hackney, London, E9 7BT ☎ (020) 8533 0040
🌐 drinkinlondon.co.uk

Brewing began in 2013 using a five-barrel plant at the Aeronaut in Acton. The brewery has three fermenters and can produce 60 firkins of beer a week. The brewing equipment is visible behind the left hand bar. A sister brewery to Laine in Brighton and the People's Park Tavern in Hackney.

Acton Ale (OG 1039, ABV 3.7%)

Porter (OG 1047, ABV 4.6%)

Random Pale Ale (OG 1046, ABV 4.6%)

IPA (OG 1051, ABV 5%)

Lancaster SIBA

Heartwick Brewery, Lancaster Leisure Park, Wyresdale Road, Lancaster, LA1 3LA
☎ (01524) 848537 🌐 lancasterbrewery.co.uk
Shop 10am-5pm daily
Tours by arrangement

Lancaster began brewing in 2005. The brewery moved to new premises in Lancaster in 2010 and installed a larger brewing plant. 12 seasonal beers are also brewed under the 'Tails from The Brewhouse' name.

Straw (OG 1035, ABV 3.5%)

Amber (OG 1038, ABV 3.7%)
Dark gold session beer with a hoppy bouquet and subtle floral and citrus aromas.

Mr Trotter's (OG 1040, ABV 4%)
Chestnuts are blended with Maris Otter barley to produce a nutty creaminess and a honeyed note with some hop spiciness.

Blonde (OG 1042, ABV 4.1%)
A crisp, hoppy flavour with a touch of caramel and a hint of citrus. Golden hued with a smooth, easy-drinking feel. Hops follow through to dominate in the aftertaste.

Black (OG 1046, ABV 4.6%)
A satisfying roast bitter beer.

Red (OG 1048, ABV 4.9%)
Sweet start with lasting roast malts leads to satisfying bitter finish.

Landlord's Friend

Kershaw House Inn, Luddenden Lane, Luddendenfoot, West Yorkshire, HX2 6NW
☎ (01422) 882222 ✉ landfriendbeers@aol.co.uk

Landlord's Friend began brewing in 2010 using a 2.5-barrel plant. Around 30 outlets are supplied direct. Around 30 outlets are supplied direct. Seasonal beers are available.

Langham SIBA

Old Granary, Langham Lane, Lodsworth, West Sussex, GU28 9BU
☎ (01798) 860861 🌐 langhambrewery.co.uk
Shop Mon-Fri 9am-5pm, Sat 10am-4pm
Tours by arrangement

Langham was established in 2006 in an 18th-century granary barn and is set in the heart of West Sussex with fine views of the rolling South Downs. It is owned by Lesley Foulkes and James Berrow who brew and run the business. The brewery is a 10-barrel steam-heated plant and more than 200 outlets are supplied.

Halfway to Heaven (OG 1035, ABV 3.5%)
A chestnut-coloured beer with a balanced biscuit maltiness and citrus and fruit hop character with a hint of spice.

Hip Hop (OG 1038, ABV 4%)
A blonde beer, clean and crisp. Loaded with floral hop aroma while the pale malt flavour is overtaken by a dry bitter finish.

Sundowner (OG 1042, ABV 4.2%)
A deep golden beer. The nose has tropical fruit, pineapple and citrus notes with a smooth maltiness in the background. There is a balanced dry and bitter finish with a floral hop aroma.

Best (OG 1043, ABV 4.5%)
A tawny-coloured classic best with well-balanced malt flavours and bitterness.

Arapaho (OG 1046, ABV 4.9%)

LSD (Langham Special Draught) (OG 1049, ABV 5.2%)
An auburn-coloured beer with rich, complex flavours and a deep red glow. The sweet maltiness is balanced with spicy hop aromas and a dry finish.

Black Swallow (OG 1055, ABV 6%)

Langton SIBA

Grange Farm, Welham Road, Thorpe Langton, Leicestershire, LE16 7TU
☎ (01858) 540116 🌐 langtonbrewery.co.uk

Tours by arrangement

Established 1999 in outbuildings behind the Bell Inn, East Langton, the brewery relocated in 2005 to a converted barn at Thorpe Langton, where a four-barrel plant was installed. Further expansion in 2010 significantly increased capacity. Seasonal beers are available.

Caudle Bitter (OG 1039, ABV 3.9%) ◆
Copper-coloured session bitter that is close to a pale ale in style. Flavours are relatively well-balanced throughout with hops slightly to the fore.

Inclined Plane Bitter (OG 1042, ABV 4.2%)
A straw-coloured bitter with a citrus nose and long, hoppy finish.

Hop On (OG 1044, ABV 4.4%)
A premium bitter, deep chestnut-coloured with a good balance of flavours and aroma.

Scarecrow (OG 1044, ABV 4.4%)
Smooth, well balanced, slightly fruity and sweet.

Bowler Strong Ale (OG 1048, ABV 4.8%)
A strong traditional ale with a deep red colour and a hoppy nose.

Bullseye (OG 1050, ABV 4.8%)
Intensely dark stout with flavours of liquorice and chocolate.

Larkins SIBA

Larkins Farm, Hampkins Hill Road, Chiddingstone, Kent, TN8 7BB
☎ (01892) 870328
Tours by arrangement (Nov-Feb)

It's been over 25 years since the farming and hop growing Dockerty family bought the original Royal Tunbridge Wells Brewery and moved it to Larkins Farm where Bob Dockerty started brewing in 1987. Production of its three main brews and two seasonal ales has steadily increased. All beers now include hops grown on Larkins Farm itself. All ales are delivered direct to around 70 freehouses within a 20-mile radius of the brewery.

Traditional Ale (OG 1035, ABV 3.4%)
Tawny-coloured, full-tasting hoppy ale with plenty of character for its strength.

Chiddingstone (OG 1040, ABV 4%)
A mid-strength, hoppy, fruity ale with a long, bittersweet aftertaste.

Best (OG 1045, ABV 4.4%) ◆
Full-bodied, slightly fruity and unusually bitter for its gravity.

Late Knights SIBA

21 Southey Street, Penge, London, SE20 7JD
lateknightsbrewery.co.uk

Originally using spare capacity at Truefitt Brewery in Middlesbrough in 2012, Late Knights began brewing using a six-barrel plant in London in 2013. Seasonal and special beers are available.

Crack of Dawn (ABV 3.9%) ◆
Amber hoppy beer with strong citrus notes. Flavour has a faint maltiness and bitterness. Aftertaste is bitter and fractionally dry.

Dawns Early Light (ABV 4%)
An American pale ale with plenty of citrus flavour.

Hop O' The Morning (ABV 4.2%) ◆
Strong black roast bitter character in the aroma and flavour with some coffee notes and fruit. Long, bitter, dry finish.

Morning Glory (ABV 4.4%)

Old Red Eyes (ABV 4.5%) ◆
Reddish brown beer with a clean hop flavour and hints of citrus and butterscotch. Finish is hoppy and dryish.

Worm Catcher (ABV 5%) ◆
Amber-coloured beer with a honey marmalade sweetness and a bitterness that builds and lingers in the slightly dry finish.

P.IPA (ABV 5.5%)
A Polish IPA.

Hairy Dog (ABV 6%)
A black IPA.

Latimer SIBA

13 South Folds Road, Oakley Hay, Northamptonshire, NN18 9EU ☎ 07812 450988

Office: 11 Meadway close, Kettering, Northamptonshire, NN15 6QG latimerales.com

Latimer is a small two-barrel brewery specialising in styles from all around the world as well as classic English beers. Brewer James Trent built the brewery himself over an 18 month period and commenced brewing in 2012. Bottle-conditioned beers are available.

Midland Mild (OG 1038, ABV 3.5%)
A light-bodied, deep auburn-coloured English ale with rich flavours of coffee and toasted malt with a slightly sweet finish.

William George IPA (OG 1045, ABV 4.4%)
A refreshing, bright golden-coloured IPA with a medium body and dry finish.

Burton Best (OG 1046, ABV 4.5%)
A chestnut-coloured, medium-bodied best bitter.

Amber Wrangler (OG 1047, ABV 4.6%)
A full-bodied, amber-coloured ale with a good balance of malt and hops and rich caramel flavours.

Uncle Sam's Pale Ale (OG 1050, ABV 5%)
A light-bodied, clear and pale ale with a crisp and fresh flavour. Finishing dry, with citrus notes.

Leadmill

Unit 3, Heanor Small Business Centre, Adams Close, Heanor, Derbyshire, DE75 7SW ☎ 07971 189915
leadmill@fsmail.net

Set up in Selston in 1999, Leadmill moved to Denby in 2001 and again in 2010 to Heanor where it shares a site with Coppice Side Brewery (qv). A sister brewery to Bottle Brook (qv), the brewery tap is the Old Oak, Horsley Woodhouse.

Langley Best (OG 1036, ABV 3.6%)

Mash Tun Bitter (OG 1036, ABV 3.6%)

Old Oak Bitter (OG 1037, ABV 3.7%)

B52 (OG 1050, ABV 5.2%)

Slumdog (OG 1058, ABV 5.9%)

Leamside SIBA

Three Horseshoes, Pit House Lane, Leamside, County Durham, DH4 6QQ

☎ (0191) 584 2394
🌐 threehorseshoesleamside.co.uk

Brewing began in 2012 using a 2.5-barrel plant. Beers are available at the Three Horseshoes as well as its two sister pubs, the Kings Arms, Sunderland, and the Courtyard, Washington.

Adventure (OG 1038, ABV 3.8%)
A deep golden-coloured session bitter. Soft fruit flavours and well-balanced medium bitterness.

Alexandrina (OG 1041, ABV 4.2%)
Light gold in colour. Initial bitterness gives way to citrus fruit flavours.

Brockwell (OG 1042, ABV 4.2%)
A straw-coloured pale ale with tropical fruit flavours.

Five Quarter (OG 1052, ABV 4.5%)
A silky smooth mouthfeel with berry fruit flavours and hints of coffee and chocolate.

Resolution (OG 1052, ABV 4.5%)
Premium pale ale brewed with a blend of American hops. Well-balanced bitterness and subtle fruit flavours.

Leatherbritches

Brewery Yard, Tap House, Annwell Lane, Smisby, Derbyshire, LE65 2TA ☎ 07976 279253
🌐 leatherbritches.co.uk
Tours by arrangement

The brewery, founded in 1993 in Fenny Bentley, has relocated and expanded over the years, moving to its current address in 2011. Both the Tap House Brewery (qv) and Leatherbritches brew on the same plant but the two businesses are separate. Seasonal and bottle-conditioned beers are available.

Goldings (OG 1036, ABV 3.6%)
A light golden beer with a flowery hoppy aroma and a bitter finish.

Lemongrass & Ginger (OG 1036, ABV 3.8%)
A pale and hoppy ale infused with lemongrass and ginger. Crisp and refreshing.

Ashbourne Ale (OG 1040, ABV 4%)
A copper-coloured bitter with a crisp, lasting taste. Fruity malt tones produce a bittersweet, lingering finish.

Doctor Johnsons (OG 1040, ABV 4%)
A mid-brown ale, not heavily hopped but full-bodied with some caramel flavour.

Scoundrel (OG 1040, ABV 4.1%)
A full-bodied, dark porter, smooth with chocolate malt and roast barley.

Dovedale (OG 1044, ABV 4.4%)
A mid-brown-coloured bitter. Well-rounded and easy drinking with a pleasant bitterness.

Ginger Helmet (OG 1047, ABV 4.7%)
As for Hairy Helmet but with a hint of China's most astringent herb.

Hairy Helmet (OG 1047, ABV 4.7%)
A pale bitter, well-hopped but with a sweet finish.

Bespoke (OG 1050, ABV 5%)
Full-bodied, well-rounded premium bitter.

Porter (OG 1055, ABV 5.5%)
A complex porter with plenty of chocolate and cara malt.

Scary Hairy (OG 1059, ABV 5.9%)

Scary Hairy Export (ABV 7.2%)
An extra strong golden IPA. Extra hops with a full-bodied taste.

Leazes Lane (NEW)

Trent House, 1-2 Leazes Lane, Newcastle upon Tyne, NE1 4QT
☎ (0191) 261 2154

Leazes Lane began brewing in 2013 using a one-barrel plant. Beer is only available in the pub.

Ledbury SIBA

Gazerdine House, Hereford Road, Ledbury, Herefordshire, HR8 2PZ
☎ (01531) 671184 🌐 ledburyrealales.co.uk
Tours by arrangement

Brewing began in 2012. Beers are produced using locally-sourced ingredients whenever possible. Distribution is generally within a 15-mile radius of the brewery.

Bitter (OG 1038, ABV 3.8%)
A traditional copper-coloured ale with a noticeably bitter start and an enjoyable finish with hints of spice and citrus.

Dark (OG 1039, ABV 3.9%)
A chocolate and coffee start with a smooth, mellow finish with notes of spice, marmalade and honey.

Gold (OG 1040, ABV 4%)
A golden bitter, well-balanced with a honey and fruit finish.

Leeds SIBA IFBB

3 Sydenham Road, Leeds, West Yorkshire, LS11 9RU
☎ (0113) 244 5866 🌐 leedsbrewery.co.uk

Production began in 2007 using a 20-barrel plant. The largest independent brewer in the city, it uses a unique strain of yeast originally used by a defunct West Yorkshire brewery. Seven pubs are owned and around 300 outlets are supplied direct. Seasonal beers: see website.

Pale (OG 1037.5, ABV 3.8%)
Well-balanced between hop and fruit, sometimes citrus, light gold in colour with a clean bitter, hoppy finish.

Yorkshire Gold (OG 1040, ABV 4%)
Plenty of zesty citrus flavours, a wallop of hops and a long-lasting bitter finish make this a refreshing beer.

Best (OG 1041, ABV 4.3%)
A pleasing mix of malt and hops makes this smooth amber-coloured bittersweet beer very drinkable.

Midnight Bell (OG 1047.5, ABV 4.8%)
A full-bodied strong mild, deep red/brown in colour. Malty caramel character with chocolate being present throughout.

Leek

See Staffordshire

THE BREWERIES

Lees IFBB

Greengate Brewery, Middleton Junction, Manchester, M24 2AX
☎ (0161) 643 2487 🌐 jwlees.co.uk
Tours by arrangement

Family owned since its foundation by John Lees in 1828, the brewery has a tied estate of around 170 pubs, mostly in north Manchester, Cheshire, Lancashire and North Wales. The vast majority serve cask beer. The current head brewer is a family member.

Brewer's Dark (OG 1032, ABV 3.5%)
Formerly GB Mild, this is a dark brown beer with a malt and caramel aroma. Creamy mouthfeel, with malt, caramel and fruit flavours and a malty finish. Becoming rare.

Manchester Pale Ale (OG 1038, ABV 3.7%)
A clean, crisp and refreshing golden ale with hop bitterness and a citrus aroma.

The Governor (OG 1038, ABV 3.8%)
Malty auburn/amber-coloured beer with floral and citrus notes and a clean, dry finish.

Bitter (OG 1037, ABV 4%)
Copper-coloured beer with malt and fruit in aroma, taste and finish.

John Willie's (OG 1041, ABV 4.5%)
A well-balanced, full-bodied premium bitter.

Moonraker (OG 1073, ABV 6.5%)
A reddish-brown beer with a strong, malty, fruity aroma. The flavour is rich and sweet, with roast malt, and the finish is fruity yet dry. Available only in a handful of outlets.

Brewed for Carlsberg:

Draught Burton Ale (OG 1047, ABV 4.8%)
Pale gold-coloured strong bitter with a rich, fruity taste.

Leila Cottage SIBA

Countryman, Chapel Road, Ingoldmells, Skegness, Lincolnshire, PE25 1ND
☎ (01754) 872268 🌐 countryman-ingoldmells.co.uk
Tours by arrangement

Leila Cottage started brewing in 2007 using a 0.5-barrel plant, which was upgraded in 2009 to a 2.5-barrel one. The brewery is situated at the Countryman pub – Leila Cottage was the original name of the building before it became a licensed club and more recently a pub. The brewery now owns its own bottling line meaning that all beers are also available bottle conditioned.

Leila's Lazy Days (OG 1040, ABV 3.6%)

Ace Ale (OG 1040, ABV 3.8%)

Lincolnshire Life (OG 1040, ABV 4.2%)

Leila's One Off (OG 1045, ABV 5.1%)

Leith Hill

c/o Plough Inn, Coldharbour Lane, Coldharbour, Surrey, RH5 6HD
☎ (01306) 711793 🌐 ploughinn.com
Tours by arrangement

Leith Hill was established in 1996 at the Plough Inn using home-made equipment and was moved to converted storerooms at the rear in 2001, increasing capacity to 2.5-barrels in 2005. All beers brewed are sold only on the premises. Bottle-conditioned beer is available.

Beautiful South (OG 1036, ABV 3.6%)
Yellowish in colour, a hoppy session beer with a little malt character.

Crooked Furrow (OG 1040, ABV 4%)
Malty beer, with some balancing hop bitterness. Pale brown with an earthy malty aroma and a long, dry and bittersweet aftertaste.

Tallywhacker (OG 1048, ABV 4.8%)
Dark, sweet and fruity old ale with good roast malt character.

Lerwick (NEW) SIBA

Staneyhill, North Road, Lerwick, Shetland, ZE1 0QA
☎ (01595) 694552 🌐 lerwickbrewery.co.uk

Lerwick Brewery was established in 2011 using a 12-barrel plant and sits at the very edge of the North Atlantic. No real ale.

Leyden SIBA

Lord Raglan, Walmersley Old Road, Nangreaves, BL9 6SP
☎ (0161) 764 6680 🌐 lordraglannangreaves.co.uk
Tours by arrangement

Leyden was established in 1999. In addition to the permanent range a number of seasonal and occasional beers are brewed.

Black Pudding (OG 1040, ABV 3.8%)
A dark brown, creamy mild with a malty flavour, followed by a balanced finish.

Nanny Flyer (OG 1040, ABV 3.8%)
A session bitter with an initial dryness, and a hint of citrus, followed by a strong, malty finish.

Balaclava (OG 1040, ABV 4.2%)
A brown-coloured session bitter with malty and hoppy flavours.

Light Brigade (OG 1042, ABV 4.2%)
Copper in colour with a citrus aroma. The flavour is a balance of malt, hops and fruit, with a bitter finish.

Rammy Rocket (OG 1042, ABV 4.2%)
A smooth, straw-coloured ale.

Forever Bury (OG 1047, ABV 4.5%)
This dark brown bitter has a distinct fruity aroma with a smooth malty finish.

Raglan Sleeve (OG 1047, ABV 4.6%)
Dark red/brown beer with a hoppy aroma and a dry, roasty, hoppy taste and finish.

Crowning Glory (OG 1068, ABV 6.8%)
A surprisingly smooth tasting beer for its strength.

Liberation SIBA

Tregear House, Longueville Road, St Saviour, Jersey, JE2 7WF
☎ (01534) 764089 🌐 liberationgroup.com
Tours by arrangement

Following the closure of the original brewery in Ann Street in 2004, the brewery is now located in an old soft drinks factory using both a 40-barrel and an eight-barrel plant. Formerly known as the Jersey Brewery it was renamed in 2010 as the Liberation

Brewery following its sale to the Liberation Group. Its flagship beer, Liberation Ale, is now regularly seen on the mainland and on the other Channel Islands. 68 pubs are owned with around two-thirds of these serving cask ale. Seasonal and one-off beers are brewed throughout the year.

Liberation Ale (OG 1039, ABV 4%)
Golden beer with a hint of citrus on the nose.

Lincoln Green SIBA

Unit 5, Enterprise Park, Wigwam Lane, Hucknall, Nottingham, NG15 7SZ
☎ (0115) 963 4233 lincolngreenbrewing.co.uk

Anthony Hughes established the Lincoln Green Brewing Company in 2012 using a 10-barrel plant. Locally-sourced ingredients are used to create five regular beers and, in addition, seasonal and special brews are available that link to local and national events. The brewery takes its name from the colour of dyed woollen cloth associated with the legend of Robin Hood.

Marion (OG 1038, ABV 3.8%)
Full-bodied pale ale, packed with citrus hop and a hint of grapefruit.

Hood (OG 1042, ABV 4.2%)
Classic English best bitter, giving a full-rounded bitterness with a gentle floral aroma.

Sherwood (OG 1044, ABV 4.4%)
An extra pale ale with orange citrus aroma and biscuit malt.

Tuck (OG 1047, ABV 4.7%)
A well-rounded porter with a hint of dark chocolate and a blackcurrant aroma.

Sheriff (OG 1055, ABV 5.5%)
An English pale ale with strong bitterness and orange citrus hop.

Linfit

Sair Inn, 139 Lane Top, Linthwaite, Huddersfield, West Yorkshire, HD7 5SG
☎ (01484) 842370

A 19th-century brewpub that started brewing again in 1982. The beer is only available at the Sair Inn.

Lion's Tale SIBA

Red Lion, High Street, Cheswardine, Shropshire, TF9 2RS
☎ (01630) 661234 cheslion96@yahoo.co.uk

The building that houses the brewery was purpose-built in 2005 and houses a 2.5-barrel plant. Jon Morris and his wife Sheila have owned the Red Lion pub since 1996. Seasonal beer is available.

Blooming Blonde (OG 1041, ABV 4.1%)

Lionbru (OG 1041, ABV 4.1%)

Chesbrewnette (OG 1045, ABV 4.5%)

Lister's (NEW)

The Old Dairy, Ford Lane, Littlehampton, West Sussex, BN18 0DF ☎ 07775 853412 listersbrewery.com

Brewing began in 2012 using a 0.25-barrel kit. The brewery relocated in 2014 and expanded to a five-barrel plant.

Little Ale Cart

c/o The Wellington, 1 Henry Street, Sheffield, South Yorkshire, S3 7EQ
☎ (0114) 249 2295

Brewing started in 2001, as Port Mahon, in a purpose-built brewery behind the Cask & Cutler. In 2007 the brewery and pub were taken over and the names of both changed to Little Ale Cart Brewing and the Wellington. Beer is brewed only for the Wellington and the Dragon pub in Worcester. The beer range varies as the brewer trials new recipes, but tends to include a 4%, 4.3% and a 5% ABV beer.

Little Beer

Building 3, 14-15 Midleton Road, Guildford, Surrey, GU2 8XW ☎ 07941 061241 littlebeer.co.uk

Little Beer Corporation is a Guildford based 10-barrel brewery that focuses on premium bottle conditioned and craft keg beers. It is run by Jim Taylor, who is also majority owner, alongside around 300 local shareholders. A monthly beer club (including beer, food and music) is for paid membership only. See website for details.

Little Brew

15-16 Auster Road, Clifton Moor, York, YO30 4XA
littlebrew.co.uk

Brewing began in 2012 using a one-barrel plant in the Camden area of London. In 2014 they relocated to Clifton Moor, York.

Little Valley SIBA

Unit 3, Turkey Lodge Farm, New Road, Cragg Vale, Hebden Bridge, West Yorkshire, HX7 5TT
☎ (01422) 883888 littlevalleybrewery.co.uk
Shop Mon-Fri 9am-5pm
Tours by arrangement

Little Valley Brewery began brewing in 2005 on a 10-barrel plant. All beers are organic and vegan, and Ginger Pale Ale uses Fairtrade ingredients. Around 100 outlets are supplied. Several beers are contract brewed for Suma Wholefoods and in 2012 the brewery was contracted by the Benedictine Order of Ampleforth Abbey to brew and bottle their Ampleforth Abbey Beer (ABV 7%). Bottle-conditioned and monthly special beers are also available.

Ginger Pale Ale (OG 1037, ABV 4%)
Full-bodied speciality ale. Ginger predominates in the aroma and taste. It has a pleasantly powerful, fiery and spicy finish.

Cragg Vale Bitter (OG 1039, ABV 4.2%)
Grainy, pale brown session bitter, light on the palate with a delicate flavour of malt and fruit and a bitter finish.

Hebden's Wheat (OG 1043, ABV 4.5%)
A pale yellow, creamy wheat beer with a good balance of bitterness and fruit, a hint of sweetness but with a lasting, dry finish.

Stoodley Stout (OG 1044, ABV 4.8%)
Dark brown creamy stout with a rich roast aroma and luscious fruity, chocolate, roast flavours. Well-balanced with a clean bitter finish.

Tod's Blonde (OG 1045, ABV 5%)

Bright yellow, grainy, speciality beer with a citrus hop start and a dry finish. Fruity, with a hint of spice. Similar in style to a Belgian blonde beer.

Python IPA (OG 1055, ABV 6%) ◆
Amber-coloured grainy beer with a complex bitter fruit palate subtly balanced by a malty sweetness, leading to a strongly lingering, bitter aftertaste.

Liverpool Craft SIBA

10 Love Lane, The Railway Arches, Liverpool, L3 7DD
☎ (0151) 236 9400 🌐 liverpoolcraftbeer.com

Liverpool Craft began brewing in 2011 using a 10-barrel plant. Beers are widely available across the north-west. The brewery regularly collaborates with arts and music events. Seasonal, speciality and bottle-conditioned beers are available.

Icon (OG 1037, ABV 3.8%)
A pale ale with a long, dry finish and citrus undertones.

Hop Beast (OG 1039, ABV 4%)
A hoppy beer with a strong hop flavour and bitterness.

American Red (OG 1047, ABV 5%)
An American ale packed with hop flavour and balanced with a subtle sweetness.

IPA (OG 1047, ABV 5%)
An IPA with a strong, hoppy finish.

Brew #56 (OG 1049, ABV 5.4%)
A strong pale ale infused with honey.

Rye Pale Ale (OG 1050, ABV 5.6%)
A crisp pale ale with a spicy rye base.

Liverpool One SIBA

82-84 Vauxhall Road, Liverpool, L3 6DL
☎ (0151) 227 2244 🌐 liverpoolonebrewery.co.uk

Liverpool One started brewing in 2010 using a five-barrel plant. Expansion took place in 2012 to cope with increased demand. Outlets are supplied throughout Merseyside as well as Chester and Warrington. Seasonal, occasional and bottle-conditioned beers are available.

Session (OG 1034, ABV 3.4%)
Chestnut-coloured, light malty bitter.

Albert Dock Amber (OG 1038, ABV 3.8%)
An amber-coloured fruity and floral ale with a hint of bitterness.

Kings Regiment (OG 1038, ABV 3.8%)
A copper-coloured malty bitter, smooth and rich. A traditional best bitter.

Mersey Mist (OG 1040, ABV 4%)
A cloudy wheat beer flavoured with fresh oranges and lemons with a touch of coriander.

Light (OG 1041, ABV 4.1%)
A pale, hoppy citrus beer.

Three Graces (OG 1042, ABV 4.2%)
Straw-coloured beer with an intense bitter bite.

Dark (OG 1050, ABV 5%)
A full-flavoured classic porter. Roasted and toasted flavours with a smoky finish.

Maharaja IPA (OG 1053, ABV 5.3%)
A classic IPA with a deep golden colour. Packed full of bitterness.

Liverpool Organic SIBA

39 Brasenose Road, Liverpool, L20 8HL
☎ (0151) 933 9660 🌐 liverpoolorganicbrewery.com
Tours by arrangement

Liverpool Organic started brewing in 2009. Outlets are supplied around the extended Merseyside area with its cask and bottle-conditioned beers. The brewery also supports many local beer festivals and also run festivals of its own including the largest beer event in Liverpool. Beers are also brewed under the name of the now defunct Cambrinus brewery.

Cascade (OG 1038, ABV 3.8%)
An intensely hopped light session bitter.

Joseph Williamson (OG 1039, ABV 4%)
Traditional malty bitter flavours with floral elements building to a smooth, satisfying finish.

Liverpool Pale Ale (OG 1039, ABV 4%)
Dry hoppy notes with floral complexity giving way to spicy tones and a slightly creamy malt finish.

Bier Head (OG 1040, ABV 4.1%)
Sharp, hoppy foretaste with complex spice and crisp malt tones, building to a rich, mellow aftertaste.

24 Carat Gold (OG 1041, ABV 4.2%)
Generously hopped with a bitterness that builds steadily towards a lingering finish with spicy orange notes.

Best Bitter (OG 1042, ABV 4.2%)
Good, hoppy bitterness balanced with pale malts: crisp, refreshing finish with a hint of citrus fruit.

Liverpool Stout (OG 1048, ABV 4.3%)
Strong, dark and dry stout with a smooth, spicy finish.

William Roscoe (OG 1042, ABV 4.3%)
Hoppy and fruity with a hint of dryness and bitterness building to a crisp and slightly earthy malt finish.

Honey Blond (OG 1043, ABV 4.5%)
A subtle and not cloyingly sweet honey aftertaste married to a solid malt backbone and a good hoppy character.

Josephine Butler (OG 1043, ABV 4.5%)
Initial citrus hops followed by elderflower fruit and pale, biscuity malt with a refreshing, sharp finish.

Kitty Wilkinson (OG 1047, ABV 4.5%)
Vanilla, butterscotch and chocolate combine in the roasted malty taste with a fairly dry finish and a generous cocoa note.

Empire Ale (OG 1056, ABV 5.3%)
A strong ruby ale with a slightly sweet finish.

Under the Cambrinus Brewery name:

Deliverance (OG 1042, ABV 4.2%)
Pale gold beer with a sharp, hoppy taste.

Endurance (OG 1044, ABV 4.3%)
A beer with vanilla notes made with English malt and hops.

Lizard Ales

The Old Nuclear Bunker, Pednavounder, Cornwall, TR12 6SE
☎ (01326) 281135 🌐 lizardales.co.uk
Tours by arrangement

Launched in 2004, Lizard Ales is now based at former RAF Treleaver, a massive disused nuclear bunker in the countryside near Coverack on the Lizard Peninsula. Specialising in bottle-conditioned ales, it mainly supplies west Cornwall.

Kernow Gold (OG 1037, ABV 3.7%)

Bitter (OG 1041, ABV 4.2%) ◆
Pale brown beer with aroma of ripe apples. Roast malt with fruit esters balanced by bitterness. Bitter finish with dryness.

Frenchman's Creek (OG 1042, ABV 4.8%)

An Gof (OG 1049, ABV 5.2%) ◆
Robust and smooth tawny ale dominated by malt in the mouth with a hint of smoke. Fruity hops follow on into the bitter finish.

Llangollen SIBA

Abbey Grange Brewing Ltd, Abbey Grange Hotel, Horseshoe Pass Road, Llantysilio, Llangollen, LL20 8DD
☎ (01978) 861916 🌐 llangollenbrewery.com
Shop open daily in summer; the hotel sells bottles throughout the year
Tours by arrangement

Brewing began in 2010 on a 2.5-barrel plant. All beers are also available bottle conditioned.

Grange No.1 (OG 1032, ABV 3.2%)
A fruity pale ale with a slight hoppy finish.

Wrexham Borders Bitter (OG 1039, ABV 3.9%)
A pale ale with fruity notes, haylike and distinctively hoppy.

Bitter (OG 1042, ABV 4.2%)

Holy Grail (OG 1043, ABV 4.3%)
A light citrus pale ale.

Welsh Black (OG 1055, ABV 5.5%)
Chocolate and toffee notes with a hoppy finish.

Lleu (NEW)

Unit A9, Penygroes Industrial Estate, Penygroes, LL54 6DB
☎ (01286) 882561 🌐 bragdylleu.co.uk

Brewing began in 2014 using a 1.25-barrel plant. Further beers are planned.

Lleu (ABV 4%)

Llŷn

Unit 6, Ffordd Dewi Sant, Nefyn, Gwynedd, LL53 6EG
☎ 07792 050134 🌐 cwrwllyn.com
Tours by arrangement

⊛The brewery is a co-operative of 12 friends that began brewing in 2011 producing 44 barrels per week. There are firm plans for a new brewery, incorporating a gas combustion system.

Y Brawd Houdini (OG 1036, ABV 3.8%)

Brenin Enlli (OG 1038, ABV 4%)

Seithenyn (OG 1040, ABV 4.2%)

Cochyn (OG 1043, ABV 4.5%)

Loch Leven

Criochan House, Maryburgh, Blairadam, KY4 0JE
☎ (01383) 831751 🌐 lochlevenbrewery.com

Loch Leven was established in 2009 on a four-barrel brewery. It supplies beer to most Scottish beer festivals and trades mainly with pubs in Fife and Perthshire. Seasonal beers are available.

Golden Goose (OG 1037, ABV 3.7%)
A golden, light ale; crisp and well-hopped with a dry aftertaste.

Cock Robin (OG 1041, ABV 4.1%)
A Scottish-style ale, full-bodied with a malty aftertaste.

Nightjar (OG 1042, ABV 4.2%)
A malty ale with a taste of chocolate. Lightly-hopped with a floral finish.

Falcon Hell (OG 1056, ABV 5.6%)

Loch Lomond SIBA

Block 1, Unit 5, Lomond Industrial Estate, Alexandria, G83 0TL
☎ (01389) 755698 🌐 lochlomondbrewery.com
Shop Mon-Tue, Thu-Sat 10am-5pm, closed Wed & Sun
Tours by arrangement

Established in 2011 by Fiona and Euan MacEachern, it is the only brewery around Loch Lomond.

Bonnie 'n' Bitter (OG 1036, ABV 3.6%)
An easy-drinking bitter with citrus flavours and a full-rounded bitterness.

The West Highland Way (OG 1038, ABV 3.8%)
A light ale with fruity flavours.

Bonnie 'n' Blonde (OG 1040, ABV 4%)
A light, refreshing ale with a well rounded citrus flavour.

The Ale of Leven (OG 1045, ABV 4.5%)
An amber-coloured beer with a slight sweetness and spicy bitterness.

Silkie Stout (OG 1050, ABV 5%)
A black stout with chocolate-orange spicy notes.

Kessog Dark Ale (OG 1052, ABV 5.2%)
Dark with warm spicy flavours.

Loch Ness SIBA ◉

Blarmor, Drumnadrochit, IV63 6UG
☎ (01456) 450080 🌐 lochnessbrewery.com
Tours by arrangement

⊛Brewing began in 2011 using a two-barrel plant in the grounds of the Benleva Hotel. The brewery moved in 2012 to nearby premises using an eight-barrel plant. Beers are available in the local area, central Scotland and northern England. There are plans for expansion.

LightNESS (OG 1040, ABV 3.9%) ◆
Golden refreshing hoppy bitter with a hint of peaches.

WilderNESS (OG 1040, ABV 3.9%) ◆
Fruity, hoppy beer with a slight malt background. Bitter-sweet turning to a more bitter finish.

CaithNESS (OG 1044, ABV 4%)

MadNESS (OG 1042, ABV 4%)

NESS Express (OG 1040, ABV 4%)

RedNESS (OG 1042, ABV 4.2%) ◆
Reddy brown colour with a good mix of malt and hops with a raspberry background in this sweetish brew.

LochNESS (OG 1044, ABV 4.4%) ◆
A malty, fruity, sweetish brew in the 80/- style. Hints of chocolate and blackcurrant.

DarkNESS (OG 1052, ABV 4.5%) ◆
Roasted chocolate malt with a slight blackcurrant background. Thick brown head all the way to the bottom.

HoppyNESS (OG 1050, ABV 5%) ◆
Golden smooth citrus, hoppy brew. The initial sweetness turns to a bitter finish. Does not drink its strength.

Loddon SIBA

Dunsden Green Farm, Church Lane, Dunsden, Oxfordshire, RG4 9QD
☎ (0118) 948 1111 🌐 loddonbrewery.com
Shop Mon-Fri 9am-5pm, Sat 9.30am-3pm
Tours by arrangement

This family-run brewery was established in 2002 in a brick-and-flint barn that was originally a grain store. The custom-built 17-barrel plant typically produces 120 barrels per week, and supplies more than 500 outlets far and wide. Popular open evenings are held quarterly. Seasonal beers and monthly specials: see website.

Hoppit (OG 1036.2, ABV 3.5%) ◆
Hops dominate the aroma of this drinkable, light-coloured session beer. Malt and hops create a balanced taste and a pleasant bitterness carries through to the aftertaste.

Hullabaloo (OG 1043.8, ABV 4.2%) ◆
A hint of fruit in the initial taste develops into a balance of hops and malt in this well-rounded, medium-bodied bitter with a bitter aftertaste.

Ferryman's Gold (OG 1045.8, ABV 4.4%) ◆
Golden coloured with a strong hoppy character throughout, accompanied by fruit in the taste and aftertaste.

Bamboozle (OG 1049.5, ABV 4.8%) ◆
Full-bodied and well balanced. Distinctive bittersweet flavour with hop and caramel to accompany.

Forbury Lion (OG 1056.5, ABV 5.5%)
A malty IPA with a strong, complex hop finish.

London Beer Factory (NEW)

Unit 4, 160 Hamilton Road, West Norwood, London, SE27 9SF
☎ (020) 8670 7054 🌐 thelondonbeerfactory.com

The London Beer Factory started brewing in 2014 using a 20-barrel plant. Local outlets are supplied.

London Session (ABV 3.8%)
A dry-hopped, easy-drinking session ale.

Chelsea Blonde (ABV 4.3%)
A light, refreshing blonde ale, full-bodied with a fruity aroma.

London Brewing

Bull, 13 North Hill, Highgate, London, N6 4AB
☎ (020) 8341 0510 🌐 londonbrewing.com

London Brewing Co began brewing in 2011 at the Bull in Highgate using a 2.5-barrel plant. In 2014 it acquired its second pub, the Bohemia in North Finchley, at which a brew plant is also planned. Seasonal and special beers are available.

High Rise (OG 1040, ABV 3.9%) ◆
A fruity, yellow-coloured ale with a bitter character balanced by a fudge sweetness and a touch of lemon/lime peel.

Beer Street (OG 1039, ABV 4%) ◆
Well-balanced copper-brown best bitter with the hoppy bitterness underpinned by the caramelised malt character. Fruit is present throughout.

Waterlow Gold (OG 1042, ABV 4.3%)

Vista (OG 1040, ABV 4.5%) ◆
Smooth brown best bitter. Some nutty notes with hints of chocolate balanced by fruit. Lingering, dry bitter finish.

Ginger (OG 1046, ABV 5.1%)

Skyline (OG 1053, ABV 5.3%) ◆
Pale brown beer with a honey sweetness and some soft fruit notes. Sweetness is balanced by a bitter dryness.

London Fields SIBA

365-366 Warburton Street, Hackney, London, E8 3RR
☎ (020) 7254 7174 🌐 londonfieldsbrewery.co.uk
Tours by arrangement

London Fields was first established in 2011, operating from a railway arch beneath London Fields Railway Station. 2012 saw considerable expansion of brewery capacity at a site nearby. London pubs are supplied, as well as events at the brewery itself.

Pale Ale (ABV 3.7%) ◆
A hoppy, yellow-coloured bitter with some citrus and apple fruitiness.

Hackney Hopster (OG 1042, ABV 4.2%) ◆
Amber beer that is malty sweet with traces of honey but is balanced by mixed fruits and a bitter dryness.

Love Not War (OG 1044, ABV 4.2%) ◆
Peppery hop character and some citrus is present throughout this copper beer with a dry finish and increasing bitterness.

Long Itch SIBA

Unit 5a, Manor Farm, Hunningham Lane, Offchurch, Warwickshire, CV33 9AG ☎ 07780 900699

Office: Walnut House, Leamington Road, Long Itchington, Warwickshire, CV47 9PL
🌐 longitchbrewery.co.uk

Long Itch Brewery commenced brewing in 2013 on a 5.5-barrel plant housed in a converted barn among the outbuildings of Manor Farm just outside Offchurch. It regularly supplies outlets in a 30-miles radius plus beer festivals. Seasonal and bottle-conditioned beers are available.

Fiesta (OG 1035, ABV 3.5%)

Light Relief (OG 1038, ABV 3.8%)

Honey Trap (OG 1041, ABV 4.1%)

Backscratcher (OG 1045, ABV 4.5%)

Dark Side (OG 1048, ABV 4.8%)

Dubbel Trubbel (OG 1059, ABV 5.9%)

Long Lane

Matchless Home Brewing, 48 Belvoir Road, Coalville, Leicestershire, LE67 3PP
☎ (0153) 813800 ⊕ matchlesshomebrewing.co.uk

This small 100-litre brewery was established in 2010, with beers brewed by passionate brewster Ann Saunders, and is based in the Matchless Homebrew shop. Beers are mostly bottle-conditioned but cask beers can be produced to order.

Long Man SIBA

Church Farm, Litlington, East Sussex, BN26 5RA
☎ (01323) 871850 ⊕ longmanbrewery.com
Tours by arrangement

Long Man began brewing in 2012 using a 20-barrel stainless steel plant. Hops and grain are sourced locally with a view to using barley currently being grown on the farm, as well as a traditional strain of Sussex yeast.

Long Blonde (OG 1039, ABV 3.8%)
A light-coloured golden ale with a distinctive hoppy aroma and crisp, clean bitterness on the finish. Smooth, light and refreshing.

Best Bitter (OG 1040, ABV 4%)
Well-balanced with a complex bittersweet malty taste, fragrant hops and a long deep finish. A traditional Sussex-style best bitter.

Old Man (OG 1048, ABV 4.3%)
Dark beer with soft malt notes of coffee and chocolate combined with a pleasant light hoppiness creating a rich, full tasting old ale.

Sussex Pride (OG 1045, ABV 4.5%)
A classic strong pale ale. Bronze-coloured with a fruity nose and full round flavours. A good balance between malt and hops.

American Pale Ale (OG 1046, ABV 4.8%)
Made with US hops, this triple-hopped beer has a pleasant citrus fruit aroma and robust bitterness.

Longden (NEW) SIBA

Red Lion, Longden Common, Shropshire, SY5 8AE
☎ 07958 007551 ⊕ longdenbrewing.co.uk

Longden Brewing Company has been brewing since 2013 using a five-barrel plant. Beer names are inspired by local legends. The regular beers are usually available at the Red Lion (the brewery tap) and in a number of free houses in Shropshire, including several in Shrewsbury town centre. Seasonal beer is available.

The Golden Arrow (OG 1038, ABV 3.8%)
A pale ale with an abundance of hop character giving lemon, lime, tropical fruit and gentle spice flavours.

Sawn Off (OG 1042, ABV 4%)
A copper-coloured best bitter, well-balanced with a gentle bitterness from a mix of traditional British hops.

Spire Dancer (OG 1044, ABV 4.2%)
A golden ale, well-balanced and refreshing with flavours of honey, orange and sweet-spicy floral notes.

Longdog SIBA

Unit A1, Moniton Trading Estate, West Ham Lane, Worting, Basingstoke, Hampshire, RG22 6NQ
☎ (01256) 324286 ⊕ longdogbrewery.co.uk
Shop Fri 2-7pm, Sat 10am-1pm
Tours by arrangement

Longdog was established in 2011 using a six-barrel plant. The name is inspired by the owner's greyhound. Seasonal beers are available.

Bunny Chaser (OG 1036, ABV 3.6%)
A dark copper-coloured session bitter with plenty of malt in the mouth and a good whack of bitterness.

Hare of the Dog (OG 1036, ABV 3.6%)
A sweet, malty mild.

Golden Poacher (OG 1038, ABV 3.9%) ◆
A fruity nose with plenty of hops, balanced by a malty sweetness in the flavour. The hops build to a faint astringent finish.

Brindle Bitter (OG 1041, ABV 4.2%) ◆
Well-crafted best bitter. Malt nose with caramel hints and berry fruits. Maltiness leads into a moderate hop flavour with bitter aftertaste.

Ale Dorado (OG 1045, ABV 4.5%)
An American pale ale brewed with El Dorado hops, giving it tropical fruit flavours.

Lamplight Porter (OG 1048, ABV 5%) ◆
Splendid porter, smoky and drier than many, with strong roast flavours giving way to a blackberry taste and slightly vinous finish.

Longhill

Longhill Cottage, Whitstone, Cornwall, EX22 6UG
☎ (01288) 341466

Longhill began brewing in 2011 using a 0.5-barrel plant, upgraded in 2012 to a four-barrel plant to meet demand. The beers are named with a wind theme. Eight outlets are supplied direct. Seasonal beers are available.

Whistler (OG 1038, ABV 3.8%)

Westerly (OG 1040, ABV 4%)

Gale Force (OG 1048, ABV 4.8%)

Hurricane (OG 1048, ABV 4.8%)

Loose Cannon SIBA

Unit 6, Suffolk Way, Abingdon, Oxfordshire, OX14 5JX
☎ (01235) 531141 ⊕ lcbeers.co.uk
Shop Mon-Sat 9am-5pm
Tours by arrangement

Loose Cannon began production in 2010 using a 15-barrel brew plant, reviving Abingdon's brewing history after the Morland Brewery closed in 2000. Beers can be found in an increasing number of local pubs. Seasonal beers are available, often named after an event of local historic interest.

Gunners Gold (OG 1034.5, ABV 3.5%)
Golden, easy-drinking session ale with a subtle peach flavour.

Abingdon Bridge (OG 1041, ABV 4.1%)
Full-flavoured and smooth, with well-rounded bitterness and a light citrus and floral finish.

Bandwagon (OG 1041.5, ABV 4.2%)

THE BREWERIES

Full-flavoured, copper-coloured bitter. Rounded malty body. Mixed berry finish.

Dark Horse (OG 1042, ABV 4.3%)
Dark beer with a fruity hop aroma.

Lord Conrad's

Unit 21, Dry Drayton Industrial Estate, Scotland Road, Dry Drayton, Cambridgeshire, CB23 8AT ☎ 07736 739700 🌐 lordconradsbrewery.co.uk
Shop Mon-Sat 10am-5pm
Tours by arrangement

Lord Conrad's was established in 2007 and moved to Dry Drayton in 2011 using a 2.5-barrel plant. One permanent outlet is supplied, the Abbot's Elm, Abbots Ripton, along with other local free houses and beer festivals. The brewery adheres strongly to 'green' principles, using low energy systems, recycled materials and local ingredients.

Stoat Warbler (OG 1035, ABV 3.4%)

Zulu Dawn (OG 1037, ABV 3.5%)

Hedgerow Hop (OG 1039, ABV 3.7%)
An amber-coloured ale made with locally-picked hops and supporting the RSPB.

Lickety Split (OG 1038, ABV 3.8%)
Sweet, malty brown ale, light but not overly hoppy.

Conkerwood (OG 1044, ABV 4%)
Dark porter with hints of liquorice.

Gubbins (OG 1040, ABV 4%)
A real mixed bag, much like its name, with a hint of spice.

Slap N' Tickle (OG 1042, ABV 4.3%)
A summer blonde with a huge hit of bitterness followed by subtle hoppiness.

Zulu (OG 1047, ABV 4.5%)
A strong black bitter.

Pheasant's Rise (OG 1050, ABV 5%)
Smoky, woody traditional strong ale commemorating the brewer's gamekeeper grandfather.

Stubble Burner (OG 1050, ABV 5%)
A straw-like beer with a good earthy nose and a well-balanced fruity bitterness.

Lovibonds

Rear of 19-21 Market Place, Henley-on-Thames, Oxfordshire, RG9 2AA
☎ (01491) 576596 🌐 lovibonds.com
Tours by arrangement

Lovibonds Brewery was founded by Jeff Rosenmeier in 2005 and is named after Joseph William Lovibond, who invented the Tintometer to measure beer colour. No real ale.

Luckie

Haig Business Park, Balgonie Road, Markinch, KY7 6AQ
☎ (01333) 352801 🌐 luckie-ales.com

Luckie Ales was established by Stuart McLuckie in 2009. Brewing moved to Haigs Business Park in 2012 using a one-barrel plant. The brewery specialises in handcrafted Scottish beers and historic British ales. Beers are brewed on demand.

Ludlow SIBA

The Railway Shed, Station Drive, Ludlow, Shropshire, SY8 2PQ
☎ (01584) 873291
🌐 theludlowbrewingcompany.co.uk
Shop Mon-Thu 10am-5pm, Fri 10am-6pm, Sat 10am-4pm
Tours by arrangement

Established in 2006, the brewery operates from a converted railway sidings shed utilising a 20-barrel brewing plant. The premises also function as a brewery tap, visitor centre and events area.

Best (OG 1037, ABV 3.7%)
A golden amber-coloured, well-balanced session beer with a banana, pineapple and toffee aroma and a resinous, dry finish.

Gold (OG 1041, ABV 4.2%)
A golden ale with a papaya, pineapple and lemon aroma and a soft, full-bodied, creamy taste.

Black Knight (OG 1045, ABV 4.5%)
A ruby black stout with a smoky, liquorice aroma and sweet, roasted nutty flavour.

Boiling Well (OG 1047, ABV 4.7%)
An auburn beer with a grassy aroma of autumn fruit with a full-bodied sweet then dry taste.

Stairway (OG 1049, ABV 5%)
A grassy, citrus floral aroma with a sharp, sweet, full-bodied taste.

LWC

Beers brewed under the Gray's brand. See Marston's

Lymestone SIBA

The Brewery, Mount Road, Stone, Staffordshire, ST15 8LL
☎ (01785) 817796 🌐 lymestonebrewery.co.uk
Shop Mon-Fri 8am-5pm, Sat & Sun by arrangement
Tours by arrangement

Lymestone commenced brewing in 2008. Rapid growth has seen the beers supplied direct to 300 outlets, with beer also being available via wholesalers. The brewery opened its first pub in 2012, the Lymestone Vaults, Newcastle-under-Lyme.

Stone Cutter (OG 1037, ABV 3.7%)
Hoppy and grassy aroma, clean, sharp and refreshing. A hint of caramel start then intense bitterness emerges with a good bitter aftertaste and a touch of mouthwatering astringency.

Stone Faced (OG 1040, ABV 4%)
Subtle citrus and toffee flavours balanced by a hoppy aroma and bitter finish.

Foundation Stone (OG 1047, ABV 4.5%)
An IPA-style beer with pale and crystal malts. Faint biscuit and chewy, juicy fruits burst on to the palate then the spicy Boadicea and Pilot hops pepper the taste buds to leave a dry bitter finish.

Ein Stein (OG 1052, ABV 5%)
A pale, citrus, hoppy ale.

Stone the Crows (OG 1056, ABV 5.4%)

A rich dark beer from chocolate malts. Fruit, roasts and hops abound to leave a deep lingering bitterness from the Styrian Goldings and Millennium hop mix.

Lymm (NEW)

18 Bridgewater Street, Lymm, Cheshire, WA13 0AB
☎ (0161) 929 0663

Lymm is a small, family-run brewery, launched in 2013. Located in an old post office, the brewing equipment is downstairs in what used to be the mess rooms with a brewery tap upstairs in what was the sorting office/post office counter. A sister brewery to Dunham Massey (qv), a joint bar opened in 2013, Costello's Bar, Stockton Heath.

Bitter (OG 1040, ABV 3.8%)
A light, refreshing, medium-bodied session bitter with a good balance of malt and hops.

Bridgewater Blond (OG 1041, ABV 4%)
Light, delicate, hoppy, subtle and refreshing.

Slitten Brook Stout (OG 1043.5, ABV 4%)
A smooth, creamy, all-malt session stout.

Heritage Trail Ale (OG 1046, ABV 4.5%)
An easy-drinking, well-balanced best bitter, fruity with a light crisp hop.

Lytham SIBA

8 Cambell's Court, Lord Street, St Annes, Lancashire, FY8 2DF
☎ (01253) 725440 lythambrewery.co.uk
Tours by arrangement

Lytham started brewing in 2008, upgrading from a 2.5-barrel to a 10-barrel plant in 2010 to cope with increased demand. Seasonal beers are available.

Amber (OG 1037, ABV 3.6%)
A traditional malty beer using English hops.

Blonde (OG 1038, ABV 3.8%)
A pale golden beer with a subtle hop aroma and a smooth, dry finish.

Gold (OG 1042, ABV 4.2%)
A golden beer with a fruity aroma and lasting bitter finish.

Royal (OG 1044, ABV 4.4%)
A full-bodied English ale with a crisp fruity aroma and a smooth, dry finish.

Dark (OG 1047, ABV 5%)
Dark chocolate malt with a hint of vanilla and a smooth, dry finish.

IPA (OG 1054, ABV 5.6%)
A pale bitter with a fresh, sweet, hoppy flavour leading to a long, dry finish.

McGivern

c/o The Bridge End Inn, 5 Bridge Street, Ruabon, LL14 6DA
☎ (01978) 810881 mcgivernales.co.uk

The brewery was established in 2008 and was originally based at the brewer's home in Wrexham but moved in 2011 to the Bridge End Inn in Ruabon using a 2.5-barrel plant.

Bridge Bitter (OG 1039, ABV 3.9%)

Bridge Pale (OG 1039, ABV 3.9%)

Pyramid Porter (OG 1045, ABV 4.5%)
A hoppy porter with chocolate undertones.

Gambit (OG 1047, ABV 4.7%)

Enigma (OG 1050, ABV 5%)

McMullen SIBA IFBB

26 Old Cross, Hertford, SG14 1RD
☎ (01992) 584911 mcmullens.co.uk
Tours by arrangement

McMullen, Hertfordshire's oldest independent brewery, was founded in 1827. A new brewhouse opened in 2006, giving the company flexibility to produce its regular cask beers and up to eight seasonal beers a year. All 140 pubs, now spread across south east England, serve cask beer.

AK (OG 1035, ABV 3.7%)
A pleasant mix of malt and hops leads to a distinctive, dry aftertaste that isn't always as pronounced as it used to be.

Cask Ale (OG 1039, ABV 3.8%)
A refreshing, well-balanced beer with a subtle biscuity flavour.

Country Bitter (OG 1042, ABV 4.3%)
A full-bodied beer with a well-balanced mix of malt, hops and fruit throughout.

IPA (OG 1047, ABV 4.8%)
A strong bitter with deep rich flavours created with specially kilned amber malts.

Maclay

See Clockwork

Mad Cat SIBA

Brogdale Farm, Brogdale Road, Faversham, Kent, ME13 8XZ
☎ (01795) 597743 madcatbrewery.co.uk
Shop Sat & Sun 10am-2pm

Mad Cat was established in 2012 by Peter Meaney in a refurbished cold store using an eight-barrel plant.

Auburn Copper Ale (ABV 4.2%)

Platinum Blonde Ale (ABV 4.2%)

Golden India Pale Ale (ABV 4.6%)

Jet Black Stout (ABV 4.6%)

Mad Hatter

8 Watkinson Street, Liverpool, L1 0BE
☎ (0151) 739 ☎ (1702) 07474 797450
madhatterbrewing.co.uk

Mad Hatter began brewing in 2013 combining traditional techniques with new flavours and approaches to brewing. Most of their output is bottled or keg with cask-conditioned beers making an occasional appearance round Merseyside. In 2014 the brewery relocated to the Baltic Triangle.

Madcap SIBA

Office: Greenknowe Avenue, Annan, DG12 6ER
☎ (01461) 203495 madcapbrewery.com

Madcap began brewing in 2009. It concentrates on the production of bottle-conditioned beers.

Magic Rock SIBA

The Bed Factory, Quarmby Mills, Tanyard Road, Oakes, Huddersfield, West Yorkshire, HD3 4YP
☎ (01484) 649823 ⊕ magicrockbrewing.com

Magic Rock began brewing in 2011 in the Old Bed Factory attached to the Rockshop Wholesale Company in Huddersfield. Bottle-conditioned and special beers are available.

Curious (OG 1038, ABV 3.9%)
Pale ale with a floral/grassy aroma and citrus hops.

Rapture (OG 1044.5, ABV 4.6%)
Full-bodied red-coloured ale with grapefruit and pine aromas, with pithy orange and a rich, malty body.

High Wire (OG 1051, ABV 5.5%)
West Coast style pale ale, with mango, lychee and grapefruit flavours.

Dark Arts (OG 1057, ABV 6%)
Chocolate, liquorice, blackberry and fig flavours with a long, roasted bitter finish.

Magpie SIBA

Unit 4, Ashling Court, Ashling Street, Nottingham, NG2 3JA ☎ 07738 762897 ⊕ magpiebrewery.com

Launched in 2006, this six-barrel plant only uses British hops and malt. The brewery maintain a large core range, plus seasonal and one-off beers. Bottle-conditioned beers are available.

Hoppily Ever After (OG 1035, ABV 3.8%)
Blonde refreshing beer with a distinct hop flavour.

Flyer (OG 1038.8, ABV 4.1%)
Single-hopped, light golden ale with a fruity and slightly spicy flavour.

Best (OG 1040.7, ABV 4.2%)
A malty traditional pale brown best bitter, with balancing hops giving a bitter finish.

Raven Stout (OG 1044, ABV 4.4%)
Rich and full-bodied, roast and smoky flavoured smooth, dark stout

Thieving Rogue (OG 1042, ABV 4.5%)
A hoppy golden ale with a long-lasting, bitter finish.

Midnight Porter (OG 1049.4, ABV 5%)
Rich and creamy dark porter with coffee, raisins and chocolate flavours.

JPA (OG 1048.6, ABV 5.2%)
Mature hops, citrus fruit nose with a balance of hops and malt in the mouth with a smooth, hoppy aftertaste.

Maidstone (NEW)

Unit 11, The Old Brewery, Rocky Hill, London Road, Maidstone, Kent, ME16 0DZ
☎ (01622) 757705

A four-barrel brewery situated in the former stable block of the old Style & Winch brewery in Maidstone. Test brewing commenced in 2013 and the first beer went on sale in the Flower Pot pub in 2014. Further beers are planned.

MBC-1 (OG 1038, ABV 3.8%)
A highly hopped light golden beer.

MBC-2 (OG 1038, ABV 3.8%)

Slight Stout (OG 1040, ABV 4%)
An easy going stout with a hop twist.

Maldon SIBA

Stable Brewery, Silver Street, Maldon, Essex, CM9 4QE
☎ (01621) 851000 ⊕ maldonbrewing.co.uk
Shop Mon-Fri 9am-4pm, Sat 10am-2pm
Tours by arrangement

Established in 2002, this family-run brewery is tucked away behind the 14th-century Blue Boar Hotel, which serves as the brewery tap. The eight-barrel plant is at full production serving over 50 outlets including many Gray & Sons houses. All cask beers are available in bottle-conditioned form. Seasonal beers: see website.

Farmer's IPA (OG 1036, ABV 3.6%)
A crisp, traditional IPA.

Drop of Nelson's Blood (OG 1038, ABV 3.8%)
An easy-drinking bitter originally brewed for Trafalgar Day. A tot of brandy is added to each cask.

Hotel Porter (OG 1041, ABV 4.1%)
A classic stout with a smoky tang produced by a good amount of roast barley.

Pucks Folly (OG 1038, ABV 4.2%)
A pale golden ale with a spicy character and pineapple in the aroma and taste.

Farmer's Golden Boar (OG 1050, ABV 5%)
An amber-coloured beer with a hoppy aroma.

Dark Horse (OG 1064, ABV 6.6%)
A chestnut-coloured bitter, smooth but with spice in the finish.

The Wallet (OG 1070, ABV 7.4%)
A pale, aromatic strong ale.

Mallard SIBA

Unit A, Maythorne, Nottinghamshire, NG25 0RS
☎ 07811 193930
Tours by arrangement

Phil Mallard built and installed a two-barrel plant in a shed at his home and started brewing in 1995. The brewery was taken over by Steve Hussey in 2010 and moved to its current address. There are plans to expand the plant, increase the range of beers and introduce bottle-conditioned ales. Bespoke and seasonal ales are available.

Duck 'n' Dive (OG 1039, ABV 3.7%)
A bitter, pale golden beer, with a dry finish.

Greet Ale (OG 1037, ABV 3.7%)

Golden Duck (OG 1039, ABV 3.9%)

Quacker Jack (OG 1040, ABV 4%)

Feather Light (OG 1040, ABV 4.1%)
A straw-coloured lager style beer with a hoppy taste and aroma.

Duckling (OG 1041, ABV 4.2%)
A dry-hopped, golden ale. Extremely bitter; hops dominate in the aroma and aftertaste.

Specduckular (OG 1042, ABV 4.2%)

Mallinson's

Unit 1, Waterhouse Mill, 65-71 Lockwood Road, Huddersfield, West Yorkshire, HD1 3QU
☎ (01484) 654301 ⊕ drinkmallinsons.co.uk
Tours by arrangement

The brewery was originally set up in 2008 on a six-barrel plant by CAMRA members Tara Mallinson and Elaine Yendall. The company moved to new premises in 2012 after trial brewing its core beers on a new 15-barrel plant for several weeks. For beer range including seasonal and special beers: see website.

Malmesbury (NEW) SIBA

Whitehill Industrial Estate, Royal Wootton Bassett, Wiltshire, SN4 7DB ☎ 07920 776274
malmesburybrewery.com

The brewery was founded in 2013 by a husband and wife team. Beers are available in a number of free houses in the North Wiltshire area. Beers are named after local locations or historic figures.

Burnivale Hop (OG 1041, ABV 3.8%)

Day Star (OG 1041, ABV 4.1%)

Athelstan (OG 1042, ABV 4.3%)

Westport (OG 1051, ABV 4.8%)

King's Wall (OG 1055, ABV 5.6%)

Malt SIBA

Collings Hanger Farm, 100 Wycombe Road, Prestwood, Buckinghamshire, HP16 0HP
☎ (01494) 865063 maltthebrewery.co.uk
Shop Fri 12-6pm, Sat 10am-6pm
Tours by arrangement

Opened in 2012 in a converted dairy, the 10-barrel brewery has conservation at its heart; from the use of local ingredients, to spent grain sent to the local farm. The ales are also used in pies and fish batter.

Golden Ale (OG 1038, ABV 3.9%)
Mellow, malty and a little fruity.

Malt Dark Ale (OG 1038, ABV 3.9%)
Smooth and drinkable. Full of deep malt tones.

Best Bitter (OG 1043, ABV 4.4%)
Full-flavoured with a refreshing finish. Made with traditional British hops.

IPA (OG 1048, ABV 5%)
Aromatic with a bitter finish.

Malvern Hills SIBA

15 West Malvern Road, Malvern, Worcestershire, WR14 4ND
☎ (01684) 560165 malvernhillsbrewery.co.uk
Tours by arrangement

Founded in 1998 in an old quarrying dynamite store and now an established presence in the Three Counties, Birmingham and the Black Country. The core brews are supplemented by a rolling programme of monthly specials.

Feelgood (OG 1037, ABV 3.8%)

Cyneweard (OG 1038, ABV 3.9%)
Pale blond and hoppy.

Swedish Nightingale (OG 1039, ABV 4%)

Dodgy Banker (OG 1040, ABV 4.1%)

Priessnitz Plzen (OG 1040, ABV 4.3%)
A mix of soft fruit and citrus give this straw-coloured brew its quaffability, making it ideal for quenching summer thirsts.

Black Pear (OG 1042, ABV 4.4%)
A sharp citrus hoppiness is the main constituent of this golden brew that has a long, dry aftertaste.

Mantle (NEW) SIBA

Unit 16, Pentood Industrial Estate, Cardigan, SA43 3AG
☎ (01239) 623898 mantlebrewery.com

Mantle began brewing in 2013 using a 10-barrel plant. Honing their skills brewing traditional beers for the local market, Ian and Dominique Kimber have now branched out into New World hops to extend their portfolio. Pubs throughout South and West Wales are supplied direct, select wholesalers delivering further afield. Seasonal beers are available.

Rock Steady (OG 1038, ABV 3.8%)

Moho (OG 1043, ABV 4.3%)

Cwrw Teifi (OG 1045, ABV 4.5%)

Dark Heart (OG 1052, ABV 5.2%)

Marble SIBA

41 Williamson Street, Manchester, M4 4JS
☎ (0161) 819 2694 marblebeers.com
Tours by arrangement

Marble began brewing in 1997 at the Marble Arch Inn in Manchester but now brew at a larger 12-barrel plant in a nearby unit, producing vegan beers. It supplies its own three pubs and more than 70 other outlets. Bottle-conditioned and regular seasonal beers are available.

Draft (OG 1039, ABV 3.9%)
Yellow beer with a hoppy, fruity aroma. Grapefruit and a bitter hoppiness dominate throughout.

Pint (OG 1038.5, ABV 3.9%)
A dry session bitter with notes of citrus and grapefruit. Plenty of character.

Manchester Bitter (OG 1041.7, ABV 4.2%)
Yellow beer with a fruity and hoppy aroma. Hops, fruit and bitterness on the palate and in the finish.

Ginger (OG 1046, ABV 4.5%)
Full-bodied, copper-coloured ale with a delicate blend of cloves, coriander and heaps of ginger.

Stouter Stout (OG 1046.5, ABV 4.7%)

Lagonda IPA (OG 1048, ABV 5%)
Golden yellow beer with a spicy, fruity nose. Fruit, hops and malt in the mouth, with a dry fruitiness continuing into the bitter aftertaste.

Chocolate Marble (OG 1054.5, ABV 5.5%)
A strong, stout-like ale.

Dobber (OG 1055.5, ABV 5.9%)
A dark golden IPA with pronounced hop character and smooth biscuit base offset by fruit aroma.

Earl Grey IPA (OG 1065, ABV 6.8%)
A smooth beer with a citrus fruit aroma. Hop notes are complemented by bergamot and a light tannic finish.

Marlpool

5 Breach Road, Marlpool, Heanor, Derbyshire, DE75 7NJ
☎ (01773) 711285 ☎ 07963 511855
marlpoolbrewing.co.uk

Tours by arrangement

Marlpool was set up by brothers Andy and Chris McAuley in 2010 using a 2.5-barrel plant situated in an old slaughterhouse. The majority of the beer is sold through its own micro pub, built into the old butcher's shop attached to the brewery. The remainder is usually supplied to pubs within a 10-mile radius. Seasonal beer: see website. Occasional bottle-conditioned beers are sold only at the micro pub.

Blind Boris (OG 1038, ABV 3.5%)
Traditional dark mild.

Otters Pocket (OG 1040, ABV 4%)
Easy-drinking, smooth amber-coloured ale.

Scratty Ratty (OG 1044, ABV 4.4%)
A pale ale, lightly hopped with a bitter, dry finish.

Derbyshire Classic (OG 1048, ABV 4.8%)
Premium amber bitter.

Owd Sowj (OG 1050, ABV 5%)
Full-bodied traditional dark bitter.

Marston Moor

See Rudgate

Marston's SIBA

Shobnall Road, Burton upon Trent, Staffordshire, DE14 2BW
☎ (01283) 531131 marstons.co.uk
Shop Mon-Fri 10am-5pm, Sat 9.30am-12pm (excluding Bank Holidays)
Tours by arrangement

Marston's, formerly Wolverhampton & Dudley, has grown with spectacular speed in recent years. It became a super regional in 1999 when it bought both Mansfield and Marston's breweries, though it quickly closed Mansfield. In 2005 it bought Jennings of Cockermouth and has invested £250,000 in Cumbria to expand fermenting and cask racking capacity. In total, Marston's owns 2,200 pubs and supplies some 3,000 free trade pubs and clubs throughout the country. It no longer has a stake in Burtonwood Brewery (qv). It added a further 70 pubs in 2006 when it bought Celtic Inns for £43.6 million. In 2007 it paid £155 million for the 158-strong Eldridge Pope pub estate. In 2007 it bought Ringwood in Hampshire and in the same year added Brakspear and Wychwood in Witney, Oxfordshire. Marston's has been brewing cask beer in Burton since 1834 and the current site is the home of the only working Burton Union fermenters, housed in rooms known as the Cathedral of Brewing. Burton Unions were developed in the 19th century to cleanse the new style of pale ale of yeast. Only Pedigree is fermented in the unions but yeast from the system is used to ferment the other beers. Pedigree celebrated its 60th anniversary in 2012.

EPA (OG 1036, ABV 3.6%)

Burton Bitter (OG 1037, ABV 3.8%)
Overwhelming sulphurous aroma supports a scattering of hops and fruit with an easy-drinking sweetness. The taste develops from the sweet middle to a satisfyingly hoppy finish.

Pedigree New World Pale Ale (OG 1038, ABV 3.8%)
The hops impart a mellow, understated bitterness, complemented by a blast of tropical fruit flavours – peach, apricot, melon and passionfruit. A light citrus tingle follows, leading to a fragrant and refreshing finish.

Pedigree (OG 1043, ABV 4.5%)
Pale brown with a sweet hoppy aroma. Malt with a dash of hop flavours give a satisfying tasty finish.

Old Empire (OG 1057, ABV 5.7%)
Sulphur dominates the gentle malt aroma. Malty and sweet to start but developing bitterness with fruit and a touch of sweetness. A balanced aftertaste of hops and fruit leads to a lingering bitterness.

Brewed for LWC Drinks Ltd:

Gray's Best Bitter (OG 1038, ABV 3.8%)
A dark brew with a toffee, malty flavour and hop and bitterness in the aftertaste.

Gray's Celtic Gold (OG 1040, ABV 4%)
A golden bitter with a pleasant balance of hops and malt. Hops continue from the taste to a smooth bitter finish.

Gray's England's Pride (OG 1045, ABV 4.5%)
A dark brew with a toffee, malty flavour with hop and bitterness and the aftertaste.

Gray's Champion (OG 1051, ABV 5.1%)
A strong dark brown ale with complex balance of fruit, malt and roast flavours through to the finish.

For AB InBev:

Draught Bass (OG 1043, ABV 4.4%)
Hints of caramel aroma and taste, lightly hopped for a short bitter finish.

MASH (NEW) SIBA

Middle Barn, Burcot Farm, East Stratton, Hampshire, SO21 3DZ
☎ (01962) 795023 mashbrewery.com

MASH began brewing in 2013 using a one-barrel plant. A new 10-barrel plant was installed in 2014. All beers are also available bottle conditioned.

Pale (OG 1035, ABV 3.8%)
A pale ale with a subtle aroma and a long bitter finish.

Bitter (OG 1037, ABV 3.9%)
A copper-coloured beer with fruity, peachy aromas and a dry bitter flavour.

Gold (OG 1039, ABV 4%)
A refreshing beer with zesty citrus flavours.

Amber (OG 1042, ABV 4.3%)
A well-balanced beer with floral aromas.

Chocolate Stout (OG 1047, ABV 5%)
A rich, black stout with roasted malt and burnt coffee flavours.

Masters

Unit 8, Greenham Business Park, Greenham, Somerset, TA21 0LR
☎ (01823) 674444
richard@mastersbrewery.co.uk
Tours by arrangement

The brewery was established in 2006 but had to close in 2009. In 2011 it was reopened using a 2.5-barrel plant.

Devon's Pride (OG 1043, ABV 3.8%)

Spypost Bitter (OG 1040, ABV 4%)

Whiteball (OG 1038, ABV 4%)

Immenstadt Weiss (OG 1043, ABV 4.3%)

Thunderbridge Ale (OG 1047, ABV 4.7%)

Mauldons SIBA

Black Adder Brewery, 13 Church Field Road, Sudbury, Suffolk, CO10 2YA
☎ (01787) 311055 ⊕ mauldons.co.uk
Shop Mon-Fri 9.30am-4pm
Tours by arrangement

The Mauldon family started brewing in Sudbury in 1795. The brewery with 26 pubs was bought by Greene King in the 1960s. The current business, established in 1982, was bought by Steve and Alison Sims in 2000. They relocated to a new brewery in 2005, with a 30-barrel plant that has doubled production. Two pubs are owned and around 150 outlets are supplied. There is a rolling programme of seasonal beers: see website.

Micawber's Mild (OG 1035, ABV 3.5%)
Light, easy-drinking mild. Malty smoothness with a rich roast flavour turns into a caramel liquorice aftertaste.

Moletrap Bitter (OG 1038, ABV 3.8%)
Pleasant fulfilling ale, with a dark fruity aroma, sticky toffee mouthfeel and a sweetness that gives depth to the flavour.

Silver Adder (OG 1042, ABV 4.2%)
Light fruity aroma, dry hoppiness and citrus fruit with rich honey in the taste, and a long, fruity, sweet aftertaste. Refreshing and well-balanced.

Suffolk Pride (OG 1048, ABV 4.8%)
A full-bodied, copper-coloured beer with a good balance of malt, hops and fruit in the taste.

Suffolk Punch (OG 1048, ABV 4.8%)

Black Adder (OG 1053, ABV 5.3%)
Malty, roast aroma leads to a well-balanced full-bodied beer, malty with roast and dark soft fruit overtones.

Maxim SIBA

1 Gadwall Road, Rainton Bridge South, Houghton-le-Spring, DH4 5NL
☎ (0191) 584 8844 ⊕ maximbrewery.co.uk
Shop Tue-Fri 12-6pm
Tours by arrangement

Rising from the ashes of Sunderland brewer Vaux, Maxim was set up with a 20-barrel plant in Houghton le Spring in 2007. In 2013 the Houghton site reached the 1,000 brews milestone. More than 100 outlets are supplied direct and four pubs are owned. Seasonal beers are available.

Lambtons (OG 1039, ABV 3.8%)
Smooth golden ale with citrus and hoppy flavors.

Samson (OG 1040, ABV 4%)
Traditional best bitter, chestnut brown in colour with a caramel taste and English hops adding a balance of bitterness.

Ward's Best Bitter (OG 1040, ABV 4%)
Brewed to a traditional process, a tawny, copper-coloured best bitter with a sweet, toasted biscuit flavour, slightly hoppy and fruity.

Swedish Blonde (OG 1042, ABV 4.2%)
A smooth beer, light in colour with refreshing hoppy and complex grapefruit flavours on the palate.

Double Maxim (OG 1048, ABV 4.7%)
A brown ale with a fruity, caramel, malty, nutty taste and a hint of sweetness. Smooth and well-balanced.

American Pride IPA (OG 1055, ABV 5.2%)
A hoppy American-style IPA.

Maximus (OG 1062, ABV 6%)
Dark ruby-coloured, full-bodied premium ale. Sweet with a liquorice flavour, caramel and dark fruits.

May Hill

See Hillside

Mayfields SIBA

No. 8, Croft Business Park, Leominster, Herefordshire, HR6 0QF
☎ (01568) 611197 ⊕ mayfieldsbrewery.co.uk
Shop Mon-Fri 10am-4pm (other times by appt)
Tours by arrangement

This small family brewery was established in 2005 at Mayfields Farm near Bishops Frome, a major hop growing region. 2008 saw a move to a business park in Leominster. Seasonal beers are brewed on a monthly basis: see website.

Copper Fox (OG 1037, ABV 3.8%)
A copper-coloured ale with fruity, hoppy flavours and a bitter malt finish.

Priory Pale Ale (OG 1039, ABV 4%)
A light golden ale with a refreshing malt body, plenty of hops in the aroma leading to a gentle bitter finish.

Aunty Myrtle's (OG 1044, ABV 4.5%)
A dark copper-coloured ale with gentle malt flavours and strong hop finish.

Maypole

North Laithes Farm, Wellow Road, Eakring, Newark, Nottinghamshire, NG22 0AN ☎ 07971 277598
⊕ maypolebrewery.co.uk

The brewery opened in 1995 in a converted 18th-century farm building. After changing hands in 2001 it was bought by the former head brewer, Rob Neil, in 2005. Seasonal beers can be ordered at any time for beer festivals: see website for details and list.

Midge (OG 1035, ABV 3.5%)
Pale ale with a lasting bitter finish.

Little Weed (OG 1037, ABV 3.8%)
Deep golden in colour with a subtle bitterness from a blend of hops.

Celebration (OG 1038, ABV 4%)
Amber-coloured traditional English ale, slightly nutty overtones.

Gate Hopper (OG 1040, ABV 4%)
Cascade hops give this golden ale a floral aroma and lingering hoppy bitterness.

Hop Fusion (OG 1040, ABV 4.2%)
Pale golden ale.

Major Oak (OG 1042, ABV 4.4%)
A well-balanced red/brown, full-bodied bitter with hints of fruit and burned malt.

Wellow Gold (OG 1044, ABV 4.6%)
Refreshing blonde ale, citrus flavours on the nose and aftertaste.

Meantime SIBA

Units 4 & 5, Lawrence Trading Estate, Blackwall Lane, London, SE10 0AR
☎ (020) 8293 1111

Head Office: Norman House, 110-114 Norman Road, London, SE10 9EH ⊕ meantimebrewing.com
Shop: Wed-Fri 4-8pm, Sat 11am-8pm, Sun 11am-4pm
Tours by arrangement

⊗ Founded in 2000, Meantime brews a wide range of continental style beer and traditional English bottle-conditioned ales. Two pubs are owned. In 2010 the brewery relocated to larger premises in Greenwich. Bottle-conditioned beers are produced, all suitable for vegetarians and vegans. A six-barrel brewery is also owned at the Old Brewery, the Old Royal Naval College in Greenwich and is used to brew limited edition beers.

London Pale Ale (OG 1043, ABV 4.3%)
Amber-coloured best bitter with a citrus hop aroma. The malty sweetness is balanced by strong bitter hops on the palate that fade in the slightly dry finish.

Medieval

Home Farm, New Road, Colston Bassett, Nottinghamshire, NG12 3FQ ☎ 07552 798027 ⊕ medievalbeers.co.uk

⊗ Medieval started production in 2012 in Nottingham and moved to its current site at Colston Bassett later that year. The 10-barrel plant is used to produce 45 casks a week.

Chivalry (OG 1038, ABV 3.8%)
Pale session ale with a balanced combination of malt and hop.

Knighthood (OG 1042, ABV 4.2%)
Amber-coloured ale with a deep hoppy taste.

Crusader (OG 1044, ABV 4.4%)
Pale ale that is slightly sweet with a refreshing citrus finish.

Melbourn

All Saints Brewery, All Saints Street, Stamford, Lincolnshire, PE9 2PA
☎ (01780) 752186
Tours by arrangement

A famous Stamford brewery that opened in 1825 and closed in 1974. It reopened in 1994 and is owned by Samuel Smith of Tadcaster (qv). Melbourn brews four handcrafted, organic fruit beers (Cherry, Strawberry, Apricot and Raspberry) using the antique steam-driven brewing equipment. The beers are all suitable for vegans and are organic. Sold in bottles only, they are not bottle conditioned.

Melwood SIBA

7 Stanley Grange, Knowsley Park, Merseyside, L34 4AR
☎ (0151) 214 3340 ⊕ melwoodbeer.co.uk

Melwood began brewing in 2013 using a five-barrel plant. Seasonal beers are available as well as monthly specials in the Icons of Rock series.

Lovelight (OG 1038, ABV 3.8%)
Light, hoppy blonde beer. Refreshing with tons of hop aroma and a crisp biting flavour.

Equinox (OG 1040, ABV 4%)
English pale session bitter.

Deadhead (OG 1041, ABV 4.1%)
A robust, hoppy beer with a fruity flavour and aroma.

Citradelic (OG 1051, ABV 5.1%)
A light pale ale with grapefruit, lychee and gooseberry aromas.

Mercian

Tyr Add, Station Terrace, Llanybydder, Carmarthenshire, SA40 9XX
☎ (01570) 481280
✉ info@mercianbreweryltd.co.uk

Brewer Andy Abram decided to combine his profession as a medieval historian and enthusiasm for traditional, characterful beers by setting up a small, locally-based brewery in 2013. Beers are available at beer festivals and food fairs.

Warrior King (OG 1040, ABV 4%)
Pale ale, fruity with a light hoppy finish.

Leofric's Tipple (OG 1048, ABV 4.6%)
Dark, smooth beer with a distinctive roasted malt flavour and rich hop aroma.

Thirsty Lady (OG 1046, ABV 4.6%)

Merlin SIBA

3 Spring Bank Farm, Congleton Road, Arclid, Cheshire, CW11 2UD
☎ (01477) 500893 ⊕ merlinbrewing.co.uk
Tours by arrangement

Established in 2010 using an eight-barrel plant in a farm unit just outside Sandbach, Merlin is a family-run concern. The beers are principally supplied to outlets within a 30-mile radius. The plant has capacity for expansion, and helps its environment by disposing of spent grain and water on the farm. Bottle-conditioned beers are available.

King's Ale (OG 1036, ABV 3.6%)
A light brown easy-drinking bitter with a slight floral and spicy aroma.

Merlin's Gold (OG 1038, ABV 3.8%)
Light golden ale with rounded floral citrus flavours.

Excalibur (OG 1039, ABV 3.9%)
A light-coloured session ale, hoppy flavours are accompanied by a faint sweetness.

Spellbound (OG 1040, ABV 4%)
A full-flavoured bitter, light chestnut in colour with a dry finish.

The Wizard (OG 1042, ABV 4.2%)
A hoppy, bitter, golden-coloured ale with generous hints of grapefruit flavour.

Dragonslayer (OG 1056, ABV 5.6%)

A dark brew with complex flavours.

Merrimen (NEW) SIBA

Unit 12, Litchborough Industrial Estate, Northampton Road, Litchborough, Northamptonshire, NN12 8JB
☎ (01327) 831308 ⊕ merrimen.co.uk

Merrimen Brewing took over Hoggleys eight-barrel plant in Litchborough in 2013, after striking a deal for six months training from owner Roy Crutchley. Outlets include pubs and off-licences in Northampton, Coventry and surrounding areas. All beers are also available bottle-conditioned. Look out for their van, registration BOOS MEN. Further beers are planned.

Merri One (OG 1033, ABV 3.6%)
A light amber ale with medium bitterness, combining three spicy hops.

Merri Weather (OG 1038, ABV 4%)
Rich golden beer with a refreshing flavour.

Be Merri (OG 1042, ABV 4.5%)
A robust bitter.

Merry Miner

Unit 20-21, Grendon House Farm, Grendon, Warwickshire, CV9 3DT ☎ 07811 932721
⊕ merryminerbrewery.com
Tours by arrangement

Merry Miner commenced brewing in 2010. The brewery is based in farm buildings on the outskirts of the village of Grendon, near Atherstone. The brewery and beers are named after the brewer's former occupation.

Miners Best Bitter (OG 1035, ABV 3.7%)
A pale, smooth traditional best bitter with a crisp bitter aftertaste.

Warwickshire's Finest (OG 1036, ABV 3.8%)
Light amber-coloured session bitter.

Self Rescuer (OG 1039, ABV 3.9%)
Deep golden in colour with a pleasing bitterness and a smooth malty aftertaste.

Davy's Lamp (OG 1038, ABV 4%)
Pale, full-flavoured bitter.

Bevin Boys (OG 1039, ABV 4.1%)
An American-style IPA full of character and aromas with a pleasant finish.

Cap Lamp (OG 1039, ABV 4.2%)
Mid gold-coloured beer with a refreshing crisp bitterness.

Deputy Drop (OG 1040, ABV 4.3%)

Going Underground (OG 1041, ABV 4.4%)
Refreshing amber-coloured beer.

Pit Pony (OG 1041, ABV 4.5%)
Deep golden-coloured smooth bitter.

Methane (OG 1045, ABV 5%)
Light golden bitter. Citrus bitter finish.

Mersea Island

Rewsalls Lane, East Mersea, Essex, CO5 8SX
☎ (01206) 385900 ☎ 07970 070399
⊕ merseabrewery.co.uk
Shop & Café Wed-Sun 10.30am-4pm, closed Mon & Tue

The brewery was established at Mersea Island Vineyard in 2005, producing cask and bottle-conditioned beers. The brewery supplies several local pubs on a guest beer basis as well as most local beer festivals. The brewery holds its own festival of Essex-produced ales over the four-day Easter weekend.

Mersea Mud (OG 1036, ABV 3.8%)
An easy-drinking mild with a refreshingly malty flavour.

Yo Boy! (OG 1038, ABV 3.8%)
A session bitter with a long-lasting bitterness on the finish.

Lion Bitter (OG 1038, ABV 3.9%)
A pale amber-coloured bitter with nutty and caramel flavours and a smooth finish.

Gold (OG 1043, ABV 4.4%)
A refreshing golden Pilsner-style ale.

Skippers (OG 1047, ABV 4.8%)
Dark amber in colour with a malty flavour and smooth hoppy bitterness.

Oyster Stout (OG 1048, ABV 5%)
A stout with local Mersea Island oysters added, giving it a distinct, unique flavour.

Middle Earth

Rowditch Inn, 246 Uttoxeter Road, Derby, DE22 3LL
☎ 07504 304564

Office: 53 Springfield Road, Etwall, Derbyshire, DE65 6JZ ⊕ mebrewco.com

Set up in 2011, Middle Earth uses the 3.75 barrel plant based at the Rowditch Inn in Derby (also used by the Rowditch Brewery). Steve Twells (the Rowditch brewer) established Middle Earth as a separate venture to utilise spare plant capacity to produce different brews for free trade sale. He has employed someone to help with the brewing with the intention of increasing output as the customer base is developed.

Dragons Gold (OG 1041, ABV 4.1%)
A crisp and refreshing golden session bitter.

Rivendale (OG 1044, ABV 4.3%)
A well-balanced golden bitter.

Honey Dragon (OG 1044, ABV 4.5%)
Well-balanced golden bitter with subtle honey notes.

Tree Beer'd (OG 1046, ABV 4.5%)
Triple-hopped premium strength golden ale.

Black Rose (OG 1048, ABV 4.6%)
Complex malt flavours, chocolate predominates, combined with subtle ginger.

Fellowship (OG 1051, ABV 5%)
Triple-hopped golden ale.

Mount Doom IPA (OG 1053, ABV 5.3%)
A well-hopped IPA with complex hop flavours without the associated high bitterness.

IPA (OG 1058, ABV 5.9%)
A well-balanced IPA, smooth on the palate with some dark malt flavours.

Mighty Oak

14b West Station Yard, Spital Road, Maldon, Essex, CM9 6TW
☎ (01621) 843713 ⊕ mightyoakbrewing.co.uk

Shop Mon-Fri 9am-5pm
Tours by arrangement

Mighty Oak was formed in 1996 and has expanded considerably following a move to Maldon in 2001. Current capacity is 8,000 barrels per year following the acquisition of an adjacent building and enlarged plant. 350 outlets are supplied. Twelve monthly ales are brewed based on a theme, which for 2015 is Beatles songs.

IPA (OG 1031.5, ABV 3.5%)
Light-bodied, pale session bitter. Hop notes are initially suppressed by a delicate sweetness but the aftertaste is more assertive.

Oscar Wilde (OG 1039.5, ABV 3.7%)
Roasty dark mild with suggestions of forest fruits and dark chocolate. A sweet taste yields to a more bitter finish.

Captain Bob (OG 1039.5, ABV 3.8%)
A traditional deep amber bitter with a fruity and hoppy aroma. There is a slight sweet maltiness that balances an easy-going bitterness, followed by hints of gooseberry, elderflower and grape in the finish.

Maldon Gold (OG 1039.5, ABV 3.8%)
Pale golden ale with a sharp citrus note moderated by honey and biscuity malt.

Kings (OG 1042.6, ABV 4.2%)
A deep golden beer bursting with hoppy fruitiness. The orange, nectarine and passion fruit flavours last long into the finish.

English Oak (OG 1047.9, ABV 4.8%)
Strong tawny, fruity bitter with caramel, butterscotch and vanilla. A gentle hop character is present throughout.

Mile Tree SIBA

Mile Tree Lane, Wisbech, Cambrideshire, PE13 4TR
☎ 07858 930363 miletreebrewery.co.uk

Mile Tree began brewing in 2012 using a five-barrel plant. Special and bottle-conditioned beers are available. Local outlets and beer festivals are supplied.

Milestone SIBA

Great North Road, Cromwell, Newark, Nottinghamshire, NG23 6JE
☎ (01636) 822255 milestonebrewery.co.uk
Shop Mon-Fri 8am-5pm, Sat 9am-3pm
Tours by arrangement

Established in 2005, Milestone currently brew on a 12-barrel plant. More than 150 outlets are supplied. Seasonal and bottle-conditioned beers are available.

Lion's Pride (OG 1038, ABV 3.8%)
A copper-coloured session ale.

Shine On (OG 1039, ABV 4%)
A straw-coloured session ale with floral and citrus notes.

Loxley Ale (OG 1042, ABV 4.2%)
A golden ale with a subtle hint of honey.

Black Pearl (OG 1043, ABV 4.3%)
A traditional Irish-style stout.

Crusader (OG 1044, ABV 4.4%)

Rich Ruby (OG 1044, ABV 4.5%)
A rich, smooth, creamy Celtic red ale.

American Pale Ale (OG 1046, ABV 4.6%)
A blonde, hoppy, citrus ale.

Olde English (OG 1049, ABV 4.9%)
Full-bodied winter warmer with a nutty finish.

Game Keeper (OG 1052, ABV 5.2%)

Raspberry Wheat Beer (OG 1055, ABV 5.6%)
Continental-style ale infused with fresh fruit.

Milk Street SIBA

Griffin, 25 Milk Street, Frome, Somerset, BA11 3DB
☎ (01373) 467766 milkstreetbrewery.co.uk
Tours by arrangement

Milk Street was established in 1999 in a former porn cinema situated behind the pub. The cinema is long gone and now houses the brewery, which expanded in 2005 and is now capable of producing 30 barrels per week. It mainly produces for its own estate of three outlets with direct delivery to pubs in a 30-mile radius. Wholesalers are used to distribute the beers further afield. Seasonal beers are available.

Folklore (ABV 3.9%)
A dark ruby ale with flavours of caramel and dry biscuit.

Funky Monkey (OG 1040, ABV 4%)
Copper-coloured summer ale with fruity flavours and aromas. A dry finish with developing bitterness and an undertone of citrus fruit.

The Usual (OG 1045, ABV 4.4%)
Pear drops meets orange marmalade notes, offering a restrained sweetness that is counter-pointed by a dry, bitter, grainy finish.

Zig-Zag Stout (OG 1046, ABV 4.5%)
A dark ruby stout with characteristic roastiness and dryness with bitter chocolate and citrus fruit in the background.

Beer (OG 1049, ABV 5%)
A blonde beer with musky hoppiness and citrus fruit on the nose, while more fruit surges through on the palate before the bittersweet finish.

Mill Green SIBA

White Horse, Edwardstone, Sudbury, Suffolk, CO10 5PX
☎ (01787) 211118 millgreenbrewery.co.uk

Mill Green started brewing in 2008 in a new complex behind the White Horse pub in Edwardstone. It has won awards for environmental innovation. The brewing liquor is heated by solar panels and a wood-fired boiler while a wind turbine supplements power on site. A 10-barrel fermentation run is used to produce a number of seasonal and one-off brews in addition to the regular range.

Mawkin Mild (OG 1028, ABV 2.9%)
A complex mild, with a strong aroma and flavour for such a low gravity beer. Bitter coffee notes in the taste and aftertaste.

White Horse Bitter (OG 1036, ABV 3.6%)
A traditional session bitter with a spicy, bitter, lasting finish.

Loveleys Fair (OG 1040, ABV 4%)
A modern-style pale ale, golden in colour and heavily hopped with a tangy citrus bite.

Tornado Smith (OG 1042, ABV 4.3%)
Fruity pale ale, strong on hop.

Good Ship Arbella (OG 1054, ABV 5.4%)
A hoppy American-style pale ale.

Millis SIBA

St Margaret's Farm, St Margaret's Road, South Darenth, Dartford, Kent, DA4 9LB
☎ (01322) 866233 ⊕ millisbrewing.com

John and Miriam Millis started with a 0.5-barrel plant at their home in Gravesend. Demand outstripped the facility and Millis moved in 2003 to its current location – a former farm cold store – using a 10-barrel plant. They now supply around 40 outlets within a 50-mile radius. Wetherspoon's pubs are supplied within a 30-mile radius with Kentish Gold (ABV 4.8%). Seasonal and bottle-conditioned beers are available.

Gravesend Guzzler (OG 1037, ABV 3.7%)
Pale, easy-drinking, fruity session beer.

Dartford Wobbler (OG 1043, ABV 4.3%)
A tawny-coloured, full-bodied best bitter with complex malt and hop flavours and a long, clean, slightly roasted finish.

Millstone SIBA

Unit 4, Vale Mill, Micklehurst Road, Mossley, nr Oldham, OL5 9JL
☎ (01457) 835835 ⊕ millstonebrewery.co.uk

Established in 2003 by Nick Boughton and Jon Hunt, the brewery is located in an 18th-century textile mill. The eight-barrel plant produces a range of pale, hoppy beers and a traditional stout. More than 40 regular outlets are supplied.

Vale Mill (OG 1039, ABV 3.9%)
A pale gold-coloured session bitter with a floral and spicy aroma building on a crisp and refreshing taste.

Three Shires Bitter (OG 1040, ABV 4%)
Yellow beer with hop and fruit aroma. Fresh citrus fruit, hops and bitterness in the taste and aftertaste.

Tiger Rut (OG 1040, ABV 4%)
A pale, hoppy ale with a distinctive citrus/grapefruit aroma.

Stout (OG 1049, ABV 4.5%)
A traditional dry stout; pale chocolate malt, roasted barley, and a hint of sweetness to the aroma.

True Grit (OG 1040, ABV 5%)
A well-hopped strong ale with a mellow bitterness and a citrus/grapefruit aroma.

For the Rising Sun, Mossley:

Rising Sunsation (OG 1050, ABV 4.7%)
A pale dry bitter on the stronger side with hints of pine.

Milltown SIBA

The Brewery, The Old Railway Goods Yard, Scar Lane, Milnsbridge, Huddersfield, West Yorkshire, HD3 4PE
☎ 07946 589645 ⊕ milltownbrewing.co.uk
Tours by arrangement

Milltown began brewing in 2011 using a four-barrel plant. Seasonal and special beers are brewed.

Golden Hop (OG 1037, ABV 3.8%)

Slubbers Gold (OG 1040, ABV 4.2%)

Milton SIBA

Pegasus House, Pembroke Avenue, Waterbeach, Cambridgeshire, CB25 9PY
☎ (01223) 862067 ⊕ miltonbrewery.co.uk
Tours by arrangement

The brewery has grown steadily since it was founded in 1999 and now operates pubs in Cambridge, London, Peterborough and Norwich through a sister company. In 2012 the brewery moved to larger premises in the village of Waterbeach.

Minotaur (OG 1035, ABV 3.3%)
A dark ruby mild with liquorice and raisin fruit throughout. Light dry finish.

Dionysus (OG 1037, ABV 3.6%)
Yellow bitter with good balance of biscuity malt and citrus hop. Some malt and hops linger on long, dry aftertaste.

Tiki (OG 1038, ABV 3.8%)
Straw-coloured golden ale with passion fruit, grapefruit and lemon hop character. Dry, slightly astringent aftertaste.

Justinian (OG 1039, ABV 3.9%)
Straw-coloured bitter with pink grapefruit hop character and light malt softness. Very dry finish.

Pegasus (OG 1043, ABV 4.1%)
Malty amber medium-bodied bitter with faint hops. Bittersweet aftertaste.

Sparta (OG 1043, ABV 4.3%)
A yellow/gold best bitter with floral hops, kiwi fruit and balancing malt softness which fades to leave long dry finish.

Nero (OG 1050, ABV 5%)
A complex black beer comprising a blend of milk chocolate, raisins and liquorice. Roast malt and fruit completes the experience.

Cyclops (OG 1055, ABV 5.3%)
Deep copper-coloured ale, with a rich hoppy aroma and full body; fruit and malt notes develop in the finish.

Marcus Aurelius (OG 1075, ABV 7.4%)
A powerful black brew brimming with raisins and liquorice. Big balanced finish.

Mitchell Krause SIBA

The Tractor Shed, Calva Brow, Workington, Cumbria, CA14 1DB
☎ (01900) 68860 ☎ 07825 580694
⊕ mkbrewing.co.uk

Mitchell Krause was set up in 2009, originally with its beers contract brewed. A new brewery opened in 2013 in an old tractor shed on the family farm. A cold store was fitted in 2014. The brewery focuses on keg and bottled continental-style beers although Hefe Weiss (ABV 5%) is also available bottle-conditioned. Its first cask-conditioned beer was produced in 2014.

Mithril

Mithril, Aldbrough St John, Richmond, North Yorkshire, DL11 7TL

THE BREWERIES

☎ (01325) 374817 🌐 mithrilales.co.uk

Mithril started brewing in 2010 in an old stables opposite the brewer's house on a 2.5-barrel plant. Owner/brewer Pete Fenwick. a well-known craft brewer, brews twice a week to supply the local area of Darlington and Richmond. A new beer is brewed every week.

Dere Street (OG 1039, ABV 3.8%)
An amber, fruity and malty session beer with a bitter finish.

A66 (OG 1041, ABV 4%)
A crisp, refreshing, satisfying golden beer. A dry bitterness, with a lingering citrus and spicy hop taste and aroma.

Flower Power (OG 1044, ABV 4.3%)
A pale ale with a massive citrus, fruity hop flavour. Hints of grapefruit and floral notes on the tongue from the late addition of elderflowers.

Mix (NEW)

3 Cemmaes Court Road, Hemel Hempstead, Hertfordshire, HP1 1ST 🌐 mixbrewery.co.uk

A small brewery established in 2013 and based in a domestic garage. Beer is produced in small batches allowing for an ever-changing range.

Mobberley SIBA

Dairy Farm, Church Lane, Mobberley, Cheshire, WA16 7RA
☎ (01565) 873601 🌐 mobberleyfineales.co.uk

Mobberley began brewing in 2011 in an old milking parlour on a working farm in the heart of the Cheshire countryside.

CropCutter (OG 1026, ABV 2.6%)
A fruity, golden ale with a lingering aftertaste.

HedgeHopper (OG 1039, ABV 3.8%)
A golden refreshing fine ale, light and aromatic.

RoadRunner (OG 1039, ABV 3.8%)
A light-coloured pale ale with a delicate, light spicy finish.

WhirlyBird (OG 1040, ABV 4%)
Pale ale, sweet, full-bodied and complex with a smooth, subtle zesty finish.

BarnBuster (OG 1042, ABV 4.2%)
A rich amber-coloured ale, full-bodied yet smooth. Rich in colour and taste, mildly bitter with a distant hint of spiciness.

Moles SIBA

5 Merlin Way, Bowerhill, Melksham, Wiltshire, SN12 6TJ
☎ (01225) 708842 🌐 molesbrewery.com
Shop Mon-Fri 9am-5pm, Sat 9am-12pm
Tours by arrangement

Moles was established in 1982 by Roger Catte, a former Ushers brewer, using his nickname for the brewery. 10 pubs are owned, all serving cask beer. More than 200 outlets are supplied direct. Seasonal beers: see website.

Tap Bitter (OG 1035, ABV 3.5%)
A session bitter with a smooth, malty flavour and clean bitter finish.

Gold (OG 1038, ABV 3.8%)
Golden refreshingly hoppy beer with a citrus zest flavour and tropical fruit aroma.

Best Bitter (OG 1040, ABV 4%)
A well-balanced, amber-coloured bitter, clean, dry and malty with some bitterness, and delicate floral hop flavour.

Elmo's Fire (OG 1044, ABV 4.4%)
Medium-bodied pale ale. Refreshingly bitter with a fruity, spicy aroma and a long bitter finish.

Landlords Choice (OG 1045, ABV 4.5%)
A dark, strong, smooth porter, with a rich fruity palate and malty finish.

Rucking Mole (OG 1045, ABV 4.5%)
A chestnut-coloured premium ale, fruity and malty with a smooth bitter finish.

Mole Catcher (OG 1050, ABV 5%)
A copper-coloured ale with a spicy hop aroma and taste, and a long bitter finish.

Molson Coors SIBA

Molson Coors (Burton): 137 High Street, Burton upon Trent, Staffordshire, DE14 1JZ
☎ (01283) 511000

Molson Coors (Alton): Manor Park Brewery, Alton, Hampshire, GU34 2PS

Molson Coors (Tadcaster): Tower Brewery, Wetherby Road, Tadcaster, North Yorkshire, LS24 9SD
🌐 molsoncoorsbrewers.com

Molson Coors is the result of a merger between Molson of Canada and Coors of Colorado, US. Coors established itself in Europe in 2002 by buying part of the former Bass brewing empire, when Interbrew (now AB InBev) was instructed by the British government to divest itself of some of its interests in Bass. Coors owns several cask ale brands. It brews 110,000 barrels of cask beer a year (under licensing arrangements with other brewers) and also provides a further 50,000 barrels of cask beer from other breweries. In 2011 Molson Coors bought Sharp's brewery in Cornwall in a bid to increase its stake in the cask beer sector. No cask ale is produced in Burton. Home of the multi award winning Worthington White Shield.

Moncada SIBA

Unit 1, Buspace Studios, Conlan Street, London, W10 5AT
☎ (020) 8964 0829 🌐 moncadabrewery.co.uk

Moncada began brewing in 2011 using a six-barrel plant. Bottle-conditioned and seasonal beers are available.

Notting Hill Bitter (ABV 3.7%)
Brown bitter with a good balance of hops and sweetness and a pleasant finish.

Notting Hill Blonde (ABV 4.2%)
Continental-style golden beer with a smooth mouthfeel, sweetish with a touch of honey and fruity hops. Short, crisp finish.

Notting Hill Amber (ABV 4.7%)
Full-bodied creamy amber-coloured beer with the citrus aroma and flavour well balanced by the sweet biscuit character.

Notting Hill Porter (ABV 5%)

Rich black porter with dark roast bitterness and black treacle flavours, which linger in the finish. Some faint hoppy notes.

Notting Hill Stout (ABV 5%)
A dry malty beer with roast, caramel and a little malty sweetness. The pleasant aftertaste is long and lingering.

Notting Hill Ruby Rye (ABV 5.2%)
Sweetish ruby red beer with a full fruity aroma, a creamy mouthfeel and a little roast throughout.

Monty's SIBA

Unit 1, Castle Works, Hendomen, Montgomery, Powys, SY15 6HA
☎ (01686) 668933 montysbrewery.co.uk

Monty's began brewing in 2009 and was the first brewery in Montgomeryshire since the Eagle brewery in Newtown closed in 1990. Three pubs are owned by the brewery's sister company, Hophouse Inns; the Sportsman in Newtown, the Red Lion in Caersws and the Abermule in Abermule. Seasonal and bottle-conditioned beers are available.

Old Jailhouse (OG 1039.5, ABV 3.9%)

Midnight (OG 1040, ABV 4%)
A dark, smooth, creamy stout.

Moonrise (OG 1040, ABV 4%)
A copper-coloured, gently malty, well-balanced traditional brew.

MPA (OG 1040.5, ABV 4%)

Sunshine (OG 1041, ABV 4.2%)
A golden, hoppy, floral/citrus ale with a pleasantly dry finish.

Masquerade (ABV 4.6%)
A gluten-free premium golden bitter with tropical fruit flavour and Citra hop aroma.

Mischief (OG 1050, ABV 5%)
Strong golden ale with a good balance of malt and hop bitterness.

Moonshine

Hill Farm, Shelford Road, Fulbourn, Cambridgeshire, CB21 5EQ ☎ 07906 066794

Office: 28 Radegund Road, Cambridge, CB1 3RS
moonshinebrewery.co.uk

Established in 2004, the brewery moved in 2010 to larger premises incorporating a five-barrel plant. Locally-produced ingredients are used including water from the brewery's own well. It mainly concentrates on supplying CAMRA beer festivals, with 20 outlets supplied direct. Bottle-conditioned beers are available.

Trumpington Tipple (OG 1038, ABV 3.6%)

Cambridge Pale Ale (OG 1038, ABV 3.8%)
Golden beer, light with a semi dry, citrus finish.

Shelford Crier (OG 1038, ABV 3.8%)

Harvest Moon Mild (OG 1040, ABV 3.9%)

Barton Bitter (OG 1040, ABV 4%)
Pale brown with red and amber highlights, balanced malt and hops and a fruity backdrop on both nose and palate. A bittersweet flavour dries as fruit and sweetness diminish.

Heavenly Matter (OG 1041, ABV 4.1%)

Reach for the Moon (OG 1040, ABV 4.1%)
Deep ruby-coloured bitter with a hoppy aroma and aftertaste.

Blueberry Ale (OG 1040, ABV 4.2%)

Cambridge Best Bitter (OG 1041, ABV 4.2%)

Nightwatch Porter (OG 1043, ABV 4.5%)

Black Hole Stout (OG 1048, ABV 5%)

Hot Numbers Coffee Stout (OG 1057, ABV 5.5%)
Dark roasted malt with balanced coffee and hops. The addition of lactose adds sweetness to the flavour

Chocolate Orange Stout (OG 1068, ABV 6.7%)

Ison (OG 1074, ABV 8%)

Wheat Wine Ale (OG 1091, ABV 10.5%)
A barley wine produced using wheat instead of barley.

Moonstone

Ministry of Ale, 9 Trafalgar Street, Burnley, Lancashire, BB11 1TQ
☎ (01282) 830909 moonstonebrewery.co.uk
Tours by arrangement

A small, three-barrel brewery, based in the front room of the Ministry of Ale pub. Brewing started in 2001 and beer is only available in the pub.

Black Star Dark (OG 1037, ABV 3.4%)

Moor SIBA

Days Road, Bristol, BS2 0QS ☎ 07887 556521
moorbeer.co.uk
Tours by arrangement

Moor Beer was founded in 1996, originally brewing in Long Sutton. Since being relaunched in 2007 the brewery has gone through a steady expansion programme, resulting in the relocation to larger premises in central Bristol featuring a shop and brewery tap. All beers are produced without isinglass finings and are naturally hazy. Specials and bottle-conditioned beers are available.

Revival (OG 1038, ABV 3.8%)
A hoppy and refreshing pale ale.

Nor'Hop (OG 1041, ABV 4.1%)
Pale, hoppy, modern ale showcasing northern hemisphere hops.

So'Hop (OG 1041, ABV 4.1%)
Pale, hoppy, modern ale showcasing southern hemisphere hops.

Raw (OG 1043, ABV 4.3%)
Dark amber-coloured, complex, full-bodied beer with fruity notes.

Amoor (OG 1045, ABV 4.5%)
Dark brown/black beer with an initially fruity taste leading to roast malt with a little bitterness. A slightly sweet malty finish.

Dark Alliance (OG 1045, ABV 4.5%)
Hoppy coffee stout.

Illusion (OG 1045, ABV 4.5%)
Session strength version of a Black IPA, powerfully hopped.

Confidence (OG 1046, ABV 4.6%)
Hoppy American-style red ale.

Ported Amoor (OG 1047, ABV 4.7%)

Amoor with added Reserve Port.

Radiance (OG 1048, ABV 5%)
Continental blonde. Unfined and naturally hazy.

Hoppiness (OG 1065, ABV 6.5%)
All the rich malt and fruit flavours of a barley wine combined with the hoppy crispness of a pale ale.

Old Freddy Walker (OG 1073, ABV 7.3%)
Rich, dark, strong ale with a fruity complex taste, leaving a fruitcake finish.

JJJ IPA (OG 1085, ABV 9%)
Copper-coloured, new world triple IPA. Immensely hoppy and malty.

Moorhouse's SIBA

The Brewery, Moorhouse Street, Burnley, Lancashire, BB11 5EN
☎ (01282) 422864 moorhouses.co.uk
Tours by arrangement

Established in 1865 as a soft drinks manufacturer, the brewery started producing cask-conditioned ale in 1978. A new 40,000-barrel brewhouse and visitor centre opened in 2012. The company owns six pubs. Monthly special beers: see website.

Black Cat (OG 1036, ABV 3.4%)
A dark mild-style beer with delicate chocolate and coffee roast flavours and a crisp, bitter finish.

Premier Bitter (OG 1036, ABV 3.7%)
A clean and satisfying bitter aftertaste rounds off this well-balanced hoppy, amber session bitter.

Pride of Pendle (OG 1040, ABV 4.1%)
Well-balanced amber best bitter with a fresh initial hoppiness and a mellow, malt-driven body.

Blond Witch (OG 1045, ABV 4.5%)
Light ale, fruity with lasting finish.

Pendle Witches Brew (OG 1050, ABV 5.1%)
Well-balanced, full-bodied, malty beer with a long, complex finish.

MòR SIBA

Old Mill, Kellas, Angus, DD5 3PD ☎ 07884 346351
morbrewing.co.uk
Tours by arrangement

Retired lifeboat coxswain Jim Hughan teamed up with family friend Ross Niven to establish this 2.5-barrel brewery in 2012. In 2014 this was expanded to a 4.3-barrel plant with six fermenters. Seasonal, special and bottle-conditioned ales are available.

MòR-Calm and Wise! (OG 1034, ABV 3.4%)
A yellow-coloured ale bursting with zingy hops. A pepper and lemon flavour with a smooth aftertaste.

MòR Tea, Vicar? (OG 1038, ABV 3.8%)
A pale amber bitter with a pleasant balance of malt and hops. With a malty, fruity aroma and a pronounced bitter finish, this is a well-balanced, refreshing session ale.

MòR-Bidly Dark! (OG 1039, ABV 3.9%)
A dark, chocolate, malty mild, lightly hopped with an aromatic vanilla aftertaste.

MòR-Scode! (OG 1040, ABV 4%)
A light citrus session ale with overtones of grapefruit and a smooth finish.

MòR-Ish! (OG 1042, ABV 4.2%)
A bright amber ale with a malty, fruity aroma and a well-balanced and controlled bitter finish.

MòR Please! (OG 1045, ABV 4.5%)
This clean-tasting, full-bodied golden bitter is bursting with malt and hops with just a hint of honey and a good hoppy finish.

Mordue SIBA

Units D1 and D2, Narvic Way, Tyne Tunnel Estate, North Shields, Tyne & Wear, NE29 7XJ
☎ (0191) 296 1879 morduebrewery.com
Shop: see website for opening times
Tours by arrangement

In 1995 the Fawson brothers revived the Mordue Brewery name (the original closed in 1879). High demand required moves to larger premises and replacing the original five-barrel plant with a 20-barrel one. The beers are distributed nationally and 300 outlets are supplied direct. Seasonal beers: see website.

Five Bridge Bitter (OG 1038, ABV 3.6%)
Crisp, golden beer with a good hint of hops, the bitterness carries on in the finish. A good session bitter.

Northumbrian Blonde (OG 1040, ABV 4%)
A blonde beer with a citrus aroma and hoppy finish.

A'l Wheat Pet (OG 1041, ABV 4.1%)
Well-balanced and hoppy copper-coloured brew with a long, bitter finish.

Workie Ticket (OG 1045, ABV 4.5%)
Complex tasty bitter with plenty of malt and hops, long satisfying bitter finish.

Radgie Gadgie (OG 1048, ABV 4.8%)
Strong, easy-drinking bitter with plenty of fruit and hops.

IPA (OG 1051, ABV 5.1%)
Easy-drinking golden ale with plenty of hops; the bitterness carries on in the finish.

Morland

See Greene King

Morton

Unit 10, Essington Light Industrial Estate, Essington, Staffordshire, WV11 2BH ☎ 07988 69647

Office: 96 Brewood Road, Coven, Staffordshire, WV9 5EF mortonbrewery.co.uk
Tours by arrangement

Morton was established in 2007 on a three-barrel plant. The brewery moved to Essington in 2008 to increase production. Essington Ale was introduced to celebrate the move and became so popular with the locals that a full range of Essington beers is brewed regularly. 30 outlets are supplied direct plus various beer festivals and a selection is always available at the brewery's own micropub, Hail to the Ale. Seasonal, special and bottle-conditioned beers: see website.

Essington Dark Mild (OG 1036, ABV 3.6%)

Essington Bitter (OG 1037, ABV 3.8%)
Fruity, hoppy session ale.

Merry Mount (OG 1037, ABV 3.8%)

A traditional bitter.

Essington Blonde (OG 1039, ABV 4%)
Thirst quenching pale ale using American hops.

Essington Ale (OG 1041, ABV 4.2%)
A refreshing golden session ale.

Jelly Roll (OG 1041, ABV 4.2%)
A dry hopped best bitter.

Essington Gold (OG 1044, ABV 4.4%)
A refreshing golden ale.

Essington Supreme (OG 1046, ABV 4.6%)
A premium brown ale, dark and sweet.

Scottish Maiden (OG 1045, ABV 4.6%)
A malty premium bitter.

Essington IPA (OG 1046, ABV 4.8%)
Pale, hoppy and bitter.

Moulin

2 Baledmund Road, Moulin, Pitlochry, Perthshire, PH16 5EL
☎ (01796) 472196

Office: Moulin Hotel, 11-13 Kirkmicheal Road, Moulin, Pitlochry, PH16 5EH 🌐 moulinhotel.co.uk
Tours by arrangement

The brewery opened in 1995 to celebrate the Moulin Hotel's 300th anniversary. Two pubs are owned and four outlets are supplied. Bottle-conditioned beer is available.

Light (OG 1036, ABV 3.7%)
Thirst-quenching, straw-coloured session beer, with a light, hoppy, fruity balance, ending with a gentle, hoppy sweetness.

Braveheart (OG 1039, ABV 4%)
An amber bitter, with a delicate balance of malt and fruit and a Scottish-style sweetness.

Ale of Atholl (OG 1043.5, ABV 4.5%)
A reddish, quaffable, malty ale, with a solid body and a mellow finish.

Old Remedial (OG 1050.5, ABV 5.2%)
A distinctive and satisfying dark brown old ale, with roast malt to the fore and tannin in a robust taste.

Mountain Hare (NEW)

Mountain Hare Inn, Brynna Road, Brynnau Gwynion, CF35 6PG
☎ (01656) 860453 🌐 mountainhare.co.uk

Paul Jones, licensee of the Mountain Hare, finally realised his ambition of installing a brewery in his family-owned pub. A 1.5-barrel custom-built brewing plant was installed in the pub and the beer first went on sale in 2013. Further beers are planned.

First Gold (OG 1041, ABV 4.1%)
A golden, well-hopped bitter. The blend of three hops provides initial citrus fruit in the mouth giving way to a satisfying bitter finish.

Mouselow Farm

3 Mouselow Farm, Dinting, Derbyshire, SK13 7QQ
☎ 07920 048252 ✉ glossopowl@btinternet.com

Mouselow Farm began brewing in 2013 using a 2.5-barrel plant housed in a converted barn. Brewing is on a part-time basis, with regular monthly specials adding to the regular range. Local free houses and beer festivals are supplied.

Golden Gosling (OG 1037, ABV 3.6%)
Light, delicately-hopped bitter.

Udder the Influence (OG 1041, ABV 4%)
Medium-hopped session bitter.

Mr Grundy's SIBA

Georgian House Hotel, 34 Ashbourne Road, Derby, DE22 3AD
☎ (01332) 349806 🌐 mrgrundysbrewery.co.uk

The brewery opened in 2010 using a four-barrel plant constructed from made-to-measure vessels to fit into a converted bedroom. Beers are produced for the company's own tavern (Mr Grundy's) and hotels.

Trench Foot (OG 1038, ABV 3.8%)
Dark in colour with strong malt flavours with some bittering using traditional hops.

Passchendaele (OG 1039, ABV 3.9%)
An English straw-coloured, pale, sharp bitter with citrus overtones.

Bullet (OG 1043, ABV 4.3%)
Dark ale with a treacle aroma and a smooth rounded taste.

The Red Baron (OG 1043, ABV 4.3%)
A rich, malty, dark red-coloured bitter with strong caramel overtones, lightly hopped to allow the malt flavours to permeate.

No Man's Land (OG 1045, ABV 4.5%)
Dark in colour, yet hoppy, retaining the soft malty flavours of a traditional bitter.

Muirhouse

Unit 1, Enterprise Court, Manners Avenue, Manners Industrial Estate, Ilkeston, Derbyshire, DE7 8EW
☎ 07916 590525 🌐 muirhousebrewery.co.uk
Tours by arrangement

Muirhouse was established in 2009 in a domestic garage in Long Eaton, it expanded in 2011 to an industrial unit in Ilkeston where brewing takes place up to four times a week. Bottle-conditioned beers are available. The brewery tap is in Ilkeston.

Shunters Pole (OG 1040, ABV 3.8%)
A pale, refreshing, hoppy bitter.

Ruby Jewel (OG 1040, ABV 3.9%)
A ruby-coloured malty beer with tastes of toffee.

Shopping for Hops (OG 1040, ABV 3.9%)
Pale session beer with a citrus bitterness.

Buzzard Bitter (OG 1040, ABV 4%)

Fully Fitted Freight (OG 1041, ABV 4%)
A premium bitter with a fine blend of malt and hops and a distinctive finish.

Tick Tock (OG 1041, ABV 4%)

Magnum Mild (OG 1045, ABV 4.5%)
Dark, smooth, strong mild.

Pirate's Gold (OG 1045, ABV 4.5%)
Pale golden beer with hint of caramel.

Tractor Spotter (OG 1045, ABV 4.5%)

Lurch's Liquor (OG 1050, ABV 5%)
Sweet, smooth stout packed with dark malts.

Foundries IPA (OG 1052, ABV 5.2%)

Deceptive in strength, a blend of English and American hops.

Hat Trick IPA (OG 1052, ABV 5.2%)
Bittered with a citrus hop and finished with a hat trick of American hops.

Stumbling Around (OG 1050, ABV 5.2%)
Dark red, strong, malty beer.

Mulberry Duck

Elan Portway, Burghill, Herefordshire, HR4 8NF
☎ 07740 468675 🌐 mulberryduck.co.uk

Mulberry Duck opened in 2012 in a former dairy using a 3.75-barrel plant. Three beers are brewed, supplied to the local free trade.

Golden Sparkle (ABV 3.8%)

Amber Sparkle (ABV 4.1%)

The Wildfowler (ABV 4.1%)

Mumbles SIBA

Pilot Inn, 726 Mumbles Road, Mumbles, Swansea, SA3 4AQ ☎ 07897 895511 🌐 mumblesbrewery.co.uk

⊗ Mumbles Brewery was established in 2011 and began brewing in 2013 at the back of the Pilot Inn. Director/brewer Rob Turner supplies numerous pubs, mostly in the Swansea area. Seasonal beers may be available.

Mile (OG 1039, ABV 3.8%)
A session bitter, light in colour with lingering hop flavours.

Gold (OG 1043, ABV 4.3%)
A light, refreshing, thirst-quenching pale ale, golden in colour. Well-hopped, the lemon and lime flavours linger well.

Oystermouth Stout (OG 1045, ABV 4.4%)
A rich creamy head and dark roasted malt flavours distinguish this classic oyster stout.

Lifesaver Strong Bitter (OG 1052, ABV 5.1%)
A smooth, malty, bronze-coloured ale, deceptively easy-drinking, with a clean, rewarding hop finish.

India Pale Ale (OG 1054, ABV 5.3%)
A traditional IPA, light gold in colour. The beer is rounded and full-bodied.

Musket (NEW) SIBA

Loddington Farm, Loddington Lane, Linton, Kent, ME17 4AG ☎ 07967 127278 🌐 musketbrewery.co.uk

Musket began production in 2013 in refurbished mushroom sheds at Loddington Farm, in the heart of the Kent countryside. Seasonal beers: see website.

Fife & Drum (OG 1034, ABV 3.8%)
A golden ale with tastes and aromas of spice, honey, marmalade and a hint of wild blackcurrant.

Flintlock (OG 1037, ABV 4.2%)
A best bitter with spicy orange undertones and just a hint of marmalade.

Nailsworth SIBA

Village Inn, The Cross, Nailsworth, Gloucestershire, GL6 0HH ☎ 07963 200768
🌐 nailsworth-brewery.co.uk
Tours by arrangement

After 96 years commercial brewing returned to Nailsworth in 2004 in the form of a six-barrel microbrewery. Beers are mainly sold at the Village Inn above the brewery. Seasonal and bottle-conditioned beers are also available.

Alestock (OG 1036, ABV 3.6%)
A light-coloured ale full of elderflower notes.

Mayor's Bitter (OG 1042, ABV 4.3%)
A best bitter with malt textures complemented by a long-lasting taste of blackcurrant.

Old Rocky (OG 1044, ABV 4.4%)
Light IPA-style beer with loads of grapefruit flavour.

Town Crier (OG 1046, ABV 4.5%)
A premium ale with delicate grassy and floral overtones.

Red October (OG 1049, ABV 4.9%)
A ruby-coloured, rich and malty, well-balanced strong bitter.

Naked Beer (NEW) SIBA

Unit F, MMBC, 2-3 Commerce Way, Lancing, West Sussex, BN15 8TA
☎ (01903) 791230 🌐 nakedbeer.co.uk

Naked Beer began brewing in 2013. Established by Robert Thomas (previously with Ascot Brewery) and Deniz Oz, using a five-barrel plant.

Streaker (ABV 4%)
A session pale ale with a slight sweetness, fruit aromas and a dry finish.

Indecent Exposure (ABV 4.5%)
A slightly bitter porter with notes of dark fruit and roasted malts.

Freudian Slip (ABV 6.5%)
A dark-coloured beer with a smooth yet smoky nose, carrying a slightly nutty body, followed by a lasting sweetness.

Naked Brewer

Corner Pin, Palmerston Street, Westwood, Nottinghamshire, NG16 5HY ☎ 07908 531901
✉ cornerpinwestwood@hotmail.co.uk
Tours by arrangement

The brewery was set up in 2010 in a skittle alley behind the Corner Pin pub and can be viewed from the function room. Due to demand the skittle alley may need to be moved to allow for increased production. Beer is mainly brewed for the pub but is occasionally supplied to beer festivals or for swaps with other brewpubs.

Hopsession (OG 1038, ABV 3.8%)
A light amber bitter retaining a smooth creamy head, with a malty/strawlike aroma and crisp bitter finish.

Blush (OG 1045, ABV 4.5%)
A dark ruby bitter with caramel undertones and a mid bitter finish.

Palindrome (OG 1048, ABV 4.7%)

Nant SIBA

Penrhwylfa, Maenan, Llanrwst, LL26 0UA ☎ 07723 36862 🌐 bragdynant.co.uk

Nant commenced brewing in 2007 with a plant purchased from the Yorkshire Dales Brewery. Capacity is currently 10-15 nine gallon firkins a week. Seasonal and one-off beers are also produced.

Brenin (OG 1038, ABV 3.8%)
A light golden session ale with balanced hops and malt.

Cennin (OG 1039, ABV 3.9%)
A pale gold-coloured bitter brewed with fennel infusion.

Cwrw Coryn (OG 1042, ABV 4.2%)
Traditional amber-coloured beer. Slightly malty with good bitter overtones.

Chwaden Aur (OG 1043, ABV 4.3%)
Golden-coloured ale with a citrus aroma and full mouthfeel. Grapefruit and lemon citrus taste balance with biscuity malt for a long, fruity finish.

Rwster (OG 1046, ABV 4.6%)
Deep copper-coloured, sweet and malty ale.

Mwnci Nel (OG 1055, ABV 5.5%)
A special dark ale not excessively sweet but dominated by burnt chocolate flavours, balanced with hops.

Navigation SIBA

Trent Navigation Inn, 17 Meadow Lane, Nottingham, NG2 3HS
(0115) 986 9877 navigationbrewery.com
Tours by arrangement

Brewing began in 2012 in the old stable block of the Trent Navigation Inn. The brewery is owned by sister company Great Northern Inns and supplies cask beers to the pubs in its estate with guest beers being provided by brewery swaps.

Traditional (OG 1038, ABV 3.8%)
Traditional-style, amber-coloured, smooth, malty beer, well-balanced giving a mellow finish.

Pale Ale (OG 1039, ABV 3.9%)
Pale straw in colour, with a distinctive fruity nose, well hopped, which blends itself to a refreshing, sharp finish.

Golden (OG 1041.8, ABV 4.3%)
Medium-bodied and clean-tasting refreshing ale, fruit and malt on the nose, satisfying biscuit flavours with a lasting malty aftertaste.

Stout (OG 1043.5, ABV 4.4%)
Traditional, robust stout with liquorice, roast almonds and chocolate flavours perfectly balanced with a tight creamy head.

Classic IPA (OG 1050, ABV 5.2%)
Straw-coloured with powerful citrus fruit balanced with malty sweetness and robust bitter flavours.

Apus (OG 1053.5, ABV 5.5%)
American-style IPA brewed with lager malts and balanced with a full American hop. Deceptively drinkable with a lasting aftertaste.

Naylor's SIBA

Midland Mills, Station Road, Cross Hills, North Yorkshire, BD20 7DT
(01535) 637451 naylorsbrewery.com
Shop Mon-Fri 10am-5pm, Sat 10am-3pm
Tours by arrangement

Naylors started brewing in 2005 at the Old White Bear pub in Cross Hills. Expansion required a move to the current site in 2006 and included a rebranding of the beers. Further expansion in 2009 gave bigger facilities for brewing as well as a shop and bar. Around 200 outlets are supplied. Bottle-conditioned ales are available, suitable for vegetarians. Annual community cider pressing and fermentation is undertaken.

Velvet (OG 1039, ABV 3.9%)
Chocolate and roast aromas and flavours predominate in this dark brown mild which has an increasingly roast bitter finish.

Neath

Endeavour Close, Port Talbot, SA12 7PT 07772 468436 neathales.co.uk

Neath Ales was established in 2009 and produces a range of single hop variety cask and bottle-conditioned beers (the latter suitable for vegans). Specials beers and one-off brews are also available with some beers being released under the Black Falls brand name.

Firebrick (OG 1042, ABV 4.2%)
Amber-coloured best bitter with British hop flavour and aroma.

Witch Hunter (OG 1042, ABV 4.2%)
Well-balanced ruby ale with roasted malt and hop fruit flavours.

Deliverance (OG 1045, ABV 4.5%)
Smooth bronze-coloured beer.

Gold (OG 1050, ABV 5%)
Citrus/grapefruit hop aroma and flavour dominate this golden ale.

Black (OG 1055, ABV 5.5%)
Dark malt flavours are balanced by aggressive hopping rates making this strong black ale dangerously drinkable.

Nelson SIBA

Unit 2, Building 64, The Historic Dockyard, Chatham, Kent, ME4 4TE
(01634) 832828 nelsonbrewery.co.uk
Shop Mon-Fri 11am-4pm
Tours by arrangement

Based in Chatham's Historic Dockyard and brewing with a nautical theme, the brewery supplies award-winning ales direct to more than 300 outlets. Many of the cask ales are also available bottle conditioned. Seasonal and occasional beers: see website.

Pieces of Eight (OG 1040, ABV 3.8%)
A light, refreshing ale with full-flavoured hops and a hint of chocolate aftertaste.

Admiral IPA (OG 1040, ABV 4%)
A traditional IPA with a combination of citrus flavours on the palate.

Midshipman Dark Mild (OG 1040, ABV 4%)
A dark mild with a roasted aftertaste on the palate.

Trafalgar Bitter (OG 1040, ABV 4.1%)
A light golden ale that has a balanced taste of hops and malt giving a sweet and nutty finish.

Powder Monkey (OG 1043, ABV 4.3%)
A golden ale with a smooth aftertaste which leaves a sweetness on the palate.

Dogwatch Stout (OG 1044, ABV 4.5%)
A smooth, creamy stout that has a strong hop taste, leaving a smoky chocolate aftertaste.

Friggin' in the Riggin' (OG 1046, ABV 4.5%)
Drinkable premium bitter with smooth malt flavour and bittersweet aftertaste.

Pursers Pussy Porter (OG 1051, ABV 4.8%)
A traditional porter.

Nelson's Blood (OG 1062, ABV 6%)
A strong malty ale with mellow roast tones, slightly nutty and fruity, with a warm aftertaste.

Nene Valley SIBA

Oundle Wharf, Station Road, Oundle, Northamptonshire, PE8 4DE
☎ (01832) 272776 🌐 nenevalleybrewery.com
Shop Fri 4-7pm, Sat 10am-6pm (shop is manned by brewery staff in normal office hours)
Tours by arrangement

⊠ Nene Valley began brewing in 2011. As sales quickly outstripped supply, larger premises and new vessels were bought to increase capacity and the brewery moved to Oundle Wharf using a 15-barrel plant. Sales have expanded into London as well as Northamptonshire, Cambridgeshire and Lincolnshire. There are plans for a restaurant and brewery tap on site.

Simple Pleasures Ale (OG 1036, ABV 3.6%)
A light, clean and refreshing beer with a pleasing citrus hop aroma and flavour.

Blonde Session Ale (OG 1038, ABV 3.8%)

Dark Mild (OG 1038, ABV 3.8%)
A dark ruby mild with roasted grains giving hints of chocolate, coffee and liquorice.

Jim's Little Brother (OG 1038, ABV 3.8%)
A session strength IPA, warmly golden with pleasant passion fruit and grapefruit hop flavours.

Bitter (OG 1040, ABV 4.1%)

Australian Pale (OG 1044, ABV 4.4%)
A rich golden ale with a floral aroma preceding citrus and tropical fruit flavours.

Starless and Bible Black (OG 1046, ABV 4.5%)
Initial rich and fruity flavours give way to a chocolate and roasted finish.

Special Bitter (OG 1044, ABV 4.6%)
Chestnut in colour with plenty of maltiness. Balanced with late-hopped spicy character.

Big Bang Theory (OG 1051, ABV 5.3%)
A heavily-hopped strong bitter.

Jim Irving Pale (OG 1053, ABV 5.6%)
Full-bodied, with a big malty taste backed with zesty hop flavour. Named for the late Jim Irving who ran Smith's brewery in Oundle until its closure in 1962.

Fenland Farmhouse Saison (OG 1068, ABV 7.2%)
Refreshing with a hint of spice.

Nethergate SIBA

The Street, Pentlow, Essex, CO10 7JJ
☎ (01787) 283220 🌐 nethergatebrewery.co.uk
Shop 9am-5pm daily
Tours by arrangement

⊠ Starting at Clare in 1986 the brewery moved to Pentlow, Essex in 2005, where after large growth there is still room to expand. Seasonal beers are available. The brewery name, under new owners, was changed to Growler but in 2014 original owner Dick Burge returned and restored Nethergate.

IPA (OG 1036, ABV 3.5%) ◆
Bitter-tasting session beer with some fruit and malt balancing the predominate hop character. Dry aftertaste.

Priory Mild (OG 1036, ABV 3.5%) ◆
A 'black bitter' rather than a true mild. Strong roast and bitter tastes dominate throughout.

Umbel Ale (OG 1039, ABV 3.8%) ◆
Pleasant, easy-drinking bitter, infused with coriander, which dominates.

Growler Bitter (OG 1040, ABV 3.9%) ◆
Light tasting, sweetish and fruity session beer.

Lemon Head (OG 1041, ABV 4%)
A union of lemon and ginger creates an unmistakable thirst-quenching surprise.

Hound Dog (OG 1043, ABV 4.2%)
Light golden beer, smooth and refreshing at the start with a well-rounded bitterness before the hop explosion leaves a slightly fruity taste at the end.

Essex Border (OG 1049, ABV 4.8%)
A pale golden summer ale, fruity and spicy with a pleasant malty finish; an easy-drinking beer.

Old Growler (OG 1051, ABV 5%) ◆
Well-balanced porter in which roast grain is complemented by fruit and bubblegum.

Umbel Magna (OG 1051, ABV 5%) ◆
Old Growler flavoured with coriander. The spice is less dominant than in Umbel Ale, with some of the weight and body of the beer coming through.

Essex Beast (OG 1063, ABV 6.2%)
Strong, dark, complex and robust ale with chocolate and rich toffee flavours. Brewed in memory of Essex CAMRA stalwart Andrew Clifton.

New Bristol (NEW)

20a Wilson Street, Bristol, BS2 9HH ☎ 07837 976871
🌐 newbristolbrewery.co.uk

Tom and Noel commenced brewing on a five-barrel plant in 2013. Three regular beers are brewed along with a selection of stouts and porters. There are plans for the brewery to relocate.

Oolala (OG 1040, ABV 4.2%)
An amber-coloured ale.

365 (OG 1041, ABV 4.3%)
A session bitter with plenty of up front malt and toffee married with hops.

India (OG 1064, ABV 6.5%)
A sugar and spice ale.

New Inn

New Inn, 112 Roberttown Lane, Roberttown, Liversedge, West Yorkshire, WF15 7NP
☎ (01924) 402069

Brewing commenced in 2012 using a half-barrel brew plant located in the cellar of the New Inn, Liversedge. The beer is produced in wood-clad vessels by Joe Kenyon, the ex-brewer at Riverhead Brewery.

Pale Bob (OG 1038, ABV 3.8%)

Golden Bob (OG 1040, ABV 4%)

Rusty Bob (OG 1045, ABV 4.5%)

Bobcastle Brown (OG 1046, ABV 4.6%)

Bobmeister (OG 1049, ABV 4.9%)

Bombay Bob (ABV 6%)

New Lion (NEW) SIBA

Station Road, Totnes, Devon, TQ9 5JR
☎ (01803) 226277 🌐 lioncraftbrewery.com

The original Lion Brewery closed in 1926 and was restarted in 2013 by four local business people. The only memorabilia found for the old brewery is a mirror for the 'Celebrated Totnes Stout' so the brewery hopes to revive this. There is a commitment to providing apprenticeship opportunities and work experience for people with learning difficulties.

Mane Event (OG 1038, ABV 3.8%)
A well-balanced, modern session bitter.

Pandit IPA (OG 1046, ABV 4.9%)
A citrus and floral nose. These flavours appear again on the palate, complemented by a well-defined, biscuity malt character.

New Plassey

Eyton, Nr Wrexham, LL13 0SP ☎ 07769 155874
🌐 plassey.com/brewery.php

Plassey brewery was founded in 1985 on the 250-acre Plassey Estate. Following the merger of Plassey and the Gertie Sweet Brewery in 2012, the New Plassey Brewery was formed.

New World Pale (OG 1039, ABV 3.9%)
A pale beer, well-balanced with a hoppy bite.

Plassey Bitter (OG 1040, ABV 4%) ◆
Smooth and malty best bitter, reddish brown in colour, with a good hop and fruit balance and a dry finish.

Midnight Mild (OG 1042, ABV 4.2%)
A medium strength mild with a real fullness of character and flavour. Dark and subtle.

Offa's Dyke (OG 1043, ABV 4.3%)
Pale, crisp and refreshing bitter.

Dusky Maiden Stout (OG 1044, ABV 4.4%)
A dark, complex flavoured stout.

Deep Porter (OG 1045, ABV 4.5%)
A smooth, deep brown porter.

Cherry Diva (OG 1047, ABV 4.7%)
A pale beer with a subtle flavour of Maraschino cherry.

Cwrw Tudno (OG 1050, ABV 5%)
A pale strong bitter.

Dragons Breath (OG 1060, ABV 6%) ◆
Well-balanced strong bitter. Plum fruit in aroma with the initial sweetness followed by a powerful smack of hops and fruit.

Newark SIBA

77 William Street, Newark, Nottinghamshire, NG24 1QU ☎ 07879 885000 🌐 newarkbrewery.co.uk

Newark Brewery was established in 2012 on the site of a former maltings using an eight-barrel plant. The bulk of production is supplied to local pubs.

Phoenix (ABV 1.8%)
A dark beer with a hint of ruby. Late hops lift the deep malt sweetness without being overly bitter, giving a smooth, mature beer.

Best (OG 1038, ABV 3.7%)
Ruby-coloured, well-balanced session bitter.

Pale (OG 1039, ABV 3.8%)
Clear bright and hoppy. Refreshing with a good head and a long, clean bitter aftertaste.

BLH4 (ABV 4%)
A bright, light and hoppy beer.

Summer Gold (OG 1045, ABV 4.5%)
Refreshing and tasty. Light malt balanced with three citrus hops and lime.

5.5 (ABV 5.5%)
A complex beer balancing deep malt with a citrus burst.

Newby Wyke SIBA

Unit 24, Limesquare Business Park, Alma Park Road, Grantham, Lincolnshire, NG31 9SN
☎ (01476) 565682 🌐 newbywyke.co.uk
Tours by arrangement

⊗ The brewery is named after a Hull trawler skippered by brewer Rob March's grandfather. It started life in 1998 as a 2.5-barrel plant in a converted garage then moved to premises behind the Willoughby Arms, Little Bytham. In 2009 it moved back to Grantham with a brew length of 10 barrels. Seasonal beers: see website.

Banquo (OG 1036, ABV 3.8%)
Pale blonde in colour with a full hoppy taste and a long fruity finish.

Orsino (OG 1037, ABV 4%)
A blonde ale with a bright, fruity citrus and mango taste moving to a soft citrus hop finish.

Kingston Topaz (OG 1039, ABV 4.2%)
A single-hopped ale with floral undertones.

Bear Island (OG 1043, ABV 4.6%)
A blonde beer with a hoppy aroma and a crisp, dry finish.

White Squall (OG 1044, ABV 4.8%) ◆
Amber-hued with a hoppy aroma. Generous amounts of hop are well-supported by a solid malty undercurrent. An increasingly bittersweet tang makes itself known towards the finish.

Newmans

See Celt Experience

Nine Standards

See Settle

Nobby's SIBA

c/o Ward Arms, High Street, Guilsborough, Northamptonshire, NN6 8PY
☎ (01604) 740785 🌐 nobbysbrewery.co.uk
Shop Mon-Fri 9am-5pm
Tours by arrangement

THE BREWERIES

Paul 'Nobby' Mulliner started commercial brewing in 2004 on a 2.5-barrel plant at the rear of the Alexandra Arms, Kettering. The brewery relocated to the Ward Arms, Guilsborough, in 2007 where a 14-barrel plant was installed at the rear. This has subsequently been expanded. The full range of beers are bottled in-house.

Claridges Crystal (OG 1036, ABV 3.6%)
Pale summer ale, crisp and fresh with a slightly citrus hop finish.

Guilsborough Guzzler (OG 1036, ABV 3.6%)
An easy-drinking, malty auburn-coloured ale with a gentle hop finish.

Best (OG 1037, ABV 3.8%)
A fine session ale with a hop finish.

Guilsborough Gold (OG 1041, ABV 4%)
Full-bodied, well-balanced golden ale with a traditional hop finish.

Wild West (OG 1046, ABV 4.6%)
Mahogany-coloured beer, full and flavoursome.

Tow'd Navigation (OG 1067, ABV 6.1%)
Dark strong ale from years gone by. Warming, with rich malt and hops.

Nook SIBA

Riverside, 7b Victoria Square, Holmfirth, West Yorkshire, HD9 2DN
☎ (01484) 682373 🌐 thenookbrewhouse.co.uk
Tours by arrangement

The Nook Brewhouse is built on the foundations of a previous brewhouse dating back to 1752, next to the River Ribble, behind the Nook pub. Brewing commenced in 2009 and two brewery taps are supplied. A history room with renovated archives dating back to the 1700s and a brewery shop are planned.

Yorks (OG 1037, ABV 3.7%) ◆
A well-balanced bitter with light malt and hop aroma, and hop and fruit in the taste, developing in strength. A good session beer.

Baby Blond (OG 1038, ABV 3.8%)

Rescue Red (OG 1038, ABV 3.8%)

Spring into Spring (OG 1038, ABV 3.8%)

Bee's Knees (OG 1039, ABV 3.9%)

Best (OG 1040.5, ABV 4.2%) ◆
An easy-drinking best bitter with hints of malt and floral hops in the aroma. The taste has an abundance of hops and fruit and a pleasant, crisp, malty aftertaste.

Blond (OG 1042.5, ABV 4.5%) ◆
A golden ale with intense fruit and hop tastes, which lessen in the aftertaste.

Red (OG 1044, ABV 4.5%) ◆
Complex tastes of fruit and roasted malt throughout, enhanced by a strong, fruity aroma.

Nook'y Brown Ale (OG 1049, ABV 4.9%)

Oat Stout (OG 1052, ABV 5.2%)

Norfolk SIBA

Moon Gazer Barn, Harvest Lane, Hindringham, Norfolk, NR21 0PW
☎ (01328) 878495 🌐 norfolkbrewhouse.co.uk
Tours by arrangement

Brewing began in 2012 using a 10-barrel plant. The brewery is owned and run by Rachel and David Holliday. Chalk-filtered water is used from the brewery's own well.

Dewhopper Lager (ABV 3.8%)

Moongazer Amber (ABV 4%)
An amber-coloured ale combining a full-bodied bitterness with fruity overtones with a smooth, lasting finish.

Moongazer Golden (ABV 4%)
A golden ale with a fresh, citrus aroma and a well-hopped character, with fruit and hop flavour carrying through to the refreshing, crisp, dry finish.

Moongazer Ruby (ABV 4%)
A ruby-coloured bitter with a rich, spicy, roasted aroma and a full malty body, resulting in a full-bodied mouthfeel.

Moongazer Dark (ABV 4.9%)
A strong dark mild with a subtle blackcurrant aroma, full-bodied with a rich, fruity, sweet finish.

Stubblestag Lager (ABV 5%)

Norfolk Square

Japonica House, Mill Road, Stokesby, Norfolk, NR29 3AL
☎ (01493) 751975 🌐 norfolksquarebrewery.co.uk

Norfolk Square began brewing in 2008 using a 2.5-barrel brewery and has increased since. The brewery is located in the broadland village of Stokesby and supplies both cask and bottle-conditioned beers, including the Maverik range.

Scroby (OG 1042, ABV 4.2%)
A refreshing pale ale with a floral and spicy hop aroma.

Sunshiny (OG 1044, ABV 4.2%)
A golden ale with a honey twist. Full-bodied and smooth with a citrus character.

B52 (OG 1046, ABV 4.8%)
A creamy russet-coloured best bitter. Smooth on the palate with a light hoppy aroma and a blackcurrant undertone.

North Cotswold SIBA

Unit 3, Ditchford Farm, Stretton-on-Fosse, Warwickshire, GL56 9RD
☎ (01608) 663947 🌐 northcotswoldbrewery.co.uk
Shop Mon-Thu 10am-4pm, Sat 10am-1pm

North Cotswold started in 1999 as a 2.5-barrel plant, which was upgraded in 2000 to 10 barrels. Seasonal beers are available.

Windrush Ale (OG 1036, ABV 3.6%)
A thirst-quenching, amber-coloured session bitter. A malty, slightly sweet palate.

Cotswold Best (OG 1040, ABV 4%)
An easy-drinking, straw-coloured best bitter.

Shagweaver (OG 1045, ABV 4.5%)
A pale, hoppy bitter.

Hung, Drawn 'n' Portered (OG 1050, ABV 5%)
Strong, dark coloured porter with a malty finish.

North Curry SIBA

The Old Coach House, Gwyon House, Church Road, North Curry, Somerset, TA3 6LH ☎ 07928 815053
🌐 thenorthcurrybrewerycouk.com

The brewery opened in 2006 and is attached to one of the oldest properties in North Curry where brewing last took place in the village in the 1920s. Beers are available at farmers markets in Taunton and Minehead and in local shops. All beers are also available bottle conditioned. Seasonal beer: see website.

Howzat (OG 1036, ABV 3.7%)
A golden-coloured beer with fruity hop flavours and a smooth aftertaste.

Curry Gold (OG 1038, ABV 3.9%)
A golden ale with a fruity aroma. Maize flakes are added to give it a smooth sweetness in contrast to the bitter hops.

Red Heron (OG 1041, ABV 4.3%)
A full-bodied, malty ale, balanced by the bitterness of Golding hops.

The Withyman (OG 1042, ABV 4.6%)
The malty flavour has a bitterness and punch from the fruity hops.

Level Headed (OG 1043, ABV 4.7%)
A dark, ruby-coloured, traditional old English ale made with chocolate malt. Rich and full of flavour.

Alfred's Stout (OG 1047, ABV 5.1%)
A black, dry stout with a good, robust flavour. A rounded body is balanced by the bitterness of roasted barley and Northern Brewer hops.

North Riding

North Marine Road, Scarborough, North Yorkshire, YO12 7HU
☎ (01723) 370004 🌐 northridingbrewpub.com

Brewing commenced in 2011 using a two-barrel plant situated in the cellar of the pub. A new beer is brewed every week. Seasonal and bottled-conditioned beers are available.

Neilsons Sauvin (OG 1039, ABV 3.7%)
A pale, hoppy session beer with a wine like finish and a taste of crushed gooseberries.

Peasholm Pale Ale (OG 1042, ABV 4.3%)
Pale and hoppy with a citrus bitterness and a long, smooth finish.

Fat Lads Mild (OG 1044, ABV 4.5%)
A strong dark mild with roast and chocolate undertones.

North Star SIBA

Unit 6, Gallows Industrial Park, off Furnace Road, Ilkeston, Derbyshire, DE7 5EP
🌐 northstarbrewery.co.uk
Tours by arrangement

North Star was established in 2012 by a long-term home brewer using a purpose-built 10-barrel plant. Now supplying numerous local outlets and distributing widely through wholesalers, production has increased to a level where several family members are now involved in the process. Seasonal, occasional and bottle-conditioned beers: see website.

Sentinel (OG 1039, ABV 3.8%)
A pale, American-style ale with citrus undertones.

Helmsman (OG 1041, ABV 4.2%)
A pale ale with a full malt flavour and a delicate hop balance with a satisfying fruit finish.

Pathfinder (OG 1045, ABV 4.5%)
A special bitter with full roast malt and rich orange peel overtones. The malt is balanced by four hop varieties.

Astronomer (OG 1048, ABV 4.8%)
A stout with rich roast malt flavour and dark chocolate overtones which lead to a dry biscuit finish.

Polaris (OG 1049, ABV 5%)
A dark ruby porter with chocolate, liquorice and coffee aromas. The flavours lead to a hoppy, bitter finish.

Endeavour (OG 1053, ABV 5.4%)
A dark beer with complex fruit flavours and notes of pepper, culminating in full malt flavouring and a toffee and wine-like finish.

North Wales

Tan-y-Mynydd, Moelfre, Abergele, LL22 9RF
☎ (0800) 083 4100 🌐 northwalesbrewery.net

John Wood established his brewery in 2007. In 2012 a bore hole was drilled to supply water for brewing. Bottle-conditioned beers are available, and mead and soft drinks are produced.

Bodelwyddan Bitter (OG 1038, ABV 3.8%)

Chilli Beer (OG 1040, ABV 4%)

Dandelion & Burdock (OG 1040, ABV 4%)
Alcoholic dandelion & burdock, brewed with lager malt.

Abergele Ale (OG 1050, ABV 5%)

Welsh Stout (OG 1052, ABV 5.2%)

North Yorkshire SIBA

Pinchinthorpe Hall, Pinchinthorpe, North Yorkshire, TS14 8HG
☎ (01287) 630200 🌐 nybrewery.co.uk
Shop Mon-Fri 9am-5pm
Tours by arrangement

Founded in Middlesbrough in 1989 the brewery moved to Pinchinthorpe Hall, a moated, listed medieval estate near Guisborough in 1998. Its own spring water produces a distinctive flavour. More than 100 trade outlets are supplied. Most cask beers are organic with some occasional beers not so. Bottle-conditioned beers are available.

Best Bitter (OG 1036, ABV 3.6%)
Refreshing session beer. Clean tasting, well-hopped, copper-coloured.

Golden Ginseng (OG 1036, ABV 3.6%)
Clean-tasting, well-hopped traditional beer with ginseng.

Prior's Ale (OG 1036, ABV 3.6%) ◆
Light, refreshing and surprisingly full-flavoured for a pale, low gravity beer, with a complex, bittersweet mixture of malt, hops and fruit carrying through into the aftertaste.

Archbishop Lee's Ruby Ale (OG 1040, ABV 4%)
Maltiness is predominant with some hops in the taste.

Boro Best (OG 1040, ABV 4%)
Mid brown with a malty aroma. A full-bodied beer.

Crystal Tips (OG 1040, ABV 4%)
A full-bodied ruby bitter.

Love Muscle (OG 1040, ABV 4%)
A thirst quenching, crisp golden ale.

Honey Bunny (OG 1042, ABV 4.2%)
Golden bitter with a hoppy finish and a hint of honey.

Mayhem (OG 1043, ABV 4.3%)
Refreshing, clean-tasting, well-hopped pale ale.

Cereal Killer (OG 1045, ABV 4.5%)
Light-coloured clear wheat bitter with a distinctive hop nose.

Fools Gold (OG 1046, ABV 4.6%)
Pale, refreshingly complex golden ale. Fruity aroma with a bittersweet flavour.

Golden Ale (OG 1046, ABV 4.6%) ◆
A well-hopped, lightly-malted, golden premium bitter, using Styrian Goldings and Goldings hops.

Flying Herbert (OG 1047, ABV 4.7%)
Smooth, full-flavoured premium bitter with a malty, fruity and dry finish.

Lord Lee's (OG 1047, ABV 4.7%) ◆
A refreshing, red/brown beer with a hoppy aroma. The flavour is a pleasant balance of roast malt and sweetness that predominates over hops. The malty, bitter finish develops slowly.

White Lady (OG 1047, ABV 4.7%)
A hoppy, strong, pale-coloured beer.

Dizzy Dick (OG 1048, ABV 4.8%)
Strong, smooth, dark ale with plenty of hops.

Rocket Fuel (OG 1050, ABV 5%)
A strong golden ale.

Valhalla (OG 1055, ABV 5.5%)
Strong traditional bitter with plenty of hops and a subtle hint of malt.

Northern

See Blakemere

Northern FC

McCracken Park, Great North Road, Gosforth, Newcastle upon Tyne, NE3 2DT
☎ (0191) 236 3369 ⊕ northernfootballclub.co.uk

Established in 2012 to supply the clubhouse for the Northern RUFC, the range is developing.

Northern Monk

See Hambleton

Northumberland SIBA

Accessory House, Barrington Road, Bedlington, Northumberland, NE22 7AP
☎ (01670) 822112 ⊕ northumberlandbrewery.co.uk
Tours by arrangement

Brewing began in 1996 in Ashington using a five-barrel plant. Relocation and expansion mean that the brewery now use a 10-barrel plant and has an on-site brewery tap, Fuggles. 30-40 barrels are brewed per week of a wide range of ales including seasonals: see website.

Pit Pony (OG 1039, ABV 3.8%)

Fog on the Tyne (OG 1040.5, ABV 4.1%)

Norton

Norton Priory, Tudor Road, Manor Park, Runcorn, Cheshire, WA7 1SX
☎ (01928) 716971 ⊕ nortonbrewing.com

Norton Brewing was created in 2009 by Halton Borough Council as a social enterprise to provide employment opportunities for people with learning disabilities, autism and other disabilites. It is situated in the grounds of Norton Priory and uses a 2.5-barrel plant.

Priory Ale (OG 1045, ABV 4.5%)

Norwich Bear

Ketts Tavern, 29 Ketts Hill, Norwich, NR1 4EX
☎ (01603) 628520 ⊕ norwichbear.co.uk

Norwich Bear was launched in 2010. It brews bespoke ales exclusively for the Ketts Tavern.

Teddy Bear (OG 1037, ABV 3.7%) ◆
Rolling malt and hop aroma introduces similar flavours with an added hint of strawberries. A gently tapering finish turns woody.

Classic (OG 1038, ABV 3.8%) ◆
A crisp hoppy backbone is heightened by a tangy grapefruit edge. A short, noticeably drier, finale.

Pooh (OG 1042, ABV 4.2%)
Amber-gold, a grassy citrus aroma flows into an easy-drinking mix of malt, caramel, hop and grapefruit. Well-rounded with a lingering fruity ending.

Legend (OG 1044, ABV 4.3%) ◆
Tawny-hued, grainy mouthfeel with a swirling malty and hop nose. Initial chocolate orange explosion fades into a bittersweet dryness.

Boudicca (OG 1045, ABV 4.5%) ◆
Caramel is dominant in aroma and taste. Malt, vine fruit, and marmalade add to the complex intermingling of flavours.

NPA (Norwich Pale Ale) (OG 1047, ABV 4.7%) ◆
Golden-coloured with a grassy hoppy nose. Easy-drinking mix with hops flowing over a bittersweet citrus base.

Platinum Blonde (OG 1050, ABV 5%) ◆
Light, crisp, and refreshing with a miasma of interlinked flavours. Elderflower, grapefruit, and hops mix well against a gentle sweet, malty background. Fragrant aroma.

Noss Beer Works SIBA

Unit 6, Ash Court, Pennant Way, Lee Mill, Devon, PL21 9GE ☎ 07977 479634 ⊕ nossbeerworks.co.uk
Tours by arrangement

Brewing began in 2012 using a six-barrel plant. Local outlets are supplied.

Church Ledge (OG 1040, ABV 4%)
A late-hopped blonde IPA; light, hoppy and zesty.

Mew Stone (OG 1043, ABV 4.3%)
A copper-coloured, well-balanced and refreshing best bitter.

Ebb Rock (OG 1049, ABV 4.9%)
A dark copper-coloured, full-bodied beer.

Nottingham SIBA

Plough Inn, 17 St Peter's Street, Radford, Nottingham, NG7 3EN
☎ (0115) 942 2649 nottinghambrewery.co.uk
Tours by arrangement

The former owners of the Bramcote and Castle Rock Breweries re-established the Nottingham Brewery in 2000 in a purpose-built brewhouse behind the Plough Inn. Philip Darby and Niven Balfour set out to revive the brands of the original Nottingham Brewery, closed by Whitbread in the 1950s, with a view to supplying local outlets within the LocAle ethos.

Rock Ale Bitter Beer (OG 1038, ABV 3.8%)
A pale and bitter, thirst-quenching hoppy beer with a dry finish.

Rock Ale Mild Beer (OG 1038, ABV 3.8%)
A reddish-black malty mild with some refreshing bitterness in the finish.

Legend (OG 1040, ABV 4%)
A fruity and malty pale brown bitter with a touch of sweetness and bitterness.

Extra Pale Ale (OG 1042, ABV 4.2%)
A hoppy and fruity golden ale with a hint of sweetness and a long-lasting bitter finish.

Dreadnought (OG 1045, ABV 4.5%)
Well-balanced best bitter. Blend of malt and hops give a rounded fruity finish.

Bullion (OG 1047, ABV 4.7%)
A refreshing premium golden ale. Brewed with a single malt variety, it is triple-hopped and exceptionally bitter.

Supreme (OG 1052, ABV 5.2%)
A strong amber fruity ale. A touch of malt in the taste is followed by a sweet and slightly hoppy finish.

Brewed for the Broadway Cinema Cafébar, Nottingham:

Broadway Reel Ale (OG 1044, ABV 4.4%)
A hoppy, amber-coloured best bitter.

Brewed for the Trent Bridge Inn, Nottingham:

Trent Bridge Inn Ale (OG 1038, ABV 3.8%)
A tawny, traditionally-hopped bitter.

Nutbrook SIBA

6 Hallam Way, West Hallam, Derbyshire, DE7 6LA
nutbrookbrewery.com
Shop Mon-Fri 10am-6pm (by invite only); Sat 9am-5pm at Oakfield Farm (open to all)
Tours by arrangement

Nutbrook was established in 2007 on a one-barrel brewery in the owners' garage. This was supplemented in 2010 with a six-barrel plant at Oakfield Farm, Stanley Common. Beers are brewed to order for domestic and corporate clients, and customers can design their own recipes. All beers are available bottle conditioned.

Or8 (OG 1041.4, ABV 3.8%)

Bitlyke (OG 1040.6, ABV 4.2%)

Banter (OG 1040.8, ABV 4.5%)

Midnight (OG 1048.4, ABV 4.5%)

Mongrel (OG 1046.9, ABV 4.5%)

O'Hanlon's

See Hanlons

Oakham SIBA

2 Maxwell Road, Woodston, Peterborough, Cambridgeshire, PE2 7JB
☎ (01733) 370500 oakhamales.com
Shop Mon-Thu 9am-5pm, Fri 9am-4pm
Tours by arrangement

The brewery started in 1993 in Oakham, Rutland, and moved to Peterborough in 1998. The brewery's main production site is a 75-barrel plant. An additional six-barrel plant is located at its city-centre brewpub, which makes special and one-off brews. Around 350 outlets are supplied and three pubs are owned. Seasonal beers: see website.

Jeffrey Hudson Bitter (OG 1038, ABV 3.8%)
Straw-coloured golden ale dominated by citrus hop character throughout. Long, dry, slightly astringent finish.

Inferno (OG 1039, ABV 4%)
The citrus hop character of this straw-coloured brew begins on the nose and builds in intensity on the palate. Clean, dry, citrus finish.

Citra (OG 1042, ABV 4.2%)
Refreshing grapefruit and peach aroma and flavour characterise this golden ale. Bittersweet palate gives way to a long dry aftertaste.

Scarlet Macaw (OG 1043, ABV 4.4%)
Tart gooseberry and soft peach on the nose and intense bitter finish.

Bishops Farewell (OG 1046, ABV 4.6%)
Powerfully citrus, the hops and fruit on the aroma of this golden/yellow beer become bittersweet on the palate. Zesty citrus aftertaste.

Oakleaf SIBA

Unit 7, Clarence Wharf Industrial Estate, Mumby Road, Gosport, Hampshire, PO12 1AJ
☎ (023) 9251 3222 oakleafbrewing.co.uk
Shop Tue-Thu 11am-5pm, Fri & Sat 11am-6pm
Tours by arrangement

Ed Anderson set up Oakleaf with his father-in-law, Dave Pickersgill, in 2000. The brewery stands on the side of Portsmouth Harbour. Some 350 outlets are supplied direct with national deliveries via wholesalers. Seasonal beers: see website. Bottle-conditioned beers are available.

Heart of Gold (OG 1038, ABV 3.8%)
An easy-drinking golden ale with a hint of spices and balanced sweetness.

Quercus Folium (OG 1040, ABV 4%)
A traditional mid-brown bitter with an initial malty flavour leading to a long hoppy finish.

Nuptu'ale (OG 1042, ABV 4.2%)
An intense spicy, floral aroma leads to a complex hoppy taste. Well-balanced with malts and citrus flavours and a hint of sweetness.

Hole Hearted (OG 1048, ABV 4.7%)

THE BREWERIES

Amber-coloured with a strong floral hop aroma continuing into the flavour, with some malt, leading to a long, bittersweet finish.

I Can't Believe It's Not Bitter (OG 1048, ABV 4.9%)
Clean and crisp with a fruity aftertaste. The use of Saaz hops gives this lager a citrus finish that lingers on.

India Pale Ale (OG 1053, ABV 5.5%)
This beer is initially dry and bitter. Full-flavoured and complex marmalade/aniseed notes to follow, which leaves a lingering bitterness on the palate.

Brewed for Suthwyk Ales:

Old Dick (OG 1038, ABV 3.8%) ◆
Pleasant, clean-tasting pale brown bitter. Easy-drinking and well-balanced.

Liberation (OG 1042, ABV 4.2%)
Light-coloured with a soft, berry fruit flavour.

Skew Sunshine Ale (OG 1046, ABV 4.6%) ◆
An amber-coloured beer. Initial hoppiness leads to a fruity taste and finish with a slightly cloying mouthfeel.

Palmerston's Folly (OG 1050, ABV 5%)
A clear wheat and barley beer. Slightly dry with a hint of honey in the aftertaste.

Oates SIBA

4 Ladyship Business Park, Mill Lane, Halifax, West Yorkshire, HX3 6TA
☎ (01422) 320100 ⊕ oatesbrewing,co,uk

Oates was founded in 2011 by former landlord Mark Oates and Master Brewer Richard Munro. Four core beers are produced on a six-barrel plant. Seasonal beers: see website.

O.M.T. (OG 1038, ABV 3.8%)
A light, straw-coloured beer with a floral and hoppy aroma and delicate hints of lemon and pineapple in taste.

Caragold (OG 1041, ABV 4.1%)
Well-balanced beer with caramel and honey in the aroma and a long bitter finish.

Wild Oates (OG 1043, ABV 4.3%)
A full bodied amber-coloured beer. Well-balanced with a rich floral fragrance and lingering bitterness to the finish.

Summit (OG 1045, ABV 4.5%)
Hints of tropical fruit on the palate, balanced by a sweet, malty backbone, which develops into a smooth bitter finish.

Oban Bay

See Argyll

Odcombe

Masons Arms, 41 Lower Odcombe, Lower Odcombe, Somerset, BA22 8TX
☎ (01935) 862591 ⊕ masonsarmsodcombe.co.uk
Tours by arrangement

Odcombe opened in 2000 and closed a few years later. It re-opened in 2005 with assistance from Shepherd Neame (qv). Brewing takes place once a week and beers are only available at the pub. Seasonal beers are also available.

No. 1 (OG 1040, ABV 4%)
Traditional best bitter flavoured with East Kent Golding hops.

Spring (OG 1042, ABV 4.1%)
Amber ale, light and hoppy with floral notes.

Roly Poly (OG 1042, ABV 4.3%)
Autumn ruby-coloured beer with juniper berries and star anise. A slightly stronger tasting beer.

Offa's Dyke SIBA

Chapel Lane, Trefonen, Shropshire, SY10 9DX
☎ (01691) 656889 ⊕ offasdykebrewery.com
Shop Mon-Fri 5-11pm, Sat & Sun 12pm-midnight
Tours by arrangement

Established in 2007, the brewery and adjoining pub straddle the old England/Wales border, Offa's Dyke. The owner has small-scale hop cultivation. The Olde Vaults and adjacent Ironworks in Oswestry, serve as alternative brewery taps.

Barley Gold (OG 1038, ABV 3.6%)

Offa's Pride (OG 1040, ABV 3.8%)

Thirst Brew (OG 1042, ABV 4%)

Grim Reaper (OG 1050, ABV 5%)

Offbeat SIBA

Unit 6, Thomas Street, Crewe, Cheshire, CW1 2BD
☎ 07502 096438 ⊕ offbeatbrewery.com
Tours by arrangement

Offbeat began brewing in 2010, quickly expanding to a six-barrel plant. Brewery open nights (usually first Friday of the month) are a regular occurrence. Specials and bottle-conditioned beers are available. The beers can be found in many local outlets and around the north west.

Outlandish Pale (OG 1037.8, ABV 3.9%)
A session beer with a lemon hoppiness.

Kooky Gold (ABV 4.1%)
Light, golden session ale, easy drinking with low bitterness.

Odd Ball Red (OG 1040.4, ABV 4.2%)
A ruby red ale with a spicy flavour and finish and a bold fruitiness.

Way Out Wheat (OG 1043.6, ABV 4.5%)
A naturally cloudy wheat beer with oranges and coriander.

Out of Step IPA (OG 1055.3, ABV 5.8%)
A well-balanced American-style IPA. Generously hopped with abundant citrus flavours leading to a dry, bitter finish.

Okells SIBA

Kewaigue, Douglas, Isle of Man, IM2 1QG
☎ (01624) 699400 ⊕ okells.co.uk
Tours by arrangement

Founded in 1874 by Dr Okell, this is the main brewery on the island and moved in 1994 to a new, purpose-built plant at Kewaigue. All the beers are produced under the Manx Brewers' Act. Seasonal beers: see website.

MPA (Manx Pale Ale) (OG 1036, ABV 3.6%)
Pale gold in colour and fruity with a dry finish.

Bitter (OG 1035, ABV 3.7%) ◆

A golden beer, malty and hoppy in aroma, with a hint of honey. Rich and malty on the tongue, it has a dry, malt and hop finish. A complex but rewarding beer.

Olaf (OG 1040, ABV 3.9%)
Deep black in colour with aromas of coffee and liquorice.

Dr Okell's IPA (OG 1044, ABV 4.5%)
A light-coloured beer with a full-bodied taste. The sweetness is offset by strong hopping that gives the beer an overall roundness with spicy lemon notes and a fine dry finish.

Alt (OG 1050, ABV 4.9%)
A copper-coloured beer with a crisp, elegant and fresh flavour, with hints of gooseberry and citrus.

Steam (OG 1052, ABV 5%)
A dark gold beer with a citrus, herb, sherbet and resin aroma. Drying with a spicy bitter palate.

Old

See Meantime

Old Bear

See Bridgehouse

Old Bog

Masons Arms, 2 Quarry School Place, Oxford, OX3 8LH
☎ (01865) 764579 ✉ theoldbog@hotmail.co.uk

Established in 2005 on a one-barrel plant behind the Masons Arms, brewing only takes place at weekends. The beers, when available, are sold at the pub (generally at weekends) and occasionally at local beer festivals. A number of one-off brews appear throughout the year.

Quarry Gold (OG 1041, ABV 4.1%)
Clean-tasting golden bitter with well balanced sweet and bitter characteristics.

Half Wit (ABV 4.5%)
A malty dark amber wheat beer.

Quarry Goldish (ABV 4.6%)
Golden ale with mild fruit notes and a sweet finish.

Wheat Beer (ABV 5%)
Pale gold in colour with a light citrus hoppiness.

Monstrous Mild (ABV 5.6%)
Strong, smooth dark mild with fruity and malty tastes.

Old Cannon SIBA

86 Cannon Street, Bury St Edmunds, Suffolk, IP33 1JR
☎ (01284) 768769 oldcannonbrewery.co.uk
Tours by arrangement

The St Edmunds Head pub opened in 1845 with its own brewery. Brewing ceased in 1917, and Greene King closed the pub in 1995. It re-opened in 1999 as the Old Cannon brewery complete with a unique state-of-the-art brewery housed in the bar area. A growing number of local outlets are supplied. Seasonal beers are available.

Best Bitter (OG 1037, ABV 3.8%)
Traditional East Anglian bitter. Rich hoppy aroma and bitterness dominate throughout with just a hint of sweetness in the aftertaste.

Hornblower (OG 1038, ABV 4%)
Light in colour with an IPA hoppiness.

Gunner's Daughter (OG 1052, ABV 5.5%)
A well-balanced strong ale with a complexity of hop, fruit, sweetness and bitterness in the flavour, and a lingering hoppy, bitter aftertaste.

Old Chimneys

Hopton End Farm, Church Road,, Market Weston, Diss, Suffolk, IP22 2NX
☎ (01359) 221411/221013
oldchimneysbrewery.com
Shop Fri 2-7pm, Sat 11am-2pm
Tours by arrangement

Old Chimneys opened in 1995, moving to a converted farm building in 2001. Most of the beers are named after rare species of wildlife found nearby. Seasonal, special and bottle-conditioned beers are also available, along with a small quantity of cider.

Military Mild (OG 1035, ABV 3.3%)
A rich, dark mild with good body for its gravity. Sweetish toffee and light roast bitterness dominate, leading to a dry aftertaste.

Great Raft Bitter (OG 1040, ABV 4%)
Pale copper-coloured bitter bursting with fruit. Malt and hops add to the sweetish fruity flavour, which is rounded off with hoppy bitterness in the aftertaste.

Black Rat Stout (OG 1048, ABV 4.4%)
Roast malt and coffee flavours with body and sweetness from added lactose.

Golden Pheasant (OG 1044, ABV 4.5%)
Pale, dry bitter with citrus, apple and malt, balanced with robust hop bitterness.

Arrowhead (ABV 4.8%)
A premium ale.

Old Cross

Old Cross Tavern, 8 St Andrew Street, Hertford, SG14 1JA
☎ (01992) 583133

The microbrewery was set up in 2008 and is located within the pub. Owner Nigel Beviss brews solely for the Old Cross Tavern. There are two regularly-available beers plus special single-hop brewed ales, with one always available at the bar.

Laugh 'n' Titter (OG 1037, ABV 3.7%)

Gertcha! (OG 1039, ABV 3.9%)

Old Dairy SIBA

Units 2 & 3, Tenterden Station Estate, Station Road, Tenterden, Kent, TN30 6HE
☎ (01580) 763867 olddairybrewery.com
Shop Mon-Fri 10am-4pm
Tours by arrangement

Old Dairy was founded in 2009. It relocated from Rolvenden in 2014 to larger premises near the Kent & East Sussex Railway in Tenterden in order to increase brewing capacity. There is a brewery shop offering discounts to CAMRA members along with a loyalty card scheme. Seasonal and bottle-conditioned beers are available.

Red Top (OG 1038, ABV 3.8%) ◆
A sweetish copper-coloured bitter with hints of caramel and a subtle hop character.

Copper Top (OG 1041, ABV 4.1%)
Dark, full-flavoured best bitter.

Gold Top (OG 1043, ABV 4.3%) ◆
A well-balanced golden ale with a good blend of malt and hops followed by a long, bittersweet finish.

Silver Top (OG 1046, ABV 4.5%) ◆
A well-crafted complex stout with a good balance of dark malts, roast barley and caramel, and a long finish.

Blue Top (OG 1048, ABV 4.8%) ◆
Rich and full bodied, this pale brown ale has a long bittersweet finish and a hint of aroma hop.

Old Forge

Radnor Arms, 32 Coleshill, Coleshill, Oxfordshire, SN6 7PR
☎ (01793) 873915 oldforgebrewery.co.uk
Tours by arrangement

Old Forge began brewing in a converted outbuilding at the Radnor Arms in 2010 using a four-barrel plant. Rick Sullivan is head brewer and also brews at the Halfpenny Brewery (qv) in Lechlade. Visitors can view the plant through several glass windows opposite the entrance to the pub.

Anvil Ale (OG 1037, ABV 3.8%)
Light session ale, amber-coloured with traditional bitterness.

Blacksmith's Gold (OG 1042, ABV 4%)
Refreshing straw-coloured ale with citrus notes and a hoppy floral finish.

Hammer & Tongs (OG 1043, ABV 4.2%)
Ruby in colour, bitter yet mellow in taste.

Sledgehammer (OG 1048, ABV 5%)
Deep red, full-bodied premium ale with hints of chocolate and caramel.

Old Inn

Old Inn, Flowerdale Glen, Gairloch, IV21 2BD
☎ (01445) 712006 theoldinn.net

Brewing began in 2010 using a 150-litre plant. Seasonal beers are available.

Erradale IPA (OG 1041, ABV 4.2%)

The Blind Piper (OG 1046, ABV 4.6%)

Old Laxey

Shore Hotel Brew Pub, Old Laxey, Isle of Man, IM4 7DA
☎ (01624) 863214 shorehotel.im
Tours by arrangement

Beer brewed on the Isle of Man is brewed to a strict Beer Purity Act. Additives are not permitted to extend shelf life, nor are chemicals allowed to assist with head retention. Old Laxey's beer is mostly sold through the adjacent Shore Hotel.

Bosun Bitter (OG 1038, ABV 3.8%)
Crisp and fresh with a hoppy aftertaste.

Old Luxters

Chiltern Valley Vineyard, Hambleden, Henley-on-Thames, Oxfordshire, RG9 6JW
☎ (01491) 638330 chilternvalley.co.uk
Shop Mon-Fri 9am-6pm, Sat-Sun 11am-6pm (5pm winter)
Tours by arrangement

Situated in a 17th-century barn beside the Chiltern Valley Vineyard, Old Luxters is a traditional brewery established in 1990 and was awarded a Royal Warrant of Appointment in 2007. The core range is bottle-conditioned beers.

Old Mill SIBA

Mill Street, Snaith, East Yorkshire, DN14 9HU
☎ (01405) 861813 oldmillbrewery.co.uk
Tours by arrangement

Opened in 1983 in a 200-year-old former malt kiln and corn mill, the brew-length is 60 barrels. The brewery is building a tied estate, now standing at 19 houses. Beers can be found nationwide through wholesalers and around 80 free trade outlets are supplied direct. Seasonal beers and monthly specials: see website.

Traditional Mild (OG 1034, ABV 3.4%) ◆
A satisfying roast malt flavour dominates this easy-drinking, quality dark mild.

Traditional Bitter (OG 1038.5, ABV 3.8%) ◆
A malty nose is carried through to the initial flavour. Bitterness runs throughout.

Blonde Bombshell (OG 1042, ABV 4%)
A straw-coloured, easy-drinking beer with delicate and refreshing fruity flavours.

Red Goose (OG 1042, ABV 4.2%)
A rich, ruby-coloured, malty beer.

Old Curiosity (OG 1044.5, ABV 4.5%) ◆
Slightly sweet amber brew, malty to start with. Malt flavours all the way through.

Bullion (OG 1047.5, ABV 4.7%) ◆
The malty and hoppy aroma is followed by a neat mix of hop and fruit tastes within an enveloping maltiness. Dark brown/amber in colour.

Old Pie Factory SIBA

Montague Road, Warwick, CV34 5LW
☎ (01926) 402100 oldpiefactorybrewery.co.uk

Old Pie Factory began brewing in 2011 using a 5.5-barrel plant. The brewery is located at Underwood Wines and is a joint venture between Underwood Wines, the Old Fourpenny Shop Hotel in Warwick and the Case is Altered in Five Ways.

Bitter (OG 1038.5, ABV 3.9%)
Classic English session bitter with only English ingredients.

Pale (OG 1040, ABV 4.1%)
Light and refreshing straw-coloured ale with pleasing hoppy notes.

Old Sawley SIBA

White Lion, 352 Tamworth Road, Sawley, Derbyshire, NG10 3AT ☎ 07722 311209

Office: 22 Park Street, Long Eaton, Derbyshire, NG10 4NA
✉ oldsawleybrewingcompany@gmail.com

Old Sawley Brewing Company was established in 2013. Brewing takes place on a half-barrel plant upstairs at the White Lion pub in Sawley, but a 10-barrel brew plant at the rear of the pub is expected to be in operation during 2015. The brewery supplies Midland beer festivals and two local pubs.

Tollbridge Porter (OG 1043, ABV 4.5%)
A dark porter with subtle flavours of coffee and vanilla and a finishing bite.

Old School SIBA

Holly Bank Barn, Crag Road, Warton, Lancashire, LA5 9PL
☎ (01524) 735005 🌐 oldschoolbrewery.co.uk
Tours by arrangement

A 12-barrel brewery, founded in 2012, located in a renovated 400-year-old former school outbuilding overlooking the picturesque village of Warton. Beer is mainly sold to free houses within a 40-mile radius. Regular open nights are held: see website. Five-litre mini casks are available direct from the brewery.

Blackboard (OG 1037, ABV 3.7%)
Dominant malts and a short finish characterise this lightly-hopped, dark mild.

Hopscotch (OG 1037, ABV 3.7%)
A yellow-coloured pale ale. It balances a crisp taste with a delicate lasting note of citrus fruits.

Detention (OG 1041, ABV 4.1%)
Light, malty bitter, sweetish middle with a gentle, hoppy bitter finish.

Headmaster (OG 1045, ABV 4.5%)
A dark, strong best bitter. It mixes a complex malty flavour with a blackcurrant aroma, leaving a subtle, sweet, nutty aftertaste.

Old Spot

Manor Farm, Station Road, Cullingworth, Bradford, West Yorkshire, BD13 5HN
☎ (01535) 691144 🌐 oldspotbrewery.co.uk
Tours by arrangement

Old Spot, named after the owner's sheepdog, started brewing in 2005. Five regular beers are available complemented by seasonal and one-off brews. The beers are available locally with the George Hotel, Cullingworth, being the main outlet and de facto brewery tap.

Light But Dark (OG 1043, ABV 4%)
Chestnut-coloured bitter with a slight malty taste and pleasant bitter finish. An ideal session beer.

Spot Light (OG 1040, ABV 4.2%)
This smooth-drinking golden ale has a slightly fruity, hoppy aroma leading to a well-balanced fruit hop flavour with hints of pineapple and a long bittersweet finish.

Inn-Spired (OG 1043, ABV 4.3%)
Light-coloured bitter with a light, hoppy taste and a slight fruity finish.

OSB (OG 1042, ABV 4.5%)
A golden-coloured, full-bodied bitter.

Spot O'Bother (OG 1060, ABV 5.5%)
Porter with a chocolate ice cream taste and slight liquorice bitterness to finish. A very complex brew.

Olde Potting Shed (NEW)

Collingdon Buildings, Collingdon Road, High Spen, Tyne & Wear, NE39 2EQ

Brewing began in 2013 using a five-barrel plant.

Cygnet (ABV 4%)

Dark Wing (ABV 4.3%)

Swan Song (ABV 4.8%)

Olde Swan

89 Halesowen Road, Netherton, Dudley, West Midlands, DY2 9PY
☎ (01384) 253075
Tours by arrangement

A famous brewpub best known as Ma Pardoe's after the matriarch who ruled it for years. The pub has been licensed since 1835 and the present brewery and pub were built in 1863. Brewing continued until 1988 and restarted in 2001. Seasonal beers are available.

Original (OG 1034, ABV 3.5%)
Straw-coloured light mild, smooth but tangy, and sweetly refreshing with a faint hoppiness.

Dark Swan (OG 1041, ABV 4.2%)
Smooth, sweet dark mild with late roast malt in the finish.

Entire (OG 1044, ABV 4.4%)
Faintly hoppy, amber premium bitter with sweetness persistent throughout.

Bumble Hole Bitter (OG 1052, ABV 5.2%)
Sweet, smooth amber ale with hints of astringency in the finish.

Oldershaw SIBA

Heath Lane, Barkston Heath, Grantham, Lincolnshire, NG32 2DE
☎ (01476) 572135 🌐 oldershawbrewery.com
Shop Mon-Fri 10am-4pm
Tours by arrangement

Oldershaw Brewery has been brewing since 1997. Owned and run by brewster Kathy Britton, it is a nine-barrel plant and brews in the region of 300,000 pints a year. The brewery produces around 25 different beers of varying styles. Seasonal beers are available.

Barkston Bitter (OG 1036, ABV 3.6%)
A mellow amber session bitter, softly spiced citrus and a smooth malt base.

Mowbray's Mash (OG 1037, ABV 3.7%)
A gold-tinted amber ale. The hops add a zesty, fruity edge to a softly nutty base. A fine session ale.

Heavenly Blonde (OG 1038, ABV 3.8%)
Pale blonde session beer, packed with zesty, refreshing tropical fruits with a crisp, dry finish.

Newton's Drop (OG 1041, ABV 4.1%)
Balanced malt and hops but with a strong bitter, lingering taste in this mid-brown beer.

Caskade (OG 1042, ABV 4.2%)
A gentle blend of flavours combine into a smooth, undemanding pint. Malt vies with a hoppy bitterness for initial recognition. Traces of caramel and sulphur appear before the short, sharp finish.

Great Expectations (OG 1040, ABV 4.2%)

A pale gold-coloured beer incorporating citrus-rich Galaxy and Cascade hops.

Grantham Stout (OG 1043, ABV 4.3%)
Dark brown and smooth with rich roast malt flavour, warming fruity complex flavours. A long, moderately dry finish.

Mosaic Blonde (OG 1041, ABV 4.3%)
Satisfying lager-style beer featuring three hop varieties. Powerfully citrus and tropical.

Posh Blonde (OG 1041, ABV 4.3%)
Crisp lager-style beer, enhanced by fruity floral and citrus-infused notes.

Regal Blonde (OG 1042, ABV 4.4%) ◆
Straw-coloured, lager-style beer with a good malt/hop balance throughout; strong bitterness on the taste lingers.

Old Boy (OG 1047, ABV 4.8%) ◆
A full-bodied amber ale, fruity and bitter with a hop/fruit aroma. The malt that backs the taste dies in the long finish.

Blonde Volupta (OG 1050, ABV 5%)
Straw-coloured zesty premium beer packed with complexity and intense tropical fruit flavours leading to a crisp, dry finish.

Alchemy (OG 1052, ABV 5.3%)
A premium golden bitter, easy-drinking and well-balanced with tropical citrus notes and subtle French toast malts.

Ole Slewfoot SIBA

Unit 1b, Gaymers Way, North Walsham, Norfolk, NR28 0AN
☎ (01603) 279927 🌐 oleslewfootbrewery.co.uk
Shop 12pm-5pm daily (please phone ahead)
Tours by arrangement

Ole Slewfoot was established in 2009. Five outlets are supplied direct.

Cabarrus Gold (OG 1036, ABV 3.6%) ◆
Citrus and hop flavours follow an elderflower aroma. Increasingly bitter finish.

January 8th (OG 1040, ABV 4.2%)

Orange Blossom Special (OG 1042, ABV 4.4%)

Fox on the Run (OG 1046, ABV 4.8%)

Devil's Dream (OG 1048, ABV 5%)

On the Edge

Nether Edge, Sheffield, South Yorkshire ☎ 07975 989654 ✉ ontheedgebrew@gmail.com

On the Edge started brewing commercially in 2012 using a 0.5-barrel plant in the brewer's home. Brewing takes place once a week. Three local pubs are supplied as well as beer festivals. There is no regular beer list as new brews are constantly being tried.

One Mile End (NEW) SIBA

White Hart Brew Pub, 1-3 Mile End Road, London, E1 4TP
☎ (020) 7790 2894 ☎ 07912 411147
🌐 the-white-hart.co.uk

Previously known as Mulligans, Simon McCabe took over as head brewer in 2014 and relaunched the brewery as One Mile End Brew Co. Capacity is 2,500 litres per week. The beers are available at the White Hart and its sister pub the Alma in Pentonville.

Opa Hay's

Glencot, Wood Lane, Aldeby, Norfolk, NR34 0DA
☎ (01502) 679144 🌐 engelfineales.com

Opa Hay's began brewing in late 2008. It is a small, family-run microbrewery, taking its name from the brewer's great grandfather. Only traditional brewing methods are used, with ingredients that are, where possible, sourced locally.

Engels Fruity Little Number (ABV 3.6%) ◆
Powerful citrus/grapefruit aroma with malt and hops. Smoky sweetish flavours with fruit notes, and a fruity, hoppy aftertaste.

Engel's Best Bitter (ABV 4%)
A triple-hopped aromatic beer, an old-fashioned traditional English ale.

Matilda's Revenge (ABV 4.3%)
Golden ale originally brewed to commemorate the resident ghost that haunts the Kings's Head Hotel.

Samuel Engels Meister Pils (SEMP) (ABV 4.8%)
A Pilsner-style beer, light in colour with a hoppy aroma.

Liquid Bread (ABV 5.2%)
Bavarian-style wheat beer, naturally cloudy, with a distinct aroma of cloves and banana.

Ordnance City SIBA

The Old Brewery, Whitley Farm, Aschott, Somerset, TA7 9QW
☎ (01458) 210050 🌐 ordnancecitybrewery.co.uk
Tours by arrangement

Established in 2012, this award-winning five-barrel brewery is situated in a special effects workshop where beer is brewed by explosives engineers and has been known to be delivered to local pubs in an armoured personnel carrier.

Detonator (OG 1039, ABV 3.8%)

Ordnance Pale Mild (OG 1040, ABV 3.8%)

Mortar Bomb (OG 1043, ABV 4.4%)

Claymore Porter (OG 1046, ABV 4.5%)

Sidewinder (OG 1048, ABV 4.7%)

Orkney SIBA 👁

Quoyloo, Stromness, Orkney, KW16 3LT
☎ (01667) 404555

Office: Sinclair Breweries Ltd, Cawdor, IV12 5XP
🌐 sinclairbreweries.co.uk
Shop & visitor centre – ring for opening hours
Tours by arrangement

Orkney was established in 1988 in an old village school building. Having incorporated sister brewery Atlas (qv) it moved next door in 2010 to enable an increase in capacity and the completion of an award-winning visitor centre in 2012. Seasonal beers are available.

Raven (OG 1038, ABV 3.8%) ◆
A well-balanced quaffable bitter. Malty fruitiness and bitter hops last through to the long, dry aftertaste.

Dragonhead (OG 1040, ABV 4%) ◆

A strong, dark malt aroma flows into the taste in this Scottish stout. The roast malt continues to dominate the aftertaste, and blends with chocolate to develop a strong, dry finish.

Northern Light (OG 1040, ABV 4%)
A well-balanced golden ale with a real smack of fruit and hops in the taste and an increasing bitter aftertaste.

Red MacGregor (OG 1040, ABV 4%)
This tawny red ale has a powerful smack of fruit and a clean, fresh mouthfeel. Generally a well-balanced bitter.

Corncrake (OG 1042, ABV 4.1%)
A straw-coloured beer with soft citrus fruits and a floral aroma.

Dark Island (OG 1045, ABV 4.6%)
The roast malt and chocolate character varies, making the beer hard to categorise as a stout or an old ale. A sweetish roast malt taste leads to a long-lasting roasted, slightly bitter, dry finish.

Skull Splitter (OG 1080, ABV 8.5%)
An intense velvet malt nose with hints of apple, prune and plum. The hoppy taste is balanced by satiny smooth malt with fruity spicy edges, leading to a long, dry finish with a hint of nut.

For Atlas Brewery:

Latitude (OG 1036, ABV 3.6%)
This straw-coloured ale has a light citrus taste with a smack of hops and grapefruit in the light bitter finish.

Three Sisters (OG 1043, ABV 4.2%)
Malt, summer fruits and caramel on the nose and blackcurrant in the taste, followed by a short, hoppy, bitter finish.

Nimbus (OG 1050, ABV 5%)
A full-bodied golden beer using some wheat malt and three types of hops. Sweet and fruity at the front, it becomes slightly astringent with lasting fruit and a pleasant, dry finish.

Ossett SIBA

Kings Yard, Low Mill Road, Ossett, West Yorkshire, WF5 8ND
☎ (01924) 261333 ossett-brewery.co.uk
Shop Mon-Fri 9am-4.30pm
Tours by arrangement

Osset began brewing in 1998, moving to a new site in 2005. Capacity is now 230 barrels per week. The brewery owns 22 pubs, three with microbreweries; the Riverhead (qv) was purchased in 2006, Fernandes (qv) in 2007 and brewing commenced at the Rat Brewery (qv) in 2011. See website for monthly seasonal beers and one-off specials.

Pale Gold (OG 1038, ABV 3.8%)
A light, refreshing pale ale with a light, hoppy aroma.

Yorkshire Blonde (OG 1040, ABV 3.9%)
A pale, full-bodied and well-rounded ale. Slightly sweet on the palate, with a generous late addition of Mount Hood hops for aroma.

Big Red Bitter (OG 1042, ABV 4%)
Deep red, malty Yorkshire bitter.

Silver King (OG 1041, ABV 4.3%)
A lager-style beer with a crisp, dry flavour and citrus fruit aroma.

Premium Yorkshire Blonde (OG 1045, ABV 4.5%)
Stronger, slightly fuller-bodied version of Yorkshire Blonde, low in bitterness, slightly sweet on the palate with a delicate floral hop aroma.

Treacle Stout (OG 1050, ABV 5%)
A rich and robust stout. The addition of black treacle gives intense depth and roasted malts impart a coffee flavour. Generous amounts of hops add a dry citrus finish to this complex black ale.

Excelsior (OG 1051, ABV 5.2%)
A strong pale ale with a full, mellow flavour and a fresh, hoppy aroma with citrus/floral characteristics.

Otley SIBA

Unit 39, Albion Industrial Estate, Pontypridd, Mid Glamorgan, CF37 4NX
☎ (01443) 480555 otleybrewing.co.uk
Tours by arrangement

Otley Brewing was established in 2005 and since then the brewery has almost tripled in size, taking over adjacent industrial units. Seasonal beers: see website. Bottle-conditioned beers are available.

01 (OG 1038, ABV 4%)
A pale golden beer with a hoppy aroma. The taste has hops, malt, fruit and a thirst-quenching bitterness. A satisfying finish completes this beer.

02 Croeso (OG 1040, ABV 4%)
Light golden ale full of citrus hop aromas.

04 Colombo (OG 1038, ABV 4%)
A golden, hoppy beer.

03 Boss (OG 1042, ABV 4.4%)
Chestnut red bitter using American hops for bitterness and aroma.

12 Thai Bo (OG 1045, ABV 4.6%)
Clear wheat beer with lemongrass, lime leaf and galangal.

05 Hop Angeles (OG 1047, ABV 4.8%)
An American red ale.

09 Blonde (OG 1047, ABV 4.8%)
Clear wheat beer flavoured with roasted orange peel, coriander and cloves.

07 Weissen (OG 1048, ABV 5%)
Cloudy German-style wheat beer.

10 Oxymoron (OG 1047, ABV 5.5%)
A black IPA-style bitter.

06 Porter (OG 1063, ABV 6.6%)

11 Motley Brew (OG 1072, ABV 7.5%)
Double IPA with big hop aromas and high bitterness giving a classic IPA mouthfeel.

Otter SIBA

Mathayes, Luppitt, Honiton, Devon, EX14 4SA
☎ (01404) 891285 otterbrewery.com
Tours by arrangement

Otter Brewery is family-run brewery (five generations of brewers) set high up in the Blackdown Hills. Environmental responsibility lies at the heart of the brewery's ethos. Otter's eco cellar has been built underground and is naturally chilled. The beers are made from the brewery's own springs and locally-sourced ingredients.

Bitter (OG 1036, ABV 3.6%)

Well-balanced amber session bitter with a fruity nose and bitter taste and aftertaste.

Amber (OG 1038.5, ABV 4%)
A well-balanced bitter with hints of tropical fruit and spice – sometimes with an impression of ginger.

Bright (OG 1039, ABV 4.3%)
Pale yellow/golden ale with a strong fruit aroma, sweet fruity taste and a bittersweet finish.

Ale (OG 1043, ABV 4.5%)
A full-bodied best bitter. A malty aroma predominates with a fruity taste and finish.

Head (OG 1054, ABV 5.8%)
Fruity aroma and taste with a pleasant bitter finish. Dark brown and full-bodied.

Ouseburn Valley

c/o The Brandling Villa, Haddricks Mill Road, South Gosforth, Tyne & Wear, NE3 1QL ☎ 07932 677899 ouseburnvallleybrewery.co.uk

Ouseburn Valley started in the owner's garage in 2010, and in 2011 the plant was moved to the cellar of the Brandling Villa pub where both capacity and beer range were increased. After a flood in 2012, brewing is back in the owner's garage.

Armstrong Bitter (OG 1042, ABV 4.1%)
Pleasant rich yellow colour, light spicy aroma with soft caramel overtones and a long bitter finish.

Golden Ale (OG 1044, ABV 4.4%)
Dark gold in colour with light hop aroma, sweet malty taste and a smooth finish.

India Pale Ale (OG 1047, ABV 4.7%)
Pale gold in colour with a strong hop aroma and a long dry finish.

Milk Stout (OG 1047, ABV 4.7%)
Dark in colour with a liquorice aroma, sweet liquorice and slightly coffee taste.

American Honey (OG 1049, ABV 5%)
Dark gold in colour with a sweet honey taste and strong dry hop aroma.

Out There SIBA

Unit 4, Foundry Lane Industrial Estate, Newcastle upon Tyne, NE6 1LH ☎ 07946 579534 outtherebrewing.com

Out There was established in 2012 by Steve Pickthall. Branding and beer names are themed around the 1950s space race.

Space is the Place (OG 1034, ABV 3.5%)
An amber-coloured beer with a cream head. The aroma is digestive biscuits and brown bread with a sweet malt flavour and floral notes.

Laika (OG 1049, ABV 4.8%)
A straw-coloured cloudy beer. The aroma is citrus with a hint of custard cream biscuits and the flavour of orange peel and spices liven the pale malt base.

Celestial Love (OG 1051, ABV 5.1%)
A rich red beer. The aroma is caramel with a hint of malt loaf and the taste is sweet malt with floral and grapefruit hop flavours.

Outlaw

See Roosters

Outstanding SIBA

Britannia Mill, Cobden Street, Bury, Lancashire, BL9 6AW
☎ (0161) 764 7723 outstandingbeers.com

Born of an aspiration to create outstanding beers and established in 2008, the brewery operates a dual system, brewing on a 15-barrel plant and utilising a 2.5-barrel plant for special and experimental brews. Selective free trade accounts are supplied nationally.

3.9 (OG 1036, ABV 3.9%)
Pale, light and hoppy.

Red (OG 1045, ABV 4.4%)
Copper-coloured, mellow and biscuity.

Blond (OG 1044, ABV 4.5%)
Pale, citrus and refreshing.

IPA (OG 1058, ABV 5.5%)
Golden, dry and bitter.

Stout (OG 1061, ABV 5.5%)
Jet black and roasty with liquorice notes.

Owenshaw Mill

Owenshaw Works, Old Cawsey, Sowerby Bridge, West Yorkshire, HX6 2AJ
☎ (01422) 839010 owenshawmillbrewery.co.uk

Owenshaw Mill began production in 2011 using an eight-barrel plant. Beers are available in pubs and clubs around Halifax and Huddersfield, and at beer festivals.

Katy's Blonde (OG 1036, ABV 3.6%)
A fruity, full-bodied blonde session beer.

Skinny Duck (OG 1037, ABV 3.7%)

Better than Best (OG 1039, ABV 3.9%)
Tanwy beer with a nutty and fruity taste combined with pleasant, long, hoppy bitterness.

Salt Road Blonde (OG 1039, ABV 3.9%)
A strong blonde ale with a distinct aroma.

Gollum's Revenge (OG 1040, ABV 4%)

Black Lightning (OG 1045, ABV 4.5%)
Strong dark mild.

Oxfordshire Ales SIBA

12 Pear Tree Farm Industrial Units, Bicester Road, Marsh Gibbon, Bicester, Buckinghamshire, OX27 0GB
☎ (01869) 278765 john@oxfordshireales.co.uk
Tours by arrangement

The company first brewed in 2005 and now supplies over 100 outlets as well as several wholesalers. Seasonal beers are produced on the 15-barrel plant. There is a bottling line onsite. The Baby Ox Brewery produces interesting one-off ales.

Triple B (OG 1037, ABV 3.7%)
This pale amber beer has a huge caramel aroma. The caramel diminishes in the initial taste, which changes to a fruit/bitter balance. This in turn leads to a long, refreshing, bitter aftertaste.

Pride of Oxford (OG 1042, ABV 4.1%)

An amber beer, the aroma is butterscotch/caramel, which carries on into the initial taste. The taste then becomes bitter with sweetish/malty overtones. There is a long, dry, bitter finish.

Blenheim (OG 1042, ABV 4.2%)
A refreshing golden ale with a fresh zesty, spicy hop aroma, biscuity malt taste and pleasant dry finish.

Churchill IPA (OG 1045, ABV 4.5%)
A full-bodied beer with a balance of malt, hop and fruit undertones. Dry, fruity bitter aftertaste.

Marshmellow (OG 1047, ABV 4.7%) ◆
The slightly fruity aroma in this golden-amber beer leads to a hoppy but thin taste, with slight caramel notes. The aftertaste is short and bitter.

Padstow SIBA

The Brewery, Unit 4a, Trecerus Industrial Estate, Padstow, Cornwall, PL28 8RW
☎ (01841) 532169 ⊕ padstowbrewing.co.uk
Tours by arrangement

⊗ The brewery began commercial brewing in 2013 using a 0.5-barrel plant. Owners Des and Caron Archer, Caron being the brewster, have since installed a custom-built 10-barrel plant. Beer festivals and local outlets are supplied. Bottle-conditioned beers are available.

Pale Ale (OG 1037, ABV 3.6%)
Well-hopped golden ale with a good balanced bitterness.

Pilot (OG 1040, ABV 4%)
Well-balanced amber ale with distinctive aroma and long finish.

Pride (OG 1044, ABV 4.5%)
Amber-coloured best bitter with a touch of honey.

IPA (OG 1046, ABV 4.8%)
Strong, traditional-style IPA, refreshing and satisfying.

May Day (OG 1048, ABV 5%)
An extra pale ale that is both crisp and smooth. Aroma hopping gives citrus and tropical notes on a long finish.

Palmers SIBA IFBB

The Old Brewery, West Bay Road, Bridport, Dorset, DT6 4JA
☎ (01308) 422396 ⊕ palmersbrewery.com
Shop Mon-Sat 9am-6pm
Tours by arrangement

⊗ Palmers is Britain's only thatched brewery and dates from 1794. It is situated in Bridport, the heart of the Jurassic Coast in south-west Dorset. The company continues to make substantial investment in its 54 tenanted pubs, all serving cask ale. An additional 400 outlets are supplied within the free trade.

Copper Ale (OG 1036, ABV 3.7%) ◆
Beautifully balanced, copper-coloured light bitter with a hoppy aroma.

Best Bitter (OG 1040, ABV 4.2%) ◆
Hop aroma and bitterness stay in the background in this predominately malty best bitter, with some fruit on the aroma.

Dorset Gold (OG 1046, ABV 4.5%) ◆
More complex than many golden ales thanks to a pleasant banana and mango fruitiness on the aroma that carries on into the taste and aftertaste.

200 (OG 1052, ABV 5%) ◆
This is a big beer with a touch of caramel sweetness adding to a complex, hoppy fruit taste that lasts from the aroma well into the aftertaste.

Tally Ho! (OG 1057, ABV 5.5%)

Panther

Unit 1, Collers Way, Reepham, Norfolk, NR10 4SW
☎ 07766 558215 ⊕ pantherbrewery.co.uk
Shop Mon-Fri 9am-6pm, Sat 10am-3pm
Tours by arrangement

⊗ Panther began brewing in 2010 on an industrial estate near the old railway station, formerly the home of Reepham Brewery. Beer and other merchandise can be purchased direct from the brewery or online from the brewery website.

Cub Panther (OG 1036, ABV 2.5%) ◆
Caramel and hop aroma. A malty beginning slowly fades to a grainy bittersweet dryness. Long, sustained bitter finish.

Ginger Panther (OG 1037, ABV 3.7%)
A ginger wheat beer with a fiery and distinct ginger flavour and subtle lemon flavour notes.

Golden Panther (OG 1037, ABV 3.7%) ◆
A hoppy, bitter beer with some caramel in the nose. Quick finishing, grainy and one dimensional.

Panther Honey (OG 1040, ABV 4%) ◆
A gentle flowing brew with honey and malt throughout. Malt, caramel and hop. Amber-coloured with a tapering bittersweet finale.

Pink Panther (OG 1039, ABV 4%)
This pink ale has a range of fruit flavours and aromas. A refreshingly balanced wheat beer with a bittersweet fruity finish. Refreshingly fruity ale with bite.

Red Panther (OG 1041, ABV 4.1%) ◆
Full flavoured brew. Solidly malty in both aroma and taste. Hops, and a residual sweetness, provide balance.

Black Panther (OG 1047, ABV 4.5%)
A dark, rich, smooth ale with a complex full flavour and a bittersweet balance which leads to a dry finish.

Paradise

Bird in Hand, Trelissick Road, Hayle, Cornwall, TR27 4HY
☎ (01736) 753974
✉ birdinhand@paradisepark.org.uk
Tours by arrangement

⊗ Brewing first started in 1981 under the name Paradise Brewery, named after its location, the Paradise Park. The name was changed to Wheal Ale in 1995. Brewing ceased in 2004 but re-started in 2009 under the original Paradise Brewery name.

Bitter (OG 1043, ABV 4.3%) ◆
Gentle malt and fruit on the nose, followed by a dominantly bitter flavour balanced by sweet malt and fruity hop. The finish is bitter.

Artist (OG 1055, ABV 5.2%) ◆
Full-bodied tawny ale with faint aroma of malt. Heavy sweet malt and bubblegum esters in the

THE BREWERIES

mouth with a balance of hops. Dryness and bitterness in the finish.

Parish

6 Main Street, Burrough on the Hill, Leicestershire, LE14 2JQ
☎ (01664) 454801 ✉ bazbrewery@gmail.com
Tours by arrangement

Parish began in 1983 and now operates on a 20-barrel plant, with capacity to brew a further 12 barrels. The brewery is located in a 400-year-old building next to Grants Freehouse, which stocks the full range of beers. Other local outlets are also supplied and one-off brews are produced for beer festivals. Baz's Bonce Blower is also available bottle conditioned.

PSB (OG 1038, ABV 3.8%)
Hoppy session beer with a malty aftertaste.

Burrough Bitter (OG 1047, ABV 4.8%)
Darker version of PSB with a good balance of malt and hops. Reddish brown in colour.

Poachers Ale (ABV 6%)
Deep ruby red, full-bodied, malty blended beer.

Baz's Bonce Blower (OG 1098, ABV 12%)
Strong, dark beer with a rich, malty character. A Christmas pudding ale.

Parker (NEW)

1 Alderson Crescent, Formby, Merseyside, L37 3LY
☎ 07949 797889 🌐 theparkerbrewery.co.uk

Parker was established in 2014 using a 25-litre plant. Operated on a part-time basis at present there are plans for expansion to a full-time, five-barrel plant plus the production of cask-conditioned beers. At present bottle-conditioned beers are produced, supplied to local restaurants and bars.

Partizan

8 Almond Road, South Bermondsey, London, SE16 3LR
☎ (020) 8127 5053 🌐 partizanbrewing.co.uk

Partizan began brewing in 2012. Only bottle-conditioned beers are produced. Each brew is different, but they are based on a variety of international styles and all are vegan-friendly and bottled by hand on site.

Partners SIBA

Unit 12, Saville Bridge Mill, Mill Street East, Dewsbury, West Yorkshire, WF12 9AG
☎ (01924) 457772 🌐 partnersbrewery.co.uk
Tours by arrangement

Partners was formed in 2011 following the purchase of the long-established Anglo Dutch Brewery by Richard Sharp. The brewery now has an annual capacity of 3,600 barrels following significant investment in new equipment during the past few years. Seasonal beers: see website.

J.Y.B. (OG 1035, ABV 3.5%)
An easy-drinking session beer brewed with four different malts creating a complex character.

Working Class Hero (OG 1038, ABV 3.8%)
A bitter tasting session beer with a strong, hoppy aftertaste.

Blond (OG 1039, ABV 3.9%)
A blonde, crisp, aromatic session beer.

Triple Hop (OG 1042, ABV 4.2%)
A triple-hopped pale ale producing a refreshing brew with high bitterness and a hoppy aftertaste.

Ghost (OG 1043, ABV 4.5%)
A pale, full-bodied bitter with a fresh, gentle nose, taken over by a smooth hop and citrus finish.

Tabatha (OG 1054, ABV 6%)
Golden Belgian-style Tripel with a strong fruity, hoppy and bitter character. Powerful and warming, slightly thinnish, with a bitter, dry finish.

Patriot

Norman Knight, Whichford, Shipston-on-Stour, Warwickshire, CV36 5PE
☎ (01608) 684621 🌐 thepatriotbrewery.co.uk
Tours by arrangement

Patriot began brewing in 2010 using a four-barrel brew plant. It is located next to the Norman Knight pub, where the beers are regularly available. Seasonal beers are available.

Morris (OG 1038, ABV 3.8%)

Kiwi (OG 1041, ABV 4.1%)

Pug IPA (OG 1057, ABV 5.6%)

Peak SIBA

Barn Brewery, Cunnery Barn, Chatsworth, Derbyshire, DE45 1EX
☎ (01246) 583737 🌐 peakales.co.uk
Tours by arrangement

Peak Ales opened in 2005 in former derelict farm buildings on the Chatsworth estate aided by a DEFRA Rural Enterprise Scheme grant and support from trustees of Chatsworth Settlement. The brewery supplies numerous local outlets. Seasonal beers: see website.

Swift Nick (OG 1038, ABV 3.8%)
Easy-drinking, copper-coloured bitter with balanced malt and hops and a gentle, hoppy, bitter finish.

Bakewell Best Bitter (OG 1041, ABV 4.2%)
Full-bodied tawny bitter with a hoppy bitterness against a malty background, leading to a hoppy dry aftertaste.

Chatsworth Gold (OG 1045, ABV 4.6%)
Speciality beer made with honey, which gives a pleasant sweetness leading to a hop and malt finish.

DPA (OG 1045, ABV 4.6%)
Subtle pale ale that is deceptively strong. Flavours of fruit, hops and malt build slowly towards a well-balanced bittersweet finish.

Peakstones Rock SIBA

Peakstones Farm, Cheadle Road, Alton, Staffordshire, ST10 4DH ☎ 07891 350908 🌐 peakstonesrock.co.uk
Tours by arrangement

Peakstones Rock was established in 2005 with a five-barrel brewery located on a farm in the Peak District National Park. The plant was expanded to 10-barrel capacity in 2009. The brewery supplies an expanding free trade market in the North Midlands and surrounding areas.

Nemesis (OG 1042, ABV 3.8%)
Biscuity aroma with some hop background. Sweet start, sweetish body then hops emerge to give a fruity middle. Bitterness develops slowly to a tongue-tingling finish.

Chained Oak (OG 1045, ABV 4.2%)
A copper-coloured beer with a bitter finish and hop aroma.

Alton Abbey (OG 1051, ABV 4.5%)

Black Hole (OG 1048, ABV 4.8%)

Oblivion (OG 1055, ABV 5.5%)

Peerless SIBA

The Brewery, 8 Pool Street, Birkenhead, Merseyside, CH41 3NL
☎ (0151) 647 7688 peerlessbrewing.co.uk
Tours by arrangement

Peerless began brewing in 2009 and is under the directorship of Steve Briscoe. Beers are sold through festivals, local pubs and the free trade. Seasonal beers are available.

Pale (OG 1036, ABV 3.8%)
Pale session ale. Good initial bitterness and a hint of grapefruit on the finish.

Jinja Ninja (OG 1040, ABV 4%)
Ginger Beer made with fresh root ginger, chilli and lemon. There is an aroma of fresh ginger followed by a kick from the ginger aftertaste.

Triple Blonde (OG 1040, ABV 4.1%)
A blonde beer with a fruity citrus finish.

Viking Gold (OG 1044, ABV 4.6%)
A well-balanced golden ale with initial hop bitterness and a citrus finish. The distinct citrus fruit and hop aroma leads to a crisp, dry finish.

Storr Lager (OG 1042, ABV 4.8%)
A continental-style lager with a fresh citrus hop finish and pleasant malt backbone.

Oatmeal Stout (OG 1050, ABV 5%)
Full-bodied black stout with toffee and caramel tones. An element of sweetness balances the bitterness from the roast malts.

Red Rocks (OG 1047, ABV 5%)
Full-bodied ruby ale. Rich malt flavours combine with hops for a beer with fruity overtones.

Full Whack (OG 1054, ABV 6%)
The high level of alcohol is complemented by increased bitterness and a fruity hop finish.

Penlon Cottage

Penlon Farm, Pencae, Llanarth, SA47 0QN
☎ (01545) 580022 penlon.biz

Penlon opened in 2004 on a smallholding with a strong focus on sustainability and self-sufficiency. Only bottle-conditioned beers are produced.

Pennine SIBA

Well Hall Farm, Well, North Yorkshire, DL8 2PX
☎ (01677) 470111 pennine-brewery.co.uk

Pennine began brewing in Batley in 2012 using an 18-barrel lager plant complete with lauter tun. In 2013 the brewery relocated to Well, near Masham and now produces four core beers plus seasonals: see website. A visitor centre opened in 2014.

Amber Necker (OG 1039, ABV 3.9%)
A session beer with a smooth and creamy texture and a hoppy aftertaste.

Best Bitter (OG 1040, ABV 3.9%)

Real Blonde (OG 1041, ABV 4%)
Well-balanced blonde ale with a fruity aftertaste.

Natural Gold (OG 1043, ABV 4.2%)

Penpont SIBA

Inner Trenarrett, Altarnun, Launceston, Cornwall, PL15 7SY
☎ (01566) 86069 penpontbrewery.co.uk
Shop at brewery (please ring first)
Tours by arrangement

Penpont opened in 2008 and has steadily increased the range and production since then. The brewery has also won a number of awards. Its beers are available in pubs across Cornwall. Seasonal beers: see website.

St Nonna's (OG 1037, ABV 3.7%)
Malt and apple fruitiness dominate the initial aroma of this brown beer. Hop bitterness is quickly apparent in the taste and lingers in the long aftertaste.

Cornish Arvor (OG 1040, ABV 4%)
Well-balanced tawny best bitter. Principally bitter with fruity sweetness and some malt. Bitter hop-fruit finish.

Shipwreck Coast (OG 1044, ABV 4.4%)
Light aroma of orange citrus. Hops dominate with marmalade and green apples. Malt emerges with a bitter and dry finish.

Roughtor (OG 1047, ABV 4.7%)
Malt dominates aroma and taste balanced by sweetness and rising hop bitterness. Strong flavour slowly fades in the dry finish.

Penzance

Star Inn, Crowlas, Penzance, Cornwall, TR20 8DX
☎ (01736) 740375
penzancebrewing.wordpress.com
Tours by arrangement

Owner Peter Elvin began brewing in 2008 on a self-built five-barrel plant in the old stable block of the Star Inn. The fermentation capacity has since been expanded, increasing the volume and range of beers produced. Production is now at full capacity of 780 barrels per year. Besides the pub, selected outlets and beer festivals are supplied.

Crowlas Bitter (OG 1037, ABV 3.8%)
Perfectly balanced session bitter with malt, hops, bitterness and a hint of fruit and biscuit. Lingering finish of malty bitterness.

Jolly Farmer (OG 1036, ABV 3.9%)
Hoppy golden ale with a citrus finish.

Potion No. 9 (OG 1039, ABV 4%)
Floral and grapefruit hops dominate the nose and taste. Big bitter taste which grows into a complex grapefruit, apricot finish.

Brisons Bitter (OG 1043, ABV 4.5%)
Dominant malt in aroma and taste, balanced by fruity hops, sweetness and bitterness. Long malty finish becoming dry and bitter.

Trink (OG 1048, ABV 5.2%)
Well-balanced golden ale, tropical fruit flavour with a citrus bite finish.

Mellow (OG 1050, ABV 5.5%) ◆
Powerful citrus hop and malt in aroma and taste leading to an astringent finish balanced by subtle lemon fruitiness.

IPA (OG 1058, ABV 6%)
A strong, traditional-style IPA.

Scilly Stout (OG 1067, ABV 7%) ◆
Full-bodied and powerful dark brown sweet stout. Roast coffee, chocolate and rich fruity malt throughout. Long roast finish.

Pheasantry SIBA

High Brecks Farm, Lincoln Road, East Markham, Nottinghamshire, NG22 0SN
☎ (01777) 872728 🌐 pheasantrybrewery.co.uk
Shop Tue-Sun 11am-5pm
Tours by arrangement

Pheasantry began brewing in 2012 using a 10-barrel plant from Canada. Situated in a listed barn on a farm, the brewery and visitor centre incorporates a restaurant, tearooms and bar, with the brewery visible through glass partitions. It supplies some 200 pubs and retail outlets in Nottinghamshire, Lincolnshire and South Yorkshire.

Best Bitter (OG 1038, ABV 3.8%)
Smooth-tasting, copper-coloured beer, with medium bitterness and low to medium sweetness. It has a light spicy aroma.

Pale Ale (OG 1040, ABV 4%)
A pale-coloured, smooth-tasting beer with floral and citrus notes and a dry finish.

Ringneck Amber Ale (ABV 4.1%)

Dark Ale (OG 1042, ABV 4.2%)
A smooth, soft. satisfying dark ale with malty flavours, balanced bitterness and a velvety texture.

Pilsner (ABV 4.2%)

Dancing Dragonfly (ABV 5%)

Phipps SIBA

The Albion Brewery, 54 Kingswell Road, Northampton, NN1 1PR
☎ (01604) 946606 🌐 phipps-nbc.co.uk

Originally founded in Towcester in 1801, Phipps had been brewing in Northampton since 1817 until taken over by Watney Mann which closed the brewery in 1974. The company name and recipes were acquired and in 2008 the first Phipps draught beer reappeared after 40 years, brewed to the original recipe at Grainstore Brewery (qv) in Oakham. The Albion Brewery site, once owned by Phipps, was acquired and a new 15-barrel brewing plant installed in 2014 to enable Phipps beers to be once again brewed in the town. Hoggleys brewery, which was established in 2002, merged with Phipps NBC at the end of 2013 and all Hoggleys beers are now brewed on the Phipps plant, with the former Hoggleys plant sold to Merrimen Brewing (qv).

Diamond Ale (OG 1037, ABV 3.7%)
A light amber-coloured harvest ale.

Red Star (OG 1038, ABV 3.8%)
A pre-WWII session beer; maltier, sweeter and darker than present day versions.

IPA (OG 1042, ABV 4.2%)
Recreated from old recipes, it has characteristic hop flavours and aromas. This pale amber beer has a residual malt sweetness which, when coupled with the grapefruit note from the hops, gives a fine, fresh, crisp finish.

Ratliffe's Celebrated Stout (OG 1043, ABV 4.3%)
A creamy, well-balanced stout with a pleasant aftertaste with just a hint of bitterness.

Gold Star (OG 1050, ABV 5.2%)
An export-style pale ale.

Brewed for Hoggleys Brewery:

Albion Bitter (OG 1040, ABV 4%)
A complex beer with deep malty tones balanced with a fresh, hoppy finish.

Mill Lane Mild (OG 1040, ABV 4%)

Northamptonshire Bitter (OG 1040, ABV 4%)
A straw-coloured bitter.

Reservoir Hogs (OG 1042, ABV 4.3%)
Mid gold, hoppy and refreshing.

Pump Fiction (OG 1045, ABV 4.5%)
Light copper-coloured beer, complex but easy-drinking.

India Pale Ale (OG 1050, ABV 5%)
A full-bodied, hoppy IPA.

Solstice Stout (OG 1050, ABV 5%)
A rich, full-flavoured stout.

Phoenix SIBA

Green Lane, Heywood, Lancashire, OL10 2EP
☎ (01706) 627009 ✉ tony@phoenixbrewery.co.uk

Established in Ellesmere Port in 1982, Oak Brewery moved to the old Phoenix Brewery in Heywood and adopted the name in 1991. It now supplies 400-500 outlets plus wholesalers. Many seasonal beers are produced throughout the year. Restoration of the old brewery, built in 1897, is ongoing.

Hopsack (OG 1038, ABV 3.8%)
A light-drinking, hoppy session beer.

Navvy (OG 1039, ABV 3.8%) ◆
Amber beer with a citrus fruit and malt nose. Good balance of citrus fruit, malt and hops with bitterness coming through in the aftertaste.

Monkeytown Mild (OG 1039, ABV 3.9%)
Dark-coloured mild with fruitiness, bitterness and a smooth, full malt finish.

Arizona (OG 1040, ABV 4.1%) ◆
Yellow in colour with a fruity and hoppy aroma. A refreshing beer with citrus, hops and good bitterness, and a shortish dry aftertaste.

Spotland Gold (OG 1041, ABV 4.1%)
A pale, hoppy beer with a lingering bitter finish.

Pale Moonlight (OG 1042, ABV 4.2%)
Quite bitter with lingering grassy hop finish.

Black Bee (OG 1045, ABV 4.5%)
Brewed with honey this porter has a malty aroma, which tastes of dark fruit, honey and a hint of coffee.

White Monk (OG 1045, ABV 4.5%) ◆

Yellow beer with a citrus fruit aroma, plenty of fruit, hops and bitterness in the taste, and a hoppy, bitter finish.

Thirsty Moon (OG 1046, ABV 4.6%) ◆
Tawny beer with a fresh citrus aroma. Hoppy, fruity and malty with a dry, hoppy finish.

West Coast IPA (OG 1046, ABV 4.6%) ◆
Golden in colour with a hoppy, fruity nose. Strong hoppy and fruity taste and aftertaste with good bitterness throughout.

Double Gold (OG 1050, ABV 5%)
Full-bodied, premium bitter.

Wobbly Bob (OG 1060, ABV 6%) ◆
A red/brown beer with malty, fruity aroma and creamy mouthfeel. Strongly malty and fruity in flavour, with hops and a hint of herbs. Both sweetness and bitterness are evident throughout.

For Brunning & Price Pub Co:

Original Bitter (ABV 3.8%)

Pictish

Unit 9, Canalside Industrial Estate, Rochdale, OL16 5LB
☎ (01706) 522227 🌐 pictish-brewing.co.uk

The brewery was established in 2000 and supplies around 60 free trade outlets in the north-west and West Yorkshire. Seasonal beers: see website.

Brewers Gold (OG 1038, ABV 3.8%) ◆
Yellow in colour, with a hoppy, fruity nose. Soft maltiness and a strong hop/citrus flavour lead to a dry, bitter finish.

Alchemists Ale (OG 1043, ABV 4.3%) ◆
Yellow beer with generous hop and fruit on the nose and palate. Good bitter hop finish.

Piddle

Unit 7, Enterprise Park, Piddlehinton, Dorset, DT2 7UA
☎ (01305) 849336 🌐 piddlebrewery.co.uk

Piddle began brewing in 2007 and in 2011 moved to larger adjacent premises where it brews on an eight-barrel plant, five days a week. The brewery supplies pubs and other outlets across Dorset and beyond. Seasonal beers are available.

Jimmy (OG 1040, ABV 3.7%) ◆
Pale brown session beer with a good depth of malty flavours for its strength.

Piddle (OG 1043, ABV 4.1%) ◆
An enjoyable, well-balanced bitter with a lingering bitter finish.

Yogi Beer (OG 1052, ABV 4.9%)
Smooth with a hint of red, an easy drinking beer with a rounded fruitiness giving way to a hint of blackcurrant, liquorice and toffee.

Slasher (OG 1053, ABV 5.1%)
Blonde, lager-style beer. Light, with a floral aroma and flavour and a sweet and refreshing dry bitter finish.

Pied Bull

Pied Bull Hotel, 57 Northgate Street, Chester, CH1 2HQ
☎ (01244) 325829 🌐 piedbull.co.uk

Pied Bull began brewing in 2011 using a one-barrel plant. Beer is mainly for in-house consumption but local beer festivals are supplied and occasional brewery swaps occur. Seasonal and special ales are available.

Sensibull (OG 1039, ABV 3.8%)
A session ale.

Pied Eyed (OG 1040, ABV 4%)

Quaffabull (OG 1039, ABV 4%)
A summer pale ale.

Bulls Hit (OG 1055, ABV 4.3%)

Matador (OG 1049, ABV 5%)

Sitting Bull (OG 1050, ABV 5%)
An American pale ale.

Black Bull Porter (OG 1060, ABV 5.2%)

Redbull (OG 1057, ABV 5.5%)
A red-coloured ale.

Pig & Porter (NEW)

18h Chapman Way, Tunbridge Wells, Kent, TN2 3EF
☎ (01424) 893519 🌐 pigandporter.co.uk

Originally brewing at several microbreweries in Sussex and Kent, brewing has taken place on its own plant in Tunbridge Wells since 2013 using a 10-barrel plant. Seasonal beers: see website.

Ashburnham Pale Ale (ABV 3.8%)

Starvation Point Porter (ABV 4.5%)

Red Spider Rye (ABV 5.5%)

Pig Pub

Pig In Muck, Manor Road, Claybrooke Magna, Leicestershire, LE17 5AY
☎ (01455) 202859 🌐 piginmuck.com/brewery

Brewing began in 2013 using a two-barrel plant. Beers are available in the Pig in Muck and the Criterion in Leicester. Special beers are brewed for the pub by customers.

Weiner Bitter (ABV 3.8%)
A straw-coloured session bitter. Hoppy and fruity throughout with a compounding bitterness culminating in a distinct dryness at the finish.

Pig Out (ABV 3.9%)
Dark amber-coloured beer with a pleasant bitterness and a fruity citrus finish.

Claybrooke Bitter (ABV 4.2%)
A full-bodied, dark amber beer with a malty aroma. Bitter at the start with a hint of fruit in the middle of the palate and a soft hop flavour to finish.

Pigs Best Bitter (ABV 4.2%)
A golden brown beer with a hint of citrus. The fresh hoppiness comes through at the end with a malt finish.

Pigeon Fishers (NEW)

Unit B1 & B2, Devonshire Buildings, Works Road, Hollingwood, Derbyshire, S43 2PE ☎ 07506 000989 🌐 pigeonfishers.com

Pigeon Fishers was founded by Managing Director Ade Cole in 2014 with the help of co-directors Neil Turner and Kathy Chadwick. Originally using a one-barrel plant donated by Thornbridge Brewery, it upgraded to a 2.5-barrel plant from Barlow

Brewery later in the year. Seasonal beers are available.

Poacher's Thirst (ABV 4%)
An easy-drinking amber ale, full of malt and hops.

Cynosure (ABV 4.6%)
A smooth-drinking floral and citrus beer with a strawberry and cherry finish.

Pikefields (OG 1052, ABV 5.2%)
An American-style pale ale, hoppy with malty middle notes and a citrus finish.

Pilgrim SIBA

11 West Street, Reigate, Surrey, RH2 9BL
☎ (01737) 222651 ⊕ pilgrim.co.uk
Tours by arrangement

⊗ Surrey was bereft of breweries when Dave Roberts started brewing in Woldingham in 1982. The brewery moved to larger premises in Reigate two years later. The brewery has two seasonal beer ranges; the Alia experimental range changes slightly each year to take advantage of new ingredients. There is now a beer counter for the collection of pre-orders or refills.

Quench (OG 1037, ABV 3.6%)
A pale beer with a delicate lemon/lime hop character. The firm malt backbone is supported by fine carbonation and a hint of sweetness.

Surrey Bitter (OG 1038, ABV 3.7%) ◆
Pineapple, grapefruit and spicy aromas. Biscuity maltiness with a hint of vanilla balanced by a hoppy bitterness and refreshing bittersweet finish.

Progress (OG 1041.5, ABV 4%) ◆
Well-rounded tawny-coloured bitter. Predominantly sweet and malty with an underlying fruitiness and hint of toffee, balanced with a subdued bitterness.

Quest (OG 1043, ABV 4.3%)
A robust, pale gold premium ale with clean bitterness and a refined floral hop character.

Pilot (NEW)

22 Jane Street, Leith, EH6 5HD
☎ (0131) 561 4267 ✉ getintouch@pilotbeer.co.uk

Pilot began brewing in 2013 in an industrial unit in Leith using a salvaged five-barrel plant. Distribution is to the Edinburgh area at present but is becoming more widespread.

Blond (OG 1047, ABV 4%)
A modern, fresh and zesty pale ale with a smooth, fully body. Generously hopped for a huge tropical fruit hit.

Vienna Pale (ABV 4.6%)
Light and dry with a delicate yet earthy, herbal flavour followed by an easy, rounded bitterness.

Iced Tea Ale (ABV 5%)
A refreshing amber-coloured beer brewed with a uniquely produced tea blend. Orange and peach tones to the tea and malt base are lifted by crisp hops.

Mochaccino Stout (OG 1069, ABV 5.5%)
A rich, dark milk stout infused with an exclusive coffee roast, organic cocoa nibs and Madagascan vanilla.

India Pale (OG 1060, ABV 6.4%)
Complex spice, maple and caramel flavours with huge floral, pine and grassy notes from the hops, finished off with a powerful yet smooth bitterness.

Pin-Up SIBA

Unit 3, Block 3, Chalex Industrial Estate, Manor Hall Road, Southwick, Brighton, West Sussex, BN42 4NH
☎ (01273) 411127 ⊕ pinupbrewingco.com

⊗ Brewing began in 2011. The brewery moved from Crowborough to Southwick near Brighton in 2014 and uses a five-barrel plant. Most of the output is sold through wholesalers to London and beyond.

Natural Blonde (OG 1037, ABV 3.8%)

Honey Brown (OG 1039, ABV 4%)

Red Head (OG 1041, ABV 4.2%)

Milk Stout (OG 1044, ABV 4.5%)

Pale Ale (OG 1051, ABV 5.1%)

Pitfield

See Dominion

Pixie Spring

Unit C1, Coedcae Lane Industrial Estate, Pontyclun, CF72 9HG ☎ 07814 255943 ⊕ pixiespring.com
Tours by arrangement

Pixie Spring began brewing in 2011 in the cellar of the Wheatsheaf, Llantrisant. In 2012 there was a joining of forces with Gazza Prescott of Steel City Brewery to form Hopcraft – Pixie Spring with a move to new premises and a 12-barrel plant. A traditional range of beers is marketed under the Pixie Spring name and a range of experimental, extremely hoppy beers is brewed as Hopcraft. A separate 0.75-barrel plant is used for specials.

Golden Pixie (OG 1035, ABV 3.8%)

Boss (OG 1043, ABV 4.4%)

Deliverance (OG 1044, ABV 4.5%)

Prince of Bengal IPA (OG 1053, ABV 5.5%)

Under Hopcraft Brewing:

Napoleon Complex (OG 1037.3, ABV 3.9%)

Tidy (OG 1039, ABV 4.1%)

Mosaic Plus (OG 1047.2, ABV 5%)

Citra Plus (OG 1048, ABV 5.4%)

The Beast (OG 1058, ABV 6.5%)

Plain SIBA

17c Deverill Trading Estate, Sutton Veny, Wiltshire, BA12 7BZ
☎ (01985) 841481 ⊕ plainales.co.uk
Tours by arrangement

Plain Ales started production in 2008 on a 2.5-barrel plant in a garage, and expanded to a 20-barrel plant in 2011.

Sheep Dip (OG 1040, ABV 3.8%)

The Wife's Bitter (OG 1041, ABV 3.8%)

Arty Farty (OG 1039, ABV 3.9%)

Innocence (OG 1042, ABV 4%)

A straw-coloured, fragrant bitter.

Innspiration (OG 1042, ABV 4%)
A traditional, copper-coloured, easy-drinking bitter.

Inntrigue (OG 1044, ABV 4.2%)

Inndulgence (OG 1055, ABV 4.5%)
A dark ruby porter with coffee, chocolate and a hint of smoke.

Inncognito (OG 1053, ABV 4.8%)

India Pale Ale (OG 1052, ABV 5.2%)

Plassey

See New Plassey

Platform 5 SIBA

Railway Inn, 197 Queen Street, Newton Abbot, Devon, TQ12 2BS
☎ (01626) 354166 🌐 platform5brewing.co.uk

Platform 5 began brewing in 2006 using a six-barrel plant. The Railway Inn is supplied along with Molloys in Teignmouth and St Marychurch. The brewery is situated in part of an enclosed alley under the disused Platform 5 of Newton Abbot station, with the other part housing the pub's skittle alley.

Wheeltappers Bitter (OG 1040, ABV 4%)

Molloy's Best (OG 1042, ABV 4.2%)

Western Gold (OG 1048, ABV 4.8%)

Whistleblower (OG 1048, ABV 4.8%)

Plockton

5 Bank Street, Plockton, Ross-shire, IV52 8TP
☎ (01599) 544276 🌐 theplocktonbrewery.com
Tours by arrangement

The brewery started trading in 2007 and expanded to a 2.5-barrel plant in 2009. Bottle-conditioned beers are available and are suitable for vegetarians.

Ciste Dhubh (OG 1040, ABV 3.9%) ◆
Excellent mix of malts and hops in this dark brew. Initially bitter turning bittersweet.

Fiddlers Fancy (OG 1046, ABV 4.6%) ◆
Refreshing grapefruit aroma and taste turning to a more malty finish.

Plockton Bay (OG 1047, ABV 4.6%) ◆
A well-balanced, tawny-coloured best bitter with plenty of hops and malt which give a bittersweet fruity flavour.

Plymouth SIBA

HQ Business Centre, 237 Union Street, Stonehouse, Plymouth, Devon, PL1 5QG
☎ (01752) 660837 🌐 plymouthbeercompany.com

⊗ Set up in the old Point's West Brewery at City College by Millfields Trust as a Community Brewery. The concept is to put the profits back into local youth projects in Stonehouse. The five-barrel plant was bought by college lecturer Roger Pengelly from the Bitter End Brewery of Cockermouth, Cumbria.

Mayflower (OG 1044, ABV 4.2%)

Pilgrim Ale (OG 1046, ABV 4.4%)
Traditional dark ruby-coloured bitter with a hint of rye malt.

Poachers SIBA

439 Newark Road, North Hykeham, Lincolnshire, LN6 9SP
☎ (01522) 807404 🌐 poachersbrewery.co.uk
Tours by arrangement

⊚ Brewing started in 2001 on a five-barrel plant. In 2006 it was downsized to 2.5-barrel and relocated to outbuildings at the rear of the brewer's home. 2011 saw capacity returned to five barrels. Regular outlets in Lincolnshire and surrounding counties are supplied direct; outlets further afield via wholesalers.

Trembling Rabbit Mild (OG 1034, ABV 3.4%)
Rich, dark mild with a smooth malty flavour and a slightly bitter finish. Local honey is used.

Shy Talk Bitter (OG 1037, ABV 3.7%)
A crisp-tasting session beer pale golden in colour, refreshing with citrus overtones.

Rock Ape (OG 1038, ABV 3.8%)

Poachers Pride (OG 1040, ABV 4%)
Amber bitter with a fine flavour and an aroma that lingers.

Bog Trotter (OG 1042, ABV 4.2%)
An amber, full-flavoured, malty beer with a bitter aftertaste.

Lincoln Best (OG 1042, ABV 4.2%)
A flowery hop-nosed, brown beer with a well-balanced but bitter taste that stays with the malt, becoming more apparent in the drying finish.

Billy Boy (OG 1044, ABV 4.4%)
A rich, full-flavoured brown beer. Named after the brewery dog, a Border Collie.

Imp Ale (OG 1044, ABV 4.4%)

Black Crow Stout (OG 1045, ABV 4.5%)
A full-bodied stout that has an aftertaste that lingers. Burnt toffee and caramel flavours come to the fore.

Hykeham Gold (OG 1045, ABV 4.5%)
A cask-conditioned lager that has both flavour and taste.

Monkey Hanger (OG 1045, ABV 4.5%)
A ruby-red bitter. Smooth, fruity flavour balanced by the bitterness of the hops.

Jock's Trap (OG 1050, ABV 5%)
A strong, pale brown bitter with a hoppy flavour and aroma and a slightly dry, fruit finish.

Trout Tickler (OG 1055, ABV 5.5%)
A strong ruby bitter with intense flavour and character, sweet undertones with a hint of chocolate. A rich, malty beer.

Pocket

La Croix Farm, La Rue de la Croix, St Ouen, Jersey, JE3 2HA ☎ 07797 771931
✉ jerseybeer@jerseymail.co.uk

⊗ As the name implies, Pocket Brewery began in 2011 on a small scale. Brewing is undertaken occasionally as demand grows but the beers are available locally in bottle-conditioned form and occasionally in cask at local free houses and beer festivals.

Pope's

73a Blackpole Trading Estate West, Worcester, WR3 8TJ
☎ (01905) 755016 ✉ popesbrew@btconnect.com
Shop Fri 5-10pm
Tours by arrangement

Pope's is a family-run brewery established in 2012. A 4.5-barrel brew plant is used with brewing taking place twice a week, supplying the local free trade and further afield. Beer names are influenced by the local area. Seasonal and bottle-conditioned beers are available.

Cavalier (OG 1036, ABV 3.6%)

Hop Market (OG 1038, ABV 3.8%)

Worcester Gold (OG 1040, ABV 4%)

Hope & Glory (OG 1046, ABV 4.6%)

Pope's Yard

Unit 12, Riverside Road, Watford, Hertfordshire, WD19 4HY
☎ (01923) 224182 🌐 popesyard.co.uk

Pope's Yard began commercial brewing in 2012 using a one-barrel plant. Cask and bottle-conditioned beers are available but no regular beers are produced.

Poppyland

46 West Street, Cromer, Norfolk, NR27 9DS
☎ (01263) 513992 🌐 poppylandbeer.com

Established in 2012 by museum curator and geologist Martin Warren as a working retirement project, Poppyland brews and bottle-conditions small batches of beer, especially saisons, IPAs, porters and fruit beers. Beers are unfiltered, vegan-friendly and gluten free.

George N Porter

Whitley Bay, Tyne & Wear, NE26 1AP
☎ (0191) 290 2134 ✉ gnporterbrewing@gmail.com

George N Porter is a 2.5-barrel microbrewery established in 2012. Seven core beers are brewed. Brewing is currently suspended.

The Twitcher (ABV 3.8%)
A citrus blonde bitter.

Super Twitcher (ABV 4.8%)
A strong blonde bitter.

The Astronomer (ABV 5%)
An Irish-style stout.

The Full Wood (ABV 5.2%)
A dark porter.

Portobello SIBA

Unit 6, Mitre Bridge Industrial Estate, Mitre Way, Kensington, London, W10 6AU
☎ (020) 8969 2269 🌐 portobellobrewing.com

Portobello began brewing in 2012 using a 10-barrel plant. Seasonal beers are available.

Pale (OG 1040, ABV 4%) ◆
Golden, well-balanced best bitter with a citrus character, some spiced hops and some malty sweetness that fades.

Star (OG 1044, ABV 4.3%) ◆
Pale brown malty best bitter with a sweetish nose and a strong bitter finish. Hints of nut on the palate.

APA (OG 1050, ABV 5%) ◆
Full-bodied, straw-coloured strong ale. The honey sweetness and soft citrus fruit are balanced by bitter hops. Dry aftertaste.

Potbelly SIBA

25-31 Durban Road, Kettering, Northamptonshire, NN16 0JA
☎ (01536) 410818 🌐 potbelly-brewery.co.uk
Tours by arrangement

Potbelly started brewing in 2005 on a 10-barrel plant and supplies some 200 outlets. The brewery has won numerous awards for its beers. Seasonal beers: see website. Bottle-conditioned beers are available.

Best (OG 1036.9, ABV 3.8%)
A traditional chestnut-coloured bitter.

Hop Trotter (OG 1041, ABV 4.1%)

Beijing Black (OG 1045, ABV 4.4%)
A strong dark mild.

Pigs Do Fly (OG 1041, ABV 4.4%)
A light golden ale.

Bellowhead Hedonism (OG 1045, ABV 4.5%)
A light-coloured bitter with a citrus hoppy finish. Brewed with the help of Bellowhead, a local band.

Captain Pigwash (OG 1050, ABV 5%)
An easy-drinking dark porter.

Crazy Daze (OG 1050, ABV 5.5%)
A light golden bitter with hidden strength.

Potton SIBA

10 Shannon Place, Potton, Bedfordshire, SG19 2SP
☎ (01767) 682258
Tours by arrangement

Bedfordshire Breweries took over ownership and management of the Potton Brewery in 2013. The core range of Potton beers is still available but new brews are being developed. Around 100 outlets are supplied direct.

Shannon IPA (OG 1034, ABV 3.6%)
A well-balanced session bitter with good bitterness and fruity late-hop character.

Buck Off (OG 1043, ABV 4.3%)
Traditional dry-hopped bitter.

Shambles Bitter (OG 1043, ABV 4.3%)
A robust pale and heavily hopped beer with a subtle dry hop character.

Village Bike (OG 1043, ABV 4.3%) ◆
Classic English premium bitter, amber in colour, heavily late-hopped.

American Mistress (OG 1048, ABV 4.8%)
An easy-drinking beer for its strength with a pleasant aftertaste.

Prescott SIBA

Unit 1, The Bramery Business Park, Alstone Lane, Cheltenham, Gloucestershire, GL51 8HE ☎ 07526 934866 🌐 prescottales.co.uk
Tours by arrangement

Prescott Ales was established in 2008, and brews on a 25-barrel plant. It takes its name from the famous Prescott Hill Climb, which is also the home of the Bugatti Owners Club UK. Beer names are inspired by the golden age of motoring. Seasonal beers: see website.

Hill Climb (OG 1039.5, ABV 3.8%)

Chequered Flag (OG 1041, ABV 4.1%)

Track Record (OG 1044, ABV 4.4%)

Grand Prix (OG 1050, ABV 5.2%)

Preseli

Unit 15, The Salterns, Tenby, Pembrokeshire, SA70 8EQ ☎ 07824 512103 🌐 preseli-brewery.co.uk

Preseli began brewing in 2009 using a six-barrel plant. Demand has led to bottled beers being supplied to numerous cafés, restaurants, hotels and pubs throughout Pembrokeshire and Carmarthenshire. Seasonal beers are available.

Even Keel (OG 1038, ABV 3.8%)

Old Mariners (OG 1040, ABV 4%)

Rocky Bottom (OG 1040, ABV 4%)

Pressure Drop

Unit 19, Bohemia Place, Hackney, London, E8 1DU ☎ (020) 8533 0614 🌐 pressuredropbrewing.co.uk

Pressure Drop is run by three partners who were home brewers but began commercial brewing in 2013 using a five-barrel plant and a small pilot kit. Bottle-conditioned beers are available.

Street Porter (ABV 5.2%)

Prior's Well

The Old Kennels, Clumber Park, Hardwick Village, Nottinghamshire, S80 3PB ☎ 07971 277598 🌐 priorswell.co.uk

Prior's Well was established in a National Trust building in Hardwick Village on the Clumber Park Estate . The five-barrel plant uses natural clumber water from the estate in the brewing process. The brewery was closed for much of 2013 and the decision was made in 2014 to suspend production while the future of the business is decided, possibly with new owners.

Private Brewery of Bob

c/o Farmers Boy, 134 London Road, St Albans, Hertfordshire, AL1 1PQ ☎ 07880 743357 🌐 bob-brewery.co.uk

The Private Brewery of Bob is run by Martin Slaughter who produces a range of bottle-conditioned beers for the off-trade and some local pubs. Four regular beers are brewed, as well as several seasonals and specials.

Privateer

Unit 80, Temperance Street, Ardwick, Manchester, M12 6HU ☎ (0161) 273 7077 ☎ 07969 771102

Privateer began brewing in 2012 using a 6.5-barrel plant. Only American hops are used and all beers are brewed under 5% ABV. Seasonal beers are also available.

Roebuck (ABV 3.8%)
A light, amber ale.

Dainty Blonde (ABV 4.2%)
A blonde ale.

Dark Revenge (ABV 4.5%)
A dark stout.

Red Duke (ABV 4.8%)
A ruby red beer.

Problem Child (NEW)

Wayfarer Inn, Alder Lane, Parbold, Lancashire, WN8 7NL ☎ (01257) 464600 🌐 problemchildbrewing.co.uk

Problem Child began brewing in 2013, at the Wayfarer Inn, Parbold, owned by Johnny and Rachel Birkett. The name originates from the family history of the Wayfarer. Once a problem child, prodigal daughter Rachel is now home and happily married to Johnny the head brewer. Obi, aged seven, is apprentice brewer and problem child.

Scallywag (OG 1037, ABV 3.7%)

Raspcallion (ABV 4.2%)

Good Spankin' (ABV 4.4%)

Scoundrel (OG 1046, ABV 4.6%)

Prospect SIBA

Unit 11, Bradley Hall Trading Estate, Bradley Lane, Standish, Wigan, WN6 0XQ ☎ (01257) 421329 🌐 prospectbrewery.com
Tours by arrangement

Prospect brewery was founded in 2007. A 12-barrel plant is used and the premises feature a brewery bar. One pub is jointly owned with Daniel Thwaites, the Silver Tally, Standish.

Silver Tally (OG 1037, ABV 3.7%)
A clean, pale golden bitter with citrus aromas and a full hop flavour with a dry bitter finish.

Whatever! (OG 1040, ABV 3.8%)
Pale bitter packed with hop flavour and aroma.

Nutty Slack (OG 1039, ABV 3.9%)
Dark brown mild ale with malt and fruit on the aroma. Creamy and chocolatey on the palate, with both malt and fruit in evidence. Malty and moderately bitter finish.

Hopper (OG 1040, ABV 4%)
A pale golden beer with citrus hops and a satisfying sweet balance.

One Twenty (OG 1039, ABV 4%)
A yellow/gold beer with zesty citrus notes; clean tasting and refreshing.

Pioneer (OG 1040, ABV 4%)
A light-bodied amber beer with aromas of dry pale malt and earthy hops.

Blinding Light (OG 1042, ABV 4.2%)
A pale refreshing beer with citrus and spicy notes.

Gold Rush (OG 1045, ABV 4.5%)
A deep golden ale with hoppy and bitter flavours, light fruity notes and a grassy floral finish.

Big John (OG 1047, ABV 4.8%)
A dark stout bursting with smoky liquorice flavour with a satisfying bitter aftertaste.

Publisher

c/o Saxon City Ales, Glebe Farm Industrial Estate, Stoke Edith, Herefordshire, HR1 4HG ☎ 07795 244060

Office: Hillkroft, Bromfield Road, Ludlow, Shropshire, SY8 1DW

Publisher Ales is the brewing arm of Doghouse magazine, a quarterly about the British pub. Established in 2013 it uses spare capacity at several breweries in the Herefordshire, Shropshire and Worcestershire area supplying pubs and beer festivals in those counties. Brewing is currently suspended.

Purity SIBA

The Brewery, Upper Spernal Farm, Spernal Lane, Great Alne, Warwickshire, B49 6JF
☎ (01789) 488007 ⊕ puritybrewing.com
Shop Mon-Fri 8am-5pm, Sat 10am-1pm
Tours by arrangement

Brewing began in 2005 in a purpose-designed plant housed in converted barns. The brewery incorporates an environmentally-friendly effluent treatment system. It supplies the free trade within a 70-mile radius and delivers to more than 500 outlets.

Pure Gold (OG 1039.5, ABV 3.8%)
An easy-drinking beer with a dry and bitter finish.

Mad Goose (OG 1042.5, ABV 4.2%)
Light copper in colour with a zesty hop character with citrus overtones.

Pure Ubu (OG 1044.8, ABV 4.5%)
A distinctive premium amber-coloured beer with a balanced, full flavour.

Purple Moose SIBA

Madoc Street, Porthmadog, LL49 9DB
☎ (01766) 515571 ⊕ purplemoose.co.uk
Shop Mon-Fri 9am-5pm, summer Sat 12-4pm
Tours by arrangement

Purple Moose opened in 2005 using a 10-barrel plant in a former iron works in the coastal town of Porthmadog. In 2013 a new 40-barrel plant was installed, significantly increasing production. The names of the beers reflect local history and geography. Seasonal beers: see website.

Cwrw Eryri/Snowdonia Ale (OG 1035.3, ABV 3.6%)
Golden, refreshing bitter with citrus fruit hoppiness in aroma and taste. The full mouthfeel leads to a long-lasting, dry, bitter finish.

Cwrw Madog/Madog's Ale (OG 1037, ABV 3.7%)
Full-bodied session bitter. Malty nose and an initial nutty flavour but bitterness dominates. Well-balanced and refreshing with a dry roastiness on the taste and a good dry finish.

Cwrw Ysgawen/Elderflower Ale (OG 1039, ABV 4%)
A pale and refreshing elderflower beer with a good citrus fruit aroma, bittersweet taste, and a zesty, hoppy, mouthwatering finish.

Cwrw Glaslyn/Glaslyn Ale (OG 1040.5, ABV 4.2%)
Refreshing light and malty amber-coloured ale. Plenty of hop in the aroma and taste. Good smooth mouthfeel leading to a slightly chewy finish.

Ochr Tywyll y Mws/Dark Side of the Moose (OG 1045, ABV 4.6%)
A dark, complex beer quite hoppy and bitter with roast undertones. Malt and fruit flavours also feature in the smooth taste and dry finish.

Quantock SIBA

Unit E, Monument View, Summerfield Avenue, Chelston Business Park, Wellington, Somerset, TA21 9ND
☎ (01823) 662669 ⊕ quantockbrewery.co.uk

Quantock is a family-run brewery that started trading in 2008 on an eight-barrel plant. The brewery supplies beers to outlets throughout the south west and further afield via wholesalers. Beers are available to the public direct from the brewery and via online sales from the website. Bottle-conditioned beers are available.

Ale (OG 1036, ABV 3.8%)
An amber-coloured beer with a fruity, full-bodied flavour and a dry finish to the palate. The blend of English hops creates a balanced, fruity character with a delicate spicy aroma.

Ginger Cockney (OG 1037, ABV 4%)
A copper-coloured ale, generously hopped with American varieties with a hint of fresh ginger.

Rorke's Drift (OG 1039, ABV 4.2%)
A light, refreshing lager-style beer, a fruit-filled experience with a delicate citrus aroma. Brewed in support of The Royal Engineers Association (REA) with five pence from every pint being donated to the association.

Sunraker (OG 1039, ABV 4.2%)
A pale straw-coloured beer, light and refreshing with a delicate, clean grassy hop finish.

Wills Neck (OG 1040, ABV 4.3%)
A bright golden ale with a rich malty flavour. Late hopped to produce a prominent aroma with hints of grapefruit and cherries and a lasting bitterness on the palate.

White Hind (OG 1042, ABV 4.5%)
A chestnut-coloured best bitter with a full-bodied, malty flavour with the roast malt coming through and a dry finish. The beer is generously hopped with a blend of English hops producing a biscuity, spicy aroma.

Royal Stag IPA (OG 1056, ABV 6%)
A copper-coloured beer with a malty and fruity flavour and smoky aroma with hints of banana and toffee.

UXB (OG 1088, ABV 9%)
A strong beer, slightly sweet with a full malty flavour.

Quantum

Unit 4 Victoria Works, Hempshaw Lane, Stockport, Greater Manchester, SK1 4LG ☎ 07976 032465
🌐 quantumbrewingcompany.co.uk
Tours by arrangement

The brewery was established in 2011 using a five-barrel plant on the site of the former Shaws Brewery. A number of seasonal beers, one-offs and specials are brewed: see website. Bottle-conditioned beers are available.

American Light (OG 1033, ABV 3.6%)
A light golden ale.

Beagle Best (OG 1037, ABV 3.8%)

Bitter (OG 1038, ABV 3.8%)

Golden Globe (OG 1040, ABV 4.1%)
Yellow beer with a modest hoppy/fruity aroma. Biscuity malt and tart fruits on the palate and in the bitter aftertaste.

Pale Ale (OG 1045, ABV 4.5%)

Quartz SIBA

Archers, Alrewas Road, Kings Bromley, Staffordshire, DE13 7HW
☎ (01543) 473965 🌐 quartzbrewing.co.uk
Shop Thu & Sat 10am-1.30pm, Fri 10am-6pm
Tours by arrangement

Quartz was established in 2005 by Scott and Julia Barnett. There are five regular beers produced in cask, bottle and mini-cask, supplemented with seasonal specials. Around 50 outlets are supplied direct.

Blonde (OG 1038, ABV 3.8%)
Little aroma, gentle hop and background malt. Sweet with unsophisticated sweetshop tastes.

Crystal (OG 1040, ABV 4.2%)
Sweet aroma with some fruit and yeasty Marmite hints. Hoppiness begins but dwindles to a bittersweet finish.

Extra Blonde (OG 1042, ABV 4.4%)
Sweet malty aroma with a touch of fruit. Sweet start, smooth with a hint of hops in the sugary finish.

Heart (OG 1045, ABV 4.6%)
Pale brown with some aroma of fruit and malt. Gentle tastes of fruit and hops eventually appear to leave a bitter finish.

Cracker (OG 1050, ABV 5%)
Chestnut in colour with a slight roasted aroma, smooth fruit notes leaving a dry hop finish.

Queen Inn (NEW) SIBA

28 Kingsgate Road, Winchester, Hampshire, SO23 9PG
☎ (01962) 853898 🌐 thequeeninnwinchester.com

Brewing began in 2014 using a 1.5-barrel brew plant. At present beers are only brewed for the pub.

Quercus SIBA

Unit 2M, South Hams Business Park, Churchstow, Devon, TQ7 3QH
☎ (01548) 854888 🌐 quercus-brewery.com
Shop Mon-Fri 10am-4pm (please call on Sat)

Quercus began trading in 2007, using an eight-barrel brew plant. The brewery was sold in 2007 by the founder Peter Walker to local residents John Tiner and Mike George. Beers are available in local pubs and shops.

Best Bitter (OG 1040, ABV 4%)
An amber-coloured bitter with balanced malt and bitterness.

Prospect (OG 1040, ABV 4%)
Subtle bitterness and sweet malt flavour with a rich aroma and colour.

Shingle Bay (OG 1042, ABV 4.2%)
A light, golden, easy-drinking ale with fruity citrus aroma and taste giving a subtle, crisp bite to refresh the palate.

Harry's (OG 1046, ABV 4.6%)
A rich, dark ale, with sweet malty chocolate aromas leading to a complex finish of sweet malt and lingering hops.

Radnorshire SIBA

Timberworks, Brookside Farm, New Radnor, LD8 2SU
☎ (01544) 350456
🌐 radnorhillsholidaycottages.com
Tours by arrangement

Radnorshire is a microbrewery set up in 2012 in the grounds of a farm offering holiday cottage accommodation.

Whimble Gold (OG 1038, ABV 3.8%)
Light and hoppy golden ale.

Four Stones (OG 1040, ABV 4%)
A light amber ale with a subtle maltiness.

Smatcher Tawny (OG 1042, ABV 4.2%)
Mellow, tawny-coloured best bitter.

Water-Break-Its-Neck (ABV 5.7%)

Rail Ale

Schooner, South Shore Road, Gateshead, Tyne & Wear, NE8 3AF
☎ (0191) 477 7404

Office: 115 Brighton Road, Gateshead, Tyne & Wear, NE8 1XS

Established in 2013, and based at the Schooner pub, Rail Ale is the first microbrewery in Gateshead. Beers are available at the Schooner and other local outlets, and are named with a railway theme.

Amber Aspect (OG 1039, ABV 3.8%)
A traditional, refreshing amber-coloured bitter.

Night Train (OG 1040, ABV 4%)
A dark beer with a smooth velvet taste.

Railway Tavern

58 Station Road, Brightlingsea, Essex, CO7 0DT
Tours by arrangement

The brewery started life as a kitchen-sink affair in 1998. In 2012 the brewery was completely refurbished; a two-barrel plant is used to create a selection of dark beers suitable for vegetarians.

Crab 'n' Winkle Mild (OG 1036, ABV 3.6%)
Thin-bodied mild with a pear drop aroma and a roasty taste. The aftertaste is slightly ash-like with suggestions of bitter chocolate.

Bladderwrack Stout (OG 1047, ABV 4.7%) ◆
Full-bodied stout with an intense roast grain character that is initially underpinned by subtle sweetness, which subsides to leave a drier finish.

Ramsbottom Craft SIBA

1 Heapworth Avenue, Ramsbottom, BL0 9EH
☎ 07976 263344 ⊕ ramsbottombrewery.com

Brewer Matt Holmes has been brewing from a microbrewery in his converted garage since 2011 using a 2.5-barrel plant, and has doubled his fermenting capacity. Cask ales are supplied throughout the north west and to beer festivals further afield. Bottle-conditioned beers are available and suitable for vegetarians and vegans.

Bumble's Honeyed Ale (OG 1039, ABV 4%)
Elderflower and honey based pale ale.

Rammy Ale (OG 1041, ABV 4%)
A session bitter using Styrian and Goldings hops.

Chocolate Porter (OG 1043, ABV 4.2%)
A brown-coloured porter with mocha notes.

Fat Lady Stout (OG 1043, ABV 4.3%)
Dark brown, almost black stout with a hint of roast in the aroma and a smooth taste.

Oh Sunny Day (OG 1046, ABV 4.5%)
A pale yellow-coloured mellow ale with balanced malt sweetness and fruitiness.

Mango Beach (OG 1054, ABV 5.5%)
American-style pale ale using Amarillo hops.

Ramsbury SIBA

Stockclose Farm, Aldbourne, Wiltshire, SN8 2NN
☎ (01672) 541407

Head Office: Ramsbury Estates Ltd, Priory Farm, Axford, Wiltshire, SN8 2HA ⊕ ramsburybrewery.com
Shop Mon-Fri 8am-4.30pm
Tours by arrangement

Ramsbury started brewing in 2004 using a 10-barrel plant and is situated high on the Marlborough Downs in Wiltshire. The brewery uses home-grown barley from the Ramsbury Estate. Expansion in 2014 saw an upgrade to a 30-barrel plant with a visitor centre, a well to provide the liquor and a distillery to follow.

Bitter (OG 1036, ABV 3.6%)
Amber-coloured beer with a smooth, delicate aroma and flavour.

Deerstalker (OG 1040, ABV 4%)
An amber best bitter with a smooth bitter finish.

Kennet Valley (OG 1041, ABV 4.1%)
A light amber, hoppy bitter with a long, dry finish.

Flint Knapper (OG 1042, ABV 4.2%)
Rich amber in colour with a malty taste.

Gold (OG 1045, ABV 4.5%)
A rich golden-coloured beer with a light hoppy aroma and taste.

Silver Pig Stout (OG 1047, ABV 4.7%)
A full-flavoured stout with a coffee chocolate finish.

Chalk Stream (OG 1050, ABV 5%)

Deerhunter (OG 1050, ABV 5%)

Belapur IPA (OG 1055, ABV 5.5%)

Ramsgate SIBA

1 Hornet Close, Pyson's Road Industrial Estate, Broadstairs, Kent, CT10 2YD
☎ (01843) 868453 ⊕ ramsgatebrewery.co.uk
Shop Mon-Fri 10am-5pm, Sat 10am-1pm
Tours by arrangement

Ramsgate was established in 2002 at the back of a Ramsgate pub. In 2006 the brewery moved to its current location, allowing for increased capacity and bottling. Bottle-conditioned beers are available. Seasonal and monthly specials: see website.

Gadds' No. 7 Bitter Ale (OG 1037, ABV 3.8%)

Gadds' Seasider (OG 1042, ABV 4.3%)

Gadds' No. 5 Best Bitter Ale (OG 1043, ABV 4.4%)

Gadds' No. 3 Kent Pale Ale (OG 1047, ABV 5%)

Gadds' Faithful Dogbolter Porter (OG 1054, ABV 5.6%)

Randalls SIBA

La Piette Brewery, St Georges Esplanade, St Peter Port, Guernsey, GY1 2BH
☎ (01481) 720134 ⊕ randallsbrewery.com
Tours by arrangement

Randalls has been brewing since 1868 and until recently was the only brewery on Guernsey (White Rock being the other one). A new 36-barrel brewhouse was installed in 2008. 18 pubs are owned and a further 50 outlets are supplied.

Patois (OG 1045, ABV 4.5%)
Chestnut brown best bitter with a subtle hop aroma and balanced bitterness.

Rat

Rat & Ratchet, 40 Chapel Hill, Huddersfield, West Yorkshire, HD1 3EB
☎ (01484) 542400 ✉ ratandratchet@ossett-brewery.co.uk

The Rat & Ratchet was originally established as a brewpub in 1994. Brewing ceased and it was purchased by Ossett Brewery (qv) in 2004. Brewing re-started in 2011 with a capacity of 30 barrels per week. Six times a year head brewer Paul Spencer produces a special one-off experimental beer under the Project Rat brand.

Dirty Rat (OG 1038, ABV 3.5%)
A velvety dark brown mild. Low bitterness with a sweet malty finish from a blend of three roasted malts. The delicate hop aroma is not overpowering.

Attack (OG 1038, ABV 3.8%)
A pale golden session beer packed full of hops. Generous dry hopping gives a powerful citrus aroma.

White Rat (OG 1040, ABV 4%)
This pale hoppy ale has an intensely aromatic and resinous finish.

Rattus Rattus (OG 1045, ABV 4.3%)
In this characteristically hazy wheat beer, flavours of banana and cloves are dominant. Fresh coriander gives a herbal spicy aroma.

Black Rat (OG 1047, ABV 4.5%)
A porter with burnt, coffee and chocolate malt character. Slightly sweet on the palate, but

moderate bitterness and a fruity/spicy aroma from the hops.

King Rat (OG 1050, ABV 5%)
A hoppy beer with a white wine aroma. Bitterness is high, but balanced nicely by a residual malty sweetness.

Against the Machine (OG 1071, ABV 7%)
A massively-hopped IPA.

Raw SIBA

Units 3 & 4, Silver House, Adelphi Way, Staveley, Derbyshire, S43 3LJ
☎ (01246) 475445 rawbrew.com
Tours by arrangement

Raw began brewing in 2010 using a five-barrel plant from Prospect Brewery of Wigan. Six core beers and a seasonal special are always available.

Blonde Pale (OG 1039, ABV 3.9%)

JR Best (OG 1042, ABV 4.2%)

Dark Peak (OG 1045, ABV 4.5%)

Edge Pale (OG 1045, ABV 4.5%)

Anubis (OG 1051, ABV 5.2%)

Grey Ghost (OG 1056, ABV 5.9%)

RCH SIBA

West Hewish, Somerset, BS24 6RR
☎ (01934) 834447 rchbrewery.com

The brewery was originally installed in the early 1980s behind the Royal Clarence Hotel, Burnham-on-Sea. Since 1993 brewing has taken place in a former cider mill at West Hewish. A 30-barrel plant was installed in 2000. RCH supplies 150 outlets and the award-winning beers are available nationwide through its own wholesaling company, which also distributes beers from other small independent breweries. Seasonal and bottle-conditioned beers are also available.

Hewish IPA (OG 1036, ABV 3.6%)
Thinnish session bitter with plenty of hops and some grapefruit. Some astringency in the finish. Pitchfork's little brother.

Hewish Mild (OG 1036, ABV 3.6%)
Black mild with light roast nose. Hints of roast malt and slight apple taste with an astringent finish.

PG Steam (OG 1039, ABV 3.9%)
A tawny beer with a hint of unripe fruit and some malt in the flavour. Bitterness and astringency throughout.

Pitchfork (OG 1043, ABV 4.3%)
Some citrus aroma is followed by a very bitter, hoppy taste with grapefruit notes. Finishes with an astringent and bitter aftertaste.

Old Slug Porter (OG 1046, ABV 4.5%)
Powerful aroma of roast and dark fruit which continues into the roast malt flavours. Bitter, slightly astringent finish.

East Street Cream (OG 1050, ABV 5%)
Full-bodied malty ale with strong malt and hops on the nose. Fruity flavours mellow into a smooth bittersweet finish.

Double Header (OG 1053, ABV 5.3%)
A strong, full-bodied golden bitter with a citrus taste and fruity hop nose. Has a bitter astringent finish.

Firebox (OG 1060, ABV 6%)
Strong golden bitter with complex hoppy and fruity aroma. Sweet malty flavours give way to a lingering bitter aftertaste

Reality

127 High Road, Chilwell, Nottingham, NG9 4AT
☎ 07801 539523
alandenismonaghan@hotmail.com

Reality began brewing in 2010 in the unused space of an IT business, hence the pun on Real-ITy. Beers are themed around the brewery name and are available in select local outlets and nationally at beer festivals.

Virtuale Reality (OG 1039, ABV 3.8%)
A pale session brew.

No Escape (OG 1043, ABV 4.2%)
Pale ale with Maris Otter malt and Cascade hops.

Bitter Reality (OG 1044, ABV 4.3%)
A copper-coloured bitter.

Stark Reality (OG 1046, ABV 4.5%)
An amber-coloured bitter with a hint of rum.

Reality Czech (OG 1047, ABV 4.6%)
Pale beer with Czech hops.

Rebel SIBA

Century House, Kernick Industrial Estate, Penryn, Cornwall, TR10 9EP
☎ (01326) 378517 rebelbrewing.co.uk

Rebel began brewing in 2011. In 2012 it expanded to a 15-barrel plant with visitor centre, shop and museum. The beers are available in local outlets.

Bal Maiden (OG 1041, ABV 4%)

Cornish Sunset (OG 1041, ABV 4%)

Penryn Pale Ale (OG 1043, ABV 4.3%)
Sweet best bitter with caramel, hop notes and banana/butterscotch flavours. Long, mellow, bitter finish and a light, fruity aroma.

Black Rock Bitter (OG 1049, ABV 4.8%)
Brown bitter with faint malt nose. Full roasted and biscuit malt flavour with fruity sweetness. Long grainy and bitter finish.

Bullhorn Black Lager (OG 1049, ABV 4.9%)

80/- Scotch Ale (OG 1051, ABV 5%)
Dark brown porter with roast malt aroma. Burnt chestnut and malt flavour with gentle bitterness and rich berry fruit sweetness.

Rebellion SIBA

Marlow Brewery, Bencombe Farm, Marlow Bottom, Buckinghamshire, SL7 3LT
☎ (01628) 476594 rebellionbeer.co.uk
Shop Mon-Sat 8am-7pm
Tours by arrangement

Established in 1993, Rebellion has grown steadily with one site move and several expansion projects, including a new on-site shop. The brewery currently brews approximately 70,000 pints per week, supplying over 400 local pubs and

THE BREWERIES

clubs within a 30-mile radius of Marlow. The shop provides customers with fresh real ale, bottled beers, merchandise and local produce and the ever-popular membership club now has over 4,000 active members. Monthly and seasonal beers: see website.

IPA (OG 1039, ABV 3.7%) ◆
Copper-coloured bitter, sweet and malty, with resinous and red apple flavours. Caramel and fruit decline to leave a dry, bitter and malty finish.

Smuggler (OG 1042, ABV 4.1%) ◆
A red-brown beer, well-bodied and bitter with an uncompromisingly dry, bitter finish.

Mutiny (OG 1046, ABV 4.5%) ◆
Tawny in colour, this full-bodied best bitter is predominantly fruity and moderately bitter with crystal malt continuing to a dry finish.

Rectory SIBA

Streat Hill Farm, Streat Hill, Streat, Hassocks, East Sussex, BN6 8RP
☎ (01273) 890570 ✉ rectoryales@hotmail.com
Tours by arrangement

⊗ Rectory was founded in 1995 by the Rev Godfrey Broster to generate funds for the maintenance of his three parish churches. 107 parishioners are shareholders. Production is split between the Streat Hill Farm, where seasonal and specials beers are brewed, and the micro-plant at Harvey's brewery (qv).

Rector's Light Relief (OG 1045, ABV 4.5%)
Golden ale with a fresh, floral aroma and distinctly hoppy, bitter characteristics.

The Rector's Revenge (OG 1050, ABV 5%)
Traditional style mid-brown coloured strong bitter with good balance of malt and hops and a long bitter finish.

Red

Unit 1, The Orchard, Garden Farm, The Town, Great Staughton, Cambridgeshire, PE19 5BE ☎ 07827 294229 ⊕ redbrewery.com

Red Brewery was established in 2012 in a converted farm building in the village of Great Staughton.

Little Orca Stout (OG 1040, ABV 4.1%)
A modern stout. Floral and slightly sweet.

Pathfinder (OG 1045, ABV 4.8%)
An amber/blonde ale with lemon citrus notes.

Sundial Gold (OG 1044, ABV 4.8%)
A golden ale, citrus with a light hop finish.

White Duck IPA (OG 1045, ABV 4.8%)
Pale, highly hopped ale with grapefruit flavours.

Staughton Bitter (OG 1048, ABV 5.2%)
Copper-coloured hoppy bitter with light fruit on the palate.

Kangaroo Ale (OG 1049, ABV 5.4%)
A bronze-coloured, malty bitter with plum and dark fruit notes.

Juggernaut Porter (OG 1056, ABV 6%)
Smooth, dark porter with a hint of chocolate and blackcurrant.

Missoula Floods APA (OG 1055, ABV 6%)
An IPA with subtle lemon and lime notes.

Red Cat (NEW) SIBA ◉

Unit 10, Sun Valley Business Park, Winnall Close, Winchester, Hampshire, SO23 0LB
☎ (01962) 863423 ⊕ redcatbrewing.co.uk

Red Cat began brewing in 2014 using a 10-barrel brew plant. The two owners/brewers are from Flowerpots Brewery and the Fulflood Arms brewpub.

Prowler Pale (ABV 3.6%)

Bitter (ABV 3.7%)

TomCat (ABV 4.7%)

Red Even (NEW)

Unit 53, Coleshill Industrial Estate, Station Road, Coleshill, Warwickshire, B46 1JT
☎ (01675) 464762 ✉ redeven@hotmail.co.uk

Red Even began brewing in 2013. It currently produces cask-conditioned beers plus beers bottled on its own facility.

Shooting Dice (OG 1042, ABV 4.2%)
An American-style pale ale with a firm malt base and biscuit notes leading to a light hop finish.

Red Fox SIBA

The Chicken Sheds, Upp Hall Farm, Salmons Lane, Coggeshall, Essex, CO6 1RY
☎ (01376) 563123 ⊕ redfoxbrewery.co.uk
Tours by arrangement

Red Fox began brewing in 2008 and has continued to expand in line with increasing demand. Around 35 outlets are supplied direct. Several local pubs now stock the beers. Seven core beers plus a number of seasonal and one-off beers are brewed throughout the year. Bottle-conditioned beers are available. Mini-pins and pins can be purchased direct from the brewery.

Mild (OG 1037, ABV 3.6%)
A classic, dark, full-flavoured mild with hints of chocolate and a deep roast barley flavour.

IPA (OG 1038, ABV 3.7%)
An East Anglian-style copper-coloured beer with a delicate flavour.

Bitter (OG 1039, ABV 3.8%)
A traditional style bitter which perfectly balances malt and fruit flavours.

Hunter's Gold (OG 1040, ABV 3.9%)
A golden beer with a delicate citrus aroma.

Best Bitter (OG 1041, ABV 4%)
A classic light brown bitter with a full flavour and a malty backbone.

Coggeshall Gold (OG 1044, ABV 4%)
An aromatic golden beer, packed full of citrus and exotic fruit flavours. Unusually for a beer of this style it does not have a bitter finish.

Surrex Gold (OG 1040, ABV 4.1%)
A highly-hopped, aromatic beer. Pink grapefruit and peach aromas abound leading to a slightly bitter finish.

Black Fox Porter (OG 1046, ABV 4.8%)
A rich-flavoured black beer packed with malty flavour with undertones of chocolate.

Wily Ol' Fox (OG 1050, ABV 5.2%)

An aromatic amber ale with a soft fruity palate. Dangerously easy to drink.

Red Rock SIBA

Higher Humber Farm, Bishopsteignton, Devon, TQ14 9TD
☎ (01626) 879738 🌐 redrockbrewery.co.uk
Shop Mon-Fri 9am-4pm (phone for weekend hours)
Tours by arrangement

Red Rock first started brewing in 2006 with a four-barrel plant and upgraded in 2011 to a 7.5-barrel one. It is based in a converted barn on a working farm using locally-sourced malt, fresh hops and the farm's own spring water. It has a bar and can accommodate private functions. Bottle-conditioned and seasonal beers also available.

Red Rock (OG 1041, ABV 4.2%)

Red Shoot

Toms Lane, Linwood, Ringwood, Hampshire, BH24 3QT
☎ (01425) 475792 🌐 redshoot.co.uk

The 2.5-barrel brewery was commissioned in 1998. About half the output is sold in the pub, the remainder to other local outlets distributed by Wadworth (qv), who also monitor the whole brewing process.

New Forest Gold (OG 1038, ABV 3.8%)
A refreshing golden ale with a light floral citrus taste, moving to a burnt toffee finish.

Red White & Brew (OG 1040, ABV 4%)
A hoppy fresh golden ale, with increasing bitterness.

Muddy Boot (OG 1042, ABV 4.2%)
A dark mild, brewed using Goldings hops, molasses and some chocolate malt.

Tom's Tipple (OG 1048, ABV 4.8%)
A copper-coloured strong malty bitter, brewed using Golding hops to give some fruit balance to the toffee and malt flavours.

Red Squirrel SIBA

Unit 24, Boxted Farm, Berkhamsted Road, Potten End, Hertfordshire, HP1 2SQ
☎ (01442) 256970 🌐 redsquirrelbrewery.co.uk
Tours by arrangement

Red Squirrel started brewing in Hertford in 2004 using a 10-barrel plant. In 2011 it moved to Potten End near Hemel Hempstead to brand new premises and has subsequently expanded production. The core beers are complemented by seasonal brews and occasional specials: see website.

Red Dawn Mild (OG 1037.7, ABV 3.7%)
Dark red in colour with mellow and nutty overtones and a smooth and rounded palate.

Hopfest (OG 1037, ABV 3.8%)
Pale, golden ale with a floral/citrus aroma and elderflower notes.

Legally Blonde (OG 1040, ABV 4%)
Hops give a fresh, citrus flavour with herbal, floral and buttery notes.

Conservation Bitter (OG 1040, ABV 4.1%)
A chestnut brown traditional bitter with a hoppy, fruity bitterness and biscuit flavours with a hint of spice and chocolate.

Mr Squirrel (OG 1042.9, ABV 4.3%)
A chestnut red bitter, lightly hopped with a creamy texture. Hints of caramel and vanilla complement the slightly hoppy and malty overtones.

Jack Black (OG 1047.7, ABV 4.8%)
A black IPA featuring the hop profile of an IPA and the dark colour of a porter.

London Porter (OG 1048, ABV 5%)
Dark brown/black porter with a good balance of chocolate and roasted barley. Full bodied on the palate with bittersweet liquorice and rich chocolate flavours and a creamy finish.

Redwood American IPA (OG 1051, ABV 5.4%)
Based on a secret Michigan recipe, golden orange in colour, with complex hoppy aromas, floral/citrus tones and a long, lingering finish.

Redball (NEW)

Kash Bar, 121 Brook Street, Chester, CH1 3DU
☎ (01244) 401777 ✉ redballbrewery@gmail.com

Redball was started at Alex Haycraft's Kash Bar in Chester in 2014. A sister brewery to Blueball (qv), the purpose was to brew strong premium beers for consumption at the Kash Bar in Chester and at Kash 22 in Frodsham.

Redchurch

275-276 Poyser Street, Bethnal Green, London, E2 9RF ☎ 07968 173097
🌐 theredchurchbrewery.com
Shop Thu & Fri 6-11pm, Sat 1-6pm

Redchurch was established in 2011 by Gary Ward using an eight-barrel plant and is situated in a unit under the railway arches in Bethnal Green. The brewery produces seven beers at present, in key casks and bottles, for both the domestic and export markets. There are ongoing plans for expansion. Special beers: see website.

Redemption SIBA

Unit 2, Compass West Industrial Estate, 33 West Road, Tottenham, London, N17 0XL
☎ (020) 8885 5227 🌐 redemptionbrewing.co.uk
Shop Mon-Fri 9am-6pm
Tours by arrangement

Redemption began brewing in 2010 on a 12-barrel plant. Six beers are brewed regularly, with occasional seasonals. Most of the beer is supplied in casks to pubs in north and central London and to beer festivals. Beers are available bottle-conditioned and in polypins from the brewery.

Trinity (OG 1036.6, ABV 3%)
Refreshing golden beer with strong citrus notes throughout. The strong bitterness is softened by a little sweet malt character.

Pale Ale (OG 1037.5, ABV 3.8%)
Well-balanced amber bitter with hops and citrus orange throughout. The sweet maltiness fades leaving a slightly dry bitter finish.

Hopspur (OG 1044.5, ABV 4.5%)

THE BREWERIES

Hoppy bitter notes are present in this tawny brown best bitter which has a hint of coffee roast throughout and some caramelised citrus notes.

Urban Dusk (OG 1044.5, ABV 4.6%) ◆
Full-bodied brown best bitter; chocolate and fudge in the aroma and flavour overlaid with citrus. Lingering dry bitter finish.

Friendship Porter (OG 1051.5, ABV 5.1%) ◆
Sweetish smooth porter with a mix of liquorice, caramel and roast notes. A pleasant burnt roast gives dry bitter overtones.

Big Chief (OG 1052.5, ABV 5.5%) ◆
Golden ale with a smooth mouthfeel and a strong fruity aroma, flavour and finish, which is also dry and bitter.

Redscar SIBA

c/o The Cleveland Hotel, 9-11 High Street West, Redcar, North Yorkshire, TS10 1SQ
☎ (01642) 513727 ⊕ redscar-brewery.co.uk
Tours by arrangement

Redscar first brewed in 2008. In early 2014 it increased its capacity to a five-barrel plant. The brewery supplies the hotel, local pubs and beer festivals. For occasional specials and seasonal beers see website.

Jazz (OG 1040, ABV 4%)
Light-coloured session beer delicately hopped with three varieties.

Poison (OG 1040, ABV 4%)
A dark, full-bodied ale.

Sands (OG 1043, ABV 4.2%)
A hoppy golden ale brewed with Pioneer and Fuggles hops.

Pier (OG 1046, ABV 4.5%)
A dark, full-bodied ale with a rich, fruity flavour.

Rocks (OG 1045, ABV 4.5%)

Beach (OG 1050, ABV 5%)

Redstone

Tynwllyd Farm, Llangorse, Powys, LD3 7UA ☎ 07581 878604 ⊕ redstone-brewery.com
Tours by arrangement

Redstone started brewing in 2012 using the remnants of the Tudor Brewery, formerly based in Abergavenny. A four-barrel plant has been installed in a converted Edwardian granary to supply both cask and bottled beer to the local area.

Olivers Twist (ABV 4%)

Malthouse (ABV 4.5%)

Bois Bach (ABV 5%)

Olivers Twisted (ABV 5%)

Redwell (NEW) SIBA

7 The Arches, Bracondale, Norwich, Norfolk, NR1 2EF
☎ (01603) 624072 ⊕ redwellbrewing.com

Redwell began brewing in 2013 using a 10-barrel plant. Production is mostly keg or bottled but occasional cask-conditioned ales are produced for beer festivals or by special request for local outlets.

RedWillow SIBA

Sutton Mill, Gunco Lane, Macclesfield, Cheshire, SK11 7JL
☎ (01625) 502315 ⊕ redwillowbrewery.com

RedWillow began brewing in 2010 from a unit within Sutton Mill. The award-winning beers are distributed nationwide and are available in cask and bottle-conditioned form. Seasonal beers are brewed, and experimental brews are branded under the Faithless label: see website. One bar is owned, the RedWillow Bar in Macclesfield.

Seamless (OG 1034, ABV 3.6%)
A light and hoppy pale ale.

Headless (OG 1038, ABV 3.9%)
A hoppy pale ale.

Mirthless (OG 1038, ABV 3.9%)

Feckless (OG 1041, ABV 4.1%)
A classic English bitter.

Directionless (OG 1041, ABV 4.2%)

Wreckless (OG 1046, ABV 4.8%)
A fruity pale ale.

Heartless (OG 1051, ABV 4.9%)
A chocolate stout.

Smokeless (OG 1055, ABV 5.7%)
A smoked porter infused with smoked chipotles

Shameless (OG 1057, ABV 5.9%)
An American-style IPA.

Ageless (OG 1067, ABV 7.2%)

Reedley Hallows SIBA

Unit B3, Farrington Close, Farrington Road Industrial Estate, Burnley, Lancashire, BB11 5SH ☎ 07749 414513 ⊕ reedley-hallows-brewery.co.uk

Brewing started on this four-barrel plant in 2012. Having moved to larger premises the brewery now has nine fermenters to cope with the production of its six core beers, one of which contributes £3 per firkin to the local Pendleside Hospice.

Old Laund Bitter (OG 1038, ABV 3.6%)
A good session beer, smooth and creamy with a distinctive hoppy aftertaste.

Filly Close Blonde (OG 1040, ABV 3.9%)
A well-balanced ale, bitter and spicy with a good fruity finish.

Pendleside (OG 1042, ABV 4%)
A light-coloured beer with hints of tropical fruits and a spicy aftertaste.

Monkholme Premium (OG 1042, ABV 4.2%)
A premium golden ale, smooth with a hoppy taste throughout.

New Laund Dark (OG 1044, ABV 4.4%)
A dark stout, sweet with a smoky, bitter finish.

Nook of Pendle (OG 1050, ABV 5%)

Revolutions SIBA

Unit B7, Whitwood Enterprise Park, Speedwell Road, Whitwood, Castleford, West Yorkshire, WF10 5PX
☎ (01977) 552649 ⊕ revolutionsbrewing.co.uk
Tours by arrangement

Revolutions began brewing in 2010. All beers are musically inspired, reflecting musical formats from the analogue era mainly brewed to 3.3% (33 rpm),

3.9% (EP), 4.5% (45 rpm) and 6.0% (C60). The Rewind 33 series of monthly specials references music from 33 years ago.

EP Session Pale (OG 1040, ABV 3.9%)
A pale ale with balanced levels of sweetness and bitterness with a crisp lemon hop finish.

Clash London Porter (OG 1045, ABV 4.5%)
A complex dark malty beer rounded off with a smooth hop finish.

Go-Go American Pale (OG 1045, ABV 4.5%)
A golden pale ale hopped with three American citrus/floral hops.

Pretender Blonde (OG 1045, ABV 4.5%)
A blonde ale with medium levels of bitterness and with pine, lemon and lime hop notes.

Manifesto (OG 1059, ABV 6%)
A rich, dark and elegant stout.

Rhymney SIBA

Gilchrist Thomas Industrial Estate, Blaenavon, Torfaen, NP4 9RL
☎ (01685) 722253 ridgesidebrewery rhymneybreweryltd.com
Shop Sat 10am-2pm
Tours by arrangement

Rhymney first brewed in 2005. The 75-hl plant was sourced from Canada. Around 220 outlets are supplied. In 2012 the brewery relocated to Blaenavon with a new brewing centre and visitor facility.

Best (OG 1037, ABV 3.7%)

Hobby Horse (OG 1038, ABV 3.8%)

Dark (OG 1040, ABV 4%)

Bevans Bitter (OG 1042, ABV 4.2%)

Bitter (OG 1043, ABV 4.3%)

General Picton (OG 1043, ABV 4.3%)

Export Ale (OG 1050, ABV 5%)

Richmond SIBA

The Station Brewery, Station Yard, Richmond, North Yorkshire, DL10 4LD
☎ (01748) 828266 richmondbrewing.co.uk
Shop 10.30am-4.30pm daily (may open outside these hours)
Tours by arrangement

Richmond opened in 2008 in the Victorian station complex beside the River Swale. The brewery's output is split between cask-conditioned (60%) and bottled ales (40%) with seasonal beers also being produced throughout the year. Beers are available in the local area in the Hildyard Arms in Colburn, Bolton Arms in Downholme and the Ralph Fitz Randal in Richmond. Ownership changed in 2013.

SwAle (OG 1035, ABV 3.7%)
Dark mild with slightly more bitterness than a traditional mild.

Station Ale (OG 1039, ABV 4%)
Light golden bitter brewed using hedgerow hops.

Pale Ale (OG 1044, ABV 4.6%)

Ridgeside SIBA

Unit 24, Penraevon 2 Industrial Estate, Meanwood, Leeds, West Yorkshire, LS7 2AW ☎ 07595 380568
ridgesidebrewery.co.uk

Ridgeside began brewing in 2010 using a four-barrel plant, which is set to expand. Special brews are produced monthly alongside an extensive core range. Regular outlets are supplied around Leeds, and the Junction in Castleford serves Ridgeside beers from oak casks.

Jailbreak (OG 1038, ABV 3.8%)
A pale session beer.

Cascade (OG 1041, ABV 4.1%)
Grapefruit flavours define this beer with a strong presence of hops and bitterness throughout.

Templar (OG 1042, ABV 4.2%)

Rushmore (OG 1043, ABV 4.3%)
A pale ale brewed using American hops.

Desert Aire (OG 1048, ABV 4.8%)
This yellow-coloured beer is fruity, hoppy and bitter; the citrus hops dominate but there is some sweetness.

Stargazer (OG 1049, ABV 4.9%)

Black Night (OG 1050, ABV 5%)
A strong dark oatmeal stout with a complex malt character and smooth mouthfeel.

Long Way From Home (OG 1050, ABV 5%)

Eliminator (OG 1060, ABV 6%)

Ridgeway

Beer Counter Ltd, South Stoke, Oxfordshire, RG8 0JW
☎ (01491) 873474
peter.scholey@beercounter.co.uk

Set up by ex-Brakspear head brewer Peter Scholey, Ridgeway specialises in bottle-conditioned beers, although cask beers are occasionally offered. At present the beers are brewed by Peter using his own ingredients on plants at Hepworth's brewery (qv) and Cotswold brewery (qv).

Bitter (OG 1040, ABV 4%)

Organic Beer/ROB (OG 1043, ABV 4.3%)

Blue (OG 1050, ABV 5%)

Ivanhoe (OG 1050, ABV 5.2%)

IPA (OG 1055, ABV 5.5%)
Golden ale with a citrus aroma, a bitter hoppy flavour and a long bitter aftertaste.

Ringway Brewery SIBA

16 Station Road Industrial Estate, Reddish, SK5 6ND
☎ (0161) 443 1818 ringwaybrewery.co.uk

Ringway started brewing in 2012 in a modern industrial estate unit, using a six-barrel kit. Brewing takes place twice a week, supplying the local trade and distributors. Extensive use is made of English hops in all beers.

Session (OG 1038, ABV 3.8%)
A light hoppy pale ale packed with hops to give a citrus punch.

Single Bramling (OG 1039, ABV 4%)
A pale, single-hopped session bitter.

Best Bitter (OG 1041, ABV 4.2%)

A classic English bitter using all English hops to give good bitterness with a delicate aroma.

Wor Stout (ABV 4.3%)
A traditional full-bodied sweet English stout.

IPA (OG 1048, ABV 4.8%)
Full-bodied deep golden ale with a good balance of hops and pale malt with a lingering bitter aftertaste.

Ringwood

Christchurch Road, Ringwood, Hampshire, BH24 3AP
☎ (01425) 471177 ⊕ ringwoodbrewery.co.uk
Shop Mon-Sat 9.30am-5pm
Tours by arrangement

⊗ Ringwood was bought in 2007 by Marstons for £19 million. Production has been increased to 50,000 barrels a year. Some 750 outlets are supplied. Ringwood beers are now available in Marston's pubs all over the country. Seasonal beers are available: see website. Part of Marston's PLC.

Best Bitter (OG 1038, ABV 3.8%) ◆
A malty session bitter with strong toffee notes in the aroma, leading to a short, bittersweet finish. Malt tends to dominate throughout.

Boondoggle (ABV 4%)

Fortyniner (OG 1049, ABV 4.9%) ◆
A caramel, biscuity aroma, with hints of damson, lead to a sweet but well-balanced taste with malt, fruit and hop flavours.

Old Thumper (OG 1055, ABV 5.1%) ◆
A powerful, sweet, copper-coloured beer. A fruity aroma preludes a sweet, malty taste with fruit and caramel and a bittersweet aftertaste.

Ripple Steam Brewery SIBA

Parsonage Farm, Vale Road, Sutton, Kent, CT15 5DH
☎ 07917 037611 ⊕ ripplesteambrewery.co.uk

Ripple Steam began brewing commercially on a farm in Kent in 2012. Seasonal beers are available.

Milk Stout (ABV 3.5%)

Best Bitter (ABV 4.1%)

Green Hopped IPA (ABV 4.5%)

IPA (ABV 4.5%)

River Leven

Lab Road, Kinlochleven, PH50 4SG
☎ (01855) 831519 ☎ 07901 873273
⊕ riverlevenales.co.uk

River Leven was established 2011 in a former aluminium factory building in Kinlochleven. Only pure malt cask-conditioned ale is produced.

Blonde (OG 1040, ABV 4%)

Dark (OG 1040, ABV 4%)

Traditional IPA (OG 1040, ABV 4%)

Riverhead

▤ 2 Peel Street, Marsden, Huddersfield, West Yorkshire, HD7 6BR
☎ (01484) 841270 (Pub) ⊕ ossett-brewery.co.uk
Tours by arrangement (through Ossett Brewing Co)

⊛ Riverhead is a brewpub that opened in 1995. Ossett Brewing (qv) purchased the site in 2006 but runs it as a separate brewery. It has since opened the Dining Room on the first floor, which uses Riverhead beers in its dishes. There are many rotating beers produced as well as seasonals.

Riverside

Bee's Farm, Wainfleet, Lincolnshire, PE24 4LX
☎ (01754) 881288
Tours by arrangement

⊗ Riverside started brewing in 2003 on a five-barrel plant, moving to its present site in 2008. Since 2014 the brewery has operated on a part time basis, mainly at weekends, with a reduced level of production. It supplies a small number of regular local outlets. Seasonal beers are brewed occasionally.

Dixon's Major Bitter (OG 1038, ABV 3.9%)
A traditional English bitter with a reddish hue.

Glory Hunter (OG 1042, ABV 4.3%)
A rich golden ale.

Robin Hood

Unit 3, Northgate Place, High Church Street, New Basford, Nottingham, NG7 7JT ☎ 07804 499462
⊕ robinhoodbrewery.com

Robin Hood began brewing in 2012, originally using spare capacity at another brewery. It moved to its own premises in 2013 using a 5.5-barrel plant producing the Robin Hood and His Outlaws range of beers. Seasonal and special beers are also available.

Maid Marian Extra Pale (OG 1039, ABV 3.9%)
Pale straw-coloured ale with overtones of honey, balanced with a hint of hop aroma and bitterness.

Robin Hood (OG 1040, ABV 4%)
A traditional English ale, light brown in colour with the distinctive aroma and taste of English hops and malt, with a smooth, dry finish.

Will Scarlet (OG 1042, ABV 4.2%)
Red-coloured ale with spicy hop overtones and port like flavours.

Friar Tuck Stout (OG 1044, ABV 4.4%)
Dark and malty, with coffee and chocolate flavours balanced out with a hint of hop background.

Outlaw (OG 1044, ABV 4.4%)
Golden ale with floral citrus hop aroma and crisp hop finish.

The Sheriff Of Nottingham (OG 1046, ABV 4.6%)
A tawny-coloured special ale, initial fruity hop flavour developing into a satisfying bitterness to finish.

Little John Strong (OG 1050, ABV 5%)
Deep gold-coloured strong ale. Full-bodied with an aroma and taste of barley wine to start, then developing a bitter, hoppy but balanced finish.

Robinsons SIBA IFBB

Unicorn Brewery, Frederic Robinson Ltd, Stockport, Cheshire, SK1 1JJ
☎ (0161) 612 4061 ⊕ robinsonsbrewery.com
Visitor centre & shop: Mon 10.30am-6pm (large tour bookings only), Tue-Sat 10.30am-6pm, Sun 10.30am-5pm

Tours by arrangement

Robinsons has been brewing since 1838 and the business is still owned and run by the family. It has an estate of 370 pubs stretching from Cheshire to Cumbria and out to North Wales. Seasonal beers: see website.

1892 (OG 1032, ABV 3.3%)
Brewed to the original recipe since 1892 (thus the name) it is an easy-drinking nut brown Cheshire ale with a dry roasted nutty malt palate and a delicate dry hop aroma.

1892 Dark (OG 1032, ABV 3.3%)
1892 with added caramel.

Dizzy Blonde (OG 1037, ABV 3.8%)
A straw-coloured summer ale with a distinctive hop aroma. A light, refreshing beer with a clean, zesty, hop-dominated palate complemented by a crisp, dry finish.

Hartleys XB (OG 1040, ABV 4%)
An overly sweet and malty bitter with a bitter citrus peel fruitiness and a hint of liquorice in the finish.

Cumbria Way (OG 1040, ABV 4.1%)
A pronounced malt aroma with rich fruit notes. Rounded malt and hops in the mouth, long dry finish with citrus fruit notes. Brewed for the Hartley's estate in Cumbria.

Cwrw'r Ddraig Aur (OG 1041, ABV 4.1%)

Unicorn (OG 1041, ABV 4.2%)
Amber beer with a fruity aroma. Malt, hops and fruit in the taste with a bitter, malty finish.

Trooper (OG 1048, ABV 4.8%)
Dark golden hoppy beer brewed in conjunction with Iron Maiden's Bruce Dickinson.

Double Hop (OG 1050, ABV 5%)
Pale brown beer with malt and fruit on the nose. Full hoppy taste with malt and fruit, leading to a hoppy, bitter finish.

Old Tom (OG 1079, ABV 8.5%)
A full-bodied, dark beer with malt, fruit and chocolate on the aroma. A complex range of flavours includes dark chocolate, full maltiness, port and fruits and lead to a long, bittersweet aftertaste.

Rock & Roll SIBA

Lamp Tavern, 157 Barford Street, Birmingham, B5 6AH
☎ (0121) 688 1220
markwshepherd@btinternet.com
Tours by arrangement

Owned and operated by Mark Shepherd, former head brewer at Weatheroak Hill and the Old Pie Factory, Rock & Roll is Birmingham's only rooftop pub brewery. The two-barrel plant was hand-crafted in Birmingham to fit into the limited space available. Due to the brewery's compact size, specials and experimental beers are regularly available.

Lamplight (OG 1039, ABV 3.9%)
Pale ale brewed with American hops.

Instant Calmer (OG 1040, ABV 4%)

Brew Springsteen (OG 1042, ABV 4.2%)
A pale ale with honey.

Rocket Science

73 Firgrove Crescent, Yate, BS37 7AJ ☎ 07759 271993 rocketscienceales.co.uk

Rocket Science is a nanobrewery, which commenced brewing in 2013. The range is currently only available bottle conditioned.

Rockin' Robin SIBA

Campfield Farm, Haste Hill Road, Boughton Monchelsea, Kent, ME17 4LR ☎ 07779 986087
robin.smallbone@delphi.com
Tours by arrangement

Brewing began in 2011 using a one-barrel plant in a garden shed. It moved to its current location in 2014. Local outlets are supplied.

Hoppin' Robin (OG 1036, ABV 3.7%)
A traditional English session bitter. A complex ale with full malt, fruit in the mouth and Kentish hops on the tongue.

RPA (OG 1036, ABV 3.7%)
A light but refreshing pale ale.

Reliant Robin (OG 1041, ABV 4.2%)
An auburn-coloured classic best bitter with traditional hop notes on the palate and a fresh, spicy finish.

Reckless Robin (OG 1044, ABV 4.5%)
A strong bitter that delivers a fresh hoppy punch, well-balanced with soft fruit malt.

Really Rockin (OG 1052, ABV 5%)
A classic, full-bodied pale ale, dry hopped to deliver tropical fruit flavours.

Rockingham

c/o 25 Wansford Road, Blatherwycke, PE8 6RZ
☎ (01832) 280722 rockinghamales.co.uk

Rockingham is a small brewery established in 1997 that operates from a converted farm building near Blatherwycke, Northamptonshire, with a two-barrel plant producing a prolific range of beers. It supplies half a dozen local outlets. Seasonal beers are available.

Forest Gold (OG 1039, ABV 3.9%)
A hoppy blonde ale with citrus flavours. Well-balanced and clean finishing.

Hop Devil (OG 1040, ABV 3.9%)
Six hop varieties give this golden ale a bitter start and fruity finish.

White Rabbit (OG 1040, ABV 4%)
Light golden ale brewed with Australian and New Zealand hops. Bitter start and a tropical fruit finish.

Saxon Cross (OG 1041, ABV 4.1%)
A golden red ale with a nutty coffee aroma and fruit and blackcurrant undertones.

Fruits of the Forest (OG 1043, ABV 4.3%)
A multi-layered beer in which summer fruits and several spices compete with a big hop presence.

Dark Forest (OG 1050, ABV 5%)
A dark and complex beer, similar to a Belgian Dubbel, with malty/smoky flavours that give way to a fruity bitter finish.

Rocky Head

Unit 16, Glenville Mews, Kimber Road, Southfields, London, SW18 4NJ
☎ (020) 8875 9917 🌐 sites.google.com/site/rockyheadbrewery

Rocky Head is a microbrewery set up in 2012 by a group of friends inspired by the American craft brewing scene. A range of vegan-friendly bottle-conditioned beers is brewed on a five-barrel plant.

Rooster's SIBA

Unit 3, Grimbald Park, Wetherby Road, Knaresborough, North Yorkshire, HG5 8LJ
☎ (01423) 865959 🌐 roosters.co.uk
Tours by arrangement

Rooster's was founded in 1993 by Sean and Alison Franklin. The brewery was acquired by the Fozard family in 2011 when Sean and Alison retired. One-off and occasional experimental brews are also brewed under the Outlaw Brewing Co name.

Buckeye (OG 1035.5, ABV 3.5%)
An easy-drinking, well-hopped pale ale, brewed with a blend of American and New Zealand hops, producing an orange, citrus fruit aroma and a refreshing level of bitterness.

Wild Mule (OG 1037, ABV 3.9%)
A session-strength pale ale with a white wine fruitiness backed up by a lasting grapefruit bitterness.

YPA (Yorkshire Pale Ale) (OG 1039.5, ABV 4.1%)
A pale, aromatic summer ale that offers up delicate peachy and berry fruit flavours.

Yankee (OG 1041, ABV 4.3%)
A straw-coloured beer with a delicate, fruity aroma leading to a well-balanced taste of malt and hops with a slight evidence of sweetness, followed by a refreshing, fruity/bitter finish.

Fort Smith (OG 1048, ABV 5%)
A big, bold IPA with tropical and passion fruit aromas and a lasting bitter finish.

Londinium (OG 1054, ABV 5.5%)
A dark beer with a hint of coffee on the finish due to the addition of Taylors of Harrogate After Dark coffee.

Roseland

c/o Roseland Inn, Philleigh, nr St Mawes, Truro, Cornwall, TR2 5NB
☎ (01872) 580254

Roseland was established in 2009 by its owner/brewer at the Roseland Inn. The beers are mostly named after local birds and are generally only available in the pub or the Victory Inn, St Mawes, and occasionally at local beer festivals. Bottle-conditioned beers are available.

Cornish Shag (OG 1037, ABV 3.8%)
A copper-coloured session bitter.

Rossendale

Griffin Inn, 84 Hud Rake, Haslingden, Lancashire, BB4 5AF
☎ (0333) 210 4021 🌐 rossendalebrewery.co.uk

Formerly known as Pennine Ales, the brewery acquired the brew plant previously used by Porter Brewing Co in 2007 and is based in the cellar of the Griffin Inn in Haslingden. It produces seven regular cask ales.

Floral Dance (OG 1040, ABV 3.8%)
A pale and fruity session beer.

Hameldon Bitter (OG 1040, ABV 3.8%)
A dark traditional bitter with a dry and assertive character that develops in the finish.

Glen Top (OG 1040.5, ABV 4%)

Rossendale Ale (OG 1045, ABV 4%)

Halo Pail (OG 1045, ABV 4.5%)

Pitch Porter (OG 1050, ABV 5%)
A full-bodied, rich beer with a slightly sweet, malty start, counter balanced with sharp bitterness and a roast barley dominance.

Sunshine (OG 1055, ABV 5.3%)
A hoppy and bitter golden beer with a citrus character. The lingering finish is dry and spicy.

Rother Valley SIBA

Gate Court Farm, Station Road, Northiam, East Sussex, TN31 6QT
☎ (01797) 252922
Tours by arrangement

Rother Valley Brewing Co was established in Northiam in 1993, overlooking the Rother Levels and the Kent & East Sussex Railway. Established and new hop varieties are grown on the farm and also sourced locally. Brewing is split between cask and an ever-increasing range of filtered bottled beers. Around 100 outlets are supplied direct and through wholesalers. A monthly seasonal ale is available.

Honeyfuzz (OG 1038, ABV 3.8%)
A pale bitter flavoured with Sussex honey, subtle but not sweet with a citrus twang on the finish.

Smild (OG 1038, ABV 3.8%)
A full-bodied, dark, creamy mild with hints of chocolate.

Level Best (OG 1040, ABV 4%)
Full-bodied tawny session bitter with a malt and fruit aroma, malty taste and a dry, hoppy finish.

Hoppers Ale (OG 1044, ABV 4.4%)
A copper-coloured ale. The initial burst of hop is followed by a pleasant caramel taste.

Boadicea (OG 1045, ABV 4.5%)
A straw-coloured beer with a delicate, fruity flavour.

Rotters

Tower Hotel, Talgarth, Powys, LD3 0BW
☎ (01874) 711253 🌐 rottersbrewery.co.uk
Tours by arrangement

Rotters Brewery opened in 2010. Seasonal beers are also available: see website.

Utter Rotter (OG 1040, ABV 3.9%)

Grounds For Divorce (OG 1048, ABV 4.7%)
A premium ruby ale.

Round Tower SIBA

Unit 11a, Robjohns House, Navigation Road, Chelmsford, Essex, CM2 6ND
☎ (01245) 807343 🌐 roundtowerbrewery.co.uk

Round Tower began brewing in 2013, the first brewery in Chelmsford since Grays & Sons ceased brewing in 1974. Former home brewer Simon Tippler started on a small scale but has now expanded to a brew length of five barrels. Several local pubs are supplied and the beers can also be found in the Grays & Sons estate and other selected free houses. The Solo range of beers showcase single hop varieties. Bottle-conditioned beer is available.

Citra Galaxy (ABV 4%)
A crisp and bitter golden ale.

Point to Point (ABV 4%)
A dark brown bitter with mild bitterness.

Solo Bramling Cross (ABV 4%)

Solo Cascade (ABV 4%)

The Mix (ABV 4%)
A golden ale with a hit of citrus and a bitter finish.

Tippler's Gold (ABV 4.1%)
A golden-coloured, refreshing session beer with a bitter finish.

Cascade Galaxy (ABV 4.2%)
A crisp golden ale.

Solo Galaxy (ABV 4.3%)
Subtle notes of citrus and tropical fruits with a malty backbone and a long-lasting bitterness.

Stout (ABV 4.6%)
Complex and rich.

Rectory Stout (ABV 4.8%)
Rich and smooth, crafted from six different malts to deliver a deep and complex stout.

Square Peg (ABV 4.9%)
A black IPA.

Lucky 7 (ABV 6.1%)
Strong and hoppy.

Rowditch

Rowditch Inn, 246 Uttoxeter New Road, Derby, DE22 3LL
☎ (01332) 343123

The Rowditch Brewery was established in 2010 and is a 3.75-barrel plant situated on the premises of the Rowditch pub. Various one-off and seasonal ales are periodically available.

St Stephens (OG 1038, ABV 3.6%)
Citrus flavoured, golden, bitter ale.

St Andrew's (OG 1042, ABV 3.9%)
A golden bitter with citrus flavours.

RPA (OG 1047, ABV 4.7%)
A well-balanced bitter.

Rowton SIBA

Stone House, Rowton, Telford, Shropshire, TF6 6QX
☎ 07746 290995 🌐 rowtonbrewery.com

Rowton was established in 2008 on a four-barrel plant in an old cow shed on the owner's farm. Barley grown on the farm is sent for malting and returned for use in the brews and water is from a borehole on site.

Bitter (OG 1040, ABV 3.9%)

Galaxy (OG 1044, ABV 4.3%)

Dark Side Stout (OG 1045, ABV 4.5%)

Rtwo Dtoo (NEW)

The Steamhouse, Station Road, Urmston, M41 9SB
☎ (0161) 748 6487 ✉ info@thesteamhouse.co.uk

The unusual name of this brewery comes from the triumvirate who run it – Rob, Ron and Danny (two 'R's and a 'D' too). Established in 2013 and located at the Steamhouse pub in Urmston, space constraints and demand for the beers in the pub means that it is unlikely that the beers will ever be made available to other pubs or beer festivals.

Best Red (ABV 4.2%)
A dark bitter with a hint of hazelnut in the taste.

Steamhopper IPA (ABV 4.9%)

Ruddles

See Greene King

Rudgate SIBA

2 Centre Park, Marston Moor Business Park, Tockwith, York, North Yorkshire, YO26 7QF
☎ (01423) 358382 🌐 rudgatebrewery.co.uk

Rudgate began brewing in 1992 on a disused WWII airfield that was chosen because of its water suitability. Traditional methods are followed using a full mash infusion system and fermentation is achieved using its own strain of Yorkshire brewing yeast. Four seasonal beers are available each month: see website.

Jorvik Blonde (OG 1036, ABV 3.8%)
Blonde ale with a balanced hoppy bitterness and a crisp, fruity finish.

Viking (OG 1036, ABV 3.8%)
An initially warming and malty, full-bodied beer, with hops and fruit lingering into the aftertaste.

Battleaxe (OG 1040, ABV 4.2%)
A well-hopped bitter with slightly sweet initial taste and light bitterness. Complex fruit character gives a memorable aftertaste.

Ruby Mild (OG 1041, ABV 4.4%)
Nutty, rich ruby ale, stronger than usual for a mild.

Volsung (OG 1046, ABV 5%)
A premium bitter, golden-coloured with distinctive lemon on the nose.

York Chocolate Stout (OG 1049, ABV 5%)
Deep, rich stout with complex balanced flavours and a subtle chocolate finish.

IPA (OG 1053, ABV 5.2%)
Moderately bitter leading to a citrus, hoppy finish.

Brewed for Marston Moor Brewery:

Matchlock Mild (OG 1038, ABV 4%)
Traditional, full-flavoured dark mild.

Mongrel (OG 1038, ABV 4%)
A balanced bitter with plenty of fruit character.

Fairfax Special (OG 1039, ABV 4.2%)

THE BREWERIES

A full-bodied premium bitter, pale in colour with a well-balanced slightly citrus aroma.

Merriemaker (OG 1042, ABV 4.5%)
A premium straw-coloured ale.

Brewers Droop (OG 1045.5, ABV 5%)
A powerful golden ale with a sweet taste.

Runaway (NEW)

Unit 4, Millgate, Dantzic Street, Manchester, M4 4JW
☎ (0161) 832 2628 🌐 therunawaybrewery.com

Runaway began brewing in 2014 using a 5.5-barrel plant producing bottle-conditioned beers. Seasonal and special beers are planned.

Rydale (NEW) SIBA

Evergreen, Malton Road, York, North Yorkshire, YO32 9TN
☎ (01904) 400303 🌐 rydalebrewing.co.uk

Rydale began brewing in 2013 using a four-barrel plant, supplying pubs in the local area. Further beers and a bottling line are planned.

Gold (ABV 3.8%)

Pale (ABV 3.8%)

Bitter (ABV 4%)

Stout (ABV 4.3%)

S&P (NEW)

Drayton Lane, Horsford, Norwich, NR10 3AN ☎ 07552 300768 🌐 spbrewery.co.uk
Tours by arrangement

Production commenced in 2013 using a 10-barrel plant constructed upon land once owned by prominent Norfolk brewers Steward & Patteson (1800-1965), hence the name. Locally produced malts are used as is water from the brewery's own borehole.

Barrack Street Bitter (OG 1041, ABV 4%)
A refreshing amber ale. A gentle hop aroma sits comfortably with the malty biscuit flavour. An increasingly bitter finish.

First Light (OG 1042, ABV 4.1%)
A light golden beer. A strong citrus aroma and deep hoppy flavour is complemented by a lingering bitter finish.

Eve's Drop (OG 1046, ABV 4.3%)
A well-balanced golden brown ale. Hops and malts dominate with a peppery mouthfeel giving way to lingering sweetness.

Saddleworth

Church Inn, Church Lane, Uppermill, Oldham, OL3 6LW
☎ (01457) 820902/872415
Tours by arrangement

Saddleworth started brewing in 1997 in a 120-year old brewhouse at the Church Inn. Brewery and inn are set above a valley overlooking Saddleworth Moor. Brewing capacity was significantly expanded in 2011 with a new 13-barrel plant. Seasonal beers are available.

Mild (OG 1038, ABV 3.6%)

More (OG 1038, ABV 3.8%)
A mild ale, badged by the brewery as a bitter.

St George's Bitter (OG 1038, ABV 3.8%)
Dry and bitter, with some citrus and nutty notes.

Honey Smacker (OG 1042, ABV 4.1%)
Hoppy and slightly sharp, with citrus notes.

Hop Smacker (OG 1042, ABV 4.1%)
A hoppy golden ale.

Slap & Tickle (OG 1045, ABV 4.3%)
A golden ale.

Shaftbender (OG 1060, ABV 5.4%)
Aroma and flavours of liquorice, roast malt, chocolate and coffee.

Sadler's SIBA

7 Stourbridge Road, Lye, Stourbridge, West Midlands, DY9 7DG
☎ (01384) 895230 🌐 sadlersales.co.uk
Tours by arrangement

Third and fourth generation brewers John and Chris Sadler re-opened this historic brewery in its current location in 2004. The brewery tap house, the Windsor Castle, was built and opened next to the brewery in 2006. Around 250 outlets are supplied.

JPA (OG 1038, ABV 3.8%)
A pale, hoppy bitter with a crisp and zesty lemon undertone.

Mellow Yellow (OG 1041, ABV 4.1%)
A pale ale brewed with plenty of hops and honey.

Worcester Sorcerer (OG 1043, ABV 4.3%)
Brewed with English hops and barley with hints of mint and lemon, creating a floral aroma and crisp bitterness.

Thin Ice (OG 1045, ABV 4.5%)
A pale ale. Bitter but with an orange and lemon finish.

Boris Citrov (OG 1046, ABV 4.7%)
An orange marmalade ale with a sweet, crisp and fruity finish.

Hop Bomb (OG 1050, ABV 5%)
A powerful IPA. A balanced malt sweetness supports the hop aroma and flavour explosion.

Red IPA (OG 1057, ABV 5.7%)

Mud City Stout (OG 1066, ABV 6.6%)
Rich, full-bodied strong stout brewed with raw cocoa, fresh vanilla pods, oats, wheat and dark malts.

Saffron SIBA

The Cartshed, Parsonage Farm, Henham, Essex, CM22 6AN
☎ (01279) 850923 🌐 saffronbrewery.co.uk
Tours by arrangement

Founded in 2005, the brewery was upgraded to a 15-barrel plant in early 2008 and re-located to a converted barn at Parsonage Farm, with a purpose-built reed bed for environmentally-friendly disposal of waste products. 40 outlets are supplied direct. Seasonal and bottle-conditioned beers are available.

IPA (OG 1036, ABV 3.6%)

Ramblers Tipple (OG 1040, ABV 3.9%)

A rich, copper-coloured bitter with toffee and caramel flavours.

Brewhouse Bell (OG 1041, ABV 4%)
Golden amber in colour with citrus and hop flavours balancing well for a clean, fresh finish.

Littlebury Lighthouse (OG 1043, ABV 4.2%)

Blonde (OG 1044, ABV 4.3%)
A light golden ale with a delicate balance of citrus and smooth, malty flavours and a crisp finish.

Squires Gamble (OG 1044, ABV 4.3%)
Traditional style copper ale; soft, mellow, full-flavoured and hoppy with citrus and biscuit hints.

Flying Serpent (OG 1046, ABV 4.5%)

Henham Honey (OG 1047, ABV 4.6%)

Tiddly Vicar (OG 1051, ABV 5%)
Dark copper nutty beer with a light, spicy finish.

Silent Night (OG 1053, ABV 5.2%)

St Andrews SIBA

Unit 7, Bassaguard Business Park, St Andrews, KY16 8AL ☎ 07879 399441
standrewsbrewingcompany.com

Established in 2012, St Andrews Brewing Company produces bottle-conditioned beers that are available across Fife and Scotland. Beers are brewed in small batches of just 750 bottles. Seven regular beers are supplemented with monthly guest ales. Cask beers are supplied to a number of local outlets including the brewery tap in St Andrews, opened in 2013. The brewery relocated to new premises in St Andrews in 2014.

St Austell SIBA

63 Trevarthian Road, St Austell, Cornwall, PL25 4BY
☎ (01726) 74444 staustellbrewery.co.uk
Shop Mon-Fri 9am-5pm, Sat 10am-4pm
Tours by arrangement

Founded by Walter Hicks in 1851, St Austell Brewery remains family owned. Its cask beers are available in all its 170 pubs, as well as the free trade and throughout the UK and including exclusive brews for the Nicholson's pub company. The brewery hosts its own Celtic beer festival late in the year. Seasonal and bottle-conditioned beers: see website.

Dartmoor Best Bitter (OG 1035, ABV 3.5%)
Easy-drinking, copper-coloured session bitter. Smooth and balanced sweet malt, fruit and spicy hop bitterness flavours with some astringency throughout.

Trelawny (OG 1039, ABV 3.8%)
Tawny bitter with aroma of hops and stone fruits. Hop bitterness and some citrus develop into caramel-malt sweetness. Refreshing, crisp finish.

Tribute (OG 1043, ABV 4.2%)
Fruity aroma with trace of tangy ester. Dominant citrus hop bitterness with elderflower notes and biscuit malt, ending refreshingly dry.

Proper Job (OG 1046, ABV 4.5%)
Resinous hop aroma gold beer. Copious citrus fruits with bitterness leading to crisp hop bitter and grapefruit finish, becoming dry.

HSD (Hicks Special Draught) (OG 1052, ABV 5%)
Malt and stone fruit aroma leads into rich, balanced fruit, caramel, bitterness and malt which lasts into the long finish.

Brewed for the Nicholson's Pub Company:

Nicholson's Pale Ale (OG 1040, ABV 4%)

St George's SIBA

The Old Bakery, Bush Lane, Callow End, Worcestershire, WR2 4TF
☎ (01905) 831316 stgeorgesbrewery.co.uk
Tours by arrangement

The brewery was established in 1998 in old village bakery premises and acquired in 2006 by Duncan Ironmonger, who owns three nearby pubs. The brewery supplies local free houses and wholesalers for a wider distribution. At least two monthly specials are usually available.

Liquid Gold (ABV 3.9%)
A golden ale with a floral aroma and clean, crisp citrus flavour.

Friar Tuck (OG 1040, ABV 4%)
A golden bitter, smooth and refreshing with a citrus character.

Midas (ABV 4%)
A gold-coloured beer with a gentle maltiness and floral, citrus fresh hop fruitiness. The finish is bittersweet with hints of citrus fruit.

Charger (OG 1046, ABV 4.6%)
A light golden beer with a citrus blast and a hint of grapefruit.

Dragons Blood (OG 1048, ABV 4.8%)
A ruby-coloured beer with a hint of chocolate with an earthy and slightly spicy aroma.

St Peter's SIBA

St Peter's Hall, St Peter South Elmham, Suffolk, NR35 1NQ
☎ (01986) 782322 stpetersbrewery.co.uk
Shop Mon-Fri 9am-5pm, Sat & Sun 11am-4pm (may close at weekends)
Tours by arrangement

St Peter's Brewery is based adjacent to a moated medieval hall near Bungay, Suffolk. Established in 1996 it concentrates in the main on bottled beer/keg (85% of capacity) but has a rapidly increasing cask market. Two pubs are owned. 45% of production is exported to 32 countries worldwide. Seasonal beers are available.

Best Bitter (OG 1038, ABV 3.7%)
A complex but well-balanced hoppy brew. A gentle hop nose introduces a singular hoppiness with supporting malt notes and underlying bitterness. Other flavours fade to leave a long, dry, hoppy finish.

Mild (OG 1037, ABV 3.7%)
Heady aroma of caramelised blackberries and black toffee. Complex flavours with caramel, blackberries, hops and an astringent bitterness. Long, sustained finish with a roast coffee bitterness; increasingly dry.

Organic Best (OG 1041, ABV 4.1%)
A dry and bitter beer with a growing astringency. Pale brown in colour, it has a gentle hop aroma which makes the definitive bitterness surprising. One for the committed.

Ruby Red (OG 1043, ABV 4.3%)
A tawny red ale with subtle malt undertones and a distinctive spicy hop aroma.

Organic Ale (OG 1045, ABV 4.5%) ◆
A rich toffee apple aroma and a smooth grainy feel. Malt and caramel initially match the dry hoppy bitterness. As the flavours mature, liquorice dryness develops. Full-bodied.

Golden Ale (OG 1047, ABV 4.7%) ◆
Amber-coloured, full-bodied, robust ale. A strong hop bouquet leads to a mix of malt and hops combined with a dry, fruity hoppiness. The malt quickly subsides, leaving creamy bitterness.

Grapefruit Beer (OG 1047, ABV 4.7%) ◆
With a strong aroma and taste of grapefruit, this refreshing beer is exactly what it says on the tin. A superb example of a fruit beer.

IPA (OG 1055, ABV 5.5%)
A full-bodied, highly hopped pale ale with a zesty character.

Salamander SIBA

22 Harry Street, Dudley Hill, Bradford, West Yorkshire, BD4 9PH
☎ (01274) 652323 salamanderbrewing.co.uk
Tours by arrangement

Salamander first brewed in 2000 in a former pork pie factory. An expansion in 2004 increased capacity to 40 barrels per week. Direct deliveries are made to about 100 outlets in Cumbria, Lancashire, North and East Yorkshire, Manchester and Derbyshire.

Axolotl (OG 1038, ABV 3.9%)

Mudpuppy (OG 1042, ABV 4.2%) ◆
A well-balanced, copper-coloured best bitter with a fruity, hoppy nose and a bitter finish.

Golden Salamander (OG 1045, ABV 4.5%) ◆
Citrus hops characterise the aroma and taste of this golden premium bitter, which has malt undertones throughout. The aftertaste is dry, hoppy and bitter.

Salopian SIBA

67 Mytton Oak Road, Shrewsbury, Shropshire, SY3 8UQ
☎ (01743) 248414 salopianbrewery.co.uk
Shop Mon-Fri 9am-4pm
Tours by arrangement

The brewery was established in 1995 in an old dairy on the outskirts of Shrewsbury and, having grown steadily, now produces more than 145 barrels a week. Salopian also brews under the Blackwater Brewery name: see website. The brewery is planning to move to bigger premises.

Shropshire Gold (OG 1037, ABV 3.8%)
A light, copper-coloured ale with an unusual blend of body and dryness.

Oracle (OG 1040, ABV 4%)
A crisp golden ale with a striking hop profile. Dry and refreshing with a long, balanced aromatic finish.

Darwin's Origin (OG 1042, ABV 4.3%)
A light copper ale with a striking hop profile balanced by a refined malt finish.

Hop Twister (OG 1044, ABV 4.5%)
A premium bitter with a citrus flavour and complex hop finish. Refreshing and crisp.

Lemon Dream (OG 1043.5, ABV 4.5%)
A light gold ale brewed with wheat malt and subtly flavoured with fresh lemons.

Golden Thread (OG 1048, ABV 5%)
A bright gold ale. Strong and quite bitter but well-balanced.

Saltaire SIBA

Unit 6, County Works, Dockfield Road, Shipley, West Yorkshire, BD17 7AR
☎ (01274) 594959 saltairebrewery.co.uk
Tours by arrangement

Launched in 2006, Saltaire is an award-winning brewery based in a former Victorian power station. A mezzanine bar gives visitors views of the brewing plant and the chance to taste the beers. More than 300 pubs are supplied across West Yorkshire and the north of England.

Blonde (OG 1040, ABV 4%) ◆
Thirst quenching and quaffable, this straw-coloured beer is slightly sweet and well rounded with fruit, malt and hops in the taste and a fruity, hoppy finish.

Elderflower Blonde (OG 1040, ABV 4%) ◆
An easy-drinking, smooth, golden-coloured ale with subtle elderflower aroma leading to a pleasant elderflower fruit taste and a long, refreshing finish.

Raspberry Blonde (OG 1040, ABV 4%)
Refreshing blonde ale infused with a hint of raspberries.

Cascade Pale Ale (OG 1047, ABV 4.8%) ◆
A well-balanced golden bitter with smooth mouth feel, floral hop aromas and pronounced bitterness, culminating in a long, dry finish and dry aftertaste.

Triple Chocoholic (OG 1048, ABV 4.8%) ◆
A creamy, dark brown, roast, chocolate stout with a dry bitter finish and a rich chocolate aroma.

Sambrook's SIBA

Units 1-3, Yelverton Road, Battersea, London, SW11 3QG
☎ (020) 7228 0598 sambrooksbrewery.co.uk
Shop Mon-Fri 10am-6pm, Sat 10am-1pm
Tours by arrangement

Sambrook's was founded by Duncan Sambrook and David Welsh in 2008, supplying its award-winning ales throughout London. Seasonal beers are available and quarterly Saturday all-day events are held at the brewery to introduce each new seasonal ale.

Wandle Ale (OG 1038.5, ABV 3.8%) ◆
Dryness balances the rounded sweetish malt flavour of this fruity, quaffable pale brown bitter. Some peach and citrus notes.

Pumphouse Pale Ale (OG 1041.5, ABV 4.2%) ◆
Refreshing golden beer with a hint of citrus aroma becoming more pronounced on the palate, lingering into the bitter finish.

Junction Ale (OG 1045.5, ABV 4.5%) ◆
Well-balanced best bitter with soft fruit and figs aroma. The flavour is a little more citrus plus creamy toffee.

Powerhouse Porter (OG 1050, ABV 4.9%) ◆
Dark brown porter with a pleasant roasted malt nose with some sultana, blackcurrant and treacle character. Dry roasted finish.

Sandstone SIBA

Unit 5, Wrexham Enterprise Park, Preston Road, off Ash Road, North Wrexham Industrial Estate, Wrexham, LL13 9JT ☎ 07851 001118
sandstonebrewery.co.uk
Tours by arrangement

Sandstone Brewery was established as a four-barrel plant in 2008. More than 60 outlets in North Wales and North West England are supplied. The brewery was taken over by new owners in 2013 with the existing portfolio retained and a number of new beers added.

Edge (OG 1039, ABV 3.8%) ◆
A satisfying session ale, this pale, dry, bitter beer has a full mouthfeel and a lingering hoppy finish that belies its modest strength.

Onyx (OG 1040, ABV 4%)

Post Mistress (OG 1046, ABV 4.4%) ◆
A full-bodied, smooth premium bitter, ruby-red in colour, with a rich, mellow taste. Good combination of malt, hops and fruit in aroma and initial taste leading to a lasting, satisfying finish.

Racing Dragon (OG 1044, ABV 4.4%)

Sawbridgeworth SIBA

81 London Road, Sawbridgeworth, Hertfordshire, CM21 9JJ
☎ (01279) 722313 thegatepub.net
Tours by arrangement

Set up in 2000 by owners Tom and Gary Barnett, the brewery is situated behind the Gate Inn. Tom is a former professional footballer whose clubs included Crystal Palace. Brewing is carried out by ex-Nethergate brewer Bob Renvoise. Special or one-off beers are regularly brewed.

Manor Mild (OG 1034, ABV 3.4%)

IPA (OG 1038, ABV 3.8%)

Selhurst Park Flyer (OG 1038, ABV 3.8%)

Gold (OG 1040, ABV 4%)

Is It Yourself (OG 1042, ABV 4.2%)

Dragon's Blood (OG 1043, ABV 4.3%)

Saxon City

Glebe Farm Industrial Estate, Stoke Edith, Hereford, HR1 4HG
☎ (01432) 890688 herefordcasks.co.uk

Brewing began in 2010 in a vacant unit adjoining a cask factory using a six-barrel plant by PBC Brewery Installations. Three beers are produced on demand and are available in pins and firkins. Brewing is currently suspended.

Scarborough SIBA

Unit 1B, Stadium Works, Barry's Lane, Scarborough, North Yorkshire, YO12 4HA
☎ (01723) 241495 scarboroughbrewery.co.uk

Scarborough Brewery was established in 2010 using a one-barrel plant. In 2011 commercial brewing began using a 10-barrel plant from Wold Top Brewery. Beers can be found at its brewery tap, Valley Bar in Scarborough, and nationwide via wholesalers. One-off and seasonal beers are available.

Blonde (OG 1038, ABV 3.8%)
Easy-drinking pale session beer with a subtle citrus flavour and hoppy aroma.

Mild (OG 1039, ABV 3.9%)

Cascades (OG 1041, ABV 4.1%)
Pale straw-coloured beer with a zesty citrus flavour and floral hoppy aroma.

Chinook (OG 1041, ABV 4.1%)
Straw-coloured pale beer with spicy bitter flavours and a fruity, hoppy aroma.

Citra (OG 1042, ABV 4.2%)
Refreshing and light pale golden beer with light citrus aromas.

Stout (OG 1046, ABV 4.6%)
Full-bodied dark stout brewed using five malts giving depth of flavour and a bitter chocolate aroma.

American Pale (OG 1050, ABV 5%)
American-style golden beer wth a crisp, hoppy taste and floral aroma.

Scottish Borders SIBA

Lanton Mill, Jedburgh, TD8 6ST
☎ (01835) 830387 scottishbordersbrewery.com
Shop 10am-5pm daily
Tours by arrangement

Scottish Borders is Scotland's original plough-to-pint brewery, and started brewing in 2011 using barley from its own farm. Beyond the core range of six ales, recent projects include the brewery's 'Wild Harvest' initiative, which investigates the use of locally foraged ingredients for its ales. The brewery has recently launched its 'Born in the Borders' Visitors' Centre, offering brewery tours, a café/restaurant and retail units featuring Borders beer, produce and food.

Wee Beastie (OG 1037, ABV 3.6%)
A hint of dark malt and an unusual mash technique create a light session ale with real body and a surprisingly rich taste for a beer with a low ABV.

Foxy Blonde (OG 1037.5, ABV 3.8%)
A golden ale bursting with citrus and floral flavours.

Game Bird (OG 1039.5, ABV 4%)
An amber ale with a balance of malty sweetness and late summer fruit with a long and easy finish.

Holy Cow (OG 1041, ABV 4.2%)
Hints of dark malt combine with a long floral finish.

Gold Dust (OG 1041.5, ABV 4.3%)
A light IPA with a big burst of hop aroma.

Dark Horse (OG 1044, ABV 4.5%)
A classic dark ale that has overtones of coffee and chocolate with a spicy finish that lingers on the tongue.

Scribbler's (NEW) SIBA

7 Lime Grove, Stapleford, Nottinghamshire, NG9 7GF
☎ (0115) 875 1759 scribblers-ales.com

THE BREWERIES

Scribbler's was established in 2014 by two published authors, Richard Nettleton and Roger Frost, hence the name. The 4.5-barrel plant was constructed by the owners from old ice cream vessels, although the copper came from Grafton Brewing Co (qv). Beer names are based on classic book titles and bottle-conditioned ales are planned.

Masher In The Rye (ABV 4.8%)

One Brew Over The Cuckoo's Nest (ABV 5.2%)

Seren (NEW) SIBA

Syfnau House, Rosebush, Pembrokeshire, SA66 7QY
☎ (01437) 532098 🌐 serenbrewing.com

Seren is an award-winning nanobrewery on the edge of the Preseli mountains in North Pembrokeshire. Beers are crafted on a small scale.

Bluestone IPA (OG 1042, ABV 4.2%)
A gold-coloured beer with citrus and tropical hop aromas and flavours.

Factory Steam (OG 1045, ABV 4.5%)
A steam brewed, full-bodied, copper-coloured best bitter. Fruity with a firm bitterness and biscuity malt notes.

Ink Spot (OG 1050, ABV 5%)
A session version of Indian Ink.

Indian Ink (OG 1062, ABV 6.5%)
A black IPA. Citrus and pine plays over a touch of roast.

West Wales IPA (OG 1062, ABV 6.5%)
A full-strength American-style IPA. Gold-coloured with citrus and tropical hop aroma and flavour.

Settle SIBA

Unit 8, The Sidings, Settle, North Yorkshire, BD24 9RP
☎ (01729) 824936 🌐 settlebrewery.co.uk
Tours by arrangement

Settle Brewery is located in a small industrial unit adjacent to Settle railway station. Brewing started in 2013 using a new 12-barrel kit. Brewer Ian Simkins originally brewed at Nine Standards Brewery in Kirkby Stephen. Outlets across Cumbria, Yorkshire and Lancashire are supplied. The beers are also available through wholesalers.

Light (OG 1036, ABV 3.6%)
A delicate straw-coloured beer with a subtle blend of fruit and spice flavours and citrus overtones.

Mainline (OG 1037, ABV 3.8%)
A refreshing, delicately fruity golden beer with a little bit of sweetness.

Classic (OG 1039, ABV 4%)
A rich, floral, one-hop bitter.

Contract brewed for Nine Standards Brewery:

Original Standard (OG 1037, ABV 3.7%)
A dark amber bitter with a fruity, spicy nose.

Gold Standard (OG 1040, ABV 4.1%)
A flavoursome golden ale with a hint of blackcurrant.

Silver Standard (OG 1042, ABV 4.3%)
A classic pale ale with a strong hoppy aroma.

Double Standard (OG 1048, ABV 4.7%)
A robust porter with caramel and coffee notes and smoky undertones.

Royal Standard (OG 1052, ABV 5.5%)
A fruity golden ale flavoured with five different hop varieties.

Severn Vale SIBA

Woodend Lane, Cam, Dursley, Gloucestershire, GL11 5HS
☎ (01453) 547550 🌐 severnvalebrewing.co.uk
Shop: Please ring first
Tours by arrangement

Severn Vale started brewing in 2005 in an old milking parlour using a new five-barrel plant. Warminster malted barley is used and mainly Herefordshire hops. Around 80 outlets are supplied. Seasonal beers are available.

Nibley Ale (OG 1039, ABV 3.8%)
A light and refreshing ale.

Vale Ale (OG 1039, ABV 3.8%)
A rich amber beer with full-bodied malt flavours and complex nose and taste.

Dursley Steam Bitter (OG 1043, ABV 4.2%)
A refreshing golden ale full of flowery hops.

Freeride (OG 1043, ABV 4.2%)
A golden best bitter using New Zealand hops which produces a soft fruity flavour.

Luverley Jub'lee (OG 1043, ABV 4.2%)
A well-balanced golden best bitter with bold fruity hops in the finish.

Severn Sins (OG 1053, ABV 5.2%)
A jet-black stout with a dry roast malt flavour with hints of chocolate and liquorice.

Shalford SIBA

c/o PO Box 10411, Braintree, Essex, CM7 5WP
☎ (01371) 850925 🌐 shalfordbrewery.co.uk

Shalford began brewing in 2007 on a five-barrel plant at Hyde Farm in the Pant Valley in Essex. More than 50 outlets are supplied direct. Bottle-conditioned beers are available.

1319 Mild (OG 1037, ABV 3.7%)
Roast malt and chocolate sweetness with a slight bitter finish.

Barnfield Pale Ale (OG 1038, ABV 3.8%) ◆
Pale-coloured but full-flavoured, this is a traditional, hoppy bitter rather than a golden ale. Malt persists throughout, with bitterness becoming more dominant towards the end.

Braintree Market Ale (OG 1040, ABV 4%)
Traditional, easy-drinking session ale with a hoppy, lingering, dry finish.

Levelly Gold (OG 1040, ABV 4%)
Golden, summery bitter with a pleasant finish.

Stoneley Bitter (OG 1042, ABV 4.2%) ◆
Dark amber session beer whose vivid hop character is supported by a juicy, malty body and a dry finish.

Hyde Bitter (OG 1047, ABV 4.7%) ◆
Stronger version of Barnfield, with a similar but more assertive character.

Levelly Black (OG 1048, ABV 4.8%)
A dark, heavy, well-hopped ale with a grainy toffee taste topped with a thick creamy head.

Rotten End (OG 1065, ABV 6.5%)
Strong beer with slightly sweet, nutty undertones and a bitter edge to finish.

Shardlow

The Old Brewery Stables, British Waterways Yard, Cavendish Bridge, Leicestershire, DE72 2HL
☎ (01332) 799188 ✉ nev@shardlowbrewery.co.uk
Tours by arrangement

On a site associated with brewing since 1819, Shardlow delivers to more than 100 outlets throughout the East Midlands and is also one of the largest UK cider distributors. Reverend Eaton is named after a scion of the Eaton brewing family, Rector of Shardlow for 40 years. The brewery tap is the Blue Bell Inn at Melbourne, Derbyshire. Seasonal, bottle-conditioned beers and cask-conditioned five-litre canned beer are also available. Prolific supplier of beers to local beer festivals.

Chancellors Revenge (OG 1036, ABV 3.6%)
A light-coloured, refreshing, full-flavoured and well-hopped session bitter.

Cavendish Dark (OG 1037, ABV 3.7%)
A mild, well-balanced beer with a hoppy aftertaste.

Golden Hop (OG 1041, ABV 4.1%)
Golden, sweet tasting beer, dry-hopped with East Kent Goldings for added aroma.

Kiln House (OG 1041, ABV 4.1%)
A refreshing golden ale with a lingering bitter finish.

Narrow Boat (OG 1043, ABV 4.3%)
A pale amber bitter, with a short, crisp hoppy aftertaste.

Cavendish Bridge (OG 1045, ABV 4.5%)
Pale amber premium bitter. Refreshing, clean and fruity with a pleasing bitter finish.

Cavendish Gold (OG 1045, ABV 4.5%)
Pale gold, bright and clean tasting. A full-bodied ale with pronounced bitterness and complexity.

Reverend Eaton (OG 1045, ABV 4.5%)
A smooth, medium-strong bitter, full of malt and hop flavours with a sweet aftertaste.

Mayfly (OG 1048, ABV 4.8%)
Fruit notes predominate together with a pronounced malty aroma. Easy drinking but strong.

Five Bells (OG 1050, ABV 5%)
Dark, rich, ruby-coloured ale, powerful and bittersweet to the palate. Coffee notes complete the profile.

Whistlestop (OG 1050, ABV 5%)
A smooth and surprisingly strong pale beer.

Sharp's

Pityme Business Centre, Rock, Cornwall, PL27 6NU
☎ (01208) 862121 🌐 sharpsbrewery.co.uk
Shop Mon-Fri 9am-5pm

⊗ Sharp's was bought for £20 million by Molson Coors in 2011. The brewery was founded in 1994 and within 15 years had grown from producing 1,500 barrels a year to 60,000. £7.5 Million of investment from Molson Coors has brought the capacity up to 200,000 barrels per year. The company delivers beer to more than 1,200 outlets across the south of England via temperature-controlled depots in Bristol and London. One pub is owned, the Mariners in Rock. Molson Coors has stressed that it will maintain production in Cornwall. Seasonal beer: see website. Bottle-conditioned beer is available.

Cornish Coaster (OG 1035.2, ABV 3.6%) ◆
Refreshing copper bitter. Gentle balance of biscuit malt, fruit and sweetness. Fruit in the finish with bitterness and faint dryness.

Doom Bar (OG 1038.5, ABV 4%) ◆
Gentle hop aroma. Refreshing brown bitter with vine fruit and hops throughout. Biscuit malt with light bitterness and dry finish.

Atlantic IPA (OG 1040, ABV 4.2%)

Own (OG 1042.5, ABV 4.4%) ◆
Gentle malt aroma and brown colour. Sweet and light roast malt with hoppy bitterness, finishing gently dry with apple fruit.

Special (OG 1048.5, ABV 5%) ◆
Rich red ale with a malty nose. Sweet fruit and malt dominate the taste, fading slowly. Caramel and roast hints.

Shed Ales

Broadfields, Pewsey, Wiltshire, SN9 5DT
☎ (01672) 564533 🌐 shed-ales.com

Shed Ales was launched in 2012 operating from a one-barrel plant in a converted garden shed. A house beer is produced for the Bell, Winterbourne Stoke and the Royal Oak, Great Wishford. Seasonal beers: see website.

Dig It (OG 1037.5, ABV 3.7%)
A light amber-coloured session ale.

Patrick's Best (ABV 3.8%)

Shed Some Light (OG 1041, ABV 3.8%)
A refreshing blonde beer with a light earthy hop aroma and flavour.

Forkin' Best (OG 1042, ABV 4.1%)
A dark amber-coloured traditional English ale, with a toffee and spicy orange aroma and a clean, bittersweet taste from start to finish.

Pail Ale (OG 1045, ABV 4.3%)
Clean-tasting and pale with hops dominating the aroma and taste of this strong ale.

Shed Brewery

2232 Stratford Road, Hockley Heath, West Midlands, B94 6NU ☎ 07910 004041
✉ perryclarke1961@gmail.com

⊗ Brewing for nearly three years, beers are available at several pubs and clubs in Solihull and Birmingham. Production is 140 bottles per week plus single casks for specific outlets. Currently eight regular beers are brewed including a seasonal porter. All beers are suitable for vegetarians and vegans.

Session Bitter (OG 1039, ABV 3.8%)
A copper-coloured session bitter with a long hoppy taste.

Archers Ale (OG 1040, ABV 4%)
A blonde ale with a creamy malt taste and a burst of hops in the mouth followed by a long, hoppy finish.

Hemlingford Ale (OG 1040, ABV 4%)
Copper-coloured hoppy ale with a malty, creamy taste.

Hockley Citrus (ABV 4%)
A blonde ale, full of citrus hops and bitter in the mouth with a lingering hoppy taste.

Warwick Bear (OG 1040, ABV 4%)
Refreshing, light and hoppy ale with a lingering hop taste.

Executioners Porter (OG 1048, ABV 4.6%)
Dark, creamy, smooth and dry with a late roast malt character and nutty finish.

Shed Gold (OG 1048, ABV 5%)
A golden beer with a smooth, easy taste and caramel notes.

Spotted Cock (OG 1050, ABV 5%)
A strong copper-coloured beer, malty in the mouth.

Dark Knight (OG 1058, ABV 5.8%)
Dark ruby in colour with a mild bitterness and chocolate taste.

Sheelin

178 Derrylin Road, Bellanaleck, County Fermanagh, BT92 2BA ☎ 07730 432232 🌐 sheelin.com

Sheelin was established by brewer and chemist Dr George Cathcart in 2013. Beer is mainly available in bottles.

Sheffield SIBA

Unit 111, JC Albyn Complex, Burton Road, Sheffield, South Yorkshire, S3 8BT
☎ (0114) 272 7256 🌐 sheffieldbrewery.com
Tours by arrangement

Sheffield began brewing in 2007 in the former Blanco polish works using a 10-barrel plant. The brewery operates on the tower principal in premises which are also used as a venue for corporate or social gatherings. More than 50 outlets are supplied direct.

Crucible Best (OG 1038, ABV 3.8%)
A complex traditional bitter.

Five Rivers (OG 1038, ABV 3.8%)
An easy-drinking, straw-coloured session ale with a hoppy aroma.

Blanco Blonde (OG 1042, ABV 4.2%)
A continental lager-style beer.

Seven Hills (OG 1041, ABV 4.2%)
A premium bitter.

Sheffield Porter (OG 1045, ABV 4.4%)
A rich, chocolatey, malty porter with caramel flavours.

Shepherd Neame IFBB

17 Court Street, Faversham, Kent, ME13 7AX
☎ (01795) 532206 🌐 shepherdneame.co.uk
Shop Mon-Sat 10am-4.30pm
Tours by arrangement

Shepherd Neame traces its history back to 1698, making it the oldest continuous brewer in the country, though brewing probably began even earlier. The same water source is still used today and 1914 oak mash tuns are still operational. The company has 350 tied houses in the South East, nearly all selling cask ale. More than 2,000 other outlets are also supplied. The cask beers are made with Kentish hops, barley and water from their own artesian well. The company also brew cask ales under the Faversham Steam Brewery and No. 18 Yard Brewhouse names. Seasonal and special beers are available.

Master Brew (OG 1032, ABV 3.7%)
A distinctive bitter, mid-brown in colour, with a hoppy aroma. Well-balanced, with an aggressive bitter taste from its hops, it leaves a hoppy/bitter finish, tinged with sweetness.

Whitstable Bay (OG 1038, ABV 3.9%)
A full-bodied, fruity ale with a subtle bitterness and grapefruit and pine aromas.

Kent's Best (OG 1036, ABV 4.1%)
A robust bitter which merges the biscuity sweetness of English malt with the fruity, floral bitterness of hops.

Spitfire (OG 1036, ABV 4.2%)
A commemorative Battle of Britain brew for the RAF Benevolent Fund's appeal, now the brewery's flagship ale.

Bishops Finger (OG 1046, ABV 5%)
A strong ale with a complex hop aroma reminiscent of lemons, oranges and bananas combined with malt, molasses and toffee. Refreshing with a good malt character tinged with a lingering bitterness.

Sherborne

257 Westbury, Sherborne, Dorset, DT9 3EH
☎ (01935) 812094 🌐 sherbornebrewery.co.uk

Sherborne started brewing in 2005 on a 2.5-barrel plant. It moved in 2006 to new premises at the rear of the brewery's pub, Docherty's Bar. Following a serious arm injury sustained by the owner/brewer, no brewing has taken place for several years. It is possible that brewing will resume at some stage in the future.

Sherfield Village SIBA

Goddards Farm, Goddards Lane, Sherfield on Loddon, Hampshire, RG27 0EL ☎ 07906 060429
🌐 sherfieldvillagebrewery.co.uk

Sherfield Village started brewing in 2011, based in a converted barn on a working dairy farm. The brewery uses a five-barrel plant, supplying local pubs and regional festivals. As well as its regular beers, numerous seasonal and one-off specials are available. Extensive use is made of New World hops, particularly those from New Zealand. Dry-hopped versions of single-hop beers are usually available. Bottle-conditioned beers are also produced.

Threesome (OG 1030, ABV 3%)
Copper-coloured session beer with a long, hoppy finish.

Southern Gold (OG 1040, ABV 4%)
A golden beer with a citrus flavour and a floral nose.

Green Bullet (OG 1042, ABV 4.3%)
A pale golden beer with a complex hoppy flavour. Powerfully floral.

Single Hop (OG 1042, ABV 4.3%)
A golden ale which uses a single hop variety that changes every month.

Hoppy Harrington (OG 1046, ABV 4.7%)
A mid-brown strong bitter using five different hops. It has a complex, sweetish flavour and a satisfying hoppy finish.

Pioneer Stout (OG 1048, ABV 5%)

A black stout, packed with chocolate malt and Pioneer hops, and a hint of vanilla.

Brewed for Art Brew:

Monkey IPA (OG 1058, ABV 6.4%)
Massively hopped proper IPA.

ShinDigger (NEW)

c/o Outstanding Brewery, Britannia Mill, Cobden Street, Bury, BL9 6AW

Office: 170 Vie Building, 185 Water Street, Manchester, M3 4JU 🌐 shindiggerbrewing.co

ShinDigger was established in 2013, and currently uses spare capacity at Outstanding Brewery in Bury. A project of two former Manchester University students, their output is predominantly keg but occasionally cask ales make an appearance.

Shiny SIBA

Furnace Inn, 9 Duke Street, Derby, DE1 3BX
☎ (01332) 385981

After being made redundant, brewer Pedro Menon bought the Furnace Inn and installed a purpose-built 5.5-barrel brewery at the rear. Brewing began in 2012 with a steady stream of different ales available at the Furnace Inn. Wider distribution is planned. All beers are named to fit the shiny theme.

New World (OG 1037, ABV 3.7%)
Light and hoppy with citrus flavours.

Launch Pad (OG 1038, ABV 3.8%)

Obsidian (OG 1040, ABV 4%)
A dark mild with a sweet malt character, hints of treacle and coffee.

Golden Man (OG 1041, ABV 4.1%)
Golden ale with a delicate floral aroma.

4 Wood (OG 1045, ABV 4.5%)
Traditional, well-balanced, light chestnut ale with a delicate hop finish.

Reflection IPA (OG 1051, ABV 5.1%)
A strong, well-hopped citrus-led IPA.

Ship Inn

Ship Inn, Newton Square, Low Newton-by-the-Sea, Northumberland, NE66 3EL
☎ (01665) 576262 🌐 shipinnnewton.co.uk

Brewing commenced in 2008 on a 2.5-barrel plant; the brewery now produces 7.5 barrels per week. All regular beers are brewed in rotation but are only available on the premises. Seasonal and bottle-conditioned beers are also available. A special beer (4.2% ABV) is brewed for every 100 brews.

Sandcastles at Dawn (OG 1038, ABV 3.8%)
A pale session beer, light and crisp with a delicate floral finish.

Sea Coal (OG 1040, ABV 4%)
A dark wheat beer with a mild coffee, bittersweet chocolate, berry fruit finish.

Sea Wheat (OG 1040, ABV 4%)
A pale, crisp, sharp English-style wheat beer with a citrus burst of strong grapefruit.

Ship Hop Ale (OG 1042, ABV 4.2%)
A light copper-coloured ale, dry with hints of orange and marmalade, balanced and rounded.

Dolly Daydream (OG 1043, ABV 4.3%)
A classic premium bitter, slight toffee edge, subtle vine fruit finish.

Shipstone's

See Belvoir

Shires

16 Tweedale Court, Madeley, Shropshire, TF7 4JZ
☎ 07977 900212 🌐 shiresbrewery.co.uk

Shires Brewery was launched in 2009. Mike Handley supervises the 10-barrel plant that supplies the historic All Nations tap house nearby as well as other trade outlets. Seasonal beers: see website.

Best Bitter/Dabley Ale (OG 1039, ABV 3.8%)
Pale in colour with fruity undertones and a hint of citrus. A tasty session beer. Sold in the All Nations as Dabley Ale.

OBJ (Oh Be Joyful!) (OG 1043, ABV 4.2%)
A light and sweet bitter; delicate flavour belies the strength.

Severn Gorgeous (OG 1048, ABV 4.8%)
A light-bodied ale with full hop bitterness accompanying pine and citrus aromas.

Dabley Gold (OG 1050, ABV 5%)
Produced from the same recipe as Dabley Ale but brewed to a higher gravity giving a sweeter, fuller flavour.

Shoes SIBA

Three Horseshoes Inn, Norton Canon, Hereford, HR4 7BH
☎ (01544) 318375
Tours by arrangement

Established in 1994. The beers are brewed from malt extract and are normally only available at the Three Horseshoes. Each September Canon Bitter is brewed with green hops fresh from the harvest. All beers are available bottle conditioned.

Norton Ale (OG 1038, ABV 3.6%)

Canon Bitter (OG 1040, ABV 4.1%)

Peploe's Tipple (OG 1060, ABV 6%)

Farrier's Ale (OG 1114, ABV 15%)

Shortts Farm SIBA

Shortts Farm, Thorndon, Suffolk, IP23 7LS ☎ 07900 268100 🌐 shorttsfarmbrewery.com

Shortts Farm Brewery was established in 2012 by Matt Hammond on what has been the family farm for over a century. A five-barrel brewing plant is used. All of the beers are based around a musical theme inspired by a love of real ale and music. Pubs, festivals and private functions are catered for. Bottle-conditioned beer is available.

Strummer (ABV 3.8%)
An amber ale. Easy drinking, light and hoppy bitter with a malty character.

Blondie (ABV 4%)

THE BREWERIES

Skiffle (ABV 4.5%)
Chestnut in colour. A complex and malty, rich bitter with a good balance of hops over malt, creating a full-flavoured premium ale.

Indie (ABV 4.8%)
A golden IPA. Subtle but refreshing citrus fruit followed by a spicy, almost honey-like lingering finish.

Shotover SIBA

Coopers Yard, Manor Farm Road, Horspath, Oxfordshire, OX33 1SD
☎ (01865) 876770 🌐 shotoverbrewing.com
Shop: please ring or email first
Tours by arrangement

⊗ A family-owned and -run brewery four miles from Oxford city centre. It began brewing in 2009 and supplies outlets in the Oxford area. Bottle-conditioned beers are available and suitable for vegetarians. Cask ale suitable for vegetarians can also be supplied.

Prospect (OG 1040, ABV 3.7%)
A pale copper-coloured, hoppy session bitter with a big mouthfeel and striking dry hoppiness.

Scholar (OG 1047, ABV 4.5%)
A copper-coloured bitter combining a silky malt base with a mixture of oranges, grapefruit and spiciness. It delivers a satisfying bitter finish.

Shottle Farm SIBA

School House Farm, Lodge Lane, Shottle, Derbyshire, DE56 2DS
☎ (01773) 550056 🌐 shottlefarmbrewery.co.uk

Located in the hills above Belper, the grade II-listed farm is part of the Chatsworth Estate. Family-run, Shottle Farm Brewery has been in production since 2011 with a 10-barrel plant and uses its own natural spring water and local honey. One-off and occasional beers are available and all regular beers are available bottle conditioned. Its brewery tap is the nearby Bulls Head, Belper Lane End and the George & Dragon, Belper is regularly supplied along with several other outlets.

Shottlecock (OG 1034.9, ABV 3.6%)
A single malt beer with local honey. Created from an old Victorian recipe for Breakfast Beer, in the summer the honey is replaced with elderflower syrup for a more summery taste.

Black Peggy (OG 1037.8, ABV 3.9%)
A smooth, easy-drinking oatmeal stout with pleasant hints of liquorice.

Shottle Pale Ale (OG 1037.8, ABV 4%)
Mid-bodied premium pale ale with a soft, hoppy hit and a little taste of citrus tangerine.

BOB (Best of Both) (OG 1038.8, ABV 4.1%)
A cask-conditioned lager with a delicate aroma, grassy notes and a spiced aftertaste.

Eight Shilling (OG 1038.8, ABV 4.1%)
A rich, dark beer. Smooth and malty. Full-bodied with a pleasant aftertaste with undertones of treacle and caramel.

Shottle Gold (OG 1041.7, ABV 4.3%)
Floral aroma with a fruity hint of citrus lemon. Easy on the palate with a crisp and a clean white head.

Dilks (OG 1048.4, ABV 5%)
A slight sweetness and good hop balance. A smooth, mature beer with a hint of citrus.

Shugborough SIBA

Shugborough Estate, Milford, Staffordshire, ST17 0XB
☎ (01782) 823447 🌐 shugborough.org.uk
Tours by arrangement

Brewing in the original brewhouse at Shugborough, home of the Earls of Lichfield, restarted in 1990 but a lack of expertise led to the brewery being a static museum piece until Titanic Brewery of Stoke-on-Trent (qv) began helping in 1996.

Miladys Fancy (OG 1048, ABV 4.6%)

Lordships Own (OG 1052, ABV 5%)

Signature Brew (NEW)

Office: Workshop 45, Hackney Downs Studios, Hackney Downs, London, E8 2BT
☎ (020) 7684 4664 🌐 signaturebrew.co.uk

Signature Brew was established in 2011 using spare capacity at a number of breweries, originally brewing beers in collaboration with music artists. In 2014 it launched a range named Signature Brew Originals. Beers are available cask-conditioned, in bottles (including bottle-conditioned ales) and keg. For the full range of beers including collaborations, see website. Seasonal beers are available.

Session (ABV 4%)

Signature Pale (ABV 4.1%)

Black Vinyl Stout (ABV 4.2%)

Red Wedge (ABV 4.7%)

Signature Lager (ABV 5%)

Backstage IPA (ABV 5.6%)

Silhill SIBA

Oak Farm, Hampton Lane, Solihull, West Midlands, B92 0JB
☎ (0845) 519 5101 ☎ 07977 444564

Office: PO Box 15739, Solihull, West Midlands, B93 3FW 🌐 silhillbrewery.co.uk

⊗ Established in 2010, Silhill is a small independent brewery which is now based in premises just outside Solihull town centre using a 10-barrel plant.

Gold Star (OG 1039, ABV 3.9%)
A golden ale, malty and smooth, finishing with a delicate honey note.

Stars & Stripes (OG 1039, ABV 3.9%)
An American pale ale with a grapefruit aroma. Silky smooth leading to a dry finish.

Blonde Star (OG 1041, ABV 4.1%)
A refreshing, sweet, citrus pale ale.

Dark Star (OG 1043, ABV 4.3%)
A chestnut-coloured ale, warm and well-balanced, with a hint of chocolate.

Silver Street (NEW)

Clarence Hotel, 2 Silver Street, Bury, BL9 0EX
☎ (0161) 763 6432 🌐 theclarence.co.uk

Beers were originally contract brewed at Outstanding Brewery (qv). Silver Street began brewing in 2014 at the Clarence Hotel in Bury.

One (OG 1040, ABV 4%)
A pale ale with plenty of New Zealand hops.

Silverstone

Kingshill Farm, Syresham, nr Silverstone, Northamptonshire, NN13 5TH
☎ (01280) 850629
silverstonebrewingcompany.com
Tours by arrangement

The brewery, which is located near the celebrated motor racing circuit, opened in 2008. In keeping with its motor racing theme, the brewery is the proud sponsor of Formula V10. 60 outlets are supplied direct. Seasonal and bottle-conditioned beers are available.

Pitstop (OG 1038, ABV 3.8%)

Pole Position (OG 1041, ABV 4.1%)

Skidmark (ABV 4.2%)

Chequered Flag (OG 1043, ABV 4.5%)

Simpsons

White Swan, Eardisland, Herefordshire, HR6 9BD
☎ (01544) 388635 simpsonsfineales.co.uk

Tim Simpson acquired the White Swan in 2011 and set up the brewery at the rear of the pub in 2013. Beers are currently served in the White Swan, and locally to the free trade. A small bottling facility is now in operation to supply local county shows. Seasonal beers are available.

Golden Cockerel (OG 1037, ABV 3.7%)

Red Leg (OG 1043, ABV 4.3%)

Black Grouse (OG 1045, ABV 4.5%)

Old English (OG 1047, ABV 4.7%)

Sinclair

See Orkney

Siren Craft SIBA

Unit 1 Hogwood Industrial Estate, Weller Drive, Finchampstead, Berkshire, RG40 4QZ
☎ (0118) 973 0929 sirencraftbrew.com

Siren is a 40-barrel brewery, established in 2013. Four core beers are available, with many seasonal beers also produced. The American head brewer is influenced by the US and European craft brewing movement. An extensive barrel-ageing programme commenced in 2013 with many interesting beers produced. The brewery boasts an eight-tap tasting room. A balance of cask, keg and bottles are distributed throughout Europe.

Undercurrent Oatmeal Pale Ale (OG 1042, ABV 4.5%)
A pale ale with spicy, grassy aromas and a taste of grapefruit and apricot.

Soundwave IPA (OG 1056, ABV 5.6%)
An American-style IPA: golden, immensely hoppy and with grapefruit, peach and mango flavours.

Liquid Mistress Red IPA (OG 1061, ABV 5.8%)
An American-style bright red ale: burnt raisins and crackers balanced by a citrus grapefruit and peach spark.

Broken Dream Breakfast Stout (OG 1072, ABV 6.5%)
A breakfast stout with a gentle touch of smoke, coffee and chocolate. Deep and complex.

Six Bells SIBA

Church Street, Bishop's Castle, Shropshire, SY9 5AA
☎ (01588) 638930 sixbellsbrewery.co.uk
Tours by arrangement

The Six Bells brewery started in 1997 with a five-barrel plant. It supplies customers both within Shropshire and over the border in Wales. A new 12-barrel plant opened in 2010. In addition to the three core beers, an ale of the month is also brewed.

Big Nev's (OG 1037, ABV 3.8%)
A pale, fairly hoppy bitter.

Ow Do! (OG 1040, ABV 4%)
Rich amber in colour, full of spicy, fruity character.

Cloud Nine (OG 1043, ABV 4.2%)
Golden ale well hopped with citrus notes throughout.

six°north

The Workshop, Cowgate, Stonehaven, AB39 2LD
☎ 07840 678243 sixdnorth.co.uk

The brewery brews beers in the Belgian tradition, using a purpose-built 20-hectolitre (approx 12.5-barrel) plant. Depending on beer style, the beers are supplied as cask or keg as appropriate. Brewing started in 2013.

Prototype (ABV 4.2%)

Maes (ABV 4.6%)

66 IBU (ABV 6.6%)

Six O'Clock (NEW)

Gould Street, Manchester, M4 4RN
sixoclockbeer.co.uk
Tours by arrangement

Six O'Clock Beer began brewing in 2013. Three core beers are available.

Overtime (OG 1042, ABV 4.2%)
A light, hoppy pale ale.

Union (OG 1048, ABV 5%)
A robust IPA with a unique flavour from the use of rare Sussex hops.

Bolt (OG 1054, ABV 5.6%)
A balance between the body of a dark beer and the hoppiness of an IPA.

Sixpenny SIBA

The Dairy Building, Manor Farm, Sixpenny Handley, Dorset, SP5 5NU
☎ (01725) 762006 sixpennybrewery.co.uk
Shop Wed & Thu 4.30-6pm, Fri 4-6.30pm, Sat 11.30am-1pm
Tours by arrangement

⊗ Established in 2007, Sixpenny relocated to Dorset from Surrey in 2009 and now operates from a 20-barrel brewery on a farm site close to the village of Sixpenny Handley. It has its own onsite shop and bar, the Sixpenny Tap. More than 50 outlets are supplied including house beers to local Wetherspoon's pubs. Seasonal beers: see website.

6D Best Bitter (OG 1042, ABV 3.8%)
A well-balanced ale with a rounded malt flavour that leads to a pleasantly bitter and hoppy finish.

106 Jack FM Ale (OG 1042, ABV 4%)
An IPA-style golden ale. Rounded malt matched by a delicate citrus and spicy hop edge with good bitterness which finishes on gentle notes of lemon and elderflower.

Addlestone Ale (OG 1044, ABV 4.2%)
Copper-coloured premium best bitter with a good balance of malt and hops.

Gold (OG 1044, ABV 4.2%)
A golden ale, slightly citrus flavoured with a distinct hoppy floral aroma.

IPA (OG 1053, ABV 5.2%)
Traditional IPA with a powerful hop character and a long, rounded malt finish.

Skinner's SIBA

Riverside, Newham Road, Truro, Cornwall, TR1 2DP
☎ (01872) 271885 skinnersbrewery.com
Shop Mon-Sat 10am-5pm
Tours by arrangement

Award-winning brewery established in 1997. The brewery moved to bigger premises in 2003, opening a shop and visitor centre. The 25-barrel plant produces 25,000 hectolitres per annum. Some speciality beers are brewed and marketed under the Cornish Beer & Surf Co brand. For full beer range plus seasonals: see website.

Cornish Trawler (OG 1038, ABV 3.8%)
Light, golden hoppy bitter. Well-balanced with a smooth bitter finish.

Ginger Tosser (OG 1038, ABV 3.8%)
Distinctly hoppy amber beer. Crisp citrus aroma and a short, bitter, dry finish with a faint ginger sting.

Betty Stogs (OG 1040, ABV 4%)
Refreshing tawny ale with balance of bitter hops, apple fruit and malt, finishing bitter. Faint aroma of malt and hops.

Heligan Honey (OG 1040, ABV 4%)
Light copper-coloured beer containing Cornish honey. Sweet caramel balanced by bitterness and hops. Lingering bittersweet and dry aftertaste.

River Cottage English Pale Ale (OG 1040, ABV 4%)
Gentle citrus hops, bitterness and faint malt to balance. Floral hop nose. Long sweet finish with rising bitterness and dryness. Brewed in association with Hugh Fearnley-Whittingstall of River Cottage in Dorset.

Lushingtons Ale (OG 1041, ABV 4.2%)

Cornish Knocker Ale (OG 1044, ABV 4.5%)
Amber colour with persistent citrus hops. Spice and fruit flavours balanced by bitterness and malt. Clean and lasting hoppy finish.

Hunny Bunny (OG 1045, ABV 4.5%)
Premium strength golden ale with subtle notes of Cornish honey. Clean tasting with a hoppy aroma.

Porthleven (OG 1048, ABV 4.8%)
Zingy golden citrus ale with bite. Refreshing and smooth with bitter grapefruit and gooseberry and a hoppy, bitter aftertaste.

Slater's SIBA IFBB

St Albans Road, Common Road Industrial Estate, Stafford, ST16 3DR
☎ (01785) 257976 slatersales.co.uk
Shop Mon-Fri 9am-5pm, Sat 10am-12pm
Tours by arrangement

The brewery was opened in 1995 and in 2006 moved to new, larger premises. It has won numerous awards from CAMRA and SIBA and supplies a large number of outlets. One pub is owned, the George at Eccleshall, which serves as the brewery tap.

Bitter (OG 1035.5, ABV 3.6%)
A pale bitter with a fine, earthy, spicy hop character allied to juicy malt and tart fruit.

Original (OG 1040, ABV 4%)
Amber bitter. Malty aroma with caramel notes, hoppy taste develops into a dry hoppy finish with a touch of sweetness.

Top Totty (OG 1039, ABV 4%)
A yellow colour with a fruit and hop nose. Hop and fruit balanced taste leads to citrus hints with mouth-watering edges. Dry finish with tangs of lemon.

Premium (OG 1043, ABV 4.4%)
Pale brown bitter with malt and caramel aroma. Malt and caramel taste supported by hops and some fruit provide a warming descent and satisfyingly bitter mouthfeel.

Supreme (OG 1044, ABV 4.7%)
A traditional copper-coloured beer with a pungent citrus fruit note, balanced by punchy hops and biscuit malt.

Haka (OG 1049, ABV 5.2%)
New Zealand hops give distinctive aroma and taste to this beer.

Slaughterhouse SIBA

Bridge Street, Warwick, CV34 5PD
☎ (01926) 490986 slaughterhousebrewery.com
Tours by arrangement

Production began in 2003 on a four-barrel plant in a former slaughterhouse. Around 30 outlets are supplied. The brewery premises are licensed for off-sales direct to the public. In 2010 Slaughterhouse opened its first pub, the Wild Boar in Warwick.

Saddleback Best Bitter (OG 1038, ABV 3.8%)
Amber-coloured session bitter with a distinctive hop flavour.

Pale Ale (OG 1041, ABV 4.1%)
A classic English pale ale with a dry, quenching balance of malt and hops and a long finish with light fruit notes.

Extra Stout Snout (OG 1044, ABV 4.4%)

Boar D'eau (OG 1045, ABV 4.5%)

Wild Boar (OG 1052, ABV 5.2%)
A robust dark beer produced using both dark crystal and chocolate malts.

Sleaford SIBA

21 Pride Court, Enterprise Park, Sleaford, Lincolnshire, NG34 8GL ☎ 07530 559322 🌐 sleafordbrewery.com
Shop opening times vary – ring for details

Sleaford was established in 2010 and came under new ownership in 2013. It is a family-run brewery creating small batch craft beers on a one-barrel plant. The brewery produces a wide range of styles and is constantly planning to expand its range, with specials and seasonal beers available: see website. Bottle-conditioned beers are available.

Tropico (OG 1036, ABV 3.5%)
A golden beer with tropical fruit aromas and a bitter tropical fruit taste.

Pale Partridge (OG 1041, ABV 3.9%)
A pale yellow beer, light and spicy aroma with an easy-drinking balanced flavour.

Hedgerow Silver (OG 1042, ABV 4%)
A pale beer with floral and elderflower aroma leading to a spicy finish.

Pleasant Pheasant (OG 1043, ABV 4.2%)
A copper-coloured best bitter. Earthy and spicy aroma with a malty caramel bitter finish.

Hedgerow Gold (OG 1045, ABV 4.4%)
A pale golden beer with honey and spices giving a spicy aroma and finish.

Screaming Eagle Stout (OG 1050, ABV 4.8%)
A complex deep red stout with coffee, sweet chocolate and roasted aroma and taste.

Old Albert ESB (OG 1051, ABV 5%)
Copper brown special bitter with a toffee aroma and a bittersweet caramel finish.

Midnight Runner (OG 1053, ABV 5.2%)
Deep black old ale with a complex spicy hop and roasted aroma and a deep roasted taste.

Slightly Foxed SIBA

Unit 25, Asquith Bottom Mill, Sowerby Bridge, West Yorkshire, HX6 3BS ☎ 07412 008221
🌐 slightlyfoxedbrewery.co.uk

Slightly Foxed launched in 2011 as a venture between an award-winning landlord and a local businessman. Originally using spare capacity at Brass Monkey Brewery, Slightly Foxed bought the brewery in 2012. Seasonal and special beers are also available.

Howlin' Fox (OG 1035, ABV 3.5%)
Pale beer with a clean dry flavour and full hop aromas.

Slightly Foxed (OG 1038, ABV 3.8%)
Pale golden light and refreshing beer with a grapefruit flavour, a light, fruity floral aroma and a clean, dry finish.

Fox Glove (OG 1043, ABV 4.3%)
A golden-coloured premium best bitter with a full-bodied fruity flavour and fruit aromas.

Bengal Fox (OG 1052, ABV 5.2%)
A bright golden beer with a complex combination of pine, citrus and vanilla flavours.

Small Paul's

27 Briar Close, Gillingham, Dorset, SP8 4SS
☎ (01747) 823574 ✉ smallbrewer@btinternet.com

⊗ Launched in 2006, this half-barrel brewery is located in the owner's garage. There are usually two brews a month but consideration is being given to increasing capacity following success at beer festivals. A small number of local pubs and clubs are supplied direct and beers can be designed and brewed to order. Seasonal beers are available.

Gylla's Gold (OG 1039, ABV 3.8%) ◆
Drinkable session ale. Mild fruit hop aromas lead to bitter hop flavours and a lingering dry hop aftertaste.

Invicta (OG 1042, ABV 4.2%)
Aromatic and hoppy with a long bitter finish.

Challenger II (OG 1045, ABV 4.3%)
A copper-coloured malty bitter.

Wyvern (OG 1044, ABV 4.4%) ◆
Red-brown, well-balanced best bitter with malt and caramel flavours and short, bittersweet finish.

Gillingham Pale (OG 1045, ABV 4.5%) ◆
Fruity, caramel aromas lead to complex bitter flavours and short, dry finish.

Small World (NEW)

Unit 10, Barncliffe Business Park, Near Bank, Shelley, West Yorkshire, HD8 8LU
☎ (01484) 602805 🌐 smallworldbeers.com
Tours by arrangement

The brewery is situated in the picturesque Barncliffe valley in rural Shelley. The beers are brewed on a 10-barrel plant using spring water from an on-site bore hole. There is a small bar on the premises and the brewery offers tours and tastings on request.

Barncliffe Pale (OG 1037, ABV 3.7%)

Shelley's Gold (OG 1040, ABV 4%)

American Pale Ale (OG 1048, ABV 4.8%)

Joseph Herbert Smith

Fox Inn, Hanley Broadheath, Worcestershire, WR15 8QS
☎ (01886) 853189 ☎ 07527 066474
✉ jhsbrewery@yahoo.co.uk
Tours by arrangement

◎ The brewery was established in Staffordshire in 2007 by Jonathan Smith. In 2008 it relocated to barns adjacent to the Fox Inn. All equipment is gas fired and ingredients are sourced locally where possible. Seasonal and monthly beers: see website.

Amy's Rose (OG 1040, ABV 4%)
A traditional mild.

Snooty Fox (OG 1042, ABV 4.1%)
A copper-coloured best bitter.

Foxy Lady (OG 1043, ABV 4.3%)
A premium light bitter.

Teddy's Tipple (OG 1044, ABV 4.4%)
Medium-coloured sweetish bitter.

Samuel Smith

High Street, Tadcaster, North Yorkshire, LS24 9SB
☎ (01937) 832225 🌐 samuelsmithsbrewery.co.uk

◎ Fiercely independent, family-owned company. Tradition, quality and value are important, resulting in brewing without any artificial additives. All real ale is supplied in wooden casks. A bottle-conditioned beer (Yorkshire Stingo, ABV 8%) is only available in specialist off-licences.

OBB (Old Brewery Bitter) (OG 1040, ABV 4%) ◆
Malt dominates the aroma, with an initial burst of malt, hops and fruit in the taste, which is sustained in the aftertaste.

Tom Smith

13 South Folds Road, Oakley Hay, Northamptonshire, NN18 9EU
☎ (01536) 399859 ✉ orders@pigsandbeer.co.uk

Tom Smith Brewery was established in 2012 by Mark Smith in an industrial unit in the back streets of Kettering. In 2013 the brewery moved to the site of Latimer Ales (qv) in Oakley Hay to share brewing facilities.

Tom's Tipple (OG 1036, ABV 3.5%)
A dark mild, quite sweet but well balanced with bittering hops.

Goat Sanctuary (OG 1040, ABV 4%)
A dry and hoppy bitter, clear and straw-coloured. An easy-drinking, light summer session ale.

Jamaican Tom (OG 1044, ABV 4.4%)
Delicately spiced ginger beer, dark amber in colour, with subtle ginger, chilli and orange flavours.

Optical Delusion (OG 1044, ABV 4.9%)

Golden Tom (OG 1047, ABV 5.2%)
Dark golden-coloured strong bitter.

John Smith's

The Brewery, Tadcaster, North Yorkshire, LS24 9SA
☎ (01937) 832091 🌐 heineken.com

The brewery was built in 1879 by a relative of Samuel Smith (qv). John Smith's became part of the Courage group in 1970 before being taken over by S&N and now Heineken UK. Major expansion has taken place, with 11 new fermenting vessels installed. Traditional Yorkshire Square fermenters have been replaced by conical vessels. John Smith's cask Magnet has been discontinued. John Smith's Bitter in cask form is brewed under contract by Cameron's (qv) in Hartlepool.

Snaggletooth (NEW)

Rear of 11 Pole Lane, Darwen, Lancashire, BB3 3LD
☎ 07810 365701 🌐 snaggletoothbrewing.com

Snaggletooth was established in 2012 by three beer geeks with a passion for crafting ales. A 2.5-barrel plant is used at the Hopstar Brewery (qv) in Darwen, Lancashire.

Allotropic Pale Ale (ABV 3.8%)
A pale ale with floral and citrus notes.

Deja Brewed (OG 1040, ABV 4%)
Refreshing ale made with American and German hops to give floral, spicy and citrus flavours.

'Cos I'm a Lobster (ABV 4.2%)
A summery red ale with subtle roasted malts.

Storm Brewing (ABV 5%)
A rich, full-bodied black ale with a tart elderberry fruitiness.

Snowdonia

Snowdonia Parc Brewpub & Campsite, Waunfawr, Caernarfon, LL55 4AQ
☎ (01286) 650409 🌐 snowdonia-park.co.uk

Snowdonia started brewing in 1998 in a two-barrel brewhouse. The brewing is now carried out by the owner, Carmen Pierce. The beer is brewed solely for the Snowdonia Park pub and campsite.

Gwyrfai (OG 1037, ABV 3.8%)

Gold (OG 1040, ABV 4%)

Theodore Stout (OG 1040, ABV 4.1%)

Carmen Sutra (OG 1043, ABV 4.4%)

Cais (OG 1045, ABV 4.8%)

Dark & Delicious (OG 1046, ABV 5%)

Welsh Highland Bitter (OG 1048, ABV 5.2%)

Son of Sid

Chequers, 71 Main Road, Little Gransden, Bedfordshire, SG19 3DW
☎ (01767) 677348 🌐 sonofsid.co.uk
Tours by arrangement

⊗ Son of Sid was established in 2007. The three-barrel plant is situated in a separate room at the back of the pub and can be viewed from a window in the lounge bar. It is named after the father of the current landlord, who ran the pub for 42 years. His son has carried the business on for the past 19 years as a family-run enterprise. Beer is sold in the pub and at local beer festivals.

English Ale (OG 1035, ABV 3.5%)
Traditional English ale with a clean, malty taste and a good hop character.

Muck Cart Mild (OG 1035, ABV 3.5%) ◆
Black mild with a resounding roast malt presence and a caramel background in aroma and taste. There is some sweetness but the balance is predominantly dry and bitter, with increasing bitterness in the aftertaste.

Golden Shower (OG 1039, ABV 3.9%)
Full-bodied golden beer with a light hop character and a defined maltiness.

Songbird (NEW)

Stumble Inn, 37 Tamworth Rd, Long Eaton, Derbyshire, NG10 1JF
☎ (0115) 972 4529 🌐 songbirdbrewery.co.uk

Songbird was founded in 2013 by father and daughter, Martin and Samantha Dodsworth, using a two-barrel plant situated at the rear of the Stumble Inn. Production commenced in 2014.

Bitter Sweet Symphony (OG 1040, ABV 4%)

Double Bass (OG 1042, ABV 4.2%)
Pale ale with a citrus and caramel taste and a light bitterness.

Mild Thing (OG 1042, ABV 4.2%)

Melody Pale (OG 1044, ABV 4.5%)
A light and fruity ale with citrus aromas.

Ale House Rock (OG 1047, ABV 4.8%)
Traditional porter, rich and dark with an outstanding depth of flavour.

Sonnet 43 SIBA

Durham Road, Coxhoe, County Durham, DH6 4HX
☎ (0191) 377 3039 🌐 sonnet43.com
Shop Mon-Fri 9am-5pm

Sonnet 43 began brewing in 2013. The name and brewing ethos is inspired by the most famous work of poet Elizabeth Barratt Browning. Six core beers are available with an ever-changing, cask-conditioned limited edition range: see website.

Steam Beer (OG 1038, ABV 3.8%)
A refreshing amber-coloured ale with a well-balanced malt and hop aroma with sourdough and nut notes. Medium-bodied with a slightly bitter aftertaste.

Blonde Beer (OG 1041, ABV 4.1%)
A straw-coloured wheat-style beer with a sweet, delicate, floral aroma.

Bourbon Milk Stout (OG 1046, ABV 4.3%)
Bourbon, cocoa and oats give this dark beer a rich, full-bodied, chocolatey bitterness.

India Pale Ale (OG 1044, ABV 4.4%)
Classic strong pale ale, light gold in colour with a complex hoppy aroma and delicate fruity malt taste.

Brown Ale (OG 1046, ABV 4.7%)
A rosy brown beer. Mild and fruity with flavours of malt and toffee blending well with a pleasant light bitterness.

American Pale Ale (OG 1055, ABV 5.4%)
Pale bronze in colour with a full-bodied complex character and a spicy and peppery aroma. A fragrant bouquet with a fruity, malty and spicy flavour.

South Hams SIBA

Stokeley Barton, Stokenham, Kingsbridge, Devon, TQ7 2SE
☎ (01548) 581151 🌐 southhamsbrewery.co.uk
Tours by arrangement

The brewery moved to its present site, a milking parlour, in 2003, with a 10-barrel plant and plenty of room to expand. A family-run brewery, it supplies more than 60 outlets in Plymouth and South Devon. Wholesalers are used to distribute to other areas. Three pubs (one being the brewery tap) are owned. Seasonal beers: see website. Bottle-conditioned beers are available.

Devon Pride (OG 1039, ABV 3.8%)
A dark amber-coloured beer, smooth to drink with a malty palate.

XSB (OG 1043, ABV 4.2%) ◆
Amber nectar with a fruity nose and a bitter finish.

Wild Blonde (OG 1044, ABV 4.4%)

Eddystone (OG 1050, ABV 4.8%)
A golden IPA with a distinct fruity aroma and a fruity palate.

Southbourne (NEW)

c/o 26 Boreham Road, Bournemouth, Dorset, BH6 5BW ☎ 07845 795464 🌐 southbourneales.co.uk

Southbourne started brewing in 2014 using spare capacity at the Town Mill Brewery (qv), until it has sufficient funding to establish its own brewhouse. Seasonal beers: see website.

Paddler (ABV 3.6%)
A light session bitter.

Sunbather (ABV 4%)
A red-coloured ale with gentle hops. An easy-drinking, malty bitter.

Beach Comber (ABV 5.7%)
A full-flavoured brown ale with a good malt and hop balance.

SouthDowns

See Downlands

Southport SIBA

Unit 3, Enterprise Business Park, Russell Road, Southport, Merseyside, PR9 7RF ☎ 07748 387652
🌐 southportbrewery.co.uk

Southport Brewery was established in 2004 on a five-barrel plant. Outlets are supplied in Southport, North-west England and nationally. Seasonal beers: see website.

Cyclone (OG 1039.5, ABV 3.8%)
A bronze-coloured bitter with a fruity blackcurrant aftertaste.

Sandgrounder Bitter (OG 1039.5, ABV 3.8%)
Pale, hoppy session bitter with a floral character.

Dark Night (OG 1040.5, ABV 3.9%)
A dark traditional mild.

Carousel (OG 1041.5, ABV 4%)
A refreshing, floral, hoppy best bitter.

Golden Sands (OG 1041.5, ABV 4%)
A golden-coloured, triple hopped bitter with citrus flavour.

Natterjack (OG 1043.5, ABV 4.3%)
A premium bitter with fruit notes and a hint of coffee.

Spa Town

See Harrogate

Spencer's SIBA

Unit 5, Ashford Works, Brunswick Road, Cobbs Wood, Ashford, Kent, TN23 1EH 🌐 spencersbrewery.co.uk

Spencer's was set up in 2012 using an eight-barrel plant by Brian Spencer, a retired space rocket fuel engineer.

Blonde (OG 1042, ABV 4.2%)

Bitter (OG 1044, ABV 4.4%)

Galaxy (OG 1047, ABV 4.7%)

Sperrin SIBA

Birmingham Road, Ansley, Warwickshire, CV10 9PQ
☎ (024) 7639 2305 🌐 sperrinbrewery.co.uk
Tours by arrangement

Sperrin began brewing in 2012 and is situated by the side of the Lord Nelson Inn. A brewery was first established there in 1868.

Brewed under the Victory Beers brand:

Ansley Mild (OG 1035, ABV 3.5%)

Brewed to an old, traditional recipe, giving a rich, roast, malty flavoured moreish mild.

Head Hunter (OG 1038, ABV 3.8%)
Triple hopped amber ale with slight fruity hints and a pleasant dry finish.

Band of Brothers (OG 1042, ABV 4.2%)
Hoppy and full-flavoured golden ale with long-lasting smooth, citrus and refreshing overtones.

Third Party (OG 1048, ABV 4.8%)
Malty ruby ale with a floral aroma and hints of fruit and spice.

Thick as Thieves (OG 1068, ABV 6.8%)
A strong stout, rich in hops with an array of roasted chocolate malts giving a smooth liquorice, well-balanced finish.

Spey Valley

Mains of Mulben, Mulben, Keith, AB55 6YH ☎ 07780 655199 🌐 speyvalleybrewery.co.uk

Spey Valley began brewing in 2007 and operates on a part-time basis. In 2013 it upgraded to a two-barrel plant. Beers are available locally and at beer festivals.

David's Not So Bitter (OG 1046, ABV 4.4%)

Stillman's IPA (OG 1047.6, ABV 4.6%)

Spey Stout (OG 1055, ABV 5.4%)

Speyside Craft SIBA

2 Greshop Road, Forres, IV36 2GU
☎ (01309) 358082 🌐 speysidecraftbrewery.com

Based in a traditional whisky-producing area, Speyside Brewery uses the same water that goes into the production of Scottish whiskies. A number of local outlets are supplied. A donation from sales of Bottlenose Bitter goes to help support the work of the Whale and Dolphin Conservation Society.

Bow Fiddle Blonde (OG 1038, ABV 3.8%)

Bottlenose Bitter (OG 1041, ABV 4.1%)

Randolph's Leap (OG 1049, ABV 4.9%)

Moray IPA (OG 1055, ABV 5.5%)

Spire SIBA

Unit 4, Deepdale Close, Hartington Industrial Estate, Staveley, Derbyshire, S43 3YF
☎ (01246) 476005 🌐 spirebrewery.co.uk
Shop Mon-Fri 9.30am-4.30pm
Tours by arrangement

The brewery was set up by ex-Scots Guards musician and teacher David McLaren in 2006 and moved to larger premises in 2012. More than 100 outlets are supplied direct, including the Three Tuns, Dronfield. Seasonal beers: see website.

Brassed Off (OG 1036, ABV 3.7%)
Easy-drinking session bitter combining malt and fruit flavours, balanced by a long, bitter finish.

Whiter Shade of Pale (OG 1039, ABV 4%)
Pale straw-coloured session bitter with a subtle lemon hop finish. It is refreshingly smooth with a well-balanced malt flavour.

Dark Side of the Moon (OG 1042, ABV 4.3%) ◆
Complex and satisfying ruby mild with coffee aroma and toffee flavours. Dark and sweet but not too strong.

Chesterfield Best Bitter (OG 1043, ABV 4.5%) ◆
Classic brown strong bitter with malt and fruit flavours and a hint of caramel and chocolate in the finish. There is a little bitterness in the aftertaste.

Coal Porter (OG 1045, ABV 4.5%)
A smooth dark beer combining coffee and bitter chocolate, becoming increasingly dry, leading to a bitter finish and aftertaste.

Land of Hop & Glory (OG 1044, ABV 4.5%) ◆
An excellent example of a clean, crisp-tasting golden ale. Easy to drink with grapefruit and lemon flavours developing. These complex citrus hop flavours lead to a bitter, dry aftertaste.

Twist and Stout (OG 1044, ABV 4.5%) ◆
Creamy and dark with flavours of bitter chocolate and coffee. Easy drinking.

Sovereigns Escort IPA (OG 1051, ABV 5.2%)
Strong amber-coloured IPA, with a delicate orange flavour, leading to a bitter finish. Full-bodied and easy to drink despite its strength.

Sgt Pepper Stout (OG 1053, ABV 5.5%) ◆
Unique full-flavoured stout brewed with ground black pepper. Liquorice and pepper flavours dominate on both aroma and taste in this original, complex dark and delicious beer.

Enigma (OG 1061, ABV 6.4%) ◆
Strong, complex beer to be savoured and appreciated. Full bodied, with hints of marmalade tartness and fruit, leading to a dry, slightly bitter finish.

Spitting Feathers SIBA

Common Farm, Waverton, Cheshire, CH3 7QT
☎ (01244) 332052 🌐 spittingfeathers.org
Tours by arrangement

Spitting Feathers was established in 2005. The brewery is located in a sandstone building set around a cobbled yard. Around 200 local outlets are supplied. A range of seasonal and special beers are produced, including those sold under the Heritage Ales and Ministry of Beer brands: see website.

Farmhouse Ale (OG 1035, ABV 3.6%)
A golden session bitter.

Thirstquencher (OG 1038, ABV 3.9%) ◆
Powerful hop aroma leads into the taste. Bitterness and a fruity citrus hop flavour fight for attention. A sharp, clean golden beer with a long, dry, bitter aftertaste.

Special Ale (OG 1041, ABV 4.2%) ◆
Complex tawny-coloured beer with a sharp, grainy mouthfeel. Malty with good hop coming through in the aroma and taste. Hints of nuttiness and a touch of acidity. Dry, astringent finish.

Old Wavertonian (OG 1043, ABV 4.4%) ◆
Creamy and smooth stout. Full-flavoured with coffee notes in aroma and taste. Roast and nut flavours throughout, leading to a hoppy, bitter finish.

Basket Case (OG 1046, ABV 4.8%) ◆
Reddish, complex beer. Sweetness and fruit dominate the taste, offset by hops and bitterness that follow through into the aftertaste.

Sportsman

1-3 St John's Road, Huddersfield, West Yorkshire, HD1 5AY ✉ info@sportsmanbrewingcompany.co.uk

The brewery opened in 2011 in the cellars of the Sportsman pub on a two-barrel plant where the beers are generally available along with the West Riding Refreshment Rooms, Dewsbury and the Cricketers Arms, Horbury. Due to restricted capacity, brewing is split between the brewpub and Golcar Brewery (qv) to meet demand.

Springhead SIBA

Robin Hood Site, Main Street, Laneham, Nottinghamshire, DN22 0NA
☎ (01777) 228080 springhead.co.uk
Shop 9am-6pm daily
Tours by arrangement

Springhead Brewery opened in 1990, and relocated to its current address in 2011. Around 500 outlets are supplied direct and the brewery owns three pubs. Six regular beers are brewed plus bi-monthly seasonals. Drop O'The Black Stuff is suitable for vegans. Brewery tours start and finish at Meg's Bar, which is part of the brewery building, where you can also watch the brewery in operation from the bar. The Bees Knees pub is adjacent to the brewery, where the core beers plus the current seasonal brew are always available.

Outlawed (OG 1040, ABV 3.8%)

Drop O'The Black Stuff (OG 1041, ABV 4%)

Robin Hood (OG 1041, ABV 4%)
A dark traditional bitter with a good head and plenty of hops.

Maid Marian (OG 1045, ABV 4.5%)
A pale golden beer with a fruity orange aroma and a dry finish.

Leveller (OG 1047, ABV 4.8%)
A dark, smoky intense flavour with a toffee finish. Brewed in the style of Belgian Trappist ale.

Roaring Meg (OG 1052, ABV 5.5%)
Smooth with a sweet, citrus honey aroma and a dry finish.

Stables

Beamish Hall Country House Hotel, Beamish, County Durham, DH9 0YB
☎ (01207) 288750 beamish-hall.co.uk/stables
Tours by arrangement

Stables was established as part of a £1 million development of an old stable block, converting a disused building to a restaurant and eight-barrel microbrewery. Seasonal and festival beers are available as are mini casks and bottles. The brewery also brews under the Bull Lane Brewing Co name.

Beamish Hall Best Bitter (OG 1038, ABV 3.8%)

Old Miner Tommy (OG 1037, ABV 3.8%)

Bobby Dazzler (OG 1042, ABV 4.2%)

Coppy Lane (OG 1043, ABV 4.2%)

Silver Buckles (OG 1044, ABV 4.4%)

Beamish Burn (OG 1045, ABV 4.5%)

Bell Tower (OG 1052, ABV 5%)

Brewed under the Bull Lane Brewing Co name:

SOL (Stadium of Light) (ABV 3.8%)

Butcher's Brew (ABV 4.4%)
Brewed for the Butchers Arms in Sunderland.

Staffordshire

12 Churnet Court, Cheddleton, Staffordshire, ST13 7EF
☎ (01538) 361919 staffordshirebrewery.co.uk
Tours by arrangement

No real ale. Brewing started in 2002 and the brewery has steadily increased in capacity since. A 20-barrel brew plant was completed in 2011. The brewery was renamed from Leek Brewery in 2013 at which time cask production ceased being replaced with filtered, pasteurised bottled beers only. Also brews for Wicked Hathern Brewery Ltd.

Stamps

The Basement, 17 Boundary Street, Everton, Liverpool, L5 9UB ☎ 07779 000094
stampsbrewery.co.uk
Tours by arrangement

Brewing began in 2012 on an environmentally-friendly brew plant: power for brewing comes from 52 solar panels and a biomass boiler, used grain is sent to a local city farm for animal feed and rainwater is recycled and used for floor cleaning. The beers are named after famous world postage stamps.

Blonde Moment (OG 1037, ABV 3.6%)
A pale-coloured session beer with a smooth floral and citrus aroma and flavour.

Bondi Blonde (OG 1037, ABV 3.7%)
A pale, full-flavoured blonde beer, flowers and citrus evident.

Flying Cloud (OG 1037, ABV 3.7%)
A dry, lager-style session beer, refreshing and pale.

Mail Train (OG 1042, ABV 4.2%)
Traditional bitter with a noticeable bitterness and a delightful malt character

The Russian (OG 1040, ABV 4.2%)
A copper-coloured ale with a hoppy finish.

Swedish Blonde (OG 1041, ABV 4.3%)
A quaffable session ale with a strong hint of citrus.

Inverted Jenny (OG 1046, ABV 4.6%)
Golden in colour with a grassy and floral bouquet and a noticeable tinge of caramel.

Stancill (NEW) SIBA

Unit 2, Oakham Drive, Off Rutland Road, Sheffield, South Yorkshire, S3 9QX
☎ (0114) 275 2788 ☎ 07809 427716

Stancill began brewing in 2014 and is named after the head brewer and co-owner. Situated on the door step of the late Cannon Brewery, taking advantage of the soft Yorkshire water.

Tom's Mild (OG 1034, ABV 3.4%)

Barnsley Bitter (OG 1038, ABV 3.8%)

Blonde (ABV 3.9%)

No. 7 (ABV 4.3%)

Porter (ABV 4.4%)

Stanway

Stanway House, Cheltenham, Gloucestershire, GL54 5PQ
☎ (01386) 584320 stanwaybrewery.co.uk

Stanway is a small brewery founded in 1993 with a five-barrel plant that confines its sales to the Cotswolds area (15 to 20 outlets). The brewery is the only known plant in the country to use wood-fired coppers for all its production. Seasonal beers: see website.

Stanney Bitter (OG 1042, ABV 4.5%)
A light, refreshing, amber-coloured beer, dominated by hops in the aroma, with a bitter taste and a hoppy, bitter finish.

Star (NEW) SIBA

Unit D, Bentley Business Park, Northfields Industrial Estate, Market Deeping, Lincolnshire, PE6 8LD
☎ (01778) 380480 starbrewco@gmail.com
Tours by arrangement

Star commenced production in 2014 using a 10-barrel brew plant. Three core beers are available plus rotating seasonal ales.

Comet (OG 1038.5, ABV 3.8%)
Well-hopped blonde ale.

Meteor (OG 1040, ABV 4%)
Traditional amber ale, brewed with English malt and hops.

Galaxy (OG 1044, ABV 4.4%)
Crisp, golden best bitter.

Star Inn

Star Inn, Starcliff Ltd, 2 Back Hope Street, The Cliff, Higher Broughton, M7 2PD ☎ 07789 175219
starinnbrewery@gmail.com

A small on-site brewhouse was built in 2010 by the cooperative that own the pub. Former Bazens' brewer, Richard Bazen, runs the four-barrel plant.

Golden Crown (OG 1039, ABV 3.8%)

Starry Night (OG 1040, ABV 4%)
Pale amber bitter with moderate and distinctive floral and citrus hop flavours.

Tall Toad (OG 1043, ABV 4.3%)
A golden ale.

Steamin' Billy

See Belvoir

Steel City

c/o Toolmakers Brewery, 6-8 Botsford Street, Sheffield, South Yorkshire, S3 9PF
steelcitybrewing.co.uk

Steel City was established in 2009 and brews once or twice a month. Brewing activity was originally based at the Brew Company before moving on to Little Ale Cart's premises for three years. It currently uses spare capacity at Toolmakers Brewery (qv).

Stewart SIBA

26a Dryden Road, Bilston Glen Industrial Estate, Loanhead, EH20 9LZ
☎ (0131) 440 2442 stewartbrewing.co.uk
Shop Mon-Thu 10am-5pm, Fri 10am-6pm, Sat 10am-4pm
Tours by arrangement

Established in 2004 by Steve Stewart, a qualified master brewer. The brewery moved to a larger, custom-built brewery in 2013 with a brand new 50-hectolitre plant from Bavarian Brewing Technologies. Seasonal and bottle-conditioned beers supplement the regular range along with Natural Selection beers brewed by Herriot Watt students. Beers are distributed throughout the UK, although they are mainly sold in South-east Scotland.

Zymic (OG 1039, ABV 3.8%)
Straw-coloured hoppy golden ale.

Pentland IPA (OG 1040, ABV 3.9%)
A pleasing, hoppy, golden session ale. The dry bitter taste is well balanced by sweetness from the malt and fruit flavours. The aftertaste is dry with a lingering bitterness.

Copper Cascade (OG 1041, ABV 4.1%)
This tawny-coloured beer is born from American hops and Scottish malt. The hop character overlays a solid malt base. Hints of roast and substantial fruitiness give a complex character. A bittersweet taste leads to a dry bitter finish.

Edinburgh No.3 Premium Scotch Ale (OG 1043, ABV 4.3%)
An excellent example of a Scottish Heavy ale. Full-bodied and dark with a predominantly malt character, fruit notes and a gentle infusion of hop. A bittersweet beer with a dry finish.

80/- (OG 1044, ABV 4.4%)
Superb traditional Scottish heavy. The complex profile is dominated by malt with fruit flavours giving the sweetish character typical of this beer style. Hops provide a gentle balancing bitterness that intensifies in the dry finish.

Edinburgh Gold (OG 1048, ABV 4.8%)
A full-bodied but easy-drinking Continental-style golden ale. Bitterness from the hop character is strong in the finish and complemented in the taste by a little sweetness from malt and fruit flavours.

Sticklegs

Unit 7, Old Forge Court, Colchester Road, Elmstead Market, Essex, CO7 7EA ☎ 07962 12906
sticklegs.co.uk
Shop Mon-Sat 9.30am-4.30pm, closed Sun
Tours by arrangement

Sticklegs was established in 2008 at the Cross Inn, Great Bromley. It has since moved and expanded and is now based on a two-barrel and six-barrel plant in Elmstead.

Malt Shovel Mild (OG 1032, ABV 3.4%)

Old Forge Bitter (OG 1038, ABV 3.8%)

Stour Gold (OG 1040, ABV 3.8%)

Tendring 100 (OG 1041, ABV 4%)

Elmstead Stout (OG 1046, ABV 4.8%)

Nemesis (OG 1048, ABV 5%)

Stocklinch SIBA

Unit 3, Manor Farm, Stocklinch, Somerset, TA19 9JG
☎ 07711 479917 🌐 stocklinchales.co.uk
Tours by arrangement

⊗ Established in 2012 in a converted farm building, Stocklinch uses a five-barrel plant supplying a number of local outlets. The brewery is licensed to open for a few days each month, which compensates for the lack of a village pub.

Ramblers Gold (OG 1038, ABV 3.8%)
Refreshing light golden beer with a slight aftertaste of grapefruit.

Jakes (OG 1040, ABV 4%)

Jakes Special (OG 1045, ABV 4.5%)

Rusty Boiler (OG 1045, ABV 4.5%)
Mid-brown best bitter, strong fruity flavours with a lick of caramel.

Gunner Boyce (OG 1048, ABV 4.8%)

Black Smock (OG 1050, ABV 5%)
Dark beer with a strong rich taste of chocolate, liquorice and coffee with a hint of blackcurrant.

Ramblers Gold Extra (OG 1050, ABV 5%)

Stod Fold (NEW) SIBA

Stod Fold Farm, Hays Lane, Halifax, West Yorkshire, HX8 2UL
☎ (01224) 245951 🌐 stodfoldbrewing.com

Stod Fold was founded by childhood friends Paul Harris and Angus Wood. They designed and built the brewery themselves and the result is a fully integrated, bespoke, computer-controlled, state of the art 10-barrel plant. The brewery is not open to the public but once a month is open to trade partners only.

Gold (OG 1038, ABV 3.8%)
Gold-coloured beer with a light bitter finish.

Amber (OG 1042, ABV 4.2%)
Amber brown best bitter with balanced bittersweet aroma and flavour.

Blonde (OG 1045, ABV 4.5%)
Pale blonde aromatic best bitter with a refreshing finish.

Pils (OG 1048, ABV 4.8%)
Cask lager style beer brewed with lager malts and Hersbrucker hops.

Stokesley

See Wainstones

Stonehenge SIBA

The Old Mill, Mill Road, Netheravon, Salisbury, Wiltshire, SP4 9QB
☎ (01980) 670631 🌐 stonehengeales.co.uk
Tours by arrangement

The brewery was founded in 1984 (as Bunce's Brewery) in what was originally a water-driven mill built in 1914 to generate electricity. In 1993 the company was bought by Danish master brewer Stig Anker Andersen and now supplies more than 300 outlets, wholesalers and pub companies. From 2013 a new borehole, accessing the Salisbury Plain Aquifer, has been supplying the water for the brewery. Seasonal beers: see website.

Spire Ale (OG 1037, ABV 3.8%) ◆
A pale golden-coloured session bitter with an initial bitterness giving way to a well-rounded bitter aftertaste with discernible fruit balance.

Pigswill (OG 1039, ABV 4%) ◆
A tawny-coloured session bitter with an initial pleasant hop aroma and slight bitterness to the initial taste moving to a well-rounded bitter finish with slight malt and fruit in the finish.

Heel Stone (OG 1042, ABV 4.3%) ◆
A copper-coloured best bitter with some malt and fruit in the aroma continuing into the initial taste along with pleasant hoppiness. Medium bodied with plenty of flavour in the aftertaste with noticeable malt, fruit and hops.

Great Bustard (OG 1046, ABV 4.8%) ◆
A copper-coloured strong bitter. Complex malt and fruit flavours at first with a long fruit and bitter aftertaste.

Danish Dynamite (OG 1048, ABV 5%) ◆
Golden-coloured strong bitter with good hop and fruit aromas. Complex flavours in the initial taste with a beautifully balanced full-bodied aftertaste with hops and fruit to the fore.

Stonehouse SIBA

Stonehouse, Weston, Oswestry, Shropshire, SY10 9ES
☎ (01691) 676457 🌐 stonehousebrewery.co.uk
Shop Mon-Thu 9am-5pm, Fri 9am-7pm, Sat 10am-5pm
Tours by arrangement

Stonehouse was established in 2007 on a 15-barrel plant. The brewery was based in former chicken sheds and is next to the old Cambrian railway line. A new building has expanded brewing capacity and includes a visitor centre. More than 120 local outlets are supplied direct.

Sunlander (OG 1037, ABV 3.7%)

Station Bitter (OG 1041, ABV 3.9%)

Cambrian Gold (OG 1042, ABV 4.2%)

Wheeltapper's Wheatbeer (OG 1043, ABV 4.5%)

KPA (OG 1047, ABV 4.6%)

Off the Rails (OG 1048, ABV 4.8%)

Storm SIBA

2 Waterside, Macclesfield, Cheshire, SK11 7HJ
☎ (01625) 431234 🌐 stormbrewing.co.uk

Storm Brewing was founded in 1998, operating from an old ICI boiler room. It 2001 it moved to its current location, which until 1937 was a pub called the Mechanics Arms. More than 60 outlets are supplied. Seasonal and bottle-conditioned beers are available.

Ale Force (OG 1042, ABV 4.2%) ◆
Amber, smooth-tasting, complex beer that balances malt, hop and fruit on the taste, leading to a roasty, slightly sweet aftertaste.

PGA (OG 1044, ABV 4.4%) ◆
Light, crisp, lager-style beer with a balance of malt, hops and fruit. Moderately bitter and slight dry aftertaste.

Stowey

Old Cider House, 25 Castle Street, Nether Stowey, Somerset, TA5 1LN
☎ **(01278) 732228** 🌐 **stoweybrewery.co.uk**
Tours by arrangement

Stowey was established in 2006, primarily to supply the owners' guesthouse and to provide beer to participants on 'real ale walks' run from the accommodation. The brewery also runs brewery workshop courses and supplies seasonal brews to the village pubs on a guest beer basis.

Nether Ending (OG 1044, ABV 4.2%)

Strands

Strands Inn, Nether Wasdale, Cumbria, CA20 1ET
☎ **(01946) 726237** 🌐 **strandshotel.com**
Tours by arrangement

Strands Brewery is a six-barrel plant with a 30-barrel fermentation capacity. The majority of beers are available bottle conditioned, and the brewery plans to sell them online. Six of the beers are available on the bar of the Strands Inn at all times.

Pied Piper (OG 1030, ABV 2.7%)
Lots of traditional mild characteristics: malty, caramel, roast, sweet and fruity.

Green Bullet (OG 1037, ABV 3.5%)
A light and creamy wheat beer.

Responsibly (OG 1038, ABV 3.7%)
Clean-tasting, heavily-hopped and lightly smoked beer.

Brown Bitter (OG 1039, ABV 3.8%)
A complex tasting brown beer with a lingering bitter aftertaste.

Errmmm... (OG 1039, ABV 3.8%)
A complex, traditional bitter.

Low Flyer (OG 1044, ABV 4.3%)
Autumnal seasonal beer with a dark biscuity malt flavour with a touch of whisky on the finish.

Red Screes (OG 1047, ABV 4.5%)
An interesting, rich-tasting, smooth, strong bitter; full-flavoured with plenty of roast and malt tastes.

T'errmmm-inator (OG 1050, ABV 5%)
A smooth, dark brown, roast-led beer. Full-bodied and well-balanced.

Brewed for Independent Lakeland Breweries:

Gold Wing (OG 1040, ABV 4%)
A clean, crisp and dry golden ale with delicate citrus aromas and a moreish finish.

Dark Knight (OG 1050, ABV 5%)
A deep, dark, well-balanced beer.

Strathaven SIBA

Craigmill Brewery, Sandford Road, Strathaven, ML10 6PB
☎ **(01357) 520419** 🌐 **strathavenales.com**
Shop Mon-Fri 9am-5pm (phone at weekend)
Tours by arrangement

Strathaven Ales is a 10-barrel brewery on the River Avon close to Strathaven and was converted from the remains of a 16th-century mill. The range is distributed throughout Scotland and the north of England. Seasonal beers: see website.

Craigmill Mild (OG 1035, ABV 3.5%)

Clydesdale (OG 1038, ABV 3.8%)

Avondale (OG 1048, ABV 4%)

Old Mortality (OG 1046, ABV 4.2%)

Claverhouse (OG 1046, ABV 4.5%)

Strathbraan SIBA

Deanshaugh, Amulree, PH8 0EB
☎ **(01350) 725264**
✉ **strathbraan.bry@btinternet.com**

Straathbraan began brewing in 2012 using a 10-barrel plant. Two beers are brewed.

Due South (OG 1038, ABV 3.8%)

Head East (OG 1042, ABV 4.2%)

Strawman (NEW)

Arch 75, 876 Old Kent Road, Peckham, London, SE15 1NQ
☎ **(020) 7112 9102** 🌐 **strawmanbrewery.com**

Strawman began brewing in 2013.

Stringers SIBA

Unit 3, Low Mill Business Park, Ulverston, Cumbria, LA12 9EE
☎ **(01229) 581387** 🌐 **stringersbeer.co.uk**

Stringers is a small family-run brewery. Brewing started in 2008 on a five-barrel plant run on 100% renewable energy. A small number of seasonal beers are produced. No. 2 Stout and Dark Country are suitable for vegans. Plan B is gluten free.

Plan B (OG 1036, ABV 3.7%)
An easy-drinking, zingy, pale thirst quencher.

No. 2 Stout (OG 1042, ABV 4%)
A robust drying stout full of roast and hop bitterness.

Yellow Lorry (OG 1039, ABV 4%)
A gold-coloured beer using Amarillo hops.

Best Bitter (OG 1041, ABV 4.2%)
Well-crafted and well-balanced with a clean hoppy bitterness.

West Coast Blond (OG 1042, ABV 4.4%)
A golden beer with a hoppy fruity aroma and taste that fades to a bitter, slightly astringent aftertaste.

Victoria IPA (OG 1053, ABV 5.5%)
Spicy, tropical fruit from the hops, then some bitter marmalade, with a definite bitter finish.

Stroud SIBA

Unit 11, Phoenix Works, London Road, Thrupp, Stroud, Gloucestershire, GL5 2BU
☎ **(01453) 887122** 🌐 **stroudbrewery.co.uk**
Shop Mon-Thu 9am-3pm, Fri 9am-5pm, Bar Fri 3-11pm
Tours by arrangement

Established in 2006, Stroud Brewery supports the local economy and does not sell its organic bottled beers through supermarkets. The ales are sold in 40-50 pubs, independent retailers and the brewery shop. Seasonal and bottle-conditioned beers are available.

Tom Long (OG 1039, ABV 3.8%)

Amber session beer with a spicy citrus aroma. Good body for low ABV.

Organic Ale (OG 1041, ABV 4%)
A refreshing, golden organic ale with a delicate apple aroma.

Budding (OG 1045, ABV 4.5%)
Pale ale with a grassy bitterness, sweet malt and floral aroma.

Stumptail

North Street, Great Dunham, Norfolk, PE32 2LR
☎ (01328) 701042 ✉ stumptail@btinternet.com

Stumptail began commercial home-brewing in 2011 using a 100-litre plant. Bottle-conditioned beers are produced with cask-conditioned versions brewed to order. Only the west Norfolk area is supplied.

Stumpy's

See Yates'

Suddaby's

See Brown Cow and Four Thorns

Sulwath SIBA

The Brewery, 209 King Street, Castle Douglas, DG7 1DT
☎ (01556) 504525 🌐 sulwathbrewers.co.uk
Shop Mon-Sat 10am-6pm
Tours by arrangement

Sulwath started brewing in 1995. The beers are supplied to markets as far away as Devon in the south and Aberdeen in the north. The brewery has a fully licensed brewery tap. Cask ales are sold to around 100 outlets and four wholesalers. Seasonal and occasional beers are available.

Cuil Hill (OG 1039, ABV 3.6%)
Distinctively fruity session ale with malt and hop undertones. The taste is bittersweet with a long-lasting dry finish.

The Grace (OG 1044, ABV 4.3%)
A refreshing, rich ale with a full-bodied flavour that balances the caramel undertones.

Black Galloway (OG 1046, ABV 4.4%)
A robust porter/stout that derives its colour from the abundance of Maris Otter barley and chocolate malts used in the brewing process.

Criffel (OG 1044, ABV 4.6%)
Full-bodied beer with a distinctive bitterness. Fruit is to the fore of the taste with hops becoming increasingly dominant in the taste and finish.

Galloway Gold (OG 1049, ABV 5%)
A cask-conditioned lager that will be too sweet for many despite being heavily hopped.

Knockendoch (OG 1047, ABV 5%)
Dark, copper-coloured, reflecting a roast malt content, with bitterness from Challenger hops.

Solway Mist (OG 1052, ABV 5.5%)
A naturally cloudy wheat beer. Sweetish and fruity.

Summer Wine

The Old Furnace, Unit 15, Crossley Mills, New Mill Road, Honley, Holmfirth, West Yorkshire, HD9 6QB
☎ (01484) 665466 🌐 summerwinebrewery.co.uk

Brewing commenced in 2006 on a 10-gallon kit with an emphasis on bottle-conditioned beer. A 2007 upgrade saw a 0.5-barrel plant installed and in 2008 the brewery expanded to a six-barrel plant. Over 500 outlets are supplied direct. Two differing specials are available each month.

Resistance (OG 1037, ABV 3.7%)
Dark ruby mild with a malty body and hints of caramel, cocoa and bitter roasted barley combined with a light, fruity hop character.

Zenith (OG 1040, ABV 4%)
Pale golden beer with a floral aroma and a crisp bitter finish.

Barista (OG 1048, ABV 4.8%)
A rich coffee-flavoured stout.

Teleporter (OG 1050, ABV 5%)
A porter with a creamy body and cocoa, caramel and vanilla flavours.

Oregon (OG 1055, ABV 5.5%)
American-style pale ale with grapefruit, sherbet, spicy and floral aroma, malty body and hop finish.

Rogue Red Hop Ale (OG 1058, ABV 5.8%)
Deep ruby red beer with good body and strong flavour and finish.

Diablo (OG 1060, ABV 6%)
A strong IPA with tropical fruit aroma and flavours.

Summerskills SIBA

15 Pomphlett Farm Industrial Estate, Broxton Drive, Billacombe, Plymouth, Devon, PL9 7BG
☎ (01752) 481283 🌐 summerskills.co.uk

Established in a vineyard in 1983 at Bigbury-on-Sea, Summerskills moved to its present site in 1985. Production has expanded to meet demand from wholesalers, who perform nationwide distribution, and national pub companies. Seasonal and bottle-conditioned beers are available.

Start Point (OG 1036, ABV 3.7%)

Westward Ho! (OG 1040, ABV 4.1%)

Best Bitter (OG 1042, ABV 4.3%)
A mid-brown beer, with plenty of malt and hops through the aroma, taste and finish. A good session beer.

Tamar (OG 1043, ABV 4.3%)
A tawny-coloured bitter with a fruity aroma and a hop taste and finish.

Devon Dew (OG 1044, ABV 4.5%)

Menacing Dennis (OG 1045, ABV 4.5%)

Sunbeam

Leeds, West Yorkshire ☎ 07772 002437
🌐 sunbeamales.co.uk

Sunbeam Ales was established in a back-to-back house in Leeds in 2009. Brewing began commercially in 2011, with only bottled beers being produced. Capacity has increased since the brewer moved and the brewery now offers both cask-conditioned and bottled beers.

THE BREWERIES

Sunny Republic SIBA

The Old Grain Barn, North West Farm, West Street, Winterborne Kingston, Dorset, DT11 9AT
☎ (01929) 471600 🌐 sunnyrepublic.com
Shop Fri 5-8pm (ring for other times)
Tours by arrangement

Located just outside the village of Winterbourne Kingston on a barley farm in two converted Georgian grain barns. Brewing began in 2012 using a state of the art 30-barrel custom-built plant. Beers are available nationally and exported to six countries.

Bay Amber (OG 1040, ABV 3.7%)
Traditional copper-coloured best bitter based on a 1920s recipe from the Dolphin Brewery in Poole.

Huna Red (OG 1042, ABV 4.2%)
Red-hued ale with fruit and berry aromas, brewed with hibiscus flowers.

Beach Blonde (OG 1043, ABV 4.4%)
Straw-coloured blonde ale with tropical aromas of mango, grapefruit and lychee. Upfront bitterness yields to a light malt body.

Dorset Cross (OG 1052, ABV 5%)
Copper red ale with a sweet body and a balanced bitterness. Complex malt tastes, with hints of roasted hazelnut, toffee and caramel.

Hop Dog IPA (OG 1055, ABV 5.5%)
Citrus-dominated IPA with an enduring bitter finish.

Surrey Hills SIBA

Denbies Wine Estate, London Road, Dorking, Surrey, RH5 6AA
☎ (01306) 883603 🌐 surreyhills.co.uk
Shop Mon-Wed 10am-3pm, Thu-Sat 10am-5pm
Tours by arrangement

Surrey Hills began brewing in 2005 near Shere, moving to Dorking in 2011. Nearly 95% of production is sold within 15 miles of the brewery. The beers have won several local and national awards. Seasonal beers: see website.

Ranmore (OG 1039, ABV 3.8%)
A light flavoursome session beer. An earthy hoppy nose leads into a grapefruit and hoppy taste and a clean, bitter finish.

Shere Drop (OG 1043, ABV 4.2%)
A hoppy ale with some balancing malt. A pleasant citrus aroma and a noticeable fruitiness in the taste, with some sweetness.

Gilt Complex (OG 1047, ABV 4.6%)

Greensand IPA (OG 1047, ABV 4.6%)
A strong flavoured and easily drinkable IPA, with intense grapefruit and hops in the aroma and taste and soft citrus finish.

Suthwyk

See Oakleaf

Swan

Swan on the Green, West Peckham, Maidstone, Kent, ME18 5JW
☎ (01622) 812271 🌐 swan-on-the-green.co.uk
Tours by arrangement

The brewery was established in 2000 in an old coal shed behind the Swan on the Green pub using a two-barrel plant.

Fuggles Pale (OG 1037, ABV 3.6%)

Trumpeter Best (OG 1041, ABV 4%)

Cygnet (OG 1048, ABV 4.2%)

Bewick (OG 1052, ABV 5.3%)

Swansea SIBA

Joiners Arms, 50 Bishopston Road, Bishopston, Swansea, SA3 3EJ
☎ (01792) 232658/290197 (Office)
Tours by arrangement

Opened in 1996, Swansea was the first commercial brewery in the area for almost 30 years. Two regular outlets are supplied along with other pubs in the South Wales area. Seasonal beers are available.

Deep Slade Dark (OG 1034, ABV 4%)
A dark brown-coloured beer with a reddish hue with a nutty, malty taste. The aroma is malty with a little roast.

Bishopswood Bitter (OG 1043, ABV 4.3%)
A delicate aroma of hops and malt in this pale brown colour. The taste is a balanced mix of hops and malt with a growing hoppy bitterness ending in a lasting bitter finish.

Three Cliffs Gold (OG 1042, ABV 4.7%)
A golden beer with a hoppy and fruity aroma, a hoppy taste with fruit and malt, and a quenching bitterness. The pleasant finish has a good hop flavour and bitterness.

Original Wood (OG 1046, ABV 5.2%)
A full-bodied, pale brown beer with an aroma of hops, fruit and malt. A complex blend of these flavours with a firm bitterness ends with increasing bitterness.

Taddington

Blackwell Hall, Blackwell, Buxton, Derbyshire, SK17 9TQ
☎ (01298) 85734

No real ale. Taddington started brewing in 2007, and brews one Czech-style unpasteurised lager in two different strengths: Moravka (ABV 4.4% and 5%), which is available on draught. Taddington also supplies an unfiltered version of Moravka called Moravka Kvasnicove.

Talke O' Th' Hill

Merelake Road, Talke, Staffordshire, ST7 1UE
☎ 07875 951399 🌐 talkeothhill.co.uk

Talke O' Th' Hill began brewing in 2011 using a two-barrel plant on a family farm on the Staffordshire border. The brewery is based on two floors in old farm buildings. Many seasonal beers are produced.

First Porter Call (OG 1045, ABV 4.5%)

Pitch (OG 1045, ABV 4.5%)

Tap East SIBA

7 International Square Montficet Road, Westfield Stratford City, Stratford, London, E20 1EE

☎ (020) 8555 4467 ⊕ tapeast.co.uk
Shop Mon-Sat 11am-11pm, Sun 12-11pm

⊗ Tap East began brewing in 2011 and is located in the Westfield shopping centre next to the Olympic Park.

Tonic Ale (OG 1032, ABV 3%) ◆
A refreshing golden ale with strong citrus throughout. Faint biscuit notes and a bitter dry aftertaste.

East End Mild (OG 1037, ABV 3.5%) ◆
Dark mild that has roast and a little fruit and treacle on the palate fading in the shortish dry finish.

Jim Wilson Bitter (JWB) (OG 1040, ABV 3.8%)
Bitter, malty backbone with a good dose of hops.

APA (OG 1046, ABV 4.4%) ◆
Yellow-coloured beer with citrus throughout and a dash of pineapple. Bitterness grows on drinking, balanced by a little sweetness.

Coffee in the Morning (OG 1059, ABV 5.3%) ◆
Black porter with coffee dominating the aroma and flavour and lingering in the dry bitter finish. Trace of liquorice.

IPA (OG 1054, ABV 5.3%)
Series of IPAs with different hops used each time.

Tap House

Tap House, Annwell Lane, Smisby, Derbyshire, LE65 2TA
☎ (01530) 413604 ⊕ taphouse-smisby.co.uk

⊗ Established in 2010, this purpose-built brewery supplies beers to its two pubs; the Tap House, Smisby and the Kings Arms, Coleorton, as well as pubs across Derbyshire and Leicestershire. Tap House and Leatherbritches share the same brewery plant and brewer, but the two businesses are run independently.

Ashby Pride (OG 1038, ABV 3.8%)
A light, quaffable session beer.

Gold (OG 1042, ABV 4%)
A light, hoppy golden ale.

Kingdom (OG 1046, ABV 4.5%)
A chestnut-coloured beer with a hint of caramel.

Malt Teaser (OG 1046, ABV 4.6%)
A rich crimson beer full of malt flavours with a light toffee aftertaste.

Dark & Dangerous (OG 1048, ABV 5%)
A delicious dark and complex porter with subtle chocolate flavours.

Tapped

Sheffield: Sheffield Tap, Platform 1b, Sheffield Station, Sheaf Street, Sheffield, South Yorkshire, S1 2BP

Leeds: Leeds Tap, 51 Boar Lane, Leeds, West Yorkshire, LS1 5EL ☎ (0113) 244 1953
⊕ tappedbrewco.com

Brewing began in 2013 after the old Edwardian dining rooms were converted into an onsite brewery with a viewing gallery at the Sheffield Tap pub. The beer is also supplied to the Euston Tap, York Tap, and Pivni, York. A further on-site brewery opened at the Leeds Tap in 2014.

Ale (OG 1035, ABV 3.5%)
A session bitter.

Mojo (OG 1036, ABV 3.6%)
A clear, crisp, light pale ale.

Bramling (OG 1042, ABV 4.2%)
Golden best bitter taking its character from the classic hop variety.

Liberty (OG 1052, ABV 5.2%)
Rich, dark, sweet beer with subtle bitterness and hop aroma.

Miami Weisse (OG 1055, ABV 5.5%)
Fresh tasting Hefe Weiss-style beer with banana and clove aromas.

Bullet (OG 1059, ABV 5.9%)
Strong IPA with fruit candy aroma.

Tatton SIBA

Unit 7, Longridge Trading Estate, Knutsford, Cheshire, WA16 8PR
☎ (01565) 750747 ⊕ tattonbrewery.co.uk
Shop Mon-Fri 9am-4pm (other times by arrangement)
Tours by arrangement

◎ Tatton is a family-run business based in the heart of Cheshire. Brewing commenced in 2010 using a steam-fired, custom-built 15-barrel brewhouse. Seasonal and occasional beers are available. Pubs are supplied throughout Cheshire and the north-west.

Ale (OG 1036, ABV 3.7%)
An easy-drinking session ale with a rich copper colour. It has a full malty/toffee flavour balanced by a soft bitterness and hoppy, fruity taste and aroma.

Blonde (OG 1039, ABV 4%)
A clean-tasting, smooth pale ale with a fine hop aroma.

Best (OG 1040.5, ABV 4.2%)
A classic light amber-coloured best bitter with a clean malt flavour and fine hop character derived from a blend of aroma hops.

Gold (OG 1046, ABV 4.8%)
A golden special ale with a maltiness backed by a robust hop character.

Tavernale (NEW)

Bridge Tavern, 7 Akenside Hill, Newcastle upon Tyne, NE1 3UF
☎ (0191) 232 1122 ⊕ thebridgetavern.com

Brewing since 2013 in association with the Wylam Brewery (qv), a two-barrel plant supplies beers to the Bridge Tavern with the in-house brewer creating bespoke 360-pint batches of ale.

Tavy SIBA

Unit 9, Porsham Close, Beliver Industrial Estate, Roborough, Devon, PL6 7DB ☎ 07966 522266

Office: Jasmine Cottage, Peter Tavy, Tavistock, Devon, PL19 9NN ⊕ tavyales.co.uk
Tours by arrangement

⊗ The brewery was formed in 2012 and is located in Roborough, on the outskirts of Plymouth, with a six-barrel plant. To keep things local its spent barley goes to feed local cattle, pigs and chickens.

Best Bitter (OG 1043, ABV 4.3%)

THE BREWERIES

A full-bodied chestnut brown beer with a well-rounded complex malt flavour and early bitterness.

Ideal Pale Ale (OG 1048, ABV 4.8%)
A pale golden beer loaded with citrus flavour, balanced bitterness and body with a strong floral and hoppy aroma.

Porter (OG 1052, ABV 5.2%)
A dark stout with a roasted, bittersweet flavour and an intense chocolate finish.

Timothy Taylor SIBA IFBB

Knowle Spring Brewery, Keighley, West Yorkshire, BD21 1AW
☎ (01535) 603139 timothy-taylor.co.uk

An independent, family-owned company established in 1858, Timothy Taylor has occupied the Knowle Spring site since 1863. Pennine spring water is used to brew its award-winning ales that are served in 18 tied pubs as well as more than 300 directly delivered outlets. Expanded brewing facilities opened on the main site in 2011.

Dark Mild (OG 1034, ABV 3.5%)
Malt and caramel dominate throughout in this sweetish beer with background hop and fruit notes.

Golden Best (OG 1033, ABV 3.5%)
Refreshing, amber-coloured traditional Pennine light mild. Malty throughout. Fruit in the nose increases to complement the delicate hoppy taste.

Boltmaker (OG 1038, ABV 4%)
Tawny bitter combining hops, fruit and nutty malt. Lingering, increasingly bitter aftertaste. Formerly, and sometimes still, sold as Best Bitter.

Landlord (OG 1042, ABV 4.3%)
A full-bodied best bitter combining citrus peel aromas, rich malt, spicy hops, an underlying marmalade sweetness and long bitter finish.

Ram Tam (OG 1043, ABV 4.3%)
A black beer with red highlights topped by a coffee-coloured head. Roast coffee bitterness is balanced by fruit and malt with burnt caramel coming through in the dry and bitter finish.

Taylors (NEW)

London Tavern, Church Street, Attleborough, Norfolk, NR17 2AH
☎ (01953) 457415 taylorsattleborough.com

Brewing began in 2014, primarily to supply the owner's two pubs in Attleborough; the London Tavern and Ry's Bar (formerly the Bear).

Number One (ABV 3.9%)

Stitched Up (ABV 4.7%)
A refreshing golden ale.

Teignworthy SIBA

The Maltings, Teign Road, Newton Abbot, Devon, TQ12 4AA
☎ (01626) 332066 teignworthybrewery.com
Shop Mon-Fri 10am-5pm at Tuckers Maltings
Tours by arrangement

Teignworthy Brewery opened in 1994 within the historic Tuckers Maltings building. The 20-barrel plant produces 50 barrels a week using malt from Tuckers and supplies around 300 outlets in Devon and Somerset. Seasonal and bottle-conditioned beers: see website.

Neap Tide (OG 1038, ABV 3.8%)
A pale, fruity bitter.

Reel Ale (OG 1039.5, ABV 4%)
Clean, sharp-tasting bitter with lasting hoppiness; predominantly malty aroma.

Gun Dog (OG 1043.5, ABV 4.3%)
A light bronze-coloured ale. Golding hops give it a flowery, fruity, aromatic finish.

Spring Tide (OG 1043.5, ABV 4.3%)
An excellent, full and well-rounded, mid-brown beer with a dry, bitter taste and aftertaste.

Old Moggie (OG 1044.5, ABV 4.4%)
A golden, hoppy and fruity ale.

Beachcomber (OG 1045.5, ABV 4.5%)
A pale brown beer with a light, refreshing fruit and hop nose, grapefruit taste and a dry, hoppy finish.

Teme Valley SIBA

Talbot, Bromyard Road, Knightwick, Worcestershire, WR6 5PH
☎ (01886) 821235 temevalleybrewery.co.uk
Tours by arrangement

Established in 1997 to brew beer for the Talbot, Knightwick. Only hops grown in Worcestershire are used in brewing. Some 30 outlets are supplied throughout the Marches and West Midlands. Seasonal beers: see website. Bottle-conditioned beers are available.

T'Other (OG 1035, ABV 3.5%)
Refreshing amber beer offering an abundance of flavour in the fruity aroma, followed by a short, dry bitterness.

This (OG 1037, ABV 3.7%)
Dark gold brew with a mellow array of flavours in a malty balance.

That (OG 1041, ABV 4.1%)
A rich, fruity nose and a wide range of hoppy and malty flavours in this copper-coloured best bitter.

Talbot Blond (OG 1042, ABV 4.4%)
A smooth, rich pale beer well hopped with Worcestershire Northdown hops.

Tempest

Winchester Row, Kelso, TD5 7DT
☎ (01573) 229664 tempestbrewingco.com
Tours by arrangement

Based in a former dairy, Tempest was set up in 2010 by Gavin Meiklejohn, brewer and co-proprietor of the Cobbles Inn in Kelso, which is the brewery tap. Gavin's focus is on bold flavours and ingredients to produce interesting styles based on classic and New World beers. There are plans for expansion and changes to the beer range. Seasonal and bottle-conditioned beers: see website.

Into the Light Blonde (OG 1039, ABV 4.1%)
A golden ale with light and refreshing fruit salad overtones complemented by a hefty dose of hops.

Emanation Pale Ale (OG 1044, ABV 4.5%)
An easy-drinking, copper-coloured ale with a light caramel sweetness and a rich hop and citrus character.

Elemental Porter (OG 1049, ABV 5.1%)

A smooth black porter with a controlled roast character, hints of coffee and chocolate on the side followed by a charge of palate-cleansing hops.

Temptation

18D Cherry Way, Dubmire Industrial Estate, Houghton-le-Spring, Tyne & Wear, DH4 5RJ ☎ 07932 774745 🌐 temptationbrewingcompany.co.uk

Temptation began brewing in 2011 using a 2.5-barrel plant upgrading to a six barrels in 2013. Local outlets are supplied in a 20-mile radius of the brewery.

New Zealand Pale Ale (ABV 4.3%)

Vanilla Bourbon Porter (ABV 4.8%)

Cascadian Dark (ABV 5%)

American Amber Ale (ABV 5.5%)

Terrace

Sandford Terrace, Aylburton, Gloucestershire, GL15 6DW
☎ (01594) 840100 🌐 terracebrewery.co.uk

Temptation was established in 2012 in a shed in the brewer's garden, producing bottle-conditioned beers from a 0.5-barrel plant. Beers are available in local farm shops: see website for details.

Thame

East Street, Thame, OX9 3JS
☎ (01844) 218202
✉ thamebrewery@btinternet.com

This one-barrel brewery was set up in 2009 by Peter Lambert and Oak Taverns in the old stables at the Cross Keys. Beer is produced for the Cross Keys and beer festivals, and includes many one-off brews.

Mr Splodge's Mild (OG 1040, ABV 4%)
A dark mild named after the pub cat.

Hoppiness (OG 1042, ABV 4.2%)
A golden ale.

That Little Brewery

c/o Farmers Boy, 134 London Road, St Albans, Hertfordshire, AL1 1PQ
☎ (01582) 768925

Correspondence: 5 Station Road, Harpenden, Hertfordshire, AL5 4SN 🌐 thatlittleplace.co.uk

That Little Brewery produces two bottle-conditioned beers available at That Little Place restaurant in Harpenden. Cask-conditioned beer is available at the Farmer's Boy in St Albans, and at beer festivals.

Theakston

The Brewery, Masham, North Yorkshire, HG4 4YD
☎ (01765) 680000 🌐 theakstons.co.uk
Tours by arrangement

After several years under the control of other companies, Theakston is now owned by four brothers, grandsons of Thomas Theakston, the son of the company's founder, who built the brewery in 1875. A new fermentation room was built in 2004 to provide additional flexibility and capacity, and further capacity was added in 2006. Seasonal beers: see website.

Best Bitter (OG 1038, ABV 3.8%)
A golden-coloured beer with a full flavour that lingers pleasantly on the palate. With a good bittersweet balance, this beer has a robust hop character, citrus and spicy.

Black Bull Bitter (OG 1037, ABV 3.9%)
A distinctively hoppy aroma leads to a bitter, hoppy taste with some fruitiness and a short bitter finish.

Lightfoot (OG 1041, ABV 4.1%)

XB (OG 1044, ABV 4.5%)
A sweet-tasting bitter with background fruit and spicy hop. Some caramel character gives this ale a malty dominance.

Old Peculier (OG 1057, ABV 5.6%)
A full-bodied, dark brown, strong ale. Slightly malty but with hints of roast coffee and liquorice. A smooth caramel overlay and a complex fruitiness leads to a bitter chocolate finish.

Thirstin (NEW)

60 Thirstin Road, Honley, West Yorkshire, HD9 6JR
🌐 thirstinbrewhouse.co.uk

Thirstin is a small 2.5-barrel brewery situated in the Holme valley, set up by Stewart Horn.

Mild Thirst (OG 1036, ABV 3.6%)
A dark mild.

Four (OG 1040, ABV 4%)
A pale session bitter.

Thirst Quencher (OG 1050, ABV 5%)
A strong pale ale.

Abraham Thompson

Flass Lane, Barrow-in-Furness, Cumbria, LA13 0AD
☎ 07708 191437
✉ abraham.thompson@btinternet.com

The half-barrel plant was set up in 2005 to return Barrow-brewed beers to local pubs. Distribution is limited to a few outlets in the Low Furness area but beer can usually be found at Ulverston Beer Festival.

John Thompson

Ingleby, Melbourne, Derbyshire, DE73 7HW
☎ (01332) 862469 🌐 johnthompsoninn.com
Tours by arrangement

The brewery was established by John Thompson in 1977 and is now run by his son Nick. Seasonal beers are available.

JTS XXX (OG 1041, ABV 4.1%)

Gold (OG 1045, ABV 4.5%)

Thornbridge SIBA

Riverside Business Park, Buxton Road, Bakewell, Derbyshire, DE45 1GS
☎ (01629) 641000 🌐 thornbridgebrewery.co.uk
Shop Mon-Fri 9am-5pm
Tours by arrangement

The first Thornbridge beers were produced in 2005 using a 10-barrel brewery, housed in the grounds of Thornbridge Hall. The beers have gained considerable success with over 300 consumer and industry awards being won. A 30-barrel brewery opened in Bakewell in 2009. The original site continues to develop new, seasonal and speciality beers. 200 outlets are supplied direct. 12 pubs are managed and owned. Unfiltered and bottle-conditioned beers are available.

Wild Swan (OG 1035, ABV 3.5%)
Extremely pale yet flavoursome and refreshing beer. Plenty of lemony citrus hop flavour, becoming increasingly dry and bitter in the finish and aftertaste.

Brother Rabbit (OG 1035, ABV 4%)
Yellow in colour with a clean, hoppy aroma, a resinous finish and some bitterness.

Lord Marples (OG 1041, ABV 4%)
Smooth, traditional, easy-drinking bitter. Caramel, malt and coffee flavours fall away to leave a long, bitter finish.

Ashford (OG 1043, ABV 4.2%)
A brown ale with a floral hoppiness, a smooth, malty kick and a delicate coffee finish.

Kipling (OG 1050, ABV 5.2%)
Golden pale bitter with aromas of grapefruit and passion fruit. Intense fruit flavours continue throughout, leading to a long bitter aftertaste.

Jaipur IPA (OG 1055, ABV 5.9%)
Flavoursome IPA packed with citrus hoppiness that's nicely counterbalanced by malt and underlying sweetness and robust fruit flavours.

Saint Petersburg (OG 1073, ABV 7.7%)
Good example of an imperial stout. Smooth and easy to drink with raisins, bitter chocolate and hops throughout, leading to a lingering coffee and chocolate aftertaste.

Three B's SIBA

Black Bull, Brokenstone Road, Tockholes, Blackburn, Lancashire, BB3 0LL
(01254) 581381 threebsbrewery.co.uk
Tours by arrangement

Robert Bell acquired the Black Bull in 2011 and the brewpub now supplies 50 outlets. A bottling plant has been installed and bottle-conditioned beers are now available.

Bee Thrifty (OG 1036, ABV 3.4%)
A light and refreshing amber-coloured beer.

Stoker's Slake (OG 1038, ABV 3.6%)
Lightly roasted coffee flavours are in the aroma and the initial taste. A well-rounded, dark brown mild with dried fruit flavours in the long finish.

Honey Bee (OG 1039, ABV 3.7%)
A golden honey beer with honey apparent in both aroma and taste.

Bobbin's Bitter (OG 1038, ABV 3.8%)
A golden bitter with warm aromas of nutty grain and a full, fruity flavour with a light, dry finish.

Bee Blonde (OG 1041, ABV 4%)
A distinctive, pale bitter with a light, dry, balance of grain and hops and a delicate finish with citrus fruits.

Black Bull (OG 1042, ABV 4%)
A dark ruby red bitter. Rich in character with a hint of chocolate.

Tackler's Tipple (OG 1044, ABV 4.3%)
A dark best bitter with full hop flavour, biscuit tones on the tongue and a deep, dry finish.

Doff Cocker (OG 1045, ABV 4.5%)
Yellow with a hoppy aroma and initial taste giving way to subtle malt notes and orchard fruit flavours. Crisp, dry finish.

Pinch Noggin (OG 1046, ABV 4.6%)
A dark, strong best bitter with full hop flavour and a long aftertaste.

Knocker Up (OG 1047, ABV 4.8%)
A smooth, rich, creamy porter. The roast flavour is foremost without dominating and is balanced by fruit and hop notes.

Shuttle Ale (OG 1050, ABV 5.2%)
A rustic-coloured traditional strong pale ale.

Three Blind Mice (NEW)

Unit W10, Black Bank Business Park, Black Bank Road, Little Downham, Cambridgeshire, CB6 2UA
07912 875825

Three Blind Mice began brewing in 2014 using a five-barrel plant, supplying outlets in Cambridgeshire. An ever-changing range of beers is brewed throughout the year.

Corombo (ABV 4%)

Pale Ale No. 1 (ABV 4.5%)

Three Castles SIBA

Unit 12, Salisbury Road Business Park, Pewsey, Wiltshire, SN9 5PZ
(01672) 564433 threecastlesbrewery.co.uk
Shop Mon-Fri 9am-4pm, Sat 9am-1pm
Tours by arrangement

Three Castles is an independent, family-run brewery, established in 2006. Seasonal beers: see website. Bottle-conditioned beers are available.

Barbury Castle (OG 1039, ABV 3.9%)
A balanced, easy-drinking pale ale with a hoppy, spicy palate.

Saxon Archer (OG 1040, ABV 4%)

Heritage (OG 1042, ABV 4.2%)

Vale Ale (OG 1043, ABV 4.3%)
Golden-coloured with a fruity palate and strong floral aroma.

Corn Dolly (OG 1047, ABV 4.7%)

Three Daggers SIBA

Westbury Road, Edington, Wiltshire, BA13 4PG
(01380) 830940 threedaggersbrewery.com
Tours by arrangement

Three Daggers Brewery was established in 2013 using a 2.5-barrel brew plant in a farm shop next to the pub. Malt is sourced locally from Warminster Maltings and hops from Charles Faram in Herefordshire. Beer is available in the pub and selected other local outlets. Bottled beers are available in the farm shop.

Daggers Ale (OG 1041, ABV 4.1%)

Daggers Edge (OG 1047, ABV 4.7%)

Three Kings SIBA

14 Prospect Terrace, North Shields, Tyne & Wear, NE30 1DX ☎ 07580 004565 🌐 threekingsbrewery.co.uk

Three Kings started in 2012 using a 2.5-barrel plant, upgrading to a five-barrel one in 2013. A core range of beers is now available with previous occasional beers being brewed again on request.

Billy Mill (OG 1040, ABV 4%)

Gallowgate Raw (OG 1045, ABV 4.4%)

Ring of Fire (OG 1048, ABV 4.5%)

Three Peaks

**Scar Top Brewery, Buck Haw Brow, Settle, North Yorkshire, BD24 0DJ
☎ (01729) 822939**

Office: 7 Craven Terrace, Settle, North Yorkshire, BD24 9DB 🌐 threepeaksbrewery.co.uk

⊗ Formed in 2006 using a five-barrel plant, Three Peaks is run by husband and wife team Colin and Susan Ashwell, assisted by Andrew Murphy. The brewery is located on Buck Haw Brow, Settle. Three regular beers are brewed along with an occasional beer.

Pen-y-Ghent Bitter (OG 1040, ABV 3.8%) ◆
The malty character of this mid-brown session bitter is balanced by fruit in the aroma and taste. The finish is malty and hoppy.

Ingleborough Gold (OG 1041, ABV 4%) ◆
This golden-coloured best bitter is hoppy throughout with fruit in the aroma and taste and a hoppy, bitter finish.

Whernside Pale Ale (OG 1042, ABV 4.2%)

Three Tuns SIBA

**16 Market Square, Bishop's Castle, Shropshire, SY9 5BN
☎ (01588) 638392 🌐 threetunsbrewery.co.uk**
Shop Mon-Fri 9am-5pm
Tours by arrangement

Brewing on this site started in the 16th century and was licensed in 1642. A small scale tower brewery from the late 19th century survives as one of the Famous Four pub breweries still running since the 1970s. Seasonal beers: see website.

Mild (OG 1040, ABV 3.4%)
Tawny-coloured beer, richly malty with burnt and roast flavours.

1642 Bitter (OG 1042, ABV 3.8%)
A golden ale with a light, nutty maltiness and spicy bitterness.

XXX (OG 1046, ABV 4.3%) ◆
A pale, sweetish bitter with a light hop aftertaste that has a honey finish.

Stout (OG 1048, ABV 4.4%)
Old fashioned-style stout.

Cleric's Cure (OG 1059, ABV 5%)
A light tan-coloured ale with a malty sweetness. Strong and spicy with a floral bitterness.

Steampunk (OG 1065, ABV 6.5%)
Rich, dark and fiery smooth barley wine with flavours of liquorice, ginger, caramel and roasted malts lasting through into a strong, bitter finish.

Thurstons (Horsell) SIBA

**The Courtyard, 102c High Street, Horsell, Surrey, GU21 4ST
☎ (01483) 771719 🌐 thurstonsbrewery.com**

⊗ Established in 2012 and originally based in the Crown pub, Thurstons moved next door in 2014 when the brewery upgraded to a four-barrel plant.

Horsell Best (OG 1040, ABV 3.8%)
A balanced, full-bodied session bitter.

Horsell Gold (OG 1040, ABV 3.8%)
A golden beer with a rounded bitterness, caramel and spice on the palate, and a hoppy aroma. A fine session ale.

Milk Stout (OG 1055, ABV 4.5%) ◆
Smooth, sweet stout, with a chocolatey flavour. A sweet malty flavour with a pleasant sharpness and a slightly dry finish.

Festival (OG 1048, ABV 4.7%)
A full-bodied amber ale with dark malt on the nose, toffee and caramel notes and a hoppy, bitter finish.

Thwaites IFBB

**Star Brewery, PO Box 50, Blackburn, Lancashire, BB1 5BU
☎ (01254) 686868 🌐 danielthwaites.com**
Tours by arrangement

⊛ Established in 1807, Thwaites is still controlled by the Yerburgh family, descendants of the founder, Daniel Thwaites. The company owns around 320 pubs, with over two thirds selling real ale. Thwaites is seeking to move to a new brewery site. In the interim period most of its cask beer is being brewed by Marston's in Wolverhampton apart from approximately 100 barrels a week, which are being brewed on its microbrewery at the existing Blackburn site.

Nutty Black (OG 1036, ABV 3.3%) ◆
A sweet, fruity mild with gentle roast bitterness and residual hops. A well-balanced, low strength mild.

Original (OG 1036, ABV 3.6%)
Hop driven, yet well-balanced amber session bitter. Hops continue through to the long finish.

Wainwright (OG 1042, ABV 4.1%)
A straw-coloured bitter with soft fruit flavours and a hint of malty sweetness.

Lancaster Bomber (OG 1044, ABV 4.4%)
Well-balanced, copper-coloured best bitter with firm malt flavours, a fruity background and a long, dry finish.

Ticketybrew (NEW) SIBA

16 Waterloo Court, Stalybridge, SK15 2AU ☎ 07970 093665 🌐 ticketybrew.co.uk

Ticketybrew is a husband-and-wife-run brewery that opened in 2013 and focuses on vegan-friendly bottled beers.

Blonde (ABV 5%)
Soft floral and fruit on the nose with a spicy, fruity and yeasty flavour.

Pale Ale (ABV 5.5%)
American bittering and aroma hops balanced with a sweetness provided by Belgian yeast.

Tigertops

22 Oakes Street, Flanshaw, Wakefield, West Yorkshire, WF2 9LN
☎ (01229) 716238
✉ tigertopsbrewery@hotmail.com

Tigertops was established in 1995 by Stuart Johnson and his wife Lynda who, as well as owning the brewery, run the Foxfield brewpub in Cumbria (qv). The brewery is run on their behalf by Barry Smith, supplying five regular outlets. Beers are brewed on demand with seasonal and experimental beers also available.

Tillingbourne SIBA

Old Scotland Farm, Staple Lane, Shere, Surrey, GU5 9TE
☎ (01483) 222228 🌐 tillybeer.co.uk
Shop Fri 1-6.30pm, Sat 10am-3.30pm (other times by arrangement)
Tours by arrangement

Tillingbourne began brewing in 2011 on a farm site previously used by Surrey Hills Brewery using its old 17-barrel plant. Around 25 local outlets are supplied. Seasonal beers: see website.

The Source (OG 1033, ABV 3.3%)

Black Troll (OG 1035, ABV 3.7%)
A black bitter in which initial roast notes are eventually overpowered by citrus hop through to the finish.

AONB (OG 1036, ABV 4%)
Golden ale in which citrus hop dominates throughout. Some balancing malt in the aroma and taste, however.

Falls Gold (OG 1037, ABV 4.2%)
While hops dominate, balancing malt is evident throughout. Hints of grapefruit in the aroma and taste lead to a dry finish.

Hop Troll (OG 1045, ABV 4.8%)
American-style IPA with plenty of hops.

Time and Tide (NEW)

Office: 10 Herschell Road, East Walmer, Kent, CT14 7SQ ☎ 07840 327265
🌐 timeandtidebrewing.co.uk

Time and Tide began brewing in 2013 using spare capacity at Ripple Steam Brewery (qv). Bottle-conditioned and specials beers are available.

Spratwaffler Pale Ale (ABV 3.7%)

Smugglers Stout (ABV 5.2%)

Calista IPA (ABV 6.1%)

Tindall

Toad Lane, Seething, Norfolk, NR35 2EQ
☎ (01508) 483844

Tindall Ales began brewing in 1998. The brewery was originally based in Ditchingham but moved to its current location towards the end of 2001.

Best Bitter (OG 1037, ABV 3.7%)

Fuggled Up (OG 1037, ABV 3.7%)

Mild (OG 1037, ABV 3.7%)

Liberator (OG 1038, ABV 3.8%)

Alltime (OG 1040, ABV 4%)

Mundham Mild (OG 1040, ABV 4%)

Ditchingham Dam (OG 1042, ABV 4.2%)

Seething Pint (OG 1043, ABV 4.3%)

Norwich Dragon (OG 1046, ABV 4.6%)

Honeydo (OG 1050, ABV 5%)

Tinpot

Allanwater Brewhouse, Queens Lane, Bridge of Allan, Stirlingshire, FK9 4NY
☎ (01786) 834555 🌐 tinpotbrewery.co.uk
Shop 12-5pm daily
Tours by arrangement

Tinpot opened in 2009 using a one-barrel plant designed to brew speciality beers and started supplying CAMRA beer festivals in 2010. Bottle-conditioned beers are available. The beer range varies depending on season and demand.

Gold Pot 70/- (OG 1042, ABV 3.9%)
A pale golden best bitter.

Choc Pot 80/- (OG 1046, ABV 4.5%)
A brown best bitter.

Pot Black (OG 1052, ABV 5%)

Procrastination (OG 1060, ABV 6%)
A hoppy IPA brewed by the Stirling University Craft Beer Society.

Tintagel SIBA

Condolden Farm, Tintagel, Cornwall, PL34 0HJ
☎ (01840) 213371 🌐 tintagelbrewery.co.uk
Shop 9am-5pm (phone ahead to confirm)

This 7.5-barrel brewery was established in 2009 in a redundant milking parlour on the highest farm in Cornwall. Some 80 outlets are supplied direct. Bottle-conditioned and seasonal beers are available.

Black Knight (OG 1040, ABV 3.8%)

Castle Gold (OG 1038, ABV 3.8%)

Cornwall's Pride (OG 1040, ABV 4%)
Malt and toffee on the nose. Full-bodied, copper-coloured and tasting mainly malty with sweet plum fruit, hop bitterness, finishing dry.

Castle Gold Extra (OG 1042, ABV 4.2%)
Golden ale with light hop aroma. Citrus hop bitterness balanced by fruit sweetness. Long, bittersweet, dry finish with hop fruit.

Gull Rock (OG 1042.6, ABV 4.2%)
Tawny-coloured best bitter. Malt aroma with some berry fruit. The taste is malt sweetness with traces of hop bitterness and caramel, finishing the same but with a little dryness.

Arthur's Ale (OG 1044, ABV 4.4%)
Combination of a best bitter and golden ale. Marmalade aroma leading to malty sweetness, grapefruit citrus bitterness and stone fruit.

Harbour Special (OG 1048.9, ABV 4.8%)
Brown ale with ripe fruity, malty aroma. Rich malt, stone fruits and esters in the mouth, finishing bitter and dry.

Tiny Rebel SIBA

Unit 12 & 12a, Maes Glas Industrial Estate, Greenwich Road, Newport, NP20 2NN
☎ (01633) 547378 🌐 tinyrebel.co.uk
Shop Mon-Fri 8am-5pm

Tiny Rebel opened in 2012. It operates on a 12-barrel brew plant consisting of six fermentation and four conditioning tanks.

Flux (OG 1039, ABV 4%)

Hank (OG 1038, ABV 4%)

Fubar (OG 1041, ABV 4.4%)

Beat Box (OG 1042, ABV 4.5%)

Loki (OG 1042, ABV 4.5%)

Billabong (OG 1045, ABV 4.6%)

Cwtch (OG 1045, ABV 4.6%)

The Full Nelson (OG 1046, ABV 4.8%)

Zool (OG 1046, ABV 4.8%)

Dirty Stopout (OG 1052, ABV 5%)

Urban IPA (OG 1051, ABV 5.5%)

Chocoholic (OG 1065, ABV 6.8%)

Hadouken (OG 1069, ABV 7.4%)

Tipples SIBA

Unit 3, The Mill, Wood Green, Salhouse, Norfolk, NR13 6NY
☎ (01603) 721310 🌐 tipplesbrewery.com

Tipples was established in 2004 on a six-barrel brew plant. An extensive range of bottled beers is produced, which can be found in some farmers markets and supermarkets in Norfolk.

Hanged Monk (OG 1038, ABV 3.8%)
Strong roast and malt notes dominate the aroma and follow through to the taste. A slightly grainy mouthfeel is softened by a hint of caramel and a growing vinous finish.

Sundown (OG 1040, ABV 3.9%)
A barrage of berries and malt introduce this smooth creamy bitter. A muted bitterness gives depth to the fruity malt core as it slowly sweetens.

Redhead (OG 1042, ABV 4.2%)
Malt and hops are well matched in both nose and palate. Toffee in the nose and initial taste soon gives way to an increasing bitterness. A fine finale retains the mix of flavours.

Brewers Progress (OG 1046, ABV 4.6%)
A solid malty, tawny beer with strong caramel and vanilla support. The smooth creamy character is given added depth by a blackcurrant fruitiness. Some bitterness in the finish.

Moonrocket (OG 1050, ABV 5%)
A complex golden brew with an earthy aroma. Malt hop bitterness and a fruity sweetness swirl round in an ever-changing kaleidoscope of flavours. A satisfying finish with hops finally emerging on top.

Tipsy Angel

Lower Angel, 27 Buttermarket Street, Warrington, Cheshire, WA1 2LY
☎ (01925) 653326 🌐 lowerangel.co.uk
Tours by arrangement

Tipsy Angel began brewing in 2011 using a one-barrel plant. The brewery was founded to recreate the brews from the original recipes of Walkers of Warrington. Beers are mainly produced for the Lower Angel pub, but are also occasionally available at beer festivals. Seasonal beers: see website.

Angelic Mild (OG 1037, ABV 3.6%)
A dark mild.

Angelic Blonde (OG 1044, ABV 4.4%)
A modern blonde bitter using traditional British ingredients.

Angel's Folly (OG 1052, ABV 5.2%)
Flagship beer from the old Walker's recipes, rich, complex and flavoursome.

Tír Dhá Ghlas

Cullins Yard, 11 Cambridge Road, Dover, Kent, CT17 9BY
☎ (01304) 211666 🌐 cullinsyard.co.uk

Brewing began in 2012 using a two-barrel plant. Beers are available in the bar/restaurant, and occasionally at the nearby Royal Cinque Ports Yacht Club, particularly when they are holding festivals.

Tirril SIBA

Red House, Long Marton, Cumbria, CA16 6BN
☎ (01768) 361846 🌐 tirrilales.co.uk
Tours by arrangement

Established in 1999, Tirril has twice outgrown its premises. Capacity has grown to 60 barrels. More than 100 outlets are supplied, 30 of which regularly stock the beer. One pub is owned.

Bewsher's Best Bitter (OG 1038.5, ABV 3.8%)
A lightly-hopped, golden brown session beer, named after the landlord and brewer at the Queen's Head in the 1830s.

Nameless Ale (OG 1038.5, ABV 3.8%)
A golden, easy-drinking session beer.

Brougham Ale (OG 1039, ABV 3.9%)
A gently-hopped, amber bitter.

Eden Valley Pale Ale (OG 1040, ABV 4%)
A pale session bitter with a fresh taste.

Old Faithful (OG 1040, ABV 4%)
Initially bitter, a gold-coloured ale with an astringent finish.

1823 (OG 1041, ABV 4.1%)
A full-bodied session bitter with a gentle bitterness.

Academy Ale (OG 1041.5, ABV 4.2%)
A dark, full-bodied, traditional rich and malty ale.

Red Barn Ale (OG 1043, ABV 4.4%)
A ruby red ale with a strong hop finish.

Titan (NEW)

Golden Eagle, 6 St Katherine's Court (off Agard Street), Derby, DE22 3AY
☎ (01332) 298465 🌐 titanbrewery.co.uk

Set up by the former Mr Grundy's brewers in 2014 with plans to install a brewery at the rear of the pub. At present beers are being brewed at Mr Grundy's (qv).

Bitter (OG 1036.8, ABV 3.8%)

THE BREWERIES

Pale (OG 1038.7, ABV 4%)

Gold (OG 1043.5, ABV 4.5%)

Stout (OG 1047, ABV 4.8%)

IPA (OG 1048.5, ABV 5%)

Titanic SIBA

Unit 5, Callender Place, Burslem, Stoke-on-Trent, Staffordshire, ST6 1JL
☎ (01782) 823447 tïtanicbrewery.co.uk
Tours by arrangement

Founded in 1985 and named after Captain Smith, a Potteries man and the Captain of the Titanic. The brewery supplies more than 600 free trade outlets and has a small, constantly expanding tied house estate. Monthly seasonals and bottle-conditioned beers are available.

Mild (OG 1036, ABV 3.5%)
Fresh fruity hop aroma leads to a caramel start then a rush of bitter hoppiness ending with a lingering dry finish.

Steerage (OG 1036, ABV 3.5%)
Pale yellow bitter. Flavours start with hops and fruit but become zesty and refreshing in this light session beer with a long, dry finish.

Lifeboat (OG 1040, ABV 4%)
Dark brown with fruit, malt and caramel aromas. Sweet start, malty and caramel middle with hoppiness developing into a fruity and dry lingering finish.

Anchor Bitter (OG 1042, ABV 4.1%)
Amber beer with a spicy hint to the fruity start followed by a rush of hops in the dry bitter finish.

Iceberg (OG 1042, ABV 4.1%)
Yellow gold sparkling wheat beer with a flowery start leading to a massively hoppy, zesty finish.

Chocolate & Vanilla Stout (OG 1047, ABV 4.5%)
Chocoholic paradise with real coffee and vanilla support. Cocoa, sherry and almonds lend depth to this creamy, drinkable 'heaven in a glass' stout.

Stout (OG 1046, ABV 4.5%)
Roasty, toasty with tobacco, autumn bonfires, chocolate and hints of liquorice; perfectly balanced with a bitter, dry finish reminiscent of real coffee.

White Star (OG 1050, ABV 4.8%)
Hints of cinnamon apple pie are found before the hops take over to give a bitter edge to this well-balanced, refreshing, fruity beer.

Plum Porter (OG 1051, ABV 4.9%)
Dark brown with a powerful fruity aroma. A sweet plum fruitiness gives way to a gentle bitter finish.

Captain Smith's Strong Ale (OG 1054, ABV 5.2%)
Red brown and full bodied, lots of malt and roast with a hint of honey but a strong bittersweet finish.

Toll End

c/o Waggon & Horses, 131 Toll End Road, Tipton, West Midlands, DY4 0ET ☎ 07903 725574
Tours by arrangement

The four-barrel brewery opened in 2004. With the exception of Phoebe's Ale, named after the brewer's daughter, all brews commemorate local landmarks, events and people. Occasional beers are available.

William Perry (OG 1043, ABV 4.3%)

Black Bridge (OG 1044, ABV 4.4%)

Tipton Pride (OG 1046, ABV 4.6%)

Phoebe's Ale (PA) (OG 1047, ABV 4.7%)

Power Station (OG 1049, ABV 4.9%)
Cask-conditioned lager.

Lil Devil Stout (OG 1058, ABV 5.4%)

Tollgate SIBA

Unit 1, Southwood House Farm, Staunton Lane, Calke, Leicestershire, LE65 1RG
☎ (01283) 229194 tollgatebrewery.com
Tours by arrangement

This family-run six-barrel brewery was founded in 2005 on the site of the old Brunt & Bucknall Brewery in nearby Woodville, but relocated to new premises on the National Trust's Calke Park estate in 2012. Around 150 outlets are supplied direct. Some seasonal beers and occasional specials are produced. Bottle-conditioned beer is available (suitable for vegans) and constitutes nearly 40% of production.

California Steam (OG 1041, ABV 4.2%)
Brewed in the style of a US West Coast lager to produce a pale golden colour.

Bitter (OG 1041, ABV 4.3%)
A smooth, easy-drinking bitter.

Ashby Pale (OG 1043, ABV 4.5%)
A light, refreshing beer with a citrus finish.

Red Star IPA (OG 1043, ABV 4.5%)
A classic hoppy IPA.

Billy's Best Bitter (OG 1044, ABV 4.6%)
Dark amber best bitter.

Red McAdy (OG 1048, ABV 5%)
Whisky-conditioned northern ale.

Tolly Cobbold

See Greene King

Tombstone (NEW) SIBA

20 Estcourt Road, Great Yarmouth, Norfolk, NR30 4JQ
☎ 07584 504444 tombstonebrewery.co.uk

Tombstone was established in 2013 and is run by former home brewer Paul Hodgson. It is named after the town cemetery which backs onto it. All the beers have a Wild West theme. 10 outlets are supplied in Yarmouth and one in Norwich.

Arizona (ABV 3.9%)

Gunslinger (ABV 4.3%)
Golden hoppy ale with a malty finish.

Stagecoach (ABV 4.4%)

Lone Rider (ABV 4.8%)

Tomos & Lilford (NEW)

Unit 14, Heritage Business Park, Wick Road, Llantwit Major, CF61 1YU
☎ (01446) 796905

Office: 117 Boverton Road, Llantwit Major, CF61 1YA
✉ **tomos.lilford@gmail.com**

⊗ Launched in 2013 by keen experimental home brewers Rolant Tomos and brothers Rob and James Lilford. The brewery supplies small amounts of beer for local and take-home trade. Expansion is planned. Seasonal beers are available.

Personal Best (ABV 4.5%)
Malty session beer with creamy, nutty notes.

Rosemary Ale (ABV 5%)
Pale, refreshing ale, bursting with the flavours of honey and rosemary.

Bragawd (ABV 5.1%)
Unhopped ale, flavoured with yarrow. Mellow orange flavours.

Local Legend (ABV 5.5%)
Amber/golden ale. Sweet, citrus and satisfying.

Cwrw Du Porter (ABV 6.5%)
Classic porter, chocolatey, rich and dangerously drinkable.

Tonbridge SIBA

Unit 19, Branbridges Industrial Estate, East Peckham, Kent, TN12 5HF
☎ **(01622) 871239** 🌐 **tonbridgebrewery.co.uk**
Tours by arrangement

⊗ Tonbridge Brewery was launched in 2010 using a four-barrel brew kit, expanding in 2013 to a 12-barrel plant. Owned and run jointly by Paul Bournazian and Mark Gardner, it produces cask-conditioned ales using predominantly Kent-grown hops. The full range of ales is available in five-litre mini casks. Pubs and shops are supplied throughout Kent as well as parts of Surrey, Sussex, Essex and South-east London.

Traditional Ale (OG 1038, ABV 3.6%)
Easy-drinking and refreshing ale with a light fruity taste and hop aroma.

Copper Nob (OG 1039.5, ABV 3.8%)
A fairly dry, rich copper-coloured ale with taste in depth. Robust fruity flavour from the hops.

Alsace Gold (OG 1041.5, ABV 4%)
Golden ale with a light caramel maltiness balanced with a delicate floral hoppiness.

Rustic (OG 1041.5, ABV 4%)
Deep bronze-coloured, rich tasting country ale. Lightly hopped giving a delicate spicy taste and aroma.

Ebony Moon (OG 1044, ABV 4.2%)
A rich porter with a pronounced maltiness balanced with a light bitterness.

Union Pale (OG 1047, ABV 4.7%)
An American-style pale ale with rich malt flavours balanced by citrus and tropical fruit aromas.

Toolmakers SIBA

6-8 Botsford Street, Sheffield, South Yorkshire, S3 9PF
☎ **07956 235332** 🌐 **toolmakersbrewery.co.uk**

Toolmakers is a family-run brewery established in 2012. Beers are brewed on a five-barrel plant and are available in local pubs.

G. Philips Driver (ABV 4.2%)

Razmataz (ABV 4.2%)

Fine Finish (ABV 4.3%)

Pin Hammer (ABV 4.3%)

Black Edge (ABV 5.2%)

Top Out (NEW)

Unit 3, 6B Dryden Road, Loanhead, EH20 9LZ
☎ **(0131) 440 0270** 🌐 **topoutbrewery.com**

Brewing began in 2013 using a six-barrel plant. Production is mostly bottle-conditioned but cask-conditioned beers are becoming increasingly available.

Staple (ABV 4%)

Smoked Porter (ABV 5.6%)

The Cone (ABV 6.8%)

Top-Notch (NEW)

Haywards Heath, West Sussex, RH16 1UQ ☎ **07963 829368** 🌐 **topnotchbrewing.co.uk**

The 0.5-barrel brewery is situated in a converted residential outbuilding in Haywards Heath.

Hop Festival (OG 1039, ABV 3.9%)

Royal Fanfare (OG 1046, ABV 4.6%)

Topsham SIBA

Globe Hotel, Fore Street, Topsham, Devon, EX3 0DP
☎ **(01392) 873471** 🌐 **topsham-ales.co.uk**
Tours by arrangement

Topsham Ales has operated since 2010. It is run solely by volunteers, and is one of only a handful of co-operatively owned breweries in the UK. The beer is sold locally in Exeter and East Devon.

Black Oar Hard (ABV 4.2%)
A smooth, medium-strength stout with full roasted flavours and a dry finish.

Trucklebed Alley (ABV 4.2%)
Refreshingly light, fruity malty beer with a dry and slightly citrus finish.

The Terror (ABV 4.3%)
Complex malt character with hoppy, slightly sweet and spicy flavours.

Toffles Ale (ABV 4.3%)
A well-hopped, amber-coloured bitter with hints of a slightly sweet and toffee flavour.

Devil's Walkabout (ABV 8.1%)
Vinous and deep toffee aroma, complex fruit character with a peppery hop finish.

Totally Brewed (NEW)

Unit 10, Meadow Lane Fruit 'n' Veg Market, Clarke Road, Nottingham, NG2 3JJ ☎ **07702 800639**
🌐 **totallybrewed.com**

Totally Brewed began brewing in 2014 using a seven-barrel plant previously used at White Dog Brewery. A diverse range of hop-forward beers are produced including seasonal and one-off brews.

Slap in the Face (OG 1040, ABV 4%)
A hoppy, blonde session ale.

Papa Jangle's Voodoo Stout (OG 1046, ABV 4.5%)
A complex, flavoursome dark stout.

Punch in the Face (OG 1047, ABV 4.8%)

A hoppy IPA brewed with American hops.

Four Hopmen of the Apocalypse (OG 1047, ABV 5.2%)
A hoppy IPA with four hop varieties.

Captain Hopbeard (OG 1050, ABV 5.5%)
A Pacific IPA utilising Australian and New Zealand hops.

Towcester Mill (NEW)

The Mill, Moat Lane, Towcester, Northamptonshire, NN12 6AD
☎ (01327) 437060 🌐 towcestermillbrewery.co.uk

⊗ A five-barrel brew plant, formerly at Whittlebury Brewery, now situated at the Old Mill in Towcester, brewing the former Whittlebury beers and a new range of Towcester Mill ales. There is a brewery tap and a shop on site. Seasonal and bottle-conditioned beers are available.

Golden Vale (OG 1039, ABV 3.7%)
Pale golden session ale with crisp lemon, citrus hop aromas and a delicate bitterness.

Mill Race (OG 1040, ABV 3.9%)

Old Tun (OG 1042, ABV 4.1%)
Chestnut bitter with a rich bitterness and slightly spicy, almost sweet hop finish.

Bell Ringer (OG 1044, ABV 4.4%)

Green Dragon (OG 1045, ABV 4.4%)
Premium amber ale, full-flavoured with a strong bitter finish.

Dark Fire (OG 1050, ABV 5.2%)

Tower SIBA

Old Water Tower, Walsitch Maltings, Glensyl Way, Burton upon Trent, Staffordshire, DE14 1PZ
☎ (01283) 562888 🌐 towerbrewery.co.uk
Shop Mon-Thu 9am-5pm, Fri 9am-11.30pm
Tours by arrangement

◎ Tower was established in 2001 by John Mills in a converted derelict water tower of Thomas Salt's Brewery. The conversion was given a Civic Society award for the restoration of a historic building in 2001. Tower has 20 regular outlets. Seasonal beers: see website.

Thomas Salt's Burton Ale (OG 1035, ABV 3.5%)

Bitter (OG 1042, ABV 4.2%) ◆
Gold-coloured with a malty, caramel and hoppy aroma. A full hop and fruit taste with the fruit lingering. A bitter and astringent finish.

Malty Towers (OG 1044, ABV 4.4%)

Gone for a Burton (OG 1046, ABV 4.6%)

Imperial Pale Ale (OG 1050, ABV 5%)

Towles' SIBA

Unit 11, Circuit 32, Easton Road, Easton, Bristol, BS5 0DB
☎ (0117) 321 3188 🌐 towlesfineales.co.uk
Shop Mon-Fri 9.30am-2pm (other times by arrangement)
Tours by arrangement

⊗ Towles' is a 10-barrel brewery built in the tower style and run by Andrew and Anna Towle. Berrow Brewery was purchased in 2011 and brewing commenced on the site in Easton in 2012. The Berrow beers continue to be brewed. The brewery includes a shop and tasting room. Bottle-conditioned beer is available.

Old Smiler (OG 1041, ABV 4.1%) ◆
Slight aroma of malt. Taste is malty with a little pale fruit. Malty aftertaste.

Berrow Copper Leaf (OG 1042, ABV 4.2%) ◆
Malt and fruit on the tongue follow a slight malt aroma with a hint of hop in the lingering aftertaste.

Ma Beese's Chocolate Stout (OG 1065, ABV 6.9%) ◆
Powerfully bittersweet stout brewed with cocoa nibs. A balanced palate of sweetness, bitterness and dark chocolate lasts into a long aftertaste.

Town Mill SIBA

Mill Lane, Lyme Regis, Dorset, DT7 3PU
☎ (01297) 444354 🌐 townmillbrewery.com
Shop & brewery tap Mon-Fri 9am-5pm, Sat & Sun 11am-5pm
Tours by arrangement

⊗ Town Mill began brewing in 2010 using a four-barrel plant in a part of the mill that at one time had housed the Lyme Regis electricity generator, although historic use of the building was as a brewer's malthouse. The outside area of the brewery is now licensed, which is proving popular in the summer and holiday times due to the location near the town centre.

Cobb (OG 1041, ABV 3.9%)
An amber/brown bitter with a full flavour and fruity hop finish.

Lyme Gold (OG 1042, ABV 4.2%)
A pale summer ale, easy drinking with a refreshing citrus aroma.

Best (OG 1045, ABV 4.5%)
A reddish brown bitter with a fruit and nut flavour.

Black Ven (OG 1050, ABV 5%)
A dark brown porter with a pronounced depth of flavour, enhanced with the blackcurrant fruitiness of the hops.

Revenge (OG 1052, ABV 5.3%)
A traditional IPA with a well-balanced hop and spiced fruit flavour.

Townes

Speedwell Inn, Lowgates, Staveley, Derbyshire, S43 3TT
☎ (01246) 472252 ✉ townesbrew@gmail.com

Townes started in 1994 and was the first brewery in Chesterfield for more than 40 years. In 1997 the Speedwell Inn at Staveley was bought and the five-barrel plant was moved to the rear of the pub. Over the next 16 years brewer Alan Wood produced many memorable and award-winning beers before retiring in 2013. New owners Lawrie and Nicoleta Evans are continuing the traditional brewing ethos. Seasonal beers are occasionally available.

Speedwell Bitter (OG 1039, ABV 3.9%) ◆
Straw-coloured session bitter with little aroma. Initially quite sweet leading to a bitterness developing in the long, slightly astringent aftertaste.

Staveley Cross (OG 1043, ABV 4.3%) ◆

Amber gold best bitter with a faint banana aroma. Hoppy with bitterness present throughout, culminating in a short, dry, slightly astringent aftertaste.

Pynot Porter (OG 1045, ABV 4.5%) ◆
Red-brown porter with a faint malt and roast coffee aroma. Roast malt flavours combine with vine fruit, becoming increasingly bitter towards the finish.

Townhouse

Units 1-4, Townhouse Studios, Townhouse Farm, Alsager Road, Audley, Staffordshire, ST7 8JQ ☎ 07976 209437 ✉ j.nixon2@btinternet.com
Tours by arrangement

Townhouse was set up in 2002 with a 2.5-barrel plant. In 2004 the brewery scaled up to five barrels. Demand is growing rapidly and in 2006 two additional fermenting vessels were added. Bottling is planned.

Traditional Scottish Ales

See Black Wolf

Traquair House SIBA

Traquair House, Innerleithen, EH44 6PW
☎ (01896) 830323 🌐 traquair.co.uk/brewery
Shop Easter-Oct 12-5pm daily (Jun-Aug 10.30am-5pm)
Tours by arrangement

The 18th century brewhouse is based in one of the wing of the 1,000 year old Traquair House, Scotland's oldest inhabited house. All the beers are oak-fermented and 60% of production is exported. Seasonal and occasional beers are available.

Bear Ale (OG 1050, ABV 5%)

Treboom SIBA

Millstone Yard, Main Street, Shipton-by-Beningbrough, North Yorkshire, YO30 1AA
☎ (01904) 471569

Correspondence: Nova Scotia Cottage, Acaster Malbis, North Yorkshire, YO23 2PY 🌐 treboom.co.uk

Treboom began in 2011 using a 10-barrel plant with production going mainly to pubs within a 50-mile radius.

Drum Beat (OG 1038, ABV 3.8%)
A copper-coloured session bitter, easy drinking with a balance of malt and hops.

Tambourine Man (OG 1038.5, ABV 3.9%)
A deep golden ale with a hint of maltiness complemented by fruit flavours from the hops.

Yorkshire Sparkle (OG 1039, ABV 4%)
A pale ale with a fresh citrus taste.

Kettle Drum (OG 1042, ABV 4.3%)
Copper coloured with a distinct fruitiness and robust hop flavours leading to a clean finish.

Hop Britannia (OG 1050, ABV 5%)
A hoppy strong pale ale brewed using only British hops. Honey in colour with intense citrus fruit and spice notes.

Tring SIBA

Dunsley Farm, London Road, Tring, Hertfordshire, HP23 6HA
☎ (01442) 890721 🌐 tringbrewery.co.uk
Shop closed Sun, Mon-Tue 11am-5pm, Wed-Thu 9am-6pm, Fri 9am-7.30pm, Sat 9am-5pm
Tours by arrangement

Founded in 1992, Tring Brewery moved to its present site in 2010. It brews more than 130 barrels a week, producing a core range of nine beers augmented by monthly and seasonal specials, most taking their names from local myths and legends. The brewery continues its practice of using experimental hop varieties from around the world in its monthly specials.

Side Pocket for a Toad (OG 1035, ABV 3.6%)
A straw-coloured ale with citrus notes and floral aroma with a crisp, dry finish.

Brock Bitter (OG 1036, ABV 3.7%)
A mid-brown quaffing ale with a hint of sweetness and caramel.

Mansion Mild (OG 1036, ABV 3.7%)
Smooth and creamy dark ruby mild with a fruity palate and gentle late hop.

Blonde (OG 1039, ABV 4%)
A refreshing blonde beer with a fruity palate, balanced with a lingering hop aroma.

Ridgeway (OG 1039, ABV 4%)
Balanced malt and hop flavours with a dry, flowery hop aftertaste.

Moongazing (OG 1042, ABV 4.2%)
Amber, red-hued beer with a rounded bitterness and hoppy aftertaste.

Tea Kettle Stout (OG 1047, ABV 4.7%)
Rich and complex traditional stout with a hint of liquorice and moderate bitterness.

Colley's Dog (OG 1051, ABV 5.2%)
Dark but not over-rich, strong yet drinkable, this premium ale has a long dry finish with overtones of malt and walnuts.

Death or Glory (OG 1074, ABV 7.2%)
A strong, dark, aromatic barley wine.

Trinity

Church Road, Gisleham, Suffolk, NR33 8DS
☎ (01502) 743121 🌐 trinityales.co.uk

⊗ Trinity Ales was launched in 2009 using a four-barrel plant. Pure spring water is used from an ancient well along with Suffolk hops and barley from local farms. Outlets are supplied within a 30-mile radius of the brewery. Bottle-conditioned beers are available.

Wishing Well (OG 1039, ABV 3.8%)

High Light (OG 1040, ABV 4%)

Black Street Smithy (OG 1045, ABV 4.5%)

Gisleham Gold (OG 1045, ABV 4.5%)

Triple fff SIBA

Magpie Works, Station Approach, Four Marks, Alton, Hampshire, GU34 5HN
☎ (01420) 561422 🌐 triplefff.com
Shop Mon-Thu 9am-5pm, Fri 9am-6pm, Sat 10am-4pm

Tours by arrangement

⊗ Established in 1997 close to a stop on the Watercress Line, the brewery and all the beers except Alton's Pride are named following a musical theme. The fff refers to fortissimo, meaning louder or stronger. Brewing on a 50-barrel plant since 2006, multiple CAMRA awards have been won. Quarterly seasonals, monthly specials and bottle-conditioned beers are available. Two pubs are owned: the Railway Arms, Alton, and the White Lion, Aldershot.

Alton's Pride (OG 1039, ABV 3.8%)
Full-bodied session bitter. An initially malty flavour fades as citrus notes and hoppiness take over, leading to a lasting hoppy/bitter finish.

Pressed Rat & Warthog (OG 1039, ABV 3.8%)
Toffee aroma with hints of blackcurrant and chocolate lead to a well-balanced flavour with roast, fruit and malt vying with the hoppy bitterness.

Moondance (OG 1045, ABV 4.2%)
An aromatic citrus hop nose, balanced by bitterness and sweetness in the mouth. Bitterness increases in the finish as fruit declines.

Trossachs Craft

See Tryst

Truefitt

3 Carcut Road, Lawson Industrial Estate, Middlesbrough, TS3 6QL ☎ 07883 072389
truefittbrewing.co.uk

Truefitt began brewing in 2012 using a four-barrel plant producing up to 16 barrels a week. Vegan beers are available to order. Seasonal and bottle-conditioned beers: see website.

Erimus Pale Ale (OG 1041, ABV 3.9%)
A pale session beer with, a crisp aroma, floral and citrus notes and a bitter finish.

North Riding Bitter (OG 1043, ABV 4%)
A traditional bitter loaded with hops, giving the beer an earthy nuttiness.

Ironopolis Stout (OG 1051, ABV 4.7%)
A bold stout packed full of chocolate and roast malt.

Mydilsburgh IPA (OG 1052, ABV 5%)
A well-hopped IPA with a spicy, dry finish.

Truman's SIBA

The Eyrie, 2 & 3 Stour Road, London, E3 2NT
☎ (020) 8533 3575 trumansbeer.co.uk

The legendary East London brewery, Truman's, was reborn in 2013 – 24 years after the original Brick Lane brewery's closure in 1989. The new brewery is a 40-barrel plant in Hackney Wick, just a stroll down the Roman Road from the original site. The original Truman's yeast, recovered from the National Collection of Yeast Cultures, is used. Seasonal beers: see website.

Swift (OG 1040.5, ABV 3.9%)
Well-balanced golden bitter with hops and a trace of grapefruit on the nose and palate and a bitter finish.

Runner (OG 1040, ABV 4%)
Traditional brown best bitter with spicy hoppy aroma and flavour fading in the dry aftertaste. Some marmalade fruity notes.

Eyrie (ABV 4.3%)
A combination of British hops give zesty, citrus flavours.

Tryst SIBA

Lorne Road, Larbert, Stirlingshire, FK5 4AT
☎ (01324) 554000 trystbrewery.co.uk
Tours by arrangement

Tryst started production in 2003. A large range of beers is produced, all available in cask and bottles.

Brockville Dark (OG 1039, ABV 3.8%)
A full-tasting session ale with hints of liquorice and roasted grains.

Brockville Pale (OG 1039, ABV 3.9%)
A pale golden session ale, smooth on the palate.

Hop Trial (OG 1040, ABV 3.9%)
Lager malt with a variable hop profile.

Bla'than (OG 1041, ABV 4%)
A strong floral nose and refreshing taste enhanced with elderflower and pale malts.

Drovers 80/- (OG 1041, ABV 4%)
A traditional, well-malted 80/- with an element of sweetness. A gentle nose complements a smooth finish.

Carronade Pale Ale (OG 1043, ABV 4.2%)
A pale ale bursting with citrus flavours.

Sherpa Porter (OG 1044, ABV 4.4%)

German Hops Pils (OG 1045, ABV 4.5%)

V.I.P. (OG 1046, ABV 4.5%)
Light brown best bitter with a deep hop taste and floral nose.

Zetland Wheatbier (OG 1046, ABV 4.5%)
Refreshing with a distinctive banana nose, a typical European cloudy wheat beer.

RAJ IPA (OG 1055, ABV 5.5%)
Exclusively English hopped with balanced flavours, with a hoppy aroma and palate.

Contract brewed for Trossach's Craft Brewery:

Waylade (OG 1040, ABV 3.9%)

LadeBack (OG 1048, ABV 4.5%)

LadeOut (OG 1055, ABV 5.1%)

Tudor SIBA

Unit 1, Llanhilleth Industrial Estate, Llanhilleth, NP13 2RX
☎ (01876) 851696 ☎ (01495) 214808
tudorbrewery.co.uk

Tudor is a family-run, four-barrel plant that began brewing in 2012. Several pubs are supplied locally, with others further afield.

Blorenge (OG 1038, ABV 3.8%)
A light, pale session ale with a fresh citrus undertone.

Black Mountain Stout (OG 1039, ABV 4%)

IPA (OG 1039, ABV 4%)
A classic IPA with a sharp, hoppy, grapefruit finish.

Skirrid (OG 1040, ABV 4.2%)
A full-flavoured dark beer.

Sugarloaf (OG 1044, ABV 4.7%)
A medium dry beer, rounded and full bodied with smooth caramelised undertones.

Winter Cheer (OG 1046, ABV 5%)
A dark ale infused with ground ginger, lemon rind, honey, cinnamon and nutmeg.

Black Rock (OG 1050, ABV 5.6%)
Bordering on a porter, this dark ale has a rich aroma and dark appearance with a smooth chocolate-coffee aftertaste.

Tunnel SIBA

Old Stable Block, Red House Farm, Nuneaton Road, Ansley, Warwickshire, CV10 0QU
☎ (024) 7639 4386 🌐 tunnelbrewery.co.uk
Shop Mon-Fri 9am-3pm
Tours by arrangement

This six-barrel brewery, established in 2005 at the Lord Nelson Inn, relocated to the picturesque stable block at Red House Farm in 2011. Beers are also brewed under the Battlefield Brewery name. Tasting sessions are available in the Belgian-style beer café. Seasonal, special and bottle-conditioned beers: see website.

Percheron (OG 1037, ABV 3.7%)
Refreshing citrus pale golden ale.

Late Ott (OG 1040, ABV 4%)
Dark golden session bitter with a fruity nose and perfumed hop edge. The finish is dry and bitter.

Meadowlands (OG 1040, ABV 4%)
Pale golden in colour with a fruity, citrus taste and light, hoppy aroma.

Trade Winds (OG 1045, ABV 4.6%)
An aromatic, copper-coloured beer with an aroma of Cascade hops and a clean, crisp hint of citrus, followed by fruity malts and a dry finish full of scented hops.

Parish Ale (OG 1047, ABV 4.7%)
A reddish-amber, malty ale with a slight chocolate aroma enhanced by citrus notes. It becomes increasingly fruity as the English hops kick in. Smooth, gentle hop bitterness in the finish.

Shadow Weaver (OG 1046, ABV 4.7%)
A dark stout starting with chocolate and roasted coffee on the tongue, developing through slight fruit into a dry, mellow, bitter finish.

Fields of Gold (OG 1048, ABV 5%)
Pale in colour with a hoppy taste and floral nose.

Nelson's Column (OG 1051, ABV 5.2%)
A ruby red, strong old English ale.

East India Pale Ale (OG 1058, ABV 5.9%)
Robust in flavour with a good hit of hops.

Tunnfield

Santley Farm, Hope Valley, Minsterley, Shropshire, SY5 0LD ☎ 07828 053065

Office: 3 Butcher Row, Condover, Shropshire, SY5 7AE 🌐 tunnfieldbrewery.co.uk

Tunnfield is an artisan brewery established in 2012, set in the heart of the Shropshire Hills near Hope Valley, Minsterley. The brewery was hand-built by two Shropshire engineers with a passion for real ale. Most of the beer is distributed locally but it is also available nationally through a main distributor. Seasonal and bottle-conditioned beers are available. Brewing is currently suspended.

Stiperstones (OG 1037, ABV 3.7%)
A smooth session ale, light and refreshing with grapefruit aromas and a crisp bitterness.

Devils Chair (OG 1041, ABV 4%)
A traditional ruby bitter with a full-bodied malt flavour.

Cannon Rock (OG 1042, ABV 4.2%)
An IPA-style beer, golden-coloured with a crisp finish.

Turners SIBA

Highfield Farm, The Broyle, Ringmer, East Sussex, BN8 5AR
☎ (08456) 892689 🌐 turnersbrewery.com

⊗ Turners began brewing in 2012, initially as a guest at a brewery in Hampshire, but moving to its own premises in Ringmer in 2013.

Golden Ale (OG 1035, ABV 3.5%)
A fruity and hoppy beer with a pleasant aftertaste.

Blonde (ABV 3.8%)
A refreshing fruity beer with a crisp, dry finish. Full of subtle malty flavours.

East Sussex Bitter (OG 1039, ABV 3.9%)
A light, refreshing beer with a floral nose and a fruity and hoppy palate.

Best (OG 1041, ABV 4.1%)
A caramel-coloured traditional best bitter with a smooth yet complex flavour profile and a fruity aroma.

Ruby Mild (OG 1046, ABV 4.6%)
A fruity body with a smooth and subtle chocolatey finish.

American Pale Ale (ABV 4.7%)
A light-coloured, strongly-hopped and bitter tasting pale ale.

Porter (ABV 4.9%)
A silky body with rich malty flavours.

IPA (ABV 5.1%)
A smooth and hoppy IPA with a balanced flavour.

Turpin (NEW)

Turpins Lodge, Lodge Farm, Tadmarton Heath Road, Hook Norton, Oxfordshire, OX15 5DO ☎ 07779 447769 ✉ turpinbrewery@btconnect.com

⊗ Brewing started in 2013. A number of local pubs and the golf club are supplied regularly, as well as a few pubs further afield in Rugby and Birmingham. Seasonal beers are available.

Bitter (ABV 3.4%)

Citrus Golden (ABV 4.2%)

Twickenham SIBA

Unit 6, 18 Mereway Road, Twickenham, TW2 6BG
☎ (020) 8241 1825 🌐 twickenham-fine-ales.co.uk
All products: Thu 3-6pm, Fri 12-6pm, Sat 10am-1pm Bottles & Merchandise only: Mon-Fri 9-6pm, Sat 10am-1pm
Tours by arrangement

⊗ The brewery was set up in 2004 using a 10-barrel brew plant and was the first brewery in

Twickenham since the 1920s. It expanded to a 25-barrel plant in larger premises in 2012. Pubs and clubs are supplied within 25 miles of the brewery, including central London. Seasonal beers: see website.

Sundancer (OG 1037, ABV 3.7%) ◆
Light zesty golden ale with citrus notes dominating from beginning to end. Finish is bitter but balanced by biscuity sweetness.

Grandstand Bitter (OG 1037, ABV 3.8%) ◆
Pale brown beer with peach, citrus and malt on the palate, fading in the bitter, slightly dry finish,

Redhead (OG 1040, ABV 4.1%)
A red beer with a gentle maltiness and a spicy hop character.

Naked Ladies (OG 1044, ABV 4.4%) ◆
Refreshing dark golden ale with a touch of spicy hop in the flavour but fruit dominates with a lasting bitterness.

Twisted (NEW) SIBA

Unit 8, Commerce Business Centre, Commerce Close, Westbury, Wiltshire, BA13 4LS
☎ (01373) 864441 🌐 twisted-brewing.com

⊠ Twisted began brewing in 2014 using a six-barrel plant. Outlets in west Wiltshire and north Somerset are supplied. Seasonal beers are available.

Gaucho (OG 1039, ABV 3.6%)
A pale ale with a lasting aroma and clean finish.

Conscript (OG 1044, ABV 4.2%)
A golden-coloured ale with a fragrant, grassy aroma.

Pirate (OG 1045, ABV 4.2%)
An English bitter with a lasting taste.

Rider (OG 1041, ABV 4.2%)
A well-balanced, traditional American red ale.

Twisted Oak SIBA

Yeowood Farm, Iwood Lane, Wrington, Somerset, BS40 5NU ☎ 07917 457797
🌐 twistedoakbrewery.co.uk

⊠ Twisted Oak began brewing in 2012 using a five-barrel plant. Seasonal and bottle-conditioned beers are available.

Fallen Tree (OG 1038, ABV 3.8%) ◆
Superb bittersweet session bitter. Aroma and flavour of hops and ripe fruit. Complex and satisfying bitter astringent finish.

Old Barn (OG 1045, ABV 4.5%) ◆
Fruity red ale. Well-balanced flavour with a long bitter finish.

Spun Gold (OG 1045, ABV 4.5%) ◆
Classic golden ale with a soft mouthfeel. Slightly spicy notes to the fruity malt aroma and flavour. Hops begin in the aroma and gradually develop into a bitter finish.

Two Beach (NEW) SIBA

Ness Cove, Shaldon, Devon, TQ14 0HP
🌐 odetruefood.com/brewery

Two Beach began brewing in 2013 using the plant previously used at Ringmore Craft Brewery.

Odeale (ABV 4.2%)

Oarsome (ABV 4.7%)

Two Bridges

c/o Fox & Hounds, 51 Gosbrook Road, Caversham, Reading, Berkshire, RG4 8BN
☎ (0118) 375 9205

Two Bridges was founded in 2009 by husband and wife Kevin and Kerri Durkan. It is named after the bridges spanning the Thames between Caversham and Reading. The 2.5-barrel plant is currently located in the brewer's garage and brewing is suspended until the move to the Fox & Hounds can be completed.

Two Cocks SIBA

Church Lane, Enborne, Berkshire, RG20 0HB
☎ (01635) 47351 🌐 twococksbrewery.com

⊠ The brewery was established in 2011 after wild hops were found growing in the farm's hedgerows. A 180-feet deep borehole supplies water for the brewery. Many local and regional outlets are regularly supplied. Most beer names refer to the 1st Battle of Newbury in the English Civil War.

Diamond Lil (OG 1035, ABV 3.2%)
A light and fruity golden ale.

1643 Cavalier (OG 1039, ABV 3.8%)
A light, refreshing, thirst-quenching golden ale with a combination of hops.

1643 Leveller (OG 1040, ABV 3.8%)
A malty session bitter brewed with a single variety of English hop.

1643 Roundhead (OG 1042, ABV 4.2%)
A full-bodied, smooth best bitter.

1643 Puritan (OG 1049, ABV 4.5%)
A dark stout with notes of caramel and chocolate.

1643 Viscount (OG 1054, ABV 5.6%)
An unusually fruity strong beer.

Two Crowns (NEW)

c/o Unit 25, Asquith Bottom Mill, West Street, Sowerby Bridge, West Yorkshire, HX6 3BS

Following the sale of the Brass Monkey Brewery in 2012 the former owners now use spare capacity at the Slightly Foxed Brewery (qv) on their old equipment.

Two Rivers SIBA

2 Sluice Bank, Denver, Downham Market, Norfolk, PE38 0EQ ☎ 07518 099868
✉ denverbrewco@hotmail.com.

The two Rivers' brewer has a background in pharmacology and fermentation technology. All the beers are currently bottle-conditioned; expansion into cask production is planned.

Two Roses SIBA

Unit 9, Darton Business Park, Barnsley Road, Darton, South Yorkshire, S75 5QX ☎ 07780 701254
🌐 tworosesbrewery.co.uk
by arrangement
Tours by arrangement

⊗ Two Roses started brewing in 2011 using an eight-barrel plant installed in a former carpet factory. Four core beers are brewed, supplemented during the year with special brews.

Full Nelson (OG 1040, ABV 3.8%)

Galaxy (OG 1040, ABV 4%)

Heron Porter (OG 1040, ABV 4.2%)

Two Towers SIBA

Unit 1, Mott Street Industrial Estate, 51 Mott Street, Hockley, Birmingham, West Midlands, B19 3HE
☎ (0121) 439 7253 🌐 twotowersbrewery.co.uk
Tours by arrangement

⊗ Established in 2010, the brewery profile and products draw heavily on the heritage, historical characters and features of Birmingham and has a very active brewery tour programme. It is a 10-barrel plant with about half of its production being bottle-conditioned. Specials are brewed for various events and all bottles and some cask beers can be delivered unfined and suitable for vegans.

Baskerville Bitter (OG 1038, ABV 3.8%)
Full-bodied bitter with a blend of four hops, providing a complex but well-balanced ale.

Chamberlain Pale Ale (OG 1042, ABV 4.5%)
A crisp light ale loaded with grapefruit flavours with a long hoppy finish.

Jewellery Porter (OG 1049, ABV 5%)
A full-bodied wholesome stout with a thick and slightly chocolate texture underlined with long, fulfilling English hops.

Birmingham Special Ale (OG 1043, ABV 5.4%)
Maltly strong bitter with a full body, reflecting the flavours and characteristics of traditional English ales.

Tydd Steam SIBA

Manor Barn, Kirkgate, Tydd Saint Giles, Cambridgeshire, PE13 5NE
☎ (01945) 871020 ☎ 07932 726552
🌐 tyddsteam.co.uk
Tours by arrangement

⊗ Tydd Steam Brewery opened in 2007 in a converted agricultural barn, using a 15-barrel plant since 2011. The brewery is named after two farm steam engines. Around 70 outlets are supplied direct. Seasonal/occasional beers are available.

Barn Ale (OG 1038, ABV 3.9%)
A golden bitter that has good biscuity malt aroma and flavour, balanced by spicy hops. Long, dry, fairly astringent finish.

Piston Bob (OG 1044, ABV 4.6%)
Malt and faint hops on the aroma progress through to a malty flavour complemented by a balance of hops and fruit. A long, dry finish rounds off this amber strong bitter.

Tyne Bank SIBA

Unit 11, Hawick Crescent Industrial Estate, St Lawrence Road, Newcastle upon Tyne, NE6 1AS
☎ (0191) 265 2828 🌐 tynebankbrewery.co.uk
Shop Tue-Thu 9am-5pm, Fri 9am-4pm
Tours by arrangement

⊗ Tyne Bank began brewing in 2011. In addition to its core range, monthly specials and seasonal beers are available.

Single Blonde (OG 1037, ABV 3.5%)
Light ale, slightly dry bitterness with hints of vanilla.

Pacifica Pale (OG 1041, ABV 4%)
Pale ale with mellow bitterness and a citrus twist.

Monument Bitter (OG 1042, ABV 4.1%)
Smooth, balanced bitter with a berry and fruit character.

Silver Dollar (OG 1051, ABV 4.9%)
Hoppy American ale with lasting bitterness and a citrus kick.

Southern Star (OG 1051, ABV 5%)
A New Zealand IPA with a bold fruity aroma and crushed grapefruit flavour.

Uffa

White Lion Inn, Lower Street, Lower Ufford, Suffolk, IP13 6DW
☎ (01394) 460770 🌐 uffabrewery.com

Uffa began brewing in 2010 using a 2.5-barrel plant. It is situated next to the White Lion pub in a converted coach house. Seasonal and bottle-conditioned beers are available.

Fox (OG 1037, ABV 3.7%)

Golden Hoard (OG 1038, ABV 3.7%)

Raedwald's Tipple (OG 1037, ABV 3.7%)

Longboat (OG 1051, ABV 4.7%)

Uley

The Old Brewery, 31 The Street, Uley, Gloucestershire, GL11 5TB
☎ (01453) 860120 🌐 uleybrewery.com

⊗ Brewing at Uley began in 1833 as Price's Brewery. After a long gap, the premises were restored and Uley Brewery opened in 1985. It has its own spring water, which is used to mash Tucker's Maris Otter malt and boiled with Herefordshire hops. Uley serves 40-50 free trade outlets in the Cotswold area and is brewing to capacity. Seasonal beers are available.

Hogshead Cotswold Pale Ale (OG 1035, ABV 3.5%)
A pale-coloured, hoppy session bitter with a good hop aroma and a full flavour for its strength, ending in a bittersweet aftertaste.

Bitter (OG 1040, ABV 4%)
A copper-coloured beer with hops and fruit in the aroma and a malty, fruity taste, underscored by a hoppy bitterness. The finish is dry, with a balance of hops and malt.

Laurie Lee's Bitter (OG 1045, ABV 4.5%)
A copper-coloured, full-flavoured, hoppy bitter with some fruitiness and a smooth, long, balanced finish.

Old Ric (OG 1045, ABV 4.5%)
A full-flavoured, hoppy bitter with some fruitiness and a smooth, balanced finish. Distinctively copper-coloured, this is the house beer for the Old Spot Inn, Dursley.

Old Spot Prize Strong Ale (OG 1050, ABV 5%)

A distinctive full-bodied, ruby coloured ale with a fruity aroma, a malty, fruity taste, with a hoppy bitterness, and a strong, balanced aftertaste.

Pig's Ear Strong Beer (OG 1050, ABV 5%) ◆
A deceptively strong pale-coloured beer with a light hop balance leads to a hoppy, fruity aroma and a smooth bitter finish.

Ulverston

Lightburn Road, Ulverston, Cumbria, LA12 0AU
☎ (01229) 586870
ulverstonbrewingcompany.co.uk
Tours by arrangement

The brewery was established in 2006, and in 2010 moved to new premises with a bespoke 12-barrel plant occupying the octagonal bull ring of the old livestock market on the outskirts of Ulverston. There is a shop on site selling local products and craftwork, and a bar that overlooks the brew plant. Seasonal beers are available. Many of the beers have a Laurel and Hardy theme; Stan Laurel came from Ulverston.

Flying Elephants (OG 1037, ABV 3.7%) ◆
Clean, refreshing yellow bitter, sweet and fruity with a dry citrus finish.

Celebration Ale (OG 1039, ABV 3.9%) ◆
Yellow fruity bitter with hints of tangerine and a notably sustained dry finish.

Harvest Moon (OG 1039, ABV 3.9%) ◆
A well-balanced, pale, hoppy bitter.

Another Fine Mess (OG 1040, ABV 4%) ◆
A refreshing gold-coloured bitter. Initially fruity but with a rising bitterness.

Laughing Gravy (OG 1040, ABV 4%) ◆
Smooth and grainy brown bitter with a good mix of flavours.

Lonesome Pine (OG 1042, ABV 4.2%) ◆
A fresh and fruity pale gold beer; honeyed, lemony and resiny with an increasingly bitter finish.

Fra Diavolo (OG 1043, ABV 4.3%)

Uncle Stuarts

The Little Beer Shop, The Leisure Village, 58 Yarmouth Road, Blofield, Norwich, NR13 4LQ
☎ (01603) 713261
unclestuartsbrewery@btconnect.com
Shop Tue & Thu-Sun 10am-4pm, closed Mon & Wed

The brewery started in 2002. In 2009 it moved to Wroxham Barns Craft Centre and in 2013 relocated again to a brewery shop in Blofield, where the beers are available in both cask and bottle-conditioned form. Local pubs are supplied on request.

North Norfolk Beauty (OG 1039, ABV 3.8%)

Pack Lane Mild (OG 1042, ABV 4%)

Broadland Bitter (ABV 4.1%)

Nut Brown Ale (ABV 4.1%)

Stout (ABV 4.4%)

Excelsior (OG 1044, ABV 4.5%)

Local Hero (OG 1047, ABV 4.7%)

Wroxham Barns Bitter (OG 1044, ABV 4.8%)

Ginger (OG 1048, ABV 5%)

Norwich Castle (OG 1048, ABV 5%)

Porter (OG 1053, ABV 5%)

Buckenham Woods (OG 1054, ABV 5.6%) ◆
Spicy with more than a hint of raisin and sultana. Heavy aroma translates into a richly-flavoured ale with a surprisingly light and creamy mouthfeel.

Strumpshaw Fen (OG 1057, ABV 5.7%)

Norwich Cathedral (OG 1059, ABV 6.5%)

Winter Ale (OG 1060, ABV 7%)
A dark, strong winter warmer.

Unsworth's Yard SIBA

4 Unsworth's Yard, Cartmel, Cumbria, LA11 6PN
☎ 07810 461313 unsworthsyardbrewery.co.uk
Tours by arrangement

Opened in 2011, the 1.5-barrel plant was upgraded in 2014 to a five-barrel one. The brewery produces beers named after historic figures and legends. Beers are available in Cartmel pubs and other local outlets as well as the brewery's own tasting room and fully-licensed bar.

JC Dickinson's The Land of Cartmel (OG 1038, ABV 3.7%)
Light but hoppy with grapefruit notes on a zesty bitter finish.

Cartmel Peninsula (OG 1039, ABV 3.8%)

Pride of Cartmel 1643 The Cromwell Door (OG 1038, ABV 3.9%)
A mildly bitter but full-flavoured amber ale.

Sir William Marshal's Crusader Gold (OG 1041, ABV 4.1%)
A crisp and refreshing golden ale.

Sir Edgar Harrington's Last Wolf (OG 1045, ABV 4.5%)
Deep red, mellow but bitter with blackcurrant and raisin flavours.

Untapped SIBA

Unit 6, Little Castle Farm Business Park, Raglan, Monmouthshire, NP15 2BX ☎ 07988 199794

Correspondence: 80 Carlisle Street, Cardiff, CF24 2PF
untappedbrew.com

Untapped was established in 2009 and is owned and run by Owen Davies and Martyn Darby. Beers were intitally brewed at Whittingtons Brewery in Newent, Gloucestershire, but in 2013 they moved to their own plant in Raglan. Bottle-conditioned beers are also available. The Whittingtons range of beers are also brewed here.

Border (OG 1036.8, ABV 3.8%)

Sundown (OG 1038.8, ABV 4%)

Eclipse (OG 1042.5, ABV 4.4%)

UPA (OG 1043.6, ABV 4.5%)

Triple S (OG 1048.4, ABV 4.9%)

Ember (OG 1050, ABV 5.2%)

Crystal (OG 1052.3, ABV 6%)
A wheat beer.

Upham SIBA

Stakes Farm, Cross Lane, Upham, Hampshire, SO32 1FL

☎ (01489) 861383 🌐 uphambrewery.co.uk
Shop Mon-Fri 10am-3pm
Tours by arrangement

Upham began brewing in 2009 and expanded to a 30-barrel plant in 2013. It owns nine pubs and supplies to more than 60 other outlets. A seasonal beer is brewed every three months. Bottled beers, beer boxes and casks are available from the brewery shop.

Tipster (OG 1036, ABV 3.6%)
An easy-drinking and light golden ale. Initial hoppiness and fruit is balanced by maltiness that lasts into the finish.

Punter (OG 1039, ABV 4%)
Light amber ale with sweet and floral hop aroma. A balanced flavour of refreshing bitterness and maltiness with a dry fruity finish.

Stakes (OG 1045, ABV 4.8%)
Full-bodied ale with striking bitterness, tastes of grapefruit and toffee, and a hoppy finish.

Vale SIBA

Tramway Business Park, Ludgershall Road, Brill, Buckinghamshire, HP18 9TY
☎ **(01844) 239237** 🌐 **valebrewery.co.uk**
Shop Mon-Fri 9am-5pm, Sat 9.30-11.30am, closed Sun & bank hols
Tours by arrangement

Established in 1994 and initially based in Haddenham, Vale moved to Brill in 2007. In 2010 it expanded to 20-barrel brew plant. Four pubs are owned, including the Hop Pole where sister brewery the Aylesbury Brewhouse (qv) opened in 2011. Bottle-conditioned beers are produced. Monthly specials and occasional beers: see website.

Best Bitter (OG 1036, ABV 3.7%)
This pale amber beer starts with a slight fruit aroma. This leads to a clean, bitter taste where hops and fruit dominate. The finish is long and bitter with a slight hop note.

Black Swan Mild (OG 1038, ABV 3.9%)
Dark and smooth with hints of chocolate and coffee on the nose and a malty, dry finish.

Wychert Ale (OG 1038, ABV 3.9%)
A traditional Thames Valley beer. Woody flavours are notable in this malty beer with a finish of port and berries on the nose.

Red Kite (OG 1040, ABV 4%)
Refreshing, chestnut beer with a bitter finish.

VPA (Vale Pale Ale) (OG 1042, ABV 4.2%)
An assertive, dry, hoppy ale with a citrus nose, combined with a pronounced malt background.

Special (OG 1046, ABV 4.5%)
Premium ale with a rich, complex and satisfying finish.

Grumpling Premium Ale (OG 1046, ABV 4.6%)
A rich, warming ruby brown traditional English bitter with mellow fruity malt flavours accompanied by a subtle dry, hoppy finish.

Gravitas (OG 1047, ABV 4.8%)
A strong pale ale packed with hop and citrus flavours, rounded off by a dry, malty, biscuit finish. A pronounced hop aroma throughout.

Vale of Glamorgan SIBA

Unit 8a, Atlantic Trading Estate, Barry, CF63 3RF
☎ **(01446) 730757** 🌐 **vogbrewery.co.uk**

Founded in 2005 using a 10 barrel plant, Vale of Glamorgan has developed a reputation locally for its range of high quality beers. Local pubs and clubs are supplied, and the beers are available nationwide via swap deals with other brewers. A recent overhaul of the beer range has seen some welcome new additions to the portfolio. Bottle-conditioned beers are available.

Light Headed (OG 1040, ABV 4%)
A light, easy-drinking ale.

Original No. 1 (OG 1042, ABV 4.2%)
Classic-style best bitter, thirst quenching and flavoursome.

Grog-y-Vog (OG 1042, ABV 4.3%)
A typical Welsh-style bitter.

Dark Matter (OG 1044, ABV 4.4%)
A deeply satisfying, complex, robust, blackcurrant porter with a fruity aftertaste balanced with liquorice, chocolate and coffee.

Dakota Red (OG 1045, ABV 4.5%)
American-style red ale, bitter and well-balanced with good hop flavours.

Rorke's Draught (OG 1046, ABV 4.6%)
A traditional best bitter, hops dominate but a good maltiness sits in the background.

Cwrw Dewi (OG 1050, ABV 5%)
Strong and satisfying with initial malt flavours balanced with powerful hopiness to follow.

Valhalla

Haroldswick, Unst, Shetland, ZE2 9TJ
☎ **(01957) 711658** 🌐 **valhallabrewery.co.uk**
Tours by arrangement

The brewery started production in 1997, set up by husband and wife team Sonny and Sylvia Priest. A bottling plant was installed in 1999. A new brewery building was opened in 2012, converted from part of the former RAF SaxaVoord camp at Haroldswick.

White Wife (OG 1038, ABV 3.8%)
Predominantly malty aroma with hop and fruit, which remain on the palate. The aftertaste is increasingly bitter.

Old Scatness (OG 1038, ABV 4%)
A light bitter, named after an archaeological dig at the south end of Shetland where early evidence of malting and brewing was found. One of the ingredients is an ancient strain of barley called Bere which used to be common in Shetland until the middle of the last century.

Simmer Dim (OG 1039, ABV 4%)
A light golden ale, named after the long Shetland twilight. The sulphur features do not mask the fruits and hops of this well-balanced beer.

Auld Rock (OG 1043, ABV 4.5%)
A full-bodied, dark Scottish-style best bitter, it has a rich malty nose but does not lack bitterness in the long dry finish.

Sjolmet Stout (OG 1048, ABV 5%)
Full of malt and roast barley, especially in the taste. Smooth, creamy, fruity finish, not as dry as some stouts.

Vens

Unit 3, Clovelly Works, Chelmsford Road, Rawreth, Essex, SS11 8SY
☎ (01268) 574477

Office: 28 Main Road, Hockley, Essex, SS5 4QS
✉ info@vensbrewing.co.uk

Microbrewery started in Essex in 2010 with production of 15 barrels per week. Five regular beers are produced and the brewery now supplies 50 pubs in Essex. Bottle-conditioned beers are available via the brewery shop based in Hockley. Brewing is currently suspended.

Mild (OG 1038, ABV 3.8%)
A smooth, malty dark mild bursting with plenty of roasted flavours and a satisfying finish.

Gold (OG 1040, ABV 4%)
A thirst-quenching refreshing pale golden beer with a well-balanced hop aroma.

Best (OG 1042, ABV 4.2%)
A classic best bitter with well-balanced malt flavours and bitterness.

Suze V (OG 1042, ABV 4.2%)

V4 (OG 1044, ABV 4.4%)

Verulam

Farmers Boy, 134 London Road, St Albans, Hertfordshire, AL1 1PQ
☎ (01727) 860535 farmersboy.co.uk
Tours by arrangement

Established in 1997, Verulam is situated at the rear of the Farmer's Boy and produces beers for the pub, where a selection is always available. Beer is supplied locally and to CAMRA festivals. All beers are also available bottle conditioned. It also brews for the free trade under the Ale Craft name. The brewery is home to two 'cuckoo' breweries: the Private Brewery of Bob and That Little Brewery (qv).

Half Nelson (OG 1029, ABV 2.8%)
A straw-coloured, low gravity beer with a big hop flavour and character.

Black Mild (OG 1033, ABV 3.3%)
Easy-drinking dark mild with rich dark malt tones.

Farmer's Delight (OG 1036, ABV 3.9%)
Straw-coloured beer with a distinct hop aroma and flavour.

Run o't' Mill (OG 1041, ABV 3.9%)
Copper-coloured session beer with a balanced flavour.

Farmer's Joy (OG 1043, ABV 4.5%)
Ruby, almost black beer, with a combination of dark malt roast and citrus hop flavours.

Citra Hit (OG 1046, ABV 4.6%)
Pale ale with a big US West Coast hop character throughout.

High Five (OG 1056, ABV 5.9%)
A combination of five hop varieties gives this IPA a big, generous hop character.

Vibrant Forest SIBA

Unit 3, Gordleton Business Park, Lymington, Hampshire, SO41 8JD
☎ (023) 8066 9204 vibrantforest.co.uk
Shop Mon-Sat 10am-7pm

Located in the New Forest, Vibrant Forest began brewing commercially in 2011 using a one-barrel plant. This award-winning brewery has progressed to a 10-barrel capacity and now produces bottle-conditioned ales as well as cask ales.

Nova Foresta (OG 1038, ABV 3.8%)
An amber, hoppy bitter.

Flying Saucer (OG 1042, ABV 4.3%)
A full-flavoured golden ale with fruity, floral and citrus-like flavours. Fresh and hoppy with a long bitter finish.

Farmhouse Ale (ABV 5%)
A light golden ale with slightly peppery and spicy aromas, subtle bitter and fruity flavours and a dry finish.

Pale Ale (OG 1046, ABV 5%)
A bitter and crisp blonde ale with distinctive tropical notes of lychee, mango and passion fruit.

Victory Beers

See Sperrin

Village Brewer

See Hambleton

Violet Cottage

Gwaelod-y-Garth Inn, Main Road, Gwaelod-y-Garth, CF15 9HH
☎ (029) 2081 0408

Brewery established in 2012 in a converted outbuilding at the rear of the Gwaelod-y-Garth Inn, within the grounds of the licensee's private house. Licensees, brewers and owners Richard and Barbara use a number of recipes that are subject to experimentation so beer range and availability may change. Most of the production is sold within the pub.

VIP SIBA

Unit E, Hawkshill Business Park, Lesbury, Alnwick, Northumberland, NE66 3PG
☎ (01665) 570268 ☎ 07545 885352
vipbrewery.co.uk

Brewing began in 2012 using a five-barrel plant to serve the owner's pub, the Village Inn in Longframlington, and the local free trade. About 150 outlets are supplied. Further beers are planned.

Village Bike (ABV 4%)
A traditional bitter with a slightly sweet mouthfeel and mild bitter aftertaste.

Village Copper (ABV 4.2%)
A well-balanced, smooth ruby bitter with subtle hints of ginger.

Village Ghost (ABV 4.5%)
A full-flavoured, rich stout with a strong bitterness and coffee and caramel aftertaste.

Wadworth SIBA IFBB

Northgate Brewery, Devizes, Wiltshire, SN10 1JW
☎ (01380) 723361 wadworth.co.uk
Shop Mon-Sat 10am-5pm

Tours by arrangement

Established in 1885 by Henry Wadworth, this impressive market town brewery is one of few remaining producers to sell beer locally in oak casks. Traditional horse-powered drays deliver beer daily around Devizes. It has 250 pubs throughout southern England. Seasonal beers: see website.

Henry's IPA (OG 1035, ABV 3.6%)
A classic session beer with malt-led flavours.

Horizon (OG 1039, ABV 4%)
A pale gold beer with zesty citrus and hop aromas and a crisp, tangy finish on the palate.

6X (OG 1040.5, ABV 4.1%)
Copper-coloured ale with a malty and fruity nose, and some balancing hop character. The flavour is similar, with some bitterness and a lingering malty, but bitter finish.

Bishops Tipple (OG 1048, ABV 5%)
A golden brew giving well-balanced hop bitterness and a clean finish.

Swordfish (OG 1049, ABV 5%)
A full-bodied, deep copper coloured ale flavoured with Pussers Rum.

Waen SIBA

Unit 7, Maesyllan Industrial Estate, Llanidloes, Powys, SY18 6YU
(01686) 627042 thewaenbrewery.co.uk
Shop Fri-Sat 10am-5pm
Tours by arrangement

Waen began brewing in 2009 on a five-barrel plant in Penstrowed. Increased demand saw the brewery move to its current address. 100 outlets are supplied direct. Seasonal beers are available.

TWA (Traditional Welsh Ale) (OG 1036, ABV 3.7%)
A complex yet balanced pale ale.

Pamplemousse (OG 1040, ABV 4.2%)
A pale ale, fresh and zingy with a lingering finish.

Landmark (OG 1052, ABV 5.5%)
An IPA with full on hop bitterness and a crisp citrus bite.

Chilli Plum Porter (OG 1065, ABV 6.1%)
A fruity porter with rich, dark fruit flavours and a warm chilli tingle.

Wagtail

New Barn Farm, Wilby Warrens, Old Buckenham, Norfolk, NR17 1PF
(01953) 887133 wagtailbrewery.com

Wagtail Brewery went into full-time production in 2006. All beers are now only available bottle-conditioned and all are suitable for vegetarians and vegans: see website for full range.

Wainstones SIBA

Unit 9, Terry Dicken Industrial Estate, Station Road, Stokesley, North Yorkshire, TS9 7AE 07885 240226
stokesleybrewing.co.uk

Wainstones began brewing in 2010 using a 2.5 barrel plant set up in a small industrial unit in Stokesley, trading as the Stokesley Brewing Company.

Amber (OG 1038, ABV 3.8%)
Distinctive light golden ale with moderate bitterness and a pleasant floral nose.

Sandstone (OG 1040, ABV 4%)
Traditional brown-coloured ale with moderate bitterness and a pleasant aftertaste.

Ironstone (OG 1042, ABV 4.2%)
A classic rich and full-flavoured ale made with English malts and complex hops giving a smooth aftertaste.

Copper (OG 1043, ABV 4.3%)
A copper-coloured ale hopped with Cascade and Galena hops.

Steel River (OG 1043, ABV 4.3%)
Traditional chestnut-coloured ale with medium bitterness, full of flavour from the American hops.

Jet (OG 1045, ABV 4.5%)
An unusual black ale full of flavour with a hoppy aftertaste.

Transporter (OG 1045, ABV 4.5%)
A dark porter with a creamy head and a deep malty taste.

Wall's

1 Binks Close, Standard Way Business Park, Northallerton, North Yorkshire, DL6 2YB
(01609) 258226 info@wallsbrewery.co.uk
Tours by arrangement

Brewing began in 2011 on a 5.5-barrel plant. Beers can be found in more than 100 local outlets along with a range of bottle-conditioned ales. Seasonal beers are available.

County Best (OG 1034, ABV 3.2%)

Summer Gold (OG 1036, ABV 3.6%)

Gun Dog Bitter (OG 1039, ABV 3.8%)

Keepers Gold (OG 1039, ABV 3.9%)

Brewers Gold (OG 1039, ABV 4%)
A golden, malty-flavoured session beer.

Northallerton Dark (OG 1040, ABV 4.4%)
Dark ale brewed with chocolate malt and First Gold hops for an orange finish.

The Darkside (OG 1040, ABV 4.4%)
A milk stout, creamy with a soft, sweet taste followed by a light bitterness.

Beaters Choice (OG 1050, ABV 4.6%)

Explorer IPA (OG 1050, ABV 4.7%)

Wantsum SIBA

Units 22 & 23, Sparrow Way, Lakesview International Business Park, Hersden, Kent, CT3 4AL
(0845) 040 5980 wantsumbrewery.co.uk
Tours by arrangement

Wantsum was established in 2009 by James Sandy and takes its name from the nearby Wantsum Channel. In 2012 a new plant was installed which increased brewing capacity to 12 barrels. Around 60 outlets are supplied mainly in East Kent. Seasonal and bottle-conditioned beers are available.

More's Head (OG 1034, ABV 3.5%)
A chestnut-coloured bitter with malt and roasted grains balanced against fruit and floral hops with a hint of citrus.

1381 (OG 1036, ABV 3.8%)
A light amber-coloured IPA with delicate citrus and herbal aromas.

Black Prince (OG 1036.5, ABV 3.9%)
A rich, full-bodied Kent mild, smooth on the palate with subtle hop notes.

Imperium (OG 1037, ABV 4%)
A deep amber best bitter; smooth biscuit malts and rich hoppy nose balance this beer perfectly.

Fortitude (OG 1039, ABV 4.2%)
This bitter combines four types of malt to give depth of body with a pronounced hop finish.

Miller's Mirth (OG 1039, ABV 4.2%)
A copper-coloured floral and spicy bitter with a smooth hop finish.

Turbulent Priest (OG 1041, ABV 4.4%)
A full-bodied best bitter offering chocolate and coffee notes on top of a sweet malt base. New World hops give the beer bitterness tempered with deep fruity hop aromas.

One Hop (OG 1042, ABV 4.5%)
Single-hop beer – changes every couple of months.

Dynamo (OG 1043, ABV 4.6%)
A crisp, light, golden ale, fruity and floral with an orange citrus twist.

Black Pig (OG 1044, ABV 4.8%)
Adapted from a Russian Imperial porter recipe, this beer is smooth with burnt chocolate and smoky malt notes mixed with delicate hop bitterness and floral notes.

Hengist (OG 1045, ABV 5%)
A golden pale ale with flavours of biscuit malt balancing a long, deep, mellow fruity nose.

Golgotha (OG 1047, ABV 5.5%)
A rich, deep and broad malt base gives this stout a long smooth finish. Hops are prominent on the nose with blackcurrant, liquorice and cedar.

Ravening Wolf (OG 1052, ABV 5.9%)
A light amber strong pale ale; toasted biscuit and rye malt flavours support a pine lemon hop crispness with a hint of vanilla.

Wapping

Baltic Fleet, 33a Wapping, Liverpool, L1 8DQ
☎ (0151) 709 3116 ⊕ balticfleetpubliverpool.com

Wapping brewery was established in 2002 in the cellars of the pub on the waterfront in Liverpool using the old Passageway Brewery plant. Stan Shaw, the brewer since inception stood down in 2014, with his assistant Angus Morrison stepping into the role.

Bitter (OG 1036, ABV 3.6%)

Baltic Gold (OG 1039, ABV 3.9%) ◆
Hoppy golden ale with plenty of citrus hop flavour. Refreshing with good body and mouthfeel.

Warcop

c/o 9 Nellive Park, St Brides Wentlooge, NP10 8SE
☎ (01633) 680058 ⊕ warcopales.com
Tours by arrangement

A small brewery based in a converted milking parlour. Beers are also available bottle conditioned. The brewery has a portfolio of 28 beers that are made on a cyclical basis, with two to four beers normally in stock at any one time. Brewing is currently suspended.

Warwickshire SIBA

The Bakehouse Brewery, Queen Street, Cubbington, Warwickshire, CV32 7NA
☎ (01926) 450747 ⊕ warwickshirebeer.co.uk
Shop open most days inc Sat am (please ring first)

A six-barrel brewery in a former village bakery that has been in operation since 1998. Beers are available in more than 100 outlets and the brewery's four pubs.

Castle Mild (OG 1034, ABV 3.4%)
A dark mild with fruity overtones and a hoppy finish.

Shakespeare's County (OG 1034, ABV 3.4%)
A refreshing low gravity golden ale.

Bottoms Up (OG 1036, ABV 3.6%)
A light, easy-drinking beer with a slightly spicy and delicate floral smooth bitterness.

Lazy Cow (OG 1036, ABV 3.6%)

Best Bitter (OG 1039, ABV 3.9%)
An easy-drinking golden brown session beer, with a malty flavour and a gentle bitterness which becomes more assertive in the aftertaste.

Darling Buds (OG 1041, ABV 4%)

Fat Pug (OG 1042, ABV 4.2%)

I Am Angus (OG 1047, ABV 4.7%)

Golden Bear (OG 1049, ABV 4.9%)
An assertive golden brown beer characterised by a long-lasting slightly resiny bitterness. The finish is fruity and warming with hints of spice and orange.

Kingmaker (OG 1055, ABV 5.5%)
A rich, fruity Christmas cake of a beer, ruddy brown in colour. A grainy spirit-like aroma leads onto a palate with overtones of whisky, orange and dark chocolate. A warming alcoholic finish.

Watermill SIBA

Ings, Cumbria, LA8 9PY
☎ (01539) 821309 ⊕ lakelandpub.co.uk
Tours by arrangement

Watermill was established in 2006 in a purpose-built extension to the inn. The beers have a doggie theme, dogs being very welcome in the pub. The brewery was extended in 2008 with a new brewery planned within the grounds. The beers are also sold under the Windermere Brewing Co name.

Collie Wobbles (OG 1037.5, ABV 3.7%)
A pale gold bitter with a slight citrus taste. A good hop and malt balance gives way to a dry finish.

Black Beard (OG 1038, ABV 3.8%)
A dark mild with bags of fruit and malt flavours.

A Bit'er Ruff (OG 1041.5, ABV 4.1%) ◆
Copper-coloured, balanced fruity beer with a lingering, bitter aftertaste.

Ruff Justice (OG 1041, ABV 4.2%)
A malty golden ale, well-balanced with caramel, light floral hops and a fresh, dry finish.

Windermere Blonde (OG 1041.5, ABV 4.2%)

Isle of Dogs (OG 1044, ABV 4.5%)

A golden bitter with a fresh, malty aroma and a distinctive citrus fruity flavour with an intense, dry aftertaste.

Wruff Night (OG 1047.5, ABV 5%) ◆
Straw-coloured, sweet and fruity, uncomplicated beer with bitterness in a short-lived aftertaste.

Dogth Vader (OG 1050, ABV 5.1%)
A dark, hoppy ale with a refreshing, dry finish.

Brewed under the Windermere Brewing Co name:

Orrest Head (OG 1037.5, ABV 3.7%)

Golden (OG 1041.5, ABV 4.2%)

Belle Isle Bitter (OG 1044, ABV 4.5%)

Tomos Watkin SIBA

Unit 3, Alberto Road, Century Park, Valley Way, Swansea Enterprise Park, Swansea, SA6 8RP
☎ (01792) 797300 🌐 tomoswatkin.com
Shop Mon-Fri 9am-5pm
Tours by arrangement

Brewing started in 1995 in converted garages in Llandeilo using a 10-barrel plant. The brewery moved to bigger premises in Swansea in 2000 and the plant increased to a 50-barrel capacity. Over 60% of production is bottled beers (not bottle conditioned). More than 600 outlets are currently supplied.

Cwrw Braf (OG 1038, ABV 3.7%)
A clean-drinking, amber-coloured ale with a light bitterness and gentle hop aroma.

Blodwens Beer (OG 1045, ABV 4.5%)
Light blonde beer with delicate creamy finish with a hint of citrus.

Old Style Bitter (OSB) (OG 1045, ABV 4.5%) ◆
Amber-coloured with an inviting aroma of hops and malt. Full bodied; hops, fruit, malt and bitterness combine to give a balanced flavour continuing into the finish.

Waveney

Queen's Head, Station Road, Earsham, Norfolk, NR35 2TS
☎ (01986) 892623 ✉ lyndahamps@aol.com

Established at the Queen's Head in 2004, the five-barrel brewery produces three beers, regularly available at the pub along with other free trade outlets. Occasional and seasonal beers are also brewed.

East Coast Mild (OG 1037, ABV 3.8%) ◆
A traditional mild with distinctive roast malt aroma and red-brown colouring. A sweet, plummy malt beginning quickly fades as a dry roasted bitterness begins to make its presence felt.

Lightweight (OG 1039, ABV 3.9%) ◆
A gentle beer with a light but well-balanced hop and malt character. A light body is reflected in the quick, bitter finish. Golden hued with a distinctive strawberry and cream nose.

Welterweight (OG 1042, ABV 4.2%)

Weard'ALE

Hare & Hounds, 24 Front Street, Westgate, County Durham, DL13 1RX
☎ (01388) 517212

Brewing commenced in the Hare & Hounds in 2010. The beers are mainly sold on the premises but some has found its way to nearby beer festivals and other local pubs.

Challenger (OG 1038, ABV 3.8%)
A sharp and tasty bitter.

Gold (OG 1038, ABV 3.8%)
Refreshing beer, light in colour but with surprising body.

Fell Over (ABV 4%)
A mellow and refreshing session bitter.

Chilled Nights (ABV 4.4%)
Dark and full flavoured.

Weatheroak SIBA

Unit 7, Victoria Works, Birmingham Road, Studley, Warwickshire, B80 7AP
☎ (0121) 445 4411 (eve)

Office: Victoria Works, 33 Redditch Rd, Studley, B80 7AU 🌐 weatheroakbrewery.co.uk

The brewery was set up in 1997 at Weatheroak Hill. It is now in a spacious factory unit in Studley. Weatheroak supplies 40 outlets. Seasonal beers are brewed on a regular basis. Its brewery tap is the nearby Victoria Works pub.

St Udley Mild (OG 1034, ABV 3.4%)

Light Oak (OG 1036, ABV 3.6%) ◆
This straw-coloured quaffing ale has lots of hoppy notes on the tongue and nose, and a fleetingly sweet aftertaste.

Tillerman's Tipple (OG 1039, ABV 3.9%)

Ale (OG 1041, ABV 4.1%) ◆
The aroma is dominated by hops in this golden-coloured brew. Hops also feature in the mouth and there is a rapidly fading dry aftertaste.

Victoria Works (OG 1043, ABV 4.3%)
A pale hoppy bitter with a citrus finish.

Redwood (OG 1047, ABV 4.7%)
A rich, tawny-coloured strong but mellow beer with a short-lived sweet fruit and malt balance.

Keystone Hops (OG 1050, ABV 5%) ◆
A golden yellow beer that is surprisingly easy to quaff given the strength. Fruity hops are the dominant flavour without the commonly associated astringency.

Weatheroak Hill SIBA

Coach & Horses, Weatheroak Hill, Worcestershire, B48 7EA
☎ (01564) 823386 (pub)
Tours by arrangement

Weatheroak Hill brews at the busy Coach & Horses pub and restaurant near Alvechurch. The range has increased significantly over the past two years, and currently includes around 10 beers in a wide variety of styles, both regular and seasonal. The beers are brewed mainly for the pub (which usually stocks five), although there are plans to make the beers available more widely.

Gold (OG 1035, ABV 3.5%)

Icknield Pale Ale (OG 1038, ABV 3.8%)

Radford Ale (OG 1040, ABV 4%)

Indian Summer (OG 1042, ABV 4.2%)

WHB (Weatheroak Hill Bitter) (OG 1042, ABV 4.2%)

Dark Horse (OG 1046, ABV 4.6%)

King O' the Hill (OG 1054, ABV 5.4%)

Weetwood SIBA

The Brewery, Common Lane, Kelsall, Cheshire, CW6 0PY
☎ (01829) 752377 ⊕ weetwoodales.co.uk

One of the original Cheshire microbreweries set up at an equestrian centre in 1993. In 2011/12 a new 30-barrel brewery was built on a site around the corner. More than 300 outlets are supplied regularly.

Best Bitter (OG 1038.5, ABV 3.8%) ◆
Pale brown beer with an assertive bitterness and a lingering dry finish. Despite initial sweetness, peppery hops dominate throughout.

Mad Hatter (OG 1038.5, ABV 3.9%)
A red-brown beer with fruity and malty flavours throughout. Brewed with American Amarillo hops to give spicy and floral notes.

Cheshire Cat (OG 1040, ABV 4%) ◆
Pale, dry bitter with a spritzy lemon zest and a grape aroma. Hoppy aroma leads through to the initial taste before fruitiness takes over. Smooth creamy mouthfeel and a short, dry finish.

Eastgate Ale (OG 1043.5, ABV 4.2%) ◆
Well-balanced and refreshing clean amber beer. Citrus fruit flavours predominate in the taste and there is a short, dry aftertaste.

Old Dog Bitter (OG 1045, ABV 4.5%) ◆
Robust, well-balanced amber beer with a slightly fruity aroma. Rich malt and fruit flavours are balanced by bitterness. Some sweetness and a hint of sulphur on nose and taste.

Ambush Ale (OG 1047.5, ABV 4.8%) ◆
Full-bodied malty, premium bitter with initial sweetness balanced by bitterness and leading to a long-lasting dry finish. Blackberries and bitterness predominate alongside the hops.

Oasthouse Gold (OG 1050, ABV 5%) ◆
Straw-coloured, crisp, full-bodied and fruity golden ale with a good dry finish.

Weighbridge SIBA

Penzance Drive, Swindon, Wiltshire, SN5 7JL
☎ (01793) 881500 ⊕ weighbridgebrewhouse.co.uk
Tours by arrangement

⊗ The Weighbridge Brewery forms part of the Weighbridge Brewhouse restaurant and bar, based in the former home of Archer's brewery and once part of Swindon Railway Works. Established in 2011 under the ownership of Anthony and Allyson Windle and with the brewing skills of Mark Wallington, formerly of Archers Brewery, and his assistant Tim Sherod, this microbrewery continues to offer an increasing diverse mix of ales to supplement its core range. Take outs are available.

Brinkworth Village (OG 1038, ABV 3.6%)
A light, hoppy, refreshing ale with a floral, spicy aroma. Easy-drinking session beer.

Best (OG 1044, ABV 4.3%)
Pale with a spicy aroma. A good bitter ale but with a malty aftertaste.

Pooley's Golden (OG 1048, ABV 4.7%)
A robust golden ale, full bodied with plenty of bitterness and an unusual gooseberry aroma. The aftertaste is a good balance of malt and hop.

Weird Beard

Unit 5, Boston Business Park, Trumpers Way, Hanwell, London, W7 2QA
☎ (020) 3645 2711 ⊕ weirdbeardbrewco.com

⊗ Brewing began in 2013 using a 10-barrel plant with two dedicated fermenters on an industrial estate in Hanwell. Beer is mostly bottled, but some is available cask conditioned.

Little Things That Kill (OG 1044, ABV 3.8%)

Black Perle (OG 1058.5, ABV 4.5%) ◆
Coffee milk stout with roast notes throughout this full-flavoured sweetish black beer. Finish has some black roast bitter dryness.

Mariana Trench (OG 1049.3, ABV 5.3%) ◆
Passion fruit and citrus are noticeable throughout this malty, sweet golden beer. Bitterness builds and lingers, overlaid by dryness.

K*ntish Town Beard (OG 1051, ABV 5.4%)

Decadence Stout (OG 1062, ABV 5.5%)

Hit The Lights (OG 1058.8, ABV 5.8%)
A clean, bitter IPA with loads of fruity hop character.

Fade to Black (OG 1064.5, ABV 6.3%) ◆
Balanced black IPA with some fruitiness. The beer contains crystal rye and chocolate malt, which gives roast coffee notes throughout.

Welbeck Abbey SIBA

Lower Motor Yard, Welbeck, Nottinghamshire, S80 3LT
☎ (01909) 512539 ⊕ welbeckabbeybrewery.co.uk
Tours by arrangement

The microbrewery is housed in a listed barn at the centre of the Welbeck Estate – the brew plant was previously used at Kelham Island. The brewery, which opened in 2011, produces a range of different styles of beers. Head brewer Claire Monk trained at the Kelham Island Brewery after studying microbiology at Sheffield University.

Henrietta (OG 1035, ABV 3.6%)
Full of hop character with bitter notes balanced by a citrus and grassy nose.

Red Feather (OG 1040, ABV 3.9%)
A traditional dark amber ale with subtle notes of caramel and toffee.

Harley (OG 1038, ABV 4.3%)

Portland Black (OG 1043, ABV 4.5%)
A rich and smooth black beer, smooth with smoke, liquorice and burnt toffee flavours and a distinctly vanilla nose.

Cavendish (OG 1046, ABV 5%)
A blonde beer laced with zesty notes of grapefruit.

Charles Wells IFBB

Bedford Brewery, Havelock Street, Bedford, MK40 4LU
☎ (01234) 272766 ⊕ charleswells.co.uk
Merchandise available online

Tours by arrangement

Charles Wells has been brewing in Bedford since 1876 when the founder built a brewery on the banks of the Ouse River. It relocated to a new site in Havelock Street in 1976. In 2006 Wells merged its brewing and brands division with Young's of Wandsworth when the London brewery closed and the company became known as Wells & Young's. Both run their own pub estates under their family names. In 2014, however, the brands became wholly owned by Charles Wells, which has restored its original company name. It runs an estate of 200 pubs and brews beers for the Young's pub company. In 2007, Wells bought the Courage brands from Scottish & Newcastle (now Heineken UK) and added the former McEwan's and Younger's brands in 2011. Seasonal beers include Wells Waggle Dance. Bottle-conditioned beers are also available.

Wells Eagle IPA (OG 1035, ABV 3.6%)
A refreshing, amber session bitter with pronounced citrus hop aroma and palate, faint malt in the mouth, and a lasting dry, bitter finish.

Courage Best Bitter (OG 1038.3, ABV 4%)
Malty nose followed by a bitter/fruity palate, finished off with a well-balanced mouthfeel.

McEwans IPA (ABV 4%)

McEwans Amber (ABV 4.1%)

Wells Bombardier (OG 1042, ABV 4.1%)
A heavy aroma of malt and raspberry jam. Traces of hops and bitterness are quickly submerged under a smooth, malty sweetness. A solid, rich finish.

Wells Bombardier Burning Gold (ABV 4.1%)

DNA (ABV 4.5%)
A beer brewed in collaboration with Dogfish Head Brewery in the United States.

Courage Directors (OG 1045.5, ABV 4.8%)
A rich, fruity and full-bodied chestnut-coloured ale.

McEwans Signature (ABV 4.8%)

Brewed under the Young's Brewery name:

Bitter (OG 1036, ABV 3.7%)
This light drinking amber bitter has citrus initially on the palate with sweet malt and a hint of hops that linger into a slightly dry and bitter finish.

London Gold (OG 1038, ABV 4%)
A dark gold beer with a smooth mouthfeel. Citrus and malt in the low aroma, coming through more strongly on the palate and aftertaste with a little peach. Dry finish.

Special (OG 1044, ABV 4.5%)
Pale brown in colour, this rounded best bitter has citrus throughout plus some slight creamy toffee, which balances the bitterness that grows in the aftertaste.

Weltons SIBA

1 Mulberry Trading Estate, Foundry Lane, Horsham, West Sussex, RH13 5PX
(01403) 242901/251873 weltonsbeer.co.uk
Tours by arrangement

Ray Welton moved the brewery into a factory unit in 2003. Over 70 different beers are brewed every year. Pubs throughout the South-east and London are supplied. Bottle-conditioned beers are available and are suitable for vegetarians and vegans.

Pride 'n' Joy (OG 1028, ABV 2.8%)
A light brown bitter with a slight malty and hoppy aroma. Fruity with a pleasant hoppiness and some sweetness in the flavour, leading to a short malty finish.

Horsham Bitter (OG 1038, ABV 3.8%)
Amber-coloured, bitter but with a huge aroma.

Export Stout (OG 1047, ABV 4.7%)
Hints of burnt toast, balanced by good levels of hops with a long finish.

Wensleydale SIBA

Unit F, Manor Road, Bellerby, North Yorkshire, DL8 5QH
(01969) 622463 wensleydalebrewery.co.uk
Shop Mon-Fri 9am-5pm
Tours by arrangement

Wensleydale Brewery was set up in 2003 and currently operates on a five-barrel plant. It was taken over by Geoff Southgate and Carl Gehrman in 2013. Around 100 outlets are supplied direct and most of the regular beers are available in bottles. Seasonal beers: see website.

Lidstone's Rowley Mild (OG 1032, ABV 3.2%)
Chocolate and toffee aromas lead into what, for its strength, is an impressively rich and flavoursome taste. The finish is pleasantly bittersweet.

Bitter (OG 1036, ABV 3.7%)
Intensely aromatic, straw-coloured ale offering a superb balance of malt and hops on the tongue.

Falconer Session Bitter (OG 1038, ABV 3.9%)
A fruity, malt-based session ale, copper in colour, with a long, bitter, dry finish.

Semerwater Summer Ale (OG 1040, ABV 4.1%)
Pale ale with citrus aromas. The clean, hoppy nose is balanced by a light, malty sweetness.

Stuka (OG 1045, ABV 4.2%)
An amber-coloured, well-balanced ale.

Coverdale Gamekeeper (OG 1042, ABV 4.3%)
A copper-coloured best bitter with huge spicy hop flavours and a juicy malt flavour.

Black Dub Oat Stout (OG 1043, ABV 4.4%)
Black, silky and nourishing with a rich concentration of four different malts and oats.

Gold (OG 1044, ABV 4.5%)
Aromatic and spicy hop flavours combine with kilned malts to make a highly quaffable, light golden best bitter.

Coverdale Poacher IPA (OG 1048, ABV 5%)
Citrus flavours dominate both aroma and taste in this pale, smooth, refreshing beer; the aftertaste is quite dry.

Wentwell

Unit 22, Perkins Industrial Estate, Mansfield Road, Derby, DE21 4AW wentwellbrewery.com

Wentwell Brewery is a three-barrel plant established in 2011. Eight regular beers are produced, with occasional seasonals. Several local outlets are supplied, with beers regularly available at the Little Chester Ale House, Derby's first micropub. All beers are available bottle conditioned.

Jeremiah Mild (OG 1035, ABV 3.3%)
Smooth, dark and malty, with a lot of body.

Derby Pale Ale (OG 1039, ABV 3.8%)
A pale, straw-coloured, hoppy bitter.

Derbyshire Gold (OG 1039, ABV 3.9%)
A light, refreshingly hoppy and zesty session beer.

Justice for Gingers (OG 1040, ABV 4%)
A pale bitter infused with ginger.

Little Tick (OG 1040, ABV 4%)
Straw-coloured bitter, triple hopped for a fuller flavour.

Farm Hands' Bitter (OG 1042, ABV 4.1%)
A rich copper-coloured best bitter with a smooth rounded flavour and nicely balanced bitterness.

Barrel Organ Blues (OG 1046, ABV 4.5%)
Golden brown full-bodied premium bitter with a rich malty flavour and aroma.

Nellie's Best (OG 1050, ABV 5.3%)
A full-flavoured best bitter.

Wentworth SIBA

Power House, Gun Park, Wentworth, South Yorkshire, S62 7TF
☎ (01226) 747070 🌐 wentworthbrewery.co.uk
Tours by arrangement

Founded in 1999 in the power house in the grounds of Wentworth Woodhouse, a custom-built 30-barrel brewery was commissioned in 2006, now producing about 4,300 barrels per year. Bottled beers are brewed under the Wentworth and Barnsley Beer Company brands in addition to the seasonal cask range and two monthly specials: see website.

WPA (OG 1039.5, ABV 4%)
A well hopped IPA-style beer that leads to some astringency. An extremely bitter beer.

Wessex

Rye Hill Farm, Longbridge Deverill, Wiltshire, BA12 7DE
☎ (01985) 844532
✉ wessexbrewery@tinyworld.co.uk

The brewery went into production in 2001 and moved to its current location in 2004. 15 local outlets are supplied. Beers are also available through selected wholesalers. Seasonal beers are available. Beers are occasionally contract brewed for the Isle of Avalon brewery.

Potter's Ale (OG 1038, ABV 3.8%)
A classic bitter.

Longleat Pride (OG 1040, ABV 4%)
A pale, hoppy bitter.

White Dwarf (OG 1040, ABV 4%)

Crockerton Classic (OG 1041, ABV 4.1%)
A full-bodied, tawny, full-flavoured bitter; fruity and malty.

Merrie Mink (OG 1041, ABV 4.2%)
A full-flavoured best with a strong hop aroma.

Deverill's Advocate (OG 1046, ABV 4.5%)
A well-balanced golden premium ale.

Warminster Warrior (OG 1045, ABV 4.5%)
Full-flavoured premium bitter.

Golden Apostle (OG 1048, ABV 4.8%)

Galaxy (OG 1050, ABV 5%)

Russian Stoat (OG 1080, ABV 9%)

WEST SIBA

Binnie Place, Glasgow Green, Glasgow, G40 1AW
☎ (0141) 550 0135 🌐 westbeer.com
Tours by arrangement

No real ale. Brewery-bar and restaurant, producing German-style beer to the Bavarian Purity Law. Beers are usually served under pressure, but not pasteurised. Four regular beers are produced along with seasonals.

West Berkshire SIBA

The Flour Barn, Frilsham Home Farm Units, Yattendon, Berkshire, RG18 0XT
☎ (01635) 202968 🌐 wbbrew.com
Shop Mon-Sat 10am-4pm
Tours by arrangement

Established in Frilsham in 1995 and now based on the edge of Yattendon, having moved to a new 50-barrel brewhouse, with office and shop, in 2011. Expanding following investment, brewing is carried out in a sustainable way, with an emphasis on British ingredients. A core range of cask ales supplies the south of England, as well as core and monthly bottled beers available online and in the brewery shop. In 2014, David Bruce, founder of the Firkin brewpub chain and then Slug & Lettuce bars, took over as chairman.

Old Father Thames (OG 1038, ABV 3.4%)
A classic copper-coloured bitter with a yeasty, sweetish, biscuity aroma and a slightly fruity, but bitter flavour. The finish is long, dry and bitter. A complex beer for its strength.

Mr Chubb's Lunchtime Bitter (OG 1040, ABV 3.7%)
A drinkable, balanced session bitter. A malty caramel note dominates aroma and taste and is accompanied by a bittersweet nuttiness and a hoppy aftertaste.

Maggs' Magnificent Mild (OG 1041, ABV 3.8%)
Silky, full-bodied, dark mild with a creamy head. Roast malt aroma is joined in the taste by caramel, sweetness and mild, fruity hoppiness. Aftertaste of roast malt with balancing bitterness.

Mr Swift's Pale Ale (OG 1041.5, ABV 3.8%)
Straw-coloured with fruity aroma and taste. Bitter finish.

Good Old Boy (OG 1043, ABV 4%)
Well-rounded, tawny bitter with malt and hops dominating throughout. A balancing bitterness accompanies the taste and aftertaste.

Dr Hexter's Wedding Ale (OG 1044, ABV 4.1%)
Fruit and hops dominate the aroma and are joined in the taste by a hint of malt. The aftertaste has a pleasant bitter hoppiness.

Full Circle (OG 1047, ABV 4.5%)
A golden ale with a pleasing aroma and taste of bitter hops with a hint of malt. The aftertaste is hoppy and bitter with a rounding note of malt.

Dr Hexter's Healer (OG 1052, ABV 5%)
An amber strong bitter with malt, caramel and hops in the aroma. Taste is a balance of malt, caramel, fruit, hops and bittersweetness. Caramel, fruit and bittersweetness dominate the aftertaste.

Westerham SIBA

Grange Farm, Pootings Road, Crockham Hill, Kent, TN8 6SA
☎ (01732) 864427 🌐 westerhambrewery.co.uk
Shop: Mon-Fri 10am-5pm; Beer Discoveries: Mon-Thu 10am-8pm, Fri-Sat 10am-9pm, Sun 11am-8pm
Tours by arrangement

The brewery was established in 2004 at the National Trust's Grange Farm, and is housed in a former dairy. Around 200 outlets are supplied in Kent, Surrey, Sussex and South London. Monthly specials: see website. Bottle-conditioned beers are available.

Finchcocks Original (OG 1036.2, ABV 3.5%)
Mid-gold session beer. Citrus notes on the palate with a hint of biscuit and resiny hoppiness.

Grasshopper (OG 1039, ABV 3.8%)
A dark, malty bitter with nutty, roasted notes from the chocolate malt.

William Wilberforce Freedom Ale (OG 1040, ABV 4%)
Deep golden ale with a mellow bitterness and long, hoppy finish.

British Bulldog (OG 1043.5, ABV 4.3%)
A rich, full-bodied best bitter with a massive aroma and palate of jammy fruit, biscuity malt and bitter hop resins.

1965 (OG 1047.5, ABV 4.8%)
A clean, refreshing bitter with a full-bodied flavour.

Hop Rocket IPA (OG 1047, ABV 4.8%)
Traditional IPA with plum jam and blackcurrant aroma and palate, balanced by sappy malt and a long, lingering bitter, fruity finish.

Audit Ale (OG 1061, ABV 6.2%)
Hoppy, strong and bitter.

Brewed for the Spirit Pub Company:

1730 Special Ale (OG 1040, ABV 4%)
Flavours of lemon balm, honey and blackcurrant merged with grassy, earthy and botanical tones to create a well-balanced ale. Brewed to an old Taylor Walker recipe.

Whale SIBA

Unit 5b, Brailes Industrial Estate, Brailes, Warwickshire, OX15 5JW
☎ (01608) 686974 🌐 whaleale.co.uk

Whale Ale started brewing in 2013 using 100% British ingredients with no artificial additives.

Pale Whale (ABV 3.6%)
A grapefruit, zesty blonde ale with honey, citrus and tropical fruit aroma.

Ruby Moby (ABV 4%)
A nutty, sweet session ale with a malty, fruity aroma.

Premium Amber (ABV 4.3%)

Whalebone

163 Wincolmlee, Hull, East Yorkshire, HU2 0PA
☎ (01482) 226648

The Whalebone pub, which dates from 1796, was bought by Hull CAMRA founding member Alex Craig in 2002. He opened the brewery the following year and his beers have names connected with the former whaling industry on the adjoining River Hull. Two or three outlets are supplied as well as the pub.

Diana Mild (OG 1037, ABV 3.5%)

Neckoil Bitter (OG 1039, ABV 3.9%)

Whaley Bridge (NEW)

Elnor Avenue, Whaley Bridge, Derbyshire, SK23 7JR
☎ 07890 455279 🌐 whaleybridgebrewery.co.uk

Whaley Bridge Brewery was set up by a former home brewer and launched commercially in 2012. A one-barrel, purpose-built plant was installed in a workshop at the rear of the owner's premises supplying local free houses and eateries. Bottle-conditioned beers are available.

Hockerley Old Ale (OG 1040, ABV 4%)
A ruby ale, fruity with a hoppy aroma and a hint of treacle.

Bugsworth Ale (OG 1042, ABV 4.2%)
Fruity and flowery, with a hint of spice and a hoppy finish.

Goyt Valley Gold (OG 1044, ABV 4.4%)
A golden ale, earthy with slightly spicy notes.

Stoneheads (OG 1047, ABV 4.8%)
American and Slovenian hops and a blend of malt and wheat give a taste of citrus, a honey finish and a hoppy aroma. Complex.

Rapa Nui (OG 1047, ABV 4.9%)
A pale amber ale with subtle spice and a hint of orange.

Wharfe Bank SIBA

Unit 4, Pool Business Park, Pool Road, Pool-in-Wharfedale, West Yorkshire, LS21 1EG
☎ (0113) 284 2392 🌐 wharfebankbrewery.co.uk
Tours by arrangement

Wharfe Bank commenced brewing in 2010 using a 20-barrel plant in a converted paper mill on the banks of the River Wharfe. The regular range of beers is complemented by two distinct series of monthly specials often featuring unusual ingredients or rare beer styles. A separate range of beers is also brewed under the Firestorm Brewing Company brand name.

Printers Ink (OG 1037.5, ABV 3.7%)
Rich dark mild with caramel flavours and subtle hops notes.

Washburn Best (OG 1036, ABV 3.7%)
A balance of malt and hop flavours along with bitterness is present throughout this subtle copper-coloured beer.

Tether Blond (OG 1039, ABV 3.8%)
A moderately hopped smooth, fruity light ale with some sweetness, the fruit flavours continue to the gentle finish.

Slingers Gold (OG 1038, ABV 3.9%)
Golden-coloured session ale with fruit and hops carrying some fruity bitterness to the short finish.

Othelia Gold (OG 1046, ABV 4.5%)
Strong golden ale with floral aroma, balanced malt and hop flavour and a refreshing finish.

Yorkshire IPA (OG 1052, ABV 5.1%)
Strong IPA brewed using only English hops.

Wharfedale SIBA

Back Barn, 16 Church Street, Ilkley, West Yorkshire, LS29 9DS
☎ (01943) 609587 wharfedalebrewery.com

Wharfedale began brewing in 2012 using spare capacity at Five Towns Brewery in Wakefield. Brewing moved to Ilkley in 2013 using a 2.5-barrel plant. Further beers are planned.

Black (OG 1037, ABV 3.7%)
A smooth, well-balanced beer with lasting flavour. Subtle hints of chocolate, coffee and liquorice come together in this rich dark mild.

Blonde (OG 1039, ABV 3.9%)
A straw-coloured session blonde ale with lingering citrus/grapefruit flavours and a fresh, satisfying, bitter finish

Best (OG 1040, ABV 4%)
A traditional chestnut-coloured Yorkshire bitter. Subtle malt flavours give way to a floral spicy hoppiness and a mild bitter finish.

Whim SIBA

Whim Farm, Hartington, Derbyshire, SK17 0AX
☎ (01298) 84991 info@whimales.co.uk

Whim opened in 1993 in outbuildings at Whim Farm. The beers are available in 50-70 outlets and the brewery's tied house, Wilkes Head in Leek. Occasional/seasonal beers are available.

Arbor Light (OG 1035, ABV 3.6%)
Light-coloured bitter, sharp and clean with lots of hop character and a delicate light aroma.

Hartington Bitter (OG 1039, ABV 4%)
A light, golden-coloured, well-hopped session beer. A dry finish with a spicy, floral aroma.

Hartington IPA (OG 1045, ABV 4.5%)
Pale and light-coloured, smooth on the palate allowing malt to predominate. Slightly sweet finish combined with distinctive light hop bitterness. Well rounded.

Flower Power (OG 1053, ABV 5.3%)
Light, golden-coloured beer with a flowery hop aroma, citrus with mild spice on the palate and a dry, bitter finish.

Whistling Kite SIBA

35a Buccleuch Street, Kettering, Northamptonshire, NN16 9EE ☎ 07891 956055

Office: 23 New Road, Geddington, Northamptonshire, NN14 1AT phillipsjez@aol.com

Whistling Kite was established by Jez Phillips in 2013 using a six-barrel plant.

Wet Your Whistle (OG 1040, ABV 3.8%)
Flavoursome, mahogany-coloured session bitter.

Eleanor's Ise (OG 1041, ABV 4.2%)
Pale golden ale brewed with lager hops.

Whitby SIBA

Unit 2b, Larpool Lane Industrial Estate, Whitby, North Yorkshire, YO22 4LX ☎ 07516 116377
whitby-brewery.com

Whitby Brewery was established in 2012 under the Conquest name by a local team who built the brewery from scratch. Local outlets are supplied.

Abbey Blonde (OG 1036, ABV 3.6%)
A golden blonde ale with a zesty finish and strong notes of toffee.

Whaler (OG 1040, ABV 4%)
A fruity pale ale with a malty, citrus flavour and a bitter finish.

Saltwick Nab (OG 1044, ABV 4.2%)
A full-bodied ruby red ale with a pleasantly fruity finish.

Black Death (OG 1045, ABV 4.5%)

Jet Black (OG 1047, ABV 4.5%)
A well-balanced porter packed with liquorice, coffee and sweet toffee.

Brewed for the Station Inn, Whitby:

Platform 3 (OG 1038, ABV 3.6%)
Nutty pale ale with a smooth citrus finish.

White Horse SIBA

3 Ware Road, White Horse Business Park, Stanford-in-the-Vale, Oxfordshire, SN7 8NY
☎ (01367) 718700 breweryoxfordshire.co.uk
Shop Mon-Fri 9am-5pm, Sat 8am-12pm
Tours by arrangement

White Horse was founded in 2004. The brewery now has its own pubs in Oxford and Banbury as well as supplying outlets nationally. Four seasonal beers are brewed: see website.

Bitter (OG 1038.7, ABV 3.7%)
Golden bitter, well-hopped with a clean, fruity finish.

Black Beauty (OG 1043.2, ABV 3.9%)
Rich, deep ruby mild.

Village Idiot (OG 1041.8, ABV 4.1%)
A blonde ale with a complex hop aroma and taste.

Wayland Smithy (OG 1047.1, ABV 4.4%)
A red-brown ale with a biscuit flavour that is balanced with a spicy hop finish.

Black Horse Porter (OG 1048.5, ABV 5%)
Dark red porter with a chocolate character and a fruity/berry hop aroma and taste.

Guv'nor (OG 1063.1, ABV 6.5%)
A light golden strong ale with a fruity finish.

White Park SIBA

Perry Hill Farm, Bourne End Road, Cranfield, Bedfordshire, MK43 0BA
☎ (01223) 911357 whiteparkbrewery.co.uk

White Park is a family business established in 2007 on a five-barrel plant. Spent malt is recycled as feed for rare breed cattle. 60 outlets are supplied direct. In 2009 the brewery began bottling and supplies pubs and local stores including Budgens. Seasonal beers: see website.

First Flight (OG 1036, ABV 3.7%)

White Gold (OG 1037, ABV 3.8%)

Bedford Best (OG 1040.5, ABV 4.1%)
Traditional best bitter, smooth and slightly biscuity with a balanced bitterness.

Cranfield Bitter (OG 1042.5, ABV 4.4%)
Amber and malty full-flavoured bitter.

Kellyhopter (ABV 4.8%)

Light yellow-coloured malt-based ale with four varieties of hop.

GB (OG 1047, ABV 5%)

Moonshine (OG 1050, ABV 5.2%)

White Rock (NEW)

Units 6 & 7, Dysons Complex, Southside, St Sampson, Guernsey, GY2 4QJ ☎ 07911 760302
🌐 whiterockbrewery.gg

White Rock began brewing in 2013, making it the second brewery on Guernsey along with Randalls. It prides itself on using locally-sourced ingredients.

Wonky Donkey (ABV 4.7%)

Lost Tourist (ABV 5.3%)
A hoppy IPA.

White Rose SIBA

c/o 119 Chapel Road, Burncross, Chapeltown, Sheffield, South Yorkshire, S35 1QL
☎ (0114) 297 6150
✉ whiterose.brewery@btinternet.com
Tours by arrangement

Gary Sheriff, former head brewer at Wentworth brewery, set up White Rose in 2007. It shares the Little Ale Cart Brewery's premises behind the Wellington in Sheffield. Some equipment is used jointly but White Rose uses its own fermenters.

Original Blonde (OG 1040, ABV 4%)

Stairway to Heaven (OG 1044, ABV 4.3%)

Raven (ABV 4.6%)

Whitewater

40 Tullyframe Road, Kilkeel, Co Down, Northern Ireland, BT34 4RZ
☎ (028) 4176 9449 🌐 whitewaterbrewery.com
Tours by arrangement

Set up in 1996, Whitewater is now the biggest brewery in Northern Ireland. One pub is owned, the White Horse in Saintfield, Co. Down. An expanding range of occasional and seasonal beers is available.

Copperhead (OG 1037, ABV 3.7%)

Crown & Glory (OG 1038, ABV 3.8%)

Belfast Black (OG 1042, ABV 4.2%)

Belfast Ale (OG 1046, ABV 4.5%)

Clotworthy Dobbin (OG 1050, ABV 5%)

Whitstable SIBA

Little Telpits Farm, Woodcock Lane, Grafty Green, Kent, ME17 2AY
☎ (01622) 851007 🌐 whitstablebrewery.info

Whitstable Brewery was founded in 2003. It currently provides all the beer for the Whitstable Oyster Company's three restaurants and hotel as well as a brewery tap plus supplying pubs in Kent, London and Surrey.

Native Bitter (OG 1036, ABV 3.7%) ◆
A classic copper-coloured Kentish session bitter with hoppy aroma and a long, dry bitter hop finish.

Renaissance Ruby Mild (OG 1038, ABV 3.7%)
Deep ruby in colour, this classic mild has a nutty taste with a gentle roast malt aroma.

East India Pale Ale (OG 1040, ABV 4.1%) ◆
A well-hopped golden IPA with good grapefruit hop character and lingering bitter finish.

Oyster Stout (OG 1045, ABV 4.5%)
Rich, dry, deep chocolate and mocha flavours.

Pearl of Kent (OG 1043, ABV 4.5%)
A light-coloured, well-rounded premium beer with tropical fruit flavours.

Winkle Picker (OG 1042, ABV 4.5%)
A well-balanced amber best bitter. Pleasant maltiness offset by a firm but not overpowering bitterness and orange flavours.

Kentish Reserve (OG 1047, ABV 5%)
Reddish amber-coloured strong bitter. Malty notes with flavours of peaches and plums, ending on a note of rich ruby port.

Whittingtons SIBA

Three Choirs Vineyards Ltd, Newent, Gloucestershire, GL18 1LS
☎ (01531) 890555 🌐 three-choirs-vineyards.co.uk/wine/beers
Shop 9am-5pm daily (later during summer)
Tours by arrangement

Whittingtons started in 2003 using a purpose-built, five-barrel plant producing 20 barrels a week. The legendary Dick Whittington came from nearby Pauntley, hence the name and feline theme. The beers are available cask conditioned, in Party 9s and as bottle-conditioned ales, from the onsite shop, online and from local outlets.

Whittlebury

See Towcester Mill

Whitworth SIBA

c/o 34 Dunard Road, Shirley, West Midlands, B90 2HR
☎ (0121) 347 6450 🌐 whitworthbrewing.co.uk

Whitworth is a family-run brewery established commercially in 2012 using a five-barrel plant, brewing twice a week. It supplies local pubs and beer festivals and is expanding into the Black Country area. The brewery was inspired by CAMRA's LocAle scheme.

Sobriety Blonde (OG 1037, ABV 3.6%)
A light blonde ale packed with American hops, with a fruity taste and tangerine notes. Refreshing and light.

Sobriety MPH (OG 1037, ABV 3.7%)
A refreshing dark brown mild with roast malt notes.

Crooked Elbow (OG 1039, ABV 3.9%)
A roasted chestnut brown beer with warm roasted malt notes.

Sobriety (OG 1040, ABV 4%)
A golden beer with floral hops and sweet toffee notes. Full-bodied with citrus flavours and a lasting finish.

Doolally Tap (OG 1058, ABV 5.7%)
A well-rounded yet delicate dark amber ale with a bittersweet, lasting hop finish.

Why Not

27 Redfern Road, Norwich, NR7 9RB
☎ (01603) 300786 ⊕ thewhynotbrewery.co.uk

Why Not opened in 2006 with equipment located in a custom-built wooden unit. The brewery can produce up to two barrels per brew. All beers are available in bottle-conditioned form and are occasionally put into casks to order.

Wally's Revenge (OG 1040, ABV 4%) ◆
A bitter beer with a hoppy background. The bitterness holds on to the end as an increasing astringent dryness develops.

Roundhead Porter (OG 1045, ABV 4.5%)
A traditional old-style London porter.

Cavalier Red (OG 1047, ABV 4.7%) ◆
Explosive fruity nose belies the gentleness of the taste. The summer fruit aroma dominates this red-gold brew. A sweet, fruity start disappears under a quick, bitter ending.

Norfolk Honey Ale (OG 1050, ABV 5%)
A golden beer with a honey nose. A definite hop edge leaves a honey aftertaste.

Chocolate Nutter (OG 1056, ABV 5.5%)

Wibblers SIBA

Joyces Farm, Southminster Road, Mayland, Essex, CM3 6EB
☎ (01621) 772044 ⊕ wibblers.com
Shop Mon-Fri 9am-4pm
Tours by arrangement

⊗ Wibblers was established in 2007 and expanded to a 20-barrel plant in 2009. Production is currently 45 barrels per week. More than 100 outlets are supplied including many of the Gray & Sons pubs. Seasonal and special beers: see website. Bottle-conditioned beers are available.

Dengie IPA (OG 1037, ABV 3.6%)
Malty and full flavoured with gentle bitterness and balanced sweetness.

Apprentice (OG 1039, ABV 3.9%)
Amber session beer with a hoppy aroma and light, malty taste.

Dengie Dark (OG 1039, ABV 4%)
Smooth, light malty beer with subtle bitterness and balancing sweetness.

Dengie Gold (OG 1040, ABV 4%)
Golden with a refreshing hop punch providing a citrus aroma and balanced bitterness.

Hop Black (OG 1041, ABV 4%)
A dark bitter that tastes light and hoppy.

Dengie Best (OG 1041, ABV 4.1%)
A pale ale with a balance of malty mouthfeel and peppery bitterness.

Crafty Stoat (OG 1056, ABV 5.3%)

Wicked Hathern

See Staffordshire

Wickwar SIBA

Old Brewery, Station Road, Wickwar, Gloucestershire, GL12 8NB
☎ (01454) 292000 ⊕ wickwarbrewing.com
Shop Tue-Fri 10am-6pm, Sat 10am-4pm (Tel 01454 299592)
Tours by arrangement

Wickwar was established as a 10-barrel brewery in 1990. In 2004 it expanded to 50 barrels. 350 outlets are supplied on a regular basis and the beers are available nationally through most distributors and SIBA. Seasonal beers are brewed.

Coopers WPA (OG 1036, ABV 3.5%) ◆
Golden-coloured, this well-balanced beer is light and refreshing, with hops, citrus fruit, apple/pear flavour and notable pale malt character. Bitter, dry finish.

Bankers Draft (OG 1040, ABV 4%)
This amber-coloured beer has a fruity citrus aroma. A biscuit malt flavour leads to a floral, crisp and clean finish.

BOB (Brand Oak Bitter) (OG 1040, ABV 4%) ◆
Amber-coloured with a distinctive blend of hop, malt and apple/pear citrus fruits. The slightly sweet taste turns into a fine, dry bitterness, with a similar malty-lasting finish.

Real Stout (OG 1041, ABV 4%)
A smooth, dark and drinkable stout. The coffee and chocolate notes from roasted grain support hints of fresh mown grass and mint delivered by English hops.

Cotswold Way (OG 1042, ABV 4.2%) ◆
Amber-coloured, it has a pleasant aroma of pale malt, hop and fruit. Good dry bitterness in the taste with some sweetness. Similar though less sweet in the finish, with good hop content.

Rite Flanker (OG 1043, ABV 4.3%)
A powerful fruity body is supported by a hoppy nose.

Gold (OG 1046, ABV 4.5%)
A clean, fresh blonde ale. Blackcurrant and spicy palate with a herbal and floral aroma.

Wild Beer (NEW) SIBA

Lower Westcombe Farm, Evercreech, Somerset, BA4 6ER
☎ (01749) 838742 ⊕ wildbeerco.com

Brewing began in 2012 using a 24-hectolitre plant. Cask, keg and bottle-conditioned beers are available including seasonal brews.

Bibble (ABV 4.2%)

Scarlet Fever (ABV 4.8%)

Fresh (ABV 5.5%)

Madness IPA (ABV 6.8%)

Wild Boar (NEW) SIBA

Wild Boar, Crook Road, Bowness-on-Windermere, Cumbria, LA23 3NF ☎ 08458 504604
✉ thewildboar@englishlakes.co.uk

Large, traditional Lakeland Inn in a luxury hotel style with its own microbrewery, on which brewing began in 2013.

Wild Card

Unit 7, Ravenswood Industrial Estate, Shernhall Street, Walthamstow, London, E17 9HQ ☎ 07982 402650 ⊕ wildcardbrewery.co.uk

Wild Card began brewing in 2013, initially using spare capacity at several breweries in and around London, now using its own six-barrel plant in Walthamstow.

Jack of Clubs (ABV 4.5%)
Initially malty but the hops and bitter flavours develop on drinking in the red-coloured beer. Traces of blackberries.

Queen of Diamonds (ABV 5%)
An IPA with complex citrus flavours and a bitter edge.

Wild Weather SIBA

Unit 19, Easter Park, Benyon Road, Silchester, Hampshire, RG7 2PQ
☎ (0118) 970 1837 ⊕ wildweatherales.com
Shop Fri pm, Sat am

Wild Weather was established in 2013 on the Hampshire/Berkshire border. American and New World hops are used to create distinctive ales. Bottle-conditioned beers are available.

Sundowner (OG 1035, ABV 3.4%)
A light golden beer with subtle floral and fruity notes.

Big Muddy (OG 1038, ABV 3.8%)
Tawny session beer where smooth malty bitterness combines with floral spicy and mild citrus hoppy overtones.

Black Night (OG 1039, ABV 3.9%)
A dark mild with a light taste that rapidly develops into a complex blend of rich malt and hop flavours and a hint of caramel. The aftertaste is long, dry, hoppy and toasty.

Little Wind (OG 1042, ABV 4.2%)
A deep amber ale with a touch of copper.

Stormbringer (OG 1044, ABV 4.5%)
Malty and hoppy.

Shepherd's Warning (OG 1056, ABV 5.6%)
A smooth, rich IPA with a hit of hoppy grapefruit, peach and mango flavours.

Williams SIBA

New Alloa Brewery, Kelliebank, Alloa, FK10 1NT
☎ (01259) 725511 ⊕ williamsbrosbrew.com
Tours by arrangement

Brothers Bruce and Scott Williams started brewing Heather Ale in 1993. A range of indigenous, historic ales have since been added. Hundreds of cask ale outlets are supplied worldwide. Seasonal beers: see website.

Gold (OG 1040, ABV 3.9%)
Golden session beer with a crisp mouthfeel and lemon hop aromas.

Harvest Sun (OG 1041, ABV 3.9%)
A straw-coloured beer with a pleasant citrus aroma that gives way to a balanced and satisfyingly bitter finish.

Fraoch Heather Ale (OG 1041, ABV 4.1%)
The unique taste of heather flowers is noticeable in this beer. A fine floral aroma and spicy taste give character to this drinkable speciality beer.

80/- (OG 1046, ABV 4.2%)
A rich mahogany ale, with malt and butter aroma, biscuit texture, orange peel infusion, and a clean, satisfyingly sweet finish.

Black (OG 1042, ABV 4.2%)
A light-bodied, rich dark ale in the style of Czech dark lagers. Aromatic and full-flavoured with coffee and chocolate undertones and a blackcurrant aroma.

Roisin (OG 1040, ABV 4.2%)
A sweetish, fruity light pink beer with a distinct soft fruity aroma and flavour.

Birds & Bees (OG 1044, ABV 4.3%)
A bright, golden ale with a late infusion of fresh elderflowers and lemon zest. Fruity, aromatic and refreshing.

Cock o' the Walk (OG 1042, ABV 4.3%)
A classic red ale.

Kelpie (OG 1045, ABV 4.4%)
A rich, dark chocolate-coloured ale, which has the aroma of a fresh Scottish sea breeze and a distinctive malty texture.

Red (OG 1045, ABV 4.5%)
A rich amber-coloured beer with a bouquet of caramel, amber malts and sweet berries giving way to a palate of biscuit malts, woody and fruity hops that deliver a medium dry finish. Toffee flavours and citrus hop aromas.

Good Times (OG 1050, ABV 5%)
A golden yellow in colour with a refreshing botanical aroma. Refreshing, fruity, malty and aromatic.

Grozet (OG 1050, ABV 5%)
Lagered gooseberry beer. Crisp, fresh and clean tasting.

Joker IPA (OG 1050, ABV 5%)
A well-balanced IPA. Gold-coloured and fruity on the nose with hints of cedar.

Seven Giraffes (OG 1051, ABV 5.1%)
Classic IPA with a late infusion of elderflower. Gold-coloured with aromas of elderflower and citrus hops, followed by sweet caramel. On the tongue the biscuity malts are well balanced with the bitterness of the hops, freshness of the lemon and lingering floral elderflower aftertaste.

Midnight Sun (OG 1058, ABV 5.6%)
A rich, black, smooth porter with an after bite of fresh root ginger.

Ebulum (OG 1062, ABV 6.5%)
Rich and dark, brewed with hops and bog myrtle then cold conditioned with fresh elderberries from a recipe taken from a 16th-century historic record in the Scottish Highlands. A dark, rich, fruity beer with a strong hop aroma and satisfying bitter conclusion.

Profanity Stout (OG 1068, ABV 7%)
Black in colour with full, floral, fruity aromas and a huge roasted malt character that gives way to a dry hopped and bitter finish.

Alba Scots Pine Ale (OG 1075, ABV 7.5%)
A traditional Highland recipe spiced with spruce and pine with a complex wood flavour and a lingering finish. Rich and tawny-coloured.

Willy Good Ale

The Old Forge, Hartley Farm, Winsley, Wiltshire, BA15 2JB ⊕ willygoodale.com
Shop Mon-Sat 9.30am-5.30pm, Sun & bank hols 10am-4pm

Award-winning Willy Good Ale was set up by head brewer Will Southward in 2010 inspired by the hoppy, often strong beers he discovered during a trip to the US. The brewery upgraded to a six-barrel plant in 2011 due to demand. Shops, pubs, cafés and restaurants are supplied in the local area as well as beer festivals, parties and wedding around the country.

Willy Hop (OG 1040, ABV 4%)
Pale ale, dry hopped providing a fuller flavored beer.

Beerier Beer (OG 1042, ABV 4.2%)
An English single hop amber ale.

High Fives (OG 1048, ABV 5%)
A strong IPA.

Hopadelic (OG 1048, ABV 5%)
Dry hopped pale ale with a floral aroma and hints of passion fruit.

Willy Brown (OG 1048, ABV 5%)
A nut brown ale dedicated to the legendary blues singer Robert Johnson.

Wheat a Second (OG 1050, ABV 5.2%)
A refreshing wheat beer with a hint of orange and coriander.

Willy's

17 High Cliff Road, Cleethorpes, Lincolnshire, DN35 8RQ
☎ (01472) 602145
Tours by arrangement

The brewery opened in 1989 to provide beer mainly for its in-house pub in Cleethorpes, although some beer is sold in the free trade. It has a five-barrel plant with maximum capacity of 15 barrels a week. The brewery can be viewed at any time from pub or street.

Original (OG 1039, ABV 3.9%)
A light brown 'sea air' beer with a fruity, tangy hop on the nose and taste, giving a strong bitterness tempered by the underlying malt.

Wilson Potter SIBA

Unit E2, Hanson Close, Middleton, M24 2QZ
☎ (0161) 654 6446 wilsonpotterbrewery.co.uk

Wilson Potter was established in 2011 by two former home brewers, Kathryn Harrison and Amanda Seddon. A full range of cask and bottle-conditioned beers is available.

Cascale (OG 1038, ABV 3.7%)
A pale and hoppy beer.

Don't Fall (OG 1039, ABV 3.9%)
A light, hoppy pale ale made using lager malt.

Tandle Hill (OG 1040, ABV 3.9%)
A blonde beer with strong citrus flavours and aroma.

Triple Gem (OG 1040, ABV 3.9%)
A pale ale with oaken flavours and distinct notes of fresh blackberry.

Bon Don Doon (OG 1042, ABV 4.2%)
A refreshing pale ale with hints of lemon.

In the Black (OG 1048, ABV 4.2%)
Fruity, with roast malt and liquorice notes, with a sweet liquorice and roast finish.

Ruby Red (OG 1047, ABV 4.4%)
An easy-drinking rich ruby ale with a full-bodied malty berry taste and a floral hop finish.

In Shreds (OG 1047, ABV 4.7%)
A pale ale with notes of lemon and pine.

Wincle SIBA

Tolls Farm Barn, Dane Bridge, Wincle, Cheshire, SK11 0QE
☎ (01260) 227777 winclebeer.co.uk
Shop 10am-4pm daily
Tours by arrangement

Wincle was set up in 2008 on a working farm in a redundant milking parlour set within the Peak District National Park. In 2011 it relocated to a new 15-barrel plant in Wincle. Bottle-conditioned and seasonal beers are available: see website.

Waller (OG 1038, ABV 3.8%)
A pale and refreshing beer with a distinctive hop character.

Sir Philip (OG 1041, ABV 4.2%)
Amber in colour, this premium bitter has light malty overtones, balanced with the classic pairing of Fuggles and Target hops.

Wibbly Wallaby (OG 1043, ABV 4.4%)
A full-bodied golden beer with fruity hoppy overtones and a dry, slightly biscuity finish.

Under Taker (OG 1044, ABV 4.5%)
A dark-coloured bitter, complex, nutty and fruit undertones last to the bitter end.

Windermere

See Watermill

Windsor & Eton SIBA

Unit 1, Vansittart Estate, Duke Street, Windsor, Berkshire, SL4 1SE
☎ (01753) 854075 webrew.co.uk
Shop Mon-Fri 8am-6pm, Sat 10am-2pm (often later, check website)
Tours by arrangement

Four friends, including two fully-qualified brewers, set up the brewery in 2010 though their brewing experience goes back to the original Courage Brewery. The purpose-built plant is 18 barrels, which produces cask, keg and bottled beers for around 250 outlets in London and the Thames Valley area. Seasonal and one-off beers: see website.

ParkLife (OG 1037, ABV 3.2%)
A full-flavoured light ale with a citrus aroma and taste.

Knight of the Garter (OG 1036.5, ABV 3.8%)
A straw-coloured golden ale with a distinctive fresh citrus hop aroma.

Windsor Knot (OG 1039, ABV 4%)
Amber ale with a grapefruit aroma. An initially sweet malt and fruit taste followed by a mild bitter finish.

Guardsman (OG 1041, ABV 4.2%)
A tangy best bitter, tawny in colour, with a fresh hoppy finish mellowed with the use of oak during conditioning.

Conqueror (OG 1049, ABV 5%)

A complex black IPA, with a full roasted taste and intense hop aroma and flavour.

Windswept SIBA

Unit B, 13 Coulardbank Industrial Estate, Lossiemouth Moray, Lossiemouth, IV31 6NG
☎ (01343) 814310 🌐 windsweptbrewing.co.uk
Shop Mon-Fri 10am-5.30pm, Sat 10am-5pm
Tours by arrangement

Windswept began brewing in 2012 using a 10-barrel plant installed by John Trow of Oban Ales. It is situated near the gates of RAF Lossiemouth and run by two former Tornado pilots who are CAMRA members.

Blonde (OG 1039, ABV 4%)
A gold-coloured, refreshing session beer with citrus hops and smooth malts.

APA (OG 1046, ABV 5%)
A well-balanced maltiness leads to a long, tangy finish.

Wolf (OG 1064, ABV 6%)
A dark and powerful brew named after the Wolf of Badenoch. Sweet malts balanced with smooth chocolate bitterness. Hides its strength well.

Windy SIBA

Volunteer Inn, New Road, Seavington St Michael, Somerset, TA19 0QE
☎ (01460) 240126 🌐 thevolly.co.uk

Windy Brewery was established in 2011. The name of the brewery stems from the time when alterations were carried out to the back of the pub and the workmen suffered extremes of varying weather conditions.

Tornado (OG 1039, ABV 3.9%)
A traditional brown bitter.

Southerly (OG 1042, ABV 4%)

Flurry (OG 1042, ABV 4.1%)

Fresh Breeze (OG 1043, ABV 4.1%)

Hurricane (OG 1043, ABV 4.2%)

Northerly (OG 1050, ABV 4.8%)

Winning Post (NEW)

Winning Post, 6 Pope Iron Road, Worcester, WR1 3HB
☎ (01905) 21178

A small pub brewery established in 2014.

Ken Porter (ABV 3.7%)

Kevin Tully (ABV 3.9%)

Tick Tack Tommy Moore (ABV 4%)

John Mason (ABV 4.2%)

Winster Valley SIBA

Brown Horse Inn, Winster, Cumbria, LA23 3NR
☎ (01539) 443443 🌐 winstervalleybrewery.co.uk
Tours by arrangement

Winster Valley was established in 2009 using a 2.5-barrel plant at the Brown Horse Inn in Winster.

Dark Horse (OG 1035, ABV 3.5%)

Hurdler (OG 1035, ABV 3.5%)

Best Bitter (OG 1036, ABV 3.7%)

Old School (OG 1037, ABV 3.9%)

Chaser (OG 1041, ABV 4.1%)

Winter's

8 Keelan Close, Norwich, NR6 6QZ
☎ (01603) 787820 🌐 wintersbrewery.com

Winter's was established in 2001 by David Winter, who had previous award-winning success as brewer for both Woodforde's and Chalk Hill breweries. Winter's ales have won many awards with David now passing his brewing knowledge to his son, Mark, an award-winning brewer in his own right. Seasonal beers are available.

Mild (OG 1036.5, ABV 3.6%)
Classic red-brown mild with a nutty roast character. A well-balanced mix of malt caramel, and roast. Lingering bitter finish.

Cloudburst (OG 1037, ABV 3.7%)
Copper coloured with a malty nose. A bitter begining with malt and hop notes ends in a long, dry finale.

Bitter (OG 1039.5, ABV 3.8%)
A well-balanced amber bitter. Hops and malt are balanced by a crisp citrus fruitiness. A pleasant hoppy nose with a hint of grapefruit. Long, sustained, dry, grapefruit finish.

Genius (OG 1040, ABV 4.1%)
A dark brown stout that has a smooth mouthfeel with a grainy edge. Roast dominates throughout but is balanced by a mix of malt, a bittersweet fruitiness and an increasingly nutty finish.

Golden (OG 1041, ABV 4.1%)
Just a hint of hops in the aroma. The initial taste combines a dry bitterness with a fruity apple buttress. The finish slowly subsides into a long, dry bitterness.

Revenge (OG 1047, ABV 4.7%)
Blackcurrant notes give depth to the inherent maltiness of this pale brown beer. A bittersweet background becomes more pronounced as the fruitiness gently wanes.

Storm Force (OG 1053, ABV 5.3%)
A well-defined, sweetish brew. Hops and vine fruit give depth to the malty backbone of this pale brown strong beer. All flavours hold up well as the finish develops a warming softness.

Wiper and True (NEW)

Unit 2, 6 – 8 York Street, St Werburghs, Bristol, BS2 9XT ☎ 07739 017636 🌐 wiperandtrue.com

Launched in 2012 and originally using spare capacity at other breweries, it has shared premises with Ashley Down Brewery (qv) since 2014. Most of its production is bottled or keg with a small amount going into casks, primarily for beer festivals.

Wirksworth SIBA

25 St John Street, Wirksworth, Derbyshire, DE4 4DR
☎ (01629) 824011 🌐 wirksworthbrewery.co.uk

Jeff Green started brewing in 2007 with a 2.5-barrel plant in a converted stone workshop. Wirksworth supplies Derbyshire pubs with six core beers and supplements these with at least one seasonal offering. Every September there is a brew house open weekend giving visitors the opportunity to gain an insight into the brewing process and taste the beers.

Sundance (OG 1039, ABV 4%)
An easy-drinking, straw-coloured beer with a dry hoppy finish.

First Brew (OG 1041, ABV 4.2%)
Pale bitter with a rich, hoppy aroma and light amber colour.

T'owd Man (OG 1048, ABV 4.9%)
A classic bitter, amber in colour with a well-hopped dry finish.

Snowfield (OG 1049, ABV 5%)

Wissey Valley

1 High Street, Downham Market, Norfolk, PE38 9DA
☎ (01366) 386658
✉ thehopandhog@btconnect.com

After several moves since starting up in 2002 (as Captain Grumpy's), the brewery is now located at the rear of the local produce store, tea room and restaurant, the Hop & Hog.

Captain Grumpy's Best Bitter (OG 1039, ABV 3.9%)

Khaki Sargeant Strong Stout (OG 1059, ABV 6%)

Witham (NEW)

7 Church Street, Witham, Essex, CM8 2JP
☎ (01376) 511195 ✉ glenn.ackerman@orange.net

Brewing started in 2012 using a 0.5-barrel plant. The brewery is at the back of the Woolpack Inn. Beer is only available at the pub, and is served under gravity. One-off beers are occasionally brewed.

No Name (OG 1043, ABV 4.3%)

Wizard SIBA

Unit 4, Lundy View, Mullacott Business Park, Ilfracombe, Devon, EX34 8PY
☎ (01271) 867260 wizardbrewery.co.uk
Tours by arrangement

Established in 2003 in Warwickshire and moving to Devon in 2007, the brewery was recently taken over by Bruce Huton and his team who have revamped pumpclips and bottle labels, introduced new beers and taken on the Pier Brewery Tap & Grill in Ilfracombe to promote them. Seasonal beers are available.

Young Apprentice (OG 1038, ABV 3.6%)

Lundy's Gold (OG 1042, ABV 4.1%)

The Phoenix (ABV 4.2%)

Druid's Fluid (OG 1048.5, ABV 5%)

Thirst Borne (ABV 5%)

Wobbly SIBA

Unit 22c, Beech Business Park, Tillington Road, Hereford, HR4 9QJ
☎ (01432) 355496 ☎ 07753 128092
wobblybrewing.co.uk

Wobbly began brewing in 2013 using a 2.5-barrel plant and is an off-shoot of AJP Process Pipework. Currently brewing three times a week; most of the beers are brewed on demand.

Welder (OG 1046.5, ABV 4.8%)
A golden-coloured strong bitter.

Wold Top SIBA

Hunmanby Grange, Wold Newton, Driffield, East Yorkshire, YO25 3HS
☎ (01723) 892222 woldtopbrewery.co.uk

An integral part of Hunmanby Grange Farm, Wold Top brewed its first ale in 2003 and uses home and Wolds-grown malting barley and chalk filtered water from the farm's own borehole. The beer range includes special edition cask and bottled beers plus a gluten free beer, Against the Grain. The brewery installed a bottling line in 2008 and contract bottles for other breweries.

Bitter (OG 1036, ABV 3.7%)
A crisp, clean, aromatic session bitter. Full-flavoured with a long, hoppy finish.

Anglers Reward (OG 1039, ABV 4%)
A refreshing golden pale ale with a fruity bitterness and lingering aftertaste.

Hello Velo (OG 1042, ABV 4.2%)
A sparkling crisp ale with an earthy spiciness and honeyed marmalade overtones.

Headland Red (OG 1042, ABV 4.3%)
A beer with a mellow, malty flavour.

Wold Gold (OG 1046, ABV 4.8%)
A light-coloured summer beer with a soft, fruity flavour with a hint of spice.

Wolf SIBA

Decoy Farm, Old Norwich Road, Besthorpe, Attleborough, Norfolk, NR17 2LA
☎ (01953) 457775 wolfbrewery.com
Shop Mon-Fri 9am-5pm

The brewery was founded in 1996 on a 20-barrel plant, which was upgraded to a 25-barrel one in 2006. The brewery also has a bottling plant with an output capability of 2,000 bottles per hour. More than 300 outlets are supplied. Seasonal beers: see website.

Edith Cavell (OG 1037, ABV 3.7%)
A hoppy, thirst-quenching beer with a fruity finish.

Golden Jackal (OG 1039, ABV 3.7%)
A hoppy, citrus nose mirrors the initial taste. Citrus notes remain to the end as a dry bitterness increases.

Lavender Honey (OG 1037, ABV 3.7%)
Malty caramel aroma leads into a bittersweet first taste with background honey notes. A long drying finish.

Wolf In Sheep's Clothing (OG 1039, ABV 3.7%)
A malty aroma with fruity undertones . Malt, with a bitter background, is the dominant flavour of this clean-tasting beer.

Ale (ABV 3.9%)
A copper-coloured, full-bodied ale

RAF Collection Battle of Britain (OG 1039, ABV 3.9%)

Unashamedly malty throughout, a complex brew with caramel, vine fruit, and an initial sweetness. Singularly quick bitter finale.

Lupus Lupus (OG 1042, ABV 4.2%)
Hops, with a citrus edge, dominate the aroma and taste. A biscuity background disappears quickly in a short, sharp finish.

Poppy Ale (OG 1042, ABV 4.2%)
Pale golden ale infused with honey and fruity hops to give a delicate flavour. Brewed to support the Royal British Legion's work. A 10p donation is made to the RBL for every pint sold.

Coyote Bitter (OG 1044, ABV 4.3%)
A well-balanced golden brew with a hop and citrus aroma. The dominant hoppy bitterness is countered by a malty, slightly sweet backdrop. Complex flavours continue to mix as the dry, bitter ending slowly fades.

Sirius Dog Star (OG 1044, ABV 4.4%)
Unique flavoured, lightly hopped red ale. A smooth beer with a soft, fruity finish.

Straw Dog (OG 1045, ABV 4.5%)
A delicately flavoured brew with a fruity nuance. An aroma reminiscent of redcurrants gives way to a low key marmalade and hop beginning. A stronger finish with increasing bitterness.

Silver Fox (OG 1047, ABV 4.6%)
A refreshingly zesty grapefruit flavoured beer with a bitter aftertaste

Granny Wouldn't Like It (OG 1049, ABV 4.8%)
Complex with a malty bouquet. Increasing bitterness softened by malt and a gentle, fruity sweetness that adds depth.

Woild Moild (OG 1048, ABV 4.8%)
Heavy and complex with malt, vine fruit, bitterness and roast notes vying for dominance. Much drier finish.

Contract brewed for City of Cambridge Brewery:

Boathouse (OG 1037, ABV 3.7%)
A light copper-coloured session bitter with a pleasant aroma from the unique blend of hops and malt.

Hobson's Choice (OG 1041, ABV 4.1%)
A pale-coloured ale with a refreshing hoppy aftertaste.

Atom Splitter (OG 1045, ABV 4.5%)
A golden ale bursting with hoppy flavours.

Parkers (OG 1050, ABV 5%)
A chestnut-coloured fruity beer with the long lasting bitterness of Goldings hops.

Wollaton

Unit 4, Balloon Woods Industrial Estate, Coventry Lane, Wollaton, Nottinghamshire, NG9 3GJ ☎ 07879 664702

Office: Lenton Business Centre, Nottingham, NG7 2BY
thewollatonbreweryco.co.uk

Wollaton is a 1,000 litre brewery that started production in 2013 initially producing just bottle-conditioned beers, although cask-conditioned beer is being considered.

Wood 

Wistanstow, Craven Arms, Shropshire, SY7 8DG
☎ (01588) 672523 woodbrewery.co.uk
Tours by arrangement

The brewery opened in 1980 in buildings next to the Plough Inn, still the brewery's only tied house. Steady growth over the years included the acquisition of the Sam Powell Brewery and its beers in 1991. Around 200 outlets are supplied.

Parish Bitter (OG 1040, ABV 4%)
A blend of malt and hops with a bitter aftertaste. Pale brown in colour.

Shropshire Lass (OG 1041, ABV 4.1%)
A golden ale with zesty bitterness.

Special Bitter (OG 1042, ABV 4.2%)
A tawny brown bitter with malt, hops and some fruitiness.

Shropshire Lad (OG 1045, ABV 4.5%)
A strong, well-rounded bitter.

Wood Farm SIBA

Coalpit Lane, Willey, Warwickshire, CV23 0SL
☎ (01788) 833469 woodfarmbrewery.co.uk
Tours by arrangement

Wood Farm was established in 2011. The brewery can be viewed from the bar of the visitor centre. Outside there is a patio area with tables set in 36 acres of Warwickshire countryside. Tours and food are available.

1823 Mild (OG 1035, ABV 3.5%)

Twickers (OG 1037, ABV 3.7%)

Webb Ellis (OG 1038, ABV 3.8%)

Best Bitter (OG 1042, ABV 4.2%)

Victorious (OG 1042, ABV 4.2%)

Union (OG 1046, ABV 4.6%)

No. 8 (OG 1050, ABV 5%)

Wood Street SIBA

Hillsborough Hotel, 54-58 Langsett Road, Sheffield, South Yorkshire, S6 2UB
☎ (0114) 234 8307 woodstreetbrewery.co.uk
Tours by arrangement

Formally the Crown Brewery, Wood Street opened in 2012 under new ownership at the re-named Hillsborough Hotel in Sheffield. The brewery uses a four-barrel plant and has doubled output since it began.

Wood Street Pale Ale (OG 1038, ABV 3.9%)
A session beer with citrus notes, a fresh and hoppy taste and a crisp, refreshing aftertaste.

Woodstreet Bitter (OG 1039, ABV 4%)
A traditional amber-coloured bitter, smooth on the palate.

Golden Larch (OG 1043, ABV 4.5%)
A full-bodied, well-rounded golden ale with a crisp fruitiness.

Honey Locust (OG 1045, ABV 4.6%)
A golden mild beer with local honey added to give a well balanced ale with a touch of sweetness.

Ebony Stout (OG 1050, ABV 5%)
Dark stout with a ruby edge, with coffee and chocolate undertones and a big, deep aroma.

Yellow Wood IPA (OG 1049, ABV 5.1%)

A well-balanced strong pale bitter, smooth tasting with a distinct hoppy flavour and a long, refreshing finish.

Tom Wood's SIBA

Melton High Wood Farm, Melton High Wood, Melton Ross, Lincolnshire, DN38 6AA
☎ (01652) 680001 tom-wood.com

The Tom Wood range of beers is brewed in the 6-barrel Highwood plant, which the brewery took over in 2011. The range consists of three permanent beers and quarterly seasonal beers: see website.

Best Bitter (OG 1035.5, ABV 3.5%)
A good citrus, passion fruit hop dominates the nose and taste, with background malt. A lingering hoppy and bitter finish.

Lincoln Gold (OG 1041, ABV 4%)
Pale bitter with a fruity aroma and slightly zesty flavour but retaining malt characteristics.

Bomber County (OG 1046, ABV 4.8%)
An earthy malt aroma but with a complex underlying mix of coffee, hops, caramel and apple fruit. The beer starts bitter and intensifies to the end.

Wooden Hand SIBA

Unit 3, Grampound Road Industrial Estate, Grampound Road, Truro, Cornwall, TR2 4TB
☎ (01726) 884596 woodenhand.co.uk

Wooden Hand was founded in 2004, and now supplies around 50 outlets with a high percentage of production being sold further afield via wholesalers. A bottling line was installed in 2005, which also contract-bottles for other breweries.

Pirates Gold (OG 1040.6, ABV 4%)
A slightly tart pale session bitter with hop aroma, light fruit yet malty underlying flavour and tangy fruit finish.

Cornish Gribben (OG 1041.6, ABV 4.1%)
A distinctive well-hopped beer, with citrus fruit notes. Well-balanced bittersweet finish.

Cornish Buccaneer (OG 1043.6, ABV 4.3%)
A golden beer with full flavour hop character, good fruit and hop balance and a long, dry finish.

Black Pearl (OG 1050.6, ABV 4.5%)
A rich, nutty stout with good hop balance and dry chocolate finish.

Cornish Mutiny (OG 1048.6, ABV 4.8%)
Rich, full-bodied strong ale with distinctive full hop character. Slightly biscuity and complex flavour with full mouth finish.

Woodforde's SIBA

Broadland Brewery, Woodbastwick, Norfolk, NR13 6SW
☎ (01603) 720353 woodfordes.co.uk
Shop Mon-Fri 10.30am-4.30pm, Sat & Sun 11.30am-4.30pm (01603 722218)
Tours by arrangement

Founded in 1981 in Drayton, Woodforde's moved to Erpingham in 1982, and then to a converted farm complex in Woodbastwick, with greatly increased production capacity, in 1989. Major expansion in 2001 saw a further increase in fermentation capacity and a new brewery shop and visitor centre. In 2008 a new Brigg's brewhouse, complete with hopback, was added. Woodforde's runs two tied houses, with around 600 outlets supplied on a regular basis.

Mardler's (OG 1036, ABV 3.5%)
Chocolate and roast aromas introduce this well-balanced dark mild. Swathes of vanilla, caramel and malt boost the dominant roast and chocolate flavours. A fine, flavoursome finish.

Wherry (OG 1037.5, ABV 3.8%)
Amber-coloured with an orange citrus nose. Complex, well-balanced but easy-drinking, the swirling mix of malt, hops, citrus and bitterness combine into a tangy marmalade dryness.

Once Bittern (OG 1040, ABV 4%)
A light malty nose with a hint of sulphur. A dark marmalade tang gives an edge to the dominant malt character. Complex, grainy, but easily drinkable with a bittersweet ending.

Sundew (OG 1039, ABV 4.1%)
Hops emerge from a competing fusion of malt, fruit and bitterness to provide a cutting edge to both taste and aroma. Smooth-drinking with a long ending.

Bure Gold (OG 1043, ABV 4.3%)
A well-balanced blend of malt and hop with significant banana, caramel and bitter contributions. Crisp and easy drinking.

Nelson's Revenge (OG 1045, ABV 4.5%)
An infusion of vine fruit, malt and hops provide a rich, rewarding experience. The aromas and flavours bounce merrily along to a sweet, Madeira-like finale.

Woodlands SIBA

Unit 3, Meadow Lane Farm, London Road, Stapeley, Cheshire, CW5 7JU
☎ (01270) 841511 woodlandsbrewery.co.uk
Shop Mon-Fri 9am-4.30pm
Tours by arrangement

The brewery opened in 2004 and moved to larger premises in 2008. An extension in 2010 allowed for increased production. The beers are brewed using water from a spring that surfaces on a nearby peat field at Woodlands Farm. More than 100 outlets are supplied including the brewery's tied houses. Seasonal and bottle-conditioned beers are available.

Mild (OG 1035, ABV 3.5%)
A dark mild ale.

Old Faithful (OG 1036, ABV 3.6%)
A pale session bitter.

Red Squirrel (OG 1038, ABV 3.8%)
A session bitter with a hint of blackcurrant.

Hop as Hell (OG 1040, ABV 4%)
A pale beer made with a long-lasting bitter finish.

Ash Blonde (ABV 4.1%)
A blonde, fruity ale with a lingering crisp aftertaste.

Oak Beauty (OG 1042, ABV 4.2%)
Malty, sweetish, copper-coloured bitter with toffee and caramel flavours. Long-lasting and satisfying bitter finish.

Best Bitter (OG 1044, ABV 4.4%)

Midnight Stout (OG 1044, ABV 4.4%)

Classic creamy dry stout with roast flavours to the fore. Well-balanced with bitterness and good hops on the taste and a good dry, roasty aftertaste. Some sweetness.

Generals Tipple (OG 1055, ABV 5.5%)
A refreshing, medium-hopped IPA.

Worcester (NEW)

Arch 49, Cherry Tree Walk, Worcester, WR1 3AU
☎ 07906 432049

A six-barrel brewery in the heart of Worcester. The brewer is keen to only use traditional British hops.

Gyle 2 (OG 1040, ABV 4%)
A pale gold bitter packing a hop punch.

Gyle 1 (OG 1045, ABV 4.5%)
A light amber-coloured, fruity ale.

Worcestershire SIBA

Hartlebury Brewery, Station Road, Hartlebury, Worcestershire, DY11 7YJ
☎ (01299) 253617
🌐 worcestershirebrewingcompany.co.uk
Tours by arrangement

Worcestershire Brewing Company is the new name for Attwood Ales, established in 2011 at the rear of Hartlebury railway station. Four regular beers are brewed on the 10-barrel plant at the rear of the Tap House, a conversion of the original ticket office at the station and one of the five tied Worcestershire Brewing pubs. Beers are sold direct to free houses, clubs and pub companies in the Worcestershire and West Midlands areas.

Gold (OG 1038, ABV 3.8%)
A refreshing golden beer with fruity, hoppy flavours and a malty, herbal aroma with a hint of orange.

Attwood's Pale Ale (OG 1039, ABV 4%)
A crisp, light and refreshing IPA with a clean bitterness and hoppy aroma.

Farmers Dark Ale (OG 1043, ABV 4.2%)
A smooth, dark session ale; slightly smoky with a caramel finish.

Nectar Bitter (OG 1043, ABV 4.2%)
A light, golden bitter. Well-balanced with a gentle sweetness throughout that counters the hops.

Attwood's Bitter (OG 1049, ABV 5%)
A tawny, copper-coloured premium bitter with dried fruit aromas, rich and warming on the palate with a bite.

World's End

Crown Inn, 60 Wilcot Road, Pewsey, Wiltshire, SN9 5EL
☎ (01672) 562653 🌐 thecrowninnpewsey.com
Tours by arrangement

World's End Ales was established in 2009 on a one-barrel plant at the rear of the Crown Inn in Pewsey. World's End is the 18th-century name for the area in which the brewery is located.

Mercian Incursion (OG 1039, ABV 4%)
A golden-coloured ale.

Bitterus Magnus (OG 1041, ABV 4.1%)
A well-balanced chestnut ale hopped with a good malt, low bitter flavour and a sweet finish.

Barbed & Tangled (ABV 4.2%)

Pewsey Mild (OG 1048, ABV 4.8%)
A dark-coloured mild full of roasted malt flavours with a sweet finish.

Worsthorne SIBA

Unit 4, Oxford Mill, Burnley Road, Briercliffe, Burnley, Lancashire, BB10 2HQ ☎ 07815 708289
🌐 worsthornebrewingcompany.co.uk

Worsthorne began brewing in 2011 using a 5.5-barrel plant. 20 outlets are supplied direct. Seasonal beers are available and there are plans for expansion.

Chestnut Mare (OG 1038, ABV 3.5%)
Chestnut-coloured mild with liquorice undertones and a dry, blackcurrant finish.

Gold (OG 1036, ABV 3.6%)
Lightly bittered golden ale with a spicy aroma.

Packhorse (OG 1039, ABV 3.7%)
Pale amber ale with subtle earthy bitterness and a floral, spicy finish.

Foxstones (OG 1041, ABV 3.9%)
Traditional-style amber bitter with a well-balanced hoppy aroma and lingering floral aftertaste.

Some Like It Blond (OG 1041, ABV 3.9%)
A blonde beer brewed with a lingering dry aftertaste.

Old Trout (OG 1047, ABV 4.5%)
Well-flavoured red/brown ale.

Worth SIBA

Royal British Legion Club, George's Road West, Poynton, Cheshire, SK12 1JY
☎ (01625) 873120/878526
🌐 poyntonlegionclub.co.uk
Tours by arrangement

Based alongside the Royal British Legion Club, Worth brews traditional English session beers for sale at the club and throughout Cheshire. The beer names celebrate Poynton's history and the pumpclips are painted by a local artist.

Coppice (OG 1035, ABV 3.5%)
A true black mild beer with a surprising depth of flavour.

Shared Space (OG 1036, ABV 3.6%)
A full-flavoured, light session ale.

Nimrod (OG 1037, ABV 3.7%)
A bright copper-coloured session beer.

Blythe's Spirit (OG 1038, ABV 3.8%)
A traditionally-hopped beer with a hint of sweetness and a bright golden colour.

Anson (OG 1040, ABV 4%)
A pale hoppy blonde bitter beer with a clean palate and a lingering bitter finish.

Redacre (OG 1040, ABV 4%)
A rich ruby red beer, malty in style with hints of fruit and a smooth finish.

Seam Cutter (OG 1042, ABV 4.2%)
A rich, dark beer, full-flavoured with a creamy tan head. Smoky and chocolate overtones with a clean finish.

Worthington's

National Brewery Centre, Horninglow Street, Burton upon Trent, Staffordshire, DE14 1NG
☎ (01283) 511000 🌐 molsoncoors.co.uk
Tours by arrangement

Molson Coors invested £1 million on this brewing plant in 2011, set within the brewery centre; the brewery is named after one of the famous Burton brewers from the 18th and 19th centuries who developed the pale ale style that transformed brewing in Britain. Based on possibly Britain's oldest microbrewery, this new brewing plant and its predecessor can be seen by visitors to the National Brewery Centre. Seasonal beers are available. Part of Molson Coors. Brewing was suspended in 2014 while the plant was refurbished.

Red Shield (OG 1040, ABV 4.2%)
Hay and straw bales aroma. Old corner sweetshop taste with malt, too. Sweet aftertaste with hints of fruit and hop bitterness for a perfect balance.

E (OG 1044, ABV 4.8%)
Grassy hop start with a bittersweet touch to follow. Bitterness grows with a dry edge and good hoppy finish.

White Shield (OG 1049, ABV 5.6%)
Sweet aroma and woody tastes with angelica, nettles and sharp apples. Ever-changing tastes but a long, hoppy finish.

Wrekin

Pheasant, 54 Market Street, Wellington, Telford, Shropshire, TF1 1DT
☎ (01952) 260683 ☎ 07795 517903

Wrekin Brewing Company (formerly Ironbridge Brewery) was established in 2014 at the Pheasant in Wellington, having relocated from Ironbridge where it was first established in 2008. A 12-barrel plant is used. Wenlock Stout is on limited supply and is stored for four weeks and supplied in oak casks.

Best Bitter (OG 1039, ABV 3.9%)

Pale Ale (OG 1040, ABV 4%)

Ironbridge Gold (OG 1045, ABV 4.4%)

Wenlock Stout (OG 1052, ABV 5.1%)

Wrexham Lager

43a St Georges Crescent, Wrexham, LL13 8DB

No real ale. Lager was first brewed in Wrexham in 1882 and returned to the town in 2011 following the closure in 2000 of the original Wrexham Lager brewery. This new German-built 50-hectolitre brewery produces keg and bottled lagers but no cask beers.

George Wright SIBA

Unit 11, Diamond Business Park, Sandwash Close, Rainford, Merseyside, WA11 8LY
☎ (01744) 886686 🌐 georgewrightbrewing.co.uk
Shop Tue-Fri 10am-4pm
Tours by arrangement

George Wright started production in 2003. The original 2.5-barrel plant was replaced by a five-barrel one, which has since been upgraded again to 25 barrels with production of 200 casks a week.

Black Swan (OG 1039, ABV 3.8%)
A dark, distinctive ale, creamy with a hint of fruit.

Drunken Duck (OG 1040, ABV 3.9%)
Fruity gold-coloured bitter beer with good hop and a dry aftertaste. Some acidity.

Long Boat (OG 1040, ABV 3.9%)
Good hoppy bitter with grapefruit and an almost tart bitterness throughout. Some astringency in the aftertaste. Well-balanced, light and refreshing with a good mouthfeel and long, dry finish.

Blonde Moment (OG 1040, ABV 4%)
A premium blonde beer. Light in colour, herbal nose with a sweet aftertaste.

Pipe Dream (OG 1044, ABV 4.3%)
Refreshing hoppy best bitter with a fruity nose and grapefruit to the fore in the taste. Lasting dry bitter finish.

Pure Blonde (OG 1045, ABV 4.6%)
A premium blonde ale, light and hoppy with an earthy hop flavour.

Cheeky Pheasant (OG 1047, ABV 4.7%)
Light amber in colour, distinctive fruit, malty taste with a sweet aftertaste.

Roman Black (OG 1047, ABV 4.8%)
A dark premium ale, smooth and creamy leaving a long, malty, sweet taste.

Blue Moon (OG 1048, ABV 5%)
Easy-drinking strong, gold-coloured beer. Good malt/bitter balance and well hopped.

Mocne Piwo (OG 1051, ABV 5.1%)
Strong ale, light amber in colour with a hoppy aftertaste.

Northern Lights (OG 1049, ABV 5.1%)
Strong ale, amber in colour. A strong citrus taste balanced by the bitter hop.

Wychwood

Eagle Maltings, The Crofts, Witney, Oxfordshire, OX28 4DP
☎ (01993) 890800 🌐 wychwood.co.uk
Shop Mon-Sat 10am-5pm
Tours by arrangement

Wychwood brewery is located in the Cotswold market town of Witney. The brewers take inspiration from the myths and legends associated with the ancient medieval Wychwood forest to create a range of award-winning, characterful ales. Monthly seasonal beers are produced and bottle-conditioned beers are available. Part of Marston's PLC.

Hobgoblin (OG 1045, ABV 4.5%)
A well-balanced blend of smooth, rich and satisfying flavours combined with a crisp, refreshing bitterness.

Wye Valley SIBA

Stoke Lacy, Herefordshire, HR7 4HG
☎ (01885) 490505 🌐 wyevalleybrewery.co.uk
Shop Mon-Fri 9am-5pm
Tours by arrangement

Founded in 1985 in Canon Pyon, the award-winning brewery is now situated in Stoke Lacy. Regarded as a successful regional brewery, a new brewhouse was commissioned in 2013 and is now operational. Bottle-conditioned beers are available and are bottled on site.

Bitter (OG 1037, ABV 3.7%) ◆
A beer whose aroma gives little hint of the bitter hoppiness that follows right through to the aftertaste.

HPA (OG 1040, ABV 4%) ◆
A pale, hoppy, malty brew with a hint of sweetness before a dry finish.

Dorothy Goodbody's Golden Ale (OG 1042, ABV 4.2%)
A light, gold-coloured ale with a good hop character throughout.

Butty Bach (OG 1046, ABV 4.5%)
A burnished gold, full-bodied premium ale.

Dorothy Goodbody's Wholesome Stout (OG 1046, ABV 4.6%) ◆
A smooth and satisfying stout with a bitter edge to its roast flavours. The finish combines roast grain and malt.

Wylam SIBA

South Houghton Farm, Heddon on the Wall, Northumberland, NE15 0EZ
☎ (01661) 853377 ⊕ wylambrewery.co.uk
Shop Mon-Fri 9am-5pm, Sat 11am-3pm
Tours by arrangement

Wylam started in 2000 on a 4.5-barrel plant. New premises and a 20-barrel plant were built on the same site in 2006 which now has a visitor area and shop, with further expansion planned. The brewery delivers to more than 200 local outlets. Seasonal beers: see website.

Bitter (OG 1039, ABV 3.8%) ◆
A refreshing, copper-coloured, hoppy bitter with a clean, bitter finish.

Gold Tankard (OG 1040, ABV 4%) ◆
Fresh clean flavour, full of hops. This golden ale has a hint of citrus in the finish.

Collingwood Festival Ale (OG 1041, ABV 4.1%)
Honey-coloured with a sweet tangerine aroma. Light and soft-bodied with a citrus zest/fresh pinewood flavour and a dry and bitter finish.

Angel (OG 1044, ABV 4.3%)
A pale copper-coloured, well-balanced bitter with a citrus character in the aroma and finish.

Northern Kite (OG 1046.5, ABV 4.5%)
A ruby ale where the hops are balanced by residual maltiness to give subtle hop character and a rich palate.

Haugh (OG 1046, ABV 4.6%) ◆
A dark, satisfying porter, smooth, full of character and complex flavours – hints of chocolate, liquorice and malt.

Rocket (OG 1048, ABV 5%) ◆
A pale, copper-coloured best bitter with a clean, bitter finish.

Wyre Piddle

See Ambridge

XT SIBA

Notley Farm, Chearsley Road, Long Crendon, Buckinghamshire, HP18 9ER
☎ (01844) 208310 ⊕ xtbrewing.com
Shop Sat 9.30am-12.30pm, Mon – Fri please ring first
Tours by arrangement

XT started brewing in 2011 with a British-built 18-barrel plant. It supplies direct to pubs in Buckinghamshire, Oxfordshire and the Midlands. The brewery shop sells its bottle-conditioned beers and locally-made cider. Seasonal beers: see website. The brewery also produces a range of limited edition, one-off brews under the Animal Brewing Co name.

Four (OG 1038, ABV 3.8%)
An amber beer with a special Belgian malt and a fruity mix of American and European hops.

Three (OG 1041, ABV 4.2%)

Two (OG 1041, ABV 4.2%)
A refreshing golden ale.

Six (OG 1044, ABV 4.5%)
Ruby red beer, malty and smooth with a hoppy finish.

Xtreme (NEW)

67 Red Barn, Turves, Cambridgeshire, PE7 2DZ
☎ 07427 661839 ✉ xtremeales@gmail.com

Xtreme began brewing in 2013 using a one-barrel plant supplying local outlets and beer festivals. Seasonal and special beers are available.

Pigeon Ale (ABV 4.3%)

Yard of Ale SIBA

Surtees Arms, Chilton Lane, Ferryhill, County Durham, DL17 0DH
☎ (01740) 655724 ⊕ thesurteesarms.co.uk
Tours by arrangement

Established in 2008, the 2.5-barrel microbrewery supplies ales to its brewery tap, the Surtees Arms, beer festivals and to a growing number of pubs from North Tyne to South Tees. Seasonal specials are available as are bottle-conditioned beers.

One Foot In The Yard (OG 1044, ABV 4.5%)
Premium golden ale. Fruity on the nose and palate with a sweet finish.

Yates SIBA

Ghyll Farm, Westnewton, Cumbria, CA7 3NX
☎ (01697) 321081 ⊕ yatesbrewery.co.uk
Tours by arrangement

The first of Cumbria's new generation of breweries, established in 1986 and bought by Graeme and Caroline Baxter in 1998. It brews using a 20-barrel brewhouse and reed bed effluent system, and utilises a limited number of site-grown hops in its beers. Seasonal beers: see website.

Bitter (OG 1036, ABV 3.7%) ◆
A well-balanced, full-bodied bitter, golden in colour with complex hop bitterness. Good aroma and distinctive flavour.

Golden Ale (OG 1038, ABV 3.9%) ◆

Skilful use of lager malt and hops results in a pale beer with a light bitterness; melon fruit and a clean, refreshing finish.

Sun Goddess (OG 1041, ABV 4.2%) ◆
A complex, full-bodied beer, packed with tropical fruit.

Yates' SIBA

Unit 4C, Langbridge Business Centre, Newchurch, Isle of Wight, PO36 0NP
☎ (01983) 867878 🌐 yates-brewery.co.uk
Tours by arrangement

Brewing started in 2000 on a five-barrel plant at the Inn at St Lawrence. In 2009 the brewery moved to Newchurch and upgraded to a 10-barrel plant. Stumpy's Brewery was bought out by Yates' in 2009 and Old Stumpy (ABV 4.5%) and Tumbledown (ABV 5%) are now produced by Yates' on request. Seasonal and bottle-conditioned beers are available.

Best Bitter (OG 1039, ABV 3.8%)

Golden Bitter (OG 1040, ABV 4%)

Undercliff Experience (OG 1040, ABV 4.1%)
An amber ale with a bittersweet malt and hop taste with a dry, lemon edge that dominates the bitter finish.

Sunfire (OG 1042, ABV 4.3%)
A full-bodied beer, rich orange/red in colour with strong citrus aromas and a bitter taste.

Blonde Ale (OG 1045, ABV 4.5%)

Holy Joe (OG 1050, ABV 4.9%)

Dark Side of the Wight (OG 1049, ABV 5%)
Malty milk chocolate at first in the nose, then plenty of orange fruit. It is bitter, malty and toasted to taste, with perfumed bitter orange notes always present. Bitter, roasted, perfumed finish.

TropicAle (OG 1050, ABV 5%)
Beer brewed using hops grown at the Ventnor Botanic Gardens on the Isle of Wight.

Special Draught (OG 1056, ABV 5.5%)

Y.S.D. (OG 1056, ABV 5.5%)
Golden in colour, with a tart fruit nose, this strong beer has a dry hoppy bitter taste. Fruit notes emerge and linger in the dry, bitter, hoppy aftertaste.

Wight Old Ale (OG 1060, ABV 6%)
A deep ruby ale with a smooth taste.

Yule Be Sorry (OG 1072, ABV 7.2%)
A rich, dark-coloured beer.

Yelland Manor (NEW)

Lower Yelland Farm, Yelland, Devon, EX31 3EN
☎ (01271) 860355 ✉ yellandmanor@gmail.com

Yelland Manor began brewing in 2013 using a five-barrel plant situated in a converted milking parlour. Around a dozen local pubs and hotels are supplied.

Standard (OG 1043, ABV 4.2%)

Classic (OG 1045, ABV 4.4%)

Yeovil SIBA 👁

Unit 5, Bofors Park, Artillery Road, Lufton Trading Estate, Yeovil, Somerset, BA22 8YH
☎ (01935) 414888 🌐 yeovilales.com
Sales counter Fri 12-5.30pm
Tours by arrangement

Yeovil Ales was established in 2006 using an 18-barrel plant. Seasonal beers: see website. Bottle-conditioned beers are available.

Glory (OG 1039, ABV 3.8%)
A well-balanced bitter with citrus hop notes.

Star Gazer (OG 1042, ABV 4%)
Dark copper bitter with late-hopped floral bouquet.

Summerset (OG 1043, ABV 4.1%)
Blonde ale with fruity hop finish.

Lynx Wildcat (OG 1044, ABV 4.3%)

Stout Hearted (OG 1048, ABV 4.3%)

Ruby (OG 1047, ABV 4.5%)
Red bitter with rich malt depth.

P.O.S.H. (OG 1054, ABV 5.4%)
A strong IPA with a fruity body and hoppy finish.

Yetman's

Bayfield Farm Barns, Bayfield Brecks Farm, Bayfield, Norfolk, NR25 7DZ ☎ 07774 809016 🌐 yetmans.net

A 2.5-barrel plant built by Moss Brew was installed in restored medieval barns in 2005. The brewery supplies local free trade outlets. Bottle-conditioned beers are available.

Yellow (OG 1035, ABV 3.5%)

Red (OG 1036, ABV 3.8%)

Orange (OG 1040, ABV 4.2%) ◆
Well-balanced and smooth-drinking. A light fruity aroma leads into a stirring mix of malt and hops supported by a bittersweet background.A big finish combines malt and a vinous fruitiness.

Green (OG 1044, ABV 4.8%)

York SIBA 👁

12 Toft Green, York, North Yorkshire, YO1 6JT
☎ (01904) 621162 🌐 york-brewery.co.uk
Shop Mon-Sat 12-9pm
Tours by arrangement

York started production in 1996, it was the first brewery in the city for 40 years and was acquired by Mitchell's of Lancaster in 2008. Five pubs are owned in York and Leeds. The brewery is open for guided tours: the 20-barrel plant has a viewing platform overlooking the conditioning and fermenting rooms. Seasonal beers: see website.

Guzzler (OG 1036, ABV 3.6%) ◆
Refreshing golden ale with dominant hop and fruit flavours developing throughout.

Yorkshire Terrier (OG 1041, ABV 4.2%) ◆
Refreshing and distinctive amber/gold brew where fruit and hops dominate the aroma and taste. Hoppy bitterness remains assertive in the aftertaste.

Centurion's Ghost Ale (OG 1051, ABV 5.4%) ◆
Dark ruby in colour, full-tasting with mellow roast malt character balanced by light bitterness and autumn fruit flavours that linger into the aftertaste.

Yorkshire SIBA

70 Humber Street, Kingston upon Hull, HU1 1TU

☎ (01482) 329999 ✉ guy@blueprint.uk.com
Tours by arrangement

Brewing started in 2012 in the Old Fruit Market using a six-barrel plant. Two of the beers are named in honour of the Holy Trinity Church in Hull. A bottling plant, tours and a retail outlet are established.

Tyger Tyger (OG 1036, ABV 3.6%)
A light refreshing bitter with a fruit twist aftertaste.

Supernatural Blonde (OG 1041, ABV 4.1%)
A refreshing blonde ale with a citrus taste.

True North (OG 1041, ABV 4.1%)
A classic Yorkshire bitter.

Yorkshire Dales

Seata Barn, Elm Hill, Askrigg, North Yorkshire, DL8 3HG
☎ (01969) 622027 yorkshiredalesbrewery.com

Situated in the heart of the Yorkshire Dales, brewing started in a converted milking parlour in 2005. Installation of a five-barrel plant increased capacity to 20 barrels a week. More than 150 pubs are supplied throughout the North of England. Four monthly specials and bottle-conditioned beers are available: see website.

Butter Tubs (OG 1037, ABV 3.7%)
A pale golden beer with a dry bitterness complemented by strong citrus flavours and aroma.

Askrigg Bitter (OG 1038, ABV 3.8%)

Leyburn Shawl (OG 1038, ABV 3.8%)
A crisp, dry, pale ale with an underlying sharpness.

Buckden Pike (OG 1040, ABV 3.9%)
A refreshing blonde beer with a crisp, fruity finish.

Nappa Scarr (OG 1041, ABV 4%)
A golden ale brewed with a trio of American hops for citrus and peach flavours throughout.

Muker Silver (OG 1041, ABV 4.1%)
A blonde lager-style ale, crisp with a sharp, hoppy finish.

Askrigg Ale (OG 1043, ABV 4.3%)
A pale golden ale with an intense aroma that generates a crisp, dry flavour with a long, bitter finish.

Garsdale Smokebox (OG 1057, ABV 5.6%)
A complex ale created by smoked and dark malts. Deep, rich chocolate and coffee flavours are complemented by the smokiness.

Yorkshire Heart SIBA

The Vineyard, Pool Lane, Nun Monkton, YO26 8EL
☎ (01423) 330716 yorkshireheart.com
Tours by arrangement

Yorkshire Heart began brewing in 2011 and is situated adjacent to the Yorkshire Heart vineyard and winery, not far from York. Six regular ales are produced and a new, larger brewhouse is now in use.

Lightheart (OG 1033, ABV 3.3%)
A pale ale full of fresh citrus flavours.

Hearty Bitter (OG 1037, ABV 3.7%)
A sparkling amber brown bitter full of the aromas of roasted malt.

Hearty Mild (OG 1039, ABV 4%)
A rich-flavoured mild with hints of nuts and chocolate with a natural residual sweetness.

SilverHeart IPA (OG 1039, ABV 4%)
An IPA with a slight citrus taste.

J.R.T. Best Bitter (OG 1041, ABV 4.2%)
Refereshing golden ale with flavours associated with long summer days.

Blackheart Stout (OG 1047, ABV 4.8%)
A stout with a chocolate liquorice flavour.

Young's

See Charles Wells (under W)

Zerodegrees

Blackheath: 29-31 Montpelier Vale, Blackheath, London, SE3 0TJ
☎ (020) 8852 5619

Bristol: 53 Colston Street, Bristol, BS1 5BA ☎ (0117) 925 2706

Cardiff: 27 Westgate Street, Cardiff, CF10 1DD
☎ (029) 2022 9494

Reading: 9 Bridge Street, Reading, Berkshire, RG1 2LR ☎ (0118) 959 7959 zerodegrees.co.uk
Tours by arrangement

Brewing started in 2000 in Greenwich, London, and now four brewpubs are owned, each incorporating a state-of-the-art, computer-controlled, German plant producing unfiltered and unfined ales and lagers. All beers use natural ingredients and are suitable for vegetarians, and are served from tanks using air pressure (not CO2). There are regular seasonal specials including fruit beers: see website.

Mango Wheat Ale (OG 1040, ABV 4%)
Hazy, yellow wheat beer with sweet mango flavour. Syrupy texture and flavour with a short aftertaste.

Wheat Ale (OG 1045, ABV 4.2%)
Powerful wheat aroma, flavour and mouthfeel. Substantial coriander aroma with hints of lemon and a clean finish.

Black Lager (OG 1048, ABV 4.6%)
Dark roast aromas and flavour. Hint of sweetness with a light body and a long bitter finish.

Pale Ale (OG 1046, ABV 4.6%)
Amber ale with dry hop on the nose and palate and a bitter finish. A move away from the classic American pale ale that it was.

Pilsner (OG 1048, ABV 4.8%)
Sweet tasting golden lager with a short bittersweet finish.

R.I.P.

The following breweries have closed, gone out of business or suspended operations since the 2014 Guide was published:

Adventure, Sutton, Greater London
Baldy, Pulborough, West Sussex
Barley Bottom, Silsden, West Yorkshire
Batch Brew, Hampshire
Bees, Walcott, Norfolk
Big River, Brough, East Yorkshire
Blacker & Son, Saltney, Cheshire
Botanist, Kew, Greater London
Breconshire, Brecon, Mid Wales
Brew Wharf, SE1: Borough, Greater London
Brupond, E10: Leyton, Greater London
Cains, Liverpool, Merseyside
Complete Pig, Britwell Salome, Oxfordshire
Cuerden, West Yorkshire
DB, Runcorn, Cheshire
Devil's Dyke, Reach, Cambridgeshire
East Coast, Filey, North Yorkshire
Ellenberg's, W7: Hanwell, Greater London
Farnham, Upper Hale, Surrey
Front Street, Binham, Norfolk
Fry's, Boyton, Cornwall
Full Moon, Battle, East Sussex
Fyfe, Kirkcaldy, Kingdom of Fife
Great Gable, Egremont, Cumbria
Green Room, St Austell, Cornwall
Green Tye, Green Tye, Hertfordshire
Hebridean, Stornoway: Isle of Lewis, Highlands & Western Isles
Hensting, Owslebury, Hampshire
Hereward, Ely, Cambridgeshire
Hogswood, St Agnes, Cornwall
Hopping Mad, Olney, Buckinghamshire
Hoppy Collie, W6: Fulham, Greater London
Justice, Mansfield, Nottinghamshire
Lamb, W4: Chiswick, Greater London
Llangorse, Llangorse, Mid Wales
Malthouse, Ossett, West Yorkshire
Mighty Hop, Lyme Regis, Dorset
Nomad, Newthorpe, Nottinghamshire
Rainbow, Coventry, West Midlands
Rodham's, Otley, West Yorkshire
Salisbury, Dinton, Wiltshire
Wellington Inn, Hull, East Yorkshire
White Dog, Eastwood, Nottinghamshire
Whittlebury, Whittlebury, Northamptonshire

FUTURE

The following new breweries have been notified to the Guide and will start to produce beer during 2014/2015. In a few cases, they were in production during the summer of 2014 but were too late for a full listing:

Aardvark, Sheffield, South Yorkshire
Against the Grain, WC1X: Kings Cross, Greater London
Ainsty, North Yorkshire
Big Beer, Bristol, Gloucestershire & Bristol
Black Dog Beers, Machynlleth, West Wales
Black Tap, Stafford, Staffordshire
Bloomsbury, WC1N: Bloomsbury, Greater London
Bohemia, N12: North Finchley, Greater London
Borough Arms, Neath, Glamorgan
Bow Wave, Bowness-on-Windermere, Cumbria
Brew On, Whitbourne, Herefordshire
Bridge, Holmfirth, West Yorkshire
Bridgnorth, Bridgnorth, Shropshire
Calderdale, Wainstalls, West Yorkshire
Chew Valley, Pensford, Somerset
Connoisseur, St Helens, Merseyside
Dancing Men, Happisburgh, Norfolk
De Brus, Dunfermline, Kingdom of Fife
East Wickham, SE10: Greenwich, Greater London
Farmageddon, Comber, Northern Ireland
Fleetwood, Fleetwood, Lancashire
Fuggle Bunny, Sheffield, South Yorkshire
Golden Valley, Hereford, Herefordshire
Grey Friars, Featherstone, Staffordshire
Gun, Heathfield, East Sussex
Hale's, Worksop, Nottinghamshire
Hercules, Holywood, Northern Ireland
Hops & Glory, N1: Islington, Greater London
Kettledrum, Rochester, Kent
Kew, Kew, Greater London
Laine @ Candlemaker, SW11: Battersea, Greater London
Leighton Buzzard, Leighton Buzzard, Bedfordshire
Liquid, Leith, Edinburgh & the Lothians
Littondale, Litton, North Yorkshire
Mad Dog, Southampton, Hampshire
Mad Dog, Cwmbran, Gwent
Med, Cambridge, Cambridgeshire
Moorside, Kirkbymoorside, North Yorkshire
Newbridge, Bilston, West Midlands
Orbit, SE17: Walworth, Greater London
Pokertree, Carrickmore, Northern Ireland
Red Hand, Donaghmore, Northern Ireland
Salisbury, Bournemouth, Dorset
Southwark, SE1: Southwark, Greater London
Stanley, Portslade, East Sussex
Thorn Dhu, Lochgair, Greater Glasgow & Clyde Valley
Three Friends, Kent
Wimbledon, SW19: Wimbledon, Greater London
Zoo, Sunderland, Tyne & Wear

Indexes & Further Information

Places index

C

D

PLACES INDEX

N

O

PLACES INDEX

T

PLACES INDEX

Beers index

These beers refer to those in bold type in the breweries section (beers in regular production) and so therefore do not include seasonal, special or occasional beers that may be mentioned elsewhere in the text.

A

BEERS INDEX

BEERS INDEX

C

D

BEERS INDEX

H

K

L

M

N

O

P

Q

R

BEERS INDEX

S

T

U

X

Y

Z

Award winning pubs

Local CAMRA Pubs of the Year

The Pub of the Year competition is judged by CAMRA members. Each of the CAMRA branches votes for its favourite pub: criteria include the quality and choice of real ale, atmosphere, customer service and value. The pubs listed below are current winners of the title; look out for the 🏆 symbol next to the entries in the Guide.

England

🏆 Bedfordshire
Albion, Ampthill
Burnaby Arms, Bedford
Stone Jug, Clophill
Engineers Arms, Henlow

🏆 Berkshire
Nag's Head, Reading
Rose & Crown, Sandhurst
Five Bells, Wickham
Carpenter's Arms, Windsor

🏆 Buckinghamshire
Ship Ashore, Milton Keynes: Willen

🏆 Cambridgeshire
King of the Belgians, Hartford
Plough, Little Downham
Ploughman, Peterborough
Chestnut Tree, West Wratting

🏆 Cheshire
Cellar, Chester
Young Pretender, Congleton
Hops, Crewe
Helter Skelter, Frodsham
Lion Hotel, Runcorn

🏆 Cornwall
Star Inn, Vogue

🏆 Cumbria
Midland Hotel, Appleby-in-Westmorland
Brook House Inn, Boot
George & Dragon, Dent
Prince of Wales, Foxfield
Fetherstone Arms, Kirkoswald

🏆 Derbyshire
Travellers Rest, Apperknowle
Smith's Tavern, Ashbourne
Tramway Tavern, Brampton
Black Horse, Coton-in-the-Elms
Furnace Inn, Derby
Butchers Arms, Langley
MoCa Bar, Matlock
Angler's Rest, Millers Dale
Black Bull's Head, Openwoodgate
Devonshire Arms, South Normanton
Old Hall Inn, Whitehough

🏆 Devon
Queen's Arms, Brixham
Foxhound Inn, Brixton
Pony & Trap, Cullompton
Red Lion, Exbourne
Fortescue Hotel, Plymouth

🏆 Dorset
Chaplin's & The Cellar Bar, Boscombe
Bottle Inn, Marshwood

🏆 Durham
Quakerhouse, Darlington
Victoria Inn, Durham
Fisherman's Arms, Hartlepool Headland
Ship Inn, Middlestone
George & Dragon, Norton

🏆 Essex
Prince of Wales, Broxted
Orange Tree, Chelmsford
Old Lifeboat House, Clacton-on-Sea
Victoria Inn, Colchester
Mayflower, Leigh-on-Sea
Traitor's Gate, Little Thurrock (Grays)
Hurdlemakers Arms, Woodham Mortimer

🏆 Gloucestershire & Bristol
Plough Inn, Cold Aston
Salutation Inn, Ham

🏆 Hampshire
George, Alton
Prince of Wales, Farnborough
Hole in the Wall, Portsmouth
Guide Dog, Southampton

🏆 Herefordshire
Prince of Wales, Ledbury

🏆 Hertfordshire
Rising Sun, Berkhamsted
Land of Liberty, Peace & Plenty, Heronsgate
Rising Sun, High Wych
Half Moon, Hitchin
Woodman, Wild Hill

🏆 Isle of Wight
Anchor Inn, Cowes

🏆 Kent
Unicorn Inn, Canterbury
Firkin Ale House, Folkestone
Stile Bridge, Marden
Three Hats, Milton Regis
Windmill, Sevenoaks
George & Dragon, Swanscombe
King's Arms, Upper Upnor
Berry, Walmer
Bake & Alehouse, Westgate-on-Sea

🏆 Lancashire
Derby Arms, Aughton
Black Bull, Blackburn
Snug, Carnforth
Horn's Inn, Goosnargh
Taps, Lytham
Swan with Two Necks, Pendleton

🏆 Leicestershire & Rutland
Cherry Tree, Catthorpe
Queens Head, Hinckley
Rose & Crown, Hose
Salmon, Leicester
Noel's Arms, Melton Mowbray
Chandlers Arms, Shearsby
Free Trade, Sileby
Crown Inn, Uppingham

🏆 Lincolnshire
Nottingham House, Cleethorpes
Nobody Inn, Grantham
Dog & Bone, Lincoln
Brown Cow, Louth
Malt Shovel, Scunthorpe
Cross Swords, Skillington
Half Moon, Willingham by Stow

🏆 Greater London
Snooty Fox, Canonbury
Hope, Carshalton
Queen's Head, Downe
Olde Mitre, Hatton Garden
Old Mitre Inn, High Barnet
JJ Moons, Hornchurch
Ivy House, Nunhead
Lamb, Surbiton
Sussex Arms, Twickenham
Queen's Head, Uxbridge
Door Hinge, Welling
Hand in Hand, Wimbledon

🏆 Greater Manchester
Bank Top Brewery Tap, Bolton
Harewood Arms, Broadbottom
Hare & Hounds, Holcombe Brook
White Lion, Leigh
City Arms, Manchester
Port Street Beer House, Manchester

Carrion Crow, Oldham
Crooke Hall Inn, Standish Lower Ground
Hope Inn, Stockport: Heaton Norris

Merseyside
Fox & Hounds, Barnston
Liverpool Pigeon, Crosby
Freshfield, Freshfield
Cricketers Arms, St Helens

Norfolk
Coach & Horses, Dersingham
Fat Cat, Norwich

Northamptonshire
Lamplighter, Northampton

Northumberland
John Bull Inn, Alnwick

Nottinghamshire
White Lion, Bingham
Queen's Hotel, East Markham
Just Beer Micropub, Newark
Horse & Jockey, Selston
Horse & Jockey, Stapleford

Oxfordshire
Nag's Head on the Thames, Abingdon
Chequers, Churchill
Bird in Hand, Henley-on-Thames
Cross Keys, Thame
Shoulder of Mutton, Wantage

Shropshire
Mytton Arms, Habberley
Old Fighting Cocks, Telford: Oakengates

Somerset
Three Horseshoes Inn, Batcombe
Bell, Bath
Plough, Congresbury
Ring of Bells, Taunton

Staffordshire
Roebuck Inn, Burton upon Trent
Huntsman, Cheadle
Codsall Station, Codsall
Cat Inn, Enville
Cross Keys Hotel, Hednesford
Holy Inadequate, Stoke-on-Trent: Etruria
Royal Exchange, Stone
Robert Peel, Tamworth

Suffolk
Queen's Head, Hawkedon
Vine, Hopton
St Jude's Brewery Tavern, Ipswich
Stanford Arms, Lowestoft

Surrey
Thyme at the Tavern, Chertsey
Running Horse, Leatherhead
Surrey Oaks, Newdigate

East Sussex
Dolphin, Hastings
Gardener's Arms, Lewes

West Sussex
Wilkes' Head, Eastergate
Jolly Tanners, Staplefield
Parsonage Bar & Restaurant, Worthing

Tyne & Wear
Bodega, Newcastle: City Centre
Isis, Sunderland

Warwickshire
Holly Bush, Alcester
Lord Nelson Inn, Ansley
Royal Oak, Kenilworth
Victoria Inn, Rugby
Griffin Inn, Shustoke
Victoria Works, Studley
Punch Bowl, Warwick

West Midlands
Old Moseley Arms, Birmingham: Balsall Heath
Bishop Vesey, Boldmere
Nursery Tavern, Coventry
Red Lion, Knowle
Beacon Hotel, Sedgley
Black Country Arms, Walsall
Graham's Place, Wollaston
Lych Gate Tavern, Wolverhampton

Wiltshire
Three Crowns, Chippenham
Earl of Normanton, Idmiston
Village Freehouse, Salisbury
Hop Inn, Swindon

Worcestershire
Weighbridge, Alvechurch
Coach & Horses, Harvington
Old Seven Stars, Kidderminster
Paul Pry, Worcester

North Yorkshire
Birch Hall Inn, Beck Hole
Wheatsheaf, Burn
Crown, Manfield

East Yorkshire
Telegraph, Bridlington
Plough, Hollym
Admiral of the Humber, Hull

South Yorkshire
Old No. 7, Barnsley
Corner Pin, Doncaster
Beehive, Harthill
Kelham Island Tavern, Sheffield: Kelham Island

West Yorkshire
Corn Dolly, Bradford
West Riding Refreshment Rooms, Dewsbury
Cross Keys, Halifax
King's Head, Huddersfield
Brown Cow, Keighley
Harry's Bar, Wakefield

Wales

Glamorgan
Landsdowne, Cardiff
Fagin's Ale & Chop House, Glan-y-Lynn
Pilot Inn, Mumbles
Red Fox, Penllyn
Pontadawe Inn, Pontadawe

Gwent
Clytha Arms, Clytha

Mid-Wales
Star Inn, Talybont-on-Usk

North-East Wales
Halcyon Quest Hotel, Prestatyn
Bridge End Inn, Ruabon

North-West Wales
Albion Ale House, Conwy
Snowdonia Park, Waunfawr

West Wales
Druid Inn, Goginan
Vine Inn, Johnston
White Horse, Llandeilo

Scotland

Aberdeen & Grampian
Moorings, Aberdeen

Borders
Cobbles, Kelso

Dumfries & Galloway
Cavens Arms, Dumfries
Steam Packet Inn, Isle of Whithorn

Greater Glasgow & Clyde Valley
Laurieston Bar, Glasgow
Corkers Bar, Paisley

Edinburgh & the Lothians
Stockbridge Tap, Edinburgh
Volunteer Arms (Staggs), Musselburgh

Highlands & Western Isles
Braeval Hotel, Nairn

Kingdom of Fife
Commercial Inn, Dunfermline

Loch Lomond, Stirling & The Trossachs
Inn & Bistro, Strathyre

Tayside
Phoenix, Dundee

Channel Islands

Guernsey
Cornerstone Cafe Bar, St Peter Port

Jersey
Lamplighter, St Helier

Readers' recommendations

Suggestions for pubs to be included or excluded

All pubs are regularly surveyed by local branches of the Campaign for Real Ale to ensure they meet the standards required by the *Good Beer Guide*. If you would like to comment on a pub already featured, or on any you think should be featured, please fill in the form below (or a copy of it), and send it to the address indicated. Alternatively, email **gbgeditor@camra.org.uk**. Your views will be passed on to the branch concerned. Please mark your envelope/email with the county where the pub is, which will help us to direct your comments efficiently.

Pub name:

Address:

Reason for recommendation/criticism:

Pub name:

Address:

Reason for recommendation/criticism:

Pub name:

Address:

Reason for recommendation/criticism:

Your name and address:

Please send to: [Name of county] Section, Good Beer Guide,
230 Hatfield Road, St Albans, Hertfordshire AL1 4LW

Have your say

Feedback on the Good Beer Guide

We are always trying to improve the *Good Beer Guide* for our readers and we welcome your feedback. If you have any suggestions for how the *Good Beer Guide*, Good Beer Guide Mobile Edition or sat-nav POI could be improved, please let us know. Simply fill out the form below (or a copy of it) and send it to the address indicated, or make your comments on our website at: **www.camra.org.uk/gbgfeedback**. Thank you.

Colour sections:

Pubs section:

Brewery section:

Good Beer Guide e-book:

Good Beer Guide Mobile:

Good Beer Guide sat-nav POI:

What other suggestions do you have?

Please send to: Good Beer Guide – Have your say,
230 Hatfield Road, St Albans, Hertfordshire AL1 4LW

Outside Influences

National boundaries have been breached as foreign beers make their mark in Britain

Good beer knows no boundaries. In the early days of the *Good Beer Guide*, the 40 or so breweries in operation concentrated almost entirely on two traditional British beers, Mild and Bitter, and their Scottish variants Light and Heavy. But the beer revolution of the past few decades has thrown up an array of new styles.

Many of them – Golden Ale in particular – are British originals but others bear the imprints of foreign brewers. Without question, the greatest input has come from Belgium, which has both a large range of beers and also benefits from proximity and easy accessibility across the Channel courtesy of Eurostar.

It's a modern truism that any British beer lover traversing the Grand Place in Brussels is likely to bump into a fellow countryman diligently reading Tim Webb's *Good Beer Guide Belgium* before heading to the nearest recommended bar. Many of the British visitors will be brewers, eager to both sample and also reflect on the amazing diversity of beers brewed in Belgium and the possibility of recreating them back at home.

There are some powerful similarities in style between the beers of both countries. Belgian pale ale and brown ales are stronger than their British counterparts but are not difficult to replicate. A number of new British Mild Ales, for example, are stronger in alcohol than is the norm and are clearly influenced by Belgian practice.

The world-famous Trappist ales from six Belgian monasteries are protected by protocols and are not easy to reproduce in Britain due to the absence of Trappist communities here. But the commercial spin-offs from the style – known as abbey ales – have made their mark. The Cistercian monks at Ampleforth Abbey in Yorkshire brew a strong bottle-conditioned dark ale in collaboration with Little Valley Brewery, while Nethergate in Essex produces an Augustian Ale in association with the monks at Clare Priory. Several breweries based in cities with strong ecclesiastical roots, such as Durham and York, brew beers that pay homage to the tradition.

Styles that emanate from one of Belgium's biggest Trappist breweries, Westmalle near Antwerp, have made a solid mark here. The monks dub their brown and golden ales Dubbel and Trippel and there is no shortage of British brewers inspired to make their own Doubles and Triples. Stuart Howe, the former head brewer

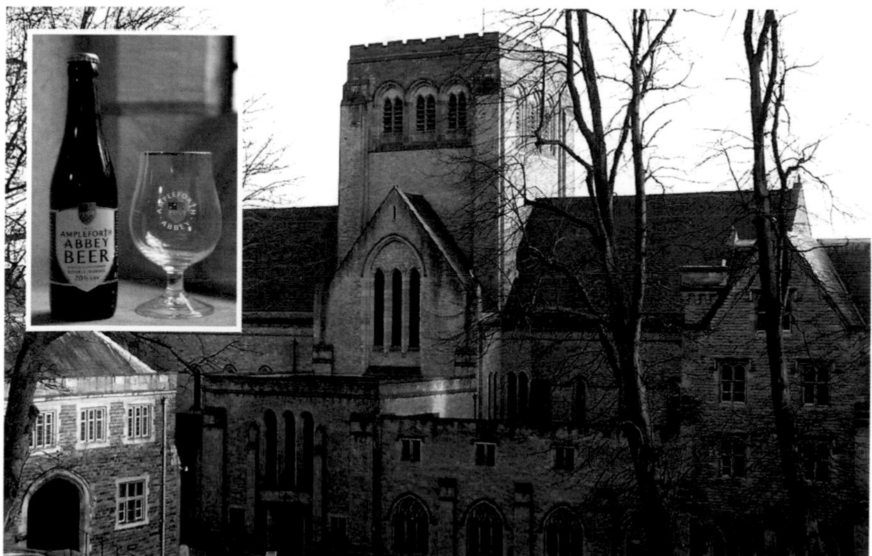

The monks at Ampleforth Abbey in Yorkshire have been inspired by their Belgium brothers to brew an abbey beer

at Sharp's in Cornwall and now in charge of all Molson Coors specialist breweries, is a regular visitor to Belgium and has created a range of bottle-conditioned ales inspired by the Trappist tradition, Westmalle's in particular.

British brewers have also picked up on the Belgian habit of producing wheat beer made with the addition of herbs and spices. The habit stems from the time when traders from the Low Countries would return home with ships laden with exotic spices and fruits. The best-known Belgian 'white' or wheat beer, Hoegaarden – now a shadow of its former self in the hands of AB InBev – was created by the legendary brewer Pierre Celis with the addition of coriander seeds and curacao orange peel. Otley in south Wales had a tongue-in-cheek O-Garden with a similar make-up but has had to change this to O-9 Blonde following lawyers' letters while St Austell's Clouded Yellow is brewed with vanilla pods, cloves and coriander.

One Belgian style that was considered to be impossible to brew elsewhere is lambic. It's made by a system known as 'wild' or 'spontaneous' fermentation, allowing yeasts in the atmosphere – instead of carefully cultivated brewers' yeast strains – to enter the brewery and start the transformation of sugary extract into finished beer. Lambic is protected by both Belgian and EU law and the term cannot be used outside Brussels and Payottenland.

But a growing number of brewers in both Britain and the United States are producing beers they label 'sour', inoculated with a yeast culture called *Brettanomyces*, the main wild strain used in lambic production. Kernel in London and Thornbridge in Derbyshire are just two of the British breweries making sour beer while Elgood's, a long-standing family brewery in Cambridgeshire, is making lambic in the true Belgian manner. The brewhouse has two copper 'cool ships' or cooling trays where the hopped extract rests after leaving the boiling copper. Windows are left open to encourage wild yeasts to enter and start fermentation. The finished beer is then aged in oak casks for several months.

Drinkers who find lambic beers too assertively acidic can try Belgian fruit lambics, traditionally made with the addition of cherries and raspberries. A large number of British brewers have taken up this challenge and add even more exotic ingredients, including coffee beans, chocolate, blackcurrants, cinnamon, fennel, root ginger and chillis.

Belgium is not the only European influence. While Germany is viewed as a major producer of properly made lager beers, Bavaria has a rich tradition of a quite different type of style – wheat beer, a member of the ale family. Bavarian wheat beers are quite different to the Belgian versions: Germany's strict Purity law, the 16th century Reinheitsgebot, bans the use of herbs, spices and fruit: only barley and wheat malts, hops, yeast and water, can be used in beer production. The result is beer brewed with a blend of both grains and fermented with a special yeast culture that adds notes of banana, Juicy Fruit bubblegum and cloves. Unfiltered wheat beers are labelled 'mit Hefe' – with yeast – and several British brewers are now producing this variant. They include Bristol Beer Factory's Bristol Hefe, Mitchell Krause's Hefe Weiss and Stewart's HefeWeizen.

A newer source of influence for British brewers comes from the United States. The development of the craft brewing movement in the U.S. owes much of its inspiration to British brewing practice. Many aspiring American brewers visited these shores and returned home to fashion their own interpretations of pale ale, IPA, brown ale, barley wine, porter and stout. Over the years those styles have changed and mutated, due in no small measure to the robust hops grown in the U.S. American hops deliver big citrus aromas and flavours, with grapefruit, orange and lemon to the fore, with additional notes of cedar and pine.

The popularity, in particular, of American pale ales and IPAs that positively zing with citrus and pine character has encouraged a raft of British brewers to import hops in order to brew beers with characteristic American flavours. Both Dark Star's award-winning American Pale Ale and Oakham's Citra, for example, deliver precisely what their pump clips promise.

Pale or dark, hoppy or malty, there are amazing beers bearing the hallmarks of brilliant artisan brewers from abroad waiting in a pub near you.

Books for beer lovers

300 More Beers to Try Before You Die!

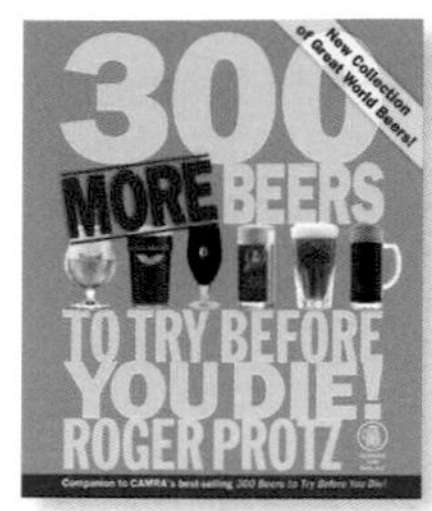

Roger Protz

300 More Beers to Try Before You Die! takes beer lovers on an exciting new odyssey through 300 of the best beers from around the world. A companion volume to the best-selling *300 Beers to Try Before You Die!*, award-winning beer writer Roger Protz selects 300 more beers that represent the most interesting products of the brewer's art available today. The book charts the world-wide beer revival and features new ales from America, rediscovered classics like English abbey beer and inventive new twists on age-old recipes from experimental brewers in Europe and beyond, plus much, much more.

£14.99 ISBN 978-1-85249-295-3 CAMRA members' price £12.99

Good Bottled Beer Guide

Jeff Evans

A pocket-sized guide for discerning drinkers looking to buy bottled real ales and enjoy a fresh glass of their favourite beers at home. The new eighth edition of the *Good Bottled Beer Guide* is completely revised, updated and redesigned to showcase the very best bottled British real ales now being produced, and detail where they can be bought. Everything you need to know about bottled beers; tasting notes, ingredients, brewery details, and a glossary to help the reader understand more about them.

£12.99 ISBN 978-1-85249-309-7 CAMRA members' price £10.99

London Pub Walks

Bob Steel

CAMRA's pocket-size walking guide to London is back. This fantastic second edition is packed with interesting new routes, fully updated classic routes from the first edition, new pubs and a special selection of routes that take full advantage of London's public transport network. With 30 walks around more than 190 pubs, CAMRA's *London Pub Walks* enables you to explore the entire city while never being far from a decent pint.

£9.99 ISBN 978-1-85249-310-3 CAMRA members' price £7.99

Great British Pubs

Adrian Tierney-Jones

Great British Pubs is a practical guide that takes you around the very best public houses in Britain and celebrates the pub as a national institution. Every kind of pub is represented in these pages with categorised listings featuring full-colour photography illustrating a host of excellent pubs from the seaside to the city and from the historic to the ultra-modern. Articles on beer brewing, cider making, classic pub food recipes and traditional pub games are included to help the reader fully understand what makes a pub 'Great'.

£14.99 ISBN 987-1-85249-265-6 CAMRA members' price £12.99

Britain's Best Real Heritage Pubs

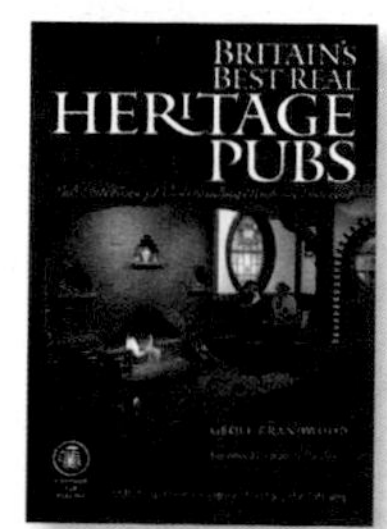

Geoff Brandwood

This new full-colour guide lists 270 pubs throughout the UK that have interiors of real historic significance – some over a century old. Illustrated with high quality photography, the book's extensive listings are the product of years of surveying and research by CAMRA's Pub Heritage Group, which is dedicated to preserving and protecting our rich pub heritage. The book features a forward by Simon Thurley, Chief Executive of English Heritage.

£9.99 ISBN 978-1-85249-304-2 CAMRA members' price £7.99

Brew Your Own British Real Ale

Graham Wheeler

The perennial favourite of home-brewers, *Brew Your Own British Real Ale* is a CAMRA classic. This new edition is enhanced and illustrated. Written by homebrewing authority Graham Wheeler, Brew Your Own British Real Ale includes detailed brewing instructions for both novice and more advanced home-brewers, as well as comprehensive recipes for recreating some of Britain's best-loved beers at home.

£14.99 ISBN 978-1-85249-319-6 CAMRA members' price £12.99

The Beer Select-o-Pedia

Michael Larson

The Beer Select-O-Pedia is a an enthusiast's guide through the delicious world of beer, demystifying scores of traditional and innovative new styles from Britain & Ireland, Continental Europe and America. Organised into families of beer styles according to their origins, it is easy to look up the style of beer you are drinking and discover more. Much more than a list of recommended brews and breweries, this book gives beer lovers all the information they need to navigate the ever-expanding world of beer and find new brews to excite their tastebuds.

£12.99 ISBN 978-1-85249-318-9 CAMRA members' price £10.99

101 Beers Days Out

Tim Hampson

101 Beer Days Out is the perfect handbook for the beer tourist wanting to explore beer and brewing culture in their local area and around the UK. From historic city pubs to beer festivals; idyllic country pub walks to rail ale trails; tourist brewery tours to serious brewing courses – Britain has beer and brewing experiences to rival any in the world. *101 Beer Days Out* brings together for the first time the best of these experiences, ordered geographically and with full visitor information, maps and colour photography – the best way to celebrate Britain's national drink.

£12.99 ISBN 978-1-85249-288-5 CAMRA members' price £10.99

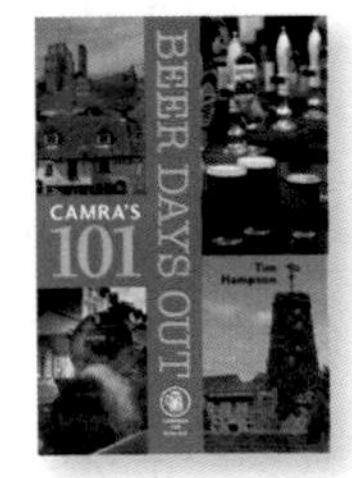

Good Beer Guide Belgium

Tim Webb & Joe Stange

The *Good Beer Guide Belgium* is CAMRA's iconic guide to the world-renowned home of serious beers. Completely revised and updated, this is the indispensible work for all Belgian beer lovers, even in Belgium itself. The definitive, totally independent guide to understanding and finding the best that Belgian brewing has to offer. The Guide is an essential companion for any visit to Belgium or for seeking out quality Belgian beer around the world.

£14.99 ISBN 978-1-85249-311-0 CAMRA members' price £12.99

Britain's Beer Revolution

Roger Protz & Adrian Tierney-Jones

UK brewing has seen unprecedented growth in the last decade. Breweries of all shapes and sizes are flourishing. Established brewers applying generations of tradition in new ways rub shoulders at the bar with new micro-brewers. Headed by real ale, a 'craft' beer revolution is sweeping the country. In *Britain's Beer Revolution* Roger Protz and Adrian Tierney-Jones look behind the beer labels and shine a spotlight on what makes British beer so good.

£14.99 ISBN 978-1-85249-265-6 CAMRA members' price £12.99

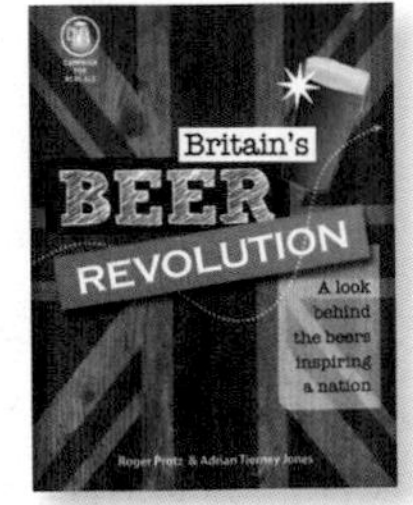

Order these and other CAMRA books online at **www.camra.org.uk/books**, ask your local bookstore, or contact: CAMRA, 230 Hatfield Road, St Albans, AL1 4LW. Telephone 01727 867201.

Good Beer Guide digital editions

The *Good Beer Guide* is also available in digital formats, including an e-book, mobile app and sat-nav download. Together, these offer the perfect solution to pub-finding on the move. To discover more, scan the QR code or visit **www.camra.org.uk/gbgdigital**.

Good Beer Guide e-book

The *Good Beer Guide 2015* e-book will be available from autumn 2014 in the widely compatible ePUB and Kindle formats. The e-book provides all the benefits of portable, searchable and adaptable digital content while also making the Guide fully interactive, taking advantage of GPS, mobile and Internet connectivity to bring exciting new features.

- Portable, electronic version of the printed Guide
- Fully interactive, searchable content in ePUB and Kindle formats, compatible with iPad, Kindle and many other e-readers
- Includes full colour features and images from the printed book as well as complete pubs and breweries listings*
- Active e-mail and web links within entries*
- Postcode links to Google maps to help you navigate*

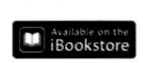

Visit **www.camra.org.uk/gbg** for further information and for details of where to buy.

*Where e-reader allows.

Good Beer Guide Mobile

The Good Beer Guide Mobile app for Apple and Android™ devices provides detailed information on local *Good Beer Guide* pubs, breweries and beers wherever you are or wherever you are going. Features include:†

- Search results with full pub descriptions and detailed visitor information
- Detailed information on all UK real-ale breweries and their beers
- CAMRA tasting notes for hundreds of regular beers
- Interactive maps help you find your way
- Search by postcode, pub or place name, or auto-locate
- Custom functions allow you to mark your favourite pubs and write your own personal reviews

To download, visit the Apple **App Store** or **Google Play** store. For more information visit: **www.camra.org.uk/gbgmobile**

†App is free to download with an in-app suscription required for full features. Subscription-free use allows for sinlge, auto-locate search results only. NOTE: Standard network charges apply when using the app.

Good Beer Guide sat-nav download

Priced at just £2.99, the Good Beer Guide POI (Points of Interest) file allows users of TomTom, Garmin and Navman sat-nav systems to see the locations of all the 4,500 current *Good Beer Guide* pubs and all the UK's real-ale breweries and plan routes to them. So, no more wasting time getting lost down country lanes – now, wherever you are, there is no excuse for not finding your nearest *Good Beer Guide* pub.

- For more information and to download visit: **www.camra.org.uk/gbgpoi**

An offer for CAMRA members
Good Beer Guide annual subscription

Being a CAMRA member brings many benefits, not least a big discount on the *Good Beer Guide*. Now you can take advantage of an even bigger discount on the Guide by taking out an annual subscription.

Simply fill in the form below and the Direct Debit form on p975 (photocopies will do if you don't want to spoil your book), and send them to CAMRA at 230 Hatfield Road, St Albans, Hertfordshire AL1 4LW. You will then receive the **Good Beer Guide** automatically every year. It will be posted to you before the official publication date and before any other postal sales are processed. You won't have to bother with filling in cheques every year and you will receive the book at a lower price than other CAMRA members (for instance, the **2014** Guide was sold to annual subscribers **for just £10** including postage & packing). So sign up now and be sure of receiving your copy early every year.

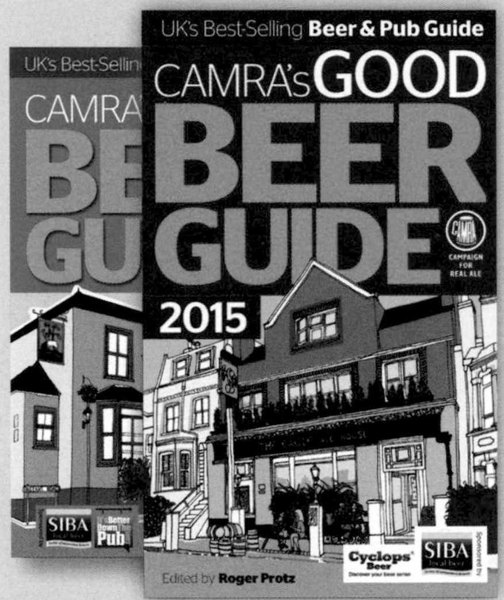

Note: This offer is open only to CAMRA members and is only available through using a Direct Debit instruction to a UK bank. This offer applies to the **Good Beer Guide 2016** onwards.

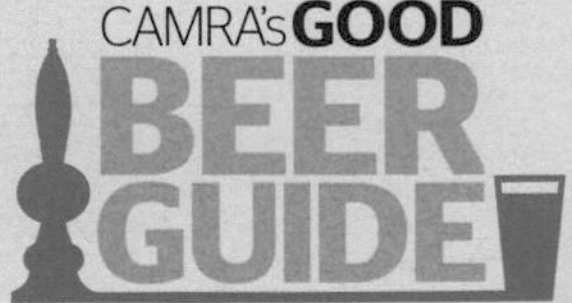

Name ____________________________________

CAMRA Membership No. ____________________________________

Address and Postcode ____________________________________

I wish to purchase the *Good Beer Guide* annually by Direct Debit and I have completed the Direct Debit instructions to my bank which are enclosed.

Signature __________________ Date __________

CAMPAIGN FOR REAL ALE

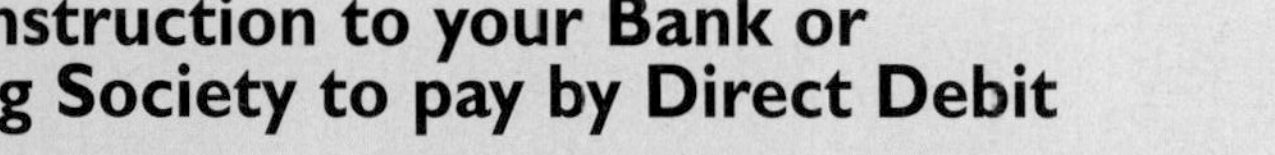

Instruction to your Bank or Building Society to pay by Direct Debit

Please fill in the form and send to: Campaign for Real Ale Ltd. 230 Hatfield Road, St. Albans, Herts. AL1 4LW

Name and full postal address of your Bank or Building Society

To The Manager — Bank or Building Society

Address

Postcode

Name (s) of Account Holder (s)

Bank or Building Society account number

Branch Sort Code

Reference Number

Originator's Identification Number

9	2	6	1	2	9

FOR CAMRA OFFICIAL USE ONLY
This is not part of the instruction to your Bank or Building Society

Membership Number

Name

Postcode

Instruction to your Bank or Building Society
Please pay CAMRA Direct Debits from the account detailed on this Instruction subject to the safeguards assured by the Direct Debit Guarantee. I understand that this instruction may remain with CAMRA and, if so, will be passed electronically to my Bank/Building Society

Signature(s)

Date

Banks and Building Societies may not accept Direct Debit Instructions for some types of account

detached and retained this section

This Guarantee should be detached and retained by the payer.

The Direct Debit Guarantee

- This Guarantee is offered by all Banks and Building Societies that take part in the Direct Debit Scheme. The efficiency and security of the Scheme is monitored and protected by your own Bank or Building Society.
- If the amounts to be paid or the payment dates change CAMRA will notify you 10 working days in advance of your account being debited or as otherwise agreed.
- If an error is made by CAMRA or your Bank or Building Society, you are guaranteed a full and immediate refund from your branch of the amount paid.
- You can cancel a Direct Debit at any time by writing to your Bank or Building Society. Please also send a copy of your letter to us.

Join the Campaign!

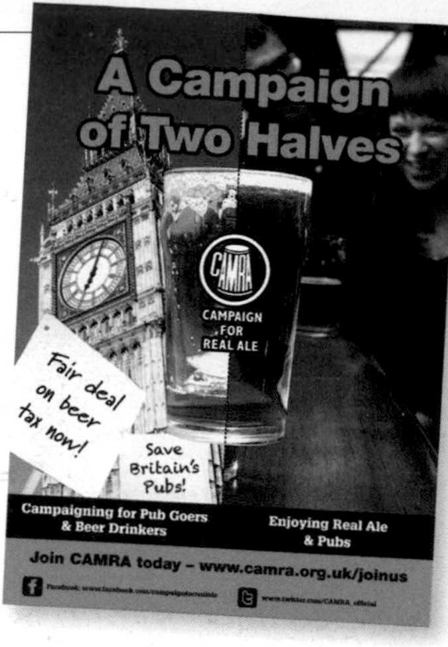

CAMRA, the Campaign for Real Ale, is an independent not-for-profit, volunteer-led consumer group. We promote good-quality real ale and pubs, as well as lobbying government to champion drinkers' rights and protect local pubs as centres of community life.

CAMRA has over 165,000 members from all ages and backgrounds, brought together by a common belief in the issues that CAMRA deals with and their love of good quality British beer. From just £23 a year – that's less than a pint a month – you can join CAMRA and enjoy the following benefits:

- A monthly colour newspaper and quarterly magazine informing you about beer and pub news and detailing events and beer festivals around the country.
- Free or reduced entry to over 160 national, regional and local beer festivals.
- Money off many of our publications including the *Good Beer Guide* and the *Good Bottled Beer Guide*.
- A 10% discount on all holidays booked with Cottages4you and Hoseasons, a 10% discount with Beer Hawk, plus much more.
- £20-worth of JD Wetherspoon real ale vouchers (40 x 50 pence off a pint).
- For more details please visit **www.camra.org.uk/benefits**.

If you feel passionately about your pint, here is how to join us...

Just fill in the application form below (or a photocopy of it) and the Direct Debit form on the previous page to receive 15 months membership for the price of 12!*

(If you wish to join but do not want to pay by Direct Debit, please fill in the application form and send along with a cheque, payable to CAMRA. Please note than non-Direct Debit payments will incur a £2 surcharge.)

Please send applications to: CAMRA, 230 Hatfield Road, St Albans, Hertfordshire, AL1 4LW

Please tick appropriate box	**Direct Debit**		**Non Direct Debit**	
Single membership (UK & EU)	£23.00	☐	£25.00	☐
Concessionary membership (under 26 or 60 and over)	£15.50	☐	£17.50	☐
Joint membership	£28.00	☐	£30.00	☐
Concessionary joint membership	£18.50	☐	£20.50	☐

Life membership information is available on request.

Title ____ Forename(s) ____________________ Surname ____________________

Address ____

____ Postcode __________

Date of Birth ________________ Email address ____________________

Signature ____

Partner's details (for Joint Membership)

Title ____ Forename(s) ____________________ Surname ____________________

Date of Birth ________________ Email address ____________________

CAMRA will occasionally send you e-mails related to your membership. We will also allow your local branch access to your email. If you would like to opt-out of contact from your local branch please tick here ☐ (at no point will your details be released to a third party).

Find out more at **www.camra.org.uk/join** or telephone **01727 867201**

*15 months membership for the price of 12 is only available the first time a member pays by Direct Debit.

NOTE: Membership prices will be increasing in January 2015. Benefits are subject to change.

REF: GBG2015